Streptococcus A

E. coli O157:H7

Influenza A

AIDS

Hantavirus

Vancomycin–resistant *Enterococcus*

Lyme disease

Drug-resistant pneumococcus

Cryptosporidiosis

Venezuelan hemorrhagic fever

Dengue

Pandemic cholera

PRINCIPLES OF MICROBIOLOGY

PRINCIPLES OF
MICROBIOLOGY

RONALD M. ATLAS, PhD
University of Louisville
Louisville, Kentucky

St. Louis Baltimore Berlin Boston Carlsbad Chicago
London Madrid Naples New York Philadelphia
Sydney Tokyo Toronto

Editor-In-Chief: James M. Smith
Editor: Robert J. Callanan
Developmental Editor: Diana Lyn Laulainen
Project Manager: Carol Sullivan Wiseman
Production Editor: Florence Achenbach
Interior Designer: Jeanne Wolfgeher
Design Manager: Betty Schulz
Art Designer: E. Rohne Rudder
Art: Pagecrafters, Inc.
Cover Designer: E. Rohne Rudder
Cover Illustrations: Hank Morgan, Photo Researchers; Lou Jones, Image Bank; Secchi-Lecaque-Roussel-UCLAF/CNRI/Science Photo Library, Photo Researchers; Jeff Spielman, Image Bank.

FIRST EDITION

Printed in the United States of America
Composition by Graphic World, Inc.
Color film by Accu-Color
Printing/binding by Von Hoffmann Press, Inc.

Mosby–Year Book, Inc.
11830 Westline Industrial Drive
St. Louis, Missouri 63146

Library of Congress Cataloging in Publication Data

Atlas, Ronald M.
Principles of microbiology / Ronald M. Atlas.
p. cm.
Includes index.
ISBN 0-8016-7790-4
1. Microbiology. I. Title.
QR41.2.A843 1994
576—dc20 93-48867
CIP

95 96 97 98 99 / 9 8 7 6 5 4 3 2

PREFACE

The study of microorganisms has had a major impact on all the biological sciences and on the quality of life for humankind. Great strides have been made using microorganisms to understand the principles that govern life. Many of the discoveries made by microbiologists have spawned new fields of science, such as molecular biology and biotechnology. The discovery of DNA as the molecular basis of heredity was made using microorganisms, laying the foundation of genetic engineering and its application in biotechnology. Controlling microorganisms has become a fundamental part of modern health practices. The maintenance of environmental quality depends largely on the metabolic activities of microorganisms. Microorganisms have become the mainstays of many technologies. The seemingly overwhelming and ever expanding state of knowledge about microorganisms—their diversity, activities and uses—makes it difficult to define the appropriate scope of microbiology. The successes of microbiology have created a dilemma for teaching microbiology. What are the central themes of microbiology? What are the basics that students should learn about microorganisms?

Principles of Microbiology presents an insightful discussion of modern microbiology. It brings together over 100 years of discoveries that place the scientific discipline of microbiology at its current state of the art. It focuses on the microorganisms—the unifying theme of this field of science. It captures the excitement of this contemporary and dynamic science, bringing forth the latest information available about microorganisms—their activities and relevance. It shows how microorganisms have evolved numerous strategies for carrying out essential life functions and how the activities of microorganisms contribute to the overall health and welfare of humans and the environment. It explains why some of the diverse and ubiquitous microorganisms are beneficial to humankind—describing the essential role of microorganisms for the maintenance of life on Earth, and why others are harmful, causing diseases of plants and animals—with a major impact on human health.

This book is about the scientific study of microorganisms. It is intended to provide the foundation for understanding and learning microbiology as a biological science. A major goal of the book is to extend the principles of biology to cover the microorganisms. It is designed to provide comprehensive, although not encyclopedic, coverage of microbiology. It provides an in-depth view of microbiology, giving sufficient detail to grasp concepts, yet not so much detail that the unifying principles of microbiology are obscured. The subjects covered and the detailed discussion on those topics reveal the breadth of microbiology and how far this science has developed—microbiology is at the cutting edge of scientific exploration leading into the twenty-first century.

Contents and Organization of the Book

Principles of Microbiology is designed to help instructors teach microbiology and to help students learn about microorganisms. The textbook is designed to be flexible; the order of chapters and topics can be subject to the instructor's creativity. Topics may be selected from the various chapters to meet individual course needs. Students can supplement their coursework by reading topics of interest that are omitted by the instructor from the formal class presentation.

Each chapter has the following general structure:

- Overview
  The overview sets out the scope of information that will be covered in the chapter.
- Text of chapter
  To develop an understanding of a topic, the text is designed to reveal the principles related to the topic of each chapter. Key terms are shown in boldface or italics. Boxes within each chapter cover current topics of special interest, topics of historical interest, and methodologies used in the study of microbiology. Elaborate illustrations supplement the written text.
- Suggested supplementary readings
  The suggested readings are meant to supplement the text for more advanced courses and to sustain interest in a particular topic relevant to the student's purpose for having enrolled in an introductory microbiology course.
- Study questions
  The set of review questions is intended to allow students to test their comprehension of the material they have just examined.
- Situational problems
  The situational problems are intended to challenge a student's creativity, to challenge him or her to think, and to aid in the development of an in-depth understanding of microbiology.

The book is organized into major parts arranged from the subcellular to the entire organism, from the fundamental to the pragmatic. Each part contains an essay written by a prominent microbiologist describing his or her view of that field of microbiology and his or her contribution to the scientific development of that field. The essays provide unique insights into why some of us chose careers as microbiologists and how we pursued our career goals.

Part One

This section reviews the scientific study of microorganisms. It introduces the microorganisms and the methods and methodologies used for their study. It presents a brief overview of the microbial world, exploring the realm of studies on microorganisms. Students reading this section gain a perspective on microbiology with its many vistas.

Chapter 1 This chapter provides an overview of the microorganisms that are the focus of the textbook. It traces the development of microbiology as a scientific discipline, showing how scientists think and how they use the scientific method for studies on microorganisms. It gives a historical perspective to microbiology, highlighting the contributions of noteworthy microbiologists such as Louis Pasteur and Robert Koch.

Chapter 2 This chapter reviews methodologies used by microbiologists. The science of microbiology depends on the ability to make observations. The chapter discusses the various forms of microscopy that are used to view microorganisms, the culture methods employed for studying microorganisms, and the development of molecular methodologies that have contributed to the understanding of microorganisms.

Part Two

This section on microbial physiology and cell biology examines the structure and function of cells of microorganisms. It explores many of the fundamental properties of living systems, showing how microorganisms have developed diverse solutions for meeting essential requirements for life.

Chapter 3 This chapter covers the organization of prokaryotic and eukaryotic cells of eubacteria, archaebacteria, and eukaryotic microorganisms. The emphasis is on prokaryotic cells, which are often only covered cursorily in general biology classes. The chapter compares structures that have evolved in different organisms to serve similar functions, emphasizing the differences between prokaryotic and eukaryotic cells, many of which have important practical implications. It highlights the design of cellular structure and reveals how cells meet the essential requirements for life.

Chapter 4 This chapter treats the bioenergetics of cellular metabolism, indicating how the principles of chemistry apply to biological systems. It focuses on the flow of energy through cellular metabolism and diverse strategies that occur among microorganisms for generating ATP.

Chapter 5 This chapter covers the metabolic reactions involved in forming cell biomass by autotrophic and heterotrophic metabolisms. It treats the transformations of materials that are necessary for the formation of new cells and shows how cells can use simple starting substrates to make complex cell structures.

Part Three

This section about microbial genetics and molecular biology covers topics of great contemporary interest. It focuses on the structure and functioning of DNA, showing that the basic revelations of the structure of DNA have led to recombinant DNA technology.

Chapter 6 This chapter examines the role of DNA in heredity and control of cellular functions. It demonstrates the discovery of the structure of DNA and the revolution in our understanding of the functioning of cells. It examines the molecular basis of heredity and how DNA controls protein synthesis, relating genetics to the functioning of the cell.

Chapter 7 This chapter discusses the genetic changes that alter hereditary information. It shows the molecular events involved in recombination. It establishes the principles underlying the development of recombinant DNA technology, giving the basis for genetic engineering and its practical importance.

Part Four

This section examines microbial growth and replication, shows that microorganisms have enormous potentials for population growth, and examines the factors that control the rates of microbial reproduction.

Chapter 8 This chapter is about viruses. It covers the replication of viruses, distinguishes viruses from living organisms, and shows why viruses depend on host cells for their replication. It describes the stages of viral replication and the strategies employed for the replication of different viruses.

Chapter 9 This chapter discusses bacterial growth and reproduction; examines the consequences of bacterial reproduction by binary fission, showing that exponential increases of bacterial cell numbers occur due to reproduction by binary fission; and discusses the influences of various environmental factors, such as temperature, on bacterial growth rates.

Chapter 10 This chapter deals with the basis for control of microbial growth and the abilities of physical and chemical factors to kill or prevent the growth of microorganisms. It relates the modes of action of various antimicrobial agents to fundamental properties of microbial physiology.

Part Five

This section about microorganisms and human disease covers topics of importance related to human health. It emphasizes relationships between the defenses of the human body and virulence factors of pathogenic microorganisms. It describes how diseases are spread and how the transmission of pathogens can be controlled.

Chapter 11 This chapter introduces immunology and the defenses of the body against infections and diseases. It discusses the innate and specific defense systems that protect the human body from infection, highlighting the complex nature of the body's lines of defense against disease. It shows the underlying molecular basis for the body's resistance to invasion by foreign substances. It also describes the consequences of failures of the immune system.

Chapter 12 This chapter gives an epidemiological perspective to selected human diseases caused by microorganisms. It examines the underlying principles of disease transmission and how understanding the basis of infectious disease can be used to block disease transmission. It includes a discussion of how vaccines are used to control and to eliminate specific diseases.

Chapter 13 This chapter covers the basis of pathogenesis of infectious diseases. It examines properties of pathogenic microorganisms that contribute to their abilities to cause disease and physiological changes that occur as a result of microbial infections. It also examines the basis for diagnosing various diseases.

Part Six

This section examines applied and environmental microbiology, emphasizing some of the practical aspects of microbiology. It shows the essential functions of microorganisms in ecology and the practical uses of microorganisms in biotechnology.

Chapter 14 This chapter examines interactions among microorganisms and the roles of microorganisms in global biogeochemical cycling. It also discusses the importance of microorganisms for maintenance of environmental quality, including essential uses of microorganisms for degrading wastes and pollutants.

Chapter 15 This chapter is about biotechnology, including the economic uses of microorganisms for producing foods, antibiotics, and numerous other products; recombinant DNA technology; and traditional practices employed in industrial microbiology.

Part Seven

This section is a survey of microorganisms that describes their great diversity.

Chapter 16 This chapter provides a survey of the prokaryotic bacteria and archaebacteria. It explains microbial systematics and the approaches used in taxonomy. It also characterizes the diverse groups that comprise the eubacteria and archaebacteria.

Chapter 17 This chapter gives a brief overview of eukaryotic microorganisms, including fungi, algae, and protozoa.

Part Eight

Additional material provides a framework for review and study.

Study Outlines The detailed study outlines for each chapter are included to aid in learning the material covered in each chapter. The outlines should be especially helpful in preparing for examinations.

Appendix: Chemistry for the Microbiologist The appendix provides an overview of organic chemistry and biochemistry as it relates to biological systems.

Glossary of Microbiological Terms An extensive glossary has been included to help understand the terminology used by microbiologists.

Illustration Program

The figures included in this text were carefully selected to enhance student understanding of key information. A color coding scheme was used throughout the text whereby specific chemicals and structures are a specific color. This will enable students to readily identify the identical structures in different organisms. The key to the color coding is presented below.

KEY TO COLOR CODE OF CHEMICALS AND STRUCTURES

Color	Chemical	Structure	Microorganism
	Protein, lipoprotein	Viral capsid, bacterial pili, flagella	Virus
	Peptidoglycan	Bacterial cell wall	Bacteria
	Carbohydrate glycoprotein, lipopolysaccharide	Bacterial outer membrane, glycocalyx, capsule	
	DNA	Bacterial chromosome, plasmas, chloroplasts	
	RNA, ATP	Ribosomes, nucleus	
	Lipid, phospholipid	Membranes, mitochondria	Eukaryotes

ACKNOWLEDGMENTS

Many individuals contributed to the writing and development of *Principles of Microbiology*. Some informally shared ideas about teaching microbiology that augmented my own two decades of teaching introductory microbiology and bacteriology courses. Others formally reviewed drafts of the manuscript and illustrations. Yet others wrote essays highlighting the excitement of being a microbiologist.

The following individuals provided essays:

Alice S. Huang, *New York University*
Moselio Schaechter, *Tufts University*
Holger W. Jannasch, *Woods Hole Oceanographic Institution*
David Schlessinger, *Washington University*
Gail Houston Cassell, *University of Alabama—Birmingham*
Rita R. Colwell, *University of Maryland*
R.G.E. Murray, *University of Western Ontario*

The following individuals provided content reviews:

Robert K. Antibus, *Clarkson University*
Prakash H. Bhuta, *Eastern Washington University*
James L. Botsford, *New Mexico State University*
Michael Dalbey, *University of California, Santa Cruz*
Michael W. Dennis, *Eastern Montana College*
Alan A. DiSpirito, *Iowa State University*
Linda E. Fisher, *University of Michigan—Dearborn*
Harold F. Foerster, *Sam Houston State University*
William Gibbons, *South Dakota State University*
Van H. Grosse, *Columbus College*
Patricia Hartzell, *University of California, Los Angeles*
George D. Hegeman, *Indiana University—Bloomington*
Scott W. Hooper, *University of Mississippi*
Douglas I. Johnson, *University of Vermont*
John J. Lee, *City College of New York*
Alan C. Leonard, *Florida Institute of Technology*
Banadakoppa T. Lingappa, *College of the Holy Cross*
Ann G. Matthysee, *University of North Carolina*
Richard L. Myers, *Southwest Missouri State University*
David R. Nelson, *University of Rhode Island*
Nina T. Parker, *Minot State University*
Kenneth Pidock, *Wilkes University*
Deborah D. Ross, *Indiana University—Purdue*
Garriet W. Smith, *University of South Carolina at Aiken*
Henry G. Spratt Jr, *Southeast Missouri State University*
Gary R. Wilson, *McMurry University*
Steven Woeste, *Scholl College*

The following individuals provided technical reviews:

Robert E. Andrews, Jr, *Iowa State University*
Marcia Cordts, *Cornell University*
Merrill Emmett, *University of Colorado—Denver*
John G. Holt, *Michigan State University*
Valeria Howard, *Bismarck State College*
David Kafkewitz, *Rutgers University*
Scott T. Kellogg, *University of Idaho*
Arthur L. Koch, *Indiana University—Bloomington*
Robert J.C. McLean, *Southwest Texas State*
Robert G.E. Murray, *University of Western Ontario*
Sara Silverstone, *California State University—Bakersfield*
Robert G. Taylor, *Eastern New Mexico University*
Bruce A. Voyles, *Grinnell College*
Eugene D. Weinberg, *Indiana University—Bloomington*

Larry Parks, a microbial physiologist by training, worked exhaustively with me, debating what was essential to include in the book—helping to define the scope of microbiology and how best to provide students with a clear understanding of the principles underlying the scientific study of microorganisms; he served as a valued reality check and helped focus the presentation of material. A debt of gratitude is also owed to Bill Page, a professor at the University of Alberta, for his extensive review of the figures to ensure accuracy. Michel Atlas, my wife and health sciences reference librarian, also read each new draft for clarity of presentation; she provided daily updates of relevant articles and reviews on which the book is based. Anne Little and Barbara Turgeon painstakenly typed each new version as the book developed.

Ronald M. Atlas

CONTENTS IN BRIEF

CONTENTS

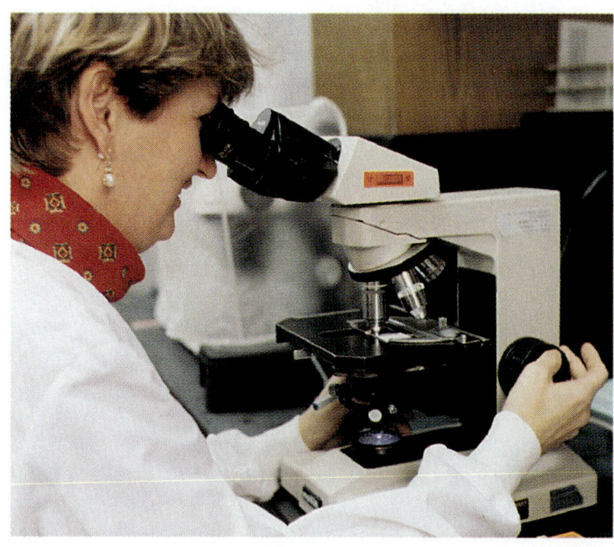

PART ONE SCIENTIFIC STUDY OF MICROORGANISMS

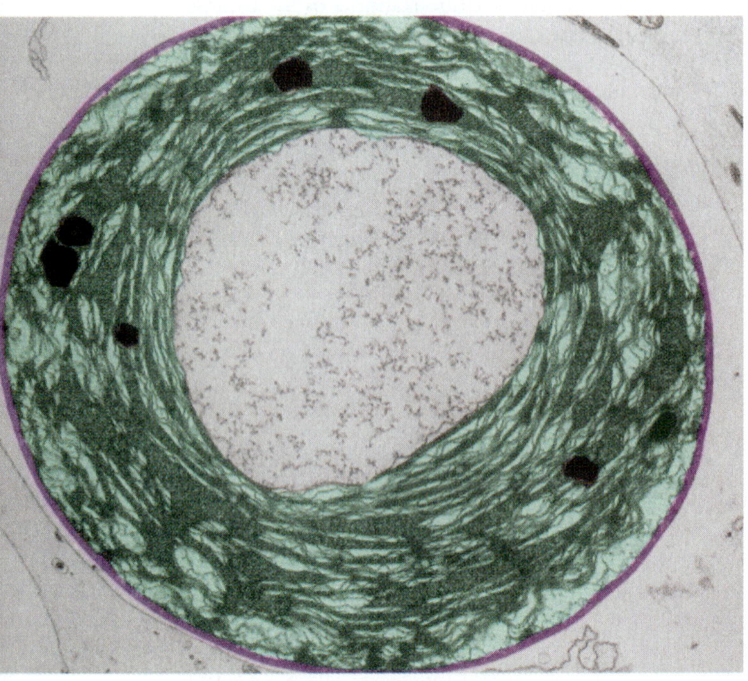

PART THREE MICROBIAL GENETICS—MOLECULAR BIOLOGY

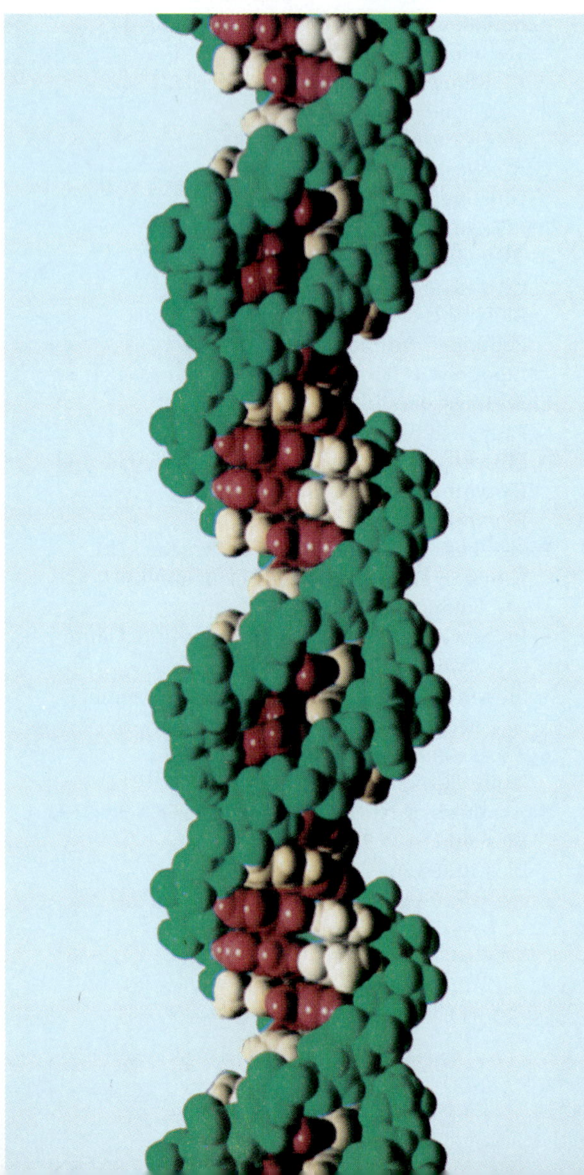

PART FOUR MICROBIAL REPLICATION AND GROWTH

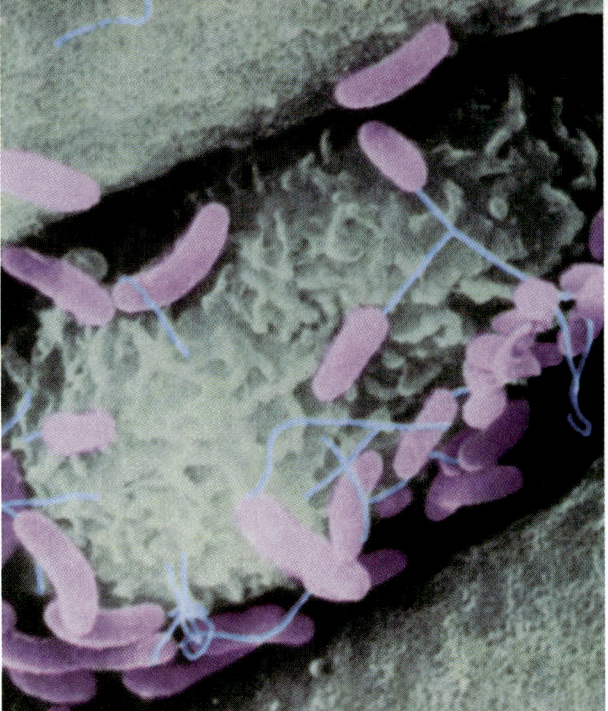

PART FIVE MICROORGANISMS AND HUMAN DISEASES

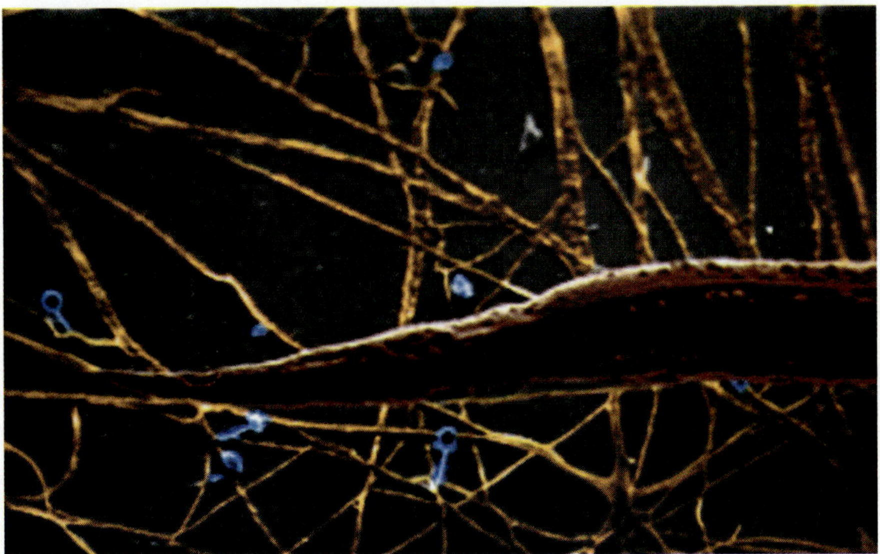

PART SIX APPLIED AND ENVIRONMENTAL MICROBIOLOGY

14 Microbial Ecology, 524

15 Biotechnology, 597

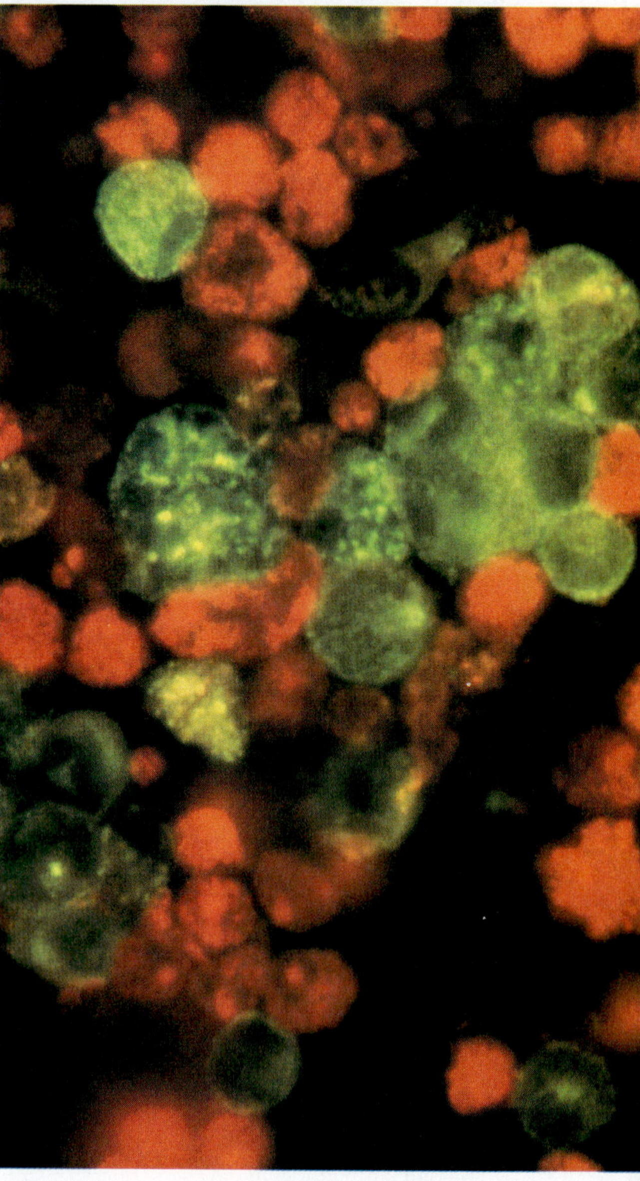

PART SEVEN SURVEY OF MICROORGANISMS

PART ONE

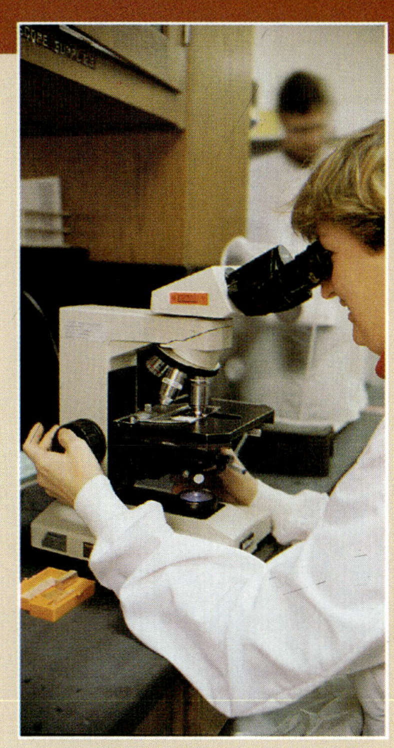

Scientific Study of Microorganisms

CHAPTER 1

Development of Microbiology as a Scientific Discipline

Chapter Outline

Microbiology is the field of science that studies microorganisms—viruses, archaebacteria, eubacteria, fungi, algae, and protozoa. Although the microbial world is highly ubiquitous, it was not until the seventeenth century that microorganisms were first observed through primitive microscopes. At first there was little notion of the importance of microorganisms and their relationships to other living organisms. By posing and testing hypotheses using scientific methodologies, including the use of controlled experiments, nineteenth century microbiologists such as Louis Pasteur and Robert Koch extended the breadth of science to the examination of the microbial world.

Today's microbiologists use microorganisms as research tools to unravel molecular mysteries and to solve practical problems in diverse fields from medicine to waste management. Microbiology has developed within the last 100 years into a major scientific discipline that is at the forefront of science leading into the twenty-first century.

1.1 CONTEMPORARY MICROBIOLOGY

The scope of modern **microbiology** (the science that deals with microorganisms) covers many fields and many diverse organisms. Microorganisms, the unifying focus of microbiology, are very small life forms that generally require magnification to be observed. For the most part, they represent an unseen, invisible world, but their small size belies their importance. Some microorganisms cause diseases, with which all of us have at some time been confronted. Others carry out the metabolic processes that are responsible for the chemical transformations that maintain the ecological balance necessary for life on Earth.

Microbiology is at the cutting edge of the biological sciences. This field of science extends into areas such as basic molecular and cellular biology, largely because the nature of microorganisms makes them suitable for use as model organisms in many basic scientific studies. Microorganisms reproduce rapidly so that large numbers of organisms with the same genetic composition can easily be grown. Because microorganisms are simpler than plants and animals, both genetically and biochemically, microbial systems are easier to deal with and understand than those of higher, more complex organisms. Accordingly, our fundamental understanding of molecular genetics and the relationship of genetics and metabolism has been developed primarily by studying microorganisms.

Furthermore, while many biologists today face growing popular concern about the use of animals and humans in scientific experiments, microbiologists do not confront this problem for microorganisms. Although some Japanese microbiologists have established a memorial to microorganisms in which they buried a Buddhist prayer scroll and the ashen remains of the bacterium *Bacillus subtilis,* microorganisms generally do not engender the same protectionist sentiments in people as do higher organisms. This makes microorganisms better suited for experimental use in scientific studies.

Besides its central position in basic biological studies, microbiology is an applied science at the center of biotechnology and genetic engineering. Many practical aspects of microbiology affect our daily lives and influence the overall quality of life. Applications of microbiology are important in medicine, industry, agriculture, and ecology. The health of humans and the existence of life on Earth depend on microorganisms, making microbiology a relevant and pragmatic science.

Medical microbiology (the medical science relating to microorganisms and human diseases) represents an important applied area in the study of microbiology. Because microorganisms are involved in causing infectious diseases, the field of microbiology logically has been extended to include the response of diseased humans and other animals. As such, the discipline of **immunology** (the study of the immune [host defense] response of higher animals) is included in the study of microbiology. An understanding of the causative agents of disease and the body's defenses against infectious agents has led to preventive and treatment methods that have reduced *morbidity* (disease) and *mortality* (death) arising from certain diseases, resulting in an increase in life expectancy (Table 1-1).

Microbial ecology, the study of the environmental relationships of microorganisms, includes the examination of biogeochemical cycling reactions, which are important in maintaining air, water, and soil quality. The maintenance of soil fertility, the role of microorganisms in causing plant diseases, and the interactions of microorganisms with pesticides and fertilizers are important considerations in **agricultural microbiology,** the study of the role of microorganisms in agriculture. **Plant pathology** (the study of diseases of plants) is also an important area of microbiological study. The ability of microorganisms to degrade waste materials extends microbiology into the field of **sanitary engineering**, which is concerned with processes for waste removal.

TABLE 1-1 Comparison of Life Expectancies and Causes of Mortality in the United States

	1920	1940	1960	1990
Life expectancy (years)	54.1	62.9	69.7	75.4
Mortality rate (deaths per 100,000) due to:				
Pneumonia and influenza	207.3	70.3	37.3	28.4
Tuberculosis	113.1	45.9	6.1	<0.1
Syphilis	16.5	14.4	1.6	<0.1
Diphtheria	15.3	1.1	<0.1	<0.1
Whooping cough	12.5	2.2	0.1	<0.1
Measles	8.8	0.5	0.2	<0.1
Other nonmicrobial causes	925.4	942.0	909.4	843.5

Industrial applications of microorganisms are a fundamental part of **biotechnology** (the modern use of biological systems for economic benefit). Microbiology is an integral part of many industrial processes, and microorganisms have great economic importance. Various products, including many pharmaceuticals and food products such as beer, cheese, wine, and spirits, are produced by microbial fermentation. Quality control in many industries is concerned with preventing microbial contamination that could lead to the spoilage of products, reducing their economic value. The proper handling of food products is based on an understanding of microbiology.

It is thus apparent that microbiology encompasses a very broad field. Some microbiologists are concerned with the basic sciences and the development of a fundamental understanding of living systems; others are concerned with the application of basic scientific knowledge. Microbiology overlaps several other scientific disciplines, including biochemistry, genetics, zoology, botany, ecology, pharmacology, medicine, food science, agricultural science, industrial science, and environmental science. The broad scope of microbiology attests to the diversity of microorganisms themselves, their ubiquitous distribution in nature, and the importance of microorganisms in virtually all aspects of life; the unity of microbiology rests with its central subject matter: the organisms that are considered to be microorganisms.

The vistas and challenges for the student of microbiology are virtually limitless, and new discoveries are being made daily. Improvements in scientific communication allow microbiologists to capitalize rapidly on scientific advances, hastening the rate of development in the field of microbiology. Today, there are numerous journals and publications through which worldwide distribution of microbiological information is made possible. Additionally, the news media carry almost daily reports of microbiological interest ranging from outbreaks of disease to court cases involving biotechnological patents. The field of microbiology promises to continue its rapid development for many years. It is an exciting and challenging field of science for students and professionals alike.

1.2 MICROORGANISMS

The microorganisms include the archaebacteria, eubacteria, fungi, algae, protozoa, and viruses. These diverse organisms are differentiated by their cellular structures and functions. Cellular organization, growth, metabolism, reproduction, and heredity are the critical functions that comprise the essential characteristics of life.

TABLE 1-2 Organizational Structure of the Major Groups of Microorganisms

MICROBIAL GROUP	STRUCTURAL ORGANIZATION
Viruses	No cell
Archaebacteria	Prokaryotic cell
Eubacteria	Prokaryotic cell
Fungi	Eukaryotic cell
Algae	Eukaryotic cell
Protozoa	Eukaryotic cell

Structural Organization of Microorganisms

The *cell* is the fundamental organizational unit of all living systems, including microorganisms. It is bounded by a cytoplasmic membrane that separates the cell contents from the external surroundings. Materials are selectively exchanged across the cytoplasmic membrane that is the delimiting boundary of the cell. This exchange of materials between the living cell and its surroundings is essential to life. Within the cell, materials are chemically modified and energy is transferred so that life processes can occur. Additionally, a cell responds to environmental stimuli, that is, it interacts with its environment. As a population, cells also are capable of changing so that cells with new combinations of hereditary information are formed, and hence new organisms can evolve.

Many microorganisms are *unicellular;* each organism is composed of a single cell. Some microorganisms form *multicellular* groups of associated cells but none form integrated units, called *tissues,* that serve different functions. It is this latter characteristic that distinguishes the microorganisms from plants, which generally lack tissues, and animals, which are multicellular and form differentiated tissues. This fundamental difference between microorganisms and higher organisms (plants and animals) was recognized in 1866 by Ernst Häckel when he defined microorganisms, which he called *protists,* as organisms lacking tissue differentiation.

Prokaryotic and Eukaryotic Cells

There are two architecturally different types of cells: **prokaryotic cells** and **eukaryotic cells,** which are distinguished based on structural organization (Table 1-2). These cells and their biology are examined in Chapter 3. Prokaryotic and eukaryotic cells have some common properties. Both (1) are highly organized, (2) are capable of growth and reproduction, and (3) contain the same hereditary molecule—DNA (deoxyribonucleic acid)—that passes hereditary information to offspring cells. Both express the hereditary information in DNA by the processes of transcription and translation. Both carry out cellular metabolism in which they utilize energy and transform materials into the structures of the cell.

Although they carry out the same overall functions, prokaryotic and eukaryotic cells differ in their structures that enable them to sustain these essential life functions. A prokaryotic cell has a much simpler internal structure than a eukaryotic cell (FIG. 1-1). It does not have membrane-bound compartments, called *organelles,* that serve specialized functions in eukaryotic cells. Eukaryotic cells have numerous organelles, including the *nucleus,* which contains the cell's DNA— its hereditary information. A prokaryotic cell does not have a nucleus, and the hereditary information of a prokaryotic cell is not separated from the other constituents within the cell. The fact that the DNA in a prokaryotic cell is *not* separated within a specialized organelle from the rest of the cell contents is of prime importance in distinguishing prokaryotic from eukaryotic cells. Thus differences in their internal organization distinguish prokaryotic from eukaryotic cells (Table 1-3).

Until a decade ago, the fundamental structural differences between eukaryotic and prokaryotic cells led most scientists to believe that there were two primary

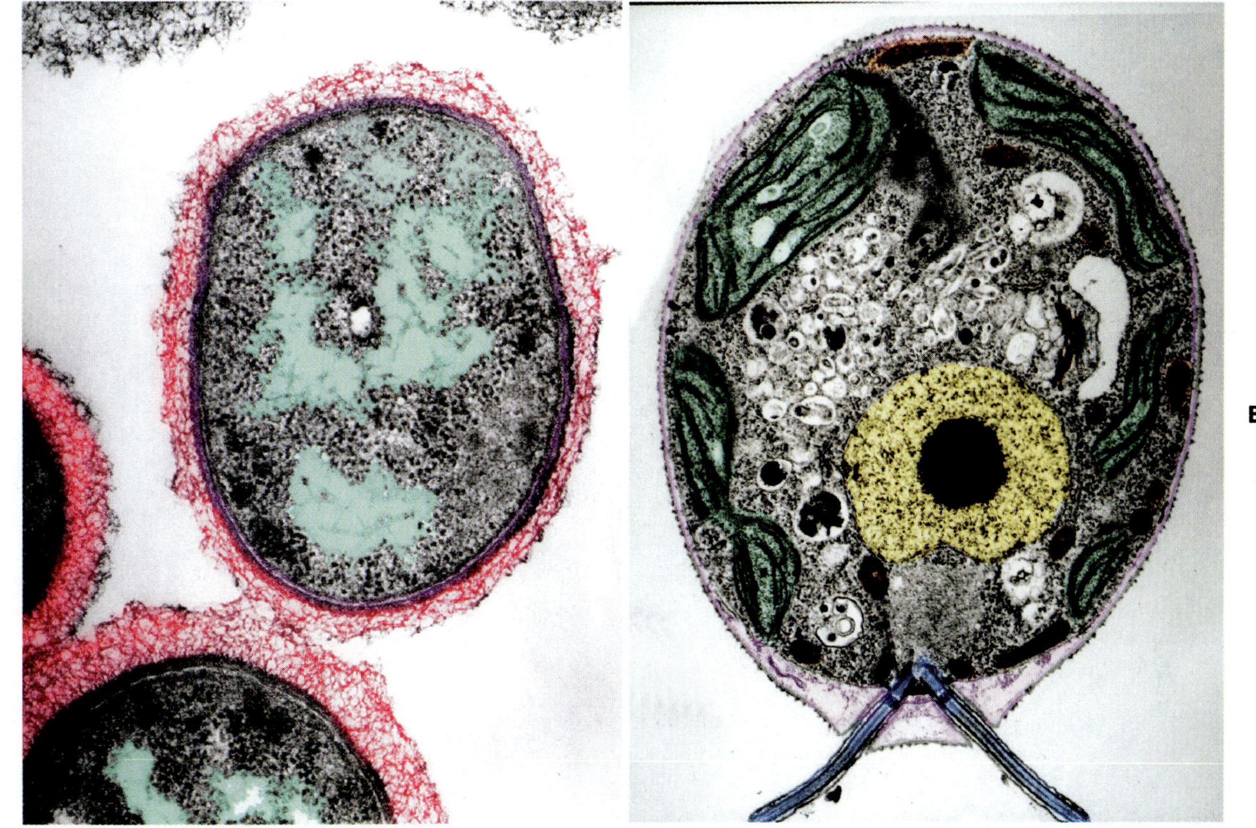

FIG. 1-1 A comparison of structural organization reveals that the eukaryotic cell has far more internal organization than the prokaryotic cell; the membrane-bound organelles found in eukaryotic cells do not occur in prokaryotic cells. **A,** Colorized micrograph of a prokaryotic cell of the bacterium *Pseudomonas aeruginosa.* (78,000×). **B,** Colorized micrograph of a eukaryotic cell of the green alga *Chlamydomonas reinhardtii.* (11,250×).

lines of evolution: one leading to organisms with prokaryotic cells—the bacteria—and the other to all other organisms. All organisms with prokaryotic cells were considered to be bacteria. The terms *bacteria* and *prokaryote* were thought to be synonymous. This view changed radically in the 1980s when molecular biologists, led by Carl Woese, began to analyze the informational molecules that directly reflect the heredity of a cell. Analyses and comparisons of similarity of RNA (ribonucleic acid) molecules of ribosomes (structures found in both prokaryotic and eukaryotic cells where proteins are synthesized) revealed that there were three principal lines of evolution that formed three separate domains of cellular evolution: *archaebacterial* (archaeal), *eubacterial,* and *eukaryotic* (FIG. 1-2). Also, it became clear that the origins of the major energy-processing organelles—mitochondria and chloroplasts—of eukaryotic cells were eubacterial prokaryotic cells that had been acquired during eukaryotic cellular evolution and that had lost the capacity of independent life. Thus the current view is that all organisms evolved from a common ancestor along three distinct paths to form the great diversity of microorganisms that exist today.

Text continued on p. 8

TABLE 1-3 Comparison of Eukaryotic and Prokaryotic Cell Structures

STRUCTURE	PROKARYOTIC CELLS	EUKARYOTIC CELLS
Cytoplasmic membrane	+	+
Nucleus containing a nuclear membrane surrounding DNA arranged as true chromosomes with associated histone proteins	−	+
Ribosomes	70S	80S
Cell wall	+	±
Internal organelles	−	+
Chloroplasts	−	±
Mitochondria	−	+
Endoplasmic reticulum	−	+
Golgi apparatus	−	+
Vacuoles	−	±
Flagella	+	+
9 + 2 microtubular arrangement	−	+
Cytoskeleton	−	+

BOX 1-1

Evolution of Microorganisms

About 3.8 billion years ago, Earth was a mass of molten rock surrounded by swirling gases. Temperature on the surface of Earth probably was well over 100° C, the temperature at which water boils. Water, which is required for life, could have been produced from the breakdown of rocks during volcanic eruptions and released into the atmosphere, but it is unlikely that much water could have accumulated on the surface of the planet because any water reaching the planet surface would have been transformed into steam and returned to the atmosphere. Because of lack of water and high temperatures, life could not have existed under the conditions that initially characterized the planet. Slowly, however, temperatures on the planet's surface cooled as heat energy radiated into space. Violent storms would have brought torrential rains, further cooling the Earth's surface and leading to the accumulation of water and the formation of the oceans.

The primitive atmosphere of Earth probably contained large amounts of hydrogen (H_2), methane (CH_4), ammonia (NH_3), and water (H_2O) but probably did not contain much, if any, carbon dioxide (CO_2), molecular oxygen (O_2), or organic compounds (chemicals containing carbon and hydrogen) other than methane, making it similar to the current atmosphere surrounding the Earth's neighboring planet of Venus. The absence of oxygen may have been critical for the occurrence of chemical changes in the atmosphere that could have permitted the evolution of life on Earth. In the absence of molecular oxygen, organic compounds found in living organisms will form from hydrogen, methane, ammonia, and water—if there is an electrical spark (see FIG.).

Stanley Miller and Harold Urey in the 1950s experimentally modelled what some hypothesize happened when electrical discharges from lightning sparked chemical reactions that produced organic compounds from

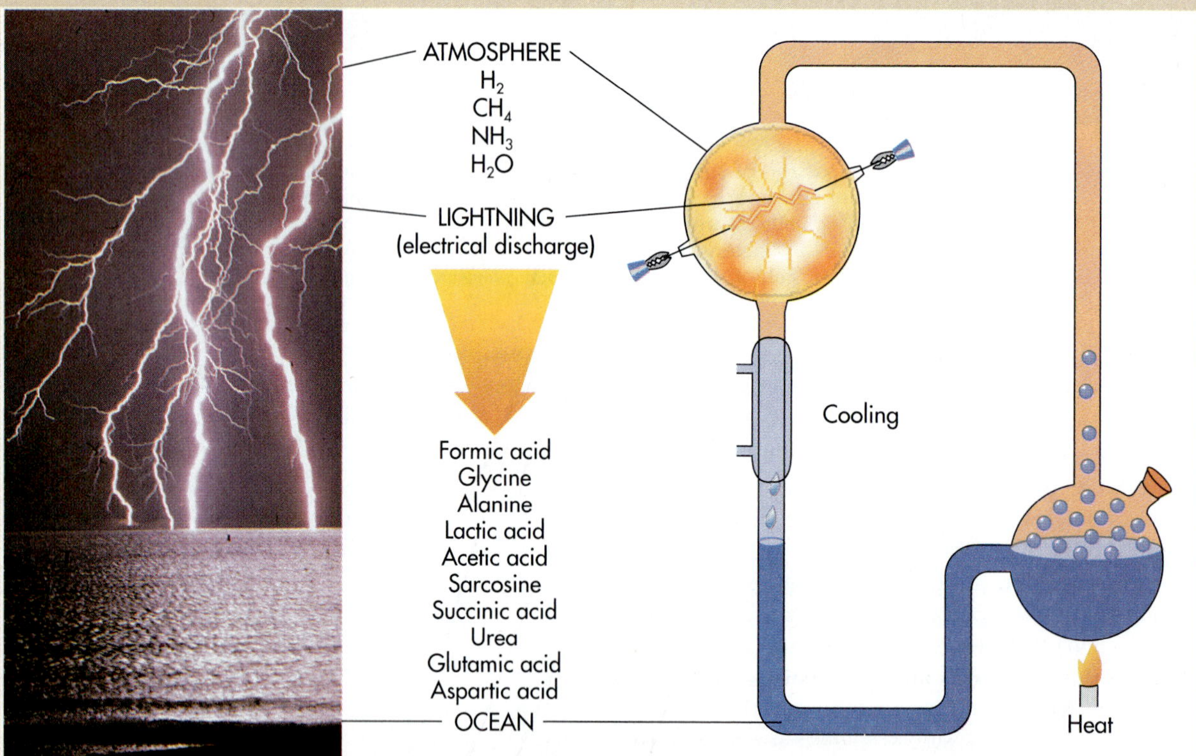

The apparatus used in the Miller-Urey experiment consisted of two connected chambers. The upper chamber contained a mixture of gases thought to resemble the earth's atmosphere. Molecules that formed collected in the lower chamber containing liquid. Organic molecules that occur in living systems were formed and accumulated in the liquid (simulating oceans) when electrical discharges (simulating lightning) reacted with the mixture of gases (representing the primitive atmosphere). These included the amino acids glycine, alanine, glutamic acid, and aspartic acid, and other organic compounds.

the gases in the atmosphere surrounding the planet. These and later experiments produced sugars, amino acids, lipids, and nucleotides, which are the building blocks of the organic chemicals that compose all living systems. The *abiotic* (nonliving) production of these organic chemicals would have provided the usable forms of materials for energy generation, growth, and reproduction necessary for life.

Thus, after perhaps a billion years of physical and chemical change, conditions could have reached a point where life could exist on Earth. Temperatures would have been below 100° C, water would have covered large portions of the planet, and organic compounds would have formed that could be used as energy sources for growth and reproduction of living systems.

An alternate hypothesis is that life on Earth began at deep ocean thermal vents. There, hot, mineral-rich water emerges through pyrite (iron sulfide)–containing rock. Some scientists hypothesize that this environment provided the right mixture of chemicals and catalysts that were needed for the formation of life. Today, the thermal vents and the unique assemblages of organisms that live there are the subjects of intensive scientific investigation.

Although we do not know exactly how the first living organism developed, we do know from laboratory experiments that when wet with water some of the organic chemicals believed to have accumulated in the primitive atmosphere of Earth could have spontaneously aggregated into spheres called *micelles.* The structure of the micelle resembles the cell. A micelle is like a hollow ball, with an internal cavity that is separated from the surrounding environment by a chemical boundary layer. The structure of the micelle allows restricted exchange of materials with the surroundings while permitting the maintenance of a high degree of organization within its center. The chemicals that make up the boundary layer of a micelle are lipids (fats), much like the lipids that make up the boundary layer of a cell. Molecules could accumulate and chemical reactions could take place within the central cavity of the micelle, protected from the surroundings.

At some point it appears that the chemicals that accumulated within a micelle permitted life functions to occur, namely, the ability to process materials and energy and to reproduce. Thus the first living microorganism would have evolved on Earth. Reproduction of this microbial cell would have produced other living cells.

These first microorganisms would have had to tolerate harsh conditions, including the relatively high temperatures, acidity, and salinity, that still characterized Earth at that time. There would have been no molecular oxygen in the primitive Earth's atmosphere and, therefore, the first microorganisms would have been anaerobes (organisms that grow without using molecular oxygen). The earliest microorganisms probably used the organic compounds that accumulated spontaneously in the primordial atmosphere or on the Earth's surface to obtain the energy and materials needed for growth and reproduction. Some contemporary microorganisms still retain properties that would have permitted their survival when life began on Earth. These descendants, closely resembling the first inhabitants of Earth, are classified in the Kingdom Archaea, which are physiologically highly specialized microorganisms, many of which grow in hot environments under acidic and otherwise harsh conditions.

Very slowly, the metabolic activities of some of the earliest microorganisms would have changed the Earth's atmosphere, so that other organisms could survive. Adaptations to the changing environmental conditions would lead to the evolution of new microorganisms. Some of the microorganisms that evolved, called *autotrophs* (self-feeding organisms that use CO_2 as a primary carbon source), were able to synthesize complex organic compounds from the gas carbon dioxide (CO_2) that was present in the atmosphere. Photoautotrophic (photosynthetic) microorganisms are able to obtain their energy for synthesizing organic compounds from light energy, another abundant available resource. The organic compounds produced by the photosynthetic microorganisms provided a continuing source of organic carbon for other microorganisms, called *heterotrophs* (other feeding), that require organic compounds as their source of energy.

Although the first photosynthetic microorganisms were obligate anaerobes (organisms growing in the absence of O_2-containing air), evolution produced new photosynthetic microorganisms that could form molecular oxygen (O_2) from water (H_2O). Geologic evidence based on chemical analyses of rocks suggests that this event occurred about 2 billion years ago. The development of oxygen-producing photosynthesis and the introduction of molecular oxygen into the Earth's atmosphere would have a profound influence on the future evolution of life. In the presence of molecular oxygen, organic compounds could no longer form abiotically. Aerobic respiration, on the other hand, the life process that uses molecular oxygen in the metabolism of organic compounds, was now possible.

After 3 billion years during which only microorganisms lived on Earth, the pace of evolution apparently quickened, and over the next 600 million years a plethora of new organisms developed, including many different types of plants, animals, and microorganisms. The diverse organisms inhabiting the Earth today continue to evolve so that new organisms are formed that potentially will proliferate.

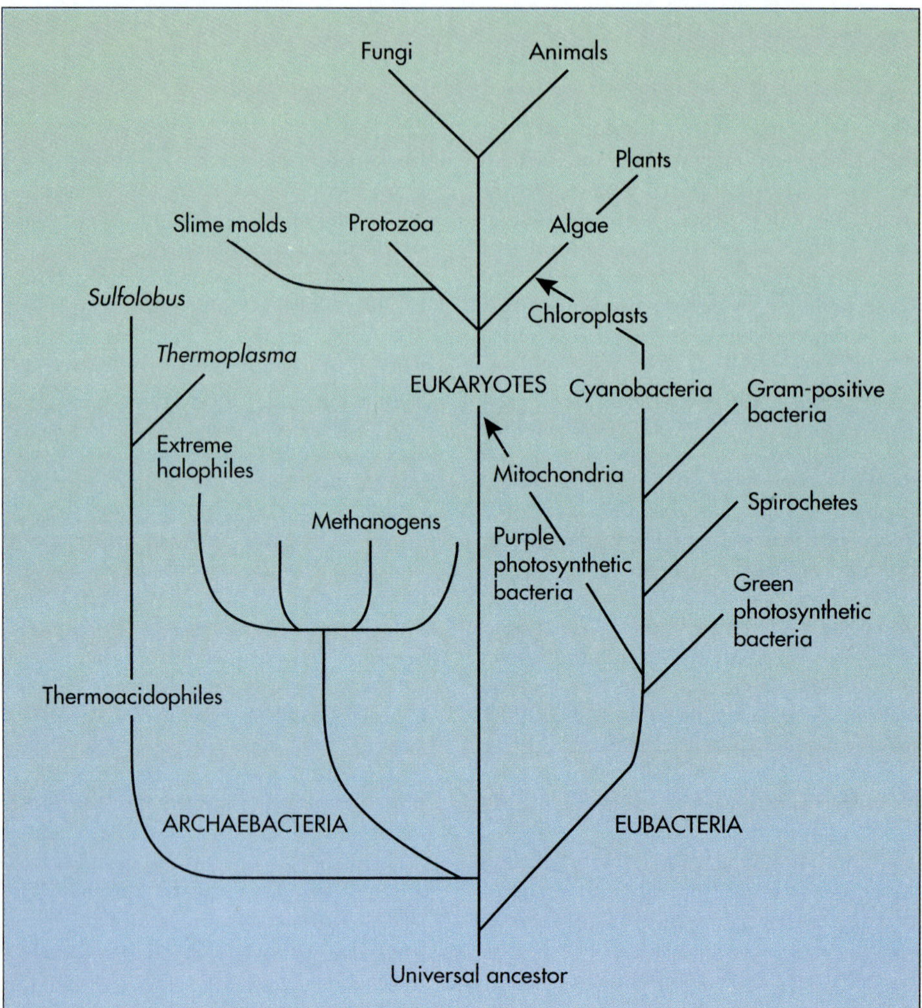

FIG. 1-2 The three-Kingdom classification system proposed by Carl Woese was developed using the modern techniques of molecular biology and, in particular, the examination of the RNA macromolecules of ribosomes. Unlike previous classification systems, the analysis of conserved gene products permits a direct assessment of genetic and, thus, evolutionary relatedness. Based on rRNA analyses, Woese found that there were three primary lines of evolution leading to the archaebacteria (Archaea), eubacteria, and eukaryotes. Modern eukaryotes have cells that incorporated mitochondria (derived from purple photosynthetic bacteria) and chloroplasts (derived from cyanobacteria); mitochondria and chloroplasts became organelles of eukaryotic cells by endosymbiosis.

Microorganisms with Prokaryotic Cells—Eubacteria and Archaebacteria

The *archaebacteria,* which are classified in the Kingdom *Archaea,* and the *eubacteria,* which are usually simply called the *bacteria,* have prokaryotic cells. The diversity of these prokaryotes is discussed in Chapter 16. Neither the cells of the archaebacteria nor those of the eubacteria have a nucleus nor other membrane-bound organelles. There are, however, significant structural differences that distinguish the cells of archaebacteria from those of eubacteria; these are discussed in Chapter 3. The difference between eubacterial and archaebacterial cells are of fundamental importance.

The **archaebacteria** (Archaea) consist of several highly specialized physiological types of prokaryotic microorganisms. Some are extremely *thermophilic* (high temperature-loving) and live only at very high temperatures (ca. 90° C) where most other organisms cannot survive. Some, called *thermoacidophiles,* grow only under very hot and highly acidic conditions. Others, called *methanogens,* produce methane from carbon dioxide and live only in places where molecular oxygen is completely absent. Yet others, *halophilic* (salt-loving) archaebacteria, grow only in brines and other highly saline environments. Still others are *acidophilic* (acid-loving) and grow in environments where the pH is that of concentrated sulfuric acid.

BOX 1-2

Largest Prokaryotic Cells

Prokaryotic cells often are described as being smaller than eukaryotic cells. The lack of internal membrane-bounded organelles in the prokaryotic cell is cited as a reason that prokaryotic cells must be smaller than eukaryotic cells. Although eukaryotic cells typically are 100 to 1,000 times larger than prokaryotic cells, some overlap of cell size has been known for some time. The eukaryotic alga *Nanochlorum eukaryotum*, which has a nucleus and a chloroplast, has a cell size of 1 to 2 μm. The prokaryotic cells of some bacteria become very long, greater than 200 μm, when growing under certain conditions.

The recent discovery of large, almost macroscopic prokaryotic cells of *Epulopiscium fishelsoni*, a bacterium that grows in the intestines of sturgeonfish from the Red Sea, has shown that size is an incorrect criterion for differentiating between eukaryotes and prokaryotes. The 80 × 600 μm cell size of *E. fishelsoni* is so much greater than other prokaryotic cells that all theories that attempt to explain why prokaryotic cells were smaller than eukaryotic cells must be re-examined. The larger size of most eukaryotic cells was thought to depend on the development of internal compartments so that the transport of substances could be contained and on the evolution of a cytoskeleton system to support the eukaryotic cell that is not present in prokaryotic cells. The absence of large cells from the fossil record before 1.5 to 2.0 billion years ago is cited as evidence that eukaryotic cells evolved after that time and that only organisms with small prokaryotic cells evolved earlier. The existence of the small eukaryote *Nanochlorum* and the giant prokaryote *E. fishelsoni* indicates that size differences between eukaryotic and prokaryotic cells are of little value in assessing the time course of evolution.

The **eubacteria** are an extremely diverse collection of prokaryotic microorganisms. They exhibit greatly differing morphologies and physiologies. Eubacterial cells are spherical (coccoid), cylindrical (rods), spirals (spirilla), and pleomorphic (irregularly shaped) (FIG. 1-3). Some eubacteria are photosynthetic, obtaining their energy from sunlight and their carbon for cellular biomass from carbon dioxide. Among these are the cyanobacteria, which previously were called blue-green algae. Other eubacteria obtain energy from the metabolism of inorganic compounds such as ammonia and elemental sulfur. Yet others can degrade organic compounds, ranging in complexity to simple sugars such as glucose to the multitude of hydrocarbons found in petroleum. Some are fastidious (nutritionally and physiologically demanding) and can grow only in very specific environments such as the tissues of the human body, where they sometimes cause disease.

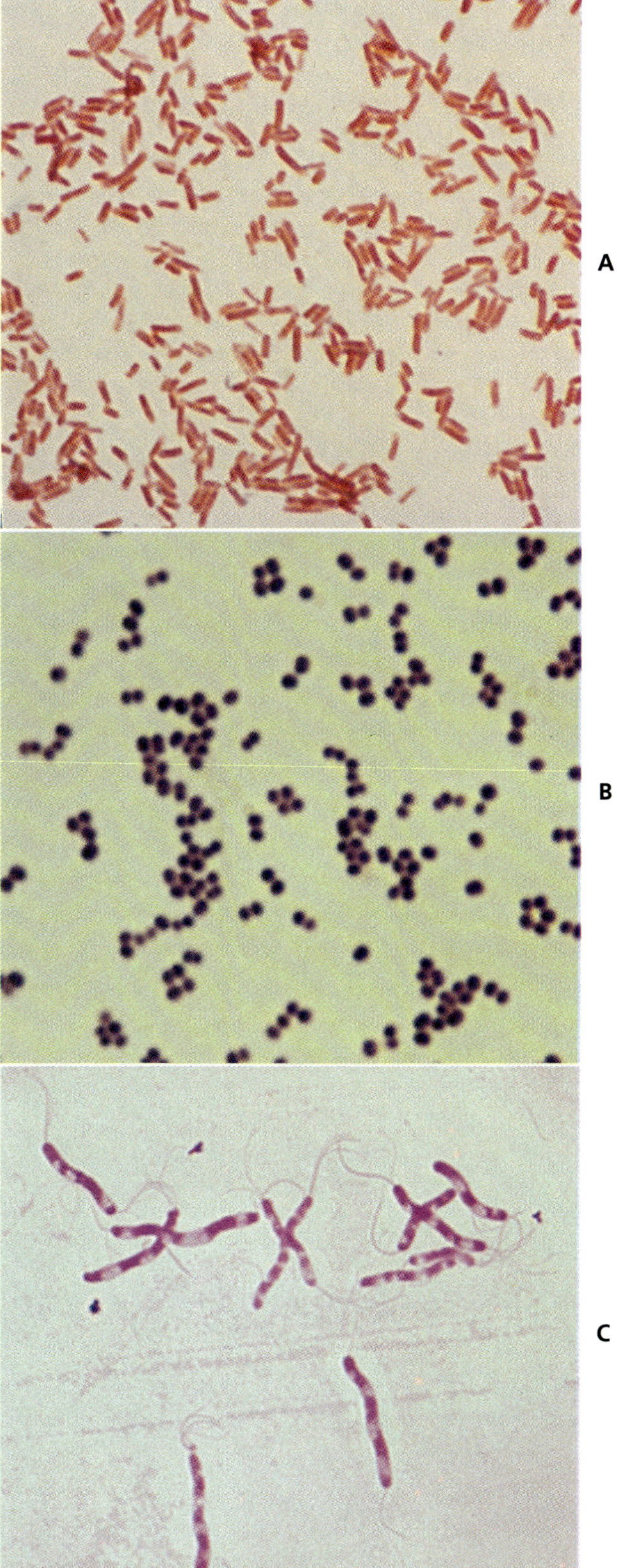

FIG. 1-3 Bacteria have characteristic shapes. **A,** Micrograph showing the rod-shaped cells of *Escherichia coli*. This bacterium lives in the human gut and is the most commonly studied (180×). **B,** Micrograph showing the coccal-shaped cells of *Staphylococcus epidermidis*, which lives on the human skin C, Micrograph showing the spiral shaped cells of the aquatic bacterium *Spirillum volutans* (180×).

MICROORGANISMS WITH EUKARYOTIC CELLS—FUNGI, ALGAE, AND PROTOZOA

Fungi, algae, and protozoa are microorganisms with eukaryotic cells. The cells of these organisms are structurally similar to those of plants and animals, which are multicellular organisms with eukaryotic cells and differentiated tissues. The diversity of the eukaryotic microorganisms is examined in Chapter 17.

Fungi are eukaryotic microorganisms that obtain their nutrition from organic compounds. Their cells are usually surrounded by protective cell walls composed of chitin or other polysaccharides. They produce spores, which are specialized cells involved in reproduction, dissemination, and survival. Some fungi, called **yeasts**, are unicellular (FIG. 1-4). Other fungi, called **molds** or **filamentous fungi**, form multicellular filaments called *hyphae* (FIG. 1-5).

Algae are photosynthetic eukaryotic microorganisms. Many are unicellular but some form multicellular filaments and other multicellular forms (FIG. 1-6). Some organisms that traditionally have been considered algae have been reclassified based on their cellular structure and organization. As indicated earlier, the blue-green algae are now considered cyanobacteria because their cells are prokaryotic. Also, the brown

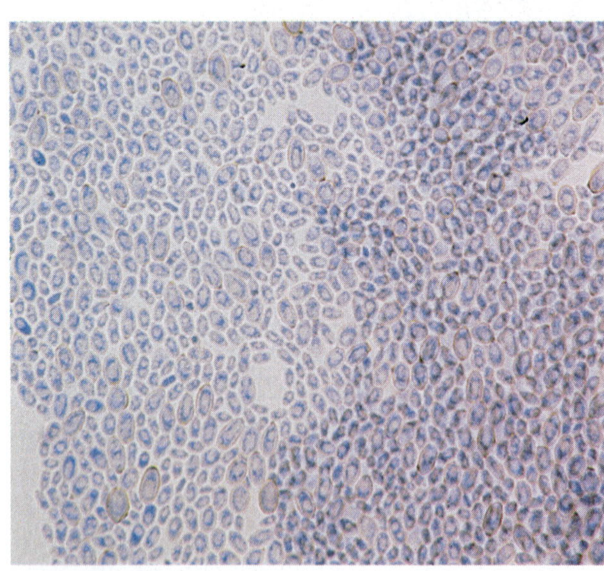

FIG. 1-4 Micrograph of the yeast-like cellular growth of the fungus *Wangiella dermatitidis.*

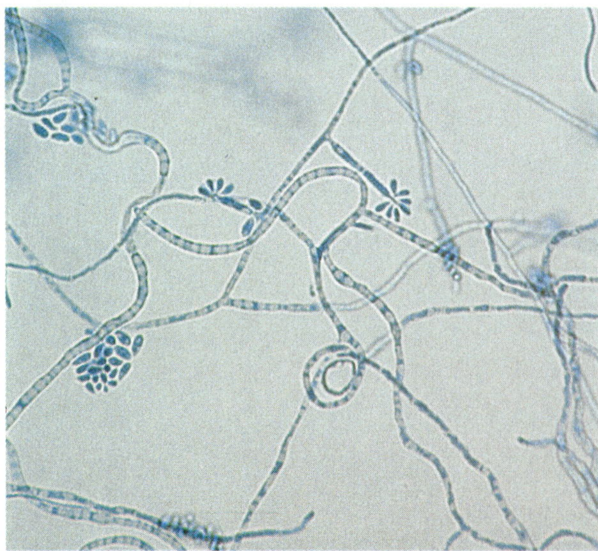

FIG. 1-5 Micrograph of the fungus *Exophiala jeanselmei* that, like other molds, forms long filaments of intertwined mycelia.

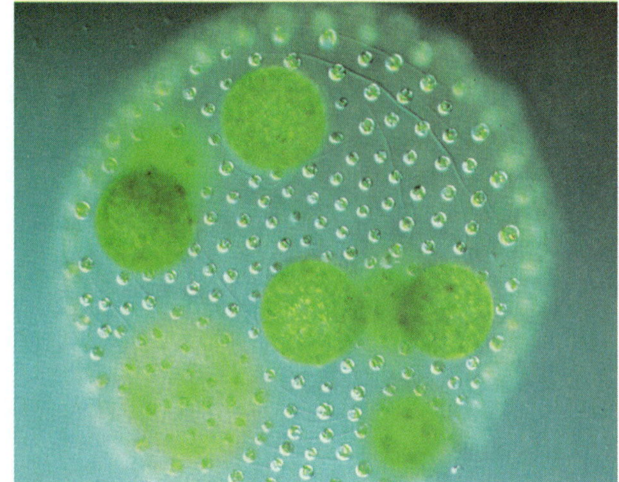

FIG. 1-6 **A,** Micrograph of various single-celled diatoms. (211×). **B,** Micrograph of the colony-forming alga *Volvox.* (211×).

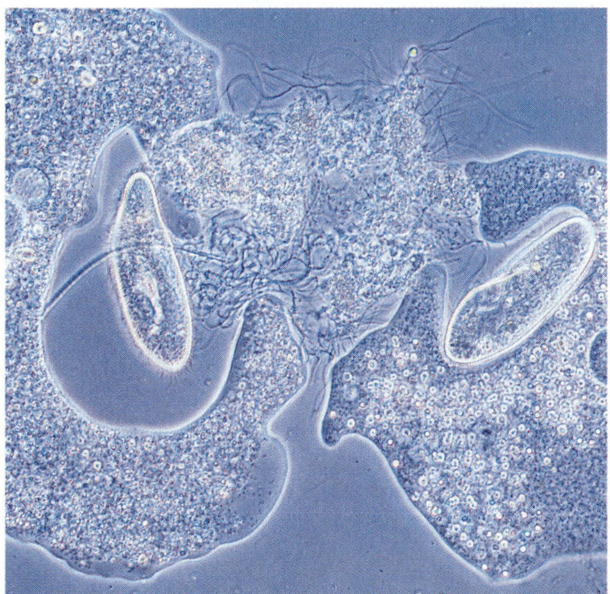

FIG. 1-7 Micrograph of the protozoan *Amoeba* consuming the ciliate protozoan *Paramecium*. (260×).

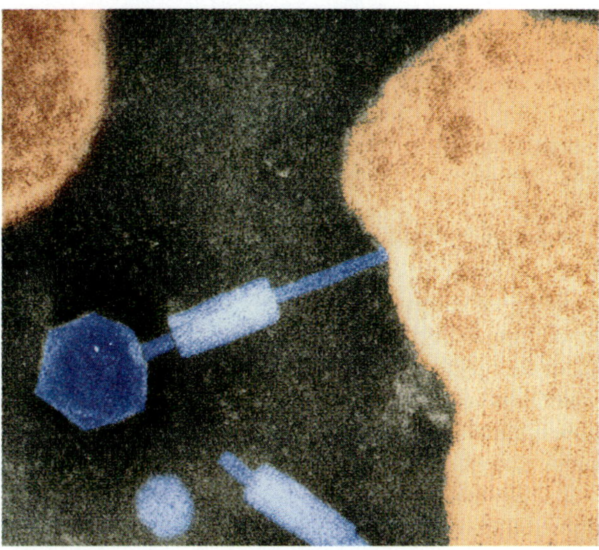

FIG. 1-8 Colorized micrograph of a bacteriophage that infects and replicates within cells of the bacterium *Chromatium violaceum*. Phage *(blue)* is attached to bacterial cell surface *(tan)*.

and red algae are now considered plants because they are multicellular organisms that exhibit tissue differentiation.

Protozoa are unicellular, nonphotosynthetic, eukaryotic microorganisms. Various groups of protozoa exhibit differing strategies of locomotion. Some, such as *Amoeba*, can change their cell shape, extending the cell so that it migrates along, whereas others, such as *Paramecium*, are propelled by numerous beating structures called *cilia* (FIG. 1-7).

MICROORGANISMS LACKING CELLS—VIRUSES

Viruses, which traditionally are considered microorganisms, lack the fundamental structure of living organisms (FIG. 1-8). No functioning cytoplasmic membrane separates the virus from its surroundings, and viruses have no means of independent life-support activities. Viruses have a genetic molecule, which may be DNA or RNA, and a protein coat. Although the viral genetic molecule is capable of directing viral reproduction (one of life's characteristics), viruses do not have the cellular support structures and metabolic machinery necessary to perform life functions. Viruses rely entirely on the metabolic activities of living cells to provide energy and materials for their replication. The replication of viruses is examined in Chapter 8.

On their own, viruses are inanimate objects that passively interact with their environment and are unable to replicate themselves. They do not transform energy, carry out metabolism, or actively respond to their environment, all of which are essential characteristics of living systems. Therefore viruses can be considered as nonliving. However, when viruses are able to enter (infect) living cells, the viral nucleic acid molecule has the capability of directing the replication of the complete virus. Within a living cell, the viral nucleic acid assumes control of the metabolic activities of that cell. In many cases, this leads to the replication of the virus and the death of the host cell. Some microbiologists therefore view viruses as genetic extensions of the host cells in which they replicate.

1.3 SCIENCE OF MICROBIOLOGY

The emergence of microbiology as a major field of science depended on developing methodologies for the study of microorganisms. Science demands objectivity. Microbiologists had to be able to make and record observations that could be confirmed by others. They had to be able to ask questions and to test the validities of potential answers to the questions.

SCIENTIFIC METHOD

Like scientists in all fields, microbiologists use an approach in their studies called the **scientific method**. It is this approach that sets the sciences apart from other fields of study. The scientific method was developed by the seventeenth-century English philosopher

Francis Bacon. It relies on observations and deductive reasoning. Using *deductive reasoning* a microbiologist says *if* this happens *then* that will happen; if I observe this, then I will observe that; if I observe a person with German measles, then I will find objective evidence that the person has been infected with the rubella virus.

Through a process of observation, questioning, and experimentation, scientists develop an understanding of cause-and-effect relationships. They learn to recognize relationships that enable them to make accurate predictions. From this they are able to use *inductive reasoning* to develop principles from repeated observations. It is in this way that scientists define cause-and-effect relationships.

In the scientific method a scientist first poses a question (FIG. 1-9). The scientist then proposes a tentative answer, called a **hypothesis**, to that question. The hypothesis makes a prediction that should be testable through objective observations. The validity of the hypothesis typically is tested by **experiments** in which systematic observations are made so that the hypothesis can be supported or refuted. An experiment examines the truthfulness of a hypothesis. Hypotheses that are not consistent with experimental observations are rejected. Hypotheses that are consistent with the data collected in experimental observations are tentatively accepted and subjected to repeated experimental testing to establish that they are indeed consistent with observed data.

Hypotheses often are tested using **controlled experiments**. The design of a controlled experiment includes a **control group** and an **experimental group.** The control group serves as the reference. It maintains (operates under) a set of conditions that does not vary. In contrast, in the experimental group, some factor or factors vary. A scientist often regulates the factors so that he or she can maintain the consistency of a control factor and change the experimental factor. By comparing the experimental group to the con-

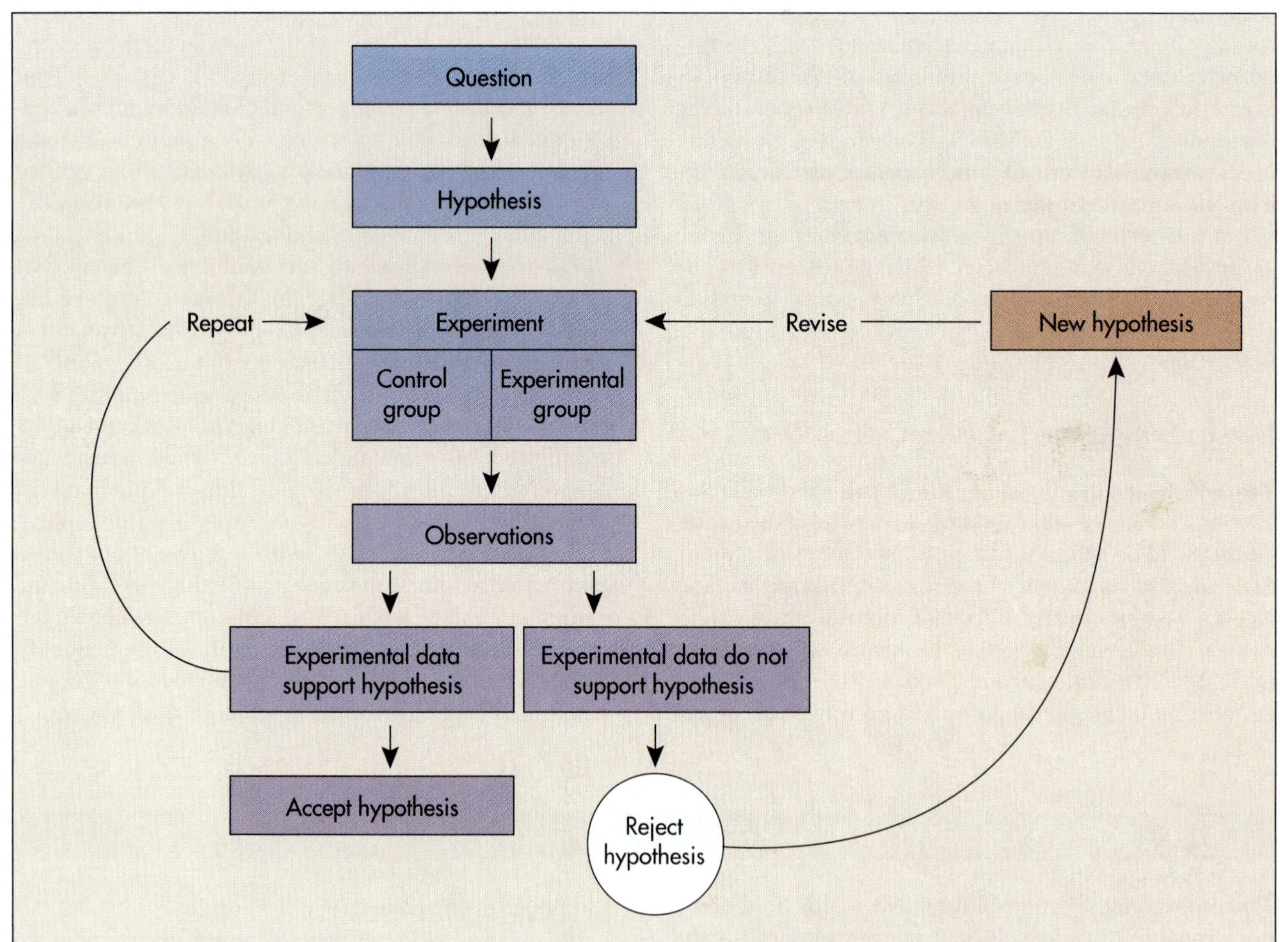

FIG. 1-9 In the scientific method, a hypothesis is proposed that can be tested. Experiments typically are run to determine whether predictions based on the hypothesis are accurate. The hypothesis is rejected if the predictions are not validated by experimental observations (data). An alternate new hypothesis may then be proposed and new experiments performed to assess its validity. When predictions based on a hypothesis are experimentally confirmed, the hypothesis is accepted.

trol group, the scientist determines the effect(s) of the factor(s) that is (are) varied on some other parameter(s). By using properly designed controlled experiments, microbiologists may determine cause-and-effect relationships.

The scientific method demands that conclusions be subjected to thorough testing to develop objective evidence that can be evaluated before their credibility is accepted. Repeatability of observations leading to the same conclusions is essential before the conclusions are accepted as accurate by scientists.

Early Observation of Microorganisms

The ability to observe microorganisms is a necessary prerequisite for applying the scientific method to microbiological studies. The invention of the microscope in the mid-sixteenth century made the observation of microorganisms possible. The first recorded observations of bacteria, yeasts, and protozoa were made in the seventeenth century by the Dutchman **Anton van Leeuwenhoek** (FIG. 1-10). Leeuwenhoek, a cloth maker and tailor, was also a surveyor and the official wine taster of Delft, Holland. As a draper, he used magnifying glasses to examine fabrics. Leeuwenhoek made simple microscopes with which he magnified objects too small to be seen with the naked eye. He made numerous observations of microscopic organisms in drops of water. Leeuwenhoek transmitted his findings in a series of letters, from 1674 to 1723, to the Royal Society in London, through which his observations were widely disseminated. These letters contained detailed drawings, some of which clearly show microorganisms (FIG. 1-11). Unfortunately, although Leeuwenhoek shared his observations with the scientific community, he never revealed the details of his methods of microscopy nor how he constructed his hundreds of microscopes.

The early microscopes of Leeuwenhoek permitted only a fuzzy view of microorganisms. Many advances in microscope-making and the science of microscopy were needed before observations could be made on the fine details of the structures of microorganisms. As microscopes were made that permitted greater magnification and viewing of more detail, scientists performed increasingly complex studies on microorganisms. As the questions raised in these studies exceeded the capabilities of the instruments, new developments in microscope-making were mandated. The major advances made in microscopy in the late nineteenth century went hand-in-hand with a period of great advancement in microbiology. During this period, Ernst Abbe, a German physicist, developed microscope lenses that corrected for *aberrations* (distortions) inherent in magnifying lenses, which had limited ability to view microorganisms. Abbe also

FIG. 1-10 Anton van Leeuwenhoek (1632-1723), here seen holding one of his microscopes, opened the door to the hidden world of microorganisms when he described bacteria. Although he was only an amateur scientist, Leeuwenhoek's keen interest in optics and diligence allowed him to make this important discovery.

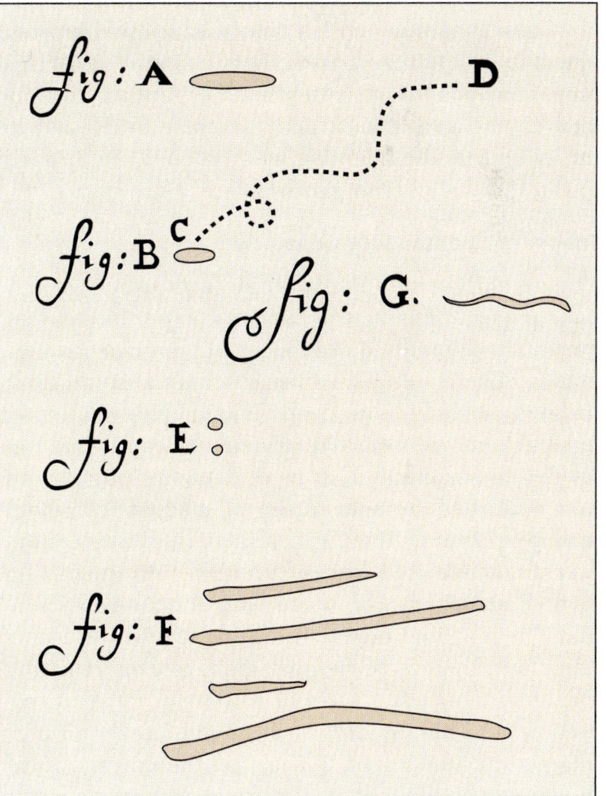

FIG. 1-11 Leeuwenhoek's sketches (including his own handwriting) of bacteria from the human mouth illustrate several common types of bacteria, including rods and cocci. **A,** A motile *Bacillus;* B, *Selenomonas sputigena;* **C** and **D,** the path of *S. sputigena's* motion; **E,** micrococci; **F,** *Leptothrix buccalis;* **G,** a spirochete.

developed the oil immersion lens, which allowed improved *resolution* (ability to see detail) in light microscopy and the use of higher magnifications for viewing bacteria clearly.

Microscopic visualization of bacteria was greatly improved by the 1881 introduction by Paul Ehrlich of vital staining of bacteria with methylene blue and the development of a differential staining method for bacteria by Hans Christian Gram in 1884. The Gram stain technique, which exploits the difference between two basic variations in cell wall structure (described in Chapter 3), is essential to the classification of bacteria today, and the microscope continues to be the essential observational tool of the microbiologist because it allows the differentiation of microorganisms based on fundamental structural differences. Modern light and electron microscopes and the current art of microscopy is discussed in Chapter 2. Throughout this book, micrographs illustrate the types of information that can be obtained about microorganisms by using different microscopic techniques.

ESTABLISHING THAT MICROORGANISMS ARE LIVING ORGANISMS

Although the microscope permitted microorganisms to be seen as early as the seventeenth century, it was not until the nineteenth century that microbiology began to develop as a truly scientific discipline. At this time, methods for observing microorganisms and objectively measuring their activities were developed to the point that the scientific method could be applied to the study of microorganisms.

Theory of Spontaneous Generation

The development of the scientific approach in microbiology is evident in the series of experiments that eventually discredited the **theory of spontaneous generation**, which held that living organisms could arise spontaneously from nonliving matter. This was a long held, commonly believed principle. People had observed, for example, that meat becomes putrid with time and that the appearance of maggots coincides with putrefaction. In the seventeenth century, however, Francisco Redi showed that flies do not spring forth from the rotting meat. In a controlled experiment, he covered one portion of meat with a loose-knit cloth, thereby preventing the flies from reaching the meat, and left a second portion of meat uncovered, so that flies could reach it. The observation of flies on the uncovered but not on the covered meat disproved the theory that *macroorganisms* arise spontaneously from decaying meat. However, the theory of spontaneous generation of *microorganisms* remained a viable idea throughout the eighteenth century and into the early nineteenth. To disprove the theory of spontaneous generation, several major advances in the field were necessary.

The relationship between the growth of what was then called *infusoria* (microorganisms in organic broths) and the onset of chemical changes that caused souring of wine and spoilage of meats, respectively known as *fermentation* (meant here as the transformation of sugar into alcohol) and *putrefaction* (spoilage of meat and other protein-containing foods with the production of foul-smelling decay products), had frequently been observed. To demonstrate that the putrefaction of organic substances is caused by microorganisms that multiply by reproductive divisions rather than arise by spontaneous generation, Lazzarro Spallanzani—an eighteenth-century priest who had an exceptionally inquiring mind and the daring to challenge the conventional wisdom of his time—sealed flasks containing meat broths that had been heated to destroy the microbes in the broth and thus prevented spoilage indefinitely.

Nineteenth-century advocates of spontaneous generation, though, claimed that the elimination of oxygen by heating and sealing the flasks compromised these experiments because it eliminated the *vital force* needed for life to arise spontaneously. Noted chemists such as Justus von Liebig, Jöns Jakob Berzelius, and Friedrich Wöhler lent support to this view, arguing that changes in organic chemicals such as the putrefaction of proteins and the transformation of sugar into alcohol occurred by strictly chemical processes without the intervention of living organisms. This premise was opposed in the 1830s by Charles Cagniard de Latour of France, Theodor Schwann, and Friedrich Kützing of Germany, each of whom separately proposed and conducted experiments to demonstrate that the products of fermentation (ethanol and carbon dioxide) were produced by microscopic forms of life. Schwann used a flame, and de Latour and Kützing used cotton plugs, to prevent microorganisms from entering heat-sterilized broth. Each of these experiments was aimed at showing that living forms were responsible for fermentation; each was criticized by chemists for destroying or eliminating some essential component in air that was supposedly needed for the spontaneous generation of the fermentation products.

Pasteur and the Final Refutation of Spontaneous Generation—Birth of Microbiology as a Science

It took several more decades of debate and experimentation before **Louis Pasteur** (FIG. 1-12) succeeded in definitively discrediting the theory of spontaneous generation and establishing that living microorganisms are responsible for the chemical changes that occur during fermentation. Pasteur had been trained as a chemist and this training had a marked influence on his approach to scientific questions. Pasteur followed the same investigative approach throughout his long scientific career: he identified the problem, sought out all available information on the topic, formed a hypothesis, and devised experiments to test the validity of his theory.

Much of Pasteur's work arose from the requests of local manufacturers to help solve the practical problems of their industrial processes. He loyally responded to these requests, attempting to solve these problems in order to improve the economy of France and to demonstrate French superiority. He was concerned with problems such as why French beer was inferior to German beer. The answer to this practical question eventually led him to the basic discovery of the existence of **anaerobic life** (life in the absence of air, or more specifically life in absence of molecular oxygen).

In 1854 Pasteur was appointed dean of the Faculty of Science at the University of Lille. Following his appointment, one of the first problems Pasteur attacked was at the request of a local industrialist and concerned the souring of alcohol produced from sugar beets. Pasteur's decision to help solve this problem of the wine industry led his scientific career from chemistry to microbiology. By comparing, with the aid of a microscope, samples taken from vats with good wine and sour wine, Pasteur observed budding yeast cells in the vats of good wine and rod-shaped bacterial cells in the vats with sour wine. He demonstrated that these two organisms determined the course of the chemical processes that result in different fermentations. The yeasts were responsible for the production of alcohol, and the rod-shaped bacteria produced the lactic acid that caused the production of sour wine. This discovery showed the versatility and importance of microbial metabolism. It also fundamentally changed the view that life depended on oxygen by showing that some microorganisms carry out anaerobic metabolism.

FIG. 1-12 Louis Pasteur (1822-1895) began as a chemist but soon became a pioneer microbiologist. Pasteur's work encompassed pure research and many areas of applied science that produced several important practical discoveries. Among his many accomplishments, Pasteur discredited the theory of spontaneous generation, introduced vaccination to treat rabies, and solved industrial problems related to the production and spoilage of foods.

Pasteur went on to explore the use of heat to destroy microorganisms in food products. In 1857 Pasteur demonstrated that the souring of milk was also caused by the action of microorganisms, and about 1860 he showed that heating could be used to kill microorganisms in wine and beer. This process of **pasteurization** (heating at moderate temperatures to reduce the number of living microorganisms), as it has come to be known, is based on these experiments.

Pasteur used heat-killing of microorganisms in a series of experiments that, for the most part, ended the controversy concerning spontaneous generation. In these experiments, Pasteur demonstrated that liquids subjected to boiling remain sterile, that is, free from any living microorganisms, as long as microorganisms in the air are not allowed to contaminate the liquid. By using a specially designed flask, called a **swan-necked flask** (FIG. 1-13), Pasteur could leave a vessel containing a fermentable substrate open to the air and show that fermentation did not occur. The shape of the flask prevented airborne microorganisms from

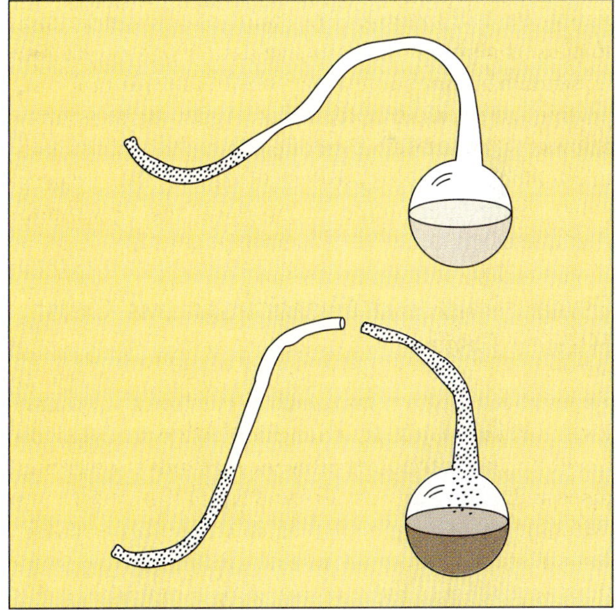

FIG. 1-13 To discredit the theory of spontaneous generation, Pasteur used various shapes in the design of his swan-necked flasks. Pasteur boiled the liquid containing nutrients to kill any microorganisms that were already there. He then left the flasks open to the air. The curved necks of the flasks trapped dust particles, preventing them from carrying microorganisms to the liquid broth growth medium so that the broth remained clear and free of microorganisms (*top*). These experiments demonstrate that spontaneous generation does not occur. When he broke the necks of some of the flasks (*bottom*), dust carried a microorganism into the broth growth medium. The microorganism grew in the broth, making it turbid (cloudy).

entering the liquid because the dust particles carrying microorganisms settled in the depressions of the curved neck of the flask. The fact that air containing oxygen could enter the flask overcame the main argument of chemists against earlier studies using sealed flasks, namely, that oxygen was essential for the chemical reactions involved in the formation of alcohol.

Despite Pasteur's eloquent disproof of spontaneous generation, attempts to repeat his experiments occasionally failed. Sometimes heating at 100° C prevented generation of new organisms and sometimes it did not: after a time, some boiled flasks were found to contain microorganisms, indicating that the "prevention" had not been permanent. Since repeatability by others is an essential part of the scientific method, these failures were problematic.

The English physicist John Tyndall, trying to confirm the results of Pasteur's experiments, determined that the variability of the results of heating was due to the capacity of bacteria to exist in two forms: a *heat-labile form* (likely to be changed or destroyed by exposure to heat) that was killed by exposure to elevated temperatures, and a *heat-resistant form* that could survive at high temperatures. He found that intermittent heating at 100° C could eliminate viable microorganisms and thus **sterilize** solutions, that is, completely eliminate living organisms from them, thereby validating Pasteur's disproof of spontaneous generation. Repeated heating on successive days, a process known as **tyndallization**, successfully sterilizes solutions containing bacteria that form heat-resistant structures known as *endospores.* Tyndallization presumably succeeds because endospores that survive one heating subsequently germinate to produce vegetative cells that are killed by the next heating.

Establishing that Microorganisms Cause Human Disease

Throughout history, humankind has had to contend with disease. Lack of scientific understanding has never impeded trials of different methods for treating disease. Lacking any understanding of the underlying microbiological cause of plague or any other infectious disease, many unscientific and ineffective practices were tried to halt the spread of contagion. In the Middle Ages people turned to self-flagellation, beating themselves in an effort to drive out the force causing the "black death" during a severe outbreak of plague that left more than 25 million dead in Europe.

A more scientifically relevant method of dealing with plague was to prevent those suspected of having the disease from coming into contact with the general public, a method known as **quarantining** that is still sometimes used today. The practice of isolating the sick dates back to biblical times, but the term *quarantine* (from the Italian *quaranta,* meaning forty) originated at the height of the fourteenth-century plague epidemic when sea voyagers coming into Sicily had to wait 40 days before entering the city. Fortunately, plague is now effectively controlled by sanitary measures that limit urban rodent populations (the primary reservoirs of plague-causing bacteria) and by the use of antibiotics to treat this disease.

Germ Theory of Human Disease

Two centuries after the major outbreaks of plague in Europe, Girolamo Fracastoro of Verona, a contemporary of the astronomer Copernicus, published a work on contagious diseases and their treatment in 1546. *De Contagione* was largely philosophical and Fracastoro did not recognize the true nature of microorganisms. Nevertheless he did hypothesize that some diseases were caused by the passage of "germs" from one thing to another, and he described three processes for their transmission: direct contact, indirect transmission via inanimate objects such as clothing, and transmission from a distance via air. Fracastoro recognized the similarity between contagion (disease processes) and putrefaction (decomposition of organic matter). He further recognized that disease-causing germs exhibit specificity, indicating that different diseases occur in different hosts and that different processes of transmission occur for different germs.

Koch and the Scientific Demonstration that Microorganisms Cause Disease

During the same period that Pasteur's studies were disproving spontaneous generation, **Robert Koch** (FIG. 1-14) was developing methods for growing individual types of microorganisms in the laboratory so that they could be studied separately. These pure culture methods permitted him to establish unequivocally the relationship between a microorganism and an infectious disease. Koch, a German country physician, was well aware of the diseases of humans and other animals. From 1873 to 1876, he studied the cattle disease anthrax and conducted experiments to show that the spores of anthrax bacilli isolated from pure cultures could infect animals. In his studies on anthrax, Koch demonstrated for the first time that germs grown outside a body could cause disease and that specific microorganisms caused specific diseases. Recognizing that to be of real use his findings would have to be published, Koch contacted Ferdinand Cohn, the esteemed director of the Botanical Institute at Breslau, Germany. Cohn quickly saw the significance of Koch's studies and arranged for their publication. This publication was the beginning of Koch's illustrious career. He went on to determine the causative organisms for several other diseases, including tuberculosis and cholera.

Koch's studies were an extension of the ideas of Jacob Henle, a professor of anatomy and advocate of

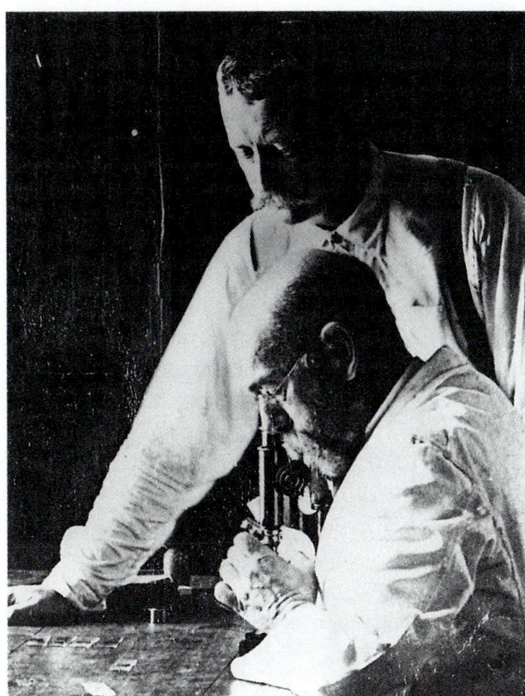

FIG. 1-14 Robert Koch *(seated)* (1843-1910) pioneered studies in medical microbiology and developed many of the basic methods essential for the study of microbiology. Koch's postulates for establishing the etiology of infectious diseases and the methodological techniques he developed are still used today in scientific investigations.

the **germ theory of disease,** who had been one of Koch's mentors at the University of Göttingen. Henle proposed that contagion was due to organized living matter that could be transmitted by direct contact or through the air and that could multiply in the body. He reasoned that to establish the cause of a specific disease, the agent would have to be found regularly in the host during the disease, the agent would have to be isolated, and the isolated agent would have to be shown to be capable of producing the disease. In his report on the **etiology** (cause) of tuberculosis, Koch reviewed his studies on anthrax and tuberculosis that permitted him to establish a cause-and-effect relationship between a given microorganism and a specific disease. Koch was able to fulfill this set of basic criteria experimentally, thus establishing their validity:

> "To obtain a complete proof of a causal relationship, rather than mere coexistence of a disease and a parasite, a complete sequence of proofs is necessary. This can only be accomplished by removing the parasites from the host, freeing them of all tissue elements to which a disease-inducing effect could be ascribed, and by introducing these isolated parasites into a healthy animal with the resulting reproduction of the disease with all its characteristic features. An example will clarify this type of approach. When one examines the blood of an animal that has died of anthrax one consistently observes countless colorless, non-motile, rod-like structures. When minute amounts of blood containing such rods were injected into normal animals, these consistently died of anthrax, and their blood in turn contained rods. This demonstration did not prove that the injection of the rods transmitted the disease because all other elements of the blood were also injected. To prove that the bacilli, rather than other components of blood produce anthrax, the bacilli must be isolated from the blood and injected alone. This isolation can be achieved by serial cultivation. The serial transfers can be continued for 3 or as many as 50 passages and in this manner the other blood components can be eliminated with certainty. Such pure bacilli produce fatal anthrax soon after injection into a healthy animal, and the course of the disease is the same as if produced with fresh anthrax blood or as in naturally occurring anthrax. These facts proved that anthrax bacilli are the unique cause of the disease." (From Robert Koch's memoir, 1884, *The Etiology of Tuberculosis*).

Koch is credited with establishing the steps that are necessary for identifying the etiologic agent of a disease. These steps, known as **Koch's postulates** (FIG. 1-15), are the following:

1. The organism should be present in all animals suffering from the disease and absent from all healthy animals.
2. The organism must be grown in pure culture outside the diseased animal host.
3. When such a culture is inoculated into a healthy susceptible host, the animal must develop the symptoms of the disease.
4. The organism must be reisolated from the experimentally infected animal and shown to be identical to the original isolate.

These four postulates, which are applicable to plant as well as animal diseases, still form the basic method for determining that a particular disease is caused by a given microorganism. For example, the search for the cause of Legionnaire's disease in 1976 followed Koch's 1890 postulates, resulting in the eventual identification of the bacterial etiologic agent. After many attempts, the bacterium *Legionella pneumophila* was isolated from patients with this disease, grown in the laboratory, inoculated into test animals, caused the onset of disease symptoms, and was reisolated from the experimentally infected animals.

Some modifications of Koch's postulates are required in some cases, such as when:

1. The disease is caused by *opportunistic pathogens* (organisms that are normally associated with healthy animals and cause disease only under specific conditions). Many urinary tract infections are caused by *Escherichia coli*, a bacterium that occurs in the intestines of all healthy individuals but causes disease if it accidentally enters the urinary tract. *E. coli* also causes meningitis if it enters the spinal column.

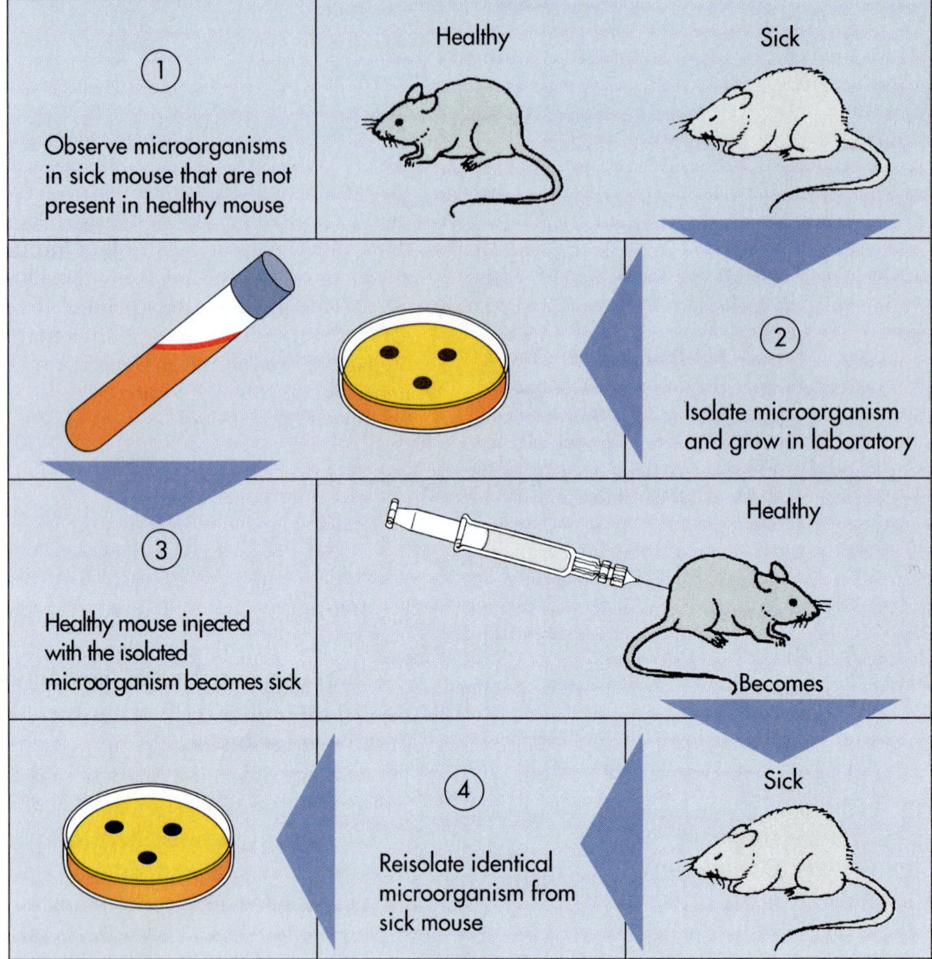
1
Observe microorganisms in sick mouse that are not present in healthy mouse
Healthy
Sick
2
Isolate microorganism and grow in laboratory
3
Healthy mouse injected with the isolated microorganism becomes sick
Healthy
Becomes
Sick
4
Reisolate identical microorganism from sick mouse

FIG. 1-15 Koch's postulates are used to define a causal relationship between a pathogenic microorganism and a specific disease. There are four postulates that make up the four steps needed to prove that a particular microorganism causes that disease: **1,** The organism should be present and observed in all sick animals with the disease and absent from all healthy animals. **2,** The organism must be isolated from the sick animals and grown in pure culture in the laboratory. **3,** When the pure culture is inoculated into a healthy animal, that animal must become sick and develop symptoms of the disease. **4,** The organism must be reisolated from the experimentally infected animal that had become sick.

2. The experimental host is *immune* (nonsusceptible due to host resistance) to the particular disease. For example, individuals who have had measles or who have been successfully vaccinated can be exposed to the measles virus and will not develop the disease.
3. The disease process involves *cooperation* between multiple organisms. An example of such a disease process is impetigo, a skin disease, which often is caused by a combined infection of *Streptococcus* and *Staphylococcus* species.
4. The causative agent cannot be grown in *pure culture* (in the absence of any other organisms) outside of host cells.

In general, however, the philosophy of Koch's postulates for identifying the causes of infectious diseases remains intact.

ESTABLISHING THAT CHEMICALS CAN CONTROL MICROBIAL INFECTIONS

Antiseptic Principles

The discovery in the early 1850s of anesthesia and its administration to patients made surgery much easier but, of course, did nothing to reduce the incidence of postsurgical infection and disease, which often was as high as 90%, especially in military hospitals. Responding to the growing awareness that microorganisms are associated with disease processes, **Joseph Lister,** an English physician, revolutionized surgical practice in 1867 by introducing **antiseptic principles**. Lister knew that in the 1840s, Ignaz Semmelweis, a Hungarian physician who worked in maternity wards in Vienna, had shown that physicians who went from one patient to another without washing their hands

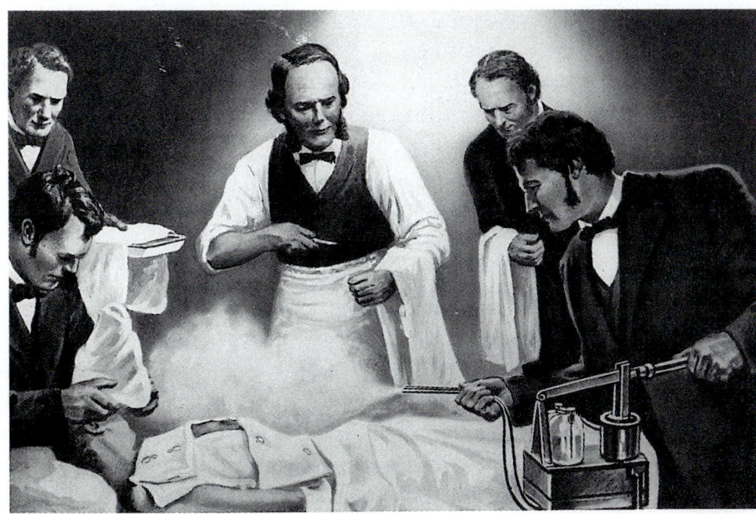

FIG. 1-16 Joseph Lister (1827-1912) recognized the importance of preventing the contamination of wounds to curtail the development of infection. He developed antiseptic methods for preventing infection using carbolic acid (phenol) to treat wounds.

were responsible for transmitting puerperal fever (childbed fever). He was also aware that Pasteur had demonstrated that microorganisms are present in the air. From the work of these men, Lister reasoned that since microorganisms could be prevented from contaminating a liquid in a flask (shown by Pasteur) and since unclean hands could spread infections to women during childbirth (shown by Semmelweis's work) that something could be done to block the spread of infection during surgery. He set forth the hypothesis that infection could be prevented by using chemicals to kill airborne microbes before they reached the wound. He carried out controlled experiments to test this hypothesis.

Lister used carbolic acid (phenol) as an antiseptic during surgery. He first used bandages soaked in carbolic acid to dress wounds caused by compound fractures to diminish the likelihood of infection. He treated some patients with carbolic acid-soaked bandages and used plain bandages on a control group (FIG. 1-16). He observed much lower rates of infection in the experimental patient group than in the control group. This experiment allowed him to conclude that carbolic acid was effective in preventing infections from wounds caused by fractures. He subsequently extended this finding to infections from other surgical procedures.

First Synthetic Antimicrobial Drugs

Various chemical formulations for preventing microbial growth and infection subsequently were described by Koch and his disciples, including **Paul Ehrlich.** From 1880 to 1896, Ehrlich worked in Koch's laboratory, and in 1896 he became director of the first of his own institutes, which he dedicated to finding "substances which have their origin in the chemist's retort," that is, substances produced by chemical synthesis, to cure infectious diseases. Ehrlich's research between 1880 and 1910 established the early basis for modern **chemotherapy.**

An arsenic-containing compound, salvarsan, proved to be effective in treating syphilis. Sahachiro Hata, a Japanese expert on the type of bacteria known as spirochetes, came to Ehrlich's laboratory and discovered that neosalvarsan (another arsenic-containing substance) could be used to cure syphilis and relapsing fever. The use of neosalvarsan in 1912 represents the first widespread use of a synthetic antimicrobial drug. These antimicrobial drugs became known as "magic bullets" and were portrayed as being able to find and kill disease-causing germs.

Discovery of Antibiotics

A major breakthrough in the development of antimicrobial drugs occurred in 1929 when the Scottish bacteriologist **Alexander Fleming,** working in a London teaching hospital, reported on the antibacterial action of cultures of a *Penicillium* species (FIG. 1-17). Fleming observed that the mold *Penicillium notatum* killed his cultures of the bacterium *Staphylococcus aureus* when the fungus accidentally contaminated some culture dishes. It is likely that the fungal contaminant of Fleming's cultures, which was to bring medical practice into the modern era of drug therapy, blew into his laboratory from the floor below where an Irish mycologist was working with strains of *Penicillium.* Such a serendipitous event can change history, but in science it takes a special individual like Fleming to recognize the significance of the observation. As Pasteur said, "Chance favors the prepared mind." After growing the fungus in a liquid medium and separating the fluid from the cells, Fleming discovered that the cell-free liquid was an inhibitor of many bacterial species. His publication on the active ingredient, which he called penicillin, was the first report of the production of an **antibiotic,**

FIG. 1-17 Sir Alexander Fleming (1881-1955) discovered the antibiotic penicillin. He had the insight to recognize the significance of the inhibition of bacterial growth in the vicinity of a fungal contaminant when most other scientists probably would have simply discarded the contaminated plates.

that is, a substance produced by microorganisms that inhibits or kills other microorganisms.

Fleming did not isolate pure penicillin, nor did he demonstrate its chemotherapeutic effects. Ten years after Fleming's initial report, Howard Florey and Ernst Chain successfully isolated and purified penicillin. Other scientists established the therapeutic value of penicillin, and just after World War II penicillin was introduced widely into medical practice. It soon was saving lives from pneumonia and other diseases. Penicillin remains a cornerstone of the modern medical treatment of many infectious diseases.

In the early 1940s a Russian immigrant soil microbiologist, **Selman Waksman,** and his co-workers at Rutgers University in New Jersey expanded the range of antibiotic substances and the range of microorganisms that produce them. They found that various bacteria of the actinomycetes group produced antibacterial agents. Streptomycin, produced by *Streptomyces griseus,* became the best known of the new antibiotic wonder drugs. The antibiotics produced by actinomycetes generally have a broader spectrum of action than penicillin and thus can be used for treating numerous diseases against which penicillin is ineffective. Most antibiotics in current use are produced by actinomycetes. The importance of penicillin and the subsequently discovered antibiotics in treating diseases of microbial origin cannot be overestimated. The use of antibiotics to control microbial growth is discussed in Chapter 10. The search for new drugs from microorganisms continues today.

Establishing the Immune Response

In addition to examining microorganisms themselves, microbiologists also examine how the human body mounts a defense against disease-causing microorganisms. The defenses of the human body against infection are known collectively as the **immune response**. Microbiologists have had a long-standing interest in the body's immune response and the field of immunology developed as a branch of microbiology. Today, immunologists are unraveling the molecular basis for the immune response. Their studies have led to the development of various immunological treatments for disease, including gene therapy to alter the body's genetic basis for mounting an immune response and the development of new vaccines for disease prevention.

Although countless microorganisms inhabit the body (some on which we depend to synthesize certain nutrients), most do not cause infection or disease because they are held in check by the body's defense system. When the immune defense system fails, as in the case of acquired immunodeficiency syndrome (AIDS), the human body is unable to defend against microorganisms that normally do not cause disease.

Development of Immunization

Immunization (also known as **vaccination**) is used for preventing infectious diseases. Immunization is an artificial means of stimulating the natural immune defense system of the body. The modern use of immunization is discussed in Chapter 12. The early development of immunization was based on the observation that individuals who survived smallpox were immune to that disease, that is, they were protected from that disease even if they were exposed to individuals with smallpox. Chinese healers in the tenth century sought to artificially transfer this immunity to others to protect them against smallpox. By the sixteenth century the Chinese had perfected *variolation,* a procedure in which scabs were collected from selected children with smallpox; the scabs, which contained the unseen smallpox viruses, were stored for a period of time (a process that reduced the disease-causing capacity of the viruses) and pulverized dried scabs were then blown into the nostrils of susceptible individuals.

This practice of variolation to protect against smallpox was first introduced in England in 1718 by Lady Mary Montagu, whose husband had been the British Ambassador to Turkey. Lady Mary used her considerable influence at the court of King George I to gain publicity for the increased use of immunization. She even arranged for testing of her idea, although she had no scientific explanation or proof of how or why it worked. Immunization was first tested on prisoners and orphans, then a common practice. Despite these efforts, variolation was not accepted by the scientists and physicians of the time as a useful practice for preventing disease. One reason was that the results were variable. In some cases it failed to protect against smallpox and in other cases it actually was responsible for the transmission of the disease.

The use of immunization against smallpox was aided by the work of **Edward Jenner,** a middle-class English country doctor, whose interest in science, like that of Leeuwenhoek, was scholarly but amateur—based on careful, methodical observation but lacking a controlled experimental scientific approach. He observed that individuals who tended cows with cowpox, a disease of cattle caused by a similar virus, rarely contracted smallpox. He recognized that exposure to the infective material of cowpox lesions could artificially stimulate the body's defenses against the related disease, smallpox. Jenner used inductive reasoning to initiate a vaccination program against smallpox that has led to the elimination of this once dreaded disease. Inductive reasoning develops general principles based on the observation of specific cases. It was through the observation of individuals who did not contract smallpox that Jenner developed the principle that exposure to a specific disease agent through vaccination will make an individual immune, that is nonsusceptible, to a specific disease. Jenner's 1798 report to the Royal Society in London on the value of vaccination with cowpox as a means of protecting against smallpox established the basis for the immunological prevention of disease (FIG. 1-18). His lack of a scientific understanding of vaccination and the fact that variable results occurred with Jenner's cowpox vaccine, however, still left questions about the effectiveness of vaccination for preventing disease. Immunization in the eighteenth century was still not based on controlled scientific experimentation.

Much work was needed beyond Jenner's 1798 report to make the use of vaccines widespread for preventing diseases. It was essential that a scientific approach be taken to create the convincing evidence for the principle that immunity could be achieved using vaccines before widespread support for vaccination was gained in official scientific and bureaucratic governmental offices. Controlled experiments were needed with objective observations. This necessary transformation of vaccination and immunology to scientific disciplines was accomplished in large part by Louis Pasteur and colleagues.

Pasteur significantly furthered the development of vaccines when in 1880 he reported that attenuated microorganisms, that is, microorganisms modified to reduce their ability to cause disease, could be used to develop effective vaccines against chicken cholera. The production of attenuated vaccines that were effective against fowl cholera depended on prolonging the time between transfers of the cultures grown in the laboratory to fresh growth media, a fact accidentally discovered through an error by Charles Chamberland, who used an old culture during one of the experiments he was conducting with Pasteur. Following his work on chicken cholera, Pasteur directed his attention to the study of anthrax, which culminated in a very dramatic public demonstration to test the effectiveness of his anthrax vaccine. Witnesses to the demonstration were amazed to see that the 24 sheep, 1 goat, and 6 cows that had received the attenuated vaccine were in good health, but that all the animals that had not been vaccinated were dead of anthrax.

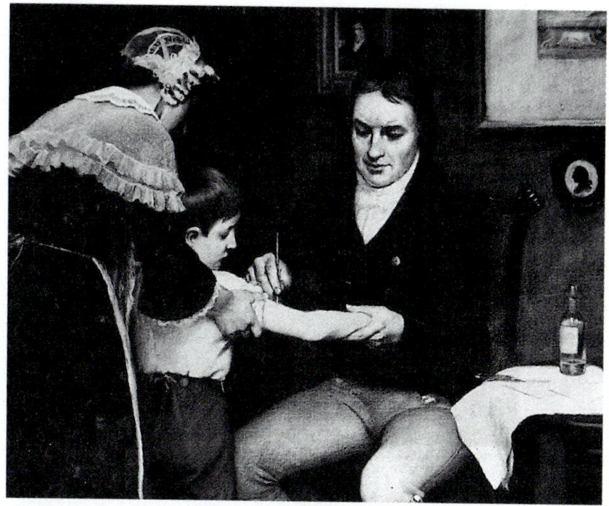

FIG. 1-18 Edward Jenner (1749-1823) vaccinated James Phipps (in about 1800) with cowpox material, resulting in the development of resistance to smallpox infection by the boy and thereby establishing the scientific credibility of vaccination to prevent disease.

Pasteur's greatest success in developing vaccines occurred in 1885 when he announced to the French Academy of Sciences that he had developed a vaccine for preventing rabies. Although he did not understand the nature of the causative organism, Pasteur developed a vaccine that worked. Pasteur's motto was "seek the microbe," but the microorganism responsible for rabies is a virus, which could not be seen under the microscopes of the 1880s. He nevertheless was able to weaken the rabies virus by drying the spinal cords of infected rabbits and allowing oxygen to penetrate the cords. The treatment of the spinal cords altered the rabies virus, eliminating its ability to cause the infection that would lead to disease, but did not eliminate the ability to induce immunity by exposure to the treated viruses. Thirteen inoculations of successively more virulent pieces of rabbit spinal cord

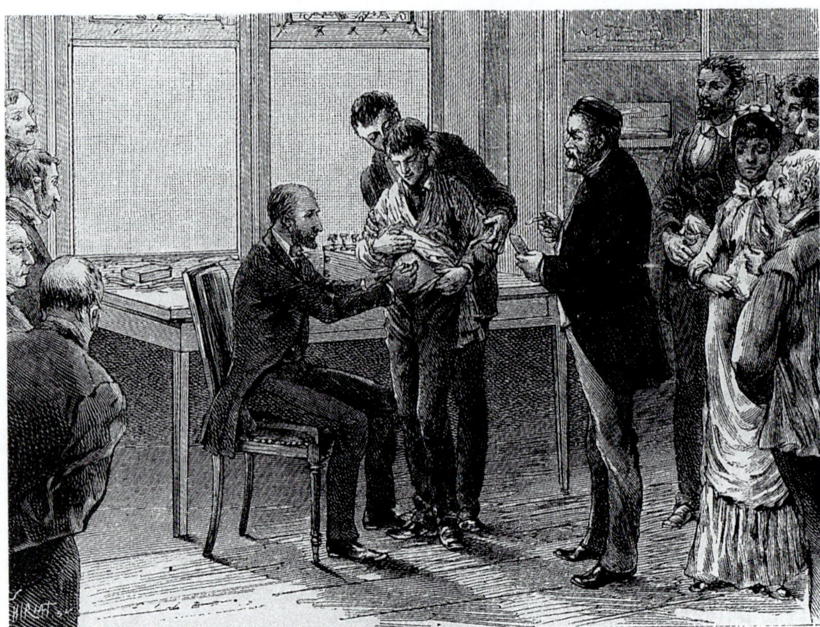

FIG. 1-19 In 1885 Pasteur announced to the French Academy of Sciences that he had developed a vaccine for preventing another dread disease, rabies. Although he did not understand the nature of the causative organism, Pasteur had developed a vaccine that worked. Pasteur's motto was "Seek the microbe," but the microorganism responsible for rabies is a virus, which could not be seen under the microscopes of the 1880s. Pasteur, nevertheless, was able to weaken the rabies virus by drying the spinal cords of infected rabbits and allowing oxygen to penetrate the cords. Thirteen inoculations of successively more virulent pieces of rabbit spinal cord were injected over a period of 2 weeks during the summer of 1885 into Joseph Meister, a 9-year-old boy who had been bitten by a rabid dog. "Since the death of the child was almost certain, I decided in spite of my deep concern to try on Joseph Meister the method which had served me so well with dogs. . . . I decided to give a total of 13 inoculations in ten days. Fewer inoculations would have been sufficient, but one will understand that I was extremely cautious in this first case. Joseph Meister escaped not only the rabies that he might have received from his bites, but also the rabies which I inoculated into him." With the successful development of a vaccine for preventing rabies, crowds flocked to Pasteur's laboratory. The development of the rabies vaccine crowned Pasteur's distinguished career.

were injected over a period of 2 weeks during the summer of 1885 into Joseph Meister, a 9-year-old boy who had been bitten by a rabid dog (FIG. 1-19). This vaccination prevented rabies. Without it Joseph Meister would have developed the disease and died. This treatment met with a highly publicized, personal success for Pasteur. The development of the rabies vaccine was the culmination of Pasteur's distinguished career. Donations sent to Pasteur as a consequence of his discoveries were used to erect l'Institute Pasteur in Paris, the first aim of which was to provide the proper facilities for the production of vaccines.

Developing an Understanding of the Immune Response

The development of vaccines demonstrated that the immune response could prevent infections but did not elucidate the mechanisms of immunity, that is, the underlying basis of the immune response. **Eli Metchnikoff** sought to establish the principle that the activity of phagocytes, white blood cells that engulf foreign particles, was responsible for the protection of animals against infectious diseases and for the development of acquired immunity. He was the first to describe the phenomenon of **phagocytosis** (1884). A Russian, Metchnikoff meticulously reported his microscopic observations of how a microbe intruding into an organism is dealt with by that organism; he began by watching starfish larvae stuck with thorns and then the transparent water flea *Daphnia* diseased with a microbial infection. Metchnikoff saw mobile cells, which he called phagocytes, migrate to the area of infection and destroy the infecting microbes by digesting them. This pioneering work established the role of cellular components of the blood in destroying disease-causing microorganisms and was the basis for the field of cellular immunology.

Koch and his disciples also made significant contributions to the field of immunology and our understanding of the complexities of the immune response. Workers in Koch's laboratory were dominated by Koch's strong personality. Koch's desire for secrecy fostered competitiveness and limited cooperation between the scientists working in his laboratory. Koch's assistants, Emil von Behring and Shihasaburo Kitasato, however, jointly discovered that substances in blood sera could neutralize foreign materials. They found that **antitoxin**, a substance from the serum of infected animals, could neutralize the effects of some bacterial toxins and could be used to cure some diseases. Their studies on diphtheria and tetanus established the existence of **antibodies,** which are substances made by the body that defend against foreign substances. Kitasato and von Behring published a joint paper on their results for tetanus, but von Behring, having learned Koch's zealotry for individual recognition, only a week later published his experiments on diphtheria toxin, which he had kept secret from Kitasato. Von Behring engineered an agreement with a dye works company and the Ministry of Culture to commercially produce diphtheria antitoxin and was able to obtain the rights to its effective production. Thus he was one of the few scientists of his time to gain substantial financial rewards for his discoveries.

Another student in Koch's laboratory, Paul Ehrlich, also worked on developing an understanding of the immune response. In 1891 he published a paper in which he differentiated *active immunity*, which occurs when one's own body develops antibodies as a result of a prior interaction with pathogens or their products, from *passive immunity*, which occurs when one receives antibodies from another person (or animal). The development of active immunity provides long-term protection against disease, whereas passive immunity, such as that transferred from mother to fetus, provides only temporary *prophylaxis* (protection) against infectious microorganisms.

Koch was not to be outdone by his assistants. Although his research was far from complete, the popular media of the day interpreted Koch's talk before the Tenth International Medical Congress in 1890 as stating that he had found a method for developing resistance against tuberculosis. Koch had been under extreme pressure from the German government to demonstrate Germanic intellectual supremacy by producing a breakthrough in tuberculosis research prior to the Medical Congress that was held in Berlin. In this case, Koch's lifelong habit of secrecy to ensure his own priority of discovery prevented a thorough, impartial examination of the treatment; yet so powerful was the force of his reputation that even scientists of international renown did not challenge the lack of specific detail in the presentation and allowed the premature and indiscriminate use of his tuberculin vaccine on patients. Koch originally tested his tuberculin vaccine on guinea pigs, but humans proved to be far more sensitive to the vaccine, incurring serious side effects within hours of vaccination. The indiscriminate use of tuberculin by physicians and the fatalities caused by the vaccine turned the tide of public opinion against Koch. When data, accumulated on 2,000 cases, showed tuberculin to be ineffective, its use as a therapeutic agent was abandoned. The development of tuberculin for preventing tuberculosis represents one of Koch's few failures. It also demonstrates the necessity of open communication and independent verification in scientific studies.

The work in Koch's laboratory, with the discoveries of Metchnikoff, established the foundations for understanding the basis for the humoral immune response, which is antibody-mediated, and the cellular immune response, which involves cell components. These two mechanisms of the immune response system represent major defenses of higher vertebrate animals against infectious agents.

Significant advances in our basic understanding of the defense mechanisms of animals against microbial infection are still being made in the late twentieth century. In the late 1950s Alick Issacs found that cells infected by a virus produce a substance called *interferon* that inhibits viral replication. The discovery of interferon was a significant advance in determining how animals recover from viral diseases. The potential use of interferon for treating viral and other diseases of humans, including cancer, is being actively investigated and may prove to be a breakthrough, comparable to the discovery of penicillin, in treating these diseases. So far, however, the potential benefits of interferon as a therapeutic agent have not been realized.

ESTABLISHING THE ROLES OF MICROORGANISMS IN NATURE

Besides their importance in human health, microorganisms play critical roles in nature and in maintaining ecological balance. Microbial ecology examines the interactions of microorganisms with their biotic and abiotic surroundings. The field of microbial ecology is relevant today, since the metabolic activities of microorganisms are essential for maintaining life on Earth and for the destruction of numerous pollutants. Understanding the essential roles of microorganisms in environmental processes began in the late nineteenth century with the independent studies of **Sergei Winogradsky,** a Russian who worked mainly in France and Switzerland, and **Martinus Beijerinck** in the Netherlands. Their studies linked microbial physiology (the activities of microorganisms, including their metabolism) and microbial ecology (the interrelationships of microorganisms with their surrounding environment).

Whereas Pasteur concentrated on the microbial use of organic compounds, Winogradsky and Beijerinck made significant discoveries concerning microbial transformations of inorganic compounds. The works of Beijerinck and Winogradsky were primarily concerned with soil processes, but the microbial transformations that they discovered formed the basis for understanding biogeochemical cycling reactions and the critical role of microorganisms in transforming elements on a global scale. These microbially mediated cycling reactions are essential for maintaining environmental quality and are necessary for supporting life on Earth as we know it.

Winogradsky isolated and described the *nitrifying bacteria,* which are bacteria that convert ammonium ions (NH_4^+) to nitrite ions (NO_2^-) and nitrite ions to nitrate ions (NO_3^-). He showed that the nitrifying bacteria are responsible for transforming ammonium ions to nitrate ions in soil, an important process because the change from the positively charged ammonium ion to the negatively charged nitrate ion leads to leaching of nitrate from soil and its loss as a nutrient for plants. He demonstrated that microorganisms can derive energy from inorganic chemical oxidation reactions such as these, while obtaining their carbon from carbon dioxide. Winogradsky also described the microbial oxidation of sulfur, hydrogen sulfide, and ferrous iron and anaerobic nitrogen-fixing bacteria.

Beijerinck reported on symbiotic and nonsymbiotic aerobic *nitrogen fixation* by bacteria, the process by which atmospheric nitrogen is combined with other elements to make this essential nutrient available to plants, animals, and other microorganisms. Beijerinck also isolated *sulfate-reducing* bacteria, which are important in the cycling of sulfur compounds in soil and sediment. All of these reactions form the basis of important transformations and movements of elements in soil ecosystems and determine the fertility of soil. Another particularly significant advance made by Beijerinck was the development of the technique of enrichment culture, which permits the isolation of a bacterium with a particular metabolic activity by adjusting incubation conditions.

During the early twentieth century, major advances were made in the understanding of biochemistry and microbial metabolism. Albert Kluyver followed Beijerinck, both as director of the Delft school and in the biochemical direction of his study, continuing the great tradition in the small town of Delft of microbiological study that had begun with Leeuwenhoek 300 years earlier. Kluyver examined the unity and diversity in metabolism of microorganisms, emphasizing the unifying features of microbial metabolism, correctly recognizing the nature of intermediary metabolism, and establishing that hydrogen transfer (oxidation-reduction reactions) is a basic feature of all metabolic processes. The flow of carbon and energy through a series of metabolic transformations is an essential feature of living microorganisms. Kluyver was instrumental in developing an understanding of the role of central metabolic pathways in microbial metabolism. C. B. van Niel, a student of Kluyver, continued the tradition of advancing microbial physiology. He made important contributions to our understanding of photosynthesis, recognizing the similar roles of H_2S and H_2O in the photosynthetic processes of anaerobic photosynthetic sulfur bacteria and in higher plants.

Important later discoveries, which emphasized the unity of intermediary metabolism, include (1) the elucidation of the citric acid cycle, for which Sir Hans Krebs received a Nobel prize in 1953, and (2) the elucidation of the chemical steps in carbon dioxide fixation during photosynthesis, for which Melvin Calvin received a Nobel prize in 1961. In 1978 a Nobel prize was awarded to Peter Mitchell for the development of chemiosmotic theory to explain how the biochemical reactions occurring at membranes generate energy in the form of ATP. Although these Nobel prizes were awarded in chemistry, they represent fundamental advances in our understanding of microbial metabolism.

ESTABLISHING THE BASIS OF HEREDITY

Our understanding of microbial genetics did not begin until the middle of the twentieth century. In 1941 **George Beadle** and **Edward Tatum** published studies on the genetic control of biochemical reactions in the fungus *Neurospora* (FIG. 1-20). The experiments of Beadle and Tatum established that specific segments of the DNA, called *genes,* encoded the information for making specific proteins. Their studies supported the *one gene–one enzyme hypothesis.* Beadle and Tatum introduced changes (mutations) in the DNA by exposing spores of *Neurospora* to X-rays. They then identified mutants that had undergone such changes in their DNA based on metabolic changes that they could observe. By adding known nutrients to the medium on which the strains of *Neurospora* were grown, they were able to identify specific points of blockage in the metabolism of the cells. For each enzyme in the biosynthetic pathway of an amino acid or vitamin, Beadle and Tatum were able to isolate mutant strains that produced a nonfunctional form of an enzyme in that pathway. They could pinpoint the location within the chromosomes of *Neurospora* where the mutation had occurred, finding, for example, that mutants that required additional amino acids or vitamins for growth had changes in the same region of the chromosome. Each mutant strain they observed had a mutation at one, and only one, site coding for a specific enzyme. They concluded that each gene encodes the information for a single enzyme with each gene of the DNA coding for the protein structure of that enzyme. Other researchers extended the findings of Beadle and Tatum to bacteria. Strains of *Escherichia coli* called *arg* mutants, for example, could not grow on a

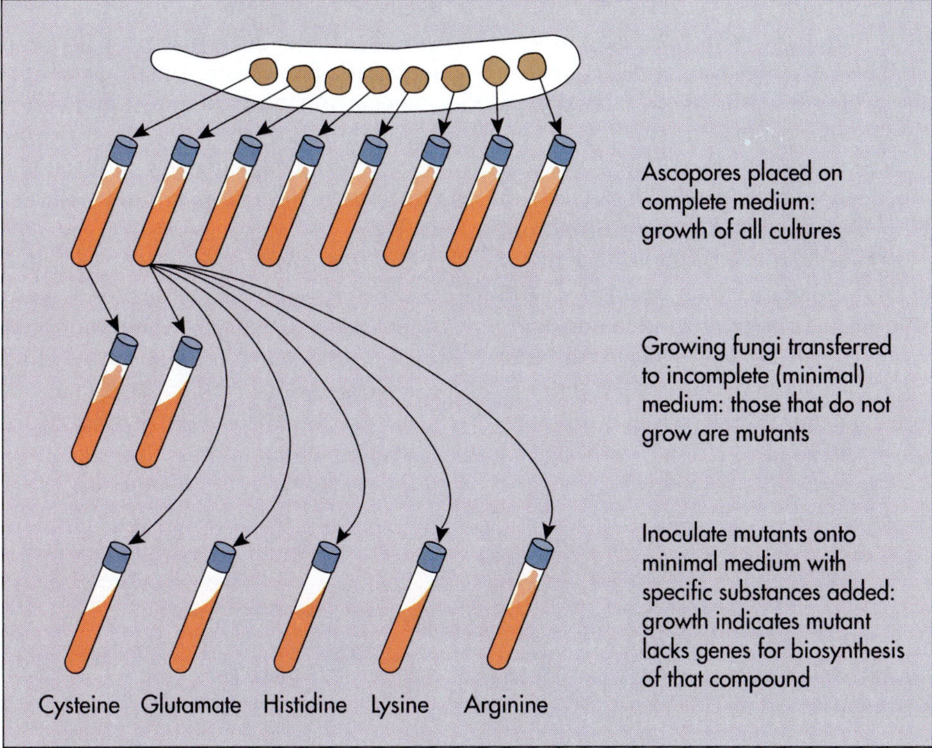
Ascopores placed on complete medium: growth of all cultures
Growing fungi transferred to incomplete (minimal) medium: those that do not grow are mutants
Inoculate mutants onto minimal medium with specific substances added: growth indicates mutant lacks genes for biosynthesis of that compound
Cysteine
Glutamate
Histidine
Lysine
Arginine

FIG. 1-20 The one gene–one enzyme hypothesis was experimentally demonstrated by Beadle and Tatum. They studied the fungus *Neurospora,* which forms spores that have single sets of genes. They were able to collect individual spores and to culture them so that they could observe any changes in the genes of the fungus that altered its nutritional requirements. Mutants that were unable to carry out complete biosynthetic pathways could grow on complete media but not on minimal media. The minimal media lacked the nutrients required for growth that the mutants could no longer synthesize. Growth on minimal media with specific compounds added, such as vitamins and amino acids, enabled them to determine which compounds the mutant fungi could not synthesize. In this manner they were able to identify the genetic changes that occurred and to associate specific genes with specific metabolic activities.

medium lacking arginine because these strains had a mutation in the gene that codes for an enzyme needed to synthesize arginine. Adding arginine to the medium enabled strains of *arg* mutants to grow.

Tatum also showed in 1945 that exposure to X-rays increased the mutation rate in the bacterium *Escherichia coli.* Other researchers, including Joshua Lederberg, showed that the same principles of heredity and genetic control of protein synthesis applied to bacteria. In 1958 George Beadle, Edward Tatum, and Joshua Lederberg shared a Nobel prize for their studies on microbial genetics. Their pioneering experiments led to the flourishing of work aimed at using genetic recombination processes to map the genomes of microorganisms.

Of course, much of the development of microbial genetics hinged on elucidation of the mechanism by which cells direct their synthesis of protein and transmit hereditary information. Science's unraveling of the mystery of DNA is a fascinating tale and perhaps one of the greatest intellectual achievements of this century.

Proving that DNA is the Hereditary Molecule

The discovery that DNA is the hereditary substance was made in the 1940s as a result of work explaining the nature of the substance that could transform some nondisease-causing strains of the bacterium *Streptococcus pneumoniae* into ones that caused pneumonia. In the late 1920s a British scientist, Fred Griffith, observed that disease-causing strains of *S. pneumoniae* produce a polysaccharide capsule and that avirulent (nondisease causing) strains do not. Mice infected with even minimal doses of the capsulated strains died a few days after exposure to the bacteria, whereas injection of even massive doses of the nonencapsulated strains did not cause death. Griffith injected mixtures of heat-killed capsule-producing strains and live nonencapsulated strains into mice; surprisingly, the mice died, and Griffith isolated live encapsulated strains from their corpses (FIG. 1-21). The nonencapsulated strains had been *transformed* into a new encapsulated, pathogenic strain.

Oswald Avery, Colin M. McCarty, and **Maclyn MacLeod** provided the molecular explanation for this event in 1941 by separating the classes of molecules in the debris of the dead capsule-producing cells and testing each one for its ability to cause transformation. First, they showed that it was not the polysaccharides in the capsules themselves that transformed the nondisease-causing strains into pathogenic ones. They found that only one class of molecules, DNA, induces transformation. Avery, McCarty, and MacLeod deduced that DNA is the agent that determines the polysaccharide character and hence the pathogenic characteristic, and that providing noncapsule-producing cells with DNA from capsule-producing ones was the same as providing them with the genes, that is, the genetic-hereditary information, for producing capsules. The unavoidable conclusion of this classic work is that the genetic information of the cell is contained within its DNA.

In 1944, Avery, MacLeod, and McCarty published their studies on the nature of the substance that induces transformation of pneumococcal types and concluded that a nucleic acid of the deoxyribose type is the fundamental unit of the transforming principle of *Streptococcus pneumoniae.* Their conclusion was not

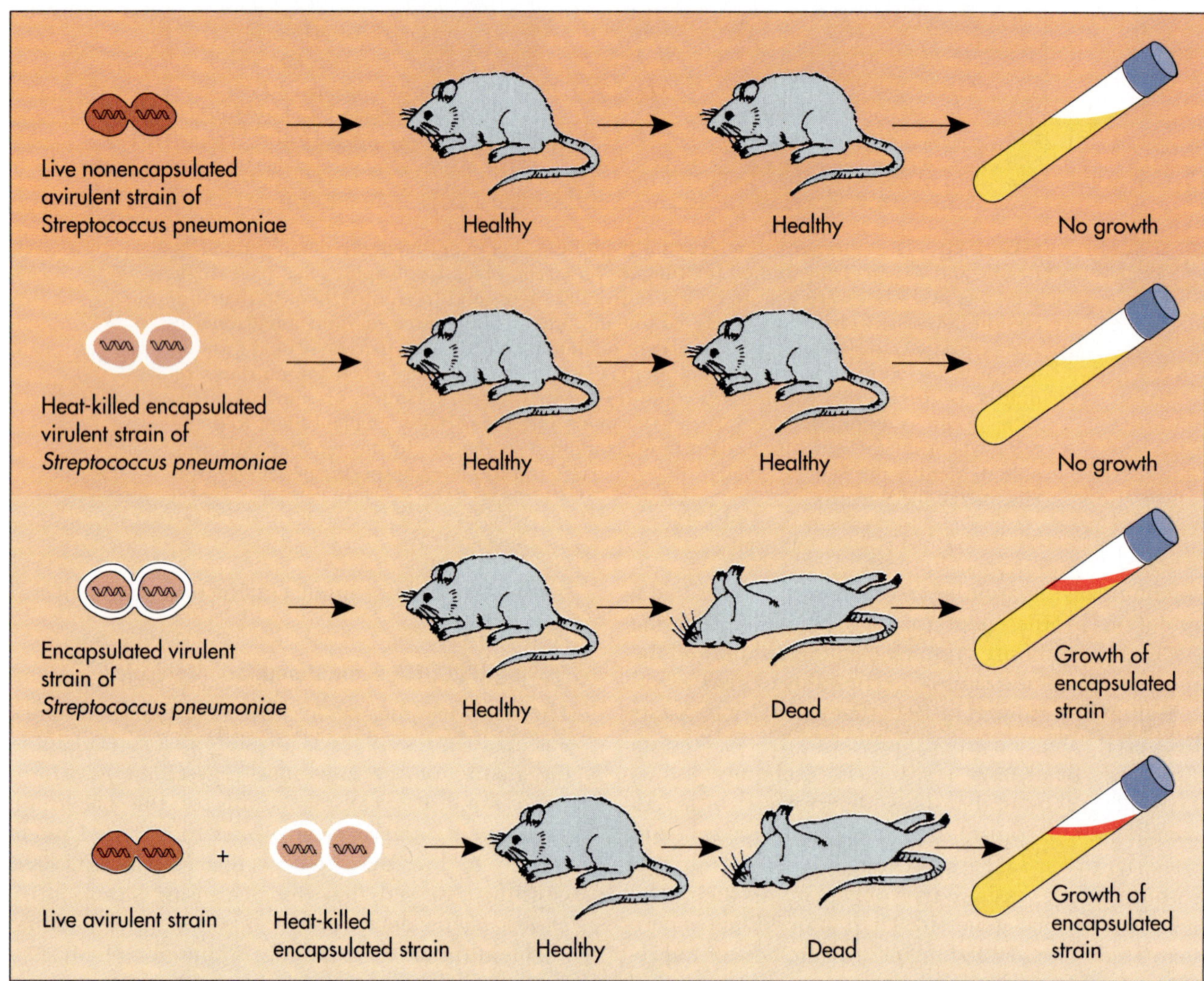

FIG. 1-21 The transformation of *Streptococcus pneumoniae* shows how the properties of a bacterial strain can be altered by a hereditary substance that was later identified as DNA. When cells of *S. pneumoniae* are heat killed they leak DNA, which can be picked up by other cells and incorporated into the genetic information of those cells. In this manner, avirulent (nonpathogenic) strains of *S. pneumoniae* that lack the gene for capsule production (virulence factor that contributes to their ability to cause fatal disease) can acquire the gene (DNA) that encodes for capsule production. When this occurs, an avirulent noncapsule-producing strain of *S. pneumoniae* is transformed into a virulent strain that produces a capsule.

widely accepted at the time and the majority of workers continued to believe that the most likely molecular identity of the genetic material was protein.

Over the next decade, other scientists added evidence that DNA is the heredity substance responsible for the genetics of all living organisms. Joshua Lederberg and co-workers, between 1946 and 1956, studied genetic exchange processes in bacteria and made the first reports on *conjugation,* in which DNA is transferred by direct contact from one bacterial cell to another, and *transduction,* in which DNA is transferred from one bacterial cell to another via a viral carrier. These studies showed that several natural processes can transmit hereditary information via DNA.

Demonstrating the Structure of DNA

A major breakthrough in our understanding of the molecular basis of heredity occurred in 1953 when **James Watson** and **Francis Crick** proposed the double-helical structure of DNA (FIG. 1-22). This particular scientific breakthrough was not accomplished through the research we often think of as involving test tubes and Petri plates, guinea pigs, and bubbling chemical retorts, but rather was the product of a great deal of thought, discussion, examination of evidence already available, and intuition, as exemplified by the decision to build two-chain models simply because of the "repeated finding of twoness in biological systems." Watson and Crick knew that they had to rely on the simple laws of structural chemistry. "The essential trick was to ask which atoms like to sit next to each other." Although they did not perform controlled experiments, they used the if/then logic of the scientific method. They would pose hypotheses and see whether existing experimental data supported or refuted the hypotheses. For example, they hypothesized that DNA was a helical molecule and used DNA X-ray diffraction patterns generated by Rosalind Franklin to test the correctness of that hypothesis. The X-ray patterns were consistent with the hypothesis that DNA is a double helical molecule, that is, a molecule with the shape of a spiral staircase.

Watson and Crick built models to test their hypotheses; their main working tools were a set of molecular models superficially resembling the toys of preschool children. After getting the structural forms of guanine and thymine serendipitously corrected by a visiting scientist, who pointed out that the structures in the organic chemistry books were wrong, Watson and Crick began shifting the bases in and out of various pairing possibilities. In the next step, their tools were a plumb line and a measuring stick to determine the relative positions of all the atoms in a single nucleotide. By assuming a helical symmetry, it became clear that the locations of the atoms in one nucleotide would automatically generate the other position.

The revelation of the structure of DNA truly opened the field of molecular genetics for major new

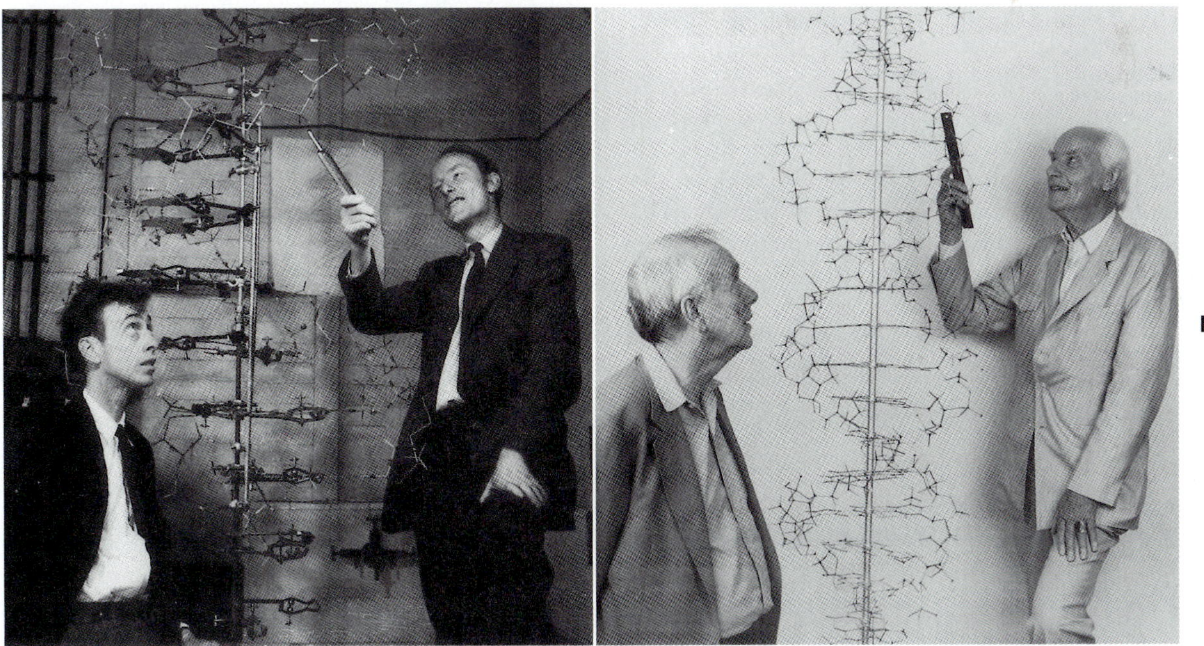

FIG. 1-22 **A,** James Watson at age 23 and Francis Crick at age 34 developed a model for the structure of DNA while working at the Cavendish Laboratory at Cambridge University, England. The model explained how DNA can transmit hereditary information. They announced their discovery of the molecular structure of DNA in 1953 and shared the Nobel prize for Medicine in 1962 with Maurice Wilkins. **B,** In 1993, on the fortieth anniversary of their discovery, they again posed with their model of DNA, which has proven to be correct.

investigations. The establishment of the structure of the molecule housing the genetic information of living organisms permitted the unraveling of the ways in which genetic information is stored and expressed.

Determining How DNA Controls Cellular Metabolism

With the establishment of the structural and biochemical nature of the genetic material of the cell, the time was right for a unification of concepts in microbial genetics and biochemical metabolism. Crick and co-workers correctly proposed that a sequence of three nucleic acid bases in a DNA strand code for one amino acid. Several research groups determined which triplet base sequences specify which amino acids. The genetic code was broken and verified by synthesizing specific sequences of DNA bases and determining which amino acids resulted. These genetic studies during the early 1960s established the basis for understanding how genetic information is stored in the DNA molecule and how that information is transcribed and translated into proteins that act as enzymes in determining the metabolic activities of microorganisms. This is discussed in further detail in Chapter 6.

DNA stores hereditary information for the production of specific proteins and the mechanisms for controlling the expression of specific genes. In 1960 Francois Jacob and Jacques Monod proposed the **operon theory**, which explains how the genetic information controls protein synthesis, that is, the nature of the control regions of the DNA molecule that act as switches, turning on and off the synthesis of enzymes.

Developing Recombinant DNA Technology

By the early 1970s the genetics of bacteria was sufficiently understood to perform experiments that could create new organisms. Methods were developed that could recombine genes from diverse sources (FIG. 1-23). These methods relied on the development of enzymes, called restriction endonucleases, derived from bacteria that cut DNA at specific sites and other enzymes, called ligases, that splice fragments of DNA together. These enzymes can be used to study genetic organization (genetic mapping) and to manipulate DNA for genetic engineering. This led to recombinant DNA methodology to clone genes, opening up an entirely new area of applied microbiology and spurring the formation of many genetic engineering companies. This topic is discussed in Chapter 7. Genes from bacteria have been placed into human cells; those from humans similarly have been transferred to bacteria. Genetic engineering, using recombinant DNA technology, holds the promise of solving many important problems, including the ability to produce drugs for treating currently incurable diseases, to produce sufficient food to feed the world's population, and to solve problems of environmental pollution.

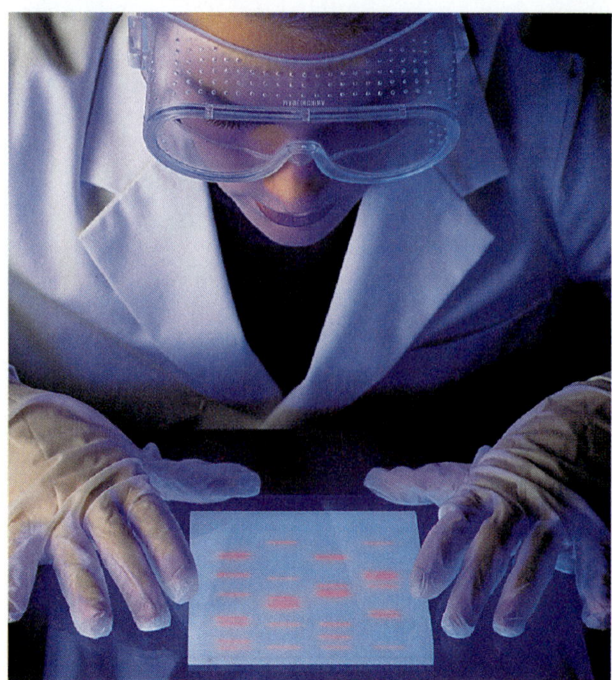

FIG. 1-23 Molecular biologists are able to isolate genes from one organism and recombine them with genes from another organism. Human genes can be transferred to bacteria, bacterial genes to human cells, and so forth. Here a molecular biologist has used electrophoresis to isolate individual fragments of DNA that can be recombined to create new genetic combinations.

CHAPTER REVIEW

Study Questions

1. What is a microorganism?
2. What organisms do we consider as microorganisms?
3. What is the scientific method?
4. How can the scientific method be applied to discovering a treatment for AIDS?
5. Why were Leeuwenhoek's observations the critical first step in the development of microbiology?
6. What was the theory of spontaneous generation?
7. How was spontaneous generation disproved and what is the significance of having disproved this theory?
8. What are Koch's postulates? What is their significance to medical microbiology?
9. Discuss a recent use of Koch's postulates to determine the cause of a disease outbreak.

CHAPTER REVIEW

STUDY QUESTIONS—CONT'D

10. What major contributions to microbiology were made by:
    a. Louis Pasteur
    b. Robert Koch
    c. Joseph Lister
    d. Edward Jenner
    e. Sergei Winogradsky
    f. Martinus Beijerinck
    g. Paul Ehrlich
    h. James Watson and Francis Crick
    i. George Beadle and Edward Tatum
    j. Oswald Avery, Maclyn MacLeod, and Colin M. McCarty
    k. Alexander Fleming
    l. Selman Waksman

SITUATIONAL PROBLEMS

1. Searching the Literature

Progress in science occurs through a step-by-step progression, building on knowledge previously attained. Students of microbiology and professional microbiologists spend many hours in library research and reading journals. Through these readings, they learn of methodological advances that can be applied to their own research and learn how their own activities mesh with those of others. The specialized journals in one's own field usually are read on a regular basis. Others are examined only during a search of the literature for specific information. The journal *Current Contents* often is used to review titles of recent articles that may be of interest. It is one of several guides to the literature.

All scientists must be able to retrieve information from the published literature. Such information gathering often is tedious. Data may be retrieved manually or with computer assistance. Only data in the accessible or open literature can be obtained. Proprietary secret data are increasingly common in this age of biotechnology and access is restricted to a very few scientists.

Biological Abstracts is the main vehicle of literature searching for microbiologists and most others involved in the biological sciences. Abstracts are published every 2 weeks and are cumulated twice a year. When manual searches are carried out, each biweekly or semiannual volume must be consulted separately. Abstracts come from almost 10,000 serials. They are numbered and arranged by major subject headings such as ecology, immunology, and medical and clinical microbiology. The abstract entry includes a full bibliographic citation of the article and a paragraph summary of the work described. Articles can be searched by author as well as subject. They are also indexed biosystematically by taxonomic category, including the genus and species names. The subject index employs a permuted keyword approach, with keywords arranged alphabetically and with additional keywords that describe the articles listed to the left and right. The reference number, which leads from the index volume to the abstract of the article, is listed at the right.

Because searching the literature is such a fundamental aspect of the work of a microbiologist, you should respond to the following situational problems by going to the library and retrieving the requested information. If you encounter problems, feel free to consult the reference librarian. At many libraries, computers can be used to search the literature.

Begin with the author index of *Biological Abstracts* by looking up the name of a scientist and see what s/he published in the last cumulated year. You may want to choose the author of this textbook, your instructor, or a microbiologist in the news. Next, pick a topic such as a specific disease and search for the articles on that topic. Ask your instructor to suggest some topics for which you could look. For each entry that you find, record the number. Then read some of the abstracts indicated. See if you can find some of the articles listed so that you learn where the journals of microbiological interest are located in your institution's library. This exercise will give you an idea of how science is communicated.

If your library has computer search facilities, you may also be able to ask for a demonstration that will enable you to verify the thoroughness of your search.

2. Designing a Science Fair Project

You have probably been required to do a science fair project many times in elementary and high school. Many of the projects that students do are scientific models or demonstrations of scientific principles. Often they are not true science experiments because they do not employ the scientific method.

Assume that a high school freshman calls and asks you to help design a science fair project concerning the effects of food preservatives on microbial growth. If you examine some packaged foods you will find the preservatives added listed on the labels. You have access to the microbiology laboratory and can grow pure cultures of bacteria and fungi. How would you design the experiment? What hypotheses would you pose? How would you test the hypotheses?

Suggested Supplementary Readings

Ainsworth GC: 1976. *Introduction to the History of Mycology*, Cambridge University Press, London.

Allen GE: 1978. *Life and Science in the Twentieth Century*, Cambridge University Press, London.

Bibel DJ: 1988. *Milestones in Immunology: A Historical Exploration*, Science Tech Publishers, Madison, WI.

Brock TD (ed.): 1975. *Milestones in Microbiology*, American Society for Microbiology, Washington, D.C.

Brock T: 1988. *Robert Koch, a Life in Medicine and Bacteriology*, Science Tech Publishers, Madison, WI.

Bulloch W: 1938. *The History of Bacteriology*, Oxford University Press, London. (1979. Dover Publications, Inc., New York.)

Clark PF: 1961. *Pioneer Microbiologists of America*, University of Wisconsin Press, Madison.

Crick F: 1988. *What Mad Pursuit: A Personal View of Scientific Discovery*, Basic Books, New York.

De Kruif P: 1926. *Microbe Hunters*, Harcourt, Brace and Co., New York. (1966. Harcourt Brace Jovanovich, Inc., New York.)

Dobell C (ed.): 1932. *Antony van Leeuwenhoek and his "Little Animals,"* Constable and Co., Ltd., London. (1960. Dover Publications, Inc., New York.)

Girard M: 1988. The Pasteur Institute's contributions to the field of virology, *Annual Review of Microbiology* 42:745-764.

Hill L: 1985. Biology, philosophy, and scientific method, *Journal of Biological Education* 19:227-231.

Holt JG, MA Bruns, BJ Caldwell, CD Pease (eds): 1992. *Stedman's/Bergey's Bacteria Words*, Williams & Wilkins, Baltimore.

Hooke R: 1665. *Micrographia*. Royal Society, London. (1961. Dover Publications, Inc., New York.)

Latour B: 1988. *The Pasteurization of France*, Harvard University Press, Cambridge, MA.

Lechevalier HA and M Solotorovsky: 1965. *Three Centuries of Microbiology*, McGraw-Hill Book Co., New York. (1974. Dover Publications, Inc., New York.)

Lederberg J (ed.): 1992. *Encyclopedia of Microbiology*, 4 volumes, Academic Press, San Diego.

Postgate J: 1992. *Microbes and Man*, Cambridge University Press, Cambridge, England.

Racker E: 1980. From Pasteur to Mitchell: A hundred years of bioenergetics, *Federation Proceedings* 39:210-215.

Reid R: 1975. *Microbes and Men*, Saturday Review Press, New York.

Singleton P and D Sainsbury: 1988. *Dictionary of Microbiology and Molecular Biology*, John Wiley & Sons, New York.

Waksman SA: 1954. *My Life with the Microbes*, Simon & Schuster, NY.

Waterson AP and L Wilkinson: 1978. *An Introduction to the History of Virology*, Cambridge University Press, New York.

Watson JD: 1968. *The Double Helix*, Atheneum Publishers, New York.

Whittaker RH: 1969. New concepts in kingdoms of organisms, *Science* 163:150-160.

Woese CR: 1981. Archaebacteria, *Scientific American* 244(6):98-122.

CHAPTER 2

Methods for Studying Microorganisms

The study of microbiology requires appropriate methods for observing microorganisms. Microscopy and the culture of microorganisms are fundamental methodologies that enable microbiologists to study the structures of microorganisms and to measure their physiological properties, including metabolism, growth, and taxonomy. Improved microscopic, pure culture, molecular, and immunological methods permit new discoveries about microorganisms. Advances in these methodologies allow greater understanding of the fundamental properties of microorganisms and the applied aspects of microbial technologies.

CHAPTER OUTLINE

2.1 MICROSCOPY

Microscopy is the use of a **microscope** (an instrument that magnifies the size of the image of an object) to view objects too small to be visible with the naked eye. Microscopes, of which there are many types (Table 2-1), are the basic tools employed by microbiologists for the observation of microorganisms. With the aid of the microscope, numerous microorganisms can be observed from many sources such as soil and water. Each drop of water we drink, for example, contains hundreds or thousands of harmless bacteria, which remain unseen unless viewed with a microscope.

The size of a microorganism or a microbial structure determines the degree of magnification needed to see it. At magnifications of 1,000×, bacteria and larger microorganisms (fungi, algae, and protozoa) can be viewed. These organisms can be seen with a light microscope used in virtually all microbiology laboratories. Visualization of smaller microorganisms, like viruses, as well as the internal structures of bacterial cells, requires the use of higher magnifications (10,000× to 100,000×) and better resolution (the ability to see smaller details). Such high magnifications can be achieved with electron microscopes that use electrons instead of visible light. Electron microscopes can magnify images up to 1,000,000×.

LIGHT MICROSCOPY

Light microscopy uses visible or ultraviolet light to illuminate an object. The light passes through several glass lenses that alter the path of the light and produce a magnified image of the object. As we will see,

TABLE 2-1 Comparison of Various Types of Microscopes

TYPE OF MICROSCOPE	MAXIMUM USEFUL MAGNIFICATION	RESOLUTION	DESCRIPTION
Bright-field	1,500×	100–200 nm	Extensively used for the visualization of microorganisms; usually necessary to stain specimens for viewing
Dark-field	1,500×	100–200 nm	Used for viewing live microorganisms, particularly those with characteristic morphology; staining not required; specimen appears bright on a dark background
Ultraviolet	2,500×	100 nm	Improved resolution over normal light microscope; largely replaced by electron microscopes
Fluorescence	1,500×	100–200 nm	Uses fluorescent staining; useful in many diagnostic procedures for identifying microorganisms
Phase contrast	1,500×	100–200 nm	Used to examine structures of living microorganisms; does not require staining
Nomarski differential interference	1,500×	100–200 nm	Used to examine structures of microorganisms; produces sharp, multicolored image with three-dimensional appearance
Confocal scanning	1,500×	100–200 nm	Used to examine structures of microorganisms and individual microorganisms within mixtures of various types of microorganism; uses fluorescence staining; produces blur-free image; used to produce three dimensional images
TEM	500,000–1,000,000×	1–2 nm	Used to view ultrastructure of microorganisms, including viruses; much greater resolving power and useful magnification than can be achieved with light microscopy
SEM	10,000–1,000,000×	1–10 nm	Used for showing detailed surface structures of microorganisms; produces a three-dimensional image

the quality of the image and the magnification that can be achieved depend on the properties of visible light and those of the glass lenses of the microscope.

Properties of Light

The physical properties of light and how light interacts with objects is of major importance in light microscopy. Visible light is a narrow range of the spectrum of electromagnetic radiation with wavelengths of approximately 400 to 700 nm that we are able to see (FIG. 2-1). A nanometer (nm) is 10^{-9} meters. The wavelength of visible light corresponds to its color. Blue light, for example, has a wavelength of about 480 nm, whereas red light has a wavelength of about 680 nm. Ultraviolet light has shorter wavelengths of 100 to 400 nm.

When light strikes an object, several things may occur that have a direct bearing on how the object will appear and how effectively the image of that object may be magnified by using a microscope (FIG. 2-2). Light may pass through a substance, a phenomenon known as *transmission.* In other cases light bounces off an object, that is, the light is *reflected.* We see the colors of objects based on the wavelengths of light reflected by the surfaces of objects. Light that passes through a fine opening, called an aperture, is *diffracted,* meaning that the light is broken up into light of differing wavelengths. In microscopy, diffraction that occurs when light passes through the aperture of a microscope lens is a problem that can cause blurring of an image.

The energy of light can be *absorbed* by objects. The energy absorbed from light may be converted to heat energy. Black objects that absorb rather than reflect light will gain heat more rapidly than white objects, which reflect rather than absorb light. In some cases a substance that absorbs light of one wavelength will emit light of a different wavelength, that is, of a lower energy level. This phenomenon is called *fluorescence.* Various dyes used in microscopy are fluorescent and some, for example, will emit blue light in the range of visible wavelengths when illuminated with ultraviolet light.

Light will be bent or *refracted* as it moves through a medium of one density into a medium of another density, such as from air into a glass microscope lens. The degree of bending of the light depends on the

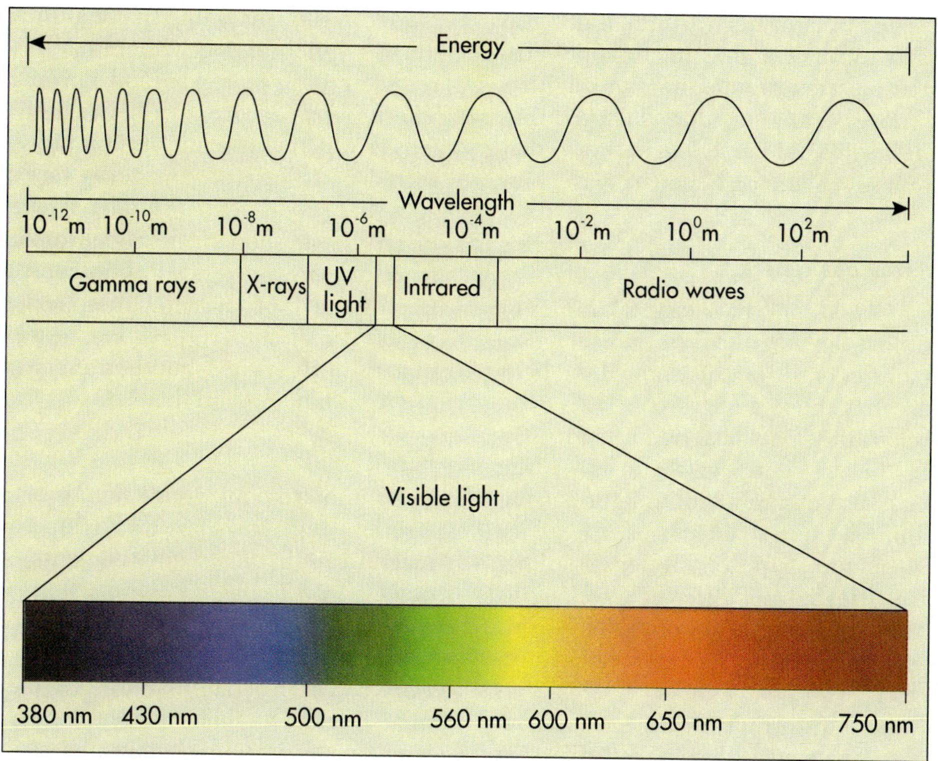

FIG. 2-1 The electromagnetic spectrum is divided into categories of radiation with differing wavelengths and energy levels. The shorter the wavelength, the greater the energy. The wavelength of visible light corresponds to its color: blue light has short wavelength and red light has long wavelength within the visible light spectrum. Visible and ultraviolet light are used in light microscopy.

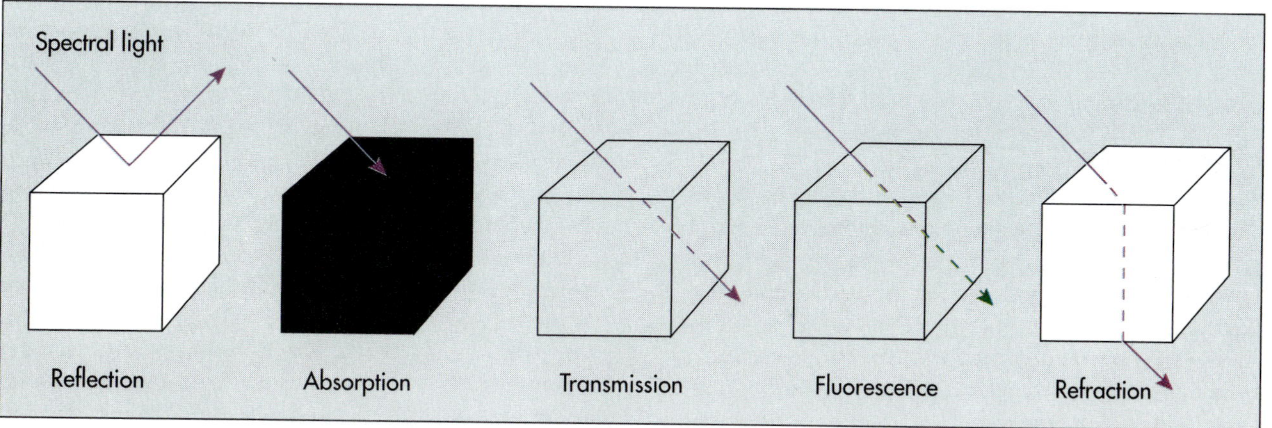

FIG. 2-2 Light interacts with objects it strikes in various ways. Light may be reflected back from the object; the wavelengths of light that are reflected back by an object determine the color that object will be perceived by the eye. When white light (which contains all visible wavelengths) is reflected, the object appears white. Light may be absorbed or taken up by the object. When white light is totally absorbed by an object, the object appears black. Light may be transmitted directly through the object. Light absorbed by an object may be reemitted as longer wavelengths, a phenomenon known as fluorescence. Light passing through an object may also be refracted or bent by it. The refraction of light by glass lenses is important for magnification in microscopy.

relative refractive indices of the media. The *refractive index* is the ratio of the speed of light in a given medium to the speed of light in a vacuum. Light also is bent as it passes through a glass microscope lens. The shape of the lens determines how the light is bent. A convex-convex lens (lens that is curved outward on both sides) will bend parallel light rays so that the light theoretically is focused at a single point called the *focal point.*

Distortions of Microscope Lenses

Lenses used in microscopes have several inherent problems that distort the magnified images they produce. Distorted images occur because not all the light from parallel rays that enters a microscope lens actually focuses at exactly the same focal point. Light passing through the thicker center of a convex-convex lens does not focus at the same point as light passing through the thinner outer edges of the lens. Distortion based on the shape of the lens is called *spherical aberration.* Also, light of differing wavelengths will focus at slightly differing focal points. This leads to distortion based on the color of light, called *chromatic aberration.*

To overcome these distortions, lenses, called *compound lenses,* are constructed with lenses of differing shapes and glass composition (FIG. 2-3). The *achromatic lens* is a compound objective lens used on many microscopes intended for routine observations of microorganisms, including many of those used in introductory microbiology laboratory courses, that corrects for both spherical and chromatic aberrations. The *apochromatic lens* is a better and more expensive lens in which chromatic aberration is more finely corrected and therefore produces very high-quality images that reveal the true colors of a specimen without distorting its shape. The apochromatic lens is excellent for *photomicrography* (photography through the microscope). Modern microscope lenses, called *flat field lenses,* also correct for curvature of field so that objects in the center and periphery of a field of view are simultaneously in focus.

Magnification

In light microscopy, visible light is bent (refracted) by a series of ground glass microscope lenses to achieve **magnification**, that is, enlargement of the image of an object. A *compound light microscope* uses multiple lenses to refract light to achieve magnification (FIG. 2-4). By using two convex-convex lenses, an *ocular lens* and an *objective lens,* in combination, the image of the specimen formed is much larger than the object itself. Such magnification permits the structure(s) of the specimen to be seen.

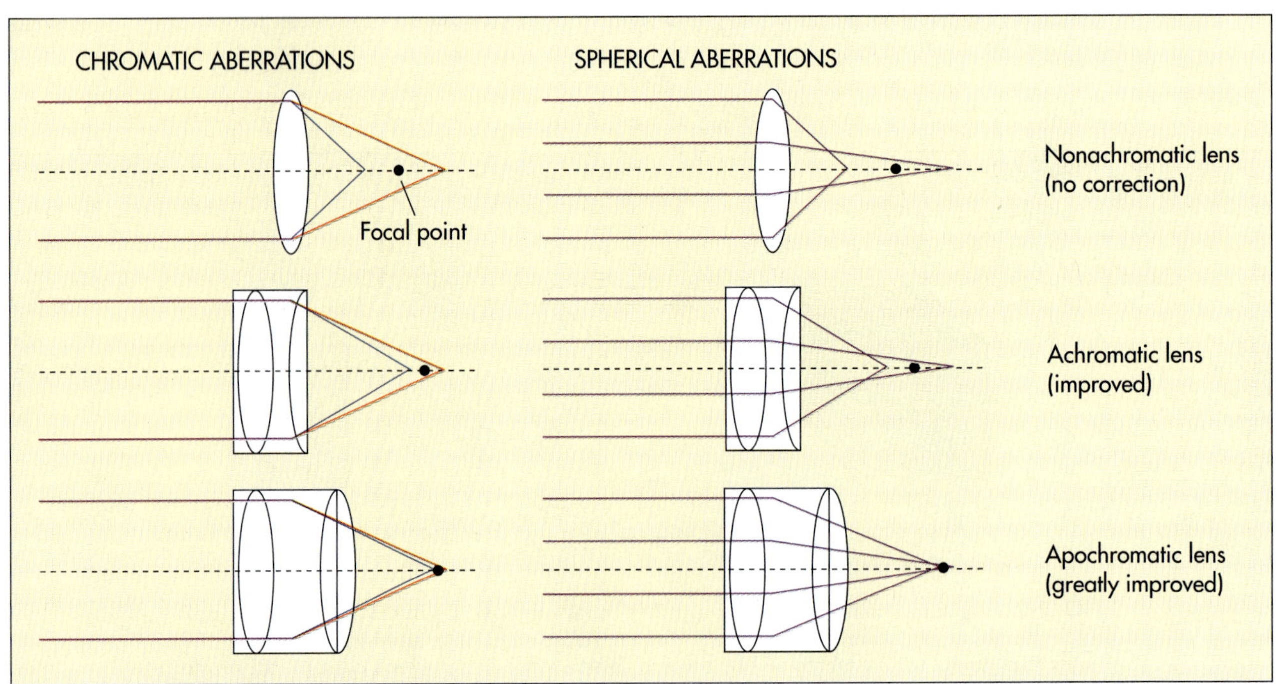

FIG. 2-3 A convex-convex lens theoretically focuses light at a single focal point. However, red light (long wavelength light) focuses more distantly from the lens than blue light (short wavelength light), causing chromatic aberrations. Also, light rays passing through the periphery of the lens (axial rays) focus more distantly from the lens than light rays that pass through the center of the lens (marginal rays), causing spherical aberrations. Achromatic lenses improve and apochromatic lenses greatly improve the performance of the microscope lens by correcting for these aberrations.

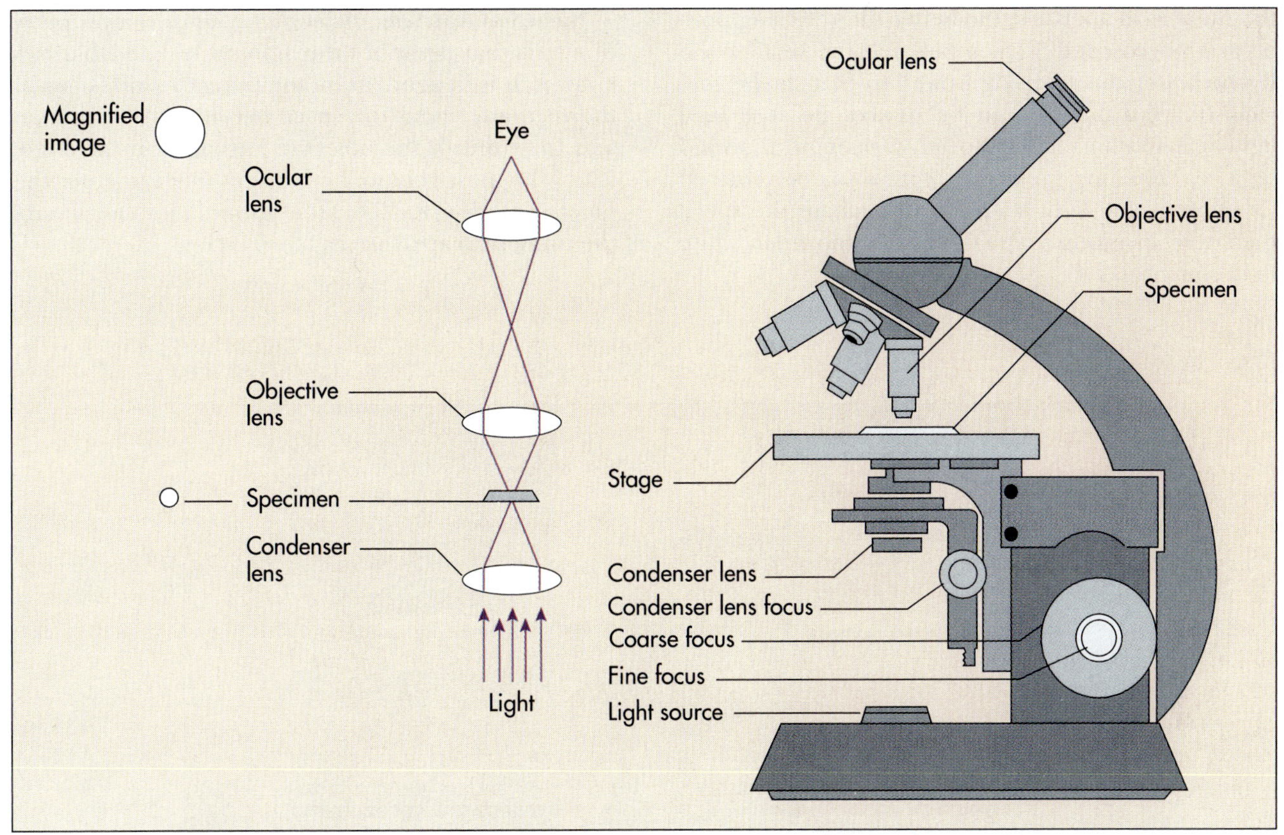

FIG. 2-4 A light microscope allows the formation of an enlarged image of a specimen. Light is refracted as it moves through a series of lenses. In a bright-field microscope the condenser lens focuses light on a specimen; the light then passes through the ocular and objective lenses to produce a magnified image.

Total magnification is the product of the magnifying powers of the individual lenses. The magnifying capability of a compound microscope is the product of the individual magnifying powers of the **ocular lens** (the lens nearest the eye) and the **objective lens** (the lens nearest the specimen). The light microscopes commonly used to observe bacteria have a 10× ocular lens and a 100× objective so that the overall magnification is 1,000×.

Resolution

Resolution is the degree to which the detail in the specimen is retained in the magnified image. The ability to see detail is essential lest everything appear as an unresolved blur. Magnifying an image by using a microscope is only useful if detail can be accurately preserved and observed.

The **resolving power** (R) of a microscope is the closest spacing between two points at which the points can still be seen clearly as separate entities; it is the distance between two structural entities of a specimen at which the entities can still be seen as individual structures in the magnified image (FIG. 2-5). The smaller the value for resolving power, the smaller the object that can be seen distinctly. The best theoretical resolving power of a light microscope is approximately 200 nanometers (nm) or just below the size of many bacterial cells. This means that bacterial cells can be observed with the light microscope but that for the most part their internal structures can not be seen.

The resolving power of a light microscope depends on the wavelength of light (λ) and a property of the objective lens, called the numerical aperture (NA). The formula for calculating the approximate resolving power of a light microscope is:

$$R = 0.5\lambda/NA$$

Wavelength The shorter the wavelength of light illuminating the specimen and the greater the value for

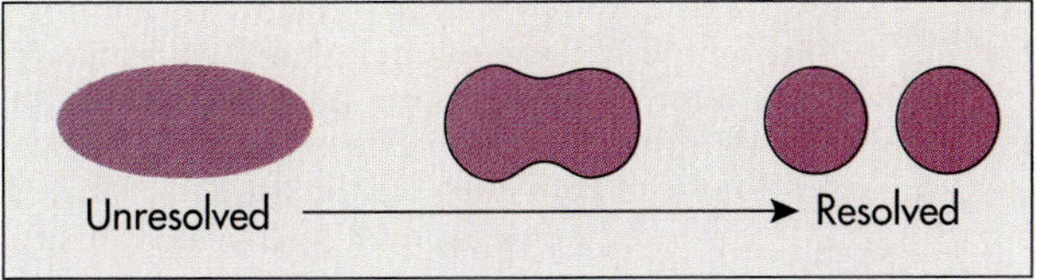

FIG. 2-5 Microscopy depends on the ability to see detail, that is, to resolve distinct points. At low resolution, structures blur together; the greater the resolution, the more detail that can be observed.

the numerical aperture, the better the resolving power of a microscope. Remember that the smaller the R, the better the resolving power, so that smaller objects (finer structure) can be viewed. Because blue light (ca. 400 nm) has a shorter wavelength than red light (ca. 700 nm), greater resolution can be achieved by using a blue light source to illuminate the specimen or by inserting a blue filter over a normally white light source.

Numerical Aperture *Numerical aperture* is a property of a lens that describes the amount of light that can enter it. It is dependent on the refractive index (η) of the medium filling the space between the specimen and the front of the objective lens and on the angle (θ) of the most oblique rays of light that can enter the objective lens (FIG. 2-6). The formula for calculating the numerical aperture is:

$$NA = \eta \times \sin \theta$$

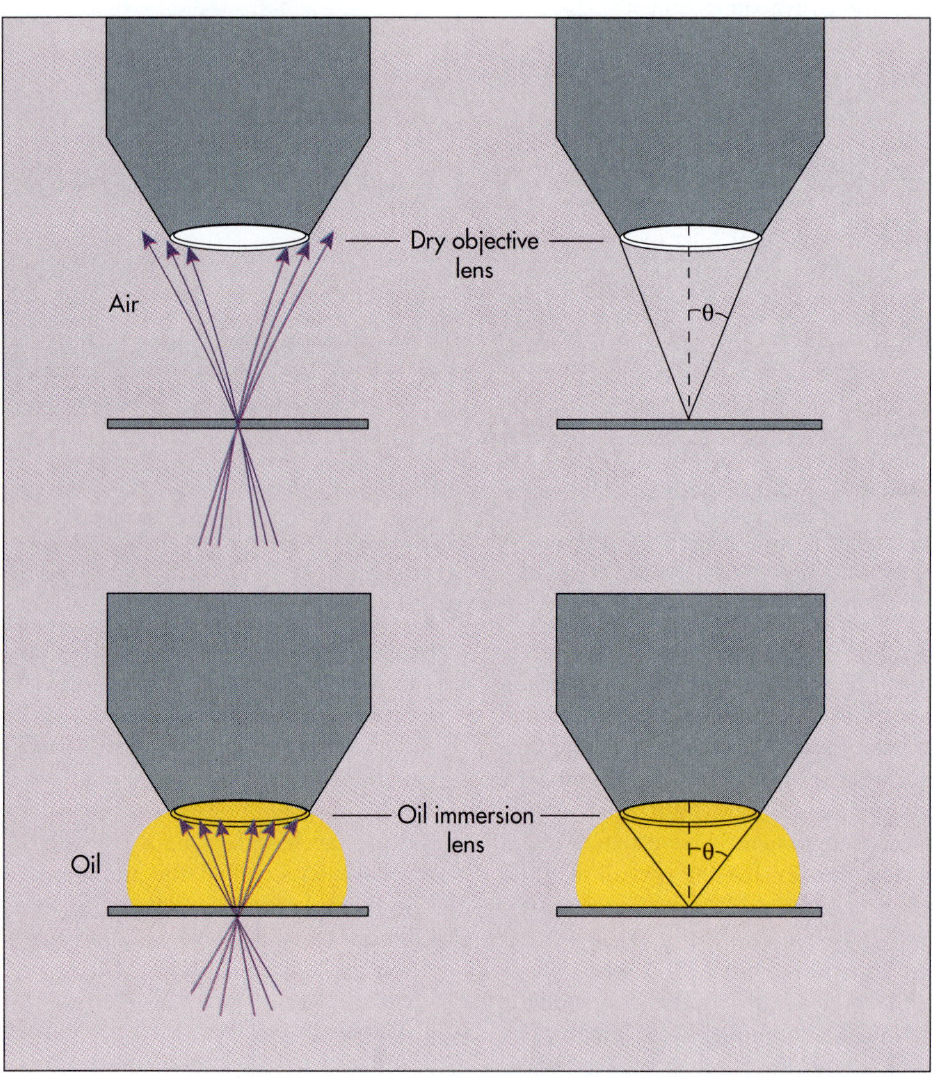

FIG. 2-6 When light passes from glass into air, refraction causes the light to bend because of the difference in refractive index. Light passing from glass through oil does not bend much because oil and glass have similar refractive indices. The resolving power of the microscope depends on the numerical aperture of the lens, which is described as $\nu\sin\theta$, where ν is the refractive index and θ is the angle of peripheral light entering the lens (one half the cone of light entering the objective lens). The numerical aperture of a lens can be improved by using immersion oil to replace the air between the objective lens and the specimen. An oil immersion lens has a greater numerical aperture than a dry objective lens, because the angle of the cone of light entering the oil immersion objective lens is greater compared to the dry objective lens.

Air has a refractive index of 1, which limits the resolution that can be achieved, but NA can be increased by placing immersion oil between the specimen and the objective lens, thus improving the resolving power of the microscope.

The numerical aperture affects the useful magnification that can be achieved. As a rule, the available magnification of a microscope is 1,000 times the NA being used, and so it is possible with an oil immersion lens with an NA of 1.4 to achieve a useful magnification of approximately 1,400×. At higher magnifications the quality of the image deteriorates and the magnification is therefore considered to be *empty*.

Oil Immersion Lens Because immersion oil has a refractive index closer to that of a glass lens than the refractive index of air, the use of immersion oil increases the cone of light that enters the objective lens (see FIG. 2-6). Using immersion oil with a refractive index of about 1.5 considerably increases the numerical aperture and thus improves the resolving power of the microscope. The observation of fungi, algae, and protozoa can be achieved with dry objectives, that is, with air occupying the space between the specimen and the objective. The viewing of bacteria in sufficient detail to determine the shape and arrangement of cells, however, normally requires the use of an **oil immersion lens**, in which immersion oil fills the space between the specimen and the objective.

The use of an oil immersion lens as the objective lens has several practical effects on microscopy. An oil immersion lens has a short *focal length*, that is, the plane of focus is near the lens, and therefore there is a short working distance between the objective lens and the specimen. The short working distance requires that the lens and the specimen be very close to one another for the image to be in focus. Another consequence of the short focal length is a very shallow *depth of field*, which means only a very thin section of the specimen can be in focus at any one time. Because of the short working distance and shallow depth of field of oil immersion lenses, many students at first have difficulty trying to focus the microscope on a specimen of bacteria without breaking the slide and scratching the objective lens, but with a little practice and proper instruction this problem is easily overcome.

Contrast

Contrast is necessary to discern an object from the surrounding background. Microorganisms are largely composed of water, as is the medium in which they are normally suspended. Viewing microorganisms with a light microscope without performing procedures to increase contrast can be likened to trying to see a white object on a white background. Staining with a colored compound is used to increase the contrast between the specimen and the background. Commonly used stains include methylene blue (blue), crystal violet (purple), and safranin (red).

Simple Staining Procedures In a **simple staining procedure**, a single stain is used and all cells and structures generally stain the same color, regardless of type. The staining procedure may be positive, in which the stain is attracted to the cells and takes on the color, or negative, in which the stain is repelled by the cells and the background takes on the color.

In **positive staining procedures** for light microscopy, the stain, which is basic, has a positively charged chromophore (from Greek *chroma*, meaning color; colored portion of the stain molecule) that is attracted to the negatively charged outer surface of the microbial cell. A stain such as methylene blue has a blue chromophore, resulting in positive blue staining of the microorganisms. The general procedure of positive staining is illustrated in FIG. 2-7.

In **negative staining procedures** for light microscopy, the stain, which is acidic, has a negatively

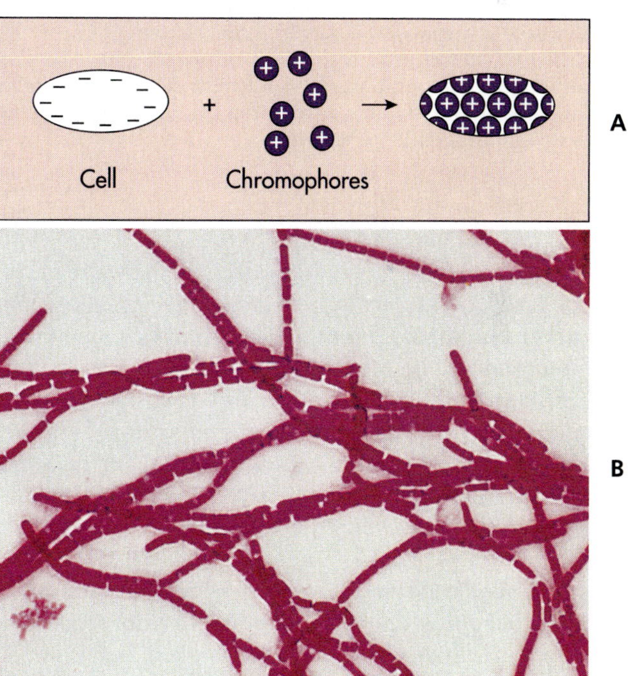

FIG. 2-7 **A,** In a simple staining procedure, microorganisms are affixed to a glass slide and stained with an appropriate dye (colored chromophore). This increases the contrast between the cells and the background so they can easily be seen using a light microscope. Because the outer layer of a cell is negatively charged, a positively charged stain chromophore is attracted to the cell; this is the basis of positive staining procedures. **B,** Micrograph of the bacterium *Bacillus cereus* after simple positive staining with carbol fuchsin. (1,300×). The cells appear red in contrast to the clear background.

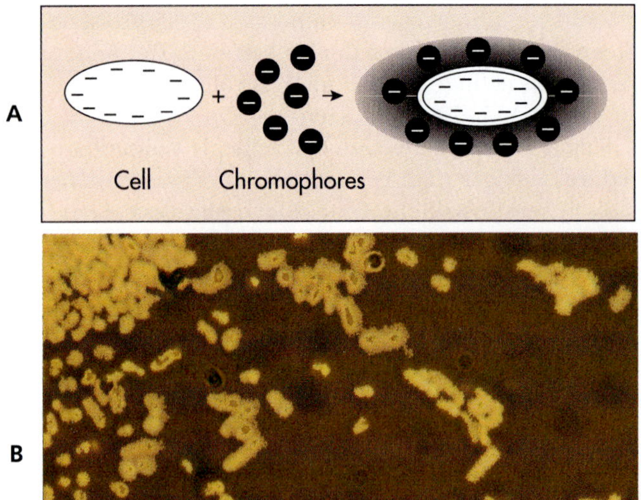

FIG. 2-8 **A,** Because the outer layer of a cell is negatively charged, a negatively charged stain chromophore is repelled by the cell; this is the basis of negative staining procedures. **B,** Micrograph of the bacterium *Escherichia coli* after simple negative staining with India ink. The cells appear clear against a dark background.

charged chromophore that is repelled by the negatively charged microorganisms so that it colors the background, resulting in the apparent negative or indirect staining of the microbial cell (FIG. 2-8). Nigrosine and India ink are frequently used for negative staining of microbial cells. Negative staining is particularly useful for viewing capsules and other structures that surround some bacterial cells. For electron microscopy, negative stains include heavy metal salts, such as uranyl acetate.

Differential Staining Procedures In **differential staining procedures**, multiple staining reactions are employed that take advantage of the fact that specific types of microorganisms and/or particular structures of a microorganism exhibit different staining reactions that can be readily distinguished by their different colors. Once a specimen is stained, the stain must be "fixed," which means the dyed specimen is treated in some way (for example, with heat or chemicals) so that the stain is tightly bound to the microbial structures with which it reacts. This permits unbound stain to be washed away and facilitates subsequent staining with different dyes.

Gram Staining The **Gram stain procedure** is the most widely used differential staining procedure in bacteriology. This staining procedure begins with **pri-**

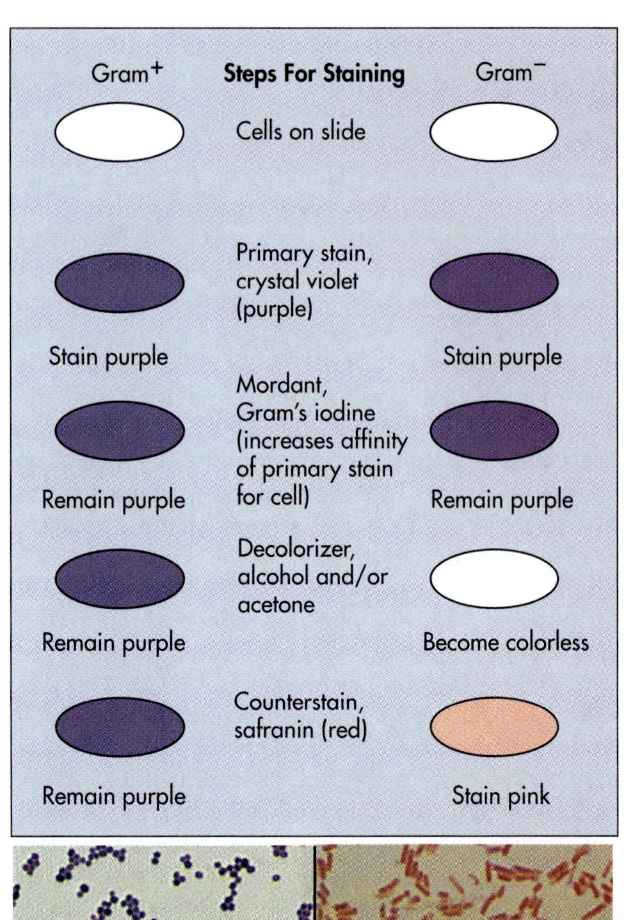

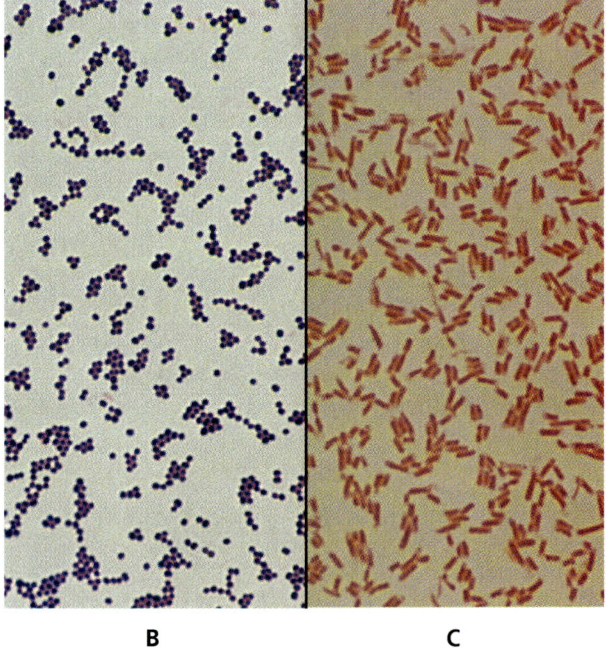

FIG. 2-9 **A,** The Gram stain procedure is widely used to differentiate major groups of bacteria. Gram-positive bacteria stain purple and Gram-negative bacteria stain pink-red by this staining procedure. Gram-positive and Gram-negative bacteria stain purple with the primary stain. The primary stain is removed from Gram-negative cells by the decolorizer and they are then stained pink by the counterstain. Gram-positive cells retain the primary stain and remain purple. **B,** Cells of the Gram-positive bacterium *Staphylococcus enterocolitis* appear as purple-blue cocci; **C,** those of the Gram-negative bacterium *Veillonella* appear as pink-red cocci.

mary staining with crystal violet, which stains all bacterial cells blue-purple, followed by application of Gram's iodine—a **mordant** (a substance that fixes the primary stain in the bacterial cells)—then **decolorization** with acetone-alcohol or some other decolorization agent (a substance that attempts to remove the primary stain), and finally **counterstaining** by application of the red stain safranin, which stains the bacteria that were decolorized in the previous step so that they can be easily visualized (FIG. 2-9).

After completion of the Gram stain procedure, the Gram-positive bacteria appear blue-purple and the remaining Gram-negative bacteria appear red-pink. This occurs because Gram-positive bacterial cells are not decolorized in step 3, whereas Gram-negative cells are decolorized. The Gram stain procedure has great diagnostic value, because of its ability to easily differentiate among bacterial species, and therefore is a key feature employed in many bacterial classification and identification systems. The distinction between Gram-negative and Gram-positive bacteria result from the differences in cell wall structure, which is discussed in Chapter 3.

ACID-FAST STAINING Another differential staining procedure frequently used in bacteriology is **acid-fast staining**. In this procedure cells are initially stained with carbol fuchsin and then decolorization is performed with acid alcohol. Acid-fast bacteria retain the red color of the carbol fuchsin and are not decolorized. Non-acid-fast bacteria are decolorized, counterstained with methylene blue, and appear blue. The acid-fast stain procedure is especially useful in identifying the causative organism of tuberculosis—*Mycobacterium tuberculosis,* which is acid fast (FIG. 2-10).

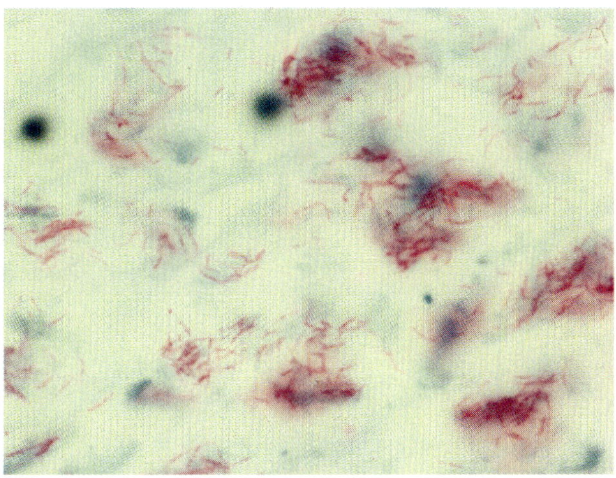

FIG. 2-10 Micrograph of *Mycobacterium tuberculosis* in a sputum sample of an individual with tuberculosis (300×). The appearance of red rods after acid-fast staining indicates the presence of mycobacteria and is diagnostic of tuberculosis.

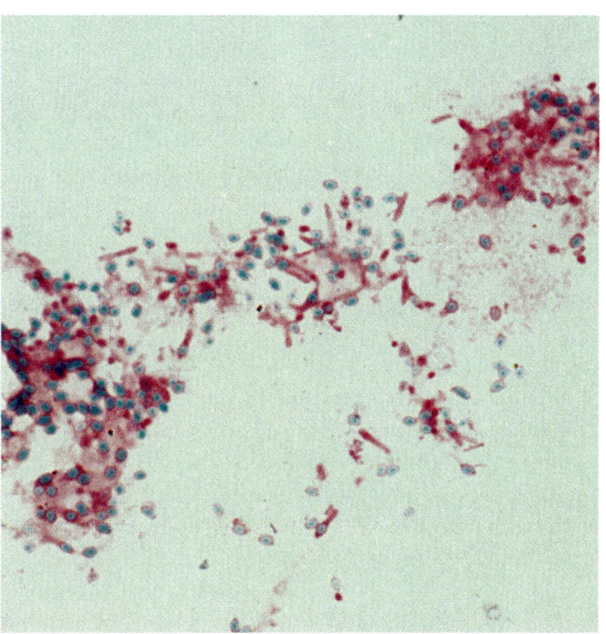

FIG. 2-11 Micrograph of *Clostridium tetani* after endospore staining. (1,400×). The spores appear green and the bacterial cells are stained red.

ENDOSPORE STAINING Another key differential staining procedure reveals the presence or absence of bacterial endospores. A bacterial **endospore** is a heat resistant structure that forms within the cell; endospores are even resistant to boiling water. In the endospore-staining procedure, the bacterial endospore typically is stained green and the rest of the bacterial cell is stained pink, permitting differentiation of the endospore from the vegetative cell (FIG. 2-11). Endospores are produced by members of the aerobic bacterial genus *Bacillus* and the anaerobic bacterial genus *Clostridium.* These are important bacterial genera because of their resistance to high temperatures. For example, *C. botulinum* sometimes survives the heat treatment of canning and causes the food poisoning disease known as botulism when contaminated food is eaten.

TYPES OF LIGHT MICROSCOPES

Many types of microscopes have varying applications in microbiology. The choice of a particular microscope depends on the size of the object, the degree of detail that must be viewed, the nature of the specimen, and the overall purpose of the microscopic observations. Some light microscopes are only useful for viewing stained specimens. Others are designed to achieve contrast without staining so that live microorganisms can be observed. Still others rely on fluorescent stains that are useful for detecting specific microorganisms or structures.

Bright-field Microscope

The most common type of microscope in microbiology laboratories is the **bright-field microscope**, a light microscope in which visible light is transmitted through the specimen. This microscope usually requires staining of specimens and rarely is used to observe live microorganisms. The specimen generally appears dark (colored) on a bright background. It has a light source, a condenser lens that focuses the light on the specimen, and two sets of lenses (objective and ocular) that contribute to the magnification of the image (FIG. 2-12).

A typical microscope used in bacteriology has objective lenses that magnify 10×, 40×, and 100× and an ocular lens of 10× and thus is capable of magnifying the image of a specimen 100, 400, and 1,000 times, respectively. If the various lenses are adjusted so that once the specimen is focused with one lens it remains in focus when one switches to other objective lenses, the microscope is said to be *parfocal.* The resolution of the typical bright-field microscope for viewing bacte-

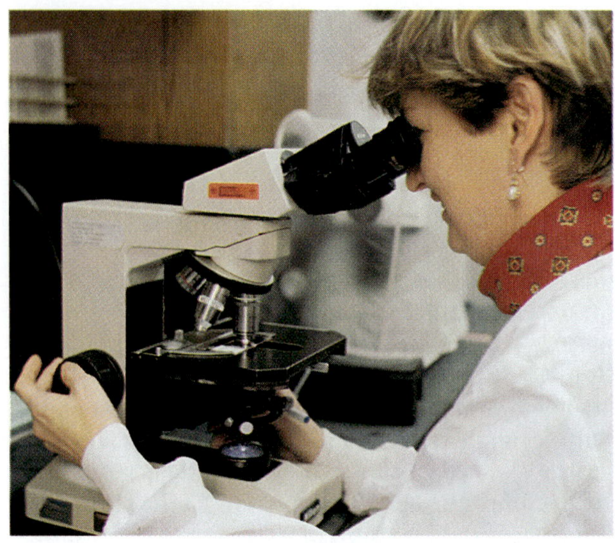

FIG. 2-12 The bright-field microscope is used routinely by students of microbiology and practicing microbiologists, such as the technician in the clinical microbiology laboratory seen here.

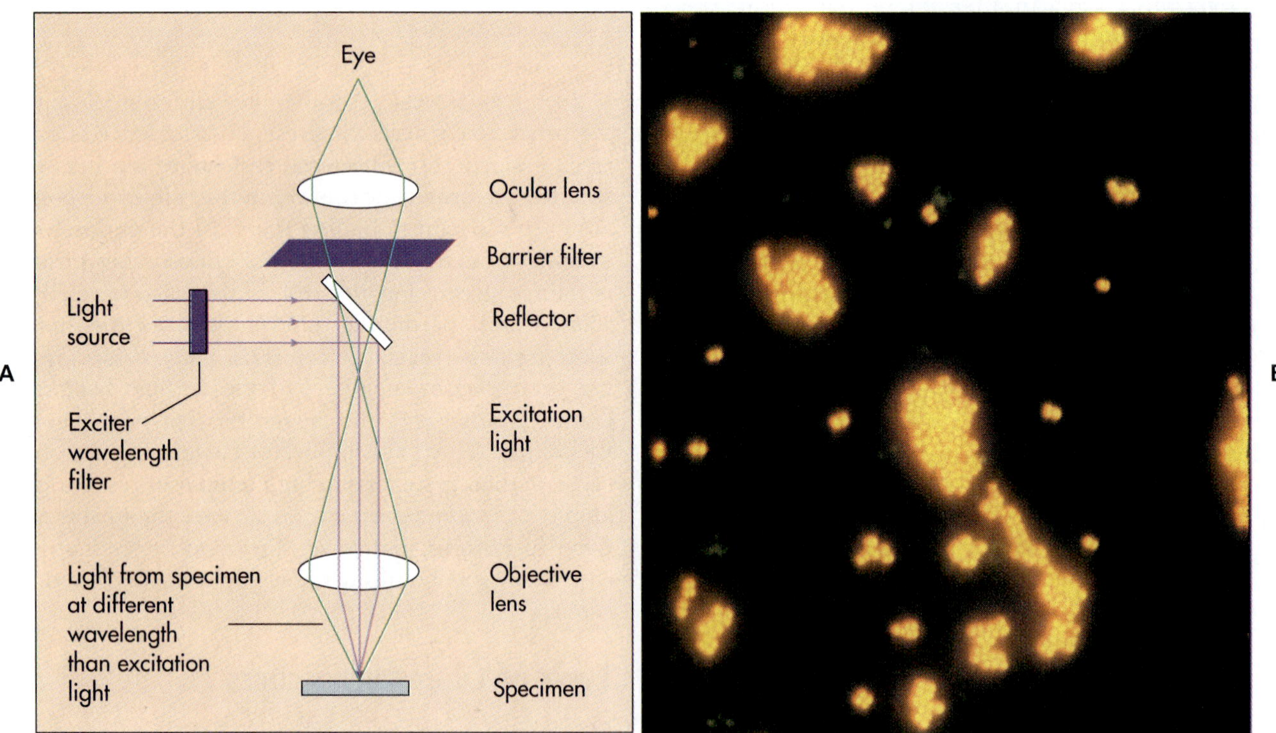

FIG. 2-13 **A,** Diagram of an epifluorescence microscope showing the light path. This type of microscope does not use a condenser. Rather, the objective lens focuses light on the specimen. The illuminating light is at one wavelength, which often is in the ultraviolet to blue wavelength range, and the light emitted from the fluorescent dye-stained specimen is at a different wavelength, which must be in the visible light range. A series of exciter and barrier filters are used to ensure that the specimen is illuminated with a particular wavelength and that the viewing is restricted to a different wavelength that corresponds to the emission wavelength of the fluorescent dye. **B,** Micrograph of staphylococci in blood after staining with acridine orange; the cells of this coccal-shaped bacterium fluoresce orange.

ria is 200 nm. Bacteria almost always are stained before viewing with the bright-field microscope.

Fluorescence Microscope

The **fluorescence microscope** is designed so that the specimen can be illuminated at one wavelength of light and observed by a light emitted at a different wavelength (FIG. 2-13, *A*). This permits the use of fluorescent stains because when a fluorescent dye is illuminated by light of one wavelength (the *excitation wavelength*) it gives off light at a different wavelength (the *emission wavelength*). For example, when the fluorescent dye, fluorescein isothiocyanate, is illuminated with blue light, it emits green light. Fluorescence microscopy has become especially important in microbiology because fluorescent dyes can be conjugated (linked) with antibodies (specific proteins produced as part of the immune response), providing great specificity in staining procedures because of the nature of immunological reactions. Immunofluorescent procedures are very useful for identifying specific microorganisms (FIG. 2-13, *B*).

Fluorescence microscopes are equipped with various excitation filters that permit the passage of the wavelength used to illuminate the specimen and barrier filters that prevent all but the emission wavelengths from passing through it. The wavelength of the light used to excite the dye may be in the UV range but the emitted light that is to be viewed must be in the visible range. When UV wavelengths are used, it is particularly important to use barrier filters to block any UV light from reaching the eye. Otherwise, blindness may result. The excitation light may be transmitted from below the specimen, in which case it is called *transmitted fluorescence,* or to the specimen through the objective lens, in which case the system is referred to as *epifluorescence* (*epi* from the Greek word meaning *upon*).

Dark-field Microscope

The **dark-field microscope** is designed to eliminate the need for staining to achieve contrast between the specimen and the background. The condenser lens of the dark-field microscope does not permit light to be transmitted directly through the specimen and into the objective lens. The dark-field condenser lens focuses light on the specimen at an oblique angle, such that, light that does not reflect off an object does not enter the objective lens (FIG. 2-14, *A*). Therefore only the light that reflects off the specimen will be seen, and the light simply passing through the slide will not enter the objective. The field will appear dark. Microorganisms that are viewed with a dark-field microscope appear very bright on a dark (black) background (FIG. 2-14, *B*).

Phase Contrast Microscope

The **phase contrast microscope** is designed so that staining is not required to view microbial structures. It is used for visualizing living microorganisms because staining usually kills cells. Light that passes through a cell or a cell structure is slowed down relative to the light that passes directly through the less dense surrounding medium. The greater the refrac-

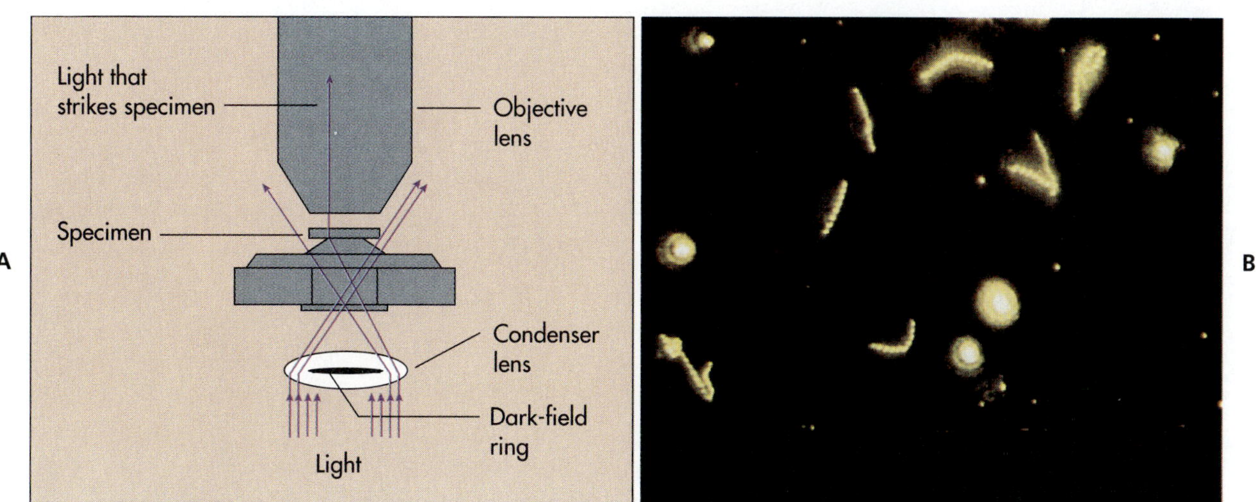

FIG. 2-14 **A,** Diagram of a dark-field microscope showing the path of light. The dark-field ring in the condenser blocks the direct passage of light through the specimen and into the objective lens. Only light that is reflected off a specimen will enter the objective lens and be seen. **B,** Micrograph of the helical-shaped bacterium *Treponema pallidum,* which causes syphilis, viewed by dark-field microscopy.

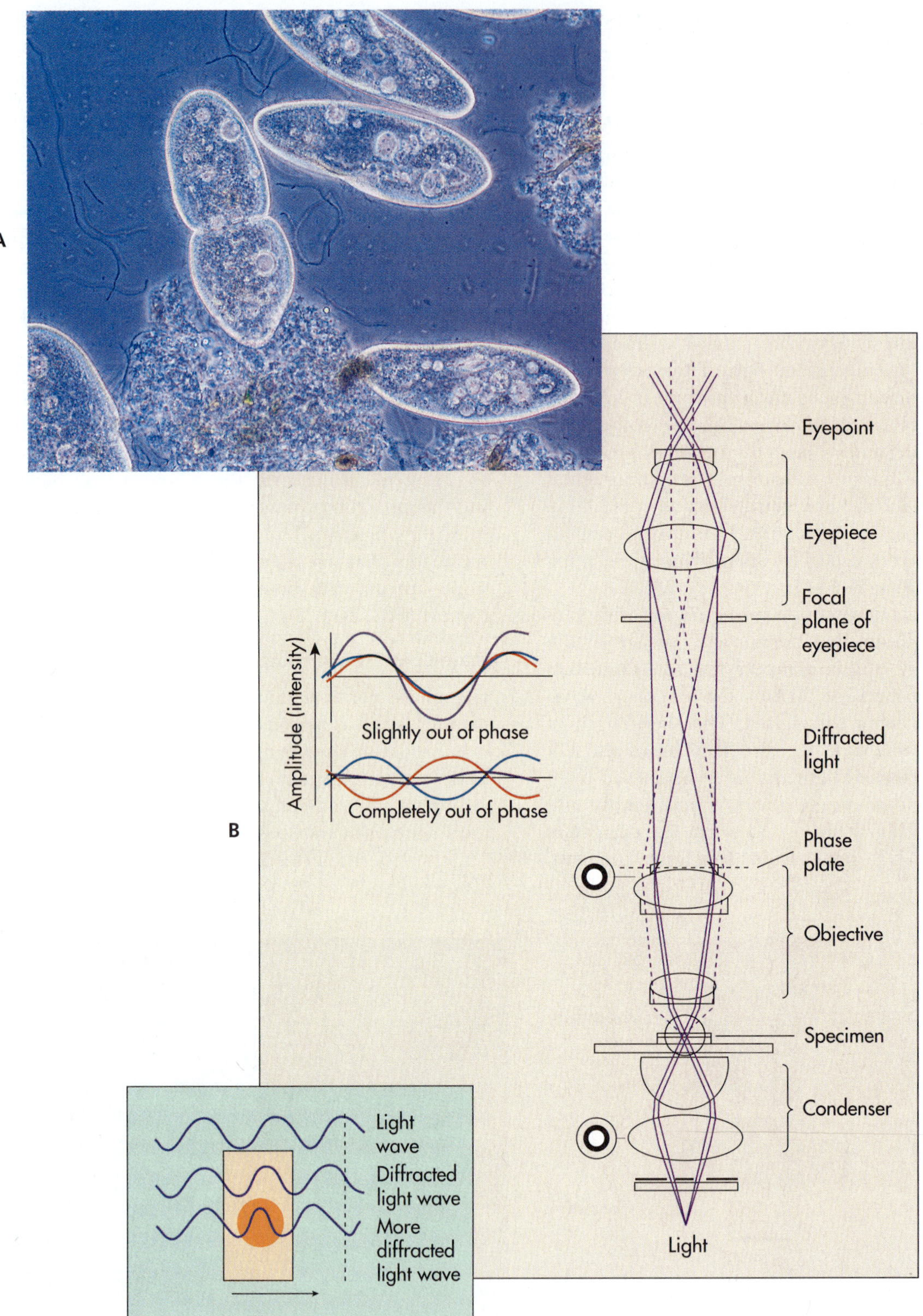

FIG. 2-15 **A,** Micrograph of the protozoan *Paramecium caudatum* viewed by phase contrast microscopy. (300×). **B,** The phase contrast microscope is designed to convert differences in the phases of light waves into visible differences in contrast. A specimen diffracts light differently than the light passing through the background. The diffracted light (*dashed line*) passes through a region of a phase plate that alters its phase. Recombination of light of differing wavelengths alters the amplitude (intensity) of the light wave, resulting in a visible difference in contrast between the specimen and the background.

tive index (ability to change the speed of a ray of light) of the cell or cellular structure, the greater the retardation of the light wave. Even difficult-to-stain structures often are conspicuous under a phase contrast microscope (FIG. 2-15, *A*). The phase contrast microscope optically changes differences in phase into differences in intensity that produce differences in contrast (FIG. 2-15, *B*).

Nomarski Differential Interference Contrast Microscope

The **Nomarski differential interference microscope** (NDIC) makes use of the fact that combining light waves that are out of phase with each other produces interference that alters the amplitude of the light wave. It produces high-contrast images of unstained, transparent specimens in what appear to be three dimensions.

The NDIC microscope has three special features: a polarizing filter, an interference contrast condenser, and a prism-analyzer plate (FIG. 2-16, *A*). In the NDIC microscope, polarized light with its defined pattern of aligned light waves is split into two beams at right angles to each other that travel closely parallel to each other through the specimen. The two beams of light are then combined and pass through an analyzer. When the two light rays that are differentially diffracted by the specimen are recombined, they produce an interference pattern.

The pseudo-three-dimensional image of NDIC is produced because the two beams of light traveling very close to each other through the specimen produce a stereoscopic effect. The degree of three-dimensional appearance is a function of the refractive index differences at the boundary surfaces of the specimen. Contrast in NDIC depends on the rate of change of the refractive index across a specimen; consequently, especially good contrast is produced at the edges of the specimen, where there is a large refractive index differential. Structures such as cell walls and spores are well defined when viewed with interference microscopes. Different structures of microorganisms appear in different colors that are related to the phase changes in the light passing through each structure, and images seen through the interference microscope are normally brilliantly colored. Interference microscopes are very useful for qualitative observations of unstained cells because they produce images with high contrast and striking topographic relief (FIG. 2-16, *B*).

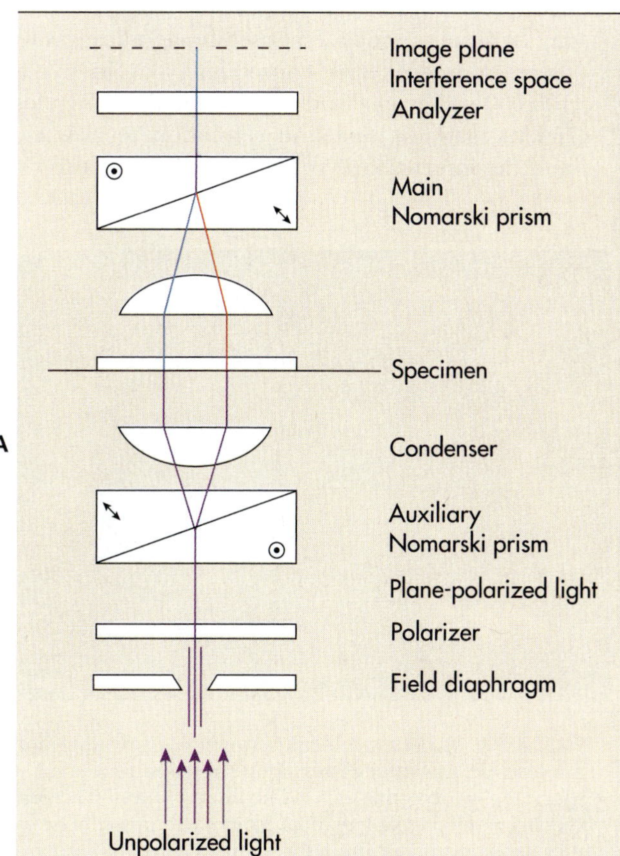

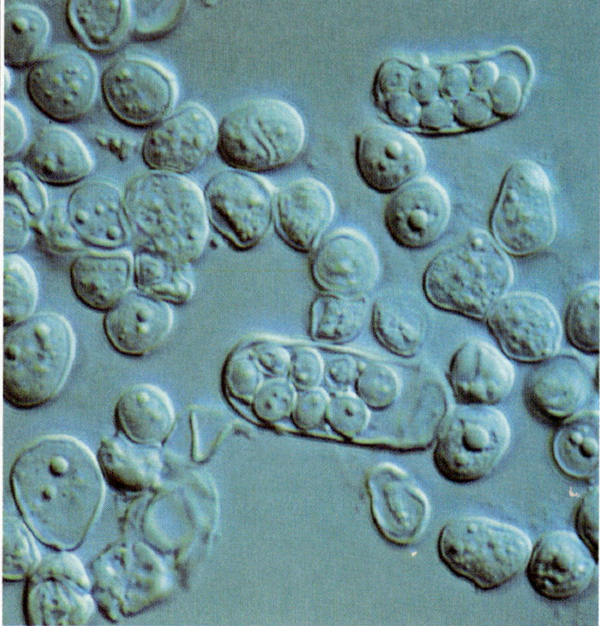

FIG. 2-16 **A,** Diagram of Nomarski interference microscopy, showing the path of light. Recombination of light that passes through the specimen with light that does not pass through produces differences in intensity and color that give a three-dimensional appearance of the specimen. **B,** Micrograph of the yeast *Schizosaccharomyces* viewed by Nomarski interference microscopy. (1,200×).

Confocal Scanning Microscope

The **confocal scanning microscope** is a new type of light microscope that does not form a two-dimensional optical image of the specimen, as occurs in a conventional microscope. Rather, a beam of light from a laser is focused to a point by an objective lens and is scanned through the sample. Scanning of the laser beam across the specimen is achieved by two mirrors: one scans in the X direction and the second mirror scans in the Y direction. A second objective lens magnifies the image, and a light detector is used to measure the interaction with each point in the object as it is scanned through a specimen. Only the light from the specific point of focus in the specimen is detected so that diffracted light from other points is not detected at all. This totally eliminates the diffracted light that tends to blur the image in a conventional light microscope.

Epifluorescence scanning optical microscopy uses an excitatory laser light from the illuminating aperture that passes through an excitation filter, is reflected by a dichroic mirror, and is focused by a microscope objective to a spot at the focal plane within the specimen (FIG. 2-17, *A*). Fluorescence emissions that are in-focus pass through an imaging aperture to be detected by a photomultiplier. Fluorescence emissions from regions above and below the focal plane have different primary image plane foci and are thus severely attenuated by the imaging aperture, which has the same focus as the illuminating light. This eliminates out-of-focus glare in the specimen by spatial filtering using a point source of light for excitation and an aperture confocal with the excitation point source. The specimen is either in focus such that structures are visible or out of focus so that absolutely no structure is seen. This is the key to the confocal microscope. The scanned images are used to generate optical sections of fluorescent dye–labeled specimens and to produce a three-dimensional image with a virtual absence of out-of-focus blur (FIG. 2-17, *B*).

Electron Microscopy

The **electron microscope**, which employs a beam of electrons rather than a beam of light, permits much greater resolution and thus much higher useful magnifications than the light microscope. The greater resolution is possible because the wavelength of an electron beam, generated at a high accelerating voltage, is much shorter than that of light in the visible range of the electromagnetic spectrum. At 60,000 volts, a typical accelerating voltage used in an electron microscope, the wavelength of the electron beam is approximately 0.005 nm, permitting a theoretical resolution of approximately 0.2 nm. This resolution is about a thousand times better than can be achieved when using light microscopy. The useful magnification for an electron microscope, consequently, is in excess of 100,000×. The electron microscope thus provides sufficient magnification and resolution to view viruses and the internal structures of all microorganisms.

A

Observer or camera
Ocular lens
Aperture array I
Objective II
Specimen
Objective I
CRT display
Aperture array I
Condenser lens
Laser

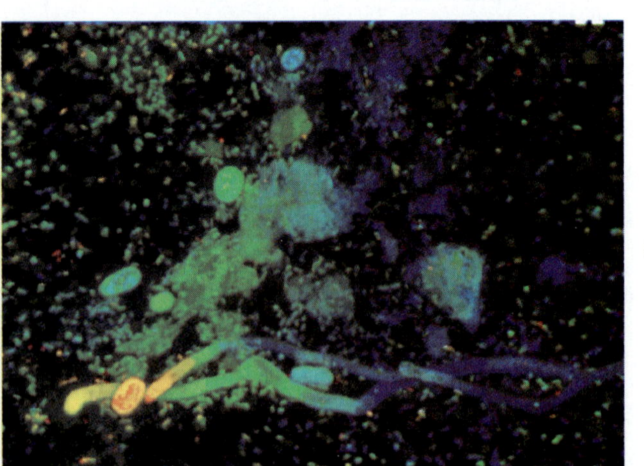

B

FIG. 2-17 **A,** In a confocal fluorescence scanning optical microscope, excitatory laser light is focused to a point on a specimen by objective lens I. The light is scanned across the specimen. Objective lens II magnifies the image. The aperture arrays compare the light intensity and produce an image on a CRT display screen. **B,** Micrograph of a bacterial biofilm viewed by confocal fluorescence scanning microscopy. (350×). The color spectrum indicates depth in the biofilm—red is deep and blue is surface.

Preparation of Specimens

There are several problems in preparing biological specimens, including microorganisms, for viewing by electron microscopy. There is great potential for creating artifacts that could be mistakenly viewed as microbial structures in electron micrographs. An **artifact** is the appearance of something in an image that is not a true representation of the features of the specimen on view. Improper sample preparation can cause the formation of artifacts.

Before viewing a microorganism with transmission electron microscopy, it is necessary to dehydrate the specimen and to fix (preserve intact) the structures in their natural orientation. The fixation and dehydration process must be carried out carefully in stages, because during the fixation process it is possible to shrink, stretch, or otherwise distort the microorganisms and alter the image.

Staining Staining is used to improve the contrast between the specimen and the background, but instead of the dyes used in light microscopy, the stains used for electron microscopy contain electron-dense heavy metal salts. The heavy metal stains scatter the electron beam and the stained areas thus appear dark (black), permitting visualization of the detailed ultrastructure of microorganisms. As in light microscopy, positive stains are attracted to microorganisms and negative stains are repelled by them (FIG. 2-18).

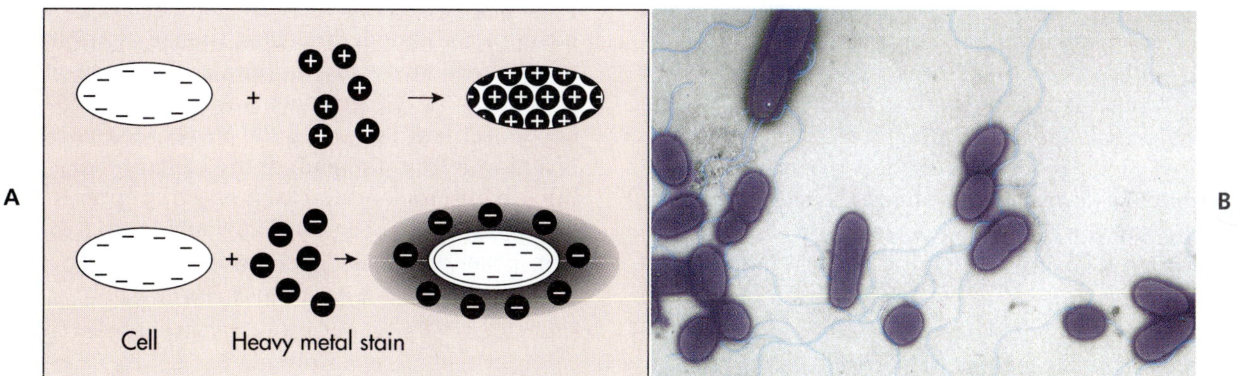

FIG. 2-18 **A,** Stains for electron microscopy use heavy metals that are electron dense. Positive stains are attracted to microorganisms and negative stains are repelled by the surfaces of microorganisms. **B,** Colorized micrograph of the bacterium *Pseudomonas aeruginosa* stained with phosphotungstic acid and viewed by electron microscopy. (5,000×).

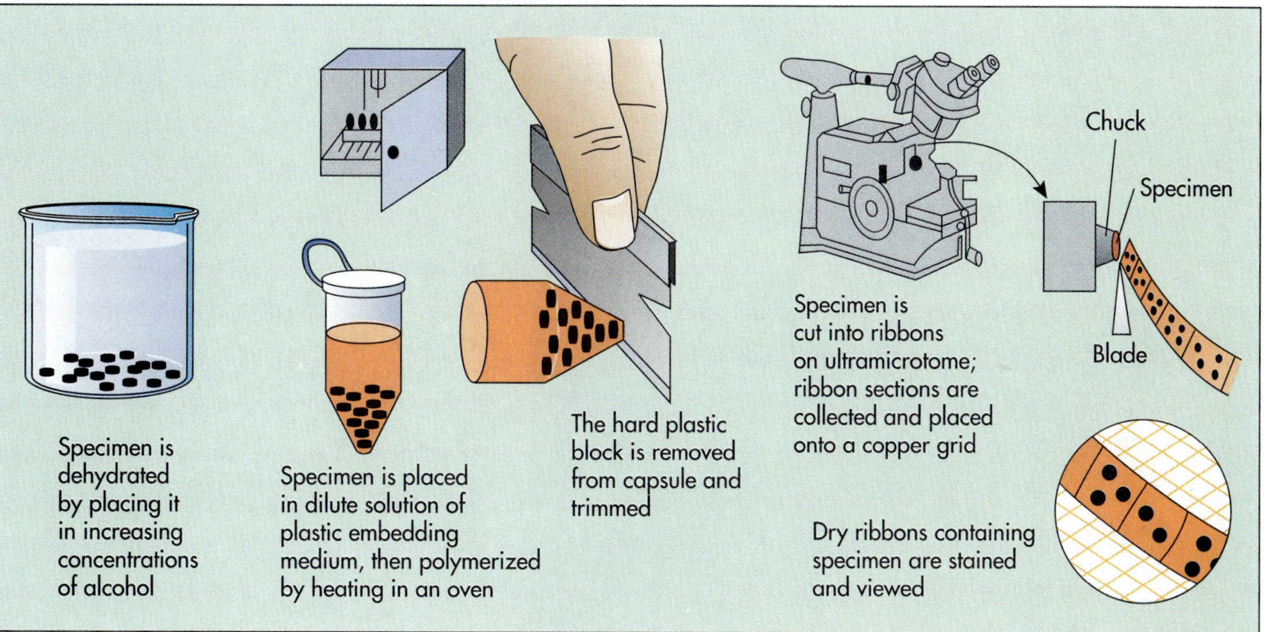

FIG. 2-19 Extensive preparation of a specimen is generally needed for viewing by transmission electron microscopy. Water must be removed; this dehydration of the specimen usually is achieved using alcohol. Many specimens must be cut into thin sections before they can be viewed in the electron microscope. Sectioning is accomplished by placing the specimen in a plastic and then cutting the sections with an ultramicrotome.

Thin Sectioning It is sometimes necessary to slice microorganisms into thin sections before staining to view their internal ultrastructures with an electron microscope. **Thin sectioning** of microorganisms is achieved by using a *microtome*, which is a mechanical instrument that advances a specimen in small increments across a knife surface, usually diamond or glass, to be sliced (FIG. 2-19). The resulting specimens are 600 to 700 nm in depth. Microorganisms typically are embedded in a plastic resin to facilitate handling during thin sectioning. The thin sections are then stained with heavy metal-containing compounds, such as phosphotungstic acid that contains the heavy metal tungsten.

Freeze Etching **Freeze etching** is a technique used to reveal the various biochemically defined layers of a microorganism, including organelle structures (FIG. 2-20). In this procedure, a specimen is first frozen at −196° C and is fractured by striking it with a knife blade (*freeze fractured*). The fractured specimen is then etched, which raises part of the surface layer of the specimen. The specimen is then exposed to vapors of a heavy metal while being held at an angle to produce a shadow effect; after which it is rotated and exposed to vaporized carbon at a 90° angle to produce a replica of the surface. Any adhering biological material is removed, and the carbon replica is then viewed with an electron microscope. The freeze-etching method reveals much detail of both internal and external surface structures and also eliminates some problems with artifacts that arise through chemical fixation and sectioning of biological specimens.

Transmission Electron Microscope

The **transmission electron microscope** (TEM) is a type of electron microscope that uses an electron beam that passes through the specimen (FIG. 2-21, *A*). The source of the electrons is a hot tungsten filament in an electron gun. The heat draws electrons from the filament and causes them to accelerate as a fine electron beam past an anode by a high voltage established between the filament and the anode. The electron beam is focused on the specimen with an electromagnetic condenser lens by varying the current to the lens. Air is removed from the path of the electron beam by using a high efficiency vacuum system to prevent collisions with gas molecules that would scatter the electron beam and make it impossible to resolve a high-

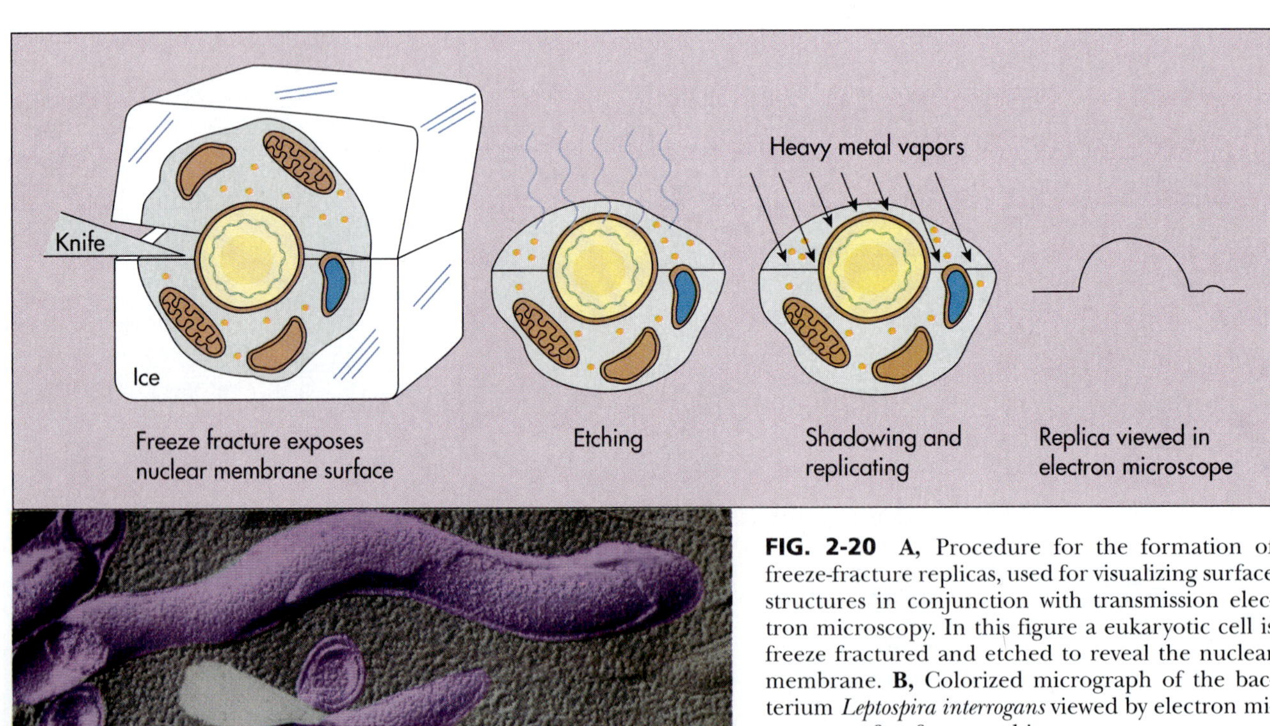

FIG. 2-20 **A,** Procedure for the formation of freeze-fracture replicas, used for visualizing surface structures in conjunction with transmission electron microscopy. In this figure a eukaryotic cell is freeze fractured and etched to reveal the nuclear membrane. **B,** Colorized micrograph of the bacterium *Leptospira interrogans* viewed by electron microscopy after freeze etching.

A

LIGHT MICROSCOPE
Lamp
Condenser lens
Specimen
Objective lens
Eyepiece
Final image seen by eye

TRANSMISSION ELECTRON MICROSCOPE
Cathode filament
Anode
Electron gun
Condenser lens magnet
Specimen
Objective lens magnet
Projector lens magnet
Final image on fluorescent screen

B

C

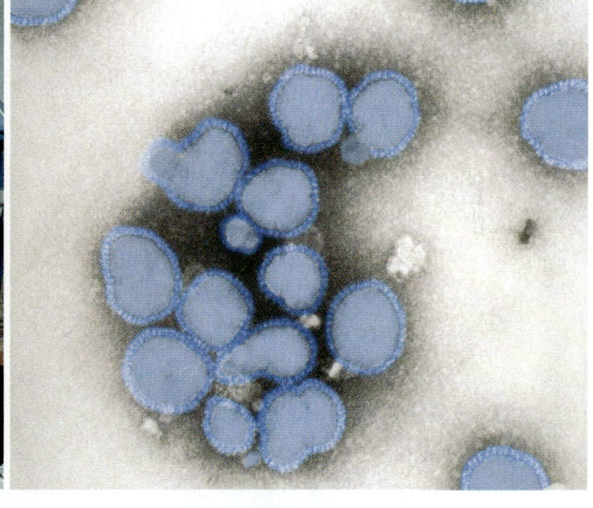

FIG. 2-21 **A,** The TEM (transmission electron microscope) allows visualization of the fine detail of the microbial cells and viruses. (An inverted light microscope is shown for comparison.) The TEM uses an electron beam and electromagnets instead of the light source and glass lenses used in light microscopy. **B,** Photograph of a TEM with its viewing screen. **C,** Colorized micrograph of the virus that causes influenza, viewed using a TEM. (360,000×).

magnification image. Fine details, even to the level of molecular arrangements, can be seen with the transmission electron microscope (FIG. 2-21, *B*).

Scanning Electron Microscope

The **scanning electron microscope** (SEM) uses an electron beam that is scanned across the surface of a specimen (FIG. 2-22, *A*). The primary electron beam knocks electrons out of the specimen surface, and the secondary electrons produced in this process are transmitted to a collector. Some of the primary electrons are also reflected or backscattered from the specimen surface, but the number of backscattered electrons is far fewer than the number of secondary electrons emitted from the specimen surface. Because the number of low-energy secondary electrons reach-

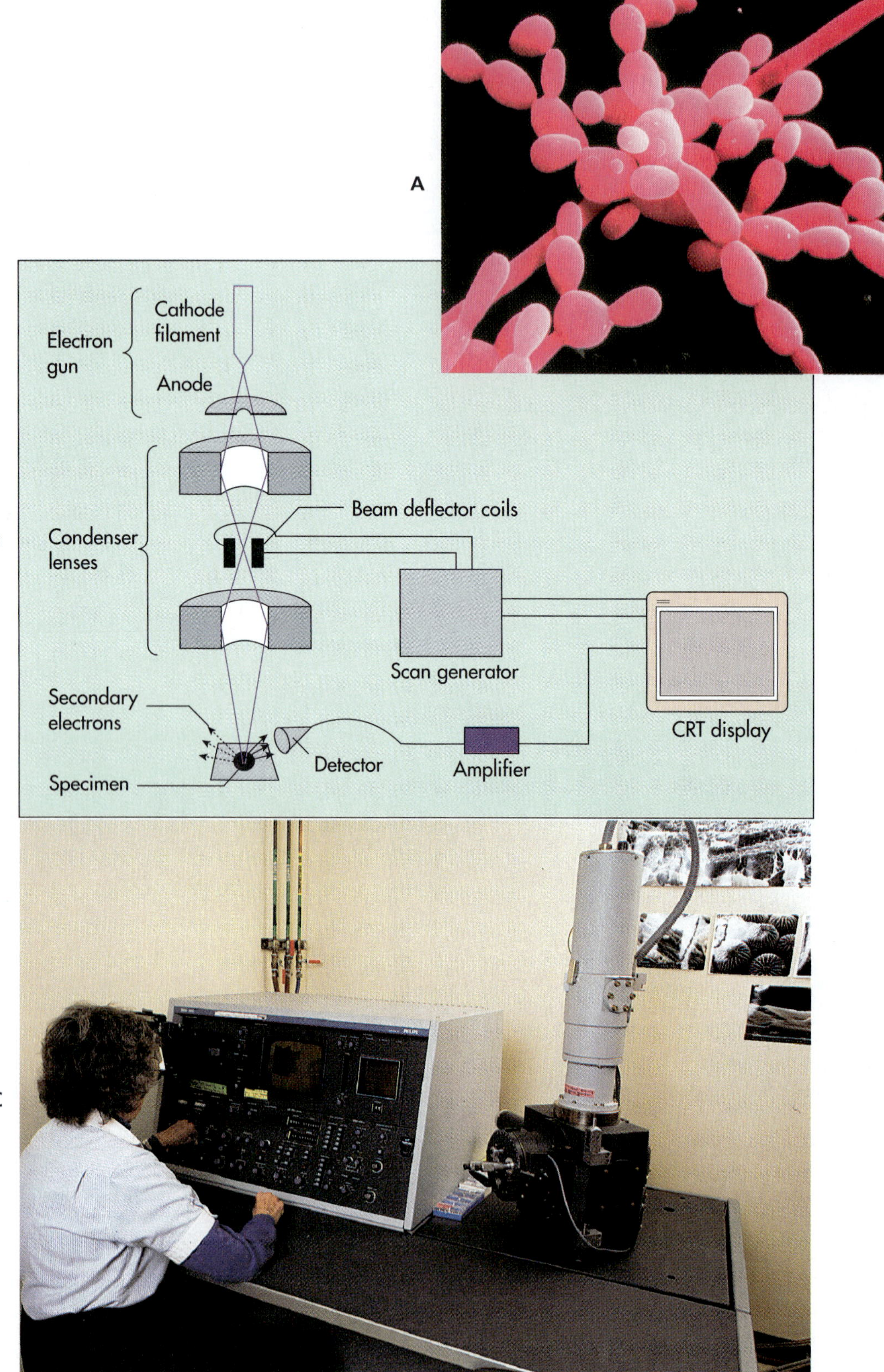

FIG. 2-22 **A,** Colorized micrograph of the fungus *Candida albicans,* viewed using a SEM. (2,200×). **B,** The SEM (scanning electron microscope) is used for viewing surface structures and their three-dimensional spatial relationships. An electron beam is scanned across a specimen. The electrons emitted from the surface of the specimen determine the intensity of the image. The relative lengths of the scans across the specimen and the CRT display determine the magnification. **C,** Photograph of a scanning electron microscope.

ing the collector is far greater than the number of backscattered electrons, a more intense signal is developed by secondary electrons than by backscattered electrons. Electrons reaching the collector are transmitted to a detector consisting of a substance that emits light when struck by electrons. The emitted light is converted to an electrical current that is used to control the brightness of an image on a cathode ray tube (CRT) screen, like that of a television.

The secondary electrons emitted from each point on the specimen are characteristic of the surface at that point. The intensity of the image on the CRT screen thus reflects the composition and topography of the specimen surface. Contrast in the SEM is primarily determined by surface topography, which controls the number of secondary electrons reaching the detector. The shadowed image shown on the CRT screen gives a three-dimensional appearance, highlighting the topography of the specimen surface as seen with the SEM (FIG. 2-22, *A*).

2.2 CULTURE OF MICROORGANISMS

The ability to examine and to study the characteristics of microorganisms, including obtaining organisms for microscopic visualization, depends in large part on being able to grow (culture) microorganisms in the laboratory. **Pure cultures** contain only one kind of microorganism. They are free from all other types. Several different methods are used for the establishment of pure cultures of microorganisms.

The isolation of pure cultures involves separating samples of microorganisms into individual cells that are then allowed to reproduce to form clones of single microorganisms. Each clone represents a pure culture. Isolation is achieved by the physical separation of the microorganisms but the success of an isolation method also depends on the ability to maintain the viability and growth of a pure culture of the microorganism. Care must be taken to ensure that the microorganisms are not killed during the isolation procedure, which can easily occur by exposing the microorganisms to conditions they cannot tolerate, such as air in the case of obligately anaerobic microorganisms that are sensitive to oxygen. The success of an isolation method also depends on the ability to grow the microorganism, that is, to define the growth medium and to establish the appropriate incubation conditions that permit its growth.

CULTURE MEDIA

Microorganisms require a suitable **culture medium** that can support their nutritional needs. Additionally, the culturing of microorganisms requires careful control of various environmental factors, such as temperature, pH, and oxygen levels. By understanding the growth requirements of a given microbial species, it is possible to establish the necessary conditions *in vitro* to support the optimal growth of that microorganism. Often, the task of defining the proper medium for growing microorganisms is tedious and taxes the creativity of the microbiologist; this is especially true for microorganisms with rigorous growth requirements, so-called "fastidious" microorganisms.

Defined and Complex Media

Different types of media are used for growing bacteria and fungi as pure cultures. Many bacterial species can be grown in the laboratory on a **defined medium**, that is, on a medium in which all components are known. Some microorganisms require a **complex medium**, that is, a medium made with constituents whose composition is not totally known and may vary. Commonly used complex media contain beef extract obtained by extracting the water-soluble components from beef tissue (a complex mixture of proteins, carbohydrates, lipids, and other biochemical constituents), peptones (an enzymatic digest of protein-containing amino acids and other nitrogen-containing compounds, as well as vitamins and other compounds), and yeast extract (an aqueous extract of yeast cells containing vitamins and other growth factors).

A typical growth medium normally contains a source of nitrogen (such as ammonium nitrate), phosphate, sulfate, iron, magnesium, sodium, potassium, and chloride ions. These inorganic chemicals are required for the biosynthesis of various cellular biochemicals and for the maintenance of transport activities across the cytoplasmic membrane. Microorganisms generally have many other specific inorganic nutritional requirements: various metals such as zinc, manganese, and copper, among others, are generally required as trace elements. Some growth factors such as vitamins and amino acids may also be included.

For the culture of heterotrophic microorganisms, specific organic carbon compounds, such as glucose, are included in the culture medium as **growth substrates** to meet the carbon and energy requirements for growth. For the growth of autotrophic microorganisms, the organic carbon source is omitted from the growth medium, and an inorganic source of carbon (carbon dioxide or carbonate) is supplied as a source of carbon for growth.

Not all microorganisms can be cultured in the laboratory. The nutritional requirements of many microorganisms are simply not known. These microorganisms reproduce in nature, where their nutritional needs are met, but we do not understand their growth requirements well enough to define the appropriate laboratory conditions. We are typically able to culture less than 1% of the microorganisms that are present in a natural soil or water sample.

Selective and Differential Media

Some media have compounds added that favor the growth and/or detection of specific microorganisms and are relatively inhibitory to others (Table 2-2). As an example, methylene blue is sometimes added to

TABLE 2-2 Some Differential and Selective Media

MEDIUM	DESCRIPTION
MacConkey agar	MacConkey agar is a differential plating medium for the selection and recovery of Enterobacteriaceae and related enteric Gram-negative rods. Bile salts and crystal violet are included to inhibit the growth of Gram-positive bacteria and some fastidious Gram-negative bacteria. Lactose is the sole carbohydrate. Lactose-fermenting bacteria produce colonies that are varying shades of red because of the conversion of the neutral red indicator dye (red below pH 6.8) from the production of mixed acids. Colonies of nonlactose-fermenting bacteria appear colorless or transparent.
Eosin methylene blue (EMB) agar	EMB agar is a differential plating medium that can be used in place of MacConkey agar in the isolation and detection of the Enterobacteriaceae and related coliform rods from specimens with mixed bacteria. The aniline dyes (eosin and methylene blue) in this medium inhibit Gram-positive and fastidious Gram-negative bacteria. They also combine to form a precipitate at acid pH, thus also serving as indicators of acid production.
Desoxycholate-citrate (DCA) agar	DCA agar is a differential plating medium used for the isolation of members of the Enterobacteriaceae from mixed cultures. The medium contains about three times the concentration of bile salts (sodium desoxycholate) of MacConkey agar, making it most useful in selecting species of *Salmonella* from specimens overgrown or heavily contaminated with coliform bacteria or Gram-positive organisms. Sodium and ferric citrate salts in the medium retard the growth of *Escherichia coli*. Lactose is the sole carbohydrate, and neutral red is the pH indicator and detector of acid production.
Endo agar	Endo agar is a solid plating medium used to recover coliform and other enteric organisms from clinical specimens. The medium contains sodium sulfite and basic fuchsin, which serve to inhibit the growth of Gram-positive bacteria. Acid production from lactose is not detected by a pH change but rather from the reaction of the intermediate product, acetaldehyde, which is fixed by the sodium sulfite.
Salmonella-Shigella (SS) agar	SS agar is a highly selective medium formulated to inhibit the growth of most coliform organisms and to permit the growth of species of *Salmonella* and *Shigella* from clinical specimens. The medium contains high bile salts concentration and sodium citrate, which inhibit all Gram-positive bacteria and many Gram-negative organisms, including coliforms. Lactose is the sole carbohydrate and neutral red is the indicator for acid detection. Sodium thiosulfate is a source of sulfur, and any bacteria that produce H_2S gas are detected by the black precipitate formed with ferric citrate.
Hektoen (HE) enteric agar	HE agar is devised as a direct plating medium for fecal specimens to increase the yield of species of *Salmonella* and *Shigella* from the heavy numbers of normal microbiota. The high bile salt concentration of this medium inhibits the growth of all Gram-positive bacteria and retards the growth of many strains of coliforms. Acids may be produced from three carbohydrates, and acid fuchsin reacting with thymol blue produces a yellow color when the pH is lowered. Sodium thiosulfate is a sulfur source, and H_2S gas is detected by ferric ammonium citrate, producing a black precipitate.
Xylose lysine desoxycholate (XLD) agar	XLD agar is less inhibitory to the growth of coliform bacteria than HE and was designed to detect *Shigella* species in feces after enrichment in Gram-negative broth. Bile salts in relatively low concentration make this medium less selective than the other media included in this table. Three carbohydrates are available for acid production, and phenol red is the pH indicator. Lysine-positive organisms, such as most *Salmonella enteriditis* strains, produce initial yellow colonies from xylose utilization and delayed red colonies from lysine decarboxylation. The H_2S detection system is similar to that of HE agar.

inhibit the growth of Gram-positive bacteria while permitting the growth of Gram-negative bacteria. These **selective media** are widely used for the isolation of pathogenic microorganisms from clinical specimens. **Differential media** contain substances that permit the detection of microorganisms with specific metabolic activities. For example, a pH indicator dye is sometimes added to detect the production of acids from the metabolism of carbohydrates.

ENRICHMENT CULTURE

By considering the metabolic capabilities of specific microorganisms, it is possible to design growth media that will favor the growth of particular microorganisms. This principle is the basis of the **enrichment culture technique**, a method used to isolate specific groups of microorganisms based on a design of culture medium and incubation conditions that preferentially support the growth of a particular microorganism. The enrichment culture technique mimics many natural situations in which the growth of a particular microbial population is favored by the chemical composition of the system and by environmental conditions. Enrichment media tend to select the microorganisms that grow best among all of the microbes introduced into the media. For example, to isolate microorganisms capable of metabolizing petroleum hydrocarbons, one can design a culture medium containing a hydrocarbon as the sole source of carbon and energy. By doing so, one establishes conditions whereby only microorganisms that are capable of metabolizing hydrocarbons can grow (FIG. 2-23). Because other microorganisms cannot reproduce in this medium, one thereby preferentially selects for hydrocarbon-utilizing microorganisms. Similarly, a culture medium that favors the growth of autotrophic microorganisms that derive their energy from the oxidation of ammonium ions and their carbon from inorganic carbon could be designed by providing ammonium ions and carbonate in the medium.

The design of an enrichment procedure takes into account the composition of the medium and environmental factors such as temperature, aeration, pH, and so forth. For example, the temperature can be adjusted to 5° C to favor the growth of microorganisms

A

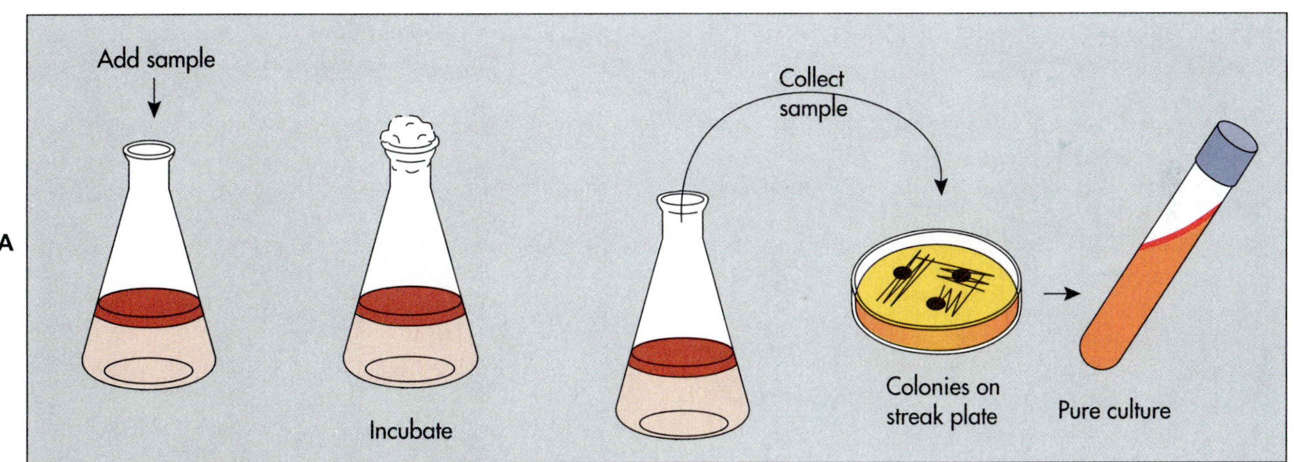

B

FIG. 2-23 **A,** To establish an enrichment, a medium is inoculated with a sample, for example, soil or water, that may contain microorganisms with specific characteristics. The medium and the incubation conditions are designed to favor the growth of the microorganisms, for example, microorganisms capable of degrading petroleum hydrocarbons. The desired microorganisms should be able to outcompete others in the sample and increase in number so they then can be isolated and pure cultures established. **B,** Enrichment cultures are designed to selectively support the growth of specific microorganisms. In a medium with petroleum hydrocarbon as the sole source of carbon and energy, hydrocarbon-degrading microorganisms are selectively enriched. *(Right flask),* Control showing oil slick and lack of enrichment for hydrocarbon degraders. *(Left flask),* Growth of the hydrocarbon-degrading microorganisms emulsifies the oil so that it disperses through the medium in the flask. A pure culture of the hydrocarbon degrader can be isolated from the enrichment culture.

that live at low refrigerator temperatures, or to 37° C to "enrich" for microorganisms capable of growth at human body temperature. Cultures may be aerated by shaking or by sparging with air to favor the growth of aerobes, or oxygen may be totally excluded to enrich for anaerobes.

ESTABLISHING A PURE CULTURE

Sterilization

To establish a pure microbial culture, it is necessary to eliminate unwanted microorganisms. There are various ways of eliminating microorganisms from the liquids, containers, and instruments used in pure culture procedures, including exposure to elevated temperatures, toxic chemicals, or radiation to kill microorganisms and filtration to remove them from liquids. Removal of microorganisms by filtration generally is accomplished by passage through a filter with 0.2 to 0.45 μm diameter pores; most bacteria are trapped on the filter, but viruses and some very small bacteria may pass through it.

Heat sterilization at a temperature that kills all microorganisms, including their endospores, is often used to eliminate unwanted microorganisms. Dry heat sterilization requires high temperatures and long exposure periods to kill all of the microorganisms in a sample. Exposure in an oven for 2 hours at 170° C (328° F) is generally used for the dry heat sterilization of glassware and other laboratory items.

Culture media preparation usually employs an autoclave that uses steam under pressure for sterilization (FIG. 2-24). An **autoclave** is an instrument that exposes substances to steam at elevated temperatures. Steam has a high penetrating power and a much higher heat capacity than dry heat. Thus it is very effective at killing microorganisms. Generally, exposure for 15 minutes at 121° C, achieved by using a pressure of 15 lb/in^2 (SI equivalent = 103.4 kPa), is used to sterilize microbiological culture media.

Aseptic Technique

Aseptic technique involves avoiding any contact of the pure culture, sterile medium, and sterile surfaces of the growth vessel with contaminating microorganisms. To accomplish this task, (1) the work area is cleansed with a disinfectant to reduce the number of potential contaminants; (2) the transfer instruments are sterilized, for example, by heating a transfer loop in a Bunsen burner flame before and after transferring; and (3) the work is accomplished quickly and efficiently to minimize the time of exposure during which contamination of the culture or laboratory worker can occur.

The steps for transferring a culture from one vessel to another are shown in FIG. 2-25: (1) flame the inoc-

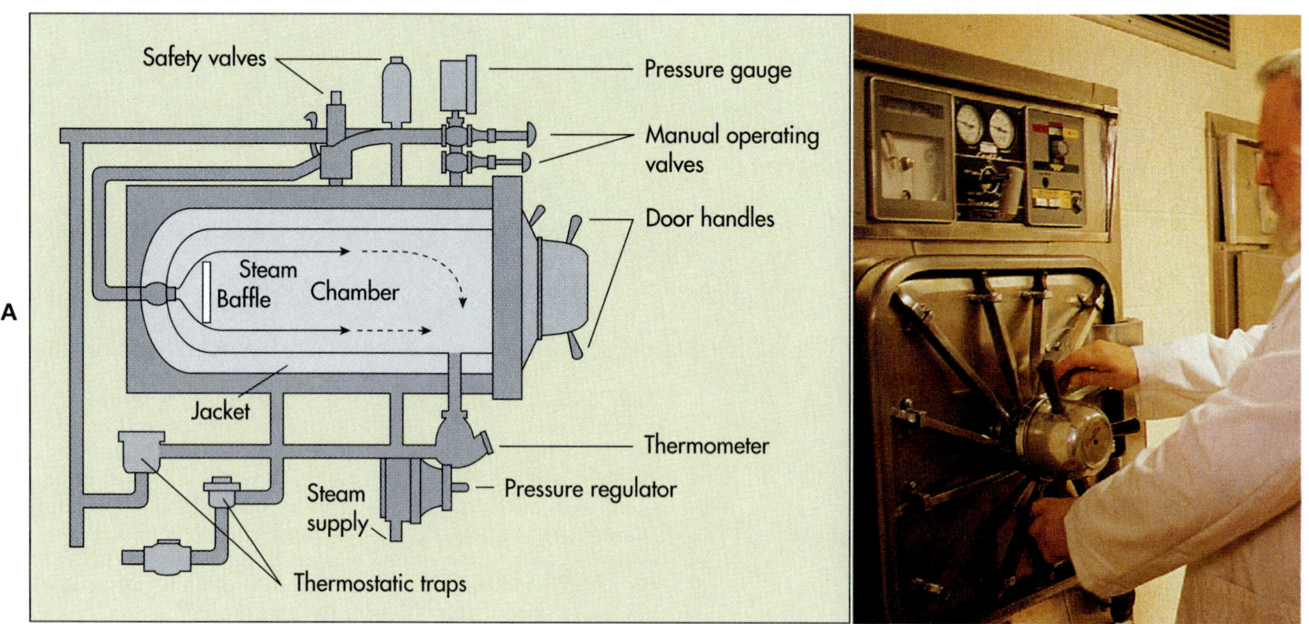

FIG. 2-24 **A,** Diagram of an autoclave. This instrument is routinely used for sterilization of media and other items in the microbiology laboratory. In an autoclave, steam is introduced under pressure into a chamber containing the material to be sterilized. The pressure generally is adjusted to 15 lb/in.^{2} so that a temperature of 121° C (250° F) is reached. The valving of the autoclave permits the rapid entry of steam from a preheated jacket into the chamber and the subsequent slow exhausting of steam from the chamber; this process permits rapid heating of the material and prevents liquids from boiling out of their containers, as would happen if the pressure was suddenly reduced. **B,** A technician is loading an autoclave with media for sterilization. This is a routine operation in most microbiology laboratories.

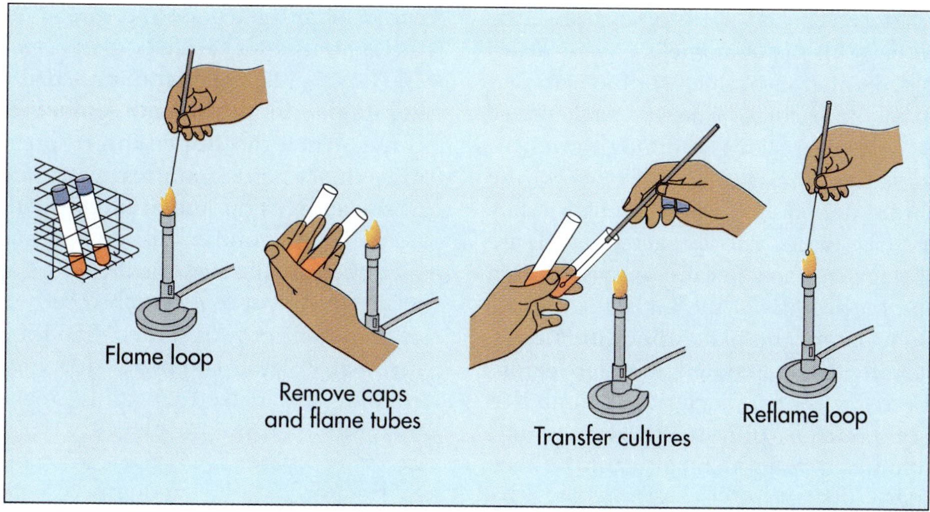

FIG. 2-25 Steps in the aseptic transfer of bacteria. Aseptic transfer procedures are essential for preventing contamination of cultures and for ensuring that the microorganisms being cultured do not escape into the laboratory.

ulating or transfer loop; (2) open and flame the mouths of the culture tubes; (3) pick up some of the culture growth and transfer it to the fresh medium; (4) flame the mouths of the culture vessels and reseal them; and (5) reflame the inoculating loop. Essentially the same technique is used for inoculating Petri dishes, except that the dish is not flamed, and for transferring microorganisms from a culture vessel to a microscope slide.

Streak Plate

In the **streak plate technique** for isolating pure cultures of bacteria, a loopful of bacterial cells is streaked across the surface of a sterile solidified agar plate that contains a nutrient medium (FIG. 2-26). Many differ-

A

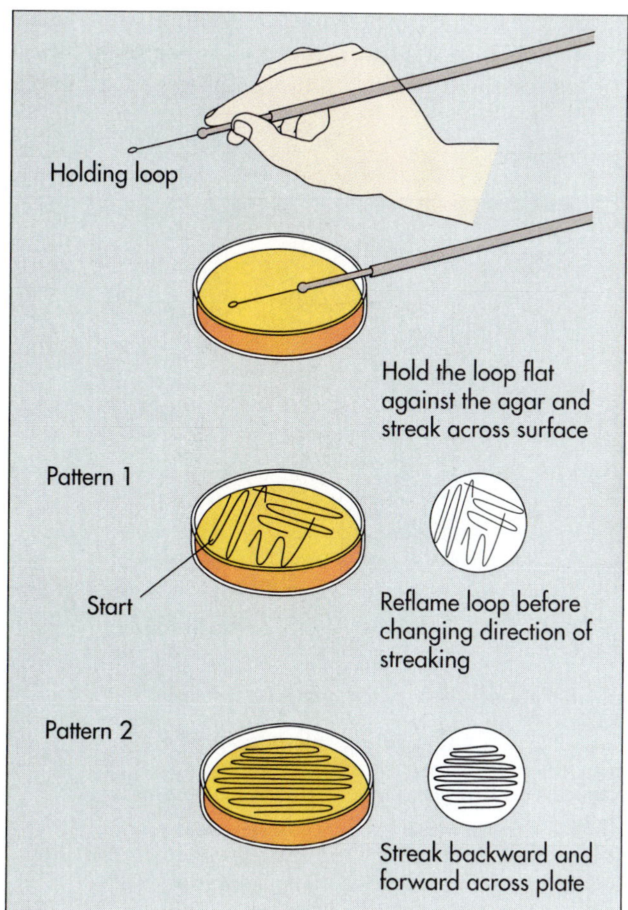

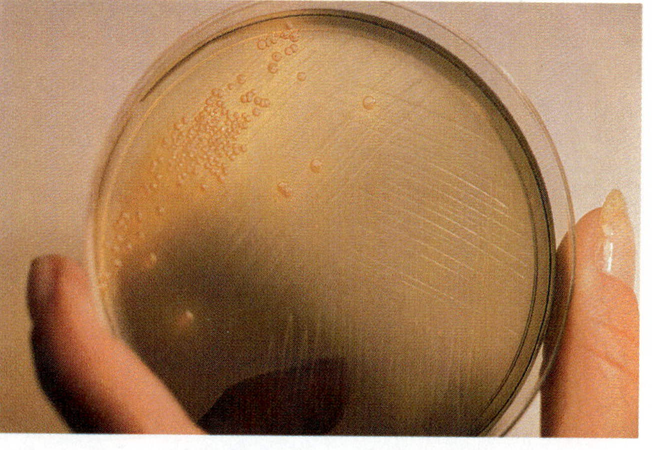

B

FIG. 2-26 **A,** Streaking for the isolation of pure cultures, showing two different streaking patterns. In this procedure, a culture is diluted by drawing a loopful of the organism across a medium. For a dilute culture, only a single streak may be used (Pattern 2). For more concentrated cultures, a second streak is drawn across the first streaks so that some cells are picked up and further diluted; several additional streaks are made to ensure sufficient dilution so that only single cells are deposited at a given location (Pattern 1). The growth of each isolated individual cell results in the formation of a discrete colony. **B,** Streak plate of *Vibrio cholerae* on thiosulfate citrate bile salts sucrose (TCBS) agar.

ent streaking patterns can be used to separate individual bacterial cells on the agar surface. The plates are then incubated under favorable conditions to permit the growth of the bacteria. The key principle of this method is that, by streaking, a dilution gradient (numbers of cells decrease as they move across the agar and away from the point of inoculation) is established across the face of the plate as bacterial cells are deposited on the agar surface. Because of this dilution gradient, *confluent growth* (from the Latin for flow together) occurs on part of the plate where the bacterial cells are not sufficiently separated; in other regions of the plate where few enough bacteria are deposited to permit space between individual cells, separate macroscopic colonies develop that can easily be seen with the naked eye.

Each well-isolated colony is assumed to arise from a single bacterium and therefore to represent a clone of a pure culture. If this important premise is not sustained, for example, because two bacterial cells are deposited at the same location on the plate, the method fails to produce a pure culture. Assuming that each colony comes from a single cell, samples of the isolated colonies can be picked up, using a sterile inoculating loop, and restreaked onto a fresh medium to ensure purity. A new sample colony is then picked up and transferred to an agar slant or other suitable medium for maintenance of the pure culture.

Spread Plate

In the **spread plate method** a drop of liquid containing a suspension of microorganisms is placed on the center of an agar plate and spread over the surface of the agar, using a sterile hockey stick-shaped glass rod (FIG. 2-27). The glass rod is normally sterilized by being dipped in alcohol and ignited to burn off the alcohol. When the suspension is spread over the plate, individual microorganisms are separated from others in the suspension and are deposited at discrete locations. To accomplish this separation, it is often necessary to dilute the suspension before application to the agar plate to prevent overcrowding and the formation of confluent growth rather than the desired development of isolated colonies. After incubation, isolated colonies are picked up and streaked onto a fresh medium to ensure purity.

Pour Plate

In the **pour plate technique**, suspensions of microorganisms are added to tubes containing melted agar cooled to approximately 42° to 45° C (FIG. 2-28). The bacteria and agar medium are mixed well, and the suspensions are poured into sterile Petri dishes using aseptic technique. The agar is allowed to solidify, trapping the bacteria at separate discrete positions within the medium. While the medium holds bacteria in place, it is still soft enough to permit the growth of bacteria and the formation of discrete isolated colonies within the gel and on the surface of the agar. As with the other isolation methods, individual colonies are then picked up and streaked onto another plate for purification. In addition to its use in isolating pure cultures, the pour plate technique is used for the quantification of numbers of viable bac-

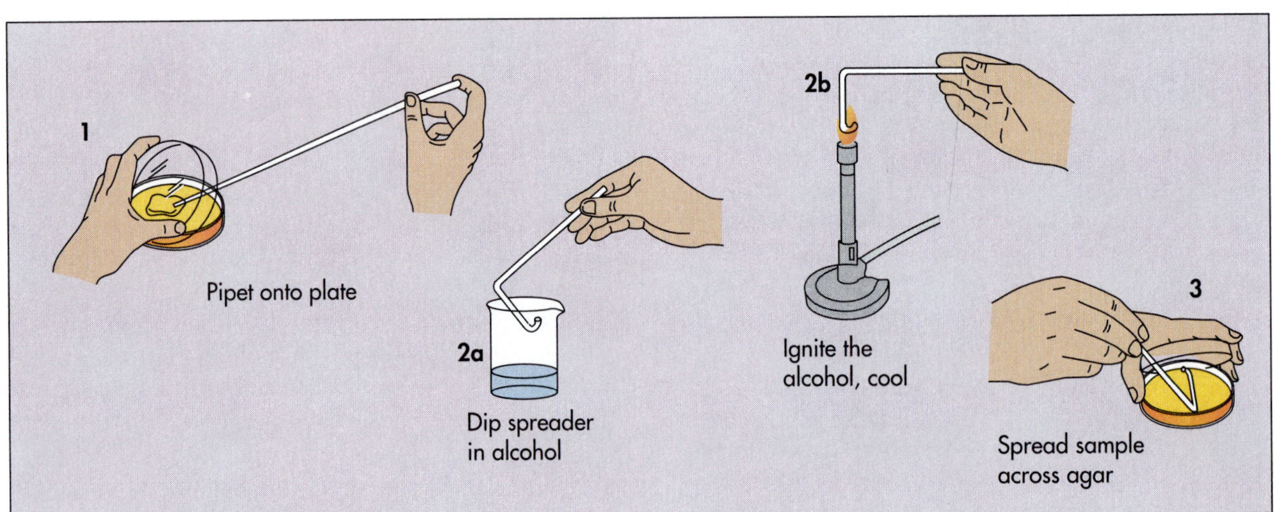

FIG. 2-27 The spread plate technique for isolating and enumerating microorganisms. **1,** A sample is aseptically pipetted onto an agar medium; **2a** and **b,** a spreading rod is sterilized by dipping in alcohol and flaming; **3,** the sterile rod is used to spread the suspension over the surface of the medium.

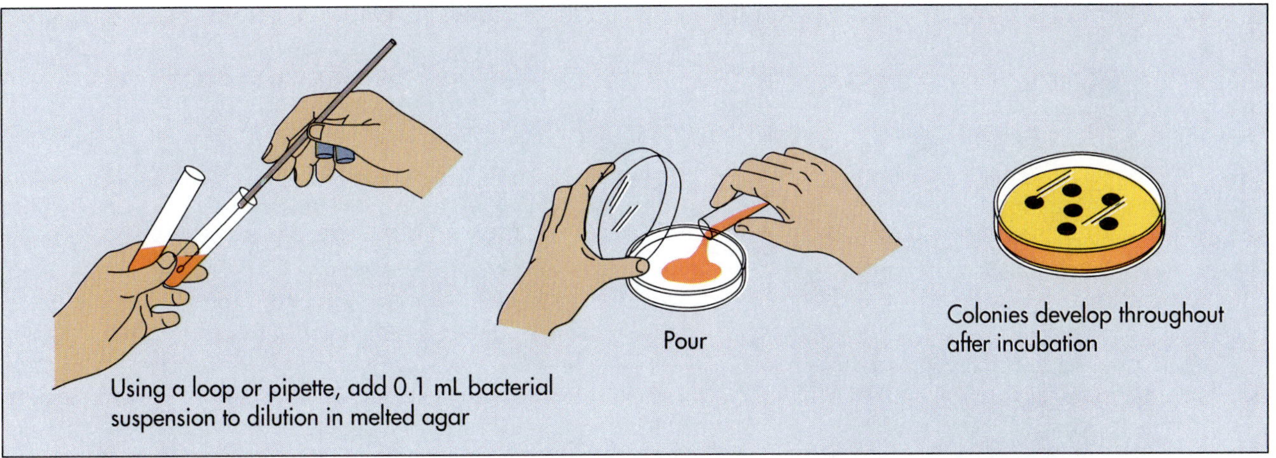
Using a loop or pipette, add 0.1 mL bacterial suspension to dilution in melted agar
Pour
Colonies develop throughout after incubation

FIG. 2-28 The pour plate technique for isolating and enumerating microorganisms. A sample of a known dilution is mixed with a liquefied agar medium that has been cooled to 45° to 50° C and poured into a Petri plate. After incubation the numbers of colonies that develop are counted and the concentration of microorganisms in the original suspension is calculated.

teria. The facts that agar solidifies below 42° C and that many bacteria survive at these temperatures ensure the success of this isolation technique. Because in some cases, such as in marine samples, significant numbers of bacteria are killed under these conditions, this method cannot always be used.

MAINTAINING AND PRESERVING PURE CULTURES

Once a microorganism has been isolated and grown in pure culture, it is necessary to maintain the viable culture, free from contamination, for some period of time. There are several methods available for maintaining and preserving pure cultures. The organisms may simply be subcultured periodically onto or into a fresh medium to permit continued growth and to ensure the viability of a stock culture. Proper aseptic technique must be used each time the organism is transferred, and there is always a risk of contamination. Furthermore, repeated subculturing is extremely time-consuming, making it difficult to maintain large numbers of pure cultures successfully for indefinite periods of time. Additionally, genetic changes (mutations) are likely to occur when cultures are repeatedly transferred.

Therefore various methods besides subculturing have been developed for preserving pure cultures of microorganisms. These methods include refrigeration at 0° to 5° C for short storage times, freezing in liquid nitrogen at −196° C for prolonged storage, and **lyophilization** (also known as freeze-drying) to dehydrate the cells (FIG. 2-29). In lyophilization, the culture is frozen at a very low temperature and placed under a high vacuum. Under these conditions, the water in the culture and microbial cells goes directly from the frozen solid state to the gaseous state (sublimates), thereby drying the cells without disrupting them. By sufficiently lowering the temperature or by removing water, microbial growth is precluded but viability in a dormant state is maintained, permitting preservation of microorganisms for extended periods of time.

Often, valuable cultures are deposited in centralized culture collections, such as the American Type Culture Collection in Rockville, Maryland, where they are preserved. It is especially important that all new microbial species be deposited in such culture collections to ensure their indefinite preservation and to make them available for scientific study. The choice of the preservation method depends on the nature of the culture and the facilities available. When freezing is used to preserve microorganisms, the rates of freezing and thawing must be carefully controlled to ensure the survival of the microorganisms because ice crystals formed during freezing can disrupt membranes. Glycerol is often employed as an "antifreeze" agent to prevent damage due to ice crystals and to ensure the ability to recover viable microorganisms when frozen cultures are thawed.

FIG. 2-29 Lyophilization, or freeze-drying, is used to preserve microbial cultures. The instrument used for this process uses a high vacuum and low temperature so that water sublimes (goes from the solid frozen state directly to a gas). This removes water from the specimen without disrupting cellular structures. Therefore the viability of lyophilized cells is maintained.

2.3 CHARACTERIZATION AND IDENTIFICATION

Modern methods for the characterization and identification of microorganisms involve growing pure cultures and determining various physiological growth parameters and metabolic characteristics, serological tests that use antibodies produced as part of the immune response, and gene probes to detect specific diagnostic genes.

Identification Based On Physiological and Metabolic Characteristics

Characterization and identification of microorganisms traditionally relies on the determination of phenotypic characteristics that are observed by growing microorganisms on various media and under various growth conditions. The abilities of microorganisms to grow at various temperatures, oxygen levels, salt concentrations, and so forth, are determined in this manner. Metabolic characteristics such as which substrates will support growth and which will be fermented to produce acids are determined (FIG. 2-30). The pattern of physiological and metabolic characteristics distinguishes one microbial species from another, forming the basis for identification.

Serological Identification

Serological tests to identify microorganisms are based on running immunological reactions in test tubes. These tests use antibodies that are protein made as part of the immune response against foreign substances called antigens. Antibodies react with antigens with an extraordinary degree of specificity. Some antigens occur on the surfaces of microorganisms, and it

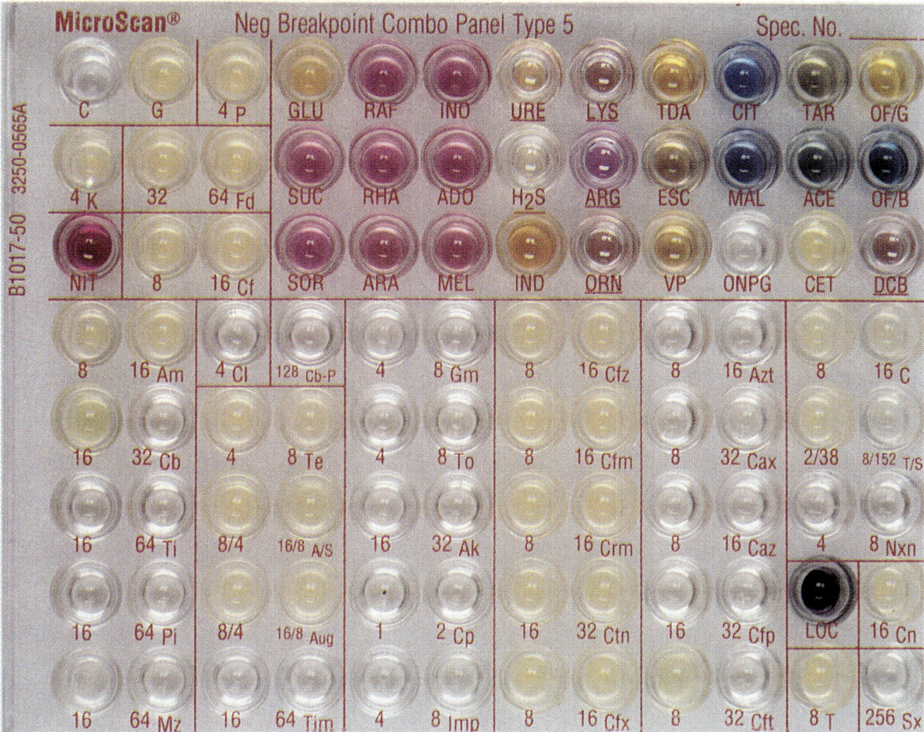

FIG. 2-30 Microtiter plate used in clinical microbiology laboratories for determination of metabolic characteristics of isolated bacteria. The color reactions indicate utilization of specific substances.

is these antigens that typically are the targets for the antigen-antibody reactions that are used to identify microorganisms. To identify microorganisms based on the reactions of antibodies with antigens, the antigens detected must be specifically associated with the target microorganism. The specificity of association of certain antigens with specific microorganisms and the unequivocal detection of the diagnostic antigens by antibodies is critical for serological identification.

Methods have been developed that make it easy to observe the reactions between specific antibodies and antigens when they occur (FIG. 2-31). These methods label the antibody so that it can be readily detected. In some methods the antibody is labelled with a fluorescent dye and is called a *fluorescent conjugated antibody*; cells stained with a fluorescent conjugated antibody can easily be seen using a fluorescence microscope. In other methods the antibody is linked to an enzyme of the substrate for an enzyme. This forms the basis for the *enzyme linked immunosorbant assay (ELISA)* that is widely used for the identification of microorganisms.

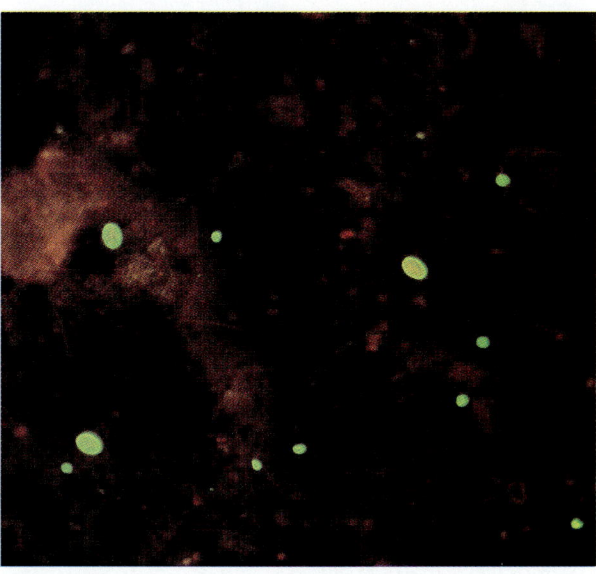

FIG. 2-31 Cysts of the pathogenic protozoa *Cryptosporidium* and *Giardia* stained with antibody conjugated fluorescent dyes. Only these specific protozoa fluoresce green.

Gene Probe Identification

To determine whether specific genes are present in the DNA of an organism, a method called *hybridization* is frequently used. **Hybridization** is the artificial construction of a double-stranded nucleic acid by complementary base pairing of two single-stranded nucleic acids (FIG. 2-32, *A*). The method is based on the fact that DNA is a double helical molecule composed of two complementary nucleotide strands held together by hydrogen bonds. Raising the temperature to 94° to 100° C breaks the hydrogen bonds without destroying the primary chains to form individual strands of DNA. This process is called *DNA melting*. If the temperature is lowered, complementary segments of the DNA reassociate. The process that reestablishes double-stranded DNA is called **reannealing**.

To detect specific DNA sequences, a small molecule of single-stranded RNA or DNA with a known sequence of nucleotides, called a **gene probe**, is added and the temperature is adjusted so that reannealing will occur. The gene probe will only reanneal to the target organism's DNA if most of the bases of the two strands are complementary. The procedures are designed so that the nonhybridized probe is washed away. If the hybridization occurs, the presence of the labelled gene probe can be detected (FIG. 2-32, *B*). Using gene probes, specific diagnostic genes can be detected and thereby used to identify various microorganisms.

A

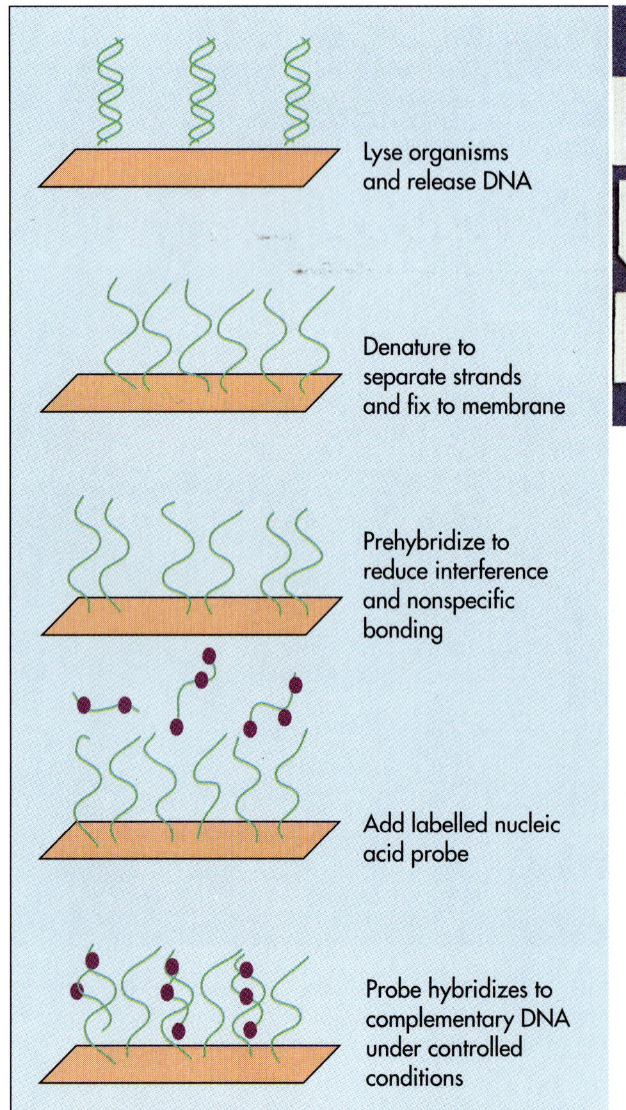
Lyse organisms and release DNA
Denature to separate strands and fix to membrane
Prehybridize to reduce interference and nonspecific bonding
Add labelled nucleic acid probe
Probe hybridizes to complementary DNA under controlled conditions

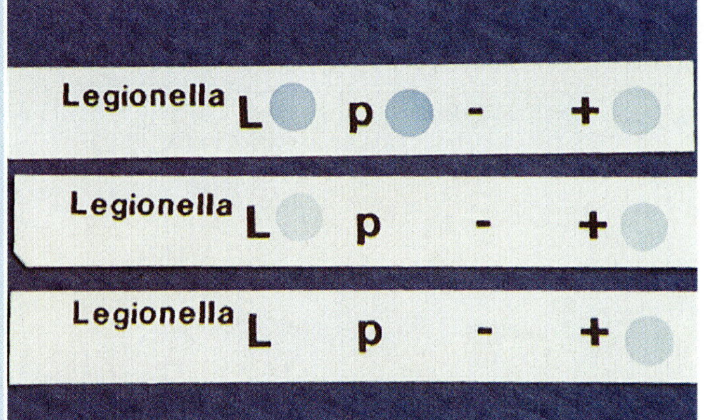
Legionella L p - +
Legionella L p - +
Legionella L p - +

B

FIG. 2-32 **A,** In DNA hybridization procedures for gene probe detection, cells are lysed to release double-stranded DNA. The DNA is denatured to convert it to single-stranded target DNA. The single-stranded DNA is affixed to a membrane. A prehybridization solution is used to prevent nonspecific binding to the membrane. A labelled nucleic acid probe (gene probe) is added. (The label may be a dye or a radioactive element.) The labelled probe hybridizes to complementary regions (if any) of the target DNA. **B,** Nucleic acid hybridization for detection of *Legionella*. The blue dots indicate where hybridization has occurred. The dots at the + are the positive control; these must be blue to read the test result. The dots at the − are the negative control; these must remain white to read the test result. A blue dot at the *L* indicates the presence of *Legionella* species. A blue dot at the *p* indicates the presence of *Legionella pneumophila*.

2.4 ENUMERATION OF BACTERIA

To assess the rate of microbial reproduction, it is necessary to determine the numbers of microorganisms present. There are various methods that can be employed for counting bacteria. Some of these methods count only live bacteria that are capable of reproducing in laboratory culture media. Others count all microbes in a sample, whether alive or dead.

Viable Count Procedures

Viable Plate Count

The **viable plate count method** is a common procedure for the enumeration of living bacteria (FIG. 2-33). Serial dilutions of a suspension of bacteria are plated onto a suitable solid growth medium. In streak or spread plate techniques the serial dilutions of the suspension are spread over the surfaces of solid agar plates, hence their general name of "spread surface techniques." In the pour plate technique, the serial dilutions are mixed with melted agar in separate tubes and then poured into culture plates where the agar solidifies. The plates are then incubated so that the bacteria can reproduce.

Bacterial reproduction on a solid medium results in the formation of a macroscopic colony visible to the naked eye. The formation of visible colonies generally

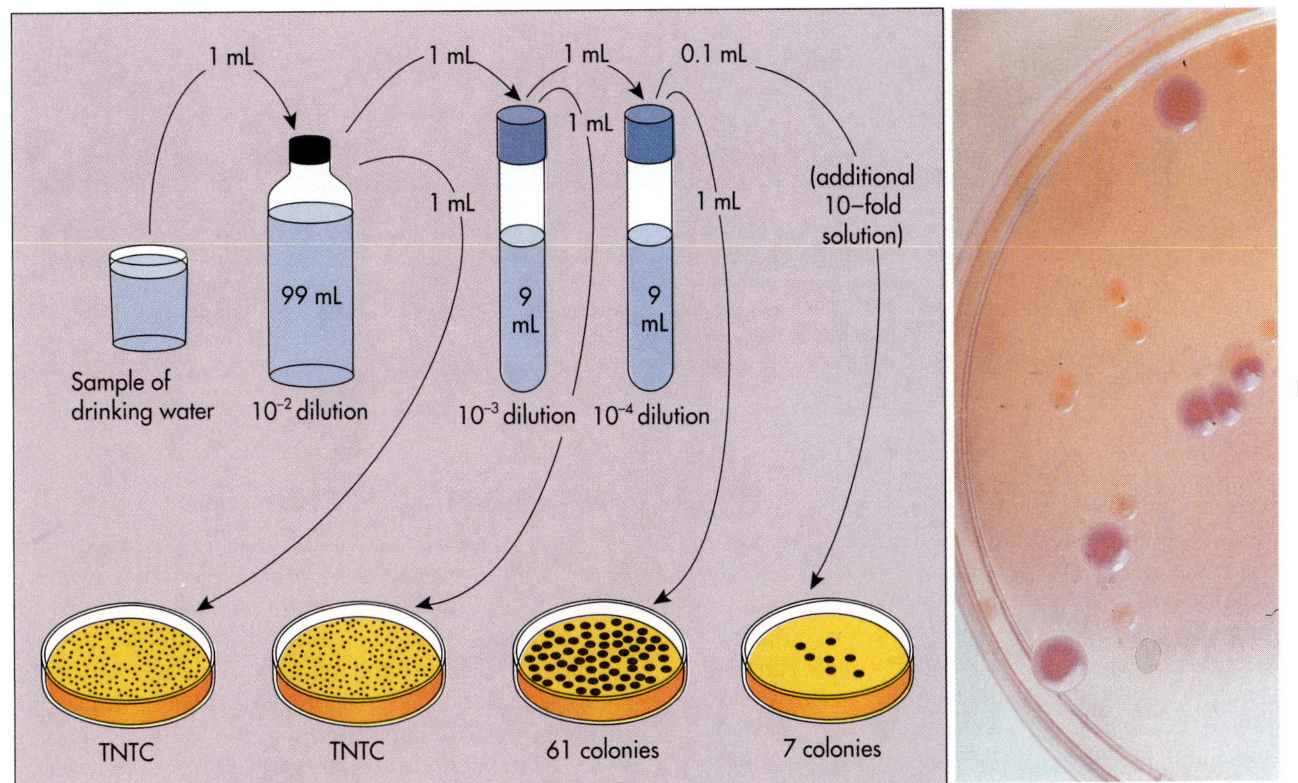

FIG. 2-33 **A,** The plate count procedure is used to determine the viable population in a sample containing bacteria. Dilutions are achieved by adding an aliquot of the specimen to a sterile water dilution tube. If 1 mL of a sample is added to 99 mL of sterile water, the dilution is 1:100 (10^{-2}). (The same dilution could also have been achieved by adding an 0.1 mL sample to 9.9 mL of sterile water). Greater dilutions are achieved by sequentially diluting the sample in series. Adding 1 mL from the first dilution to 9 mL of sterile water achieves an additional tenfold dilution, so that the total dilution is 1:1000 (10^{-3}). Adding 1 mL from that second dilution to 9 mL of sterile water achieves a further tenfold dilution, so that the total dilution is 1:10000 (10^{-4}). Transferring 1 mL samples from each tube to agar media maintains these dilution factors. Transferring 0.1 mL samples increases the dilution by a factor of 10. After incubation the number of colonies are counted. Counts on the plates in the range of 30 to 300 colonies are used to calculate the concentration of bacteria. The standard notation "TNTC" means too numerous to count (greater than 300 colonies). In this example the plate with 61 colonies would be used to calculate the number of bacteria in the original water sample. Because these colonies developed on a plate in which 1 mL from a 1:10000 dilution was added, the number of bacteria per mL in the original sample is calculated as 6.1×10^5 (61×10^4). **B,** Colonies of lactose fermenting bacteria growing on MacConkey agar.

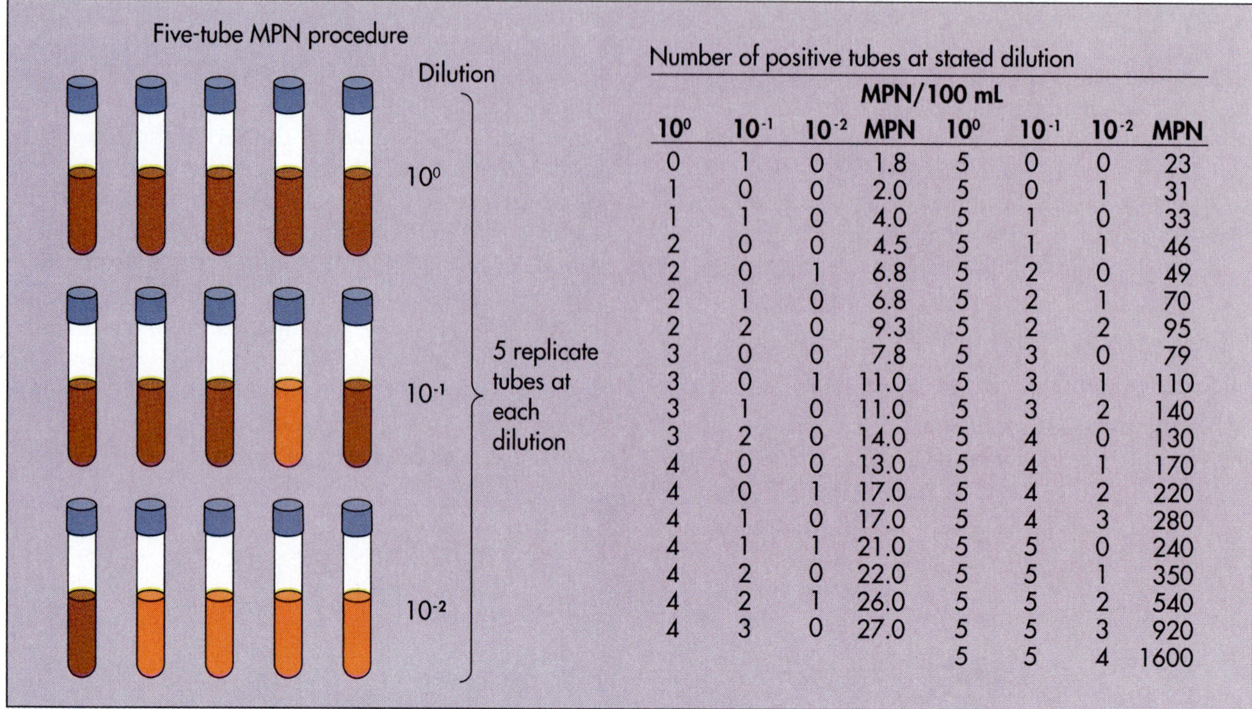

Number of positive tubes at stated dilution

MPN/100 mL							
10^0	10^{-1}	10^{-2}	MPN	10^0	10^{-1}	10^{-2}	MPN
0	1	0	1.8	5	0	0	23
1	0	0	2.0	5	0	1	31
1	1	0	4.0	5	1	0	33
2	0	0	4.5	5	1	1	46
2	0	1	6.8	5	2	0	49
2	1	0	6.8	5	2	1	70
2	2	0	9.3	5	2	2	95
3	0	0	7.8	5	3	0	79
3	0	1	11.0	5	3	1	110
3	1	0	11.0	5	3	2	140
3	2	0	14.0	5	4	0	130
4	0	0	13.0	5	4	1	170
4	0	1	17.0	5	4	2	220
4	1	0	17.0	5	4	3	280
4	1	1	21.0	5	5	0	240
4	2	0	22.0	5	5	1	350
4	2	1	26.0	5	5	2	540
4	3	0	27.0	5	5	3	920
				5	5	4	1600

FIG. 2-34 The most probable number (MPN) procedure involves inoculation of multiple tubes with replicate samples of dilutions. The pattern of tubes that show growth (*brown*) and those that do not (*red*) are compared with a statistical table to calculate the MPN of bacteria in the original sample. In this example, all 5 tubes at the 10^0 dilution show growth; 4 of 5 tubes at the 10^{-1} dilution show growth; and only 1 of 5 tubes at the 10^{-2} dilution show growth. Therefore the MPN bacteria in the original sample is 170 per 100 mL.

takes 16 to 24 hours. It is assumed that each colony arises from an individual bacterial cell. Therefore by counting the number of colonies that develop, **colony-forming units (CFUs)**, and by taking into account the dilution factors, the concentration of bacteria (number of bacteria/mL) in the original sample can be determined. Countable plates are those having between 30 and 300 colonies. Fewer than 30 colonies are not acceptable for statistical reasons, and more than 300 colonies on a plate are likely to produce colonies too close to each other to be distinguished as individual CFUs.

A limitation of the viable plate count procedure in enumerating bacteria from natural environments is its selectivity. There is no set of incubation conditions and medium composition that permits the growth of all bacterial types. The nature of the growth medium and the incubation conditions determine which bacteria can grow and thus be counted. Viable counting measures only cells that are capable of growth on the given plating medium under the set of incubation conditions that are used. Sometimes bacterial cells are *viable but nonculturable* in the medium and incubation conditioning chosen by the experimenter.

Most Probable Number (MPN) Procedures

Another approach to viable bacterial enumeration, determination of the **most probable number** (MPN), is a statistical method based on probability theory. In an MPN enumeration procedure, multiple serial dilutions are performed to reach a point of extinction, that is, a dilution level at which not even a single cell is deposited into one or more of the multiple tubes at that dilution level. A criterion, such as the development of cloudiness or turbidity in a liquid growth medium, is established for indicating whether a particular dilution tube contains bacteria. The pattern of positive and negative test results is then used to estimate the concentration of bacteria in the original sample, that is, the MPN of bacteria, by comparing the observed pattern of results with a table of statistical probabilities for obtaining those results (FIG. 2-34).

Direct Count Procedures

Bacteria can be enumerated by **direct counting procedures**, that is, counting without the need to first grow the cells in culture. These procedures generally count *all* bacterial cells whether they are viable or not.

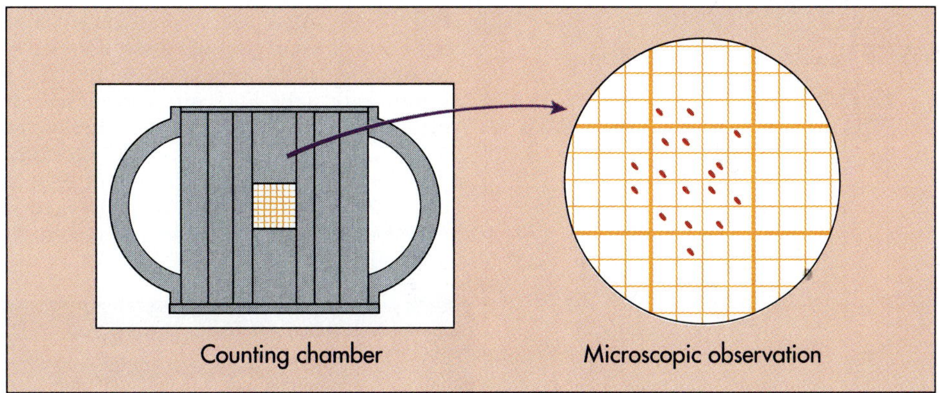

FIG. 2-35 The direct counting procedure, using the Petroff-Hauser counting procedure. The sample is added to a counting chamber of known volume. The slide is viewed and the number of cells determined in an area delimited by a grid. In the counting chamber shown, the entire grid has 25 large squares for a total area of 1 mm^2 and a total volume of 2×10^{-5} mL. There are 12 cells within the single large grid (composed of 16 smaller boxes) in this example. Assuming the number of cells in this single grid is representative of all the grids, the number of cells within the total area under the grids is 12×25 cells. The concentration of cells is therefore $300/2 \times 10^{-5}$ mL = 1.5×10^7 cells/mL.

In one type of direct counting procedure, dilutions of samples are observed under a microscope and the number of bacterial cells in a given volume of sample is counted and used to calculate the concentration of bacteria in the original sample. Special counting chambers such as a hemocytometer or Petroff-Hausser chamber are sometimes used (FIG. 2-35). These chambers are ruled with squares of known area and are so constructed that a film of liquid of known depth can be introduced between the slide and the cover slip. Consequently, the volume of liquid overlying each square is known. To help visualize bacterial cells, it is often desirable to stain the cells. Alternatively, a known volume of a sample containing a suspension of bacteria is passed through a filter, for example, a bacteriological filter with a 0.2 μm pore size. The bacteria are stained on this filter and counted under a microscope. Fluorescent dyes are frequently used to stain bacteria in direct counting procedures. However, such dyes stain all of the cells, making it impossible to differentiate living bacteria from dead bacteria. The difficulty in establishing the metabolic status of the observed bacteria, that is, whether the cells are living or dead, is a major limitation of this procedure.

Some procedures can be used with direct microscopic observations to distinguish viable from nonviable cells. Cells can be incubated with nalidixic acid prior to direct microscopic observation. Nalidixic acid blocks cell division and so in its presence viable cells become elongated. The observation of elongated cells is objective evidence of cell viability, and cells that are not elongated show no sign of the growth that characterizes viable bacterial cells. Alternately, cells can be incubated with chemicals that change color when acted on by specific enzymes that are active in viable cells. INT, for example, forms pink-red deposits in cells when acted on by dehydrogenases. The observation of cells with pink-red inclusions after treatment with INT indicates that those cells were metabolically active (viable); the observation of cells lacking such inclusions indicates that those cells were metabolically inactive (nonviable).

Another approach to direct counting is to use an electronic particle counter such as a Coulter counter. This instrument can register the magnitude and duration of the changes in conductivity of a suspension of bacterial cells as they pass through a small orifice and thus can register and record both the number and distribution of the size of a cellular population. Such instruments permit the discrimination of particles based on size so that particles the size of bacteria can be counted automatically. If there are no nonliving interfering particles in the same size range of bacteria, this is a rapid counting method.

TURBIDIMETRIC PROCEDURES

When a beam of light passes through a suspension of particles the size of bacteria, the light is scattered. In effect, the *turbidity* of the solution reduces the amount of light that can pass through. Measuring the amount of light that passes through a suspension of microorganisms with a spectrophotometer (FIG. 2-36) or other optical measuring device can be used for estimating cell mass, since the amount of light absorbed or scattered by the microorganisms is proportional to the concentration of cells.

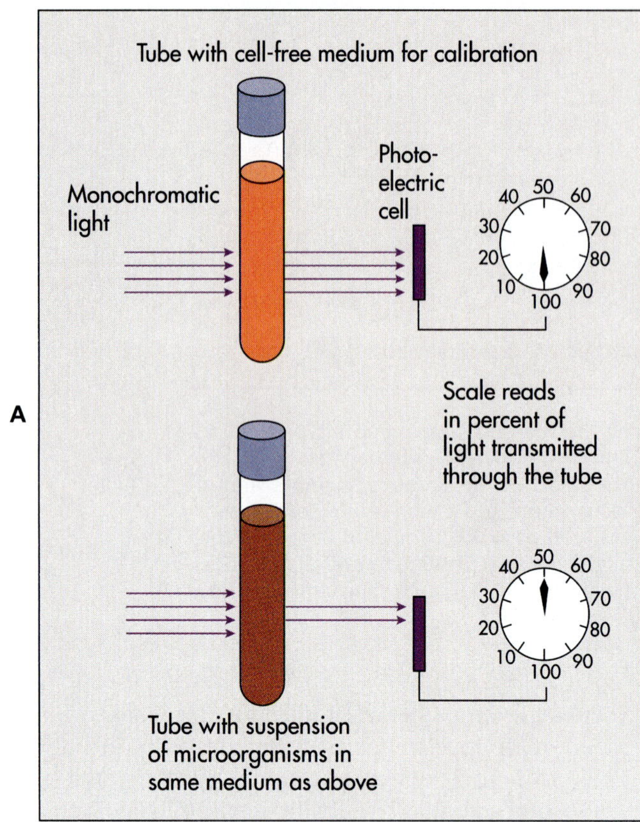

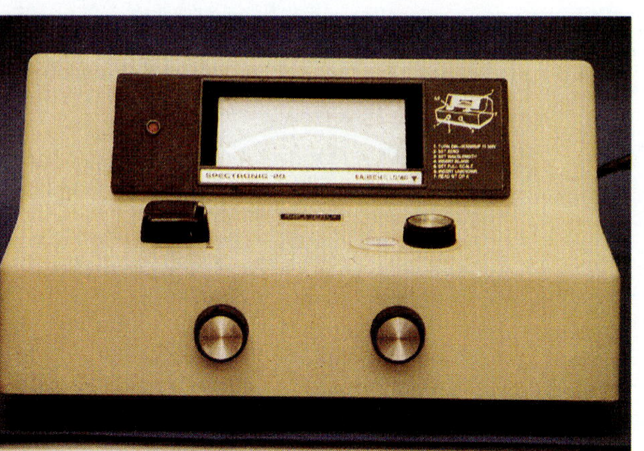

FIG. 2-36 **A,** A spectrophotometer is used to measure light transmission through a solution. Particles such as bacterial cells in the suspension reduce the amount of light transmission. The lower the percent light transmission, the greater the number of cells. **B,** A spectrophotometer is used in microbiology laboratories to determine cell numbers. The reading of light transmission or light absorbance made using the spectrophotometer is compared with standard curves to estimate the number of cells in the microbial suspension.

Spectrophotometers measure absorbency units (A), which follows the log of (I_0/I) where I_0 is the intensity of light striking a suspension and I is the intensity of light transmitted by the suspension. The absorbency or optical density (OD) of a solution is related to the percentage of light transmitted ($\%T$) through the solution according to the formula:

$$\text{OD} = \log 100 - \log \%T$$

When calibrated against bacterial suspensions of known concentration, a requirement for estimating cell concentrations, spectrophotometers provide an accurate and rapid way to estimate the dry weight (mass) of bacteria per unit volume of culture. An increase in cell mass, which can be equated with increases in the number of bacterial cells, is useful for establishing a growth curve for a bacterium.

Because bacteria are in suspension, not in solution, a measure of the absorbency of a bacterial suspension is not a direct measure of the bacterial cell concentration. In fact, because light scattering also contributes so significantly to the determination, the measured value of A depends on the precise geometry of the instrument used. The value of A of a bacterial suspension measured on one instrument will not be the same as that measured on a different instrument. The instrument must be calibrated for the particular bacterium and medium being studied by directly determining the number of bacteria in a dense suspension and by measuring its absorbance A, as well as the absorbance of known dilutions of the suspension. At low densities A is roughly proportional to the cell number, but at higher densities there is a significant deviation from linearity. Such deviation is a consequence of double scattering; at high culture densities the probability of a scattered ray of light being scattered back so that it strikes the photodetection system is increased.

CHAPTER REVIEW

STUDY QUESTIONS

1. What is resolution, and why is it important in microscopy? What factors influence resolution, and why do we consider an electron microscope superior to a light microscope?
2. What organisms and structures can be seen with a light microscope? What organisms and structures can be seen with a TEM?
3. What is meant by the term *useful magnification*?

CHAPTER REVIEW

STUDY QUESTIONS—CONT'D

4. Why do we stain microorganisms before viewing them with a microscope?
5. What is the difference between a simple and a differential stain?
6. Name five types of microscopes, and discuss the advantages and disadvantages of each.
7. How does a scanning electron microscope differ from a transmission electron microscope? What are the different applications for each of these electron microscopes?
8. What is a pure culture? Why do we place such importance on obtaining and maintaining pure cultures?
9. What is aseptic transfer technique? Why must you master this technique to work in a microbiology laboratory?
10. Discuss three methods for isolating pure cultures of microorganisms.
11. Why are so many types of microbiological media employed in laboratories for the culture of microorganisms?
12. How are selective and differential media used in the clinical laboratory?
13. Discuss three approaches to the enumeration of bacteria. What are the advantages and disadvantages of each?
14. What is a gene probe and how is it used in molecular biology?
15. Discuss why you might want to determine a sequence of DNA or RNA.

SITUATIONAL PROBLEMS

1. Selecting a Microscope

As a microbiologist, you may need to purchase a microscope. Microscopes have a wide price range and many options. When purchasing a microscope, you must determine the applications for which it will be used and the technical requirements for those applications. Performance and cost depend largely on the objective lenses and any special applications such as phase contrast capability. Once your own requirements for a microscope are established, consult the microscope catalogs available from your departmental office, scientific buyer or purchasing department, and/or a scientific supply house to obtain the necessary information concerning available options and costs.

If you go to medical school, you will likely be required to purchase your own microscope. To determine your microscope requirements, assume that you will be taking courses in histology and microbiology. Based on the sorts of microscopic observations you anticipate being required to make in these courses, you can determine the resolving and magnifying capabilities needed and whether you should add special options such as phase contrast. You will then be able to choose the lenses that you need and add up the costs. Pay careful attention to the extra cost needed to obtain increased resolution. Don't be shocked by the total cost.

2. Ensuring Drinking Water Safety

Based on your expertise in bacteriology, you have a part-time summer job working with the municipal board of health to perform routine tests on the bacteriological quality of food and water. Your job involves performing tests to determine the number of bacteria in samples sent to the health department and reviewing test results from independent laboratories. Your main concern is with enteric pathogens, which are bacteria that cause disease when they enter the gastrointestinal tract and which tend to be shed with fecal matter. To test for the presence of such bacteria, you look for coliform bacteria (*Escherichia coli*), which are found in high numbers in human fecal matter. By using this indicator organism, you provide a margin of safety because the actual enteric pathogens generally are present in much lower numbers than coliforms and hence might be missed.

To detect coliforms, your laboratory uses eosin methylene blue (EMB) agar (see Table 2-2) because it is selective for Gram-negative bacteria and because coliforms produce colonies with a green metallic sheen due to their ability to use the lactose in this medium. The standard that you are using for determining the safety of the water supply is a maximal permissible coliform count of 4/100 mL. To detect coliforms in this concentration, you filter a water sample to collect the bacteria on the filter and place the filter on the surface of an agar plate. The nutrients diffuse through the filter and colonies develop directly on the surface of the filter. The procedure that you use is as follows. You filter 1 liter, 100 mL, and 10 mL water samples through separate 0.45 μm Nuclepore filters and place them on EMB agar plates. After they incubate for 24 hours, you examine the filters and count only the colonies with a green metallic sheen.

You fail to detect more than five colonies on any of the plates on samples from the municipal water supply. On one well water sample from a rural farm, the 1 liter filter is completely overgrown, the 100 mL filter has 80 colonies with a green metallic sheen, and the 10 mL filter has 13 colonies with a green metallic sheen. What recommendations would you make?

Suggested Supplementary Readings

Aldrich HC and WJ Todd (eds.): 1986. *Ultrastructure Techniques for Microorganisms,* Plenum Press, New York.

Atlas RM: 1993. *Handbook of Microbiological Media,* CRC Press, Boca Raton, FL.

Ausubel FM, R Brent, RE Kingston, DD Moore, JA Smith, JG Sideman, K Struhl: 1987. *Current Protocols in Molecular Biology,* John Wiley and Sons, Inc., New York.

Badbury S: 1984. *An Introduction to the Optical Microscope,* Oxford University Press, Oxford, England.

Balows A: 1991. *Manual of Clinical Microbiology,* ed. 5, American Society for Microbiology, Washington, D. C.

Boatman ES, MW Berns, RJ Walter, JS Foster: 1987. Today's microscopy, *BioScience* 37:384-394.

Clark G (ed): 1980. *Staining Procedures,* ed. 4, Williams & Wilkins, Baltimore, MD.

Collins CH: 1989. *Microbiological Methods,* ed. 6, Butterworth-Heinemann, Stoneham, MA.

Delly JB: 1988. *Photography Through the Microscope,* ed. 9, Eastman Kodak Company, Rochester, NY.

Ferris FG and TL Beveridge: 1985. Functions of bacterial cell surface structures, *BioScience* 35(3):172-177.

Ford TC and JM Graham: 1991. *An Introduction to Centrifugation,* BIOS Scientific, Oxford, England.

Gerhardt P (ed.): 1993. *Manual of Methods for General Bacteriology,* American Society for Microbiology, Washington, D.C.

Glauert AM: 1975. *Fixation, Dehydration and Embedding of Biological Specimens: Practical Methods in Electron Microscopy,* Elsevier Science Publisher, Amsterdam, The Netherlands.

Harris JR (ed): 1991. *Electron Microscopy in Biology: A Practical Approach,* IRL Press, Oxford, England.

Hayat MA: 1978. *Introduction to Biological Scanning Electron Microscopy,* University Park Press, Baltimore.

Howells MR, J Kirz, W. Sayre: 1991. X-ray microscopes, *Scientific American* 264(2):88-97.

Labeda DP: 1990. *Isolation of Biotechnological Organisms from Nature,* McGraw-Hill, New York.

Laskin A and HA Lechevalier: 1977-1981. *Handbook of Microbiology,* 4 volumes, CRC Press, Boca Raton, FL.

Norris JR and DW Ribbons (eds.): 1969-. *Methods in Microbiology,* Academic Press, New York.

Rash J and CS Hudson: 1982. *Electron Microscopy Methods and Applications,* Praeger Publishers, New York.

Rochow TG and EG Rochow: 1979. *An Introduction to Microscopy: By Means of Light, Electrons, X-Rays or Ultrasound,* Plenum Publishing Co., New York.

Sambrook J, EF Fritsch, T Maniatis: 1989. *Molecular Cloning: A Laboratory Manual,* Volumes 1-3, Cold Spring Harbor Laboratory, Cold Spring Harbor, New York.

Schatten G and JB Pawley: 1988. Advances in optical, confocal and electron microscopic imaging for biomedical researchers, *Science* 239:164-165.

Scherrer R: 1984. Gram's staining reaction: Gram types and cell walls of bacteria, *Trends in Biochemical Science* 9:243-245.

Shih G and R Kessel: 1982. *Living Images: Biological Microstructures Revealed by Scanning Electron Microscopy,* Jones and Bartlett Publishers, Inc., Boston.

Wang Y and DL Taylor (eds): 1989. *Fluorescence Microscopy of Living Cells in Culture,* Academic Press, San Diego, CA.

Wischnitzer S: 1981. *Introduction to Electron Microscopy,* Pergamon Press, New York.

MICROBIOLOGY IN THE 1990S AND BEYOND: CHALLENGES AND REWARDS

ALICE S. HUANG
NEW YORK UNIVERSITY

Alice Shih-Hou Huang was born in Kiangsi, China, in 1939. She received her education at Johns Hopkins University. Dr. Huang was professor of microbiology and molecular genetics at Harvard Medical School and currently serves as dean of science at New York University. Her research is on the replication of RNA in animal viruses. She was president of the American Society for Microbiology (1987-1988).

Since I was 7 years old I thought that saving lives and helping humankind would be a wonderful way to spend the rest of my life, but during medical school when I got into my first research laboratory I was surprised. Instead of finding slimy molds and smelly germs all over the place or bubbling cauldrons tended by mad scientist types, the laboratory was spanking clean. It was then that I discovered that there was a whole area of science called microbiology that dealt with microorganisms.

The history of microbiology began in 1677 when Antony van Leeuwenhoek, a Dutch cloth merchant and amateur scientist, put a drop of water under a light microscope and saw, magnified 150 times, small dots and dashes that appeared to be swimming around. He called these "animalcules." This was the first proof that in the world, beyond what we can see with the naked eye, there lay numerous organisms of an unimaginable diversity that populate every corner of the earth. Of course, even without our seeing them, their manifestations were well known in ancient times. Diseases such as leprosy, poliomyelitis, and rabies and the ability to ferment wines and make cheeses, all dependent on microorganisms, were well documented from the earliest of recorded history. But knowing the effects produced by these microorganisms did not lead to their recognition until many centuries later.

Today, microbiology as a science has extended into so many fields that it has a problem identifying itself as one discipline. It encompasses not only bacteria and viruses but also other microorganisms such as yeast and parasites. The single cell, whether it is a small self-contained organism like the paramecium or a building block of a human being, falls within the province of microbiology and is studied as a microorganism. From a rather limited definition, microbiology has enlarged so that it now provides the essential basic underpinning of almost all the life sciences.

The widening scope of microbiology has become particularly obvious during the last 10 years. Such fast moving areas of the life sciences such as molecular biology and molecular genetics depend on a thorough understanding of microbiology and the ability to manipulate microorganisms in the laboratory. For example, the study of genetics depends on the identification of genes as individual pieces of DNA and cloning them in bacterial or eucaryotic systems. The use of yeast artificial chromosomes (YACS) provides rapid means of isolating any desired gene, once its map position is known. The selection and amplification of rare nucleic acid sequences by the polymerase chain reaction (PCR) is now done on a routine basis. This is made possible by the use of a heat-resistance enzyme obtained from a microorganism. The cascade of events involved in the regulation of gene expression are analyzed using sophisticated manipulations of bacterial products.

Viruses, long studied as the simplest replicating systems, have become probes for dissecting the functions of the cell, thus moving the study of cell biology from microscopic observations to defined molecular analyses. Genetic loci responsible for human hereditary diseases are now mapped, using microbiology based DNA isolation methodologies such as restriction enzyme fragment-linked polymorphism (RFLPs) made possible because of sequence-specific DNA cutting enzymes obtained from bacteria. Their products are measured with highly specific antibodies, now also generated in bacteria.

Almost every area of medicine from diagnosis and prevention to potential cure depends in some way on microbiology. This represents much more than the simple use of recombinant DNA technology. Infectious diseases provide many classical examples. For these, any hope of combating a disease depends on identifying the causative agent, which often turns out to be a microorganism. Diagnosis has moved from traditional methods involving isolation and culture of the organism to rapid identification by immunofluorescense using monoclonal antibodies or the PCR. Prevention depends on the development of vaccines, which are microorganisms that are altered in their disease-causing potential and which, instead, can be used to stimulate the host's protective responses.

Microorganisms are being tested in many of the newer vaccines—examples are (1) the engineering of a vaccine normally used to protect against smallpox to carry an additional gene, that of the human immunodeficiency virus (HIV), the agent that causes AIDS, and (2) the addition to *Salmonella* bacteria, which normally resides in the gut, of another surface property so that it elicits host defense mechanisms that are active in the gut. Because of microorganisms' natural inclination to compete for similar ecological niches by defending themselves with a range of antibiotics we can harvest these antibiotics to combat microbial diseases of humans.

Even in noninfectious diseases, such as atherosclerosis or dwarfism, powerful enzymatic or hormonal products fashioned and made possible by microbial biotechnology are making a difference in the lives of afflicted individuals. Genetic analysis of hereditary disease, early diagnosis, and treatment are leading gradually to the elimination of some of the worst diseases that plague mankind. Autoimmune or allergic reactions, themselves often triggered by microbial infection, reflect natural host defense mechanisms that appear to have gone awry. These examples represent only the beginning. The practice of medicine will continue to be changed by the ever new tools provided through microbiology. A general acknowledgement of this trend in clinical medicine is shown by the establishment of new research centers of molecular medicine at several of the most prestigious universities.

The growing commercial area that takes advantage of microbiology, biotechnology, is based historically in industrial and agricultural scientific interests. Traditionally the antibiotics and the enzymes produced were genetically prescribed by microorganisms and the microorganisms themselves served as factories for the mass production of these valuable products. Now, in addition, microorganisms produce new biologically important substances from genes that we provide them. Added to these now classic uses of microorganisms, it is noteworthy that there are now numerous examples of microorganisms trained, mutated, and selected in the laboratory to solve some of the important environmental problems now facing our planet. Microorganisms to reduce carbon dioxide levels, to eat up oil spills, and to reduce toxic wastes are or will become realities. Microorganisms will contribute to alternative and cheap sources of energy someday. The world's nutritional needs may be met by harnessing microorganisms. On the other hand, the same genetic engineering techniques developed with microorganisms have led to a new agricultural revolution, which is only just beginning. The possibilities are numerous and limited only by our imaginations.

An often forgotten part of microbiology is its importance as an educational tool. Because genetically identical microorganisms grow to large numbers in a short period of time, they provide ideal populations for the novice to study and manipulate. For a beginning student, microorganisms are used to demonstrate genetics and biostatistics. Training in microbiology not only provides an understanding of the individual microorganisms and their biosynthetic pathways, it also encompasses training in quantitative reasoning and molecular concepts important to many other fields. Understanding such basic concepts becomes important to the future decision-making process of every adult, whether they become scientists or not.

Knowing all this, how could someone not become engaged in microbiology at some time in his or her life? I certainly could not resist. That entry into my first research laboratory led me into discovering viruses. After I started purifying viruses, I recognized that even viruses had their parasites, and I named them defective interfering virus particles. Now it remains for future generations of scientists to find out how these particles affect disease processes and how they might be harnessed to benefit humankind.

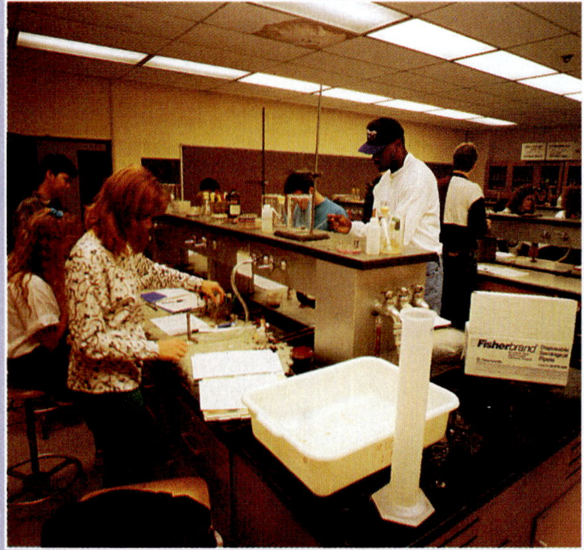

The excitement of the science of microbiology grows from the laboratory where scientific enquiry pursues new knowledge.

PART TWO

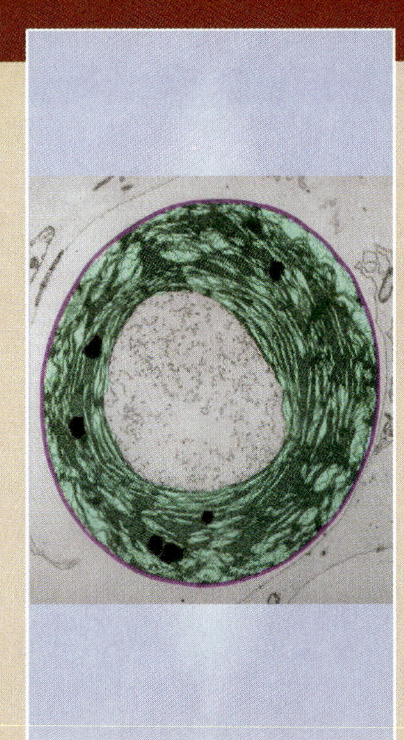

Microbial Physiology—Cellular Biology

CHAPTER 3

Organization and Structure of Microorganisms

Chapter Outline

Living systems are characterized by the ability to exist in a highly ordered state while interacting dynamically with their environment. From their surroundings, living organisms acquire energy and materials, which they use to assemble their structural components and to maintain their structural integrity. When they fail to do so, they die and their highly organized state disappears. In this chapter we consider the properties of the functional and structural unit of all living organisms—the cell—and how this basic unit of organization permits an organism to obtain and process the energy and materials it requires for life. Structural and functional components of the cell are compared, and the similarities and differences of eubacterial, archaebacterial, and eukaryotic cells are highlighted.

3.1 CELLS: THE BASIC ORGANIZATIONAL UNITS OF LIVING SYSTEMS

The **cell** is the fundamental structural unit of all living organisms. A cell is a self-contained unit separated from its surroundings by a cytoplasmic membrane that serves as its limiting boundary. Within the cytoplasmic membrane, the cell contains a fluid called *cytoplasm.* The cell has hereditary information in molecules of DNA, processes genetic information using RNA intermediates to form proteins at ribosomes, and uses ATP as the central cellular form of energy. This genetic information permits each cell to reproduce its own organizational pattern by itself. Enzymatic reactions within the cell generate ATP and form new substances for cellular growth and reproduction.

UNIFYING PROPERTIES OF CELLS

All cells have certain common functional and structural properties:

1. Each cell has a **cytoplasmic membrane** that surrounds it, forming a boundary between the living cell and the surroundings. The cytoplasmic membrane regulates the passage of materials into and out of the cell. Such regulation allows the cell to maintain a more organized internal state than the cell's external surroundings.
2. Each cell contains a fluid substance, called the **cytoplasm.** Chemical reactions that transform the energy and material needed for cell growth and reproduction take place in the cytoplasm. The cytoplasm consists of a solution, called the *cytosol,* and various particulate structures. The concentrations of dissolved substances, such as amino acids and sugars, within the cytosol are very different from those of the outside environment.
3. Each cell contains hereditary information stored in double helical macromolecules of **DNA (deoxyribonucleic acid).** DNA, which directs the activities of the cell, is copied and transferred to new cells formed as a result of cellular reproduction, and thereby hereditary information is passed to succeeding generations.
4. Each cell has thousands of small structures called **ribosomes** where proteins are made. The actual transfer of genetic information from DNA into proteins involves the formation of another informational molecule, **RNA (ribonucleic acid).** RNA carries the genetic information to the ribosomes where that information is used to direct the synthesis of proteins. Proteins that act as enzymes are the molecules that actually perform the metabolic functions of the cell.
5. Each cell utilizes energy from **ATP (adenosine triphosphate),** the "universal energy currency" of living cells. Energy is needed to convert raw materials obtained from the cell's surroundings into cellular structures. The processes of metabolism capture the energy stored in nutrient molecules and convert it to a more usable energy molecule, ATP.

PROKARYOTIC AND EUKARYOTIC CELLS

There are two distinct organizational patterns among living cells that distinguish the *prokaryotic cells* of the eubacteria and archaebacteria from the *eukaryotic cells* of all other living organisms. The differences between prokaryotic and eukaryotic cells represent an important division of living systems. Because of their differences in cellular organization, eukaryotic and prokaryotic microorganisms possess different structures and strategies for carrying out essentially the same physiological and reproductive functions, which include the generation of energy in the form of ATP—and the storage and expression of genetic information. Table 3-1 lists the structures in prokaryotes and eukaryotes.

The **prokaryotic cell** is a simply organized cell, lacking specialized internal membrane-bound compartments known as **organelles** that characterize the more complex and larger eukaryotic cell (Table 3-2). In particular, the DNA of a prokaryotic cell is not contained within the specialized organelle called the *nucleus* (FIG. 3-1). In contrast, the **eukaryotic cell** has a nucleus (FIG. 3-2). In fact, by definition, all eukaryotic cells at some time have a nucleus, whereas prokaryotic cells never possess this organelle; *eukaryotic* means "true nucleus" and *prokaryotic* means "before the nucleus." Eukaryotic cells also have numerous other organelles that serve specialized functions. Presumably, as cells evolved into more advanced forms, greater separation of function was needed to carry out the operations of the cell efficiently; hence, the eukaryotic cell acquired organelles from prokaryotic cells by endosymbiotic evolution. Comparable functions are not so structurally separated within prokaryotic cells.

The structural differences between the prokaryotic cells of bacteria and the eukaryotic cells of plants and animals have great practical importance. For example, the ability to use an antimicrobial agent such as penicillin to treat human bacterial diseases depends on targeting such agents against specific structures found only in prokaryotic bacterial cells. Otherwise, we would be killing eukaryotic human cells at the same time. It is more difficult to target agents selectively against disease-causing fungi and protozoa, which, like humans, have eukaryotic cells. Therefore we have far fewer drugs of therapeutic value and more difficulty in treating infections when eukaryotic microorganisms invade the human body.

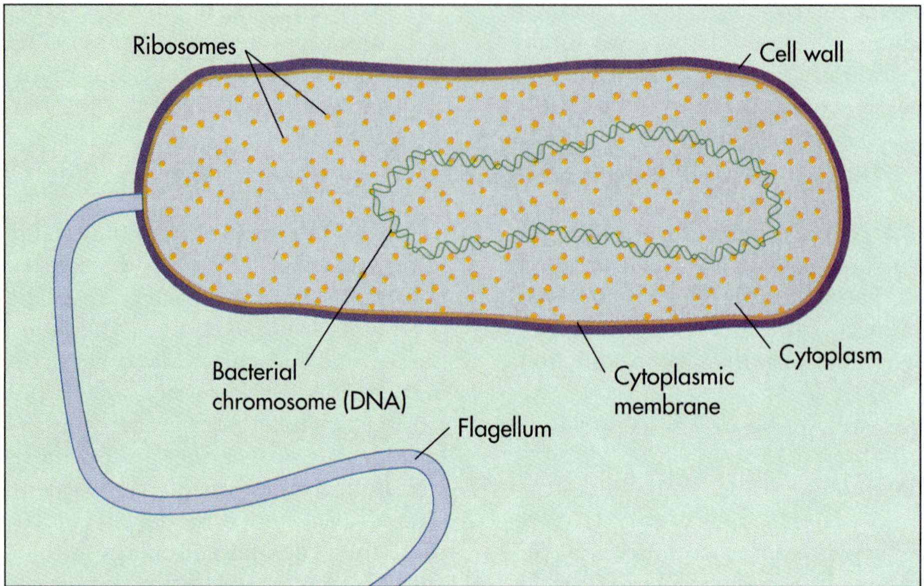

FIG. 3-1 The prokaryotic cell has a cytoplasmic membrane enclosing the cytoplasm within which there is a bacterial chromosome made of DNA that stores the hereditary information. There are numerous membrane-bound ribosomes in the cytoplasm where proteins are synthesized. Almost all bacterial cells have a cell wall that surrounds the cytoplasmic membrane and protects the cell. Some prokaryotic cells have a flagellum that rotates and propels the cell so that it can move from place to place.

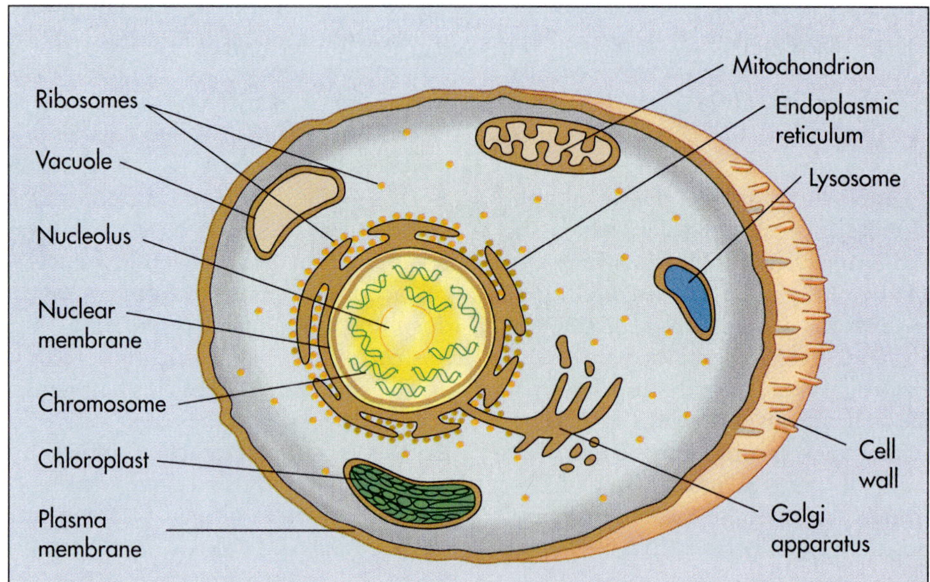

FIG. 3-2 The eukaryotic cell has far more internal organization than the prokaryotic cell; it has numerous membrane-bound organelles that do not occur in prokaryotic cells, including a nucleus within which chromosomes store the hereditary information.

TABLE 3-1 Comparison of Structures Found in Prokaryotic and Eukaryotic Cells

		PROKARYOTIC CELLS		EUKARYOTIC CELLS				
STRUCTURE	FUNCTION	ARCHAEBACTERIA	EUBACTERIA	FUNGI	ALGAE	PROTOZOA	PLANTS	ANIMALS
Cytoplasmic membrane	Semipermeable barrier; regulation of substances moving into and out of cell	+	+	+	+	+	+	+
Cell wall (with peptidoglycan)*	Protects cell against osmotic shock	−	+	−	−	−	−	−
Cell wall (without peptidoglycan)	Protects cell against osmotic shock or physical damage	+	−	+	+	−	+	−
Flagella	Cell movement	+	+	+	+	+	−	+
Cilia	Cell movement; movement of materials	−	−	−	−	+	−	+
Nucleoid	Region of DNA concentration; heredity control	+	+	−	−	−	−	−
Nucleus	Membrane-bound organelle containing DNA; region of heredity control	−	−	+	+	+	+	+
Nucleolus	Formation of ribosomal subunits	−	−	+	+	+	+	+
Bacterial chromosome	Circular molecule of DNA that contains genome (hereditary information)	+	+	−	−	−	−	−
Chromosomes	Linear molecules that contain the genome; DNA stores the hereditary information; protein establishes structure of the chromosome essential for gene expression	−	−	+	+	+	+	+
Ribosome	Translation of genetic information carried by mRNA into proteins; protein synthesis	+	+	+	+	+	+	+
Endoplasmic reticulum	Processing and transport of proteins and other substances through cell; communication of chemicals and coordination of functions within cell	−	−	+	+	+	+	+
Golgi body	Processing and packaging of chemicals for transport out of cell	−	−	+	+	+	+	+
Lysosome	Containment of digestive enzymes; controlled degradation of substances	−	−	+	+	+	+	+
Cytoskeleton	Organization and support of organelles within cell	−	−	+	+	+	+	+
Mitochondrion	Respiratory chemiosmotic generation of ATP	−	−	+	+	+	+	+
Chloroplast	Photosynthetic chemiosmotic generation of ATP	−	−	−	+	−	+	−
Endospore†	Survival; heat resistance	−	+	−	−	−	−	−

*Lacking in some eubacteria. †Present in only a few eubacteria.

TABLE 3-2 Descriptions of Some Membrane-bound Organelles Found in Eukaryotic Cells that do not occur in Prokaryotic Cells

ORGANELLE	DESCRIPTION
Nucleus	Stores the genetic information (genome) of the eukaryotic cell; within the nucleus, genetic information is processed before it is sent out for use in directing protein synthesis.
Mitochondrion	Site of respiratory ATP generation. Hydrogen ions are translocated across the inner membrane of the mitochondrion to establish the electrochemical gradient needed for driving the generation of ATP.
Chloroplast	Site of photosynthetic ATP generation. Chlorophyll and auxiliary pigments in the chloroplast trap light energy, which is used to generate ATP. In this process, hydrogen ions are translocated across the inner membrane of the chloroplast to establish the electrochemical gradient needed for driving the generation of ATP.
Endoplasmic reticulum	Extensive membrane network used to coordinate the flow of material within the cell. Proteins made at ribosomes attached to the surface of the endoplasmic reticulum move through its tubular structure to other organelles.
Golgi apparatus	Associated with the endoplasmic reticulum, this organelle is involved with packaging of materials for export from the cell.
Vacuoles	Various types of vacuoles occur in different cells, where they serve different functions. Some vacuoles store reserve materials, others are involved with digestive functions, and one type—the contractile vacuole—pumps water out of the cell.
Lysosomes	Organelles that contain digestive enzymes.
Microbodies	Organelles that contain degradative enzymes that generate hydrogen peroxide during the metabolic transformations they catalyze.

3.2 CYTOPLASMIC MEMBRANE: MOVEMENT OF MATERIALS INTO AND OUT OF CELLS

The survival of a cell depends on its ability to meet its physiological needs by exchanging materials with its surroundings. The primary function of the cytoplasmic membrane is to regulate the flow of material into and out of the cell. The cytoplasmic membrane is a *differentially permeable barrier,* meaning that the movement of molecules across the cytoplasmic membrane is selectively restricted. Some small, neutrally-charged molecules such as water (H_2O), oxygen (O_2), and carbon dioxide (CO_2) move across the membrane quite readily, but larger molecules and ions such as glucose or small, charged molecules such as a proton (H^+) do not move across the cytoplasmic membrane freely, although they can cross the cytoplasmic membrane via specific transport systems—discussed later in this chapter.

BOX 3-1

CELL SIZE

Most cells are quite small. Many eubacterial cells have a radius of only 0.1 μm. It had been considered that the maximal radius for any prokaryotic cell was only a few times this value. Why is this so? The surface area of the cytoplasmic membrane limits the rate of exchange between a cell and its surroundings. You may recall from your geometry classes that the volume of a sphere is $\frac{4}{3}\pi r^3$ and the surface area of a sphere is $4\pi r^2$. Therefore as the size (radius) of a spherical cell increases, its volume increases much more rapidly than its surface area. In other words, as a cell grows larger, the ratio of surface area to volume decreases. If a cell is too large, it does not possess sufficient surface area to permit adequate exchange across its limiting boundary to acquire its required nutrients and remove its waste products. Eukaryotic cells tend to be larger than prokaryotes because of their internal compartmentalization and because they have specialized mechanisms for transporting substances into the cell without actually going through the membrane.

Recently, however, the view of how large a bacterial cell could be was radically changed with the discovery of very large bacterial cells of *Epulopiscium fishelsoni* in the guts of sturgeonfish. These bacteria have cells 1,000,000 times larger in volume than the typical bacterial cell. The width of these cells is about 0.5 mm (for comparison, *Escherichia coli,* a bacterium found in the human gut, has a width of about 0.5 μm). The discovery of these large prokaryotic cells is forcing a rethinking of the size restriction for bacterial cells. It will require a thorough examination of how these cells acquire all their materials across the cytoplasmic membrane and how the cell is able to function without the internal compartmentalization that characterizes eukaryotic cells.

STRUCTURE AND CHEMICAL COMPOSITION OF THE CYTOPLASMIC MEMBRANE

Structure and chemical composition of the cytoplasmic membrane is key to its selectivity that regulates the specific transport processes and determines which molecules can enter and leave the cell. The structure and chemical composition of the cytoplasmic membranes of archaebacterial cells are distinct from those of eubacterial and eukaryotic cells. The major differences in the cytoplasmic membranes of archaebacteria, eubacteria, and eukaryotes are summarized in Table 3-3.

Cytoplasmic Membranes of Eubacterial and Eukaryotic Cells

Lipids Cytoplasmic membranes found in eubacterial and eukaryotic cells contain **phospholipids,** which are molecules containing two functional portions: a phosphate group and a fatty acid joined together by glycerol. The phosphate group is negatively charged and hence is hydrophilic (literally meaning "water loving" because such groups are attracted to water). The fatty acid portion is nonpolar and therefore hydrophobic (literally meaning "afraid of water" because such molecules are repelled by water). Typically, the fatty acids are unbranched and contain 16 to 18 carbon atoms. Two fatty acids and one phosphate are bonded to glycerol to form the phospholipid (FIG. 3-3). The actual fatty acids in the cytoplasmic membranes vary depending on species and environmental conditions. The major fatty acid profiles can be used to identify specific microorganisms grown under a standardized set of conditions. Under different environmental conditions microorganisms alter the lipid composition of their cytoplasmic membranes. For example, when a cell grows at higher temperatures, the cytoplasmic membrane has an increased proportion of unsaturated fatty acids in the phospholipids that enhance the ability of the cytoplasmic membrane to function as a semipermeable barrier.

Within an aqueous environment, phospholipid molecules tend to aggregate spontaneously such that their hydrophobic portions face one another and their hydrophilic portions are exposed to the water. This arrangement results in a phospholipid bilayer, which is the basic structure of all eukaryotic and eubacterial cytoplasmic membranes (see FIG. 3-3).The hydrophilic portions of the cytoplasmic membrane occur at the outer and inner surfaces, those directly contacting the exterior of the cell and the cytoplasm respectively; the hydrophobic portions occur within the internal matrix of the cytoplasmic membrane.

When thin sections of cells are viewed with the electron microscope, the cytoplasmic membrane has a railroad track appearance; the dark, rail-like portions

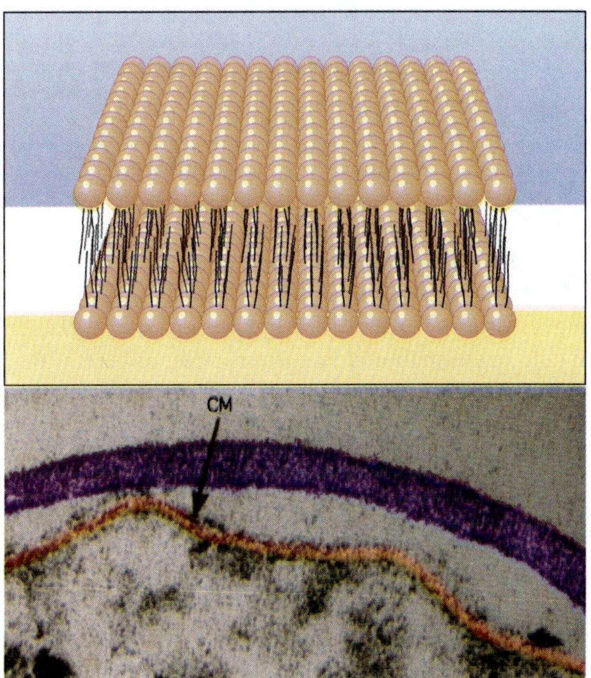

FIG. 3-3 **A,** The typical cytoplasmic membrane of prokaryotic and eukaryotic cells is a lipid bilayer, as illustrated here showing the orientations of the hydrophilic *(tan spheres)* and hydrophobic (*black*) ends of phospholipids that make up this structure. The hydrophilic portions (phosphate groups) occur near the water inside and outside the cell. The hydrophobic portions (formed from fatty acids) are sequestered in the interior of the membrane. **B,** Colorized electron micrograph of the cytoplasmic membrane (*CM*) of the bacterium *Bacillus subtilis* reveals the characteristic railroad track appearance of this lipid bilayer.

TABLE 3-3 Comparison of Archaebacterial, Eubacterial, and Eukaryotic Cytoplasmic Membranes

CHARACTERISTIC	ARCHAEBACTERIA	EUBACTERIA	EUKARYOTIC
Protein content	High	High	Low
Lipid composition	Phospholipids, sulfolipids, glycolipids, nonpolar isoprenoid lipids	Phospholipid	Phospholipid
Lipid Structure	Branched	Straight chain	Straight chain
Lipid Linkage	Ether-linked (diethers and tetraethers)	Ester-linked	Ester-linked
Sterols	Absent	Absent*	Present

*Some eubacteria in the genus *Mycoplasma* contain sterols in their cytoplasmic membranes.

of the membrane correspond to the electron-dense hydrophilic portions of the phospholipid molecule (see FIG. 3-3). The fact that the phospholipid has hydrophobic and hydrophilic portions contributes to the ability of the cytoplasmic membrane to regulate selectively the flow of material into and out of the cell.

The cytoplasmic membranes of eukaryotic cells are like those of eubacterial cells, but they also contain **sterols.** Sterols, such as cholesterol, make up as much as 25% of the lipids in the cytoplasmic membranes of some eukaryotic cells. Generally, the cytoplasmic membranes of eubacterial cells do not contain sterols. The eubacterial genus *Mycoplasma,* however, has sterols that it acquires from the cytoplasmic membranes of eukaryotic cells. *Mycoplasma* also differs from other eubacteria in that it lacks the outer protective cell wall layer found in almost all other eubacteria. Polyene antibiotics are effective against *Mycoplasma* because they interact with sterols and disrupt the integrity of the cytoplasmic membrane.

Proteins—Fluid Mosaic Model In addition to phospholipids, the cytoplasmic membrane also contains proteins, which are integrated into the lipid bilayer. The membrane proteins of eukaryotic and eubacterial cells are distributed in a mosaic-like pattern within the lipid bilayer structure of the membrane (FIG. 3-4). Proteins and lipids can "float" laterally within the phospholipid matrix of the membrane, although proteins move to a lesser extent than the phospholipid molecules. The structure and movement of proteins

TABLE 3-4 Functions of Some Cytoplasmic Membrane Proteins

LOCATION IN MEMBRANE	FUNCTION	EXAMPLE
Inside surface	Energy transformation	ATPase F_1
	Transport of molecules	HPr
	Protein export	Docking protein
	Association of DNA with membrane	DNA-binding protein
Both sides	Transport of molecules	Permease
	Chemotaxis	Methyl-accepting chemotaxis proteins
	Electron and proton transport	Flavoprotein
Outside surface	Penicillin-binding proteins	Cell wall biosynthesis
	Flagellar activity	M protein of basal body of flagellum

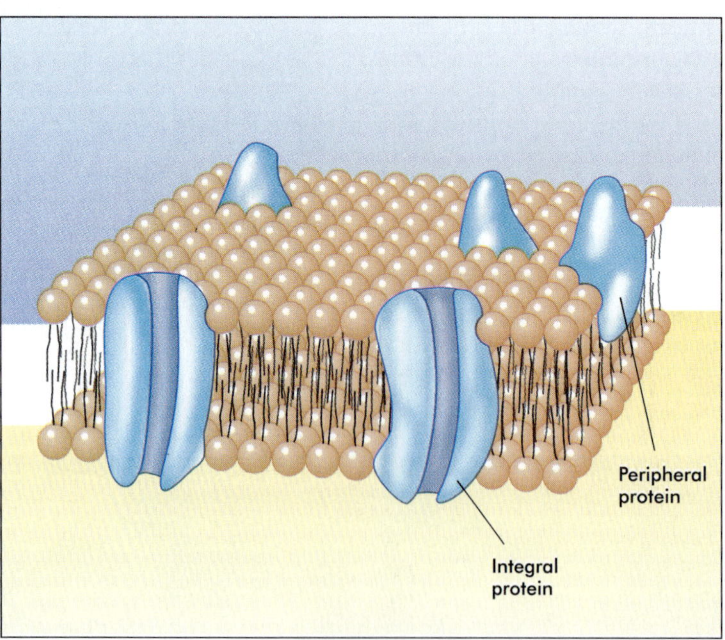

FIG. 3-4 The fluid mosaic model of membrane structure accounts for the facts that proteins *(blue)* and lipids (*beige* and *black*) comprise an integral part of membranes and that the structure is dynamic as opposed to static. Some proteins extend through the membrane (integral proteins) and others are associated with one side or the other (peripheral proteins).

and phospholipids is described by the *fluid mosaic model* of the cytoplasmic membrane.

Some of the proteins of the cytoplasmic membrane are confined to the membrane surfaces *(peripheral proteins)*, and others are partially or totally buried within the membrane matrix *(integral proteins)*, often spanning the entire membrane matrix. Most integral proteins span the entire lipid bilayer of the cytoplasmic membrane, exposing portions to the internal cytoplasm and the external surroundings. The distribution of proteins contributes to the definite sidedness of the cytoplasmic membrane, which gives the membrane a distinguishable inside and outside with differing functional roles. Some of the roles of these membrane proteins are outlined in Table 3-4.

Proteins are interspersed in the matrix of the cytoplasmic membrane. Eubacterial cytoplasmic membranes tend to contain a higher proportion of proteins than eukaryotic cytoplasmic membranes. Some of these proteins are involved in ATP generating metabolism that occurs at the cytoplasmic membranes of eubacterial cells and within the mitochondria and chloroplast membranes of eukaryotic cells.

Cytoplasmic Membranes of Archaebacterial Cells

Differences in the cytoplasmic membranes represent one of the major features that distinguish the archaebacteria from the eubacteria and eukaryotes (FIG. 3-5). The cytoplasmic membranes of eubacterial and eukaryotic cells contain straight chain fatty acids

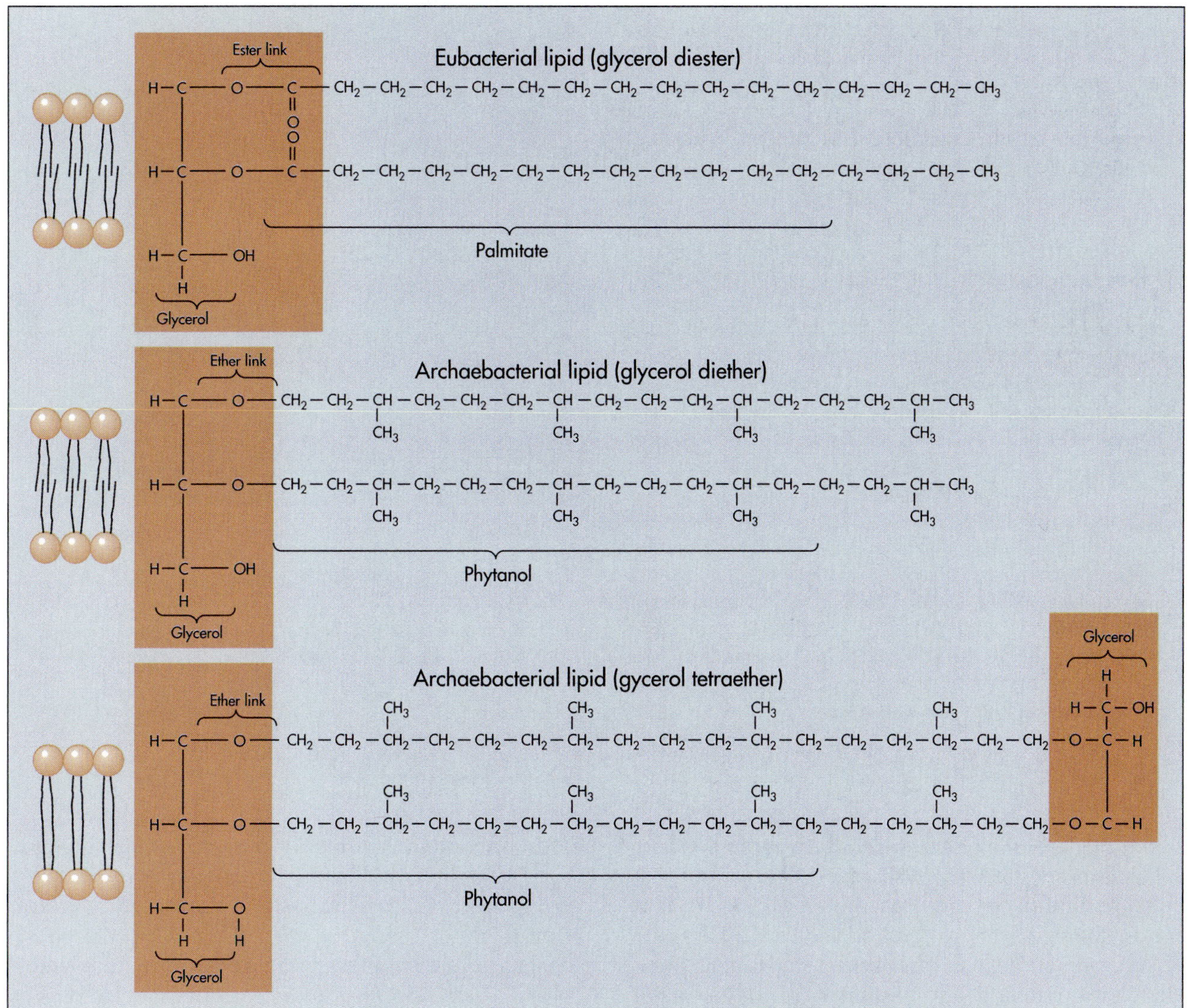

FIG. 3-5 Unlike the lipids that make up the cytoplasmic membranes of eubacterial cells, which are glycerol diesters *(top structure)*, major lipids of archaebacteria are glycerol diethers *(middle structure)*, diglycerol tetraethers *(bottom structure)*, and tetrapentacyclic diglycerol tetraethers (not shown). The glycerol diethers, like the phospholipids (glycerol diesters) of eubacterial and eukaryotic cells, form a lipid bilayer. Diglycerol tetraethers form a single layer with the two glycerols on the outside.

BOX 3-2

RECOVERY OF CELLS AND ANALYSIS OF CELLULAR CONSTITUENTS

To study cell structures and cellular biochemical constituents it is often necessary to work with large numbers of cells. A concentrated mass of cells can be obtained by centrifugation. A centrifuge is an instrument that rotates at variable speeds so that the centrifugal force generated causes sedimentation of particles. The rate of sedimentation per unit of centrifugal force is called the sedimentation coefficient and is generally expressed as Svedberg (S) units. This rate of sedimentation depends on the centrifugal force, the size of the particle, the density of the particle, and the density of the liquid in which the particle is suspended. Because microorganisms and cellular constituents are of differing sizes, they can be separated by centrifugation (FIG. *A*). Larger particles tend to sediment faster than smaller ones; increasing centrifugal force causes greater sedimentation rates; increasing the density difference between the particle and the liquid increases the rate of sedimentation; sedimentation doesn't occur when the density of the particle is equal to the density of the liquid in which it is suspended.

A high speed centrifuge rotates at speeds up to 25,000 rpm, which can produce forces of over 100,000 × *g*, that is, over 100,000 times the force of gravity. This type of centrifuge is especially useful for sedimenting whole cells, as well as some cell constituents. Centrifugation at speeds of 1,000-5,000 × *g* for 10 minutes is generally adequate to recover prokaryotic and eukaryotic cells. The supernatant (liquid above the sedimented material) can be examined for extracellular substances or discarded. The sedimented material that contains the cells can be resuspended and resedimented to wash away any extracellular substances.

An ultracentrifuge can spin faster (85,000 rpm) and produce higher centrifugal forces (>500,000 × *g*). An ultracentrifuge is particularly useful for sedimenting cellular particles, such as the ribosomes and membranes, and also various cellular macromolecules, such as proteins and nucleic acids. To obtain cellular components, cells are disrupted by physical or chemical means: after centrifugation in a high speed centrifuge to pellet the larger

A, Centrifuges are used to separate cells and various cellular components and chemicals. High-speed centrifuges sediment cells and large particles. Ultracentrifuges sediment smaller particles such as membranes and ribosomes. Using support gradients, such as sucrose and cesium chloride, specific chemical components, such as lipids and nucleic acids, can be separated into bands of differing molecular weights.

linked to glycerol by *ester* bonds, whereas the cytoplasmic membranes of archaebacterial cells contain lipids that are branched and linked to glycerol by *ether* bonds. Many of the glycerol molecules in the cytoplasmic membranes of archaebacteria lack a phosphate group; that is, phospholipids are *not* the major lipids of archaebacterial cytoplasmic membranes. Moreover, the configuration around the central atom of glycerol in archaebacterial lipids is the mirror image of the configuration in eubacterial and eukaryotic lipids. In many archaebacterial membranes the glycerol is bonded to two branched hydrocarbons and the remaining hydroxyl group of glycerol is unbonded. This unbonded hydroxyl group makes the glycerol somewhat hydrophilic. In some cases a more polar group replaces the hydroxyl group of the glycerol. Due to these "replacements," the polar lipids in archaebacterial cytoplasmic membranes include phospholipids, sulfolipids, and glycolipids; even various nonpolar lipids, including squalene derivatives, other isoprenoid hydrocarbons, sterols, and carotenoids have been found. Thus there are diverse lipids in the cytoplasmic membranes of various archaebacteria.

Many archaebacteria have lipid bilayers composed of glycerol diether lipids, which are analogous to the lipid bilayers of eubacterial and eukaryotic mem-

cell components, the supernatant solution is centrifuged at 100,000 × *g* for 1 hour to pellet membranes; further centrifugation at 150,000 × *g* for 3 hours will form a pellet containing ribosomes and other cytoplasmic constituents.

To further separate macromolecules, ultracentrifugation is used with a gradient of sucrose or cesium chloride. This type of centrifugation is called buoyant density centrifugation because macromolecules move downward in the gradient until they reach a density equal to their own, where they remain even with further centrifugation. Centrifugation in a gradient for several hours at high speeds causes separation of macromolecules and particles of varying size and density. Proteins, which differ in their molecular weights and densities, typically are separated on sucrose gradients. DNA and RNA are most often separated using cesium chloride gradients. Ethidium bromide, which binds to DNA and fluoresces, often is added to preparations so that DNA can be observed after buoyant density ultracentrifugation.

Electrophoresis is a method that uses an electric field to achieve the separation of macromolecules (FIGS. *B* and *C*). In an electric field, molecules migrate at characteristic rates based on their size, shape, and electronic charge. Electrophoresis is especially useful for separating proteins and nucleic acids, which are highly charged molecules. The solution containing the macromolecules is added to a support gel made of agarose or polyacrylamide and a high voltage electric field is placed across the gel. After allowing migration to occur for a specified period of time, the locations of proteins or DNA molecules in the gel are determined by staining or by using radioactive tracers.

The molecular weights of proteins can be determined by electrophoresis according to how far they migrate in a gel. This is accomplished by treatment with certain detergents such as sodium dodecyl sulfate (SDS) that alter the shape and charge of the proteins so that they migrate in an electric field according to their size. The migration distance is then compared to the migration distances of standard molecules of known size.

B

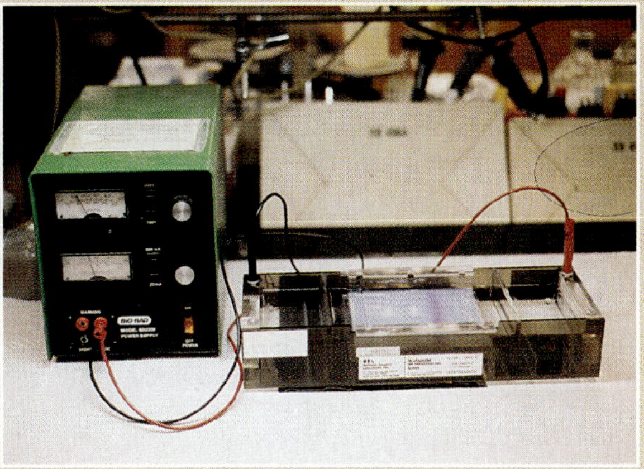

B, Electrophoresis unit for analysis of nucleic acids. The power source is shown on the left; the gel for separating nucleic acids on the right.

C

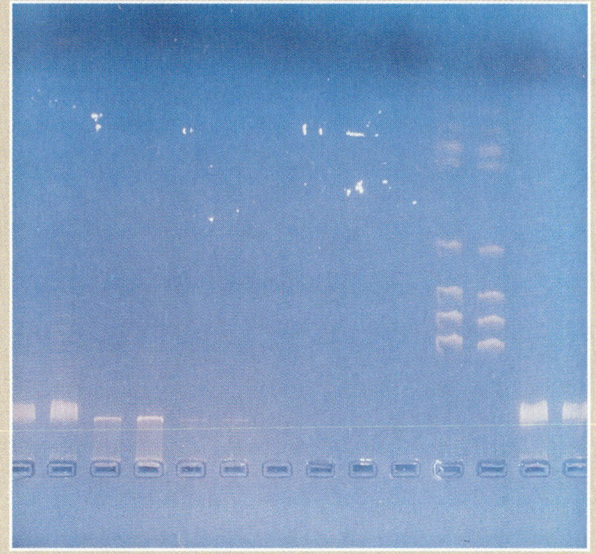

C, Gel showing electrophoretic separation of DNA stained with ethidium bromide and viewed with ultraviolet light. The fluorescing bands show fragments of DNA of specific molecular weights. The heaviest fragments of DNA move the least and are near the bottom wells where the DNA was added to the gel. The lightest fragments of DNA move the furthest and are near the top blue band.

branes. The cytoplasmic membranes of some archaebacteria, however, have monolayers composed of glycerol tetraether lipids. These monolayers still have hydrophilic portions (glycerol) at the cytoplasm and external interfaces and an internal hydrophobic portion (hydrocarbons).

The diversity of archaebacterial cytoplasmic membranes appears related to the diverse locations in which archaebacteria live. Many archaebacteria live in extreme environments where unusual, physiologically specialized cytoplasmic membranes are needed for survival. For example, *Sulfolobus* (an archaebacterium that lives at high temperatures [up to 90° C] in acidic environments [as low as pH 2]) has a cytoplasmic membrane that contains long chain branched hydrocarbons twice the length of the fatty acids in the cytoplasmic membranes of eubacteria. Similar unusual cytoplasmic membrane structures occur in archaebacteria living in other extreme habitats, including *Thermoplasma,* which lives at high temperatures, and *Halobacterium,* which lives in habitats with high salt concentrations. The structure of these cytoplasmic membranes makes them very resistant to conditions that would disrupt the function of a normal bilipid layer, thereby enabling them to remain as semipermeable barriers in extreme habitats.

TRANSPORT ACROSS THE CYTOPLASMIC MEMBRANE

Because cells must acquire substances from their surroundings and excrete waste products to survive, the cytoplasmic membrane must be *permeable;* that is, it must allow substances to pass through it. However, indiscriminate passage of materials would not allow the cell to maintain its highly ordered state. Many substances are 1,000 times higher in concentration within the cell than in the surroundings. Therefore the cytoplasmic membrane must *selectively* regulate the movement of materials into and out of the cell, that is, it must be semipermeable.

Cells have various transport mechanisms for moving molecules across the cytoplasmic membrane. Some substances cannot move across the cytoplasmic membrane; others can move across the cytoplasmic membrane simultaneously by several different mechanisms. Transport mechanisms are distinguished by whether molecules pass directly through the bilipid layer or via membrane channels, whether or not the molecule is altered as it passes through, or whether or not the process requires cellular energy.

Passive Processes: Diffusion

Transport mechanisms that do not require any expenditure of cellular energy are considered passive processes. These processes include passive diffusion, osmosis, and facilitated diffusion.

Movement of molecules from a region of higher concentration to one of lower concentration is known as **diffusion.** When the concentrations of a substance are different on opposing sides of a cytoplasmic membrane, there is a *concentration gradient* of that substance across the membrane. In this case, unless their transport is restricted by the structure of the cytoplasmic membrane (FIG. 3-6), the molecules will move across the cytoplasmic membrane by diffusion until equilibrium occurs, that is, until equal concentrations exist on both sides of the membrane. Equilibrium represents an energetically favorable condition.

Passive Diffusion Unassisted movement from areas of high to areas of low concentration is called **passive diffusion.** Various small solute molecules can diffuse passively across the cytoplasmic membrane. The rates of passive diffusion are determined by the concentration gradient and the permeability of the cytoplasmic membrane. The greater the concentration difference across a membrane and the greater the membrane permeability, the more rapid the rate of passive diffusion.

In some cases, when a substance moves into a cell it binds with other substances, forming complexes, or it is metabolically transformed. Such processes prevent the buildup in concentration of the transported substance within the cell, and thereby maintain the concentration gradient. This allows a substance to diffuse into the cell at a faster rate than would otherwise occur, but the rates of passive diffusion across the cytoplasmic membrane are still relatively slow. Sugars such as glucose and amino acids such as tryptophan, for example, have diffusion rates across the cytoplasmic membrane 1/10,000 that of water. Not surprisingly, cells have difficulty in obtaining sufficient material for growth and reproduction through passive diffusion.

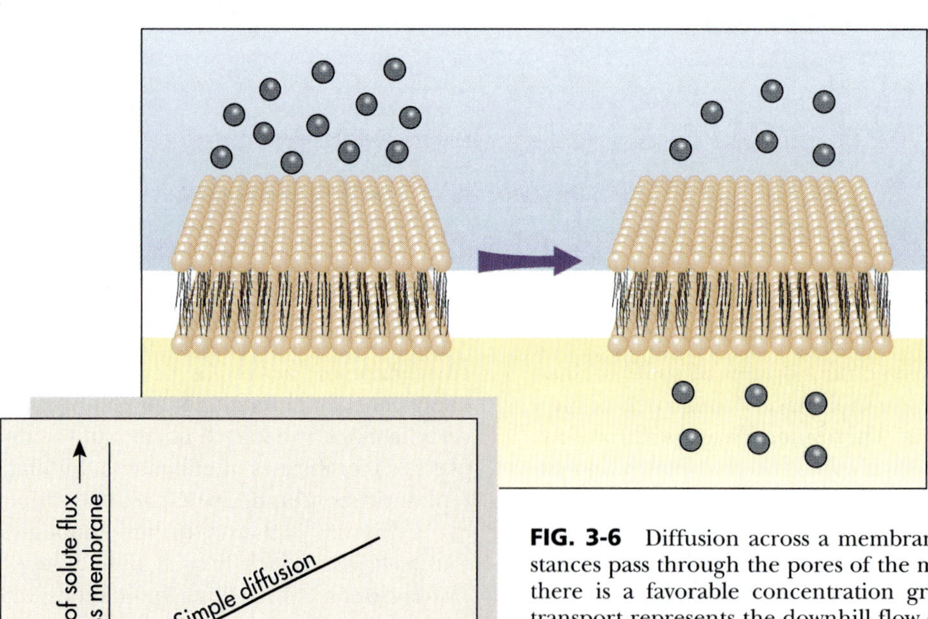

FIG. 3-6 Diffusion across a membrane occurs when substances pass through the pores of the membrane and when there is a favorable concentration gradient; this type of transport represents the downhill flow of a substance along a concentration gradient.

Osmosis The process by which water crosses the membrane in response to the concentration gradient of the solute (which in cells refers to substances dissolved in water) is known as **osmosis.** Osmosis occurs because the movement of solutes is restricted by the cytoplasmic membrane. Some solutes cannot move across the cytoplasmic membrane. Water moves across the cytoplasmic membrane in an attempt to balance the concentration of the solutes, since the solutes cannot. A dilute solution has a lower concentration of solute and, hence, a higher concentration of water than a concentrated solution. Water moves via osmosis across semipermeable membranes from the region of higher water concentration to the region of lower water concentration.

Water will move across the cytoplasmic membrane from the region of lower to the region of higher solute concentration until the concentrations of the solute are equalized on both sides of the membrane or until a pressure force prevents further flow of the water. In a medium in which the solute concentration inside the cell is equal to the solute concentration outside the cell (isotonic), water will flow equally in both directions across the membrane (FIG. 3-7). However, in a medium in which the solute concentration is higher outside than inside the cell (hypertonic), water will flow out of the cell and the cell will shrink, a process called *plasmolysis.* The reverse is true if the cell is in a medium in which the solute concentration is lower outside the cytoplasmic membrane than inside the cell (hypotonic), in which case the cell will expand and burst unless it is otherwise protected.

The movement of water by osmosis, which generally is into the cell because there is a higher concentration of solute within the cytoplasm, exerts a pressure on the cytoplasmic membrane, known as **osmotic pressure.** This osmotic pressure represents the force that must be exerted to maintain the concentration differences between solutions on opposite sides of the membrane. The osmotic pressure can be great enough to cause the cell to rupture, that is, for the cell to lyse. Cell lysis due to excess osmotic pressure is called **osmotic shock.** To survive in hypotonic environments, microorganisms have developed various strategies—discussed later in this chapter—as protection against osmotic shock.

Facilitated Diffusion **Facilitated diffusion** is diffusion at an enhanced rate, that is, solute movement from a region of high concentration to one of low concentration that occurs more rapidly than it would based only on that solute's concentration gradient. Facilitated diffusion is common in eukaryotic cells but rare in prokaryotic cells. In fact, glycerol is the only known substrate to be transported through the membrane by facilitated diffusion in some bacteria.

The enhanced rate of diffusion depends on specific proteins, called **facilitator proteins** or membrane transport proteins, within the cytoplasmic membrane.

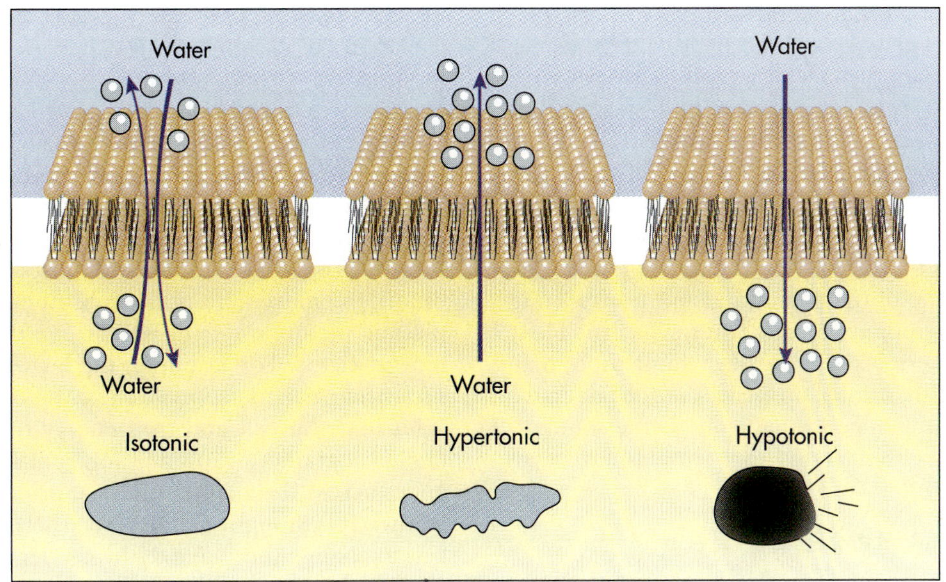

FIG. 3-7 Cells respond to osmotic pressure because water can move across the cytoplasmic membrane by osmosis and cause the cell to expand or shrink. Under isotonic conditions (equal concentrations of solute on both sides of the cytoplasmic membrane), cell shape is maintained. Under hypertonic conditions (higher solute concentration outside cell), the cell loses water and shrivels. Under hypotonic conditions (lower solute concentration outside cell), water moves into the cell, pressing the cell to expand; because the cell has very limited ability to increase volume without new synthesis of cell wall and cytoplasmic membrane components, osmotic pressure increases and the cell lyses due to osmotic shock.

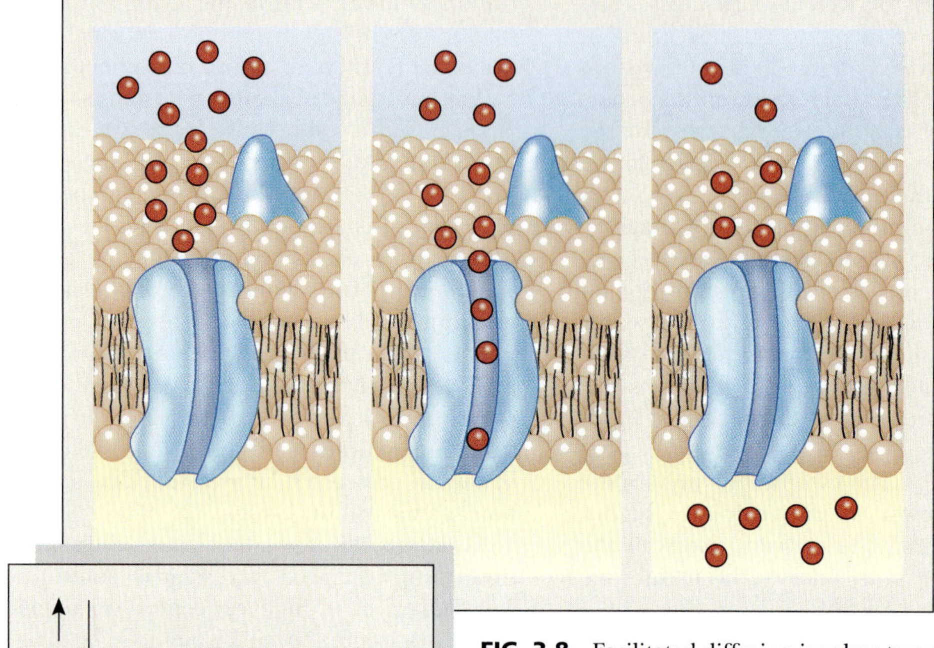

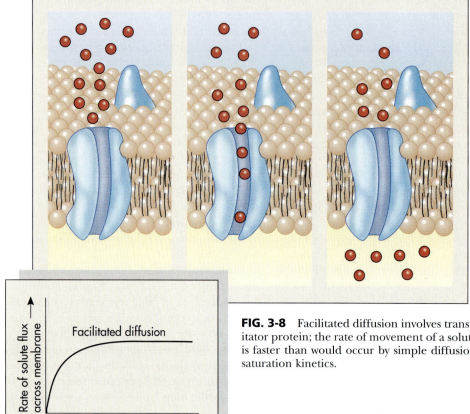

FIG. 3-8 Facilitated diffusion involves transport via a facilitator protein; the rate of movement of a solute (solute flux) is faster than would occur by simple diffusion and exhibits saturation kinetics.

These facilitator proteins selectively increase the permeability of the membrane for specific solutes, that is, the degree of ease with which that substance can cross the membrane. These proteins are quite specific, but some can transport multiple compounds of a particular class; others transport only one type of molecule, for example, glucose. It is thought that facilitator proteins form paths through which facilitated diffusion occurs and that they act as carriers, picking up a molecule on one side of the membrane and transporting it across the membrane to the other side. It is likely that the binding of a solute to a facilitator protein alters the three-dimensional properties of the facilitator protein and this change in shape allows the solute to be moved or carried across the cytoplasmic membrane (FIG. 3-8).

Active Energy Linked Processes

Transport mechanisms that require expenditure of cellular energy are considered active processes. These processes include active transport, group translocation, binding protein transport, and cytosis.

Active Transport Cells often use metabolic energy to move substances across the cytoplasmic membrane against a concentration gradient, that is, from a region of low concentration on one side of the membrane to a region of high concentration on the other. Membrane transport requiring the expenditure of energy and in which the substance is not chemically modified as it is transported across the membrane is called **active transport**.

In active transport, **permeases,** which are transmembrane proteins within the cytoplasmic membrane, act as carriers to move substances across the membrane. Different permeases transport specific substrates or a few chemically similar substrates. In addition, the movement of the substrate across the cytoplasmic membrane is driven by energy from ATP or ion gradients. For example, the lactose permease of *Escherichia coli* transports lactose or other β-galactosides into the cell and uses energy from an electrochemical gradient caused by ion concentration differences across the membrane (see protonmotive force below). It is thought that the electrochemical gradient acts to change the shape of the carrier so that the substrate can be moved across the membrane. In eukaryotic cells, active transport is driven by hydrolysis of ATP or by ion gradients.

Some permeases carry only one substance at a time and are referred to as **uniporters;** others can carry more than one substrate and are called **co-transporters** (FIG. 3-9). Of the latter variety, two substrates may be carried across the membrane in the same direction simultaneously. For example, lactose is trans-

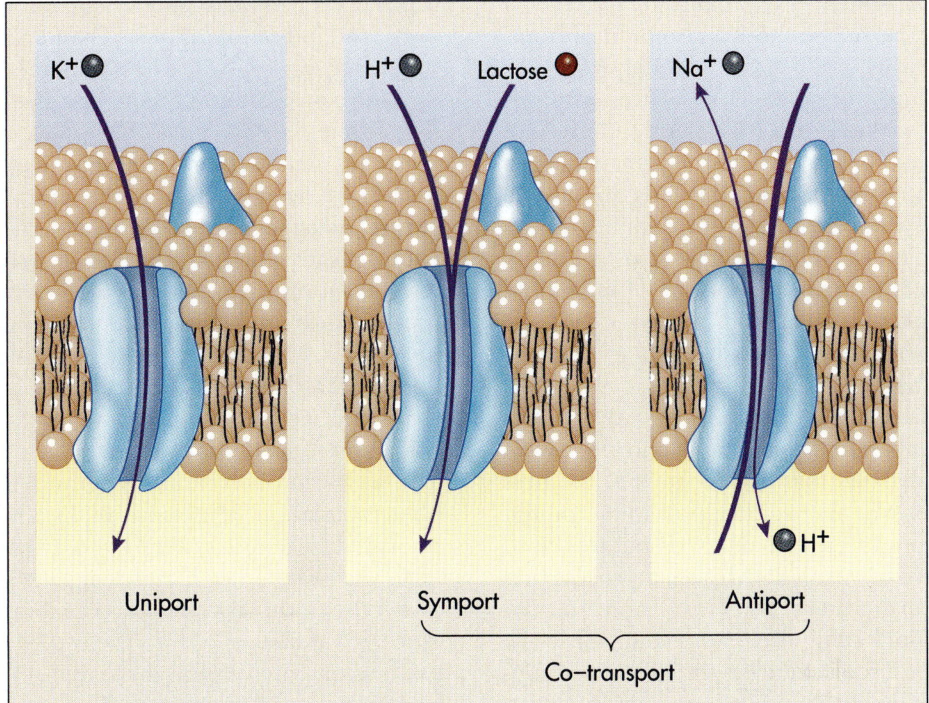

FIG. 3-9 Uniport involves the movement of a single substance by a permease. Co-transport involves the simultaneous movement of two substances. Symport occurs when the substances move together in the same direction. Antiport occurs when they move in opposite directions.

ported across the cytoplasmic membrane at the same time that a proton (H^+) is transported. This is called **symport** ("carried together"). Other substrates may be transported across the membrane in opposite directions; sodium ions (Na^+) are pumped outside the cell at the same time that H^+ is transported inside the cell. This mechanism is referred to as **antiport** ("carried opposite").

Protonmotive Force The energy for active transport in archaebacterial, eubacterial, and algal cells generally comes from the **protonmotive force;** the protonmotive force is the energy that comes from the separation of protons (hydrogen ions, H^+) across the cytoplasmic membrane (FIG. 3-10). This is in contrast to protozoan, fungal, plant, and animal cells—where the energy for active transport typically is supplied by ATP. The metabolism of bacterial cells is used to translocate protons out of the cell so that there is a greater concentration of protons outside than inside the cell. The higher concentration of protons (H^+) outside the cell creates an excess of hydrogen and positive ions on the outer side of the cytoplasmic membrane—a situation that strongly favors the movement of protons or other cations back into the cell.

Potassium ions (K^+), for example, are transported by uniporters and co-transporters due to the protonmotive force, moving down their electrochemical gradients from an area of greater positive charge to an area of greater negative charge. On the other hand,

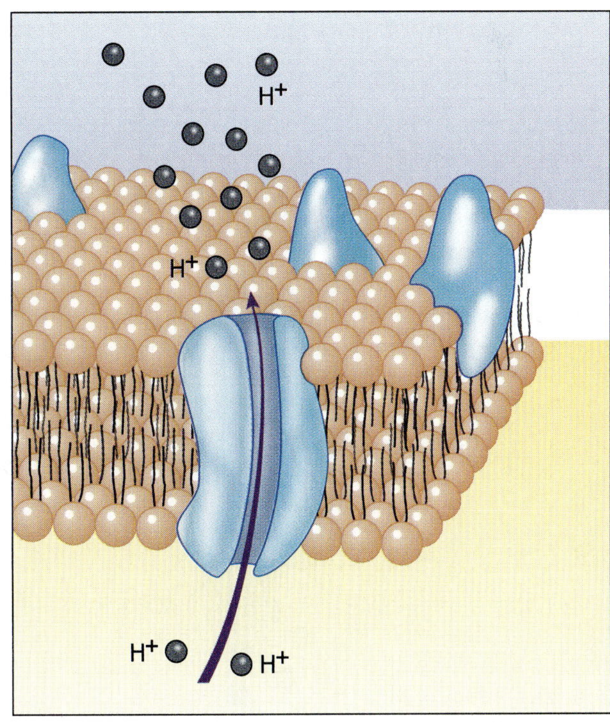

FIG. 3-10 Hydrogen ions (protons) are translocated across a membrane via a proton transporter to form a gradient of protons (H^+). This establishes a protonmotive force across the membrane that can be used to drive the formation of ATP.

anions such as phosphate (PO_4^{3-}) and sulfate (SO_4^{2-}) can be bound to permeases, which also bind protons. Because the proton's positive charge effectively neutralizes the anion's negative charge, this symport mechanism allows transport of anionic molecules against their electrochemical gradient. Uncharged molecules such as sugars and amino acids can also be transported with protons. The protonmotive force is vital to the function of all bacterial cytoplasmic membranes, as well as the inner membranes of mitochondria and chloroplasts in eukaryotes. The various metabolic means by which cells establish a proton gradient is explored in Chapter 4.

Sodium-Potassium Pump In many eukaryotic cells a gradient between sodium ions (Na^+) and potassium ions (K^+) is established that is analogous to the protonmotive force. Via the **sodium-potassium pump,** Na^+ is pumped out of the cell and K^+ is pumped into the cell by the enzyme Na^+-K^+ ATPase, a process that requires ATP. Furthermore, for every three sodium ions pumped out, only two potassium ions are pumped in. By this mechanism then, the sodium-potassium pump establishes not only a higher Na^+ concentration outside the cell and a higher K^+ concentration within the cell but also an unequal distribution of positive charge (FIG. 3-11). The result is a powerful electrochemical gradient that is used for the active uptake of many substances. For example, a symport protein that binds glucose and Na^+ results in the uptake of glucose with the simultaneous lowering of the Na^+ concentration gradient across the cytoplasmic membrane.

Group Translocation—Phosphoenolpyruvate:Phosphotransferase System In the transport process called **group translocation** that occurs in the **phosphoenolpyruvate: phosphotransferase system (PEP:PTS),** the transported substance is chemically altered during passage through the membrane by the addition of phosphate. This process occurs exclusively in prokaryotic cells. Molecules transported via group translocation into bacterial cells include carbohydrates, fatty acids, and some of the building blocks of nucleic acids. The well-known example of group transport is the phosphorylation of glucose in *Escherichia coli* by the phosphotransferase system.

In the PEP:PTS of *E. coli,* a sugar is phosphorylated as it crosses the cytoplasmic membrane. Thus when glucose is transported into the cell by the PEP:PTS, it exists as glucose outside the *E. coli* cell but as glucose 6-phosphate within the cell (FIG. 3-12). Because carbohydrate substrates, such as glucose, are normally phosphorylated as part of their metabolism, the chemical modification that occurs during group transport provides an efficient mechanism for initiating

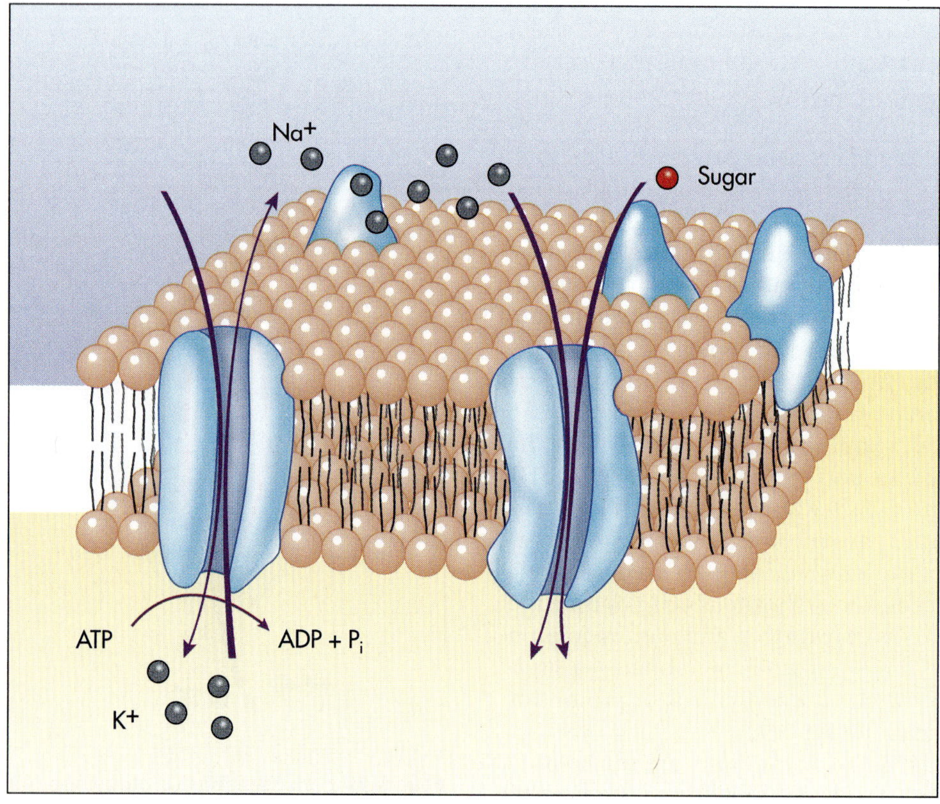

FIG. 3-11 The sodium-potassium pump moves potassium ions (K^+) into the cell and sodium ions (Na^+) out of the cell. The transport requires energy from ATP.

the metabolism of these compounds as they are brought into the cell. Furthermore, group translocation prevents any change in the concentration gradient because the substance does not exist in the same chemical state on both sides of the membrane.

The PEP:PTS system is found only in some prokaryotic cells and does not occur in eukaryotic cells. Generally, PEP:PTS transport is associated with bacteria that grow in the absence of molecular oxygen, whereas aerobic bacteria transport substrates by active transport. The evolution of this transport system by bacteria allows them to use their energy resources efficiently by coupling transport with the initiation of energy-generating metabolism.

The PEP:PTS system involves a series of steps and enzymes (see FIG. 3-12). A phosphate group is initially transferred from phosphoenolpyruvate (PEP) to a low molecular weight histidine-containing protein (HPr) found in the bacterial cytoplasm. This reaction is catalyzed by Enzyme I. The phosphorylated-HPr then transfers the phosphate group to Enzyme III, which in turn transfers the phosphate group to Enzyme II, which is an integral membrane bound permease. In the last step of this mechanism, the phosphate group is transferred to a substrate as the substrate is simultaneously being translocated or transported through the cytoplasmic membrane by Enzyme II. Typically, simple sugars such as glucose and fructose are transported by this mechanism. For other substrates, mannitol for example, the phosphorylation of Enzyme II is accomplished directly from phosphorylated HPr (without the intervening Enzyme III).

Some components of the PEP:PTS are specifically required for the transport of particular substrates, but others are nonspecific, that is, they are necessary for the PEP:PTS mechanism to work in general. Enzyme I and HPr are nonspecific and so mutations in the genes coding for Enzyme I (*pts*I) or HPr (*pts*H) lead to general failure of transport of all substrates by the PTS. On the other hand, Enzymes II and Enzymes III

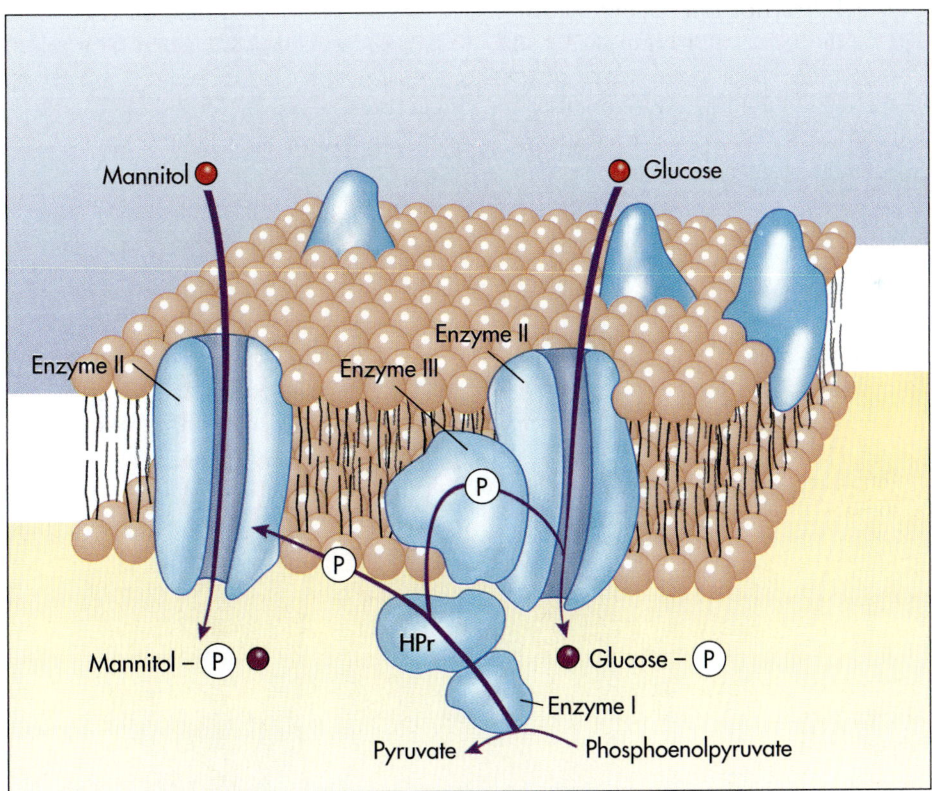

FIG. 3-12 The phosphoenolpyruvate-phosphotransferase (PEP:PTS) group transport system transfers phosphate from PEP (phosphoenolpyruvate) to a sugar as it is transported across a membrane. The transfer of phosphate occurs in a sequence of reactions. The initial step in this process is catalyzed by enzyme I, which involves the transfer of phosphate from PEP to a heat-stable protein molecule (HPr). This reaction occurs in the cytoplasm or at the inner surface of the membrane. Within the membrane, the phospho-HPr molecule then transfers phosphate to the sugar being transported. Three phosphate transfers are needed for the phosphorylation and transport of glucose, while only two are needed for mannitol. There are two enzymes, II and III, involved in the transfer of phosphate from the phospho-HPr molecule to glucose. Only enzyme II is needed for the transfer of phosphate from the phospho-HPr molecule to mannitol.

are substrate specific. For example, Enzyme II^{glu} in *E. coli* is involved only in the transport of glucose, glucosamine, and 2-deoxyglucose and a few other minor sugars. Similarly, Enzyme II^{fru} is predominantly involved in fructose uptake. Mutations in the genes that code for Enzyme II or Enzyme III therefore lead to failure of transport only of the specific substrate handled by that carrier.

Binding Protein Transport **Binding protein transport** is a specialized transport system that occurs only in Gram-negative bacteria. It involves a complex of proteins associated with a second membrane, called the outer membrane, that surrounds Gram-negative bacterial cells (see FIG. 3-13). The space between the outer membrane and the cytoplasmic membrane is called the *periplasmic space.* For example, maltose transport in *E. coli* involves an outer membrane protein (LamB) that functions as a pore (porin) to transport maltose from outside the cell into the periplasmic space. There, the maltose molecule interacts with a soluble periplasmic maltose-binding protein. The binding protein acts as a shuttle, carrying the maltose from the outer membrane. At the cytoplasmic membrane there is an additional complex of proteins—MalF, MalG, and MalK—involved in maltose transport. MalF and MalG act as a permease to transport the maltose through the cytoplasmic membrane and MalK is involved in obtaining energy from ATP for the transport process. Binding protein transport is also called **shock-sensitive transport** because cells that are osmotically shocked lose proteins that are involved in the transport of some substances.

Cytosis Some substances enter and leave eukaryotic cells by **cytosis,** a transport process in which a substance is engulfed by the cytoplasmic membrane to form a **vesicle** (a membrane-bounded sphere) (FIG. 3-14). Cytosis effectively allows transport of substances around rather than through the cytoplasmic mem-

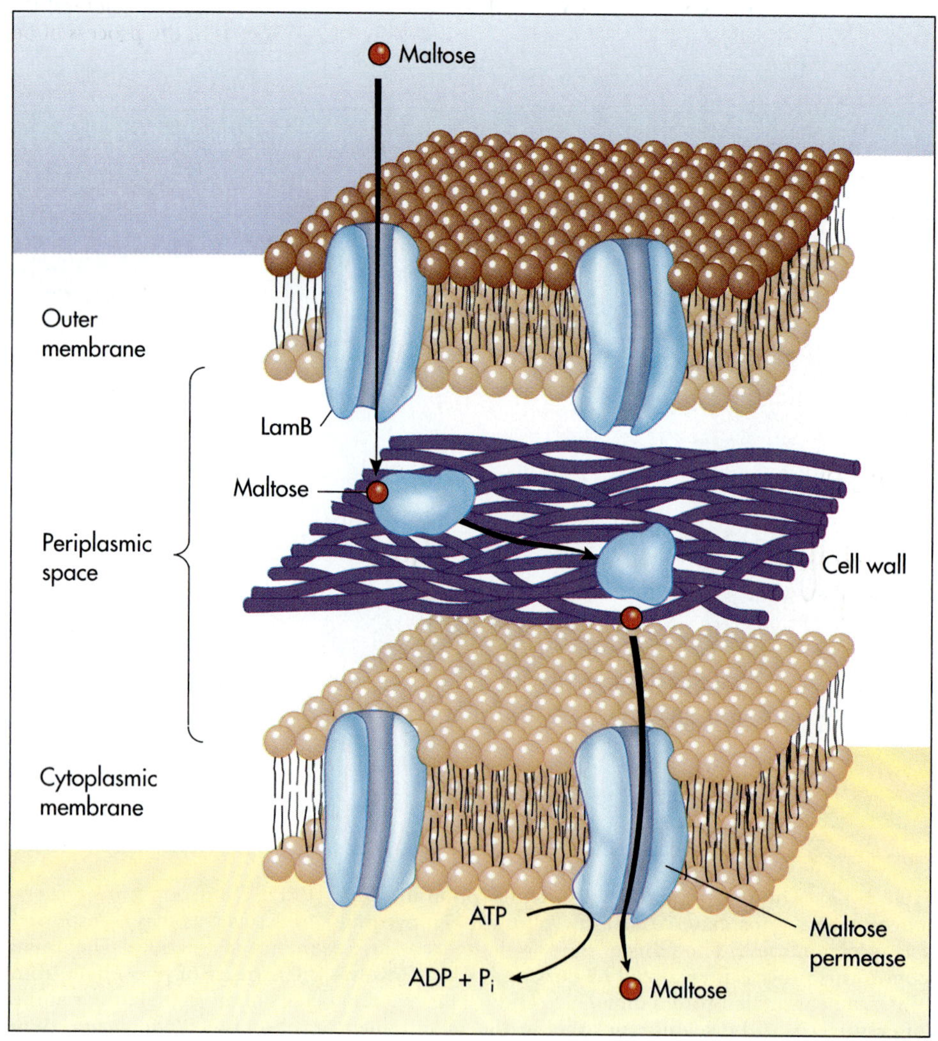

FIG. 3-13 In binding protein transport of maltose across the Gram-negative cell wall, a binding protein in the periplasmic space picks up maltose as it comes through the pores in the outer membrane; the binding protein shuttles the maltose through the cell wall across the periplasmic space to a maltose permease in the cytoplasmic membrane. This maltose permease transports maltose across the cytoplasmic membrane using energy from ATP.

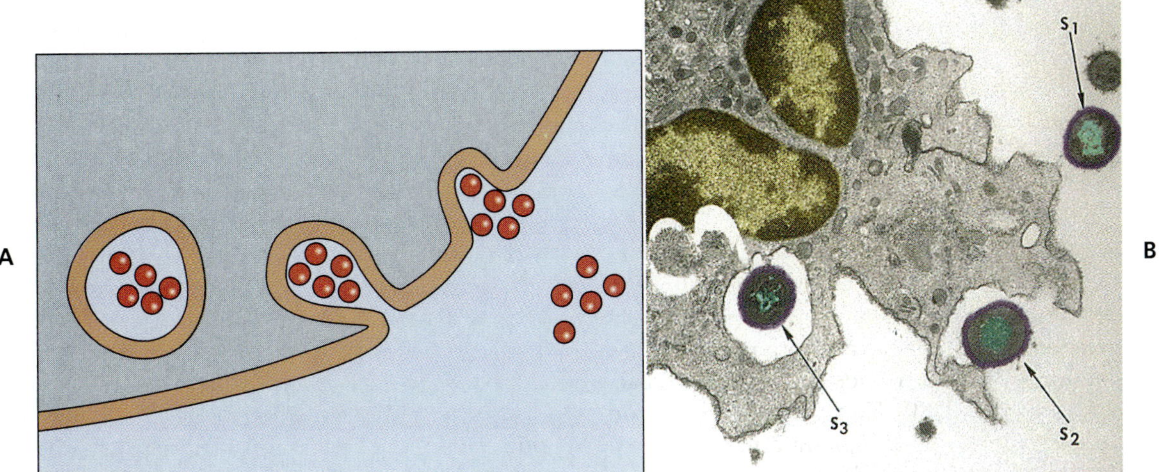

FIG. 3-14 **A,** In cytosis, which only occurs in eukaryotic cells, a substance is transported into or out of the cell without actually passing through the membrane. This is important for the movement of large substances and large quantities of substances into and out of the cell. **B,** Colorized micrograph showing the phagocytosis of the bacterium *Streptococcus pyogenes* by a human polymorphonuclear leukocyte, which is a white blood cell that helps defend the body against infection. (14,000×). One bacterial cell is free *(S_1)*. One is in the process of being phagocytized *(S_2)*, and one has been phagocytized *(S_3)*.

BOX 3-3

MESOSOMES: REAL STRUCTURES OR ARTIFACTS?

When thin sections of bacteria are viewed by electron microscopy, extensive invaginations (infoldings) of the cytoplasmic membrane often are seen (see FIG.). These extensively invaginated portions of the cytoplasmic membrane have been called *mesosomes*. Careful observations indicate that mesosomes are continuous with the cytoplasmic membrane. They are often seen in the region where cell division occurs during bacterial reproduction, but they are not always seen when bacterial cells divide, nor, when they are present, do they always occur near the site of cell division. Having observed mesosomes in many routine electron microscopic preparations, several investigators set out to determine their function(s), assuming that, as with other cell structures, a structure–function relationship would be elucidated.

An observed structure must be correlated with a function for it to be considered a true cellular structure. Although many functions have been proposed for mesosomes, including a role in cell division, various metabolic processes, enzyme secretion, and the possibility that they provide additional necessary membrane surface within bacterial cells for functions accomplished by membranes of organelles in eukaryotic cells, the role of mesosomes is elusive. For each proposed function, cells were found with no apparent mesosomes that were not defective for that function. After many studies, it became necessary to reevaluate the evidence for the existence of mesosomes, focusing on why they were only sometimes observed.

When mesosomes were observed, they were almost always attached to or closely associated with DNA within the cell. Some investigators hypothesized that the DNA might be shrinking due to dehydration or fixation during preparation for electron microscopy, stretching an attached region of the cytoplasmic membrane as this occurred. To see if this was the case, cells were frozen in liquid nitrogen and exposed to X radiation to break up the DNA before the cells were fixed and dehydrated for electron microscopic viewing. When this procedure was followed, no mesosomes were observed. This suggests that these observed structures are artifacts of preparation for electron microscopic observation rather than real structures of the bacterial cell, formed by DNA pulling on the cytoplasmic membrane when the cells are dehydrated. The current view is that mesosomes are artifacts rather than real cell structures with definable functions.

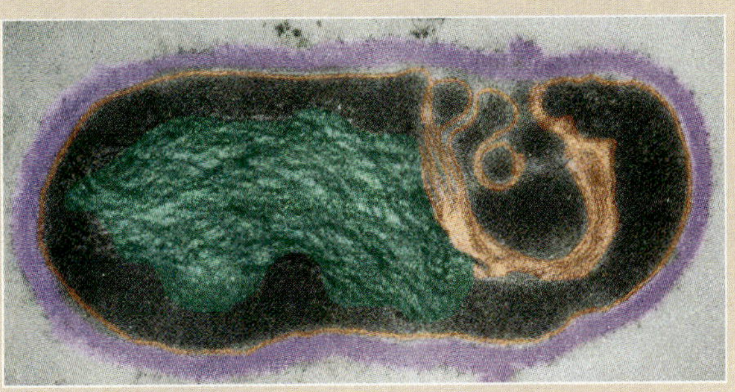

Colorized micrograph of the bacterium *Corynebacterium parvum* shows the invaginated membrane *(tan)* that has been called a mesosome.

brane. Whether the substance is entering or leaving a cell by cytosis is designated by using the prefixes *endo-* (into) or *exo-* (out of). **Endocytosis** refers to the movement of materials into the cell and **exocytosis** denotes movement out of the cell. Endo- and exocytosis require energy and are important in moving substances too large to be transported through a membrane into and out of eukaryotic cells. **Phagocytosis** is a specific example of this mechanism in which one cell engulfs a smaller cell or particle. This transport mechanism is particularly important for many protozoa, such as *Paramecium,* that feed on bacteria and for certain white blood cells that engulf and digest bacteria as part of the immune response. *Pinocytosis* occurs when a cell engulfs a fluid containing dissolved substances. In some cases a receptor on the cell surface binds to a substance, initiating the transport of that substance in to the cell via *receptor-mediated endocytosis.* The uptake of some viruses by host cells is an example of this mechanism.

3.3 EXTERNAL STRUCTURES THAT PROTECT THE CELL

Protecting the cytoplasmic membrane against damage is essential for the survival of a living cell. The cytoplasmic membrane is often surrounded by a protective layer, such as a cell wall. Cell walls serve different protective functions in the cells of different organisms. The cell walls of eubacterial cells protect against osmotic shock, whereas the cell walls of eukaryotic cells typically protect against physical damage. Besides the cell wall, various other structures may surround and help protect the cell to ensure its survival.

EUBACTERIAL CELL WALL

The **cell wall** of the eubacterial cell is a strong, firm, but flexible external structure that surrounds most eubacterial cells (FIG. 3-15). The cell wall is relatively porous so that it does not greatly restrict the flow of small molecules to or from the cytoplasmic membrane; very large molecules, however, usually are unable to pass across it. Because eubacteria normally exist in dilute aqueous (that is, hypotonic) environments, most eubacterial cells would burst from the osmotic pressure exerted on their cytoplasmic membranes were it not for their cell walls. If the cell wall structure is disrupted, or if its manufacture by the cell is inhibited, eubacterial cells typically burst. This forms the basis for the action of some antibiotics such as penicillin.

Eubacterial Cell Shape

The cell wall establishes the shape of a bacterial cell. Bacteria exist as spheres called **cocci** (Greek *coccus,* meaning "berry"), cylinders called **rods** or **bacilli** (Latin *bacillus,* meaning "little walking stick"), and spiral shapes called **spirilli** (Greek *spirillum,* meaning "little coil") (FIG. 3-16). These and other forms typify different bacterial species; the diversity of bacterial forms can be seen in the micrographs throughout this book.

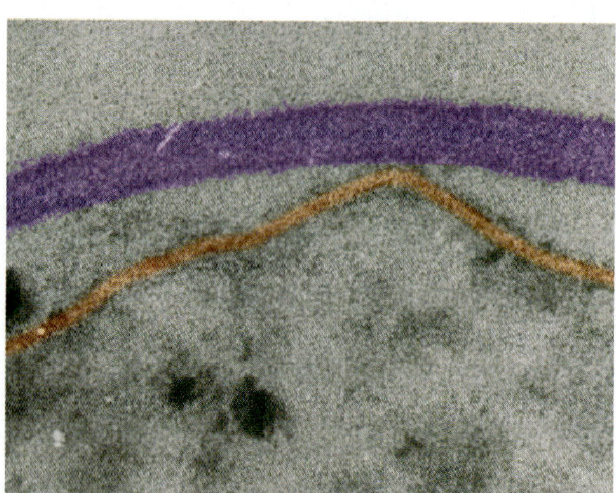

FIG. 3-15 Colorized micrograph of the cell wall of the Gram-positive bacterium *Bacillus subtilis* shows the thick peptidoglycan layer *(purple).* This cell wall completely surrounds and protects the cytoplasmic membrane.

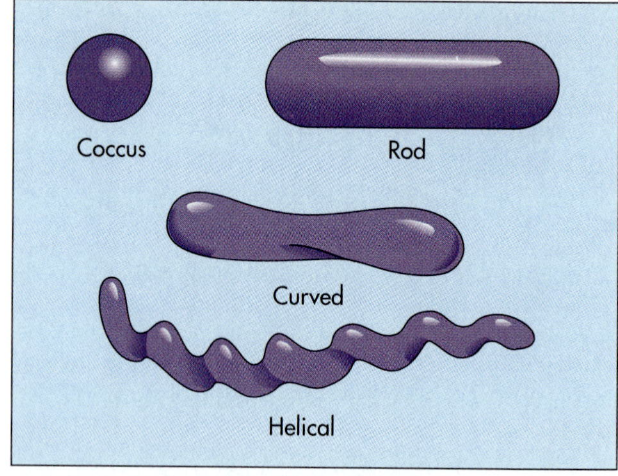

FIG. 3-16 The cells of each bacterial species have characteristic shapes. The most common shapes of bacterial cells are rods (cylindrical), cocci (spheres), and helical (corkscrew shaped).

Chemical Composition of the Eubacterial Cell Wall: Peptidoglycan

The cell wall of almost every eubacterial cell contains **peptidoglycan,** also known as **murein** or **mucopeptide,** which is largely responsible for protecting the cell against osmotic shock. This peptidoglycan layer occurs only in eubacteria; it is not found in any archaebacterial or eukaryotic cell. As the name implies, there are two parts to the peptidoglycan molecule: a peptide portion, which is composed of amino acids connected by peptide linkages, and a glycan (sugar) portion. The glycan portion, which forms the backbone of the molecule, is composed of alternately repeating units of the amino sugars *N*-acetylglucosamine and *N*-acetylmuramic acid linked to each other by β 1-4 glycosidic bonds. Attached to most of the *N*-acetylmuramic acid units are short peptide chains with four amino acids *(tetrapeptides)* (FIG. 3-17).

Some of the amino acids occurring in the peptide portion of the molecule are relatively unusual in biological systems. These include D-amino acids and diaminopimelic acid (DAP), which occur in peptidoglycan but not in proteins. The tetrapeptide usually includes L-alanine, D-glutamic acid (which may have a hydroxyl group added in some organisms), either L-lysine or diaminopimelic acid, and D-alanine. The major variation that occurs is the substitution of lysine and diaminopimelic acid, with lysine occurring in most Gram-positive bacteria and diaminopimelic acid occurring in all Gram-negative bacteria.

The tetrapeptide chains are interlinked by a peptide bridge between the carboxyl group of an amino acid in one tetrapeptide chain and the amino group of an amino acid in another tetrapeptide chain (see FIG. 3-17). The greatest variation in the peptidoglycan occurs in these cross-linkages. In the Gram-positive bacterium *Staphylococcus aureus,* for example, the cross-linkage is a pentapeptide composed entirely of the amino acid glycine. In Gram-negative bacteria, cross-linkage almost always occurs by the direct bonding of diaminopimelic acid of one chain to the terminal D-alanine of another chain. The cross-linkage can

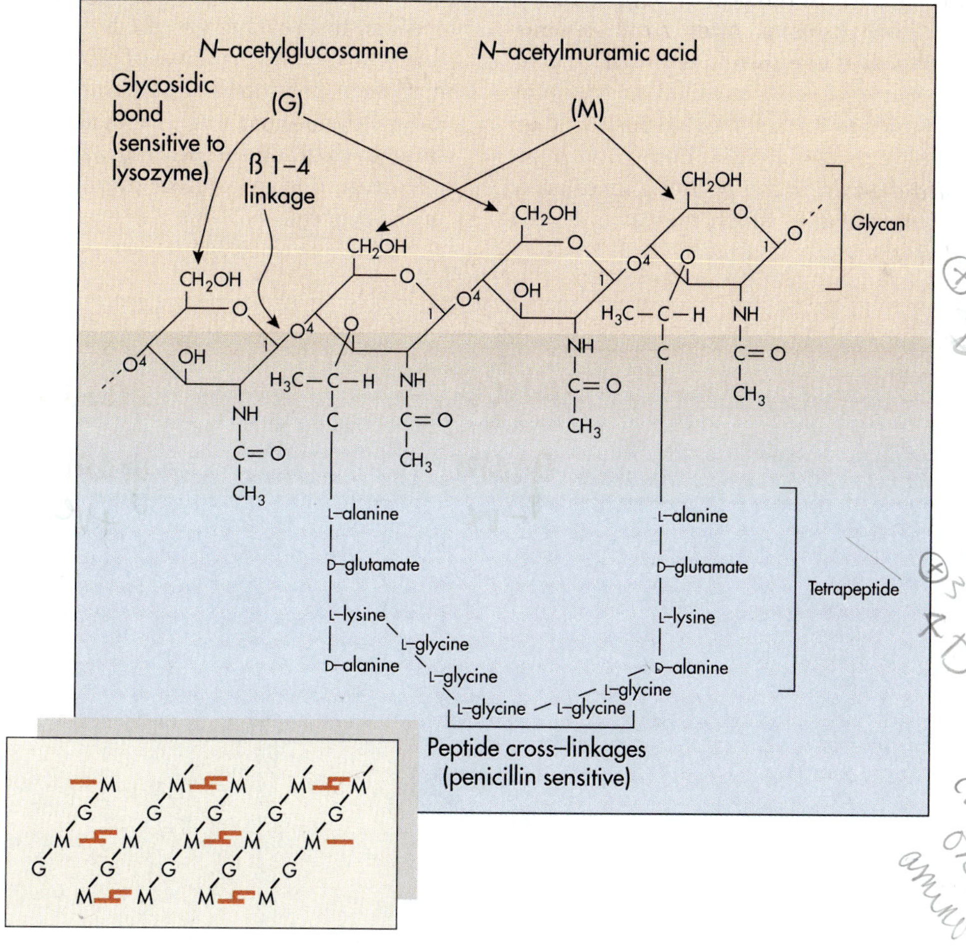

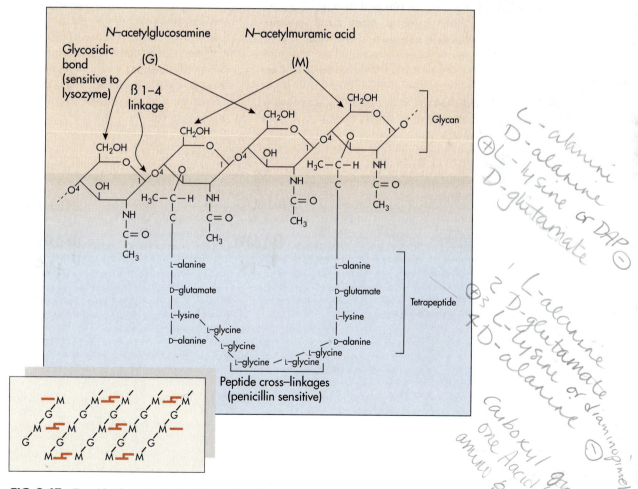

FIG. 3-17 Peptidoglycan is the backbone chemical of the bacterial cell wall; it is composed of repeating alternating units of *N*-acetylglucosamine (G) and *N*-acetylmuramic acid (M) and has cross-linked, short peptide chains, some of which have unusual amino acids such as D-alanine. The cross-links provide the needed structural support of the wall. The structure shown here is for *Staphylococcus aureus* and may differ in other bacteria.

occur between tetrapeptides in different chains, as well as directly between adjacent tetrapeptides, so that the peptidoglycan forms a strong, multilayered sheet. In fact, the peptidoglycan may be viewed as one large cross-linked molecule, or **sacculus,** (Latin *sacculus,* meaning "little sac") that entirely surrounds the eubacterial cell.

Effect of Lysozyme on the Cell Wall

Lysozyme is an enzyme that breaks the bonds of the glycan backbone portion of the peptidoglycan molecule—it breaks the β 1-4 bonds between *N*-acetylmuramic acid and *N*-acetylglucosamine. This enzyme, produced by various organisms that consume bacterial cells, aids in the digestion of the bacteria by such larger organisms. Lysozyme also occurs as part of various normal body secretions such as tears and saliva and is found in high concentration in egg white, providing protection against would-be bacterial invaders.

Lysozyme can destroy all or part of the cell wall structure (FIG. 3-18). If a portion of the bacterial cell wall remains after lysozyme treatment, the remaining cell is called a *spheroplast.* Treatment of Gram-negative eubacterial cells with lysozyme often forms spheroplasts. If the cell wall is completely removed, the remaining intact bacterial cell is called a *protoplast.* Protoplasts are easier to form for Gram-positive than for Gram-negative eubacterial cells. Both protoplasts and spheroplasts can exist in a supporting medium of high solute concentration in which the osmotic pressure is high enough to prevent lysis. If the supporting medium is removed the cell bursts.

Effect of Penicillin on the Cell Wall

Breaking down the cell wall is one way to destroy a bacterial cell; preventing proper wall formation in the first place is another. Penicillin, an antibiotic commonly used to treat bacterial infections, acts by preventing the formation of a strong interlinked peptidoglycan layer. Cells growing in the presence of penicillin produce defective cell walls that cannot protect against osmotic shock. Specifically, penicillin prevents the formation of cross-linkages between the tetrapeptides of the cell wall.

Penicillin works by binding irreversibly to certain proteins in the cytoplasmic membrane called **penicillin-binding proteins** (PBPs). PBPs are enzymes responsible for some of the reactions of peptidoglycan biosynthesis, therefore binding to them stops cell wall synthesis (FIG. 3-19). In addition to PBPs, bacteria contain a number of diverse enzymes, probably located in the cell wall, called **autolysins.** The function of autolysins is the restructuring or reshaping of the cell wall by breaking specific bonds in the peptidoglycan. Thus, in the presence of penicillin, many bacteria have their peptidoglycan biosynthetic machinery shut down or inhibited while their autolytic enzymes continue to degrade the existing wall. The result is often cell death due to cell lysis due to the weakened state of the cell wall.

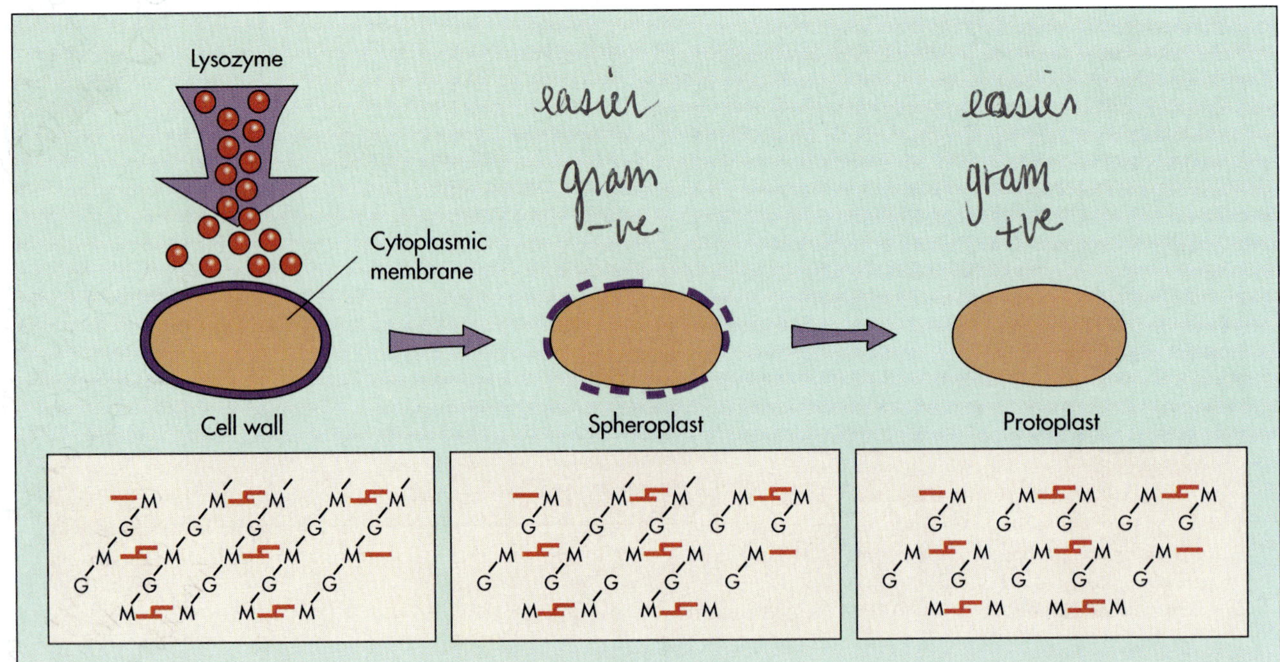

FIG. 3-18 Lysozyme cleaves β 1-4 bonds in the glycan portion of the peptidoglycan. The wall is degraded but as long as there is an osmotic support (such as a 0.5 M sucrose solution) the cells do not lyse. Spheroplasts have some residual wall, whereas protoplasts have none. If the osmotic support is removed, both spheroplasts and protoplasts lyse.

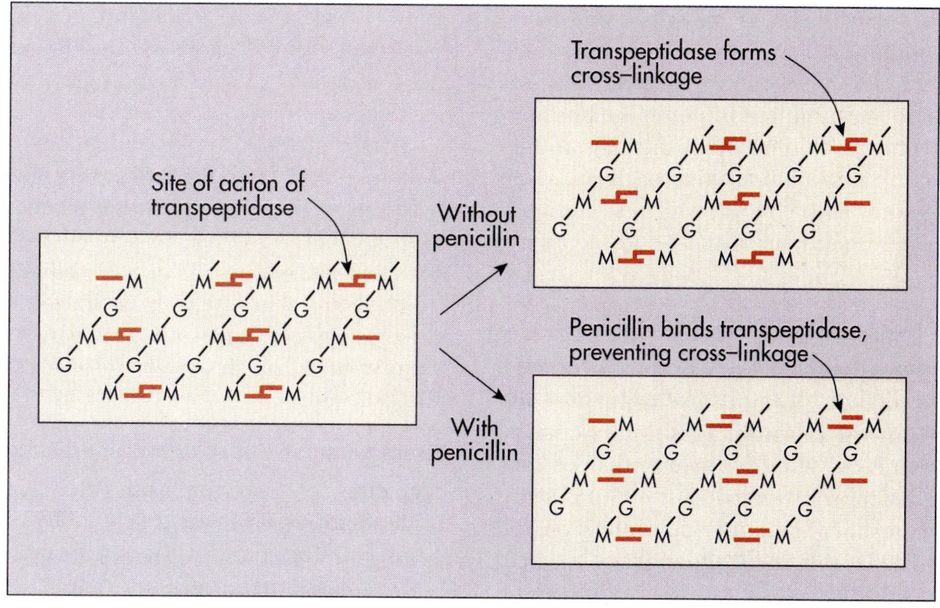

FIG. 3-19 The mode of action of penicillin involves inhibition of the formation of the normal cross-linkages in the peptidoglycan layer of the bacterial cell wall. Penicillin forms an inactive complex with transpeptidase, a key enzyme in cell-wall synthesis, so that the peptide cross-linkages do not form.

BOX 3-4

DEVELOPMENT OF THE GRAM STAIN PROCEDURE

The development of the Gram stain procedure by the Danish physician Hans Christian Gram remains one of the most important methodological contributions in bacteriology. At the time Gram published the description of his staining method, most bacteriologists were concerned with simply trying to see difficult-to-detect bacteria and with differentiating infecting bacteria from mammalian nuclei. Gram's paper describing the staining technique, "The Differential Staining of *Schizomycetes* in Sections and in Smear Preparations," was published in 1884. In this paper, Gram described primary staining with aniline-gentian violet, treatment with iodine-potassium iodide (Gram's iodine mordant), and decolorization with absolute alcohol followed by further decolorization with clove oil: "Bacteria are stained intense blue while the background tissues are light yellow." Gram observed that not all bacteria were stained in this procedure and suggested that counterstaining was possible. It was the detailed reporting of which bacteria were stained and which were not that was crucial to the recognition of the value of this staining procedure. "I. The following forms of *schizomycetes* retain the aniline-gentian violet after treatment with iodine followed by alcohol: (a) cocci of croupous pneumonia (19 cases) . . . (k) tubercule bacilli (5 cases). . . . II. The following *schizomycetes* are decolorized by alcohol subsequent to treatment with iodine: (a) encapsulated cocci from croupous pneumonia . . ."

Gram undoubtedly was disappointed with his procedure. He wanted to stain all bacteria, not the surrounding mammalian tissues. It is not known who thought of using the Gram stain procedure to differentiate bacteria, as routinely employed in bacteriology laboratories today. Gram died in 1935 without further developing his staining procedure but with the hope, stated in the conclusion to his paper, that "the method would be useful to other workers." Frequently in science, the discoverer of a method does not recognize the full potential of the discovery, and it remains for later scientists, working in an era of different concerns and enlightened by later discoveries, to realize the significance of the original finding.

Since the advent of the Gram stain, many investigations have been carried out to determine the basis for differential staining of bacteria in this procedure. The most recent investigations have used electron microscopy and heavy metal–labeled stains to see where the stains were going and what was happening to the cell. Based on such observations, it now appears that thick walls are able to trap the stain within the cell, whereas thin walls become porous when treated with a decolorizing agent, allowing the stain to wash out of the cell. Thus a eubacterial cell with a Gram-positive wall with its thick peptidoglycan layer traps the stain; one with a Gram-negative wall with its thin peptidoglycan layer does not.

Penicillin will work only on growing cells that contain peptidoglycan. A few eubacterial genera lack a cell wall entirely. Members of the genera of cell wall-less bacteria will not be inhibited by penicillin because they lack the biochemical component that this antibiotic affects. In contrast, Gram-positive bacteria, such as *Staphylococcus* and *Streptococcus,* which sometimes cause infections in humans, are usually quite sensitive to penicillins.

Gram-positive Eubacterial Cell Wall

The **Gram-positive cell wall** has a peptidoglycan layer that is relatively thick (ca. 40 nm) and comprises approximately 90% of the cell wall. This thick peptidoglycan layer, which is considerably hydrated, accounts for the staining reaction observed in the Gram stain procedure. The primary stain (crystal violet) passes across the wall freely and is firmly attached to cell structures by the addition of the mordant (Gram's iodine). The decolorizing agent (ethanol or acetone) dehydrates the wall, causing it to shrink and trap the primary stain-iodine complex. Thus Gram-positive bacterial cells retain the primary stain and appear blue-purple following Gram staining.

The cell walls of most Gram-positive eubacteria also have **teichoic acids,** which are acidic anionic polysaccharides (FIG. 3-20). Teichoic acids contain a carbohydrate such as glucose, phosphate, and an alcohol (either glycerol or ribitol). The teichoic acids are bonded to the peptidoglycan, making them an integral part of the Gram-positive cell wall structure. Teichoic acids can bind protons, thereby maintaining the cell wall at a relatively low pH. This low pH prevents autolysins from degrading the cell wall. Teichoic acids also bind cations such as Ca^{2+} and Mg^{2+} and act as receptor sites for some viruses.

When phosphate concentrations are low, Gram-positive bacteria replace the phosphate-rich teichoic acids of the cell wall with **teichuronic acids.** This enables them to conserve phosphate that is essential for ATP, DNA, and other cellular components. Teichuronic acids are polysaccharide chains of uronic acids and *N*-acetylglucosamine, which fulfill the cell's requirement for an acidic, anionic polysaccharide in the cell wall.

Gram-negative Eubacterial Cell Wall and Cell Envelope

The **Gram-negative cell wall** is far more complex than its Gram-positive counterpart. The peptidoglycan layer of the Gram-negative cell wall is very thin (ca. 2 nm) and often comprises only 10% or less of the cell wall. The Gram-negative staining reaction occurs because the wall is too thin to retain the crystal-violet iodine complex when treated with the decolorizing agent. Teichoic acids do not occur in Gram-negative bacterial cell walls. Rather, lipoproteins (lipids linked to protein molecules) are bonded to the peptidoglycan, forming an integral part of the Gram-negative bacterial wall (FIG. 3-21). Additionally, there are layers of lipopolysaccharide (lipids linked to carbohydrate molecules), phospholipids, and proteins outside the peptidoglycan layer. Although these layers sometimes are considered part of the cell wall, it is now more common to view the peptidoglycan layer as the

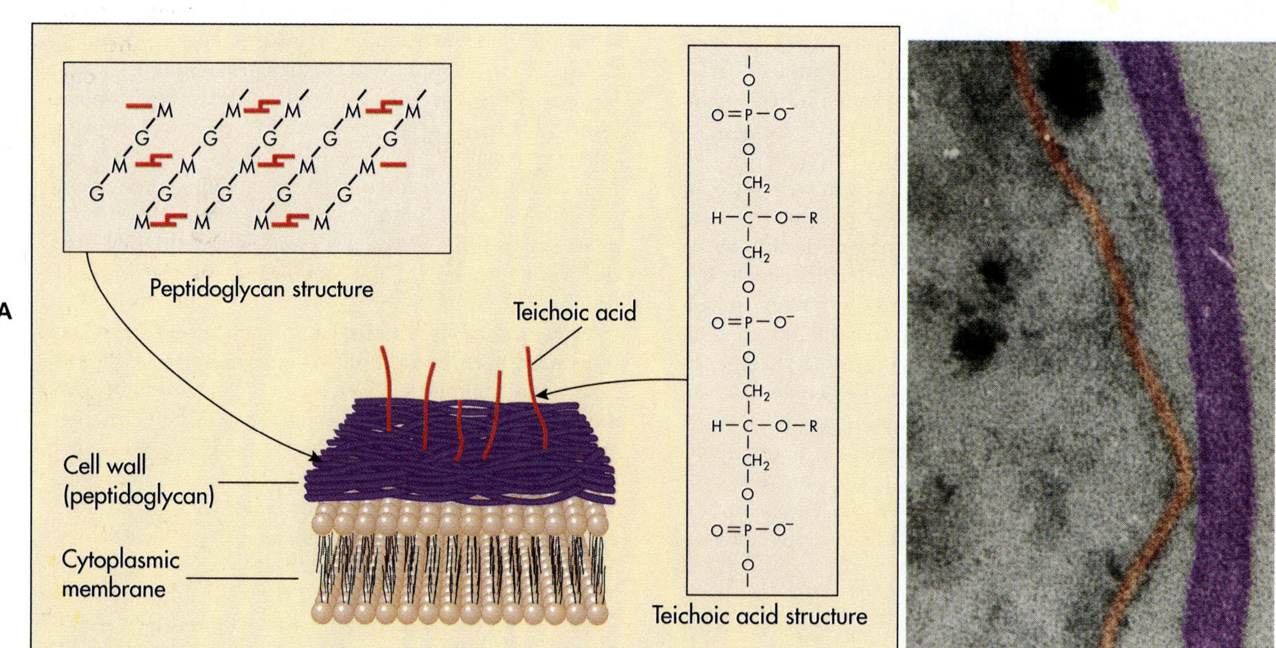

FIG. 3-20 **A,** The Gram-positive cell wall that surrounds and protects the cytoplasmic membrane has a relatively thick peptidoglycan layer. It also has teichoic acids, which are polymers of glycerol or ribitol phosphate. The techoic acid structure shown here is the glycerol type, and *R* may be D-alanine or glucose. **B,** Colorized micrograph of a Gram-positive cell wall (purple).

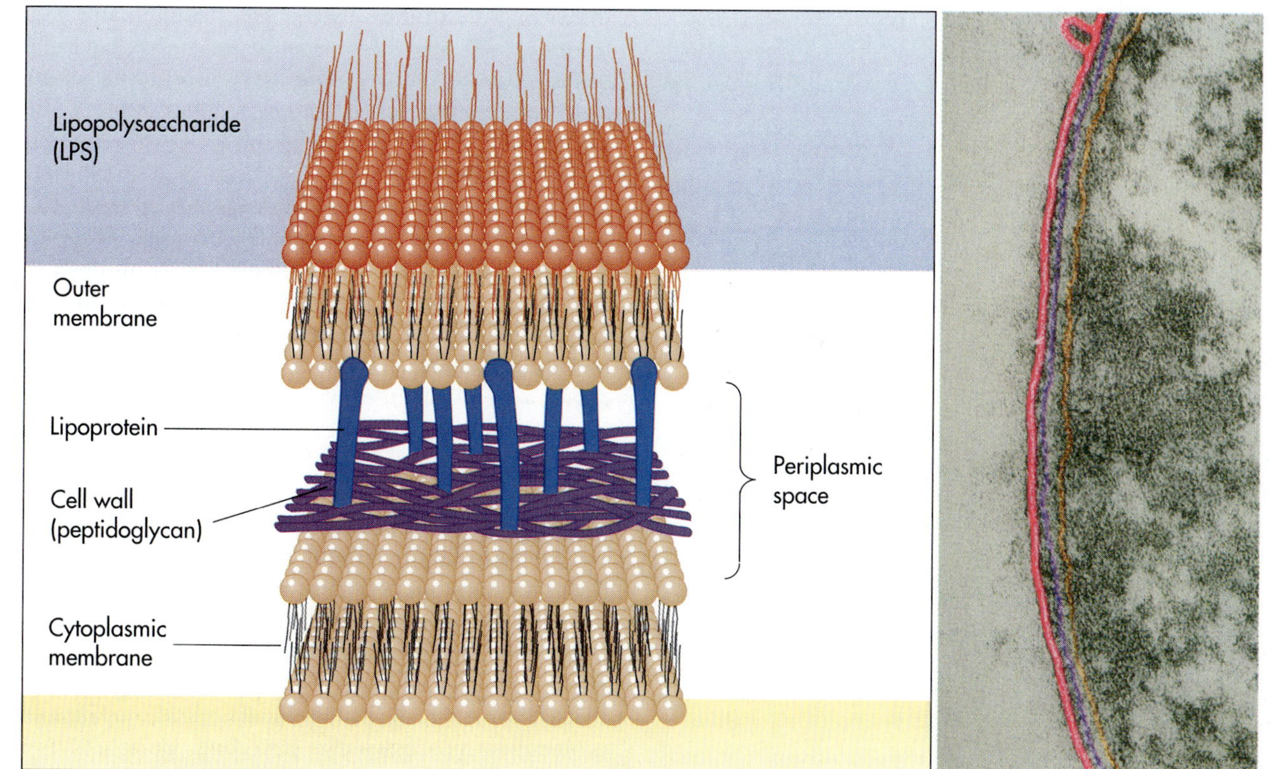

FIG. 3-21 **A,** The Gram-negative cell wall is a thin layer attached to an outer membrane via lipoproteins. The outer membrane contains phospholipid on its inner surface and lipopolysaccharide (LPS) on its outer surface. The space between the outer membrane and the cytoplasmic membrane is called the periplasmic space. **B,** Colorized micrograph of the cell wall of the Gram-negative bacterium *Escherichia coli.* (110,000×) The outer membrane encloses the peptidoglycan. The entire cell wall surrounds the cytoplasmic membrane.

wall component of a larger, more complex structure, called the **cell envelope,** of the Gram-negative bacterial cell.

Outer Membrane The cell envelope of the Gram-negative eubacterial cell extends outward from the cytoplasmic membrane to a second membrane—the **outer membrane.** The outer membrane is a lipid bilayer containing phospholipids, proteins, lipoproteins, and lipopolysaccharides; unlike the cytoplasmic membrane, it is relatively permeable to most small molecules.

Electron microscopic analyses of *E. coli* and *Salmonella* reveal that the cytoplasmic membranes and outer membranes of these Gram-negative rod-shaped bacteria are joined or fused at several points around the cell. These so-called **adhesion sites,** or **Bayer junctions** (named for their discoverer, Mannfred Bayer), are purportedly sites at which some material, such as excreted polysaccharide, is moved from the inside of the cell where it is first synthesized to the outside of the cell.

On the inner surface of the outer membrane in many Gram-negative bacteria is a lipoprotein that anchors or bridges the outer membrane to the peptidoglycan layer (see FIG. 3-21). The lipoprotein molecule contains fatty acids, which associate with the hydrophobic portion of the outer membrane. The protein portion of some of the lipoprotein molecules (about 35%) is bonded to the backbone of the peptidoglycan layer. The lipoprotein molecule in *E. coli* and *Salmonella* is the most abundant protein in the cell and probably confers stability to the outer membrane.

The outer membrane contains **lipopolysaccharides (LPS),** which are not found in cytoplasmic membranes. LPS is often called **endotoxin** because when this molecule is introduced into animals it causes fever and can lead to shock and death. It is called endotoxin because it is within or part of the cell (*endo* means inside).

LPS is a complex molecule composed of distinct regions (FIG. 3-22). The innermost portion of LPS is a lipid, called lipid A, that anchors the LPS to the hydrophobic portion of the outer membrane. Lipid A consists of *N*-acetylglucosamine disaccharide linked via ester and amide bonds to unusual fatty acids such as β-hydroxymyristic, caproic, and lauric acids. The toxic portion of LPS lies in the lipid A.

The polysaccharide portion of the LPS, which is external to lipid A, consists of a core polysaccharide and a repeat polysaccharide called the O-antigen or

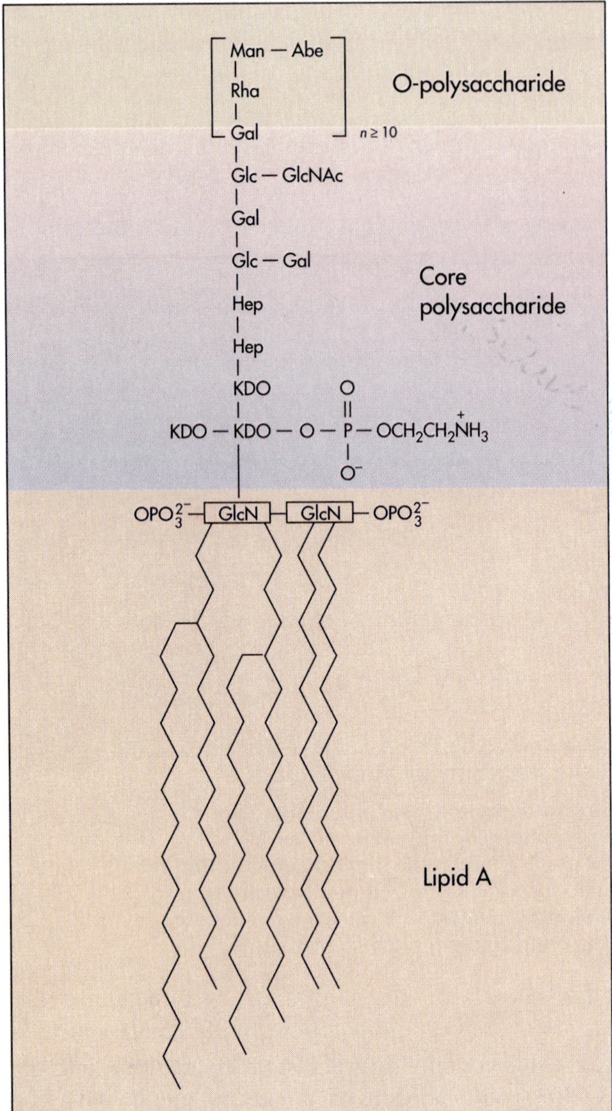

FIG. 3-22 LPS (lipopolysaccharide) is composed of lipid A containing abequose (Abe), mannose (Man), rhamnose (Rha), and galactose (Gal), a core polysaccharide that contains 2-keto-3-deoxyoctulosonic acid (KDO) and L-glycero-D-mannoheptose (Hep), phospholipid, lipoprotein, and repeat polysaccharide units.

O-polysaccharide. The core polysaccharide is fairly consistent for most Gram-negative bacteria and contains glucose, galactose, *N*-acetylglucosamine, and unusual sugars such as the 8-carbon sugar ketodeoxyoctulosonic acid (KDO) and heptoses (7-carbon sugars). The repeat polysaccharide consists of 3 to 5 sugars whose sequence is repeated up to about 25 times. The O-polysaccharide typically contains glucose, galactose, rhamnose, mannose, and several dideoxy sugars such as abequose, colitose, paratose, and tyvelose. The composition of the sugars and their arrangement varies from one Gram-negative bacterium to another or even from one subspecies to another. Generally, the LPSs of Gram-negative bacteria living in animal intestinal tracts, such as *Salmonella* and *E. coli,* have elaborate repeat structures. The LPSs of other Gram-negative bacteria that live in different environments, such as *Neisseria* and *Pseudomonas,* tend to lack these repeat polysaccharides.

Functionally, the outer membrane of the Gram-negative bacterial cell is a coarse molecular sieve. The permeability of the outer membrane to nutrients is due in part to proteins, collectively called **porins.** The porins, usually in aggregates of three, form cross-membrane channels through which some molecules can diffuse. Molecules with molecular weights up to about 800 for *E. coli* and even higher (3,000 to 10,000) for *Pseudomonas* and *Neisseria* species, can pass through the outer membrane. Hydrophilic and hydrophobic molecules can diffuse through the outer membrane, but the cytoplasmic membrane excludes almost all hydrophilic substances except water.

The outer membrane, however, is more restrictive than the cytoplasmic membrane to certain substances. It is less permeable than the cytoplasmic membrane to hydrophobic (nonpolar molecules) and amphipathic molecules (molecules that have both polar and nonpolar ends), such as phospholipids. For this reason, Gram-negative bacteria are less sensitive than Gram-positive bacteria to some antibiotics because the outer membrane prevents the drugs from reaching their targets in the cytoplasm. One of the first tests performed in the clinical microbiology laboratory is to determine whether an infection is due to a Gram-negative or a Gram-positive bacterium so that the physician knows which antibiotics should be considered for treatment.

Periplasmic Space The region between the cytoplasmic and outer membranes is known as the **periplasmic space** (see FIG. 3-21). Recent studies suggest that the term *periplasmic space* should be replaced with the term *periplasmic gel* to indicate that the peptidoglycan may actually fill the region between the cytoplasmic and outer membranes. The term *periplasmic gel* implies that the peptidoglycan is relatively porous and that proteins can migrate through its gel-like composition.

Several proteins are found in the periplasmic space. These include binding proteins, chemoreceptors, and enzymes—such as oxidases and dehydrogenases. The binding proteins facilitate the transport of substances into the cell by delivering substances to carriers that are bound to the cytoplasmic membrane. The periplasmic space also contains chemoreceptors, which are proteins that bind with substances and direct the cell's movement toward or away from those substances. Hydrolytic enzymes in the periplasmic space break down large molecules so that the smaller products can be transported across the cytoplasmic membrane where they are metabolized to produce ATP and cellular constituents.

CELL WALLS OF ARCHAEBACTERIA

The archaebacteria do not contain peptidoglycan in their cell walls as occurs in eubacteria. *N*-acetylmuramic acid and D-amino acids are not found in the cell walls of archaebacteria. Some archaebacteria have walls composed of **pseudopeptidoglycan,** which resembles the peptidoglycan of eubacteria but contains *N*-acetyltalosaminuronic acid instead of *N*-acetylmuramic acid and L-amino acids instead of the D-amino acids in eubacterial cell walls (FIG. 3-23). Also, the bonds between the carbohydrates in pseudopeptidoglycan are β 1-3 instead of β 1-4 as in peptidoglycan. Cell walls with pseudopeptidoglycan occur in some methanogenic (methane-producing) and extremely halophilic (high salt-requiring) archaebacteria. Other archaebacteria have cell walls composed of proteins; others contain polysaccharide cell walls; still others have walls with different chemical compositions.

Although there is no unifying structural composition, archaebacterial cell walls can protect the cytoplasmic membranes even in hot, acidic, and saline environments in which many archaebacteria live. The cell walls of *Halobacterium,* for example, contain glycoproteins with a high abundance of negatively charged (acidic) amino acids. The cell walls of *Halobacterium* are stabilized by the interaction between its acidic amino acids and the high abundance of positively charged sodium ions (Na^+) in the very saline environments in which this organism lives; if the sodium chloride concentration surrounding the cell drops below 15%, the cell wall loses its integrity and the cells may lyse due to osmotic shock.

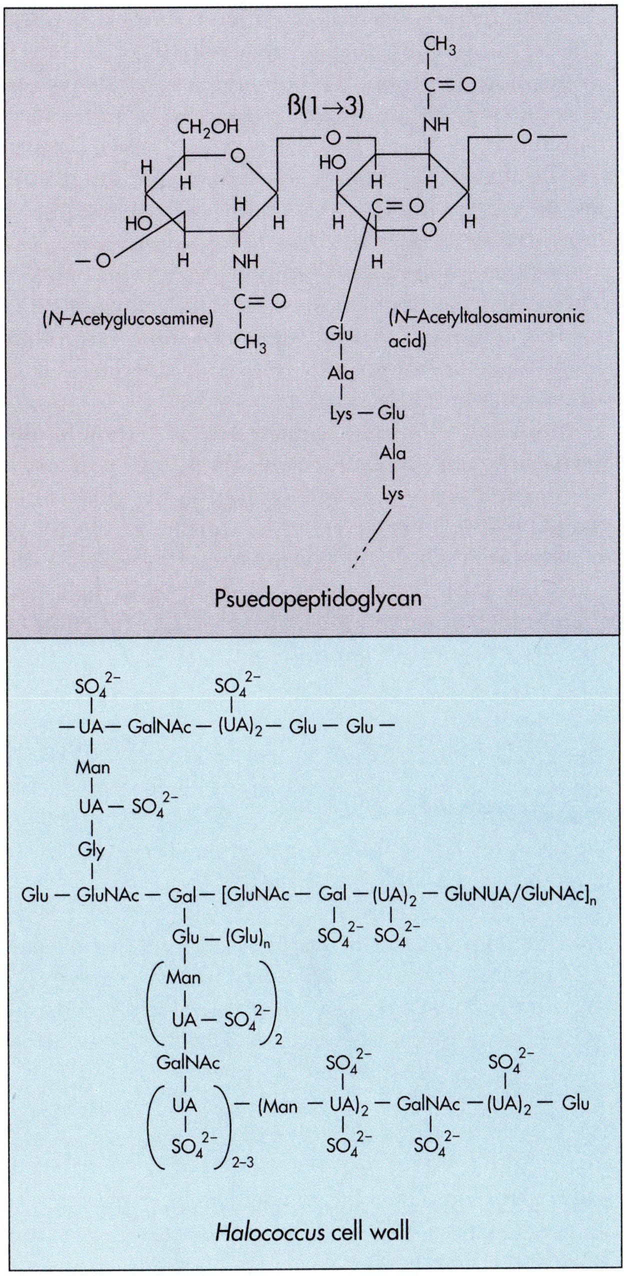

β(1→3)
(*N*-Acetyglucosamine)
(*N*-Acetyltalosaminuronic acid)
Glu – Ala – Lys – Glu – Ala – Lys

Psuedopeptidoglycan

Halococcus cell wall

FIG. 3-23 Archaebacterial cell walls are composed of polysaccharides other than the peptidoglycan of eubacterial cells. Some, such as those of *Methanobacterium,* contain pseudopeptidoglycan (*top*) which has β 1-3 bonds and *N*-acetyltalosaminuronic acid not found in peptidoglycan. Others, such as *Halococcus,* which grows in brines, have more complex wall structures (*bottom*) that permit them to live in extreme environments (UA, uronic acid; Man, mannose).

CELL WALLS OF EUKARYOTIC MICROORGANISMS

Algal Cell Walls

Many algae have cell walls of cellulose, but various other polysaccharides are found as major components of some algae. Some algae have cell wall structures containing calcium or silicon, sometimes called the *test* or *frustule.* The diatoms, for example, have frustules that are cell walls composed of silicon dioxide, protein, and polysaccharide. The frustule has two overlapping halves and distinctive markings that give these organisms their characteristically symmetric and beautiful shapes (FIG. 3-24). The coral algae deposit calcium carbonate in their wall structures, forming

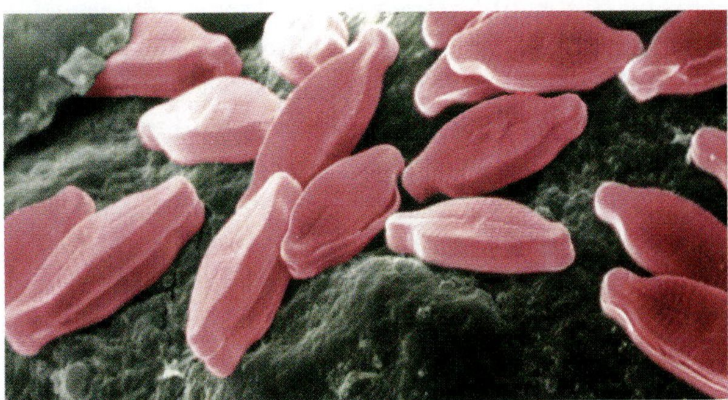

FIG. 3-24 Colorized micrograph of the diatom *Achnanthes exigna.* (860×). The frustule, composed of silicon dioxide, has two overlapping halves.

the basis of coral reefs. These structures protect the cell against physical damage rather than against osmotic shock, and the cell walls of these organisms are preserved long after the organisms die.

Fungal Cell Walls

Most fungi, including yeasts, have cell walls. The chemical composition of fungal cell walls is reflected in taxonomic relationships and is a useful criterion in fungal classification systems. The cell walls of many fungi are composed of chitin, a nitrogen-containing polysaccharide. The hard shells of crabs and the exoskeletons of arthropods are also composed of this substance. Chitin is relatively resistant to microbial decomposition.

Protozoan Cell Walls

The protozoa usually do not have a true cell wall surrounding their membranes, and many protozoa have developed alternative mechanisms for protection against osmotic pressure that are based on the exclusion of water. Many protozoa have a thin *pellicle* surrounding the cell that maintains the shape of the organism. If the pellicle of a ciliate protozoon such as *Paramecium* is removed, the cell becomes spherical. The pellicle does not protect the protozoan cell against osmotic shock. Some protozoa form an outer wall or shell, composed of calcium carbonate (as in the foraminifera) or silicon dioxide or strontium sulfate (as in the radiolaria), that physically protects the organism. These shells are not a basis for protection against osmotic pressure, and, in fact, many foraminifera extend their cytoplasm beyond the shell.

BACTERIAL CAPSULES AND SLIME LAYERS

Some bacteria form a protective structure called a **capsule** (FIG. 3-25). The capsule surrounds the cell wall. Chemical composition of the capsule varies among species of bacteria. It often is composed of polysaccharides attached externally to the cell wall. Such polysaccharide capsules occur in pneumonia-causing strains of *Streptococcus pneumoniae, Haemophilus influenzae,* and *Klebsiella pneumoniae.* Some *Bacillus* species, in contrast, produce capsules composed exclusively of glutamic acid, largely in the D form, rather than polysaccharide capsules.

The capsule is especially important in protecting bacterial cells against phagocytosis by eukaryotic cells, such as by various protozoa and human white blood cells. Having a capsule can be a major factor in determining the *pathogenicity* of a bacterium, that is, the ability of a bacterium to cause disease in the organism that it infects. In some cases, a bacterial species will have two variants, one that forms a capsule and is a virulent pathogen, and a nonencapsulated form that does not cause disease. The nonencapsulated bacteria are subject to phagocytosis by blood cells involved in the immune response of the infected host organism. On the other hand, phagocytizing blood cells involved in the immune response are unable or less able to adhere to, engulf, and digest those bacteria that have capsules.

Although capsules and slime layers are often similar in composition, a distinction is made between them. **Slime layers** are not as tightly bound to the cell as capsules. Most are composed of polysaccharides. These external layers may protect the cell against dehydration and a loss of nutrients. In some cases, they act as traps for nutrients by restricting the flow of substrates away from the cell.

In addition to these layers some eubacteria have a crystalline protein layer, called the **S layer** surrounding the cell. This layer occurs outside the cell wall of Gram-positive eubacteria and external to the outer membrane of Gram-negative eubacteria. It also is the only layer observed surrounding the cytoplasmic membranes of some archaebacteria. The function of the S layer is not yet known.

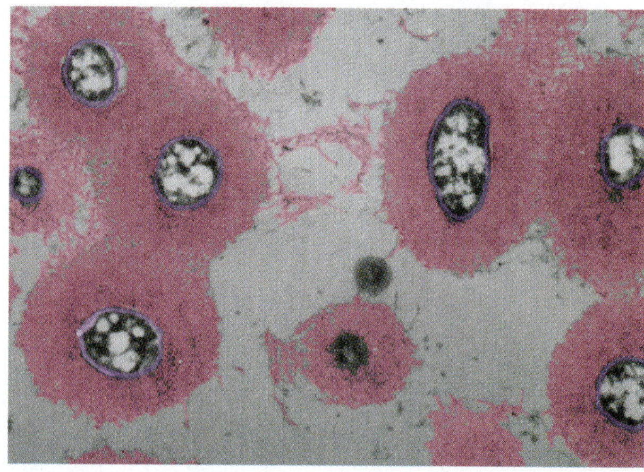

FIG. 3-25 Colorized micrograph showing the capsule *(pink)* of the bacterium *Alcaligenes faecalis.* The capsule surrounds and protects the cell.

3.4 CELLULAR GENETIC INFORMATION

The hereditary information of a cell is contained in double helical macromolecules of DNA (deoxyribonucleic acid). The DNA is composed of nucleotides, the sequence of which determines the properties of the cell. The maintenance of DNA within a cell for storage and expression of genetic information and the passage of DNA to progeny cells as the hereditary macromolecule is essential for living systems.

BACTERIAL CHROMOSOME

Most of the genetic information of a bacterial cell—both for archaebacteria and eubacteria—is contained within a single **bacterial chromosome.** The bacterial chromosome is a circular DNA macromolecule except in *Streptomyces* where it is linear and *Rhodobacter sphaeroides,* which has two separate chromosomes. There are about 4.7×10^6 nucleotide base pairs in the bacterial chromosome of *Escherichia coli.* The average bacterial cell contains 5×10^{-15} g of DNA, which is far less than the average eukaryotic cell. Some bacteria, such as archaebacteria, typically have few nucleotides; others, such as myxobacteria, have greater numbers of nucleotides. The molecular weight of the DNA in the average fungal cell is an order of magnitude higher, and algae have even larger amounts of DNA.

The bacterial chromosome occupies a region within the cell referred to as the **nucleoid region** (FIG. 3-26). Some sequences of the DNA are associated or complexed to the cytoplasmic membrane, but the nucleoid region is not separated from the rest of the cell within a membrane-bound organelle. The bacterial chromosome, therefore, is sometimes referred to as "naked DNA."

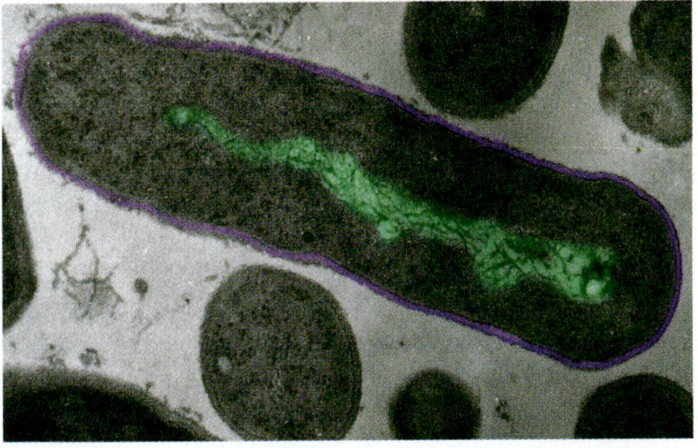

FIG. 3-26 Colorized micrograph of the bacterium *Mycobacterium phlei* showing the nucleoid region *(green)* within the cytoplasm where the bacterial chromosome occurs.

FIG. 3-27 Colorized micrograph of the bacterial chromosome released from a lysed cell of *Escherichia coli* shows that this (green) DNA macromolecule must be tightly coiled to fit within the bacterial cell.

The DNA of the bacterial chromosome is highly twisted *(negatively supercoiled),* but the nature of the forces maintaining this very condensed form are not fully understood and do not appear to be equivalent to the specific winding patterns observed in eukaryotic organisms. If the bacterial chromosome were not supercoiled it would expand to about 1 millimeter in linear length, which is far longer than the bacterial cell (FIG. 3-27). As a supercoiled molecule, the bacterial chromosome is condensed so that it occupies only a fraction of a bacterial cell that is 1 micrometer long.

The bacterial chromosome lacks the basic proteins, called *histones,* that are responsible for the coiling of the DNA in eukaryotic chromosomes. Histone-like proteins have been reported in only a few archaebacteria and eubacteria. The proteins normally associated with the bacterial chromosome are those involved in DNA replication, transcription of the information in the DNA molecule to RNA, and regulation of genetic expression.

Reproduction of a bacterial cell requires the replication of the bacterial chromosome so that each daughter cell receives a complete bacterial chromosome (FIG. 3-28). Hence, cell division must be syn-

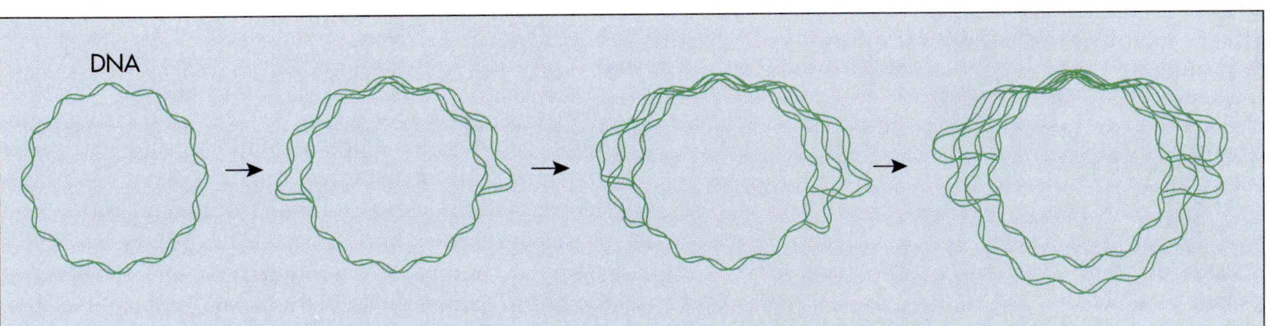

FIG. 3-28 The replication of a bacterial chromosome showing the sequence of synthesis of new circular loops of double helical DNA. Every time the cell divides, a new cycle of DNA synthesis begins, so that there is a completed copy of the bacterial chromosome and several copies of partially completed copies passed to the progeny cells.

chronized with replication of the bacterial chromosome. Because it can take longer to duplicate the bacterial chromosome, the bacterium initiates a new round of DNA replication every time the cell divides, even though the previously initiated replication of the DNA has not been completed. Thus in addition to the complete copy of the bacterial chromosome, a bacterial cell may have several partially completed bacterial chromosomes.

By initiating a new round of DNA replication every time the cells divide, the bacteria produce completely duplicated genomes in time for cell division, with DNA replication occurring at the same frequency as cell reproduction. The regulatory mechanism is such that cell division occurs at a specified time after completion of the replication of the bacterial chromosome. Completion of the replication of the bacterial chromosome is a prerequisite for cell division; if the termination of DNA replication is blocked, cell division that normally occurs 20 minutes later is prevented. The expression of specific genes required for cell division occurs at or immediately after the termination of replication of the bacterial chromosome.

Bacteria normally reproduce by **binary fission,** a process in which a cell divides to produce two equal-sized daughter cells (FIG. 3-29). In binary fission the inward movement of the cytoplasmic membrane and cell wall, **septum formation,** pinches off and separates the two complete bacterial chromosomes, providing each of the progeny cells with a complete set of genetic (hereditary) information. The formation of **septa,** or **cross walls,** physically cuts apart the bacterial chromosomes and distributes them to the two daughter cells. On completion of cross wall formation, there are two equal-sized cells that can separate, each having an identical bacterial chromosome.

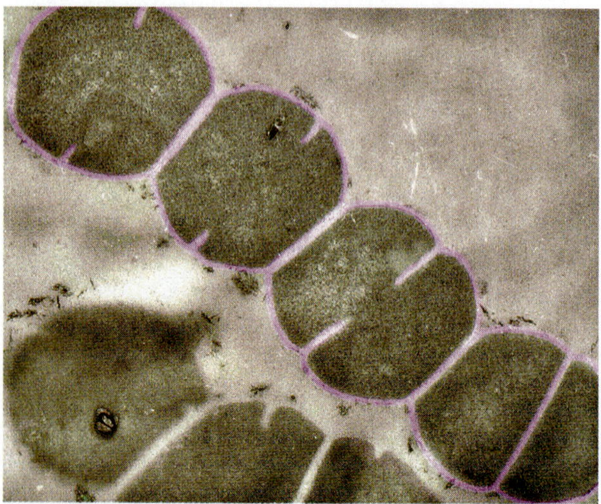

FIG. 3-29 Colorized micrograph showing the reproduction of *Streptococcus pyogenes* by binary fission. The inward growth of the septum divides the parent cell to produce two equal-sized progeny cells.

PLASMIDS

In addition to the bacterial chromosome, bacteria may contain one or more small, circular macromolecules of DNA known as **plasmids.** All bacterial cells have a bacterial chromosome, but not all bacteria have plasmids. Plasmids contain a limited amount of specific genetic information that supplements the essential genetic information contained in the bacterial chromosome. This supplemental information can be quite important, establishing such things as mating capabilities, resistance to antibiotics, production of toxins, and tolerance to toxic metals. Such supplemental genetic capability can permit the survival of the bacterium under conditions that are normally unfavorable. Although plasmids usually contain no more than 1% to 5% of the DNA in the bacterial chromosome, the effect of this limited amount of DNA can mean 100% versus 0% survival if the plasmid, for example, contains an antibiotic resistance gene.

Pathogenic bacteria containing plasmids that code for multiple drug resistance have become a particular problem in treating some infectious diseases of humans. These bacteria are resistant to many antibiotics and can continue to grow in the body despite antibiotic treatment. On the other hand, plasmids can be quite useful and are employed in genetic engineering as carriers of genetic information from various sources. Because of their relatively small size, plasmids are easy to manipulate. They can be isolated, genetic information from other sources can be spliced into them, and then they can be implanted into viable bacterial cells, permitting expression of the genetic information they contain in the newly created organisms into which they are placed.

NUCLEUS AND CHROMOSOMES OF EUKARYOTIC CELLS

Nucleus

The **nucleus** is an organelle in eukaryotic cells within which the cell maintains its genetic information. DNA within the nucleus is separated from the rest of the cell by the nuclear membrane (FIG. 3-30). The **nuclear membrane** is a double layer with an inner and an outer membrane, each of which is a phospholipid bilayer; there is a distinct space between the inner and outer membranes. Pores through the nuclear membrane permit exchange of relatively large molecules between the nucleus and the cytoplasm of the cell.

Separation of the DNA from the rest of the cell is necessary because there is much greater processing of genetic information before it can be expressed in a eukaryotic cell than in a prokaryotic cell. In prokaryotic cells, where there is no nucleus, the information in the bacterial chromosome is not separated; the information coding for specific proteins occurs as a contiguous sequence of nucleotides within the DNA

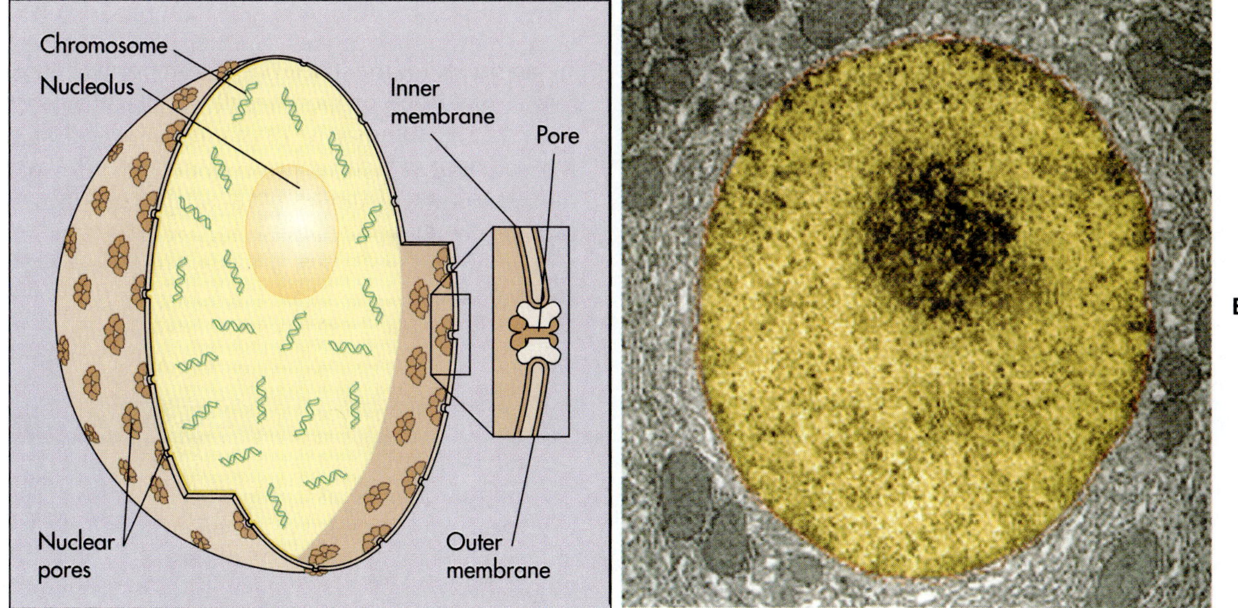

FIG. 3-30 **A,** The nucleus that contains the hereditary information in a eukaryotic cell is surrounded by two membranes: an inner and an outer membrane. The nucleolus within the nucleus is the site where ribosomal subunits are made. There are pores in the membranes through which materials can move, including messenger RNA that carries information from the DNA within the nucleus to the ribosomes in the cytoplasm. **B,** Micrograph of the nucleus of a eukaryotic cell shows the double membrane structure and the pores of this organelle that contains the chromosomes of eukaryotic cells.

macromolecule. Thus, the genetic information of prokaryotes does not have to be extensively processed before it can be used to code for the synthesis of proteins.

Chromosomes

The genetic information within the nucleus is stored in a distinct set of **chromosomes,** made up of **chromatin** consisting of DNA and protein. The chromosomes of eukaryotic cells contain linear DNA macromolecules arranged as a double helix and associated proteins. The DNA encodes hereditary information and the proteins help establish structure of the chromosomes. Chromosomes are visible with a light microscope only when the cell is undergoing division and the DNA is in a highly condensed form. Under these conditions the chromosomes appear as distinct threadlike structures in the nucleus; at other times the chromosomes are not condensed and thus are not visible. All of the genetic information resides in the DNA. The more abundant protein component maintains the coiled structure of the chromatin.

Chromatin proteins consist primarily of five cationic (basic) proteins, called **histones,** that bind to the DNA by ionic interactions. The DNA coils around the histones to form subunits of the chromatin known as **nucleosomes** (FIG. 3-31). Each nucleosome is com-

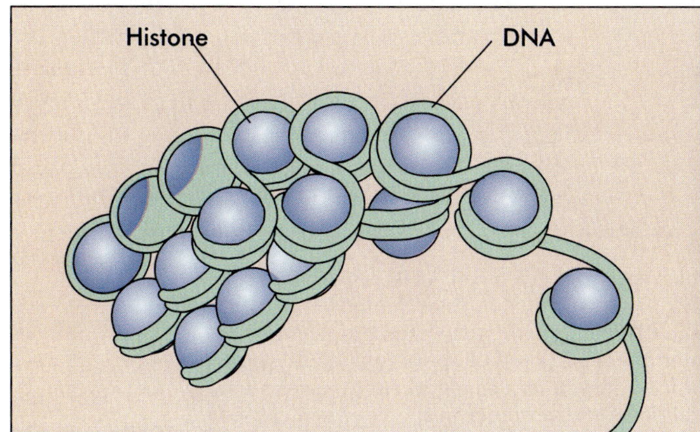

FIG. 3-31 **A,** A nucleosome showing that DNA is wrapped around histones (basic proteins), establishing coiling of DNA within the nucleus of eukaryotic cells. **B,** Micrograph of a region of a chromosome showing the bead-like appearance of nucleosomes.

posed of about 200 *nucleotides* (the structural units of nucleic acid) coiled around the histones. The resulting structures appear as spherical particles, looking like beads on a string when viewed by electron microscopy. The nucleosomes, which establish the structural configuration of eukaryotic chromosomes, are fundamental units of eukaryotic genetic material but are absent in bacterial chromosomes.

An exception to the usual eukaryotic chromosomal arrangement occurs in the dinoflagellate algae. These organisms are eukaryotic, and the DNA is contained within their nuclei, but the DNA is not associated with histones and is not supercoiled as it is in the chromosomes of other eukaryotic organisms. The DNA within the nucleus of dinoflagellates resembles the nucleoid region of prokaryotic cells; except for this feature the structure of dinoflagellates conforms to that of eukaryotic cells. Dinoflagellates may represent an evolutionary link between eubacteria and eukaryotic algae.

3.5 RIBOSOMES AND PROTEIN SYNTHESIS: INFORMATION FLOW IN CELLS

Although DNA of an organism stores the genetic information, enzymes of the cell actually mediate the expression of that information. The cell uses the information stored in the DNA macromolecules to direct the synthesis of functional proteins, with the information stored in the DNA determining the sequence of amino acids in a protein. Genetic expression depends on protein synthesis.

Synthesis of proteins within all cells occurs at the **ribosomes**. In both prokaryotic and eukaryotic cells the functional ribosomes have two subunits (FIG. 3-32). Ribosomes are functional and synthesize proteins only when the two subunits are combined. The formation of functional ribosomes depends on the presence of magnesium ions and chemical energy for binding the subunits.

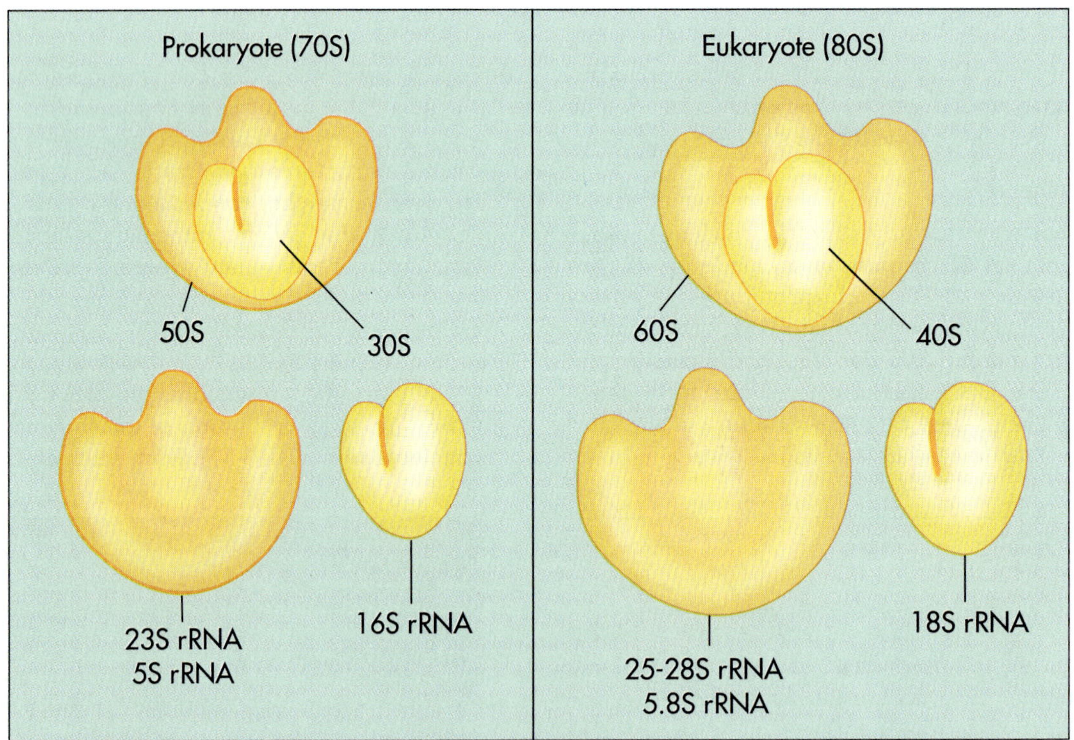

FIG. 3-32 A basic difference between prokaryotic and eukaryotic cells is the nature of the ribosomes in the cytoplasm. The prokaryotic cell has 70S ribosomes composed of 30S and 50S subunits. The 30S subunit contains about 21 proteins and a 16S rRNA molecule, having approximately 1,540 nucleotides; the 50S subunit is composed of approximately 34 proteins, a 23S rRNA, having approximately 2,900 nucleotides, and a small 5S rRNA species having only about 120 nucleotides. A eukaryotic cell has 80S ribosomes in its cytoplasm composed of 60S and 40S subunits. The 40S subunit contains proteins and an 18S rRNA, and the larger 60S subunit has proteins, 25-28S rRNA, and 5.8S rRNA. These differences form the basis for the specificity of action of some antibiotics that inhibit protein synthesis.

A typical prokaryotic cell may have 10,000 or more ribosomes, and eukaryotic cells contain considerably more. During protein synthesis, the information stored in the DNA is transferred to a messenger RNA molecule (mRNA) in a process called *transcription.* The mRNA carries the information to the ribosomes located in the cell's cytoplasm. There, the information is *translated* to direct the synthesis of a protein.

Ribosomes are intracellular particles composed of *ribosomal ribonucleic acid (rRNA)* and proteins. In *E. coli,* about two thirds of the ribosome is rRNA and the remainder is protein. The ribosomes of eukaryotic cells are larger and contain different-sized rRNA molecules than the ribosomes of prokaryotic cells. The sizes of ribosomes are given in Svedburg (S) units, which represent a measure of how rapidly particles or molecules sediment in an ultracentrifuge. Generally, the larger a substance, the greater its S value. However, the rate of sedimentation in a centrifuge depends on shape as well as size. Therefore when the subunits of a ribosome combine to form the functional ribosome, the intact ribosome has a lower S value than would have been calculated based on the S values of the individual subunits.

Prokaryotic cells have **70S ribosomes** composed of 30S and 50S subunits. The 30S subunit contains about 21 proteins and a 16S rRNA molecule, having approximately 1,540 nucleotides. The 50S subunit is composed of approximately 34 proteins, a 23S rRNA, having approximately 2,900 nucleotides, and a small 5S rRNA species having only about 120 nucleotides.

Eukaryotic cells have **80S ribosomes** composed of 40S and 60S subunits. The 40S subunit contains 18S rRNA, and the larger 60S subunit has 25-28S rRNA and 5.8S rRNA. In eukaryotic cells, the ribosomal subunits are synthesized within the nucleus in a region known as the **nucleolus.** They are transported through the pores of the nuclear membrane to the cytoplasm, where assembly of the 80S ribosomes occurs.

In addition to their 80S ribosomes, eukaryotic cells have 70S ribosomes within their mitochondria and chloroplasts. The 70S ribosomes of these organelles are very similar to the ribosomes of prokaryotic cells, giving strong credence to the endosymbiotic theory that mitochondria and chloroplasts evolved from prokaryotic cells.

Differences in the structural composition of prokaryotic 70S and eukaryotic 80S ribosomes forms another important basis for using antibiotics in the treatment of animal and plant diseases caused by bacteria. Protein synthesis that occurs at the ribosomes is essential for cells to carry out life-supporting metabolism, and any disruption of ribosomal conformation can disrupt this process. Many antibiotics such as erythromycin and streptomycin are effective because they bind to and alter the shape of 70S ribosomes. Such antibiotics are useful therapeutically because they selectively attach to 70S ribosomes and hence disrupt protein synthesis in bacteria, but do not exhibit any affinity for 80S ribosomes and therefore do not severely disrupt protein synthesis in eukaryotic human cells. Here we can see the practical application of a fundamental difference in the cellular structures of eukaryotes and prokaryotes.

3.6 SITES OF CELLULAR ENERGY TRANSFORMATIONS WHERE ATP IS GENERATED

All living cells transform energy, with ATP generation and utilization being the central focus of cellular energy transformation. There are two mechanisms by which cells can generate ATP. In one, mechanisms called *substrate level phosphorylation,* no specialized structure is involved and the reactions take place in the cytoplasm. In the other mechanism, called *chemiosmosis,* a membrane-bound ATPase is required. Chemiosmosis requires membranes. Chemiosmotic ATP generation involves two distinct processes: generation of a proton gradient and use of energy stored in the gradient to drive the phosphorylation of ADP by ATPase. The relationship between metabolism and cellular energy is the subject of Chapter 4. Here, we discuss the general locations and structures involved in ATP-generating reactions. Some ATP-generating reactions occur within the cell's cytoplasm. Additionally, some cell membranous structures are key to the cell's ability to generate ATP.

SITES OF ATP GENERATION IN PROKARYOTIC CELLS

Bacterial Cytoplasmic Membrane

Cytoplasmic membranes of some eubacteria and archaebacteria are involved in energy transformations: generation of ATP and protonmotive force (FIG. 3-33). As a result of cellular metabolism, protons (hydrogen ions) can be expelled across the cytoplasmic membrane to establish a concentration gradient where the concentration of protons is greater on the outside of the membrane than within the cell. Protons cannot move freely across the cytoplasmic membrane because of their charge, but they can move into pores in the membrane that are specifically associated with an enzyme system, adenosine triphosphatase (ATPase), for generating chemical energy in the form of ATP. The generation of ATP by the flow of protons across a membrane is known as **chemiosmosis.** Using

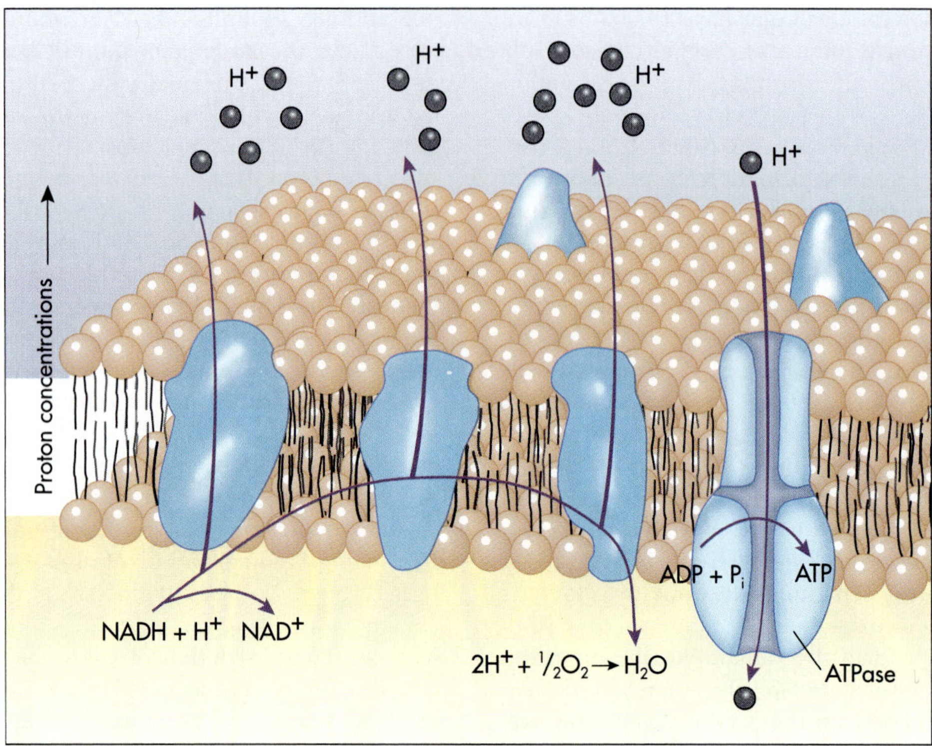

FIG. 3-33 The protonmotive force drives the formation of ATP by chemiosmosis. Protons are translocated across the membrane to establish a proton gradient. The membrane is impermeable to protons, which can only move back across the membrane through protein channels associated with ATPase. As the protons move by diffusion through these channels energy is transferred to form ATP.

chemiosmosis, bacteria that carry out respiration generate relatively large amounts of ATP from metabolism of sugars and other substrates.

Bacterial Internal Membranes

A few specialized groups of bacteria contain extensive internal membranes that are similarly involved with chemiosmotic generation of ATP. Such groups of bacteria include some nitrifying bacteria, which oxidize inorganic nitrogen-containing compounds to generate ATP, and the photosynthetic bacteria, which use light energy to generate ATP (FIG. 3-34). In nitrifying bacteria, the internal membranes are simple invaginations of the cytoplasmic membrane. These invaginations have the same general protein and lipid as the nonvaginated regions of the cytoplasmic membrane. In photosynthetic bacteria the internal membranes are sites where light is converted to chemical energy in the form of ATP during photosynthesis. These **photosynthetic membranes,** or **chromatophores,** can be simple extensions of the cytoplasmic membrane, as in the purple sulfur bacteria; cylindrically shaped vesicles, as in the green photosynthetic bacteria; or extensive multilayered membrane structures, known as **thylakoids,** in the cyanobacteria. This structural diversity suggests an evolutionary development sequence of photosynthetic membranes in these organisms.

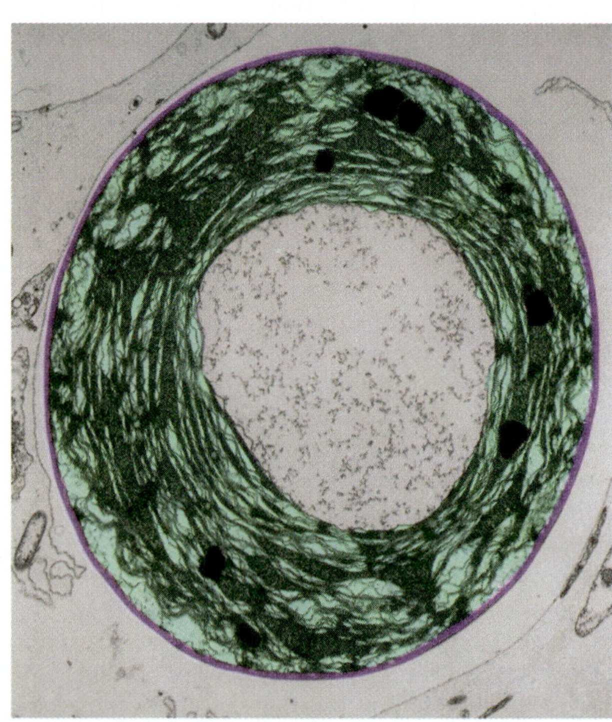

FIG. 3-34 Colorized micrograph of the photosynthetic bacterium *Prochloron* reveals that it has extensive internal membranes. (7,900×). These membranes are the sites of chemiosmotic generation of ATP by this bacterium, which derives the energy for ATP formation from light energy.

SITES OF ATP GENERATION IN EUKARYOTIC CELLS

Mitochondria

Mitochondria of eukaryotic cells are organelles in which chemiosmotic generation of ATP occurs (FIG. 3-35). A mitochondrion has an interior membrane that is extensively folded and an outer membrane that acts as the boundary between it and the cell cytoplasm. Convolutions of the inner membrane that extend into the interior of the mitochondrion are called **cristae.** This inner membrane has a higher proportion of protein associated with it than the outer mitochondrial membrane. Many of these proteins are involved in energy-transferring metabolic reactions. As a result of electron transport through a series of carriers embedded asymmetrically within the membrane and the resultant expulsion of protons, a proton gradient across the inner membrane drives the synthesis of ATP.

Chloroplasts

Chloroplasts occur in algal and plant cells, where they are the sites of photosynthetic ATP synthesis and carbon dioxide fixation. Chloroplasts are one form of **plastids,** which are large cytoplasmic organelles occurring within the cytoplasm of algae that contain pigments or other cellular products. Like mitochondria, chloroplasts contain an outer membrane, which separates the organelle from the cytoplasm, and an inner membrane. The interior compartment of the chloroplast, defined by the inner membrane and called the **stroma,** is where the fixation of carbon dioxide occurs during photosynthesis (FIG. 3-36).

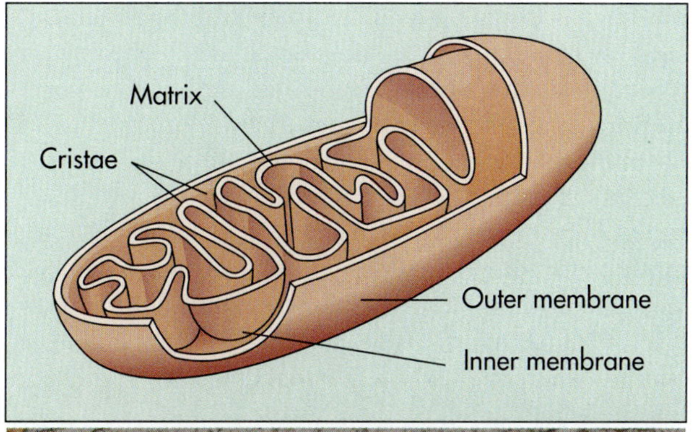

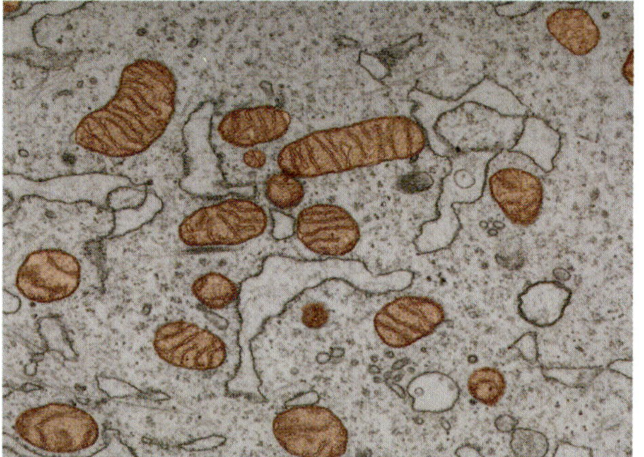

FIG. 3-35 **A,** A mitochondrion is the site of ATP generation by chemiosmosis in eukaryotic cells. There are two distinct membranes and extensive folding of the internal membrane. Protons are translocated across the inner membrane into the space between the inner and outer membranes. This establishes the protonmotive force that drives the formation of ATP. **B,** Colorized micrograph of mitochondria of a human cell. (14,500×).

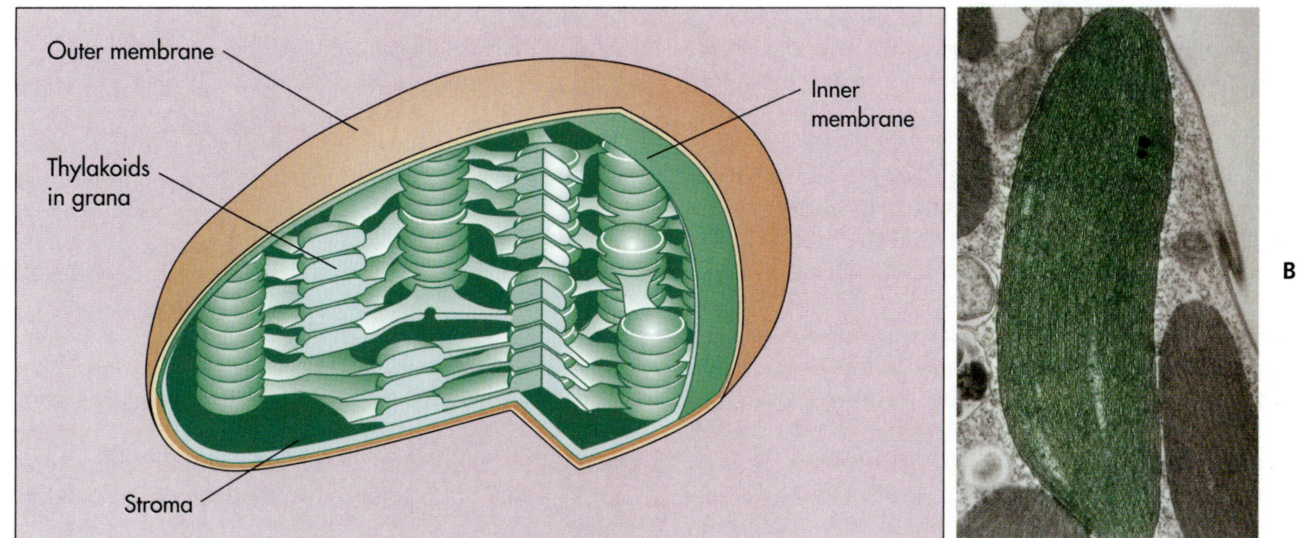

FIG. 3-36 **A,** A chloroplast is the site of ATP generation by chemiosmosis in eukaryotic photosynthetic cells. Light energy is trapped by the chlorophyll in the chloroplast. There are two distinct membranes. Protons are translocated inward across the inner membrane. This establishes the protonmotive force that drives the formation of ATP. The return flow of protons into the space between the inner and outer membranes passes through a protein channel associated with ATPase. **B,** Colorized micrograph of a chloroplast of the alga *Euglena proxima.* (17,600×).

The chloroplast has a complex internal membranous system known as the **thylakoids.** Within the chloroplast, the thylakoids, which are sac-like membranous vesicles, may be stacked to form **grana** that normally are densely packed piles of individual thylakoids. Although there are variations in the structures of chloroplasts in different algae, in general, the subunits of the chloroplast structure are less organized than the highly specialized structures characteristic of higher plants. The brown algae, for example, contain no grana and their thylakoid membranes are not stacked.

The establishment of a proton gradient across the thylakoid membranes drives the synthesis of ATP by chemiosmosis. This is analogous to the synthesis of ATP in the mitochondria, except that the flow of protons is inward for chloroplast and outward for mitochondria. The photosynthetic pigments in the thylakoid membranes, including the chlorophylls, trap light energy and initiate the photosynthetic generation of ATP. The auxiliary pigments within the chloroplast confer characteristic colors on the algae and determine which wavelengths of light can be used for initiating photosynthetic ATP generation.

3.7 COORDINATED MATERIAL MOVEMENT AND STORAGE IN CELLS

In addition to energy generation, another task cells must accomplish is the movement of substances from one place to another within the cell. In prokaryotes this is relatively simple because the lack of internal membrane-bound organelles allows substances to mix freely within the cell's cytoplasm. In eukaryotic cells, however, materials must move from one organelle to another within the cell. The compartmentalization of the eukaryotic cell makes a system of coordinated movement within them necessary. Thus the eukaryotic cell contains extensive networks of membranes and cytoskeleton components (to be discussed later in this chapter), but the prokaryotic cell has none of these structures.

MATERIAL MOVEMENT OUT OF PROKARYOTIC CELLS

Prokaryotes do not have elaborate physical structures to aid in the packaging and transport of materials out of the cell; however, they have means to effect transfer of substances. In some cases, it is necessary for bacterial cells to chemically "earmark" materials for export from the cell. The secretion of extracellular enzymes is a good example. Because some large nutrient molecules, such as cellulose, are too big to transport through the pores of the cytoplasmic membrane into the cell, bacterial cells must secrete extracellular enzymes that can break down such substances. These extracellular enzymes, called *exoenzymes,* degrade the large molecules outside the cell, forming smaller molecules that can then be transported across the cell membrane and metabolized within the cell. In addition to their role in converting substances that cannot be transported through a membrane into usable substrates, exoenzymes are involved in destroying substances that are harmful to the cell.

The secretion of extracellular enzymes represents an interesting regulatory mechanism whereby the cell recognizes which proteins to export. Many enzymes that are designed to be secreted contain a segment at the amino terminal end of the molecule that acts as a signal to initiate the secretion process. This **signal sequence** contains about 20 predominantly hydrophobic amino acids that react with the membrane, initiating the translocation of the protein across the cell membrane barrier (FIG. 3-37). During transport across the cytoplasmic membrane, the signal sequence of the protein is cleaved by an enzyme within the membrane matrix, so that the exoenzyme released is smaller. In many cases, the secretion of the exoenzyme is initiated before the synthesis of the protein is complete and secretion continues while protein synthesis is proceeding. The chemical composition of the synthesized exoproteins and their interactions with the components of the cytoplasmic membrane provide the mechanism for the selective secretion of these extracellular enzymes.

MATERIAL STORAGE IN PROKARYOTIC CELLS: INCLUSION BODIES

Bacteria store various chemicals within the cell under some conditions, such as when there are excess nutrients or there is an imbalance in the types of nutrients available—for example, lots of carbon-containing carbohydrates and no nitrogen for protein synthesis. Some of the substances accumulated within the cell act as nutrient reserves to be used in times of need. In prokaryotic cells, these reserve materials accumulate as cytoplasmic **inclusion bodies** that are not separated by a boundary membrane from the rest of the cytoplasm. The separation of the reserve inclusions is generally based on differential solubility, with the reserve material typically being relatively insoluble in water.

Many bacteria accumulate granules of **polyphosphate,** which are reserves of inorganic phosphates that can be used in the synthesis of ATP (FIG. 3-38). Polyphosphate granules can be seen using light microscopy after staining. These granules are sometimes

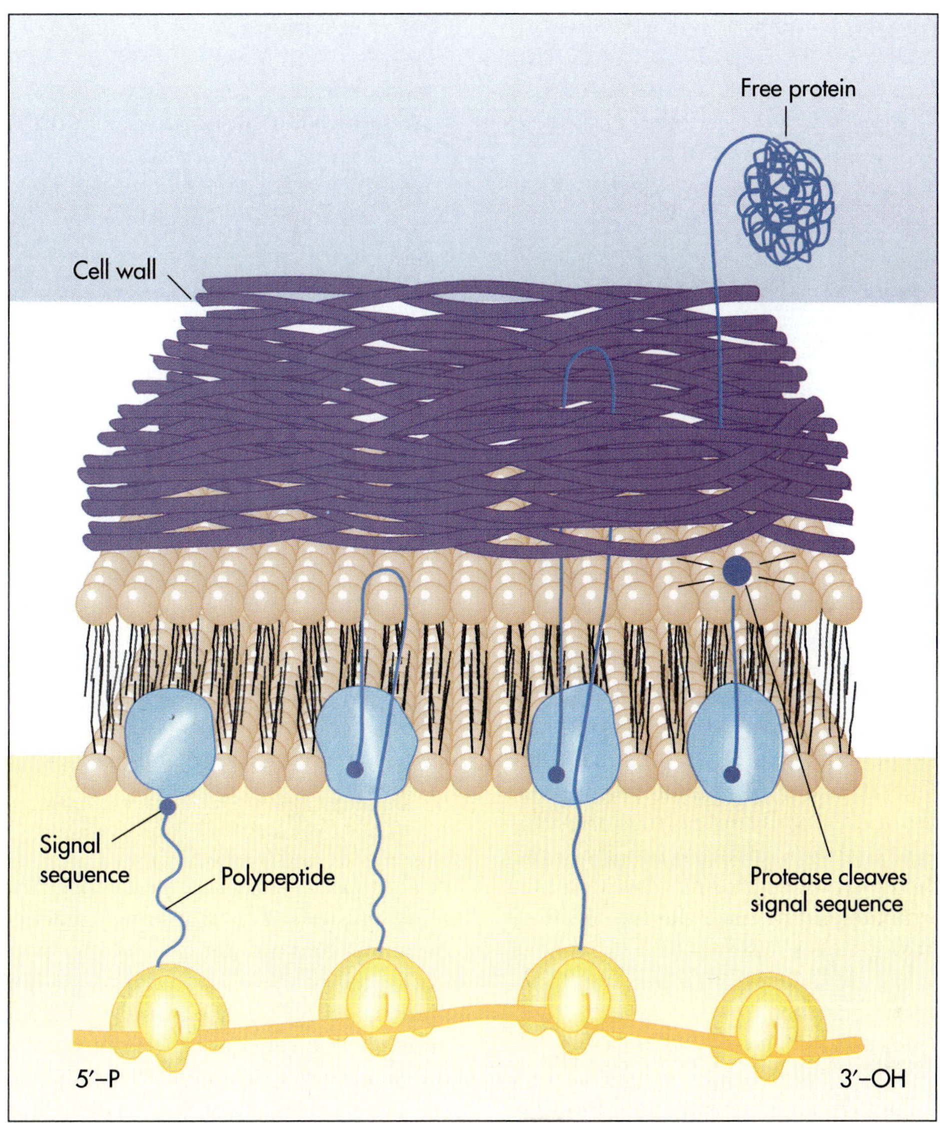

FIG. 3-37 A signal sequence on the polypeptide chain synthesized at the ribosome indicates that the protein containing that polypeptide should move across the cytoplasmic membrane and be excreted from the cell. This is important for the secretion of exoenzymes that function outside the cell to break down large substances into molecules small enough to be transported across the membrane.

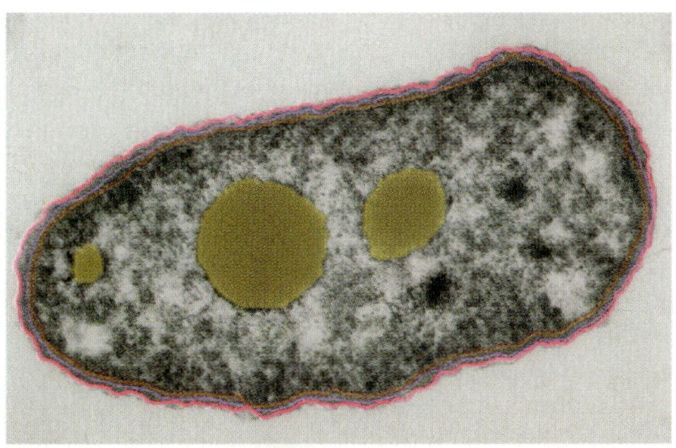

FIG. 3-38 Polyphosphate accumulates in some bacterial cells such as *Pseudomonas aeruginosa* (colorized; gold). (44,000×).

called **volutin** or **metachromatic granules.** These accumulated reserves can be metabolized at a later time for the generation of ATP and cell constituents. Some bacteria, including many photosynthetic bacteria, accumulate elemental **sulfur granules** as a result of their metabolism.

In many cases the substances that accumulate are synthesized as reserve materials by the cell. The most common bacterial carbon reserve material is **poly-β-hydroxybutyric acid (PHB),** a lipid-like molecule that accumulates in the cytoplasm (FIG. 3-39). Its nonpolar hydrophobic nature causes it to accumulate as a distinct inclusion body. PHB inclusions are surrounded by proteins thought to be involved with the metabolism of this carbon reserve.

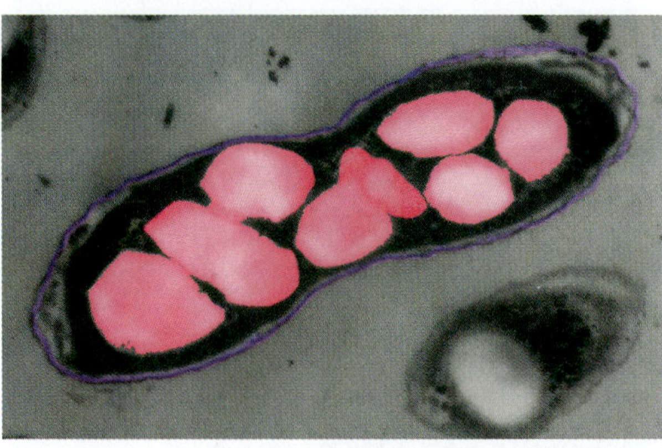

FIG. 3-39 The polyhydroxybutyrate inclusions of a *Vibrio* species nearly fill the cells of this colorized bacterium. (32,500×).

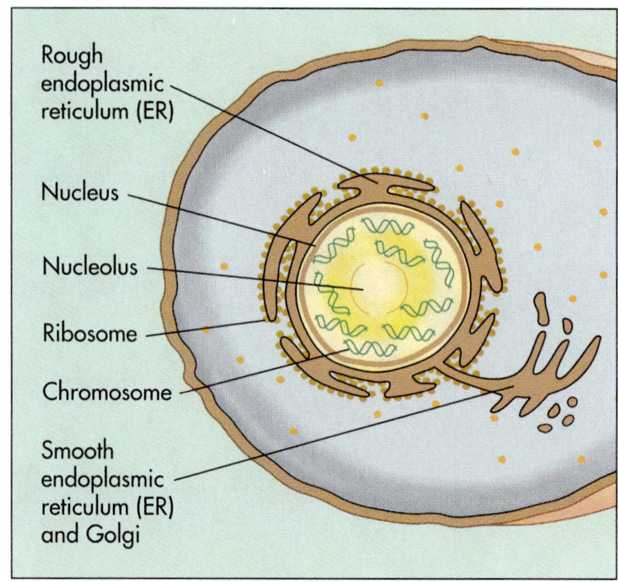

FIG. 3-40 The endoplasmic reticulum (ER) is an extensive membrane network that runs throughout the eukaryotic cell. Regions of the ER that have attached ribosomes are called rough ER; those lacking ribosomes are called smooth ER. These names are derived from the appearances of the ER when viewed by electron microscopy.

NETWORK OF MEMBRANE-BOUND ORGANELLES IN EUKARYOTIC CELLS

In marked contrast to the prokaryotic cell, the eukaryotic cell is filled with membranous organelles involved with the processing and storage of materials within the cell. The extensive internal membrane system of eukaryotic microorganisms permits the efficient segregation of function, adding versatility to the metabolism of the eukaryotic cell, and also increases the need to coordinate and manage the functions of the cell's subunit organelles. Many of the organelles of the eukaryotic cell are linked so that they can function in a coordinated manner.

Endoplasmic Reticulum

Eukaryotic cells contain an extensive membranous network known as the **endoplasmic reticulum** (FIG. 3-40). The appearance of the endoplasmic reticulum varies among different eukaryotic cells but always forms a system of fluid-filled sacs enclosed by the membrane network. The endoplasmic reticulum may form a continuum with the outer nuclear membrane and may provide a communication network for coordinating the metabolic activities of the cell.

The endoplasmic reticulum shows two distinct morphologies when examined by electron microscopy. In one case, the endoplasmic reticulum looks rough and has attached ribosomes **(rough ER);** in the other case, it appears smooth and is not associated with ribosomes **(smooth ER).** Smooth ER is where vesicles (membrane-bounded sacs) are discharged within the cell.

The attachment of ribosomes to the endoplasmic reticulum that forms rough ER allows for coordinated activity whereby proteins made at the ribosomes can immediately be sent through the channels of the endoplasmic reticulum to other organelles within the cell for use, packaging, or export. Many of the proteins synthesized by ribosomes attached to the endoplasmic reticulum are destined to be transported out of the cell or incorporated into membranes. Proteins synthesized on free ribosomes not associated with the endoplasmic reticulum are not transported through the channels of this membranous network and generally are used within the cytoplasm of the cell. Rough ER is involved in the production of secretory proteins and the production of new membranes by assembling proteins and phospholipids.

The endoplasmic reticulum also provides a large surface for enzymatic activities, as well as a source of lipids and membranes for the other organelles of the eukaryotic cell. No analogous membrane structure exists in prokaryotic cells to which ribosomes could attach, and bacteria have no system comparable to the endoplasmic reticulum for coordinated material movement within the cell.

Golgi Apparatus

The **Golgi apparatus** of the eukaryotic cell forms a continuous network with the rough endoplasmic reticulum (FIG. 3-41). Normally, four to eight Golgi bodies, which are flattened membranous sacs, are stacked to form the Golgi apparatus. The Golgi apparatus is sometimes referred to as the Golgi complex and the individual stacks of membranes as **dictysomes.** Golgi bodies are the sites of various synthetic activities

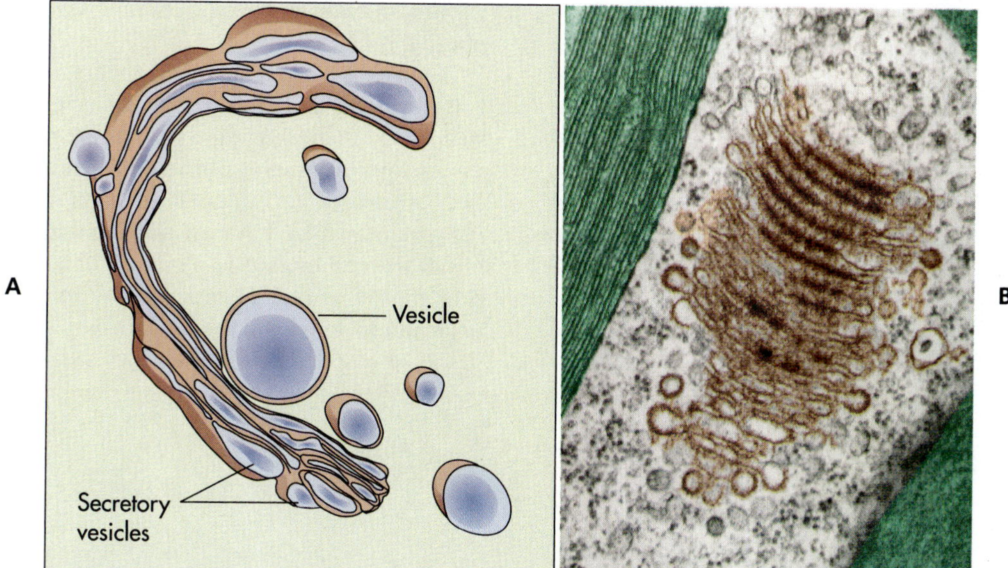

FIG. 3-41 **A,** The Golgi apparatus is involved in the packaging of substances for export from the cell. Secretory vesicles are formed at the Golgi apparatus that carry substances out of the cell. **B,** Colorized micrograph of the Golgi apparatus of the alga *Euglena.* (27,000×).

by which polysaccharides and lipids can be added to proteins to form lipoproteins, glycoproteins, and various polysaccharide derivatives that are essential for the synthesis of various cell parts.

Proteins and lipids are transferred directly from the endoplasmic reticulum to the Golgi apparatus, where repackaging into **secretory vesicles** occurs. Proteins transported through the rough endoplasmic reticulum are transferred to the Golgi apparatus by a process of vesicular budding called *blebbing.* The secretory vesicles are formed by the Golgi apparatus and then move to the cytoplasmic membrane, where they release their contents through exocytosis. Such a process is important for the construction of structures external to the cytoplasmic membrane, such as the cell wall of a eukaryotic cell.

Lysosomes

Lysosomes are specialized membrane-bound organelles of eukaryotic cells, probably produced in the Golgi apparatus, that contain various digestive enzymes. Some of the digestive activities of eukaryotic cells occur within the lysosome. Indeed, one of the functions of the enzymes within the lysosomes is to digest prokaryotic cells that have been ingested by phagocytosis. The lysosome membrane is impermeable to the outward movement of digestive enzymes and is also resistant to their action. This segregation of certain enzymes within the lysosome is necessary because these enzymes often are capable of digesting many of the cell's structural components.

Microbodies

Microbodies, which are smaller than lysosomes, isolate metabolic reactions that involve hydrogen peroxide. Microbodies contain catalase, an enzyme that breaks down hydrogen peroxide to oxygen and water. The **peroxisome,** a type of microbody found in eukaryotic microorganisms, is a site where some amino acids are oxidized with the production of hydrogen peroxide. If the peroxides formed in these reactions were not contained or destroyed, they could oxidize several essential biochemicals within the cell, resulting in the death of the cell. Their isolation within the peroxisome protects the cell.

Vacuoles

Various types of membrane-bound organelles, called **vacuoles,** serve different purposes within the cells of eukaryotic microorganisms. The **storage vacuole** is involved in maintaining accumulated reserve materials segregated from the cytoplasm in eukaryotic cells. For example, yeasts can store polyphosphate, amino acids, and uric acid as reserve materials within storage vacuoles. Other organisms store other forms of organic carbon, nitrogen, and phosphate reserves for times of need. Other vacuoles are involved in the movement of materials out of the cell. These vacuoles can unite with the cytoplasmic membrane during endo- and exocytosis. In some cases, a vacuole formed when the cell engulfs a food source fuses with lysosomes, establishing a digestive vacuole that permits digestion of the contents.

Cytoskeleton

The eukaryotic cell has a **cytoskeletal network,** which consists of microtubules and microfilaments, that helps determine the ability of the cell to move and to maintain its shape (FIG. 3-42). This cytoskeletal network links the various components of the cytoplasm into a unified structure called the **cytoplast,** that provides the rigidity needed to hold the various structures in their appropriate locations. The microtubular-microfilament arrangement of the cytoskeleton runs throughout the eukaryotic cell, connecting membrane-bound organelles with the cytoplasmic membrane.

The cytoskeletal structure appears to be involved in the support and movement of membrane-bound structures, including the cytoplasmic membrane and the various organelles of the eukaryotic cell. It apparently provides an important basis for membrane movement involved in transporting materials into and out of the cell by cytosis. The lack of a cytoskeleton in prokaryotic cells may explain why bacteria have not been found to be capable of cytosis.

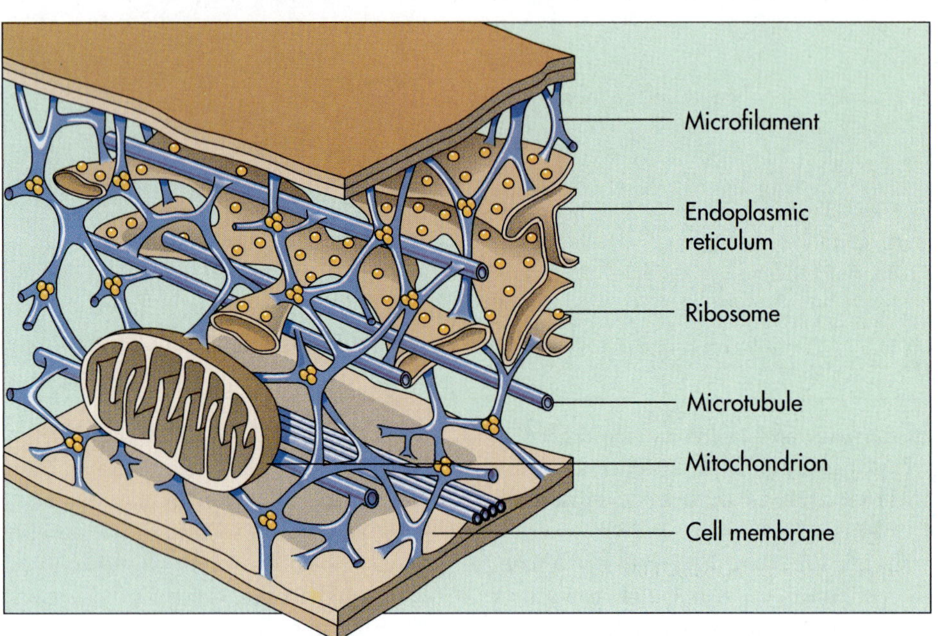

FIG. 3-42 The cytoskeleton is a complex network that links the organelles of the eukaryotic cell. Organelles are attached to microfilaments of the cytoskeleton.

3.8 STRUCTURES INVOLVED WITH MOVEMENT OF CELLS

Motility of microbial cells is important because it allows them to move from place to place to obtain nutrition to grow, reproduce, or escape from noxious microenvironments. In some cases, the cytoskeletal structure plays a role in the movement of an organism. For example, the movement of microtubules permits the extension of the cytoplasmic membrane to form the "false feet" (pseudopodia) used by some protozoa, like *Amoeba,* that move by extending their cytoplasm in a particular direction as they continuously change shape. More commonly, though, microorganisms move by means of flagella or cilia, which are specialized structures that project from the cell surface and propel the cell. Although flagella serve the same function of locomotion in prokaryotes and eukaryotes, the flagella of bacteria and those of eukaryotic cells are markedly different in mechanism and structure.

BACTERIAL FLAGELLA

Arrangement

Bacterial flagella are relatively long projections extending outward from the cytoplasmic membrane that propel bacteria from place to place (FIG. 3-43). In some bacteria, such as *Pseudomonas,* the flagella are known as **polar flagella** because they originate from the end or pole of the cell. A bacterial cell may have one or more polar flagella, which they use to swim rapidly in what is generally described as a corkscrew motion. In contrast to polar flagella that emanate from an end of the cell, **peritrichous flagella** such as those of the bacterial genus *Proteus* surround the cell. The specific number of flagella varies but there are always multiple flagella emanating from lateral points around a cell with peritrichous flagella. The arrangement of the flagella is characteristic of a bacterial

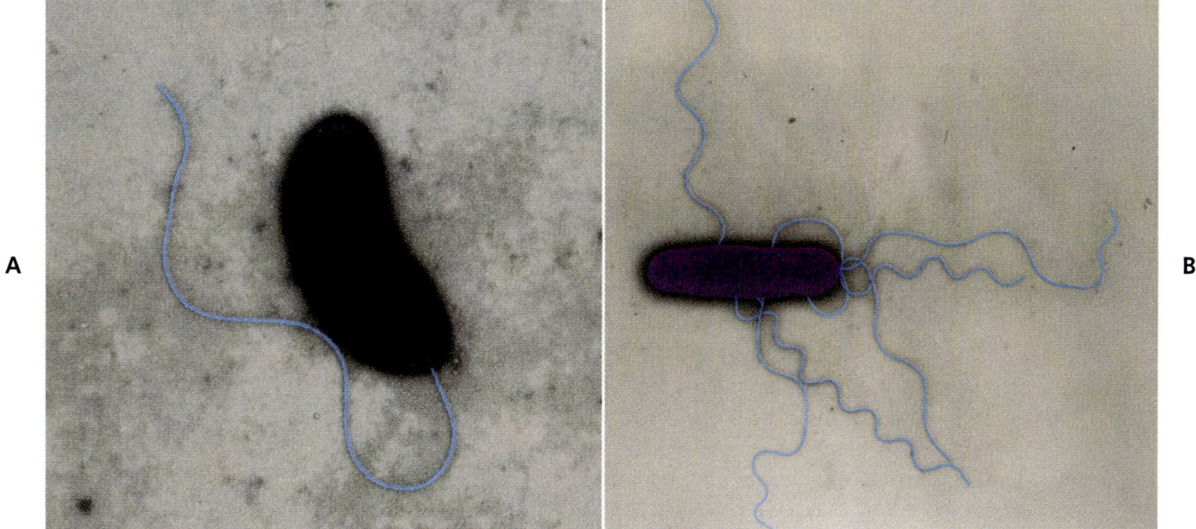

FIG. 3-43 **A,** Colorized micrograph of the bacterium *Vibrio* shows a single polar flagellum emanating from the end of the cell. (21,000×). **B,** Colorized micrograph of the bacterium *Salmonella* shows that peritrichous flagella surround the cell. (30,000×).

genus and is an important diagnostic characteristic used in classifying bacteria.

Structure

The bacterial flagellum consists of a single filament composed of many subunits of the protein **flagellin.** It is a nonflexible structure. During growth of a bacterial flagellum, the flagellin protein subunits are transported through the hollow core of the flagellum. At the tip of the flagellum the subunits self-assemble so that the flagellum is continuously growing. If a piece of a flagellum breaks off it immediately begins to regenerate itself.

The bacterial flagellum is attached to the cell by a hook and a basal body, which has a set of rings that attach to the cytoplasmic membrane and a rod that passes through the rings to anchor the flagellum to the cell (FIG. 3-44). In Gram-negative bacteria the

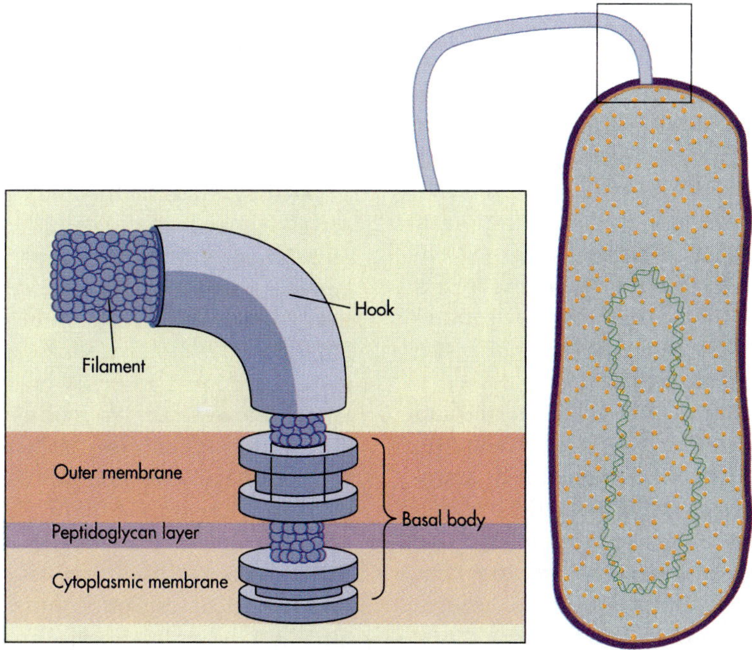

FIG. 3-44 The flagellum is anchored to the cell via a hook and basal body structure. There are rings that attach the flagellum to the outer and cytoplasmic membranes of a Gram-negative cell. This structure permits the flagellum to rotate. The energy for rotation comes from the protonmotive force.

basal body has a second set of rings that attaches to the outer membrane of the cell envelope. In Gram-positive bacteria there is only one set of rings that attaches to the cytoplasmic membrane. The hook structure attaches the filament of the bacterial flagellum to the rod of the basal body.

The structure of the bacterial flagellum allows it to spin like a propeller and thereby to propel the bacterial cell. Rotation of the flagellum requires energy, which is supplied by the proton gradient across the cytoplasmic membrane. Approximately 256 protons must cross the cytoplasmic membrane to power a single rotation of the flagellum. The flagellum can rotate at speeds of 1200 revolutions per minute. This enables bacterial cells to move at speeds up to 100 μm/second (0.0002 mile/hour). Considering that a typical bacterial cell has a maximal length of 2 μm, a rapidly swimming bacterial cell can move 50 times its body length per second—or in relative terms, twice as fast as a cheetah.

Chemotaxis

The bacterial flagellum provides the bacterium with a mechanism for swimming toward or away from chemical stimuli, a behavior known as **chemotaxis.** By controlling the duration and direction in which their flagella rotate, bacteria move toward certain chemicals, **(chemoattractants)** and away from others **(chemorepellents).** Chemosensors or receptors in the periplasmic space or the cytoplasmic membrane can bind to these chemicals and send a signal to the flagella.

Bacterial cells are too small to detect spatial chemical concentration differences directly; they do not have different chemosensors on the ends of the cell that indicate which way to move (spatial sensing). Rather, bacteria have a memory system that allows them to compare chemical concentrations periodically as they swim through the environment (temporal sensing). As motile bacteria move through the environment, they compare the present concentration of chemoattractants or chemorepellents with the previous environment. This memory system is based on a complex system of interactions of receptors, predominantly in the cytoplasmic membrane, with the chemoattractant or chemorepellent.

To understand how chemotaxis works, we need to recognize that, when bacteria move, they change direction rather than reaching the destination by swimming in a straight line (FIG. 3-45). Initially, bacteria rotate their flagella counterclockwise. In peritrichous bacteria, when the flagella rotate counterclockwise, they come together in a uniform bundle that causes the cell to move forward smoothly. This is called a *run.* After a period of smooth swimming, the direction of flagellar rotation is reversed; clockwise rotation causes the cell to *tumble* or *twiddle* without apparent direction because the flagellar bundle flies apart.

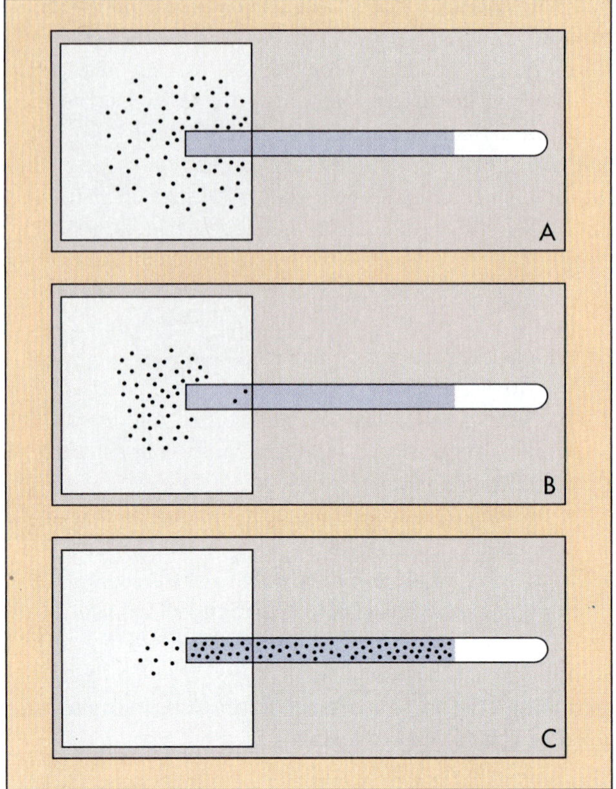

FIG. 3-45 Chemotactic behavior is readily demonstrated and measured by placing the tip of a thin capillary tube containing an attractant solution in a suspension of motile *Escherichia coli* bacteria. The suspension is placed on a slide, under a cover slip. **A,** At first, the bacteria are distributed at random throughout the suspension. **B,** After 20 minutes, they have congregated at the mouth of the capillary tube. **C,** After about an hour, many cells have moved up into the capillary tube. If the capillary tube had contained a repellant, few bacteria, if any, would have entered. Using this technique, it is possible to show which chemicals attract bacteria and which do not.

Bacterial flagella-mediated movement, therefore, results from alternating runs and tumbles through the environment. Runs last about 1 to 2 seconds and tumbles about 0.1 to 0.2 seconds under normal conditions. When a cell encounters a chemoattractant, it lengthens the time of its runs (counterclockwise flagellar rotation); when it encounters a chemorepellent, it shortens the time of its runs. Thus it is the relative durations of runs and tumbles that determine whether a bacterial cell moves toward or away from a particular chemical environment.

There are several systems in bacteria that control the direction in which the flagella rotate. The Enzymes II of the phosphotransferase transport system and other receptors in the cytoplasmic membrane, which detect O_2 and light, can alter the direction of flagellar rotation. Additionally, there are receptors in the periplasmic space, which are the same binding proteins that are involved in shock-sensitive transport systems, that affect the direction of flagella rotation.

In the cytoplasmic membrane of *E. coli* and *Salmonella typhimurium*, there also are several proteins, called **methyl-accepting chemotaxis proteins** (MCPs), that can control the direction of flagellar rotation. The MCPs are transmembrane proteins that interact with the chemorepellents and chemoattractants or indirectly with receptors in the periplasmic space. The MCPs are sometimes called transducers because they translate the signals from a chemoreceptor to the direction of rotation of the bacterial flagellum.

The MCPs alternate between an *excited state* in which they can detect an increasing concentration gradient of a chemoeffector molecule (chemoattractant), which leads to smooth runs. The MCPs then reach an *adapted state* in which they cannot distinguish the concentration gradient. The MCPs become methylated by a methyl transferase with the methyl group coming from the donor *S*-adenosylmethionine. Up to four methyl groups can be added to an MCP. Methylation of an MCP reduces the sensitivity to an attractant, up to 100-fold, and this leads to clockwise rotation of the flagellum and tumbling. Demethylation of the MCP by a methyl esterase returns the molecule to the excited state and smooth swimming runs.

The specific nature of how the degree of methylation of the MCPs communicates with the flagellum to alternate the direction of rotation is still unclear. Several proteins actually control the rotation of the flagellum. The MCPs appear to control phosphorylation of these proteins. The methylated MCP initiates phosphorylation of a protein designated CheA. The phosphate is transferred to a second protein designated CheY. When phosphate is added to CheY proteins the flagellum rotates in a clockwise direction and the cell tumbles. Removal of phosphate from CheY, which occurs when the MCP is demethylated, leads to counterclockwise rotation of the flagellum and straight runs.

Magnetotaxis

Some motile bacteria contain structures that enable them to respond to environmental stimuli other than chemical concentration differences. One fascinating group of bacteria contains inclusions of crystalline magnetic iron oxide (Fe_3O_4) called **magnetosomes.** These crystals are surrounded by a protein layer rather than a membrane and can be easily isolated from lysed bacteria with a magnet. Magnetosomes permit these bacteria to orient their movement in response to magnetic fields, a phenomenon known as magnetotaxis (FIG. 3-46). Magnetotactic bacteria can use these granules to navigate along the Earth's magnetic field. Some bacteria move predominantly north, and others move south. Magnetotaxis allows some bacteria to orient themselves so that as they move they point downward into the sediment where there are richer sources of nutrients. Interestingly, if magnetotactic bacteria collected in one hemisphere are transferred to the other hemisphere, as they move, they point the body of the cell upward instead of orienting it downward.

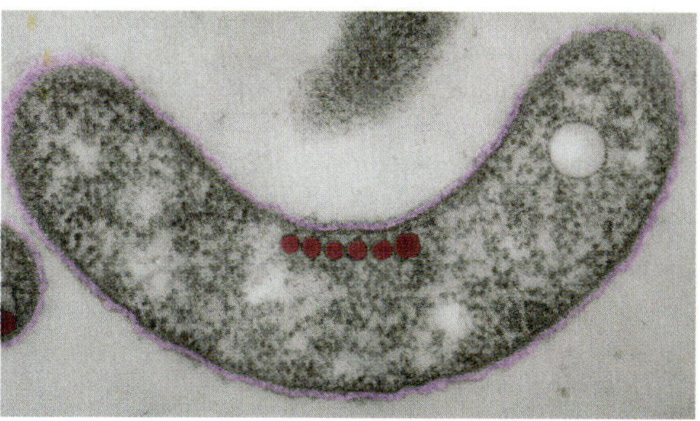

FIG. 3-46 Colorized micrograph of *Aquaspirillum magnetotacticum* shows characteristic magnetosomes *(red granules)* that allow this bacterium to respond to a magnetic field. (29,000×).

Phototaxis

Some bacteria detect and respond to differences in light intensity, a phenomenon called **phototaxis.** In some bacteria this process is similar to chemotaxis, and the bacteria use flagella to swim to areas of particular light intensities.

Other bacteria form **gas vacuoles** that enable them to respond to light (FIG. 3-47). The formation of gas vacuoles by aquatic bacteria provides a mechanism for

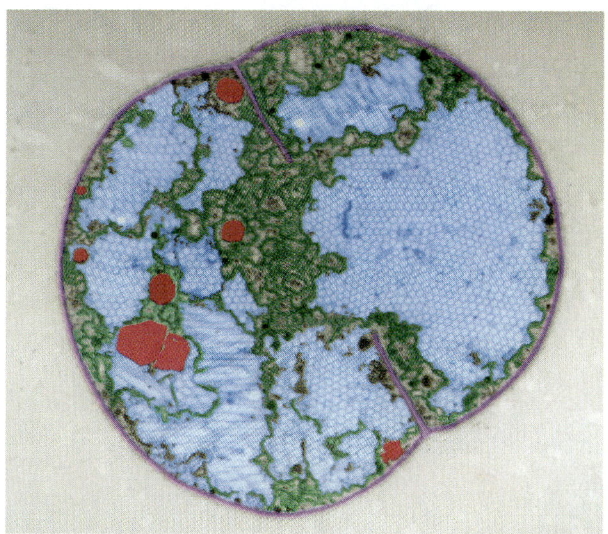

FIG. 3-47 Colorized micrograph of the gas vacuoles (*blue*) and storage granules *(red)* of the cyanobacterium *Microcystis.* Changing the gas content of the gas vacuole permits this bacterium to adjust its buoyancy. (12,600×).

adjusting the buoyancy of the cell. The gas vacuoles are filled with buoyant hydrogen gas. This allows bacteria with gas vacuoles to adjust their height in a water column. Many aquatic cyanobacteria, for example, use their gas vacuoles to move up and down in the water column, depending on light irradiation levels, to achieve optimal conditions for carrying out their photosynthetic metabolism. Although the gas vacuoles appear to be membrane bound, the boundary layers of these vacuoles are not true membranes but rather are composed exclusively of protein. The "membrane" layer appears to be only one protein molecule thick. The protein composing the boundary layer of these vacuoles has both hydrophilic and hydrophobic properties built into it.

FLAGELLA AND CILIA OF EUKARYOTIC CELLS

The cilia and flagella of eukaryotic cells undulate in a wavelike motion to propel the cell (FIG. 3-48). They are flexible structures that act with a whiplike motion and do not rotate to propel the cell.

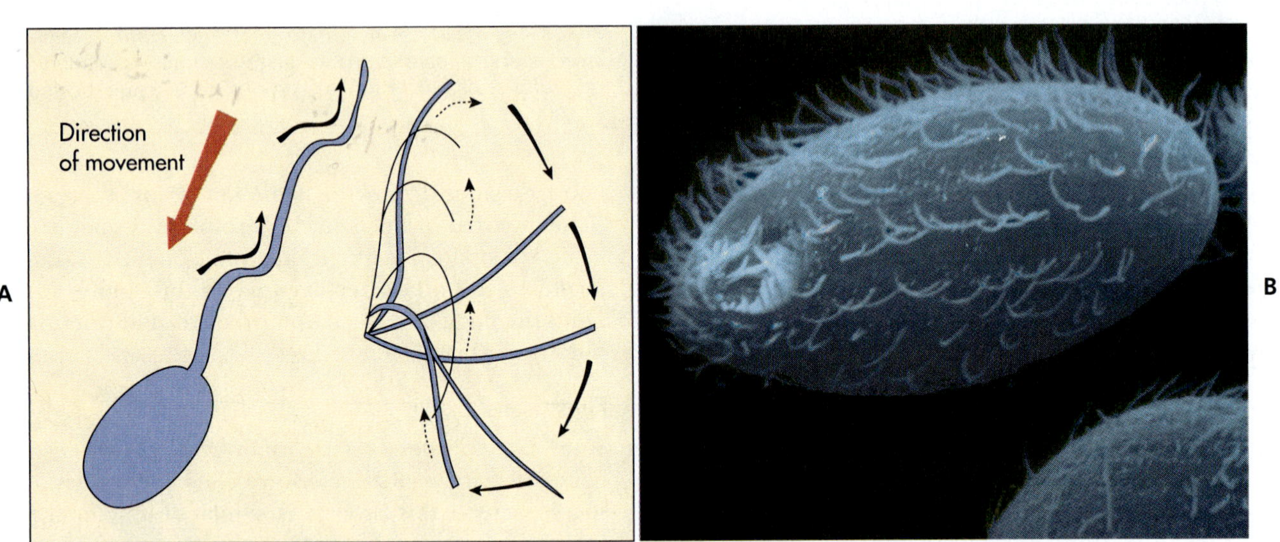

FIG. 3-48 **A,** The eukaryotic flagellum moves with a whiplike motion that propels the cell forward. **B,** Colorized micrograph of the ciliate protozoan *Tetrahymena*.

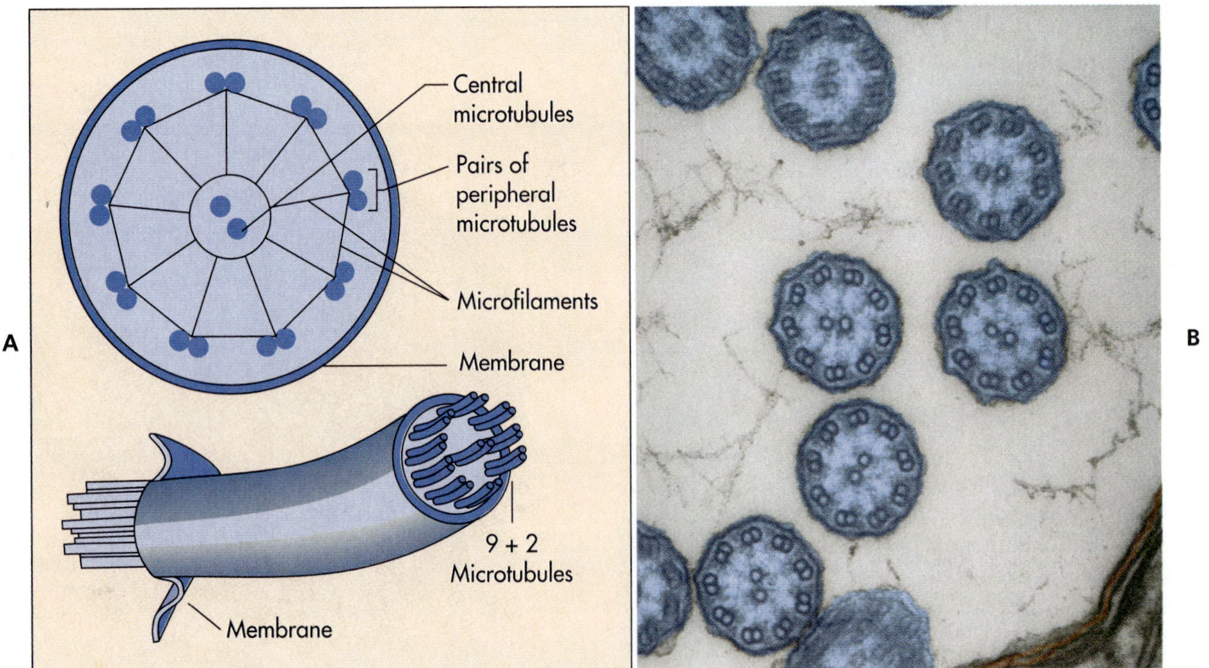

FIG. 3-49 **A,** The structure of the eukaryotic flagellum and cilia has nine pairs of peripheral microtubules surrounding a central pair of microtubules. The microtubules are connected by microfilaments. The peripheral microtubules slide past the central microtubules, causing the flagellum or cilia to bend. **B,** Colorized cross section of the cilia of the ciliate protozoan *Mesodinium*. (74,500×).

Eukaryotic **flagella** emanate from the polar region of the cell. **Cilia,** which are somewhat shorter than flagella, surround the cell. The flagella and cilia of eukaryotic microorganisms are important taxonomic characteristics. Among the protozoa, the Ciliophora are grouped taxonomically because of the presence of cilia, and the Mastigophora are grouped on the basis of the presence of flagella. Both cilia and flagella are generally involved in cell locomotion but cilia may also be involved in moving materials, such as food particles, past the cell surface while the organism or cell remains stationary.

In contrast to the rather simple structure of the bacterial flagellum, the flagella and cilia of eukaryotic microorganisms are far more complex and larger. The eukaryotic flagella and cilia consist of a series of microtubules—hollow cylinders composed of proteins (tubulin)—surrounded by membrane. The arrangement of microtubules in eukaryotic flagella and cilia is known as the *9 + 2 system* because it consists of nine peripheral pairs of microtubules surrounding two single central microtubules (FIG. 3-49). The nine pairs of microtubules form a circle surrounding the central microtubules. The peripheral microtubule doublets are linked to the central microtubules by radial spokes of protein microfilaments; they are also similarly linked to each other to form a circular network based on a sliding microtubule mechanism in which the peripheral doublet microtubules slide past each other, resulting in bending of the flagella or cilia. The peripheral spokes of the microtubular network contain a protein (dynein), which has ATPase activity and is involved in coupling ATP utilization to the movement of the flagella or cilia.

3.9 STRUCTURES INVOLVED IN ATTACHMENT

Microbial cells often attach to surfaces via specific structures. When attached, cells express different genes and have different physiological functions. The ability to attach to surfaces is important in the overall survival of microorganisms. It allows them to interact with other cells and in some cases to initiate the process of infection that permits their reproduction within other organisms.

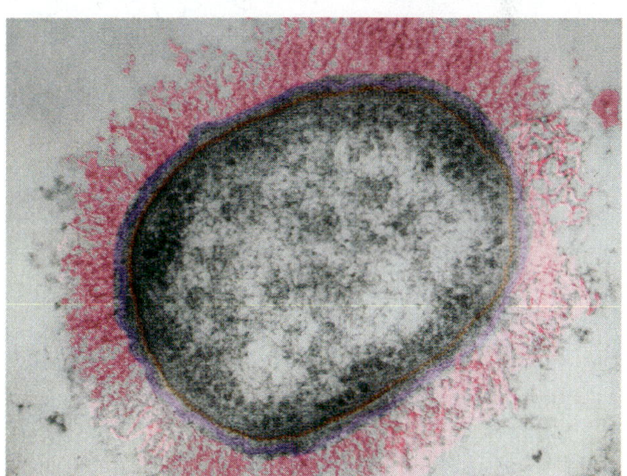

FIG. 3-50 Colorized micrograph of the glycocalyx *(red)* of a Gram-negative bacterium. (59,000×).

GLYCOCALYX

Many bacterial cells are surrounded by a structure called the **glycocalyx,** which plays a role in attachment processes. The glycocalyx is a mass of tangled fibers of polysaccharides or branching sugar molecules surrounding an individual cell or colony of cells (FIG. 3-50). It often is indistinguishable from a slime layer. The glycocalyx may act to bind cells together, forming multicellular aggregates. Additionally, the glycocalyx of some bacteria are involved in attachment to solid surfaces. Some bacteria, for example, adhere to the animal tissues they invade via a glycocalyx. Other bacteria in aquatic habitats seem to be held to rocks through the slime layers they secrete. Bacteria occurring in the oral cavity on the surfaces of teeth form an extensive polysaccharide slime, dental plaque, which enables them to adhere to the tooth. This adherence to the tooth surface is important in the formation of dental caries.

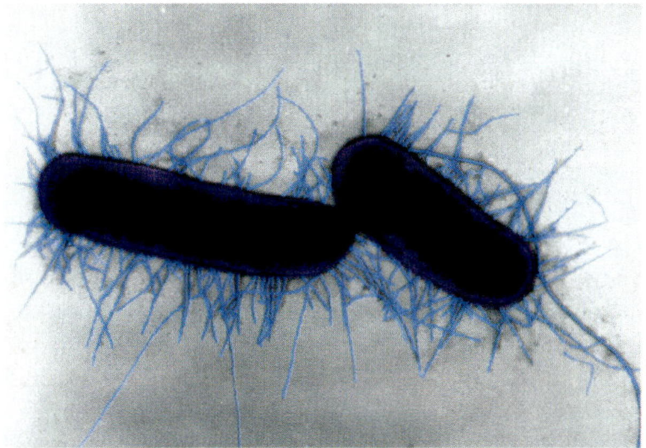

FIG. 3-51 Colorized micrograph of pili *(blue)* emanating from the surface of a cell of *Escherichia coli.* (18,500×).

PILI

Pili are short, thin, straight, hairlike projections that emanate from the surface of some bacteria and are involved in attachment processes (FIG. 3-51). Pili are phosphate–carbohydrate–protein complexes containing a single type of peptide subunit called *pilin*. There are several types of pili associated with the bacterial surface, each serving a different function. Sometimes a distinction is made between types of attachment processes, with the term *pilus* referring only to attachment between mating bacterial cells and the term *fimbriae* referring to all other attachment processes.

The **F pilus (fertility pilus)** is involved in bacterial mating and is found exclusively on the cells that donate DNA during this process. Mating requires cell to cell contact that depends on the F pilus (FIG. 3-52). Mating pairs of bacteria cannot form in the absence of an F pilus or if the bridge established by the F pilus between the DNA donor and recipient cells is interrupted. Although the F pilus is a hollow cylinder, the transfer of DNA during mating probably occurs directly through the cell wall rather than through the pilus. After pilus contact, there is direct cell wall to cell wall contact established between the mating pair that allows direct DNA transfer.

Pili also act as receptor sites for some bacteriophage (viruses that replicate within bacterial cells). The bacteriophage attach to the pili and subsequently transfer their genetic information to the bacterial cell. Pili have also been implicated in the ability of bacteria to recognize specific receptor sites that enable them to attach to the cytoplasmic membranes of eukaryotic cells. The pili seem to play the role of adhesins by allowing bacteria to attach to and colonize host cells, sometimes leading to colonization and disease in the host organism. For example, *Neisseria gonorrhoeae* (the etiologic agent of gonorrhea) attaches to the surfaces of cells of the human genitourinary tract via its pili when it initiates colonization and the subsequent disease process. Some pathogens, such as enteropathogenic *Escherichia coli*, attach to the lining of the gastrointestinal tract, similarly initiating an infection. In such processes, the pili act as points of specific contact and attachment between the bacterial cell and another surface.

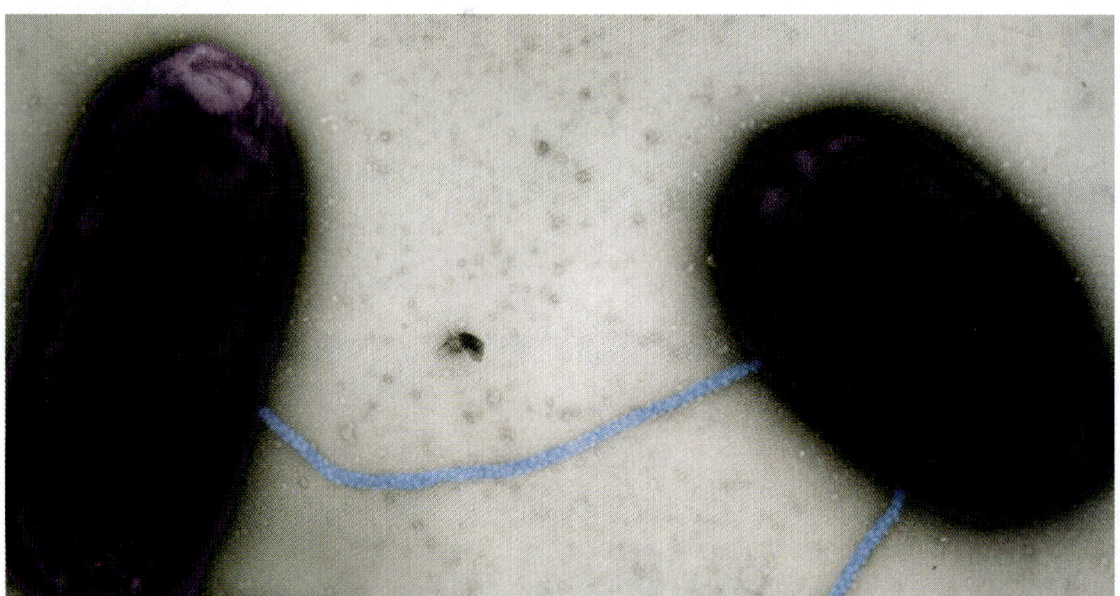

FIG. 3-52 Colorized micrograph of mating cells of *Escherichia coli*. The cells are joined via the F pilus *(blue)* of the donor cell.

3.10 SURVIVAL THROUGH THE PRODUCTION OF SPORES

Some microorganisms produce specialized resistant structures, called **spores,** to enhance their survival potential. Spores typically are involved in reproduction, dispersal, or the ability of the organism to withstand adverse environmental conditions. Each of these functions is involved in the overall survival of the organism. The spores involved in reproduction are metabolically quite active, whereas those involved in dispersal or survival of the microorganism often are metabolically dormant. Spores involved in the dispersal of microorganisms usually are quite resistant to desiccation (drying), and the production of such spores is an important adaptive feature that permits the survival of microorganisms for long periods of time during transport in the air. The spread of many fungi, for example, depends on the successful transport of fungal spores from one place to another. Unfortunately, many of these fungi are plant pathogens and cause great agricultural damage as a result of their ability to move from field to field.

BACTERIAL ENDOSPORES

The **bacterial endospore** is a heat resistant spore formed within the cells of a few bacterial genera (FIG. 3-53). The endospore is a complex, multilayered structure containing peptidoglycan within its complex spore coat and **calcium dipicolinate** within its core. The endospore is highly refractory, that is, it is resistant to elevated temperatures and desiccation, retaining its viability over long periods of time under conditions that do not permit growth of the organism. Endospores can survive exposure to high temperatures for extended periods, whereas bacterial vegetative cells (actively growing cells) are killed by brief exposures to such high temperatures. Endospores survive being placed in boiling water for hours! The absence of water and the presence of calcium dipicolinate are involved in conferring heat resistance on the endospore. Cells growing in a medium lacking calcium and mutant strains that cannot form calcium dipicolinate produce endospores that are not particularly resistant to elevated temperatures.

Only a few bacterial genera form endospores; the most important endospore producers are *Bacillus* and *Clostridium*. Members of both genera are Gram-positive rods that form endospores; *Bacillus* is aerobic, grow in the presence of oxygen, and *Clostridium* is obligately anaerobic, grow only in the absence of oxygen. That members of these genera form endospores presents special problems for the food industry, which employs processes that rely on heat to prevent spoilage of products. Because some endospores can withstand boiling (100° C) for more than 1 hour, it is necessary to heat liquids to higher temperatures to ensure the killing of endospores; a temperature >121° C maintained for at least 15 minutes is used with steam under pressure to kill endospores, as well as viable vegetative cells; dry materials require several hours at this temperature to ensure sterilization.

ENDOSPORE FORMATION

Endospores are formed when conditions are unfavorable for continued growth of the bacterium. **Sporulation,** that is, the formation of spores, can be initiated under conditions of starvation (see FIG. 3-53). Once started, the process at some point becomes irreversible, and sporulating bacteria continue to form spores even when starvation is relieved and conditions suitable for growth are restored.

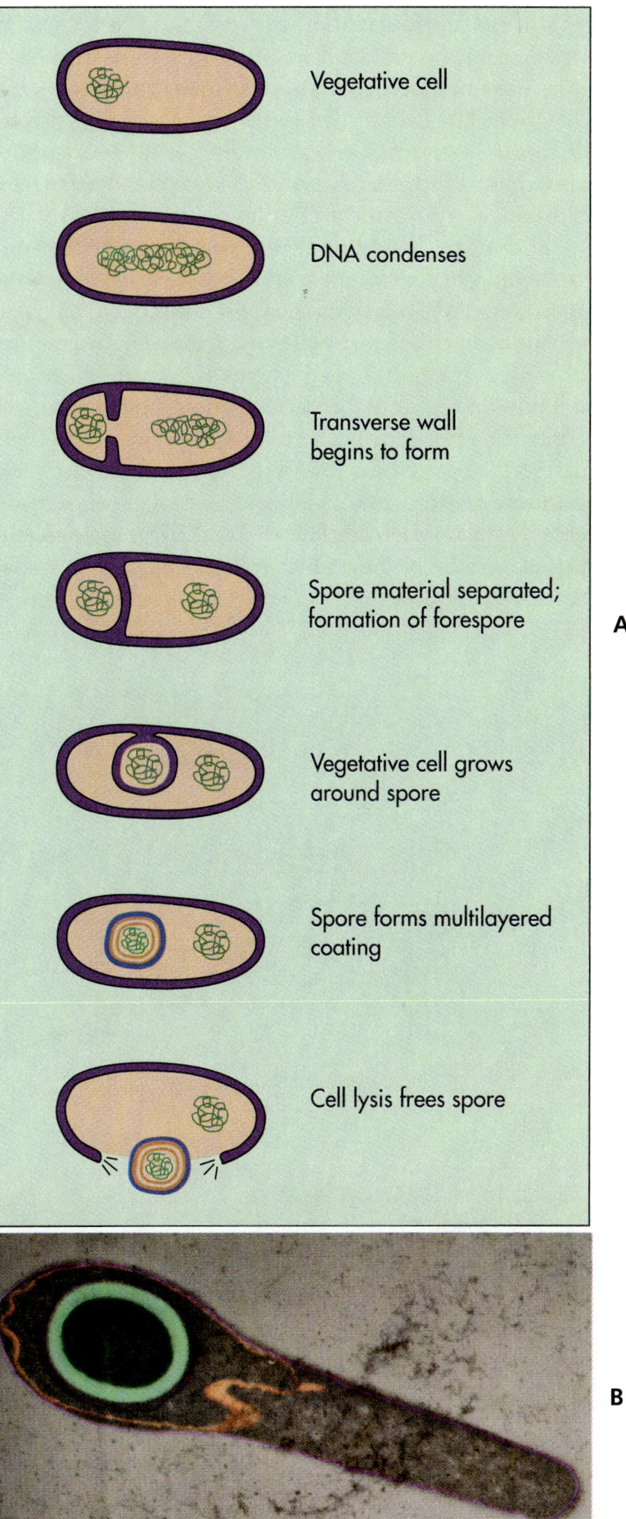
Vegetative cell
DNA condenses
Transverse wall begins to form
Spore material separated; formation of forespore
Vegetative cell grows around spore
Spore forms multilayered coating
Cell lysis frees spore
A
B

FIG. 3-53 **A,** The formation of an endospore is a complex process that occurs in stages. The spore contains a copy of the bacterial chromosome, which is separated from the rest of the cell by several layers that contain peptidoglycan. There is also a layer containing calcium dipicolinate that contributes to the heat resistance of the spore. **B,** Colorized transmission electron micrograph of an endospore of *Clostridium tetani* shows the complex multilayers of this heat-resistant body. (20,000×).

During the sporulation process, there is an invagination of the cytoplasmic membrane within the cell to establish the site of endospore formation. A copy of the bacterial chromosome is incorporated into the endospore, and the various layers of the endospore are then synthesized around the bacterial DNA. Substances are synthesized that are specifically related to endospore formation; these include dipicolinic acid, involved in conferring heat resistance to the spore, and polypeptides composed almost exclusively of single amino acids, such as cystine. The formation of the completed spore involves the synthesis of two wall-like layers and the formation of a spore cortex. Once the endospore is formed within the parent cell, it can be released by lysis of the parent cell. Endospores can retain viability for millennia, and viable endospores have been found in geological deposits in which they must have been dormant for thousands of years.

ENDOSPORE GERMINATION

Under favorable conditions, such as when water and nutrients are available and the temperature is permissive of growth, the endospore can germinate and give rise to an active vegetative cell of the bacterium (FIG. 3-54). During **germination** the spore swells, breaks out of the spore coat, and elongates. One of the striking features of spore germination is the speed with which metabolism shifts from a state of dormancy to the high activity levels that characterize a germinating spore. This shift in metabolic activity can occur within minutes. The endospore is metabolically self-sufficient, and during germination, ATP generation and protein synthesis can take place for at least 15 minutes, using the energy and substrates, principally phosphoglycerate, contained within the spore. After spore germination, the organism renews normal vegetative growth.

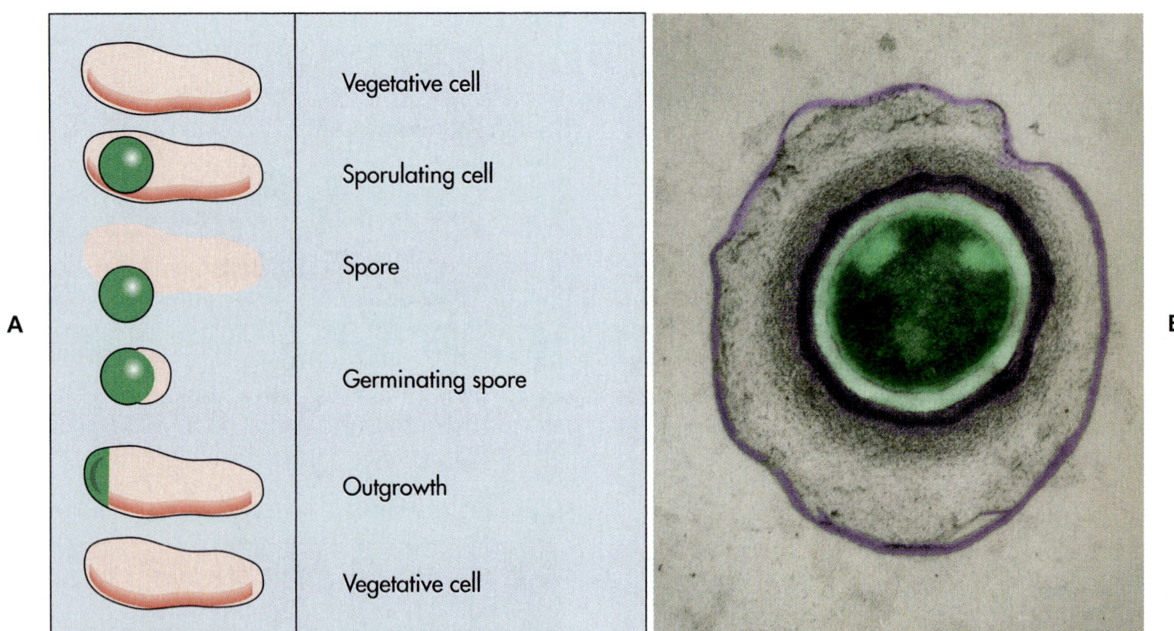

FIG. 3-54 **A,** The endospore is a multilayered structure that is heat resistant. It is formed within a vegetative cell and released when the cell lyses. Subsequently, an endospore can germinate under favorable conditions to form new vegetative cells. **B,** Colorized micrograph of an endospore of *Bacillus sphaericus.* (50,000×). The central core *(dark green)* is surrounded by the cortex *(light green)* and spore membrane/spore coat *(inner purple)*. The outermost purple layer covering the endospore is the exosporium.

CHAPTER REVIEW

STUDY QUESTIONS

1. What are the fundamental properties of a cell?
2. Which groups of microorganisms are prokaryotic, and which are eukaryotic?
3. What are the fundamental differences between prokaryotic and eukaryotic cells?
4. What are the structural differences between archaebacteria and eubacteria?
5. What structures occur in eukaryotic cells that are not found in prokaryotic cells? What structures are found in prokaryotic cells and not in eukaryotic cells? What

CHAPTER REVIEW

STUDY QUESTIONS—CONT'D

structures occur in both prokaryotic and eukaryotic cells?

6. What is osmotic pressure and what strategies have microorganisms evolved for protection against this force?
7. Discuss how materials move into and out of cells. What are the different transport mechanisms in prokaryotic and eukaryotic cells?
8. How is the structure of the cytoplasmic membrane related to transport processes?
9. How is energy supplied to drive a concentration gradient across the membranes of cells?
10. Describe the differences in cell wall structure between Gram-negative and Gram-positive bacteria.
11. What is the mode of action of penicillin? Why is penicillin generally more effective against Gram-positive bacteria than Gram-negative bacteria?
12. How does a capsule protect bacterial cells?
13. Where is ATP produced in prokaryotic cells and in eukaryotic cells?
14. What are the similarities between a mitochondrion and a bacterial cell?
15. What are the differences between bacteria and fungi in terms of how the genetic information is stored?
16. What are the similarities and differences between prokaryotic and eukaryotic flagella?
17. What is chemotaxis? How do bacteria respond to chemoattractants?
18. What is a bacterial endospore, and what is the significance of this structure?
19. Which structures are used by bacteria to attach to other surfaces?
20. What type of specialized membranes do some bacteria synthesize? What is the relationship between these membranes and the cytoplasmic membrane?

SITUATIONAL PROBLEMS

1. Debating the Origins of Eukaryotic Flagella

The question "Has the endosymbiont hypothesis been proven?" appears to have been answered in the affirmative through the use of RNA analyses, at least as it relates to the evolution of mitochondria and chloroplasts. It now seems certain that chloroplasts and mitochondria evolved from an endosymbiotic relationship between a primitive eukaryotic cell and a eubacterial prokaryotic cell. Before molecular genetic-level analyses, however, this topic remained unresolved and was still the subject of argumentative debates even when the structural similarities between these eukaryotic organelles and the prokaryotic cell were known. The reason is that appearance alone cannot be the sole proof of a scientific hypothesis. It had been logically argued that even though mitochondria and chloroplasts appear to be more eubacterial than eukaryotic (nuclear), this was because the traits being considered were primitive ones and because mitochondria and chloroplast genomes changed more slowly than nuclear genomes after evolutionary divergence from a common ancestor occurred.

Even though the 16S rRNA analyses settled part of the debate on the endosymbiotic theory, it did not resolve the argument over the origins of eukaryotic flagella. Did eukaryotic flagella and cilia, with their 9 + 2 organization, arise from an endosymbiotic eubacterium? Let us consider the interesting organism *Mixotricha paradoxa.* This protozoan lacks its own mitochondria but harbors endosymbiotic eubacteria that carry out the essential metabolism that provides the protozoan with necessary ATP as an energy source. The protozoan swims along, apparently propelled by bacterial cells attached to the surface. These attached bacteria are spirochetes, which have a central axial filament connecting the two ends of the cell. The filament enables the spirochetes, which are approximately the same size as a eukaryotic flagellum, to contract and move with a creeping motion similar to that of a caterpillar. The filaments connecting the ends of the spirochete resemble the filaments of the eukaryotic flagellum, although they do not have the typical 9 + 2 arrangement. There may be as many as 50,000 spirochetes attached to the surface of a single cell of *M. paradoxa.* There are also four eukaryotic flagella with a 9 + 2 arrangement that appear to steer rather than to propel the protozoan. Clearly, as its name implies, this organism is a biological paradox.

Now let us assume that you are a member of the university debating team and the topic of the next contest is the origin of the eukaryotic flagellum, a topic certain to attract all biology students. Choose a side in the debate and begin to prepare your arguments. Consider whether the evidence supports the view that flagella and cilia of eukaryotes originated from spirochetes, what additional lines of evidence you might require, and exactly how you could resolve this question. In preparing for this debate, you may want to read L. Margulis (1982), *Symbiosis in Cell Evolution,* W. H. Freeman, San Francisco; L. Margulis and D. Sagan (1986), *Micro-Cosmos: Four Billion Years of Microbial Evolution,* Summit Books, New York; M. W. Gray and W. F. Doolittle (1982), Has the endosymbiont hypothesis been proven?, *Microbiological Reviews* 46:1-2; M. A. Sleigh (1985), Origin and evolution of flagella movement, *Cell Motility* 5:137-173, and more recent relevant articles that you can find in the library. Be sure to consider the alternate views so that you are prepared for the opposition.

Continued.

SITUATIONAL PROBLEMS—CONT'D

2. Mission to Recognize Extraterrestrial Life Forms

Defining life and recognizing living systems is not always easy, as evidenced by the debate over whether viruses should be considered living organisms. Because life on Earth is so diverse, we have difficulty in recognizing the unifying structural and functional properties common to *all* living organisms. Living systems are highly organized, but so is an ice crystal; they exchange materials with their surroundings, but so does a mailbox; they transform energy, but so does a solar cell; they process information, but so does a computer; they reproduce themselves, but so does the robot that has been programmed to make more robots. No one would ever claim that the crystal, the mailbox, the solar cell, the computer, or the robot is alive, so we feel safe in proclaiming, "We know life when we see it," believing that we have little difficulty in recognizing living organisms, even microorganisms.

Since we can't decide exactly what to tell a laymen to look for when searching for life, you as a student of microbiology have been chosen to travel on the next mission to planet X to search for life. You have been chosen with the confidence that you will know what to look for and will know how to discriminate between living organisms, inanimate objects, and extraplanetary artifacts. Previous space missions to planet X have failed to detect any visible forms of macroscopic life, but there is available water and environmental conditions are within the tolerance limits in which living microorganisms are found on Earth. The chemical composition of the planet and the atmosphere, however, is quite different from that of Earth. Therefore if microbial life exists on planet X, the microbes there need not have the same structures as microbes on Earth, both in terms of their biochemical composition and their physical arrangement. Your spacecraft is outfitted with the best light and electron microscopes. The ship has a computer available for your use, and you may bring up to 50 pounds of additional scientific equipment to assist you in your quest for life forms.

Before embarking, you should establish your observational and experimental plan and the criteria that you are going to use to define living organisms. Begin now by entering in your logbook what you are going to look for and how you are going to know if whatever you find is or is not a life form.

Suggested Supplementary Readings

Alberts B, D Bray, J Lewis, M Raff, K Roberts, JD Watson: 1989. *Molecular Biology of the Cell,* ed. 2, Garland Publishing, New York.

Allen MM: 1984. Cyanobacterial cell inclusions, *Annual Review of Microbiology* 38:1-26.

Ames GF-L: 1986. Bacterial periplasmic transport systems: Structures, mechanism, and evolution, *Annual Review of Biochemistry* 55: 397-426.

Anderson JM and B Andersson: 1982. The architecture of photosynthetic membranes: Lateral and transverse organization, *Trends in Biochemical Sciences* 7:288-292.

Armitage JP and JM Lackie (eds.): 1990. *Biology of the Chemotactic Response,* Cambridge University Press, Cambridge, England.

Attardi G and G Schatz: 1988. Biogenesis of mitochondria, *Annual Review of Cell Biology* 4:290-335.

Avers CJ: 1986. *Molecular Cell Biology,* Benjamin-Cummings, Menlo Park, CA.

Becker WM and DW Deamer: 1991. *World of the Cell,* Benjamin-Cummings, Menlo Park, CA.

Beveridge TL and LL Graham: 1991. Surface layers of bacteria, *Microbiological Reviews* 55(4):684-705.

Bishop WR and RM Bell: 1988. Assembly of phospholipids into cellular membranes: Biosynthesis, transmembrane movement and intracellular translocation, *Annual Review of Cell Biology* 4:580-610.

Blakemore RP: 1982. Magnetotactic bacteria, *Annual Review of Microbiology* 36:217-238.

Campbell A: 1981. Evolutionary significance of accessory DNA elements in bacteria, *Annual Review of Microbiology* 35:55-84.

Carraway KL and CAC Carraway (eds): 1992. *The Cytoskeleton: A Practical Approach,* IRL Press, Oxford, England.

Costerton JW, RT Irwin, K-J Cheng: 1981. The bacterial glycocalyx in nature and disease, *Annual Review of Microbiology* 35:299-324.

Csonka LN and AD Hanson: 1991. Prokaryotic osmoregulation: Genetics and physiology, *Annual Review of Microbiology* 45: 569-606.

Darnell J: 1990. *Molecular Cell Biology,* W. H. Freeman, New York.

Darnell J, H Lodish, D Baltimore: 1990. *Molecular Cell Biology,* Scientific American Books, New York.

Deisenhofer J and H Michel: 1991. Structures of bacterial photosynthetic reaction centers, *Annual Review of Cell Biology* 7:1-24.

Doetsch RN and RD Sjoblad: 1980. Flagellar structure and function in eubacteria, *Annual Review of Microbiology* 34:69-108.

Drlica K and M Riley: 1990. *The Bacterial Chromosome,* American Society for Microbiology, Washington, D. C.

Findlay JBC and WH Evans (eds.): 1987. *Biological Membranes: A Practical Approach,* IRL Press, Oxford, England.

Ford TC and JM Graham: 1991. *An Introduction to Centrifugation,* BIOS Scientific Publishers, Oxford, England.

Forst S and M Inouye: 1988. Environmentally regulated gene expression for membrane proteins in *Escherichia coli, Annual Review of Cell Biology* 4:21-42.

Gray MW and F Doolittle: 1982. Has the endosymbiont hypothesis been proven? *Microbiological Reviews* 46:1-42.

Hancock REW: 1984. Alterations of outer membrane permeability, *Annual Review of Microbiology* 38:237 266.

Hill WE, A Dahlberg, RA Garrett, PB Moore, D Schlessinger, JR Warner: 1990. *The Ribosome: Structure, Function, and Evolution,* American Society for Microbiology, Washington, D. C.

Inouye M (ed.): 1979. *Bacterial Outer Membranes: Biogenesis and Functions,* John Wiley & Sons, Inc., New York.

Koch AL: 1990. Growth and form of the bacterial cell wall, *American Scientist* 78:327-341.

Kornberg RD and A Klug: 1981. The nucleosome, *Scientific American* 244(2):55-72.

Lake JA: 1981. The ribosome, *Scientific American* 245(2):84-97.

Lindquist S and EA Craig: 1988. The heat-shock proteins, *Annual Review of Genetics* 22:631-678.

Macnab RW and S Aizawa: 1984. Bacterial motility and the bacterial flagellar motor, *Annual Review of Biophysics and Bioengineering* 13:51-84.

Moat AG and JW Foster: 1988. *Microbial Physiology,* John Wiley & Sons, New York.

Moir A and DA Smith: 1990. The genetics of bacterial spore germination, *Annual Review of Microbiology* 44: 531-554.

Neidhardt FC, JL Ingraham, M Schaechter: 1990. *Physiology of the Bacterial Cell: A molecular Approach,* Sinauer, Sunderland, MA.

Newport JW and DJ Forbes: 1987. The nucleus: Structure, function, and dynamics, *Annual Review of Biochemistry* 56:535-565.

Nikaido H and M Vaara: 1985. Molecular basis of bacterial outer membrane permeability, *Microbiological Reviews* 49:1-32.

Paranchych W and LS Frost: 1988. The physiology and biochemistry of pili, *Advances in Microbial Physiology* 29:53-114.

Pelham HRB: 1989. Control of protein exit from the endoplasmic reticulum, *Annual Review of Cell Biology* 5:1-24.

Raetz CRH: 1990. Biochemistry of endotoxins, *Annual Review of Biochemistry* 59:129-170.

Reusch VM: 1984. Lipopolymers, isoprenoids, and the assembly of the Gram-positive cell wall, *CRC Critical Reviews in Microbiology* 11:129-156.

Rogers HJ: 1983. *Bacterial Cell Structure,* American Society for Microbiology, Washington, D.C.

Schaechter M, FC Neidhardt, JL Ingraham, NO Kjeldgaard: 1985. *Molecular Biology of the Bacterial Cell,* Jones & Bartlett, Boston.

Schmidt MB: 1988. Structure and function of the bacterial chromosome, *Trends in Biochemical Science.* 13(4):131-135.

Sharpe PT: 1988. *Methods of Cell Separation,* Elsevier Science Publishing Co., Inc., New York.

Sheeler P and DE Bianchi: 1987. *Cell and Molecular Biology,* ed. 3, John Wiley and Sons, New York.

Shockman GD and JF Barrett: 1983. Structure, function, and assembly of cell walls of Gram-positive bacteria, *Annual Review of Microbiology* 37:501-528.

Singer SJ: 1990. The structure and insertion of integral proteins in membranes, *Annual Review of Cell Biology* 6:247-296.

Sleytr UB and P Messner: 1983. Crystalline surface layers on bacteria, *Annual Review of Microbiology* 37:311-340.

Sutherland IW: 1985. Biosynthesis and composition of Gram-negative bacterial extracellular and wall polysaccharides, *Annual Review of Microbiology* 39:243-270.

Widnell C: 1990. *Essentials of Cell Biology,* Williams & Wilkins, Philadelphia.

Wittmann HG: 1983. Architecture of prokaryotic ribosomes, *Annual Review of Biochemistry* 52:35-65.

Woese CR: 1981. Archaebacteria, *Scientific American* 244(6):98-122.

Yatis GT: 1986. How microorganisms move through water, *American Scientist* 74:358-365.

CHAPTER 4

Cellular Metabolism: The Generation of ATP

The flow of energy through a cell is one of the most fundamental characteristics of life. The formation and utilization of ATP is essential to the energy flow within living cells. ATP is the key molecule of cellular energy transformations and is the central focus of cellular metabolism. Various metabolic strategies for generating ATP have evolved and diverse metabolic pathways are used by different microorganisms to achieve this end. These include chemoorganotrophic (heterotrophic) metabolism using organic compounds as energy sources, chemoautotrophic metabolism using inorganic compounds as energy sources, and photoautotrophic metabolism using light as the energy source for ATP generation.

Chapter Outline

4.1 CELLULAR ENERGY AND METABOLISM—UNDERLYING CHEMICAL PRINCIPLES

Living cells maintain their organization by utilizing energy. Without a flow of energy through the cell, life ceases. Cells capture and utilize energy through a series of chemical reactions. These chemical reactions involve the rearrangement of electrons within the molecules involved in the reaction, accompanied by the redistribution of the energy those molecules contain. *Energy* is the ability to bring about change or do work. Matter contains energy in two basic forms: *kinetic energy* (energy due to movement, such as the movement of molecules, atoms, and electrons); and *potential energy* (energy due to the positions the positively charged atomic nuclei and negatively charged electrons occupy relative to one another within molecules). As chemical reactions proceed, the kinetic and potential energy of the molecules involved in those reactions becomes redistributed. Some molecules end up with more energy than they began with, some with less. Energy may flow into the molecules from the environment or out of them to the environment, depending on what reaction is proceeding. Such exchanges of energy occur within all living cells and between living cells and their environments.

As energy flows through living cells, it becomes transformed and redistributed in ways that allow the cells to grow and to multiply. The chemical reactions accompanying this flow of energy collectively form the process known as **cellular metabolism.** The word metabolism is derived from the Greek, meaning to change. Cellular metabolism consists of a complex network of reactions that captures the energy and raw materials of the environment and allows them to be changed into forms that are used to sustain cells.

At the heart of cellular metabolism lie reactions that transform energy into the form of chemical energy stored within molecules of ATP (adenosine triphosphate). The energy within ATP can then serve to drive forward the various energy-requiring reactions on which all cells depend. All living organisms use ATP as the "central currency of energy." A growing bacterial cell of *Escherichia coli,* for example, synthesizes approximately 2.5 million molecules of ATP per second to support its energy needs.

CONSERVATION OF ENERGY

During all the rearrangements of matter and energy involved in chemical reactions, energy is never created or destroyed. This is known as the **principle of energy conservation,** or the **conservation of energy.** While energy is always conserved, it is readily transformed between its various forms. Energy can be converted during cellular metabolism between its various forms, such as chemical energy, heat energy, light energy, electrical energy, and mechanical energy, but the total amount of energy always remains unchanged. Chemical energy, for example, can be transformed into heat energy during the chemical reactions of cellular metabolism that give out heat. Chemical energy means the mixture of kinetic and potential energy stored within the structure of atoms, molecules, or ions; heat energy means the kinetic energy due to the overall motion of the atoms, molecules, or ions.

Free Energy

All chemical reactions are accompanied by a net energy change, whose value depends on how much energy is taken in by the chemicals to break chemical bonds during the reaction and how much energy is released when new chemical bonds form. In a chemical reaction there is a net balance between the energy required to break chemical bonds, the energy released by new bonds that are formed, and the energy—such as heat energy—that is exchanged with the surrounding environment. As a result of a chemical reaction there is an overall loss of usable energy.

The **change in free energy** (ΔG) describes the change in the usable energy that is available for doing work. A reaction with a negative free energy change can proceed spontaneously and is able to do work on the surroundings. A reaction with a positive free energy change will not proceed spontaneously unless work is done on it by the surroundings.

The change in the free energy of a reaction is a function of the change of the heat of reaction or enthalpy (ΔH), the absolute temperature in degrees Kelvin (T), and the change in the entropy (ΔS) between the reactants and the products of a chemical reaction as indicated by the equation:

$$\Delta G = \Delta H - T\Delta S$$

The Kelvin scale of temperature begins at $-273°$ C (absolute zero—the temperature at which no movement of molecules occurs); each degree Kelvin has the same magnitude as each degree Celsius. Therefore degrees Kelvin (°K) are related to Celsius (°C) according to the equation:

$$°K = °C + 273°$$

The ΔH (enthalpy) of the reaction is the change in the stored energy between the amount contained in the bonds of the reactants and that stored in the products of a chemical reaction. It is the amount of heat energy given out by or taken in by a reaction. Negative ΔH values indicate that energy is given out to the surroundings by the chemicals during the reaction; positive values indicate energy is taken in by the chemicals from the surroundings.

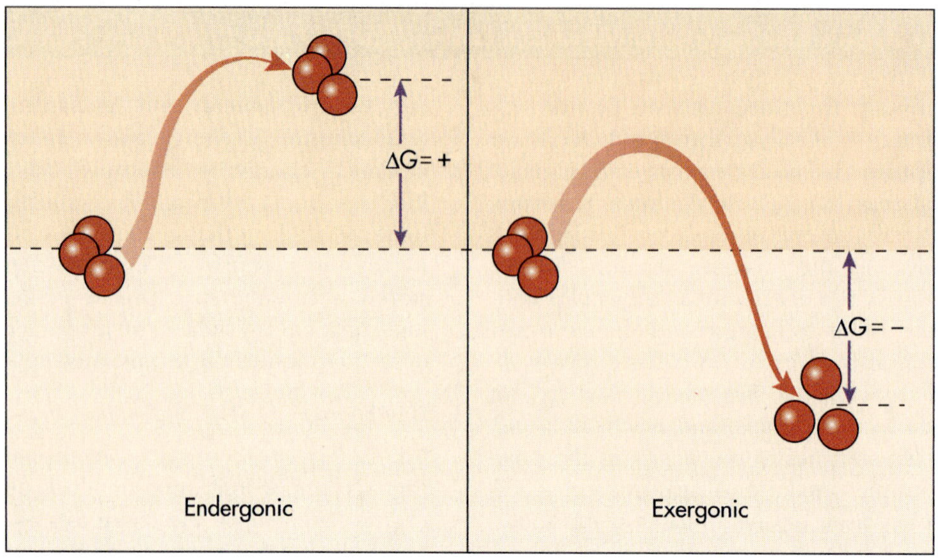

FIG. 4-1 In an endergonic reaction the products have more energy than the starting substances; the reaction therefore has a positive change in free energy (ΔG). In an exergonic reaction the products have less stored energy than the starting substances; the reaction therefore has a negative ΔG.

The ΔS (entropy) of the reaction describes the change in the state of order or degree of randomness of the reactants and products. Positive ΔS values indicate that the chemicals have become more disordered (more random) during the reaction; negative ΔS values indicate the chemicals have become more ordered.

To proceed spontaneously, meaning without any outside assistance, a reaction must have a negative ΔG value. Reactions that release free energy, and so have a negative ΔG value, are called **exergonic reactions.** They release their free energy as they spontaneously "run downhill" from the free energy level of their reactants to the free energy level of their products (FIG. 4-1). Reactions that only proceed if supplied with free energy from another source, and so have a positive ΔG value, are called **endergonic reactions.** Endergonic reactions are described as requiring free energy to "drive them uphill" from the free energy level of their reactants to that of their products.

The ΔG of a reaction is a function of the relative concentrations of reactants and products and the standard free energy change ($\Delta G°$) of the reaction at 1 atmosphere (atm) pressure and 1 molar concentrations of reactants. The $\Delta G°$ is the difference between the standard free energies of the products and the standard free energies of the reactants:

$$\Delta G°_{\text{reaction}} = \Sigma\Delta G°_{\text{products}} - \Sigma\Delta G°_{\text{reactants}}$$

If a chemical reaction is allowed to proceed to completion, it will reach a point where there is no further change in the relative concentrations of the reactants and products. This is called the point of *equilibrium.* Each chemical reaction moves toward the point of equilibrium, with the net flow of the reaction shifting toward the products or reactants, depending on their relative concentrations. Adding or removing reactants can alter the direction of the reaction.

The **equilibrium constant (K_{eq})** of a chemical reaction at a given temperature is the product of the concentrations of the molecules formed in the reaction divided by the product of the concentrations of the reactants. For the chemical reaction:

$$A + B \rightleftarrows C + D$$

$$K_{eq} = [C][D]/[A][B]$$

At equilibrium the free energy will be at a minium and no further change in the reaction will occur. For each chemical reaction the standard free energy ($\Delta G°$) at equilibrium is given by the equation:

$$\Delta G° = -RT\ln K_{eq}$$

where R is the gas constant (1.99 cal/mole/deg) and T is the temperature in degrees Kelvin.

The $\Delta G°$ for an overall reaction is the same regardless of the number of steps required to go from reactants to products. Although the $\Delta G°$ values themselves depend on the chemical nature of the reactants and products, each overall reaction has its own $\Delta G°$ value, and this value remains the same regardless of what chemical route the reaction takes.

The free energy released by an exergonic reaction can serve to drive forward another reaction that is endergonic. If two or more reactions become *coupled,* meaning that they are somehow made to proceed together, a reaction with a negative $\Delta G°$ value can drive forward a coupled reaction with a smaller positive $\Delta G°$ value. This is one of the central principles of the

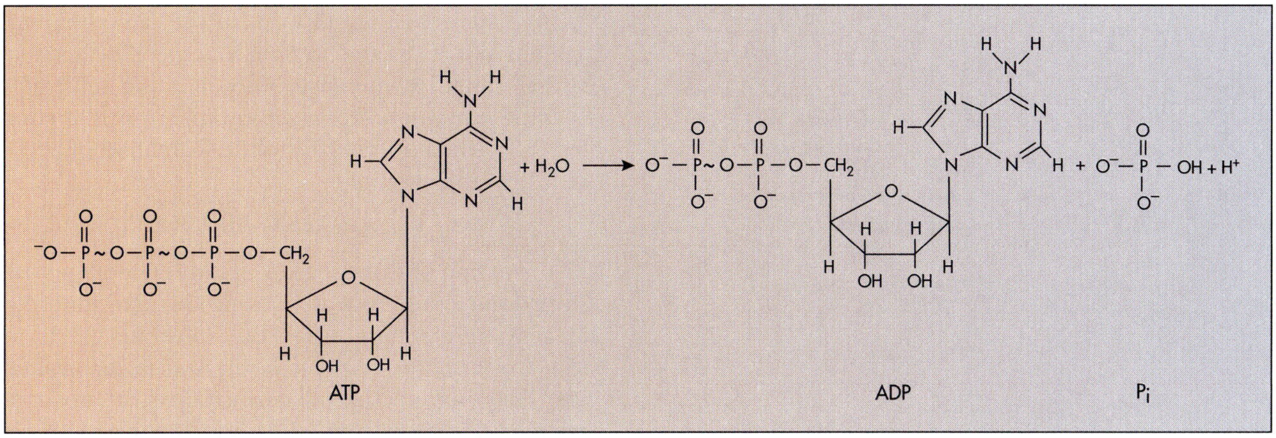

FIG. 4-2 ATP is a compound with high energy phosphate bonds. When adenosine triphosphate (ATP) is converted to adenosine diphosphate (ADP) a high energy phosphate bond is cleaved, releasing about 7.5 kcal/mole that can be used to drive other chemical reactions.

energetics of metabolism in living cells where the energy released by an exergonic reaction is used to drive an endergonic reaction.

ATP and Free Energy

Some molecules—like ATP—contain bonds that are called *high energy phosphate bonds* (FIG. 4-2). When a high energy phosphate bond is broken,. a large amount of free energy is released. It should be noted that although we say that energy is released when the high energy phosphate bond of ATP is broken, the actual bond-breaking process—like all bond-breaking processes—requires an input of energy. Bond-breaking requires energy and bond-making releases energy. In the case of breaking the high energy phosphate bond of ATP, however, the immediate formation of the new bonds of the products releases considerably more energy than was taken in to break the original bond. When ATP is converted to ADP, the electrostatic repulsion between the negatively charged phosphate groups is reduced, and this accounts for the relatively large release of free energy associated with this reaction. Thus the conversion of ATP to ADP and P_i releases energy overall, and this energy is referred to as the energy given out when the high energy phosphate bond "breaks." Breaking the terminal phosphate bond in ATP releases −7.3 kcal/mole of free energy.

Many of the metabolic pathways of a cell are involved with coupling exergonic reactions with the endergonic conversion of ADP and inorganic phosphate (P_i) to ATP, which can then serve as a common "energy currency" within the cell. Many other metabolic pathways require inputs of ATP and use the energy of ATP to drive forward endergonic reactions, splitting the ATP to ADP and phosphate ions as they do so. The cycling of ADP and ATP within the cell is fundamental to cellular energetics, and a living cell continuously forms and consumes ATP.

ATP is particularly useful for cellular metabolism because of its intermediate position in terms of stored energy, making it possible for cells to generate, as well as to use this molecule as a currency of free energy (Table 4-1). The constant transformation of ADP and phosphate into ATP, and of ATP back into ADP and phosphate, is the most fundamental process of cellular energetics. The importance of ATP to the cell is indicated by the fact that coupling an endergonic reaction to the exergonic utilization of ATP can shift the ratio of products to reactants by a huge factor, of the order of 10^8. This helps explain why cells continuously form and consume vast numbers of ATP molecules.

TABLE 4-1 Free Energies of Hydrolysis of Some Phosphorylated Compounds

COMPOUND	ΔG°(KCAL/MOLE)
Phosphoenolpyruvate	−14.8
Carbamyl phosphate	−12.3
Acetyl phosphate	−10.3
Creatine phosphate	−10.3
Pyrophosphate	−8.0
ATP to ADP	−7.3
Glucose 1-phosphate	−5.0
Glucose 6-phosphate	−3.3
Glycerol 3-phosphate	−2.2

Enzymes and Activation Energy

All chemical reactions begin with an input of energy, regardless of whether they eventually take in or release energy overall (FIG. 4-3). This initial input energy, called the *activation energy of the reaction,* starts the reaction; it is required to rearrange the electrons of the reactants in whatever way allows the rest of the reaction to proceed. The energy required to initiate a chemical reaction comes from the energy of the colli-

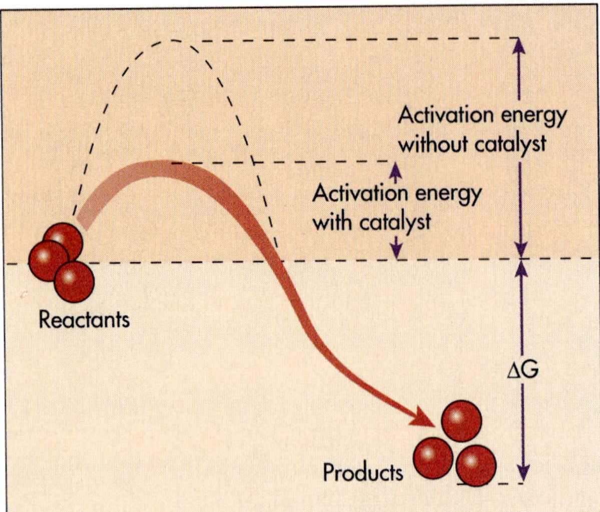

FIG. 4-3 An input of energy called the activation energy is needed to start a chemical reaction. A catalyst lowers the activation energy. In biological systems, enzymes serve as the catalysts to lower the activation energy.

sion between the reacting chemicals, during which some of the kinetic energy of the chemicals' movement is transformed into energy stored within the reacting chemicals. The **activation energy,** thus, is the energy required in a collision between two molecules to initiate a chemical reaction between those molecules.

Chemical reactions can be made to proceed more quickly by increasing the average kinetic energy of the reactants, or by using an alternative reaction pathway with a lower activation energy. In chemistry laboratories, reactions are often speeded up by heating the reactants (to increase their kinetic energy) with a Bunsen burner. In cells, however, the reactions needed to sustain life are speeded up or *catalyzed* by chemicals that lower the activation energies of the reactions they catalyze.

The chemicals that perform almost all of these acts of catalysis within cells are a class of protein molecules called *enzymes.* **Enzymes** are proteins that act as biological catalysts to speed up the rates at which chemical reactions occur by lowering the activation energy. Only a very few specific cellular chemical reactions are catalyzed by RNA, rather than proteins, in which case, the term *ribozyme* is used. Ribozymes are involved in the synthesis of proteins at ribosomes and the processing of DNA within the nucleus of eukaryotic cells.

The enzymes within cells allow the chemistry of life to proceed at high rates at moderate temperatures. Enzymes can make chemical reactions proceed at rates more than a billion times faster than they would otherwise proceed. Without the assistance of enzymes most of the chemical reactions of metabolism would barely proceed at all. Enzymes catalyze specific chemical reactions (Table 4-2).

Enzymatic reactions all work in the same manner. Each enzyme (E) is able to bind to a specific chemical or small range of chemicals known as the substrates (S) of the enzyme to form an enzyme-substrate complex (ES), which then leads to the formation of products (P) of the reaction:

$$E + S \rightleftarrows ES \rightleftarrows E + P$$

The formation of this complex greatly encourages the conversion of the substrate into products by lowering the activation energy. After the substrate reacts to form products, the enzyme is released in its original state. Thus enzymes, like all true catalysts, are not consumed or modified during the overall course of the reactions they catalyze. One enzyme molecule can catalyze its associated reaction over and over again.

Enzyme-substrate Specificity

Enzymes exhibit very precise **substrate specificity,** meaning that each enzyme can bind to and catalyze the reaction of only a very small range of molecules. Within cells, many enzymes catalyze reactions involving one particular substrate, although they may be able to accept a small range of related substrates.

The key to the specificity of enzymes for particular substrates lies in the precise structure of each enzyme's **active site.** This is the site on the enzyme molecule at which the substrate binds and the catalyzed reaction actually proceeds (FIG. 4-4). It is thought that the binding of a substrate molecule to an enzyme slightly alters the three-dimensional configuration of the enzyme, inducing it to adopt the form in which the substrate properly fits. The substrate is held in place by various kinds of weak bonds between it and the enzyme, and sometimes by short-lived full covalent bonds as the catalyzed reaction proceeds. These bonds and other interactions impose strains on the

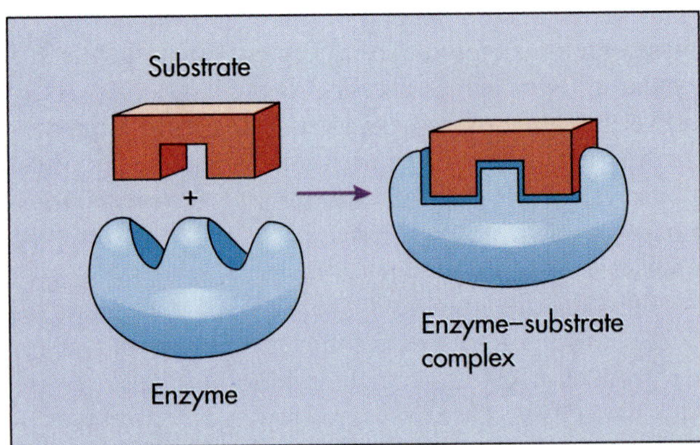

FIG. 4-4 The fit between the enzyme and the substrate to form an enzyme-substrate complex has been likened to that of a lock and key. Actually, this interaction modifies the three-dimensional structure of the enzyme so that the substrate induces its fit to the enzyme. The precision of fit is responsible for the high degree of specificity of enzymes for particular substrates.

TABLE 4-2 Some Types of Enzymes and the Reactions They Catalyze

ENZYME	REACTION	EXAMPLES
Isomerase	Rearranges groups within a molecule	
Racemase		*Alanine racemase* L-Alanine ⇌ D-alanine
Mutase		*Phosphoglucomutase* Glucose-1-phosphate ⇌ glucose-6-phosphate
Hydrolase	Hydrolyzes a molecule by adding H_2O	*Enolase* 2-phosphoglycerate ⇌ phosphoenolypyruvate + H_2O
Ligases	Joins two molecules together using energy from ATP or other nucleotide triphosphates	*DNA ligase* Joins 5′-OH to 3′-phosphate in deoxyribonucleotides
Transferase	Transfers a part of one molecule to another molecule	
Methyltransferase	Transfers C-1 groups	*Methyl transferase* Methyl-tetrahydrofolate + homocysteine → methionine
Aminotransferase	Transfers *N*-containing groups	*Alanine transaminase* L-Alanine + α-ketoglutarate ⇌ pyruvate + L-glutamate
Oxidoreductase	Carries out oxidation-reduction reactions	
Oxidase	Uses O_2 as electron acceptor	*Glucose oxidase* Glucose + O_2 → D-gluconolactone + H_2O_2
Dehydrogenase	Removes a pair of electrons and one or more protons from a molecule	*Lactate dehydrogenase* Pyruvate + NADH + H^+ ⇌ lactate + NAD^+
Lyase	Removes groups from a molecule to form double bonds or adds groups to double bonds	
Carboxy lyase	Removes carboxyl groups	*Pyruvate decarboxylase* Pyruvate + H^+ → acetaldehyde + CO_2
Aldehyde lyase	Removes aldehyde groups	*Aldolase* Fructose-1,6-bisphosphate ⇌ dihydroxyacetone phosphate + glyceraldehyde-3-phosphate

substrate molecule that are sufficient to greatly encourage some specific reaction to take place. If more than one substrate molecule is involved in the reaction, their binding to the enzyme effectively positions them in exactly the right spatial orientation required for the reaction to occur. The main point is that the precision of the fit between enzyme and substrate molecule(s) is crucial to the catalytic process.

Enzyme Kinetics

The study of the rates at which enzymatic reactions proceed is called **enzyme kinetics.** The rate of an enzyme-catalyzed reaction depends on the temperature, the concentrations of the enzyme and substrate, and the affinity of the enzyme for the substrate.

Enzymatic reactions are very sensitive to temperature. Increasing the temperature by 10° C up to a maximum of around 40° C generally doubles the rate of an enzymatic reaction; reducing the temperature by 10° C will halve it. Above about 40° C, many enzymes begin to be structurally altered by a process known as heat **denaturation.** This damages and can ultimately destroy the activity of the enzyme molecules, with an associated decrease in the rate of the enzymatic reaction. The sensitivity of enzymatic reactions to temperature changes may have a great impact on the rate of reactions within microorganisms, which are subject to the temperature fluctuations of their environment. It is less relevant within complex multicellular organisms such as humans, whose body temperatures fluctuate very little.

Raising the concentration of substrates can also increase the rate of an enzymatic reaction. At some point, however, a phenomenon known as **saturation** occurs. At the saturation concentration of substrate there is so much substrate present that all of the en-

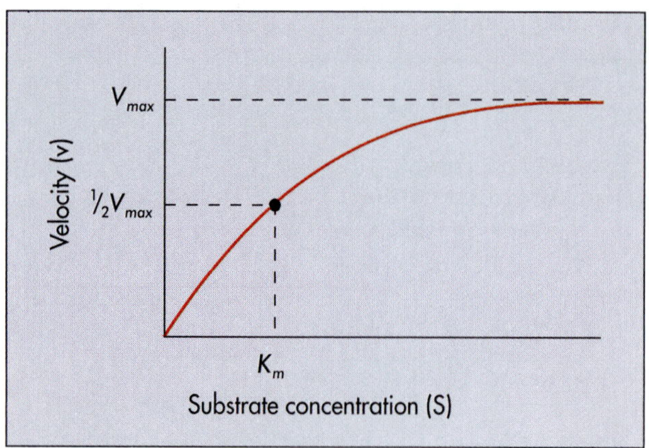

FIG. 4-5 The relationship between the velocity of an enzymatic reaction and the substrate concentration. The maximal velocity (rate) of the reaction is V_{max}. The substrate concentration at half the maximal velocity is called K_m.

zyme active sites are occupied. Only a limited number of these sites are available (whose value depends on the enzyme concentration) and each site takes a certain amount of time to perform its enzymatic reaction. Once a substrate concentration is reached that ensures that all the active sites are occupied all the time, increasing the substrate concentration further will not increase the rate of the reaction. The system cannot work any faster.

The maximal rate of an enzymatic reaction is called its V_{max}, and the substrate concentration that results in a reaction rate at one half of V_{max} is termed the K_m (FIG. 4-5). Each substrate is associated with a different K_m value, which is also known as the *Michaelis constant.* This value is a measure of the affinity of the enzyme for a particular substrate: the greater the affinity, the lower the K_m. The mathematical relationship between V_{max}, K_m, the substrate concentration [S], and the rate or "velocity" (v) of an enzymatic reaction is described by the Michaelis-Menten equation:

$$v = \frac{V_{max}\,[S]}{K_m + [S]}$$

When all the active sites of all the molecules of a particular enzyme of an organism are occupied, saturation occurs, and the reaction proceeds at the maximal rate.

Enzyme Regulation

In addition to the factors considered already, the rate of enzymatic reactions can be altered by molecules that can act as **allosteric effectors.** Each allosteric effector can bind to a particular enzyme at a site some distance away from the active site. The binding of the effector then induces changes in the three dimensional structure of the enzyme molecule that alters the shape of the distant active site (FIG. 4-6). The fit between the enzyme and its substrate is changed. The binding of an allosteric effector may increase (activate) or decrease (inhibit) the activity of an enzyme, depending on the effector and the enzyme concerned.

Particular groups of enzymes tend to operate sequentially within the cell, forming **metabolic pathways** that perform specific multistep chemical changes. A metabolic pathway is a particular set of chemical reactions that follows a defined route from substrate to product molecules.

The end products of such metabolic pathways may act as allosteric effectors able to bind to and inhibit some crucial enzyme of the pathway. This sets up a self-regulatory system, because there is a feedback mechanism that slows the pathway down when the

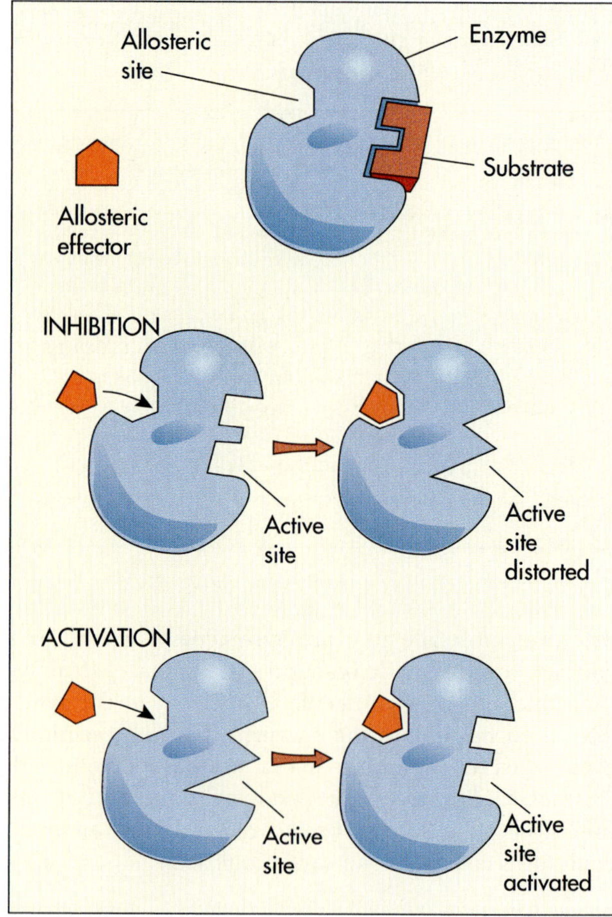

FIG. 4-6 The activities of enzymes can be increased or decreased by the binding of a substance other than the substrate to allosteric effector sites. Some substances inhibit enzymes by distorting the active site. Other substances activate enzymes by changing the active site so that the enzyme and substrate bind efficiently.

concentration of the end-product increases. This type of allosteric inhibition is called **feedback inhibition** or **end product inhibition.** If, on the other hand, a chemical acts as an allosteric activator of a pathway, then a process of **allosteric activation** is set up, causing the pathway to accelerate. Allosteric inhibition and activation are important processes that regulate the activities of enzymes and thus the rates of cellular metabolic reactions.

OXIDATION-REDUCTION REACTIONS

Many metabolic reactions, including those involved in energy capture and utilization, are **oxidation-reduction reactions** (FIG. 4-7). This means that they can be viewed as *electron transfer* reactions. They involve the loss of electrons from one substance and the gain of these electrons by another substance. A loss or removal of electrons is defined as an *oxidation;* a gain or addition of electrons is defined as a *reduction.* When two electrons are removed from a hydrogen molecule, for example, the hydrogen is oxidized and produces two hydrogen ions or protons (H^+):

$$H_2 \rightarrow 2e^- + 2H^+$$

When an electron is added to an oxygen atom, the oxygen is reduced to form O^{2-}:

$$\tfrac{1}{2}O_2 + 2e^- \rightarrow O^{2-}$$

Because the electrons lost from the oxidized substance have to go somewhere, the oxidation of one substance must always be accompanied by the reduction of some other substance. Thus the oxidation of hydrogen can be combined with the reduction of oxygen to form water:

$$2H^+ + O^{2-} \rightarrow H_2O$$

The overall oxidation-reduction reaction can be expressed as:

$$H_2 + \tfrac{1}{2}O_2 \rightarrow H_2O$$

In this case, hydrogen is the *electron donor* and the substance that is oxidized, and oxygen is the *electron acceptor* and the substance that is reduced.

The two oxidation and reduction *half reactions* of an oxidation-reduction reaction are always coupled together in this manner, and the number of electrons lost from the substance that is oxidized must equal the number of electrons gained by the substance that is

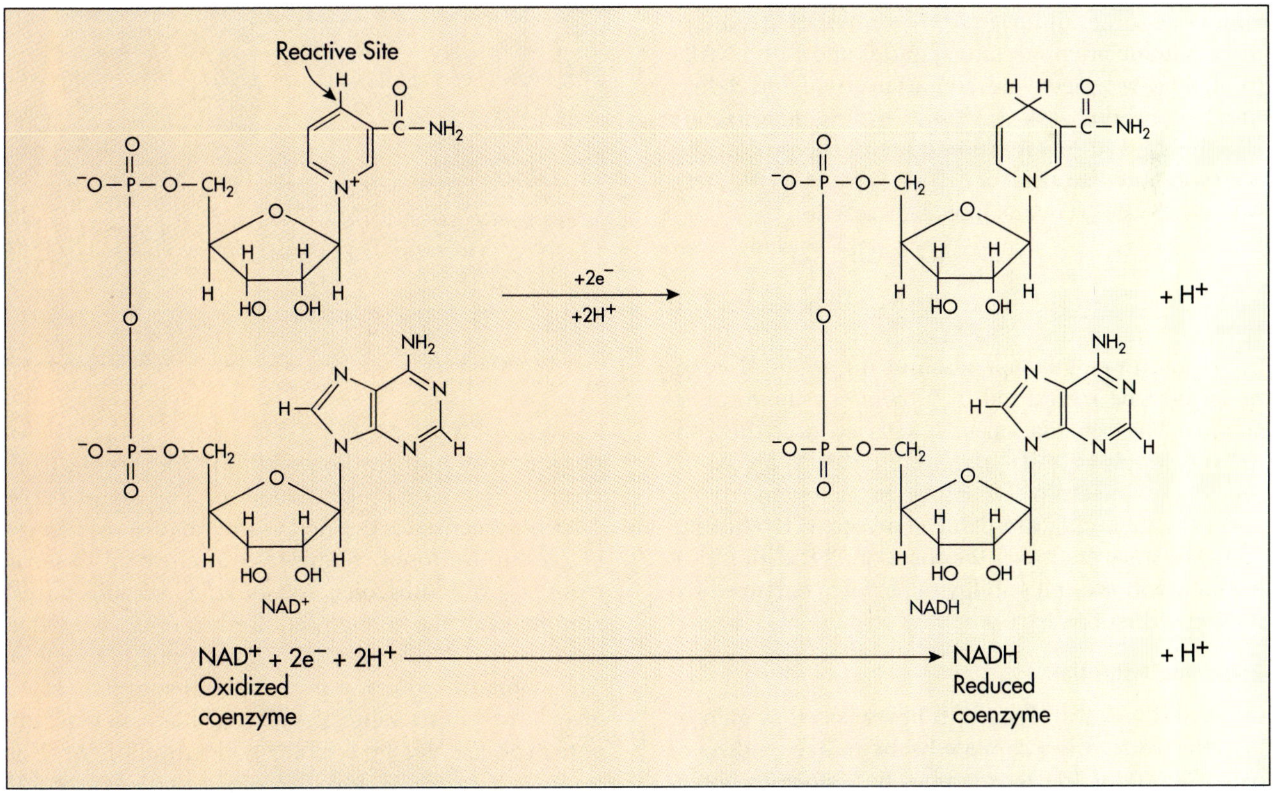

FIG. 4-7 The reduction of the oxidized coenzyme NAD^+ to the reduced coenzyme $NADH + H^+$ is a critical reaction that often is coupled with the oxidation of substrates within a cell. This reaction can be written several ways, for example $NAD^+ \rightarrow NADH$.

reduced. The source of electrons (electron donor) in an oxidation-reduction reaction is called the *reducing agent,* since it reduces some other chemical and becomes oxidized (loses electrons) in the process. The electron acceptor in an oxidation-reduction reaction is called the *oxidizing agent,* since it oxidizes some other chemical and becomes reduced in the process.

Coenzymes

Many enzymatic oxidation-reduction reactions require **coenzymes,** which are small non-protein organic substances that bind loosely to specific enzymes and assist in their catalytic function. They can accept a chemical group (including an individual electron) produced by one enzymatic reaction, hold on to it for a short time, and then donate it to the substrate of another enzymatic reaction. Coenzymes differ from **cofactors,** which are inorganic substances such as minerals required for enzymatic activity. A coenzyme is also distinct from a prosthetic group, which is a non-protein organic substance that binds tightly to an enzyme, forming a permanent part of the enzyme.

The oxidation of a substrate is often coupled to the simultaneous reduction of a coenzyme, which briefly holds the electron or electrons until they are transferred onto another substrate. For example, the reduction of the coenzyme NAD^+ (oxidized nicotinamide adenine dinucleotide) to NADH (reduced nicotinamide adenine dinucleotide) allows the NAD^+ to pick up two electrons from a substrate and deliver them elsewhere. Two protons (hydrogen ions) are also involved in this reaction. One of the protons becomes bonded to the coenzyme (written as NADH), while the other remains free. This reaction is:

$$NAD^+ + 2e^- + 2H^+ \rightleftarrows NADH + H^+$$

The reduced form of this coenzyme will be referred to as NADH rather than NADH + H^+.

To sustain cellular metabolism the reduced coenzyme must be reoxidized in subsequent chemical reactions. The reoxidation of NADH ensures the continuous supply of NAD^+ required for use as an oxidizing agent (electron acceptor) in many metabolic pathways, including those that generate ATP. Thus the ability to store energy in the form of ATP is inextricably linked to the cell's ability to perform balanced oxidation-reduction reactions.

Reduction Potential

Molecules vary with regard to how easily they gain or lose electrons. A key concept in the understanding of oxidation-reduction reactions is the **reduction potential** of a substance, which is a value indicating how readily a substance accepts electrons and thereby undergoes reduction, or how readily it donates electrons and thereby undergoes oxidation. The standard reduction potential is defined as the relative voltage (or electromotive force) required to remove an electron from a given substance (or mixture of substances) compared to the voltage required to remove an electron from H_2 under the same conditions (Table 4-3). The standard reduction potential of hydrogen (H_2) is given an arbitrary value of 0.00 volts when all reactants and products are at 1 molar concentration or 1 atmosphere pressure and the pH is 0.0. At pH 7.0, which is more typical of biological systems, the reduction potential of hydrogen is −0.42 volts.

TABLE 4-3 Biologically Important Half Reactions and Their Reduction Potentials

REDOX COUPLE	E'_0 (VOLTS)
SUBSTRATE REDOX COUPLES	
Succinate + CO_2 + $2H^+$ + $2e^-$ → α-ketoglutarate + H_2O	−0.67
Acetyl-CoA + CO_2 + $2H^+$ + $2e^-$ → pyruvate + CoA	−0.48
α-Ketoglutarate + CO_2 + $2H^+$ + $2e^-$ → isocitrate	−0.38
Acetaldehyde + $2H^+$ + $2e^-$ → ethanol	−0.20
Pyruvate + $2H^+$ + $2e^-$ → lactate	−0.19
Oxaloacetate + $2H^+$ + $2e^-$ → malate	−0.17
Fumarate + $2H^+$ + $2e^-$ → succinate	+0.03
ELECTRON-TRANSPORT CHAIN REDOX COUPLES (AEROBIC RESPIRATION)	
$2H^+ + 2e^- \rightarrow H_2$	−0.42
Ferredoxin (Fe^{3+}) + e^- → ferredoxin (Fe^{2+})	−0.42
NAD^+ + H^+ + $2e^-$ → NADH	−0.32
$NADP^+$ + H^+ + $2e^-$ → NADPH	−0.32
FAD + $2H^+$ + $2e^-$ → $FADH_2$	−0.18
Cytochrome *b* (Fe^{3+}) + e^- → cytochrome *b* (Fe^{2+})	+0.08
Ubiquinone + $2H^+$ + $2e^-$ → ubiquinone H_2	+0.10
Cytochrome *c* (Fe^{3+}) + e^- → cytochrome *c* (Fe^{2+})	+0.25
Cytochrome a_3 (Fe^{3+}) + e^- → cytochrome a_3 (Fe^{2+})	+0.55
$O_2 + 4H^+ + 4e^- \rightarrow 2H_2O$	+0.82
ELECTRON-TRANSPORT CHAIN REDOX COUPLES (ANAEROBIC RESPIRATION)	
$SO_4^{2-} + 3H^+ + 2e^- \rightarrow HSO_3^- + H_2O$	−0.52
$NO_3^- + 2H^+ + 2e^- \rightarrow NO_2^- + H_2O$	+0.42
$NO_2^- + 8H^+ + 6e^- \rightarrow NH_4^+ + 2H_2O$	+0.44
$Fe^{3+} + e^- \rightarrow Fe^{2+}$	+0.77

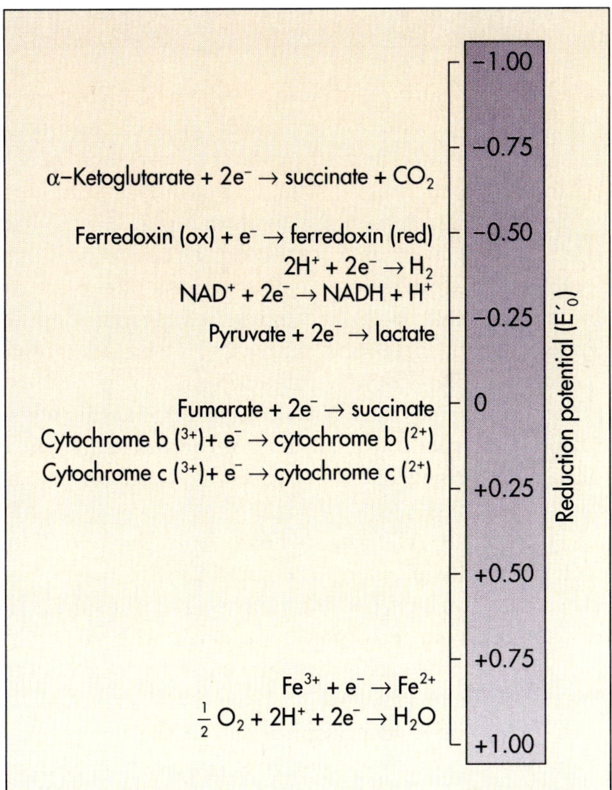

FIG. 4-8 The reduction potentials for half-reactions can be shown as an electron tower, with the reactions most likely to donate electrons (most negative E'_0) at the top and those most likely to accept electrons (most positive E'_0) at the bottom. In an oxidation-reduction reaction, the difference in E'_0 values between the electron donor and the electron acceptor determines the free energy of the reaction.

The more positive the reduction potential value, the more readily the substance concerned accepts electrons. The more negative the reduction potential value, the more readily the substance concerned donates electrons. Thus the reducing agent in an oxidation-reduction reaction will be the substance with the more negative reduction potential; the oxidizing agent will be the substance with the more positive reduction potential. The standard reduction potentials of some common chemical species are shown in FIG. 4-8.

An overall oxidation-reduction reaction consists of two half reactions. In one half reaction, electrons are added to a chemical (the reduction half reaction) and in the other half reaction, electrons are removed from another chemical (the oxidation half reaction). By convention, equations for the half reactions are both written as reductions, even though one of the half reactions must be an oxidation that proceeds in the reverse direction from which it is written. For example, consider the reaction between hydrogen and oxygen to form water:

$$H_2 + \frac{1}{2}O_2 \rightarrow H_2O$$

We can view this as an oxidation-reduction reaction whose two half reactions are:

$$2H^+ + 2e^- \rightarrow H_2 \quad \text{reduction potential } -0.42V$$

$$\frac{1}{2}O_2 + 2e^- \rightarrow O^{2-} \quad \text{reduction potential } +0.82V$$

The hydrogen (H_2) donates electrons, since it has the more negative reduction potential, while the oxygen (O_2) accepts electrons, since it has the more positive reduction potential. This electron transfer from hydrogen to oxygen generates $2H^+ + O^{2-}$, which can combine to form H_2O:

$$2H^+ + O^{2-} \rightarrow H_2O$$

Half reactions with more negative reduction potentials are likely to donate electrons and those with more positive reduction potentials are likely to accept electrons; for example, the half reactions shown in FIG. 4-8 at the top of the scale have the most negative reduction potentials and are the most likely to donate electrons. The half reactions in the middle of the scale can accept electrons from those above them or donate electrons to those below. For example, the half reaction SO_4^{2-}/H_2S has an intermediate reduction potential of −0.22. Therefore, SO_4^{2-} can accept electrons from hydrogen and become reduced to H_2S, or alternatively, H_2S can donate electrons to oxygen and become oxidized to SO_4^{2-}.

An important aspect of reduction potentials is their relationship to the free energies of chemical reactions. The greater the difference in voltage between the half reactions, the greater the free energy of the reaction. Reduction potential (E'_0) is related to free energy according to the equation:

$$\Delta G^{\circ\prime} = -nF\Delta E'_0$$

where $\Delta G^{\circ\prime}$ is the standard free energy change at pH 7.0, n is the number of electrons transferred, F is the Faraday constant (23,000 cal/volt), and $\Delta E'_0$ is the difference between the potentials of the two half reactions involved in an oxidation-reduction reaction. For example, based on E'_0 values of −0.32 volt for the half reaction $NAD^+/NADH$ and +0.82 for the half reaction $\frac{1}{2}O_2/H_2O$, the oxygen-linked oxidation of NADH to NAD^+ has an $\Delta E'_0 = 1.14$, which is equivalent to a free energy for this reaction of −52.4 kcal. This particular exergonic reaction $NADH \rightarrow NAD^+$ is very important in the generation of cellular energy by respiration.

4.2 METABOLIC STRATEGIES FOR GENERATING ATP

Microorganisms exhibit various strategies for converting chemical and light energy into the energy stored within ATP, as well as for obtaining the carbon they need to synthesize cellular constituents (Table 4-4). Although unified in purpose to generate cellular energy as ATP, diversity is the hallmark of microbial metabolism. The synthesis of ATP can be achieved through the metabolism of inorganic substrates, through the conversion of light energy to chemical energy, or through the utilization of organic substrates. The amount of ATP synthesized in these processes varies greatly, and microorganisms accordingly show great variation in the efficiency with which they synthesize ATP to meet their energy requirements. Chemolithotrophic metabolism, which uses inorganic chemicals to generate ATP, for example, is relatively inefficient energetically; cells of chemolithotrophs must metabolize numerous inorganic substrate molecules to generate enough ATP for their metabolic needs during growth and reproduction because of the relatively small E_0 difference between the electron donor and acceptor, which limits the available energy.

As a consequence of their metabolic activities, cells are capable of channeling energy into the synthesis of ATP. The metabolism of a cell occurs via a specific series of chemical reactions, called **metabolic pathways,** in which energy is transformed to generate ATP. A metabolic pathway has discrete steps between a starting substance (substrate molecule) and the products of the chemical reactions (end products). All of the ATP-generating strategies involve metabolic pathways consisting of multiple discrete enzyme-catalyzed steps that operate in sequence to convert an initial substrate or substrates into the end product or products of the pathway, accompanied by the formation of ATP.

Several central metabolic pathways play key roles in the metabolism of microbial cells. The reactions that lead to ATP generation involve various intermediary metabolites that are linked in a series of small steps to form unified metabolic pathways. These metabolic pathways are precisely regulated, so that they accelerate when supplies of ATP are low and decelerate when supplies are plentiful. Allosteric inhibition and activation of the activity of key enzymes plays a major part in such regulation.

To generate ATP, organisms couple the release of free energy by an exergonic reaction with the endergonic reaction that combines inorganic phosphate or phosphate from an organic molecule with ADP. Organisms have two different mechanisms for generating ATP: *substrate-level phosphorylation* and *chemiosmosis.*

In **substrate-level phosphorylation** the free energy required to combine inorganic phosphate (P_i) or phosphate from an organic molecule and ADP to form ATP is derived from the release of free energy of an exergonic reaction to which the ATP-forming reaction is directly coupled. Substrate level phosphorylation occurs by coupling an exergonic reaction in the catabolic pathway of an organic molecule with the endergonic conversion of ADP to ATP.

An example of substrate-level phosphorylation is the coupling of the exergonic conversion of phospho-

TABLE 4-4 Terms Used to Describe Metabolism Based on Sources of Energy and Carbon

PHYSIOLOGICAL TYPE	ENERGY SOURCE	CARBON SOURCE	ELECTRON SOURCE
TERM			
Autotroph		CO_2	
Heterotroph		Organic molecule	
Photo-	Light		
Chemo-	Chemical		
Organotroph			Organic molecule
Lithotroph			Inorganic molecule
TYPE OF METABOLISM*			
Chemoorganotrophic (heterotrophic)	Organic molecule	Organic molecule	Organic molecule
Chemolithotrophic (chemoautotrophic)	Inorganic molecule	Inorganic CO_2	Inorganic molecule
Photolithotrophic (Photoautotrophic) (photosynthetic)	Light	Inorganic CO_2	Inorganic molecule
Photoorganotrophic (photoheterotrophic)	Light	Organic molecule	Organic molecule

*The first part of the name refers to the energy source (chemo = chemical; photo = light); the second part of the name refers to the carbon source (lithotrophic = inorganic CO_2; organotrophic = organic compounds).

enolpyruvate to pyruvate with the endergonic conversion of ADP to ATP:

Phosphoenolpyruvate + ADP → Pyruvate + ATP

In **chemiosmosis** the formation of ATP is also coupled to an exergonic process, but not a chemical reaction. Instead, the exergonic process almost always is the movement of protons down a proton gradient (an imbalance in proton concentrations) set up across a membrane. In one case, a sodium ion gradient is used. For the chemiosmotic generation of ATP, the energy released by the metabolism of the cell is used to expel protons in one direction across a membrane so that a proton gradient is established. The proton gradient generates a force that would push the proton through the membrane if it were not impermeable to protons. The proton gradient is a electrochemical gradient. It is composed of two components: (1) an electrical gradient due to the fact that the membrane becomes more positively charged on one side and more negatively charged on the other because protons carry a positive charge and (2) a pH gradient due to the fact that the accumulation of protons (H^+) results in a more acidic environment outside and a more alkaline environment inside the membrane.

This electrochemical gradient across the membrane establishes a force, called the **protonmotive force,** that drives the formation of ATP. The protonmotive force is coupled to ATP synthesis by a proton-conducting membrane-bound enzyme called **ATPase.** As a proton moves back across the membrane by diffusion, it passes through the ATPase, so that its energy is captured and transferred to form ATP.

AUTOTROPHIC METABOLISM

Autotrophic metabolism literally means self-feeding metabolism. Organisms capable of this form of metabolism do not need preformed organic substances as a source of carbon. Instead, they use inorganic CO_2 as a carbon source. Autotrophs also obtain the required energy for cellular functions either by the metabolism of inorganic substrates or by the conversion of light energy to chemical energy (Table 4-5). **Photoautotrophic metabolism (photosynthetic metabolism** or **photolithotrophic metabolism**) captures light energy and transforms it into the chemical energy of ATP. **Chemoautotrophic metabolism (chemolithotrophic metabolism)** uses energy derived from inorganic chemicals to supply the free energy needed to generate ATP. Both photoautotrophic and chemolithotrophic metabolism are based on the establishment of a proton gradient across a membrane and the subsequent chemiosmotic generation of ATP.

HETEROTROPHIC METABOLISM (CHEMOORGANOTROPHIC METABOLISM)

Heterotrophic metabolism (chemoorganotrophic metabolism), in contrast to autotrophic metabolism (photolithotrophic and chemolithotrophic metabolism), requires a supply of preformed organic matter for production of cellular biomass and as a source of the chemical energy used to form ATP. It involves the conversion of the organic substrate molecule to end products via a metabolic pathway that releases sufficient free energy for it to be coupled to the formation of ATP. This process involves the breakdown of an organic molecule to smaller molecules—such breakdown processes form a part of metabolism known as **catabolism.**

Sugar molecules are major substrates of the catabolic energy-releasing reactions of heterotrophic metabolism. In sugar catabolism, there are several ways in which cells can break down a sugar into small molecules that can serve as substrates for other metabolic reactions. The process of breaking down a sugar is called **glycolysis** (from the Greek *glyco,* sweet or sugar, and *lysis,* breaking down) and the catabolic pathways of sugar metabolism are called **glycolytic pathways.** The enzymatic reactions of a glycolytic pathway end with the formation of pyruvate and are accompanied by ATP synthesis brought about by substrate level phosphorylations.

Glycolysis and a second metabolic pathway, the **tricarboxylic acid cycle,** represent the central core of cel-

TABLE 4-5 Types of Autotrophic Microbial Metabolism Used to Generate ATP

TYPE OF METABOLISM	DESCRIPTION
Oxygenic photosynthesis	Uses two connected photosystems and results in evolution of oxygen, as well as generation of ATP; carried out by algae and cyanobacteria
Anoxygenic photosynthesis	Uses one photosystem and does not result in evolution of oxygen; carried out by anaerobic photosynthetic bacteria, e.g., green and purple sulfur bacteria, and under some conditions by cyanobacteria
Chemoautotrophic (chemolithotrophic)	Uses oxidation of inorganic compounds such as sulfur, nitrite, nitrate, and hydrogen to establish an electrochemical gradient across a membrane that results in generation of ATP by chemiosmosis

TABLE 4-6 Types of Heterotrophic Microbial Metabolism Used to Generate ATP

TYPE OF METABOLISM	DESCRIPTION
Respiration	Uses complete oxidation of organic compounds, requiring an external electron acceptor to balance oxidation-reduction reactions used to generate ATP; much of the ATP is formed as a result of chemiosmosis based on establishment of a proton gradient across a membrane
Aerobic Respiration	Uses oxygen as the terminal electron acceptor in the membrane-bound pathway that establishes the proton gradient for chemiosmotic ATP generation
Anaerobic Respiration	Uses compounds other than oxygen, e.g., nitrate or sulfate, as the terminal electron acceptor in the membrane-bound pathway that establishes the proton gradient for chemiosmotic ATP generation
Fermentation	Does not require an external electron acceptor, achieving a balance of oxidation-reduction reactions using the organic substrate molecule; various fermentation pathways produce different end products

lular metabolism. The tricarboxylic acid cycle is a cyclical pathway that involves various carboxylic acid intermediates. It is the pathway where carbon dioxide is produced during respiration. Many different organic substrates are transformed into the intermediate chemicals of the glycolytic and tricarboxylic acid pathways to generate ATP and to provide the chemicals needed for biosynthesis. The metabolism of carbohydrates, lipids, proteins, and nucleic acids are all interconnected through these central core pathways.

There are two basic types of heterotrophic metabolism in which cells generate ATP: *fermentation* and *respiration* (Table 4-6). The distinction between these two types is made in the nature of the final electron acceptor of the pathways. Fermentation uses a terminal electron acceptor derived from the organic substrate, whereas respiration requires an external terminal electron acceptor not derived from the organic substrate.

Respiration

In **respiration** an external molecule, not derived from the initial organic substrate, is needed to act as the final electron acceptor whose reduction balances the oxidation of the initial substrate. Therefore in respiration the initial organic substrate molecule (electron donor) undergoes a net oxidation, while the external electron acceptor is reduced to form a balanced oxidation-reduction process. The most common external electron acceptor in respiration pathways is molecular oxygen, but some bacteria use alternate terminal electron acceptors (Table 4-7).

When molecular oxygen serves as the terminal electron acceptor of respiration the process is known as **aerobic respiration** (meaning it requires the presence of air). When another inorganic chemical, such as nitrate or sulfate, serves as the terminal electron acceptor the process is known as **anaerobic respiration** (meaning it does not require the presence of air). Some microorganisms can use oxygen or some other inorganic chemical as the terminal electron acceptor and so can carry out both aerobic and anaerobic respiration. The bacterium *Paracoccus denitrificans,* for example, can use either oxygen or nitrate as the terminal electron acceptor. Many other bacterial species are restricted to one or the other form of respiration, but many others can perform both aerobic and anaerobic respiration.

TABLE 4-7 Electron Acceptors Used in Respiratory Metabolism

TYPE OF METABOLISM	ELECTRON ACCEPTOR	PRODUCTS FORMED	MICROORGANISMS (EXAMPLES)
Aerobic respiration	O_2	H_2O	*Escherichia coli, Pseudomonas aeruginosa,* and numerous other bacteria, fungi, algae, and protozoa.
Anaerobic respiration	NO_3^-	NO_2^-	*Escherichia coli* and other enteric bacteria
	NO_3^-	NO_2^-, N_2O, or N_2	*Paracoccus denitrificans*
	SO_4^{2-}	H_2S	*Desulfovibrio desulfuricans*
	CO_2	CH_4	*Methanobacterium autotrophicum*
	S°	H_2S	*Desulfuromonas acetoxidans*
	Fe^{3+}	Fe^{2+}	*Bacillus licheniformis*

Fermentation

In **fermentation** an organic substrate acts as an electron donor and a product of that substrate acts as an electron acceptor. Both the electron donor and the acceptor are *internal* to the organic substrate in a fermentation pathway, meaning that the eventual acceptor is derived from the original substrate. There is no net change in the oxidation state of the products relative to the starting substrate molecule in fermentation pathways. In fermentation pathways no external electron acceptor is reduced and there is no net change in the oxidation state of the products relative to the initial substrate molecule. The oxidized products are exactly counterbalanced by the reduced products, and thus the required oxidation-reduction balance is achieved. Coenzymes that are reduced at the beginning of a fermentation pathway are reoxidized later in the pathway, so that they are in fact not consumed in the process. Fermentation pathways can occur in the absence of air because there is no requirement for oxygen or another electron acceptor to achieve a balance in the oxidation-reduction reaction; the organic substrate provides both the electron donor and the acceptor needed to achieve this balance.

Fermentation yields less ATP per substrate molecule than respiration. This is because in fermentation the organic substrate molecule must serve as both the internal electron donor and internal electron acceptor. Thus the carbon and hydrogen atoms of the organic substrate cannot be fully oxidized to carbon dioxide and water but are simply rearranged into a form containing less chemical energy than with which they began. In respiration the carbon and hydrogen atoms of the substrate molecule are completely oxidized to carbon dioxide and water, with the accompanying release of far more free energy, much of which becomes trapped within ATP. The $\Delta G°$ for the complete oxidation of glucose to carbon dioxide and water is -686 kcal/mol. By contrast, when glucose is only partially oxidized during fermentation to two molecules of the fermentation product lactic acid, the $\Delta G°$ value is only -58 kcal/mol. This dramatic difference makes it clear why far less ATP is generated by the fermentation of glucose than by its complete respiration.

Because fermentation generates fewer ATP per molecule of substrate than respiration, more substrate molecules must be metabolized during fermentation than during respiration, to achieve equivalent growth. So from the viewpoint of both bioenergetics and utilization of available organic nutrient sources, respiration is more beneficial than fermentation. Cells that have the ability to perform both types of catabolic metabolism will generally use the energetically more favorable pathway when conditions permit. They will rely on fermentation only when there is no available external electron acceptor that they can use.

4.3 RESPIRATORY METABOLISM

The pathway of aerobic respiration begins with an organic substrate molecule and typically combines it with oxygen in an oxidation-reduction process that ends with the formation of carbon dioxide and water. In the process, a substantial amount of ATP is also formed. The classic equation that describes this pathway for aerobic respiration of glucose is:

$$C_6H_{12}O_6 + 6O_2 \rightarrow 6CO_2 + 6H_2O$$

The oxidation of glucose by this pathway can generate up to 38 molecules of ATP for each molecule of glucose converted to carbon dioxide and water.

The overall pathway of respiratory metabolism for glucose and other substrates can be divided into three distinct phases:

1. A catabolic pathway, during which the organic molecule is broken down into smaller molecules usually with the generation of some ATP and reduced coenzymes; in the case of carbohydrates, a substrate molecule such as glucose is initially broken down to pyruvate via a pathway of glycolysis.
2. The tricarboxylic acid cycle (TCA), during which the small organic molecules produced in the first phase are oxidized to inorganic carbon dioxide and water, accompanied by the production of more ATP and reduced coenzymes.
3. A process known as oxidative phosphorylation, during which the reduced coenzymes are reoxidized; the electrons they release are transported through a series of membrane-bound carriers to establish a proton gradient across a membrane; a terminal acceptor such as oxygen is reduced, and ATP is synthesized.

CONVERSION OF CARBOHYDRATES TO PYRUVATE—GLYCOLYTIC PATHWAYS

Embden-Meyerhof Pathway

Glucose is converted to pyruvate in eukaryotic cells and a large number of anaerobic and facultatively anaerobic eubacteria via the **Embden-Meyerhof pathway** of glycolysis (also known as the **Embden-Meyerhof-Parnas pathway**) (FIG. 4-9). In this pathway, glu-

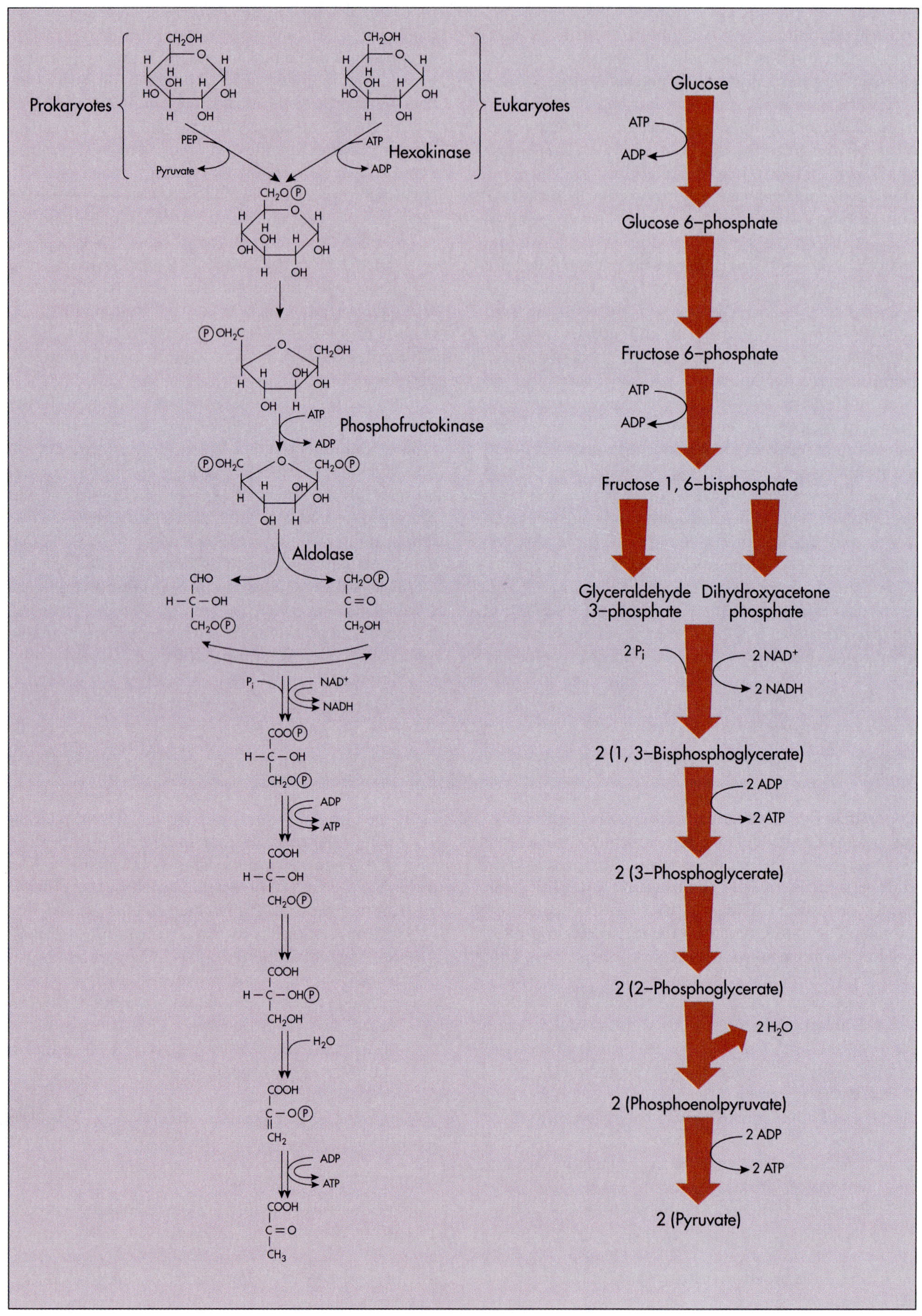
Prokaryotes
Eukaryotes
PEP
Pyruvate
ATP
Hexokinase
ADP
Phosphofructokinase
Aldolase
NAD+
NADH
H2O
Glucose
ATP
ADP
Glucose 6–phosphate
Fructose 6–phosphate
ATP
ADP
Fructose 1, 6–bisphosphate
Glyceraldehyde 3–phosphate
Dihydroxyacetone phosphate
2 Pi
2 NAD+
2 NADH
2 (1, 3–Bisphosphoglycerate)
2 ADP
2 ATP
2 (3–Phosphoglycerate)
2 (2–Phosphoglycerate)
2 H2O
2 (Phosphoenolpyruvate)
2 ADP
2 ATP
2 (Pyruvate)

TABLE 4-8 Free Energies of Glycolysis Reactions

REACTION	ENZYME	ΔG° (Kcal/mole)	ΔG (Kcal/mole)
Glucose + ATP → glucose 6-phosphate + ADP + P_i	Hexokinase	−4.0	−8.0
Glucose 6-phosphate → fructose 6-phosphate	Phosphoglucose isomerase	+0.4	−0.6
Fructose 6-phosphate + ATP → fructose 1,6-bisphosphate + ADP + P_i	Phosphofructokinase	−3.4	−5.3
Fructose 1,6-bisphosphate → dihydroxyacetone phosphate + glyceraldehyde 3-phosphate	Aldolase	+5.7	−0.3
Dihydroxyacetone phosphate → glyceraldehyde 3-phosphate	Triose phosphate isomerase	+1.8	+0.6
Glyceraldehyde 3-phosphate + P_i + NAD → 1,3-bisphosphoglycerate + NADH	Glyceraldehyde 3-phosphate dehydrogenase	+1.5	−0.4
1,3-bisphosphoglycerate + ADP → 3-phosphoglycerate + ATP	Phosphoglycerate kinase	−4.5	+0.3
3-Phosphoglycerate → 2-phosphoglycerate	Phosphoglyceromutase	+1.1	+0.2
2-Phosphoglycerate → phosphoenolpyruvate	Enolase	+0.4	−0.8
Phosphoenolpyruvate + ADP → pyruvate + ATP	Pyruvate kinase	−7.5	−4.0

cose is first converted in a series of reactions to form fructose 1,6-bisphosphate. The 1,6-bisphosphate, in turn, is cleaved to form two interconvertable 3-carbon sugars that enter a common set of catabolic reactions to form two pyruvates. The breakdown of one molecule of glucose to two molecules of pyruvate by this pathway releases sufficient free energy to permit a net synthesis of two ATP molecules (Table 4-8). The conversion of glucose to form pyruvate also is accompanied by the formation of two reduced coenzyme (NADH) molecules.

The initial steps in the Embden-Meyerhof pathway of glycolysis involve endergonic reactions that require coupling with energy releasing exergonic reaction to drive them. Therefore the pathway starts with the use, rather than the synthesis, of ATP. Cells initiate the Embden-Meyerhof pathway either by coupling the conversion of glucose to glucose 6-phosphate with the conversion of ATP to ADP or, in the case of eubacterial cells, by using the phosphoenolpyruvate:phosphotransferase system (PEP:PTS) that converts glucose to glucose 6-phosphate during transport across the cytoplasmic membrane. The energy balance of the PEP:PTS is roughly equivalent to that of the direct conversion of glucose into glucose-6-phosphate using ATP. Glucose 6-phosphate is then isomerized to fructose 6-phosphate, which is converted to fructose 1,6-bisphosphate in a reaction that requires input of energy from ATP. The conversion of fructose 6-phosphate to fructose 1,6-bisphosphate, is catalyzed by **phosphofructokinase,** which is a key enzyme in regulating the rate of glycolysis. Thus the initial steps of glycolysis that convert glucose to fructose 1,6-bisphosphate require an input of energy equivalent to the utilization of two ATP to ADP conversion reactions.

Although the initial series of reactions of the Embden-Meyerhof pathway require the input of the energy equivalent of two ATP molecules, subsequent to the formation of fructose 1,6-bisphosphate, each individual reaction is exergonic and, thus, further utilization of ATP is not required. In fact, sufficient ATP is synthesized in two of the later steps to yield a net gain of ATP from glycolysis as a whole.

The result of the first steps of glycolysis is the formation of a compound that can be broken down into two phosphorylated 3-carbon units without loss of energy. Fructose 1,6-bisphosphate, which contains six carbon atoms, is split into two 3-carbon molecules—glyceraldehyde-3-phosphate and dihydroxyacetone phosphate—by the action of the enzyme aldolase. This splitting of 1,6-bisphosphate into two 3-carbon units is called the *aldolytic reaction.* Dihydroxyacetone

FIG. 4-9 The Embden-Meyerhof pathway of glycolysis is a central metabolic pathway in various eukaryotic and prokaryotic cells for the conversion of carbohydrates to pyruvate and the formation of ATP. In the Embden-Meyerhof pathway a molecule of glucose is converted to two molecules of pyruvate, with the net production of two molecules of ATP and two molecules of reduced coenzyme NADH. Although the reactions involved are virtually identical in prokaryotic and eukaryotic cells, the mechanism for the initial phosphorylation of glucose can differ. In some prokaryotes, the conversion of glucose to glucose 6-phosphate occurs during transport of the substrate across the membrane; this group transport process involves three enzyme systems and is driven by the hydrolysis of phosphoenolpyruvate. In eukaryotes, hexokinase catalyzes the formation of glucose 6-phosphate from glucose; the reaction is coupled with the hydrolysis of ATP and occurs within the cytoplasm.

phosphate, which is not in the direct glycolytic pathway, can be converted to glyceraldehyde-3-phosphate. The equilibrium between dihydroxyacetone phosphate and glyceraldehyde-3-phosphate favors the formation of dihydroxyacetone phosphate. However, the constant removal of glyceraldehyde-3-phosphate, which is in the direct glycolytic pathway, shifts the balance of reactants and products so that the dihydroxyacetone is converted to glyceraldehyde-3-phosphate. Thus, for each 6-carbon glucose substrate molecule, two molecules of glyceraldehyde-3-phosphate are formed.

After the formation of glyceraldehyde-3-phosphate, the next portion of the glycolytic pathway is concerned with using the energy stored in this compound to drive the synthesis of ATP. It is important to keep in mind that two phosphorylated 3-carbon molecules are formed for each 6-carbon carbohydrate substrate molecule to keep track of the net yield of ATP and reduced coenzyme (NADH) molecules formed during the overall pathway. Each of the steps subsequent to the formation of glyceraldehyde-3-phosphate occurs twice for each 6-carbon glucose molecule that is metabolized.

BOX 4-1

REGULATION OF PHOSPHOFRUCTOKINASE ACTIVITY

Even though ATP is required for the conversion of fructose 6-phosphate to fructose 1,6-bisphosphate, phosphofructokinase is inhibited by excess ATP because ATP is an allosteric inhibitor of the enzyme. If the cell has a sufficient supply of ATP, the inhibition of this enzyme slows down the glycolytic pathway near its beginning, decreasing the rate of ATP synthesis. When ATP is depleted, the cell has a relatively high concentration of adenosine monophosphate (AMP)—the monophosphate formed by the hydrolysis of ADP. AMP is an allosteric activator for phosphofructokinase; thus when the cell really needs to generate ATP, the key rate-limiting reaction of glycolysis is stimulated, leading to increased synthesis of ATP.

The allosteric control of phosphofructokinase is responsible for the paradoxical observation that, in the presence of oxygen, less carbohydrate substrate disappears during the growth of many microorganisms than during the growth of the same organisms in the absence of air. This phenomenon, known as the *Pasteur effect,* occurs because during aerobic respiration a high level of ATP accumulates within the cell and inhibits phosphofructokinase, greatly slowing the rate of substrate conversion. In the absence of oxygen, when the cell is using fermentative metabolism, less ATP is produced and glycolysis proceeds without inhibition.

Each glyceraldehyde-3-phosphate molecule is converted to 1,3-bisphosphoglycerate by the incorporation of inorganic phosphate (P_i) into the molecule during an exergonic reaction. The oxidative conversion of glyceraldehyde-3-phosphate to form 1,3-bisphosphoglycerate is coupled with the conversion of oxidized NAD^+ to the reduced coenzyme NADH. Because there are two molecules of 1,3-bisphosphoglycerate generated from each glucose molecule, there is a net production of two NADH molecules per molecule of glucose.

The 1,3-bisphosphoglycerate is converted to 3-phosphoglycerate, an exergonic reaction that can be coupled with the synthesis of ATP. The formation of ATP in this coupled reaction is a substrate-level phosphorylation reaction, so designated because ATP is formed from ADP by the direct transfer of a high-energy phosphate group from the 1,3-bisphosphoglycerate, an intermediate substrate in the pathway. Because this reaction occurs for each of the two 3-carbon molecules generated from glucose, two molecules of ATP are generated per glucose molecule. Therefore the synthesis and utilization of ATP are balanced at this point in the metabolic pathway. So at this point in the glycolytic pathway the net production of ATP by the pathway is 0.

The 3-phosphoglycerate is then further converted to phosphoenolpyruvate and finally to pyruvate. The conversion of phosphoenolpyruvate to pyruvate is coupled with the synthesis of additional ATP. Thus this glycolytic pathway results in the conversion of the 6-carbon molecule glucose to two molecules of the 3-carbon molecule pyruvate, with the net production of two molecules of reduced coenzyme, NADH, and the net synthesis of two ATP molecules. The overall equation for glycolysis by the Embden-Meyerhof pathway can be written as follows:

$$\text{Glucose} + 2\ \text{ADP} + 2\ P_i + 2\ \text{NAD}^+ \rightarrow 2\ \text{pyruvate} + 2\ \text{NADH} + 2\ \text{ATP}$$

Glucose is not the only carbohydrate that can be converted to pyruvate by glycolysis (Table 4-9). Many cells use other monosaccharides, disaccharides, and polysaccharides as substrates for ATP-generating metabolism. Common disaccharides that can be used by microorganisms are maltose, which can be broken down by maltase to form glucose; sucrose, which can form glucose and fructose by the action of sucrase; and lactose, which can form galactose and glucose by the action of β-galactosidase. The monosaccharides formed from these disaccharides can enter the pathways of glycolysis. For example, the galactose derived from lactose can be converted to glucose 1-phosphate, which can then be transformed to glucose 6-phosphate, an intermediate in the Embden-Meyerhof glycolytic pathway. The glucose derived from lactose similarly can react to form glucose 6-phosphate.

TABLE 4-9 Examples of Carbohydrate Conversions to Intermediates of Glycolytic Pathways

CARBOHYDRATE	ENZYME	END PRODUCTS
Maltose	Maltase	Glucose + glucose
Maltose	Maltose phosphorylase	Glucose + β-D-glucose 1-phosphate
Cellobiose	Cellobiose phosphorylase	Glucose + α-D-glucose 1-phosphate
Sucrose	Sucrase	Glucose + fructose
Sucrose	Sucrose phosphorylase	Fructose + α-D-glucose 1-phosphate
Lactose	β-Galactosidase	Glucose + galactose
Fructose	Fructokinase	Fructose 6-phosphate
Fructose	Fructokinase	Fructose 1-phosphate
Galactose	Galactokinase, glucose:galactose 1-phosphate uridylyltransferase, UDP-glucose epimerase	Glucose 1-phosphate + UDP galactose

When sucrose or glycogen is used, the glucose that is formed reacts with inorganic phosphate to produce glucose 1-phosphate. The glucose 1-phosphate is then transformed, by the action of phosphoglucomutase, to glucose 6-phosphate, which enters the Embden-Meyerhof pathway. Because of the initiation of glycolysis without the need for ATP to form the phosphorylated carbohydrate, there is an increase in the net production of ATP.

Entner-Doudoroff Pathway

The **Entner-Doudoroff pathway** of glycolysis is an alternate pathway used by many aerobic eubacteria, such as *Pseudomonas* species (FIG. 4-10, p. 136). The net equation for the Entner-Doudoroff pathway of glycolysis is:

$$\text{Glucose} + 2\ \text{NADP}^+ + \text{ADP} + \text{P}_i \rightarrow 2\ \text{pyruvate} + 2\ \text{NADPH} + \text{ATP}$$

These eubacteria that carry out the Entner-Doudoroff pathway lack the key enzyme 6-phosphofructokinase of the Embden-Meyerhof pathway. In the Entner-Doudoroff pathway, glucose 6-phosphate is oxidized to 6-phosphogluconate and then converted to 2-keto-3-deoxy-6-phosphogluconate (KDPG). KDPG is then cleaved to yield glyceraldehyde-3-phosphate and pyruvate directly. Since pyruvate is formed directly, some of the ATP generating steps are lost. The catabolism of glucose via the Entner-Doudoroff pathway results in the net production of only one ATP molecule per molecule of glucose because the glucose 6-phosphate is oxidized to pyruvate before aldolytic cleavage.

Another difference between the Entner-Doudoroff pathway and the Embden-Meyerhof pathway is that in the Entner-Doudoroff pathway the reduced coenzyme NADPH is generated from $NADP^+$, rather than NADH from NAD^+. NADPH is a phosphorylated form of NADH. Generally, NAD^+ and its reduced form NADH are used in metabolic reactions that generate ATP, whereas $NADP^+$ and NADPH are used in biosynthetic reactions that build up molecules needed by the cell from simpler substrates.

The Entner-Doudoroff pathway provides an important mechanism for producing NADPH and 3-carbon building blocks that are used in biosynthetic reactions when the need for them is greater than that for ATP. NADPH can be formed from NAD^+ by the reaction:

$$\text{NAD}^+ + \text{ATP} \rightarrow \text{NADP}^+ + \text{ADP}$$

The two forms of reduced nicotinamide adenine dinucleotide coenzyme also can be interconverted by the reaction:

$$\text{NADPH} + \text{NAD}^+ \rightleftharpoons \text{NADP}^+ + \text{NADH}$$

Archaebacterial Glycolytic Pathways—Modified Entner-Doudoroff Pathways

Some archaebacteria have evolved glycolytic pathways that differ from their eubacterial counterparts. Halophilic archaebacteria (archaebacteria that live in highly saline environments) possess a modified Entner-Doudoroff pathway that does not begin with phosphorylated intermediates. These archaebacteria oxidize glucose to gluconate, which is then converted to 2-keto-3-deoxygluconate (KDG). Phosphorylation subsequently occurs to form KDPG. The KDPG is split into pyruvate and glyceraldehyde-3-phosphate with the generation of one molecule of ATP per molecule of glucose, as in the classical Entner-Doudoroff pathway.

Thermoacidophilic archaebacteria (archaebacteria that live in very hot, acidic environments) possess an Entner-Doudoroff pathway in which only the terminal steps of the pathway involve phosphorylated compounds. This nonphosphorylated pathway begins in the same way as that of the halophilic archaebacteria, until 2-keto-3-deoxygluconate is split into pyruvate and glyceraldehyde. The glyceraldehyde is then oxidized to glycerate, which is phosphorylated to 2-phosphoglycerate, dehydrated to phosphoenolpyruvate, and finally dephosphorylated to pyruvate. This nonphosphorylated pathway does not yield any ATP from the conversion of one molecule of glucose to two molecules of pyruvate; ATP is generated from further oxidation of pyruvate.

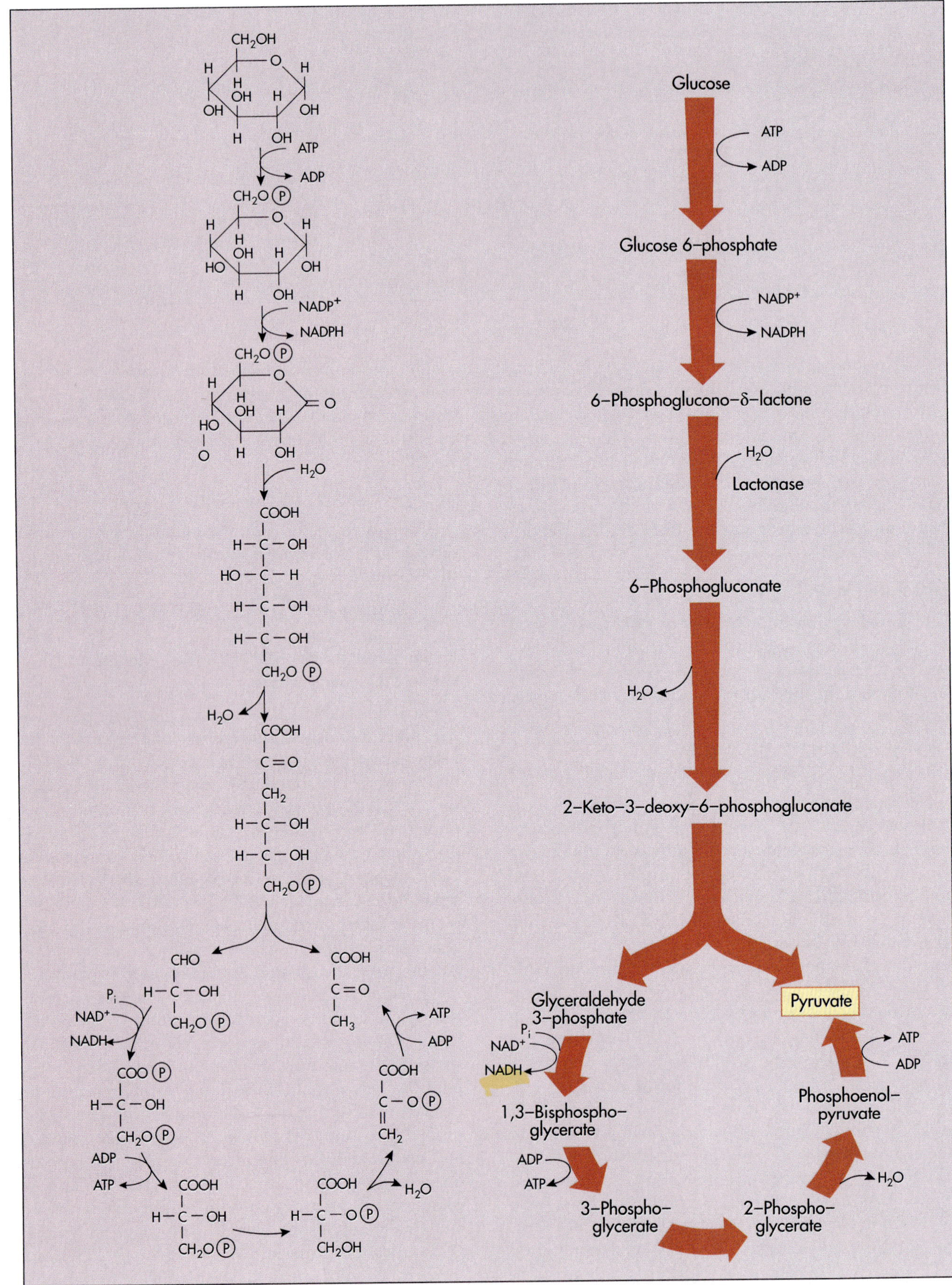

FIG. 4-10 The Entner-Doudoroff pathway is one of several types of glycolysis. Compared to the Embden-Myerhof pathway, less ATP is generated when this metabolic pathway is used.

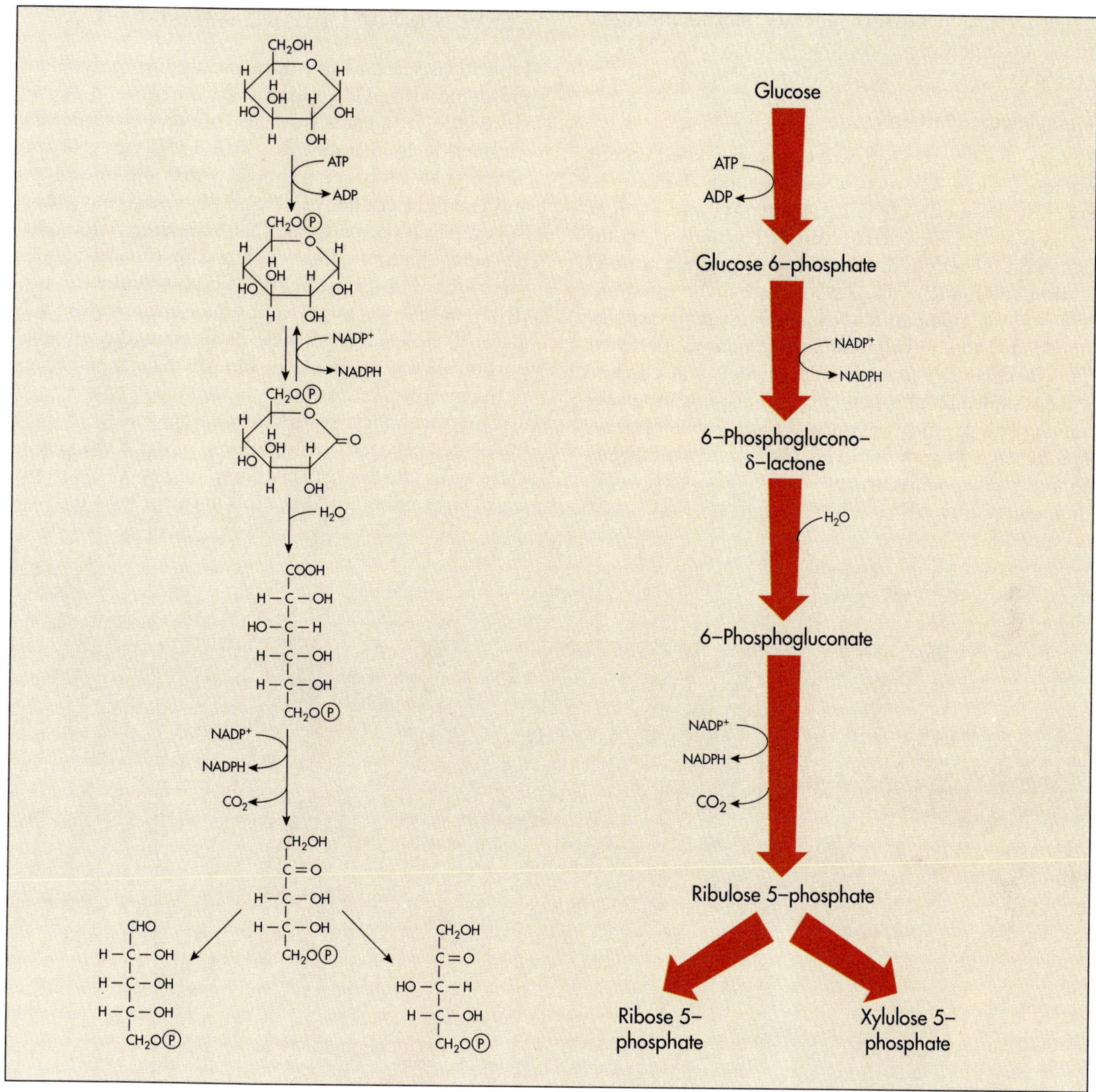

FIG. 4-11 The pentose phosphate pathway connects the metabolism of 6-carbon and 5-carbon carbohydrates. This pathway forms five carbon-containing compounds, such as ribose 5-phosphate required for incorporation into nucleic acids such as DNA and RNA.

Pentose Phosphate Pathway

The **pentose phosphate pathway** generates ATP, and reduced coenzymes and small molecules that are needed for biosynthesis (FIG. 4-11). This pathway is essential for providing ribose for incorporation into the nucleotides of DNA, RNA, ATP, NAD^+, and $NADP^+$. Several different variations in the pentose phosphate pathway are possible, depending on the need for NADPH, ATP, and small precursor molecules for incorporation into macromolecules.

In one version of the pentose phosphate pathway, glucose is converted into ribulose 5-phosphate and carbon dioxide, a process that requires the use of one ATP molecule and results in the generation of two NADPH molecules. When a large amount of reduced coenzyme is required, the glucose molecule can be completely metabolized to carbon dioxide, with the production of 12 molecules of reduced coenzyme NADPH. This series of reactions really involves a cyclic pathway in which glucose 6-phosphate is broken down and resynthesized, providing a large amount of reduced coenzymes needed by microorganisms during times of active growth. When the cell requires both NADPH and ATP, phosphoglycerate can be converted to pyruvate, with NADPH generated during the initial steps of the pentose phosphate pathway and ATP generated as a result of the oxidation of the pyruvate.

Methylglyoxal Pathway

In some eubacteria (*Escherichia coli* and related enteric bacteria, some *Clostridium* species, and *Pseudomonas* species) the methylglyoxal pathway operates as an alternate to the Embden-Meyerhof pathway when the cell experiences conditions of low phosphate concentration (FIG. 4-12). When phosphate is the rate-limiting reagent, this pathway converts dihydroxyacetone phosphate to methylglyoxal and then to pyruvate. This bypasses the phosphorylation step that converts glyceraldehyde-3-phosphate to 1,3-bisphosphoglycerate, yet still produces pyruvate, which can be further metabolized to generate ATP. Overall, the methylglyoxal pathway consumes two ATP molecules rather than generating ATP.

CONVERSION OF LIPIDS TO ACETYL-COA

Lipids can serve as substrates to support the cellular production of ATP. **Lipases** are enzymes that can cleave the fatty acids from the glycerol portion of a triglyceride lipid molecule (FIG. 4-13). Glycerol can be metabolized to form dihydroxyacetone phosphate and then glyceraldehyde 3-phosphate, thereby entering the glycolytic pathways that have already been discussed for carbohydrate metabolism (FIG. 4-14). In the case of a phospholipid, a **phospholipase** can cleave the fatty acid and phosphate groups from the glycerol molecule, similarly converting the glycerol portion of the molecule to intermediate metabolites of the glycolytic pathways.

The metabolism of the fatty acid portions of lipid molecules proceeds by a pathway called **β-oxidation.** Fatty acids can be broken down into small 2-carbon acetyl Coenzyme A (CoA) units in the process of β-ox-

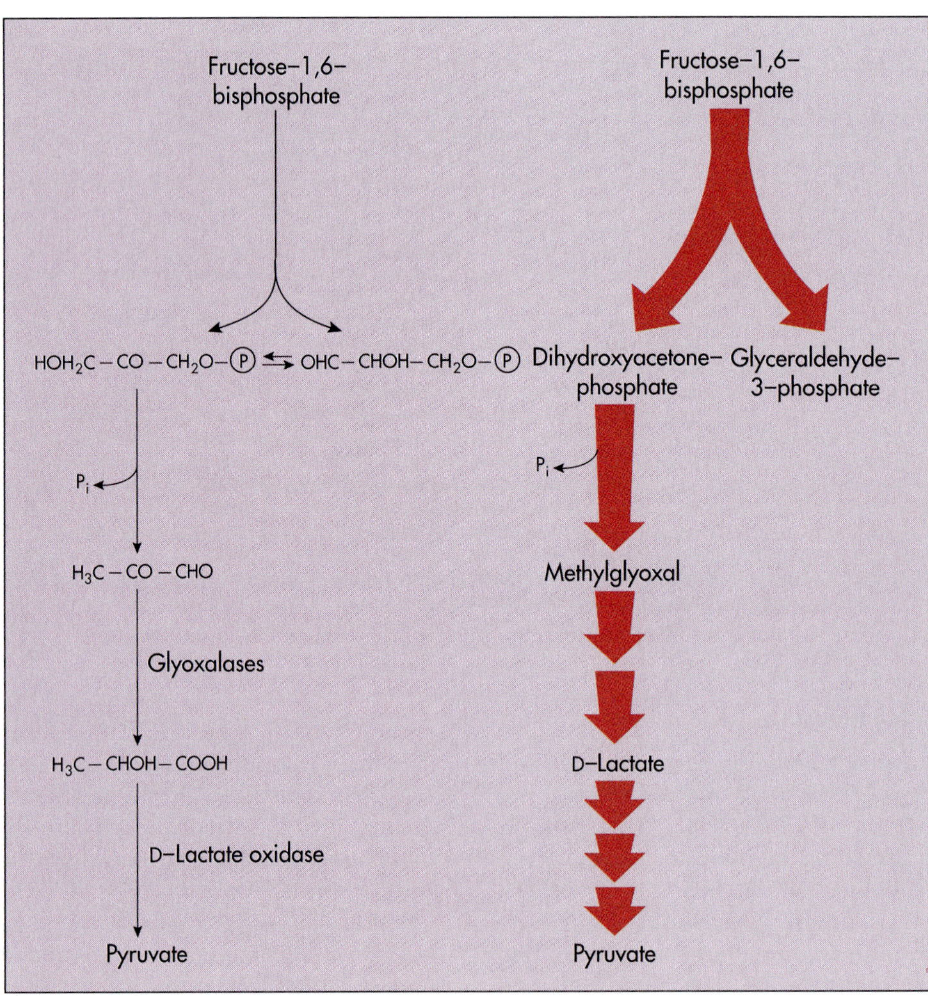

FIG. 4-12 The methylglyoxal pathway varies from the Embden-Myerhof pathway in the steps after formation of dihydroxyacetone phosphate. This pathway, in which methylglyoxal is an intermediate, does not produce ATP.

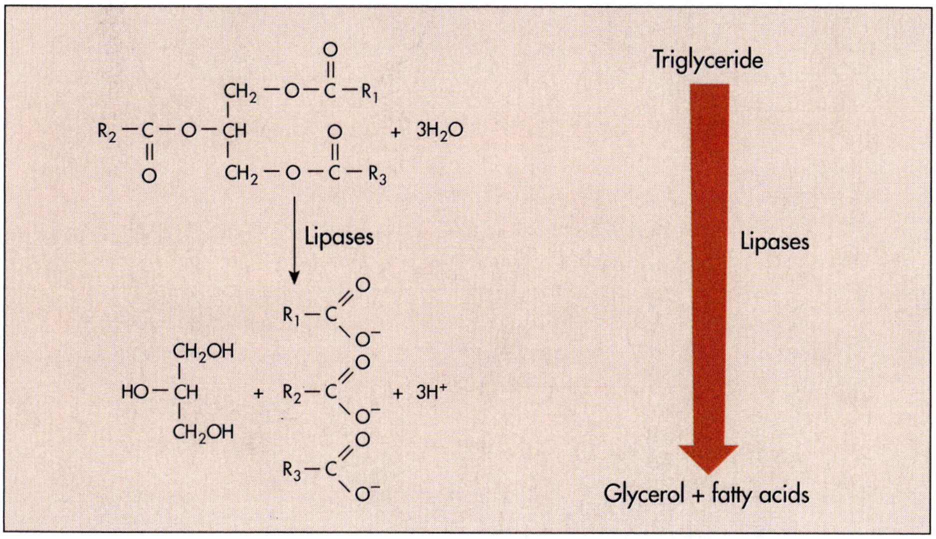

Triglyceride

$$\begin{array}{l} CH_2-O-C(=O)-R_1 \\ R_2-C(=O)-O-CH \\ CH_2-O-C(=O)-R_3 \end{array} + 3H_2O$$

Lipases

$$\begin{array}{l} CH_2OH \\ HO-CH \\ CH_2OH \end{array} + \begin{array}{l} R_1-COO^- \\ R_2-COO^- \\ R_3-COO^- \end{array} + 3H^+$$

Glycerol + fatty acids

FIG. 4-13 The metabolism of triglycerides is initiated by lipases that cleave the triglyceride lipid molecule into glycerol and fatty acids.

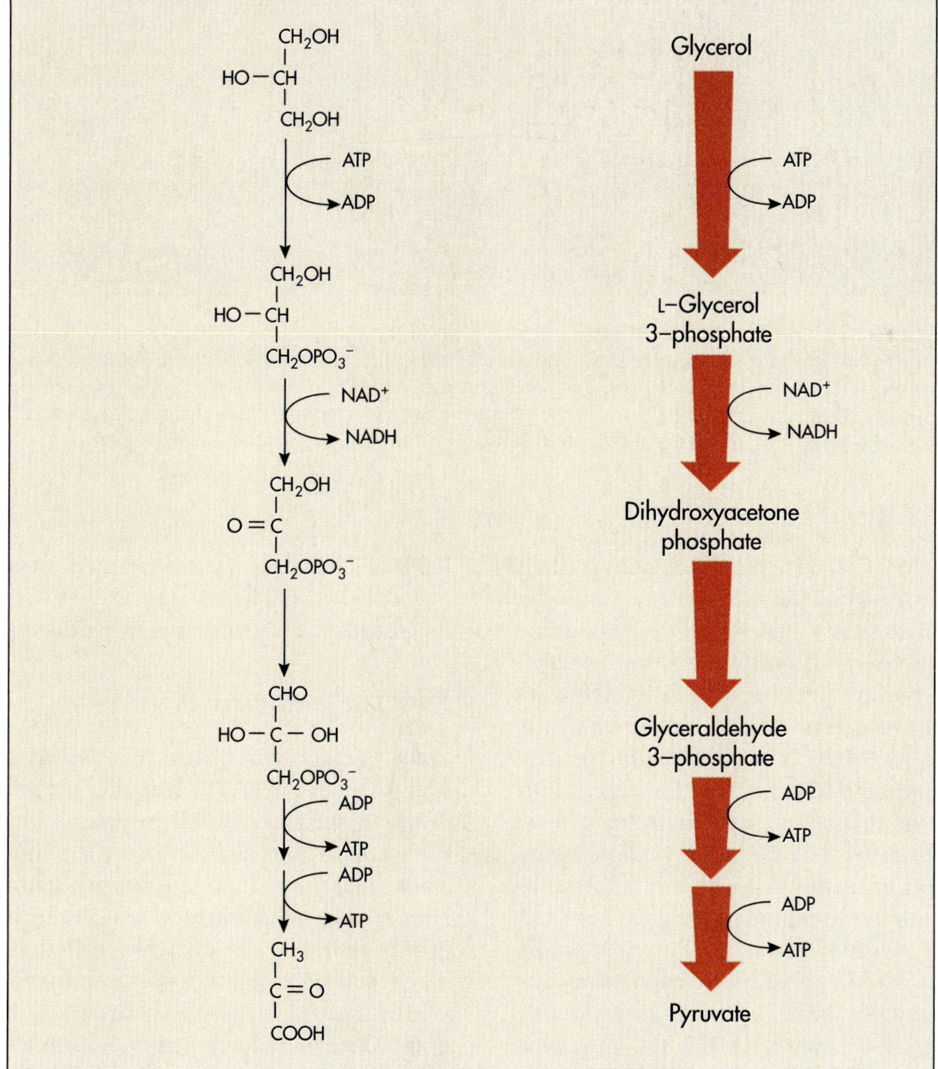

FIG. 4-14 Glycerol can enter a glycolytic pathway via the ATP-driven formation of glycerol phosphate and the NADH-coupled reduction to form dihydroxyacetone phosphate. Glycerol is metabolized to glyceraldehyde 3-phosphate, an intermediary metabolite of glycolysis. The glyceraldehyde 3-phosphate then is metabolized to pyruvate with the formation of ATP.

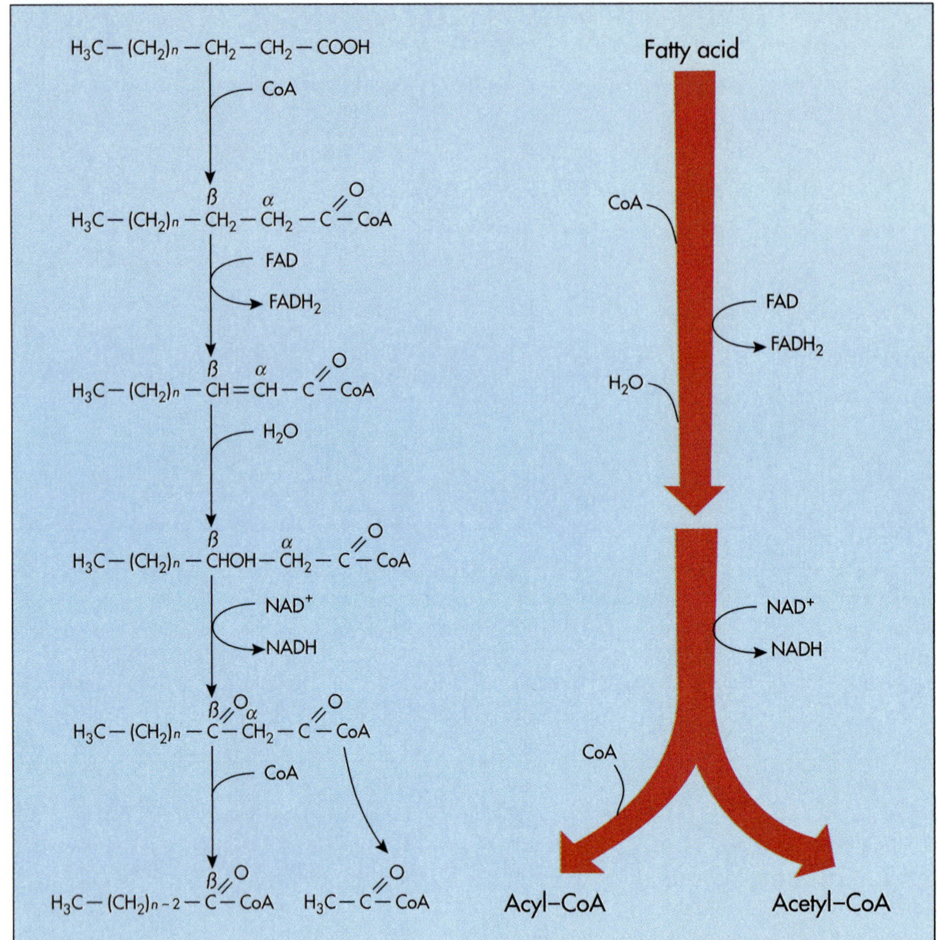

FIG. 4-15 The metabolism of fatty acids occurs via the β-oxidation pathway, which forms acetyl-CoA and acyl-CoA molecules. The acetyl-CoA can release the CoA and form acetate, which contains two carbon atoms. The acyl-CoA molecules can release the CoA and form a fatty acid that is two carbon atoms shorter than the parent fatty acid. This process is repeated so that it progressively forms acetate and fatty acids that are two carbon atoms shorter.

idation (FIG. 4-15). The fatty acid molecule initially reacts with CoA to form a fatty acid–CoA molecule. The activation of the fatty acid with CoA is coupled with utilization of energy from ATP. Further metabolism releases acetyl-CoA and forms a fatty acid–CoA molecule that is two carbon atoms shorter than the parent fatty acid molecule. The β-oxidation process then repeats the same basic reaction, forming a fatty acid–CoA molecule that is four carbon atoms shorter than the original fatty acid, then six carbon atoms shorter and so on until the original fatty acid molecule has been completely degraded.

The release of acetyl-CoA from the fatty acid is coupled with the formation of reduced coenzyme: one molecule of reduced flavin adenine dinucleotide ($FADH_2$) and one molecule of NADH. The process is repeated continuously, forming fatty acid molecules that are successively two carbon atoms shorter, with the production each time of acetyl-CoA, NADH, and $FADH_2$. The acetyl-CoA produced during β-oxidation of fatty acids is passed into the TCA cycle to be oxidized with the accompanying synthesis of ATP.

Protein Catabolism

Many bacteria can utilize proteins as a source of energy to generate ATP. Initially, proteins are broken down by enzymes called **proteases** into smaller peptides and amino acids (FIG. 4-16). Individual amino acids then have their amino group removed by enzymes called **deaminases** and their carboxylic acid group removed by enzymes called **decarboxylases.** The resulting molecules are then further metabolized via the central metabolic pathways of the cell to generate ATP. Their further metabolism also provides the intermediary metabolite for biosynthesis. For example, the amino acids alanine, glycine, and serine can all be converted to pyruvate (FIG. 4-17).

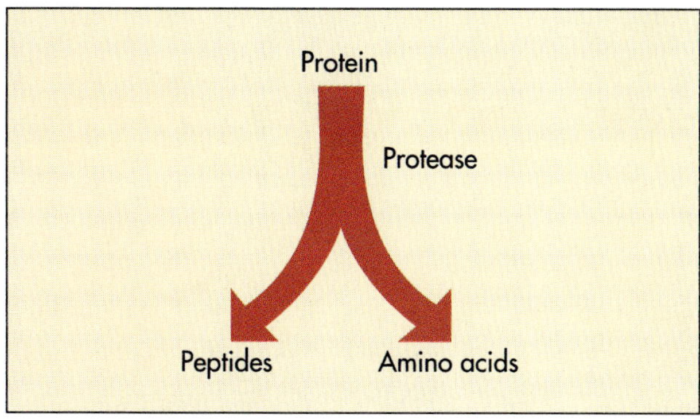

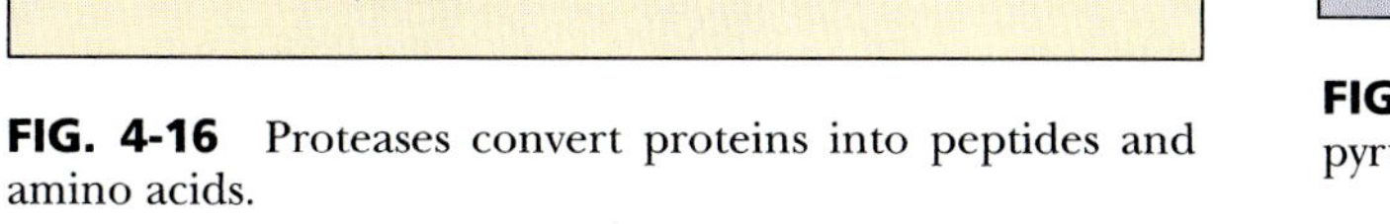
FIG. 4-16 Proteases convert proteins into peptides and amino acids.

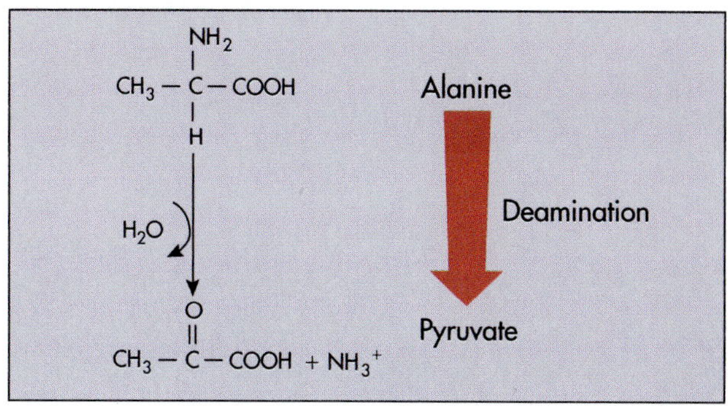

FIG. 4-17 Deamination of the amino acid alanine to form pyruvate.

TRICARBOXYLIC ACID CYCLE

We now turn our attention to the second phase of the respiratory metabolism of glucose and other substrates. This phase of metabolism feeds acetyl-CoA from β-oxidation of fatty acids or pyruvate from carbohydrate or protein catabolism via acetyl-CoA into the **tricarboxylic acid cycle (TCA cycle)** and results in the production of carbon dioxide, water, reduced coenzymes, and ATP.

To enter the TCA cycle, which is also known as the **citric acid cycle** or the **Krebs cycle,** pyruvate molecules generated during glycolysis or protein catabolism first react with CoA in a reaction catalyzed by the pyruvate dehydrogenase complex. Pyruvate dehydrogenase is a multi-enzyme complex that has 48 polypeptides. The decarboxylation of pyruvate, which is coupled with the conversion of the coenzyme NAD^+ to reduced NADH, forms acetyl-CoA and carbon dioxide:

$$\text{Pyruvate} + NAD^+ + \text{CoA} \rightarrow \text{Acetyl-CoA} + NADH + CO_2$$

The acetyl-CoA formed from pyruvate decarboxylation, or by β-oxidation of fatty acids, can then feed its acetyl group into the TCA cycle (FIG. 4-18).

In the first step of the TCA cycle, acetyl-CoA reacts with oxaloacetate to form citrate and release CoA. Through a series of reactions involving carboxylic acids, the TCA cycle then regenerates oxaloacetate. During the TCA cycle, two reactions liberate carbon dioxide: the conversion of the 6-carbon compound isocitrate to the 5-carbon compound α-ketoglutarate, and the subsequent conversion of α-ketoglutarate to succinyl-CoA (succinate is a 4-carbon compound). Reduced coenzyme NADH is generated during three reactions of the TCA cycle. The coenzyme flavin adeine dinucleotide (FAD) is also reduced to $FADH_2$ during the conversion of succinate to fumarate.

Only one of the exergonic reactions of the TCA cycle, the conversion of succinyl-CoA to succinate, is directly coupled with the generation of a high-energy phosphate-containing compound. In this reaction in some bacteria, ATP is formed in a substrate-level phosphorylation by transfer of energy from the high energy succinate–CoA bond to ADP and P_i. In eukaryotic cells, a different reaction occurs within the mitochondria in which guanosine triphosphate (GTP) is synthesized from guanosine diphosphate (GDP) and P_i. Some bacteria similarly form GTP rather than ATP in the metabolic reaction. The GTP formed in this reaction can be used directly or transferred to ATP. GTP is the energy source used in some specific cellular reactions, most importantly during the synthesis of protein at the ribosomes. The energy stored within GTP is equivalent to that stored within ATP and the high energy phosphate group of GTP can be transferred onto ADP to form ATP by the reaction:

$$GTP + ADP \rightleftharpoons GDP + ATP$$

For energy accounting purposes, the GTP generated in this reaction will be treated as if it is all transformed to ATP.

An important aspect of the TCA cycle is that the reaction intermediates are reused. The two carbon atoms that originated from acetyl- CoA are completely oxidized to CO_2. The other carbon atoms of the reactants are conserved as the cycle repeats itself and picks up another two carbons from a new acetyl-CoA molecule.

The net reaction of the TCA cycle, starting with the pyruvate generated by the glycolysis of glucose, can be summarized as:

$$2\ \text{pyruvate} + 2\ ADP + 2\ FAD + 8\ NAD^+ \rightarrow 6CO_2 + 2ATP + 2\ FADH_2 + 8\ NADH$$

At the end of the TCA cycle, all of the carbon from the original glucose molecule has been converted to carbon dioxide. Assuming the pyruvate that fed into the TCA cycle was generated by the Embden-Meyerhof pathway, there will have been a net synthesis of four ATP molecules: two from the Embden-Meyerhof pathway and two from the TCA cycle. Ten reduced

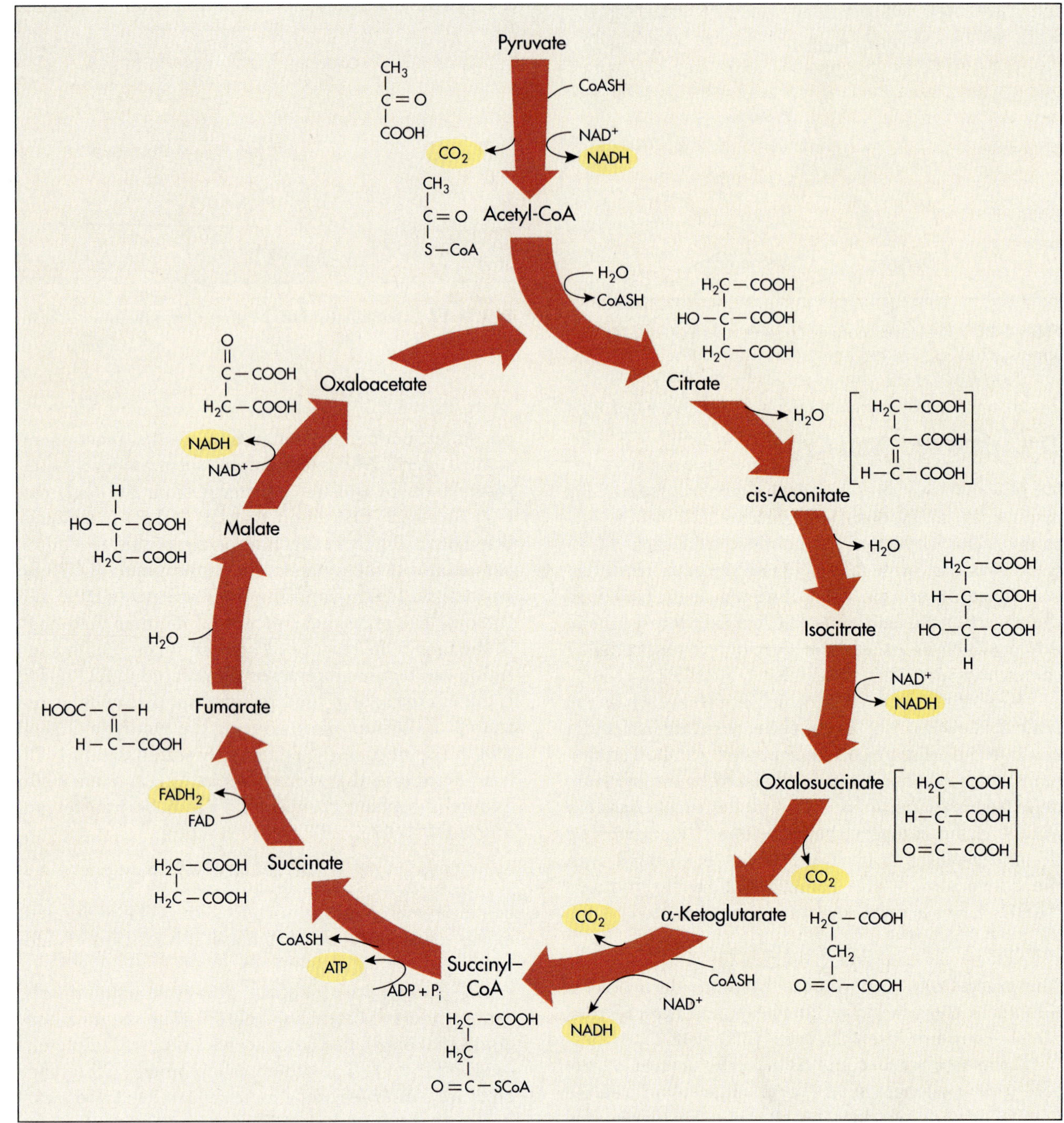

FIG. 4-18 The tricarboxylic acid cycle is a metabolic pathway central to respiratory metabolism and provides a critical link between the metabolism of the different classes of macromolecules. The metabolism of pyruvate through the tricarboxylic acid cycle results in the generation of ATP and reduced coenzymes and the formation of CO_2. When the pathway is completed, the intermediate carboxylic acids are regenerated and continue to cycle throughout the reactions. The tricarboxylic acid cycle begins when oxaloacetate reacts with acetyl-CoA and H_2O to yield citrate and CoA. Citrate is next isomerized into isocitrate to enable the 6-carbon unit to undergo oxidative decarboxylation. The next step, which is the first of four oxidation-reduction reactions in the tricarboxylic acid cycle, results in the conversion of isocitrate to NADH. The conversion of isocitrate into oxidative decarboxylation reaction results in the formation of succinyl-CoA, CO_2, and NADH. The cleavage of the thioester bond of succinyl-CoA produces succinate and is coupled to the phosphorylation of ADT to form ATP in prokaryotic cells or guanosine diphosphate (GDP) to form guanosine triphosphate (GTP) in eukaryotic cells. Succinate is converted into oxaloacetate in three steps—an oxidation, a hydration, and a second oxidation reaction—thereby regenerating the oxaloacetate for another round of the cycle and simultaneously generating $FADH_2$ and NADH.

coenzyme molecules will have been generated in the form of NADH (two from the Embden-Meyerhof pathway and eight from the TCA cycle), while two reduced coenzyme molecules in the form of $FADH_2$ will have come from the TCA cycle.

In addition to its role in the overall respiratory generation of ATP, the TCA cycle also plays a central role in the flow of carbon through the cell. It supplies organic precursor molecules to many biosynthetic pathways, as discussed in Chapter 5. Because some of the intermediates in the TCA cycle are siphoned out of it for use in biosynthesis, some of the intermediates must be resynthesized to maintain TCA cycle activity. Many microorganisms oxidize only part of their substrate molecules for the production of ATP, using the remainder for biosynthesis. Similarly, the reduced coenzymes generated by the TCA cycle and glycolysis can either be used for generating ATP, which is examined in the next section, or used to synthesize the reduced coenzyme NADPH for use in biosynthesis.

OXIDATIVE PHOSPHORYLATION

In the third and final phase of the respiratory metabolism of glucose and other substrates, called **oxidative phosphorylation,** reduced coenzymes generated earlier in glycolysis and the TCA cycle are reoxidized, the electrons they release are transported through a series of membrane-bound carriers to establish a proton gradient across a membrane, a terminal acceptor such as oxygen is reduced, and ATP is synthesized by chemiosmosis.

Electron Transport Chain

During oxidative phosphorylation, electrons from the reduced coenzymes NADH and $FADH_2$ are transferred through a series of membrane-bound carriers that form an **electron transport chain.** The reduced coenzymes are reoxidized in this process and can be reused in cellular metabolism as electron acceptors. The transfer of electrons during the electron transport chain involves a series of oxidation-reduction reactions of the membrane-bound carrier molecules and the eventual reduction of a terminal electron acceptor.

The carriers in the electron transport chain participate in a series of reactions of increasing reduction potential difference ($\Delta E'_0$) between that of the primary electron donor and the terminal electron acceptor (FIG. 4-19). Flavoproteins (containing flavin mononucleotide) and iron-sulfur proteins (non-heme iron proteins) transfer hydrogen from NADH to coenzyme Q (quinone). Electrons from coenzyme Q reduce a series of cytochromes, usually beginning with cytochrome *c* or cytochrome *b*. Cytochromes contain a central iron ion, which can be cycled between the oxidized ferric state (Fe^{3+}) and the reduced ferrous state (Fe^{2+}). Ultimately, electrons are passed to a cytochrome *a*/cytochrome oxidase (cytochrome *o*) complex and then to O_2 in aerobic respiration or to an alternate inorganic final electron acceptor in anaerobic respiration.

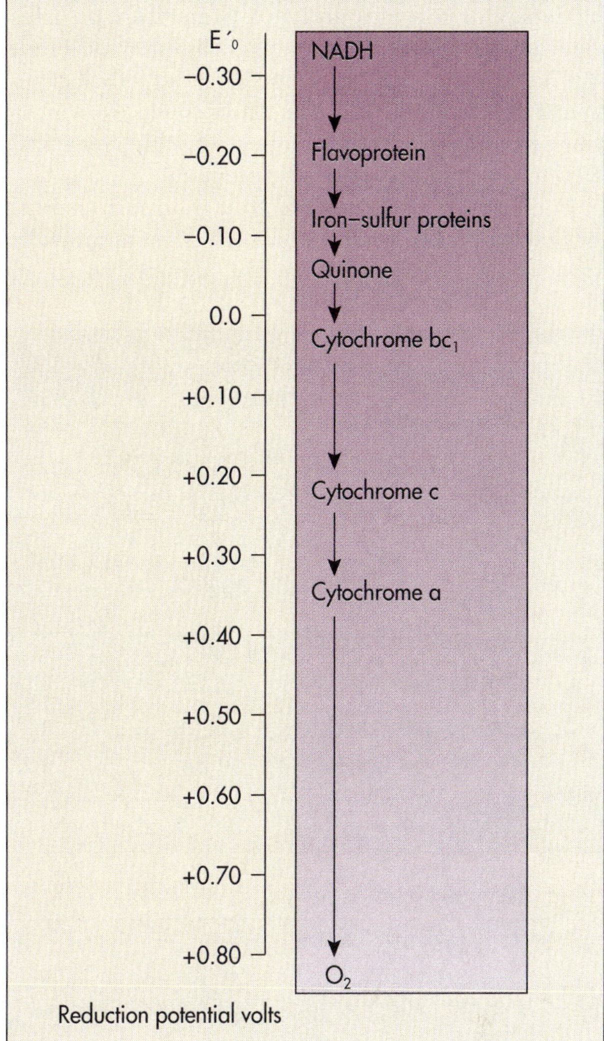

FIG. 4-19 The electron transport chain involves sequential transfers of electrons from carriers with low reduction potentials (E'_0) to carriers with higher reduction potentials.

The transport of electrons from reduced coenzymes to a terminal electron acceptor can be blocked by various agents, resulting in the inability of a cell to generate ATP so that the cell dies. Cyanide can bind to the iron of certain cytochromes, blocking their ability to transfer electrons and turn over oxygen. Carbon monoxide can bind to the terminal cytochrome, blocking the reduction of oxygen.

Within the electron transport chain, some carriers transport hydrogen atoms (an electron plus a proton), whereas others transport only electrons (Table 4-10). Flavoproteins and quinones are hydrogen atom carriers. Cytochromes and non-heme iron proteins are electron carriers. Different cells have different specific carriers but the general series of electron transfers is from NADH to a flavoprotein, to a non-heme iron protein, to a quinone, to cytochromes, and then to the terminal electron acceptor.

In eukaryotic cells, the electron transport chain is located within the inner mitochondrial membrane. In mitochondria, two protons are transferred from NADH to a flavoprotein, which expels the protons across and outside the inner membrane as electrons are transferred to a non-heme iron protein (FIG. 4-20). The reduced non-heme iron transfers its electron to the quinone, coenzyme Q, and two protons are picked up from the cytoplasm to form reduced coenzyme Q ($CoQH_2$). The $CoQH_2$ transfers its electrons to a cytochrome *b*–cytochrome c_1 complex, whereas protons are expelled outside the membrane. The electrons then pass from the cytochrome *b*–cytochrome c_1 complex to cytochrome *c* and then to cytochrome *a*. In the final step of the pathway, the electrons from cytochrome *a* are used to reduce O_2 to H_2O.

Bacterial electron transport chains can be even more complex. Different bacterial species contain various components that make up their electron transport chains, and the components found within a particular species of bacterium vary depending on the environmental conditions in which the cell is growing (FIG. 4-21). For example, in *E. coli* the electrons from NADH are transferred to flavoprotein, non-heme iron, and coenzyme Q. Then, depending on environmental conditions, the electron is transferred to a distinct cytochrome *b*, cytochrome *d*, and oxygen, or to a different cytochrome *b*, cytochrome *o*, and oxygen. Cytochrome *o* is used under high oxygen concentrations. Cytochrome *d* is used under low oxygen con-

TABLE 4-10 Components of Bacterial Electron Transport Systems

COMPONENT	TYPE OF MOLECULE	FUNCTION
NADH dehydrogenase	Protein, enzyme	Transfers H^+ and e^- from NADH
Flavoproteins	Flavin-containing protein	H^+ acceptor; e^- transfer
Cytochromes	Heme-containing protein	e^- donor and acceptor
Non-heme iron sulfur proteins	Iron–sulfur-containing proteins	e^- donor and acceptor
Quinones	Lipid	H^+ acceptor; e^- transfer

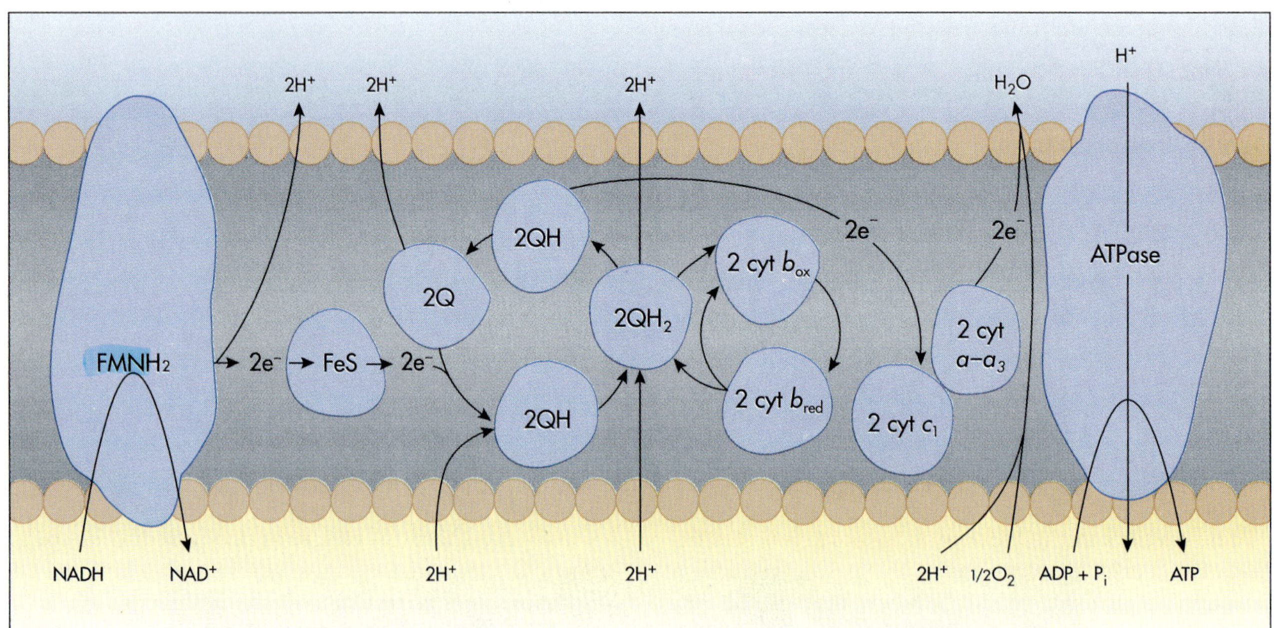

FIG. 4-20 The electron transport chain is a membrane-embedded series of reactions that results in the reoxidation of reduced coenzymes. The transport of electrons through the cytochrome chain of this pathway results in the expulsion of protons across the inner membrane of the mitochondrion, and the return flow of hydrogen ions resulting from this proton gradient drives the generation of ATP. Electrons that enter the system from NADH are transported through flavin mononucleotide (FMN) to coenzyme Q; those that enter from $FADH_2$ go directly to coenzyme Q. Electrons then flow through a series of cytochromes, designated cyt *b*, *c*, *a*, and a_3, to the terminal electron acceptor. As the electron is transported through each carrier, there is an oxidation-reduction reaction, so that in the case of the cytochromes, for example, iron within the cytochrome alternates between the oxidized Fe^{3+} and reduced Fe^{2+} states. At three locations, protons are transported out of the cell.

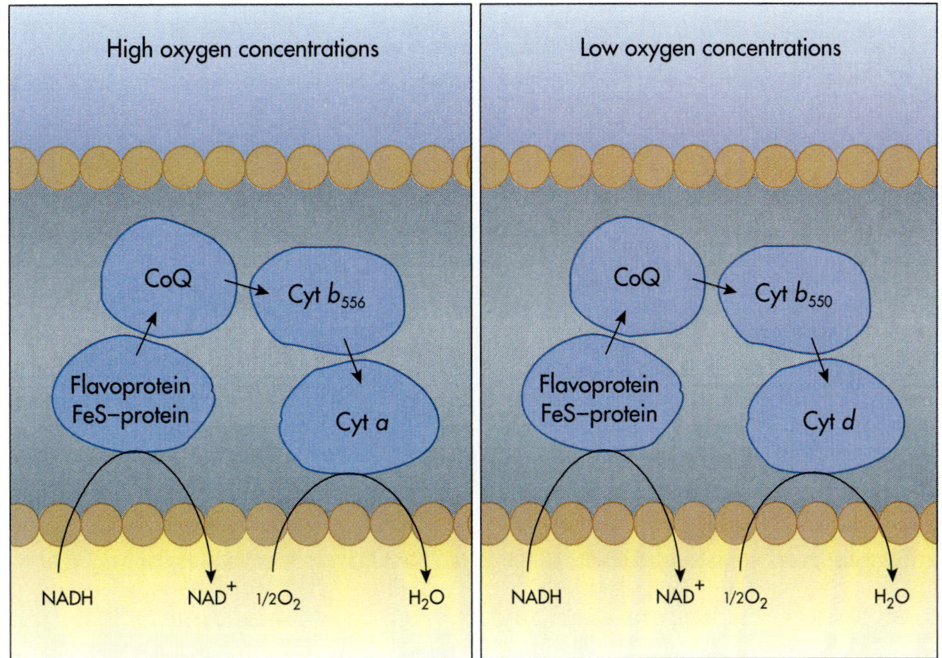

FIG. 4-21 The actual carriers of electrons involved in this transport system vary among microorganisms. What is critical is the establishment of a sequence of oxidation-reduction reactions that establish a link between the electron donor and the terminal electron acceptor. In some cases, such as within *Escherichia coli,* the electron transport carriers can vary under different conditions.

centrations. In the absence of oxygen, another cytochrome *b* can transfer electrons to nitrate to complete the electron transport chain.

When nitrate serves as the terminal electron acceptor during anaerobic respiration, the products of its reaction are also capable of serving as terminal electron acceptors. This establishes a series of anaerobic respirations: nitrate reduced to produce nitrite, nitrite reduced to produce nitrous oxide, and nitrous oxide reduced to molecular nitrogen (FIG. 4-22). This denitrification process returns N_2 to the atmosphere. Similarly, when sulfate acts as a terminal electron acceptor a series of reactions can eventually produce hydrogen sulfide and water.

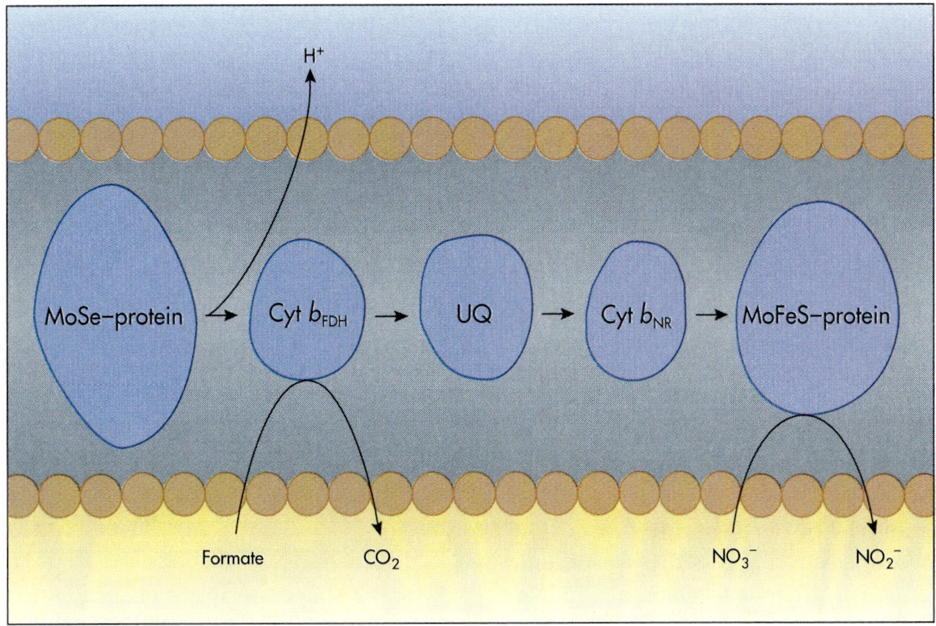

FIG. 4-22 Anaerobic respiration in which nitrate serves as the terminal electron acceptor has specific electron carriers, including cytochrome *b*:formate dehydrogenase (cyt b_{FDH}) and cytochrome *b*:nitrate reductase (cyt b_{NR}). The electron transfer results in the formation of nitrite from nitrate.

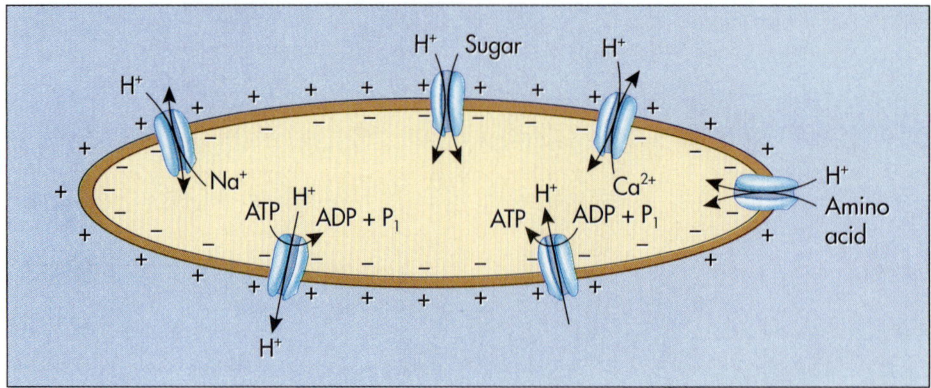

FIG. 4-23 The establishment of a protonmotive force (hydrogen ion gradient) across a membrane is needed to generate ATP by chemiosmosis. As a result of the reactions of the electron carriers, protons are transported across the membrane, establishing a hydrogen ion (proton) gradient across it. The force that results from this concentration and electrical difference, the protonmotive force, is used to generate ATP and to do other work, such as the active transport of some substrates.

Protonmotive Force—Chemiosmotic ATP Generation

The transfer of electrons from the reduced coenzyme to the terminal electron acceptor and the coupled transfers of protons establishes the proton gradient across the membrane that powers the formation of ATP (FIG. 4-23). The electron carriers of the electron transport chain are asymmetrically distributed through the membrane, and the movement of protons across the membrane, as a result of electron transport, forms an electrochemical proton gradient that is used for generating ATP. In the case of eukaryotic cells, this electrochemical gradient is established across the inner mitochondrial membrane, whereas for bacteria it is formed across the cytoplasmic membrane.

The orientation of the carriers in the bacterial cytoplasmic membrane is such that proton carriers transport toward the outside of the cell and electron carriers transport toward the inside. At each conjunction in the chain of a hydrogen atom carrier and an electron carrier, one or more protons (H^+) are transported out of the cell. It is unclear as to the exact number of protons that are expelled across the membrane during electron transport from NADH to O_2. As many as 10 protons may be transported across a membrane for each NADH molecule. A portion of the chemical energy released by the net reaction of the electron transport chain (oxidation of the primary electron donor by the terminal electron acceptor) is thereby trapped in the form of a protonmotive force that can be used to generate ATP or perform other work. The protonmotive force measured across the cytoplasmic membrane of *E. coli* is sufficient to generate the formation of the high-energy phosphate bond of ATP.

The generation of ATP by chemiosmosis depends on the fact that protons cannot simply diffuse back across the membrane but can only recross it via a specific proton channel, such as the one established by a membrane-bound adenosine triphosphatase (ATPase). Electron transport can be uncoupled from ATP generation by agents such as dinitrophenol, which allow leakage of protons across a membrane and hence destroy the proton gradient and its associated protonmotive force.

ATPase is a multicomponent enzyme system containing two major polypeptide complexes called F_0

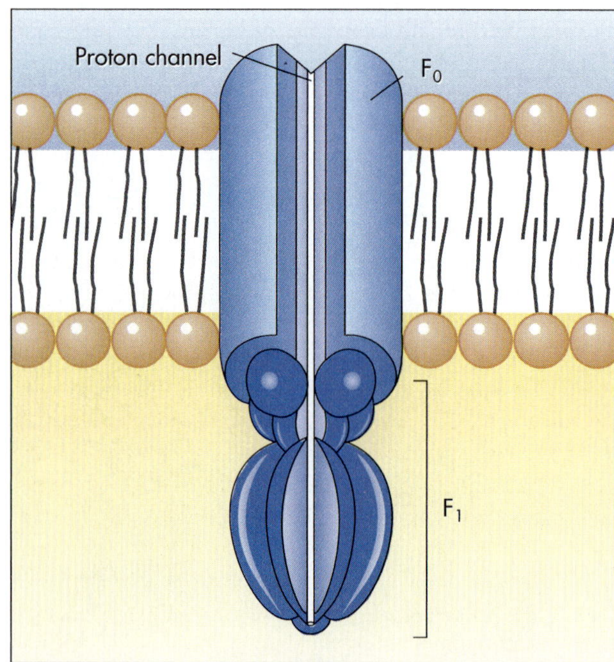

FIG. 4-24 ATPase is a multicomponent enzyme system composed of two major complexes designated F_0 and F_1. The F_0F_1 components link the protonmotive force with ATP synthesis. Protons are channeled by the F_0 component of the system to F_1, where the conversion of ADP to ATP is catalyzed.

and F_1 (FIG. 4-24). The F_0F_1 complex couples the synthesis of ATP with proton diffusion. The F_1 polypeptides sit on the inner surface of the membrane, whereas the F_0 polypeptides are embedded in the membrane. F_0 forms a channel across the membrane through which protons flow to F_1. Then F_1 catalyzes the synthesis of ATP from ADP. F_1 is also capable of catalyzing the conversion of ATP to ADP + P_i.

As a consequence of the protonmotive force established by the electron transport chain, three ATP molecules can be synthesized for each NADH molecule oxidized to NAD^+, and two ATP molecules can be made for each $FADH_2$ molecule oxidized to FAD. The difference between the amount of ATP that can be generated from NADH compared to $FADH_2$ occurs because the oxygen-linked oxidation of NADH liberates 52.4 kcal/mole compared to only 42 kcal/mole for the oxygen-linked oxidation of $FADH_2$. For a bacterial cell, the 10 NADH molecules generated during glycolysis and the TCA cycle, therefore, can be used to synthesize 30 ATP molecules during oxidative phosphorylation; the 2 $FADH_2$ molecules generated during the TCA cycle can generate 4 ATP molecules.

The chemiosmotic synthesis of ATP during oxidative phosphorylation is in addition to the ATP formed during glycolysis and the TCA cycle. Thus the overall reaction for the respiratory metabolism of glucose by a bacterial cell using the Embden-Meyerhof pathway of glycolysis can be expressed as follows:

$$\text{Glucose} + 6\ O_2 + 38\ \text{ADP} + 38\ P_i \rightarrow 6\ CO_2 + 6\ H_2O + 38\ \text{ATP}$$

The production of 38 ATP molecules from glucose is a theoretical maximal yield. It may occur in the bacterium *Paracoccus denitrificans,* which has an electron transport chain that can yield 3 ATPs for each NADH and 2 ATPs for each $FADH_2$. The electron transport chains of other bacteria, such as *E. coli,* may only produce 2 ATPs for each NADH and 1 ATP for each $FADH_2$. Such bacterial cells produce only 26 ATPs from the respiratory metabolism of each glucose molecule.

Anaerobic respiration, which occurs in some bacteria, often yields less ATP than aerobic respiration, producing only about one third the ATP made by aerobes. This is because a complete tricarboxylic acid cycle does not function in the absence of molecular oxygen and because there is less of a free energy difference between NADH and nitrate or sulfate than between NADH and molecular oxygen. Therefore two ATPs are made for each NADH in anerobic respiration rather than three ATPs made as in aerobic respiration.

In mitochondria the overall respiratory metabolism can only produce 36 ATP molecules per glucose. This is because glycolysis takes place in the cytoplasm of a eukaryotic cell. The transport of the two NADH molecules produced during glycolysis into the mitochondrion, where the tricarboxylic acid cycle and oxidative phosphorylation occur, requires active transport that consumes ATP. One ATP is consumed per NADH entering the mitochondrion from the cytoplasm, so that the NADH formed in glycolysis produces a net gain of only 2 ATP compared to the 3 ATPs produced from the NADH formed subsequently. Thus only 36, rather than 38, ATP molecules can be produced from each glucose molecule in eukaryotic cells.

4.4 FERMENTATION

Some cells can perform catabolism of substrates by a mechanism other than respiration, known as fermentation. In fermentation the organic substrate acts as an electron donor, and an organic molecule derived from that substrate acts as an electron acceptor. No external electron acceptor, such as oxygen, is involved. There is no net change in the oxidative state of the coenzymes involved in the fermentation pathway, and so they do not appear in the overall equation for fermentation.

The synthesis of ATP in fermentation is due to substrate-level phosphorylations and is largely restricted to the amount formed during glycolysis. Oxidative phosphorylation and chemiosmotic generation of ATP do not occur in fermentation. Because they do not require oxygen, all fermentation pathways are anaerobic, and microorganisms that generate their energy by fermentation carry out anaerobic metabolism, even if the organism is growing in the presence of molecular oxygen.

Obligately fermentative bacteria, such as *Streptococcus* species, do not use oxidative phosphorylation to generate ATP, but they do have an F_0F_1-ATPase system in their cytoplasmic membranes. In such bacteria, ATP is used to pump protons through the F_0F_1 complex in the reverse direction. In this process, ATP generated by substrate-level phosphorylation in a fermentation pathway is converted to ADP and P_i by the ATPase, and the energy of this reaction is coupled with the export of protons from the cell. The F_0F_1-ATPase system thereby generates a protonmotive force across the cytoplasmic membrane. This maintains the intracellular pH at the appropriate value and provides a mechanism for driving processes that depend on the protonmotive force across the membrane, such as active uptake of sugars and other substances, export of Na^+ and Ca^{2+}, and rotation of flagella.

A complete fermentation pathway begins with a substrate, includes glycolysis, and terminates with the

TABLE 4-11 Types of Fermentative Metabolism

FERMENTATION PATHWAY	END PRODUCTS
Homolactic acid	Lactate
Heterolactic acid	Lactate + ethanol + CO_2
Ethanolic	Ethanol + CO_2
Propionic acid	Propionate + acetate + CO_2
Mixed acid	Ethanol + acetate + lactate + succinate + formate + H_2 + CO_2
Butanediol	Butanediol + CO_2
Butyric acid	Butyrate + butanol + acetone + CO_2
Amino acid	Acetate + NH_4^+ + CO_2
Methanogenesis	CH_4 + CO_2

formation of end products (Table 4-11). Considering the actual way in which ATP is generated in fermentative bacteria, the initial metabolic steps of the fermentation pathway are identical to those of a respiration pathway. The metabolic pathway for carbohydrate fermentation, for example, begins with glycolysis. If a cell uses the Embden-Meyerhof glycolytic pathway for the fermentation of glucose, it generates two pyruvate molecules, two reduced coenzyme NADH molecules, and two ATP molecules for each molecule of glucose. In general, the two ATP molecules formed during glycolysis represent the total energy yield of the fermentation pathway, although some bacterial fermentation pathways subsequently generate additional ATP. The remainder of the fermentation pathway is usually concerned with reoxidizing the coenzyme.

In fermentation, the reoxidation of NADH to NAD^+ depends on the reduction of the pyruvate molecules formed during glycolysis, which balances the oxidation-reduction reactions. This happens in different ways in different microorganisms, and produces various end products, depending on which pathway is used. The different fermentation pathways generally are named for the characteristic end products that are formed.

LACTIC ACID FERMENTATION

In the lactic acid fermentation pathway, pyruvate is reduced to lactic acid, with the coupled reoxidation of NADH to NAD^+. This fermentation pathway is carried out by bacteria that, by virtue of their fermentation end products, are classified as lactic acid bacteria. Two important genera of lactic acid bacteria are *Streptococcus* (Gram-positive cocci that tend to form chains) and *Lactobacillus* (Gram-positive rods that tend to form chains).

Homolactic Fermentation

When the Embden-Meyerhof pathway of glycolysis is used in the lactic acid fermentation pathway, the overall pathway is a **homolactic fermentation** because the only end product formed is lactic acid (FIG. 4-25). The overall lactic acid fermentation pathway can be expressed as follows:

$$\text{Glucose} + 2\ \text{ADP} + 2\ \text{P}_i \rightarrow 2\ \text{lactic acid} + 2\ \text{ATP}$$

Homolactic fermentation is carried out by *Streptococcus, Pediococcus, Lactococcus, Enterococcus,* and various *Lactobacillus* species.

The homolactic acid fermentation pathway is important in the dairy industry. It is the pathway responsible for souring milk and is used in the production of numerous types of cheese, yogurt, and various other dairy products.

Streptococci living on tooth surfaces in the oral cavity (mouth) produce lactic acid by the homolactic acid pathway. The lactic acid is held against the tooth by dental plaque and gradually eats through the enamel of the tooth, creating caries (cavities). Even though they can grow in the mouth, *Streptococcus* species are metabolically obligate anaerobes using only fermentative metabolism.

Lactobacillus species occur in the human digestive tract and aid in the digestion of milk. These species are the initial colonizers of the intestinal tract. Some adults lack the ability to digest the carbohydrates in

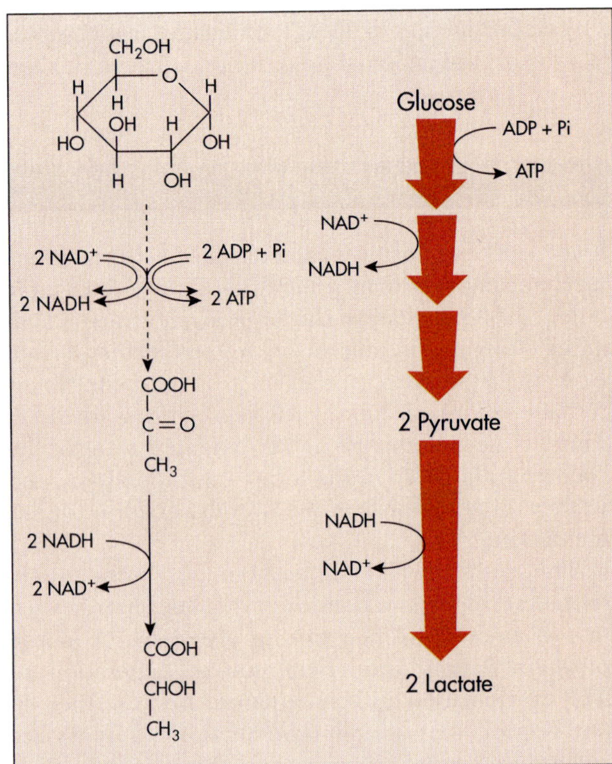

FIG. 4-25 The homolactic acid fermentation pathway results in the production of lactate (lactic acid).

milk and suffer disease symptoms (lactose intolerance) if they consume milk. *Lactobacillus acidophilus* is added to various commercial milk products (acidophilus milk) to aid individuals who are unable to digest milk products adequately. The enzymes produced by *L. acidophilus* convert milk sugars to products that do not accumulate and cause gastrointestinal problems.

Heterolactic Fermentation

Some microorganisms carry out a **heterolactic acid fermentation,** using the pentose phosphate pathway rather than the Embden-Meyerhof pathway of glycolysis. Heterolactic acid fermentation is so named because ethanol and carbon dioxide are produced in addition to lactic acid (FIG. 4-26). The ethanol and carbon dioxide come from the glycolytic portion of the pathway. The overall reaction for the heterolactic fermentation can be expressed as follows:

$$\text{Glucose} + \text{ADP} + \text{P}_i \rightarrow \text{lactic acid} + \text{ethanol} + \text{CO}_2 + \text{ATP}$$

The heterolactic fermentation pathway produces only one molecule of ATP per molecule of glucose substrate metabolized. This fermentative pathway is carried out by *Leuconostoc* species, which are used to produce sauerkraut, and by various *Lactobacillus* species.

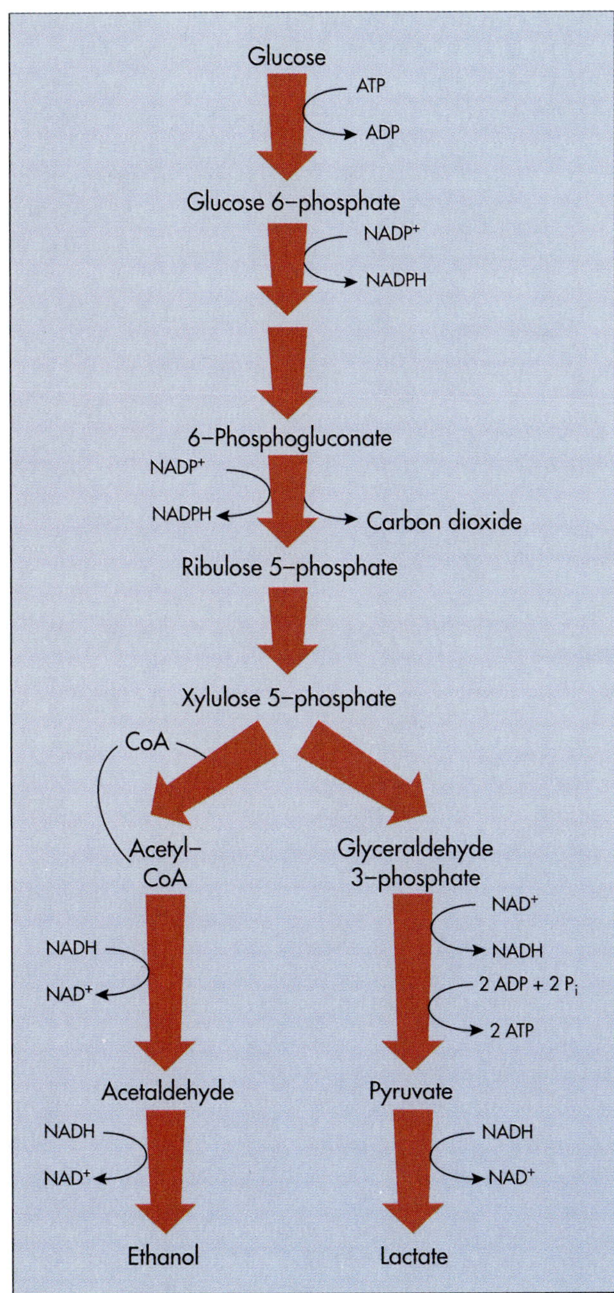

FIG. 4-26 The heterolactic acid fermentation pathway results in the production of lactate (lactic acid), ethanol, and carbon dioxide.

ETHANOLIC FERMENTATION

The **ethanolic fermentation pathway** derives its name from the fact that ethanol is one of the end products. In this fermentation pathway, pyruvate is converted to ethanol and carbon dioxide (FIG. 4-27). This terminal reaction of the ethanolic fermentation pathway is coupled with the conversion of NADH to NAD^+. The equation for ethanolic fermentation when glucose is

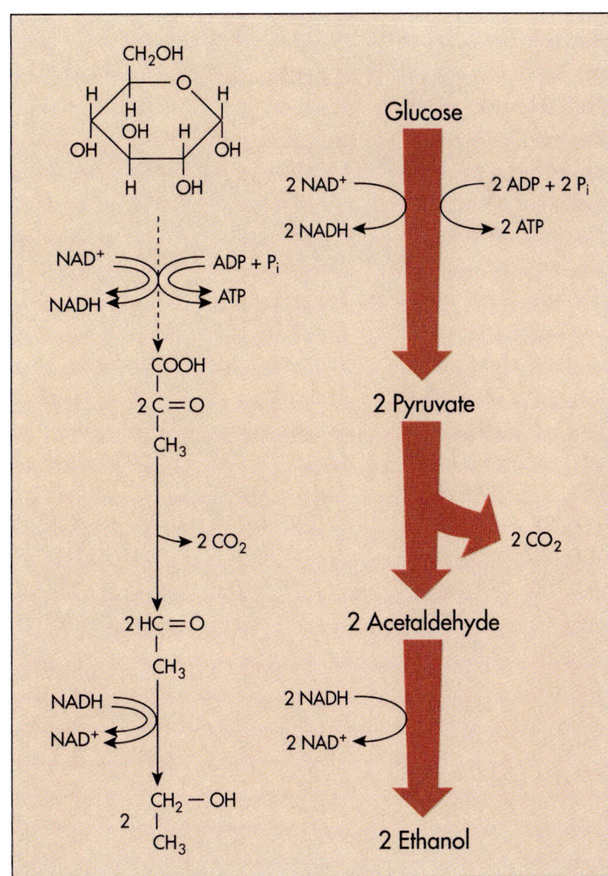

FIG. 4-27 The ethanolic fermentation pathway results in the formation of ethanol and carbon dioxide. The fermentation of carbohydrates to these end products forms the basis of the beer, wine, and spirits industries.

the substrate and the Embden-Meyerhof pathway is followed is:

$$\text{Glucose} + 2\ \text{ADP} + 2\ \text{P}_i \rightarrow 2\ \text{ethanol} + 2\ \text{CO}_2 + 2\ \text{ATP}$$

Ethanolic fermentation is carried out by many yeasts, such as *Saccharomyces cerevisiae* (baker's and brewer's yeast), but by relatively few bacteria. This fermentation pathway is important in food and industrial microbiology and is used to produce beer, wine, and distilled spirits. Besides its importance in alcoholic beverages, ethanol produced by *S. cerevisiae* in this fermentation is used as a fuel in gasohol. In addition to its use for ethanol formation, *S. cerevisiae* is used in the production of bread, in which the carbon dioxide released by the ethanolic fermentation causes the bread to rise. All of these uses of the ethanolic fermentation pathway have considerable economic importance.

PROPIONIC ACID FERMENTATION

In the **propionic acid fermentation** pathway the end product is propionic acid. This fermentation pathway is carried out by the propionic acid bacteria (propionibacteria). The bacterial genus *Propionibacterium* is defined as a group of Gram-positive rods that produce propionic acid from the metabolism of carbohydrates and lactate.

Propionibacteria utilize lactic acid as a substrate for the propionic acid fermentation. The ability to utilize the end product from another fermentation pathway

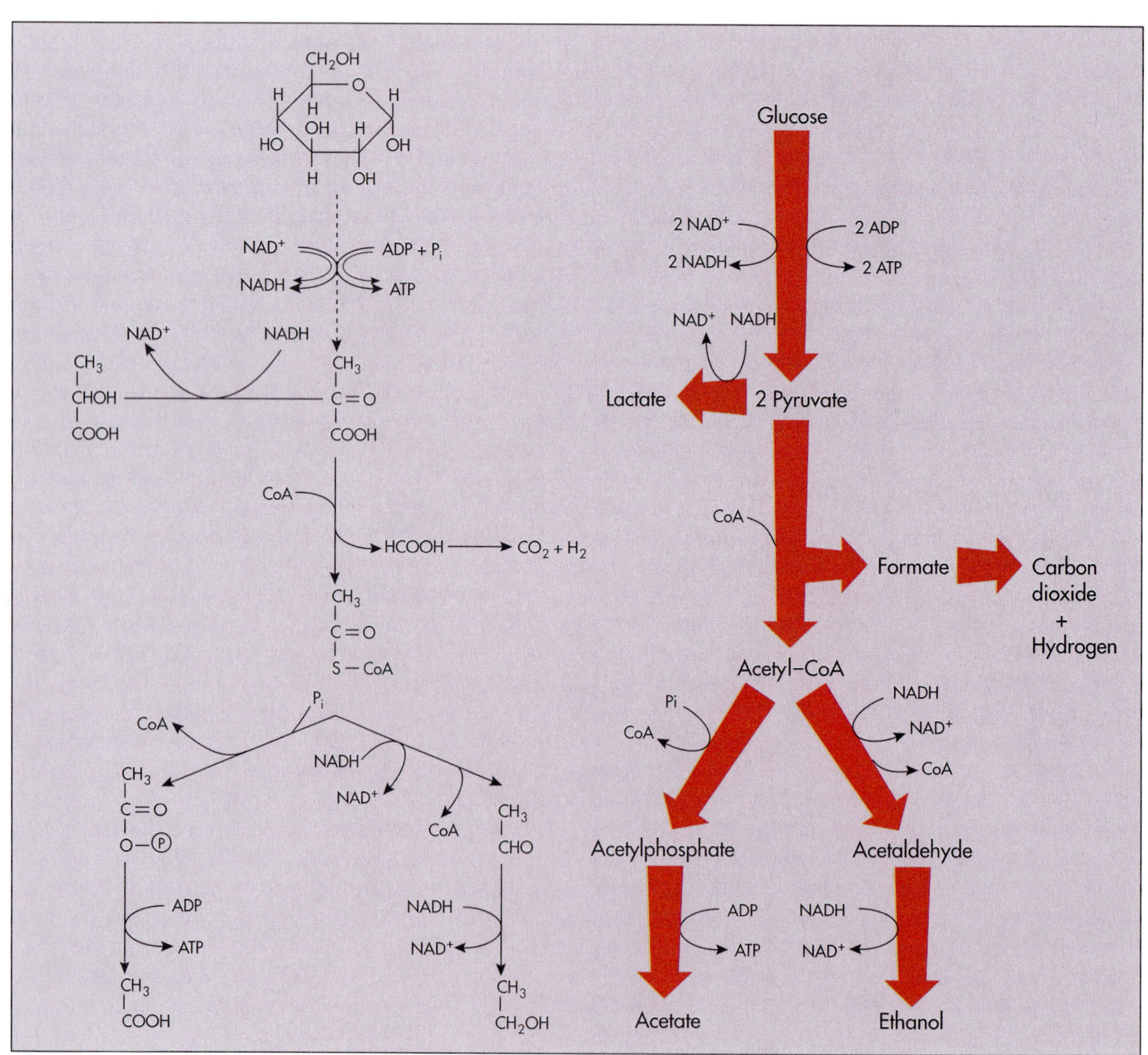

FIG. 4-28 The mixed acid fermentation pathway, which is carried out by enteric bacteria such as *Escherichia coli*, results in the production of carbon dioxide, hydrogen gas, acetic acid, lactic acid, formic acid, and ethanol.

is unusual, and it permits species of *Propionibacterium* to carry out late fermentation during the production of cheese. The lactic acid bacteria convert the initial substrates in the milk to lactic acid. The propionic acid bacteria subsequently convert the lactic acid to propionic acid and carbon dioxide. The propionic acid bacteria begin their fermentation only after the cheese curd forms through the action of lactic acid bacteria. The release of carbon dioxide during this late fermentation forms gas bubbles in the semisolid cheese curd, which we recognize as Swiss cheese holes. The propionic acid formed during this fermentation contributes to the characteristic flavor of Swiss cheese.

MIXED ACID FERMENTATION

The **mixed acid fermentation** pathway is so named because of the mixture of end products that are formed (FIG. 4-28). It is carried out by members of the family Enterobacteriaceae, a large family of bacteria that includes *E. coli* and hundreds of other bacterial species. In this metabolic pathway the pyruvate formed during glycolysis is converted to various products, including ethanol, acetate, succinate, formate, molecular hydrogen, and carbon dioxide. The overall proportions of the products vary, depending on the bacterial species, but there are equimolar concentrations of CO_2 and H_2 formed by the mixed acid fermentation pathway. This is because CO_2 is produced exclusively from formate in this pathway by the enzyme formic hydrogen lyase of the pyruvate: formate lyase enzyme system. This reaction produces equal amounts of CO_2 and H_2:

$$HCOOH \rightarrow CO_2 + H_2$$

During formation of these various products, the reduced NADH is reoxidized to NAD^+. The formation of acetate is also accompanied by a substrate-level phosphorylation that forms additional ATP.

The end products of the mixed acid fermentation can be detected by the **Methyl Red (MR) test,** which is based on the color reaction of the pH indicator Methyl Red (FIG. 4-29). This is because the concentrations of acidic products formed in the mixed acid fermentation pathway typically are four times greater than those of neutral products. The Methyl Red test is one of several tests typically employed in identification systems, including miniaturized commercial identification systems used in clinical laboratories for the identification of bacteria, such as *E. coli,* that can cause urinary tract and other infections.

FIG. 4-29 The Methyl Red test is useful for differentiating various bacterial species, including *Enterobacter aerogenes* and *Escherichia coli.* Negative test for *Enterobacter aerogenes* is on left. Positive test result for *Escherichia coli,* indicating production of acid, is on right.

BUTANEDIOL FERMENTATION

The end product of the **butanediol fermentation** pathway is the neutral substance butanediol. During this fermentation pathway, carbon dioxide is released and NADH is reoxidized to NAD^+, but no additional ATP is generated (FIG. 4-30). An intermediate metabolite, acetoin (acetyl methyl carbinol), of the butanediol pathway in a cell can be detected by the **Voges-Proskauer (VP) test** (FIG. 4-31). The VP test classically has been used with the MR test to distinguish between *Enterobacter aerogenes,* which is VP^+ and MR^-, and *E. coli,* which is VP^- and MR^+. Among other reasons, the ability to make this distinction is very important because *E. coli* is used as an indicator of human fecal contamination in processes that assess the safety of water supplies.

Some bacteria, such as members of the genus *Klebsiella,* carry out both the butanediol and mixed acid fermentations. Such bacteria show a positive VP test but a negative MR test because they are producing acetoin and not enough acid to cause the Methyl Red indicator to undergo its color change. The typical ratio of neutral (butanediol and ethanol) products to acidic products (acetate, formate, lactate, and succinate) in an organism carrying out both the butanediol and mixed acid fermentation pathways is 6:1. CO_2 and H_2 are also produced by such organisms, typically in a ratio of about 5:1, since CO_2 is produced at several steps and H_2 is produced only from the decomposition of formate.

BUTYRIC ACID FERMENTATION

Members of the genus *Clostridium* carry out a **butyric acid fermentation** pathway, also known as the **butanol fermentation** pathway. Different *Clostridium* species form various end products via this fermentation pathway, with pyruvate being converted to either acetone and carbon dioxide, isopropanol and carbon dioxide, butyrate, or butanol. Many of these fermentation products are good organic solvents that have com-

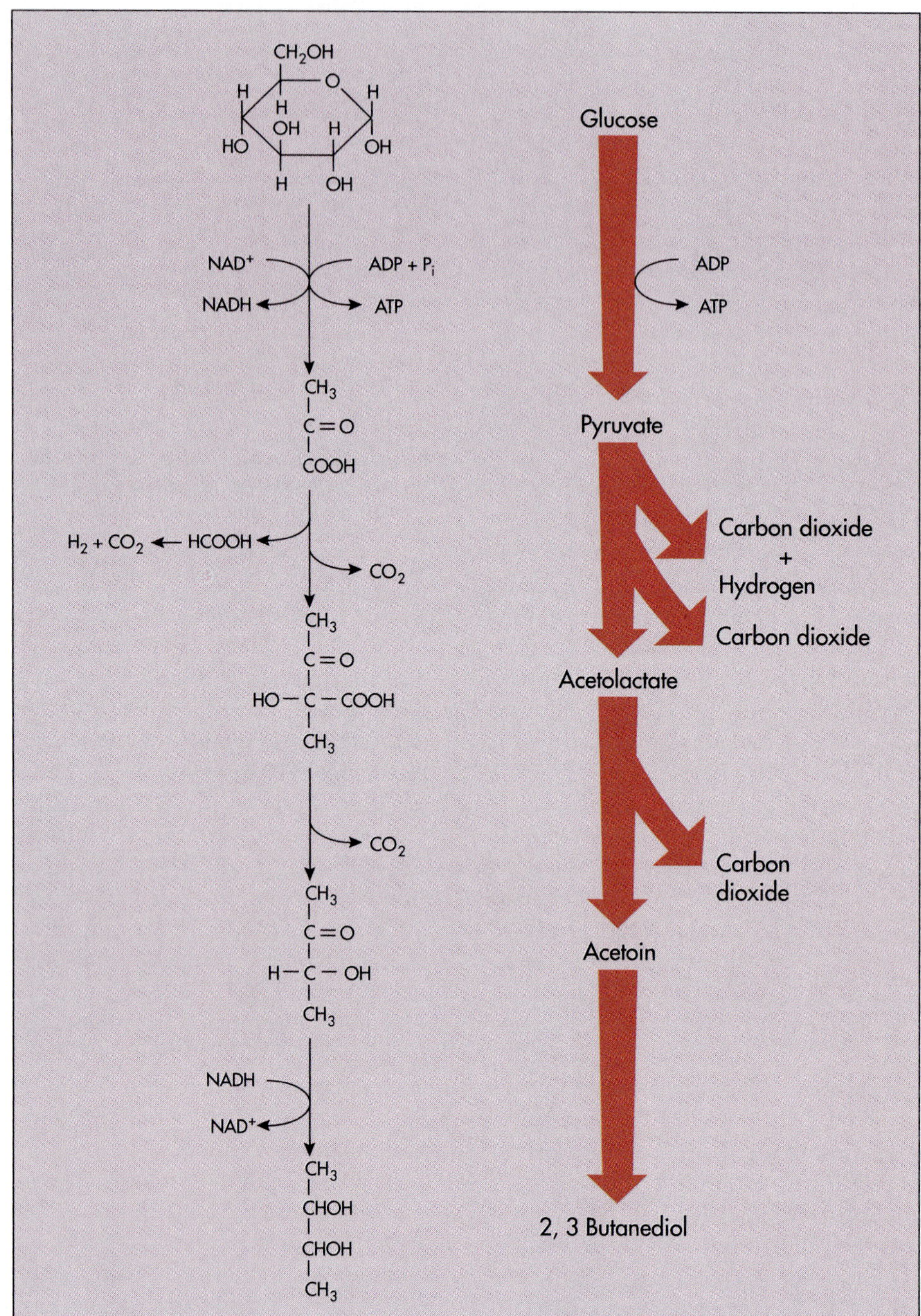

FIG. 4-30 The butanediol fermentation pathway results in the production of the neutral product 2,3 butanediol. The production of acetoin, an intermediary metabolite, is diagnostic of this pathway.

mercial applications, such as the use of acetone for nail polish remover. Today, the choice of using microbial or organic-synthetic means to produce solvents is based on economic factors. When the butanol fermentation pathway was first discovered by Chaim Weizmann, it was particularly important because it allowed Britain to produce acetone for use in the manufacture of munitions during World War I. This discovery in microbiology was instrumental in determining the outcome of the war.

AMINO ACID FERMENTATIONS

In addition to various pathways for the fermentative metabolism of carbohydrates, a number of individual amino acids can serve as energy and carbon sources for many anaerobic microorganisms. Arginine is fermented by *Clostridium, Streptococcus,* and *Mycoplasma* species to ornithine, CO_2, and NH_3 (ammonia) by an arginine dihydrolase pathway. In this pathway, arginine is deaminated to citrulline. Then, citrulline is phosphorylated and split into ornithine and carbamyl

FIG. 4-31 The Voges-Proskauer test that determines the production of acetoin is useful for differentiating various bacterial species, including *Enterobacter aerogenes* and *Escherichia coli.* Negative test result for *Escherichia coli* is on left. Positive test result for *Enterobacter aerogenes* is on right.

phosphate. Carbamyl phosphate contains a high-energy phosphate bond, which can be utilized in a substrate-level phosphorylation to synthesize ATP from ADP. Similarly, fermentation of glycine to acetate by *Peptococcus anaerobius* leads to the formation of acetyl phosphate, which can be utilized in a substrate-level phosphorylation to generate ATP. Other amino acids that can be fermented by various anaerobes, although without the additional synthesis of ATP, are threonine, glutamate, lysine, and aspartate.

Some bacteria, especially the clostridia, metabolize multiple amino acids by a **mixed amino acid fermentation pathway.** This fermentation occurs when there is extensive protein degradation and involves one amino acid serving as an electron donor and another amino acid acting as an electron acceptor in an oxidation-reduction reaction. The coupling of oxidation-reduction reactions between pairs of amino acids is called the **Stickland reaction** (FIG. 4-32). This reaction results in the deamination and decarboxylation of the amino acids. For example, a mixture of alanine and glycine can yield the end products acetate, carbon dioxide, and ammonia. The mixed amino acid fermentation pathway contributes to the pleasant odors

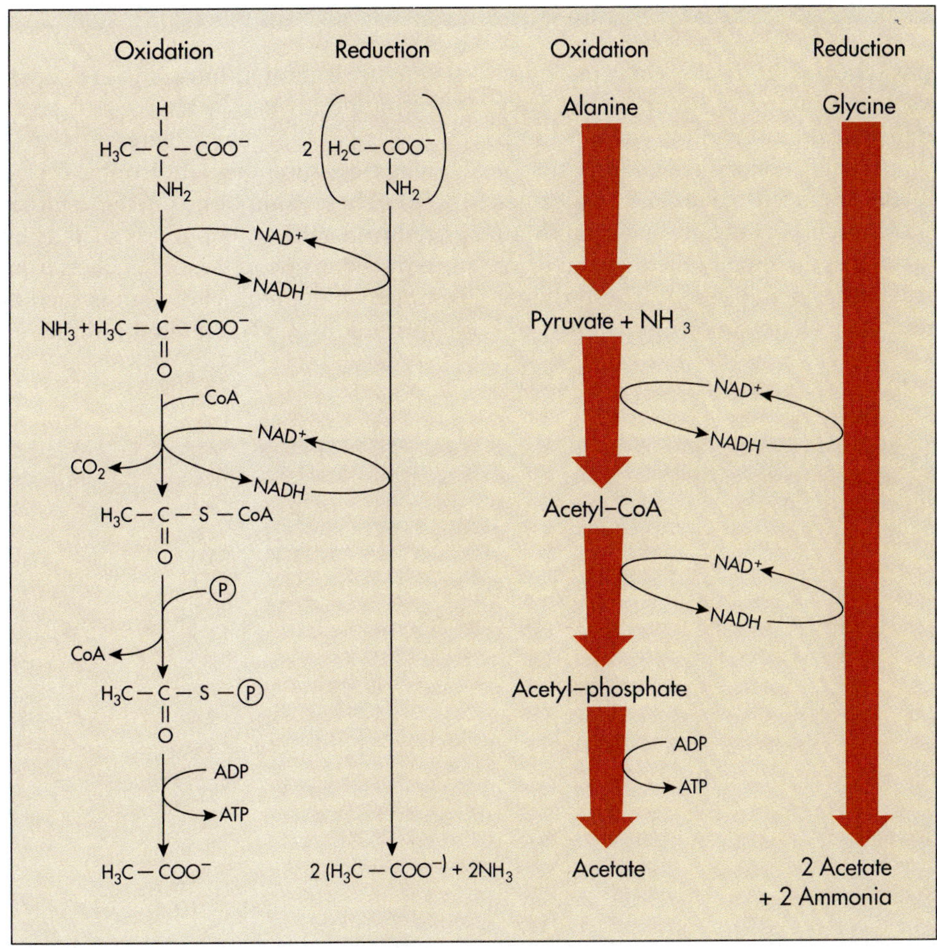

FIG. 4-32 The coupled oxidation-reduction reaction (Stickland reaction) between alanine and glycine in *Clostridium sporogenes* results in the formation of acetate.

of some wines and cheeses but is also partly responsible for the horrible smell of a gangrenous wound.

FERMENTATION OF ACETATE TO METHANE: METHANOGENESIS

Some archaebacteria are **methanogens,** so named because they form methane (CH_4) in a type of metabolism called **methanogenesis.** Some methanogens are chemoautotrophs because they use electrons from molecular hydrogen or formate and reduce inorganic CO_2 to form CH_4 and compounds for cell biomass. Others that produce methane from the fermentation of acetate are chemoorganotrophs. About one third of the methane formed in nature is produced by chemoautotrophic methanogenesis and about two thirds is formed from the fermentation of acetate by chemoorganotrophic methanogens.

The fermentation of acetate involves the reduction of the methyl group to form methane and the oxidation of the carboxyl group to form carbon dioxide:

$$CH_3COO^- + H^+ \rightarrow CH_4 + CO_2$$

This pathway of methane formation begins with the reaction of acetate and coenzyme A to form acetyl-CoA, which requires an input of energy from ATP. A nickel/cobalt-containing carbon monoxide dehydrogenase (CODH) cleaves the acetyl-CoA into coenzyme A, which can be recycled; carbon monoxide (CO), which is oxidized to CO_2; and a methyl group, which is attached to 2-mercaptoethanesulfonic acid (HS-CoM.) The resulting CH_3-S-CoM is subsequently reduced with two electrons from 7-mercaptoheptanoylthreonine phosphate (HS-HTP) to form methane and a disulfide of CoM-S-S-HTP. This disulfide is reduced using electrons that are obtained from the oxidation of CO to CO_2. It is not certain how these methanogens generate energy for growth, especially since the first step of methanogenesis from acetate involves utilization of ATP. However, a fairly high electrochemical potential has been measured across the cytoplasmic membranes of methanogens, and it is quite likely that electron transport and chemiosmotic generation of ATP occurs in these archaebacteria.

4.5 CHEMOAUTOTROPHY (CHEMOLITHOTROPHY)

Chemoautotrophs (chemolithotrophs) carry out respiration by metabolizing inorganic compounds. They couple the oxidation of an inorganic compound with the reduction of a suitable coenzyme. The transfer of electrons from the reduced coenzyme molecules through an electron transport chain then establishes a proton gradient across the membrane that can drive the synthesis of ATP by chemiosmosis. The terminal electron acceptor for chemoautotrophs most frequently is oxygen but some are capable of anaerobic respiration.

Various inorganic compounds can serve as the raw materials for chemoautotrophic metabolism (Table 4-12). These compounds include molecular hydrogen, reduced sulfur compounds such as hydrogen sulfide, reduced iron compounds such as iron sulfide, and nitrogen-containing compounds such as ammonia and nitrite ions. Only a limited number of specific eubac-

TABLE 4-12 Chemolithotrophic Metabolism: Energy Sources and Yields

REACTION	ELECTRON DONOR	ELECTRON ACCEPTOR	$\Delta G^{\circ\prime}$ (KCAL/MOLE)	BACTERIA
$H_2 + \frac{1}{2}O_2 \rightarrow H_2O$	H_2	O_2	−56.6	*Alcaligenes eutrophus*
$NO_2^- + \frac{1}{2}O_2 \rightarrow NO_3^-$	NO_2^-	O_2	−17.4	*Nitrobacter winogradskyi*
$NH_4^+ + 1\frac{1}{2}O_2 \rightarrow NO_2^- + H_2O + 2H^+$	NH_4^+	O_2	−65.0	*Nitrosomonas europaea*
$S^\circ + 1\frac{1}{2}O_2 + H_2O \rightarrow H_2SO_4$	S°	O_2	−118.5	*Thiobacillus denitrificans*
$S_2O_3^{2-} + 2O_2 + H_2O \rightarrow 2SO_4^{2-} + 2H^+$	$S_2O_3^2$	O_2	−223.7	*Sulfolobus acidocaldarius*
$2Fe^{2+} + 2H^+ + \frac{1}{2}O_2 \rightarrow 2Fe^{3+} + H_2O$	Fe^{2+}	O_2	−11.2	*Thiobacillus ferrooxidans*
$CO + O_2 + 2H^+ + 2e^- \rightarrow CO_2 + H_2O$	CO	O_2	—	*Hydrogenomonas carboxydovorans*

teria and archaebacteria can carry out chemoautotrophic metabolism. The metabolism of each is restricted to specific inorganic compounds.

To generate the amount of ATP needed for growth and reproduction, the chemoautotrophic microorganisms must oxidize very large amounts of reduced nitrogen-, sulfur-, or iron-containing compounds. This makes them ecologically important. Their metabolic activities form critical links in biogeochemical cycling reactions, including those that transfer nitrogen and sulfur compounds between the air, water, and soil.

HYDROGEN OXIDATION

Some chemoautotrophic eubacteria, such as *Alcaligenes eutrophus,* produce an enzyme called *hydrogenase.* This is a nickel-containing enzyme that oxidizes molecular hydrogen to form water and the reduced coenzyme NADH (FIG. 4-33). Organisms containing hydrogenase are referred to as hydrogen-oxidizing bacteria. There are two distinct forms of hydrogenase in *A. eutrophus.* A membrane-bound hydrogenase transports protons (H^+) and electrons through a series of membrane-bound carriers, including quinones and cytochromes to O_2. The membrane-bound electron transport chain establishes a proton gradient across the membrane and is used to generate three molecules of ATP per H_2 molecule. A distinct cytoplasmic hydrogenase transfers protons from hydrogen to NAD^+, forming NADH that is needed for its reducing capability in the synthesis of carbon skeleton intermediates. Some hydrogen-oxidizing bacteria only have the membrane-bound hydrogenase and, in these organisms, reducing capability is generated by other mechanisms. Some of these bacteria can use NADH rather than NADPH for biosynthesis and others convert the NADH to NADPH.

Homoacetogenic bacteria, such as *Clostridium aceticum* and *Acetobacterium woodii,* can couple the oxidation of hydrogen to the reduction of carbon dioxide to form acetate. The reduction of CO_2 to acetate in these bacteria occurs via the acetyl-CoA pathway (FIG. 4-34). This pathway involves special coenzymes, including tetrahydrofolate and vitamin B_{12}. Two molecules of CO_2 are combined in this pathway to form acetate. In the final step of this pathway, the conversion of acetyl-CoA to acetate releases sufficient free energy to generate ATP. Additional ATP is made by chemiosmosis driven by the protonmotive force generated from the oxidation of hydrogen.

Many extremely thermophilic archaebacteria (that is, archaebacteria that grow at very high temperatures) can oxidize hydrogen. *Pyrodictium,* which lives in deep sea thermal vent regions, can grow at 110° C. This archaebacterium links the oxidation of hydrogen with the reduction of elemental sulfur. It generates ATP by chemiosmosis, using hydrogen as the electron donor and elemental sulfur as a terminal electron acceptor.

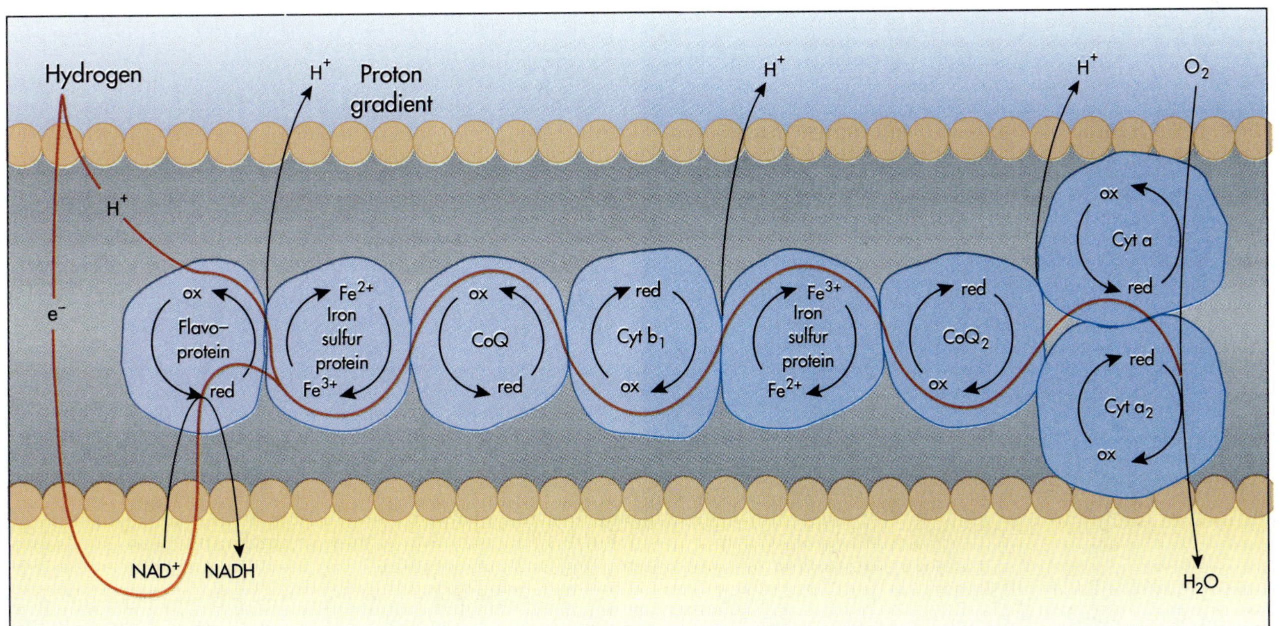

FIG. 4-33 Hydrogenase splits hydrogen into protons and electrons that are transported via a membrane-bound electron transport system. This transport establishes a proton gradient.

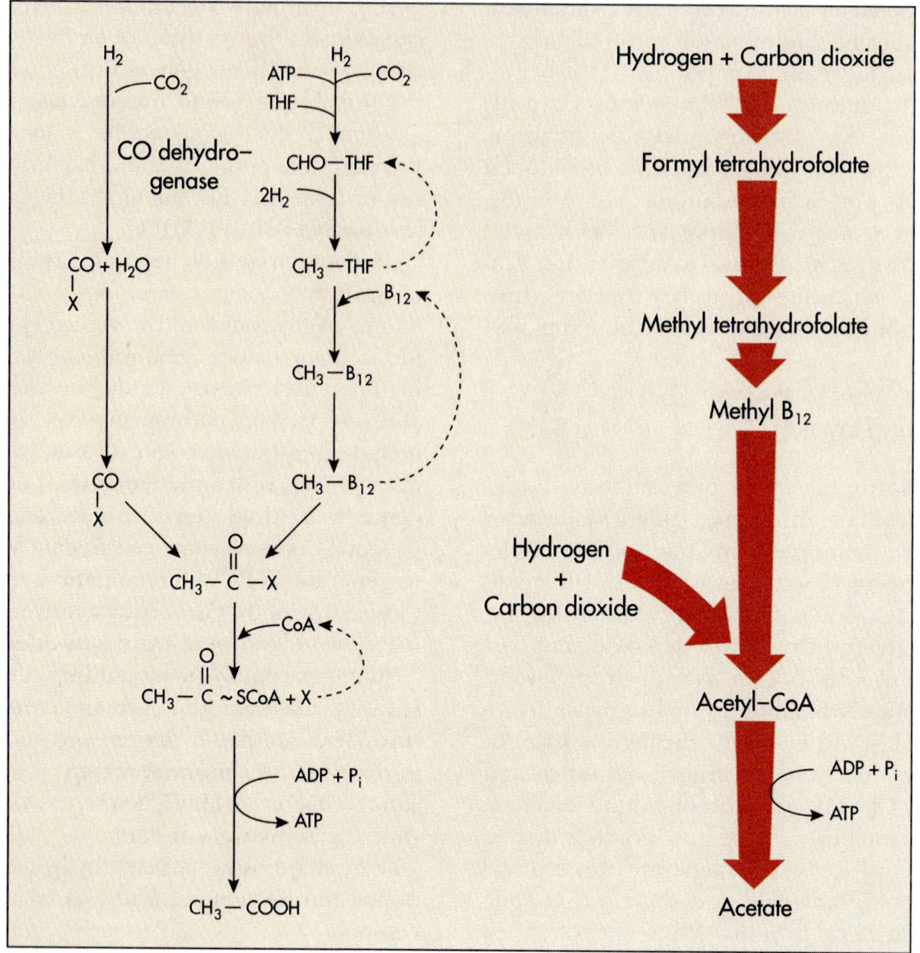

FIG. 4-34 The acetyl-CoA pathway carried out by homoacetogenic bacteria results in the formation of acetate.

AUTOTROPHIC METHANOGENESIS

Some methanogens generate methane during autotrophic metabolism, using electrons from molecular hydrogen to reduce CO_2 to CH_4. These methanogenic archaebacteria may have been among the earliest organisms on earth because they can grow autotrophically on hydrogen and carbon dioxide under anaerobic conditions, similar to those presumed to have prevailed on the early earth.

The methanogens use a specialized anaerobic respiration pathway to convert CO_2 to CH_4 (FIG. 4-35). They are strict anaerobes that are killed on exposure to air. Several cofactors that seem unique to methanogenesis have been identified (Table 4-13). Coenzyme F_{420} accepts two electrons from hydrogen or NADPH

TABLE 4-13 Coenzymes of Methanogenic Bacteria

COMPONENT	TYPE OF MOLECULE	FUNCTION
Coenzyme F_{420}	Flavin-containing coenzyme	Transfers $2H^+$ and $2e^-$
Coenzyme F_{430}	Nickel-containing tetrapyrrole	Involved in terminal step of reduction to methane
Methanofuran	Phenol-glutamate-dicarboxylic acid-furan complex	Binds CO_2 in the initial stage of methanogenesis
Methanopterin	Pterin-containing coenzyme	C-1 carrier for most of the reductive pathway of methanogenesis
Coenzyme M	Mercapto-containing coenzyme	Methyl carrier involved in terminal step of reduction to methane
HS-HTP	7-Mercaptoheptanoylthreonine phosphate	e^- donor involved in terminal step of reduction to methane

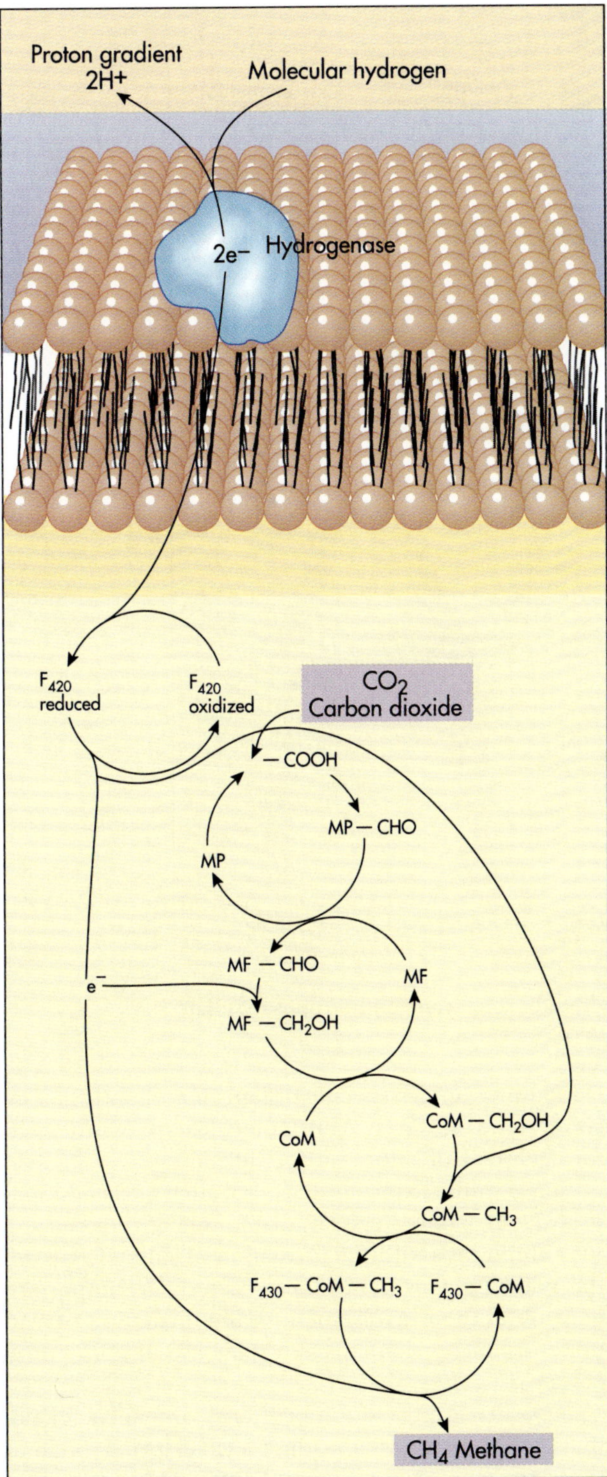

FIG. 4-35 The conversion of CO_2 to CH_4 (methane) is carried out by a specialized group of archaebacteria. This is a strictly anaerobic pathway involving the flow of electrons from a hydrogen donor. Several unique electron carriers are involved in the transfer of electrons in this pathway, including factor 420 (F_{420}), factor 430 (F_{430}), coenzyme M (CoM), methanopterin (MP), and methanofuran (MF). The oxidation of hydrogen, which occurs outside of the cell, produces hydrogen ions and supplies electrons for the reduction of F_{420}, which occurs inside the cell. Because the reduction of F_{420} inside the cell also consumes protons, whereas the oxidation of hydrogen produces protons outside the cell, the net result is the establishment of a proton gradient (protonmotive force) across the membrane.

and its oxidized form has a characteristic blue-green fluorescence at 420 nm, which helps identify an organism as a methanogen.

Methanofuran, the initial acceptor of CO_2, is reduced to a formyl group using electrons from Coenzyme F_{420} in the first step of methanogenesis. The formyl group is passed to methanopterin, which is similar to folic acid and carries the C_1 group in its reduction from formyl through metheneyl to methyl carbon.

The methyl group is transferred to Coenzyme M and further reduced to yield methane with electrons donated from 7-mercaptoheptanoylthreonine phosphate (HS-HTP). Coenzyme M is a 2-mercaptoethanesulfonic acid molecule that is directly involved in the last step of methanogenesis. It carries the methyl group as it is reduced to methane by electrons from the methyl reductase-Coenzyme F_{430} complex. Coenzyme F_{430} is a nickel-containing molecule that absorbs light at 430 nm but, unlike Coenzyme F_{420}, does not fluoresce. Coenzyme F_{430} works in conjunction with HS-HTP. In the terminal step of methanogenesis, HS-HTP donates an electron to the methyl group, which is carried by Coenzyme M, thus reducing methyl to methane and forming an oxidized disulfide complex between HS-HTP and Coenzyme M. This latter complex is then reduced by H_2 back to the free mercapto forms of both HS-HTP and Coenzyme M. During this last step, as the methyl group is reduced to methane, a proton is pumped to the outside of the membrane to establish a protonmotive force. This protonmotive force drives the synthesis of ATP via a membrane-bound ATPase.

The conversion of carbon dioxide to methane, using molecular hydrogen as the electron donor, is an exergonic reaction with a $\Delta G°$ of −31 kcal/mole and an actual ΔG under cellular concentrations of about −15 kcal/mole. About one molecule of ATP can be synthesized for every molecule of CO_2 converted to CH_4. During the conversion of CO_2 to CH_4, NADPH is also generated. This NADPH is used for the incorporation of CO_2 into the macromolecules of the cell. Approximately 90% to 95% of the CO_2 used by methanogens is converted to CH_4, presumably supporting ATP and NADPH synthesis, and the remainder is incorporated into cellular carbon.

SULFUR AND IRON OXIDATION

Sulfur-oxidizing Bacteria

Some bacteria, such as *Thiobacillus* and *Sulfolobus,* can grow using reduced sulfur compounds as their source of energy (FIG. 4-36). The reduced sulfur compounds most commonly oxidized by chemoautotrophs are hydrogen sulfide, elemental sulfur, and thiosulfate. When hydrogen sulfide is used, elemental sulfur is often deposited, with some bacteria producing sulfur

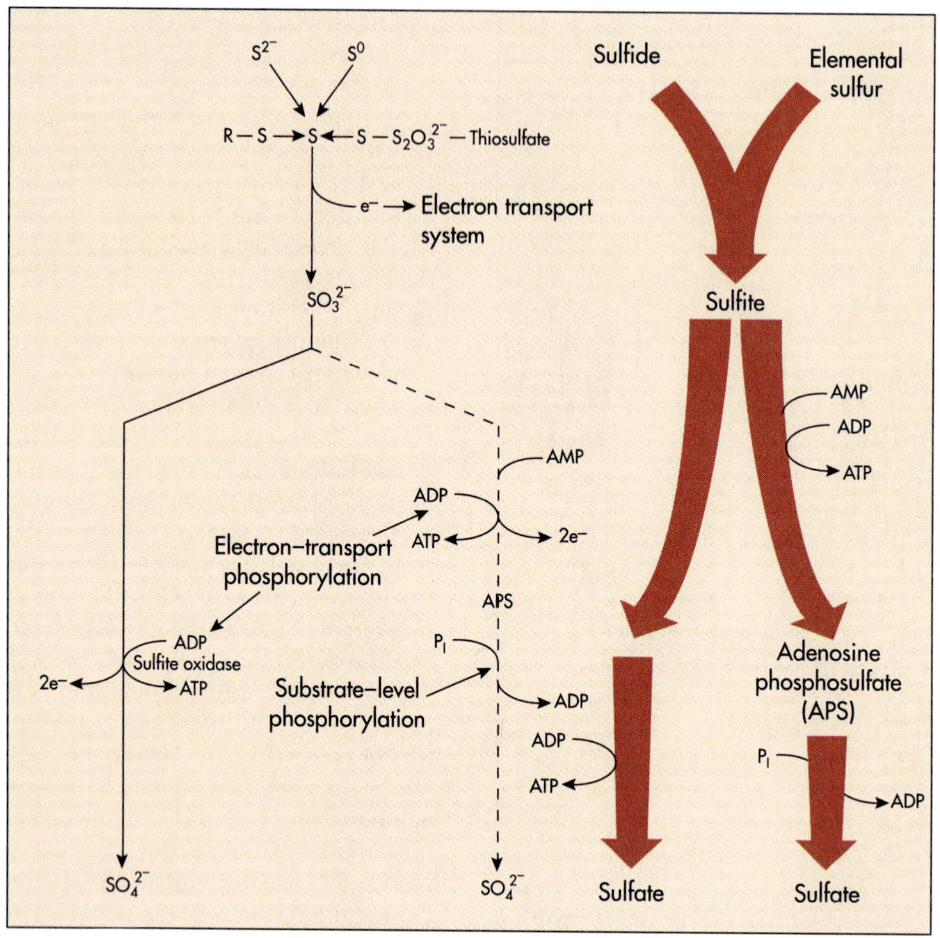

FIG. 4-36 Sulfides and elemental sulfur are oxidized by some chemolithotrophs to sulfate.

granules within their cells and others depositing elemental sulfur outside of the cells.

The oxidation of reduced sulfur compounds does not produce a sufficient change in reduction potential to drive the reduction of NAD^+ to NADH. The electrons derived from the oxidation of reduced sulfur compounds therefore enter the electron transfer chain at an intermediate point. They enter via one of the cytochrome carriers that are at a lower energy level than NADH. Some of the electrons flow toward the terminal electron acceptor, oxygen, establishing a proton gradient across the membrane that can drive the synthesis of ATP. Other electrons flow in the reverse direction to produce reduced coenzymes needed in biosynthesis.

Some thiobacilli perform an additional substrate-level phosphorylation to synthesize ATP. In this process, sulfite combines with adenosine monophosphate (AMP) to form adenosine phosphosulfate. Adenosine phosphosulfate then reacts with inorganic phosphate to form ADP and sulfate. ATP is then formed by the reaction:

$$\text{ADP} + \text{ADP} \rightleftarrows \text{ATP} + \text{AMP}$$

Depending on the specific organism and pathways involved, two or three ATP molecules are synthesized for each pair of sulfite units oxidized.

Some sulfur-oxidizing bacteria, such as *Thiobacillus thiooxidans,* can oxidize large amounts of reduced sulfur compounds with the formation of sulfate. The sulfur-oxidizing activities of these bacteria are important because of their involvement in the formation of acid mine drainage problems and their use in mineral recovery processes.

Sulfolobus is an acidophilic thermoarchaebacterium that lives in sulfur-rich acidic thermal springs such as those in Yellowstone National Park. This archaebacterium grows at temperatures up to 90° C and pH values as low as 1. It can oxidize hydrogen sulfide or elemental sulfur to form sulfuric acid using molecular oxygen as the terminal electron acceptor.

The chemoautotrophic activities of sulfur-oxidizing bacteria have received considerable attention as a result of the discovery that a highly productive submarine area off the Galapagos Islands is supported by the productivity of chemoautotrophs growing on reduced sulfur released from thermal vents in the ocean floor.

The finding of an ecosystem driven by chemoautotrophic metabolism is unique; most ecosystems depend on the primary productivity of photoautotrophs: higher plants, algae, or photosynthetic bacteria.

Iron-oxidizing Bacteria

Thiobacillus ferrooxidans oxidizes both reduced sulfur and reduced iron for generating ATP. It often is found in acid mine drainage streams, where it has an available source of reduced sulfur and reduced iron that it can utilize for the chemolithotrophic generation of ATP. The reduction potential of ferric to ferrous (Fe^{3+}/Fe^{2+}) iron is so high (+0.77 volts) that it cannot be used to reduce NAD^+ or other electron transport components. Electrons from Fe^{2+} pass to an iron-sulfur protein that uses cytochrome *c* as an electron acceptor; electrons are subsequently transported to the cytochrome a_1–cytochrome *o* complex, which donates electrons to molecular oxygen to form water. The protons for the reduction of molecular oxygen come from the cytoplasm. *T. ferrooxidans* generates ATP by using the acid environment (high H^+ concentration) in which it lives to generate its protonmotive force. The protons enter the cell as a result of the hydrogen ion gradient between the acidic environment and the less acidic interior of the cell, passing through ATPase and generating ATP as they do so. This is different from other bacteria where the proton gradient must be established by the metabolic extrusion of protons across the membrane.

AMMONIUM AND NITRITE OXIDATION—NITRIFICATION

Some eubacteria oxidize either ammonia or nitrite ions to generate ATP by chemiosmosis. These bacteria are called **nitrifying bacteria** (FIG. 4-37).

Some nitrifying bacteria, such as *Nitrosomonas,* oxidize ammonia to nitrite. The $\Delta G°$ for this reaction is −65 kcal/mole. This reaction occurs best at high pH because the initial enzyme uses ammonia rather than ammonium ions. The first product of ammonia oxidation is hydroxylamine. The formation of this intermediate does not generate ATP and in fact consumes NADH. Hydroxylamine is oxidized to nitrite. This reaction initiates an electron transport chain that establishes a protonmotive force across the membrane. Oxygen is the terminal acceptor for the electrons and ATP is produced by chemiosmosis.

Other nitrifyers, such as *Nitrobacter,* oxidize nitrite to nitrate. The $\Delta G°$ for this reaction is −18 kcal/mole. The oxidation of nitrite to nitrate is accomplished by nitrite oxidase, which transfers electrons from the electron donor to cytochromes within the membrane-bound electron transport system, and then on to O_2. This generates a protonmotive force across the membrane that generates ATP by chemiosmosis.

These forms of ammonium and nitrite oxidation yield only a rather limited amount of ATP, because some of the electrons are used to generate reduced coenzymes for biosynthesis rather than a proton gra-

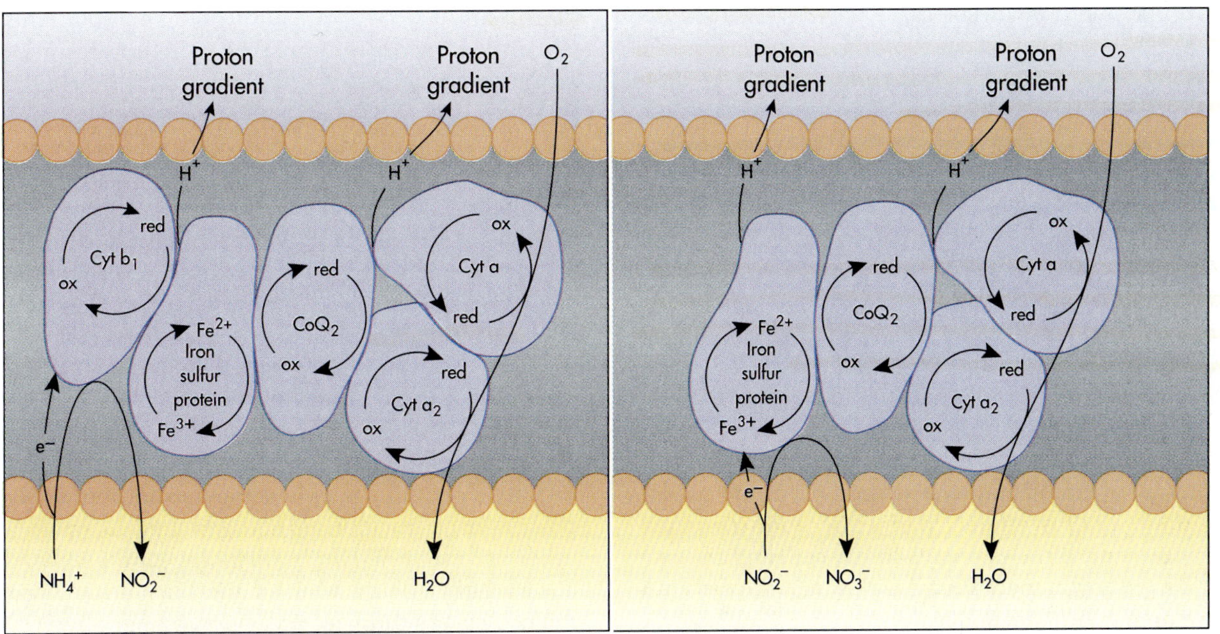

FIG. 4-37 Nitrifying bacteria are chemolithotrophs that oxidize inorganic nitrogen compounds to generate ATP. Some, such as *Nitrosomonas,* oxidize ammonium ions (NH_4^+) to nitrite ions (NO_2^-) *(left);* others, such as *Nitrobacter,* oxidize nitrite ions to nitrate ions (NO_3^-) *(right).*

dient for chemiosmotic ATP production. It appears that only one ATP molecule is generated for each ammonium ion or nitrite ion oxidized.

Because the chemoautotrophic oxidation of reduced nitrogen compounds yields relatively little energy, chemoautotrophic bacteria carry out extensive transformation of nitrogen compounds in soil and water to generate the ATP they require. The activities of these bacteria are important in soil because the alteration of the oxidation state of the nitrogen-containing compounds radically changes their mobility in the soil column. Nitrifying bacteria have a marked influence on soil fertility, because positively charged ammonium ions bind to negatively charged soil clay particles, but negatively charged nitrite and nitrate ions do not bind and so are leached from soils by rainwater.

4.6 PHOTOAUTOTROPHY

Microorganisms with a **photoautotrophic metabolism** obtain their energy supplies directly from the energy of the sun, which they use to drive the production of ATP. The conversion of light energy from the sun into chemical energy within ATP occurs by a process known as **photophosphorylation.** This process is initiated when light energy excites a photoreactive molecule, a pigment molecule able to absorb particular wavelengths of sunlight. This absorption of the sun's energy causes release of an electron from the photoreactive pigment molecule. The electron is then transferred through a series of membrane-bound carriers, which are collectively known as a **photosystem.** Electron transfer by the photosystem drives the formation of a proton gradient across the membrane, which in turn serves to drive the formation of ATP by chemiosmosis.

Algae and cyanobacteria (formerly known as blue-green algae) have two photosystems. These photoautotrophic microorganisms carry out **oxygenic photosynthesis,** meaning that they produce oxygen in addition to ATP and reduced coenzymes as a result of their photoautotrophic metabolism. During oxygenic photosynthesis, H_2O is split to serve as a source of electrons needed in reduction reactions and oxygen is liberated as a product.

Other photoautotrophic eubacteria carry out **anoxygenic photosynthesis** in which ATP is produced but oxygen is not. They do not use H_2O as an electron donor for generating reducing power but use alternate electron donors such as H_2 or H_2S. These anaerobic photoautotrophic eubacteria have only one photosystem. The differences between the oxygenic photosynthetic algae and cyanobacteria and the anoxygenic photoautotrophic eubacteria lie in the nature of their photosynthetic pigments, the structural arrangement of the pigments in the cell, and the oxidation-reduction mechanisms with which the cells balance their biochemical reactions.

ABSORPTION OF LIGHT ENERGY

Photoautotrophic microorganisms have pigment molecules, including chlorophylls or bacteriochlorophylls, associated with their specialized photosynthetic membranes (Table 4-14, p. 162). These pigment molecules trap the light energy to initiate the process that results in the conversion of some of that energy into chemical energy. The general strategy of light energy capture involves the initial capture of the light by light-harvesting "antennae" pigments, which then transfer the photons of light to a "photochemical reaction center" (which is just a particular pigment molecule) where the process of electron flow begins. Ultimately, this electron flow results in the chemiosmotic synthesis of ATP.

Pigments of various colors permit different photoautotrophic microorganisms to trap light energy of different wavelengths. These pigments include red, orange, and yellow carotenoids (molecules that have a cyclic ring with a side chain of alternating single and double carbon-carbon bonds) and green chlorophylls (molecules with porphyrin rings containing magnesium [FIG. 4-38]). Photoautotrophic microorganisms are often stratified within lakes, with the stratification pattern determined by the particular wavelengths of light that each type of microorganism can absorb. The anoxygenic photoautotrophic eubacteria, such as the purple sulfur bacteria, absorb light of longer wavelengths and live well below the water's surface; algae, cyanobacteria and prochlorobacteria absorb light of shorter wavelengths and live nearer the surface.

Cyanobacteria, prochlorobacteria, and algae possess chlorophyll *a* as the predominant reaction center pigment and chlorophylls, carotenoids, or phycobiliproteins and other accessory molecules as antenna pigments. The prochlorobacteria synthesize chlorophyll *b* in addition to the chlorophyll *a*.

The green and purple photoautotrophic bacteria possess bacteriochlorophylls, generally *a* or *b,* and other accessory pigments, including carotenoids, that absorb light energy. Most of the bacteriochlorophyll molecules function as accessory or light-harvesting antenna pigments that absorb light and pass photons to reaction center pigments. Carotenoids also function as accessory antenna pigments. Some of the green photoautotrophic bacteria produce vesicles called **chlorosomes** that are filled with antenna pig-

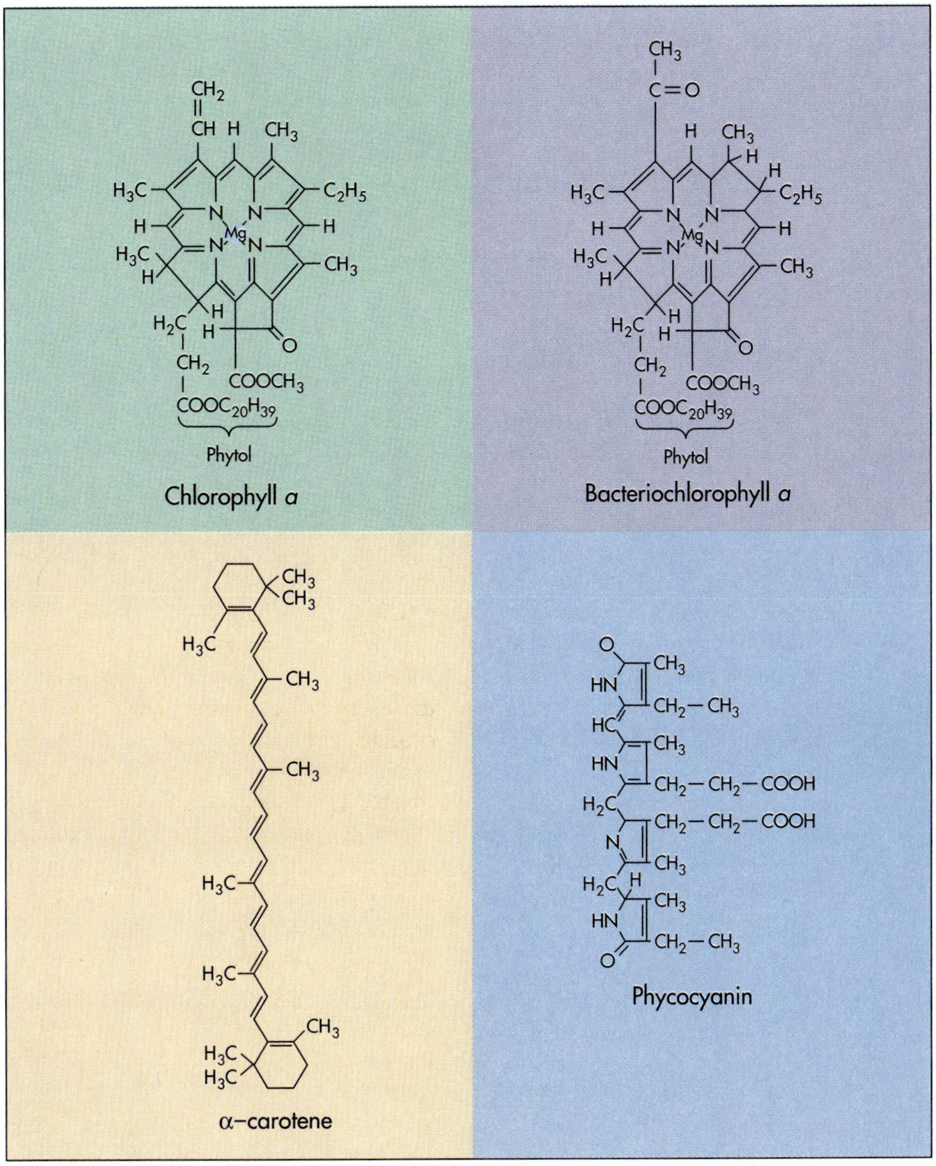

FIG. 4-38 Various chlorophylls and auxiliary pigments are involved in the capture of light energy and its conversion to ATP. The various photosynthetic pigments absorb light energy of differing wavelengths. Chlorophyll *a* is the primary photosynthetic pigment in cyanobacteria and algae. Various bacteriochlorophylls, such as bacteriochlorophyll *a*, shown here, are the primary photosynthetic pigments in noncyanobacterial photosynthetic bacteria. Carotenoids, such as the α-carotene shown here, are widely found accessory pigments in many photosynthetic microorganisms. These molecules, which have long hydrocarbon chains with repeating double bonds and are typically yellow in color, are able to absorb light energy, usually blue light, and transfer it to chlorophyll molecules. Cyanobacteria and some algae contain phycobiliproteins, such as phycoerythrin, (which has a red color) and phycocyanin (which has a blue color). The structure shown here is part of the phycocyanin.

TABLE 4-14 Characteristics of Photoautotrophic Microorganisms

GROUP AND EXAMPLES	DESCRIPTION	BACTERIOCHLOROPHYLLS (BCHL) OR CHLOROPHYLLS (CHL) AND CAROTENOIDS	PHOTOSYNTHETIC MEMBRANES
Purple sulfur bacteria (Chromatiaceae) *Chromatium, Ectothiorhodospira*	Gram-negative anoxygenic eubacteria that grow only in the absence of air; depend on sulfide as an electron donor for generating reduced coenzymes; purple-red to red-brown in color	Bchl *a* or Bchl *b*, Lycopenol, Spirilloxanthin, Okenone	Vesicles, tubules, or lamellae that are continuous with the cytoplasmic membrane
Purple nonsulfur bacteria (Rhodospirillaceae) *Rhodospirillum, Rhodopseudomonas, Rhodobacter*	Gram-negative anoxygenic eubacteria; can utilize sulfide only at very low concentrations, otherwise use organic acids as electron donors; purple-red in color	Bchl *a* or Bchl *b*, Spheroidene, Spirilloxanthin, Lycopenol	Vesicles, tubules, or lamellae that are continuous with the cytoplasmic membrane
Green sulfur bacteria (Chlorobiaceae) *Chlorobium* *Pelodictyon*	Gram-negative anoxygenic eubacteria that grow only in the absence of air; depend on sulfide or thiosulfide as an electron donor to generate reduced coenzymes; fix carbon dioxide but grow better on simple organic acids, such as acetate; typically form the lowest layer of photoautotrophs growing in a stratified lake; green to brown in color	Bchl *c*, Bchl *d*, or Bchl *e*; some Bchl *a*, Chlorobactene	Photosynthetic apparatus in cytoplasmic membrane; light harvesting pigments in chlorosomes
Green nonsulfur (Chloroflexaceae) *Chloroflexus* *Chloronema*	Gram-negative anoxygenic eubacteria that flex and glide and usually occur as a golden mat under a layer of cyanobacteria; typically found in hot springs; capable of photoheterotrophic growth using light energy to generate ATP and organic compounds to generate reduced coenzymes and cellular macromolecules; green to golden in color	Bchl *a* and Bchl *c* or Bchl *d*, β-Carotene, γ-Carotene	Photosynthetic apparatus in cytoplasmic membrane only
Heliobacteria, Heliobacterium, Heliobacillus	Gram-positive anoxygenic eubacteria that are relatively tolerant of air; green-golden in color	Bchl *g* Neurosporene	Photosynthetic apparatus in cytoplasmic membrane only
Cyanobacteria *Anabaena, Nostoc*	Oxygenic photosynthetic eubacteria	Chl *a* phycobiliproteins	Thylakoid membranes
Prochlorobacteria *Prochloron*	Oxygenic photosynthetic eubacteria	Chl *a* and Chl *b* phycobiliproteins, β-carotene	Thylakoid membranes
Algae	Oxygenic photosynthetic eukaryotes; green, golden, red, or brown	Chl *a*, Chl *b*, Chl *c* or Chl *d* β-Carotene, Phycoerythrin Phycocyanin, Xanthophylls, Fucoxanthin	Thylakoid membranes of chloroplasts

ments: bacteriochlorophylls *c, d,* or *e,* bacteriochlorophyll *a,* and carotenoids. Chlorosomes serve as light-harvesting complexes in addition to the photosynthetic pigments that are found in the cytoplasmic membrane.

The reaction center bacteriochlorophylls and chlorophylls are directly involved in the photochemical oxidation-reduction reactions of photosynthesis. These bacteriochlorophylls and chlorophylls emit electrons when they absorb light energy. The primary photoreaction center in the purple bacteria is bacteriochlorophyll P_{870}; in the green bacteria, it is bacteriochlorophyll P_{840}; and in the heliobacteria, it is bacteriochlorophyll P_{798}. The cyanobacteria and algae have two photoreaction centers, one with chlorophyll P_{680} and the other with chlorophyll P_{700}. The subscript numbers refer to the wavelengths at which the particular bacteriochlorophyll or chlorophyll molecules maximally absorb light.

The electrons emitted by the varying bacteriochlorophylls or chlorophylls have differing energy levels. All have sufficient energy to generate a protonmotive force to drive the formation of ATP. Most have adequate energy to also drive the direct reduction of $NADP^+$ to NADPH. However, the electrons released by bacteriochlorophyll P_{870} of the purple photoautotrophic bacteria do not directly lead to the formation of NADPH. Additional energy input from the protonmotive force by reverse electron flow is required to drive the formation of NADPH in the purple photoautotrophic bacteria.

A few nonphotosynthetic, heterotrophic eubacteria also possess bacteriochlorophylls. *Erythrobacter longus* and *Protomonas* species contain bacteriochlorophylls that stimulate their aerobic growth in the light. The function of bacteriochlorophylls and its evolutionary significance in these species is unclear.

OXYGENIC PHOTOSYNTHESIS

The cyanobacteria, prochlorobacteria, and the algae—like green plants—have two photosystems that are involved in the generation of ATP and NADPH. Each photosystem has its own photoreaction center. Photosystem I has a reaction center with chlorophyll *a* P_{700}; photosystem II has a reaction center composed of a modified chlorophyll *a* P_{680}. Photosystems I and II are normally linked into a unified pathway, the **Z pathway of oxidative photophosphorylation,** that generates ATP and reduced coenzyme for biosynthesis

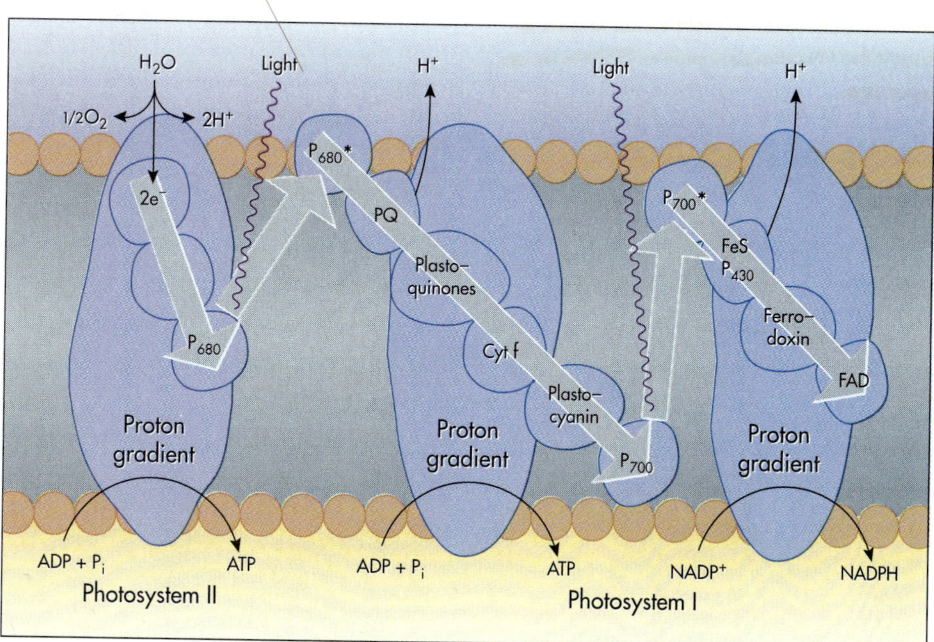

FIG. 4-39 The Z pathway of oxidative photophosphorylation combines two separate photosystems into a unified pathway. Two separate photoactivation steps (photosystems) are needed to complete this pathway. These are the excitation of P_{680} to P_{680}* and the excitation of P_{700} to P_{700}*. The P_{680} has a sufficiently positive reduction potential to use H_2O as an electron donor. The resulting P_{680}* is at a considerably more negative reduction potential, such that the resulting electrons can "fall down" a potential gradient in which protons are translocated across the membrane. The electrons are passed to the P_{700} complex, which when excited is at a potential more negative than that of the $NADP^+$/NADPH redox pair and is thereby capable of reducing $NADP^+$ to NADPH. The pathway is called the *Z pathway* because when these reactions are plotted as a function of reduction potential the resulting figure resembles a Z.

(FIG. 4-39). The operation of the Z pathway requires two separate photoacts, that is, the absorption of light energy at two different photo-activation centers.

In photosystem II, which is a **noncyclic photophosphorylation pathway,** electrons are transferred in one direction (unidirectionally) through a series of membrane-bound electron carriers. The electron flow is initiated when chlorophyll *a* P_{680} absorbs light energy, causing an energetically excited state that results in the release of an electron. The P_{680} chlorophyll becomes oxidized as a result of the electron release. This oxidation reaction is balanced by the splitting of water to form oxygen, hydrogen ions, and the electrons that are donated to the oxidized P_{680} chlorophyll to reduce it back to its original state. Because oxygen is produced, the process is called **oxygenic photosynthesis.**

Electrons from photosystem II are transferred through a series of membrane-bound carriers to the P_{700} chlorophyll reaction center molecule of photosystem I. The overall process that transfers an electron from an excited P_{680} chlorophyll molecule of photosystem II to the P_{700} chlorophyll molecule of photosystem I establishes a sufficient proton gradient across the membrane to synthesize one molecule of ATP. The electron transport chain then continues when a molecule of P_{700} absorbs light energy, initiating the electron transfer sequence of photosystem I. Each electron that is transferred from photosystem II balances an electron ejected from the excited P_{700} molecule of photosystem I. The electrons transferred through photosystem I are normally eventually used to reduce the coenzyme $NADP^+$ to NADPH, providing an essential source of reducing power for biosynthetic metabolic reactions.

The movement of electrons through the entire Z pathway is normally noncyclic, with a unidirectional electron flow from the electron donor H_2O to the electron acceptor $NADP^+$ but electrons can also flow cyclically through photosystem I. When this occurs, reduced coenzyme NADPH is not generated but ATP is synthesized. At low light intensities, many cyanobacteria can carry out non-oxygen-evolving photosynthesis, during which photosystem I follows this cyclic photophosphorylation pathway. No oxygen is generated because photosystem II is inoperative and therefore not splitting water to generate oxygen. When only photosystem I is active, the cyanobacteria derive their reducing power from the oxidation of hydrogen sulfide, which is coupled with coenzyme reduction. When cyanobacteria utilize hydrogen sulfide as a reducing agent in this process, they form elemental sulfur granules that are deposited outside of the cells.

ANOXYGENIC PHOTOSYNTHESIS

In **anoxygenic photosynthesis,** light energy is captured and used to generate ATP but oxygen is not produced. In the anaerobic green and purple photosynthetic bacteria and the heliobacteria, there is only one photosystem, known as **photosystem I** or **cyclic oxidative photophosphorylation** (FIG. 4-40). An electron is initially removed from a bacteriochlorophyll molecule as a result of light excitation—thus oxidizing it—and ultimately returns to that molecule to reduce it. The exci-

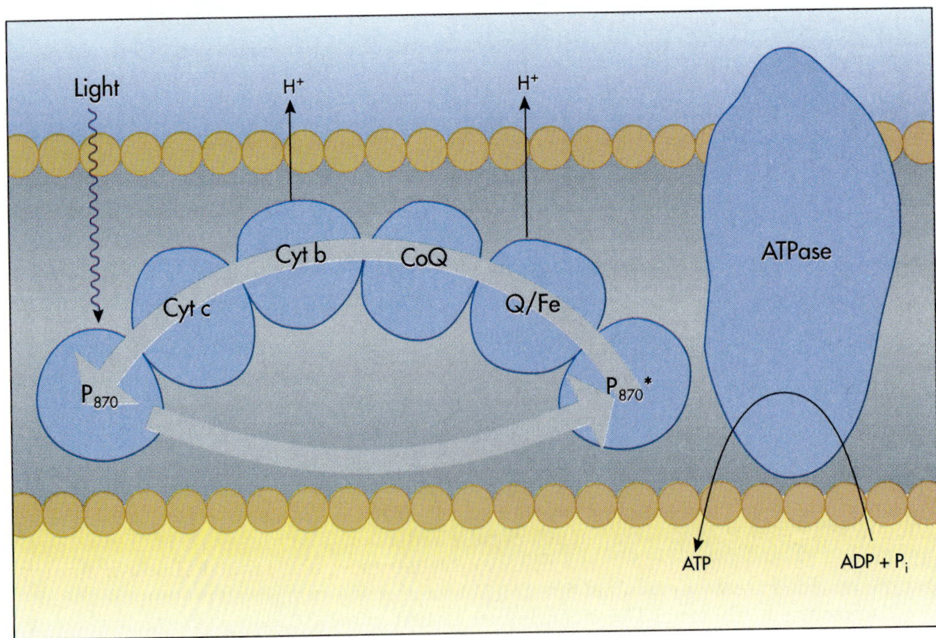

FIG. 4-40 Cyclic oxidative photophosphorylation of anaerobic photosynthetic bacteria uses P_{870}. This pathway generates the proton gradient needed to drive the formation of ATP and does not produce reduced coenzyme.

BOX 4-2

ATP Generation by the Purple Membrane of *Halobacterium*

Halobacterium is an archaebacterium that can generate ATP by respiration using an organic substrate and light energy (see FIG.). In the presence of oxygen, halobacteria use aerobic respiration to generate ATP, including oxidative phosphorylation for chemiosmotic ATP synthesis. The mediators of the electron transport chain in this process are located in a portion of the cytoplasmic membrane that is red in color and hence is called the *red membrane.*

In the absence of oxygen, these bacteria turn to a form of oxidative photophosphorylation for synthesizing ATP. Light energy is converted to chemical energy by a mechanism different from the ones already discussed for photoautotrophic microorganisms. This alternate pathway is based on a purple membrane portion of the cytoplasmic membrane that contains bacteriorhodopsin, a protein that has a chemical structure similar to that of the rhodopsin pigment of the human eye. When illuminated by light, bacteriorhodopsin pumps protons to the outside of the membrane, establishing a proton gradient across the membrane. The counterflow of protons drives the synthesis of ATP by chemiosmosis. The ATPase enzyme used for converting ADP + P_i to ATP is contained in a separate red membrane fraction so that the same ATP-synthesizing system used for oxidative photophosphorylation is used for oxidative phosphorylation. The halobacterial membrane system for using light energy to establish a proton gradient that can drive the synthesis of ATP provides firm evidence for the essential role of chemiosmosis in the synthesis of ATP.

Establishing the role of the purple membrane in light-coupled ATP synthesis was accomplished largely through the work of Walter Stoeckenius and his co-workers. In studying *Halobacterium* they observed that the medium around suspensions of the bacteria became acidic when the suspensions were exposed to light. They also found that exposure of the intact cells to light slowed their respiration. Because they were aware of Peter Mitchell's chemiosmotic hypothesis, they postulated that in the intact cell the purple membrane acts as a proton pump, and that under light illumination, protons move from the inner side of the cytoplasmic membrane to the outer side and on into the medium. To show that light exposure was coupled with ATP generation, they suspended the bacteria in the dark in a salt solution without nutrients and bubbled nitrogen through the medium. Under these conditions, the intracellular ATP concentration decreased to about 30% of its original level because the cells could not perform either aerobic respiration or light-coupled ATP generation. Adding oxygen in the dark led to reestablishment of the original ATP level, as did illuminating the cells in the absence of oxygen. This indicated that both aerobic respiration and light-coupled photophosphorylation could be used by *Halobacterium* to form ATP. Examining the effect of the wavelength of light revealed that only light of wavelengths absorbed by the purple membrane was effective in powering ATP synthesis.

These observations were consistent with the hypothesis that respiration and light generate an electrochemical

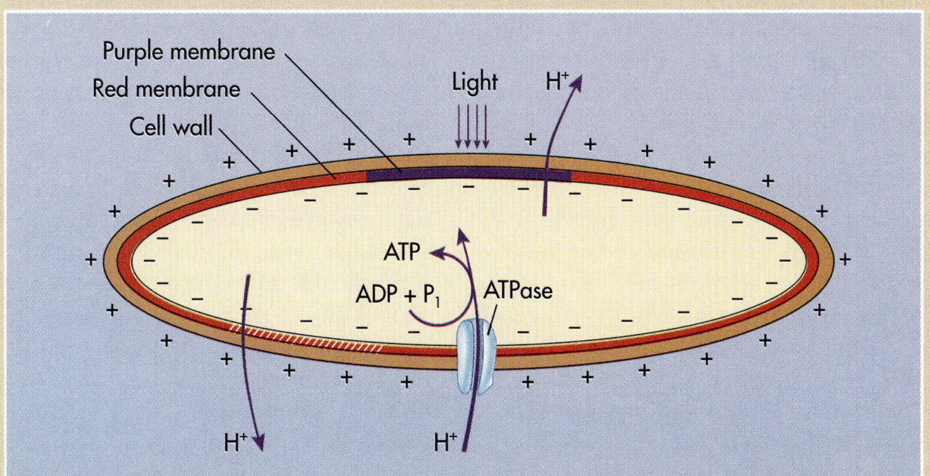

Regions of the cytoplasmic membrane of *Halobacterium* contain bacteriorhodopsin and have a purple color. The purple membrane is involved with light-coupled generation of ATP. A larger portion of the cytoplasmic membrane is red in color and contains ATPase and mediators of the respiratory electron transport chain *(hatched portion of red membrane).* When illuminated with light or supplied with an organic substrate in the presence of oxygen, protons are pumped across the cytoplasmic membrane, establishing an electrochemical and hydrogen ion gradient across the membrane. The protonmotive force and backflow of protons through the enzyme ATPase result in the formation of ATP.

Continued.

BOX 4-2—CONT'D

proton gradient across the cytoplasmic membrane and that the gradient drives the synthesis of ATP by membrane ATPase. To verify this hypothesis, Stoeckenius and co-workers used inhibitors of membrane ATPase, showing that they prevented the accumulation of ATP driven by light or respiration. They also used electron transport uncouplers, substances that permit electron transport to proceed but make the membrane very permeable to protons, preventing the generation of an electrochemical gradient. The uncouplers inhibited ATP accumulation driven by light or respiration and blocked acidification of the surrounding medium. Finally, they used substances that interfere specifically with the respiratory electron transport chain, all of which blocked respiratory, but not light-driven, ATP formation.

To establish definitively that bacteriorhodopsin in the purple membrane is responsible for the light-coupled protonmotive force, Stoeckenius and his co-workers made artificial vesicles from the halobacterial membrane. When the vesicles, which were free of substances from the cytoplasm of the archaebacterial cell, were exposed to light, an electrochemical proton gradient formed across the membrane. This finding excluded the possibility that enzyme systems in the cell cytoplasm were responsible for the formation of the proton gradient. Working with Efraim Racker, Stoeckenius next removed the red portion of the cytoplasmic membrane and replaced it with membrane derived from artificial phospholipid vesicles. This left the bacteriorhodopsin-containing purple membrane as the only source of protein. When the resulting preparation was exposed to light the medium became acidic, indicating that protons were being pumped across the membrane. Because bacteriorhodopsin was the only protein in these preparations, and because it worked in vesicles composed of various lipids, there was no longer any doubt that bacteriorhodopsin converts light energy into the electrochemical energy stored within a proton gradient across the cell membrane. This established the unusual photochemical mechanism of ATP generation by *Halobacterium.*

tation of the bacteriochlorophyll by absorbtion of light energy causes it to emit an electron. When the electron is emitted from the bacteriochlorophyll it is transported to a primary electron acceptor and then passes along an electron transport chain. A series of carriers takes it back to reduce the bacteriochlorophyll molecule from which it came. Thus there is no need for an external donor or acceptor of electrons. The bacteriochlorophyll molecule acts as an internal electron donor and acceptor mediating the cyclic flow of electrons around the photosystem. In essence, the energy of light drives electrons around the cycle repeatedly, with some of the energy being used to drive the synthesis of ATP. This ATP can be made because during the passage of electrons through the carriers of photosystem I, four protons are picked up from the cytoplasm of the cell, two of them being used to reduce an oxidized carrier, known as the secondary quinone carrier, and two being extruded to the outside of the membrane. This causes a proton gradient and associated protonmotive force to be set up, which is used to generate ATP via chemiosmosis through membrane bound ATPase (FIG. 4-41).

In the purple bacteria, photons (light energy) are initially absorbed by the antenna pigments and transferred to the photochemical reaction center pigments, which consist of four bacteriochlorophyll molecules, two molecules of bacteriopheophytin (bacteriochlorophyll, which lacks magnesium atoms) and two ubiquinone molecules. Two of the bacteriochlorophyll molecules of the reaction center behave as a pair, and the initial interaction of the photon from the antenna pigments produces an excited singlet state in this pair as an electron is released from these molecules. The electron is rapidly transferred to the bacteriopheophytin and then to a primary ubiquinone. In the last step of the reaction center sequence, the electron is passed from the primary quinone to a secondary quinone. The reduced secondary quinone can transfer its electron to a cytochrome bc_1 complex. The cytochrome bc_1 complex transfers the electron to cytochrome c_2 that, in turn, passes the electron back to the oxidized bacteriochlorophyll pair.

Not all anoxygenic photoautotrophic bacteria contain this identical pathway of cyclic electron flow and electron carriers. Variations in different bacteria include different numbers of reaction center pigment molecules, substitutions of bacteriochlorophyll *b* for bacteriochlorophyll *a*, and substitutions of menaquinones for ubiquinones. Reaction center bacteriochlorophylls absorb maximally at 840 nm in the green bacteria and at 798 nm in the heliobacteria.

Cyclic oxidative photophosphorylation generates ATP without generating reduced coenzymes. The anaerobic photosynthetic bacteria, however, require the reduced coenzyme NADH for biosynthetic reactions. To generate NADH, phototrophic anoxygenic bacteria utilize reduced inorganic compounds such as H_2S, H_2, or organic acids as electron donors. When bacteria utilize an organic compound such as malate as an electron donor, growth is said to be **photoheterotrophic (photoorganotrophic).** The electrons from the initial oxidation of bacteriochlorophyll are used to reduce NAD^+ to NADH and the electrons from the external organic electron donor can then be used to rereduce the oxidized bacteriochlorophyll molecule.

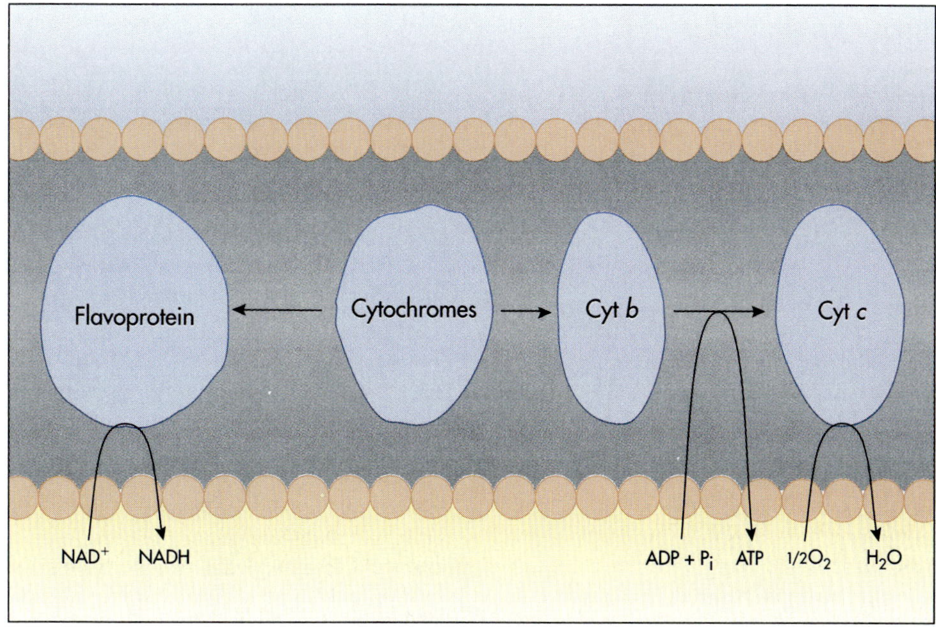

FIG. 4-41 In some photosynthetic organisms there is a reverse flow of electrons and protons through a membrane-bound transport chain so that some electrons and protons are used to produce reduced coenzyme and others are used to generate the proton gradient across the membrane needed to drive the formation of ATP by chemiosmosis.

The flow of electrons from the external electron donor to form the reduced coenzyme may pass through photosystem I in a noncyclic pathway. In the purple sulfur and green nonsulfur photosynthetic bacteria, the reduction potential of the primary electron acceptor is not sufficient to reduce NAD^+. In these bacteria, reverse electron flow up the electron transport chain driven by energy from the electrochemical potential of the membrane is used to drive the formation of reduced coenzyme.

CHAPTER REVIEW

STUDY QUESTIONS

1. What is autotrophic metabolism? Discuss the different ways in which autotrophs generate ATP. Consider photoautotrophs and chemolithotrophs.
2. What is heterotrophic or chemoorganotrophic metabolism?
3. What is the difference between fermentation and respiration?
4. What individual pathways are involved in respiratory metabolism?
5. What is a terminal electron acceptor?
6. What is the difference between aerobic and anaerobic respiration?
7. Name five different fermentation pathways. For each pathway, what are the metabolic end products, and what organisms characteristically carry out the pathway?
8. What is the difference between oxygenic and anoxygenic photosynthesis?
9. How do different photosynthetic pigments in different organisms allow these organisms to co-exist in the same environment?
10. Based only on their metabolism, should the blue-greens be considered bacteria or algae?
11. What is chemiosmosis, and how does it explain the generation of ATP in oxidative phosphorylation and in photophosphorylation?
12. Where do the following processes occur?
    a. Oxidative phosphorylation in bacteria
    b. Oxidative phosphorylation in fungi
    c. Photophosphorylation in algae
    d. Photophosphorylation in cyanobacteria
    e. The TCA cycle in bacteria
13. What are the basic differences between the Embden-Meyerhof and the Entner-Doudoroff pathways of glycolysis? How much ATP/glucose is generated by each pathway?
14. How can bacteria generate ATP from carbon sources other than glucose?
15. What are the important differences between chemiosmotic mechanisms and substrate-level phosphorylation mechanisms for generation of ATP?
16. What are the two main forms of metabolism by which methane is produced in the environment?

SITUATIONAL PROBLEMS

1. Determining the Pathways of ATP Generation in Newly Discovered Bacteria

You work in a research laboratory that received sample sediments from the deep ocean thermal vent regions. Working as part of a team, you isolated three distinct bacteria that appear to be new species. They all grow at elevated temperatures. Two of the three will grow on a medium with glucose as the sole source of carbon and energy, provided that mineral nutrients are also added. One of these bacteria will grow in the presence or absence of oxygen and produces acid and gas when growing on glucose. Another bacterium will also grow in the presence or absence of oxygen; it produces gas only when growing in the absence of oxygen and does not produce acid in either case. The third bacterium will not grow with added glucose but will grow if bicarbonate and thiosulfate are added.

Because these are newly discovered bacteria from a unique and very interesting ecosystem, you decide to determine how they are generating their required ATP. Specifically, you want to know whether they are autotrophs, heterotrophs, or mixotrophs (organisms capable of both autotrophic and heterotrophic growth). You also want to know about the specific pathways that are involved in ATP generation, for example, whether the bacteria carry out one or more fermentation and/or respiration pathways. Before initiating actual experimental studies, you, like all competent scientists, must design an experimental protocol that will provide unequivocal answers. The laboratory in which you are working is well equipped with pH meters to measure hydrogen ion concentrations, oxygen meters to measure oxygen concentrations, balances, spectrophotometers, and other routine equipment. There are also nonspecialty chemicals such as glucose, iorganic salts, and the like. You also have a budget of $500 with which to purchase additional supplies. You could buy substrates, metabolic inhibitors such as uncoupling reagents, analytical standards, and so forth.

Design an experiment that would reveal the metabolic pathway(s) used by each of these organisms to generate ATP. Be specific in your design. If appropriate, consult chemical supply catalogs to determine the costs of the specific reagents you intend to use and make sure that their cost is within the allotted budget.

2. Determining the Pathways of ATP Generation Based on Measurements of ATP Concentrations Under Different Conditions

ATP concentrations can be measured using a relatively simple assay known as the *luciferin-luciferase assay.* It is based on the reaction that produces light in the tail of a firefly and uses the intensity of light as a quantitative measure of ATP concentration. In this assay, ATP is extracted from cells by boiling in Tris buffer, pH 7.75. The heating disrupts the cytoplasmic membranes of the cells, permitting ATP to diffuse out of the cells. After cooling, the extracted ATP is added to a mixture of reduced luciferin and luciferase in a buffer containing magnesium ions. Under these conditions, the reduced luciferin reacts with oxygen in a luciferase-catalyzed reaction to produce oxidized luciferin. In this reaction, light is emitted, and its intensity is directly proportional to the concentration of ATP, which is the limiting factor in this reaction. The amount of light emitted can be measured with a commercial instrument that has a photodetector and a photomultiplier. Using a standard curve, it is thus easy to measure the ATP in the bacterial cells.

Using the luciferin-luciferase assay, you have measured the ATP concentration for samples of a bacterial culture grown under several different conditions. When the culture is illuminated in the presence of oxygen without any added organic carbon source, the measured ATP concentration is 200 μg per milliliter of culture. When the light source is turned off, the ATP concentration drops to 5 μg/mL. After glucose is added in the dark, the concentration of ATP goes up to 100 μg/mL. Sparging the culture with nitrogen again lowers the ATP concentration to 5 μg/mL. Illuminating the culture again raises the ATP concentration to 200 μg/mL.

Based on these data, what conclusions can you draw about the way(s) in which this bacterium generates ATP?

Suggested Supplementary Readings

Altman S: 1989. Ribonuclease P: An enzyme with a catalytic RNA subunit, *Advances in Enzymology* 62:1-36.

Anraku Y: 1988. Bacterial electron transport chains, *Annual Review of Biochemistry* 57:101-132.

Battley EH: 1987. *Energetics of Microbial Growth,* John Wiley & Sons, New York.

Capaldi RA: 1990. Structure and function of cytochrome *c* oxidase, *Annual Review of Biochemistry* 59:569-596.

Danson MJ: 1988. Archaebacteria: The comparative enzymology of their central metabolic pathways, *Advances in Microbial Physiology* 29:166-232.

Darnell J, H Lodish, D Baltimore: 1986. *Molecular Cell Biology,* Scientific American Books, New York.

Dawes EA: 1986. *Microbial Energetics,* Chapman, New York.

Dawes EA and IW Sutherland: 1992. *Microbial Physiology,* ed. 2, Blackwell Scientific Publications, London.

Ferguson SJ and MC Sorgato: 1982. Proton electrochemical gradients and energy transduction processes, *Annual Review of Biochemistry* 51:185-218.

Gottesman S: 1989. Genetics of proteolysis in *Escherichia coli, Annual Review of Genetics* 23:163-198.

Gottschalk G: 1986. *Bacterial Metabolism,* ed. 2, Springer-Verlag, NY.

Jones CW: 1982. *Bacterial Respiration and Photosynthesis,* American Society for Microbiology, Washington, D.C.

Kalckar HM: 1991. 50 years of biological research-from oxidative phosphorylation to energy requiring transport regulation, *Annual Review of Biochemistry* 60:1-38.

Kashket ER: 1985. The proton motive force in bacteria: A critical assessment of methods, *Annual Review of Microbiology* 39:219-242.

Kornberg A: 1989. Never a dull enzyme, *Annual Review of Biochemistry* 58:1-30.

Kraut J: 1988. How do enzymes work? *Science* 242:533-539.

Krebs HA: 1970. The history of the tricarboxylic acid cycle, *Perspectives in Biology and Medicine* 14:154-170.

Lehninger AL: 1988. *Principles of Biochemistry,* Worth Pub., NY.

Lessie TG and PV Phibbs Jr: 1984. Alternative pathways of carbohydrate utilization in *Pseudomonas, Annual Review of Microbiology* 38:359-388.

Lidstrom ME and DI Stirling: 1990. Methylotrophs: Genetics and commercial applications, *Annual Review of Microbiology* 44:27-58.

Lin ECC and S Iuchi: 1991. Regulation of gene expression in fermentative and respiratory systems in *Escherichia coli* and related bacteria, *Annual Review of Genetics* 25:361-387.

Mandelstam J, K McQuillen, IW Dawes: 1982. *Biochemistry of Bacterial Growth,* Blackwell Scientific Publications, Oxford, England.

Mathews CK and KE van Holde: 1990. *Biochemistry,* Benjamin/Cummings, Menlo Park, CA.

McNeil B and LM Harvey: 1990. *Fermentation: A Practical Approach,* IRL Press, Oxford, England.

Meadow ND, DK Fox, S Roseman: 1990. The bacterial phospheoenolpyruvate:glucose phosphotransferase system, *Annual Review of Biochemistry* 59:497-542.

Meyer H, O Kappeli, A Fiechter: 1985. Growth control in microbial cultures, *Annual Review of Microbiology* 39:299-319.

Neidhardt FC, JL Ingraham, M Schaechter: 1990. *Physiology of the Bacterial Cell: A Molecular Approach,* Sinauer Associates, Sunderland, MA.

Nicholls DG: 1982. *Bioenergetics: An Introduction to the Chemiosmotic Theory,* Academic Press, New York.

Okamura MY and G Fehr: 1992. Protein transfer in reaction centers from photosynthetic bacteria, *Annual Review of Biochemistry* 61:861-896.

Penefsky HS and RL Cross: 1991. Structure and mechanism of F_0F_1-type ATP synthesis and ATPases, *Advances in Enzymology* 64:173-214.

Postgate J: 1989. Trends and perspectives in nitrogen fixation research, *Advances in Microbial Physiology* 30:1-22.

Schlegel HG and B Bowien: 1981. Physiology and biochemistry of aerobic hydrogen-oxidizing bacteria, *Annual Review of Microbiology* 35:405-452.

Scott T and M Eagleson: 1988. *Concise Encyclopedia Biochemistry,* ed. 2, Walter de Gruyter, Inc., Hawthorne, NY.

Stenesh J: 1989. *Dictionary of Biochemistry and Molecular Biology,* ed. 2, John Wiley and Sons, New York.

Stoeckenius W and RA Bogomolni: 1982. Bacteriorhodopsin and related pigments of halobacteria, *Annual Review of Biochemistry* 51:587-616.

Stryer L: 1988. *Biochemistry,* ed. 3, W. H. Freeman and Company, New York.

Sukalski KA and RC Nordlie: 1989. Glucose-6-phosphatase: Two concepts of membrane-function relationship, *Advances in Enzymology* 62:93-118.

Symons RH: 1992. Small catalytic RNAs, *Annual Review of Biochemistry* 61:641-672.

Voet D and JG Voet: 1990. *Biochemistry,* John Wiley and Sons, New York.

Werner R: 1992. *Essential Biochemistry and Molecular Biology: A Comprehensive Review,* ed. 2, Elsevier, New York.

Youvan DC and BL Marrs: 1987. Molecular mechanisms of photosynthesis, *Scientific American* 256(6):42-48.

Zubay G:1993. *Biochemistry,* ed. 3, William C. Brown Communications, Inc., Dubuque, IA.

CHAPTER 5

Cellular Metabolism: Biosynthesis of Macromolecules

Chapter Outline

The metabolic pathways of the cell form an interlocking network of chemical reactions through which organic chemicals flow, their structures being altered as they go. Through these reactions, a cell synthesizes its component structures with their diverse chemical compositions. A main theme of cellular metabolism is the breaking down of substrate molecules into smaller organic compounds, which then, sometimes with inorganic substrates, serve as the precursors for the biosynthesis of many different macromolecules. There are many variations, involving the major products of biosynthesis: carbohydrates, lipids, proteins, and nucleic acids. The metabolism of these various macromolecules is interconnected via the central metabolic pathways of the cell, allowing carbon and other elements to be readily moved from one class of compound to another.

5.1 BIOSYNTHESIS (ANABOLISM)

The pathways of cellular metabolism that build up macromolecules from smaller precursors collectively form the process known as **biosynthesis** or **anabolism** (FIG. 5-1). From simple substrates, cells synthesize the various types of macromolecules needed to allow the cells to live and to grow. The substrates may be the inorganic compounds such as CO_2 used by autotrophs or the organic compounds such as glucose used by heterotrophs. The compounds formed from these substrates include proteins (which act as enzymes, structural proteins, membrane carriers, receptors and so on); lipids (which serve as the main components of membranes); carbohydrates (which form much of the structure of cell walls), and nucleic acids (which store

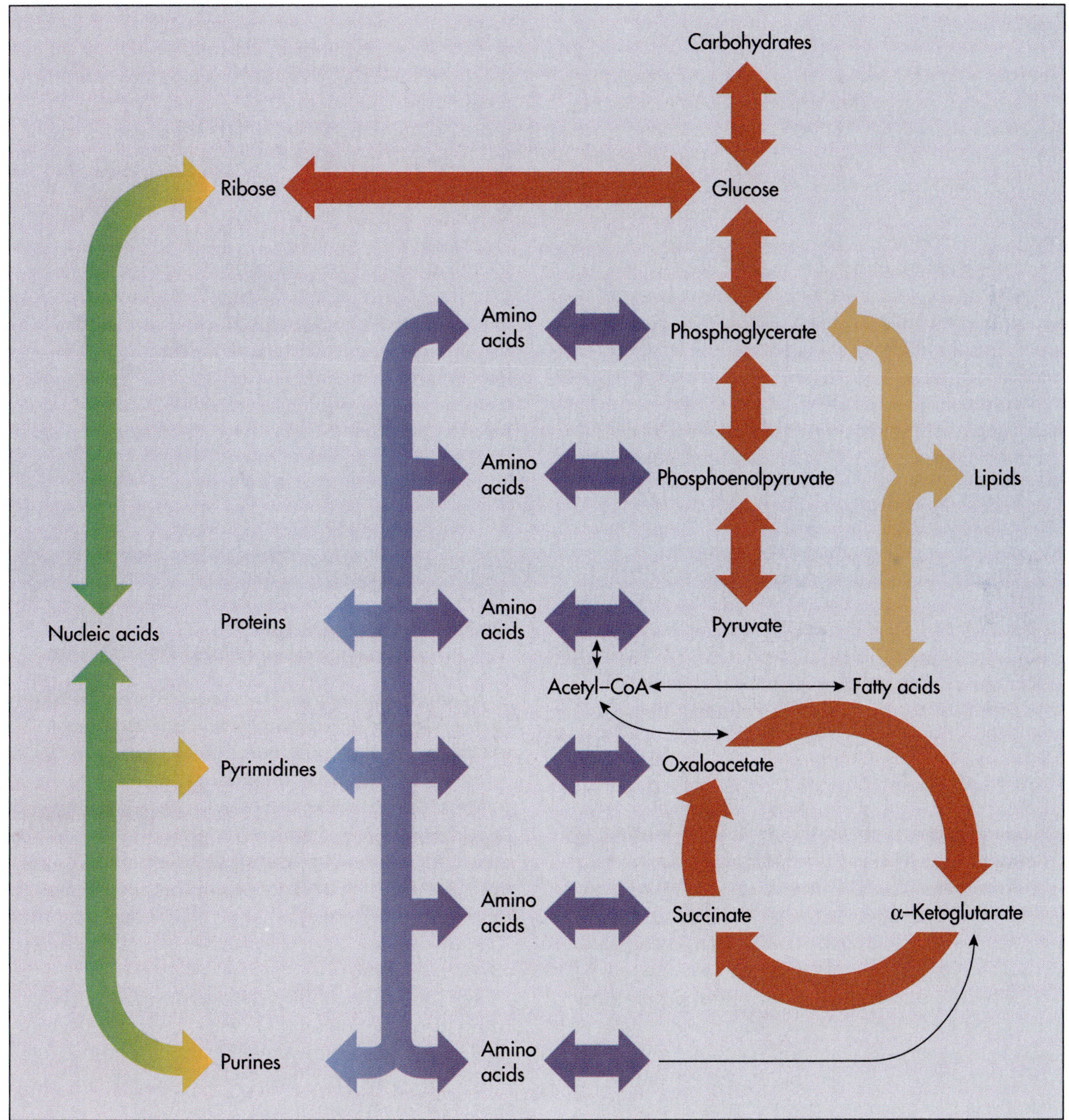

FIG. 5-1 The central metabolic pathways are interconnected so that carbon flows through the cell via a unified network of metabolic reactions. This network connects all of the major classes of macromolecules. Small carbon molecules formed from the breakdown of one macromolecular class can be used for the biosynthesis of compounds of the same or other classes of macromolecules.

and express genetic information). All of these compounds are based on *carbon skeletons* composed of chains or rings of linked carbon atoms, joined in places by other types of atoms such as oxygen, nitrogen, and phosphorus. The basic strategy of cellular metabolism in terms of carbon flow—the movement of carbon between substrates and cell components—is to employ a core set of relatively small organic molecules as the central building blocks for the manufacture of various large macromolecules.

REDUCING POWER

The macromolecules of a cell are generally in a more reduced oxidation state than the starting substrate molecules; therefore, anabolic pathways require reducing power. The coenzyme NADPH provides this reducing power or, in other words, acts as the reducing agent needed in biosynthetic pathways. It is converted to its oxidized form, $NADP^+$, as it performs its reduction. The use of the coenzyme $NADPH/NADP^+$ system in anabolism contrasts with the use of the related coenzyme $NAD^+/NADH$ system in catabolism. Some central metabolic activities of cells serve to generate the reducing power in the form of NADPH needed for biosynthesis; $NADP^+$ can be formed from NAD^+ in an ATP-requiring reaction. ATP is also required for many other steps of anabolism, because anabolic pathways are endergonic overall, again in contrast with catabolic pathways, which are exergonic.

CENTRAL (AMPHIBOLIC) METABOLIC PATHWAYS

Central metabolic pathways, such as the tricarboxylic acid cycle, play key roles in both catabolism and anabolism. Carbon can flow in either direction along at least parts of these pathways, allowing them to act as a source of precursors for biosynthesis and a route by which high-energy substrates can be broken down and their energy trapped in chemicals such as ATP. In recognition of this versatility such pathways are called **amphibolic** pathways (dual-purpose pathways). ATP, reduced coenzymes, and small molecules such as pyruvate and acetyl-CoA formed during the catabolic activities of these pathways are used for the synthesis of other molecules when the flow of materials is reversed during anabolism. The amphibolic pathways permit the necessary metabolic connections between the breakdown of one class of compound and the biosynthesis of another class of compound. They allow the metabolism of carbohydrate, lipid, protein, and nucleic acid to be linked into the extended network of metabolism as a whole (see FIG. 5-1). Compounds are regularly siphoned from the central metabolic pathways to make new materials for the cell (biomass).

5.2 CARBON DIOXIDE FIXATION

The fixation of CO_2 is the process by which inorganic carbon dioxide becomes incorporated (fixed) into the structure of organic compounds within cells. This is the principle basis of autotrophic metabolism.

CALVIN CYCLE

CO_2 fixation occurs within many autotrophic microbial and plant cells via a metabolic pathway known as the **Calvin cycle.** The Calvin cycle is a complex series of reactions that synthesizes glyceraldehyde-3-phosphate from CO_2 (FIG. 5-2). It effectively takes three turns of the Calvin cycle to synthesize one molecule of glyceraldehyde-3-phosphate, with one CO_2 molecule entering at each turn to build the 3-carbon glyceraldehyde-3-phosphate molecule. Because glyceraldehyde-3-phosphate contains three carbon atoms, the Calvin cycle is sometimes referred to as a C_3 pathway.

CO_2 is the most oxidized form of carbon, and its conversion to glyceraldehyde-3-phosphate via the Calvin cycle requires a great deal of energy (as ATP) and reducing power (as NADPH), as can be seen from the overall equation for the process:

$$3\ CO_2 + 9\ ATP + 6\ NADPH \rightarrow \text{glyceraldehyde-3-phosphate} + 9\ ADP + 6\ NADP^+$$

In photoautotrophs, the ATP and NADPH come from the light reactions of photosynthesis. In chemoautotrophs (chemolithotrophs), the ATP and NADPH come from the oxidation of inorganic compounds. The Calvin cycle is known as a *dark reaction* because, although it requires ATP and NADPH and can be a part of the overall process of photosynthesis, it does not involve any reactions directly coupled to the input of light energy. If there is an adequate supply of ATP and NADPH, the Calvin cycle can proceed in the absence of light.

The initial metabolic step in the Calvin cycle involves the reaction of CO_2 with ribulose-1,5-bisphosphate to form an unstable 6-carbon compound that immediately splits to form two molecules of 3-phosphoglycerate. This reaction is highly exergonic, with a ΔG° of −12.4 kcal/mole. The reaction of CO_2 with ribulose-1,5-bisphosphate is catalyzed by **ribulose-1,5-bisphosphate carboxylase (RuBisCo),** a key enzyme in the Calvin cycle. Many autotrophic bacteria store ribulose-1,5-bisphosphate carboxylase as inclusions within

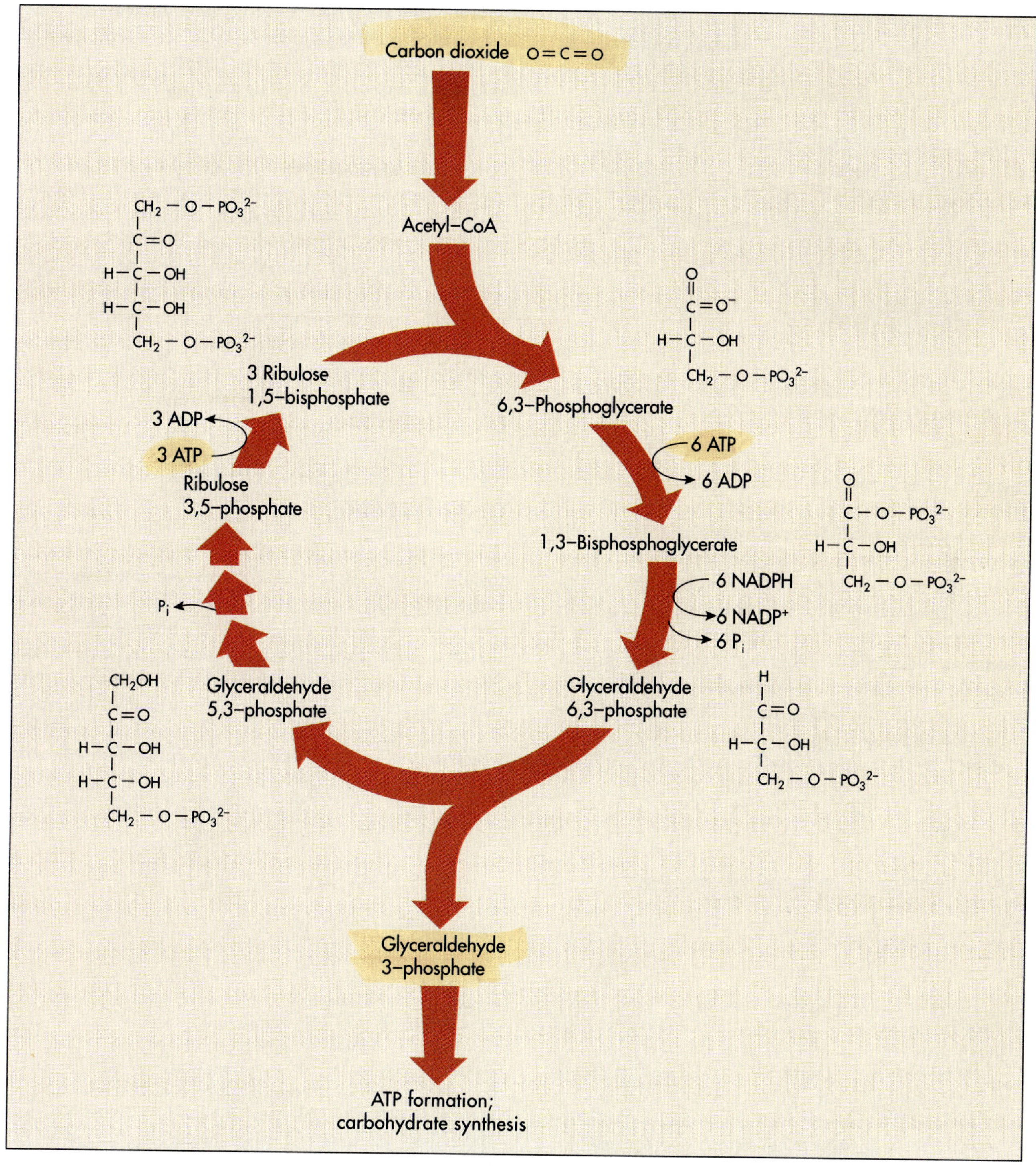

FIG. 5-2 The Calvin, or carbon reduction, cycle is the main metabolic pathway used by autotrophs for the conversion of carbon dioxide to organic carbohydrates. The pathway, which is active in photoautotrophs and chemolithotrophs, requires the input of carbon dioxide, ATP (energy), and NADPH (reducing power).

the cell. These inclusion bodies, called **carboxysomes,** are polyhedral structures that contain insoluble, crystalline ribulose-1,5-bisphosphate carboxylase (FIG. 5-3). Carboxysomes are found in nitrifying bacteria, the photosynthetic cyanobacteria, and in many of the sulfur-oxidizing autotrophic bacteria.

When the reaction catalyzed by ribulose-1,5-bisphosphate carboxylase occurs three times, it allows three molecules of CO_2 to react with three molecules of ribulose-1,5-bisphosphate, and generates a total of six molecules of 3-phosphoglycerate. Five of the six molecules of 3-phosphoglycerate go through a series

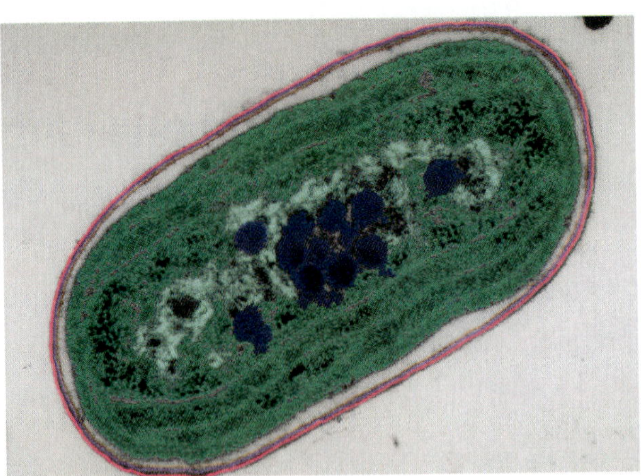

FIG. 5-3 Colorized micrograph of the cyanobacterium *Synechococcus* showing carboxysomes *(blue)*. (42,000×).

of reactions that regenerate the original three molecules of ribulose-1,5-bisphosphate. The remaining 3-phosphoglycerate molecule is reduced to form the net product of the cycle, the glyceraldehyde-3-phosphate molecule. It is because the ribulose-1,5-bisphosphate is regenerated that this pathway is called a cycle. The only net carbon flow is the entry of three CO_2 molecules, accompanied by the production of one molecule of glyceraldehyde-3-phosphate. Carbon dioxide continually flows into the Calvin cycle and glyceraldehyde-3-phosphate continually flows out, all mediated by the interconversion of the cycle's intermediates.

The glyceraldehyde-3-phosphate molecules that are formed during the Calvin cycle can further react to form glucose and polysaccharides composed of linked glucose units, such as starch and cellulose. It takes six turns of the Calvin cycle to form one 6-carbon carbohydrate such as glucose. The overall conversion of CO_2 to glucose is highly endergonic and requires 114 kcal/mole. For this conversion, the net input of energy as ATP and of reducing power as NADPH is 18 ATP molecules and 12 NADPH molecules. In algae and cyanobacteria, to meet the ATP and NADPH requirements of this process, eight photo-acts (reactions in which a photon is absorbed), four each in photosystems I and II, are needed. Since 1 mole of photons is approximately equivalent to 47 kcal, the efficiency of photosynthesis is about 114/(47 × 8), or 30%.

REDUCTIVE TRICARBOXYLIC ACID CYCLE PATHWAY

Some photoautotrophs, such as the green sulfur bacterium *Chlorobium,* fix CO_2 via a **reverse (reductive) tricarboxylic acid cycle** (FIG. 5-4). In these cells, oxaloacetate is reduced to malate, converted to fumarate, and then reduced again to succinate. Succinate is activated to succinyl-CoA with the input of energy from ATP. Next, CO_2 is added to the succinyl-CoA by a reduced-ferredoxin-linked enzyme, which forms α-ketoglutarate. A second molecule of CO_2 is then reductively added to the α-ketoglutarate

BOX 5-1

REGULATION OF RIBULOSE 1,5 BISPHOSPHATE CARBOXYLASE

Ribulose-1,5-bisphosphate carboxylase is the key enzyme that determines the rate of the Calvin cycle. It catalyzes the reaction of CO_2 with ribulose-1,5-bisphosphate. This enzyme is the most abundant protein in the world. It is found on the surfaces of the thylakoid membranes of photosynthetic microorganisms. In the chloroplasts of some eukaryotic microorganisms it constitutes about 15% of the total protein.

Ribulose-1,5-bisphosphate carboxylase is subject to allosteric control, which provides the mechanism by which CO_2 fixation via the Calvin cycle is regulated. The rate of the enzymatic reaction is increased by NADPH, an allosteric activator of the enzyme. Thus when the light reactions are generating large amounts of NADPH, the dark reactions that use the NADPH to fix CO_2 are stimulated. When reducing power is not available, the Calvin cycle ceases to function. Ribulose-1,5-bisphosphate carboxylase also becomes activated at alkaline pH values. Proton expulsion across the membrane of photosynthetic and chemoautotrophic bacteria increases the intracellular pH. This activates ribulose-1,5-bisphosphate carboxylase, increasing the rate of carbon fixation in general. Similarly, in eukaryotic photosynthetic organisms, the pumping of hydrogen ions across the photosynthetic membrane during the light reactions of photosynthesis raises the pH in the stroma of chloroplasts where the Calvin cycle occurs, and hence activates the cycle. Having the Calvin cycle regulated at its first step allows the cell to efficiently conserve its metabolic energy and reducing power.

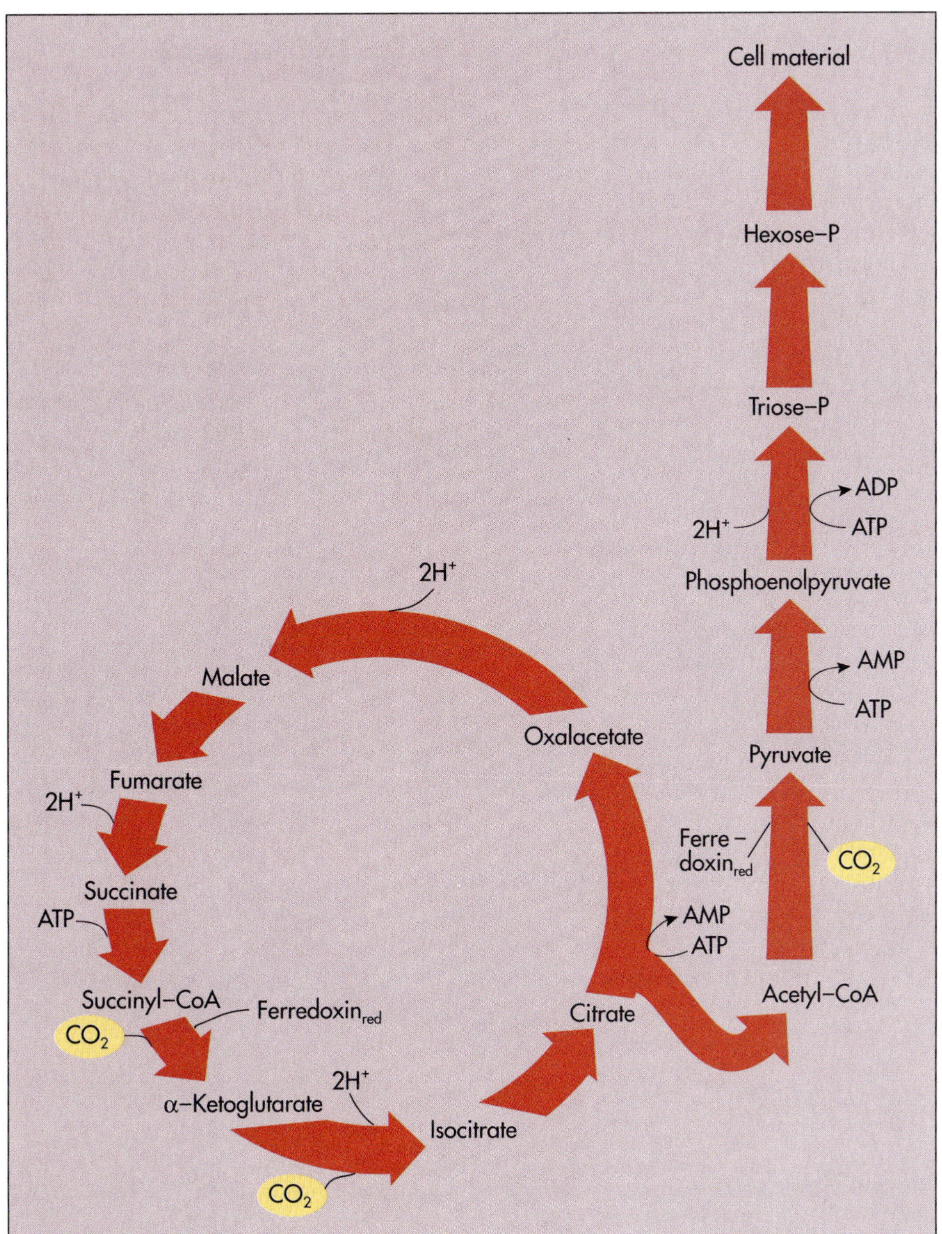

FIG. 5-4 The reductive tricarboxylic acid cycle of some photoautotrophs converts CO_2 molecules into an oxaloacetate molecule for incorporation in cell biomass.

to form isocitric acid and then citric acid. The citric acid is split into oxaloacetate and acetyl-CoA in an ATP dependent step. The oxaloacetate is available to repeat the process once more. The acetyl-CoA formed by this reverse TCA cycle, containing the two fixed carbon atoms, can be reductively carboxylated by another reduced-ferredoxin-linked enzyme to form pyruvate. The pyruvate is activated to phosphoenolpyruvate in an ATP-dependent step, and in the final step, another CO_2 molecule is fixed to convert the pyruvate into oxaloacetate. Thus four CO_2 molecules are fixed overall, into the form of oxaloacetate, which can be channeled into biosynthetic reactions. This is achieved at the expense of three ATP molecules.

In most of the reactions in the reductive TCA cycle in *Chlorobium,* the normal enzymes of the TCA cycle work in reverse of the normal oxidative direction of the cycle. One exception is that the enzyme citrate lyase cleaves citrate into acetyl-CoA and oxaloacetate in the reductive TCA cycle pathway. In the oxidative direction, citrate is produced from acetyl-CoA and oxaloacetate by the enzyme citrate synthase.

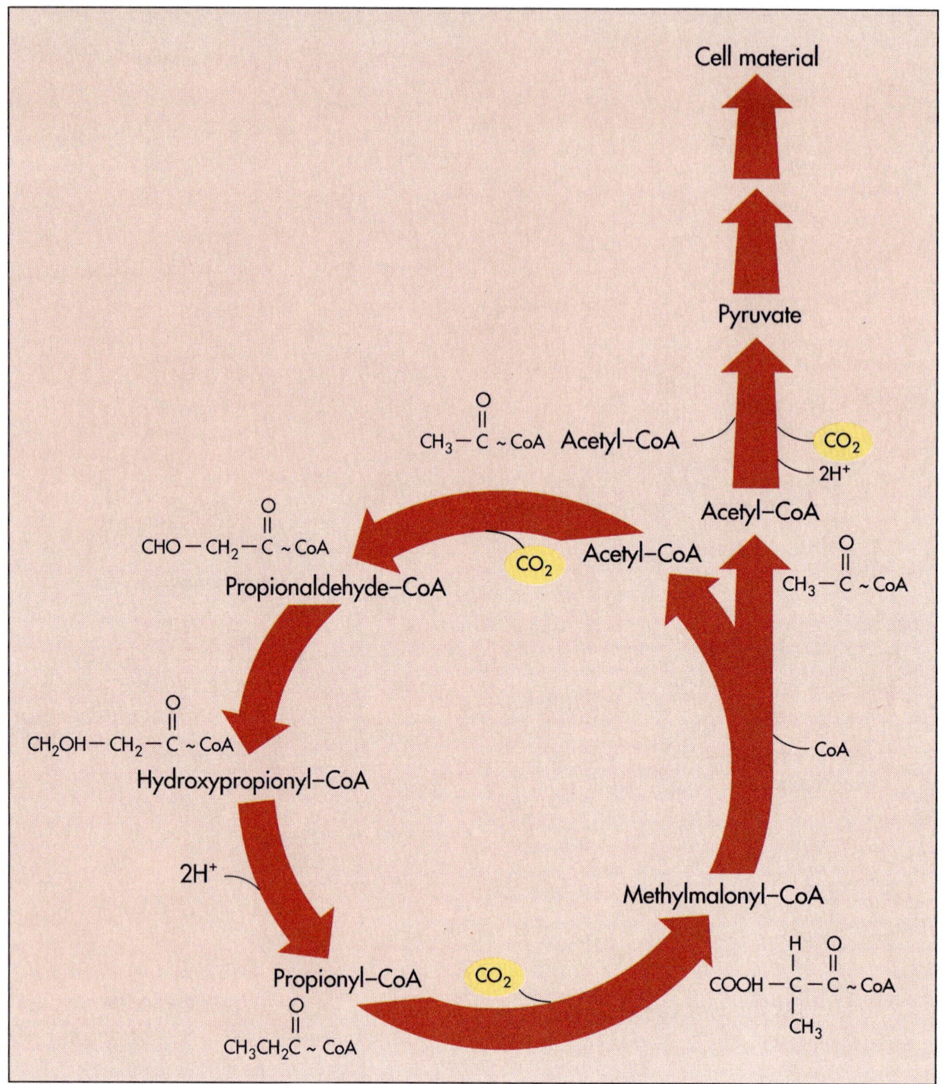

FIG. 5-5 The hydroxypropionate pathway of *Chloroflexus* converts CO_2 into acetyl-CoA for incorporation into cell biomass.

HYDROXYPROPIONATE PATHWAY

The green nonsulfur bacterium, *Chloroflexus,* grows autotrophically using H_2 or H_2S as an electron donor, but it does not use the Calvin cycle or reverse TCA cycle to fix CO_2 into organic carbon. Instead, two CO_2 molecules are fixed and converted into one acetyl-CoA via the **hydroxypropionate pathway** (FIG. 5-5). All of the specific steps of this pathway have not been elucidated but hydroxypropionyl-CoA is probably a key intermediate. The acetyl-CoA formed by this pathway can then be reduced and carboxylated to form pyruvate. The net result is that three CO_2 molecules are converted into one pyruvic acid molecule.

C_4 PATHWAY

A common pathway for the fixation of CO_2 in both heterotrophs and autotrophs is the **C_4 pathway,** so designated because the product formed via this pathway,

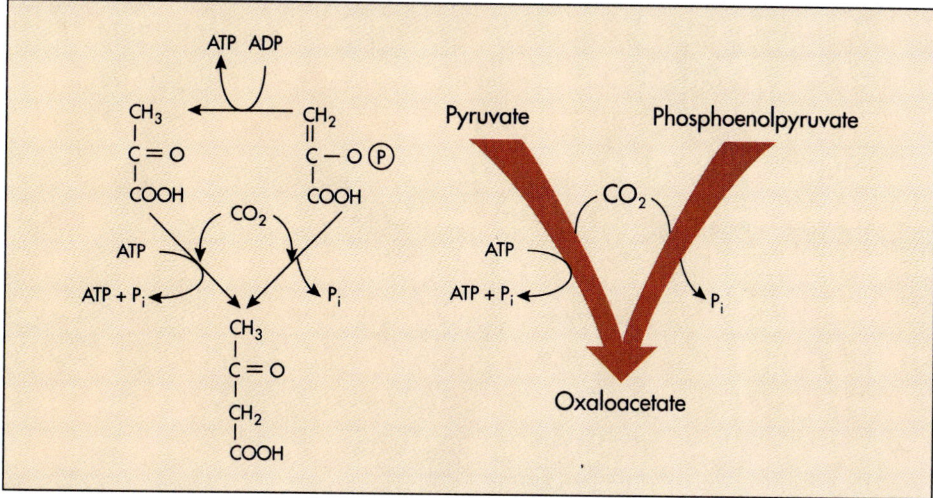

FIG. 5-6 The C_4 pathway adds CO_2 to either pyruvate or phosphoenolpyruvate to produce oxaloacetate.

oxaloacetate, is a 4-carbon molecule (FIG. 5-6). In this metabolic pathway, pyruvate or phosphoenolpyruvate (metabolites of the glycolytic pathway) react with CO_2 to form oxaloacetate, an intermediate metabolite of the TCA cycle. The oxaloacetate formed in this pathway can then be used in amino acid and nucleic acid biosynthesis, which is discussed later in this chapter. Although all organisms fix CO_2 as part of their metabolism, heterotrophic organisms are unable to form a significant portion of their macromolecules from the C_4 pathway alone, and so remain dependent on organic compounds as substrates for cellular growth.

5.3 ASSIMILATION OF ORGANIC C-1 COMPOUNDS

Specialized metabolic pathways are required to convert C-1 compounds, such as methanes, into intermediates of the central metabolic pathways.

METHANOTROPHY

Bacteria that have the ability to use methane (CH_4)—the most reduced form of carbon—as their sole carbon source are called **methanotrophs**. Methane is an organic compound with only one carbon, or, in other words, a C-1 compound. All methanotrophs are obligate aerobes that require O_2; they are obligate C-1 utilizers. Some methanotrophs such as *Methylomonas, Methylococcus,* and *Methylosinus* can grow on various C-1 compounds—methanol, for example—rather than only methane.

The initial step in the utilization of methane is its oxidation by reaction with O_2, catalyzed by the enzyme **methane monooxygenase.** This enzyme has a wide range of substrate specificity and can also catalyze the oxidation of ammonium ions, chloromethane, bromoethane, ethane, propane, trichloroethylene, and various other compounds. It is a "mixed function" oxidase in the sense that it can catalyze both oxidation and reduction. It catalyzes the incorporation of a single oxygen atom from O_2 into the substrate (an oxidation), as well as the reduction of the other oxygen atom to water. The reduction process uses electrons from NADH or cytochrome *c,* and when methane is a substrate of the oxidation process, methanol (CH_3OH) is produced:

$$CH_4 + O_2 + NADH \rightarrow CH_3OH + H_2O + NAD^+$$

$$CH_4 + O_2 + \text{cytochrome } c_{(reduced)} \rightarrow CH_3OH + H_2O + \text{cytochrome } c_{(oxidized)}$$

Ribulose Monophosphate Cycle

The methanol formed by methane monooxygenase is further oxidized to formaldehyde. Type I methanotrophs, such as *Methylomonas* and *Methylococcus,* then feed the formaldehyde into the **ribulose monophosphate cycle** (FIG. 5-7). In this pathway, the formalde-

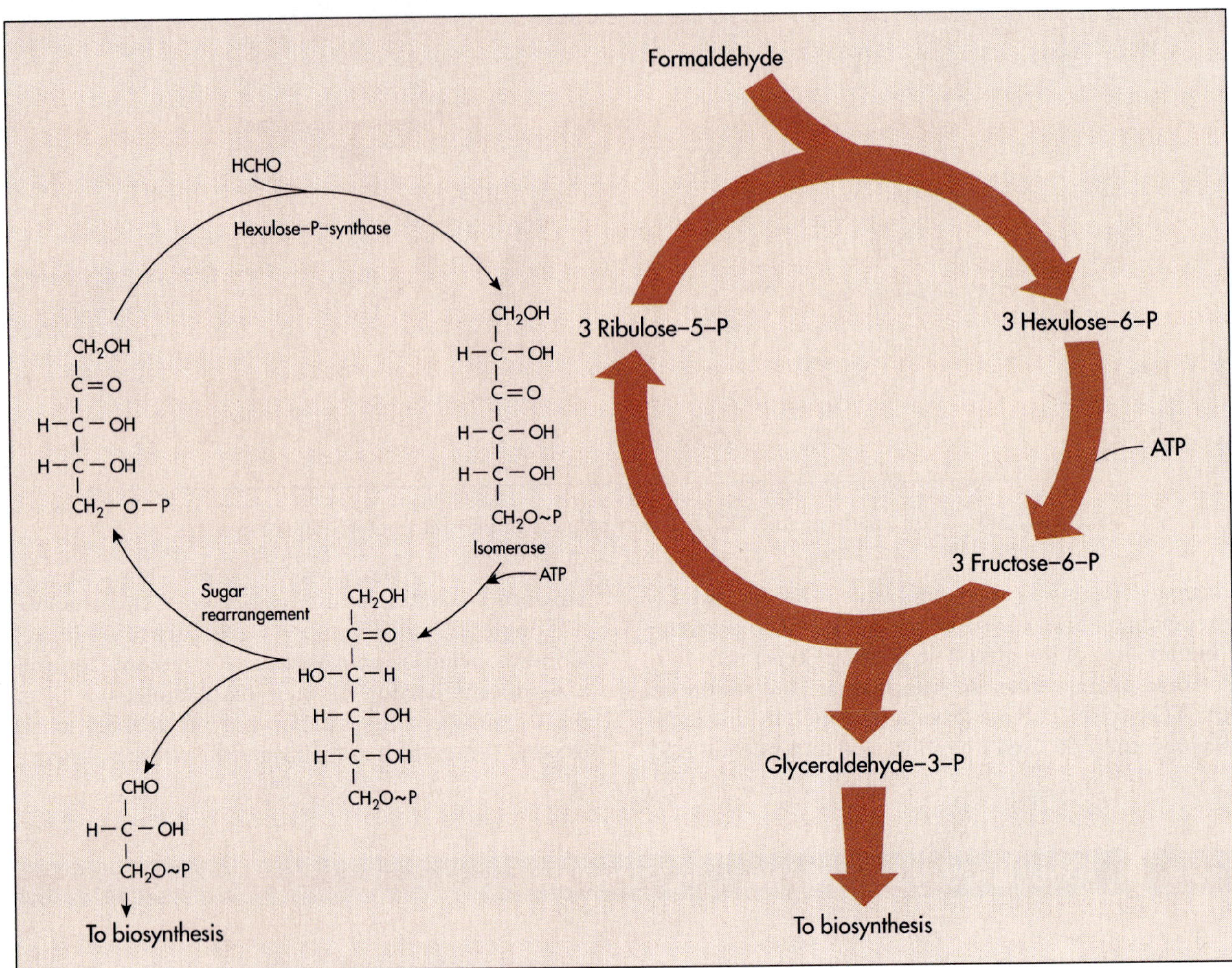

FIG. 5-7 The ribulose monophosphate cycle incorporates formaldehyde and produces glyceraldehyde 3-phosphate for biosynthesis.

hyde initially reacts with ribulose-5-phosphate to form hexulose-6-phosphate, with the consumption of ATP. The hexulose-6-phosphate is split to form glyceraldehyde-3-phosphate. Rearrangement reactions similar to those of the pentose phosphate pathway regenerate ribulose-5-phosphate and allow the cycle to turn again. Overall, six formaldehyde molecules can be used to generate two new glyceraldehyde-3-phosphate molecules:

6 formaldehyde + 2 ATP →
2 glyceraldehyde-3-phosphate + 2 ADP

The glyceraldehyde-3-phosphate can be used in biosynthetic pathways.

Serine Pathway

Type II methanotrophs, such as *Methylosinus,* utilize the **serine pathway** for carbon assimilation (FIG. 5-8). The first step in this pathway is the reaction of formaldehyde with glycine to form serine. The serine is deaminated to form pyruvate, which is then reduced by NADH to form glycerate. The input of energy from ATP serves to convert the glycerate to phosphoenolpyruvate. The 3-carbon phosphoenolpyruvate reacts with CO_2 to form oxaloacetate. Further reduction of oxaloacetate via malate results in the production of acetyl-CoA and glyoxylate. The acetyl-CoA is the net synthetic product of this pathway. The glyoxylate is aminated to form glycine, which completes the cycle. The overall equation is:

formaldehyde + CO_2 + CoA + 2 NADH + 2 ATP →
acetyl-CoA + 2 NAD^+ + 2 ADP + 2 P_i + 2 H_2O

The serine pathway of C-1 fixation is less efficient than the ribulose monophosphate cycle because it has greater energy requirements. The ribulose mono-

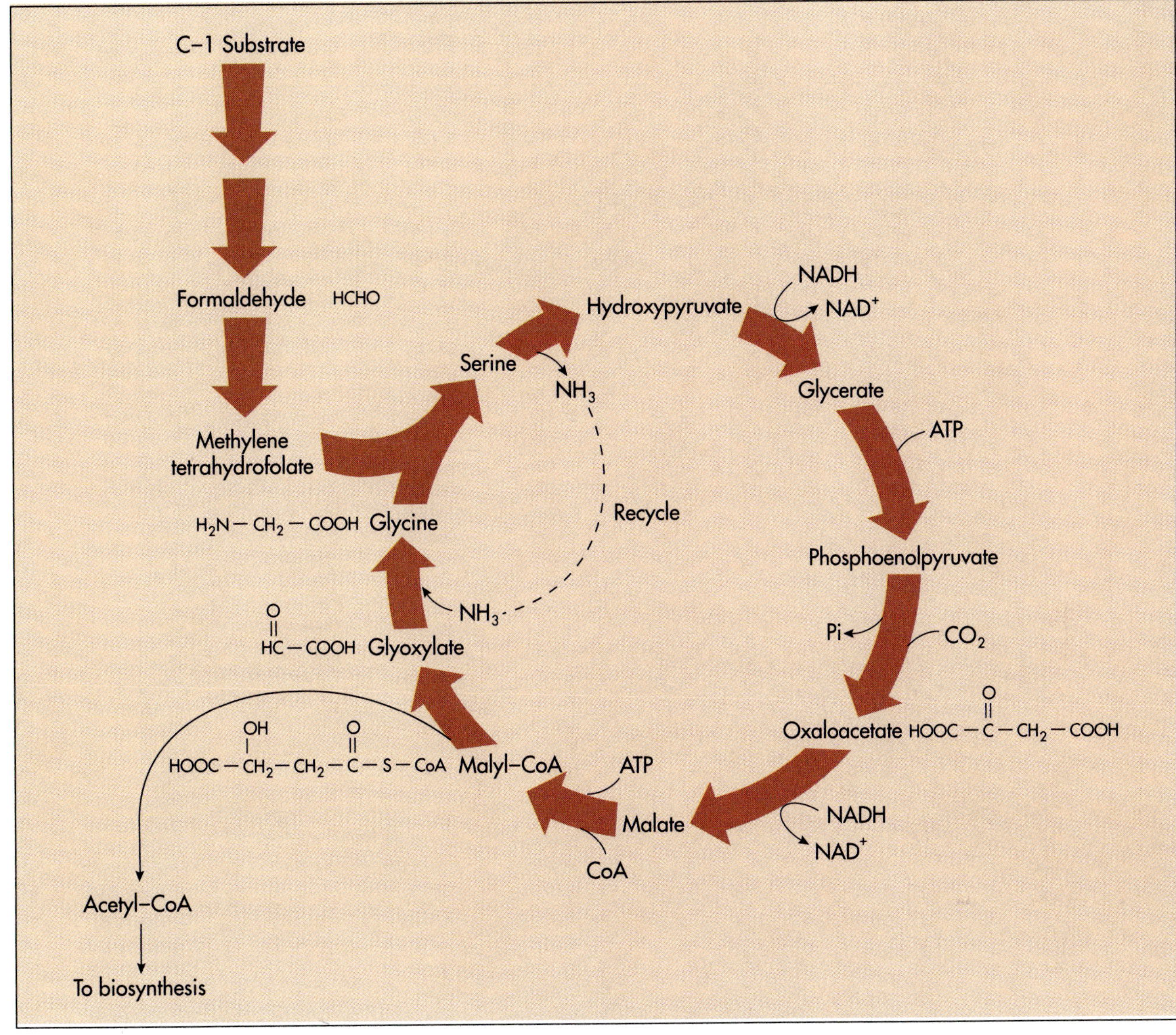

FIG. 5-8 The serine pathway for the assimilation of C-1 units into cell material by Type II methylotrophic bacteria.

phosphate cycle only requires one ATP to form a glyceraldehyde-3-phosphate, whereas, alternatively, the serine pathway requires two ATP for the formation of acetyl-CoA.

Methylotrophy

The more general class of heterotrophic aerobes that can utilize one-carbon organic molecules other than methane, are called **methylotrophs.** Some *Pseudomonas, Bacillus,* and *Vibrio* species use methanol, formate, or methylamine as a carbon source. These organisms are diverse in nature and are grouped by the common property that they can synthesize carbon-carbon bonds from substrates that contain no carbon-carbon bonds. The methylotrophs use the serine pathway for assimilating C-1 compounds into organic molecules.

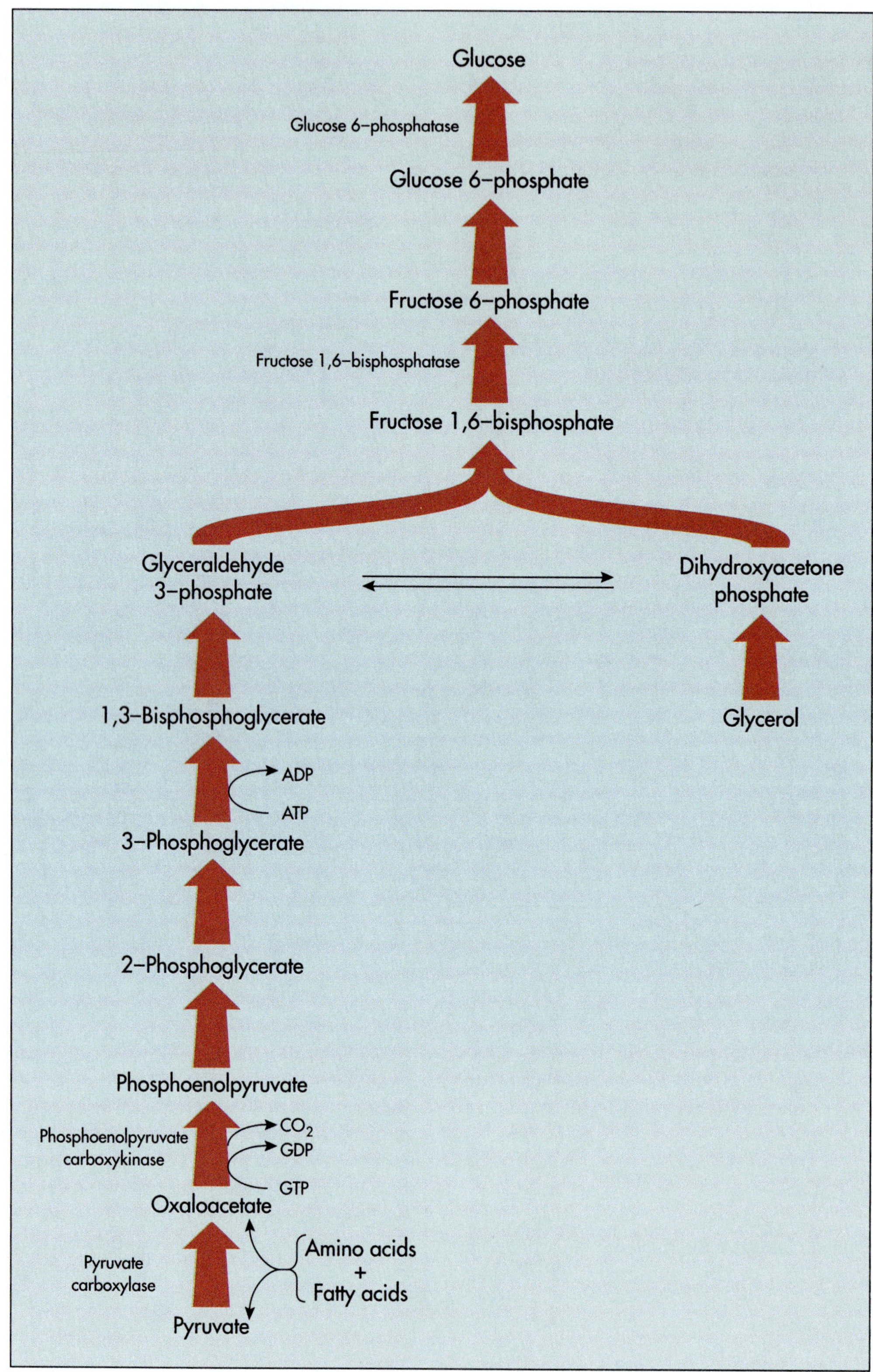

FIG. 5-9 The conversion of noncarbohydrate substrates, for example, amino acids to carbohydrates such as glucose, is accomplished via a gluconeogenic pathway.

5.4 CARBOHYDRATE BIOSYNTHESIS

GLUCONEOGENESIS

The biosynthesis of glucose from noncarbohydrate molecules is called **gluconeogenesis** (FIG. 5-9). The biosynthesis of glucose is essential because carbohydrates comprise portions of the macromolecules in a cell, including DNA and RNA, and the carbohydrate parts of glycoproteins. Once formed, glucose can feed into the pentose phosphate pathway to supply 5-carbon carbohydrate molecules such as ribose and deoxyribose needed for the synthesis of nucleic acids.

Typically, gluconeogenesis involves the conversion of a substrate into pyruvate or another intermediate in the pathway, which is then converted to glucose. Amino acids derived from proteins, for example, can be converted into pyruvate or phosphoenolpyruvate, which are intermediary metabolites of the entire gluconeogenic pathway. Similarly, lipids in some organisms can be broken down into the 3-carbon intermediates of the gluconeogenic pathway.

The pathway of gluconeogenesis effectively reverses the flow of carbon that occurs during glycolysis, and the intermediary metabolites of gluconeogenesis are identical to those of the glycolytic pathway. Although the intermediates are the same, the pathways are actually different, involving different enzymes. In each direction there is a critical enzymatic step that is irreversible, meaning that the enzyme concerned catalyzes the reaction in one direction only. For example, during the Embden-Meyerhof pathway of glycolysis, the conversion of fructose-6-phosphate to fructose-1,6-bisphosphate is catalyzed irreversibly by the enzyme phosphofructokinase. During gluconeogenesis, the conversion of fructose-1,6-bisphosphate to fructose-6-phosphate is catalyzed irreversibly by the enzyme fructose-1,6-bisphosphatase. These enzymes have different allosteric inhibitors that regulate the rate of carbon flow in either direction. The biosynthesis of carbohydrates is favored when the cell has an adequate supply of ATP. The catabolism of carbohydrates is favored when ATP concentrations are relatively low.

BOX 5-2

REGULATING CARBON FLOW IN AMPHIBOLIC PATHWAYS

Amphibolic pathways serve a dual purpose within the cell because carbon can flow along them in both directions (catabolic and anabolic), with the predominant direction at any one time determined by the circumstances of substrate supply, product need, etc. Because the same intermediary metabolites in these amphibolic pathways serve for both catabolism and anabolism, there must be very effective mechanisms to regulate the direction of carbon flow. Differences between the pathways when operating in catabolic or anabolic mode involve the use of different coenzymes and different enzymes at key points in the catabolic and anabolic pathways. Elucidating the controlling mechanisms has provided insight into the fundamental functioning of the cell at a molecular level.

The major distinction in the use of coenzymes is that nicotinamide adenine dinucleotide coenzyme (NAD^+ when oxidized, NADH when reduced) is involved in catabolic pathways, and the related coenzyme nicotinamide adenine dinucleotide phosphate ($NADP^+$ when oxidized, NADPH when reduced) is involved in anabolic pathways. The use of different coenzymes forms an important distinction between the two directions of carbon flow achieved via the same intermediary metabolites. It allows reductive biosynthesis to occur at the same time as the cell is generating ATP through catabolic pathways such as glycolysis.

Of even greater importance in regulating bidirectional carbon flow is the fact that anabolic and catabolic pathways contain irreversible steps catalyzed by different enzymes (see Table below). Thus carbon cannot simply flow freely in both directions. The enzymes catalyzing the key irreversible reactions are generally controlled by al-

Some Key Reactions in the Glycolytic and Gluconeogenic Pathways and the Enzymes that Catalyze Those Reactions

GLYCOLYSIS REACTION (ENZYME)	GLUCONEOGENESIS REACTION (ENZYME)
Glucose → glucose 6-phosphate (hexokinase)	Glucose 6-phosphate → glucose (glucose 6-phosphatase)
Fructose 6-phosphate → fructose 1,6-bisphosphate (phosphofructokinase)	Fructose 1,6-bisphosphate → fructose 6-phosphate (fructose 1,6-biphosphatase)
Phosphoenolpyruvate → pyruvate (pyruvate kinase)	Pyruvate → phosphoenolpyruvate (pyruvate carboxylase/ phosphoenolpyruvate carboxykinase)

Continued.

BOX 5-2—CONT'D

losteric effectors that can activate or inhibit the enzymes, depending on the effectors and enzymes concerned. In this way, the chemistry of the cell can "fine tune" the flow of carbon, balancing catabolic activities involved in generating ATP and anabolic activities involved in the synthesis of essential macromolecules. In particular, feedback inhibition, whereby an end product of a pathway allosterically inhibits an enzyme catalyzing an early step of the pathway, often plays a critical role in the regulation of cell metabolism.

A major factor controlling the direction of carbon flow through amphibolic pathways is the energy status of the cell, one measure of which is the energy charge. The **energy charge** is a numerical value dependent on the relative proportions of ATP, ADP, and AMP (adenosine monophosphate) in the cell. It is defined as follows:

$$\text{Energy charge} = \frac{[\text{ATP}] + \frac{1}{2}[\text{ADP}]}{[\text{ATP}] + [\text{ADP}] + [\text{AMP}]}$$

The energy charge in a cell varies between 0 and 1, although at an energy charge <0.5, cells begin to die. As a rule, ATP-generating pathways are inhibited by a high energy charge, whereas ATP-utilizing pathways are stimulated by a high energy charge. The reason for this is that ATP generally acts as an allosteric inhibitor of a key enzyme in an energy-generating pathway—for example, phosphofructokinase, which catalyzes the conversion of fructose 6-phosphate to fructose-1,6-bisphosphate in the Embden-Meyerhof pathway of glycolysis. In contrast, AMP is an allosteric inhibitor of fructose-1,6-bisphosphatase, which catalyzes the reverse reaction that converts fructose-1,6-bisphosphate to fructose-6-phosphate in the energy-requiring gluconeogenic pathway. Thus when the catabolic ATP-generating pathway is active, the reverse anabolic ATP-requiring pathway is inhibited, and vice versa, so that the flow of carbon through an amphibolic pathway at any point in time is unidirectional, regulated by differences in enzymes, their allosteric inhibitors, and the energy charge of the cell.

GLYOXYLATE CYCLE

Some cells use a pathway, called the **glyoxylate cycle,** to permit the flow of carbon from fatty acids or acetate to carbohydrates. This pathway is a shunt or "short circuit" across the tricarboxylic acid cycle that serves to replenish oxaloacetate in the cell (FIG. 5-10). This type of pathway is important because key intermediates of the tricarboxylic acid cycle may be used for the biosynthesis of other organic molecules. Reactions in a cell that serve to replenish the supplies of key molecules are called **anaplerotic sequences** (meaning filling up).

In the glyoxylate cycle, isocitrate is split by isocitrate lyase into succinate and glyoxylate. Malate is then formed from the reaction of glyoxylate and acetyl-CoA. The malate is converted via oxaloacetate to phosphoenolpyruvate, an intermediary metabolite of the gluconeogenic pathway. This links the pathway of fatty acid metabolism with the pathway of carbohydrate metabolism, allowing four molecules of acetyl-CoA to participate in the formation of glucose as follows:

$$\text{4 acetyl-CoA} \rightarrow \text{2 oxaloacetate} \rightarrow \text{2 phosphoenolpyruvate} + 2\ CO_2$$

$$\text{2 phosphoenolpyruvate} \rightarrow \text{glucose}$$

BIOSYNTHESIS OF POLYSACCHARIDES

The carbohydrates formed by gluconeogenesis can be converted to polysaccharides. Some polysaccharides, such as starch and glycogen, are synthesized when the cell experiences nutritionally-rich conditions. They are used to store carbon and energy within the cell. These polysaccharides can later be broken down, especially when the cell is nutritionally deprived, to form glucose-l-phosphate or glucose-6-phosphate, which can enter the pathways beginning with glycolysis that generate ATP.

The synthesis of glycogen in bacteria occurs in two reactions (FIG. 5-11). First, glucose-l-phosphate is activated using ATP, to form ADP-glucose and pyrophosphate. The activated glucose is then transferred from ADP-glucose to the non-reducing end (carbon 4) of an oligosaccharide chain that contains at least four glucose molecules. This reaction is performed by glycogen synthetase and leads to formation of chains composed of $\alpha(1\rightarrow4)$ linkages. Later, $\alpha(1\rightarrow6)$ branched chain linkages are formed by the action of a transglucosylase. In contrast to bacterial glycogen synthesis, eukaryotic cells use uridine triphosphate (UTP) to activate glucose-l-phosphate. Starch is synthesized by a similar mechanism using UDP-glucose.

A few bacteria, notably *Streptococcus mutans* and *Leuconostoc mesenteroides,* produce dextran from sucrose. Dextran is a "sticky" polymer of glucose molecules linked together in $\alpha(1\rightarrow6)$ linkages with some $\alpha(1\rightarrow3)$ branches. It is produced outside of bacterial cells by the enzyme dextransucrase (glycosyl transferase). This enzyme splits sucrose into glucose and fructose and links the glucose molecules into a dextran polymer. The dextran is deposited as a thick glycocalyx around the cell and is partially responsible for the ability of *S. mutans* to stick to teeth.

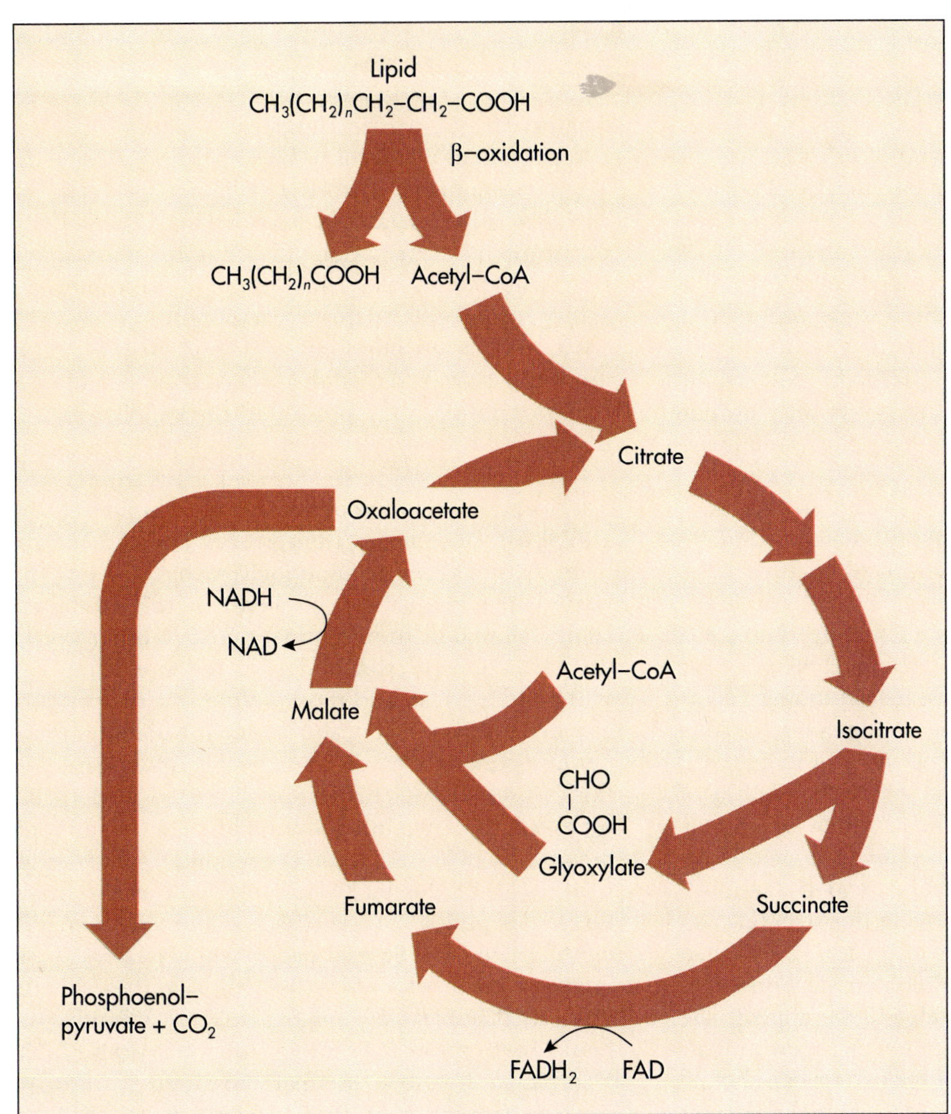

FIG. 5-10 The glyoxylate cycle is a shunt across the normal tricarboxylic acid cycle. This pathway is needed to maintain the tricarboxylic acid cycle intermediates when lipids are metabolized. It also provides a way of converting lipids into carbohydrates.

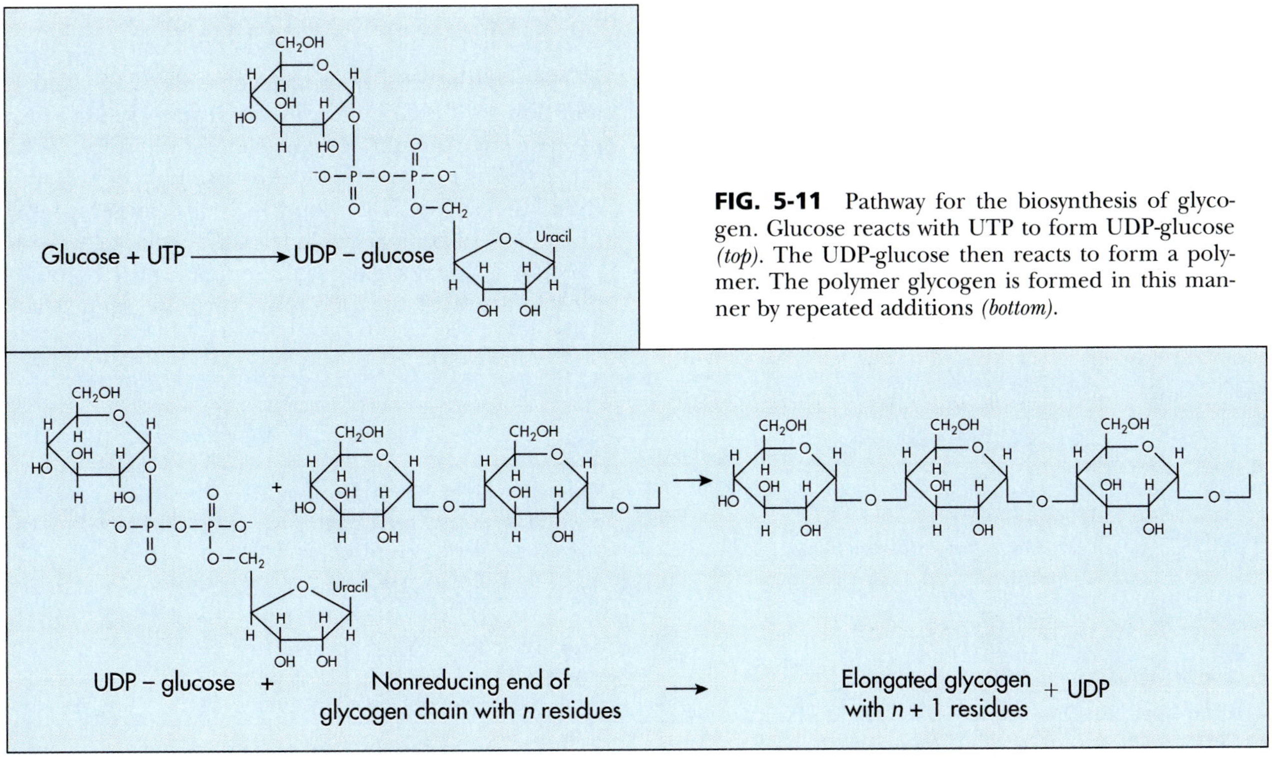

Glucose + UTP ⟶ UDP – glucose

UDP – glucose + Nonreducing end of glycogen chain with *n* residues ⟶ Elongated glycogen with *n* + 1 residues + UDP

FIG. 5-11 Pathway for the biosynthesis of glycogen. Glucose reacts with UTP to form UDP-glucose *(top)*. The UDP-glucose then reacts to form a polymer. The polymer glycogen is formed in this manner by repeated additions *(bottom)*.

PEPTIDOGLYCAN BIOSYNTHESIS

The biosynthesis of peptidoglycan is essential for cell growth and division of eubacteria. The glycan portion of the eubacterial cell wall peptidoglycan is a disaccharide composed of *N*-acetylglucosamine and *N*-acetylmuramic acid. The formation of *N*-acetylglucosamine involves the conversion of glucose to fructose-6-phosphate and subsequent reactions with glutamic acid and acetyl-CoA. To form *N*-acetylmuramic acid, *N*-acetylglucosamine reacts with uridine triphosphate (UTP) to form *N*-acetylglucosamine-uridine diphosphate (UDP), which then reacts with phosphoenolpyruvate to form *N*-acetylmuramic acid-UDP. The enzyme that adds phosphoenolpyruvate to *N*-acetylglucosamine-UDP is inhibited by the antibiotic phosphonomycin (fosfomycin).

During the first stage of cell wall synthesis, the precursors of peptidoglycan are assembled in the cytoplasm to form a UDP–*N*-acetylmuramic acid–pentapeptide (FIG. 5-12). The pentapeptide is composed of a tetrapeptide that occurs in the cell wall and an additional D-alanine at the carboxyl end of the chain. In *E. coli* and *Bacillus subtilis* the pentapeptide would be UDP–*N*-acetylmuramic acid–L-alanine–D-glutamate–diaminopimelic acid–D-alanine–D-alanine. The peptide bonds linking this structure are synthesized by enzymes in the cytoplasm rather than on ribosomes where most other peptide bonds are formed. Each amino acid is added in the appropriate place by specific adding enzymes or ligases whose activity requires ATP. D-Alanine is formed from L-alanine by alanine racemase and then two D-alanine molecules are connected to form a D-alanine–D-alanine dipeptide by D-alanine–D-alanine synthetase. Both of these reactions are inhibited by the antibiotic cycloserine. In a separate series of reactions that also occur in the cytoplasm, the cell forms a UDP–*N*-acetylglucosamine precursor.

The *N*-acetylmuramic acid–pentapeptide is transferred to a carrier molecule in the second stage of peptidoglycan biosynthesis. The carrier is called the *C_{55} carrier lipid, undecaprenylphosphate,* or *bactoprenol.* It is located within the cytoplasmic membrane, which is where the second stage of cell wall biosynthesis occurs. The C_{55} carrier lipid exists in the cell as a pyrophosphate that must be dephosphorylated by a pyrophosphatase before it can act as a carrier. The pyrophosphatase is specifically inhibited by the antibiotic bacitracin. The *N*-acetylglucosamine is transferred to the bactoprenol–*N*-acetylmuramic acid–pentapeptide to form bactoprenol–*N*-acetylglucosamine–*N*-acetylmuramic acid–pentapeptide. This molecule moves across the cytoplasmic membrane (translocation) to the outside of the cell. There it is transferred to a growing chain of cell wall precursors within the cell wall called *nascent peptidoglycan.* The translocation step of peptidoglycan is inhibited by the antibiotics vancomycin, tunicamycin, and ristocetin.

In the final stage of peptidoglycan biosynthesis, the nascent peptidoglycan is covalently bound to the existing cell wall by transpeptidation or, in other words, the formation of cross-bridges between existing cell wall peptidoglycan and those on the nascent peptidoglycan. In this reaction, the terminal D-alanine of the pentapeptide is cleaved and the energy released by this is used to attach the fourth amino acid (D-alanine) of the remaining tetrapeptide to diaminopimelic acid of an adjacent tetrapeptide, which is already part of the wall. Thus the nascent or newly formed peptidoglycan chains become added to the existing cell wall. Several enzymes involved in peptidoglycan synthesis bind to penicillin and are therefore called *penicillin-binding proteins* (PBPs). Binding of penicillin to these PCPs inhibits their activities (Table 5-1), blocking various essential steps in the synthesis of the bacterial cell wall.

LIPOPOLYSACCHARIDE (LPS) BIOSYNTHESIS

The biosynthesis of lipopolysaccharide (LPS) and its addition to the Gram-negative cell wall occurs at the cytoplasmic membrane in successive steps (FIG. 5-13) that are analogous to the assembly of cell wall. As in the synthesis of peptidoglycan, undecaprenylphosphate or bactoprenol serves as the lipid carrier to which individual sugars of the repeat unit (the outermost portion of the LPS molecule) are sequentially

TABLE 5-1 Penicillin-binding Proteins (PBPs) in *Escherichia coli*

PBP	ENZYME ACTIVITY	FUNCTION
1A and 1B	Transglycosylase-transpeptidase	Cell wall synthesis (elongation) during cell reproduction
2	Transpeptidase	Cell wall synthesis during cell growth; cell shape; rod growth
3	Transglycosylase-transpeptidase	Cell wall synthesis during cross wall formation
4	DD-endopeptidase/DD-carboxypeptidase	Hydrolysis of D-amino acids during transpeptidation
5	DD-carboxypeptidase	Hydrolysis of pentapeptide containing D-amino acids; peptidoglycan maturation
6	DD-carboxypeptidase	Hydrolysis of unused pentapeptide containing D-amino acids

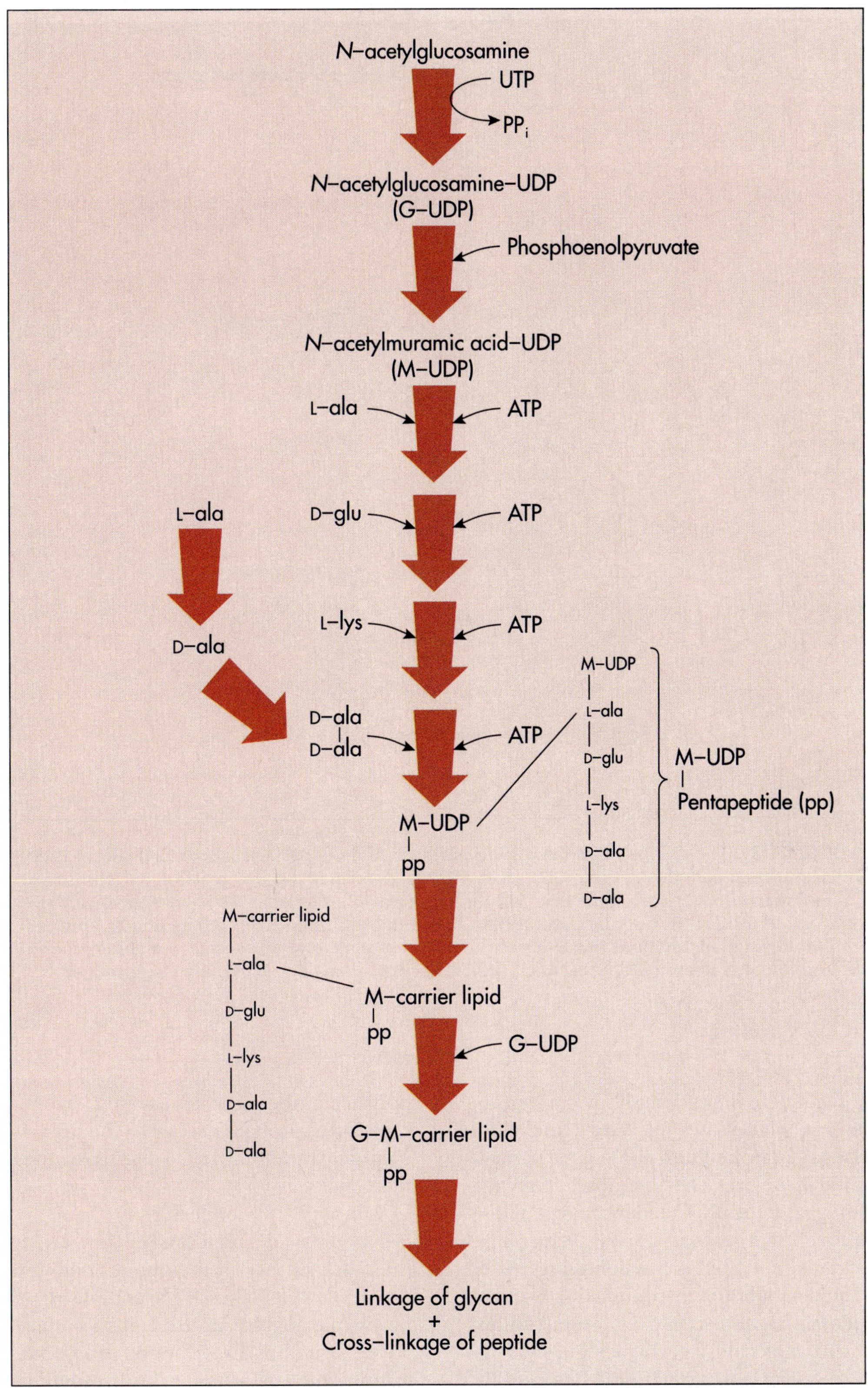

FIG. 5-12 The synthesis of peptidoglycan by bacteria is important to provide the backbone material of the cell wall. Uridine triphosphate (UTP) activates *N*-acetyl glucosamine and reacts with phosphoenolpyruvate to form *N*-acetylmuramic acid-UDP. To form peptidoglycan, amino acids must be added to *N*-acetylmuramic acid, a repeating and alternating glycan chain of *N*-acetylmuramic acid and *N*-acetylglucosamine must be formed, and the peptide chains must be cross-linked.

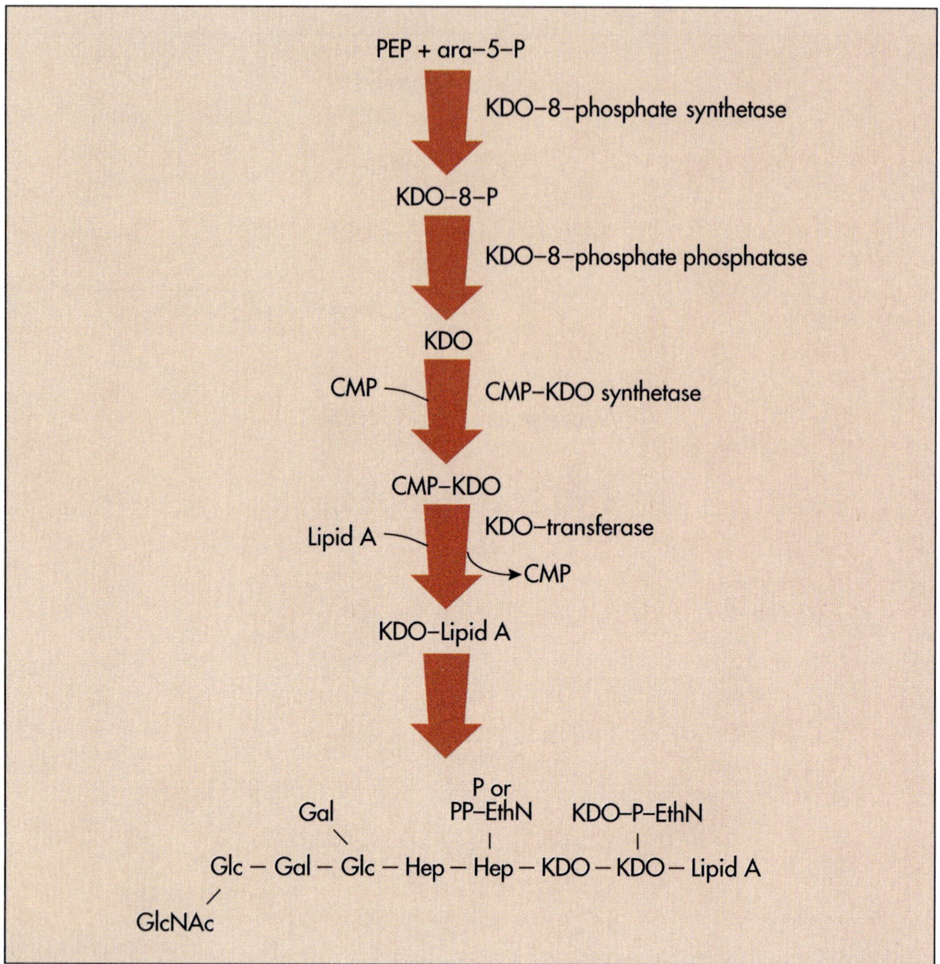

FIG. 5-13 The synthesis of core polysaccharide linked to lipid A is an essential part of LPS biosynthesis. Ketodeoxyoctulosonic acid (KDO) is formed by the reaction of phosphoenolpyruvate (PEP) and arabinose 5-phosphate (ara-5-P). Cytosine monophosphate (CMP) is added to KDO during the pathway and later removed when KDO is attached to lipid A. Two subsequent additions of KDO and the inclusion of several other sugars, including heptose (Hep), glucose (Glc), galactose (Gal), and ethanoloamine (EthN) are also needed.

added. These sugars are first activated by condensing with nucleotide triphosphates to form nucleotide diphosphate–sugar intermediates such as GDP–mannose, UDP–galactose, or CDP–abequose. The activated sugars are enzymatically added in a particular sequence, thus forming a polysaccharide chain of repeating sugar units. The lipid A fraction is assembled in the cytoplasmic membrane by condensing two molecules of glucosamine phosphate and then adding several fatty acid molecules, particularly β-hydroxymyristic acid. The core polysaccharide is built on the lipid A fraction by the sequential enzymatic addition of core sugars such as KDO (2-keto-3-deoxyoctulosonic acid), heptose, and glucose. The lipid A-core polysaccharide is translocated to the outer surface of the cytoplasmic membrane; after which the repeat polysaccharide is transferred from the undecaprenylphosphate carrier to the lipid A-core polysaccharide, thus completing the biosynthesis of the LPS molecule.

Although LPS molecules are initially assembled in the cytoplasmic membrane, they are transferred to the outer surface of the outer membrane. The mechanism by which the cell accomplishes this is unclear but it may involve transfer of molecules through the Bayer junctions or adhesion sites that connect the cytoplasmic membrane and outer membrane in Gram-negative bacteria. It has been shown that newly synthesized LPS molecules first appear in the outer membrane at adhesion sites, suggesting that it is transported through the Bayer junctions to the outer layer of the Gram-negative cell wall.

5.5 LIPID BIOSYNTHESIS

FATTY ACID BIOSYNTHESIS

The biosynthesis of fatty acids proceeds by the sequential addition of 2-carbon units derived from acetyl-CoA (FIG. 5-14). A key intermediate in the synthesis of fatty acids is malonyl-CoA, which is formed from the reaction of acetyl-CoA with CO_2. The formation of malonyl-CoA requires ATP and biotin. The requirement for biotin in this reaction is one reason that many organisms require biotin in trace quantities as a growth factor. Malonyl-CoA contributes successive 2-carbon units to the elongation of a growing fatty acid with the accompanying release of CO_2. During these reactions, the substrates are bound to a protein known as the *acyl carrier protein* (ACP).

The synthesis of fatty acids requires energy in the form of ATP and reducing power in the form of NADPH. The synthesis of a C_{16} saturated fatty acid, palmitic acid (a common component of membrane phospholipids) requires 7 ATP and 14 NADPH.

8 acetyl-CoA + 7 ATP + 14 NADPH → palmitic acid + 14 $NADP^+$ + 8 CoA + 6 H_2O + 7 ADP + 7 P_i

The saturated fatty acids palmitic (C_{16}) and stearic (C_{18}) serve as precursors of the monounsaturated fatty acids palmitoleic acid and oleic acid, respectively. The double bond is formed by the action of the enzyme fatty acyl-CoA oxygenase in an oxidation reaction. In this reaction, NADPH is oxidized to $NADP^+$. Fatty acyl-CoA oxygenase is a *mixed function oxidase* because two different groups are oxidized by the same enzyme.

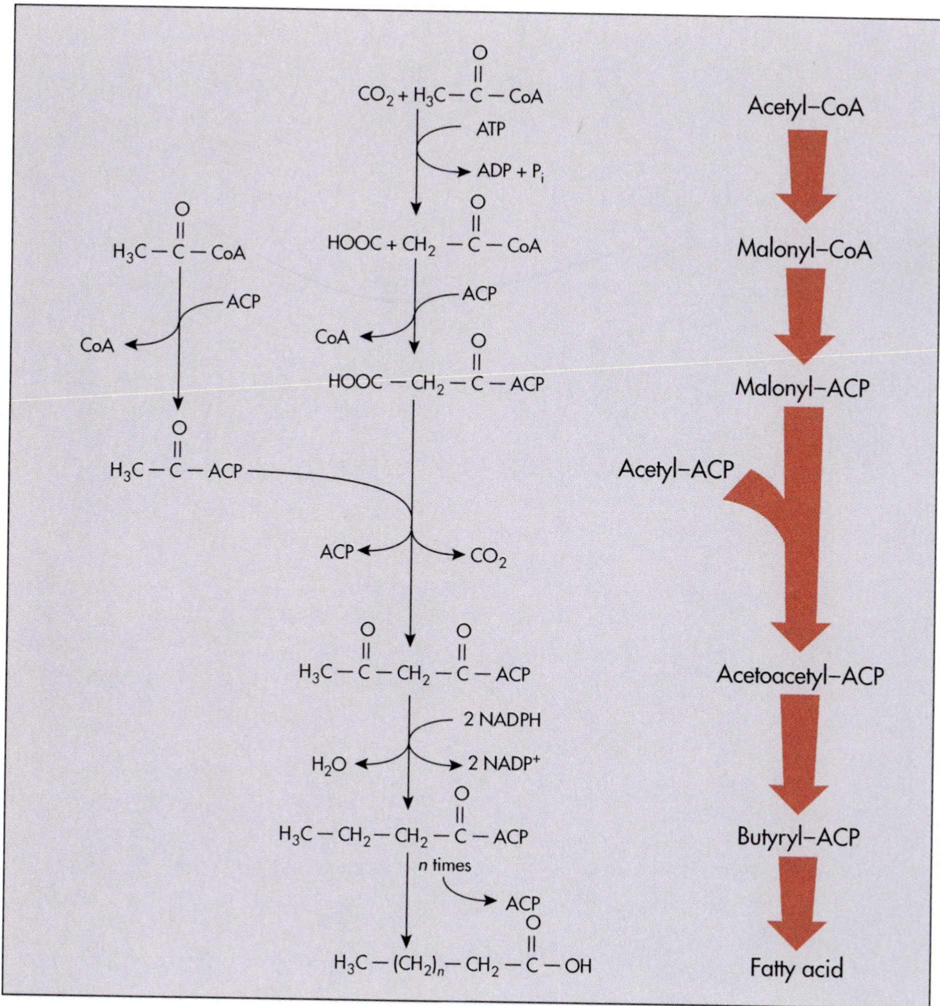

FIG. 5-14 The synthesis of fatty acids involves two carbon additions from acetyl-CoA and an acyl carrier protein (ACP). Fatty acid biosynthesis is not a simple reversal of *β*-oxidation used for the catabolism of fatty acids.

BIOSYNTHESIS OF POLY-β-HYDROXYBUTYRIC ACID

The pathway for the synthesis of poly-β-hydroxybutyric acid, a common storage product of bacteria, is similar to the pathway for fatty acid biosynthesis (FIG. 5-15). Acetyl-CoA reacts to form acetoacetyl-CoA (a 4-carbon derivative of CoA that can be reduced with NADH to form β-hydroxybutyryl-CoA). Repetitive sequential addition of acetyl-CoA results in chain length elongation, and subsequent removal of the CoA portion of the molecule forms the poly-β-hydroxybutyric acid, which can accumulate in large amounts in bacteria. Interestingly, unlike other biosynthetic reactions, the formation of poly-β-hydroxybutyrate uses the coenzyme NADH rather than NADPH.

BIOSYNTHESIS OF PHOSPHOLIPIDS

The biosynthesis of phospholipids, which are essential components of membranes, involves the addition of fatty acids to glycerol-3-phosphate (FIG. 5-16). Dihydroxyacetone phosphate, which is a readily available intermediate of glycolysis, is reduced by NADPH to glycerol-3-phosphate. The glycerol-3-phosphate then reacts with acylated-ACP to form phosphatidic acid, a common intermediary metabolite in the synthesis of phospholipids and triglycerides. The phosphatidic acid is activated by cytosine triphosphate (CTP) to form a CDP-diacylglycerol molecule, and the CDP is finally displaced by alcohols such as serine, inositol, or glycerol to produce a completed phospholipid as phosphatidyl serine, phosphatidyl inositol, or phosphatidyl glycerol respectively.

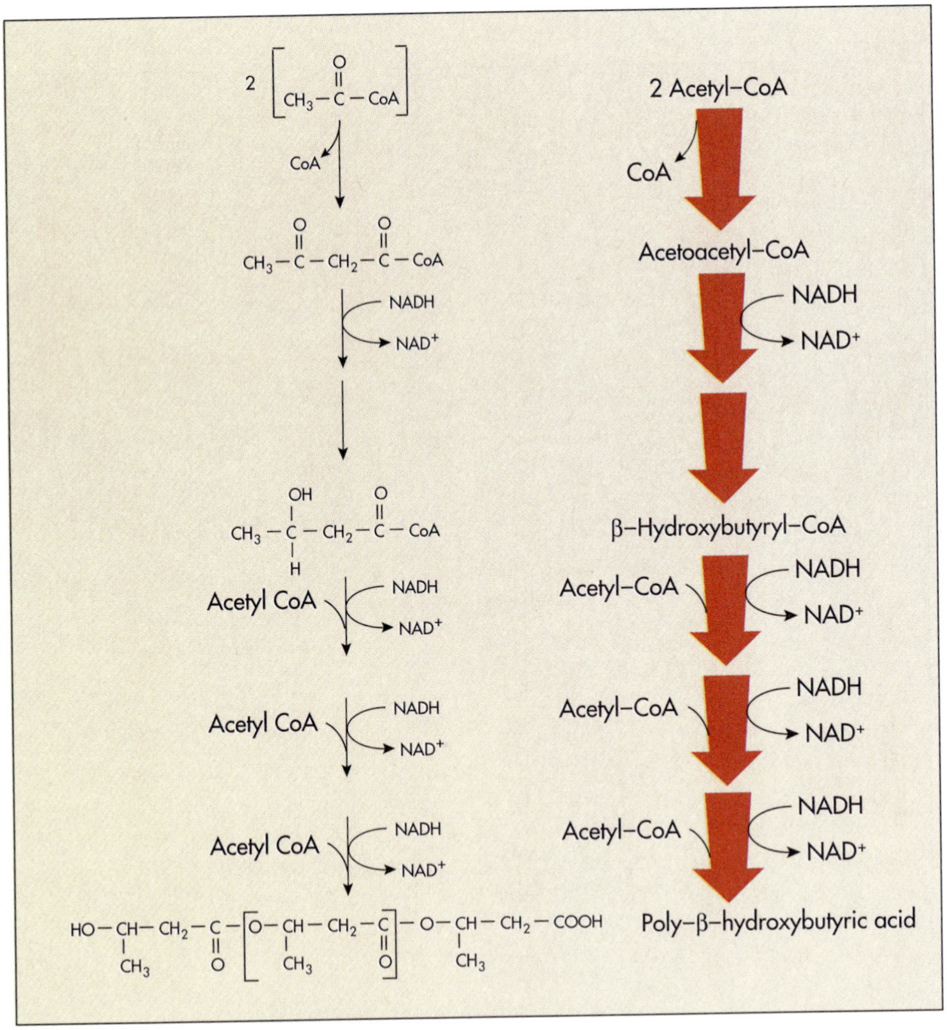

FIG. 5-15 The synthesis of poly-β-hydroxybutyric acid (poly-β-hydroxybutyrate) is used by bacteria to store carbon and energy reserves. This is an unusual biosynthetic pathway in that NADH, rather than NADPH, is used as a source of reducing power.

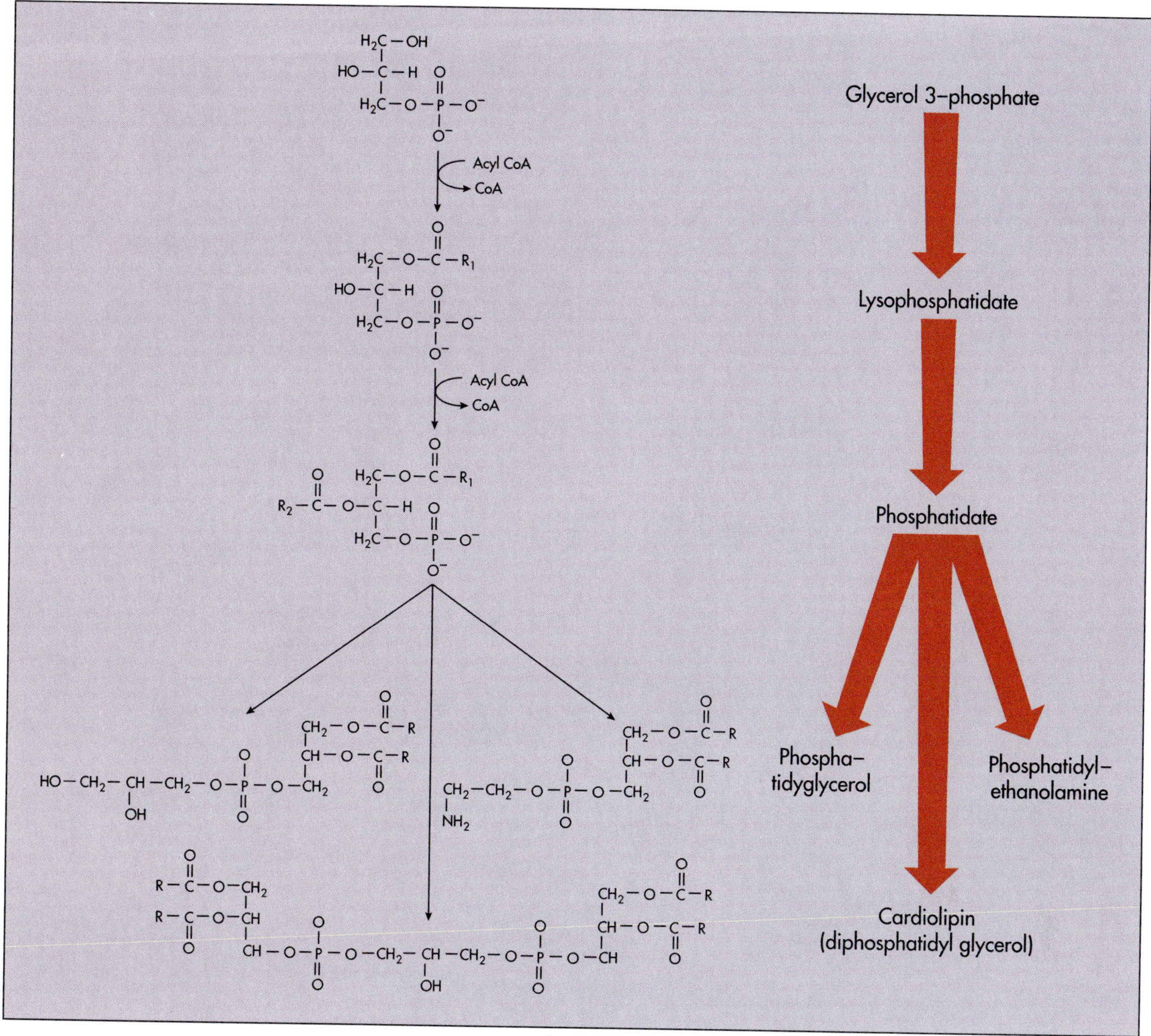

FIG. 5-16 The formation of phosphatidate and lipids, starting with glycerol 3-phosphate, is necessary for the formation of phospholipids for cellular membranes.

BIOSYNTHESIS OF STEROLS

The membranes of many eukaryotic cells contain sterols, such as cholesterol, that are made up of repeating units of the unsaturated hydrocarbon isoprene (isoprenoid hydrocarbons). Isoprenoid hydrocarbons are synthesized from acetyl-CoA molecules in an ATP-requiring reaction. The synthesis of isoprenoid hydrocarbons differs from fatty acid biosynthesis in the mechanism of chain elongation.

The synthesis of mevalonic acid from 3-hydroxy-3-methylglutaryl-CoA—derived from the reaction of acetyl-CoA with acetoacetyl-CoA—is the key step in the formation of cholesterol. The activity of the enzyme 3-hydroxy-3-methylglutaryl-CoA reductase regulates the rates of cholesterol biosynthesis. The biosynthesis of cholesterol exemplifies the fundamental mechanisms of long chain carbon skeleton formation from 5-carbon isoprenoid units (FIG. 5-17).

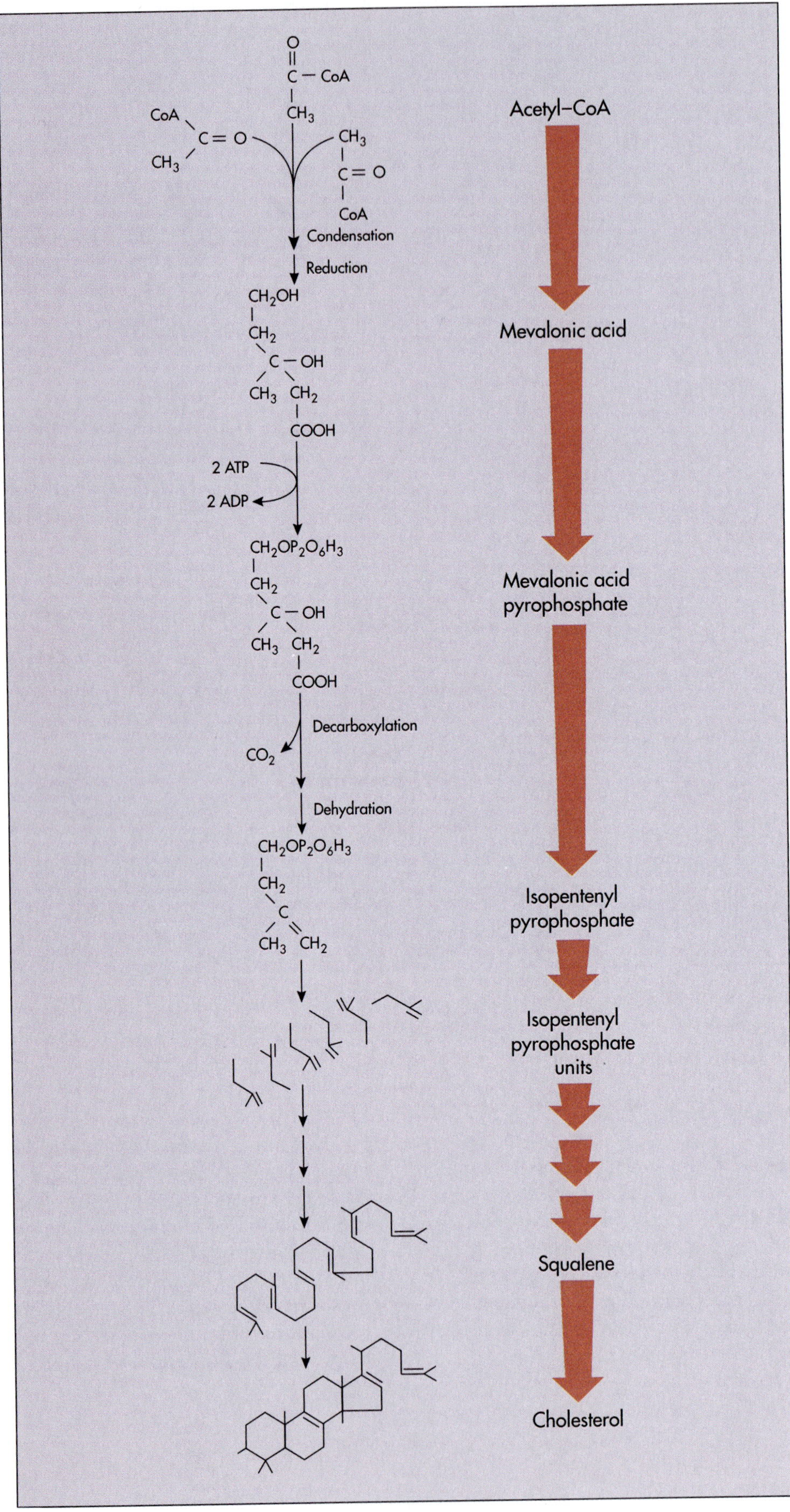

FIG. 5-17 The synthesis of cholesterol involves the formation and subsequent condensation of isopentenyl pyrophosphate units from acetyl-CoA.

5.6 BIOSYNTHESIS OF AMINO ACIDS FOR PROTEINS

Protein biosynthesis can be viewed as occurring in two parts: (1) formation of the 20 amino acids that serve as the basic chemical building blocks of proteins and (2) linkage of the amino acids in the proper sequence to form the primary structure of a protein molecule. The sequential ordering of amino acids to form the primary protein structure is under the direct control of the genetic informational macromolecules, DNA and RNA; that aspect of protein biosynthesis is covered in Chapter 6 as part of the discussion of genetic expression. In this section we consider the biosynthetic pathways for the amino acids that become linked into protein chains.

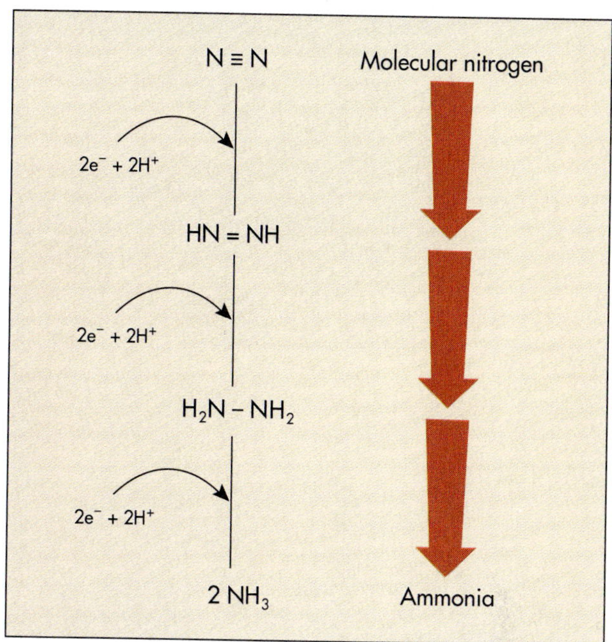

FIG. 5-18 Nitrogen fixation involves a series of sequential reductions of nitrogen compounds, all of which are catalyzed by the nitrogenase enzyme complex.

NITROGEN FIXATION AND THE FORMATION OF AMMONIUM IONS

The incorporation of inorganic nitrogen into organic molecules is needed for the synthesis of amino acids, which all contain at least one nitrogen atom per molecule. Although molecular nitrogen (N_2) is abundant in the atmosphere, most organisms are unable to use it as a source of nitrogen for incorporation into amino acids and the other nitrogen-containing compounds of the cell. Most cells require a supply of "fixed" forms of nitrogen, which can be ammonium, nitrate or nitrite ions, or organic nitrogen-containing compounds formed by other cells.

A limited number of eubacteria and archaebacteria have the ability to perform **nitrogen fixation,** the transformation of molecular nitrogen into ammonium nitrogen (that is, nitrogen combined within ammonium ions). These microorganisms possess **nitrogenase,** an enzyme complex that catalyzes their nitrogen-fixing abilities (FIG. 5-18). The process is highly endergonic and requires reducing power from reduced ferredoxin and energy from ATP. The equation for this reaction is:

$$N_2 + 6e^- + 6H^+ \rightarrow 2NH_3 \qquad (\Delta G = +150 \text{ kcal/mole})$$

The ammonia (NH_3) forms ammonium ions (NH_4^+) in water and is further assimilated into amino acids. Amino acids can be combined to form proteins or used to synthesize nucleic acid, which are also nitrogen-containing organic molecules.

Nitrogenase is a complex of two coproteins. One coprotein, **dinitrogenase,** has an attached cofactor that contains iron and molybdenum **(FeMoco)** or vanadium in some bacteria. It is responsible for reducing N_2 to NH_3. The other coprotein, **dinitrogenase reductase,** contains only iron atoms in its cofactor. This iron-containing coprotein transfers electrons from reduced ferredoxins and channels them to the dinitrogenase protein (FIG. 5-19). The reduction of the extremely stable N≡N triple bond is thought to occur in sequential steps on the dinitrogenase coprotein, forming N═N double bond and N—N single bond intermediates with each pair of electrons that is added. Therefore at least six electrons are required to completely reduce N_2 to NH_3. The breaking of bonds during the conversion of N_2 to NH_3 requires the input of energy, and hydrolysis of 12 to 15 ATP molecules are required.

Nitrogen fixation is a reductive process and is inhibited by O_2. This is because the dinitrogenase reductase is inactivated by O_2. In aerobically growing bacteria that can fix nitrogen it is thought that the cells create an anaerobic environment within the cytoplasm to maintain the activity of this enzyme. Other bacteria and cyanobacteria only fix nitrogen under anaerobic conditions.

Nitrogen-fixing organisms are important because they provide a supply of fixed nitrogen that can be assimilated by other organisms for incorporation into amino acids and other essential nitrogen-containing biochemicals. Biological nitrogen fixation is restricted to several bacterial genera such as *Rhizobium, Brady-*

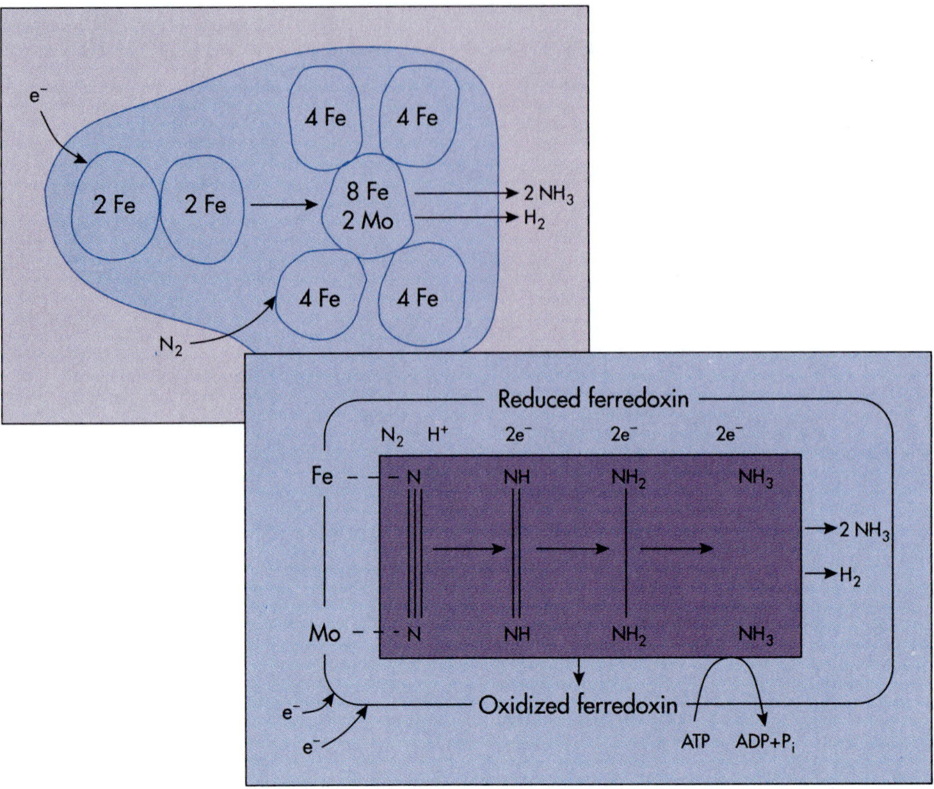

FIG. 5-19 Nitrogenase is an enzyme system composed of dinitrogenase and dinitrogenase reductase. In this system, electrons are transferred from reduced ferredoxins to convert molecular nitrogen, with its triple bond, into ammonia. The reaction center of dinitrogenase has an iron-molybdenum cofactor, containing 2 Mo atoms and 24 to 32 Fe atoms, that is critical in the conversion of nitrogen to ammonia.

rhizobium, Azotobacter, Frankia, Anabaena, and *Nostoc* (FIG. 5-20). These nitrogen-fixing bacteria are the only natural source of fixed nitrogen, and their nitrogen-fixing activity is necessary to support the growth of non-nitrogen-fixing organisms, including plants and humans. Nowadays, however, large amounts of industrially produced nitrogenous fertilizers supplement the natural bacterial supply.

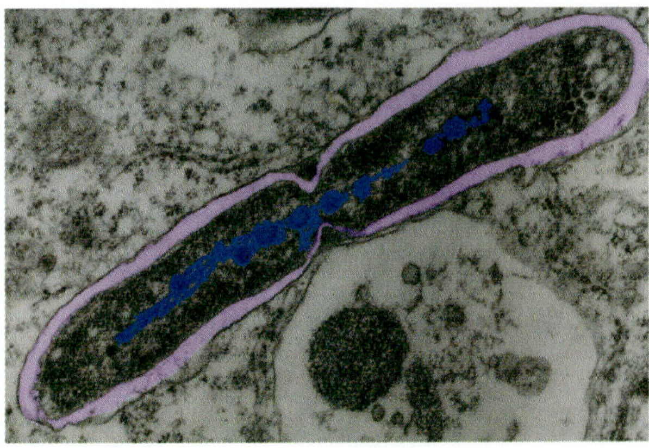

FIG. 5-20 Colorized micrograph of the nitrogen-fixing bacterium *Bradyrhizobium japonicum.* (22,000×).

INCORPORATION OF AMMONIUM IONS INTO AMINO ACIDS

The amino acid L-glutamate can be formed from the reaction of ammonium ions with α-ketoglutarate, a TCA cycle intermediate, in a pathway known as **reductive amination.** This pathway is catalyzed by the enzyme glutamate dehydrogenase and requires reducing power in the form of NADPH or NADH. When the concentration of ammonium ions is relatively high the process of reductive amination proceeds via their direct combination with an α-ketocarboxylic acid such as α-ketoglutarate.

For most microorganisms, however, this does not appear to be the main pathway incorporating ammonium ions into amino acids, since the concentration of ammonium ions is usually relatively low. Under these conditions microorganisms resort to another pathway for the formation of L-glutamate, the **glutamine synthetase/glutamate synthase pathway.** In this pathway, a pre-existing molecule of L-glutamate reacts with ammonium ions to form L-glutamine. This reaction is catalyzed by glutamine synthetase and requires energy in the form of ATP. The L-glutamine then reacts with α-ketoglutarate to form two molecules of L-glutamate in a reaction that is catalyzed by glutamate synthase and requires the reducing power of NADPH. Thus the net reaction catalyzed by the enzymes glutamine synthetase and glutamate synthase is:

$$\alpha\text{-Ketoglutarate} + NH_4^+ + \text{NADPH} + \text{ATP} \rightarrow \text{L-glutamate} + \text{NADP}^+ + \text{ADP} + P_i$$

The enzyme glutamine synthetase plays a key role in regulating the rates of intermediary metabolism because of the regulatory control it exerts on the flow of nitrogen into amino acids and consequently into proteins and nucleic acids.

Glutamine synthetase is subject to cumulative feedback inhibition by each of the products of glutamine metabolism, that is, a series of different feedback inhibitors can act additively to reduce the enzyme's activity. Inhibitors of glutamine synthetase include tryptophan, histidine, alanine, glycine, carbamoyl phosphate, glucosamine-6-phosphate, cytidine triphosphate (CTP), and AMP. Each of these allosteric inhibitors appears to have its own binding site on the enzyme, and when all eight inhibitors are bound to the enzyme its activity is virtually shut off. AMP plays a particularly important role in this system of inhibition because when AMP is bound to the enzyme it makes the enzyme more susceptible to the cumulative feedback effects of other inhibitors.

BIOSYNTHESIS OF THE MAJOR FAMILIES OF AMINO ACIDS

The assimilation of nitrogen to form the amino acid L-glutamate establishes the basis for the biosynthesis of the other essential amino acids in protein macromolecules, as well as for the biosynthesis of other essential nitrogen-containing compounds. The 20 L-amino acids in proteins originate from 6 different non-amino acid precursors, and as a result, there are only six biosynthetic families of amino acids (FIG. 5-21).

L-Glutamate is the parent molecule of the amino acid family that also contains L-glutamine, L-proline,

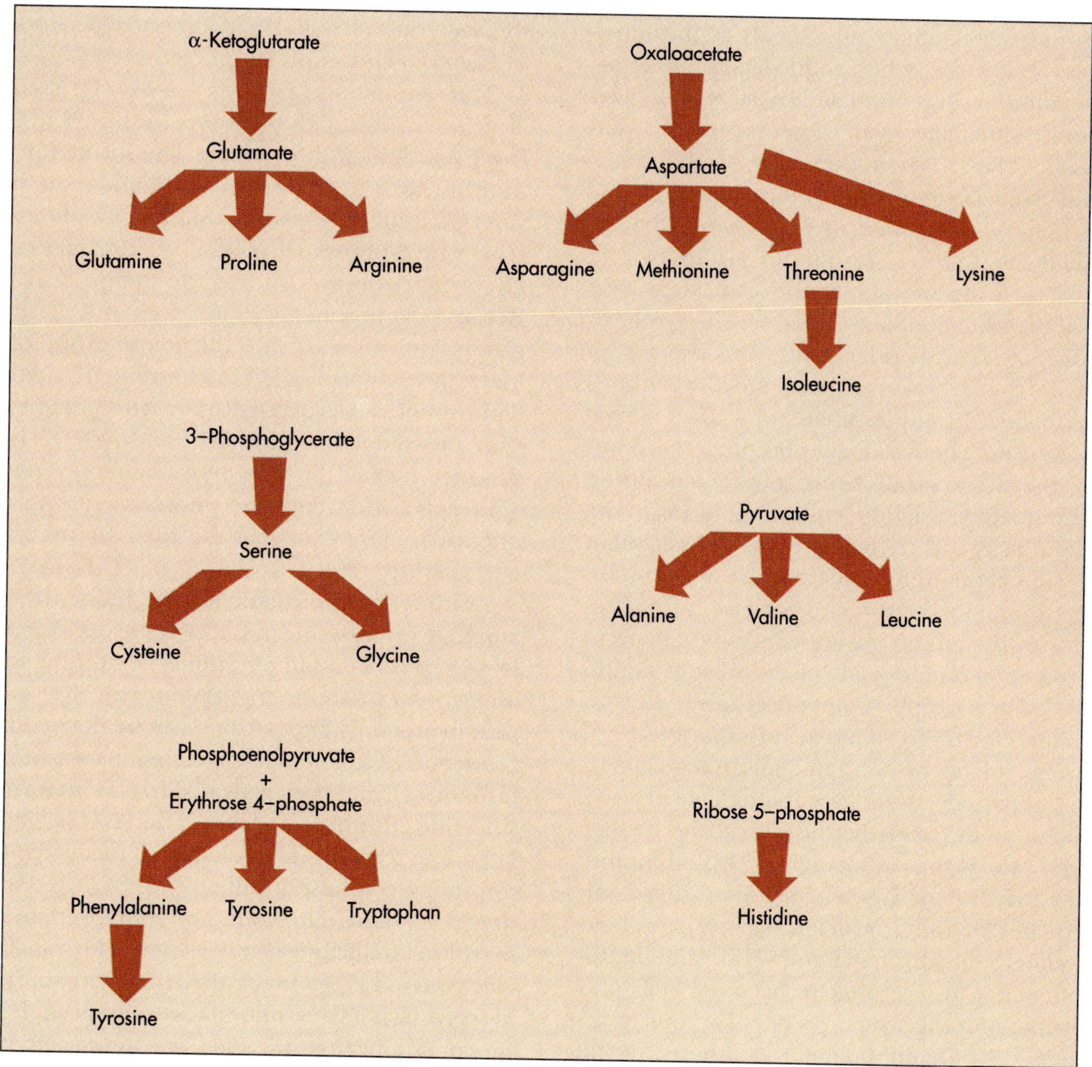

FIG. 5-21 The biosynthesis of the 20 L-amino acids in proteins represents the formation of six families of related amino acids.

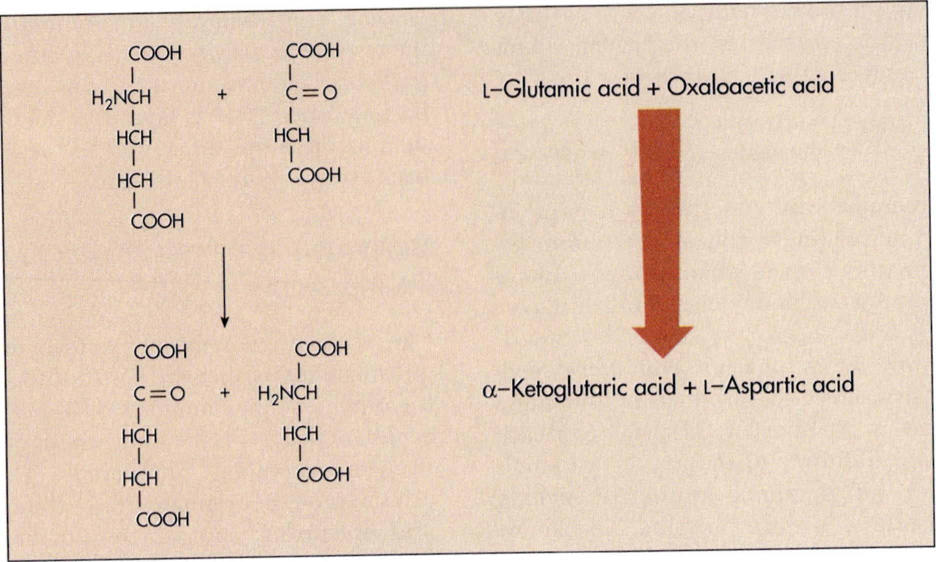

FIG. 5-22 Once nitrogen is incorporated into an amino acid, such as L-glutamic acid, the amino group can be transferred in a transamination reaction to form a new amino acid, such as L-aspartic acid.

and L-arginine. L-Glutamate also serves as the nitrogen source for all the other amino acids. In other words, the amino group of all amino acids is derived from that of L-glutamate, even those not in the L-glutamate family. The carbon skeletons of the other amino acids come from various intermediates of the glycolytic, pentose phosphate, or TCA cycle pathways.

The ability to transfer the amino group of one amino acid to form another amino acid, a process known as **transamination,** is essential for the synthesis of all of the amino acids (FIG. 5-22). This process involves specific transaminase enzymes and also requires the coenzyme pyridoxal phosphate, which is a derivative of vitamin B_6. The pyridoxal phosphate becomes bonded to the amino group being transferred during the transamination reaction collecting it from the donor amino acid and passing it on to the recipient molecule. Glutamate transaminase is the most important of the transaminase enzymes because it catalyzes the transfer of the amino group from L-glutamate to form the parental amino acids of the various amino acid families. For example, L-glutamate can react with oxaloacetate to form the amino acid L-aspartate.

L-Aspartate, made by transamination of oxaloacetate with L-glutamate, is the parent molecule of a second family of amino acids because it can be further metabolized to form L-asparagine, L-methionine, L-threonine, L-lysine, or L-isoleucine. Two intermediary metabolites in the conversion of L-aspartate to L-lysine, namely dihydrodipicolinic acid, and meso-diaminopimelic acid, are used in bacterial cells and do not form part of the structures of eukaryotic or archaebacterial cells. Diaminopimelic acid is one of the unusual amino acids that forms part of the peptide portion of the peptidoglycan molecule that makes up the bacterial cell wall. Dipicolinic acid occurs uniquely in bacterial endospores.

Transamination reactions can also be used to generate the amino acids L-alanine, L-valine, and L-leucine from reactions with pyruvate. The formation of L-alanine involves a single-step transamination that converts pyruvate to L-alanine. Similarly, L-glutamate can react with 3-phosphoglycerate, an intermediate of the glycolytic pathway, to form the amino acid L-serine. Because 3-phosphoglycerate does not have a keto group that can react with the amino group of L-glutamate, the 3-phosphoglycerate must first be oxidized to 3-phosphohydroxypyruvate, a reaction that is coupled with the reduction of NAD^+ to NADH. The initial product formed by the transamination reaction is 3-phosphoserine, and the phosphate group is subsequently removed to yield the final amino acid product, L-serine.

L-Serine is a precursor for the biosynthesis of the amino acids L-glycine and L-cysteine. L-Cysteine is one of the sulfur-containing amino acids, and the transformation of L-serine to L-cysteine involves a reaction with hydrogen sulfide, which can be derived from the reduction of sulfate. First, sulfate ions are transported into the cell and then activated by ATP to form adenosine phosphosulfate (APS). The APS is phosphorylated by a second ATP molecule to form adenosine-3′-phosphate-5′-phosphosulfate (PAPS). The PAPS is reduced to sulfite and AMP. The sulfite is then reduced by sulfite reductase using 3 NADPH (transferring 6 electrons) to H_2S. Finally, the H_2S is incorporated into *O*-acetyl serine to form L-cysteine and acetate. The sulfur-containing amino acids are important in determining the secondary structure of proteins, particularly due to the ability of two cysteine molecules in dif-

BOX 5-3

DETERMINING THE STEPS OF A BIOSYNTHETIC PATHWAY

Several approaches are useful in determining the steps in a biosynthetic pathway. One approach relies on the premise that every enzyme, including each enzyme in a biosynthetic pathway, is specified by a single gene (see FIG.). Although there are exceptions, in which multiple genes contribute to the formation of a single enzyme, it holds for most enzymes and was useful in elucidating many biosynthetic pathways. If a single enzyme is genetically encoded by a single gene, one can search for mutants, or in other words, strains of genetically altered microorganisms whose genetic changes only affect specific enzymes. In particular, one looks for mutants carrying alterations only in the gene that codes for an enzyme in a biosynthetic pathway. Assuming that the product of that pathway is necessary for growth, such a mutant will have a nutritional requirement for the biosynthetic product that it would otherwise synthesize for itself. Supplying the specific compound that cannot be synthesized because of the loss of the enzyme (not the end product of the pathway), will permit the mutant organisms to grow and will identify the supplied compound as an intermediate of the pathway that leads to formation of the end product. By repeating this process with other mutants all the intermediates of the pathway can be identified, provided a full set of mutants, each deficient in a different enzyme of the pathway, can be found. The eight steps in the biosynthesis of arginine from glutamate were identified in this way using mutants of *Salmonella typhimurium*.

Fortunately, the search for possible intermediary metabolites is not a process of random chance. Blockage

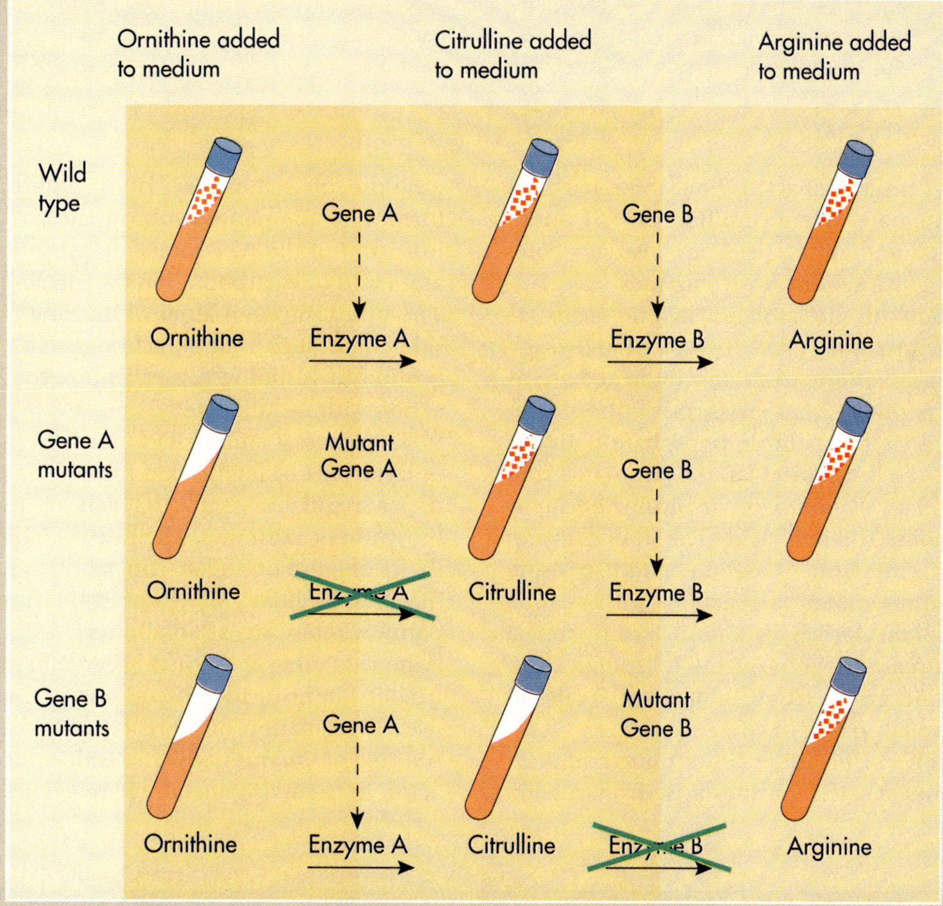

The one gene–one polypeptide hypothesis was experimentally demonstrated. Mutant strains were unable to carry out complete biosynthetic pathways. For example, a wild type *Escherichia coli*, which has a complete pathway for the synthesis of arginine, could grow on ornithine, citrulline, or arginine. A mutant strain with a mutation in gene A fails to produce enzyme A that is needed for the conversion of ornithine to citrulline; such gene A mutants could grow on citrulline and arginine but not ornithine. A mutant strain with a mutation in gene B fails to produce enzyme B; such gene B mutants could only grow on arginine but not ornithine or citrulline. This experiment confirmed that one gene codes for the production of individual enzymes. It also allowed the pathway ornithine → citrulline → arginine to be deduced.

Continued.

BOX 5-3—CONT'D

of a pathway at a particular point causes intermediates of the pathway produced prior to the blocked step to accumulate and to be excreted into the surrounding medium. The metabolites that accumulate in the medium can permit the growth of other strains if they are blocked at a point earlier in the pathway than the supplied intermediate, but not if they are blocked at a point later than the supplied intermediate. Therefore the positions in a pathway of the enzymes missing from a series of different mutant strains can be determined by fairly straightforward deduction. Alternatively, the abilities of substances whose biochemical structures make them seem likely intermediates in a pathway can be tested to see if they overcome the metabolic blockages in various mutants. Such empirical (experimental) testing of compounds deduced to be likely intermediates (or in other words, educated guessing) has frequently been successfully employed in the search for intermediates in biosynthetic pathways.

A quite different approach is the use of radioactively labelled (radiolabeled) compounds as so-called "tracers" to trace the flow of the radiolabeled atoms through the various intermediates of a pathway. A radiolabeled compound is supplied in the growth medium, sometimes continuously, sometimes for only a short time. After allowing the organisms to grow and so incorporate the atoms of the radiolabeled compound into their biochemicals, the cells are chemically fractionated and the compounds now containing the radiolabeled atoms identified. This makes it possible to determine what chemicals the radiolabeled compound is transformed into. Also, examining the varying levels of radioactivity in the various intermediates can reveal the order in which the newly identified intermediates are formed within the pathway under study. For example, when glutamate labelled with radioactive carbon-14 atoms (^{14}C-radiolabeled glutamate) is added to growing bacterial cells, the radioactive carbon atoms are incorporated into protein. Analysis of the protein reveals that the labelled atoms are concentrated in the amino acids glutamate, proline, and arginine. This indicates that glutamate is a biosynthetic precursor of proline and arginine. Various biosynthetic pathways have been elucidated using such radiotracer methods.

ferent parts of a protein chain to hold these parts together by forming a covalent disulfide (S—S) bond. The sulfur-containing amino acids are also key components of the active sites of many enzymes.

The formation of the aromatic amino acids, L-phenylalanine, L-tyrosine, and L-tryptophan, originates with phosphoenolpyruvate (an intermediate of the glycolytic pathway) and erythrose-4-phosphate, which is formed via the pentose phosphate pathway. The details of the formation of the aromatic ring structure are relatively complex, involving the intermediate metabolite shikimic acid. The amino group of the amino acids L-phenylalanine and L-tyrosine arise through transamination reactions with L-glutamate. L-Tryptophan derives its amino group from a transamination reaction with L-serine (although L-serine gets its amino group from L-glutamate, as do all amino acids, directly or indirectly).

The formation of L-histidine also is quite complex. Histidine and nucleic acid purines arise from a common precursor molecule, ribose-5-phosphate, which is formed by the pentose phosphate pathway. The adenine unit of the ATP molecule provides one nitrogen atom and one carbon atom for the ring of L-histidine. The other nitrogen atom of the ring comes from the side chain of the amino acid L-glutamate. The amino group of L-histidine comes from a transamination reaction with L-glutamate.

The rates of amino acid biosynthesis are regulated in large part by feedback inhibition. Usually there is a major regulatory step in each of the amino acid biosynthetic pathways. The rates of amino acid biosynthesis depend on the activities of the enzymes catalyzing these regulatory steps, and the final product of a pathway often acts as an allosteric inhibitor of the enzyme catalyzing the critical regulatory step. The control of amino acid biosynthesis is important in the overall regulation of metabolism because of the central role of enzymes, which are all composed of amino acids, in catalyzing metabolic reactions.

5.7 BIOSYNTHESIS OF NUCLEOTIDES FOR NUCLEIC ACIDS

The nucleic acids DNA and RNA lie at the very heart of the activities of the cell, holding the genetic information needed to construct and maintain a cell and allowing it to be expressed as required. These nucleic acids are composed of nucleotides, themselves composed of chemicals known as nitrogenous bases, linked to sugar groups and phosphate groups.

There are two classes of nitrogenous bases in nucleotides, the **purines** and **pyrimidines.** The pathways for the biosynthesis of the purine and pyrimidine ring structures of nucleic acid bases are quite complex, so only a cursory overview will be given here. The ribonucleotides of RNA are made first and then subsequently modified enzymatically to form the deoxynu-

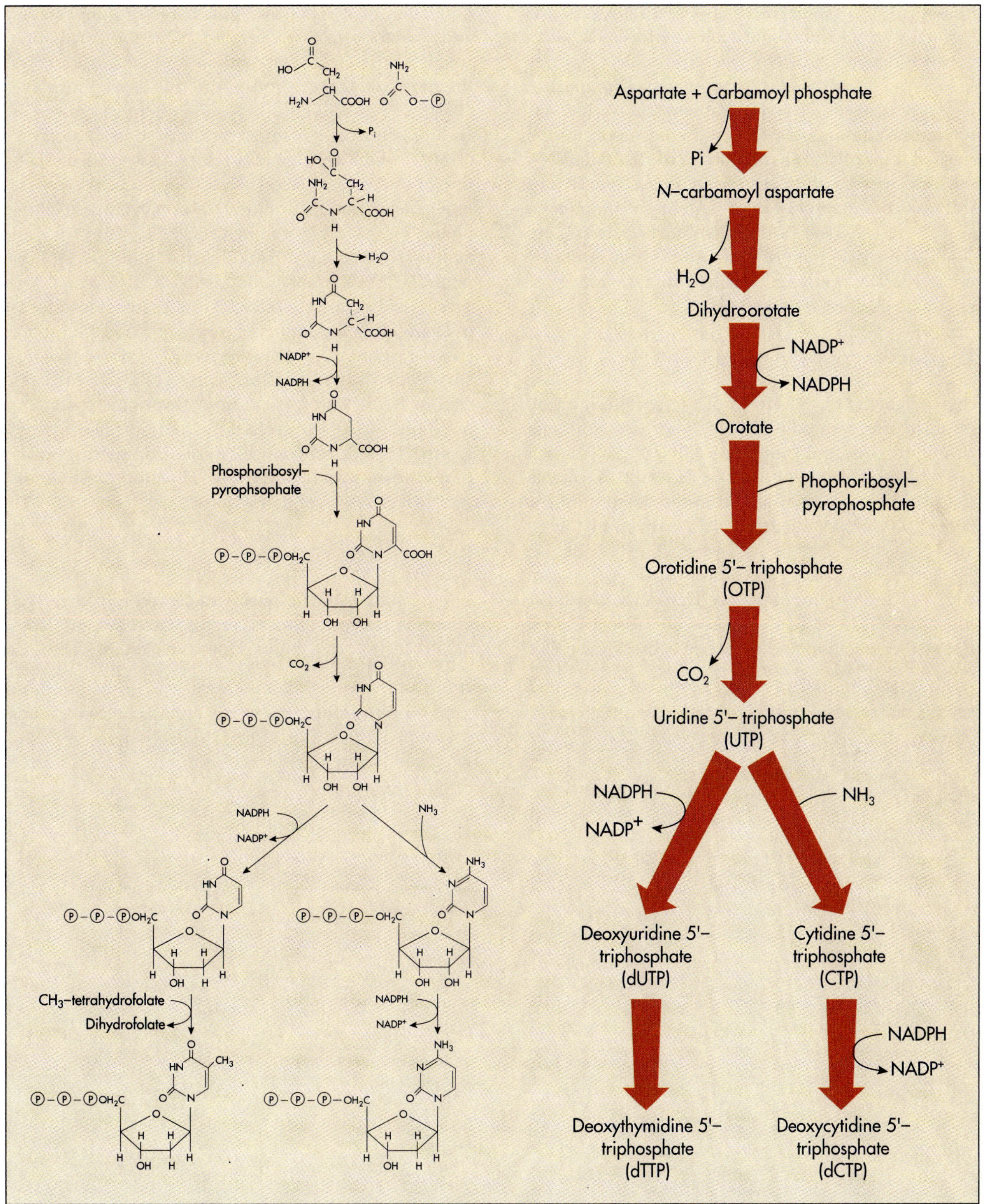

FIG. 5-23 The formation of a pyrimidine ring is necessary for the biosynthesis of nucleic acids. This pathway results in the formation of uridine triphosphate (UTP) from aspartate and carbamoyl phosphate. The conversion of uridine triphosphate to cytidine triphosphate forms the nucleotide found in RNA (CTP), and the conversion of ribose to deoxyribose produces the cytidine triphosphate of DNA (dCTP). UTP also is converted to thymidine triphosphate (dTTP) found in DNA.

cleotides of DNA. This may reflect the fact that RNA is a more primitive molecule than DNA. RNA probably existed as an informational molecule for cells before the evolution of the DNA macromolecules that now serve as the hereditary informational macromolecules of all living cells. The biosynthesis of purine and pyrimidine-containing nucleotides is important because of their role as the precursors of DNA and RNA, but also because they are found in ATP, ADP, and AMP (all adenine nucleotides) and in the major coenzymes NAD^+/NADH, $NADP^+$/NADPH, and CoA. Nucleotides are also important activators and inhibitors of many key enzymes that regulate the rates of various metabolic reactions within cells.

BIOSYNTHESIS OF PYRIMIDINES

The precursors of the atoms of the **pyrimidine ring,** found in the pyrimidine nucleotides, are ammonia, carbon dioxide, and L-aspartate (FIG. 5-23). The synthesis of the pyrimidine ring begins with the formation of carbamoyl aspartate, from the reaction of carbamoyl phosphate and aspartate, catalyzed by the enzyme aspartate transcarbamoylase. This is the key regulatory step in the biosynthesis of the pyrimidine ring, and the enzyme aspartate transcarbamoylase is subject to allosteric feedback inhibition by the products of the reaction, and allosteric activation by ATP. The succeeding steps in the formation of the pyrimidine ring involve dehydration, cyclic ring formation, and oxidation to form orotate. After the pyrimidine ring is synthesized, ribose and phosphate are added to the molecule using 5-phosphoribosyl-l-pyrophosphate (PRPP). A carboxyl group is subsequently removed as carbon dioxide, forming uridine monophosphate (UMP), which is then phosphorylated to form UTP, one of the nucleotides of RNA.

The UTP can be modified to form cytidine triphosphate, by the replacement of a keto group with an amino group in the pyrimidine ring. Cytidine triphosphate (CTP) is a nucleotide in both RNA and DNA. The ribose sugar is reduced to the deoxyribose form in DNA, using the reducing power of NADPH and the enzyme ribonucleoside reductase. UTP is also the precursor for thymidine triphosphate (TTP), which occurs in DNA. The formation of thymidine for incorporation into DNA involves the addition of a methyl group, derived from serine, to the uridine ring structure to form thymine, and the reduction of ribose using NADPH to form deoxyribose.

BIOSYNTHESIS OF PURINES

The formation of the **purine nucleotides,** which contain two rings joined together, is somewhat more complex than that of the pyrimidine nucleotides (FIG. 5-

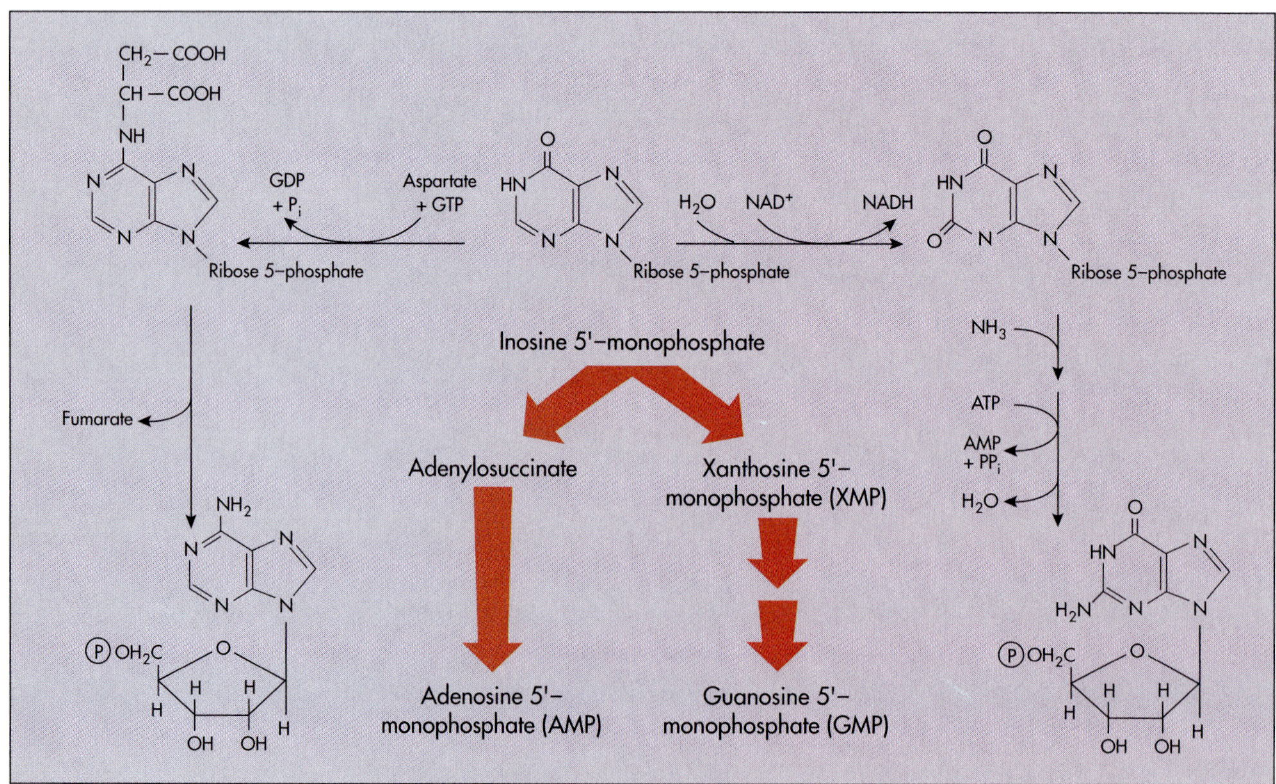

FIG. 5-24 The pathway leading to the biosynthesis of the purine nucleotides adenosine and guanosine for incorporation into RNA and DNA are complex. The carbons involved in the formation of a purine ring are derived from several sources.

24). Ten metabolic steps are involved in the formation of the basic purine ring structure. It is synthesized from various amino acids, including L-aspartate, L-glycine, and L-glutamine. Carbon dioxide and a methyl group donated from folic acid are also essential for the formation of the purine ring skeleton. The initial step in the synthesis of the purine ring involves the addition of an amino group to a phosphorylated ribose molecule. The pathway then continues with the phosphorylated ribose of the eventual nucleotide already attached. This is in contrast to the synthesis of the pyrimidine ring and eventual pyrimidine nucleotides, in which the ribose group is added after formation of the ring structure. Once the basic purine ring is completed, it is modified to form the adenine and guanine nucleotides.

Biosynthesis of the adenine ring involves the substitution of an amino group for a keto group. The biosynthesis of the guanine ring involves the addition of an amino group without the removal of a keto group. The adenosine phosphate molecule that is formed serves not only as a nucleotide base in RNA and DNA, but also in the ATP, NAD^+/NADH, $NADP^+$/NADPH, CoA, and FAD molecules. Thus the synthesis of purine nucleotides is crucial for the biosynthesis of many of the most important molecules that act as energy carriers and coenzymes in the biochemical reactions of cellular metabolism.

CHAPTER REVIEW

STUDY QUESTIONS

1. What is the Calvin cycle, and what is its function? Why is it called a *dark reaction cycle?*
2. What is an amphibolic pathway? What is a catabolic pathway? What is an anabolic pathway?
3. What is gluconeogenesis? How would a cell make glucose starting with a protein?
4. What is the problem with metabolizing compounds containing only two carbons, such as acetate?
5. How is nitrogen incorporated into organic compounds to form amino acids?
6. How is sulfur incorporated into organic compounds to form amino acids?
7. How are allosteric effectors involved in regulating the flow of carbon through a cell?
8. What is the general strategy of a cell in terms of carbon flow?
9. What is the relationship of the reductive TCA cycle to the regular TCA cycle?
10. How do cells incorporate C-1 compounds into organic molecules?
11. What is energy charge? How does it effect the overall metabolism of the cell?
12. Where do the three stages of peptidoglycan biosynthesis occur? What are the main features of each stage?
13. What is nitrogen fixation? Why is it so important?
14. What is the overall organization of a cell's biosynthesis of the amino acids?
15. Explain the importance of ATP as a precursor molecule used in cell biosynthesis.

SITUATIONAL PROBLEMS

1. Determining What is Needed to Synthesize a Cell

We have seen that given the necessary enzymes, cells can transform a starting substrate molecule into all of its macromolecular constituents. Let us consider the composition of a simple hypothetical bacterial cell. The cell has 2,000,000 protein molecules, 200,000 RNA molecules, 1 DNA molecule, and 20,000,000 lipid molecules. It has no cell wall and hence no peptidoglycan. Besides lacking a cell wall, this bacterial cell is very unusual in several other ways. Its proteins are composed only of the amino acids proline (an amino acid with five carbon atoms) and glycine (an amino acid with two carbon atoms), which occur in equal concentrations. There are 10 different types of proteins. Each protein has 300 amino acids. The DNA and RNA contain only cytidine (a nucleotide containing 9 carbon atoms) and guanidine (a nucleotide containing 10 carbon atoms), which also occur in equal concentrations. The DNA molecule contains 1,000 nucleotide kilobase pairs. There are 30 types of RNA molecules. The RNA molecules each have 1,000 nucleotides. The lipids are all phospholipids containing glycerol and two attached chains of palmitic acid, which is a straight chain, saturated fatty acid containing 16 carbon atoms. The bacterium can grow on glucose as its sole source of carbon and energy.

1. Considering only the flow of carbon (ignore the need for ATP), draw the pathways needed to convert glucose into the macromolecules of this cell. (You may wish to consult one of the biochemistry texts listed in the Suggested Supplementary Readings.)
2. Based on the composition of this cell, and again considering only the flow of carbon (ignore the need for ATP), determine how many glucose molecules are needed to synthesize the macromolecules required for this cell to divide and produce an exact replicate.

Suggested Supplementary Readings

Carman GM and SA Henry: 1989. Phospholipid biosynthesis in yeast, *Annual Review of Biochemistry* 58:635-670.

Crawford IP: 1989. Evolution of a biosynthetic pathway: The tryptophan paradigm, *Annual Review of Microbiology* 43:567-600.

Doyle RJ, J Chaloupka, V Vinter: 1988. Turnover of cell walls in microorganisms, *Microbiological Reviews* 52(4):554-567.

Gottschalk G: 1986. *Bacterial Metabolism,* ed. 2, Springer-Verlag, New York.

Lechner J and F Wieland: 1989. Structure and biosynthesis of prokaryotic glycoproteins, *Annual Review of Biochemistry* 58:173-194.

Lehninger L: 1982. *Principles of Biochemistry,* Worth Publishers, Inc., New York.

Magasanik B: 1982. Control of nitrogen assimilation in bacteria, *Annual Review of Genetics* 16:135-168.

Mandelstam J, K McQuillen, IW Dawes: 1982. *Biochemistry of Bacterial Growth,* Blackwell Scientific Publications, Oxford, England.

Mathews CK and KE van Holde: 1990. *Biochemistry,* Benjamin/Cummings, Menlo Park, CA.

Neidhardt FC, JL Ingraham, M Schaechter: 1990. *Physiology of the Bacterial Cell: A Molecular Approach,* Sinauer Associates, Sunderland, MA.

Scolnik PA and BL Marrs: 1987. Genetic research with photosynthetic bacteria, *Annual Review of Microbiology* 41:703-726.

Smith EL, RL Hill, IR Lehman, RJ Lefkowitz, P Handler, A White: 1983. *Principles of Biochemistry: General aspects,* ed. 7, McGraw-Hill, New York.

Stewart WDP: 1980. Some aspects of structure and function in N_2-fixing cyanobacteria, *Annual Review of Microbiology* 34:497-536.

Stryer L: 1988. *Biochemistry,* ed. 3, W. H. Freeman Co., San Francisco.

Vanden Boom T and JE Cronan Jr: 1989. Genetics and regulation of bacterial lipid metabolism, *Annual Review of Microbiology* 43:317-344.

Voet D and JG Voet: 1990. *Biochemistry,* John Wiley and Sons, New York.

Zubay G: 1993. *Biochemistry,* ed. 3, William C. Brown Communications, Inc., Dubuque, IA.

WHY I AM AMAZED BY SIMPLE THINGS

MOSELIO SCHAECHTER
TUFTS UNIVERSITY

Moselio Schaechter was born in Milan, Italy, in 1928, and was raised in Quito, Ecuador. He received degrees from the Universities of Kansas and Pennsylvania and currently is chair of the department of molecular biology and distinguished professor of microbiology at Tufts University in Boston. He was president of the American Society of Microbiology from 1985 to 1986. He studies the role of the cell membrane in bacterial DNA replication and segregation.

As is true for other researchers, a new result in the lab produces for me a surge of excitement and renewed enthusiasm. It is hard to describe the high that accompanies even a modest discovery. Sometimes this comes about in a simple way, such as by looking at colonies on a Petri dish or at an X-ray film of an elecrophoresis gel and realizing that here is an answer to a question that had not been asked before. Other times, the breakthrough follows the use of complex technology. Still, I reserve my sense of primordial awe not only for discovery as such but also for one of the simplest experiments in bacterial physiology, one that is done over and over in many laboratories. What I am referring to is the measurment of the growth of a bacterial culture in liquid medium. One can get an instantaneous reading simply by determining the turbidity of the culture at different times using a common light-metering device as a spectrophotometer. With time, as the bacteria grow, the turbidity increases and the readings go up apace. What is so spectacular to me is that in a rich medium the bacterial mass doubles in 20 minutes! And it does it every time, like clockwork. I find it hard to imagine how everything that goes into making bacteria—their enzymes, genes, structural elements—doubles so precisely and so rapidly. No wonder when I feel down I go to the bench and "run a growth curve!"

In our age, most experiments depend on sophisticated technology, appropriately so. Let me, nevertheless, try to explain, using my experience from a simpler age, why I still get excited about running growth curves. Until the mid-1950s, the growth of bacteria was something of a mystical subject. Cultures were known to go through stages: a lag phase, an exponential phase of rapid growth, and a stationary phase. Drawn on logarithmic paper, this looks like an S-shaped curve, which, in the old days, invited much theorizing about its deeper meaning. Many models were proposed based on the idea that these various phases of growth were inevitable and that a bacteria culture had to undergo all of them in order to make it. This, it turns out, is the wrong way to look at it. I was involved in the dispelling of these myths and in attempting to clarify what really goes on when bacteria grow, at least in the laboratory.

In the 1950s, I was working in the laboratory of a distinguished Danish microbiologist, Ole Maaløe. Besides enjoying the delights of Copenhagen, including Danish beer and *real* Danish pastry, I became involved in research on bacterial growth physiology using the enteric bacterium, *Salmonella typhimurium.* We based our work on a known fact that a given species of bacteria will grow more rapidly in a nutritionally complex medium, a so-called "rich medium," than in a "minimal medium" in which the only organic substance may be a simple sugar such as glucose. We wanted to know what happens when the cells find themselves abruptly in a different medium. How do they adjust? One of the experiments we did consisted of adding concentrated rich medium to a culture in the poor medium and following the turbidity as well as the cell number. What we learned is that after such a nutritional shift the cellular mass increases at the new rate, starting immediately, but that the increase in the number of cells lags behind. The simplest explanation was that cells growing in the poor medium were smaller than those growing in the concentrated medium and that the lag represented the time required for them to become larger. In other words, the cells grew in mass but for a while did not divide, hence the delay in the increase in numbers.

Why would cells of the same species differ in size? We wondered if this was an intrinsic property, dependent on the rate of growth alone rather than on the composition of the medium. We set up cultures in a collection of different media that supported various growth rates, from the slowest to the fastest attainable in the laboratory. The range of generation times was from 2 hours to 20 minutes per doubling at 37°. What we found is that there is a simple relationship between mass and growth rate and that the cells are indeed larger when they grow faster. Provided that the medium supports unhindered growth, its acutal composition influences cell size only as it determines the growth rate. In other words, cells growing in two different media but at the same growth rate have the same cell size.

This finding, which removed much of the mystery surrounding bacterial growth, led to the next question.

What is it about size of the cells that is influenced by the growth rate? How should one think about it? Bacteria consist mainly of proteins, which account for half or more of their dry weight. We wondered if fast-growing cells weren't larger because of having to accommodate more of the protein synthesizing apparatus, the ribosomes. We measured the content of ribosomes in cells growing at different rates and found, to our joy, that there was a simple relationship here too. The faster the growth rate, the more ribosomes per cell mass. In other words, the concentration of ribosomes is a linear function of the growth rate. As an aside, this relationship breaks down at very slow rates, which makes sense because otherwise cells growing infinitely slowly would have no ribosomes! Such cells would not be able to make proteins when placed in a better medium.

What does this linear relationship between ribosome content and growth rate tell us? First of all, the rate of protein synthesis is proportional to the growth rate, as long as cells grow unhindered. This means that the concentration of ribosomes is proportional to the rate of protein synthesis. In turn, this tells us that ribosomes operate at a single unit of efficiency, regardless of whether they find them selves in a small, slow-growing cell, or a large, fast-growing one. Another way of expressing this is that the rate of polymerization of proteins (the *chain growth rate*) is constant as long as cells are growing under what is known as balanced growth conditions. This was eventually measured directly by others, and it turns out that at 37°, bacteria hook together, on average, 14 amino acids per second, regardless of the medium. In time, it was found that this concept, that the polymerizing machinery of bacteria perform at unit rates, is also true for the biosynthesis of DNA, RNA, and cell wall constituents. This demonstrates the economy that bacteria exhibit in adapting to different growth environments. Instead of making the same amount of biosynthetic machinery under all conditions, which would be a burdensome strain on their economy, they make only what they actually need in a given condition. Thus, bacteria in different media are different. They obey the maxim of the Spanish philosopher Ortega y Gasset: "I am I and my circumstance" (*Yo soy yo y mi circunstancia*).

This way of thinking has led others to further experiments that have revealed a great deal the mechanisms that control gene expression in bacteria. How is the synthesis of the RNA of the ribosomes regulated? What about the synthesis of ribosomal proteins? What does this have to do with the general aspects of regulation of gene expression? Questions of this sort probe the central problems of biological regulation, and much has been learned from sophisticated and elaborate experiments that take advantage of a combination of physiological thinking and genetic tools. I have participated in this work and, as I stated at the beginning of this essay, derive much pleasure from this work. I still stand in awe at the ability of such seemingly simple cells to grow in such perfect rhythm.

Microbiologists routinely culture microorganisms to study their physiology.

PART THREE

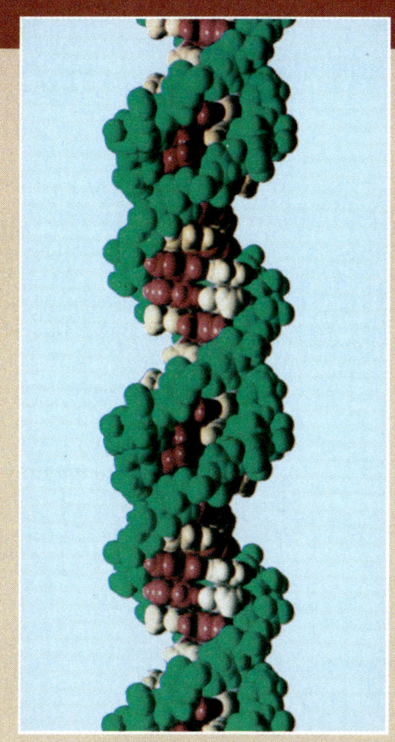

Microbial Genetics—Molecular Biology

CHAPTER 6

DNA Replication and Gene Expression

Chapter Outline

The genetics of the cell encompasses the replication and expression of its hereditary information. The hereditary information of all living cells is encoded in the cell's deoxyribonucleic acid molecule(s) (DNA). The information within the DNA determines the metabolic and structural nature of the organism. Expression of genetic information involves using information encoded within the DNA to direct the synthesis of proteins. By specifying and regulating protein synthesis, the genetic informational macromolecules define and control the metabolic capabilities of microorganisms.

The order of nucleotides in the DNA is used to specify the order of amino acids in a protein. The information in the DNA molecule is initially transferred to ribonucleic acid (RNA) molecules in a process called *transcription* (Transcription = DNA → RNA). The information encoded in the mRNA molecule is then translated into the sequence of amino acids that comprise the protein (Translation = RNA → protein). The DNA contains regulatory genes that control gene expression. The elucidation of the molecular-level events involved in the transmission and expression of genetic information has revolutionized our understanding of microbial genetics.

6.1 DNA REPLICATION

Replication of the hereditary information of a cell involves synthesizing new DNA molecules that have the same nucleotide sequence as the genome of the parental organism, a process that requires great precision (Replication = DNA → DNA). The genome of the progeny must contain the appropriate information to permit the survival and growth of the organism. Because changes in the sequence of nucleotides can greatly alter the characteristics of an organism, the process of DNA replication requires great fidelity. The process of DNA replication is designed to ensure that the progeny receive an accurate copy of the genetic information of the parent cell.

The double helical nature of the DNA macromolecule is critical for its replication. The discovery of the DNA double helix by James Watson and Francis Crick in 1953 revolutionized biology. The elucidation of the structure of DNA almost instantly revealed how hereditary information is transmitted from one generation to the next.

DNA (DEOXYRIBONUCLEIC ACID)

DNA is the macromolecule that stores the hereditary information of the cell. It is composed of subunits, called *nucleotides*, that are like the letters of the "genetic alphabet." The order of the nucleotides specifies the genetic information of the cell. The sequence of nucleotides within the DNA molecule encodes all the potential properties of that cell, determining the sequence of amino acids in a particular protein. This is like saying that the letters of a word create that word and hence its meaning. The genetic code, based on only the "few letters" (nucleotides) in its "alphabet," provides the necessary chemical basis for encoding the genetic information of the great diversity of living organisms.

Just as we have a convention for reading the letters of words (left to right in the English language), reading the sequence of nucleotides in the appropriate order is essential for converting stored genetic information into the functional activities of the organism. The structure of a DNA gives the macromolecule directionality. The directional nature of nucleic acid molecules is critical for establishing the necessary direction of reading the genetic information.

Within the double helical DNA macromolecule there are two polynucleotide chains that run in opposite direction. A consequence of this antiparallel nature of the DNA molecule is that different information is stored in each of the chains. This further means that for a given region of stored information, there must be some mechanism for designating which of the complementary chains is running in the appropriate manner for extracting the correct information coding for a particular function. As discussed later, there are indeed recognition sequences encoded within the DNA molecule that designate which chain to read, where to begin, and where to end.

Composition of DNA: Nucleotide Subunits

DNA macromolecules are made up of numerous subunits called *deoxyribonucleotides*. These deoxyribonucleotides generally are referred to as *nucleotides*, a generic term that also describes the ribonucleotides found in RNA. Each deoxyribonucleotide consists of a nucleic acid base, the sugar deoxyribose, and phosphate (FIG. 6-1).

Four different nucleic acid bases occur in the nucleotides of DNA: adenine, guanine, cytosine, and thymine. **Adenine (A)** and **guanine (G)** are **purines**, which are molecules composed of two fused rings. **Cytosine (C)** and **thymine (T)** are **pyrimidines**, which have only one ring. Both purines and pyrimidines are heterocyclic molecules; their rings contain two kinds of atoms, carbon and nitrogen instead of just carbon. The nucleic acid bases are attached to the deoxyribose sugars to form deoxyribonucleosides, and the deoxyribonucleosides are joined to a phosphate group on carbon 5′ of the sugar to form the deoxyribonucleotide subunits of DNA (Table 6-1).

The deoxyribonucleotides in DNA are linked by 3′–5′ phosphodiester bonds (FIG. 6-2). Consequently, at one end of the nucleic acid molecule, there is no phosphodiester bond to the 3′-carbon of the monosaccharide; thus there is an unattached, or

TABLE 6-1 Names of the Most Common Bases in DNA and RNA and Corresponding Names of Nucleosides and Nucleotides Containing These Bases

NUCLEIC ACID BASE	NUCLEOSIDE*	NUCLEOTIDE*
Adenine (DNA or RNA)	Adenosine	Adenylate (or adenylic acid)
Cytosine (DNA or RNA)	Cytidine	Cytidylate (or cytidylic acid)
Guanine (DNA or RNA)	Guanosine	Guanylate (or guanylic acid)
Thymine (DNA)	Thymidine	Thymidylate (or thymidylic acid)
Uracil (RNA)	Uridine	Uridylate (or uridylic acid)

*The prefix deoxy- or deoxyribo- is added to nucleosides or nucleotides of the deoxyribose type. The prefix ribo- is added to nucleosides or nucleotides of the ribose type.

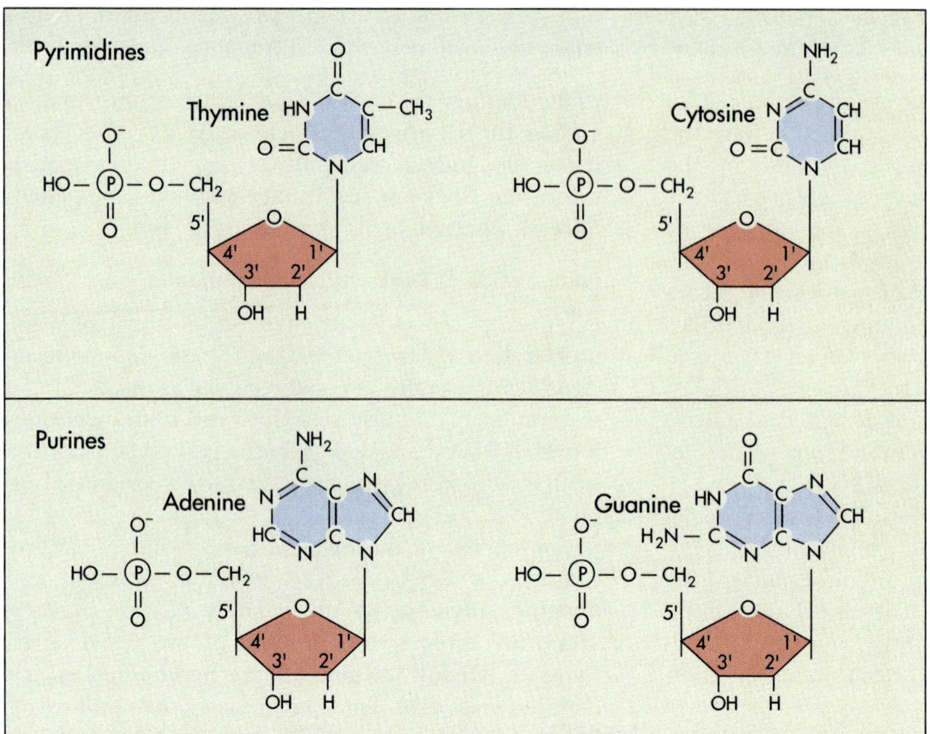

FIG. 6-1 Four different deoxyribonucleotides comprise the subunit molecules of DNA. These have differing nucleic acid bases: thymine, cytosine, adenine, and guanine.

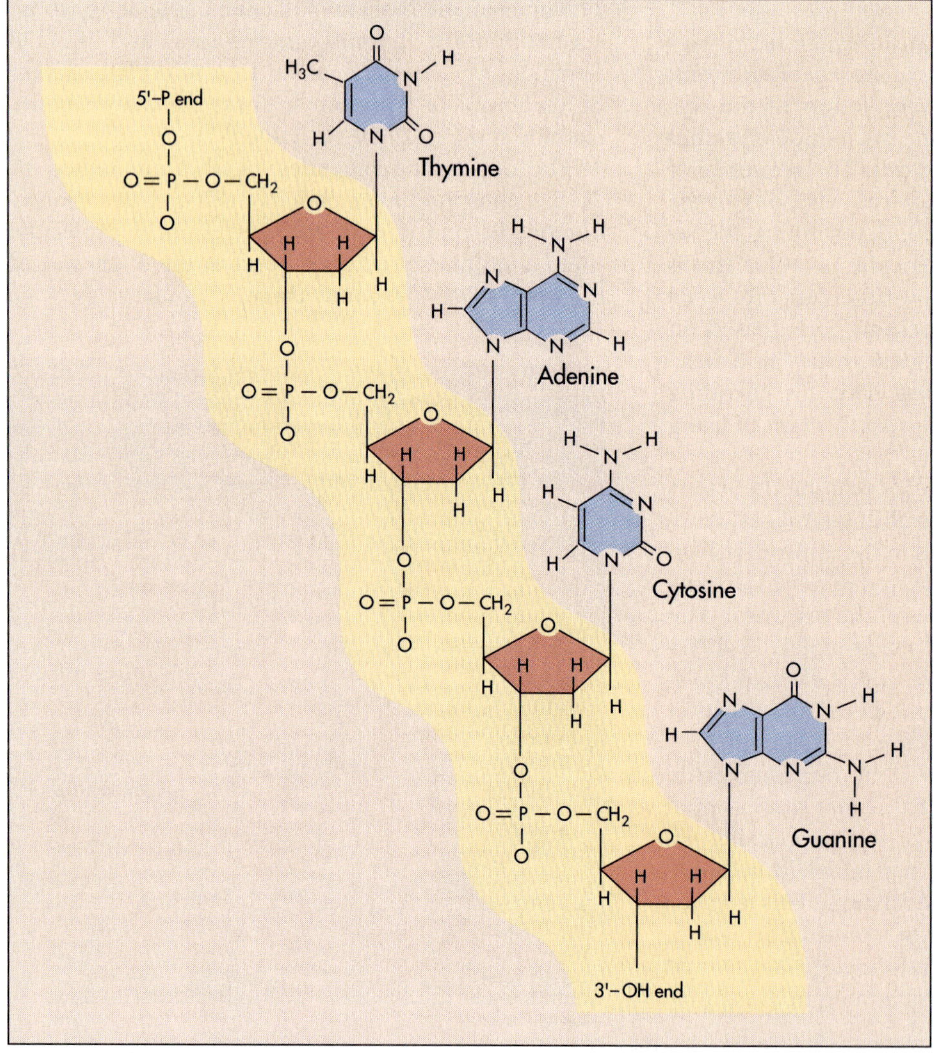

FIG. 6-2 Nucleotides are joined together by phosphodiester bonds between the 3′-OH and 5′-P positions. There is a free 5′-P at one end of the polynucleotide chain and a free 3′-OH at the other end.

free, hydroxyl group at the 3′-carbon position, and it is called the **3′-OH free end**. At the other end of the molecule, the 5′-carbon is not involved in forming a phosphodiester linkage, and there is a free phosphate ester group at the 5′-carbon position so that it is called the **5′-P free end**. The fact that the ends of the DNA macromolecule differ is extremely important because this permits directional recognition at the biochemical level in the same sense that we can recognize left and right. This is essential for the DNA to perform its principal function in biological systems, which is to store and transmit the genetic information of the cell.

Structure of DNA: The Double Helix

The DNA macromolecule is a **double helix** composed of two primary polynucleotide strands held together by **hydrogen bonding** (FIG. 6-3). A hydrogen bond is a weak linkage based on charge separations within molecules due to the electronegativity of specific atoms in that molecule. This type of bond occurs when a more positively charged hydrogen atom that is covalently bonded to an oxygen or nitrogen atom within a molecule is simultaneously attracted to a more negatively charged nitrogen or oxygen atom of a neighboring molecule. The hydrogen bonds that hold together the chains occur between complementary nucleic acid bases. Adenine usually pairs with thymine, and guanine usually pairs with cytosine. Two hydrogen bonds form between adenine and thymine base pairs while three hydrogen bonds occur between guanine and cytosine base pairs. This means that the greater the number of guanine-cytosine base pairs in a DNA double helix, the more tightly the two strands are held together.

In addition to hydrogen bonding the DNA double helix is stabilized by hydrophobic interactions. The nitrogen-containing nucleic acid bases are stacked almost horizontally along the interior axis of the double helix and these hydrophobic groups are therefore kept away from water. In contrast the hydrophilic deoxyribose sugar–phosphate backbone is on the out-

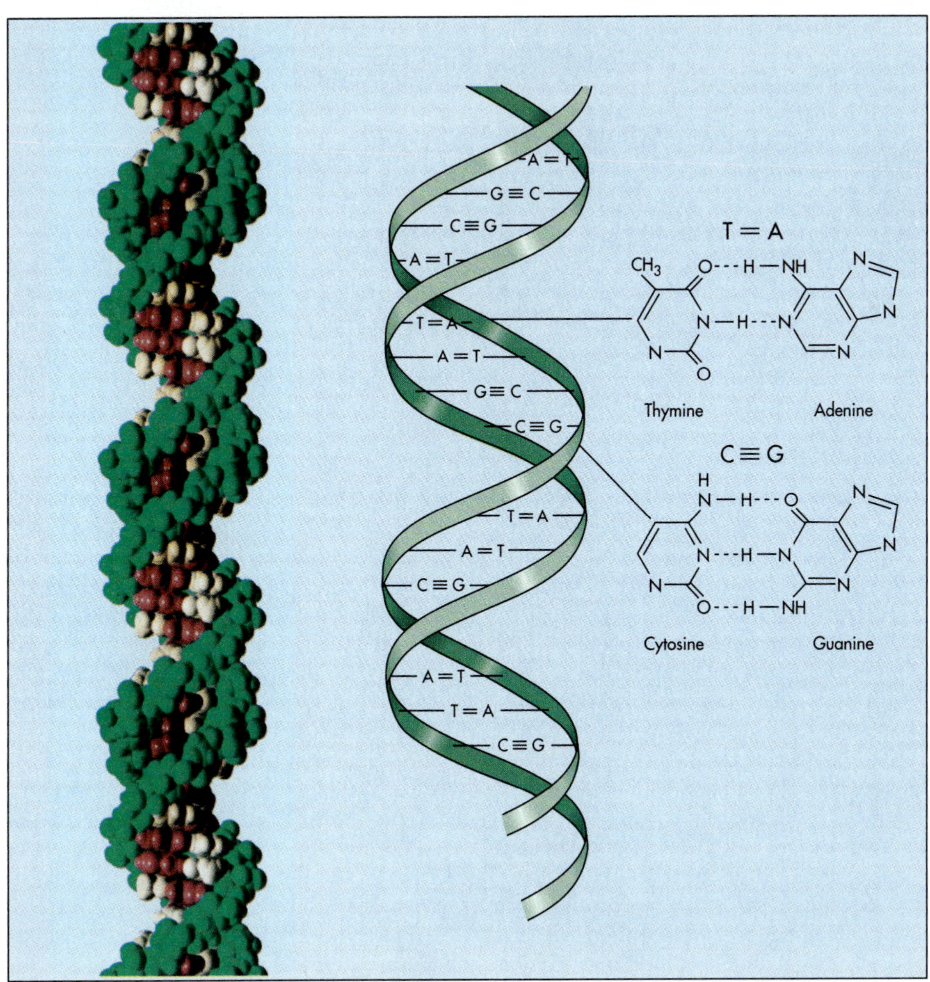

FIG. 6-3 The double helix is the fundamental structure of the DNA macromolecule. The two strands are held together by hydrogen bonding between complementary base pairs. There are three hydrogen bonds between the base pairs guanine and cytosine and two hydrogen bonds between the base pairs adenine and thymine.

BOX 6-1

DETERMINING THE NUCLEOTIDE SEQUENCE OF DNA

The sequence of nucleotides in DNA encodes the information and, thus, determines its hereditary information. Therefore determining the nucleotide sequence reveals critical information about cellular genetics. Automated units have been developed that facilitate the sequencing of nucleotides in DNA. The entire sequences of some bacterial plasmids and bacterial viruses are already available. A project is currently under way (the human genome project) that is attempting to completely sequence the nucleotides in human chromosomes. Knowledge of the nucleotide sequence of the human genome will allow detection and treatment of hereditary diseases.

The sequencing of DNA depends on generating DNA fragments that end specifically with one of the four nucleotides of the DNA macromolecule. The fragments are tagged, usually by radiolabeling with ^{32}P, or by using fluorescent dyes so that they can be detected. Gel electrophoresis is used to separate the fragments based on the numbers of nucleotides they contain. This technique can resolve DNA molecules between 15 to 600 nucleotides that differ by only one nucleotide in length.

Four separate lanes in the electrophoresis gel are used to generate a *ladder gel* that has all the possible fragments, each fragment being one nucleotide longer than the previous one—like the rungs of a ladder. One lane is for fragments terminating at adenine, one for those terminating at guanine, one for the fragments that end with cytosine, and one for the fragments that terminate with thymine. By determining the positions of each fragment in the ladder and by knowing that one lane represents a nucleotide with the nucleic acid base adenine, one with cytosine, one with guanine, and one with thymine, the exact order of nucleotides in the DNA being sequenced is readily determined (FIG. *A*). For large DNA molecules, multiple gels are run so that overlapping segments of the DNA are sequenced.

There are two different procedures for sequencing DNA: the Maxam-Gilbert procedure and the more commonly used Sanger dideoxy procedure. The Maxam-Gilbert procedure generates fragments of DNA based on breaking DNA at specific nucleotides (FIG. *B*). The Sanger dideoxy method generates the DNA fragments required for sequencing based on synthesizing a new strand of DNA with the synthesis terminating at specific positions corresponding to the four nucleotides in DNA.

To sequence DNA by the Maxam-Gilbert method the DNA is first labelled, typically with ^{32}P. The DNA is then subjected to chemical conditions that form one break per chain. This involves the modification of a specific base by methylation, removal of the methylated base, and, finally, cleavage of the residual sugar. The chemical digestion permits preferential breaking of the DNA at a specific nucleotide. Four separate reactions are run, one each for breaking the chain at adenine, thymine, guanine, and cytosine. The reactions are not run to completion. Instead, only one or a few of the specific bases are randomly modified, thus generating a mixture of ladder fragments that end with specific nucleotides. Electrophoresis is used to separate the fragments. The distance migrated corresponds to the size of the fragment and hence the position of the specific nucleotide in the DNA. If ^{32}P is used to label the DNA, autoradiography is used to identify the positions of the fragments. The sequence of nucleotides is read directly from the positions of the bands in the four lanes of the electrophoresis gel.

A, The nucleotide sequence of a DNA molecule is determined using sequencing gels. The sequencing procedures produce polynucleotide chains that are separated on these gels by electrophoresis based on the length of that polynucleotide. Each band corresponds to a polynucleotide ending with a specific nucleotide in the DNA so that the length of that band indicates the position of that specific nucleotide in the DNA. The lanes of the gel specify the nucleotide: G (*red*), A (*green*), T (*yellow*), and C (*blue*).

In the Sanger dideoxy procedure, an enzyme is used to make a single stranded copy of the DNA being sequenced (FIG. *C*). Instead of using just the deoxyribonucleotides normally incorporated during DNA replication, this procedure uses dideoxyribonucleotides, which lack a 3′-OH group. The lack of the 3′-OH group means that the chain cannot be extended. Thus the incorporation of a dideoxyribonucleotide acts as a specific chain terminator. By using dideoxyribonucleotide analogs for each of the normal deoxyribonucleotides, the synthesis of DNA can be terminated at a specific kind of nucleotide. One of the usual deoxyribonucleotides is labelled with ^{32}P and added to the reaction. As a result, radioactivity is incorporated into the newly synthesized DNA and can be detected following electrophoresis. The reactions can be run separately and the order of nucleotides determined using four separate electrophoresis lanes. Alternately, four different color fluorescent dyes can be used to label the four different dideoxyribonucleotides. In this case, one electrophoresis lane can be employed and the order of the four colors read directly as the nucleotide sequence in the DNA.

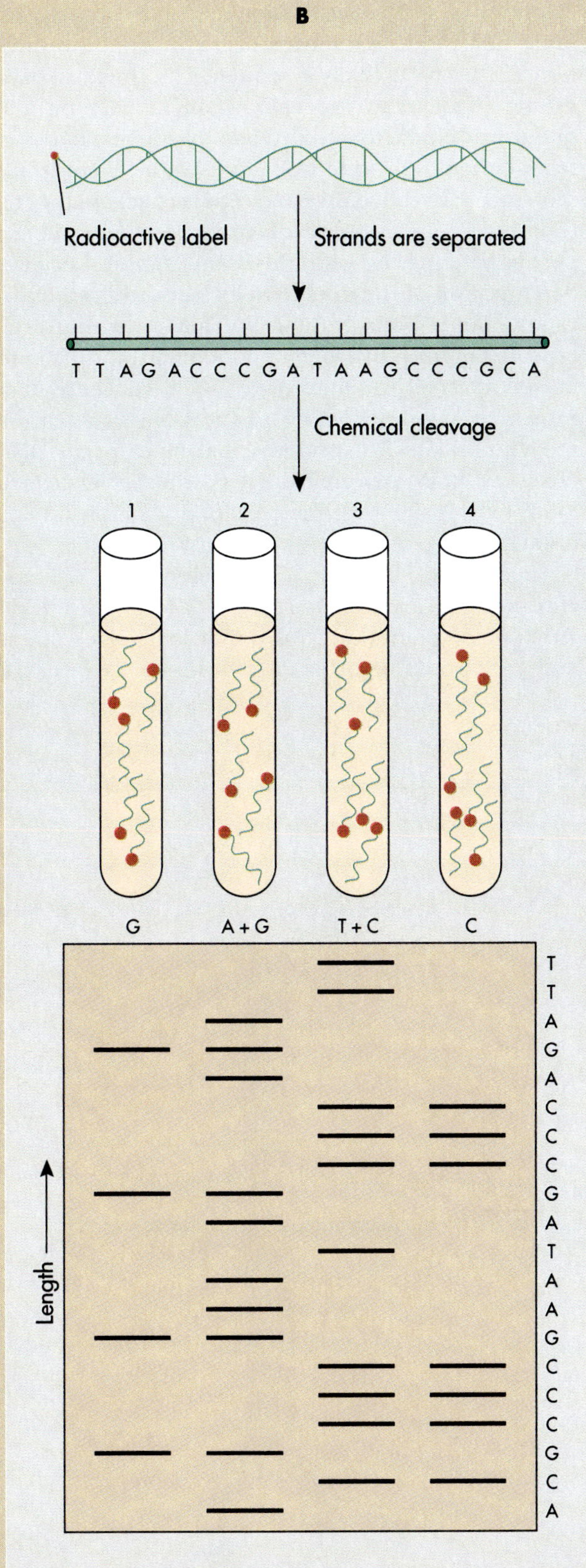

B, The nucleotide sequence of DNA can be determined by the Maxam-Gilbert sequencing procedure. This procedure involves chemically breaking the DNA at specific positions. The fragments produced are analyzed using electrophoresis and a sequencing gel to determine the positions of the nucleotides.

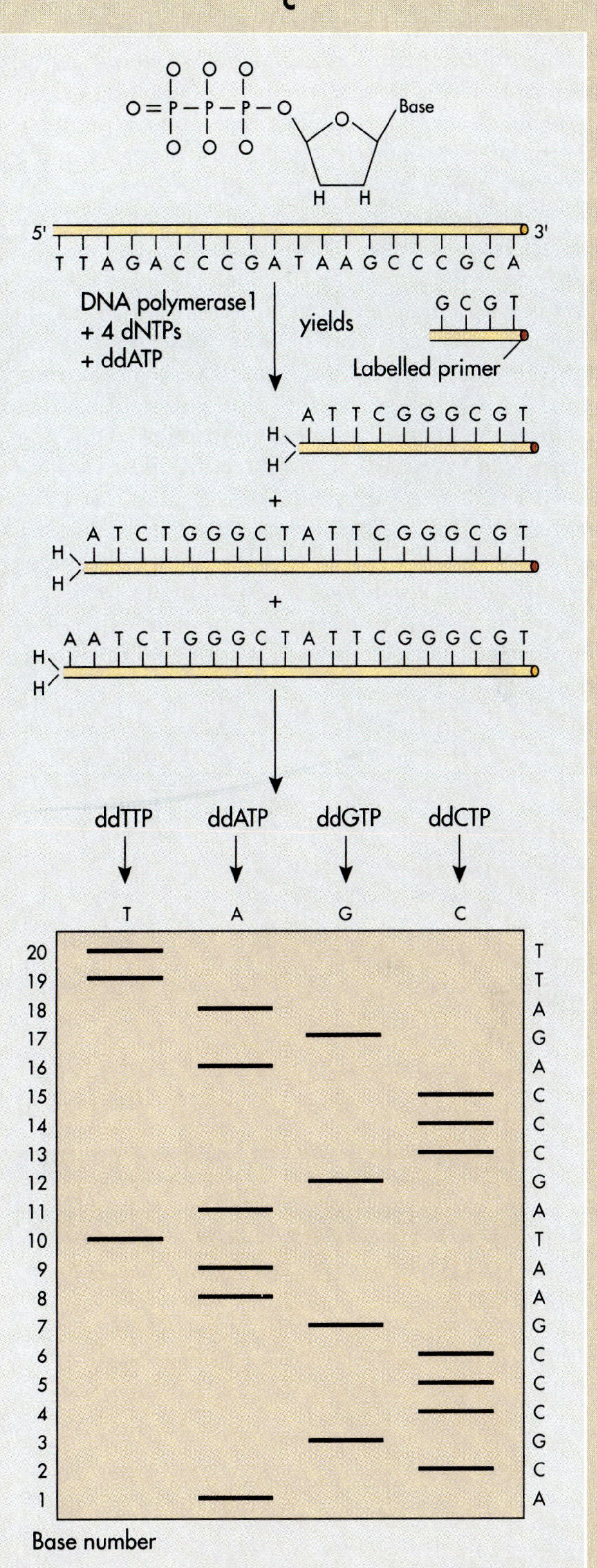

C, The nucleotide sequence of DNA can be determined by the Sanger dideoxy sequencing procedure. This procedure involves copying a single strand of DNA and using dideoxynucleotides to terminate formation of the DNA. Four dideoxynucleotides are used in separate reactions and four lanes are run on a sequencing gel to determine the nucleotide sequence of the DNA.

side of the axis of the double helix and interacts with water. This arrangement helps maintain the double helix arrangement of the DNA macromolecule.

The double helix has a diameter of about 2 nm. Each complete turn of the helix is 3.4 nm long so that there are about 10 nucleotides in each chain per turn. Along the axis there are a wider major groove and a narrower minor groove. These grooves, particularly the major groove, where base pairs are more accessible, are important for DNA-protein interactions. The most common form of the DNA helix is called B-DNA. This is a right-handed form (the helix rotates clockwise as it proceeds away from an observer looking down the axis). Under different physiological conditions the DNA may assume different right-handed forms with altered tightness of twisting. Differing numbers of bases per turn of the DNA occur in these forms, which are designated A-, C-, D-, and E-DNA. A left-handed DNA helical form, called Z-DNA, also has been observed to occur in regions of the DNA under certain cellular conditions. These different forms appear to be related to differences in gene expression but their ultimate significance is not well understood.

In some regions of the DNA, the sequence of nucleotides is symmetrical about an axis because the same nucleotide sequences occur in opposite directions (FIG. 6-4). Such a sequence is called a **palindrome** (Greek, "to run back again"), meaning a sequence of characters that reads the same when read from either right to left or left to right. Palindromic sequences are called **inverted repeats** because they are repeated in inverse order. Inverted repeat sequences permit base pairing within the same strand. Localized denaturation of the double helix leads to strand separation, and regions in the DNA that contain inverted repeats can form hydrogen-bonded hairpin structures known as **cruciform loops** (see FIG. 6-4). These structures may stabilize folding of the DNA and serve as recognition sites for proteins that bind or cut DNA. However, it is currently unclear whether cruciform loops exist inside of living cells or are simply a manifestation of isolated DNA in the test tube.

Supercoiling Because a representative bacterial chromosome, that of *Escherichia coli*, contains 4.5 × 10^3 kilobase pairs (kb), this rather large DNA macromolecule would be difficult to fit inside a typical bac-

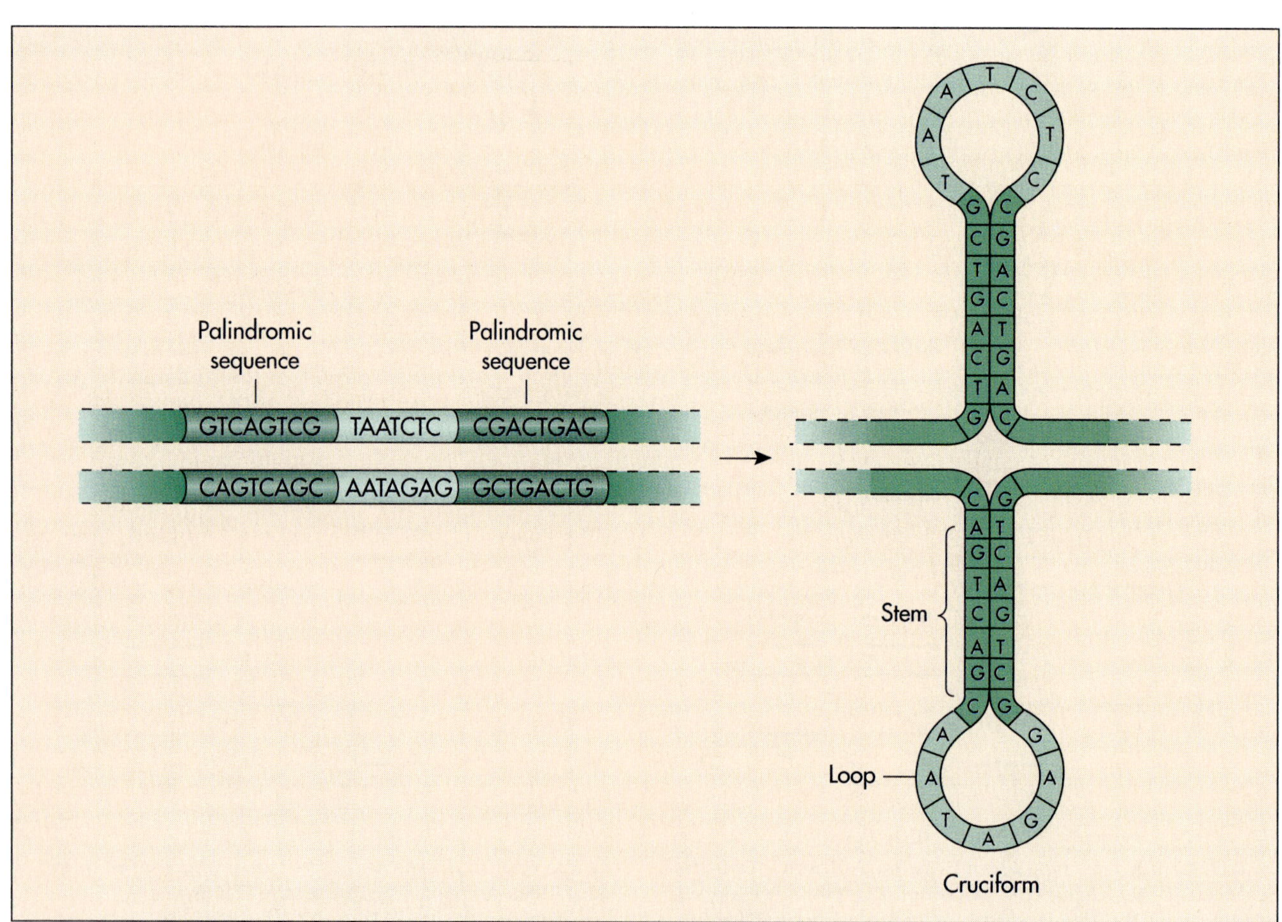

FIG. 6-4 Regions with a palindrome sequence can denature and reanneal to form a stem and loop (cruciform structure)

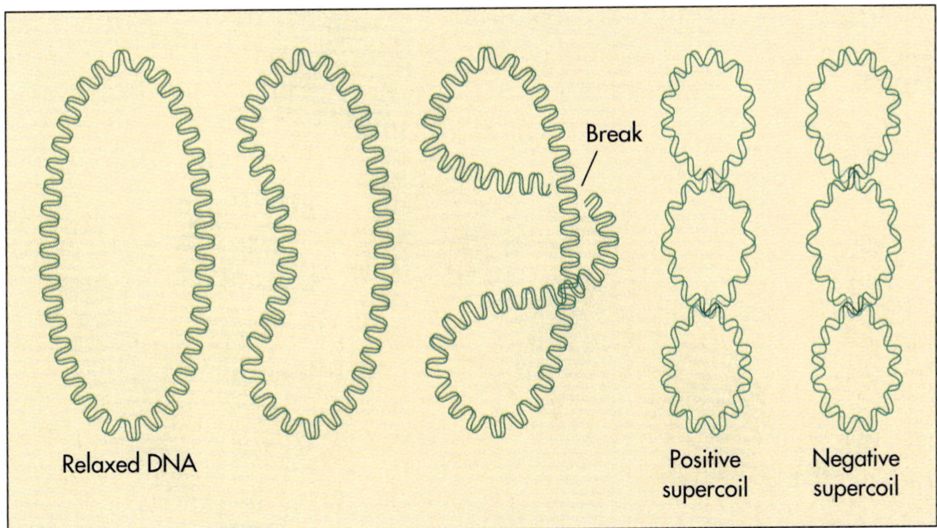

FIG. 6-5 Relaxed DNA has a simple circular form. The DNA can be overwound (positively supercoiled) or underwound (negatively supercoiled). Within cells the DNA is compacted by negative supercoiling.

terial cell if it were linear or in a simple circular form (see FIG. 3-27). To partially resolve this problem, bacterial DNA is supercoiled or tightly wound so that it forms kinks or knots and twists around itself much like an overwound telephone cord. DNA in simple circular form is said to be **relaxed DNA**. When relaxed circular DNA has one strand broken, twisted in the direction of the helix turns, and is then resealed, the DNA becomes overwound or **positively supercoiled**. Conversely, when relaxed DNA has one strand broken, twisted in the opposite direction of the helix turns, and is then resealed, the DNA becomes underwound or **negatively supercoiled** (FIG. 6-5). DNA is normally found in the cell in a negatively supercoiled state.

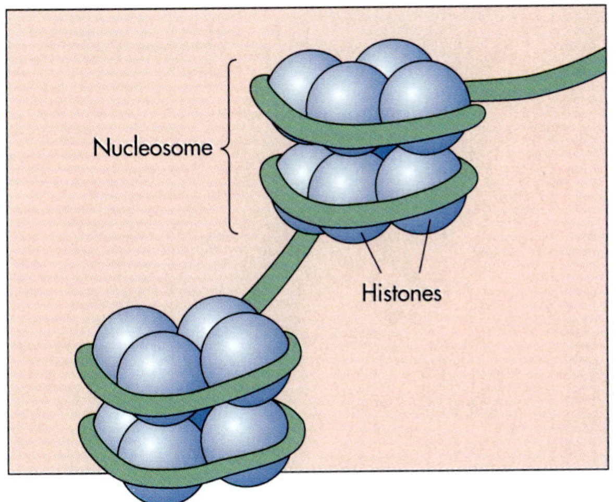

FIG. 6-6 In eukaryotic cells, histones (basic proteins) stabilize the coiled DNA. These form units called nucleosomes.

Histones and Nucleosomes The supercoiling of DNA in eukaryotic cells is stabilized by a group of basic proteins called **histones** (FIG. 6-6) and also by nonhistone proteins. Eukaryotic chromosomes contain a large amount of protein, about twice as much as nucleic acid. There are five types of histone molecules; H1, H2A, H2B, H3, and H4. The histones interact to form an octomer that consists of two molecules each of H2A, H2B, H3, and H4. This octomer is the basis for a core around which the DNA strands are wound, similar to a thread wrapped around a spool. The DNA-histone (nucleohistone) complex is a beadlike structure that is visible in the electron microscope and is called a **nucleosome**. The DNA in each nucleosome has about 140 base pairs wrapped around the histone core in slightly less than two turns. Histone H1 forms a complex with the DNA immediately adjacent to each nucleosome. Histones are associated with all eukaryotic nuclear DNA, but they are absent from prokaryotic cells. Some bacteria have been found to possess basic proteins—histone-like proteins—that complex with the bacterial DNA. However, these histone-like proteins and DNA do not lead to nucleosome formation.

The chromosomes are found in eukaryotic cells in a dispersed form called **chromatin**. When chromatin is extracted under conditions of low salt concentration the fiber resembles a string of beads when viewed in the electron microscope. Under normal conditions in the cell, the chromatin is probably wound into a secondary helix with about six nucleosomes per turn. This structure is called a **solenoid** (FIG. 6-7). It is also probable that within the chromosome the solenoids are further organized into larger supercoils.

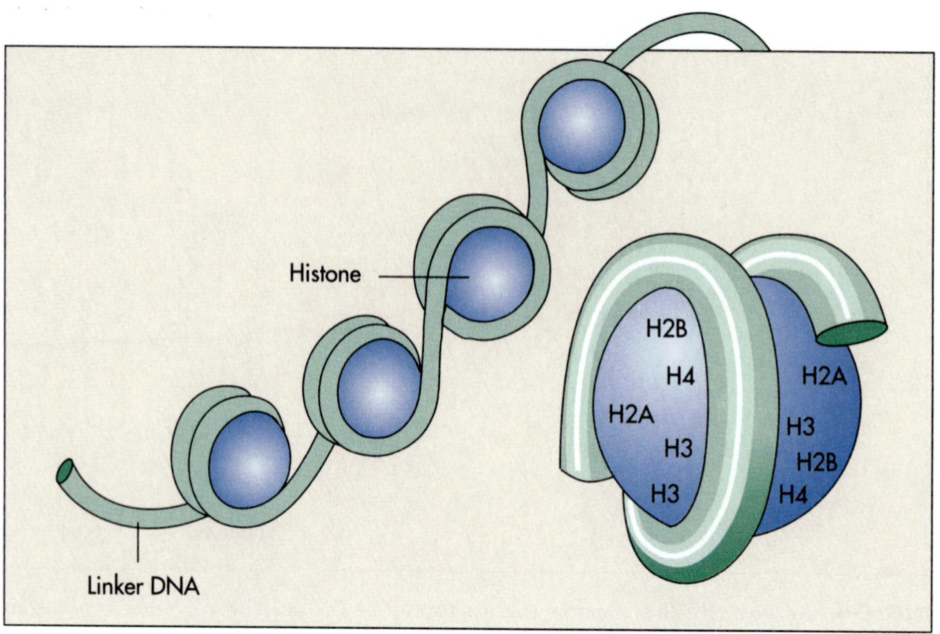

FIG. 6-7 Winding of DNA around histones forms a secondary helical structure.

SEMICONSERVATIVE NATURE OF DNA REPLICATION

The replication of the double helical DNA molecule is a **semiconservative** process, so-called because when double-stranded DNA is replicated, each of the two new daughter DNA double helices contains one intact (conserved) strand from the parental double helical DNA and one newly synthesized complementary strand (FIG. 6-8).

Semiconservative DNA replication of the bacterial chromosome begins at the origin of replication (*ori*C), a region of the DNA where specific initiation proteins attach. Once replication is initiated, the process of copying parental DNA into daughter DNA proceeds uninterrupted. Initially, the double helix must be unwound and separated into single strands so that each strand is used as a **template** for the assembly of a complementary strand.

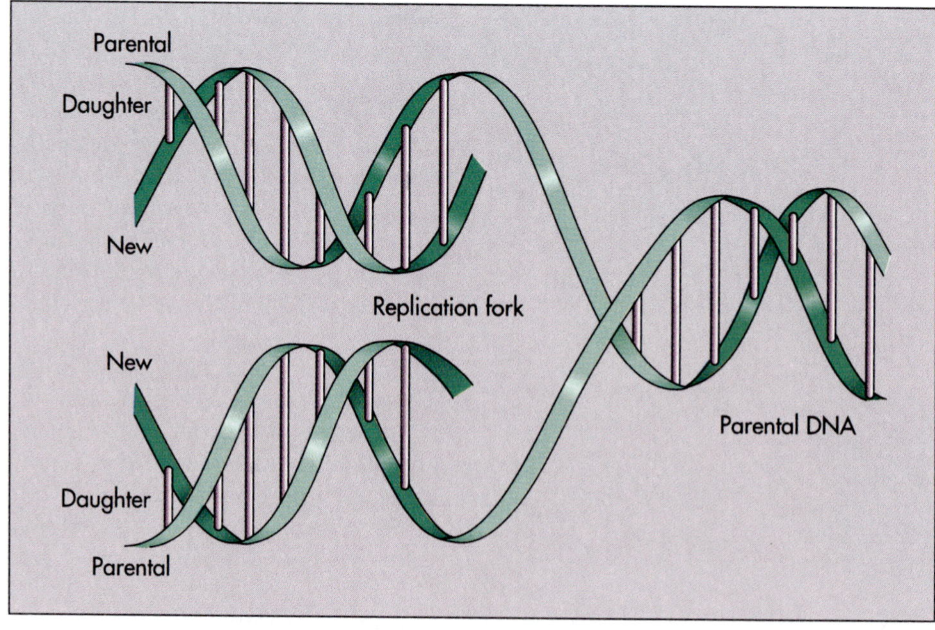

FIG. 6-8 DNA replication is semiconservative, so that each double helical daughter DNA molecule has one parental and one newly synthesized strand.

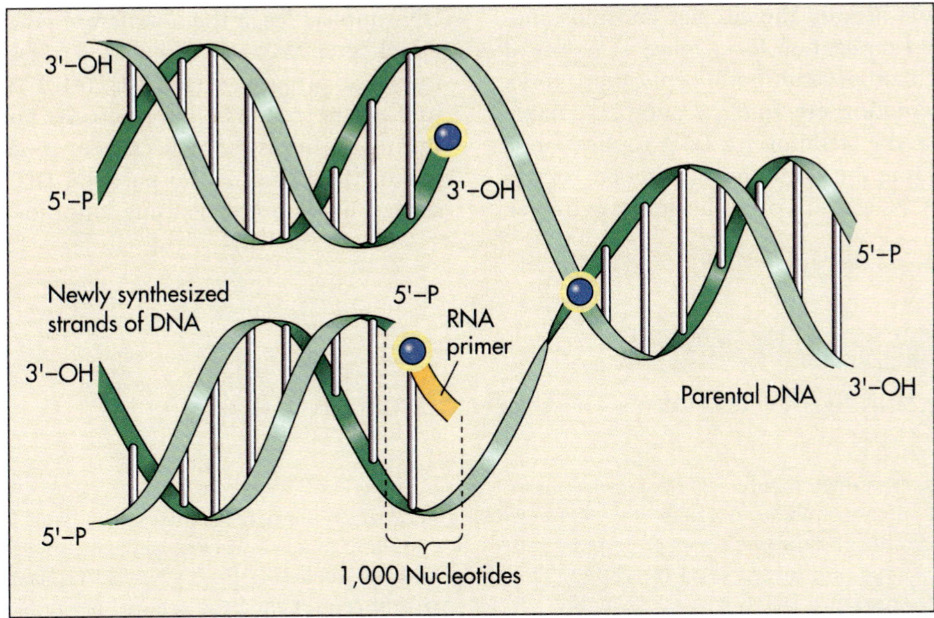

FIG. 6-9 A localized unwinding of the double helical DNA catalyzed by helicases occurs during DNA replication to form a replication fork. An RNA primer is synthesized to initiate DNA replication. Deoxyribonucleotides align opposite their base pairs and DNA polymerase adds them to the 3′-OH ends of the newly synthesized strands of DNA.

The region of DNA helix unwinding, strand separation, and DNA synthesis is localized and referred to as the **replication fork** (FIG. 6-9) where free nucleotide bases are aligned opposite their base pairs in the parental DNA molecules, A opposite T and G opposite C. At the replication forks there are four strands of DNA, two are conserved and two are newly synthesized.

DNA Replication in Prokaryotic Cells

All bacterial chromosomes that have been studied have a single point of origin of DNA replication (*ori*C) (FIG. 6-10). DNA polymerases move bidirectionally from the origin to the terminus of DNA replication (*tre*), so that there are two replication forks moving in opposite directions. Both forks move along the double helix away from the origin of replication in oppo-

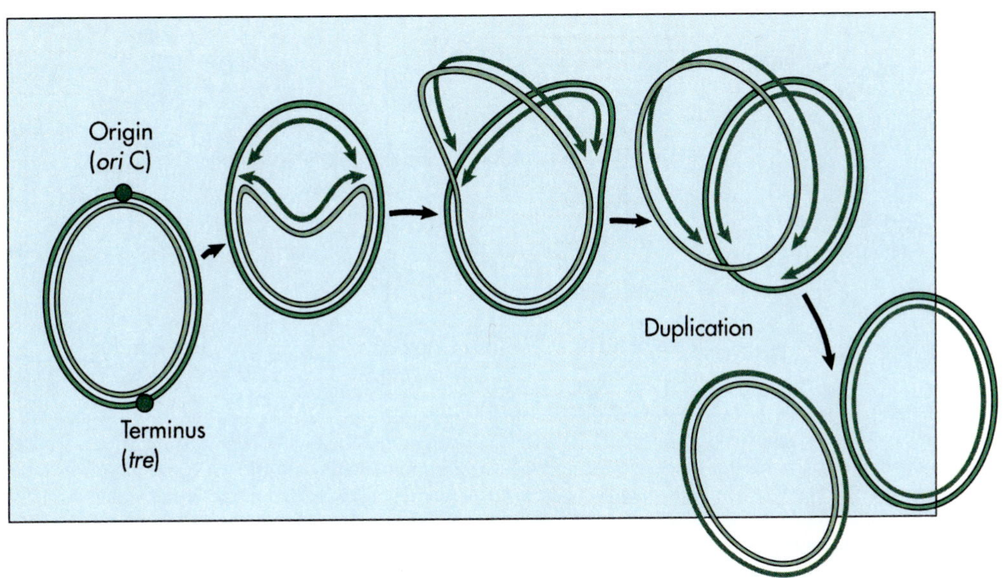

FIG. 6-10 The replication of DNA begins at an origin *(oriC)* and the two replication forks proceed in opposite direction around the circular bacterial chromosome to the terminus of replication *(tre)* until two complete duplicate daughter molecules are produced.

site directions and around the circular chromosome. The bidirectional replication forks move at identical speeds after initiation, and both replication forks meet at the termination site. In *E. coli* and presumably in other bacteria, the terminus for DNA replication is not exactly opposite the origin in the circular bacterial chromosome. As a result of replication of circular DNA molecules, a **theta structure** is formed (like the Greek letter theta, θ) with a loop of DNA that appears in planar projection (see FIG. 6-10). The circular nature of the bacterial chromosome and the fact that during synthesis the new circular loop of DNA grows out of the plane of the parental DNA were demonstrated by John Cairns using autoradiography. In this

BOX 6-2

DEMONSTRATING SEMICONSERVATIVE DNA REPLICATION

The semiconservative nature of DNA replication was elegantly demonstrated in 1958 by Matthew Meselson and Franklin Stahl in a series of experiments that used the isotope of nitrogen (^{15}N) (see FIG.). This isotope is non-radioactive but is heavier than the ^{14}N atom. In these experiments, *Escherichia coli* was initially grown in a medium with a sole nitrogen source of ^{15}N ammonium ions. The bacteria incorporated the heavy nitrogen into their nucleic acids. The bacterial culture was then transferred to a medium with a nitrogen source of ^{14}N ammonium ions. During incubation the bacterial DNA was replicated and the bacterial cells were reproduced. Cells were collected for analysis of the DNA after they were allowed to grow for different generation times, and the DNA was then analyzed for the presence of ^{15}N and ^{14}N using buoyant density gradient ultracentrifugation. In this analytical method, heavy molecules move to a denser part of the gradient than lighter molecules; thus DNA containing ^{15}N moves a greater distance than DNA containing only ^{14}N. When Meselson and Stahl performed this experiment, all of the initial DNA formed as a single band, corresponding to heavy DNA. After one generation, a single sedimentation band formed, corresponding to a hybrid DNA molecule of a mixture of ^{14}N- and ^{15}N-labelled DNA. If DNA was replicated so that the parent cell retained the original bacterial chromosome, and the progeny received a totally newly synthesized DNA macromolecule, there would have been two bands after the first generation.

After two generations, two bands formed, one corresponding to light DNA (containing only ^{14}N) and the other corresponding to the ^{14}N–^{15}N hybrid DNA. These results are consistent with our understanding of a semiconservative mode of DNA replication.

In the first generation, the *E. coli* cells each had one parental strand of DNA that contained ^{15}N and one newly synthesized strand of DNA that contained ^{14}N. In the second generation, some of the cells contained the ^{15}N-labelled parental strand of DNA and a newly synthesized ^{14}N strand and other cells contained the parental ^{14}N strand and a newly synthesized ^{14}N-containing strand.

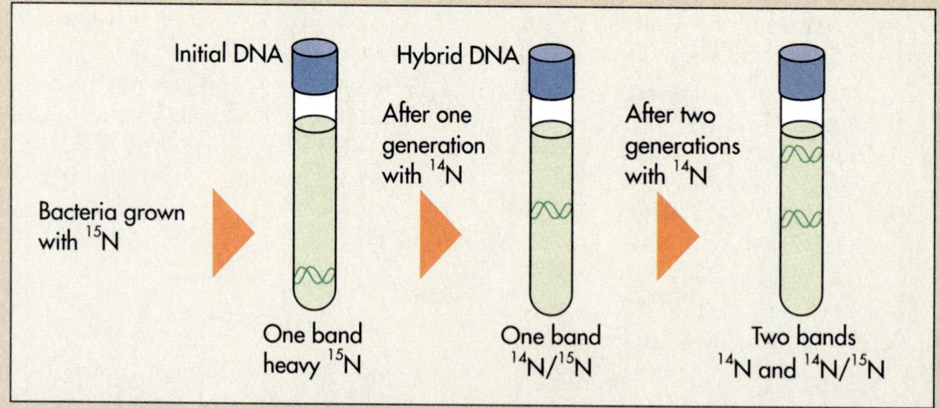

The semiconservative nature of DNA replication was demonstrated by labelling DNA by the incorporation of heavy nitrogen (^{15}N) and following the fate of this tagged DNA from one generation to the next, using density gradient ultracentrifugation. The location of the bands obtained by ultracentrifugation, that is, the distance that the DNA moves (which is a function of the molecular weight of the DNA) permitted the tracking of the fate of the heavy DNA when the cells were grown in the presence of normal light (^{14}N). The banding pattern obtained in these experiments, illustrated in the figure, proved that DNA replication occurs by a semiconservative method.

method, bacteria were grown in the presence of a radioactive compound, e.g., tritiated (^{3}H) thymidine, which was incorporated into the DNA. The bacterial cells were lysed, releasing the radioactive DNA molecules. A fine-grained photographic emulsion was placed over the unfolded bacterial chromosomes and incubated in the dark. When radioactive material decays, it releases particles that strike the film and expose it. The areas of radioactivity were detected when the film was developed. The visualization of the bacterial chromosome by autoradiography leaves no doubt as to its circular nature.

DNA Replication in Eukaryotic Cells

The replication of eukaryotic DNA begins at multiple points of origin within each chromosome and proceeds bidirectionally. The rate of synthesis of DNA along a replicating fork may be slower in eukaryotic than in prokaryotic cells, and although the replication of DNA in prokaryotes proceeds at a uniform rate, the rate of DNA synthesis can vary in a eukaryote. Despite these potential differences in the rates of DNA synthesis within a particular region of DNA, the overall rate of DNA replication is higher in eukaryotes than in prokaryotes. This is because the DNA of eukaryotes has multiple **replicons** (segments of a DNA macromolecule having their own origin and termini) compared to the single replicon of the bacterial chromosome. Consequently, even though there is much more DNA in a eukaryotic chromosome than in a bacterial chromosome, the eukaryotic genome can be replicated much faster (25 to 30 minutes in yeast) than the bacterial genome (40 minutes in *E. coli*) because of these multiple initiation points for DNA synthesis. Bacteria must initiate several new rounds of DNA replication to keep pace with the rate of reproduction. The distinction between single and multiple origins of DNA synthesis is a fundamental difference between prokaryotic and eukaryotic microorganisms.

ENZYMES INVOLVED IN DNA REPLICATION

The replication of the DNA macromolecule involves a complex series of coordinated enzymatic reactions. These enzymes first untwist and unwind a segment of DNA so that a replication fork is established. Then, following alignment of free nucleotides opposite their corresponding base pairs in the template DNA, other enzymes join the nucleotides into a newly synthesized DNA strand.

Topoisomerases

Since the DNA helix is negatively supercoiled, the strands must be uncoiled or "relaxed" before it can be replicated; this is accomplished by **topoisomerase I.** This enzyme breaks the phosphodiester linkage of one of the strands and passes the strand through the other, which results in a localized uncoiling effect. Surprisingly, no energy is needed to break the bond, and the topoisomerase I enzyme uses the energy of the tightly wound DNA strand to function.

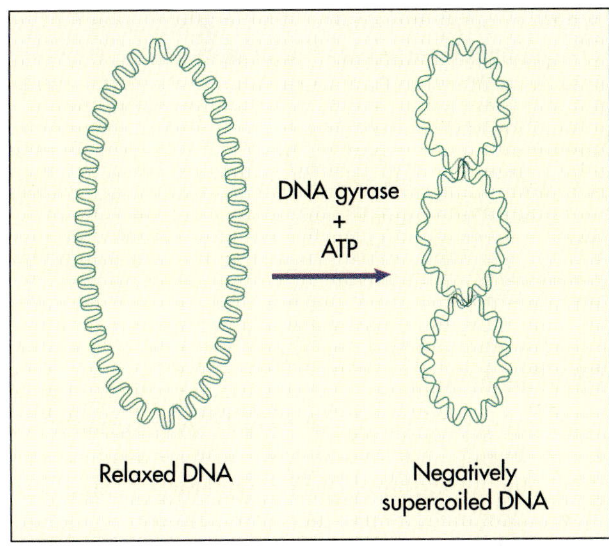

FIG. 6-11 DNA gyrase catalyses the formation of negatively supercoiled DNA during replication of the bacterial chromosome.

Another enzyme that functions in relationship to DNA winding is **topoisomerase II**, or **DNA gyrase.** This enzyme introduces negative supercoiling into relaxed DNA and therefore is important after replication has taken place to return the DNA into its negatively supercoiled, condensed state. DNA gyrase of *E. coli* is composed of four protein subunits: two A subunits and two B subunits. The A subunits are responsible for the nicking-closing function of the enzyme and are inhibited by the antibiotics nalidixic acid and ciprofloxacin. The gyrase nicks or hydrolyzes both strands of DNA, passes the strands around another part of the double helix (thus introducing a supercoil), and covalently links the nicks (FIG. 6-11). Energy, obtained from ATP, is required to nick and reseal the DNA strands. This activity (ATPase) is contained in the B subunits, which are inhibited by the antibiotics coumermycin and novobiocin.

Helicases

The double helix must be separated into single-stranded regions before each single strand can be used as a template. **DNA helicases** and **Rep protein** (collectively known as unwinding proteins) catalyze the breaking of hydrogen bonding that holds the two strands of DNA together. This reaction requires energy from ATP. Once the strands are separated, the strands are prevented from reassociating by **single-stranded binding proteins** that attach to single-stranded regions of the DNA and stabilize them.

TABLE 6-2 Characteristics of Various Bacterial DNA Polymerases

PROPERTY	POLYMERASE I	POLYMERASE II	POLYMERASE III
Initiation of chain synthesis	−	−	−
5′-P → 3′-OH elongation of primer	+	+	+
3′-OH → 5′-P exonuclease activity	+	+	+
5′-P → 3′-OH exonuclease activity	+	−	+
Molecular weight	190,000	120,000	380,000
Molecules/cell	400	75	15

DNA Polymerases

The newly synthesized strands of DNA are established by linking the nucleotide bases with phosphodiester bonds by the action of **DNA polymerases** (Table 6-2). The action of DNA polymerase results in the elongation of the nucleotide chain of the synthesized DNA molecule and can be likened to a zipper where the teeth of the zipper are initially aligned and progressively linked together in a continuous motion. DNA polymerases have several interesting properties.

All DNA polymerases add deoxyribonucleotides only to the free 3′-OH end of an existing nucleic acid polymer (FIG. 6-12). These enzymes require an RNA primer molecule with a 3′-OH free end for DNA synthesis. The RNA primer is synthesized by **RNA polymerase** or another enzyme, **DnaG protein.** The DnaG

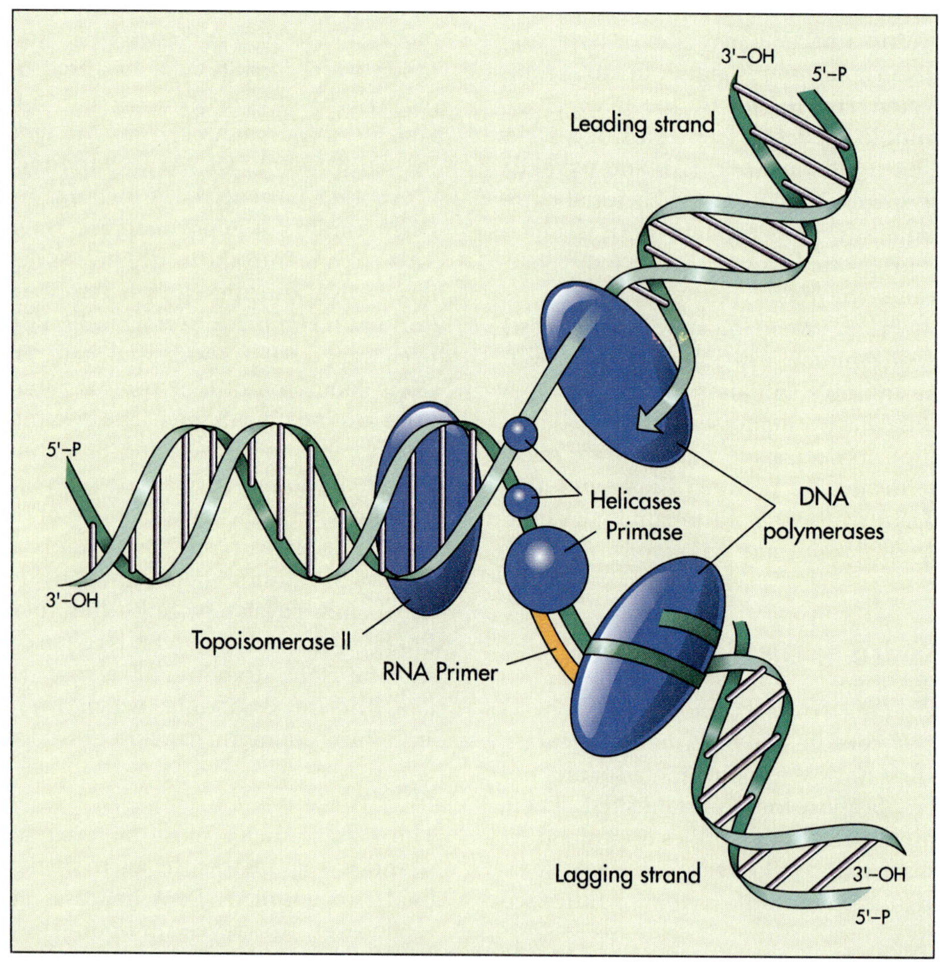

FIG. 6-12 Several enzymes are involved in the replication of DNA. Topoisomerases alter the supercoiling; helicases unwind the double helix, RNA primase adds an RNA primer, and DNA polymerase adds nucleotides to the newly synthesized DNA polynucleotide chains. The action of DNA polymerase results in the formation of a diester linkage and the elongation of the DNA chain. This reaction is pulled in the direction of DNA synthesis by the splitting of PP_i to P_i, an essentially irreversible reaction that results in the removal of the products of the polymerase reaction.

protein, sometimes called *primase,* or RNA polymerase, makes an RNA primer of about 3 to 5 bases long. After the primer has been synthesized, the strand is extended by DNA polymerases, which are DNA dependent and require an existing DNA molecule to act as a template. The enzymatic dependence on an existing template molecule is exceptional among biochemical reactions.

DNA Polymerases in Prokaryotic Cells Several different DNA-dependent DNA polymerases have been isolated from prokaryotic cells, each serving somewhat different functions during DNA synthesis. In *E. coli* and *Bacillus subtilis,* three different DNA polymerases have been discovered: DNA polymerase I or PolI, DNA polymerase II or PolII, and DNA polymerase III or PolIII. DNA polymerases I and II are a single polypeptide, whereas DNA polymerase III is composed of at least three polypeptides for functional activity and as many as four additional polypeptide coenzymes. Initially, when PolI was discovered by Arthur Kornberg in 1958, it was thought to be the enzyme responsible for DNA replication in the cell. However, in 1969, DeLucia and Cairns isolated a mutant of *E. coli* that had no demonstrable PolI activity—although it retained sufficient PolI activity for viability of the cells—and yet replicated its DNA. Subsequent investigations led to the discovery of PolII and PolIII in bacteria. It remains unclear how PolII functions physiologically in the cell, but PolIII appears to be the major enzyme involved in DNA replication.

Since DNA polymerases can add nucleotides only to a 3′-OH free end, at one time this caused a paradox in our understanding of the replication of DNA (FIG. 6-13). The two strands of the double helical DNA molecule are antiparallel, one strand running from the 5′-P to the 3′-OH free end and the other complemen-

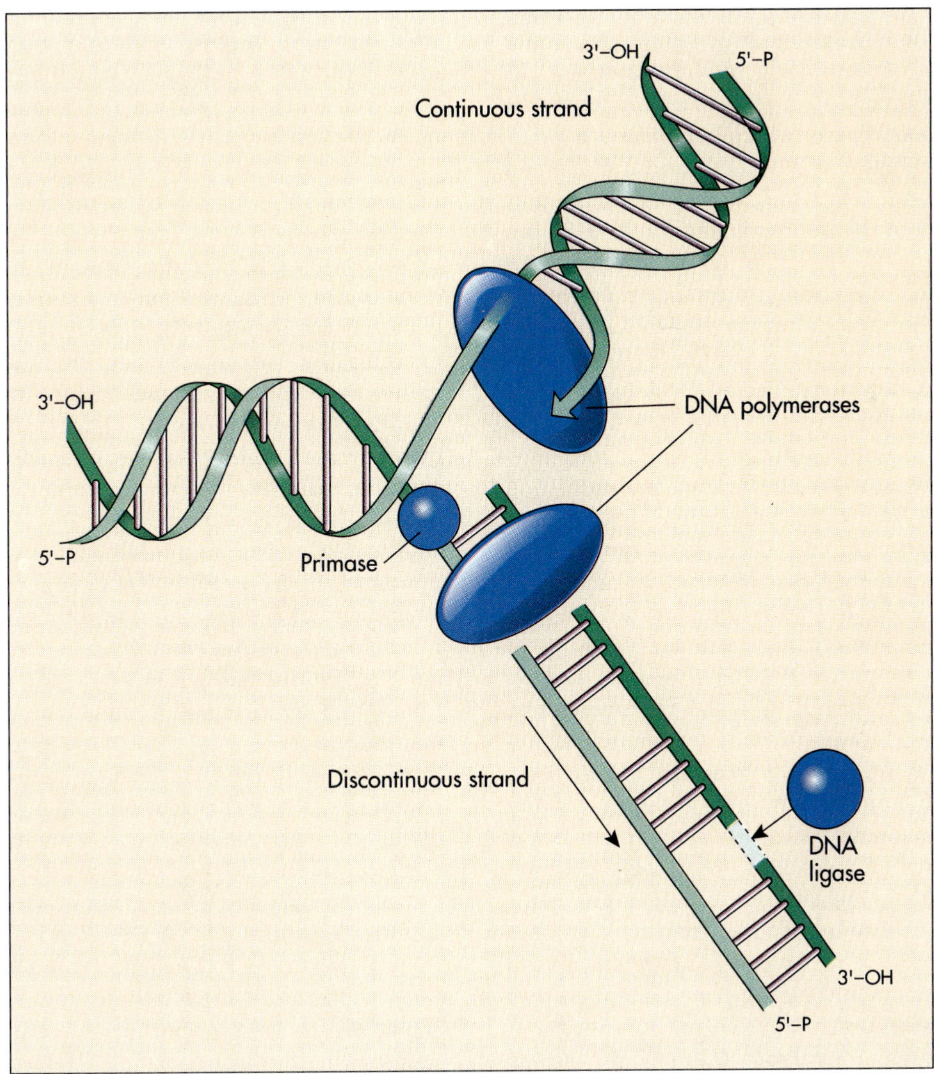

FIG. 6-13 DNA polymerases add nucleotides only to the 3′-OH ends of the newly synthesized DNA polynucleotide chains. One chain is elongated continuously along the direction of formation of the replication fork. The other strand is synthesized as discontinuous segments (Okazaki fragments) that are then joined together by DNA ligase.

tary strand running from the 3′-OH to the 5′-P free end. Therefore synthesis of complementary strands requires that DNA synthesis proceed in opposite directions, while the double helix is progressively unwinding and replicating in only one direction. One of the DNA strands is continuously synthesized because it is elongated in the same direction as the advancing replication fork. This strand is the **continuous**, or **leading strand of DNA**. The other strand of DNA, however, must be synthesized discontinuously in segments. The initiation of the synthesis of the **discontinuous strand of DNA** begins only after some unwinding of the double helix and therefore lags behind the synthesis of the continuous strand; it is referred to as the **lagging strand**. Because the leading strand is replicated continuously and the lagging strand is replicated discontinuously, DNA replication is referred to as **semidiscontinuous**.

Short segments of DNA (about 2,000 nucleotides long in prokaryotic cells and about 200 nucleotides long in eukaryotic cells) known as **Okazaki fragments** are formed by the DNA polymerase running opposite to the direction of unwinding of the parental DNA molecule. The Okazaki fragments are later joined by the action of **DNA ligase**, which establishes a phosphodiester bond between the 3′-OH and 5′-P ends of chains of nucleotides. In *E. coli*, the energy needed by DNA ligase to form the bond comes from NADH, but in eukaryotic cells it comes from ATP. Ligases are not involved in chain elongation; rather, they act as repair enzymes for sealing "nicks" within the DNA molecule. Thus, through the combined actions of DNA polymerase III, DNA polymerase I, and DNA ligase, both complementary strands of the DNA can be synthesized during DNA replication.

It is more efficient for the cell to replicate long stretches of DNA by enzymes that form a complex that stays together as it moves along the helix synthesizing new DNA. The DNA polymerase and its associated proteins move along the DNA template adding nucleotides without dissociating and reassociating at each step. The complex of DNA polymerase and accessory proteins is referred to as the **replisome**. The fact that enzymes involved in DNA replication stay together is unlike most enzymatic reaction, in which enzymes dissociate immediately after catalysis. Having the enzymes remain as a replisome complex makes the process more efficient and, hence, more rapid. This aspect of DNA replication is known as **processivity**. It is the mechanism in which an enzyme or enzyme complex that copies a long message maintains an uninterrupted contact with the template until the copying is terminated.

DNA Polymerases in Eukaryotic Cells Four types of DNA polymerases, α, β, γ, and δ, have been identified in eukaryotic cells; these differ from the DNA polymerases I, II, and III of prokaryotic cells. The α DNA polymerase functions in replication of DNA within the nucleus. The δ DNA polymerase also appears to function in DNA replication within the nucleus. The γ DNA polymerase functions in the replication of mitochondrial DNA, and the β form appears to be involved in DNA repair.

Proofreading

In addition to polymerization (synthesis) activity, bacterial DNA polymerases also exhibit exonuclease activity, that is, the ability to degrade or depolymerize a nucleic acid chain. Exonuclease activity is not associated with the DNA polymerases of eukaryotic organisms. All bacterial DNA polymerases (polI, polII, and polIII) can remove bases from the 3′-OH end; only polI and polIII have exonuclease activity from the 5′-P end. Given the potential for mutations from incorrect nucleotide insertions, this activity is critical.

The exonuclease activity of bacterial DNA polymerases allows them to correct errors in the DNA molecule. If an inappropriate nucleotide base is inserted during DNA synthesis, the DNA polymerase can reverse direction, remove nucleotide bases from the free end of the DNA molecule, and then renew its polymerization activity. An inappropriate base is recognized because improper insertion causes base pairing instability. This $3' \rightarrow 5'$ exonuclease activity of DNA polymerases is referred to as **proofreading**. It allows the bacterial cell to correct errors in base pairing that occur during DNA synthesis due to improperly added nucleotides. This mechanism explains, in part, how bacterial DNA replication has remarkable fidelity. By excising the "wrong" nucleotide, the proofreading ability of DNA polymerases lowers the frequency of spontaneous mutations or changes in the DNA sequence that might occur during replication. It ensures that the information in copies of those hereditary molecules is correct.

Another activity exhibited by bacterial DNA polymerases is the removal of RNA primers from the DNA strand. In eukaryotes, the removal of the RNA primer is accomplished by a ribonuclease. Some bacteria also have a ribonuclease, RNase H, that can recognize DNA–RNA hybrids and remove the ribonucleotides from them.

When nucleotides have been removed from one strand of DNA, either through DNA polymerase exonuclease or ribonuclease activity, the result is a **gap**—a region of the double helix in which there are no complementary nucleotide bases opposite one of the strands. Gaps in the DNA are filled in by the action of DNA polymerase I. Thus polI plays a large role in DNA replication, especially in primer removal and gap filling. It is also important in repairing DNA damaged by chemicals or radiation. There are several ways that bacteria can recognize and excise damaged sections of DNA. These mechanisms lead to the formation of a gap after excision of altered deoxyribonucleotides; the gap is repaired by DNA polymerase I.

BOX 6-3

POLYMERASE CHAIN REACTION

The understanding of how DNA replication occurs within cells facilitated the development of an *in vitro* method for the replication of specific sequences of DNA (FIG. *A*). This method, called the polymerase chain reaction (PCR), revolutionized molecular biology. Using PCR it is possible to amplify a region of DNA so that there is enough DNA to study. PCR permits the production of sufficient quantities of DNA segments within a few hours so that diagnoses of the presence or absence of specific genes can be made, the nucleotide sequences of genes can be determined, and DNA can be produced for use in genetic engineering.

The key features of DNA replication that permit PCR amplification of DNA are: (1) DNA replication is semiconservative so that a chain of parental DNA serves as the template that specifies the sequence of nucleotides in a newly synthesized chain; (2) during replication, the two chains of the DNA separate; (3) primers attach to the region at the replication fork, and DNA replication extends from those primers by the addition of nucleotides to the 3′-OH ends; and (4) the addition of nucleotides is catalyzed by a DNA polymerase.

Within a cell the separation of DNA at the replication fork is enzymatic but it is possible to break the hydrogen bonds that hold double helical DNA together by heating to 90° to 100° C without breaking the phosphate diester bonds that hold together the primary chains of the DNA molecule. Thus by placing DNA in a boiling water bath the DNA is denatured, that is, the two chains of the double helix separate without being broken apart.

Short segments of DNA, called oligonucleotides, can easily be synthesized with nucleotide sequences complementary to a segment of DNA one wishes to amplify. These oligonucleotides can act as primers for DNA replication. Commercial services using automated DNA synthesizers supply oligonucleotides for use in PCR with overnight delivery. At low temperatures, oligonucleotides will rapidly and specifically bind to complementary regions of a DNA chain, a process called annealing.

Once oligonucleotide primers attach to a segment of DNA, nucleotides can be added to the 3′-OH ends by a DNA polymerase. All one need do is add a supply of the four nucleotides needed for incorporation of DNA, a buffer with magnesium ions that facilitate binding of primers and base pairing of free nucleotides, template DNA, and DNA polymerase. Unfortunately, most DNA polymerases are denatured and hence inactivated at high temperatures, so that if the DNA was heated to separate the chains, new DNA polymerase would have to be repeatedly added. This would make *in vitro* amplification of DNA impractical on a routine basis.

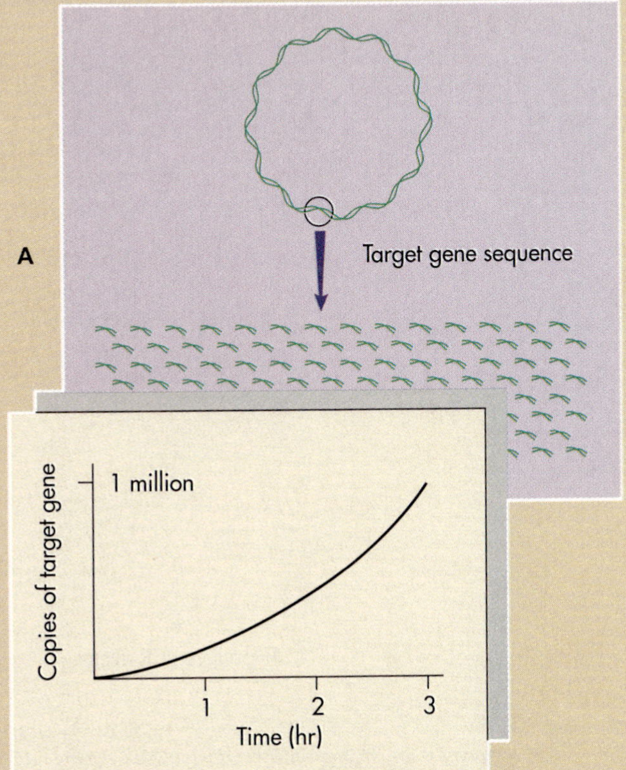

A, The polymerase chain reaction (PCR) is an *in vitro* method for replicating DNA. A target nucleotide sequence is copied repeatedly so that a million copies can be made in less than an hour.

Continued.

BOX 6-3—CONT'D

POLYMERASE CHAIN REACTION—CONT'D

The key discovery that makes PCR routinely possible was the discovery of a thermostable DNA polymerase from the thermophilic bacterium *Thermus aquaticus*. This enzyme functions optimally at 70° to 72° C, which are temperatures that denature the DNA polymerases of most organisms. The stability of *T. aquaticus* DNA polymerase (*taq* DNA polymerase) is taken advantage of in PCR. Other thermostable DNA polymerases are also used in PCR.

The PCR includes three steps: (1) DNA denaturation, (2) primer annealing, and (3) chain elongation by the action of *taq* or another thermostable DNA polymerase (FIG. *B*). The stages are controlled by regulating the temperature. For DNA denaturation the temperature is raised to 94° to 95° C. For primer annealing the temperature is lowered to 37° to 70° C, depending on the specific nucleotide sequence of the primer. For DNA chain elongation the temperature is adjusted to 60° to 72° C to permit the action of the thermostable DNA polymerase.

By repetitive cycling of the three PCR steps the target DNA sequence is amplified. Each cycle results in a doubling of the target sequence defined by the region where the primers anneal. Beginning with a single copy of a gene sequence, it takes only twenty PCR cycles to make about a million copies. Automated thermal cyclers make it simple to cycle between the temperatures needed for denaturation, primer annealing, and chain elongation. At about 2 minutes for a complete PCR cycle, a millionfold increase in target DNA takes less than an hour. Given the simplicity and power of the reaction it is no wonder that PCR has revolutionized the study of the molecular basis of heredity.

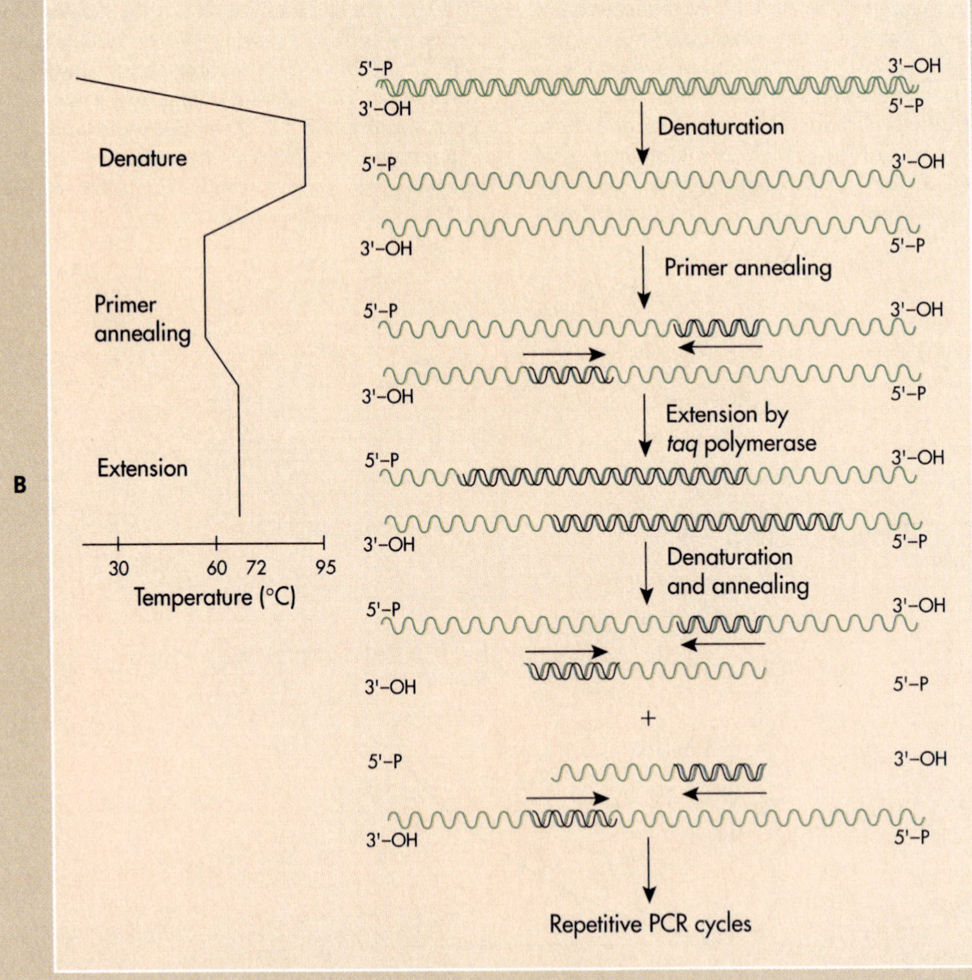

B, PCR involves three stages. First the DNA is denatured. This is accomplished by heating to convert the double helical DNA to single-stranded DNA. Then primers complementary to the nucleotide sequence's flanking target region are annealed. This is accomplished by lowering the temperature to permit primer annealing. Then the DNA is extended by the action of *taq* polymerase. Because *taq* polymerase is heat stable, the process can be repeated to increase the number of copies of the target sequence.

Post-replication Modification of DNA

After DNA has been replicated, the two newly synthesized strands are subject to enzymatic modification. These changes usually involve the addition of certain molecules to specific sites along the double helix. In this way, the cell tags or labels the DNA so that it can distinguish its own genetic material from any foreign DNA that may enter the cell. Post-replication modification of DNA may also influence the way in which the molecule is folded.

Subsequent to its replication, DNA is subject to modification, particularly by the addition of methyl groups to some adenine and cytosine residues. The methyl groups are added by **DNA methylases** after the nucleotides have been incorporated by DNA polymerases. The addition of methyl to cytosine forms 5-methylcytosine and the methylation of adenine forms 6-methyladenine. Methyladenine is more common than methylcytosine in prokaryotic cells, whereas in eukaryotic cells, methyl groups are almost exclusively added to cytosine. The methylation occurs only at a few specific nucleotide sequences. In eukaryotic cells, for example, methylation generally occurs at a cytosine that is adjacent to a guanine on its 3′-OH side (5′P–CG–3′OH).

The pattern of methylation is specific for a given species, acting like a signature for the DNA of that species. This is critical because methyl groups protect the DNA against digestion by specific enzymes called **restriction endonucleases** (FIG. 6-14). Foreign DNA is digested by restriction endonucleases. In a particular cell, the restriction endonuclease can cut the DNA at the same specific site where the DNA methylase adds a methyl group. The methylation pattern protects the DNA from digestion by a cells' own endonucleases but not against the restriction enzymes produced by cells of other species. This restricts the natural exchanges of DNA among cells of different species. Restriction endonucleases are discussed further in Chapter 7 when considering recombination and genetic engineering.

The methylation of DNA at specific sites may result in the localized conversion of B-DNA into the Z-DNA form. In the B-DNA form, the hydrophobic methyl groups protrude into the hydrophilic environment of the major groove; this arrangement is destablizing. By switching to the Z form, the methyl groups form hydrophobic regions that help stabilize the DNA. The localized conversion of B-DNA to Z-DNA may influence the functioning of some genes.

Enzyme	Source organism	Restriction site	Enzyme	Source organism	Restriction site
EcoRI	*Escherichia coli*	C-T-T-A-A↓-G-5' 5'-G↑-A-A-T-T-C-	*HpaII*	*H. parainfluenzae*	-G-G-C-C-5' 5'-C↑-C-G-G-
EcoRII	*E. coli*	-C-G-G-A-C↓-C-G-5' 5'-G↑-C-C-T-G-G-C-	*PstI*	*Providencia stuartii*	-G↓-A-C-G-T-C-5' 5'-C-T-G-C-A↑-G-
HindII	*Haemophilus influenzae*	-C-A-Pu-Py-T↓-G-5' 5'-G-T-Py↑-Pu-A-C-	*SmaI*	*Serratia marcescens*	-G-G-G↓-C-C-C-5' 5'-C-C-C↑-G-G-G-
HindIII	*H. influenzae*	-T-T-C-G-A↓-A-5' 5'-A-A↑-G-C-T-T-	*BamI*	*Bacillus amyloliquefaciens*	-C-C-T-A-G↓-G-5' 5'-G↑-G-A-T-C-C-
HaeIII	*H. aegyptius*	-C-C-G-G-5' 5'-G↑-G-C-C-	*BglII*	*B. globiggi*	-T-C-T-A-G↓-A-5' 5'-A↑-G-A-T-C-T-

FIG. 6-14 Restriction enzymes cut DNA at specific sites, often palindromic sequences. These enzymes protect against the entry of foreign DNA. The site of cutting typically is a site of methylation within a species, which is how that species protects its own DNA against degradation. (Py indicates any pyrimidine and Pu any purine.)

6.2 TRANSCRIPTION: TRANSFERRING INFORMATION FROM DNA TO RNA

The process of using the information in the DNA to direct the synthesis of proteins employs intermediary RNA molecules. If the DNA is likened to an encyclopedia that contains the full scope of information and is housed in the reference room of a library, the RNA would be a photocopy of a segment of that encyclopedic information. Multiple copies of RNA can be made from segments of the cell's total genome and be used without threatening potential damage to the reference information housed in the DNA.

Transcription is the process in which the information stored in the DNA is used to code for the synthesis of RNA. Transcription is similar in several ways to DNA replication, but there are some major differences between RNA and DNA synthesis. The RNA that is synthesized is single-stranded. Thus, for a given region, only one strand of DNA serves as a template; the strand of DNA coding for the synthesis of RNA is known as the **sense strand**. Different regions of both strands of the DNA can serve as sense strands. The term *sense strand* is applied only to the specific region of the DNA that is being transcribed. In transcription, the sense strand of DNA serves as a template for synthesis of RNA, accomplishing a critical transfer of information for the eventual expression of genetic information.

RIBONUCLEIC ACID (RNA)

In all living cells, RNA macromolecules act as informational mediators between the DNA where the genetic information is stored and the proteins that functionally express that information. RNA is involved in the expression of hereditary information, acting as a carrier of genetic information within a cell.

RNA is chemically similar to DNA in that it is a macromolecule composed of nucleotides (FIG. 6-15). RNA is a strand of ribonucleotides linked by 3′-5′ phosphodiester bonds with a 3′-OH free end and a 5′-P free end. Ribose instead of deoxyribose occurs in the nucleotides of RNA. The extra hydroxyl group that occurs in ribose as compared to deoxyribose makes RNA a less stable structure than DNA. RNA, like DNA, contains adenine, guanine, and cytosine, but RNA contains the pyrimidine **uracil (U)** and uridine nucleotides (uridylate) instead of thymine.

RNA exists mainly as a single strand as opposed to the double helix of DNA. However, portions of the RNA chain can fold back on themselves and form G–C hydrogen-bonded base pairs similar to those in DNA, as well as hydrogen-bonded base pairs between A and U. RNA molecules contain single-stranded regions and double-stranded regions with structures called

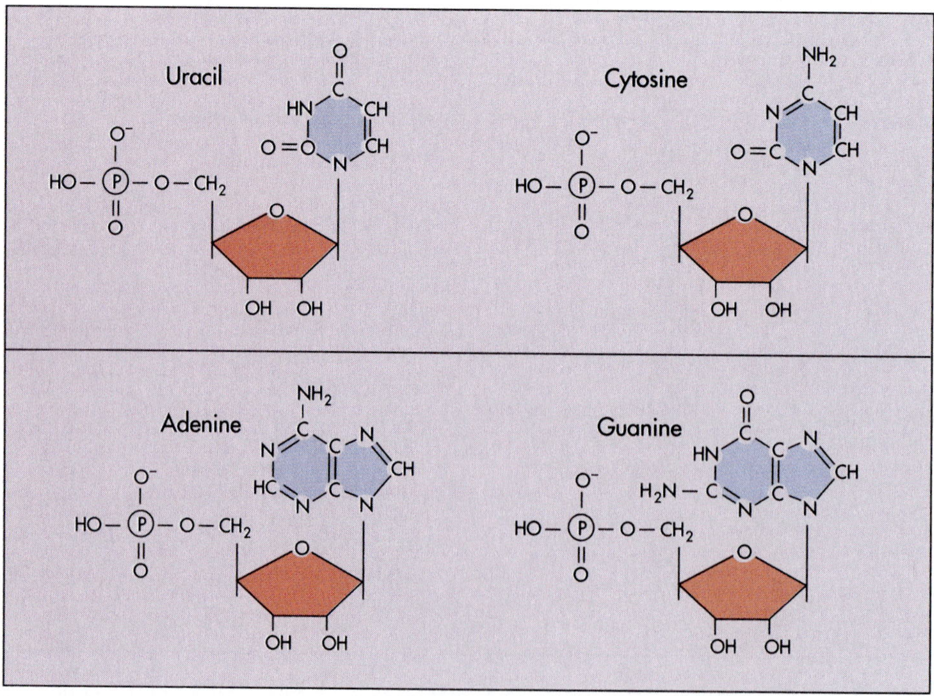

FIG. 6-15 Ribonucleic acid (RNA) is composed of ribonucleotides that have the sugar ribose, a phosphate group, and one of four nucleic acid bases: uracil, cytosine, adenine, or guanine.

TABLE 6-3 Characteristics of Various Types of RNA

TYPE OF RNA	ABBREVIATION	SEDIMENTATION COEFFICIENT	MOLECULAR WEIGHT	NUMBER OF NUCLEOTIDES
Messenger RNA	mRNA	6-50S	25,000-1,000,000	100-10,000
Transfer RNA	tRNA	4S	23,000-30,000	75-90
Prokaryotic ribosomal RNA	rRNA	5S	48,000	120
		16S	616,000	1540
		23S	1,200,000	3000
Eukaryotic ribosomal RNA	rRNA	5S	48,000	120
	rRNA	5.8S	64,000	160
		18S	760,000	1900
		28S	1,920,000	4800

hairpin loops created by their three-dimensional topology.

The transcription of DNA results in the production of three classes of RNA: rRNA, tRNA, and mRNA, each of which serves a different function (Table 6-3). Each of these RNA molecules is transcribed from different regions of the DNA.

Messenger RNA (mRNA)

Messenger RNA (mRNA) contains the code that is transcribed from the DNA genetic information and is then used to specify a sequence of amino acids in protein synthesis. In prokaryotic cells, there is usually only one DNA sequence coding for a particular mRNA, whereas in eukaryotic cells there often are multiple copies of genes coding for the same mRNA molecules. In both prokaryotic and eukaryotic cells, however, there can be multiple copies of a particular mRNA macromolecule, allowing multiple sites of protein synthesis for the same product.

The longevity of prokaryotic and eukaryotic mRNA differs drastically. In prokaryotic cells the mRNA molecules last for only a few minutes, whereas in eukaryotic cells an mRNA molecule can remain functional for hours or days. The long period of activity of an mRNA molecule in a eukaryotic cell imparts relative stability to the protein complement compared to the changing situation in a prokaryotic cell where the mRNA molecules are quickly degraded. The bacterial cell, as a result, can rapidly alter its metabolism in response to changing environmental conditions, whereas eukaryotic microorganisms are better adapted for continuous metabolism in a stable environment.

Transfer RNA (tRNA)

Transfer RNA (tRNA) decodes the mRNA sequence or translates it into a correct amino acid sequence. It carries a specific amino acid to the ribosome where protein synthesis occurs. Transfer RNA molecules are relatively short, containing about 70 to 80 ribonucleotides (FIG. 6-16). Although RNA molecules are

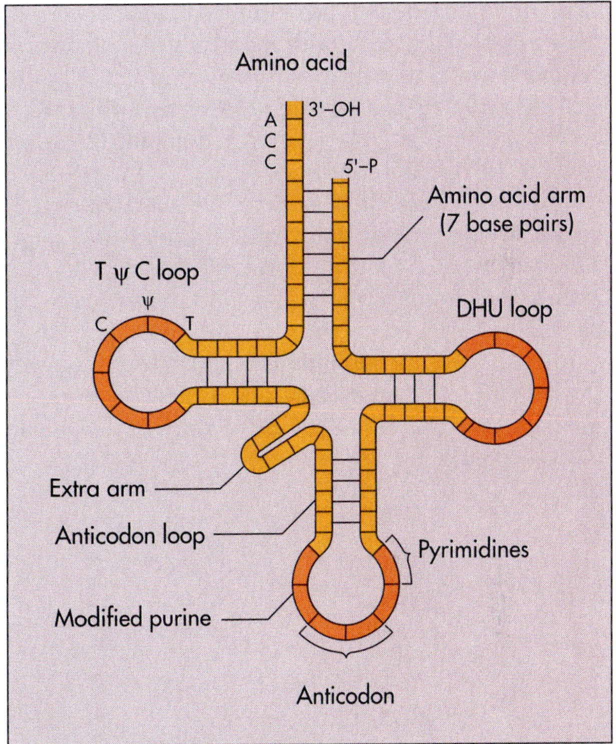

FIG. 6-16 All tRNA molecules have a characteristic four-lobe structure that results from internal base pairing of some of the nucleotides. Each lobe of the tRNA molecule has a distinct function. Several of the lobes are characterized by the inclusion of unusual nucleotides. These nucleotides are formed by enzymatic modification of the nucleotides directly coded for by the DNA; that is, the DNA does not have additional nucleotides that directly call for the insertion of nucleic acid bases other than adenine, uracil, cytosine, and guanine into the RNA. One of the lobes, designated the *DHU* or *D loop,* contains dihydrouracil (DHU). This lobe binds to the enzyme involved in forming the peptide during translation. The TΨC loop contains pseudouracil (Ψ). The third loop, which also contains modified purines, is designated the *anticodon loop* because it is complementary to the region of the mRNA, the codon, that specifies the amino acid to be incorporated during protein synthesis. The 3′-OH end always has the terminal sequence ACC, which is where the amino acid binds. This terminal sequence is usually referred to as the *CCA end,* reading from the 5′-P end of the tRNA molecule.

single-stranded, they can fold back on themselves, establishing double-stranded regions. tRNA molecules have extensive double-stranded regions that arise from the folding of the primary RNA chain. These molecules are elaborately folded into three-dimensional structures that resemble a four-leaf clover. Each of the four lobes of tRNA has characteristic nucleotide sequences and functions. The four parts of the RNA molecule fold back on themselves by G–C and A–U base pairing to form stable double-stranded regions called stems. Extending from three of the four stems are hairpin loops. This stem–loop structure is further folded three-dimensionally to form an L-shaped structure.

The nucleic acids in tRNA molecules are enzymatically modified after the RNA molecule has been synthesized. Specific nucleotides are methylated, hydrogenated, or rearranged to form unusual ribonucleotides such as pseudouridine (Ψ), thymidine (T), and dihydrouridine (D), which are not found in other types of RNA. These changes in the tRNA sequence are fairly constant for all tRNA molecules. They contain a D loop, a TΨC loop, and an anticodon loop. The fourth stem of the cloverleaf structure is the amino acid stem, to which a specific amino acid is attached and carried to the ribosome during protein synthesis. The anticodon loop contains three adjacent nucleotides, the anticodon, that can form complementary base pairs with the three nucleotides in the mRNA codon.

Ribosomal RNA (rRNA)

Ribosomal RNA (rRNA) combines with various ribosomal proteins to form a ribosome; rRNA is important in the structural arrangement of the ribosomal proteins to form a functional particle: the ribosome (FIG. 6-17). In prokaryotic cells, the 30S small ribosomal subunit contains one 16S rRNA molecule, which contains about 1,540 nucleotides, and the 50S large ribosomal subunit contains one 23S rRNA molecule (2,900 nucleotides) and one 5S rRNA (120 nucleotides). In eukaryotes, the 40S small subunit contains one 18S (1,900 nucleotides) rRNA and the 60S large subunit contains one each of 28S (4,800 nucleotides), 5.8S (160 nucleotides), and 5S (120 nucleotides) rRNA molecules. Recent research has led to structural three-dimensional maps and a further understanding of the relationship between the individual proteins and the rRNA molecules that comprise the ribosome and their function in protein synthesis. RNA does not play only a structural role in the ribosome. It also is important in positioning tRNAs on the ribosome and has been shown to contain peptidyl transferase activity involved in peptide bond formation.

Synthesis of RNA

The molecule of RNA that is synthesized in transcription is antiparallel to the strand of DNA that serves as a template. The synthesis of RNA during transcription

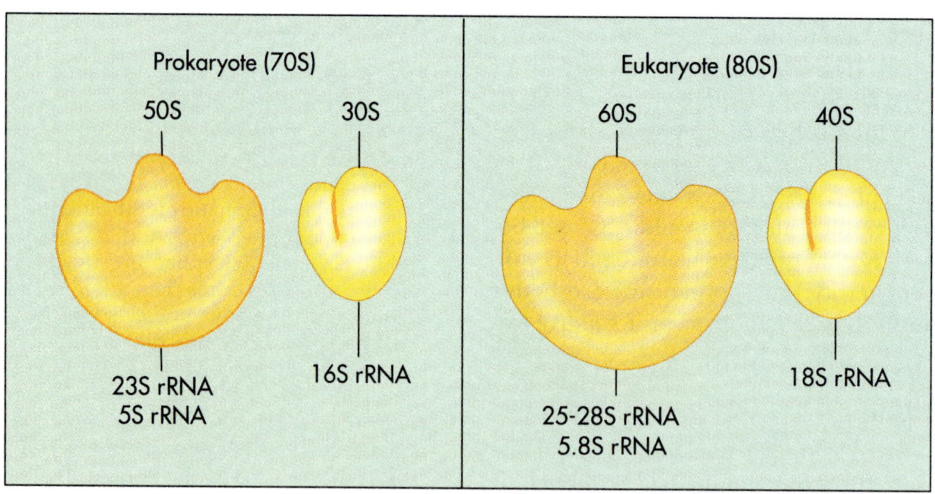

FIG. 6-17 Ribosomes are composed of proteins and RNA. The ribosomal subunits have several ribosomal RNA (rRNA) molecules of differing molecular weights. For example, the 30S subunit in prokaryotic cells has 16S rRNA and the 40S subunit in eukaryotic cells has 18S rRNA.

involves unwinding of the double helical DNA molecule for a short sequence of nucleotide bases, alignment of complementary ribonucleotides by base pairing opposite the nucleotides of the DNA strand being transcribed, and linkage of these nucleotides with phosphodiester bonds by a DNA-dependent RNA polymerase. Binding of RNA polymerase to DNA may also be involved in localized unwinding and proper alignment of complementary RNA nucleotides. RNA polymerases are able to link nucleotides only to the 3′-OH free end of the polymer; thus the synthesis of RNA, like that of DNA, occurs in a 5′-P → 3′-OH direction.

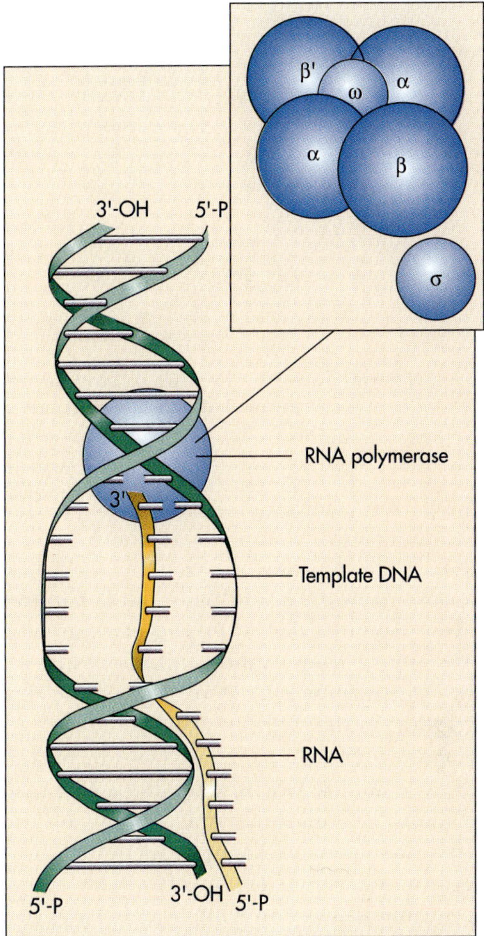

FIG. 6-18 Transcription produces RNA using one of the strands of DNA as a template. The formation of the RNA is catalyzed by RNA polymerase. In eubacteria, this enzyme is composed of several subunits.

RNA Polymerases

The enzyme that synthesizes RNA from ribonucleotides is **RNA polymerase**. This enzyme is capable of forming phosphodiester bonds between two ribonucleotides only as long as they are aligned opposite the complementary DNA template nucleotides; therefore, unlike DNA replication, RNA synthesis does not require a primer.

Eubacteria have one basic type of RNA polymerase that produces all three classes of RNA molecules. In *E. coli* there is only one form, although other bacteria may possess several variants of the basic type of RNA polymerase.

Eubacterial RNA polymerase is actually a complex of four protein subunits that form the core enzyme (FIG. 6-18). In *E. coli*, these subunits are labelled α, β, and β'; there are two copies of the α subunit in the core enzyme and one copy each of the β and β' subunits. In addition to the core proteins is a sigma (σ) factor, which is involved in the initiation of RNA synthesis, and an omega (ω) factor, whose function in transcription is not clear at this time.

Archaebacteria appear to have their own unique RNA polymerases. These contain 7 to 12 polypeptides but differ in the size and number of copies of each subunit in the core enzyme in different archaebacteria. All archaebacterial RNA polymerases examined so far seem to be insensitive to rifampicin and streptolydigin and show a greater similarity to eukaryotic RNA polymerases than to eubacterial RNA polymerases.

Eukaryotic cells have three distinct RNA polymerase enzymes that are responsible for the synthesis of the three different classes of RNA. These enzymes are more complex than those of eubacteria and are composed of 9 to 12 or more subunits. RNA polymerase I synthesizes rRNA, RNA polymerase II synthesizes mRNA, and RNA polymerase III synthesizes tRNA and 5S rRNA. RNA polymerase I is insensitive to α-amanitin, whereas RNA polymerase II has a low sensitivity, and RNA polymerase III has a high sensitivity to chemicals produced by some fungi. All eukaryotic RNA polymerases are insensitive to rifampicin and streptolydigin.

Initiation and Termination of Transcription

The transfer of information from DNA to RNA requires that transcription begin at precise locations. There are multiple initiation sites for transcription along the DNA molecule in both prokaryotes and eukaryotes. Different initiation sites are needed to begin the synthesis of different classes of RNA and the synthesis of RNA for different polypeptide sequences. There are also specific sites for the termination of transcription. By examining the DNA sequence for specific transcription start and stop signals it is possible to locate a region called an *open reading frame* (nucleotide sequence coding for a polypeptide). The open reading frame is equivalent to a gene.

Promoters What in the DNA molecule signals where to start reading a specific gene? DNA contains specific sequences of nucleotides, known as **promoter regions**, that serve as signals for the initiation of transcription. The promoter region of DNA is the site

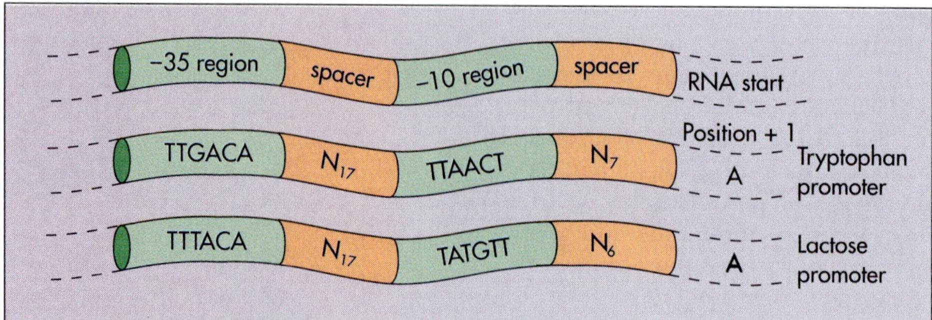

FIG. 6-19 The site of binding of RNA polymerase to the promoter region is specified by the Pribnow sequence. This sequence occurs several nucleotides upstream (toward the 5′-P region) of the actual start of transcription. The Pribnow sequence that begins at the −10 region has a conserved region (nearly identical sequence of nucleotides) at that region and at the −35 region. There is a spacer of about 17 nucleotides (N_{17}) between the −10 and −35 region that is not conserved.

where RNA polymerase initially binds for transcription. The presence of the promoter region specifies both the site of transcription initiation and which of the two DNA strands is to serve as the sense strand for transcription in that region.

The promoter regions in the DNA of bacteria that have been examined consist of about 40 nucleotides and contain a seven-nucleotide sequence, known as the **Pribnow sequence**, that appears to be a key part of the recognition signal (FIG. 6-19). The Pribnow sequence occurs about 5 to 8 nucleotide bases upstream (in the 5′-P direction) from the actual start of transcription. The designation upstream indicates that it is transcribed prior to later downstream nucleotides. Since the Pribnow sequence has seven nucleotides, it overlaps the −10 position, that is, a location 10 nucleotides upstream from the initial nucleotides of the gene that is transcribed. The Pribnow sequence contains a sequence of nucleotides that is the same or almost the same as TATAAT for most of the bacterial promoters that have been examined. This type of conserved DNA sequence is called a **consensus sequence** (meaning regions of general agreement, that is, high nucleotide sequence homology). The Pribnow consensus sequence starts at the −10 position on the DNA (counting nucleotides backward or upstream from the start site of transcription which is +1 and excluding 0.) A second consensus sequence, TTGACA, is located on the promoter at about position −35.

Role of Sigma Factor The initial binding of eubacterial RNA polymerase core enzyme ($\alpha_2\beta\beta'$) to the promoter region depends on the presence of sigma factor (σ factor) (see FIG. 6-19). Without the sigma subunit, the RNA polymerase fails to exhibit the necessary specificity for recognizing the initiation sites for transcription. The sigma factor ensures that RNA synthesis begins at the correct site.

The complete RNA polymerase (core + sigma unit) is the *holoenzyme.* The RNA polymerase holoenzyme first binds to the DNA promoter at the −35 consensus sequence, forming a *closed complex.* The RNA polymerase holoenzyme then shifts its binding to the −10 Pribnow sequence. As it does so, the DNA helix is unwound to form a single-stranded region and an *open complex.* The RNA polymerase holoenzyme is now poised to begin transcription. The first nucleotide added is usually a purine (adenosine or guanosine). After formation of about 10 phosphodiester bonds between ribonucleotides, the sigma subunit dissociates from the RNA polymerase and the remainder of the RNA molecule is synthesized or elongated by the core RNA polymerase. The sigma subunit is then free to associate with another RNA polymerase molecule, completing that molecule and establishing the necessary specificity for the recognition of a new transcriptional initiation site.

Eubacteria actually have multiple σ factors, each of which is responsible for the recognition of specific promoter initiation sequences. The main σ factor in *E. coli* is σ^{70} with σ^{54}, σ^{32} and σ^{28} normally present in lower concentrations. The superscript associated with each σ factor represents the molecular weight of the protein $\times$ 10^{-3}. Under certain changes in environmental conditions, σ^{54} or σ^{32} increase in concentration and direct the RNA polymerase to bind at other promoter consensus sequences (TTGCA for σ^{54} and CCCCAT for σ^{32}), which are both different than the Pribnow sequence recognized by σ^{70}. As a result of this control mechanism, regulation of the concentrations of the different σ factors in the cell leads to the specific or preferential transcription of certain genes and not others.

Transcription Factors in Eukaryotic Cells An analogous consensus sequence for initiation of transcription has been found in eukaryotic cells. Eukaryotic RNA polymerases, however, do not utilize σ factor to initiate RNA synthesis as in bacterial cells. Instead, **transcription factors (TFs)** bind to DNA at specific promoter sites independently of the RNA polymerases. TFI, TFII, and TFIII are responsible for binding the correct RNA polymerases of eukaryotic cells to their correct promoters.

The transcription of RNA polymerase II promoters in eukaryotic cells requires the binding of TFIID, also called TATA factor. The TATA factor is a protein transcription factor that preferentially binds to a conserved A-T rich DNA sequence (TATAXAX, where X can be either A or T) called the **TATA box**. This conserved consensus sequence is centered about −25 nucleotides upstream from the start nucleotide and is analogous to the −10 consensus sequence in prokaryotic cells. Since RNA polymerase II synthesizes mRNA, the TATA box is an important recognition site for initiation of transcription that leads to synthesis of the proteins of the cell.

Termination of Transcription The rate of RNA polymerization is not constant during the elongation phase of synthesis. Actually, the polymerase stops synthesis or pauses after certain sequences have been transcribed and may continue on in the elongation process or end biosynthesis in a termination step.

There are specific **termination sites** that act as a signal to stop transcription. The termination sequence of nucleotides in the DNA contains a region with an abundance of GC bases followed by a region with an abundance of AT bases (FIG. 6-20). The GC-rich region exhibits a symmetry that enables the synthesized RNA to fold back on itself, forming a stem and loop. The A bases in the AT-rich region code for a terminal sequence of several U (uridine) nucleotides. These sequences cause the RNA polymerase to pause and terminate RNA synthesis.

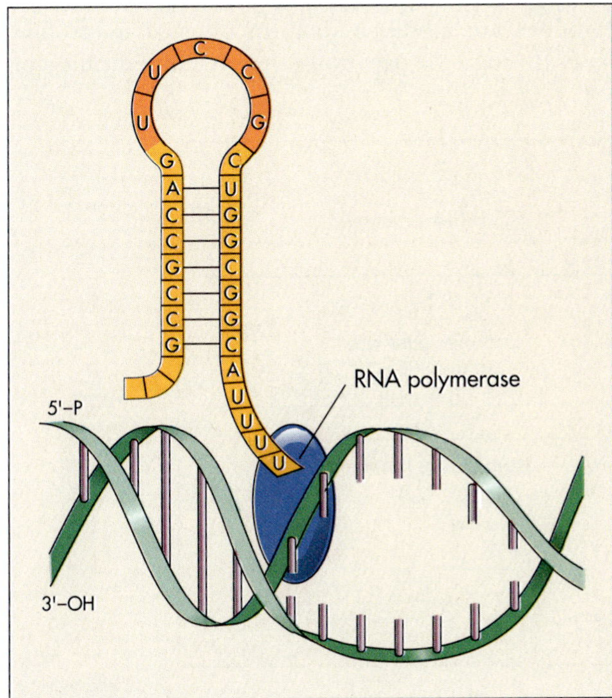

FIG. 6-20 The transcription termination site is characterized by a GC-rich nucleotide sequence so that the RNA forms a hairpin loop and a polyA sequence that causes the RNA polymerase to pause and release from the RNA.

In some cases, termination of transcription requires the presence of an additional factor called **rho (ρ) protein**. This ρ-dependent termination does not require the presence of a sequence of uridines to function. It is believed that the ρ protein binds to the nascent RNA strand and travels along it toward the RNA polymerase, that is, in the 5′-P → 3′-OH direction. When the RNA polymerase pauses at a termination sequence, the ρ protein catches up with it and causes the release of the nascent transcript.

POST-TRANSCRIPTIONAL MODIFICATION OF RNA

RNA formed by transcription can be subsequently modified to produce various RNA molecules. This occurs in the synthesis of rRNA and tRNA in both prokaryotic and eukaryotic cells. It also occurs for the production of mRNA in eukaryotic cells. The mRNA molecule in prokaryotic cells is not extensively modified between the time it is synthesized, through transcription of the DNA, and the time it is translated into the amino acid sequence of a poly-peptide at the ribosome. In bacteria, the mRNA molecule is transcribed directly from a contiguous sequence of DNA (FIG. 6-21).

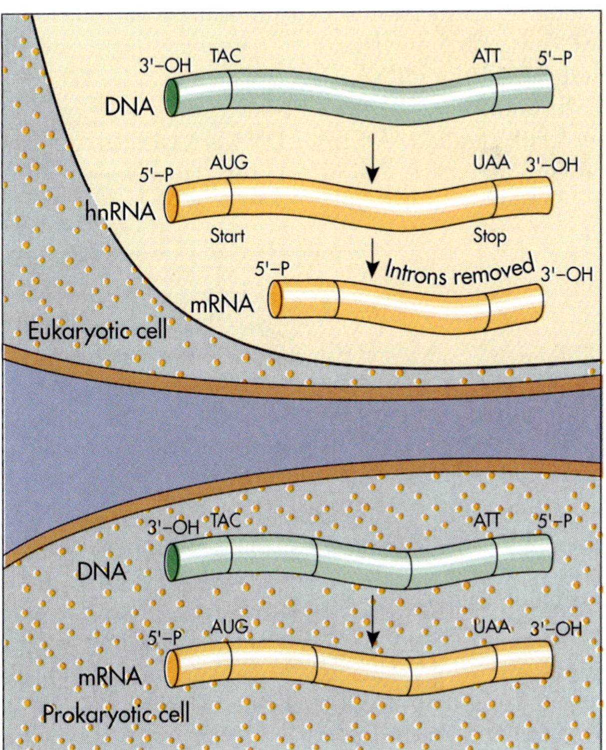

FIG. 6-21 In eukaryotic cells the primary transcript (hnRNA) is extensively modified within the nucleus to produce mRNA. The conversion of hnRNA to mRNA involves the removal of introns. Each mRNA usually encodes only a single gene. In prokaryotic cells the primary transcript serves as the mRNA. It often encodes several genes.

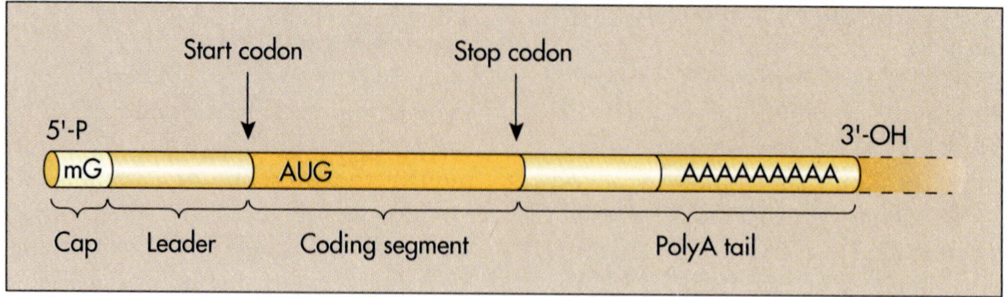

FIG. 6-22 Post-transcriptional modification of eukaryotic RNA molecules involves addition of a polyA tail, a leader sequence, and a cap of 7-methyl guanosine (mG).

Often, bacterial mRNA is **polycistronic**, containing the information for several proteins, usually with related functions. There may be spacer regions that are not translated between the regions of DNA coding for the different proteins.

rRNA and tRNA

rRNA and tRNA molecules are substantially modified in both prokaryotic and eukaryotic cells. There are leader, spacer, and trailer sequences for rRNA and tRNA that do not get translated (FIG. 6-22). The leader sequence of 25 to 150 nucleotides is located just upstream of the initiation codon. The trailer sequence is involved in the termination of transcription and is located downstream from the termination codon. A polyuridine trailer following a hairpin loop will cause RNA polymerase to terminate transcription and release the mRNA.

In both prokaryotic and eukaryotic cells, the RNA molecules transcribed from DNA are larger than the rRNA molecules found in the ribosomes (FIG. 6-23). The precursor rRNA molecules must therefore be processed to form the rRNA molecules. The ribosomes of prokaryotic cells contain 5S, 16S, and 23S RNA, but the initial transcript from the DNA is a large 30S molecule that can be cleaved by nuclease enzymes to form these different-size RNA molecules. In some cases, a separate large precursor is used for the production of the 5S rRNA molecules. In eukaryotic cells a large precursor RNA molecule similarly is cleaved to form the 28S, 18S, and 5.8S rRNA molecules that make up the RNA portions of the ribosomes.

The tRNA molecules are similarly synthesized as high molecular weight precursors that are then processed to produce the mature tRNA molecules. All tRNA molecules have a 3′-OH terminus with the nucleotide sequence CCA that may be encoded in the primary nucleotide sequence or added enzymatically as a cap after transcription from the DNA template.

Within the tRNA molecule, several of the nucleotides are modified to form unusual nucleotide bases through the post-transcriptional modification of

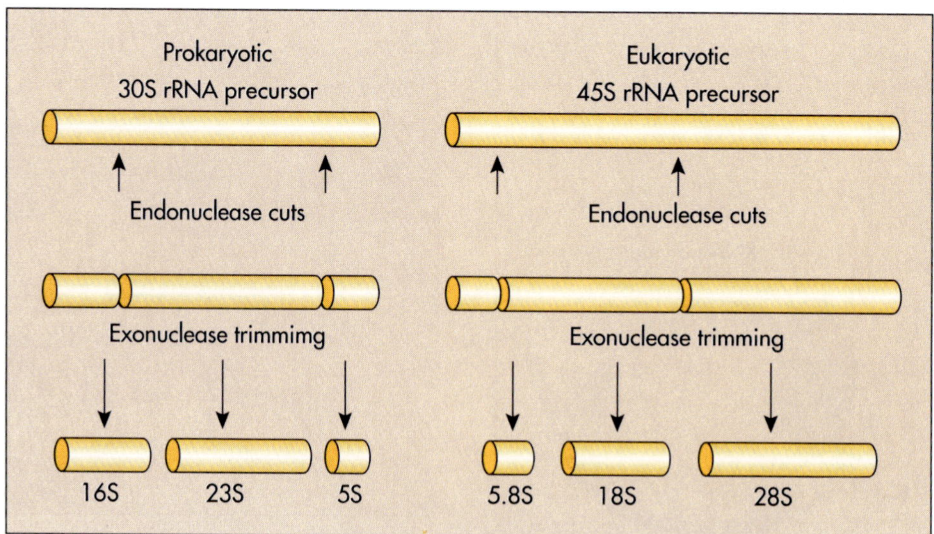

FIG. 6-23 The rRNA molecules of the ribosomal subunits are made by endonuclease cutting of a precursor RNA and exonuclease trimming of the segments to produce the necessary rRNAs. In prokaryotes 16S, 23S, and 5S rRNAs, and in eukaryotes 5.8S, 18S, and 28S rRNAs, are made for inclusion in ribosomes.

the normal RNA nucleotides by specific enzymes. Some of the unusual nucleotide bases found in tRNA are pseudouridine, dihydrouridine, ribothymidine, and inosine. The specific functions of the unusual bases are not completely established (although some modified nucleotides in the anticodon loop have been shown to reduce wobble), but their hydrophobic nature may be important in the interactions of tRNA and ribosomes. The presence of the unusual nucleotides and the specific multilobed configuration of the tRNA molecule distinguish it from other classes of RNA molecules.

Split Genes in Eukaryotic Cells

The RNA molecules of eukaryotic cells are generally modified extensively after transcription from DNA to form mRNA. The precursor of mRNA in eukaryotes, known as **heterogeneous nuclear RNA (hnRNA)**, is several times larger than the final mRNA molecule and is subjected to substantial post-transcriptional modification within the nucleus to form the mRNA. The processing of the hnRNA involves removing and adding sequences of nucleotides. The 5′-P end of the hnRNA is capped with an inverted guanosine triphosphate (GTP) residue, some of the terminal adenine bases are methylated, and the 3′-OH end of the hnRNA molecule is modified by the addition of a sequence of adenosine nucleotides (polyA tail). Instead of the normal 3′-5′ phosphodiester bond, the 7-methyl guanosine cap is added as a 5′-5′ bond. It appears that guanosine is first added and then methylated. The adjacent two nucleotides may also be methylated at the 5′-P end.

Perhaps the most surprising discovery concerning the transcription of DNA and the processing of hnRNA is the occurrence of intervening sequences, or **introns** (see FIG. 6-21). (The regions that code for amino acid sequences are known as **exons**.) Introns do not code for amino acid sequences, and the reason for their existence is unknown. In one case in yeast mitochondria, an intron within the gene for one protein has been found to code for the removal of introns from genes that are subsequently transcribed, suggesting that introns are important regulators of gene function. Part of the processing of hnRNA involves the excision of introns to form the mature mRNA molecule. Exon-intron junctions have a GU rich sequence at the 5′-P end of the intron and an AG rich sequence at its 3′-OH end. This permits recognition of the boundaries between introns and exons so that appropriate regions are removed and the necessary splicing occurs.

The rearrangement of RNA molecules transcribed from DNA to form a mature mRNA molecule involves cutting out and splicing together pieces of RNA to form a functional mRNA. Thus the eukaryotes are said to have **split genes** because the nucleotides that comprise the gene that codes for a specific protein are separated in the DNA. The splicing of the pre-mRNA involves a complex of small nuclear RNAs (snRNAs) and small nuclear ribonucleoprotein particles (snRNPs). The snRNPs (SNURPS) are formed from snRNAs and proteins. The complex of snRNAs and snRNPs involved in forming the spliced mRNA is called a **spliceosome.** The snRNPs recognize the sites where splicing should occur, some snRNPs recognizing the 5′-P and others the 3′-OH end. In some cases the ribozymes catalyze the splicing.

As a result of post-transcriptional processing, RNA molecules of eukaryotic microorganisms generally are not colinear with the DNA molecule. The sequence of nucleotide bases in an mRNA of a eukaryotic cell is not complementary to the specific contiguous linear sequence of bases in a DNA molecule. The mRNA that is formed in eukaryotic cells is *monocistronic* (contains only the information for one polypeptide sequence), and the transcriptional and translational processes are spatially and temporally separated.

6.3 PROTEIN SYNTHESIS: TRANSLATION OF THE GENETIC CODE

The expression of this functional activity is largely mediated by proteins, which—acting as enzymes—determine the metabolic capacity and, hence, the phenotype (appearance, behavior, metabolism, etc.) of the cell. The DNA macromolecule that comprises the bacterial chromosome of *E. coli* theoretically contains enough information to encode 3,500 different proteins. The information in RNA, obtained from DNA during transcription, directs the sequence of amino acids in a protein.

Translation of the genetic information into protein molecules, which can functionally express genetic information, occurs on the ribosomes. Ribosomes provide the spatial framework and structural support for aligning the translational process of protein synthesis. Distortion of the proper configuration of the ribosome can prevent the proper informational exchange and expression of the genetic information, forming the basis for the action of many antibiotics.

All three types of RNA (rRNA, tRNA, and mRNA) are involved in transferring the information obtained from the sequence of nucleotides in DNA to the sequence of amino acids in the polypeptide chain of a protein. tRNA molecules carry the amino acids to the site of protein synthesis and properly align amino acids for incorporation into the polypeptide chain. It is the mRNA molecule, however, that actually contains the coded information that specifies the sequence of amino acids in the polypeptide chain.

The mRNA molecule of bacteria usually contains a sequence of nucleotides at the beginning and end of the molecule that do not code for specific amino acids in a polypeptide sequence. Rather, the beginning, or **leader sequence**, of nucleotides in the mRNA molecule is involved in the initiation of protein synthesis at the ribosomes. The nontranslated leader promotes binding of mRNA to the ribosomes. The attachment of mRNA to the ribosomes in prokaryotic cells often occurs before transcription of the mRNA is complete, indicating the close proximity of the transcriptional and translational processes.

GENETIC CODE

Within the mRNA, three sequential nucleotides are used to code for a given amino acid; the **genetic code** therefore is called a **triplet code** (Table 6-4). Each triplet nucleotide sequence is known as a **codon**. Because there are 4 different nucleotides, there are 64 possible codons; that is, there are 64 possible three-base combinations of the 4 different nucleotides. The genetic code, which is almost universal, can therefore be said to have 4 letters in the alphabet and 64 words in the dictionary, each word containing 3 letters. Although there are 64 possible codons, proteins in biological systems normally contain only 20 L-amino acids. Some proteins do contain other amino acids, but in such cases the unusual amino acids are usually formed by post-translational enzymatic modification of the chemical structure rather than by coding sequences that specify the unusual amino acids. Thus there are many more codons than are needed for the translation of genetic information into functional proteins.

More than one codon can code for the same amino acid, and therefore the genetic code is said to be **degenerate**. Stated another way, the genetic code is redundant, with several codons coding for the insertion of the same amino acid into the polypeptide chain.

Additionally, there are three **termination codons**, or **nonsense codons**, so named because they do not code for any amino acid. Termination codons, however, serve a very important function; they act as punctuators that signal the termination of the synthesis of a polypeptide chain.

The genetic code as shown in Table 6-4 is nearly universal. The codons listed in the table function in both eukaryotic and prokaryotic cells. However, a few exceptions, principally in mitochondrial DNA, have been found, forcing an alteration to the principle of a

TABLE 6-4 Codons of the Genetic Code (mRNA shown in 5′-P → 3′-OH direction)

FIRST NUCLEIC ACID (5′-P END)	SECOND NUCLEIC ACID U		C		A		G		THIRD NUCLEIC ACID (3′-OH END)
U	UUU	Phenylalanine	UCU	Serine	UAU	Tyrosine	UGU	Cysteine	U
	UUC	Phenylalanine	UCC	Serine	UAC	Tyrosine	UGC	Cysteine	C
	UUA	Leucine	UCA	Serine	UAA	STOP	UGA	STOP	A
	UUG	Leucine	UCG	Serine	UAG	STOP	UGG	Tryptophan	G
C	CUU	Leucine	CCU	Proline	CAU	Histidine	CGU	Arginine	U
	CUC	Leucine	CCC	Proline	CAC	Histidine	CGC	Arginine	C
	CUA	Leucine	CCA	Proline	CAA	Glutamine	CGA	Arginine	A
	CUG	Leucine	CCG	Proline	CAG	Glutamine	CGG	Arginine	G
A	AUU	Isoleucine	ACU	Threonine	AAU	Asparagine	AGU	Serine	U
	AUC	Isoleucine	ACC	Threonine	AAC	Asparagine	AGC	Serine	C
	AUA	Isoleucine	ACA	Threonine	AAA	Lysine	AGA	Arginine	A
	AUG	Methionine	ACG	Threonine	AAG	Lysine	AGG	Arginine	G
G	GUU	Valine	GCU	Alanine	GAU	Aspartate	GGU	Glycine	U
	GUC	Valine	GCC	Alanine	GAC	Aspartate	GGC	Glycine	C
	GUA	Valine	GCA	Alanine	GAA	Glutamate	GGA	Glycine	A
	GUG	Valine	GCG	Alanine	GAG	Glutamate	GGG	Glycine	G

TABLE 6-5 Exceptions to the Universal Code

CODON	NORMAL TRANSLATION	ALTERED TRANSLATION	LOCATION WHERE ALTERED CODON FUNCTIONS
UGA	Stop	Tryptophan	Human and yeast mitochondria *Mycoplasma*
CUA	Leucine	Threonine	Yeast mitochondria
AUA	Isoleucine	Methionine	Human mitochondria
AGA, AGG	Arginine	Stop	Human mitochondria
UAA	Stop	Glutamine	*Tetrahymena* *Paramecium* *Stylonychia*
UAG	Stop	Glutamine	*Paramecium*

universal genetic code. The termination codon UGA, for example, codes for tryptophan in human and yeast mitochondria and also in the bacterium *Mycoplasma capricolum.* Several other aberrations to the normal code are listed in Table 6-5. These changes occur in distinct species that evolved over a long period of time and are distantly related.

Translation of the information in the mRNA molecule, that is, reading of the codons, is a directional process. mRNA is read in a 5′-P to 3′-OH direction, and the polypeptide is synthesized from the amino terminal to the carboxyl terminal end. The mRNA molecule is read one codon (three nucleotides) at a time. There are no spaces between the codons and they are non-overlapping. Therefore establishing a reading frame, that is, determining which nucleotide is used to initiate the reading of the three-nucleotide sequences, is critical for extracting the proper information. Within the mRNA molecule there are sequences of nucleotides that define the beginning and end of each encoded polypeptide chain. Here we see the importance of having a mechanism for recognizing direction in the informational macromolecules. Just as we establish a convention for reading the English language from left to right, the correct interpretation of the information stored in the mRNA molecule requires that it be read from the 5′-P to the 3′-OH free end.

INITIATING THE TRANSLATION OF MRNA

The reading of an mRNA molecule begins from a fixed starting point. The first codon normally read is AUG, which codes for the amino acid methionine. In eukaryotic microorganisms, methionine is always the first amino acid of the polypeptide sequence. In prokaryotic cells the codon AUG codes for *N*-formylmethionine (f-Met) to initiate the polypeptide chain, although the same codon (AUG) codes for methionine (Met) when it occurs elsewhere in the mRNA molecule. In some bacteria the codon GUG acts as the initiator codon that specifies f-Met to begin the polypeptide chain, although when GUG occurs at an internal position in the mRNA molecule, it codes for valine. Whereas either Met or f-Met is the first amino acid in all peptide chains when they are initially synthesized, these terminal amino acids can later be enzymatically modified. Deformylase can remove the formyl group from formylmethionine, and methionine amino peptidase can remove methionine from the amino terminus of the peptide. Therefore not all polypeptides in microorganisms have f-Met at their amino terminal ends.

The initiating (start) codon establishes the **reading frame** (three-nucleotide sequences) for the rest of the mRNA molecule (FIG. 6-24, p. 232). Because the nucleotide bases are read three at a time along a continuous chain of nucleotides, shifting the reading frame by inserting or deleting a single nucleotide base within a gene can dramatically alter the amino acid sequence of the protein it can produce.

Several proteins are required as initiating factors to begin the translational process. In prokaryotic cells, three initiation factors, IF1, IF2, and IF3, and in eukaryotic cells, at least nine eukaryotic initiation factors (eIF1 to eIF6) are needed to start protein synthesis. Although translation occurs on 70S or 80S ribosomes in prokaryotes and eukaryotes, respectively, the initiation process requires that the ribosomes dissociate into their respective subunits. Ribosomes are normally in equilibrium between their associated and dissociated forms. Part of the role of the initiation factors (IF3 and eIF6) is to prevent reassociation of the small subunits (30S or 40S) with their respective large subunits (50S or 60S). The binding of IF3 to the 30S ribosomal subunit is necessary for the subunit to bind mRNA, f-Met tRNA, and GTP. In eukaryotic cells, an initiation complex is formed between eIF2, GTP, and Met-tRNA that can bind to free 40S ribosomal subunits. This initiation complex can then bind to the 5′-P end of mRNA and move to the initiation site.

Whereas initiation of eukaryotic protein synthesis begins at the 5′-P end of the mRNA molecule, initiation of protein synthesis in prokaryotic cells may begin at internal start sites on the mRNA, since most prokaryotic mRNAs are polycistronic.

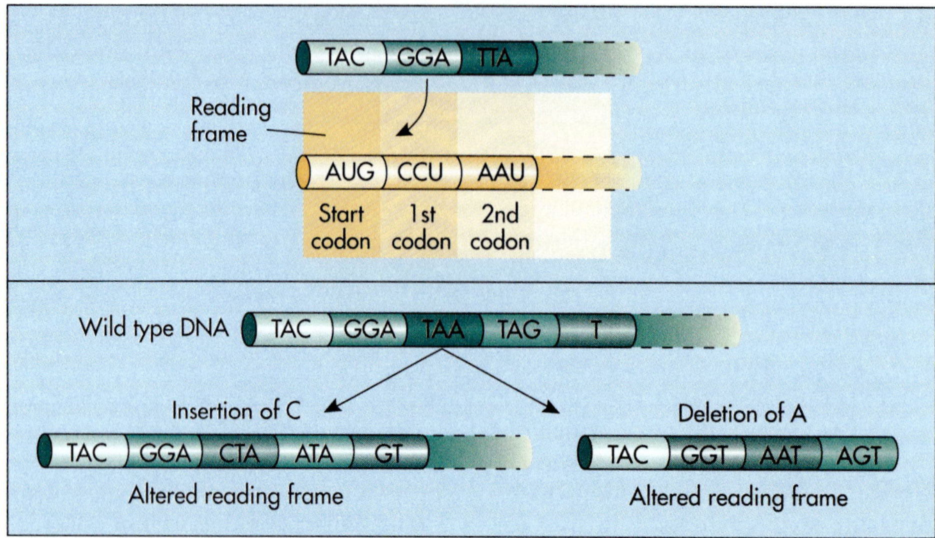

FIG. 6-24 The start codon establishes the reading frame. In prokaryotes, AUG is the start codon. Codons are read as three nucleotide sequences. Adding or deleting a single nucleotide alters the reading frame so that altered codons are read.

In prokaryotic cells, positioning the 30S ribosomal subunit at the appropriate initiation sites usually depends on a consensus ribonucleotide sequence of UCCUCC at the 3′-OH end of the 16S rRNA that is found in the 30S subunit. About 7 bases upstream (toward the 5′-P end) of the AUG start codon on the mRNA is a polypurine consensus sequence, AGGAGG, known as the **Shine-Dalgarno sequence** (FIG. 6-25). The Shine-Dalgarno sequence is complementary to the consensus sequence on the 16S rRNA and thus forms a base-paired region of double-stranded RNA between the 16S rRNA and the mRNA. In this way the 30S ribosomal subunit is properly oriented just upstream from the initiator codon, which signals where translation of the mRNA should start. Not all Shine-Dalgarno sequences contain the complete hexamer but usually 4 to 5 bases that are complementary to the 16S rRNA are present.

After the initiation complexes have formed in prokaryotic cells the 50S subunit binds to the 30S–mRNA–f-Met tRNA complex. This is accompanied by the hydrolysis of GTP to GDP and P_i and the release of the initiation factors. Likewise, in eukaryotic cells the 60S subunit binds to the 40S-ternary complex, which releases all the initiation factors and hydrolyzes GTP to GDP.

Role of tRNA in Protein Synthesis

Before continuing, we need to consider the role of tRNA in the translation process. A tRNA molecule contains approximately 80 nucleotides, about half of which exhibit base pairing. The tRNA molecule forms four lobes, some of which are characterized by the presence of unusual nucleotides. tRNA brings the amino acids to the ribosomes and properly aligns them during translation. The binding of the amino acid to the tRNA molecule occurs at the 3′-OH end of the tRNA molecule. Attachment of an amino acid to its specific tRNA molecule is called **charging**; a tRNA molecule with its attached amino acid is said to be *charged.* Charging tRNA molecules requires ATP and an aminoacyl synthetase. There is at least one aminoacyl synthetase for each of the 20 amino acids. There are at least 20 different types of tRNA molecules, with each of the 20 amino acids that occur in proteins

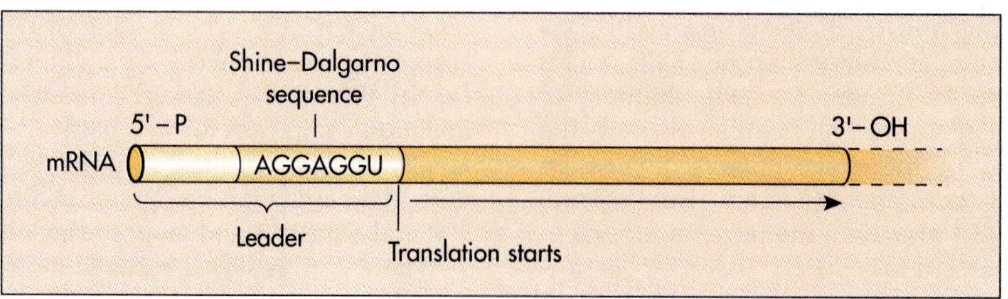

FIG. 6-25 The Shine-Dalgarno sequence occurs before the start sequence of the mRNA. This nucleotide sequence allows the mRNA to align with the 30S ribosomal subunit of the prokaryotic cell.

binding with a different tRNA molecule. The structure of the tRNA molecule plays a role in establishing the proper alignment of molecules during translation. One of the four lobes is attached to the amino acid; one contains a nucleotide sequence that interacts with the rRNA, establishing the proper orientation to the ribosome; one interacts with aminoacyl synthetase; and one contains a region, the *anticodon*, that interacts with mRNA.

The **anticodon** has three nucleotides that are complementary to the three-based nucleotide sequence of the codon. It is the pairing of the codons of mRNA molecules and the anticodons of tRNA molecules that determines the order of the amino acid sequence in the polypeptide chain. The third base of the anticodon does not always properly recognize the third base of the mRNA codon. As a result, base pairing between the first two nucleotides of the anticodon to the mRNA codon are more significant than the third base in codon-anticodon recognition. This phenomenon is known as **wobble**. Because of wobble and the degeneracy of the genetic code, the cell does not have to synthesize a different tRNA for each of the 61 sense codons. For example, only two different tRNA anticodons are needed to recognize four different glycine codons.

FORMING THE POLYPEPTIDE—ELONGATION

Returning to the sequence of events during translation, there are two sites on the ribosome involved in protein synthesis, the **peptidyl site** and the **aminoacyl site** (FIG. 6-26). The aminoacyl site is the location where tRNA molecules bring individual amino acids to be sequentially inserted into the polypeptide chain. The peptidyl site is the location where the growing peptide chain is aligned. At the initiation of protein synthesis, the f-Met tRNA or Met tRNA occupies the peptidyl site on the ribosome rather than the aminoacyl site, which is normally where the charged tRNA molecules associate with the ribosome.

In prokaryotes, the placement of charged tRNA molecules into the aminoacyl site depends on an **elongation factor**, EF-Tu. EF-Tu initially forms a complex

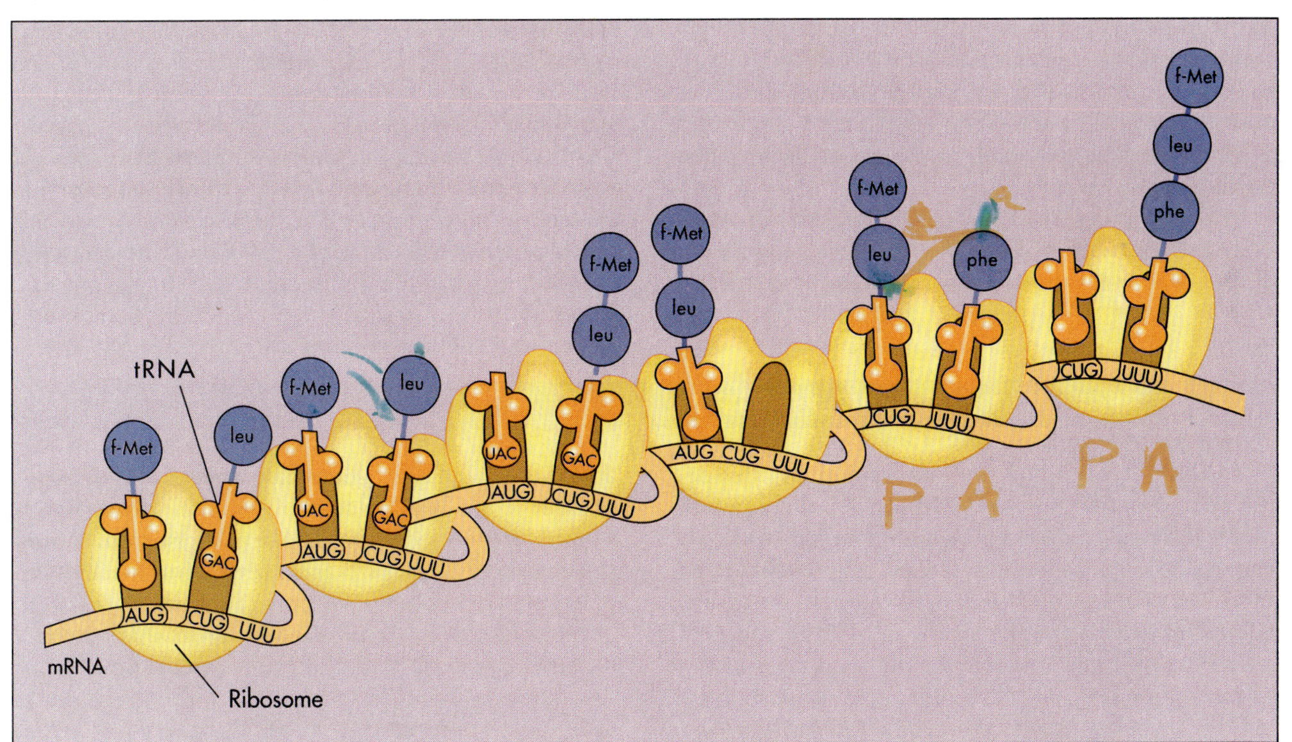

FIG. 6-26 During protein synthesis the codons of the mRNA are translated into an amino acid sequence at the ribosome. Each codon of the mRNA matches an anticodon of a tRNA so that the proper amino acid sequence is formed. The start codon AUG specifies the insertion of formyl methionine (f-Met) at the peptidyl site. A second amino acid is aligned at the aminoacyl site by the pairing of a tRNA with the codon. Formyl methionine is transferred to the amino acid at the aminoacyl site with the formation of a peptide bond. The mRNA then moves along the ribosome so that the tRNA with its two attached amino acids moves to the peptidyl site. A new amino acid is aligned at the aminoacyl site, again by pairing of the appropriate tRNA with the codon. The two amino acids are transferred to the amino acid with the formation of a new peptide bond so that the peptide chain now has three amino acids. The process is repeated over and over to form the long polypeptide chain of amino acids joined by peptide bonds in the sequence specified by the mRNA.

with GTP, which then binds to charged tRNA to form a ternary complex of aminoacyl-tRNA–EF-Tu–GTP. This ternary complex can enter the aminoacyl site on the ribosome. Then, after GTP hydrolysis to GDP, EF-Tu–GDP is released. An additional elongation factor, EF-Ts, is required to recycle the EF-Tu–GDP back to EF-Tu–GTP. In eukaryotes, eEF1 is the elongation factor responsible for bringing the charged tRNA to the aminoacyl site on the ribosome; this reaction also requires the hydrolysis of GTP to GDP.

When tRNA molecules move to the aminoacyl site, the proper anticodon pairs with its matching codon on the mRNA. The polypeptide chain is then transferred from the tRNA occupying the peptidyl site to the aminoacyl site. A peptide bond is formed between the amino group of the amino acid attached at the aminoacyl site and the carboxylic acid group of the last amino acid that had been added to the peptide chain. This reaction is mediated by peptidyl transferase, which is intimately associated with the 50S or 60S subunit and may be inherent in the rRNA of the large subunits. Energy is not required to form this peptide bond, since two high energy bonds have already been expended to form the aminoacyl tRNAs. At the initiation of protein synthesis, f-Met in prokaryotes and Met in eukaryotes are transferred to the aminoacyl site, forming a peptide bond with the second amino acid coded for by the mRNA molecule. The mRNA then moves along the ribosome by three nucleotides.

The movement of the mRNA, tRNA, and growing polypeptide chain along the ribosome, a process known as **translocation**, requires the input of energy from GTP. This is an unusual biochemical reaction that requires a specific energy carrier other than ATP. Translocation moves the tRNA molecule with an attached peptide chain to the peptidyl site, leaving the aminoacyl site open for the anticodon of the next charged tRNA molecule to pair with the next codon of the mRNA. Translocation requires an additional elongation factor, EF-G in prokaryotes or eEF-2 in eukaryotes. During translocation, the tRNA molecule that has transferred its attached amino acids, and is thus no longer charged, returns to the cytoplasm, where it can be recycled, that is, where it can once again be charged with an amino acid and returned to the aminoacyl site.

TERMINATION OF PROTEIN SYNTHESIS

The process of peptide elongation is repeated over and over, resulting in the formation of the polypeptide chain. Eventually, one of the termination codons appears at the aminoacyl site. Because no charged tRNA molecule pairs with the termination codon, the aminoacyl site is empty when the peptide chain tries to transfer to that site. In addition, in bacteria, two **release factors** (RF1 and RF2) help to catalyze **termination** of peptide bond formation. RF1 acts on UAA or UAG termination codons and RF2 acts on UGA. In eukaryotic cells, there is only a single release factor, eRF, involved in termination. At termination, the carboxyl end of the nascent protein is transferred to H_2O. This causes the polypeptide chain to be released into the cytoplasm where it can play a functional role in mediating the metabolism and structure of the organism.

6.4 REGULATION OF GENE EXPRESSION

In addition to encoding the information for the specific polypeptide sequences of proteins, the genome of the cell codes the information that regulates its own expression. The genome is divided into sequences of DNA, known as *genes*, that have specific functions. Some genes code for the synthesis of RNA and proteins, determining, respectively, the sequences of the subunit ribonucleotide bases and amino acids in these macromolecules. Genes that code for proteins are known as *structural genes*, or *cistrons*. Other genes have regulatory functions (*regulatory genes*) and act to control the expression of the structural genes. Together the structural and regulatory genes constitute the genotype and determine the *phenotype*, that is, the actual appearance and activities of the organism.

By controlling which of the genes of the organism are to be converted into functional enzymes, the cell regulates its metabolic activities. Some regions of DNA are specifically involved in regulating transcription, and these regulatory genes can control the synthesis of specific enzymes. In some cases, gene expression is not subject to specific genetic regulatory control, and the enzymes coded for by such regions of the DNA are **constitutive**, that is, they are continuously synthesized.

Some enzymes are synthesized only when the cell requires them. Such enzymes are **inducible**, that is, they are made only in response to a specific inducer substance, or **repressible**, that is, they are made unless stopped by the presence of a specific repression substance. Often, several enzymes that have related functions are controlled by the same regulatory genes.

Induction and repression are based on **regulatory genes** producing a regulator protein that controls transcription by binding to a specific site on the DNA (FIG. 6-27). Regulation of transcription may be under *negative control*, that is, mRNA for a particular set of genes is synthesized unless it is turned off by the regulatory protein. Alternately, transcriptional regulation

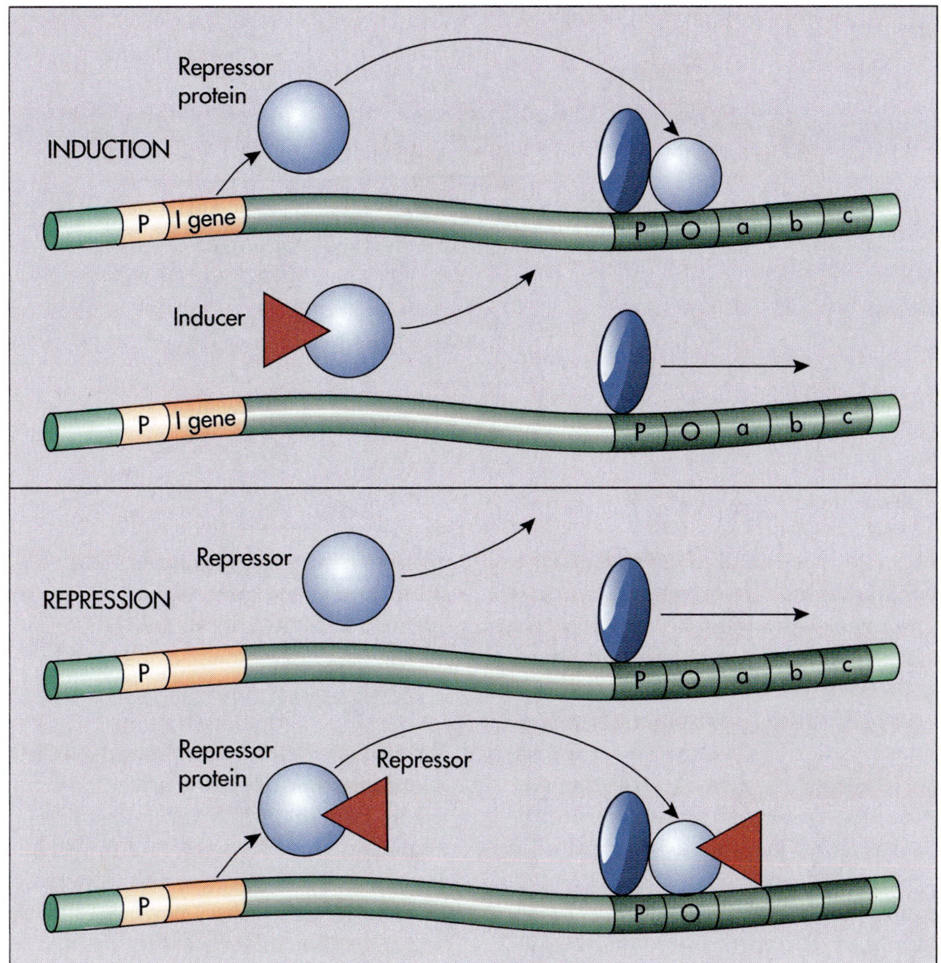

FIG. 6-27 Some genes are inducible and others repressible. Induction occurs when a repressor protein, encoded by the I gene, that normally binds to the operator region of the DNA reacts with an inducer substance so that it no longer binds to the operator region. This results in the ability of RNA polymerase to move past the operator region so that structural genes under the control of that operator are transcribed. Repression occurs when a repressor protein, encoded by the I gene, that normally does not bind to the operator region of the DNA reacts with a repressor substance so that it then binds to the operator region. This results in the inability of RNA polymerase to move past the operator region so that structural genes under the control of that operator no longer are transcribed.

of a different set of genes may be under *positive control*, that is, mRNA is synthesized only in the presence of a regulatory protein that binds to the DNA.

REGULATING THE METABOLISM OF LACTOSE: THE *LAC* OPERON

One of the best-studied regulatory systems concerns the enzymes produced by *Escherichia coli* strain K-12 for the metabolism of lactose (FIG. 6-28). Three enzymes are specifically synthesized by *Escherichia coli* for the metabolism of lactose: β-galactosidase, galactoside permease, and thiogalactoside transacetylase. The β-galactosidase cleaves the disaccharide lactose into the monosaccharides galactose and glucose. Permease is required for the active transport of lactose across the bacterial cytoplasmic membrane, and transacetylase acetylates galactosides, allowing them to escape from the cell so they do not accumulate to toxic levels. The structural genes that code for the production of these three enzymes occur in a contiguous segment of the DNA, which codes for polycistronic DNA. Although there is some basal level of gene expression in the absence of an inducer, these structural genes are appreciably transcribed only in the presence of an inducer.

Control of the expression of these structural genes for lactose metabolism is explained in part by the **operon model**, which demonstrates how the transcription of mRNA directing the synthesis of these enzymes is regulated. An **operon** is a DNA sequence that codes for one or more polypeptides (**structural genes**), usually of related function, and a DNA sequence that regulates the expression of these genes.

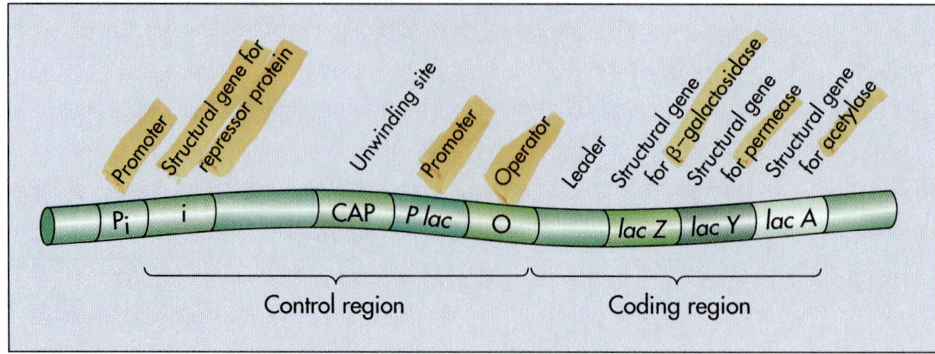

FIG. 6-28 The *lac* operon controls the utilization of lactose. Three structural genes under the control of the *lac* promoter (P *lac*) code for the synthesis of the enzymes needed for lactose utilization. These enzymes are made only when lactose is present.

The operon for lactose metabolism, the ***lac* operon**, includes a **promoter region (p)** where RNA polymerase binds, a **regulatory gene (i)** that codes for the synthesis of a repressor protein, and an **operator region (o)** that occurs between the promoter and the three structural genes involved in lactose metabolism. The regulatory gene codes for a repressor protein, which in the absence of lactose binds to the operator region of the DNA. The binding of the repressor protein at the operator region blocks the transcription of the structural genes under the control of that operator region. In some operons, the operator region nucleotide sequence and the promoter region nucleotide sequence overlap each other. Other operons may have more than one, or multiple, promoters.

In the case of the *lac* operon, the three structural *lac* genes that code for the three enzymes involved in lactose metabolism are not transcribed in the absence of lactose. The operator region of the *lac* operon is adjacent to or overlaps the promoter region. Binding of the repressor protein at the operator region interferes with binding of RNA polymerase at the promoter region. An *inducer* such as allolactose (a derivative of lactose) binds to the repressor protein and alters the conformation of the repressor protein; that is, it acts as an allosteric effector, so that it is unable to interact with and bind at the operator region. Thus in the presence of an inducer that binds with the repressor protein, transcription of the *lac* operon is derepressed, and the synthesis of the three structural proteins needed for lactose metabolism proceeds.

As the lactose is metabolized and its concentration diminishes, the concentration of the derivative allolactose, produced from lactose by low levels of β-galactosidase, also declines, making it unavailable for binding with the repressor protein; therefore, active repressor protein molecules are again available for binding at the operator region, and the transcription of the *lac* operon is repressed, ceasing further production of the enzymes involved in lactose metabolism that are controlled by this regulatory region of the DNA. The *lac* operon is typical of negatively-controlled, inducible operons that regulate catabolic pathways; in the presence of an appropriate inducer, the system is derepressed.

CATABOLITE REPRESSION

When *E. coli* grows in a medium that contains glucose and lactose, it does not utilize both sugars simultaneously. Instead, it preferentially utilizes glucose first until that sugar is depleted and only then switches to utilization of lactose as the carbon source. This results in a biphasic (two phase) pattern of growth known as **diauxie** or **diauxic growth** (FIG. 6-29).

In the first phase of growth on glucose, the genes that code for the enzymes that metabolize lactose are shut off. After glucose depletion, there is a lag phase in growth during which the genes that code for the enzymes that metabolize lactose are turned on and are transcribed and translated into proteins. Then, the cells can resume optimal growth using lactose. The mechanism that allows bacteria to discriminate between utilization of two different carbon sources is largely due to catabolite repression.

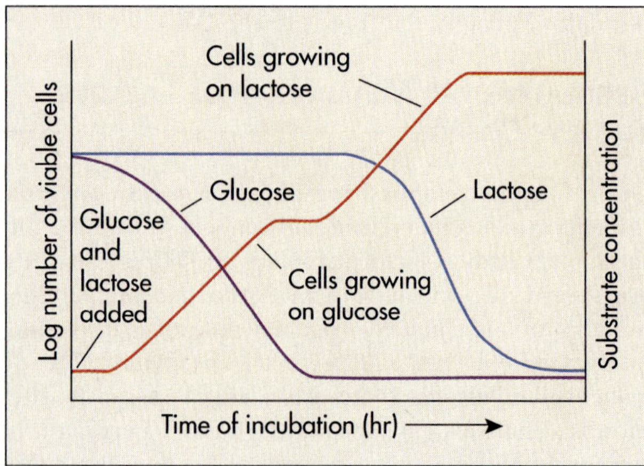

FIG. 6-29 *Escherichia coli* preferentially utilizes glucose and only uses lactose when the glucose supply is exhausted. This results in biphasic growth and the phenomenon of diauxie.

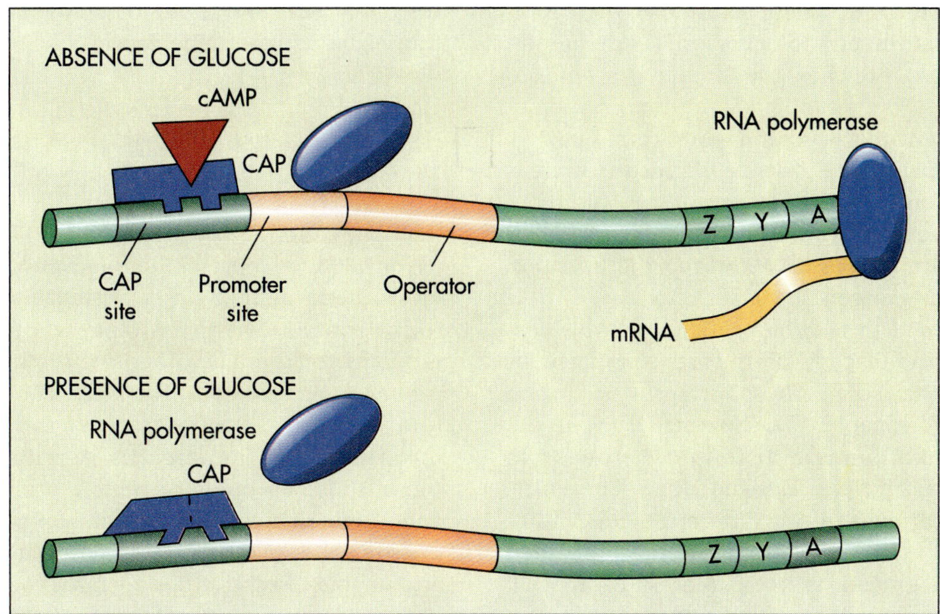

FIG. 6-30 Catabolite repression explains why several catabolic pathways are shut off in the presence of glucose. Catabolite repression is based on the need for cyclic AMP (cAMP) to form an activated complex with catabolite activator protein (CAP) at the promoter site that enhances the binding of RNA polymerase. When glucose is metabolized, there is inadequate cAMP to facilitate RNA polymerase binding. Therefore transcription at several promoters ceases. When there is inadequate glucose, there is enough cAMP to bind with CAP and so that transcription occurs at those promoters.

Catabolite repression is a generalized type of repression that simultaneously shuts off several operons (FIG. 6-30). In the presence of an adequate concentration of glucose, for example, some catabolic pathways are repressed by catabolite repression, including those involved in the metabolism of lactose, galactose, and arabinose. When glucose is available for catabolism in the glycolytic pathway, other monosaccharides and disaccharides need not be used by the cell to generate ATP, and by blocking the metabolism of these other carbohydrates, the cell conserves its metabolic resources.

Catabolite repression is an example of regulation by positive control. It acts via the promoter region of DNA, and by doing so it complements the control exerted by the operator region. The efficient binding of RNA polymerase to promoter regions subject to catabolite repression requires the presence of a catabolite activator protein (CAP), also called cyclic AMP receptor protein (CRP). In the absence of the CAP, the RNA polymerase has a greatly decreased affinity to bind to the promoter region. The CAP, in turn, cannot bind to the promoter region unless it is bound to cyclic adenosine monophosphate (cAMP).

There is an inverse relationship between the concentrations of cAMP and ATP, and levels of cAMP respond to the state of cellular metabolism. Molecules of cAMP are formed from ATP by the enzyme adenyl cyclase (FIG. 6-31). Intracellular levels of cAMP are low when rapidly metabolizable substrates, such as

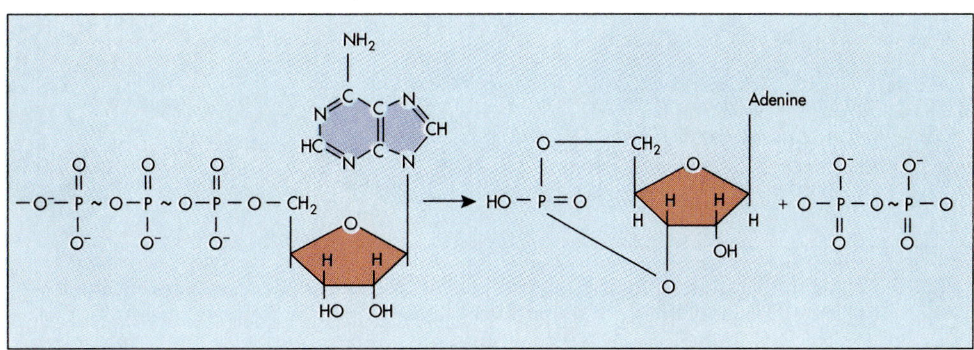

FIG. 6-31 Conversion of ATP to cyclic AMP by adenylcyclase is important in the regulation of gene expression and control by catabolite repression.

glucose, are used. Under these conditions, the CAP is unable to bind at the promoter region. Consequently, RNA polymerase enzymes are unable to bind to catabolite repressible promoters, and transcription at a number of regulated structural genes ceases in a coordinated manner. In the absence of glucose, there is an adequate supply of cAMP to permit the binding of RNA polymerase to the promoter region. Thus, when glucose levels are low, cAMP stimulates the initiation of many inducible enzymes.

Adenylcyclase activity, which effects the concentration of intracellular cAMP, is partly regulated by the phosphoenolpyruvate:phosphotransferase system (PEP:PTS) (see Chapter 3). Enzyme III^{glc} of the PEP:PTS functions to shuttle a phosphate group from phosphorylated HPr to Enzyme II^{glc}. Therefore, Enzyme III^{glc} can exist in two different forms, either phosphorylated ($EIII^{glc}{\sim}P$) or nonphosphorylated ($EIII^{glc}$). When glucose is present outside the cell, Enzyme III^{glc} continually transfers a phosphate group to Enzyme II^{glc} and then to glucose as the sugar is transported through the cytoplasmic membrane. Therefore, when glucose is present, the $EIII^{glc}$ form predominates. When glucose is absent, phosphate groups are not transferred and the $EIII^{glc}{\sim}P$ form predominates.

$EIII^{glc}$ (but not $EIII^{glc}{\sim}P$) is an allosteric inhibitor of adenyl cyclase. This means that when glucose is present, and $EIII^{glc}$ levels are high, adenyl cyclase activity is inhibited and cAMP levels become reduced. Conversely, when glucose is absent and lactose is present, $EIII^{glc}{\sim}P$ levels are high, adenyl cyclase activity is not inhibited, and cAMP levels increase. Adequate concentrations of cAMP allow the cell to transcribe its catabolite repressible operons such as the *lac* operon.

REGULATING THE BIOSYNTHESIS OF TRYPTOPHAN: THE TRP OPERON

Regulatory genes can be shut off under specific conditions. Such **repressible operons** control specific biosynthetic pathways. For example, the ***trp* operon**, which contains the genes that code for the enzymes required for the biosynthesis of the amino acid tryptophan, is repressible (FIG. 6-32). There are five structural genes in the *trp* operon that are responsible for the synthesis of five enzymes. As with other operons there is also an operator region, a promoter region, and a gene that codes for a regulator protein in the *trp* operon. The *trp* repressor protein is normally inactive and unable to bind at the operator region, but tryptophan can act as an allosteric effector or corepressor. In the presence of excess tryptophan, the *trp* repressor protein binds with tryptophan and, as a result, is also then able to bind to the *trp* operator region. When the *trp* repressor protein tryptophan complex binds at the *trp* operator region, the transcription of the enzymes involved in the biosynthesis of tryptophan is repressed.

In the case of the *trp* operon, tryptophan acts as the repressor substance that shuts off the biosynthetic pathway for its own synthesis when there is a sufficient supply of tryptophan. This is an example of **end product repression**—the process of shutting off transcription by a by-product of the metabolism coded for by

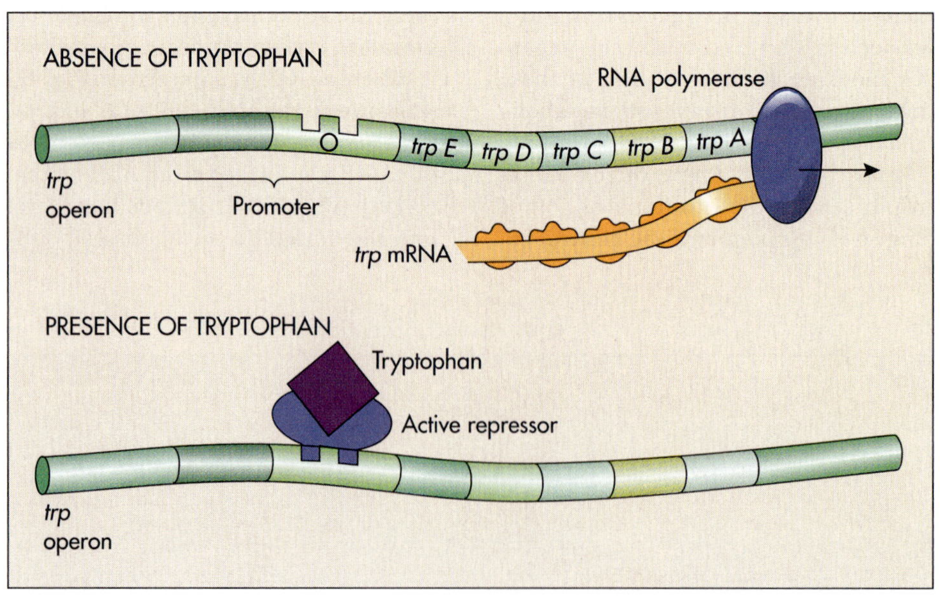

FIG. 6-32 The operation of the *trp* operon permits the cell to stop synthesizing the enzymes involved in the biosynthesis of tryptophan when there is a sufficient concentration of this amino acid. Tryptophan interacts with a repressor protein, altering its conformation so that it can bind to the operator gene controlling the synthesis of several enzymes needed for the biosynthesis of tryptophan. Thus, when there is enough tryptophan, the enzymes needed for tryptophan biosynthesis are not made, thereby regulating this pathway.

the genes in that operon. When the level of tryptophan in the cell declines, there is insufficient tryptophan to act as corepressor, and the transcription of the genes for the biosynthesis of tryptophan, therefore, resumes. The *trp* operon is typical of anabolic pathways, where in the presence of a sufficient supply of the biosynthetic product of the pathway, the system is repressed.

ATTENUATION: REGULATION OF TRANSCRIPTION BY TRANSLATION

Attenuation is a mode of regulating gene expression in which the events that occur during translation affect the transcription of an operon region of the DNA (FIG. 6-33). As indicated earlier, translation in prokaryotes normally begins before transcription of the

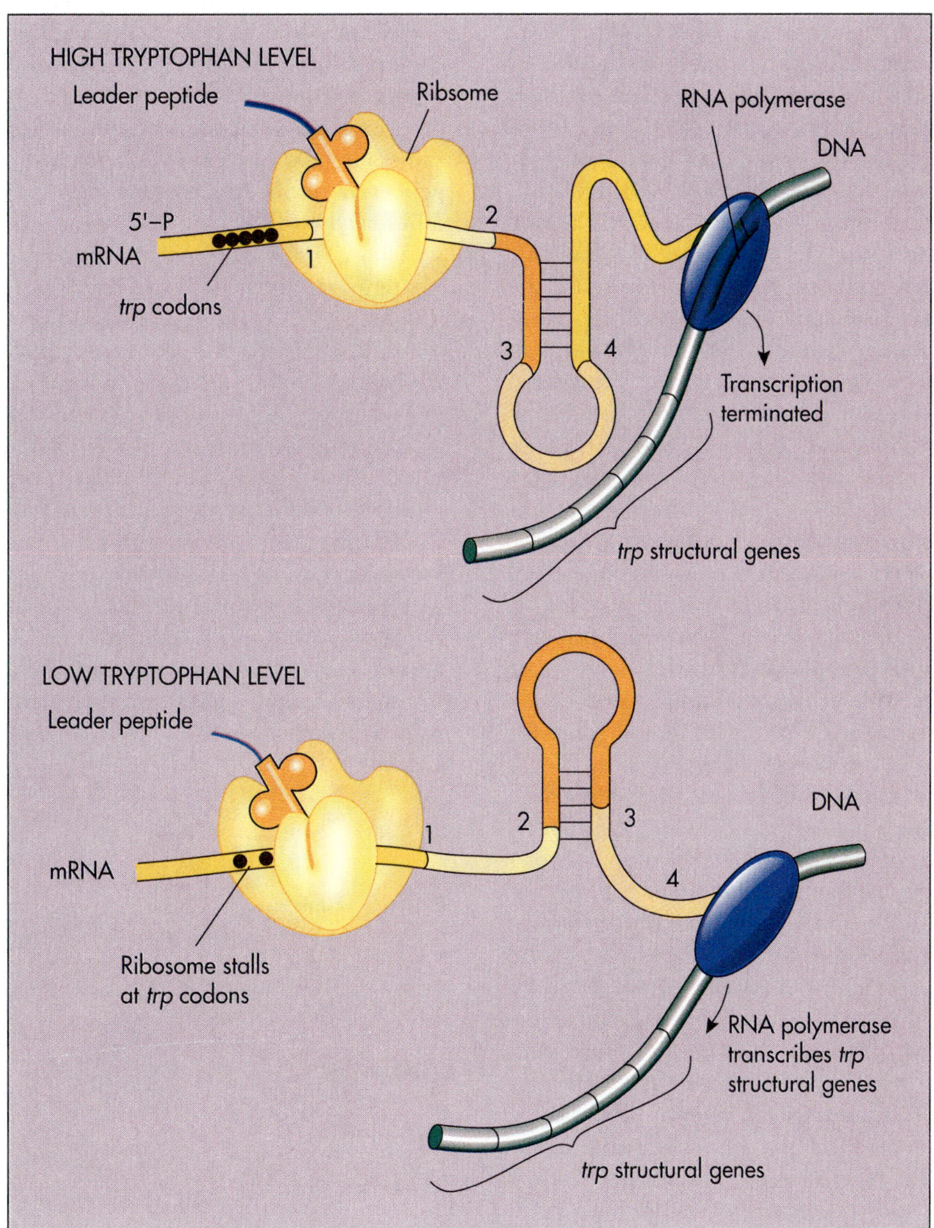

FIG. 6-33 Attenuation permits translational control of transcription of the *trp* operon. The phenomenon of attenuation depends on the intramolecular interactions within the leader sequence of the mRNA. The occurrence of base pairing results in the formation of a double-stranded segment that forms a hairpin loop. When sufficient tryptophan is present, translation of the leader sequence, which calls for a high proportion of tryptophan insertion, occurs rapidly and the portion of the leader sequence that has not yet been translated folds into a specific stem loop structure—shown in the top portion of the figure. This structure results in termination of transcription of the *trp* genes. If, on the other hand, sufficient tryptophan is not present, translation of the leader sequence does not occur rapidly and a different stem loop structure—shown in the lower portion of the figure—occurs. This structure does not expose the terminator sequence for the *trp* operon genes, and, hence, transcription continues.

mRNA is completed, with the leader portion of the mRNA attaching to the ribosome and translation beginning before the complete mRNA is transcribed. The leader sequence in prokaryotes occurs between the operator and the first structural genes. In the case of the *trp* operon, there is an **attenuator site** between the operator region and the first structural gene of the operon (at or near the end of the leader sequence) where transcription can be interrupted.

Whether or not termination occurs is determined by the secondary structure of the mRNA at the attenuator region. There are two possible structures of mRNA. In one form, mRNA folds to establish a double-stranded region, known as the *terminator hairpin*, that causes termination of transcription. The particular structure that forms depends on the availability of tryptophan because tryptophan is one of the amino acids coded for in the leader sequence. When tryptophan is available for incorporation into proteins, the peptide sequence coded for by this leader sequence can be successfully translated. When tryptophan reaches very low concentrations, however, translation is delayed at the leader codons that code for the insertion of tryptophan into the polypeptide because sufficient tryptophan and charged tryptophyl-tRNA are not available. When the translational process is slowed, the mRNA is in the form that permits transcription to proceed through the entire sequence of the *trp* operon. However, if there is sufficient tryptophan to permit rapid translation to proceed through the attenuator site, the mRNA forms the terminator hairpin structure and further transcription of the *trp* operon ceases, so that none of the structural genes for tryptophan metabolism are transcribed.

In addition to the tryptophan operon, the histidine and phenylalanine operons in *E. coli* also contain attenuator regions. In histidine, there is a sequence of 7 contiguous codons in the leader sequence; in phenylalanine, there are 15. Only when the concentrations of these amino acids are very low does translation stall, allowing transcription to proceed through the attenuator site. The attenuator complements the regulation of gene expression by the operator gene; thus there is a redundancy in the control mechanisms for the biosynthesis of amino acids such as tryptophan. The leader sequence and the associated attenuator site thus provide a mechanism for even finer control of transcription and the expression of genetic information than does the operator region.

Relaxed-Stringent Control of Transcription

Some bacteria have a unique mechanism for regulating the transcription of specific operons and DNA sequences that code for rRNA and tRNA, especially when they experience a depletion of the amino acid pool (amino acid starvation) and temperature shifts in their environment. Under these poor growth conditions the cell has the ability to shut down a number of energy-draining activities as a survival mechanism. This is called the **stringent response** and involves the production of unusual guanosine phosphates, guanosine pentaphosphate (pppGpp) and guanosine tetraphosphate (ppGpp) (sometimes referred to as Magic Spot I and Magic Spot II for their sudden appearance in *E. coli* cell extracts run on paper chromatography).

Bacteria that exhibit the stringent response produce a protein called stringent factor that is a product of the *relA* gene. Stringent factor is normally associated with the bacterial ribosome at a ratio of about 1 molecule/200 ribosomes. Under conditions of amino acid starvation, uncharged tRNAs can enter the aminoacyl site on the ribosome. When this occurs, stringent factor catalyzes the transfer of a pyrophosphate group from ATP to either GTP or GDP, which are involved in protein synthesis. The pyrophosphorylation of GTP (pppG) produces pppGpp and the pyrophosphorylation of GDP (ppG) or dephosphorylation of pppGpp produces ppGpp (FIG. 6-34).

The effector molecule ppGpp may work in several ways. It may specifically bind to promoters of rRNA and tRNA sequences and inhibit their transcription by RNA polymerase. Alternately, ppGpp causes increased idling or pausing of the translation process and therefore premature termination of specific polypeptides. Some bacterial strains that have mutations in the *relA* gene do not exhibit a stringent response under conditions of amino acid starvation. Such strains are said to be **relaxed strains**.

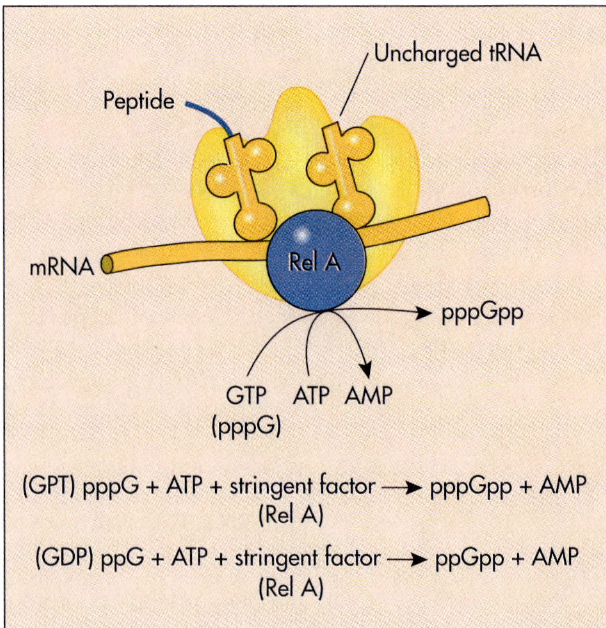

FIG. 6-34 During amino acid starvation the *RelA* gene product (stringent factor) causes formation of ppGpp and pppGpp, which suppresses gene expression.

GENE EXPRESSION IN EUKARYOTIC MICROORGANISMS

The regulation of genetic expression in eukaryotic microorganisms is more complex than in bacteria, and many of the mechanisms described may not operate in the same manner in prokaryotic and eukaryotic cells. Some enzymes in eukaryotic microorganisms are clearly inducible and others are repressible, but the expression of these enzyme systems may not be under the control of mechanisms comparable to the *lac* operon in *E. coli*.

Each mRNA of a eukaryotic cell generally contains the information for only one protein and hence is monocistronic rather than polycistronic. Thus control over several different mRNA molecules may be required to achieve coordinated control in eukaryotes, whereas control of a single mRNA molecule, carrying the information for the expression of several contiguous and sequential genes in a prokaryotic cell, can regulate the synthesis of several enzymes with related functions. Additionally, in almost all cases, the sequence of codons of a given gene in eukaryotic microorganisms is not colinear with the mRNA molecule or with the polypeptide sequence of the protein. It is, therefore, unlikely that in eukaryotic microorganisms an operator region could regulate the transcription of a series of genes that are contiguous with the region of the regulator gene. This effectively precludes the existence of a unified operon region, such as occurs in prokaryotic microorganisms, although an analogous type of operon control over a gene cluster can still exist in eukaryotic cells.

A series of different control mechanisms may be present in eukaryotic microorganisms to control genetic expression. These include the loss of genes, gene amplification, rearrangement of genes, differential transcription of genes, post-transcriptional modification of RNA, and translational control.

Some cells of organisms lose genes. For example, in the protozoan *Oxytricha*, elimination of most of the DNA (gene loss) occurs in the vegetative cells. The elimination of some of the genetic information restricts the number of genes that can be expressed, and this mechanism allows for specialization in vegetative cells—analogous to differentiation of somatic cells in higher organisms. Most higher eukaryotic organisms do not seem to use gene elimination, although several insects use it as a means of differentiation.

Some eukaryotic cells are capable of **amplifying gene expression**, thereby producing large amounts of the enzyme coded for by a given gene. Eukaryotes do so by increasing the amount of rRNA and thus the number of ribosomes that can be used to translate a stable mRNA molecule. The ribosomes line up along the same mRNA so that translation results in multiple copies of the synthesized protein. In the protozoan, *Tetrahymena*, for example, there are hundreds of copies of the genes for rRNA in the vegetative cell that provide a mechanism for gene amplification. Within the eukaryotic genome, the position of some genes can be changed, thereby rearranging the location of genes within the eukaryotic chromosome.

The **rearrangement of genes** (change in relative position within the chromosome) can alter the expression of the information contained in those genes. For example, the rearrangement of genes results in altered mating types in yeasts and the production of altered surface proteins in protozoa. This phenomenon has also been observed in prokaryotes, as for example in the case of flagellin protein synthesis in *Salmonella*.

In addition to these mechanisms, promoter regions in eukaryotic organisms are involved in the binding of RNA polymerase enzymes, and these may be sites for genetic regulation of the type exhibited in catabolite repression by prokaryotes. It is also likely that post-transcriptional modification of hnRNA is involved in the control of genetic expression in eukaryotes. The leader sequences, introns, and trailer sequences of RNA molecules in eukaryotes probably affect the expression of genetic information in eukaryotic microorganisms. Different strains of *Tetrahymena* have different introns in the genes that code for their rRNA. Further, the regulation of translation may be more important in controlling gene expression in eukaryotes than in prokaryotes because of the relative longevity of mRNA in eukaryotic cells.

It is thus clear that there are several mechanisms for regulating gene expression in eukaryotic microorganisms that do not exist in prokaryotes. Unraveling the complexity of gene regulation in eukaryotes and developing a better understanding of genetic regulation in prokaryotes remain prime challenges for the microbial geneticist.

CHAPTER REVIEW

STUDY QUESTIONS

1. How was the semiconservative nature of DNA replication demonstrated?
2. What is a DNA polymerase enzyme? An RNA polymerase enzyme? How are these enzymes different from the enzymes involved in microbial metabolism?
3. How is DNA structurally organized in prokaryotic cells? In eukaryotic cells?
4. What are the functions of topoisomerases and gyrases in DNA replication? What would happen if a cell lacked these activities?

CHAPTER REVIEW

Study Questions — cont'd

5. What are the similarities and differences between DNA replication in prokaryotes and eukaryotes?
6. What are the roles of σ factors and TFs in prokaryotic and eukaryotic transcription respectively? How do they function to provide specificity to transcription?
7. How are RNA polymerases different from and similar to DNA polymerases?
8. What are the important structural, compositional and functional differences between tRNAs, mRNAs, and rRNAs?
9. What are the steps in protein synthesis? What roles do different nucleic acids have in the expression of genetic information?
10. How is information encoded within nucleic acid molecules? What are the essential properties of the genetic code that permit the storage and extraction of genetic information?
11. With respect to the genetic code, what is meant by codons, wobble, and degeneracy?
12. Why is it important that DNA and RNA have distinct 3′-OH and 5′-P ends?
13. What signals the initiation and termination of transcription? Of translation?
14. How is the expression of DNA regulated at the level of transcription? What is the difference between positive and negative control of transcription?
15. How are operons and promoters involved in gene expression?
16. Discuss the functioning and control of the *lac* and *trp* operons.
17. What is the glucose effect, and how does catabolite repression help explain its molecular basis?
18. What is the relaxed-stringent response in bacteria? How and why does it function in controlling transcription?
19. What is a split gene, and why does it represent a fundamental difference between prokaryotes and eukaryotes?
20. Which RNA molecules are post-transcriptionally modified in prokaryotes and in eukaryotes? What type of changes occur in the RNA molecules as a result of these modifications?

SITUATIONAL PROBLEMS

1. Constructing a DNA Sequence for a Polypeptide

Today, automated systems are available for determining the sequence of amino acids in a polypeptide and for synthesizing DNA molecules with a specified order of nucleotides. You are assisting in a laboratory that has instruments for amino acid sequencing and DNA synthesis. You have isolated a bacterium that produces a surface polypeptide that acts to initiate ice crystal formation. The bacterium, a strain of *Pseudomonas syringae*, was isolated from the surface of a leaf. In this entrepreneurial era, you decide that there may be commercial value in producing this polypeptide; for example, it might be useful in increasing the efficiency of artificial snow production at ski resorts. You have been reading about the future of biotechnology and the power of genetic engineering, and you decide to produce a sequence of nucleotides that codes for this ice-nucleation polypeptide with the expectation of later introducing it into a bacterium, such as *E. coli*, and producing it in commercial quantities.

The first thing you do is to isolate and purify the polypeptide. Then you slip into the laboratory after hours and run it through the amino acid analyzer, with the following results for a segment of the polypeptide:amino terminal-phe-phe-his-trp-lys-lys-lys-lys-asp-arg-lys-ser-ser-trp-his-ile-phe-met-asp-glu-glu-glu-gly-gly-pro-gly-gly-val-leu. Based on these data, you program the DNA synthesizer for the desired sequence of nucleotides. Using a table of mRNA codons (see Table 6-4), write an appropriate sequence of DNA nucleotides that would code for this polypeptide.

2. Determining the Regulatory Mechanisms of a Bacterial Isolate

As part of an undergraduate research project, you have been given a bacterial strain that can use carbohydrates and hydrocarbons as growth substrates. You discover that the strain uses glucose following a minimal lag period after culture inoculation, regardless of the other carbohydrates and hydrocarbons in the growth medium. Lactose, however, is not used until much later if glucose is present. In the absence of glucose, lactose is used after a lag period about three times as long as the lag period for glucose utilization, but well before it would have been used if glucose had been present. The presence of hydrocarbons does not affect the lag period for the utilization of lactose. The utilization pattern for all hydrocarbons is similar to that of lactose, that is, there is an intermediate lag period in the absence of glucose and a long delay before any utilization occurs if glucose is initially present. The presence of lactose does not affect the lag period before hydrocarbon utilization occurs. Also, it is observed that branched hydrocarbons are not immediately used if straight chain hydrocarbons are initially present but they are used much sooner in the absence of straight chain hydrocarbons.

As part of your research project report, you have been asked to explain these data. What regulatory mechanisms are consistent with the observed patterns of carbohydrate and hydrocarbon utilization?

Suggested Supplementary Reading

Adolph KW (ed.): 1993. *Methods in Molecular Genetics,* Academic Press, New York.

Andersson SGE and CG Kurland: 1990. Codon preferences in free-living microorganisms, *Microbiological Reviews* 54:198-210.

Atlas RM: 1991. Environmental applications of the polymerase chain reaction, *ASM News* 57:630-632.

Ausubel PM: 1988. *Current Protocols in Molecular Biology,* John Wiley & Sons, New York.

Bachmann BJ: 1990. Linkage map of *Escherichia coli* K-12, edition 8, *Microbiological Reviews* 54:130-197.

Birge EA: 1981. *Bacterial and Bacteriophage Genetics,* Springer-Verlag, New York.

Campbell JL: 1986. Eukaryotic DNA replication, *Annual Review of Biochemistry* 55:733-772.

Cattaneo R: 1991. Different types of messenger RNA, *Annual Review of Genetics* 25:71-88.

Cech TR: 1983. RNA splicing: Three themes with variations, *Cell* 34:713-716.

Chambon P: 1975. Eucaryotic nuclear RNA polymerases, *Annual Review of Biochemistry* 44:613-638.

Chambon P: 1981. Split genes, *Scientific American* 244(5):60-71.

Chase JW and KR Williams: 1986. Single-stranded DNA binding proteins required for DNA replication, *Annual Review of Biochemistry* 55:103-136.

Darnell JE: 1982. Variety in the level of gene control in eukaryotic cells, *Nature* 297:365-371.

Darnell JE: 1983. The processing of RNA, *Scientific American* 249:90-100.

Darnell J, H Lodish, D Baltimore: 1986. *Molecular Cell Biology,* Scientific American Books, New York.

Dynan WS and R Tijan: 1985. Control of eukaryotic messenger RNA synthesis by sequence-specific DNA-binding proteins, *Nature* 316:774-778.

Erlich HA (ed.): 1989. *PCR Technology: Principles and Applications for DNA Amplification.* Stockton Press, NY.

Erlich HA, D Gelfand, JJ Sninsky: 1991. Recent advances in the polymerase chain reaction, *Science* 252:1643-1651.

Fasman GD (ed.): 1989. *Practical Handbook of Biochemistry and Molecular Biology,* CRC Press Boca Raton, FL.

Firshein W: 1989. Role of the DNA/membrane complex in prokaryotic DNA replication, *Annual Review of Microbiology* 43:89-120.

Gardner EJ, MJ Simmons, DP Snustad: 1991. *Principles of Genetics,* ed. 8, John Wiley and Sons, New York.

Genetics: Readings from Scientific American: 1981. W. H. Freeman Co., San Francisco.

Gold L, D Pribnow, T Schneider, S Shinedling, BS Singer, G Stormo: 1981. Translational initiation in prokaryotes. *Annual Review of Microbiology* 35:365-403.

Goldstein L, and DM Prescott (eds.): 1980. *Gene Expression: The Production of RNA's,* Academic Press, New York.

Hames BD and SJ Higgins (eds.): 1985. *Nucleic Acid Hybridisation: A Practical Approach,* IRL Press, Oxford, England.

Howe CJ, ES Ward (eds.): 1989. *Nucleic Acids Sequencing: A Practical Approach,* IRL Press, Oxford, England.

Innis MA, DH Gelfand, JJ Sninsky, TJ White (eds.): 1990. *PCR Protocols: A Guide to Methods and Applications,* Academic Press, San Diego, CA.

Kaplan AS (ed.): 1982. *Organization and Replication of Viral DNA,* CRC Press, Inc., Boca Raton, FL.

Kornberg A: 1980. *DNA Replication,* W. H. Freeman Co., San Francisco.

Kornberg A: 1988. DNA Replication, *Journal of Biological Chemistry* 263:1-4.

Kornberg A and TA Baker: 1991. *DNA Replication.* ed. 2, W. H. Freeman and Company, NY.

Lewin B: 1990. *Genes IV,* John Wiley & Sons, Inc., New York.

Matthews KS: 1992. DNA looping, *Microbiological Reviews* 56:123-136.

McClure WR: 1985. Mechanism and control of transcription initiation in prokaryotes, *Annual Review of Biochemistry* 54:171-204.

McPherson MJ, P Quirke, GR Taylor (eds.): 1991. *PCR: A Practical Approach,* IRL Press, Oxford, England

Miller JH (ed.): 1991. *Methods in Enzymology: Vol. 204, Bacterial Genetic Systems,* Academic Press, NY.

Miller JH and WS Reznikoff (eds.): 1980. *The Operon,* Cold Spring Harbor Laboratory, Cold Spring Harbor, N.Y.

Miller RV and TA Kokjohn: 1990. General microbiology of *recA*: Environmental and evolutionary significance, *Annual Review of Microbiology* 44:365-394.

Mullis KB: 1990. The unusual origin of the polymerase chain reaction, *Scientific American* 262:56-65.

Neidhardt FC (ed.): 1987. *Escherichia coli and Salmonella Typhimurium: Cellular and Molecular Biology,* Volumes 1 and 2, American Society for Microbiology, Washington, D.C.

Noller HF: 1991. Ribosomal RNA and translation, *Annual Review of Biochemistry* 60:191-228.

Novick RP: 1989. Staphylococcal plasmids and their replication, *Annual Review of Microbiology* 43:537-566.

Osawa S, TH Jukes, K Watanabe, A Muto: 1992. Recent evidence for evolution of the genetic code, *Microbiological Reviews* 56:229-264.

Padgett RA, PJ Grabowskii, MM Konarska, S Seiler, PA Sharp: 1986. Splicing of message RNA precursors, *Annual Review of Biochemistry* 55:1119-1150.

Platt T: 1986. Transcription termination and the regulation of gene expression, *Annual Review of Biochemistry* 55:339-372.

Raibaud O and M Schwartz: 1984. Positive control of transcription in bacteria, *Annual Review of Genetics* 18:173-206.

Reznikoff WS, DW Cowing, C Gross: 1985. The regulation of transcription initiation in bacteria, *Annual Review of Genetics* 19:355-388.

Sanger F: 1988. Sequences, sequences, and sequences, *Annual Review of Biochemistry* 57:1-28.

Silver S and TK Misra: 1988. Plasmid-mediated heavy metal resistances, *Annual Review of Microbiology* 42:717-743.

Simons RW and N Kleckner: 1988. Biological regulation by antisense RNA in prokaryotes, *Annual Review of Genetics* 22:567-600.

Streips UN and RE Yasbin (eds.): 1991. *Modern Microbial Genetics,* Wiley-Liss, Inc., New York.

Stryer L: 1987. *Biochemistry,* W. H. Freeman Co., San Francisco.

Walker JM (ed.): 1988. *New Nucleic Acid Techniques: Methods in Molecular Biology,* Vol 4, Humana Press, Clifton, NJ.

Watson JD, N Hopkins, J Roberts, J Steitz, A Weiner: 1987. *Molecular Biology of the Gene,* ed. 4, Benjamin/Cummings Publishing Co., Menlo Park, CA.

Yanofsky C: 1981. Attenuation in the control of expression of bacterial operons, *Nature* 289:751-758.

Zubay G: 1987. *Genetics.* Benjamin/Cummings Publishing Co., Menlo Park, CA.

CHAPTER 7

Genetic Variation: Mutation and Recombination

Changes in the sequence of nucleotides of a cell's DNA occur by mutation (from Latin *mutare,* meaning to change). Various types of mutations introduce modifications into DNA with varying degrees of frequency. Mutations produce multiple allelic forms of the same gene. Recombinational processes permit further redistribution of genetic information. Recombination involves exchange of DNA segments from differing genomes. This establishes new combinations of genes. Heritable changes in the sequences of nucleotides of cells introduce variability into the gene pool of microbial populations. Diversity within the gene pool establishes the basis for the selective evolution of microorganisms. Recombinant DNA technology also permits the directed formation of cells with specific genes that may come from divergent sources.

CHAPTER OUTLINE

7.1 GENETIC VARIATION

Genetic variability typically occurs within a population or cells of a given organism. The genes of one bacterial cell may differ slightly, for example, from the genes of another bacterial cell within the same species. Heterogeneity within the gene pool may give some organisms a competitive advantage for survival. This forms the basis for evolution according to the Darwinian principle of survival of the fittest.

ALLELES

Eukaryotic cells generally have pairs of matching chromosomes. Such cells are **diploid,** because they have two sets of genes. Corresponding genes of the pairs of chromosomes in a diploid cell are called **alleles** (FIG. 7-1). Alleles may be identical or can contain different genetic information. Allelic forms of a

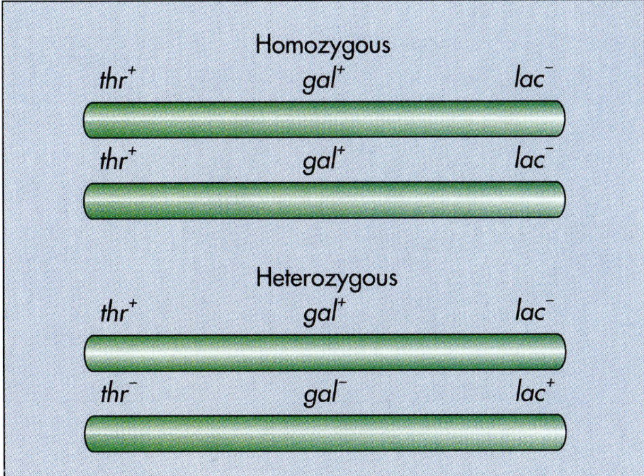

FIG. 7-1 Diploid cells have two sets of genes, which may be identical (homozygous alleles) or different (heterozygous alleles).

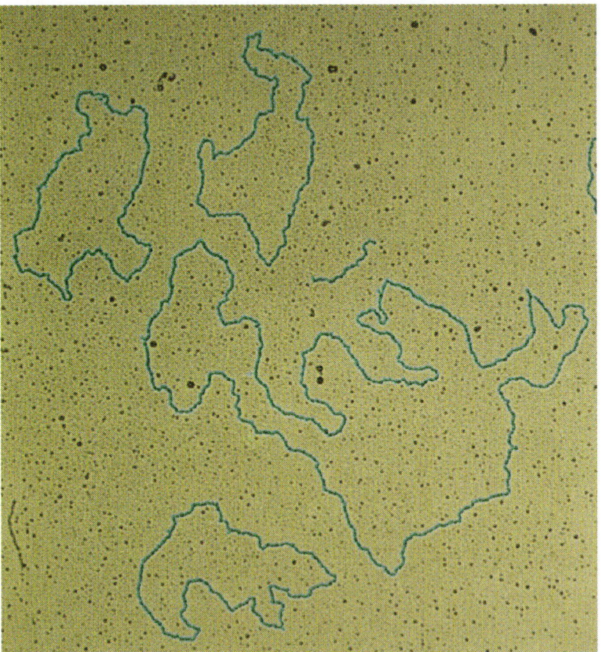

FIG. 7-2 Colorized micrograph of plasmid pBF4 (*larger molecules*) from *Bacillus fragilis* and pSC101 (*smaller molecules*) from *Escherichia coli.*

gene often code for different amino acid sequences in polypeptides. When both copies of the gene are identical, the cell is **homozygous.** When the corresponding copies of the gene differ, the cell is **heterozygous.**

The information encoded in one of the alleles may dominate over the information in the other allele; that is, one gene may be *dominant* and the other *recessive.* For example, a **recessive allele** may code for an inactive enzyme, whereas the **dominant allele** codes for a fully active enzyme. In some cases, alleles may exhibit **codominance,** producing a hybrid state within an intermediate phenotype. For example, cells with homozygous dominant alleles may appear red, those with homozygous recessive alleles may appear white, and those with heterozygous alleles (codominance) may appear pink.

Even though a single diploid cell can have no more than two alleles, there may be more than two allelic forms of a given gene in the entire population. The number of alleles determines the number of potential genotypes for a given gene locus. If there are two alleles, there are three possible genotypes—two homozygotes and one heterozygote. If there are 4 alleles, however, there are 10 possible genotypes—4 homozygotes and 6 heterozygotes. The number of different genotypes that can arise from multiple alleles raises the potential degree of heterogeneity within the gene pool of a population.

PLASMIDS

Although a prokaryotic cell has a single bacterial chromosome and is *haploid* because it has only a single set of genes, such a cell may have small extrachromosomal genetic elements called **plasmids** (FIG. 7-2). Plasmids do not normally contain the genetic information for the essential metabolic activities of the cell, but they generally do contain genetic information for specialized features, such as resistance to heavy metals and antibiotics. Plasmids are a source of genetic variability, because cells that possess plasmids contain different genetic information than those that lack plasmids.

Plasmids are small genetic elements relative to the bacterial chromosome. They typically have 1 to 30 kb pairs (the range is 2 to 100 kb) and are, at most, 20% of the bacterial chromosome. Plasmids are capable of self-replication. There is an origin of replication and the same mechanisms usually operate for plasmid replication as for replication of the bacterial chromosome. A replication fork forms and DNA polymerases add nucleotides. Cells may accumulate a few or many copies of a plasmid.

Plasmids can be exchanged between cells. Transmissibility of some plasmids is controlled by *tra* genes (transfer genes) that occur within the plasmid. The transmission of plasmids is a mechanism by which specialized information can be transferred from one cell to another. Cells may acquire or lose plasmids so that within a population of cells some will have different genetic information than others. The loss of plasmids is called **curing.** Various agents, such as acridine dyes, ultraviolet light, and heavy metals, increase the rates of plasmid curing.

Maintenance of Plasmids

Retention or loss of plasmids often depends on whether there is selective pressure to possess the

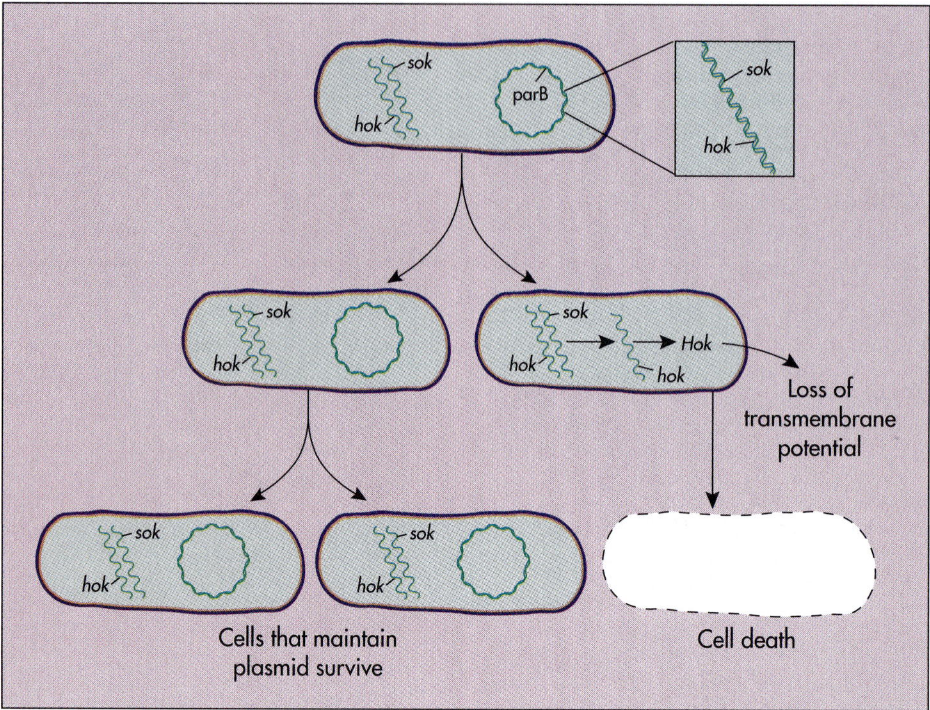

FIG. 7-3 The parB locus of a plasmid in *Escherichia coli* acts as a suicide gene so that the plasmid must be maintained for the cells to survive. One strand of the DNA has the *hok* gene that encodes a polypeptide that kills the cell; if *hok* is expressed the cells die. The other strand of the DNA has the *sok* gene, which produces an antisense mRNA. If the *sok* RNA binds to the *hok* mRNA, the Hok polypeptide is not produced. If *sok* RNA is not there, hok is translated. Because the *sok* RNA has a shorter-half life than the hok mRNA, if the plasmid with parB is lost, Hok polypeptide is produced and the cell dies. As long as the cell maintains the plasmid with parB, the cell production of *sok* RNA blocks the translation of *hok* mRNA.

genes encoded within that plasmid. For example, some plasmids contain genes that encode resistance to antibiotics. When there is excessive use of antibiotics, such as sometimes occurs in clinical settings, there tends to be a high prevalence of bacterial cells with such resistance plasmids. In places where antibiotics do not occur, few bacterial cells will have plasmids with genes that encode for resistance to antibiotics.

An interesting specialized mechanism has been discovered in *Escherichia coli* for the retention of certain plasmids within a population that otherwise might be lost (FIG. 7-3). The genes for plasmid maintenance occur at the parB locus of the plasmid. One gene at that locus, the *hok* gene (host killing gene), encodes a short polypeptide that disrupts functioning of the cell's plasma membrane. When *hok* is expressed the cell dies.

A second gene, the *sok* gene (suppression of killing gene), can block the expression of the *hok* gene. It does so by encoding an **antisense mRNA,** that is, *sok* encodes a mRNA that is complementary to the mRNA encoded by the *hok* gene. The *sok* mRNA and the *hok* mRNA form a double-stranded RNA that is not translated. This occurs as long as the cell retains the plasmid with the parB locus.

If the cell loses the plasmid with the parB plasmid it ceases to produce *sok* and *hok* mRNAs. The *sok* mRNA is degraded faster than *hok* mRNA so that after a very short period the *hok* mRNA is translated. The production of the Hok polypeptide results in death of the cell. This *suicide system* is a powerful selective factor for the retention of the plasmid with the parB locus *hok* and *sok* genes.

Incompatibility of Plasmids

Bacterial cells may contain more than one plasmid, but certain pairs of plasmids cannot be stably replicated in the same bacterial cell. **Incompatible plasmids** do not co-exist in the same cell and are said to belong to an **incompatibility group** (Table 7-1). The incompatibility group of a plasmid is designated *Inc* followed by a capital letter and sometimes also a number, for example, *Inc*P1. It appears that plasmids of the same incompatibility group are closely related and have similar replication-partition systems. The property of incompatibility is encoded within the genes of the plasmid.

Functions of Plasmids

Several different types of plasmids serve different functions (Table 7-2). Plasmids can contain, among

TABLE 7-1 Plasmid Incompatibility Groups

INCOMPATIBILITY GROUP	PLASMIDS IN GROUP	INCOMPATIBILITY GROUP	PLASMIDS IN GROUP
IncL/M	R471a, R69-2, R69, pIP171, pIP135, R446b, pTH1	IncHI1	TP123, pIP522, TR6, pIP523, R27, R726
IncN	R46, RPC3, pIP113, N3, N3T, R390	IncHI2	R477, R478, R826, TP116, pIP235, pSD114
IncP	RP1, RP4, R702, R751, R906	IncX	R6K, R485, TP228, TP231, pHH1187
IncT	R402, Rts1, R394, R401		
IncU	R1460, RA3	IncA/C	pIP55, pIP55-1, pIP218, pIP216, R16a, RA1, pIP40a, R666, R707, R714b, R807, P-*lac*, pHH1350
IncW	RS-a, pIP100b, pIP339, R388, R7K, pIP356		
IncY	MIP231, P1Cm		
IncB/O	RRIP185, R16, R16-1, R723	IncD	R711b
IncFII	R1*drd*-19, pIP24, pIP187, pIP100, R1, R1-16, R136, R222Jap, R494, R538-1	IncFIV	R124*drd*-2
		IncFV/FO	Folac
		IncFVI	pSU104
IncI1	RIP112, RIP186, R144*drd*-3, R64, R144, R483, R648, JR66a	IncH13	MIP233
		IncHII	pHH1508a
		Inc12	R175, TP114, MIP241, pHH721, R821a
IncK	R387		
IncFI	*F'lac*, pIP180, pIP174, R386, R453, pHH507, R773, R455, R456, pIP162-1, pIP162-2, RGN238, ColV, ColV2-K94, ColV3-K30, pIP234, P307	IncIγ	R621a, R621a-la
		IncJ	R391, R391-3b-1
		IncV	R753, R905

other things, (1) the information that determines the ability of bacteria to mate and whether a bacterial strain acts as a "male," donating DNA during mating; (2) the information that codes for resistance to antibiotics and other chemicals, such as heavy metals, which are normally toxic to microorganisms; (3) the information for the degradation of various complex organic compounds, such as the aromatic hydrocarbons in petroleum; (4) the information for toxin production that renders some bacteria pathogenic to humans; and (5) the genes responsible for nitrogen fixation and the formation of root nodules on leguminous plants.

The **F Plasmid (fertility plasmid)** codes for mating behavior in *E. coli.* Strains of *E. coli* that have the F plasmid are donor strains, and those that lack the F plasmid are recipient strains. Bacteria that have the F plasmid form pili of the F type that are involved in establishing mating pairs. The F plasmid may exist as an independent circular molecule of double helical DNA or may become incorporated into the bacterial chromosome.

TABLE 7-2 Cell Functions Coded For by Some Plasmids

GROUP	FUNCTION	EXAMPLE
Fertility plasmids	Transfer of DNA from one cell to another via conjugation	F plasmid
Resistance plasmids	Resistance to various antibiotics	R plasmids, RP4, R1, pSH6
	Resistance to cadmium or mercury	R100
	Resistance to ultraviolet radiation	
Col plasmids	Bacteriocin production	ColE1, ColE2
Virulence Factor plasmids	Enterotoxin production	LT plasmid (in *E. coli*)
	Fimbriae production	K88 plasmid
	Antibiotic production	Methylenomycin plasmid (in *Streptomyces*)
Metabolic plasmids	Utilization of camphor	CAM
	Utilization of toluene	TOL
Transformation plasmids	Formation of spores in streptomycetes	
	Formation of crown gall tumors in plants	Ti plasmid (in *Agrobacterium*)

Colicinogenic plasmids carry the genes for a protein that is toxic only to closely related bacteria. For example, when strains of *E. coli* containing colicinogenic plasmids are mixed with other strains of *E. coli*, only one strain can survive. The toxins produced by *E. coli* are called *colicins*. In addition to the genes for toxin production, colicinogenic plasmids have genes that protect the host cell; they also may carry the information necessary for bacterial conjugation, that is, mating involving cell–cell contact. The acquisition of colicinogenic plasmids enables bacterial strains to enter into antagonistic relationships with other bacterial strains.

The **R Plasmids (resistance plasmids)** carry genes that code for antibiotic resistance (FIG. 7-4). Some R factor plasmids also carry genes for mating. The enzymes coded for by the genes of some R plasmids are able to degrade antibiotics, rendering them inactive and thus conferring resistance on bacterial strains that possess such R plasmids. R factors can be passed among bacteria, for example, from *E. coli* to pathogenic strains of *Shigella* or *Salmonella*. Antibiotic-resistant strains of bacteria have become a serious health problem because R plasmids can occur in pathogenic bacteria, and the treatment of human bacterial diseases is complicated by the occurrence of these pathogens that are resistant to multiple antibiotics.

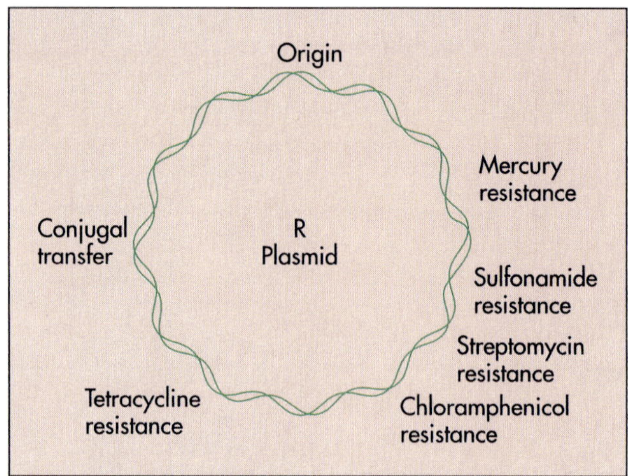

FIG. 7-4 R plasmids encode genes for resistance to multiple antibiotics.

7.2 MUTATIONS

A **mutation** is a heritable change in the nucleotide sequence of a cell's DNA. Changes in the cell's hereditary molecules sometimes occur as a result of mistakes made during DNA replication. Mutations sometimes occur during DNA replication despite the mechanisms that are designed to ensure the fidelity of DNA replication, which include the proofreading activities of DNA polymerases. Mutations alter a cell's **genotype,** that is, its genetic composition specified by the ordered nucleotides of the DNA. Changing the nucleotide sequence of the DNA even slightly can alter the ability of the cell to produce proteins that function properly. This may change the functions of regulatory or structural genes. Mutations can be reflected in the gene products that are produced and the control of their production. Mutations can alter the sequence of bases in the promoter or operator regions of the DNA, changing the ability of the cell to regulate protein synthesis at the level of transcription. Thus a mutation may change an inducible or repressible enzyme system to a constitutive enzyme system and vice versa. Deletions of large numbers of base pairs, called **deficiencies,** can result in the loss of genetic information for one or more complete genes.

TYPES OF MUTATIONS

Mutations are described based on the nature of the changes in the DNA or on the effects of those changes on the observed phenotype. Mutations, for example, can be described based on the changes in the DNA sequence, as additions, deletions, or substitutions of nucleotides. They can also be described based on phenotypic changes that result from the mutation. Morphological mutations alter the shape of individual cells or effect colonial characteristics. Lethal mutations result in the death of a cell. Keep in mind that the classification of mutations is artificial and an individual mutation can be placed in more than one category. For example, the addition of a single base to the nucleotide sequence may be classified as a frameshift mutation or a lethal mutation if those classifications are appropriate.

Mutations may arise in the cell as a result of naturally occurring changes **(spontaneous mutations)** in the DNA sequence as a result of mismatched base insertion or slippage errors (leading to small additions or deletions) by DNA polymerases (Table 7-3). These spontaneous mutations are minimized by the proofreading function of the DNA polymerases but nevertheless occur at a frequency of approximately 10^{-9}. Other spontaneous mutations may be due to lesions that occur when the bond between a sugar and base is broken or when deamination of cytosine forms uracil. **Induced mutations** result from the exposure of the cell to exogenous DNA modifiers such as radiation or chemical substances.

Cells that contain the most common form of DNA sequences are referred to as **wild type.** The introduction of genetic changes in wild type cells leads to **for-**

TABLE 7-3 Rates of Spontaneous Mutations at Various Loci in Different Organisms

ORGANISM	PHENOTYPE	GENE	RATE
Escherichia coli	Lactose fermentation	$lac^- \rightarrow lac^+$	2×10^{-7}
	Lactose fermentation	$lac^+ \rightarrow lac^-$	2×10^{-6}
	Phage T1 resistance	$T1^s \rightarrow T1^r$	2×8^{-8}
	Histidine requirement	$his^+ \rightarrow his^-$	2×10^{-6}
	Histidine independence	$his^- \rightarrow his^+$	4×10^{-8}
	Streptomycin dependence	$str^s \rightarrow str^d$	1×10^{-9}
	Streptomycin sensitivity	$str^d \rightarrow str^s$	1×10^{-8}
	Radiation resistance	$rad^s \rightarrow rad^d$	1×10^{-5}
	Leucine independence	$leu^- \rightarrow leu^+$	7×10^{-10}
	Arginine independence	$arg^- \rightarrow arg^+$	4×10^{-9}
	Tryptophan independence	$try- \rightarrow try^+$	6×10^{-8}
Salmonella typhimurium	Tryptophan independence	$try^- \rightarrow try^+$	5×10^{-8}
Streptococcus pneumoniae	Penicillin resistance	$pen^s \rightarrow pen^r$	1×10^{-7}
Chlamydomonas reinhardtii	Streptomycin sensitivity	$str^r \rightarrow str^s$	1×10^{-6}
Neurospora crassa	Inositol requirement	$inos^- \rightarrow inos^+$	8×10^{-8}
	Adenine independence	$ade^- \rightarrow ade^+$	4×10^{-8}

ward mutations. Sometimes second mutations occur in a mutant cell that cancel the phenotypic effects of a first mutation. These genotypically double mutants appear phenotypically like wild type cells and are called **reversion mutations.**

Base Substitutions

A **base substitution mutation** occurs when one pair of nucleotide bases in the DNA is replaced by another (FIG. 7-5). There are two general types of base substitution: transitions and transversions. **Transitions** involve the replacement of a purine on one strand by a different purine and the replacement of a pyrimidine on the other strand by a different pyrimidine, that is, the replacement of an adenine-thymine (AT) pair by a guanine-cytosine (GC) pair or vice versa. **Transversions,** on the other hand, are base substitutions in which purines replace pyrimidines and pyrimidines replace purines. The conversion of an AT pair to a TA or CG pair represents a transversion mutation. Similarly, the change of a GC pair to a CG or TA pair also establishes a transversion mutation. Because only one strand of the DNA acts as the sense strand, a transversion, such as from a GC to a CG pair, changes the sequence of nucleotides in the mRNA molecule that is transcribed.

Missense Mutations

Most base substitutions are **missense mutations,** so named because they result in a change in the amino acid inserted into the polypeptide chain specified by the gene in which the mutation occurs. Missense mutations can result in the production of an inactive enzyme or may have no effect on the phenotype. Changes in a single amino acid within a polypeptide often do not drastically reduce the activity of an enzyme and are rarely fatal to the microorganism.

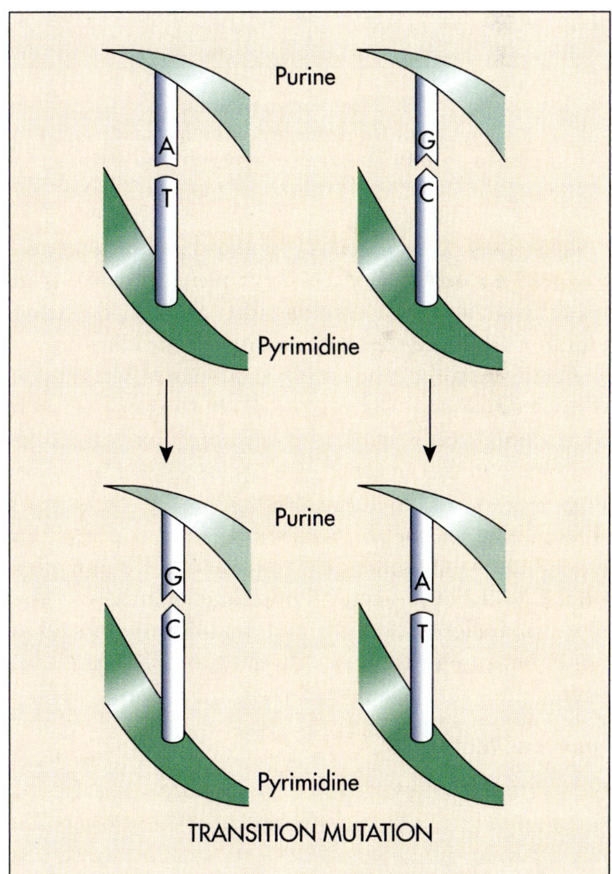

FIG. 7-5 Transitions occur when an AT pair is replaced with a GC pair, or vice versa.

Silent Mutations

Because the genetic code is degenerate, the substitution of one nucleotide base for another may not change the amino acid specified by the codon (FIG. 7-6). Such mutations are called **silent mutations**

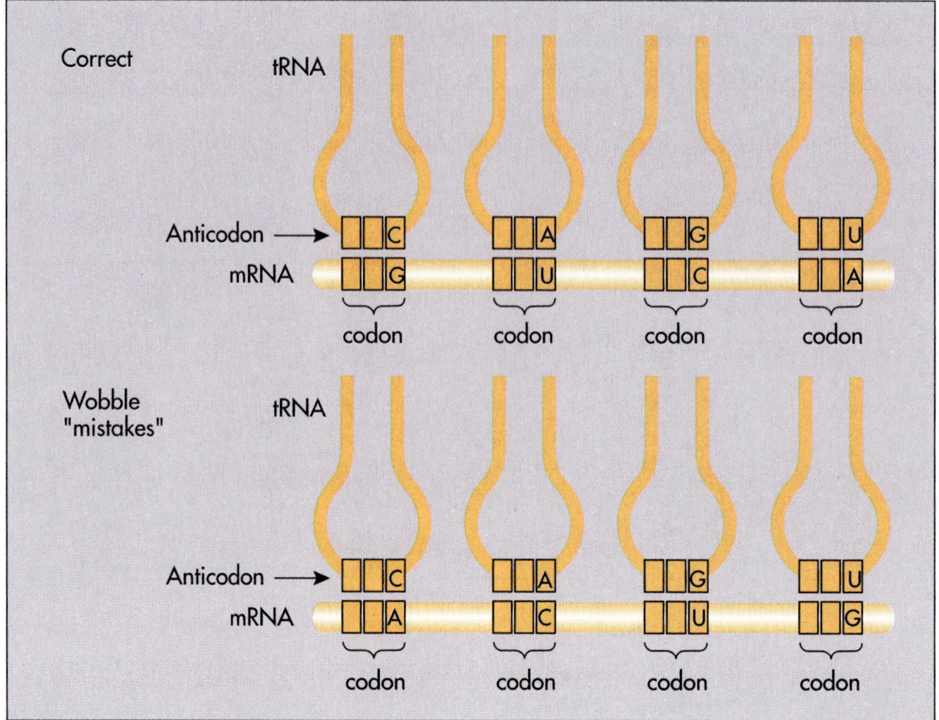

FIG. 7-6 Some mutations are silent because the change in nucleotide sequence does not alter the sequence of amino acids. According to the wobble hypothesis, silent mutations are most common on the third nucleotide of a codon.

because they do not alter the phenotype of the organism and go undetected. A silent mutation results in the production of proteins with exactly the same amino acid sequences as the nonmutant cell.

Changes in the nucleotide sequence that alter the third base of codon are most likely to produce such silent mutations because this is where most of the redundancy in the genetic code occurs. This phenomenon is described by the *wobble hypothesis*, which states that changes in the third position of the codon often do not alter the amino acid sequence of the polypeptide. The tRNA molecules sometimes match only the first two nucleotides of the codon and thus are said to *wobble* because of the variability in the third base position.

Nonsense Mutations

A mutation that often has a major effect on the expression of the genetic information occurs when the alteration in the base sequence of the DNA results in the formation of a codon that does not code for an amino acid. This type of mutation is called a **nonsense mutation.** Because nonsense codons act as terminator signals during protein synthesis, formation of a nonsense codon often signals premature termination of a polypeptide chain, preventing the formation of a functional enzyme molecule. In bacteria, where the mRNA molecule often is polycistronic, a nonsense mutation can affect the synthesis of several polypeptides.

Polar Mutations

Mutations that prevent the translation of subsequent polypeptides coded for in the same mRNA molecule are said to be **polar mutations.** The degree to which a mutation within one gene affects the expression of other genes depends on the degree of polarity, which is highly dependent on the relative locations of the nucleotide sequences involved in initiation and termination of the specific genes. Nonsense mutations near the beginning of translation (the 5′-P end) will terminate translation of all the successive genes, whereas nonsense mutations farther down will have fewer effects. In contrast, nonsense mutations at the 3′-OH end will generally have a lesser effect because they have no effect on genes transcribed at the 5′-P end.

Frameshift Mutations

Perhaps the greatest effect of deleting or adding a base occurs because the nature of the translation process depends on the establishment of the proper reading frame for the codons to specify the proper amino acids to be inserted into the polypeptide chain (FIG. 7-7). A **deletion mutation** involves the removal of one or more nucleotide base pairs from the DNA, and an **insertion mutation** involves the addition of one or more base pairs. Because adding or deleting a single base pair changes the reading frame of the transcribed mRNA, the deletion or addition of a single base pair can have as great an effect as a large defi-

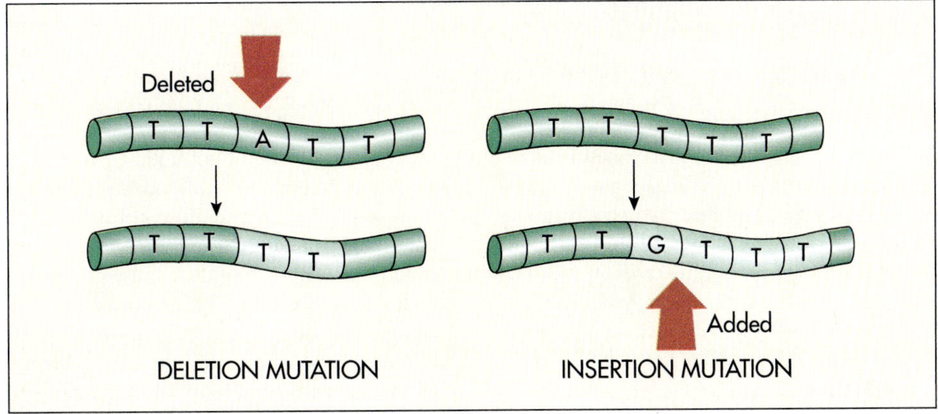

FIG. 7-7 Deletion mutations occur when one or more nucleotides are omitted during DNA replication. Addition mutations occur when one or more nucleotides are added during DNA replication. A frame shift mutation results from such nucleotide deletions or additions.

ciency. Such **frameshift mutations** can result in the misreading of large numbers of codons.

To understand how such mutations can alter the informational content of a message, consider what would happen if the English language contained only three-letter words; if we did not use spaces between words; if we used the three-letter sequence XXX instead of a period to indicate the end of a sentence; and if we changed, deleted, or added a letter. We could understand the simple sentence "THECATATETHERATXXX" as "The cat ate the rat." Changing a single letter can alter the meaning but still convey information; for example, "THECATATETHEBATXXX," translated as "The cat ate the bat," still conveys meaning, although a somewhat different meal for the cat. However, deleting a letter, for example, deleting the C, "THEATATETHERATXXX," alters the reading frame and renders the message nonsensical. In this case, we recognize only the words "THE" and "HER" in the sentence "The ata tet her atx." Similarly, adding a letter can alter the reading frame and greatly change the informational content.

Suppressor Mutations

In some cases, a second mutation can occur that reestablishes the reading frame (FIG. 7-8). A mutation that reestablishes a reading frame is called a **suppressor mutation.** For example, the addition of a base pair after the deletion of a base pair can restore the reading frame, suppressing the expression of the first mutation. An **intragenic suppressor mutation** (a mutation within one gene), such as one that reestablishes a

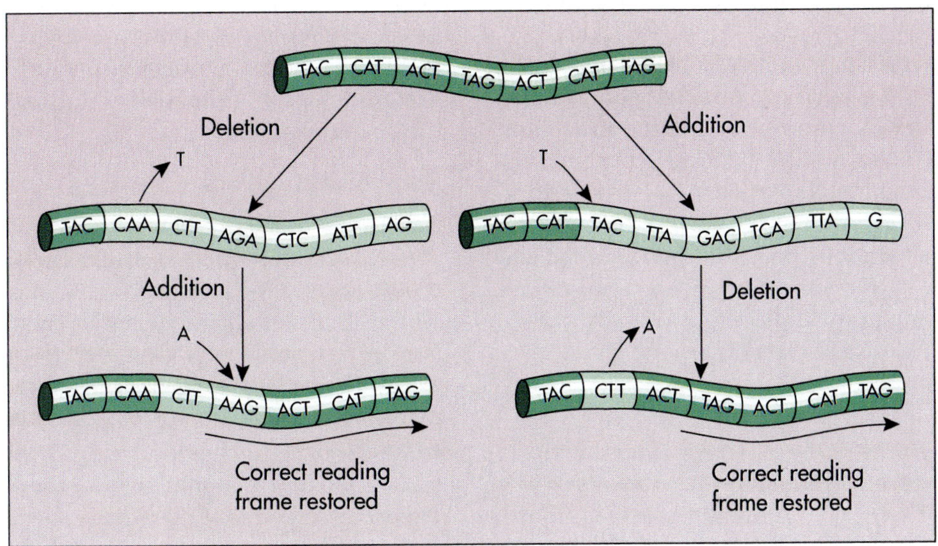

FIG. 7-8 A suppressor mutation restores the reading frame by inserting a nucleotide following a deletion, or deleting a nucleotide following an insertion.

BOX 7-1

EVIDENCE FOR DIRECTED MUTATIONS

Spontaneous mutation clearly occur as a result of errors during DNA replication. Such mutations occur randomly and can alter any gene. The rates of occurrence of such mutations increase in response to certain environmental conditions, such as exposure to radiation. Spontaneous mutations can create new genes that result in cells with altered properties that may effect their survival capacities. It is also possible that environmental conditions drive the occurrence of certain specific mutations.

Studies by John Cairns and Barry Hall indicate that environmental conditions may in some cases direct the occurrence of specific mutations. This suggests that environmental conditions can dictate the course of evolution. The experiments were designed to detect nonrandom mutations arising in response to environmental factors. Cairns used a strain of *E. coli* that was *lac*$^-$, meaning that it was a mutant strain that had lost the ability to utilize lactose as a growth substrate. The bacterium was cultured using a medium with glucose as the carbon source so that both *lac*– and spontaneous *lac*$^+$ mutants would grow. The bacterial cells were then plated onto a medium with lactose as the carbon source. The spontaneous *lac*$^+$ mutants grew and formed colonies on this medium. The *lac*$^-$ bacterial cells survived but could not reproduce and form colonies on the lactose medium. If a cell mutated to *lac*$^+$ while sitting on the lactose medium it would grow and form a colony. The distribution of colonies indicated that both spontaneous mutations and mutations with a higher frequency directed by the presence of lactose on the plates occurred. To show that the lactose was directing the frequency of mutation, Cairns followed a second mutation (*Val*^{R}) for resistance to the amino acid valine. He used an agar medium containing glucose as a growth substrate and a high concentration of valine so that only *Val*^{R} mutants could grow. If only spontaneous mutations occurred the incidence of *Val*^{R} and *lac*$^+$ mutants should be the same. They were not. There was a higher frequency of *lac*$^+$ mutants, indicating that the presence of lactose directed the frequency of a specific mutation.

A similar adaptive response to growth on salicin by *E. coli* was demonstrated by Barry Hall. He used a system in which two sequential mutations are required. Again there was a much higher mutation frequency when salicin was present in the growth medium than could be explained by spontaneous mutations alone. The mechanism for such increased rates of specific mutation are not known and require further studies.

reading frame, permits the successful synthesis of the polypeptide specified by the gene in which the mutation occurs. Returning to our English language analogy to understand this concept, we saw that deleting a letter that resulted in "THEATATETHERATXXX" formed a nonsensical sentence. An addition after the first deletion, such as "THEANTATETHERATXXX," could have created a new but interpretable informational content, in this case telling us that "The ant ate the rat."

A suppressor mutation may also be an **intergenic mutation,** which is a mutation within one gene that affects another gene. Mutations that alter the anticodon region of tRNA molecules can be involved in such intergenic suppression of mutations. For example, a mutation in the anticodon of the tRNA molecule can suppress a nonsense mutation if the change in the anticodon results in the insertion of an amino acid where the mutant nonsense codon normally causes premature termination of the polypeptide chain.

Lethal Mutations

When the mutation results in the death of the microorganism or its inability to reproduce, it is said to be a **lethal mutation.** Such mutations may be conditional, causing the death of the organism only under certain environmental conditions, or unconditional, being lethal to the organism regardless of the environmental conditions.

A **conditionally lethal mutation** causes a loss of viability only under some specified conditions in which the organism would normally survive. **Temperature-sensitive mutations,** for example, alter the range of temperatures over which the microorganism may grow when using specific substrates. A temperature-sensitive mutation of *E. coli* that alters the stability of the enzymes involved in lactose utilization can prevent that strain of *E. coli* from growing on lactose at elevated temperatures, while not altering its ability to grow on lactose at a lower temperature or its ability to grow on glucose at the temperature at which it can no longer use lactose.

Nutritional Mutations

Nutritional mutations occur when a mutation alters the nutritional requirements for the progeny of a microorganism. Often, nutritional mutants are unable to synthesize essential biochemicals, such as amino acids. Nutritional mutants that require growth factors, such as specific amino acids, that are not needed by the parental or wild-type **(prototroph)** strain are called **auxotrophs.**

DETECTION OF MUTATIONS

Several approaches are used to detect mutations. In some cases, a colony growing on an agar plate can easily be seen to be different from the normal parental

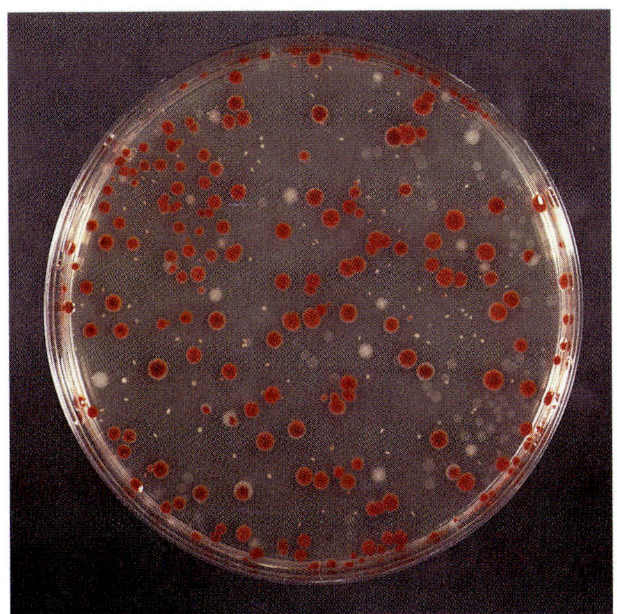

FIG. 7-9 Plate of *Serratia marcescens* showing growth of wild type colonies (*red*) and mutant colonies (*gray*).

type. For example, if the parental strain is pigmented, the observation of nonpigmented colonies may indicate the presence of mutations (FIG. 7-9). Indicators can also be incorporated into the medium to detect organisms with and without particular metabolic capabilities, or various incubation conditions can be used. For example, pH indicators can be incorporated into the medium to detect the production of acidic products. Acid production by one strain and not another strain of the same organism growing under identical conditions indicates the presence of a mutant.

Replica Plating

Nutritional mutants (organisms with a mutation that alters the nutritional requirement), as well as various other types of mutants, are often detected using the **replica plating technique** (FIG. 7-10). This method allows the observation of microorganisms under a series of growth conditions. In replica plating, a piece of sterile velvet is touched to the surface of an agar plate containing surface bacterial colonies. The fibers of the velvet act as fine inoculating needles, picking up bacterial cells from the surface of this master plate. The velvet with its attached microorganisms is then touched to the surface of a sterile agar plate, inoculating it. In this manner, microorganisms can be repeatedly stamped onto media of differing composition. The distribution of microbial colonies should be exactly replicated on each plate unless the colonies represent strains of differing genetic composition. If a colony that develops on a complete medium fails to develop on a minimal medium that lacks a specific growth factor, the occurrence of a nutritional mutation is indicated. The microorganisms that do not grow on the minimal medium represent *auxotrophic strains.* By determining which biochemicals permit the growth of the auxotroph, the step in the metabolic pathway and the genetic site of the metabolic blockage can be determined.

The replica plating technique was developed by Joshua and Esther Lederberg in 1952 to provide direct evidence for the existence of pre-existing mutations. Their experiment consisted of replicating master plates of sensitive cells to two or more plates containing either streptomycin or a virus that infects bacteria. When the replicas were grown, they were compared to the locations of colonies on the master plate, and any resistant bacterial colonies that appeared at the same position on all of the replica plates were marked. The area of the master plate corresponding to the marked areas was cut out, and the bacteria on it were resuspended in a liquid medium. If the hypothesis of pre-existing mutations was correct, the culture derived from these cells would be enriched for resistant mutants because only a very few cells from a small area in the agar were removed from the master plate. The enriched culture could then be used to prepare a new master plate and the entire process repeated. The final result was a master plate

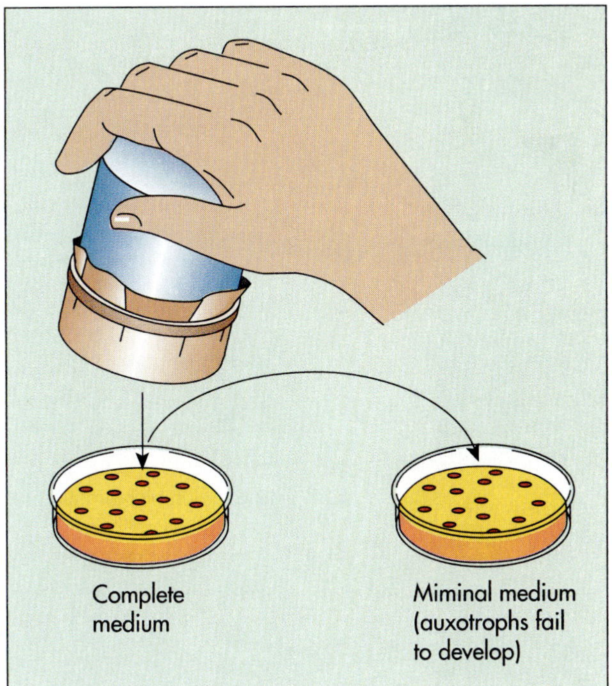

FIG. 7-10 Replica plating is used to identify mutants by transferring identical colonies to different types of media and comparing the colonies that develop on the respective plates. This method is critical in identifying auxotrophic mutants. All colonies develop on a complete medium that satisfies the nutritional needs of both the parental and mutant strains. Colonies of the auxotrophic mutant fail to develop on a minimal medium lacking the specific nutritional growth factors required by the mutant.

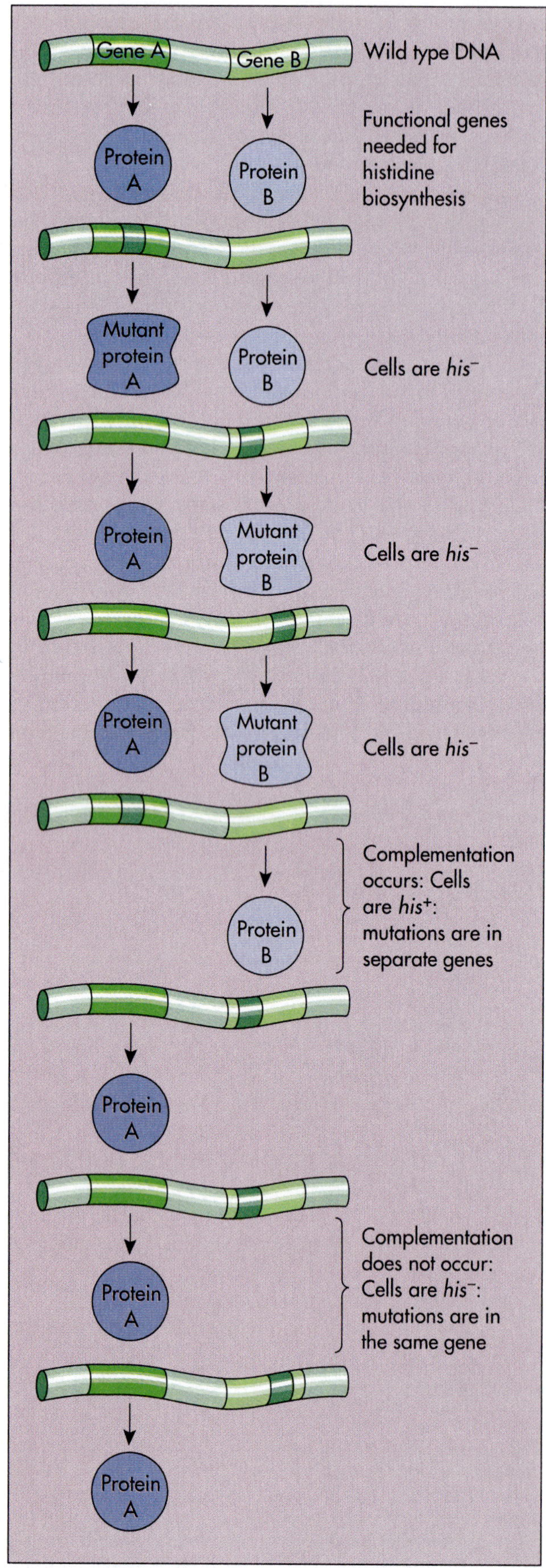

FIG. 7-11 Complementation distinguishes between mutations in *cis* configuration (within the same DNA molecule) or *trans* configuration (on separate DNA molecules).

containing nothing but resistant bacteria, even though the cells and their progenitors had never been directly subjected to selection.

The replica plating method has been applied in numerous experiments to identify the occurrence of mutations. The method permits the detection of mutations and the retention of viable colonies of mutant strains that can be readily identified and cultured for further study. Many biochemical pathways have been elucidated in this way by using nutritional mutations based on examining the growth requirements of auxotrophic strains to determine the sequential order of intermediary metabolites in a metabolic pathway.

Complementation

Complementation is a method for determining whether mutations are in the same or in different locations (FIG. 7-11). The complementation test procedure involves genetically crossing (mating) two different mutant strains. It aims at determining whether the two mutations complement each other. If the two mutations are in the same gene, the resulting progeny of the genetic cross should still be mutant. On the other hand, if the mutations are in different genes, the mutant phenotype should be eliminated in the progeny.

A ***cis/trans complementation test*** is used to determine whether two mutations are in the same gene and on the same DNA molecule. If the two mutations are on separate DNA molecules, they are in the ***trans*** configuration, and if they are on the same molecule, they are in the ***cis*** configuration. Behavior is different for two mutants in *cis* or *trans* configuration, depending on whether they code for the same proteins. If the two mutants affect the same protein, then they fail to complement each other when in *cis* configuration, but would complement each other in *trans* because in *trans* there is a functional gene for each mutation.

MUTATION RATES AND MUTAGENIC AGENTS

The **mutation rate** is the probability that any one cell will mutate during the period of time required by a cell to divide to form a new generation of cells. It is equal to the average number of mutations per cell generation. The relationship of mutation rate to cell number is given in the following equation:

$$\text{Mutation rate} = \frac{(0.69)\,m}{(n - n_0)}$$

where m is the average number of mutations occurring when n_0 cells increase in number to n cells. The mutation rate of a given culture can be determined by growing a population of cells on a solid medium where each mutation gives rise to a mutant clone that can be detected as a single colony.

Mutations occur spontaneously only at relatively low rates (see Table 7-3). In *E. coli*, for example, the spontaneous mutation rate is approximately one change per billion nucleotide pairs replicated. This spontaneous rate varies among different bacterial species. Additionally, various chemical and physical agents can increase the incidence of mutation. Such agents are called **mutagens.**

Radiation

High-energy radiation, such as X-rays, causes mutations because it produces breaks in the DNA molecule. Exposure to gamma radiation, such as that emitted by ^{60}Co, can be used to sterilize objects, including plastic Petri plates, because sufficient exposure to ionizing radiation results in lethal mutations and the death of all exposed microorganisms. The time and intensity of exposure determine the number of lethal mutations that occur and thus establishes the required exposures when ionizing radiation is employed in sterilization processes.

Ultraviolet light also can cause base substitutions by creating covalent linkages between adjacent thymidines on the same strand of the DNA (FIG. 7-12). A **thymine dimer** cannot act as a template for DNA polymerase, and the occurrence of such dimers therefore prevents the proper functioning of polymerases. Exposure to ultraviolet light can cause lethal mutations and is sometimes used to kill microorganisms in sterilization procedures. UV light does not penetrate well but is useful for sterilizing surfaces, such as the work surfaces of the microbiology laboratory.

Chemical Mutagens

Various chemicals modify nucleotides and act as **chemical mutagens,** increasing rates of mutations. Hydroxylamine, for example, chemically modifies cytosine to uracil so that it pairs with adenine instead of its normal complementary base guanine. After one generation this change results in the replacement of a GC pair with an AT pair, that is, in a transition. Nitrosoguanidine and several other chemical mutagens can alkylate nucleotide bases, causing transitions that

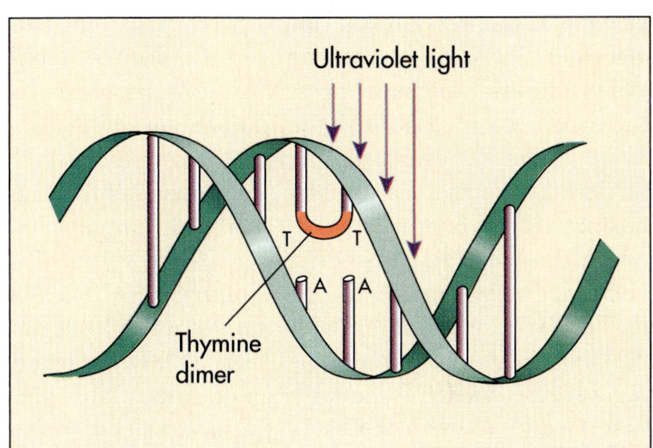

FIG. 7-12 Exposure of DNA to UV light results in the formation of thymine dimers.

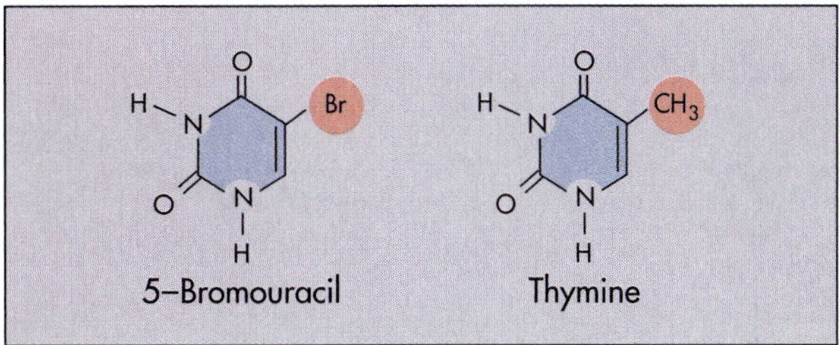

FIG. 7-13 Exposure to a base analog results in mutation; for example 5-bromouracil, which is a base analog of thymine, causes mutations.

result in the substitution of GC for AT in the second generation. Nitrous acid oxidizes the amino group of cytosine or adenine, forming keto (–CO–) groups, converting cytosine to uracil and adenine to hypoxanthine. This results in a base substitution mutation.

Some chemicals are **base analogs,** meaning that they resemble DNA nucleotides. Although a base analog structurally resembles a DNA nucleotide, and therefore may substitute for it, it does not function in the same manner (FIG. 7-13). For example, 5-bromouracil can replace thymine and pair with adenine or replace cytosine and pair with guanine, thus producing base substitutions in the DNA.

Several chemical mutagens, such as acridine, result in base deletion or base addition mutations and cause frame shift mutations. Others, such as mitomycin C, form covalent cross-linkages between base pairs, preventing the replication of the DNA molecule. Thus exposure to various chemicals that act in different ways can greatly increase mutation rates.

Ames Test

The **Ames test** is a procedure used to detect chemical mutagens and carcinogens (FIG. 7-14, p. 256). It is based on determining whether exposure to a particular chemical alters the mutation rate of microorganisms. It is easy to expose huge numbers of microorganisms, perhaps a billion, to the chemical in a single Petri plate so that mutation rates can be rapidly and accurately determined. To expose this number of macroorganisms, say rabbits or mice, to the chemical for mutagenicity testing would be impossible.

The Ames test procedure typically uses strains of the bacterium *Salmonella typhimurium* for determining chemical mutagenicity. The *S. typhimurium* strains employed in the Ames test procedure are auxotrophs that require the amino acid histidine for growth. Several different strains are used, each specific for a type of mutation, such as frame shift, deletion, and so forth. The reason for using different strains is that they differ in their responses to different types of chemicals. For example, one strain may have greater permeability to large molecules than another and may hence be a better organism to use when testing large

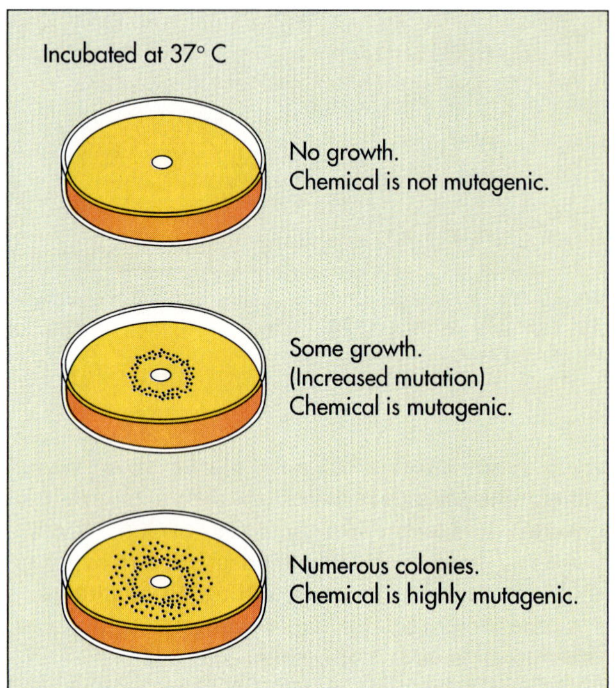

Incubated at 37° C
No growth.
Chemical is not mutagenic.
Some growth.
(Increased mutation)
Chemical is mutagenic.
Numerous colonies.
Chemical is highly mutagenic.

FIG. 7-14 The Ames test procedure is used to screen for mutagens and potential carcinogens. The auxotrophic strain used in this procedure, generally a histidine-requiring mutant of *Salmonella typhimurium*, will not grow on a minimal medium. Mutants that revert to the prototrophic wild type will grow on this medium. The number of colonies that develop after exposure to a chemical indicates the effect of that chemical on mutation rate and therefore its degree of mutagenicity. The development of many colonies indicates that the chemical is highly mutagenic.

molecules. Often five different strains are used in the test protocol.

The organisms are exposed to a concentration gradient of the chemical being tested on a solid growth medium that contains only a trace of histidine. The amount of histidine in the medium is only enough to support the auxotrophs long enough for the potential mutagenic chemicals to act. Normally, the test strain bacteria cannot grow sufficiently to form visible colonies because of the lack of histidine. Therefore, in the absence of a chemical mutagen, no colonies develop. If the chemical is a mutagen, many mutations will occur in the areas of high chemical concentration. It is likely that no growth will occur in these areas because of the occurrence of lethal mutations. At lower chemical concentrations along the concentration gradient, fewer mutations will occur. Some of the mutants will be revertants to the prototrophs that do not require histidine. Since histidine prototrophs synthesize their own histidine, they grow and produce visible bacterial colonies on the histidine-deficient medium. The appearance of these colonies demonstrates that histidine prototrophs have been produced, and a high rate of formation of such mutants suggests that the chemical has mutagenic properties.

The Ames test is also useful to determine if a chemical is a potential carcinogen (cancer-causing agent) because there is a high correlation between mutagenicity and carcinogenicity. Even though the Ames test does not actually establish whether a chemical causes cancer, determining whether a chemical has mutagenic activity is useful in screening large numbers of chemicals for potential carcinogenicity. In testing for potential carcinogenicity in the Ames test procedure, the chemical is incubated with a preparation of rat liver enzymes to simulate what normally occurs in the liver, where many chemicals are inadvertently transformed into carcinogens in an apparent effort by the body to detoxify the chemical. Following this activation step, various concentrations of the transformed chemical are incubated with the *Salmonella* auxotroph to determine whether it causes mutations and is a potential carcinogen. Further testing for carcinogenicity is done on those chemicals that have tested positive for mutagenicity.

DNA REPAIR MECHANISMS

To prevent mutations, cells have evolved several mechanisms for repairing damaged or altered DNA. This decreases the frequency of mutation and promotes the fidelity of DNA replication. These repair mechanisms provide a mechanism for proofreading and repairing damaged DNA. Some are general repair mechanisms; others function to repair specific types of damage to the DNA. They limit changes in the DNA but are unable to prevent totally the occurrence of mutations.

Mismatch Repair

Although DNA polymerases have proofreading functions that can correct improperly inserted bases during DNA replication, they still leave errors in the DNA sequence. Another mechanism, called **mismatch repair,** is responsible for recognizing and correcting these residual errors. The gene products of *mut*H, *mut*L, *mut*S, and *mut*U form a **mismatch correction enzyme** that recognizes improperly inserted nucleotides that lead to distortions in the double helix. When mutations arise as a result of replication errors, the incorrect nucleotide is found in the newly synthesized strand, whereas the "correct" complementary nucleotide is found in the older template strand. The mismatch correction enzyme can discriminate between these two strands because the older strand has been tagged by the specific DNA methylases that are a part of the restriction-modification system in bacteria. For example, in *Bacillus subtilis* the DNA methylase recognizes –GGCC– sequences and methylates the first cytosine to form –GGC*C– (the asterisk represents a methyl group). The modification of specific residues in a DNA sequence occurs after replication but there is a lag between replication and methylation. During this lag period, the mismatch repair mechanism can operate. The mismatch correction enzyme binds preferentially to the unmethylated strand and excises the mismatch. Then, DNA polymerases can fill in the gap with another opportunity to insert the correct nucleotide.

Excision Repair

Excision repair corrects damaged DNA by removing nucleotides and then resynthesizing the region (FIG. 7-15). This mechanism is particularly important in recognizing thymine dimers that form as a result of exposure to ultraviolet radiation. Cells with mutations in *uvr*A, *uvr*B or *uvr*C show increased sensitivity to UV light. Thymine dimers and other mutations that lead to distortion of the double helix are excised by a repair endonuclease or UvrABC nuclease that also removes nucleotides on either side of a nicked site in a DNA macromolecule. This creates a single-stranded gap about 12 nucleotides long that is filled by DNA polymerase I. DNA ligase then joins the fragments. Specialized excision repair systems specifically excise sites on the DNA where the bases have been removed to form "nucleotides" lacking the nucleic acid bases while the sugar phosphate backbone remains intact. Specific endonucleases recognize these locations and nick the backbone at these sites, allowing excision repair to begin with the excision of a short stretch of nucleotides.

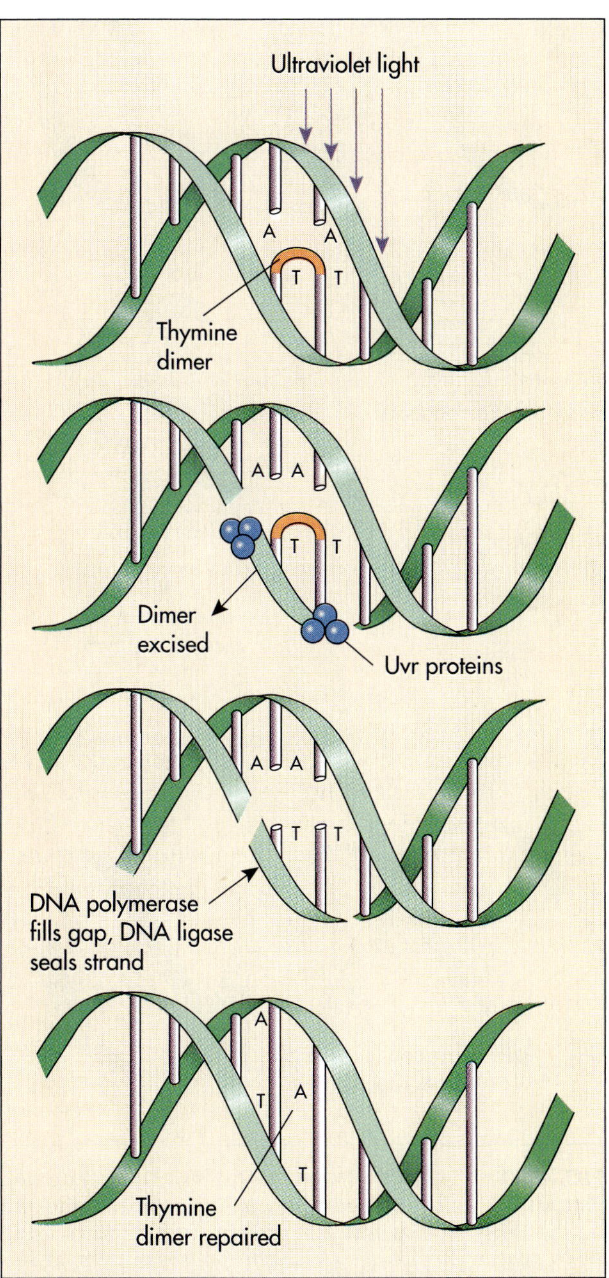

FIG. 7-15 In excision repair, the segment of DNA containing a thymine dimer is removed by Uvr proteins. The gap is then filled by DNA polymerase I and sealed by DNA ligase.

Photoreactivation

Thymine dimers can also be removed by a **photoreactivation** mechanism that breaks the covalent linkages between the thymine bases (FIG. 7-16). The mechanism depends on a photoreactivation enzyme (PRE)

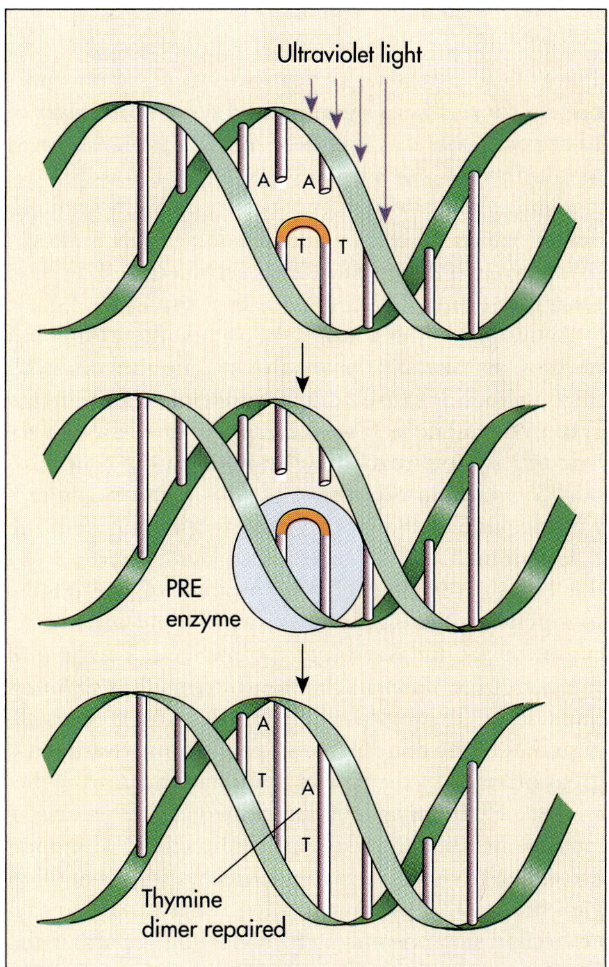

FIG. 7-16 Photoreactivation repair uses a photoreactivation enzyme (PRE) that obtains its energy from light.

that functions only in the presence of light. The ability to remove thymine dimers that occur as a result of exposure to UV radiation is a particularly important adaptation in microorganisms that are normally exposed to high levels of solar radiation. The PRE can recognize and bind to thymine dimers in the dark but it must absorb a light photon to cleave the bonds forming the dimer. This enzyme reverses the damaging effects of UV light without requiring excision and gap filling as in other repair mechanisms.

Recombinational Repair

Damaged DNA for which there is no remaining template can be restored by **recombination repair**. If both nucleotide base pairs at a site are damaged, or if there is a gap opposite a lesion, recombination repair can restore the nucleotide sequence of the DNA. In recombination repair the RecA protein cuts a piece of template DNA from a complementary molecule and puts it into the gap or uses it to replace a damaged strand. Another copy of the damaged segment is often available, even though bacteria are haploid, because it has been replicated as the cell is growing rapidly. There are more than one partially replicated bacterial chromosome in growing bacterial cells.

SOS System

The **SOS system** is a complex, error-prone multifunctional process that is a generalized system for repair of damaged DNA. It is a radical repair system designed to save the cell when there is persistent DNA damage. The induction of this system occurs only after a delay during which incomplete replication of DNA has occurred. When the SOS system is activated, cell division ceases, resulting in filamentous growth.

Activation of the SOS system occurs when the RecA protein is altered, probably by interaction with oligonucleotides formed as a result of DNA damage (FIG. 7-17). The activated RecA protein has proteolytic activity and attacks several DNA-binding proteins that function as repressors of transcription. Proteolytic cleavage of these repressor proteins turns on the SOS system. The SOS system is normally repressed by the LexA protein—a protein product of the regulatory gene *lex*A. LexA is inactivated by the proteolytic action of the RecA protein. Both the *rec*A gene and the genes for UvrA nuclease, which excises thymine dimers, are expressed when the LexA protein is digested. The increase in RecA production results in a great increase in the rate of DNA modification.

Once the SOS system is activated, DNA repair occurs in the absence of template direction. The damage to the DNA activates repair mechanisms that fill in gaps in the DNA without copying the template so that errors are not promulgated. Following repair of the DNA damage, the SOS system is switched off and further modifications of DNA cease.

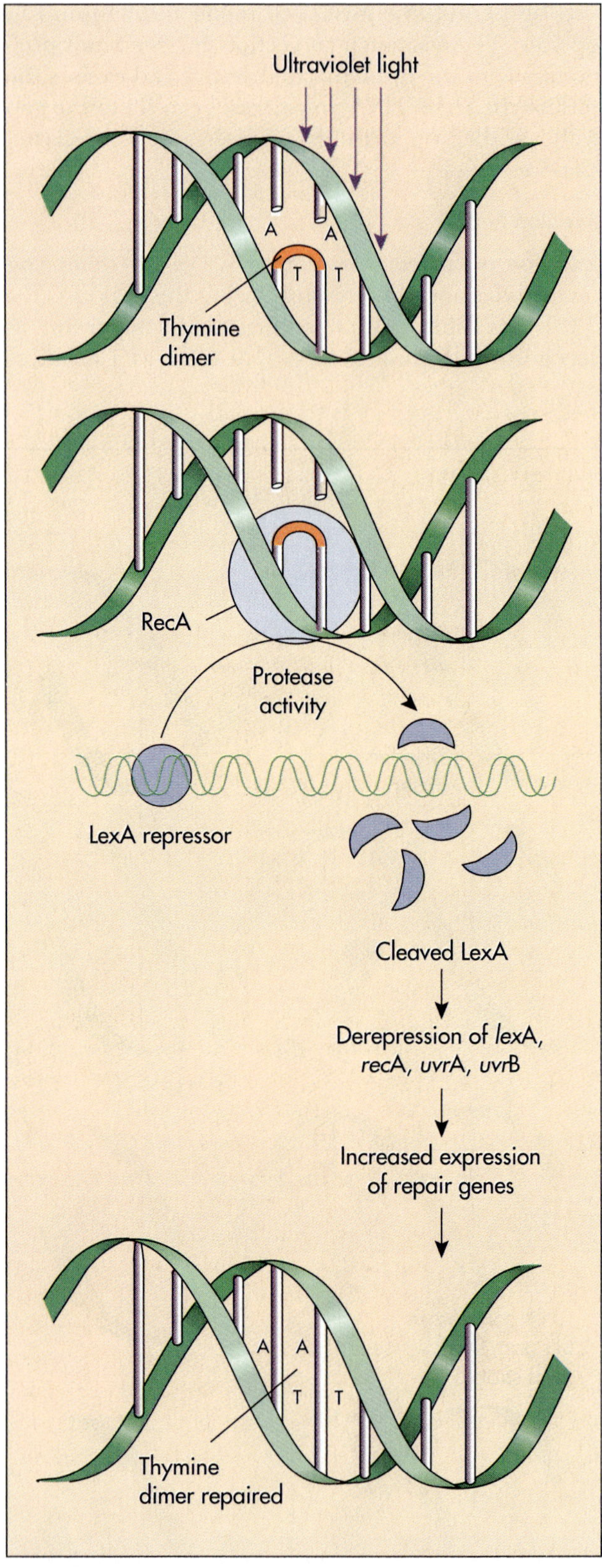

FIG. 7-17 The SOS system is an extensive, integrated repair system. It is initiated when *rec*A is activated and the bound RecA protein acts as a proteolytic enzyme, cleaving LexA protein. Because LexA is the repressor protein for several genes, including *lex*A, *rec*A, *uvr*A, and *uvr*B, cleavage of LexA derepresses these genes and thereby activates DNA repair. The synthesis of Uvr proteins, for example, repairs the DNA by excising thymine dimers.

7.3 RECOMBINATION

Recombination occurs when there is an exchange of genetic information among different DNA molecules that results in a reshuffling of genes. This process can produce numerous new combinations of genetic information. Recombination of genetic information from two different cells produces progeny that contain genetic information derived from two potentially different genomes.

Recombination results in an exchange of allelic forms of genes that can produce new combinations of alleles. In eukaryotic cells, genetic exchange during sexual reproduction affords a mechanism for gene reassortment within the population and maintenance of genetic heterogeneity. Even in prokaryotic cells, where reproduction is asexual (not involving mating of two cells) or parasexual mating (not involving gamete formation or a long-lasting diploid state), there are genetic exchange processes that lead to the recombination of genetic information.

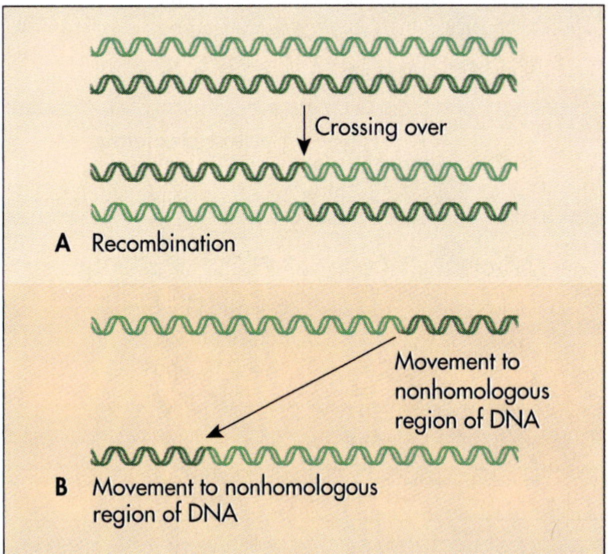

FIG. 7-18 There are two processes of genetic recombination, one with extensive homology between the nucleotide sequences that are recombining (homologous recombination) and another with relatively little homology (nonhomologous recombination). Each process is important in redistributing genetic information and maintaining genetic diversity. **A,** Chromosomal crossing-over, which results in the recombination of genes, is a classic example of homologous recombination. **B,** The movement of transposons, which are sometimes called *jumping genes,* is an example of nonhomologous recombination.

TYPES OF RECOMBINATIONAL PROCESSES

Homologous Recombination

The classic type of genetic exchange, called **homologous recombination,** is a recombination process that occurs between regions of DNA containing the same or nearly the same nucleotide sequences (FIG. 7-18). This process can be considered a general or reciprocal exchange of DNA. Homologous recombination is seen in the crossing over of chromosomes where pairs of chromosomes containing the same gene loci pair and exchange allelic portions of the same chromosomes. The term *homologous* implies that the exchange is between alleles of the same gene and is not meant to imply that the exchanged DNA segments have exactly the same nucleotide sequences.

In homologous recombination, there is relatively good base pairing of corresponding regions of the DNA, and the aligned chromosomes may establish duplexes between homologous DNA regions. In eukaryotic cells this often occurs during meiosis, the process whereby homologous chromosome pairs are separated and one member of each pair is distributed to each of the two daughter cells. Meiosis results in the conversion of a diploid cell into a haploid cell. A similar homologous alignment of DNA molecules can occur when a bacterial chromosome or portion thereof is transferred from a donor to a recipient bacterial cell.

Molecular Basis of Homologous Recombination

Single-stranded regions of DNA are involved in homologous recombination. Recombination can be initiated by an endonuclease. The endonuclease produces a short single-stranded segment by nicking one of the strands of DNA. A helix-destabilizing protein (cleaving a phosphodiester bond) combines at the site where the nick occurs and aids in opening up of the DNA double helix. The free 3′-OH end of the DNA molecule that results from endonuclease activity acts as a primer for DNA synthesis, involving a DNA polymerase that produces a single strand of DNA.

The newly synthesized region of the DNA pairs with the corresponding region of the homologous chromosome, establishing a *heteroduplex* (FIG. 7-19). A heteroduplex forms when two strands of DNA that are complementary over only part of their lengths join together. The homologous regions form a duplex (double-stranded complementary segment) and the noncomplementary segments remain single-stranded. Because there are duplex and nonduplex regions, the term heteroduplex is used. An endonuclease cleaves out the unpaired section of the DNA macromolecule, and finally, ligases join the free ends of the DNA strands.

The formation of the heteroduplex is catalyzed by enzymes coded for by ***rec*** **genes (recombination genes).** Some of these are the same genes involved in the SOS repair system discussed earlier. Recombina-

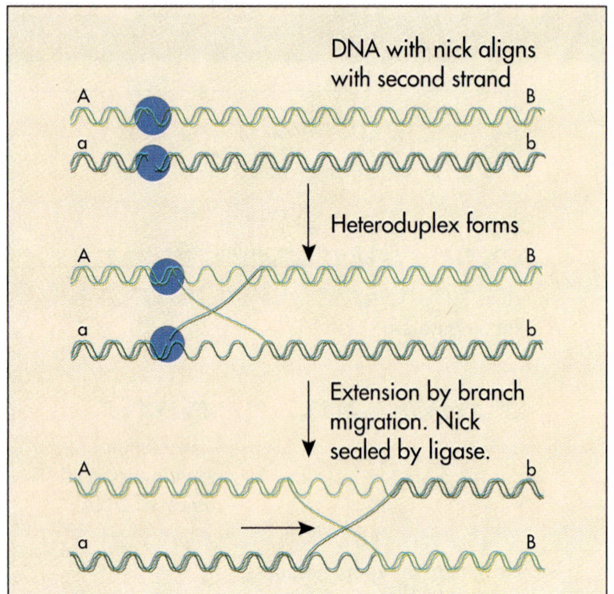

FIG. 7-19 Nonhomologous recombination involves formation of a heteroduplex, followed by excision and ligase resealing to form new recombined DNA molecules. In this case, the genes in the original DNA molecules are designated AB and ab; the recombined molecules have gene combinations Ab and aB.

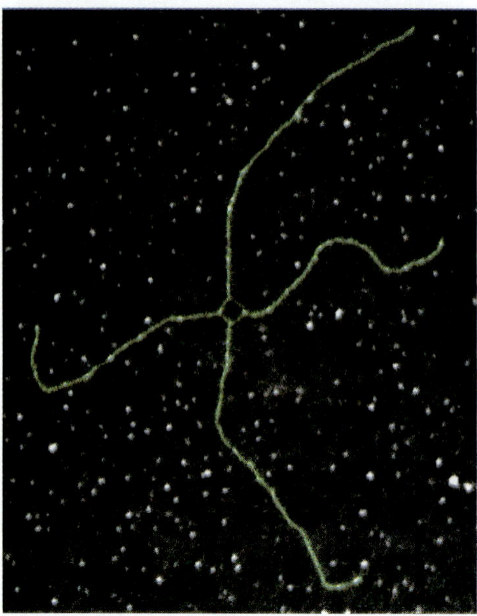

FIG. 7-20 Micrograph of the chi form of a heteroduplex during homologous recombination.

tion does not occur in cells lacking *rec* genes. The result of this enzymatic action is the formation of a bridge between the two homologous DNA strands. The joining of chromosomes at a homologous region establishes a **chi form** (FIG. 7-20). The chromosomes then rotate so that the two strands no longer cross each other but are still held together by covalent linkages. An endonuclease cleaves the DNA strands, breaking the heteroduplex and establishing two independent chromosomes. In some cases, cleavage by the endonuclease results only in the exchange of DNA in the short region where the heteroduplex formed; this type of exchange does not establish recombinant DNA molecules. In other cases, the action of the endonuclease results in the formation of chromosomes that exchanged large portions of homologous DNA regions. Recombinant DNA is formed by such exchanges.

In *E. coli*, homologous recombination depends on the enzymes coded for by three recombination genes—designated *rec*A, *rec*B, and *rec*C. These enzymes generate single-stranded DNA that can then interact with a double-stranded DNA macromolecule. In this process the single-stranded DNA locates a region of homology within the duplex, pairs with the complementary strand, and displaces the other strand.

Mutations in the *rec* genes greatly reduce the frequency of recombination. The first relevant observation in this case involved a series of mutant genes labeled *rec*A, *rec*B, *rec*C, and *rec*D. The first mutant gene, *rec*A, was found to diminish genetic exchange in bacteria 1,000-fold, nearly eliminating it altogether. The other *rec* mutations reduced exchange by about 100 times. Clearly, the normal wild type products of these genes have some essential role in the process of genetic exchange.

The RecA protein catalyzes an ATP-driven assimilation reaction in which the single-stranded DNA hybridizes with a duplex (double-stranded) DNA macromolecule. The RecA protein has a strong affinity for single-stranded DNA. The enzymes coded for by the *rec*B and *rec*C genes are involved in unwinding double helical DNA and breaking the chains into small fragments. The binding creates a DNA-protein complex that migrates until the single-stranded DNA reaches its homologous region within the duplex. When the homologous region is encountered, the single-stranded DNA replaces its counterpart in the initial duplex. Once the hybrid duplex is formed, the RecA protein is released.

Nonhomologous Recombination

Exchanges of DNA can also occur between segments of DNA having quite different nucleotide sequences. This type of recombination, called **nonhomologous recombination,** occurs when the extent of homology between the regions of DNA that are exchanged is limited. Nonhomologous recombination, which also is called **nonreciprocal recombination,** can be a site-specific exchange process, that is, a process in which DNA exchange occurs only at a given location within the genome. Nonhomologous recombinations permit the joining of DNA molecules from different sources. For example, viral DNA may become incorporated into a bacterial chromosome, plasmids may enter into bacterial chromosomes, and the locations of DNA segments may be transposed within chromosomes.

There probably are several mechanisms that can bring about nonreciprocal recombination. Some enzymes that are different from those involved in reciprocal recombination appear to be involved in the site-specific transposition of genetic information. The *rec* genes are not involved in nonreciprocal recombination, and microorganisms deficient in these enzymes that are needed for homologous recombination still carry out nonreciprocal transpositions. In nonreciprocal exchanges of DNA, the lack of large regions of DNA homology suggests that DNA–protein interactions, rather than base pairing, have a particularly important role in the insertion process.

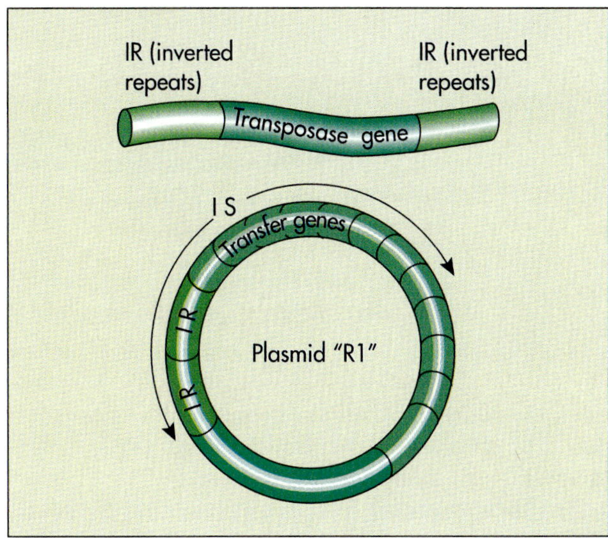

FIG. 7-21 An insertion sequence (IS) has inverted repeats that facilitate its nonreciprocal recombination; an IS may also code for a transposase.

TRANSPOSABLE GENETIC ELEMENTS

Transposable genetic elements have nucleotide sequences that enable them to undergo nonreciprocal recombination. Genes on such transposable elements move from one location to another and are therefore sometimes called "jumping genes." The ends of the transposable genetic elements often contain inverted repetitive sequences of nucleotide bases that permit the folding of DNA stabilized by hydrogen bonding between complementary bases within the DNA macromolecule. The occurrence of these inverted sequences appears to be important in establishing the ability of genetic elements to exhibit nonreciprocal recombination.

Insertion Sequences

An **insertion sequence (IS)** is one type of transposable genetic element (FIG. 7-21). An IS can move around bacterial chromosomes, so that at different times it occurs at different locations on the chromosome. ISs are small, transposable genetic elements with about 1,000 nucleotide bases (Table 7-4). An IS is not homologous with the regions of the plasmids or the chromosomes into which it is inserted. It has an identical nucleotide sequence repeated at each end. The occurrence of inverted terminal repeats allows for base pairing that is essential for transposition to occur. The nucleotide bases in the IS regions often do not appear to code for structural proteins but may have a regulatory function and may be involved in specifying the locations at which site-specific recombination occurs. ISs, for example, can alter a promoter site and thereby affect the expression of nearby genes. They may also code for *transposase,* an enzyme that is required for transposition.

Transposons

Transposons, like ISs, have identical nucleotide sequences that are repeated at each end of the DNA molecule, and these terminal nucleotide sequences appear to establish the basis for their enzymatic insertion (Table 7-5). **Transposons** are transposable ge-

TABLE 7-4 Properties of Insertion Sequences

DESIGNATION	SIZE (BASE PAIRS)	DIRECT REPEAT AT TARGET (BASE PAIRS)	TERMINAL REPEATS (BASE PAIRS)
IS*1*	768	9	30, inverted
IS*2*	1,327	5	32, inverted
IS*3*	1,400	3–4	32, inverted

TABLE 7-5 Properties of Some Transposons

DESIGNATION	SIZE (BASE PAIRS)	DIRECT REPEAT AT TARGET (BASE PAIRS)	CORE ENCODES	TERMINAL REPEATS (BASE PAIRS)
Tn*1*	5,000	5	Ampicillin resistance	38; inverted
Tn*5*	5,700	9	Kanamycin resistance	1,400; inverted
Tn*9*	2,600	9	Chloramphenicol resistance	768 (IS*1*); direct
Tn*10*	9,300	9	Tetracycline resistance	1,400 (IS*10*); inverted

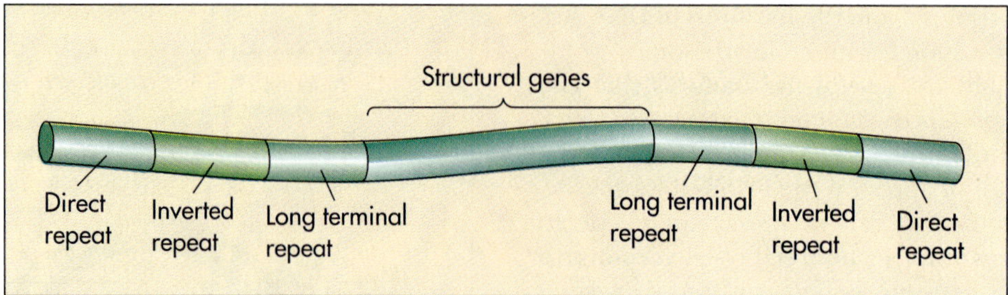

FIG. 7-22 A transposon has repeat sequences and a series of structural genes.

netic elements that contain genetic information for the production of structural proteins (FIG. 7-22). Many code for antibiotic resistance.

The distinction between transposons and ISs is not always clear, and some ISs may code for proteins whose functions have yet to be recognized. In some cases, transposons may be constructed by the attachment of ISs to structural genes. Recombination can occur between an IS on a bacterial chromosome and an IS on a transposon. For example, the F plasmid may be incorporated into the bacterial chromosome by recombination between the IS on the F plasmid and a homologous IS on the bacterial chromosome.

In **conservative transposition,** the transposon is excised from one location and inserted at another. There is no change in copy number in this process, only a change in location. Transposon Tn5 is an example of a transposable genetic element that exhibits conservative transposition. In contrast, bacteriophage Mu exhibits **replicative transposition.** In this process, a copy of the transposable DNA is made and inserted at a new location. The source transposon is retained and does not move from its site. The copy number of the transposon increases as a result of this process.

In some cases, the transposon inserts at the same site but in the reverse direction. This inverts the order of nucleotides and may alter gene expression. The flip flop or phase inversion of genes is involved in flagella protein production in some Gram-negative bacteria, including *Salmonella.* Different functional flagella proteins are made depending on the orientation of a transposon.

Transposon Mutagenesis

Transposons provide a mechanism for obtaining mutants because the insertion of a transposon within a gene alters the nucleotide sequence of the gene (FIG. 7-23). This establishes a mutation in the gene into which the transposon inserts. Often a transposon eliminates the activities of the gene into which it inserts. If the transposon contains the genes for antibiotic resistance it is very easy to select strains into which the transposon has inserted. Tn 5 has the genes for

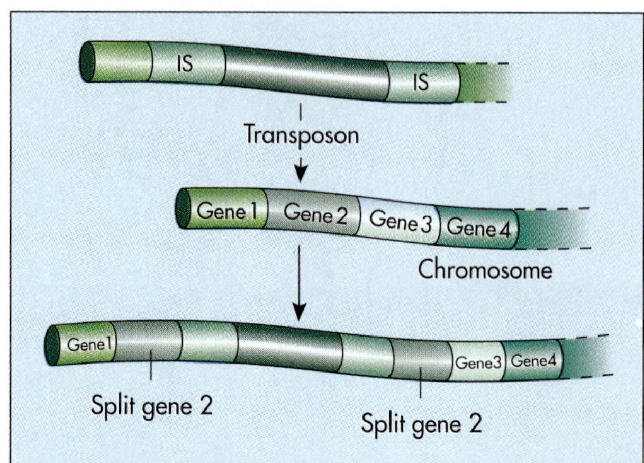

FIG. 7-23 A transposon can insert within a gene, splitting that gene. In this manner the transposon can cause a mutation by altering the nucleotide sequence of that gene. Transposon mutagenesis often results in the inactivation of genes.

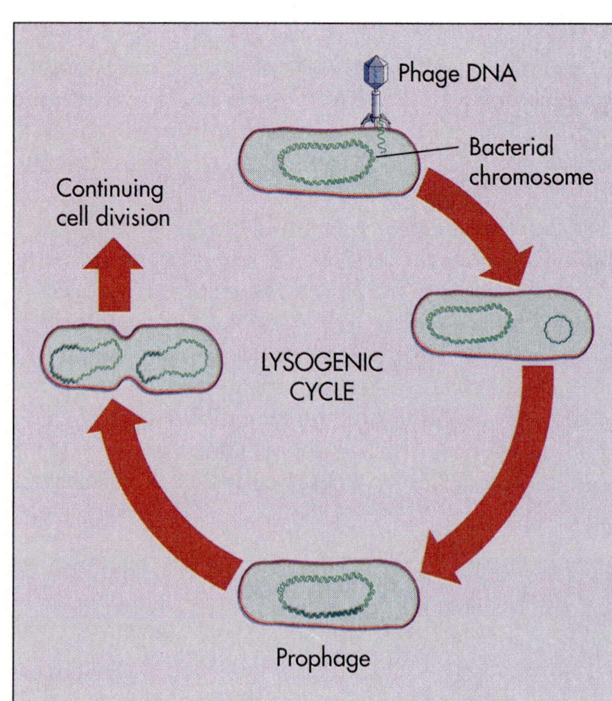

FIG. 7-24 Lysogenic conversion occurs when a temperate phage transfers bacterial DNA that it has acquired and that DNA recombines with the DNA of the host cell. The bacterial cell then replicates the phage DNA along with the bacterial chromosome DNA.

neomycin and kanamycin resistance and Tn10 has the gene for tetracycline resistance. Plating onto a medium containing tetracycline cells containing Tn10 can be selected and, likewise, plating onto a medium with either kanamycin or neomycin can be used to select cells containing Tn5. Subsequent screening on various media of those selected strains of cells can be employed to detect auxotrophic mutants.

Lysogeny

A viral genome may be incorporated into a bacterial chromosome in the process called **lysogeny** (FIG. 7-24). The genes of temperate bacterial viruses (viruses that are capable of lysogeny) can be expressed by the bacterial host, with the bacterium producing proteins that are coded for by the viral genes. This process is called **lysogenic conversion**. In *Corynebacterium diphtheriae*, the presence of a temperate phage renders the bacterium pathogenic. Strains of *C. diphtheriae* that contain the viral genome produce proteins that are toxins and cause the disease symptoms of diphtheria, whereas strains of *C. diphtheriae* that lack the incorporated viral genome are harmless nonpathogens.

7.4 DNA TRANSFER IN PROKARYOTES

In bacteria, genetic exchange followed by recombination occurs principally by three mechanisms that differ in the way DNA is transferred between a donor and a recipient cell (FIG. 7-25). Transformation occurs when free, or naked, DNA moves from a donor to a recipient cell. Transduction happens when DNA is carried from a donor to a recipient bacterial cell by a virus. Conjugation, or mating, requires cell–cell contact for transfer of DNA from a donor to a recipient cell.

TRANSFORMATION

In **transformation** a free DNA molecule is transferred from a donor to a recipient bacterium. The donor bacterium leaks its DNA, generally as a result of lysis of the bacterium, and the recipient bacterium takes up the DNA. Transformation is an example of a reciprocal recombinational event, and if the allelic forms of the donor and recipient genes are not identical, the progeny of the recipient cell may have a composite

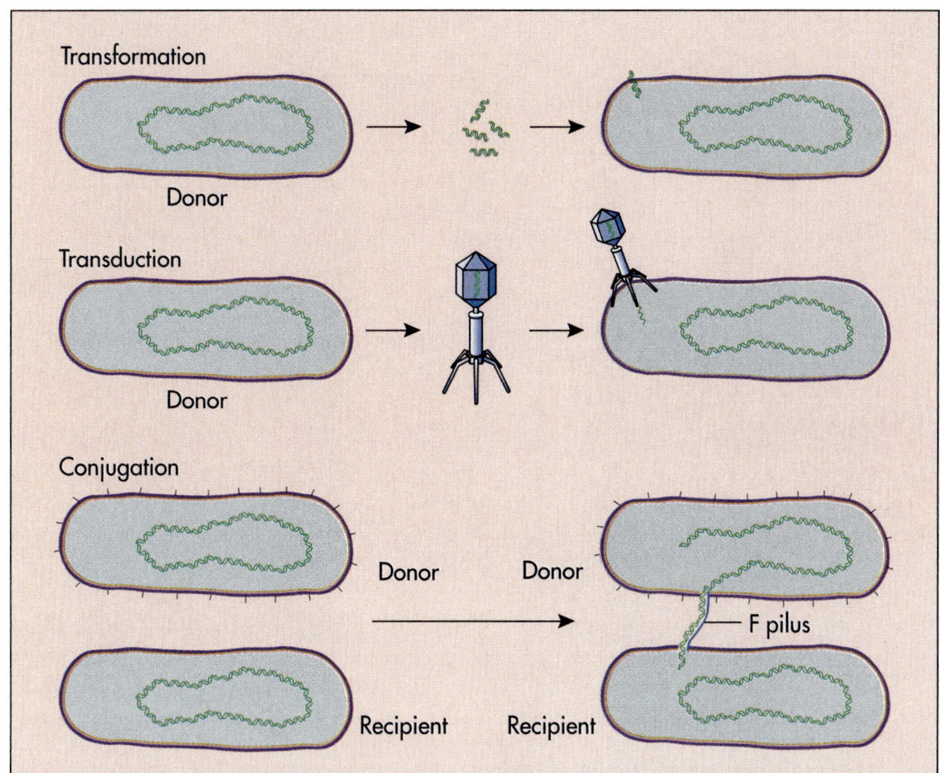

FIG. 7-25 Three natural processes lead to movement of DNA from a donor to a recipient cell and the formation of a recombinant cell: transformation (transfer of naked DNA); transduction (transfer of DNA via a phage); and conjugation (transfer by direct mating contact).

(hybrid) genome different from that of either the donor or the recipient strain.

To take up DNA, a recipient cell must be **competent,** that is, it must have a site for binding the donor DNA at the cell surface and its plasma membrane must be in a state so that free DNA can pass across it. Competent cells have a limited number of binding sites at the surface to which donor DNA can attach. DNA is then transported across the plasma membrane. A short 10 to 12 base pair specific nucleotide sequence in the donor DNA often serves as a signal for uptake. Transformation is favored in strains lacking DNase, which are enzymes that degrade DNA. Treatment with DNase eliminates transformation and is one way of demonstrating that naked DNA is involved in the transfer from donor to recipient cell.

The competency of a cell, that is, the ability to take up and not to degrade naked DNA, depends on its growth phase and environmental conditions. Temperature and cation concentration have a marked influence on the efficiency of transformation. Treating *E. coli* with high concentrations of magnesium or calcium ions and incubating at 5° C for 12 hours greatly enhances the uptake of DNA. Such treatments alter the properties of the cell wall so that it is more accessible to interaction with transforming DNA. They may shield the transforming DNA from phosphate groups of the outer membrane that otherwise restrict the binding and uptake of the free DNA.

Relatively few bacterial genera are capable of taking up naked DNA. When DNA is taken up by *Haemophilus,* one strand of the double helical DNA is enzymatically degraded. *Bacillus, Streptococcus,* and *E. coli* take up only single-stranded DNA. A competence specific protein associates with the intact DNA and protects it from nuclease digestion. The intact strand of DNA forms a heteroduplex with the bacterial chromosome of the recipient bacterium. A nuclease degrades the corresponding region of DNA in one of the strands of the recipient cell, and ligases join the donor DNA with the DNA of the recipient bacterial chromosome.

The classic example of transformation involves the bacterium *Streptococcus pneumoniae* (FIG. 7-26). One strain of this bacterium produces a capsule and is a virulent pathogen (disease-causing microorganism),

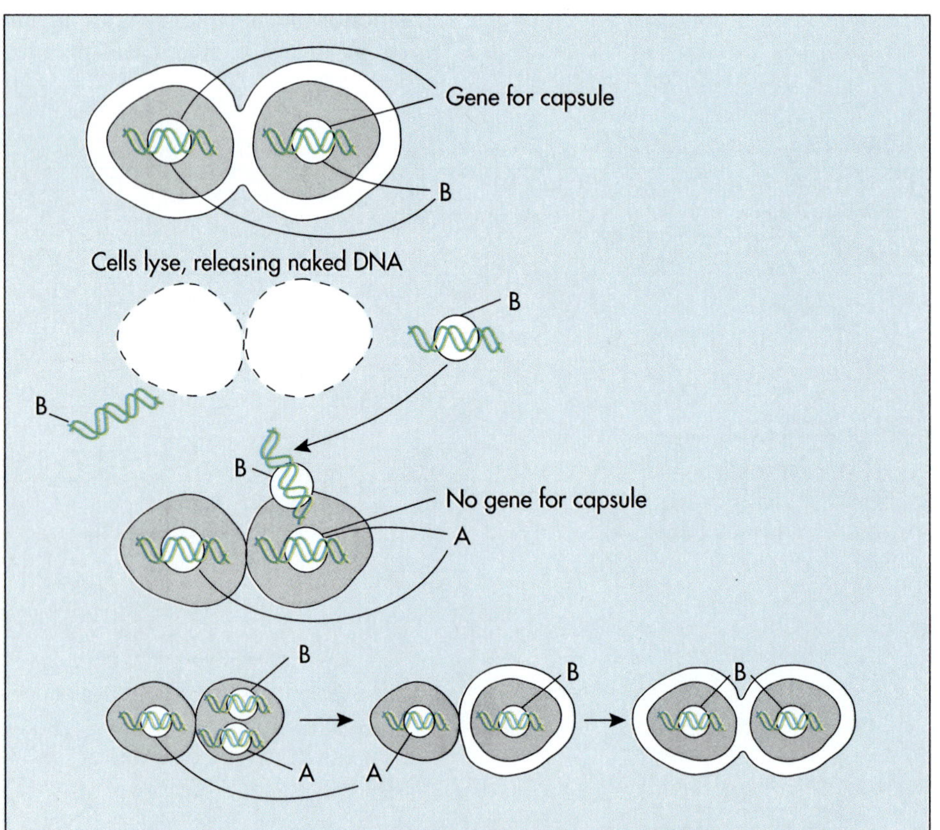

FIG. 7-26 The transformation of *Streptococcus pneumoniae* is the classic example showing that the properties of a bacterial strain can be altered by the transfer of naked DNA. The gene for capsule production (designated B) is released from cells that lyse and taken up by nonencapsulated bacterial cells that have an inactive gene (designated A). Recombination results in the replacement of the inactive A form of the gene with the active B form so that the recombinant cells acquire the ability to produce capsules.

whereas another strain of the same bacterium lacks the genetic information for capsule production and is avirulent (non-disease-causing microorganism). When dead cells of the virulent strain are mixed with avirulent live bacteria, transformation occurs, producing a mixture of avirulent and virulent bacteria. The DNA containing the genes for capsule production leaks out of the dead bacteria and is taken up by the living bacteria that normally lack the genetic information for capsule production. Recombination occurs and the progeny of the transformed bacteria become capable of producing capsules. In this manner, nonpathogenic strains are transformed into deadly pathogens.

Transduction

In **transduction**, DNA is transferred from a donor to a recipient cell by a viral carrier. For transduction a virus must acquire genes of the host cell in which it reproduces. A bacteriophage, for example, can acquire bacterial DNA when it infects a bacterial host cell and can then transfer this acquired bacterial DNA to another bacterial cell.

Generalized Transduction

Generalized transduction brings about the general transfer of genes. This process results in the exchange of any of the homologous alleles. In generalized transduction, pieces of bacterial DNA are accidentally acquired by developing bacteriophage during their normal replication within a host bacterial cell (FIG. 7-27). The normal replication of bacteriophage involves the invasion of a host cell, the replication of the virus within the host, and the lysis (bursting) of the host cell to release the newly formed phage.

If a bacteriophage carries bacterial instead of viral DNA, it cannot cause lysis in a recipient bacterium. Such phage are called **defective phage,** since they do not cause death of a host cell. Defective phage, however, can attach to and inject DNA into a recipient bacterium, permitting it to carry bacterial DNA from a donor cell and inject it into a recipient bacterial cell. Once inside the recipient cell, the DNA may be degraded by nucleases, in which case, genetic exchange does not occur. The injected DNA, however, may undergo homologous recombination. If recombination occurs, the transduced recipients may possess new combinations of genes.

Specialized Transduction

Specialized transduction results in transmission of a specific bacterial DNA region. The incorporation of the phage DNA into the bacterial chromosome is an example of nonhomologous recombination (FIG. 7-28). Lambda (λ) and mu (μ) bacteriophage are capable of establishing *lysogeny*, in which the phage

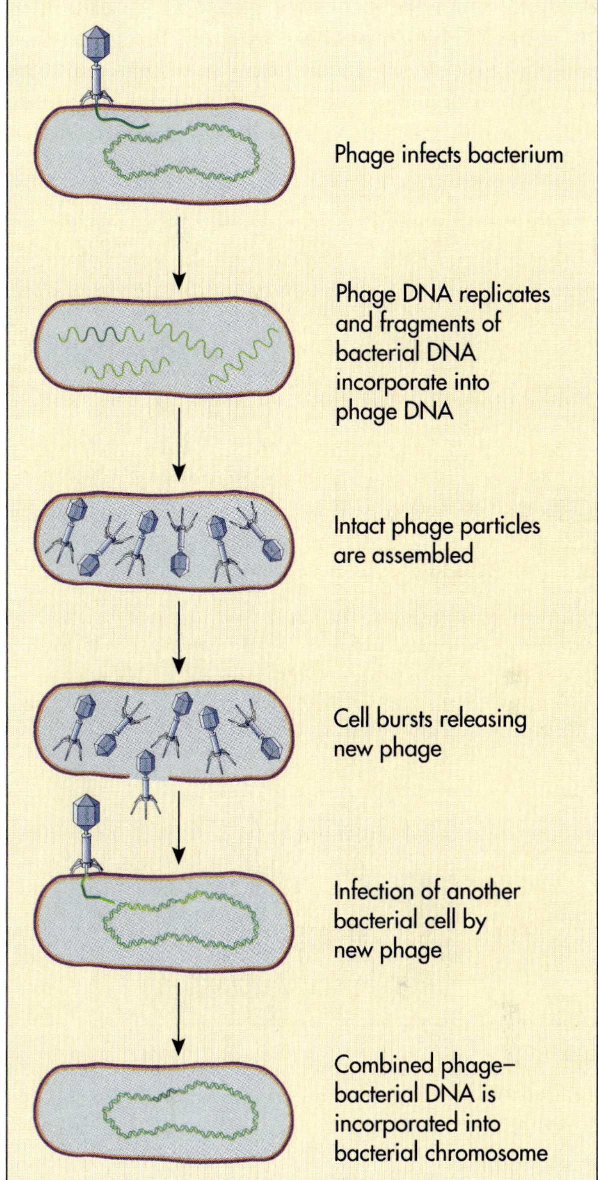

FIG. 7-27 Transduction transfers bacterial DNA via a phage. Bacterial DNA is mixed with phage DNA during phage replication within a bacterial host cell. The phage carries the bacterial DNA along with phage genes to another host cell, where recombination (transduction) occurs.

genome is incorporated into the bacterial genome. When this occurs, the phage DNA occasionally carries with it adjacent bacterial genes when viral replication occurs and leaves behind some of the viral genes. This makes the phage defective in some viral genes. The formation of defective phage establishes a viral carrier of bacterial DNA.

Because there is a specific site for incorporation of the phage DNA into the bacterial chromosome, only the genes that are adjacent to the site of insertion of the viral genome may be transferred by specialized transduction. As an example, the λ phage of *E. coli* transfers either the genes for galactose utilization or the genes for biotin synthesis by specialized transduction, because these are the two genes that flank the site where this phage inserts its DNA into the bacterial chromosome. Lambda phage containing *E. coli* DNA may infect new host cells but are unable to insert DNA into the bacterial chromosome in the normal manner because they lack the necessary insertion sequence. However, successful insertion can occur in the presence of a second normal bacteriophage. This type of recombination produces a bacterial chromosome with a section containing both normal and defective phage DNA molecule and two loci for either the galactose or biotin genes. In this manner, the recipient bacterium becomes diploid for either galactose or biotin. If these genes are of different allelic forms, the organism produced by specialized transduction is heterozygous.

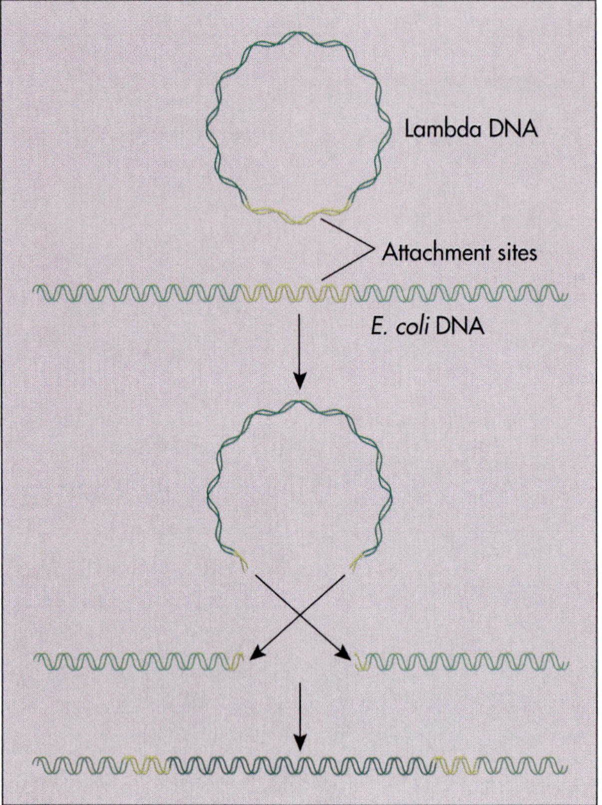

FIG. 7-28 Specialized transduction by λ phage results in the transfer of a limited number of specific genes by nonhomologous recombination.

CONJUGATION

Conjugation (mating) requires the establishment of physical contact between the donor and recipient bacterial cells of the mating pair. To demonstrate that contact is needed for mating, two different auxotrophic strains can be placed in a U-shaped tube separated by only a glass disk barrier that is impermeable to cells. The barrier blocks physical contact, and thus conjugation. Free DNA and phages, however, can pass through the membrane, and thus the other recombinational processes of transduction and transformation can still occur.

Formation of Mating Pairs

The physical contact between mating cells of *E. coli* is established by the F pilus (FIG. 7-29). The F plasmid confers the ability to produce the F pilus needed to form mating pairs of *E. coli* and other Gram-negative bacteria. It is one of several conjugative plasmids. Gram-negative bacterial strains that produce F pili act as donors during conjugation, whereas those lacking the F plasmid are recipient strains. The F plasmid con-

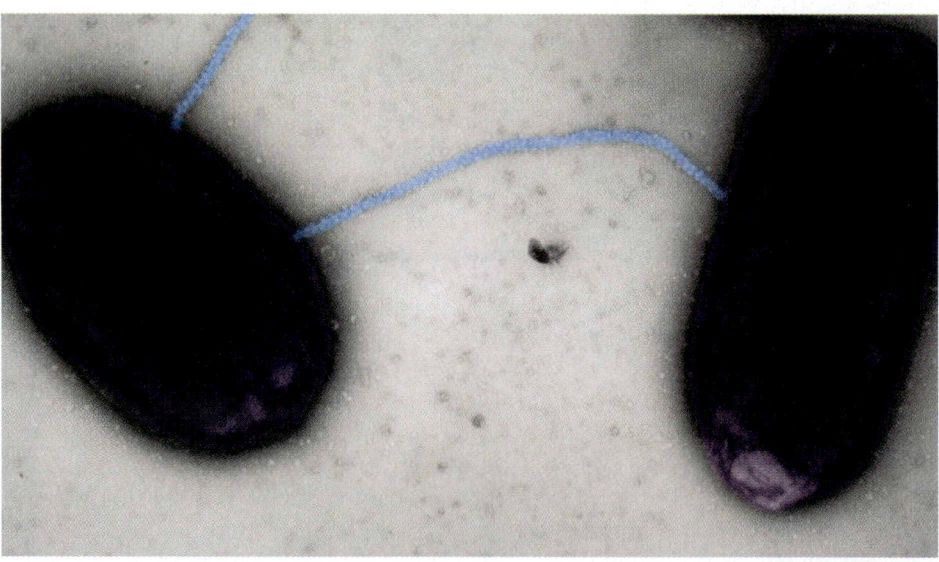

FIG. 7-29 Colorized micrograph of mating cells of *Escherichia coli.* The cells are joined by the F pilus *(blue)* of the donor strain. (24,800×).

tains certain genes (*rep* genes) that allow it to be replicated by the host cell. The F plasmid belongs to the *Inc*F1 incompatibility group; that is, the F plasmid is not replicated when another plasmid of this incompatibility group is present.

Recipient bacterial strains are designated F⁻ and donor strains are designated either F⁺ if the F plasmid is independent or **Hfr (high frequency recombination strain)** if the F plasmid DNA is incorporated into the bacterial chromosome (FIG. 7-30). The F plasmid may incorporate at different specified sites within the bacterial chromosome. It may also later become detached from the bacterial chromosome, reestablishing itself and sometimes carrying genes from the chromosome, in which case the plasmid is called an F′ plasmid. For example, the F′ lac plasmid contains genes from the *lac* locus (genes involved in lactose utilization) of the bacterial chromosome.

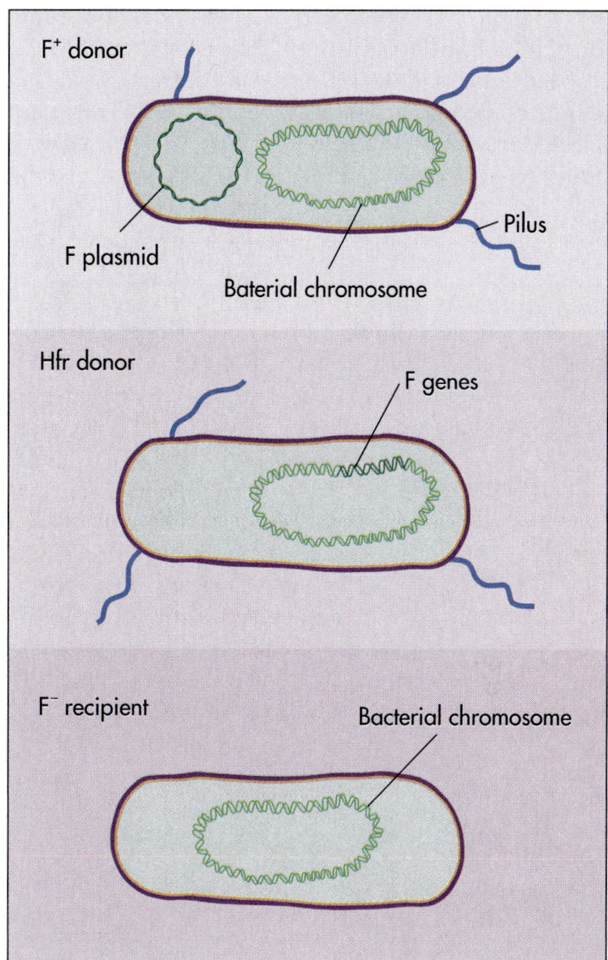

FIG. 7-30 Donor bacteria that have the fertility gene (F gene) produce F pili. In F⁺ strains the F gene is on a plasmid. The F gene can be incorporated into the bacterial chromosome to produce donor strains designated Hfr (high frequency recombination strains).

Conjugative Gene Transfer

The F plasmid and several others, collectively known as **conjugative plasmids,** encode for self-transfer. When F⁻ cells are mixed with F⁺ cells, virtually all become F⁺ because the transfer of the F plasmid occurs at a high frequency. Chromosomal genes are transferred to the F⁻ cell along with the F plasmid, but at a lower frequency. The donor cell replicates one strand of DNA using *rolling circle DNA replication,* a process in which one of the strands of the double helical DNA is nicked and replicated using the unnicked strand as a template. The original nicked strand becomes displaced as the replication fork "rolls" around the circular DNA. Rolling circle replication of DNA does not result in semiconservative replication because the daughter molecules of newly synthesized DNA do not contain any of the original parental strands.

In addition to mediating self-transfer, the F plasmid mediates the transfer of other plasmids that are incapable of self-transfer. The ability of the F plasmid to mobilize chromosomal DNA rests with its complement of insertion sequences. The F plasmid occasionally interacts with the chromosome or another plasmid, causing some or all of this other element also to be transferred. The F plasmid can replicate only in Gram-negative enteric bacteria, but other conjugative plasmids can self-transfer in other Gram-negative bacteria. Some conjugative plasmids have a broad host range, replicating in most Gram-negative bacteria. Not all conjugative plasmids, however, readily mobilize the transfer of chromosomal DNA.

Normally, only a portion of the donor bacterial chromosome is transferred during bacterial mating. The precise portion of the DNA that is transferred depends on the time of mating, that is, on how long the F pilus maintains contact between the mating cells. When an F⁺ cell is mated with an F⁻ cell, the F plasmid DNA is usually transferred from the donor to the recipient (FIG. 7-31). The F plasmid does not normally recombine with the bacterial chromosome of the recipient bacterium. Instead, the single-stranded linear DNA molecule that is transferred acts as a template for the synthesis of a complementary strand of DNA, and the double-stranded DNA then reestablishes a circular form. The independent circular F plasmid confers the genetic information for acting as a donor strain, and the offspring of the recipient of such a cross, therefore, are mostly donor strains.

When an Hfr strain is mated with an F⁻ strain, the bacterial chromosome with the integrated F plasmid begins rolling circle DNA replication in response to attachment of the F pilus, that is, replication of the DNA in which a single strand is copied and "rolls" off the circular chromosome (FIG. 7-32). A single strand of DNA is transferred from the donor Hfr cell to the F^- bacterium, and the DNA that is transferred may undergo homologous recombination with the recipient DNA. Only part of the F plasmid DNA normally is transferred in this type of mating cross, and as a result, the recipient cell normally remains F^-. However, a relatively large portion of the bacterial chromosome is transferred from the donor to the recipient, and this results in a relatively high frequency of recombination of genes of the bacterial chromosome when Hfr strains are mated with F^- strains.

Conjugational genetic exchange has not been as well studied in Gram-positive bacteria. In one Gram-positive bacterium examined, *Enterococcus faecalis*, pili do not play a role in this process. Instead, plasmid-containing cells form clumps with cells that lack the plasmid, and plasmid transfer occurs within these clumps. Clumping results from the interaction between an aggregation substance on the surface of the plasmid-containing cell and a binding substance on the surface of a plasmid-lacking recipient. The aggregation substance is produced only when a plasmid-containing (donor) cell is in close proximity to a cell that lacks that particular plasmid (recipient cell).

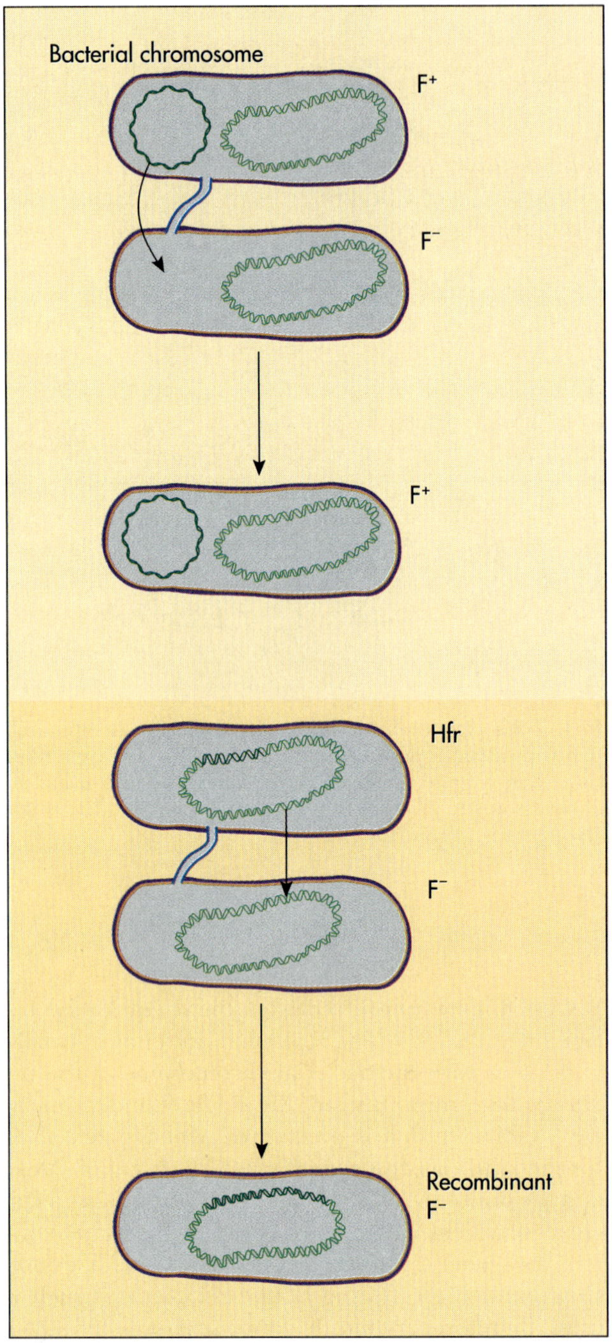

FIG. 7-31 The mating of a donor F^+ strain with a recipient F^- strain (top) results in transfer of the F plasmid and the production of F^+ progeny; there is relatively little recombination. The mating of an Hfr strain with an F^- strain (bottom) results in transfer of many genes from the bacterial chromosome and a high frequency of recombination; the F gene is not transferred so that the progeny are F^- recipient strains.

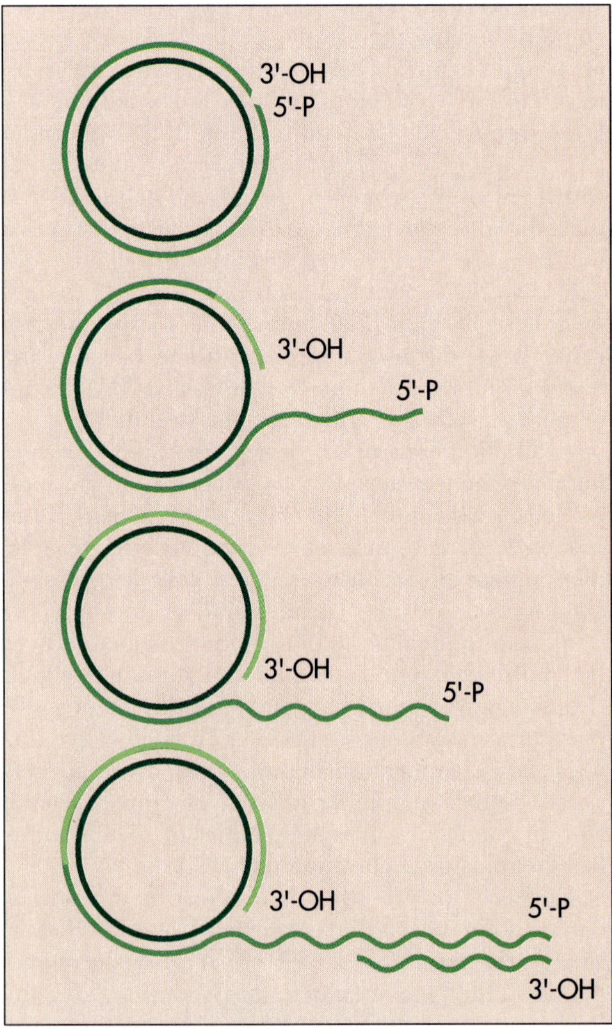

FIG. 7-32 The transfer of DNA from an Hfr strain involves copying of a single strand of DNA by the rolling circle mechanism; the single strand then moves to the recipient cell.

7.5 GENETIC MAPPING

Recombinants formed from different allelic forms of multiple genes can be used to determine the relative locations of genes (FIG. 7-33). This is called **genetic mapping.** The occurrence of recombinants that result from mating is used to establish a map showing the order and relative locations (loci) of genes. In *E. coli*, mating between Hfr and F$^-$ strains has been used to map large sections of the bacterial chromosome. By vibrating a culture of mating bacteria, one can interrupt mating by breaking the F pilus, which stops further transfer of DNA. Such interruption of mating can be done at various times after conjugational cell–cell contact begins. The order of genes on the bacterial chromosome can be determined by examining the times at which recombinants for given genes are found.

In mating experiments aimed at mapping the order of genes, the recovery of recombinants of marker genes is normally used as a reference point for establishing the fine structure of the genome. If a gene of unknown location shows a high frequency of recombination along with the marker gene, it is likely that the marker and unknown genes are closely associated in the chromosome. If, however, the genes are far apart, it is less likely that recombinants of both the marker gene and the gene of unknown location will occur in the progeny.

Transduction similarly can be used to establish the fine structure of the bacterial genome. In generalized transduction, it is unlikely that genes will undergo cotransduction unless they are closely associated in the bacterial chromosome because the transducing phage carry a very small piece of the bacterial chromosome. Conversely, if two genes are closely linked, it is more likely that they will be cotransduced and recombine than if they are not located adjacently on the bacterial chromosome. Cotransformation can similarly be used to map the microbial genome. Using various processes to achieve genetic exchange, the rates of recombination can be measured and the relative locations of the genes deduced, thus producing a detailed genetic map.

The locations of genes can be determined by the transfer times for recombination as determined by interrupted mating (FIG. 7-34). For example, when an Hfr strain that is Thr$^+$, Leu$^+$, Az^S, T1^S, Lac$^+$, Gal$^+$, Str^S is mated with an F$^-$ strain that is Thr$^-$, Leu$^-$, Az^R, T1^R, Lac$^-$, Gal$^-$, Str^R the genetic markers are threonine biosynthesis (Thr), leucine biosynthesis (Leu), azide sensitivity (Az), phage T1 sensitivity (T1), lactose utilization (Lac), galactose utilization (Gal), and streptomycin sensitivity (Str). The superscript plus ($^+$) indicates that the organism has the genes for biosynthesis or utilization, whereas the superscript minus ($^-$)

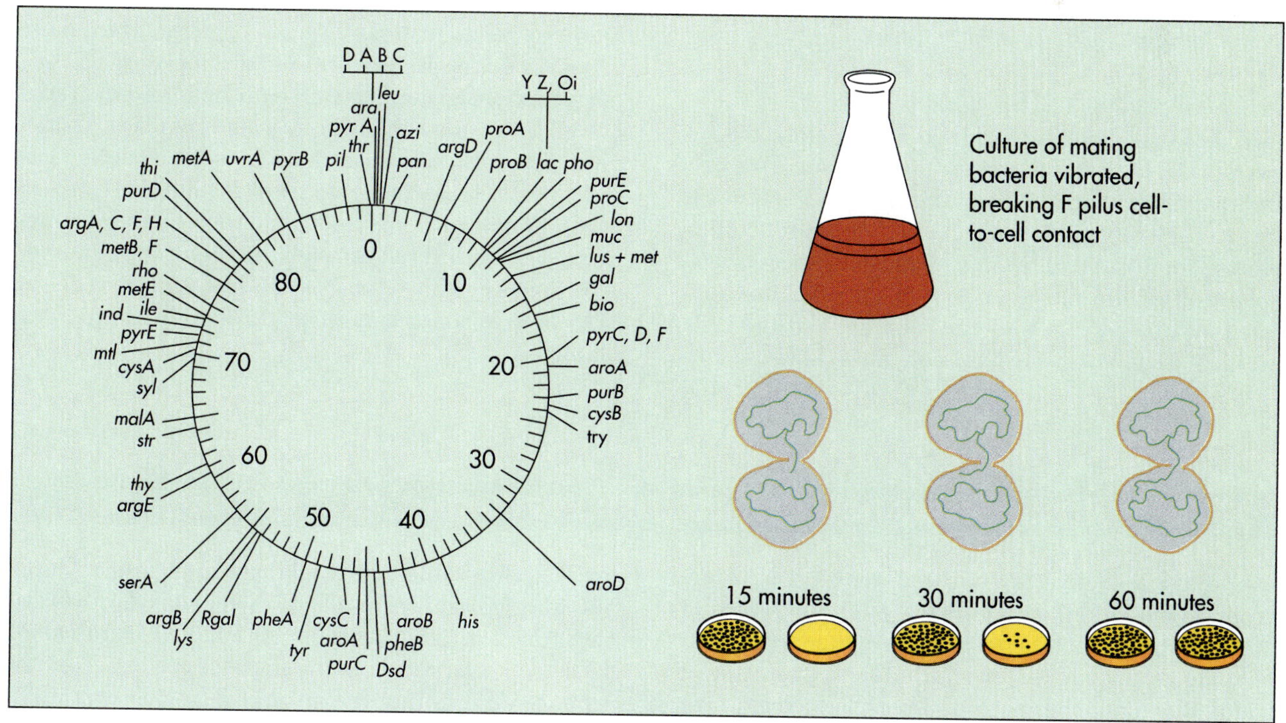

FIG. 7-33 A genetic map showing the relative positions of the genes can be established by mating bacteria for varying times and interrupting the mating to halt further gene transfer. The Petri plate on the left of each pair shows the uninterrupted conjugation frequency, and each plate on the right shows the frequency of gene transfer at the time of interruption.

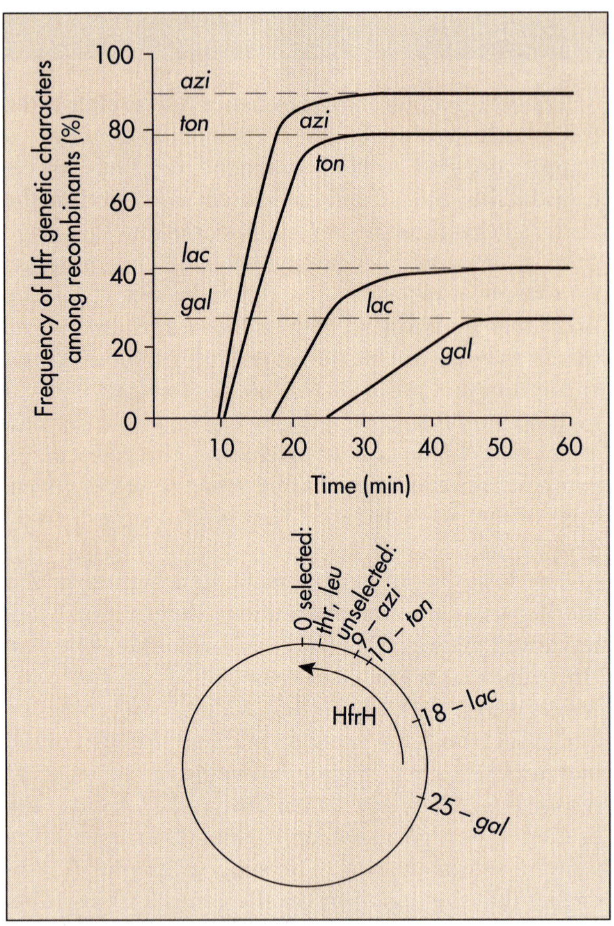

FIG. 7-34 The transfer times of genes and the frequency of recombination indicates the relative positions of genes. Graphs like this are used for gene mapping.

indicates that the organism lacks these genes; the superscript R indicates resistance, and the superscript S indicates sensitivity. Mating of the Hfr and F⁻ strains is initiated by mixing the two cultures at time t_0. After mating for 10, 15, 20, 25, 30, 40, 50, and 60 minutes, a portion of the mixed culture is removed and agitated in a blender to interrupt mating, and the cells are then plated on a medium containing glucose and streptomycin. On this medium, Thr^+ Leu^+ Str^R recombinants are selected, with the respective selected markers of thr^+, leu^+, and str^R. Azide sensitivity (*azi*), phage T1 sensitivity (*ton*), lactose utilization (*lac*), and galactose utilization (*gal*) are unselected markers because this medium does not specifically detect the different alleles of these genes. The Thr^+ Leu^+ Str^R recombinants that form colonies are scored for the alleles of the unselected markers that are present in the selected recombinants by replica plating on media that individually select for *azi, ton, lac,* and *gal.* As shown in FIG. 7-34, the frequencies of unselected markers among Thr^+ Leu^+ Str^R selected recombinants are plotted as a function of time until mating is physically interrupted. Extrapolation of the frequency of each unselected marker to zero indicates the earliest time at which markers become available for recombination with the chromosome of the F^- cell. These times permit the ordering of genes, that is, construction of a genetic map, with the assignment of distances between genes based on the time (in minutes) elapsed from the initiation of conjugation until the earliest time at which a marker from the Hfr strain is detected as a recombinant with the F^- strain.

Based on such determinations, genetic maps have been developed for several bacteria. About 1,400 out of an estimated 3,000 gene loci have been mapped for *E. coli* K12, probably the most studied bacterium. Extensive maps have also been developed for *Salmonella typhimurium, Bacillus subtilis, Pseudomonas aeruginosa, P. putida,* and *Streptomyces coelicolor.* The maps of *E. coli* and *S. typhimurium* reflect the close evolutionary relationship of these bacteria, with most genes occurring in identical relative locations. *B. subtilis* also shows groupings of biosynthetic and degradative genes consistent with integrated regulatory functions. *Pseudomonas* species have biosynthetic and central metabolic pathways located in only half of the bacterial chromosome and numerous catabolic functional genes scattered through the rest of the genome. This suggests that *Pseudomonas* has acquired genes from diverse sources, perhaps through integration of plasmids.

7.6 GENETIC MODIFICATION AND MICROBIAL EVOLUTION

Introduction of diversity into the gene pools of microbial populations establishes a basis for selection and evolution, that is, a basis for the better adaptation of some organisms for survival under a given set of conditions and therefore favored (selected) over other less well-adapted organisms. The basis of evolution lies in the ability to change the gene pool and to maintain favorable new combinations of genes. Mutation and general recombination appear to provide a basis for the gradual selection of adaptive features. In particular, reciprocal recombinations are expected to produce an evolutionary link between closely related organisms, and nonreciprocal recombinational events appear to provide a mechanism for rapid, stepwise evolutionary changes. The fact that unrelated genomes can recombine suggests that different lines of evolution can suddenly merge.

Mutations introduce variability into genomes, resulting in changes in the enzymes that the organism synthesizes. Variations in the genome are passed from one generation to another and are disseminated through populations. Because of their relatively short generation times compared to higher organisms, changes in the genetic information of microorganisms can be widely and rapidly disseminated. Although in some cases the modification of the genome is harmful to the organism (some mutations are lethal or conditionally lethal), a mutation may change the genetic information in a favorable way.

The occurrence of favorable mutations introduces information into the gene pool that can make an organism more fit to survive in its environment and compete with other microorganisms for available resources. Over many generations, natural selective pressures may result in the elimination of unfit variants and the continued survival of organisms possessing favorable genetic information. Change toward more favorable variants in a particular environment is the essence of evolution. Recombination creates new allelic combinations that may be adaptive. Altering the organization of genetic information within populations provides a basis for directional evolutionary change. The exchange of genetic information can produce individuals with multiple attributes that favor the survival of a microbial population. The long-term stability of a population depends on its incorporating adaptive genetic information into its chromosomes.

Plasmids and other transposable genetic elements may contribute to rapid changes in the genetic composition of a population, but the evolutionary stability of such changes is not clear. For example, the incidence of bacteria-containing plasmids that code for antibiotic resistance has certainly increased since the widespread use of antibiotics in medicine, particularly in hospital settings where antibiotic use is extensive (FIG. 7-35). Possession of the genetic information that encodes for antibiotic resistance is adaptive for microorganisms trying to survive in the presence of various antibiotics. The information contained in plasmids, however, can be readily lost, especially if selective pressure diminishes. It is too early to say whether possessing the information for antibiotic resistance will be of long-term evolutionary advantage to bacteria and, if so, whether this information will be permanently incorporated into the bacterial chromosome.

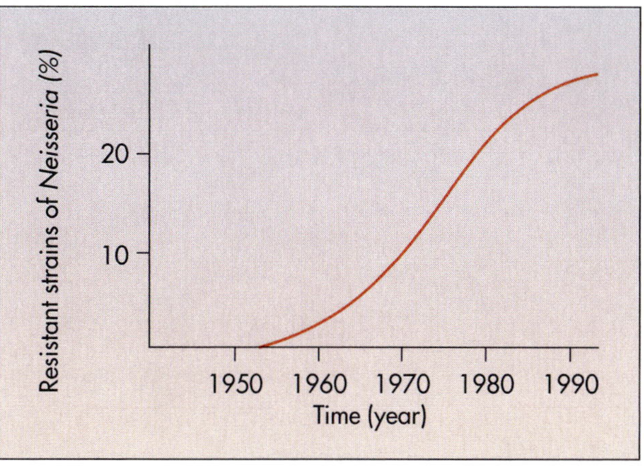

FIG. 7-35 The incidence of antibiotic resistance in some bacterial pathogens has been increasing since the widespread clinical use of antibiotics. The graph shows the incidence of strains of *Neisseria gonorrhoeae* which are resistant to 0.5 unit penicillin/mL.

7.7 RECOMBINANT DNA TECHNOLOGY

Recombinant DNA technology is the intentional recombination of genes from different sources by artificial means. This is the basis for the creation of new genetic varieties of organisms known as **genetic engineering** (FIG. 7-36). It is the foundation of the "biotechnological revolution." Recombinant DNA technology promises to be a powerful tool for understanding basic genetic processes, and genetic engineering has tremendous potential industrial applications. The development of an understanding of the molecular basis of genetics spawned the new and exciting field of genetic engineering, and applications of genetic engineering promise to revolutionize the industrial applications of microorganisms, as well.

The identity of DNA as the hereditary macromolecule in all living cells, the fundamental strategy of DNA replication using the existing DNA as a template, and the universality of the genetic code are critical for recombinant DNA technology. In principle, a specific nucleotide sequence of DNA carries the same genetic information regardless in which cell it occurs. A DNA template from any source should be able to be replicated within any cell into which it is placed. Further, DNA can be altered *in vitro* and placed back into living cells where DNA replication will occur. This results in the formation of a clone of the gene. It permits, in theory, the artificial colony of genes from divergent sources in any cell—human genes in *E. coli, E. coli* genes in human cells, and so forth.

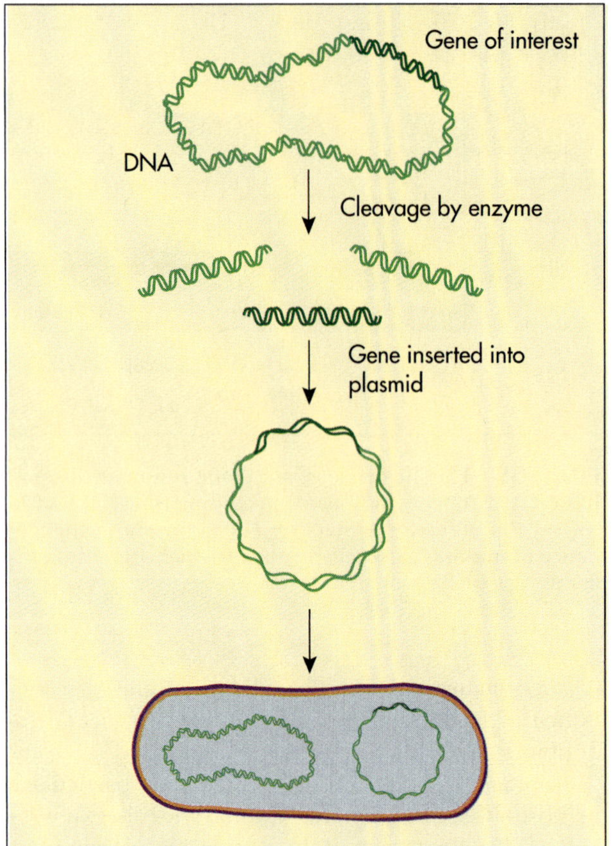

FIG. 7-36 Genetic engineering uses enzymes to cut out target genes and to join DNA to form recombinant DNA molecules. The recombinant DNA contains DNA that may come from diverse sources; for example, bacterial and human DNA can be combined in a recombinant DNA molecule by genetic engineering.

GENE CLONING

The replication of recombinant DNA can be accomplished by **gene cloning.** A collection of clones of individual genes from a specific organism can constitute a **genomic library.** Construction of a genomic library involves obtaining copies of the nucleotide sequences of the genome and cloning these into a suitable vector. Since each cloned DNA segment is relatively small, many separate clones must be constructed to include even a small portion of the total genome of an organism.

In many cases, the nucleotide sequence of DNA to be used for cloning is known or can be deduced from the amino acid sequence of a protein product and knowledge of the genetic code. In other cases, if the sequence of DNA to be used for cloning is unknown, a technique of **shotgun cloning** can be used. The shotgun method involves using restriction endonucleases that break the entire genome into fragments that are each about 20 kb. Each fragment is individually cloned into a suitable vector. Statistically, by examining a high number of clones (about 900 in *E. coli,* which has a total genome length of about 4,000 kb) one of the fragments should contain the sequence in which you are interested. Genes that are isolated in this manner can later be sequenced.

The process of cloning genes typically involves (1) isolation of the DNA to be cloned, (2) incorporation of the source DNA into a segment of DNA used for replication of foreign DNA fragments to form a recombinant DNA molecule, (3) incorporation of the recombinant DNA in the cloning vector into a recipient cell that can replicate the cloning vector, (4) detection of the newly transformed cells containing recombinant DNA, and (5) growth of cultures of cells containing the cloned DNA fragment.

Protoplast Fusion

In some cases, DNA is directly transferred between cells that are artificially fused. Cell fusion is achieved using protoplasts, which are cells that had their walls removed by enzymatic and/or detergent treatment. The protoplasts are protected against lysis due to osmotic shock by suspension in a buffer containing a high concentration of a solute such as sucrose. The membranes of protoplasts can fuse to form a single cell. Protoplast fusion is a particularly useful technique for achieving gene transfer and genetic recombination in organisms with no efficient, natural gene transfer mechanism. Interestingly, more than two strains can be combined in one fusion, generating recombinants that have inherited genes from all parents in the fusion. The basic procedure involves polyethylene glycol–induced fusion of protoplasts followed by the regeneration of normal cells. Protoplast fusion establishes a transient quasi-diploid state during fusion. This permits recombination to occur between complete bacterial chromosomes, as opposed to fragments of the donor bacterial chromosome and the recipient bacterial chromosome.

DNA for Cloning

DNA is isolated from bacterial cells for cloning by lysing the cells and recovering and purifying the DNA. Lysozyme treatment readily releases DNA from Gram-negative bacterial cells. Gram-positive cells are more difficult to lyse and in some cases physical disruption, such as sonication or freezing and thawing, is used to break open Gram-positive cells. Once the DNA is released it is often treated with ribonuclease (RNase) to remove any contaminating RNA and phenol to denature and separate contaminating proteins. The DNA is precipitated with cold ethanol. Repeated washing and reprecipitation is employed to produce purified DNA, free of proteins and other cellular components. The DNA sometimes is further purified by cesium-chloride buoyant density ultracentrifugation, electrophoresis, or column chromatography. The purified DNA can then be used for genetic engineering.

In some cases mRNA rather than DNA is isolated as a template, and a copy DNA (cDNA) is then synthesized. This is necessary for cloning some eukaryotic genes because the nucleotide sequences in eukaryotic cells often are discontinuous. cDNA is made by using reverse transcriptase. This enzyme uses an RNA template and synthesizes a complementary DNA strand. The cDNA can then be used for cloning.

DNA sequences can also be produced by chemical or automated nucleotide synthesizing systems. These procedures can produce DNA sequences up to several hundreds of nucleotides in length.

Formation of Recombinant DNA

The ability to manipulate DNA for genetic engineering depends largely on the use of bacterial enzymes called **restriction endonucleases** or **restriction enzymes** that can cut double-stranded DNA at specified locations and **ligases** that can attach segments of double-stranded DNA (FIG. 7-37). These enzymes permit the cutting and splicing of DNA. Restriction endonucleases normally function with DNA methylases (see Chapter 6) to prevent the incorporation of foreign DNA into the genome of a cell by cutting both strands of a foreign DNA molecule. Bacteria usually protect themselves against their own endonucleases by methylating DNA bases at the recognition sites where the endonucleases act, using specific DNA methylases for this purpose.

Restriction endonucleases are named using a system whereby the first letter indicates the genus of the cell from which it was isolated, the next two letters indicate the species, the fourth letter (when needed) indicates the strain, and the number indicates the order of discovery of endonucleases from that strain. For example, the restriction enzyme *Eco*RI was isolated from the genus *Escherichia* (E), species *E. coli* (co), strain R, and it was the first (I) endonuclease isolated from that strain.

Different types of endonucleases vary with respect to the site at which they cut DNA (Table 7-6, p. 274). Type I restriction endonucleases cleave DNA 1-5 Kb away from a recognition site in the DNA nucleotide sequence at a random site. Type II restriction endonucleases cleave the DNA at the recognition site. Type III endonucleases cut the DNA at some precise distance from the recognition site. A type II restriction endonuclease cuts the DNA at a **palindromic sequence** of bases, which is a sequence of nucleotide bases that can be read identically in both the 3′-OH → 5′-P and 5′-P → 3′-OH directions; type II restriction endonucleases frequently produce DNA with staggered single-stranded ends. The ends of the cut DNA that are staggered can act as cohesive or sticky ends during re-

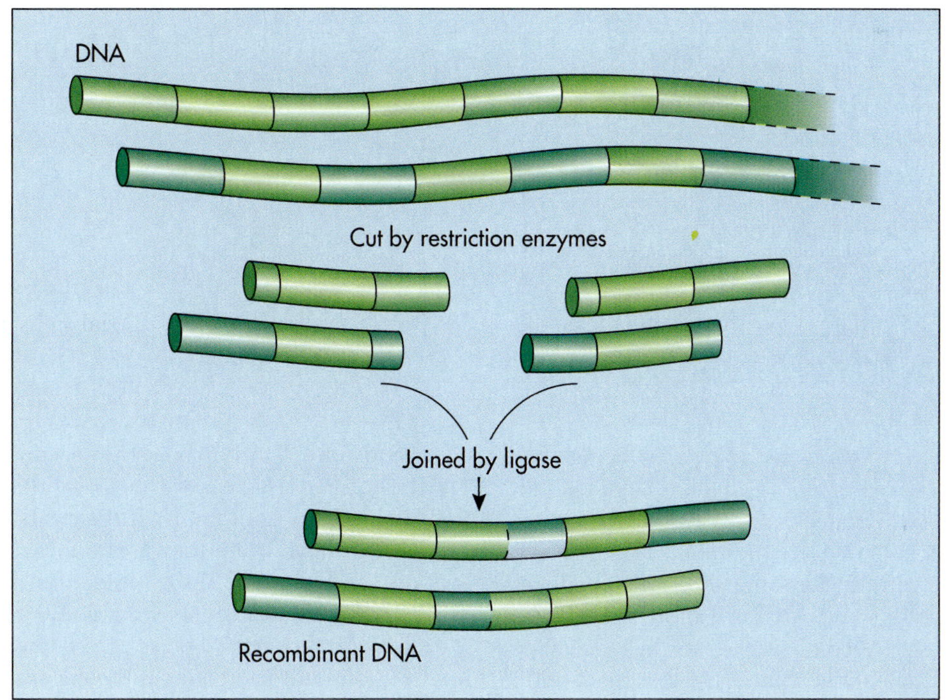

FIG. 7-37 In recombinant DNA technology, restriction enzymes are used to cut fragments of DNA containing specific genes, and ligases are used to join donor and recipient DNA fragments so that recombinant DNA is formed. The recombinant DNA contains DNA that may come from diverse sources; for example, bacterial and human DNA can be combined in a recombinant DNA molecule.

TABLE 7-6 Some Type II Restriction Endonucleases and Their Recognition Sequences

ENZYME	MICROBIAL SOURCE	SEQUENCE	ENZYME	MICROBIAL SOURCE	SEQUENCE
*Alu*I	*Arthrobacter luteus*	5′AGCT3′ 3′TCGA5′	*Kpn*I	*Klebsiella pneumoniae* OK8	5′GGTACC3′ 3′CCATGG5′
*Ava*I	*Anabaena variabilis*	5′CPyCGPuG′ 3′GPuGCPyC5′	*Not*I	*Nocardia otitidis-caviarum*	5′GCGGCCGC3′ 3′CGCCGGCG5′
*Bam*HI	*Bacillus amyloliquefaciens* H	5′GGATCC3′ 3′CCTAGG5′	*Pma*CI	*Pseudomonas maltophila* CB50P	5′CACGTG3′ 3′GTGCAC5′
Bcl I	*Bacillus caldolyticus*	5′TGATCA3′ 3′ACTAGT5′	*Pst*I	*Providencia stuartii* 164	5′CTGCAG3′ 3′GACGTC5′
BglI	*Bacillus globigii*	5′GCCNNNNNNGGC3′ 3′CGGNNNNNNCCG5′	*Pvu*I	*Proteus vulgaris*	5′CGATCG3′ 3′GCTAGC5′
Bgl II	*Bacillus globigii*	5′AGATCT3′ 3′TCTAGA5′	*Pvu* II	*Proteus vulgaris*	5′CAGCTG3′ 3′GTCGAC5′
*Cla*I	*Caryophanon latum* L	5′ATCGAT3′ 3′TAGCTA5′	*Sal*I	*Streptomyces albus* G	5′GTCGAC3′ 3′CAGCTG5′
*Eco*RI	*Escherichia coli* RY13	5′GAATTC3′ 3′CTTAAG5′	*Sau*3A	*Staphylococcus aureus* 3A	5′GATC3′ 3′CTAG5′
*Eco*RV	*Escherichia coli* J62(pLG74)	5′GATATC3′ 3′CTATAG5′	*Sma*I	*Serratia marcescens* Sb	5′CCCGGG3′ 3′GGGCCC5′
*Fok*I	*Flavobacterium okeanokoites*	5′GGATG3′ 3′CCTAC5′	*Sst*I	*Streptomyces stanford*	5′GAGCTC3′ 3′CTCGAG5′
*Hae*III	*Haemophilus aegyptius*	5′GGCC3′ 3′CCGG5′	*Taq*I	*Thermus aquaticus* YTI	5′TCGA3′ 3′AGCT5′
*Hind*III	*Haemophilus influenzae* d	5′AAGCTT3′ 3′TTCGAA′	*Xba*I	*Xanthomonas badrii*	5′TCTAGA3′ 3′AGATCT5′
*Hpa*I	*Haemophilus parainfluenzae*	5′GTTAAC3′ 3′CAATTG5′	*Xho*I	*Xanthomonas holcicola*	5′CTCGAG3′ 3′GAGCTC5′
*Hpa*II	*Haemophilus parainfluenzae*	5′CCGG3′ 3′GGCC5′			

*Methylation site; ↓ or ↑ Endonuclease cleavage site; *Pu,* purine; *Py,* pyrimidine; *N,* any base.

combination, making them suitable for splicing with segments of foreign source DNA that has been excised using the same endonuclease.

Some type II restriction endonucleases cut the DNA in both strands at the same site. This produces fragments with blunt ends that are more difficult to work with to create recombinant DNA. The enzyme terminal deoxynucleotidyl transferase can be used to create artificial homology at the terminal ends of two different DNA molecules. This can be accomplished by adding polyA (polyadenosine) tails to one fragment and polyT (polythymidine) tails to the other. Pairing occurs between homologous regions of complementary bases.

Blunt end ligation is also encountered when two different endonucleases are used: one to open a plasmid ring and another to form a segment of donor DNA. Artificial homology at the terminal ends of the donor and plasmid DNA molecules must be synthesized using the transferase reaction. Pairing occurs between homologous regions of complementary bases, and ligases are used to seal the circular plasmid. The tails left by the action of the endonuclease are cleaved *in vitro,* using exonucleases. By adding a polyT tail to the donor DNA after its excision with an endonuclease, the donor DNA can be made complementary to the polyA tails of the plasmid DNA, permitting the formation of a circular plasmid molecule.

If the same restriction endonuclease is used to cut both the donor and recipient plasmid DNA, the strands will have homologous ends and it will be unnecessary to add polyA and polyT tails. The sealing of the ends of the DNA molecules is accomplished by using ligases. This forms a circular loop of DNA, which contains a foreign segment of DNA that can be replicated *(cloned)* within a suitable host cell.

Using different restriction endonucleases with different cleavage sites in separate reactions on a large sequence of DNA, fragments are generated that have overlapping nucleotide sequences. By identifying the nucleotide sequences and comparing the overlaps, the restriction fragments can be ordered into a **restriction map.** Restriction mapping allows you to determine the sites at which DNA can be cut. This is important in formulating locations where foreign DNA can be inserted in genetic engineering.

Cloning Vectors

A **cloning vector** typically is used to clone a segment of DNA (FIG. 7-38). DNA is commonly cloned in both bacteriophages and plasmids. Plasmid vectors are usually much smaller than phage λ DNA molecules. The insertion of large fragments of foreign DNA into plasmids may cause instability. Therefore plasmids are usually limited to cloning of fragments that contain less than 5,000 base pairs. However, plasmids may be more convenient to use as vectors than phage λ DNA molecules, since plasmid DNA often contains only one restriction site for a particular endonuclease. The amount of foreign DNA inserted into the plasmid DNA is relatively large and the insertion of foreign DNA can easily be observed by ultracentrifugation as an increase in the molecular weight of the plasmid.

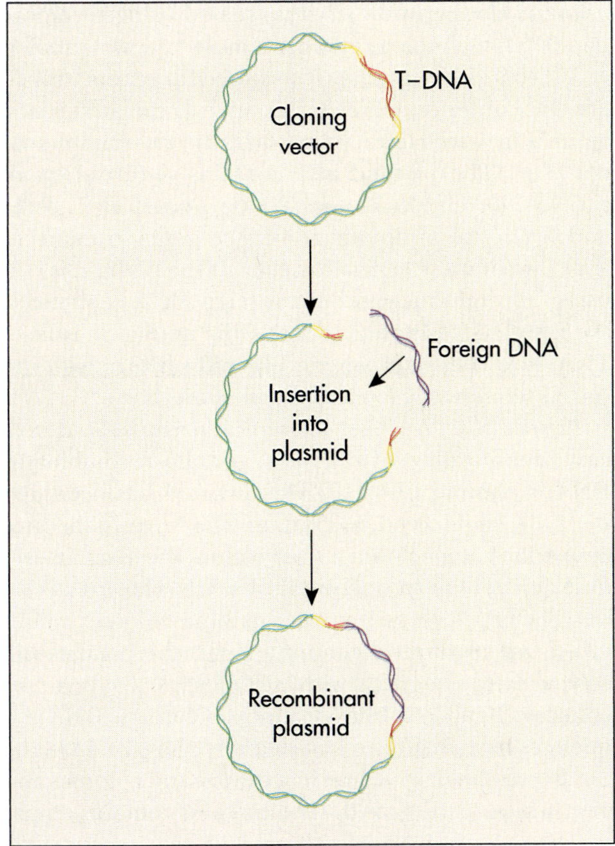

FIG. 7-38 Plasmids commonly are used as cloning vectors for the production of recombinant DNA molecules.

The cloning vector should have certain properties. It should replicate autonomously in a suitable host cell. It should be separable from the host DNA so that it can be purified and should have regions that can accept source DNA without losing self-replication capacity. It should also be able to enter a host cell and replicate to a **high copy number** (large number of repetitive copies of the genes, such as can be achieved by having multiple identical plasmids). It should be stable in the host. Plasmids, bacteriophage (such as λ phage), and phage–plasmid artificial hybrids **(cosmids)** that have these properties are frequently used as cloning vectors.

The cloning vector usually has several single restriction enzyme cleavage sites. These sites permit circular DNA to be opened (linearized) without breaking the DNA into several small pieces. The linearized DNA of the cloning vector can be joined with the DNA to be cloned by ligation. Plasmid pBR322, a commonly used cloning vector, has 26 different single restriction cleavage sites, including sites for *Eco*R1, *Eco*RV, *Sal*I, and *Hind*III. pBR322 also has genes for ampicillin resistance and tetracycline resistance so that it is easily selected on agar plates containing antibiotics. If the insertion occurs at the antibiotic resistance site, resistance is lost because the nucleotide sequence of the antibiotic resistance gene is disrupted, an event known as *insertional inactivation* that is useful for detecting the presence of foreign DNA within a plasmid.

Bacteriophage λ Bacteriophage λ has several properties that make it a good choice for use as a cloning vector. When dealing with a mixture of DNA fragments, λ phage can be used to clone segments of a particular size range from 38.5 to 52.0 kilobase pairs (Kbp). Some λ DNA has been modified so that it contains one or two EcoRI restriction sites; when exposed to EcoRI restriction endonuclease, the DNA yields two or three fragments. The middle fragment contains the genes needed for the incorporation of the phage DNA into the host DNA (lysogeny). The end fragments contain the genes needed for the replication of the phage DNA, packaging of the DNA into the viral protein coat, and death of the host cell (lysis). Lysogeny and lytic death are discussed in greater detail in Chapter 8. If the two end fragments are introduced into *E. coli*, replication of phage DNA can occur but no phage progeny are formed, since the fragments do not form a molecule that is large enough to be packaged. But, if the end fragments are enzymatically ligated to pieces of foreign DNA, the resultant composite DNA may be large enough to be packaged. The recombinant DNA can be introduced into host cells by packaging the DNA *in vitro* and subsequently infecting the cells with the λ phage. Special techniques may be used to detect the inserted DNA.

Various λ phage that are used as vectors have been named Charon after the character in Greek mythology who ferried the spirits of the dead across the River Styx. Charon phage differ in the restriction sites they contain and by the size of the fragment of DNA that can be inserted. A particularly useful λ variant is Charon 16A, in which the β-galactosidase gene, *lacZ*, from *E. coli* is inserted into a nonessential region of λ DNA. Bacteria infected with these Charon phage form blue plaques on agar plates that contain an indicator dye, Xgal (5-bromo-4-chloro-3-indolyl-β-D-galactoside). The *lacZ* also contains a restriction site, so that if foreign DNA is inserted into this site, the recombinant phage that result produce white plaques because a functional β-galactosidase is not made. Other Charon phage such as Charon 27 have mutations in an essential gene to promote biological containment.

Bacteriophage M13 M13 is a filamentous bacteriophage that contains single-stranded DNA as its genetic material. It does not result in lytic cell death as does λ phage. Since several recombinant DNA techniques, such as sequencing by the Sanger method, require the use of single-stranded DNA, phage M13 is ideal for use as a cloning vector.

The single strand of circular DNA contained in the M13 phage particle is called the (+) strand. However, after infection of the host cell, the (+) strand is converted to a double-stranded replicating form (RF) by the synthesis of a complementary (−) strand. Multiple copies of the RF are synthesized. Later, the (+) strands of the RF are packaged and viral progeny are released from the bacterial cell by budding (see Chapter 8). M13 phage differs from most other phage by not being limited to the amount of DNA that is packaged in the mature particle; packaging of larger DNA molecules simply results in the formation of longer phage filaments. Although the host bacteria are not lysed to release progeny M13 phage, they grow more slowly than noninfected cells; infected cells are thereby identified as a plaque or zone of low turbidity in a turbid lawn of noninfected cells.

In the use of bacteriophage M13 as a cloning vector, foreign DNA is inserted into the RF because there is no convenient way to insert foreign sequences into single-stranded DNA. The RF is cut using a restriction endonuclease, combined with foreign DNA fragments, and then the mixture is ligated. The orientation of the foreign DNA into the RF is important because only the (+) strand of the RF will ultimately be packaged into progeny phage particles. Because foreign DNA is inserted in either orientation into individual RFs, both strands of the foreign DNA can be cloned from separate plaques.

Site-directed mutagenesis is a technique in which bacteriophage M13 is frequently used for cloning. In this technique a single and specific base is altered in a gene sequence, producing a mutation at a desired site. After transcription and translation of the gene, the properties of the modified or mutant protein product can be compared to the original or wild type protein. Site-directed mutagenesis can be used to produce a mutant protein with enhanced or diminished enzyme activity, or structural changes in the folding of the protein as a result of amino acid substitutions at a single site. In site-directed mutagenesis, the original DNA sequence is inserted into the (+) strand of M13 DNA (FIG. 7-39). A short, synthetically produced DNA that contains a single base difference from the original sequence is annealed to the insert; the synthetic oligonucleotide will hybridize to the original sequence except at the single base mismatch. DNA polymerases and ligase can then extend the synthetic oligonucleotide to form a complete helix that behaves like a RF. The RF can then be transformed into a bacterial cell and the gene containing the mutant sequence is cloned.

Plasmids pPBR322 and pBR325 Derivatives of plasmid pBR322, most commonly plasmid pBR325, are used for cloning. pBR325 was created using recombinant DNA technology and has a molecular weight of 4×10^6 (5,995 base pairs). It has specific genetic markers that confer on the cell resistance to the antibiotics ampicillin *(amp)*, tetracycline *(tet)*, and chloramphenicol *(cap)*. The plasmid also contains one restriction site for the endonucleases *Eco*RI, *Bam*HI *Bgl*I, *Pst*I, and *Sal*I. The antibiotic resistance genes contain at least one of these restriction sites. If the plasmid is cut using an endonuclease and foreign DNA sequences are inserted, resistance to a specific antibiotic is lost. Therefore cells that contain plasmid pBR325 with inserted sequences can easily be identified.

Plasmid pUC Another vector that permits rapid and easy identification of cells that contain recombinant DNA is plasmid pUC119. This plasmid has been genetically engineered to contain *amp*^{R} (resistance to ampicillin) and cloning sites within the β-galactosidase gene of the *lac* operon. If pUC119 is inserted into *lac*$^-$ bacteria, they will appear as blue colonies when grown on medium containing Xgal; the β-galactosidase activity associated with pUC119 can convert the colorless Xgal to a blue product. If foreign DNA sequences have first been inserted into the pUC119 vector, β-galactosidase will be inactivated and colonies appear white. If the growth medium also contains ampi-

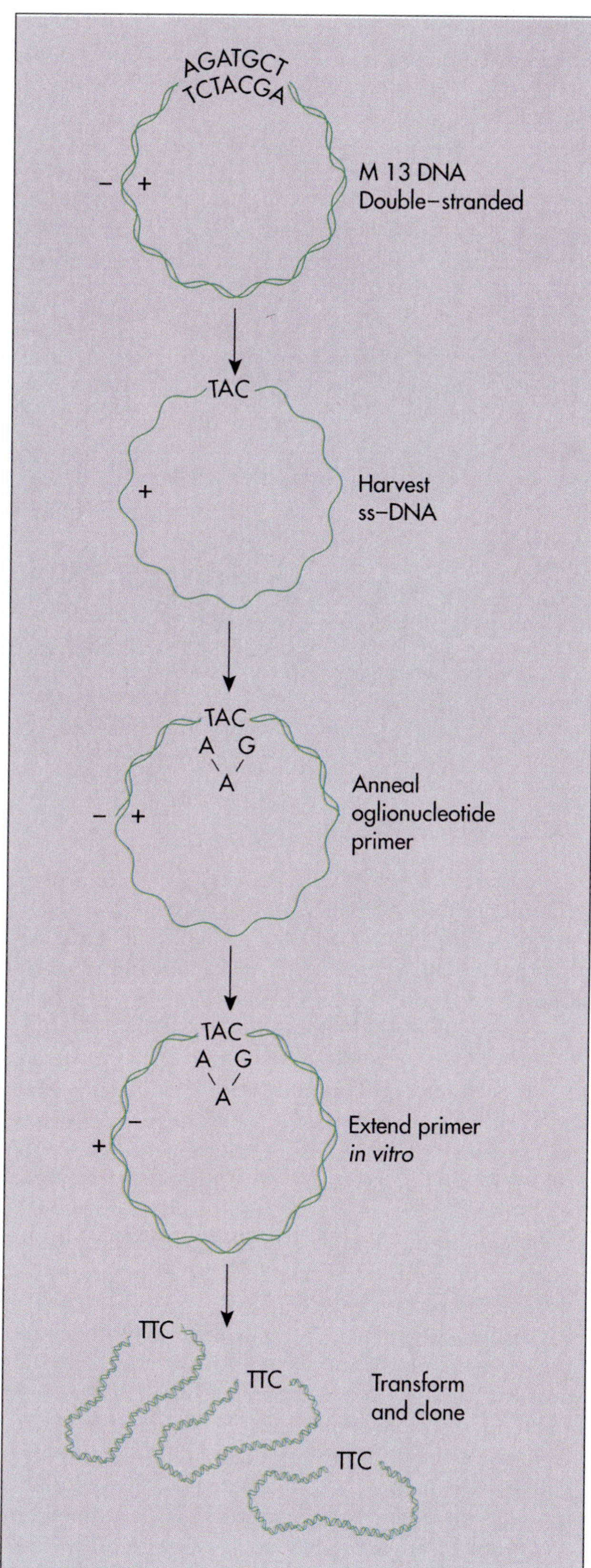

FIG. 7-39 M13 phage are used for site directed mutagenesis. The phage is used as a template for DNA synthesis. An oligonucleotide primer introduces a point mutation because it is designed to have a single base mismatch.

cillin, then the colonies that grow should contain the plasmid, and the color of an individual colony indicates whether it contains recombinant DNA.

Plasmids as Shuttle Vectors Often, cloning vectors are constructed to function in several different types of cells. Such vectors, called **shuttle vectors,** permit the transfer of recombinant DNA from one cell type to another, such as from *Pseudomonas* to *E. coli.* Some vectors have been genetically engineered from yeast DNA and *E. coli* plasmids. These can serve as shuttle vectors that allow the transfer of DNA sequences between *E. coli* and *Saccharomyces cerevisiae,* a yeast. YIp vectors (yeast integrating plasmids) contain a bacterial origin of DNA replication with yeast chromosomal sequences. They can replicate in *E. coli* but not in *S. cerevisiae.* However, these plasmids can integrate into the yeast chromosome. Other plasmids that have been developed include YEp vectors (yeast episomal plasmids), YRp vectors (yeast replicating plasmids), and YCp vectors (yeast centromere plasmids). These allow the incorporation and expression of bacterial genetic sequences in a eukaryotic cell.

Expression Vectors

The ability to clone a gene does not necessarily ensure the production of a useful product. Production requires that a cloned gene be expressed. Because the genetic code is essentially universal, the information encoded in the DNA sequence theoretically can be expressed, and the polypeptide chain specified by the foreign DNA segment can be transcribed and translated to form an active protein molecule. The expression of the foreign genetic information, however, requires that the appropriate reading frame be established and the transcriptional and translational control mechanisms turned on to permit the expression of the DNA.

Often the genes produced using a cloning vector must be transferred to an **expression vector** that contains the desired gene and the necessary regulatory sequences that permit control of the expression of that gene. Several factors influence the level of expression of a gene. In general, more product is made if multiple copies of the gene are present, and expression vectors should be able to obtain a high copy number.

There should be a strong promoter associated with the gene to ensure binding of RNA polymerase (Table 7-7, p. 278). Strong *E. coli* promoters used in the construction of expression vectors include *lacuv*5, which normally controls β-galactosidase expression; *trp,* which controls tryptophan biosynthesis; and *omp*F, which regulates production of outer membrane protein. An especially strong promoter called *tac* has been constructed from part of the *lac* promoter and part of the *trp* promoter. The *lac* promoter contains a Prib-

TABLE 7-7 Some Promoters Used in Expression Vectors

			OPERATIONAL CONTROL	
PROMOTER	FUNCTIONAL IN	SOURCE	OFF	ON
λpL, λpR	*Escherichia coli*	Leftward and rightward early promoters of λ	30° C	>37° C (in cI_{857} host)
lac	*E. coli*	*E. coli lac* operon		IPTG in medium
trp	*E. coli*	*E. coli trp* operon	Tryptophan in medium	Indoleacetic acid in medium
tac	*E. coli*	*trp*-35 region *lac*-10 region hybrid		IPTG in medium
*pho*A	*E. coli*	*E. coli* alkaline phosphatase operon		Phosphate-limited medium
*rec*A	*E. coli*	*E. coli rec*A gene	Excess phosphate in medium	Mitomycin C in medium
tet	*E. coli*	Tn10 tetracycline-resistance gene		Tetracyclines in medium
bla	*B. subtilis*	*Bacillus licheniformis* β-lactamase gene		β-lactams in medium
cat	*B. subtilis*	*Bacillus pumilis* chloramphenicol acetyl transferase		Chloramphenicol in medium
gyl	*Streptomyces*	*Streptomyces coelicolor* glycerol operon	Glucose in medium	Glycerol in medium
ADH	*S. cerevisiae*	Yeast repressible alcohol dehydrogenase (ADR) gene	High glucose in medium	Low glucose in medium
GAL 1	*S. cerevisiae*	Yeast galactose utilization operon	Glucose in medium	Galactose in medium
GPD-PH05	*S. cerevisiae*	Hybrid between yeast glyceraldehyde 3-phosphate dehydrogenase and alkaline phosphatase gene promoters	Excess phosphate in medium	Phosphate-limited medium

now sequence at −10 but no −35 consensus sequence. The *trp* promoter contains a −35 consensus sequence but no Pribnow sequence. The newly constructed *tac* promoter contains both consensus sequences, which makes it highly efficient with respect to initiating transcription.

Besides a strong promoter, it is important that the early part of the RNA transcript contain a ribosome-binding site that establishes the appropriate reading frame. The ideal condition allows the culture containing the expression vector to grow until a large population of cells is obtained, each containing a large copy number of the vector; then all copies would be expressed simultaneously. To this end, plasmids have been engineered with the *lac* promoter, ribosome-binding site, and operator such that the *lac* inducer can initiate production of the protein(s) encoded by the gene(s) engineered into the organism.

Detection of Recombinant DNA

After the segment of DNA is transferred to an appropriate vector, there must be suitable methods to detect its presence.

Gene Probes One way of detecting specific DNA sequences is to use **gene probes.** A gene probe is a segment of DNA or RNA that contains a sequence that is complementary to one you are interested in detecting. Hybridization of a radiolabeled gene probe to a region of DNA isolated from a specific clone readily indicates that the DNA sequence of interest is present.

An important technique that separates DNA fragments by gel electrophoresis was developed in 1975 by E. M. Southern and is called **Southern blotting** (FIG. 7-40). In this procedure, DNA is first digested with restriction enzymes and the resulting fragments are separated by size on gels using electrophoresis. The DNA fragments are transferred from the gel to a nitrocellulose membrane filter by "blotting," and specific sequences are identified on the filter by hybridization using a radiolabeled probe.

An analogous procedure, **Northern blotting,** permits the separation and identification of specific RNA sequences. The RNA is isolated from cells and separated by gel electrophoresis. It is then transferred from the gel to an RNA-binding membrane filter. Specific RNA sequences are identified by hybridization using a radiolabeled single-stranded DNA probe. The Northern blotting procedure can be useful in determining if DNA sequences are transcriptionally active.

Another technique that can be used to detect the presence of a specific DNA sequence in a cell is **colony hybridization.** This method first involves replica plat-

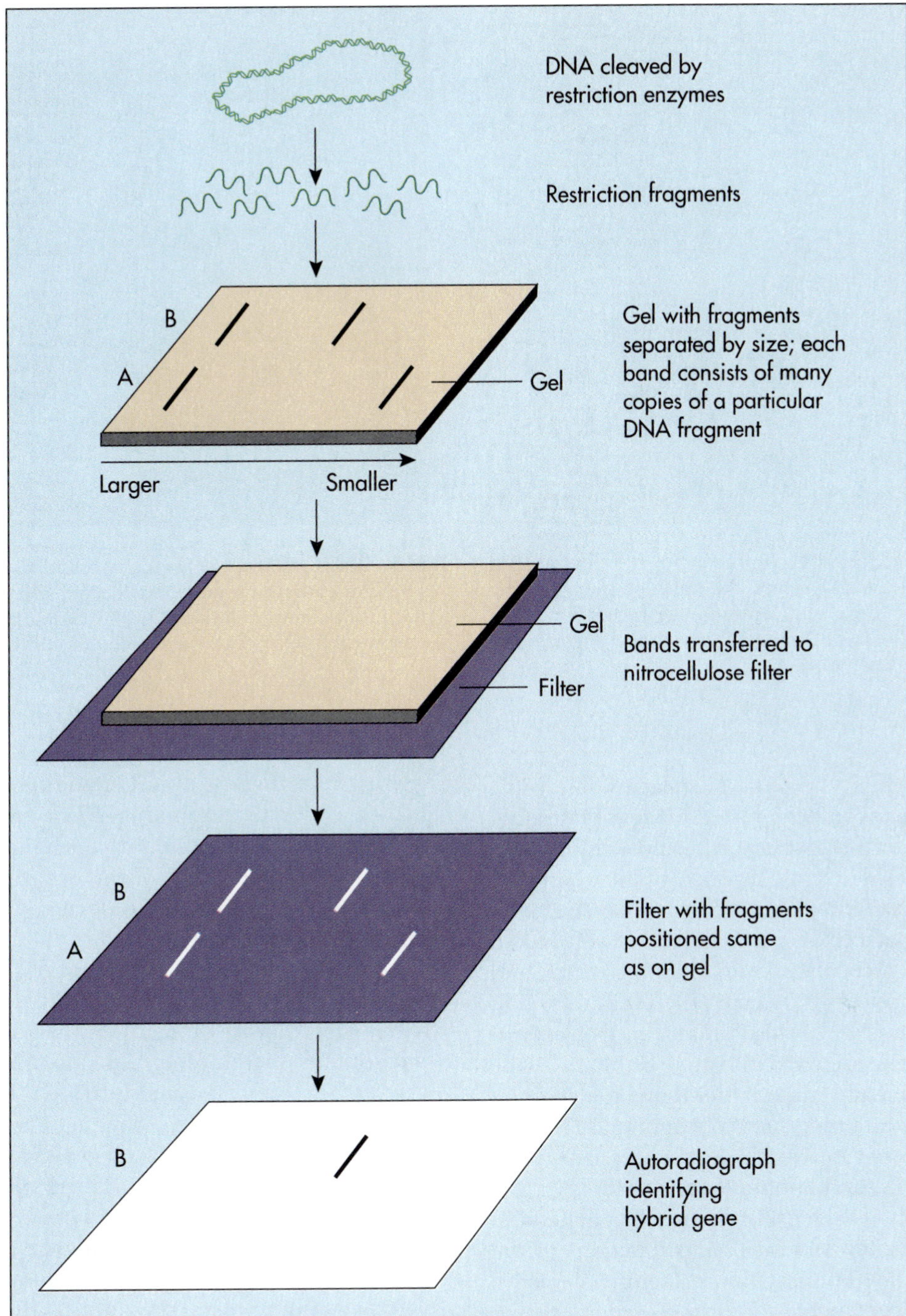
DNA cleaved by restriction enzymes
Restriction fragments
B
A
Gel
Gel with fragments separated by size; each band consists of many copies of a particular DNA fragment
Larger
Smaller
Gel
Filter
Bands transferred to nitrocellulose filter
B
A
Filter with fragments positioned same as on gel
B
Autoradiograph identifying hybrid gene

FIG. 7-40 In Southern blotting, digested fragments of DNA are separated by gel electrophoresis. The bands of separated DNA are transferred to nitrocellulose filter, retaining their positions according to the number of nucleotides in each fragment. A radiolabeled gene probe is then used to identify specific genes.

ing to transfer colonies from an agar plate to a nitrocellulose filter. The cells are lysed, thus releasing the DNA, which can be denatured with 0.5 N NaOH. The single-stranded DNA is fixed to the filter and then identified by hybridization with a radiolabeled probe and autoradiography. Colonies can be selected from the original plate that correspond to the radioactive spots that are visible on the exposed film.

Reporter Genes Recombinant DNA can also be detected using **reporter genes** that code for an easily detectable trait in the cell in which they are placed. The most frequently used reporter system uses the *lacZ*

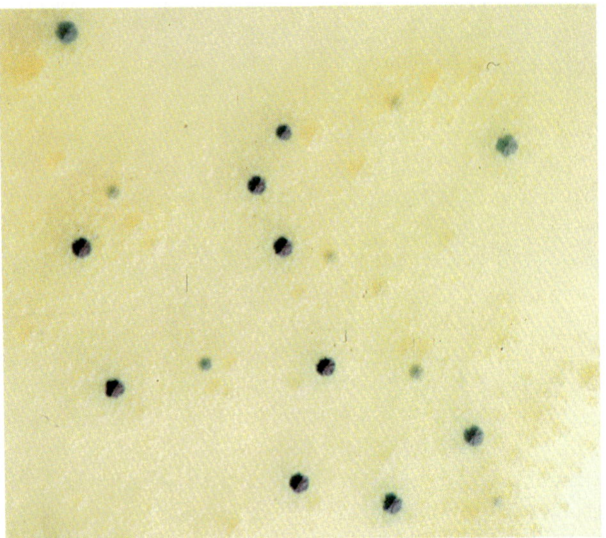

FIG. 7-41 Detection of recombinants can easily be seen when the *lacZ* gene is used. Here, the blue colonies have the active *lacZ* gene and the white colonies are recombinants in which the *lacZ* gene has been inactivated due to insertion of recombinant DNA.

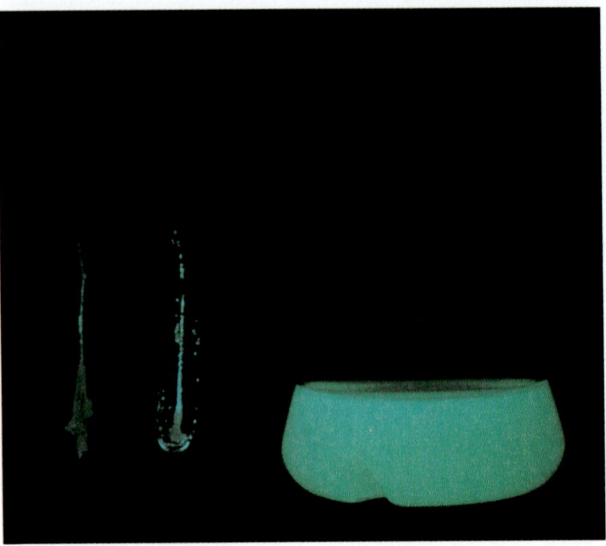

FIG. 7-42 Detection of recombinants and gene expression can easily be seen when the *lux* genes are used. Here the luminescent colonies are expressing the *lux* genes that have been incorporated into recombinant DNA.

gene of *E. coli*, which codes for a β-galactosidase (FIG. 7-41). This activity can be detected on agar plates that contain the indicator chemical 5-bromo-4-chloro-3-indolyl-β-D-galactoside (Xgal) that turns blue when split by β-galactosidase. If a recombinant molecule is constructed such that a DNA sequence is physically linked to the *lacZ* sequence, placed into a cloning vector, and β-galactosidase activity is detected then it is likely that the first DNA sequence is also present in that cell. In cases where a gene is cloned into a site within *lacZ*, the *lacZ* is inactivated and white rather than blue colonies form on Xgal-containing media. Additional reporter genes include other enzymatic activities such as β-glucuronidase (GUS) and antibiotic resistance.

Detection can also be based on the *trxA* gene of *E. coli*, which codes for *thioredoxin* and functions in the reduction disulfide bonds within proteins. The active site of thioredoxin contains two cysteines that can easily form a disulfide bond. In the dithiol form, thioredoxin reduces a disulfide bond in a protein and, in its active site, forms a disulfide bond that can be reduced by *thioredoxin reductase* and NADPH + H^+. Therefore, in *E. coli* and many other bacteria, intracellular proteins have reduced thiols in spite of being in an oxidizing environment.

E. coli has another system that maintains protein thiols in a reduced state. The tripeptide glutathione, with the enzymes glutathione reductase and glutaredoxin, function to maintain the reduced state of protein thiols. In addition, methionine sulfoxide reductase can specifically reduce methionine sulfoxide to methionine. A methionine *auxotroph* (methionine-requiring strain) can grow on methionine sulfoxide that is then converted to methionine by methionine sulfoxide reductase and thioredoxin. Thioredoxin is necessary for the reduction of the disulfide bond before the methionine sulfoxide reductase can be recycled. However, a methionine auxotroph that is also deficient in thioredoxin (*trxA*$^-$) does not grow well on methionine sulfoxide. This double mutant (*metE*$^-$, *trxA*$^-$) forms tiny colonies on medium that lacks methionine but contains methionine sulfoxide. Alternatively, cells that incorporate a plasmid bearing the *trxA* gene and perhaps foreign DNA sequences will form large colonies. In this way the *trxA* gene can be used as an indicator of the presence in a cell of a plasmid that may contain recombinant sequences.

A relatively new reporter system involves the luciferase operon *(lux)* of *Photobacterium fischeri*. This marine bacterium possess the unusual property of bioluminescence due to its *lux* genes. By linking a DNA sequence to the *lux* genes, the presence of the desired DNA sequence will be detected or reported in cells that emit light (FIG. 7-42).

Cloning Eukaryotic Genes in Bacteria

The construction of bacterial DNA sequences, containing complete gene sequences derived from eukaryotic organisms, is complicated by the fact that eukaryotic genes are generally split by introns. In eukaryotic organisms, post-transcriptional modification of the hnRNA is required to produce a mature mRNA molecule that can be properly translated, but bacteria do not possess the capacity to remove introns

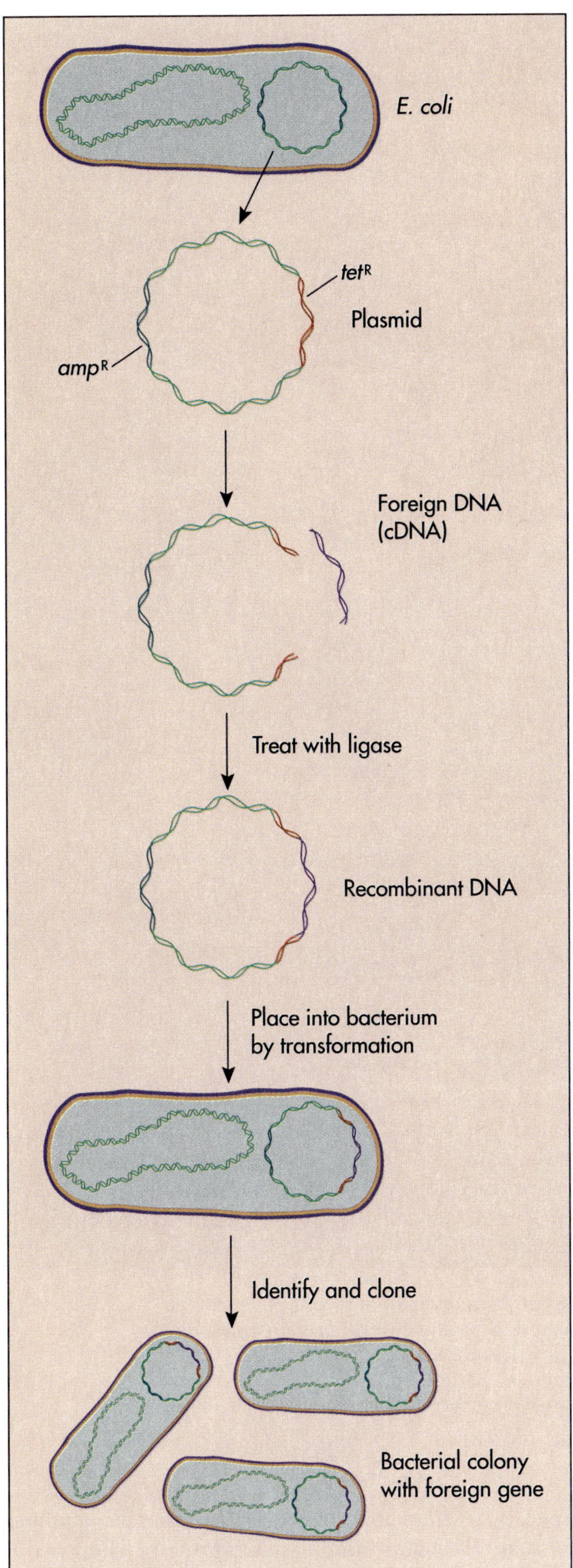

FIG. 7-43 Eukaryotic DNA can be incorporated into a bacterial plasmid and expressed by the bacterial cell. In this manner some recombinant bacteria have been genetically engineered to produce human proteins.

from eukaryotic DNA to form the mRNA needed for producing a functional protein molecule. Therefore it is necessary to cut and splice eukaryotic DNA artificially or to use an alternative procedure to establish a contiguous sequence of nucleotide bases to define the protein that is to be expressed (FIG. 7-43). The problem of the discontinuity of the eukaryotic gene can be overcome by using an mRNA molecule and a reverse transcriptase enzyme to produce a DNA molecule that has a contiguous sequence of nucleotide bases containing the complete gene. A major advantage of using mRNA is that the noncoding information in the DNA (introns) has been removed. The single-stranded DNA molecule that is formed in this procedure is complementary to the complete mRNA molecule and is therefore called **complementary DNA** or **copied DNA (cDNA).** The RNA can be removed using ribonuclease and the second complementary strand of DNA synthesized. The double-stranded DNA molecule formed in this manner can then be inserted into a carrier plasmid.

In addition to overcoming problems with sequencing the gene itself, when cloning eukaryotic genes in prokaryotic cells, it is necessary to take steps to ensure proper expression and stability of the product. One method of providing a ribosome-binding site in the proper reading frame when a mammalian DNA sequence is added to a bacterial host cell is to establish a nucleotide sequence that produces a fusion protein that contains a short prokaryotic sequence at the amino end and the desired eukaryotic sequence at the carboxyl end. Fusion proteins are often more stable in bacteria than unmodified eukaryotic proteins. Also, the bacterial portion can contain the bacterial sequence coding for the signal peptide that enables transport of the protein across the cell membrane, making possible the development of a bacterial system that synthesizes the mammalian protein and actually excretes it.

Using these methods, many eukaryotic genes can be cloned in prokaryotic cells. Several human proteins, including insulin, are now being commercially produced using genetically engineered bacteria (FIG. 7-44). Diabetes, a disease resulting from an insulin deficiency, can be treated by injection of insulin extracted from cattle pancreas, which occasionally elicits an allergic reaction, or by injection of humulin, human insulin produced by genetically engineered bacteria. Insulin consists of two polypeptides, labeled A and B, that are coded for by separate parts of a single insulin gene. The genetic engineering of bacteria for the production of human insulin involved synthesizing the DNA sequence coding for A and B polypeptide chains that were elucidated by analyzing the amino acid sequences of the insulin molecule and determining the corresponding codons. Because the insulin protein is fairly small, it was more convenient to

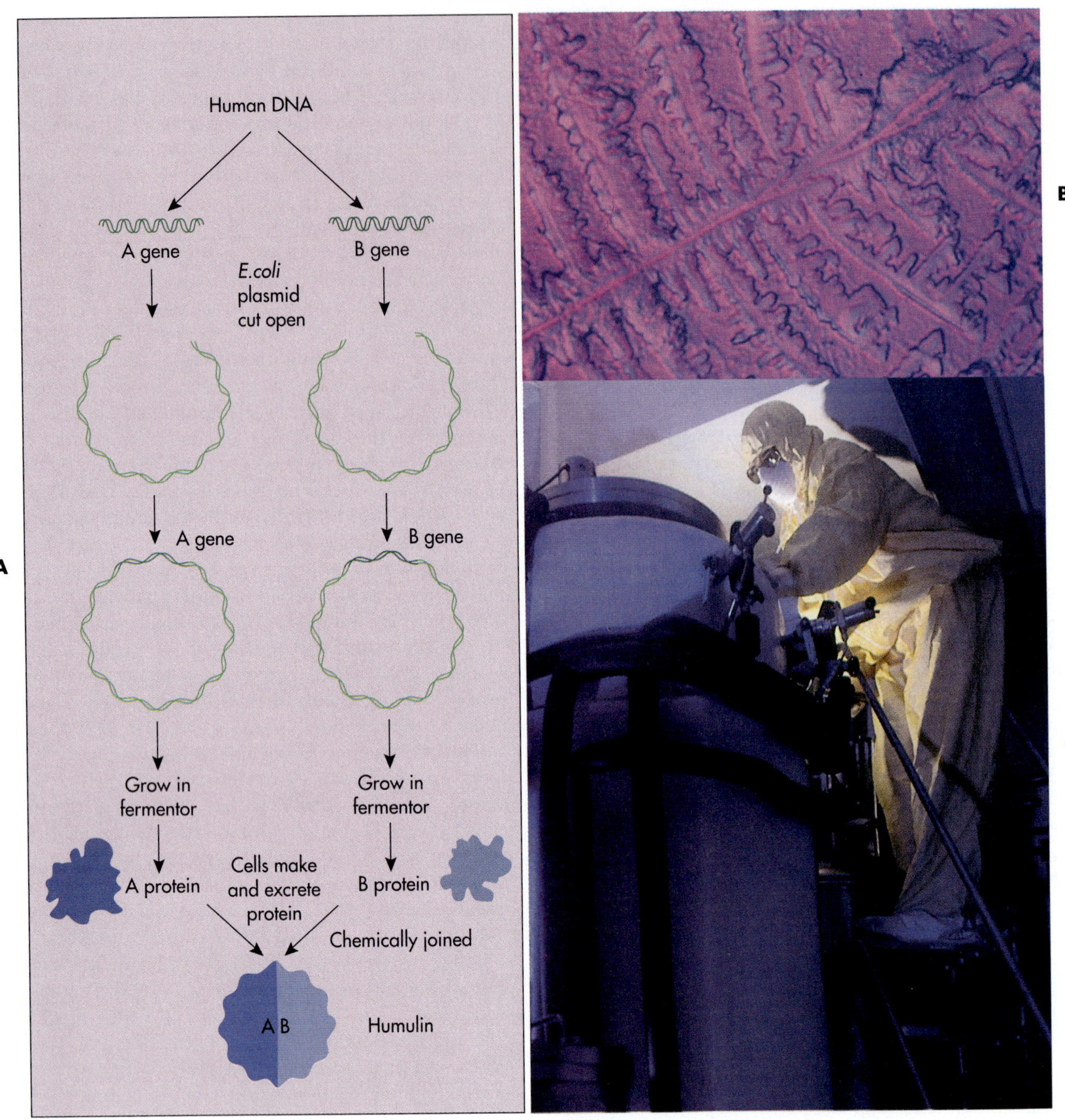

FIG. 7-44 **A,** Human insulin (humulin) is produced by recombinant strains of *Escherichia coli.* One recombinant strain is genetically engineered to produce the A protein and a second recombinant strain, the B protein. The two proteins are then chemically combined to produce commercial humulin. **B,** Crystals of humulin. **C,** Large fermentors are used to grow recombinant *E. coli* containing the genes for human interferon and human interleukin-2 hormone for commercial production.

synthesize the proper DNA sequence chemically rather than to isolate the insulin gene from human tissue. Each DNA sequence was added separately to an expression vector, plasmid pBR322, containing the *trp* promoter and the bacterial ribosome-binding site, which was cloned in separate cultures of *E. coli.* The two bacterial cultures were grown in large-scale fermentors, where they produced commercial qualities of A and B chains fused to a Trp protein. The fused A and B proteins were purified and the A and B portions separated from the Trp protein by cleavage using cyanogen bromide. Finally, the A and B peptides were chemically joined to produce human insulin. The humulin produced functions as normal human insulin.

POTENTIAL BENEFITS AND RISKS OF RECOMBINANT DNA TECHNOLOGY

Recombination involving plasmids, as well as other vectors, provides a mechanism for the particularly rapid dissemination of genes through a population. Plasmids are quite useful as carriers of foreign genetic information in genetic engineering. Recombinant DNA technology can be employed to create organisms that contain combinations of genetic information that do not occur naturally. In addition, for example, bacteria containing genetically engineered plasmids can synthesize proteins that are normally produced only in eukaryotic organisms. In theory, recombinant DNA technology can be used to engineer organisms that can produce any desired combination of proteins. As a result, genetic engineering holds great promise in industry and medicine because various proteins of economic importance or use in curing disease may be produced.

The potential of genetic engineering to short-circuit evolution has raised numerous ethical, legal, and safety questions. The Supreme Court of the United States has ruled, in a landmark decision, that genetic engineering can create novel living systems that can be patented as inventions. This ruling establishes the precedent for future genetic engineering efforts. The problem of safety has been temporarily solved by using mutation and selection procedures to develop a fail-safe strain of *E. coli* that is unable to grow outside a carefully defined culture medium. A committee was established in the United States by the National Institutes of Health—the Recombinant DNA Advisory Committee (RAC)—to oversee proposed government-sponsored research using recombinant DNA technology. Gradually the stringent guidelines established by this committee relaxed as it became apparent that many of the initial concerns regarding the unintentional escape of genetically engineered organisms from the laboratory were exaggerated.

A new concern, however, focuses on the development of genetically engineered organisms designed for deliberate release into the environment. Environmentalists question the safety of such a procedure, and new governmental regulations have been developed amid a series of court cases concerning safety and regulatory issues. The questions of whether novel genomes will survive in the environment, whether they will transfer to other microorganisms and spread, and whether this dissemination could represent a serious biological hazard to human health and the environment are being actively debated. The debate also continues as to whether it is ethical to clone DNA in all cases and whether recombinant DNA technology will permit the cloning of higher eukaryotic organisms, including plants and animals.

One must weigh these ethical questions against the benefits that can be derived through genetic engineering. There is little question that through genetic engineering the quality of human life can be improved. However, scientists have a responsibility to see that the public is informed about genetic engineering; to see that research remains within acceptable guidelines; to use this powerful technique for examining basic questions about molecular-level genetics; and to develop genetically engineered organisms of agricultural, ecological, medical, and economic importance that can be safely used.

CHAPTER REVIEW

STUDY QUESTIONS

1. How are plasmids related to the prevalence of multiple drug resistance? Why does the overuse of antibiotics increase the prevalence of drug resistant bacterial strains?
2. How are plasmids maintained in bacterial populations? Explain how the parB locus works.
3. Why do some bacteria have multiple plasmids and others none?
4. What is a mutation?
5. How do mutations occur naturally?
6. What effect does exposure to ionizing radiation or chemical mutagens have on rates of mutation?
7. What is a plasmid? What are some functions associated with plasmids?
8. How would you go about increasing the rate of mutations?
9. How could you recognize the occurrence of a mutant?
10. How could you design an experiment to select mutants?
11. How is the Ames test used to determine whether a chemical is a likely carcinogen?
12. What is recombination?
13. Compare homologous and nonhomologous recombination.
14. How is recombination involved in maintaining heterogeneity within the gene pool?
15. What is a transposable genetic element?
16. What is the difference between an insertion element and a transposon?
17. How is DNA exchanged in prokaryotes?
18. How would you experimentally distinguish transformation, transduction, and conjugation?
19. How could you determine the role of the F pilus in conjugation?
20. Compare general and specialized transduction.
21. How can transformation and transduction be used to map genes in a bacterial chromosome?

Continued.

CHAPTER REVIEW

STUDY QUESTIONS—CONT'D

22. How is DNA repaired and how is the fidelity of DNA replication ensured?
23. What is the difference between a genetic map and a restriction map?
24. How can transposons be used to introduce mutations?
25. How is genetic variability related to the evolution of microorganisms?
26. What is recombinant DNA technology?
27. How can genetic engineering create new organisms?
28. What are the advantages and risks of deliberately releasing genetically engineered microorganisms into the environment?
29. How can the survival of genetically engineered organisms in the environment be limited?

SITUATIONAL PROBLEMS

1. Testing Potential Carcinogenicity of Water Supplies

You have just begun working part-time for an analytical laboratory that services the municipal water company. Most of the work concerns chemical analyses for heavy metals and toxic chemicals. The water company requested that tests be added to determine the mutagenicity and potential carcinogenicity of the water before and after disinfection. Because of your expertise in bacteriology, you have been asked to perform these tests. You decide to employ the Ames test as a routine screening procedure, using two histidine-requiring, auxotrophic strains of *Salmonella typhimurium.*

You collect 100-L water samples and pass the water through an ion exchange column to concentrate organic chemicals. You then elute the organics with a solvent, which is then evaporated. The concentrated organics are dissolved in 10 mL dimethyl sulfoxide (DMSO) for use in the Ames test procedure. You add a series of volumes—2 to 20 μL—of the concentrated organics to suspensions of the *Salmonella* strains suspended in liquefied agar. A control suspension with only DMSO and no organic concentrate is also prepared. A microsomal preparation of rat liver homogenate is added to the suspensions to activate potential mutagens. The agar suspensions are then poured onto minimal media (lacking histidine) and incubated for 48 hours. A replicate sample is also streaked onto a complete medium to ensure viability of the bacteria in the suspension.

Having done this you observe the numbers of colonies shown in the Table below.

Based on these data, what specific conclusions can you reach, and based on these conclusions, what recommendations would you make to the water company in your report?

MEDIUM	*Salmonella typhimurium* STRAIN	DMSO ALONE	2 μL ORGANIC CONCENTRATE	10 μL ORGANIC CONCENTRATE	20 μL ORGNANIC CONCENTRATE
		NUMBER OF COLONIES			
WATER SAMPLE A					
Minimal	1	75	140	230	380
Comlete	1	400	400	400	400
Minimal	2	10	75	150	300
Complete	2	300	300	300	300
WATER SAMPLE B					
Minimal	1	65	80	35	0
Complete	1	400	400	350	150
Minimal	2	10	25	0	0
Complete	2	200	200	180	0
WATER SAMPLE C					
Minimal	1	65	70	67	72
Complete	1	400	400	400	400
Minimal	2	25	30	30	25
Complete	2	300	300	300	300
WATER SAMPLE D					
Minimal	1	60	120	260	375
Complete	1	400	400	400	400
Minimal	2	10	15	12	10
Complete	2	300	300	300	300

SITUATIONAL PROBLEMS—cont'd

2. Mapping a Genome Based On Interrupted Mating Data

You are preparing for the next bacteriology exam, which will contain a problem on genetic mapping. To make sure you can handle this problem, you construct the following hypothetical data. Suppose you mated an Hfr strain that is $Leu^+Gal^+Trp^+His^+Str^S$ and an F^- strain that is $Leu^-Gal^-Trp^-His^-Str^R$ and used a medium that selected for Leu^+Str^R. You then screened the isolates for Gal, Trp, and His, with the results shown in the Table below.

Using these data, graph the results and construct the genetic map for these genes.

GAL⁺ TIME (MIN)	STR^R RECOMBINANTS PER 100 HFR	TRP⁺ TIME (MIN)	STR^R RECOMBINANTS PER 100 HFR	HIS⁺ TIME (MIN)	STR^R RECOMBINANTS PER 100 HFR
0	0	0	0	0	0
5	2	6	0	16	0
7	9	8	0	18	0
9	15	10	0	20	0
11	21	12	0	22	0
13	27	14	2	24	0
15	33	16	3	26	0
17	39	18	7	28	0
19	45	20	11	30	0
21	46	22	14	32	2
23	46	24	14	34	15
25	46	26	18	36	24
27	46	28	22	40	46
		30	27		
		32	30		
		43	38		

3. Engineering a Bacterial Strain to Degrade Herbicide 2,4,5-T

2,4,5-T is an herbicide that is persistent in soil because of the limited capacity of microorganisms to degrade this synthetic organic compound. You isolated two bacterial strains that will partially degrade 2,4,5-T, but neither strain alone will completely detoxify it. Therefore you decide to use recombinant DNA technology to engineer genetically a single bacterial strain that will accomplish this environmentally important task.

Complete degradation of 2,4,5-T involves sequential cleavage of the acetic acid residue, removal of the three chlorine atoms, and cleavage of the phenol ring. The number 5 chlorine residue is the most difficult to remove and is cleaved only after all other substitutions are removed. Of the two organisms you isolated, organism A is capable of cleaving the acetic acid residue and the number 4 chlorine. Organism B is capable of cleaving the remaining chlorines and the phenol ring. Electron microscopic analysis of DNA preparations from organism A reveals the presence of two plasmids: 4.5 kb (plasmid A1) and 6.5 kb (plasmid A2) kb in size. Organism B contains only one plasmid (B1) of 10.5 kb. When removed from the two organisms, the plasmids no longer have the ability to degrade 2,4,5-T.

The restriction fragments produced by digesting the three plasmids with the restriction endonuclease enzymes *Bam*HI and *Bgl*II are as follows:

BAMHI			*BGLII*		
A1	A2	B1	A1	A2	B1
2.5	3.0	5.0	3.3	4.1	6.9
2.0	3.5	4.0	1.2	2.4	3.6
		1.5			

By incorporating the individual restriction fragments into the multiple cloning site of the 2.9-kb *Pseudomonas cepacia* cloning vector pRS101, you can demonstrate that the 3.0-kb fragment from A2 codes for cleavage of the acetic acid residue of 2,4,5-T. None of the other fragments from A1 and A2 produced changes in the herbicide. When the 6.9-kb fragment of B1 was cloned into pRS101 containing the 3.0-kb fragment from A2, the organism was capable of degrading benzene and removing the acetic acid residue and number 2 chlorine from 2,4,5-T. Cloning the 1.5-kb fragment from B1 into pRS101 also resulted in degradation of phenol.

Based on these results, how would you complete the construction of a plasmid that would enable the common soil bacterium *P. cepacia* to degrade 2,4,5-T completely?

Suggested Supplementary Readings

Andrews AT: 1986. *Electrophoresis: Theory, Techniques, and Biochemical and Clinical Applications,* ed. 2, Oxford University Press, Oxford, England.

Ansubel FM, R Brent, RE Kingston, DD Moore, JG Seidman, JA Smith, K Struhl, SG Bonitz: 1992. *Short Protocols in Molecular Biology, A Compendium of Methods from Current Protocols in Molecular Biology,* ed. 2, Academic Press, San Diego, CA.

Bennett JW and LL Lasure: 1991. *More Gene Manipulations in Fungi,* Academic Press, New York.

Berg DE: 1989. *Mobile DNA,* American Society for Microbiology, Washington, D.C.

Berger SL and AR Kimmel (eds.): 1987. *Guide to Molecular Cloning Techniques: Methods in Enzymology, Volume 152,* Academic Press, San Diego, CA.

Bickle TA and DH Krüger: 1993. Biology of DNA Restriction, *Microbiological Reviews* 57:434-450.

Birge EA: 1981. *Bacterial and Bacteriophage Genetics,* Springer-Verlag, New York.

Birge EA: 1988. *Bacterial and Bacteriophage Genetics—An Introduction,* ed. 2, Springer-Verlag, New York.

Bishop MJ and CJ Rawlings (eds.): 1987. *Nucleic Acid and Protein Sequence Analysis: A Practical Approach,* IRL Press, Oxford, England.

Campbell A: 1981. Evolutionary significance of accessory DNA elements in bacteria, *Annual Review of Microbiology* 35:55-83.

Clewell DB: 1993. *Bacterial Conjugation,* Plenum Publishing, NY.

Cohen SN and JA Shapiro: 1980. Transposable genetic elements, *Scientific American* 242(2):40-49.

Collins MKL (ed.): 1991. *Methods in Molecular Biology: Vol. 8, Practical Molecular Virology, Viral Vectors for Gene Expression,* Humana Press, Clifton, NJ.

Dale JW: 1989. *Molecular Genetics of Bacteria,* John Wiley & Sons, NY.

Genetics: Readings from Scientific American: 1981. W. H. Freeman & Co., San Francisco.

Gardner EJ, MJ Simmons, DP Snustad: 1991. *Principles of Genetics,* ed. 8, John Wiley & Sons, NY.

Glass RE: 1982. *Gene Function:* E. coli *and Its Heritable Elements,* University of California Press, Berkeley, CA.

Grindley NDF and RR Reed: 1985. Transpositional recombination in prokaryotes, *Annual Review of Biochemistry* 54:863-890.

Hackett PB, JA Fuchs, JW Messing: 1988. *An Introduction to Recombinant DNA Techniques: Basic Experiments in Gene Manipulation,* The Benjamin/Cummings Publishing Co., Menlo Park, CA.

Hardy K: 1986. *Bacterial Plasmids,* ed. 2, American Society for Microbiology, Washington, D. C.

Higgins IJ, DJ Best, J Jones: 1985. *Biotechnology: Principles and Practice,* Blackwell Scientific Publications, Oxford, England.

Hopwood DA: 1981. Genetic studies with bacteria protoplasts, *Annual Review of Microbiology* 35:237-272.

Innis MA, DH Gelfand, JJ Snissky: 1990. *PCR Protocols: A Guide to Methods and Applications,* Academic Press, New York.

Kingsman SM and AJ Kingsman: 1988. *Genetic Engineering—An Introduction to Gene Analysis and Exploitation in Eukaryotes,* Blackwell Scientific Publications, Oxford, England.

Kleckner N: 1990. Regulation of transposition in bacteria, *Annual Review of Cell Biology.* 6:297-327.

Kolodny GM (ed.): 1981. *Eukaryotic Gene Regulation,* CRC Press, Inc., Boca Raton, FL.

Kreigler M: 1990. *Gene Transfer and Expression: A Laboratory Manual,* Stockton Press, NY.

Kucherlapatri RS and GR Smith: (eds.): 1988. *Genetic Recombination,* American Society for Microbiology, Washington, D. C.

Lederberg J: 1987. Genetic recombination in bacteria: A discovery account, *Annual Review of Genetics* 21:23-46.

Levy SB and RV Miller (eds.): 1989. *Gene Transfer in the Environment,* McGraw-Hill Publishing Company, New York.

Lewin B: 1990. *Genes IV,* Oxford University Press, New York, and Cell Press, Cambridge, MA.

Maniatis T, EF Fritsch, J Sambrook: 1989. *Molecular Cloning: A Laboratory Manual,* ed 2, Cold Spring Harbor Laboratory, Cold Spring Harbor, NY.

Margulis L and D Sagan: 1986. *Origin of Sex: Three Billion Years of Genetic Recombination,.* Yale University Press, New Haven, CT.

McPherson MJ (ed.): 1991. *Directed Mutagenesis: A Practical Approach,* IRL Press, Oxford England.

Miller RV and TA Kokjohn: 1990. General microbiology of *recA*: Environmental and evolutionary significance, *Annual Review of Microbiology* 44:365-394.

Murray EJ (ed.): 1991. *Methods in Molecular Biology, Vol 7, Gene Transfer and Expression Protocols,* Humana Press, Clifton, NJ.

Murrel JC and LM Roberts: 1989. *Understanding Genetic Engineering,* Halsted Press, New York.

Novick R: 1980. Plasmids, *Scientific American* 243(6):103-123.

Old RW and SB Primrose: 1987. *Principles of Gene Manipulation: An Introduction to Genetic Engineering,* ed. 4, Blackwell Scientific Publications, Oxford, England.

Old RW and SB Primrose: 1989. *Principles of Gene Manipulation,* ed. 4, Blackwell Scientific Publications, Boston.

Oliver SG and JM Ward: 1985. *A Dictionary of Genetic Engineering,* Cambridge University Press, Cambridge, England.

Peters P: 1993. *Biotechnology: A Guide to Genetic Engineering,* William C. Brown, Dubuque, IA.

Rickwood D and BD Hames (eds.): 1990. *Gel Electrophoresis of Nucleic Acids: A Practical Approach,* ed. 2, IRL Press, Oxford, England.

Scaife J, D Leach, A Galizzi (eds.): 1985. *Genetics of Bacteria,* Academic Press, New York.

Setlow JK: 1992. *Genetic Engineering,* Plenum Publishing, New York.

Smith GR: 1987. Mechanism and control of homologous recombination in *Escherichia coli, Annual Review of Genetics* 21:179-202.

Smith HO, DB Danner, RA Deich: 1981. Genetic transformation, *Annual Review of Biochemistry* 50:41-68.

Stewart-Tull DE and M Sussman (eds.): 1992. *The Release of Genetically Modified Microorganisms—REGEM 2,* Plenum Publishing Corp., New York.

Streips UN and RE Yasbin (eds.): 1991. *Modern Microbial Genetics,* Wiley-Liss, Inc., New York.

Sussman MC, H Collins, FA Skinner, DE Stewart-Tull: 1988. *The Release of Genetically-Engineered Microorganisms,* Academic Press, Harcourt Brace Jovanovich, Publishers, New York.

Suzuki DT, AJF Griffiths, JH Miller, RC Lewontin: 1986. *An Introduction to Genetic Analysis,* W. H. Freeman & Co., San Francisco.

Walker GC, C Marsch, LA Dodson: 1985. Genetic analyses of DNA repair: Inference and extrapolation, *Annual Review of Genetics* 19:103-126.

Watson JD, N Hopkins, J Roberts, J Steitz, A Weiner: 1987. *Molecular Biology of the Gene,* Benjamin/Cummings Publishing Co., Menlo Park, CA.

Watson JD, M Gilman, J Witkowski, M Zoller: 1992. *Recombinant DNA,* ed. 2, W. H. Freeman, San Francisco.

Weising K, J Schell, G Kahl: 1988. Foreign Genes in Plants: Transfer, Structure, Expression, and Applications, *Annual Review of Genetics* 22:421-477.

Wild JR and ME Wales: 1990. Molecular evolution and genetic engineering of protein domains involving aspartate transcarbamoylase, *Annual Review of Microbiology* 44:193-218.

Wu R: 1992-1993. *Methods in Enzymology: Vols. 216-218, Recombinant DNA,* Academic Press, New York.

Wu R, L Grossman, K Moldave (eds.): 1989. *Recombinant DNA Methodology,* Academic Press, San Diego, CA.

Zyskind JW and SI Bernstein: 1992. *Recombinant DNA Laboratory Manual,* Academic Press. New York.

DAVID SCHLESSINGER
WASHINGTON UNIVERSITY SCHOOL OF MEDICINE

David Schlessinger was born in Toronto, Canada, in 1936. He received his education at the University of Chicago and Harvard University. He worked at the Pasteur Institute in Paris in the early 1960s before coming to the department of microbiology at the School of Medicine at Washington University in St. Louis. He was president of the American Society for Microbiology from 1994 to 1995. Dr. Schlessinger studies cell physiology and biochemistry. His pioneering studies have helped elucidate the role of RNA in cellular functions.

As a very-wet-behind-the-ears 16-year-old high school graduate, I arrived at the College of the University of Chicago in September, 1953. The Natural Sciences syllabus had just added the newly published *Nature* paper of Watson and Crick to its usual lineup of Newton and Mendel. The impact of the structure of DNA on a freshman chemistry major was not inconsiderable.

By my fourth year as an undergraduate, I found that organic chemistry was the branch of chemistry that was easiest for me, and most interesting, but it was dispiritingly full of memorization of complex name reactions with poor yields. In contrast, the simplicity and power of the DNA model continued to be fascinating. I had also started to work in the lab of Eugene Goldwasser as a part-time technician, and had done the initial steps in the purification of erythropoietin: an entire field of hormone action and chemistry opening up, among so many others! Also, I had been reading that bacteria could modify intermediary metabolites, including lactate, in many ways—and in high yields—just by using appropriate enzymes.

The attraction of biochemistry and microbiology became increasingly great, and I applied to Harvard University for graduate study. There, I was one of the first graduate students with James D. Watson.

Molecular biology is so young a set of techniques and ideas that a number of current practitioners have lived through its entire development. I was fortunate to follow much of its embryonic period in Watson's laboratory and to see "from below" the interactions of the greats who defined the first rash of ideas. It was easy to make discoveries and get jobs and grants in those days because everything was wide open and everyone was a raw recruit. It is a source of wistful amusement to think that I made the first pure preparations of 30S, 50S, and 70S ribosomes from *Escherichia coli* and measured their molecular weights and that my Ph.D. research also included one of the first functional *in vitro* systems for bacterial protein synthesis.

Results that I obtained with subcellular systems provided some of the indications that RNA was involved in directing protein formation. At the time, the notion of messenger RNA was just being formulated, in large part, in the group of Jacob and Monod in Paris. Again I was privileged to work in a postdoctoral "stage" with a remarkable group—that of Jacques Monod at the Institut Pasteur. There, I realized more fully the wide-open domains that were added to microbiology by the French school: much of microbial genetics, growth control, and scrupulous attention to the balance of physiological processes.

When I arrived at Washington University in St. Louis in 1962 as an instructor, I determined to begin an independent career by attacking a new problem: the analysis of bacterial membranes. At that time, membranes were a nonexistent field of study, and I soon found out why. After a year, the only substantive progress I made was to determine that my membrane preparations were always highly contaminated with RNA. However, the contaminating RNA, released with nonionic detergents, soon proved to be ribosomes (in fact, the first bacterial polyribosomes to be observed), and I realized that RNA must be my research fate.

In other work at the time, I participated in the comparable discovery of mammalian polysomes and stable mRNA in reticulocytes and initiated two long-term projects in *E. coli:* (1) studies of messenger RNA turnover in subcellular systems that identified several of the enzymes involved and provided some of the early hypotheses about the control of turnover and (2) formulation and analysis of the ribosome cycle in protein synthesis. With my colleagues, David Apirion and Giorgio Mangiaretti, I analyzed the dynamics of ribosome metabolism, facilitating the study with fragile mutants of *E. coli* that could be lysed gently enough to preserve the polysomal structures.

The formulation of the ribosome cycle was extended to the analysis of the action of antiribosome antibiotics, and with Lucio Luzzatto, I discovered the specific block of polysome function at initiation that explains the bactericidal action of streptomycin. That work led to the recognition of the Eli Lilly Award in Microbiology.

Throughout the next decades, as I continued to teach and conduct research in Microbiology, gradually rising in the professorial ranks, I sustained an interest in infectious diseases, which centered on antibacterial

on nucleic acid metabolism followed my discovery with Nikolai Nikolaev of the role of double-stranded RNases in the formation of mature RNA species and subsequent analyses of ribosome formation.

In recent years I have continued the adroit choice of collaborators who were initiating pioneering ventures. Seven years ago, an increasing interest in long-range chromatin organization led me to join forces with Maynard Olson and my long-term associate Michele D'Urso in the development and exploitation of yeast artificial chromosomes (YAC) technology for the Human Genome Project. Although X chromosome mapping and technology development for gene searches may seem a far cry from traditional microbiology, it can be recalled that cell biology, genome mapping, and biotechnology are all disciplines derivative from classical microbiology, and they continue to depend on classical microbiology. One can note that the human genetics community would have found it unlikely that genome studies would become essentially totally dependent on the use of yeast hosts, clones, and genetics—in addition to the more traditional bacterial systems that already dominated the approaches to positional cloning.

After almost 40 years of research work, working with new ideas and students who become colleagues remains fun, and I am somewhat envious of those who are just starting out in microbiology as a career. Genome analysis and the study of X-linked diseases provide the current focus of my work but I have maintained an avid interest in all the branches of microbiology. The great renaissance of "real" microbiology is now just beginning, with the application of genome approaches to topics of the greatest scientific and practical interest—the understanding of evolution by the comparative analysis of microbial biochemistry, the use of microbial agents to solve environmental pollution problems, and the analysis of microbial pathology to conquer infectious diseases.

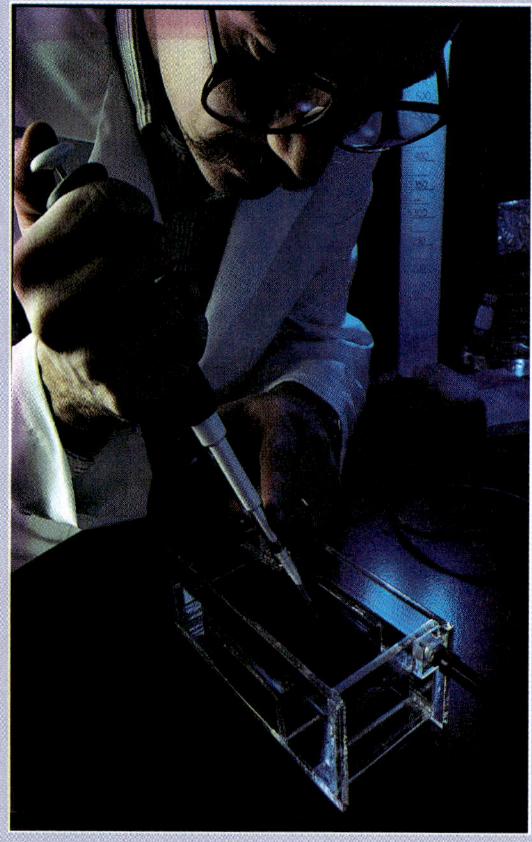

Molecular analyses often involve separation of nucleic acids by electrophoresis.

PART FOUR

Microbial Replication and Growth

CHAPTER 8

Viral Replication

Chapter Outline

Replication of viruses differs significantly from reproduction of the cells of living organisms. Because viruses lack cell structures such as a functional cytoplasmic membrane and ribosomes, they are incapable of independent activity outside of a host cell; viral replication can only occur within a host cell. There is great specificity between a virus and its host cell. Viruses depend on contact with a compatible host cell for replication. Animal viruses replicate within animal cells, plant viruses replicate within plant cells, and bacteriophage replicate within bacterial cells.

Replication of a virus consists of making copies of the viral genome and protein coat and assembling these into new viruses. During replication, the components of the virus (capsid, viral genome, and envelope if present) separate so that there is not a complete virus (virion) until after replication produces new virions. The nucleic acid and protein capsid structures—the essential components of a virus—are synthesized separately and then assembled before release from the host cell.

Viral replication begins with attachment of the virus to a host cell. This is followed by entry of the viral genome into the host cell where it begins to direct the synthesis of viral proteins and nucleic acid molecules. New viruses are assembled within the host cell by packaging viral genomes into protein coats. The completed viral progeny exit the host cell, sometimes killing it and sometimes acquiring a piece of host cell membrane as a viral envelope. The replicated viruses remain inert unless they attach to the surface of another compatible host cell.

8.1 STRUCTURE OF VIRUSES

Most viruses are too small to be seen under the light microscope. Observing the structure of a virus generally requires the use of an electron microscope. The smallest viruses, such as bacteriophage *ϕX174*, are about 27 nm in diameter. The largest viruses, the poxviruses, are about 300 nm in diameter, which is about the size of the smallest bacterial cell.

Viruses do not have cells, which are the fundamental structural units of all living organisms. Structurally, all viruses consists of an RNA or DNA core *genome* surrounded by a protein coat *capsid.* The combined viral genome and capsid is called the **nucleocapsid.** The nucleocapsid structures of viruses have characteristic morphologies (FIG. 8-1).

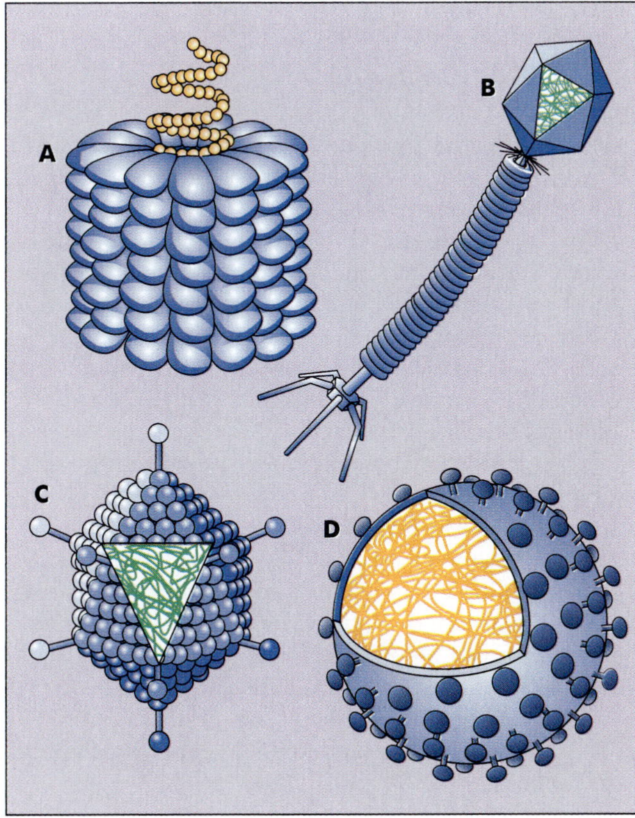

FIG. 8-1 Viruses have a central nucleic acid core, which may be RNA *(gold)* or DNA *(green)* surrounded by a protein coat called a capsid *(blue).* **A,** Some viruses, such as tobacco mosaic virus, have a helical symmetry with the capsid surrounding an RNA genome. **B,** Many viruses that infect bacteria, such as the T-even bacteriophage, have a complex capsid with DNA contained within the head structure. **C,** Some animal viruses, such as adenovirus, have isometric symmetry and a DNA genome. **D,** Yet others, such as coronavirus, have complex capsids and an envelope with protruding proteins surrounding an RNA genome.

CAPSID

The viral coat structure surrounding the nucleic acid genome of a virus is called the **capsid** (FIG. 8-2). The capsid may be composed of a single type of protein or may contain several different proteins. There are two basic types of symmetry in viral capsids: helical and isometric. The capsid symmetry is an important taxonomic criterion used in classifying viruses. The capsid of a helical virus, such as tobacco mosaic virus, forms a coil around the nucleic acid. The capsid of an isometric virus, such as poliovirus, often is a geometric polyhedral structure known as an icosahedron.

A capsid is composed of protein subunits called **capsomers.** The capsomers of isometric viruses with polyhedral structure typically are composed of five, six, or more protein subunits. In the simplest cases, capsid proteins aggregate into pentamers, which have five subunits, or hexamers, which have six subunits. The capsids of SV40 viruses consist only of pentamers. In most other isometric viruses, both hexamers and pentamers bind together to form more complex capsids (FIG. 8-3); a pentamer is located at each of the 12 vertices and hexamers comprise the surfaces of the capsid between the vertices. For example, adenoviruses have four hexamers on each edge, six hexamers on each face, and one pentamer at each vertex. Because this virus has an icosahedral capsid with 20

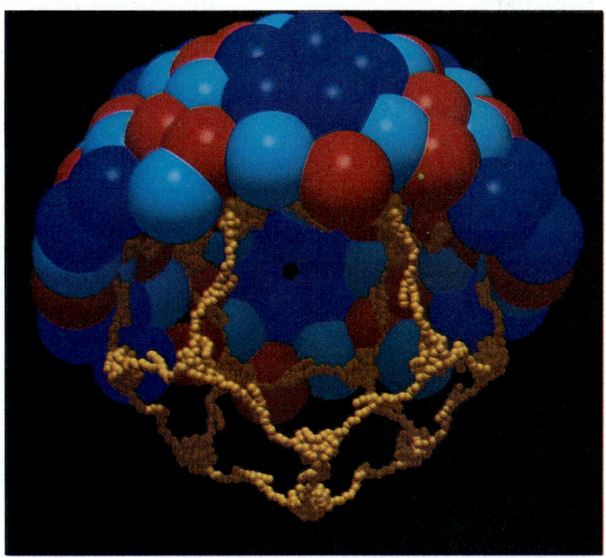

FIG. 8-2 Computer-generated photograph of the capsid of tomato bushy stunt virus. Red and blue spheres represent groups of amino acids and yellow spheres represent individual amino acids; the colors portray the varying symmetries of the proteins in the capsid.

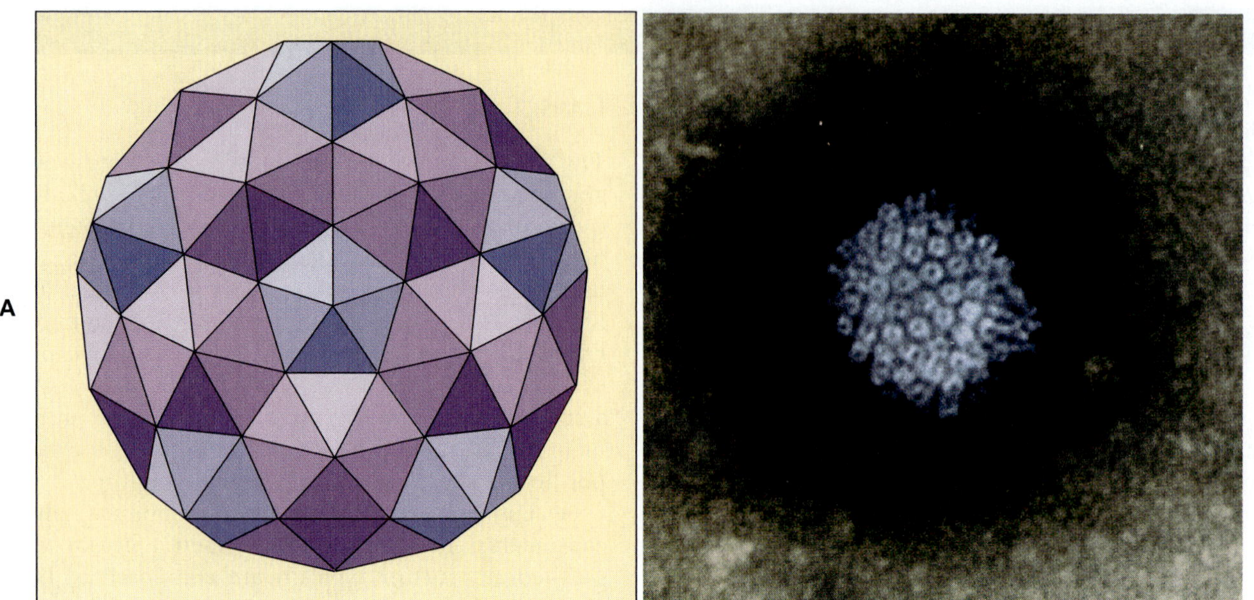

FIG. 8-3 **A,** Capsid of an isometric virus has capsomers joined as pentamer and hexamer units. **B,** Colorized micrograph of the capsid of a herpesvirus with no envelope present. (300,000×).

faces, there are 30 edges and 12 vertices. Adenoviruses, therefore, have 240 hexamers in addition to 12 pentamers.

In some viruses, such as the T-even bacteriophage that replicate in *Escherichia coli,* the capsid structures are even more complex. T-even bacteriophage have a head structure that is isometric and a tail structure that is helical. This combined structure is termed *binal* and is common among the bacteriophage.

GENOME

Unlike living cells, where double helical DNA is always the hereditary molecule comprising the genome of the cell, a **viral genome** may consist of linear or circular double-stranded DNA, single-stranded DNA, single-stranded linear RNA, or double-stranded linear RNA. As examples of viruses that replicate within bacterial cells, bacteriophage T4 has a linear double-stranded DNA genome, bacteriophage T7 has a linear double-stranded DNA genome, bacteriophage $\phi X174$ has a single-stranded DNA genome, bacteriophage Qβ has a single-stranded linear RNA genome, and bacteriophage $\phi 6$ has a linear double-stranded RNA genome. The ability of nucleic acid molecules other than double-stranded DNA to store the genetic information of an "organism" is unique among biological systems and suggests that different viruses evolved from diverse host cells.

The viral genome must be small and compact to fit within the viral capsid but must still code for a large number of gene products and regulatory functions. The genetic maps of several viruses show that genes are clustered according to their function. Some viruses maximize the amount of information that is stored within the genome by using overlapping genes and transcription of both strands of the DNA in opposite directions to code for different protein products. This is particularly important for the small viral genome to encode all the essential proteins for replication of the virus.

The genes of a virus may be contained within a single nucleic acid molecule (one segment) or the virus may have a **segmented genome,** that is, the viral genome may be made up of several nucleic acid molecules (multiple segments). Reovirus, for example, is a double-stranded RNA virus, with a segmented genome consisting of 10 separate RNA molecules (10 segments). Influenza viruses have single-stranded segmented RNA genomes. Measles and rabies viruses, in contrast, have single-stranded RNA genomes with only one segment.

ENVELOPE

Some viruses have a membrane layer called an **envelope** surrounding the outside of the capsid. These viruses are called *enveloped viruses.* The envelope of a virus does not function to regulate the flow of materials, nor does it exhibit any of the other physiological activities associated with the membranes of living cells. The presence of an envelope surrounding a viral par-

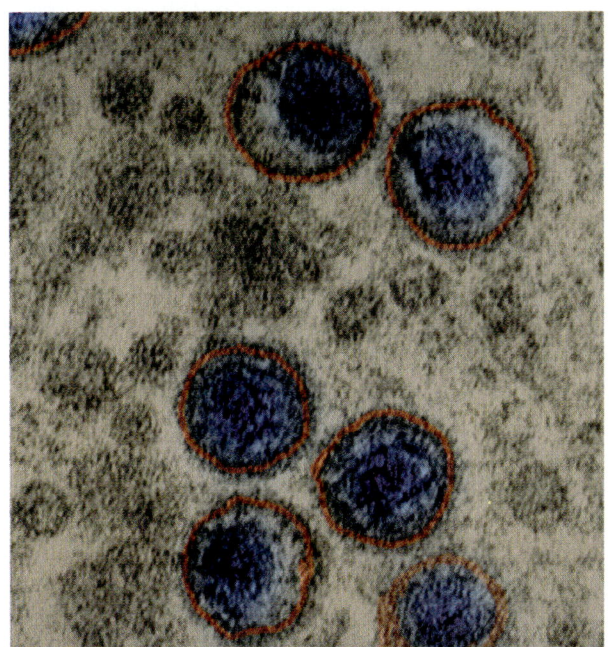

FIG. 8-4 Colorized micrograph of mouse mammary tumor viruses (MMTV), which like many animal viruses is surrounded by an envelope acquired from the host cell. (200,000×).

ticle, however, can alter recognition by host defense mechanisms designed to recognize and destroy foreign substances. The envelope may also have an important role in the initial attachment of a viral particle to the host cell in which it replicates.

The viral envelope is composed of phospholipid and proteins. Some of the envelope proteins are glycosylated (sugar added), and the hydrophilic carbohydrate ends of such proteins may protrude from the viral particle (FIG. 8-4). Such glycoproteins often occur as spikes on the outer surface of the virus. Some of these proteins are involved in binding the virus to a host cell, and others cause cell lysis (rupture of the host cell). In addition to the glycoproteins, other proteins of the viral envelope form a matrix layer that attaches the envelope to the capsid.

The proteins of the envelope are specified by the viral genome, but the carbohydrate portions of the glycoproteins and the lipid components of the viral envelope are obtained from the host cell. When the virus leaves the host cell, it picks up a portion of the nuclear or cytoplasmic membrane and that piece of host cell membrane can surround the viral capsid, forming the lipid portion of the envelope.

BOX 8-1

History of Virology

The word *virus* was used by the ancient Romans to mean poison, venom, or secretion—all unpleasant meanings. When the field of bacteriology began to develop, the medical use of the term *virus* implied any microscopic etiologic agent of disease. It was not until the invention of bacterial filters in 1884 by Charles Chamberland, Louis Pasteur's co-worker, who also invented the autoclave, that the field of virology really began to develop. In 1882, when Dmitrii Ivanowski reported that the agent responsible for tobacco mosaic disease could pass through a bacteriological filter, it became apparent that the microbial world contained even smaller members (viruses) than had been previously recognized.

While the observation of most viruses awaited a further advance in microscopy, that is, the development of the electron microscope in the 1940s, the field of virology continued to progress. In 1898, Friedrich Loeffler and Paul Frosch reported that foot and mouth disease was caused by an agent that passed through a bacteriological filter, and they suggested that the causal agents of many other infectious diseases, including smallpox, cowpox, and measles, might be similar filterable agents (viruses). Their discoveries opened up the field of animal virology. Also in 1898, Martinus Beijerinck, unaware of Ivanowski's work, ascribed tobacco mosaic disease to a "contagious living liquid." In 1911, Peyton Rous demonstrated that a cell-free filtrate could cause malignant growths in animals, showing that some viruses cause cancer. The work of Beijerinck and Rous established the basis for tumor virology. The work of Walter Reed and others on yellow fever in the early 1900s showed that this disease was caused by a filterable agent (virus) that could be transmitted by a mosquito carrier (vector); this work demonstrated that viruses could infect more than one animal species and that viral diseases could be transmitted to humans by biting arthropods. Bacteriophage, viruses that infect bacteria, were discovered by Frederick Twort and Felix d'Herelle separately. Consequently, it was known by 1915 that viruses could infect even the smallest organisms observed to that date.

In the mid-1920s, F. Parker and R. N. Nye successfully cultivated viruses using tissue culture techniques. Further advances were made by others during the following three decades, including the culture of viruses by Ernest Goodpasture and colleagues, using chick embryos (1931), and the establishment of the HeLa cell line (isolated from a cervical carcinoma of Henrietta Lacks) by G. O. Gay and co-workers (1952) that could be used for cultivating viruses. The ability to grow viruses in culture to facilitate the study of these organisms and permit various experiments with viruses was a significant milestone in the advancement of microbiology.

8.2 VIRAL REPLICATION

The replication of a virus within a host cell depends on the ability of the viral genome to enter the host cell, to remain functional, and to direct the host cell to produce viral macromolecules. For a specific virus to replicate within a host cell, (1) the host cell must be permissive, and the virus must be compatible with the host cell; (2) the host cell must not degrade the virus; (3) the viral genome must possess the information for modifying the normal metabolism of the host cell; and (4) the virus must be able to use the metabolic capabilities of the host cell to produce new virus particles containing replicated copies of the viral genome.

The virus or only its nucleic acid enters the host cell, where the viral nucleic acid—free of the viral protein coat—codes the alteration of normal host cell metabolism and the production of viral proteins and nucleic acid. When the viral genome is released from the capsid, the virus loses its identity, so that shortly after a host cell is infected with a virus, there are no complete viruses within the host cell. This loss of identity distinguishes viral replication from the reproduction of cellular organisms, including cellular organisms that reproduce within host cells. (Loss of cellular integrity is equated with cell death.)

HOST CELLS AND VIRAL REPLICATION

A cell within which a virus replicates is called a **host cell.** Cells in which a virus can replicate are termed *permissive* or *compatible host cells.* Only some cells are susceptible to infection with a virus. Cells in which the virus cannot replicate are *nonpermissive.* The **host cell range** of a virus is defined by the types of cells within which replication of that virus occurs. Some viruses have broad host ranges and can replicate within several types of cells and the cells of various plant species, animal species, or bacterial species. Other viruses have a narrow host range and may be able to replicate only within a single cell type of a single species.

There is enormous specificity between viruses and their compatible host cells. Some viruses called **bacteriophage,** or simply **phage,** replicate only within bacterial cells. Phage are further restricted to replication only within certain bacterial species. Other viruses,

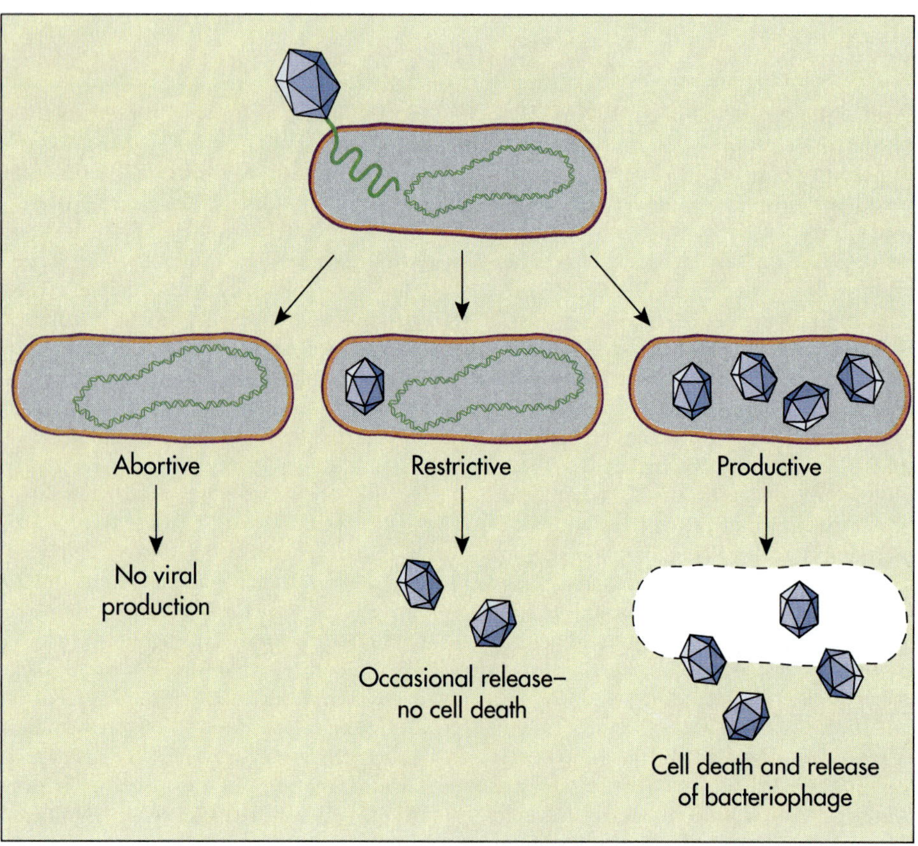

FIG. 8-5 Different possible outcomes of a viral infection range from no viral replication and no effect on the host cell to production of viruses and death of the host cell.

the **animal viruses,** replicate only within animal cells. Other viruses, called **plant viruses,** only replicate within plant cells. Yet others replicate within fungal, algal, and protozoan cells.

Within the host cell, the viral genome achieves control of the cell's metabolic activities. Either transcription of host cell genes is inhibited or viral mRNAs are translated more efficiently than host cell mRNAs so that viral protein synthesis dominates over synthesis of normal host cell proteins. In many cases, the viral genome actually codes for the shutdown of metabolic activities normally involved in host cell reproduction. The virus then uses the metabolic capacity of the host cell for the production of new viruses. In particular, the virus employs the host cell's ribosomes for producing viral proteins and the cell's ATP and reduced coenzymes for carrying out biosynthesis. Often the replication of a virus causes changes in the host cell, usually causing the death of that cell.

Viral infection of a host cell can have various outcomes (FIG. 8-5). **Productive infection,** which occurs in permissive cells, results in viral replication with the production of viruses that can infect other compatible host cells. The complete infective viruses produced in such infections are called *virions.* **Abortive infections** occur because the host cell is nonpermissive so that viral replication does not occur or because viral replication produces viral progeny that are incapable of infecting other host cells. Host cells may be only transiently permissive and the consequences are that the virus persists in the cell until the cell becomes permissive or that only a few of the cells in a population produce viral progeny at any time. **Restrictive infections** occur when the host cell is transiently permissive so that infective viral progeny are sometimes produced and at other times the virus persists in the infective cell without the production of infective viral progeny. In some cases, a viral genome will persist within an infected cell without destroying the host cell.

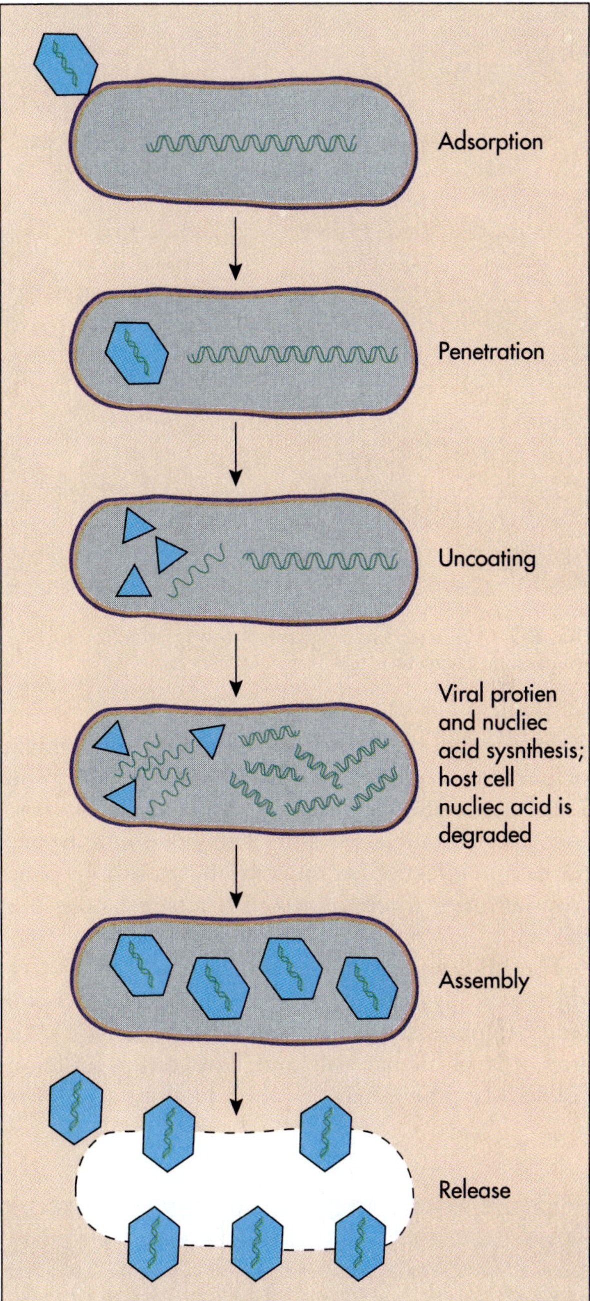

FIG. 8-6 Viral replication begins with adsorption to a host cell. Within the host cell the viral nucleic acid is released from the capsid and directs the synthesis of viral proteins and nucleic acids. When viruses infect bacterial cells, penetration and uncoating occur simultaneously and only the viral (phage) nucleic acid enters the host cell. Viral progeny are assembled and subsequently released from the host cell.

STAGES OF VIRAL REPLICATION

Although the specific details of viral replication vary from one virus to another, the general strategy for replication is the same for most viruses (FIG. 8-6). The stages in viral replication include (1) attachment of the virus to the outer surface of a suitable host cell, a process called adsorption; (2) penetration of the virus into the host cell; (3) release of the viral genome from the capsid, a process called uncoating that sometimes occurs simultaneously with penetration; (4) synthesis of viral proteins; (5) synthesis of viral nucleic acid; (6) assembly of viral progeny called virions; and (7) release of viruses from the host cell. This *viral replication cycle* is repeated when a virus encounters another suitable host cell.

Attachment to Host Cells

Viral replication begins with the attachment (adsorption) of a virus to the surface of a susceptible host cell (FIG. 8-7). Attachment of a virus to a host cell involves the binding of specific sites on the surface of the virus

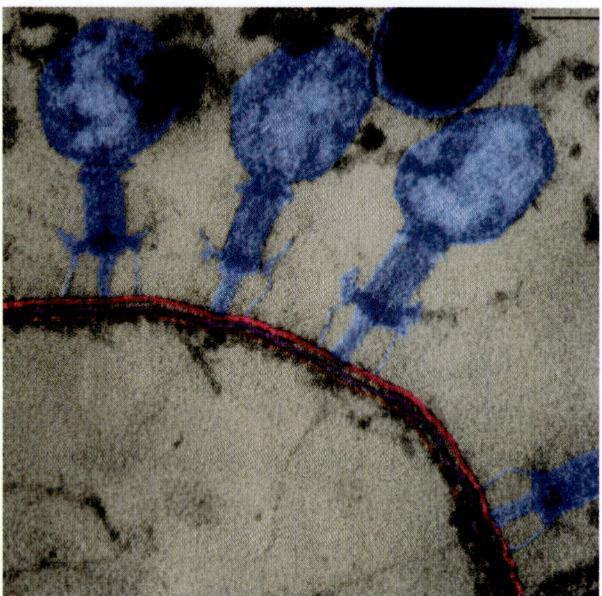

FIG. 8-7 Colorized micrograph showing attachment of T-even phage (*blue*) to a cell of *Escherichia coli*.

to specific sites on the surface of the host cell. Viral attachment to a cell surface does not require energy but does require ions in sufficient concentrations to reduce electrostatic repulsion. The susceptibility of a cell to viral infection is limited by the availability of appropriate sites where a virus can attach to the host cell.

The binding constituent on the host cell surface, which typically is a glycoprotein, is called the **receptor.** Viral receptors are part of the normal surface structure of a particular cell and have other functions (Table 8-1). There may be more than one type of receptor on a cell surface involved in the attachment of viruses. In some cases the receptors are on specific cell surface structures, such as the pili of donor bacterial cells. Some receptors are specific molecules such as the CD4 glycoprotein, which serves as the receptor for human immunodeficiency virus (HIV), on human T lymphocytes. Others occur on various cells, such as the neuraminic acid receptor for influenza viruses and the heparan sulfate receptor for herpesviruses. The ability of a virus to attach to a host cell only at a particular receptor explains in part the high degree of specificity between the virus and the host cell.

TABLE 8-1 Examples of Host Cell Surface Proteins that Serve as Virus Receptors

VIRUS	CELL SURFACE PROTEIN
Epstein-Barr virus	Receptor for the C3d complement protein on human B lymphocytes
Hepatitis A virus	Alpha 2-macroglobulin
Herpes simplex virus, type 1	Fibroblast growth factor receptor
Human immunodeficiency virus	CD4 protein on T-helper cells, macrophages, and monocytes
Poliovirus	Neuronal cellular adhesion molecule (NCAM)
Rabies virus	Acetylcholine receptor on neurons
Rhinovirus	Intercellular adhesion molecules (ICAMs) on the surface of respiratory epithelial cells
Reovirus, type 3	β-adrenergic receptor
Vaccinia virus	Epidermal growth factor receptor

Attachment of viruses to cells in many instances leads to irreversible changes in the structure of the virion. In many cases, once a virus attaches to a cell surface it cannot detach. In some instances, however, when penetration does not proceed, the virus can detach and readsorb to a different cell. Orthomyxoviruses and paramyxoviruses, as examples, have neuraminidases on their surfaces that can cleave neuraminic acid from the polysaccharides of the glycoprotein receptors, thereby releasing the attached virus.

Entry into Host Cells: Penetration and Uncoating

Entry of a virus into a host cell occurs very shortly after attachment (FIG. 8-8). The entry of the virus into the host cell may involve (1) transfer of only the viral genome across the cytoplasmic membrane; (2) transport of the entire virus across the cytoplasmic membrane by endocytosis, so that viruses accumulate within vacuoles in the cell; or (3) fusion of a viral envelope with the cytoplasmic membrane of the host cell.

Bacteriophage inject their DNA genomes into the host cell while their capsids remain outside the cell. In this case, **penetration** (entry of the phage genome into the host cell) and **uncoating** (release of the phage genome from the capsid) occur simultaneously. Similarly, the capsid of a poliovirus loses its structural integrity as a poliovirus is transported across the cytoplasmic membrane of a host cell. Other plant and animal viruses are engulfed by host cell and remain intact until inside the host cell. In such cases, penetration precedes uncoating.

Most enveloped viruses, such as influenza viruses, enter cells by endocytosis. After attachment of the viruses to the cell surface, an invagination of the cytoplasmic membrane, called a *clathrin-coated pit,* is formed. Clathrin is a membrane-bound protein that may be a receptor for specific attachment. The clathrin-coated pit with its attached virion moves into the cell and pinches off, forming a clathrin-coated vesicle. This vesicle then fuses with cytoplasmic vesicles called *endosomes.* Acidification of the interior of the vesicle follows and the pH drops, so that a hydrophobic portion of a viral surface protein is exposed. This hydrophobic region promotes fusion be-

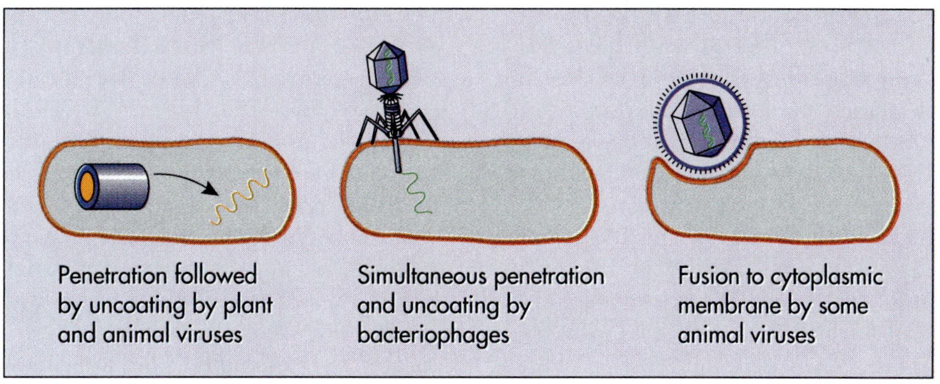

FIG. 8-8 Viruses can enter host cells in several ways.

tween the viral lipid envelope and the vesicle membrane, releasing the nucleocapsid into the cytoplasm.

In various animal viruses, such as orthomyxoviruses and paramyxoviruses, the capsid is removed as soon as the virus enters the host cell. In other cases, such as the replication of herpesviruses, the intact virus moves from the site of penetration to the nucleus. The cytoskeleton of the eukaryotic cell appears to play a critical role in such transport of the viral nucleocapsid to the nucleus. Uncoating occurs at the nuclear pores and the viral DNA or a DNA-protein complex is transported into the nucleus. The capsid breaks down and is eliminated in this process so that the genome is uncoated. Uncoating of poxviruses involves removal of the capsid by host cell enzymes and then further release of viral DNA from the core by enzymes coded for by the virus after infection.

A few enveloped viruses, exemplified by herpesviruses, enter the host cell by fusion of their envelopes with the cytoplasmic membrane of the host cell. Fusion of viral envelopes with the cytoplasmic membrane of the host cell involves the interaction of specific viral fusion proteins in the envelope of the virus with specific protein components of the cytoplasmic membrane. Surface fusion leaves the virion envelope surface proteins on the cell surface as part of the host cell cytoplasmic membrane, whereas entry of viruses by endocytosis leads to internalization of viral surface proteins.

Expression and Replication of Viral Genomes

The expression of the viral genome to synthesize viral proteins and the replication of the viral genome within the host cell are essential for viral replication. Viral proteins are made that alter host cell functions. In addition, the host cell produces viral capsid proteins, proteins for the replication of viral genomes, and proteins for the packaging of the genome into virus particles. Some viruses, such as papovaviruses and papillomaviruses, rely on host enzymes to replicate the viral genome. Most viruses, such as herpesviruses, use viral proteins to replicate the viral genome.

Viruses may stimulate transcription of their own genes within the infected cell by encoding a viral transcription factor that directly binds to DNA, or by modifying the number or activity of cellular transcription factors. Infection with many viruses leads to an inhibition of transcription of cellular protein-coding genes by host RNA polymerase II. Usually after viral infection, inhibition of host-cell mRNA translation also occurs. Inhibition of host-cell mRNA translation or degradation of host mRNA provide the viral mRNA with increased availability of ribosomal subunits, translation factors, tRNAs, and amino acid precursors for protein synthesis.

DNA Viruses The replication of a DNA viral genome can occur in many ways. Some viruses act like the bacterium *E. coli,* exhibiting bidirectional DNA replication from a single point of origin. In some cases, however, the terminus for DNA replication is offset from the origin. Some linear viruses exhibit multiple initiation points for DNA synthesis and thus resemble DNA replication in eukaryotic cells. In other cases, the replication of viral DNA follows a rolling circle model in which a circular DNA molecule is used to spin off unidirectionally a linear DNA molecule. The rolling circle replication of a DNA molecule requires an endonuclease that can nick the circular DNA molecule, establishing a free end of the nucleotide chain that can *roll off* the circle. A variation of the rolling circle model of DNA replication appears in the synthesis of single-stranded DNA for those DNA viruses that lack the normal double helical DNA molecule.

The genes of some DNA viruses are expressed within the nuclei of eukaryotic host cells. Viruses, such as adenoviruses and herpesviruses, use host cell DNA-dependent RNA polymerases for transcription to produce viral mRNAs. In other viruses, such as the poxviruses, the initial transcriptional events and most events in viral replication occur in the cytoplasm. The poxviruses encode the factors necessary for transcription. The initial transcription occurs within the core of the virion and the protein products of these transcripts function to release the viral genome from the core. A few DNA viruses require the help of a second virus to complete their replication. The adeno-associated virus is a defective DNA virus requiring the help of adenoviruses or herpes simplex viruses.

Single-Stranded (+) RNA Viruses Some viruses have single-stranded RNA genomes. The genomes of all such RNA viruses are linear. Viruses whose RNA genomes can serve as mRNAs are called **plus (+) strand viruses.** The RNA genome of the single-stranded (+) RNA viruses also serves as a template for synthesis of a complementary minus (−) strand RNA that is used for viral genome replication.

Picornaviruses, such as polioviruses, are examples of single-stranded (+) RNA viruses. Because the RNA genome serves as mRNA, these viruses need not carry an RNA polymerase within the virion to initiate viral gene expression. Following penetration via endocytosis and uncoating, poliovirus RNA binds to ribosomes and is translated in its entirety to produce a large polypeptide that is subsequently cleaved by virus-encoded proteases into smaller functional proteins. The synthesis of the (−) strand RNA is performed by a viral RNA-dependent RNA polymerase that is derived from cleavage of the polypeptide. An RNA-dependent RNA polymerase is called an **RNA replicase.** The (−) strand RNA serves as a template for the viral RNA replicase to make more (+) strands. The progeny (+) strands can function as mRNAs, templates to make more (−) strands, and genomes of progeny virions. Compared to a DNA-dependent polymerase, an RNA primase is less accurate and hence there is a relatively high rate of spontaneous mutations during replication of RNA viruses.

Single-stranded (−) RNA Viruses RNA viruses whose genome does not function as an mRNA are called (−) viruses. The genome of the single-stranded (−) RNA viruses (rabies, for example) does not serve as a mRNA. Rather, transcription using the minus strand as a template must occur to form (+) mRNAs. To accomplish transcription, all (−) RNA viruses carry an RNA polymerase within the virion. Uncoating of the (−) RNA virus introduces both the viral RNA genome and the necessary RNA polymerase for its expression into the host cell.

Transcription of the (−) viral genome is the first event after entry into a host cell. The process yields functionally monocistronic mRNAs that are (+) strands, each specifying a single protein. The (−) strand RNA alternately serves for the transcription of specific mRNAs and as a complete template for the synthesis of (+) RNA that can serve as the template for the production of (−) RNA genomes. Splicing of the (+) RNA can produce multiple mRNAs, each specifying a different protein. Thus the (+) transcript that functions as mRNA can be different from the (+) strand RNA that serves as the template for production of RNA genomes for viral progeny.

Retroviruses Retroviruses are RNA viruses that produce DNA by reverse transcription during their replication. These viruses have a genome consisting of two identical single-stranded (+) RNA molecules. Retroviruses are *diploid* because they have two copies of all genes. The two identical RNA molecules of the genome are partially held together by hydrogen-bonding between complementary palindromic sequences located near one end of the RNA molecules.

The key steps in the replication of a retrovirus are (1) binding of the primer–reverse transcriptase complex to the genomic RNA, (2) synthesis of a DNA copy complementary to the RNA to produce a DNA-RNA hybrid, (3) digestion of RNA in the DNA-RNA hybrid by ribonuclease H activity of the reverse transcriptase, and (4) synthesis of the complementary strand of the viral DNA to produce linear double-stranded DNA.

The genomic RNA of a retrovirus, such as the human immunodeficiency virus (HIV) that causes AIDS, serves as the template for the synthesis of viral DNA. Besides the RNA genome, a retrovirus contains an RNA-dependent DNA polymerase (reverse transcriptase), a primer to initiate DNA synthesis, and a mixture of tRNAs that can function as primers within the host cell. The linear double-stranded DNA formed by reverse transcription moves into the nucleus of the host cell and is integrated into the host cell genome. The products of transcription are genome-length RNA molecules and mRNAs that are translated to form viral polypeptides that are subsequently cleaved to produce individual viral proteins.

Double-stranded RNA Viruses Only a few viruses, such as reoviruses, have double-stranded RNA genomes. The double-stranded RNAs of reoviruses are transcribed by an RNA-dependent RNA polymerase contained within the virion. The RNAs formed serve as mRNAs for protein synthesis and also serve as templates for synthesis of the complementary strands of RNA so that double-stranded RNA genome segments are formed for incorporation into viral progeny.

Assembly and Maturation

Once sufficient proteins for capsids and copies of the viral genome are synthesized, new viruses are assembled within the host cell (FIG. 8-9). **Assembly** involves the packaging of the nucleic acid genome into the capsid to form the nucleoprotein. Many viruses usually are assembled at the same time and completed viruses accumulate within the host cell.

Viruses have evolved several strategies for their assembly (FIG. 8-10). Generally a portion of the capsid is assembled first and the nucleic acid genome is then added. The capsid structure is then completed, sealing the genome within it.

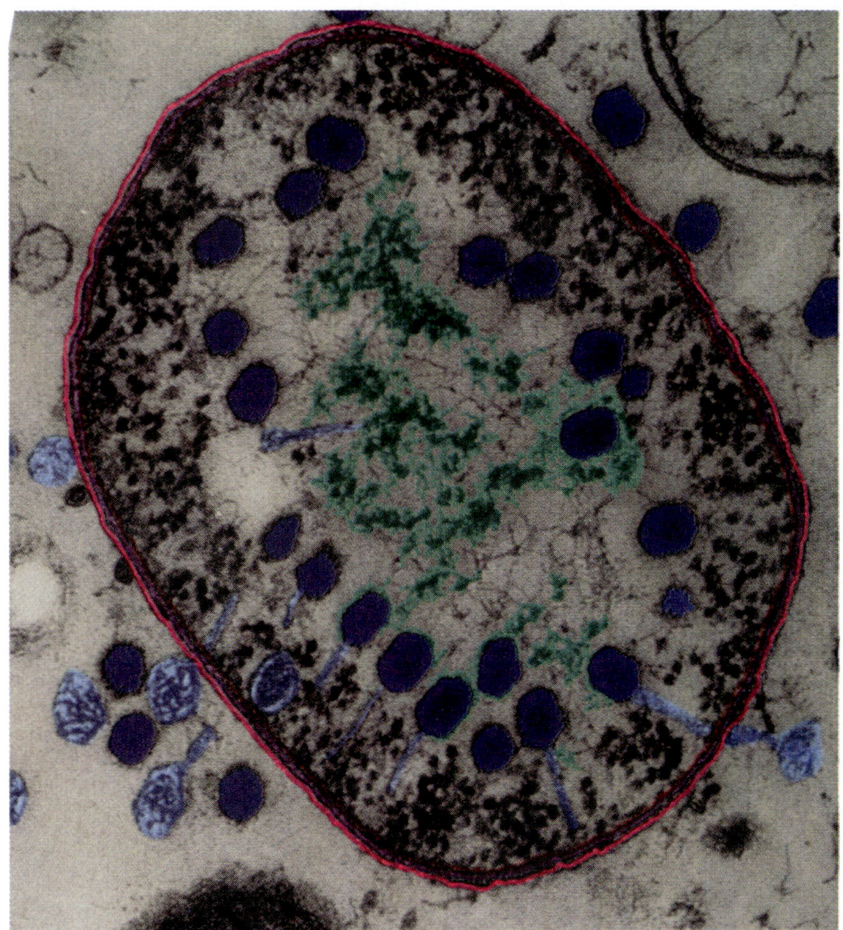

FIG. 8-9 Colorized micrograph of *Escherichia coli* with assembled bacteriophage *(blue)* inside the bacterial host cell.

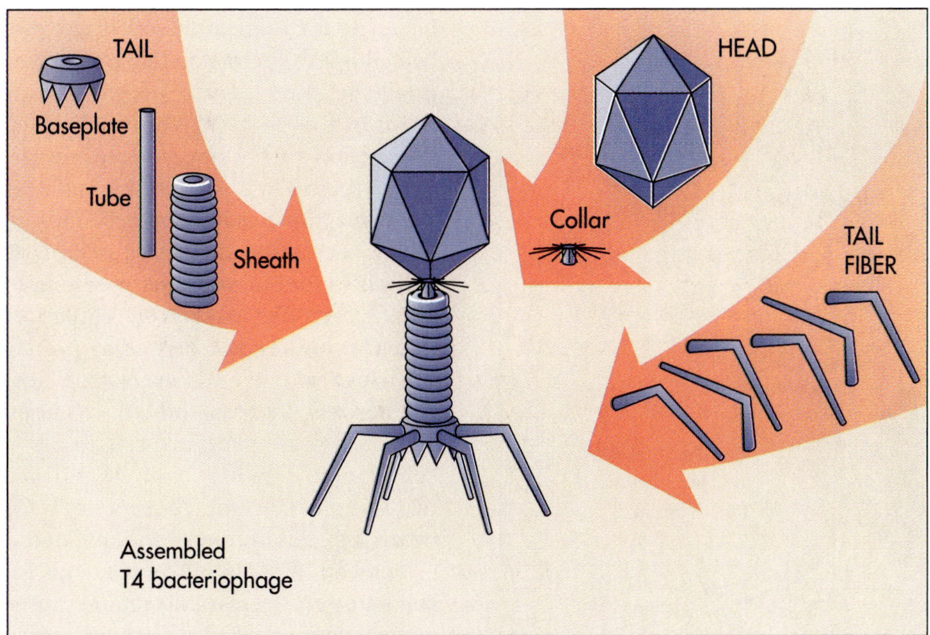

FIG. 8-10 Assembly of a T-even bacteriophage requires attachment of many different capsid protein components that surround the DNA genome. Only the head surrounds the genome; the tail parts are for host recognition and DNA injection.

Assembly of some viruses, such as adenoviruses, occurs within the nucleus. Assembly of other viruses, such as poxviruses, occurs in the cytoplasm. Bacteriophage, obviously, also are assembled in the cytoplasm because prokaryotic cells lack a nucleus.

Assembly can be a complex process. In picornaviruses, for example, 60 copies each of the virion proteins designated VP0, VP1, and VP3 assemble in the cytoplasm to form a procapsid. Viral RNA then wraps around inside the procapsid, and, in the process, VP0 is cleaved to yield two polypeptides: VP2 and VP4. The cleavage probably causes rearrangement of the capsid into a stable structure in which the RNA is shielded from access by nucleases.

In the enveloped viruses the virus undergoes further modifications, including the addition of the envelope from the host cell. This process is called **maturation** (FIG. 8-11). In many cases, maturation occurs at membrane sites with added viral proteins for the phospholipid envelope obtained from the host cell. This often occurs as the virus is released from the host cell. The last step of virion maturation for all of the (−) strand RNA viruses (such as influenza viruses) is linked with release of the virus from the infected cell. Assembled viral nucleocapsids become wrapped up by portions of the cytoplasmic membrane of the host cell to complete viral maturation as the virus particle is released from the cell.

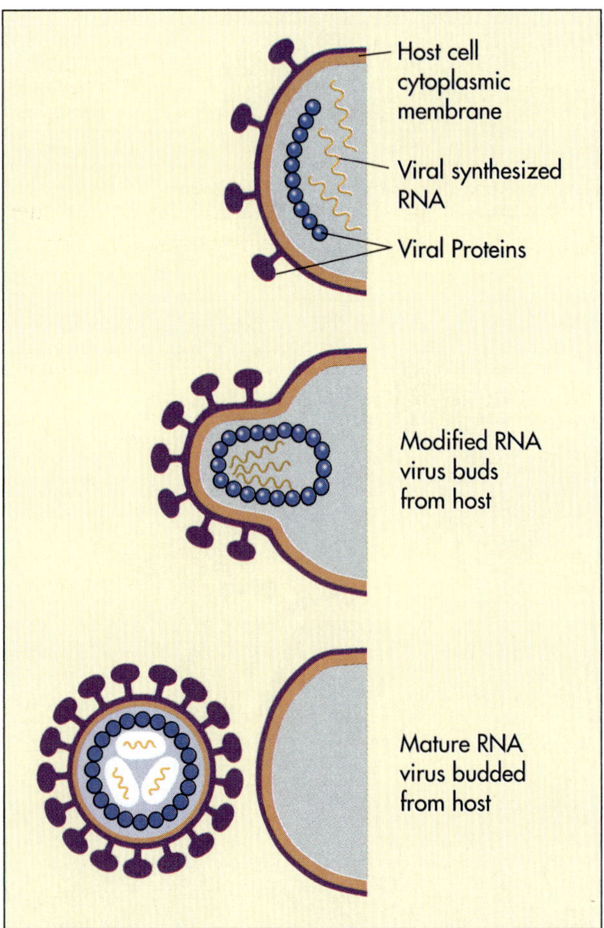

FIG. 8-11 Enveloped viruses acquire the envelope as they pass across the nuclear or cytoplasmic membrane of the host cell.

Viral replication proteins and assembled virions often accumulate in specific regions of the nucleus or cytoplasm. The envelopment and maturation of herpesviruses occur at the inner nuclear membrane. Mature enveloped herpesviruses accumulate in the space between the inner and outer nuclear membranes, within the endoplasmic reticulum, and in vesicles carrying the virus to the cell surface. The assembly of these new structures in the infected cell often displaces host-cell components from specific regions of the cell and leads to one form of cytopathic effect. The inclusion bodies or areas of altered staining are useful in diagnostic virology because they are found at locations in the cytoplasm or nucleus that are characteristic of specific groups of viruses.

Release

Generally, many viruses are produced within a single host cell and are released together. The complete viruses that are released are called **virions.** The release of viruses from the host cell often kills the host cell. In some cases, during release, viruses acquire a portion of host cell cytoplasmic membrane as an envelope surrounding the virus.

Cell Lysis The release of many viruses occurs through cell lysis. All the viruses assembled within the host cell are released simultaneously, when the host cell lyses. The host cell is killed in the process. Most bacteriophage are released from their bacterial host by cell lysis. One of the late proteins coded for by the phage genome is lysozyme, which catalyzes the breakdown of the peptidoglycan wall structure of bacteria. The action of the lysozyme results in sufficient damage to the cell wall so that the wall is unable to protect the cell against osmotic shock. This results in the lysis of the bacterial cell and the release of the phage particles into the surrounding medium. Lysozyme activity is subject to phage-directed regulation, which ensures that the wall is not degraded prematurely before a sufficient number of phage particles are completely synthesized and assembled. Nonenveloped animal viruses also are generally released by lysis of the host cell. Proteins coded for by these viruses inhibit host macromolecular metabolism and this leads to the death and disruption of the infected cell.

Budding Enveloped viruses exit from the infected cell through the cytoplasmic membrane by exocytosis or by fusion of vesicles containing virus particles with the cytoplasmic membrane of the host cell (FIG. 8-12). This mode of release is called **budding.** Some viral proteins, including proteins that are gly-

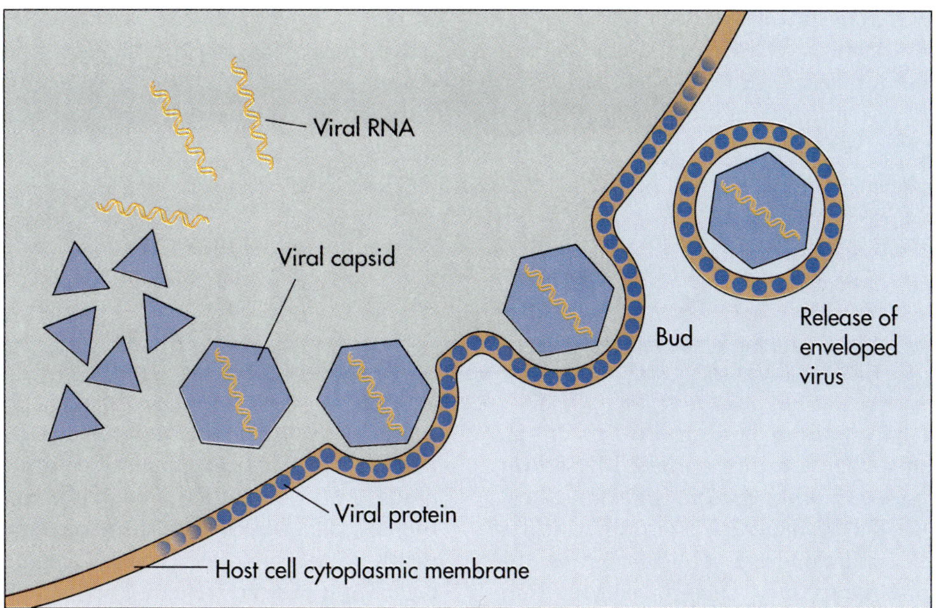

FIG. 8-12 Some enveloped viruses are released from the host cell by budding.

cosylated, become inserted into the cytoplasmic membrane during budding release from the host cell. The membrane proteins aggregate and displace host membrane proteins.

Some viruses, including retroviruses, are released from host cells when their assembled nucleocapsids bud directly through the cytoplasmic membrane. This produces enveloped virions during the release process (FIG. 8-13). Other viruses bud through internal membranes such as the endoplasmic reticulum or Golgi apparatus (rotaviruses), or inner nuclear membrane (herpesviruses), forming vesicles. These viruses obtain their envelopes from the membranes of the vesicles rather than from the cytoplasmic membrane surrounding the host cell. The vesicles containing the assembled viruses migrate to the inner surface of the cytoplasmic membrane and fuse with it, effectively releasing intact virions to the outside.

Viruses that are released by budding vary considerably in their effects on host cell metabolism and in-

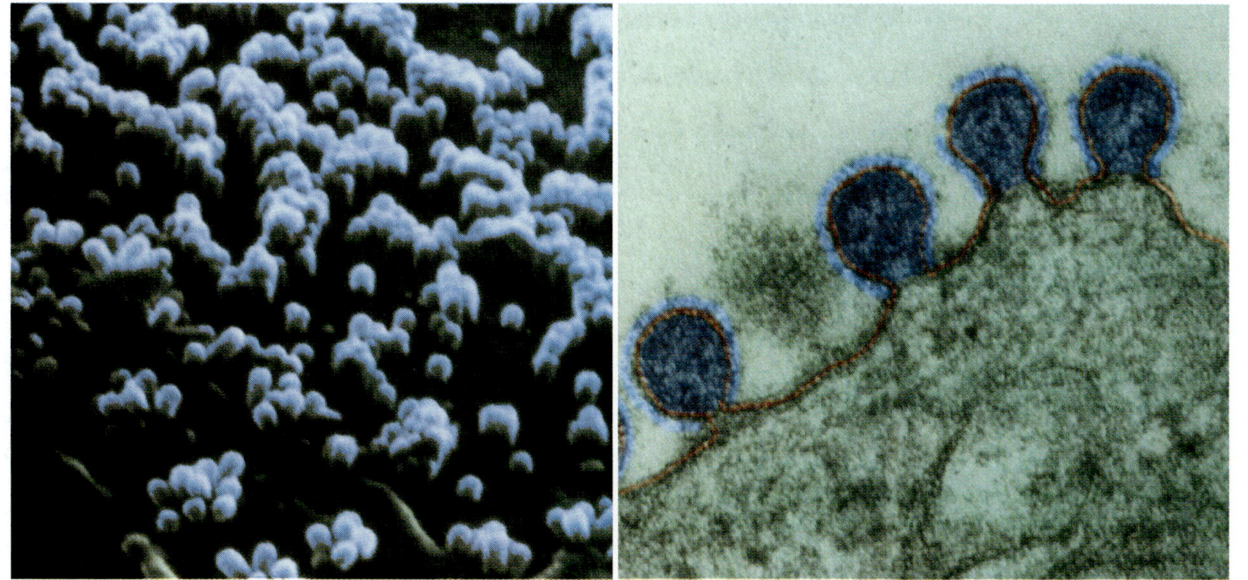

FIG. 8-13 **A,** Scanning electron micrograph (colorized) showing budding release of human immunodeficiency virus. **B,** Transmission electron micrograph (colorized) showing budding release of human immunodeficiency virus *(blue)*.

tegrity. Some, such as herpesviruses, cause host cell lysis, whereas others, such as retroviruses, do not immediately disrupt the integrity of the host cell. However, by virtue of the insertion of the viral glycoproteins into the cell surface, these viruses impart to the cell new specificity surface proteins and glycoproteins, and the infected cell can and does become a target for the immune defenses of the host.

Some enveloped virions, such as Sendai virus, have cell-surface proteins that facilitate the fusion of the virion envelope with the host cell–surface membrane. Viral glycoproteins that are inserted into the host membrane surface promote fusion between neighboring cells, leading to multinucleated cell formation. The fusion of the neighboring cells allows efficient cell-to-cell spread of the virus.

8.3 REPLICATION OF BACTERIOPHAGE

The bacteriophage replicate within host bacterial cells. The bacteriophage are differentiated based on their morphologies, genomic nucleic acids, and host cell ranges (Table 8-2). Some replicate only within a specific host cell strain. Others replicate in various Gram-negative or Gram-positive bacterial cells. Within the host bacterial cell the phage uses the cells molecules (e.g., ATP and nucleotides) and structures (including ribosomes) to make new phage. In most cases the complete replication cycle of the phage results in death of the host cell. Phage that kill host bacterial cells when they are released are called **lytic phage.**

TABLE 8-2 Characteristics of Some of the Groups of Bacteriophage

BACTERIOPHAGE	DESCRIPTION
Tailed bacteriophage	Genome: DNA, double-stranded. Virion: complex shape, binary symmetry, variable number of capsomers. The tails of the phage are long and contractile in group A (Myoviridae), long and noncontractile in group B (Styloviridae), and very short in group C (Pedoviridae). Example: T-even coliphages.
Cubic bacteriophage	Group 1 (Microviridae) Genome: DNA, single-stranded. Virion: icosahedral, cubic symmetry, 12 capsomers. Example: ϕX174 Group 2 (Corticoviridae) Genome: DNA, double-stranded. Virion: cubic symmetry, enveloped. Example: PM-2. Group 3 (Leviviridae) Genome: RNA, single-stranded. Virion: icosahedral, cubic symmetry, 32 capsomers. Example: f_2. Group 4 (Cystoviridae) Genome: RNA, double-stranded. Virion: cubic symmetry, enveloped. Example: ϕ6.
Filamentous bacteriophage (Inoviridae)	Genome: DNA, single-stranded. Virion: rod-shaped, helical symmetry. Example: fd.

The replication of lytic phage can be observed as plaques (zones of clearing) when permissive bacteria are grown on a solid medium (see Box 8-2). In the absence of phage infection, the bacterial growth is confluent, forming a "lawn" of bacterial cells. Several kinds of mutations can occur during the replication cycle of a bacteriophage that alter its host cell range or the appearance of the plaques it forms (Table 8-3).

Some bacteriophage are capable of **lysogeny,** an alternate replication strategy in which the phage genome is incorporated into the bacterial chromosome. Such phage are called **temperate bacteriophage** because only the integrated phage genome is replicated along with the replication of host cell DNA. Phage capsids are not made and complete phage progeny are not produced. The host cell is not killed by lysis in this mode of phage replication.

In lysogeny, the phage genome is usually incorporated into the bacterial chromosome by nonreciprocal recombination. Once incorporated into the bacterial chromosome, the phage genome (referred to as a **prophage**) is replicated with the bacterial DNA during normal host cell DNA replication. At a later time, the prophage can be excised from the bacterial chromosome or plasmid DNA, reestablishing a lytic replicative cycle.

BOX 8-2

ASSAYING FOR LYTIC BACTERIOPHAGE

To assay for infective bacteriophage, a lawn of bacteria is prepared on a suitable solid nutrient medium, and dilutions of the phage suspension are then spread over the same surface. In the absence of lytic bacteriophage, the bacteria form a confluent lawn of growth.

In regions where phage replication occurs, the bacteria are killed due to the lytic release of the phage. Lysis by bacteriophage is indicated by the formation of a zone of clearing or plaque within the lawn of bacteria (see FIG.). Each plaque corresponds to the site where a single bacteriophage acted as an infectious unit and initiated its lytic replicative cycle. The spread of infectious phage from the initially infected bacterial cell to the surrounding cells results in the lysis of the bacteria in the vicinity of the initial phage particle and hence this zone of clearing. The number of plaques that develop and the appropriate dilution factors can be used to calculate the number of bacteriophages in a sample. The medium used in these assays has a relatively low percentage of agar and therefore is called *soft agar;* it permits diffusion of phage to nearby uninfected cells but does not permit the phages that are produced to move to remote parts of the plate.

Plaques do not continue to spread indefinitely. With T4 phage, the plaque size is limited because when a cell is heavily reinfected with phage before the time of normal lysis, the lysis of the cell is inhibited, a phenomenon known as *lysis inhibition,* which is actually an extension of the period of phage synthesis. In other phage, plaques are limited in size because the host bacterial cells are no longer in a growth phase in which phages can be produced.

Replication of lytic bacteriophage causes the formation of plaques in a lawn of bacterial cells growing on an agar surface.

TABLE 8-3 Types of Mutations in Bacteriophage

TYPE OF MUTATION	DESCRIPTION
Host range	Change the range of host cells that the phage can infect that is due to a change in receptor sites of the host cell, a change in the phage or host enzymes involved in replication, or in the restriction enzymes or modification of the phage genome.
Plaque morphology	Change in the characteristics of the plaques (zones of clearing due to host cell lysis) formed by the phage growing on host bacterial cells spread on a solid surface that may be seen as a change in size of the plaque or whether the plaque is clear or turbid; plaque morphology is characteristic of the rate of phage replication and the efficiency of host cell lysis.
Temperature sensitive	Change in range of temperatures over which the phage can replicate such that the phage remains able to replicate at one temperature but not at a higher temperature due to a change in a phage protein that makes the protein unstable at the higher temperature; this is an example of a conditionally "lethal" mutation because the phage is unable to replicate at the higher temperature, but replicates at the lower temperature.
Nonsense	Change in the nucleotide sequence of the phage genome that forms a stop codon, causing termination of the synthesis of a phage-coded protein; in some host cells the nonsense codon is suppressed and the phage will replicate, whereas in other host cells lacking a suppressor the phage is unable to replicate; this limits the host cell range of the phage.

Growth Curve of Lytic Phage

The lysis of the bacterial cell releases a large number of phage simultaneously. Consequently, the lytic replication cycle exhibits a **one-step growth curve** with high numbers of phage released periodically (FIG. 8-14). The growth curve for lytic phage begins with an **eclipse period** during which there are no complete infective phage particles and the naked DNA within the host cell is unable to infect other cells to initiate a new replicative cycle. The end of the eclipse period is the time at which an average of one infectious unit is produced for each productive cell. The eclipse period, thus, is the time between entry of the phage DNA and formation of the first complete phage within the host cell.

The eclipse period is part of a longer period, the **latent period,** which, like the eclipse period, begins when the phage injects DNA into a host cell, but which does not end until the first assembled phage from the infected cells appear extracellularly. The latent period for a T-even phage typically is about 15 minutes. During the time between the end of the eclipse period and the end of the latent period, assembled phage accumulate within the bacterial cell. Completely assembled phage accumulate within the bacterial cell until the cell lyses, releasing the phages into the extracellular fluid.

The **burst size,** which varies from cell to cell, represents the average number of infectious phage units produced per cell; a typical burst size for a T-even phage may be as high as 200. As a result of the simultaneous release of infective phage, the number of phages that can initiate a lytic replication cycle increases greatly in a single step. The entire lytic growth cycle for some T-even phage can occur in less than 20 minutes under optimal conditions.

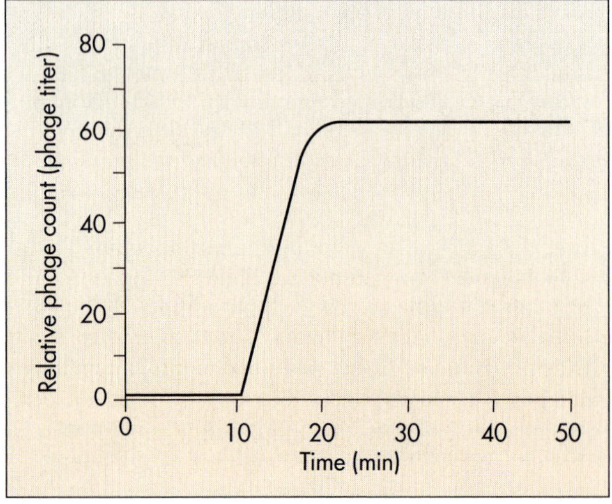

FIG. 8-14 Because many viruses are released simultaneously when a host cell lyses, lytic viruses exhibit a one-step growth curve.

Lytic T-even Phage

The general developmental sequence of the T-even phage is exemplified by the replication of phage T4, a bacteriophage with an icosahedral head capsid that contains the genome and a tail portion of the capsid that is involved in attachment to the host cell. The genome of phage T4 is a large double-stranded linear DNA macromolecule that is highly folded within the head of the phage (FIG. 8-15). The replication of T4 results in lysis of the host cell.

Attachment and Penetration

Replication of bacteriophage T4 begins with the attachment of phage tail fibers to the outer surface of a host cell, such as *E. coli* (FIG. 8-16). Bacteriophage T4, like other T-even phages of *E. coli*, use cell wall lipopolysaccharides or proteins as receptors. Variation in receptors on different strains of *E. coli* results in differing host cells for T4 phage. The entire phage does not penetrate the bacterial cell. Rather, after the baseplate of the phage is attached to the surface of the host cell, conformational changes occur in the baseplate and sheath, and the tail sheath appears to contract because it is reorganized from 24 to 12 rings. The sheath contains deoxy-ATP that provides the energy for the powerful contraction. The central core of the tail structure is forced through the bacterial wall and the phage DNA is pushed into the periplasmic space by the contraction of the sheath. The phage tail penetrates the cell wall but not the cytoplasmic membrane. Subsequently, the phage DNA migrates across the cytoplasmic membrane and into the cell.

When phage T4 DNA enters a compatible *E. coli* cell, it is not degraded by the endonucleases of that host cell. This is because the DNA of T4 phage contains glucosylated 5-hydroxymethylcytosine instead of cytosine, a chemical modification of the DNA that prevents the endonucleases of the bacterium from degrading the phage genome. T4 phage code for enzymes that synthesize 5-hydroxymethylcytosine and subsequently add glucose to this nucleotide. The glucosylation of the T4 phage genome requires uridine diphosphoglucose. If T4 phage is grown on a host cell that does not produce uridine diphosphoglucose, the phage DNA will not be glucosylated and it can not replicate in other host cells because its DNA genome will be destroyed by restriction endonucleases.

Early Gene Expression

Phage T4 codes for over 20 new proteins that are synthesized early after infection. The production of these proteins represents the early developmental steps of phage replication. Collectively the enzymes involved in these steps are referred to as **early proteins** (proteins that are made soon after phage penetration). These early proteins bring about the stoppage of host cell macromolecular synthesis. An early protein of T4

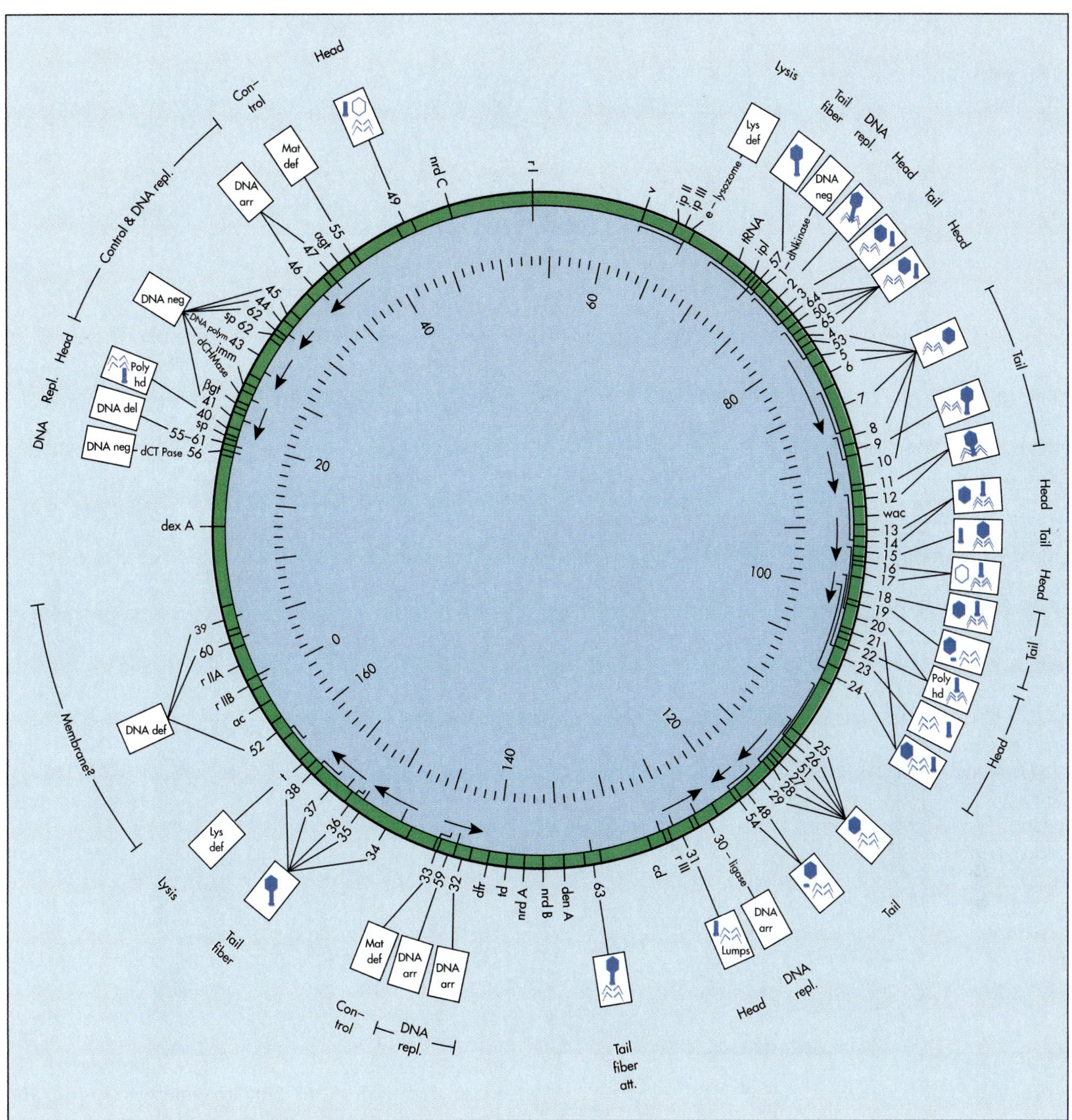

FIG. 8-15 The genome of T-even phage encodes the information for phage DNA replication and synthesis of numerous proteins. The genome is transcribed in differing directions *(arrows)* for the production of the phage structures.

phage is a nuclease that degrades the host cell DNA; the deoxynucleotides released by the degradation of the bacterial chromosome are used as precursors for the synthesis of phage DNA. The genome of T4 also codes for enzymes that break down the precursor for the normal host cell nucleotide deoxycytidine triphosphate. Several new tRNAs are also produced that read phage T4 mRNA more efficiently. The entire sequence of penetration, shutting off host cell transcription and translation, and the degradation of the bacterial chromosome takes only a few minutes.

Phage T4 DNA is initially transcribed by a bacterial RNA polymerase, and among the first proteins synthesized are ones for the modification of the *E. coli* RNA polymerase. The phage-coded polypeptides replace or modify the sigma subunits of the *E. coli* RNA polymerase. By doing so, they alter the recognition sequence so that the RNA polymerase no longer binds at the normal Pribnow sequences of the *E. coli* DNA. When this occurs, the RNA polymerase from the host cell binds at sites that control the transcription of other genes required for phage replication.

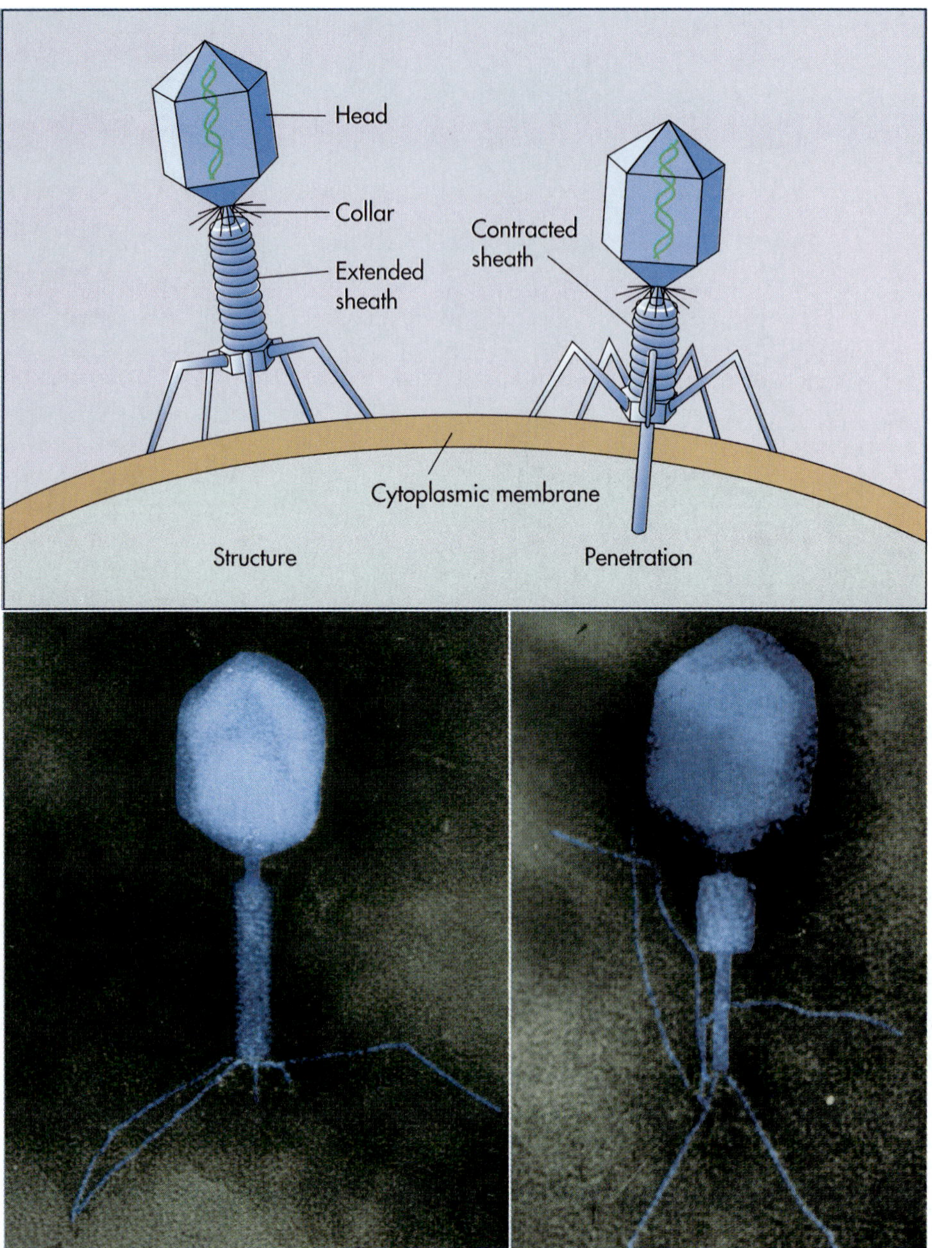

FIG. 8-16 The tail structure of a T-even bacteriophage is involved in adsorption and penetration. Contraction of the tail sheath forces the phage through the cytoplasmic membrane of the host cell and injects the phage DNA.

The early genes coded for by the phage genome include enzymes involved in the replication of the phage DNA. These enzymes are made in large amounts so that synthesis of phage T4 DNA occurs rapidly. T4 DNA contains hydroxymethylcytosine, which is synthesized by two phage-encoded enzymes. After T4 DNA is synthesized, it is glucosylated by the addition of glucose to the hydroxymethylcytosine.

The linear DNA of T4 has terminal redundancy, that is, a nucleotide sequence is repeated at both ends of the molecule. This redundancy occurs because the virus has more than one set of genes. It also makes the genome map circular even though the viral genome is linear. Following replication of phage DNA, an enzymatic reaction joins 6 to 10 copies of the phage DNA via terminally redundant ends to form *concatemers.* During assembly, concatemers are cleaved to produce the phage genome.

Late Gene Expression

After these early events in the phage replication cycle, there is a further modification of the RNA polymerase, resulting in the cessation of further synthesis of the early phage proteins. RNA polymerase cores combine with new phage-specific sigma factors that control transcription of late genes. This shift in the recognition site of the RNA polymerase coincides with the beginning of the synthesis of **late proteins.**

The late phage genes code for the various proteins that make up the capsid structure of the phage. The tail, tail fiber, and head structures of the phage are made up of proteins coded for by different phage genes, with at least 32 genes involved in the formation of the tail structure and at least 55 genes involved in the formation of the head structure.

The transition from early to late gene transcription in T4 phage involves a shift with regard to which of the two DNA strands of the phage genome serves as the sense strand. Early genes are transcribed in a leftward direction; late genes are transcribed in a rightward direction. Alteration of the recognition subunit of the RNA polymerase accounts for the change in the base sequences of the DNA recognized as promoter sites for transcription of the phage genome and permits changes in the DNA strand that acts as the sense strand. By altering reading frames and by changing the DNA strand that serves as the sense strand, the phage genome can encode the almost 150 genes involved in the replication of T4 phage.

Assembly

The assembly of the T-even phage capsid is a complex process that follows a sequential pathway. Assembly of the head and tail structures requires several enzymes that are coded for by the phage genome. The head, tail, and tail fiber units of the T-even phage capsid are assembled separately, and the tail fibers are added after the head and tail structures are combined. Because of the small size of the virion, the DNA must be tightly packed within the phage head assembly. Packaging DNA into the head structure involves stuffing the head with DNA and cutting away the excess. When the head structure is completely filled with DNA, any extra DNA is cleaved by a nuclease. The specific mechanism that is responsible for filling the phage head with DNA and folding the DNA within the assembled phage particle has not been totally elucidated.

Lytic Release

A lytic enzyme—T4 lysozyme—that is coded for by the phage attacks the peptidoglycan of the host cell and causes cell lysis. The number of phage progeny released when the host cell lyses depends on how rapidly lysis occurs. Lower numbers of phage progeny are associated with early lysis. Slower lysis leads to higher numbers of phages released from the host cell. Typically the T4 phage lytic cycle takes about 25 minutes. Lysis inhibition is exhibited by wild type phage so that when lysis occurs there is a release of large numbers of phages. Rapid lysis mutants have lesser numbers of progeny because lysis occurs early before many phage are assembled.

LYTIC T-ODD PHAGE

Gene Expression

Bacteriophage T7, a representative T-odd phage, has a small linear double-stranded DNA genome (FIG. 8-17). The DNA is injected linearly into bacterial cells after the phage attaches to a host cell, most commonly *E. coli.* Transcription of the T7 genome begins immediately after penetration. Host cell RNA polymerase initiates RNA synthesis at closely spaced promoters of the phage DNA end. Host RNA polymerase is used to copy the first few phage genes, called early genes. It also makes mRNA for the phage-specific RNA polymerase that is used in the major RNA transcription process that occurs during replication of this phage.

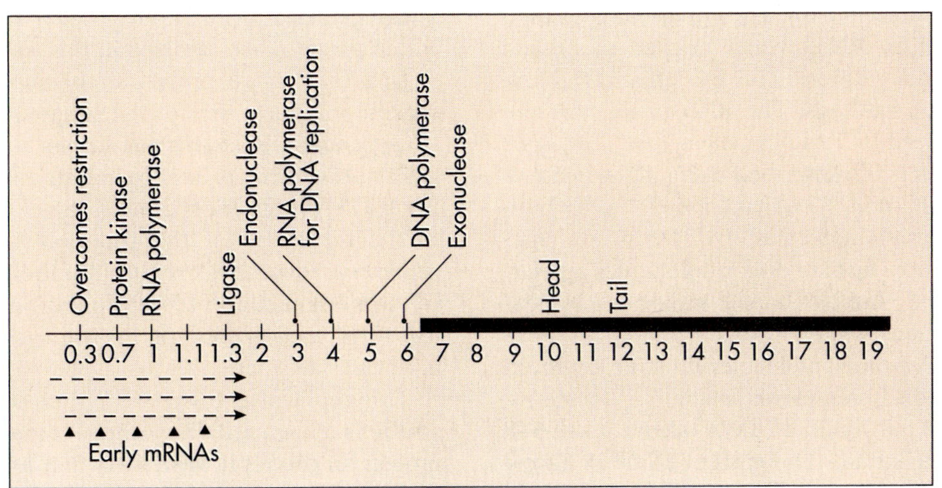

FIG. 8-17 Linear genome of T7 bacteriophage.

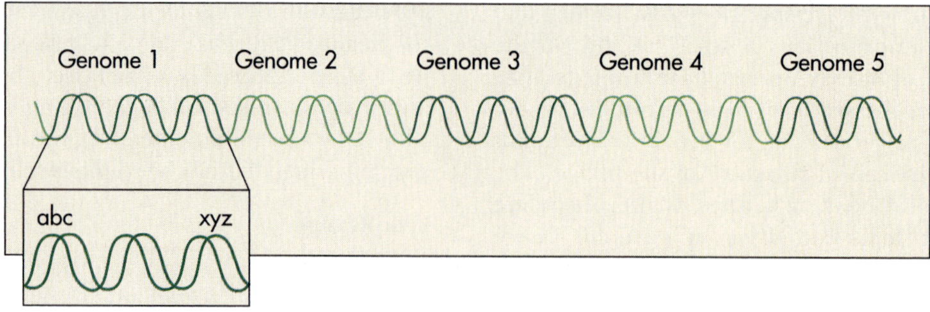

FIG. 8-18 A concatamer is a linear molecule in which multiple copies of the genome (shown here as genomes 1 to 5) are joined together.

Transcription generates a set of overlapping polygenic mRNA molecules. These mRNA molecules are then cut by a host-specified RNaseIII that acts at several sites. This generates smaller mRNA molecules that code for one to four proteins each. One of these proteins is an RNA polymerase that copies double-stranded DNA. Two others code for proteins that stop host RNA polymerase action. This turns off early gene transcription and translation of host genes.

The T7 phage strongly affects host transcription and translation processes by producing proteins that turn off transcription of host genes. This phage has genes coding for enzymes that degrade host cell DNA. Nucleotides from degraded DNA are incorporated into phage progeny. Late genes expressed, beginning 6 minutes after infection, code for enzymes involved in DNA replication. Regulation of T7 gene expression is both positive and negative. Negative control is by means of the formation of proteins that stop host RNA polymerase and shut off early T7 gene transcription. Positive control is by the formation of new RNA polymerase that recognizes the rest of the T7 promoters.

Genome Replication

T7 DNA replication begins at an origin of replication and proceeds bidirectionally. The enzymes involved in the synthesis of an RNA primer needed to initiate DNA replication are different for the left and right directions of DNA synthesis. The RNA primer for the right is synthesized by T7 RNA polymerase. The RNA primer for the left is transcribed using T7 primase, a phage-specific enzyme. T7 polymerase elongates both primers. Replicating molecules of T7 DNA have characteristic structures that are discernible under an electron microscope. Bubble-shaped molecules appear early in replication.

Because RNA primer molecules must be removed before replication is completed at the 5′-P terminus, an unreplicated portion of T7 DNA occurs at the 5′-P terminus of each strand. The ends of T7 DNA have a 160 bp terminal repeat sequence so that complimentary single-stranded regions occur at the ends of the opposing strands. The complementary 3′-OH ends on separate DNA molecules pair with these 5′-P ends to form a DNA molecule that is twice as long as the original T7 DNA. The action of DNA polymerase and ligase completes the unreplicated portions of this end-to-end bimolecular structure. The product is a linear bimolecule, called a concatamer, that can become very long through continued replication (FIG. 8-18). An endonuclease cuts each concatamer at a specific site, producing linear molecules with repetitious ends.

BACTERIOPHAGE $\phi X174$

The genome of phage $\phi X174$ consists of a circular single-stranded 5.3 kb DNA molecule. The single-stranded DNA of such phages is called a plus sense strand. The phage plus strand genome separates from the protein coat after infection of the host cell.

The single-stranded DNA genome of $\phi X174$ is converted into a doubled-stranded form called **replicative form (RF) DNA** (FIG. 8-19). Replicative form is a closed, supercoiled, double-stranded circular DNA. RNA primase, DNA polymerase, ligase, and gyrase are cell-coded proteins involved in the conversion of phage genomic DNA into replicative form. No phage-coded proteins are involved in this conversion.

In $\phi X174$ phage, replication begins at one or more specific initiation sites of the single-stranded circular DNA genome. RNA primase brings about the synthesis of a short RNA primer to initiate replication of this DNA. DNA replication around the closed circle leads to the formation of the complete double-stranded replicative form. DNA replication then occurs by conventional semiconservative replication of the replicative form so that new replicative form DNA macromolecules are made.

The replicative form DNA directs phage mRNA synthesis. Phage mRNA synthesis begins at several promoters on the replicative form and terminates at several sites. Polygenic mRNA is translated into various

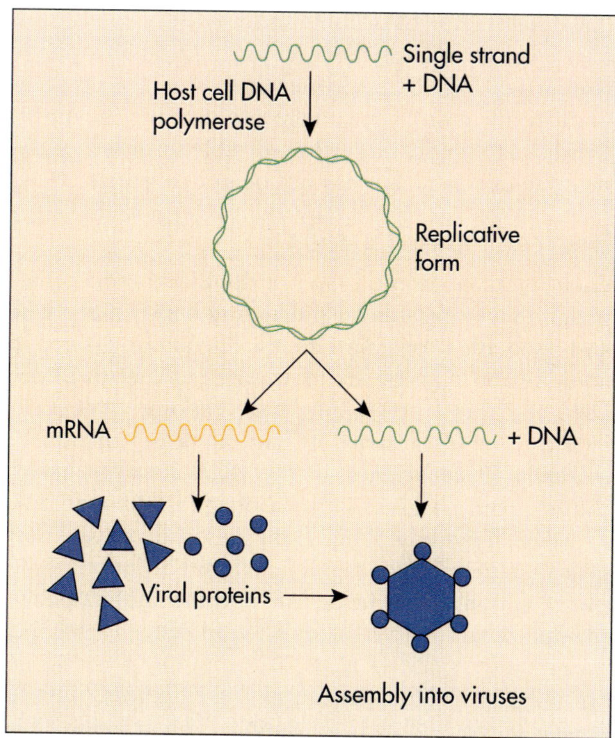

FIG. 8-19 Replication of single-stranded DNA phage can involve formation of a double-stranded replicative form that is used for production of mRNA and single-stranded DNA phage genomes.

phage proteins, including protein A, which is involved in formation of single-stranded DNA genomes for phage progeny. Formation of single-stranded phage progeny begins with a single-stranded cleavage of the phage (+) strand of the replicative form at the origin of replication catalyzed by protein A. Asymmetric rolling circle replication produces single-stranded phage progeny. Protein A cleaves and ligates the two ends of the newly synthesized strand to give a circular single-stranded DNA when the growing phage strand reaches unit length. After single-stranded DNA genome and capsid protein production, new phage are assembled. Lysis of host cells then occurs, releasing phage progeny.

FILAMENTOUS M13

Filamentous DNA phages have circular DNA and a capsid with helical symmetry. They attach to the specific receptor on the pilus of a donor host cell. The adjacent halves of the genome run up and down the phage and form loops at the ends. They exhibit little base pairing. The replication events of the filamentous phage M13 are similar to $\phi X174$. Uniquely, however, bacteriophage M13 virion is released without killing the host cell. The release of M13 phage from a host cell occurs by a budding mechanism with capsid proteins first being inserted into the cytoplasmic membrane of the host cell. The M13 phage genome then moves into the matrix of the cytoplasmic membrane where assembly occurs. Assembled phage are released (secreted) from the cytoplasmic membrane. Phage M13 infection slows cell growth but cells infected with phage M13 can continue to grow while releasing phage particles.

BACTERIOPHAGE MS2

Bacteriophage MS2 has a single-stranded RNA genome. After penetration and uncoating, phage MS2 RNA goes to a host cell ribosome, where it is translated into four proteins: maturation protein (A-protein), coat protein, lysis protein, and RNA replicase. The RNA replicase of bacteriophage MS2 is composed partly of a phage-encoded polypeptide and partly of host cell–encoded polypeptides. The host cell polypeptides that make up part of the viral replicase include ribosomal protein S1 that is part of the 30S host cell ribosome and elongation factors used by the host cell during translation. Thus the phage employs host cell proteins for an entirely distinct function than they normally serve.

The phage RNA, which is a (+) strand, can act as a mRNA. It is translated to produce a phage RNA polymerase. This RNA polymerase or RNA replicase can synthesize (−) strand RNA using infecting RNA as the template. More (+) RNA is made from this (−) RNA. New (+) RNA strands serve as mRNAs for continued phage protein synthesis. Complete phage assembly requires a maturation protein encoded at the 5′-P end of the RNA. Translation of maturation protein gene occurs only from the nascent form of the (+) strand as the replication process occurs. This limits the amount of maturation protein needed. As the phage RNA is made, it folds into a complex extensive secondary and tertiary structure.

The most accessible AUG start site for the translation process is that for the coat protein. Coat protein molecules increase in number and combine with the RNA around the AUG start site for the replicase RNA, which shuts off synthesis of RNA replicase. The major phage protein then synthesized is coat protein. One hundred eighty copies per RNA of coat protein is needed to complete assembly of a new phage.

The lysis protein needed for release of phage MS2 is coded by a gene that overlaps with both the coat protein gene and the replicase gene. A shift in the reading frame occurs as the ribosome passes over the coat protein genes. Only when this occurs is the lysis gene read. The efficiency of the translation is thus limited, preventing premature cell lysis. Lysis begins when sufficient coat protein is available for mature phage particle assembly.

Bacteriophage Qβ

Bacteriophage Qβ has a small single-stranded RNA genome. The genome of the bacteriophage Qβ (designated as a (+) RNA strand) is used as a template for forming a replicative double-stranded form that has both (+) and complementary (−) RNA strands. When the RNA-dependent RNA polymerase uses the replicative form as a template, the product includes mostly (+) RNA that goes into the genomes of the phage progeny. The complete assembly of the phage is followed by lysis of the host cell, catalyzed by a phage-coded lytic enzyme.

Bacteriophage ϕ6

Bacteriophage ϕ6 is an enveloped, icosahedral, double-stranded RNA phage that replicates in host cells of *Pseudomonas phaseolicola.* It is the only phage discovered with a double-stranded RNA genome. There are three segments of double-stranded RNA, each of which directs the synthesis of an mRNA. This phage contains its own RNA polymerase that may be involved in the replication of the phage genome, but the mechanism of replicating the double-stranded RNA genome of this phage has not been elucidated.

Bacteriophage Lambda

Bacteriophage lambda (λ) is a double-stranded DNA phage that is capable of alternating between the lytic and lysogenic replication cycles. The amino groups of adenine and cytosine are methylated in lambda phage DNA and this protects the phage genome against destruction by the restriction endonucleases of host *E. coli* cells. If methylation of the DNA does not occur, the host cell range of lambda phage is changed. For example, if lambda phage replicates in *E. coli* K12 host cells that are methionine deficient, methylation of the phage genome does not occur, and the lambda phage produced are unable to replicate in other *E. coli* K12

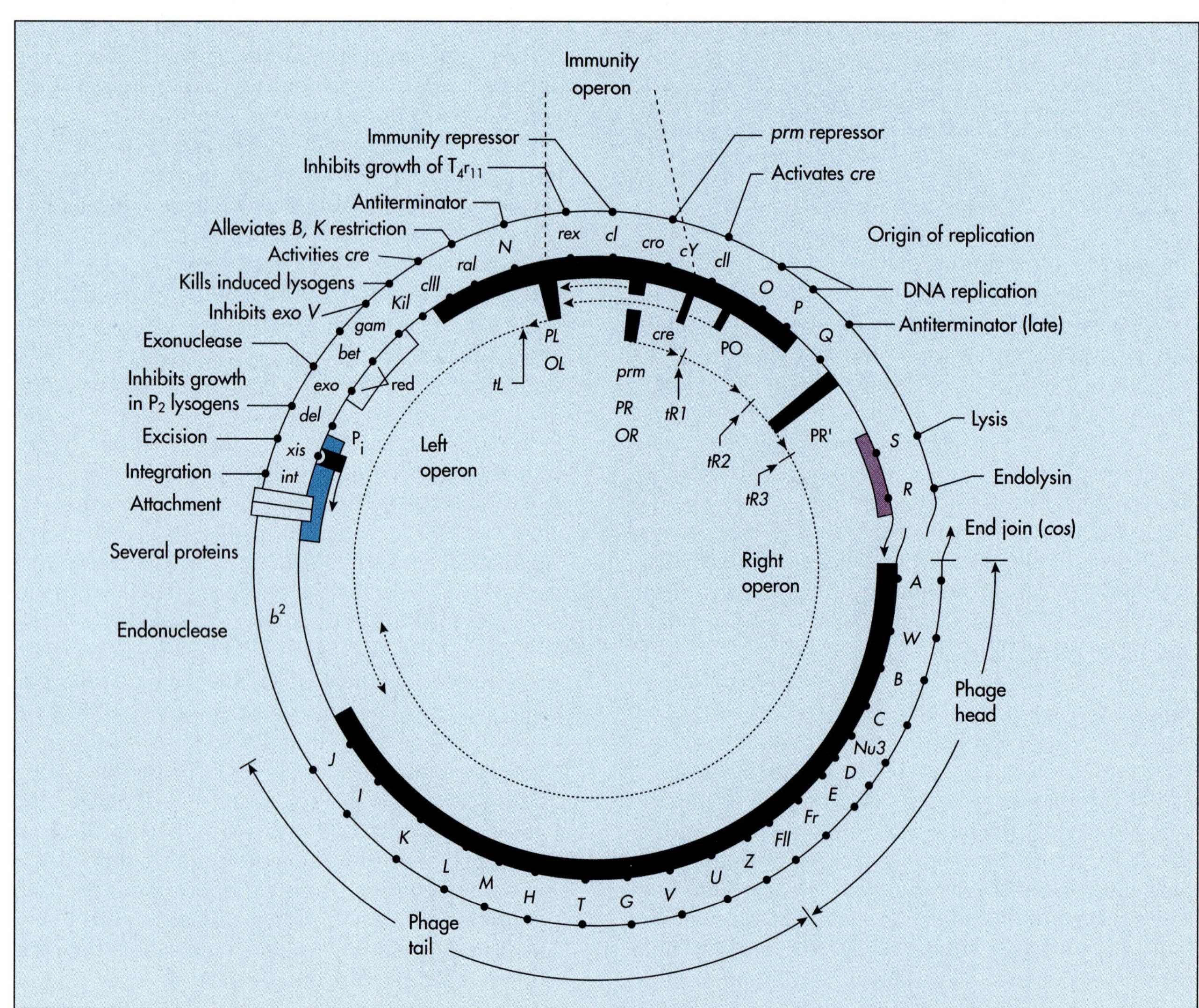

FIG. 8-20 Replication of bacteriophage lambda involves two operons that are transcribed in opposite directions. Expression of the genes in each operon occurs at different times for production of early and late proteins.

host cells. However, such lambda phage lacking methylated genomes could still replicate in *E. coli* C host cells because that bacterial strain does not produce restriction endonucleases that degrade the phage DNA. Lambda phage that replicate in *E. coli* C host cells do not produce modified (methylated) genomes and, therefore, although they can replicate in *E. coli* C, they are unable to replicate in *E. coli* K12 host cells.

The regulation of lambda phage replication, which determines whether the replication cycle is lytic or lysogenic, is an interesting example of molecular-level control of gene expression (FIG. 8-20). During the lytic replication cycle of lambda, transcription begins at two promoter sites during the early phase of replication. One of the promoter sites initiates rightward transcription; the other initiates leftward transcription. The completion of the rightward transcription of the phage genome requires the expression of a *Q* gene, which codes for a Q protein required for late gene expression. The complete counterclockwise transcription of the lambda genome requires expression of the *N* gene that codes for an N protein. Both the *N* and *Q* genes must be expressed for the transcription of the complete genome.

The lambda phage genome contains a *cI* gene, which codes for a repressor protein that binds to the operator that controls the expression of the N protein. In the absence of N protein synthesis, the replication of lambda phage DNA cannot proceed. The repressor protein also binds to another operator region, blocking the rightward transcription of the lambda phage DNA and, thus, the production of the Q protein. This leads to a conversion to lysogenic replication.

For integration of the lambda phage genome, homologous overlapping ends of the linear lambda genome join to form a circular DNA molecule. This circular DNA then is integrated into a specific site of the *E. coli* bacterial chromosome. Integration requires a site-specific topoisomerase that is coded for by the *int* gene. During cell growth, the lambda repression system prevents the expression of the integrated lambda genes except for the gene *cI*, which codes for the lambda repressor. The integrated lambda phage DNA is replicated with host cell DNA during reproduction of the host cell.

The expression of the *cI* gene is itself subject to regulation. Transcription of *cI* increases when the lambda repressor is present in low concentrations and high concentrations of repressor protein inhibit further transcription. If the concentration of lambda repressor protein declines sufficiently to permit further transcription of the phage genome, a protein, coded for by the *cro* gene, is produced. The cro protein represses further transcription of the *cI* gene, thus stopping synthesis of the repressor protein responsible for preventing complete expression of the phage genome. When this occurs, the phage can carry out a lytic replication cycle. The lambda phage genome is excised from the bacterial chromosome by the action of an excisionase that is coded for by the *xis* gene. Expression of the lambda phage genes then leads to formation of complete phages and their lytic release from the host cell.

BACTERIOPHAGE MU

Mu is a temperate DNA bacteriophage that can act as a transposon within a host cell (FIG. 8-21). When the Mu genome enters an *E. coli* host cell it is not digested

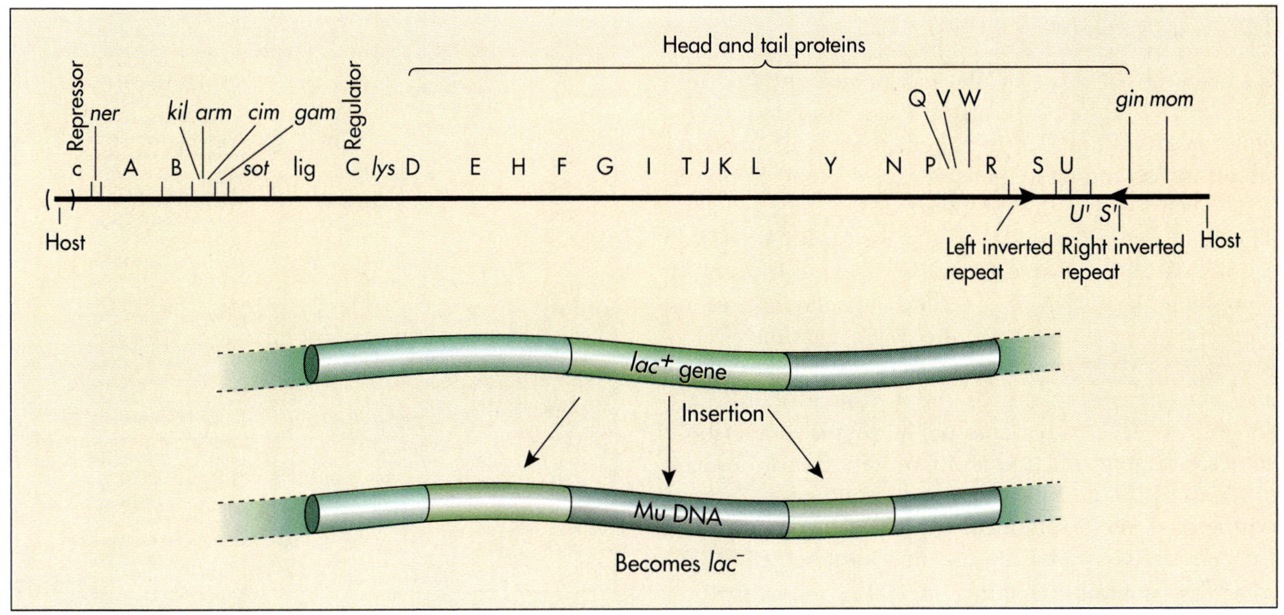

FIG. 8-21 Bacteriphage Mu can act as a transposon, and by inserting within a gene such as the *lac* gene it can cause mutations.

by nucleases because its DNA has a high proportion of adenine that is acetoamidated. Integration of the Mu genome into the bacterial chromosome occurs through the action of a transposase that is encoded by the phage. Mu DNA is transposed to multiple sites of the bacterial chromosome. When Mu integrates its genes around the bacterial chromosome, it inserts phage DNA within bacterial genes, causing mutations (Mu stands for mutator phage). At each insertion site there is a 5 base pair duplication of host cell DNA. The resultant single-stranded regions are subsequently converted to double-stranded DNA. Production of a *c* gene repressor prevents complete expression of the Mu genome that would lead to phage progeny production and lysis of the host cell. As long as the C protein production is repressed, the Mu phage DNA is maintained as a prophage and replicated with host cell DNA during bacterial cell reproduction.

BACTERIOPHAGE P1

Phage P1 is a temperate bacteriophage. Its DNA does not become integrated into the bacterial chromosome following infection of an *E. coli* host cell. Rather, phage P1 genome is maintained in the prophage state like a plasmid within the cytoplasm. Only one copy of the prophage is maintained in a host cell because the phage repressor genes closely coordinate the replication of the phage genome with the replication of host cell DNA.

8.4 REPLICATION OF PLANT VIRUSES

Many plant viruses exhibit a replicative cycle similar to the lytic replication cycle of bacteriophage. The stages of plant viral replication involve (1) penetration by the virus of a susceptible plant cell—generally through abrasions or insect bites, (2) uncoating of the viral nucleic acid within the plant cell, (3) assumption by the viral genome of control of the synthetic activities of the host cell, (4) expression of the viral genome so that viral nucleic acid and capsid components are synthesized, (5) assembly of the viral particles within the host cell, and, (6) release of the complete viral particles from the host plant cell. Most plant viruses exhibit great host cell specificity and cause various symptoms in the plants they infect. The plant viruses are typically named on this basis (Table 8-4).

TABLE 8-4 Groups of Plant Viruses

PLANT VIRUS	DESCRIPTION
Bromovirus (brome mosaic virus)	Small, icosahedral RNA viruses
Cauliflower mosaic virus (DNA virus of higher plants)	Double-stranded DNA; reproduces in cytoplasm
Cucumovirus (cucumber mosaic virus)	Naked, icosahedral, RNA viruses
Luteovirus (barley yellow dwarf virus)	Small isometric virus, RNA genome
Nepovirus (tobacco ringspot virus)	Polyhedral, nematode transmitted, RNA viruses
Potexvirus (potato virus X)	Flexous rods, 480-580 nm, RNA genome
Potyvirus (potato virus Y)	Flexous, rod-shaped, helical symmetry, single-stranded RNA
Tobacco necrosis virus	Isometric RNA viruses
Tobamovirus (tobacco mosaic virus)	Rod-shaped, helical symmetry, single-stranded RNA
Tobravirus (tobacco rattle virus)	Rod-shaped, nematode transmitted, plus-stranded RNA viruses, segmented genome
Tombusvirus (tomato bushy stunt virus)	Small RNA viruses, cubic symmetry, resistant to elevated temperatures and organic solvents
Tymovirus (turnip yellow mosaic virus)	Icosahedral virus, RNA genome, transmitted by flea beetles
Watermelon mosaic virus	Flexous rods, 700–950 nm, RNA genome

TOBACCO MOSAIC VIRUS

Tobacco mosaic virus (TMV) is a plant virus that infects tobacco plants. It has a single-stranded RNA genome contained within a helical array of protein subunits that comprise the viral capsid. Replication of TMV occurs within the cytoplasm of the infected cell. The RNA genome of TMV codes for an RNA-dependent RNA replicase that is used for the synthesis of a complementary RNA ([−] strand) to serve as a template for the synthesis of the RNA genome ([+] strand) of TMV. The complementary (−) strand RNA also acts as a template for the synthesis of mRNA, which is subsequently translated at the plant cell ribosomes for the production of the protein coat subunits. Once the RNA and protein components of TMV are synthesized, the assembly of the protein coat around the central RNA core can proceed spontaneously; that is, TMV is self-assembled.

The initiation of TMV assembly involves the attachment of the viral RNA to a protein disc subassembly of

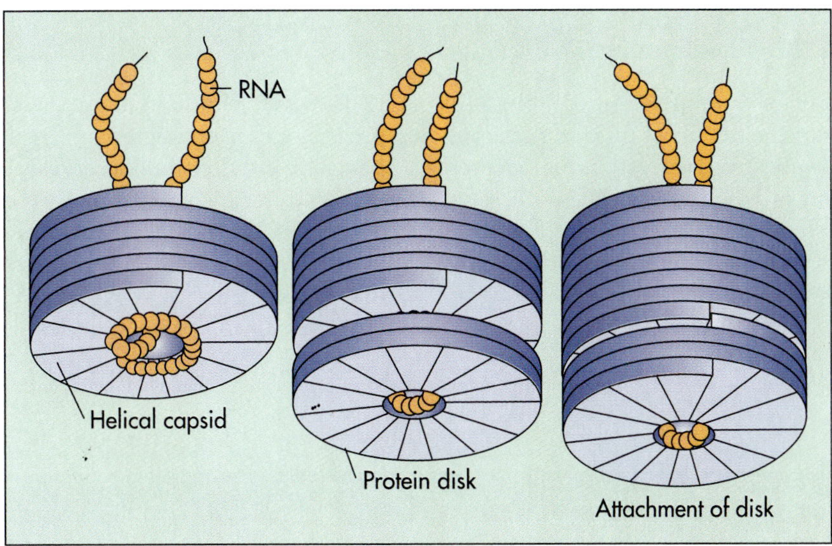

FIG. 8-22 The assembly of tobacco mosaic virus involves sequential addition of protein discs to surround the viral RNA genome.

the core structure (FIG. 8-22). The TMV RNA is capable of binding with amino acids to initiate the assembly of the virus. The RNA molecule forms a loop, and the protein disk subunits are added continuously to the looped end of the RNA. The RNA overcomes the electrostatic forces that prevent binding of the protein subunits, and without the RNA the protein subunits will not bind at physiological pH and low ionic strength. Thus, in the absence of the RNA core, the protein units will not assemble, whereas with the RNA, self-assembly occurs.

Within infected plant cells, the replicated TMV particles form cytoplasmic inclusions. These viral inclusions are crystalline in nature. The chloroplast of a TMV-infected leaf becomes chlorotic (yellow due to loss of chlorophyll), leading to the death of the cell. The death of the plant cell releases completely assembled TMV particles and viral nucleic acid that has not been packaged with the protein subunits. Within plants, completely assembled viral particles and viral RNA can move from one cell to another, establishing new sites of infection. As a consequence of the viral replication within the plant cells, the plant develops characteristic disease symptoms, including the appearance of a mosaic pattern of chlorotic spots on the leaves that gives both the disease and the virus their names (FIG. 8-23).

FIG. 8-23 Leaf infected with tobacco mosaic virus.

VIROIDS

Viroids are small RNA genomes. Unlike true viruses they lack a capsid. In essence, a viroid is simply an RNA macromolecule that can be preserved and transmitted to cells, where it is replicated. Compared to viruses, viroids introduce far less genetic information.

The presence of viroids sometimes manifests as disease symptoms in the host organism, and certain plant diseases have been identified as caused by viroids. Diseases caused by viroids include, among others, potato spindle tuber, citrus exocortis, chrysanthemum stunt, cucumber pale fruit, avocado sunblotch, and coconut cadang-cadang.

Viroid RNA is replicated within host cells, using host cell enzymes and the viroid RNA as a template. Viroid RNA does not appear to be translated into viroid-specified polypeptides. It is not yet clear how these molecules survive outside of host cells or how they are transmitted to compatible host cells. That such macromolecules can be transmitted and cause infectious diseases of higher organisms is a relatively new finding, the ramifications of which have yet to be fully appreciated. While the origin of viroids is unclear, some have been found to have nucleotide sequences in common, suggesting a common ancestry.

8.5 REPLICATION OF ANIMAL VIRUSES

There are many types of animal viruses (Table 8-5) and many variations in the details of their replication. In some cases, the replicative cycle of animal viruses closely resembles that of lytic bacteriophage. In such instances, there is a stepwise growth curve with a burst of numerous viruses released simultaneously. Unlike bacteriophage, however, the single-step growth curve for viruses occurs within hours rather than minutes (FIG. 8-24). Although many viruses exhibit single-step growth curves characterized by the lytic death of the host cell and the simultaneous release of a large number of viruses, some animal viruses characteristically do not kill the host cell and instead reproduce with a gradual, slow release of intact viruses. Also, some animal viruses transform the host cells, resulting in tumor formation rather than death of the host cells.

TABLE 8-5 Characteristics of Various Animal Viruses

				VIRIONS WITH CUBIC SYMMETRY			VIRIONS WITH HELICAL SYMMETRY			
VIRUSES	NUCLEIC ACID	SYMMETRY	NUCLEOCAPSID	NUMBER OF CAPSOMERS	DIAMETER OF THE NUCLEOCAPSID (NM)	DIAMETER OF THE ENVELOPE (NM)	DIAMETER AND LENGTH OF THE NUCLEOCAPSID (NM)	DIMENSIONS OF THE ENVELOPED VIRUSES (NM)	MOL WT ($\times 10^6$) OF NUCLEIC ACID	NUMBER OF NUCLEIC ACID STRANDS
Inoviruses	D	H	N				0.5 × 85		1.7-3	1
Poxviruses	D	H?	E				?	250 × 160 300 × 230	160-240	2
Microviruses	D	C	N	12	25				1.7	1
Parvoviruses	D	C	N	32	22				1.8	1
Densoviruses	D	C	N	42	20				160-240	1
Papillomaviruses (papovaviruses)	D	C	N	72	45-55				3-5	2
Adenoviruses	D	C	N	252	70				20-25	2
Iridoviruses	D	C	N	812	130				126	2
Herpesviruses	D	C	E	162	77	150-200			54-92	2
Uroviruses	D	BC	N							2
Rhabdoviruses	R	H	N				2 × 13 1 × 125			1
Myxoviruses	R	H	E				9 × ?	100	2-3	1
Paramyxoviruses	R	H	E				18 × ?	120	7.5	1
Stomatoviruses (rhabdoviruses)	R	H	E				18 × ?	175 × 68	6	1
Thylaxoviruses	R	H	E				?	1000	10	1
Napoviruses	R	C	N	32	22-27		?		1.1-2	1
Reoviruses	R	C	N	92	70				10	2
Cyanoviruses	R	C	N	32 or 42	54					2
Encephaloviruses	R	C	E	?	?		60-80		2-3	1

Based on Lwoff A and Tourneir P: Remarks on the classification of viruses. In Maramorosch K and Kurstak E (eds.): *Comparative Virology*, Academic Press, New York.

D, DNA; *R*, RNA; *H*, helical; *C*, cubic; *B*, binal; *N*, naked; and *E*, enveloped.

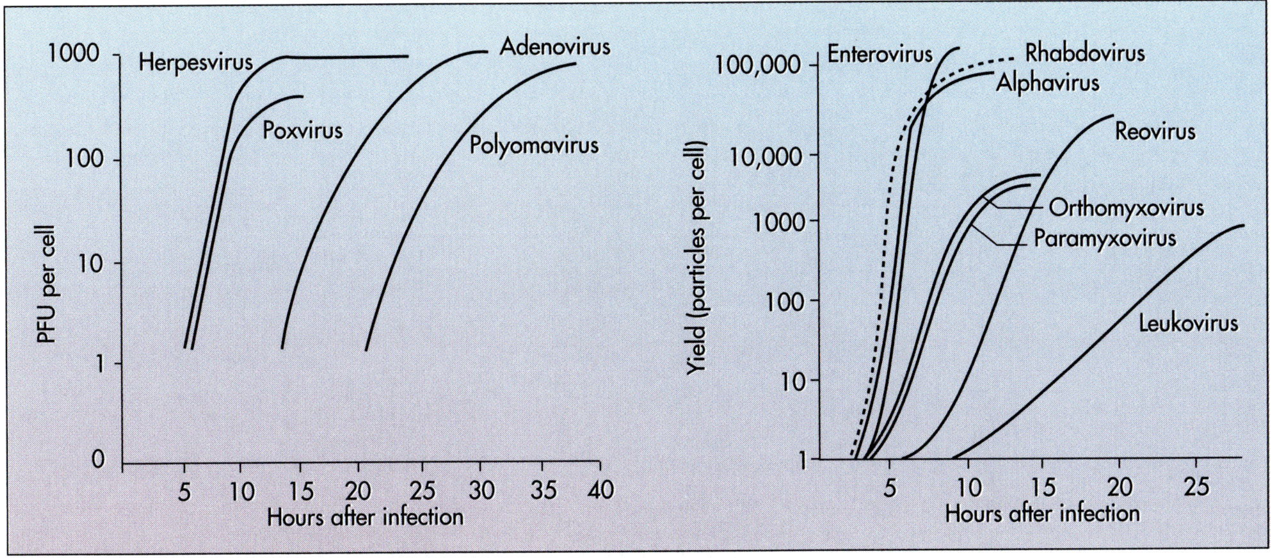

FIG. 8-24 Replication of animal viruses often takes hours, as shown as the time needed to increase the plaque forming units (PFU) or yield of viral particles.

EFFECTS OF VIRAL REPLICATION ON HOST ANIMAL CELLS

Cytopathic Effect

Virus-infected animal cells often develop abnormally, with visible change in their appearance, known as the **cytopathic effect (CPE)** (FIG. 8-25). Some of the more common morphological changes are (1) cell rounding and detachment from the substrate, (2) cell lysis, (3) syncytium formation (a mass of fused cells), and (4) inclusion body formation. Many of these host-cell alterations by virus infection can now be explained as changes in the host cell that permit necessary steps in viral replication. Thus many of the CPEs, which are also called cell injuries, are secondary effects of the virus doing what is necessary to replicate and are not simply toxic effects of viral gene products on the host cell.

Transformation of Animal Cells

The DNA produced during the replication of retroviruses, as well as the DNA of some other viruses (such as herpesviruses), can also be incorporated into the host cell's chromosomes. This process is analogous to lysogeny in bacterial cells. Within the chromosomes of the host cell, the viral genome can be transcribed, resulting in the production of virus-specific RNA and viral proteins. The DNA coded for by the virus, which is incorporated into the host cell genome, can be passed from one generation of animal cells to another. It is, therefore, possible for animals to inherit a viral genome. The presence of virus-derived DNA within the host cell can transform the animal cell.

Transformed cells, which are produced *in vitro*, have altered surface properties and continue to grow even when they contact a neighboring cell. *In vitro* infections that result in virus-derived DNA can result in the formation of a tumor. Viruses that transform cells and cause cancerous growth are called **oncogenic viruses.** Oncogenic DNA viruses replicate in permissive hosts but not in nonpermissive host cells. In nonpermissive host cells, part of the viral genome is incorporated into the host cell genome, resulting in the transformation of the host cell. Several different retroviruses produce malignancies within infected cells when this occurs. Rous sarcoma virus, for example, is an RNA tumor retrovirus that causes malignancies in chickens. HTLV (human T cell leukeumia virus) also is a retrovirus that produces malignancies in humans. Some DNA viruses, such as Simian virus 40 (SV40) and polyomavirus, also are capable of transforming host cells and producing malignant tumors. At least one form of cervical cancer may result from transformation of cells by certain papillomaviruses.

REPLICATION OF DNA ANIMAL VIRUSES

Within the host cell, uncoating varies from one animal virus to another. The viral nucleic acids may be released at the cytoplasmic membrane, as occurs in the single-stranded RNA enteroviruses; the virus may be uncoated in a series of complex steps within the host cell, as occurs in the large, double-stranded DNA poxviruses; or the virus may never be completely uncoated, as occurs in the double-stranded RNA reoviruses. After uncoating, the genome of a DNA ani-

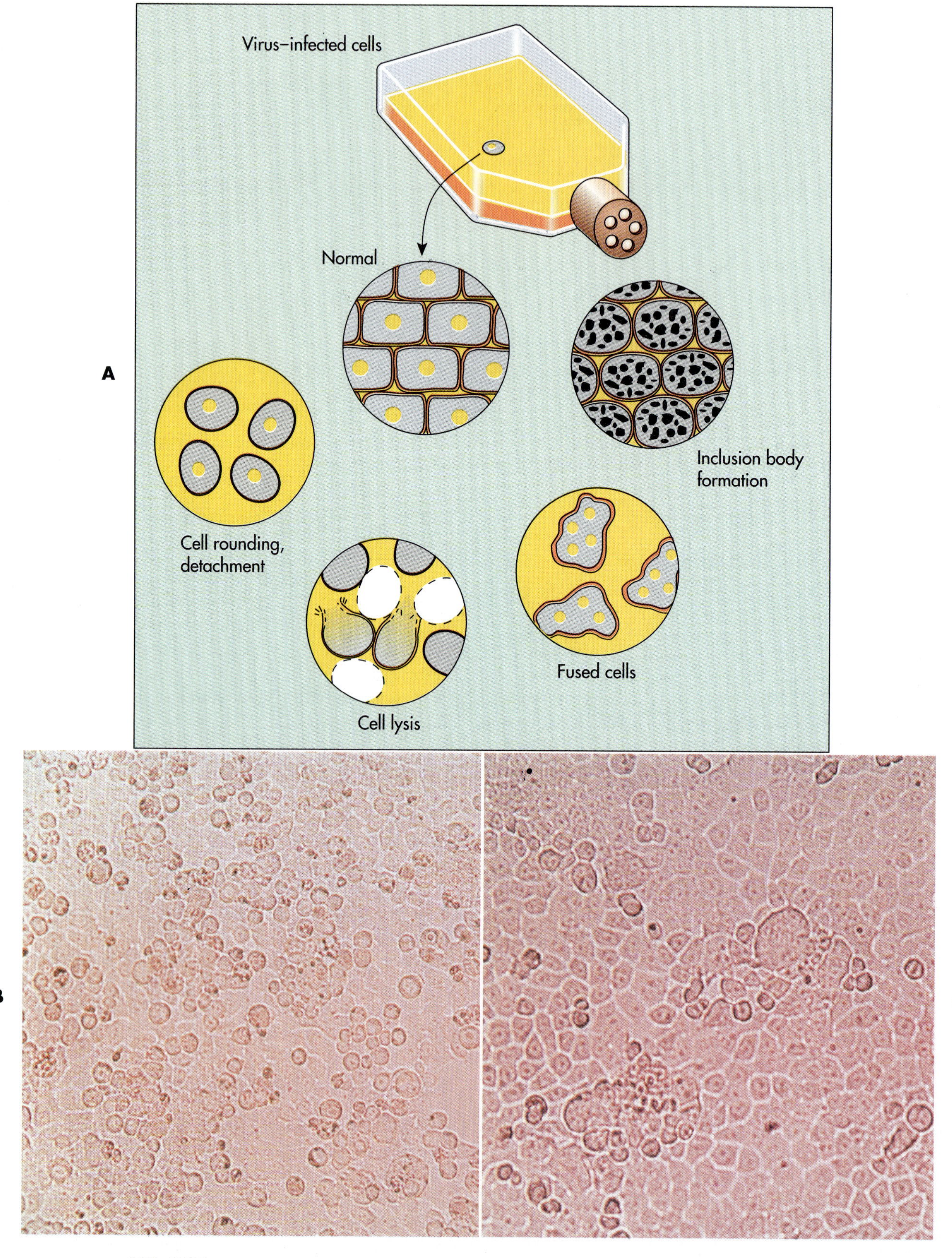

FIG. 8-25 **A,** Infections of animal cells can result in various abnormalities known as cytopathic effects. **B,** Micrograph showing the cytopathic effect on HEp-2 cells grown in tissue culture by an infection with adenovirus. **C,** Micrograph showing the cytopathic effect on HEp-2 cells grown in tissue culture by an infection with respiratory syncytial virus.

BOX 8-3

QUANTITATIVE ASSAYS FOR ANIMAL VIRUSES

Several specialized techniques have been developed for the cultivation of animal viruses. Growth of viruses in the animal host is not always feasible or ethically possible (especially for viruses that can only be grown in human cells). Some viruses can be grown in embryonated tissues of chicken or duck eggs (FIG. *A*). Virus suspensions can be injected through the egg shell and appropriately incubated to allow viral replication.

Animal cells from many organs can be grown *in vitro* by tissue culture techniques (FIG. *B*). The tissue from an animal is separated into individual cells by treatment with the enzyme trypsin. The cells are transferred to an appropriate container where they flatten out and attach to the container surface. These cells are supplied with a rich growth medium. The cells divide until they occupy all the available surface of the container and then stop growing. The cells do not overlap each other—a phenomenon referred to as contact inhibition. The growing layer of animal cells constitutes the tissue culture.

Animal cells cultured *in vitro* from the original tissues lead to primary cell lines. After confluent growth, the cells can be dislodged from the container's surface and transferred or passaged to new containers. These transferred cells can be grown and form secondary cell lines. Normal cells can only be passaged for a limited number of times and then the cells stop growing, even with appropriate nutrients. Malignant cells, on the other hand, give rise to continuous cell lines that can be passaged an infinite number of times. The HeLa cell line derived from a human cervical carcinoma is often used for cultivating viruses.

It is possible to assay quantitatively for animal viruses using tissue cultures in a method analogous to the plaque assay for enumeration of bacteriophage. In a typical procedure, a tissue culture monolayer of animal cells growing on a plate surface is inoculated with dilutions of a viral suspension and incubated for various periods of time. Viral infection of the animal tissue culture cells may result in plaque formation, indicative of localized death of animal cells, which can be observed microscopically, or, more commonly, with the naked eye. The number of plaques that form and the dilution factors are used to determine the concentration of viruses in the sample. It is also possible to observe microscopically the cytopathic effect (CPE) in animal cell cultures and to determine the number of infecting virus particles by counting the number of cells exhibiting the characteristic morphological changes. Different viruses produce cytopathic effects in tissue culture that are diagnostic for that particular virus.

By using an appropriate method to quantitate the number of infectious animal viruses, a growth curve can be established. Many animal viruses exhibit a single-step growth curve for normal replication that includes an eclipse period during which infectious viruses disappear and replication of viral particles occurs. At the end of the eclipse period, new viral progeny appear within the host cell, but often there is a further delay before they are released, except for viruses released by budding. Thus the latent period, the time from the adsorption of the virus onto the host cell until the release of new viruses, generally exceeds the eclipse period.

A
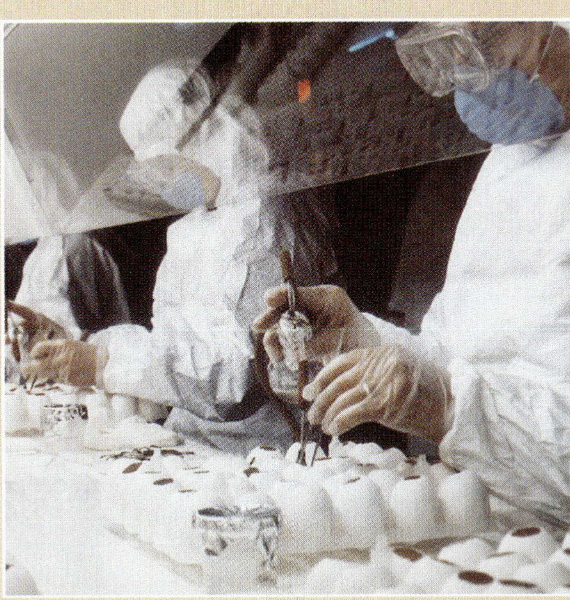

B
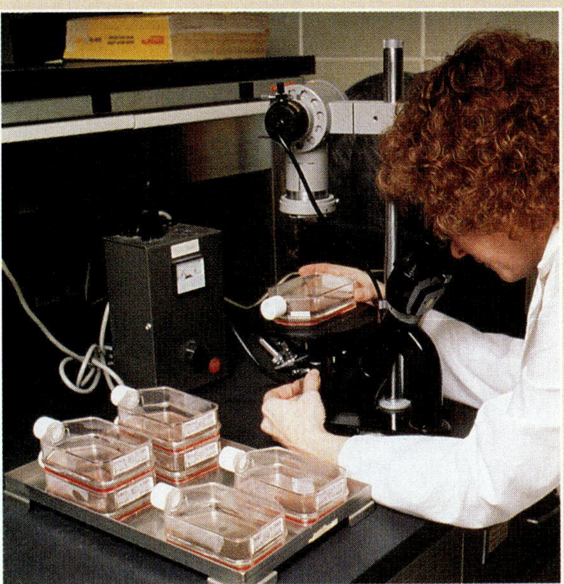

A, Viruses being cultured in eggs for influenza vaccine production. **B**, Viruses being grown in tissue culture and observed with an inverted microscope to detect CPEs in the cell culture.

mal virus generally enters the nucleus, where it is replicated. The genome of most RNA animal viruses, in contrast, only enters the cytoplasm of the animal cell to be replicated.

Replication of Adenoviruses

Adenoviruses are medium-sized viruses containing double-stranded DNA. They exhibit cubic symmetry and have 252 capsomers. Adenoviruses normally have spikes projecting from the capsid that give these viruses a characteristic shape. The spikes are involved in the adsorption of the virus to the host cell. Adenoviruses are associated with acute respiratory tract infections.

In the replication of adenovirus, the host cell continues its normal metabolic activities for a short period of time after viral penetration. Uncoating of the virus takes several hours, and during this period the viral nucleic acid is released from the capsid, entering the nucleus through a nuclear pore. Within the nucleus, the viral genome codes for the inhibition of normal host cell synthesis of macromolecules. The viral genome also acts as a template for its own replication. Viral genes are transcribed and the resulting mRNA is translated to make viral proteins at the ribosomes within the cytoplasm. The assembly of the adenovirus particles, however, occurs within the nucleus; therefore the nucleus of an infected animal cell contains inclusion bodies consisting of crystalline arrays of densely packed adenovirus particles (FIG. 8-26). With lysis of the host cell, numerous adenovirus progeny are released.

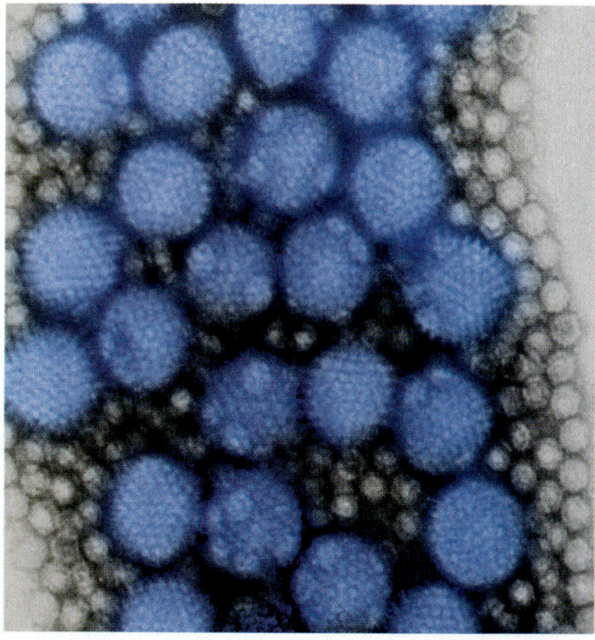

FIG. 8-26 Colorized micrograph of densely packed adenoviruses. (200,000×).

Replication of Hepadnaviruses

Hepatitis B virus (HBV) is a hepadnavirus that has a double-stranded DNA genome composed of a complete (−) strand and an incomplete (+) strand. The virions also contain a DNA polymerase. The HBV polymerase completes the synthesis of a closed circular (+) strand DNA. The negative strand is transcribed into (+) strand RNA and mRNA. The mRNAs are translated into the respective proteins of the virus and the (+) strand RNA then gets packaged into cores. Within the core, the (+) strand RNA is transcribed into (−) strand DNA by the HBV polymerase and the RNA template is degraded. The DNA polymerase of HBV is functionally similar to the reverse transcriptase of retroviruses—it reverse transcribes RNA into DNA. It is therefore possible that hepadnaviruses and retroviruses share a common ancestor.

Replication of Herpesviruses

Herpesviruses are medium-sized viruses containing linear, double-stranded DNA. The capsid has cubical symmetry with 162 capsomers. The capsid is surrounded by a lipid-containing envelope. Herpesviruses are composed of more than 33 proteins—6 have been identified in the nucleocapsid and 8 have been located in the envelope.

Herpesviruses exhibit a complex life cycle. They probably enter the host cell by fusion of the cytoplasmic membrane of the cell with the viral envelope, mediated by one of the surface proteins. The double-stranded DNA is uncoated at the nuclear pores and the viral genome proceeds into the nucleus. The viral DNA is replicated by a virus-specified DNA polymerase but the genome is transcribed and translated by host-specified RNA polymerase II and ribosomes respectively. After the protein capsids are assembled, the newly synthesized DNA is spliced and packaged into them.

The DNA-containing capsids become attached to the nuclear membrane where patches of virus-specified protein have been inserted. The enveloped herpesviruses are assembled in the nucleus and accumulate in the space between the inner and outer lamellae of the nuclear membrane, in the cisternae of the cytoplasmic reticulum, and in vesicles carrying the virus to the cell surface. The virions bud out of the nuclear membrane and are transported through the cytoplasm of the cell to the cell surface. These viruses are uniquely shielded from contact with the cytoplasm. It is not clear how they get to the cell surface or how they are released by the cell.

Herpesviruses can establish latent and recurrent infections within host animals that can last for the entire life of the host. A distinctive feature of herpes simplex virus and varicella-zoster virus is their ability to alternate in the host between periods of active infection and viral replication and periods of latency. The virus

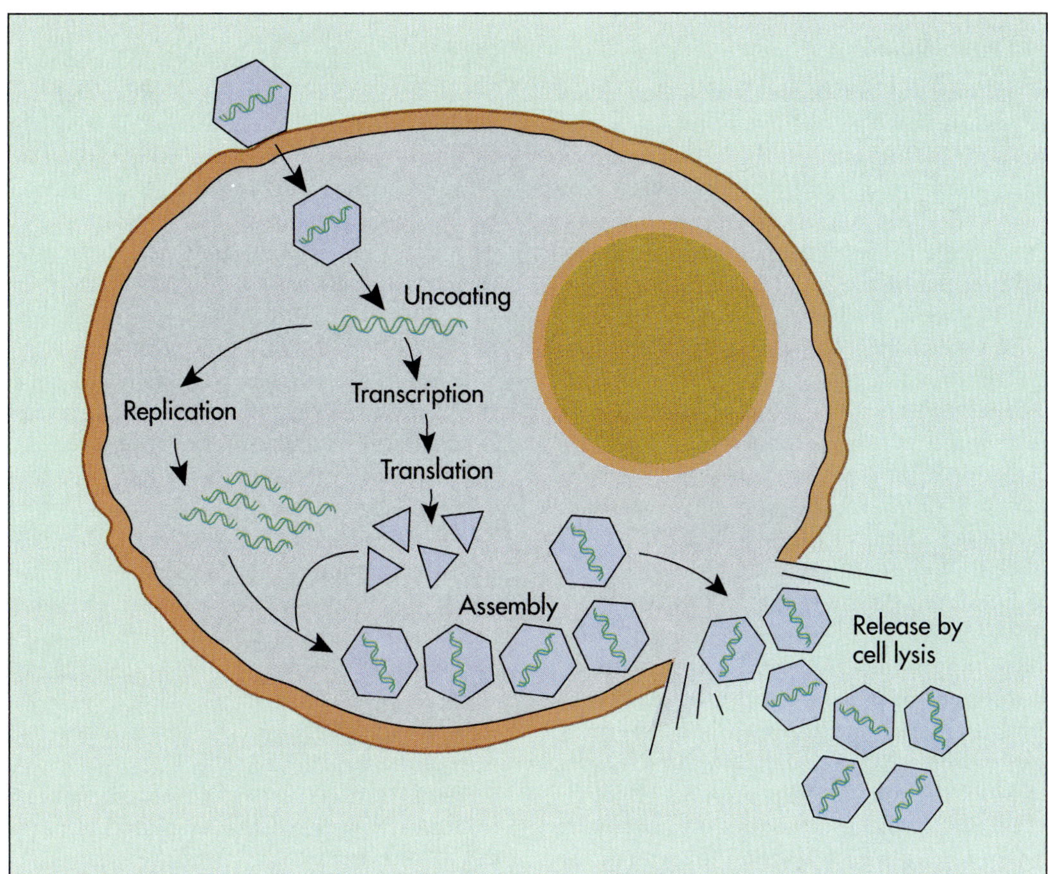

FIG. 8-27 Poxviruses are DNA viruses that replicate within the cytoplasm of a host cell.

migrates from infected epithelial cells to sensory nerves that innervate the infected area. In the nerve cells, the virus is not replicated and its DNA may exist in a circular form. Only one viral protein is known to be expressed in nerve cells and this protein may act as a regulator to maintain the latent infection. The virus remains in this dormant phase until an appropriate stimulus causes the virus to move down the neuron to epithelial cells and reestablish or reactivate the infection.

Replication of Poxviruses

Poxviruses are the largest and most complex of the animal viruses (FIG. 8-27). Their capsids contain over 100 proteins. They are DNA viruses that multiply in the cytoplasm and therefore must code for their own transcription enzymes, including an RNA polymerase and several DNA processing enzymes. Many poxviruses are human pathogens that reproduce primarily within skin tissues. The formation of vesicular lesions in superficial body tissues is symptomatic of many diseases caused by poxviruses. Smallpox, cowpox, monkeypox, and fowlpox are examples of diseases caused by members of the poxvirus group.

Poxviruses are taken up into the cell by coated pits in the cytoplasmic membrane and liberated into the cytoplasm. The viral DNA is uncoated by a viral specified protein. Vaccinia viruses are poxviruses that begin to replicate their DNA about 1½ hours after infection and have completed replication in about 5 hours. Since the poxviruses code for their own replication and transcription proteins, they tend to form complexes in the cytoplasm in which viral synthesis occurs. These complexes can be seen microscopically inside the host cell as inclusions. After packaging of the replicated DNA into their complex cores, outer coats, envelopes, and surface fibers, they are released from the cell when it disintegrates.

REPLICATION OF RNA ANIMAL VIRUSES

RNA animal viruses exhibit many diverse strategies for replication. In some cases, the RNA genome of the virus acts as an mRNA on entering the host cell, coding for the production of capsid proteins and an RNA-dependent RNA polymerase. Other viruses such as the rhabdoviruses, paramyxoviruses, and orthomyxoviruses contain an RNA genome that cannot serve as mRNA. In these viruses, the first step in the replication cycle must be the transcription from (−) strand RNA to (+) strand RNA. These viruses carry their own RNA-dependent RNA polymerases, which enter the host cell with the viral genome to initiate viral replication.

Replication of Picornaviruses

The picornaviruses are small, single-stranded RNA viruses. The nucleocapsid has cubical symmetry and is nonencapsulated. Maturation of the picornaviruses occurs in the cytoplasm of the host cell. Enterovirus and rhinovirus have members that infect humans. Species of rhinovirus cause 25% of all common colds in adults. The enteroviruses include poliovirus, echovirus, hepatitis A virus, and coxsackievirus. Diseases caused by members of this group include poliomyelitis, infectious hepatitis, and foot and mouth disease. Picornaviruses also cause mild infections of the gastrointestinal and respiratory tracts.

The most studied picornavirus, poliovirus, is very specific in its adsorption to cells (FIG. 8-28). It is mediated by the viral protein, VP1. The poliovirus virions are internalized by endocytosis and RNA is released into the cytoplasm. Interestingly, the poliovirus single-stranded RNA codes for a very large polypeptide chain, a polyprotein, which is cleaved by proteases to form many different proteins. The proteases are encoded by both the virus and the host cell. The proteins formed by protease cleavage include an RNA-dependent RNA polymerase and four proteins of the viral capsid. The RNA polymerase is used to produce a complementary replicative RNA strand that can act as a template for the synthesis of new viral genomes. The capsomer proteins assemble into pentamers that condense into capsids. The assembly of the capsid and insertion of the RNA genome is followed by the release of numerous viral particles. Release of the poliovirus occurs because blockage of cellular protein synthesis by the poliovirus leads to breakdown of lysosomes. The digestive enzymes released from the lysosomes causes cell lysis.

Replication of Orthomyxoviruses

The orthomyxoviruses, such as influenza viruses, are single-stranded, enveloped (−) RNA viruses that exhibit helical symmetry. Many influenza viruses are referred to by common names that indicate their geographic origins, such as *Hong Kong flu virus.*

The genome of the influenza viruses is a segmented genome composed of eight different RNA molecules that code for a different monocistronic mRNA molecule (segments 7 and 8 are spliced together and each codes for two proteins). One of the RNA genome segments specifically codes for the RNA-dependent RNA polymerase required for transcription of the viral genome.

There are two types of protein spikes on the influenza virus envelope, designated H and N (FIG. 8-29). There are at least 13 different types of H proteins and 9 types of N proteins found on different influenza

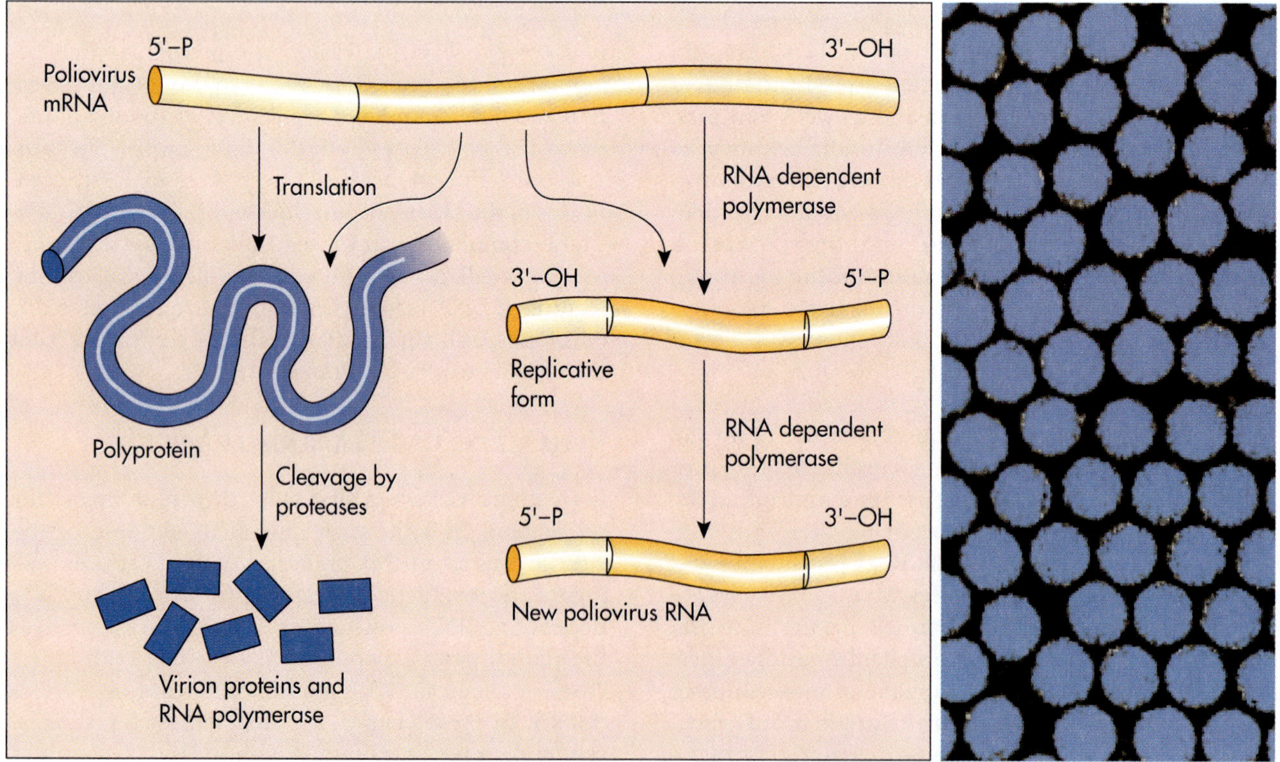

FIG. 8-28 In poliovirus (colorized micrograph, *blue*), RNA serves as a messenger for production of a polyprotein that is then cleaved to form capsid proteins and RNA polymerase. The RNA also serves as the template for producing a replicative form that in turn is the template for new poliovirus genomic RNA.

A

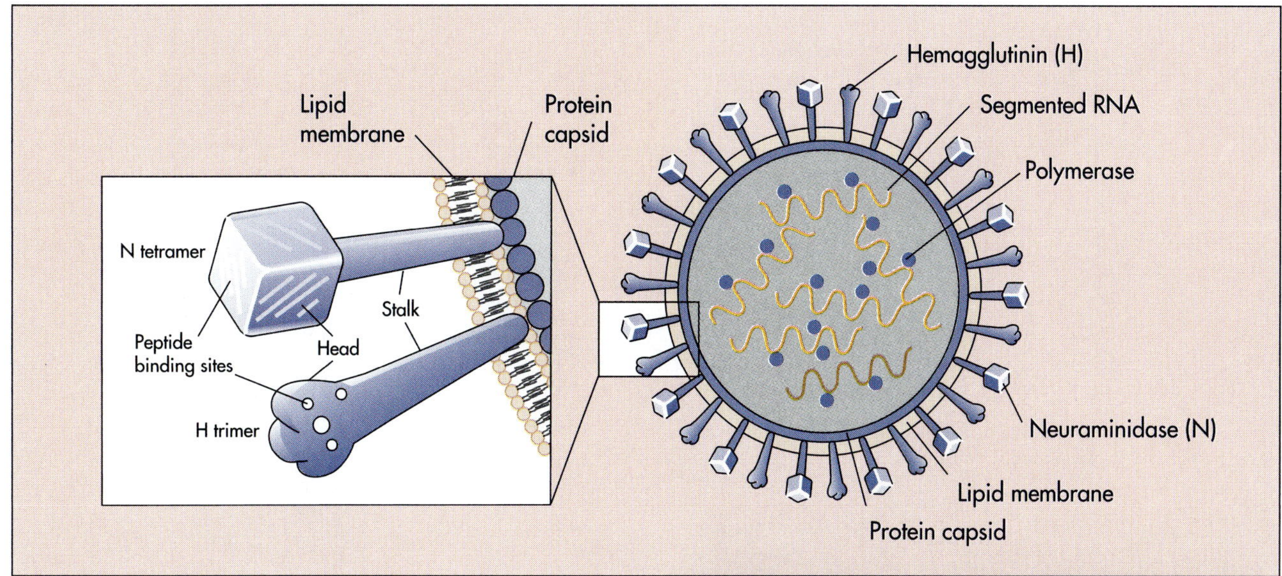

B

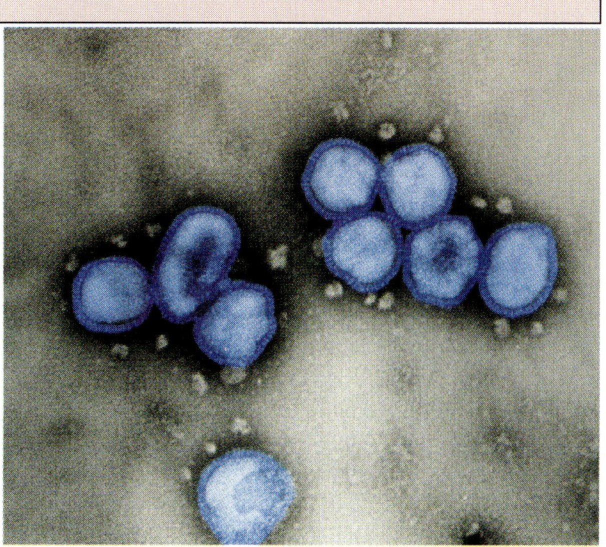

FIG. 8-29 **A,** Influenza viruses have envelope proteins called H and N spikes that protrude from the surface. **B,** Colorized micrograph of influenza viruses. (81,000×).

virus strains. The hemagglutinin (H) spikes are responsible for the attachment of the viral particle to the cell. Hemagglutinin brings about the fusion of the viral envelope with the cytoplasmic membrane of the host cell. The cell receptor is neuraminic acid residues found on cell surface glycoproteins. The second type of protein spike is a neuraminidase (N) that cleaves neuraminic acid residues from the cell surface and may facilitate the release of newly formed virus from the host cell.

Influenza virus is transported inside the host cell by endocytosis. The low pH of the endosomal vesicle causes a change in the H spikes that results in the viral envelope fusing with the vesicle membrane. This releases viral cores into the cytoplasm. The RNA-protein complex then migrates to the host cell nucleus.

Influenza viruses are unique in that they are the only RNA-containing viruses that replicate in the cell nucleus (FIG. 8-30, p. 322). Influenza mRNA transcription from the genomic RNA segments occurs in the host-cell nucleus. Host-cell nascent transcripts are cleaved by a virus-encoded endonuclease, and the 5′-P end of the host transcript is used as a primer for synthesis of viral mRNA from the viral genome. Thus influenza virus transcription complexes intervene in the host mRNA maturation pathway to obtain primer molecules for the viral transcription process.

Replication of the viral (−) strand RNA genome involves the production of a complementary (+) strand RNA that then serves as a template for the synthesis of new viral (−) strand RNA genomes. The viral-specified RNA polymerase also synthesizes viral mRNAs but requires primer molecules and uses the host cell's own mRNAs to initiate transcription of (+) strand mRNA. The newly synthesized (−) strand RNAs are assembled by random assortment of the eight different RNA segments into capsid proteins. Not all influenza viral progeny contain the correct arrangement of genome segments and therefore many are noninfectious after their release. Mature particles exit the host cell by budding, which slowly releases encapsulated (lipid-enveloped) influenza viruses from infected host cells.

Replication of Reoviruses

Reoviruses contain segmented double-stranded RNA genomes. Reoviruses initially attach to cells via a hemagglutinin and a surface protein that interacts mainly with cells of the immune system. Only portions of the capsid are removed, and the viral genome expresses all its functions even though it is never fully re-

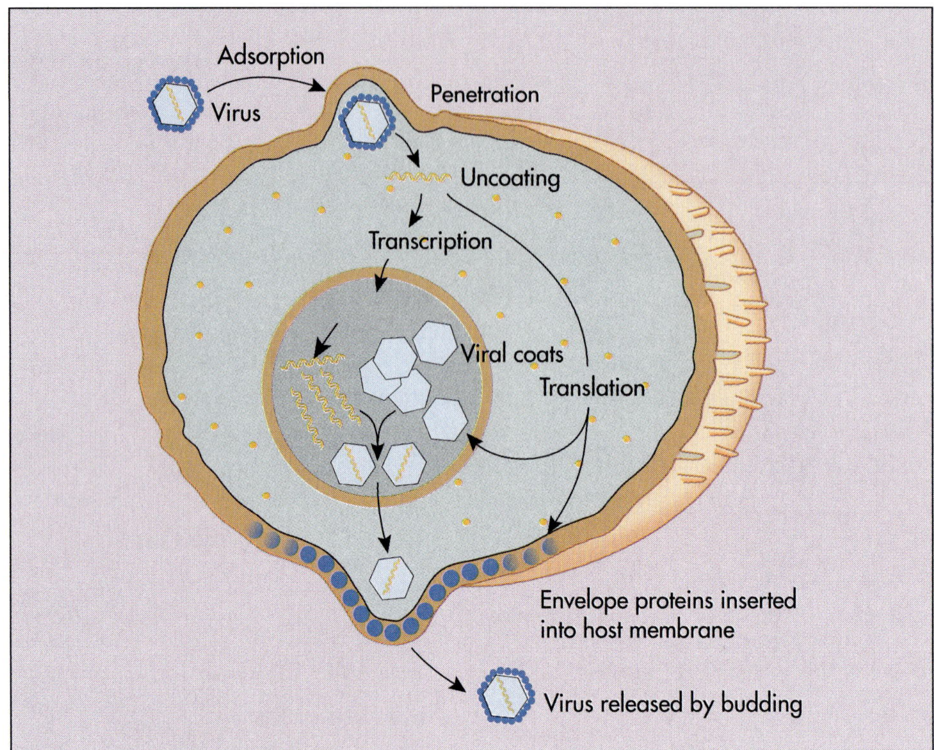

FIG. 8-30 Influenza viruses replicate within the cell nucleus.

leased from the capsid. The reovirus genome is segmented, containing 10 different double-stranded RNA genome molecules. The double-stranded genome cannot be expressed in cells until it is transcribed to (+) strand RNA that is translated. Reovirus carries in its core an RNA polymerase that is used for the synthesis of new viral genomes. The (+) RNA molecules are placed into capsids and integral capsid-RNA replicase uses this as a template to form the (−) strand of the double-stranded RNA genome.

Replication of Retroviruses

Retroviruses, such as the human immunodeficiency viruses (HIVs) that cause acquired immunodeficiency syndrome (AIDS), are RNA viruses that use a reverse transcriptase to produce a DNA molecule within the host cell (FIG. 8-31). The production of the DNA molecule requires an RNA-dependent DNA polymerase (reverse transcriptase) to carry out reverse transcription of the viral RNA. The DNA molecule "transcribed" from the viral RNA genome by reverse transcriptase codes for viral replication within the host cell. Reverse transcriptase is a DNA polymerase that has additional enzymatic activities. It can synthesize DNA with an RNA template (reverse transcription). It also can synthesize DNA with a DNA template (normal DNA polymerase activity). It also has ribonuclease H activity, which removes RNA from RNA/DNA hybrid molecules.

Retroviruses contain a central capsid core surrounded by an inner protein coat and an outer lipid-containing envelope to which protein spikes are attached. Two proteins that form the envelope spikes are coded for by the *env* gene. Several other structural proteins are coded for by the *gag* gene, which is translated into a primary protein product and then proteolytically cleaved into individual proteins. The enzyme that cleaves this protein is itself coded for by a *pro* gene. Retroviruses also contain two proteins coded for by the *pol* gene. Like the *gag* gene product, the *pol* gene product is proteolytically cleaved into two proteins: (1) the reverse transcriptase, which can transcribe RNA or DNA into DNA and also contains RNase activity and (2) an integrase protein, which is probably responsible for the integration of the viral-specified DNA into the host DNA.

Retroviruses adsorb to specific receptors on host cells. HIV binds to CD4 receptors of cells of the immune system and to glial cells of the brain. Penetration occurs by fusion of the viral envelope with host cell cytoplasmic membrane. Single-stranded RNA genome is transcribed by reverse transcriptase into double-stranded DNA. This DNA, called proviral DNA, is transported into the host cell nucleus where it becomes integrated with the host genome at specific sites on the chromosome. The integrated viral genome is called a **provirus.**

Integrated proviral DNA is transcribed by the host's own RNA polymerase II into mRNA and then translated into the polyproteins of the *gag* and *pol* genes and the *env* gene products. Some of the transcripts are also incorporated into maturing viral particles. Ma-

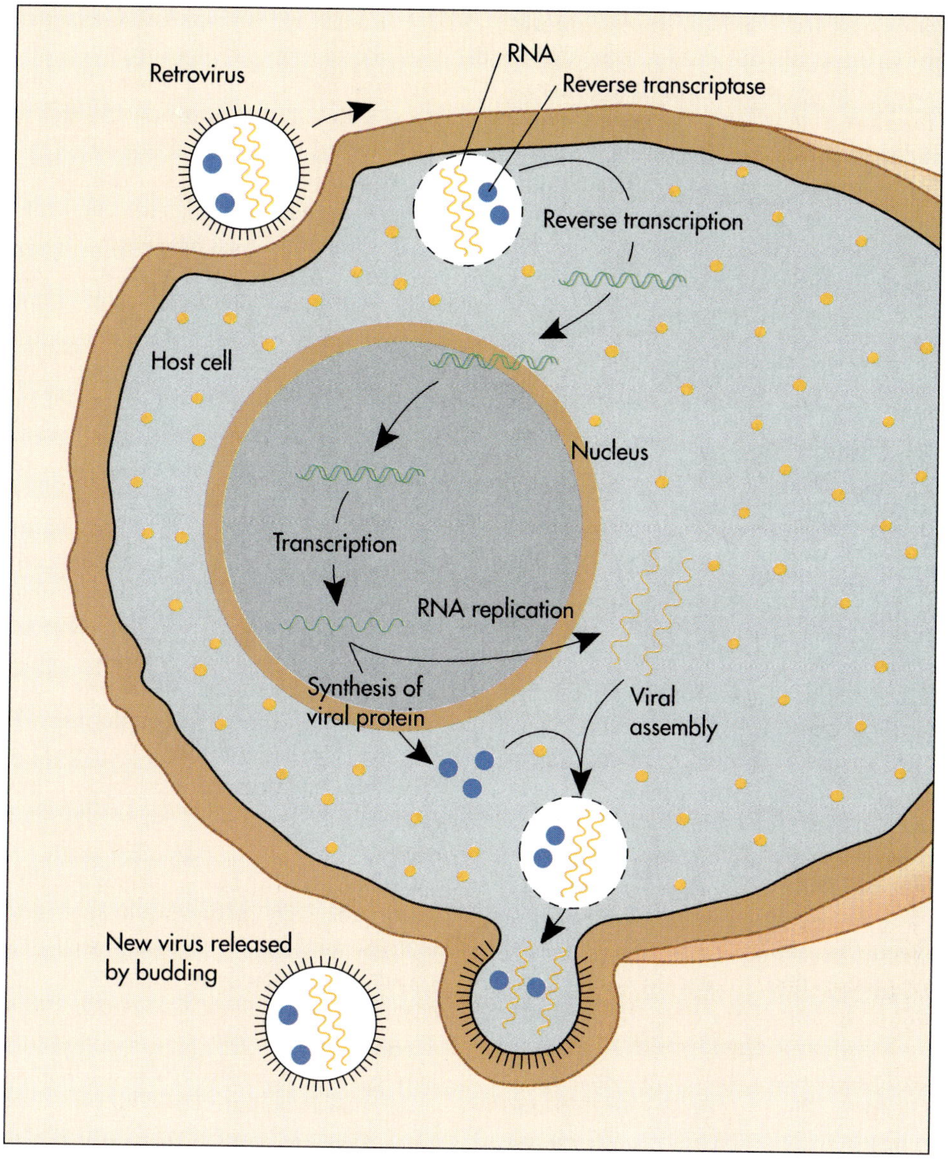

FIG. 8-31 Retroviruses replicate using reverse transcriptase to form DNA that is used to produce viral proteins and RNA genomes for viral progeny.

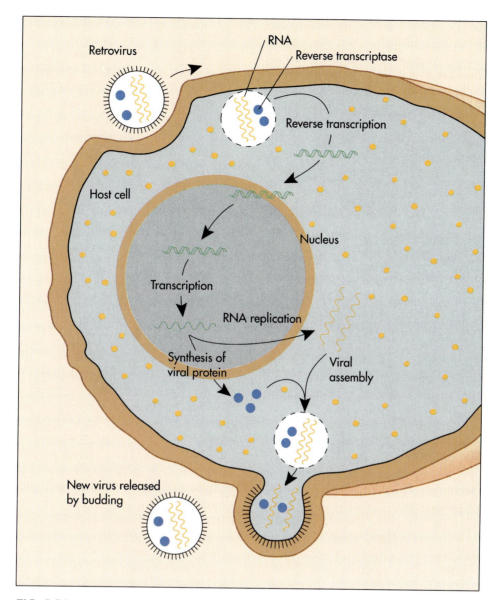

ture viral particles are released slowly and continuously from infected host cells by budding (FIG. 8-32).

The HIV genome codes for 7 genes in addition to those in common with all retroviruses. These genes code for proteins that function to regulate the expression of the HIV genome. Two of these genes are *tat*, which codes for a *trans*-activator protein, and *rev*. The Tat protein binds to an RNA sequence on the genome—TAR, the *trans*-activation response element—which increases the amount of RNA transcripts formed.

Some other retroviruses carry an additional gene that codes for a protein that causes the host cell to be transformed from a normal cell into a cancer cell. These retroviruses are said to be v-*onc*$^{+}$, that is, oncogenic. Oncoviruses are retroviruses that cause animal

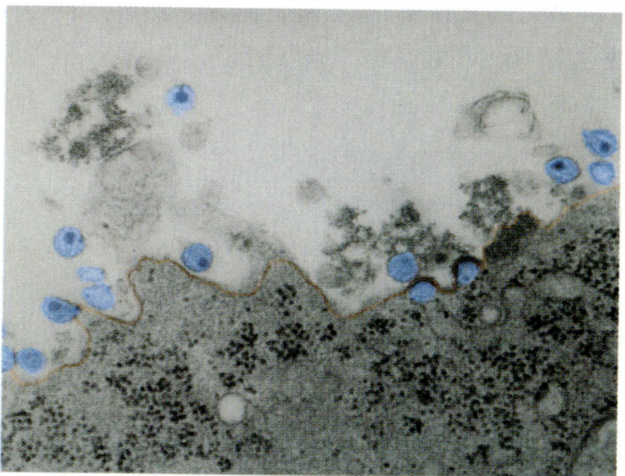

FIG. 8-32 Human immunodeficiency viruses (colorized; *blue*) are released by budding from infected cells. (40,200×).

cell transformations and its members were formerly called RNA tumor viruses; they are known to be oncogenic, that is, to cause malignancies in birds and mammals, including humans. The specific *onc* gene carried by each oncogenic retrovirus varies from virus to virus and includes, for example, *v-src,* in Rous sarcoma viruses; *v-myc,* in avian myelocytomatosis viruses; and *v-ras,* in murine sarcoma viruses. These viruses can form sarcomas and leukemias in the hosts they infect.

Prions

The most recently discovered and least understood microorganisms are the **prions,** which may be "infectious proteins." The discovery of prions in 1983 was unexpected, and their nature is very controversial. What is so unusual is that some analyses of prions indicate that they may be composed only of protein. If these "organisms" are nothing more than specific infectious protein molecules that contain the information that codes for their own replication, they are unique entities that violate the accepted dogma that nucleic acids are the conveyers of information.

The discovery of prions indicates an exception to the universal characteristic of living systems, viruses, and viroids—their genetic information is stored in nucleic acid molecules. All other organisms store genetic information in nucleic acids, DNA or, less commonly, RNA. We know how the genetic information in these nucleic acid molecules is replicated so that it can be passed from one generation to the next. We also broke the genetic code and know how the information contained within nucleic acid molecules is expressed. What we do not know is how a protein can direct its own replication. Thus we do not understand how prions replicate. Prions actually could be encoded by host cell chromosomal genes.

Although we do not know exactly how prions reproduce or how prevalent they are, we recognize their potential importance. Prions were discovered during the search for the cause of scrapie. Scrapie is an infectious and usually fatal disease of sheep. It is a neurological disease that is characterized by wild facial expressions, nervousness, twitching of the neck and head, grinding of the teeth, and scraping of portions of the skin against rocks with subsequent loss of wool. This disease is caused by an agent that can pass through a bacteriological filter and, therefore, was believed to be a virus. It was designated as a *slow virus* because of the slow development of the disease. However, no virus could be found, and eventually the cause of scrapie was attributed to a prion. It is likely that other diseases, including some human diseases such as kuru, result from the reproduction of prions within host cells. Kuru is a degenerative neurological disease that is associated with cannibal rituals in New Guinea; ingestion of infected brains results in transmission of the prions and kuru to the cannibal. Other diseases that are ascribed to prion infections include transmissible mink encephalopathy, chronic wasting disease, Creutzfeldt-Jakob disease, and Gerstmann-Straüssler syndrome. Several of these diseases are characterized by slow degeneration of the nervous system.

Prions and the consequences of their reproduction within the cells of the organisms they infect may explain several other diseases that still have no known cause. Some scientists suggest that Alzheimer's disease, a degenerative disease of the nervous system that afflicts many people over 40 years old, is caused by a prion. This is one of several hypotheses to explain the etiology of degenerative nervous disorders. Much more research is needed to reveal the importance of the discovery of prions.

CHAPTER REVIEW

Study Questions

1. Compare the lytic and lysogenic viral reproductive cycles. What are the similarities and differences in these two modes of replicating viral genomes?
2. How do we assay for lytic bacteriophage?
3. Discuss two ways that an RNA virus can replicate its genome.
4. How can viruses transform animal cells? What are oncogenes?
5. Is there a situation in animal viruses that is analogous to lysogeny in bacteria?
6. How does the structure of a viroid differ from that of an RNA virus?
7. How do viroids and RNA viruses compare with respect to their mode of replication?
8. How does a prion differ from a virus? How could a prion reproduce in a host cell?
9. What are the similarities and differences between animal, plant, and bacterial viruses? How could viral classification be unified?
10. How do retroviruses differ from other viruses?
11. What are the different mechanisms by which viruses are released from their host cells?
12. How are animal viruses replicated in the laboratory for study?

CHAPTER REVIEW

STUDY QUESTIONS—CONT'D

13. What advantages do enveloped viruses have over nonenveloped viruses?
14. Compare the replication mechanisms of the RNA-containing animal viruses. What specialized enzymes do these viruses contain?
15. What kinds of changes occur in host animal cells as a result of infection by viruses?
16. Compare viruses to bacteria in terms of structure and function.
17. Describe the growth curve for a bacteriophage, indicating what is occurring at each stage.
18. How is gene expression controlled in lambda phage?
19. How is genetic information efficiently stored in viruses?
20. Why is it difficult to find therapeutically useful antiviral drugs?

SITUATIONAL PROBLEMS

1. Debating Whether Viruses are Alive

Microbiologists often argue about whether or not acellular microorganisms should be considered as living entities. Geneticists may consider that information flow is the principal life function and accordingly view viruses as alive because they store and use genetic information to specify their own replication. Physiologists, on the other hand, may consider viruses as nonliving entities because of their inability to carry out physiological functions, such as ATP generation. Thus the perspective of an individual can bias the opinion on whether viruses should be viewed as living or not. A philosophical or scientific discussion of whether viruses are alive requires a fundamental understanding of the meaning of life and the ability to examine the processes that distinguish living from nonliving entities.

Consider that you are a member of the university debate team and that the topic for the next debate is "Viruses: Are They alive?" As in any formal debate, you must be prepared to argue either side of this issue. Prepare notes for debate, making sure that you consider both sides. Think about how the properties of viruses can be viewed as evidence for determining whether they are alive or not. Also, decide what experiments could be designed to help resolve this issue.

2. Determining the True Nature of Prions

Prions are the most recently discovered major group of microorganisms, and their nature is extremely controversial. You are asked to review a journal article on prions that proposes that (1) prions are composed exclusively of proteins and (2) a prion interacts with its host cell genome via a regulator gene, such that a structural gene controlled by that regulator gene is turned on by the presence of the prion protein, with that structural gene coding for the production of a protein identical to the prion protein.

1. To accept the arguments regarding these structural and reproductive properties of prions, what lines of evidence would you consider necessary? Consider structural data gathered by electron microscopic observation, chemical data obtained by enzymatic analyses, and genetic data determined by recombinant methods and the examination of mutants.
2. Having established the criteria to accept or reject the validity of an article on prion structure and mode of reproduction, go to the library and find a recent article on prions, perhaps one by Stanley Prusiner and his colleagues. Read the article and, using the criteria that you developed, see whether the information in that article supports or refutes the previous discussed properties of prions.
3. Next, go to the library and read "The Game of the Name Is Fame. But Is It Science?" by Gary Taubes in the December 1986 issue of *Discover* magazine. In this article, the author describes the controversy about the evidence concerning the nature of prions. See whether the criteria that you developed permits resolution of the issues raised in the article and whether, in fact, recent articles on prions have helped resolve this controversy.

Suggested Supplementary Readings

Aiken JM and RF Marsh: 1990. The search for scrapie agent nucleic acid, *Microbiological Reviews* 54(3):242-46.

Berns KI: 1990. Parvovirus replication, *Microbiological Reviews* 54(3):316-29.

Braun MM, WL Heyward, JW Curran: 1990. The global epidemiology of HIV infection and AIDS, *Annual Review of Microbiology* 44:555-77.

Buck KW: 1986. *Fungal Virology*, CRC Press, Boca Raton, FL.

Casjens S: 1985. *Virus Structure and Assembly*, Jones & Bartlett, Boston.

Crowell RL and K Lonberg-Holm: 1986. *Virus Attachment and Entry into Cells*, American Society for Microbiology, Washington, D.C.

Diener TO: 1981. Viroids, *Scientific American* 224:66-73.

Diener TO: 1982. Viroids and their interactions with host cells, *Annual Review of Microbiology* 36:239-258.

Diener TO, MP McKinley, SB Prusiner: 1982. Viroids and prions, *Proceedings of the National Academy of Sciences, U.S.A.* 79:5220-5224.

Dimmock NJ and SB Primrose: 1987. *Introduction to Modern Virology*, ed. 3, Blackwell Scientific Publications, London.

Dulbecco P: 1980. *Virology*, Harper & Row Publishers, Hagerstown, MD.

Dulbecco R and HS Ginsberg: 1988. *Virology*, ed. 2, J. B. Lippincott. Philadelphia.

Fields BN: 1991. *Fundamental Virology*, ed. 2, Raven Press, New York.

Fields BN, DM Knipe, RM Chanock, MS Hirsch, JL Melnick, TP Monath, B Roizman (eds.): 1990. *Fields Virology*, ed. 2, Raven Press, New York.

Fraenkel-Conrat H: 1985. *The Viruses: Catalogue, Characterization, and Classification*, Plenum Press, New York.

Fraenkel-Conrat H and PC Kimball: 1982. *Virology*, Prentice-Hall, Inc., Englewood Cliffs, NJ.

Fraenkel-Conrat H, PC Kimball, JA Levy: 1988. *Virology*, ed. 2, Prentice-Hall, Englewood Cliffs, NJ.

Francki RIB and RG Milne: 1985. *Atlas of Plant Viruses*, CRC Press, Inc., Boca Raton, FL.

Geiduschek EP: 1991. Regulation of expression of the late genes of bacteriophage T4, *Annual Review of Genetics* 25:437-460.

Kaplan AS (ed.): 1982. *Organization and Replication of Viral DNA*, CRC Press, Inc., Boca Raton, FL.

Katz RA and AM Shalka: 1990. Generation of diversity in retroviruses, *Annual Review of Genetics* 24:409-446.

Lin ECC, R Goldstein, M Syvanen: 1984. *Bacteria, Plasmids, and Phages*, Harvard University Press, Cambridge, MA.

Maramorosch K and JJ McKelvey Jr (eds.): 1985. *Subviral Pathogens of Plants and Animals: Viroids and Prions*, Academic Press, Inc., Orlando, FL.

Marsh M and A Helenius: 1989. Virus entry into animal cells, *Advances in Virus Research* 367:107-51.

Mathews C, E Kutter, G Mosig, P Berget (eds.): 1983. *Bacteriophage T4*, American Society for Microbiology, Washington, D.C.

Matthews R: 1985. Viral taxonomy for the nonvirologist, *Annual Review of Microbiology* 39:451-474.

Matthews REF: 1991. *Plant Virology*, ed. 3, Academic Press, New York.

Murialdo H: 1991. Bacteriophage lambda DNA maturation and packaging, *Annual Review of Biochemistry* 60:125-154.

Oldstone MBA: 1990. *Animal Virus Pathogenesis: A Practical Approach*, IRL Press, Oxford, England.

Palmer EL and ML Martin: 1982. *An Atlas of Mammalian Viruses*, CRC Press, Inc., Boca Raton, FL.

Prince AM: 1983. Non-A, non-B hepatitis viruses, *Annual Review of Microbiology* 37:217-232.

Prusiner SB: 1984. Prions, *Scientific American* 251(4):50-60.

Ptashne M, AD Johnson, CO Pabo: 1982. A genetic switch in a bacterial virus, *Scientific American* 247(5):128-140.

Rao VC and JL Melnick: 1986. *Environmental Virology*, American Society for Microbiology, Washington, D.C.

Reanney DC: 1982. The evolution of RNA viruses, *Annual Review of Microbiology* 36:47-73.

Riesner D and HJ Gross: 1985. Viroids, *Annual Review of Biochemistry* 54:531-561.

Sherker AH and PL Marion: 1991. Hepadnaviruses and hepatocellular carcinoma, *Annual Review of Microbiology* 45:475-508.

Simons K, H Garoff, A Helenius: 1982. How an animal virus gets into and out of its host cell, *Scientific American* 246(2): 58-66.

Steffy K and F Wong-Staal: 1991. Genetic regulation of human immunodeficiency virus, *Microbiological Reviews* 55(2):193-205.

Stephens EB and RW Compans: 1988. Assembly of animal viruses at cellular membranes, *Annual Review of Microbiology* 42:489-516.

Strauss JH and EG Strauss: 1988. Evolution of RNA viruses, *Annual Review of Microbiology* 42:657-83.

Varmus H: 1988. Retroviruses, *Science* 249:1427-35.

Voyles BA: 1993. *The Biology of Viruses*, Mosby, St. Louis.

Webster RG, WJ Bean, OT Gorman, TM Chambers, Y Kawaoka: 1992. Evolution and ecology of influenza A viruses, *Microbiological Reviews* 56(1):152-79.

White DO and FJ Fenner: 1986. *Medical Virology*, Academic Press, Orlando, FL.

CHAPTER 9

Bacterial Growth and Reproduction

Chapter Outline

Bacterial reproduction by binary fission results in a doubling of the number of viable cells in a population. The growth of bacteria is most often equated with cell reproduction. Bacteria growing in cultures double their numbers regularly; growth is exponential, with the rate of increase depending on the doubling time. In batch culture, bacteria exhibit a characteristic growth curve consisting of periods of adaptation, reproduction, no net growth, and decline. Many factors influence bacterial growth rates. These include temperature, salinity, pH, oxygen, and various other physical and chemical factors. Bacteria exhibit ranges of tolerance for these factors that determine the limits of growth. Outside the range of environmental conditions under which a given bacterium can reproduce, it may either survive in a relatively dormant state or lose viability; that is, it may lose the ability to reproduce and will subsequently die. Bacteria also have optimal growth rates. Some environmental conditions favor rapid bacterial reproduction and others permit slow or no bacterial growth. Conditions permitting the growth of one bacterium may preclude the growth of another. Not all bacteria can grow under identical conditions.

9.1 BACTERIAL GROWTH

Growth may be generally defined as a steady increase in all of the chemical components of an organism. Growth usually results in an increase in the size of a cell and frequently results in cell division (except for some filamentous microorganisms). There is an important distinction between the growth of multicellular versus unicellular organisms: growth in multicellular organisms leads to an increase in the size of the organism; growth in unicellular organisms leads to an increase in the number of individuals in the population. Because cell division is usually a tightly related consequence of cell growth in bacteria, measuring the change in cell number in a population is often used to assess growth. Methods for enumerating numbers of bacterial cells are discussed in Chapter 2.

The life cycle of a single bacterial cell may be taken as the time of division of a mother cell into two daughter cells until one of the daughter cells divides into two more daughter cells. The cell cycle in eukaryotic cells involves separate phases for cell enlargement, replication of the genome, separation of the replicated genomes by mitosis, and cell division (cytokinesis) that are separated by gaps (Table 9-1). The bacterial cell cycle is characterized by continuous macromolecular synthesis and cell elongation occurs while the genome is being replicated. The replicated bacterial chromosomes are not pulled apart by microtubules as in mitosis of eukaryotic cells but appear to be attached to the cytoplasmic membrane. In essence the cytoplasmic membrane of the prokaryotic cell replaces the mitotic spindle fibers of the eukaryotic cell. The cell cycle in bacteria thus is relatively simple.

TABLE 9-1 Cell Cycle in Eukaryotic Cells

$G_1 \rightarrow S \rightarrow G_2 \rightarrow M \rightarrow C$

PHASE	DESCRIPTION
G_1	Primary growth phase of the cell during which cell enlargement occurs; a gap phase separating cell growth from replication of the genome
S	Phase in which replication of the genome occurs
G_2	Phase in which the cell prepares for separation of the replicated genomes; this phase includes synthesis of microtubules and condensation of DNA to form coherent chromosomes; a gap phase separating chromosome replication from mitosis.
M	Phase called mitosis during which the microtubular apparatus is assembled and subsequently used to pull apart the sister chromosomes
C	Phase of cytokinesis during which the cell divides to form two daughter cells

Reproduction of Bacterial Cells—Binary Fission

Most bacterial cells reproduce asexually by **binary fission**, a process in which a cell divides to produce two nearly equal-sized progeny cells (FIG. 9-1). Binary fission involves three processes: increase in cell size (cell elongation), DNA replication, and cell division. Not all bacteria reproduce by binary fission but use other mechanisms such as yeast-like budding for reproduction. Even among the bacteria that do reproduce by binary fission, there is considerable variability in the overall process.

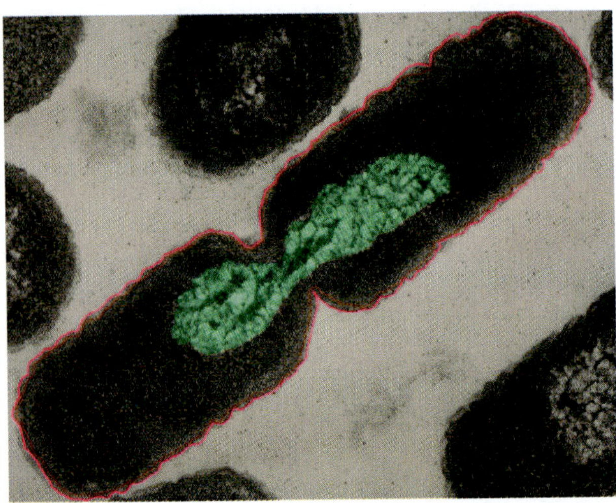

FIG. 9-1 Colorized micrograph of *Escherichia coli* dividing by binary fission. The cell wall and cytoplasmic membrane are growing inward to separate the cells and the replicated bacterial chromosomes *(green)*.

Cell Elongation

Increase in cell size requires growth of the cell wall. The biosynthesis of new cell surface occurs at specific sites (FIG. 9-2). Newly synthesized cell wall material in cocci is inserted at specific sites of the pre-existing cell wall. In the coccal bacterium *Enterococcus*, for example, cell wall synthesis begins at a band that circles the cell perpendicular to a line running from cell pole to cell pole. As additional cell wall material is added the nascent wall is forced away from the site laterally to form an elongated cell. Incorporation of radioactive cell wall precursors and autoradiographic analyses suggest that rod-shaped bacteria also incorporate new wall at discrete sites. In Gram-negative rod-shaped bacteria, cell wall is added all around the cylindrical region and outer membrane material is inserted at the specific adhesion sites between the cytoplasmic membrane and outer membrane.

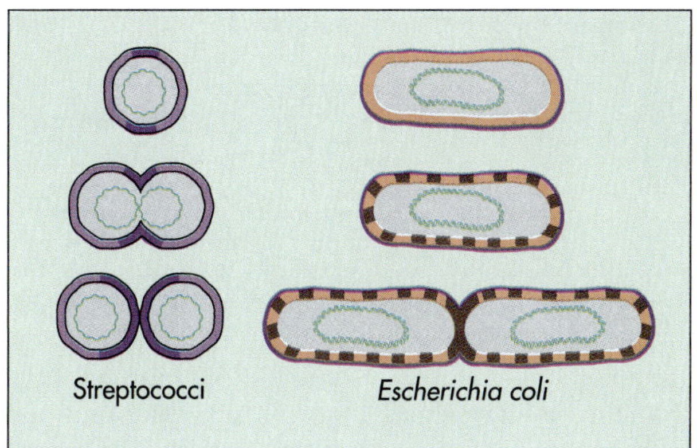

FIG. 9-2 Cell growth occurs at specific sites *(dark purple)* so that the cell elongates prior to division.

DNA Replication

DNA replication in *Escherichia coli* takes 40 minutes to completely copy the bacterial chromosome. In *E. coli* and other bacteria that can reproduce every 20 minutes, new DNA synthesis is initiated before a previously initiated round of DNA synthesis is completed. This means that rapidly growing bacteria have multiple initiation forks of DNA synthesis simultaneously on their bacterial chromosome. When a bacterial cell divides into two cells, each cell receives a complete genome and an additional portion of the genome whose synthesis was initiated part of the way through the life cycle of that cell.

A new round of replication of the bacterial chromosome is initiated every time the cell divides. Thus the initiation of DNA replication is actually controlled with the rate of cell division. It is not clear what regulates the initiation step, although the product of the *dnaA* gene is required for initiation to proceed. Surprisingly, this gene product appears to be self-regulated. When DnaA protein is present in the cell in high concentration it initiates DNA synthesis more frequently but also binds to the *dnaA* gene to shut off its own synthesis.

Septum Formation

At some time during the cell cycle the cell must partition the DNA and cytoplasmic components by synthesizing a **septum,** or crosswall, consisting of cytoplasmic membrane and cell wall peptidoglycan (and outer membrane in Gram-negative bacteria) (FIG. 9-3). In most bacteria the septum is initiated by invaginations of the cell envelope layers, which leads to formation of a ring-shaped constriction, generally in the center of the cell and perpendicular to the outer surface of the cell. The opening in the ring gradually becomes smaller and smaller as new cell envelope material is added until it completely walls off one compartment of the cell from the other.

In many bacteria, the septum is separated after cell division by autolysins, which leads to two independent daughter cells. In other bacteria, such as streptococci, septum separation usually is incomplete and the cells remain attached to one another to form chains (FIG. 9-4). In other bacteria, such as *Thiopedia,* cells divide in one division plane in the first generation, and in the next generation the daughter cells synthesize a septum perpendicular to the first. This leads to the formation of sheets of cells. Yet other bacteria, such as *Sarcina,* divide in three-dimensional division planes and form cubical arrangements of cells called octads.

What triggers the initiation of septum formation or what ties septum formation to DNA replication is not known. At least 12 proteins in *E. coli* are responsible for septation to occur. One of these is a cytoplasmic membrane protein, penicillin-binding protein 3, and is believed to be involved in the septation process. The

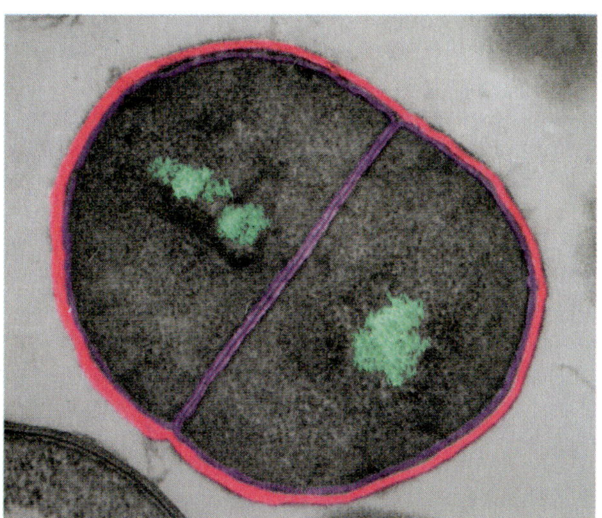

FIG. 9-3 Colorized micrograph of dividing *Sporosarcina ureae* with a completed septum separating the two daughter cells.

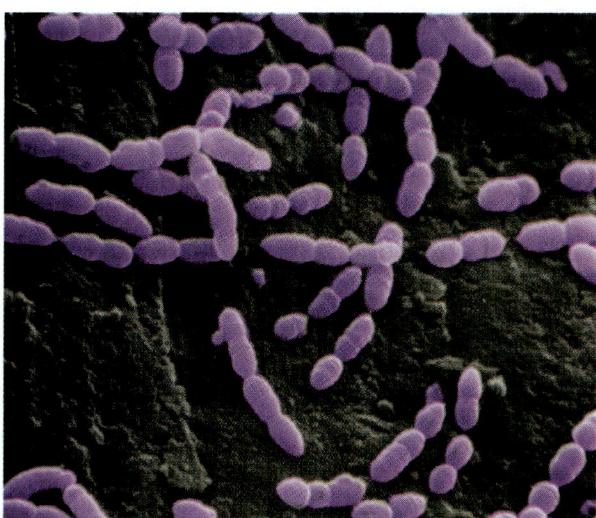

FIG. 9-4 Scanning electron micrograph of a chain of cells of *Streptococcus mutans.* (colorized; 7,600×).

antibiotic cephalexin preferentially binds to and inhibits penicillin-binding protein 3, which leads to filamentous growth of *E. coli* cells (long cells that lack septa). Another important protein is the product of the *ftsZ* gene, since mutations in this gene lead to the formation of elongated cells with multiple chromosomes. The FtsZ protein and SulA proteins act to block septation and cell division.

Another unknown factor in the bacterial cell cycle is how the DNA is segregated into the two daughter cells before septation is complete. There is no mitotic apparatus (centromere, spindle fibers, and microtubule contraction) in prokaryotic cells to assure the separation of replicated chromosomes. One explanation may lie in the attachment of the DNA to the cytoplasmic membrane. As the membrane and cell wall grow laterally, the DNA is swept along by virtue of its attachment.

Kinetics of Bacterial Reproduction

Reproduction by binary fission results in doubling of the number of viable bacterial cells. Therefore, during active bacterial growth, the bacterial population is continuously doubling. The time required to achieve a doubling of the population size, known as the **doubling time** or **generation time,** is the unit of measure of the bacterial growth rate (Table 9-2).

Because the bacterial population doubles every generation, if the initial population size is N_0, then after one generation of growth:

$$N_1 = 2 \times N_0$$

after two generations of growth:

$$N_2 = 2 \times 2N_0 = 2^2N_0$$

after three generations of growth:

$$N_3 = 2 \times 2^2N_0 = 2^3N_0$$

and after *n* generations of growth:

$$N_n = 2^nN_0$$

This relationship can be expressed in terms of the generation time. If N_0 is the initial population number; N_t, the population at time *t*; and *n*, the number of generations in time, then:

$$N_t = N_0 \times 2^n$$

Solving for *n* (the number of generations):

$$\log N_t = \log N_0 + n \times \log 2$$

$$n = \frac{\log N_t - \log N_0}{\log 2} = \frac{\log N_t - \log N_0}{0.301}$$

The growth rate of a bacterial culture can also be expressed as a function of the **reciprocal of the doubling time,** *k:*

$$k = \frac{n}{t} = \frac{\log N_t - \log N_0}{0.301\, t}$$

TABLE 9-2 Growth Rates for Some Representative Bacteria under Optimal Conditions

ORGANISM	TEMPERATURE (°C)	GENERATION TIME (MIN)
Bacillus stearothermophilus	60	11
Escherichia coli	37	20
Bacillus subtilis	37	27
Bacillus mycoides	37	28
Staphylococcus aureus	37	28
Streptococcus lactis	37	30
Pseudomonas putida	30	45
Lactobacillus acidophilus	37	75
Vibrio marinus	15	80
Mycobacterium tuberculosis	37	360
Bradyrhizobium japonicum	25	400
Nostoc japonicum	25	570
Anabaena cylindrica	25	840
Treponema pallidum	37	1980

The growth rate constant represents the number of generations per time and is usually described as generations per hour. A useful calculation, the **mean generation time (*g*)** or **doubling time** for a population that is actively reproducing, is:

$$k = \frac{\log(2N_0) - \log N_0}{0.301\, g} = \frac{\log 2 + \log N_0 - \log N_0}{0.301\, g} = \frac{0.693}{g}$$

$$g = \frac{0.693}{k}$$

This mathematical formula for the bacterial growth rate is based on the premise that the rate of increase is proportional to the number or mass of cells present at any given time and that the doubling time is constant during a period of growth.

By determining cell numbers during the period of active cell division, the generation time can be estimated. In comparing generation times, one finds that bacteria reproduce more rapidly than higher organisms. A bacterium such as *E. coli* can have a generation time as short as 20 minutes under optimal conditions, although in nature many bacteria have generation times of several hours. One cell of a bacterium with a 20-minute generation time could multiply to 1,000 cells in 3.3 hours and to 1,000,000 cells in 6.6 hours.

Phases of Bacterial Growth

If an old culture of bacteria is inoculated or added to a fresh medium and the cell concentration is periodically measured, then a curve describing the change in cell number against time can be drawn. This curve,

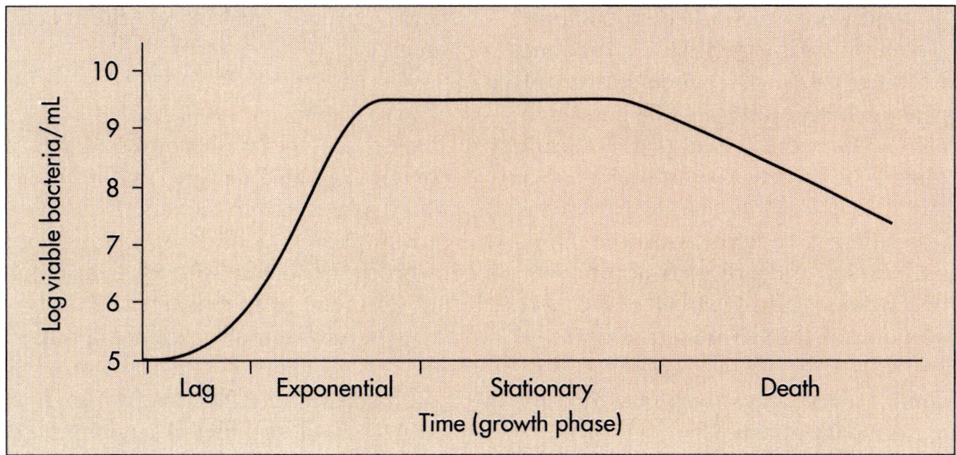

FIG. 9-5 Growth curve for bacteria has four distinct phases: lag, exponential (log), stationary, and death.

called the **growth curve,** will be hyperbolic due to the exponential nature of bacterial growth (FIG. 9-5).

Lag Phase

The typical growth curve of a bacterial culture begins with the **lag phase.** During the lag phase there is little increase in cell numbers. Rather, during this phase the bacteria are transporting nutrients inside the cell from the new medium, preparing for reproduction, and synthesizing DNA and various inducible enzymes needed for cell division. They increase in size during this process but the number of cells does not increase.

Exponential Phase

In the **log growth phase,** also called the **exponential growth phase,** bacterial cell division begins and proceeds as a geometric progression. One cell divides to form two, each of these cells divides to form four, and so forth in a geometric progression (FIG. 9-6).

During the log phase of growth, so named because the logarithm of the bacterial biomass increases linearly with time, bacterial reproduction occurs at a maximal rate for the specific set of growth conditions. This growth phase is better called the exponential growth phase because the number of cells is increasing as an exponential function of time. Growth during much of the exponential growth phase is said to be balanced, that is, the concentrations of all macromolecules of the cell are increasing at the same rate. The average composition of the cells, therefore, remains constant. During the log phase of the growth curve, the growth rate of a bacterium is proportional to the biomass of bacteria that is present.

The growth rate during the log phase is described by the equation:

$$\frac{dB}{dt} = \alpha B$$

where B is the bacterial biomass, t is time, and α is the instantaneous growth rate constant. During this period the generation time of the bacterium is determined. If a bacterial culture in the exponential growth phase is inoculated into an identical fresh medium, the lag phase is usually bypassed and exponential growth continues. This occurs because bacteria are already actively carrying out the metabolism necessary for continued growth. If, however, the chemical composition of the new medium differs significantly from that of the original growth medium, the bacteria go through a lag phase wherein they synthesize the enzymes needed for growth in the new medium before entering the logarithmic growth phase.

Stationary Phase

A growing bacterial culture eventually reaches a phase during which there is no further net increase in bacterial cell numbers. This is called the **stationary growth phase.** The transition between the exponential

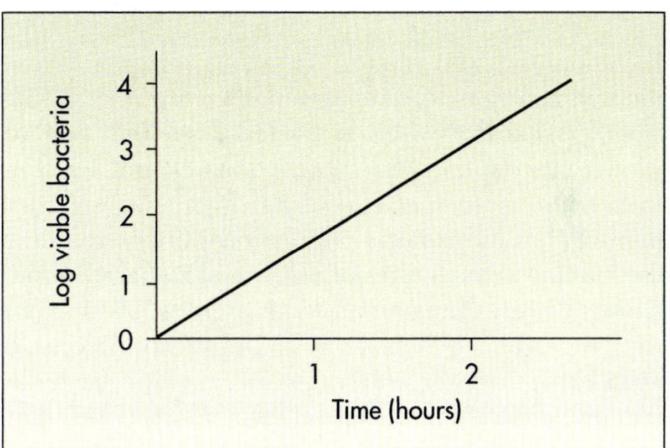

FIG. 9-6 During exponential growth the number of cells doubles each generation time; a graph of the log number of bacteria versus time is linear.

and stationary phases involves a period of unbalanced growth during which the various cellular components are synthesized at unequal rates. Consequently, cells in the stationary phase have a different chemical composition from cells in the exponential phase. During the stationary phase, the growth rate is exactly equal to the death rate. A bacterial population may reach stationary growth when a required nutrient is exhausted, when inhibitory end products accumulate, or when physical conditions change. In all cases, there are feedback mechanisms that regulate the bacterial enzymes involved in key metabolic steps. The duration of the stationary phase varies; some bacteria exhibit a very long stationary phase.

The physiological changes between the exponential and stationary phases often are very significant so that cells in stationary phase have distinct characteristics. When *Arthrobacter,* for example, reaches stationary phase there is a change from rod-shaped cells to coccoid cells. These coccoid cells are called arthrospores or cystites. The formation of arthrospores represents the beginning of a regular life cycle that is characteristic of eukaryotic microorganisms but is rare among prokaryotes. The sequence of morphological changes in the growth cycle distinguishes *Arthrobacter* from other genera.

Death Phase

Eventually the number of viable bacterial cells begins to decline, signaling the onset of the **death phase.** The kinetics of bacterial death, like those of growth, are exponential because the death phase really represents the result of the inability of the bacteria to carry out further reproduction. The rate of the death phase need not, however, be equal to the rate of growth during the exponential phase. The rate of death is proportional to the number of survivors. Modifying environmental conditions can alter the rate of exponential growth and the death rate of a bacterium.

Growth of Bacterial Cultures

In laboratory and natural situations, some environmental parameter or interaction of environmental parameters controls a given bacterial specie's rate of growth. In nature, where conditions cannot be controlled and many species co-exist, fluctuating environmental conditions favor population shifts because of the varying growth rates of individual bacterial populations within the community at a given location. In the laboratory, it is possible to adjust conditions to achieve optimal growth rates for a given bacterial species. Similarly, in industrial fermentors, conditions can be adjusted to optimize bacterial growth rates, thereby maximizing the accumulation of desired metabolic products. Many laboratory and industrial applications use pure cultures of bacteria, facilitating the adjustment of the growth conditions so that they favor optimal growth of the particular bacterial species.

Batch Culture

The normal bacterial growth curve is characteristic of bacteria in **batch culture,** that is, under conditions in which a fresh medium is simply inoculated with a bacterium. A flask containing a liquid nutrient medium or broth inoculated with a bacterium such as *E. coli* is an example of a batch culture. In batch culture growth, nutrients are expended, and metabolic products accumulate in the closed environment. The batch culture models situations such as occur when a canned food product is contaminated with a bacterium.

During exponential growth in a batch culture the instantaneous growth rate constant (μ) is related to the generation time (g) by the equation:

$$\mu = \frac{0.693}{g}$$

This equation is derived from the fact that during exponential growth the rate of change of a population of cells from a given cell number (N) is described by the equation:

$$\frac{dN}{dt} = \mu N$$

The generation time represents the average time that it takes a population to double in size, whereas the instantaneous growth rate constant more closely resembles the growth (reproduction) of individual cells.

As a batch culture approaches stationary phase it is necessary to modify the equation describing growth because there is a maximal obtainable population:

$$\frac{dN}{dt} = \mu N - \frac{\mu}{N_{max}} N^2$$

According to this logistics equation, as the population size (N) approaches its maximal obtainable limit (N_{max}) the change in population size (dN/dt) approaches zero, which is what occurs during the stationary growth phase.

Continuous Culture

In continuous culture systems, fresh medium replaces some of the spent medium, thus permitting continuous growth of a culture. In a **turbidostat** the system includes an optical sensing device that measures the turbidity of the culture in the growth vessel and generates an electrical signal that is used to regulate the flow of fresh medium into the vessel and the flow of spent medium and cells out of it. Thus, in a turbidostat, the number of cells in the culture controls the flow rate, and the rate of growth of the culture adjusts to this flow rate.

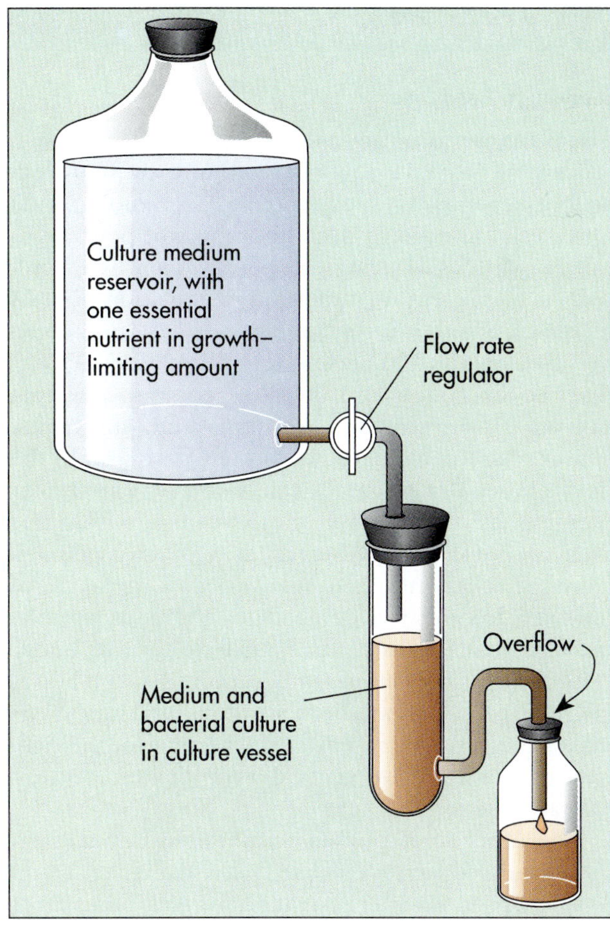

FIG. 9-7 A chemostat continuously provides nutrients with a growth-rate-limiting factor to a flow-through culture chamber in which bacteria grow.

In a **chemostat** the flow rate from a reservoir of a growth medium is set at a particular value and the rate of growth of the culture adjusts to this flow rate (FIG. 9-7). Because end products do not accumulate and nutrients are not completely expended, the bacteria never reach stationary phase in a chemostat. Bacteria grown in a chemostat, in which nutrients are supplied and end products continuously removed, are maintained in the exponential growth phase. Continuous growth of bacteria is accomplished in this device by continuously feeding a liquid medium into the bacterial culture. The liquid medium contains some nutrient in growth-limiting concentrations, and the concentration of the limiting nutrient in the growth medium determines the rate of bacterial growth. During steady-state operation of a continuous culture device, the concentration of the limiting nutrient remains constant because the rate of addition of the nutrient equals the rate at which it is used by the culture, plus that lost through overflow.

Even though bacteria are continuously reproducing, a number of bacterial cells are continuously being washed out and removed from the culture vessel. Thus a constant number of bacterial cells are maintained in the chemostat culture vessel.

The instantaneous growth rate of the bacterial population in the chemostat is:

$$\frac{dN}{dt} = \mu N$$

The rate at which cells are lost as a result of being washed out of the chemostat is:

$$\frac{dN}{dt} = \mu N - DN = (\mu - D)N$$

where N is the size of the steady state population and D is the rate of dilution.

Because the rate of cell washout is equal to the growth rate, the dilution rate is equal to the growth rate of a bacterium growing in a chemostat.

The relationship between the culture generation time and the concentration of the limiting substrate is:

$$\mu = \mu_{max} \frac{s}{(k_s + s)}$$

where μ is the culture generation time, μ_{max} is the maximal growth rate at saturating concentrations of substrate, s is the substrate concentration, and k_s is the saturation constant defined as the substrate concentration at $\frac{1}{2}\ \mu_{max}$. Cell numbers and the concentration of the limiting nutrient change little at low dilution rates. As the dilution rate approaches k_s, the cell concentration drops rapidly to zero, and the concentration of the limiting nutrient approaches its concentration in the reservoir. A chemostat is a good model for bacterial growth in open systems such as rivers and oceans, and by using chemostats and the appropriate mathematical calculations, the growth rates of bacteria in nature can be estimated.

Synchronous Culture

Synchronous growth of bacteria occurs when all cells divide at the same time. Adjusting environmental conditions, such as by repeatedly changing the temperature or by adding fresh nutrients to cultures as soon as they enter the stationary phase, can induce synchronous growth. A synchronous population of bacterial cells also can be obtained by physical separation procedures. For example, an unsynchronized culture of bacteria can be filtered through a membrane filter. The loosely associated bacteria are washed from the filter, leaving some cells tightly adsorbed to it. The filter is inverted and fresh medium allowed to flow through it. New bacterial cells that arise through cell division are not tightly bound to the membrane and are washed into the effluent. All of the cells in the effluent are newly formed and are therefore at the same stage of the cell cycle. Such synchronous growth, however, can be maintained for only a few generations.

9.2 EFFECTS OF NUTRIENT CONCENTRATIONS ON BACTERIAL GROWTH

To grow, bacteria utilize various substances called **nutrients.** They obtain nutrients from their environment and use them for the production of energy and for the biosynthesis of cellular macromolecules. Water comprises a large part of the cell by weight, about 80% to 90%, and therefore is an essential nutrient. The remaining solids of the cell are largely composed of hydrogen, oxygen, carbon, nitrogen, phosphorus, and sulfur. Also vital for proper cell functioning, although in substantially smaller amounts, are metal cations of potassium, magnesium, calcium, iron, manganese, cobalt, copper, molybdenum, and zinc; as well as anions such as chloride; and, for some microorganisms, growth factors such as vitamins. Each nutrient plays an important role in the overall growth of the cell (Table 9-3).

General Strategies for Coping with Periods of Low Nutrient Availability

Most natural ecosystems are characterized by low concentrations of usable organic matter. Because periods of starvation are probably experienced by most free-living bacteria, starvation survival is important for most bacteria. Bacteria preferentially growing at low nutrient concentrations are called **oligotrophs.** Most oligotrophs have slow growth rates. In contrast to oligotrophs, bacteria that grow at high nutrient concentrations exhibit high rates of reproduction. Bacteria that grow at high nutrient concentrations, such as the nutrient concentration in most culture media, are called **copiotrophs.**

Starvation Response

The response to nutrient or energy starvation in heterotrophic bacteria is often rapid and pronounced. Within seconds after exposure to starvation conditions, cells shut down RNA, protein, and peptidoglycan biosynthesis. During this period, the rate of proteolysis or protein turnover and degradation of RNA increases. There is a concomitant increase in the synthesis of ppGpp (guanosine tetraphosphate). This is likely to be coupled to the stringent response that shuts down transcription and translation and makes amino acids available for new protein synthesis. In the next phase, ppGpp levels fall and macromolecular synthesis increases as cells deplete storage polymers such as poly-β-hydroxybutyric acid or glycogen. Finally, the cells continue to survive for a long period of time at a low metabolic rate. They synthesize specific proteins that enhance their ability to survive under conditions of starvation. In addition, the half-life of mRNA greatly increases. The synthesis of new proteins makes the cell a more efficient scavenger of the deficient nutrient. The proteins also confer a more stress-tolerant phenotype.

The number of proteins synthesized depends on the specific nutrient depleted. *E. coli* synthesizes about 30 novel proteins after starvation for a carbon source and 26 to 32 proteins when deprived of nitrogen. *Bacillus subtilis* produces several new proteins in response to carbon, nitrogen, oxygen, or phosphate limitation. Iron deprivation in Gram-negative bacteria leads to the induction of high-affinity iron chelators called siderophores. Some of these proteins may be

TABLE 9-3 Principal Elements of the Cell and their Physiological Functions

ELEMENT	PERCENTAGE OF CELL DRY WEIGHT	PHYSIOLOGICAL FUNCTIONS
Carbon	50	Constituent of all organic cell components
Oxygen	20	Constituent of cellular water and most organic cell components; molecular oxygen serves as an electron acceptor in aerobic respiration
Nitrogen	14	Constituent of proteins, nucleic acids, coenzymes
Hydrogen	8	Constituent of cellular water and organic cell constituents
Phosphorus	3	Constituent of nucleic acids, phospholipids, coenzymes
Sulfur	1	Constituent of some amino acids in proteins and some coenzymes
Potassium	1	Important inorganic cation and cofactor for some enzymatic reactions
Sodium	1	One of the principal inorganic cations in eukaryotic cells and important in membrane transport
Calcium	0.5	Important inorganic cation and cofactor for some enzymatic reactions
Magnesium	0.5	Important inorganic cation and cofactor for many enzymatic reactions
Chlorine	0.5	Important inorganic anion
Iron	0.2	Constituent of cytochromes and some proteins
All Others	~0.3	—

part of a larger global control by which the cell responds to stress.

The outcome of these cellular events leads to the formation of smaller-than-normal size cells. There appears to be a correlation between slow growth rate and small cell size. The unsaturated fatty acids in the cytoplasmic membrane phospholipids of minicells are converted to cyclopropane fatty acids. This renders the lipids more resistant to oxidation. Many Gram-positive bacteria synthesize phosphorus-rich teichoic acids as cell wall accessory molecules. Under conditions of phosphate limitation, phosphate is more importantly required for DNA, RNA, and ATP; teichoic acids in the cell wall are replaced by phosphorus-free teichuronic acids.

Viable Nonculturable Cells

Often, cells in the environment are viable but nonculturable. These cells exhibit active metabolism in the form of respiration or fermentation, incorporate radioactive substrates, and have active protein synthesis but cannot be cultured or grown on conventional laboratory media. They have been detected by observing discrepancies between plate count enumeration of bacterial populations and direct staining and microscopic counts. These cells may be particular problems in the environment if they are pathogens; viable nonculturable cells of *Vibrio cholerae,* enteropathogenic *E. coli,* and *Legionella pneumophila* have been shown to regain culturability after they have entered the intestinal tracts of animals.

Specific Strategies for Coping with Periods of Low Nutrient Availability

Oligotrophic Bacteria

Oligotrophic bacteria, which are also called **low-nutrient bacteria,** possess physiological properties that permit them to use efficiently the limited nutrient resources available to them. Substrate uptake characteristics of oligotrophs permit acquisition of growth substrates against steep concentration gradients between the cell and its surrounding. They conserve available resources.

Many oligotrophic bacteria have appendages or form very small cells so that they have a high surface area to volume ratio. This enables them to accumulate nutrients efficiently from dilute solutions. One morphologically distinct group forms appendages called **prosthecae.** The prosthecae increase the surface area to volume ratio. For many appendage-forming bacteria in dilute aquatic environments, this is an important adaptation for acquiring adequate nutrients.

Some bacteria, such as *Caulobacter,* form a **stalk,** which is a prosthecal structure by which they attach to solid substrates (FIG. 9-8). The tip of the stalk establishes a holdfast through which the cell can affix to a surface. This enables *Caulobacter* to conserve energy, remaining sessile (nonmoving) while nutrients flow by its surface and can be absorbed. *Caulobacter* can grow in very dilute solutions, including distilled water (even double-distilled water contains low concentrations of organic molecules that are absorbed from the air). In nature, *Caulobacter* grows in aquatic environments, often attached to plant or microbial cells. The stalks of *Caulobacter* cells can attach to each other to form rosettes.

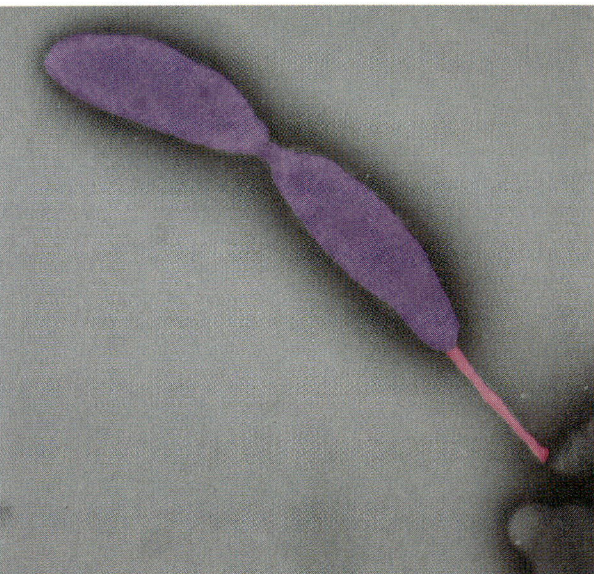

FIG. 9-8 Colorized micrograph of *Caulobacter crescentus* showing the stalk (*pink*). This bacterium can grow at very low nutrient concentrations.

Cell division in *Caulobacter* occurs by elongation of the cell followed by fission. The cell that forms at the pole opposite the stalk has a single flagellum. The cell with the flagellum, called a swarmer cell, swims away from the nonmotile mother cell. The swarmer cell eventually settles at a surface where nutrients may be concentrated and the flagellum is then lost. A stalk is synthesized by this cell and the cell division process is repeated.

Endospore-forming Bacteria

A few bacterial genera, such as *Bacillus* and *Clostridium,* form endospores when an essential growth nutrient is exhausted (FIG. 9-9, p. 336). Endospore formation is initiated when exhaustion of a growth substrate causes exponential growth to cease. The formation of endospores and normal reproduction are mutually exclusive processes. Endospore formation represents a cellular differentiation to a non-

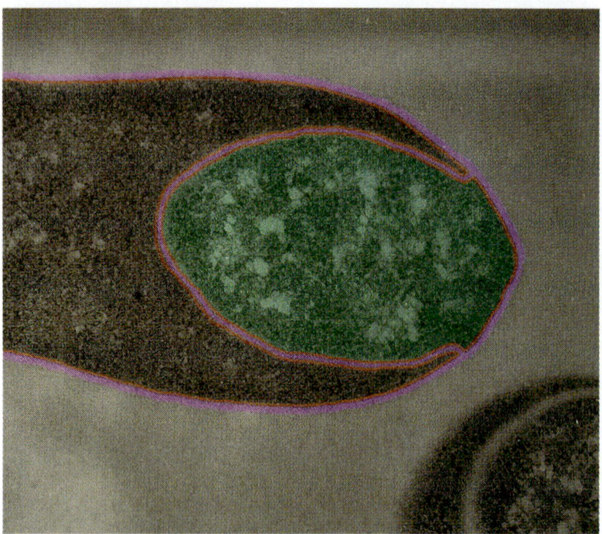

FIG. 9-9 Colorized micrograph of *Bacillus* during formation of an endospore. (40,600×).

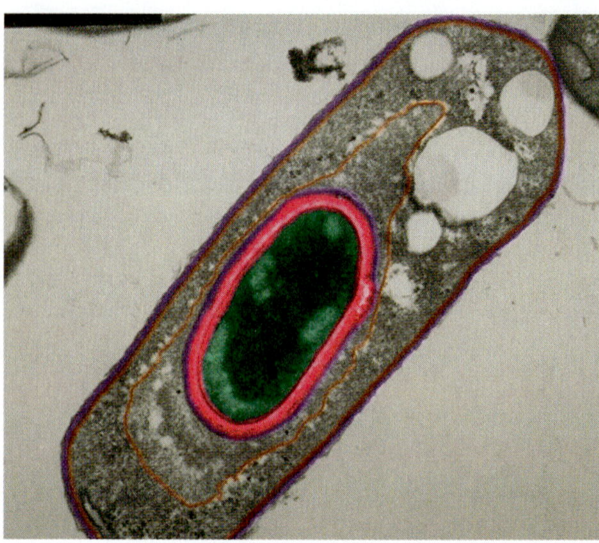

FIG. 9-10 Colorized micrograph of *Bacillus* after formation of an endospore. (32,400×).

reproducing form. Glucose and other growth substrates repress endospore formation. Sporulation of a culture of *Bacillus* begins immediately after guanine nucleotide levels rise in the medium as a result of growth substrate exhaustion. The energy for sporulation comes from cellular protein and poly-β-hydroxybutyrate. The actual formation of the endospore takes about 8 hours.

Once started, the process of endospore formation is irreversible, and sporulating bacteria continue to form spores even when starvation is relieved and conditions suitable for growth are restored (FIG. 9-10). During the sporulation process, there is an invagination of the cytoplasmic membrane within the cell to establish the site of endospore formation. A copy of the bacterial chromosome is incorporated into the endospore, and the various layers of the endospore are then synthesized around the bacterial DNA. Dipicolinic acid, which is involved in conferring heat resistance to the spore, and polypeptides composed almost exclusively of single amino acids, such as cystine, are made.

Endospore-forming bacteria, such as *Bacillus* and *Clostridium,* have numerous spore-specific genes, and there is a shift in protein synthesis to spore-specific gene expression as endospore formation begins. During sporulation, the cell makes spore-specific proteins rather than synthesizing proteins involved in cell growth. *Bacillus subtilis,* which has been extensively studied, has at least 45 separate sporulation genes.

Expression of spore-specific genes involves production of new sigma factors that alter the promoter recognition sites of RNA polymerase. Vegetative cells of *Bacillus subtilis* contain σ^{55}, σ^{37}, σ^{32}, and σ^{28}. During sporulation there is a cascade of different sigma factors that sequentially activate transcription of spore-specific genes. When starvation conditions occur, endospore formation is initiated when σ^{37} and σ^{32} combine with the core RNA polymerase so that a few new proteins are synthesized. A new σ factor (σ^{29}) is among these proteins. Many spore-specific genes are then transcribed because σ^{29} recognizes spore-specific promoters. Sporulation, thus, is controlled by sequential activation of sigma factors, each sigma factor directing the synthesis of a particular set of genes. As new sigma factors become active, old sigma factors may become inactive, so that the expression of some genes ceases as others are transcribed.

An endospore is a very resistant body that can withstand adverse conditions of desiccation and elevated temperature. Endospores can retain viability for millennia, and viable endospores have been found in geological deposits where they must have been dormant for thousands of years.

Under favorable conditions, such as when water and nutrients are available and temperature is permissive of growth, the endospore can germinate and give rise to an active vegetative cell of the bacterium. During germination the spore swells, breaks out of the spore coat, and elongates. One of the striking features of spore germination is the speed with which metabolism shifts from a state of dormancy to the high activity levels that characterize a germinating spore. This shift in metabolic activity can occur within minutes. The endospore is metabolically self-sufficient. During germination, ATP generation and protein synthesis can take place for at least 15 minutes, using the energy and substrates—principally phosphoglycerate—contained within the spore. After spore germination, the organism renews normal vegetative growth.

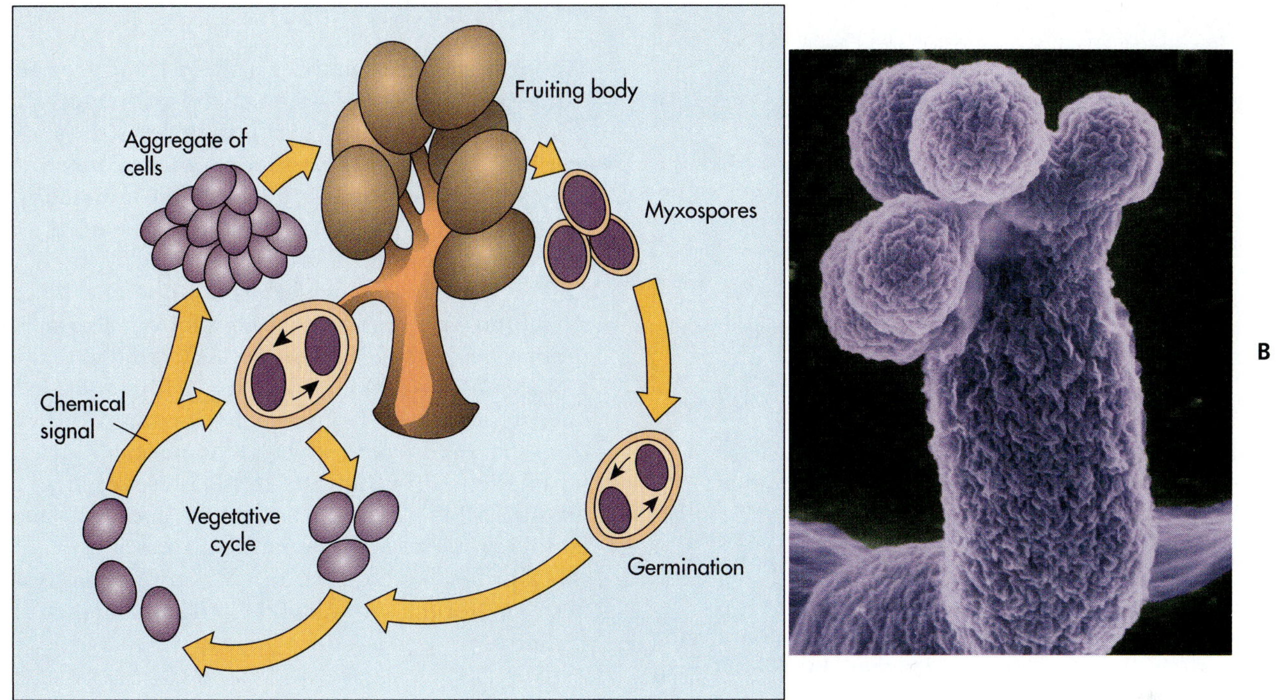

FIG. 9-11 **A,** Myxobacteria exhibit a life cycle during which a fruiting body is formed. **B,** Colorized micrograph of the fruiting body of the myxobacterium *Stigmatella aurantiaca.*

Myxobacteria

Several bacteria have developed complex life cycles to cope with alternating conditions of sufficient nutritional resources and starvation. Myxobacteria commonly grow on rotting plant materials or animal wastes. These are gliding Gram-negative bacteria that can consume bacterial cells, as well as obtain nutrients from dead plants or animals. During growth on the nutrient-rich animal or plant material, vegetative cells divide by binary fission. The cells glide over the surface of the rotting material, growing and consuming nutrients.

At a point prior to total consumption of a nutrient source, which would lead to starvation, binary fission ceases and up to a million cells fuse to form a fruiting body (FIG. 9-11). The formation of the fruiting body is initiated by a chemical signal from a myxobacterial cell. The fruiting body rises up from the surface and myxospores form within it. Myxospores are cells surrounded by a thick layer of polysaccharide that makes them resistant to desiccation. Myxospores are released from the fruiting body and are disseminated into the surrounding environment. They can survive for prolonged periods. When a myxospore reaches a nutrient-rich environment that is favorable for growth, the myxospores germinate and produce vegetative cells. These vegetative cells reproduce and the process is repeated. This life cycle strategy permits survival and movement between discrete and widely dispersed sources of nutrients.

9.3 EFFECTS OF TEMPERATURE ON BACTERIAL GROWTH RATES

Temperature is one of the most important factors that influences growth of cells. Cells grow within a well-defined **temperature growth range** (FIG. 9-12, p. 338). This growth range is defined by a minimum temperature below which cells are metabolically inactive and a maximum temperature above which cells do not grow. Within this range of extremes is an optimal growth temperature at which cells exhibit their highest rates of growth and reproduction.

Enzymatic Response to Temperature

Temperature influences the rate of chemical reactions and the three-dimensional configuration of proteins, thereby affecting the rates of enzymatic activities. As long as the enzyme is not denatured, that is, as long as its three-dimensional structure is not disrupted, a rise of 10° C generally results in the approximate doubling of the rate of its reaction. The $\mathbf{Q_{10}}$ of a reac-

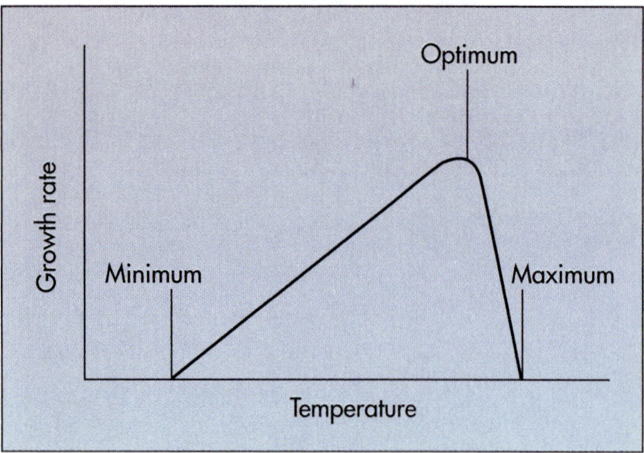

FIG. 9-12 Bacteria grow over a range of temperatures; they do not reproduce below the minimum growth temperature nor above the maximum growth temperature. Within the temperature growth range there is an optimum growth temperature at which bacterial reproduction is fastest.

tion describes the change in reaction rate that occurs when the temperature is increased by 10° C (FIG. 9-13). Enzymatic reactions typically exhibit Q_{10} values of 2 to 3.

Enzymes have optimal temperatures, that is, at some temperature each enzyme exhibits maximal activity. Optimal temperatures vary among enzymes, and even the same enzyme from different organisms can have different optimal temperatures. At some temperature above optimal, denaturation occurs. Enzymatic activities decline above the specific temperature that is characteristic of the heat stability of the particular enzyme. Because of protein denaturation at elevated temperatures and the resultant change in membrane fluidity, there is an upper temperature limit for bacterial growth. At temperatures above that limit, bacteria do not survive because they cannot carry out their life-supporting metabolic activities.

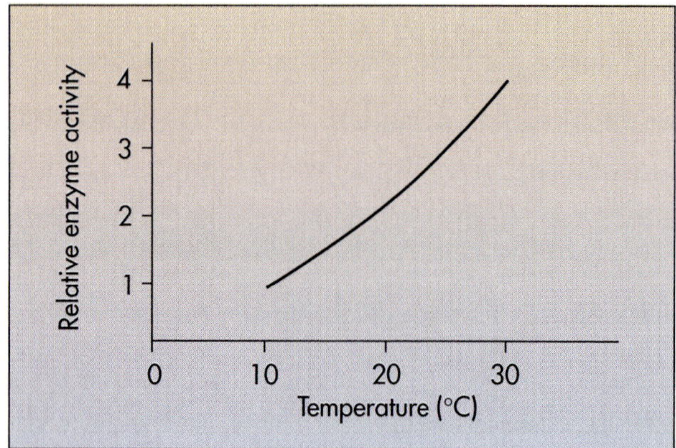

FIG. 9-13 Enzymes exhibit a Q_{10} so that within a suitable temperature range the rate of enzyme activity doubles for every 10° C rise in temperature.

Heat Shock Response

The **heat shock response** is a rapid change in gene expression that occurs when there is a temperature shift to an elevated temperature. Between 10 and 30 new proteins, called **heat shock proteins,** are synthesized at the higher temperature that are not otherwise expressed. In *E. coli,* 24 heat shock proteins are induced abruptly after a change from 30° C to 42° C. Most of these heat shock proteins are under the control of the *rpoH* gene, which codes for σ^{32}, a sigma factor that causes the RNA polymerase to bind to the promoters of heat shock genes. The −10 consensus sequence of heat shock promoters is entirely different from that used by σ^{70}, which is the normal sigma factor of *E. coli.* σ^{32} is induced by the presence of an additional σ^{24}. The production of σ^{32} increases about tenfold when the temperature increases. The heat shock proteins, which perform diverse functions, are necessary for the survival of the cell at the higher temperature.

Growth Range and Optimal Growth Temperatures

Within the growth range for a particular microorganism there is an **optimal growth temperature** at which the highest rate of reproduction occurs. The optimal growth temperature is defined by the maximal growth rate, not the maximal cell yield. Sometimes greater cell or product yields are achieved at lower or higher temperatures. Because the generation time is the reciprocal of the instantaneous growth rate, the shortest generation time occurs at the optimal temperature.

Bacteria that grow best at low temperatures (<20° C) are called **psychrophiles,** those that reproduce fastest at moderate temperatures (20° to 40° C) are called **mesophiles,** and those with fastest growth rates at high temperatures (>40° C) are called **thermophiles** (FIG. 9-14). As a rule, the maximal growth rates of thermophiles are greater than those of mesophiles, which in turn are greater than those of psychrophiles. The differences in optimal growth temperatures and temperature growth ranges among bacteria result in a spatial separation of these different classes of organisms in nature. A bacterium can proliferate only when the environmental temperatures are within the temperature growth range of that organism. The ability of a bacterium to compete for survival in a given system is increased when temperatures are near its optimal growth temperature.

Some bacteria, known as **stenothermal bacteria,** grow only at temperatures near their optimal growth temperature, whereas **eurythermal bacteria** grow over a wider range of temperatures. Laboratory incubators, which are simply controlled-temperature chambers,

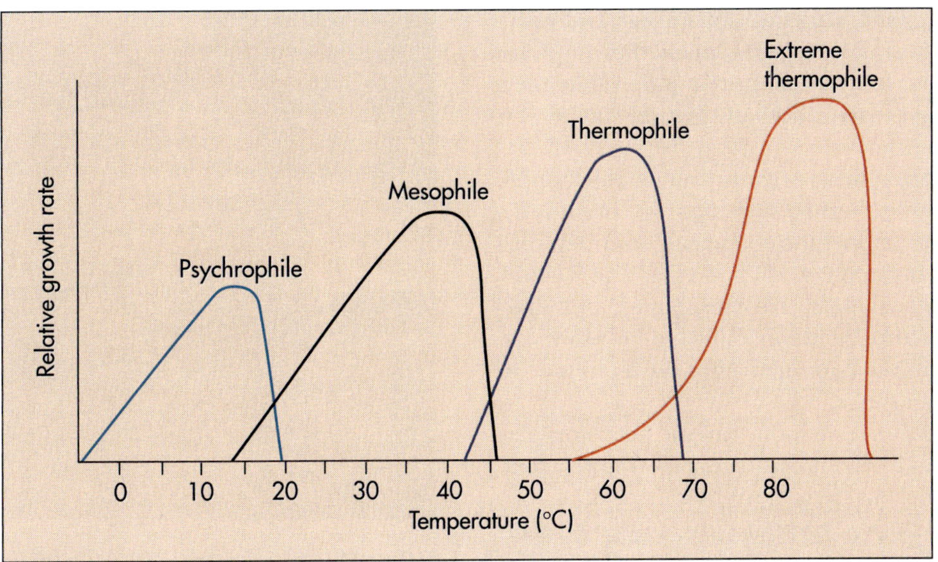

FIG. 9-14 Microorganisms are classified as psychrophiles, mesophiles, thermophiles, and extreme thermophiles based on their optimal growth temperatures.

are normally used to establish conditions that permit the growth of a bacterial culture at temperatures favoring optimal growth rates.

Psychrophiles

Psychrophiles have optimal growth temperatures below 20° C. Some psychrophilic bacteria can grow below 0° C, as long as liquid water is available. Psychrophilic bacteria are commonly found in Arctic and Antarctic environments, in the world's oceans, and occasionally in household refrigerators (5° C), where they are important agents of food spoilage.

Psychrophilic bacteria have several physiological characteristics that allow them to function at low temperatures. Their enzymes and ribosomes are active at low temperatures and many psychrophiles have enzymes that are inactivated at even moderate temperatures, of about 25° C. Membrane function is also sensitive to cold; membrane lipids containing saturated fatty acids tend to form a more crystalline array at lower temperatures. This results in a more rigid membrane that has a decreased ability to transport material into the cell. Psychrophiles maintain membrane fluidity by incorporating more lipids with unsaturated or short chain fatty acids into their membranes. These membranes stay in a semifluid state in the cold. Many psychrophiles cannot tolerate higher temperatures because their cell membranes become leaky under these conditions.

It is not known whether there is an absolute low-temperature limit to the metabolic activity of psychrophiles. The limit may simply be the freezing temperature of the cell and its environment—liquid water is required for metabolic function. In an Antarctic pond kept from freezing by its high $CaCl_2$ content, active metabolism of microorganisms has been observed to about -10° C.

Mesophiles

Mesophiles have optimal growth temperatures between 20° C and 40° C. Most of the bacteria grown in introductory microbiology laboratory courses are mesophilic. Many mesophiles have an optimal temperature of about 37° C, which corresponds to human body temperature. All of the normal resident bacteria of the human body, such as *E. coli,* are mesophiles. Similarly, most human pathogens are mesophiles and thus are able to grow rapidly and establish an infection within the human body. Although some bacteria are restricted to growth near the optimal growth temperature, others can grow over a range of temperatures. Bacteria can generally actively reproduce over a wider range of temperatures below the optimal growth temperature than above it. For example, psychrotrophic bacteria are eurythermal mesophiles; their optimal growth temperature is between 20° and 50° C (making them mesophiles), but they are capable of growth at low temperatures, such as in a refrigerator.

Thermophiles

Thermophiles have optimal growth temperatures above 40° C. Thermophiles such as *Bacillus stearothermophilus* grow at relatively high temperatures (55° to 70° C). The upper growth temperature for most thermophilic bacteria, though, is about 99° C. Many thermophilic bacteria have optimal growth temperatures of about 55° to 60° C. **Extreme thermophiles** have optimal temperatures above 80° C. Thermophiles are found in such exotic places as hot springs and effluents from laundromats. However, many thermophiles can survive very low temperatures and viable thermophilic bacteria are routinely found in frozen Antarctic soils.

The classification of an organism as a psychrophile, mesophile, or thermophile refers to the organism's optimal growth temperature and the temperature range at which it can grow. Many *Bacillus* and *Clostridium* species, for example, are mesophiles, not thermophiles, even though their ability to produce endospores permits them to survive in a dormant state at very high temperatures.

The archaebacteria include extreme thermophiles that grow only at high temperatures. The highest temperature at which bacterial growth can occur is not known. **Cauldoactive bacteria** are extreme thermophiles that often fail to grow at temperatures below 50° C and are able to grow at temperatures above 100° C. The prevailing theory is that the critical determining factor is the availability of liquid water rather than the actual temperature, and that as long as liquid water exists, temperatures up to some quite elevated limit need not preclude the existence of life. Archaebacteria isolated from hot areas such as those surrounding thermal vents in the deep oceans can grow under very high pressure at 110° C.

Obligate thermophiles are restricted to growth at high temperatures. These thermophilic bacteria have adaptive features that allow them to carry out active metabolism at temperatures over 60° C. Many thermophilic bacteria produce enzymes that are not readily denatured at high temperatures. Sometimes unusual amino acid sequences occur within the proteins of thermophiles, stabilizing these proteins at elevated temperatures. The membranes of thermophilic bacteria possess a major proportion of high molecular weight and branched fatty acids that permit them to maintain their semipermeable properties at high temperatures. Thermophiles have relatively high proportions of guanine and cytosine in their DNA that raise the melting point and add stability to the DNA molecules of these organisms. Their DNA polymerases are thermally stable and are used in the polymerase chain reaction in recombinant DNA technology.

Obligate thermophiles occur in high-temperature habitats, such as in areas of volcanic activity. Steam vents in such areas may reach a temperature of 500° C. Hot springs, which occur throughout the world, including Yellowstone National Park in the United States, have temperatures near 100° C. Bacteria living in hot springs obviously must be adapted to function at such high temperatures (FIG. 9-15). The growth of bacteria in hot springs is often limited by low concentrations of organic matter, oxygen, and, depending on the particular hot spring, acid or alkaline pH values. Despite these extreme conditions, several bacteria possess the adaptive features necessary to live in such habitats. For example, as water overflows the hot spring, it flows down channels, establishing a temperature gradient, with a clear zonation of bacteria occupying habitats of differing maximal temperatures along this temperature gradient; bacteria are the most tolerant of elevated temperatures. At temperatures above 75° C, only a few bacterial species, including members of the genera *Thermus* and *Sulfolobus,* appear to grow. *Bacillus stearothermophilus* is often the dominant bacterial species in hot springs in temperature zones of 55° to 70° C, but many other bacteria, including cyanobacteria and algae, also occur in such

FIG. 9-15 Bacteria grow within the streaming effluents of hot springs in Yellowstone National Park. Many of the bacteria are brightly pigmented and color the water.

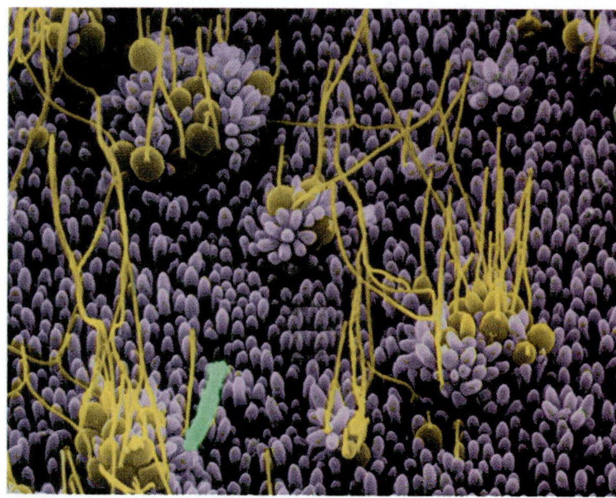

FIG. 9-16 Colorized micrograph of deep sea thermal vent bacterial community; stalks of *Beggiatoa (yellow)* are abundant.

hot spring habitats. Cyanobacteria occur in layers of growth within specific zones of thermal ponds. The cyanobacteria grow in higher temperature zones than algae, which are restricted to growth below 55° C. Prokaryotes are often more tolerant of extreme environments than eukaryotes.

Thermal vent communities are located at depths of 800 to 1,000 m, where spreading of the sea floor allows seawater to percolate deeply into the crust and to react with hot core materials. These vent regions receive no sunlight and minimal organic nutrient input from the low-productivity surface water. Nevertheless, bacterial growths cover all available surfaces on and near the vents, and high densities of unique clams, mussels, vestimentiferan worms, and other invertebrates cluster in the vicinity (FIG. 9-16). The entire vent community is supported energetically by the chemoautotrophic oxidation of reduced sulfur, primarily by *Beggiatoa, Thiomicrospira,* and additional sulfide or sulfur oxidizers of great morphological diversity.

9.4 EFFECTS OF OXYGEN CONCENTRATION—REDUCTION POTENTIAL

The presence or absence of oxygen in the environment is important in the growth of microorganisms. In some cases, the type of metabolism used by a particular bacterium may differ according to the concentration of oxygen. Oxygen has limited solubility in water. Therefore, in still aqueous environments, availability of oxygen may be a limiting factor in the growth of microorganisms. Many cells may utilize O_2 for their metabolism, and since O_2 cannot easily diffuse back into the solution, the environment becomes oxygen-depleted.

OXYGEN RELATIONSHIPS OF MICROORGANISMS

Microorganisms can be grouped into categories based on their requirement or intolerance of O_2. **Aerobes** grow in the presence of air that contains molecular oxygen. Obligate aerobes require O_2 for growth and carry out aerobic respiration.

Other microorganisms, called **microaerophiles,** grow only at reduced concentrations of molecular oxygen. Such organisms require O_2 for growth but only at concentrations (∽5%) reduced from that of atmospheric levels (20%). Generally, microaerophilic organisms will not grow in air. Some microaerophiles grow at elevated CO_2 concentrations (5% to 10%) and are called **capnophiles.**

Facultative anaerobes can grow in the presence or absence of air. Many facultative anaerobes, such as *E. coli,* switch between aerobic respiration and fermentation depending on the availability of molecular oxygen; they usually carry out fermentative metabolism in the absence of O_2 and aerobic respiration in the presence of O_2. This group of facultative anaerobes also includes strictly fermentative bacteria, such as streptococci, that are insensitive to oxygen *(oxyduric)* and hence can grow in the presence of O_2.

Other bacteria are **anaerobes** and grow only in the absence of air. **Obligate anaerobes** carry out fermentative metabolism. Only a few genera of bacteria (for example, methanogenic archaebacteria and sulfate-reducing eubacteria) and protozoa are obligate anaerobes. **Strict anaerobes** are sensitive to oxygen and even a brief exposure to O_2 will kill such organisms. *Clostridium* species can be classified as obligate, strict anaerobes.

OXYGEN TOXICITY AND ENZYMATIC DETOXIFICATION

The different relationships between microorganisms and O_2 are due to several factors, including the formation of toxic O_2 products and the presence or absence of enzymes in the cell that can eliminate these toxic products. Oxygen can exist in several electronic states (Table 9-4). In atmospheric O_2 (triplet oxygen) a pair of electrons in the outer orbitals spin in parallel directions. O_2 is a highly electronegative molecule and can readily accept additional energy or electrons. Reduced flavoproteins (and other electron donors) or radiation may lead to the reduction of O_2. This may cause the outer orbital electrons to spin in antiparallel directions, forming singlet oxygen (O_2^*).

TABLE 9-4 Electronic States of Oxygen

FORM	FORMULA	SIMPLIFIED ELECTRONIC STRUCTURE	SPIN OF OUTER ELECTRONS
Triplet oxygen (normal atmospheric form)	$^3O_2$	$\dot{O}—\dot{O}$	(↑) (↑)
Singlet oxygen	$^1O_2$	$\dot{O}—\dot{O}$	(↓↑) ( ) or (↑) (↓)
Superoxide free radical	O_2^-	$\ddot{O}—\dot{O}$	(↓↑) (↑)
Peroxide	O_2^{2-}	$\ddot{O}—\ddot{O}$	(↓↑) (↓↑)

Singlet oxygen has a higher energy than triplet oxygen and is more toxic to microorganisms. In addition, the reduction of O_2 can lead to the formation of superoxide radicals (O_2^-) and peroxides (O_2^{2-}). Hydroxyl free radicals, OH•, which are very toxic, are formed by the reduction of hydrogen peroxide. These reactions can be represented as:

$$O_2 + e^- \rightarrow O_2^-$$

$$O_2^- + e^- + 2H^+ \rightarrow H_2O_2$$

$$H_2O_2 + e^- + H^+ \rightarrow H_2O + OH\cdot$$

Single oxygen, hydroxyl free radicals, peroxides, and superoxides are toxic because they are strong oxidizing agents; they can oxidize sulfhydryl groups and inactivate the active sites of enzymes, denature structural proteins, and cause damage to DNA.

Many cells synthesize enzymes that help them break down these toxic derivatives of O_2. Catalase and peroxidase catalyze the degradation of peroxides in the following reactions:

$$2H_2O_2 \xrightarrow[\text{catalase}]{} 2H_2O + O_2$$

$$H_2O_2 + NADH + H^+ \xrightarrow[\text{peroxidase}]{} 2H_2O + NAD^+$$

Superoxides are degraded by the action of superoxide dismutase:

$$2O_2^- + 2H^+ \xrightarrow[\text{superoxide dismutase}]{} H_2O_2 + O_2$$

Catalase and superoxide dismutase are usually found in aerobic and facultatively anaerobic microorganisms and these enzymes protect the cells from damage in the presence of O_2. Microaerophiles may or may not have catalase but usually have superoxide dismutase. In contrast, strict anaerobes generally do not synthesize these enzymes or only produce them at low levels. Since they cannot detoxify toxic forms of oxygen, anaerobes cannot grow in the presence of O_2.

OXIDATION-REDUCTION (REDOX) POTENTIAL

The oxygen concentration also has a major affect on the reduction potential that influences whether oxidation or reduction reactions are likely to occur. A positive reduction potential (E_h) value favors oxidation, whereas a negative E_h indicates a reducing environment (FIG. 9-17). In a complex system, such as soil, the reduction potential is influenced by the strongest oxidant or reductant in that system, as well as by the concentration of that compound. The reduction potential is greatly influenced by the presence or absence of molecular oxygen. Environments in equilibrium with atmospheric oxygen have an E_h of around +800 mV; environments with reduced oxygen tensions have reduction potentials well below +800 mV. Some essential nutrient elements, such as iron and manganese, are soluble at low reduction potentials and precipitate in oxidizing environments.

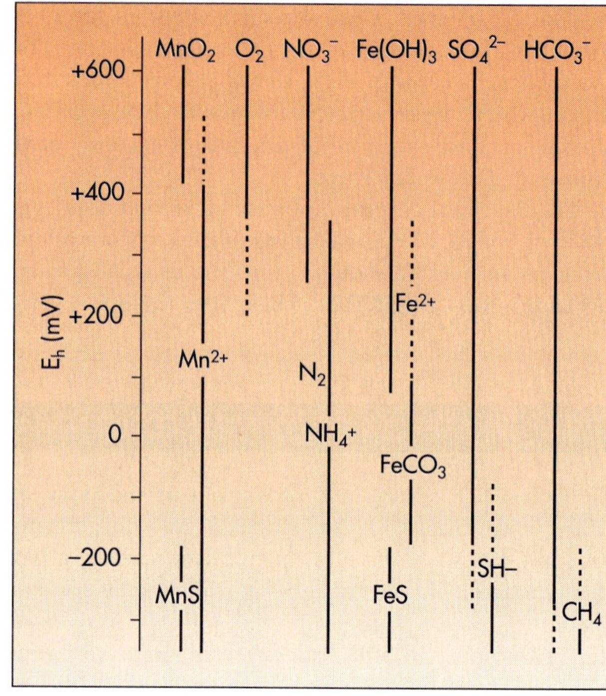

FIG. 9-17 Ranges of E_h values for various substances.

Lower reduction potentials may be caused by the extensive growth of heterotrophic bacteria that scavenge all available oxygen. Such is often the case in highly polluted ecosystems, where bacteria utilize the available oxygen for decomposition processes. The reduction potential of sediments rich in organic matter can be as low as −450 mV. At these low E_h values, obligate anaerobes can reduce sulfate to H_2S and archaebacterial methanogens can reduce CO_2 to CH_4 (FIG. 9-18).

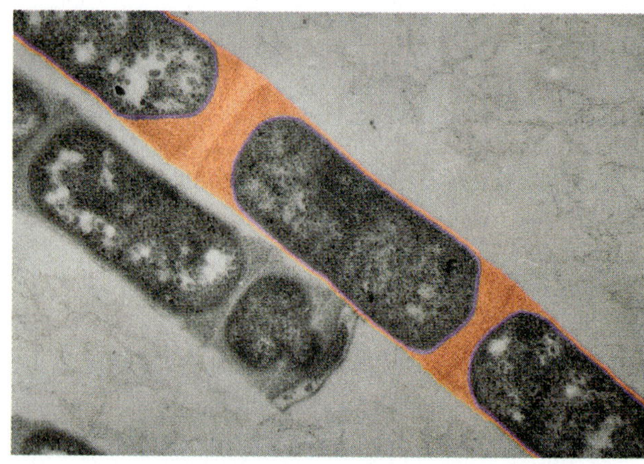

FIG. 9-18 Colorized micrograph of the methanogen *Methanothrix concilii*. There is a spacer *(orange)* between cells. This archaebacterium, like other methanogens, is strictly anaerobic. (25,500×).

9.5 EFFECTS OF WATER ACTIVITY

All bacteria require water for growth and reproduction. Water is an essential solvent and is needed for all biochemical reactions in living systems, and the availability of water has a marked influence on bacterial growth rates. Pure distilled water has a **water activity (A_w)** of 1.0. Water activity is an index of the amount of water that is free to react. It is equivalent to the atmospheric measure of water availability known as *relative humidity.* Adsorption and solution factors, however, can reduce the availability of water and thus lower the water activity. Water, for example, may be bound by a solute and hence unavailable to the bacteria. A saturated solution of NaCl has an A_w of 0.8. Seawater, though, which has a salt concentration of only about 3%, has an A_w of 0.98.

In the atmosphere, the availability of water is expressed as **relative humidity (RH)**. RH = 100 A_w and thus a relative humidity of 90% corresponds to an A_w of 0.90. The relatively low availability of water in the atmosphere accounts for the inability of bacteria to grow in the air. Bacteria likewise are unable to grow on dry surfaces except when the relative humidity is high. Bacterial growth on surfaces is a problem in tropical zones, where the available water in the atmosphere can support bacterial growth, permitting bacteria to grow on clothing, tents, and numerous other surfaces where this normally does not occur in temperate regions.

Water activity is an index of the water that is actually available for utilization by bacteria. Most bacteria require an A_w above 0.9 for active metabolism (Table 9-5). Some bacteria, however, known as **xerotolerant** organisms, can grow at much lower water activities. Some yeasts grow on concentrated sugar solutions with an A_w of 0.60. As a rule, fungi can grow at lower water activities than bacteria. Fungi, therefore, grow on many surfaces where the available water will not support bacterial growth. This is why fungal, not bacterial, growth is commonly observed on bread.

TABLE 9-5 Approximate Limiting Water Activities for Microbial Growth

WATER ACTIVITY (A_W)	BACTERIA	FUNGI	ALGAE
1.00	*Caulobacter*		
	Spirillum		
0.90	*Lactobacillus*	*Fusarium*	
	Bacillus	*Mucor*	
0.85	*Staphylococcus*	*Debaromyces*	
0.80		*Penicillium*	
0.75	*Halobacterium*	*Aspergillus*	*Dunaliella*
	Halococcus	*Chryosporum*	
0.60		*Saccharomyces rouxii*	
		Xeromyces bisporus	

The ability to withstand drying can have important consequences for disease transmission. *Mycobacterium tuberculosis* is a classic example of an organism capable of withstanding severe desiccation and still remain infective. This characteristic obviously has important public health implications. Whereas some bacteria are

BOX 9-1

MICROBIAL GROWTH IN EXTRATERRESTRIAL HABITATS

The planets in our solar system, other than Earth, are hostile habitats for living organisms, lacking water and organic carbon and having toxic concentrations of various gases in their atmospheres to make life as we know it impossible. The planet Mars, however, contains some water; therefore, experimental life detection systems were sent there as part of the U. S. National Aeronautics and Space Administration's Viking Mission in the early 1970s. Martian bacteria would have to have adaptations that permit their existence under Mar's harsh conditions; a Martian microorganism would have to be hardy.

The life detection systems of the Viking Mars lander were designed to detect bacterial life. More specifically, they could detect the increased turbidity associated with bacteria growing in solution, as well as the exchange of gases between bacteria and the overlying atmosphere, including the production of volatile products from the degradation of organic matter and the fixation of carbon dioxide in organic compounds. Soils from the dry Antarctic valleys were used to test these life detection systems because conditions in these terrestrial Earth habitats are most similar to those of the dry, cold soils of Mars. The results of the Viking mission were initially confusing. They showed apparently positive test results indicating the presence of living bacteria but the results appear to have been due to strictly chemical reactions. The rapid release of carbon dioxide was characteristic of a chemical reaction; it was too fast and had no lag period, which is associated with biological growth and metabolism. The Viking exploration project scientists concluded that there are no living organisms in the Martian soils examined.

relatively resistant to drying, others are unable to survive desiccating conditions for even a short period of time. For example, *Treponema pallidum,* the bacterium that causes syphilis, is extremely sensitive to drying and dies almost instantly in the air or on a dry surface. Many bacteria produce specialized spores that can withstand the desiccating conditions of the atmosphere. Such spores generally have thick walls that retain moisture within the cell. Many fungal spores can be transmitted over long distances through the atmosphere (some spores even travel from one continent to another). The transmission of fungal spores through the air is a serious problem in agriculture because it permits the spread of fungal diseases of plants from one field to another.

Bacteria living in dry desert soils must be able to tolerate long periods of desiccation. In the dry valleys of Antarctica, bacteria must also tolerate very low temperatures and, during part of the year, high irradiation levels. In such environments, many bacteria develop adaptations that allow them to survive in a dormant state during unfavorable conditions and to grow actively during the brief periods when conditions are favorable, such as after a rainstorm. Many of the bacteria and fungi living in desert soils form spores that allow them to exist, if necessary, for decades between growth periods. When there is adequate moisture, the spores germinate and for a brief period the organisms can actively grow and reproduce. The lichen symbiosis, a mutually dependent association between fungi and photosynthetic bacteria or algae, is an adaptive association between microorganisms that permits growth under conditions of severe desiccation (FIG. 9-19). Lichens are important in the dry habitats of Antarctica, where they can grow slowly during the relatively warm summer months. The slow growth rates and the ability to retain water permit lichens to exist in such extremely dry habitats.

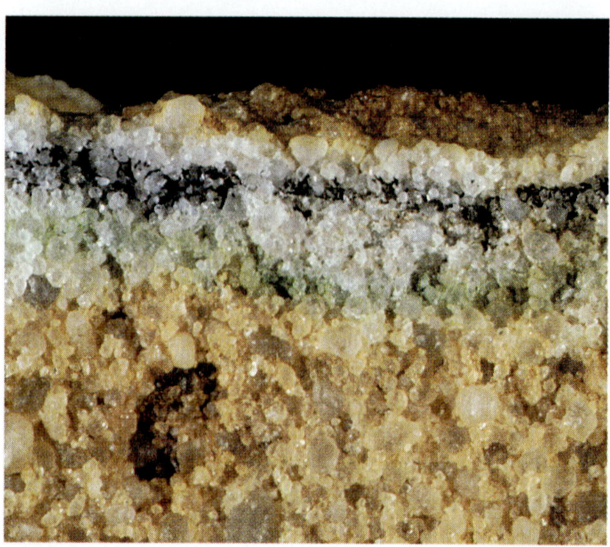

FIG. 9-19 A lichen growing within a rock in an Antarctic dry valley. The black, white, and green zones represent differentiated parts of the lichen thallus.

9.6 EFFECTS OF PRESSURE

The growth of all cells is affected by the external and internal pressures they experience. These forces include osmotic pressure and hydrostatic pressure. Hydrostatic pressure results from the weight of a column of water on cells such as those found in the deepest parts of the ocean. Osmotic pressure results from water diffusing across the cell membrane in response to solute concentrations. Solute concentration affects the availability of water and also the osmotic pressure. This often is associated with the salt concentration (salinity) surrounding the cell.

Osmotic Pressure and Salinity

The cell-wall structures of bacteria make them relatively resistant to changes in osmotic pressure, but extreme osmotic pressures can result in the death of bacteria. In hypertonic solutions, bacteria may shrink and become desiccated, and in hypotonic solutions the cell may burst. Organisms that can grow in solutions with high solute concentrations are called **osmotolerant**. These organisms can withstand high osmotic pressures and also grow at low water activities. Some microorganisms are **osmophiles,** requiring a high solute concentration for growth. For example, the fungus *Xeromyces* is an osmophile, with an optimum A_w of approximately 0.9. Additionally, solutions with high sugar concentrations are used in laboratory procedures to protect protoplasts (cells with their cell walls completely removed) and spheroplasts (cells with their cell walls partially removed) against rupture due to osmotic pressure.

Salinity has an important effect on osmotic pressure. Some bacteria also have specific responses to concentrations of salt. Bacteria, known as **halophiles,** require NaCl for growth (FIG. 9-20). Moderate halophiles, which include many marine bacteria, grow best at salt concentrations of about 3%. The outer membranes of marine bacteria require at least 1.5% NaCl to maintain their integrity. Extreme halophiles exhibit maximal growth rates in saturated brine solutions. These organisms grow well at salt concentra-

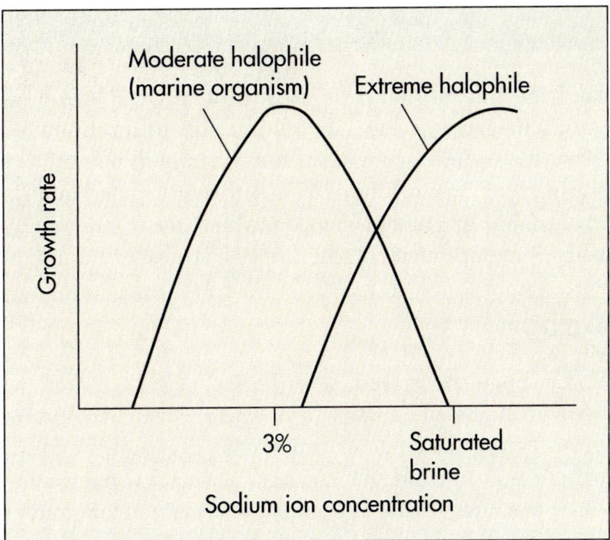

FIG. 9-20 Halophiles require sodium chloride for growth. Marine bacteria typically grow best near 3% NaCl. Some extreme halophiles grow best near 15% NaCl.

FIG. 9-21 Halophiles growing within salt lakes often turn the water pink; this sometimes occurs in Great Salt Lake, Utah.

tions of greater than 15% and can grow in places like salt lakes and pickle barrels (FIG. 9-21). High salt concentrations normally disrupt membrane transport systems and denature proteins, and extreme halophiles must possess physiological mechanisms for tolerating high salt concentrations. For example, the extreme halophilic bacterium, *Halobacterium,* possesses an unusual plasma membrane and many unusual enzymes that require a high salt concentration for activity.

Most bacteria, however, do not possess these physiological adaptations and are not tolerant of high salt concentrations. The degree of sensitivity to salt varies among different bacterial species. Many bacteria will not grow at a salt concentration of 3%. Some strains of *Staphylococcus,* however, are salt tolerant and grow at salt concentrations greater than 10%. This physiological adaptation in *Staphylococcus* is important because some members of this genus grow on skin surfaces where salt concentrations can be relatively high.

Relatively few organisms can grow in highly saline waters, such as those of salt lakes, and often the biota of salt lakes is restricted to a few halophiles (salt-requiring) and salt-tolerant bacteria. Halophilic bacteria have high internal concentrations of potassium chloride, and their enzymes must have a greater tolerance of salt than the enzymes of bacteria that are not salt tolerant. In many cases, high concentrations of salt are required by halophiles to maintain their enzymatic activities. Many halophiles have unusual membranes, such as the purple bilayer membranes of *Halobacterium.* The cell wall of *Halobacterium* lacks peptidoglycan and appears to be stabilized by sodium ions. The ribosomes of *Halobacterium* require high concentrations of potassium for stability. These types of adaptive features permit halophiles to live in the saturated brine environments of salt lakes.

HYDROSTATIC PRESSURE

Hydrostatic pressure, the pressure exerted by a water column as a result of the weight of the column, can influence bacterial growth rates. Each 10 m of water depth is equivalent to approximately 1 atm. Most bacteria are relatively tolerant of the hydrostatic pressures in most natural systems but cannot withstand extremely high hydrostatic pressures. Hydrostatic pressures of more than 200 atm generally inactivate enzymes and disrupt membrane transport processes. However, some bacteria—referred to as **barotolerant**—can grow at high hydrostatic pressures, and there even appear to be some bacteria—referred to as **barophiles**—that grow best at such pressures.

High hydrostatic pressures are found in the deep regions of the oceans. It is here that barophilic and barotolerant bacteria occur. Very low numbers of bacteria and low rates of metabolism characterize most of these deep ocean regions. In most cases the deep oceans are also cold, so that the low rates of metabolism may reflect the combined effects of low temperature and high hydrostatic pressure. When the deep sea submersible *Alvin* sank, the lunches of the crew that went to the bottom with the vessel remained undecomposed for months. In contrast the hot thermal vent regions, where the high hydrostatic pressures maintain water in the liquid state at temperatures well above 100° C, are highly biologically active.

9.7 EFFECTS OF ACIDITY AND pH

The pH of a solution describes the hydrogen ion concentration H^+ (FIG. 9-22). The pH is equal to $-\log H^+$ or $1/\log H^+$. A neutral solution has a pH of 7.0, acidic solutions have pH values below 7, and alkaline or basic solutions have pH values greater than 7. Bacterial growth rates are greatly influenced by pH values and are based largely on the nature of proteins. Charge interactions within the amino acids of a polypeptide chain strongly influence the secondary structure and folding of a protein. This change in shape of the active site of enzymes effects their function; enzymes are normally inactive at very high and very low pH values. Also, bacteria are less tolerant of higher temperatures at low pH values than they are at neutral pH values.

In culture media and industrial fermentors, pH values are controlled to achieve optimal growth rates. This is normally accomplished by buffering the solution.

Buffers are used to maintain the pH value within a range, permitting continued bacterial growth. Buffers are salts of weak acids or bases that keep the hydrogen ion concentration constant by maintaining an equilibrium with the hydrogen ions of the solution. Buffers thus dampen changes in pH. At neutral pH values, a phosphate buffer may be used; at alkaline pH values, borate buffers are often employed. Citrate buffers are frequently used for maintaining acidic conditions.

Bacteria vary in their pH tolerance ranges (Table 9-6). Most bacteria grow well over a range of 6 to 9 pH. Fungi generally exhibit a wider pH range, growing within a range of 5 to 9 pH. Most bacteria can be considered **neutralophiles** because they tend to thrive under neutral pH conditions. Similarly, some fungi grow well at lower pH values, as low as 0. Some other eukaryotic microorganisms, including protozoa and algae, can grow at low pH values; the lower limit for growth of some protozoa is approximately 2, and, for some algae, approximately 1. Although most bacteria are unable to grow at low pH values, there are exceptions. Certain bacteria tolerate pH values as low as 0.8.

TABLE 9-6 Table of pH Tolerances of Various Bacteria

ORGANISM	MINIMUM pH	OPTIMUM pH	MAXIMUM pH
Thiobacillus thiooxidans	1.0	2.0-2.8	4.0-6.0
Lactobacillus acidophilus	4.0-4.6	5.8-6.6	6.8
Escherichia coli	4.4	6.0-7.0	9.0
Proteus vulgaris	4.4	6.0-7.0	8.4
Entrobacter aerogenes	4.4	6.0-7.0	9.0
Clostridium sporogenes	5.0-5.8	6.0-7.6	8.5-9.0
Pseudomonas aeruginosa	5.6	6.6-7.0	8.0
Erwinia carotovora	5.6	7.1	9.3
Nitrobacter spp.	6.6	6.6-8.6	10.0
Nitrosomonas spp.	7.0-7.6	8.0-8.8	9.4

ACIDOPHILES

Some bacteria, called **acidophiles,** are restricted to growth at low pH values. The cytoplasmic membrane of an acidophilic bacterium breaks down and cannot function at neutral pH values. *Thiobacillus* species, for example, are acidophilic and grow only at pH values

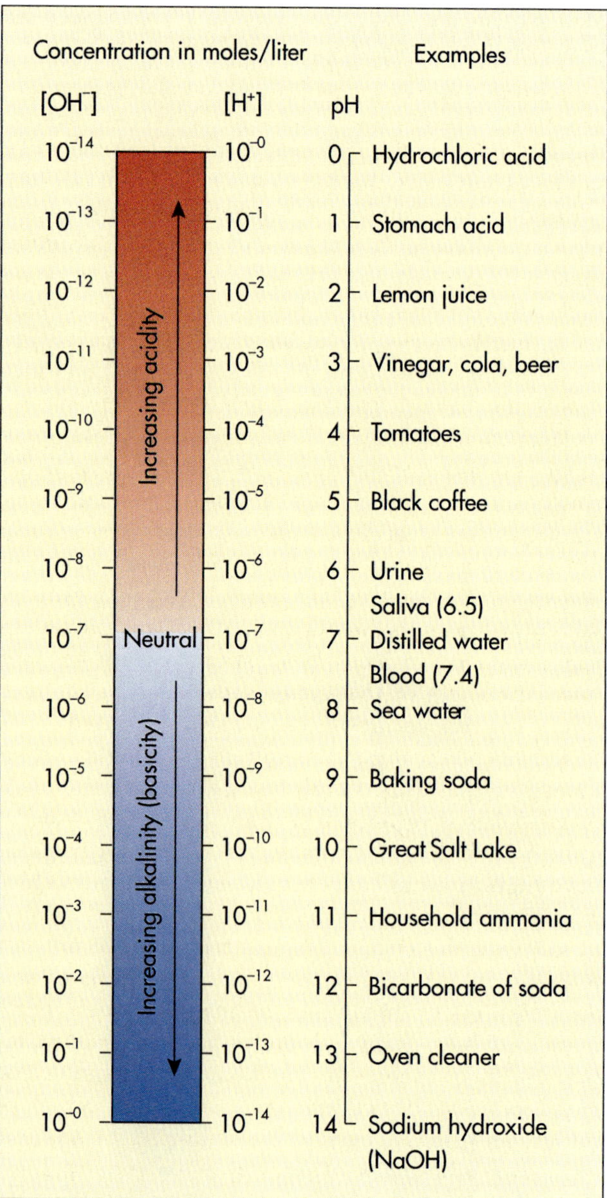

FIG. 9-22 pH scale showing pH values of some common substances.

near 2. *Sulfolobus* and *Thiobacillus* species possess physiological adaptations that permit enzymatic and membrane transport activities.

An important factor that regulates bacterial growth under any condition is the protonmotive force. This essential energy source is derived from the separation of protons (H^+) across the cytoplasmic membrane. The protonmotive force is actually composed of two interchangeable components: a ΔpH due to the H^+ ion gradient and a $\Delta\Psi$ (membrane potential) due to the charge separation across the membrane. Bacteria can use either of these components to drive protons back across the membrane and perform work (ATP synthesis, flagellar rotation, and active transport).

All cells try to maintain their internal pH near neutrality. As a result of living in a low pH environment, acidophiles have a very large ΔpH across the membrane. Many acidophiles have a $\Delta\Psi$ which is reversed from that of neutralophiles—the outside of the membrane is negatively charged while the inside is positively charged. These two features in acidophiles (a large naturally occuring ΔpH and reversed $\Delta\Psi$) produce a protonmotive force that supports cell function.

Differences in tolerance to acidic pH values can be used in designing selective growth media. A growth medium with a pH of 5.5 is favorable for the growth of most fungi but does not permit the growth of most bacteria. This factor is used in clinical isolation procedures; it is also employed in industry, where lowering the pH of a medium designed to support the growth of a fungus, such as *Saccharomyces,* can eliminate unwanted bacterial growth.

ALKALOPHILES

A small group of bacteria prefer growth under very alkaline conditions. Environments with high sodium concentrations such as some salt lakes or soils high in sodium carbonate can have pH values in the range of 9 to 11. Bacteria that live at these pH extremes, **alkalophiles,** have developed mechanisms for keeping sodium ions outside the cell.

Alkalophiles have a distinct problem in generating a protonmotive force in an alkaline environment. They do not have the naturally occurring ΔpH as seen in acidophiles. In contrast, the ΔpH across the membrane of alkalophiles is reversed—the internal pH is about 7 to 9 while the external pH is between 9 to 11. To accommodate this feature, alkalophiles use a Na^+/H^+ antiporter or K^+/H^+ antiporter to maintain a sufficiently high $\Delta\Psi$ to drive the protonmotive force. The Na^+/H^+ antiporter in alkalophilic bacteria is largely responsible for returning protons to the cytoplasm during growth at alkaline pH.

9.8 EFFECTS OF LIGHT

Photosynthetic bacteria require light to carry out their photoautotrophic generation of ATP. These bacteria function optimally at specific light intensities. They utilize specific light wavelengths. Certain photosynthetic bacteria move through their environment in response to light, called **phototaxis.** Some of these phototactic bacteria have mechanisms that regulate flagellar rotation in response to changing intensities of light. Bacteria may also respond to specific wavelengths of light.

Visible light as well as ultraviolet light can cause structural damage to proteins and DNA. Many bacterial cells that are exposed to bright light in their environment protect themselves from harmful radiation damage by synthesizing carotenoids and other pigments. These pigments absorb light of certain wavelengths before the light can cause damage.

Many phototactic bacteria that live in aquatic environments can adjust their vertical position in the water column by synthesizing gas vesicles (FIG. 9-23). Gas vesicles are intracytoplasmic vacuoles that contain gas. The amount of gas in the vesicles determines the buoyancy of the cell. When light intensities are low, the bacteria form gas vesicles so they can float closer to the surface of the lake or pond and hence brighter light. When light intensities are high, the bacteria collapse their gas vesicles and sink to a lower level.

FIG. 9-23 Colorized micrograph of freeze fracture preparation of *Nostoc* showing cylindrical gas vacuoles (*blue*) that allow this cyanobacterium to adjust its buoyancy in response to light intensity. (34,600×).

CHAPTER REVIEW

STUDY QUESTIONS

1. What is the effect of temperature on microbial growth rates? What is the difference between optimal and maximal growth temperatures?
2. What is a mesophile? Psychrophile? Thermophile?
3. What effect does a high salt concentration have on bacteria? What is the difference between a halophile and a salt tolerant organism?
4. What mechanisms have bacteria evolved for protection against radiation exposure?
5. Discuss the adaptation and zonal separation of bacteria in a hot spring habitat.
6. Why were the Antarctic dry valleys used as models for the design of the Mars Viking lander?
7. Why are bacterial growth and reproduction considered synonymous?
8. How do we measure microbial growth? What units do we use to express it?
9. Discuss three approaches to the enumeration of bacteria. What are the advantages and disadvantages of each for determining growth rate?
10. Describe the typical bacterial growth curve. What is occurring during each of the growth phases?
11. Compare batch and continuous culture methods for growing bacteria.
12. Calculate the growth rate for a bacterium at 37° C based on the following data. At the time of inoculation the bacterial concentration is 10/ml; after 1 hour it is still 10/ml; after 2 hours it is 30/ml; after 3 hours it is 480/ml; and after 4 hours it is 7,680/ml.

SITUATIONAL PROBLEMS

1. Designing a School Science Fair Project

Science fair projects are a routine part of the elementary and high school curricula. Many times students grow bacteria on various sugar-containing substances, such as jams and jellies, to demonstrate visible microbial growth and to describe the bacteria that they observe with the aid of a microscope. Another common project is to observe the effects of various disinfectant substances, such as mouthwashes, on microbial growth. In most cases, elementary and high schools lack the necessary facilities, and their teachers the needed expertise, to perform such projects safely. Every year, students faced with the task of doing such projects turn to college students and professors for advice.

In advising such students, it is important to make sure that they understand basic microbiological methods, especially aseptic technique and how to transfer and dispose of bacteria safely. Too often the students developing such elementary projects fail to recognize that the microorganisms they are working with are living organisms; they do not realize that bacteria require specific growth conditions; and they ignore the fact that growth-supporting substances will dry out and that cultures must be repeatedly transferred to be maintained. They simply open the containers containing extensive microbial growth and hold the contents up to their faces to see and smell.

Suppose that you have been asked by a high school student to help with a project for the school science fair. This student is specifically interested in bacteria and the effects of environmental factors on the distribution of bacteria in nature. The interest stems from an article in *National Geographic* on bacteria growing in deep-sea vents at extremely high temperatures. The student would really like to study these thermal vent microbes but realizes that this is beyond the scope of available resources and therefore he would like to do something similar. What project would you suggest?

Although the project must be the student's own work, you can help with its design and can ensure that the right methods are used. Assuming that the student wants to do the project that you suggest, what are the next steps? What books would you recommend that the student consult as references? Develop a specific set of hypotheses and methods that would support the determination of their validity. Make sure that the methods are within the scope of the available resources and that the experiments can be concluded within 1 to 3 months.

2. Searching for Life on Other Planets

If life exists on other planets, bacteria most likely would be present, even if higher forms of life also exist, because of the ubiquitous role of bacteria in transforming elements into forms that can support the continued requirements of living organisms. An unmanned probe sent to Mars failed to detect living bacteria, but new analyses of the composition of the Martian surface, and of other planets and their atmospheres, has raised new questions about where to search for extraterrestrial life. Assuming that you could help direct the search for extraterrestrial microbial life, what chemical and physical properties would you look for in the surface and atmospheric composition of potential planetary exploration sites? What conditions would you expect to favor life? What conditions would you view as precluding life?

Suggested Supplementary Readings

Atlas RM and R Bartha: 1993. *Microbial Ecology: Fundamentals and Applications,* ed. 3, Benjamin/Cummings, Menlo Park, CA.

Baross JA and JW Deming: 1983. Growth of "black smoker" bacteria at temperatures of at least 250° C, *Nature* (London) 303:423-426.

Blakeman JP (ed.): 1981. *Microbial Ecology of the Phylloplane,* Academic Press, London.

Blakemore RP: 1982. Magnetotactic bacteria, *Annual Review of Microbiology* 36:217-238.

Brock T: 1978. *Thermophilic Microorganisms and Life at High Temperatures,* Springer-Verlag, New York.

Brock T (ed.): 1986. *Thermophiles: General Molecular and Applied Microbiology,* John Wiley & Sons, Inc., New York.

Brown M and P Williams: 1985. The influence of environment on envelope properties affecting survival of bacteria in infections, *Annual Review of Microbiology* 49:527-556.

Burns RG and JH Slater (eds.): 1982. *Experimental Microbial Ecology,* Blackwell Scientific Publications, Oxford, England.

Button DK: 1985. Kinetics of nutrient-limited transport and microbial growth, *Microbiological Reviews* 49:270-297.

Codd GA (ed.): 1984. *Aspects of Microbial Metabolism and Ecology,* Academic Press, London.

Edwards C: 1981. *The Microbial Cell Cycle,* American Society for Microbiology, Washington, D.C.

Fletcher M and GD Floodgate (eds.): 1985. *Bacteria in Their Natural Environments,* Academic Press, London.

Friedman EI: 1982. Endolithic microorganisms in the Antarctic cold desert, *Science* 215:1045-1053.

Gould GW and JEL Corry (eds.): 1980. *Microbial Growth and Survival in Extremes of Environment,* Academic Press, New York.

Griffin DM: 1981. Water and microbial stress, *Advances in Microbial Ecology* 5:91-136.

Herbert RA and GA Codd (eds.): 1986. *Microbes in Extreme Environments,* Academic Press, London.

Jannasch HW and MJ Mottl: 1985. Geomicrobiology of deep-sea hydrothermal vents, *Science* 216:1315-1317.

MacLeod RA: 1985. Marine microbiology far from the sea, *Annual Review of Microbiology* 39:1-20.

Mandelstam J, K McQuillen and IW Dawes: 1982. *Biochemistry of Bacterial Growth,* Blackwell Scientific Publications, Oxford, England.

Rheinheimer G: 1981. *Aquatic Microbiology,* John Wiley & Sons, Inc., New York.

Russell AD, WB Hugo, GAJ Ayliffe: 1982. *Principles and Practice of Disinfection, Preservation and Sterilization,* Blackwell Scientific Publications, Oxford, England.

Skujins J: 1984. Microbial ecology of desert soils, *Advances in Microbial Ecology* 7:49-91.

Slater JH, R Whittenbury, JWT Wimpenny: 1983. *Microbes in Their Natural Environments,* Thirty-Fourth Symposium of the Society for General Microbiology, Cambridge University Press, Cambridge, England.

CHAPTER 10

Control of Microbial Growth

Control of microbial growth is equated with preventing microbial reproduction. This is accomplished by killing microorganisms or creating conditions under which they can not grow. Exposure to high temperatures, ionizing radiation, and various chemicals are routinely employed to kill microorganisms. Low temperatures, high solute concentrations, and desiccation are employed to prevent microbial growth. Killing and limiting growth of microorganisms is especially important in preserving and maintaining the safety of foods. It is also key to modern medical practice and the use of antimicrobics to treat infectious diseases. Antimicrobial agents that exhibit toxicities to microorganisms have greatly reduced death rates from such diseases.

CHAPTER OUTLINE

10.1 STERILIZATION AND DISINFECTION

There are many situations in which the presence or growth of microorganisms is undesirable or even harmful to animal and plant populations. Therefore the ability to control microbial populations is an important concern of microbiology. For example, when you open a can of food to eat you assume that you are not being exposed to microorganisms or their toxic products that may cause illness. The canned food is treated to eliminate microorganisms or inhibit their growth. Similarly, procedures that invade body tissues as in dentistry and surgery require that foreign microorganisms are not introduced into the body and potentially result in disease in a patient.

In some circumstances, it is important to eliminate all forms of microorganisms. In the process of **sterilization** (Latin *sterilis,* meaning unfruitful), all living cells, spores, viruses, and viroids are killed, inactivated, or removed from a specific object or environment. Objects that are sterile are completely free from these microbial forms. Sterilization can be accomplished by various chemical or physical procedures. In other cases, it may be desirable to eliminate only microorganisms that can cause disease (pathogens).

The process of killing, inactivating, or removing pathogenic microorganisms from an environment is called **disinfection.** An agent that is used to carry out disinfection is called a **disinfectant.** Most disinfectants are chemicals. They are generally too harsh to be applied to body tissues and are strictly applied to inanimate objects or surfaces. Although disinfectants can remove pathogens from an environment, they may have no effect on spores, some nonpathogenic microorganisms, and viruses. Therefore disinfected objects are not sterile. Sometimes, chemicals can be used to clean inanimate objects and lower the overall number of microorganisms, a process called **sanitization.**

Many situations call for the use of chemicals that control microorganisms on body tissues. These chemicals, called **antiseptics,** are safe to apply to living tissues. Antiseptics prevent sepsis (Greek *sepsis,* meaning decay) or growth of pathogens on these tissues. Some chemicals, such as ethanol, can be used as a disinfectant (for example, to clean a laboratory bench top) or as an antiseptic to prevent infection through breaks in the skin (for example, to clean skin surfaces before giving injections).

10.2 PHYSICAL CONTROL OF MICROORGANISMS

Several physical agents can be used to control microbial populations. Some of these, such as high temperatures and ionizing radiation, kill microorganisms by damaging essential cell components. Enzymes, DNA, and cytoplasmic membranes often are disrupted by these physical agents. Other physical treatments, such as filtration, remove microorganisms without killing them. Still others, such as low temperature and removal of oxygen, prevent microbial growth. These physical treatments for the control of microorganisms are widely used, for example, in the food industry. Many foods are preserved by physical treatments. Similarly physical treatments are widely used in microbiology laboratories for the preparation of culture media and labware. They are also used in medicine and dentistry for sterilization of instruments and materials contaminated with microorganisms.

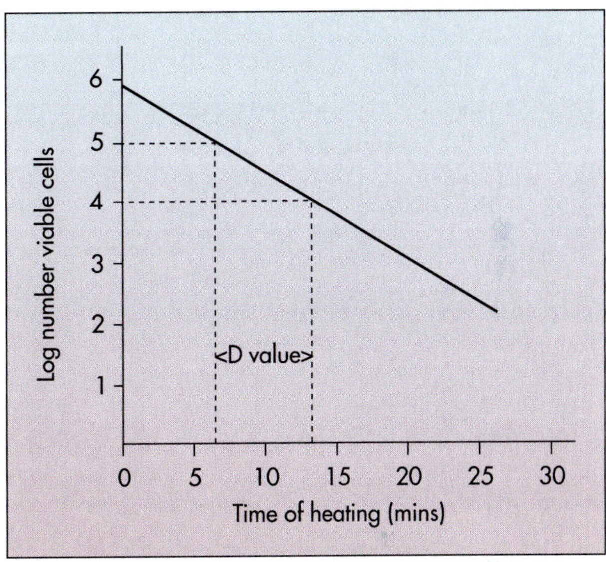

FIG. 10-1 The D value is the time in minutes needed to reduce the number of viable microorganisms by a factor of ten (one log unit).

HIGH TEMPERATURE

Exposure at high temperatures kills microorganisms because proteins are denatured and hence microbial structures and metabolism cease to function. Temperatures much above the optimal growth temperature for a given microorganism generally produce death rates greater than growth rates. The exposure time at a given temperature needed to reduce the number of viable microorganisms by 90% is called the ***D* value (decimal reduction time)** (FIG. 10-1). The death rate increases with higher temperature. Thus relatively short exposure times at high temperatures are necessary to greatly reduce the numbers of viable microorganisms.

High temperature exposure methods to kill microorganisms include incineration, dry heat, and moist heat. Incineration involves complete combustion of the material concerned. This is used for sterilization of platinum or nichrome wires used for inoculation of microbial cultures. Incineration may also be used for decontamination of disposable materials such as bedding or plasticware. Moist heat and dry heat involve exposure to high temperatures with or without water.

Moist heat is more effective than dry heat in killing microorganisms because water at elevated temperatures (steam) can penetrate into microbial structures more readily than dry air at elevated temperatures and steam causes hydrogen bond rearrangement.

Dry heat methods use the conventional convection oven. Since dry heat is not as effective in killing microorganisms as is moist heat, conditions of 2 hours at 180° C may be required to sterilize, especially for the killing of endospores. Dry cells are more resistant than moist cells. Inert materials such as glassware and metals are sterilized by this method. Also, materials such as some jellies, oils, and powders, which do not lend themselves to steam sterilization, may be sterilized by this method.

Exposure at 100° C in boiling water for just a few minutes usually is effective at killing all vegetative cells of most microorganisms in a sample. However, endospores survive such temperatures. Higher tempera-

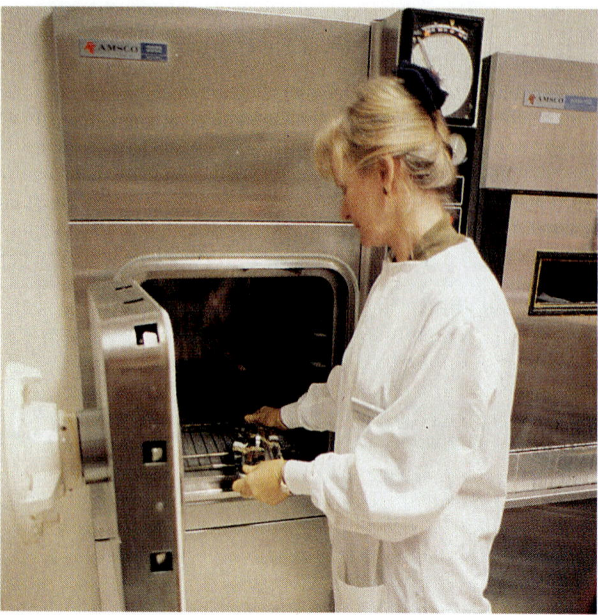

FIG. 10-2 An autoclave is used to sterilize materials by exposure to steam under pressure.

tures of 121° C, achieved in an autoclave at 15 pounds per square inch (psi) pressure, are needed to kill endospores (FIG. 10-2). The preferred method for moist heat sterilization involves the use of steam under pressure because it kills microorganisms more rapidly and at lower temperatures. At 100° C, it takes about 5.5 hours to inactivate spores of *Clostridium botulinum;* at 121° C, it only takes about 4 to 5 minutes (FIG. 10-3). Steam sterilization is carried out in an autoclave, which is like a large pressure cooker. Typical conditions used with the autoclave involve steam at 121° C under 15 psi of pressure, which ensures its penetrating capability.

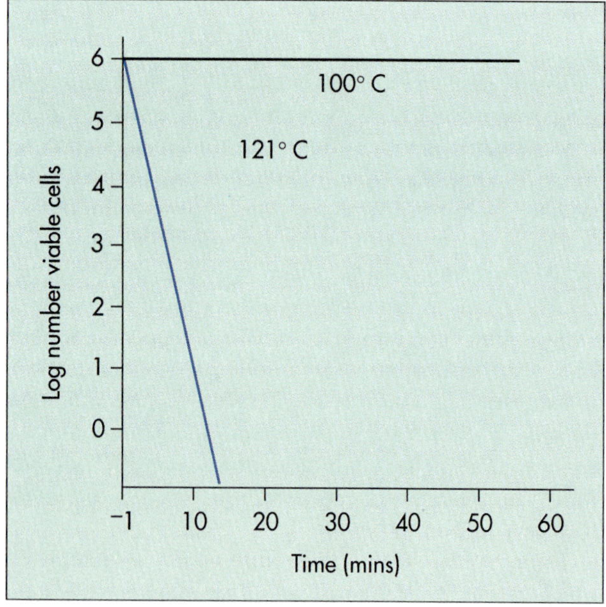

FIG. 10-3 Boiling water at a temperature of 100° C would take hours to kill endospores, whereas steam at 121° C is effective at rapid endospore killing.

Many products are sterilized by using high temperature treatments. Media for microbiology laboratories for the most part is sterilized by autoclaving. Many medical instruments are rendered free of living microorganisms that could cause disease in this manner. Foods are routinely cooked to reduce numbers of microorganisms that could cause foodborne disease. Killing foodborne microorganisms by exposure to high temperatures is a very effective means of preventing food spoilage. The nature of the environment in which the organisms reside may influence the killing rate by heating. Microorganisms die more rapidly under acidic conditions, and the presence of proteins, sugars, or fats may increase the resistance of the cells to heat.

The ability to use high-temperature preservation methods for a given food depends on the temperature sensitivity of that food. If a food is destroyed by exposure to the high temperatures necessary to kill its associated microorganisms, high-temperature methods obviously cannot be used. Very high temperatures and short exposure times sometimes are used to sterilize a food without destroying the value of that food. Exposure to 141° C for 2 seconds can be used to sterilize milk without destroying its flavor or texture, a process known as **ultra high-temperature (UHT) sterilization.**

Canning

Canning uses heat to sterilize food and hermetic sealing to drive out oxygen; this prevents spoilage (FIG. 10-4). High-temperature exposure kills all of the microorganisms in the product, the can or jar acts as a physical barrier to prevent recontamination of the product, and the anaerobic conditions inside prevent

FIG. 10-4 Canning is widely used to preserve foods and keep them free of pathogenic microorganisms. Canning involves heat killing of microorganisms and hermetic sealing under anaerobic conditions to prevent recontamination and spoilage.

TABLE 10-1 Classification of Canned Foods and Their Processing Requirements

ACIDITY CLASS	pH	REPRESENTATIVE FOODS	SPOILAGE AGENTS	PROCESSING
Low acid	7	Ripe olives, eggs, milk, poultry, beef, oysters	Mesophilic, *Clostridium* spp.	High temperature (121° C)
	6	Beans, peas, carrots, beets, asparagus, potatoes	Thermophiles, plant enzymes	High temperature (121° C)
Medium acid	5	Figs, tomato soup, ravioli	Limit of growth of *C. botulinum*	High temperature (121° C)
Acid	4	Potato salad, pears, peaches, oranges, apricots, tomatoes	Aciduric bacteria	Boiling water (100° C)
		Sauerkraut, apple, pineapple, grapefruit, strawberry	Plant enzymes	Boiling water (100° C)
Highly acid	3	Pickles, relish, lemon juice, lime juice	Yeasts and other fungi	Boiling water (100° C)

oxidation of the chemicals in the food. In commercial canning, *Bacillus stearothermophilus* or *Clostridium sporogenes* PA 3679 is used to determine an acceptable *D* value . Exposure to 115° C for 15 minutes is generally considered necessary in home canning to ensure killing of endospore formers. Somewhat lower temperatures, for example, exposure to 100° C for 10 minutes, are often employed in home canning of acidic (pH <4.5) foods, in part because of the lowered thermal resistance of microorganisms under acidic conditions and because *Clostridium botulinum* is unable to grow at low pH values (Table 10-1).

Endospores of *C. botulinum* have a *D* value of 0.21 minute at 121° C. Heating a food for 2.52 minutes at 121° C reduces the probability of the survival of *C. botulinum* endospores to 10^{-12}. Thus, if there were one spore in every can, the probability of contamination remaining after processing should be reduced to one in every trillion cans. Heating at 121° C for 2.52 minutes therefore should ensure the safety of canned foods with respect to possible contamination with *C. botulinum.*

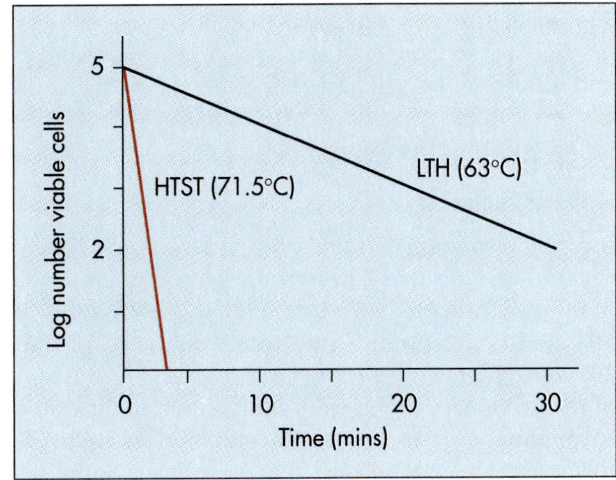

FIG. 10-5 The same reduction of viable microorganisms is achieved by two different pasteurization processes: the low temperature–hold (LTH) process uses 63° C and the high temperature–short time (HTST) process uses 71.5° C.

Pasteurization

Pasteurization is a process that uses relatively brief exposures to moderately high temperatures to reduce the number of viable microorganisms and to eliminate human pathogens (FIG. 10-5). Pasteurization does not eliminate all viable microorganisms—it is not a sterilization process. There are two different pasteurization processes. The **low temperature–hold or LTH process** employs exposure to 62.8° C for 30 minutes. The **high temperature–short time or HTST process** uses 71.7° C for 15 seconds. Both the LTH and HTST pasteurization processes achieve identical reductions of viable microorganisms.

Pasteurization is widely used for reducing numbers of microorganisms in milk, both to increase its shelf life and to ensure its safety. It eliminates several non-spore-forming pathogenic bacteria, namely, *Brucella* species, *Coxiella burnetii,* and *Mycobacterium bovis,* that are associated with the transmission of disease via contaminated milk. Pasteurization of milk has been very effective in curbing the spread of diseases caused by these pathogenic microorganisms and has virtually eliminated the foodborne spread of tuberculosis.

Low Temperature

Refrigeration and freezing are widely used for the preservation of foods. Low temperatures restrict the rates of growth and enzymatic activities of microorganisms. Most pathogenic microorganisms are mesophilic and thus unable to grow in refrigerated foods at 5° C. *Clostridium botulinum* type E can grow and produce toxin at 5° C. Refrigeration extends the shelf life of the product, but it does not do so indefinitely, since psychrophilic and psychrotrophic microorganisms are able to grow slowly at 5° C. Freezing at temperatures of −20° C or less precludes microbial growth entirely.

Freezing does not kill all microorganisms. Some microbial death occurs during freezing and thawing as a result of ice crystal damage to microbial membranes. Therefore, when food is thawed, the surviving microorganisms can grow, leading to food spoilage and potential accumulation of microbial pathogens and toxins if the food is not promptly prepared or consumed. Once food products have been frozen, it is generally not advisable to thaw and refreeze them. When thawed a second time, refrozen food products are even more prone to microbial spoilage than foods that are allowed to thaw only once.

RADIATION

All cells, including microorganisms and viruses, are sensitive to exposure to electromagnetic radiation. The main forms of radiation that can cause cellular damage or viral inactivation are ionizing radiations and ultraviolet light. These radiations can be used under controlled conditions to eliminate microorganisms from some environments.

Ionizing Radiation

Ionizing radiations interact with atoms and cause them to lose electrons, or ionize. The two main forms of ionizing radiations are gamma rays (wavelengths of 10^{-3} to 10^{-1} nm) and X-rays (wavelengths of 10^{-3} to 10^{-1} nm). These high energy, short wavelength forms of radiation have high penetrating power and are able to kill microorganisms within a sample by inducing or forming toxic free radicals. Free radicals are highly reactive and can lead to polymerization and other chemical reactions that disrupt the chemical organization of microorganisms. Ionizing radiation destroys hydrogen bonds, double bonds, and ring structures in various molecules. In the presence of oxygen, these radiations form hydroxyl free radicals (OH•) that are quite toxic to the cell. Although different components of a microorganism are affected by ionizing radiation, the critical factor that leads to cell death or viral inactivation is most likely the destruction of DNA (or RNA in some viruses). Ionizing radiation increases the death rate of microorganisms and is used in various sterilization procedures to inactivate viruses and to kill other microorganisms.

Sensitivities to ionizing radiation vary among microorganisms (Table 10-2). Endospores are more resistant than the vegetative cells of many bacterial species. Exposure from 0.3 to 0.4 Mrad is necessary to cause a tenfold reduction in the number of viable bacterial endospores. *Micrococcus radiodurans* is particularly resistant to ionizing radiation. Vegetative cells of *M. radiodurans* tolerate as much as 1 Mrad of exposure with no reduction in viable count. Efficient repair mechanisms are responsible for the high resistance to radiation exhibited by this bacterium.

Exposure to ionizing radiation is useful in sterilizing materials that are destroyed by heat, such as plastics. Many of the Petri plates used in microbiology laboratories are radiation sterilized by using gamma radiation. Radiation exposure can be used to increase the shelf life of various foods, including seafoods, vegetables, and fruits (Table 10-3). In addition to killing spoilage organisms, radiation can inactivate enzymes involved in autocatalytic spoilage. Most food sterilization procedures involving exposure to radiation employ gamma radiation from ^{60}Co or ^{137}Ce at levels of 100 to 200 krads. Radiation exposures that kill *M. radiodurans* ensures a margin of safety against spores, in-

TABLE 10-2 Radiation Tolerances for Various Microorganisms

ORGANISM	DOSE (Mrad)
BACTERIA	
Clostridium botulinum (type E)	1.5
Enterobacter aerogenes	0.16
Escherichia coli	0.18
Micrococcus radiodurans	6.0
Mycobacterium tuberculosis	0.14
Salmonella typhimurium	0.33
Staphylococcus aureus	0.35
Streptococcus faecalis	0.38
VIRUSES	
Polio virus	3.8
Vaccinia virus	2.5

TABLE 10-3 Potential Useful Radiation Dosages for Extending the Shelf Life of Food Products

PRODUCT	DOSE (krads)	SHELF LIFE (days)
FISHERY PRODUCTS		
Atlantic haddock fillets	100-250	30-37
Fresh shrimp	100-250	21-28
Pacific cod fillets	100	16-18
Pacific oysters	100	31
King crab meat	100	21
MEATS AND POULTRY		
Fresh meat and poultry	50-100	21
FRUITS		
Cherries	250	14-20
Oranges	200	90
Peaches, nectarines	200	14
Pineapples	300	14
Strawberries	200	14-18

cluding those of *Clostridium botulinum.* Exposure to radiation does not leave any residual radioactivity in the food, but the method is still controversial. Labels are placed on foods that have been radiation treated to inform consumers.

Ultraviolet Light

Ultraviolet (UV) radiation (wavelengths of 4 to 400 nm) does not have high penetrating power. It is useful for killing microorganisms only on a surface or near the surface of a clear solution. The greatest effectiveness for killing microorganisms occurs at a wavelength of 260 nm. This coincides with the absorption maxima of DNA, suggesting that a principal mechanism by which UV light exerts its lethal effect is through mutations, such as those resulting from the formation of thymine dimers in the DNA. Exposure to 340-nm UV light also has a powerful killing effect on microorganisms, although DNA does not strongly absorb light of this wavelength. This indicates that UV radiation has other mechanisms of killing microorganisms.

FILTRATION

Gases and liquids that contain microorganisms can be sterilized by passing them through porous filters. The filters do not kill the microorganisms. If the pores are small enough, the particulate microorganisms are trapped in the filter and physically removed from the gas or liquid. Filters used to remove microorganisms are composed of cellulose acetate, cellulose nitrate, polycarbonate, teflon, or other suitable synthetic materials. They may vary in the size of the pores but generally pore diameters of about 0.2 μm are effective in removing microorganisms (except viruses) from solutions. Viruses and the smallest bacteria, mycoplasmas, may not be removed from solutions by filtration. When viruses were first discovered, they were referred to as filterable agents because they passed through bacteriological filters (filters with pore sizes less than 0.2 μm).

Air is commonly filtered to sterilize it. Many microbiological techniques requiring strictly sterile conditions are performed in a laminar flow hood. This semi-contained work space directs sterile air across the opening of the cabinet. This restricts contamination of the work space from outside and also prevents the escape of dangerous material or microorganisms into the room. The air in laminar flow hoods is sterilized by being passed through high-efficiency particulate air filters (HEPA). These HEPA filters remove particulate material larger than about 0.3 μm from the air.

Air is also filtered through cotton plugs that are used in flasks for growing microorganisms and in pipettes for the transfer of sterile liquids. Hospital or surgical masks act as filters to prevent the exchange of microorganisms from one person to another or from the environment to an individual.

TABLE 10-4 Minimum A_W Values for the Growth of Various Food Spoilage Fungi

ORGANISM	MINIMUM A_W
Candida utilis	0.94
Botrytis cinerea	0.93
Rhizopus nigricans	0.93
Mucor spinosus	0.93
Candida scottii	0.92
Trichosporon pullulans	0.91
Candida zeylanoides	0.90
Endomyces vernalis	0.89
Alternaria citri	0.84
Aspergillus glaucus	0.70
Aspergillus echinulatus	0.64

DESICCATION

Since microorganisms require water for growth, **desiccation** (drying) is effective for preventing microbial reproduction. Drying, however, does not kill microorganisms and freeze drying is used for preservation of microbial cultures. Bacteria generally will not grow below an A_w (water activity) level of 0.9, and fungi generally will not grow below an A_w value of 0.65 (Table 10-4). Maintenance at an A_w value of 0.65 or less prevents microbial growth. Foods preserved by drying do not spoil for years.

Food preservation by desiccation is an ancient natural practice where food is placed outdoors in the sunlight. It is still used in warm, dry climates and for preservation of fruits such as raisins, prunes, and figs. Milk can be dehydrated by using spray drying or heated drum processes. Evaporated milk is prepared by removing 60% of the water from whole milk. In powdered milk, over 85% of the water is generally removed. Freeze drying is less destructive and yields higher-quality foods than drying at elevated temperatures but is much more expensive. This process, which sublimes water directly from frozen foods under a high vacuum, is used only for high-value products such as meats, camping rations, and coffee.

OXYGEN

Although oxygen is a chemical, we discuss it in this section because the removal of oxygen from an environment is a physical process. Oxygen is required for the growth of aerobic microorganisms but is toxic to strict anaerobes (FIG. 10-6). Therefore the removal of oxygen can be used to prevent the growth of aerobic microorganisms. Packaging of food products under

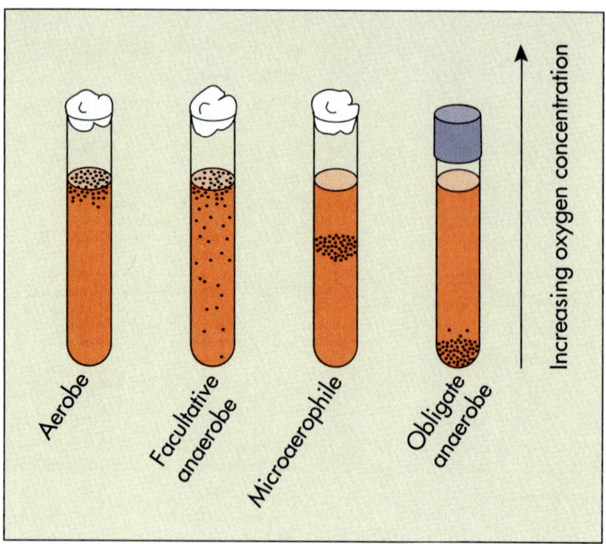

FIG. 10-6 Oxygen is required for growth by aerophiles (aerobes) but must be excluded for the growth of obligate anaerobes. Facultative anaerobes grow in the presence and absence of oxygen. Microaerophiles grow only at reduced oxygen concentrations.

anaerobic conditions (anaerobiosis) is effective in preventing aerobic spoilage processes. Vacuum packing in an airtight container eliminates air; ground coffee, for example, is preserved by this method. The absence of oxygen prevents the growth of aerobic microorganisms and also autoxidation of the food as a result of intrinsic enzymatic activities, greatly increasing product shelf life. Establishing anaerobic conditions, however, also creates ideal conditions for the growth of obligate anaerobes, such as *C. botulinum,* and therefore is normally used in conjunction with additional preservation methods. For example, in canning, heat sterilization precedes packaging under anaerobic conditions.

Oxygen concentrations can be raised to kill strict anaerobes. **Hyperbaric oxygen** (pure oxygen under pressure) is used for the treatment of gas gangrene. This disease is caused by the strict anaerobe *Clostridium perfringens.* By forcing 100% oxygen into the infected tissues at 3 atmospheres pressure in repeated treatments the bacterial infection sometimes can be controlled so that radical surgery can be avoided.

10.3 CHEMICAL CONTROL OF MICROORGANISMS

Many chemicals kill or prevent growth of microorganisms. Such chemicals have been called **antimicrobial agents,** and they have various applications. Some common types of antimicrobial agents used to control microbial growth and prevent infections are listed in Table 10-5.

Concentration and contact time are critical factors that determine the effectiveness of an antimicrobial agent against a particular microorganism. Microorganisms vary in their sensitivity to particular antimicrobial agents. Generally, growing microorganisms are more sensitive than organisms in dormant stages, such as spores. Many antimicrobial agents block active metabolism and prevent the organism from generating the macromolecular constituents needed for reproduction. Because resting stages are metabolically dormant and are not reproducing, they are not affected by such antimicrobial agents. Similarly, viruses are more resistant than other microorganisms to antimicrobial agents because they are metabolically dormant outside host cells.

Antimicrobial agents are classified according to their application and spectrum of action. Agents that kill microorganisms are given the suffix *-cide* (Latin *caedere,* meaning to kill). **Germicides** are antimicrobial agents that kill microorganisms but not necessarily bacterial endospores. Such chemicals may exhibit selective toxicity and, depending on their **spectrum of action,** may act as **viricides** (killing viruses), **bactericides** (killing bacteria), **algicides** (killing algae), or **fungicides** (killing fungi).

Agents that inhibit growth of microorganisms are given the suffix *-static* (Greek *statikos,* meaning to make stand). A bacteriostatic agent inhibits the growth of bacteria. A fungistatic agent inhibits fungal growth. When such microstatic agents are removed, microorganisms resume their growth.

DISINFECTANTS

Disinfectants are antimicrobial agents that kill or prevent the growth of pathogenic microorganisms; they may be microbicidal or microbiostatic. Household cleaning agents often contain disinfectants to control the growth of microorganisms. In general, agents that oxidize biological macromolecules, such as hypochlorite, are effective disinfectants. Disinfectants are not, however, considered safe for use on living tissue and are applied only to inanimate objects. Ammonia and bleach (hypochlorite) are widely used disinfectants. Ethylene oxide gas has been widely used as a sterilizing agent, particularly for prepackaged disposable plasticware such as pipettes and Petri dishes, surgical supplies, respiratory therapy, and anesthesia equipment. This gas is fairly toxic to humans and is also flammable, so that its general use is limited. Exposure of materials to ethylene oxide gas must be performed in special sealed chambers.

TABLE 10-5 Summary of Chemical Agents Used to Control Microbial Growth

ANTIMICROBIAL AGENT	DESCRIPTION
Phenolics	Phenol is no longer used as a disinfectant or antiseptic because of its toxicity to tissues. Derivatives of phenol such as *o*-phenylphenol, hexylresorcinol, and hexachlorophene are used as disinfectants and antiseptics.
Halogens	Chlorination is extensively used to disinfect water; drinking water, swimming pools, and waste treatment plant effluent are disinfected by chlorination. Iodine is an effective antiseptic; iodophors are used as disinfectants and antiseptics; the soaps used for surgical scrubs often contain iodophors.
Alcohols	Alcohols are bactericidal and fungicidal but are not effective against endospores and some viruses; ethanol and isopropanol are commonly used as disinfectants and antiseptics. Thermometers and other instruments are disinfected with alcohol, and the skin is swabbed with alcohol before injections.
Heavy metals	Heavy metals such as silver, copper, mercury, and zinc have antimicrobial properties and are used in disinfectant and antiseptic formulations. Silver nitrate was used to prevent gonococcal eye infections. Mercurochrome and merthiolate are applied to skin after minor wounds. Zinc is used in antifungal antiseptics. Copper sulfate is used as an algicide.
Dyes	Several dyes, such as gentian violet, inhibit microorganisms and are used as antiseptics for treating minor wounds.
Surface-active agents	Soaps and detergents are used to remove microorganisms mechanically from the skin surface. Anionic detergents (laundry powders) remove microorganisms mechanically; cationic detergents, which include quaternary ammonium compounds, have antimicrobial activities. Quaternary compounds (quats) are used as disinfectants and antiseptics.
Acids and alkalies	Organic acids can control microbial growth and are frequently used as preservatives. Sorbic, benzoic, lactic, and propionic acids are used to preserve foods and pharmaceuticals. Benzoic, salicylic, and undecylenic acids are used to control fungi that cause diseases such as athlete's foot.

Effectiveness of Disinfectants

Several standardized test procedures are employed for evaluating the effectiveness of disinfectants. The classic test procedure, used until a few decades ago, is the **phenol coefficient.** The phenol coefficient test compares the activity of a given product with the killing power of phenol under the same test conditions. To determine the phenol coefficient, dilutions of phenol and the test product are added separately to test cultures of *Staphylococcus aureus* or *Salmonella typhi.* The tests are run in liquid culture. After exposure for 5, 10, and 15 minutes, a sample from each tube is collected and transferred to a nutrient broth medium. After incubation for 2 days, the tubes from the different disinfectant dilutions are examined for visible evidence of growth. The phenol coefficient is defined as the ratio of the highest dilution of a test germicide that kills the test bacteria in 10 minutes, but not in 5 minutes, to the dilution of phenol that has the same killing effect. For example, if the greatest dilution of a test disinfectant producing a killing effect is 1:100 and the greatest dilution of phenol showing the same result is 1:50, the phenol coefficient is 100/50 or 2.0.

The phenol coefficient indicates the relative antimicrobial activity of various disinfectants but does not establish the appropriate concentration that should be used for disinfecting surfaces. The Association of Official Analytical Chemists' (AOAC) **use-dilution method,** which has replaced the phenol coefficient as the standard method for evaluating the effectiveness of disinfectants, establishes appropriate dilutions of a germicide for actual conditions. The use-dilution test is superior to the phenol-coefficient test because (1) it gauges the effects of disinfectants by comparing them to each other, not to phenol; and (2) it tests non-phenol-like disinfectants. In this procedure, disinfectants are tested against *Staphylococcus aureus* strain ATCC 6538, *Salmonella choleraesuis* strain ATCC 10708, and *Pseudomonas aeruginosa* strain ATCC 15442. Small stainless steel cylinders are contaminated with specified numbers of the test bacteria. After the cylinders are dried, they are placed in a series of specified dilutions of the test disinfectant. At least 10 replicates of each organism at the test dilutions of the disinfectant are used. The cylinders are exposed to the disinfectant for 10 minutes, allowed to drain, transferred to appropriate culture media, and incubated for 2 days. After incubation the tubes are examined for growth of the test bacteria. No growth should occur if the disinfectant was effective at the test concentration. An acceptable use dilution is one that kills all test organisms at least 95% of the time.

Disinfection of Water

Chlorination is the traditional method employed for disinfecting municipal water (FIG. 10-7). Chlorine is widely used for the disinfection of water supplies. Swimming pools are regularly treated with chlorine. This treatment method is relatively inexpensive, and the free residual chlorine content of the treated water represents a built-in safety factor against pathogens surviving the actual treatment period and causing recontamination.

The disadvantage of chlorination is the incidental production of trace amounts of organochlorine compounds, particularly trihalomethane (THM), a suspected carcinogen. The U.S. Environmental Protection Agency established in 1979 a maximal THM limit in drinking water of 100 μg/L. To stay within this limit using traditional chlorine disinfection, organic compounds would have to be removed by sand filtration or other methods that are impractical and expensive.

Chloramination, the use of chloramines as drinking water disinfectants, is the least expensive way to reduce THM formation, and this practice is spreading rapidly. Disinfection by monochloramine is effective and produces much lower amounts of THMs than treatment with chlorine. As an example, traditional chlorination of Ohio River water produced 160 μg THM/L, but chloramine treatment produced THM levels consistently below 20 μg/L. Monochloramine may be generated right in the water to be disinfected by adding ammonium prior to or simultaneously with chlorine or hypochlorite.

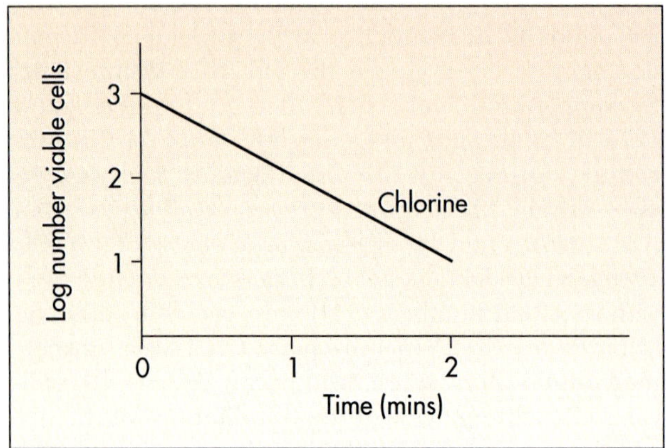

FIG. 10-7 Chlorine rapidly kills microorganisms and is widely used for the disinfection of water.

Ozone (O_3) is a more expensive alternative for disinfecting water supplies that has sometimes been used for water disinfection, with good results, in Europe and the United States. Ozone treatment **(ozonation)** kills pathogens reliably and does not result in the synthesis of any undesirable trace organochlorine contaminants. However, because ozone is an unstable gas, water treated with it does not have any residual antimicrobial activity and is more prone to chance recontamination than chlorinated water. Ozone has to be generated from air on site in ozone reactors, using an electrical corona discharge. Only about 10% of the electricity is actually generating ozone; the rest is lost as heat, making disinfection by ozone considerably less cost effective than chlorination.

FOOD PRESERVATIVES

The use of chemical preservatives to prevent unwanted growth of microorganisms in foods is an important means of preventing food spoilage and protecting against the growth of pathogens in foods (Table 10-6). Although there is concern today over the addition of any chemicals to foods because of the finding that some chemicals that have been used as food additives, such as red dye number 2, are potential carcinogens, it must be remembered that the effective preservation of food prevents spoilage and the transmission of foodborne diseases. In the United States the FDA is responsible for determining and certifying the safety of food additives and must approve any chemicals that are added to foods as preservatives.

Salt

The addition of salt (NaCl) to a food reduces the amount of available water and alters the osmotic pressure. High salt concentrations, such as occur in saturated brine solutions, are bacteriostatic, and the shrinkage of microorganisms in brine solutions can cause loss of viability. European voyages of exploration in the fifteenth century relied on salting to preserve foods. Salting is effectively used for the preservation of fish, meat, and other foods. However, because of the association of high levels of salt in the diet with high blood pressure and heart disease, there is currently great interest in lowering the salt content of foods. Nevertheless, various foods are currently preserved in brines.

Sugar

The high osmotic pressure and low water availability of a high sugar solution prevents microbial growth. Sugars such as sucrose act as preservatives and are effective in preserving fruits, candies, and other foods. Some foods, including maple syrup and honey, are preserved naturally by their high sugar content.

TABLE 10-6 Some Representative Chemical Food Preservatives

PRESERVATIVES	MAXIMUM	TARGET ORGANISMS	FOODS
Propionic acid and propionates	0.32%	Fungi	Bread, cakes, some cheese
Sorbic acid and sorbates	0.2%	Fungi	Cheeses, syrups, jellies, cakes
Benzoic acid and benzoates	0.1%	Fungi	Margarine, cider, relishes, soft drinks, catsup
Sulfur dioxide, sulfites, bisulfites, metabisulfites	200-300 ppm	Microorganisms	Dried fruits, grapes, molasses
Ethylene and propylene oxides	700 ppm	Fungi	Spices
Sodium diacetate	0.132%	Fungi	Bread
Sodium nitrite	200 ppm	Bacteria	Cured meats, fish
Sodium chloride	None	Microorganisms	Meats, fish
Sugar	None	Microorganisms	Preserves, jellies
Wood smoke	None	Microorganisms	Meats, fish

Organic Acids

Various low molecular weight carboxylic acids are inhibitors of microbial growth. The effectiveness of a particular acidic compound depends on the pH of the food, which determines the degree of dissociation of the acid. For example, at the same pH, the order of effectiveness as a preservative is citric acid < lactic acid < acetic acid.

Lactic, acetic, propionic, citric, benzoic, and sorbic acids or their salts are effective food preservatives. Propionates are primarily effective against filamentous fungi and are used as preservatives in bread, cake, and various cheeses. Cheeses, pickles, and sauerkraut contain concentrations of lactic acid that normally protect the food against spoilage. Vinegar contains acetic acid, an effective inhibitor of bacterial and fungal growth. Benzoates, including sodium benzoate, methyl *p*-hydroxybenzoate (methylparaben), and propyl-*p*-hydroxybenzoate (propylparaben), are extensively used as food preservatives in fruit juices, jams, jellies, soft drinks, salad dressings, fruit salads, relishes, tomato catsup, and margarine.

Nitrates and Nitrites

Nitrates and nitrites are added to cured meats to preserve the red meat color and to protect against the growth of food spoilage and poisoning microorganisms. Nitrates effectively inhibit *Clostridium botulinum* in meat products such as bacon and ham. There is concern, however, over the addition of nitrates and nitrites to meats because these salts can react with secondary and tertiary amines to form nitrosamines, which are highly carcinogenic.

Sulfur Dioxide, Ethylene Oxide, and Propylene Oxide

Sulfur dioxide and various sulfites have antimicrobial activities. Such fruit products as lemon juice, wine, and dried fruit can be preserved by fumigating with sulfur dioxide or by adding liquid sulfites. Ethylene and propylene oxides are microbicidal and can be used to sterilize food products. These compounds are used as fumigating agents in the food industry and are primarily applied to dried fruits, nuts, and spices as antifungal agents.

ANTISEPTICS

Antiseptics are antimicrobial agents that can be applied safely to living tissues. They are used for topical (surface) applications and are not necessarily safe for ingestion. The use of antiseptics in surgical practice was introduced by Joseph Lister (see FIG. 1-16). Before the introduction of antiseptics, infections following compound fractures and surgical procedures often were fatal.

Effectiveness of Antiseptics

There are two factors that determine the effectiveness of antiseptics: (1) the antimicrobial activity of the agent and (2) the toxicity to living tissues. A particularly meaningful approach for comparing antiseptics that encompasses both of these factors is the generation of a **toxicity index.** In the tissue toxicity test, germicides are tested for their ability to kill bacteria and their toxicity to chick-heart tissue cells. The toxicity index is defined as the ratio of the greatest dilution of the product that can kill the animal cells in 10 minutes to the dilution that can kill the bacterial cells in the same period of time under identical conditions. For example, if a substance is toxic to chick-heart tissue at a dilution of 1:1,000 and is bactericidal for *Staphylococcus aureus* at a dilution of 1:10,000, the toxicity index would be 1,000/10,000, or 0.1. Typical toxicity values for tincture of iodine solution and tincture of merthiolate are 0.2 and 3.3, respectively. Ideally, an antiseptic should have a toxicity index of less than 1.0, that is, it should be more toxic to bacteria than to human tissue.

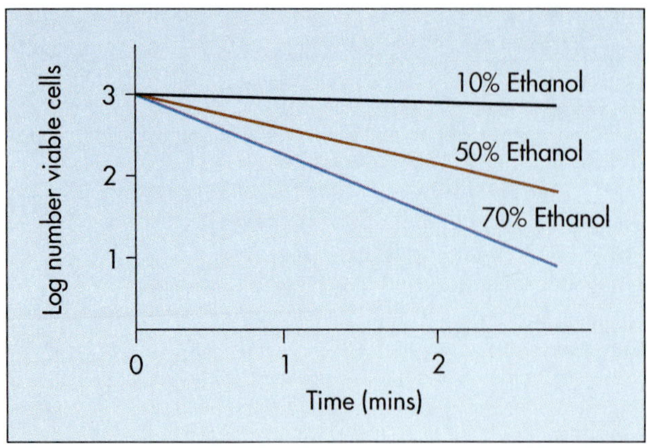

FIG. 10-8 Alcohol is a widely used antiseptic for killing microorganisms on skin. Its effectiveness is concentration dependent.

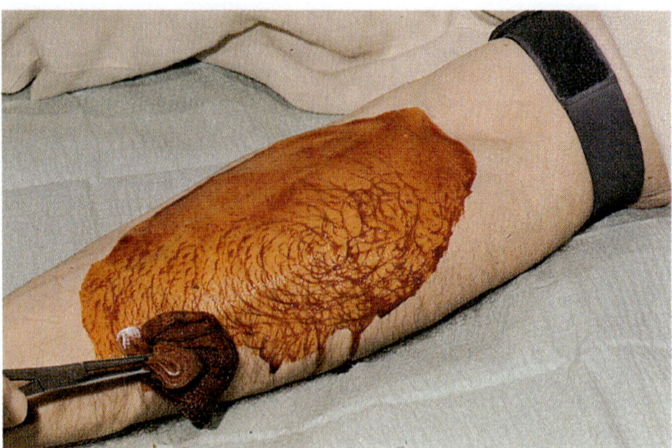

FIG. 10-9 Iodine being applied before a surgical procedure.

Antiseptic Agents

Alcohol is probably the most widely used antiseptic and is used to reduce the number of microorganisms on the skin surface in the area of a wound (FIG. 10-8). Alcohol denatures proteins, extracts membrane lipids, and acts as a dehydrating agent, all of which contribute to its effectiveness as an antiseptic. Even viruses are inactivated by alcohol. The drawbacks of alcohol are that it evaporates too quickly and that it dries and sometimes cracks the skin.

Iodine is another effective antiseptic agent, killing all types of bacteria, including spores. Iodine-containing soaps are commonly used for preoperative scrubbing. It is frequently applied to minor wounds to kill microorganisms contaminating the surface, preventing infection, but is not used by diabetics because it causes localized tissue damage (FIG. 10-9). Various dyes in selective media, such as crystal violet, are similarly used as antiseptic agents. Such stains are normally effective bactericidal agents in concentrations of less than 1:10,000.

Heavy metal ions are also used in antiseptic formulations. Mercuric chloride, copper sulfate, and silver nitrate are examples of heavy metal–containing compounds that are used to kill microorganisms. Silver nitrate, for example, was once applied to the eyes of newborn human infants to kill possible microbial contaminants to preclude the transmission of gonococcal infections from an infected mother to the infant's eyes. It has been replaced with the antibiotic erythromycin. Zinc oxide is sometimes used as an antifungal agent.

Phenolics and related compounds are often used as surgical scrubs. Both cationic and anionic detergents are also used as antiseptics; various detergents are quite effective, particularly those containing quaternary ammonium salts.

10.4 ANTIBIOTICS (ANTIMICROBICS)

Antibiotics are antimicrobial substances produced by microorganisms. Antibiotics were discovered by Sir Alexander Fleming (see FIG. 1-17). They have been used in medicine only since the mid-1940s. Although many of the antibiotics used today are in fact produced by microorganisms, and therefore are true antibiotics, some are produced partly or entirely by chemical synthesis. To avoid problems in terminology the all-inclusive term **antimicrobic** often is used to include the antimicrobial agents produced by microorganisms and those made by chemists.

Some antimicrobics are produced by several companies under several different trade names (Table 10-7). Many municipalities now require pharmacies to fill a prescription with its generic brand, to encourage competitive pricing, unless a specific brand name is required. Such laws are controversial because the pharmaceutical manufacturers lose the incentive to develop new antibiotics and to maintain high and costly quality control when a less stringently regulated and less expensive product will be used to fill a prescription. The public wants cost-effective but high-quality antibiotics.

Some antimicrobial agents are **microbicidal** (killing microorganisms) and others are **microbiostatic** (inhibiting the growth of microorganisms but not actually killing them). Microbiostatic agents prevent the proliferation of infecting microorganisms, holding populations of pathogens in check until the normal immune defense mechanisms eliminate the invading pathogens. Antibiotics represent a major class of antimicrobial agents. By definition, antibiotics are biochemicals produced by microorganisms that inhibit the growth of, or kill, other microorganisms. By their very nature, antibiotics and synthetic antimicrobics must exhibit selective toxicity because they are produced by one microorganism and exert varying degrees of toxicity against others. The discovery and use of antibiotics have revolutionized medical practice in the twentieth century.

To be of therapeutic use, an antimicrobic must exhibit **selective toxicity.** It must inhibit infecting microorganisms and exhibit greater toxicity to the infecting pathogens than to the host organism. A drug that kills the patient is of no use in treating infectious diseases, whether or not it also kills the pathogens. Even selective, therapeutically useful antimicrobics, though, can produce side effects (Table 10-8). As a rule, antimicrobics are most useful in medicine when their mode of action involves physiological features of the invading pathogens not possessed by normal host cells.

TABLE 10-7 Generic and Trade Names of Some Common Antibiotics

GENERIC NAME	TRADE NAME
Tetracycline	Achromycin, Panmycin, Tetracyn, Tetrachel, Rexamycin
Oxytetracycline	Terramycin
Chlorotetracycline	Aureomycin
Demeclocycline	Declomycin
Methacycline	Rondomycin
Doxycycline	Vibramycin
Minocycline	Minocin, Vectrin
Penicillin G	Crysticillin, Duracillin
Ampicillin	Amcill, Omnipin, Penbritin, Polycillin
Cephalothin	Keflin
Cephalexin	Keflex
Chloramphenicol	Chloromycetin, Mychel
Gentamicin	Garamycin
Kanamycin	Kantrex
Erythromycin	Ilotycin
Nystatin	Mycostatin, Nilstat
Trimethoprim-sulfamethoxazole	Bactrin, Septra
Chloroquine	Aralen, Avloclor, Resochin

TABLE 10-8 Major Toxicities of Selected Antimicrobics

ANTIMICROBIC AGENT	MECHANISM	SIGNS
Aminoglycosides	Binds hair cells of organ of Corti	Deafness
	Binds vestibular cells	Vertigo
	Competitive neuromuscular blockage	Respiratory paralysis
	Tubular necrosis	Nephrotoxicity
Amphotericin	Distal tubular damage	Nephrotoxicity
	Renal tubular acidosis	Nephrotoxicity
Carbenicillin	Inhibition of platelet aggregation	Bleeding
Cephalosporins	Stimulation of muscle	Myoclonic seizures
Cephaloridine	Proximal tubular damage	Nephrotoxicity
Chloramphenicol	Damages stem cells	Aplastic anemia
	Inhibits protein synthesis	Reversible anemia
Clindamycin	Proliferation of *Clostridium difficile*	Diarrhea
Emetine	Permeability changes	Hypotension
Isoniazid	Liver cell damage	Hepatitis
Neomycin	Villous damage	Malabsorption
Penicillins	Cortical stimulation	Myoclonic seizures
Polymyxins	Noncompetitive neuromuscular blockage	Nephrotoxicity
	Tubular necrosis	Hepatitis
Rifampin	Liver cell damage	Hepatitis
Sulfonamides	Glucose 6-phosphate deficiency	Hemolytic anemia
	Collecting duct obstruction	Nephrotoxicity
Tetracyclines	Liver cell damage	Hepatitis
	Degradation products	Fanconi syndrome

Selection of Antimicrobial Agents

The selection of a particular antimicrobial agent for treating a given disease depends on several factors, including (1) the sensitivity of the infecting microorganism to the particular antimicrobial agent; (2) the side effects of the antimicrobial agent with regard to direct toxicity to mammalian cells and to the microbiota normally associated with human tissues; (3) the biotransformations of the antimicrobial agent that occur *in vivo,* relative to whether the agent will remain in its active form for a sufficient period of time to be selectively toxic to the infecting pathogens; and (4) the chemical properties of the antimicrobial agent that determine its distribution within the body, relative to whether or not adequate concentrations of the active antimicrobial chemical can reach the site of infection to inhibit or kill the pathogenic microorganisms causing the infection.

Because of differential solubilities, antimicrobics exhibit specific distribution patterns within the body that must be recognized when choosing the proper agent (Table 10-9). For example, although many antibiotics possess antimicrobial activities that are effective against the pathogenic bacteria that cause urinary tract infections, only a limited number of antibiotics are effective in treating these infections because relatively few can reach and be concentrated in the tissues of the urinary tract in their active form. Additionally, one antimicrobial agent can influence the effects of

TABLE 10-9 Distribution of Antimicrobics to Specific Body Areas

Bone

Penicillins, tetracyclines, cephalosporins, lincomycin, and clindamycin antimicrobics penetrate bone and bone marrow; levels are higher in infected bone than in normal bone.

Central Nervous System

Only lipid-soluble antimicrobics cross the blood-brain barrier and reach brain tissues. In the presence of inflammation, such as brain abscess, various penicillins achieve appreciable concentrations in the brain. Levels of most antimicrobics in the cerebrospinal fluid (CSF) are low. Penicillin G and ampicillin can achieve adequate CSF levels in the presence of inflammation; oxacillin, naficillin, and methicillin can be used to treat staphylococcal meningitis. CSF levels of chloramphenicol are adequate to treat *Streptococcus, Neisseria,* and *Haemophilus* but not most Gram-negative bacteria. Cefoxamine, moxalactam, and cefoperazone enter CSF in the presence of inflammation in concentrations that are adequate to treat *Streptococcus, Neisseria, Haemophilus, Klebsiella,* and *Escherichia coli* infections.

Ears and Sinuses

Most of the penicillins reach levels in the middle ear fluid in sufficient concentrations for the treatment of otitis media. Concentrations of antimicrobics in sinuses are adequate for sulfonamides and trimethoprim to treat infections.

Eyes

Few antimicrobics penetrate the eye well. Levels of penicillins and cephalosporins in the aqueous humor are less than 10% of the peak serum levels and inhibit only highly sensitive bacteria.

Pleural and Pericardial Fluids

Most of the penicillins, cephalosporins, sulfonamides, macrolides, clindamycin, chloramphenicol, and antituberculosis drugs diffuse into serus cavities.

Pulmonary

Concentrations of most antibiotics within the lung are satisfactory, provided there is sufficient blood flow. Penicillins and tetracyclines show variable sputum concentrations. Antituberculosis agents, such as isoniazid and rifampin, achieve appreciable levels in pulmonary tissue.

Skin

Tetracyclines and clindamycin concentrate in skin tissue and are effective in treatment of acne.

Synovial Fluid

Most antibiotics used in the treatment of joint infection reach inflamed joints in adequate concentrations.

Urinary Tract

Treatment of kidney and other urinary tract infections depends largely on concentrations in the urine rather than on serum levels. Nalidixic acid and nitrofurantoin are effective in treating urinary tract infections.

another antimicrobial agent. In some cases, the use of two drugs enhances the effectiveness of the treatment. In other cases, one drug interferes with the inhibitory effects of the other.

Some antibiotics are more selective than others with respect to the bacterial species that they inhibit. A **narrow-spectrum antibiotic** may be targeted at a particular pathogen, for instance at Gram-positive cocci, or at a particular bacterial species. In contrast, the **broad spectrum antibiotic** inhibits a relatively wide range of bacterial species, including both Gram-positive and Gram-negative types. In most cases, physicians make an educated guess as to which antibiotic is appropriate for treating a particular infection, and the selection of the antibiotic is based on the most likely pathogen causing the disease symptomatology and the antibiotics generally known to be effective against this pathogen. Many times, a physician will select a broad-spectrum antibiotic to ensure timely and effective treatment. Only in special cases, such as when a patient fails to respond to a particular antibiotic and an infection persists, is an attempt normally made to isolate the pathogenic bacterium and to determine its range of antibiotic sensitivity.

However, concern is mounting in the medical field about the overuse of antibiotics because the undesired side effect is the selection for disease-causing antibiotic-resistant strains. It is now considered proper medical practice to perform culture and sensitivity studies to determine the proper antibiotic for treating a patient. Only in cases of life-threatening infections should antibiotics be used without such testing to avoid selective pressure for the development of antibiotic-resistant pathogens. The importance of this problem was recently underscored when the American Medical Association advised physicians to avoid unnecessary use of antibiotics.

The reason for concern about how we use antibiotics is that numerous bacterial strains have acquired the ability to resist the effects of some antibiotics, with some bacterial strains, generally those containing R plasmids, having **multiple antibiotic resistance** (FIG. 10-10). The basis of resistance in some cases is the ability of the particular strain to produce enzymes that degrade the antibiotic, preventing the active form of the antibiotic from reaching the bacterial cells where they could be inhibitory. For example, some bacterial strains produce penicillinase enzymes (β-lactamases) that degrade the antibiotic penicillin, making such strains resistant to penicillin. Resistance may also be due to decreased drug uptake, decreased transformation of the drug to its active form, or decreased sensitivity of the microbial structure against which the drug is directed.

Determination of the antimicrobial susceptibility of a pathogen is important in aiding the clinician to select the most appropriate agent for treating that disease. It is pointless to prescribe an antibiotic that is ineffective against the microorganism causing the disease. Additionally, physicians want to avoid indiscriminate administration of antibiotics because the selective pressures of excessive antibiotic usage can and have led to the evolution of antibiotic-resistant strains of pathogens. Such pathogens become problems

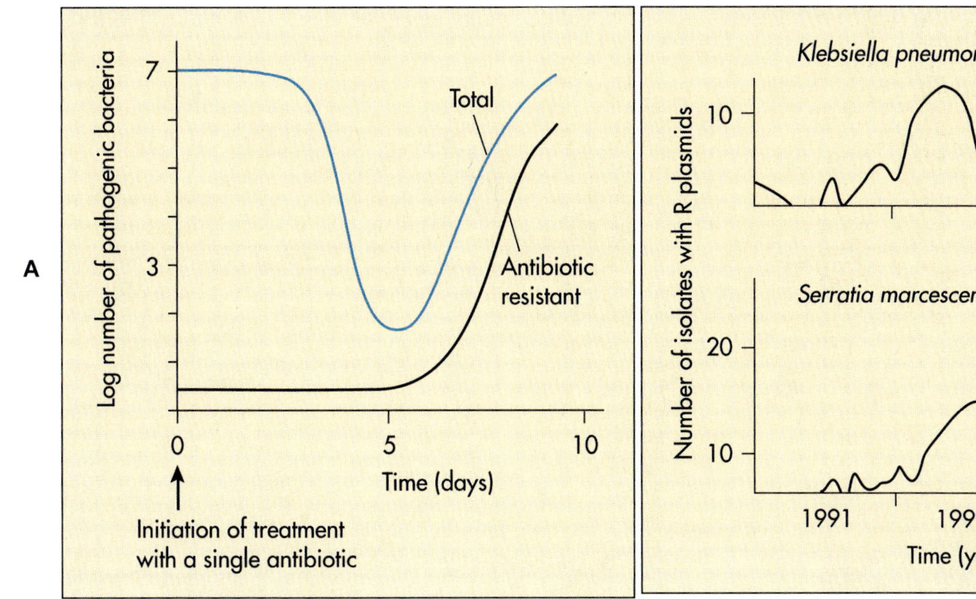

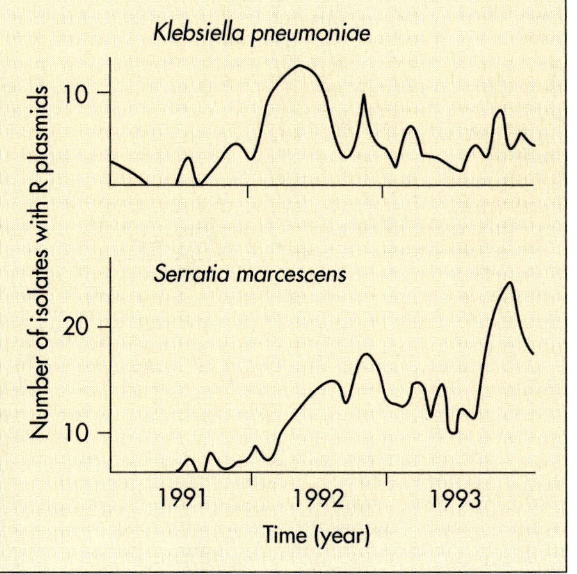

FIG. 10-10 **A,** The incidence of antibiotic resistance has been increasing, making it more difficult for physicians to treat some infections. **B,** Antibiotic resistance is seen within a hospital as the periodic occurrence of bacterial isolates containing multiple antibiotic resistant plasmids.

when they cause infections that do not respond to the antibiotics routinely used to treat specific diseases.

Clinical microbiology laboratories provide information, through standardized *in vitro* testing, with regard to the activities of antimicrobial agents against microorganisms that have been isolated and identified as the probable etiological agents of disease. Antibiotic susceptibility testing, which relies on the observation of antibiotics inhibiting the growth and/or killing cultures of microorganisms *in vitro,* provides the physician with the information needed to prescribe the proper antibiotics for treating infectious diseases.

Bauer-Kirby Test

The **Bauer-Kirby test** (also called the **Kirby-Bauer test**) is a standardized antimicrobial susceptibility procedure in which a culture is inoculated onto the surface of Mueller-Hinton agar, followed by the addition of antibiotic impregnated disks to the agar surface. The antibiotics diffuse into the agar, establishing a concentration gradient. Inhibition of microbial growth is indicated by a clear area *(zone of inhibition)* around the antibiotic disc (FIG. 10-11). The diameter of the zone of inhibition reflects the solubility properties of the particular antibiotic—that is, the concentration gradient established by diffusion of the antibiotic into the agar—and the sensitivity of the given microorganism to the specific antibiotic. Standardized zones for each antibiotic disc determine whether the microorganism is sensitive (S), intermediately sensitive (I), or resistant (R) to the particular antibiotic (Table 10-10). The results of Bauer-Kirby testing indicate whether a particular antibiotic has the potential for effectively controlling an infection caused by a particular pathogen.

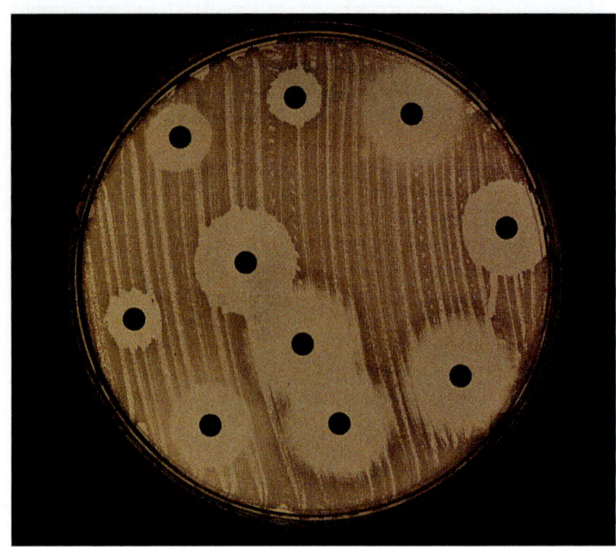

FIG. 10-11 The Bauer-Kirby test (also called the Kirby-Bauer test) is a standardized procedure for determining antibiotic susceptibility. The diameter of the zone of inhibition (clear area around antimicrobic impregnated discs) indicates the sensitivity of the microorganism to that antibiotic.

The Bauer-Kirby agar diffusion test procedure is designed for use with rapidly growing bacteria. It is not directly applicable to filamentous fungi, anaerobes, or slow-growing bacteria, although modifica-

TABLE 10-10 Interpretation of Zones of Inhibition for Bauer-Kirby Antibiotic Susceptibility Testing

		INHIBITION ZONE DIAMETER (mm)		
ANTIBIOTIC	DISC CONC.	RESISTANT (R)	INTERMEDIATE (I)	SUSCEPTIBLE (S)
Amikacin	0.01 mg	13 or less	12-13	14 or more
Ampicillin	0.01 mg	11 or less	12-13	14 or more
Bacitracin	10 units	8 or less	9-11	13 or more
Cephalothin	0.03 mg	14 or less	15-17	18 or more
Chloramphenicol	0.03 mg	12 or less	13-17	18 or more
Erythromycin	0.015 mg	13 or less	14-17	18 or more
Gentamicin	0.01 mg	13 or less	—	13 or more
Kanamycin	0.03 mg	13 or less	14-17	18 or more
Lincomycin	0.002 mg	9 or less	10-14	15 or more
Methicillin	0.005 mg	9 or less	10-13	14 or more
Nalidixic acid	0.03 mg	13 or less	14-18	19 or more
Neomycin	0.03 mg	12 or less	13-16	17 or more
Nitrofurantoin	0.3 mg	14 or less	15-16	17 or more
Penicillin G—staphylococci	10 units	20 or less	21-28	29 or more
Penicillin G—other organisms	10 units	11 or less	12-21	22 or more
Polymyxin	300 units	8 or less	9-11	12 or more
Streptomycin	0.01 mg	11 or less	12-14	15 or more
Sulfonamides	0.3 mg	12 or less	13-16	17 or more
Tetracycline	0.03 mg	14 or less	15-18	19 or more
Vancomycin	0.03 mg	9 or less	10-11	12 or more

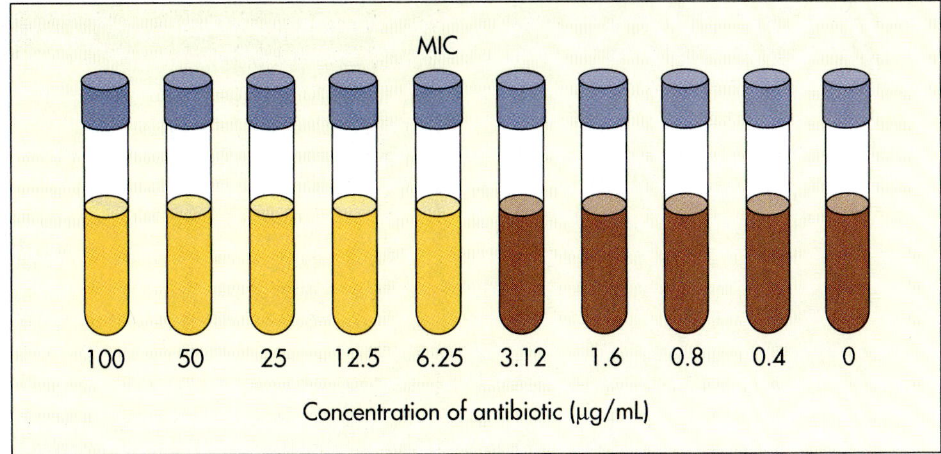

FIG. 10-12 The minimum inhibitory concentration (MIC) indicates the lowest concentration of an antimicrobic that prevents growth. In this example the MIC is 6.25 μg/mL. It is the lowest concentration that precludes growth *(clear gold)*; growth occurs at lower concentrations *(cloudy brown)*.

tions of the media composition and incubation conditions can be made for testing the antibiotic susceptibility of such microorganisms. Different standardized systems are used for performing antibiotic sensitivity testing in these cases. For example, prereduced Wilkins-Chalgren agar, anaerobic transfer techniques, and anaerobic incubation can be used for determining the antibiotic sensitivities of anaerobic bacteria.

Many clinical laboratories today use light scattering or equivalent automated liquid diffusion methods for antibiotic sensitivity testing. The concentrations of the antibiotics and the density and growth phase of the cultures are adjusted so that uniform interpretive guidelines can be used for assessing antibiotic sensitivities. A normalized light scattering index is generated to determine S, I, and R; for R this index is 0.00 to 0.50; for I, 0.51 to 0.60; and for S, 0.60 to 1.00, except for penicillin G, when it is 0.60 to 0.90. Automated systems available for performing this procedure include the Autobac, Microscan, BBL sceptre, Vitek AMS, and Abott MSII. These automated systems simplify and enhance the reliability of antimicrobial susceptibility testing, making it likely that they will be used more frequently, thereby reducing the excessive use of inappropriate antimicrobics by some physicians.

Minimum Inhibitory Concentration

The **minimum inhibitory concentration (MIC)** test uses dilutions of the antimicrobic to determine the lowest concentration of the antimicrobic (the MIC) that is effective in preventing the growth of the pathogen (FIG. 10-12). A standardized microbial inoculum is added to tubes containing serial dilutions of an antibiotic, and the growth of the microorganism is monitored as a change in turbidity. The MIC indicates the minimal concentration of the antibiotic that must be achieved at the site of infection to inhibit the growth of the microorganism being tested. By knowing the MIC and the theoretical level of the antibiotic that may be achieved in body fluids, such as blood and urine, the physician can select the appropriate antibiotic, the dosage schedule, and the route of administration (Table 10-11, p. 366). Generally, a margin of safety of 10 times the MIC is desirable to ensure successful treatment of the disease.

The use of microtiter plates (which require only a few hundred microliters per sample well) and automated inoculation and reading systems make the determination of MIC feasible for use in the clinical laboratory (FIG. 10-13).

FIG. 10-13 A microtiter plate showing the determination of an MIC.

TABLE 10-11 Achievable Levels of Some Common Antibiotics in Various Body Fluids

ANTIBIOTIC	ACHIEVABLE PEAK BLOOD LEVELS (μg/mL)	ACHIEVABLE URINE LEVELS (μg/mL)	DOSE
Clindamycin	1-4	>20	Oral 150-300 mg
	6-10	>60	IV 300-600 mg
Erythromycin	1-2	—	Oral 250-500 mg
	10-20	—	IV 300 mg
Penicillin	2-3	>300	Oral 500 mg
	6-8	>300	IM 500 mg
	4-7	>300	IV 500 mg
Ampicillin	1-3	>50	Oral 250-500 mg
	2-6	>20	IM 250-500 mg
	10-25	>100	IV 1,000-1,500 mg
Cephalothin	3-18	>100	Oral 250-500 mg
	9-24	>300	IM 500-1,000 mg
	30-85	>1,000	IV 1,000-2,000 mg
Gentamicin	2-10	>20	IV/IV 1-2 mg
Tetracycline	1-2	>200	Oral 250-500 mg
	10-20	>200	IV 500 mg
Chloramphenicol	10-12	>100	Oral 1,000 mg
	20-30	>200	IV 1,000 mg
Nitrofurantoin	—	>100	Oral 50-100 mg

IV, Intravenous; *IM,* intramuscular.

Minimum Bactericidal Concentration

The **minimal bactericidal concentration (MBC),** also known as the minimal lethal concentration (MLC), is the lowest concentration of an antibiotic that will kill a defined proportion of viable organisms in a bacterial suspension during a specified exposure period. Generally, a 99.9% kill of bacteria at an initial concentration of 10^5 to 10^6 cells/mL during an 18- to 24-hour exposure period is used to define the MBC.

To determine the minimal bactericidal concentration, it is necessary to plate the tube suspensions showing no growth in tube dilution (MIC) tests onto an agar growth medium to determine whether the bacteria are indeed killed or whether they survive exposure to the antibiotic at the concentration being tested. Although determination of the MIC is adequate for establishing the appropriate concentration of an antibiotic that should be administered to control an infection in patients with normal immune response levels, the MBC is essential in cases of endocarditis and is particularly useful in determining the appropriate concentration of an antibiotic for use in treating patients with lowered immune defense responses, such as those receiving chemotherapy for cancer.

Serum Killing Power

The **serum killing power** is determined by adding a bacterial suspension to dilutions of the patient's serum. Assuming that the patient is being treated with an antibiotic, no bacterial growth should occur. The breakpoint in the dilutions where bacterial growth occurs reflects the concentration of the antibiotic in the patient's blood and the *in vivo* effectiveness of the antibiotic in controlling the infection. Inhibition at dilutions of the patient's serum of to 1:8 or more is considered an acceptable level.

Antibacterial Antimicrobics

Most of the therapeutically useful antimicrobics are effective against bacterial infections. This is because of the significant differences between the prokaryotic cells of the infecting bacteria and the eukaryotic cells of the infected human. There are various targets in a bacterial cell that are absent from eukaryotic cells so that selective toxicity can be achieved.

Cell-wall Inhibitors

The **penicillins** and **cephalosporins** are two widely used classes of antibiotics that inhibit the formation of bacterial cell walls. Penicillins are synthesized by strains of the fungus *Penicillium.* The cephalosporins are produced by members of the fungal genus *Cephalosporium.* The penicillins and cephalosporins contain a β-lactam ring (FIG. 10-14). Various penicillin and cephalosporin antibiotics contain different substituent groups and exhibit different spectrums of antibacterial activity. Because of these different properties, various penicillins and cephalosporins are used in the treatment of specific diseases (Table 10-12, pp. 368-369).

Both the penicillins and cephalosporins inhibit the formation of peptide cross-linkages within the peptidoglycan backbone of the cell wall. These antibiotics

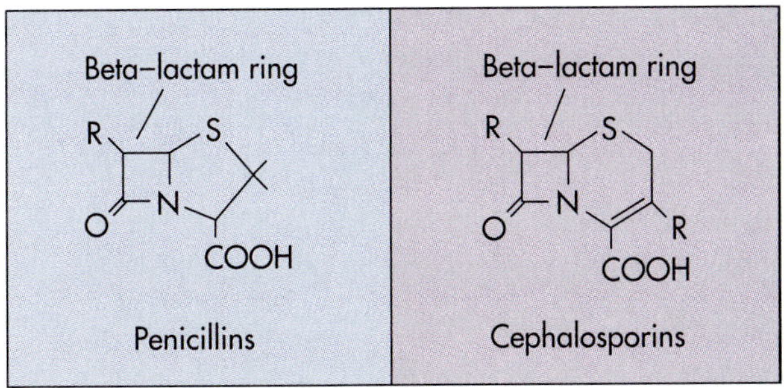

FIG. 10-14 The structures of penicillins and cephalosporins have beta lactam rings.

specifically inhibit the enzymes involved in the cross-linkage for transpeptidase reactions (FIG. 10-15). It appears that the β-lactam portion of cephalosporin and penicillin antibiotics binds to the transpeptidase enzyme, preventing the binding of the enzyme to the normal substrate, D-alanyl-D-alanine.

Bacterial cell walls lacking the normal cross-linking peptide chains are subject to attack by **autolysins,** which are autolytic enzymes produced by the organism that degrade the cell's own cell wall structures. In the presence of cephalosporins or penicillins, growing bacterial cells are subject to lysis because, without functional cell wall structures, the cells are not protected against osmotic shock. It should be noted that the penicillin and cephalosporin antibiotics do not themselves remove intact cell walls and thus are ineffective against resting or dormant cells.

Penicillins Many of the penicillins, such as penicillin G (benzylpenicillin), have a relatively narrow spectrum of activity, being most effective against Gram-positive cocci, including *Staphylococcus* species. Pharmaceutical companies have chemically modified the original parent compound to produce various *semi-synthetic penicillin derivatives.* These chemical modifications give the penicillin molecule altered chemical properties. The design of semi-synthetic drugs often improves the antimicrobial action of an antibiotic. For example, if an amino group is added to the benzylpenicillin molecule, a new compound, aminobenzyl penicillin (or ampicillin) is formed. Ampicillin has a broader spectrum of activity than penicillin G, inhibiting some Gram-negative as well as Gram-positive bacteria. Ampicillin is active against many Gram-negative rods, including *Escherichia coli, Haemophilus influenzae, Shigella* species, and *Proteus* species. To inhibit peptidoglycan synthesis effectively in Gram-negative bacteria, the antibiotic must pass through the outer lipopolysaccharide (LPS) layers to reach the peptidoglycan located at the inner layer of the cell wall. The broad spectrum activity of ampicillin appears to be based on its ability to penetrate the outer membrane to the site of action of the transpeptidase enzyme. Penicillin G is relatively inefficient at reaching this site because it cannot pass through the outer membrane of the Gram-negative cell wall.

Other semi-synthetic penicillins have been produced that are more acid stable than penicillin G. Acid stability allows a drug to be administered orally; it will not be degraded by the acid environment of the stomach. Oral administration of a drug is sometimes more convenient for the patient than other routes of administration (intravenous or intramuscular injection). Ampicillin and phenoxymethylpenicillin (or penicillin V) are examples of semi-synthetic penicillin derivatives that can be administered orally. Penicillin G must be administered by non-oral routes.

Penicillin G and various other β-lactam antibiotics are subject to inactivation by penicillinase enzymes (β-

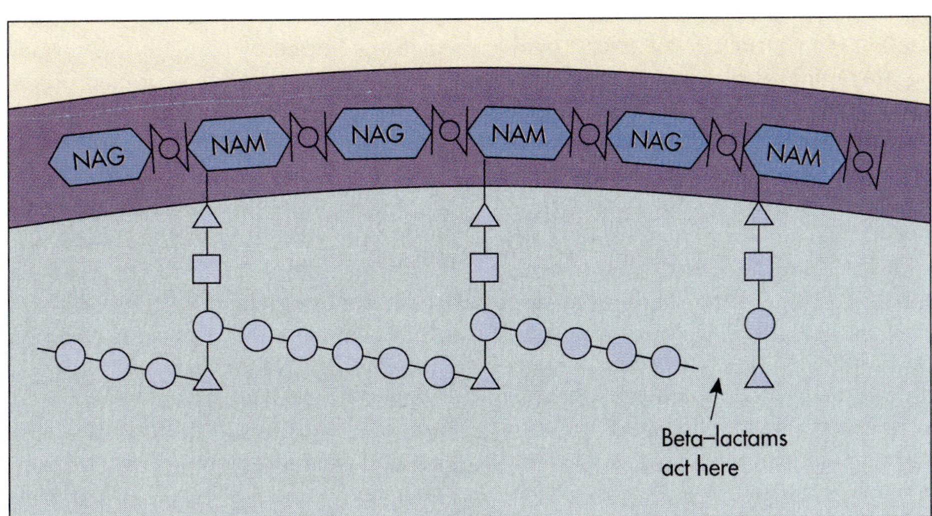

FIG. 10-15 Penicillins and cephalosporins, which are widely used antimicrobics, block synthesis of bacterial cell walls.

TABLE 10-12 Some Diseases and Their Causative Organisms for Which Penicillins and Cephalosporins Are Recommended

CAUSATIVE ORGANISM	DISEASE	DRUG OF CHOICE
GRAM-POSITIVE COCCI		
Staphylococcus aureus	Abscesses Bacteremia Endocarditis Pneumonia	Penicillin G
	Meningitis Osteomyelitis Cellulitis	A penicillinase-resistant penicillin
Streptococcus pyogenes	Pharyngitis Scarlet fever Otitis media, sinusitis Cellulitis Erysipelas Pneumonia Bacteremia Other systemic infections	Penicillin G Penicillin V
Streptococcus (viridans group)	Endocarditis Bacteremia	Penicillin G
Streptococcus faecalis (*Enterococcus faecalis*)	Endocarditis Urinary tract infection	Penicillin G Ampicillin
	Bacteremia	Penicillin G
Streptococcus bovis	Endocarditis Urinary tract infection Bacteremia	Penicillin G
GRAM-POSITIVE RODS		
Bacillus anthracis	"Malignant pustule" pneumonia	Penicillin G
Corynebacterium diphtheriae	Pharyngitis Laryngotracheitis Pneumonia Other local lesions	Penicillin G
Erysipelothrix rhusiopathiae	Erysipeloid	Penicillin G
Clostridium perfringens	Gas gangrene	Penicillin G
Clostridium tetani	Tetanus	Penicillin G
GRAM-NEGATIVE RODS		
Haemophilus influenzae	Otitis Sinusitis Bronchitis Epiglottitis	Amoxicillin Ampicillin
Enterobacter aerogenes	Urinary tract infection	Cephamandole
Klebsiella pneumoniae	Urinary tract infection Pneumonia	Cephalosporin
Pasteurella multocida	Wound infection Abscesses Bacteremia Meningitis	Penicillin G

lactamases). Penicillinase-producing bacterial strains degrade the β-lactam ring structure of many penicillins, rendering them ineffective in treating such bacterial strains. For example, penicillin G is normally effective against *Neisseria gonorrhoeae*, a Gram-negative coccus that causes gonorrhea, but some penicillinase-producing strains of *N. gonorrhoeae* have now been found, requiring the use of antibiotics other than penicillin G in the treatment of cases of gonorrhea caused by these strains (FIG. 10-16). There may also be other causes for the penicillin resistance of *N. gonorrhoeae.* About 1 in 10^9 cells of *N. gonorrhoeae* are resistant to penicillin; thus high enough antibiotic concentrations must be given for a long enough time to allow the natural body defense mechanisms to eliminate all of the infecting bacteria. Structural modifications of penicillin G, such as occur in methicillin, can render the molecule resistant to penicillinases but may also narrow the spectrum of action, limiting the primary use of such antibiotics to the treatment of infections caused by penicillinase-producing *Staphylococcus* species. There are serious problems when staphylococci become methicillin resistant (MRSA is an acronym for methicillin-resistant *S. aureus*).

Cephalosporins In contrast to the penicillins, the cephalosporins generally have a broad spectrum of action, and many of them, such as cefoxitin and cephalothin, are relatively resistant to penicillinase. As such, the cephalosporins are useful in treating various infections caused by Gram-positive and Gram-negative bacteria. Many physicians are now using broad-spectrum cephalosporins when the use of narrow-range and more specifically directed penicillins would be adequate. Cephalosporins are most prudently used as alternatives to penicillins for patients who are allergic to penicillin and for those pathogens that are not penicillin sensitive. Cephalothin is often the antibiotic of choice for treating severe staphylococcal infections,

CAUSATIVE ORGANISM	DISEASE	DRUG OF CHOICE
Streptococcus (anaerobic species)	Bacteremia Endocarditis Brain and other abscesses Sinusitis	Penicillin G
Streptococcus pneumoniae (pneumococcus)	Pneumonia Meningitis Endocarditis Arthritis Sinusitis Otitis	Penicillin G
Gram-negative Cocci		
Neisseria gonorrhoeae (gonococcus)	Genital infections	Ampicillin or amoxicillin Penicillin G
	Arthritis-dermatitis syndrome	Ampicillin or amoxicillin Penicillin G
Neisseria meningtidis (meningococcus)	Meningitis Bacteremia	Penicillin G
Bacteroides spp.	Oral disease Sinusitis Brain abscess Lung abscess	Penicillin G
Fuscobacterium nucleatum	Ulcerative pharyngitis Lung abscess Genital infections Gingivitis	Penicillin G
Streptobacillus moniliformis	Bacteremia Arthritis Endocarditis Abscesses	Penicillin G
Spirochetes		
Treponema pallidum	Syphilis	Penicillin G
Treponema pertenue	Yaws	Penicillin G
Leptospira	Weil disease Meningitis	Penicillin G
Actinomycetes		
Actinomyces israelii	Cervical, facial, abdominal, thoracic, and other lesions	Penicillin G

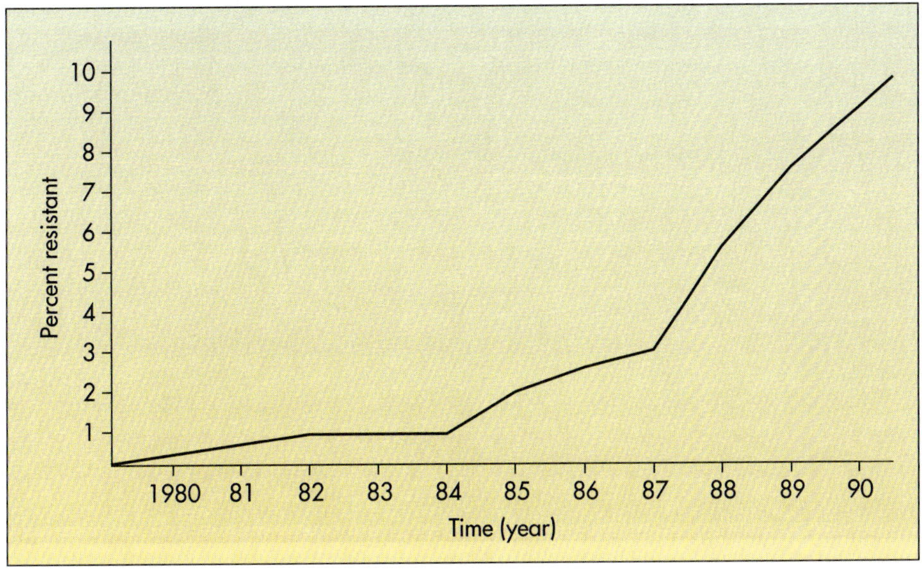

FIG. 10-16 An increasing number of isolates of *Neisseria gonorrhoeae* are resistant to penicillin.

such as endocarditis, to avoid complications in cases where the infecting *Staphylococcus* species produces β-lactamases. Cefamandole, another of the cephalosporins, is widely used in treating pneumonia because it is active against *Haemophilus influenzae, Staphylococcus aureus,* and *Klebsiella pneumoniae,* which are frequently the causative agents of respiratory tract infections resulting in pneumonia. The cephalosporins may also be used in place of penicillins for the prophylaxis of infection by Gram-positive cocci following surgical procedures.

Other Cell Wall Inhibitors In addition to the penicillins and cephalosporins, several other antibiotics inhibit cell-wall synthesis, including **vancomycin, bacitracin,** and **cycloserine.** These antibiotics do not block the enzymes involved in the formation of peptide cross-linkages in the peptidoglycan component of the wall but rather block other reactions involved in the synthesis of the bacterial cell wall. Cycloserine is a structural analogue of D-alanine and can prevent the incorporation of D-alanine into the peptide units of the cell wall. In the presence of D-cycloserine, the subunits that are necessary for cell-wall synthesis cannot be adequately synthesized. Cycloserine is a broad-spectrum antibiotic produced by *Streptomyces orchidaceus.* Its therapeutic use is limited by its toxic reactions involving the central nervous system. Cycloserine is inhibitory for *Mycobacterium tuberculosis* and has been used in conjunction with other antibiotics in the treatment of tuberculosis.

Vancomycin and bacitracin prevent the linkage of the *N*-acetylglucosamine and *N*-acetylmuramic acid moieties that compose the peptidoglycan molecule. Bacitracin is produced by strains of *Bacillus subtilis.* The use of bacitracin is restricted to topical application because this antibiotic causes severe toxicity reactions. Vancomycin is produced by *Streptomyces orientalis* and is especially effective against strains of *S. aureus.* Vancomycin is used to treat only serious infections caused by penicillin-resistant strains of *Staphylococcus* or when the patient exhibits allergic reactions to penicillins and cephalosporins.

Inhibitors of Protein Synthesis

Because proteins are essential for the functioning of living cells, chemicals that inhibit protein synthesis can be used to kill or prevent the growth of microorganisms. Various antimicrobial chemicals inhibit protein synthesis. Those that specifically disrupt protein synthesis at 70S ribosomes are effective antibacterial agents. Many of the commonly used antimicrobics, such as erythromycin and tetracycline, are therapeutically useful antibacterial agents because they specifically target 70S ribosomes, thereby blocking protein synthesis.

Aminoglycosides The **aminoglycoside antibiotics,** which include streptomycin, gentamicin, neomycin, kanamycin, tobramycin, and amikacin, are inhibitors of bacterial protein synthesis (FIG. 10-17). The aminoglycosides are used almost exclusively in the treatment of infections caused by Gram-negative bacteria. These antibiotics are relatively ineffective against anaerobic bacteria and facultative anaerobes growing under anaerobic conditions, and their action against Gram-positive bacteria is also limited. The aminoglycoside antibiotics are produced by actinomycetes. For example, streptomycin is produced by *Streptomyces griseus,* neomycin by *Streptomyces fradiae,* kanamycin by *Streptomyces kanamyceticus,* and gentamicin by *Micromonospora purpurea;* amikacin is a semi-synthetic derivative of kanamycin.

Aminoglycosides bind to the 30S ribosomal subunit of the 70S prokaryotic ribosome, blocking protein synthesis and decreasing the fidelity of translation of the genetic code. They disrupt the normal functioning of the ribosomes by interfering with the formation of initiation complexes, the first step of protein synthesis that occurs during translation. Additionally, aminoglycosides induce misreading of the mRNA molecules, leading to the formation of nonfunctional

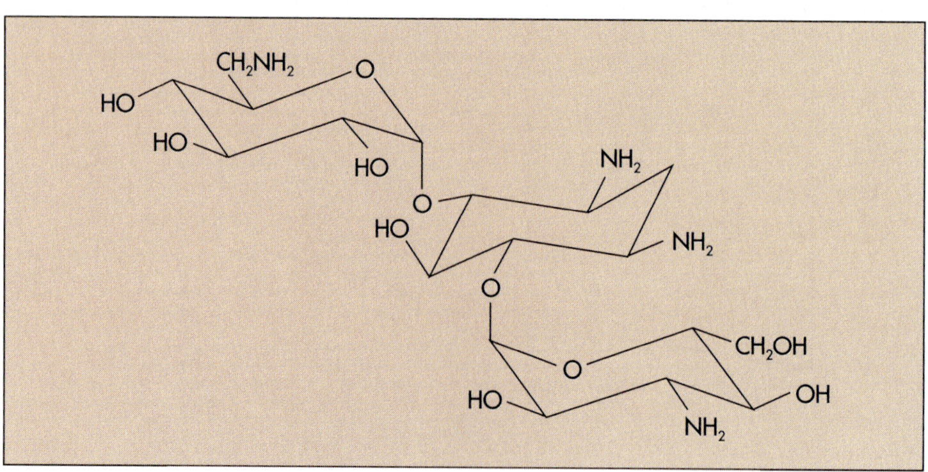

FIG. 10-17 Structure of an aminoglycoside antimicrobic.

enzymes. The interference of protein synthesis results in the death of the bacterium. Various mutations, though, can occur that reduce the effect of misreading some mRNA molecules, in some cases even leading to a dependence on streptomycin-induced misreading of the genetic information.

To be effective, the aminoglycoside antibiotics must be transported across the cytoplasmic membrane. Although sensitive bacteria transport the aminoglycosides across the cytoplasmic membrane, accumulating these antibiotics intracellularly, resistant strains may lack a mechanism for aminoglycoside transport into the cell. Resistant strains may also produce enzymes that degrade or transform the aminoglycoside molecules. For example, various enzymes associated with the plasma membranes of some bacterial strains can adenylate, acetylate, or phosphorylate aminoglycoside antibiotics. Also, mutations can occur that alter the site at which the aminoglycosides normally bind to the bacterial ribosomes. Some *Pseudomonas aeruginosa* strains, for example, possess ribosomes to which streptomycin is unable to bind.

The aminoglycosides are useful in treating various diseases (Table 10-13). Because of its serious side effect on the eighth cranial nerve that can cause deafness with prolonged usage, streptomycin is used in the treatment of only a limited number of bacterial infections. It is sometimes used in the treatment of brucellosis, tularemia, endocarditis, plague, and tuberculosis. Gentamicin is effective in treating urinary tract infections, pneumonia, and meningitis. Gentamicin is, however, extremely toxic and thus is used only in severe infections that may prove lethal if unchecked, particularly when the infecting bacteria are not sufficiently sensitive to other, less toxic, antibiotics. Tobramycin has properties similar to those of gentamicin, but *P. aeruginosa* is particularly sensitive to tobramycin. Thus, this antibiotic is sometimes used for the treatment of pneumonia and other infections caused by *Pseudomonas* species. Neomycin, which is active against many Gram-negative bacteria, is primarily used in topical application for various infections of the skin and mucous membranes. Kanamycin, a narrow-spectrum antibiotic, is frequently used by pediatricians for infections due to *Klebsiella, Enterobacter, Proteus,* and *E. coli.* Amikacin, which has the broadest spectrum of activity of the aminoglycosides, is the antibiotic of choice for treating serious infections caused by Gram-negative infections acquired in hospitals because such infections are often due to bacterial strains that are resistant to multiple antibiotics, including other aminoglycosides.

Other Protein Synthesis Inhibitors In addition to the aminoglycoside antibiotics, several other antibiotics inhibit bacterial protein synthesis. These antibiotics include the tetracyclines, chloramphenicol, erythromycin, lincomycin, clindamycin, and spectinomycin. Some recommended therapeutic uses of these antibiotics are shown in Table 10-14, p. 372. Unlike the aminoglycoside antibiotics, which are bactericidal, these inhibitors of bacterial protein synthesis are generally bacteriostatic.

TABLE 10-13 Some Diseases and Their Causative Organisms for Which Aminoglycoside Antibiotics Are Recommended

CAUSATIVE ORGANISM	DISEASE	DRUG OF CHOICE
Enterobacter aerogenes	Urinary tract; other infections	Gentamicin; tobramycin
Proteus	Urinary tract; other infections	Gentamicin; tobramycin
Pseudomonas aeruginosa	Bacteremia	Gentamicin; tobramycin
Acinetobacter	Various nosocomial infections; bacteremia	Gentamicin
Yersinia pestis	Plague	Streptomycin ± tetracycline
Serratia	Various nosocomial and opportunistic infections	Gentamicin
Mycobacterium tuberculosis	Tuberculosis	Streptomycin + other antibiotics

The **tetracyclines** bind specifically to the 30S ribosomal subunit, apparently blocking the receptor site for the attachment of aminoacyl tRNA to the mRNA ribosome complex and thus preventing the addition of amino acids to a growing peptide chain. The sensitivity to tetracyclines depends on the transport of the tetracycline molecules across the cytoplasmic membrane. Some tetracyclines, such as doxycycline, appear to pass directly across the membrane; others enter the cell only by active transport. Resistance to tetracyclines develops because of the movement of a transposon between a plasmid and the bacterial chromosome, and involves an alteration of the mechanisms of membrane transport of the tetracycline molecules.

There are various tetracycline antibiotics. For example, chlortetracycline (aureomycin) is produced by *S. aureofaciens,* oxytetracycline by *S. rimosus,* and demeclocycline by *S. aereofaciens;* methacycline, doxyclycline, minocycline, and tetracycline are all semi-synthetic derivatives. The tetracyclines are effective against various pathogenic bacteria, including rickettsia and chlamydia species. Tetracylines, for example, are used therapeutically in treating the rickettsial infections of Rocky Mountain spotted fever, typhus fever, and Q fever and the chlamydial diseases of lymphogranuloma venereum, psittacosis, inclusion conjunctivitis, and trachoma. Tetracyclines are also useful in treating various other bacterial infections, includ-

TABLE 10-14 Some Therapeutic Uses of Tetracyclines, Chloramphenicol, Erythromycin, and Clindamycin

CAUSATIVE ORGANISM	DISEASE	DRUG OF CHOICE
GRAM-NEGATIVE RODS		
Salmonella	Typhoid fever	Chloramphenicol
	Paratyphoid fever	
	Bacteremia	
Haemophilus influenzae	Pneumonia	Chloramphenicol
	Meningitis	
Haemophilus ducreyi	Chancroid	A tetracycline
Brucella	Brucellosis	A tetracycline ± streptomycin
Vibrio cholerae	Cholera	A tetracycline
Flavobacterium meningosepticium	Meningitis	Erythromycin
Pseudomonas mallei	Glanders	Streptomycin + a tetracycline
Pseudomonas pseudomallei	Melioidosis	A tetracycline ± chloramphenicol
Campylobacter fetus	Enteritis	No treatment or erythromycin
Bacterioides fragilis	Brain abscess	Chloramphenicol
	Lung abscess	Clindamycin
	Intra-abdominal abscess	
	Bacteremia	
	Endocarditis	
Legionella pneumophila	Legionnaire's disease	Erythromycin
SPIROCHETES		
Borrelia recurrentis	Relapsing fever	A tetracycline
MISCELLANEOUS AGENTS		
Mycoplasma pneumoniae	Atypical pneumonia	Erythromycin
Rickettsia	Typhus fever	Chloramphenicol
	Murine typhus	A tetracycline
	Brill disease	
	Rocky Mountain spotted fever	
Chlamydia trachomatis	Trachoma	A sulfonamide + a tetracycline
	Inclusion conjunctivitis	A tetracycline
	Nonspecific urethritis	A tetracycline

ing pneumonia caused by *Mycoplasma pneumoniae,* brucellosis, tularemia, and cholera.

Chloramphenicol acts primarily by binding to the 50S ribosomal subunit, preventing the binding of tRNA molecules to the aminoacyl and peptidyl binding sites of the ribosome. Consequently, peptide bonds are not formed when chloramphenicol is present in association with the bacterial ribosome. It is used in the laboratory as a specific inhibitor of protein synthesis. Chloramphenicol, which is produced by *Streptomyces venezuelae,* is a fairly broad-spectrum antibiotic active against many species of Gram-negative bacteria. Resistance to chloramphenicol is generally associated with the presence of an R plasmid that codes for enzymes able to transform the chloramphenicol molecule. The production of an acetyl transferase enzyme can inactivate the chloramphenicol molecule because acetylated derivatives of chloramphenicol do not bind to bacterial ribosomes. This appears to be the main mechanism by which resistance to chloramphenicol occurs. Chloramphenicol has some toxic effects, including aplastic anemia, that limit its therapeutic uses to those where the benefits outweigh the dangers associated with toxic reactions. Chloramphenicol is used for treating typhoid fever, as well as various other infections caused by *Salmonella* species; it is also effective against anaerobic pathogens and can be used in treating diseases such as brain abscesses normally caused by anaerobic bacteria.

Erythromycin acts by binding to 50S ribosomal subunits, blocking protein synthesis. Erythromycin, produced by *Streptomyces erythreus,* is a macrolide antibiotic, so named because it contains a multimembered lactone ring attached to deoxy sugar moieties that is red. This antibiotic is most effective against Gram-positive cocci, such as *Streptococcus pyogenes.* Erythromycin is not active against most aerobic Gram-negative rods but does exhibit antibacterial activity against some Gram-negative organisms such as *Pasteurella multocida, Bordetella pertussis,* and *Legionella pneumophila.* Therapeutically, erythromycin is recommended for the treatment of Legionnaire's disease and is also effective in treating diphtheria, whooping cough, and the type of pneumonia caused by *Mycoplasma pneumoniae.* Erythromycin may also be used as an alternative to penicillin in treating staphylococcal infections, streptococcal infections, tetanus, syphilis, and gonorrhea.

Lincomycin and clindamycin bind to the 50S ribosomal subunit, blocking protein synthesis. Lincomycin is produced by *Streptomyces lincolnensis,* and clindamycin is a semi-synthetic derivative of lincomycin. The use of these antibiotics is restricted by their side effects, such as severe diarrhea. Clindamycin is particularly effective against Gram-positive bacteria, including anaerobes, and in the treatment of infections due to *Bacteroides* and *Fusobacterium* species.

Several other antibiotics that inhibit protein synthesis are not useful in treating bacterial infections because they inhibit protein synthesis in mammalian cells to the same extent as in bacterial cells. If the mode of action of these antibiotics is not specific for bacteria, they are not therapeutic antibacterial agents. For example, puromycin is an analogue of tRNA molecules and can compete with them in binding to ribosomes. The mode of action of this antibiotic does not distinguish between inhibiting eukaryotic and prokaryotic protein synthesis. Similarly, dactinomycin (actinomycin D) blocks protein synthesis in both bacterial and eukaryotic cells; this antibiotic binds to double-stranded DNA, blocking transcription of the genetic information to form an mRNA molecule. Although not useful in treating bacterial infections, dactinomycin has a therapeutic role in treating some malignancies when it is desirable to block the rapid division of cancer cells.

Rifampin, a semi-synthetic derivative of rifamycin B, also blocks protein synthesis at the level of transcription. Rifampin inhibits DNA-dependent RNA polymerase enzymes and thus can block transcription. This antibiotic is more effective against bacterial RNA polymerases than mammalian RNA polymerases and therefore can be used therapeutically in treating some bacterial diseases. Rifampin is used in combination with other antibiotics in the treatment of mycobacterial diseases, such as tuberculosis.

Inhibitors of Membrane Function

The cytoplasmic membrane is the site of action of some bacterial agents. The polymyxins, such as polymyxin B, interact with the cytoplasmic membrane, causing changes in the structure of the bacterial cytoplasmic membrane and leakage of cell contents (FIG. 10-18). Polymyxin B is bactericidal, and its effectiveness is restricted to Gram-negative bacteria.

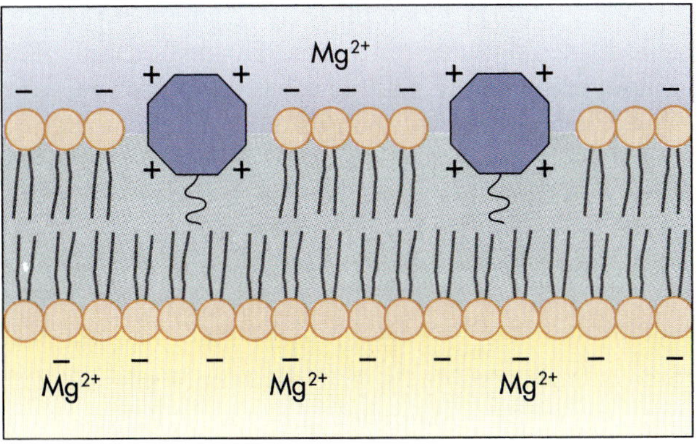

FIG. 10-18 Polymyxin B disrupts the cytoplasmic membrane, causing leakage and cell death.

The action of polymyxin B is related to the phospholipid content of the cell wall–cytoplasmic membrane complex. Sensitive bacteria take up more polymyxin B than resistant strains. The principal use of polymyxin B and colistin (polymyxin E) is in the treatment of infections caused by *Pseudomonas* species and other Gram-negative bacteria that are resistant to penicillins and the aminoglycoside antibiotics. Both polymyxin B and colistin are useful in treating severe urinary tract infections caused by Gram-negative bacteria that are resistant to other antibiotics.

DNA Inhibitors

Some bacterial agents act by blocking normal DNA replication. In particular, the **quinolones** interfere with DNA gyrase, preventing the establishment of a replication fork and the replication of DNA needed for cell multiplication (FIG. 10-19). Although DNA synthesis is blocked, transcription and translation

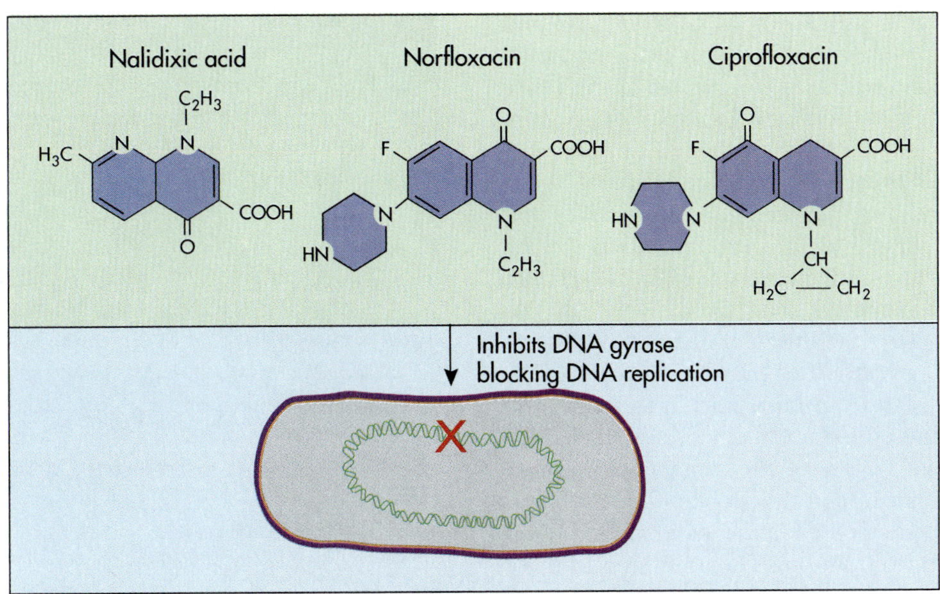

FIG. 10-19 Quinolones inhibit DNA gyrase, blocking bacterial cell reproduction.

(protein synthesis) can still occur. Bacteria exposed to quinolones elongate rather than divide normally. The quinolones include nalidixic acid, ciprofloxacin, norfloxacin, amifloxacin, and enoxacin. These antimicrobics are effective against a broad range of Gram-positive and Gram-negative bacteria, including some—such as mycobacteria—that are resistant to many other compounds.

Inhibitors with Other Modes of Action

Sulfonamides, sulfones, and para-aminosalicylic acid are structural analogues of the vitamin para-aminobenzoic acid, which makes them useful antibacterial agents. A cell mistakenly using an analogue, such as sulfonamide, in place of the normal substance, para-aminobenzoic acid in this case, results in the formation of molecules that are unable to perform their essential metabolic functions; in this case, there is a failure of critical coenzyme functions. Folic acid is an essential coenzyme composed in part of para-aminobenzoic acid. Mammalian cells are unable to synthesize folic acid; they require an intake of folic acid as part of their diet and cellular uptake via an active transport system. Bacterial cells, in contrast, normally synthesize their required folic acid and are unable to transport it across their cytoplasmic membranes. The analogues of para-aminobenzoic acid are effective competitors with the natural substrate for the enzymes involved in the synthesis of folic acid and, as such, inhibit the formation of this required coenzyme, causing a bacteriostatic effect. The sulfones are useful in treating leprosy. The use of sulfonamides and para-aminosalicylic acid has declined as a result of the development of resistant strains and of more effective antibiotics with less toxic side effects.

Trimethoprim is an inhibitor of dihydrofolate reductase, especially in bacteria. Dihydrofolic acid is a coenzyme required for 1-carbon transfers, such as those that occur in the synthesis of thymidine and purines. Trimethoprim is effective in blocking bacterial growth by preventing the formation of the active form of the required coenzyme. Its effectiveness is enhanced when coupled with sulfamethoxazole. Trimethoprim is a broad-spectrum antibacterial agent and is effective in the treatment of many urinary and intestinal tract infections. It is used primarily for the treatment of urinary infections due to *E. coli, Proteus, Klebsiella,* and *Enterobacter.*

In addition to the use of trimethoprim-sulfamethoxazole, several other compounds are used as antiseptics in treating urinary tract infections. The term *antiseptic* is used to indicate that these substances actually wash the surface of the urinary tract. These compounds, which inhibit the growth of many bacterial species, include methenamine, nalidixic acid, oxolinic acid, and nitrofurantoin. The usefulness of these drugs, though, depends on the fact that they are concentrated in the urinary tract tissues and thus can act as antiseptics at this location. Nitrofurantoin inhibits several bacterial enzymes but its mode of action is unknown. It is used only in limited cases because it is generally not as effective as other antibiotics, including sulfanomides and nalidixic acid.

Because isoniazid is not particularly effective against *Mycobacterium tuberculosis* when used alone, it is generally used in association with other antibiotics in treating tuberculosis. The specific mechanism of isoniazid is not known, but its primary action appears to involve the inhibition of mycolic acid biosynthesis. Mycolic acids are unique components of the cell walls of mycobacteria, and blockage of the biosynthesis of these compounds could specifically inhibit mycobacteria.

ANTIFUNGAL ANTIMICROBICS

There are sufficient differences between a fungal cell and a human cell so that some therapeutically useful compounds with antifungal activity have been discovered (Table 10-15). Polyene antibiotics act by altering the permeability properties of the cytoplasmic membrane, leading to the death of the affected cells. Interactions of polyenes with the sterols in the cytoplasmic membranes of eukaryotic cells appear to form channels or pores in the membrane, allowing leakage of small molecules. Differences in the sensitivity of various organisms are determined by the concentrations of sterols in the membrane. The polyene antibiotics, amphotericin B, and nystatin are used in treating various fungal diseases. Because mammalian cells, like fungi, contain sterols in their cytoplasmic membranes, it is not surprising that polyene antibiotics also cause

TABLE 10-15 Some Therapeutic Uses of Antifungal Agents

CAUSATIVE ORGANISM	DISEASE	DRUG OF CHOICE
Candida albicans	Skin and superficial mucous membrane lesions	Amphotericin B Nystatin
Cryptococcus neoformans	Meningitis	Amphotericin B + flucytosine
Candida albicans	Pneumonia	Amphotericin B
Aspergillus	Meningitis	
Mucor	Skin lesions	
Histoplasma capsulatum	Lung lesions Histoplasmosis	Amphotericin B
Coccidioides immitis	Coccidiomycosis	Amphotericin B
Blastomyces dermatitidis	Blastomycosis	Amphotericin B

alterations in the membrane permeability of mammalian cells and toxicity to mammalian tissue, as well as the death of fungal pathogens. Amphotericin B has a greater affinity for ergosterol, the major sterol of fungal membranes, than for cholesterol of human cells. This accounts for the therapeutic use of this drug.

Amphotericin B, which is produced by *Streptomyces nodosus* is a polyene antibiotic with a relatively broad spectrum of activity. It is the most effective therapeutic agent for treating systemic infections due to yeast and fungi. The potential toxic side effects of amphotericin B usage, however, such as kidney damage, require careful supervision of its administration. Patients requiring amphotericin B must be hospitalized so that the initial reaction to the therapy can be carefully supervised. Patients who receive amphotericin B almost always exhibit some toxic side effects, but without this drug, systemic fungal infections are almost invariably fatal. Amphotericin B is used in the treatment of cryptococcosis, histoplasmosis, coccidioidomycosis, blastomycosis, sporotrichosis, and candidiasis.

Imidazole derivatives such as miconazole and clotrimazole have a broad spectrum of antifungal activities and are used in the topical treatment of superficial mycotic infections. These two antimicrobial agents appear to alter membrane permeability, leading to the inhibition or death of selected fungal species.

Flucytosine, a fluorinated pyrimidine, is also effective in treating systemic fungal infections. Flucytosine is less effective, but also less toxic, than amphotericin B and is primarily used in combination with it. Within fungal cells, flucytosine is converted to fluorouracil and is further metabolized to form an inhibitor of thymidylate synthetase, causing an inhibition of normal nucleic acid synthesis. Mammalian cells do not convert as much flucytosine to fluorouracil as do fungal cells, accounting for the selective toxicity of this antifungal agent.

Griseofulvin is another antibiotic that is effective against some fungal infections. This antibiotic is produced by *Penicillium griseofulvum* and causes a disruption of mitotic spindles, inhibiting fungal mitosis. Griseofulvin is used in the treatment of fungal diseases of the skin, hair, and nails caused by various species of dermatophytic fungi, like *Microsporum, Epidermophyton,* and *Trichophyton.* These dermatophytes concentrate griseofulvin by an active uptake process, and their sensitivity is correlated directly with their ability to concentrate the antibiotic.

ANTIPROTOZOAN ANTIMICROBICS

Treatment of human protozoan diseases with antimicrobial agents presents a special problem because many of the pathogenic protozoa exhibit a complex life cycle, often including stages that develop within mammalian cells. Different antimicrobial agents are generally needed for use against different forms of the same pathogenic protozoan, depending on the stage of the life cycle and the involved tissues. For example, the protozoan species of the genus *Plasmodium* that cause malaria exhibit complex life cycles, part of which occur in the liver and blood of human beings. The erythrocytic stage of the *Plasmodium* life cycle that occurs within human blood cells is the most sensitive to antimalarial drugs. The life stages that occur within the liver are difficult to treat, and the sporozoites injected into the bloodstream by mosquitoes are not affected by antimalarial drugs. The antimalarials effective against the erythrocytic forms of the protozoan include chloroquine and amodiaquine, neither of which is effective against the stages of the *Plasmodium* that occur in the liver. These antimalarial agents appear to interfere with DNA replication. The effect of these drugs is a rapid **schizontocidal action,** that is, the rapid interruption of schizogony or multiple division, the reproductive phase that occurs within red blood cells. The sensitivity of malarial protozoa to these drugs depends on the active transport of these compounds into the protozoa and their selective accumulation intracellularly.

Chloroguanide is also used in the suppression of malaria. This drug is transformed within the body to a triazine derivative that inhibits the enzyme dihydrofolate reductase and thus interferes with the essential metabolic reactions involving this coenzyme, which are required for the proliferation of the malaria-causing protozoa. Chloroguanide is sometimes used concurrently with sulfonamide compounds that also interfere with folate metabolism. It binds more strongly to the plasmodial enzyme than to the comparable mammalian dihydrofolate reductase, accounting for its selective inhibition. In addition to affecting the schizont stage, chloroguanide influences the sterilization of gametocytes. Because resistance to the synthetic antimalarial drugs is increasing, quinine, one of the early drugs used for the treatment of malaria, is once again being used.

For the radical cure of malaria, that is, the eradication of both the erythrocytic and liver stages of the protozoan, primaquine is normally used. This drug is used in conjunction with chloroquine and chloroguanide. The precise mode of action of primaquine has not been elucidated. Because of its toxic side effects, it is primarily used in the treatment of relapsing malarial infections. Pyrimethamine, which also inhibits folic acid metabolism, has also been used in the treatment of malaria. Many *Plasmodium* strains, however, have developed resistance to this drug, limiting its usefulness in treating malaria.

Several other drugs are used in the treatment of various other protozoan infections (Table 10-16). As

TABLE 10-16 Some Drugs Used in the Treatment of Diseases Caused by Protozoan Pathogens

INFECTING ORGANISM DISEASE	DRUG OF CHOICE
Entamoeba histolytica	Diiodohydroxyquin
Asymptomatic cyst passer	
Mild intestinal disease	Metronidazole
Severe intestinal disease	Metronidazole
Hepatic abscess	Metronidazole
Giardia lamblia (giardiasis)	Quinacrine hydrochloride
Balantidium coli (balantidiasis)	Oxytetracycline
Trichomonas vaginalis (vaginitis)	Metronidazole
Pneumocystis carinii (pneumocystis pneumonia)	Trimethoprim-sulfamethoxazole
Toxoplasma gondii (toxoplasmosis)	Pyrimethamine plus trisulfapyrimidines
Leishmania donovania (kala azar, visceral leishmanisasis)	Sodium stibogluconate
Leishmania tropica (oriental sore, cutaneous leishmaniasis)	Sodium stibogluconate
Leishmania braziliensis (American mucocutaneous leishmaniasis)	Sodium stibogluconate
Trypanosoma gambiense (African trypanosomiasis)	Pentamidine
Trypanosoma rhodesiense (African trypanosomiasis)	Suramin
T. gambiense or *T. rhodesiense* in late disease with central nervous system involvement	Malarsoprol
Trypanosoma cruzi (South American trypanosomiasis; Chagas disease)	Nifurtimox

with malaria, the life cycle of the particular protozoan determines which agents will be effective in controlling the infection. Only a few of these antiprotozoan agents will be discussed here. Quinacrine hydrochloride is used to treat *Giardia lamblia,* a protozoan disease spread through contaminated water that has become a major problem in the United States. Metronidazole is also used in the treatment of *Giardia* infections, as well as in cases of dysentery caused by the protozoan *Entamoeba histolytica.* Metronidazole interferes with hydrogen transfer reactions, specifically inhibiting the growth of anaerobic microorganisms, including anaerobic protozoa. Pentamidine and related diamidine compounds are useful in treating infections by members of the protozoan genus *Trypanosoma.* Compounds of this type interfere with DNA metabolism.

Melarsoprol is an arsenical (an arsenic-containing compound) that is useful in treating some stages of human trypanosomiasis. It penetrates into cerebrospinal fluid. Arsenicals react with the sulfhydryl groups of proteins, inactivating large numbers of enzymes. It appears that mammalian cells can metabolize these compounds to nontoxic forms more rapidly than protozoan cells, accounting for the selective toxicity of melarsoprol to trypanosome protozoans. Sodium stibogluconate, an antimony-containing compound, is useful in treating diseases caused by members of the protozoan genus *Leishmania.* Antimony compounds of this type inhibit the enzyme phosphofructokinase in some life history stages of the leishmanias, accounting for its inhibitory effects. Other antiprotozoan agents useful in the chemotherapy of protozoan diseases include suramin, a nonmetallic compound that inhibits a variety of enzymes, and nifurtimox, which is effective against *Trypanosoma cruzi,* the causative organism of Chagas disease.

ANTIVIRAL ANTIMICROBICS

Relatively few antimicrobics are useful as antiviral agents (Table 10-17). Viruses replicate as obligate parasites within host cells and it is difficult to distinguish a virally-infected cell from a non-infected cell. Treatment that results in killing of virally-infected cells most likely will also kill healthy cells, resulting in the death of the host. The few antiviral antimicrobics developed thus far take advantage of distinguishing characteristics of specific viruses that allow them to be selectively inhibited without damaging host cells.

Amantadine hydrochloride (SYMMETREL) has been effective in the treatment of Influenza A virus. It is used as a prophylactic treatment for some high risk individuals such as the elderly or persons with little natural defenses. This drug is not effective in preventing infections caused by Influenza B virus or Influenza C virus. The antiviral activity of this drug is not clearly understood but it is believed to prevent the release of infectious viral nucleic acid into the host cell, that is, it blocks viral uncoating. This is a unique mode of action for an antiviral drug.

TABLE 10-17 Some Antiviral Agents and Their Therapeutic Uses

CAUSATIVE ORGANISM	DISEASE	DRUG OF CHOICE
Herpes simplex virus	Keratoconjunctivitis	Acyclovir, Vidarabine
	Encephalitis	Acyclovir
	Cold sores	Acyclovir
	Genital herpes	Acyclovir
Varicella-zoster virus	Shingles	Acyclovir
	Chickenpox	Acyclovir
Influenza virus A	Influenza	Amantadine
HIV	AIDS	Zidovudine Didanosine Zalcitabine

Vidarabine was originally developed for the treatment of leukemia but has proven to be more effective in treating herpes simplex virus encephalitis and keratoconjuntivitis. Vidarabine (Vira-A) is an adenine arabinoside, which is rapidly deaminated into arabinosylhypoxanthine after injection. Arabinosylhypoxanthine is further converted in mammalian cells into nucleotides that inhibit herpes simplex virus and varicella-zoster virus (herpes zoster) DNA polymerase. The selectivity of vidarabine is due to its inhibition of viral DNA replication to a greater extent than mammalian DNA synthesis.

Acyclovir (9-[2-hydroxyethoxymethyl]guanine; Zovirax) is the best antiherpes drug so far discovered. It is inhibitory to herpes simplex viruses, varicella-zoster virus, Epstein-Barr virus, and cytomegalovirus. Acyclovir is a nucleoside analogue that is converted *in vivo* to an acyclovir triphosphate. This triphosphate inhibits herpes simplex viral DNA polymerase, thus blocking viral DNA replication (FIG. 10-20). The activation of acyclovir is brought about by a viral-directed thymidine kinase enzyme that converts this compound to an acycloguanosine monophosphate, which is subsequently converted to the inhibitory acycloguanosine di- and triphosphates. In an uninfected cell, there is only very limited conversion of acyclovir to the phosphorylated acylguanosines. Because an enzyme coded for by the herpes virus is required to activate acyclovir, this compound exhibits selective antiviral activity, making it therapeutically valuable.

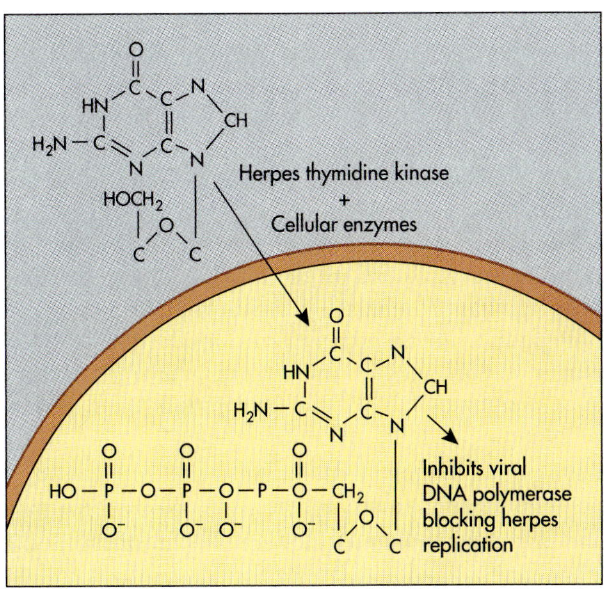

FIG. 10-20 Acyclovir is phosphorylated in cells infected with herpes simplex viruses. This activates the drug by forming compounds that inhibit viral DNA polymerase and herpes replication.

Azidothymidine (AZT) (also called zidovudine and Retrovir), dideoxyinosine (ddI) (also called didanosine and VIDEX), and dideoxycytidine (ddC) (also called zalcitabine and HIVID) are effective in the treatment of AIDS (FIG. 10-21). HIV, which causes AIDS, is a retrovirus and contains reverse transcriptase

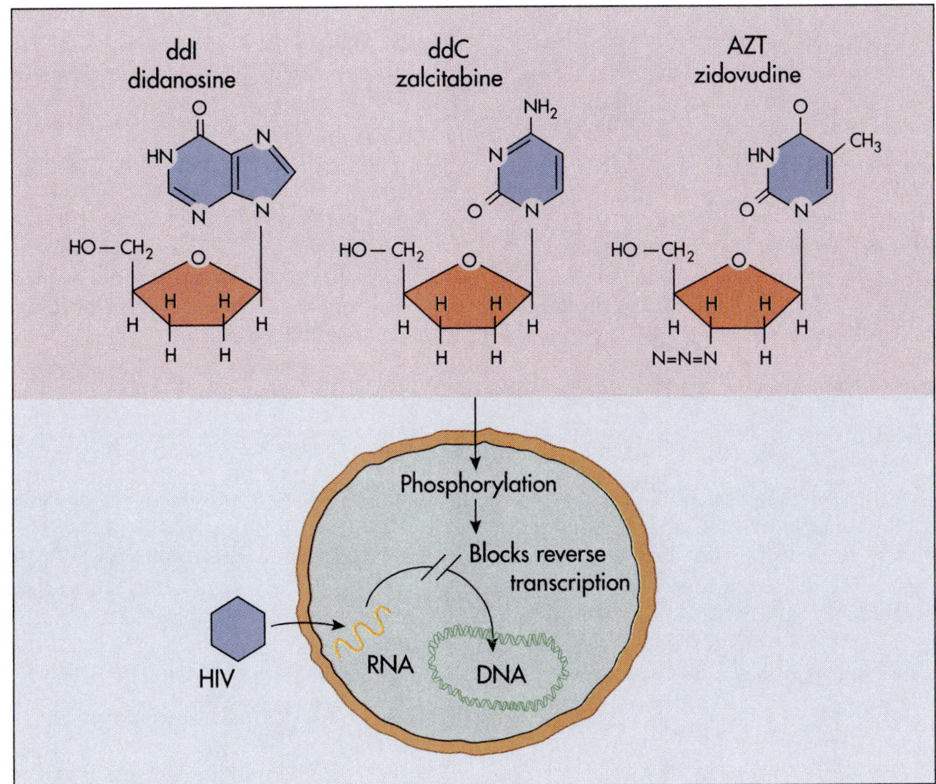

FIG. 10-21 DNA nucleotide analogs block reverse transcription by retroviruses.

that is needed for the successful replication of the virus. AZT, ddI, and ddC are DNA nucleotide analogs that prevent the formation of viral-directed DNA by retroviruses. AZT is converted by cellular thymidine kinase into azidothymidine monophosphate. Additional cellular enzymes convert the monophosphate into the di- and triphosphate forms. Azidothymidine triphosphate is an analogue of the DNA base thymidine. However, it has an azide group in the 3′-OH position that prevents the formation of a bond to the 5′-P position of an adjacent nucleotide during DNA synthesis. AZT inhibits the viral reverse transcriptase and terminates DNA chain elongation prematurely. ddI and ddC substitute for several nucleotides and these dideoxynucleotides also act as chain terminators. They prevent reverse transcription and thereby block viral replication. These three antiviral agents also interfere with normal human cell DNA replication. Furthermore, they have serious side effects with prolonged usage. Because of their side effects and conflicting results in clinical trials, there is controversy over when best to initiate the use of these drugs in treating HIV-infected individuals. AZT, ddI, and ddC are effective in limiting viral replication and delaying the onset of AIDS, but they are not cures for this deadly disease.

CHAPTER REVIEW

STUDY QUESTIONS

1. How is temperature used to control microbial growth?
2. Discuss the differences between pasteurization and heat sterilization.
3. Why is it necessary to refrigerate milk that has been pasteurized?
4. What is a food preservative? Discuss how and why food preservatives are used.
5. Discuss the differences between germicides, antiseptics, and antibiotics.
6. Discuss the differences between bactericidal and bacteriostatic agents, including why one or the other might be used?
7. Discuss how ionizing radiation is employed to control microbial growth.
8. Discuss the use of ionizing radiation as a food preservation method, giving the pros and cons.
9. Discuss the differences between broad and narrow spectrum antimicrobics.
10. Why is it essential to perform antimicrobial susceptibility testing on pathogenic isolates?
11. How does a physician select an antibiotic for treating an infectious disease? Describe several approaches used to determine the sensitivity of a pathogen to antibiotics. Is antimicrobial sensitivity the sole criterion for selecting an antibiotic? Discuss.
12. What is an MIC? Why is this an increasingly common test in clinical microbiology laboratories?
13. Is penicillin useful in treating the common cold? Explain.
14. Why is it easier to find antibacterial agents than to discover useful antifungal agents?
15. Why is it so difficult to find antimicrobial agents for treating viral diseases?
16. What antibiotics should a physician prescribe for each of the following conditions?
    a. Urinary tract infection
    b. Upper respiratory tract bacterial infection
    c. Fungal infection of the vaginal tract
    d. Herpes encephalitis
    e. Malaria
17. Discuss the mode of action of penicillin.
18. Why is penicillin ineffective against bacteria that produce β-lactamases?
19. Why is an inhibitor of transcription not useful in treating bacterial infections of humans?
20. Discuss the mode of action of streptomycin.
21. Discuss the mode of action of acyclovir.
22. Explain how information from a clinical laboratory helps in the selection of an appropriate antibiotic for treating a disease?

SITUATIONAL PROBLEMS

1. Opening a Restaurant on a Farm

Given the current economics in agriculture, many farmers are seeking additional sources of income. Some are establishing restaurants. Many such restaurants feature home-grown organic foods. Health conscious people patronize such restaurants, expecting to find tasteful and healthful foods. They expect no problems with foodborne diseases. Assuming you had a farm and wanted to open a restaurant for such a clientele, how would you go about preserving foods grown on your farm so that you could operate the restaurant year round? Make sure that you consider how you would handle eggs and poultry; vegetables such as red tomatoes, yellow tomatoes, lettuce; butter and peanut butter; and various other foods. If you were to can any foods, be specific about the procedures you would use. If you use other preservation methods, describe how they work.

SITUATIONAL PROBLEMS—CONT'D

2. Antimicrobics in Medical Practice

Health practitioners are faced with daily decisions about when to prescribe antimicrobics and which specific antimicrobics to use for particular conditions. Patients seeking physician care expect prescriptions for effective medications. Representatives of pharmaceutical companies seek physicians who will prescribe drugs their companies produce. Often physicians consult the Physician's Desk Reference (PDR) for information on antimicrobial drugs. Suppose you were a physician. What would you prescribe for patients with the following conditions:

a. Common cold
b. Sore throat
c. Ear ache
d. Tuberculosis
e. A deep cut
f. AIDS
g. Pregnancy
h. Typhoid Fever
i. Legionnaire's Disease
j. Appendicitis
k. Pneumonia
l. Influenza
m. Viral gastroenteritis

Consult the PDR as necessary.

Suggested Supplementary Readings

Berdy J (ed.): 1980-1982. *Handbook of Antibiotic Compounds,* CRC Press, Inc., Boca Raton, FL.

Block SS: 1991. *Disinfection, Sterilization and Preservation,* ed. 4, Lea and Febiger, Malvern, PA.

Brown F: 1984. Synthetic viral vaccines, *Annual Review of Microbiology* 38:221-236.

Bryan LE: 1982. *Bacterial Resistance and Susceptibility to Chemotherapeutic Agents,* Cambridge University Press, New York.

Cohen ML and RV Tauxe: 1986. Drug-resistant *Salmonella* in the United States: An epidemiological perspective, *Science* 234:964-969.

Curran JW, WM Morgan, AM Hardy, HW Jaffe, WR Dowdle: 1985. The epidemiology of AIDS: Current status and future prospects, *Science* 229:1352-1357.

Ewing WH: 1985. *Edward's and Ewing's Identification of Enterobacteriaceae,* Elsevier Publishing Co., New York.

Finegold SM and E Baron: 1986. *Diagnostic Microbiology,* C.V. Mosby Co., St. Louis.

Fundenberg HH, DP Sites, JL Caldwell, JV Wells (eds.): 1980. *Basic and Clinical Immunology,* Lange Medical, Los Altos, CA.

Gilman AG, LS Goodman, A Gilman (eds.): 1980. *Goodman and Gilman's Pharmacological Basis of Therapeutics,* Macmillan Publishing Co., Inc., New York.

Glass RI: 1986. New prospects for epidemiological investigations, *Science* 234:951-955.

Hugo WB and AD Russell: 1983. *Pharmaceutical Microbiology,* Blackwell Scientific Publications, Oxford, England.

Kagan BM: 1974. *Antimicrobial Therapy,* W.B. Saunders, Co., Philadelphia.

Koneman EW, SD Allen, VR Dowell Jr, HM Sommers (eds.): 1983. *Color Atlas and Textbook of Diagnostic Microbiology,* J.B. Lippincott Co., Philadelphia.

Lancini G and F Parenti: 1982. *Antibiotics: An Integrated View,* Springer-Verlag, New York.

Lennette EH, A Balows, WJ Hausler Jr, JP Truant (eds.): 1986. *Manual of Clinical Microbiology,* American Society for Microbiology, Washington, D.C.

Lorian V (ed.): 1986. *Antibiotics in Laboratory Medicine,* Williams & Wilkins, Baltimore.

Lynn M and M Solotorovsky (eds.): 1981. *Chemotherapeutic Agents for Bacterial Infections* (Benchmark Papers in Microbiology), Academic Press, New York.

Mandell GL, RG Douglas Jr, JE Bennett: 1985. *Anti-Infective Therapy.* John Wiley & Sons, Inc., New York.

Physician's Desk Reference: Published annually. Medical Economics Co., Oradell, NJ.

Pulverer G and J Jeljaszewicz (eds.): 1985. *Chemotherapy and Immunity,* VCH Publishers, New York.

Ravel R: 1978. *Clinical Laboratory Medicine: Clinical Application of Laboratory Data,* Year Book Medical Publishers, Inc., Chicago.

Smith JR, RJ Laudicina, RD Rufo: 1986. *Learning Guides for the Medical Microbiology Laboratory,* John Wiley & Sons, Inc., New York.

Zuckerman AJ, JE Banatvala, JR Pattison: 1987. *Principles and Practice of Clinical Virology,* John Wiley & Sons, Inc., New York.

EXPLORATORY AND (SOMETIMES) ADVENTUROUS MICROBIOLOGY

Holger W. Jannasch
Woods Hole Oceanographic Institution

Holger Winderkilde Jannasch was born in 1927 in Germany and studied at the University of Göttingen. He has been at the Woods Hole Oceanographic Institute on Cape Cod, Massachusetts, since 1963. Jannasch studies the physiology and ecology of freshwater and marine bacteria, deep water microbiology, and the growth of microorganisms at extreme temperatures and pressures, such as deep sea hydrothermal vents. His studies have greatly advanced our understanding of microbial physiology and the extreme conditions under which some microorganisms grow.

I will never forget that afternoon in January of 1977 when I got a telephone call from our port office's radio operator. It was relayed to me from the mother ship of ALVIN, our Institution's research submersible. Every day our research vessels have to call home from wherever they are to report on their well-being and scientific news if there are any. On this particular day ALVIN had been diving to 2600 m depth at the Galapagos Rift (about 200 miles north of the Galapagos Islands) to find signs of the predicted seawater circulation through the freshly formed oceanic crust and the emission of hot water near tectonic spreading centers.

The geologist, who was the lucky one to be on this dive, landed in the midst of a copious population of invertebrates. When I first spoke to him on the phone I was full of doubts, I must admit, that I heard correctly. Oceanographers knew for a long time that the deep sea floor looks like the Sahara desert: miles and miles of bare sediment with few animals here and there in permanent darkness and near freezing temperatures. This is simply because very little of the organic matter, the animals' food source, produced photosynthetically at the sea surface, reaches the deep sea through the sedimentation of particles. But now I was told about masses of mussels, huge white clams, and tube worms 6 feet long. Since they even brought some of these animals up to the surface, it must have been right. Most surprising was the high biomass of these animals, which clearly could not be living on that limited amount of photosynthetically produced organic matter. What then, if not photosynthesis, would there be to feed those massive populations?

Well, microbiologists know about chemolithoautotrophy, or, in short, chemosynthesis. Instead of using light energy, in chemosynthesis, the inorganic carbon CO_2 is reduced to organic carbon by chemical energy obtained, for instance, from the oxidation of ammonia, hydrogen, or hydrogen sulfide. This was discovered a long time ago, but in the biological carbon cycle, never considered to amount to much in the presence of photosynthesis. Could it be that these deep-sea animals living in permanent darkness developed a life support system based on chemosynthesis?

When I was told that, indeed, hydrogen sulfide was contained in the warm springs in high concentration, I went right back to the lab and wrote a proposal to study the possibility that bacterial chemosynthesis may represent the base of the food chain for the existence of the astounding biomass production at these deep-sea hydrothermal vents, as they became to be called. And, lo and behold, 2 years later (it takes considerable time to get funded for and prepare diving programs with ALVIN) a biology cruise went to the Galapagos Rift. This first expedition began a series of most exciting cruises as new vent sites with many different animal populations were discovered. We are still at it, after almost 15 years, and many new forms of hitherto unknown microorganisms and bacteria/animal interelationships have been observed and described.

The necessary cooperation in such work with colleagues of other disciplines has always attracted me. Beginning as a microbiologist among limnologists, I was fascinated by the metabolic diversity of bacteria that took care of the remineralization of nutrients in the different parts of lakes, oxic, anoxic, acidic, alkaline, etc., and I needed to know the physiography and chemistry of water bodies. Without the physical and chemical oceanographers we would never have found the hydrothermal vents and their new biological world in the deep sea. Learning from these colleagues, geochemistry has been paramount for us in understanding and predicting the extent of microbial life in the extreme corners of our biosphere. During evolution, higher forms of life became limited to just two major metabolic systems: photosynthesis of the green plants and the digestion and respiration of organic carbon by the animals. While higher forms could not exist without the metabolic abilities of the "primitive" microorganisms, the primitive microorganisms themselves could certainly exist without plants and animals. Harvard's paleontologist Stephen Jay Gould said in a lecture on evolution last summer here at Woods Hole that the 3.5-billion-years-old microorganisms will also be the ultimate survivors on this planet. Pasteur said "The microbes have the last word."

But back to the deep-sea hydrothermal vents. It never fails to amaze me how and why this co-existence between the metabolically versatile bacteria and the genetically and developmentally advanced marine invertebrates produced interrelationships that appear to maximize the production of biomass. In fact, the electron donor at the base of this so highly efficient food chain is a poison: H_2S. Furthermore, the inefficient mechanism of feeding by filtering planktonic animals on the quickly diluting bacterial suspensions in the vent plumes is "cleverly" improved by developing various symbiotic systems where the bacteria grow autolithotrophically within certain tissues of the vent invertebrates: clams and tube worms. In turn, these animals provide the microorganisms through a specially adapted blood system with everything they need, especially their source of energy, hydrogen sulfide and oxygen, and CO_2 as their source of carbon. How the microbially produced organic matter gets distributed in the animals is presently being studied in many laboratories.

It is interesting that the detour via deep-sea studies was necessary to discover these novel types of symbioses between chemosynthetic bacteria and marine invertebrates. Since many marine clams are known to occur in anoxic coastal marine sediments, a search for their symbiotic existence with chemosynthetic bacteria was immediately done. Sure enough, there is a clam living profusely in the H_2S-containing shallow sediments of Buzzard's Bay, right near Woods Hole, operating on the same principle. In the meantime, many other invertebrates have been found to make use of this symbiosis: a whole new area of research.

Another novel type of microorganism was found at the deep sea vents. Some time ago, Thomas Brock and, later, Karl O. Stetter discovered so-called hyperthermophilic microorganisms, bacteria that grow at temperatures between 80° and 100° C, at ter-

Continued.

Preparation of the research submersible ALVIN for a deep sea dive.

restrial and shallow marine hot-springs. We were soon also able to isolate many of these "extremophiles" from the deep-sea "hot smokers" where the temperature gradients range from 2° to 360° C, most of them belonging to Woese's new domain "Archaea." Today these isolates have an important role in biotechnology where highly temperature-stable enzymes, mainly polymerases and proteases, are commercially produced.

There are other even more obvious points that appear to be suitable in areas of applied microbiology. The mere observation of tremendous productivity of organic carbon (the copious animal populations on the deep sea floor) from hydrogen sulfide as the main electron donor or source of energy in the presence of free oxygen leads to the logical question: can we use a similar system for getting rid of one of our most bothersome waste materials of all mining industries and major source of acid rain (hydrogen sulfide) and at the same time use it for the production of useful biomass? We began work on this and devised a continuous flow system where bacterial biomass was harvested from a reactor fed with a H_2S/seawater mixture. We demonstrated that the produced biomass could be used for feeding mussels in aquaculture. Also, this well-defined carbohydratious material may be a useful base material for fermentations to alcohols as synfuels or other industrial applications. The oil prices are still too low to interest the government in financing the necessary upscaling of the process.

It is not difficult to see why we are fascinated by this type of microbiology: a healthy and always exciting mix of interdisciplinary activities, and classical and modern microbiological approaches—and, for anything, I wouldn't miss those dives to the deep sea floor.

The research submersible *ALVIN* being lowered over the stern of her mothership, *ATLANTIS II*. *ALVIN* can dive to a depth of 4000 m, commonly for dive durations of 7 to 8 hours. It takes three people down: the pilot and two scientists. It has two manipulators and can take 300 pounds of equipment to the bottom or samples back up to the surface.

PART FIVE

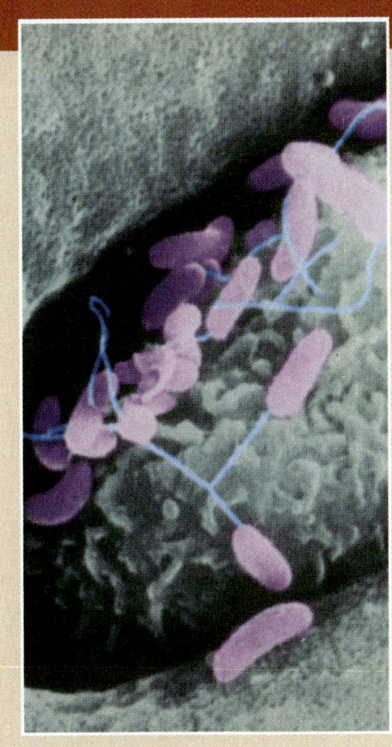

Microorganisms and Human Diseases

CHAPTER 11

Immunology

CHAPTER OUTLINE

The defense mechanisms of the human body that protect us against pathogenic microorganisms are a complex network of interactive overlapping systems. Nonspecific barriers to microbial invasion of the body, which include the skin, phagocytic cells, and various antimicrobial chemicals, form the first line of defense. These barriers block the entry of microorganisms into the body and seek out and destroy microorganisms that enter the body. The nonspecific defenses are augmented by a second line of defenses called the specific immune system. This is a learned response that recognizes specific substances that are foreign to the body, including specific strains and species of pathogens. Failure to recognize and respond to foreign substances can render one susceptible to infectious disease. The specific immune response involves (1) B lymphocytes, which contain the genetic information for producing specific antibodies and maintaining a memory system for recognizing and responding to foreign antigens; and (2) T lymphocytes, including T helper, cytotoxic T, and T suppressor cells, which are effector cells of the immune system that act to kill abnormal human cells. The specific immune response detects and reacts rapidly to antigens that are foreign, thereby protecting the body.

11.1 NONSPECIFIC DEFENSES AGAINST MICROBIAL INFECTIONS

The human body has several nonspecific lines of defense against potentially pathogenic microorganisms. These defenses guard against invasion of the body by many different microorganisms and are not geared to specific pathogenic species. Most nonspecific defenses are innate and offer protection from the moment of birth. The nonspecific defenses include physical, chemical, and cellular elements. Each is important in the overall defense network.

Some defense factors are based on genetic makeup of the individual. For example, individuals with the inherited disease sickle cell anemia are more resistant to malaria. General health and nutrition also defend the body against infection. In general, individuals who are malnourished or have some pre-existing disease condition are more susceptible to infection than a healthy individual. Age also has an effect; the very young and very old have weaker defense systems and are more prone to disease.

Physical Barriers

Intact body surfaces represent the first line of defense against microorganisms. They physically block the entry of pathogens into the body. Preventing microorganisms from entering the body precludes infection and is an effective means of disease prevention.

Skin

Intact skin is impervious to most microorganisms. Most microorganisms are noninvasive and so do not penetrate the skin. This is because the outer surface of the skin layer is composed of *keratin,* which is not readily degraded enzymatically by microorganisms. Keratin is a fibrous and insoluble protein that resists penetration of water. Since the body is frequently exposed to microorganisms in aqueous environments (as aerosols or suspensions in liquids) an impermeable keratinized layer provides a formidable external barrier to microorganisms. Additionally, the outer layer of skin consists predominantly of dead cells that are continuously being sloughed off or shed. This prevents infection by viruses that require live cells for their replication.

The importance of the skin as a protective barrier can readily be seen when breaks in the intact skin occur. Disruption of the intact skin exposes the body to numerous microorganisms that can then establish infections. Wounds disrupt the protective barrier of the skin and allow microorganisms to enter the circulatory system and deep body tissues. This results in infection unless precautionary actions are taken. To avoid entry of bacteria into a wound, the area is cleansed and usually covered with gauze to protect against contamination. Washing and antimicrobial agents are used to lower the probability of infection following wounds and burns. Care is taken in surgical procedures to prevent the entry of microorganisms into exposed tissues.

Mucous Membranes

Many body surfaces are covered with cells that secrete mucus. These linings are called *mucous membranes.* Mucus is secreted by goblet cells and subepithelial glands. The mucus accumulates on the surface of the cells, where it traps microorganisms and prevents them from penetrating into the body. The mucous membranes that line the surfaces of many body tissues are important and effective barriers to invasion by microorganisms.

The respiratory tract, for example, is protected in part against the invasion of pathogenic microorganisms by a mucous membrane lining. Some of the mucus and trapped microorganisms is swept out of the body through the oral and nasal cavities by the wavelike action of the ciliated epithelial cells that make up the lining of much of the respiratory tract. The movement of the cilia establishes an upward wave motion. This system, called the *mucociliary escalator system,* effectively acts as a filter to prevent potential pathogens from penetrating the surface tissues of the respiratory tract.

Sneezing and coughing also may remove many of these microorganisms from the respiratory tract (FIG. 11-1). When provoked, the gag reflex helps remove postnasal drip and mucus swept up by the ciliated ep-

FIG. 11-1 A sneeze showing the dispersion of droplets; aerosols carry microorganisms from the respiratory tract.

ithelium of the bronchi, with its associated microorganisms. Additionally, the swallowing reflex removes most remaining particulates from the respiratory tract, including microorganisms that become attached to mucus, moving the trapped microorganisms out of the respiratory tract and into the digestive tract. The digestive tract also is lined by a mucous membrane that makes it difficult for pathogenic microorganisms to attach to and to penetrate the gastrointestinal tract lining.

Fluid Flow

Some body tissues are protected against accumulations of microorganisms by the movement of fluids across their surfaces. For example, microorganisms that do not adhere to surfaces in the oral cavity are washed into the stomach by the fluid flow of saliva. Tears continuously remove microorganisms from the eye. Urine, which generally is a sterile body fluid, flushes microorganisms from the surfaces of the urinary tract.

Chemical Defenses

Some of the fluids that wash body tissues also contain antimicrobial chemicals. Additionally, blood and lymph contain several chemical factors that defend against microbial infections. These chemicals limit the abilities of microorganisms to infect the body. Antimicrobial chemicals may inhibit the growth of microorganisms or may kill potential pathogens.

Lysozyme

Lysozyme is an enzyme that degrades the cell walls of bacteria. It is found in some body fluids, including saliva, mucus, and colostrum. Lysozyme confers antimicrobial activity on these body fluids. Ova, which are essential for reproduction, are surrounded by lysozyme and bathed in mucus secretions, protecting them from infection. The continuous washing of the eye with tears containing lysozyme generally prevents the growth of microorganisms on the tissues of the eye. In a similar way, swallowing, coughing, and sneezing expose bacteria to body fluids that contain lysozyme, thus reducing the number of potential pathogens.

Acidity

Acids kill or prevent the growth of most microorganisms. Various body tissues are protected by the low pH environment created by acid production. The skin, for example, is bathed by sebaceous secretions that deposit lipids onto the outer surface. The indigenous microorganisms on the surface of the skin can break down these lipids into free fatty acids. This contributes to the acidity of the skin and inhibits the growth of other microorganisms.

The normal vaginal pH in postpubescent and premenopausal women (those producing estrogen) is maintained at about 4. This low pH is generally inhibitory to the growth of most microorganisms. The low vaginal pH is partially due to the presence of *Streptococcus* and *Lactobacillus* species (Döderlein's bacillus, which are nonpathogenic and acid-tolerant bacteria) that produce lactic acid from their fermentation of glycogen. The low pH is generally inhibitory for the growth of pathogens, including the bacterium *Neisseria gonorrhoeae* that causes gonorrhea.

The hydrochloric acid of the stomach provides another chemical barrier that prevents microbial invasion of the body. Most microorganisms entering the digestive tract are unable to tolerate the low pH (normally <2) of the stomach. Thus the number of viable microorganisms is greatly reduced during passage through the stomach. Microorganisms indigenous to the lower intestinal tract protect the host against invasion of pathogens by producing acidic metabolic fermentation products such as lactic acid and acetic acid; the natural microbiota of the gastrointestinal tract form antagonistic relationships with nonindigenous microorganisms. Some microorganisms produce bacteriocins (substances that are toxic to the same or similar species). As a result, most nonindigenous microorganisms entering the intestinal tract are degraded during passage through it or are removed, along with large numbers of indigenous microorganisms, in the passage of fecal material from the body.

Iron-binding Proteins

Some chemicals within the body bind iron, thereby withholding this essential growth element from pathogenic microorganisms. By limiting the amount of available iron, these compounds limit the growth of pathogens. *Lactoferrin* and *transferrin* are examples of such iron-binding compounds. Lactoferrin is present in tears, semen, breast milk, bile, and nasopharyngeal, bronchial, cervical, and intestinal mucosal secretions. Transferrin is present in serum and the intercellular spaces of many tissues and organs. Transferrin transports iron from the small intestine, where the iron is absorbed, to the tissues, where the iron is used.

Since iron is stored intracellularly in a form that is tightly bound, it is not readily available to support microbial growth within the body's tissues. The concentration of free iron in the blood and other tissues is normally less than 10^{-18}M, which is far lower than the 10^{-8}M iron concentration that is required for growth by most microorganisms. Systemic bacterial infections are precluded in large part by the lack of free iron in the blood. Conversely, when the iron supply is abun-

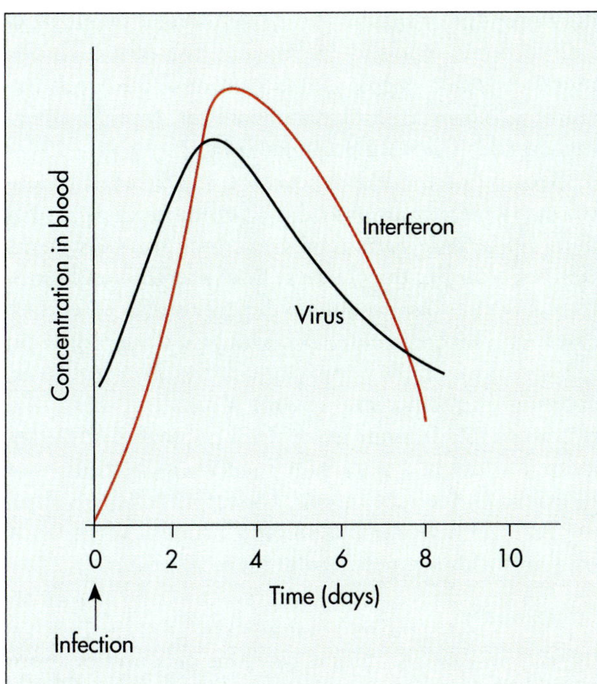

FIG. 11-2 Time course of interferon production after infection with a virus.

dant, infection is more likely; for example, during menstruation there is more free iron in the vaginal tract and during this time a woman is more likely to contract the sexually transmissible disease, gonorrhea.

Interferon

The body is protected in part against viral infections by the production of interferons, which block viral replication by rendering host cells nonpermissive. **Interferons** are a family of inducible glycoproteins produced by eukaryotic cells in response to viral infections and other microbial pathogens that reproduce within host cells. The production of interferon occurs shortly after such infections (FIG. 11-2). Interferon is produced by infected tissue cells (α and β interferons) and by certain lymphocyte blood cells (γ interferon) that are part of the body's immune defense system. These interferons limit the abilities of viruses to replicate within the cells of the body.

Interferons are of relatively low molecular weight and are normally produced only in low concentrations. These glycoproteins are released from infected cells and migrate to uninfected cells, protecting healthy cells from viral infections (FIG. 11-3). Because interferon is produced in very limited quantities, only neighboring cells are immediately protected. Interferons do not block the entry of the virus into a cell, but rather prevent the replication of viral pathogens within protected cells.

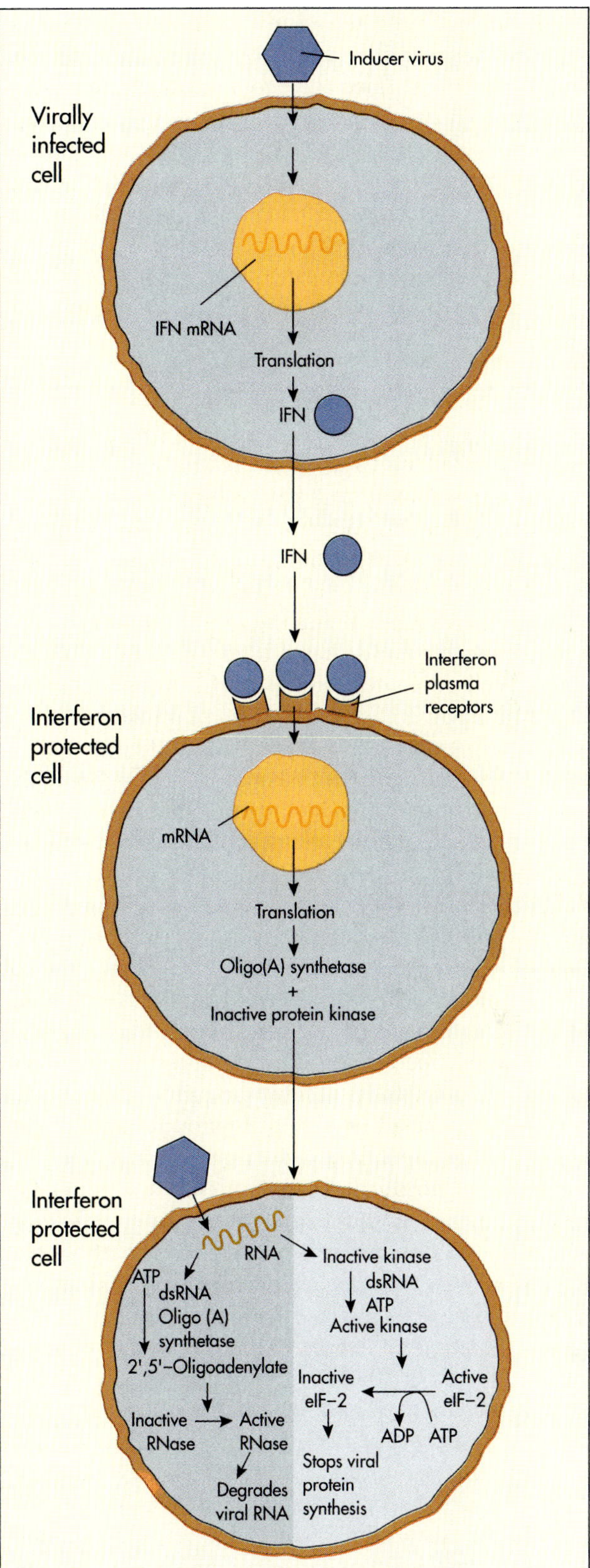

FIG. 11-3 Virally-infected cells release interferon (IFN) that protects neighboring cells from viral infections. The mechanisms of interferon action are complex and result in degradation of viral RNA and blockage of viral protein synthesis.

The action of interferons involves a series of molecular events that induce an antiviral state. Interferons bind to specific surface receptors of uninfected cells, stimulating them to produce at least two enzymes. One of these enzymes (2′,5′-oligoadenylate synthetase) catalyzes the synthesis of an unusual polymer (2′, 5′-oligoadenylate) that activates an intracellular ribonuclease. This ribonuclease cleaves the viral RNA genome, thereby inactivating viral replication. The other enzyme produced in response to interferon is a protein kinase that is activated only in the presence of double-stranded RNA. The activated protein kinase catalyzes the phosphorylation of a factor, eIF2a, that is required for the initiation of protein synthesis. The phosphorylated eIF2a is inactive; therefore protein synthesis ceases, including synthesis of viral proteins.

The synthesis of interferons is regulated at the level of transcription. An infection with a virus induces synthesis of interferon glycoproteins, with double-stranded RNA viruses being the most potent inducers of interferon synthesis. When interferons move to uninfected cells, the synthesis of specific proteins that inhibit translation is derepressed. These translational inhibitory proteins block the translation of viral mRNA without preventing the translation of host cell mRNA molecules. These events include recognition of an interferon-inducing molecule; derepression and synthesis of interferon proteins; modification and secretion of the interferon molecules; interaction of interferon with susceptible cells; activation and synthesis of previously repressed genetic information; and alteration of the cell's metabolism as expressed by some identifiable interferon interaction, such as resistance to viral infection. It should be emphasized, though, that interferons are not direct antiviral substances. They have no direct effect on viruses, and their antiviral action is mediated by cells in which they induce an antiviral state.

Interferon production is considered a nonspecific resistance factor because interferon proteins do not exhibit specificity toward a particular pathogenic virus, which means that interferon produced in response to one virus is also effective in preventing the replication of other viruses. Although interferons are not specific for a species of invading viruses or for other intracellular microbial parasites, they are specific for the host organism that produced them; that is, interferons produced by human cells are effective only in human cells and do not exert a protective effect against intracellular parasites in other animal species. Interferons appear to be an important component of the elaborate integrated defense system against viral infections, and their production has a significant role in preventing and facilitating recovery from viral infections such as the common cold.

Besides protecting against viral infections, interferon acts as a regulator of the complex defense network that protects the body against infections and the development of malignant cells. As such, gamma (γ) interferon is involved in the control of phagocytic blood cells that engulf and kill various pathogens (including bacteria) and abnormal or foreign mammalian cells (including cancer cells).

Because of the importance of interferons in controlling viral infections and the proliferation of malignant cells, their commercial production is being developed with the expectation that interferon administration will prove useful in the treatment of certain diseases. The human genes coding for the production of interferons have been cloned into *Escherichia coli*, creating by genetic engineering a bacterial strain that produces this human protein. Such genetically engineered bacteria can produce sufficient quantities of interferons for therapeutic uses. Interferons produced by genetically engineered bacteria is currently used in various experimental medical protocols.

Complement

Besides interferon, blood contains a family of more than 11 glycoprotein molecules, collectively called **complement,** that play a role in the removal of invading pathogens. Complement is especially important in preventing and limiting bacterial infections. Complement glycoproteins are designated C1, C2, C3, and so forth, with the numbers assigned based on the order of their discovery. As the name implies, complement augments or complements other defenses that protect the body against microbial infections. Complement glycoproteins work together in an autocatalytic cascade fashion so that as one component becomes activated, it in turn activates another complement component. The result of complement activation leads to various nonspecific defense responses in the host.

The nonspecific initiation of the complement system is referred to as the *alternate pathway.* The central activator of this pathway is the complement component C3 (FIG. 11-4). When activated by substances such as the lipid A component of LPS toxins (Gram-negative endotoxin), the C3 complement molecule is split into C3a and C3b. C3b becomes fixed to the cytoplasmic membrane of a bacterial cell and factors B and D become activated to split C5 into C5a and C5b. The C5b combines with the remaining complement components C6 to C9 to form a *membrane attack complex (MAC).* The MAC penetrates the cytoplasmic membrane, forming a pore that leads to osmotic lysis of the bacterial cell.

The complement cascade can also be initiated or triggered by specific antigen–antibody complexes (discussed later in this chapter). This is called the *classical pathway.* When antibodies, which are substances made by the body, combine with an antigen on a cell surface, complement C1 can bind to a region of the antibody molecule; this forms an antigen-antibody–complement complex. This complex initiates

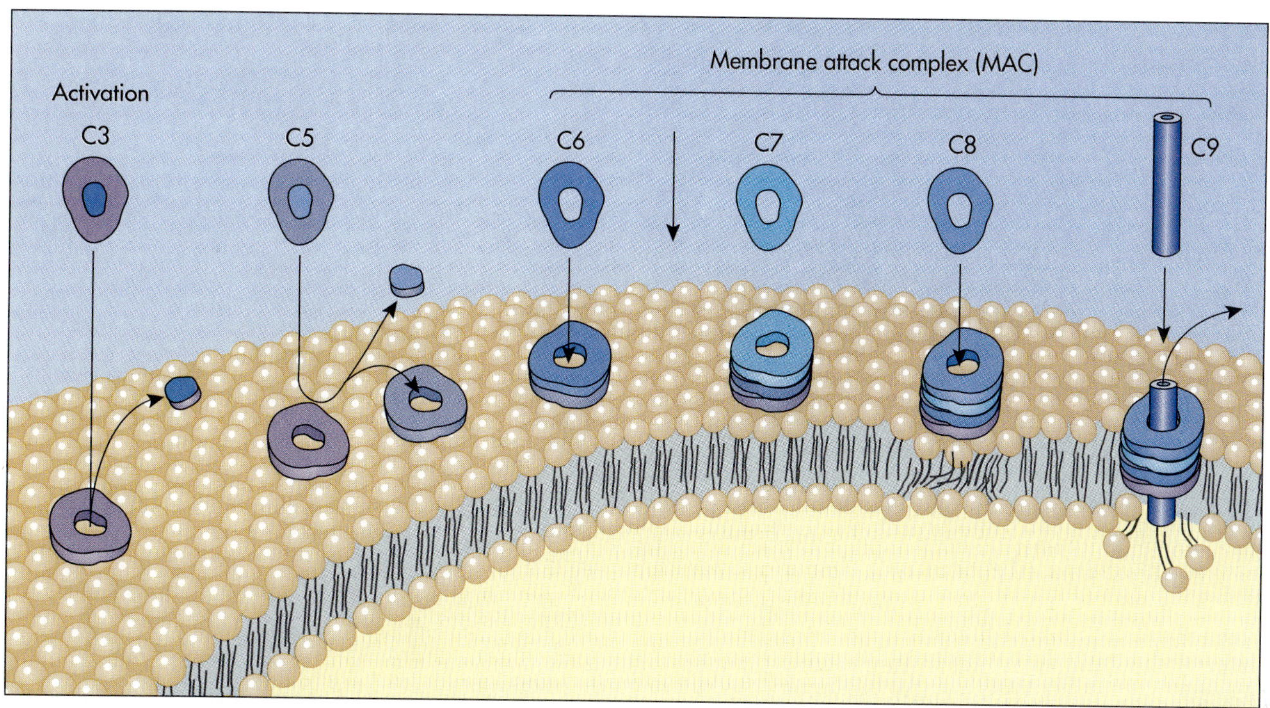

FIG. 11-4 Complement is activated in a multistep process by the complete (classical) pathway or the alternative pathway. The result of activation is a cascade of complement molecules onto a cell that produces damage to the cytoplasmic membrane and cell lysis.

the cascade of complement molecules. At each stage of the complement cascade, different complement molecules are activated, so that each in turn activates the next complement molecule in the pathway.

The initiation of the classical complement pathway involves C1, C2, and C4. Three proteins (C1q, C1r, C1s), comprising the C1 complex, are triggered by the antigen–antibody complex to become active proteases. The proteolytic action of the activated C1 complex, in turn, activates C2 and C4 and cleaves them into a C4b2a complex called *C3 convertase.* The C3 convertase splits C3 and C5 into C3a and C3b. The C3b then binds to the C3 convertase to form C5 convertase, which splits C5 into C5a and C5b. The C5b combines with the remaining complement components C6 to C9, as in the alternate pathway, to form a membrane attack complex that results in cell lysis.

In addition to bacterial cell lysis by the MAC formed in the classical or alternative pathways, initiation of the complement cascade leads to other end results. The binding of C3b to cell surfaces leads to enhanced binding to neutrophils and macrophages, which then are able to carry out phagocytosis. This coating of the bacterial cell surface that leads to enhanced phagocytosis is referred to as **opsonization.**

Enhanced phagocytosis occurs because both neutrophils and macrophages have receptors on their surfaces for complement C3b. The binding of C3b to a pathogen permits the establishment of a bridge between that pathogen and a neutrophil or macrophage so that the phagocytic cell remains in contact with the pathogen. Individuals lacking C3 complement have inadequate phagocytic activities and are particularly susceptible to bacterial infections. Bacterial cells that have been opsonized have a 1,000-fold greater chance of being engulfed by phagocytic cells than non-opsonized bacteria.

Some complement molecules act as chemotactic agents to attract phagocytic cells to the site of infection. This is particularly important in the inflammatory response, which is discussed later in this chapter. Activation of complement with subsequent production of C3a and C5a leads to the induction of chemotaxis in neutrophils, monocytes, macrophages, and lymphocytes. Attraction of these cells to the site of infection enhances the opportunity of phagocytic cells to eliminate invading bacteria from the body.

C3a and C5a complement components are also *anaphylatoxins,* that is, they induce a physiological response that results in blood vessel dilation and hypotension, increases vascular permeability, causes contraction of smooth muscle tissue, and degranulates mast blood cells. Anaphylaxis, like phagocytosis, is an evolutionarily old nonspecific immune defense mechanism. The combination of these physiological responses results in enhanced elimination of pathogenic microorganisms, especially bacteria, from the body.

TABLE 11-1 Normal Microbiota of Various Body Sites

BODY SITE	RESIDENT MICROBIOTA	FACTORS INFLUENCING MICROBIAL COMMUNITY COMPOSITION
Skin	Gram-positive bacteria *Staphylococcus* and *Micrococcus* most abundant; Gram-positive *Corynebacterium, Brevibacterium,* and *Propionibacterium* also occur; few fungi and few Gram-negative bacteria except in moist regions	Low water activity and fatty acids produced from sebum limit numbers and types of microorganisms on the skin
Oral cavity	*Streptococcus species,* such as *S. mutans* on teeth and *S. sanguis* on saliva-coated surfaces, are abundant, as are obligate anaerobes Gram-negative coccoid members of the genus *Veillonella* and Gram-positive species of *Bacteroides, Fusobacterium,* and *Peptostreptococcus*	Polysaccharide production by resident microbiota that forms plaque and allows adherence to surfaces in the oral cavity; scavenging of molecular oxygen by facultative anaerobes allows growth of obligate anaerobes
Gastrointestinal tract	Obligate and facultative anaerobes of the genera *Lactobacillus, Streptococcus, Clostridium, Veillonella, Bacteroides, Fusobacterium, Escherichia, Proteus, Klebsiella,* and *Enterobacter*	Abundance of substrates for growth of abundant resident microbiota; scavenging of molecular oxygen by facultative anaerobes allows growth of obligate anaerobes
Upper respiratory tract (nasal cavity and nasopharynx)	*Streptococcus, Staphylococcus, Moraxella, Neisseria, Haemophilus, Bacteroides,* and *Fusobacterium*	Ability to resist nonspecific defenses
Lower respiratory tract	None	Phagocytic cells prevent colonization by a resident microbiota
Upper urinary tract (kidneys and bladder)	None	Filtration and outward fluid flow prevent establishment of resident microbiota
Vaginal tract	*Streptococcus, Lactobacillus, Bacteroides,* and *Clostridium;* coliforms; spirochetes; yeasts, including members of the genus *Candida*	Large surface area and secretions of nutrients permits growth of abundant microbiota; acidity limits species within resident microbial community

Normal Human Microbiota

While the body is protected against microbial invasion by various defenses, the body surfaces of most animals, including humans, are populated by microorganisms. These surface associated microorganisms contribute to the body defenses against pathogens. Distinct microbial populations inhabit the surface tissues of the skin, oral cavity, respiratory tract, gastrointestinal tract, and genitourinary tract (Table 11-1). The average adult human has 10^{13} eukaryotic animal cells (human cells) and 10^{14} associated prokaryotic and eukaryotic cells of microorganisms. Stated another way, the normal human being is composed of just over 10^{14} cells—10% are human and the remaining 90% are microbial. Most of these are bacteria associated with the gastrointestinal tract.

The microbial populations most frequently found in association with particular tissues are referred to as **indigenous microbial populations, normal microflora,** or **normal microbiota.** Although the term *microflora* is used extensively, the term *microbiota* is preferable because it avoids any inference that microorganisms are little plants. The normal microbiota qualitatively describes the species that are generally found within the stable mixture of microbial populations (microbial community) associated with particular body tissue (FIG. 11-5). Within this microbial community the relative concentrations of individual populations can and do fluctuate throughout an individual's life and in response to numerous external environmental influences.

Although some parasites can migrate through the placenta, the human fetus is normally sterile, and colonization of body tissues actually begins during the birth process. The acquisition of a resident microbiota by humans occurs in stages and therefore is termed a *successional process.* The different tissues of the body provide distinct habitats with varying environmental conditions for the growth of differing microbial populations. The growth of microorganisms on body tissue surfaces alters the local environmental conditions, leading to the successional changes in the populations of microorganisms associated with the tissues until a relatively stable, normal microbiota is established.

Not all body tissues provide suitable habitats for the growth of microorganisms. For example, most of the urinary tract lacks a resident microbiota. Only the distal end of the urethra has a resident microbiota. Urine that has not contacted this extremity (that is,

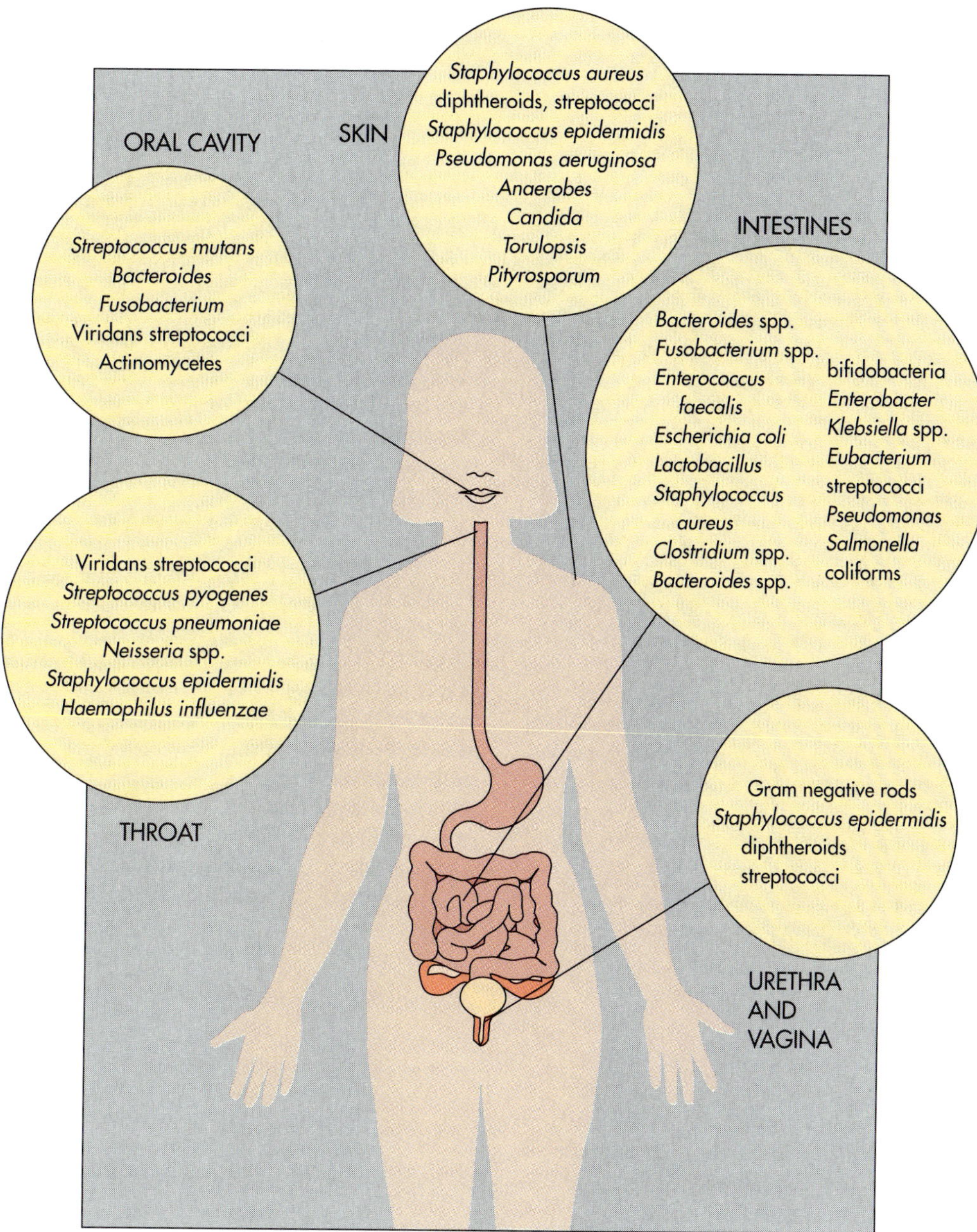

FIG. 11-5 Normal microbiota at various body sites.

urine in the kidney, ureter, and bladder) is considered a sterile body fluid. Similarly, blood is considered a sterile body fluid because the circulatory system does not possess a resident microbiota. In reality, various microorganisms frequently enter the bloodstream but normally do not establish growing populations within the circulatory system. For example, a segment of the circulatory system that is associated with the liver, the hepatic portal system, normally contains low numbers of bacteria that pass through the intestinal wall as a result of abrasions in the lining of the intestinal tract caused by food particles. These bacteria are routinely eliminated from the circulatory system by specialized leukocytes that occur in blood vessels of the liver.

Usually the normal microbiota of the human body are nonpathogenic, that is, they do not cause disease. They grow on body surfaces and do not invade the body's tissues. They contribute to the nonspecific defense of the body against infections with pathogens by producing antimicrobial substances, known as *allelopathic substances,* that act to prevent the establishment of infection by pathogenic microorganisms. Allelopathic substances are chemicals produced by an organism that kills or inhibits other organisms. Microorganisms living on the skin surface, for example, produce low molecular weight unsaturated fatty acids that have antimicrobial activities.

When the normal microbiota are adversely affected—for example, by antibiotics that are used to

BOX 11-1

Germ-free Animals

To determine the role of the indigenous microbiota, it is possible to deliver an animal by cesarean section (surgical removal of the fetus from the uterus via the abdomen) and raise that animal in the absence of microorganisms. Such *gnotobiotic* or *germ-free* animals provide suitable experimental models for investigating the interactions of animals and microorganisms. Comparing animals possessing normal associated microbiota with germ-free animals permits the elucidation of the complex relationships between microorganisms and host animals.

Germ-free experimentation extends the microbiologist's pure culture concept to *in vivo* studies. From the use of germ-free animals, it is learned that an animal's lack of exposure to microorganisms results in a complex of deleterious effects. Germ-free animals differ from other members of their species. Their metabolic rate and cardiac output are reduced. Structures that are designed to defend against bacterial invasion—such as the lymphatic system, the antibody-forming system, and the mononuclear phagocyte system—are poorly developed. Some of the animal's organs that normally have natural populations of bacteria are often reduced in size or capacity.

In most cases, the relationships between animals and their normal microbiota are mutually beneficial. Germ-free animals develop abnormalities of the gastrointestinal tract and are more susceptible to disease than animals with normal associated microbiota. The normal associated microbiota of animals contributes in part to the normal defense mechanisms that protect animals against infection by pathogens. It is important to note that some members of the normal indigenous microbiota exhibit antagonism toward potential pathogens, and their absence removes an important line of defense against pathogens. For example, acid production by the indigenous microbiota of the vaginal tract lessens the probability of infection with *Neisseria gonorrhoeae,* and the normal microbiota of this region also lessens the likelihood of overgrowth by *Candida* yeasts. Other mechanisms of antagonism by the indigenous microbiota that enhance host resistance to disease include alteration of the oxygen tension, production of antibiotics, and competition for available nutrients.

As expected, germ-free animals are more susceptible to bacterial infection. Organisms such as *Bacillus subtilis* and *Micrococcus luteus,* which are harmless to other animals, cause disease in germ-free animals. Pathogenic microorganisms such as *Vibrio cholerae* and *Shigella dysenteriae* establish infections far more readily when there are no normal microbiota that have a competitive advantage within the intestinal tract.

At the same time, though, germfree animals are resistant to *Entamoeba histolytica,* the causative organism of amoebic dysentery. This is because the protozoan *E. histolytica* requires the normal intestinal bacteria as a food source. Likewise, tooth decay is not a problem to germ-free animals, even those on high-sugar diets, because of

treat a disease—an imbalance may occur that leads to the development of disease. For example, the use of antibiotics sometimes disrupts the balance of the microbial community of the gastrointestinal tract, permitting the growth of *Clostridium difficile;* this causes a severe and sometimes fatal gastrointestinal tract infection (antibiotic-associated pseudomembranous enterocolitis). Similarly, women taking antibiotics sometimes develop vaginitis due to an overgrowth of the fungus *Candida albicans.* The yeast *C. albicans* is normally held in check by the indigenous bacteria of the vaginal tract.

Besides their role in preventing certain diseases, the indigenous microbiota contribute to the nutrition of the animal by synthesizing nutrients essential to the welfare of the host. For example, germ-free animals require vitamin K, which normally is synthesized by the resident microbiota of the gastrointestinal tract. These microbiota also synthesize biotin, riboflavin, pantothenate, and pyridoxine, supplying these vitamins to the animal host. Thus the maintenance of a healthy indigenous microbiota is essential to the maintenance of a healthy individual.

Phagocytosis

Phagocytosis involves the engulfment and ingestion of cells, generally followed by the destruction of the engulfed cells. Phagocytosis is a highly efficient host defense mechanism against the invasion of microorganisms. Microorganisms that enter the circulatory system are subject to phagocytosis by various cells of the blood, the mononuclear phagocyte system, and the lymphatic system. Various cells at fixed body sites are also capable of phagocytosis.

Several types of **leukocytes** (white blood cells) are involved in nonspecific phagocytic defenses against pathogenic microorganisms (FIG. 11-6). Some leukocytes, called *granulocytes,* contain cytoplasmic granules. These granulocytes are differentiated on the basis of staining reactions accomplished in the laboratory and include *basophils,* leukocytes that stain with basic dyes; *eosinophils,* leukocytes that react with acidic dyes, becoming red when stained with the dye eosin; and *neutrophils* (also called polymorphonuclear neutrophils, polymorphs, or PMNs) that contain granules that exhibit no preferential staining—that is, they are

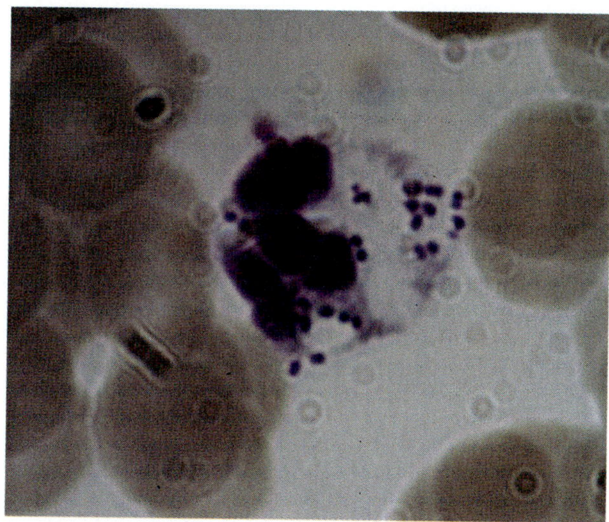

FIG. 11-6 Micrograph showing phagocytosis of *Streptococcus pneumoniae* by a polymorphonuclear neutrophil.

stained by neutral, acid, and basic dyes. The leukocytes that do not contain granular inclusions *(agranulocytes)* include the *monocytes* and *lymphocytes.* Monocytes are important in the nonspecific immune response, and lymphocytes are especially important in the specific immune response. Monocytes, macrophages, and PMNs are the main phagocytic cells, that is, "professional phagocytes" of the host defense system. Other cells in the body can be phagocytic but are not as efficient as these professional phagocytes in engulfment and destruction of particles. The phagocytic cells engulf and destroy most bacteria that attempt to invade the body.

The encounter between a phagocytic cell and a microorganism, however, does not always result in engulfment and destruction. Some bacteria and fungi produce polysaccharide capsules that make them more resistant to phagocytosis than noncapsulated microorganisms. The capsule prevents the phagocytic cell from adhering to the microbial surface. Other noncapsule producing microbes may be engulfed into the phagocyte but have developed mechanisms to evade killing and degradation. These microorganisms, such as *Mycobacterium tuberculosis* and *Salmonella typhi,* can survive as intracellular pathogens within the phagocytic cell. Other microorganisms evade phagocytosis by producing leukocidins, which are toxic proteins that destroy the phagocytic cell. Bacteria such as *Staphylococcus aureus* produce a leukocidin that leads to pus formation; pus is mainly composed of destroyed phagocytes.

Mechanism of Phagocytic Killing

Phagocytic blood cells can have numerous lysosomes that contain hydrolytic enzymes capable of digesting microorganisms. During phagocytosis, the microorganism is engulfed by the pseudopods of the phagocytic cell and is transported by endocytosis across the cell membrane, where it is contained within a vacuole called a *phagosome.* The phagosome migrates to and fuses with a lysosome, producing a *phagolysosome.* Within the phagolysosome, an engulfed microorganism is exposed to enzymes and chemicals, including degradative enzymes and enzymes that catalyze the production of toxic biochemicals (FIG. 11-7). Phagocytic cells kill or degrade engulfed microorganisms in at least three different ways: (1) oxygen-independent mechanisms, (2) oxygen-dependent mechanisms, and (3) nitrogen-dependent mechanisms.

During phagocytosis there is an increase in oxygen consumption by the phagocytic cells associated with elevated rates of metabolic activities of the hexose monophosphate shunt. This phenomenon is called the respiratory burst and results from the cell's requirement for ATP to power phagocytosis. Oxygen-dependent enzymes in the lysosome (and phagolysosome) form toxic derivatives from oxygen. Oxygen is converted to the superoxide anion, hydrogen peroxide, singlet oxygen, and hydroxyl radicals, all of which have antimicrobial activity. Phagocytosis also involves a shift in metabolism from a respiratory to a fermentative process, with the consequent production of lactic acid. This leads to a decrease in pH, which enhances the activity of many lysosomal enzymes.

Oxygen-independent mechanisms of killing by phagocytes include various degradative enzymes that are associated with lysosomes. These enzymes include lysozyme, phospholipases, proteases, RNase, and DNase, which contribute to the destruction of the ingested microorganism.

Polymorphonuclear neutrophils also synthesize *defensins,* which are a family of peptides with antimicrobial activity. These defensins are human neutrophil proteins (HPNs) and are labelled HPN-1, HPN-2,

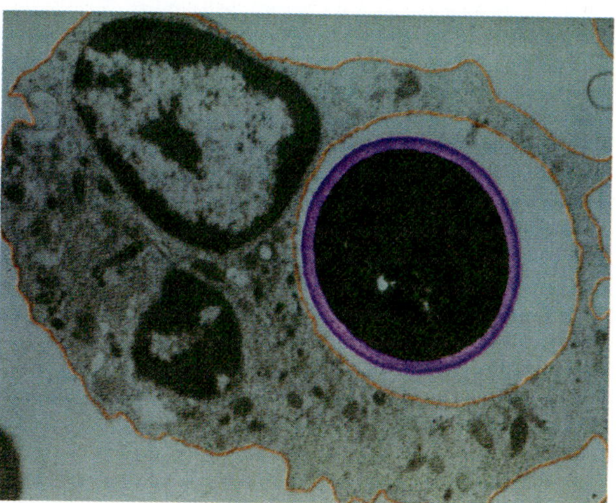

FIG. 11-7 Colorized micrograph showing lysosomes fusing with a phagosome containing a *Candida albicans* yeast cell *(purple).*

HPN-3, and HPN-4. Defensins are stored in cytoplasmic granules and delivered to phagocytic vacuoles. They can increase the permeability of bacterial and fungal cell membranes and affect enveloped viruses (but not nonenveloped viruses). Alterations in the cytoplasmic membranes of these microorganisms contribute to their death or inactivation.

Another mechanism of killing used by phagocytic cells involves *reactive nitrogen intermediates* (RNIs). These RNIs include nitric oxide (NO), nitrite (NO_2^-), and nitrate (NO_3^-). Nitric oxide is likely to be the most effective killing agent. It is produced from arginine by macrophages when they are stimulated by interferons or tumor necrosis factor. The nitric oxide can then be further oxidized to NO_2^- and NO_3^-. All of these forms of nitrogen are toxic to microorganisms.

After the engulfed microorganisms have been killed and degraded, the remaining material is transported to the cytoplasmic membrane of the human cell within a vacuole; it is removed from the phagocytic cells by exocytosis or is consumed within the phagocytic cell.

Phagocytic Cells

Neutrophils **Neutrophils,** which are the most abundant phagocytic cells in circulating blood, are produced in the bone marrow. They are continuously present in circulating blood, affording protection against the entry of foreign materials. These leukocytes exhibit chemotaxis and are attracted to foreign substances, including invading microorganisms. Neutrophils engulf and digest microorganisms and particulate matter that may be present, such as cell debris (FIG. 11-8). Neutrophils live for only a few days in the body but are replenished from the bone marrow in high numbers.

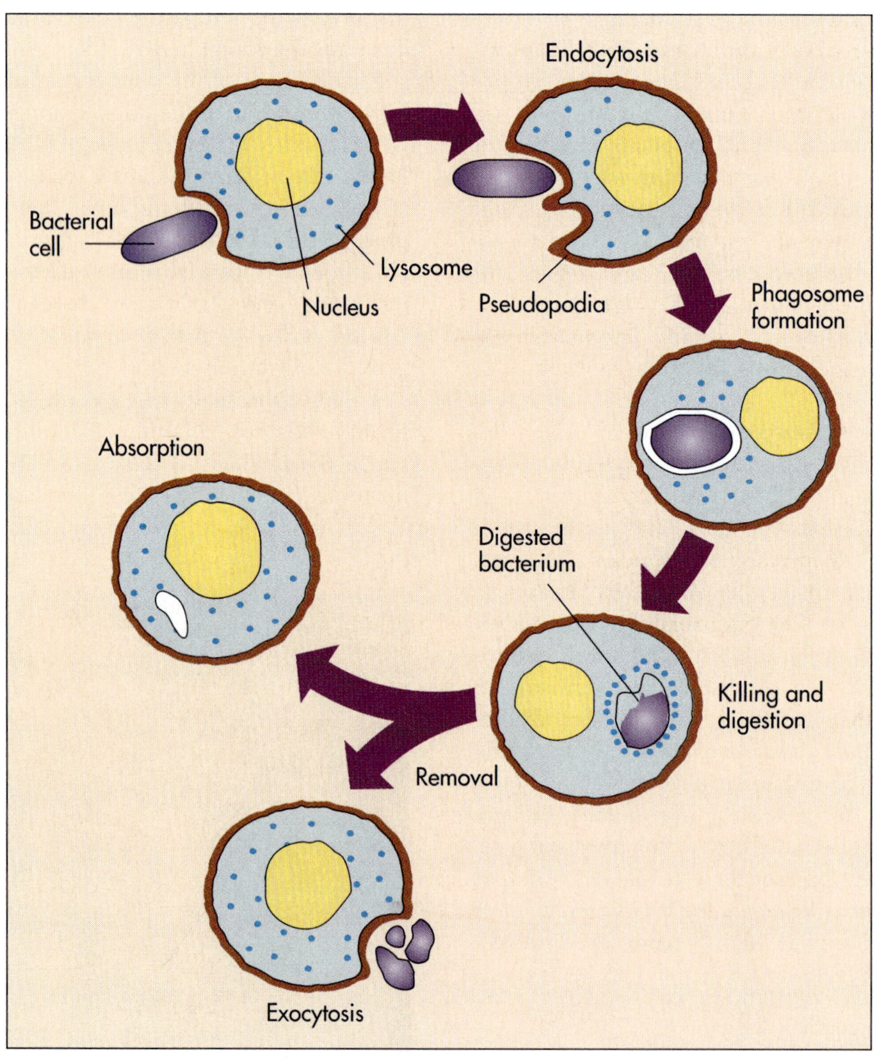

FIG. 11-8 Neutrophils phagocytize and degrade microorganisms that invade the body. The bacterial cell that has been captured by endocytosis is enclosed within the cell in a phagosome. Lysosomes fuse with the phagosome to form a phagolysosome. The lysosomal enzymes digest the bacterial cell and the cellular debris of the degraded bacterial cell are absorbed or released from the neutrophil cell.

Monocytes and Macrophages **Monocytes** are mononuclear phagocytic cells. They are (1) larger than neutrophils, (2) precursors of macrophages, and (3) able to move out of the blood to tissues that are infected with invading microorganisms. Outside the blood, monocytes become enlarged, forming phagocytic **macrophages.** Macrophages are long-lived in the body, persisting in tissues for weeks or months. Once these differentiated macrophages are formed, they are capable of reproducing to form additional macrophages. This is in contrast to neutrophils, which are terminal cells that are short-lived in the body; neutrophils are nonreproductive and must be replenished from the bone marrow. Macrophages, like neutrophils, engulf and digest microorganisms. As discussed later in this chapter, they also play an important role as antigen-presenting cells in the immune response.

Some of the lysosomal enzymes of macrophages are different from those of neutrophils. Some microorganisms are resistant to the enzymatic activities of neutrophils and macrophages. For example, *Mycobacterium tuberculosis* survives and even multiplies within macrophages. As a result, some microorganisms survive, continuing to grow and later to cause infection because of the failure of these phagocytic cells to kill the invading pathogens. This is one of the reasons that tuberculosis is a persistent disease and is difficult to treat.

Macrophages are distributed throughout the body, including fixed sites within the mononuclear phagocyte system (FIG. 11-9). The **mononuclear phagocyte**

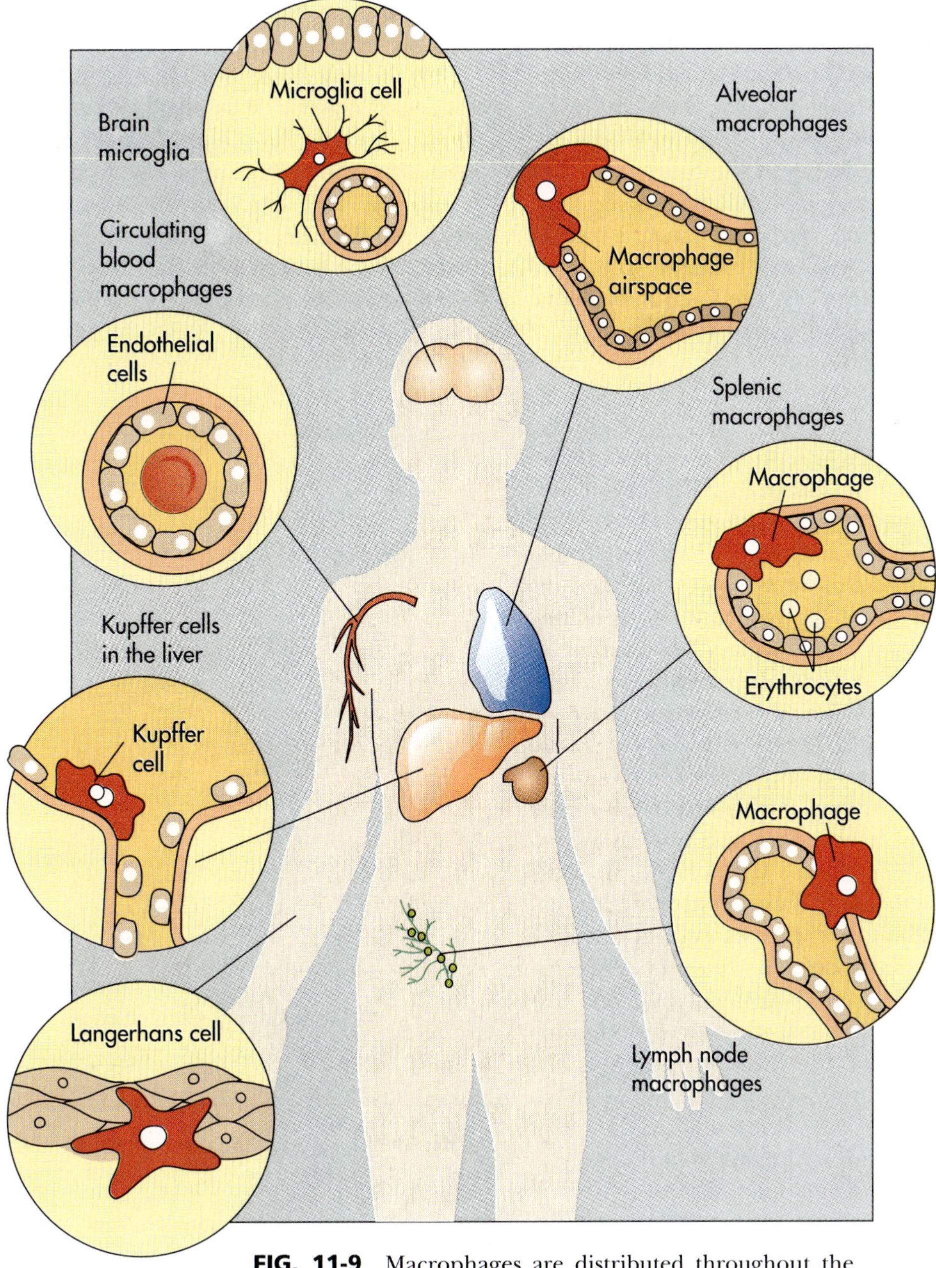

FIG. 11-9 Macrophages are distributed throughout the body, protecting different body sites from infection.

system, formerly called the *reticuloendothelial system,* refers to a systemic network of phagocytic macrophage cells distributed through a network of loose connective tissue and the endothelial lining of the capillaries and sinuses of the human body. The phagocytic cells associated with the lining of the blood vessels in bone marrow, liver, spleen, lymph nodes, and sinuses constitute this host defense system.

Some of the macrophages in the mononuclear phagocyte system occur at fixed sites and are designated with particular names. For example, **microglia** are macrophages of the central nervous system; **Kupffer cells** are phagocytic cells that line the blood vessels of the liver; **alveolar macrophage (dust cells)** are macrophages fixed in the alveolar lining of the lungs; and **histiocytes** are fixed macrophages in connective tissues. Other macrophages of the mononuclear phagocytic system are called **wandering cells** because they move freely into tissues where foreign substances have entered. Wandering macrophages are attracted to these tissues through chemotaxis by chemical stimuli elicited by the foreign material. Wandering macrophages occur in the peritoneal lining of the abdomen and the alveolar lining of the lung, as well as in other tissues. The presence of relatively high numbers of macrophages in the respiratory tract is important in preventing the establishment of both pathogens and a normal indigenous microbiota within the tissues of the lower respiratory tract.

Inflammatory Response

The **inflammatory response** represents a generalized response to infection or tissue damage and is designed to localize invading microorganisms and arrest the spread of the infection. The inflammatory response is characterized by four symptoms: reddening of the localized area, swelling, pain, and elevated temperature. *Redness* results from capillary dilation that allows more blood to flow. The term *dilation* is a misnomer because many of the capillaries remain constricted; during "dilation" there are simply fewer constricted capillaries, permitting increased blood circulation through more open (dilated) capillaries. The *elevated temperature,* which is a localized phenomenon, also occurs because capillary dilation permits increased blood flow through these vessels with the associated high metabolic activities of neutrophils and macrophage. The dilation of blood vessels is accompanied by "increased capillary permeability," causing *swelling* as fluids accumulate in the spaces surrounding tissue cells. Actually, the swelling is due to increased permeability of the venules, but the term *increased capillary permeability* is entrenched in the clinical terminology used to describe this phenomenon.

Pain, in the case of inflammation, is due to lysis of blood cells that triggers the production of bradykinin and prostaglandins. These are substances produced by human cells that alter the threshold and intensity of the nervous system response to pain. Bradykinin decreases the firing threshold for pain nerve fibers and the prostaglandins, PGE1 and PGE2, intensify this effect. Aspirin, which is often used to decrease pain, antagonizes prostaglandin formation but has little or no effect on bradykinin formation. Thus aspirin can decrease—but not eliminate—the pain associated with the inflammatory response.

The dilation of blood vessels in the area of the inflammation increases blood circulation, allowing increased numbers of phagocytic blood cells to reach the affected area. Neutrophils are initially most abundant. In the later stages of inflammation, monocytes and macrophages of the mononuclear phagocyte system predominate (FIG. 11-10). The phagocytic cells are able to kill many of the ingested microorganisms. Phagocytic blood cells migrate to the affected tissues, passing between the endothelial cells of the blood vessel by a process known as *diapedesis.* The death of phagocytic blood cells involved in combating the infection results in the release of histamine, prostaglandins, and bradykinins, which, in addition to their other effects, are vasodilators, that is, substances that increase the internal diameter of blood vessels. Additionally, specialized cells that line connective tissues, called *mast cells,* react with complement, leading to the

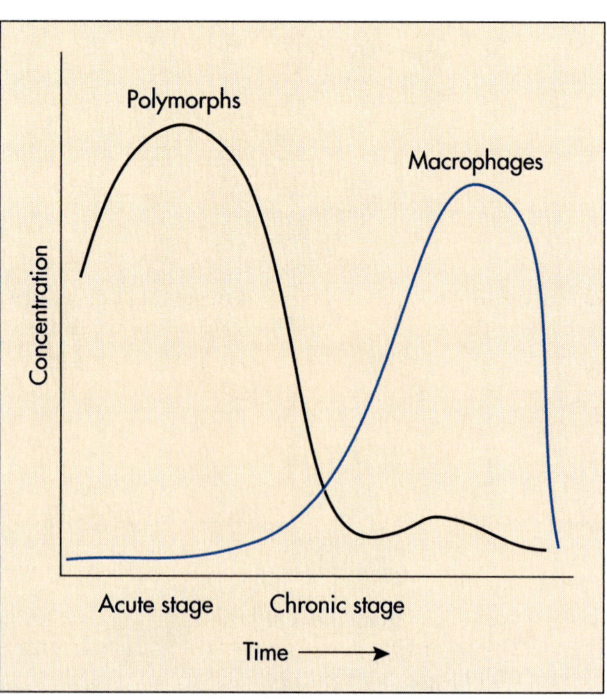

FIG. 11-10 During the inflammatory response there is an increase in polymorphs (PMNs) with fluid accumulation during the acute stage. Later there is an increase in macrophages during the chronic stage.

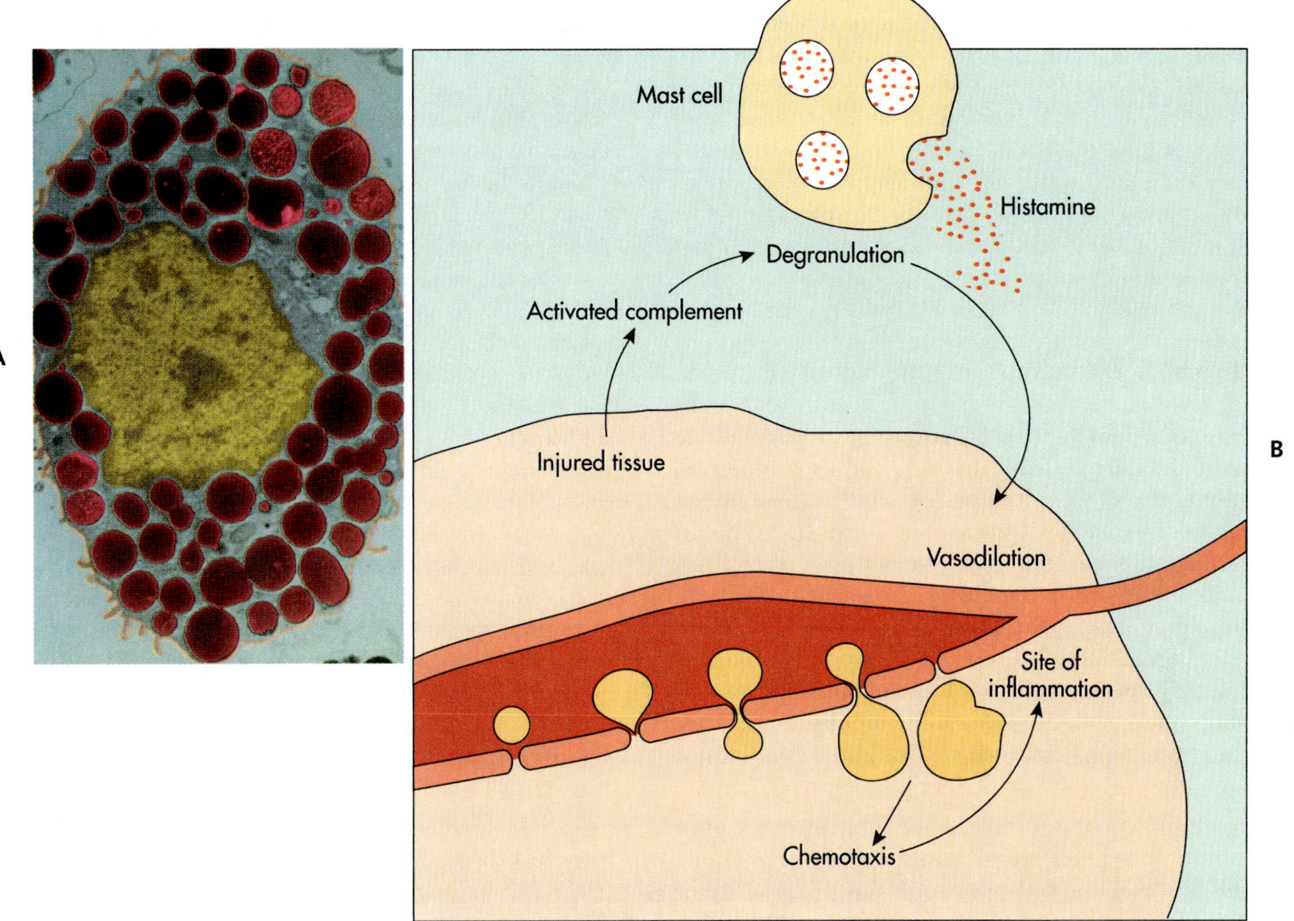

FIG. 11-11 **A,** Colorized micrograph showing a mast cell with numerous dense granules of histamine *(red)*. **B,** Degranulation of mast cells causes vasodilation, which mediates the inflammatory response. Mast cell degranulation can be triggered by tissue injury. Release of histamine granules by degranulation causes vasodilation, heightening the inflammatory response and the movement of PMNs and macrophages to the site of inflammation.

release of large amounts of histamine contained within these cells (FIG. 11-11). These substances are biochemical mediators that alter the circulation during the inflammatory response. Thus the death of some phagocytic cells and the release of certain biochemicals enhance the inflammatory response.

The area of the inflammation also becomes walled off as the result of the development of fibrinous clots. The deposition of fibrin isolates the inflamed area, cutting off normal circulation. The fluid that forms in the inflamed area is known as the inflammatory exudate, commonly called pus. This exudate contains dead cells and debris in addition to body fluids. After the removal of the exudate, the inflammation may terminate and the tissues may return to their normal function, which is why physicians, for example, often lance boils to remove the exudate. Thus the complex reactions of the inflammatory response work in an integrated fashion to contain and eliminate infecting pathogenic microorganisms. The last stage of inflammation involves repair of the damaged tissue.

FEVER

Humans are *homeothermic animals,* meaning that they maintain a body temperature within a fairly constant range. Usually during a 24 hour period, the body temperature of a healthy individual fluctuates about 1° to 1.5° C. Although "normal" body temperature is considered to be 37° C, body temperature may fluctuate around 36° C or 38° C. Part of the brain called the hypothalamus regulates body temperature.

Fever is an abnormal increase in body temperature. Many microorganisms produce substances that enter the bloodstream and result in fever by directly or indirectly stimulating the hypothalamus. Chemicals that cause fever are called **pyrogens** (Greek *pyr* + *genes,* meaning fire or heat producing). Some examples of pyrogens are: (1) the lipopolysaccharide (endotoxin) molecules of Gram-negative bacterial cell walls; (2) *N*-acetylglucosamine–*N*-acetylmuramic acid-containing fragments of the peptidoglycan molecule in the cell walls of Gram-negative and Gram-positive bacteria; and (3) specific pyrogenic exotoxins, such as the toxic-shock syndrome toxin-1, that are produced by some *Staphylococcus aureus* strains and the erythrogenic toxin produced by *Streptococcus pyogenes.*

Bacterial endotoxins and peptidoglycan cause phagocytic cells that have ingested these substances to release interleukin-1 (IL-1), also called *endogenous pyrogen.* Bacterial exotoxins that are produced during infections enter the bloodstream and also stimulate macrophages and monocytes to release IL-1. IL-1 in turn stimulates the hypothalamus to release prostaglandins. Prostaglandins cause the hypothalamus to readjust its thermostat to a higher temperature, thus causing fever. The body responds to signals from the hypothalamus by constriction of peripheral blood vessels, increased rate of metabolism, and muscular contractions (shivering). This initial condition is called a chill. The body temperature rises to the new "thermostat setting" of the hypothalamus and remains in this state of fever until the IL-1 is depleted from the blood. The body then responds with dilation of peripheral blood vessels and sweating to attempt to lose heat and return to normal temperature.

Some fevers are continuous; that is, the body temperature remains elevated during the progression of an infection. Typhoid fever is an example of a continuous fever. An intermittent or spiking fever is one in which the temperature is elevated but fluctuates widely (>1° C). A remittent fever is one that abates (returns to normal) for a short period or intervals. Malaria and many bacterial infections result in remittent fevers. Relapsing fever, caused by *Borrelia recurrentis,* is manifested by recurring episodes of fever and normal temperatures.

Fever enhances the body's natural defense mechanisms by stimulating phagocytosis, increasing the rate of enzymatic reactions that lead to degradation of microorganisms and tissue repair, intensifying the action of interferons, and causing a reduction in blood iron concentrations—iron is required by many bacteria for growth. Some pathogens are very sensitive to even slightly elevated temperatures.

11.2 SPECIFIC IMMUNE RESPONSE

The **specific immune response** (simply called the *immune response*) is a defense system that protects the body against pathogenic microorganisms. It recognizes foreign substances that are not part of the body and acts to eliminate those foreign molecules. It can recognize and attack microorganisms by responding to the specific chemicals of the microorganisms. This physiological response is especially important as a defense against infection and for protection against disease.

The immune response is characterized by specificity, memory, and the acquired ability to detect foreign substances. The ability to differentiate "self" from "nonself" at the molecular level is necessary for the development of the specific immune response. The human immune response recognizes substances that differ from the normal macromolecules of the body. The specificity of the immune response permits the recognition of even very slight biochemical differences between molecules. Consequently, the macromolecules of one microbial strain can elicit a different response from those of even a very closely related strain of the same species.

Once a response to a particular macromolecule, called an *antigen,* has occurred, a memory system is established that permits a rapid and specific secondary response on reexposure to that same substance (FIG. 11-12). Thus the body acquires immunity only after exposure to an antigen, and the specific immune response is therefore adaptive. The ability to recognize and respond rapidly to pathogenic microorganisms establishes a state of immunity that precludes infection with those specific pathogens. The ability to recognize the microorganisms that previously elicited an immune response forms the basis for acquiring or developing immunity to specific diseases. As a consequence of such *acquired immunity,* we usually suffer from many diseases, such as chicken pox, only once. We can also be exposed intentionally to specific foreign macromolecules through the use of vaccines to artificially establish a state of immunity. The use of vaccination to prevent disease is discussed in Chapter 12, after we establish the basis for its use in this chapter.

When an individual's immune system is active in responding to the foreign antigen, the immune response is called **active immunity.** Alternately, immunity may be conferred on an individual by the transfer of serum, secretions such as milk and colostrum, or immune cells from another individual. The recipient of such a transfer becomes immune to specific foreign antigens without his or her own immune system being activated. This form is called **passive immunity.** Transfer of antibodies from mother to child during breast-feeding is an example of passive immunity. The term

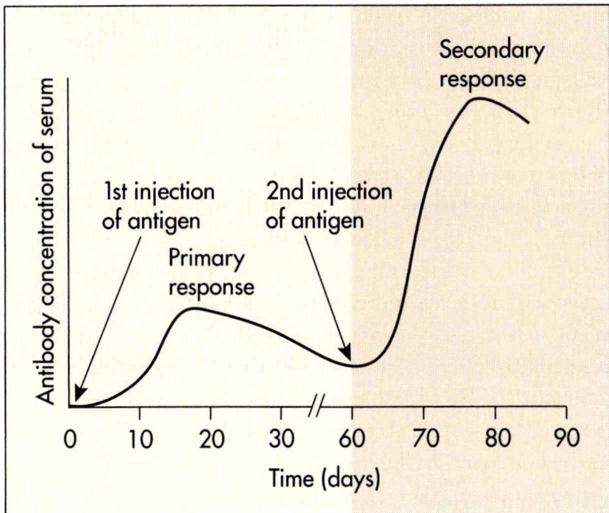

FIG. 11-12 The primary immune response, which occurs after the first exposure to an antigen, is characterized by a lag period and a slow rise in antibody production. The secondary response, which occurs on subsequent exposure to an antigen that the body "remembers," is characterized by a short lag and rapid rise in antibody concentration.

passive indicates that antibody production occurred outside the individual's body. In contrast, the term *active-acquired immunity* indicates production of antibody within the individual's body as a result of the learned (acquired) ability to recognize antigens.

Artificial immunity indicates medical treatment as opposed to natural means of acquiring passive or active immunity. Thus natural passive immunity occurs when a fetus acquires antibodies from its mother, whereas artificial passive immunity occurs when an individual is injected with serum containing antibodies.

LYMPHOCYTES

The immune defense system depends on lymphocytes that are differentiated into B lymphocytes (B cells), T lymphocytes (T cells), and natural killer cells (NK cells) (Table 11-2). B and T lymphocytes originate from bone marrow stem cells and become differentiated during maturation (FIG. 11-13, p. 400). B cells are responsible for *antibody-mediated immunity (humoral immunity)* and T cells are responsible for *cell-mediated immunity (cellular immunity)*.

The precursors of T cells pass through the liver and spleen before reaching the thymus gland, where they are processed. T cells are inactive until they mature later in the thymus. T cells are processed within specialized T-cell domains of lymphoid tissues. The thymus-dependent differentiation of T cells or thymocytes occurs during childhood, and by puberty the secondary lymphoid organs of the body generally contain their full complement of T cells. The T cells then generally circulate throughout the body.

The term *B lymphocyte* actually refers to bursa-dependent lymphocytes, so named because these lymphocytes are differentiated in chickens and other birds in the lymphoid organ known as the *bursa of Fabricius*. Even though humans do not possess a bursa of Fabricius, the designation **B lymphocyte** is applied to lymphocytes that can differentiate into antibody-synthesizing cells in the human body. Human B lymphocytes appear to develop in the bone marrow. They are found predominantly in lymphoid tissues. Like T cells, B cells undergo secondary activation within lymphatic tissues, including the spleen, tonsils, and lymph nodes. The B cells are processed within T-cell–independent regions of the lymphoid tissues. Within lymphatic tissues, B lymphocytes give rise to

TABLE 11-2 Types of Lymphocytes and Their Functions

LYMPHOCYTES	MAJOR SURFACE MARKERS	FUNCTION
T helper cells (T_H)	CD2, CD3, CD4	Help or assist other T cells and B cells to express their immune functions
Cytotoxic T cells (T_C)	CD2, CD3, CD8	Kill and lyse target cells that express foreign antigens (cells containing obligate intracellular parasites and tumor cells)
T suppressor cells (T_S)	CD3?, CD8	Suppress or inhibit the immune function of other lymphocytes
T memory cells	—	Long-lived cells that recognize previously encountered T dependent antigens
B lymphocytes	Ig	Differentiate into antibody-producing plasma cells and B memory cells in response to an antigen
Plasma cells	Ig	Actively secrete antibody
B memory cells	Ig	Long-lived cells that recognize a previously encountered antigen
Natural killer or null cells (NK)	—	Kill and lyse target cells that express foreign antigens

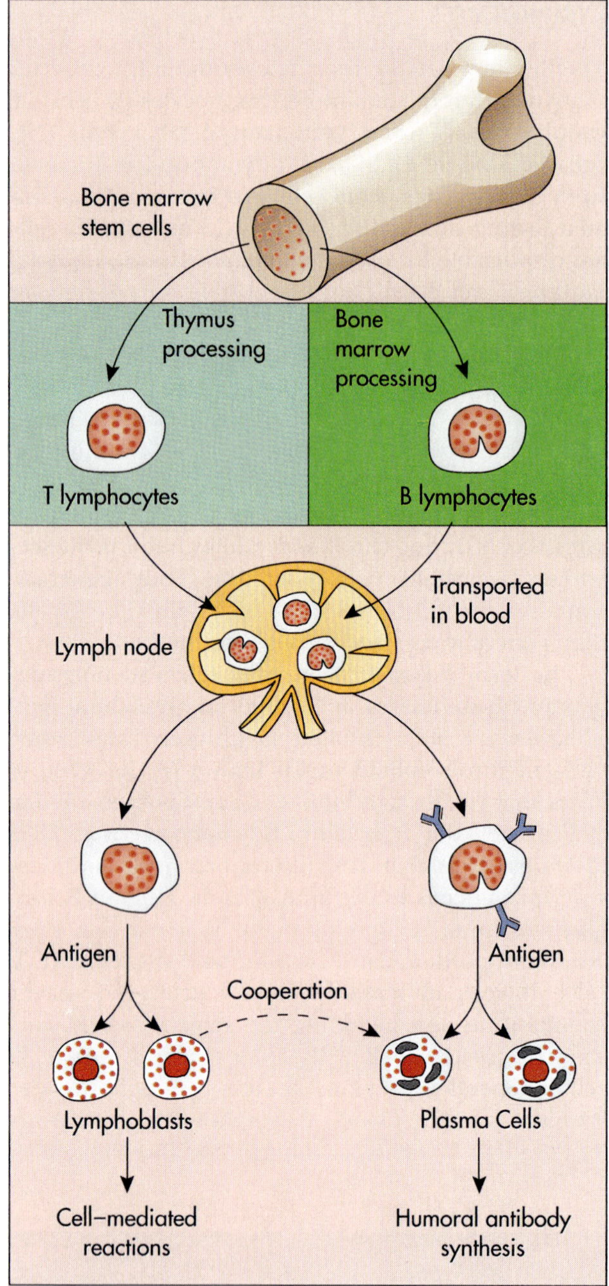

FIG. 11-13 B and T cells are differentiated at different locations in the body. Each serves distinct functions in the immune response.

antibody-secreting plasma cells in response to antigenic stimulation.

Various types of **T lymphocytes** have different functions within the immune response. These cells have surface receptors that enable them to recognize other cells. Some T lymphocytes, **T helper cells (T_H),** interact with B lymphocytes and are required for B cells to produce antibody. These T_H cells activate the immune response. Other T lymphocytes, **cytotoxic T cells (T_C)** are responsible for recognizing the body's cells that have been invaded by intracellular parasites such as viruses and some microorganisms; they also recognize tumor cells. On recognition of these "different" body cells, cytotoxic T lymphocytes can lyse and destroy them, thus providing an important mechanism in the defense against viral infection and cancer. **Suppressor T lymphocytes (T_S)** may be involved in the regulation, especially shutting down, of the immune response but their role is not clearly understood.

Finally, a subset of lymphocytes that are neither T cells or B cells, called **natural killer cells (NK cells)** are responsible for lysis of tumor cells. Natural killer cells or null cells are a special subset of lymphocytes that are neither T nor B cells. They do not express antibody, CD3, or CD4 markers on their surface. Some NK cells express CD8 on their surface. The marker on the NK cell surface that recognizes target cells is not known. NK cells do not have to be stimulated by foreign antigen. They utilize the same killing mechanisms of target cells as those of cytotoxic T lymphocytes and require cell-to-cell contact with the target cell. NK cells have been proposed to kill virally infected cells and tumor cells *in vivo.* NK cells also have an important role in graft-versus-host disease, which will be discussed later in this chapter.

Lymphocytes are differentiated based on the presence of specific cell surface proteins or antigens bound to their cytoplasmic membranes. B lymphocytes are predominantly characterized by having antibody (immunoglobulin) as surface proteins. T lymphocytes lack immunoglobulin on their surface but have other specific antigens. A surface marker that identifies a specific line of cells or a stage of cell differentiation because it interacts with a group or cluster of individual antibodies is called a CD (cluster of differentiation) antigen. CD antigens have been identified on various blood and tissue cells. Helper T cells contain CD3 and CD4 antigens and are described as being $CD3^+CD4^+CD8^-$. Cytotoxic T cells and suppressor T cells have CD3 and CD8 antigens and are designated $CD3^+CD4^-CD8^+$. Most natural killer cells lack all of these markers and therefore are sometimes called *null cells.*

Antibody-Mediated Immunity

In **antibody-mediated immunity,** specific proteins called **antibodies** or **immunoglobulins** are made when foreign antigens are detected. Antibodies are found in serum, which is the fluid portion of coagulated (clotted) blood tissue fluids and some secretions. In old medical terminology, blood and other vital body fluids were considered as "humors" after the Greek word for fluids. Thus antibody-mediated immunity is sometimes referred to as *humoral immunity* because the antibody molecules flow extracellularly through the body fluids. The key to antibody immunity is the ability of antibodies to react specifically with antigens.

Antigens

An **antigen** is any macromolecule that elicits the formation of an antibody and that can subsequently react with that antibody. Various macromolecules can act as antigens, including all proteins, most polysaccharides (especially large polysaccharides), nucleoproteins, lipoproteins, and various small biochemicals if they are attached to proteins or polypeptides. The two essential properties of an antigen are its *immunogenicity* (ability to stimulate antibody formation) and its specific reactivity with antibody molecules. The epitope, or antigenic determinant, is the portion of the antigen that reacts biochemically with the antibody molecule.

Some molecules called **haptens** have antigenic determinants but are too small to elicit the formation of antibodies by themselves. A hapten, however, can complex with a larger molecule, a carrier, and thereby become an antigen (FIG. 11-14). A hapten can react with antibody molecules but is unable to elicit the formation of antibody, whereas a complete antigen molecule both reacts and elicits the production of specific antibodies.

Antigenic molecules may be multivalent, having multiple epitopes, or monovalent, having only one epitope. Generally, multivalent antigens elicit a stronger immune response than monovalent antigens. In some cases, a multivalent antigen, variously called a *heterophile antigen, heterologous antigen,* or *Forssman antigen,* can react with antibodies produced in response to a different antigen.

In many cases, antigens are associated with cell surfaces and are therefore called *surface antigens.* Human cells have specific surface antigens; for example, human blood types are determined by the presence or absence of antigens designated A and B on the surfaces of red blood cells. Microorganisms, including viruses and bacteria, also have many surface antigens, some of which may be associated with particular structures. For example, strains of *Salmonella* have specific antigens associated with the proteins of their flagella, called *flagellar antigens* or *H antigens,* and other specific antigens associated with the surface lipopolysaccharides (LPS) of the cell wall, called *somatic antigens* or *O antigens.*

One of the reasons that the immune response is effective in preventing disease is that the toxins contributing to the virulence of pathogenic microorganisms usually have antigenic properties. Antibodies produced against toxins are referred to as *antitoxins.* Most protein toxins are highly antigenic, eliciting the synthesis of high titers (concentrations) of antibody. Similarly, bacterial LPS toxins are moderately antigenic and responsible for the initiation of antibody production against many Gram-negative bacteria. Antibodies formed against viral proteins combine with these proteins and thereby inhibit the viral particle

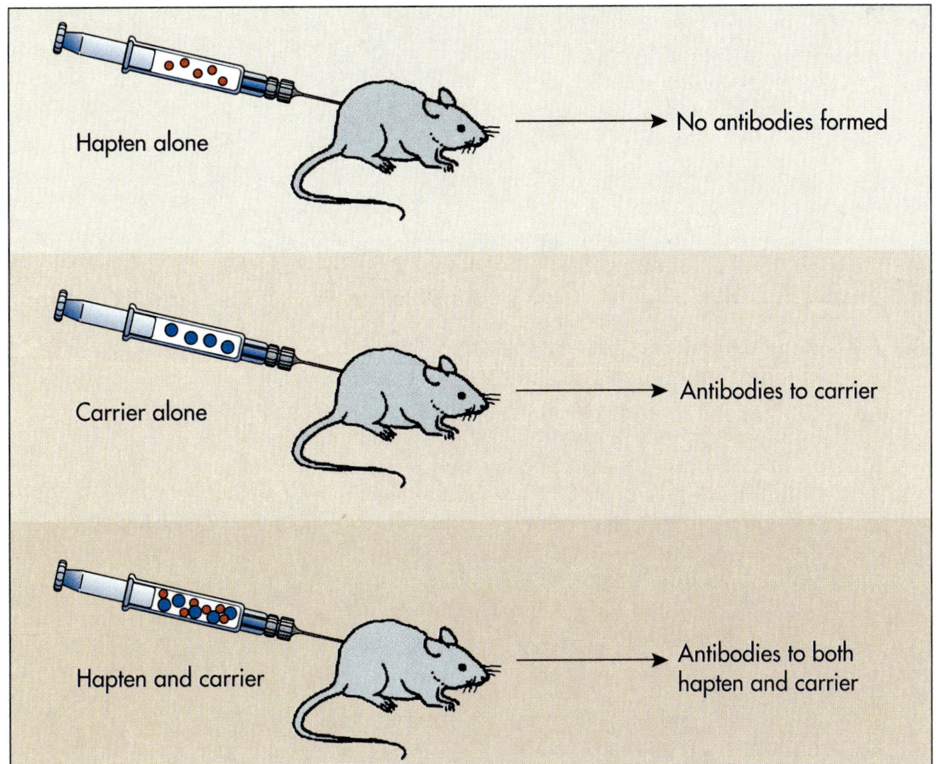

FIG. 11-14 A hapten can elicit antibody formation only when bound to a larger molecule.

from attaching to a host cell. This effectively inhibits the viral replication cycle. These antiviral antibodies are called *neutralizing antibodies.*

Classes of Immunoglobulins (Antibody Molecules)

Immunoglobulins (antibodies) are globular glycoproteins in the serum fraction of blood tissue fluids and some secretions. Plasma cells derived from activated B lymphocytes synthesize antibodies in response to the detection of a foreign antigen. They are made in response to specific antigens and react with those antigens.

There are five classes of immunoglobulins: IgG, IgA, IgM, IgD, and IgE. Each class of immunoglobulin serves a different function in the immune response. The characteristics of these five major classes of immunoglobulin molecules are summarized in Table 11-3.

IgG IgG (immunoglobulin G) is the largest immunoglobulin fraction, generally comprising approximately 80% of the body's immunoglobulins. It is the predominant circulating antibody and readily passes through the walls of small vessels (venules) into extracellular body spaces, where it reacts with antigen and stimulates the attraction of phagocytic cells to invading microorganisms. Reactions of IgG with surface antigens on bacteria activate the complement system and attract additional neutrophils to the site of the infection. IgG is the only antibody that can cross the placenta and confers immunity on the fetus that lasts for the first months after birth. IgG can combine with toxins and neutralize or inactivate them. It also helps prevent the systemic spread of infection through the body and facilitates recovery from many infectious diseases.

TABLE 11-3 Properties of the Five Classes of Immunoglobulins

PROPERTY	IgG	IgA	IgM	IgD	IgE
Molecular weight	150,000	160,000 and dimer	900,000	185,000	200,000
Number of basic four-peptide units (monomers)	1	1, 2	5	1	1
Heavy chains	γ	α	μ	δ	ϵ
Light chains	$\kappa + \lambda$	$\kappa + \lambda$	$\kappa + \lambda$	$\kappa + \lambda$	$\kappa + \lambda$
Number of antigen binding sites	2	2, 4	10	2	2
Concentration range in normal serum	8-16 mg/mL	1.4-4 mg/mL	0.5-2 mg/mL	0-0.4 mg/mL	17-450 μg/mL
Percentage of total immunoglobulin	80	13	6	0-1	0.002
Complement fixation					
Classical	+	−	++	−	−
Alternative	−	±	−	−	−
Crosses the placenta	+	−	−	−	−
Fixes to homologous mast cells and basophils	−	−	−	−	+
Binds to macrophages and neutrophils	+	±	−	−	−
Major characteristics	Most abundant Ig of body fluids; combats infecting bacteria and toxins	Major Ig in seromucous secretions; protects external body surfaces	Effective agglutinator produced early in immune response	Mostly present in lymphocyte surface	Protects external body surfaces; responsible for atopic allergies
Structure	IgG (monomer)	IgA (dimer)	IgM (pentamer)	IgD (monomer)	IgE (monomer)

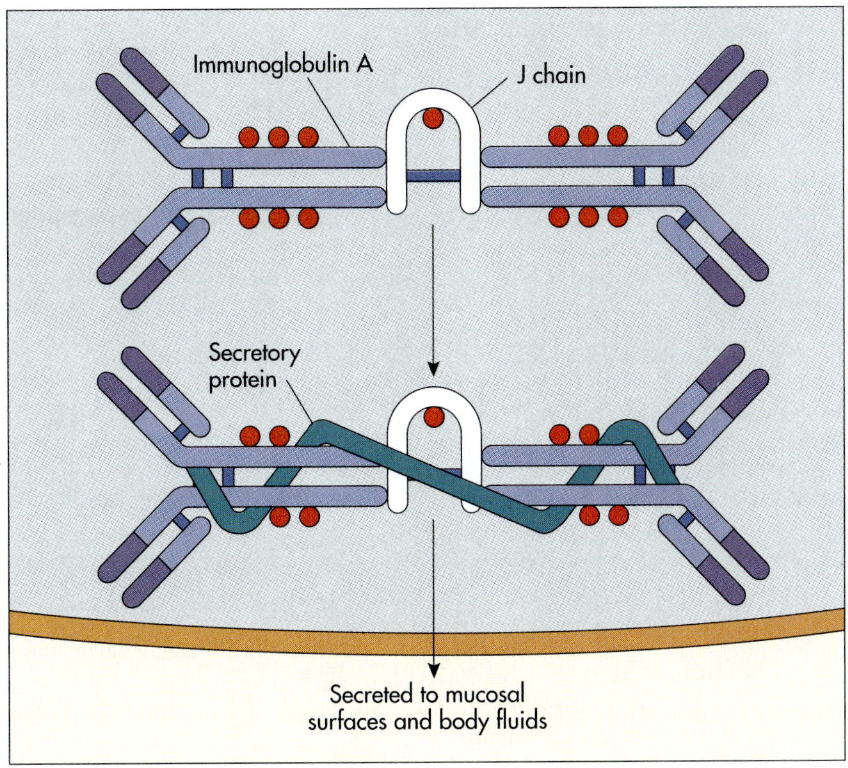

FIG. 11-15 IgA is a dimer that is secreted from plasma cells. A secretory protein binds to the IgA, allowing it to be secreted. The secreted IgA binds to mucosal membranes, protecting body surfaces from infection. (Carbohydrates, *red*.)

IgA IgA (immunoglobulin A) occurs in mucus and in secretions such as saliva, tears, and sweat. It is important in the respiratory, gastrointestinal, and genitourinary tracts, where it protects surface tissues against invasion by pathogenic microorganisms. IgA also is secreted into human breast milk and colostrum, protecting nursing newborns against infectious diseases. The IgA molecules bind with surface antigens of microorganisms, preventing the adherence of such antibody-coated microorganisms to the mucosal cells lining the respiratory, gastrointestinal, and genitourinary tracts. IgA molecules do not initiate the classical complement pathway but may activate the alternative complement pathway. Plasma contains relatively high concentrations of monomeric IgA molecules, but the dimers of IgA bind to receptors on the surface of secretory cells, leading to their secretion into body fluids (FIG. 11-15). The IgA picks up an additional secretory protein that protects it against proteases and promotes its secretion. In mucus secretions, IgA is the major immunoglobulin molecule involved in the immune response that protects external body surfaces.

IgM IgM (immunoglobulin M) is a high molecular weight immunoglobulin, occurring as a pentamer; that is, IgM contains five monomeric units of the basic four-peptide chain immunoglobulin molecule. IgM molecules are formed prior to IgG molecules in response to exposure to an antigen. Because of its high number of antigen-binding sites, the IgM molecule is effective in attaching to multiple cells that have the same surface antigens. As such, it is important in the initial response to a bacterial infection and in the activation of complement. During the later stages of infection, IgG molecules are more important. IgM molecules occur primarily in the blood serum and, with IgG molecules, are important in preventing the circulation of infectious microorganisms through the circulatory system.

IgD IgD (immunoglobulin D) antibody molecules, with monomeric IgM, are present on the surface of some lymphocyte cells. Although the precise role of IgD remains to be fully defined, it appears to play a role as an antigen receptor in lymphocyte activation and suppression. Within blood plasma, IgD molecules are short-lived, being particularly susceptible to proteolytic degradation.

IgE IgE (immunoglobulin E) molecules are normally present in the blood serum as a very low proportion of the immunoglobulins. The ratio of IgG to IgE is normally 50,000:1. IgE serum levels, though, are elevated in individuals with allergic reactions, such as hay fever, and in some persons with chronic parasitic infections. The main role of IgE appears to be the pro-

BOX 11-2

Separation of Immunoglobulins

Immunoglobulins are difficult to separate but can be differentiated by using electrophoresis. Electrophoresis is the process of separating charged particles by their migration in an electrical field. Proteins are separated by electrophoresis on the basis of the electric charge, their size, and the shape of the macromolecule (see FIG.). A protein sample is usually placed on a solid support medium such as agarose or polyacrylamide, which in turn is placed between two electrodes, a positively charged anode and a negatively charged cathode. When the current is turned on, migration takes place at a characteristic rate for each protein determined by its net charge, which is a function of pH, and its molecular weight.

When serum is subjected to electrophoresis, the rapidly migrating albumin fraction is separated from the more slowly migrating globular proteins or globulins. The globulin family is further separated into α, β, and γ globulin fractions. All antibodies are in the γ globulin fraction and sometimes referred to as gammaglobulins.

All classes of immunoglobulins form relatively broad electrophoretic bands, indicating the heterogeneity of molecules within each class and making it difficult to use some forms of electrophoresis for the quantitation of individual classes of immunoglobulins. Such analyses are useful in clinical medicine in diagnosing certain diseases, such as ones associated with deficiencies of the immune response.

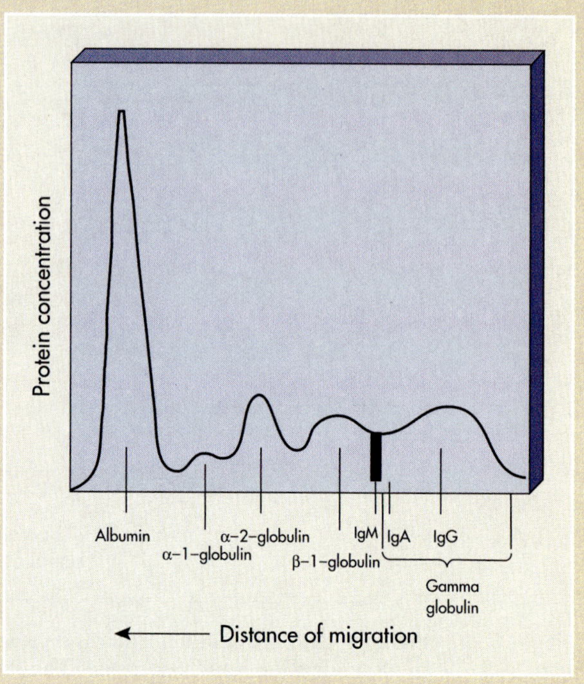

Immunoglobulins can be separated by electrophoresis into various globulins, including IgA and IgG.

tection of external mucosal surfaces by mediating the attraction of phagocytic cells and the initiation of the inflammatory response. IgE molecules are important because they bind to mast cells and basophils, where they have a role in mediating immune reactions, including, unfortunately, hypersensitivity reactions such as hay fever and other allergic responses. The tight binding of IgE to cell membranes of circulating mast cells and basophils is an unusual property of IgE.

Structure of Immunoglobulins

The five classes of immunoglobulins have the same basic molecular structure, consisting of four peptide chains, two identical heavy chains, and two identical light chains, which are joined by disulfide bridges linking the chains (FIG. 11-16; Table 11-3). The terms *heavy* and *light* refer to the relative molecular weights of the polypeptide chains. There are more amino acids in the heavy chain; hence, it has a greater molecular weight than the light chain.

Papain cleaves the immunoglobulin molecule to form two identical **Fab fragments** that contain the

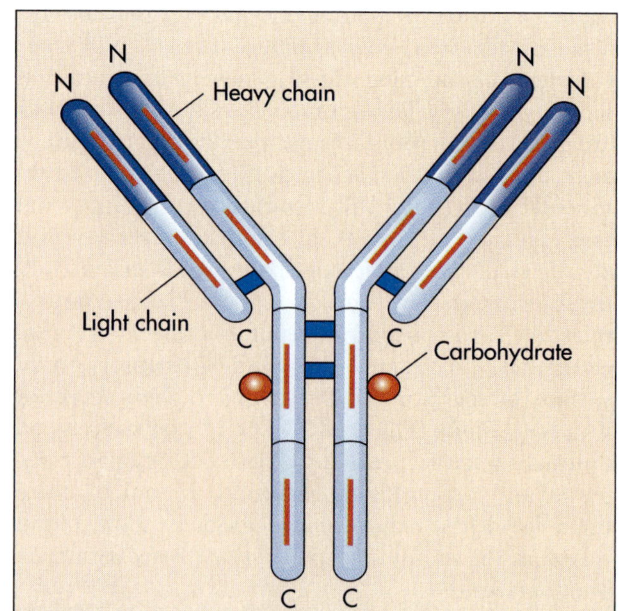

FIG. 11-16 **A,** An immunoglobulin has two heavy and two light chains joined by disulfide bonds.

B

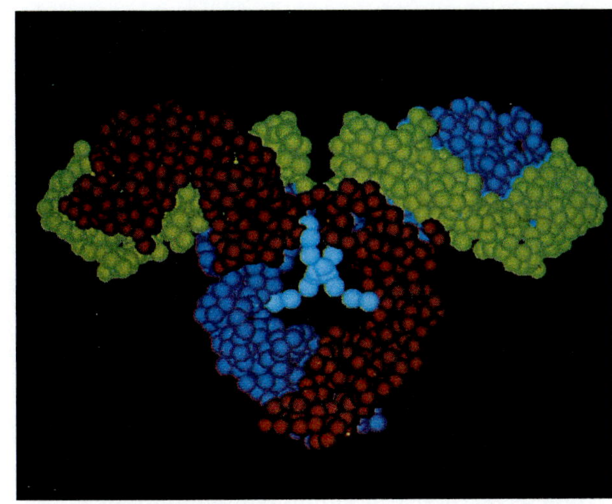

FIG. 11-16, cont'd. **B,** A computer-generated model of IgG showing one heavy chain in red, one heavy chain in blue, and the light chains in green.

antigen-combining site and an additional **Fc fragment,** which is crystallizable. The Fc portion may contain amino acid sequences that anchor the immunoglobulin molecule to the cytoplasmic membranes of cells. Pepsin cleaves the immunoglobulin molecule at another location, forming a divalent antibody-binding fragment (Fab'_2) but not forming Fc fragments (FIG. 11-17). It is the Fab fragment that actually binds to antigen molecules, whereas the Fc fragment augments the action of the immunoglobulin molecule by binding to complement molecules or phagocytic cells.

Within each of the major classes of immunoglobulins, there may be variants. For example, IgG can be grouped into four subclasses, IgG1, IgG2, IgG3, and IgG4; each subclass has differences in the heavy chains of the immunoglobulin molecule. There are two subclasses of IgA. Immunoglobulin molecules of the same class are referred to as **isotypes,** due to variations in the heavy chain constant regions. **Allotypes** refer to genetically controlled allelic forms of the immunoglobulin molecule and reflect variations in the constant regions of the heavy chains, and **idiotypes** refer to the individual specific immunoglobulin molecules that differ in certain regions of the Fab fragments. Isotype forms are present in all individuals but allotypes result from the allelic differences in immunoglobulin genes. These many variations in immunoglobulins establish the needed diversity of macromolecules for an effective immune response.

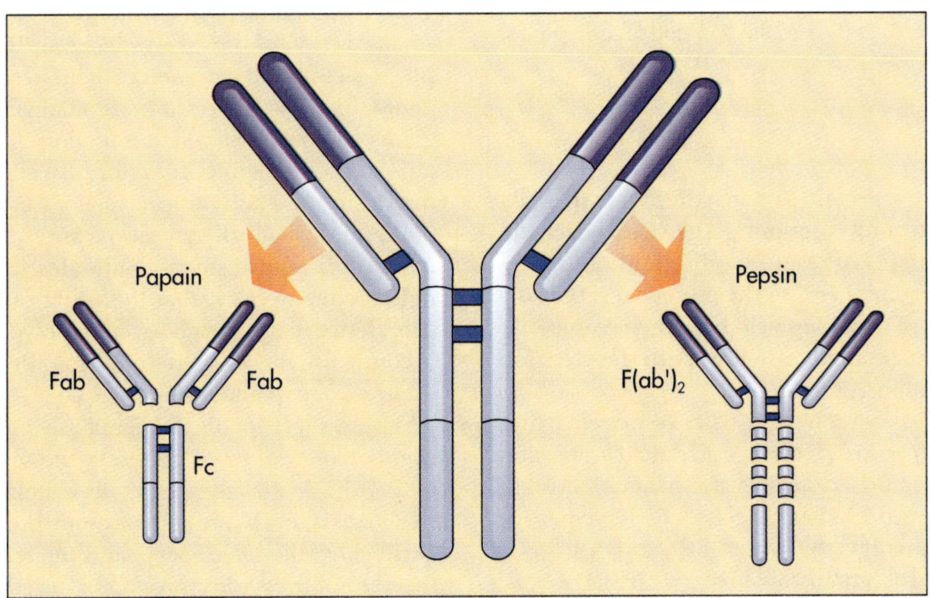

FIG. 11-17 Papain and pepsin cleave IgG into differing fragments, including Fab and Fc fragments; the Fab fragment binds to antigen.

Light Chains The light chains of the immunoglobulin molecules may be kappa (κ) or lambda (λ). Both κ and λ light chains are roughly divided into two domains, each containing about 110 amino acids (FIG. 11-18). At the amino terminal end is a **variable region (V),** so called because there is a high degree of variability in the amino acid sequence from one λ chain or one κ chain to another. Within each V region are three domains that have even greater amino acid variability than the rest of the V region. These three domains are **hypervariable regions**; together with the

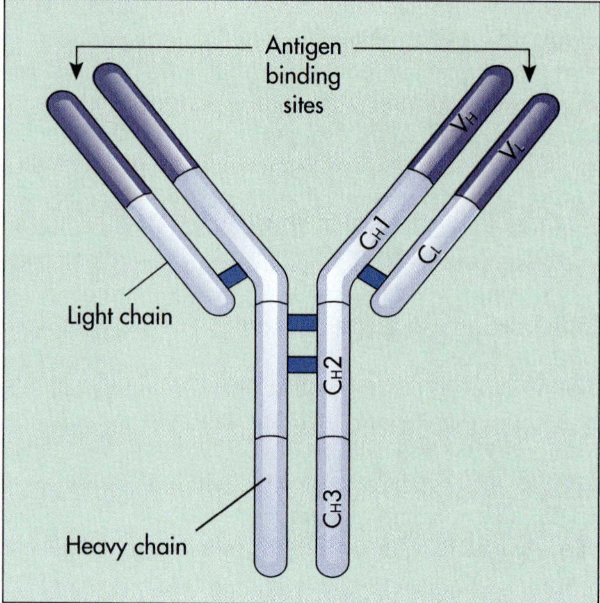

FIG. 11-18 The light chains of immunoglobulins have domains, each with about 110 amino acids. Different amino acid sequences occur at the variable (V) end accounting for the specificity of the antigen-antibody reaction.

heavy chain hypervariable regions, they form the antigen recognition and combining site. Differences in hypervariable regions result in different idiotypes. The carboxyl terminal end of the molecule is the **constant region (C)**. The amino acid sequence in the C region of one light chain is conserved with the C region of other light chains.

Heavy Chains There are five types of heavy chains, referred to as alpha (α), gamma (γ), delta (δ), epsilon (ϵ), and mu (μ). Differences in the heavy chains are responsible for the five major classes, or **isotypes,** of immunoglobulins. IgG, for example, contains two γ heavy chains; IgD contains two δ heavy chains.

Immunoglobulin heavy chains are roughly divided into domains, each containing approximately 110 amino acids. γ, δ, and α chains form three domains and μ and ϵ chains form four domains. The N terminal domain contains the variable or V region, within which are three hypervariable regions just as in light chains. The remaining two or three domains of the heavy chain form the C or constant region. The conserved nature of the heavy chain is only within a particular class. In other words, α heavy chain C regions are all similar but are different from μ heavy chain C regions. Between constant domains 1 and 2 (toward the N terminus) is a region on the heavy chain that is more flexible than the rest of the Ig molecule. This area is called the *hinge region* and may help the antibody molecule stretch to cross-link two separate antigens. μ, α, and δ heavy chains have additional amino acids at the carboxyl terminus called *tail pieces*. The tail piece allows the binding of an additional polypeptide chain, the joining chain (J). This J chain allows dimers and pentamers of these immunoglobulins to form. IgM is found as a pentamer and IgA is a dimer.

Genetic Basis for Immunoglobulin Diversity

The human immune system has a virtually unlimited capacity to generate different antibodies, which recognize and bind to millions of potential antigens. The genetic variability coding for this diversity of antibody molecules provides the basis for the immune response to many different antigens. Before the recognition that eukaryotic cells had split genes, it was difficult to understand how the genome encoded the information for the enormous diversity of antibodies.

One early theory of immunoglobulin diversity proposed that each human cell contains a separate gene encoding each antibody chain that an individual is capable of synthesizing. However, there is not enough DNA in human cells to accomplish this and still have genes that code for other functions; the human genome contains perhaps a million genes, and only a small fraction of these can specify antibodies. Another proposal was that each cell contains a small number of genes for encoding antibody chains but that these genes are so susceptible to mutation that multiple mutations accumulating in mature B cells confer on the organism the ability to produce a variety of different antibodies. This theory also cannot adequately account for the diversity of antibodies. Thus the theory, held for many years, that there is a one-to-one correspondence between genes and polypeptides cannot account for the diversity of antibodies, and another theoretical explanation is necessary.

The essence of the explanation of how a limited number of genes can generate the great diversity of antibodies is that the genes ultimately specifying the structure of each antibody are not present as such in germ cells (the male sperm and the female egg) or in the cells of the early embryo. Rather, the currently accepted theory is that there are variable and constant regions of antibodies that are encoded by separate groups of genes. Polypeptides making up the antibodies can be synthesized from information contained in several gene fragments scattered over the genome. Recombination permits shuffling and joining of the components so that billions of different combinations can be generated. The reshuffling results in numerous combinations of varieties of the light chains (kappa and lambda) and heavy chains (alpha, delta, epsilon, gamma, and mu) that make up the complete immunoglobulin molecules. There are three clusters of genes, one for heavy chain synthesis and two for light chain synthesis. Within each cluster, there are gene fragments that contain the information for the complete immunoglobulin molecules.

Light Chain Diversity The active gene for a light chain is assembled and expressed by a process of so-

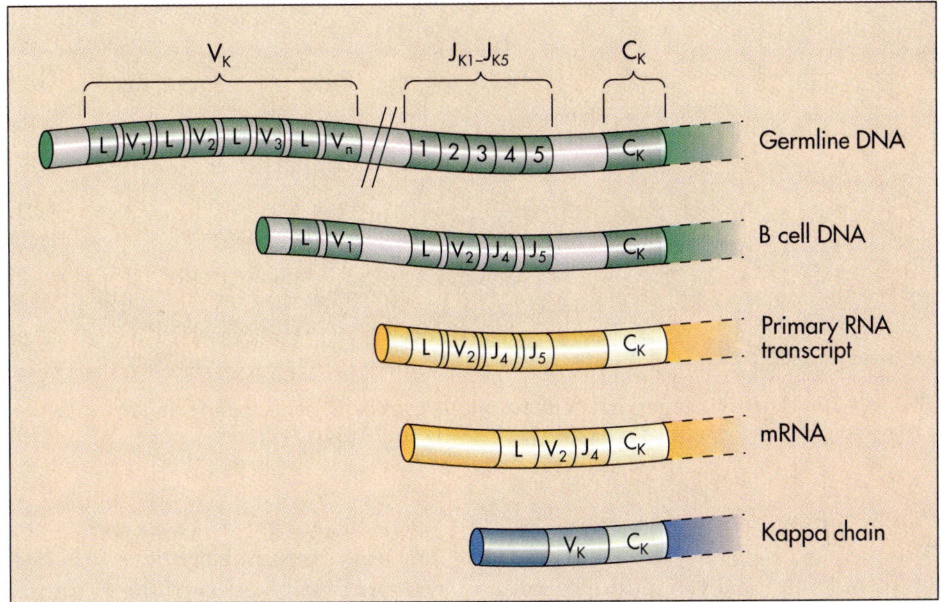

FIG. 11-19 Immunoglobulin genes that code for the light chains are split. In B cells, rearrangements result in joining of some V and J genes. Transcription followed by elimination of introns produces a functional mRNA. Translation results in the formation of one of the chains of the immunoglobulin.

matic recombination and RNA splicing (FIG. 11-19). In this system, the components of the active gene are present in the germ line in the cells of the embryo in multiple versions. Each complete light chain genetic region includes a variable region and a constant region. For the light chain, the variable region is encoded by *variable (V)* and *joining (J) sequences* and the constant region by a *C* gene. A large number of variable genes, with closely related nucleotide sequences, have been identified in embryonic DNA. There may be 150 alternative *V* sequences, each separated from a leader (*L*) sequence by a short intervening sequence. The *L* sequence specifies a hydrophobic leader that is 17 to 20 amino acids long. The other coding region of the *V* gene specifies most but not all of the variable region. The *L*/*V* segments are separated from five joining sequences by a long noncoding sequence of DNA. The *J* sequence, which codes for the remaining portion of the variable region, is a short sequence that is repeated several times, with slight but significant variations, at intervals of about 300 nucleotides. In the human light kappa-chain system, the *J* sequences, in turn, are separated from a *C* gene by another intervening sequence. In the human light lambda-chain system, the arrangement is somewhat different in having six *C* genes, each one apparently linked to its own *J* sequence.

The joining of one of 150 *V* genes to one of 5 *J* genes can generate 150 × 5, or 750, different active genes for a light-chain variable region. However, even greater light chain diversity occurs because the *V*/*J* recombination site is not precisely defined. A *V* gene and a *J* gene can apparently be joined at different crossover points, and if there are 10 alternative joining sites, there would be a tenfold increase in diversity, giving rise to 7,500 different possible combinations.

During lymphocyte development, one *V* gene with its *L* sequence is recombined with one of the *J* sequences to form, along with the single *C* gene, an active kappa gene. The entire gene is transcribed into an hnRNA transcript. The hnRNA is converted to mRNA by removing the intervening sequences (introns), including extra joining segments that may be present in the hnRNA. The mRNA is translated to form a light-chain precursor containing a leader that acts as a signal sequence to initiate the transport of the protein across the cytoplasmic membrane. The leader is cleaved away as the light-chain precursor moves across the cytoplasmic membrane to produce the mature light chain. Light chains fold up in such a way that the hypervariable region forms the antibody-antigen combining site.

Heavy Chain Diversity Formation of the variable region in the heavy chain is governed by the same principles that apply to the light chain, but the potential for diversity is even greater (FIG. 11-20, p. 408). The additional diversity comes from a sequence of embryonic DNA called the *diversity (D) gene.* The *D* gene accounts for a significant portion of the hypervariable region of the heavy chain. The heavy chain is thus a recombinational product of the *V, J, D,* and *C* genes. Active heavy-chain genes are assembled by recombination of one of the *L*/*V* sequences, a *D* gene, and a *J* gene to code for the variable region of the chain and a *C* gene to code for the constant region. In the heavy chain, there are eight separate *C* sequences, each one

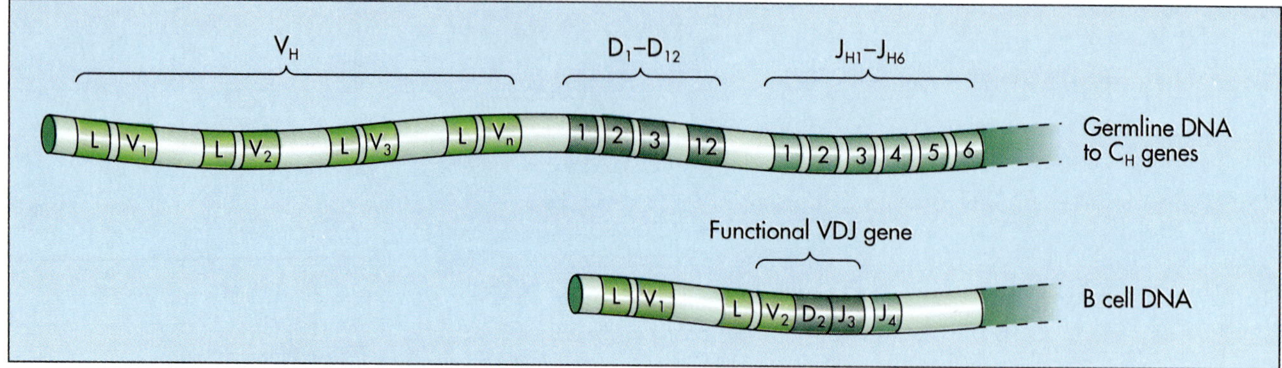

FIG. 11-20 The split genes that code for the heavy chains of immunoglobulin molecules are rearranged to form functional genes with V, D, and J gene segments.

coding for a different constant region. Assuming that there are 50 *D* sequences, 80 *V* sequences, 6 *J* sequences, and 100 recombinational variations, for embryonic human cells there are therefore 2.4 million possible different heavy chains. With the 7,500 possible combinations available to the human kappa light chain, the 2.4 million heavy chains yield a total of some 18 billion possible antibodies coded for by only about 300 separate genetic segments in the embryonic DNA. In addition, mutations within the genes encoding the variable region of the immunoglobulin also contribute to immunoglobulin diversity.

B Cell Activation

When a B lymphocyte with an immunoglobulin molecule on its surface (antigen receptor) encounters a foreign antigen for which that immunoglobulin is programmed, there is a reaction between the immunoglobulin and the antigen that initiates B cell activation. This activation leads to the formation of plasma cells that secrete antibody and to a clone of B cells, called B memory cells, that have identical surface antigen receptors as the initial B cell that is activated.

Each individual B lymphocyte cell contains the genetic information for initiating an immune response to a single specific antigen. The antigen receptor is located within the cytoplasmic membrane of the differentiated B lymphocyte. The presence of a specific antigen selects for a specific pre-existing B cell. The activation of this B cell leads to *clonal expansion,* that is, cell division of a specific B lymphocyte that leads to a population of genetically identical B lymphocytes that respond to the specific antigen that initiated B cell activation.

During B cell activation, a bivalent or multivalent antigen with more than one antigenic determinant can cross-link or bring together membrane immunoglobulin molecules. As a result of cross-linking, the antibody molecule and antigen are internalized within the B cell. The antigen is processed within the cell. If the antigen is a protein, it is proteolytically broken down into polypeptides that become associated with specific proteins of the B lymphocyte known as *major histocompatibility (MHC) class II proteins.* As a result of this interaction, the B lymphocyte becomes an **antigen presenting cell (APC).** APCs are cells with small polypeptide antigens attached to the MHC class II proteins on outer cell membrane surfaces such that the antigen is presented or shown to T_H cells.

T_H cells interact with these B lymphocyte APCs via the MHC class II antigen and T cell receptor-CD3-CD4 complex (discussed later in this chapter). The T_H cells become activated in response to binding to the B lymphocyte. The activated T_H cells then release substances called **cytokines** or **lymphokines** that specifically stimulate the B lymphocyte into cell growth and proliferation. These cytokines include γ-interferon, interleukin-2 (IL-2), interleukin-4 (IL-4), and interleukin-5 (IL-5). The γ-interferon may enhance antibody isotype switching. IgM is the first immunoglobulin made by an activated B lymphocyte. Later, the B lymphocyte can switch to making IgG or another immunoglobulin isotype.

Some antigens do not require interaction with T lymphocytes for B lymphocytes to become activated. These antigens are called *thymus-independent antigens (TI antigens).* TI antigens generally do not stimulate as strong an immune response as thymus dependent antigens. TI-1 antigens are totally T cell independent. They do not involve any interaction with immunoglobulin receptors. LPS of Gram-negative bacteria is a potent TI-1 antigen and, at high concentrations (>10 μg/mL), may stimulate B cells directly. TI-2 antigens may be partially independent of T cell help and can elicit antibody formation in mice that lack thymus glands. TI-2 antigens may induce cross-linking of membrane immunoglobulin receptors, which leads to B cell activation without T_H interaction. TI-2 antigens include polysaccharides such as dextrans and pneumococcal polysaccharide and some lipids. Both TI-1 and TI-2 antigens lead only to IgM formation, since T lymphocyte cytokines are required for isotype switching. Also, TI-1 and TI-2 antigens do not elicit a B memory cell response, which also involves cytokines.

Maturation of B Lymphocytes

Following B cell activation, there is a series of additional events that lead to antibody production and formation of a clone of B memory cells. These events are called *B cell maturation.* The steps in B lymphocyte maturation occur in response to interactions with specific antigens. An antigen binds to a receptor at the best-fitting antigen-combining site. By this interaction, the cell displaying the selected immunoglobulin is driven further along its developmental pathway (FIG. 11-21).

In the course of B-cell maturation, IgD and IgM disappear from the cell surface and, instead, IgM, IgG, IgE, or IgA is secreted by the cell. Because each heavy chain gives the antibody a different effector function, the same combining site can take part in different immune reactions. The process by which the same variable region appears in association with different heavy-chain constant regions is called **heavy-chain class switching.**

During the maturation of B lymphocytes, a precursor of the antibody-producing cells, the pre-B lymphocytes, makes a μ heavy-chain constant region linked to a specific variable region (a product of V/D/J recombination). This heavy chain at first remains inside the pre-B cell, but after the onset of light-chain and delta heavy-chain synthesis, the μ and the δ heavy chains combine with the light chains to form complete IgM and IgD molecules, with the concurrent appearance of both IgM and IgD on the cell surface. Both antibodies have the same variable regions, and so both are directed against the same antigen.

There are two mechanisms involved in class switching in B lymphocytes. One mechanism is based on differential RNA transcription and splicing, and the other mechanism is based on a version of DNA recombination. RNA transcription and splicing account for the successive appearance of membrane-bound and secreted IgM and for the simultaneous appearance of IgM and IgD. A heavy-chain class switch is accomplished by DNA recombination in which a switching signal (S) precedes each constant region. The switching signal can modify the recombination that joins a V/D/J sequence to one of the downstream constant-region sequences by changing the particular constant region that is united to the V/D/J sequence. In addition, the secretion of cytokines by T helper lymphocytes is required for class switching to occur.

As a result of its activation and maturation, B lymphocytes differentiate into *plasma cells* that secrete large amounts of antibody specific for the stimulating antigen. In addition to leading to the formation of antibody-secreting cells, the reaction of B cells with antigen results in the establishment of an increased population of memory cells. Although B lymphocyte memory cells do not secrete antibody themselves, they are the precursors of plasma cells. Plasma cells derived from the cloning and differentiation of B lymphocytes are responsible for the secretion of extracellular anti-

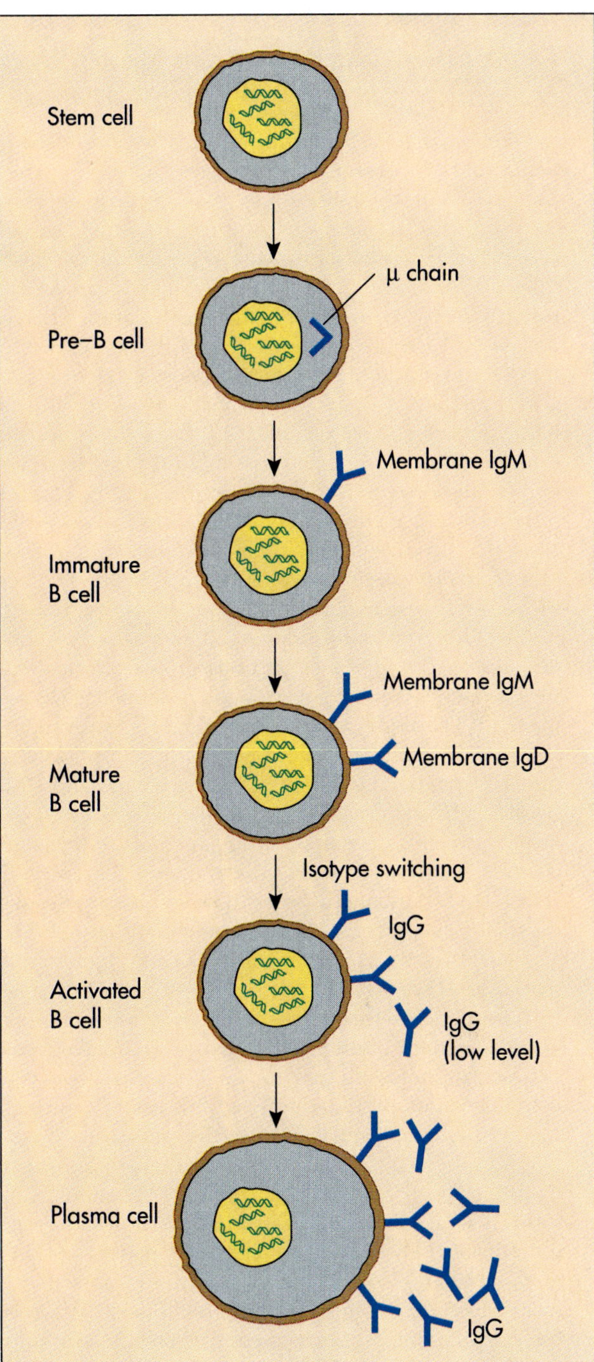

FIG. 11-21 B cell maturation involves formation of a cell with membrane-bound IgM and IgD. When stimulated by an antigen there is isotope switching to form an activated B cell with IgG surface receptors. The activated B cell gives rise to an IgG secreting plasma cell.

BOX 11-3

Culture of Hybridomas and Monoclonal Antibodies

The fact that each specific antibody is synthesized by a different cell line of B lymphocytes and their derived plasma cells makes it difficult to study antibody structure and antibody–antigen interactions. However, certain cells called *myelomas* can be used to produce large quantities of one type of antibody; *myeloma* cells can be cultured indefinitely in tissue culture techniques, whereas normal cells tend to die off after a specific number of transfers in tissue culture media. Most myelomas produce antibody of unknown specificity. However, a technique was developed in 1975 by Cesar Milstein and Georges Köhler in England that fused B lymphocytes of known antibody production with myeloma cells. This cell fusion created immortalized hybrid cells, called *hybridomas,* that produce large amounts of *monoclonal antibody* of a particular specificity. A monoclonal antibody reacts with a single type of antigen.

The formation of hybridoma cell lines is based on the development of myeloma cells that grow in normal culture medium but do not grow in a defined, selective medium. These cells lack the functional genes thymidine kinase (TK) and hypoxanthine-guanine phosphoribosyl transferase (HGPRT) required for nucleotide and DNA synthesis. In addition, these myeloma cells cannot grow in the presence of aminopterin, which also blocks nucleotide synthesis. The selective medium that is used, called HAT, contains hypoxanthine, aminopterin, and thymidine but specific myeloma mutants that are TK^- and $HGPRT^-$ die in HAT medium because they cannot synthesize DNA.

B lymphocytes that secrete antibody to a specific antigen are produced by injecting the specific antigen into a mouse. After allowing time for the B cells to respond to the antigen and produce antibody, the mouse's spleen is removed and opened to release the numerous B lymphocytes it contains (see FIG.). Hybridomas are formed by fusing the B cells with $TK^-/HGPRT^-$ myeloma cells using Sendai virus (today, hybridomas are fused with polyethylene glycol). These cells are placed in HAT medium to grow. B cells do not survive for more than 1 or 2 weeks and the myeloma cells die quickly. However, fused hybridoma cells grow well in HAT medium, since they have the TK and HGPRT genes from the normal B lymphocytes and their ability to grow in tissue culture from the myeloma cell. The hybridomas are screened and selected for the production of antibody specific for the antigen used. The clones of these hybridoma cells produce, in tissue culture, large amounts of specific monoclonal antibody.

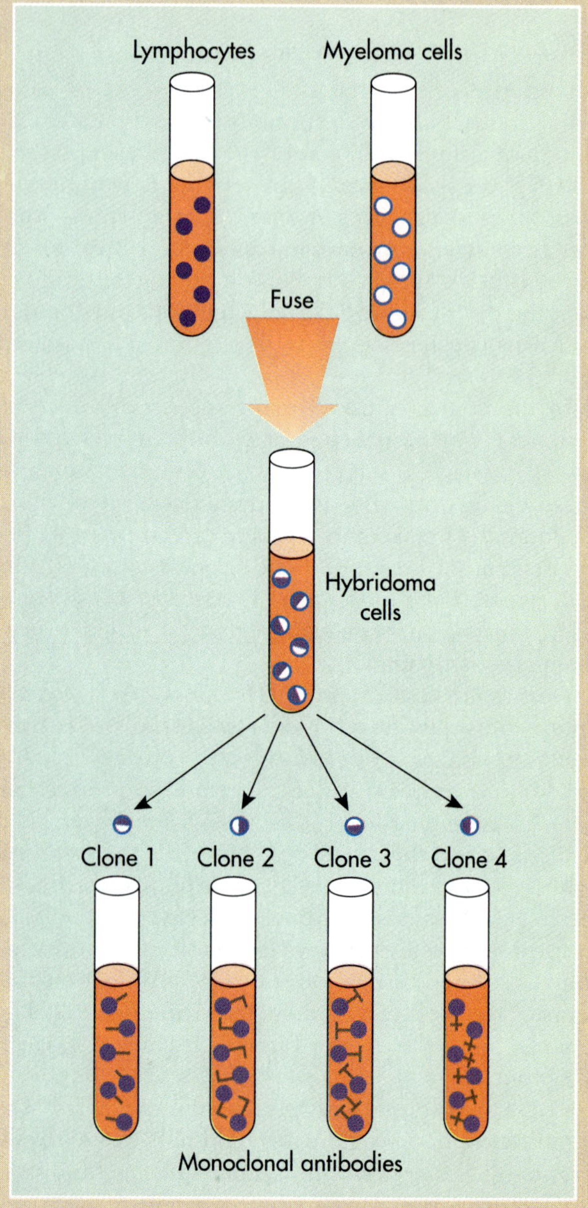

Monoclonal antibodies are produced by fusing lymphocytes with specific IgG encoding genes with myeloma cells to form hybridoma cells. Clones of these hybridoma cells reproduce rapidly and express single antibodies.

These highly specific monoclonal antibodies are useful in clinical procedures and may prove useful in the treatment of some diseases. If, for example, monoclonal antibodies could be made from antigens that are unique to particular pathogens, these antibodies could be used to treat specific diseases. Monoclonal antibodies are already used for the diagnosis of allergies and infectious diseases such as hepatitis, rabies, and some venereal diseases. Early stages of cancer may also be detectable with monoclonal antibodies because certain types of cancer cells have surface antigens that differ from those of normal cells. It is possible that, in the future, monoclonal antibodies will be used to treat cancer and infectious diseases. Monoclonal antibodies, used alone or chemically attached to drugs, could locate and destroy a cancer cell or pathogenic microorganism without damaging the healthy tissue surrounding it.

bodies into the blood serum. Each clone of a plasma cell line secretes a single specific antibody molecule.

Because relatively few B cells with the appropriate receptors are present at the first exposure to a given antigen, the primary antibody-mediated immune response is characteristically slow, producing relatively low yields of antibody. There is a long lag period in the **primary immune response,** during which selection, differentiation, and cloning of appropriate B cell lines must occur. After an antigen elicits an antibody-mediated immune response, there is an increase in the number of B lymphocytes capable of reacting with that antigen. Because antigen binds to and selects for cells having receptors of the highest affinity, this process results in an increase in the number of lymphocyte cells with receptors of high affinity for the particular antigenic molecule. The cloning of these cells establishes a bank of memory cells. Memory cells are long-lived resting cells. They do not secrete antibody. On subsequent exposure to the same antigen, perhaps years later, the memory cells are activated and rapidly divide into a clone, producing a larger population of plasma cells that can initiate the **secondary immune response** rapidly and efficiently. Subsequent exposure to the same antigen leads to a secondary immune response that is called a **memory response** or **anamnestic response.** The anamnestic response is characterized by the more rapid and extensive production of immunoglobulin.

Antigen–Antibody Reactions

Antibody-mediated immunity is important in preventing and eliminating microbial infections. The basis of these reactions depends on the reactions of antigen with antibody molecules. The reactions of IgA molecules with bacteria and viruses in the fluids surrounding surface tissues, for example, prevent the adsorption of many potential pathogens onto these surface barriers. In this way, IgA antibody molecules prevent the establishment of infections. IgG antibody molecules, acting as antitoxins, neutralize toxin molecules by combining with them, thus blocking their reactions and preventing the onset of disease symptomatology. Even poisonous cobra venom can be neutralized by reaction with appropriate antibody molecules.

Opsonization The interactions of antibody with surface antigens of bacterial cells render many pathogenic bacteria susceptible to phagocytosis. In fact, the ingestive phagocytic attack on most bacteria requires an initial antigen–antibody reaction before phagocytic blood cells can engulf the invading bacteria. Both polymorphonuclear neutrophils and macrophages express receptors for the Fc portion of antibody on their surface. The increased phagocytosis associated with antibody-bound antigen, called **opsonization,** is important in the destruction of pathogenic bacteria (FIG. 11-22). Antigen–antibody

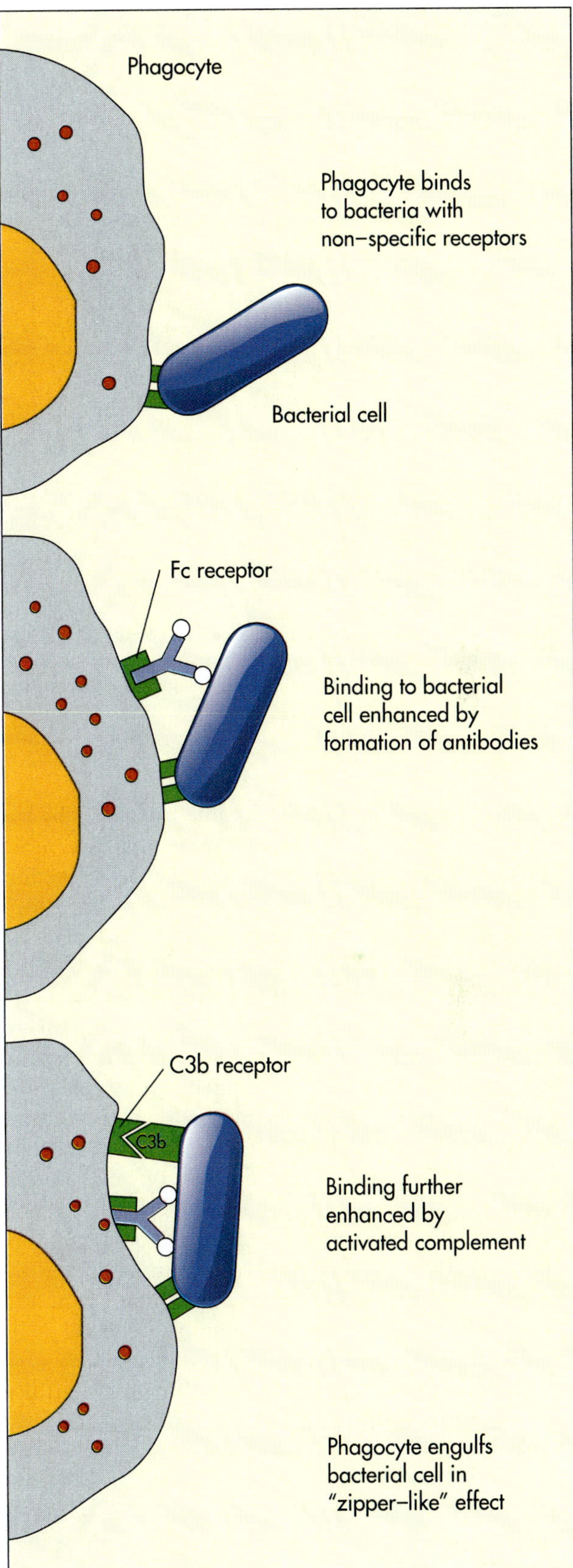

FIG. 11-22 Opsonization involves binding of a bacterial cell to the surface of a phagocyte via several mechanisms, including immunoglobulin and complement receptors. By binding to multiple receptors the bacterial cell becomes firmly attached and engulfed by the phagocytic cell. It is subsequently ingested and digested.

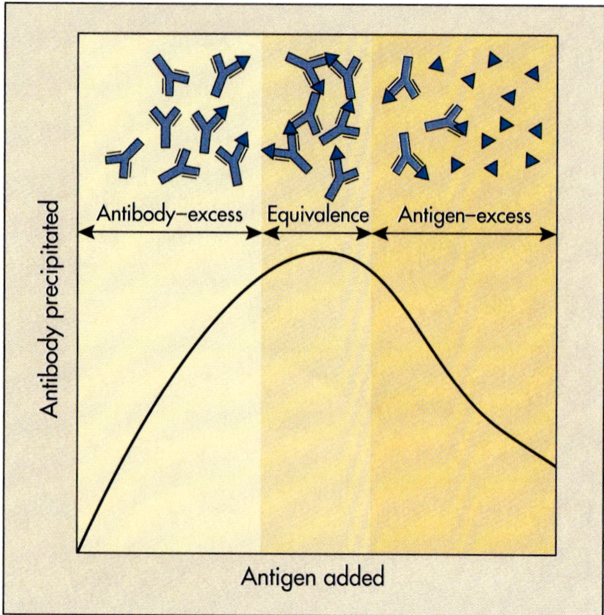

FIG. 11-23 When antibody and antigen react in the right proportions (within the equivalence zone) a precipitate forms. Less precipitation occurs when antigen or antibody are in excess.

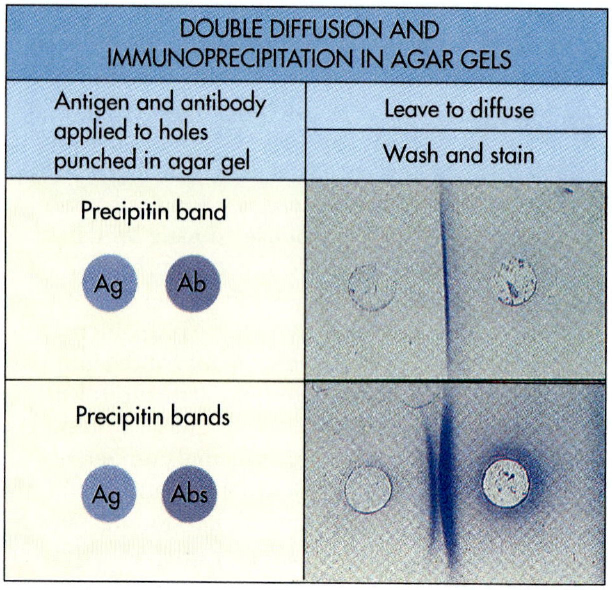

DOUBLE DIFFUSION AND IMMUNOPRECIPITATION IN AGAR GELS

Antigen and antibody applied to holes punched in agar gel

Leave to diffuse

Wash and stain

Precipitin band

Ag Ab

Precipitin bands

Ag Abs

FIG. 11-24 To achieve equivalence of antigen and antibody so that precipitaton will occur, the antigen and antibody can be allowed to diffuse toward each other from separate wells in an agar support medium. This is done in the Ouchterlony double diffusion method. If the antigen and antibody match precisely, an arc of precipitation will occur in the zone of equivalence. No precipitate occurs if there is no antigen–antibody reaction. If there is only a partial match between antigen and antibody, only a partial arc of precipitation will occur.

reactions are required to overcome infections by bacteria, such as *Haemophilus influenzae,* that are inherently resistant to phagocytosis. These *in vivo* reactions between antigen and antibody molecules constitute a major defense against invading bacteria and other microorganisms.

Precipitin Reactions Antibody molecules have two or more antigen-combining sites. Many antigens are also multivalent, that is, they contain multiple antibody combining sites. If an antigen is a soluble molecule and is multivalent, its combination with antibody can lead to aggregates or lattice formation with the resultant precipitation of the antigen out of solution. Antibodies that combine with soluble multivalent antigens are called *precipitating antibodies* or *precipitins.* Precipitation occurs when there are optimal concentrations (zone of equivalence) of both antigen and antibody rather than an excess of one or the other (FIG. 11-23).

Precipitin reactions can be used for the identification of antigen–antibody complexes by carrying out the reaction in agar or agarose gels. In the *Ouchterlony double-diffusion technique,* antigen and antibody (antiserum) are put into wells that are cut in the gel (FIG. 11-24). The antigen and antibody diffuse out of their wells. Where antigen and antibody meet they form complexes and, at their zone of equivalence, will form precipitin lines in the gel. Interpretation of the patterns of precipitin lines can often determine the similarity or difference of the reactants to each other.

Gel diffusion of antigen and antibody can also be combined with electrophoresis in an immunoelectrophoresis technique (FIG. 11-25). A sample is placed in a well cut into agar that has been poured on a glass slide. The antigens in the sample are separated from one another in an electrical field. Then a trough is cut in the agar and filled with antibody solution. The antigens and antibody diffuse through the gel toward one another and if they form antigen–antibody complexes, precipitin arcs will form in the gel.

Agglutination Antigens that are located on the surface of cells or other particles are not soluble. Reaction with antibody molecules can lead to the aggregation or clumping of these cells or particles; such a reaction is called **agglutination.** Antibodies that combine with particulate antigens are called **agglutinating antibodies** or **agglutinins.**

If the antigens are located on the surface of red blood cells and the addition of antibody leads to clumping of the cells, this is called **hemagglutination.** Hemagglutination is the basis for blood typing and distinguishing the presence of A type antigen or B type antigen on the surface of human red blood cells (FIG. 11-26). Individuals with type A blood have erythrocytes with the A antigen on their surface and these cells will be agglutinated by anti-A antibodies, whereas individuals with type B blood have erythrocytes with the B antigen on their surface and these cells will be agglutinated by anti-B antibodies. Type O erythrocytes have neither the A nor B antigen and will not be ag-

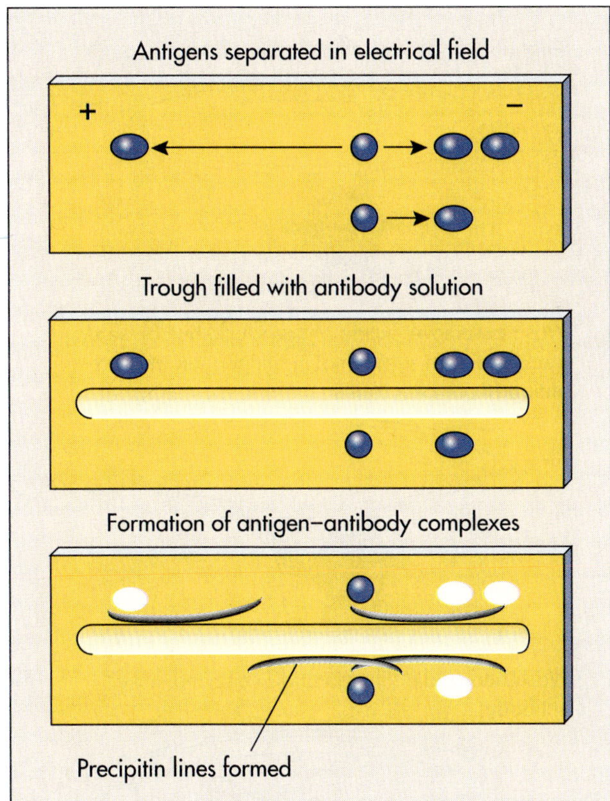

FIG. 11-25 In immunoelectrophoresis, antigens can be separated by electrophoresis on a gel. Antibody can then be allowed to diffuse into the gel. Precipitin lines form in the zones of equivalence.

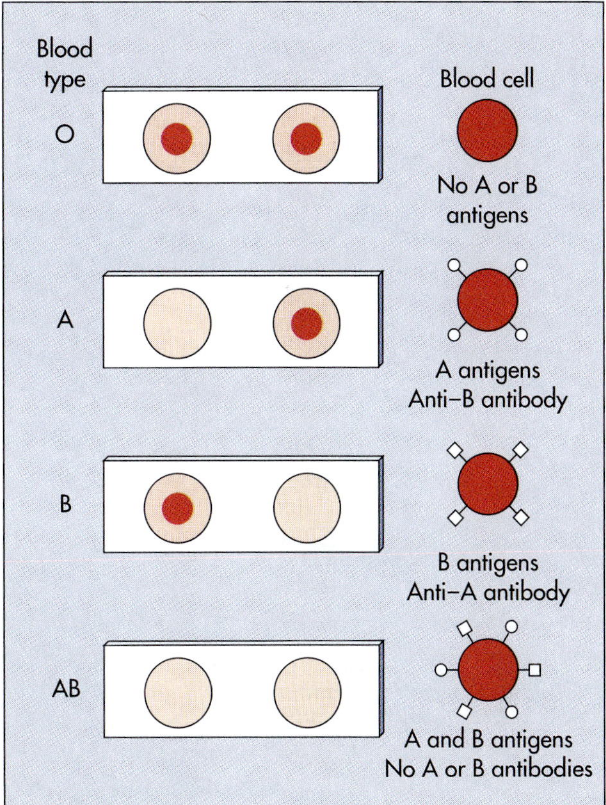

FIG. 11-26 Agglutination reactions are used to determine the major blood types. This is based on separate reactions with anti-A and anti-B antibodies to determine the presence or absence of A and B antigens on the cell surface. Agglutination is shown here as the formation of clumps of cells *(small dotted pattern)* and lack of agglutination by the presence of a pellet of unreacted cells in the center; this is how the reaction appears in the wells of a microtiter plate where many blood typing reactions are run.

glutinated by either anti-A serum or anti-B serum. Finally, type AB blood has erythrocytes with both markers and will be agglutinated by both anti-A and anti-B sera.

ELISA and RIA The identification of antigen–antibody complexes has been one of the hallmarks of immunology. Two techniques increased the sensitivity of detection of antigen–antibody complexes beyond that of precipitation and agglutination reactions. The **enzyme-linked immunosorbent assay (ELISA)** and **radioimmune assay (RIA)** utilize labels attached to antibody molecules to detect antigen–antibody reactions. These labels or ligands include enzymes for ELISA and radioisotopes for RIA.

The ELISA can be used for detecting the presence of antigen in a sample (FIG. 11-27, p. 414). Antibody specific for the antigen is bound to a well in a plastic microtiter plate. A sample that may or may not contain antigen is added to the well. If antigen is present, it will bind to the antibody. Unbound antigen is washed out of the well. A second antibody solution is added to the well, but these labelled antibodies have an enzyme molecule bound to them. Frequently used are horseradish peroxidase, glucose oxidase, and alkaline phosphatase. Excess labelled antibody is washed out of the well. Then, the substrate for the enzyme is added. The reaction of the enzyme forms a colored product that can be measured spectrophotometrically. The amount of colored product is proportional to the amount of antigen bound in the microtiter well. The direct ELISA can be used for detecting viral or bacterial proteins, hormones, drugs, and other antigens in a specimen.

Indirect ELISAs (FIG. 11-28, p. 414) are used for detecting the presence of antibody in serum. In the indirect method, antigen is bound to the microtiter well and serum (containing antibody) is added to it. Excess and unbound antibody is washed out of the well. If antibody specific to the antigen is present in the serum, it will bind to the antigen in the microtiter well. A second antibody is then added; this antibody is animal (usually goat or rabbit) anti-human IgG that has been conjugated with enzyme. If the primary antibody has bound to antigen, the secondary antibody will bind to it and can be detected by the addition of the enzyme substrate. Indirect ELISAs are used in clinical laboratories to detect the presence of antibodies

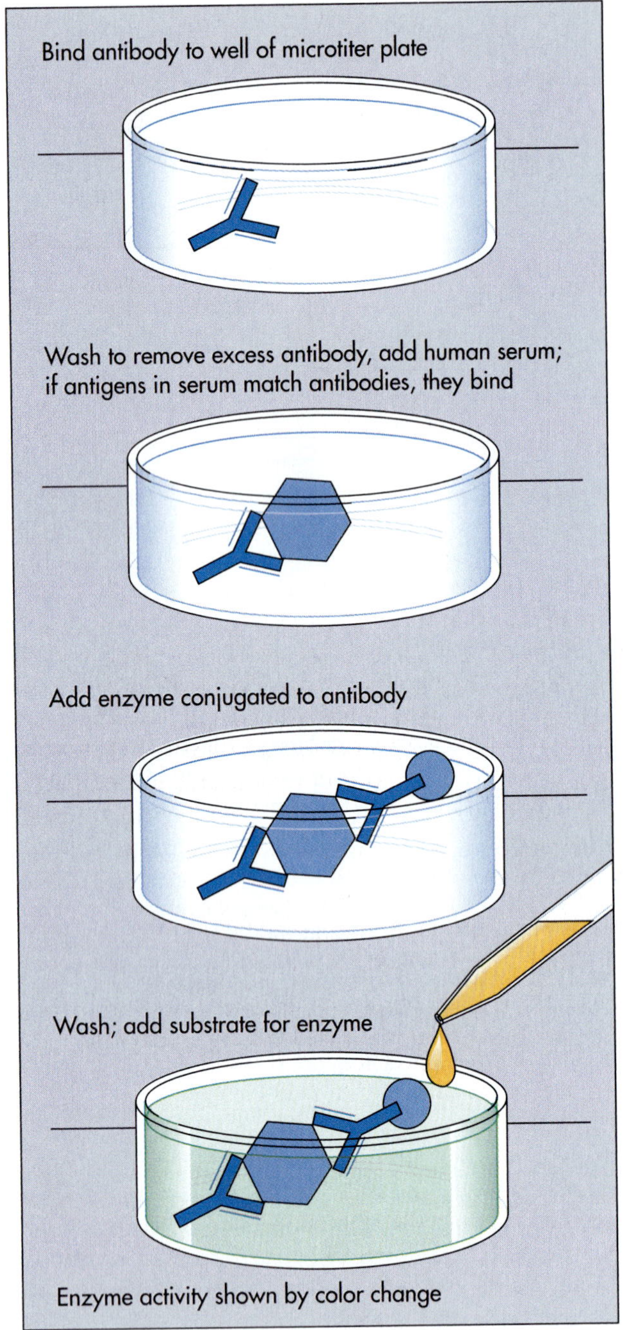
Bind antibody to well of microtiter plate
Wash to remove excess antibody, add human serum; if antigens in serum match antibodies, they bind
Add enzyme conjugated to antibody
Wash; add substrate for enzyme
Enzyme activity shown by color change

FIG. 11-27 The direct ELISA procedure uses antibody bound to the walls of a microtiter plate to trap antigen. A second antibody molecule with an attached ligand, typically a substrate for an enzymatic reaction, is added. When the enzyme is added, activity is shown by a color change indicating the reaction of the enzyme with its substrate.

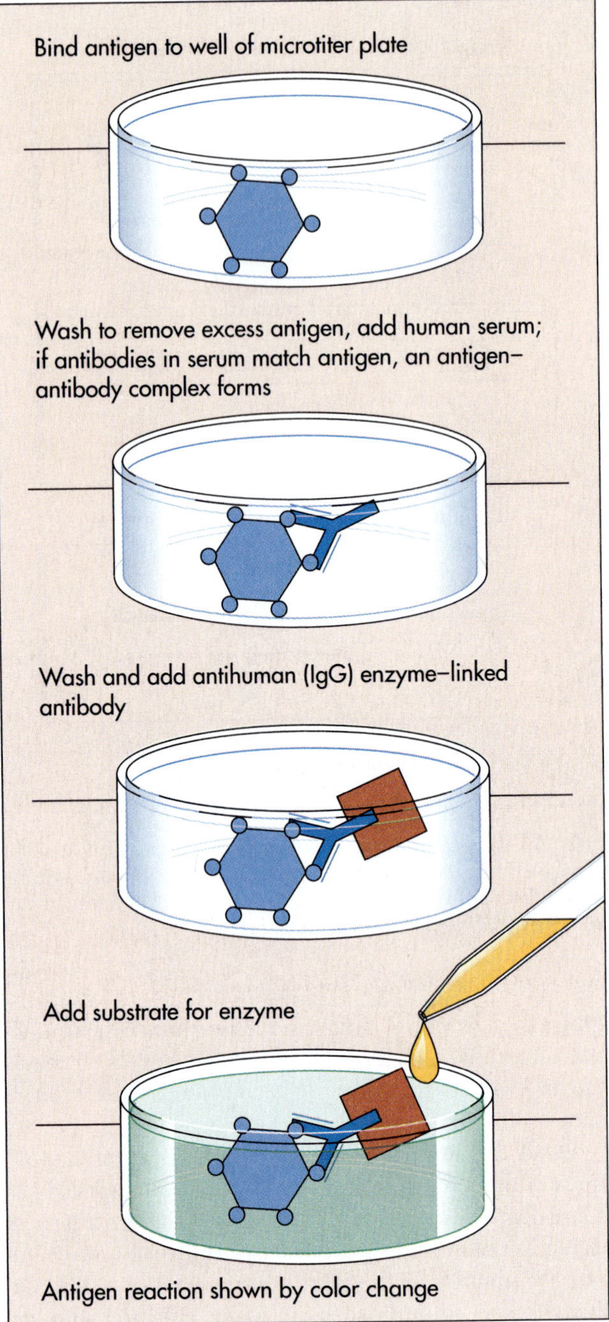
Bind antigen to well of microtiter plate
Wash to remove excess antigen, add human serum; if antibodies in serum match antigen, an antigen–antibody complex forms
Wash and add antihuman (IgG) enzyme–linked antibody
Add substrate for enzyme
Antigen reaction shown by color change

FIG. 11-28 The indirect ELISA procedure uses antigen bound to the walls of a microtiter plate to trap human antibody if it is present in serum. A second antihuman-antibody IgG molecule with an attached enzyme is added. When the enzyme substrate is added, activity is shown by a color change indicating the reaction of the enzyme with its substrate.

to HIV virus, rubella virus (German measles), *Mycoplasma pneumoniae, Helicobacter pylori,* and *Borrelia burgdorferi* (Lyme disease).

Direct and indirect radioimmunoassays can be run similarly to the ELISA procedures. The RIA is a soluble-phase, quantitative assay, and the ELISA is usually a solid-phase, qualitative assay. In the RIA, the ligand bound to the antibody molecule or antigen is a radioisotope, usually ^{125}I (FIG. 11-29). This allows an even greater sensitivity of detection than most other methods. RIA assays are used to detect Hepatitis B surface antigen and *Legionella pneumophila* antigen.

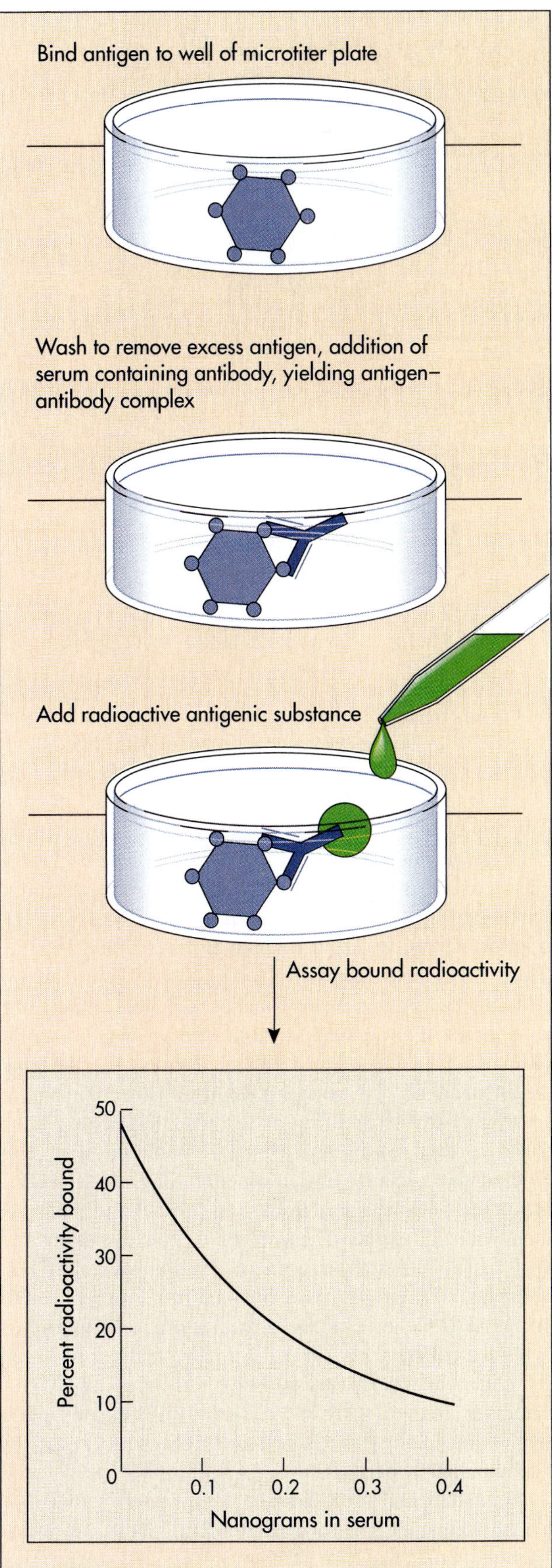
Bind antigen to well of microtiter plate
Wash to remove excess antigen, addition of serum containing antibody, yielding antigen–antibody complex
Add radioactive antigenic substance
Assay bound radioactivity
Percent radioactivity bound
50
40
30
20
10
0
0.1
0.2
0.3
0.4
Nanograms in serum

FIG. 11-29 The RIA procedure detects the ability of antibody to bind a radiolabeled antigen.

Cell-Mediated Immune Response

Whereas the antibody-mediated immune response system recognizes substances that are outside host cells, the **cell-mediated immune response** is effective in recognizing modified host cells. Cell-mediated immunity is important in controlling infections in which the pathogens can reproduce within human cells, including infections caused by viruses; some bacteria, such as rickettsias and chlamydias; and some parasitic protozoa, such as trypanosomes. In addition, the cell-mediated immune response may be important in surveillance for and destruction of naturally occurring tumor cells. Antibodies are ineffective in some intracellular viral infections. In such cases, cell-mediated immunity augments the antibody-mediated immune response. Although antibody molecules can neutralize free viruses, antibodies are unable to penetrate and attack viruses multiplying within host cells. It is the cell-mediated immune response that has the capability of eliminating cells infected with viruses. Cell-mediated immune responses include: (1) delayed hypersensitivity in response to intracellular bacteria such as *Listeria monocytogenes* and *Mycobacterium tuberculosis* and fungal infections such as *Histoplasma capsulatum* and *Cryptococcus neoformans;* (2) cytotoxic T lymphocyte response to virally infected cells, tissue transplants, and tumors; and (3) response to tumor cells and tissue grafts by natural killer (NK) cells.

Lymphocyte Activation and Function

The cell-mediated immune response is based on various T lymphocytes. When T cells are activated they recognize foreign or abnormal cells. T helper cells have a central role in the activation of this system. They, like other T cells, have specific surface receptors that mediate their interaction with other cells. Activation of T helper cells results in the secretion of *lymphokines,* which are the effector molecules of the cell-mediated immune response.

T Helper Cell Activation Antibody-mediated and cell-mediated immune responses usually depend on the activation of T_H lymphocytes (T helper cells). For T and B lymphocytes to function in response to a particular protein antigen, they must interact with the antigen, and they also require the presence and interaction with T_H lymphocytes. T_H cells are stimulated and activated by interaction with macrophages and dendritic cells of the spleen and lymph nodes; they also can be activated by B lymphocytes. *Antigen presenting cells* (APCs), for example, encounter antigens and digest them, and also attach small polypeptide antigens to their outer cell membrane surface and present or show the antigen to T_H cells.

Foreign antigen-activated T_H lymphocytes can secrete various cytokines, leading to activation of neutrophils, eosinophils, macrophages, and NK cells. Stimulation by cytokines and these activated cells causes localized inflammation. The activation of macrophages leads to destruction of bacteria, other pathogens, and damaged tissue. This response is important in the elimination of various infections, including infections with mycobacteria.

The Major Histocompatibility Complex The mechanism for T cell activation requires the presence of specific molecules in the cell membrane that are coded for by genes of the **major histocompatibility complex (MHC).** MHC proteins are found on almost all cells in the body. They were first identified as the main determinants of tissue or graft rejection when tissue from one individual is transplanted to a second individual. There are three types of MHC proteins: *class I MHC molecules, class II MHC molecules,* and *class III MHC molecules.* The first two MHC classes are involved with antigen presentation, and the third class includes some complement components and cytokines. The foreign antigens that become associated with class I MHC proteins are quite different from those that associate with class II MHC proteins.

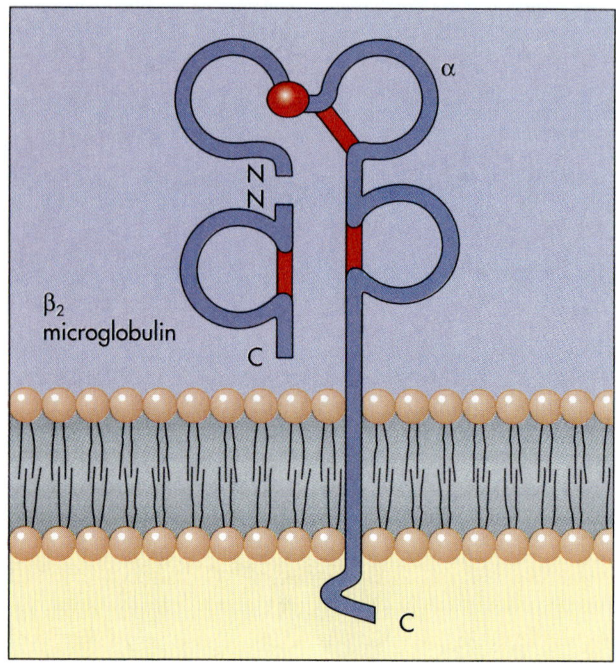

FIG. 11-30 Structure of a class I MHC protein.

Class I MHC molecules are found on the surfaces of nearly all nucleated cells. Class I MHC molecules with their bound foreign antigens are recognized exclusively by T lymphocytes carrying the CD8 marker, that is, cytotoxic T lymphocytes. This phenomenon of MHC marker/T cell specificity is referred to as *MHC restriction.* T_C cells are restricted for class I antigens, that is, T_C cells only recognize other cells that carry antigen bound to class I MHC proteins.

The class I MHC proteins are composed of two polypeptide chains (FIG. 11-30). The larger α glycoprotein chain is coded for by MHC genes located on chromosome 6. The carboxyl-terminal end is tightly anchored to the cytoplasmic membrane of the cell. The polypeptide is folded to form an immunoglobulin-like domain and a cleft at the amino-terminal end that binds processed protein antigens. In addition, class I MHC molecules contain a small polypeptide chain, β_2 microglobulin, that is not coded for by MHC genes and is noncovalently attached to the α chain.

Cytotoxic T cells respond to foreign protein antigens associated with MHC class I molecules. They are predominantly $CD8^+$ T_C cells that become activated from noncytolytic pre-T_C cells by the action of cytokines secreted by T_H lymphocytes. Direct contact of the activated T_C cell with its target cell is required for killing to occur. Therefore adjacent host cells that are healthy are not accidentally destroyed as innocent bystanders.

Cytotoxic T cells appear to kill target cells by at least two different mechanisms. Activated T_C cells produce cytoplasmic granules that contain a membrane pore-forming protein called *perforin* and toxic proteins. These proteins are directed to the point of contact between the T_C cell and target cell and lead to the osmotic lysis of the target cell. In addition, cytotoxic T cells secrete a protein toxin that causes fragmentation of nuclear DNA and produce γ-IFN, which has antiviral activity.

The foreign antigens that become associated with class I MHC molecules are those from intracellularly synthesized proteins. In general, intracellularly or endogenously synthesized foreign polypeptides, such as those from viral infections and other obligate intracellular parasites, are produced in the host cell on the ribosomes of the rough endoplasmic reticulum (ER) (FIG. 11-31). The class I MHC proteins are likewise synthesized on the rough ER. After proteolytic processing of the viral antigens into linear polypeptides, these foreign antigens become associated with the cleft of the class I MHC molecule. The class I MHC molecule with antigen then migrates to the cell surface where it displays the antigen to T_C cells. Assembly and intracellular transport of class I MHC-antigen complex depends on the protein transporters TAP1 and TAP2. Cells that present antigen to T_C lymphocytes are called *target cells* rather than antigen-presenting cells. Target cells are subsequently lysed by T_C lymphocytes. Since nearly all nucleated cells express class I MHC molecules, this is a major defense mechanism against viral infections.

Class II MHC molecules are expressed only on B lymphocytes, macrophages, dendritic cells, and endothelial cells. Class II MHC molecules are composed of two glycoprotein chains, α and β, that are noncovalently associated (FIG. 11-32). The α chain is slightly larger than the β chain. Although the three-dimen-

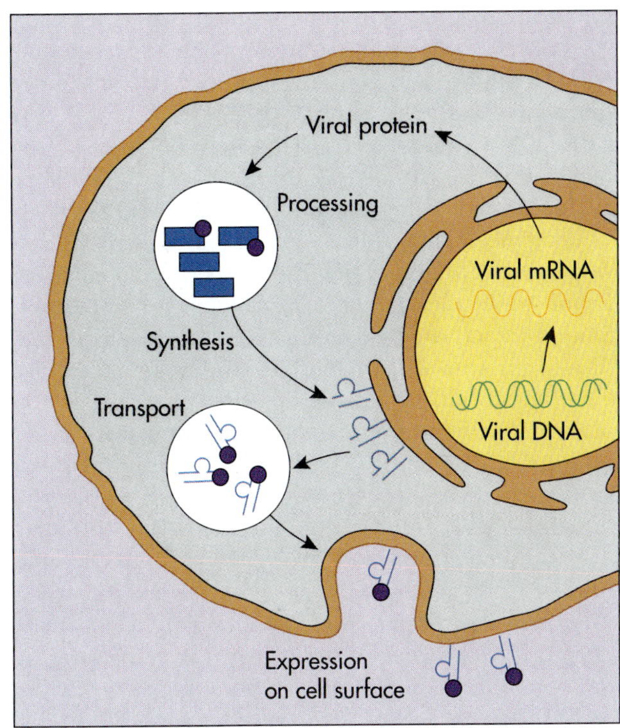

FIG. 11-31 Viral antigens that are processed within an infected cell become associated with class I MHC proteins that are produced at rough endoplasmic reticulum.

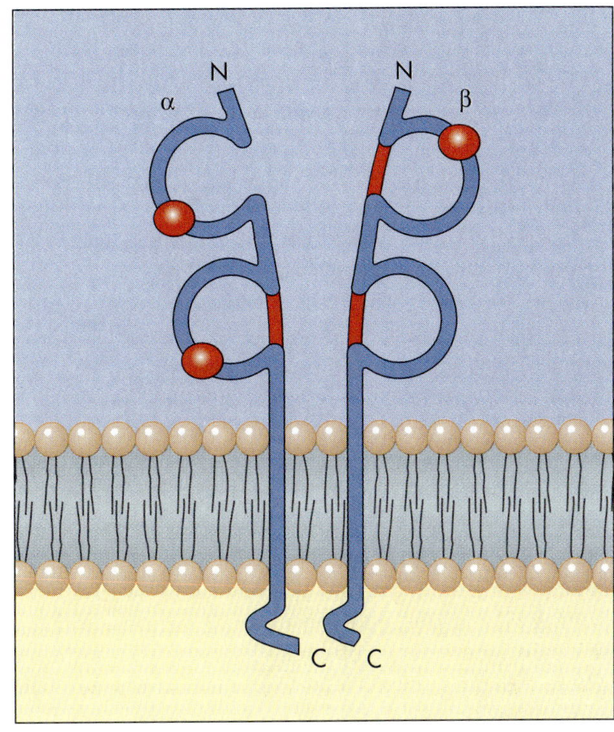

FIG. 11-32 Structure of a class II MHC protein.

sional structure of class II proteins has not been completely resolved, the amino acid sequence suggests a structure similar to that of class I proteins. The carboxyl-terminal ends of α and β chains are anchored to the cytoplasmic membrane and more than two thirds of the chains extend outward into the extracellular space. Both chains are likely to have immunoglobulin-like domains and the amino-terminal ends of both chains fold to form a cleft that binds protein antigens.

Class II MHC molecules with their bound antigen are recognized exclusively by $CD4^+$ cells or T helper cells. Therefore, T_H cells are MHC restricted for class II antigens. Class II-associated antigens are derived from extracellularly synthesized proteins such as bacterial proteins and soluble exotoxins (FIG. 11-33). These foreign proteins enter a macrophage or dendritic cell by phagocytosis or endocytosis. After protein processing, the antigens become associated with intracellular, membrane-bound endosomes. The exact site of binding of these antigens with class II MHC molecules is not clear. Class II MHC proteins are synthesized on the rough ER but may have an additional polypeptide chain, γ, that blocks the cleft and prevents class I antigens from associating with the class II polypeptides. Later, when the class II protein migrates out of the rough ER, the γ chain is released and class II antigens become associated with the cleft of the class II MHC polypeptides. The class II MHC mole-

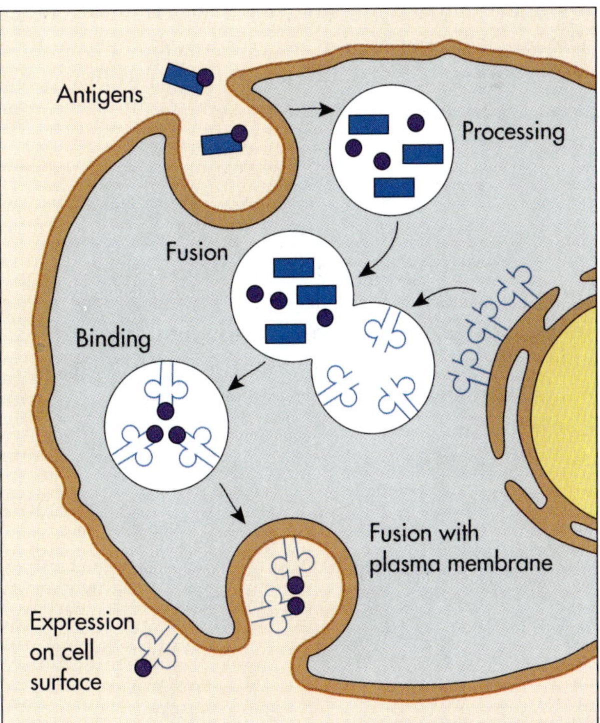

FIG. 11-33 Exogenous antigens (those synthesized outside the cell) are taken up by antigen-presenting cells. These antigens are processed and bind to class II MHC proteins. The peptide-MHC complex is displayed on the surface of the antigen-presenting cell.

cule with antigen then migrates to the cell surface where it displays the antigen to T_H cells as an APC.

T Cell Receptors The interaction of T_H cells with APCs and T_C cells with target cells involves receptors on the T cell surface. The *T cell receptor (TCR)* in association with CD4 or CD8 is responsible for MHC-restricted antigen recognition. The TCR on most cells is a heterodimer of two polypeptide chains, α and β. Both chains are anchored to the T cell membrane and contain immunoglobulin-like constant domains and amino-terminal variable domains. Because of the similarity in structures of immunoglobulin molecules, class I MHC and class II MHC molecules, TCR, CD4, CD8, and other molecules, these proteins are grouped into an *Ig gene superfamily* that may have evolutionarily originated from a common gene.

Functional TCR genes are formed by recombination of gene segments similar to the rearrangement of Ig segments. TCR genes contain variable (V) regions, joining (J) regions, and constant (C) regions, and the β chain gene also contains diversity (D) regions. These rearrangements lead to the formation of TCRs with different specificities.

In addition to the recognition of MHC molecules by the TCR, a T cell membrane-bound CD3 complex is required to recognize the signal that the APC or target cell is displaying a foreign antigen; this is needed to activate the T lymphocyte (FIG. 11-34). The CD3 complex consists of four or five polypeptides, γ (gamma), δ (delta), ϵ (epsilon), ζ (zeta), and η (eta). The complex may exist as $\gamma\delta\epsilon\zeta\eta$ or $\gamma\delta\epsilon\zeta\zeta$. These polypeptides have relatively short extracellular segments, a membrane-bound segment, and relatively long intracellular tail segments. The tail segments contain amino acid residues that may become phosphorylated after the binding of TCR-CD4 to APCs or TCR-CD8 to target cells. This may be part of the mechanism for stimulating the T cell but the molecular nature of T cell activation is still unclear.

Lymphokines (Cytokines) Activated T lymphocytes respond to antigen recognition by secreting small effector molecules called **lymphokines** or **cytokines.** Similar to activated T lymphocytes, macrophages and fibroblasts can also secrete cytokines. Cytokines are generally produced during the effector phase of natural or specific immunity and have stimulatory or inhibitory effects on other cells of the immune system. Cytokines serve as communication and regulatory functions between different immune cells.

Various lymphokines are produced by T cells (Table 11-4). These include (1) interleukin, which stimulates reproduction of T cells; (2) macrophage chemotactic factor, a lymphokine that causes the attraction and accumulation of macrophages to the site of lymphokine release; (3) migration inhibition factor, which inhibits macrophages from migrating farther once they have reached the site of lymphokine attraction; (4) macrophage activating factor (MAF), which results in an alteration of macrophage cells that increases their lysosomal activities and thus their ability to kill and ingest organisms; (5) skin reactive factor, which enhances capillary permeability and thus the movement of monocytes across the vascular spaces; (6) immune interferon (IFN), which activates

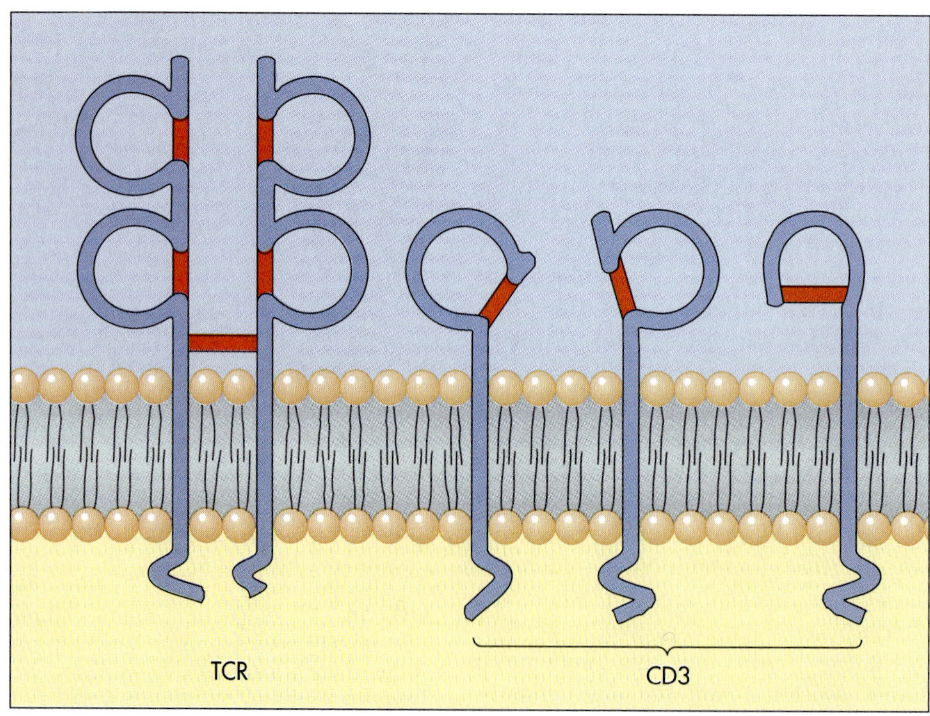

FIG. 11-34 Structure of the T cell receptor (TCR) and part of the CD3 complex.

TABLE 11-4 Effects of Lymphokines on Various Cells

LYMPHOKINE	MODE OF ACTION
Macrophage chemotactic factor	Attracts macrophages to site of lymphokine release, typically causing an accumulation of macrophages at a site of inflammation
Migration inhibition factor (MIF)	Inhibits migration of macrophages away from the site of inflammation
Macrophage activating factor (MAF)	Stimulates phagocytic activity of macrophages (γ-interferon) by enhancing their lysosomal activities
Immune interferon (IFN-γ)	Activates antiviral proteins, T cells, and macrophages
Interleukin-1 (IL-1)	Stimulates activities of T cells, B cells, and macrophages
Interleukin-2 (IL-2)	Stimulates antigen activated T-helper T-cytotoxic cells
Interleukin-3 (IL-3)	Stimulates growth and differentiation of various blood cells
Interleukin-4 (IL-4) (B cell growth factor)	Stimulates production of B cells
Interleukin-5 (IL-5)	Activates eosinophils and activates and stimulates growth of B cells
Interleukin-6 (IL-6)	Promotes B cell differentiation into plasma cells and secretion of antibody; induces acute-phase response in hepatocytes.
Interleukin-7 (IL-7)	Stimulates growth and differentiation of B cells
Leukocyte inhibitory factor	Inhibits migration of phagocytic neutrophils away from the site of infection
Leukocyte chemotactic factor (IL-8)	Attracts phagocytic neutrophils to the site of infection
Skin reactive factor	Enhances capillary permeability and movement of monocytes across vascular spaces
Platelet-activating factor	Activates platelets to aggregate
Eosinophil chemotactic factor	Attracts phagocytic neutrophils to the site of parasitic infection

antiviral proteins, preventing further intracellular multiplication of viruses (IFN and MAF may represent different activities of the same protein); and (7) macrophage colony stimulating factor (CSF), which regulates the production of macrophages.

Activated T lymphocytes secrete **interleukin-2 (IL-2)**; IL-2 is secreted and reabsorbed by the same cell. IL-2 is thus an autocrine (self-stimulator). As a result of T cell activation and cytokine production, T cell metabolism is stimulated and enhanced mitosis leads to cell division and expansion of T cell clones.

One of the specific lymphokines, **immune** or **gamma (γ) interferon (IFN-γ)** is secreted by lymphocytes in response to a specific antigen to which they have been sensitized or stimulated to divide. In some of its physiological effects, this immune interferon is different from other interferon molecules and may kill tumor cells. Like other interferons, immune interferon molecules have antiviral activities, stimulating the synthesis of antiviral proteins, including 2,5 adenylate polymerase. This polymerase, when bound to double-stranded RNA, a viral replicative intermediate, activates an endonuclease that can cleave viral RNA. The primary function of γ-interferon, though, appears to be different from that of α- and β-interferons. Immune interferon may regulate the proliferation of the lymphoid cells that are stimulated to divide in response to interactions with antigenic biochemicals. Immune interferon may also enhance phagocytosis by macrophages, as well as enhance the cytotoxicity of lymphocytes and the activities of killer T cells.

IMMUNOLOGICAL TOLERANCE

The immune system is essential for protection against "foreign substances," but it is critical that this system not attack the body's own cells. The immune system is designed to ignore *self antigens,* that is, antigens associated with one's own cells.

Unresponsiveness to self-antigens is called **immunological tolerance.** Tolerance of T helper lymphocytes is a central mediator of overall immunological tolerance because T_H cells are required for activation of other T lymphocytes as well as B lymphocytes. Tolerance in T_H and T_C lymphocytes occurs during the maturation of these cells in the thymus. Many self-reacting clones of T cells are systematically recognized and destroyed in the thymus gland and therefore never circulate in the blood or get deposited in peripheral lymphoid tissues such as the spleen. This type of tolerance is called *clonal deletion.*

Alternatively, tolerance may be induced by the development of T cells that are *anergic* or unresponsive to self antigens. **Anergy** means *without working.* Anergy shuts off self-reactive cells as a result of the way in which the antigens are presented. $CD4^+$ T helper cells require activation by antigen bound to MHC class II molecules, as well as by other stimulatory factors. Some T_H cells may recognize antigen-presenting cells that carry self-antigens but do not respond to that antigen because of a lack of accessory stimulator molecules. Anergy induction occurs when a T cell is presented with an antigen-specific signal but without a second cosignal. Such T cells fail to produce IL-2 and do not divide. They may produce other lymphokines and inhibitory proteins.

The development of immunological tolerance in B lymphocyte clones occurs by similar mechanisms as that seen in T lymphocytes. Since their maturation occurs in the bone marrow, it is likely that specific recognition and deletion of self-antigen specific B cell clones occur in that site. Also, clonal unresponsiveness may arise in B cell populations forming *anergic B cell clones,* which are B cells that do not respond to antigenic stimulation.

An alternative mechanism for tolerance of the immune system may be provided by the activities of suppressor T lymphocytes (T_S). These cells are difficult to study because they are difficult to purify, and the establishment of suppressor cell hybridomas has been unsuccessful. Suppressor T cells generally are $CD8^+$. They may secrete cytokines that have an inhibitory effect on either T or B cells. For example, transforming growth factor-β is a potent inhibitor of the proliferation of both T and B lymphocytes. Alternatively, suppressor cells may absorb stimulatory cytokines and prevent other cells of the immune system from becoming activated. The specific role of T_S cells is unclear but may modulate and suppress the immune response. Suppressor T lymphocytes may have a specific role in preventing immune responses to self-antigens but this remains to be demonstrated.

11.3 DYSFUNCTIONAL IMMUNITY

The immune system is designed to recognize foreign invaders and abnormal cells and to tolerate normal self cells. Lack of an adequate response or an excessive response both represent *dysfunctional immunity,* that is, an improper functioning of the immune system.

Failures of the immune response can compromise the ability of humans to resist infection, leaving an individual susceptible to many diseases. Indeed, infectious diseases often result from failures of the immune response to protect the individual adequately against the invasion of or toxicity associated with pathogenic microorganisms. Failures of the immune response can also result in autoimmune diseases in which the inability to differentiate between self and nonself antigens results in reactions with self-antigens and the killing of some of one's own cells. The development of tumor cells can also be viewed as a failure of the immune response, but in this case, the failure to recognize and to respond properly to inappropriate cells within the body allows malignant cells to proliferate in an uncontrolled manner. The normal active immune response can also be undesirable in some cases, such as in transplants where the immunological recognition of and response to the foreign antigens of a donor results in tissue rejection. Additionally, allergies are the result of physiological changes caused by certain types of substances in foods or dust that do not normally activate the immune system. Individuals suffering from allergies know too well that immune responses may occasionally be dysfunctional.

TABLE 11-5 Some Types of Autoimmunity

DISEASE	MAJOR ANTIGEN(S)
Hashimoto thyroiditis; primary myxedema	Thyroglobulin
Thyrotoxicosis (Grave disease)	Thyroid-stimulating hormone (TSH) receptors
Pernicious anemia	Intrinsic factor; parietal cell microsomes
Addison disease	Cytoplasm of adrenal cells
Premature onset of menopause	Cytoplasm of steroid-producing cells
Male infertility (some)	Spermatozoa
Juvenile diabetes	Cytoplasm and surface of islet cells
Goodpasture syndrome	Glomerular and lung basement membrane
Myasthenia gravis	Skeletal and heart muscle; acetylcholine receptor
Autoimmune hemolytic anemia	Erythrocytes
Idiopathic thrombocytopenic purpura	Platelets
Ulcerative colitis	Colon "LPS"
Sjögren syndrome	Ducts, mitochondria, nuclei, thyroid; IgG
Rheumatoid arthritis	IgG; collagen
Systemic lupus erythematosus	DNA; nucleoprotein; cytoplasmic soluble Ag; array of other Ag, including elements of blood-clotting factors

AUTOIMMUNITY

One should not exhibit **autoimmunity;** that is, one should not show an immune response against one's own antigens. Autoimmunity can occur, though, if B cells and T cells are not exposed to particular human antigens during fetal development. In such cases, some of these lymphocytes programmed for reacting with self-antigens may survive fetal development. For example, if B cells are not exposed during fetal development to the specific antigens that later occur on male sperm cells, male infertility can result because the body reacts to such antigens as foreign antigens. In fact, such autoimmunity is an important cause of male infertility. Additionally, autoimmunity occurs if mutations reestablish B cell or T cell lines that were properly eliminated during fetal development. Thus there are several ways in which the body can have lymphocytes programmed to react with self-antigens. In fact, it appears that some B cell lines that are genetically programmed for reacting with self-antigens are typically present in the body, but that these B cells are normally held in check by the action of T-lymphocyte suppressor cells. Thus the development of self-tolerance does not require the complete elimination of self-reactive precursor lymphocytes, but it is necessary that suppression be dominant.

Some **autoimmune diseases** result from the failure of the immune response to recognize self-antigens. Such autoimmunity diseases often result in the progressive degeneration of tissues. These diseases are summarized in Table 11-5. In **systemic lupus erythematosus,** various autoantibodies are produced that react with self-antigens, including some directed at DNA molecules. In this disease, antigen–antibody complexes often circulate and settle in the glomeruli of the kidney, causing kidney failure. In cases of **myasthenia gravis,** antibodies react with nerve–muscle junctions. In autoimmune hemolytic anemia, antibodies react with red blood cells, causing anemia. Various other disease conditions may reflect the failure of the immune system to recognize self-antigens. These diseases can be treated by using immunosuppressive drugs to prevent the self-destruction of body tissues by the body's own immune response.

IMMUNODEFICIENCIES

Several types of deficiencies can occur within the immune system, resulting in the failure of the system to recognize and respond properly to the antigens of pathogenic microorganisms. Individuals with **immunodeficiencies** are more prone to infection than those who are capable of a complete and active immune response. Immunodeficiencies can affect the cells that are interactive in the immune response system (Table 11-6, p. 422). Some immunodeficiencies result from inherited genetic defects; these are called congenital immunodeficiencies. Other immunodeficiencies may be acquired during the lifetime of an individual as a result of exposure to exogenous factors, such as viruses or radiation, or from physiological changes, such as the onset of diabetes, that affect the immune system.

BOX 11-4

GENE THERAPY FOR TREATING SCID

Gene therapy is a revolutionary new approach for treating adenosine deaminase (ADA) deficiency, an inherited genetic disorder that causes 10% to 20% of all cases of severe combined immunodeficiency. Children lacking the gene for ADA develop SCID. Gene therapy uses recombinant DNA technology to introduce the missing ADA gene.

In the absence of the gene for ADA, deoxyadenosine accumulates in many tissues, especially those of the lymphoid system where high levels of the ADA are constitutively expressed. The accumulation of deoxyadenosine and its metabolite deoxyadenosine triphosphate inhibits DNA synthesis. This causes T-cell and subsequent B-cell dysfunction. Clinically, the disease is characterized by failure to thrive and severe infections caused by bacteria, yeast/fungi, viruses, and protozoa. The onset of disease starts at 1 to 3 months after birth in the majority of cases. The course of the disease generally leads to mortality before the age of 1 year. With administration of gammaglobulin and antimicrobials, an individual with SCID due to ADA deficiency may reach an age of 1 to 2 years.

ADA deficiency–SCID can be cured with bone marrow transplantation using bone marrow cells from an HLA-genotypically identical donor. Successful bone marrow transplantation results in a long-term cure rate of 95% to 100%. However, a related HLA-identical bone marrow donor is not available for 75% of the individuals with SCID. Also there is slightly over 21% mortality related to bone marrow transplantation.

Some children with ADA-negative SCID who lack an HLA-identical bone marrow donor have been treated with infusions of purified bovine ADA linked to polyethylene glycol (PEG-ADA). The polyethylene glycol reduces the antigenicity of the ADA so that the body does not readily produce antibodies that inactivate the ADA. PEG-ADA treatment has been successful in decreasing a number of infections and partial restoration of T-cell functions. However, the formation of inactivating antibodies against the bovine ADA was observed in 3 patients who were receiving PEG-ADA for 20 months.

Based on these relatively poor results of various treatments in ADA-negative SCID patients lacking a genotypically HLA-identical bone marrow donor, a new treatment, called *somatic cell gene therapy,* has been developed. Somatic cell gene therapy is based on the ability to introduce human genes into somatic cells of the patient. In ADA-deficiency, peripheral lymphocytes or hematopoietic stem cells are the targets for introduction of the gene encoding the human ADA. Retroviral vectors appear to be the most effective vectors for gene transfer into the rare population of hematopoietic stem cells (HSCs) capable of long-term reconstitution of all myeloid and lymphoid lineages. The few children treated with gene therapy have shown marked improvement.

TABLE 11-6 Types of Immunodeficiencies

		IMMUNE RESPONSE			
DEFICIENCY	EXAMPLE	HUMORAL	CELLULAR	COMMON INFECTIONS WITH THIS IMMUNODEFICIENCY	TREATMENT
Complement	C3 deficiency	Normal	Normal	Pyogenic bacteria	Antibiotics
Myeloid cell	Chronic granulomatous disease	Normal	Normal	Catalase-positive bacteria	Antibiotics
B cells	Infantile sex-linked agammaglobulinemia (Bruton)	Absent	Normal	Pyogenic bacteria; *Pneumocystis carinii*	γ-globulin
T cells	Thymic hypoplasia (DiGeorge syndrome)	Lower	Absent	Certain viruses; *Candida*	Thymus graft
Stem cell marrow	Severe combined deficiency (Swiss type)	Absent	Absent	All of the above	Bone graft

Severe Combined Immunodeficiency (SCID)

The most dangerous type of congenital (inherited) immunodeficiency, **severe combined immunodeficiency (SCID),** results from a failure of stem cells to differentiate properly. Individuals with SCID have neither B nor T lymphocytes and are incapable of any immunological response. Exposure of such individuals to microorganisms can result in the unchecked growth of the microorganisms within the body, resulting in certain death. Almost any microorganism can cause a fatal infection in an individual with SCID. Individuals suffering from SCID can be kept alive in sterile environments where they are protected from any exposure to microorganisms (FIG. 11-35). Bone mar-

FIG. 11-35 In a widely publicized case of severe combined immunodeficiency (SCID) a boy named David was kept alive by isolating him in a sterile chamber. He was known as the bubble baby. He was delivered by Caesarian section under aseptic conditions and kept in a sterile environment. He died after an attempt to infuse his body with lymphocytes to establish an immune response. Today, gene therapy and other treatments are being used to cure or treat SCID.

row grafts may be employed to establish normal immune functions, but the grafts must come from siblings with histocompatible bone marrow. Gene therapy may also be used to treat SCID.

DiGeorge Syndrome

Less severe immunodeficiencies occur when only B cell or only T cell functions are lacking. **DiGeorge syndrome** results from a failure of the thymus to develop correctly, so that T lymphocytes do not become properly differentiated. Individuals suffering from this condition do not exhibit cell-mediated immunity and thus are prone to viral and other intracellular infections. Additionally, because T_H cells are involved in stimulating antibody production by B cells, the antigen-mediated or humoral response is depressed in individuals suffering from DiGeorge syndrome. The complete absence of the thymus is rare, and partial DiGeorge syndrome—in which some T cells are produced, although in lower numbers than in individuals with fully functional thymus glands—is more common.

Bruton Congenital Agammaglobulinemia

Bruton congenital agammaglobulinemia results in the failure of B cells to differentiate and produce antibodies but the cell-mediated response is normal. This immunodeficiency disease is a sex-limited inherited disease and affects only males. Boys with Bruton agammaglobulinemia are particularly subject to bacterial infections, including those by pyogenic (pus-inducing) bacteria such as *Staphylococcus aureus, Streptococcus pyogenes, Streptococcus pneumoniae, Neisseria meningitidis,* and *Haemophilus influenzae.* The treatment of this disease involves the repeated administration of IgG to maintain adequate levels of antibody in the circulatory system.

Late-onset Hypogammaglobulinemia

The most common form of inherited immunodeficiency is known as **late-onset hypogammaglobulinemia.** Individuals with this condition have a deficiency of circulating B cells or B cells with IgG surface receptors. Such individuals are unable to respond adequately to antigen through the normal differentiation of B cells into antibody-secreting plasma cells. Other immunodeficiencies may affect the synthesis of specific classes of antibodies. For example, some individuals exhibit IgA deficiencies, producing depressed levels of IgA antibodies. Such individuals are susceptible to infections of the respiratory tract and body surfaces normally protected by mucosal cells that secrete IgA.

Acquired Immunodeficiency Syndrome (AIDS)

Acquired immunodeficiency syndrome or **AIDS** was recognized as a disease in 1979. Individuals with this disease exhibit immunosuppression because of a viral infection. Specifically, they have depressed levels of T_H cells, which effectively shuts off the immune response network. As a result of the immunodeficiency, individuals with AIDS are subject to opportunistic infections by various disease-causing microorganisms and to the development of several forms of cancer, especially Kaposi sarcoma. Onset of the disease may be delayed for many years after initial HIV infection. Early symptoms of infection may include low-grade fever, swollen lymph nodes, night sweats, and general malaise. Generally, once AIDS begins, one infection follows another in victims of this disease until death occurs.

Since its discovery, a great deal has been learned about AIDS, and some treatments and possible vaccines for prevention hold promise in checking the future spread of this disease. However, for the near future, no cure or vaccine for preventing this disease is likely to be found. The replication of retroviruses is discussed in Chapter 8.

AIDS is caused by *human immunodeficiency virus (HIV),* which is a retrovirus. HIV initially binds via its envelope glycoprotein, gp120, to the CD4 protein that is an important surface marker on T_H cells. In addition, HIV has been found associated with macrophages and dendritic cells, which may play a role in the pathogenesis of the disease by carrying the HIV to activated $CD4^+$ cells. HIV has been shown *in vitro* to infect various cells and tissues from the brain, skin, bowel, and other body sites. The predominant infection *in vivo* nevertheless appears to be within T_H cells that results in the immunodeficiency syndrome. An important feature of AIDS is a latency period from the time of initial infection with HIV to the onset of symptoms. Latency may last for 10 to 14 years in some individuals. During this period, antibodies to HIV appear in the blood (HIV^+) but the patient appears asymptomatic.

HIV replication in host T_H lymphocytes leads to the fusion of infected cells with uninfected $CD4^+$ cells in culture. This produces multinucleated cells or syncytia. However, it is not clear whether syncytia are formed *in vivo* in the infected host. Syncytia formation and accumulation of viral DNA and proteins in host cells may lead to cell death. A primary consequence of HIV infection is depletion of $CD4^+$ T_H lymphocytes, including memory T cells. Typically, in uninfected individuals the ratio of $CD4^+$ lymphocytes to $CD8^+$ lymphocytes (T_C and T_S cells) is approximately 2. However, in patients with AIDS, $CD4^+/CD8^+$ ratios are <0.5.

Since the T_H lymphocyte population is crucial in the activation of B lymphocytes, as well as other T lymphocytes, the overall effect is the increased susceptibility of AIDS patients to many opportunistic infections. *Pneumocystis carinii* pneumonia and tuberculosis are common in individuals with AIDS. The HIV can also gain access to cells in the brain and cause central nervous system damage.

Several drugs limit the replication of HIV. These drugs delay the progression of the disease but do not eliminate the HIV from the AIDS patient. Zidovudine (formerly called AZT) is one of the most promising of these antiviral drugs (antiviral chemotherapy is discussed in Chapter 10). The use of zidovudine for prophylaxis is a controversial topic. Some studies indicate that zidovudine does not delay the onset of symptoms in HIV^+ patients. These studies indicate that AZT could prevent the development of AIDS if HIV infection was identified early. Other studies, however, indicate that AZT is ineffective in preventing AIDS once an individual is infected with HIV. These studies indicate that AZT should be used only later in the course of the disease, since AZT appears to be effective in delaying the progression of the disease once AIDS has developed.

Hypersensitivity Reactions

Whereas immunodeficiencies cause diseases, an excessive immunological response to an antigen can also result in tissue damage and a physiological state known as **hypersensitivity.** Hypersensitivity reactions occur when an individual is sensitized to an antigen, so that further contact with that antigen results in an elevated immune response. The hypersensitivity reaction may be immediate, occurring shortly after exposure to the antigen, or delayed, occurring a day or more afterward. There are several types of hypersensitivity reactions, each mediated by different aspects of the immune response (Table 11-7).

Anaphylactic Hypersensitivity

Anaphylactic hypersensitivity (type 1 hypersensitivity), a systemic, potentially life-threatening condition, occurs when an antigen reacts with antibody bound to mast or basophil blood cells, leading to disruption of these cells with the release of vasoactive mediators, such as histamine (FIG. 11-36). This condition is also known as *immediate hypersensitivity* because it occurs shortly (5 to 30 minutes) after exposure to the antigen that triggers this response. The antigens that initiate this response are called **allergens.**

Basis of Allergies In the absence of proper modulation by T cells, a clone of B lymphocytes is transformed by the binding of an allergen that would not normally elicit a response, leading to the formation of antibody-secreting plasma cells. The plasma cells make IgE antibodies against the allergen. The reason that IgE is made preferentially is not yet known, but some individuals inherit the genetic trait for producing high levels of IgE and are prone to develop type I hypersensitivities.

Allergies are specific because IgE is specific. The Fc region of the IgE binds to specific sites on the surfaces of mast and basophil cells, sensitizing the individual against the allergen. The surface of a mast cell can be covered with as many as 500,000 IgE receptors. When specific IgE antibodies are synthesized in response to an allergen, they move through the bloodstream to mast cells in connective tissue and become firmly fixed to the receptors, a process known as *sensitization.* The next time the individual is exposed to the same allergen, that allergen can react directly with the IgE fixed to mast cells rather than causing B lymphocytes to initiate antibody synthesis.

When two adjacent IgE molecules on the surface of a mast cell are bridged by two reactive sites on the allergen molecule, a sequence of events causes the cytoplasmic membrane of the mast cell to become permeable to calcium ions. The calcium ions activate en-

TABLE 11-7 Comparison of Characteristics of the Four Types of Hypersensitivity Reactions

HYPERSENSITIVITY EXAMPLE/REACTION	ALTERNATIVE NAME	DESCRIPTION
Type 1 atopic allergies; asthma	Anaphylactic hypersensitivity; IgE-mediated hypersensitivity	IgE attached to mast cell or basophil reacts with antigen, causing degranulation and release of biochemicals that are potent physiological mediators, such as histamine
Type 2 transfusion incompatibility; Rh incompatibility	Antibody-dependent cytotoxic hypersensitivity	Antigen on cell surface combines with antibody and cell dies
Type 3 serum sickness	Complex-mediated hypersensitivity; Arthus reaction	Formation of immune complex involving antigen, antibody, and complement triggers an inflammatory response, and immune complex is deposited in tissues
Type 4 contact dermatitis	Cell-mediated hypersensitivity; delayed hypersensitivity	Hypersensitivity that occurs only after a delay and involves T cells

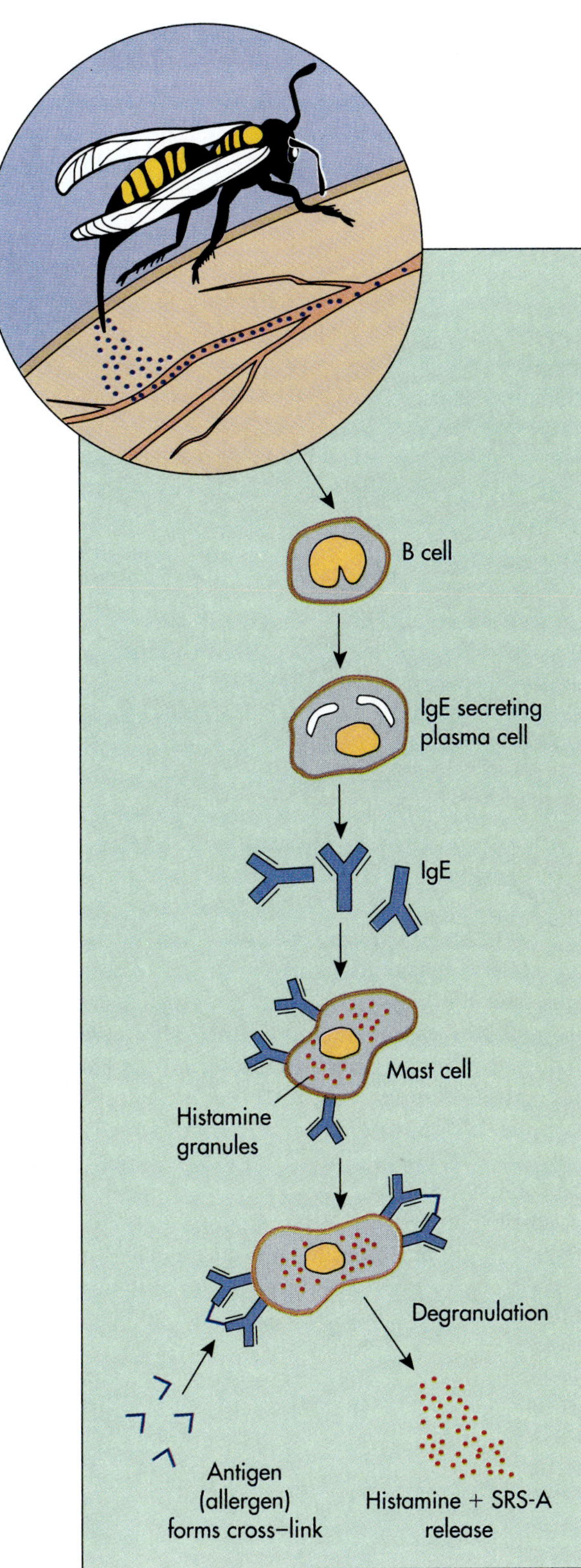

FIG. 11-36 In sensitized individuals, an allergen initiates formation of IgE, which binds to the surfaces of mast cells. When the allergen reacts with IgE on the mast cell surface, the mast cell degranulates. The release of histamine and SRS-A causes anaphylaxis.

zymes that promote ATP generation, the assembly of microtubules, and the contraction of microfilaments. These events cause the granular contents of the mast cell to migrate to the cytoplasmic membrane, with the subsequent release of histamine, heparin, serotonin, and chemical factors that activate blood platelets and attract eosinophils and phagocytic leukocytes. Each of these chemical mediators contributes in its own way to the allergic reaction.

The bridging of the mast cells by an allergen also leads to the formation of prostaglandins and leukotrienes. The interaction of an allergen with a mast cell activates serine esterase, initiating a series of reactions that generate phosphatidyl choline. When calcium ions enter the cell, the enzyme phospholipase A2 is activated, which promotes the conversion of phosphatidyl choline to lysophosphatidyl choline and arachidonic acid. Prostaglandins and leukotrienes are produced from arachidonic acid by two different enzymatic pathways. The prostaglandin pathway is initiated when the enzyme cyclooxygenase converts arachidonic acid to prostaglandins G2 and H2, which are subsequently converted to the active prostaglandins D2, E2, F2a, I2, and thromboxane A2. Prostaglandins F2a and thromboxane A2 are potent but short-lived constrictors of smooth muscle in the bronchi of the lungs. Prostaglandin E2 has the opposite effect, dilating the bronchi. These mediators of hypersensitivity are produced by different pathways that involve arachidonic acid. Members of the prostaglandin family also affect the activity of mucous glands and the stickiness of blood platelets. The alternative leukotriene pathway involves the conversion of arachidonic acid to a mixture of leukotrienes known as *slow-reacting substance of anaphylaxis,* or *SRS-A.* The leukotrienes are 100 to 1,000 times as potent as histamine or the prostaglandins in constricting bronchi.

The release of the contents of basophil or mast cells establishes the basis for a severe physiological response. The sudden release of a large amount of histamine (a potent vasodilator) and other pharmacologically active compounds—such as heparin, platelet-activating factors (PSFs), SRS-A, and serotonin—into the bloodstream can produce anaphylactic shock, causing respiratory or cardiac failure. Plant pollens, dust mites, insect stings, and some drugs and foods can trigger such *anaphylactic hypersensitivity reactions* (FIG. 11-37, p. 426). Many allergies occur as a result of low molecular weight compounds, such as penicillin, that act as haptens. Symptoms may include hives, abdominal cramps, diarrhea, nausea, vomiting, respiratory difficulties, and rapid death. Prompt administration of adrenaline (epinephrine) counters anaphylactic hypersensitivity reactions. Epinephrine raises blood pressure, thereby reversing the action of the va-

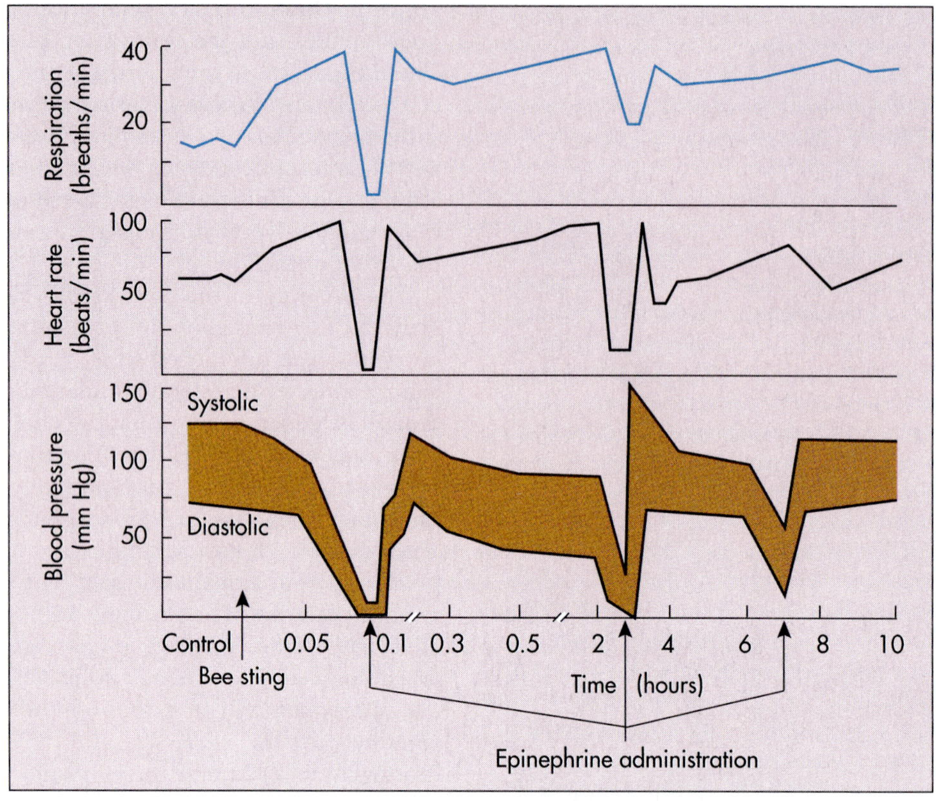

FIG. 11-37 During systemic anaphylaxis, such as occurs following allergic reactions to drugs and bee stings, blood pressure drops due to vasodilation, and breathing and heart irregularities develop. If untreated the person dies as breathing and heart beating cease. Epinephrine is administered to restore respiratory and heart function.

sodilators released as a result of the hypersensitivity reaction.

Atopic Allergies Atopic allergies result from a localized expression of type 1 hypersensitivity reactions. The interaction of antigens (allergens) with cell-bound IgE on the mucosal membranes of the upper respiratory tract and conjunctival tissues initiates a localized type 1 hypersensitivity reaction. Hay fever and allergies to certain foods are examples of such atopic allergies. When the allergen interacts with sensitized cells of the upper respiratory tract, the symptoms often include coughing, sneezing, congestion, tearing eyes, and respiratory difficulties. In cases where the allergen enters the body through the gastrointestinal tract, the symptoms often include vomiting, diarrhea, or hives. Antihistamines are useful in treating many such allergic reactions because they neutralize the main mediator of the physiological response; the antihistamine blocks the vasoactive action of the histamine released from sensitized mast and basophil cells.

In some cases, the allergic reaction primarily affects the lower respiratory tract, producing a condition known as *asthma.* Asthma is characterized by shortness of breath and wheezing. These symptoms occur because the allergic reaction causes a constriction of the bronchial tubes, producing spasms. The primary mediator of asthma is not histamine but SRS-A. Therefore antihistamines are not of therapeutic value in treating this condition and the treatment of asthma generally involves administration of epinephrine or aminophylline.

Atopic allergies can be diagnosed by skin tests (FIG. 11-38). Subcutaneous or intradermal injection of antigens results in a localized inflammation reaction if the individual is allergic to that antigen, that is, if that individual exhibits a type 1 hypersensitivity reaction. In this way, allergens for a particular individual are identified. The symptoms of atopic allergies can be controlled, at least in part, by avoiding the identified allergens and by using antihistamines.

In addition to treating the immediate symptoms of an allergic reaction, attempts can be made to desensitize the individual. Desensitization usually is achieved by identifying and then administering repeated doses of the allergen. The procedure generally is time consuming and costly. Over time, however, the allergic response can be reduced or eliminated. The mechanism by which desensitization works is not known but may

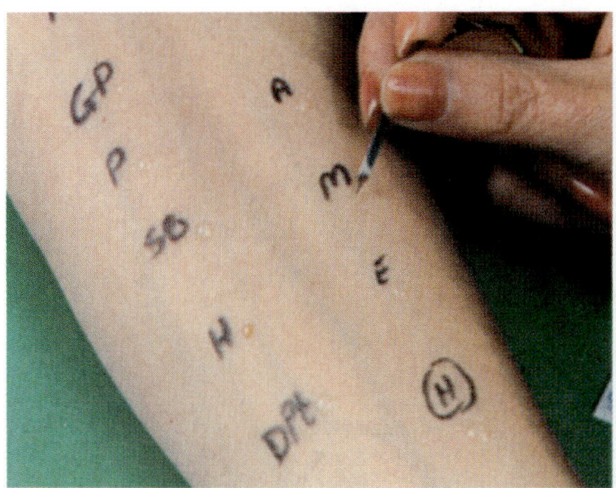

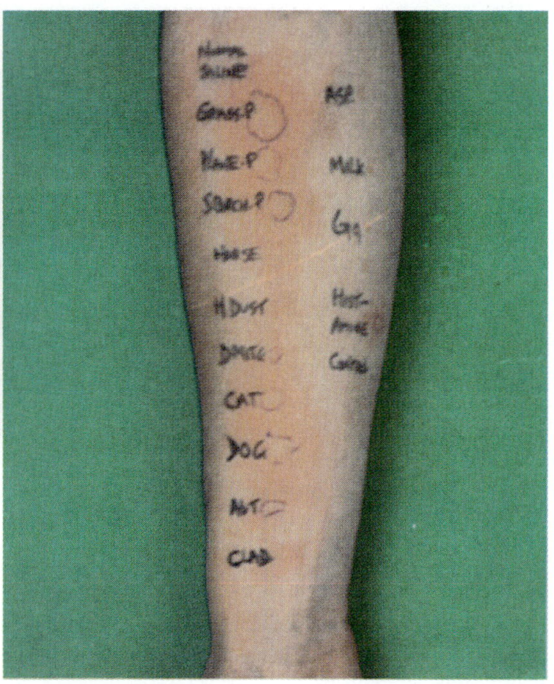

FIG. 11-38 Skin tests are used to diagnose allergies. Antigens are placed below the skin. Development of a red raised area is indicative of an allergic response.

consist of directing immunoglobulin production in the direction of IgG. Levels of IgE decrease and levels of IgG increase as a result of this treatment. Since IgG is not involved in the allergic response and IgE is the critical mediator of atopic allergies, desensitization reduces the allergic response.

Antibody-dependent Cytotoxic Hypersensitivity

Antibody-dependent cytotoxic hypersensitivity reactions *(type 2 hypersensitivity)* occur by a different mechanism. In type 2 hypersensitivity reactions an antigen on the surface of the cell combines with an antibody, resulting in the death of that cell by stimulating phagocytic attack or by initiating the sequence of the complement pathway that results in cell lysis.

Blood Group Compatibility An antibody-dependent cytotoxic response occurs after transfusions with incompatible blood types. An individual's blood serum also contains antibody to any antigens that do not occur in the cytoplasmic membranes of the red blood cells of that individual. If, for example, a person with type A blood (antigen A on blood cell surfaces and antibody B circulating) were given a transfusion with type B blood (antigen B on blood cell surface and antibody A in serum), the circulating antibodies in the recipient would react with the surface antigens of the donor cells, initiating the addition of complement molecules and the lysis of the donated cells. Symptoms of such incompatible transfusions include fever, chills, chest pain, nausea, vomiting, jaundice, and sometimes death. It is therefore essential that blood transfusions be made with compatible blood types.

With respect to compatible blood types, persons with type O blood are sometimes called *universal donors* and individuals with type AB blood are sometimes called *universal recipients.* The reason for this is that type O blood cells lack A and B antigens on their surfaces and therefore lack the antigens generally associated with transfusion incompatibility; regardless of the circulating antibodies in the recipient, the donated blood cells do not have the antigens to react, and the anti-A and anti-B antibodies in the donated blood are rapidly diluted when introduced into the larger volume of blood in the recipient. Similarly, persons with type AB blood do not have circulating antibodies against A or B antigens and therefore lack antibodies that react with the A and B antigens on blood cells that are introduced regardless of the cell type. However, the concepts of the universal donor and the universal recipient refer only to the major A and B antigens. There are other antigens on blood cell surfaces, including the Rh antigen, that can cause incompatibility reactions. Therefore, except in emergencies, transfusions are given only after adequate analysis of cell antigens and only with matching blood types.

Rh Incompatibility *Rh incompatibility* of mother and fetus is another example of type 2 hypersensitivity (FIG. 11-39). Rh incompatibility occurs when the father is Rh^+, the mother is Rh^-, and the fetus is Rh^+. In this case, the mother develops Rh antibodies in response to exposure to the Rh antigens of the fetus. Generally, the mother is exposed to the fetal Rh antigens at the time of birth, so that she does not develop an immune response until after the birth of her first Rh^+ child. In subsequent pregnancies, however, the

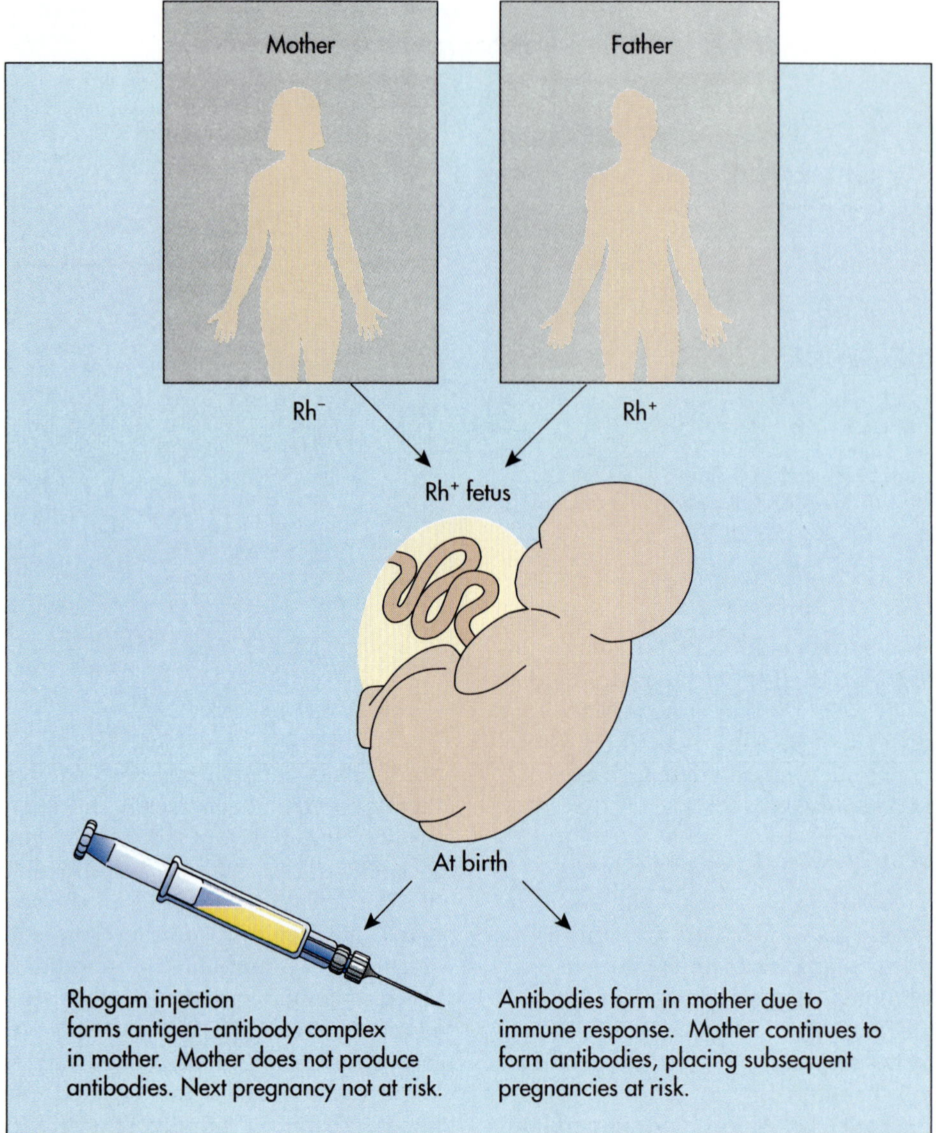

FIG. 11-39 Hemolytic disease of the newborn occurs when an Rh-negative mother becomes sensitized and produces antibodies that attack an Rh-positive fetus. Administration of Rhogam prevents the mother from developing an immune response that would produce anti-Rh antibodies that attack the fetus.

anti-Rh antibodies (IgG) circulating through the mother's body can cross the placenta and attack the cells of the fetus (if it is Rh$^+$), causing anemia. During development of the fetus, fetal blood is purified by the mother's liver (FIG. 11-40). At birth, the fetal blood is no longer purified by the maternal circulatory system and the infant develops jaundice. This disease, *hemolytic disease of the newborn* (previously called *erythroblastosis fetalis*), can be treated by removal of the fetal Rh-positive blood and replacement by transfusion with Rh-negative blood that will not be attacked by the anti-Rh antibodies that crossed the placenta and now are circulating within the newborn. At a later time, when the anti-Rh antibodies passively acquired from the mother have been diluted and eliminated, these transfused cells are later replaced by Rh-positive cells produced by the infant.

To prevent hemolytic disease of the newborn, passive artificial immunization of the Rh-negative mother with Rhogam (anti-Rh antibodies) is used at the time of birth. The anti-Rh antibodies react with the fetal Rh-positive cells that enter the mother at the time of birth through traumatized tissue. The reaction of anti-Rh antibodies with Rh-positive cells limits the development of an anamnestic (memory) immune response (active natural acquired immunity) in the mother by binding to the Rh antigens that have been introduced, thereby preventing their recognition by the immune system of the mother. Thus artificial passive immunization is used to prevent the development

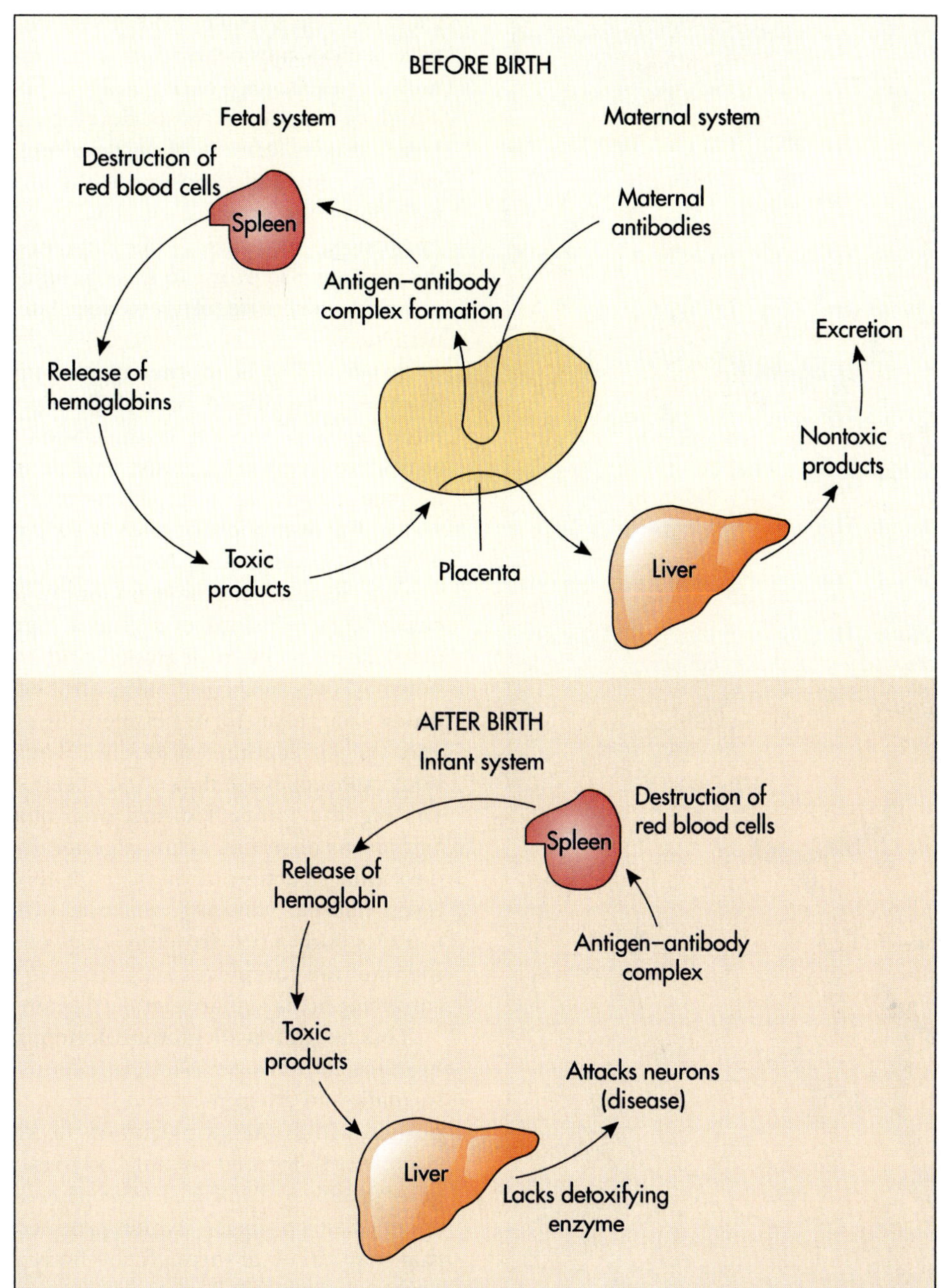

FIG. 11-40 Before birth the products formed by the attack of anti-Rh antibodies pass across the placenta and are detoxified by the maternal liver. After birth the liver of the newborn is unable to detoxify these products, which attack the nerves as well as red blood cells, causing disease.

of active natural immunity. This treatment is repeated at each birth when the baby is Rh-positive and the mother is Rh-negative. As a result of this treatment, a serious antibody-dependent cytotoxic hypersensitivity reaction can be prevented.

Immune Complex-mediated Hypersensitivity

Immune complex-mediated hypersensitivity (type 3 hypersensitivity) reactions involve antigens, antibodies, and complement that initiate an inflammatory response. These reactions occur when the formation of antibody–antigen complexes triggers the onset of an inflammatory response (FIG. 11-41, p. 430). Such an inflammatory response is part of the normal immune response, but if there are large excesses of antigen, the antigen–antibody–complement complexes may circulate and become deposited in various tissues. Inflammatory reactions from such deposition of immune complexes can cause physiological damage to kidneys, joints, and skin. Some examples of type 3 hy-

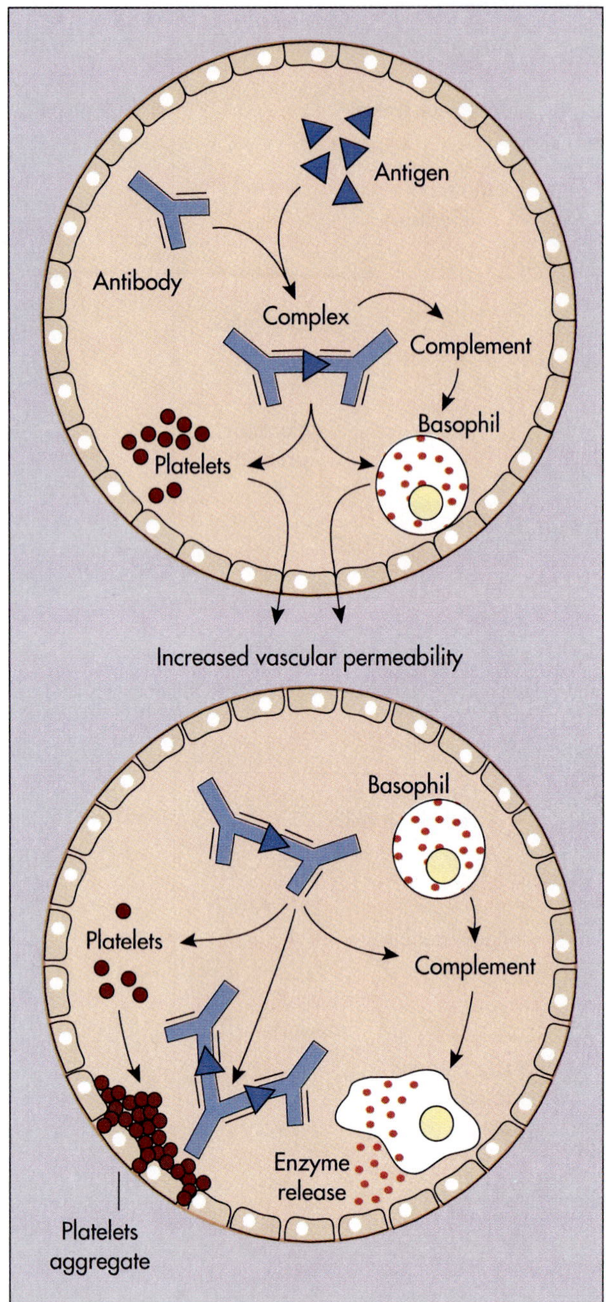

FIG. 11-41 Type 3 hypersensitivity reactions result in inflammation and deposition of immune complexes in blood vessel walls.

persensitivity or *Arthus immune-complex reactions* are listed in Table 11-8.

In the Arthus reaction, the site becomes infiltrated with neutrophils and there is extensive injury to the walls of the local blood vessels. This sometimes occurs in the lungs because of repeated exposure to antigens on the surfaces of inhaled particulate matter. When an antigen–antibody complex initiates such a reaction in the alveoli, the symptoms generally include cough, fever, and difficulty in breathing. These symptoms typically develop over a period of 4 to 6 hours, and the attack usually subsides within a few days after the removal of the source of the antigen. Some people have a high occupational risk of developing this condition. For example, farmers often develop this reaction because of repeated exposure to the airborne spores of actinomycetes growing on hay. Sugarcane workers, mushroom growers, cheesemakers, and pigeon fanciers are also prone to this condition because of exposure to airborne antigens associated with their activities.

Serum sickness is another type of immune complex disorder. This disease results when patients are given large doses of foreign serums, such as horse serum antitoxins to protect against tetanus and diphtheria—a once widely used practice—and antilymphocyte serum for immunosuppression to protect against rejection of transplanted tissues. The antigens in these foreign serums stimulate an immune response. Because large infusions of serum are given, these antigens have not been degraded and cleared from the body by the time circulating antibodies appear. Immune complexes form between the residual antigens and the circulating antibodies. These antigen–antibody complexes are deposited at certain body sites, including the joints, kidneys, and blood vessel walls. Symptoms of serum sickness generally appear 7 to 10 days after injection of the foreign serum and include fever, nausea, vomiting, malaise, hives, and pain in muscles and joints. In many cases of serum sickness, the immune complexes are carried to the kidneys and cause nephritis (inflammatory disease of the kidneys).

This condition of glomerulonephritis can also be brought about by persistent infections resulting in the formation of antigen–antibody complexes that are deposited within the glomeruli of the kidneys. Immune complexes—formed by antibody reactions with antigens produced by *Streptococcus pyogenes* (the causative agent of "strep throat," which produces protein toxins that may circulate through the body and cause other diseases), hepatitis B virus (the cause of serum hepatitis), *Plasmodium* species (protozoa that cause

TABLE 11-8 Examples of Type 3 Hypersensitivity Reactions

DISEASE CONDITION	CAUSED BY EXPOSURE TO:
Farmer's lung	Actinomycete spores
Cheese washer's disease	*Penicillium cassei* spores
Furrier's lung	Fox fur protein
Maple bark stripper's disease	*Cryptostroma* spores
Pigeon fancier's disease	Pigeon antigens
Serum sickness	Foreign blood serum

malaria), and *Schistosoma* (helminthic worms that cause schistosomiasis)—may lead to this condition. The persistence of these infections provides a continuing supply of antigen to react with circulating antibodies produced by the infected individual. The immune complexes that form accumulate in the kidneys, eventually causing nephritis due to complex-mediated hypersensitivity.

Cell-mediated (Delayed) Hypersensitivity

Cell-mediated or delayed hypersensitivity (type 4 hypersensitivity) reactions involve activated T lymphocytes. As the name implies, these reactions occur only after a prolonged delay after exposure to the antigen, often reaching maximal intensity 24 to 72 hours after the initial exposure. Delayed hypersensitivity reactions occur as allergies to various microorganisms and chemicals.

Contact dermatitis, resulting from exposure of the skin to chemicals, is a typical delayed hypersensitivity reaction. Poison ivy is one of the best-known examples of contact dermatitis (FIG. 11-42). Contact with catechols in the leaves of the poison ivy plant leads to development of a characteristic rash with itching,

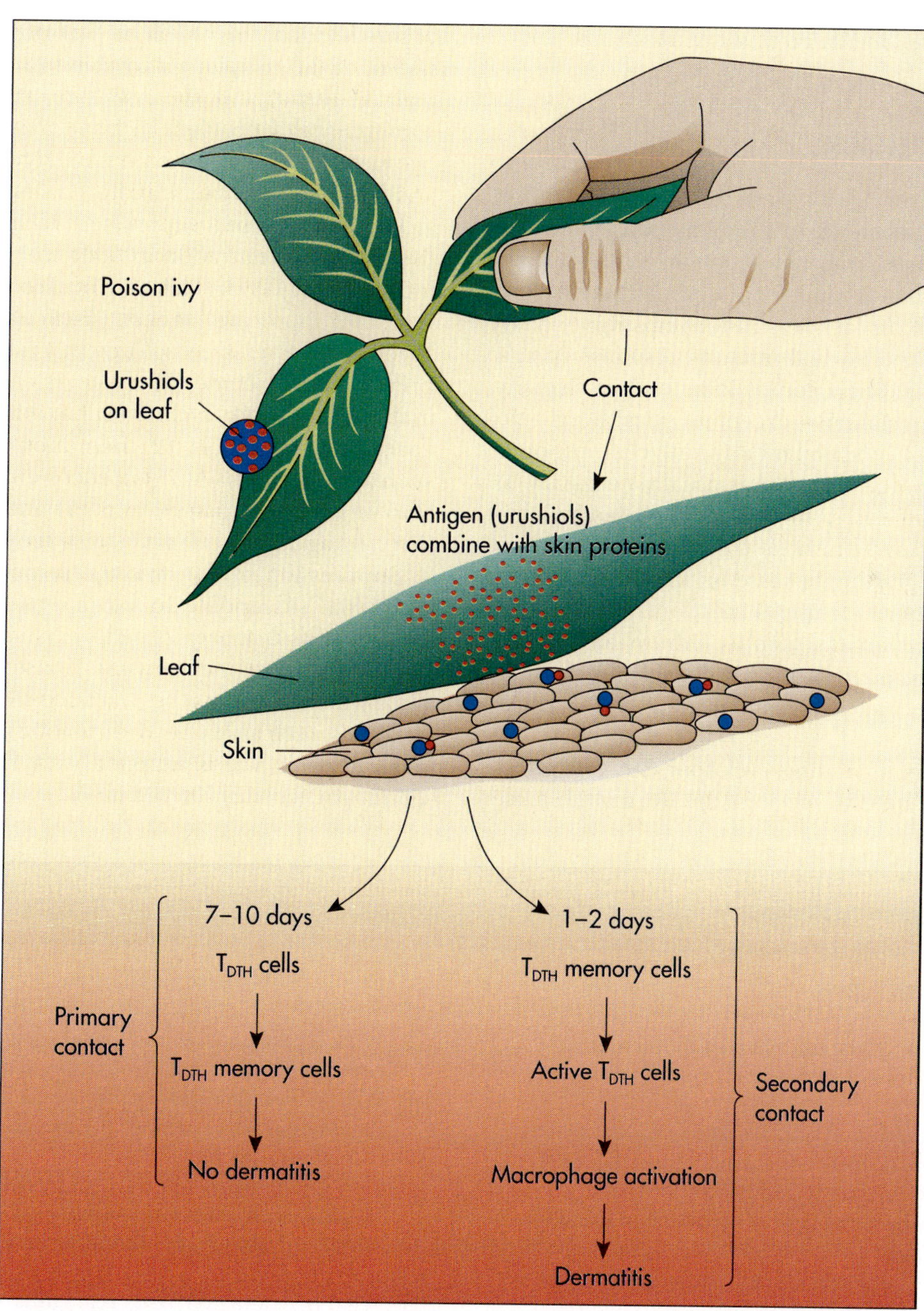

FIG. 11-42 Contact dermatitis, such as poison ivy, involves reactions of T_{DTH} cells that activate macrophage.

swelling, and blistering. Catechols appear to act as haptens, small molecules that elicit an immune response when bound to larger molecules, reacting with skin proteins to form active antigens; lipids in the skin help to retain the catechols. By combining with skin proteins, catechols bring about a cell-mediated response involving T cells. On primary exposure to poison ivy, no dermatitis (skin rash) occurs, but subsequent exposure of sensitized individuals to the oils of the poison ivy plant results in dermatitis after an initial delay of several days. Other agents, including metals, soaps, cosmetics, and biological materials, can also cause contact dermatitis. Treatment of contact dermatitis often involves administration of corticosteroids that depresses cell-mediated immune reactions.

Tissue Transplantation and Immunosuppression

Tissues contain surface antigens that are coded for by the MHC, and reactions to these antigens generally preclude successful transplantation of tissues unless the transplant tissues come from a compatible donor, that is, one with an identical histocompatibility complex, or unless the normal immune response is suppressed. Since finding a compatible donor is virtually impossible (even siblings—except identical twins—do not share many histocompatibility antigens), suppression of the immune response is usually necessary in organ transplant cases. In a sense, the normal immune defense mechanism is dysfunctional in transplantation and grafting because in these cases it does not serve the desired or useful function. The ability to transplant major organs such as kidneys and hearts depends on the ability to suppress the normal immune response and prevent rejection of the transplanted tissues.

Several drugs, including cyclosporin A and prednisone, may be used to suppress the normal immune response. The most widely used immunosuppressant for blocking rejection of major organ transplants is cyclosporin A. This drug is produced by the fungus *Tolypocladium inflatum*. It blocks rejection of the transplanted tissue by suppressing the cell-mediated immune system. Cyclosporin A, however, is extremely expensive; it currently costs $800 per month to prevent rejection of a transplanted heart. Without continued suppression of the immune system, rejection of a transplanted organ would occur.

Immunosuppression in organ transplant cases can also result in graft-versus-host (GVH) disease. This occurs when the transplanted (grafted) tissue contains immunocompetent cells that respond to the antigens of the tissues of the recipient. The depressed immune system of the recipient is unable to control the transplanted tissue, and the reaction can be fatal. This commonly is a problem in bone marrow transplants because bone marrow contains large numbers of B and T cells that can initiate an immune response against the immunosuppressed recipient. Lowering the T cell concentration in bone marrow reduces the incidence of GVH. This can be accomplished using immunosuppressive agents, particularly those that specifically attack T cells. Currently used treatments to prevent GVH include (1) cytotoxic chemicals, such as azathioprine and cyclophosphamide, that have a specificity for T cells; (2) immunosuppressive drugs such as cyclosporin A; (3) corticosteroids; (4) irradiation of lymphoid tissues; and (5) antibodies that are directed against T cell surface antigens.

Suppression of the immune response renders the individual susceptible to various pathogens or even opportunists that are normally excluded by the host's immune defense mechanisms. Consequently, extraordinary measures must be practiced to protect such individuals, such as extensive antibiotic therapy and hospitalization in wards supplied with HEPA (high efficiency particulate) filtered air.

CHAPTER REVIEW

Study Questions

1. What is meant by the normal human microbiota?
2. What body surfaces are normally colonized by microorganisms?
3. What body fluids normally are free of bacteria? Why?
4. How does the resident microbiota of the skin differ from that of the gastrointestinal tract? What are some of the major bacterial genera occurring in these two habitats?
5. What factors influence which bacterial genera can establish themselves within the indigenous microbial community of the skin?
6. How does the presence of an indigenous microbiota benefit humans?
7. What is phagocytosis and how does it contribute to our resistance to pathogenic microorganisms?
8. What is an inflammatory response and how does inflammation act to prevent the spread of pathogens throughout the body?
9. How is the respiratory tract protected against invasion by pathogenic microorganisms?
10. How is interferon involved in protection against viral infections?
11. What is an antigen? What is an antibody?
12. How does the clonal selection theory explain the ability of the immune response network to distinguish between self and nonself antigens?

CHAPTER REVIEW

STUDY QUESTIONS—CONT'D

13. Discuss the differences between a primary and a secondary (memory) immune response.
14. Discuss the differences between the antibody-mediated and cell-mediated immune response systems. Why do we need two such elaborate defense systems?
15. What is an agglutination reaction?
16. How is agglutination used in blood typing?
17. What is meant by compatible blood for transfusion purposes?
18. How does an agglutination reaction differ from a precipitin reaction?
19. How can agglutination reactions be carried out with soluble antigens?
20. What is complement?
21. How is complement involved in the immune response to a bacterial infection?
22. What are autoimmune diseases?
23. How can autoimmune diseases occur?
24. What is an allergy? How are allergies related to the immune response?
25. What is a lymphokine?
26. What functions do lymphokines have in the immune response?
27. How is the MHC region of the genome related to tissue compatibility?
28. What are the five major classes of immunoglobulins?
29. Compare the role of each immunoglobulin class in the immune response.

SITUATIONAL PROBLEM

Detecting and Treating Allergies

Many individuals in our population are hypersensitive to specific or multiple antigens, leading to allergic responses whenever exposed to specific allergens to which they have become sensitized. Thus we see seasonal episodes of allergy as sensitivity to plant and tree pollens lead to rhinitis, sinusitis, pharyngitis and bronchial asthma, as well as reactions to certain animal danders, drugs, or foods. Once an atopic allergic response to an allergen or group of allergens develops, avoidance of that allergen will prevent the occurrence of an anaphylactic response. This is feasible for food allergies or drug allergies. However, exposure to environmental allergens such as pollens and dust mites may be unavoidable and lead to considerable suffering in thousands of individuals. Some individuals treat the symptoms of allergies with antihistamines. Some allergy sufferers use allergy shots in which small amounts of highly purified allergen are injected subcutaneously over a period of weeks or months in the hope of developing an IgG response to the specific antigen.

A married couple moved to Baton Rouge from Boston 2 years ago. In the spring he developed symptoms of an allergy with sneezing and coughing. She developed allergic symptoms in the fall with tearing of the eyes. How would you determine whether they had allergies and (if they did) to what they were allergic? Assuming he had an allergy to the pollen of a plant that blooms in the spring and she to one that blooms in the fall what could they do? Would allergy shots be worth the expense and trouble of the patient? How would the allergy shots work to eliminate the allergy?

Suggested Supplementary Readings

Abbas AK, AH Lichtman, JS Pober: 1991. *Cellular and Molecular Immunology,* W. B. Saunders Co., Philadelphia.

Ada GL and G Nossal: 1987. The colonal selection theory, *Scientific American* 257(2):62-69.

Alt FW (ed.): 1992. *Immunology in the 21st Century,* Sigma Chemical Company, St. Louis.

Altman A, KM Coggeshall, T Mustelin: 1990. Molecular events mediating T cell activation, *Advances in Immunology* 48:227-360.

Atassi MZ, CJ vanOss, DR Absolom: 1984. *Molecular Immunology: A Textbook,* Marcel Dekker, New York.

Bach MK: 1982. Mediators of anaphylaxis and inflammation, *Annual Review of Microbiology* 36:371-413.

Baglioni C and TW Nilsen: 1981. The action of interferon at the molecular level, *American Scientist* 69:392-399.

Barret JT: 1983. *Textbook of Immunology: An Introduction to Immunochemistry and Immunobiology,* C.V. Mosby, St. Louis.

Beaman L and BL Beaman: 1984. The role of oxygen and its derivatives in microbial pathogenesis and host-defense, *Annual Review of Microbiology* 38:27-48.

Bellanti J (ed.): 1985. *Immunology III,* W.B. Saunders Co., Philadelphia.

Benacerraf B: 1981. Role of MNC gene products in immune regulation, *Science* 212:1229-1238.

Benjamini E and S Leskowitz: 1991. *Immunology: A Short Course,* ed. 2, Wiley-Liss, New York.

Bowry TR: 1984. *Immunology Simplified,* Oxford University Press, New York.

Brodsky FM and L Guagliardi: 1991. The cell biology of antigen processing and presentation, *Annual Review of Immunology* 9:707-744.

Brown MRW and P Williams: 1985. The influence of environment on envelope properties affecting survival of bacteria in infections, *Annual Review of Microbiology* 39:527-556.

Bullen JJ and E Griffiths: 1987. *Iron and Infection: Molecular, Physiological and Clinical Aspects,* John Wiley & Sons, Inc., New York.

Burke DC and AG Morris (eds.): 1983. *Interferons: From Molecular Biology to Clinical Applications* (Thirty-Fifth Symposium of the Society for General Microbiology), Cambridge University Press, Cambridge, England.

Burton DR and JM Woof: 1992. Human antibody effector function, *Advances in Immunology* 51:1-84.

Capon DJ and RHR Ward: 1991. The CD4-GP120 interaction and AIDS pathogenesis, *Annual Review of Immunology* 9:649-678.

Catty D (ed.): 1988. *Antibodies: A Practical Approach,* Vol I, IRL Press. Oxford, England.

Catty D (ed.): 1989. *Antibodies: A Practical Approach,* Vol II, IRL Press. Oxford, England.

Cohen IR: 1988. The self, the world, and autoimmunity, *Scientific American* 258(4):52-68.

Cooper EL: 1982. *General Immunology,* Pergamon Press, New York.

Crosa JH: 1984. The relationship of plasma-mediated iron transport and bacterial virulence, *Annual Review of Microbiology* 38:69-89.

Davies DR and H Metzger: 1983. Structural basis of antibody function, *Annual Review of Immunology* 1:87-117.

Davis MM: 1990. T cell receptor diversity and selection, *Annual Review of Biochemistry* 59:475-496.

Dodd RY and LF Barker: 1985. *Infection, Immunity and Blood Transfusions,* A.R. Liss, New York.

Doria G and A Eshkol: 1980. *The Immune System,* Academic Press, New York.

Eisen HN: 1980. *Immunology,* Harper & Row Publishers, Inc., Hagerstown, MD.

Esser C and A Radbruch: 1990. Immunoglobulin class switching: molecular and cellular analysis, *Annual Review of Immunology* 8:717-736.

Gallo R: 1987. The AIDS virus, *Scientific American* 256(1):46-72.

Goding JW: 1986. *Monoclonal Antibodies: Principles and Practice,* ed. 2, Academic Press, San Diego, CA.

Golub ES and DR Green: 1991. *Immunology: A Synthesis,* Sinauer Associates, Sunderland, MA.

Gooi HC and H Chapel (eds.): 1990. *Clinical Immunology: A Practical Approach,* IRL Press, Oxford, England.

Hamilton H and MB Rose (eds.): 1985. *Immune Disorders,* Springhouse Publishers, Springhouse, PA.

Harlow E and D Lane: 1988. *Antibodies: A Laboratory Manual,* Cold Spring Harbor Laboratory Press, Cold Spring Harbor, NY.

Herman A, JW Kappler, P Marrack, AM Pullen: 1991. Superantigens: mechanism of T-cell stimulation and role in immune responses, *Annual Review of Immunology* 9:745-772.

Hildemann WH: 1984. *Essentials of Immunology,* Elsevier Publishing Co., New York.

Honjo T: 1983. Immunoglobulin genes, *Annual Review of Immunology* 1:499-528.

Hudson L and FC Hay: 1989. *Practical Immunology,* ed. 3, Blackwell Scientific Publications, Oxford, England.

Johnson HM, JK Russell, CH Pontzer: 1992. Superantigens in human disease, *Scientific American* 266(4):92-101.

Kelso A and D Metcalf: 1990. T lymphocyte-derived colony-stimulating factors, *Advances in Immunology* 48:69-106.

Kimball JW: 1986. *Introduction to Immunology,* Macmillan, New York.

Kirkwood EM and CJ Lewis: 1984 *Understanding Medical Microbiology,* John Wiley & Sons, Inc., New York.

Klein J: 1982. *Immunology: The Science of Self-Nonself Discrimination,* John Wiley & Sons, Inc., New York.

Kroemer G, JL Andreu, JA Gonzalo, JC Gutierrez-Ramos, C Martinez-A: 1991. Interleukin-2, autotolerance, and autoimmunity, *Advances In Immunology.* 50:147-236.

Liddell JE and A Cryer: 1991. *A Practical Guide to Monoclonal Antibodies,* John Wiley & Sons, Chichester, England.

Macario CL and EC deMacario (eds.): 1985. *Monoclonal Antibodies Against Bacteria,* Academic Press, Orlando, FL.

Matis LA: 1990. The molecular basis of T-cell specificity, *Annual Review of Immunology* 8:65-82.

Matthews TJ and DP Bolognesi: 1988. AIDS vaccines, *Scientific American* 259(4):120-127.

McEvedy C: 1988. The Bubonic plague, *Scientific American* 258(2):118-123.

McNabb PC and TB Tomasi: 1981. Host defense mechanisms at mucosal surfaces, *Annual Review of Microbiology* 35:477-496.

Milstein C: 1980. Monoclonal antibodies, *Scientific American* 243(4):66-74.

Mitchison NA: 1992. Specialization, tolerance, memory, competition, latency, and strife among T cells, *Annual Review of Immunology* 10:1-12.

Miyajima A, S Miyatake, N Arai, F Lee, T Yokota: 1990. Cytokines: Coordinators of immune and inflammatory responses, *Annual Review of Biochemistry* 59:783-836.

Mizel SB and P Jaret: 1986. *The Human Immune System: The New Frontier in Medicine,* Simon & Schuster, New York.

Moss PAH, MCW Rosenberg, JI Bell: 1992. The human T cell receptor in health and disease, *Annual Review of Immunology* 10:71-96.

Myrvik QN (ed.): 1984. *Fundamentals of Immunology,* Lea & Febiger, Philadelphia.

Nahmias AJ and RJ O'Reilly (eds.): 1981. *Immunology of Human Infection,* Plenum Publishing Co., New York.

Newby TJ and CR Stokes (eds.): 1984. *Local Immune Responses of the Gut,* CRC Press, Inc., Boca Raton, FL.

Ngo TT and HM Lenhoff (eds.): 1985. *Enzyme-Mediated Immunoassay,* Plenum Publishing Co., New York.

Old LJ: 1988. Tumor necrosis factor, *Scientific American* 258(5):59-75.

Parkman R: 1991. The biology of bone marrow transplantation for severe combined immune deficiency, *Advances in Immunology* 49:381-410.

Pascual V and JD Capra: 1991. Human immunoglobulin heavy-chain variable region genes: organization, polymorphism, and expression, *Advances in Immunology* 49:1-74.

Potts E and M Morra: 1986. *Understanding Your Immune System,* Avon Books, New York.

Roitt I: 1991. *Essential Immunology,* ed. 7, Blackwell Scientific Publications, Oxford, England.

Rose NR: 1981. Autoimmune diseases, *Scientific American* 244(2):80-103.

Rothenberg EV: 1992. The development of functionally responsive T cells, *Advances in Immunology.* 51:85-214.

Schatz DG, MA Oettinger, MS Schlissel: 1992. V (D) J Recombination: Molecular biology and regulation, *Annual Review of Immunology* 10:359-384.

Schlesinger RB: 1982. Defense mechanisms of the respiratory system, *BioScience* 32(1):45-50.

Schwartz AL: 1990. Cell biology of intracellular protein trafficking, *Annual Review of Immunology* 8:195-230.

Schwartz RH: 1993. T cell anergy, *Scientific American* 269(2):62-71.

Sikora K and H Smedley: 1984. *Monoclonal Antibodies,* Blackwell Scientific Publications, Oxford, England.

Singhal SK and TL Delovitch (eds.): 1986. *Mediators of Immune Regulation and Immunotherapy,* Elsevier, New York.

Smith KA: 1990. Interleukin-2, *Scientific American* 262(3):50-57.

Steele RW: 1983. *Immunology for the Practicing Physician,* Appleton and Lange, Norwalk, CT.

Steitz JA: 1988. "Snurps," *Scientific American* 258(6):56-65.

Stites DP and AI Teer (eds.): 1991. *Basic and Clinical Immunology,* ed. 7, Appleton and Lange, Norwalk, CT.

Van Snick J: 1990. Interleukin-6: An overview, *Annual Review of Immunology* 8:253-278.

Verma IM: 1990. Gene therapy, *Scientific American* 263(5):68-84.

Vitetta ES, MT Berton, C Burger, M Kepron, WT Lee, X-M Yin: 1991. Memory B and T cells, *Annual Review of Immunology* 9:193-218.

Waldmann TA: 1989. The multi-subunit interleukin-2 receptor, *Annual Review of Biochemistry* 58:875-912.

Wysocki LJ and ML Gefter: 1989. Gene conversion and the generation of antibody diversity, *Annual Review of Biochemistry* 58:509-532.

Yague J, J White, C Coleclough, J Kappler, E Palmer, P Marrack: 1985. The T cell receptor: The alpha and beta chains define idiotype, and antigen and MHC specificity, *Cell* 42(1):81-88.

Young JD-E and ZA Cohn: 1988. How killer cells kill, *Scientific American* 258(1):38-45.

CHAPTER 12

Epidemiology

Chapter Outline

The development of a basic understanding of the interrelationships between humans and microorganisms, particularly the immune defense system and the virulence of specific microbial pathogens, has led to practices that prevent the occurrence or diminish the incidence of human diseases caused by microorganisms. Understanding the sources of pathogens and their routes of transmission is useful for controlling the spread of infectious diseases. The examination of disease transmission is part of the field of epidemiology, which studies the causes of disease and the factors involved in the transmission of infectious agents, especially in relation to populations. Epidemiologists attempt to determine the cause of a disease outbreak and how that disease outbreak in a population can be effectively controlled. Based on the epidemiology of a disease, strategies can be employed to prevent disease outbreaks. Many once deadly diseases are now prevented by practices such as vaccination and disinfection of potable waters, based on an epidemiological understanding of how to control pathogenic microorganisms.

12.1 SCIENCE OF EPIDEMIOLOGY

Epidemiology is the field of science concerned with the circumstances under which diseases occur. This science examines factors involved in the incidence and spread, and prevention and control, of infectious and noninfectious diseases. Epidemiologists consider the effects of diseases on populations and individuals within those populations. The effect of the disease in a population can be measured by the death, or *mortality rate,* it produces. The incidence of the disease, or *morbidity rate,* is usually much higher than the mortality rate; many more individuals infected with a pathogen become ill rather than die of a disease. In the United States, the Centers for Disease Control (CDC) in Atlanta, Georgia, compiles and publishes the statistics on morbidity and mortality that are necessary for monitoring outbreaks of disease (Table 12-1).

TABLE 12-1 Summary of Cases of Specified Notifiable Diseases in the United States During 1993 Reported by the Centers for Disease Control in *Morbidity and Mortality Weekly Report*

DISEASE	CASES	DISEASE	CASES
AIDS	93,282	Measles, imported	56
Anthrax	0	Measles, indigenous	221
Botulism, foodborne	21	Plague	10
Botulism, infant	55	Poliomyelitis, paralytic	0
Botulism, other	5	Psittacosis	53
Brucellosis	88	Rabies, human	2
Cholera	18	Syphilis, primary and secondary	25,875
Congenital Rubella Syndrome	7	Syphilis, congenital	1,493
Diphtheria	0	Tetanus	42
Encephalitis, post-infectious	151	Toxic shock syndrome	218
Gonorrhea	392,192	Trichinosis	40
Haemophilus influenzae (invasive disease)	1,236	Tuberculosis	22,038
Hansen Disease	170	Tularemia	120
Leptospirosis	46	Typhoid fever	341
Lyme Disease	7,760	Typhus fever, tickborne Rocky Mountain Spotted Fever	450

The underlying premise of epidemiology is that there is a statistical probability that a susceptible individual will be exposed to a particular pathogen and that such exposure will result in disease transmission. The likelihood of a disease outbreak occurring within a population depends on the concentration and virulence of the pathogen, the distribution of susceptible individuals, and the potential sources of exposure to the pathogenic microorganisms.

The science of epidemiology owes its origins to the classic studies in the mid-1800s by the British physician, John Snow. Snow sought the cause of the cholera epidemic that was devastating London. He believed that the disease was spread by contaminated food and water, not by bad air or casual contact. Snow studied medical records of patients in the Broad Street area of London who had died of cholera. He discovered that most of the victims obtained drinking water from the Broad Street water pump. He hypothesized that the water from that pump was contaminated with raw sewage containing the cause of cholera and that shutting off that source of water would end the cholera outbreak. The Broad Street pump was shut down and the number of cholera cases dropped dramatically. These important findings led the way to understanding the causes and modes of transmission of infectious diseases.

Like Snow, contemporary epidemiologists consider the *etiology of disease,* that is, the underlying cause of the disease. For infectious diseases, this means identifying the pathogen responsible for the disease. Epidemiologists also examine the factors involved in the *transmission* of infectious agents, especially in relation to populations. They identify the origin and mode of transmission of a disease and assess the microbiological safety of various substances, such as food and water, involved in this transmission. By understanding the spread of pathogens through populations, epidemiologists can develop methods to control infectious diseases (FIG. 12-1). Public health measures and safety depend on the methods and findings of the epidemiologist. The epidemiologist often acts as a detective, sometimes searching for a source of tainted food or locating infected individuals to determine the origin of a disease outbreak.

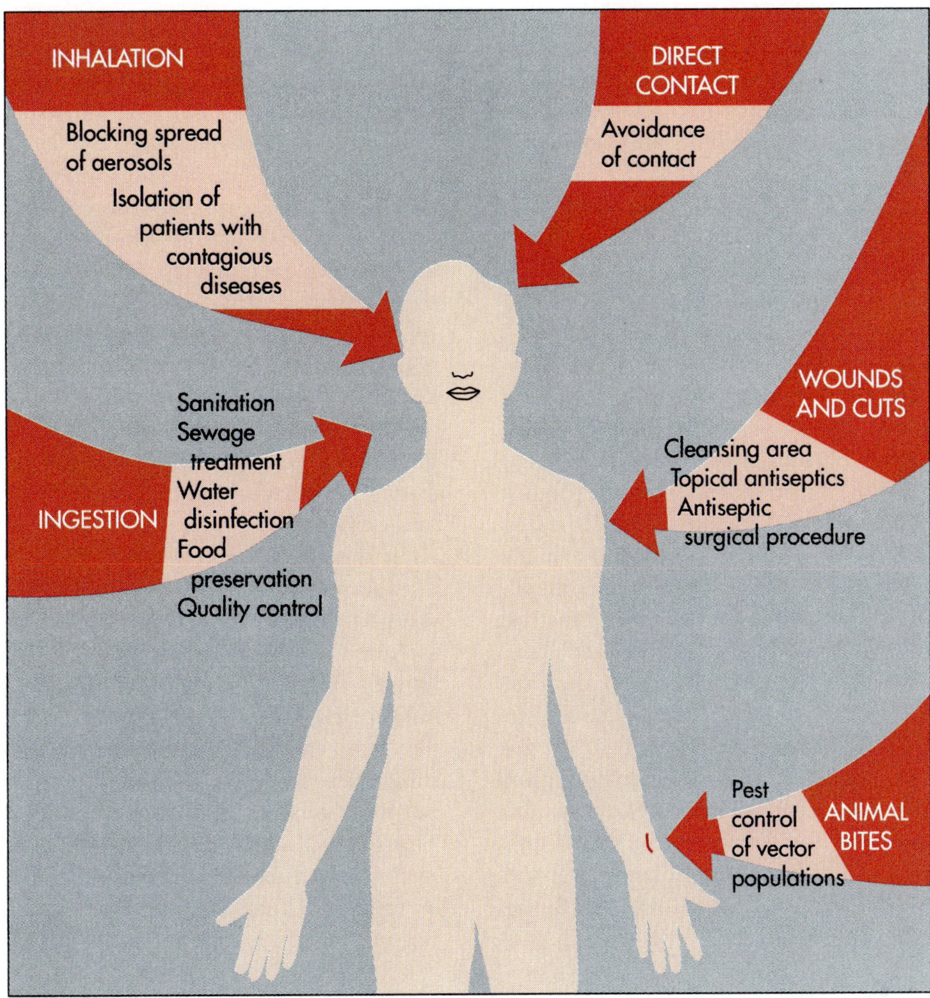

FIG. 12-1 Routes of pathogen transmission and means of blocking disease spread.

Descriptive Epidemiological Studies

Descriptive epidemiological studies are based on data that describe the pattern of disease within populations according to various demographic features such as age, gender, geographic area, and time of occurrence. Such information often reveals the factors responsible for the etiology of the disease. The epidemiologist is aided by the knowledge that disease transmission frequently occurs via the air, the ingestion of contaminated food or water, and direct contact with infected individuals or contaminated inanimate objects (fomites). By determining where and what people have eaten, where they have been, and with whom they have been in contact, the epidemiologist can establish a pattern of disease transmission.

During January 1993, for example, hundreds of individuals, many of them children, in the state of Washington developed signs of a gastrointestinal infection that included severe bloody diarrhea. Several deaths occurred from this outbreak. All of the individuals had eaten hamburgers at one fast food restaurant chain. Stool specimens from over 300 persons confirmed that the disease was the result of infections with *Escherichia coli* strain O157:H7. Meat from the same lots of beef had been distributed to several other states, and increased incidence of bloody diarrhea was reported in those states. A recall of the meat from the common source was ordered and restaurants were instructed to increase the temperature used to cook hamburgers.

Analytical Epidemiological Studies

Analytical epidemiological studies use the scientific method to test hypotheses regarding the etiology of disease and the transmission routes of infectious agents. They seek to establish cause and effect relationships between particular factors and the occurrence of disease. They set forth hypotheses, for example, that eating a particular food exposed an individual to a specific pathogen. They then test these hypotheses by making observations and rejecting hypotheses that are shown to be invalid.

The most definitive type of analytical epidemiological study is called a *cohort study.* In such a study, groups of persons (cohorts) with and without various suspected risk factors determined at the start of the study, are followed over time for the development of disease. These studies may be carried out by identifying a cohort at the present time and then following them for a period of time to see if they develop a disease or by identifying a group of persons who at some time in the past were then presumably free of the disease under investigation, as indicated by examining existing records. Studies of disease outbreaks usually begin after several individuals already have become ill, so that the exposed and unexposed cohort must be identified retrospectively and followed forward from that time. Such was the case in the study of the outbreak of a mysterious malady that occurred in Philadelphia in 1976 during a convention of the American Legion. At the time the investigation started, the involved population had already left the hotel suspected as being the source of the agent causing the disease, but this potentially exposed group could be identified, interviewed, and followed. By examining the incidence of disease in the cohort, particularly those who had spent significant time in the hotel's lobby, it was eventually established that the air-conditioning system was the source of the bacterium *(Legionella pneumophila)* that caused the outbreak of Legionnaire's disease.

In *case–control studies,* persons with the disease are compared with a disease-free control group for various possible risk factors. When a significant difference in the prevalence of a risk factor is identified, then the possibility of a causal association is considered. Analysis of an outbreak of a water or foodborne disease is a good example. The epidemiologist compares the incidence of disease in the group composed of those individuals who had eaten a specific food or imbibed water from a specific source with the incidence of that disease in a group that had not eaten food or imbibed water from those sources.

In the spring of 1993, for example, an inordinate number of individuals in Milwaukee, Wisconsin, developed signs of a gastrointestinal tract infection that included severe abdominal pain. The number of cases and the fact that individuals outside of Milwaukee who had not recently visited Milwaukee, including individuals from the Milwaukee suburbs, showed no signs of similar disease suggested that the source of the disease outbreak was the Milwaukee municipal water supply. The disease signs were consistent with an infection with the protozoan *Cryptosporidium.* Microscopic observations of fecal samples from individuals who had become ill and from the water supply confirmed that

BOX 12-1

AN OUTBREAK OF *SALMONELLA* INFECTION ASSOCIATED WITH THE CONSUMPTION OF RAW EGGS

In 1991 several individuals in a city developed symptoms of gastrointestinal infections that included diarrhea, fever, abdominal cramping, nausea, and chills. The pathogenic bacterium *Salmonella enteritidis* was isolated from the stools of 15 sick individuals, confirming an outbreak of an infectious disease. Interviews with the 15 individuals revealed that they had eaten at the same restaurant within a 9-day period. This pointed to the restaurant as the likely source of infection. Twenty-three employees of the restaurant reported that they had similar disease symptoms during the same period, supporting the view that the restaurant was the source of the outbreak.

Epidemiologists hypothesized that consumption of a particular food was responsible for the *Salmonella* infections. Fourteen of the fifteen patrons of the restaurant who became ill reported that, among other foods, they had eaten Caesar salad at the restaurant. Eleven individuals who had eaten at the restaurant during the same 9-day period and had not become ill reported that they had not eaten Caesar salad. Stool specimens of restaurant employees who had eaten the Caesar salad and become ill were positive for *Salmonella enteritidis.* Not all restaurant employees who were positive for *Salmonella enteritidis,* however, reported eating Caesar salad. Those who had not eaten Caesar salad had eaten other foods with raw eggs.

The Caesar salad dressing was prepared by combining 36 egg yolks with olive oil, anchovies, garlic, and warm water. The salad dressing generally was prepared each morning except for a 3-day period when a single batch was prepared and stored in a refrigerator that was found later to be at 15.6° C. Tracing the source of eggs used during the outbreak of the disease indicated that they all had come from a single flock of chickens. The information gained in this study points to the consumption of raw eggs as the source of *Salmonella enteritidis* infection. It highlights the risks of infection associated with the consumption of uncooked eggs.

TABLE 12-2 AIDS Patients in the United States

PATIENT GROUP	TOTAL CASES BY YEAR AND (PERCENT OF TOTAL CASES FOR EACH YEAR) 1981-1983	1986	1990	1993
Homosexual/bisexual	562 (69)	8,322 (67)	24,053 (56)	36,000 (52)
IV drug user	98 (12)	1,674 (13)	10,161 (24)	17,000 (25)
Homosexual and IV drug user	74 (9)	925 (8)	2,445 (5)	2,800 (4)
Hemophilia–coagulation disorder	7 (1)	119 (1)	369 (1)	500 (1)
Heterosexual contacts	57 (7)	470 (4)	2,799 (7)	7,000 (10)
Transfusion recipients	3 (<1)	275 (2)	884 (2)	1,500 (2)
Undetermined	17 (2)	510 (5)	1,948 (5)	4,000 (6)
Total	818	12,295	42,659	68,800

an outbreak of cryptosporidiosis had occurred and that the municipal water supply was the source of infection.

Statistical analyses are performed in a case–control study, such as *Cryptosporidium* infection in Milwaukee, to compare the prevalence of the relative risk factor in the group with the disease with the prevalence of that same risk factor in the control group. In Milwaukee the risk factor was drinking municipal water. If the frequency of the risk factor in persons with the disease is statistically significantly greater than the frequency of that risk factor in those in the group without the disease, then a cause and effect relationship may exist between that risk factor and the disease. It was in this manner that homosexual men and intravenous drug users were identified as having high risk factors that expose them to the human immunodeficiency virus that causes AIDS (Table 12-2).

12.2 DISEASE OUTBREAKS

A disease outbreak is considered to have occurred when several cases are reported in a relatively short period of time in a geographically defined area previously experiencing only sporadic cases of the disease. Disease occurrences are considered *sporadic* when individual cases of the disease are recorded in areas geographically remote from each other or can be temporally separated. Such a situation implies that the occurrences are not related.

SOURCES OF DISEASE OUTBREAKS

Epidemiologists collect data on the geographical, seasonal, and age-group distribution of a disease. They correlate this data to follow the incidence of a disease and the possible sources of the agents causing the disease. For example, there is a significant correlation between age and the specific etiologic agent in cases of meningitis (Table 12-3) By knowing the age of an individual with meningitis, the physician often makes an assumption about the etiologic agent based on the established relationship between age and the etiologic agent. This enables the physician to initiate therapy while awaiting definitive clinical diagnostic results.

In many cases, a disease outbreak can be traced to a single source of exposure with rapid onset of disease. In other cases, pathogens are transmitted from

TABLE 12-3 Correlation of Age with Etiological Agents of Meningitis

ETIOLOGICAL AGENT	PERCENT OF ISOLATES FOUND IN PATIENTS UNDER 2 MONTHS	2-60 MONTHS	5-40 YEARS	OVER 40 YEARS
Neisseria meningitidis	—	20	55	10
Haemophilus influenzae	—	60	5	2
Escherichia coli and other Enterobacteriaceae	55	—	—	10
Pseudomonas aeruginosa	2	—	—	—
Streptococcus pneumoniae and other *Streptococcus* spp.	28	12	25	55
Staphylococcus spp.	5	—	10	13
Other	10	8	10	10

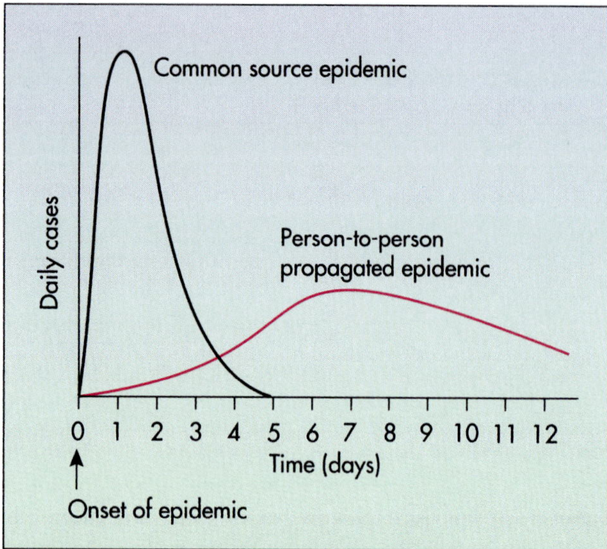

FIG. 12-2 In some cases, disease outbreaks occur when numerous individuals are exposed to a common source of the pathogen. Such outbreaks are characterized by a sudden rapid rise in the number of cases. Person to person transmission of disease results in epidemic outbreaks of disease that are characterized by a slower rise in the number of cases over a more prolonged time period.

one infected individual to another (FIG. 12-2). Pathogens can be transmitted directly from one individual to another, indirectly, by means of another living agent, called a *vector,* or from inanimate sources such as food and water. The geographical distribution of a disease may suggest a particular vector, as for example, the various types of encephalitis caused by vector-borne viruses (Table 12-4). The close association of a disease with a particular season often indicates a specific mode of transmission, such as in the case of chickenpox or measles, where the number of cases jumps sharply when children enter school and are in close contact with one another. The age-group distribution of a disease can suggest or eliminate particular routes of transmission.

The number of cases reported each day and the locations of disease occurrences enable epidemiologists to distinguish between a *common source outbreak,* which is characterized by a sharp rise and rapid decline in the number of cases, and a *person-to-person outbreak,* which is characterized by a relatively slow, prolonged rise and decline in the number of cases (see FIG. 12-2).

Reservoirs of Pathogens

The transmission of infectious agents involves the movement of pathogens from a source to the appropriate portal of entry. The source of an infectious agent is known as the *reservoir.* In some cases, the reservoirs of human pathogens are nonliving sources such as soil and water. For example, tetanus is generally acquired when spores of *Clostridium tetani,* which are widely distributed in soil, contaminate a wound. Often, diseases acquired from such sources are noncommunicable, that is, they are singular events and are not normally transmitted from an infected individual to an uninfected individual. So it is that, for example, health care workers who treat a patient with tetanus are at no greater risk of contracting this disease than the rest of the population.

Nonhuman animals are sometimes the reservoirs of human pathogens. They may also be involved in the transmission of pathogens. Humans, however, are the principal reservoirs for microorganisms that cause human diseases. People infected with a pathogen act as a source of contagion for others. The term *contagious disease* or *communicable disease* indicates that a pathogen will move with ease from one individual to the next. People who come in contact with someone suffering from a contagious disease are at risk of contracting that disease unless they are immune.

In some cases, infected individuals do not develop disease symptoms. Such individuals are called *asymptomatic carriers* or simply *carriers.* Although they do not become sick themselves, carriers are important reservoirs of infectious agents.

TABLE 12-4 Encephalitis in Humans

DISEASE	VECTOR	GEOGRAPHIC DISTRIBUTION
Eastern equine encephalitis	Mosquito	Eastern United States, Canada, Brazil, Cuba, Panama, Dominican Republic, Trinidad, Philippines
Venezuelan equine encephalitis	Mosquito	Brazil, Colombia, Ecuador, Trinidad, Venezuela, Mexico, Florida, Texas
Western equine encephalitis	Mosquito	Western United States, Argentina, Canada, Mexico, Guyana, Brazil
St. Louis encephalitis	Mosquito	United States, Trinidad, Panama
Japanese B encephalitis	Mosquito	Japan, Guam, Eastern Asian mainland, India, Malaya
Murray Valley encephalitis	Mosquito	Australia, New Guinea
Ileus	Mosquito	Brazil, Guatemala, Honduras, Trinidad
Tick-borne group (Russian spring-summer encephalitis group)	Tick	USSR, Canada, Malaya, United States, Central Europe, Finland, Japan, India, Great Britain

BOX 12-2

TYPHOID MARY

The classic case of disease transmission by an asymptomatic carrier occurred in the early 1900s when a cook, Mary Mallon, spread typhoid fever from one community to another. In 10 years Mary, never ill herself, worked in seven different households in which 50 cases of typhoid fever occurred with 3 deaths. She quit and disappeared each time a case of typhoid appeared in the household of her employer. When she was finally tracked down in 1907, she was diagnosed as a carrier of *Salmonella typhi.* She refused to undergo the surgical removal of infected tissues and was imprisoned. She was released in 1910 due to public outcry protesting her confinement, only to continue spreading typhoid to other communities, including a sanitorium in New Jersey and a hospital in New York. In 1915, she was recaptured and forcibly hospitalized for the rest of her life. Typhoid Mary, as she was known, died in 1938 at the age of 70. The forced surgery and imprisonment for having an infectious disease was instrumental in the initiation of the American Civil Liberties Union.

EPIDEMICS

A disease constantly present in a population in relatively low numbers is said to be *endemic.* **Epidemics,** in contrast, are outbreaks of disease in which unusually high numbers of individuals in a population contract a disease. A *pandemic* is an outbreak of disease that affects large numbers of people in a major geographical region or that has reached epidemic proportions simultaneously in different parts of the world. During 1918 and 1919, a pandemic of influenza resulted in the death of over 20 million people.

Common Source Epidemic

In a *common source epidemic* many individuals simultaneously acquire the infectious agent from the same source. This occurs, for example, in outbreaks of cholera in the Far East, where the pathogen is acquired from drinking water contaminated with fecal matter as a result of monsoon rains. When a common source for an epidemic outbreak of disease is identified, action can be taken to break the chain of disease transmission. For example, potentially contaminated foods can be recalled from the marketplace if foods from the same source are identified as a source of infection.

BOX 12-3

HOW NEW DISEASES ORIGINATE

Periodically, new infectious diseases emerge, challenging epidemiologists to find the origin of the pathogens. In some cases, these diseases existed for some time but were undetected. In other cases, genetic changes due to mutation or recombination may have led to new strains with altered virulence. Periodic outbreaks of influenza are due to genetic changes that result in the evolution of new strains of influenza viruses. Other theories are needed to explain the emergence of seemingly new pathogens such as the human immunodeficiency virus that causes AIDS in the late 1970s and the hantavirus that killed over 20 people, mostly Navajos, in the summer of 1993, in the southwest United States.

In recent years, epidemiologists found evidence that changing environments is a major cause of emerging infectious diseases. Construction of roadways through jungles and rain forests may allow pathogens to spread rapidly to huge numbers of people. One of the most dramatic indications that humans were disrupting the balance between pathogens and humans came when Brazil built a highway deep in the Amazonian jungle to its new capital, Brasilia. Soon after construction of the highway in the 1950s, viruses, some of which were unknown, were found in the blood of highway workers. One of these viruses, the Oropouche virus, also was found in the blood of a sloth dead at the side of the highway. Oropouche virus was not known to be responsible for epidemics in humans or animals before 1960. In 1961 the Oropouche virus was identified as the cause of a flu-like epidemic in Brazil that afflicted 11,000 people.

While it was clear that Oropouche was to blame for the epidemic, it was not clear how a virus never seen in human beings before had emerged to cause a new disease. Finding the answer took epidemiologists almost 2 decades. In 1980 the Oropouche virus was isolated from biting midges. During construction of the highway through the Amazonian jungle, the midges had undergone a population explosion. This led to a huge increase in vectors carrying the Oropouche virus. Similar environmental changes may underlie the emergence of the new viruses that cause AIDS, Ebola hemorrhagic fever, Marburg hemorrhagic fever, and yellow fever (where the viruses probably initially occurred in monkeys); Rift Valley fever (where the viruses probably initially occurred in cattle, sheep, and mosquitoes); and Hantaan (where the viruses probably initially occurred in rodents).

Person-to-Person Epidemic

In a *person-to-person epidemic* there is transmission from one infected individual to an uninfected individual, called *propagated transmission,* since the infectious agent is spread from one individual to the next in a progressive chain of infection. Propagated transmission occurs in sexually transmitted diseases such as acquired immunodeficiency syndrome (AIDS). It is the aim of the epidemiologist to identify the sources of disease outbreaks and to advise public health officials regarding the steps that should be taken to prevent them. In some cases, when person-to-person transmission is responsible for disease outbreaks in a population, steps can be taken to reduce the number of susceptible individuals, for example, by immunization, thereby breaking the chain of transmission.

Influenza outbreaks, for example, spread worldwide via person-to-person–propagated transmission from the site of an initial outbreak with a new strain. It is possible to watch the disease spread from one area to another (FIG. 12-3). Each year, epidemiologists make predictions about the severity of influenza outbreaks, and public health officials take the necessary steps of immunizing high-risk individuals with the correct antigenic type and warn the public about the dangers of this disease. Even in a nonepidemic year, influenza causes a significant number of deaths; for example, the death rate due to influenza in 1980 (a nonepidemic year) in the United States was 0.3 per 100,000 population. These periodic epidemic outbreaks are the result of genetic variation and viral gene recombination.

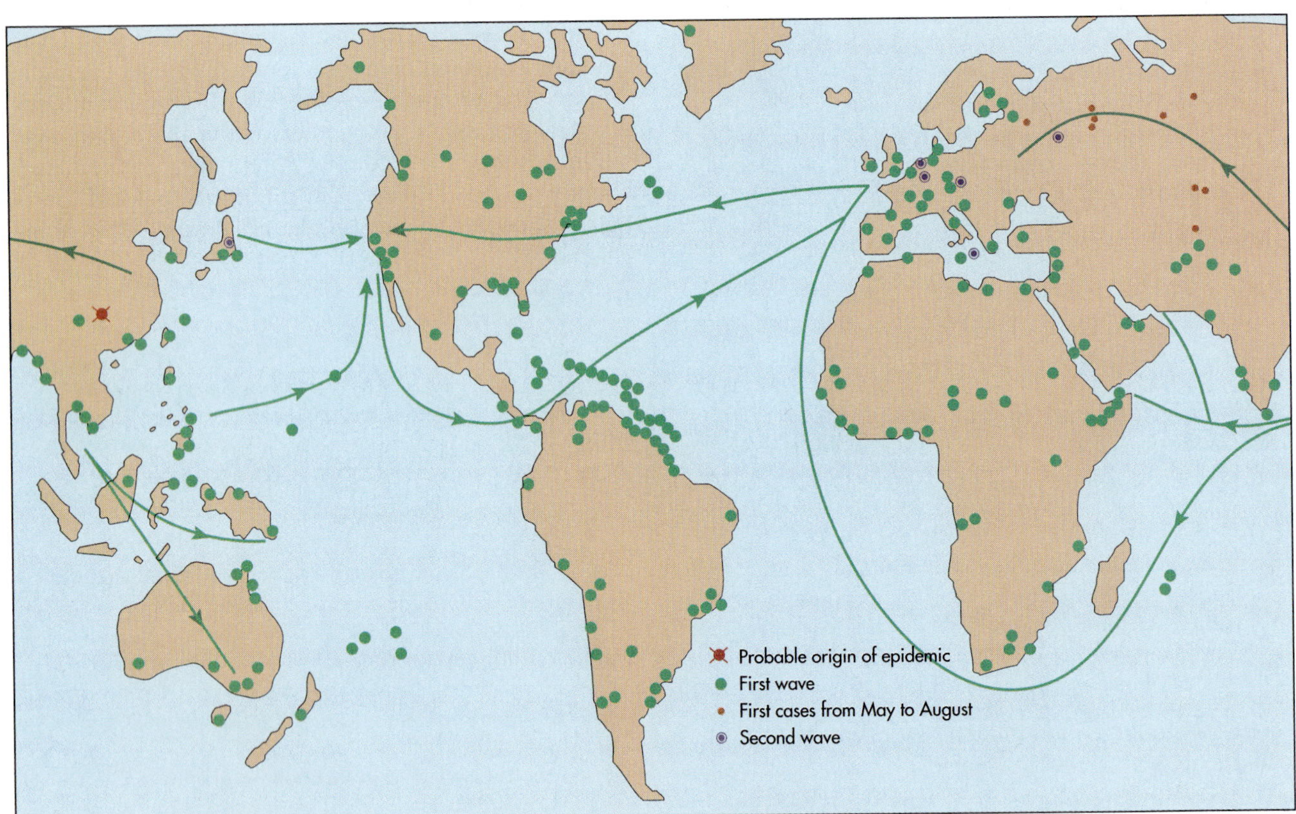

FIG. 12-3 Worldwide spread of an epidemic outbreak of influenza originated in Southeast Asia and spread in waves to other population centers of the world. Arrows indicate route of spread.

12.3 DISEASE PREVENTION

The science of epidemiology and the public health procedures based on that scientific knowledge have reduced the incidence of many important diseases. The reduced incidence of many infectious diseases is the consequence of an understanding of the modes of transmission of pathogenic microorganisms and of preventive measures to reduce exposure to disease-causing microorganisms. Many once widespread deadly diseases such as cholera and whooping cough are rare today because there is now a thorough understanding of how the infectious agents causing these diseases are spread and how they can be controlled. Public health measures based on epidemiology have resulted in the institution of hygienic practices and the development of immunization programs that have drastically reduced the incidence of certain diseases. Treatment of water and food to eliminate pathogens has virtually eliminated some diseases, such as cholera, in many developed countries. The use of vaccines for preventing disease and of antimicrobial agents for treating infectious diseases has led to greatly increased life expectancies. Vaccination protects the vaccinated individual and also helps to control the spread of the disease through the population. Indeed, the control of microorganisms pathogenic to humans is fundamental to the practice of modern medicine.

Preventing Exposure to Pathogenic Microorganisms

Total avoidance of microorganisms is not practical because we are continuously exposed to microorganisms in the air, in water and foods, and on the surfaces of virtually all objects that we contact. Only in the rarest of cases, when the immune system is totally nonfunctional, is absolute avoidance of contact with microorganisms practiced. It is possible, though, to control microbial populations and our interactions with them in ways that reduce the probability of encountering pathogenic microorganisms, thus reducing the incidence and spread of infectious diseases. Many modern sanitary practices are aimed at reducing the incidence of diseases by preventing the spread of pathogenic microorganisms or by reducing their numbers to concentrations that are insufficient to cause disease.

Removal of Pathogens from Food and Water

Methods employed for preventing exposure to specific disease-causing microorganisms vary depending on the particular route of transmission. Proper sewage treatment and drinking water disinfection programs reduce the likelihood of contracting a bacterial disease through contaminated water. The recognition that many pathogens causing serious diseases, such as those that cause typhoid and cholera, are transmitted through water contaminated with fecal material is the basis for enforcement of strict water quality control standards in the United States. Chloramination of municipal water supplies, that is, treatment with chloramines, is widely practiced to prevent exposure to the pathogenic microorganisms that occur in water supplies and thus to ensure the safety of drinking water.

Quality control measures are also applied throughout the food industry to prevent the transmission of disease-causing microorganisms through food products. Pasteurization of milk is a good example of a process designed to reduce exposure to pathogenic microorganisms that occur and proliferate in untreated milk. The purpose of washing one's hands before eating is to avoid the accidental contamination of one's food with soil or other substances that may harbor populations of disease-causing microorganisms.

Failure to maintain quality control of water and food supplies often results in outbreaks of disease; for example, cholera outbreaks often occur when sewage is allowed to mix with drinking water supplies, such as frequently occurs in the Far East when monsoon rains cause flooding, resulting in contamination of drinking water supplies. Outbreaks of botulism are associated with improperly canned food products, that is, with food products that have not been heated long enough to kill contaminating endospores of *Clostridium botulinum*. Growth of *C. botulinum* in canned food results in the exposure of individuals who ingest the inadequately cooked food to the lethal toxins produced by this bacterium. Extensive quality control testing is required in most countries to prevent outbreaks of disease associated with contaminated water and food supplies.

Vector Control

Practices are sometimes employed to control insect and other animal populations that act as vectors for the transmission of diseases caused by pathogenic microorganisms and to control the populations or nonbiological sources that may act as reservoirs of pathogens. The most notable vectors of pathogenic microorganisms are mosquitoes, lice, ticks, and fleas. Some public health measures such as mosquito control programs are aimed at reducing the sizes of these vector populations and thus lowering the probability of exposure to the pathogenic microorganisms capable of causing diseases such as plague, typhus fever, yellow fever, malaria, and various other diseases transmitted by insect vectors.

Quarantine and Isolation of Individuals with Disease

Perhaps the most effective way of preventing diseases caused by microorganisms is to avoid exposure to pathogenic microorganisms. Separating individuals with a disease from healthy individuals to control the spread of disease dates back to biblical times. The formal practice of quarantine began in 1348 in Europe during a severe outbreak of plague. The term *"quarantine"* comes from the Italian *quarantenaria,* meaning forty. Sea voyagers coming into Sicily had to wait 40 days before entering the city. Today the World Health Organization recommends quarantine for plague, yellow fever, and cholera.

Avoiding direct contact with infected individuals is important in preventing the spread of diseases when the pathogen is transmitted by direct contact. Individuals with certain diseases were isolated from the remainder of a population as early as biblical times. Historically, the isolation in remote colonies of patients with leprosy (Hansen disease) is an example of the extreme measures taken to prevent contact of such individuals with the general population. Today, this extreme practice is not needed because of the use of antimicrobial agents. We also recognize that this disease is not as infectious as once thought. However, discontinuance of sexual activity by individuals suffering from sexually transmissible diseases (venereal diseases such as syphilis, gonorrhea, and AIDS) interrupts the transmission of the pathogens that causes these diseases; abstinence by infected individuals and the proper use of prophylactic condoms are absolutely essential for controlling the spread of sexually transmitted diseases and will undoubtedly remain the main methods. Latex condoms are effective barriers against the transmission of bacteria and viruses, including the human immunodeficiency virus (HIV) that causes AIDS.

In the case of pathogens that enter the body through breaks in the skin surface, various procedures are employed to reduce the probability of exposure. Great care, for example, is taken during surgical procedures to prevent contamination by accidental introduction of microorganisms into the exposed tissues. Clean operating rooms and sterile instruments, garments, gloves, and masks are used by a hospital surgical staff (FIG. 12-4). Wounds are cleansed to prevent the introduction of foreign material that may harbor potential pathogens, and antiseptics are applied to skin surfaces to minimize the entry of pathogenic microorganisms into tissues normally protected by an intact skin covering.

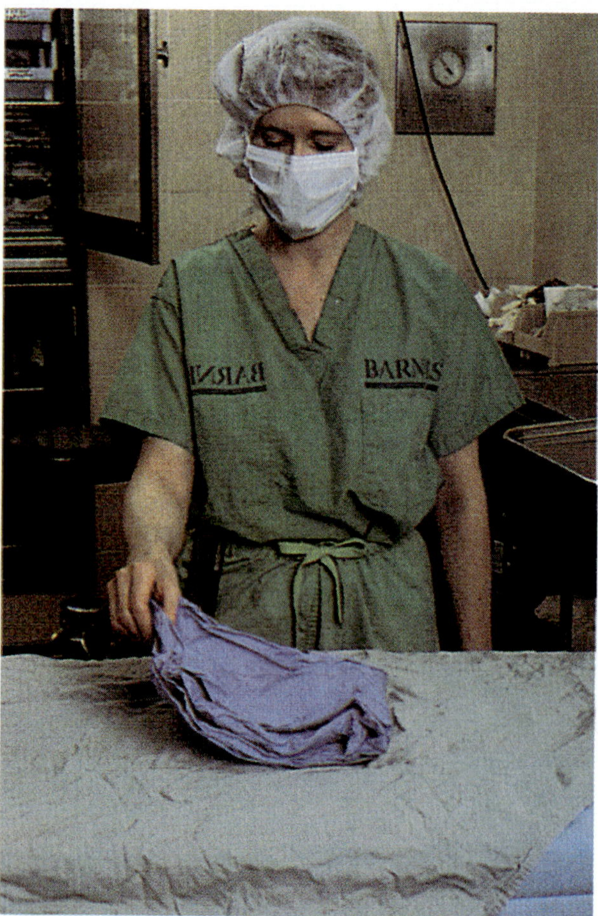

FIG. 12-4 Medical staff use gowns, masks, sterile instruments, and clean rooms to reduce the risk of infection, especially during surgical procedures.

The use of surgical masks when visiting individuals who are particularly susceptible to infections is an important precaution in preventing the spread of infectious diseases. Likewise, preventing the exposure of individuals whose immunological defense mechanisms are compromised by various conditions (such as treatment for cancer or a recent organ transplant) to airborne pathogenic microorganisms is an important aspect of patient management practice. Similarly, masks should be worn in the presence of patients with tuberculosis. Isolation of individuals with contagious microbial diseases, in which the infectious agent is airborne, is often practiced. For example, children with measles, chickenpox, or mumps are often kept away (isolated) from other children who are not immune to these diseases. Such practices decrease the probability of exposure to pathogenic organisms and prevent, or at least reduce, the transmission of disease.

IMMUNIZATION

Immunization, that is, the intentional exposure of susceptible individuals to antigens to elicit an immune response, was first formally introduced in the 1700s to control smallpox. Many societies before this time practiced variolation to obtain immunity to smallpox without knowing the mechanism of action. Immunization has since been used to prevent various diseases besides smallpox. Preparations of antigens designed to stimulate the normal primary immune response are called *vaccines*. Immunization results in a proliferation of *memory cells* and the ability to exhibit a *secondary memory* or *anamnestic response* on subsequent exposure to the same antigens. Antigens within a vaccine do not have to be associated with active virulent pathogens; they may be a purified fraction from the intact cells. They need only elicit an immune response, with the production of antibodies possessing the ability to cross-react with the critical antigens associated with the pathogens against which the vaccine is designed to protect. Vaccines are useful because they confer immunity; that is, they render an individual insusceptible to a disease without actually producing the disease, or at least not a serious form of it.

Herd Immunity

The number of individuals who must be immune to prevent an epidemic outbreak of disease is a function of the infectivity of the disease (ability of a microorganism to produce infection) *(I)*, the duration of the disease *(D)*, and the proportion of susceptible individuals in the population *(s)*. As these individuals recover from the disease, they become immune and thus no longer participate in the chain of disease transmission. When the triple product, $s\,I\,D$, is low because of a high proportion of immune individuals, that is, when approximately 70% of the population is immune, the entire population generally is protected, a concept known as **herd immunity** (FIG. 12-5). Although immunity in 70% of the population usually prevents propagation of a pathogen through the population, the proportion of the population that must be immune to prevent an epidemic varies, depending on the effectiveness with which the pathogen is transmitted and its virulence. Herd immunity can be established by artificially stimulating the immune response system through the use of vaccines, rendering individuals nonsusceptible to a particular disease and thereby protecting the entire population.

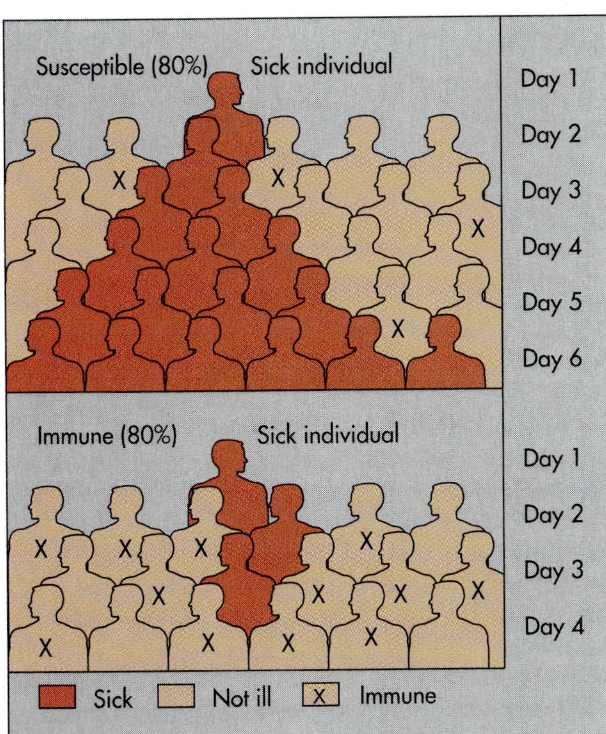

FIG. 12-5 When only a few individuals are immune, a pathogen can spread rapidly through a population, resulting in an epidemic. When over 70% of the individuals in a population are immune, the propagation from individual to individual is not sustained and epidemics do not occur. Such herd immunity is why immunization programs are effective even when not everyone is immunized or immune to a disease.

Vaccines for Disease Prevention

Infectious disease is controlled in developed countries through vaccination programs and public health measures. The administration of vaccines, **vaccination,** is used to establish a state of immunity. Children are given vaccines against many diseases, including diphtheria, pertussis, tetanus, measles, mumps, rubella, polio, hepatitis B, and *Haemophilus influenzae* b. Travelers to certain countries need to be vaccinated against the infectious diseases endemic to that area. Indiviuals who are not vaccinated are susceptible to disease. When recommended vaccination schedules are not followed, there are outbreaks of diseases such as diphtheria and polio that could have been prevented.

Vaccines may contain antigens prepared by killing or inactivating pathogenic microorganisms, attenuated (weakened) live strains that are unable to cause severe disease symptoms, or purified extracts of specific antigens. Some of the vaccines that are useful in preventing diseases caused by various microorganisms are listed in Table 12-5. The use of the inactivated (killed) virus Salk and attenuated ("live") Sabin polio

TABLE 12-5 Some Vaccines Useful in Preventing Microbial Diseases

DISEASE	TYPES OF VACCINE
Smallpox	Attenuated live virus (limited in U.S. to military personnel)
Yellow fever	Attenuated live virus (limited in U.S. to individuals who travel to foreign endemic areas)
Hepatitis B	Purified HBsAg; Recombinant HBsAg
Measles	Attenuated live virus
Mumps	Attenuated live virus
Rubella	Attenuated live virus
Polio	Attenuated live virus (Sabin)
Polio	Inactivated virus (Salk) (limited in U.S. to immunocompromised individuals)
Influenza	Inactivated virus (limited in U.S. to high risk individuals)
Rabies	Inactivated virus (limited in U.S. to high risk individuals)
Tuberculosis	Attenuated live bacteria (rarely used in U.S.)
Pertussis	Inactivated bacteria
Cholera	Inactivated bacteria (limited in U.S. to individuals who travel to foreign endemic areas)
Diphtheria	Toxoid
Tetanus	Toxoid
Haemophilus meningitis	Capsular material/protein conjugate
Pneumococcal pneumonia	Capsular material

vaccines, for example, have dramatically reduced the incidence of poliomyelitis (FIG. 12-6). It is important that preschool children be immunized because major outbreaks of poliomyelitis traditionally are associated with transmission among children in close contact in a schoolroom. Despite the ability to prevent this serious disease, many children are not immunized voluntarily, even in affluent countries such as the United States. Many school systems now require evidence of polio vaccination before a child can be enrolled. This is essential to reduce the incidence of this disease—so that there are fewer paralyzed individuals to serve as visible reminders of its seriousness. Constant efforts to reinforce parental awareness of the importance and success of vaccination against potentially fatal diseases are worthwhile. Children especially must receive several vaccines (Table 12-6).

Not all diseases can be prevented by using vaccines, and some antigens confer immunity that lasts for only weeks or months. Such short-lived immunity may be effective in preventing disease if there is a known likelihood of exposure to a given pathogen, but it is not feasible to attempt the large-scale use of vaccines that confer only short-term immunity.

Toxoids Some vaccines are prepared by modifying protein toxins produced by microorganisms; such modified toxins are called **toxoids.** Bacterial protein exotoxins are commonly inactivated and converted to toxoids by treatment with formaldehyde. This treatment denatures the proteins so that they are unable to initiate the specific biochemical reactions that cause disease conditions. Toxoids retain their antigenic properties but do not cause the onset of disease symptoms because they are no longer toxic. Toxoids elicit antibody-mediated immune responses. Therefore

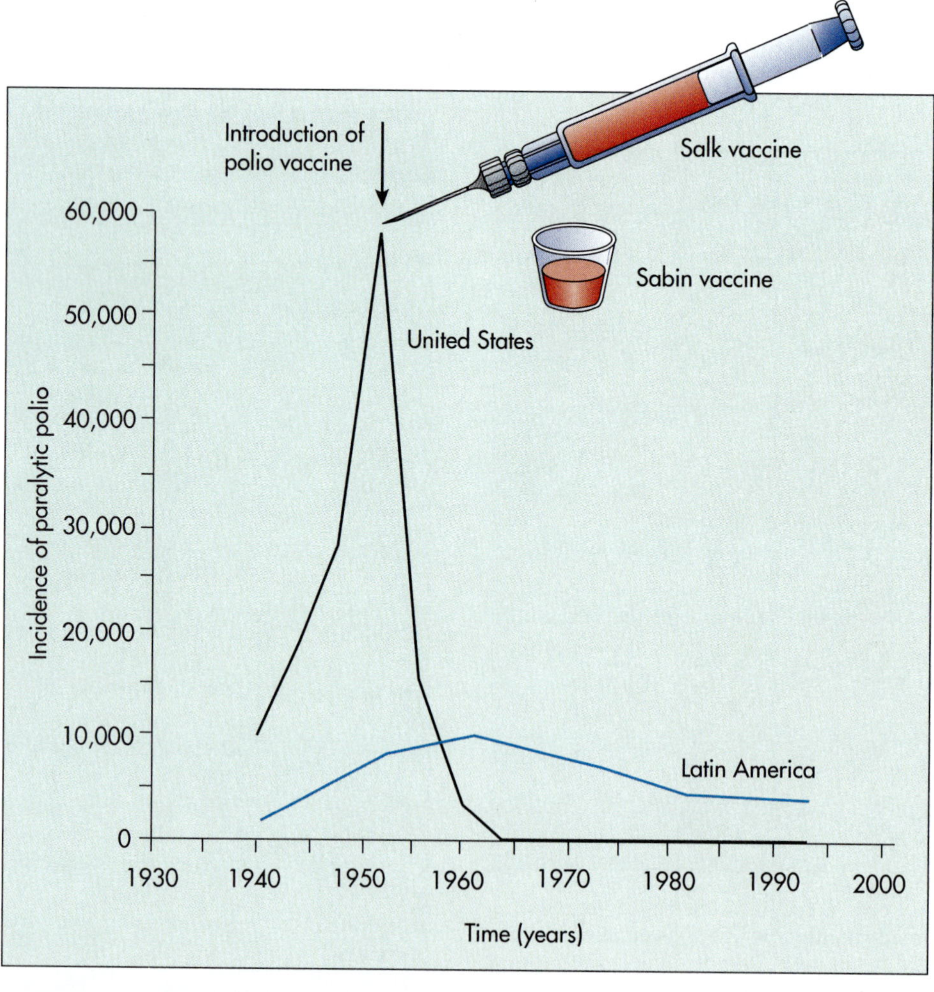

FIG. 12-6 Vaccines greatly reduce disease incidence. Paralytic polio declined dramatically in the United States after the introduction of the Salk inactivated vaccine and Sabin oral vaccine. The incidence of this disease has remained relatively constant in Latin America where vaccination against polio has not been as widely practiced.

TABLE 12-6 Recommended Schedule for Vaccine Administration

DISEASE	PRIMARY IMMUNIZATION	BOOSTER DOSES
Diphtheria, pertussis, tetanus	Intramuscular DPT injections at 2, 4, 6, and 15 months	One intramuscular booster at 3-6 years (tetanus every 10 years)
Influenza	Seasonally for high-risk elderly and chronically ill	
Measles, mumps, rubella	One subcutaneous injection at 15 months	Measles boosters are required
Polio	Sabin vaccine: oral at 2, 4, and 15 months	One oral dose at 4-6 years
	Salk vaccine: intramuscular injections at 2, 3, 4, and 16 months	Intramuscular injections every few years
Meningitis	Hib vaccine at 2, 4, 6, and 15 months; intramuscular injection	—
Hepatitis	Hepatitis B vaccine at 1 week and 2, 6, and 18 months; intramuscular injection	—

they are widely used as vaccines for protecting individuals against diphtheria, tetanus, and various other diseases caused by toxigenic (toxin-producing) microorganisms.

Vaccines with Killed or Inactivated Microorganisms In some cases, whole microorganisms rather than individual protein toxins are used for preparing vaccines. When microorganisms are killed by treatment with chemicals, radiation, or heat, the antigenic properties of the pathogen are retained without the risk that exposure to the vaccine could cause the onset of the disease associated with the virulent live pathogens. The vaccines used for the prevention of whooping cough (pertussis) and influenza are representative of the preparations containing antigens that are prepared by inactivating pathogens.

Quality control is extremely important in preparing all vaccines, particularly those using killed or inactivated strains of virulent pathogens. Some people given swine flu vaccine during the 1976 scare about an impending outbreak of this disease in the United States actually contracted flu because of the inadequate inactivation (killing) of the viruses in hastily prepared vaccines. Others developed a neurological disorder called Guillain-Barré syndrome after vaccination against swine flu. In the 1950s, several tragic cases of polio occurred in children given the Salk polio vaccine, which was prepared with inactivated polioviruses, because of the failure to fully inactivate some batches of the vaccine. Because the Salk vaccine is prepared from a particularly virulent strain of poliovirus, replication of the virus in those inoculated with the problem batches caused paralytic polio.

Even when the vaccines are properly killed cells or inactivated viruses, problems can occur in some cases. A small percentage of children, for example, have allergic reactions to the pertussis component of the standard diphtheria-pertussis-tetanus (DPT) vaccine, leading some to question the wisdom of government-mandated administration of this vaccine. Some manufacturers of this vaccine ceased producing it rather than face the liability lawsuits associated with such reactions. Enhanced quality control programs by the major remaining producer and the development of a new form of the vaccine promise to reduce the incidence of adverse reactions. Nevertheless, the relative risks of complications from exposure to a vaccine are usually better than acquiring the disease itself.

Vaccines with Attenuated Microorganisms In contrast to these vaccines, other vaccine preparations contain living but attenuated strains of microorganisms. Pathogens are attenuated by several procedures, including moderate use of heat, chemicals, desiccation, and growth in tissues other than the normal host. The Sabin vaccine for poliomyelitis, for example, uses viable polioviruses attenuated by growth in tissue culture. These viruses can multiply within the digestive tract and the salivary glands but are unable to invade the nerve tissues and thus do not produce the symptoms of paralytic polio. The vaccines for measles, mumps, rubella, and yellow fever similarly utilize viable but attenuated viral strains. Vaccines containing viable attenuated strains require relatively low amounts of the antigens because the microorganism replicates after administration of the vaccine, resulting in a large increase in the amount of antigen available within the host to trigger the immune response.

The failure of the quality control program for the Salk vaccine was partly responsible for the general switch to the live attenuated Sabin polio vaccine. The Sabin vaccine is prepared with attenuated viral strains that are not particularly virulent and that do not invade the nervous system and cause paralysis. It uses strains of poliovirus that have the three predominant antigens of the major polioviruses, designated type 1, 2, and 3 antigens. The Sabin vaccine is administered orally, and the virus multiplies within the gastrointestinal tract. Although the virus is attenuated, mutations and recombinations are possible during replication. Some recent cases of polio have been reported with the Sabin vaccine, causing some to reevaluate the relative merits of the Salk versus the Sabin vaccine.

A vaccine against chickenpox is one of the newest live attenuated vaccines. The vaccine called Varivax uses the Oka strain of varicella virus. This vaccine is expensive. It is licensed for general use in Japan and Korea. Although the vaccine has been shown to be safe and efficacious, its potential in the United States and elsewhere is controversial. The point of controversy is whether to institute a costly vaccination program to protect children against chickenpox and increase the possibility that adults will contract this disease, particularly considering that chickenpox in children is a mild disease but can be serious if it occurs in adults.

Vaccines with Individual Antigenic Components One way to avoid the problems associated with attenuated (live) and inactivated (killed) vaccines such as the Sabin and Salk vaccines is to use only individual components of the microorganism to elicit an immune response. For example, the capsule of *Streptococcus pneumoniae* is used to make a vaccine against pneumococcal pneumonia. This vaccine is used in high-risk patients, such as individuals over 50 years old who have chronic diseases such as emphysema. It is also given with influenza vaccine to prevent major complications from influenza. Another vaccine has been produced from the capsular polysaccharide of *Haemophilus influenzae* type b, a bacterium that frequently causes meningitis in children up to 3 years old. The *Hib* vaccine is being widely administered to children in the United States. In 1990 a Hib vaccine was released that is administered at 2 months, 4 months, and 6 months of age and a booster at 15 months of age. This vaccine, which is given at an earlier age, should better protect infants from *Haemophilus influenzae* type b infections than previous vaccines.

The first vaccine to provide active immunization against Hepatitis B (Heptavax-B) was prepared from Hepatitis B surface antigen (HBsAg). This antigen was purified from the serum of patients with chronic Hepatitis B. Immunization with Heptavax-B is about 85% to 95% effective in preventing Hepatitis B infection. It has been administered predominantly to individuals in high risk categories such as health care workers. Another, more recently developed Hepatitis B vaccine, Recombivax HB, is derived from HBsAg that has been produced in yeast cells by recombinant DNA technology. To produce Recombivax HB, a part of the Hepatitis B virus gene that codes for HBsAg was cloned into yeast.

Other Approaches to Vaccine Development It is not always easy to find antigens associated with pathogens that confer long-term, active immunity. Desperate efforts are now underway to formulate a vaccine that will prevent AIDS. Years of research, however, have failed to produce vaccines against other sexually transmitted diseases, such as syphilis, and other prevalent diseases, such as malaria and tooth decay. Attempts to make a vaccine against gonorrhea using pili from *Neisseria gonorrhoeae* were not successful because long-lasting immunity against *N. gonorrhoeae* does not develop; the vaccine, though, has been used by the military to achieve short-term immunity. Other vaccines are in development that use ribosomes instead of surface components of the cell. Additionally, synthetic proteins are being considered as potential antigens for protection against various diseases, and recombinant DNA technology is being used to create **vector vaccines** containing the genes for the surface antigens for various pathogens (FIG. 12-7). A vector vaccine is one that acts as a carrier for antigens associated with pathogens other than the one from which the vaccine was derived. The attenuated virus used to eliminate

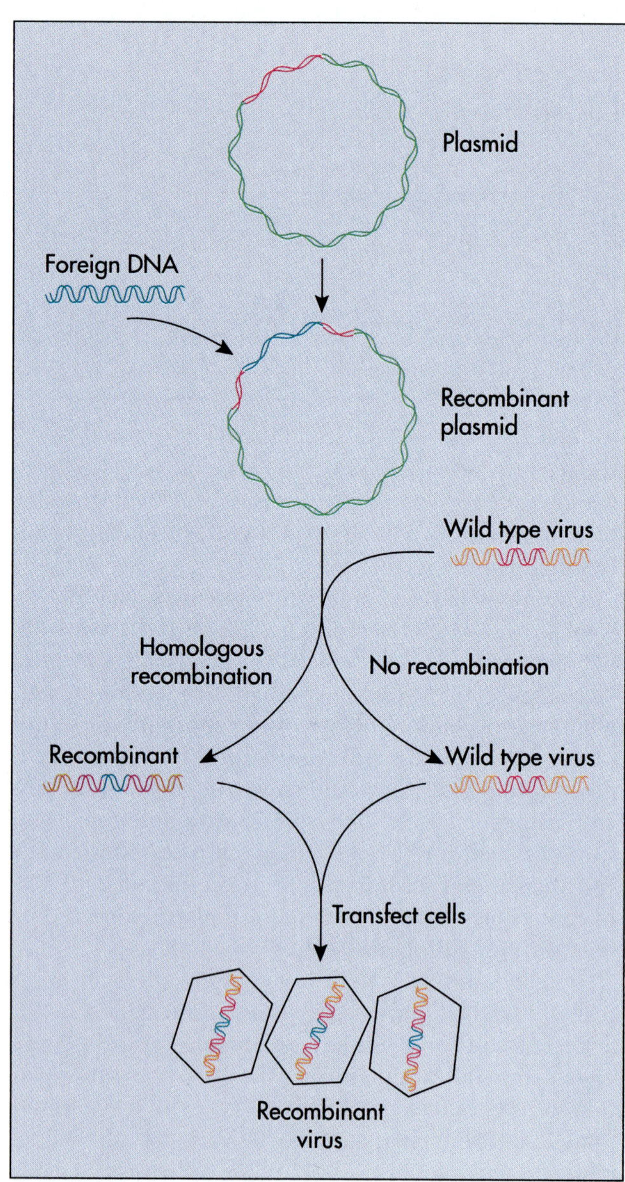

FIG. 12-7 New vaccines can be formed by using recombinant DNA technology to form vector vaccines, for example, using vaccinia virus as a carrier.

smallpox is a likely vector for simultaneously introducing multiple antigens associated with different pathogens, such as the chicken pox virus; several prototype vaccines using the smallpox vaccine as a vector have been made.

Booster Vaccines

Multiple exposures to antigens **(booster vaccinations)** are sometimes needed to ensure the establishment and continuance of a memory response. Periodic booster vaccinations are necessary, for example, to maintain immunity against tetanus. Several administrations of the Sabin vaccine are needed during childhood to establish immunity against poliomyelitis. Tetanus boosters are recommended at least every 10 years. Vaccination against measles also requires a booster that may be given as a second combined measles, mumps, and rubella (MMR) vaccine or as an individual dose of measles vaccine.

Routes of Introducing Vaccines

Vaccine antigens may be introduced into the body by several routes: *intradermally* (into the skin), *subcutaneously* (under the skin), *intramuscularly* (into the muscle), *intravenously* (into the bloodstream), into the mucosal cells lining the respiratory tract through inhalation, or *orally* into the gastrointestinal tract. The effectiveness of a given vaccine depends in part on the normal route of entry for the particular pathogen. For example, polioviruses normally enter via the mucosal cells of the upper respiratory or gastrointestinal tract; therefore the Sabin polio vaccine is administered orally, enabling the attenuated viruses to enter the mucosal cells of the gastrointestinal tract directly. It is likely that vaccines administered this way stimulate secretory antibodies of the IgA class in addition to other immunoglobulins. Intramuscular administration of vaccines, like the Salk polio vaccine, is more likely to stimulate IgG production, which is particularly effective in precluding the spread of pathogenic microorganisms and toxins produced by such organisms through the circulatory system.

Adjuvants

The effectiveness of a vaccine depends on several factors, including antigens in the vaccine, other chemicals in the vaccine, and route of administration. Some chemicals, known as **adjuvants,** enhance the antigenicity of other biochemicals (FIG. 12-8). The inclusion of an adjuvant can greatly increase the effectiveness of the vaccine. When protein antigens are mixed with aluminum compounds, for example, a precipitate is formed that is more useful for establishing immunity than are the proteins alone. Alum-precipitated antigens are released slowly in the human body, enhancing the stimulation of the immune response. The use of adjuvants eliminates the need for repeated booster doses of the antigen—which increase the intracellular exposure to antigens to establish immunity—and permits the use of smaller doses of the antigen in the vaccine.

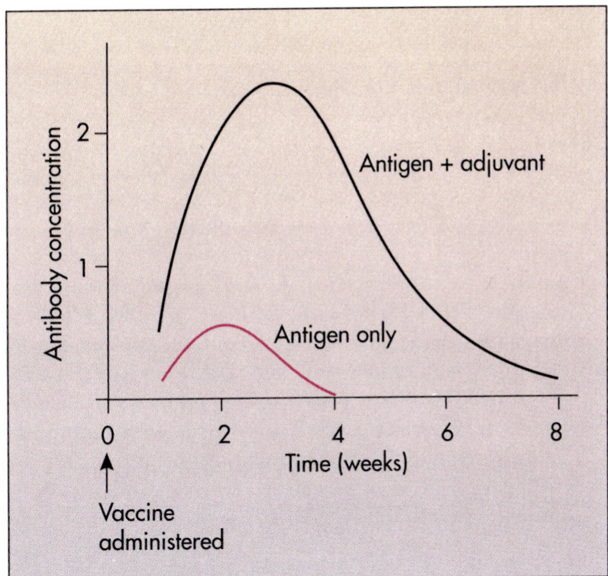

FIG. 12-8 Adjuvants enhance antigenicity and can greatly improve the effectiveness of a vaccine.

Vaccines for Disease Treatment

Although vaccines are normally administered before exposure to antigens associated with pathogenic microorganisms, some vaccines are administered after suspected exposure to a given infectious microorganism. In these cases, the purpose of vaccination is to elicit an immune response before the onset of disease symptoms. For example, tetanus vaccine can be administered after puncture wounds may have introduced *Clostridium tetani* into deep tissues, and rabies vaccine is administered after animal bites may have introduced rabies virus. The effectiveness of vaccines administered after the introduction of the pathogenic microorganisms depends on the relatively slow development of the infecting pathogen before the onset of disease symptoms and the ability of the vaccine to initiate antibody production before active toxins are produced and released to the site where they can cause serious disease symptoms.

Rabies is one of the few diseases in which active immunization is used as a treatment after suspected infection. The vaccination procedure employed for many years used a vaccine prepared from rabies viruses propagated in embryonated duck eggs and inactivated by β-propiolactone. The treatment involved 21 daily injections followed by booster inoculations 10 and 20 days later. Today, the vaccine is produced in tissue culture. The new vaccine requires only a few intramuscular injections that are administered with rabies immune globulin. The new rabies vaccine has a higher concentration of the necessary antigens for

BOX 12-4

Elimination of Smallpox

The greatest success in preventing disease through the use of vaccines can be seen in the case of smallpox (see FIG.). The vaccine used to prevent smallpox contains a live strain of pox virus. The vaccine most commonly used is prepared from scrapings of lesions from cows or sheep. The scrapings are treated with 1% formaldehyde to kill bacterial contaminants and 40% glycerol to stabilize the viral antigens. These antigens are quite labile, which is why live viral preparations are required for successful vaccination to achieve immunity. Various commercial viral strains have been used for the production of commercial vaccines. Although these strains were presumed to have been derived from cowpox virus, it now appears, based on its antigenic properties, that an attenuated strain of smallpox virus may have been inadvertently used. Because of the length of time this virus has been cultivated, it is difficult to identify its original source positively, but the pox virus used for vaccine preparation clearly differs from the cowpox viruses found in nature.

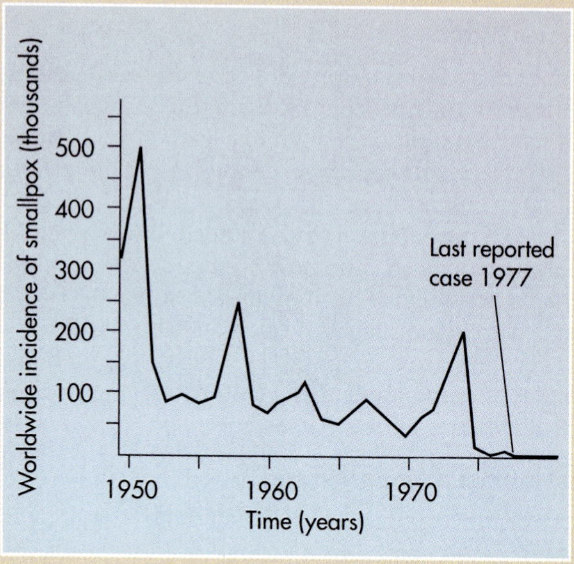

Smallpox was eliminated through a global vaccination program.

Regardless of the origins of the viral strain used in the vaccines, smallpox, a once dreaded disease, has been completely eliminated through an extensive worldwide immunization program conducted under the auspices of the World Health Organization (WHO). The success of the WHO program depended on the use of lyophilized vaccines to overcome the problem of inactivation of the viral antigens in hot climates. The program was not without risks; the virus used for vaccination was virulent enough to cause a fatality rate of 1 in 1 million vaccinations. By immunizing a sufficient portion of the world's population against smallpox, though, it was possible to interrupt the normal transmission of smallpox virus from infected individuals to susceptible hosts. A consequence of the success of this immunization program is that it is no longer necessary to vaccinate against smallpox.

The successful elimination of smallpox through a vaccination program depended on the facts that humans are the only known host for the smallpox virus and that the virus has a relatively short survival time outside human host tissues. Smallpox presumably is eliminated permanently and, as such, is the only infectious human disease known to have been eliminated through human intervention, ingenuity, and cooperation.

eliciting an immune response, and only 3 injections over a 7-day period are required to establish immunity.

Antitoxins

Several other immunological procedures in addition to vaccination may be used to prevent or to treat disease. For example, **antitoxins** (antibodies that neutralize toxins) can be used to prevent toxins of microbial or other origin from causing disease symptomatology. The administration of antitoxins establishes passive artificial immunity. Antitoxins are used to neutralize the toxins in snake venom, saving the victims of snake bites. The toxins in poisonous mushrooms can also be neutralized by administration of appropriate antitoxins. Antitoxins are administered to prevent disease after exposure to a toxin or a toxigenic infectious microorganism.

Immunoglobulins

It is also possible to establish passive immunity by the administration of IgG obtained from another individual. Passive immunity lasts for a limited period of time because IgG molecules have a finite lifetime in the body and because the administration of IgG does not involve the establishment of a memory immune response capability. Such passive immunity is conferred naturally on an infant by the passage of IgG molecules across the placenta during fetal development. IgG and IgA are found in the colostrum and milk of nursing mothers, protecting newborns against infectious diseases during the early period of life. The administration of IgG as immunoglobulin or gammaglobulin is also particularly useful therapeutically in preventing disease in persons with immunodeficiencies and other high-risk individuals.

12.4 DISEASE TRANSMISSION

Transmission of infectious agents typically involves escape from the host, travel, and entry into a new host. Different pathogens have different modes of transmission. Modes of transmission are usually related to the habitats of the organisms in the body. For instance, respiratory tract pathogens are generally airborne, and intestinal pathogens usually are spread by food or water. Pathogens often must be continuously transmitted from one host to another to survive. They have evolved features or mechanisms that permit or ensure transmittal.

Because the transmission of pathogens occurs via restricted routes, it is possible to control interactions with microbial populations in ways that reduce the probability of contracting infectious diseases. The methods employed for preventing exposure to specific disease-causing microorganisms vary, depending on the particular route of transmission. Many modern sanitary practices are aimed at reducing the incidence of diseases by preventing the spread of pathogenic microorganisms or by reducing their populations to concentrations that are insufficient to cause disease. Mosquito and rodent control, sanitary waste disposal, sewage treatment, chlorination of swimming pools and chloramination of water supplies, pasteurization, and various other methods are used to restrict the spread of pathogens. The greatly diminished incidence of many diseases caused by microorganisms is the consequence of an adequate understanding of the modes of transmission of pathogenic microorganisms and preventive measures that reduce exposure to disease-causing microorganisms.

PORTALS OF ENTRY

Pathogenic microorganisms gain access to the body through a limited number of routes known as **portals of entry** (FIG. 12-9). The portals of entry into the human body are the mucosal surfaces of the respiratory tract, gastrointestinal tract, and genitourinary tract;

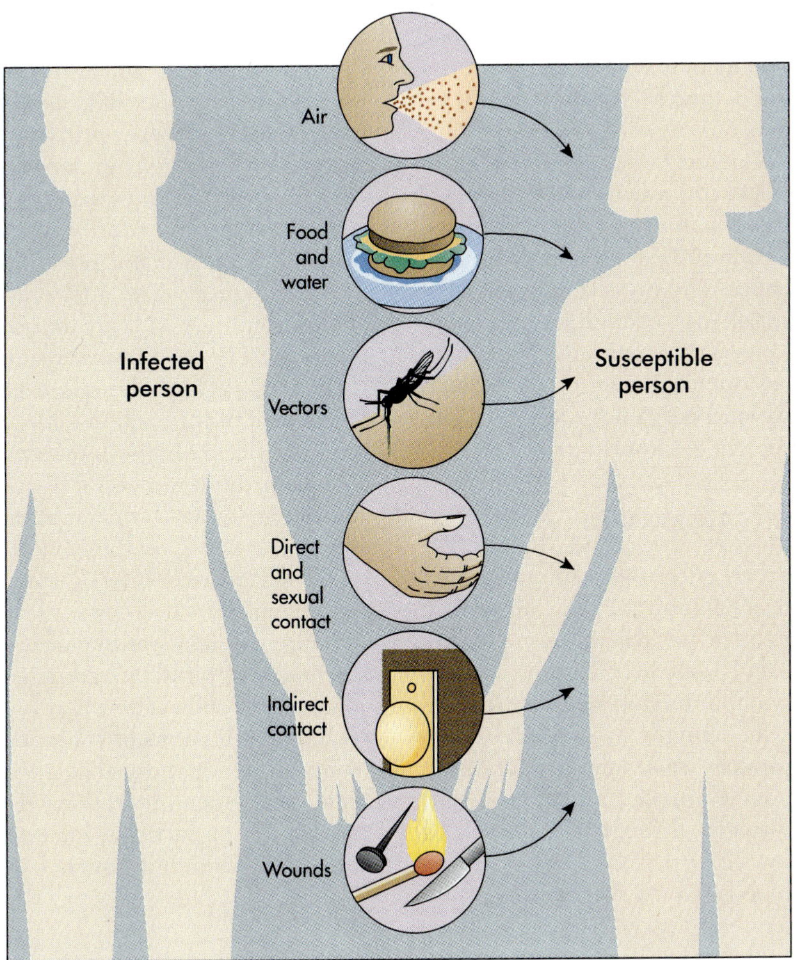

FIG. 12-9 Disease-causing microorganisms enter the body via a limited number of portals of entry. Understanding how a pathogen can be transmitted and enter the body to establish an infection permits preventive measures that limit the spread of disease.

skin; and wounds. Most pathogenic microorganisms cause disease only if they enter the body via a specific route. For example, depositing *Clostridium tetani* on the intact skin surface has no effect, but its deposit in deep wounds results in the deadly disease, tetanus. Pathogens can become established within the body in only a limited number of ways because of the nonspecific and immune defenses associated with different body tissues and the inherent properties of the microorganism.

The restrictive nature of the portals of entry also means that a sufficient number of microorganisms is necessary to initiate an infective process. The number of pathogens needed to establish a disease is known as the **infectious dose.** For some pathogens, the infectious dose is one cell, but for others, hundreds of thousands of microorganisms may be necessary to overwhelm the host defenses and allow the invading microorganisms to reproduce within the body. Various factors influence the infectious dose required to initiate a disease, including the nature of the pathogen, the portal of entry, and the state of the host defenses. In many cases, diminished host defenses permit relatively low numbers of potential pathogens to establish an infection. Malnutrition, for example, results in lowered amounts of antimicrobial body fluids and inadequate host defenses to protect against infectious microorganisms.

In many cases, pathogenic microorganisms establish localized infections in the region of the portal of entry, but in other cases, pathogens can spread systemically through the body and establish infections involving other body tissues. The invasive properties of many pathogens permit them to penetrate the body's defense mechanisms through a particular portal of entry. The normal body openings that serve as portals of entry for pathogenic microorganisms are the respiratory, gastrointestinal, and genitourinary tracts.

Airborne Disease Transmission

Potential pathogens freely enter the respiratory tract through the normal inhalation of air. We inhale 10,000 to 20,000 liters of air per day that usually contains between 10,000 and 1,000,000 microorganisms, some of which are potential human pathogens. Various viruses, bacteria, and fungi can multiply within the tissues of the respiratory tract, sometimes causing localized infections; some inhaled microorganisms enter the circulatory system through the numerous blood vessels associated with the respiratory tract and spread through the bloodstream to other sites in the body.

Transmission through the air **(airborne transmission)** is undoubtedly the main route of transmission of pathogens that enter via the respiratory tract. Airborne transmission often occurs when droplets containing pathogenic microorganisms move from an infected to a susceptible individual. Droplets regularly become airborne during normal breathing, but the coughing and sneezing associated with respiratory tract infections are primarily responsible for the spread of pathogens in aerosols and thus for the airborne transmission of disease (FIG. 12-10).

FIG. 12-10 Sneezing propels aerosols containing microorganisms. In this manner pathogens are transmitted through the air. Use of a handkerchief can block the spread of aerosols containing pathogens.

Several factors contribute to the fact that the respiratory tract is a major portal of entry for pathogenic microorganisms. The upper respiratory tract is in continuous contact with air that contains many microorganisms. The respiratory system has a very large surface area to facilitate gas exchange, and there is a great deal of interaction between the respiratory tract and the circulatory system to permit reoxygenation of blood in the lower respiratory tract. Thus the potential for respiratory infection is great, but fortunately the actual rate of disease is low.

To establish an infection via the respiratory tract, a pathogen must overcome the natural immunological defense mechanisms that are particularly extensive in the lower respiratory tract, where there are numerous phagocytic cells. The microorganisms that generally establish infections in the upper respiratory tract are different from those that are able to move past the cilia and mucus secretions designed to restrict the movement of particles, including microorganisms, to the lower respiratory tract.

Common Cold

Viruses causing the common cold, the most frequent infectious human disease, infect the cells lining the nasal passages and pharynx, producing an inflammatory response with associated tissue damage in the infected region. The etiological agents responsible for the majority of cases of the common cold have yet to be identified, but we do know that in adults approximately 25% of all colds are caused by *rhinoviruses,* compared to only about 10% of colds in children. There are over 100 immunologically distinct types of rhinoviruses capable of causing the common cold; hence it is not surprising that immunity does not offer continuous protection against all of the antigenically distinct viruses capable of causing it. Rhinoviruses can enter the respiratory tract directly from air or indirectly via tears from the eyes. Touching one's eyes or nose may be an important route of transmission for these viruses. The initial viral infection can be followed by a secondary bacterial infection as the normal microbiota of the upper respiratory tract invade the damaged tissues. Symptoms include nasal stuffiness, sneezing, coughing, headache, malaise (a vague feeling of discomfort), sore throat, and sometimes a slight fever. There is no specific treatment for the common cold, which is a self-limiting clinical syndrome. Recovery usually occurs within 1 week without complications as a result of the natural immune defense response. The common cold is the most frequent infectious human disease, and it is safe to assume that we have all had a cold at some time. More than 200 million work and school days are lost each year in the United States because of colds. Like many other respiratory diseases, colds occur primarily during the winter months, in part because of the physiological stress posed by exposure to cold temperatures and in part because of increased contact of individuals during indoor winter activities.

Influenza

Influenza is transmitted by inhalation of aerosols containing influenza viruses, which are released into the air as droplets originating from the respiratory tracts of infected individuals. The outer envelope of an influenza virus has numerous protruding spikes *(peplomers)* that affect the pathogenicity and antigenicity of the particular viral strain (see FIG. 8-29). Changes in combinations of genes and the production of new strains of influenza viruses generally are associated with changes in the structure of these peplomers. There are two types of peplomers, designated *H (hemagglutinin)* and *N (neuraminidase) peplomers.* The H peplomers cause clumping (agglutination) of red blood cells; presumably they are important in increasing the ability of the influenza virus to attach to human cells during the establishment of an infection and are also a valuable aid in the serological identification of the particular strain of influenza virus. Antibodies against the H peplomers will neutralize free virus and block attachment to cells; they are very important in the body's resistance against infection by that particular strain of influenza virus. The N peplomers appear to be involved in the release of viruses from infected cells following viral replication. Antibodies against the N peplomers are less important in increasing resistance to influenza infections and only limit the spread of the virus.

Major groups of influenza viruses are designated according to the antigens associated with their capsids. There are three major groups of influenza viruses, designated types A, B, and C. Specific strains of influenza virus are further designated by variations in the protein composition of their H and N spikes. Outbreaks of influenza are cyclical, with major outbreaks caused by type A virus occurring every 2 to 4 years, those caused by type B virus occurring every 4 to 6 years, and outbreaks caused by type C virus occurring only rarely (FIG. 12-11).

Within each of the major types of influenza virus there are various antigenic subtypes that are responsible for different outbreaks of influenza. Major antigenic changes, known as **antigenic drift,** occur because of accumulated genetic mutations and recombi-

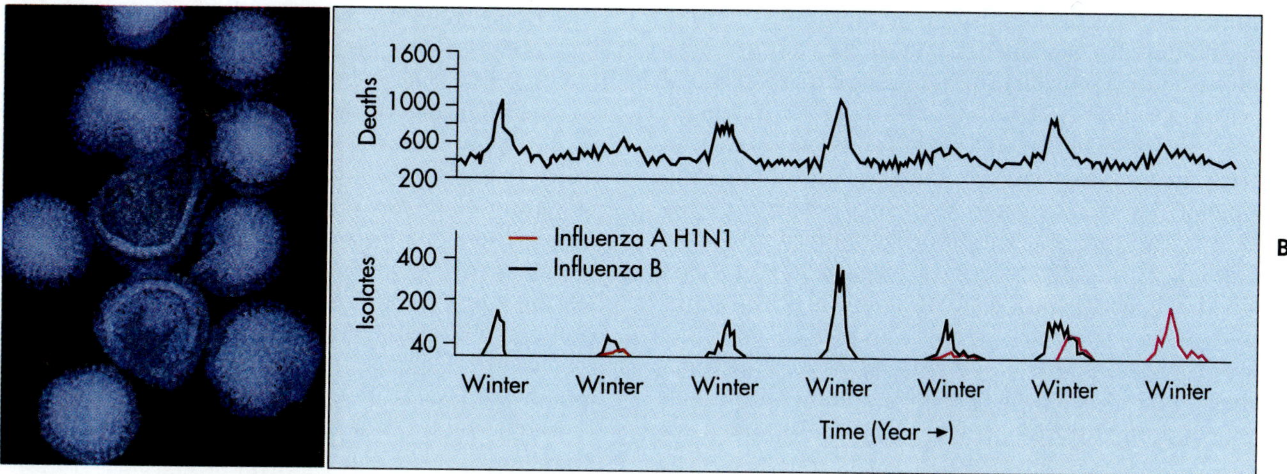

FIG. 12-11 **A,** Colorized micrograph of influenza A viruses. (108,800×). **B,** Influenza outbreaks show regular cyclic fluctuations due to antigenic changes in the influenza viruses and associated changes in the susceptibilities of individuals in the population. The highest incidence of influenza in the United States occurs during the winter.

nations that can even cause gene reassortment between an animal and a human strain. Antigenic drift is gradual and cumulative so that major antigenic changes only become apparent with time. An *antigenic shift* resulting from the addition of new genes produces new strains of influenza virus. Strains of influenza viruses are often described by the location where outbreaks of the disease associated with that particular antigenic variety of the flu virus were first detected. For example, the Taiwan strain of influenza virus, first seen in the Orient in 1986, is a type A influenza virus designated H_1N_1. The antigenic designation is important because it indicates to epidemiologists whether there has been a substantial change in the antigenic properties of the virus and whether a sufficient proportion of the population will be susceptible to that strain such that an epidemic is likely.

Influenza is characterized by the sudden onset of a fever, with temperatures abruptly reaching 102° to 104° F approximately 1 to 3 days after actual exposure, and infection. The disease is further characterized by malaise, headache, and muscle ache. In uncomplicated cases of influenza, the viral infection is self-limiting and recovery occurs within a week. However, influenza can lead to complications, such as a secondary bacterial infection, causing pneumonia. Complications associated with influenza infections are prevalent among the elderly and individuals with compromised host defense responses. Such individuals should be immunized against the prevalent strain of influenza virus before the outbreak of influenza epidemics because complications can result in death. Also, amantadine has been used as a prophylactic treatment of high risk patients.

One serious complication associated with outbreaks of influenza is the development of Reye syndrome, an acute pathological condition affecting the central nervous system. Reye syndrome also occurs after infections with other viruses, and the specific relationship to influenza virus is not clear. Occurrences of Reye syndrome are highly but inexplicably correlated with outbreaks of influenza B virus. Reye syndrome is associated principally with children. For reasons that have yet to be elucidated, there is a greater incidence of Reye syndrome when aspirin (salicylate) is used to treat the symptoms of a viral infection. Consequently, pediatricians warn against the use of aspirin for children with influenza and other viral infections of the respiratory tract. The recommended treatment for influenza is acetaminophen. Although a direct cause-and-effect relationship between aspirin use and Reye syndrome has not been established, aspirin manufacturers place warning labels on the bottles, especially on children's aspirin.

Legionnaire's Disease

The first detected outbreak of *Legionnaire's disease* occurred during a convention of the American Legion in Philadelphia during July 1976. In the investigation of this outbreak, the first 90,000 hours of investigation, costing over $2 million and employing virtually all conventional isolation procedures, failed to reveal the causative agent of the disease. The breakthrough, revealing that this disease is of bacterial etiology, involved the use of indirect immunofluorescent staining with antibodies from the sera of affected individuals (FIG. 12-12). Later it was discovered that the bacterium, subsequently named *Legionella pneumophila* (lung-loving), could be grown on a chocolate agar medium. This is a medium made with heated blood that looks as though it contains chocolate—it also contains iron and cysteine that are added as growth factors. *L. pneumophila* is a Gram-negative, fastidious, rod-shaped organism whose nutritional requirements for growth complicated early isolation attempts. *L. pneumophila* stains poorly if at all with the Gram stain and they are not found in sputum samples or lung biopsy material that is Gram stained. It was also later found, by examining stored blood sera, that a 1968 outbreak of a disease in Pontiac, Michigan, the etiology of which had not been identified, was caused by a different strain of *L. pneumophila*. Various other outbreaks of this disease have since been identified.

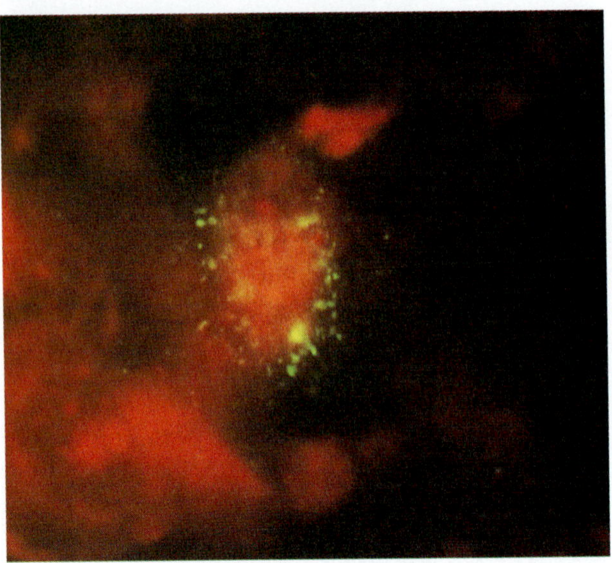

FIG. 12-12 Micrograph after fluorescent antibody staining for the specific detection of *Legionella pneumophila* (*yellow-green*).

Species of *Legionella* are natural inhabitants of bodies of water. They are routinely found in the air-conditioning cooling towers of large buildings such as hotels, factories, and hospitals. During periods of rapid evaporation, such as occur during summer, the bacteria can become airborne in aerosols, and inhalation of contaminated aerosols can lead to the onset of illness. In several cases, outbreaks of Legionnaire's disease have been traced to air-conditioning cooling systems. These bacteria multiply in the cooling system waters, which are rapidly evaporated to provide cooling, and inadvertently become airborne and circulate through air-conditioning systems. Transmission of *Legionella* species may also be due to aerosols from sink taps and showerheads, because *Legionella* may accumulate in warm water storage tanks.

In addition to the typical symptoms of pneumonia, Legionnaire's disease is often characterized by kidney and liver involvement and by an unusually high incidence of associated gastrointestinal symptoms. The fever associated with this disease starts low but then typically reaches 104° to 105° F. If untreated, the fatality rate is about one in six. *L. pneumophila* produces β-lactamase enzymes and is not sensitive to most penicillins and cephalosporins, but it is sensitive to other antibiotics, such as erythromycin and tetracycline. Erythromycin is the antibiotic of choice when Legionnaire's disease is diagnosed.

Tuberculosis

Tuberculosis, caused by *Mycobacterium tuberculosis* and related mycobacterial species, is primarily transmitted via droplets from an infected to a susceptible individual, although it can also be transmitted by the ingestion of contaminated food. Before the extensive use of pasteurization, milk contaminated with *M. tuberculosis* was associated with outbreaks of this disease. The principal portal of entry for *M. tuberculosis,* however, is through the respiratory tract because much lower numbers of bacteria are required to establish an infection compared to transmission through the gastrointestinal system.

The common form of tuberculosis involves an infection of the pulmonary system, with multiplication of *M. tuberculosis* occurring in the lower respiratory tract despite the phagocytic activity of macrophages that protect this area from infection by most potential bacterial pathogens. The pulmonary form of tuberculosis involves inflammation and lesions of lung tissue, which can be detected by chest X-rays (FIG. 12-13). The bacteria spread from the primary lesions to the draining lymph and then through lymph and blood to other parts of the body. Infection with *M. tuberculosis* elicits a cellular immune response because the bacteria are able to reproduce within phagocytic cells, and a delayed hypersensitivity reaction is typical. Dormant mycobacteria can remain within the body and the infectious process can be reactivated at a later time, with various physiological factors probably contributing to recurrence of the disease.

The course of tuberculosis varies among infected individuals. In some cases, the infection is restricted to the area of primary lesions, and in others it spreads into various other tissues. Disease symptoms, including fatigue, weight loss, and fever, generally do not appear until extensive lesions develop in the lung tissues. As a result of the slow growth rate of *M. tuberculosis* and the ineffectiveness of phagocytic cells in killing this bacterial species, tuberculosis is generally a persistent and progressive infection. Without treatment, it is often fatal. Effective treatment of tuberculosis is generally prolonged and involves the use of multiple antibiotics such as streptomycin, rifampin, and isoniazid. Malnutrition and stress are important factors relating to the resistance to tuberculosis and the course of the disease. Additionally, individuals with suppressed immune systems, notably individuals with AIDS, have a high risk for contracting tuberculosis. Infections with *Mycobacterium avium* have caused significant mortality in individuals with AIDS. The disease is referred to as MAT for *Mycobacterium avium* tuberculosis. An additional problem associated with tuberculosis in the United States is the recent emergence of multiply antibiotic-resistant strains of *M. tuberculosis.* These strains have appeared in nosocomial infections, especially in immunocompromised individuals. They may be resistant to up to 25 different antibiotics, making treatment of the disease difficult and costly.

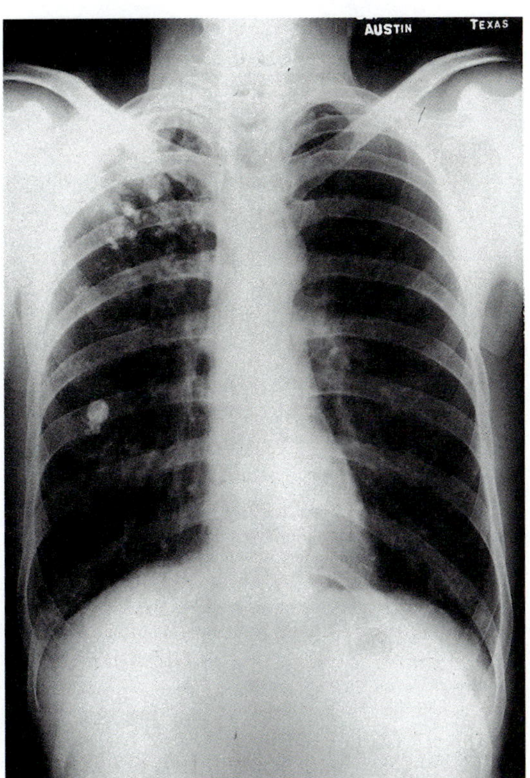

FIG. 12-13 X-rays reveal calcified areas (tubercules) where mycobacteria infect the lung in cases of tuberculosis (shown here in the right lung).

Histoplasmosis

Histoplasmosis is caused by the fungus *Histoplasma capsulatum (Emmonsiella capsulata),* which enters the respiratory tract through the inhalation of spores that are then deposited in the lungs. Histoplasmosis is endemic to certain regions of the world, such as the

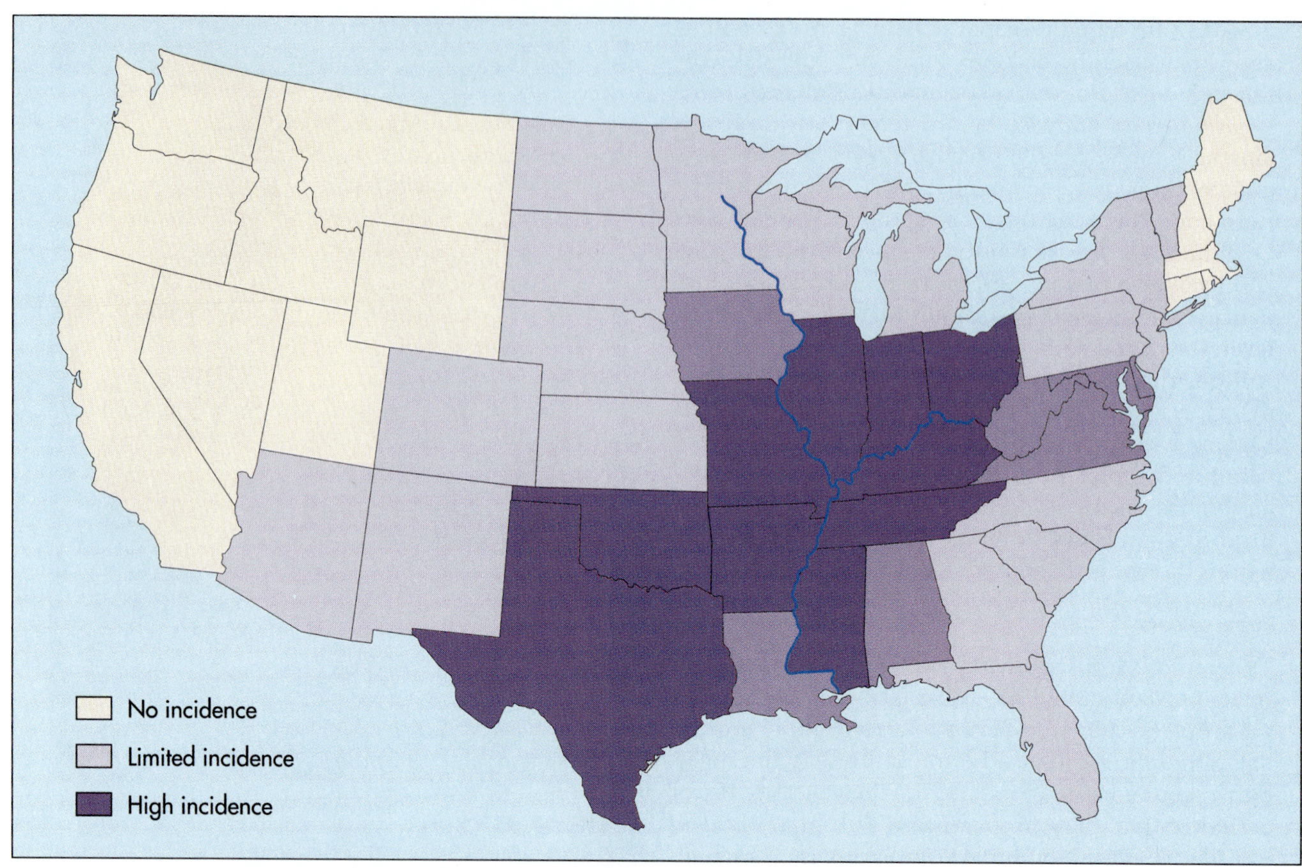

FIG. 12-14 Histoplasmosis is endemic to the Ohio and Mississippi river valleys (shown in purple). Individuals in this area show immunological evidence of a high incidence of infection with *Histoplasma capsulatum.* Over 90% of individuals tested in the region show skin reactivity to histoplasmin.

Ohio and Mississippi river valleys of the United States (FIG. 12-14). The fungus is found in soils contaminated with bird droppings, and dust particles released from abandoned bird roosts appear to be involved in some outbreaks of this disease. The apparent association of bird roosts with histoplasmosis has been used as the justification for large-scale kills of blackbirds, but the usefulness of this procedure has not been conclusively demonstrated. Normally, histoplasmosis is a self-limiting disease in which symptoms may be absent or resemble a mild cold. In some cases, however, the systemic distribution of the fungus to different organs of the body may prove fatal.

Coccidioidomycosis

Coccidioidomycosis, which is caused by *Coccidioides immitis,* is also referred to as *Valley fever* or *San Joaquin fever* because of the geographic distribution of *C. immitis* and the associated areas of occurrence of this disease. Because of the association of the spores of *C. immitis* with the arid soils of the southwestern United States, these soils must be disinfected before being shipped to other regions. Visitors to the states of Nevada, California, Utah, Arizona, and New Mexico often develop symptoms of a mild cold because of infection with *C. immitis.* Normally, *C. immitis* occurs in soil, and transmission of coccidioidomycosis involves inhalation of dust particles containing conidia (arthrospores) of this fungus. When deposited in the bronchi or alveoli, the arthrospores of *C. immitis* elicit an inflammatory response. Within host tissues, *C. immitis* appears as spherules containing multiple spores. In some cases, *C. immitis* remains localized in the area of the primary lesion, but the organism can be distributed to other parts of the body. Symptoms of coccidioidomycosis include chest pain, fever, malaise, and a dry cough. In most cases, no special treatment is required for the cure of localized coccidioidomycosis and, on recovery, the individual is immune to this disease.

Food and Waterborne Disease Transmission

Microorganisms routinely enter the gastrointestinal tract in association with ingested food and water. The large resident microbiota that develop in the human intestinal tract after birth are important for the maintenance of good health and are usually not involved in disease processes. In fact, presence of a resident microbiota provides protection in the gastrointestinal tract from outside pathogens. The resident microbiota are normally noninvasive and are associated with the surface tissues and ingested food material. Some pathogenic microorganisms, however, possess toxigenic or invasive properties that may cause disease when they enter the gastrointestinal tract.

There are two distinct processes that can initiate disease through the gastrointestinal tract. One process is food poisoning, or intoxication. The other process results from ingestion of pathogenic microorganisms that can grow in the intestinal tract and produce toxic substances.

Food Poisoning

Microorganisms growing in food or water may produce toxins, and their ingestion can initiate a disease process. Such diseases are classified as **food poisoning** or **intoxication** because the etiological agents of the disease need not grow within the body; that is, there is no true infectious process. Toxins absorbed through the gastrointestinal tract can cause neural damage and death in some cases, as well as localized inflammation and gastrointestinal upset in others.

Staphylococcal Food Poisoning Strains of *Staphylococcus aureus* that cause food poisoning reproduce in many different types of foods. Enterotoxin-producing strains of *S. aureus* often enter foods from the skin surfaces of people who handle food. Foods with high sugar or high salt concentrations (custard-filled bakery goods, dairy products, processed meats, potato salad, and various canned foods) are frequent sources for the enterotoxin-producing *S. aureus* organisms. Salads prepared for a summer picnic can easily be contaminated (inoculated) with *S. aureus,* and when salads are left in the sun in a traditional wicker picnic basket (incubated), the bacteria can multiply, producing an amount of enterotoxin sufficient to provide an unexpected nighttime encore to the day's fun.

The symptoms of staphylococcal food poisoning occur relatively rapidly after ingestion of toxin-contaminated food, usually within 2 to 4 hours. The toxin is heat stable. The symptoms generally include nausea, vomiting, and abdominal pain. Diarrhea generally occurs in <30% of patients. Symptoms usually subside within 8 hours of onset and complete recovery usually occurs within a day or two. The prevention of staphylococcal food poisoning depends on proper handling and preservation of food products to prevent contamination and subsequent growth of toxin-producing strains of *Staphylococcus.*

Botulism Botulism is caused by the ingestion of food containing toxins produced by *Clostridium botulinum,* an obligate anaerobe that can grow in canned foods. Over 90% of the cases of botulism involve improperly home-canned food. Of 236 outbreaks of this disease in the United States between 1899 and 1974, 57% were caused by contaminated vegetables, 15% by contaminated fish, and 12% by contaminated fruit. The endospores of *C. botulinum* are heat resistant and can survive prolonged exposure at 100° C. Certain canned foods provide an optimal anaerobic environment for the growth of *C. botulinum* that results in the release of toxin into the food. *C. botulinum,* though, cannot grow and produce toxin at low pH and thus is not a problem in acidic food products. Although *C. botulinum* is heat resistant, botulinum toxin is heat labile. Nanograms of the toxin are sufficient to cause death.

C. botulinum is normally incapable of establishing an infection in adults because of the low pH of the stomach and the upper end of the small intestine. However, in infants, before the colonization of the intestinal tract by *Lactobacillus species, C. botulinum* can reproduce and elaborate neurotoxin into the gastrointestinal tract tissues. Such a situation leads to toxemia or elaboration of toxin into the blood. There is evidence that some cases of sudden infant death syndrome, or crib death, can be attributed to *C. botulinum.* Accordingly, additional concern is being given to food products that infants consume, particularly honey, with respect to the possible ingestion of *C. botulinum* endospores.

Foodborne and Waterborne Infections

Some pathogens transmitted via food and water establish infections within the human body. Generally, the establishment of infection through the gastrointestinal tract requires a relatively large infectious dose; that is, a relatively large number of pathogenic microorganisms are required to successfully overcome the inherent defense mechanisms of the gastrointestinal tract. Quite different measures are required to prevent and treat infectious gastrointestinal diseases compared to those for specific microorganisms responsible for food poisoning.

Gastroenteritis and Enterocolitis Gastroenteritis involves an inflammation of the lining of the gastrointestinal tract. This disease can be caused by various bacteria and viruses. Viruses causing gastroenteritis normally replicate within cells lining the gastrointestinal tract, and large numbers of viruses are released in fecal matter. Contamination of food with fecal matter is an important route of transmission of microorganisms responsible for gastroenteritis, as well as many other diseases caused by microorganisms that enter via the gastrointestinal tract.

Various microorganisms cause infections of the upper gastrointestinal tract (stomach and upper small intestine), causing the disease *gastroenteritis.* This disease typically is characterized by abdominal pain, nausea, vomiting, and diarrhea. Bacterial infections of the lower gastrointestinal tract, lower small intestine and colon, cause *enterocolitis,* often with blood in the stools.

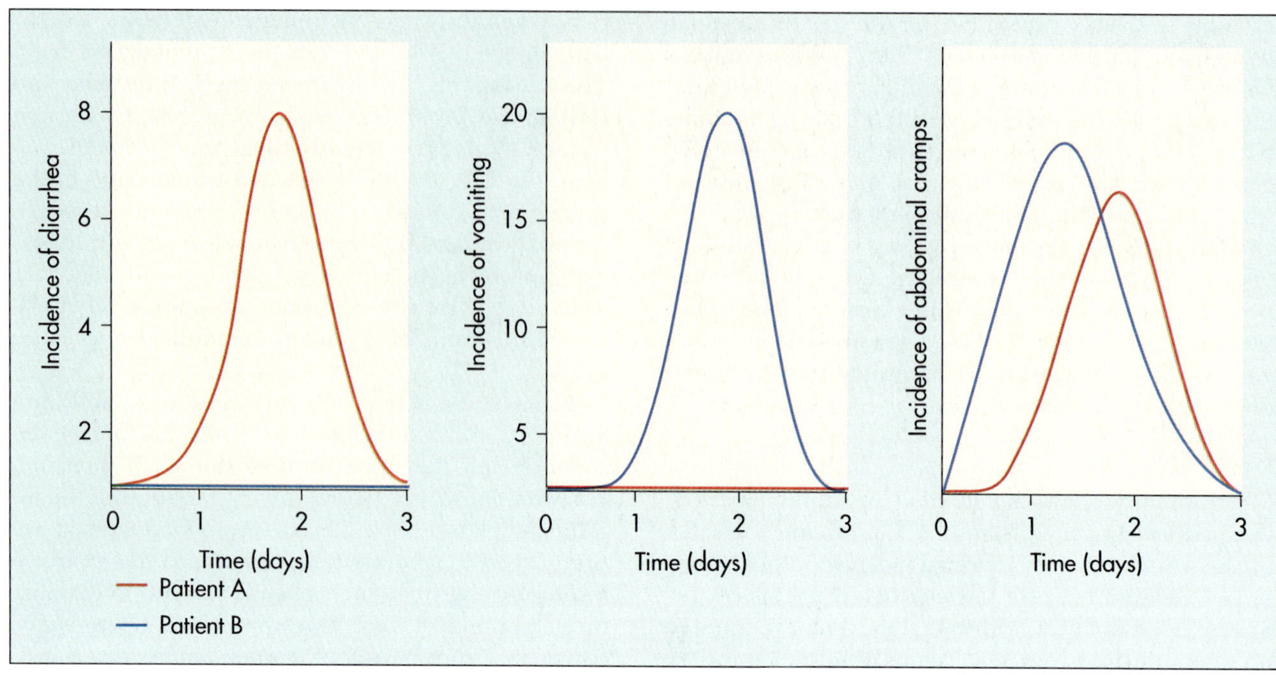

FIG. 12-15 Viruses that cause viral gastroenteritis are transmitted via contaminated food and water. Large numbers of the virus are shed in feces from infected individuals. Two volunteers were orally administered a stool filtrate from an individual infected with Norwalk agent. Both individuals developed viral gastroenteritis characterized by nausea and abdominal cramps; one individual vomited repeatedly and the other had severe diarrhea.

VIRAL GASTROENTERITIS *Viral gastroenteritis* is a self-limiting disease, often referred to as the *24-hour* or *intestinal flu.* Viral gastroenteritis is not caused by an influenza virus and is not related to true cases of flu; rather, it is due to several different viruses, including adenoviruses, coxsackieviruses, polioviruses, and members of the ECHO virus group. The Norwalk agent, a small DNA virus identified as being responsible for an outbreak of "winter vomiting disease" that occurred in Norwalk, Ohio, in 1968, appears to be an important etiological agent of various viral gastroenteritis outbreaks. Rotavirus, a large RNA virus, also appears to be a common etiological agent of diarrhea in infants, particularly in socioeconomically depressed regions of the world.

The characteristic symptoms of viral gastroenteritis include sudden gastrointestinal pain, vomiting, and diarrhea (FIG. 12-15). Recovery normally occurs within 12 to 24 hours of the onset of disease symptoms. As a result of the vomiting and diarrhea, there can be a severe loss of body fluids and dehydration. The loss of water and the resultant imbalance in electrolytes can have serious consequences, particularly in infants, where viral gastroenteritis is sometimes fatal.

BACTERIAL GASTROENTERITIS AND ENTEROCOLITIS Various *Salmonella* species, especially the numerous serotypes of *S. enteritidis,* are commonly the etiological agents of salmonellosis. Many enteropathogenic bacteria, such as *Salmonella* species and enteropathogenic *Escherichia coli,* have pili that enable them to adhere to the lining of the gastrointestinal tract (FIG. 12-16). Although *Salmonella* species can reproduce within the intestines, causing inflammation, they do not normally penetrate the mucosal lining and enter the bloodstream; in some cases, however, *Salmonella* species can gain access to the circulatory system, causing bacteremia. For example, paratyphoid fever, which is caused by strains of *S. paratyphi* and *S. typhimurium,* is characterized by

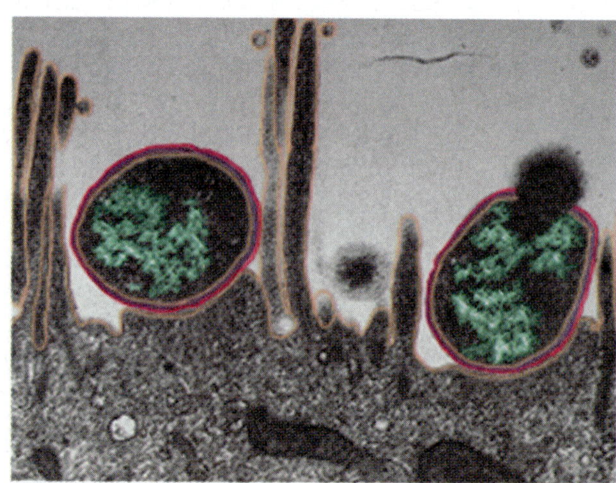

FIG. 12-16 Colorized micrograph of enteropathogenic *Escherichia coli* that have attached to the lining of the gastrointestinal tract via pili.

gastroenteritis and a relatively high rate of bacteremia. *Salmonella* species causing gastroenteritis are normally transmitted by ingestion of contaminated food. Birds and domestic fowl, especially ducks, turkeys, and chickens, including their eggs, are commonly identified as the sources of *Salmonella* infections. Inadequate cooking of large turkeys and the ingestion of raw eggs cause a significant number of cases of salmonellosis.

An infection with *Salmonella* is normally characterized by abdominal pain, fever, and diarrhea that lasts for 3 to 5 days. The onset of disease symptoms typically occurs 8 to 24 hours after ingestion of contaminated food. Nausea and vomiting may be the initial symptoms but they usually do not persist after pain and diarrhea begin. The feces may contain mucus and blood. Generally, the disease is self-limiting, with recovery occurring within 1 week. During acute salmonellosis the feces may contain 1 billion *Salmonella* cells per gram. Fecal contamination of water and food supplements can contribute to the transmission of this disease.

Campylobacter fetus var. *jejuni* has been found to be the causative agent of many cases of bacterial gastroenteritis in infants. In fact, *C. fetus* may be more important in juvenile gastroenteritis than *Salmonella* species. The transmission of *C. fetus* appears to be via contaminated food or water. *C. fetus* is a Gram-negative, motile, spiral-shaped bacterium, formerly known as *Vibrio fetus,* which also causes fetal abortion in cattle and sheep.

Vibrio parahaemolyticus is responsible for many cases of gastroenteritis in Japan and perhaps in the United States. It occurs in marine environments, and the ingestion of contaminated seafood, particularly the eating of raw fish, is the main route of transmission. Gastroenteritis caused by *V. parahaemolyticus* requires the establishment of an infection within the gastrointestinal tract, rather than simple ingestion of an enterotoxin. The symptoms generally appear 12 hours after ingestion of contaminated food and include abdominal pain, diarrhea, nausea, and vomiting. Recovery from this form of gastroenteritis normally occurs in 2 to 5 days, and the mortality rate is low.

Typhoid Fever Outbreaks of typhoid fever, a systemic infection caused by *Salmonella typhi,* are associated with contaminated water supplies and the handling of food products by individuals infected with this bacterium. Although the portal of entry for *S. typhi* normally is the gastrointestinal tract, infections with *S. typhi* do not initially cause gastroenteritis; rather, the bacteria simply enter the body via this route and cause infections at other sites. In the course of the disease, however, the intestines become involved, along with various other organs.

A relatively low infectious dose is required for *S. typhi* to establish an infection. The infecting bacteria rapidly enter the lymphatic system and are disseminated through the circulatory system. Phagocytosis by neutrophil cells does not kill *S. typhi,* and the bacteria continue to multiply within phagocytic blood cells. The surface Vi antigen of *S. typhi* apparently interferes with phagocytosis, and elimination of infecting cells depends on the antibody-mediated immune response.

After invasion of the mononuclear phagocyte system, the *S. typhi* infection becomes localized in lymphatic tissues, particularly in Peyer patches of the intestine, where ulcers can develop. Localized infections always develop and cause damage to the liver and gallbladder, and sometimes also to the kidneys, spleen, and lungs.

The symptoms of typhoid fever include fever (104° F), headache, apathy, weakness, abdominal pain, and a rash with rose-colored spots. The symptoms develop in a stepwise fashion over a 3-week period. If no complications occur, the fever begins to decline at the end of the third week. However, if it remains untreated, the mortality rate averages 10%. Chloramphenicol is effective in the treatment of typhoid fever; its use and that of other antibiotics has reduced the death rate to approximately 1%.

Shigellosis *Shigellosis,* or *bacterial dysentery,* is an acute inflammation of the intestinal tract caused by species of the Gram-negative genus *Shigella,* including *S. shiga, S. flexneri, S. sonnei,* and *S. dysenteriae. Shigella* species penetrate the mucosal cells of the large intestine and multiply in the submucosa. Areas of intense inflammation develop around the multiplying bacteria, and micro-abscesses form and spread, leading to bleeding ulceration. The symptoms of *Shigella* infections include abdominal pain, fever, and diarrhea, with mucus and blood in the excreta. Bacterial dysentery normally is a self-limiting disease, with recovery occurring 2 to 7 days after onset. The severe dehydration associated with this disease can cause shock and lead to death in children, in whom the incidence of bacterial dysentery is highest.

Yersiniosis *Yersinia enterocolitica* can be transmitted via contaminated foods. Symptoms of an infection with *Y. enterocolitica* resemble those of appendicitis. These symptoms include abdominal pain, fever, diarrhea, vomiting, and elevated white blood cell count. Often, an appendectomy is performed before this disease is properly diagnosed as yersiniosis. Outbreaks of yersiniosis are most common in Western Europe but have also been confirmed in the United States. In an outbreak of yersiniosis in New York involving over 200 school children, the infection was traced to a common source of contaminated chocolate milk. Ten children underwent unnecessary appendectomies before the true etiology of the disease was established. *Y. enterocolitica* is widely distributed and has been found in water, milk, fruits, vegetables, and seafoods. This organism is psychrotrophic and thus can reproduce within refrigerated foods, where it can multiply and reach an infectious dose. In fact, *Y. enterocolitica* grows better at 25° C than at 37° C.

Hepatitis Hepatitis type A virus is usually transmitted by the fecal-oral route and is prevalent in areas with inadequate sewage treatment. Several outbreaks of viral hepatitis have been associated with contaminated shellfish that contained concentrated viruses from sewage effluents. An infection with hepatitis type A virus affects the liver. The initial symptoms of infectious hepatitis include fever, abdominal pain, and nausea, followed by jaundice, the yellowing of the skin indicative of liver impairment caused by the virus (FIG. 12-17). Damage to liver cells also results in increased serum levels of enzymes, such as transaminases, normally active in liver cells. The detection of increased serum levels of these enzymes is used in diagnosing this disease. In most cases of infectious hepatitis, the infection is self-limiting and recovery occurs within 4 months.

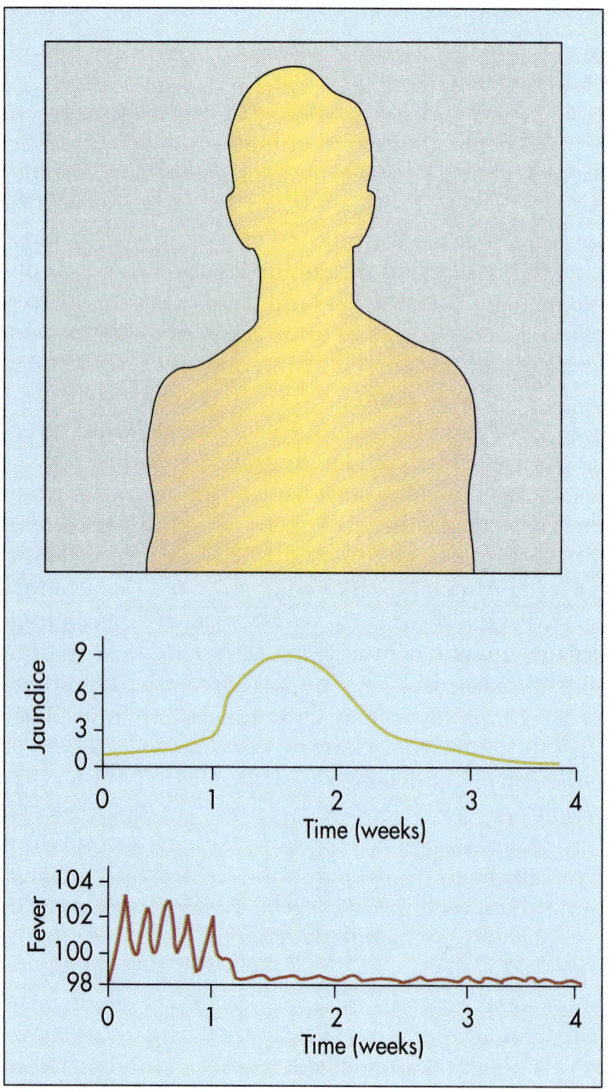

FIG. 12-17 In a case of hepatitis, fever occurs intermittently. Jaundice (indicative of liver damage) begins 1 week after the initial fever.

Giardiasis *Giardia lamblia,* a waterborne flagellated protozoan, is responsible for most cases of diarrhea caused by protozoa (FIG. 12-18). *G. lamblia* forms motile cells called trophozoites and nonmotile cysts. The cysts of *G. lamblia,* which are the infective form, can enter the gastrointestinal tract through contaminated water. A high incidence of giardiasis occurred among groups touring Leningrad during the 1970s as a result of contaminated water supplies. In 1973 a major outbreak of giardiasis occurred in upstate New York, with an estimated 4,800 individuals developing symptoms of the disease. The following year, giardiasis was the most common waterborne disease in the United States. *G. lamblia* can live within the small intestine without causing any symptoms of giardiasis, and in the United States almost 4% of the population appears to be infected by this organism. Excessive growth of the organism, however, can cause disease symptoms that include diarrhea, dehydration, mucus secretion, and flatulence. Metronidazole is generally used in the treatment of this disease.

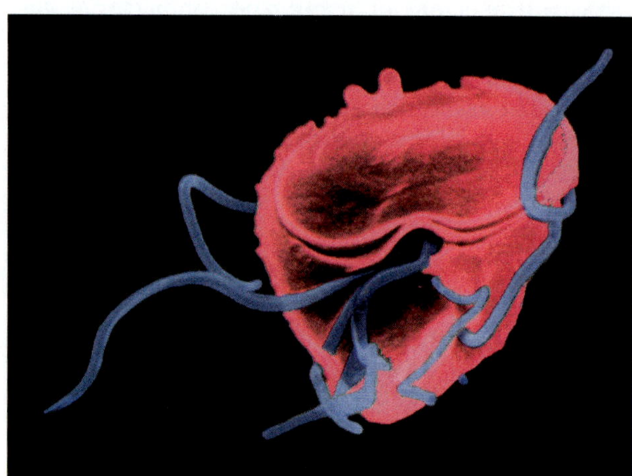

FIG. 12-18 Colorized micrograph of *Giardia lamblia,* a protozoan that is a common cause of gastrointestinal infections. (4,800×).

Sexually Transmitted Diseases

Sexually transmitted diseases (STDs) are contracted by direct sexual contact with an infected individual, generally during sexual intercourse. The physiological properties of the pathogens causing these diseases restrict their transmission, for the most part, to direct physical contact because the etiological agents of STDs have very limited natural survival times outside infected tissues. The incidence of STDs reflects contemporary sexual behavioral patterns but in part may also reflect changes in reporting and recording cases of these diseases. At present, outbreaks of some STDs are considered to be reaching epidemic proportions. The social implications of their transmission often overshadow the fact that these are infectious diseases and must be treated as medical problems, with the emphasis on curing the patient and reducing the incidence of disease by preventing the spread of the infectious agents. The overall control of STDs depends on breaking the network of transmission, which necessitates public health practices that seek to identify and to treat all sexual partners of anyone diagnosed as having one of the sexually transmitted diseases.

Acquired Immunodeficiency Syndrome (AIDS)

The incidence of AIDS has increased in epidemic fashion in the last few years (FIG. 12-19). High-risk groups include homosexual men, intravenous drug abusers, and hemophiliacs, as well as the sexual partners of persons in these groups. The disease is transmitted by sexual contact, which is the main means of transmission among homosexuals within infected communities, or by exchange of blood or blood products. Heterosexual transmission also occurs. In some regions of Africa, heterosexual transmission has resulted in up to 25% of the population, male and female, infected with HIV. HIV infections due to heterosexual transmission also are increasing among women in the United States.

If AIDS develops during pregnancy, it can be transmitted through the placenta to the fetus. Intravenous drug users also are at risk because the virus can be transmitted via blood-contaminated hypodermic needles. Although low levels of the virus have been detected in the saliva of infected individuals, direct transmission of the disease by kissing, airborne droplets, and eating utensils has not been demonstrated. AIDS is incurable at this time, but treatment with azidothymidine (AZT) or dideoxyinosine (ddI) limits replication of the HIV virus and currently is the most hopeful, albeit experimental, treatment. Patients with this disease can be treated with passive immunization and antibiotics to protect them against life-threatening secondary infections.

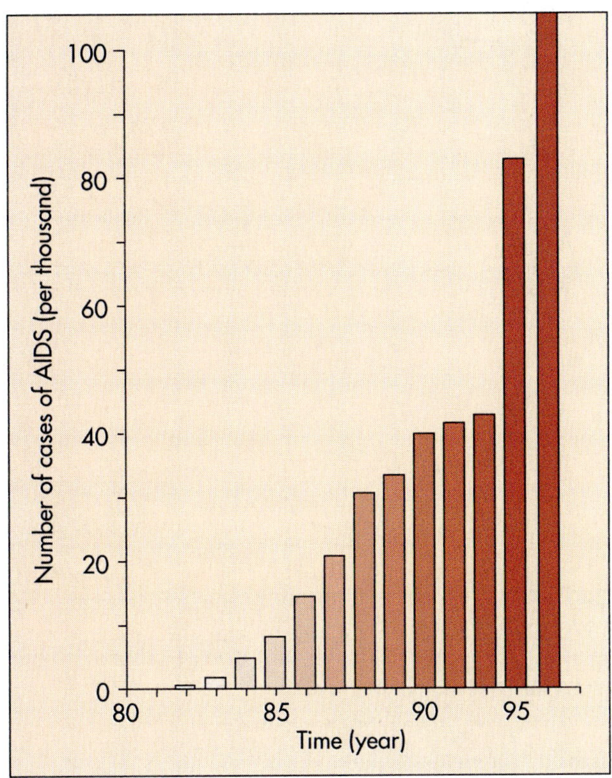

FIG. 12-19 AIDS in the United States is increasing in epidemic proportions.

Clearly, AIDS is a serious and frightening disease, and there have been some excessive public reactions. In some hospitals, staff members refused to treat patients with AIDS. Establishments in San Francisco catering to the homosexual community closed on the grounds that they constitute a public health hazard. Until we fully understand how to treat and prevent the spread of AIDS, unfounded public reactions are likely to continue. We will undoubtedly find methods to control HIV and better ways of treating AIDS, as we have for most other infectious diseases.

Genital Herpes

It is estimated that 20 million Americans now have the sexually transmitted disease, genital herpes simplex, and that there will be at least half a million new cases per year unless effective means of controlling this disease are found. In women, the primary site of herpes simplex viral infection is the cervix, but it may also involve the vulva and vagina. In men, the herpes simplex virus frequently infects the penis. The primary infection includes symptoms of genital soreness and ulcers in the infected areas. The herpes virus and manifestations of infection may be transmitted to other areas of the body, most notably the mouth and anus. Genital herpes may have particularly serious repercussions in pregnant women because the virus can be transmitted to the infant during vaginal delivery, causing damage to the infant's central nervous system and/or eyes. Herpes is lethal in up to 60% of infected newborns, and in surviving babies, there is a 50% risk of blindness or neurological damage.

The ulcers produced by herpes simplex type 2 infection generally heal spontaneously in 10 to 14 days, but because of the ability of herpes viruses to establish biological latency in the host, the infection is not eliminated when the ulcers heal; rather, a reservoir of viruses remains within the nerve cells of the body. Later multiplication of the viruses can produce new ulcers, even in the absence of additional sexual activity. It is not known exactly what initiates subsequent attacks of herpes but such recurrences may be triggered by sunlight, sexual activity, menstruation, and stress. The disease remains transmissible, which interferes with the establishment of stable sexual relationships;

there are also many adverse psychological effects associated with genital herpes. Genital herpes disrupts marital relationships, and the epidemic outbreak may contribute to a reversal of the sexual revolution. Several of the newly developed antiviral drugs should be useful in the treatment of herpes viral infections. In particular, acyclovir reduces the longevity of genital herpes lesions. Acyclovir doesn't cure genital herpes but is effective in reducing the period of symptoms and also the period during which there are open lesions with infective viruses that can be transmitted.

Genital Warts

Warts are benign tumors caused by infections with papilloma viruses. These viruses are transmitted by direct contact, normally infecting the skin and mucous membranes. Direct sexual contact usually is the source of the infecting papilloma viruses when genital warts occur. Warts generally do not appear for several weeks after infection. Chemical (e.g., acid) and physical (e.g., freezing) methods can be used to remove warts, but these benign tumors also disappear without treatment. There is increasing evidence that some of the papilloma viruses that cause genital warts can cause cancer. Previously it was thought that herpes viruses might lead to cervical cancer, but it now appears that adolescent women who have had extensive sexual contacts and have developed genital warts have an elevated rate of cervical cancer. Frequent Pap smears are suggested for such women.

Gonorrhea

Gonorrhea is a sexually transmitted disease caused by the Gram-negative diplococcus *Neisseria gonorrhoeae,* often referred to as the *gonococcus.* This bacterium adheres by its pili to the lining of the genitourinary tract during sexual transmission. *N. gonorrhoeae* infects the mucosal cells lining the epithelium. It can penetrate to the subepithelial connective tissue during spread of the infection. *N. gonorrhoeae* can also infect the urethra, cervix, rectum, pharynx, and conjunctivae.

N. gonorrhoeae is a fastidious organism readily killed by drying and exposure to metals. The sensitivity of *N. gonorrheae* to desiccation makes negligible the chances of transmission of gonorrhea through inanimate objects, such as toilet seats in public restrooms.

There was an alarming increase in the number of cases of gonorrhea in the United States from 1960 to 1970 (FIG. 12-20). This increase coincides with the sexual revolution and widespread use of oral contra-

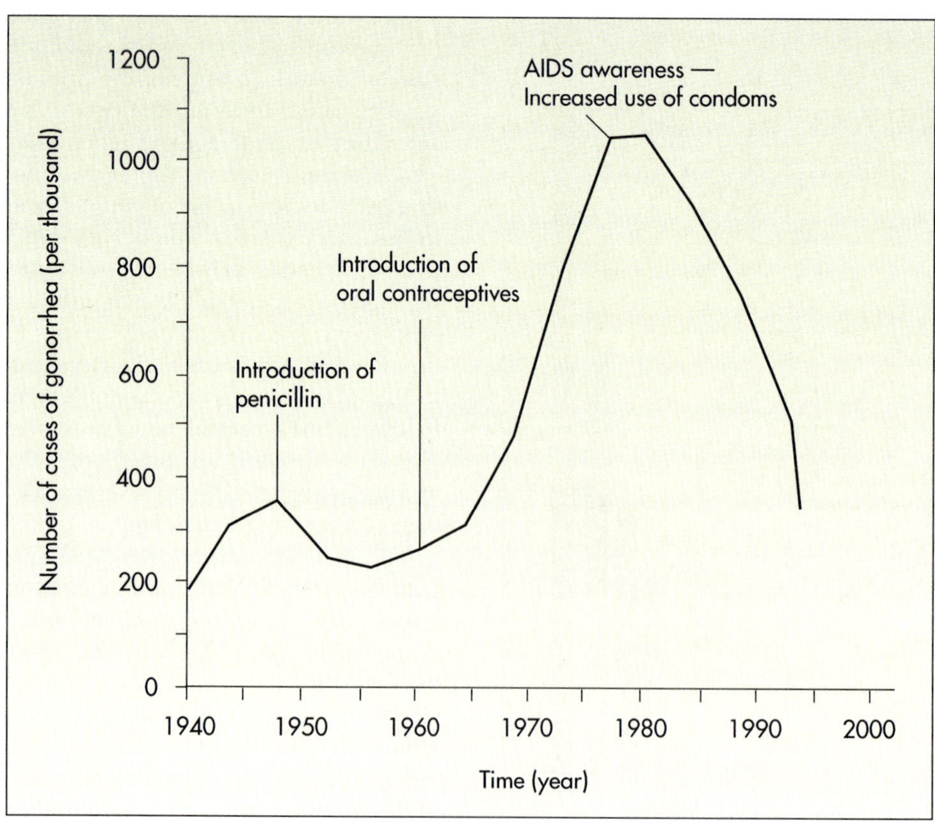

FIG. 12-20 The increase in gonorrhea from 1960 to 1970 coincides with the greater use of oral contraceptives. The decrease in this disease after 1980 probably reflects an increase in safe sex practices.

ceptives. Oral contraceptives contain hormones that cause pH values in the vaginal tract to increase. In neutralizing the acid environment of the vagina, the normal protection against infections by acid-sensitive bacteria, including *N. gonorrhoeae,* is removed. The rate of gonorrhea began to decline after 1980, probably because AIDS awareness led to an increase in the use of condoms. Gonorrhea is normally contracted from someone who is asymptomatic or who has symptoms but does not seek treatment. The rate of gonorrhea acquisition among men is about 35% after a single exposure to an infected woman and rises to 75% after multiple sexual contacts with the same individual. It can be transmitted to newborns during birth.

In most cases, gonorrhea is a self-limiting disease, but in both sexes the infection may spread to contiguous parts of the genitourinary tract and *N. gonorrhoeae* may be disseminated to other parts of the body. For example, infections with *N. gonorrhoeae* can spread to the joints, causing gonorrheal arthritis; to the heart, causing gonorrheal endocarditis; and to the central nervous system, causing gonorrheal meningitis.

Often in women, the early stages of gonorrhea are not associated with any overt symptoms, and many women with gonorrhea remain asymptomatic carriers. The cervix often is the site of gonococcal infection. Various other tissues may be involved if the infection spreads. If the infection spreads to the uterus, it causes a chronic infection of the Fallopian tubes called *salpingitis.* This condition typically is characterized by abdominal pain. Salpingitis can cause infertility. It is also the cause of implantation outside the uterus, a life-threatening situation called *ectopic pregnancy.* A gonococcal infection may spread to the urethra, causing an inflammation called *gonococcal urethritis.* Gonorrhea also can lead to *pelvic inflammatory disease* (PID), which results from a generalized bacterial infection of the uterus, pelvic organs, fallopian tubes, and ovaries (FIG. 12-21). PID may occur without the overt symptoms of gonorrhea but nevertheless may cause infertility.

In men, gonorrhea results in a characteristic painful, purulent urethral discharge. The pus results from the migration of phagocytic leukocytes to the site of infection. Symptoms of gonorrhea in men are usually apparent less than 1 week after infection. If the disease is untreated, occlusion of the vas deferens due to scarring may produce sterility.

Gonorrhea is readily treated with antibiotics, with penicillin being the drug of choice. Other antibiotics, such as tetracycline, are also effective. In recent years there has been an increase in the tolerance of *N. gonorrhoeae* to antibiotics, creating a major concern in the treatment of gonorrhea (see FIG. 10-16). The recent

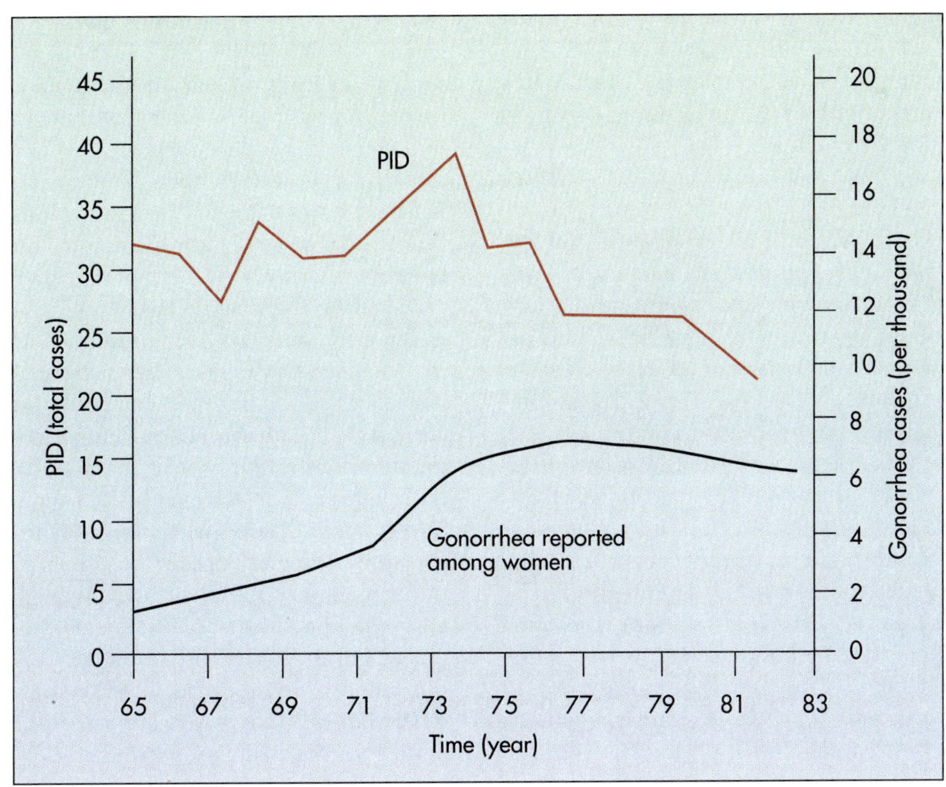

FIG. 12-21 Pelvic inflammatory disease (PID) can be a complication in women from an infection with *Neisseria gonorrhoeae* and other sexually transmitted pathogens.

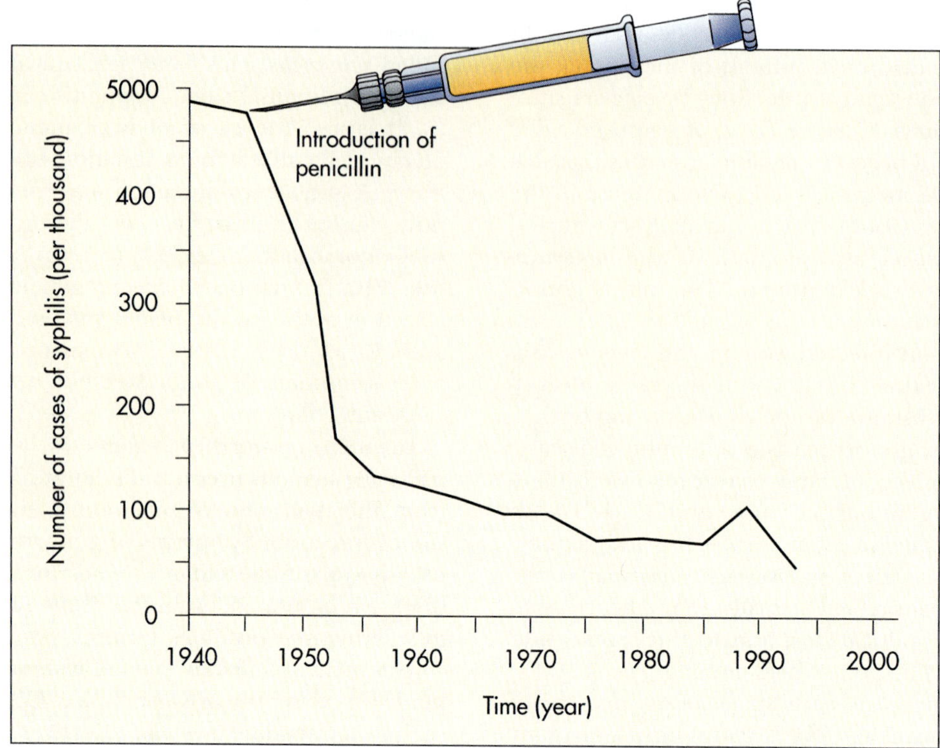

FIG. 12-22 The incidence of syphilis declined after the introduction of penicillin.

identification of β-lactamase-producing strains of *N. gonorrhoeae* in some cases may lead to a movement away from penicillin in treating gonorrhea because such strains are resistant to most penicillins. With penicillin-resistant strains of *N. gonorrhoeae,* streptomycin is the antibiotic of choice.

Syphilis

Syphilis is a sexually transmitted disease caused by *Treponema pallidum.* This organism is a bacterial spirochete, fastidious in its growth requirements and readily killed by drying, heat, and disinfectants such as soap, arsenicals, and mercurial compounds. Unlike gonorrhea, the number of cases of syphilis in the United States has been relatively constant; there was a major decline in this disease after the introduction of penicillin (FIG. 12-22). It can be detected by serological blood tests, and premarital syphilis testing was once required by many states. As with other sexually transmitted diseases, the control of syphilis depends on finding and treating all sexual contacts who may have contracted this disease and may be involved in its further transmission. No long-term immunity develops after infections with *T. pallidum,* and individuals who are cured by treatment with antibiotics remain susceptible.

Historically, hot bath spas and arsenic- and mercury-containing compounds have been used in the treatment of syphilis. The inability of *T. pallidum* to survive for long outside the body makes transmission through inanimate objects (fomites) virtually nonexistent. Transmission depends on direct contact with the infective syphilitic lesions containing *T. pallidum. T. pallidum* enters the body via abrasions of the epithelium and by penetrating mucous membranes. The bacteria migrate to the lymphatic system shortly after penetrating the dermal layers.

Syphilis manifests itself in three distinct stages. During the primary stage, a *chancre* develops at the site of *Treponema* inoculation. Primary lesions generally occur on the genitalia. The average incubation period for the manifestation of primary syphilis is 21 days after infection. The primary lesions typically heal within 3 to 6 weeks, often giving the individual the false impression that the disease has been cured. The secondary stage of syphilis normally begins 6 to 8 weeks after the appearance of the primary chancre. During this stage, there are cutaneous lesions and lesions of the mucous membranes that contain infective *T. pallidum.* Lesions may appear on the lips, tongue, throat, penis, vagina, and numerous other body surfaces (FIG. 12-23). There may be additional symptoms of

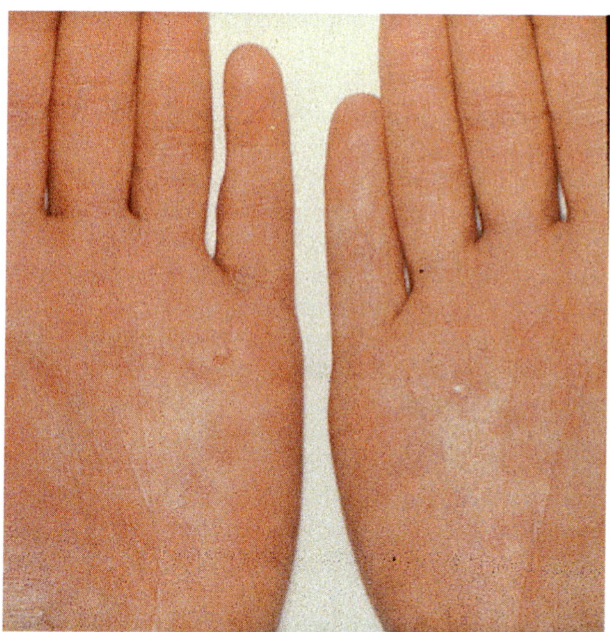

FIG. 12-23 Secondary lesions of syphilis on the palms of the hands.

systemic disease during this stage, such as headache, low-grade fever, and enlargement of the lymph nodes. After the secondary stage, syphilis enters a characteristic latent period during which there are no clinical symptoms of the disease. The latent phase marks the end of the infectious period of syphilis.

The tertiary phase of syphilis, also known as *late syphilis,* usually does not occur until years after the initial infection. During tertiary syphilis, damage can occur to any organ of the body. People with tertiary syphilis exhibit cell-mediated immunity and hypersensitivity reactions to treponemal antigens. These reactions may contribute to cellular damage. In about 10% of the cases of untreated syphilis, this phase involves the aorta, and damage to this major blood vessel can result in death. In approximately 8% of the cases of untreated syphilis, there is central nervous system involvement with various neurological manifestations, including personality changes and paralysis.

If untreated, approximately 25% of the individuals who contract syphilis will suffer one or more relapses of the secondary stage during the first 4 years of illness, 15% will develop tertiary benign lesions, 10% cardiovascular lesions, and 8% central nervous system lesions. The risks of debilitating symptoms and death make this a very serious form of sexually transmitted disease. Fortunately, syphilis can be treated with penicillin and other antibiotics, particularly during the early stages.

In addition to sexually transmitted syphilis, *T. pallidum* can be transmitted across the placenta of pregnant women with syphilis, infecting the fetus and causing stillbirth or congenital syphilis in the newborn. Stillbirth is likely if pregnancy occurs during the primary or secondary stages of syphilis. Congenital syphilis is most likely during the latent period of the disease. Congenital syphilis has very serious consequences, usually resulting in mental retardation and neurological abnormalities in the infant; the probability of survival in such infants depends on the specific nature of the neurological impairment.

Nongonococcal Urethritis

Nongonococcal urethritis (NGU) is the term used to describe sexually transmitted diseases that result in inflammation of the urethra caused by bacteria other than *N. gonorrhoeae.* This disease is also called *nonspecific urethritis* (NSU). It is estimated that between 4 and 9 million people in the United States have contracted this disease. Most cases are mild. Women often are asymptomatic; men usually notice some pain and discharge during urination. In serious cases, the inflammation associated with this condition can cause infertility. In men the epididymis may become inflamed, and in women the cervix or fallopian tubes may become blocked.

Most cases of NGU appear to be caused by *Chlamydia trachomatis,* a small, obligately intracellular, parasitic bacterium. *Mycoplasma hominis* and *Ureaplasma urealyticum* also have frequently been reported to cause NGU. These two bacterial species lack cell walls. It is difficult to diagnose the causes of NGU because of problems with culturing and identifying these bacteria. All of these bacteria are inhibited by antibiotics such as tetracyclines but not by penicillin. Compared to gonococcal urethritis, NGU has a longer incubation period. Individuals treated with penicillin for cases diagnosed as gonorrhea may later develop NGU if multiple bacteria were associated with the sexually transmitted disease.

C. trachomatis, like *N. gonorrhoeae,* can be transmitted during birth from the mother to the eyes of the newborn. *Chlamydia* infections of the eye can be serious. Because many women are asymptomatic, it is difficult to take selective measures to prevent this occurrence. Therefore erythromycin is applied to the eyes of all newborns shortly after birth to protect them against both *N. gonorrhoeae* and *C. trachomatis.* Before the prevalence of *C. trachomatis* was recognized, silver nitrate was used to treat the eyes of newborns. Silver nitrate inhibits *N. gonorrhoeae* but not *C. trachomatis,* whereas erythromycin is effective against both of these infectious agents.

Zoonoses and Vector Transmission of Human Diseases

In some cases, nonhuman animal populations are the source of an infectious agent. Diseases that primarily affect wild and domestic animals are known as **zoonoses.** Some zoonoses can be transmitted to humans by direct contact with infected animals, by ingesting contaminated meat, or, more frequently, by **vectors,** which are carriers of disease agents (Table 12-7). The vector need not develop disease; it need only transmit the causative agent from a reservoir to a susceptible individual. Arthropods, such as mosquitoes, are frequently the vectors of human disease. For example, malaria is a disease prevalent in tropical regions where the *Plasmodium* species that causes malaria are transmitted by the *Anopheles* mosquito.

Yellow Fever

Yellow fever, caused by a small RNA virus, is transmitted by mosquito vectors, predominantly *Aedes aegypti.* There are two epidemiological patterns of transmission. Urban transmission involves vector transfer by *A. aegypti* from an infected to a susceptible individual. Jungle yellow fever normally involves transmission by mosquito vectors among monkeys, with transfer via mosquito vectors to humans representing an occasional deviation from the normal transmission cycle (FIG. 12-24). Outbreaks of yellow fever were a major problem in the construction of the Panama Canal, leading to Walter Reed's instrumental work in establishing the relationship between yellow fever and mosquito vectors in 1901. Today, yellow fever occurs primarily in remote tropical regions, and current outbreaks take place primarily in Central America, South America, the Caribbean, and Africa.

The onset of yellow fever is marked by *anorexia* (loss of appetite), nausea, vomiting, and fever. The multiplication of the virus results in liver damage, causing the *jaundice* from which the disease derives its name. The symptoms generally last for 1 week, after which recovery begins or death occurs. The mortality rate for yellow fever is about 5%. There is no effective antiviral drug at present for treating the disease; however, it can be prevented by vaccination, using the 17D strain of yellow fever virus. The urban form of transmission has been largely controlled by effective mosquito eradication programs, but the jungle form of transmission cannot easily be interrupted because of the large natural reservoir of yellow fever viruses maintained within monkey populations.

TABLE 12-7 Representative Human Diseases Transmitted by Arthropod Bites

DISEASE	ETIOLOGICAL AGENT	BIOLOGICAL VECTOR	RESERVOIR
Yellow fever	Yellow fever virus	Mosquito (*Aedes aegypti, Haemagogus* spp.)	Humans, monkeys
Dengue fever	Dengue fever virus	Mosquito (*Aedes* spp., *Armigeres obturbans*)	Humans
Eastern equine encephalitis	Encephalitis viruses	Mosquito (*Aedes* spp., *Culex* spp., *Mansonia titillans*)	Humans, horses, birds
Colorado tick fever	Colorado tick fever virus	Wood ticks (*Dermacentor andersoni*)	Golden mantle ground squirrel
Plague	*Yersinia pestis*	Rodent fleas (*Xenopsylla cheopis*), human fleas (*Pulex irritans*)	Rodents (rats)
Tularemia	*Francisella tularensis*	Ticks (*Dermacentor* spp., *Amblyomma* spp.), deerflies (*Chrysops discalis*)	Rodents, ticks
Rocky Mountain spotted fever	*Rickettsia rickettsii*	Ticks (*Dermacentor* spp., *Amblyomma* spp., *Ornithodoros* spp., and others)	Rodents
Endemic typhus fever	*Rickettsia typhi*	Fleas (*Xenopsylla cheopis* and others)	Humans
Relapsing fever	*Borrelia recurrentis* and other species	Body louse (*Pediculus humanus*)	Humans, ticks
Chagas disease	*Trypanosoma cruzi*	Cone-nosed bugs (*Triatoma* spp., *Panstronglyus* spp., *Rhodnius* spp.)	Dogs, cats, opossums, rats, armadillos
African trypanosomiasis (sleeping sickness)	*Trypanosoma gambiense; T. rhodesiense*	Tsetse flies (*Glossina* spp.)	Humans, wild mammals
Malaria	*Plasmodium vivax, P. malariae, P. falciparum, P. ovale*	Mosquito (*Anopheles* spp.)	Humans
Leishmaniasis	*Leishmania donovani; L. tropica; L. braziliensis*	Sandflies (*Phlebotomus* spp.)	Dogs, foxes, rats, mice, two-toed sloth, gerbils, humans

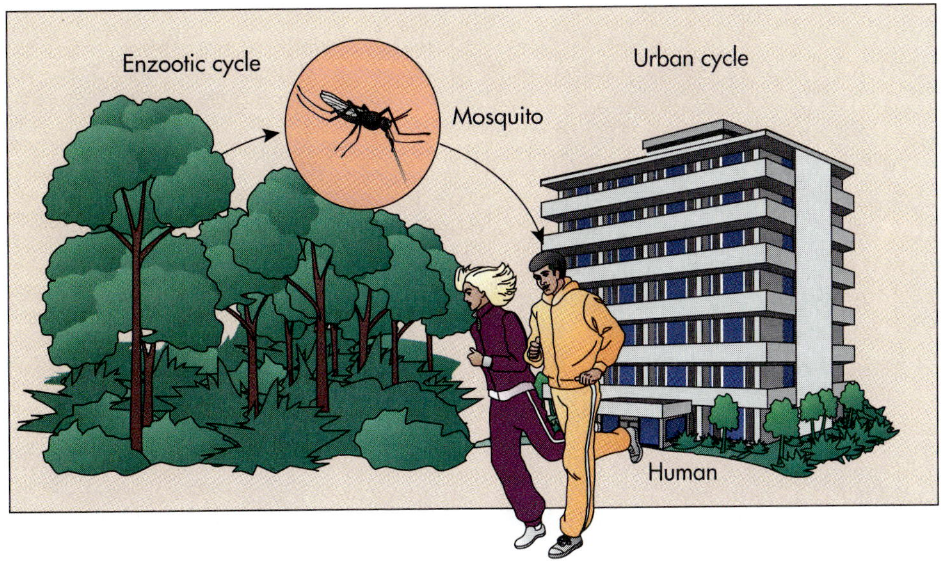

FIG. 12-24 Yellow fever virus is transmitted by the mosquito *Aedes aegypti.* It normally is transmitted to monkeys but can also be transmitted to humans, causing yellow fever.

Plague

Plague is caused by *Yersinia pestis,* a Gram-negative, nonmotile, pleomorphic rod. *Y. pestis* is normally maintained within populations of wild rodents and is transferred from infected to susceptible rodents by fleas. *Y. pestis* is able to multiply within the gut of the flea, which blocks normal digestion, causing the flea to increase the frequency of feeding attempts and so to bite more animals, increasing the probability of disease transmission. Plague is endemic to many rodent populations; for example, *Y. pestis* is permanently established in rodent populations from the Rocky Mountains to the West Coast of the United States.

The transmission of plague was extremely widespread during the Middle Ages because of poor sanitary conditions and the abundance of infected rat populations in areas of dense human habitation (FIG. 12-25). The development of rat control programs and

A

FIG. 12-25 **A,** During the Middle Ages there were major epidemics of plague. The disease followed the trade routes, as did the rats carrying the flea vectors infected with *Yersinia pestis.*

Continued.

B

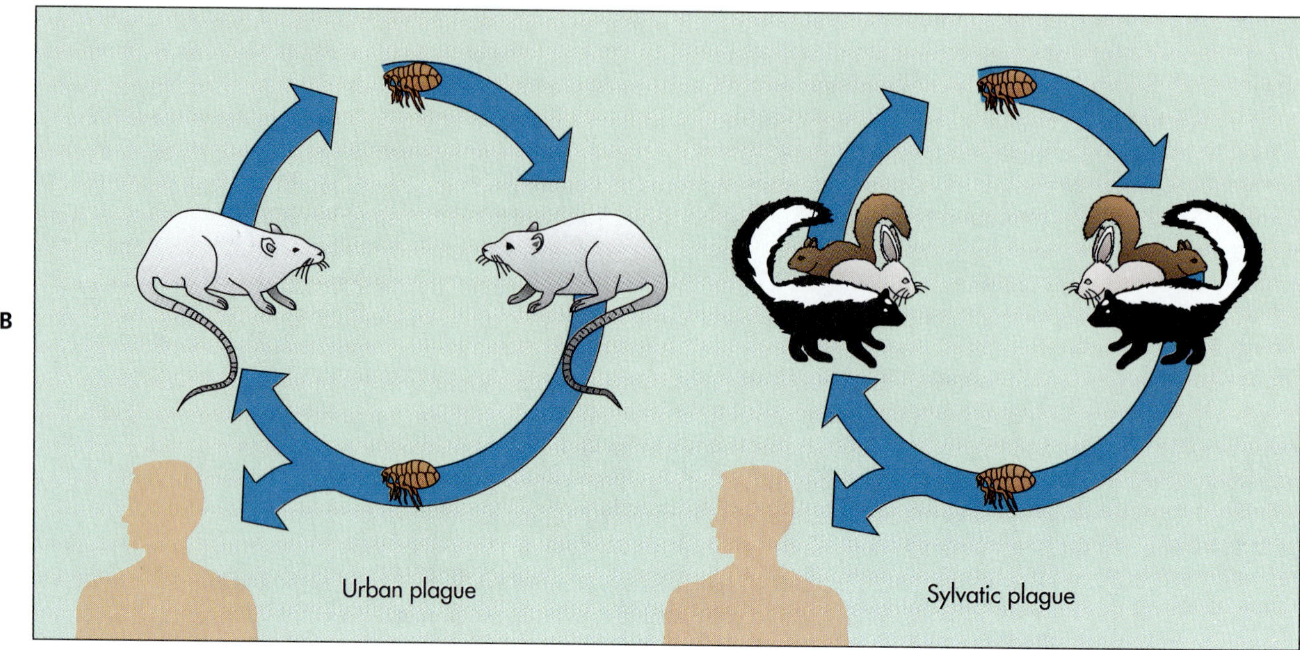

FIG. 12-25, cont'd. **B,** The natural cycle that maintains *Y. pestis* involves transfer among wild rodents by fleas (rural sylvatic plague). Rats can become infected with *Y. pestis,* leading to urban plague. If a human is bitten by infected fleas, he or she may develop bubonic plague, which is not transmitted to other humans unless the bacteria grow in the lung. *Y. pestis* released from the lungs of an infected individual can be transmitted through the air to other individuals, causing pneumonic plague.

improved sanitation methods in urban areas greatly reduced the incidence of this disease. It is not possible, however, to completely eliminate plague in humans because of the large number of alternative hosts in which *Y. pestis* is maintained. In rural environments, for example, *Y. pestis* is found in ground squirrels, prairie dogs, chipmunks, rabbits, mice, rats, and other animals. Exposure to these animals and their fleas leads to sylvatic plague.

The introduction of *Y. pestis* into humans through flea bites initiates a progressive infection that can involve any organ or tissue of the body. Phagocytosis is effective in killing many of the invading bacteria but some cells of *Y. pestis* are resistant and continue to multiply and spread through the circulatory system. In bubonic plague, *Y. pestis* becomes localized and causes inflammation of the regional lymph nodes. The enlarged lymph nodes are called *buboes,* from whence the name of the disease is derived. The symptoms of bubonic plague include malaise, fever, and pain in the area of the infected regional lymph nodes. Severe tissue necrosis can occur in various areas of the body and the skin appears blackened. It is this symptom that gave the name *black death* to the disease in the Middle Ages. As the infection progresses, the symptoms become severe, and without treatment the mortality rate is 60% to 100%.

In severe cases, patients may develop pulmonary involvement that leads to pneumonic plague. This form of plague is the most contagious and can lead to transmission of *Y. pestis* from person to person via droplet inhalation, especially within families. All forms of plague can be effectively treated with antibiotics. Streptomycin generally is the drug of choice against *Y. pestis,* although other antibiotics such as chloramphenicol and tetracycline can also be used.

Rocky Mountain Spotted Fever

Rocky Mountain spotted fever is caused by *Rickettsia rickettsii* that is transmitted to humans through the bite of a tick. *R. rickettsii* is normally maintained within various tick populations, such as the wood and dog ticks (FIG. 12-26). The bacteria multiply within the midgut of the tick and are passed congenitally from one generation of ticks to the next. Humans are accidental hosts of *R. rickettsii* as a result of occasional bites of infected ticks that allow the transfer of *R. rickettsii.*

Rocky Mountain spotted fever occurs in areas of North and South America, most commonly in the spring and summer, when ticks and humans are most likely to come in contact, and normally occur in well-defined localized regions. During the mid-twentieth century, many cases of Rocky Mountain spotted fever occurred in the United States in the region of the

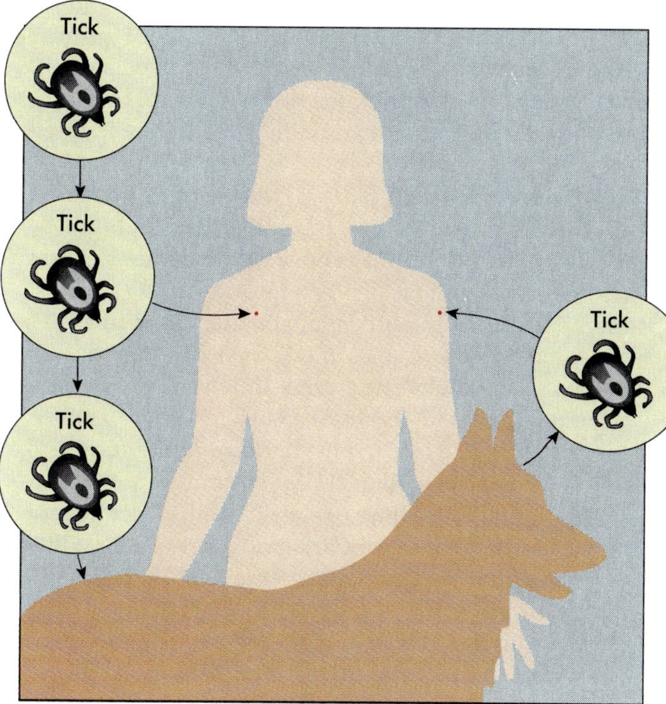

FIG. 12-26 Rocky Mountain spotted fever is transmitted by ticks.

Rocky Mountains, but relatively few cases have been reported there in recent years. On the other hand, outbreaks of this disease have risen dramatically in the eastern United States, where most cases now occur (FIG. 12-27).

When injected into humans, *R. rickettsii* multiply within the endothelial cells lining the blood vessels. Vascular lesions occur and account for the production of the characteristic skin rash associated with this disease. The rash is most prevalent on the extremities, particularly the palms of the hands and soles of the feet. In approximately 19% of Rocky Mountain spotted fever cases there is no rash, making these cases especially hard to diagnose. Lesions probably also occur in the meninges, causing severe headaches and mental confusion. If treated with antibiotics such as chloramphenicol and tetracycline, the disease is rarely fatal, but if untreated, the overall mortality rate is probably greater than 20%. Prevention of Rocky Mountain spotted fever primarily involves control of populations of infected ticks and avoidance of tick bites. However, control is difficult to achieve and there are about 1,000 cases of Rocky Mountain spotted fever in the United States each year.

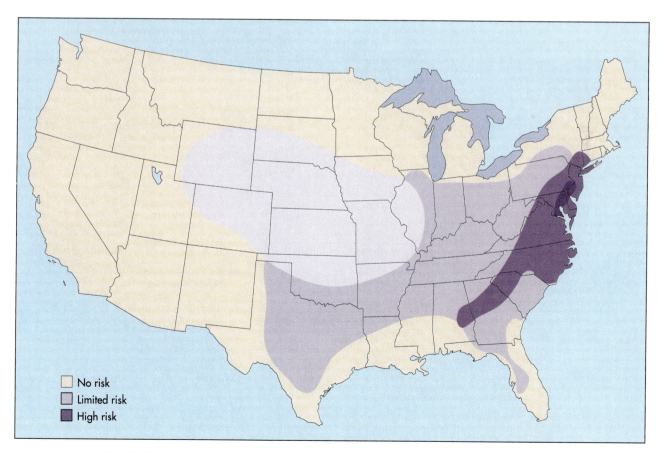

FIG. 12-27 Although initially endemic to the Rocky Mountain region, Rocky Mountain spotted fever today occurs primarily east of the Mississippi River.

Typhus Fever

There are several types of typhus fever, all of which are caused by rickettsias transmitted to humans via biting arthropod vectors (FIG. 12-28). *Infectious typhus fever* (also called *epidemic typhus* or *classic typhus fever*) is caused by *Rickettsia prowazekii* and is transmitted to humans via the body louse. The chain of transmission is restricted to humans and lice. Lice contract the disease from infected humans and pass the rickettsia to susceptible human hosts. *R. prowazekii* multiplies within the epithelium of the midgut of the louse. When an infected body louse bites a human it defecates at the same time, depositing feces containing *R. prowazekii,* which enter through the wound created by the bite. The name *epidemic typhus* is derived from the fact that this form of typhus is transmitted from person to person only by the body louse. Under crowded conditions the disease can spread easily. For example, millions of cases occurred in World War I and in the concentration camps during World War II. The onset of epidemic typhus involves fever, headache, and rash. The heart and kidneys frequently are sites of vascular lesions. If untreated, the mortality rate in persons 10 to 30 years old is approximately 50%. Chloramphenicol, tetracycline, and doxycycline are effective in treating epidemic typhus.

Murine typhus or *endemic typhus fever* is caused by *Rickettsia typhi* and is transmitted to humans by rat fleas. Murine typhus is normally maintained in rat populations endemically through transmission by rat fleas. Occasionally, rat fleas attack humans, and if they are infected with *R. typhi,* the disease can be transmitted. As with louse-borne typhus, the flea deposits pathogenic bacteria in the fecal matter, which is rubbed into the flea bite by the host because of the local irritation caused by the bite. The symptoms of murine typhus are similar to those of classic typhus fever but are generally milder. Chloramphenicol and tetracycline are effective in treating this disease, and there is a relatively low mortality rate. Prevention of murine typhus depends on limiting rat populations, which also limits the size of the vector rat flea population.

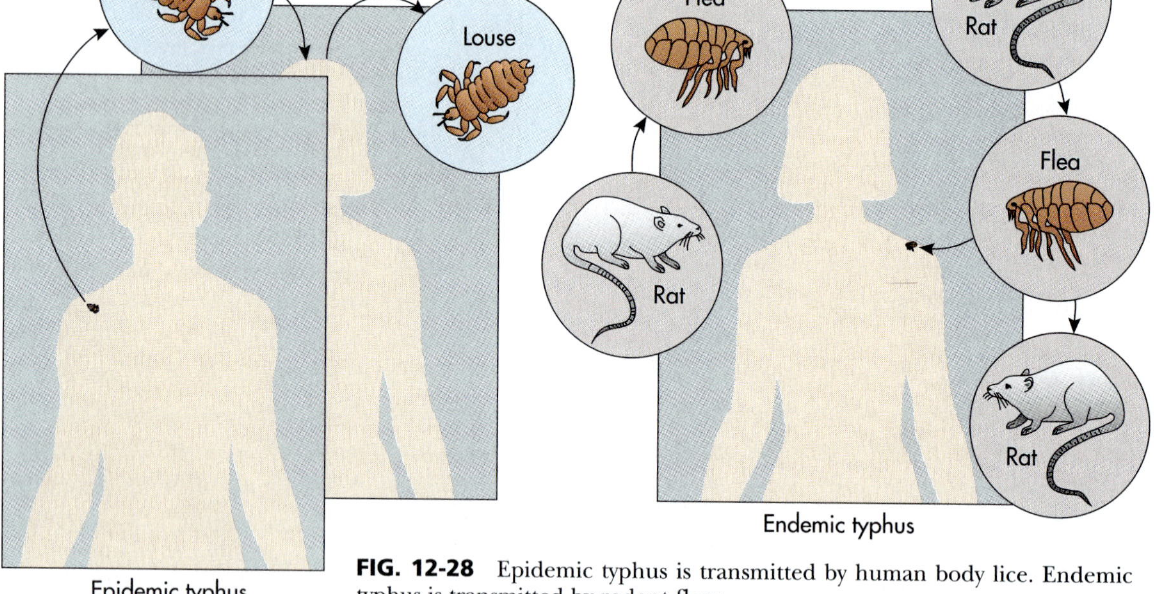

FIG. 12-28 Epidemic typhus is transmitted by human body lice. Endemic typhus is transmitted by rodent fleas.

Lyme Disease

Lyme disease was named for the small Connecticut community in which the disease was first recognized in 1975. It is an inflammatory disorder caused by a spirochete. It is characterized by the development of arthritis and neurological symptoms that result when the body's immune defenses react to infections with the spirochete. The territory over which this disease has occurred is expanding. The majority of the approximately 7,000 reported cases of Lyme disease have occurred in the Northeast, Upper Midwest, and California.

Lyme disease may be a different manifestation of erythema chronicum migrans, a syndrome long recognized in Europe. Both diseases are caused by the spirochete, *Borrelia burgdorferi,* transmitted to humans by the bites of *Ixodes* ticks (FIG. 12-29). Similar spirochetes have been recovered from the blood of Lyme disease patients and cultured from *Ixodes* ticks, and patients with Lyme disease have antibodies to the cultured spirochetes. When this disease is diagnosed, phenoxymethylpenicillin or tetracycline for 2 to 3 weeks is an effective treatment.

Lyme disease begins with a distinctive skin lesion after the initial tick bite. The circularly expanding annular skin lesions are hardened (indurated) with wide borders and central clearing. Although these lesions may reach diameters of 12 inches or more, they are painless. Accompanying symptoms may resemble a mild flu, with some patients experiencing symptoms resembling mild meningitis or encephalitis, hepatitis, musculoskeletal pain, enlarged spleen, and cough. Weeks to months later, the patient often shows signs of the second stage of the disease, developing arthritic joint pain, and sometimes neurologic or cardiac abnormalities. The neurological complications may include visual, emotional, and memory disturbances; temporary paralysis of a facial nerve; and movement difficulties. The third stage, which may appear months to years after infection, is characterized by crippling migrating arthritic symptoms in one or more joints, especially in the knees, and severe neurological symptoms that mimic multiple sclerosis. These symptoms are believed to be caused by the body's immune defense system's attempts to fight the infective agent, rather than by the organism itself. The antibody complexes produced in response to the infective agent cause the joints to become inflamed.

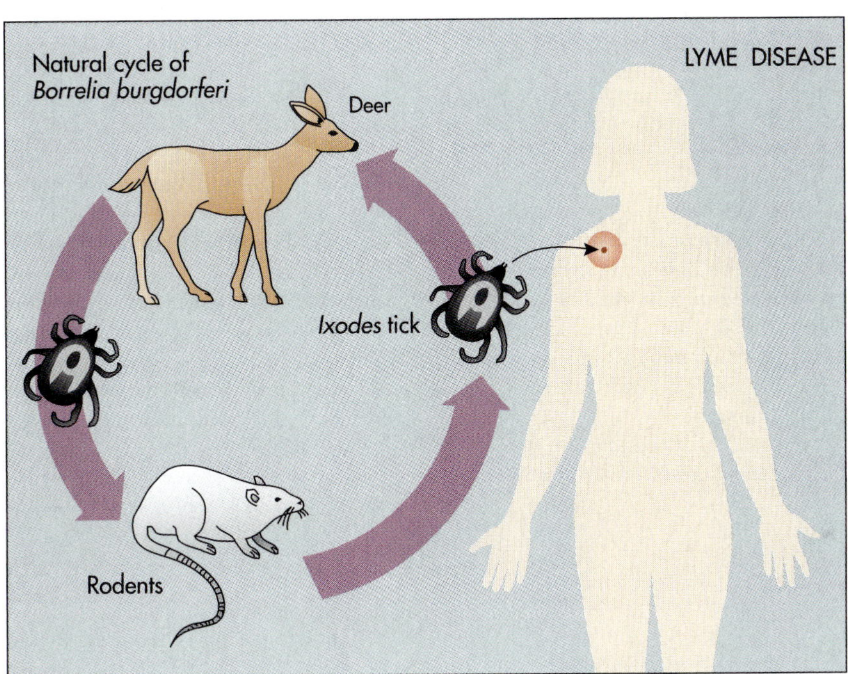

FIG. 12-29 Lyme disease is transmitted to humans by ticks, principally deer ticks.

BOX 12-5

Determining the Epidemiology of Lyme Disease

In October 1975 the Connecticut Department of Health received independent calls reporting multiple cases of what appeared to be arthritis in children in Lyme and Old Lyme, which are rural towns in that state. Despite being assured by their physicians that arthritis was not infectious, the callers were not satisfied. An epidemic investigation ensued in which the extent, characteristics, mode of transmission, and etiology of the cluster of cases were studied. Public health officials began by trying to locate all individuals who had sudden onset of swelling and pain in the knee or other large joints lasting a week to several months, an odd, large skin rash, repeated attacks at intervals of a few months of fever, and fatigue. State epidemiologists questioned parents and physicians—trying to determine if the cases were related, if there were other similar cases, and if this was an infectious form of arthritis. The epidemiologists determined the time, place, and personal characteristics of these cases. The incidence of onset of disease seemed to cluster in late spring and summer and lasted from a week to a few months. The cases were concentrated in three adjacent towns on the eastern side of the Connecticut River and most patients lived in wooded areas near lakes and streams. Of the 51 cases, 39 were children about evenly split between boys and girls and there were no familial patterns. Epidemiologists created an epidemic curve, listing the cases by the time of onset and began calling the disease "Lyme arthritis."

Continued.

BOX 12-5

DETERMINING THE EPIDEMIOLOGY OF LYME DISEASE—CONT'D

The clustering of cases, the fact that most began in late spring or summer and that they were most frequently located in wooded areas along lakes or streams, suggested a disease transmitted by an arthropod. A study was undertaken to determine if this was a communicable disease. Cases of the disease were matched with a similar group of control or unaffected persons for age, sex, and other relevant factors. It was found that affected people were more likely to have a household pet than those who weren't. Pet owners are more likely to come in contact with ticks that their dogs and cats might pick up in the woods. The importance of this finding was emphasized when combined with the fact that one fourth of the patients reported that their arthritic symptoms were preceded by an unusual skin rash that started as a red spot that spread to a 6-inch ring. A dermatology consultant recalled a similar skin outbreak reported in Switzerland in 1910 that was attributed to tick bites.

This was only suggestive evidence that a tick bite might initiate an infectious disease. The connection between the rash and the disease had to be strengthened. Now public health authorities asked if patients with such a rash always progress to develop Lyme arthritis. A prospective study looked for new patients with a rash. Of 32 new cases of the characteristic skin rash, 19 progressed to show signs and symptoms of Lyme disease. The tick connection was strengthened after an entomological study found that adult ticks were 16 times more abundant on the east side of the Connecticut River than the west. This corresponded to the proportion of incidence of the disease on each side of the river. Also, more tick bites were reported by the arthritis sufferers than by their unaffected neighbors. A surveillance network was set up in Connecticut and surrounding states to gather information about other cases. Investigations showed more adult victims than children and also more serious manifestations, including neurological and heart diseases.

The Rocky Mountain Public Health Laboratory in Montana assisted in the investigation because of their expertise in the area of tickborne disease. They found unusual spirochetes in the guts of many of the ticks sent from Connecticut. Spirochetes, which are bacteria with curved cells wound around a central filament, are often difficult to culture. Therefore they tried to infect laboratory animals with the infected ticks. The rabbits developed rashes resembling those seen in humans. A spirochete was isolated from the ticks, and when pure cultures were inoculated into rabbits, the rabbits developed the characteristic rash. The infected rabbits contained antispirochetal antibodies in their serum. The identification was complete when the spirochete was isolated from human cases. The spirochete was classified as a member of the genus *Borrelia* and named *Borrelia burgdorferi* after the entomologist who discovered the organisms in the ticks. *B. burgdorferi* is the identified cause of Lyme disease and it is transmitted primarily by deer ticks.

Malaria

Although malaria is largely eliminated from North America and Europe, it remains the most serious infectious disease in tropical and subtropical regions of the world (FIG. 12-30). The annual incidence is about 150 million cases, making malaria one of the most common human infectious diseases. It is caused by four species of *Plasmodium* (Table 12-8). *P. vivax* and *P. falciparum* are most frequently involved in human infections. The *Anopheles* mosquito is the major vector responsible for transmitting malaria to humans. *Plasmodium* species are infective for humans in the spore stage, called a *sporozoite*. After inoculation into the body, the sporozoites of *Plasmodium* begin to reproduce within liver cells (FIG. 12-31). Multiplication of *Plasmodium* sporozoites occurs by *schizogony* (multiple

TABLE 12-8 Summary of Important Characteristics of Human Malarias

	Plasmodium falciparum	*Plasmodium vivax*	*Plasmodium ovale*	*Plasmodium malariae*
Incidence	Common	Common	Uncommon	Uncommon
Cell increase during primary hepatic schizogony	1-40,000 in 5.5-7 days	1-10,000 in 6-8 days	1-15,000 in 9 days	1-2,000 in 13-16 days
Cell increase during secondary hepatic schizogony	1-8 to 24 (avg. 16) in 48 hr	1-12 to 24 (avg. 16) in 48 hr	1-6 to 16 in 48 hr	1-6 to 12 (avg. 8) in 72 hr
Incubation period	8-27 days (avg. 12)	8-27 (avg. 14) (rarely months)	9-17 days (avg. 15)	15-30 days
Mortality	High in nonimmune persons	Uncommon	Rarely fatal	Rarely fatal

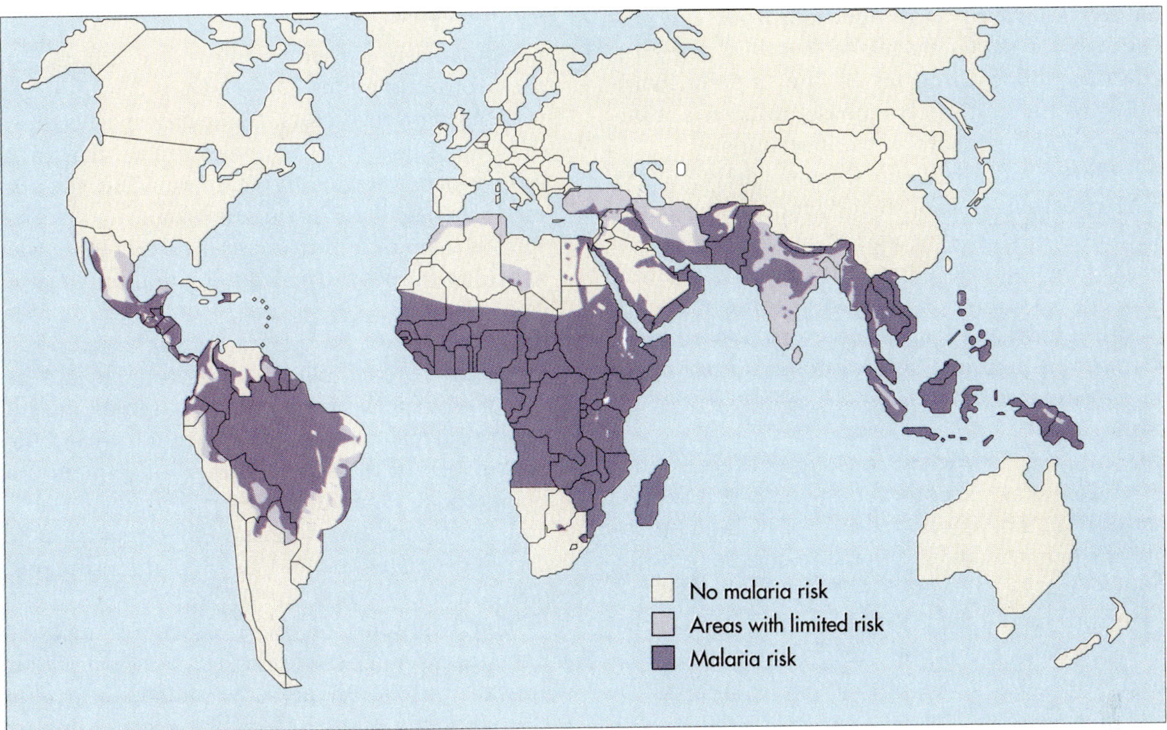

FIG. 12-30 Malaria is one of the most prevalent infectious diseases in the world. It occurs primarily in tropical and subtropical regions.

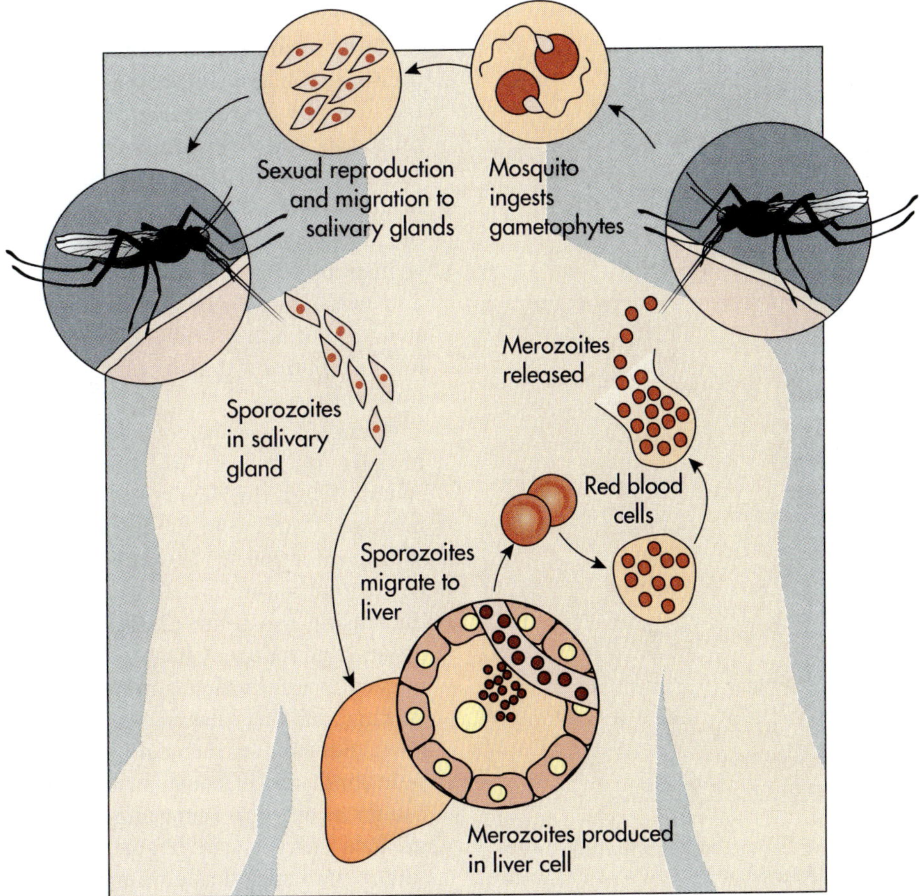

FIG. 12-31 *Plasmodium* species that cause malaria have complex life cycles, portions of which are carried out in the mosquito vector. Within the human body, different stages of the malaria-causing protozoa multiply in blood cells and the liver.

asexual fission), in which a single sporozoite can produce as many as 40,000 progeny cells called *merozoites.* The invasion of erythrocytes by the hepatic merozoites begins the erythrocytic phase of malaria, causing anemia and other severe manifestations.

Symptoms of malaria begin approximately 2 weeks after the infection is established by the mosquito bite and include chills, fever, headache, and muscle aches. These symptoms appear periodically, generally lasting for less than 6 hours. Schizogony occurs every 48 hours with *P. vivax* and *P. ovale* and every 72 hours with *P. malariae,* resulting in a synchronous rupture of infected erythrocytes that triggers the onset of disease symptoms.

Malarial infections persist for long periods of time and are rarely fatal, except when the disease is caused by *P. falciparum.* There is no vaccine for malaria but attempts are being made to engineer one genetically. The disease can be prevented by drug prophylaxis. Individuals traveling to areas with high rates of malaria, such as Southeast Asia and Africa, often use antimalarial drugs, such as chloroquine, to avoid contracting this disease. The use of insect netting and other measures to prevent being bitten by an infected mosquito is extremely important. In the United States, control measures have been effective, but periodic morbidity increases have occurred after overseas military ventures (FIG. 12-32).

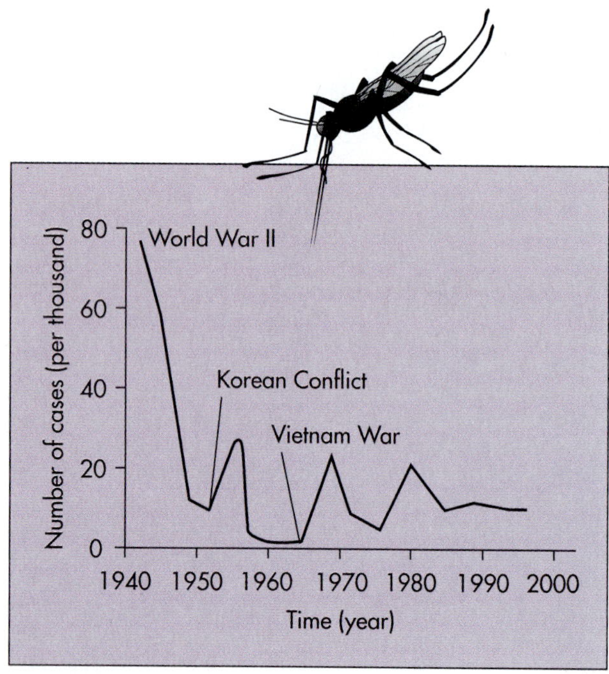

FIG. 12-32 Malaria in the United States is largely associated with the return of war veterans.

Leishmaniasis

Leishmaniasis, caused by infections with members of the protozoan genus *Leishmania,* is transmitted to humans by sand fly vectors. *Leishmania* species reproduce in humans and other animals intracellularly as a nonmotile form, the amastigote. In sand flies the protozoa exist in a flagellated form, the promastigote. The most serious form of leishmaniasis is caused by *L. donovani,* which multiplies throughout the mononuclear phagocyte system.

Leishmaniasis is geographically restricted to regions where sand flies can reproduce and acquire *Leishmania* species from infected canines and rodents. The protozoa can reproduce within the sand flies and are present in the saliva. Numerous soldiers who participated in Operation Desert Storm in the Kuwait and Saudi Arabian deserts were bitten by sand flies carrying *L. donovani* and developed Leishmaniasis after returning to the United States.

The symptoms of these infections, including fatigue, occasional fever, diarrhea, and anemia, did not appear until months after the soldiers returned to the United States. Many had differing symptoms, leading to confused diagnoses, especially because some of the veterans who returned ill had other diseases.

Trypanosomiasis

Trypanosomiasis is caused by infections with species of the protozoan *Trypanosoma.* American trypanosomiasis, or Chagas disease, occurs in Latin America and is caused by *Trypanosoma cruzi,* which is usually transmitted to humans by infected triatomid (cone-nosed) bugs. *T. cruzi* is a flagellate protozoan, but in vertebrate hosts it forms a nonflagellate form, the amastigote. Dogs and cats may be reservoirs of *T. cruzi.* The vectors of Chagas disease normally live in the mud and wood houses of South America. Therefore construction of better housing reduces the habitat for vector populations that brings them into close contact with humans.

When *T. cruzi* infects human hosts, the protozoa initially multiply within the mononuclear phagocyte system. Later, the myocardium and nervous system are invaded. Damage to the heart tissue occurs as a result of this infection. In 90% of the cases there is spontaneous remission, but 10% of the hospitalized patients die during the acute phase of the disease because of myocardial failure. Chagas disease is the leading cause of cardiovascular death in South America, and the incidence of this disease in Brazil is extraordinarily high. Several antiprotozoan drugs, such as aminoquinoline, are effective in treating Chagas disease if the symptoms are recognized early, but once the progressive stages have begun, treatment is supportive rather than aimed at eliminating the infecting agent.

African trypanosomiasis, also known as African sleeping sickness, is caused by infections with *T. gambiense* and *T. rhodesiense,* which are transmitted to humans through the tsetse fly vector. Tsetse flies acquire *Trypanosoma* species from various vertebrate animals, such as cows, that act as reservoirs of the pathogenic protozoa. Multiplication of the protozoa can damage heart and nerve tissues. Progression through the central nervous system takes months to years. If untreated, the initially mild symptoms, which include headaches, increase in severity and lead to fatal meningoencephalitis. If the disease is diagnosed before there is central nervous system involvement, it can be successfully treated with antiprotozoan agents, such as suramin. If there is central nervous system involvement, melarsoprol, an arsenical, is used. Prevention of African trypanosomiasis involves the control of the tsetse fly population, which is accomplished by clearing vegetation to destroy the natural habitats of the tsetse fly.

Diseases Transmitted Through Direct Skin Contact

In some cases, the deposition of pathogenic microorganisms on the skin surface can lead to an infectious disease. Some diseases transmitted in this manner are restricted to superficial skin infections. However, in other cases, the pathogens enter the body and spread systemically. Although relatively few microorganisms possess the enzymatic capability to establish infections through the skin surface, some microorganisms can enter the subcutaneous layers through the channels provided by hair follicles. The transmission of some *contact diseases* may follow minor abrasions that allow the pathogens to circumvent the normal skin barrier.

Warts

Warts are benign tumors of the skin that are caused by papillomaviruses, which are small icosahedral DNA viruses. Transmission of wart viruses appears to occur primarily by direct contact of the skin with wart viruses from an infected individual, although indirect transfer also may occur through fomites. The human papillomaviruses appear to infect only humans and no other animals. Children develop warts more frequently than adults. Warts can occur on any of the body surfaces; their appearance varies, depending on their location. At present there is no effective antiviral treatment for human warts, and therapy often involves destruction of infected tissues by applying acid or freezing. In general, warts are self-limiting and recovery can be expected without treatment within 2 years.

Leprosy

In 1980 there were about 3 million cases of leprosy, or Hansen disease, worldwide. This disease is caused by *Mycobacterium leprae.* There may be 1 billion viable cells of *M. leprae* per gram of skin in advanced cases of lepromatous leprosy, and prolonged direct skin contact appears to be very important in the transmission of this disease. There is an extremely long incubation period for leprosy, usually 3 to 5 years, before the onset of disease symptomatology. The symptoms of leprosy vary but the earliest detectable ones generally involve skin lesions. Unlike other mycobacterial species, *M. leprae* can reproduce within nerve tissues, damaging the nervous system by reproducing within certain nerve cells (Schwann cells).

During the course of leprosy, many organs and tissues of the body may be infected in addition to the infection of nerve cells characteristic of all forms of leprosy. In the tubercular form, relatively few nerves and skin areas are involved, but in lepromatous leprosy, multiplication of *M. leprae* is not contained by the immune defense mechanisms and the bacteria are disseminated through many tissues. Leprosy can be treated with dapsone, which is bacteriostatic, or rifampin, which is bactericidal. Prolonged treatment with antimicrobial agents is needed to control leprosy infections. Leprosy is rarely fatal, and complete recovery occurs after treatment in many cases.

Tinea

Various fungal species are responsible for several superficial infections of the skin called *tinea* or *ringworm* (FIG. 12-33). Many of the fungi that cause superficial skin infections are *dermatophytes;* that is, they infect only the skin and its appendages, such as hair and nails. These diseases are normally well localized and never fatal. The identification of the disease depends

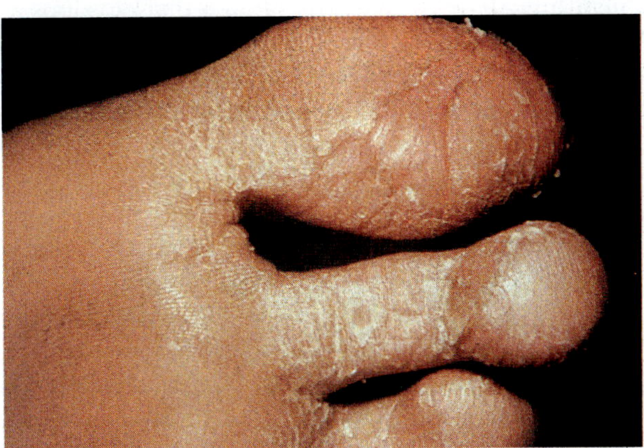

FIG. 12-33 Athlete's foot occurs when dermatophytic fungi infect the feet and grow on the moist skin surface.

TABLE 12-9 Epidemiology of Dermatomycoses

DISEASE	CAUSATIVE AGENT	TRANSMISSION	EXAMPLES OF SOURCES
Tinea capitis (ringworm of the scalp)	*Microsporum* spp., *Trichophyton* spp.	Direct or indirect contacts	Lesions, combs, toilet articles, headrests
Tinea corporis (ringworm of the body)	*Epidermophyton, Microsporum* spp., *Trichophyton* spp.	Direct or indirect contacts	Lesions, floors, shower stalls, clothing
Tinea pedis (ringworm of the feet [athlete's foot])	*Epidermophyton, Trichophyton* spp.	Direct or indirect contacts	Lesions, floors, shoes and socks, shower stalls
Tinea unguinum (ringworm of the nails)	*Trichophyton* spp.	Direct contact	Lesions
Tinea cruris (ringworm of the groin [jock itch])	*Trichophyton* spp., *Epidermophyton*	Direct or indirect contacts	Lesions, athletic supports

on which regions of the body are infected (Table 12-9). Most dermatophytic fungi are members of the genera *Microsporum, Trichophyton,* and *Epidermophyton.*

Transmission of dermatophytic fungi is enhanced by conditions of high moisture and sweating, and retention of moisture increases the probability of contracting superficial infections of the skin. The transmission of *athlete's foot,* for example, is often associated with the high moisture levels and bare feet of athletes in a locker room. Drying feet and using antifungal agents, however, can reduce the spread of this disease. It is virtually impossible to protect all body areas against potential infection with superficial dermatophytic fungi, resulting in a high incidence of dermatomycoses.

Nosocomial Infections

Medical procedures are designed to cure diseases, but some procedures used in the treatment of disease can inadvertently introduce pathogenic microorganisms into the body and initiate an infectious process. **Nosocomial infections** are hospital-acquired infections. Such infections include pneumonia that develops after surgery, urinary tract infections that develop as a result of the insertion of a catheter, and puerperal fever that develops from gynecological procedures (FIG. 12-34).

Serum Hepatitis

Serum hepatitis is caused by hepatitis B virus and hepatitis C virus (non-A, non-B hepatitis virus). An estimated 80,000 to 100,000 new cases of serum hepatitis occur in the United States each year. The incidence is much higher in Africa and Asia. The principal means of transmission of serum hepatitis involves exposure to contaminated blood or semen. There is a high rate of transmission of serum hepatitis among drug addicts, who frequently use contaminated syringe needles. Hepatitis B can also be transmitted sexually or by blood transfusions. Perhaps 10% of those infected with hepatitis B and hepatitis C virus become chronic carriers. The carrier rate of these viruses in blood donors in the United States appears to be between 0.5% and 1%, but in other countries it may be as high as 5%. It is estimated that there are 2 million carriers of serum hepatitis viruses in the world. The blood of an infected individual may remain infective for months or years.

The clinical manifestations of serum hepatitis may include the development of jaundice and generally are very similar to those described for hepatitis A infections. When the viral infection is transmitted through blood transfusions, the mortality rate associated with serum hepatitis is about 10%, reflecting the high dose of viruses normally transmitted via this route and the fact that the patient receiving the transfusion is in a debilitated state. One of the most important ways of preventing the transmission of this disease is to screen blood donors and to eliminate contaminated blood from blood banks. Avoiding the reuse of syringe needles among drug addicts also reduces the spread of this disease.

The U.S. Food and Drug Administration has approved a vaccine for hepatitis B (Heptavax) produced from viral particles isolated from the blood of human carriers of the disease. This vaccine, made available in 1982, was the first completely new viral vaccine in a decade and the first ever licensed in the United States made directly from human blood. The production of this vaccine involves a 65-week cycle of purification and safety testing to preclude inclusion of intact infectious viruses or other undesired factors from the blood of hepatitis B carriers. The cost is about $100 for the three doses required to establish immunity. Several recent advances in genetic engineering, however, have made available a second-generation hepatitis B vaccine (Recombivax) at a considerably lower price. Hepatitis B vaccines originally were administered primarily to high-risk individuals, including health care workers and drug addicts, but are now routinely administered to newborns to prevent hepatitis.

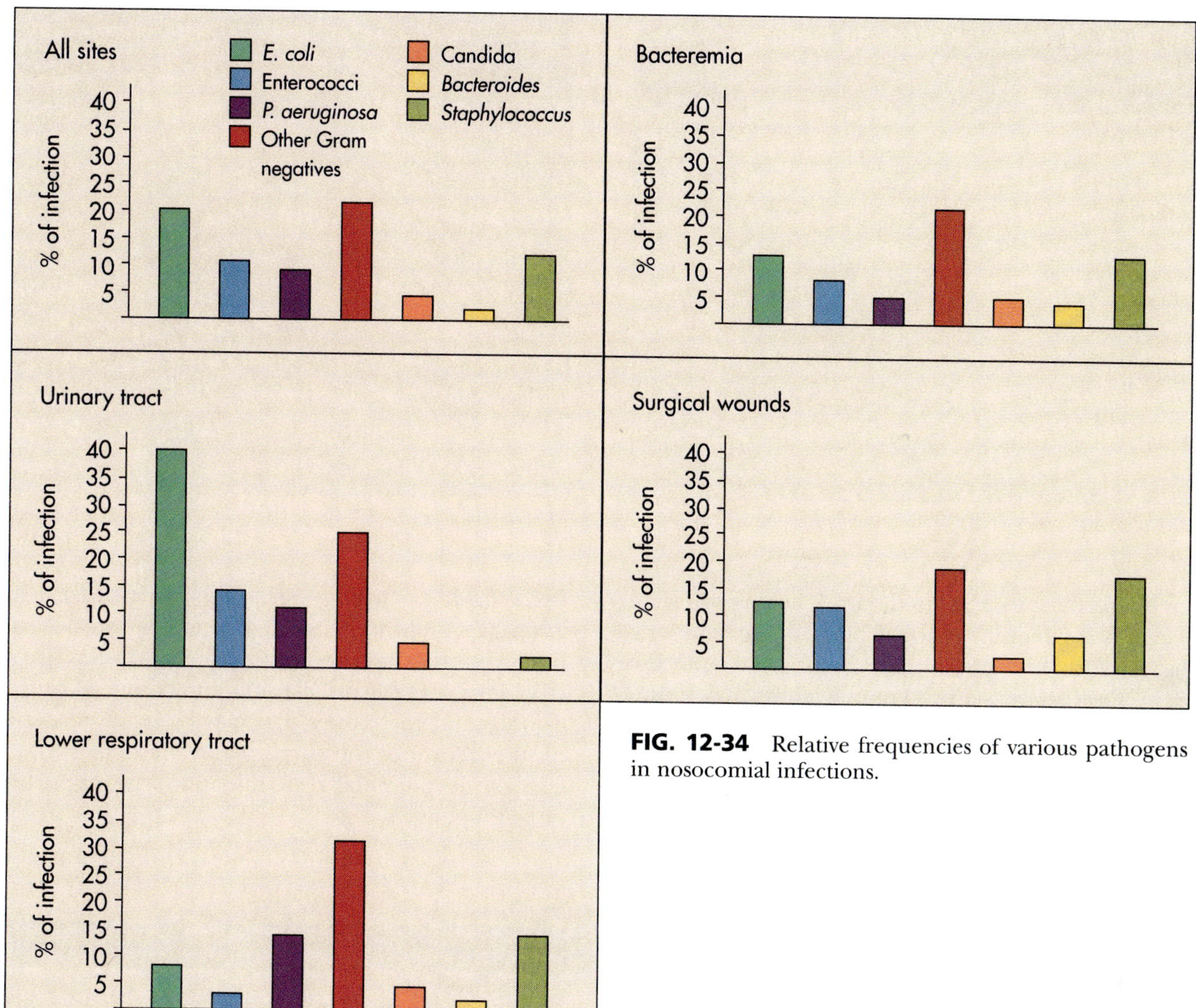

FIG. 12-34 Relative frequencies of various pathogens in nosocomial infections.

Puerperal Fever

Puerperal or childbed fever is a systemic bacterial infection that may be acquired via the genital tract during childbirth or abortion. The most frequent etiological agents of postpartum sepsis are β-hemolytic group A and B *Streptococcus* species. *Staphylococcus, Pseudomonas, Bacteroides, Peptococcus, Peptostreptococcus,* and *Clostridium* species, as well as other bacteria, can also cause this disease. The source of infection is normally the obstetrician, obstetrical instruments, or bedding. The bacteria causing puerperal fever are not normally part of the resident microbiota of the vaginal tract. Before the introduction of aseptic procedures, puerperal fever was often a fatal complication after childbirth. It remains an important complication following childbirth and abortion procedures; it was the leading cause of maternal death in Massachusetts in the mid-1960s. Penicillin is usually effective in treating postpartum sepsis. The use of proper obstetric procedures generally prevents this disease.

Post-surgical Infections

Surgical procedures often expose deep body tissues to potentially pathogenic microorganisms. A surgical incision circumvents the normal body defense mechanisms. Great care is taken in modern surgical practice to minimize microbial contamination of exposed tissues. These practices include the use of clean operating rooms with minimal numbers of airborne microorganisms; sterile instruments, masks, and gowns, all of which prevent the spread of microorganisms from the surgical staff to the patient; and the application of topical antiseptics before making the incision, to prevent accidental contamination of the wound with the indigenous skin microbiota of the patient. After many surgical procedures, antibiotics are given for several days as a prophylactic measure.

Despite all of these precautions, infections still sometimes occur after surgery (Tables 12-10 and 12-11). These infections can be serious because the pa-

TABLE 12-10 Bacterial Causes of Wound Infections Recorded at an Urban Hospital

BACTERIUM	FREQUENCY
Staphylococcus aureus	48%
Enteric and other bacteria associated with the gastrointestinal tract	49%
Escherichia coli	
Proteus spp.	
Klebsiella spp.	
Enterobacter spp.	
Bacteroides spp.	
Enterococcus faecalis	
Streptococcus pyogenes, group A	3%

TABLE 12-11 Some Factors in the Development of Surgical Wound Infections

SITUATION	*Staphylococcus aureus* (%)	*Enteric bacteria* (%)	*Streptococcus pyogenes* (%)
Emergency operation	10	21	1
In wound of second operation	11	12	0
First operation of day	17	16	0
Other	10	0	2
Total	48	49	3

tient is already in a debilitated state. The onset of such infections is generally marked by a rise in temperature. A purulent lesion may develop around the wound. Particularly serious complications may follow open heart surgery if the patient develops *endocarditis,* caused by *Staphylococcus* or *Streptococcus* species. In surgical procedures involving cutting of the intestines, the normal gut microbiota may contaminate other body tissues, causing peritonitis unless great care is taken to minimize such contamination and antibiotics are used to prevent microbial growth. The specific microorganisms causing infections of surgical wounds and the tissues that may be involved depend on the nature of the surgery and the tissues that are exposed to potential contamination with opportunistic pathogens.

CHAPTER REVIEW

STUDY QUESTIONS

1. How should you avoid exposure to airborne pathogens?
2. What is a vaccine?
3. How is vaccination used to prevent disease?
4. What is a portal of entry?
5. How are pathogens that enter the body through the gastrointestinal tract generally transmitted?
6. How do we control the transmission of waterborne and foodborne pathogens?
7. How are pathogens that enter the body through the respiratory tract generally transmitted?
8. How do we control the transmission of airborne pathogens?
9. What is a vector?
10. What are some of the common vectors of infectious diseases?
11. What is the difference between a foodborne infection and food poisoning (intoxication)? How is this difference reflected in the way we control different types of foodborne disease?
12. Name several viral, three bacterial, and three protozoan disease-causing organisms that enter the body through the respiratory tract.
13. What are some vector-borne infectious diseases?
14. For each of the following diseases, what is the causative organism, the reservoir for the etiological agent, and the vector for disease transmission?
    a. Plague
    b. Rocky Mountain spotted fever
    c. Malaria
    d. Endemic typhus
15. What is the etiological agent of malaria, and why is this disease difficult to treat?
16. Give some examples of sexually transmitted diseases and their causative organisms.
17. Why is it difficult to control the spread of sexually transmitted diseases, even though many of them are readily treated with antibiotics?
18. Name five diseases that are routinely prevented by the use of prophylactic immunization.

SITUATIONAL PROBLEMS

1. Expressing an Opinion on Government-Mandated Vaccinations

The introduction of vaccines, which started in the 1700s, was initially welcomed by the public because of the promise of the eradication of feared diseases such as smallpox. By the twentieth century, the vaccination of children against once deadly diseases, including tetanus, diphtheria, and whooping cough (pertussis), became routine practice in developed nations. Through the efforts of WHO, these vaccines were also introduced into developing nations, leading to the worldwide elimination of smallpox and better control of several other diseases. Within the past few decades, vaccines have been introduced that prevent various other diseases, including measles, mumps, rubella, influenza, polio, and others. The control of measles and polio in North America is particularly effective but requires constant vigilance to ensure that children continue to be immunized.

The effectiveness of a vaccination program depends on reducing the number of susceptible (nonimmune) individuals to such a low level that even if a case of the disease occurs it cannot spread because of the statistical improbability of a viable pathogen reaching a susceptible individual. To ensure that an adequate proportion of the population is immune to specified diseases, the governments of developed nations have instituted mandatory vaccination programs. Typically, proof of vaccination is required to attend school, making vaccination of children necessary.

In recent years, however, mandated vaccination has come under severe attack and sometimes public scrutiny. The problem arises from the fact that some children exhibit adverse reactions to vaccines. Particular problems have been encountered with the pertussis vaccine; a small proportion of children receiving the vaccine exhibit very severe side effects, including mental retardation and death. Requiring parents to have their children immunized with this vaccine, despite the knowledge that a small proportion will die or suffer severe illness as a result, raises serious ethical questions for the medical profession and the general public. These questions became frequent topics of debate on television talk shows and in Congress. Issues discussed include how to balance the interest of the health and welfare of the general public through the use of mass immunizations with the legitimate needs of individuals to whom immunization may be a threat or a violation of religious principles and the role of government in this aspect of public and personal health and safety.

Compose a letter to the editor of your local newspaper or to your congressional representative expressing your support of or dissatisfaction with government mandated vaccination. Consider the medical, ethical, and financial ramifications of your position.

2. When Should AIDS Testing be Required?

For many years, a blood test for the diagnosis of syphilis (the Wassermann test) was required in most states before a marriage license could be obtained. This requirement was based on the recognition that syphilis is a sexually transmitted disease, the presumption that protecting married couples would lead to the control of this feared disease, and the lack of adequate treatment methods. Unfortunately, the prevalence of extramarital sexual activity and the inadequacy of the most frequently used, now outdated, test failed to control the disease. With the introduction of a penicillin treatment that could cure the disease and the recognition that there are many other sexually transmitted diseases that were not being diagnosed, most states dropped the required blood test to obtain a marriage license.

Today, the fear of AIDS has caused some to propose that mandatory blood testing be required for various situations, including as a prerequisite for applying for a marriage license. The military services of the United States now require AIDS testing of new recruits. Various employers also are requiring such tests, and predictions are that over 5% of all new job positions will require such tests for all applicants. The American Civil Liberties Union and various other groups express concern that such required testing is an unwarranted infringement on personal rights.

Should AIDS testing be a requirement for employment, military service, or marriage? Under what conditions or situations do you feel AIDS testing should be required? Justify your position.

3. Trying to Help Find the Source of Diseases

If you have a job with the Department of Public Health in Peoria, Illinois, you might be in charge of recording the cases of infectious diseases as reported by local hospitals. These reports are forwarded to the Centers for Disease Control (CDC) in Atlanta. Although it is not specifically part of your job, you decide to try to identify the sources of the etiological agents for each of the diseases you report to CDC and to alert your supervisor to any cases where you feel steps should be taken on the local level to prevent additional cases of the disease.

a. One week after a family of four returned home after traveling to Africa, where they were on safari for 10 days, one of the children became quite ill, exhibiting periodic severe chills that recurred every 24 hours, serious muscle pain, and severe headache. When the pain was not severe, the child slept a great deal and, when awakened, was quite tired. None of the other family members exhibited any of these symptoms. The physician reported this as a probable case of malaria. What source of the disease would you

Continued.

SITUATIONAL PROBLEMS—cont'd

suspect, and would you recommend any local precautionary steps to preclude the development of additional cases?

b. Five men from an investment group traveled to Panama on a business trip. They stayed at a five-star hotel that had excellent restaurants and a chlorinated water supply. They all ate the same meals. Shortly after their return, one of the men found that he had little appetite. After eating very little for a day, he developed symptoms of nausea, vomiting, and fever. The next day he was jaundiced. The symptoms lasted for about a week, after which he exhibited a full recovery. The physician reported this as a probable case of yellow fever. What source of the disease would you suspect, and would you recommend any local precautionary steps to preclude the development of additional cases?

c. Because of injuries sustained in an automobile accident, a woman required transfusions with 2 units of blood. During her recovery, she developed a fever that oscillated daily for a week and then disappeared. She showed no sign of pneumonia. Just before her body temperature returned to normal, she started to experience abdominal pain and nausea. A few days later, she showed yellowing of the skin. Elevated levels of transaminases were detected in her blood at this time. Five days later, she died. The physician reported this as a probable case of hepatitis. What source of the disease would you suspect, and would you recommend any local precautionary steps to preclude the development of additional cases?

Suggested Supplementary Readings

Anderson RM and RM May: 1992. Understanding the AIDS pandemic, *Scientific American* 266(5):58-67.

Aral SO and K Holmes: 1991. Sexually transmitted diseases in the AIDS era, *Scientific American* 264(2):62-69.

Axnick KJ and M Yarbrough: 1984. *Infection Control: An Integrated Approach,* C. V. Mosby Co., St. Louis.

Ayliffe GA and LJ Taylor: 1982. *Hospital Acquired Infections: Principles and Prevention,* John Wright-PSG, Littleton, MA.

Balows A: 1991. *Manual of Clinical Microbiology,* ed. 5, American Society for Microbiology, Washington, D. C.

Baron EJ, LR Peterson, SM Finegold: 1994. *Bailey and Scott's Diagnostic Microbiology,* C. V. Mosby Co., St. Louis.

Broome CV and RR Facklam: 1981. Epidemiology of clinically significant isolates of *Streptococcus pneumoniae, Review of Infectious Diseases* 3:277-80.

Brown F: 1984. Synthetic viral vaccines, *Annual Review of Microbiology* 38:221-236.

Cohen ML and RV Tauxe: 1986. Drug-resistant *Salmonella* in the United States: An epidemiological perspective, *Science* 234:964-969.

Curran JW, WM Morgan, AM Hardy, HW Jaffe, WR Dowdle: 1985. The epidemiology of AIDS: Current status and future prospects, *Science* 229:1352-1357.

Evans AS and PS Brachman: 1991. *Bacterial Infections of Humans,* Plenum Publishing Corp. New York.

Glass RI: 1986. New prospects for epidemiological investigations, *Science* 234:951-955.

Habicht GS, G Beck, JL Benach: 1987. Lyme disease, *Scientific American* 257(1):78-83.

Hensyl WR (ed.): 1990. *Stedman's Medical Dictionary,* ed. 25, Williams and Wilkins, Baltimore, MD.

Heyward WL and JW Curran: 1988. The epidemiology of AIDS in the U. S., *Scientific American* 259(4):72-81.

Kahn HA: 1983. *An Introduction to Epidemiologic Methods,* Oxford University Press, New York.

Koneman EW, SD Allen, VR Dowell Jr, HM Sommers (eds.): 1983. *Color Atlas and Textbook of Diagnostic Microbiology,* J.B. Lippincott Co., Philadelphia.

Lennette EH, A Balows, WJ Hausler Jr, JP Truant (eds.): 1986. *Manual of Clinical Microbiology,* American Society for Microbiology, Washington, D.C.

Mandell GL, RG Douglas Jr, JE Bennett: 1985. *Anti-Infective Therapy,* John Wiley & Sons, Inc., New York.

Mann JM, J Chin, P Piot, T Quinn: 1988. The international epidemiology of AIDS, *Scientific American* 259(4):82-89.

Mausner JS and S Kramer: 1985. *Epidemiology: An Introductory Text,* ed. 2, W. B. Saunders, Philadelphia.

McConkey GA, AP Waters, TR McCutchan: 1990. The generation of genetic diversity in malaria parasites, *Annual Review of Microbiology* 44:479-498.

Milgrom F, CJ Abeyounis, K Kano (eds.): 1981. *Principles of Immunological Diagnosis in Medicine,* Lea & Febiger, Philadelphia.

Mills J and H Masur: 1990. AIDS-related infections, *Scientific American* 263(2):50-59.

Rose NR, and H Friedman (eds.): 1986. *Manual of Clinical Immunology,* American Society for Microbiology, Washington, D.C.

Tyrrell DAJ: 1988. Hot news for the common cold, *Annual Review of Microbiology* 42:35-48.

Winkler WG and K Bogel: 1992. Control of rabies in wildlife, *Scientific American* 266(6):86-93.

Zuckerman AJ, JE Banatvala, JR Pattison: 1987. *Principles and Practice of Clinical Virology,* John Wiley & Sons, Inc., New York.

CHAPTER 13

Pathogenesis of Infectious Diseases

Chapter Outline

Pathogenic microorganisms cause diseases because the growth of the pathogen in the body or toxins produced by the pathogen disrupt normal body functions. Pathogens have intrinsic properties that contribute to their potential for causing human disease. Virulence depends on the ability of the pathogens to invade body tissues and to produce toxins. Pathogenicity (the ability to cause disease), however, is not a property of the microorganism alone; the simple presence of an organism does not equal disease. The invasion or infection of the body by a microorganism, even by a pathogen that typically causes disease, results in disease only when the infecting microorganism disrupts normal body functions. In some cases, infections with potentially pathogenic microorganisms do not lead to disease because their ability to affect body functions adversely is not fully expressed. Many healthy individuals are carriers of potentially pathogenic microorganisms, that is, they are infected with the microorganisms but will not or have not developed a disease as a result of the infection.

13.1 INFECTION AND DISEASE

Infectious diseases begin when microorganisms enter the body and reproduce or replicate. The term **infection** describes the growth or replication of microorganisms within the body (Table 13-1). In some cases, an infection occurs at one site. In other cases, the infecting microorganisms become disseminated throughout the body.

The growth of microorganisms within the body does not always result in disease. Many microorganisms grow on body surfaces without invading body tissues or disrupting normal body functions. The normal microbiota of the body are usually not pathogenic but under certain conditions can become opportunistic pathogens. **Disease** results when an infection produces a change in the normal physiology of the body. Disease may also result if a toxin produced by a microorganism enters the body, as may occur if tainted food is ingested.

TABLE 13-1 Types of Microbial Infections

INFECTION	DESCRIPTION
Localized	Restricted to a confined area in the body
Systemic	An infection in which the microorganism spreads throughout the body
Primary	Caused by one type of microorganism; initial infection by a microorganism
Secondary	Caused by a microorganism as a sequel to a primary infection; occurs subsequent to first infection
Acute infection	Short and relatively severe infection (e.g., strep throat)
Chronic infection	Prolonged infection, in some cases pernament (e.g., pulmonary infections associated with cystic fibrosis)
Fulminating infection	Occurs suddenly and with great intensity (e.g., meningitis)
Mixed	An infection caused by two or more microorganisms
Subclinical	An infection that does not display any symptoms
Bacteremia	Indicating the presence of bacteria in the blood, usually transient
Septicemia	Indicating the presence of bacteria and their growth products in the blood
Viremia	Presence of viruses in the blood
Opportunistic	A microorganism that normally does not cause disease but after certain physiological changes in the host (diabetes, immunosuppressive drug therapy, AIDS) can cause infection
Nosocomial	An infection acquired while in the hospital

Virulence of Pathogenic Microorganisms

Disease-causing microorganisms **(pathogens)** possess properties, referred to as **virulence factors,** that enhance their pathogenicity and allow them to colonize or to invade human tissues and disrupt normal body functions. **Pathogenicity** refers to the qualitative ability of a microorganism to cause disease; **virulence** quantitatively describes the extent of a microorganism's ability to cause disease. The term *virulence* is derived from the Latin *virulentia,* meaning poison. The establishment of a microbially caused disease is a function of the virulence of the particular microorganism, the dosage (numbers) of that microorganism, and the resistance of the host individual.

Invasiveness

Pathogenicity depends in part on the ability of a microorganism to establish an infection within the body. **Invasiveness** refers to the ability of microorganisms to invade human cells and tissues and to multiply on or within them, that is, to establish an *infection* within the body. Most of the microorganisms of the normal microbiota of humans do not invade the tissues on whose surfaces they grow. Microorganisms that possess invasive properties are able to establish infections within host cells and tissues. Invasive microorganisms may destroy the tissues they infect. *Streptococcus pneumoniae* is an example of a pathogen that is highly invasive. The source of its virulence is its ability to disseminate rapidly throughout the lung.

Toxigenicity

The virulence of many pathogens is due to the production of substances, known as **toxins,** that disrupt the normal functions of cells or are generally destructive to human cells and tissues (Table 13-2). Some toxin-producing microorganisms can grow outside of the host and still cause disease symptoms if the toxins enter human tissues. These toxin-producing strains need not establish an infection within the human body to cause disease. *Clostridium botulinum* grows in some foods, producing botulism toxin that, if ingested, is almost always lethal. *Clostridium tetani,* which is only slightly invasive, moving little beyond the initial point of infection, is an example of a highly toxigenic pathogen. The toxin produced by *C. tetani* causes widespread effects at sites far removed from the site of infection.

Pattern of Disease

Signs and Symptoms of Disease

Reproduction of pathogenic microorganisms within the body often produces characteristic signs and symptoms that are associated with a particular disease (Table 13-3). **Signs** are objective changes, such as a rash or fever, that a physician can observe. **Symptoms** are subjective changes in body function, such as pain or loss of appetite, that are experienced by the patient. A characteristic group of signs and symptoms constitutes a *disease syndrome.* Often, the physician can diagnose a disease exclusively on the basis of the symptoms reported by the patient and the signs observed. In other cases, more elaborate laboratory tests are necessary to identify the cause of the disease.

In most cases, a microbial infection elicits an inflammatory response characterized by fever, pain, swelling, and redness. Although an inflammatory response does not necessarily reflect an infectious disease, an elevated body temperature (fever) is often considered presumptive evidence of a microbial infection. The physician observing a patient with a red, sore throat and fever assumes that the symptoms are the result of a microbial infection. In many such cases, when the presumptive evidence strongly indicates pharyngitis (infection of the pharynx), treatment is

TABLE 13-2 Some Toxins Produced by Pathogenic Microorganisms

MICROORGANISM	TOXIN	DISEASE	ACTION
Clostridium botulinum	Several neurotoxins	Botulism	Paralysis; blocks neural transmission
Clostridium perfringens	α-Toxin κ-Toxin θ-Toxin	Gas gangrene	Lecithinase Collagenase Hemolysin
Clostridium tetani	Tetanospasmin Tetanolysin	Tetanus	Spastic paralysis interferes with motor neurons Hemolytic cardiotoxin
Corynebacterium diphtheriae	Diphtheria toxin	Diphtheria	Blocks protein synthesis at level of translation
Streptococcus pyogenes	Streptolysin O Streptolysin S Erythrogenic	Scarlet fever	Hemolysin Hemolysin Causes rash of scarlet fever
Shigella dysenteriae	Neurotoxin	Bacterial dysentery	Hemorrhage, paralysis
Staphylococcus aureus	Enterotoxin	Food poisoning	Intestinal inflammation
Aspergillus flavus	Aflatoxin B_1	Aflatoxicosis	Blocks protein synthesis at level of transcription
Amanita phalloides	α-Amanitin	Mushroom food poisoning	Blocks protein synthesis at level of transcription

TABLE 13-3 Signs and Symptoms of Disease

SIGNS AND SYMPTOMS	MECHANISM
General aches and pains	Chemicals released from damaged tissue stimulate pain receptors in joints and muscles.
Localized pain	Chemicals released from pathogens or leukocytes stimulate pain receptors.
Headache	Chemicals released from tissue injury result in dilation of blood vessels in the brain.
Fever	Leukocytes release pyrogens that affect hypothalmus and cause rise in body temperature.
Swollen lymph nodes	Leukocytes release substances that stimulate cell division and fluid accumulation in lymph nodes. Some pathogens multiply in lymph nodes, which attracts phagocytic cells into nodes.
Rash	Leukocytes release substances that cause capillary damage and small hemorrhages; some pathogens invade skin cells and cause eruptive disease.
Localized redness and swelling	Pathogen damages tissues at site of infection and causes chemical substances to be released that dilate blood vessels (redness) and allow fluid from blood to enter tissues (swelling).
Nasal congestion	Pathogen (usually viruses) damages nasal mucosal cells that release fluids and increase mucous secretions.
Cough	Pathogen damages mucosal cells of the respiratory tract that release excess mucus; neural centers in the brain activate cough reflex to remove mucus.
Sore throat	Pathogens and leukocytes release inflammatory substances that result in swollen lymphatic tissue of the pharynx.
Nausea	Pathogens release toxins that stimulate neural centers.
Vomiting	Ingested toxins stimulate the brain's vomiting center.
Diarrhea	Toxins produced by pathogens cause hypersecretion of the gastrointestinal tract; some pathogens directly injure the intestinal epithelium; both toxins and pathogens stimulate peristalsis.

usually administered without rigorous clinical diagnosis and confirmation of the cause, even though it is appropriate to identify the etiologic agent by laboratory testing.

The relationship between a pathogen and its host is dynamic and varies depending on the physiological state of each. The extent of pathology varies greatly, depending on the microorganism and the physiological state of the host, that is, the properties of the specific microbial strain and the environment in which it may proliferate. Some microorganisms, such as influenza viruses, infect many individuals but the disease symptoms generally are not too severe. However, influenza can be a fatal disease in the elderly and in those who are physiologically debilitated. Rabies virus, on the other hand, causes severe disease symptoms and the death of infected individuals who do not receive preventive treatment because of the intrinsic properties of the virus, regardless of the age and general physiological condition of an infected individual.

Stages of Disease

The progress of any infectious disease in a given patient follows a characteristic pattern that occurs in distinct stages (FIG. 13-1). There is an **incubation period** after the pathogen enters the body and before any signs or symptoms appear. The incubation period varies in different diseases (Table 13-4). During this period, the microorganism has invaded the host, is migrating to various tissues, but has not yet increased to sufficient numbers to cause discomfort or infectivity.

The onset of signs and/or symptoms marks the end of the incubation period and the beginning of the

TABLE 13-4 Incubation Times of Some Viral Infections

VIRUS	DISEASE	INCUBATION TIME (DAYS)
Influenza virus	Influenza	1-2
Rhinovirus	Common cold	1-3
Enterovirus		1-3
Adenovirus		1-3
Myxovirus		1-3
Coronavirus		
Parainfluenza virus	Croup	3-5
Respiratory scyncytial virus		3-5
Dengue virus	Dengue fever	5-8
Herpes simplex virus	Cold sores	5-8
Poliovirus	Poliomyelitis	5-20
Measles virus	Measles	9-12
Smallpox virus	Smallpox	12-14
Varicella-zoster virus	Chickenpox	13-17
Mumps virus	Mumps	16-20
Rubella virus	German measles	17-20
Epstein-Barr virus	Infectious mononucleosis	30-50
Hepatitis A virus	Infectious hepatitis	15-40
Hepatitis B virus	Serum hepatitis	50-150
Rabies virus	Rabies	30-100
Papilloma virus	Warts	50-150
Human immunodeficiency virus	AIDS	365-3650

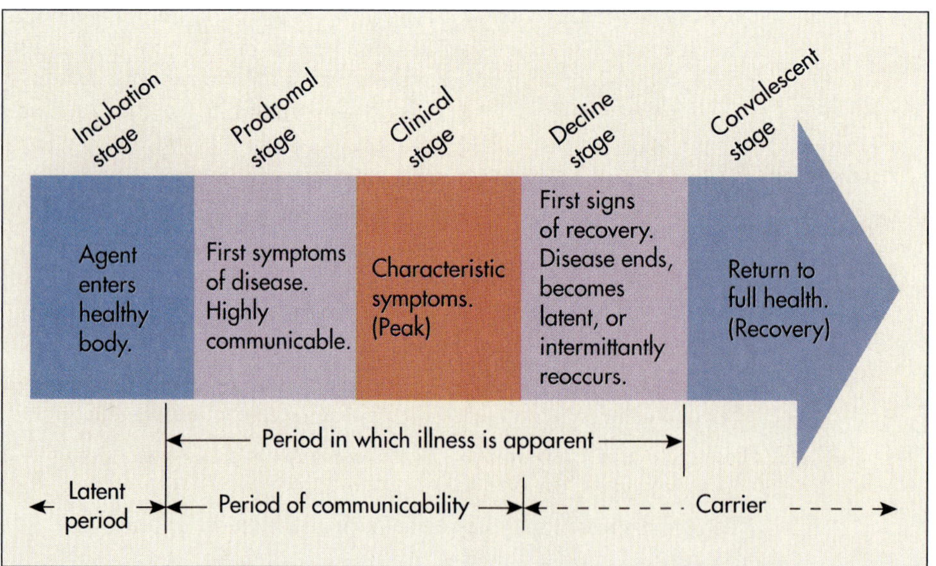

FIG. 13-1 Diseases progress through characteristic stages: from the prodromal stage following infection, during which the pathogen multiplies in the body, through the acute phase, when there are disease symptoms, to the recovery stage, during which the pathogen and disease symptoms are eliminated.

prodromal stage. Now the patient is aware of discomfort but does not have sufficient precise symptoms to permit the clinician to make a diagnosis. However, substantial replication of the pathogen has occurred to render the patient contagious to others. Moreover, the nonspecific inflammatory defenses have become operative.

The **period of illness** (acute stage) occurs next, during which time the disease is most severe. The various signs and symptoms that characterize the particular disease occur in this period. In *acute* diseases the symptoms and signs develop rapidly, reaching a height of intensity, and end fairly quickly. Measles, cholera, and influenza are all examples of acute diseases. In *chronic diseases* the symptoms persist for a prolonged period of time. The persistent cough of chronic bronchitis is typical of the long-term signs associated with a chronic disease.

During the **acute stage,** the patient often is sufficiently ill to alter normal work or school activities. Clones of B or T cells are being selected to initiate the immune defense. This phase of the disease progresses toward death or convalescence. Recovery depends on whether the immune system or medical treatments are adequate.

Assuming the disease is not fatal or chronic, signs and symptoms begin to disappear during the **period of decline.** Convalescence progresses to a carrier stage or to freedom from the pathogen. In some cases, the immune memory system may protect a person from recurrence of the infection for months, years, or life. Full recovery marks the end of the disease syndrome.

13.2 DIAGNOSIS OF INFECTIOUS DISEASES

Immunological responses of the body provide useful indicators that can aid the diagnosis of an infectious disease. Detection of antibodies to an antigen on a microorganism in an individual suggests that he or she is currently exposed or has been previously exposed to the pathogen. Alternatively, detection of specific antigens in blood, serum, or tissues by immunological techniques may indicate the presence of a pathogen. The clinical identification of a disease-causing microorganism often makes use of properties of that pathogen that contribute to its pathogenicity. For example, the selective media used in the clinical laboratory often include factors that mimic the conditions the pathogen would find in the body. In other cases, differentiation is based on the virulence factors of the pathogen, such as the production of specific toxins.

DIFFERENTIAL BLOOD COUNTS

Changes in the composition of the blood usually occur as a consequence of a microbial infection. An infection elicits nonspecific and specific immune defenses that are reflected in shifts in the relative quantities and types of leukocytes (white blood cells). Consequently, a **differential blood count** *(WBC differential),* in which the relative concentrations of different types of blood cells are determined, can be used to determine if a disease is caused by a microbial infection. The differential blood count further provides a general indication of the nature of the infecting agent, that is, if the disease is caused by a virus, bacterium, fungus, or protozoan.

A systemic bacterial infection is normally characterized by an elevated leukocyte count *(leukocytosis).* There is a progressive *neutrophilia (neutrophilic leukocytosis),* which is an increase in neutrophil cells; particularly, there is an increase in young neutrophil cells known as *stab* or *band cells* (Table 13-5). Compared to mature neutrophils, stab cells have a U-shaped nucleus that is slightly indented but not segmented. The increase in stab cells, indicative of neutrophilia, is known as a *shift to the left,* referring to a blood cell clas-

TABLE 13-5 Differential Blood Counts for Representative Bacterial Infections

	NUMBER (PER μL)				
CELL TYPE	NORMAL	SCARLET FEVER	APPENDICITIS	STAPHYLOCOCCAL SEPTICEMIA	TULAREMIA
Leukocytes, total	7,500	16,680	13,800	34,950	19,550
Basophils	0-1	2	0	0	1
Eosinophils	2-4	0	0	0	0
Immature neutrophils (myelocytes + stabs)	0-6	100	70	40	60
Mature neutrophils (segmented)	58-66	58	20	46	23
Lymphocytes	21-30	18	10	8	12
Monocytes	4-8	7	0	3	5

sification system in which immature blood cells are positioned on the left side of a standard reference chart and mature blood cells are placed on the right. The recovery phase of an infection is characterized by a reduction in fever, a decrease in the total number of leukocytes, and an increase in the number of monocytes. Gradually, the relative numbers of the various leukocytes return to their respective normal ranges.

In addition to systemic infections, some localized infections, such as abdominal abscesses, result in neutrophilia. Not all bacterial infections show this characteristic leukocytosis. Some, such as typhoid fever, paratyphoid fever, and brucellosis, actually result in a persistent depression in the number of neutrophil cells *(neutropenia)*. Many viral infections similarly result in lowered numbers of leukocytes *(leukopenia)*, particularly neutrophils. A general indication of whether a disease is of bacterial or viral origin, therefore, may be obtained by performing a leukocyte count and determining whether there is a significant shift in the quantity of neutrophils.

Changes in the quantities of eosinophils may also indicate the nature of the infection. The number of eosinophil cells generally declines during systemic bacterial infections. *Eosinophilia* (increased numbers of eosinophils) is symptomatic of allergic diseases and parasitic infections, including those mediated by protozoans. Thus the observation of elevated numbers of eosinophils is useful in the preliminary diagnosis of such diseases.

In some diseases, such as infectious mononucleosis, there are characteristic changes in the leukocytes (FIG. 13-2). In this disease, there is a transient leukocytosis because of an increase in B lymphocytes, which characteristically are enlarged (making them appear like monocytes) and show obvious changes in the nucleus, including the shape, size, and density of the nuclear region. These changes are useful in the diagnosis of this disease. A few microbial infections, malaria for example, result in decreased numbers of red blood cells *(anemia)*. Thus a simple examination of the blood often gives a preliminary indication of the etiology of a disease condition, establishing the direction of additional test procedures for positively identifying the causative agent.

Hypersensitivity Reactions—Skin Testing

Skin testing, based on delayed hypersensitivity reactions, can be used for the presumptive diagnosis of several infectious diseases. These tests, however, are merely *screening methods* used as diagnostic aids with regard to prior exposure to an infectious agent or antigen; they cannot be used for positive diagnosis of a disease. In skin testing, antigens derived from a test organism are injected intradermally. The development of induration within 24 to 72 hours is evidence of a delayed hypersensitivity reaction, indicating that the patient had previously been exposed and become sensitized to that specific antigen. A positive skin test may indicate an active infection caused by the organism from which the antigens are derived but it usually reflects an earlier exposure to that organism.

The classic skin test for a microbial infection is the *tuberculin reaction* for detecting probable cases of tuberculosis (FIG. 13-3). A purified protein derivative (PPD) extract from *Mycobacterium tuberculosis* is injected intradermally, and the area near the injection is observed for evidence of a delayed hypersensitivity reaction. A positive test results in *erythema* (reddening) and *induration* (hardening) of the skin, with the peak reaction occurring in 48 to 72 hours. A positive test is indicated when the diameter of the observed reaction is 5 mm or greater. This indicates active disease, prior exposure, or a false positive test due to cross-reacting antigen. The reliability of the tuberculin test depends on how the antigen is administered. In the Mantoux test, commonly used in the United States, an appropri-

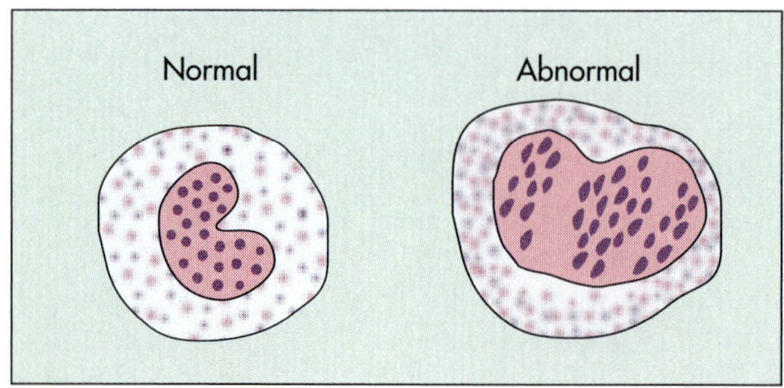

FIG. 13-2 During infectious mononucleosis the leukocytes exhibit characteristic changes that can be used to diagnose this disease. These changes are apparent in the cell size and morphology of the nucleus.

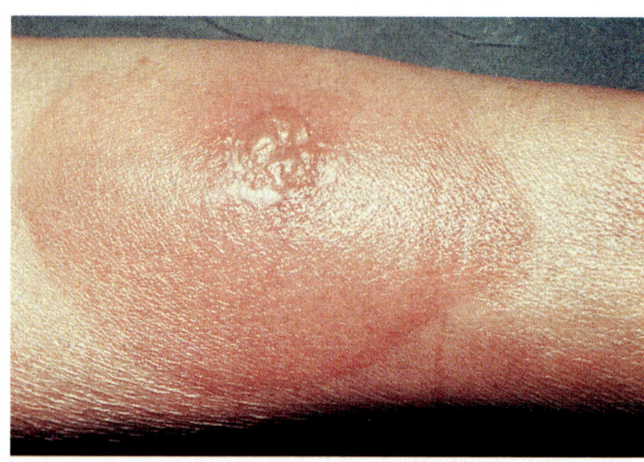

FIG. 13-3 The tuberculin test is used to diagnose potential cases of tuberculosis. The development of an indurated red area following subdermal antigen inoculation is characteristic of a positive tuberculin test.

ate dilution of PPD is injected intradermally into the superficial layers of the skin of the forearm. Other test procedures, including the once widely used Tine test, employ various mechanical devices and multiple punctures to expose the individual to the antigen. They are not as reliable as the Mantoux PPD procedure.

Similar skin tests are available for the diagnosis of coccidioidomycosis, using coccidioidin, an antigen derived from *Coccidioides immitis;* histoplasmosis, using histoplasmin, a crude filtrate from *Histoplasma capsulatum;* leprosy, using lepromin derived from *Mycobacterium leprae;* brucellosis, using brucellergen obtained from a *Brucella* species; and the sexually transmitted disease lymphogranuloma venereum, using lygranum from *Chlamydia* species. In many cases, skin tests are used to screen a population for individuals who are infected with a pathogen but who have not developed clinical symptoms; this procedure identifies persons for which additional rigorous test procedures should be performed. For example, tuberculosis testing is routinely carried out on schoolchildren to identify possible carriers of *M. tuberculosis.*

ANTIBODY TITERS

During the active phase of an infection, there is usually a rise in antibody titer against the pathogen, and this increase can be the basis of a diagnosis. When a pathogen cannot be isolated, the antibody titer to a suspected pathogen still can be measured as an indicator of disease. A series of dilutions of serum (usually twofold dilutions: 1:2, 1:4, 1:8, 1:16, 1:32, and so on) is set up and the highest dilution at which the antigen–antibody reaction occurs is determined. Diagnoses based on antibody titer are especially useful for many diseases caused by viruses. The development of the enzyme-linked immunosorbant assay (ELISA) and the use of monoclonal antibodies in particular permit highly specific, sensitive, and rapid serologic diagnoses.

ISOLATION AND IDENTIFICATION OF PATHOGENS

Determining that a disease is caused by microorganisms is only part of the job of diagnosing a disease. It is also necessary to identify the specific causative organism. When the cause of a disease is first investigated, one must identify the etiologic agent using an unambiguous procedure. For infectious diseases, Koch's postulates are used; these postulates, discussed in Chapter 1, permit the establishment of a cause-and-effect relationship between a specific pathogen and a particular disease. Once Koch's postulates are fulfilled and the causative microbial agent of a disease is known, a disease can be diagnosed based on the positive identification of that pathogen in the patient coupled with the observation of characteristic signs.

The definitive diagnosis of an infectious disease commonly requires the isolation and identification of the pathogenic microorganism or the identification of antigens specifically associated with a given microbial pathogen. Specific culture methods are used for the isolation and identification of the various pathogenic microorganisms. Traditional methods for the identification of pathogens depend on microscopic observations and the measurement of metabolic changes that occur as a result of the growth of the pathogen. Many differential media use color changes to show microbial growth. These growth-dependent methods provide rapid and reasonably accurate means of identifying the pathogen and diagnosing many infectious diseases.

Isolation and Culture Procedures

Various procedures are employed for the collection, isolation, and identification of pathogenic microorganisms from different tissues. Table 13-6, pp. 488-489, lists some examples of the different procedures that are required for the isolation of different types of microorganisms, and the clinical procedures designed to screen and facilitate the recovery of the etiologic agents of disease that predominate within specific tissues. When the manifestation of a disease suggests that the disease may be caused by a rare pathogen or routine screening fails to detect a probable causative microorganism, additional specialized isolation procedures may be required.

Upper Respiratory Tract Cultures For the isolation of pathogens from the upper respiratory tract, throat and nasopharyngeal cultures are collected using sterile cotton swabs. The cotton swabs are placed in sterile transport media to prevent desiccation during transit to the laboratory. These cultures are streaked onto blood agar plates—which were prepared by using defibrinated sheep red blood cells—and incubated in an atmosphere of 5% to 10% CO_2 for isolation of microorganisms. Human red blood cells are not used in the preparation of blood agar because the natural antibodies inhibit the recovery of bacteria, particularly *Streptococcus* species. Blood agar plates permit the detection of alpha hemolysis (greening of the blood around the colony) or beta hemolysis (zones of clearing around the colony). *Streptococcus pyogenes,* which forms relatively small colonies and demonstrates beta hemolysis on blood agar, is the predominant pathogen detected by using throat swabs and blood agar plates. The detection of β-hemolytic streptococci is important because the organisms can cause rheumatic fever. β-Hemolytic *Staphylococcus aureus* cultures, as well as any other hemolytic bacteria, may also be detected by using this procedure.

Haemophilus influenzae, Neisseria meningitidis, and *N. gonorrhoeae* can also be detected by using throat swabs and plating on various media. These organisms grow

TABLE 13-6 Some Procedures for the Diagnosis of Various Diseases

BODY PART	COLLECTION METHOD	CULTURE MEDIUM	ORGANISM	RESULT	DISEASE
Upper respiratory tract: throat and nasopharyngeal cultures	Sterile cotton swabs	Blood agar	*Streptococcus pyogenes*	Beta-hemolysis	Pharyngitis, rheumatic fever
		Chocolate agar	*Haemophilus influenzae*		Epiglottitis, meningitis
			Neisseria meningitidis		Meningitis
		Bordet-Gengou	*Bordetella pertussis*		Whooping cough
		Tellurite serum agar	*Corynebacterium diphtheriae*	Smooth, glistening gray-black colonies	Diphtheria
Lower respiratory tract	Transtracheal aspiration of sputum	Blood agar	*Streptococcus pneumoniae, Staphylococcus aureus, Haemophilus influenzae*		Pneumonia
		Chocolate agar	*Streptococcus pyogenes*		
		MacConkey agar	*Klebsiella pneumoniae, Haemophilus influenzae*		
		Stained smears	*Histoplasma capsulatum*		
		Sabouraud agar	*Coccidioides immitis, Candida albicans*		
		Lowenstein-Jensen	*Mycobacterium tuberculosis*	Buff-colored colonies	Tuberculosis
Central nervous system	Lumbar puncture for cerebrospinal fluid	Liquid enrichment media	*Streptococcus pneumoniae*		Meningitis
		Blood agar	*Neisseria meningitidis*		
		Chocolate agar	*Haemophilus influenzae*		

better on chocolate agar (a medium prepared by heating blood agar until it turns a characteristic brown color) than on plain blood agar. Thayer-Martin medium, which contains antibiotics, is preferred for the isolation of *N. gonorrhoeae* because the growth of normal throat microbiota is inhibited on this medium. Infection of the upper respiratory tract with these pathogens can lead to serious diseases—such as meningitis—if the infection spreads, making early diagnosis important. Also, *Haemophilus influenzae* may cause acute epiglottitis, the rapid diagnosis of which is important, because death can result within 24 hours. Nasopharyngeal swabs may also be used for determining the presence of *Bordetella pertussis,* the causative organism of whooping cough. The isolation of *B. pertussis* requires plating on a special medium, such as Bordet-Gengou potato medium.

When diphtheria is suspected, additional special procedures must be carried out. The presence of bacteria demonstrating typical snapping division (Chinese letter formation) indicates the possible presence of *Corynebacterium diphtheriae.* However, this is not a positive diagnosis because other bacteria with similar morphologies may be present. Usually, several media are employed in the culture of *C. diphtheriae.* Colonies of *C. diphtheriae* on tellurite serum agar (a medium used for the culture of *Corynebacterium species)* appear smooth, glistening, and gray-black. Gram stains prepared on colonies that develop on tellurite agar can confirm the presence of morphologically typical *C. diphtheriae,* giving an early indication of the presence of this bacterium before more rigorous identification procedures can be performed.

In addition to culturing for bacterial pathogens, throat swabs can be used to collect viral pathogens. The laboratory growth of viruses employs tissue cultures rather than bacteriological media. Primary rhesus monkey kidney cells are used most frequently for viral tissue culture. Antibiotics are added to the tissue culture to prevent bacterial and fungal growth.

BODY PART	COLLECTION METHOD	CULTURE MEDIUM	ORGANISM	RESULT	DISEASE
Circulatory tract blood	Renal puncture	Radiolabeled glucose medium Roll-tube streak anaerobic culture	Various		Septicemia
Urinary tract	Midstream catch of voided urine	Blood agar MacConkey agar, EMB agar	*Escherichia coli* *Klebsiella, Proteus, Pseudomonas, Salmonella, Serratia, E. coli,* and other Gram-negative rods	$>10^5$ bacteria/mL	Urinary tract infections
Genital tract	Urethral exudate (males) Swabs from cervix, vagina, and anal canal	Thayer-Martin medium and chocolate agar with inhibitors	*Neisseria gonorrhoeae*	Glistening grey colonies	Gonorrhea
Intestinal tract	Stool samples	Hektoen enteric media, xylose-lysine-deoxycholate media, brilliant green, EMB, Endo and MacConkey	*Salmonella-Shigella*		Dysentery, typhoid fever
Eyes and ears	Fluids	Blood, chocolate, MacConkey	Various		Conjunctivitis, otitis
Skin	Swabs, aspirates, or washings from lesions	Aerobic and anaerobic culture techniques	*Clostridium tetani, C. perfringens, Staphylococcus*		Tetanus, gas gangrene, impetigo

Viruses are washed from throat swabs by using appropriate synthetic medium such as Hanks' or Earls' basal salt solutions, and the solution is then added to tissue culture tubes or plates. The viral infection of the tissue culture cells normally produces morphological changes, known as **cytopathic effects** (CPE), which can be observed readily by microscopic observation. Some viruses exhibit a characteristic CPE that can be used in the identification of the virus, but in other cases, serologic procedures or electron microscopy are necessary to identify viral isolates.

Lower Respiratory Tract Cultures Isolating microbial pathogens from the lower respiratory tract is a more formidable task than culturing organisms from the upper respiratory tract. Sputum, an exudate containing material from the lower respiratory tract, is frequently used for the culture of lower respiratory tract pathogens. Unfortunately, sputum samples vary in quality and should, therefore, be examined microscopically to determine whether they are suitable for culturing lower respiratory tract organisms. Acceptable sputum samples should have a high number of neutrophils, should show the presence of mucus, and should have a low number of squamous epithelial cells. A large number of epithelial cells generally indicates contamination with oropharyngeal secretions, and such samples are not suitable.

To ensure the quality of lower respiratory tract specimens, transtracheal aspiration may be employed. In this technique, a needle is passed through the neck, a catheter is extended into the trachea, and samples are then collected through the catheter tube. An additional technique for collection of sputum is bronchoscopy in which a tube is passed through the pharynx into the lungs. Samples are collected by brushing or lavaging (washing) of the bronchial epithelium. Collection of sputum by using the transtracheal procedure or bronchoscopy avoids contact with oropharyngeal microorganisms so that the clinician is certain of the source of any isolates that are obtained.

It is important to know where the isolated strains originate because some microorganisms are not likely to be associated with disease when they occur among the normal microbiota of the upper respiratory tract, but if these same organisms are found in the lower respiratory tract they are prime candidates for the etiologic agents of disease.

The routine examination of sputum involves plating on appropriate media. For example, blood agar (an enriched medium), chocolate agar with antibiotics (an enriched and selective medium), and MacConkey agar (a selective and differential medium used for the isolation of Gram-negative enteric bacteria) are frequently used. The bacterial pathogens normally detected by using this technique include *Streptococcus pneumoniae, Staphylococcus aureus, Streptococcus pyogenes, Klebsiella pneumoniae,* and *Haemophilus influenzae* (FIG. 13-4). In cases of suspected tuberculosis and diseases caused by fungi, additional procedures are necessary. Examination of stained smears of the sputum are useful in detecting such infections. Yeast-like cells of *Histoplasma capsulatum, Coccidioides immitis,* and *Candida albicans* may be observable in such smears. In cases where these organisms appear to be present, fungal culture media, such as Sabouraud agar supplemented with antibacterial antibiotics, should be employed for culturing the suspected fungal pathogens. For the diagnosis of tuberculosis, the acid-fast stain procedure can reveal the presence of *M. tuberculosis* in sputum samples. Members of the genus *Mycobacterium* are acid-fast and appear red when stained by this procedure. Sputum showing presumptive evidence of the presence of *M. tuberculosis* should be cultured by using Lowenstein-Jensen medium—or other suitable medium that supports the growth of *M. tuberculosis*—for the positive diagnosis of this organism.

Cerebrospinal Fluid Cultures In cases of suspected infection of the central nervous system, cerebrospinal fluid (CSF) can be obtained by performing a lumbar puncture. It is important to determine rapidly whether there is a microbial infection of the cerebrospinal fluid because such infections (meningitis) can be fatal if not rapidly and properly treated. Several chemical tests can be performed immediately to determine whether a CSF infection is of probable bacterial or viral origin. Most bacterial infections of the cerebrospinal fluid greatly reduce the level of glucose, but viral infections do not alter the glucose level; this difference can be determined rapidly by measuring glucose and lactic acid concentrations in the cerebrospinal fluid.

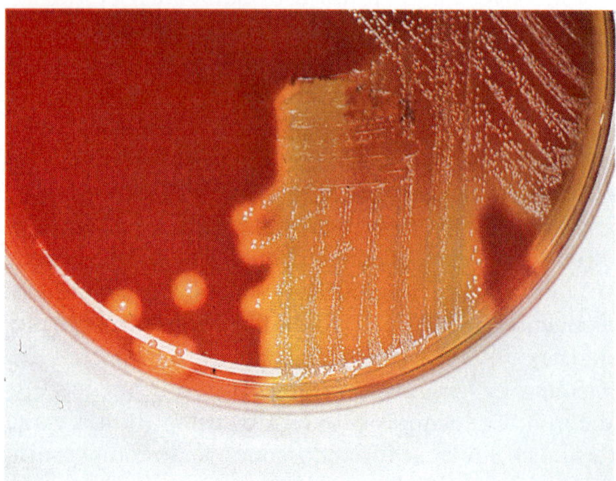

FIG. 13-4 Growth of *Streptococcus pneumoniae* colonies on blood agar showing α-hemolysis.

The cerebrospinal fluid can be screened further for possible bacterial infection by observing Gram-stained slides and by culture techniques. The growth of bacteria in a liquid enrichment medium can easily and rapidly be detected as an increase in turbidity. Cultures can also be obtained from CSF by plating on blood and chocolate agar. To provide a sufficient inoculum, the CSF is routinely centrifuged to concentrate the bacteria, and the sediment is used for inoculation. Bacteria commonly associated with cases of bacterial meningitis include *Streptococcus pneumoniae, Neisseria meningitidis, Haemophilus influenzae, Streptococcus pyogenes, Staphylococcus aureus, Escherichia coli, Klebsiella pneumoniae,* and *Pseudomonas aeruginosa. Streptococcus pneumoniae* and *Neisseria meningitidis* probably are the most frequent etiologic agents of bacterial meningitis in adults. *Haemophilus influenzae* most frequently is found in children but rarely occurs in cases of adult bacterial meningitis. It should be noted that various other microorganisms can cause meningitis, including anaerobic bacteria, fungi, and protozoa. Anaerobic bacteria can be cultured in thioglycollate broth or other media in the absence of free oxygen. Fungi and protozoa can be observed microscopically and identified by using both cultural and serologic test procedures. In cases of tubercular CSF infections, additional culture techniques are required for the isolation of *Mycobacterium tuberculosis.* Detection of neurosyphilis requires serologic diagnosis because *Treponema pallidum* cannot be cultured. In cases of suspected infections of the cerebrospinal fluid, rapid and accurate diagnosis of the infecting agent is crucial for determining the appropriate treatment.

Blood Cultures The detection of bacteria in blood is important in diagnosing various diseases, including *septicemia* (systemic bacterial infection of the bloodstream [blood poisoning]). For culturing bacteria, blood should be collected by venal puncture, using aseptic technique. The numbers of infecting bacteria in the blood are often low and may vary with time. Therefore it is necessary to collect and examine blood samples at various time intervals. For example, in respiratory infections, bacteria may follow a 45 minutes to 1 hour cycle of entry into the blood, removal, and

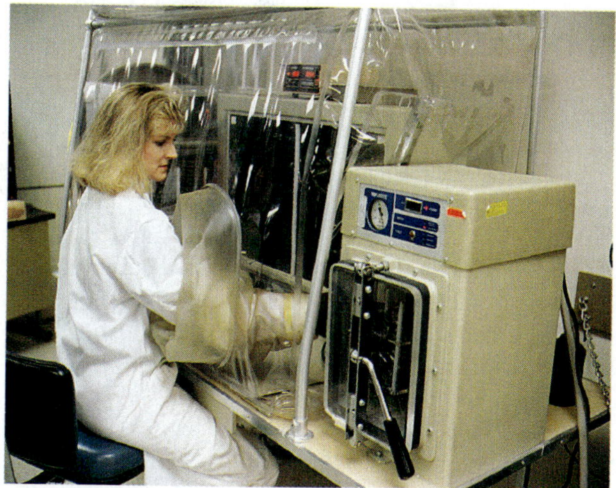

FIG. 13-5 An anaerobic hood is used in the clinical microbiology laboratory for the culture of anaerobes. The atmosphere in the hood is free of oxygen. Sealed gloves permit inoculation of cultures without exposure to air.

reentry. In contrast, in endocarditis, the numbers of bacteria in the blood generally remain relatively constant. Both aerobic and anaerobic culture techniques are needed to ensure the growth of any bacteria in the blood. There are several effective methods for isolating anaerobes to ensure that air is avoided, such as the roll tube-streak method. Anaerobic hoods are frequently used for transferring samples and culturing anaerobes (FIG. 13-5).

Another rapid screening procedure for the presence of bacteria in blood employs a medium containing radiolabeled glucose. The conversion of glucose to radiolabeled carbon dioxide is rapidly determined with great sensitivity by using automated instrumentation. Initial screening of the blood for bacterial contaminants can be accomplished in liquid media, aerobically and anaerobically, by using an assay such as increased turbidity as an index. Liquid media can also serve as an enrichment culture before plating on such solid media as blood agar, chocolate agar, and MacConkey agar. The blood sample should be diluted (blood:broth ratio of 1:10 or greater) and an inhibitor of coagulation and phagocytosis added to remove residual bactericidal factors in the blood. Additionally, if there was previous antibiotic treatment, the blood specimens may require further dilution, or an appropriate antibiotic inactivator may be added to permit growth of bacterial pathogens present in the patient's blood.

Urine Cultures To detect urinary tract infections, a midstream catch of voided urine is usually employed to minimize contamination with the normal microbiota of the genitourinary tract. Precautions are normally taken to avoid contamination with exogenous bacteria during voiding of the urine sample, for instance, by washing the area around the opening of the urinary tract. Urine, though, normally becomes contaminated with bacteria during discharge through the urethra, particularly in females. Therefore culture of the urine should be performed qualitatively and quantitatively. High numbers of a given microorganism are indicative of infection rather than contamination of the urine during discharge. In general, greater than 10^5 bacterial/mL indicates a urinary tract infection. Plating should be performed on a general medium, such as blood agar, and on selective media, such as cysteine lactose electrolyte-deficient agar (CLED), MacConkey agar, or eosin-methylene blue (EMB) agar. Bacteria of clinical significance that may be in the urine include *Escherichia coli, Klebsiella, Proteus, Pseudomonas, Salmonella, Serratia, Streptococcus,* and *Staphylococcus* species. Gram-negative enteric bacteria are most frequently the etiologic agents of urinary tract infections.

Urethral and Vaginal Exudate Cultures Examination of urethral and vaginal exudates centers on the detection of microorganisms that cause sexually transmitted diseases, most notably *Neisseria gonorrhoeae, Chlamydia* species, and *Treponema pallidum.* In males, one symptom of gonorrhea is painful urination and a urethral exudate. Gram-stained slides of the exudate are made, and if Gram-negative, kidney bean-shaped diplococci are present, this suggests a diagnosis of gonorrhea (FIG. 13-6). In females, gonorrhea is more difficult to detect because of the high numbers and variety of normal microbiota associated with the vaginal tract. Culture techniques using inoculation with swabs collected from the cervix, urethra, and anal canal can be employed for detecting *Neisseria gonorrhoeae.* Thayer-Martin medium incubated under an atmosphere of 5% to 10% carbon dioxide is employed for the culture of *N. gonorrhoeae.* Screening for pathogens

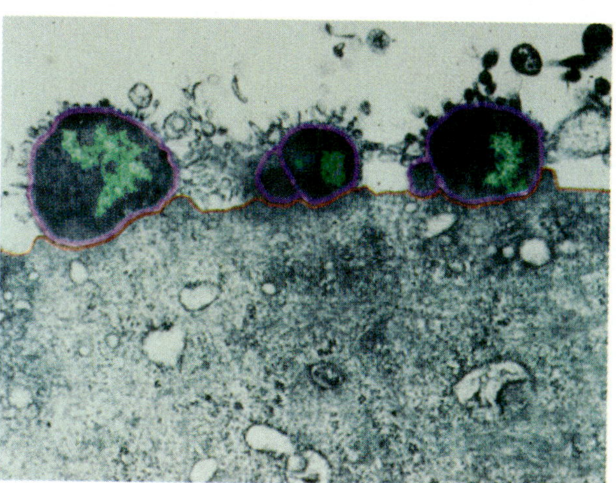

FIG. 13-6 Colorized micrograph showing diplococci of *Neisseria gonorrhoeae* on the surface of a human urethral epithelial cell.

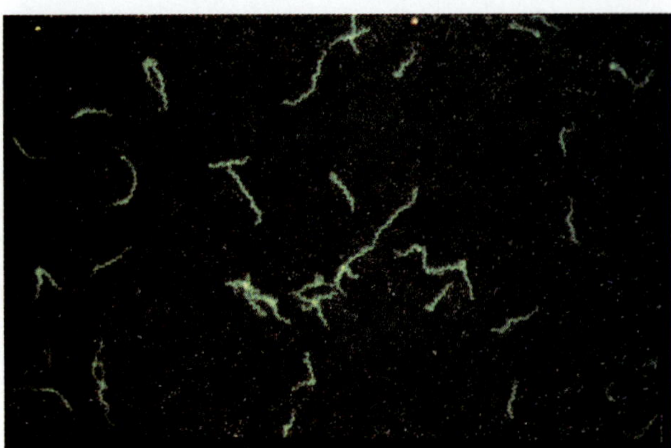

FIG. 13-7 Micrograph after fluorescent antibody staining showing the characteristically coiled cells of *Treponema pallidum* fluorescing green.

infecting the genital tract such as *Haemophilus ducreyi, Streptococcus pyogenes, Staphylococcus aureus,* and *Candida albicans* is accomplished by plating on blood agar, chocolate agar, MacConkey agar, and Sabouraud agar. *Treponema pallidum,* the causative organism of syphilis, cannot be cultured on laboratory media, but exudates from primary or secondary lesions can be examined by using dark-field microscopy and fluorescent antibody staining for the detection of *Treponema pallidum* (FIG. 13-7). The characteristic morphology and movement of spirochetes can be readily detected by dark-field microscopic observation but caution should be employed in the diagnosis because nonpathogenic spirochetes may also be present.

Fecal Cultures Stool specimens are normally used for the isolation of microorganisms that cause intestinal tract infections. The common enteric bacterial pathogens are *Salmonella* spp., *Shigella* spp., enteropathogenic *Escherichia coli, Vibrio cholerae, Campylobacter* spp., *Yersinia enterocolitica,* and *Staphylococcus aureus.* Because fecal matter contains numerous nonpathogenic microorganisms, it is necessary to employ selective and differential media for the isolation of intestinal tract pathogens. Usually, selective media contain some toxic compound that selectively inhibits some microorganisms, often preventing the overgrowth of pathogenic microorganisms that are present in low numbers by other more numerous microbial populations. Selective media contain components that select for the growth of particular microorganisms and inhibit the growth of normal flora. Differential media contain indicators that permit the recognition of microorganisms with particular metabolic activities. For example, pH indicators are often incorporated into media for the detection of acidic metabolic products.

Common selective and differential media that are employed for the isolation of intestinal tract pathogens include *Salmonella-Shigella* (SS), Hektoen enteric (HE), xylose-lysine-deoxycholate (XLD), brilliant green, eosin methylene blue (EMB), Endo, and MacConkey agars. A combination of a differential medium, such as MacConkey agar, and a selective medium, such as Hektoen enteric agar, is often used for the isolation of intestinal tract pathogens.

It is often necessary to carry out an enrichment culture before *Salmonella* and *Shigella* species can be isolated by using differential or selective solid media. For example, in cases of suspected typhoid fever, it may be necessary to carry out an enrichment in appropriate selective medium, such as GN (Gram-negative) broth or selenite F broth, before isolation of *Salmonella typhi* can be achieved.

In cases of suspected viral infections, tissue cultures can be inoculated with fecal matter for the culture of enteric viral pathogens. Characteristic cytopathic effects and serologic procedures can then be employed in the identification of viral pathogens. Additionally, electron microscopy and ELISA tests can be used for the direct detection of viruses, such as rotavirus, that cause viral gastroenteritis (FIG. 13-8).

Eye and Ear Cultures Fluids collected from eye and ear tissues can be inoculated onto blood agar, chocolate agar, MacConkey agar, or other defined media to culture bacterial pathogens commonly found in these tissues. Additionally, a Gram stain slide can be prepared and observed to identify the presence of bacteria. The microscopic observation of stained slides can indicate whether the infection is due to bacterial pathogens. In eye infections, it is particularly important to differentiate between bacterial and viral infections to determine the appropriate treatment.

Skin Lesion Cultures Material from skin lesions, including wounds and boils, can be collected for culture purposes with swabs, aspirates, or washings. Such material, though, often is contaminated with endoge-

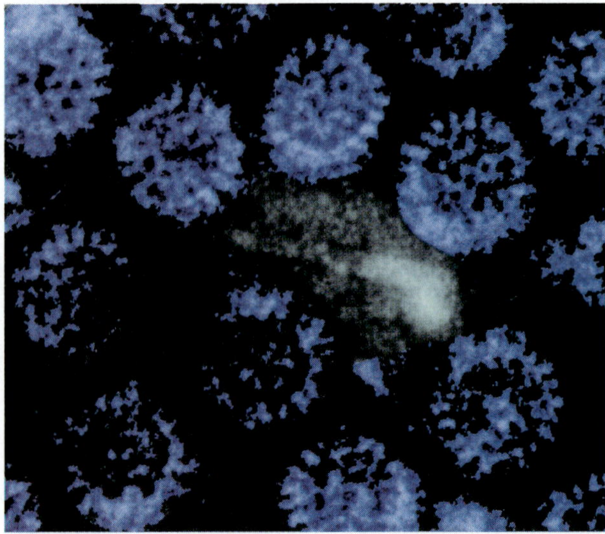

FIG. 13-8 Colorized electron micrograph of rotavirus from a patient with viral gastroenteritis.

nous bacteria. Various bacteria can infect wounds and cause localized skin infections. Both aerobic and anaerobic culture techniques are required for the screening of wounds for potential pathogens. Particular concern must be given to the possible presence of *Clostridium tetani* and *Clostridium perfringens* because these anaerobes cause serious diseases. Various fungi may also be involved in skin infections, and appropriate fungal culture media are required for the isolation of these organisms. Dermatophytic fungi and actinomycetes that cause skin infections can also be detected by direct microscopic examination of skin tissues because the characteristic morphological appearance of filamentous fungi and bacteria often permits rapid presumptive diagnosis of the disease.

Identification of Pathogenic Microorganisms

Several microscopic, metabolic, serologic, and gene probe procedures are available for the definitive identification of microbial isolates of clinical significance. Accuracy, reliability, and speed are important factors governing the selection of clinical identification protocols. The selection of the specific procedures to be employed for the identification of pathogenic isolates is guided by the presumptive identification of the organism at the genus or family level, based on the observation of colonial morphology and other growth characteristics on the primary isolation medium, and on the microscopic observation of stained specimens.

Metabolic Identification Various criteria are used to identify bacteria based on their metabolism. Bacteria are differentiated by the substrates they utilize and the products of their metabolism. Most clinical laboratories use miniaturized identification systems that permit performing about 20 tests simultaneously that can differentiate most pathogenic bacteria. Several commercial systems have been developed for the rapid identification of members of the family Enterobacteriaceae and other pathogenic microorganisms. These systems are widely used in clinical microbiology laboratories because of the frequency of isolation of Gram-negative rods indistinguishable except for characteristics determined by detailed metabolic or serologic testing.

Systems commonly used in clinical laboratories include the Enterotube II, API 20-E, Minitek, Micro-ID, Enteric Tek, and r/b enteric systems. The pattern of test results obtained in these systems is converted to a numerical code that can be used to calculate the identity of the isolate. The numerical code describing the test results obtained for a clinical isolate is compared with results in a data bank describing test reactions of known organisms. Some of the commercial systems list a series of possible identifications indicating the statistical probability that a given organism (biotype) could yield the observed test results. All of the commercial systems employ miniaturized reaction vessels, and some are designed for automated reading and computerized processing of test results. The systems differ in how many and which specific biochemical tests are included. They also differ in whether they are restricted to identifying members of the family Enterobacteriaceae or whether they can be used to identify other Gram-negative rods. The test results obtained with all of these systems show excellent correlation with conventional test procedures, and these package systems yield reliable identifications as long as the isolate is one of the organisms that the system is designed to identify.

The Enterotube II system contains twelve solid media (FIG. 13-9). Fifteen different metabolic characteristics of an isolate can be determined (Table 13-7).

TABLE 13-7 Metabolic Tests Used in the Enterotube II System

	VISUAL REACTIONS	
TEST	POSITIVE	NEGATIVE
Glucose fermentation	Yellow	Red
Gas from glucose	Bubbles	No bubbles
Lysine decarboxylase	Purple-blue	Yellow
Ornithine decarboxylase	Purple-blue	Yellow
Hydrogen sulfide production	Black media	No blackening
Indole production	Red ring	No red ring
Adonitol fermentation	Yellow	Red
Lactose fermentation	Yellow	Red
Arabinose fermentation	Yellow	Red
Sorbitol fermentation	Yellow	Red
Voges-Proskauer	Red	Colorless
Phenylalanine deaminase	Brown	Light green
Dulcitol fermentation	Yellow	Light green
Urease	Red	Light yellow
Citrate utilization	Deep blue	Light green

A

FIG. 13-9 **A,** Enterotubes for the identification of clinical isolates (*upper,* inoculated; *lower,* uninoculated).

Continued.

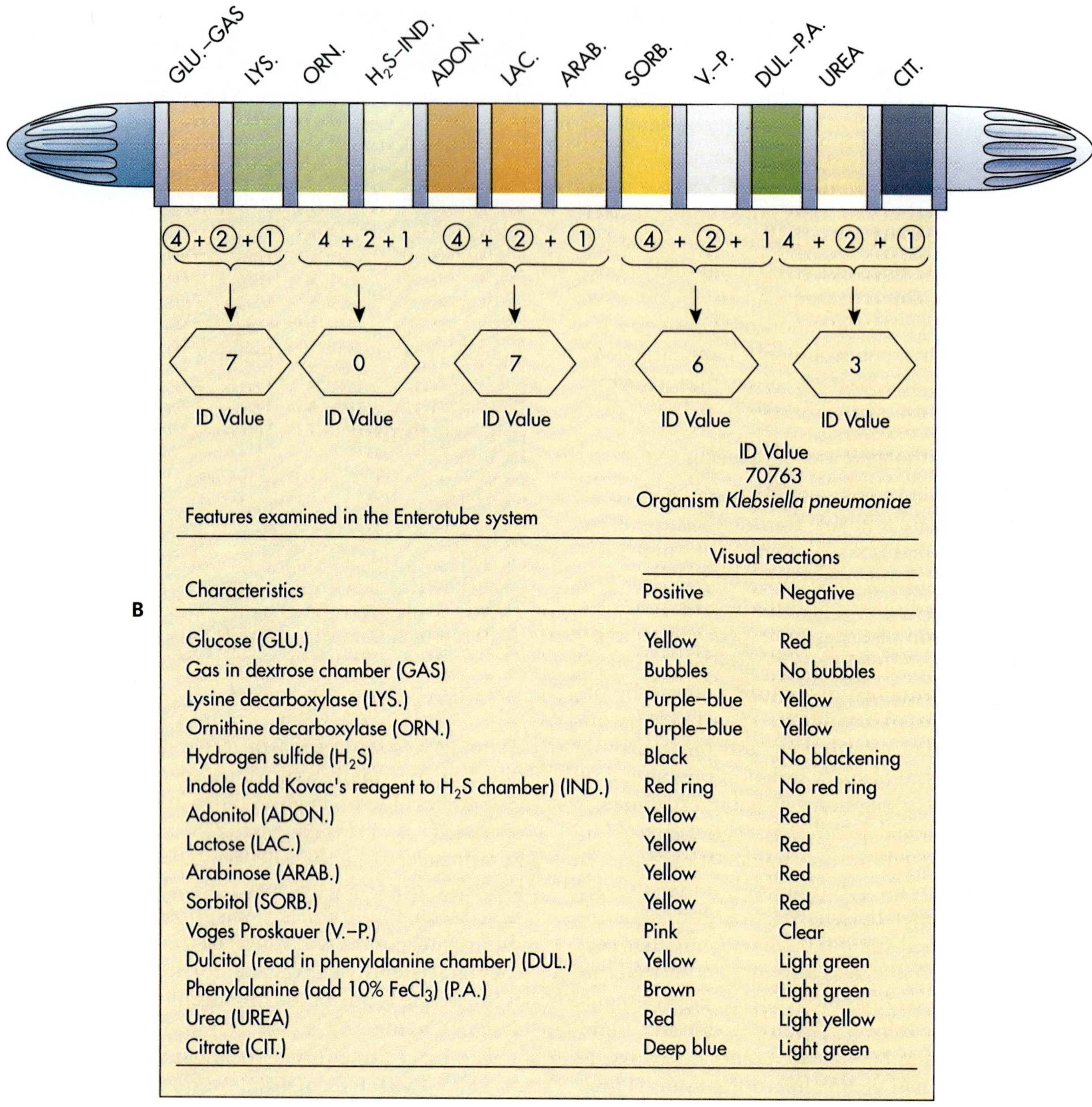

Features examined in the Enterotube system

Characteristics	Visual reactions: Positive	Visual reactions: Negative
Glucose (GLU.)	Yellow	Red
Gas in dextrose chamber (GAS)	Bubbles	No bubbles
Lysine decarboxylase (LYS.)	Purple–blue	Yellow
Ornithine decarboxylase (ORN.)	Purple–blue	Yellow
Hydrogen sulfide (H_2S)	Black	No blackening
Indole (add Kovac's reagent to H_2S chamber) (IND.)	Red ring	No red ring
Adonitol (ADON.)	Yellow	Red
Lactose (LAC.)	Yellow	Red
Arabinose (ARAB.)	Yellow	Red
Sorbitol (SORB.)	Yellow	Red
Voges Proskauer (V.–P.)	Pink	Clear
Dulcitol (read in phenylalanine chamber) (DUL.)	Yellow	Light green
Phenylalanine (add 10% $FeCl_3$) (P.A.)	Brown	Light green
Urea (UREA)	Red	Light yellow
Citrate (CIT.)	Deep blue	Light green

FIG. 13-9, cont'd. **B,** Reactions in the enterotube system for the identification of Gram-negative pathogens.

This system has a self-contained inoculating needle that is touched to a colony on the isolation plate and drawn through the tube. The characteristics determined in the Enterotube II are used to generate a five-digit biotype number from which bacterial identifications can be made. The identification is made by comparing the biotype number of an unknown organism with those of previously identified organisms.

The API 20-E system, as the name implies, uses twenty miniature capsule reaction chambers (FIG. 13-10). Twenty metabolic characteristics are determined in this system. A suspension of bacteria is used to inoculate each of the reaction chambers. The results of the API 20-E test system yield a seven-digit biotype number from which a computer-assisted identification can be made. The results of the API 20-E system can also be used in the identification of some nonfermentative, Gram-negative rods and for the identification of anaerobic bacteria. For the identification of nonfermentative, Gram-negative rods, six additional tests are run to generate a nine-digit biotype identification number. Over one hundred taxa of Gram-negative rods can be identified by using the API 20-E system.

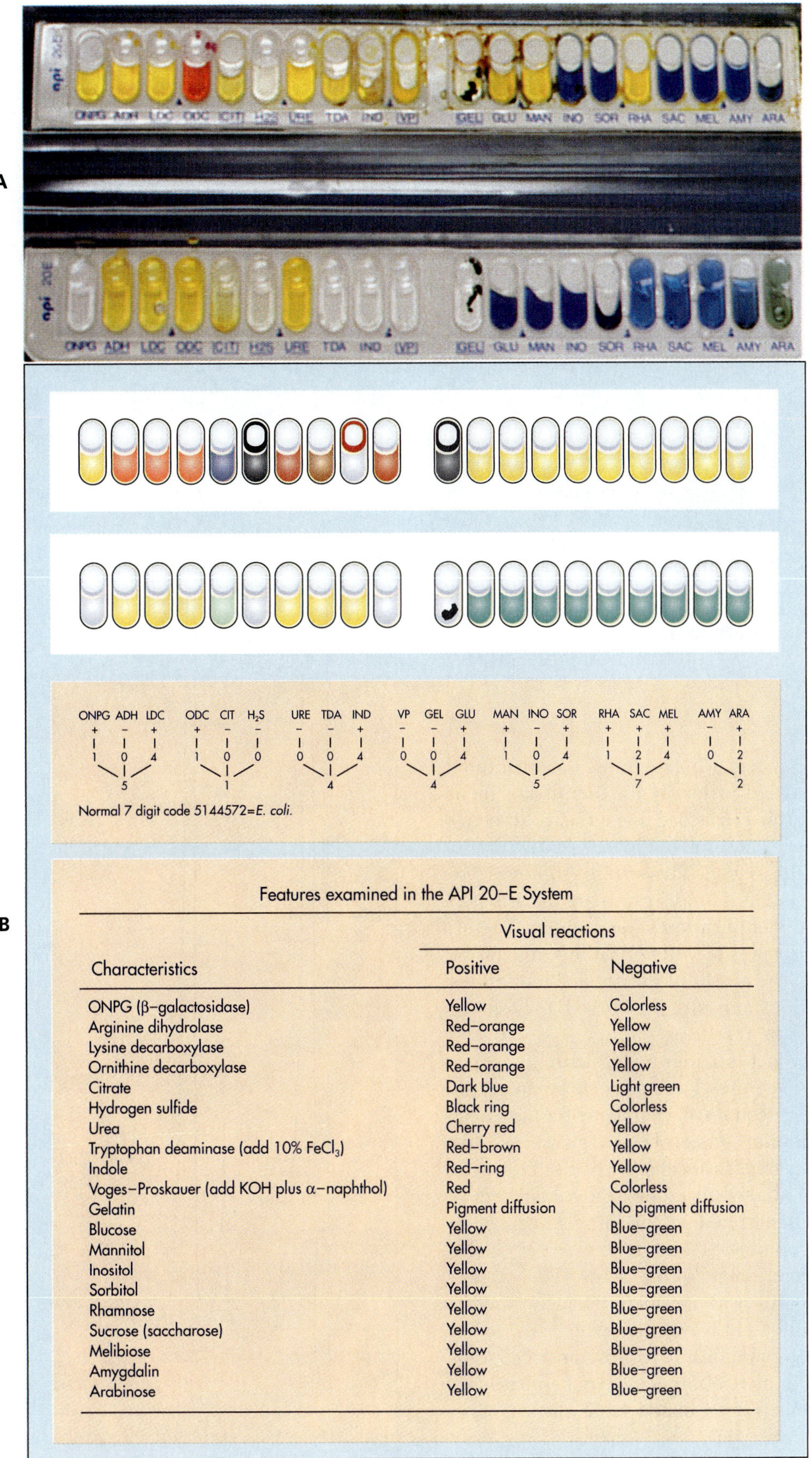

Features examined in the API 20–E System

Characteristics	Visual reactions: Positive	Visual reactions: Negative
ONPG (β–galactosidase)	Yellow	Colorless
Arginine dihydrolase	Red–orange	Yellow
Lysine decarboxylase	Red–orange	Yellow
Ornithine decarboxylase	Red–orange	Yellow
Citrate	Dark blue	Light green
Hydrogen sulfide	Black ring	Colorless
Urea	Cherry red	Yellow
Tryptophan deaminase (add 10% $FeCl_3$)	Red–brown	Yellow
Indole	Red–ring	Yellow
Voges–Proskauer (add KOH plus α–naphthol)	Red	Colorless
Gelatin	Pigment diffusion	No pigment diffusion
Blucose	Yellow	Blue–green
Mannitol	Yellow	Blue–green
Inositol	Yellow	Blue–green
Sorbitol	Yellow	Blue–green
Rhamnose	Yellow	Blue–green
Sucrose (saccharose)	Yellow	Blue–green
Melibiose	Yellow	Blue–green
Amygdalin	Yellow	Blue–green
Arabinose	Yellow	Blue–green

FIG. 13-10 **A,** API 20-E system for the identification of clinical isolates (*top,* inoculated; *bottom,* uninoculated). **B,** Reactions of the API 20-E system for the identification of pathogens.

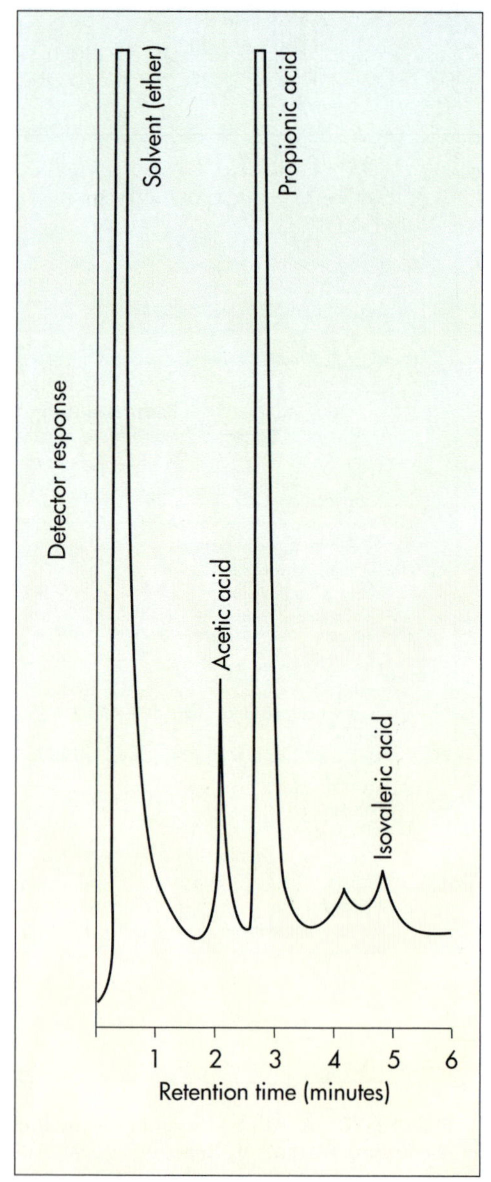

FIG. 13-11 **A,** Gas chromatograph for detecting diagnostic fatty acids in bacterial identification. **B,** Characteristic fatty acid profile used to identify anaerobic pathogens.

The Micro-ID system, which is based on constitutive enzymes, is designed primarily for identifying members of the Enterobacteriaceae. Bacteria are screened for oxidase activity, and only oxidase-negative strains are tested with this system. This system employs 15 reaction chambers, and the test results are used to generate a five-digit identification code number. The Micro-ID system lists possible identifications and probabilities based on the results of the 15 biochemical test reactions. Identifications with the Micro-ID system can be accomplished in as little as 4 hours.

Another approach for identifying pathogens, particularly anaerobes, uses gas-liquid chromatography (GLC) for the detection of characteristic fatty acids and other metabolites. Anaerobes are grown in a suitable medium and the short chain, volatile fatty acids produced are extracted in ether to identify them by GLC. Fatty acids detected in this procedure can include acetic, propionic, isobutyric, butyric, isovaleric, valeric, isocaproic, and caproic acids (FIG. 13-11). The pattern of fatty acid production can be used to differentiate and identify various anaerobes. When coupled with observations of colony and cell morphology and a limited number of biochemical tests, the common anaerobes isolated from clinical specimens can be identified.

Similarly, lipids of membranes of aerobic and anaerobic bacteria can be extracted and analyzed to give positive identifications. The Biolog System is based on the detection of specific patterns of fatty acids that are associated with the cytoplasmic membrane. This system, which is becoming quite popular, provides rapid and accurate identifications.

Serologic Identification Serum containing antibodies and purified antibodies can be used to detect bacterial antigens, viral antibodies, and viral antigens. Known (purified) antibodies and antigens can be used to detect antigens and antibodies in body fluids and tissues. Serologic tests are particularly useful in identifying pathogens that are difficult or impossible to isolate on conventional media and in identifying many varieties of pathogenic strains not easily distinguished by biochemical testing. For example, over 2,000 serotypes in the genus *Salmonella* are defined by the O (somatic cell) and H antigens (flagella), with each serotype defined by a constellation of O and H antigens. The identification of pathogenic viruses and nonculturable bacteria, such as *Treponema pallidum,* generally depends on serologic testing.

Viruses are very difficult to cultivate, and therefore diseases caused by viruses cause special diagnostic problems. Cell cultures detect the presence of some viruses but suitable cell cultures have not been developed for all viruses of interest. Most identifications of viral disease, for example, measles, rubella, or HIV, are based on the detection of viral antibodies in body fluids or tissues. Some viral infections, such as rotavirus, hepatitis B, and hepatitis C, are identified by the detection of viral particles or specific viral antigens. Because they can be used without culture, the use of nucleic acid probes and immunological reagents is increasing in the clinical laboratory for identifying viruses.

Gene Probe Identification Nucleic acid probes are used for the identification of some major microbial pathogens. Gene probes detect specific regions of DNA or RNA that are diagnostic of a specific pathogenic microorganism. Probe detection systems do not require culture of the pathogens and therefore can be used to identify pathogens directly from clinical specimens. Various hybridization procedures such as colony and Southern blot hybridization can be used. (See Chapter 6 for a discussion of hybridization methods.) Two advantages of gene probe identification are its speed and accuracy.

Before using gene probes it is possible to amplify (increase the number of copies) a region of DNA. Very sensitive and specific detection can be accomplished by using the polymerase chain reaction (PCR) to amplify a target DNA sequence before gene probe detection. This is accomplished using primers that flank the region to be amplified and a thermally stable DNA polymerase. (See Chapter 6 for a discussion of PCR.) The sensitivity of this method allows detection of a single pathogen in a specimen.

13.3 BACTERIAL TOXIGENICITY

Toxins produced by pathogenic bacteria cause discernible damage to human host systems and in some cases cause death. These toxins include the lipopolysaccharide toxins of the Gram-negative bacterial cell and the protein toxins produced by some pathogenic bacteria (Table 13-8). In the past, toxins

TABLE 13-8 Comparison of Selected Characteristics of Bacterial LPS Toxins (Endotoxins) and Protein Toxins (Exotoxins)

CHARACTERISTIC	LPS TOXIN	PROTEIN TOXIN
Chemical composition	LPS–lipid A	Protein
Source	Cell walls of Gram-negative bacteria; released after death and autolysis of the bacteria	Gram-negative and Gram-positive bacteria; excretion products of growing cells or, in some cases, substances released after autolysis and death of the bacteria
Location of genes	Chromosomal	Chromosomal or, more frequently, plasmid
Effects on host	Nonspecific	Generally affects specific tissues
Host receptor	Nonspecific	Specific
Thermostability	Relatively heat-stable (may resist 120° C for 1 hour)	Heat-labile; most are inactivated at 60° to 80° C
Toxoids	No	Yes
Lethal dose	Large	Small

produced by bacteria were classified as endotoxins if they comprised a heat-stable part of the microbial cell and as exotoxins if they were heat-labile proteins secreted by the cell. However, we now know that some exotoxins are not released until the cell is disrupted and that substances classified as endotoxins are sometimes released from the cell without lysis. Therefore a better classification system for toxins is one based on the biochemical nature of the toxin, whereby endotoxins are equated with lipopolysaccharide toxins and exotoxins are equated with protein toxins.

Lipopolysaccharide Toxin (Endotoxin)

The lipopolysaccharide (LPS) component of the Gram-negative eubacterial cell wall acts as a toxin. Because it is part of the bacterial cell structure it is called **endotoxin.** Although all Gram-negative eubacteria have LPS in their cell walls, LPS is not toxic unless it is released from the outer layer of the cell. When Gram-negative bacteria die, their cell walls disintegrate, releasing the **LPS toxin.** Some growing Gram-negative bacteria also release LPS toxin due to sloughing or "blebbing" of outer membrane; in these cases, the LPS can have a toxic effect on a host organism.

Toxicity is associated with the lipid portion of the LPS molecule, termed *lipid A,* which is composed of fatty acids, such as β-hydroxy myristic, attached by an ester or amide linkage to a diglucosamine-β-1,6 disaccharide (FIG. 13-12). LPS can trigger the complement cascade by the alternative pathway. In addition, endotoxin interacts with the blood clotting system via Hageman factor (factor XII). This may result in the inappropriate clotting of blood in the peripheral vasculature, called disseminated intravascular coagulation (DIC). The physiological effects of LPS toxins include fever, circulatory changes, and other general symptoms, such as weakness and nonlocalized aches. The injury to the circulatory system by LPS is basic to the action of this toxin but its mechanism of action is not fully understood. The effects of LPS toxins are generally the same for all species of Gram-negative bacteria because of the common nature of lipid A. Thus there are no specific characteristic disease symptoms associated with the endotoxin of a particular bacterial species. LPS toxins of *Salmonella* and *Shigella* species are responsible in part for diseases, such as

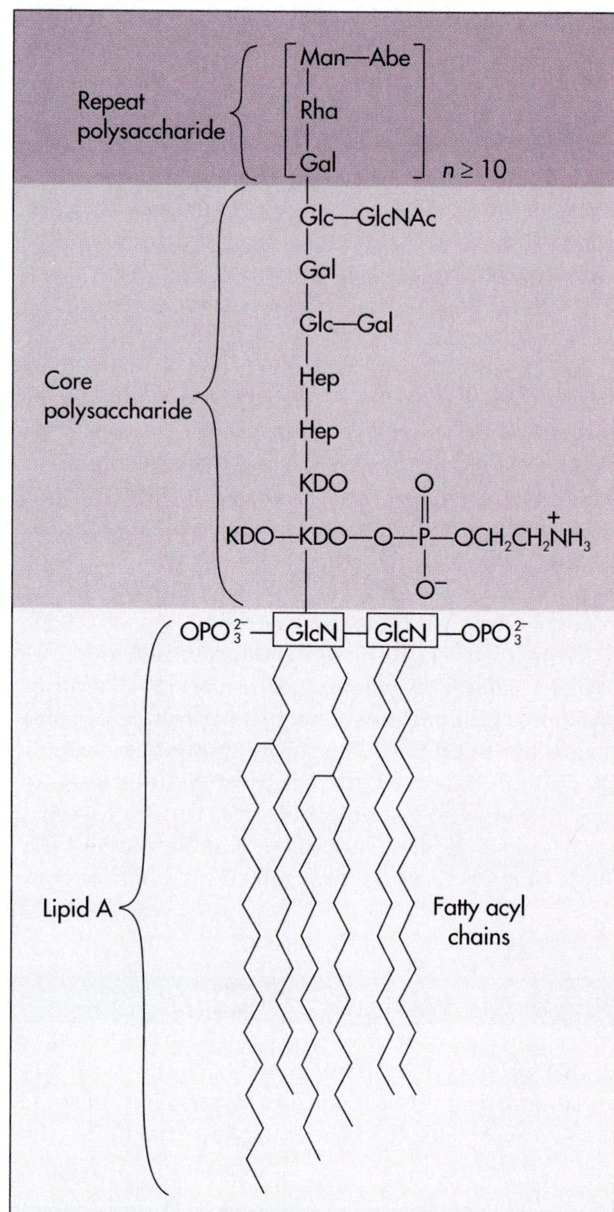

FIG. 13-12 Lipid portion of LPS that acts as endotoxin (*Abe,* abequose; *Man,* mannose; *Rha,* rhamnose; *Gal,* galactose; *Glc,* glucose; *Glc-NAc, N*-acetyl-glucosamine; *Hep,* heptose; *KDO,* ketodeoxyoctulosonic acid; *GlcN,* glucosamine).

BOX 13-1

Detection and Quantitation of Endotoxin

Endotoxin (LPS) can be assayed by the *Limulus* amoebocyte assay, which uses aqueous extracts from the blood cells (amoebocytes) of the horseshoe crab (*Limulus*). *Limulus* amoebocyte lysate specifically reacts with the lipid component of LPS, causing precipitation of the *Limulus* lysate, which increases the turbidity of the solution. The turbidity is proportional to the concentration of endotoxin and can be measured with a spectrophotometer. The assay is extremely sensitive and can detect less than 1,000 bacteria per milliliter of sample. The *Limulus* amoebocyte assay is used to detect minute quantities of endotoxin in serum, cerebrospinal fluid, water, and other substances. This assay is important in the diagnosis of Gram-negative bacterial infections of blood and cerebrospinal fluid.

gastroenteritis, caused by these pathogens, but these pathogens also produce protein toxins (exotoxins) that are largely responsible for their pathogenicity; for example, *Shigella* produces protein toxins that act on nerve cells.

PROTEIN TOXINS (EXOTOXINS)

In contrast to LPS toxins, the effects of **exotoxins** *(protein toxins)* are specific to the microorganism producing the toxin, and these toxins cause distinctive clinical symptoms. Most bacterial exotoxins are composed of a receptor protein component that attaches to a target cell and a toxic component that enters the cell and disrupts normal cell activity. Often exotoxins are referred to by the disease they cause, such as diphtheria toxin or botulinum toxin. They may also be categorized according to the symptoms they cause. As examples, neurotoxins affect the nervous system, enterotoxins cause an inflammation of the tissues of the gastrointestinal tract, and cytotoxins interfere with cellular functions. Whereas LPS toxins are produced exclusively by Gram-negative bacteria, protein exotoxins are produced by both Gram-negative and Gram-positive bacteria.

Protein exotoxins are more readily inactivated by heat than LPS toxins. A protein exotoxin can normally be inactivated by exposure to boiling water for 30 minutes, whereas LPS toxins can withstand autoclaving. Some enterotoxins, however, are proteins or peptides that are relatively heat stable. Typically, protein exotoxins are excreted into the surrounding medium. For example, *Clostridium botulinum,* the causative organism of botulism, secretes a potent exotoxin into canned food products, of which the ingestion of even minute amounts is lethal. Protein exotoxins are generally more potent than LPS toxins, and far smaller amounts are needed to produce serious disease symptoms than are required for disease symptoms due to LPS. Protein exotoxins are extremely potent: about 30 g of diphtheria toxin could kill 10 million people, and 1 g of botulinum toxin can kill everyone in the United States (over 225 million people).

Botulinum Toxin

Botulism is caused by neurotoxins (toxins that affect the nervous system) called *botulinum toxins* that are produced by *Clostridium botulinum.* Botulinum toxins are the most potent toxins known to humans. These toxins are neurotoxins because they bind to nerve synapses, blocking the release of acetylcholine from nerve cells of the central nervous system and causing the loss of motor function (FIG. 13-13). The inability to transmit impulses through motor neurons can

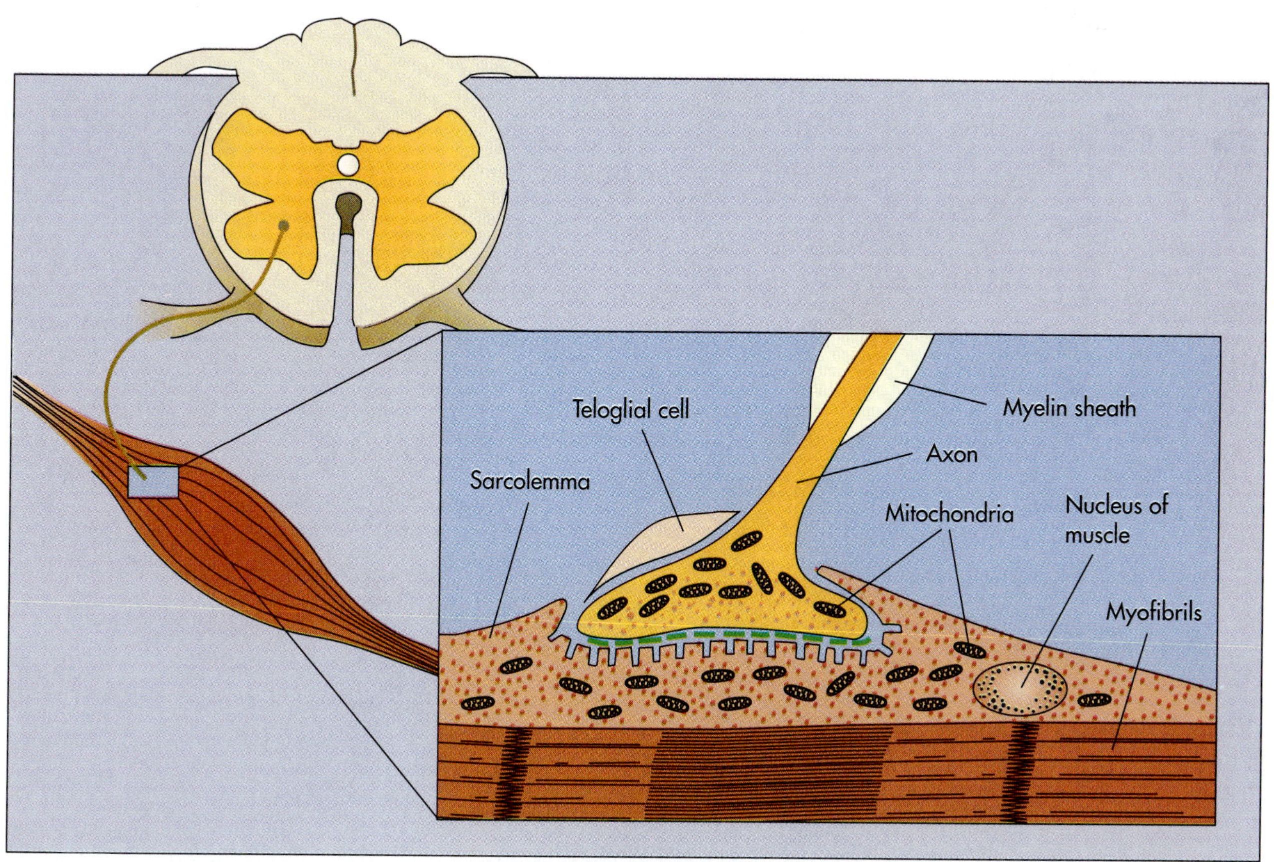

FIG. 13-13 Botulinum toxin blocks release of acetylcholine from nerve cells, causing paralysis due to blockage of motor neuron transmission.

cause respiratory failure, resulting in death. The toxins are absorbed from the intestinal tract and transported via the circulatory system to motor nerve synapses, where their action blocks normal neural transmissions.

Various strains of *C. botulinum* elaborate different botulinum toxins. Types A, B, and E toxins cause food poisoning of humans. Type E toxins are associated with the growth of *C. botulinum* in fish or fish products, and most outbreaks of botulism in Japan are caused by type E toxins because large amounts of fish are consumed there. Type A is the predominant toxin in cases of botulism in the United States, and type B toxin is most prevalent in Europe.

Symptoms of botulism can appear 8 to 48 hours after ingestion of the toxin and their early onset normally indicates that the disease will be severe. Type A toxin botulism is generally more severe than the disease caused by other types of toxin. In severe cases of botulism there is paralysis of the respiratory muscles, and despite improved medical treatment, the mortality rate is still about 25%. The use of trivalent ABE antibodies is useful in treating this disease but it is of paramount importance to ensure continued respiratory function. The trivalent ABE antibodies will only neutralize free toxin; it has no effect on botulinum toxin already bound to neurons.

Tetanospasmin

The neurotoxin, *tetanospasmin,* produced by *Clostridium tetani,* interferes with the peripheral nerves of the spinal cord (FIG. 13-14). This toxin causes tetanus with characteristic severe muscle spasms. Tetanospasmin inhibits the ability of these nerve cells to properly transmit signals to the muscle cells, causing the symptomatic spastic paralysis of tetanus. Like the neurotoxin produced by *C. botulinum,* the neurotoxin of *C. tetani* paralyzes motor neurons, but unlike botulinum toxin, tetanospasmin acts only on the nerves of the cerebrospinal axis. It is postulated that tetanus toxin inhibits the release of glycine from the inhibitory neurons (interneurons) in the anterior horn of the spinal cord. Because glycine is the inhibitory neurotransmitter in these interneurons, the result is convulsions

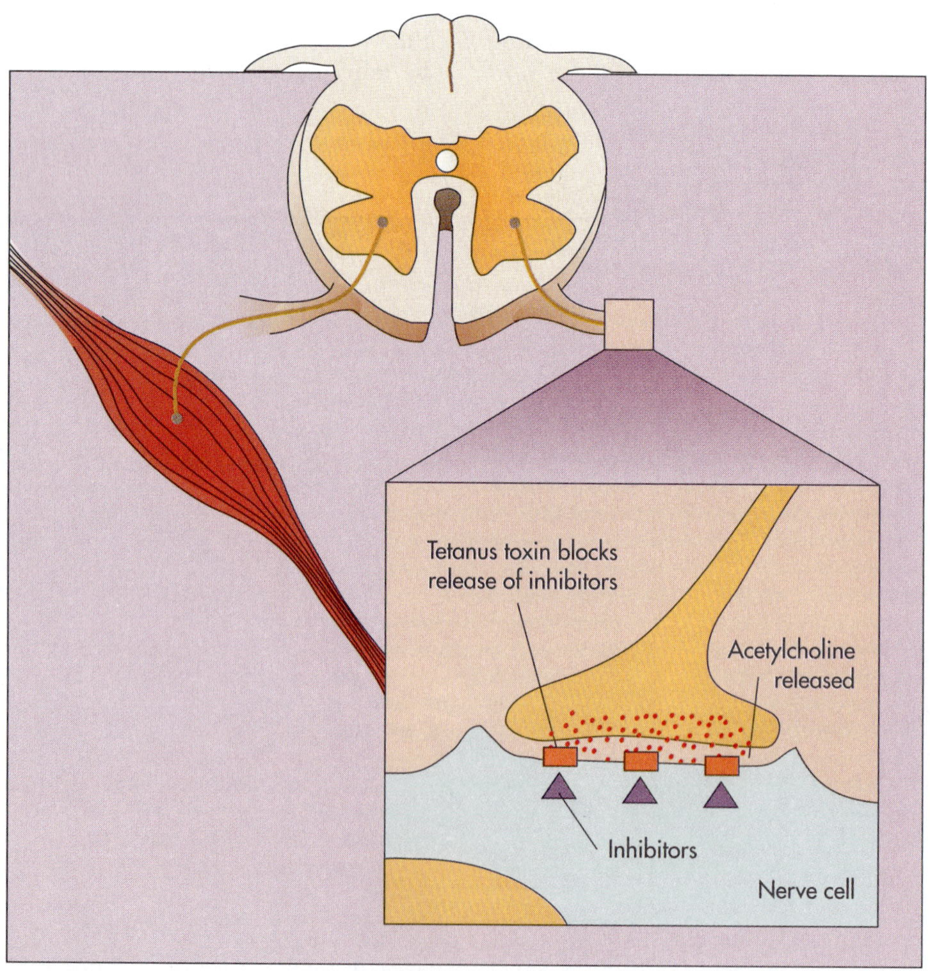

FIG. 13-14 Tetanus toxin blocks release of glycine from inhibitory neurons of peripheral nerves of the spinal cord. This results in spastic paralysis.

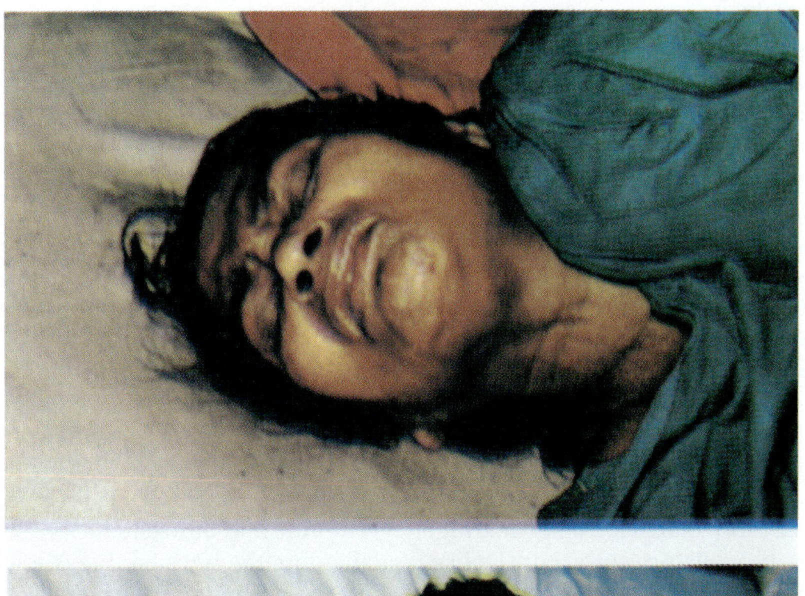

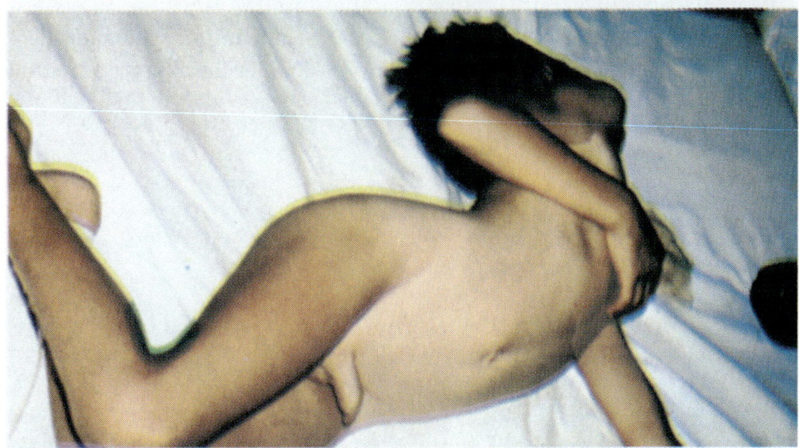

FIG. 13-15 Signs of tetanus are characterized by arching of the back and neck and "lockjaw" due to convulsive spastic paralysis.

similar to those produced by strychnine, which is known to compete with glycine for receptor sites. Tetanus is sometimes referred to as *lockjaw* or *trismus* because the muscles of the jaw and neck contract convulsively so that the mouth remains locked closed, making swallowing difficult (FIG. 13-15).

C. tetani is widely distributed in soil. Transmission to humans normally occurs as a result of a puncture wound that inoculates the body with spores of *C. tetani.* If anaerobic conditions develop at the site of the wound, the endospores of *C. tetani* germinate and the multiplying bacteria produce neurotoxin. *C. tetani* is noninvasive and multiplies only at the site of inoculation. The neurotoxin it produces, however, spreads systemically, causing the symptoms of this disease.

Virtually any type of wound into which foreign material is introduced may carry spores of *C. tetani* and lead to the development of tetanus. Tales of the association of rusty nails with this disease probably originated because farmers often developed tetanus after stepping on such nails that were contaminated with soil and endospores of *C. tetani,* but clearly the rusty nails are not the cause of this disease. If untreated, tetanus is frequently fatal, but if recovery occurs there are no lasting effects. Tetanus can be treated by the administration of tetanus antitoxin to block the action of the neurotoxin. The disease can be prevented by immunization with tetanus toxoid, and tetanus booster vaccinations are frequently given after wound injuries to ensure immunity against this disease.

Shiga Toxin

The neurotoxin produced by *Shigella dysenteriae,* the so-called "Shiga toxin," differs from the neurotoxins produced by *C. botulinum* and *C. tetani* in that it interferes with the circulatory vessels that supply blood to the central nervous system rather than affecting the nerve cells directly. The neurological effects of the shiga toxin are thus secondary to the primary action of the toxin on the vascular circulatory system.

Clostridium perfringens Toxins

Clostridium perfringens produces toxins that cause food poisoning. The ingestion of food containing toxin produced by *C. perfringens* and the adsorption of the toxin into the cells lining the gastrointestinal tract initiate this disease. Toxin type A of *C. perfringens* is associated with most cases of clostridial food poisoning, particularly with cooked meats if a gravy is prepared with the meat. The spores of *C. perfringens* type A can survive the temperatures used in cooking many meats and, if incubated in a warm gravy, there is sufficient time for the spores to germinate and the growing bacteria to produce enough toxin to cause this disease.

The symptoms of food poisoning associated with *C. perfringens* generally appear within 10 to 24 hours after ingestion of food containing the toxin. They include abdominal pain and diarrhea, but vomiting, headache, and fever normally do not occur. Unlike botulism, recovery from food poisoning caused by *C. perfringens* generally occurs within 24 hours.

Choleragen

The toxin produced by *Vibrio cholerae* causes cholera. This toxin, called *choleragen,* is an enterotoxin (toxin affecting the gastrointestinal system). Choleragen is produced by the Gram-negative, curved rod *Vibrio cholerae,* serotypes *cholerae* and *El Tor.* The toxin stimulates the conversion of ATP to cyclic AMP by increasing the activity of adenylcyclase. Adenylcyclase is activated by GTP bound to its regulatory subunit. Hydrolysis of adenylcyclase-GTP complex inactivates adenylcyclase. Choleragen transfers ADP-ribosyl to the adenylcyclase regulatory subunit, inhibiting its ability to hydrolyze GTP. Adenylcyclase, therefore, remains in the active state and continues to make cAMP.

The resulting elevated concentrations of cyclic AMP cause the release of inorganic ions, including chloride and bicarbonate ions, from the mucosal cells that line the intestine into the intestinal lumen (FIG. 13-16). Although the exact mechanism of toxin action on adenylcyclase is not understood, the change in the

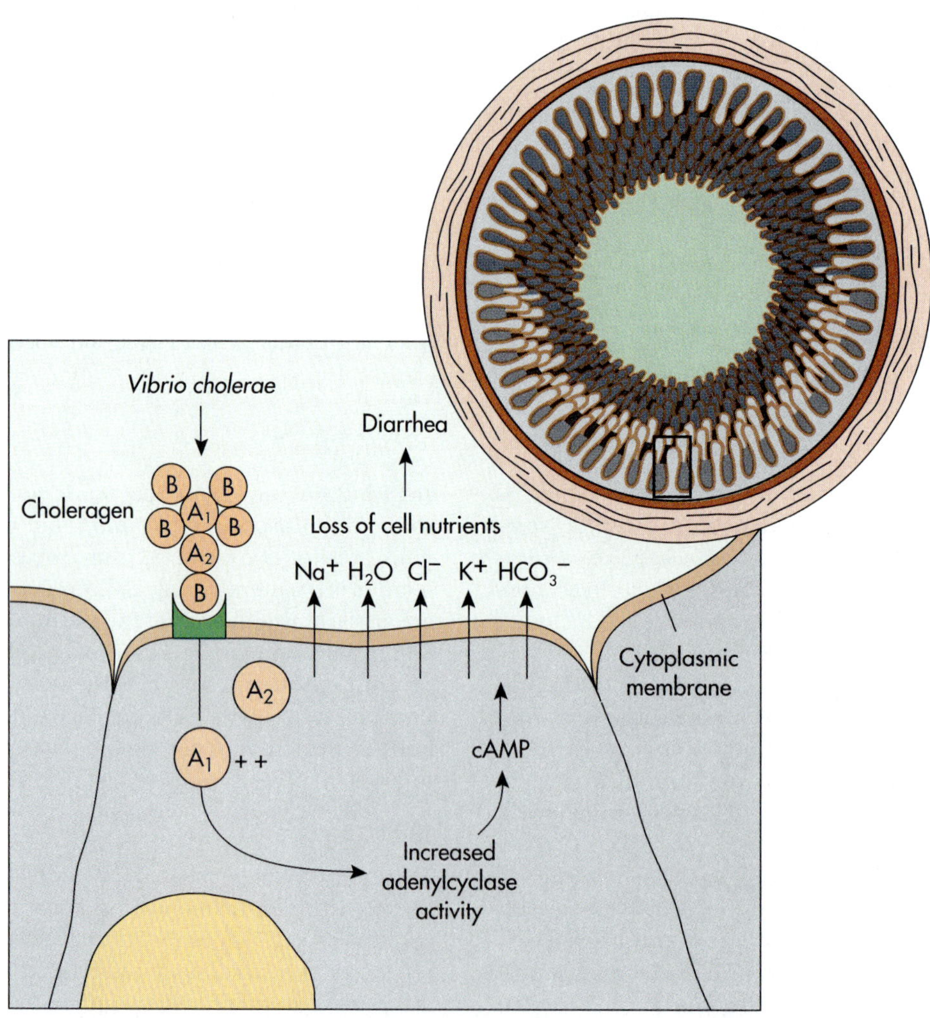

FIG. 13-16 Cholera toxin activates adenylcyclase, producing cyclic AMP; sodium ion transport is blocked and chloride ions and water move into the intestine from the blood. This causes severe diarrhea and water loss.

ionic balance resulting from the action of this toxin causes the movement of large amounts of water into the lumen in an attempt to balance the osmotic pressure. This leads to severe dehydration that sometimes results in the death of infected individuals. The rapid loss of fluid from the cells of the gastrointestinal tract associated with this disease often produces shock, and if it remains untreated, the mortality rate is high. The initial diarrhea that results from infection with *V. cholerae* can cause the loss of several liters of fluid within a few hours.

The symptoms of cholera include nausea, vomiting, abdominal pain, diarrhea with "rice water stools," and severe dehydration, followed by collapse, shock, and in many cases death. *V. cholerae* itself does not invade the body and is not disseminated to other tissues. The treatment of cholera centers on replacing fluids and maintaining the electrolyte balance, that is, on combating shock. Treatment with tetracycline generally reduces the duration of the disease.

Although we typically associate cholera with Asia, sometimes referring to the disease as *Asiatic cholera,* it also occurs in the United States, primarily in the Gulf Coast region, where cases have been traced to contaminated shellfish. Cholera is a particular problem in socioeconomically depressed countries, where there is poor sanitation and inadequate sewage and water treatment and where medical facilities have only a limited capacity to deal with outbreaks. This disease is endemic in the Ganges delta, and there are annual epidemic outbreaks of cholera in India and Bangladesh. In these endemic areas of Asia the death rate is normally 5% to 15%. Seasonal outbreaks of cholera often occur in Southeast Asia when monsoon rains wash sewage into drinking water supplies. During sudden epidemics, the mortality rate may reach 75%. Most recently, a cholera pandemic appeared in South America, notably in Peru, and the disease has spread to neighboring countries and into Central America. This disease outbreak has been especially associated with eating contaminated marinated uncooked fish and drinking contaminated water.

Escherichia coli Enterotoxin

Enterotoxin-producing strains of *Escherichia coli* are also capable of causing mild and severe forms of enterocolitis. In most cases, enterotoxin-producing strains of *E. coli* do not invade the body through the gastrointestinal tract; rather, heat-labile and heat-stable toxins released by cells growing on the surface lining of the gastrointestinal tract cause diarrhea. The heat-stable enterotoxins activate guanylate cyclase. Like cholera toxin, the heat-labile enterotoxins produced by *E. coli* stimulate adenylcyclase activity in the small intestine epithelium. This, in turn, results in increased permeability of the intestinal lining, which causes loss of fluids and electrolytes. With proper replacement of body fluids and maintenance of the essential electrolyte balance, infections with enterotoxigenic *E. coli* normally are not fatal. Aside from diarrhea, abdominal cramps are normally the only other clinical symptom of this disease. From the United States to Mexico, people often suffer severe diarrhea as a result of ingestion of strains of *E. coli* foreign to their own microbiota and, therefore, generally avoid drinking the water in different locales. Many cases of severe diarrhea in children are caused by noninvasive, enterotoxin-producing strains of *E. coli.*

In some cases, enteropathogenic strains of *E. coli* invade the body through the mucosa of the large intestine to cause a serious form of dysentery. Invasive strains of *E. coli* are primarily associated with contaminated food and water in Southeast Asia and South America. The ability to invade the mucosa of the large intestine depends on the presence of a specific K antigen in enteropathogenic serotypes of *E. coli.*

Diphtheria Toxin

Diphtheria results from the action of a protein toxin produced by strains of *Corynebacterium diphtheriae* harboring a temperate phage. Diphtheria toxin is a potent protein exhibiting toxicity against almost all mammalian cells.

Diphtheria toxin is released from the bacterial cell as a protein composed of two polypeptide chains: A and B. Fragment B is required to bind to the eukaryotic cell membrane for Fragment A to gain access to the cytoplasm of the cell. Fragment A catalyzes the transfer of adenosine diphosphoribose (ADPR) from nicotinamide adenine dinucleotide (NAD^+) to eukaryotic elongation factor 2 (EF2), which functions in protein synthesis. Thus diphtheria toxin effectively inhibits protein synthesis in the host cells. The production of diphtheria toxin is particularly interesting because only lysogenized cells of *C. diphtheriae* produce diphtheria toxin proteins. This is a good example of how phage can convert an otherwise nonpathogenic bacterium into a pathogenic one. The protein toxin is coded for by the phage genome. Thus a human infection with *C. diphtheriae* results in disease only when *C. diphtheriae* is infected with a virus.

The bacteria generally do not invade the tissues of the respiratory tract; rather, it is the dissemination of the toxin through the body that causes the severe symptoms of this disease. *C. diphtheriae* is normally transmitted via droplets from an infected individual to a susceptible host, establishing a localized infection on the surface of the mucosal lining of the upper respiratory tract.

There is generally a localized inflammatory response, pharyngitis, in the vicinity of bacterial multiplication in the upper respiratory tract. In severe infections with *C. diphtheriae,* symptoms include low-grade fever, cough, sore throat, difficulty in swallowing, and swelling of the lymph glands. Complications from diphtheria can block respiratory gas exchange and result in death due to suffocation. Death also can be due to the extensive use of vaccine to prevent diphtheria. This vaccine has greatly reduced the incidence of this disease but has not altered the fatality ratio (FIG. 13-17).

In immunized individuals, infection with toxigenic strains of *C. diphtheriae* is generally restricted to a localized pharyngitis with no serious complications. Diphtheria, however, remains a serious problem in socioeconomically depressed regions of the world where extensive immunization is not practiced. Treatment of diphtheria involves the use of antitoxin to block the cytopathic effects of diphtheria toxin, which prevents the occurrence of serious symptoms associated with this disease. This immunological treatment is augmented by antibiotics such as erythromycin to eliminate the bacterial infection.

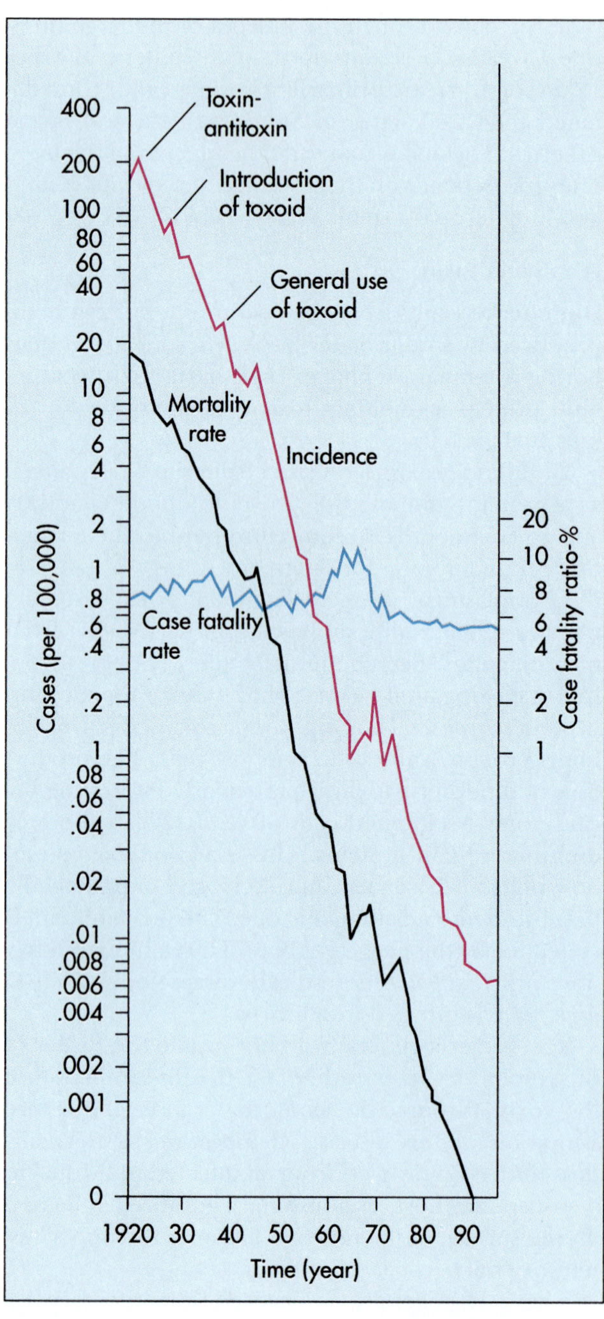

FIG. 13-17 The incidence of diphtheria and mortality due to this disease have declined because of the use of antitoxin and a toxoid vaccine.

Pertussis Toxin

Bordetella pertussis, which causes whooping cough or pertussis, produces several toxins that establish the pathogenicity of this organism. These toxins include pertussis toxin, adenylate cyclase toxin, tracheal cytotoxin, and dermonecrotic toxin. Several of these toxins are involved in the attachment of *B. pertussis* to the epithelial cells of the respiratory tract. *B. pertussis* can reproduce within the respiratory tract and high numbers of this bacterium are found on the surface tissues of the bronchi and trachea. Adenylate cyclase toxin, which catalyzes the conversion of endogenous ATP to cAMP, inhibits phagocytic cells. Pertussis toxin, which has ADP-ribosylating activity, interferes with the transfer of signals from guanine nucleotide–binding proteins on the surfaces of human cells to intracellular regulators of adenylate cyclase activity. This activity inhibits neutrophils, macrophages, and other cells of the immune response. The virulence factor, filamentous hemagglutinin, facilitates attachment of *B. pertussis* to ciliated cells. The tracheal cytotoxin inhibits cilia function and, in high concentrations, causes death of ciliated cells lining the respiratory tract. The dermonecrotic toxin causes vasoconstriction of peripheral blood vessels and probably is responsible for localized tissue destruction.

Whooping cough derives its name from the distinctive symptomatic cough associated with this disease. Other symptoms resemble those of the common cold, although vomiting often occurs after severe coughing episodes. *Bordetella pertussis* is a Gram-negative coccobacillus, which exhibits fastidious nutritional requirements. Erythromycin and tetracyclines are effective in eliminating *Bordetella pertussis* infections, although the treatment of whooping cough primarily involves maintenance of an adequate oxygen supply. Antibiotic therapy is effective only if administered before the onset of the characteristic cough. The administration of pertussis vaccine has greatly reduced the occurrence of whooping cough, and the disease is prevented by routine immunization of infants. Some children immunized with this vaccine have had serious adverse reactions that can even cause death, leading to questions about whether mandatory vaccination should continue. If immunization is discontinued, however, cases of this disease would increase.

Streptococcal Toxins

Some streptococcal species produce toxins, called *hemolysins,* that cause lysis of erythrocytes. A hemolysin is a type of *cytolysin* or cell killing toxin. When bacteria that release hemolysins are grown on blood agar plates, zones of clearing may be seen around individual colonies due to destruction of red blood cells. A complete zone of clearing around a bacterial colony growing on a blood agar plate is referred to as *beta hemolysis* and a partial zone of clearing around a bacterial colony is referred to as *alpha hemolysis* (FIG. 13-18). Alpha hemolysis involves the conversion of hemoglobin to methemoglobin, generally seen as a zone of green discoloration with partial clearing around the colony.

Streptococcus species produce various hemolysins, including streptolysin O, an oxygen-labile and heat stable protein, and streptolysin S, an oxygen-stable, acid-sensitive, and heat-labile protein. Hemolytic activity is associated with *Streptococcus* species and various other bacterial genera, including *Staphylococcus* and *Clostridium.* In addition to red blood cells, leukocytes are killed by some microbial cytotoxins. For example, leukocidin produced by *Staphylococcus aureus* causes lysis of leukocytes, contributing to the pathogenicity of this organism.

Streptococcus species, which cause various diseases, are normally transmitted through the air in contaminated droplets and establish the primary infection in the tissues of the upper respiratory tract. In some cases, the infection is limited to these tissues, causing conditions such as pharyngitis and tonsillitis. In other cases, the streptococci or protein exotoxins produced by streptococci enter the circulatory system and spread systemically. In scarlet fever, for example, the systemic spread of hemolysins produced by *S. pyogenes* manifests as a rash of pinhead red spots, and in rheumatic fever the systemic spread of *S. pyogenes* involves multiple body sites.

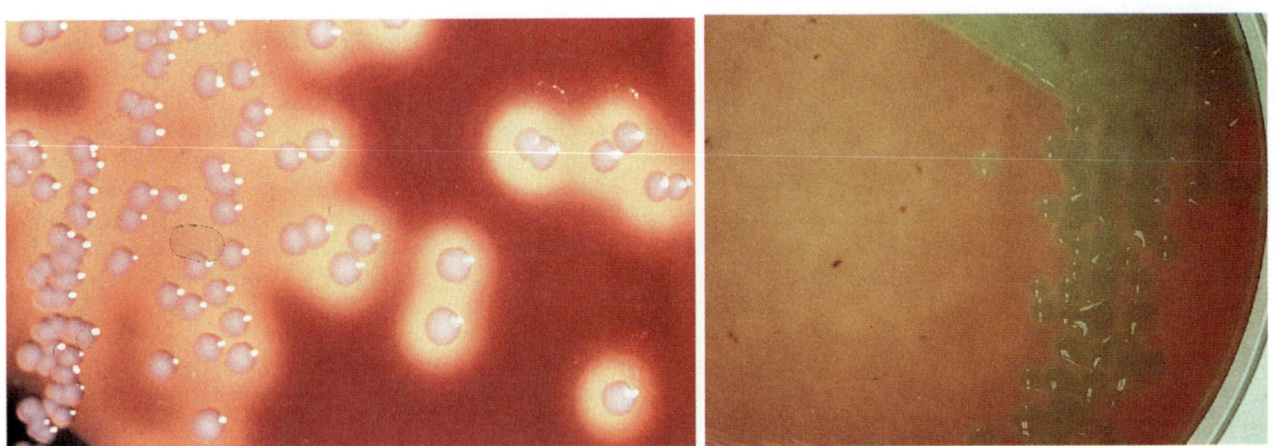

FIG. 13-18 **A,** Blood agar plate showing beta hemolysis (zones of clearing due to complete hemolysis of red blood cells) around colonies of *Streptococcus pyogenes.* **B,** Blood agar plate showing alpha hemolysis (greening due to partial hemolysis of red blood cells) around colonies of *Streptococcus pneumoniae.*

Rheumatic fever is generally the most serious consequence of *S. pyogenes* infections. In rheumatic fever the systemic production of antibodies to *S. pyogenes* toxins affects multiple body sites. The symptoms of this disease vary but characteristically there is a high fever, painful swelling of various body joints, and cardiac involvement, including subsequent development of heart murmurs from childhood occurrences. The symptoms of rheumatic fever normally begin to occur a little over 2 weeks after a characteristic sore throat associated with an upper respiratory tract infection with *S. pyogenes.* Because of the serious manifestations of rheumatic fever, it is important to diagnose the etiologic agents of sore throats in children. Throat swabs plated on blood agar can readily be screened for the presence of β-hemolytic streptococci, and when they are detected, serologic or biochemical tests are carried out to determine if group A streptococci, the group that includes *S. pyogenes,* are present. Penicillin is effective in treating group A streptococcal infections, and its use in treating streptococcal pharyngitis can prevent the occurrence of rheumatic fever.

The specific causal relationship between *S. pyogenes* and the symptoms of rheumatic fever has not been established. It is likely that antibodies produced in response to group A streptococcal cell-wall antigens are cross-reactive with cardiac antigens and that it is an autoimmune response that actually results in cardiac damage. The treatment of rheumatic fever, therefore,

BOX 13-2

Biological Warfare Agents

The capabilities of pathogenic microorganisms to cause debilitating and lethal human diseases makes them potential agents of biological warfare. There are instances where biological warfare may have been practiced. European settlers to the Americas gave Native Americans blankets contaminated with smallpox virus. The Native Americans were not immune to smallpox and the disease decimated some Native American communities. Whether or not such occurrences were accidental or acts of biological warfare will never be known. What is known is that nations have, at times, developed biological warfare agents, as well as defenses against such agents.

The former Soviet Union, as well as probably other nations, developed biological warfare programs for anthrax and other agents. An accidental release of anthrax spores occurred at a test facility in the Soviet Union during the 1980's, resulting in deaths of nearby animals. Anthrax is particularly suitable as a biological agent because endospores of *Bacillus anthracis* can be stored indefinitely and because the disease can be transmitted by aerosols. Similarly, plague, although not caused by an endospore-producing bacterium can be transmitted via the air, and hence *Yersinia pestis* is a likely candidate as a biological warfare agent. Cholera and diseases caused by toxins, such as botulinum toxin and staphylococcal enterotoxin, likewise, could have devastating effects on military and civilian populations; these agents could be disseminated via food and water.

The fear of biological weapons, their unpredictability, and their unacceptable effects on humankind, has led to an International Convention banning biological weapons. The United States led in establishing an international ban on biological weapons. By international convention, signatory nations are to cease all research and development of offensive biological weapons. By declaring that even if attacked with biological weapons, the United States would not respond by using such weapons, the United States leads in attempting to eliminate biological weapons from the arsenal of weapons of mass destruction. Many other nations have similar stances against biological warfare. The fear remains, however, that some nations will not comply with International Conventions on banning biological weapons. Unfortunately, verification of compliance with the Biological Weapons Convention is difficult. Unlike treaties limiting nuclear weapons and banning chemical weapons, biological weapons development could easily be confused with natural occurrences of disease outbreaks and with medical efforts to protect humans against pathogens. Development of vaccines against anthrax, tularemia, and other devastating diseases could serve the dual purpose of developing biological agents that could be used for offensive military purposes. An effective vaccine against a disease can, in some cases, be converted into an offensive biological weapon by simply eliminating a final inactivation step that normally renders the organism harmless. Thus the threat of biological warfare remains.

includes the use of anti-inflammatory drugs to reduce tissue damage and antibiotics to remove the infecting streptococci.

Toxic Shock Syndrome Toxin

Toxic shock syndrome is caused by toxic shock syndrome toxin-1 (TSST-1) producing strains of *Staphylococcus aureus*. This bacterium can enter the body via the genital tract, and elaboration of its toxins causes high fever, nausea, vomiting, and, in many cases, death. The toxin binds to major histocompatibility complex class II molecules on mononuclear cells and stimulates production of interleukins. Interleukin-1 is a potent pyrogen (fever inducer) and stimulates the inflammatory response.

This disease is not restricted to women and can occur after the introduction of *S. aureus* via other portals of entry, including surgical wounds. The occurrence of toxic shock syndrome, though, is especially correlated with the use of tampons during menstruation, particularly if these devices are left in place for a long period of time (FIG. 13-19). The association of this

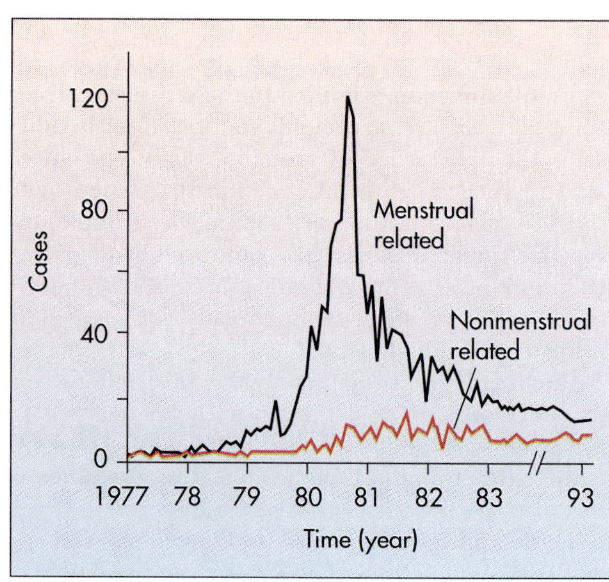

FIG. 13-19 In the early 1980s there was an increase in the incidence of menstrual-related toxic shock syndrome associated with certain tampons that fostered extensive growth of toxin-producing *Staphylococcus aureus*.

disease with the use of tampons received a great deal of publicity in the early 1980s, forcing one major manufacturer to remove its product from the market. The fibers of some tampons absorb magnesium, permitting the proliferation of *Staphylococcus* species, with the production of large amounts of toxins. The hormonal changes that occur during menstruation also favor the proliferation of bacteria in the vaginal tract.

Anthrax Toxin

Anthrax is primarily a disease of animals other than humans but it can occasionally be transmitted to people. The disease is caused by *Bacillus anthracis,* a Gram-positive, endospore-forming rod. Transmission to humans can occur by direct contact of *B. anthracis* endospores with broken or cut skin, via the respiratory tract through inhalation of spores, and via the gastrointestinal tract through the ingestion of spores. The cutaneous route of transmission accounts for 95% of the cases of anthrax in the United States. Contact with animal hair, wool, and hides containing spores of *B. anthracis* is often implicated in transmission of anthrax and the disease is therefore known as *wool sorter's disease.* Deposition of spores of *B. anthracis* under the epidermis permits germination, with subsequent production of toxin by the growing bacteria.

The major factors for the virulence of *B. anthracis* are the production of capsule and exotoxin. The localized accumulation of toxin causes necrosis of the tissue, with the formation of a blackened lesion. The toxin produces edema in experimental animals. The development of cutaneous anthrax can initiate a systemic infection, and untreated cutaneous anthrax has a mortality rate of 10% to 20%. Cutaneous anthrax can be treated with penicillin and other antibiotics, reducing the death rate to less than 1%. Avoiding contact with infected animals and preventing the development of anthrax in farm animals through the use of anthrax vaccine have effectively reduced the incidence of this disease.

13.4 BACTERIAL INVASIVENESS

ENZYMES AS VIRULENCE FACTORS

Specific enzymes produced by microorganisms contribute to the virulence of microbial pathogens. Some of these enzymes may enable the pathogens to invade body tissues and cells. Other enzymes may interfere with normal mammalian functions (Table 13-9). For example, various phospholipase enzymes produced by microorganisms can destroy animal cell membranes. Phospholipases can act as hemolysins, causing the lysis of red blood cells. Indeed, some substances that have been classified as toxins are now known to be toxic enzymes.

TABLE 13-9 Some Extracellular Enzymes Involved in Microbial Virulence

ENZYME	ACTION	EXAMPLES OF BACTERIA-PRODUCING ENZYME
Hyaluronidase (spreading factor)	Breaks down hyaluronic acid	*Streptococcus pyogenes*
Coagulase	Blood clots; coagulation of plasma	*Staphylococcus aureus*
Phospholipase	Lyses red blood cells	*Staphylococcus aureus*
Lecithinase	Destroys red blood cells and other tissue cells	*Clostridium perfringens*
Collagenase	Breaks down collagen (connective tissue fiber)	*Clostridium perfringens*
Fibrinolysin (kinase)	Dissolves blood clots	*Streptococcus pyogenes*

Clostridium perfringens Enzymes

Deep wounds provide a portal of entry for microorganisms, and tissue damage often interrupts circulation to the area, creating conditions that permit the growth of obligately anaerobic bacteria. Gas gangrene is a serious infection that may result from the growth of *Clostridium perfringens* and other *Clostridium* species. The development of gas gangrene depends on the deposition of endospores of *Clostridium* in the wound tissue and the occurrence of anaerobic conditions that permit the germination and multiplication of these obligately anaerobic bacteria.

The *Clostridium* species that cause gas gangrene produce toxins, the diffusion of which extends the area of dead and anaerobic tissues. Enzymes produced by these species are tissue necrosins and hemolysins that account, in part, for the rapid spread of infection.

The alpha toxin of *Clostridium perfringens* is a *lecithinase,* also known as *phospholipase C* or *phosphatidylcholine phosphohydrolase.* Lecithinase hydrolyzes lecithin, which is a lipid component of eukaryotic membranes. This enzyme thereby destroys the integrity of the cytoplasmic membranes of many cells. It is partly responsible for the ability of *C. perfringens* to grow, to invade tissues, and to cause gas gangrene. It is the primary cause of the extensive tissue damage seen in this disease. Lecithinase also acts as a hemolysin, causing lysis of red blood cells in addition to destroying cells of various other tissues. The release of iron from the lysed blood cells allows this pathogen to grow in an environment that normally has a very low concentration of this essential growth nutrient.

The growing *Clostridium* species produce carbon dioxide and hydrogen gases, as well as odoriferous low molecular weight metabolic products. The gas that accumulates is primarily hydrogen because it is less soluble than CO_2. In most cases, the onset of gas gangrene occurs within 72 hours of the occurrence of the wound; if untreated, the disease is fatal. Even with antimicrobial treatment, there is a high rate of mortality; therefore, radical surgery (amputation) is often employed to prevent the spread of infection. If treated rapidly enough, localized areas of necrotic tissue can be excised and high doses of penicillin administered to block the spread of the infection. The prevention of gas gangrene depends on ensuring that wounds do not provide a suitable environment for the growth of the anaerobic *Clostridium* species. This requires adequate drainage of wounds to prevent the establishment of anaerobic conditions and the removal of foreign material and dead tissue.

Staphylococcal and Streptococcal Enzymes

Some *Staphylococcus* and *Streptococcus* species produce *fibrinolysins (staphylokinase* and *streptokinase)*. These fibrinolytic enzymes catalyze the lysis of fibrin clots. The action of these two fibrinolytic enzymes may enhance the invasiveness of pathogenic strains of *Staphylococcus* and *Streptococcus* by preventing fibrin in the host from walling off the area of bacterial infection. Without the action of fibrin, the pathogens are free to spread to surrounding areas. In a somewhat different way, the production of *coagulase* enhances the virulence of some *Staphylococcus* species. The enzyme coagulase, on the other hand, converts fibrinogen to fibrin, enhancing the virulence of some *Staphylococcus* species. Some *Staphylococcus* species, such as *S. aureus*, produce this enzyme, and the deposition of fibrin around the staphylococcal cells presumably protects the cells against the circulatory defense mechanisms of the host. Coagulase-negative strains of *S. aureus*, however, still have been found to be virulent pathogens. It is thus difficult to associate virulence with the activity of a single enzyme, even though these enzymes appear to play a role in the virulence of various pathogenic microorganisms.

Several other enzymes produced by microorganisms can destroy body tissues. For example, *hyaluronidase* breaks down hyaluronic acid, the substance that holds together the cells of connective tissues. Pathogens that produce hyaluronidases spread through body tissues, and therefore hyaluronidase is referred to as the *spreading factor.* Various species of *Staphylococcus, Streptococcus,* and *Clostridium* produce hyaluronidases. Some *Clostridium* species also produce *collagenase,* an enzyme that breaks down the proteins of collagen tissues. The k toxin of *C. perfringens,* for example, is a collagenase that contributes to the spread of this organism through the human body. The breakdown of fibrous tissues enhances the invasiveness of pathogenic microorganisms. Thus the actions of some microbial enzymes contribute to the virulence of pathogens by enhancing the ability of the microorganisms to proliferate within body tissues and by interfering with the normal defense mechanisms of the host organism.

Interference with Phagocytosis

Several other factors contribute to the virulence of microorganisms, including the production of surface layers that interfere with the ability of phagocytic blood cells to engulf and destroy bacteria that invade the human body. As discussed in earlier chapters, capsules protect some bacteria against the host defense mechanism of phagocytosis. Capsules surrounding the cells of strains of *Streptococcus pneumoniae,* for example, permit these bacteria to evade the normal defense mechanisms of the host, allowing them to reproduce and causing the symptomatology of pneumonia. The virulence of other bacteria, including *Haemophilus influenzae* and *Klebsiella pneumoniae,* is also enhanced by capsule production (FIG. 13-20).

There are some instances where capsules actually mimic host molecules in structure: *Escherichia coli K1* and *Neisseria meningitidis B* (neuraminic acid) capsules mimic the neural cell adhesion molecule. This molecular mimicry of host molecules helps these

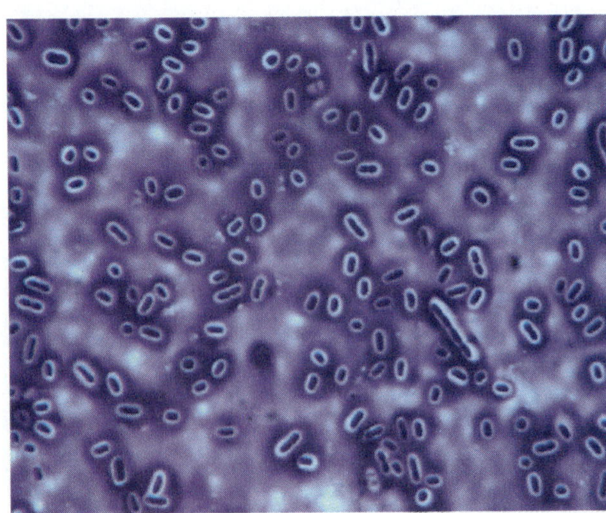

FIG. 13-20 Micrograph of *Klebsiella pneumoniae* (2,500×) surrounded by capsules that interfere with phagocytosis.

pathogens evade recognition by the immune system. It may also trigger an autoimmune response.

Many chronic infections involve the growth of infecting bacteria on surfaces as encapsulated biofilms. Here, capsules help microorganisms evade recognition and clearance by the immune system. Biofilm bacteria such as *Pseudomonas aeruginosa* and *Staphylococcus aureus* infect medical devices (for example, catheters, artificial hips, and artificial heart valves) and are also highly resistant to antibiotics due, in part, to the presence of the capsules and the slow growth of the biofilm bacteria.

Pneumonia

Pneumonia is an inflammation of the lungs involving the alveoli that can be caused by a number of viral and bacterial agents. The most frequent etiologic agent of bacterial pneumonia in adults is *Streptococcus pneumoniae* (pneumococcus), a Gram-positive, capsule-forming diplococcus. The capsule permits *S. pneumoniae* to evade the phagocytic neutrophils and macrophages of the lung. Often, pneumococcal pneumonia is an endogenous disease, originating in the individual's normal throat microbiota. Several other bacteria, including *Haemophilus influenzae* and *Klebsiella pneumoniae,* are also responsible for a significant number of cases of pneumonia. In children, *H. influenzae* type b frequently is the cause of pneumonia. These pneumonia-causing bacteria also produce capsules that enable them to evade the phagocytic defenses of the lungs.

Pneumonia is often a complication that occurs when the host defense mechanisms are compromised as a result of other diseases. Frequently, pneumonia is a nosocomial (hospital-acquired) infection occurring after surgery or during treatment for another disease, when patients are "run down" and their physiologically impaired state reduces the effectiveness of the immune response system. The lack of movement and deep breathing in postsurgical patients reduce the efficiency of the normal defense mechanisms in clearing the lungs of mucus and bacteria, and the accumulation of fluids favors the establishment of a microbial infection. There is a high rate of mortality in cases of pneumonia (FIG. 13-21); more than half of the cases of pneumonia are caused by bacteria, and this disease ranks among the top causes of death from infectious diseases. Bacteria that cause pneumonia most frequently enter the lungs via the air, although transport of pathogens to the lungs through the bloodstream can also occur.

The symptoms of pneumococcal pneumonia, which is most prevalent in men, include the sudden onset of a high fever; production of colored, purulent sputum; and congestion. In most patients, an upper respiratory tract infection with the characteristic symptom of a sore throat precedes the development of pneumococcal pneumonia. Vaccines have been developed using polysaccharides from purified capsules against both *S. pneumoniae* and *H. influenzae.*

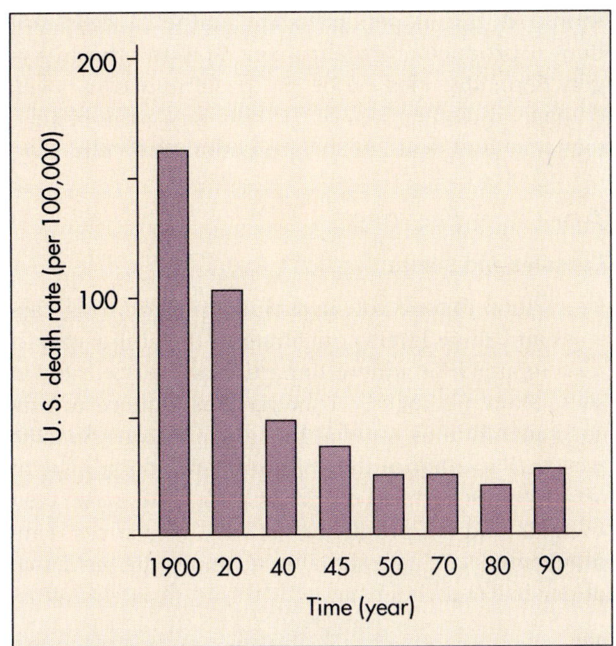

FIG. 13-21 Although the mortality rate due to pneumonia declined during the twentieth century due to the use of antibiotics and medical practices that support respiratory function, pneumonia remains a major cause of mortality.

During the development of pneumonia, bacteria reproduce in the lung tissue, forming a lesion. The phagocytic portion of this inflammatory response results in decreased numbers of bacteria within the lesion. Bacteria spread through the alveoli and into the pulmonary system. The exudate that develops during pneumonia interferes with gas exchange in the lungs. Without treatment the death rate from pneumococcal pneumonia is about 30%. Antibiotic treatment cures bacterial pneumonia, with penicillin the antibiotic of choice for treating pneumonia caused by *S. pneumoniae.* The specific antibiotic treatment for pneumonias caused by bacteria other than *S. pneumoniae* varies with their specific antibiotic sensitivities.

Primary Atypical Pneumonia

Mycoplasma pneumoniae, a bacterium lacking a cell wall, causes an atypical self-limiting pneumonia (primary atypical pneumonia) that has a low death rate. During World War II this disease became known as *walking pneumonia.* It is often the cause of pneumonia among children of school age. *M. pneumoniae* lacks a cell-wall structure and is therefore not sensitive to penicillin. This organism, however, is sensitive to tetracycline and erythromycin, which can be used effectively to treat this type of atypical pneumonia. Unlike other mycoplasmas, *M. pneumoniae* can attach to the epithelial surface of the respiratory tract. This bacterium does not penetrate the epithelial cells, nor does it produce a protein toxin; however the hydrogen peroxide released by the bacterium causes cell damage, including loss of the cilia lining the respiratory tract and death of surface endothelial cells.

Adhesion Factors

Capsules and Slimes

In addition to their role in avoiding phagocytosis, capsules and slime layers contribute to the ability of bacteria to attach or adhere to particular host cells or tissues. Many pathogenic bacteria must adhere to mucous membranes to establish an infection. Specific factors that enhance the ability of a microorganism to attach to the surfaces of mammalian cells are termed *adhesins,* and the production of such substances is another important factor that determines the virulence of particular pathogens.

Pili

The pili of several pathogenic bacteria and their associated adhesins appear to play a key role in permitting the bacteria to adhere to host cells and establish infections. For example, enteropathogenic strains of *E. coli* have particular adhesins associated with their pili that permit them to bind to the mucosal lining of the intestine. In a similar manner, *Vibrio cholerae* adheres to the mucosal cells lining the intestine, allowing the establishment of an infection (FIG. 13-22).

Pili (fimbriae) often attach to specific molecules that may be found only on particular tissue surfaces. This highly selective adhesion is one reason why a particular pathogen may infect only one region of the body.

Pili can also interfere with phagocytosis. The pili of *Neisseria,* for example, can retard phagocytosis, increasing the persistence of the pathogenic *Neisseria* species. Although not an adhesin, strictly speaking, *Neisseria* species also secrete an IgA protease that can degrade and inactivate secretory IgA. This antibody is the main protector of mucous membrane surfaces. By inactivating part of the host immune system, *Neisseria* can survive long enough for their pili to attach to mucosal epithelial cells.

Dextrans

The surfaces of the oral cavity are heavily colonized by microorganisms. Excessive growth of microorganisms in the mouth can cause diseases of the tissues of the oral cavity. One of the most common human diseases caused by microorganisms is dental caries. Caries are initiated at the tooth surface as a result of the growth of *Streptococcus* species. These streptococci can initiate caries because they have the following essential properties: (1) they can adhere to the tooth surface; (2) they produce lactic acid as a result of fermentative metabolism, thereby dissolving the dental enamel surface of the tooth; and (3) they produce a polymeric substance that causes the acid to remain in contact with the tooth surface.

Streptococcus mutans is implicated as the causative agents of dental caries. These bacteria produce dextran sucrase, which catalyzes the formation of extracellular glucans from dietary sucrose. Glucan production contributes to the formation of dental plaque

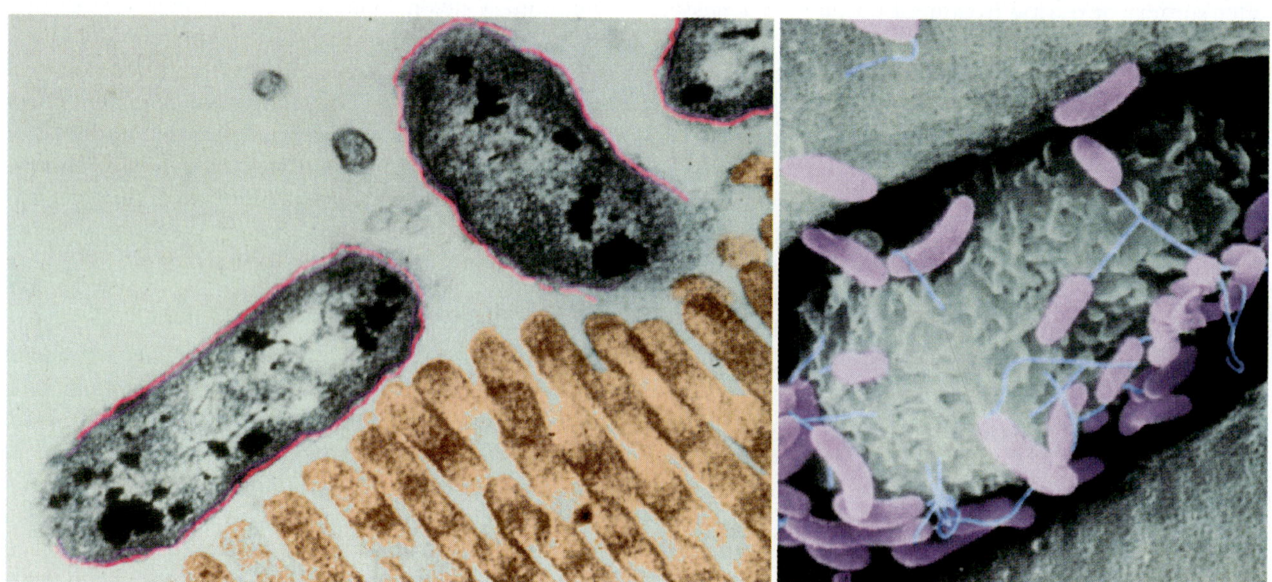

FIG. 13-22 *Vibrio cholerae* attachment to **(A)** brush border *(tan)* of rabbit villus and **(B)** Cells in human ileal mucosa. Pili *(blue)* surrounding bacterial cells permit adherence and the initiation of an infection.

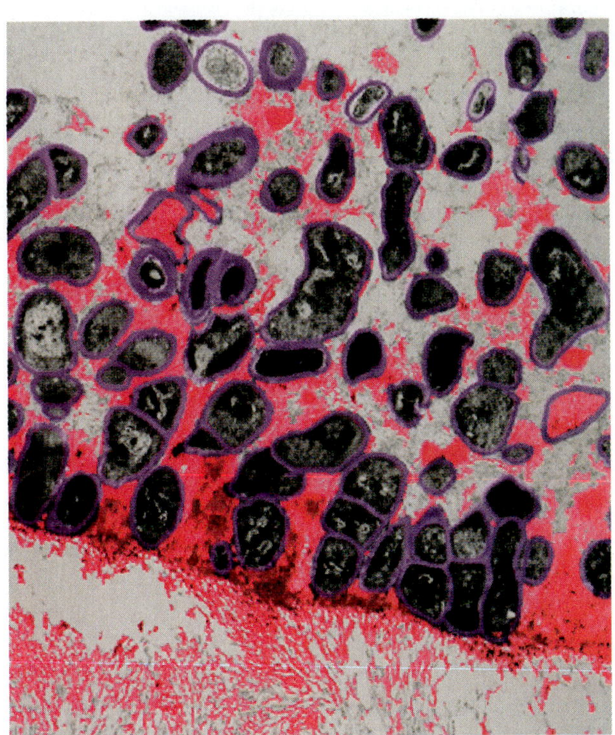

FIG. 13-23 Glucan production allows bacteria to adhere to teeth, forming dental plaque. This colorized micrograph shows bacterial cells and the dextran matrix *(red fibrils)* of plaque on a tooth surface. (11,600×).

(FIG. 13-23). Dental plaque is an accumulation of a mixed bacterial community in a dextran matrix; it may be as many as 500 cells thick. There is a high degree of structure within plaque, indicative of sequential colonization by different bacterial populations and the different positions of each population within this complex bacterial community. Many of the bacteria within plaque are streptococci and lactobacilli that produce acid from their fermentation of carbohydrates. This acid-producing microbial community, which is tightly apposed to the tooth surface by dextrans, leads to the dissolution of the tooth matrix (caries).

Dental caries can be prevented by limiting dietary sugar substrates, especially sucrose, and by removing accumulated food particles and dental plaque by periodic brushing and flossing of the teeth. Such hygienic practices are particularly effective if performed after eating meals and snacks. The development of aspartame-sweetened sugarless gums is an aid to some people in limiting exposure of teeth to sugars. Additionally, tooth surfaces can be rendered more resistant to microbial attack by including calcium in the diet, such as by drinking milk, and by fluoride treatments of the tooth surface. The administration of fluorides in the diet, such as by consumption of fluoridated water, during the period of tooth formation can reduce dental caries by as much as 50%. New methods of plaque removal, including the use of enzymes in mouthwashes and slightly acidic toothpastes, should aid in limiting dental caries.

Attempts are also being made to limit colonization of the tooth surface by using antibodies to block the sites of attachment of oral streptococci. One related new approach to preventing dental caries involves the use of low-acid–producing streptococci to preempt colonization of the oral cavity by the normal lactic acid–producing strains of *Streptococcus;* this approach is still highly experimental.

IRON UPTAKE

Most bacteria require an iron concentration above 10^{-8} M free iron, but that of most human tissue is less than 10^{-18} M. Therefore the ability of some bacteria to grow within blood and tissues may be limited by the lack of available iron. Some pathogens, however, can overcome this limitation and sequester the iron that they require from the blood. To acquire the iron needed for reproduction, such pathogens produce low molecular weight compounds involved in iron transport, called **siderophores,** that bind iron tightly. Siderophores remove iron normally bound to transferrin or other iron-binding compounds in blood.

Enteric bacteria produce two types of siderophores: enterobactin and aerobactin. Enterobactin is bound to a specific outer membrane receptor, transferred to the periplasmic space, and bound to a specific periplasmic binding protein. This binding protein shuttles the enterobactin to the cytoplasmic membrane receptor complex. The entire molecule is transported into the cytoplasm where the iron is reduced. The iron is then released from the complex and utilized in cellular metabolism. In enteroinvasive *E. coli,* enterobactin is not too important in iron acquisition from transferrin in the blood. Strains that are invasive have a virulence plasmid that codes for the production of *aerobactin,* a hydroxamate siderophore. The aerobactin–iron complex attaches to the outer membrane where a protein acts to dissociate the iron from the siderophore. This allows the iron to be transported into the cell. If *E. coli* was cured of this plasmid or the aerobactin genes are deleted, the strains are less invasive and less virulent.

Other pathogens, such as *Neisseria* and *Mycobacterium* species, sequester iron without producing siderophores by synthesizing an outer membrane protein that removes iron directly from transferrin. Thus these bacteria have virulence properties with respect to their ability to acquire iron that enable them to overcome host resistance and initiate systemic infections.

13.5 FUNGAL AND ALGAL TOXINS

FUNGAL TOXINS

Several fungi produce potent **cytotoxins,** (toxins that kill cells by interfering with their normal physiological functions). Many mushrooms are highly poisonous because of the potency of the cytotoxins they produce. Some cause ultrastructural changes in the host; others interfere with various metabolic activities of host cells. Although there is no generalized mechanism that applies to all fungal toxins, the mode of action of most of these toxins appears to be based primarily on their ability to interact with macromolecules, subcellular organelles, and organs of animals.

Mycotoxin

Mycotoxins, which are toxins produced by some fungi, are responsible for serious cases of food poisoning. Various species of mushrooms contain toxins that can be absorbed through the gastrointestinal tract and the ingestion of poisonous mushrooms is normally fatal. The cytotoxins produced by *A. phalloides* and other species of *Amanita* cause symptoms of food poisoning 8 to 24 hours after their ingestion. In the most infamous of the poisonous mushrooms *(Amanita phalloides)* the toxin (alpha amanitin) blocks transcription of DNA by interfering with RNA polymerase enzyme. Initial symptoms include vomiting and diarrhea; later, degenerative changes occur in liver and kidney cells, and death may ensue within a few days of ingesting as little as 5 to 10 mg of toxin.

Aflatoxin

Some filamentous fungi, other than mushrooms, also produce toxins that can cause human disease. *Aspergillus* species growing on peanuts and grains produce **aflatoxins,** which are potent carcinogens. Aflatoxins bind to DNA and prevent transcription of genetic information, resulting in various adverse effects on humans and other animals. They are known to cause death in sheep and cattle and may be involved in some human disease conditions. Aflatoxin exposure in humans has been associated with consumption of peanut butter, particularly peanut butter lacking preservatives. Aflatoxins are the only known carcinogens for which the United States government has set permissible levels.

Ergot Alkaloids

Ergotism results from ingesting grain containing toxic ergot alkaloids, ergometrine, ergotamine, and ergotaminine, produced by the fungus *Claviceps purpurea.* These toxins stimulate smooth muscle contraction, block nervous transmission, and cause degeneration of the capillary blood vessels. This type of food poisoning has a relatively high mortality rate. Symptoms of ergotism may include vomiting, diarrhea, thirst, hallucinations, convulsions, and lesions of the extremities. Various outbreaks of mass hallucinations have been traced to contamination of food with ergot alkaloids. There are theories that the Salem witch hunts in colonial Massachusetts were related to grain contamination and widespread ergotism.

ALGAL TOXINS

Algae are rarely considered as the etiologic agents of disease, but paralytic shellfish poisoning is caused by toxins produced by the dinoflagellate *Gonyaulax.* Blooms of *Gonyaulax* cause red tides in coastal marine environments. During such algal blooms, the algae and the toxins they produce can be concentrated in bivalve shellfish such as clams and oysters. The ingestion of shellfish containing algal toxins can lead to symptoms that resemble those of botulism. Shellfishing is banned in areas of *Gonyaulax* blooms to prevent this form of food poisoning.

13.6 VIRAL PATHOGENESIS

Pathogenic viruses have virulence factors that contribute to their ability to cause disease (Table 13-10). The adsorption of viruses onto specific receptor sites of human cells establishes the necessary prerequisite for the uptake of the viruses by host cells, leading to the replication of the viruses, the disruption of normal host cell function, and the production of disease symptoms by the invading viral pathogens.

Some viruses, such as adenoviruses, have external spikes that aid in their attachment to host cells. Similarly, the spikes of orthomyxoviruses and paramyxoviruses attach to receptors of *N*-acetylneuraminic acid on the surfaces of human red blood cells. The ability of pathogenic microorganisms, including viruses, to attach to and invade particular cells and tissues establishes specific tissue affinities for pathogenic microorganisms.

When viruses reproduce within host cells, they can also produce substances that may destroy or interfere with the normal functioning of cells. The observable

TABLE 13-10 Mechanisms of Viral Cellular Pathogenesis

MECHANISM	REPRESENTATIVE VIRUSES
Inhibition of protein synthesis	Polioviruses, herpes simplex virus, togaviruses, poxviruses
Inhibition and degradation of cellular DNA	Herpes simplex virus
Changes in structure of cell membrane	
Insertion of glycoproteins	All enveloped viruses, reoviruses
Syncytia formation	Herpes simplex virus, varicella-zoster, paramyxoviruses, human immunodeficiency virus
Disruption of cytoskeleton	Herpes simplex virus
Changes in permeability	Togaviruses, herpes viruses
Inclusion bodies	
Negri bodies (cytoplasmic)	Rabies
Owl's eye (nuclear)	Cytomegalovirus
Cowdry's type A (nuclear)	Herpes simplex virus, measles virus
Nuclear basophilic inclusion bodies	Adenoviruses
Cytoplasmic acidophilic inclusion bodies	Poxviruses
Perinuclear acidophilic inclusion bodies	Reoviruses
Toxicity of components of the virion	Adenovirus fibers

changes in the appearance of cells infected with viruses are collectively known as *cytopathic effects* (CPE). In some cases, human cells infected with viruses die. For example, polio viruses kill the human cells they infect. In other cases, infected cells develop nonlethal abnormalities. Inclusions sometimes occur within the nucleus or cytoplasm of infected cells. These inclusions may be stained with basic or acid dyes and viewed with a microscope. For example, cells infected with measles virus develop acidophilic inclusions in the nucleus and cytoplasm; cells infected with rabies virus develop acidophilic inclusions only within the cytoplasm; and cells infected with adenovirus develop basophilic inclusions within the nucleus. Some viruses, such as measles virus, cause infected cells to fuse together, forming multinuclear giant cells or syncytia. Additionally, some viruses possess genes, called *oncogenes*, that transform normal cells into malignant (cancerous) cells.

MEASLES

When the measles virus replicates within the body it causes a systemic infection. Measles virus causes infected human cells to fuse, forming giant cells and syncytia (multinucleated giant cells). Inclusion bodies that contain incomplete viral particles form within the infected cells. Many infected cells lyse and die.

Initially, measles virions adsorb to cells of the upper respiratory tract. After replication in the mucosal lining of the upper respiratory tract, they are disseminated to lymphoid tissues, where further replication occurs. Before the onset of symptoms, large numbers of measles viruses are shed in secretions of the respiratory tract and eye, and in urine, promoting the rapid epidemic spread of this disease.

Infection with measles viruses can involve various organs, and there is a high rate of mortality associated with measles in regions of the world where malnutrition and limited medical treatment facilities predominate. The disease is associated with 2 to 3 million deaths per year in developing nations. When the virus invades the central nervous system, the disease is generally fatal.

Measles is characterized by the eruption of a skin rash approximately 14 days after exposure to the measles virus. The rash generally appears initially behind the ears, spreading rapidly to other areas of the body during the next 3 days. Disease symptoms often begin a few days before the onset of the characteristic measles rash. These initial symptoms include high fever, coughing, sensitivity to light, and the appearance of Koplik spots (red spots with a white dot in the center that occur in the oral cavity, generally appearing first on the inner lip). Treatment is normally supportive, including rest and the intake of sufficient fluids. In uncomplicated cases, the fever disappears within 2 days and the individual returns to normal activities a few days later. If the fever persists for more than 2 days after the eruption of the rash, it is likely that a complication such as bronchitis or pneumonia has developed. In these cases, additional treatment is needed to cure the secondary infection. Another serious complication of measles is a progressive infectious encephalitis that has been observed in immunocompromised patients.

Measles can be prevented by childhood immunization; therefore the rate of infection in the United States, at least where immunization is practiced rou-

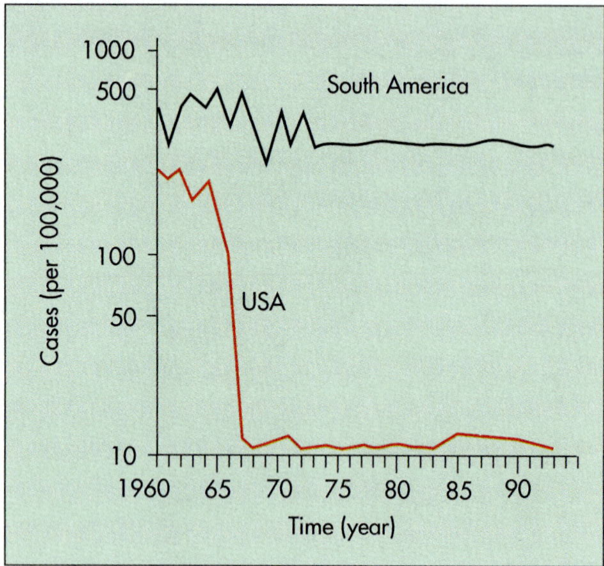

FIG. 13-24 Measles has been effectively eliminated in the United States through vaccination but the incidence of this disease remains high in other regions.

tinely, has declined regularly in recent years, although in other countries, measles has not declined in the same way (FIG. 13-24). It was predicted that measles would be eliminated from the United States by 1982, but there have been several outbreaks among college-age individuals who were not immunized and who had not contracted this disease as children. Some college campuses were quarantined in the early 1980s during severe outbreaks. Recent outbreaks of measles in the United States are due in large part to the inadequacy of a single-dose vaccine to provide lifelong immunity; a booster vaccine for measles is now recommended.

German Measles

Rubella viruses cause German measles, or rubella. After multiplication in the mucosal cells of the upper respiratory tract, rubella viruses appear to be disseminated systemically through the blood. Approximately 18 days after initiation of the infection, a characteristic rash, appearing as flat pink spots, occurs on the face and subsequently spreads to other parts of the body. Enlarged, tender lymph nodes and a low-grade fever characteristically precede the occurrence of the German measles rash. In children and adolescents, rubella is usually a mild disease.

If the rubella virus is acquired during pregnancy, the fetus can become infected with the rubella virus. This results in congenital rubella syndrome, which is characterized by the development of multiple abnormalities in the infant. There is a very high rate of mortality, exceeding 25%, in cases of congenital rubella syndrome. Vaccination has greatly reduced the incidence of rubella (FIG. 13-25) in children and is also used to confer immunity on women of childbearing age who did not contract the disease at an earlier age.

Mumps

Mumps viruses have several virulence factors that permit them to adsorb to human cells and to initiate infection. The ribonucleic acid–protein core of the mumps virus contains a complement-fixing antigen and the viral envelope has two major glycoproteins. The larger envelope glycoprotein is comprised of a hemagglutinin-neuraminidase molecule that is responsible for the adsorption of the virus particle to host cells. The smaller envelope glycoprotein is a fusion protein and effects the penetration of the viral nucleocapsid through the host cell membrane. This facilitates lytic replication of the mumps virus within the body.

The replication of the mumps virus causes enlargement of one or more of the salivary glands (usually the parotid). Swelling on both sides *(bilateral parotitis)* occurs in about 75% of patients. The average incubation period for mumps is 18 days, and the swelling of the salivary glands generally persists for less than 2 weeks. The mumps virus may spread to various body sites, and although the effects of the disease are normally not long lasting, there can be several complications; for example, mumps is a major cause of deafness in childhood. In males past puberty, the mumps virus can cause orchitis (inflammation of the testes), but old wives' tales to the contrary, mumps rarely results in male sterility.

Chickenpox

Chickenpox (varicella) is caused by the varicella-zoster virus, a member of the herpesvirus group. It has nothing to do with chickens; the name is derived from the old English *gicken,* meaning itching. Ninety percent of all cases of chickenpox occur in children under 9 years of age. In children, chickenpox is generally a relatively mild disease, but when it occurs in adults the symptoms are characteristically severe. Local lesions (vesicles) occur in the skin after dissemination of the virus through the body. These skin lesions become encrusted, and the crusts fall off in about 1 week. Vesicles also occur on mucous membranes, especially in the mouth.

In some cases, the varicella-zoster virus spreads to the lower respiratory tract, resulting in pneumonia; in this way, several other tissues, including the central nervous system, can also be involved in complicated cases of chickenpox. Effective vaccination practices have not been introduced, and outbreaks of chickenpox continue to show regular seasonal cycles of the same magnitude (FIG. 13-26).

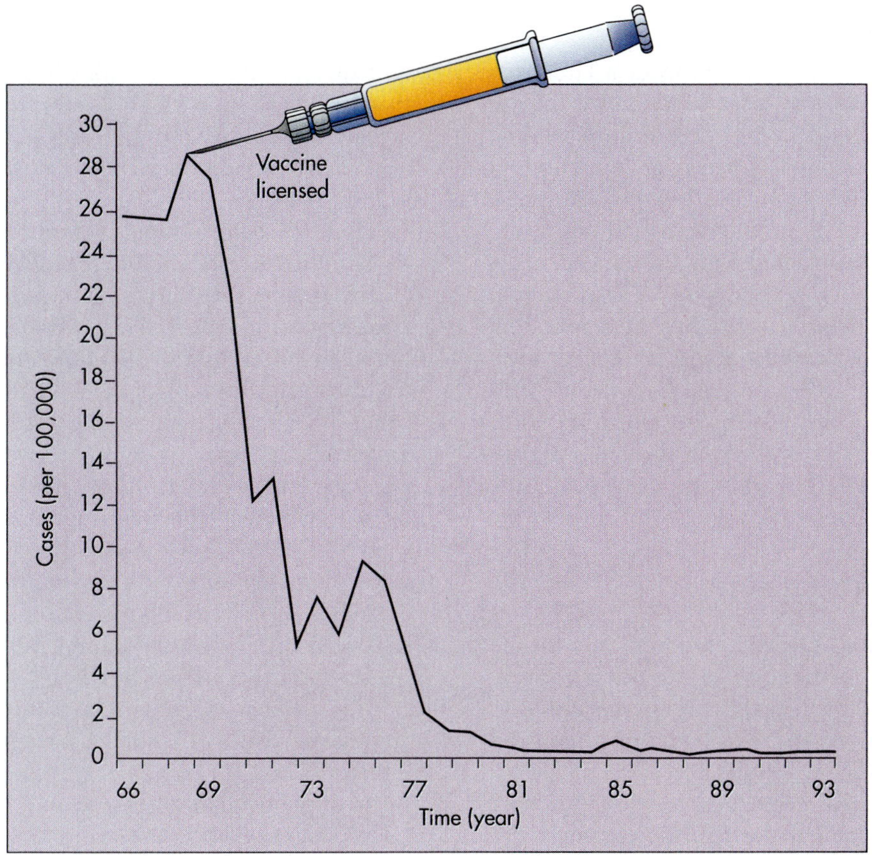

FIG. 13-25 Vaccination has resulted in the near elimination of rubella in the United States.

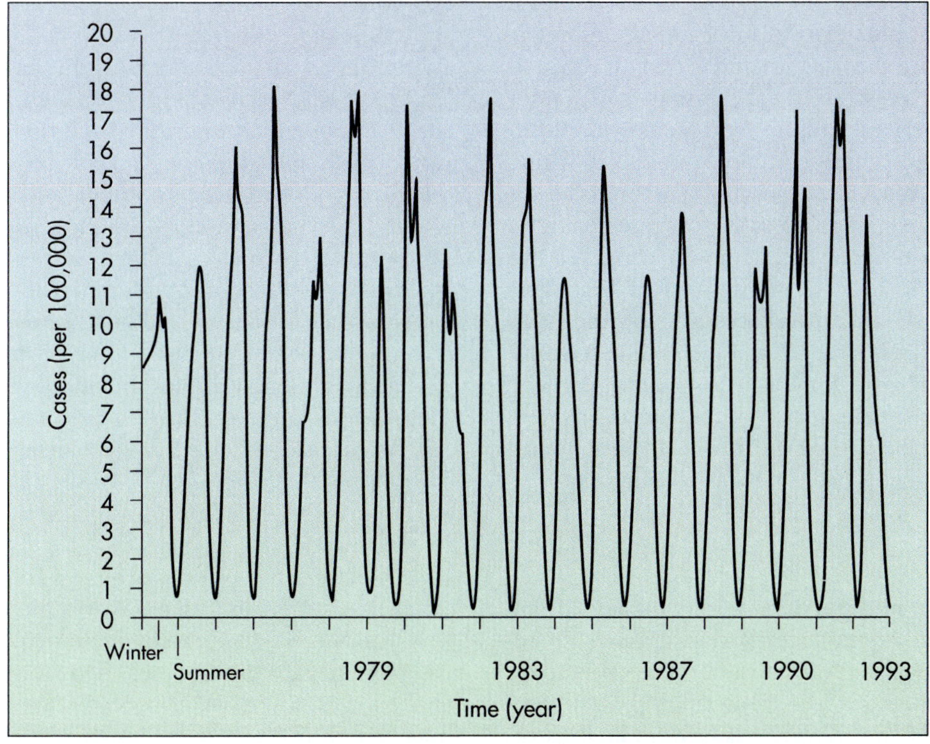

FIG. 13-26 Chickenpox shows regular yearly cyclic outbreaks, with the highest incidence occurrence during the winter and the lowest incidence occurring in the summer.

Shingles

Shingles is the result of reactivation of a latent varicella-zoster virus that may have remained within the body from a childhood case of chickenpox. Shingles affects individuals who developed circulating antibodies in response to infection with this virus. It appears to be the reaction of antibodies with body sites, such as nerve endings, associated with the emergence of the latent virus that causes the symptoms of shingles. In cases of shingles, the virus reaches the sensory ganglia of the spinal or cranial nerves, producing an inflammatory response. There is usually an acute onset of pain and tenderness along the affected sensory nerves. A rash also develops along these nerves, usually lasting for 2 to 4 weeks, but the pain may last for weeks or months.

Infectious Mononucleosis

Infectious mononucleosis is caused by the Epstein-Barr (EB) virus, a member of the herpesvirus group. The virus specifically infects B lymphocytes and some epithelial cells. The B cell viral receptor is the C3d receptor of complement. Replication of EB viruses within epithelial cells leads to formation of various antigenic proteins. One of these proteins, lymphocyte-defined membrane antigen, elicits a cell-mediated immune response. The cell-mediated T-cell response causes a swelling of the lymph glands, splenomegaly (enlargement of the spleen), and hepatomegaly (enlargement of the liver).

The symptoms and signs of infectious mononucleosis include a sore throat, low-grade fever that generally peaks in the early evening, enlarged and tender lymph nodes, general fatigue, and weakness. Infectious mononucleosis most commonly occurs in young adults 15 to 25 years of age, a fact that may be explained by the exchange of saliva during kissing, a prevalent activity often involving more partners in this age group than others. In most cases of infectious mononucleosis, the symptoms are relatively mild and the acute stage of the illness lasts for less than 3 weeks. However, the EB virus has been associated with the subsequent development of two forms of cancer: Burkitt lymphoma in certain African populations and nasopharyngeal carcinoma in Asian populations.

Poliomyelitis

Polioviruses can multiply within the tissues of the oropharynx and intestines. Poliovirus adsorbs to receptors that are located on only a few cell types: cells in the nasopharynx, intestinal tract lining, and anterior horn cells of the spinal cord have poliovirus receptors. The viral particles attach to these cell receptors via viral surface capsid proteins. Then, the poliovirus is taken up inside the cell by endocytosis. Viruses entering the bloodstream are disseminated and further viral replication occurs within lymphatic tissues. Polioviruses can cross the blood-brain barrier, where they continue to multiply within neural tissues and cause varying degrees of damage to the nervous system.

The initial symptoms of poliomyelitis, commonly referred to as *polio,* include headache, vomiting, constipation, and sore throat. In many cases, these early symptoms are followed by obvious neural involvement, including paralysis due to the injury of motor neurons. Although the paralysis can affect any motor function, in over half of the cases of paralytic poliomyelitis the arms or legs are involved. Fortunately, paralytic symptoms are 1,000 times less frequent than nonparalytic infections, and many cases of poliovirus infection fail to show any evidence of clinical symptomatology. Poliomyelitis is prevalent in children and as such is also called *infantile paralysis.* The disease also strikes adults; in fact, the fatality rate in adults is much higher than that in children.

A postpolio syndrome has surfaced in recent years among survivors of polio, occurring about 40 years after the initial attack. The symptoms are similar to those of the original disease but there is no trace of viral involvement. It is theorized that the neurological cells that took over the functions of polio-damaged tissues are now suffering the aftereffects of 40 years of overwork.

Rabies

When rabies viruses, which are bullet-shaped, single-stranded RNA viruses, enter through an animal bite, they are normally deposited within muscle tissues, where they subsequently multiply. The rabies viruses reach peripheral nerve endings and migrate to the central nervous system. Cytoplasmic inclusion bodies, known as *Negri bodies,* develop within the neurons of the brain. Replication of rabies viruses within the nervous system causes numerous abnormalities, which are manifested as the symptoms of this disease. The initial symptoms of rabies include anxiety, irritability, depression, and sensitivity to light and sound. These symptoms are followed by the development of hydrophobia (fear of water) because of difficulty in swallowing. As the infection progresses, there is paralysis, coma, and death.

In urban settings, dogs are most frequently the animal that transmits rabies. Wild animals involved in the transmission of rabies include raccoons, foxes, skunks, jackals, mongooses, squirrels, coyotes, badgers, and bats (FIG. 13-27). Raccoons are the number one reservoir for rabies in much of the U.S. today. Rabies viruses multiply within the salivary glands of infected animals and normally enter humans in the an-

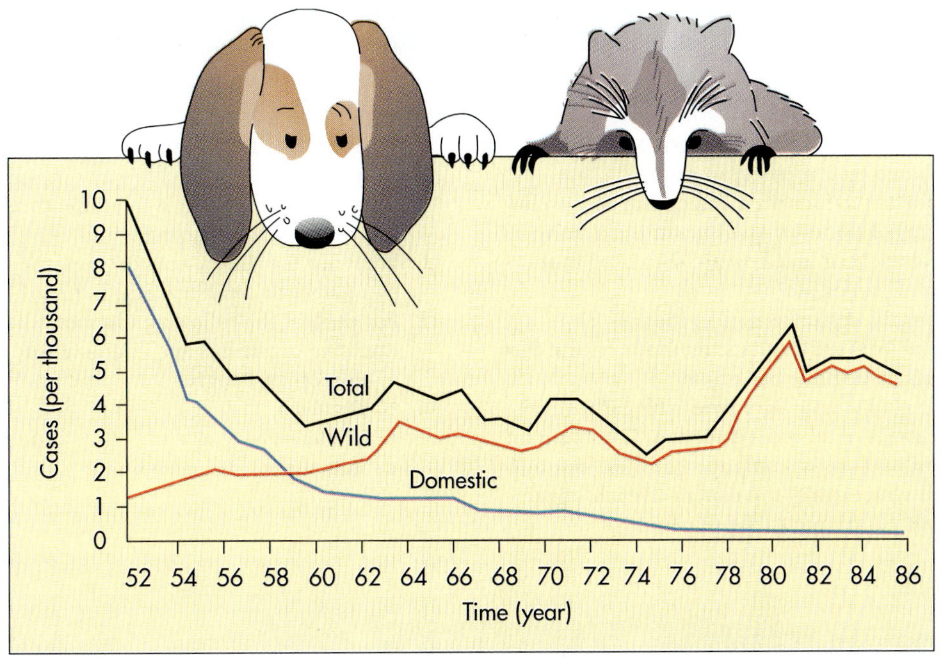

FIG. 13-27 Mandatory vaccination of domestic animals has resulted in the near elimination of rabies from dogs and other pets. The rabies virus remains endemic in many wild animals that act as vectors of this disease.

imal's saliva through the portal of entry established by the animal's bite. The rabies virus cannot penetrate the skin by itself, and deposition of infected saliva on intact skin does not necessarily result in transmission of the disease. A new live vaccine has been developed that can be added to baited foods and dropped into forests and remote areas. This would make it possible to establish immunity in wild animal populations. The new vaccine is genetically engineered using the smallpox vaccine (vaccinia virus) as a vector.

DENGUE FEVER

The dengue virus replicates within cells of the circulatory system, causing a viral infection called dengue fever, of the bloodstream that persists for 1 to 3 days during the febrile period. Replication of the dengue virus within the cytoplasm of cells of the circulatory system causes vascular damage. Immune reactions contribute to the formation of complexes that initiate intravascular coagulation (blood clotting within the blood vessels) or hemorrhagic lesions. A characteristic rash and fever develop during all forms of this disease. Previous exposure to dengue virus and the presence of a cross-reacting antibody seem to be important in determining the severity of the disease symptomatology. Damage to the circulatory vessels appears to occur when antigen–antibody complexes activate the complement system, with the release of vasoactive compounds.

ENCEPHALITIS

Encephalitis, a disease syndrome defined by an inflammation of the brain, can be caused by various viruses. The different forms of viral encephalitis include eastern equine, western equine, Venezuelan equine, St. Louis, Japanese B, Murray Valley, California, and tick-borne encephalitis, as well as several others. The specific viral etiologic agent, arthropod vector, and geographic distribution are different for each of these forms. Infections with encephalitis-causing viruses begin with viremia, followed by localization of the viral infection within the central nervous system, where lesions develop. The locations of the lesions within the brain are characteristic for each type. With the exception of St. Louis encephalitis, in which kidney damage also occurs, the pathological changes are normally restricted to the central nervous system.

Encephalitis symptoms are often subclinical. When the illness is symptomatic, encephalitis begins with fever, headache, and vomiting, followed by stiffness and then paralysis, convulsions, psychoses, and coma. Different forms of viral encephalitis have different outcomes. For example, in symptomatic cases of eastern equine encephalitis the mortality rate is approximately 80%, but in western equine encephalitis it is less than 15%. Individuals who recover from symptomatic encephalitis may have permanent neurological damage.

CHAPTER REVIEW

STUDY QUESTIONS

1. How are differential blood counts used to determine if a disease is caused by a microorganism?
2. Why is it important to identify cultures sent to the clinical microbiology laboratory quickly and accurately?
3. What are serologic tests and how are they used in the identification of pathogens?
4. How is immunofluorescence used to identify *Treponema pallidum*? Why are serologic methods critical for identifying this pathogenic bacterium?
5. How are gene probes used for identifying pathogens?
6. Describe the stages of an acute infection. Comment on the number of pathogens, components of the immune response, and symptoms of the patient at each stage.
7. What attributes contribute to the virulence of pathogens?
8. What is the difference between toxigenicity and invasiveness?
9. What is a toxin? What is the difference between an endotoxin and an exotoxin?
10. What are the differences between the toxins produced by *Clostridium botulinum* and *C. tetani?*
11. For each of the following diseases, what are the causative organisms and characteristic pathologies:
    a. Whooping cough
    b. Botulism
    c. Cholera
    d. Tetanus

SITUATIONAL PROBLEMS

1. Defining a Pathogen

United States federal regulations concerning the deliberate release of genetically engineered microorganisms into the environment established one set of guidelines for pathogens and another for nonpathogens. Other regulations concern the shipment and transport of pathogens. The guidelines fail to deal specifically with opportunistic pathogens, which are organisms that normally do not cause disease but that can do so under certain conditions. For example, *Escherichia coli,* which is part of the normal intestinal microbiota of a healthy individual, can cause serious urinary tract and spinal column infections under certain circumstances. Therefore it may be considered by some as a nonpathogen and by others as a pathogen.

Typically, when governmental regulations and guidelines are proposed, a time period is made available for public comment. Assume that we are still in that period when public comment is requested to help shape the final regulations. What definition would you propose for pathogenic microorganisms that could be applied universally for regulatory purposes? Justify your position in a cogent letter that could be sent to your congressional representative.

2. Trying to Diagnose Diseases

To help finance your college education, you have a part-time job in a physician's office. Your job includes responsibility for gathering information about the patient that may aid in making a diagnosis. Because you are a premed major, you decide to find out whether you can diagnose the disease based on the information you acquire. You keep a private record of your presumed diagnoses and later check them against the diagnoses made by the physician.

1. The first patient of the day is a 12-year-old boy who suddenly developed localized severe pain on the right side of the abdomen. At a party the previous night, he ate 12 hot dogs and various other foods. He is currently exhibiting nausea and vomiting. He weighs 130 pounds. He has a temperature of 101° F. Examination of a blood sample shows an elevated leukocyte count. Based on this information, what disease would you suspect?
2. The second patient is a 30-year-old woman who has been experiencing a series of upper respiratory tract infections. She is diabetic. Last month she had a case of pneumonia that was diagnosed as caused by *Streptococcus pneumoniae.* She was treated with a third-generation penicillin and recovered fully. Now she again has pneumonia, but this time the clinical laboratory diagnosed the causative agent as *Pneumocystis carinii.* She is being treated with metronidazole. What underlying disease do you suspect?
3. Next, you answer a phone call from one of the doctor's regular patients. The patient informs you that his entire family had gone to the beach for a summer picnic. After swimming for some time they had lunch, which included chicken salad, potato salad, lemonade, and apple pie. A few hours later, they dug up some clams, which they ate raw. By the time they reached home, they all had abdominal pain and the children were vomiting. No member of the group had a fever. What disease would you suspect?
4. The next patient to enter the office is an 18-year-old freshman at Wisconsin University who has just come home for the summer vacation. Shortly before finals for the spring semester, she noticed that she was tired and had little energy. She had an ac-

SITUATIONAL PROBLEMS–cont'd

tive social life but still maintained a high B average. She has blond hair, blue eyes, is 5 feet 5 inches tall, and weighs 124 pounds. She tells you that she has been feeling slightly feverish each evening but that the feeling always disappears by morning. Just before she left school for vacation, the university's health clinic took a blood sample and told her to have her family physician call for the test results. You call the clinic and are told that the test revealed an elevated leukocyte count and the presence of abnormal leukocytes. What disease would you suspect?

5. A female patient has several painful lesions on her genitals. She has been sexually active. She tells you that this is not the first time she has had such lesions. At each occurrence, the lesions healed within a few weeks, but shortly thereafter new lesions appeared in the same region. She does not now, nor has she previously had, lesions anywhere else on her body. The process of healing and recurrence has occurred every few weeks over the past year, and she has finally decided to see a physician about this condition. What disease would you suspect?

Suggested Supplementary Readings

Alcamo IE: 1993. *AIDS: The Biological Basis,* Wm. C. Brown Communications, Inc., Dubuque, IA.

Bhakdi S and J Tranum-Jensen: 1991. Alpha-toxin of *Staphylococcus aureus, Microbiological Reviews* 55(4):733-51.

Brubaker RR: 1985. Mechanisms of bacterial virulence, *Annual Review of Microbiology* 39:21-50.

Buller RM and G Palumbo: 1991. Poxvirus pathogenesis, *Microbiological Reviews* 55(1):80-122.

Chesney PJ, MS Bergdoll, JP Davis: 1984. The disease spectrum, epidemiology, and etiology of toxic-shock syndrome, *Annual Review of Microbiology* 38:315-38.

Costerten JW, K-J Cheng, GG Geesey, TI Ladd, JC Nickel, M Dasgupta, TJ Marrie: 1987. Bacterial biofilm in nature and disease, *Annual Review of Microbiology* 41:435-464.

DiRita VJ and JJ Mekalanos: 1989. Genetic control of bacterial virulence, *Annual Review of Genetics* 23:455-482.

Dowling JN, AK Saha, RH Glew: 1992. Virulence factors of the family *Legionellaceae, Microbiological Reviews* 56(1):32-60.

Eidels LRL and DA Hart: 1983. Membrane receptors for bacterial toxins, *Microbiological Reviews* 47:596-614.

Evans EGV and MD Richardson (eds.): 1989. *Medical Mycology: A Practical Approach,* IRL Press, Oxford, England.

Fitzgerald TJ: 1981. Pathogenesis and immunology of *Treponema pallidum, Annual Review of Microbiology* 35:29-54.

Habicht GS, G Beck, JL Benach: 1987. Lyme disease, *Scientific American* 257(3):78-83.

Hawkey PM and DA Lewis (eds.): 1989. *Medical Bacteriology: A Practical Approach,* IRL Press, Oxford, England.

Hensyl WR (ed.): 1990. *Stedman's Medical Dictionary,* ed. 25, Williams and Wilkins, Baltimore, MD.

Isenberg HD: 1988. Pathogenicity and virulence: Another view, *Clinical Microbiology Reviews* 1(1):40-53.

Jawetz E, JL Melnick, EA Adelberg: 1986. *A Review of Medical Microbiology,* Appleton and Lange, New York.

Joklik WK, HP Willett, DB Amos, CM Wilfert (eds.): 1992. *Zinsser Microbiology,* ed. 20, Appleton and Lange, Norwalk, CT.

Kenne L and B Linderg: 1983. Bacterial polysaccharides. In Aspinall GO (ed.) The polysaccharides, vol 2, Academic Press, New York.

Loesche WJ: 1986. Role of *Streptococcus mutans* in human dental decay, *Microbiological Reviews* 50:353-380.

Lyerly DM, HC Krivan, TD Wilkins: 1988. *Clostridium difficile:* Its diseases and toxins, *Clinical Microbiology Reviews* 1(1):1-18.

Mandell GL, RG Douglas Jr, JE Bennett: 1990. *Principles and Practices of Infectious Diseases,* ed. 3, John Wiley and Sons, New York.

Middlebrook JL and RB Dorland: 1984. Bacterial toxins: Cellular mechanisms of action, *Microbiological Reviews* 48:199-221.

Moss J and M Vaughan: 1990. *ADP-ribosylating Toxins and G Proteins,* American Society for Microbiology, Washington, D. C.

Murray PR, GS Kobyashi, MA Pfaller, KS Rosenthal: 1993. *Medical Microbiology,* ed. 2, Mosby, St. Louis.

Nolte WA (ed.): 1980. *Oral Microbiology,* C.V. Mosby Co., St. Louis.

Rietschel ET and H Brade: 1992. Bacterial endotoxins, *Scientific American* 267(2):54-61.

Roberts RB: 1986. *Infectious Disease: Pathogenesis, Diagnosis, and Therapy,* Year Book Medical Publishers, Inc., Chicago.

Shulman ST, JP Phair, HM Sommers: 1992. *The Biologic and Clinical Basis of Infectious Disease,* ed. 4, W. B. Saunders, Philadelphia.

Smith H: 1989. The mounting interest in bacterial and viral pathogenicity, *Annual Review of Microbiology* 43:1-22.

Sweet C and H Smith: 1980. Pathogenicity of influenza viruses, *Microbiological Reviews* 44:303-309.

Tiollais P and M-A Buenidia: 1991. Hepatitis B virus, *Scientific American* 264(4):116-123.

Todd JK: 1988. Toxic shock syndrome, *Clinical Microbiology Reviews* 1(4):432-46.

Unny SK and BL Middlebrook: 1983. Streptococcal rheumatic carditis, *Microbiological Reviews* 47:97-109.

Volk WA et al: 1986. *Essentials of Medical Microbiology,* J.B. Lippincott Co., Philadelphia.

Wick MJ, DW Frank, DG Storey, BH Iglewski: 1990. Structure, function, and regulation of *Pseudomonas aeruginosa* endotoxin A, *Annual Review of Microbiology* 44:335-364.

Gail Houston Cassell
University of Alabama at Birmingham

Gail Houston Cassell's research focuses on host–parasite relationships in mycoplasmal diseases and the role of phagocytes in host resistance. She was born in Alabama in 1946 and received her undergraduate education at the University of Alabama. Her Ph.D. is from the University of Alabama, Birmingham, where she is currently chair of the microbiology department.

When I was in the second or third grade I became fascinated with butterflies. They were so small, yet so efficient in their flight and their pursuit of food. How could that be? I lived in a small rural Alabama community so I was lucky enough to have nature as my first laboratory, and somehow early in my life I learned the skills of observation and focus, two essentials to becoming a scientist. That I ended up directing my research interests toward understanding mycoplasmas is a consequence, once again, of being fortunate enough to be in the right place at the right time but, more importantly, being there with the right skills and the desire to learn.

Mycoplasmas are the smallest known free-living microorganisms. They are known to cause arthritis, and respiratory and genitourinary diseases. My research has focused on the mycoplasma *Ureaplasma urealyticum,* which is found in the lower genitourinary tract of more than 50% of sexually active individuals. The organism is sexually transmitted and can be transferred from a pregnant woman to the fetus. Our research has shown that this organism is significantly associated with respiratory disease and meningitis in the newborn, particularly premature infants. It may also be associated with increased risk of death, particularly in very low birth weight infants.

In another area of mycoplasma research, my laboratory established *Mycoplasma pulmonis* as a major cause of respiratory and genital disease in laboratory rats and mice. Our work has led to routine screening for this organism in animal colonies used in biomedical research. In fact, before the first rats were placed on the NASA space shuttle we screened them in our University of Alabama at Birmingham laboratory for mycoplasma infection.

Mycoplasmas were first recognized as significant human pathogens in the early 1950s, so when I entered the field in the 1970s it was very exciting and still very new. It was fortuitous that I ended up working on this group of microorganisms. I majored in microbiology as an undergraduate at the University of Alabama in Tuscaloosa and was ready to move on to graduate at the University of Indiana where truly outstanding research was being conducted in bacteriology. My interest in microbiology had been nourished by a learning environment that provided opportunity and also rewarded dedication and hard work.

My interest in science peaked in the tenth grade when I first learned about the ability to grow cells in culture. I had a superb biology teacher that year. I was amazed that cells could be grown out of the body. That year I entered a project in the high school science fair on mammalian sarcomas in chickens. Sarcomas are malignant tumors of mesenchymal derivation and I was interested in the etiology of malignancy. I suppose it was at this point that I realized I wanted to pursue a science related to human health.

I continued to try to understand the phenomena of sarcoma and in the eleventh grade I won first place in the International Science Fair for my entry on the rous sarcoma virus. My project dealt with vaccination of chickens against the cancer caused by this virus, an idea that in those days was rather unconventional. I was also a Westinghouse Science Talent Search semifinalist that year. The awards were wonderful and a strong positive influence on my decision to seek a career in science but I believe I would have gone down the same path without the accolades. Winning science fairs is not a prerequisite for becoming a scientist. Science is a great adventure with abundant challenges and rewards but it is also a way of seeing the world with new eyes and giving meaning to life. I never really thought of doing anything else.

Days before I was preparing to leave for the University of Indiana I was contacted by an individual who had established a nonprofit foundation with the goal to keep the products of the Alabama science educational system in Alabama for undergraduate and graduate study. This was a marvelous piece of social and economic engineering that worked, at least in my case. The foundation made me an offer I could not refuse so I changed my plans at the last minute and enrolled at the University of Alabama in Tuscaloosa and ultimately at the University of Alabama at Birmingham as a doctoral candidate. The Birmingham campus was very small then; it is now, in 1994, only 25 years old.

There was not lot to choose from in picking a research area for study. It was my great good luck that two veterinarians had just arrived from Johns Hopkins University to conduct research in comparative medicine (the study of animal models related to human disease), specifically, naturally occurring respiratory disease in rodents. Thus began my pursuit of understanding mycoplasmas and their role in infection and disease.

Today I sit on the board of the very same foundation that persuaded me to stay in Alabama, and the academic health center of the University of Alabama at Birmingham has grown to great diversity and vitality, ranking seventeenth in overall funding of research from the National Institutes of Health. Barbara McClintock, who won the 1983 Nobel prize for her lifelong research into the genetic characteristics of maize, once said, "It might seem unfair to reward a person for having so much pleasure over the years." I certainly feel fortunate that so many opportunities were available to me and I recognize that such opportunities are increasingly limited. Young scientists today have so much more complexity to deal with and so much more information to process. Fortunately, biomedical science is also becoming more multidisciplinary, so the narrow interests of various disciplines are more able to cross over and assist each other.

As a practicing scientist I believe it is also my responsibility to train the next generation of scientists. As chair of the Department of Microbiology at the University of Alabama at Birmingham I maintain an active training pro-

Continued.

gram for students in the study of the basic mechanisms of lung diseases, and we provide summer research fellowships for medical, dental, and veterinary students. A rapidly expanding knowledge base in biology and medicine and the potential for clinical application has presented unprecedented opportunities for advances in disease prevention, diagnosis, and treatment. Now, more than ever, it is important that basic scientists and clinicians communicate and exchange information.

Communication and the exchange of information is especially true in my area of research. Although my laboratory has made great strides in understanding the structure and behavior of the ureaplasma organism, we depend on physician colleagues to help us apply this knowledge to alleviate human suffering. We have found that women infected with *Ureaplasma urealyticum* usually have no symptoms. If the organism remains confined to the lower genital tract, which is usually the case, it typically causes no problems, but if the pathogen finds its way to the upper genital tract early in pregnancy, it can cause miscarriage or premature delivery. Although ureaplasma is the most common organism isolated from the lungs of newborns with respiratory disease it is not usually looked for in sick infants. This is where physicians enter the picture because bench scientists are typically not in a position to order the necessary diagnostic tests. If a physician is not keeping up with the latest scientific developments, we all lose. Conversely, if the bench scientist is ignorant of the complexities of clinical research, time and resources are wasted.

We know that the ureaplasma organism does not have a cell wall and is not affected by a lot of the antibiotics commonly prescribed prophylactically to mothers and newborns. We also know that it does respond to the antibiotic erythromycin. Therefore, if you can recognize the pathogen, you can treat it, and if you do that early enough you can reduce the complications from it. However, we cannot prove that until we conduct some long-term collaborative studies on the pharmacokinetics of erythromycin in newborns. How safe is such therapy? Is there a chance that it's toxic? Clinical studies in humans are very complex, and physician scientists have a lot to offer the bench scientist who is accustomed to controlled experimentation in the test tube. Biomedical research will always need the most creative minds from the basic and clinical sciences to collaboratively find the causes and cures of human suffering. Patience is also required. When one is working with human subjects, considerations must always be given to the ethics and safety of the work no matter how enthusiastic and confident one is about the possible outcomes.

Just as exciting new fields in microbiology were opening up when I started my career 20 years ago, exciting new possibilities exist today, but many of these ideas are still just possibilities. They have to be tested, redefined, modified, and tested again. The work of science is never done; it just keeps changing.

Biotechnology with its possibilities to provide new antibiotics and other drugs, accurate diagnostics, and tools for bioremediation, marine biotechnology, and the production of new food products provides an enormous playing field for individuals pursuing science in academic, government, and industrial laboratories. Vaccine development is at the edge of an entire new approach to controlling disease because of new developments in molecular biology . Vaccines are even being tested against different forms of cancer. Imagine that! Never has there been such an exciting time in the life sciences. Whether we train students to becomes bench scientists, physicians, industrialists, investment bankers, or public officials, knowing the process of science, recognizing its capabilities and having an awareness of its limitations has never been more important.

PART SIX

Applied and Environmental Microbiology

CHAPTER 14

Microbial Ecology

Chapter Outline

Microbial ecology examines the interrelationships between microorganisms and their living (biotic) and nonliving (abiotic) environments. Some interactions, such as mutualism, between microorganisms are beneficial; others, such as competition and predation, often limit the development of microbial populations. These population interactions are dynamic. Competition eliminates populations that are less well adapted to conditions at a given habitat. Mutualism gives rise to essentially new organisms, such as lichens.

Microbial activities have a major influence on the environment. Microbial metabolism establishes global biogeochemical cycles of elements. Microorganisms are crucial for the biodegradation of wastes and pollutants. The treatment of sewage and municipal wastes depends on the use of microbial degradation activities. Microbial activities and interpopulation relationships have a major impact on agricultural productivity. Microorganisms are especially critical in the cycling of nitrogen, with bacterial fixation of atmospheric nitrogen, nitrification, and denitrification determining the availability of nitrogenous nutrients for the growth of plants. Biological control uses the negative interactions of microorganisms to control pests and plant pathogens.

14.1 COMMUNITIES AND ECOSYSTEMS

Microorganisms do not live alone. Individual microorganisms reproduce to form *populations* or *clones*. Often, populations of microorganisms occur as microcolonies in the environment. Populations also interact with each other to form communities. A **community** is a unified assemblage of populations that coexist and interact at a given location called a *habitat*. For microorganisms, the habitat may be spatially small and often is called a *microhabitat*. The community and habitat are part of a larger system called an *ecosystem*. An **ecosystem** is a functional self-supporting system that includes the organisms in a natural community and their environment. Energy flows through ecosystems and materials are cycled within ecosystems.

Populations within a community perform functions that contribute to the overall community and maintain the ecological balance of the ecosystem. Each population occupies a **niche** (functional role) within the community. The microbial populations that occupy the niches represent the autochthonous (indigenous) microorganisms. Theoretically, there are a limited number of niches within the community for which populations compete. The best-adapted populations win and displace those less well suited to occupy the niches of that community.

The successful populations within a community must survive and grow under the environmental conditions of the habitat. In particular, the autochthonous populations respond to the microenvironmental conditions of the microhabitat, modifying their environment as they grow. On a larger scale, microbial populations live in various habitats. Soil, freshwater, and marine habitats have differing environmental properties and distinct microbial communities. Some bacteria are considered to be marine species, others soil bacteria, and so forth. Microbial populations living in extreme environments, such as Antarctic dry valley soils, hot springs, deep sea geothermal vents, and salt lakes, have received special attention from microbial ecologists because of the special adaptive characteristics required to occupy niches in those extreme habitats. The adaptive physiological properties of various specialized groups of microorganisms are discussed in Chapter 9.

14.2 POPULATION INTERACTIONS

TYPES OF INTERACTIONS

Within a biological community, various types of interactions can occur between diverse microbial populations, between microbial and plant populations, and between plant and animal populations. In some cases, the interaction is beneficial; in other cases, the interaction is harmful to one or both populations (Table 14-1).

Positive interactions between biological populations enhance the survival capacity of the interacting populations. The development of positive interactions permits more efficient use of available resources than can be accomplished by an individual population growing alone. Sometimes populations co-exist in habitats where neither could exist alone.

Because all relationships can be viewed as beneficial in the overall sense of maintaining ecological balance, the term *symbiosis* was originally used to denote any intimate relationship between two populations, whether beneficial or not. The present use of the term *symbiosis,* however, is restricted to situations in which both organisms benefit and where the relationship is obligatory.

Negative interactions between populations act as feedback mechanisms that limit population densities. In some cases, negative interactions may eliminate a population that is not well adapted for continued existence within the community of a given habitat. Negative interactions tend to preclude the invasion of an established community composed of **autochthonous populations** *(indigenous populations)* by **allochthonous populations** *(foreign populations);* negative interactions thus act to maintain community stability. Within stable communities, negative interactions are adaptive and ensure the maintenance of a balance between popu-

TABLE 14-1 Classification of Population Interactions

NAME OF INTERACTION	EFFECT OF INTERACTION: POPULATION A	EFFECT OF INTERACTION: POPULATION B
Neutralism	0	0
Commensalism	0	+
Synergism (protocooperation)	+	+
Mutualism (symbiosis)	+	+
Competition	−	−
Amensalism	0 or +	−
Parasitism	+	−
Predation	+	−

0, No effect; +, positive effect; −, negative effect.

lations within the biological community. Negative feedback interactions limit population densities and provide a self-regulation mechanism that benefits the overall population in the long-term because it prevents overpopulation and destruction of the habitat's resources.

The intensity of both positive and negative interactions between populations generally are greatest at high population densities and when populations are actively growing. It is under these conditions that organisms living together within a community interact and compete for the available resources. In contrast, low rates of metabolic activity, which characterize the resting stages of microorganisms, favor a lack of interaction. Low population densities and the formation of resting stages permit organisms to co-exist without competing for the same available resources in the habitat. Such a lack of interaction between two populations, called *neutralism,* is more likely at low population densities so that organisms are less likely to come into contact and to compete with each other. Microorganisms in dormant resting stages are more likely to exhibit neutralism toward other microbial populations than actively growing vegetative cells.

COMMENSALISM

Commensalism is a unidirectional relationship between populations in which one population benefits and the other one is unaffected. Commensal relationships are common, often occurring when the unaffected population modifies the habitat in such a way that a second population benefits. For example, the removal of oxygen from a habitat, as a result of the metabolic activities of a population of facultative anaerobes, creates an environment favorable for the growth of obligately anaerobic populations. Many obligate anaerobes, such as *Bacteroides* species, can live in the human gastrointestinal tract because facultative anaerobes, such as *Escherichia coli,* have removed the molecular oxygen. The lowered oxygen tension favors the anaerobic bacteria, and assuming that there is lack of competition for the same available substrates, the obligate anaerobes do not affect the existence of the facultative organisms. Various other chemical modifications of the environment of a given habitat by one microbial population likewise may benefit other populations without resulting in any negative or positive feedback interactions.

In some cases, a microbial population can physically or chemically alter a habitat, permitting a second population to exist. Production of a primary bacterial film on the hull of a ship, for example, permits secondary colonization by many other microorganisms that results in fouling. In a similar manner, a primary infection caused by one microbial species may allow opportunistic pathogens to establish secondary infections, with the opportunistic pathogens benefiting from their ability to invade and multiply within the host organism without adversely affecting the primary pathogen population. Waste products of one organism may be a favorable substrate for the growth of another organism. *Coprophagous fungi,* for example, live on fecal material. The fungi benefit from the animals' deposition of fecal material, and the members of that animal population are unaffected by the relationship.

Many commensal relationships are based on the production of growth factors. Some bacterial populations produce and excrete growth factors, such as vitamins, that can be utilized by other populations. As long as the growth factors are produced in excess and are excreted from an organism, a commensal interaction can occur. For example, fastidious microorganisms often depend on growth factors released from other organisms. Some marine bacteria growing within the water column depend on specific amino acids or vitamins produced by surface algae. Often it is difficult to culture such bacteria on defined media because of a lack of understanding of the organism's growth factor requirements.

Cometabolism

Cometabolism occurs when an organism growing on a particular substrate gratuitously transforms a second substrate that it is unable to assimilate. This forms the basis for many commensal relationships. Although the organism responsible for the transformation does not

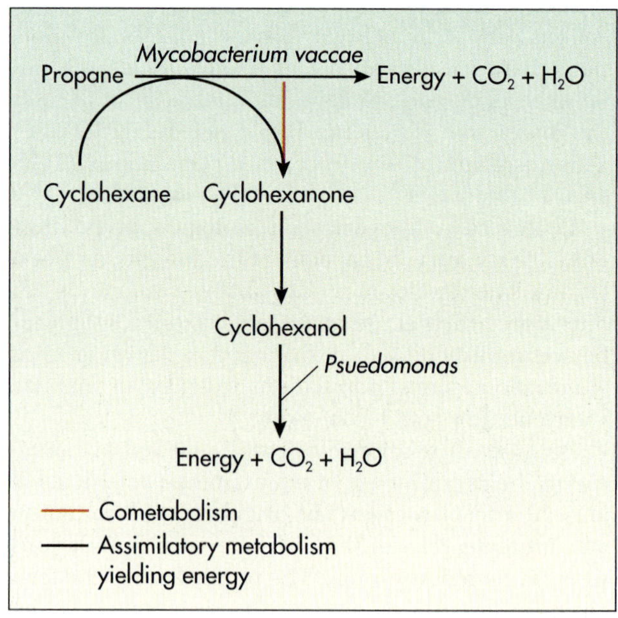

FIG. 14-1 Cyclohexane is transformed by cometabolism to cyclohexanol by *Mycobacterium vaccae* growing on propane. This is a gratuitous oxidation; *M. vaccae* gains nothing by the oxidation of cyclohexane. A *Pseudomonas* species, however, can use cyclohexanol as its source of carbon and energy. In this manner, cometabolism forms the basis for commensalism with one microorganism feeding another.

benefit, other populations may use the transformation products it forms. For example, *Mycobacterium vaccae,* growing on propane as a source of carbon and energy, will gratuitously oxidize cyclohexane to cyclohexanone (FIG. 14-1). *M. vaccae* gains no energy and assimilates no carbon from the metabolic transformation of cyclohexane to cyclohexanone. The cyclohexanone can be used by other microorganisms, such as populations of *Pseudomonas* species. In such a case, the *Pseudomonas* species benefit because they are unable to metabolize cyclohexane; the *Mycobacterium* is unaffected because it does not assimilate cyclohexanone.

Epiphytes

A commensal relationship may also be established when one organism grows on the surface of another organism. **Epiphytic bacteria** (literally growing on plant surfaces) grow as commensal populations on many plant surfaces. They colonize the surfaces of algae and plants, benefiting from the photosynthetic metabolic activities of these organisms (FIG. 14-2). Bacterial populations also grow on the skin surface, generally exhibiting a commensal relationship with human beings. (The use of the term *epiphytic* extends to include growth on the surfaces of animals and other organisms besides plants.) The normal microbiota of humans that grow on skin are epiphytes that benefit from being able to grow on a surface and from the nutrients and water provided in human sweat. Humans are not adversely affected nor do they necessarily benefit directly from the growth of various microbial populations on the skin surface. Many other animals similarly have naturally occurring surface bacterial populations.

SYNERGISM

Synergism or **proto-cooperation** between two populations indicates that both populations benefit from the relationship but that the association is not obligatory. Both populations are capable of surviving independently, although they both gain advantage from the synergistic relationship. Synergistic relationships are loose in that one member population can readily be replaced by another. In some cases, it is difficult to distinguish between commensalism and synergism.

Syntrophism

Syntrophism is a type of synergism in which the two populations supply each other's nutritional needs. The term *syntrophic* means eating together. Syntrophism is sometimes called *cross-feeding.* Two microbial populations may complete a metabolic pathway that neither organism is capable of carrying out alone because of syntrophism. As a result of such cooperative metabolism, both organisms can derive carbon and energy from a substrate.

As an example of syntrophism, *Streptococcus faecalis* and *E. coli* are able to convert arginine to putrescine together, although neither organism can carry out the transformation alone. *S. faecalis* is able to convert arginine to ornithine, which can then be used by a population of *E. coli* to produce putrescine; *E. coli* growing alone can transform arginine to produce agmatine but cannot convert arginine to putrescine. *Lactobacillus arabinosus* and *S. faecalis* similarly can establish a synergistic relationship based on the mutual exchange of required growth factors (FIG. 14-3). *L. ara-*

FIG. 14-2 Micrograph showing numerous epiphytic bacteria growing on the surface of an alga. (400×).

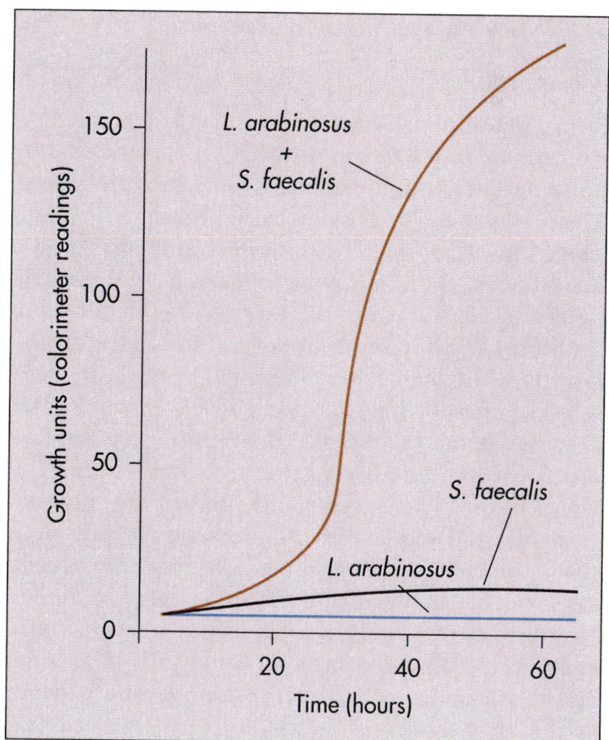

FIG. 14-3 The synergistic relationship between *Lactobacillus arabinosus* and *Streptococcus faecalis* permits each to grow on a minimal medium when both are present. The synergism is based on cross-feeding of essential growth factors. Neither can grow alone on a minimal medium.

binosus requires phenylalanine for growth, which is produced by *S. faecalis*. *S. faecalis* requires folic acid, which is produced by *L. arabinosus*. In a minimal medium, both populations can grow together, but neither population can grow alone.

Syntrophism is very important in methanogenesis. The production of methane by archaebacteria depends on *interspecies hydrogen transfer*, which is a series of reactions that results in supplying hydrogen from complex polymers for the reduction of CO_2 to CH_4. Various fermentative bacteria produce low molecular weight fatty acids that can be degraded by anaerobic bacteria to produce molecular hydrogen (H_2). H_2-producing fatty acid–oxidizing bacteria grow better when H_2 is consumed by methanogens because H_2 does not accumulate as an end-product inhibitor. Both *Syntrophomonas* and *Syntrophobacter* are H_2 producers. The names of these bacterial genera indicate their syntrophic relationships with H_2-consuming methogenic archaebacteria. *Syntrophomonas* species oxidize butyric acid and caproic acid to acetate and H_2; members of this genus also oxidize valeric acid and enanthic acid to acetate, CO_2, and H_2. *Syntrophobacter* oxidizes propionic acid to acetate, CO_2, and H_2. The acetate and H_2 produced by these bacteria are used by methanogenic archaebacteria to produce methane. The metabolism of the methanogens maintains very low concentrations of H_2. The removal of the H_2 end product draws the equilibrium of fatty acid fermentation toward additional H_2 production, increasing the growth rates of *Syntrophomonas* and *Syntrophobacter* species.

Rhizosphere Effect

Synergistic interactions between plants and microorganisms are important in providing the nutritional requirements of both members. Within the **rhizosphere,** which is the soil region in close contact with plant roots, the plant roots exert a direct influence on the soil bacteria. This influence is known as the **rhizosphere effect.** Likewise, the microbial populations in the rhizosphere have an important influence on the growth of the plant. As a consequence of these interactions, microbial populations reach much higher densities in the rhizosphere than in the free soil and plants exhibit enhanced growth characteristics. The interactions of plant roots and rhizosphere microorganisms are based largely on interactive modification of the soil chemical environment by processes such as water uptake by the plant system, release of organic chemicals to the soil by the plant root, microbial production of plant growth factors, and microbially mediated availability of mineral nutrients. The bacteria in the rhizosphere grow on the nutrients released from the plant roots. It is based on these nutrients that the high bacterial population levels in the rhizosphere occur.

Microbial populations in the rhizosphere may benefit the plant by (1) removing hydrogen sulfide, which is toxic to the plant roots; (2) increasing solubilization of mineral nutrients needed by the plant for growth; (3) synthesizing vitamins, amino acids, auxins, and gibberellins that stimulate plant growth; and (4) antagonizing potential plant pathogens through competition and the production of antibiotics. *Allelopathic substances,* which are substances formed by an organism that inhibit other organisms, are produced by microorganisms in the rhizosphere; these may allow plants to establish antagonistic relationships with other plant populations. Allelopathic substances surrounding some plants prevent invasions of that habitat by other plants, and such amensal relationships between plant populations may actually be based on synergistic relationships between plants and synergistic microbial populations.

MUTUALISM

Mutualism or **symbiosis** is an obligatory interrelationship between two populations that benefits both of them. Mutualism is an extension of synergism, allowing populations to unite and establish essentially a single unit population that can occupy habitats unfavorable for the existence of either population alone. Mutualistic relationships may lead to the evolution of new organisms. Various theories of evolution point to the structural similarities between mitochondria, chloroplasts, and prokaryotic cells to indicate that the development of eukaryotic organisms was based on the establishment of endosymbiotic relationships with bacteria. According to the theory of endosymbiotic evolution, bacterial cells began to live within the predecessors of modern eukaryotic cells; both the bacteria and eukaryotes became mutually dependent on this relationship for survival, leading to the contemporary eukaryotic cells. In a more specific example, the protozoan *Mixotricha paradoxa* is propelled by rows of attached bacterial cells (spirochetes) rather than by conventional cilia.

Lichens

Lichens are composed of a primary producer, the phycobiont, and a consumer, the mycobiont (FIG. 14-4). Lichens are formed by a mutualistic relationship between some heterotrophic fungi *(mycobiont)* and their photosynthetic algal or cyanobacterial partners *(phycobiont)*. A lichen has totally different physiological properties than either of the species of which it is composed. Lichens can grow in habitats, such as on rock surfaces, where neither algae, cyanobacteria, nor fungi can exist alone. Most lichens are resistant to extremes of temperature and desiccation, a particular advantage on exposed surface habitats. The lichen is

FIG. 14-4 **A,** Colorized micrograph of the lichen *Letharia vulpina* showing it is composed of a fungus (mycobiont) and an alga (phycobiont) living in mutualistic association. (1,000×). The fungal hyphae *(yellow)* weave around the algal cells *(green)*. **B,** Lichens growing on a rock. These organisms can grow under dry conditions.

a very self-sufficient organism. The phycobiont utilizes light energy and atmospheric CO_2 to produce the organic matter consumed by the mycobiont. In some lichens the cyanobacterial partner is also capable of fixing atmospheric nitrogen. The mycobiont provides physical protection for the lichen and produces organic acids that can solubilize rock minerals, making essential nutrients available to the lichen.

Although the mutualistic relationships of algal or cyanobacterial and fungal populations in lichens are normally stable, they can be disrupted by environmental perturbations. Lichens are extremely sensitive to air pollution; sulfur dioxide in the atmosphere is particularly inhibitory to lichens (FIG. 14-5). Exposure to sulfur dioxide reduces the efficiency of the photosynthetic activity by the phycobiont, allowing the mycobiont to overgrow it and leading to the elimination of the symbiotic relationship. Once the careful metabolic balance is interrupted, the lichen and its member algal and fungal populations disappear from the habitat.

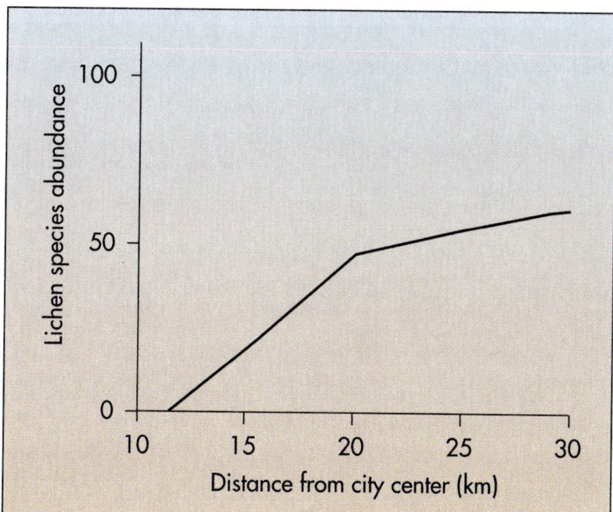

FIG. 14-5 Lichens are sensitive to air pollutants and disappear from urban areas. Contaminants in the air disrupt the delicate balance between the phycobiont and the mycobiont of the lichen.

Endosymbionts

Interesting mutualistic relationships occur between the protozoan *Paramecium aurelia* and various bacterial species. The obligately *endosymbiotic bacteria* live within protozoa. These include endosymbiotic bacteria that appear as structures, such as kappa particles. The two classes of populations of *P. aurelia* are killer strains, which contain kappa particles, and sensitive strains, which lack bacterial endosymbionts. The presence of kappa particles gives an important advantage to killer strains when they compete for available resources with sensitive strains because those with kappa particles can eliminate those that lack them. The endosymbiotic bacteria probably derive nutritional benefits from the protozoan.

Nitrogen-fixing Symbiosis

The natural ability of organisms to convert atmospheric nitrogen to ammonia is called **nitrogen fixation.** This process provides fixed forms of nitrogen, such as ammonium ions, that can be used by other organisms. The capability of fixing nitrogen is restricted to some bacterial populations. The highest rates of nitrogen fixation occur when nitrogen-fixing bacteria establish mutualistic relationships with plants. The nitrogen-fixing symbiotic relationship between members of the bacterial genera *Rhizobium* and *Bradyrhizo-*

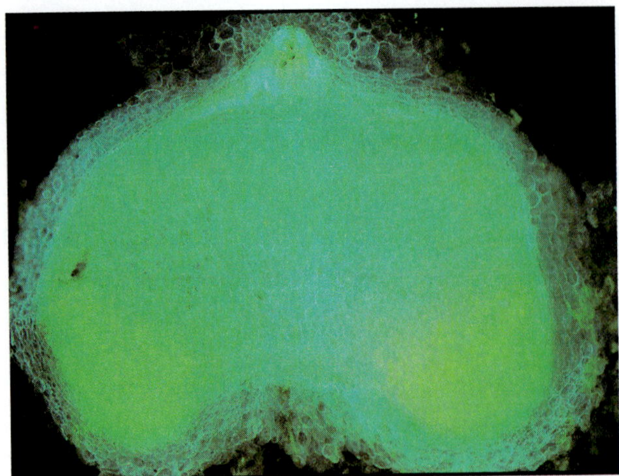

FIG. 14-6 Cross section of a nodule.

bium and leguminous plants is extremely important for maintaining soil fertility. These bacterial species invade the roots of suitable host plants, leading to the formation of **nodules.** Within nodules, *Rhizobium* and *Bradyrhizobium* are able to fix atmospheric nitrogen (FIG. 14-6). *Bradyrhizobium* species nodulate soybeans, lupines, cowpeas, and various tropical leguminous plants. *Rhizobium* species nodulate alfalfa, peas, clover, and a wide variety of leguminous plants.

The establishment of a symbiotic association between these microorganisms and a plant is very specific, with the bacteria recognizing specific binding sites on the surfaces of the plant roots. The interaction between these microbes and a leguminous plant involves (1) the attraction of the bacteria to the plant roots by amino acids secreted by the plant; (2) the binding of the bacteria to receptors (lectins) on the plant root; (3) the activity of plant growth substances, leading to curling and branching of the rootlets; (4) the entry of bacteria into the root hairs; (5) the development of an infection thread; (6) the transformation of the plant cells to form a tumorous growth; (7) the multiplication of bacteria within the nodule; and (8) the transformation of the invading bacteria into distorted (pleomorphic) forms.

Specific expression of plant and bacterial genes accompanies the development of the rhizobial-plant symbiosis. The genes involved in root nodule formation are collectively called *nodulin genes.* In the fast-growing *Rhizobium* species, most of these genes are located on large Sym plasmids, whereas the slow-growing *Bradyrhizobium* species carry the late nodulin genes on the bacterial chromosome. Genes essential for the process of nitrogen fixation include *nif* and *fix,* among which are the structural genes for nitrogenase. The rhizobial genes required for nodule formation and nodulin gene expression include the nodulation (*nod*) genes, several groups of genes concerned with the structure of the outer surface of the bacterium (the *exo, lps,* and *ndv* genes), and several less well-defined genes. The host-specific *nod* genes determine the specificity of nodulation on a particular host. The *nod*D gene is the only *nod* gene that is constitutively expressed in both the free-living and symbiotic states of *Rhizobium.* In combination with flavonoids excreted by plant roots, the NodD protein probably acts as a transcriptional activator for all other *nod* genes, and the gene is essential for nodulation as the common *nod*ABC genes. The *nod* gene clusters coding for the infection and nodulation process are generally located on the Sym plasmids, which also carry specificity genes.

Within the infected plant tissue the root-nodule bacteria multiply, forming unusually shaped pleomorphic cells called *bacteroids;* once they form bacteroids, *Rhizobium* and *Bradyrhizobium* are no longer capable of independent reproduction (FIG. 14-7). The bacteroid cells contain active nitrogenase, the enzyme complex that converts molecular atmospheric nitrogen to fixed forms of nitrogen. Nitrogenase is not generally found in free-living *Rhizobium* cells. Nitrogenase allows the bacteroid cells of *Rhizobium* and *Bradyrhizobium* to fix molecular nitrogen and provide their symbiotic plant partner with an available source of fixed nitrogen for growth. The plants provide organic compounds for the generation of required ATP by the symbiotic bacteria. Leghemoglobin in the nodule supplies oxygen to the bacteroids for their respiratory metabolism but also maintains a sufficiently low concentration of free oxygen so the nitrogenase enzymes are not inactivated. The control of oxygen is therefore critical because oxygen is both required and inhibitory for the nitrogen fixation process.

In addition to the symbiotic relationship between *Rhizobium* and *Bradyrhizobium* with leguminous plants, various other bacterial species, including cyanobacteria and actinomycetes, enter into similar mutualistic

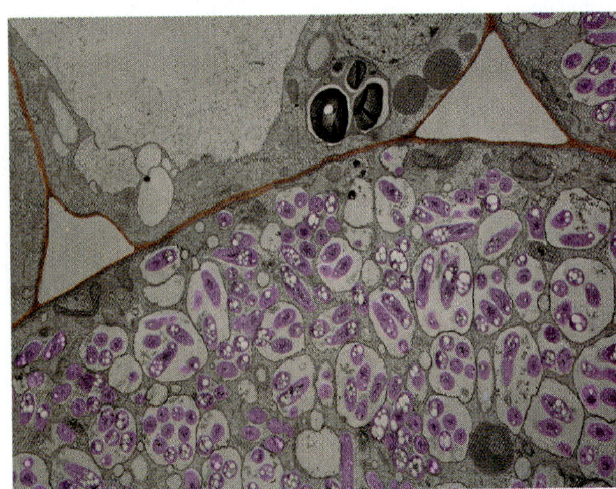

FIG. 14-7 Colorized micrograph showing bacterial cells (bacteroids) of *Bradyrhizobium japonicum* within a nodule of a soybean. (6,000×).

BOX 14-1

GENETIC ENGINEERING TO CREATE NEW NITROGEN-FIXING ORGANISMS

One of the greatest benefits that may be realized through genetic engineering is the introduction of the capacity to fix nitrogen into plants, such as wheat, corn, and rice, that are not able to utilize atmospheric nitrogen (see FIG.). Because of the inefficiency and lack of success with the mutation-screening approach, microbiologists have been studying the genetics and biochemistry of infection by *Rhizobium* with the aim of employing recombinant DNA techniques to genetically engineer plants containing the bacterial genes for nitrogen fixation. Many research groups have carried out these investigations.

In one series of studies, the genes for nitrogen fixation were first inserted into the genome of a eukaryotic yeast cell; plasmids from *Escherichia coli* and a yeast cell

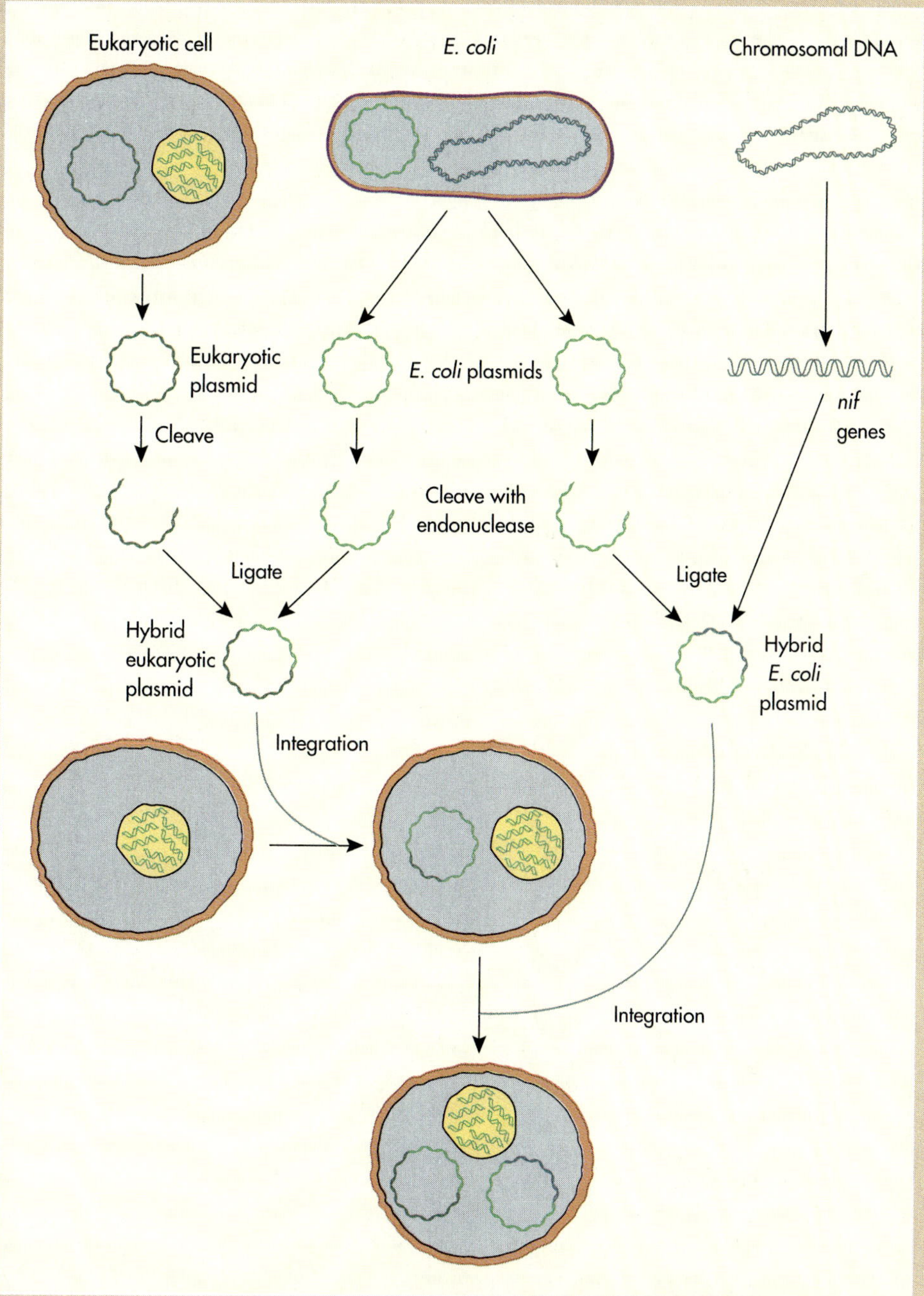

The *nif* genes can be incorporated into the genomes of eukaryotic cells through recombinant DNA technology. In this way, genetically engineered nitrogen-fixing crops may be created for future use.

BOX 14-1

GENETIC ENGINEERING TO CREATE NEW NITROGEN-FIXING ORGANISMS—CONT'D

were cleaved and then fused to form a single hybrid plasmid, which could be recognized by the yeast cell and integrated into its chromosomal DNA. In the next step, the genes introduced into the yeast were isolated from the chromosome of *Klebsiella pneumoniae,* a nitrogen fixer. The genes, collectively designated *nif,* code for some 17 proteins. Another *E. coli* plasmid was cleaved, and the isolated *nif* genes were introduced to form a second hybrid plasmid. Because of the bacterial DNA already inserted into one of the yeast chromosomes, the yeast cell recognized the hybrid *E. coli* plasmid. The plasmid was then integrated into the yeast chromosome.

Although the insertion of the prokaryotic *nif* genes into the eukaryotic yeast cell demonstrated that genetic material can be transferred between different biological systems, the nitrogen-fixing proteins were not expressed in the yeast. More studies are needed to elucidate the factors controlling expression of the *nif* genes before success is obtained. It is increasingly apparent that the ability to engineer organisms, such as eukaryotic plant cells that can fix atmospheric nitrogen, depends on a thorough understanding of the molecular biology of gene expression and knowing how to create the environmental conditions for nitrogen-fixing activity. Once the mechanisms of gene regulation in eukaryotes and the physiological requirements for nitrogen fixation are understood, this knowledge can be applied through genetic engineering to create organisms with novel properties.

relationships with a restricted number of other types of plants; this results in the formation of nodules and the ability to fix atmospheric nitrogen. An equivalent sequence of events is involved in the formation of nodules resulting from the mutualistic relationships between bacteria and nonleguminous plants, although leghemoglobin is not the specific oxygen carrier in such relationships. *Rhizobium,* for example, can fix nitrogen in association with *Trema,* a tree found in tropical and subtropical regions. Likewise, actinomycetes establish specific mutualistic relationships that permit the bacteria to fix nitrogen, such as occurs when *Frankia alni* infects the roots of the alder tree, leading to the formation of nodules. Such an actinomycete-type nitrogen-fixing symbiosis is especially important with angiosperms. The productivity of many forests depends on such nitrogen-fixing symbioses.

In agriculture, much higher crop yields and significant economic savings would be realized if plants could be grown without the need for adding artificially produced nitrogen fertilizer. The elimination of massive fertilizer applications to agricultural soils would also reduce problems associated with nitrification and groundwater contamination. For years scientists have been exploring the relationships between the root-nodule bacteria and the plants with which these nitrogen-fixing bacteria can establish symbiotic relationships. Several researchers have tried to find especially effective nitrogen-fixing strains of *Rhizobium* that could increase crop yields. Using mutagens and screening procedures, Winston Brill and colleagues at the University of Wisconsin isolated strains of *Rhizobium* that were capable of very high rates of nitrogen fixation. However, field tests with these efficient *Rhizobium* strains did not increase crop yields; the superior nitrogen-fixing strains could not successfully compete with indigenous strains.

Mycorrhizae

Mycorrhizae (fungal roots) are formed by mutualistic relationships between fungi and plant roots. The fungus derives nutritional benefits from the plant roots and contributes to the plant's nutrition. The establishment of mycorrhizal associations involves the integration of plant roots and fungal mycelia into a unified morphological unit. Some plants with mycorrhizal fungi are able to occupy habitats that they otherwise could not inhabit. The importance of this microorganism-plant interaction is attested to by the fact that 95% of all plants have mycorrhizae.

Several types of mycorrhizal associations are differentiated on the basis of the degree of integration of the fungus into the root structure (FIG. 14-8). *Ectomycorrhizae* are characterized by the formation of an external fungal sheath around the root and fungal penetration of the intercellular regions of the root. Such ectomycorrhizal associations occur in most oak,

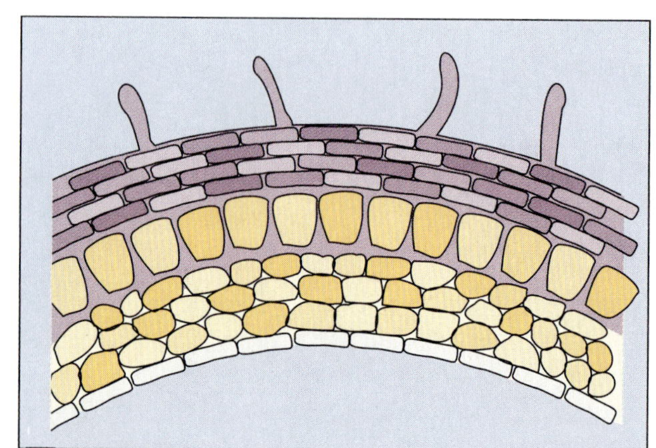

FIG. 14-8 There are several types of mycorrhizae formed between fungi *(purple)* and plant root. **A,** Ectomycorrhizae.

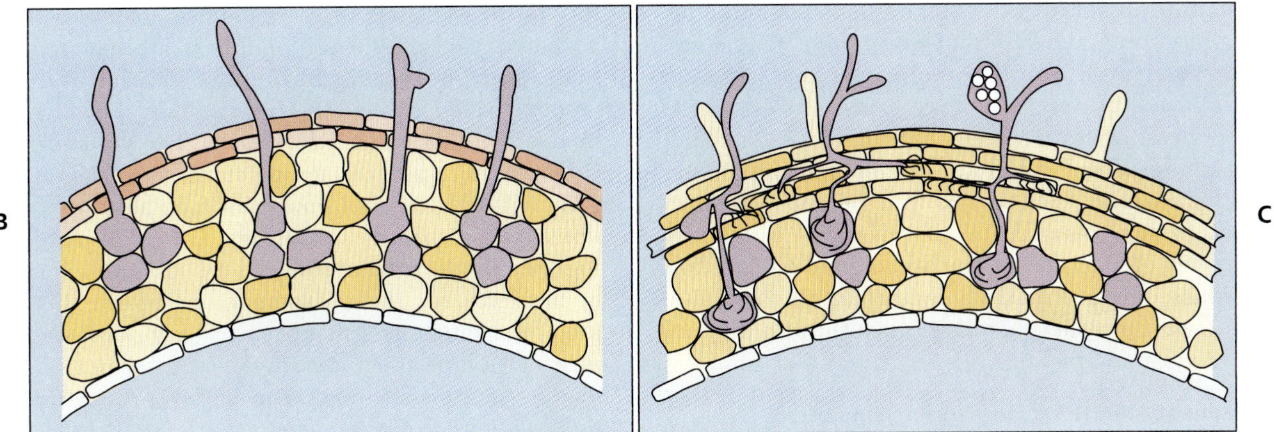

FIG. 14-8, cont'd **B,** Endomycorrhizae. **C,** Vesicular-arbuscular (VA) mycorrhizae.

beech, birch, and coniferous trees. *Endomycorrhizae* involve fungal penetration of root cells. The *vesicular-arbuscular* (VA) type of mycorrhizal association is one in which the root cortex contains specialized inclusions, called *vesicles* and *arbuscules;* VA is the most common form of mycorrhiza. This association frequently goes unnoticed because it does not have a macroscopic effect on root morphology. Most major agricultural crop plants, including wheat, maize, potatoes, beans, soybeans, tomatoes, strawberries, apples, oranges, grapes, cotton, tobacco, tea, coffee, sugar cane, sugar maple, and others, form VA endomycorrhizal associations.

Fungal Gardens of Insects

There are some particularly interesting mutualistic relationships between microorganisms and animal populations. Some plant-eating insect populations, for example, actually cultivate microorganisms on plant tissues (FIG. 14-9). The microorganisms degrade cellulosic plant residues, providing a digestible source of nutrition for the insects; the insects lack cellulase enzymes and cannot derive any nutritional benefit from simply eating plant material. The insects provide the microorganisms with a habitat in which they can proliferate. At the same time, the insects process the plant material, preparing a suitable medium for microbial growth and, in some cases, secreting substances that protect the growing microorganisms from invasion by other microbial species.

The *fungal gardens* of myrmicine ants (the attini ants) are an excellent example of an insect population growing fungi in pure culture. The ants macerate leaf

FIG. 14-9 Various animals cultivate fungi as their food sources. The fungi typically degrade cellulose that the animals cannot. The animal derives nutrition from the fungal biomass.

material, mix it with saliva and fecal matter, and inoculate the prepared substrate with a pure fungal culture. After growth of the fungus, the ants harvest a portion of the fungal biomass and the by-products they ingest. Various wood-inhabiting insects, including ambrosia beetles and some termites, maintain similar mutualistic relationships with microbial populations. In these cases, the insects rely on the cellulolytic enzymes of microbial populations to convert plant residues into nutritional sources that they can use. The insect provides the microorganism with an optimal habitat for growth.

Ruminant Animal-Microorganism Symbioses

Animals, such as cows, llamas, and camels, establish mutualistic relationships with microbial populations. Although plants are the main food sources for these animals, they do not produce cellulase enzymes themselves; instead, they depend on microbial populations for the degradation of the cellulosic materials they consume. The microbial population are maintained in the large first chamber within the stomach of these animals, which is called the *rumen.* (Animals with a rumen are called *ruminant animals.*) The rumen provides a stable, constant-temperature, anaerobic environment for the establishment of mutualistic associations with microbial populations. The plant material ingested by the animal provides a continuous source of nutrients for the microorganisms within the rumen, very much like what occurs in a continuous fermentor. Compartmentalization of cellulose-degrading microorganisms is common in herbivores, including those that are not ruminants.

Microbial populations within the rumen convert cellulose, starch, and other polysaccharides to carbon dioxide, hydrogen gas, methane, and low molecular weight organic acids (FIG. 14-10). A portion of the low molecular weight fatty acids, carbon dioxide, and

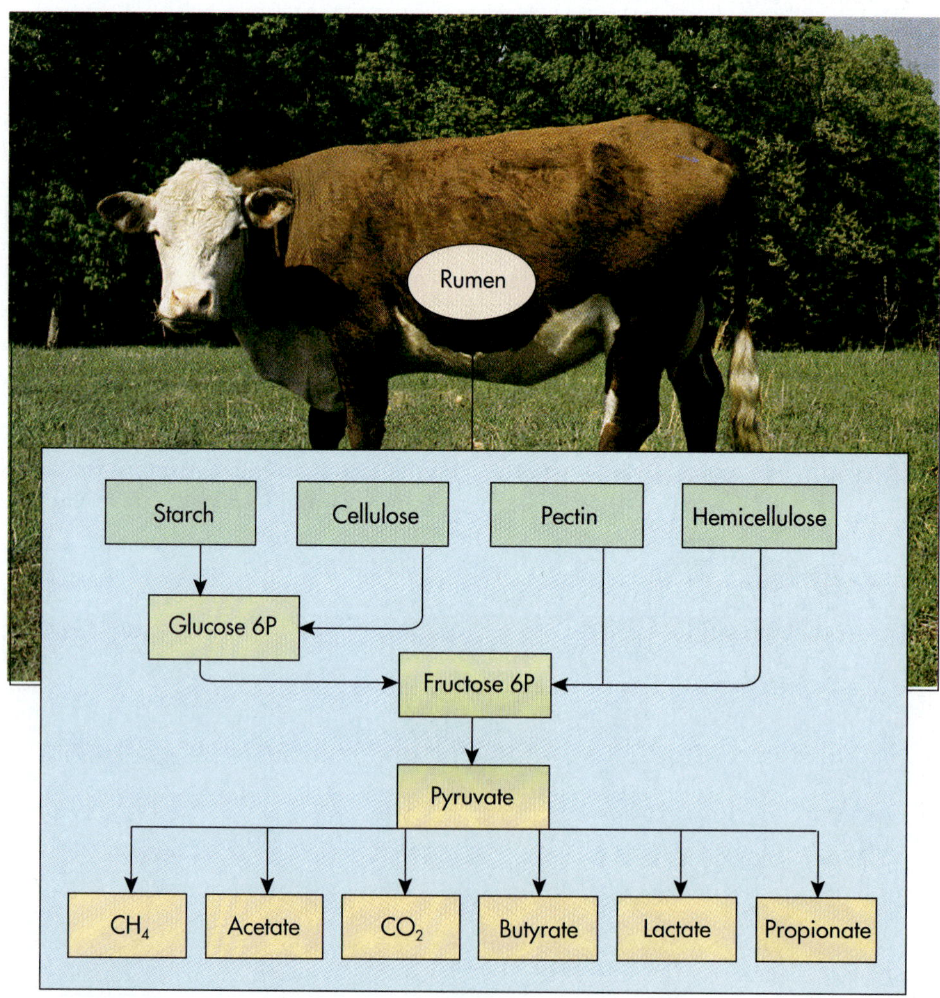

FIG. 14-10 Anaerobic microorganisms within the rumen degrade polysaccharides. The fermentation products they form serve as the nutritional sources for the ruminant animal. Methane is produced by methanogenic bacteria in the rumen.

molecular hydrogen produced by various fermentative bacteria, such as *Ruminococcus*, are converted by methanogenic bacteria to methane.

The overall equation for the fermentation that occurs in the rumen is:

$$57.5\ (C_6H_{12}O_6) \rightarrow 65 \text{ acetate} + 20 \text{ propionate} + 15 \text{ butyrate} + 60\ CO_2 + 35\ CH_4 + 25\ H_2O$$

Although hydrogen is produced by many of the fermentative bacteria in the rumen, it does not accumulate because of its rapid utilization by methanogenic bacteria. Cows burp considerable amounts of the methane generated by these bacteria within the rumen. The organic acids produced by the microbial populations are absorbed into the bloodstream of the animal, where they are oxidized aerobically to produce the ATP needed to meet the animal's energy requirements. Because the rumen is anaerobic, most of the caloric content of the ingested plants is maintained in the fatty acids transferred to the bloodstream of the animal.

A diverse bacterial and protozoan population exists within the rumen. Some of these microbial populations are found only within the specialized environment of the rumen, and others also occur in analogous environments, making this a borderline case between synergism and mutualism. Clearly, although both animal and microbial populations benefit from this relationship, there is a delicate balance among the individual populations within the complex microbial community in the rumen, with each population contributing metabolically to the conversion of substrate to fermentation products. The population balances can be upset by sudden diet changes in ruminants, leading to a condition of bloat caused by excessive gas formation. Restoration of the metabolic balance among microbial populations restores the healthy state of the animal.

Bioluminescence

The mutualistic relationship between some **luminescent bacteria** and marine invertebrates and fish is particularly interesting. The light emitted by the bacteria is blue-green and is emitted continuously, provided that oxygen is available. *Bioluminescence* by *Photobacterium* requires *luciferase,* an aldehyde (such as *dodecanal*), flavin mononucleotide (FMN), and O_2. Light production is based on the reaction of reduced flavin mononucleotide ($FMNH_2$), molecular oxygen, and the aldehyde that produces FMN in an electronically excited state. The return of the excited FMN to its ground state results in the emission of light. The reaction is catalyzed by the enzyme luciferase.

$$FMNH_2 + O_2 + RCHO \xrightarrow[\text{luciferase}]{} FMN + RCOOH + H_2O + \text{light}$$

FIG. 14-11 The flashlight fish *(Photoblepharon)* maintains populations of luminescent bacteria *(turquoise)* near the eye and elsewhere on the body. This fish lives in dark regions of the ocean and the luminescent bacteria produce blue light.

Some fish have specific organs in which they maintain populations of luminescent bacteria, including members of the genera *Photobacterium* and *Vibrio* (FIG. 14-11). Although the bacteria normally emit light continuously, the fish are able to manipulate the organs containing the luminescent bacteria and emit flashes of light. The fish supply the bacteria with nutrients and protection from competing microorganisms. The light emitted by the bacteria is used in various ways by different fish. In some cases, the pattern of light emission is used in sexual mating rituals. In deep-sea and nocturnal fish, such as the flashlight fish *Photoblepharon,* the light emitted by the bacteria aids the fish in finding food sources and warding off predators.

COMPETITION

Competition occurs when two populations are striving for the same resource. Often it focuses on a nutrient present in limited concentrations, but it may also occur for other resources, including light and space. As a result of the competition, both populations achieve lower densities than would have been achieved by the individual populations in the absence of competition. Competitive interactions tend to bring about ecological separation (exclusion) of closely related populations.

Competitive exclusion prevents two populations from occupying the same ecological niche, that is, they cannot play the same functional role at the same location. When two populations attempt to occupy the same niche, one will win the competition and the other will be excluded (FIG. 14-12). Chemostats,

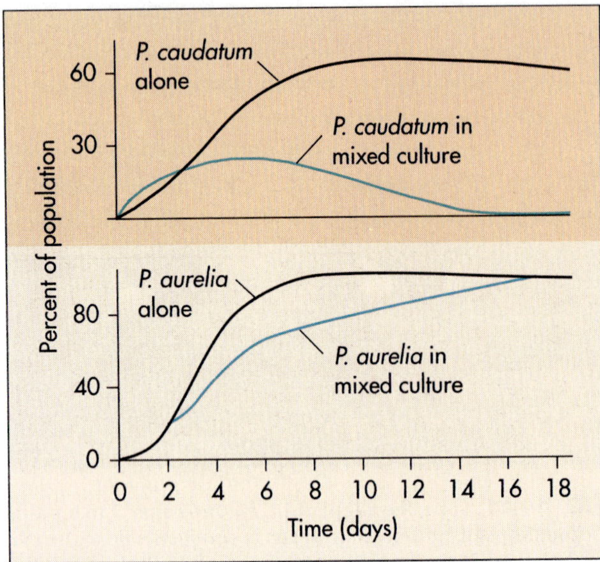

FIG. 14-12 Competition for available nutrients can lead to the exclusion of the less successful population. *Paramecium caudatum* is competitively excluded by *P. aurelia* in mixed culture.

which by definition have a growth-limiting substrate in the growth medium, are used frequently to study competition between populations under controlled conditions. As a rule, the population with the higher growth rate under the given set of environmental conditions in the habitat will win over the population with the lower growth rate. Fluctuations in environmental conditions can lead to shifts in competitive balances, resulting in population oscillations within the microbial community. Spatial separation allows microorganisms to escape competitive pressures, permitting co-existence of competitive populations.

Amensalism

Amensalism, or **antagonism,** occurs when one population produces a substance inhibitory to another population. The first population gains a competitive edge as a result of its ability to inhibit the growth of competitive populations. The production of antibiotics, for example, can give the antibiotic-producing population an advantage over a sensitive strain when competing for the same nutrient resources. The production of lactic acid by *Streptococcus* and *Lactobacillus* species similarly eliminates competitors. The preemptive colonization of food products by lactic acid bacteria precludes the invasion of that food by other bacterial species. This fact is utilized in the production and preservation of food products by the addition of lactic acid as a preservative. Various other chemicals produced by microbial populations, including inorganic compounds such as oxygen, ammonia, mineral acids, and hydrogen sulfide, and organic compounds such as fatty acids, alcohols, and antibiotics, permit the establishment of amensal relationships between microbial populations.

Predation

Predation involves the consumption of a prey species by a predatory population. The *predator* eats the *prey.* Normally, predator–prey interactions are of short duration and the predator is larger than the prey, but this is not always the case. The predatory populations derive nutrition from the prey species, and clearly, the predator population exerts a negative influence on the consumed prey population.

Many protozoa prey on bacterial species (FIG. 14-13), and the nondiscriminatory consumption of bacterial populations by protozoan predators is sometimes referred to as *grazing.* Similarly, protozoa and invertebrate animal populations graze on algal primary producers. Although the predator is normally larger than the prey, there are some interesting cases in which a small microbial predator consumes a larger organism. For example, the protozoan *Didinium* can engulf and consume the larger protozoan *Paramecium.*

Predation is an important process in establishing transfers of food within an ecosystem to support the growth of higher organisms. Various filter-feeding an-

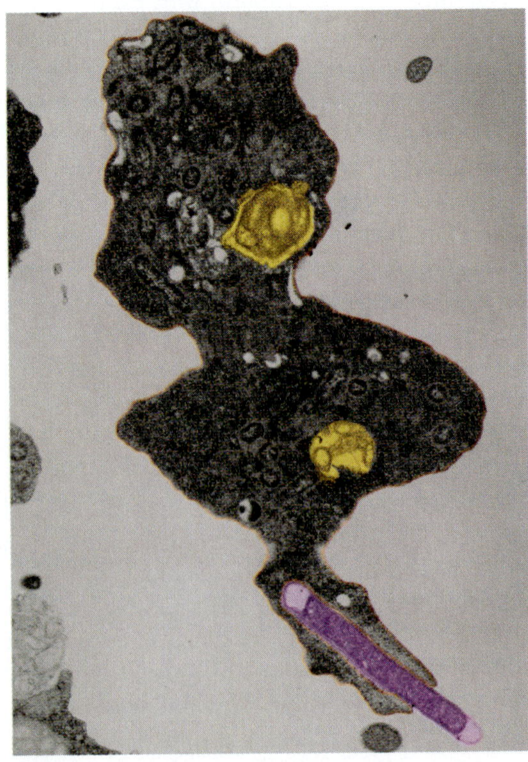

FIG. 14-13 Colorized micrograph showing the phagocytic capture of a rod-shaped bacterium by the soil protozoan *Vahlkampfia.* (5,200×). Many protozoa graze on bacteria as their food sources.

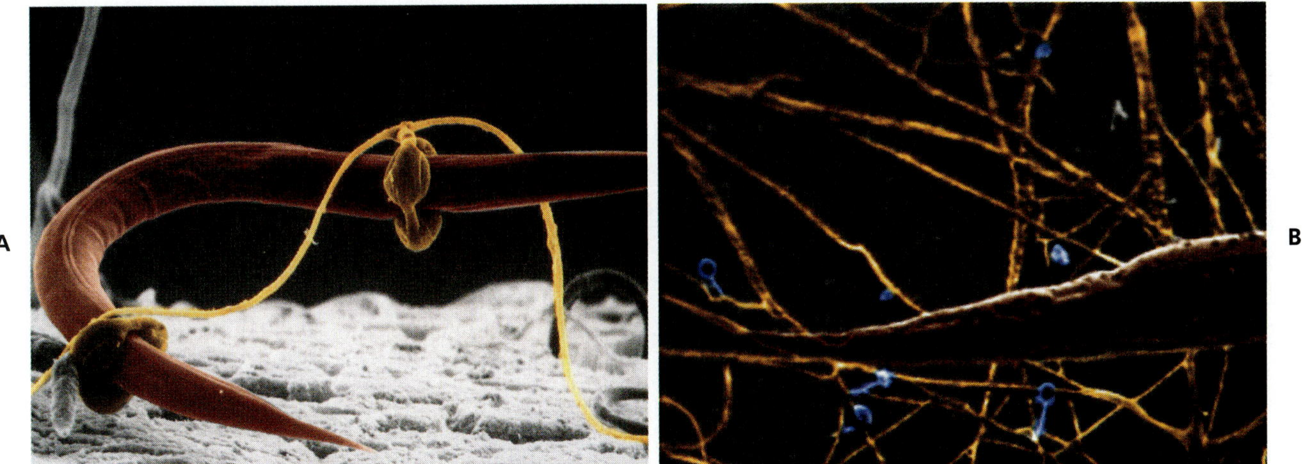

FIG. 14-14 **A,** Colorized micrograph showing hyphae of nematode-trapping fungus with a circle of cells that is the trap. When a nematode swims through this trap, the cells contract like a noose to capture the nematode. **B,** Colorized micrograph of a nematode-trapping fungus that forms a "sticky lethal lollipop." When a nematode, as shown here, contacts this trap, it adheres to the fungus *(yellow)* so tightly that, despite violent thrashing, it cannot escape.

imals are able to remove microorganisms from suspension. This grazing activity is important in transferring biomass from microorganisms to higher organisms in aquatic food webs.

Some fungi are able to trap and consume much larger nematodes (FIG. 14-14). There are several mechanisms by which these fungi capture nematode prey, including the production of networks of adhesive branches, stalk adhesive knobs, and adhesive or constrictive rings. When a nematode attempts to move past such a predacious fungus, the fungus traps it. Even violent movements by the nematode to escape the grasp of the fungus generally fail. The fungal hyphae penetrate and digest the nematode, consuming the animal.

Theoretically, interactions of predator and prey species could lead to regular cyclic fluctuations in the populations of the two species (FIG. 14-15). As the size of the prey population increases, it can support a larger predator population. The decline in the size of the prey population means that fewer predators can be supported, and therefore, the size of the predator population also declines. If either the predator or the prey were completely eliminated, the population of the other would be deleteriously affected. Without the prey as an available food resource, the predator would be eliminated, and without the control exerted by the predator, the prey population could grow too large, leading to the complete consumption of the available nutrient resources of the habitat. In reality this situation rarely occurs because disturbances and other factors dampen the cyclic oscillations and generally prevent the elimination of either the predator or the prey population.

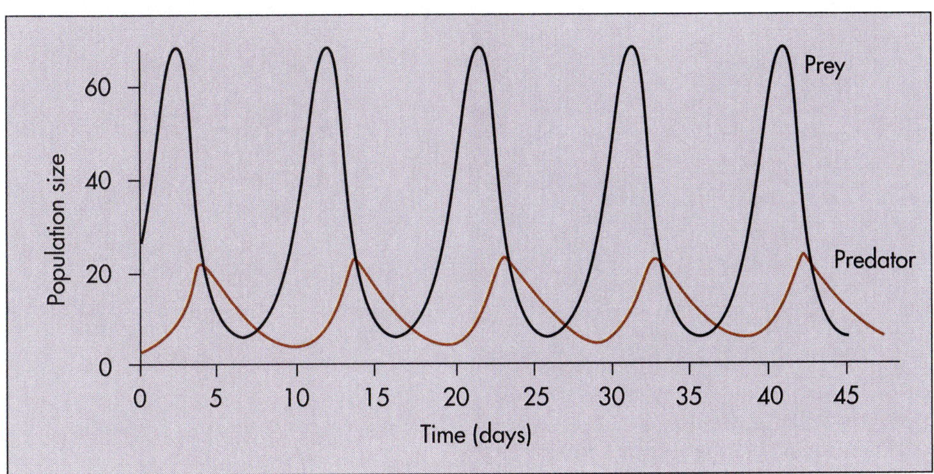

FIG. 14-15 Theoretical cycles of population sizes of a predator and its prey species.

PARASITISM

In a relationship of **parasitism,** the parasite population is benefited and the host population is harmed. As a rule, parasitic relationships are characterized by a relatively long period of contact, and the parasite is smaller than the host. This distinguishes parasitism from predation, but this distinction is not always clear. The parasite normally derives its nutritional requirements from the host cell or organism, and in the process the host is damaged.

The host–parasite relationship is typically quite specific. Some microorganisms are obligate parasites, their existence depending on the successful establishment of a parasitic relationship with a host organism. For example, viruses are obligate intracellular parasites, able to multiply only within suitable host cells. Bacteriophage invade and multiply within bacterial cells, causing lysis and death of the bacteria; viruses invade fungi, algae, and protozoa. Similarly, rickettsiae are obligately parasitic bacteria and sporozoans are obligately parasitic protozoa. Many human diseases result from infections with microbial parasites, and some diseases of plants and animals will be considered later in this chapter. Such host–parasite relationships that cause disease syndromes clearly exert a negative influence on the susceptible host and benefit the parasite.

Some bacteria are parasites of other bacteria. For example, *Bdellovibrio* is parasitic on other bacterial populations and is able to invade and multiply by binary fission within cells of *E. coli* (FIG. 14-16). As a result of such parasitic interactions, populations of host cells generally decline. Parasitism as such acts as a mechanism for controlling population densities, which in an overall sense is beneficial in maintaining ecological stability.

PLANT PATHOGENS

Plant pathogens (microorganisms that cause diseases of plants) exhibit a parasitic relationship in which the microorganism harms the plant. Plant pathogens typically weaken or destroy cells and tissues, reducing or eliminating the ability to perform their normal physiological functions and resulting in disease symptoms and reduced plant growth or death (Table 14-2; FIG. 14-17). There are tens of thousands of diseases of cul-

TABLE 14-2 Some Symptoms of Microbial Diseases of Plants

SYMPTOM	DESCRIPTION
Necrosis (rots)	Death of plant cells; may appear as spots in localized areas
Canker	Localized necrosis resulting in lesions, usually on the stem
Wilt	Droopiness due to loss of turgor
Blight	Loss of foliage
Chlorosis	Loss of photosynthetic capability due to bleaching of chlorophyll
Hypoplasia	Stunted growth
Hyperplasia	Excessive growth
Gall	Tumorous growth
Scab	Localized lesions, usually slightly raised or sunken

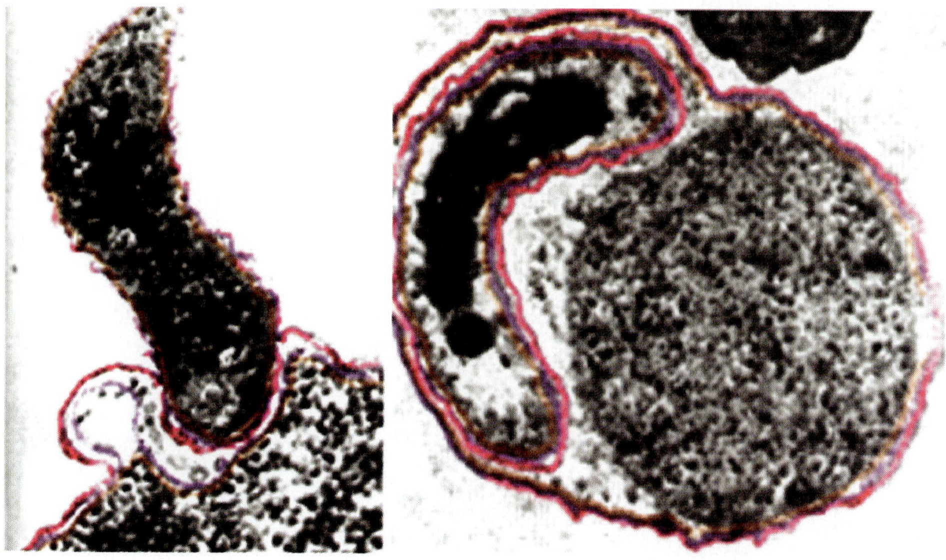

FIG. 14-16 Colorized micrograph showing *Bdellovibrio* entering an *Escherichia coli* cell and reproducing within the periplasmic space.

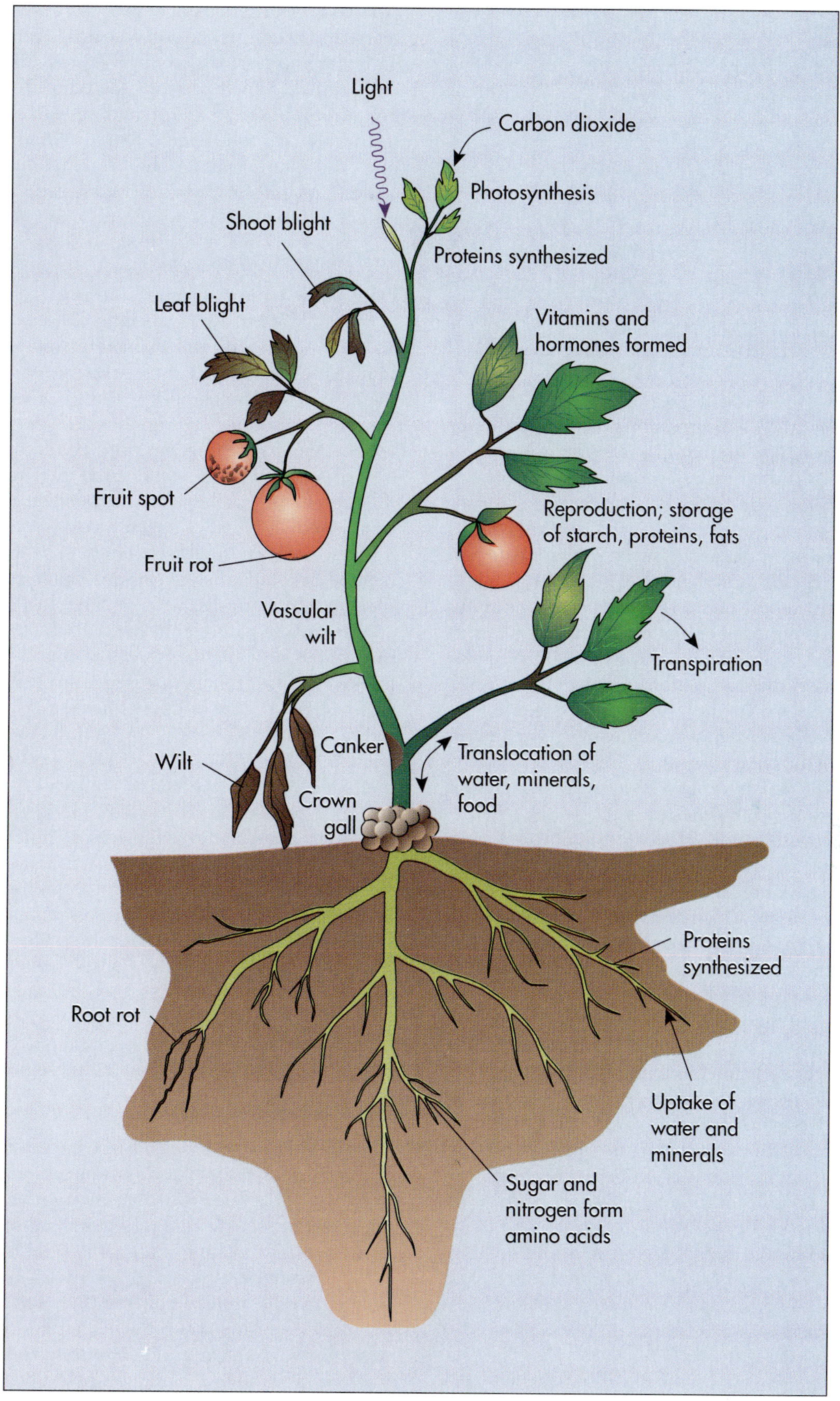

FIG. 14-17 Normal plant functions *(right)* and disease symptoms *(left)* that occur when microbial infections interfere with these functions.

TABLE 14-3 Worldwide Agriculture Crop Losses Due to Plant Diseases

CROP	LOSS (MILLIONS OF TONS)
Cereals	135
Potatoes	89
Sugar beets and sugar cane	232
Other vegetables	31
Fruits	33
Coffee, cocoa, and tobacco	3
Oil crops	14
Fiber crops and natural rubber	3

tivated plants, and each agricultural crop is generally subject to over 100 different diseases. Diseases of agricultural crops cause serious economic losses, with annual worldwide crop losses due to diseases, insects, and weeds totaling about $200 billion (Table 14-3). Outbreaks of plant diseases can cause immediate and long-lasting agricultural damage. The chestnut blight disease destroyed the native North American chestnut trees that had provided an important cash crop, especially in the Appalachian area. A leaf blight of maize in 1970 caused the destruction of more than 10 million acres of corn in the United States. Sometimes plant diseases even have far-reaching effects on masses of people. The potato blight in Ireland in 1845 resulted in mass starvation and widespread emigration from Ireland to North America.

Infected plants can develop various morphological abnormalities as a result of infection by a microbial pathogen. The kinds of cells and tissues that become infected determine which physiological functions of the plant are initially impaired, as shown when (1) infection of the root, as occurs in root rots, interferes with absorption of water and nutrients from the soil; (2) infection of the xylem vessels, which occurs in vascular wilts and certain cankers, interferes with translocation of water and minerals to the crown of the plant; (3) infection of the foliage, as occurs in leaf spots, blights, and mosaics, interferes with photosynthesis; (4) infection of the cortex, which occurs in cortical canker and viral infections of phloem, interferes with the downward translocation of photosynthetic products; (5) infections of reproductive structures, as occur in bacterial and fungal blights and microbial infections of flowers, interfere with reproduction; and (6) infections of fruit, as occur in fruit rots, interfere with reproduction and/or storage of reserve foods for the new plant (see FIG. 14-17).

Plant pathogens may alter the metabolic activities of the plant, and diseased plants sometimes show decreased growth as a result of changes in respiratory activity and rates of carbon dioxide fixation. Foliar pathogens sometimes produce *chlorosis* (bleaching of chlorophyll), which prevents the plant from carrying out photophosphorylation and producing the ATP needed for carbon dioxide fixation. Plant pathogens may also cause changes in protein synthesis. *Overgrowths* and *gall formation* involve alterations in the nucleic acid function controlling protein synthesis.

Viral Plant Pathogens

Plant pathogenic viruses are often named according to their ability to cause specific diseases. Often the only symptom of a viral plant infection is a reduced growth rate that results in some degree of dwarfing. In the case of systemic viral diseases of plants, the most common symptoms are mosaics and ringspots (FIG. 14-18). *Mosaics* are characterized by the formation of light-green, yellow, or white spots intermingled with the normal green aerial plant structures. *Ringspots* are characterized by the appearance of chlorotic or necrotic rings on the leaves. These primary symptoms may be accompanied by various other symptoms in specific viral plant diseases (see FIG. 14-17).

Many plant pathogenic viruses are transported to susceptible host plants by vectors that acquire these pathogens from soil or diseased plant tissues. Insects, such as aphids, leaf hoppers, mealy bugs, and nematodes, often act as vectors for viral diseases of plants. Even microorganisms can serve as vectors for viral pathogens. *Olpidium brassicae*, a chytrid fungus, is the vector of tobacco necrosis virus and probably of several other plant pathogenic viruses. Pollen and plant seeds are also involved in the transmission of plant viruses. For example, tobacco rattle virus is detectable on the pollen of infected petunia plants and is disseminated through the air with the pollen to susceptible plants. The spread of viruses on structures involved in the reproductive activities of the plant, such as pollen and seeds, ensures that viruses are maintained with susceptible host plant populations and that viral diseases are endemic to these populations.

Viroid Plant Pathogens

Viroids, which are discussed in Chapter 8, cause several plant diseases. They have been implicated in potato spindle tuber disease, chrysanthemum stunt, and citrus exocortis disease, as well as several other plant diseases. Potato spindle tuber disease, one of the most destructive diseases of potatoes, is caused by potato spindle tuber viroid (PSTV). PSTV is spread primarily by knives when they are used to cut potato seed tubers, as well as during handling and planting of the crop. Following inoculation of a tuber with PSTV, the viroid replicates and spreads systemically through-

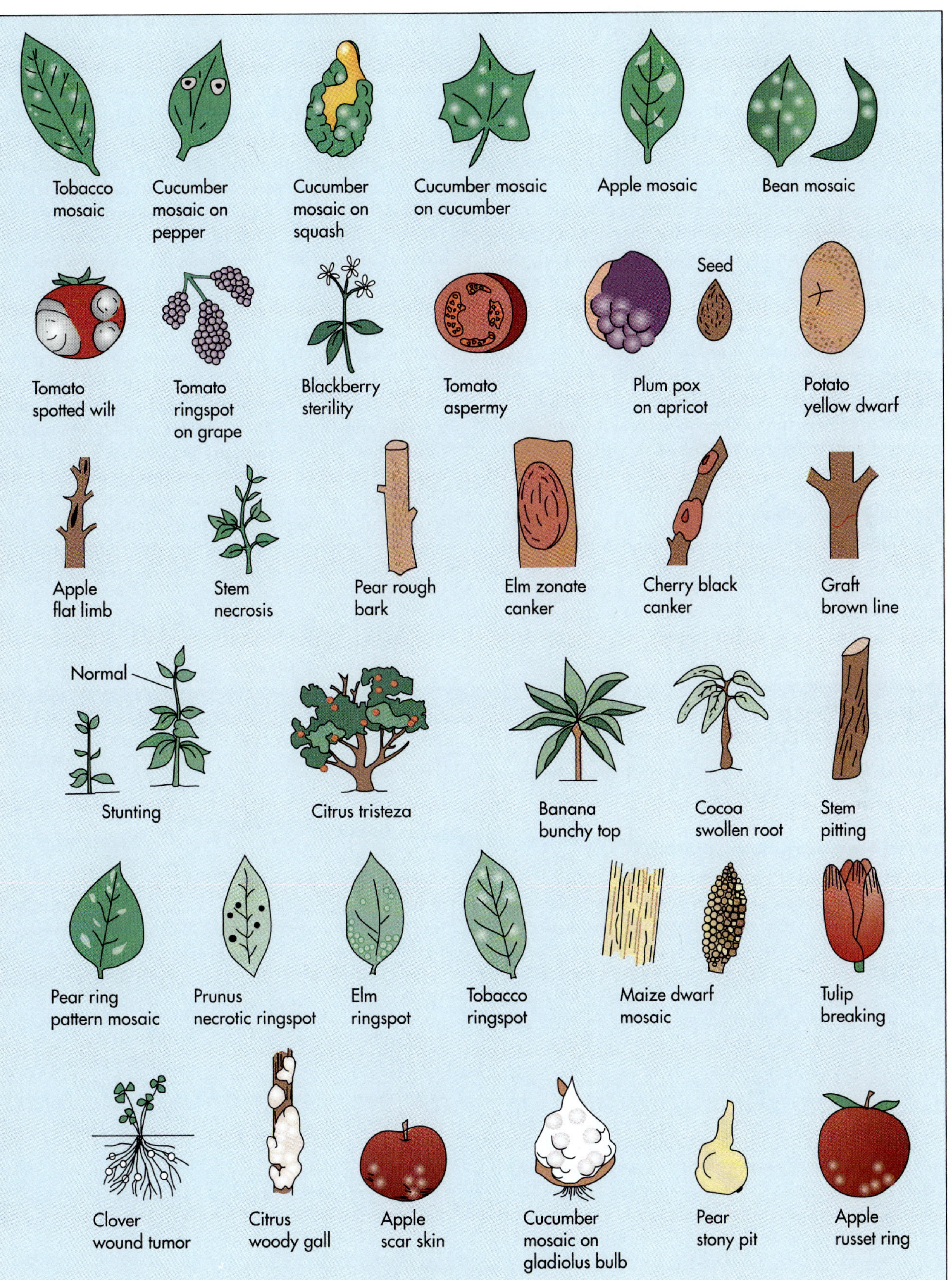

FIG. 14-18 Signs of viral diseases of plants.

out the plant. Infected potato plants appear erect, spindly, and dwarfed, and the tubers are elongated.

Citrus exocortis viroid (CEV), which is similar to PSTV, causes citrus exocortis, a disease that affects various citrus trees. Infected plants show splits in the bark and partially loosened outer bark that give the bark a cracked, scaly appearance. CEV is readily transmitted from diseased to healthy trees by cutting tools. The viroid survives on contaminated blades even after treatment with many chemical disinfectants but can be inactivated by sodium hypochlorite. The viroid appears to be associated with the nuclei and internal membranes of host cells and results in aberrations of the cytoplasmic membranes. Chrysanthemum plants infected with chrysanthemum stunt viroid (ChSV) are smaller, paler, and inferior in quality to normal ones. ChSV moves slowly through a plant, often taking 5 to 6 weeks to move from an inoculated leaf into the stem, and new symptoms develop 3 to 4 months after inoculation.

Bacterial Plant Pathogens

Plant pathogenic bacterial species (called *plant pests* by the U. S. Department of Agriculture) occur in the genera *Mycoplasma, Spiroplasma, Corynebacterium, Agrobacterium, Pseudomonas, Xanthomonas, Streptomyces,* and *Erwinia.* These bacteria are widely distributed and cause a large number of plant diseases, including hypertrophy, wilts, rots, blights, and galls (Table 14-4). Plant pathogenic bacteria cause many different disease symptoms, and most symptoms of plant disease can be caused by several different bacterial species (FIG. 14-19). Many of these plant pathogens enter the plant via the roots. A few infect the plant through the stomata of the leaf. Yet others are injected into the plant by insects. Once an infection occurs, the pathogens can spread throughout the plant, causing numerous disease symptoms.

The relationship between bacterial plant pathogens and their host plant is greatly affected by the stationary nature of the plant, the periodicity of plant growth, and the protective surfaces of the plant. Bacterial plant pathogens must possess an independent mode of dispersal to reach new host plants and must have some mechanism for entering the plant. Because most plant pathogenic bacteria do not form resting stages, they must remain within the confines of the plant tissues. Even during times of plant dormancy,

TABLE 14-4 Some Bacterial Diseases of Plants

GENUS	SPECIES	DISEASE	GENUS	SPECIES	DISEASE
Pseudomonas	*tabaci*	Wildfire of tobacco	*Corynebacterium*	*insidiosum*	Wilt of alfalfa
	angulata	Leaf spot of tobacco		*michiganese*	Wilt of tomato
	phaseolicola	Halo blight of beans			
	pisi	Blight of peas		*facians*	Leafy gall of ornamentals
	glycinea	Blight of soybeans			
	syringae	Blight of lilac	*Streptomyces*	*scabies*	Scab of potato
	solanacearum	Moko of banana		*ipomoeae*	Pox of sweet potato
	caryophylli	Wilt of carnation	*Agrobacterium*	*tumefaciens*	Crown gall of various plants
	cepacia	Sour skin of onion			
	marginalis	Slippery skin of onion		*rubi*	Cane gall of raspberries
	savastanoi	Olive knot disease			
	marginata	Scab of gladiolus		*rhizogenes*	Hairy root of apple
Xanthomonas	*phaseoli*	Blight of beans	*Mycoplasma*	sp.	Aster yellows
	oryzae	Blight of rice		sp.	Peach X disease
	pruni	Leaf spot of fruits		sp.	Peach yellows
	juglandis	Blight of walnut		sp.	Elm phloem necrosis
	campestris	Black rot of crucifers, citrus canker	*Spiroplasma*	sp.	Citrus stubborn disease
	vascularum	Gumming of sugar cane		sp.	Bermuda grass, witches' broom
Erwinia	*amylovora*	Fire blight of pears and apples		sp.	Corn stunt
	tracheiphila	Wilt of cucurbits			
	stewartii	Wilt of corn			
	carotovora	Soft rot of fruit, black leg of potato, blight of chrysanthemum			

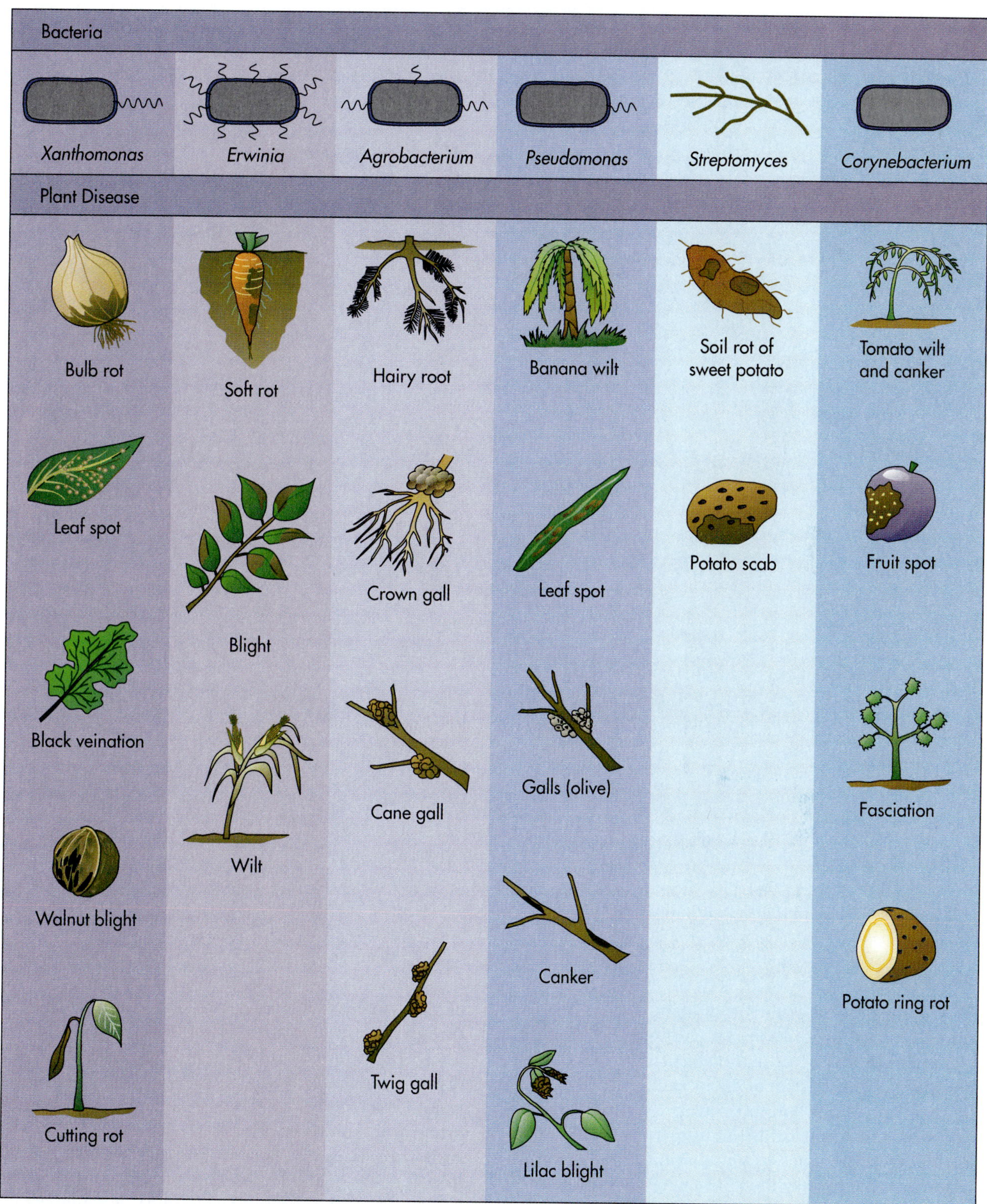

FIG. 14-19 Signs of diseases of plants caused by various bacterial plant pathogens.

many plant pathogenic bacteria can remain viable on plant seeds and other plant tissues. Some bacterial populations exhibit no significant soil phase. For example, *Erwinia amylovora,* which causes fire blight in fruit trees, remains within infected tissues and is disseminated in plant exudates by insects or raindrops (FIG. 14-20). During the winter, *E. amylovora* does not grow but remains dormant within infected tissues of the stems and branches of trees; in the spring, the bacteria are distributed to susceptible plants.

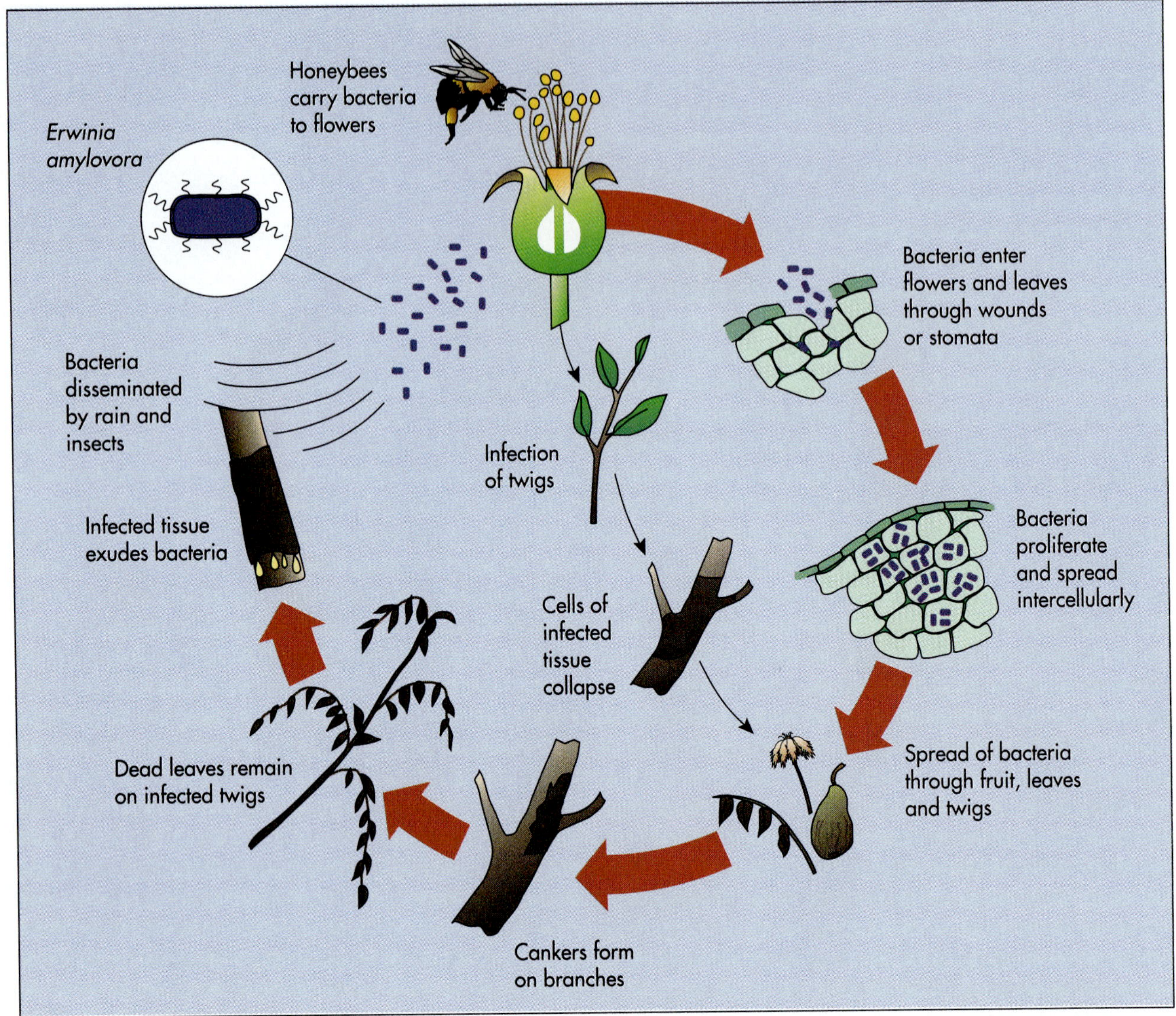

FIG. 14-20 Life cycle of *Erwinia amylovora,* the cause of fire blight, and the effect of infection with this bacterium on the plant.

A serious recent outbreak of plant disease is citrus canker, caused by *Xanthomonas campestris* var. *citrii.* Infections with this plant pathogen produce lesions on the leaves. An outbreak of citrus canker in 1913 took 20 years and $6 million to control. A new strain of *X. campestris* infected Florida citrus groves in 1984. It is distinct from previous strains, having a high level of fatty acids that protect the pathogen. Quarantine procedures and the burning of infected seedlings, about 21% of the nursery stock of Florida, were used to suppress this outbreak of the disease.

Crown gall, which is caused by *Agrobacterium tumefaciens,* is a particularly interesting plant disease (FIG. 14-21). Crown gall may occur on fruit trees, sugar beets, or other broad-leaved plants. The disease process is initiated when viable cells of *A. tumefaciens* enter wounded surfaces of susceptible dicotyledonous plants, usually at the soil–plant stem interface, either through the root or a wound. *A. tumefaciens* is able to transform host plant cells into tumorous cells, and the disease is manifested by the formation of a tumor growth, the crown gall. Once the disease is established, the tumor continues to grow even if viable *Agrobacterium* are eliminated. The tumor maintenance principle has been identified as a fragment of a large, **tumor-inducing plasmid (Ti plasmid).** A fragment of this bacterial plasmid is transferred to the plant, where it is maintained. The Ti plasmid contains *vir* genes, which code for proteins that are required for the transfer of T-DNA (transforming DNA). The *vir* genes are expressed after induction by plant-specified phenolic compounds such as *p*-hydroxybenzoic acid and vanillin. These phenolic inducer molecules are produced by damaged plant tissues.

A

B

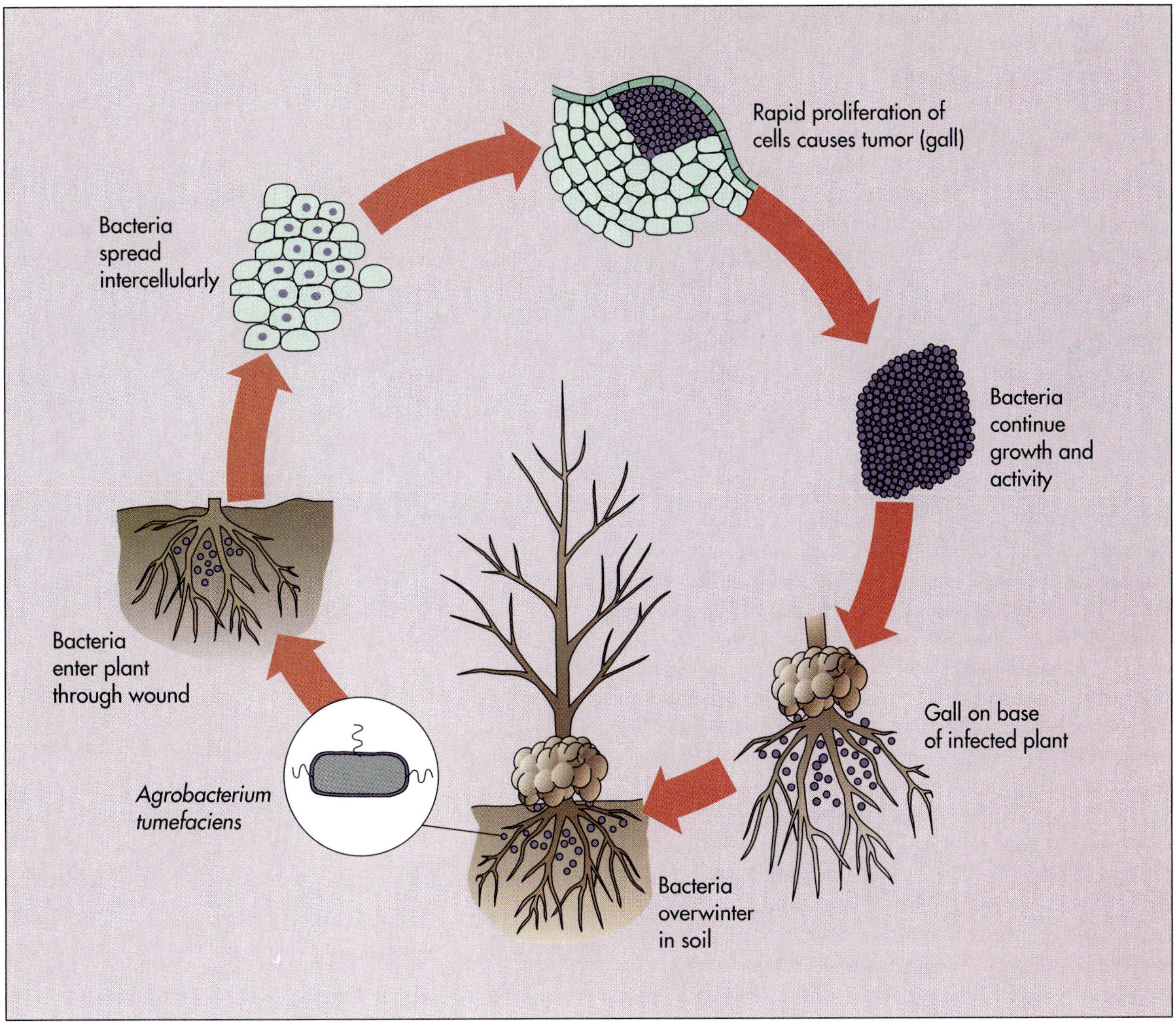

Rapid proliferation of cells causes tumor (gall)

Bacteria continue growth and activity

Gall on base of infected plant

Bacteria overwinter in soil

Agrobacterium tumefaciens

Bacteria enter plant through wound

Bacteria spread intercellularly

FIG. 14-21 **A,** A tree with crown gall (tumorous growth at base of the tree). **B,** Life cycle of *Agrobacterium tumefaciens,* the cause of crown gall, and its effect on a tree.

The activities coded for by the *vir* genes lead to the transfer of genetic information contained in the T-region from a bacterial cell to a plant cell. The *vir*A gene codes for a protein kinase that utilizes ATP to phosphorylate the VirG protein. Phosphorylation of the VirG protein converts it to an active state that, in turn, activates other *vir* genes. The VirD protein nicks the Ti plasmid DNA adjacent to the T-DNA. Then, the VirE protein, a single-stranded binding protein, complexes to the single-stranded DNA that contains the T-region. The VirE protein–T-region complex is transported into the plant cell via a mechanism similar to bacterial conjugation. The VirB protein acts like a sex pilus and may be involved in the transfer of the single-stranded DNA into the plant cell.

Once inside the plant cell, the T-region-containing DNA is transported into the nucleus and integrates into the plant chromosomes at a number of sites. The T-DNA contains oncogenes that code for either octopine or nopaline (two opines that serve as carbon and energy sources for the infecting bacteria). The expression of these oncogenes also leads to the formation of tumors in the plant.

The Ti plasmid has great potential in recombinant DNA technology to introduce desired genetic information into a wide range of plants of agricultural significance (FIG. 14-22). Plants that have gained new genetic information from foreign sources are called **transgenic plants.** Some examples of transgenic plants include tomato, potato, tobacco, soybean, alfalfa, cotton, poplar, walnut, and apple. Thus, although *Agrobacterium* possessing the Ti plasmid cause great damage to crops, the Ti plasmid itself represents a vehicle for the creation of improved transgenic crops capable of disease resistance and increased yields with decreased management.

One of the most interesting ecological relationships between bacteria and plants involves the role of certain phyllosphere bacteria in initiating ice crystal formation, which results in frost damage to the plant. Some strains of *Pseudomonas syringae* and *Erwinia herbicola* produce a surface protein that can initiate ice crystal formation. These bacteria are conditional plant pathogens, causing death due to frost damage only at temperatures that can initiate the freezing process. When ice-nucleation active populations are replaced with mutant strains that do not produce the ice-initiating proteins, laboratory experiments demonstrate that ice crystals do not form until the temperature drops to −7 to −9° C, thereby limiting frost damage. The development of genetically engineered strains of ice-minus *P. syringae,* that is, strains that do not form the ice-nucleating surface protein, and the proposal to apply such strains to field crops for frost

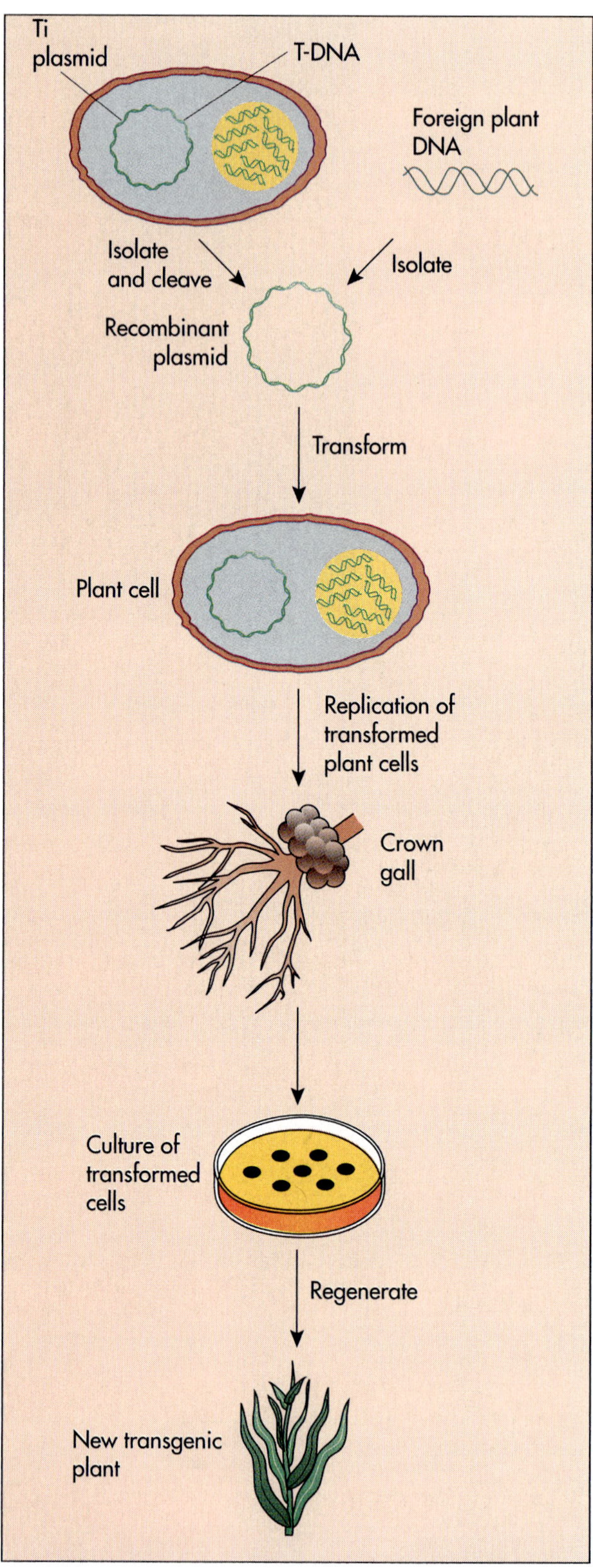

FIG. 14-22 The Ti plasmid of *Agrobacterium tumefaciens* has the ability to integrate into plant cell chromosomes. It can carry foreign genes with it and therefore is useful in genetic engineering and the formation of transgenic plants.

TABLE 14-5 Some Diseases of Plants Caused by Fungi

GROUP/GENUS	DISEASE
SLIME MOLDS	
Plasmodiphora	Clubfoot of crucifers
Plasmopara	Downy mildew of grapes
Polymyxa	Root disease of cereals
Spongospora	Powdery scab of potato
OOMYCETES	
Albugo	White rust of crucifers
Phytophthora	Late blight of potato
Pythium	Seed ecary, root rots, damping off
CHITRIDIOMYCETES	
Olpidium	Root disease of various plants
Physoderma	Brown spot of corn
Synchytrium	Black wart of potato
Urophlyctis	Crown wart of alfalfa
ZYGOMYCETES	
Rhizopus	Soft rot of fruits
ASCOMYCETES	
Ceratocystis	Dutch elm disease
Claviceps	Ergot of rye
Diaporthe	Bean pod blight
Dibotryon	Black knot of cherries
Diplocarpon	Black spot of roses
Endothia	Chestnut blight
Erysiphe	Powdery mildew of grasses
Lophodermium	Pine needle blight
Microsphaera	Powdery mildew of lilac
Mycosphaerella	Leaf spots of trees
Ophiobolus	Take all of wheat
Podosphaera	Powdery mildew of apple
Sclerotinia	Soft rot of vegetables
Taphrina	Peach leaf curl
Venturia	Apple scab
BASIDIOMYCETES	
Armillaria	Root rots of trees
Cronartium	Pine blister rust
Exobasidium	Stem galls of ornamentals
Fomes	Heart rot of trees
Marasmius	Fairy ring of turf grasses
Polyporus	Stem rot of trees
Puccinia	Rust of cereals
Sphacelotheca	Loose smut of sorghum
Tilletia	Stinking smut of wheat
Typhylai	Blight of turf grasses
Urocystis	Smut of onion
Uromyces	Rust of beans
Ustilago	Smut of corn, wheat, and others
DEUTEROMYCETES	
Alternaria	Leaf spots and blight of various plants
Aspergillus	Rots of seeds
Botrytis	Blights of various plants
Cladosporium	Leaf mold of tomato
Colletotrichum	Anthracnose of crops
Cylindrosporium	Leaf spots of various plants
Fusarium	Root rot of many plants, vascular wilt of grain and tomato
Helminthosporium	Blight of cereals
Penicillium	Blue mold rot of fruits
Phoma	Black leg of crucifers
Rhizoctonia	Root rot of various plants
Thielaviopsis	Black root rot of tobacco
Verticillium	Wilt of various plants

protection have caused great public and scientific concern about the possible environmental consequences of such uses of genetically engineered microorganisms. A field test of genetically engineered ice-minus *P. syringae* on strawberries was the first deliberate release of a microorganism created by recombinant DNA technology.

Fungal Plant Pathogens

Most plant diseases are caused by pathogenic fungi (Table 14-5). Many fungi are well adapted to act as plant pathogens. Fungal spore production permits aerial transmission between plants and allows plant pathogenic fungi to remain viable outside host plants. Survival and infectivity of most plant pathogenic fungi depend on prevailing environmental temperature and moisture conditions. Spores germinate and mycelia grow when the temperature is between −5° and +45° C and there is an adequate supply of moisture. Spores, though, can retain viability for long periods of time during environmental conditions that do not allow germination.

Plant pathogenic fungi generally exhibit a complex life cycle, spent in part in host plant infection and in part outside host plants in soil or on plant debris in the soil. As an example, the life cycle of *Rhizoctonia solani,* a fungus that causes a variety of diseases, is illustrated in FIG. 14-23. Similarly, the fungus *Monilinia*

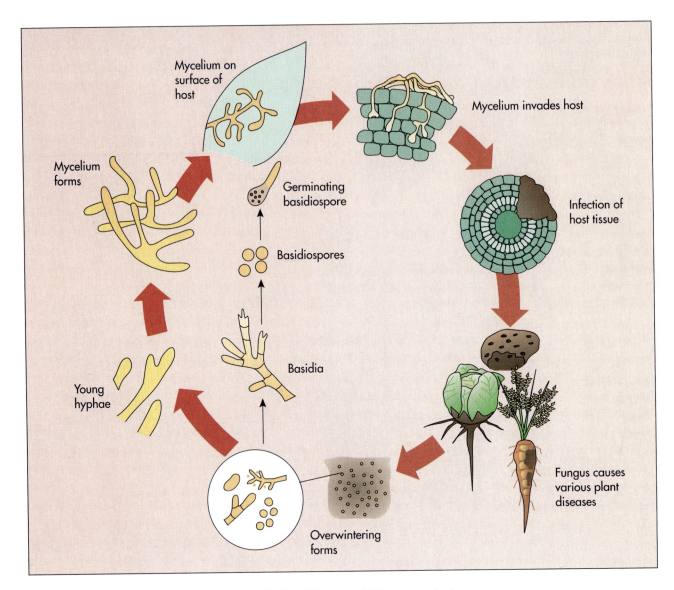

FIG. 14-23 Life cycle of *Rhizoctonia solani.*

distinct from previous strains, having a high level of fatty acids that protect the pathogen. Quarantine procedures and the burning of infected seedlings, about 21% of the nursery stock of Florida, were used to suppress this outbreak of the disease.

Crown gall, which is caused by *Agrobacterium tumefaciens*, is a particularly interesting plant disease (FIG. 14-21). Crown gall may occur on fruit trees, sugar beets, or other broad-leaved plants. The disease process is initiated when viable cells of *A. tumefaciens* enter wounded surfaces of susceptible dicotyledonous plants, usually at the soil–plant stem interface, either through the root or a wound. *A. tumefaciens* is able to transform host plant cells into tumorous cells, and the disease is manifested by the formation of a tumor growth, the crown gall. Once the disease is estab-

FIG. 14-24 Brown rot of an apricot.

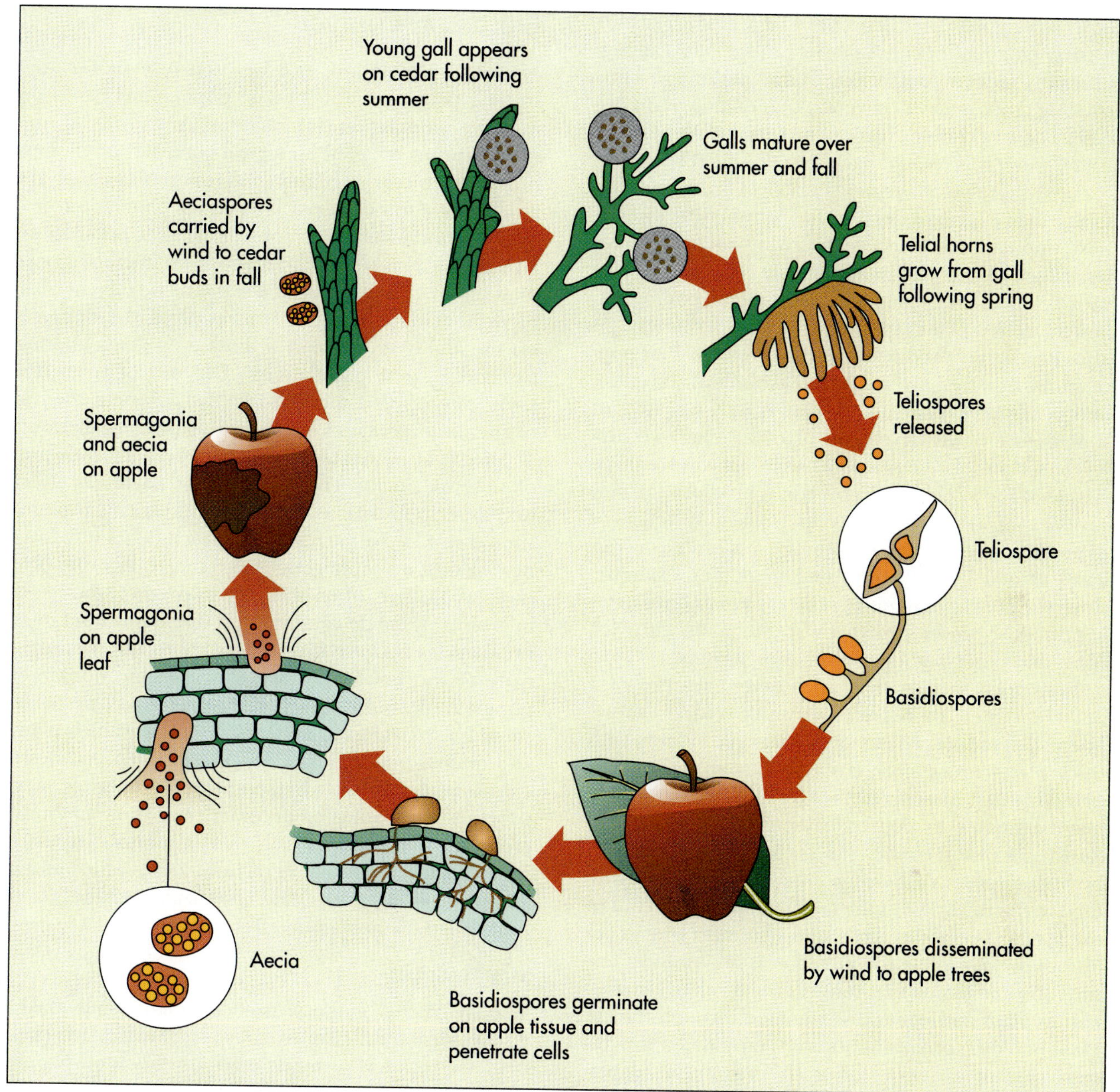

FIG. 14-25 Life cycle of the apple-cedar rust fungus *Gymnosporangium juniperi*. This fungus alternates between apple and cedar trees to complete its life cycle.

rust. The smuts are so named because they produce black, dusty spore masses resembling soot or smut. Important diseases caused by smut fungi include loose smut of oats, corn smut, bunt or stinking smut of wheat, and onion smut. Smut and rust fungi cause millions of dollars worth of crop damage annually.

CONTROL OF PLANT PATHOGENS

Since obligate plant pathogens can remain viable for only a limited period of time outside host plant tissues, appropriate management procedures can be used to control plant pathogens of agricultural crops. The most important of these are (1) *quarantine* (restriction of movement) procedures to restrict the spread of plant pathogens; (2) *sanitary practices* to prevent infection of plants with contaminated soils and tools; (3) the development and planting of *resistant crop varieties* that are not susceptible to particular plant pathogens; (4) the use of *crop rotation practices* to limit contact between the pathogen and the host plant, and (5) the use of *pesticides,* such as fungicides, to control populations of plant pathogens. Plant pathogens are normally specific for particular host plants. By periodically sowing new plant varieties that are not hosts for a particular pathogenic microorganism one can significantly reduce populations of that pathogen. Thus rotating crops is an effective way of reducing plant disease. The susceptible crop can be successfully reestablished when it is rotated back into that field later.

Agricultural management practices frequently attempt to avoid plant disease through modification of host populations. Selective breeding methods have been used extensively in agriculture to develop plant varieties that are genetically resistant to pathogens, and many new plant varieties developed in this way are also successfully producing high crop yields. Pest populations, however, are subject to evolution, selection, and geographical spread, making it only a matter of time before newly developed plant varieties are subject to serious plant diseases. Thus in agriculture there is a need for a continuous breeding program for new varieties of resistant plants to replace varieties of plants that are, or are becoming, susceptible to diseases caused by pathogens and pests. For example, since the 1930s, varieties of resistant wheat have been continuously developed to resist infections with rust fungi and other pathogenic microorganisms.

Resistance to disease is an inherent feature of a plant designed to restrict the entry and/or subsequent deleterious effects of a pathogen. Plants with thicker cuticles or cork layers are more resistant to plant diseases. Insect vectors carrying plant pathogens may be unable to penetrate these thickened layers. Resistance of some species of barberry to penetration by basidiospores of *Puccinia graminis* has been attributed to the thickness of the cuticle in the epidermis of the leaves. The ability to close the stomata when conditions are favorable for infection is an adaptive feature of some plants that renders them relatively resistant to plant pathogens disseminated through the air. Plant-breeding programs often attempt to develop disease-resistant varieties with such anatomical adaptations.

Microbial amensalism and parasitism can be used to control populations of pathogenic microorganisms. Negative interpopulation relationships protect many plants from infection with disease-causing microorganisms. The phenomenon of **soil fungistasis** (the inhibition of fungi by soil) is believed by some to be due to microbial activities. Fungistasis is widespread in soil. Some bacterial species produce antifungal substances, and the addition of *Bacillus* and *Streptomyces* species to soil has been shown to control damping off disease in cucumber, peas, and lettuce and several other diseases caused by the fungus *Rhizoctonia solani*. The addition of cellulase-producing myxobacteria to the rhizosphere of young seedlings has been found to control diseases caused by pathogenic fungi such as *Pythium*, *Rhizoctonia*, and *Fusarium*, which enter the plant through the soil.

BIOLOGICAL CONTROL

Microbial populations can be used directly for controlling plant and animal pest populations based on negative population interactions. Such use of microorganisms is called **biological control.** Populations of pathogenic or predatory microorganisms that are antagonistic toward a particular pest population provide a natural means of controlling that population, and preparations of such antagonistic microbial populations are called *microbial pesticides*. The effective use of pathogenic microorganisms as pesticides depends on the ability to establish a disease epidemic among susceptible pest populations. The use of microbial pathogens offers a method that can augment the use of chemical pesticides in controlling pest populations.

Microbial pesticides should exhibit a high degree of host specificity. They should not adversely affect nontarget populations. The host specificity, though, should not be so narrow as to preclude its effectiveness against a simple genetic variance within the pest population. It is often difficult to predict whether a microbial pesticide can establish disease in nontarget populations because it is impossible to test the infectivity of the pesticide against all possible nontarget populations. Obviously, any microbial pesticide should be harmless to humans and other valued plant and animal populations. The use of microbial pesticides is probably best when employed in an integrated program of management practices for agricultural crops and domestic animals that minimizes opportunities for infection or interaction, along with limited applications of appropriate chemical pesticides carefully timed for maximum effect.

Viral Pesticides

The specificity of the virus–host relationship makes viruses ideal for the control of specific insect pest populations, with few or no deleterious effects on people and other animals. Insect pathogenic viruses frequently cause natural disease epidemics in insect populations; these are known as *epizootics* (disease outbreak in nonhuman animals). Viruses have been used in attempts to control outbreaks of various insect pests, including gypsy moths, Douglas fir tussock moths, pine processionary caterpillars, red-banded leaf rollers (a pest of apples), spruce budworms, codling moths (a pest of apples, walnuts, and other deciduous fruits), Great Basin tent caterpillars, alfalfa caterpillars, cabbage white butterflies, cabbage loopers, cotton bollworms, corn earworms, tobacco budworms, tomato worms, army worms, and wattle bagworms, among others.

The most thoroughly studied of these viruses are the nuclear polyhedrosis viruses, cytoplasmic polyhedrosis viruses, and granulosis viruses. The *nuclear polyhedrosis viruses* develop in the host-cell nuclei; the viri-

BOX 14-2

VIRAL CONTROL OF AUSTRALIAN RABBITS

An interesting example of the use of viral pesticides was the attempt to control the rabbit populations of Australia with myxoma virus. Rabbits were introduced into Australia from Europe in 1859, and because there were no natural enemies for the rabbit in Australia, their reproduction was unchecked. Myxoma virus, occurring naturally among South American rabbits, was found to be a virulent pathogen of the European rabbit, and in an effort to achieve control of the rabbit populations in Australia, the myxoma virus was introduced. The virus rapidly spread among the rabbit populations, causing high seasonal morbidity and mortality. Initially, 99% of the infected rabbits died, but after only a few years the virulence of the myxoma virus for the surviving rabbits declined. The survivors of the initial epidemics had been selected for their resistance to the virus. The resistance of the rabbits is innate and is not due to an immunological defense system. Thus, within only a few years, an equilibrium was achieved between the virus and the Australian rabbits. Myxomatosis was effective in lowering the Australian rabbit population to about 20% of its level before the introduction of the virus, and now that the virus is firmly established within the rabbit population, there is a pathogen that controls its level. However, the introduction of the myxoma virus did not completely eliminate the rabbits, as was originally envisioned. Rather, after killing 99% of the rabbits in Australia, some rabbits developed resistance. Later the virus mutated into a less virulent form. The rabbit population rebounded.

Other means of biological control using genetically engineered myxoma viruses are being explored to further reduce the rabbit populations of Australia. Such an application of genetically engineered microorganisms is controversial. There are some who fear that once released the genetically engineered virus could not be contained and that it might reach Europe where it could devastate the rabbit populations. The genetically engineered virus proposed for controlling the Australian rabbits was formed by inserting a gene for a rabbit sperm protein into the virus. It would work by inducing sterility. Replication of the genetically engineered virus within a female rabbit would release sperm protein so that the female rabbit would develop "immunity" to male sperm. The female rabbit would produce antibodies against the male sperm protein. The antibodies of an "immune" female rabbit would attack male sperm so that reproduction could not occur. It also would work on foxes, which are also a major problem in Australia. In essence the genetically engineered virus would act as a contraceptive. This is a novel means of biological control with a genetically engineered microorganism and represents an interesting means of achieving biological control.

ons are occluded singly or in groups in polyhedral inclusion bodies. *Cytoplasmic polyhedrosis viruses* develop only in the cytoplasm of host midgut epithelial cells; the virions are occluded singly in polyhedral inclusion bodies. *Granulosis viruses* develop in either the nucleus or the cytoplasm of host fat, tracheal, or epidermal cells; the virions are occluded singly or, rarely, in pairs in small occlusion bodies called *capsules*.

Bacterial Pesticides

Bacillus thuringiensis has been extensively exploited in the bacterial control of pest insect populations. Commercial preparations of *B. thuringiensis* are registered by at least twelve manufacturers in five countries for use on numerous agricultural crops, forest trees, and ornamentals for control of various insect pests (Table 14-6). *B. thuringiensis* has been tested successfully against more than 140 insect species, including members of the Lepidoptera, Hymenoptera, Diptera, and Coleoptera. It is a crystalliferous bacterium because, in addition to endospores, it produces discrete parasporal bodies within its cell (FIG. 14-26). The proteinaceous parasporal crystal is the toxic factor. Four separate toxic substances are produced by

TABLE 14-6 Some Registered Uses for *Bacillus thuringiensis* Products in the United States

PEST	CROP
VEGETABLE AND FIELD CROPS	
Alfalfa caterpillar, *Colias eurytheme*	Alfalfa
Artichoke plume moth, *Platyptila carduidactyla*	Artichokes
Bollworm, *Heliosthis zea*	Cotton
Cabbage looper, *Trichoplusia ni*	Beans, broccoli, cabbage, cauliflower, celery, collards, cotton, cucumbers, kale, lettuce, melons, potatoes, spinach, tobacco
Diamondback moth, *Plutella maculipennis*	Cabbage
European corn borer, *Ostrina nubilalis*	Sweet corn

Continued.

TABLE 14-6 Some Registered Uses for *Bacillus thuringiensis* Products in the United States—cont'd

PEST	CROP
Vegetable and Field Crops	
Imported cabbageworm, *Pieris rapae*	Broccoli, cabbage, cauliflower, collards, kale
Tobacco budworm, *Heliothis virescens*	Tobacco
Tobacco hornworm, *Manduca sexta*	Tobacco
Tomato hornworm, *Manduca quinquemaculata*	Tomatoes
Fruit Crops	
Fruit tree leaf roller, *Archips argyurospilus*	Oranges
Orange dog, *Papilio cresphontes*	Oranges
Grape leaf folder, *Desmia funeralis*	Grapes
Shade Trees, Ornamentals	
California oakworm, *Phryganidia californica*	—
Fall webworm, *Hyphantria cunea*	—
Fall cankerworm, *Alsophila pometaria*	—
Great Basic tent caterpillar, *Malacosoma fragile*	—
Gypsy moth, *Lymantria (Porthetria) dispar*	—
Linden looper, *Erannis tiliaria*	—
Salt marsh caterpillar, *Estigemen acrea*	—
Spring cankerworm, *Paleacrita vernata*	—
Winter moth, *Operophtera brumata*	—

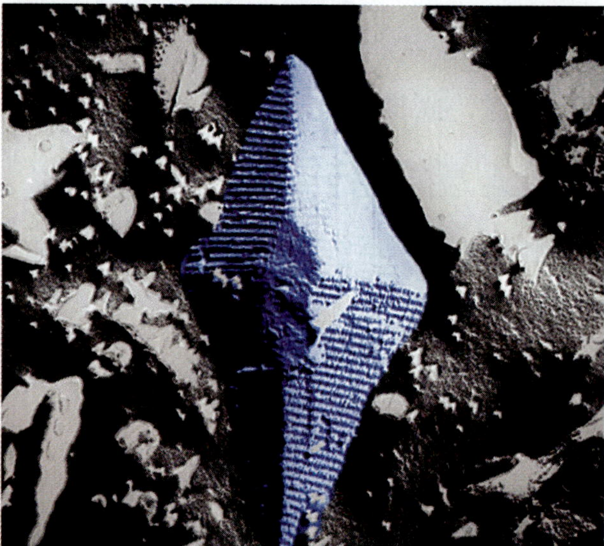

FIG. 14-26 **A,** Colorized micrograph of *Bacillus thuringiensis* showing endospores *(green)* and toxin crystals *(blue)*. **B,** A purified crystal of *B. thuringiensis* toxin *(blue)*. This toxin is an effective insecticide.

B. thuringiensis. Use of this bacterium results in commercially acceptable levels of suppression of cabbage worms, cabbage loopers, and many other pests of vegetable crops. *B. thuringiensis* also readily suppresses populations of tent caterpillars, bagworms, and canker worms, which are pests of forest trees. Gypsy moth and spruce budworm can be suppressed by *B. thuringiensis* but only when high application rates are used and uniform foliage coverage is attained.

Other *Bacillus* species cause milky disease of Japanese beetles. In Japan, where the beetle encounters natural antagonists, it is a relatively minor pest. In the United States, however, the beetle does not have any natural associated pathogens or other antagonists. The Japanese beetle feeds voraciously on some 300 species of plants and has been responsible for large economic losses. The greatest success in suppressing pest populations of Japanese beetles has been obtained by using bacteria that produce milky disease. For many years, a mixture of *Bacillus popilliae* and *Bacillus lentimorbus* has been marketed under the trade name Doom. *B. lentimorbus,* which infects mainly first and second instar grubs, does not produce parasporal crystals; *B. popilliae* produces parasporal bodies and infects a high proportion of third instar grubs. The use of these *Bacillus* species to produce milky disease in grubs of Japanese beetles is probably responsible for the control of pest beetle populations, and although in the past there have been major infestations of Japanese beetles in the United States, today there are relatively few major outbreaks.

14.3 BIOGEOCHEMICAL CYCLING

All living organisms carry out chemical transformations that influence their environment. Many of these chemical changes are a consequence of oxidation-reduction reactions that occur during microbial metabolism. Changes in the chemical forms of various elements can lead to the physical translocations of materials, sometimes mediating transfers between the atmosphere (air), hydrosphere (water), and lithosphere (land). These chemical and physical changes result in *global cycling* of substances.

Biogeochemical cycling is the movement of materials via biochemical reactions through the global biosphere. The biosphere is the portion of the Earth and its atmosphere in which living organisms occur. The activities of microorganisms within the biosphere have a direct impact on the quality of human life. Without the essential biogeochemical cycling activities of microorganisms, all forms of life, including humans, could not exist.

CARBON CYCLE

Carbon is actively cycled between inorganic carbon dioxide and the various organic compounds that compose living organisms. The **carbon cycle** primarily involves the transfer of carbon dioxide and organic carbon between the atmosphere, where carbon occurs principally as inorganic CO_2, and the hydrosphere and lithosphere, which contain varying concentrations of organic and inorganic carbon compounds (FIG. 14-27). In the lithosphere and hydrosphere, carbon dioxide reacts with water to form carbonate and bicarbonate, which are the principal inorganic forms of carbon found there.

Microbial Metabolism of Inorganic and Organic Carbon

Microorganisms have great capacities for metabolizing organic and inorganic carbon. The pathways of microbial metabolism are discussed in Chapters 4 and

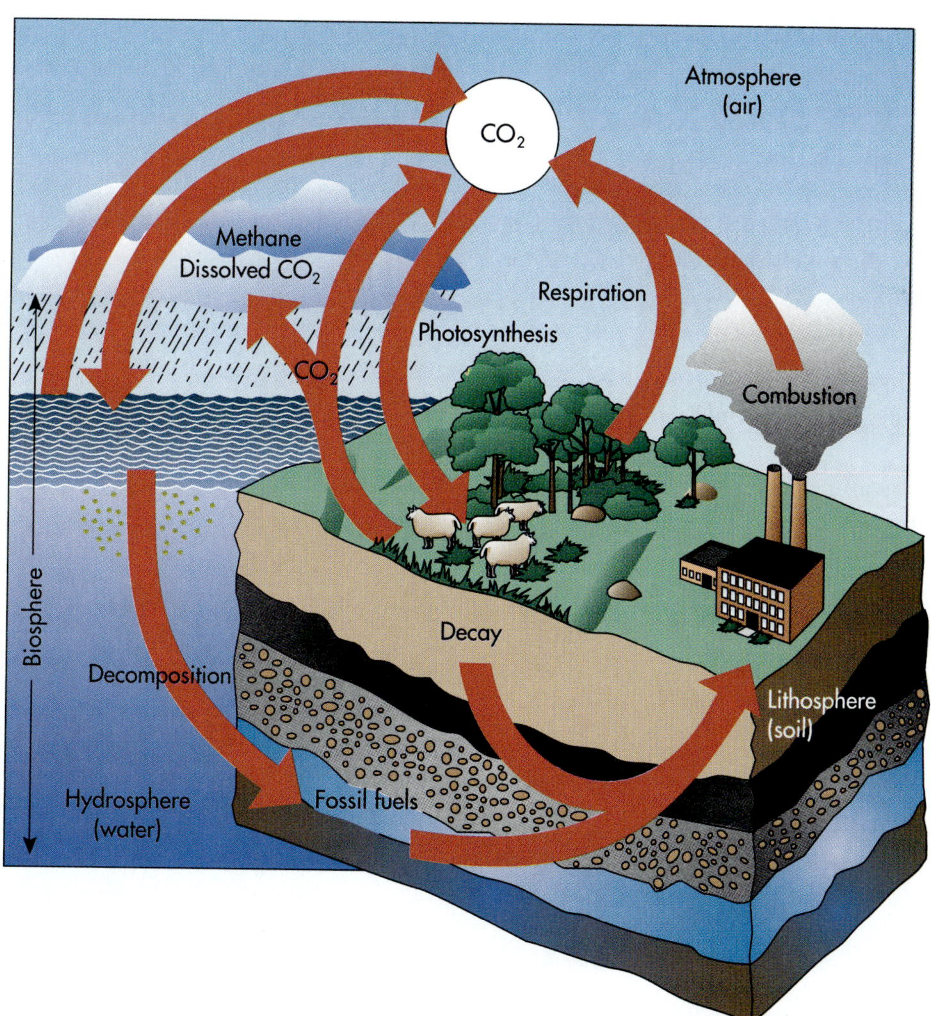

FIG. 14-27 The carbon cycle showing the dominant transfers between atmospheric carbon dioxide and organic compounds in soil and water.

5. The autotrophic metabolism of photosynthetic and chemolithotrophic organisms is responsible for **primary production:** the conversion of inorganic carbon dioxide to organic carbon. Once carbon is fixed (reduced) into organic compounds, it can be transferred from population to population within the biological community, supporting the growth of many heterotrophic organisms. The respiratory and fermentative metabolism of heterotrophic organisms returns inorganic carbon dioxide to the atmosphere, completing the carbon cycle. This represents the decay portion of the carbon cycle. The combination of carbon fixation by autotrophs and decomposition by heterotrophs cycles carbon through ecosystems.

Production of methane by a specialized group of methanogenic archaebacteria represents a shunt to the normal cycling of carbon because the methane that is produced cannot be used by most heterotrophic organisms and thus is lost from the biological community to the atmosphere. Normally, fossil fuels, such as coal and petroleum, are not actively cycled through the activities of microorganisms. Burning of fossil fuels also adds CO_2 to the atmosphere, which has led to a general rise in the concentration of atmospheric CO_2 and a resulting warming of global temperatures, a phenomenon known as the *greenhouse effect.*

The carbon dioxide converted into organic carbon by the **primary producers,** the autotrophs, in an ecosystem represents the **gross primary production** (total amount of organic matter produced) by the biological community in a given habitat. Part of the gross primary production is converted back to carbon dioxide by the respiration of the primary producers, and only the remaining organic carbon in the form of biomass and soluble metabolites—the **net primary production**—is available for heterotrophic consumers in terrestrial and aquatic habitats. The oxidative metabolism of the biological community removes organic carbon and the energy stored in such compounds from the ecosystem, and thus represents a decay of the energy stored within a given habitat. If the net primary production is greater than the community respiration, organic matter accumulates within the ecosystem. If, on the other hand, respiratory activities are greater than the net primary production, organic matter must be added from an external source or the community in that ecosystem will decline.

Most ecosystems depend on the photosynthetic fixation of carbon dioxide, that is, the input of organic matter by photosynthetic organisms, including plants, algae, and photosynthetic bacteria. The thermal rift areas of the deep ocean regions near the Galapagos Islands represent an interesting exception because the ecosystems associated with these areas are based on the input of organic carbon by sulfur-oxidizing chemolithotrophic bacteria that grow in the warm, hydrogen sulfide-rich waters that enter the ocean through thermal vents (FIG. 14-28). These organisms generate ATP and reduced coenzymes by oxidizing hydrogen sulfide and use the ATP and reduced coenzymes to drive the reduction of CO_2 via the Calvin cycle.

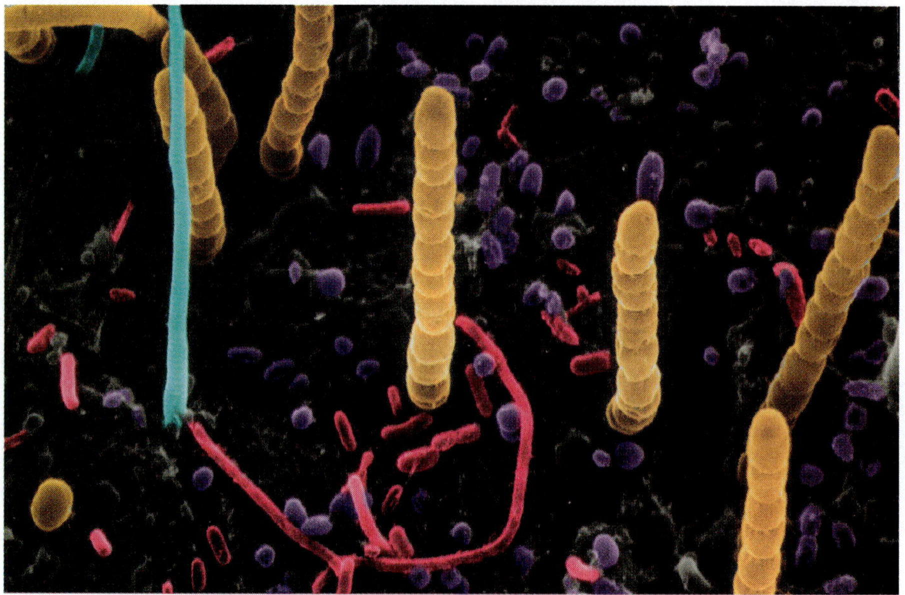

FIG. 14-28 Colorized scanning electron micrograph of a mat of bacterial growth in a deep sea vent bacterial community dominated by filamentous growth of *Thiothrix.* (yellow) Chemolithotrophic bacteria grow abundantly in the H_2S-rich waters around the thermal vents and cover almost all surfaces that are exposed to the H_2S-containing vent plumes.

Trophic Relationships

Feeding relationships between organisms establish the **trophic structure,** that is, the routes by which energy and materials are transferred within an ecosystem. This movement of carbon and energy through an ecosystem occurs in steps from one trophic level to another. Each step is called a *trophic level* (feeding level). When one organism consumes another, carbon and energy are transferred to the next higher trophic level. The carbon and energy in organic compounds that are formed by primary producers, move through the biological community of an ecosystem in this manner. Energy moves through the system in one direction while carbon is cycled. Only a portion of the energy is transferred, usually about 10%, to the next higher trophic level.

Transfer of energy stored in organic compounds between the organisms in the community forms a **food web,** an integrated feeding structure (FIG. 14-29). At the base of the food web are the *primary producers,* which form the organic matter for the system. *Grazers* are organisms that feed on primary producers. In *phytoplankton-based food webs,* algae and cyanobacteria are the primary food source for grazers. In *detrital food webs,* microbial biomass produced from growth on dead organic matter (detritus) serves as a primary food source for grazers. The grazers, in turn, are eaten by *predators,* which in turn may be preyed on by larger predators. In this manner, carbon and stored energy are moved to the higher levels of the food web. Respiration causes some of the carbon and energy to be lost during each transfer.

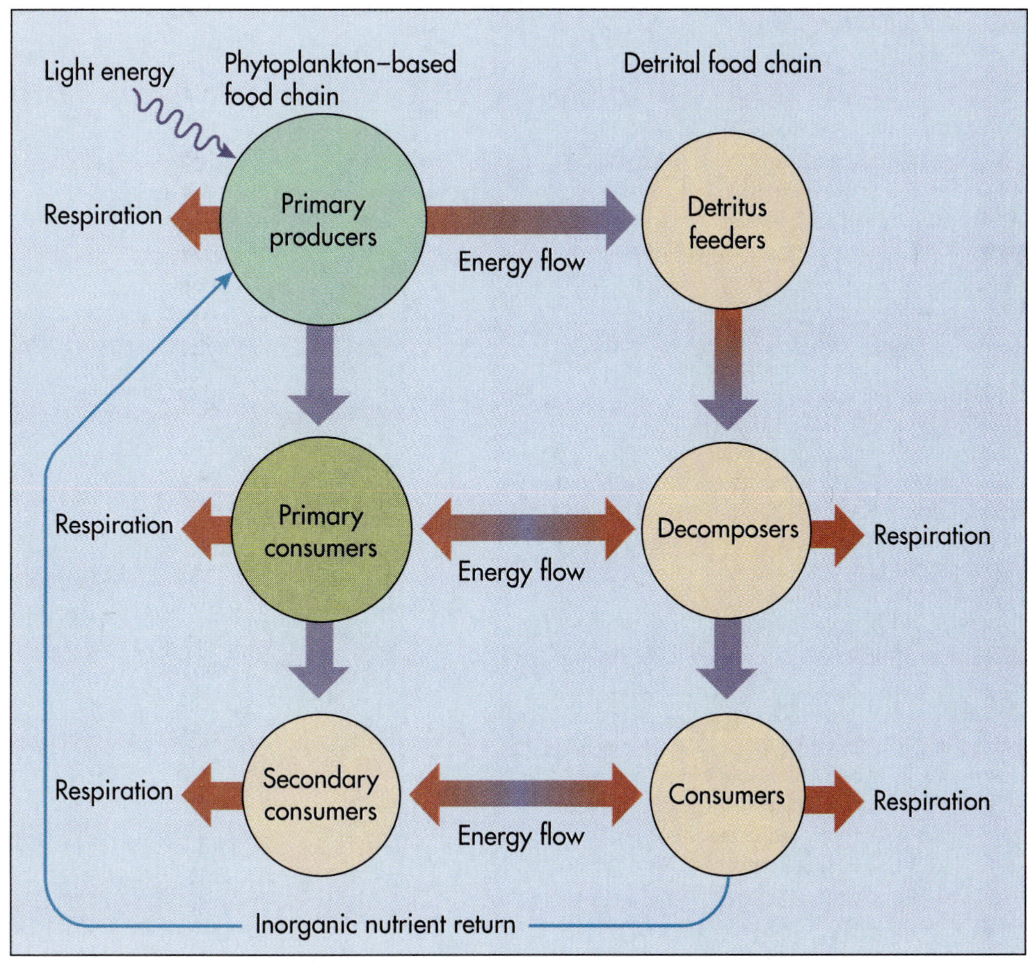

FIG. 14-29 In a food web, organic compounds formed by primary producers are transferred to higher trophic levels. Decomposers return organic biomass to carbon dioxide and minerals. In a grazing food web, primary producers feed grazers and other consumers. In a detrital food web, dead organic matter (detritus) initially feeds decomposers. The biomass of the decomposers subsequently is consumed.

The overall feeding relationships establish a pyramid of biological populations in the food web (FIG. 14-30). The pyramid shape occurs because only a small portion of the energy stored in any trophic level is transferred to the next higher trophic level. Normally, 85% to 90% of the energy stored in the organic matter of a trophic level is consumed by respiration during transfer to the next trophic level and enters the decay portion of the food web. Since only 10% of the energy is transferred to each successively higher trophic level, the higher the trophic level, the smaller its biomass.

The decay portions of food webs are dominated by microorganisms (FIG. 14-31). Microbial decomposition of dead plants and animals and partially digested organic matter is largely responsible for the conversion of organic matter to carbon dioxide and the reinjection of inorganic CO_2 into the atmosphere. The rates of organic matter mineralization depend on various factors, including environmental conditions—such as pH, temperature, and oxygen concentration—and the chemical nature of the organic matter. Some natural organic compounds, such as lignin, cellulose, and humic acids, are relatively resistant to attack and decay only slowly. Various synthetic compounds, such as DDT, may be *recalcitrant,* that is, completely resistant to enzymatic degradation. We depend on the activities of microorganisms to decompose organic wastes, and when microbial decomposition is ineffective, organic compounds accumulate. This is evidenced by the environmental accumulation of plastic materials that are recalcitrant to microbial attack. Many modern problems relating to the accumulation of environmental pollutants reflect the inability of microorganisms to degrade rapidly enough the concentrated wastes of industrialized societies.

BOX 14-3

Winogradsky Column

The Winogradsky column, which is named after the Russian microbiologist Sergei Winogradsky, is a model ecosystem that is used to study soil and sediment microorganisms (see FIG.). A Winogradsky column is a core of soil or sediment placed within a glass or clear plastic cylinder. The height of the column allows the development of an aerobic zone at the surface and microaerophilic and anoxic zones below the surface. The column is exposed to light so that various photosynthetic populations develop. The soil or sediment contains or is augmented with organic carbon substrates, sulfide, and sulfates. This permits the development of numerous heterotrophic and photoautotrophic populations, including anaerobic photosynthetic bacteria. Because numerous microorganisms with diverse physiologies flourish, the Winogradsky column is a rich source of microorganisms with varying metabolic capabilities.

Because populations of algae and cyanobacteria (oxygenic photosynthetic microorganisms) grow at the surface, the upper zone typically appears green. The oxygen produced by these microorganisms maintains an aerobic zone within which heterotropic aerobic bacterial and fungal populations grow. Consumption of oxygen by aerobic and facultatively anaerobic populations produces anoxic zones and an anaerobic subsurface region. Fermentative metabolism in these zones produces organic acids, alcohols, and H_2. These are substrates for sulfate-reducing bacteria. The sulfides produced by the metabolism of sulfate-reducers are used by anaerobic photosynthetic bacterial populations. Purple sulfur bacterial populations develop overlying growths of green sulfur bacterial populations; these are seen as purple and green zones. The purple sulfur bacteria are more tolerant of sulfide then the green sulfur bacteria, which is why they grow in the upper region that has the greater sulfide concentration. Similar colored zones associated with the growth of these anaerobic photosynthetic bacterial populations often are observed at the mud–water interfaces of ponds.

In a Winogradsky column, specific microbial populations grow at different levels because of the different environmental conditions. There, distribution of discrete populations throughout the soil transfers energy through a defined food web from primary producers to consumers and decomposers.

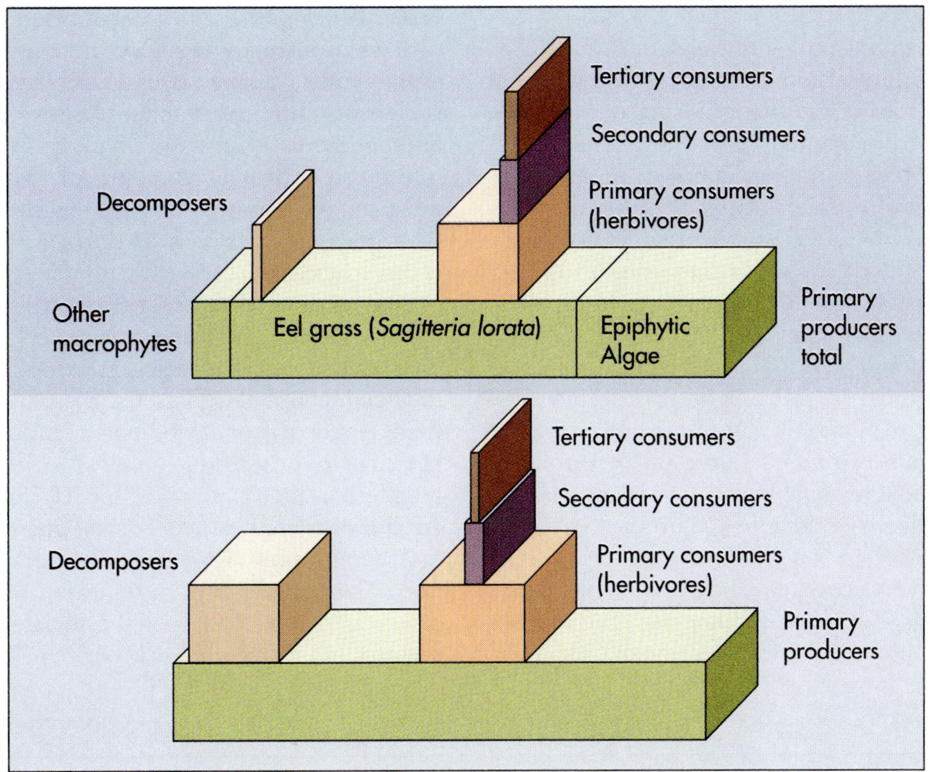

FIG. 14-30 Only a portion of the stored energy is transferred, so that each successively higher trophic level has less biomass.

A

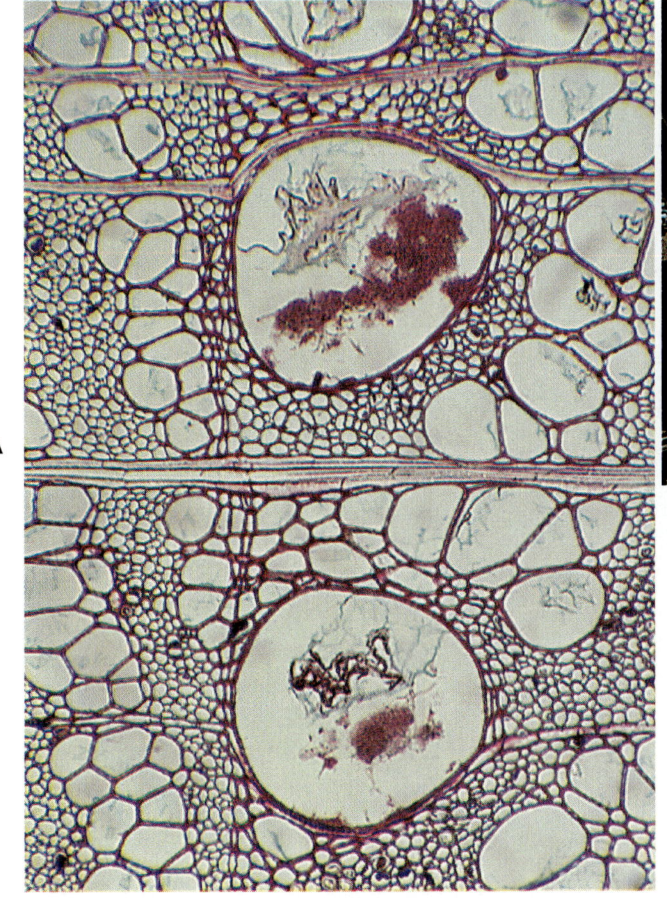

B

FIG. 14-31 **A,** Micrograph showing bacteria and fungi growing within dead plant cells. (160×). These microorganisms are decomposing the dead plant matter. **B,** The myxomycete *Fuliga septica* decomposing a dead tree.

NITROGEN CYCLE

Nitrogen can exist in various oxidation states. Molecular nitrogen, the most abundant substance in the atmosphere, is not directly usable by most organisms; only a few bacteria use molecular nitrogen directly. Microorganisms utilize other forms of nitrogen such as NH_4^+, NO_2^- and NO_3^-, as well as organic nitrogen-containing compounds such as amino acids and proteins. The conversions of nitrogen compounds, primarily by microorganisms, changes the oxidation states of nitrogenous compounds and establishes a nitrogen cycle (FIG. 14-32). As a result of the biogeochemical cycling of nitrogen, known as the **nitrogen cycle,** nitrogen moves from the atmosphere through the biota (soil and aquatic habitats).

Nitrogen Fixation

Productivity of many ecosystems is limited by the supply of fixed forms of nitrogen. Other than the industrial chemical fixation of molecular nitrogen using the Haber-Bosch process to form nitrogen fertilizers, the process of **nitrogen fixation,** the conversion of N_2 to ammonia or organic nitrogen, is restricted almost exclusively to a limited number of bacterial species. Only a few microorganisms and no plants or animals use atmospheric nitrogen directly; plants, animals, and most microorganisms depend on the availability of fixed forms of nitrogen for incorporation into their cellular biomass.

The fixation of atmospheric nitrogen depends on the **nitrogenase** enzyme system (FIG. 14-33). In this enzyme system, composed of nitrogenase and nitrogenase reductase, electrons are transferred through either ferredoxin or flavodoxin to nitrogenase reductase and then to nitrogenase, where they are used to reduce N_2 and H^+ to NH_3 and H_2. The nitrogenase enzyme system has two coproteins, one containing molybdenum plus iron and the other containing only iron. The active site of nitrogenase, where reduction of nitrogen actually occurs, is associated with a molybdenum- and iron-containing cofactor. The production

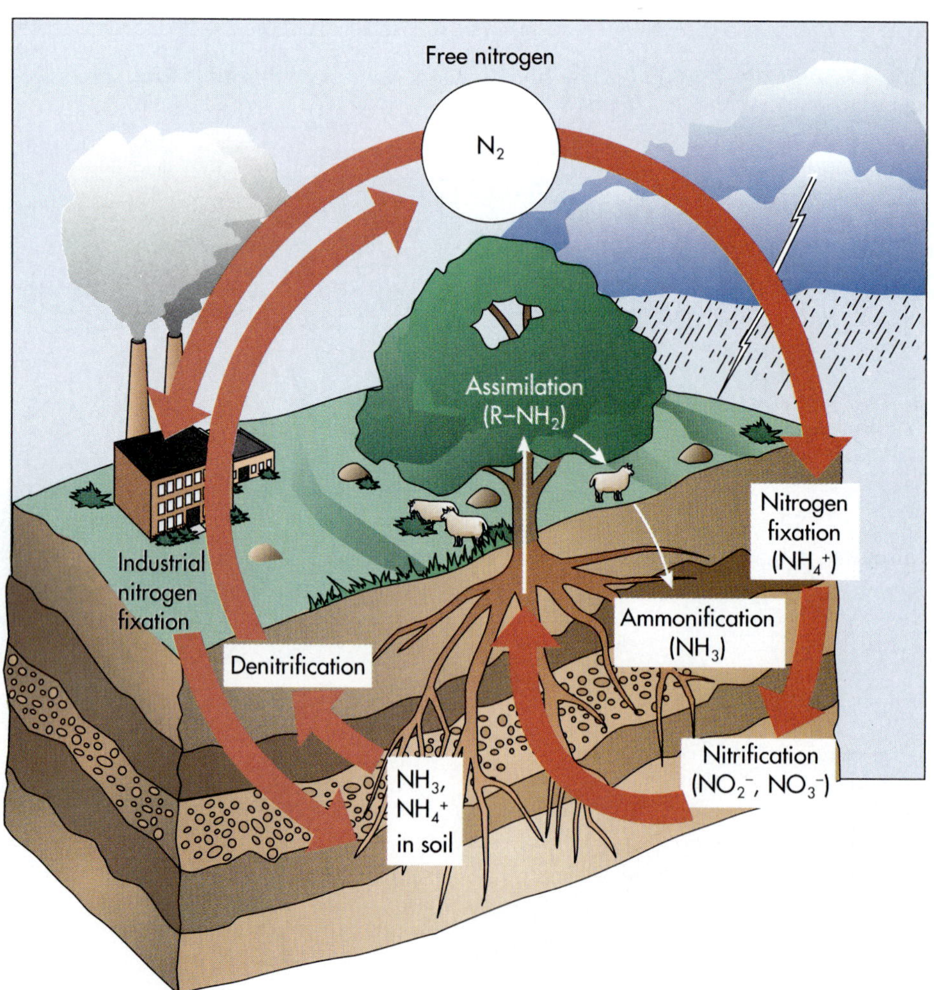

FIG. 14-32 Nitrogen cycle showing various microbial processes that move nitrogen between the atmosphere, soil, and water.

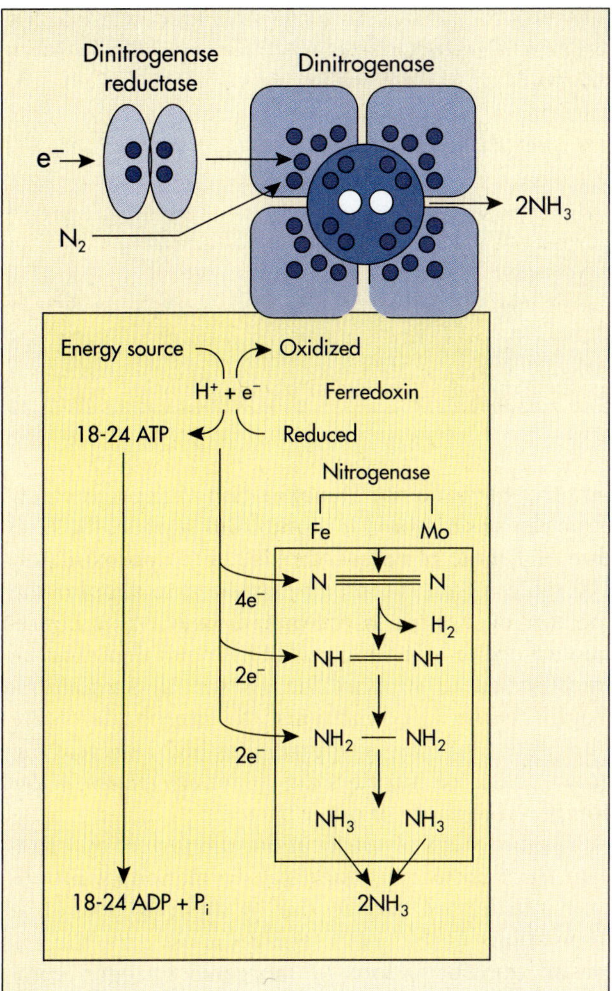

FIG. 14-33 The nitrogenase enzyme system catalyzes the reduction of molecular nitrogen to ammonia. This enzyme system has Fe and Mo at the reaction center. Nitrogen fixation brought about by nitrogenase-producing bacteria transfers atmospheric nitrogen to fixed forms of nitrogen that can be used by other microorganisms, plants, and animals.

of H_2 that accompanies the reduction of nitrogen adds to the ATP requirements of nitrogen fixation. Some nitrogen-fixing bacteria possess a hydrogenase and therefore are able to gain some energy by oxidizing hydrogen.

Nitrogenase is very sensitive to oxygen and is irreversibly inactivated on exposure to even low concentrations. Nitrogen fixation, therefore, often is restricted to habitats in which nitrogenase is protected from exposure to molecular oxygen; the nitrogenase enzyme is protected in the root nodule system by the red pigment leghemoglobin, which supplies oxygen to the organisms for respiration without denaturing the nitrogenase. Nitrogenase is also inhibited by high concentrations of ATP, but large amounts of ATP are required to drive the electron transfer reactions catalyzed by the nitrogenase enzyme system. The fixation of atmospheric nitrogen requires a high energy input (approximately 30 ATP/N_2 fixed) and in terrestrial ecosystems is largely dependent on the availability of relatively high concentrations of organic matter for use in the respiratory generation of ATP.

In terrestrial habitats, the microbial fixation of atmospheric nitrogen is carried out by free-living bacteria and by bacteria living in symbiotic association with plants. **Symbiotic nitrogen fixation** by *Rhizobium* or *Bradyrhizobium,* discussed earlier in this chapter, is most important in agricultural fields, where these bacteria live in association with leguminous crop plants. *Rhizobium* and *Bradyrhizobium* species generally exhibit rates of nitrogen fixation that are two to three orders of magnitude higher than those accomplished by free-living, nitrogen-fixing soil bacteria.

Azotobacter species, which are free-living nitrogen fixers, have exceptionally high respiratory rates far in excess of those of all other aerobic bacteria, and this may prevent molecular oxygen from reaching and inactivating the oxygen-sensitive nitrogenase. *Azotobacter* species also produce resting cells known as *cysts* that are quite resistant to desiccation but not to heat. Free-living, nitrogen-fixing members of the genera *Azotobacter, Azomonas,* and *Derxia* are common in temperate regions in neutral or alkaline soils and waters. These bacteria tend to be sensitive to low pH. In tropical regions, *Beijerinckia* species, which are more acid tolerant, are the prevalent nitrogen-fixing, free-living soil microorganisms. *Frankia* and other actinomycetes are also important symbiotic and free-living nitrogen-fixing bacteria in various terrestrial ecosystems.

In aquatic habitats, cyanobacteria, such as *Anabaena* and *Nostoc,* are very important in determining the rates of nitrogen fixation. Cyanobacteria, capable of nitrogen fixation, are distributed in both marine and freshwater habitats. These cyanobacteria couple the ability to generate ATP (through the conversion of light energy) and organic matter (through the reduction of carbon dioxide) with the ability to fix atmospheric nitrogen; this enables them to efficiently form nitrogen-containing organic compounds. In such organisms, the oxygen-sensitive nitrogenase enzyme is usually protected by thick-walled heterocysts, where oxygen-evolving photosynthesis does not occur. Cyanobacteria fix nitrogen only under low oxygen tension. In low-nutrient aquatic environments, light energy for generating ATP is critical in supplying sufficient ATP to drive the nitrogen fixation reactions. Rates of nitrogen fixation by cyanobacteria are typically 10 times higher than those shown by free-living soil bacteria; thus cyanobacteria form a very important component of aquatic food webs. Also, epiphytic cyanobacteria associated with the phyllosphere or leaf surfaces of Arctic mosses are the most important nitrogen fixers in the high Arctic ecosystem. Cyanobacteria fix nitrogen in some lichens. In some cases lichens with nitrogen-fixing cyanobacteria grow in the forest canopy. When it rains the fixed nitrogen is washed to the forest floor, where it supplies nitrogen nutrients to trees.

The ability of microorganisms to fix nitrogen is readily detected by the acetylene reduction assay. The assay is based on the fact that the nitrogenase system also catalyzes the reduction of acetylene—which, like molecular nitrogen, has a triple bond. The reduction of acetylene forms ethylene, which is easily detectable by gas chromatography. Consequently, many additional free-living bacteria have been shown to be capable of fixing atmospheric nitrogen. Most of these free-living, nitrogen-fixing bacteria exhibit nitrogen-fixing activities only at oxygen levels well below 0.2 atm. Such conditions frequently occur in subsoil and sediment environments. Although the amount of nitrogen fixed per hectare by free-living soil bacteria is considerably lower than the amount fixed by symbiotic nitrogen-fixing species, the widespread distribution of the free-living bacteria in soil makes a significant contribution to the input of nitrogen to terrestrial habitats.

Ammonification

Many microorganisms, as well as plants and animals, convert organic amino nitrogen to ammonia; this process is known as **ammonification.** Deaminases play an important role in this process of ammonification, which transfers nitrogen from organic to inorganic forms. Microbial decomposition of urea, for example, results in the release of ammonia, which may be returned to the atmosphere or may occur in neutral aqueous environments as ammonium ions. Ammonium ions can be assimilated by a number of organisms, continuing the transfer of nitrogen within the nitrogen cycle.

Nitrification

Although many organisms are capable of ammonification, relatively few are capable of **nitrification,** the process in which ammonium ions (oxidation level = −3) are initially oxidized to nitrite ions (oxidation level = +3) and subsequently to nitrate ions (oxidation level = +5). Nitrification is an example of aerobic respiration. The oxidation of ammonia to nitrite and the oxidation of nitrite to nitrate, the two steps of nitrification, are energy-yielding processes from which chemolithotrophic bacteria derive needed energy. The metabolism of the chemolithotrophic nitrifying bacteria changes the oxidation levels of the ammonium and nitrite ions when these ions serve as electron donors for chemiosmotic generation of ATP.

Relatively low amounts of ATP, however, are generated by the oxidation of inorganic nitrogen compounds. Therefore large amounts of inorganic nitrogen compounds must be transformed to generate sufficient ATP to support the growth of these chemolithotrophic bacteria. The oxidation of approximately 35 moles of ammonia is required to support the fixation of 1 mole of carbon dioxide, and approximately 100 moles of nitrite must be oxidized to support the fixation of 1 mole of carbon dioxide. As a consequence of the high amounts of nitrogen that must be transformed to support the growth of chemolithotrophic bacterial populations, the magnitude of the nitrification process is typically very high, whereas the growth rates of nitrifiers are generally relatively low compared to those of other bacteria.

TABLE 14-7 Genera of Nitrifying Bacteria

GENUS	CONVERTS	HABITAT
Nitrosomonas	Ammonia to nitrite	Soils, freshwater, marine
Nitrosospira	Ammonia to nitrite	Soils
Nitrosococcus	Ammonia to nitrite	Soils, freshwater, marine
Nitrosolobus	Ammonia to nitrite	Soils
Nitrobacter	Nitrite to nitrate	Soils, freshwater, marine
Nitrospina	Nitrite to nitrate	Marine
Nitrococcus	Nitrite to nitrate	Marine

The two steps of nitrification, the formation of nitrite from ammonium and the formation of nitrate from nitrite, are carried out by different microbial populations (Table 14-7). For the most part, the oxidative transformations of inorganic nitrogen compounds in the nitrification process are restricted to several species of autotrophic bacteria. In addition to the chemolithotrophic nitrifying bacteria, some heterotrophic bacteria and fungi are capable of oxidizing inorganic nitrogen compounds but the rates of heterotrophic nitrification are normally four orders of magnitude lower than those of autotrophic nitrification. In soils *Nitrosomonas* is the dominant bacterial genus involved in the oxidation of ammonia to nitrite, and *Nitrobacter* is the dominant genus involved in the oxidation of nitrite to nitrate. Several other autotrophic bacteria, including ammonia-oxidizing members of the genera *Nitrosospira, Nitrosococcus,* and *Nitrosolobus,* and nitrite-oxidizing members of the genera *Nitrospira* and *Nitrococcus,* are also important nitrifiers in different ecosystems. Many of the nitrifying bacteria contain extensive internal membrane networks that are probably the sites of nitrogen oxidation (FIG. 14-34).

Because relatively few microbial genera make significant contributions to the rates of nitrification, it is not surprising that this process is particularly sensitive to environmental stress. Toxic chemicals can block the nitrification process. Nitrification is an obligately aerobic process, and under anaerobic conditions, such as may exist when high concentrations of organic matter are added to soil or aquatic ecosystems, the nitrifica-

FIG. 14-34 Colorized micrograph of the nitrifying bacterium *Nitrococcus oceanus.*

tion process may cease. The process of nitrification is very important in soil habitats because the transformation of ammonium ions to nitrite and nitrate ions results in a change from a cation to an anion. Positively charged cations are bound by negatively charged soil clay particles and thus are retained in soils, but negatively charged anions such as nitrate are not absorbed by soil particles and are readily leached from the soil (FIG. 14-35). Nitrification, therefore, represents a mobilization process in soils that results in the transfer of inorganic fixed forms of nitrogen from surface soils to subsurface groundwater reservoirs. In agriculture, inhibitors of nitrification, such as nitrapyrin, sometimes are intentionally added to soils to prevent the transformation of ammonium to nitrate, ensuring better fertilization of crops.

The transfer of nitrate and nitrite ions from surface soil to groundwater supplies is critical for two reasons: (1) it represents an important loss of nitrogen from the soil, where it is needed to support the growth of higher plants, and (2) high concentrations of nitrate and nitrite in drinking water supplies pose a serious human health hazard. Nitrite is toxic to humans because it can combine with blood hemoglobin to block the normal gas exchange with oxygen. Additionally, nitrites can react with amino compounds to form highly carcinogenic nitrosamines. Further, nitrate, although not highly toxic itself, can be reduced microbially in the gastrointestinal tracts of human infants to form nitrite, causing the "blue baby syndrome"; this reduction of nitrate does not occur in adults because of the low pH of the normal adult gastrointestinal tract. Nitrate and nitrite in groundwater is a particular problem in agricultural areas such as the corn belt of the midwestern United States where high concentra-

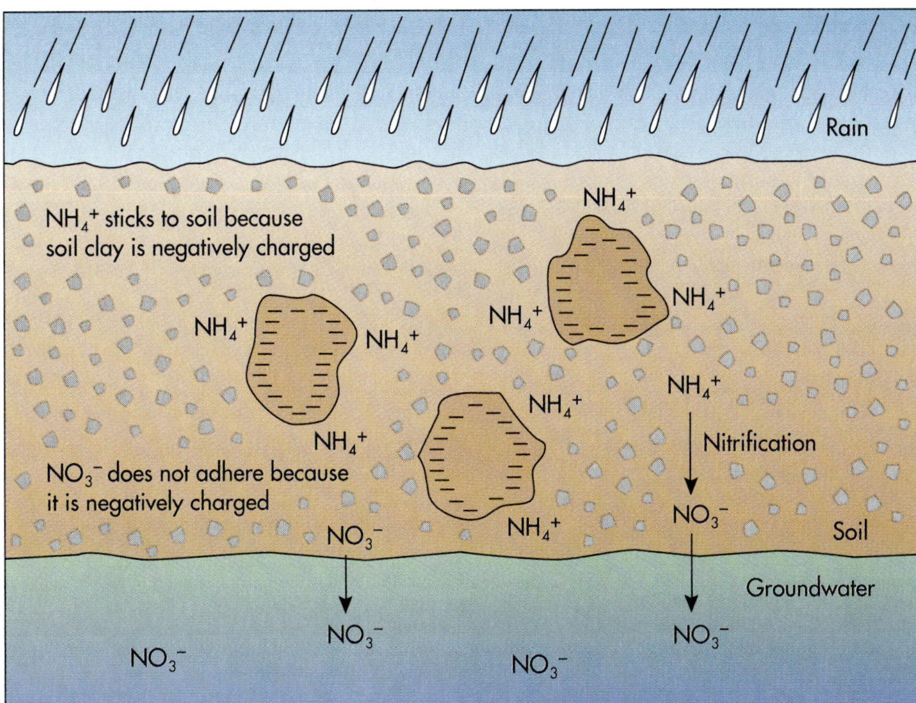

FIG. 14-35 Nitrification converts NH_4^+ to NO_3^-. Changing the charge from the positive charge of NH_4^+ to the negative charge of NO_3^- results in the leaching of nitrogen from soil because negatively charged soil particles bind positively charged ions but not negatively charged ones. Hence nitrification results in the mobilization of nitrogen and its movement from soil to ground water.

tions of nitrogen fertilizers are applied to soil. The use of nitrification inhibitors in combination with the application of ammonium nitrogen fertilizers can minimize the nitrate leaching problem, and at the same time support better soil fertility and increased plant productivity.

Nitrite Ammonification

Some bacteria, particularly *Clostridium* species, reduce nitrite to ammonium ions in a process called **nitrite ammonification.** Although involved in ATP generation, the process is not an example of anaerobic respiration. In nitrite ammonification, electrons from NADH are used to reduce nitrite rather than to reduce an organic compound. Consequently, the organic products of fermentation are more completely oxidized and the yield of ATP via substrate-level phosphorylation can be greater. Denitrification, nitrite ammonification, does not remove nitrogen from the soil. In fact, much of the nitrate added to soils is reduced to ammonia by fermentative bacteria rather than to N_2 by denitrifiers.

Denitrification

Denitrification, the conversion of fixed forms of nitrogen to molecular nitrogen, is another important process in the biogeochemical cycling of nitrogen that is mediated by microorganisms. Some aerobic bacteria

BOX 14-4

Soil Fertility and Management of Agricultural Soils

Microbial biogeochemical cycling activities are extremely important for the maintenance of soil fertility, that is, the ability of the soil to support plant growth. The nutrient in most limited supply normally is nitrogen, and thus the concentration of fixed forms of nitrogen in soil usually determines the potential productivity of an agricultural field. The natural availability of fixed forms of nitrogen in agricultural soils is determined by the relative balance between the rates of microbial nitrogen fixation and denitrification. Nitrogen-rich fertilizers are widely applied to soils to support increased crop yields, but proper application of nitrogen fertilizers must consider the solubility and leaching characteristics of the particular chemical form of the fertilizer and the rates of microbial biogeochemical cycling activities. To avoid losses caused by leaching and denitrification, nitrogen fertilizer is commonly applied as an ammonium salt, free ammonia, or urea. When nitrification proceeds too quickly, as it does in some agricultural soils, wasteful losses of nitrogen fertilizer and groundwater contamination with nitrate occur. Nitrification of ammonium compounds also yields acidic products that may have to be neutralized by liming. To prevent the undesirable microbial transformation of nitrogen fertilizers, nitrification inhibitors such as nitrapyrin are often applied with the nitrogen fertilizer. The use of nitrification inhibitors can increase crop yields by 10% to 15% for the same amount of nitrogen fertilizer applied. In addition, by decreasing the rate of nitrification, the problem of groundwater pollution by nitrate is reduced.

Crop rotation, that is, alternating the types of crops planted in a field, is traditionally used to prevent the exhaustion of soil nitrogen and to reduce the cost of nitrogen fertilizer applications. Leguminous crops such as soybeans often are planted in rotation with other crops because of their symbiotic association with nitrogen-fixing bacteria, which reduce the soil's requirement for expensive nitrogen fertilizer. Leguminous plants accumulate fixed nitrogen, particularly in root nodules. Other plants release nutrients that stimulate free-living nitrogen fixers in the rhizosphere, leading to a similar increase in soil nitrogen. Most of the combined (fixed) nitrogen is released to the soil from decomposition of the crop residues from leguminous plants that are plowed under (see Table). Soybeans and corn are often rotated every few years in the midwestern United States because corn takes up nitrogen from the soil, substantially decreasing the concentration of soil nitrogen, but during the seasons when soybeans are grown, the level of fixed nitrogen in the soil increases.

Nitrogen Gains in Soils in the United States Obtained by Planting Leguminous Crops

CROP	SOIL NITROGEN INCREASE (kg nitrogen fixed/hectare/year)
Alfalfa	100-280
Red clover	75-175
Pea	75-130
Soybean	60-100
Cowpea	60-120
Vetch	60-140

In some cases, nitrogen fixation can be enhanced by inoculation of legume seeds with appropriate *Rhizobium* strains, which increases the extent of nodule formation because of the increased numbers of rhizobia that effectively initiate the infective process that leads to nodule formation. Besides increasing the extent of nodule formation, it is possible to take steps to increase the rate of nitrogen fixation within the nodules. In molybdenum-deficient soils, a dramatic improvement in the rate of nitrogen fixation can be achieved by the application of small amounts of molybdenum because this element is a constituent of the nitrogenase enzyme complex that is required for nitrogen-fixing activities. It is important that maximal rates of nitrogen fixation be achieved to successfully replenish soil nitrogen.

can use nitrate in place of oxygen as a final electron acceptor, reducing nitrate as a result of anaerobic respiration. Some bacteria, such as *E. coli,* are only able to reduce nitrate to nitrite, but various other bacteria can carry out the two subsequent anaerobic respirations by which nitrite ion is reduced to nitrous oxide gas (N_2O) and subsequently to molecular (N_2). The process is called *denitrification* when N_2O or N_2 is produced. Some species of *Pseudomonas, Moraxella, Spirillum, Thiobacillus,* and *Bacillus* are capable of denitrification. Nitrous oxide formation occurs preferentially in habitats with high nitrate concentrations and/or low pH values. Formation of molecular nitrogen is favored when there is an adequate amount of organic matter to supply energy. Dissimilatory nitrate reductase, the enzyme involved in initiation of the denitrification process, is inhibited by oxygen, and denitrification generally occurs under anaerobic conditions. The return of nitrogen to the atmosphere by the denitrification process completes the nitrogen cycle.

SULFUR CYCLE

Sulfur can exist in various oxidation states within organic and inorganic compounds, and oxidation-reduction reactions—mediated by microorganisms—change the oxidation states of sulfur within various compounds. Microbial transformations of sulfur establish the **sulfur cycle** (FIG. 14-36). Microorganisms are capable of removing sulfur from organic compounds. Under aerobic conditions, the removal of sulfur *(desulfurization)* of organic compounds results in the formation of sulfate, whereas under anaerobic conditions hydrogen sulfide is normally produced from the mineralization of organic sulfur compounds (FIG. 14-37). Hydrogen sulfide may also be formed by sulfate-reducing bacteria that utilize sulfate as the terminal electron acceptor during anaerobic respiration. Hydrogen sulfide can accumulate in toxic concentrations in areas of rapid protein decomposition, is highly reactive, and is very toxic to most biological systems. It can react with metals to form insoluble metallic sulfides.

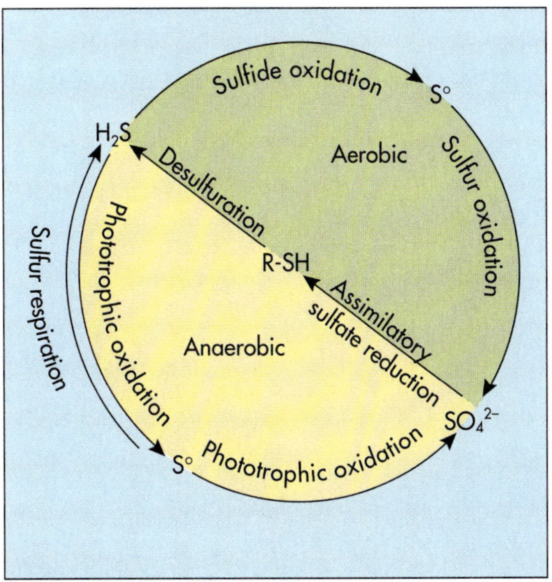

FIG. 14-36 The sulfur cycle involves conversions of sulfur in various oxidation states. Oxidation of sulfur compounds occurs in aerobic environments, and reduction of sulfur compounds occurs in anaerobic environments.

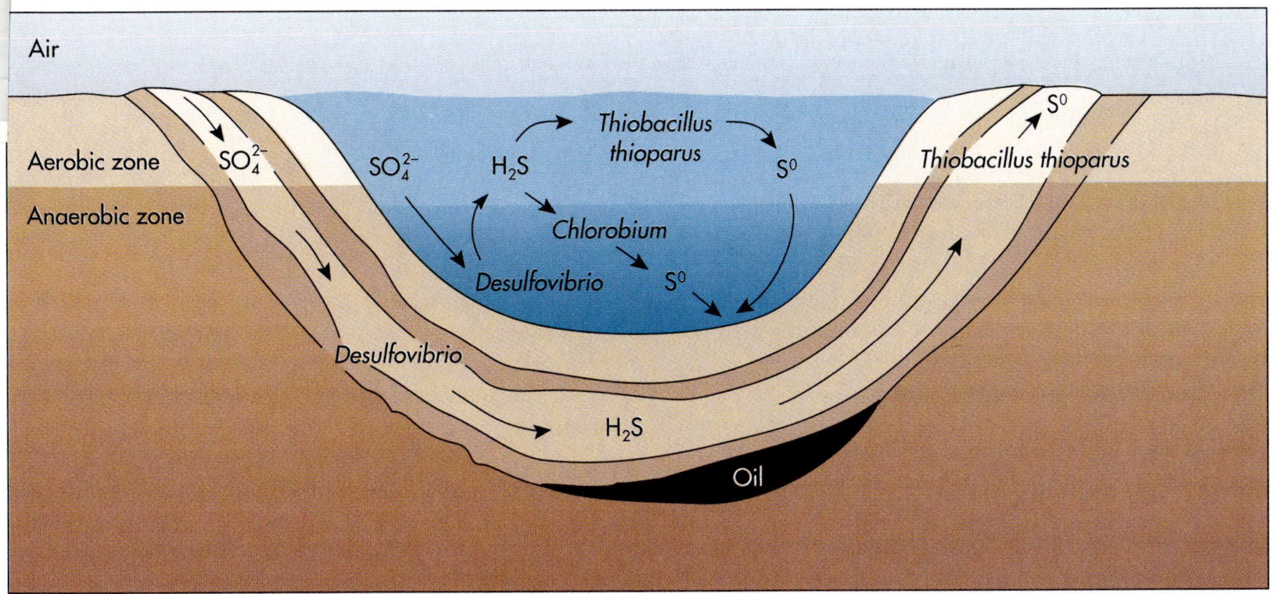

FIG. 14-37 Sulfur transformations involve the conversion of sulfate (SO_4^{2-}) to hydrogen sulfide (H_2S) by *Desulfovibrio* under anaerobic conditions and the reoxidation of H_2S to SO_4^{2-} under aerobic conditions by *Thiobacillus.*

BOX 14-5

Thermal Vent Communities and Sulfur Cycling

Thermal vents (deep sea regions of volcanic activity) harbor unique biological communites that depend on chemoautotrophic sulfur metabolism for primary production. The vent communities, located at a depth of 800 to 1,000 meters, receive no sunlight and minimal organic nutrient input from the low-productivity surface water above, yet their biomass exceeds that of the surrounding seafloor by orders of magnitude. Microbial mats cover all available surfaces on and near the vents, and high densities of unique clams, mussels, vestimentiferan worms, and other invertebrates cluster in the vicinity. Some of these graze or filter-feed on microorganisms; others are directly symbiotic with microorganisms and exhibit chemoautotrophic activity.

Energetically, the entire vent community is supported by the chemoautotrophic oxidation of reduced sulfur, primarily by *Beggiatoa, Thiomicrospira,* and additional sulfide or sulfur oxidizers of great morphological diversity. Oxidation of H_2, CO, NH_4^+, NO_2^-, Fe^{2+}, and Mn^{2+} are assumed to contribute to chemoautotrophic production, although measurements of these processes in the vent environment are yet to be accomplished. Methane, derived from reduction of CO_2 with geothermally produced hydrogen by extremely thermophilic *Methanococcus* species detected in the anoxic hydrothermal fluid, is also oxidized by methanotrophic bacteria and provides additional carbon and energy input for the vent ecosystem.

High numbers of sulfur-oxidizing bacteria are found surrounding the deep sea thermal vents; high numbers of sulfur-oxidizers have also been found living within animals in the thermal vent communities, including tube worms (see FIG.). These tube worms, which may be almost a meter in length, lack a digestive tract. They have a spongy tissue, called a trophosome, in which symbiotic sulfur-oxidizing chemolithotrophs live. The tube worms transport O_2 and H_2S using specialized hemoglobins to the trophosome, where it is used by the sulfur-oxidizing bacterial populations. The bacteria produce metabolites such as fatty acids that are used by the tube worms for their metabolism. The bacteria thus feed the tube worms. Similar sulfur-oxidizing bacterial populations occur in the gills of giant clams that also are found in abundance surrounding the thermal vents.

The tube worms *(Riftia pachyptila)* that grow extensively near deep sea thermal vents have no gut. They have extensive internal populations of chemolithotrophic sulfur oxidizing bacteria that produce the nutrients used by these animals for sustenance. The red-brown color of the worms is due to a form of hemoglobin that supples oxygen and hydrogen sulfide to the chemolithotrophic bacteria within the tissues of the tube worms. Microbial mats of *Beggiatoa* grow between strands of the tube worms at the Guaymas Basin vent site (Gulf of California) at a depth of 2010 meters.

The predominant source of hydrogen sulfide in different habitats varies. In organically rich soils, most of the hydrogen sulfide is generated from the decomposition of organic sulfur-containing compounds. In anaerobic sulfate-rich marine sediments, most of it is generated from the dissimilatory reduction of sulfate by sulfate-reducing bacteria, such as members of the genus *Desulfovibrio.* Anaerobic sulfate reduction is important in corrosion processes and in the biogeochemical cycling of sulfur.

Use of Hydrogen Sulfide by Autotrophic Microorganisms

Although hydrogen sulfide is toxic to many microorganisms, the photosynthetic sulfur bacteria use it as an electron donor for generating reduced coenzymes during their metabolism. The anaerobic photosynthetic bacteria often occur on the surface of sediments, where there is light to support their activities and a supply of hydrogen sulfide from dissimilatory sulfate reduction and anaerobic degradation of organic sulfur-containing compounds. Some photosynthetic bacteria deposit elemental sulfur as an oxidation product, whereas others form sulfate.

Some bacteria, including members of the genera *Beggiatoa* and *Thiothrix,* generate ATP by oxidizing hydrogen sulfide. These bacteria deposit elemental sulfur granules within the cell, which in the absence of hydrogen sulfide can be further oxidized to sulfate (FIG. 14-38). *Beggiatoa* and *Thiothrix* are not true

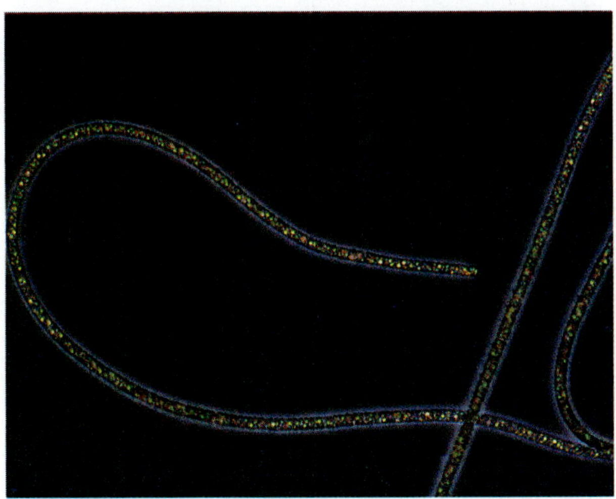

FIG. 14-38 Micrograph of *Beggiatoa* showing accumulation of sulfur granules. (500×).

chemolithotrophs, and although energy is apparently derived from the oxidation of hydrogen sulfide, these organisms require organic carbon for growth. Chemolithotrophic members of the genus *Thiobacillus* oxidize sulfur as their source of energy. *Thiobacillus* species are used in bioleaching processes for mineral recovery. Some *Thiobacillus* species are acidophilic and grow well at 2 to 3 pH. The growth of such species can produce sulfate from the oxidation of elemental sulfur, leading to the environmental accumulation of sulfuric acid.

Acid Mine Drainage

Acid mine drainage is a consequence of the metabolism of sulfur and iron-oxidizing bacteria. Coal in geological deposits is often associated with pyrite (FeS_2), and when coal mining activities expose pyrite ores to atmospheric oxygen, the combination of autoxidation and microbial sulfur and iron oxidation produces large amounts of sulfuric acid. When pyrites are mined as part of an ore recovery operation, oxidation may produce large amounts of acid. The acid draining from mines kills aquatic life and renders the water it contaminates unsuitable for drinking or for recreational uses. At present, approximately 10,000 miles of waterways in the United States are affected in this manner, predominantly in the states of Pennsylvania, Virginia, Ohio, Kentucky, Indiana, and Colorado. Strip mining is a particular problem with acid mine drainage because this method of coal recovery removes the overlying soil and rock, leaving a porous rubble of tailings exposed to oxygen and percolating water. The problem of strip mining can be alleviated by covering with soil so as to reduce the availability of oxygen. Oxidation of the reduced iron and sulfur in the tailings produces acidic products, causing the pH to drop rapidly and preventing the reestablishment of vegetation and a soil cover that would seal the rubble from oxygen. A strip-mined piece of land continues to produce acid mine drainage until most of the sulfide is oxidized and leached out; recovery of this land may take 50 to 150 years.

The overall reaction for the oxidation of pyrite can be summarized as:

$$2FeS + 7.50 + 7H_2O \rightarrow 2Fe(OH)_3 + 4H_2SO_4$$

The sulfuric acid produced accounts for the high acidity and the precipitated ferric hydroxide for the deep brown color of the effluent. The mechanism of pyrite oxidation in acid mine drainage is quite complex. At neutral pH, oxidation by atmospheric oxygen occurs rapidly and spontaneously, but below pH 4.5, autoxidation is slowed drastically. In the pH range of 4.5 to 3.5, the stalked iron bacterium *Metallogenium* catalyzes the oxidation of iron. As the pH drops below 3.5, the acidophilic bacteria of the genus *Thiobacillus* oxidize the reduced iron sulfide in the pyrite. The rate of microbial oxidation of FeS is several hundred times greater than the rate of spontaneous oxidation, and although pyrite oxidation begins spontaneously, microbial oxidation of sulfur and iron is responsible for the continued production of high levels of acid mine drainage.

OTHER ELEMENT CYCLES

Phosphorus

Phosphorus normally occurs as phosphates in both inorganic and organic compounds. Microorganisms assimilate inorganic phosphate and mineralize organic phosphorus compounds, and microbial activities are involved in the solubilization or mobilization of phosphate compounds. Unlike the other elements discussed, microorganisms normally do not oxidize or reduce phosphorus. The phosphorus cycle represents physical movement of phosphates without alteration of the oxidation level. In many habitats, phosphates are combined with calcium, rendering them insoluble and unavailable to most organisms. Various heterotrophic microorganisms are capable of solubilizing phosphates primarily through the production of organic acids. These actions of microorganisms mobilize phosphate. Activities of other microorganisms immobilize phosphorus. For example, microorganisms compete with plants for available phosphate resources because the assimilation of phosphates by microorganisms removes phosphates from the available nutrient pool required by plants.

In many habitats, productivity is limited by the availability of phosphate. When excess concentrations of phosphate enter phosphate-limited aquatic habitats, as for example when wastewater containing phosphate detergents are added to lakes, there can be a sudden increase in productivity. This process of nutri-

FIG. 14-39 Eutrophication of streams and rivers occurs when high levels of inorganic nutrients, often phosphates, permit excessive growth of photosynthetic microorganisms. The growth of algae often enriches the water with organic compounds in these situations.

ent enrichment is called **eutrophication** (FIG. 14-39). Eutrophication is an increase in organic matter concentration that often occurs when a factor that normally limits primary productivity no longer acts as a limiting factor. This results in increased production of organic matter. For example, adding phosphate to a lake in which the concentration of phosphate is the key factor limiting primary productivity allows increased formation of organic matter. If phosphate, however, was not the principal factor limiting productivity, then adding it would not increase organic matter production and would not cause eutrophication. The blooms of algae and cyanobacteria associated with eutrophication can greatly increase the concentrations of organic matter in bodies of water. During the subsequent decomposition of this organic matter, the water column can be severely depleted of oxygen, causing major fish kills. The introduction of high concentrations of phosphate from phosphate laundry detergents created such serious eutrophication problems in many water bodies that some municipalities banned their use.

Iron

The cycling of iron compounds has a marked effect on the availability of this essential element for other organisms. Iron is transformed between the ferrous (Fe^{2+}) and ferric (Fe^{3+}) oxidation states by microorganisms (FIG. 14-40). Ferric and ferrous ions have very different solubility properties: ferric compounds tend to be less soluble than ferrous compounds. Bacterial transformations of iron are important in corrosion processes and in the formation of acid mine drainage. Various bacteria, including members of the genera *Thiobacillus, Gallionella,* and *Leptothrix,* oxidize iron compounds. Some of these bacteria deposit ferric hydroxide in an extracellular sheath. Over eons of time, the accumulation of iron-oxidizing bacterial sheath material can lead to the formation of substantial iron deposits.

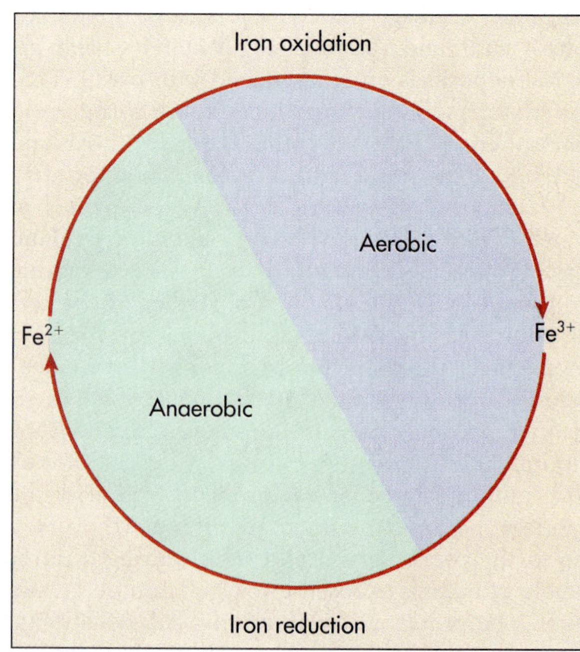

FIG. 14-40 The iron cycle produces oxidized ferric ions (Fe^{3+}) in aerobic zones and reduced ferrous ions (Fe^{2+}) in anaerobic zones.

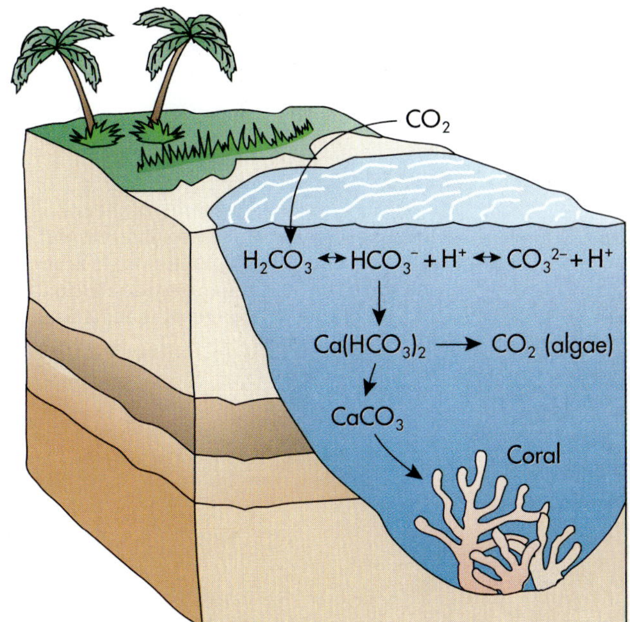

FIG. 14-41 **A,** In seawater, calcium reacts with carbon dioxide to form calcium bicarbonate. When algae consume carbon dioxide from bicarbonate in the oceans, as occurs within corals, insoluble calcium carbonate forms. **B,** The white cliffs of Dover were formed from calcium carbonate precipitated by foraminiferan protozoa. The calcium carbonate from the foraminifera form white limestone.

Calcium

Calcium also exhibits biogeochemical cycling between soluble and insoluble forms. Calcium bicarbonate is extremely soluble; calcium carbonate is much less so. The microbial production of acidic compounds solubilizes precipitated and immobilized calcium compounds. There is an interesting cycling of calcium in marine habitats in which dissolved carbon dioxide reacts with available calcium, forming calcium bicarbonate and calcium carbonate (FIG. 14-41). During the formation of coral, calcium carbonate precipitates when carbon dioxide held in solution as calcium bicarbonate is removed by algal cells of the coral. This process results in the deposition of calcium carbonate and the formation of coral reefs. Calcium carbonate is also precipitated by various algae to form an outer frustule. Accumulation of calcium carbonate by foraminiferans can lead to the formation of major limestone deposits, such as the famous white cliffs of Dover on the British coast of the English Channel.

Silicon

Various algae, most notably the diatoms, form silicon-impregnated structures (FIG. 14-42). These algae precipitate silicon dioxide to build their delicate, decorative shells. As much as 10 billion metric tons of silicon dioxide is precipitated by microorganisms in the oceans each year. The shells of these dead microorganisms accumulate and form silicon-rich oozes that later develop into extensive deposits of diatomaceous, or Fuller's, earth. These are mined for various industrial uses.

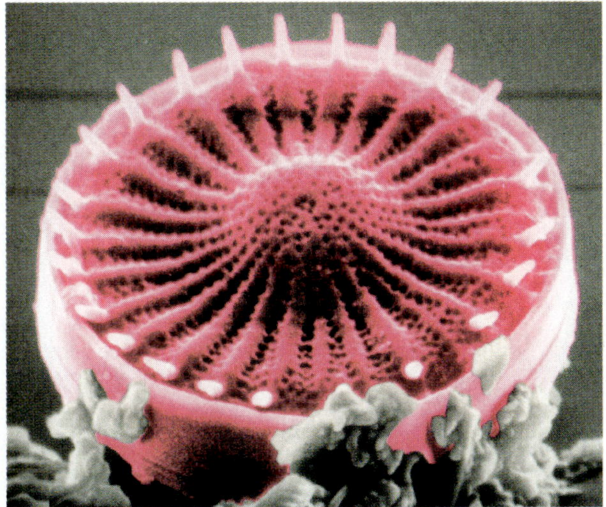

FIG. 14-42 Colorized micrograph of the diatom *Stephanodiscus* showing the elaborate cell wall structure. (1,800×). The cell walls of diatoms contain silicon dioxide.

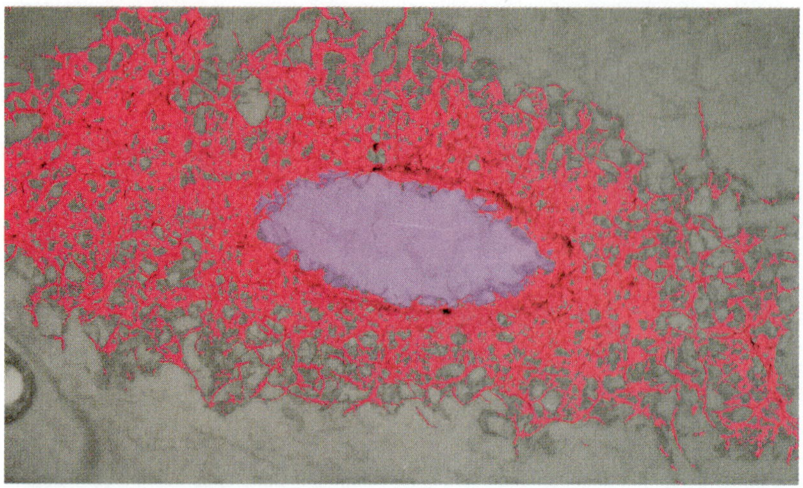

FIG. 14-43 Colorized micrograph of *Leptothrix discophora* showing a sheath of manganese oxide encrusting the cell *(red)*. Such deposits of manganese oxide accumulate to form manganese nodules that can be mined as sources of manganese.

Manganese

Manganese exists as a water-soluble divalent manganous ion and as a relatively insoluble tetravalent manganic ion. The microbial oxidation of manganous ions forms manganese oxides, which produce characteristic *manganese nodules* (FIG. 14-43). The manganese for the nodules originates in anaerobic sediments; when the manganese enters aerobic habitats, it is oxidized and precipitates to form the nodules. The farming of manganese nodules in deep ocean sediments is considered a possible method of obtaining manganese for industrial use.

Heavy Metals

Mercury, arsenic, and other heavy metals are also subject to microbial biogeochemical cycling. These transformations are important because they alter the mobility and toxicity of the metals. For example, mercury is released into the environment largely as a consequence of its widespread use in industry and the burning of fossil fuels, although some mercury is also leached from rocks. The methylation of mercury causes increased toxicity (FIG. 14-44). Mercury salts, though fairly toxic, are excreted efficiently; therefore their release into the environment was not originally viewed with much concern. In anaerobic sediments, however, some microorganisms are capable of methylating mercury, that is, adding a methyl group to mercury. The product, methylmercury, is lipophilic and is readily concentrated in filter-feeding shellfish. This accumulation is called **biomagnification.** Unlike inorganic and phenylmercury compounds, methylmercury is excreted by humans very slowly, having a half-life of 70 days, and it is highly neurotoxic. In Japan in the 1950s, the ingestion of shellfish containing methylmercury led to outbreaks of Minamata disease, a severe disturbance of the central nervous system associated with mercury poisoning. The buildup of methylmercury compounds in Scandinavian freshwater lakes and the U.S. Great Lakes forced large areas to be condemned for fishing.

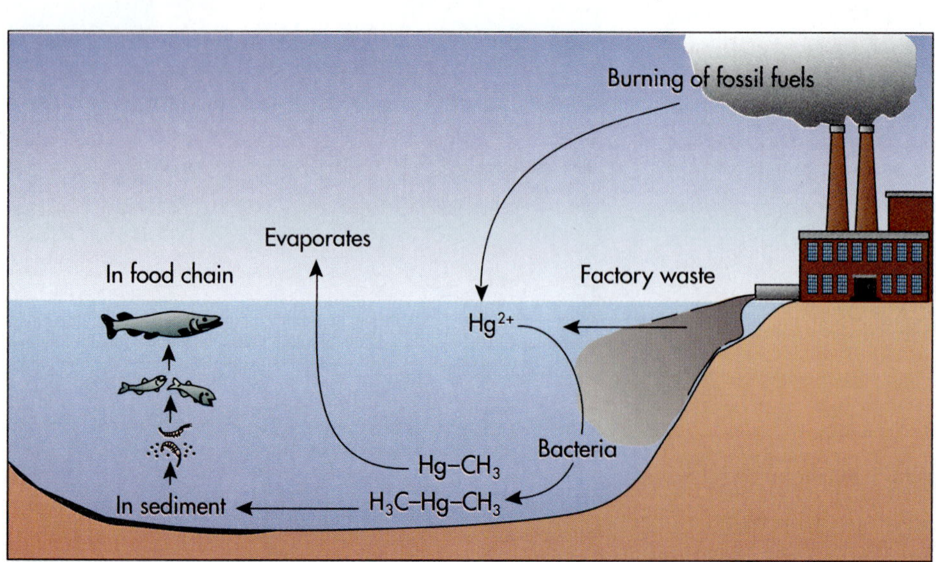

FIG. 14-44 Mercury is cycled by microbial transformations. Some microorganisms methylate mercury, producing more toxic forms of this heavy metal.

14.4 BIOLOGICAL TREATMENT OF WASTES AND POLLUTANTS

The metabolic activities of microorganisms are employed for the decomposition of wastes. Microbial degradation of wastes and pollutants is essential for maintaining environmental quality.

SOLID WASTE DISPOSAL

Urban solid waste production in the United States amounts to roughly 150 million dry tons per year. Much of this material is inert, composed of glass, metal, and plastic, but the remainder is decomposable organic waste such as household and industrial garbage. Up to 50% of municipal solid waste is organic; removal of glass, plastic, and aluminum in recycling programs improves the degradability of the remaining wastes. Sewage sludge derived from treatment of liquid wastes, animal waste from cattle feedlots, and large-scale poultry and swine farms are also major sources of solid organic waste. In traditional small family farm operations, most organic solid waste is recycled into the land as fertilizer. In highly populated urban centers and areas of large-scale agricultural production, the disposal of massive amounts of organic waste becomes a difficult and expensive problem.

There are several options for dealing with solid waste problems. Today, many of the inert components of solid waste such as aluminum and glass are recovered and recycled. Even paper, which is relatively resistant to microbial degradation, can be recovered from solid waste, and many books and newspapers are printed on recycled paper. The remaining bulk of the solid waste may be incinerated, creating potential air pollution problems, or the organic components can be subjected to microbial biodegradation in aquatic or terrestrial ecosystems. In many cases the solid waste is dumped at sea or discarded on land, allowing biodegradation to occur naturally without any special treatment, but excessive dumping of organic wastes into terrestrial and marine ecosystems can cause untoward problems unless the operation is carefully managed and monitored.

Sanitary Landfills

The simplest and least expensive way to dispose of solid waste is to place the material in **landfills** and to allow it to decompose. In a landfill, organic and inorganic solid wastes are deposited together in low-lying land that has minimal real estate value. Because exposed waste can cause aesthetic and odor problems, attract insects and rodents, and pose a fire hazard, each day's waste deposit is covered with a layer of soil, creating a **sanitary landfill** (FIG. 14-45, p. 570). For 30 to 50 years after filling a landfill, the organic content of the solid waste undergoes slow, anaerobic microbial decomposition. The products of anaerobic microbial metabolism include carbon dioxide, water, methane, various low molecular weight alcohols, and acids, which diffuse into the surrounding water and air, causing the landfill to settle slowly. Extensive amounts of methane are produced during this decomposition process, potentially providing a source of needed natural gas. At some solid waste disposal sites, such as one at Palos Verdes, California, the methane that is produced is collected and sold to nearby power plants. Eventually, the decomposition slows, signaling completion of the biodegradation of the solid waste, subsidence ceases, and the land is stabilized. Then the site can be used for recreational purposes; later it may eventually provide a foundation for construction.

Although the use of sanitary landfills is simple and inexpensive, there are several problems associated with this waste disposal method. Premature construction on a still biologically active landfill site may result in structural damage to the buildings because of movement of the land base, and an explosion hazard may exist due to methane seepage into basements and other belowground structures. Aboveground plantings may also be damaged because of methane seepage. The number of suitable disposal sites available in urban areas is very limited, often necessitating long and expensive hauling of the solid waste to available sites. The possible seepage of anaerobic decomposition products, heavy metals, and various recalcitrant hazardous pollutants from the landfill site into underground aquifers, which are used in many urban areas as water sources, has caused many municipalities to place severe restrictions on the location and operation of landfills and the types of materials that can be deposited in them. The United States Environmental Protection Agency (USEPA) now requires lining of landfills and treatment of collected leachate to prevent contamination of groundwater. Thus alternatives to the landfill technique for disposing of solid waste are being sought.

Composting

The organic portion of solid waste can be biodegraded by **composting,** the process by which solid heterogeneous organic matter is degraded by aerobic, mesophilic, and thermophilic microorganisms (FIG. 14-46, p. 570). Composting is a microbial process that converts organic waste materials into a stable, sanitary, humus-like product. Reduced in bulk, it can be used for soil improvement.

Composting, like incineration, requires sorting of the solid waste into its organic and inorganic compo-

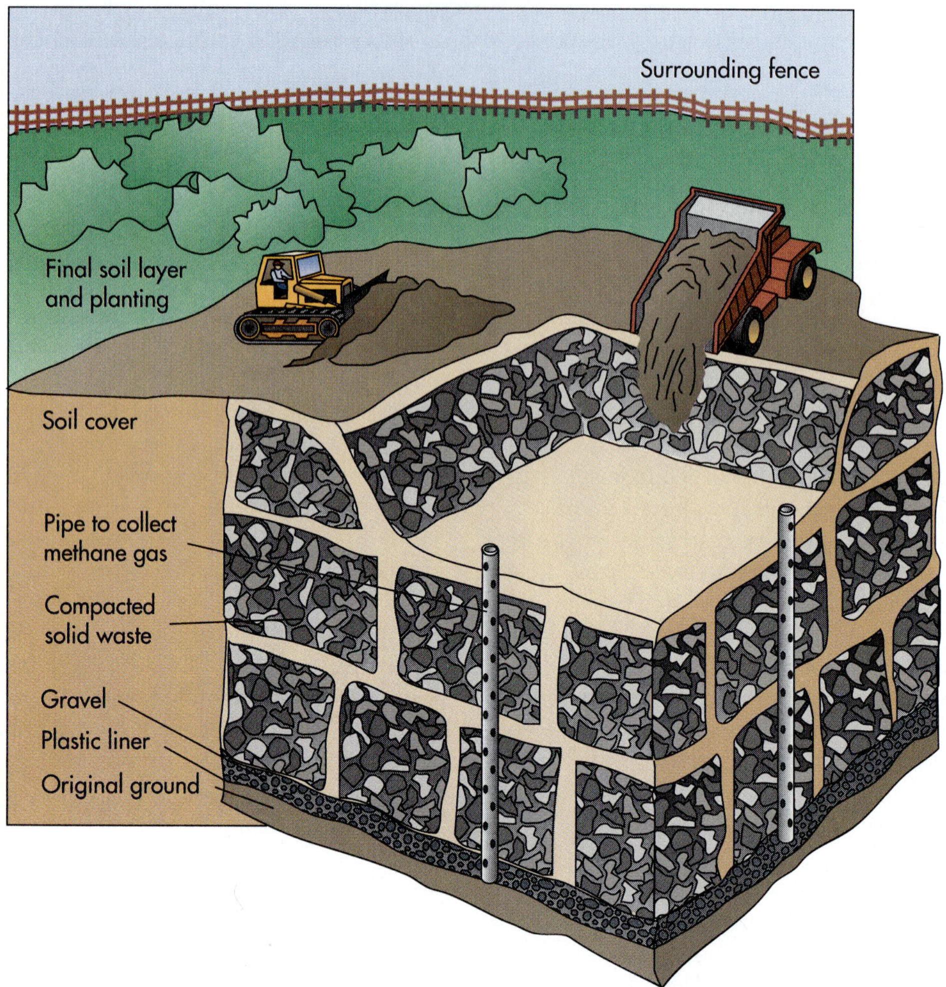

FIG. 14-45 Sanitary landfills are an inexpensive way of decomposing solid organic wastes. Many municipalities use this method of anaerobic decomposition for disposal of municipal waste. Methane is one of the products formed from decomposition of organic matter in landfills.

nents. This can be accomplished at the source, by the separate collections of garbage (organic waste) and trash (inorganic waste), or at the receiving facility, by using magnetic separators to remove ferrous metals and mechanical separators to remove glass, aluminum, and plastic materials. The remaining largely organic waste is ground up, mixed with sewage sludge or bulking agents such as shredded newspaper or wood chips, and then composted. The addition of dehydrated sewage sludge to domestic garbage improves the carbon/nitrogen balance because sewage sludge is high in nitrogen and therefore enhances microbial biodegradation activities, as well as providing a means of disposing of some sewage sludge waste and supplying a considerable number of decomposer microorganisms. The addition of 10% by weight sewage sludge to the material being composted improves its porosity. This is important because 30% air space is needed to optimize the availability of oxygen for mi-

FIG. 14-46 Compost heaps are commonly used for the aerobic decomposition of wastes. The organic matter of leaves and other dead plant matter frequently is decomposed to carbon dioxide and humus in such compost heaps.

crobial respiration in the aerobic compost process. It also is important because water must drain out of the composting material to prevent waterlogging and the development of anaerobic conditions.

The various composting methods are differentiated by the physical arrangement of the solid waste; that is, composting can be accomplished in windrows, aerated piles, or continuous-feed reactors. The *windrow method,* in which solid waste is arranged in long rows, is a simple but relatively slow process, typically requiring several months to achieve biodegradation of the metabolizable components and stabilization of the waste material. The windrow process can be speeded up by periodically mixing and restacking the waste pile. Odor and insect problems are controlled in this process by covering the windrows with a layer of soil or finished compost. Unless the decomposing material is turned several times during the process, the quality of the finished compost product is uneven. Because the process is slow, large amounts of land must be used, causing the same problems as sanitary landfills in densely populated urban areas.

Composting rates can be enhanced in the *aerated pile method,* in which waste is arranged in piles and forced aeration is used to provide needed oxygen. Perforated pipes are buried inside the compost pile and air is pumped through the pile, oxygenating and cooling it. The heat generated in the aerated pile process is used to evaporate water for the final drying of the product. The *continuous-feed composting process* uses a reactor that permits control of the environmental parameters (FIG. 14-47). The reactor is analogous to an industrial fermentor and permits the production of a relatively uniform product. Compared to other compost methods, the continuous-feed process requires a high initial financial investment. By optimizing conditions, composting in the reactor is accomplished in just 2 to 4 days, although the product requires additional curing for about a month before packaging and shipment.

In a compost of domestic garbage and sludge, numerous microbial species that come from soil, water, and fecal matter are present. The relatively high moisture content of the compost material favors the development of bacterial rather than fungal populations. In the composting of solid organic wastes, the process is initiated by mesophilic heterotrophs, which, as the temperature rises, are replaced by thermophilic microorganisms. The initial temperature increase is probably due to the growth of mesophilic bacteria in the interior portions of the composting material. Thermophilic microorganisms prominent in the composting process include the bacteria *Bacillus stearothermophilus, Thermomonospora* spp., *Thermoactinomyces* spp., and *Clostridium thermocellum* and the fungi *Geotrichum candidum, Aspergillus fumigatus, Mucor pusillus, Chaetomium thermophile, Thermoascus auranticus,* and *Torula thermophila.* In the continuous-reactor composting process, the reactor is maintained continuously at thermophilic temperatures by using the heat produced within the reactor by the biodegradation of the organic matter.

FIG. 14-47 In a continous feed compost process, solid waste is periodically added so that the compost contains a mixture of new undegraded waste, older partially degraded waste, and fully decomposed waste.

Control of several conditions is critical for achieving optimal composting. Temperatures needed to achieve maximal rates of organic matter decomposition are in the range of 50° to 60° C. Self-heating typically raises the temperature inside a static compost pile to 55° to 60° C or above in 2 to 3 days under favorable conditions, but after a few days at this optimal level, the temperature gradually declines unless the pile is turned to resupply oxygen and ensure that the thermophilic process occurs throughout the pile, instead of only at the core. Moisture must be adequate; 50% to 60% water content is optimal, but excess moisture—70% or above—interferes with aeration and lowers self-heating because of water's large heat capacity. The carbon-to-nitrogen ratio must not be greater than 40:1; a lower nitrogen content precludes the formation of a sufficient microbial biomass, and a greater nitrogen concentration, such as C:N = 25:1, would lead to volatilization of ammonia, causing odor problems and lowering the usefulness of the compost product as a fertilizer.

Although compost is a good soil conditioner and supplies some plant nutrients, it cannot compete with synthetic fertilizers for use in agricultural production. The sale of compost effectively reduces the cost of the waste disposal operation but generally does not render the waste disposal operation self-supporting. When sewage sludge is used as a major component of the original compost mixture, however, the finished product may contain relatively high concentrations of potentially toxic heavy metals, such as cadmium, chromium, and thallium. Because little is known about the behavior of these metals in agricultural soils, the use of sewage sludge-derived compost in agriculture is not widely practiced. Compost does find extensive applications in parks and gardens for ornamental plants, in land reclamation, particularly after strip mining, and as part of highway beautification projects. Although landfill operations are less expensive than composting, the long-range environmental costs in terms of groundwater contamination favor the composting process.

TREATMENT OF LIQUID WASTES

Agricultural and industrial operations—as well as everyday human activities—produce liquid wastes, including domestic sewage. These liquid waste discharges flow through natural drainage patterns or sewers, eventually entering natural bodies of water, such as groundwater, rivers, lakes, and oceans. In theory the liquid wastes disappear when they are flushed into such water bodies, according to the adage "the solution to pollution is dilution." Bodies of water into which sewage flows must also serve local communities as the source of water for drinking, household use, industry, irrigation, fish and shellfish production, swimming, boating, and other recreational purposes, mak-

BOX 14-6

BIOLOGICAL OXYGEN DEMAND (BOD)

We have developed several measures of water quality that help us manage aquatic ecosystems by indicating how much waste can safely be allowed to enter rivers and lakes without causing serious deterioration of water quality. One widely used measure of water quality, the *biological oxygen demand (BOD)*, represents the amount of oxygen required for the microbial decomposition of the organic matter in the water. The BOD procedure, which is used extensively in monitoring water quality and biodegradation of waste materials, is designed to determine how much oxygen is consumed by microorganisms during oxidation of the organic matter in the sample.

The BOD can be easily determined in the laboratory by incubating a water sample and measuring the amount of oxygen consumed during a 5-day period (see FIG.). The procedure is based on the consumption of oxygen by the microorganisms that are naturally present in the water sample. The oxygen remaining after 5 days of incubation can be determined chemically or, more commonly, with the use of oxygen electrodes. The difference between the starting concentration of oxygen and the residual oxygen represents the amount of oxygen consumed by the indigenous microorganisms in degrading the organic materials in the water sample, that is, the BOD.

Incubation at 20° C for 5 days is commonly used because the test was originally developed in Great Britain, where average water temperatures are near 20° C and where it takes a maximum of 5 days for anything entering a local river to reach the ocean. Once the organic matter reaches the ocean, it is no longer considered a threat to water quality. In the United States and other large countries, it may be useful to consider modifying the incubation period used in the standard 5-day BOD procedure to account for the extended residence time of organic matter in the waterways receiving organic pollutants. The development of appropriate modifications to the original procedure has been slow, in part because of a lack of understanding of the original assumptions used in establishing the standard 5-day incubation procedure. Appropriate modifications of the standard BOD procedure, based on actual residence times in inland waterways and desirable multiple uses of water, are presently being incorporated into water quality standards.

ing the maintenance of the acceptable high quality of these natural waters essential.

Fortunately, self-purification is an inherent capability of natural waters, based on the biogeochemical cycling activities and interpopulation relationships of the indigenous microbial populations. Organic nutrients in the water are metabolized and mineralized (converted to inorganic chemicals) by heterotrophic aquatic microorganisms. Ammonia is nitrified and, with other inorganic nutrients, used and immobilized by algae and higher aquatic plants. These are indigenous (autochthonous). Allochthonous (foreign nonindigenous) populations of enteric and other pathogens that enter aquatic ecosystems are maintained at low levels and/or eliminated by the pressures of competition and predation of the autochthonous aquatic populations. Consequently, reasonably low amounts of raw sewage can be accepted by natural waters without causing a significant decline in the level of water quality.

Human demographic patterns of densely populated areas, large-scale agricultural operations, and major industrial activities result in the production of liquid wastes on a scale that routinely overwhelms the self-purification capacity of aquatic ecosystems. This causes an unacceptable deterioration of water quality. A prominent feature of river water receiving sewage effluents is the presence of the filamentous aerobic bacterium *Sphaerotilus natans,* known as the "sewage fungus" (FIG. 14-48). A heterogeneous microbial community also develops amid the filaments of this bacterium below a sewage outfall. *S. natans* and the associated microbial community are efficient degraders of organic matter, consuming oxygen at a rate of 2 grams per hour per square meter. The bloom of the sewage fungus exemplifies the aesthetically displeasing results of excessive addition of organic matter to natural water bodies. Depending on the rate of sewage discharge, flow rate, water temperature, and other environmental factors, water may reestablish an acceptable quality level at some distance downstream from the sewage outfall, typically within 24 to 60 km. The

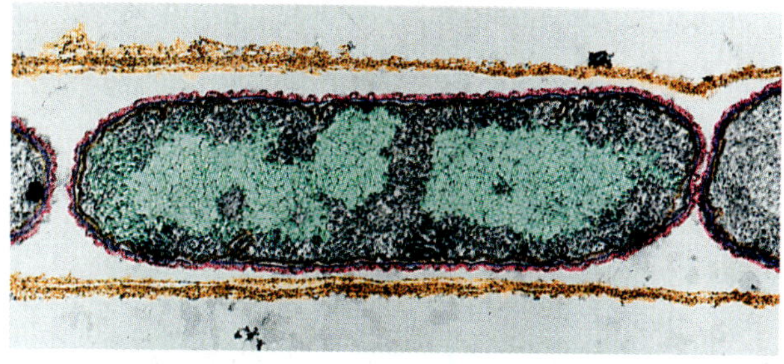

FIG. 14-48 Colorized micrograph of the filamentous bacterium *Sphaerotilus natans.* Cells of this bacterium are enclosed within a sheath *(orange).*

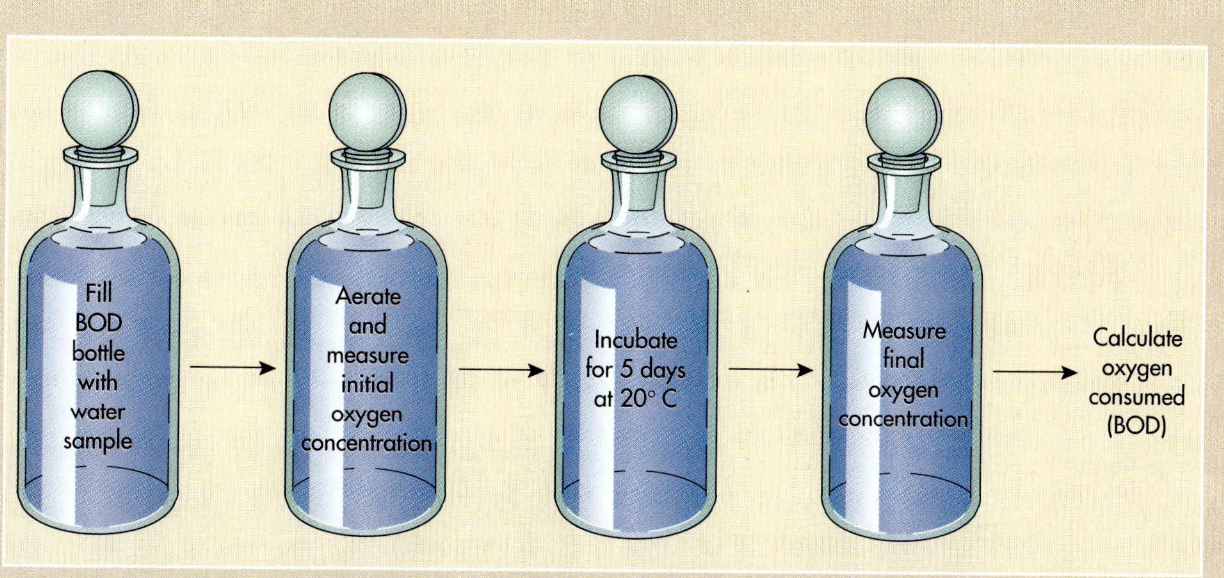

Biological oxygen demand (BOD) is determined by measuring how much oxygen is consumed by microorganisms during a 5-day incubation period. This oxygen consumption reflects the organic content of the water sample and whether the water will have a detrimental effect on animals in a receiving water. Water with too high a concentration of organic matter results in depletion of oxygen and death of animals.

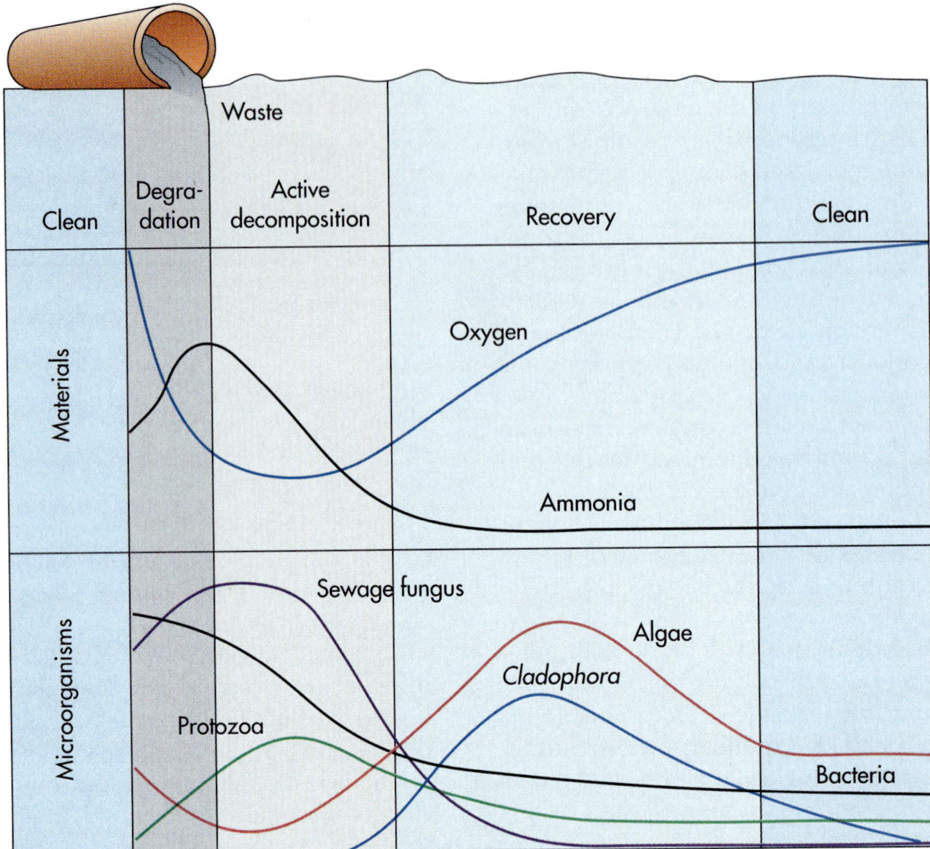

FIG. 14-49 Immediately below a sewage outfall the oxygen is depleted and the concentration of ammonia is elevated. Microbial populations are high, especially *Sphaerotilus natans:* the bacterium known as the sewage fungus because of its filamentous growth. Further downstream, oxygen concentrations, nutrient levels, and populations of microogranisms and higher animals return to normal, indicating degradation and dilution of the sewage and the return to clean water conditions.

relative changes in some environmental parameters and populations in a river receiving sewage are illustrated in FIG. 14-49. The maintenance of satisfactory water quality means that natural waters should not be overloaded with organic or inorganic nutrients or with toxic, noxious, or aesthetically unacceptable substances; that their oxygen, temperature, salinity, turbidity, or pH levels should not be altered so significantly that they lose their ability to support fish production and recreational usage of the water body; and that they should not be allowed to become vehicles of disease transmission due to fecal contamination.

Sewage Treatment

One consequence of urbanization is the need to remove sewage and other organic wastes from concentrated population centers. Waterways that are normally used for waste removal under the premise that "the solution to pollution is dilution" can be overwhelmed by concentrated inputs of organic matter. A high BOD generally indicates the presence of excessive amounts of organic carbon. The dissolved oxygen in natural waters seldom exceeds 8 mg/L because of its low solubility, and it is often considerably lower because of heterotrophic microbial activity, making oxygen depletion a likely consequence of adding wastes with high BOD values to aquatic ecosystems. The polluting power of different sources of wastes is reflected in the BOD of the material (Table 14-8). Exhaustion of the dissolved oxygen content is the principal result of a sewage overload on natural waters. Oxygen deprivation kills obligately aerobic organisms, including some microorganisms, fish, and invertebrates, and the

TABLE 14-8 Biochemical Oxygen Demand (BOD) Values for Different Types of Wastes

TYPE OF WASTE	BOD (mg/L)
Domestic sewage	200-600
Slaughterhouse wastes	1,000-4,000
Piggery effluents	25,000
Cattle shed effluents	20,000
Vegetable processing	200-5,000

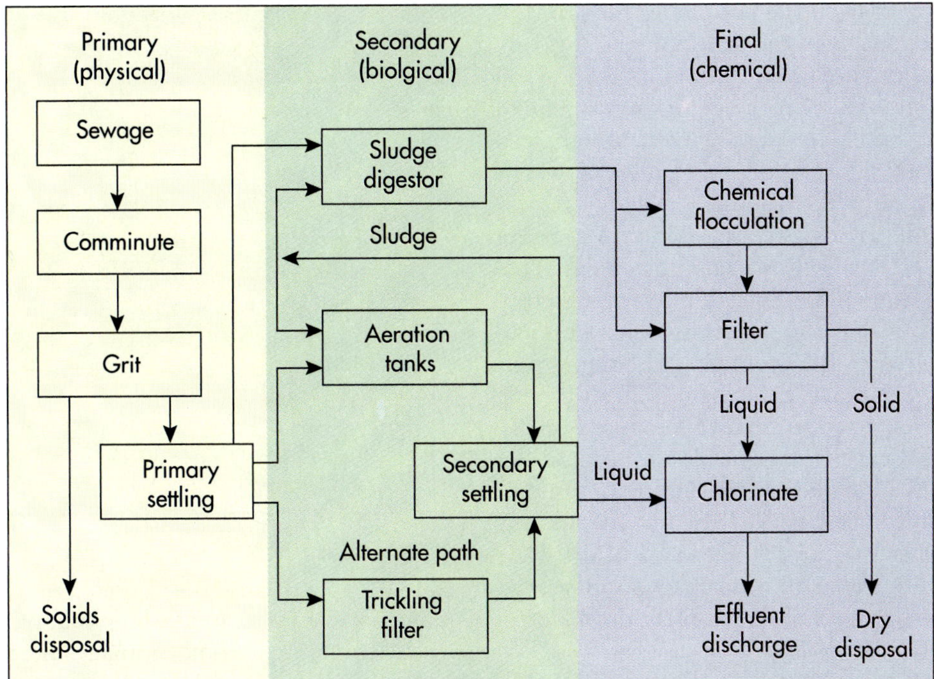

FIG. 14-50 Sewage treatment consists of primary stage (physical treatment), secondary stage (biological treatment), and a tertiary stage (chemical treatment). Microorganisms degrade wastes in the secondary stage.

decomposition of dead organisms within the body of water creates an additional oxygen demand. Fermentation products and the reduction of the secondary electron sinks of nitrate and sulfate give rise to noxious odors, tastes, and colors, making the water putrid and septic.

Modern methods of liquid waste treatment attempt to maintain acceptable water quality by reducing the BOD of the waste before it is discharged into a body of water. There are several different approaches to reducing the BOD, employing combinations of physical, chemical, and microbiological methods. Most communities in developed countries have facilities for treating sewage, which is the used water supply containing domestic waste, with human excrement and wash water; industrial waste, including acids, greases, oils, animal matter, and vegetable matter; and storm waters. The use of household garbage disposal units also increases the organic content of domestic sewage. The treatment of liquid wastes is aimed at removing organic matter, human pathogens, and toxic chemicals. The treatment of domestic sewage reduces the BOD due to suspended or dissolved organics and the number of enteric pathogens so that the discharged sewage effluent will not cause unacceptable deterioration of environmental quality.

Sewage is subjected to different treatments, depending on the quality of the effluent deemed necessary to be achieved to permit the maintenance of acceptable water quality (FIG. 14-50). **Primary sewage treatments** rely on physical separation procedures to lower the BOD; **secondary sewage treatments** rely on microbial biodegradation to further reduce the concentration of organic compounds in the effluent; and **tertiary treatments** use chemical methods to remove inorganic compounds and pathogenic microorganisms. Municipal sewage treatment facilities are designed to handle organic wastes but are normally incapable of dealing with industrial wastes containing toxic chemicals, such as heavy metals. Industrial facilities frequently must operate their own treatment plants to deal with waste materials.

Primary sewage treatment removes suspended solids in settling tanks or basins (FIG. 14-51). The

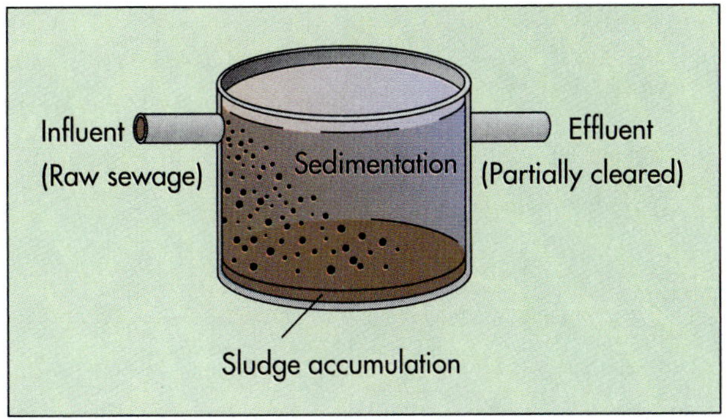

FIG. 14-51 In a settling tank, sludge accumulates as solids are removed from the waste. This primary treatment lowers the organic content of the water.

solids are drawn off from the bottom of the tank and may be subjected to anaerobic digestion and/or composting before final deposition in landfills or as soil conditioner. Only a low percentage of the suspended or dissolved organic material is actually mineralized during liquid waste treatment; most of it is removed by settling, and as a result the disposal problem is merely "displaced" to the solid waste area rather than being solved. Nevertheless, this displacement is essential because of the detrimental effects of discharging effluents with high BOD into aquatic ecosystems with naturally low dissolved oxygen contents. The liquid portion of the sewage, which contains dissolved organic matter, can be subjected to further treatment or discharged after primary treatment alone. Because liquid wastes vary in composition and may contain mainly solids and little dissolved organic matter, primary treatment may remove 70% to 80% of the BOD and may be sufficient. For typical domestic sewage (Table 14-9), however, primary treatment normally removes only 30% to 40% of the BOD.

To achieve an acceptable reduction in the BOD, secondary treatment is necessary (Table 14-10). In secondary sewage treatment, a small portion of the dissolved organic matter is mineralized and the larger portion is converted to removable solids. The combination of primary and secondary treatment reduces the original sewage BOD by 80% to 90%. The secondary sewage treatment step that relies on microbial activity may be aerobic or anaerobic. Secondary treatment can be accomplished by using various devices. A well-designed and efficiently operated secondary treatment unit should produce effluents with BOD and/or suspended solids of less than 20 mg/L.

TABLE 14-9 Characteristics of Typical Municipal Waste Water

COMPONENT	CONCENTRATION (mg/L)
Solids	
Total	700
Dissolved	500
Fixed	300
Volatile	200
Suspended	200
Fixed	50
Volatile	150
BOD (biochemical oxygen demand)	300
TOC (total organic carbon)	200
COD (chemical oxygen demand)	400
Nitrogen (as N)	
Total	40
Organic	15
Ammonia	25
Nitrate	0
Phosphorus (as P)	—
Total	10
Organic	3
Inorganic	7
Grease	100

TABLE 14-10 Efficiency of Various Types of Sewage Treatment

TREATMENT	BOD (% REDUCED)	SUSPENDED SOLIDS (% REMOVED)	BACTERIA (% REDUCED)
PRIMARY TREATMENT			
Sedimentation	30-75	40-95	40-75
SECONDARY TREATMENT			
Septic tank	25-65	40-75	40-75
Trickling filter	60-90	0-80	70-85
Activated sludge	70-96	70-97	95-99

Because the secondary treatment of sewage is a microbial process, it is extremely sensitive to the introduction of toxic chemicals that may be contained in industrial waste effluents or that accidentally may contaminate the sewerage system. The accidental introduction of the organic chemicals octachlorocyclopentene and hexachlorocyclopentadiene into the municipal sewerage system of Louisville, Kentucky, for example, poisoned the microorganisms in the sewage treatment facility, forcing the dumping of 7 billion gallons of untreated sewage into the Ohio River during a 3-month period before the toxic chemicals could be removed from the system. The accidental introduction of hexanes into the same sewerage system several years later caused a massive explosion and the disruption of normal sewage treatment for an extended period of time.

Oxidation Ponds **Oxidation ponds,** also known as **stabilization ponds** and **lagoons,** are used for the simple secondary treatment of sewage effluents in rural communities and some industrial facilities (FIG. 14-52). Heterotrophic bacteria degrade sewage organic matter within the ponds, producing cellular material and mineral products that support the growth of algae. The proliferation of algal populations in these lagoons produces oxygen that replenishes the oxygen depleted by the heterotrophic bacteria, permitting continued organic matter decomposition. Because oxygenation is usually achieved by diffusion and by the photosynthetic activity of algae, such ponds need to be shallow. Typically, oxidation ponds are less than 10 feet deep, which maximizes the euphotic zone for

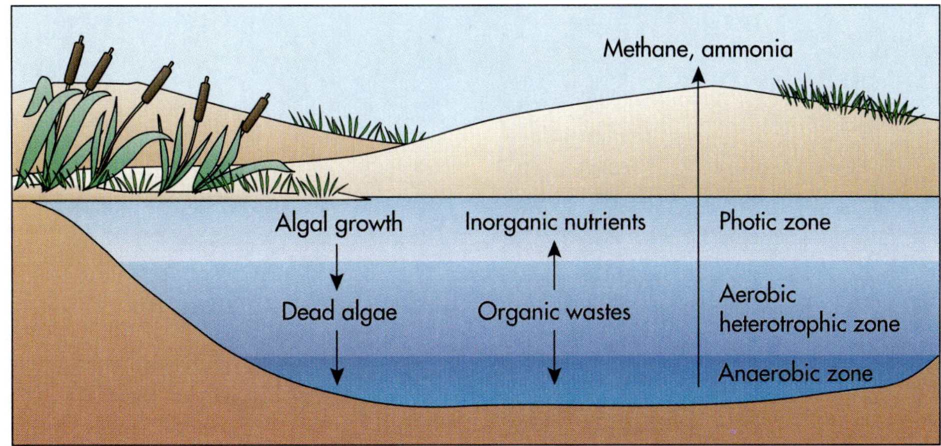

FIG. 14-52 In an oxidation pond, various microbial populations contribute to waste degradation. This is a simple system that is relatively inefficient but has low operating cost.

algal growth. Oxygenation is usually incomplete, with consequent odor problems. The performance of oxidation ponds is strongly influenced by seasonal temperature fluctuations, and their usefulness, therefore, is largely restricted to warmer climatic regions. The bacterial and algal cells formed during the decomposition of the sewage settle to the bottom, eventually filling in the pond. Oxidation ponds generally are low-cost operations but they tend to be inefficient and require large holding capacities and long retention times. The degradation of organic matter in these ponds is relatively slow, and the residence time for the treatment of domestic sewage may be as long as a week. The effluents containing oxidized products are periodically removed from the ponds, which are then refilled with raw sewage. Alternately, sewage may flow into one end of the pond and overflow may occur at another point.

Trickling Filter The **trickling filter system** is a simple and relatively inexpensive film-flow type of aerobic sewage treatment method (FIG. 14-53). The sewage is distributed by a revolving sprinkler suspended over a bed of porous material. The sewage slowly percolates through this porous bed, and the effluent is collected

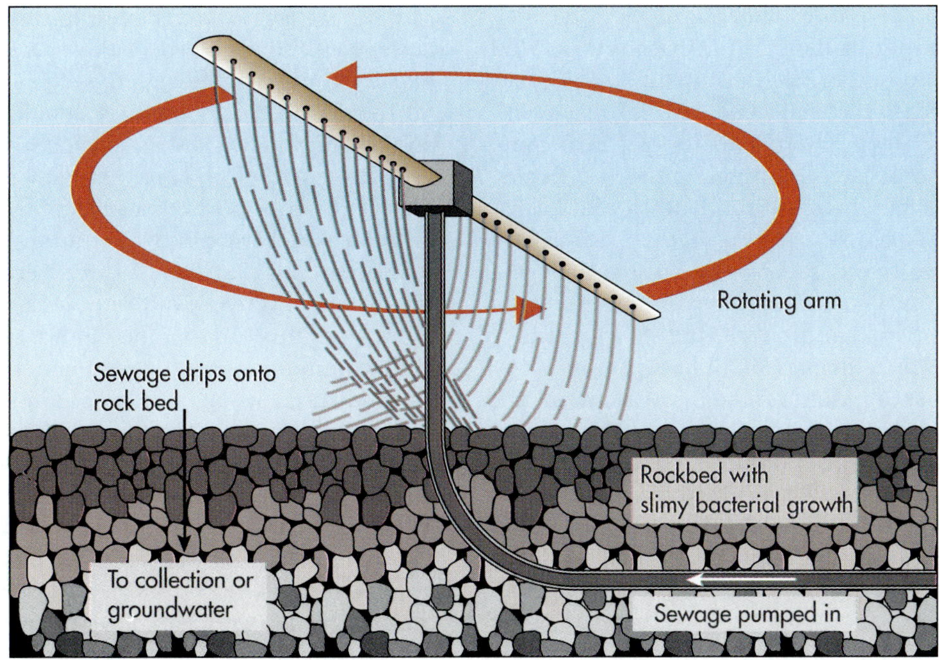

FIG. 14-53 In a trickling filter, liquid waste flows past a biofilm of microorganisms adhering to a bed of rocks. The biofilm microorganisms, many of which form slimes, aerobically degrade the organic compounds in the waste.

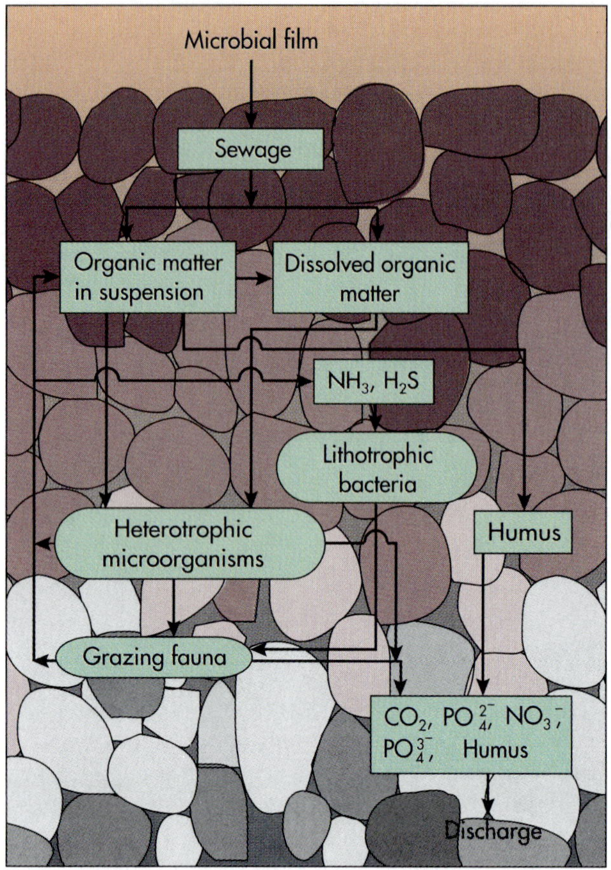

FIG. 14-54 A complex microbial community in the biofilm of a trickling filter degrades organic compounds and recycles mineral nutrients.

FIG. 14-55 The biodisc system rotates a biofilm of adhering microorganisms through a liquid waste. This is effective for treatment of wastes with relatively low concentrations of organic compounds.

at the bottom. The porous material of the filter bed becomes coated with a dense, slimy bacterial growth, principally composed of *Zooglea ramigera* and similar slime-forming bacteria. The slime matrix thus generated accommodates a heterogeneous microbial community, including bacteria, fungi, protozoa, nematodes, and rotifers. The most frequently found bacteria are *Beggiatoa alba, Sphaerotilus natans, Achromobacter* spp., *Flavobacterium* spp., *Pseudomonas* spp., and *Zooglea* spp. This microbial community absorbs and mineralizes dissolved organic nutrients in the sewage, reducing the BOD of the effluent (FIG. 14-54). Aeration occurs passively as a result of the movement of air through the porous material of the bed. The sewage may be passed through two or more trickling filters or may be recirculated several times through the same filter to reduce the BOD to acceptable levels. The effluent from the trickling filters may be clarified by allowing sloughed-off biomass to settle before discharge. A drawback of this otherwise simple and inexpensive treatment system is that a nutrient overload produces excess microbial slime, which reduces aeration and percolation rates, periodically necessitating renewal of the trickling filter bed. Also, cold winter temperatures strongly reduce the effectiveness of such outdoor treatment facilities.

Biodisc System The **rotating biological contactor** or **biodisc system** is a more advanced type of aerobic film-flow treatment system. In the biodisc system, closely spaced discs, usually made of plastic, are rotated in a trough containing the sewage effluent (FIG. 14-55). The discs are partially submerged and become coated with a microbial slime similar to the one that develops in trickling filters. Continuous rotation of the discs keeps the slime well aerated and in contact with the sewage. The thickness of the microbial slime layer in all film-flow processes is governed by the diffusion of nutrients through the film. Microbial growth on the surface of the discs is sloughed off gradually and is removed by subsequent settling. When the film becomes so thick that oxygen and nutrients fail to reach the inner portions of the film, most of the innermost microorganisms die, causing detachment of the slime layer. Patches of slime periodically fall off the surface. The slime layer immediately begins to regrow when this occurs. The biodisc system is used in some communities for the treatment of both domestic and industrial sewage effluents. This system requires less space than trickling filters and is more efficient and stable in operation but needs a higher initial financial investment.

Activated Sludge The **activated sludge process** is a widely used aerobic suspension type of liquid waste treatment system (FIG. 14-56). After primary settling, the sewage, containing dissolved organic compounds, is introduced into an aeration tank. Air injection and/or mechanical stirring provides the aeration. The rapid development of microorganisms is also stimulated by reintroduction of most of the settled

FIG. 14-56 An activated sludge treatment facility has tanks in which microorganisms degrade wastes. Extensive aeration and agitation maintain aerobic conditions that favors complete degradation of organic compounds by respiring microorganisms.

TABLE 14-11 Number of Bacteria at Different Stages of Sewage Treatment

TREATMENT	TOTAL BACTERIA (NUMBER/mL)	VIABLE BACTERIA (NUMBER/mL)
Settled sewage	7×10^8	1×10^7
Activated sludge mixed liquor	7×10^8	6×10^7
Filter slimes	6×10^{10}	2×10^9
Secondary effluents	5×10^7	6×10^5
Tertiary effluents	3×10^7	4×10^4

sludge from a previous run (FIG. 14-57); the process derives its name from this inoculation with such *activated sludge.*

During the holding period in the aeration tank, vigorous development of heterotrophic microorganisms occurs. The heterogeneous nature of the organic substrates in sewage allows the development of diverse heterotrophic bacterial populations, including Gram-negative rods, predominantly *Escherichia, Enterobacter, Pseudomonas, Achromobacter, Flavobacterium,* and *Zooglea* spp.; other bacteria, including *Micrococcus, Arthrobacter,* various coryneforms and mycobacteria, *Sphaerotilus,* and other large filamentous bacteria; and low numbers of filamentous fungi, yeasts, and protozoa, mainly ciliates. The protozoa are important predators of the bacteria, along with rotifers. The bacteria in the activated sludge tank occur in free suspension and as aggregates or flocs. The flocs are composed of microbial biomass held together by bacterial slimes, produced by *Zooglea ramigera* and similar organisms. Most of the ciliate protozoa, such as *Vorticella,* are of the attached filter-feeding type and adhere to the flocs, while feeding predominantly on the suspended bacteria. The floc is too large to be ingested by the ciliates and rotifers and acts as a defense mechanism against predation. In the raw sewage, suspended bacteria predominate, but during the holding time in the aeration tank, their numbers decrease, and at the same time those bacteria associated with flocs greatly increase in number (Table 14-11).

As a consequence of extensive microbial metabolism of the organic compounds in sewage, a signifi-

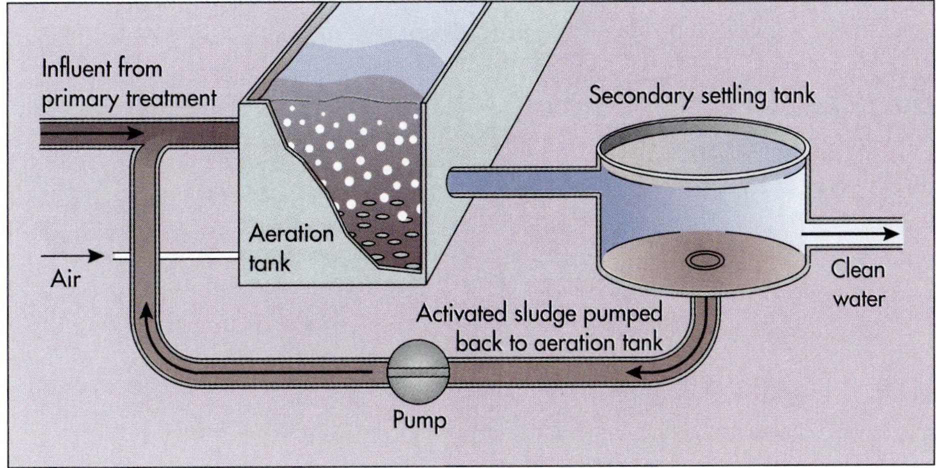

FIG. 14-57 An activated sludge treatment system has an aeration tank in which aerobic microorganisms actively degrade the wastes remaining after primary settling of sludge from influent sewage. This is run as a batch reaction. The biomass produced in the aeration tank settles in a secondary settling tank. A portion of this activated sludge containing massive populations of microorganisms is used as an inoculum for treatment of a new batch of sludge.

cant portion of the dissolved organic substrates is mineralized and another portion is converted to microbial biomass. In the advanced stage of aeration, most of the microbial biomass becomes associated with flocs that can be removed from suspension by settling. The settling characteristic of sewage sludge flocs is critical to their efficient removal. Poor settling produces "bulking" of sewage sludge, caused by proliferation of such filamentous bacteria as *Sphaerotilus, Beggiatoa, Thiothrix,* and *Bacillus* and such filamentous fungi as *Geotrichum, Cephalosporium, Cladosporium,* and *Penicillium.* The causes of bulking are not always understood but it is frequently associated with high C:N and C:P ratios and/or low dissolved oxygen concentrations. A portion of the settled sewage sludge is recycled for use as the inoculum for the incoming raw sewage; the remainder of the sludge requires additional treatment by composting or anaerobic digestion.

Combined with primary settling, the activated sludge process reduces the BOD of the effluent to 10% to 15% of that of the raw sewage. The treatment also drastically reduces the number of intestinal pathogens in the sewage. This reduction is the result of the combined effects of competition, adsorption, predation, and settling. Predation by ciliates, rotifers, and *Bdellovibrio* is probably indiscriminate and affects pathogens as well as nonpathogenic heterotrophs. Also, pathogens tend to grow poorly or not at all under the environmental conditions of an aeration tank, and nonpathogenic heterotrophs proliferate vigorously. Therefore, whereas nonpathogenic heterotrophs reproduce to compensate for their predatory removal, the pathogens are continuously decimated (Table 14-12). Settling of the flocs removes additional pathogens, and the number of *Salmonella,*

TABLE 14-12 Percentage of Reductions in the Numbers of Indicator Organisms in Different Types of Sewage Treatment Processes

TREATMENT	*Escherichia coli*	COLIFORMS	FECAL STREPTOCOCCI	VIRUSES
Sedimentation	3-72	13-86	44-66	—
Activated sludge	61-100	13-83	84-93	79-100
Trickling filter	73-97	15-100	64-97	40-82
Lagoons	80-100	86-100	85-99	95

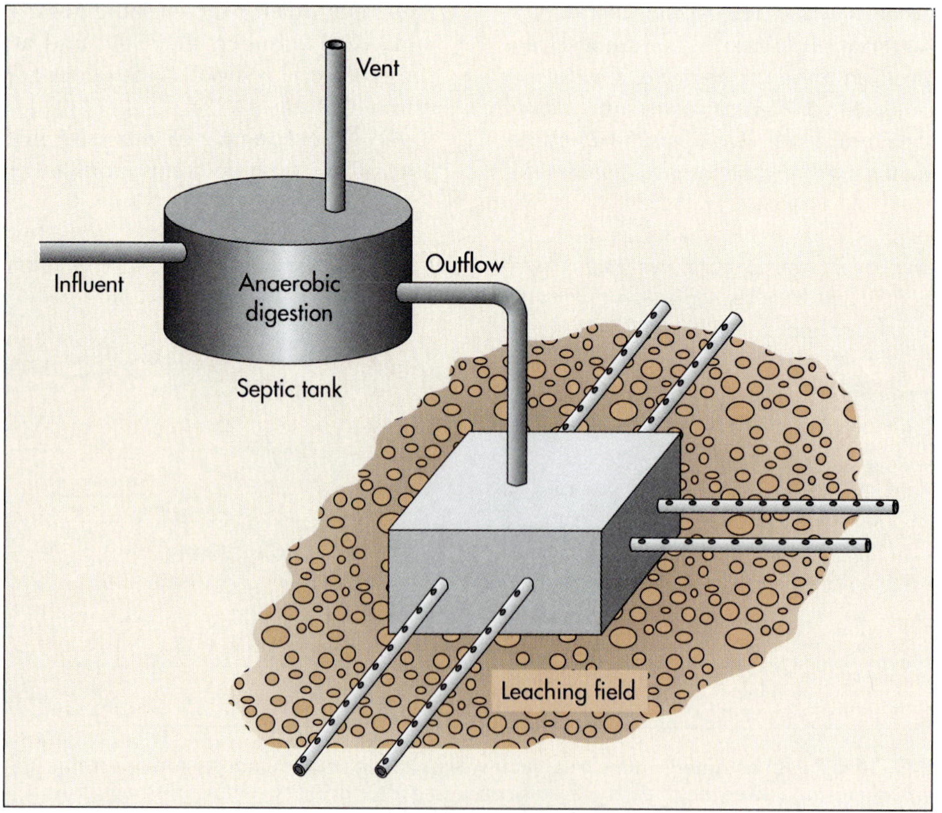

FIG. 14-58 A septic tank is a simple system that incorporates primary settling and secondary anaerobic decomposition of organic compounds.

Shigella, and *Escherichia coli* typically is 90% to 99% lower in the effluent of the activated sludge treatment process than in the incoming raw sewage. Enteroviruses are removed to a similar degree, and the principal removal mechanism appears to be adsorption of the virus particles onto the settling sewage sludge floc.

Septic Tank The simplest anaerobic treatment system, the **septic tank,** is used extensively in rural areas that lack sewage systems (FIG. 14-58). Many rural and suburban single-family dwellings use septic tanks. A septic tank acts largely as a settling tank, within which the organic components of the waste water undergo limited anaerobic digestion. The accumulated sludge is maintained under anaerobic conditions and is degraded by anaerobic microorganisms to organic acids and hydrogen sulfide. Residual solids settle to the bottom of the septic tank and the clarified effluent passes out of the tank. The effluent passes through a series of buried perforated tubes; the effluent percolates into the soil, where the dissolved organic compounds in the effluent undergo biodegradation. Septic tank treatment does not reliably destroy intestinal pathogens, and it is important that the soils receiving the clarified effluents not be in close proximity to drinking wells to prevent contamination of drinking water with enteric pathogens.

Anaerobic Digestors **Anaerobic digestors** are large fermentation tanks designed for continuous operation under anaerobic conditions. Large-scale anaerobic digestors are used for further processing of the sewage sludge produced by primary and secondary treatments (FIG. 14-59). Although anaerobic decomposition could be used for direct treatment of sewage, economic considerations favor aerobic processes for relatively dilute wastes, and the use of anaerobic digestors is restricted to treatment of concentrated organic wastes. Therefore, in practice, large-scale anaerobic digestors are used only for processing settled sewage sludge and the treatment of very high BOD industrial effluents.

Provisions for mechanical mixing, heating, gas collection, sludge addition, and drawoff of stabilized sludge are incorporated into the design of a large-scale anaerobic digestor to permit effective operation. Anaerobic digestors contain high amounts of suspended organic matter; between 20 and 100 g/L is considered favorable. Much of this suspended material is bacterial biomass, and viable counts can be as high as 10^9 to 10^{10} bacteria per milliliter. Fungi and protozoa are present in very low numbers and do not play a significant role in anaerobic digestion. A complex bacterial community is involved in the degradation of organic matter within an anaerobic digestor, with the number of anaerobic microorganisms typically two to three orders of magnitude higher than the number of aerobes.

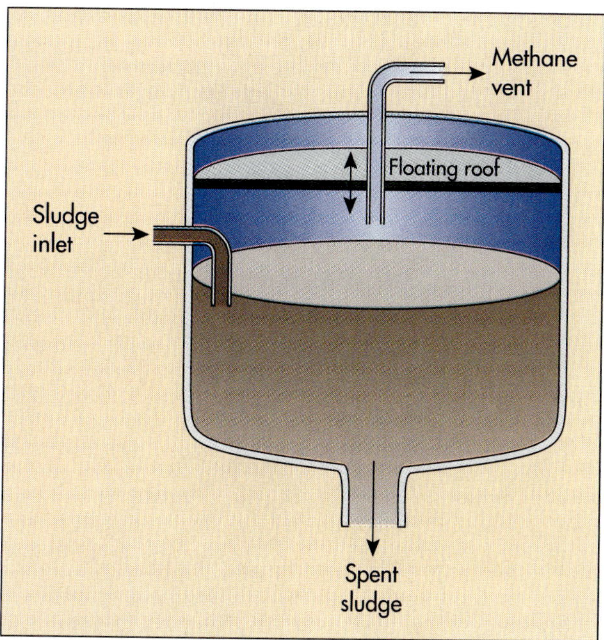

FIG. 14-59 An anaerobic sludge digestor is a tank in which anaerobic degradation processes occur, including the production of methane.

The anaerobic digestion of wastes is a two-step process in which a large variety of nonmethanogenic, obligately, or facultatively anaerobic bacteria participate. First, complex organic materials, including microbial biomass, are depolymerized and converted to fatty acids, CO_2, and H_2 (FIG. 14-60, p. 582). In the next step, methane is generated either by the direct reduction of methyl groups to methane or by the reduction of CO_2 to methane by molecular hydrogen or other reduced fermentation products, such as fatty acids. The final products obtained in an anaerobic digestor are a gas mixture, approximately 70% methane and 30% carbon dioxide, microbial biomass, and a nonbiodegradable residue.

The optimal operation of anaerobic digestors requires good control of several parameters, such as retention time, temperature, pH, and C:N and C:P ratios. The optimal performance temperature is in the range of 35° to 37° C. The pH must remain in the range of 6.0 to 8.0, with 7.0 being optimal. Variations in pH and the inclusion of heavy metals or other toxic materials in the sludge can easily upset the operation of the anaerobic digestor. In a "stuck" or "sour" digestor, methane production is interrupted, fatty acids and other fermentation products accumulate, and it is difficult to restore normal operation. It is usually necessary to clean out the reactor and charge it with large volumes of anaerobic sludge from an operational unit, a costly and time-consuming task.

A properly operating anaerobic digestor yields a greatly reduced volume of residue compared to the

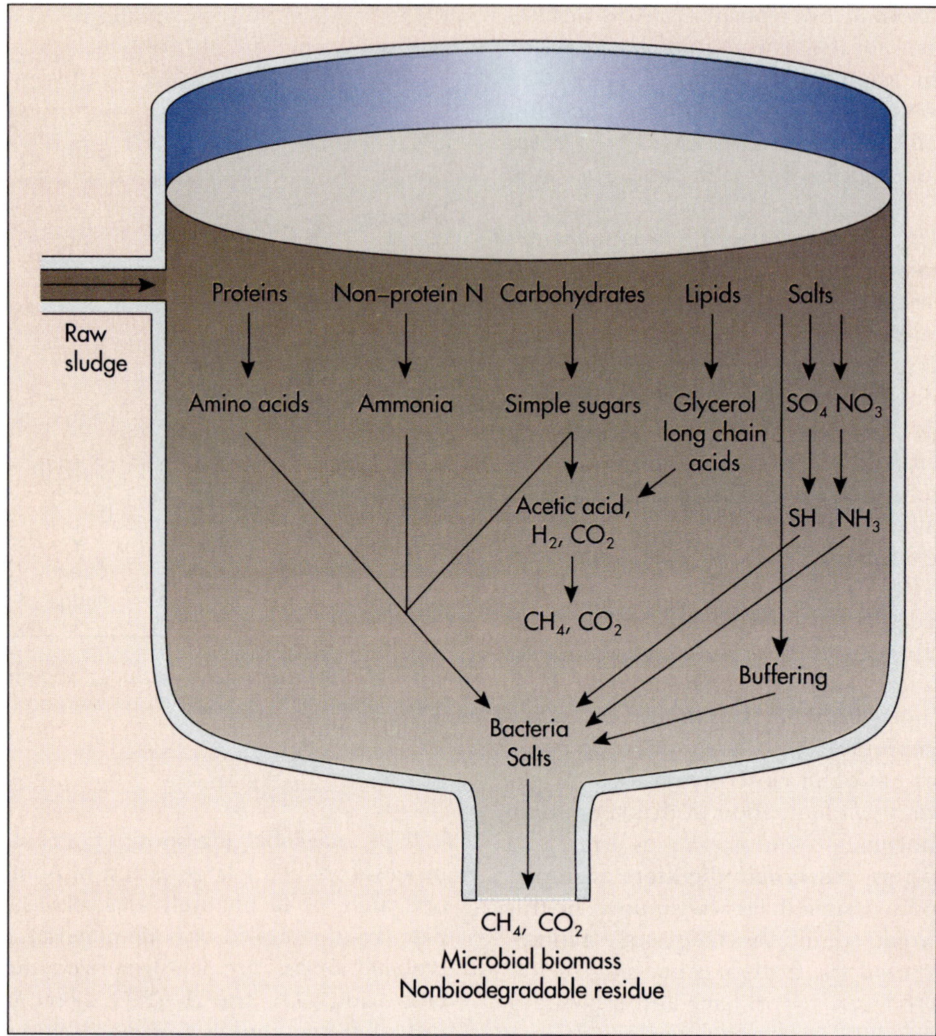

FIG. 14-60 Complex populations of fermentative bacteria degrade proteins, carbohydrates, and lipids to low molecular weight fatty acids (such as acetic acid), gases (CO_2 and H_2), and minerals. Methanogens produce methane from carbon dioxide and acetic acid.

starting waste material. The product obtained, however, still causes odor and water pollution problems and can be disposed of at only a few restricted landfill sites. Aerobic composting can be used to further consolidate the sludge, rendering it suitable for disposal in any landfill site or for use as a soil conditioner. Several gases are produced as a result of the anaerobic biodegradation of sludge, primarily methane and CO_2. The gas can be used within the treatment plant to drive the pumps and/or to provide heat for maintaining the temperature of the digestor; or after purification, it may be sold through natural gas distribution systems. Thus, in addition to its primary function in removing wastes, anaerobic digestors can produce needed fuel resources.

Tertiary Treatment The aerobic and anaerobic biological liquid waste treatment processes just discussed are designed to reduce the BOD of biodegradable organic substrates and oxidizable inorganic compounds, and all represent secondary treatment processes. **Tertiary treatment,** defined as any practice beyond a secondary one, is designed to remove nonbiodegradable organic pollutants and mineral nutrients, especially nitrogen and phosphorus salts. Secondary treatment is still required to avoid overloading this expensive treatment stage with biodegradable materials that could have been removed in more economical ways. The removal of toxic, nonbiodegradable organic pollutants, such as chlorophenols, polychlorinated biphenyls, and other synthetic pollutants, is necessary to reduce the toxicity of the sewage effluent to acceptable levels. Activated carbon filters are normally used in the removal of these materials from secondary-treated industrial effluents. Reverse osmosis is one way of eliminating organics and inorganics but there are problems with this procedure because of microbial fouling of the filters.

The release of sewage effluents containing phosphates and fixed forms of nitrogen can cause serious *eutrophication* (nutrient enrichment) in aquatic ecosystems. Sudden nutrient enrichment by sewage discharge or agricultural runoff triggers explosive algal blooms. Because of various causes—some unknown but including mutual shading, exhaustion of micronutrients, and the presence of toxic products and/or antagonistic populations—the algal population usually "crashes," and the subsequent decomposition of the dead algal biomass by heterotrophic microorganisms exhausts the dissolved oxygen supply in the water, precipitating extensive fish kills and septic conditions. Even if the process does not proceed to this extreme, algal mats, turbidity, discoloration, and shifts in the fish population from valuable species to more tolerant but less valued forms represent undesirable changes due to eutrophication.

To prevent eutrophication, phosphate is commonly removed from sewage by precipitation as calcium, aluminum, or iron phosphate. This can be accomplished as an integral part of primary or secondary settling or in a separate facility where the precipitating agent can be recycled. Nitrogen, present mainly as ammonia, can be removed by volatilization as NH_3 at a high pH. Some ammonia eliminated from the sewage in this manner, however, may return to the watershed in the form of precipitation and cause further eutrophication problems.

Breakpoint chlorination is an alternative procedure for removing ammonia. The addition of hypochlorous acid (HOCl), in a 1:1 molar ratio, results in the formation of monochloramine (NH_2Cl), and further addition of HOCl to an approximate molar ratio of 2:1 results in nearly complete oxidation of the ammonia to molecular nitrogen. As chlorination of the sewage effluent is commonly practiced for disinfection purposes, chlorination to this "breakpoint" can be accomplished in the same process. The removal of ammonium nitrogen also lowers the BOD of the effluent because the ammonia undergoes nitrification in waters receiving the sewage effluent, which consumes oxygen dissolved in the receiving water.

A highly advanced tertiary water treatment system that integrates several of these tertiary treatment processes is currently in operation in South Tahoe, California. This advanced treatment system was installed to prevent the eutrophic deterioration of scenic Lake Tahoe, an oligotrophic crater lake. In this system, after conventional primary and secondary treatments, phosphate is precipitated by liming, and ammonia is removed by stripping the high-pH effluent in a stripping tower at elevated temperature with vigorous aeration. After ammonia stripping, the pH is adjusted to neutrality. After additional settling, aided by polyelectrolyte addition and further clarification, nonbiodegradable organics are removed by filtration through activated carbon. The result of this extensive treatment procedure is a very high-quality effluent that can be released into Lake Tahoe without causing eutrophication. There is a high cost of using such chemical/physical tertiary treatments. In other locations such as Disney World in Orlando, Florida, wetland aquatic plants are used to remove nitrogen and phosphates from wastewater effluent.

Disinfection The final step in the sewage treatment process is **disinfection,** designed to kill enteropathogenic bacteria and viruses that were not eliminated during the previous stages of sewage treatment. Disinfection is commonly accomplished by *chlorination,* using chlorine gas (Cl_2) or hypochlorite ($CaOCl_2$ or NaOCl). Chlorine gas reacts with water to yield hypochlorous and hydrochloric acids, the actual disinfectants. Hypochlorite is a strong oxidant, which is the basis of its antibacterial action. As an oxidant, it also reacts with residual dissolved or suspended organic matter, ammonia, reduced iron, manganese, and sulfur compounds. The oxidation of these compounds competes for available HOCl, reducing its disinfecting power. Amounts of hypochlorite sufficient to satisfy these reactions and to allow excess-free residual chlorine to remain in solution for disinfection results in high salt concentrations in the effluent. Therefore it is desirable to remove nitrogen and other contaminants by alternative means and to use chlorination for disinfection only. A disadvantage of disinfection by chlorination is that the more resistant organic molecules such as some lipids and hydrocarbons are not completely oxidized but instead become partially chlorinated. Chlorinated hydrocarbons tend to be toxic and difficult to mineralize. Because alternative means of disinfection, such as ozonation, are more expensive, chlorination has been used as the principal means of sewage disinfection. The free residual chlorine content of the treated water is a built-in safety factor against pathogens surviving the actual treatment period and against recontamination.

The disadvantage of chlorination is the creation of trace amounts of trihalomethane (THM) compounds. The fact that THMs were formed in virtually all municipal water supplies that used chlorination for disinfection linked the formation of these contaminants to the chlorination process. Since some of the THMs are suspected carcinogens, the U.S. Environmental Protection Agency (EPA) established in 1979 a maximal THM limit in drinking water of 100 $\mu g/L$. To keep the levels within this limit using traditional chlorine disinfection, organic compounds were removed from the water meticulously by sand filtration and other tech-

BOX 14-7

COLIFORM COUNTS FOR ASSESSING WATER SAFETY

The most frequently used indicator organism is the normally nonpathogenic coliform bacterium *Escherichia coli.* Positive tests for *E. coli* do not prove the presence of enteropathogenic organisms but do establish this possibility. Because *E. coli* is more numerous and easier to grow than the enteropathogens, the test has a built-in safety factor for detecting potentially dangerous fecal contamination. *E. coli* meets many of the criteria for an ideal indicator organism but there are limitations to its use as such, and various other species have been proposed as additional or replacement indicators of water safety.

For *E. coli* to be a useful indicator organism of fecal pollution, it must be differentiated readily from nonfecal bacteria. The conventional test for the detection of fecal contamination involves a three-stage test procedure (FIG. *A*). In the first stage, lactose broth tubes are inoculated with undiluted or appropriately diluted water sam-

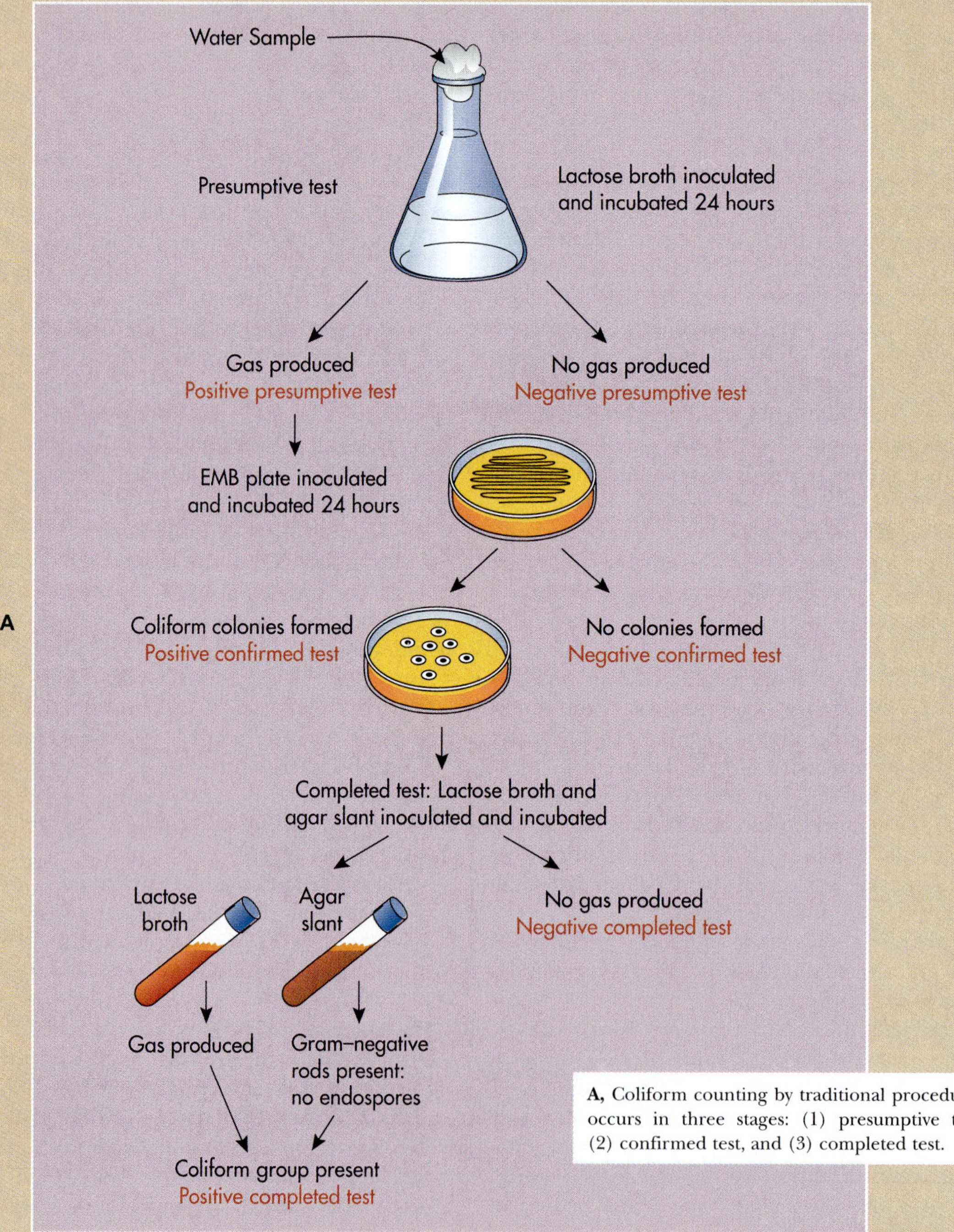

A, Coliform counting by traditional procedures occurs in three stages: (1) presumptive test, (2) confirmed test, and (3) completed test.

ples. The tubes showing gas formation are recorded as positive and are used to calculate the most probable number of coliform bacteria in the sample. Gas formation, detected in small inverted test tubes called *Durham tubes*, gives positive presumptive evidence of contamination by fecal coliforms; this is called a *presumptive test*. Gas formation in lactose broth at 37° C is characteristic not only of fecal *E. coli* strains but also of the nonfecal coliform *Enterobacter aerogenes* and some *Klebsiella* species. Therefore, in the second test stage of this procedure, the presence of enteric bacteria is confirmed by streaking samples from the positive lactose broth cultures onto a medium, such as eosin methylene blue (EMB) agar. Fecal coliform colonies on this medium acquire a characteristically greenish metallic sheen, *Enterobacter* species form reddish colonies, and nonlactose fermenters form colorless colonies, respectively; this is called a *confirmed test*. Alternatively, the confirmed test can be accomplished by using brilliant green lactose-bile broth (BGLB). If BGLB is used, it is then subcultured onto EMB. Subculturing colonies showing a green metallic sheen on EMB into lactose broth incubated at 35° C should produce gas formation, completing a positive test for fecal coliforms; this is called a *completed test*.

This three-stage test can be simplified. In the Eijkman test, suitable dilutions are incubated in lactose broth at 44.5° C, a temperature at which fecal coliforms still grow but nonfecal coliforms are inhibited. Gas formation constitutes a one-step positive test, but precise temperature control is mandatory because temperatures only a few degrees higher inhibit or kill the fecal coliforms. It is also possible to filter known volumes of diluted or undiluted water samples through 0.45 μm pore size bacteriological filters and incubate the filters directly on EMB agar, m-Endo agar, or other suitable media (FIG. *B*). Colonies of fecal coliforms appear with a characteristic metallic sheen on EMB, for example, and can be easily counted (FIG. *C*).

Before 1989 the EPA certified only two techniques for the detection of coliform bacteria in water: the multiple tube fermentation technique and the membrane filtration test. These procedures take several days to complete. In 1991, the EPA eliminated the requirement for the enumeration of coliform bacteria in water samples, instituting regulations based only on the presence or absence of coliform bacteria. This was done in response to studies that demonstrated that the level of coliform bacteria was not quantitatively related to the potential for an outbreak of waterborne disease; the presence/absence of coliform bacteria provided adequate water quality information. Culture-requiring methods for the detection of coliform bacteria, however, are limited in their ability to detect

B

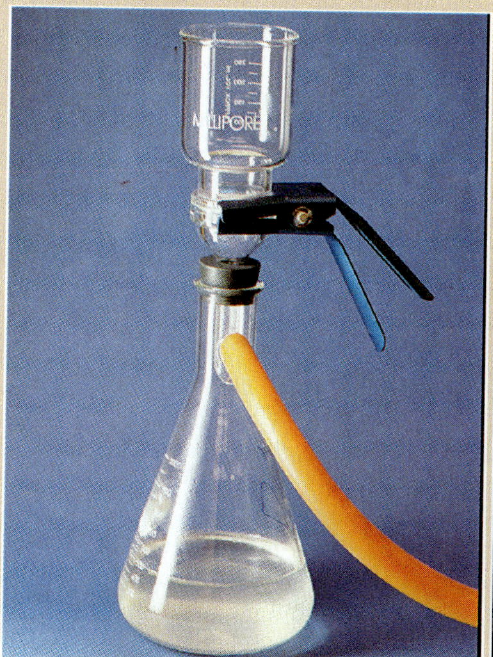

C

B, After testing, 100 mL water samples are passed through bacteriological filters (0.2 to 0.45 μm pore size) to trap bacteria. **C,** The filters with trapped bacteria are placed on a medium containing lactose as a carbon source inhibitor to suppress growth of noncoliforms and indicator substances to facilitate differentiation of coliforms. Here, colonies develop on a filter placed on an Endo medium.

Continued.

BOX 14-7

Coliform Counts for Assessing Water Safety—cont'd

viable but nonculturable bacteria. In oligotrophic situations, such as drinking water distribution systems, a proportion of the total population of coliform bacteria may be unrecoverable while in the pseudosenescent state associated with bacteria adapted to low-nutrient situations.

Several alternate procedures can provide the information necessary for determining drinking water quality in the presence/absence test format. These tests can be completed in 24 hours or less. One test uses defined substrate technology to determine enzymatic activities that are diagnostic of coliform bacteria and the fecal coliform *E. coli.* A medium containing isopropyl β-D-thiogalactopyranoside (IPTG) is used to detect β-galactosidase, which is diagnostic of total coliform bacteria, and a medium containing o-nitrophenol-β-D-galactopyranoside-4-methylumbelliferyl-β-D-glucuronide (MUG) is used to detect β-glucuronidase, which is diagnostic of *E. coli.* The defined substrate test requires only a day to complete. Gene probes and other molecular approaches may also be used to detect coliform bacteria and *E. coli.*

The drinking water standard does not absolutely exclude the possibility of ingesting enteropathogens (especially enteroviruses that are not related to *E. coli*) but seems to reduce this possibility to a statistically tolerable limit. Enteropathogens are likely to be present in much lower numbers than fecal coliforms, and a few infective bacteria are usually unable to overcome body defenses. A minimum infectious dose from several hundred to several thousand bacteria is necessary for various diseases to establish an actual infection. Drinking water supplies meeting the 1 per 100 mL coliform standard have never been demonstrated to be the source of waterborne bacterial infections.

niques. This method is often impractical and too expensive. Fortunately, disinfection by monochloramine is effective but produces much lower amounts of THMs. As an example, traditional chlorination of Ohio River water produced 160 μg THM/L, whereas chloramine treatment produced THM levels consistently below 20 μg/L. The practice of using chloramines as drinking water disinfectants, the least expensive way to reduce THM formation, is spreading rapidly.

Standards for tolerable limits of fecal contamination (Table 14-13) vary with the intended water use and are somewhat arbitrary, with large built-in safety margins. These standards are based on **coliform counts,** which are indirect indicators of fecal contamination. The most stringent standards are imposed on the municipal water supplies to be used by many people. Somewhat higher coliform counts are sometimes tolerated in private wells used by only one family because such wells would not become a source of a widespread epidemic. Maintenance of a high drinking water standard does not absolutely exclude the possibility of ingesting enteropathogens with the water but helps keep this possibility to a statistically tolerable minimum. The built-in safety factors are twofold: (1) enteropathogens are very likely to be present in much lower numbers than fecal coliforms and (2) a few infective bacteria are unlikely to be able to overcome natural body defenses. A minimum infectious dose of several hundred to several thousand bacteria is usually necessary for an actual infection to be established. Drinking water supplies meeting the 1 coliform cell/100 mL water coliform standard have never been demonstrated to be the source of a waterborne bacterial infection.

TABLE 14-13 United States Water Standards for Coliform Contamination

WATER USE	MAXIMUM PERMISSIBLE COLIFORM COUNT (NUMBER/100 mL)
Municipal drinking water	1
Waters used for shellfishing	70
Recreational waters	1,000

Fecal coliform counts are also used to establish the safety of water in shellfish harvesting and recreational areas. Because shellfish concentrate bacteria and other particles acquired through their filter-feeding activity and are sometimes eaten raw, they can become a source of infection by waterborne pathogens. Therefore there are relatively stringent standards for waters used for shellfishing. Clinical evidence for infection by enteropathogenic coliforms through recreational use of waters for bathing, wading, and swimming is unconvincing, but as a precaution, beaches are usually closed when fecal coliform counts exceed the recreational standard of 1,000/100 mL. Some regional standards require that disinfected sewage discharges not exceed this limit.

Water quality standards based on fecal coliform levels do not account for the possible transmission of viruses associated with fecal matter through municipal water supplies. There is ample evidence, of course, for destructive epidemics by enteroviruses caused by untreated drinking water in various underdeveloped countries. Enteroviruses are somewhat more resistant to disinfection by chlorine or ozone than bacteria and, occasionally, active virus particles are recovered from treated water that meets fecal coliform standards. Thus the possibility exists that water that meets accepted quality standards may still occasionally be a source of a viral infection. As many as 100 different viral types can be shed in human feces, but practical concern has been mainly with the viruses that cause infectious hepatitis, poliomyelitis, and viral gastroenteritis. Infectious hepatitis is sometimes spread by water supplies, although the more prevalent mode of infection is by the consumption of raw shellfish from fecally contaminated waters. Spread of polio infection through water supplies and/or recreational use of beaches has been suspected in many cases. The situation with regard to viral gastroenteritis is similar. At this point, we can only say that the possibility of an occasional sporadic viral infection through drinking water adequately treated by bacteriological standards cannot be excluded, but there is no hard evidence for any epidemics caused by such water.

BIODEGRADATION OF ENVIRONMENTAL POLLUTANTS

Human exploitation of fossil fuel reserves and the production of many novel synthetic compounds *(xenobiotics)* in the twentieth century have introduced into the environment many compounds that microorganisms normally do not encounter and thus are not prepared to biodegrade. Many of these compounds are toxic to living systems, and their presence in aquatic and terrestrial habitats often has serious ecological consequences, including major kills of indigenous biota. The disposal or accidental spillage of these compounds has created serious modern environmental pollution problems, particularly when microbial biodegradation activities fail to remove the pollutants quickly enough to prevent environmental damage. Sewage treatment and water purification systems are usually incapable of removing these substances if they enter municipal water supplies, where they pose a potential human health hazard.

The following are a few examples of compounds that have produced environmental problems where bioremediation has been successful or has the potential for providing an economical solution.

Alkyl Benzyl Sulfonates

Alkyl benzyl sulfonates (ABS) are the major components of anionic laundry detergents. Cleaning occurs when ABS molecules form a monolayer around lipophilic droplets or particles that make up most stains or dirt on clothing, forming an emulsion that can be rinsed out of the fabric with water. The ABS molecule is a surface active molecule, having a polar sulfonate and a nonpolar alkyl end. During laundering, ABS molecules orient their nonpolar ends toward lipophilic substances and their sulfonate ends toward the surrounding water. The alkyl portion of the ABS molecule may be linear or branched (FIG. 14-61). *Nonlinear ABS* is easier to manufacture and has slightly superior detergent properties than conventional soaps, but nonlinear ABS has proved to be resistant to biodegradation, causing extensive foaming of rivers receiving ABS-containing wastes. Some communities have banned the use of anionic detergents because of their persistence in groundwater supplies used as sources of potable water.

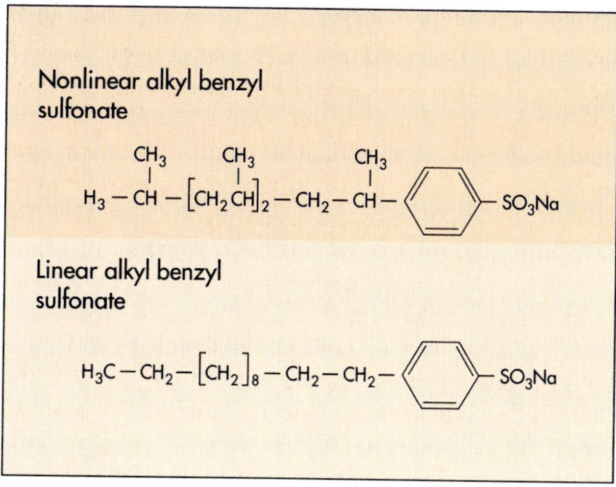

FIG. 14-61 Linear alkyl benzyl sulfates are easily biodegraded, whereas branched ABS molecules are relatively resistant to microbial attack.

It is the methyl branching of the alkyl chain that interferes with biodegradation because the tertiary carbon atoms block the normal β-oxidation sequence. By changing the design of this synthetic molecule to that of a linear ABS, the blockage can be removed. The detergent industry has switched to linear ABS, which is free from this blockage and consequently more easily biodegraded. The ABS story is particularly significant because it was one of the first instances in which a synthetic molecule was specifically redesigned to remove obstacles to biodegradation while preserving the useful characteristics of the compound.

Biodegradable polymers, for example, can be synthesized to replace or augment various plastics, including polyethylene, polystyrene, and polyvinylchloride, which are recalcitrant to microbial attack and therefore have been accumulating in the environment. By understanding the role of microbial biodegradation in maintaining environmental quality, human ingenuity has the potential to produce economically profitable synthetic compounds that are biodegradable and that can be safely disposed of in an environmentally safe manner.

Chlorinated Hydrocarbons

Even though distribution tends to dilute organo-chlorines to the low parts per billion (ppb) range, these chemicals still cause concern. They do so because of a phenomenon called **biological magnification** or **biomagnification,** which is the increase in concentration of a chemical in biological organisms compared to its concentration in the environment. Biomagnification occurs when an environmental pollutant is persistent (resistant to microbial degradation) and lipophilic (more soluble in hydrophobic substances than in water). Because of their lipophilic character, such compounds are partitioned from the surrounding water into the lipids of both prokaryotic and eukaryotic microorganisms; their concentrations in microbial cells may be one to three orders of magnitude higher than those in the surrounding environment (FIG. 14-62). When microorganisms are ingested by members of the next higher trophic level in the food web, the pollutant is neither degraded nor excreted to any significant extent; in fact, its concentration is increased by almost another order of magnitude. Thus such pollutants are concentrated as they are transferred to higher trophic levels. Consequently, their concentration is increased by almost an order of magnitude, so that the top trophic level organisms—such as birds of prey, carnivores, and large predatory fish—may carry a body burden of the environmental pollutant that exceeds the environmental concentration by a factor of 10^4 to 10^6.

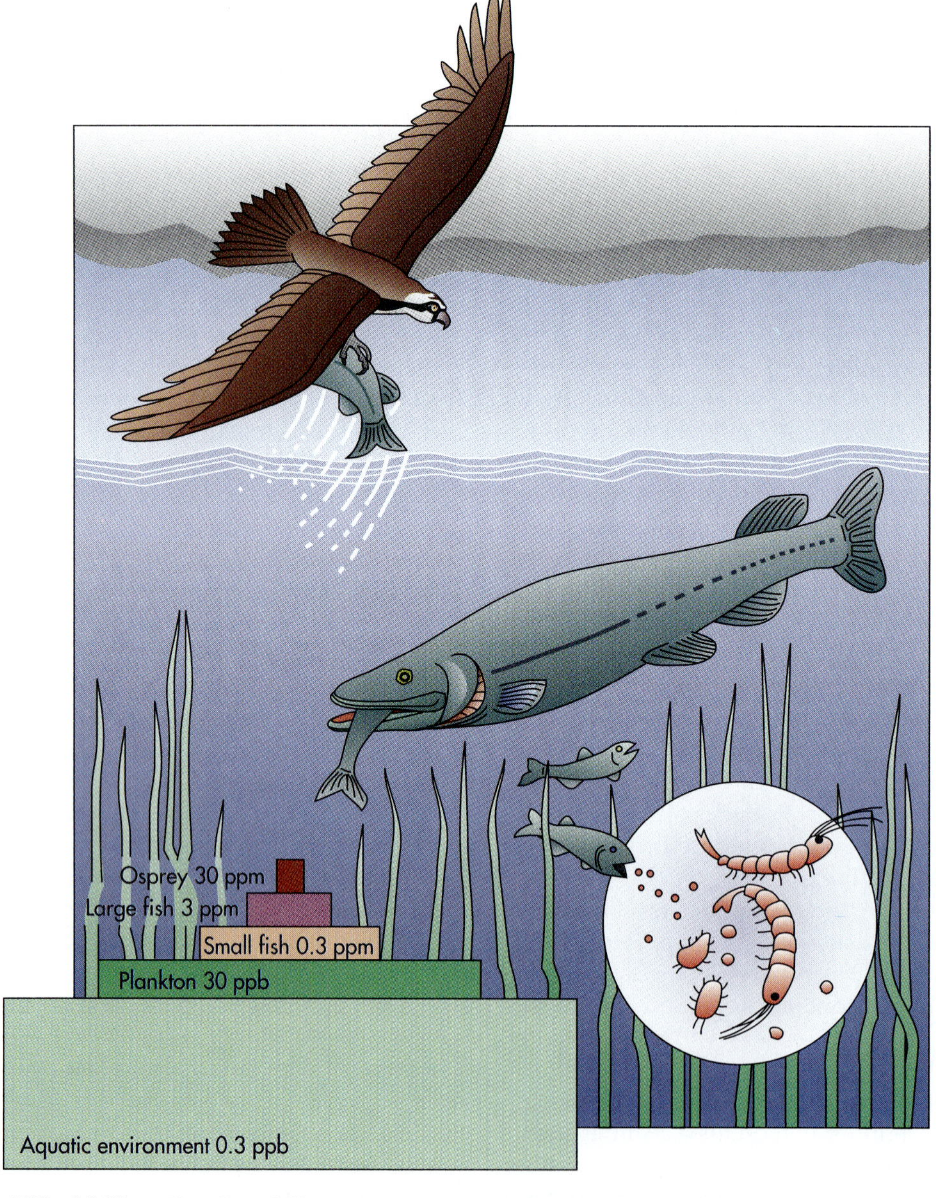

FIG. 14-62 When lipophilic compounds such as DDT are not degraded they accumulate and are passed through the food web, reaching higher concentrations in the higher levels of the food web. DDT concentrations reach concentrations in osprey 100,000 times higher than in the aquatic environment through such biomagnification.

TABLE 14-14 Environmental Persistence Times of Some Pesticides

COMMON NAME	CHEMICAL STRUCTURE	PERSISTENCE TIME
Aldrin	1,2,3,4,10,10-1,2,4a,4,8,8a,hexahydro-endo-1,4-exo-5,8-dimethanonaphthalene	>15 years
Chlordane	1,2,3,4,6,7,8,8-octachloro-2,3,3a,4,7,7a-hexahydro-4,7-methanoindene	>15 years
DDT	1,1,1-trichloro-2,2-*bis*(p-chlorophenyl)-ethane	>15 years
Dicamba	3,6-dichloro-*o*-anisic acid	4 years
2-(2,4-DP)	2-(2,4-dichlorophenyl)-1,1-dimethylurea	>15 years
Endrin	1,2,3,4,10,10-hexachloro-6,7-3poxy-1,4,4a,5,6,7,8,8a-octahydro-endo-1,4-endo-5,8-dimethanonaphthalene	>15 months
Fenac	2,3,6-trichlorophenylacetic acid	>18 months
Fluomenturon	*N'*-(3-trifluoromethylphenyl)-*N,N*-dimethylurea	195 days
Heptachlor	1,4,5,6,7,8,8-heptachloro-3a,4,7,7a-tetrahydro-4,7-endomethanoindene	>14 years
Lindane	1,2,3,4,5,6-hexachlorocyclohexane	15 years
Monuron	3-(*p*-chlorophenyl)-1,1-dimethylurea	3 years
Parathion	0,0-diethyl 0-*p*-nitrophenyl phosphorothioate	>16 years
PCP	pentachlorophenol	>5 years
Picloram	4-amino-3,5,6-trichloropicolinic acid	>5 years
Propazine	2-chloro-4,6-*bis*-(isopropylamino)-*s*-triazine	2-3 years
Simazine	2-chloro-4,6-*bis*-(ethylamino)-*s*-triazine	2 years
2,4,5-T	2,4,5-trichlorophenoxyacetic acid	>190 days
2,3,6-TBA	2,3,6-trichlorobenzoic acid	2 years
Toxaphene	chlorinated camphene	>14 years

A pesticide that is biomagnified may cause the death or serious debilitation of animals at the top of the food web. DDT and other chlorinated hydrocarbons were implicated in the death or reproductive failure of various birds of prey and other wildlife. Because human beings derive their food from various trophic levels, humans have less exposure to biomagnified pesticides than a top-level carnivore. Nevertheless, at the time of unrestricted DDT use, the average American, with no occupational exposure, carried a body burden of 4 to 6 ppm DDT and its derivatives. Although this amount was not considered dangerous, the trend toward increasing contamination of the higher trophic levels of the biosphere became sufficiently clear and led to the ban on the use of DDT in the United States and several other countries for all but emergency situations.

The majority of the currently used chlorinated organic pesticides are subject to extensive biodegradation. To maintain environmental quality, pesticide biodegradation normally should occur within a single growing season (Table 14-14). Synthetic pesticides show a bewildering variety of chemical structures but most contain relatively simple hydrocarbon skeletons with various substituents, such as halogens, amino, nitro, hydroxyl, and other functional groups. Aliphatic hydrocarbons are oxidized to fatty acids (FIG. 14-63). The fatty acids are then degraded via the β-oxidation

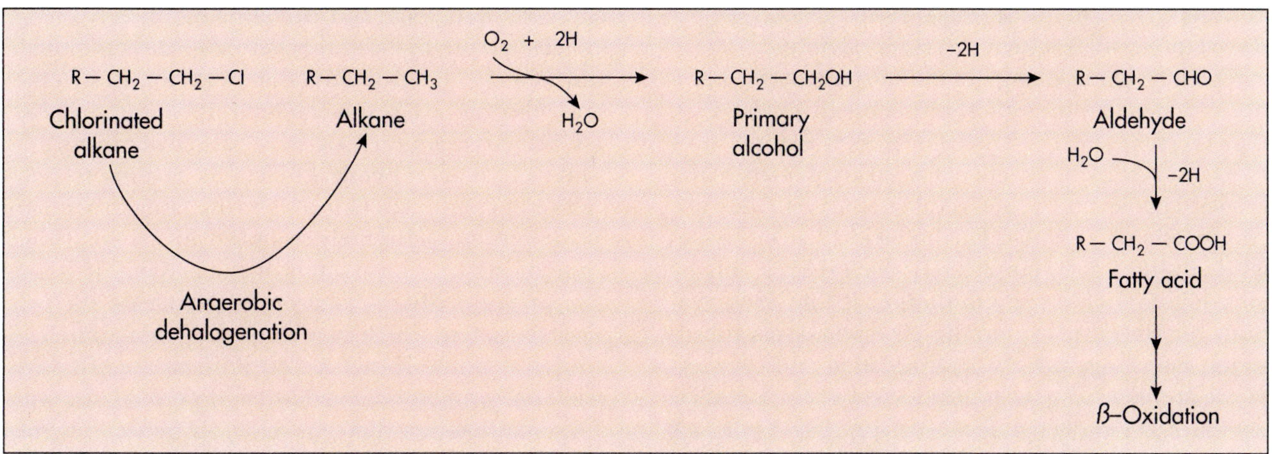

FIG. 14-63 Chlorinated hydrocarbons are dechlorinated by anaerobic dehalogenation. The hydrocarbon is then degraded to a fatty acid that is metabolized via β-oxidation.

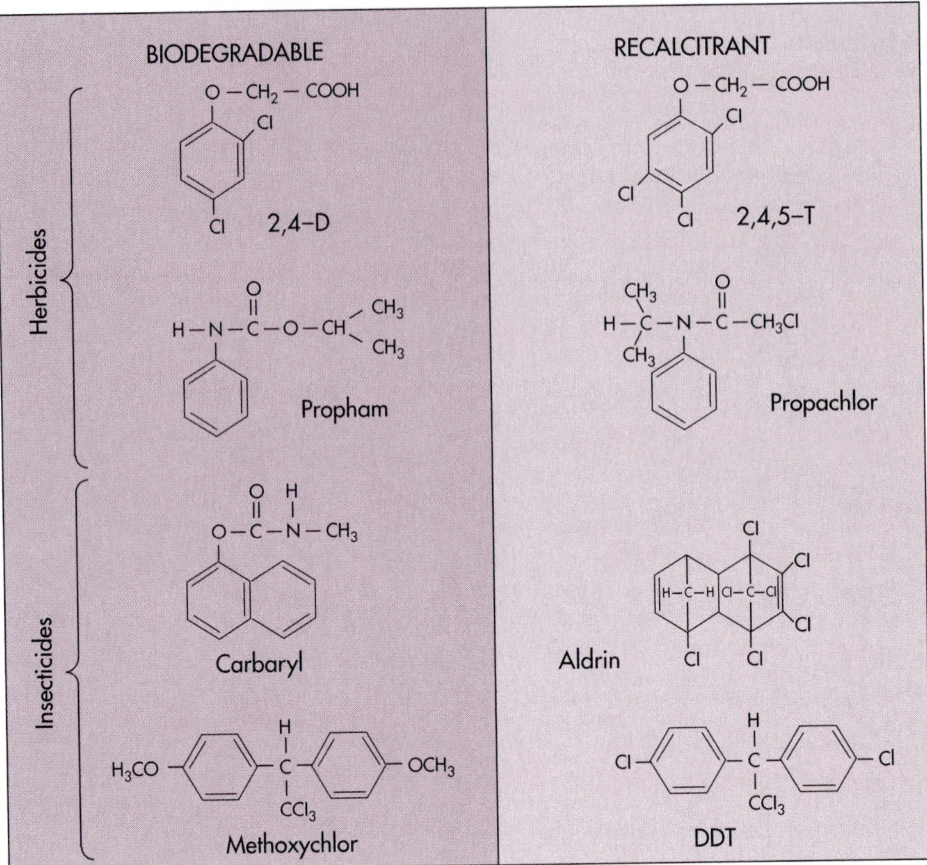

FIG. 14-64 The structure of a pesticide has a dramatic effect on its ability to be biodegraded. Some such as 2,4-D are readily degraded, whereas others such as 2,4,5-T are recalcitrant to microbial degradation.

sequence, and the resulting C_2 fragments are further metabolized via the tricarboxylic acid cycle. Aromatic ring structures are metabolized by dihydroxylation and ring cleavage mechanisms. Prior to these transformations, substituents on the aromatic ring may be completely or partially removed. Substituents uncommon in natural compounds, such as halogens, nitro, and sulfonate groups, if situated so as to impede hydroxylation, will frequently cause recalcitrance.

Often a simple change in the substituents of a pesticide may make the difference between *recalcitrance*, that is, complete resistance to biodegradation, and biodegradability. The chemical structures of some biodegradable and some recalcitrant pesticides are compared in FIG. 14-64. The herbicide 2,4-D is biodegraded within days, but 2,4,5-T, which differs only by an additional chlorine substitution in the *meta*-position, persists for many months. The additional substitution interferes with the hydroxylation and cleavage of the aromatic ring. Propham is cleaved by microbial amidases so rapidly that for some applications the addition of amidase inhibitors becomes necessary, but propachlor, which has a tertiary amine group, is not subject to attack by such amidases and persists considerably longer. Methoxychlor is less persistent than DDT because the *p*-methoxy groups are subject to dealkylation and the *p*-chloro substitution endows DDT with great biological and chemical stability.

In some cases, one portion of the pesticide molecule is susceptible to degradation and another is recalcitrant. Some acylanilide herbicides are cleaved by microbial amidases, and the aliphatic moiety of the molecule is mineralized (converted to carbon dioxide and water). The aromatic moiety, stabilized by chlorine substitutions, resists mineralization, but the reactive primary amine group may participate in various biochemical and chemical reactions, leading to polymers and complexes that render the fate of such herbicide residues extremely complex. FIG. 14-65 shows some of the transformations of the acylanilide herbicide propanil. Microbial acylamidases cleave the propionate moiety, which is subsequently mineralized. A portion of the released 3,4-dichloroaniline (DCA) is acted on by microbial oxidases and peroxidases, with the result that they dimerize and polymerize to highly stable residues, such as 3,3′,4,4′-tetrachloroazobenzene (TCAB), and related azo compounds. The reasons for such transformations are still somewhat ob-

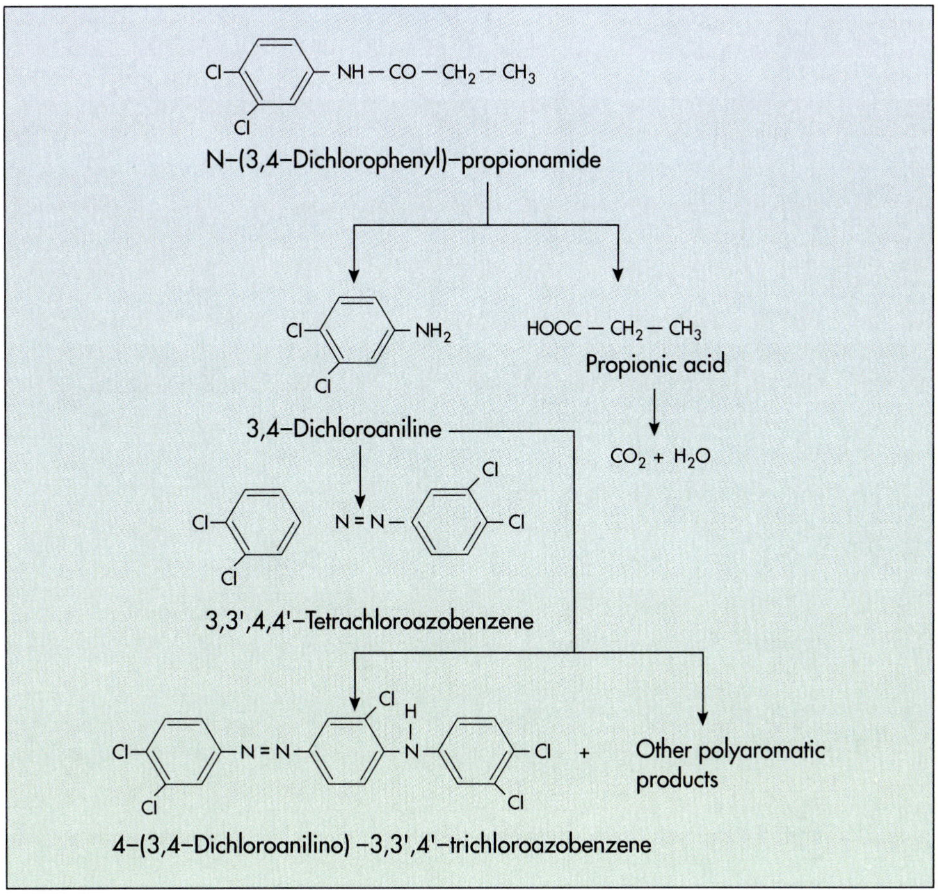

N-(3,4-Dichlorophenyl)-propionamide

3,4-Dichloroaniline

$HOOC-CH_2-CH_3$
Propionic acid

$CO_2 + H_2O$

3,3',4,4'-Tetrachloroazobenzene

4-(3,4-Dichloroanilino)-3,3',4'-trichloroazobenzene + Other polyaromatic products

FIG. 14-65 Degradation of the herbicide propanil produces polymeric products such as tetrachloroazobenzene, as well as small degradation products such as carbon dioxide, chloride, and water.

scure. They may occur by chance when a microbial enzyme that has another metabolic function recognizes and acts on the man-made residue. In some cases, the reaction seems to "detoxify" the residue (from the microorganism's point of view) but the overall persistence and environmental impact of the pesticide are increased by such synthetic transformations because some of the synthetic products may be toxic or carcinogenic to higher organisms.

Oil Pollutants

Over 10 million metric tons of oil pollutants enter the marine environment each year as a result of accidental spillages and disposal of oily wastes. Most comes from small spillages. Periodically, pictures of dead birds floundering in a sea of oil after a major oil spillage occur on the front page of the daily newspaper, evoking images of impending ecological doom. Actually, only a small portion of all marine oil pollutants comes from major oil spills; most of the oil pollution problems originate from minor spillages associated with routine operations.

Petroleum is a complex mixture composed primarily of aliphatic, alicyclic, and aromatic hydrocarbons (FIG. 14-66, p. 592). There are hundreds of individual compounds in every crude oil, the composition of each crude oil varying with its origin. As a result, the fate of petroleum pollutants in the environment is complex. The challenge for microorganisms to degrade all of the components of a petroleum mixture is immense. Nevertheless, microbial biodegradation of petroleum pollutants is a major process and is the reason that the oceans are not covered with oil today. As an example of the ability of microorganisms to degrade petroleum pollutants, measurements indicate that after the 1978 wreck of the supertanker *Amoco Cadiz* off the coast of France, microorganisms biodegraded 10 tons of oil per day in the affected area. Microbial biodegradation represented the major process responsible for the ecological recovery of the oiled coastal region.

The susceptibility of petroleum hydrocarbons to biodegradation is determined by the structure and molecular weight of the hydrocarbon molecule. *n*-Alkanes of intermediate chain length (C_{10}—C_{24}) are degraded most rapidly. Short chain alkanes (less than C_9) are toxic to many microorganisms but they generally evaporate rapidly from oil slicks. As alkane chain length increases, so does resistance to biodegradation. Branching, in general, reduces the rate of biodegra-

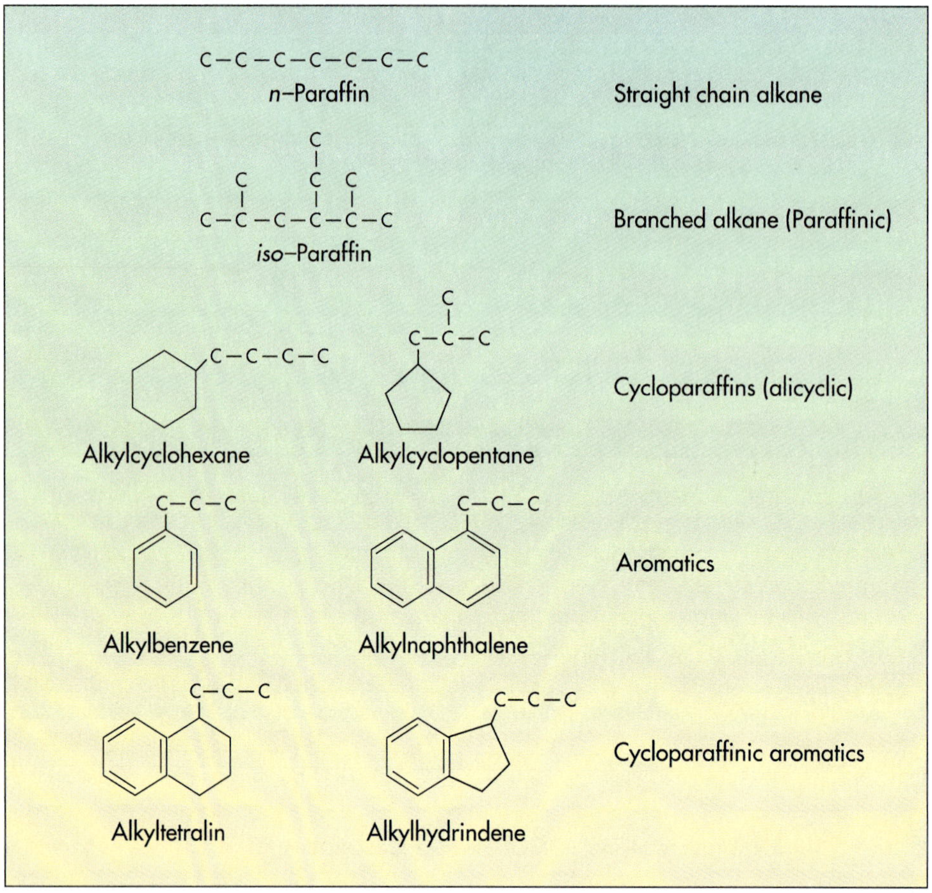

n–Paraffin — Straight chain alkane

iso–Paraffin — Branched alkane (Paraffinic)

Alkylcyclohexane, Alkylcyclopentane — Cycloparaffins (alicyclic)

Alkylbenzene, Alkylnaphthalene — Aromatics

Alkyltetralin, Alkylhydrindene — Cycloparaffinic aromatics

FIG. 14-66 Petroleum contains thousands of different compounds. Each class of hydrocarbon is subject to microbial degradation via different pathways. Many naturally occurring microorganisms are capable of hydrocarbon biodegradation.

dation because tertiary and quaternary carbon atoms interfere with degradation mechanisms or can block degradation altogether. Aromatic compounds, especially of the condensed polynuclear type, are degraded more slowly than alkanes. Alicyclic compounds are frequently unable to serve as the sole carbon sources for microbial growth unless they have a sufficiently long aliphatic side chain, but they can be degraded via cometabolism by two or more cooperating microbial strains with complementary metabolic capabilities.

Petroleum has always entered the biosphere by natural seepage but at rates much slower than those of the forced recovery of petroleum by drilling, which is now estimated to be about 2 billion metric tons per year. The production, transportation, refining, and ultimately the disposal of used petroleum and petroleum products result in inevitable environmental pollution. Because the bulk of this load is, of course, heavily centered on offshore production sites, major shipping routes, and refineries, its input frequently exceeds the self-purification capacity of the receiving waters. Petroleum pollutants in the environment are destructive to birds and marine life and, when driven ashore, cause heavy economic losses due to aesthetic damage to recreational beaches. Pictures of dead wildlife invariably spur public outrage after oil spills.

In addition to killing birds, fish, shellfish, and other invertebrates, oil pollution can have more subtle effects on marine life. Even at a low parts per billion (ppb) concentration, dissolved aromatic components of petroleum can disrupt the chemoreception of some marine organisms. Because feeding and mating responses largely depend on chemoreception, such disruption can lead to elimination of many species from a polluted area even when the pollutant concentration is far below the lethal level. Another disturbing problem is the possibility that condensed polynuclear components of petroleum, some of which are carcinogenic and relatively resistant to biodegradation, may move up marine food chains and taint fish or shellfish. Polynuclear aromatic compounds are among the components of crude oil most resistant to microbial biodegradation and become a major component of the tarry residues left in the sea when oil biodegradative activities slow.

The successful biodegradative removal of petroleum hydrocarbons from the sea depends on the enzymatic capacities of microorganisms and various abiotic factors. Microbial hydrocarbon biodegradation requires suitable growth temperatures and available supplies of fixed forms of nitrogen, phosphate, and molecular oxygen. In the oceans, temperature and nutrient concentrations often limit the rates of petroleum biodegradation. The low concentrations of nitrate and phosphate in seawater are particularly limiting to hydrocarbon biodegradation because petroleum is primarily composed of hydrogen and carbon. For example, after the IXTOC I well blowout, which in 1980 created the largest known oil pollution incident, little biodegradation of the oil–water emulsion (mousse) occurred in the surface waters of the Gulf of Mexico because of severe nutrient limitations.

Many different microorganisms can degrade petroleum. *Pseudomonas* and *Acinetobacter* species often are the dominant oil-degraders in contaminated ecosystems. Although many microorganisms can metabolize petroleum hydrocarbons, no single microorganism possesses the enzymatic capability to degrade all, or even most, of the compounds in a petroleum mixture. More rapid rates of degradation occur when there is a mixed microbial community than can be accomplished by a single species. Apparently the genetic information in more than one organism is required to produce the enzymes needed for extensive petroleum biodegradation.

Microorganisms engineered (created) by microbiologists may help cleanse the environment of pollutants made by humans. No genetically engineered microorganism has been put to the true test of expressing its potential activity in a natural ecosystem. Despite the ability to create superbugs, the usefulness of such organisms in pollution abatement depends on compatibility with the environment. In many cases, environmental factors, rather than the genetic capability of a microorganism, limit the biodegradation of pollutants. Thus, although genetically engineered organisms are a useful addition to the arsenal of antipollution measures, there is no panacea for solving human pollution problems.

CHAPTER REVIEW

STUDY QUESTIONS

1. What is a food web?
2. What are the trophic levels of a food web?
3. What functions do microorganisms play in the cycling of organic matter through food webs?
4. Discuss the role of microorganisms in the biogeochemical cycling of nitrogen; include the different processes and microbial populations involved in the global nitrogen cycle. Discuss the differences in nitrogen cycling in aquatic and soil habitats.
5. What are the problems associated with nitrification after fertilizer addition to agricultural soils?
6. How are microorganisms involved in the formation of acid mine drainage?
7. Why is neutralism favored at low population densities?
8. What is cometabolism?
9. Why can cometabolism be important in the degradation of complex organic pollutants?
10. How does commensalism differ from synergism?
11. What are the differences between predation and parasitism?
12. Discuss a mutualistic relationship between
    a. Two microbial populations
    b. Microorganisms and a plant
    c. Microorganisms and an animal population
13. Why is the nitrogen fixation symbiotic relationship so important to soil fertility?
14. How can genetic engineering extend the range of plants that can establish mutualistic relationships with nitrogen-fixing bacteria?
15. What are some of the symptoms of plant disease?
16. Discuss agricultural management practices for controlling plant diseases.
17. What is biomagnification?
18. What properties of a pesticide are important in determining its biomagnification through a food web?
19. Why must pesticides be biodegradable for their safe use in agriculture?
20. What is biological control?
21. How are insect viruses used in the control of plant diseases?
22. What are the differences between composting and sanitary landfill operations?
23. Discuss how sewage is treated. What is primary, secondary, and tertiary sewage treatment?
24. What is an indicator organism?
25. Why are coliform counts used to assess the safety of potable water supplies?
26. What is disinfection of a water supply? How is the disinfection of municipal water supplies normally achieved?
27. What is BOD?
28. Why is it important to reduce the BOD of liquid wastes before they are discharged into rivers or lakes?
29. Compare activated sludge and anaerobic digestors for treating sewage. What roles do each play in an integrated liquid waste removal system?
30. What factors influence the rates at which microorganisms degrade petroleum hydrocarbons?
31. How does the chemical structure of a compound influence its rate of biodegradation?
32. Compare the biodegradability of linear and nonlinear alkyl benzyl sulfonates.
33. How can we use the same waterways as sources of drinking water and for the disposal of liquid wastes?
34. How are the activities of microorganisms essential for the maintenance of environmental quality?

SITUATIONAL PROBLEMS

1. Establishing the Role of Antibiotics in Nature

We all recognize the importance of antibiotics in modern medicine. Antibiotics are substances produced by microorganisms that selectively inhibit or kill other microorganisms. Many antibiotics are produced by soil actinomycetes; some are produced by fungi and others by bacteria. A natural assumption is that soil microorganisms produce antibiotics in their natural habitat and use them to gain advantage over their competitors; that is, antibiotics are presumed to be involved in naturally occurring amensal relationships in the soil. However, demonstrating that antibiotics play an important role, or even a minor role, in nature has been difficult.

Antibiotics are secondary metabolites, that is, they are not involved in the primary microbial metabolism that is concerned with energy generation and biosynthesis of cell constituents. As secondary metabolites, antibiotics are produced only when conditions are very favorable for microbial metabolism. The substrate concentrations supplied in fermentors for the commercial production of antibiotics are rarely found in nature. The concentrations of readily usable substrates in soil typically are near starvation levels and are not sufficient to support the production of secondary metabolites. Free antibiotics are not detectable in soils, at least not with the analytical instruments currently in use.

Additionally, although antibiotic resistance plasmids are found in very high proportions of the microbial populations exposed to the antibiotics used in medicine—for example, in bacterial populations inhabiting hospitals, where large amounts of antibiotics are used—only small proportions of soil isolates are antibiotic resistant. Thus, whereas some soil microorganisms clearly have the potential for producing antibiotics, there is little indication that others need to respond to the antibiotics in their natural habitats to survive.

Suppose you were asked to determine whether antibiotics play a role in soil. What evidence would you consider necessary to resolve this issue, and how would you go about obtaining it? Try researching the approaches that have been used and the answers that have been proposed by searching *Biological Abstracts* to find relevant journal articles on this subject.

2. Safety Considerations for the Deliberate Release of Genetically Engineered Microorganisms in Agriculture

For many centuries, humans have selected genetically different varieties of plants and animals for various purposes. Horticulturists select and breed plant varieties for their aesthetic value. Agriculturists select and breed plants and animals for their nutritive value and resistance to disease. These practices are accepted as necessary for the production of the world's food supplies and proceed without a great deal of public attention or scrutiny. However, the development of recombinant DNA technology, with its enormous potential for genetically engineering novel plants, animals, and microorganisms, has raised many scientific and ethical questions.

In addition to the development of novel microorganisms intended to be grown in contained fermentors to produce pharmaceuticals and other industrially valuable substances, much of the effort and potential of genetic engineering lies in the area of agriculture. Specific areas with great potential include (1) the creation of new plants, particularly staple crops that, directly or in association with mutualistic microorganisms, can use atmospheric nitrogen instead of fertilizers; (2) herbicide-resistant plants, produced perhaps by the incorporation of novel rhizosphere microorganisms; (3) pesticide- and/or pest-resistant plants, again produced perhaps by the incorporation of novel rhizosphere microorganisms; (4) novel pesticide-degrading microorganisms that can eliminate toxic levels of pesticides from contaminated areas; and (5) frost-resistant plants covered with microorganisms that do not form ice-crystallization nuclei. The technical capability of producing these novel organisms is at hand and, in fact, several such organisms have already been created, and limited field testing has been carried out.

However, none of these novel organisms has ever been intentionally released into the environment on a commercial scale. The reason is concern over the ecological effects of introducing genetically engineered organisms, particularly microorganisms that cannot be readily seen and traced after their introduction into the environment. Many examples of the adverse effects of introducing new species, including the proliferation of imported rabbits in Australia and the progression of kudzu in the United States, make many environmentalists apprehensive about introducing newly created organisms. Yet we have had experience and success in introducing microorganisms to control pests, as exemplified by the use of *Bacillus thuringiensis* to control insect pests in North America and the introduction of Myxoma virus to control rabbits in Australia. Concern about the environmental risks versus the benefits of introducing organisms engineered for agricultural use has led to public and scientific debates, congressional legislation, and court rulings that make the outlook for the environmental use of any such organisms in agricultural practice uncertain. Editorials in local newspapers have called on the public and local representative bodies to become active participants in determining the future uses of engineered microorganisms for environmental and agricultural purposes in their communities.

If your community were to hold a public hearing on this issue, as many are doing, you could speak as an informed layman. Consult news media, books, and journal articles on the issues related to the safety of deliberate release of genetically engineered microorganisms into the environment to determine the stand that you will take. Then prepare a 10-minute statement expressing your informed opinion. Base your presentation on scientific principles. Be sure to include the critical issues as you see them and the ways in which uncertainties could be reduced so that the decision of the community representatives will be the correct one for your area.

SITUATIONAL PROBLEMS—cont'd

3. Designing the Waste Disposal System for a Self-Contained Residential Development

Suppose you are on the planning board for a resort retirement community in Arizona. The community is situated on a remote lake that is distant from oceans and rivers, and there are no other communities nearby. The lake is planned as a center of recreational activities and also as a major source of drinking water for the community. Additional water will come from an aquifer that is located 500 feet below the surface of the soil. The soil in this area is mostly sand. The community will have a golf course that requires water and nutrients. It is imperative that the disposal of wastes not destroy the aesthetic value of the lake or interfere with its use as a supply of potable water.

There are various options for the disposal of solid waste and sewage. The selection of a particular disposal method or methods depends in large part on the magnitude of the wastes generated, as well as the location and cost of the facility. In this case, the community is planned for a maximum of 400 residences. How would you go about selecting the appropriate waste disposal system? How would you monitor the effectiveness of the waste disposal system and foresee any deleterious effects on the multiple uses of the water supply? How could you economically link the disposal of wastes with the maintenance of the golf course? What could you do if, despite your best planning efforts, excessive waste entered the lake, leading to eutrophication and the potential introduction of enteric pathogens?

Suggested Supplementary Readings

Alexander M: 1981. Biodegradation of chemicals of environmental concern, *Science* 211:132-138.

Alexander M (ed.): 1984. *Biological Nitrogen Fixation: Ecology, Technology, and Physiology,* Plenum Press, New York.

Alexander M: 1985. Ecological constraints on nitrogen fixation in agricultural ecosystems, *Advances in Microbial Ecology* 8:163-183.

Allen MF: 1991. *The Ecology of Mycorrhizae,* Cambridge University Press, Cambridge, England.

Aronson AI, W Beckman, P Dunn: 1986. *Bacillus thuringiensis* and related insect pathogens, *Microbiological Reviews* 50:1-24.

Atlas RM (ed.): 1983. *Petroleum Microbiology,* Macmillan, New York.

Atlas RM and R Bartha: 1992. Hydrocarbon biodegradation and oil spill bioremediation, *Advances in Microbial Ecology* 12:(6)287-338.

Atlas RM and R Bartha: 1993. *Microbial Ecology: Fundamentals and Applications,* ed. 3, Benjamin/Cummings Publishing Co., Inc., Menlo Park, CA.

Austin B: 1988. *Marine Microbiology,* Cambridge University Press, New York.

Bird DF and J Kalff: 1986. Bacterial grazing by planktonic lake algae, *Science* 231:493-495.

Blackburn TH: 1983. The microbial nitrogen cycle. In *Microbial Geochemistry* (CWE Krumbein, ed.), pp. 63-89, Blackwell Scientific Publications, Oxford, England.

Blakeman JP (ed.): 1981. *Microbial Ecology of the Phylloplane,* Academic Press, London.

Brewin NJ: 1991. Development of the legume root nodule, *Annual Review of Cell Biology* 7: 191-226.

Brill W: 1980. Biochemical genetics of nitrogen fixation, *Microbiological Reviews* 44:449-467.

Brill W: 1981. Biological nitrogen fixation, *Scientific American* 245(3):68-81.

Brill W: 1981. Agricultural microbiology, *Scientific American* 245(3):198-215.

Burges HD (ed.): 1981. *Microbial Control of Pests and Plant Diseases, 1970-1980,* Academic Press, New York.

Burns RG and JH Slater (eds.): 1982. *Experimental Microbial Ecology,* Blackwell Scientific Publications, Oxford, England.

Campbell R: 1985. *Plant Microbiology,* Edward Arnold, London.

Cavanaugh CM, PR Levering, JS Maki, R Mitchell, ME Lidstrom: 1987. Symbiosis of methylotropic bacteria and deep-sea mussels, *Nature* 325:346-48.

Chakrabarty AM (ed.): 1982. *Biodegradation and Detoxification of Environmental Pollutants,* CRC Press, Inc., Boca Raton, FL.

Characklis WG and PA Wildered (eds.): 1989. *Structure and Function of Biofilms,* John Wiley & Sons, New York.

Chet I (ed.): 1993. *Biotechnology in Plant Disease Control,* Wiley-Liss, Inc., New York.

Childress JJ, H Felbeck, and GN Somero: 1987. Symbiosis in the deep sea, *Scientific American* 256(5):115-120.

Codd GA (ed.): 1984. *Aspects of Microbial Metabolism and Ecology,* Academic Press, London.

Cohen Y and E Rosenberg: 1989. *Microbial Mats. Physiological Ecology of Benthic Microbial Communities,* American Society for Microbiology, Washington, D.C.

Costerton JW, K-J Cheng, GC Geesey, TI Ladd, JC Nickel, M Dasgupta, TJ Marrie: 1987. Bacterial biofilms in nature and disease, *Annual Review of Microbiology* 41:435-464.

Dagley S: 1987. Lessons from biodegradation, *Annual Review of Microbiology* 41:1-24.

Dart RK and RJ Stretton: 1980. *Microbiological Aspects of Pollution Control,* Elsevier Publishing Co., Amsterdam.

Deacon JW: 1983. *Microbiological Control of Plant Pests and Disease* (Aspects of Microbiology No. 7), American Society for Microbiology, Washington, D.C.

Dickinson CH and JA Lucas: 1982. *Plant Pathology and Plant Pathogens,* Blackwell Scientific Publications, Oxford, England.

Ducklow HW and CA Carlson: 1992. Oceanic bacterial production, *Advances in Microbial Ecology* 12:(3)113-182.

Edwards C: 1990. *Microbiology of Extreme Environments,* McGraw Hill, New York.

Ehrlich HL: 1981. *Geomicrobiology,* Marcel Dekker, New York.

Evans WC and G Fuchs: 1988. Anaerobic degradation of aromatic compounds, *Annual Review of Microbiology* 42:289-317.

Fenchel T: 1982. Ecology of heterotrophic microflagellates: Adaptations to heterogeneous environments, *Marine Ecology Progress Series* 9:25-33.

Ferry BW: 1982. Lichens. In *Experimental Microbial Ecology* (RG Burns and JH Slater, eds.), pp. 291-319, Blackwell Scientific Publications, Oxford, England.

Finstein MS, FC Miller, PF Strom, ST MacGregor, KM Psarianos: 1983. Composting ecosystem management for waste treatment, *Biological Technology* 1:347-353.

Fletcher M and TRG Gray. (eds.): 1987. *Ecology of Microbial Communities,* 41st Symposium of the Society for General Microbiology, Cambridge University Press, New York.

Focht DD: 1982. Denitrification. In *Experimental Microbial Ecology* (RG Burns and JH Slater, eds.), pp. 194-211, Blackwell Scientific Publications, Oxford, England.

Friedmann I (ed.): 1993. *Antarctic Microbiology,* Wiley-Liss, Inc., New York.

Gaudy A and E Gaudy: 1980. *Microbiology for Environment Science Engineers,* McGraw-Hill Book Co., New York.

Gooday GW: 1990. The ecology of chitin degradation, *Advances in Microbial Ecology* 11:(10)387-430.

Greenberg A (ed.): 1992. *Standard Methods for the Examination of Water and Wastewater,* American Public Health Association, Washington, D.C.

Halvorson HO, D Pramer, M Rogul (eds.): 1985. *Engineered Organisms in the Environment: Scientific Issues,* American Society for Microbiology, Washington, D.C.

Harris K and K Maramorosch: 1981. *Pathogens, Vectors, and Plant Diseases,* Academic Press, New York.

Jannasch HW and MJ Mottl: 1985. Geomicrobiology of deep-sea hydrothermal vents, *Science* 229:717-725.

Jones JG: 1986. Iron transformations by freshwater bacteria, *Advances in Microbial Ecology* 9:149-185.

Jorgensen BB: 1980. Mineralization and the bacterial cycling of carbon, nitrogen, and sulphur in marine sediments. In *Contemporary Microbial Ecology* (DC Ellwood, JN Hedger, MJ Latham, JM Lynch, JH Slater, eds.), pp. 239-252, Academic Press, London.

Kelly DP and NA Smith: 1990. Organic sulfur compounds in the environment: Biogeochemistry, microbiology, and ecological aspects, *Advances in Microbial Ecology* 11:(9)345-386.

Krulwich TA and AA Guffanti: 1989. Alkalophilic bacteria. *Annual Review of Microbiology* 43:435-464.

Leisinger T et al. (eds.): 1982. *Microbial Degradation of Xenobiotics and Recalcitrant Compounds,* Academic Press, New York.

Levin MA, RJ Seidler, M Rogul: 1991. *Microbial Ecology: Principles, Methods and Applications,* McGraw-Hill, New York.

Lindow SE: 1983. The role of bacterial ice nucleation in frost injury to plants, *Annual Review of Phytopathology* 21:363-384.

Long S: 1989. *Rhizobium* genetics, *Annual Review of Genetics* 23:483-506.

Ljungdahl LG and KE Ericsson: 1985. Ecology of microbial cellulose degradation, *Advances in Microbial Ecology* 8:237-299.

Lynch JM and JE Hobbie: 1988. *Micro-organisms in Action: Concepts and Applications in Microbial Ecology,* Blackwell Scientific, Boston.

Lynch JM: 1982. The rhizosphere. In *Experimental Microbial Ecology* (RG Burns and JH Slater, eds.), pp. 395-411, Blackwell Scientific Publications, Oxford, England.

Lynch JM: 1982. *Soil Biotechnology: Microbiological Factors in Crop Productivity,* Blackwell Scientific Publications, Oxford, England.

Maramorosch K: 1991. *Biotechnology for Biological Control of Pests and Vectors,* CRC Press, Boca Raton, FL.

Mitchell R (ed.): 1992. *Environmental Microbiology,* John Wiley, NY.

Norris JR and R Grigorova (eds): 1990. *Methods in Microbiology: vol. 22—Techniques in Microbial Ecology,* Academic Press, New York.

Olson BH and LA Nagy: 1984. Microbiology of potable water, *Advances in Applied Microbiology* 30:73-132.

Paerl HW: 1990. Physiological ecology and regulation of N_2 fixation in natural waters, *Advances in Microbial Ecology* 11(8):305-344.

Postgate J: 1982. *Fundamentals of Nitrogen Fixation,* Cambridge University Press, New York.

Postgate J: 1984. *The Sulphate-Reducing Bacteria,* Cambridge University Press, New York.

Rheinheimer G: 1991. *Aquatic Microbiology,* ed 4, John Wiley and Sons, New York.

Sayler GS, R Fox, JW Blackburn: 1991. *Environmental Biotechnology for Waste Treatment,* Plenum Press, New York.

Sayler GS and AC Layton: 1990. Environmental application of nucleic acid hybridization, *Annual Review of Microbiology* 44: 625-648.

Stacey G, RH Burris, HJ Evans: 1991. *Biological Nitrogen Fixation,* Chapman and Hall, New York.

Steffan RJ and RM Atlas: 1991. Polymerase chain reaction: Applications in environmental microbiology, *Annual Review of Microbiology* 45:137-61.

Toerien DF, A Gerber, LH Lotter, TE Cloete: 1990. Enhanced biological phosphorus removal in activated sludge systems, *Advances in Microbial Ecology* 11:(5)173-230.

Tunnicliffe V: 1992. Hydrothermal-vent communities of the deep sea, *American Scientist* 80:336-49.

Veal DA, HW Stokes, G Daggard: 1992. Genetic exchange in natural microbial communities, *Advances in Microbial Ecology* 12:(8)383-430.

Verma DPS: 1991. *Molecular Signals in Plant-Microbe Communications,* CRC Press, Inc., Boca Raton, FL.

Ward CH, W Giger, PL McCarty (eds.): 1985. *Groundwater Quality,* John Wiley and Sons, New York.

Whipps JM and JM Lynch: 1986. The influence of the rhizosphere on crop productivity, *Advances in Microbial Ecology* 9:187-244.

Whitely HR and HE Schnepf: 1986. The molecular biology of parasporal crystal body formation in *Bacillus thuringiensis, Annual Review of Microbiology* 40:549-576.

Whitman WB and JE Rogers: 1991. *Microbial Production of Greenhouse Gases: Methane, Nitrogen Oxides, and Halomethanes,* American Society for Microbiology, Washington, D.C.

Wolf RL, NR Ward, BH Olson: 1984. Inorganic chloramines as drinking water disinfectants: A review, *Journal of the American Water Works Association* 76:74-88.

Wynn-Williams DD: 1990. Ecological aspects of Antarctic microbiology, *Advances in Microbial Ecology* 11:(3)71-146.

Zambryski P: 1988. Basic processes underlying *Agrobacterium*-mediated DNA transfer to plant cells, *Annual Review of Genetics* 22:1-30.

Zeikus JG: 1981. Lignin metabolism and the carbon cycle: Polymer biosynthesis, biodegradation and environmental recalcitrance, *Advances in Microbial Ecology* 5:211-243.

CHAPTER 15

Biotechnology

Biotechnology applies practical and economical uses of microorganisms. It encompasses the traditional uses of microorganisms for the production of foods, pharmaceuticals, and other products of economic value, and the treatment of wastes. It also includes the modern uses of recombinant DNA technology for the creation of genetically engineered microorganisms that can be used to carry out novel metabolism. It further involves improving technologies for the more efficient production of specific compounds.

Chapter Outline

15.1 BIOTECHNOLOGY AND THE FERMENTATION INDUSTRY

Biotechnology forms the basis for the fermentation industry in which the enzymatic activities of microorganisms are used to produce substances of commercial value. The term *fermentation* as used in biotechnology describes any chemical transformation of organic compounds carried out by using microorganisms and their enzymes. Raw materials (substrates), microorganisms (specific strains or microbial enzymes), and a controlled favorable environment (created in a fermentor) are brought together to produce the desired substance. The essence of a biotechnological process in the fermentation industry is to combine the right organism, an inexpensive substrate, and the proper environment to produce high yields of a desired product (FIG. 15-1).

Critical activities of industrial microbiologists include the search for microorganisms that carry out biotransformations of commercial importance, with emphasis on finding or creating specific strains of microorganisms that will yield sufficient quantities of the desired product to permit commercial production on an economically favorable basis; emphasis is also given to the design of the optimal production process. Production process technology includes defining the substrate mixture—containing the least expensive components—that will produce the highest yield of the desired product. Often the presence or absence of even trace amounts of a component will vastly alter the yield of the desired product. Fermentors are designed to optimize the environmental conditions to achieve maximal product yields. Recovery methods are developed that achieve separation of the desired product from microbial cells, residual substrate, and other metabolic products in the most economical manner.

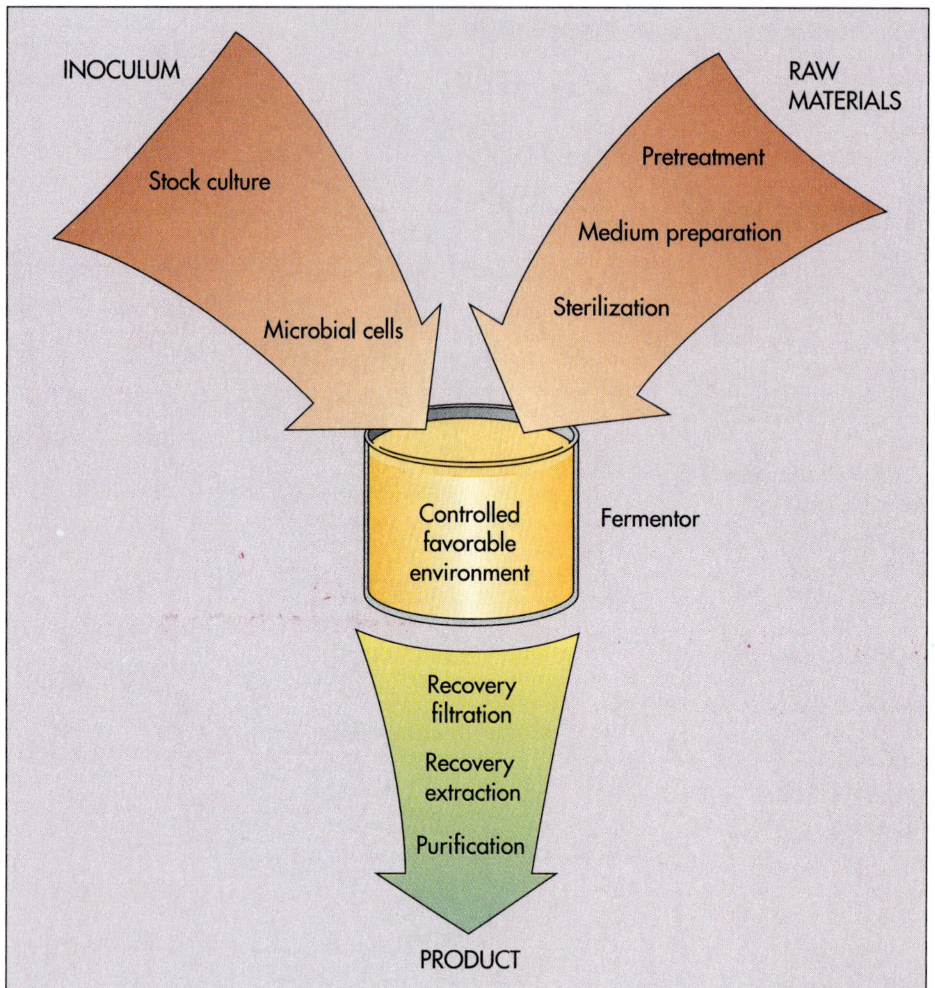

FIG. 15-1 In a fermentation process, an inoculum and a suitable growth medium are prepared and added to a fermentor. Conditions of oxygen concentration, pH, and so forth are controlled to favor growth of the microorganism and its production of the fermentation product. The fermentation product is then recovered and purified.

SCREENING MICROORGANISMS

Selection of microorganisms for use in the fermentation industry begins with **screening** to find the right microorganism. Of the many species of microorganisms, relatively few possess the genetic information needed to produce economically useful products (Table 15-1). The screening procedures employed in industry are designed to separate microorganisms that are potentially valuable in producing a commercially useful product. Large-scale industrial screening procedures incorporate assays that permit identification of these microorganisms.

The search for antibiotics in the pharmaceutical industry presents a good example of how screening procedures are employed to select microorganisms for industrial applications. The discovery of new antibiotics results from laborious searches. Samples from many sources, including soils from around the world, are examined as potential sources of antibiotic-producing microorganisms; countless strains of microbial isolates are tested by pharmaceutical laboratories. One of the best penicillin-producing strains of *Penicillium* was isolated from a fruit purchased at a roadside fruit stand; several antibiotic-producing actinomycetes were isolated from a manure-enriched pasture. Identification of compounds with antimicrobial activity is an essential step in the screening process. Of the numerous investigations, few studies yield evidence of promising new compounds of potential clinical importance.

A useful antibiotic-producing strain must produce metabolites that inhibit the growth or reproduction of pathogens. This essential property can be assayed by using test strains and examining whether the isolate being screened produces substances that inhibit the growth of these test organisms. If a suspension of the test organism is applied to the surface of an agar plate, the zone of inhibition around a colony may indicate that the organisms in that colony are producing an an-

TABLE 15-1 Some Microbial Species Used for Producing Commercial Products

INDUSTRIAL CHEMICALS	
Saccharomyces cerevisiae	Ethanol (from glucose)
Kluyveromyces fragilis	Ethanol (from lactose)
Clostridium acetobutylicum	Acetone and butanol
Aspergillus niger	Citric acid
AMINO ACIDS AND FLAVOR-ENHANCING NUCLEOTIDES	
Corynebacterium glutamicum	L-Lysine
Corynebacterium glutamicum	5′-inosinic acid and 5′-guanylic acid
Corynebacterium glutamicum	MSG
VITAMINS	
Ashbya gossypii	Riboflavin
Eremothecium ashbyi	Riboflavin
Pseudomonas denitrificans	Vitamin B_{12}
Propionibacterium shermanii	Vitamin B_{12}
ENZYMES	
Aspergillus oryzae	Amylases
Aspergillus niger	Glucamylase
Trichoderma reesii	Cellulase
Saccharomyces cerevisiae	Invertase
Kluyveromyces fragilis	Lactase
Saccharomycopsis lipolytica	Lipase
Aspergillus	Pectinases and proteases
Bacillus	Proteases
Mucor pussilus	Microbial rennet
Mucor meihei	Microbial rennet
POLYSACCHARIDES	
Leuconostoc mesenteroides	Dextran
Xanthomonas campestris	Xanthan gum
PHARMACEUTICALS	
Penicillium chrysogenum	Penicillins
Cephalosporium acremonium	Cephalosporins
Streptomyces species	Amphotericin B, kanamycins, neomycins, streptomycin, tetracyclines and others
Bacillus brevis	Gramicidin S
Bacillus licheniformis	Bacitracin
Bacillus polymyxa	Polymyxin B
Rhozopus nigricans	Steroid transformation
Arthrobacter simplex	Steroid transformation
Mycobacterium	Steroid transformation
Escherichia coli (via recombinant DNA technology)	Insulin, human growth hormone, somatostatin, interferon

tibiotic. Alternatively, the crude filtrate of a broth-grown microbial culture can be added to a culture of a test organism to determine whether substances with antimicrobial activity are produced by the organism being screened.

A positive result in such a primary screening procedure does not ensure the discovery of an industrially useful antibiotic-producing strain. It simply identifies strains of microorganisms that have the potential for further development. Secondary screening procedures are then used to determine whether the organism is indeed producing a substance of industrial interest that merits further investigation and development. These procedures may include (1) qualitative assays, to identify the nature of the substance being produced and determine whether it is a new compound not previously considered for industrial production, and (2) quantitative assays, to determine how much of the substance is being produced.

In screening for antibiotic producers, the crude filtrate from a broth culture may be separated chromatographically and the antimicrobial activities of the separated components determined. In some cases, paper chromatography is used to separate compounds for testing. In other cases, high-pressure liquid chromatography (HPLC) is employed. The individual active components can then be isolated and used for further screening against additional test organisms to determine the microbial inhibition spectrum. This additional screening helps determine whether the substance has a broad or narrow range of activity and if it is particularly effective against specific pathogens. If an organism is found to possess the potential for creating a useful new antibiotic, many additional tests are required to determine whether sufficient quantities of the substance can be produced to permit industrial production.

The screening program should identify the optimal incubation conditions for maximal economic yield of the product. Usually toxicity testing also must be performed to determine whether the product can selectively inhibit pathogens without causing severe side effects that would preclude its therapeutic use. The secondary screening procedure thus yields a great deal of information about potentially useful microorganisms, allowing emphasis on the development of processes employing microorganisms likely to produce economically valuable substances.

Both naturally occurring microorganisms and genetic variants are screened for the potential for producing industrially important substances. The classic approach used to find new antibiotic-producing strains has been to screen large numbers of isolates from soil samples for microorganisms that naturally produce antimicrobial substances. Additionally, mutations can be induced by exposure to radiation or mutagenic chemicals to increase genetic variability within the populations showing some indication for success, with the hope of isolating a unique microbial strain capable of producing a novel metabolite with the desired properties or a strain that produces large quantities of a valuable substance. Furthermore, once a microorganism is identified as possessing the genetic

BOX 15-1

GENETIC ENGINEERING

Genetic engineering has introduced many new possibilities for employing microorganisms to produce economically important substances. Whereas the mutation and selection approach is hit or miss, the use of recombinant DNA technology permits the purposeful manipulation of genetic information to engineer a microorganism that can produce high yields of a variety of products. Until the recent breakthroughs in the techniques of genetic engineering, a bacterium could produce only substances coded for in its bacterial genome. It is now possible to engineer bacterial strains that produce plant and animal gene products (see FIG.). Thus bacteria now exist that produce human interferon, insulin, and other hormones.

The use of genetic engineering has great social consequences. The ability to modify the genetic composition of all organisms—from microorganisms to humans—using genetic engineering raises serious ethical questions that society must now face. The development of microorganisms producing high yields of such substances promises to revolutionize the economics of the pharmaceutical industry. The seemingly unlimited potential for creating microorganisms capable of producing lucrative products has spawned a major new growth industry:

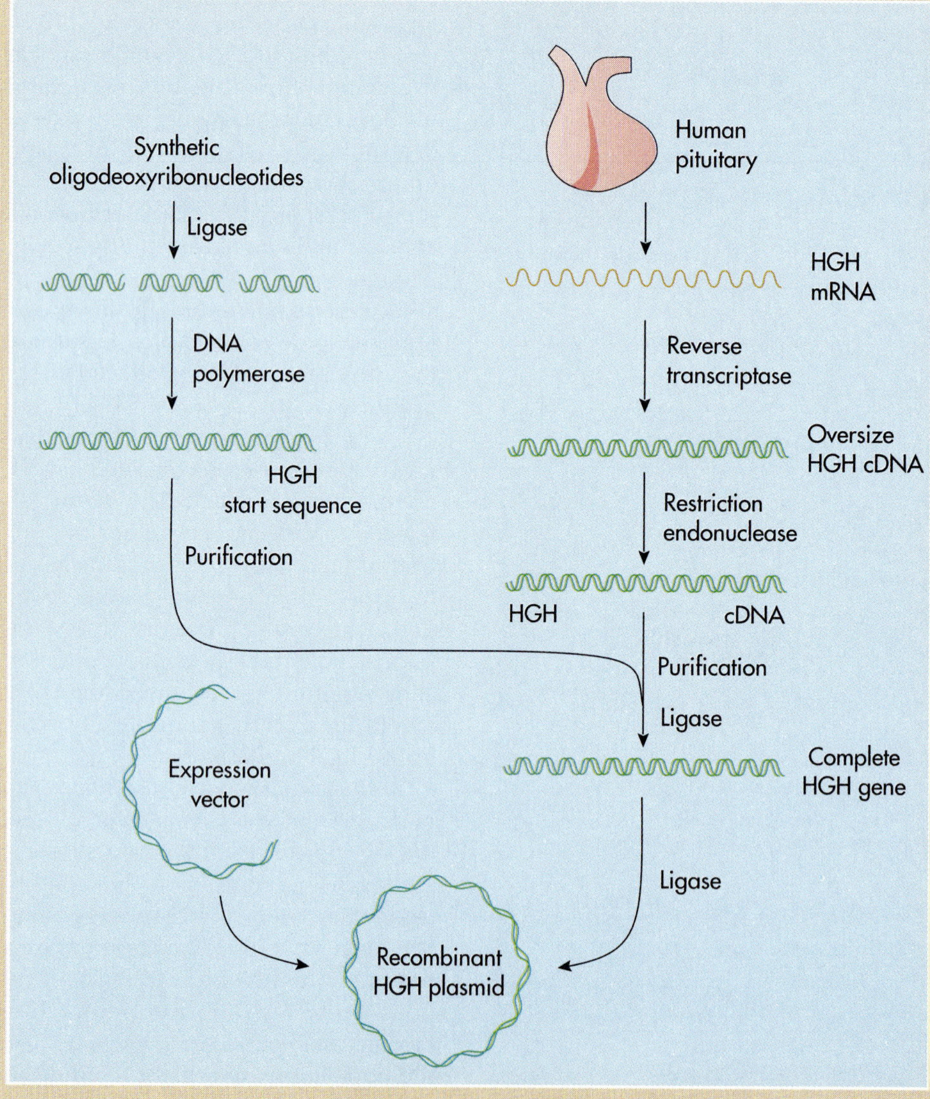

Genetic engineering was used to create a bacterial strain that produces human growth hormone (HGH).

biotechnology. The ruling of the U.S. Supreme Court that genetically engineered microorganisms can be patented also adds economic incentive for industrial applications of recombinant DNA technology.

It is critical to consider genetic regulatory mechanisms in both the mutation-screening and genetic engineering approaches to the development of microbial strains of industrial importance. The development of such strains often involves the need to overcome natural regulatory mechanisms that limit the amount of the gene product produced. In nature it is advantageous for a microorganism to produce only the needed amounts of a required substance because doing so gives that organism a competitive edge for survival; overproduction is wasteful and makes an organism less competitive. As a result, various genetic regulatory mechanisms have evolved to conserve available carbon and energy resources and to avoid production of unnecessary amounts of any product.

In the fermentation industry the valuable microbial strains produce excessively high amounts of the desired product. Many mutant or genetically engineered strains used for industrial production no longer possess the genetic regulatory mechanisms for conserving their resources and producing limited amounts of a substance. Whereas such organisms would not do well in natural environments, where competition for available resources dictates which organisms survive, they do quite well in fermentors, where competition is eliminated and optimal conditions are created to favor the growth of that microbial strain in pure culture.

information needed to produce a potentially useful substance, it is often necessary to carry out successive stages of mutation before isolating a strain of that organism that can be employed for commercial production.

For example, the *Penicillium* species observed by Alexander Fleming to inhibit the growth of *Staphylococcus* had obvious potential for commercial development but did not produce sufficient quantities of penicillin to permit industrial production. Extensive screening of soil samples from around the world led to the isolation of a potentially useful strain from soil collected in Peoria, Illinois. Multiple successive mutations, though, were necessary to develop a strain of *Penicillium chrysogenum* capable of producing nearly 100 times the concentration of penicillin produced by the original strain, making production of penicillin commercially feasible (FIG. 15-2). The mutation and screening approach has been important in the successful development of various strains of microorganisms currently used in the fermentation industry.

Because industry relies on specific microbial strains, it is important to maintain those specific genetic variants and protect against further spontaneous mutations that could alter the economics of the fermentation process. Industrial strains of microorganisms are therefore maintained in culture collections, generally in a dormant state where they are protected against mutational processes. The maintenance of these stock cultures is an essential part of industrial microbiology. Checks are periodically run on production strains to ensure that they retain their essential genetic capabilities. If undesirable alterations in the production strain are detected, new cultures are initiated from those maintained in the stock culture collection.

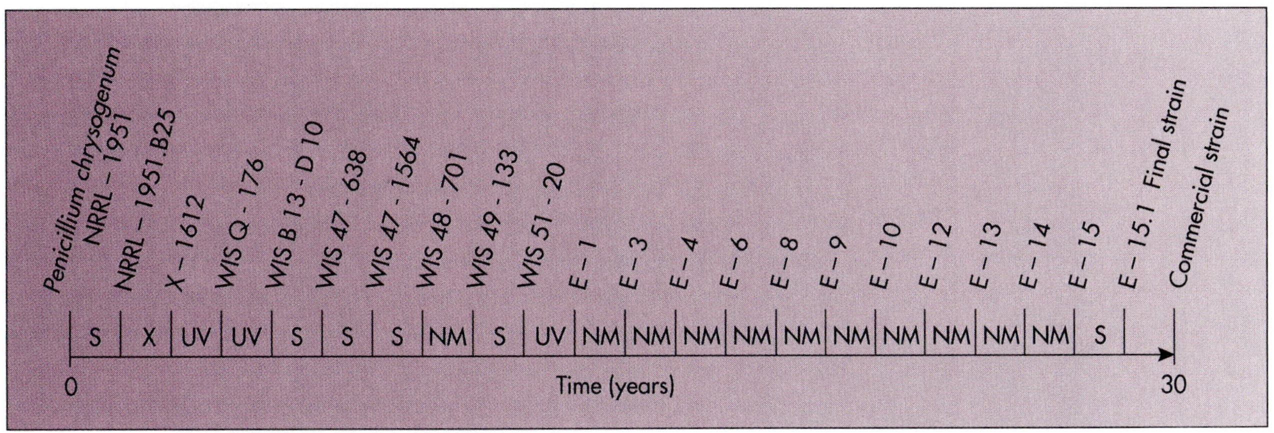

FIG. 15-2 Strains used for producing commercial quantities of fermentation products overexpress the formation of the products. Often, extensive genetic mutations are needed to achieve such overexpression, as in the case of pencillin production where numerous mutations, achieved spontaneously (S) and by UV light, X-radiation, and chemical mutagen (nitrogen mustard [NM]) exposure, were required to form the final strain that produces enough penicillin to permit commercial production.

Production Processes

The fermentation process optimizes conditions for the desired microbial activity that yields maximal amounts of product with the highest economic profit. It achieves a balance between production costs and the price of the product because excessive costs may render commercial production economically infeasible.

The development of a commercial process occurs in a stepwise fashion, initially using small flasks, then small fermentors (under 10 gallons), intermediate-size fermentors (up to several hundred gallons), and finally, large-scale fermentors (thousands of gallons) (FIG. 15-3). *Scale-up,* going from small laboratory flasks to large production fermentors, is a complex stepwise process.

The small flasks represent "lab scale" experiments in which it is easy to test many parameters. Fermentors are larger chambers in which microorganisms are grown. They are sometimes called bioreactors. There are numerous designs for fermentors that permit additions of materials, sampling, and control of environmental parameters. Oxygen concentration control is an especially important parameter in the design of a large volume fermentor. The small and intermediate-size fermentor studies are usually done at a *pilot plant.* Here only a few parameters can be manipulated because of the cost and the limited numbers of fermentors. Large scale fermentors are used for commercial production. At the production stage the process should already have been perfected so that the outcome of the fermentation is reliable. The fermentation process is monitored during production to ensure that the course of the fermentation is proper. Adjustments can be made to certain parameters, such as pH and oxygen concentration, to maintain the desired course of the fermentation and to achieve the normal yield of the fermentation product. Often, modern fermentors employ computers for monitoring and automated parameter adjustments.

At each stage of developing a fermentation process, conditions are adjusted to produce maximal yields at minimal costs. The organic and inorganic composition of the medium, as well as the pH, temperature, oxygen concentration, and agitation, are the main factors that are varied to maximize the efficiency of the production process. Even in a batch process, conditions are often varied during fermentation to achieve the maximal product yield, and conditions are monitored during the fermentation process to ensure that critical parameters remain within allowable limits. It is necessary that the reaction chambers and substrate solutions be sterilized before the addition of the microbial strain. This is particularly important because the strains of microorganisms used in industrial fermentations are selected for their ability to produce the desired product in high yield, rather than for their ability to compete with other microorganisms. Infections of fermentation reactions with microbial contaminants can easily lead to a competitive displacement of the strain being employed to produce the product, with obvious deleterious results.

Fermentation Medium

The composition of the fermentation medium must include the nutrients essential to support the growth

FIG. 15-3 The fermentors used for commercial production of antibiotics and other fermentation products are large tanks holding hundreds or thousands of gallons of fermentation culture.

of the microbial strain and the formation of the desired product. Essential nutrients for microbial growth include sources of carbon, nitrogen, and phosphorus (Table 15-2). The choice of a particular nutrient source is made on economic as well as biological grounds, making plant materials attractive choices. Depending on the nature of the fermentation process, all of the raw materials may be added at the beginning of the fermentation, or nutrients may be fed to the microorganisms gradually throughout the process. Often plant materials, such as molasses, are used as a carbon source. Some pretreatment of the raw material is frequently necessary to convert complex carbohydrate materials into relatively simple sugars that can be readily metabolized by microorganisms. Organic nitrogen, sometimes in the form of cornsteep liquor, or inorganic nitrogen, such as ammonia, may be used to meet the nutritional needs of the microbial strain. Phosphorus is usually added as an inorganic salt.

Because crude raw materials are normally employed in the medium, many of the minor nutritional requirements of microorganisms are met because they naturally occur in appropriate concentrations in the raw material. In some fermentation processes, however, trace elements, such as heavy metals, must be present in specific concentrations to achieve acceptable yields of the desired product. The quality of the water used in the fermentation and the nature of the pipes used to supply solutions to the fermentation reaction can be especially important. In some cases, metals leaching from pipes can inhibit microbial production of fermentation products, and in other cases such leached metals may be essential for achieving optimal yields of the desired product.

TABLE 15-2 Nutrient Sources for Industrial Fermentations

NUTRIENT	RAW MATERIAL
CARBON SOURCE	
Glucose	Corn sugar
	Starch
	Cellulose
Sucrose	Sugarcane
	Sugar beet molasses
Lactose	Milk whey
Fats	Vegetable oils
Hydrocarbons	Petroleum fractions
NITROGEN SOURCE	
Protein	Soybean meal
	Cornsteep liquor (from corn milling)
	Distillers' solubles (from alcoholic beverage manufacture)
Ammonia	Pure ammonia or ammonium salts
Nitrate	Nitrate salts
Nitrogen	Air (for nitrogen-fixing organisms)
PHOSPHORUS SOURCE	Phosphate salts

Aeration

Many industrial fermentations are aerobic processes; therefore it is important to achieve the optimal oxygen concentration to permit microbial growth with maximal product yield. The transfer of oxygen to microorganisms in large-scale fermentors is particularly difficult because the microorganisms must be well mixed and the oxygen dispersed to achieve relatively uniform concentrations to support maximal production rates. The development of fermentors for the growth of obligately aerobic microorganisms in a broth (submerged aerobic culture) requires careful design to achieve optimal oxygen concentrations throughout the solutions contained in high-volume fermentors. Many fermentor designs have mechanical stirrers to mix the solution, baffles to increase turbulence and ensure adequate mixing, and forced aeration to provide needed oxygen (FIG. 15-4, p. 604). It should be noted that a high concentration of microbial cells, as is achieved in a fermentor, can rapidly deplete the soluble oxygen in an aqueous solution, creating anaerobic conditions that may not be favorable to microbial production of the desired product. However, forced aeration and mechanical mixing are relatively expensive because of the high energy costs involved and must be economically justified for use in industrial fermentation processes.

pH Control

The pH of the reaction is critical. The enzymes involved in forming the desired product have optimal pH ranges for maximal activity and limited pH ranges in which activity is maintained. The rapid growth of microorganisms in a fermentor can quickly alter the pH of the reaction medium. For example, if the microorganisms produce acid, which in fact may be the desired product, the pH of a nonbuffered medium can decline precipitously. If the pH drops too far, microbial production of the desired fermentation product may cease. To prevent such changes, fermentation media are often buffered to dampen changes in the pH. Additionally, the pH of the reaction solution normally is continuously monitored, and acid or base is added as needed to maintain it within acceptable tolerance limits.

Temperature Regulation

The temperature of the reaction must be carefully regulated to achieve optimal yields of product. Rapidly growing microorganisms can generate a large

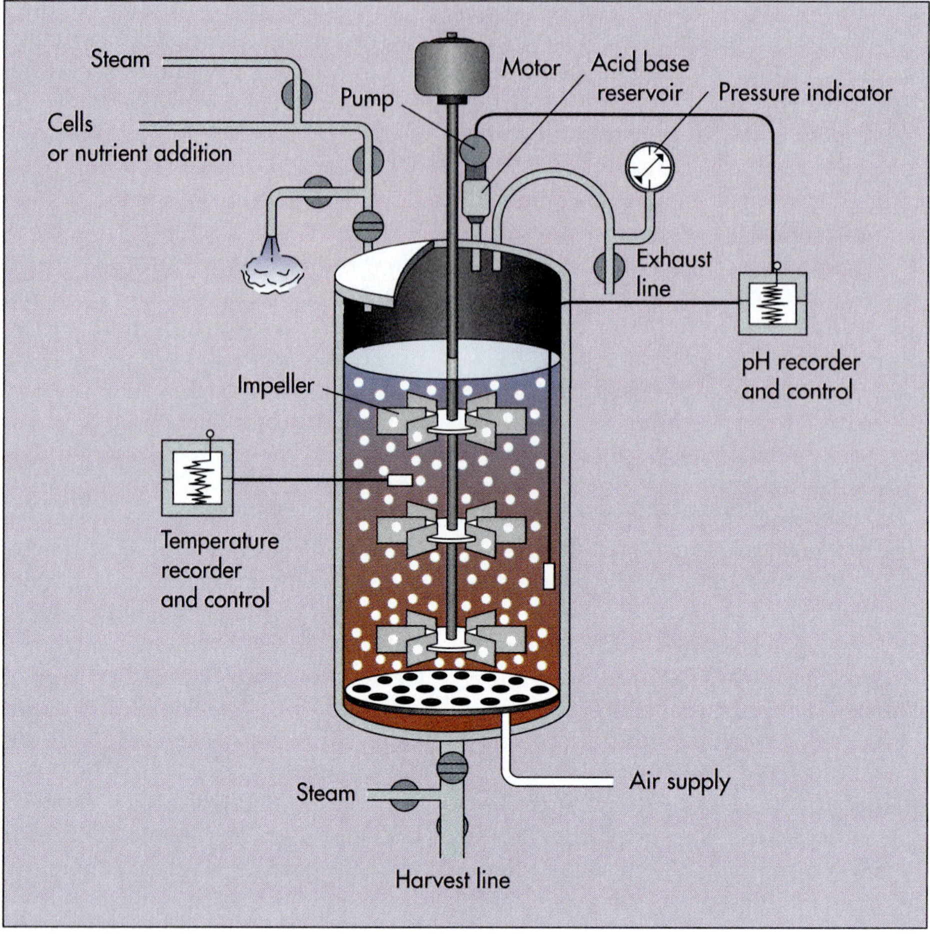

FIG. 15-4 A fermentor is designed to control environmental conditions so as to favor the growth of a specific microorganism and the yield of a fermentation product. The supply of oxygen and its mixing are critical in fermentor design. In a batch reactor, the medium and inoculum are added and, after sufficient incubation, the reaction is stopped and the fermentation product recovered.

amount of heat that must be dissipated to prevent inactivation of enzymes. Cooling coils are often employed in fermentors to regulate temperature to maximize the rate of product accumulation. Heating coils are used in some fermentors when elevated temperatures are required to achieve optimal rates of product formation. These heating coils are also used for periodic sterilization of the fermentor chamber.

Batch versus Continuous Processes

A fermentation process may be designed as a *batch process,* which is analogous to inoculating a flask containing a broth with a microbial culture, or as a *continuous flow process,* which is analogous to that of a chemostat. The choice of the process design depends on the economics of production and recovery of the desired product. Compared to batch processes, flow-through fermentors are more prone to contamination with undesired microorganisms, making quality control difficult to maintain. The flow-through design, however, has the advantage of producing a continuous supply of product that can be recovered at a constant rate for commercial distribution (FIG. 15-5). Continuous processes have higher volumetric productivity, that is, more efficient use of fermentor capacity because they are always full. In contrast, batch processes require significant startup times to initiate the fermentation process, incubation times to allow fermentation products to accumulate, and recovery times during which the product is separated from the spent medium and microbial cells. The downtime involved in filling, emptying, and cleaning reduces the volumetric efficiency of these reactors.

Immobilized Enzymes

The use of **immobilized enzymes** is an interesting alternative method for producing a desired product. In this process, microbial enzymes or microbial cells are adsorbed or bonded to a solid surface support, such as cellulose (FIG. 15-6). The bonded and thus *immobi-*

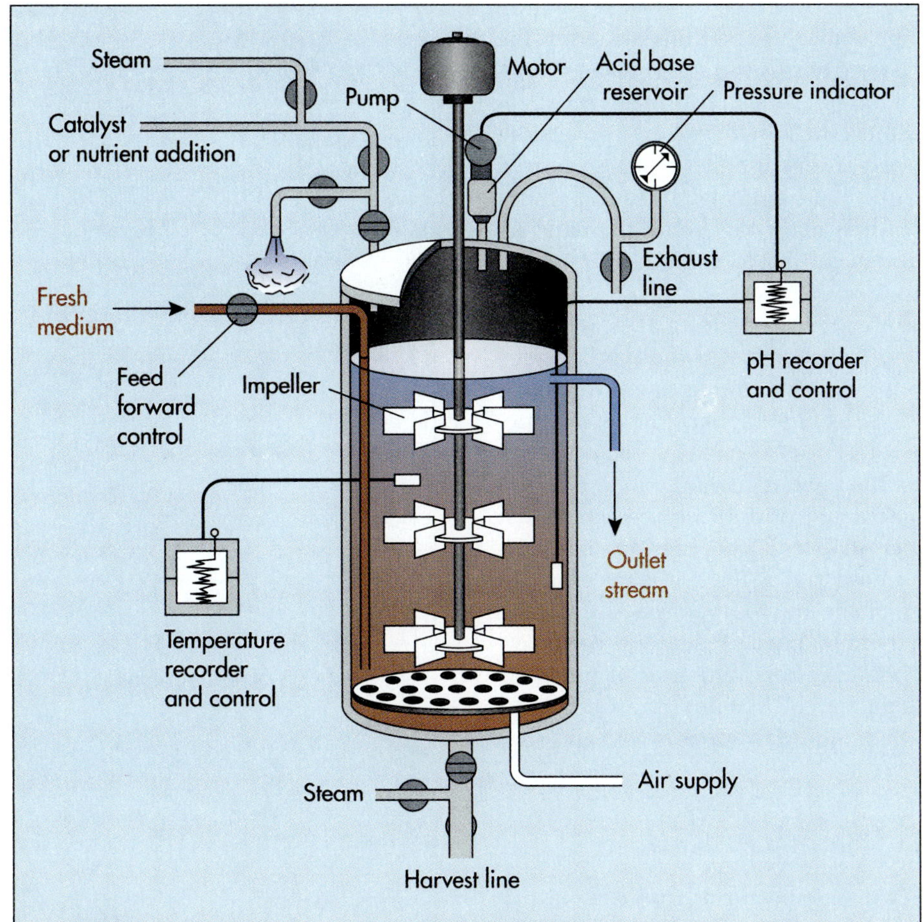

FIG. 15-5 In a flow-through fermentor, fresh medium is continuously added and products are continuously harvested from the outflow. Using such fermentors is economically favorable.

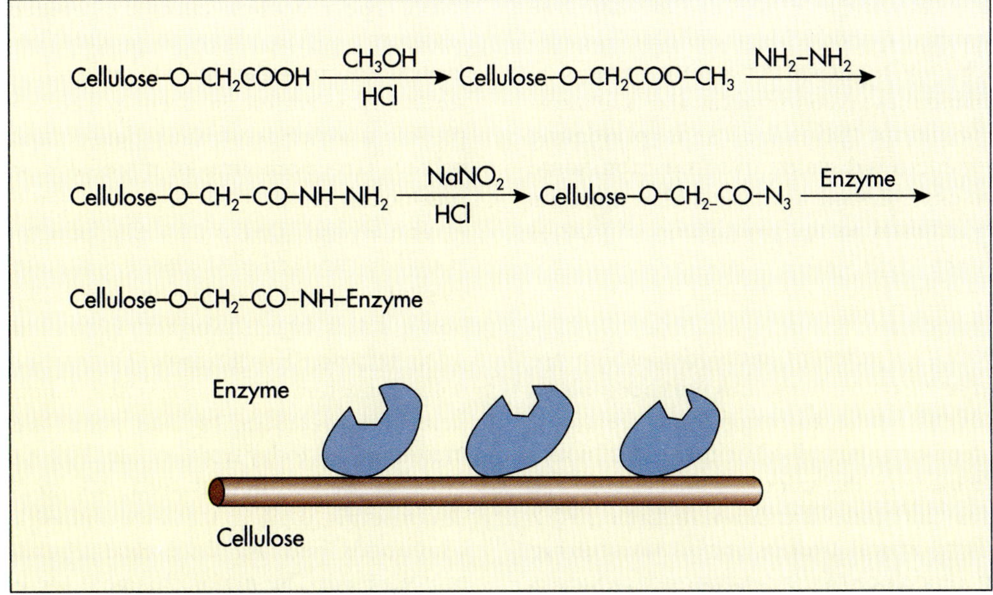

FIG. 15-6 Immobolized enzymes can be made by the enzymes reacting with carboxymethylcellulose. As a substrate flows past the immobilized enzyme it is transformed into the reaction product.

lized enzymes act as a solid-surface catalyst. A solution containing the biochemicals to be transformed by the enzymes is then passed across the solid surface. Temperature, pH, and oxygen concentration are set at optimal levels to achieve maximal rates of conversion. This type of process is very useful when the desired transformation involves a single metabolic step, but it is more complex when many different enzymatic activities are required to convert an initial substrate into a desired end product.

The use of immobilized enzymes makes an industrial process far more economical, avoiding the wasteful expense of continuously growing microorganisms and discarding the unwanted biomass. In such immobilized enzyme systems, it is essential to maintain enzymatic activity so that the enzymes are not washed off the surface or inactivated during the process. When whole cells, rather than cell-free enzymes, are employed in such immobilized systems, it is necessary to maintain viability of the microorganisms during the process. This generally involves adding necessary growth substrates, but far lower amounts of nutrients are needed to maintain the viability of immobilized cells than would be required to support actively growing cells.

TABLE 15-3 Some Antibiotics Produced by Microorganisms

ANTIBIOTIC	PRODUCED BY
Amphotericin B	*Streptomyces nodosus*
Bacitracin	*Bacillus licheniformis*
Carbomycin	*Streptomyces halstedii*
Chlorotetracycline	*Streptomyces aureofaciens*
Chloramphenicol	*Streptomyces venezuelae* or total chemical synthesis
Erythromycin	*Streptomyces erythreus*
Fumagillin	*Aspergillus fumigatus*
Griseofulvin	*Penicillium griseofulvin* *Penicillium nigricans* *Penicillium urticae*
Kanamycin	*Streptomyces kanamyceticus*
Neomycin	*Streptomyces fradiae*
Novobiocin	*Streptomyces niveus* *Streptomyces spheroides*
Nystatin	*Streptomyces noursei*
Oleandomycin	*Streptomyces antibioticus*
Oxytetracycline	*Streptomyces rimosus*
Penicillin	*Penicillium chrysogenum*
Polymyxin B	*Bacillus polymyxa*
Streptomycin	*Streptomyces griseus*
Tetracycline	Dechlorination and hydrogenation of chlortetracycline; direct fermentation in dechlorinated medium
Vira A (adenine arabinoside)	*Streptomyces antibioticus*

PRODUCTION OF PHARMACEUTICALS

The pharmaceutical manufacturing industry is primarily concerned with making drugs to control disease. The world's supply of pharmaceuticals, including many antibiotics, steroids, vitamins, and vaccines, is produced in large part by microorganisms. Microbial production of pharmaceuticals is a major industry; antibiotic sales alone accounted for approximately $5 billion in worldwide sales in 1980. The role of microorganisms in producing these pharmaceuticals is economically important for industry and is essential for making these compounds available at a cost low enough to permit their wide use in preventing and treating numerous diseases. In this section, some representative examples will be discussed to illustrate the processes involved in the production of various pharmaceuticals.

Antibiotics

Of the thousands of different **antibiotics,** which are substances made in nature by various microorganisms that inhibit or kill other microorganisms, relatively few are produced commercially. The major antibiotics used in medicine and the microorganisms used for producing these antibiotics are shown in Table 15-3.

Penicillin In a typical process for manufacturing penicillin, an inoculum of *Penicillium chrysogenum* is produced by inoculating a dense suspension of spores of the fungus onto a wheat bran nutrient solution. The cultures are allowed to incubate for approximately 1 week at 24° C and are then transferred to an inoculum tank. In some cases, these spores are germinated to produce mycelia for inoculation into these tanks. The inoculum tanks are agitated with forced aeration for 1 to 2 days to provide a heavy mycelial growth for inoculation into a production tank. In some cases, additional step-up procedures are employed in which sequentially larger tanks are used to achieve larger amounts of mycelial inoculum for the production tanks.

The typical medium for the production of penicillin has changed in the last few decades. Whereas in 1945 the typical medium contained 3.5% cornsteep liquor solids (waste product of starch manufacture), 3.5% lactose, 1% glucose, 1% calcium carbonate, 0.4% potassium phosphate, 0.25% vegetable oil, and a penicillin precursor such as phenylacetic acid, the medium used today typically uses 10% total glucose or molasses by continuous feed, 4% to 5% cornsteep liquor solids, 0.5% to 0.8% total phenylacetic acid by continuous feed, and 0.5% total vegetable oil by continuous feed. The major change is the elimination of lactose from the medium and the use of continuous feed substrate addition to increase the efficiency of penicillin production. The phenylacetic acid is the precursor used to form the benzene ring side chain of

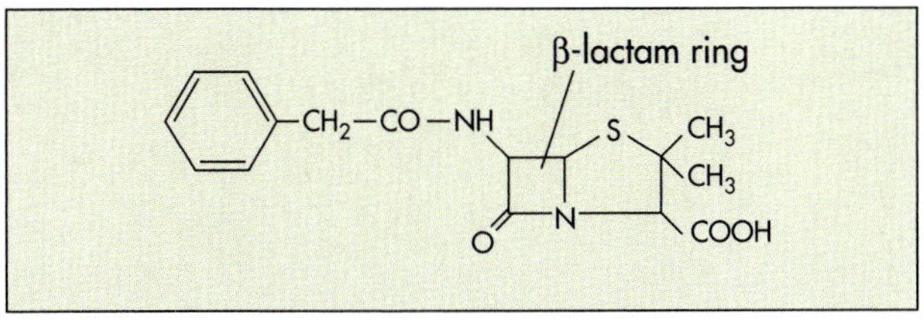

FIG. 15-7 Penicillin is composed of phenylacetic acid joined to 6-aminopenicillanic acid, which has a β-lactam ring.

the penicillin G molecule (see FIG. 15-7 for the structure of the penicillin molecule). The addition of this precursor steers the fungal metabolic reactions to form increased amounts of penicillin.

The pH of the medium after sterilization is approximately 6, which is critical because penicillin is inactivated at both low and high pH values. The pH is maintained near neutrality during the course of the fermentation by the addition of alkali to the medium as needed. The incubation temperature for the fermentations is maintained at approximately 25° to 26° C, and aeration is provided during the production process.

The typical course of a penicillin fermentation takes 7 days, although longer times may be required when very large fermentors are used (FIG. 15-8). During the first day of the fermentation, there is a large

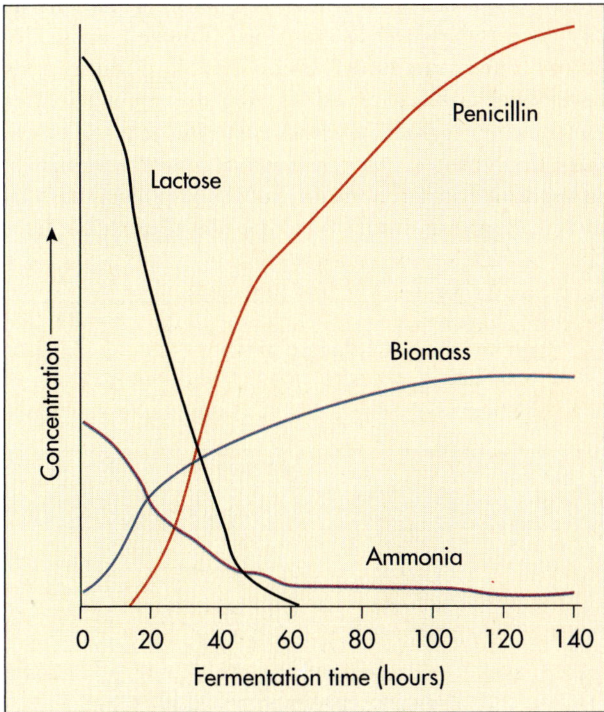

FIG. 15-8 Penicillin production can be achieved by feeding *Penicillium chrysogenum* lactose and ammonia. After sufficient fungal biomass is formed, penicillin begins to accumulate in the idiophase.

increase in the biomass of *Penicillium* mycelia. The carbohydrate substrate is rapidly used during this early phase, providing the necessary carbon and energy for the production of fungal mycelia. At a later stage, reduction of the carbohydrate concentration provides the necessary nutritional starvation conditions that favor penicillin production. The nitrogen required to support fungal growth comes from the cornsteep liquor. The production of penicillin, a secondary metabolite or **idiolite**—which is a substance not required for the growth of the fungus—lags behind the accumulation of fungal biomass. The production of fungal biomass occurs in a growth phase called the **trophophase.** The accumulation of penicillin occurs in the **idiophase,** which is the phase in which the idiolite accumulates; the idiophase begins on the second day and reaches maximal concentration a few days later (FIG. 15-9).

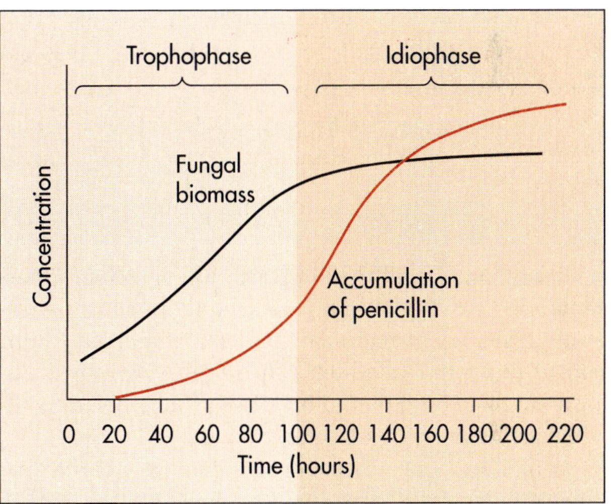

FIG. 15-9 The course of penicillin production, like other industrial fermentations, is marked by (1) a growth phase during which substrate is consumed and no product is formed (trophophase during which lactose is consumed and *Penicillium* biomass is formed in this case) and (2) a phase of limited further growth during which the product accumulates (idiophase during which penicillin accumulates in this case).

When the fermentation is completed, the concentration of penicillin having reached maximal achievable levels, the liquid medium containing the penicillin is separated from the fungal cells using a rotating vacuum filter. The fungal biomass is scraped from the surface of the filter drum, dried, and marketed as an animal feed supplement. Penicillin is recovered from the filtrate. It is extracted from the solution by using an organic solvent and then extracted back into aqueous solution. The exchange of penicillin back and forth between organic and aqueous solvents is accomplished by altering the pH and results in the partial purification of the antibiotic. Spent solvents used

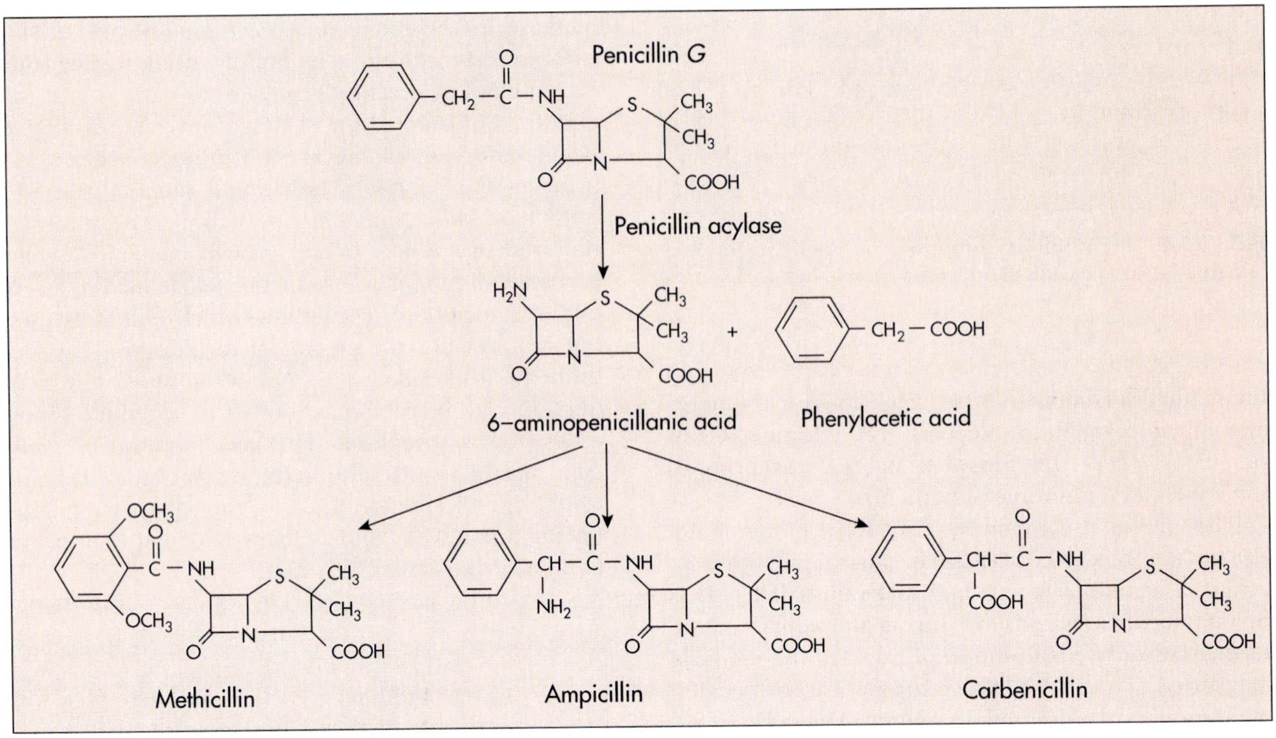

FIG. 15-10 Penicillin can be chemically or enzymatically modified to produce various other antimicrobics. These second- and third-generation penicillins have differing applications.

in the extraction of the penicillin are recycled. Potassium ions are then added to the aqueous solution, resulting in the formation of the crystalline potassium salt of penicillin G, which can be recovered by filtration or centrifugation. The filtered and dried penicillin salt is over 99.5% pure.

Penicillin G produced in this process can be further modified to form various penicillin derivatives (FIG. 15-10). The modification of penicillin may be accomplished chemically or by using microbial enzymes. For example, 6-aminopenicillanic acid (6-APA) can be formed by fermentation, using bacterial acylase enzymes in an aqueous solution at 37° C. The same transformation of penicillin G to form 6-APA can also be accomplished chemically in three steps by using various chemical solvents, anhydrous conditions, and low temperatures. Similar transformations of the basic penicillin structure can also yield other penicillin derivatives. For example, in 1981 piperacillin was approved as a broad-spectrum antibiotic, and in 1982 azlocillin was introduced for use against bacterial strains that are resistant to earlier-generation penicillins.

Cephalosporins Similar semisynthetic approaches can be used for manufacturing other antibiotics. For example, cephalosporin C is made as the fermentation product of *Cephalosporium acremonium* but this form of the antibiotic is not potent enough for clinical use. The cephalosporin C molecule, however, can be transformed by removal of an α-aminoadipic acid side chain to form 7-α-aminocephalosporanic acid, which can be further modified by adding side chains to form clinically useful products with relatively broad spectra of antibacterial action (FIG. 15-11). Various side chains can be added to, as well as removed from, 6-aminopenicillanic and 7-aminocephalosporanic acids to produce antibiotics with varying spectra of activities and varying degrees of resistance to inactivation by enzymes produced by pathogenic microorganisms. These are "third-generation" cephalosporins, such as moxalactam, that were developed to combat bacteria

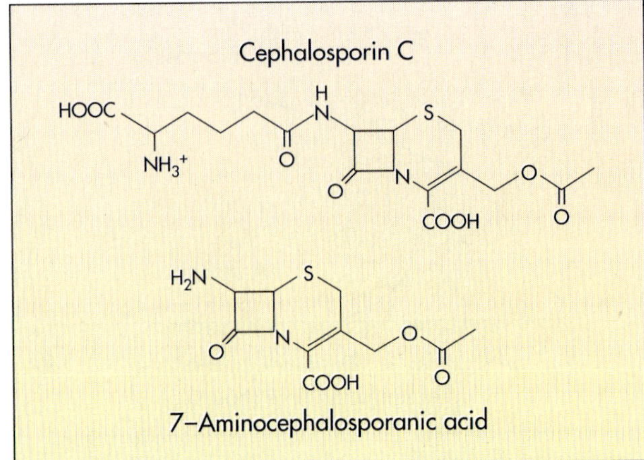

FIG. 15-11 Cephalosporin C can be converted to 7-aminocephalosporinic acid, which can be further modified to form second and third generation cephalosporins.

that produce enzymes capable of degrading penicillins and cephalosporins.

Streptomycin Streptomycin is produced using strains of *Streptomyces griseus*. *S. griseus* and other actinomycetes produce numerous other antimicrobics, most of which inhibit protein synthesis in prokaryotic cells. The discovery of streptomycin production by Selman Waksman revolutionized the search for the production of new antimicrobics by soil microorganisms, especially by actinomycetes.

As in penicillin fermention, spores of *S. griseus* are inoculated into a medium to establish a culture with a high mycelial biomass for introduction into an inoculum tank, with subsequent use of the mycelial inoculum to initiate the fermentation process in a production tank. The basic medium for the production of streptomycin contains soybean meal as the nitrogen source, glucose as the carbon source, and sodium chloride. The optimum temperature for this fermentation is approximately 28° C, and the maximal rate of streptomycin production is achieved in the pH range of 7.6 to 8.0. High rates of aeration and agitation are required to achieve maximal production of streptomycin. The fermentation process lasts for approximately 10 days and yields of streptomycin exceed 1 g/L.

The classic fermentation process for the production of streptomycin involves three phases (FIG. 15-12). During the first phase there is rapid growth of *S. griseus,* with production of mycelial biomass. Proteolytic enzymatic activity of *S. griseus* releases ammonia to the medium from the soybean meal, causing a rise in pH. During this initial fermentation phase there is little production of streptomycin. During the second phase there is little additional production of mycelia but the secondary metabolite streptomycin accumulates in the medium. The glucose added in the medium and the ammonia released from the soybean meal are consumed during this phase. The pH remains fairly constant, between 7.6 and 8.0. In the third and final phase of the fermentation, after depletion of carbohydrates from the medium, streptomycin production ceases and the bacterial cells begin to lyse. There is a rapid increase in pH because of the release of ammonia from the lysed cells, and the fermentation process normally is ended by the time the cells begin to lyse.

After completion of the fermentation, the mycelium is separated from the broth by filtration and the streptomycin is recovered. Streptomycin is a water-soluble basic substance and is insoluble in most organic solvents. One method of recovery and purification consists of adsorbing the streptomycin onto activated charcoal and eluting with acid alcohol. The antibiotic is then precipitated with acetone and further purified by using column chromatography. Several other chemical procedures can be employed for recovering and purifying streptomycin.

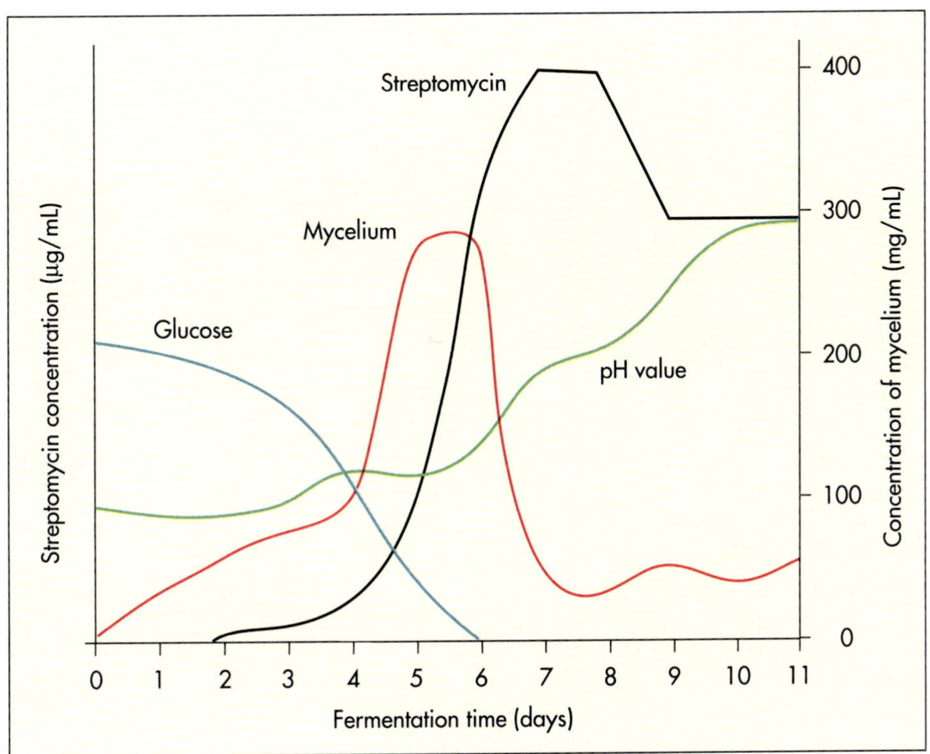

FIG. 15-12 During the trophophase of streptomycin production, glucose is consumed and *Streptomyces* biomass increases. During the idiophase the concentration of bacterial mycelia declines, pH rises, and streptomycin accumulates.

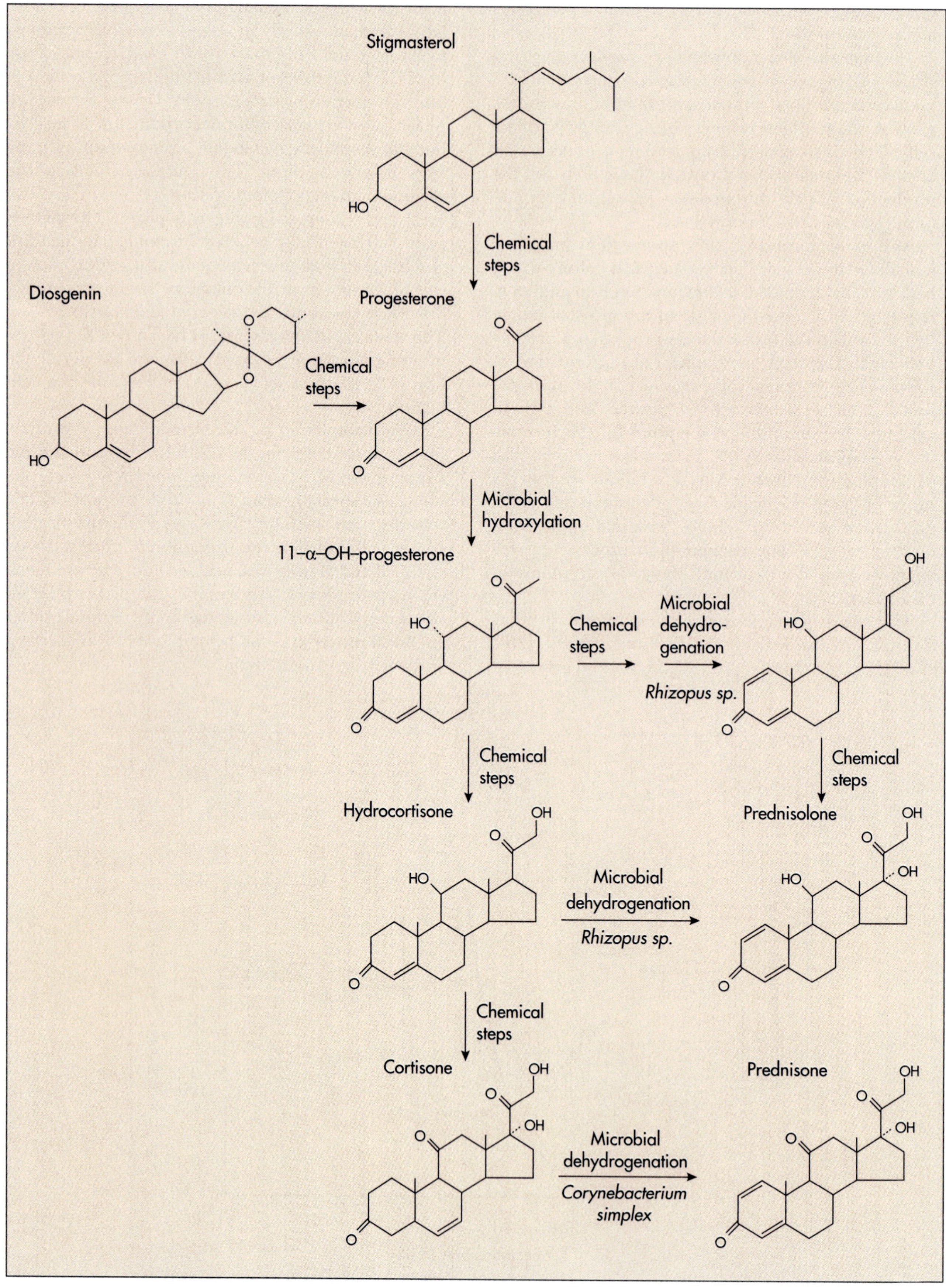

FIG. 15-13 Some microbial transformations used in the commercial production of steroids.

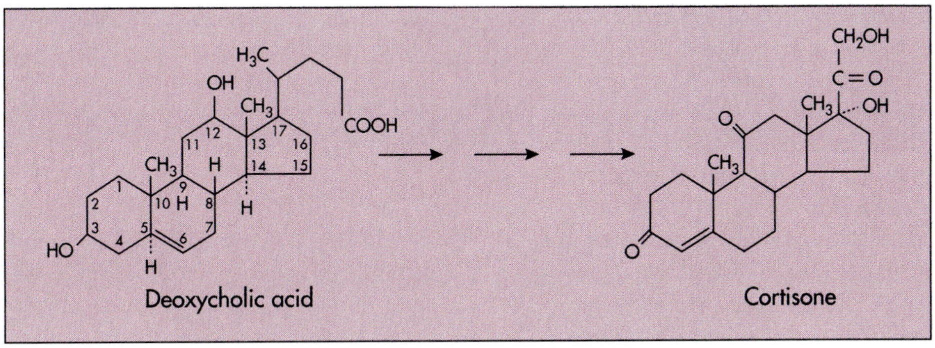

FIG. 15-14 Cortisone is synthesized from deoxycholic acid.

Steroids

The use of microorganisms to carry out biotransformations of steroids is very important in the pharmaceutical industry (FIG. 15-13). Steroid hormones regulate various aspects of metabolism in animals, including humans. One such hormone, cortisone, has been found to relieve the pain associated with rheumatoid arthritis. Various cortisone derivatives are also useful in alleviating the symptoms associated with allergic and other undesired inflammatory responses of the human body. Additionally, various steroid hormones regulate human sexuality; some of them are manufactured as oral contraceptives. The physiological properties of a steroid depend on the nature and the exact position of the chemical constituents on the basic steroid ring structure. The chemical synthesis of steroids is very complex because of the requirement to achieve the necessary precision of substituent location.

For example, cortisone can be synthesized chemically from deoxycholic acid (FIG. 15-14), but the process requires 37 steps, many of which must be carried out under extreme conditions of temperature and pressure, with the resulting product costing over $200 per gram. The major difficulty in chemically synthesizing cortisone is the need to introduce an oxygen atom at the number 11 position of the steroid ring; this can be accomplished by microorganisms. The fungus *Rhizopus arrhizus,* for example, hydroxylates progesterone, forming another steroid with the introduction of oxygen at the number 11 position (FIG. 15-15).

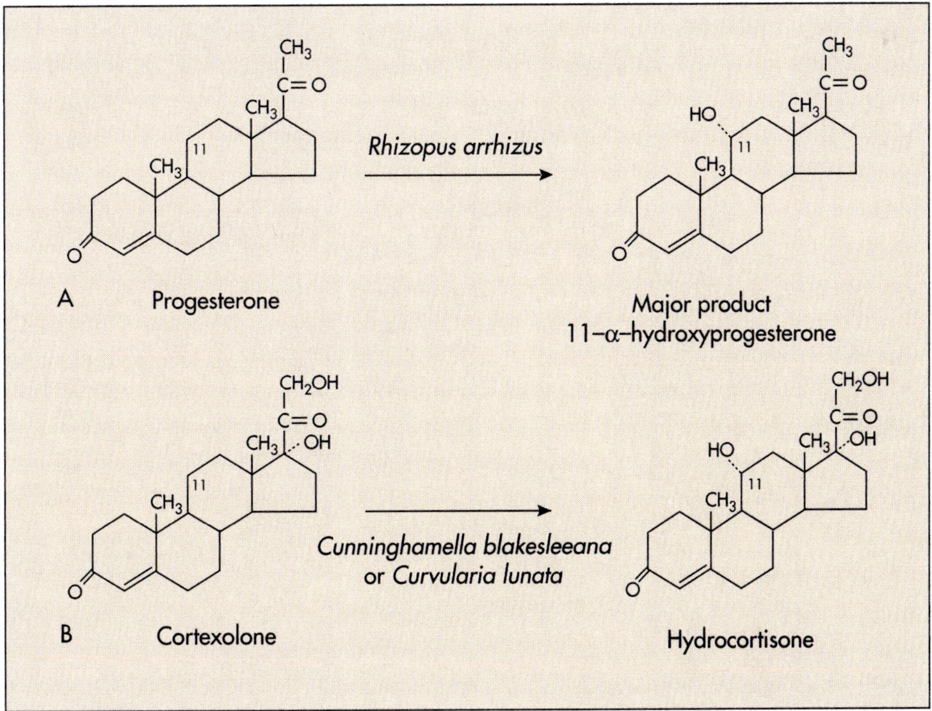

FIG. 15-15 Microorganisms are used to transform steroids. The specificity of microbial hydroxylation reaction is critical for the commercial production of various corticosteroids. **A,** Production of 11 α-hydroxyprogesterone. **B,** Production of hydrocortisone.

The fungus *Cunninghamella blakesleeana* similarly can hydroxylate the steroid cortexolone to form hydrocortisone with the introduction of oxygen at the number 11 position. Other transformations of the steroid nucleus carried out by microorganisms include hydrogenations, dehydrogenations, epoxidations, and removal and addition of side chains. The use of such microbial transformations in the formation of cortisone has lowered the original cost over 400-fold, so that in 1980 the price of cortisone in the United States was less than 50¢ per gram, compared to the original $200.

In a typical steroid transformation process, the microorganism (such as *Rhizopus nigricans*) is grown in a fermentor, using an appropriate growth medium and incubation conditions to achieve a high biomass. In most cases, aeration and agitation are employed to achieve rapid growth. After the growth of the microorganisms, the steroid to be transformed is added. For example, when progesterone is added to a fermentor containing *R. nigricans* that has been growing for approximately 1 day, the steroid is hydroxylated at the number 11 position to form 11-α-hydroxyprogesterone. The product is then recovered by extraction with methylene chloride or various other solvents, purified chromatographically, and recovered by crystallization. Numerous similar transformations are carried out to produce various steroid derivatives for different medicinal uses.

Human Proteins

In addition to its impact on many other fields of microbiology, genetic engineering has expanded the roles of microorganisms in the pharmaceutical industry to include the production of human proteins. By using recombinant DNA technology, human DNA sequences that code for various proteins have been incorporated into the genomes of bacteria. By growing these recombinant bacteria in fermentors, human proteins can be produced commercially (Table 15-4). Human insulin, for example is produced by a recombinant *Escherichia coli* strain and marketed as Humulin. Other strains are used to produce human growth hormone, tumor necrosis factor (TNF), interferon, and interleukin-2. Humulin is used to treat diabetes in cases in which the individual is allergic to insulin harvested from cattle. Human growth hormone is used to treat diseases, such as dwarfism, resulting

TABLE 15-4 Some Human Proteins Produced by Recombinant Microorganisms

PROTEIN	PRODUCT NAME	FUNCTION AND USE
Insulin	Humulin, Novolin	Hormone that regulates sugar levels in blood; used in treatment of diabetes
Human growth hormone	Protropin, Humatrope	Hormone that stimulates growth of human body; used in treatment of dwarfism
Bone growth factor	—	Stimulates growth of bone cell; used in treatment of osteoporosis
Interferon alpha	Berofor, Intron A, Wellferon, Roferon-A, human recombinant alpha interferon	Cytokine of immune system; used in treatment of cancer and viral diseases
Interferon beta	Frone, Betaseron, human recombinant beta interferon	Cytokine of immune system; used in treatment of cancer and viral diseases
Interferon gamma	Actimmune	Lymphokine of immune system; used in treatment of cancer and viral diseases
Interleukin-2	Proleukin, human recombinant interleukin-2	Lymphokine of immune system that stimulates T cells; used in treatment of immunodeficiencies and cancer
Tumor necrosis factor (TNF)	—	Lymphokine of immune system that causes death of malignant cells; used in treatment of cancer
Tissue plasminogen activator (TPA)	Actilyse	Dissolves blood clots; used in treatment of heart disease and during heart surgery
Blood clotting factor VIII	Recombinate	Stimulates blood clot formation; used in treatment of hemophiliacs
Epidermal growth factor	—	Regulates calcium levels and stimulates growth of epidermal cells; used in treatment of wounds to stimulate healing
Granulocyte colony stimulating factor	Filgrastin, Neupogen	Regulates production of neutrophils in bone marrow; used in treatment of cancer to prevent infections
Erythropoietin (EPO)	Procrit, Epogen	Stimulates red blood cell production, used in treatment of anemia in dialysis patients

from a deficiency of this hormone. Interleukin-2, interferon, and TNF are important components of the natural human immune response, and their production may prove useful in treating some diseases in which increased levels of these substances would be therapeutic. Interferon, for example, is important in the defense against viruses, and it may prove useful in treating viral infections. TNF is a natural substance produced in the body in small amounts by certain white blood cells, called *macrophages*, that appears to kill some cancer cells and infectious microorganisms without adversely affecting most normal cells. The production of large amounts of TNF by recombinant bacteria is aiding in the investigation of its potential use in the treatment of cancer.

Synthetic peptides for medical purposes have also been developed through recombinant DNA technology. These peptides include blood clotting factors and tissue healing factors, intracellular adhesin molecules for treatment of the common cold, and growth factors. This area of genetic engineering is likely to rapidly expand in the future.

Vaccines

The use of *vaccines* is extremely important for preventing various serious diseases. The development and production of these vaccines constitute an important function of the pharmaceutical industry. The production of vaccines involves growing microorganisms possessing the antigenic properties needed to elicit a primary immune response. Vaccines are produced by mutant strains of pathogens or by attenuating or inactivating virulent pathogens without removing the antigens necessary for eliciting the immune response.

For the production of vaccines against viral diseases, strains of the virus often are grown by using embryonated eggs (FIG. 15-16). Individuals who are allergic to eggs cannot be given such vaccine preparations. Viral vaccines may also be produced by using *tissue culture*. For example, the older rabies vaccine, which was produced in embryonated duck eggs and had painful side effects, has been replaced with a vaccine produced in human fibroblast tissue cultures that has far fewer side effects. The production of vaccines that are effective in preventing diseases caused by bacteria, fungi, and protozoa generally involves growing the microbial strain on an artificial medium, which minimizes problems with allergic responses. Commercially produced vaccines must be tested and standardized before use. It is critical that the vaccine not contain active forms of a virulent pathogen, lest the vaccine transmit the disease it attempts to prevent. Unfortunately, there have been several outbreaks of disease associated with improperly prepared vaccines. High standards of quality control and appropriate safety test procedures can prevent such incidents. Various vaccines, including some new vaccines produced with recombinant microorganisms, are discussed in Chapter 12.

FIG. 15-16 Vaccines are produced by growing and harvesting microorganisms. Some viral vaccines are produced by culture in eggs or tissue culture. Bacterial vaccines often are produced by growing the vaccine strains in fermentors.

TABLE 15-5 Production of Some Vitamins Using Microorganisms

VITAMIN	CULTURE	MEDIUM	FERMENTATION CONDITIONS	YIELD
Riboflavin	*Ashbya gossypii*	Glucose, collagen, soya oil, glycine	6 days at 36° C, aerobic	4.25 g/L
L-Sorbose (in vitamin C synthesis)	*Gluconobacter oxidans* subsp. *suboxidans*	D-Sorbitol, 30% cornsteep	45 hours at 30° C, aerobic	70% based on substrate used
5-Ketogluconic acid (in vitamin C synthesis)	*Gluconobacter oxidans* subsp. *suboxidans*	Glucose, $CaCO_3$, cornsteep liquor	33 hours at 30° C aerobic	100% based on substrate used
Vitamin B_{12}	*Propionibacterium shermanii*	Glucose, cornsteep, ammonia, cobalt, pH 7.0	3 days at 30° C, anaerobic, +4 days, aerobic	23 mg/L

Vitamins

Vitamins are essential animal nutritional factors. Some vitamins can be produced by microbial fermentation and used as dietary supplements (Table 15-5).

Vitamin B_{12}, for example, can be produced as a by-product of *Streptomyces* antibiotic fermentations (FIG. 15-17). A soluble cobalt salt is added to the fermentation reaction as a precursor to vitamin B_{12}. Relatively high amounts of this vitamin accumulate in the medium at concentrations that are not toxic to the *Streptomyces.* Vitamin B_{12} can also be produced commercially by direct fermentation, using *Propionibacterium shermanii* or *Paracoccus denitrificans,* and these are the organisms used today for the production of this vitamin. *P. shermanii* can be grown in anaerobic culture for 3 days and in aerobic culture for 4 days to produce vitamin B_{12}. The growth medium for vitamin B_{12} production by these organisms contains glucose, cornsteep liquor (a waste product of starch manufacture), and cobalt chloride. The medium is maintained at pH 7 by using ammonium hydroxide. *P. denitrificans* is grown for 2 days in aerated culture for vitamin B_{12} production, using a medium containing sucrose, betaine, glutamic acid, cobalt chloride, 5,6-dimethylbenzimidazole, and salts.

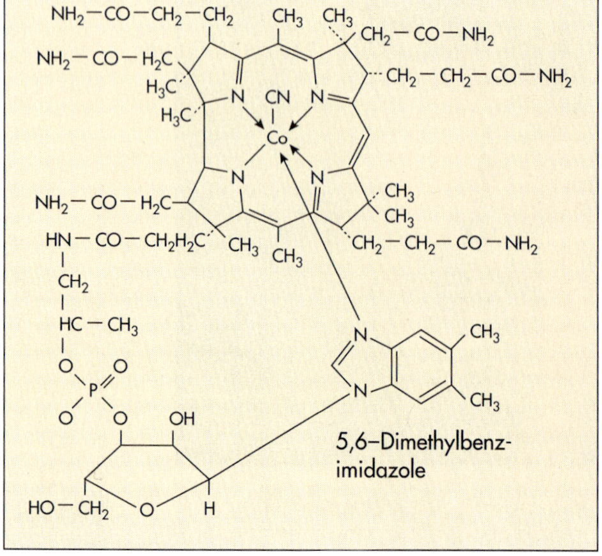

Riboflavin can also be produced as a fermentation product by using various microorganisms. Riboflavin is a by-product of acetone butanol fermentation and is produced by various *Clostridium* species. Commercial production of riboflavin by direct fermentation often uses the fungal species *Eremothecium ashbyii* or *Ashbya gossypii.* Riboflavin production using such fungi employs a medium containing glucose and/or corn oil. Corn oil may be added even when glucose is used as the primary growth substrate to increase yields of riboflavin. The fermentation using *Ashbya gossypii* to produce riboflavin is normally carried out at 26° to 28° C, pH 6 to 7.5, for approximately 4 to 5 days. After growth of the yeast, the cells are recovered and used as a feed supplement to supply needed riboflavin for animals. Various other vitamins can also be produced by fermentation but relatively low yields often limit their economic potential.

FIG. 15-17 Microorganisms are used to produce vitamins such as cobalamin (vitamin B_{12}).

PRODUCTION OF AMINO AND OTHER ORGANIC ACIDS

Several organic acids, including acetic, gluconic, citric, itaconic, gibberellic, and lactic acids, and various amino acids, including lysine and glutamic acid, are produced by microbial fermentation (Table 15-6). Microbial production of the amino acids lysine and glutamic acid presently accounts for over $1 billion in annual worldwide sales (FIG. 15-18). Animals require various amino acids in their diets. Lysine and methionine are essential amino acids but are not present in sufficient concentrations in grains to meet animal nutritional needs. Lysine produced by microbial fermentation and methionine produced synthetically are used as animal feed supplements and as additives in cereals. Glutamic acid is principally made for use as monosodium glutamate (MSG), an ingredient in soup production widely used as a flavor enhancer. The fla-

TABLE 15-6 Some Organic Acids Produced by Fermentation

PRODUCT	CULTURE	SUBSTRATE (YIELD %)	PROCESS
Acetic acid	*Acetobacter* spp.	Ethanol (98-99)	Continuous aerated reactor using an alcoholic solution containing glucose, 0.9%; ammonium phosphate, 0.4%; magnesium sulfate, 0.1%; potassium citrate, 0.1%; pantothenic acid, 0.0005%. Extraction by filtration.
Lactic acid	*Lactobacillus delbrueckii*	Milk whey, molasses, pure sugars (90)	10%-15% glucose, 5-6 days, 50° C in corrosion-resistant fermentor; pH 5.5-6.0 buffered with $CaCO_3$; no aeration, growth factors provided by malt. Extraction by precipitation after heating to 80° C and the addition of chalk (calcium lactate is formed); extraction with solvents; esterification with methanol followed by distillation.
Fumaric acid	*Rhizopus* spp.	Glucose (60)	3 days at 30° C with aeration; pH 5-6 maintained by the addition of NaOH. Extraction by acidification of media and crystallization.
Gluconic acid	*Aspergillus niger*	Glucose and corn-steep liquor (90)	36 hours at 30° C with aeration; pH 6.5. Extraction by filtration and purification using cation exchange column.

voring industry in the United States consumed more than 30,000 tons of MSG in 1980, some of which was imported from Japan (a major producer of amino acids by fermentation), Taiwan, and South Korea.

In the microbial production of amino acids, only the desired L-isomer is formed, whereas their chemical synthesis produces a racemic mixture that requires costly separation procedures to remove the biologically inactive D-isomer half of the mixture. The major problem in using microbial fermentation for commercial production of amino acids is overcoming the natural microbial regulatory control mechanisms that limit the amount of amino acid produced and released from the cells. Commercial amino acid production processes have successfully overcome these restrictions, and future genetically engineered strains with defective control mechanisms and membranes will undoubtedly permit the economic production of various amino acids by microbial fermentation.

Lysine

Direct production of L-lysine from carbohydrates uses a homoserine-requiring auxotroph of *Corynebacterium glutamicum* (FIG. 15-19). Cane molasses is generally used as the substrate, and the pH is maintained near neutrality by adding ammonia or urea. As the sugar is

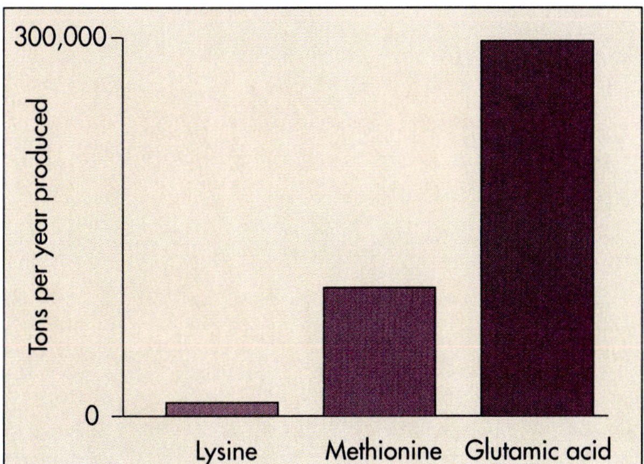

FIG. 15-18 Microbial production of amino acids account for the commercial formation of thousands of tons of lysine, methionine, and glutamic acid annually.

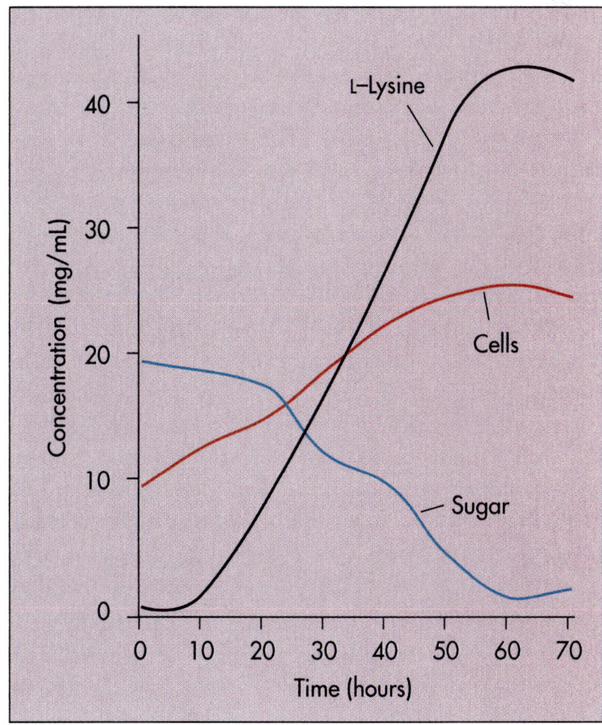

FIG. 15-19 Lysine is commerically produced by growth on sugars. Lysine production begins about 10 hours after inoculation and reaches maximal concentration after 60 hours.

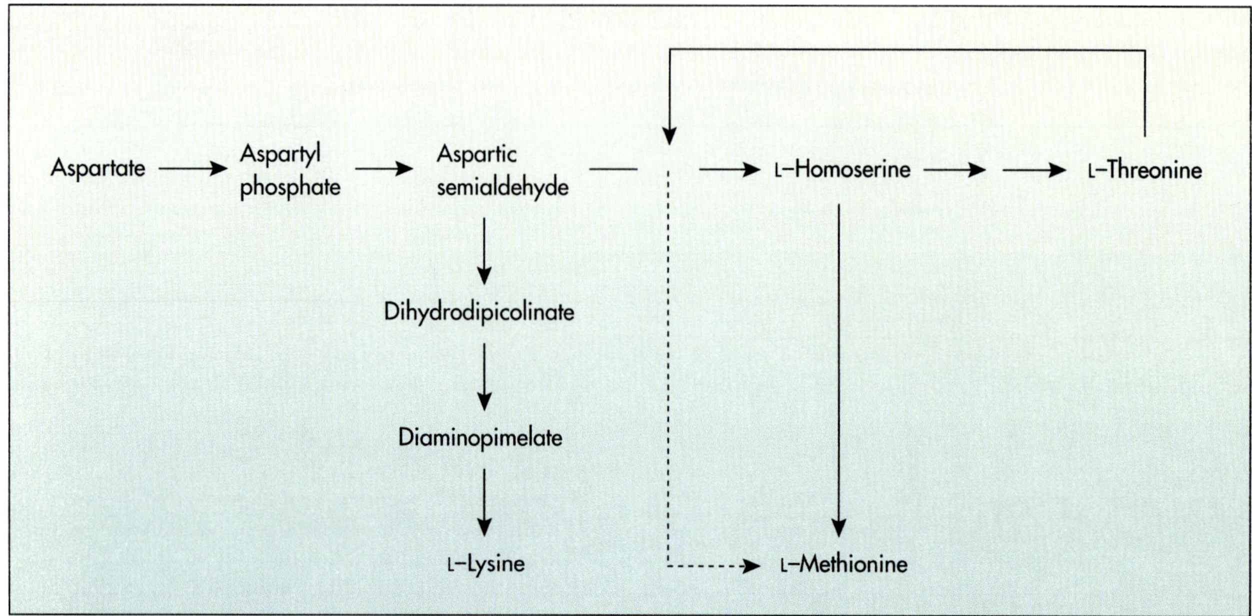

FIG. 15-20 The biosynthesis of lysine is regulated by several different mechanisms. Several feedback inhibition loops *(dotted line)* must be eliminated to get overexpression of lysine so that commercial quantities are made.

metabolized, lysine accumulates in the growth medium. The homoserine-requiring auxotroph produces about 50 g/L of lysine in 2 to 3 days (FIG. 15-19). Because lysine accumulates in this strain, homoserine synthesis is blocked at the level of homoserine dehydrogenase (FIG. 15-20).

Glutamic Acid

L-Glutamic acid and MSG can be produced by direct fermentation, using strains of *Brevibacterium, Arthrobacter,* and *Corynebacterium.* Cultures of *C. glutamicum* and *Brevibacterium flavum* are widely used for the large-scale production of MSG. The fermentation process employs a glucose–mineral salts medium and periodic additions of urea as a nitrogen source during the course of the fermentation; the pH is maintained at 6 to 8 and the temperature at about 30° C, and the medium is well aerated. The difficulty in the production of glutamic acid, as well as other amino acids, by direct fermentation is getting the cells to secrete sufficient quantities of the amino acid to permit commercial production. There are several methods for inducing leaky membranes that permit excretion of the amino acid product from the cell. One approach is to grow *C. glutamicum* in a medium with suboptimal concentrations of biotin (FIG. 15-21). Without an adequate supply of biotin, the cells form membranes that are deficient in phospholipids, and the glutamic acid is secreted through these leaky membranes. Another approach is to add fatty acids or surface active agents (detergents) to disrupt the membranes and release the glutamic acid from the cells. Still another way of causing the cell to excrete amino acids is to add penicillin to the medium during the exponential phase of growth, causing the bacteria to become leaky and release glutamic acid to the surrounding medium. Adjusting the pH and adding sodium chloride can be used to convert glutamic acid to the desired MSG.

Gluconic Acid

Gluconic acid is produced by various bacteria, including *Acetobacter* species, and by several fungi, including

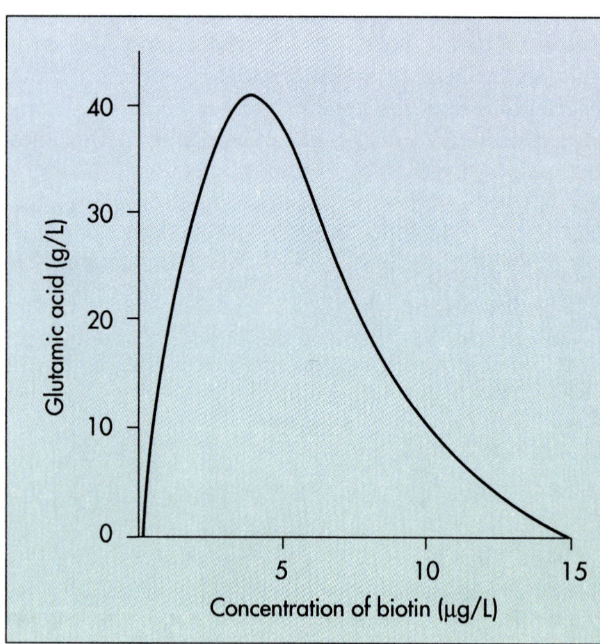

FIG. 15-21 Optimal yields of glutamic acid depend on establishing the optimal concentration of biotin.

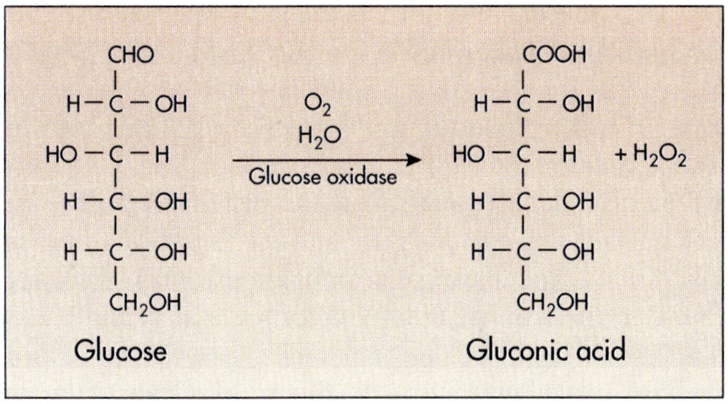

Glucose $\xrightarrow[\text{Glucose oxidase}]{O_2,\ H_2O}$ Gluconic acid $+ H_2O_2$

FIG. 15-22 Glucose is converted to gluconic acid by glucose oxidase.

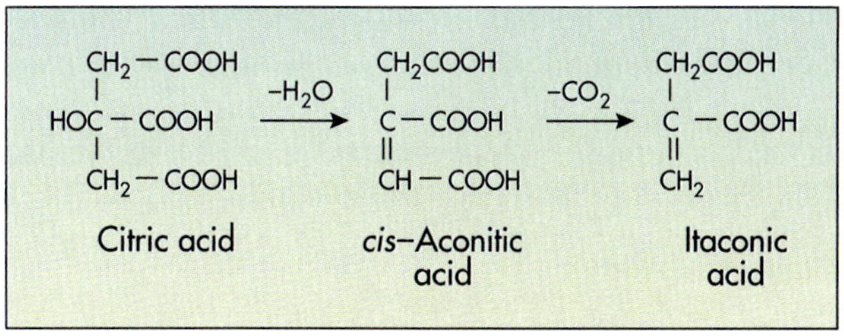

Penicillium and *Aspergillus* species. *Aspergillus niger*, for example, converts glucose to gluconic acid in a single enzymatic reaction (FIG. 15-22). Gluconic acid has various commercial uses. Calcium gluconate, for example, is used as a pharmaceutical to supply calcium to the body; ferrous gluconate similarly is used to supply iron in the treatment of anemia; and gluconic acid in dishwasher detergents prevents spotting of glass surfaces due to the precipitation of calcium and magnesium salts.

Commercial production of gluconic acid by *A. niger* employs a submerged culture process. *A. niger* is initially grown to form a sufficient amount of mycelium, after which the conversion of glucose to gluconic acid is mediated by the fungal enzyme glucose oxidase; this latter stage is purely an enzymatic reaction. A typical growth medium for the production of gluconic acid contains approximately 25% glucose, various salts, calcium carbonate, and a compound containing the element boron. Borate in the medium stabilizes calcium gluconate, maintaining this compound in solution and preventing its precipitation, permitting the use of excess calcium carbonate to neutralize most of the gluconic acid produced and keeping the pH within acceptable limits. The fermentation is conducted at 30° C with aeration and agitation. Cooling coils are used to control the heat generated in this oxidative process. The growth of fungal mycelia is limited by the concentration of nitrogen in the medium. The gluconic acid is recovered from the fermentation by addition of calcium hydroxide to form crystalline calcium gluconate. Free gluconic acid can then be recovered by the addition of acid.

Citric Acid

Citric acid is produced by cultures of *Aspergillus niger*. Commercially produced citric acid is used in various ways, including as a food additive, especially in the production of soft drinks; as a metal chelating and sequestering agent; and in the manufacture of plasticizer. The composition of the fermentation medium is critical for obtaining high yields of citric acid. It is essential to limit the growth of the fungus so that high levels of citric acid can accumulate; this can be accomplished by having a deficiency of trace metals or phosphate in the medium. A typical medium for the production of citric acid contains molasses, ammonium nitrate, magnesium sulfate, and potassium phosphate. Acid is added to achieve a low pH, and some of the metals in the medium are complexed with ferricyanide, removing them from solution; alternatively, metals are removed using cation exchange resins.

Citric acid $\xrightarrow{-H_2O}$ *cis*-Aconitic acid $\xrightarrow{-CO_2}$ Itaconic acid

FIG. 15-23 Citric acid is converted to itaconic acid in a two-step reaction.

Itaconic Acid

The transformation of citric acid by *Aspergillus terreus* can be used for the production of itaconic acid, which is used as a resin in detergents (FIG. 15-23). The fermentation process uses a well-aerated molasses–mineral salts medium at a very low pH, below 2.2. At higher pH values, *A. terreus* degrades itaconic acid and the desired product obviously would not accumulate. Iron concentrations must be limited to achieve acceptable product yields (Table 15-7). The develop-

TABLE 15-7 Effects of the Concentrations of Some Metals in the Fermentation Medium on Itaconic Acid Production by a Mutant of *Aspergillus terreus*

ELEMENT	CONCENTRATION (mg/L)	YIELD (% CONVERSION)
Zinc	0	16
	0.5	43
	6	50
Copper	0.5	55
	1	52
	3	53
	6	55
Calcium	0	9
	337	43
	2700	59
Iron	0	57
	1	25
	2	17
	4	17

ment of fungal mycelia in this fermentation is intentionally limited, often by using a low inoculum size, to produce high accumulations of itaconic acid. Recovery is accomplished by evaporation of the fermentation medium to crystallize the itaconic acid.

Gibberellic Acid

Gibberellic acid is formed by the fungus *Gibberella fujikuroi (Fusarium moniliforme)* and can be produced commercially, using aerated submerged culture. A glucose–mineral salts medium, an incubation temperature of approximately 25° C, and slightly acidic pH conditions are employed for the production of gibberellic acid. Production normally takes 2 to 3 days, with accumulation of gibberellic acid lagging behind the growth of the fungus. Gibberellic acid and related gibberellins are plant hormones and are extensively used as growth-promoting substances to stimulate plant growth, flowering, and seed germination and to induce the formation of seedless fruit. Commercially produced gibberellins can be used to enhance agricultural productivity.

Lactic Acid

Lactobacillus delbrueckii is widely used in the commercial production of lactic acid, but various other *Lactobacillus, Streptococcus,* and *Leuconostoc* species also are of industrial importance for the production of this compound. Lactic acid is used in foods as a preservative, in leather production for deliming hides, and in the textile industry for fabric treatment. Various forms of lactic acid are also used for other purposes—in resins as polylactic acid, in plastics as various derivatives, in electroplating as copper lactate, and in baking powder and animal feed supplements as calcium lactate.

The typical medium for the production of lactic acid contains 10% to 15% glucose or another fermentable sugar, 10% calcium carbonate to neutralize the lactic acid formed, and ammonium phosphate and trace amounts of other nitrogen sources. Corn sugar, beet molasses, potato starch, and whey are often used as sources of carbohydrates for this fermentation. A typical production process for lactic acid uses an incubation temperature of 45° to 50° C and a pH of 5.5 to 6.5. The fermentor is agitated to suspend the calcium carbonate but is not aerated because this is an anaerobic process. The fermentation is normally completed within 5 to 7 days, with approximately 90% of the sugar converted to lactic acid. After the fermentation, calcium carbonate is added to raise the pH to 10 and the medium is heated and filtered. This proce-

TABLE 15-8 Important Uses for Enzymes Produced by Microorganisms

INDUSTRY	APPLICATION	ENZYME	SOURCE
Analytical	Sugar determination	Glucose oxidase	Fungi
	Glycogen determination	Galactose oxidase	Fungi
	Uric acid determination	Urate oxidase	Fungi
Baking	Bread baking	Amylase	Fungi
		Protease	Fungi
Brewing	Mashing-making beer	Amylase	Bacteria
		Glucamylase	Fungi
Carbonated beverages	Oxygen removal	Glucose oxidase	Fungi
Cereals	Breakfast foods	Amylase	Fungi
Chocolate, cocoa	Syrups	Amylase	Fungi, bacteria
Coffee	Coffee bean fermentation	Pectinase	Fungi
Confectionery	Soft-center candies	Invertase	Bacteria, fungi
Dairy	Cheese production	Rennin	Fungi
Dry cleaning	Spot removal	Protease, amylase	Bacteria, fungi
Eggs, dried	Glucose removal	Glucose oxidase	Fungi
Fruit juices	Clarification	Pectinases	Fungi
	Oxygen removal	Glucose oxidase	Fungi
	Debittering of citrus	Naringinase	Fungi
Laundry	Spot removal	Protease, amylase	Bacteria
	Cold-soluble laundry starch	Amylase	Bacteria
Leather	Bating	Protease	Bacteria, fungi

dure kills the bacteria, coagulates proteins, removes excess calcium carbonate, and decomposes residual carbohydrates. The recovery of lactic acid of high enough purity for some applications is difficult to achieve, and the cost of recovery has forced the replacement of lactic acid with alternative chemicals for some commercial uses.

PRODUCTION OF ENZYMES

Enzymes have various commercial applications, some of which are shown in Table 15-8. Enzymes produced for industrial processes include proteases, amylases, glucose isomerase, glucose oxidase, rennin, pectinases, and lipases. The four extensively produced microbial enzymes are protease, glucamylase, α-amylase, and glucose isomerase (FIG. 15-24). Microbial production of useful industrial enzymes is advantageous because of the large number of enzymes and the virtually unlimited supply that can be produced by microorganisms. A generalized scheme for the microbial production of commercial enzymes is shown in FIG. 15-25.

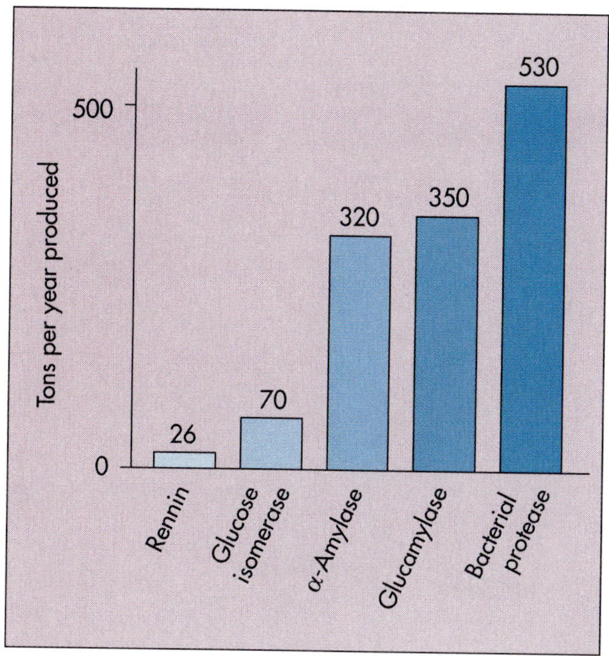

FIG. 15-24 Bacterial proteases account for the greatest commercial sales of enzymes.

INDUSTRY	APPLICATION	ENZYME	SOURCE
Meat	Meat tenderizing	Protease	Fungi, bacteria
Mayonnaise, salad dressings	Oxygen removal	Glucose oxidase	Fungi
Paper	Starch modification for paper coating	Amylase	Bacteria
Pharmaceutical and clinical	Digestive aids	Amylase	Fungi, bacteria
		Protease	Fungi, bacteria
		Lipase	Fungi
		Cellulase	Fungi
	Wound debridement (tissue removal)	Streptokinase-streptodornase	Bacteria
Photographic	Recovery of silver from spent film	Protease	Bacteria
Plumbing	Drain opener	Keratinase (protease)	Bacteria
Starch and syrup	Corn syrups	Amylase, dextrinase	Fungi
		Glucose isomerase	Fungi, bacteria
	Production of glucose	Glucamylase, amylase	Fungi, bacteria
Textile	Desizing of fabrics	Amylase, protease	Bacteria
Wine	Clarification	Pectinases	Fungi

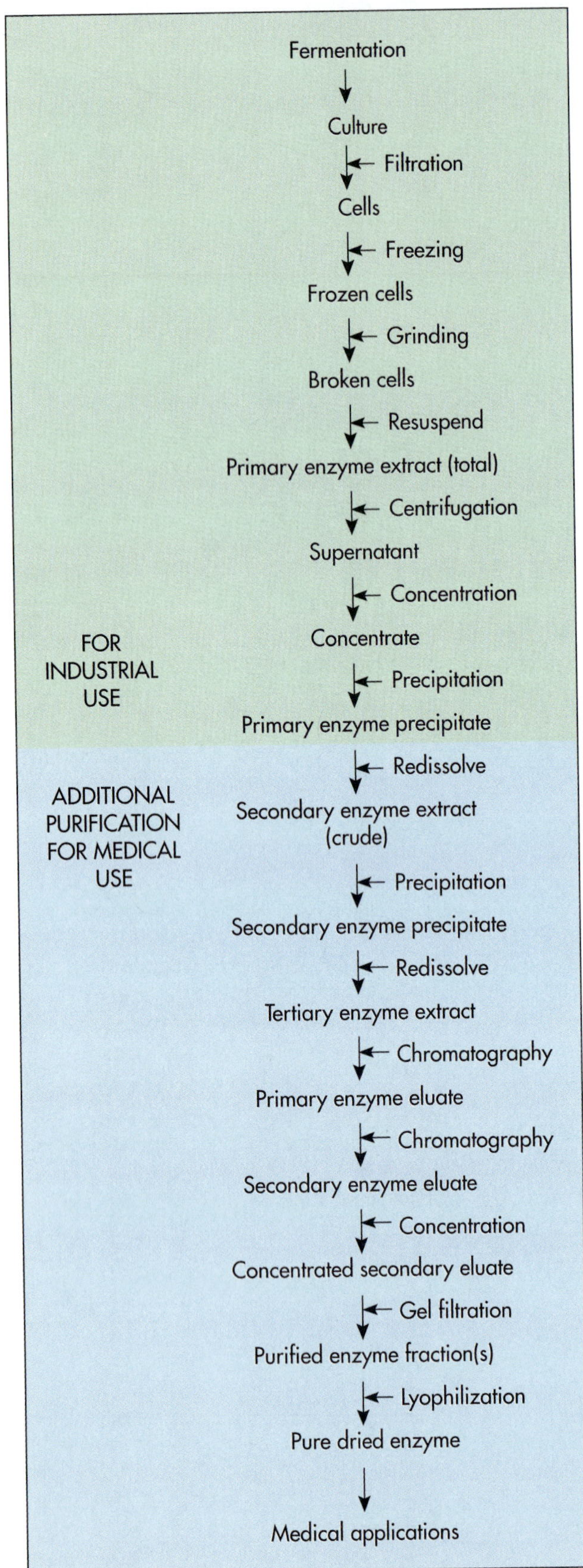

FIG. 15-25 Enzymes are produced by recovering cells from culture and releasing the enzymes by rupturing the cells. The cell-free extract undergoes minimal purification for industrial uses. Extensive additional purification is used for enzymes used in medicine.

Proteases

Proteases are a class of enzymes that attack the peptide bonds of protein molecules, forming small peptides. Proteases produced by different bacterial species are used for different industrial purposes. The largest commercial application of bacterial alkaline proteases is in the laundry industry, principally in modern detergent formulations. The general trend toward the use of nonphosphate laundry detergents that function at lower wash temperatures has led to the increasing incorporation of enzymes into liquid and powdered detergents to improve their cleaning performance. In the United States, the proportion of detergents containing enzymes increased from 2.5% in 1979 to about 25% in 1985. In the cleaning industry proteases are used as spot removers in dry cleaning, as presoak treatments in laundering, and in laundry detergents. The action of the enzyme degrades various proteinaceous materials such as milk and eggs, forming small peptide fragments that can be washed out readily. In dry cleaning, proteases are effective spot removers and are even useful in removing blood spots. These protease enzymes are relatively heat stable and are able to remain active in warm to hot water long enough for them to degrade the proteinaceous materials contaminating the fabric being washed. When used as a presoak, protease enzymes have sufficient time to act to degrade insoluble proteinaceous materials staining the fabric. Currently proteases for detergents are largely produced by *Bacillus licheniformis.* The enzymes produced by these *Bacillus* strains are active against protein molecules that make up common stains such as blood and grass.

Other alkaline proteases are being developed, using recombinant DNA technology, to function over a wide pH and temperature range. They are also being designed to remain stable under alkaline conditions and in the presence of detergent components—such as sequestering agents, surfactants, and bleach—and to exhibit long shelf life stability. One recombinant strain, *Bacillus* sp. GX6644, secretes an alkaline protease that is highly active toward the milk protein casein, with highest activity occurring at pH 11 and at moderate temperatures of 40° to 55° C. Another recombinant strain, *Bacillus* sp. GX6638, produces several alkaline proteases, one of which remains active over a broad pH range (8 to 12), exhibits exceptional stability under highly alkaline conditions (88% of the initial activity at pH 12 after 25 hours), and functions in the presence of bleach.

In addition to the development of enzymes for use in detergents, recombinant DNA technology has been employed to develop a bacterial strain that produces an enzyme, known as Kerazyme, that is used for dissolving hair and opening hair-clogged drains. Hair consists of the protein keratin, which is resistant to enzymatic attack. Agreements already guarantee over $3.8 million in product sales for Kerazyme over the next 5 years, making this the most successful product developed to date by genetic engineering.

Another major use of microbial proteases is in the baking industry. Proteases are used to alter the properties of the gluten proteins of flour. Fungal protease is added in the manufacture of most commercial bread in the United States to reduce mixing time and improve the quality of the loaf. Fungal or bacterial protease is used in the manufacture of crackers, biscuits, and cookies. Fungal proteases are principally obtained from *Aspergillus* species, and bacterial proteases are primarily produced using *Bacillus* species. Fungal proteases have a wider range of pH tolerance than bacterial proteases.

Proteases are also used for various other products, including digestive aids. Adding protease enzymes to beef can soften or tenderize it, making the meat more edible. A typical meat tenderizer contains 5% fungal protease, as well as MSG and other ingredients. In the leather industry, microbial proteases are used for bating of hides, which improves the quality by softening the leather. In the textile industry, protease enzymes are used for removing proteinaceous sizing and freeing silk fibers from the proteinaceous material in which they are embedded.

Amylases

Amylases are used for the preparation of sizing agents and the removal of starch sizing from woven cloth; preparation of starch sizing pastes for use in paper coatings; liquefaction of heavy starch pastes that form during heating steps in the manufacture of corn and chocolate syrups; production of bread; and removal of food spots in the dry cleaning industry, where amylase functions in conjunction with protease enzymes. Amylases are also sometimes used to replace or augment malt for starch hydrolysis in the brewing industry, as in the production of low-calorie beers. Light beers have become very popular.

There are various types of amylases, including (1) α-amylase, which converts starch to oligosaccharides and maltose; (2) β-amylase, which converts starch to maltose and dextrins; and (3) glucamylase, which converts starch to glucose. All three enzymes are used in the production of syrup and dextrose from starch. Fungal production of amylases uses *Aspergillus* species. For example, *A. oryzae* is used to produce amylases from wheat bran in stationary culture, and *A. niger* is used to produce amylases in aerated submerged culture, using a starch–mineral salts medium. *Bacillus subtilis* and *B. diastaticus* are used for the commercial production of bacterial amylases.

The conversion of starch to a high-fructose corn syrup sweetener, using microbial enzymes, represents an economically significant and relatively new industrial process, producing over 2 million tons of high-grade sweetener per year. This sweetener, produced in a three-step process using the enzymes alpha-amylase, glucamylase, and glucose isomerase, is rapidly replacing sucrose as the primary sweetener in soft drinks. In the final step, glucose (approximately 50%) is converted into fructose by the enzyme glucose isomerase. The use of mutation-screening methods combined with genetic recombination techniques has permitted the development of strains of *B. subtilis* with greatly enhanced abilities to produce high yields of alpha-amylase. The development of such strains markedly increases the economic feasibility of producing sweeteners for foods and beverages; it also shows how similar products can be made using microbial enzymes.

Other Enzymes

Various other microbial enzymes are produced for industrial applications. Rennin (also known as chymosin) is the milk curdling enzyme that catalyzes the coagulation of milk. It is used in the production of cheese, and *Mucor pussilus* or *M. meihei* can be used for the commercial production of rennin for curdling milk in cheese production. Fungal pectinase enzymes are used in the clarification of fruit juices. Glucose oxidase, produced by fungi, is used for removing glucose from eggs prior to drying, since powdered dried eggs brown because of the chemical reaction of proteins with glucose and removing the glucose stabilizes and prevents deterioration of the dried egg product. Glucose oxidase is also used to remove oxygen from various products such as soft drinks, mayonnaise, and salad dressings, preventing oxidative color and flavor changes.

Microbial enzymes may also be used for the production of synthetic polymers. For example, the plastics industry now uses chemical methods for producing alkene oxides used in the production of plastics. It is possible to synthesize alkene oxides by using microbial enzymes (FIG. 15-26, p. 622), and the use of genetically engineered microbial strains can make such synthesis commercially feasible. The synthesis of alkene oxides from alkenes is accomplished by the sequential action of three enzymes: pyranose-2-oxidase from the fungus *Oudmansiella mucida,* a haloperoxidase from the fungus *Caldariomyces,* and an epoxidase from a *Flavobacterium* species. The production of propylene oxide using microbial enzymes could revolutionize the plastics industry, altering the cost of producing this widely used material.

The production of thermally stable DNA polymerases is important because of their uses in amplifying DNA. The polymerase chain reaction, discussed in Chapter 6, is widely used in diagnostic medicine, forensic, and molecular biological research. Cultures of *Thermus aquaticus* and other thermophiles are used to produce thermally stable DNA polymerases. A genetically engineered strain of *E. coli* containing the gene for *taq* DNA polymerase from *Thermus aquaticus* is used to make the recombinant thermally stable DNA polymerase called Ampli*taq*.

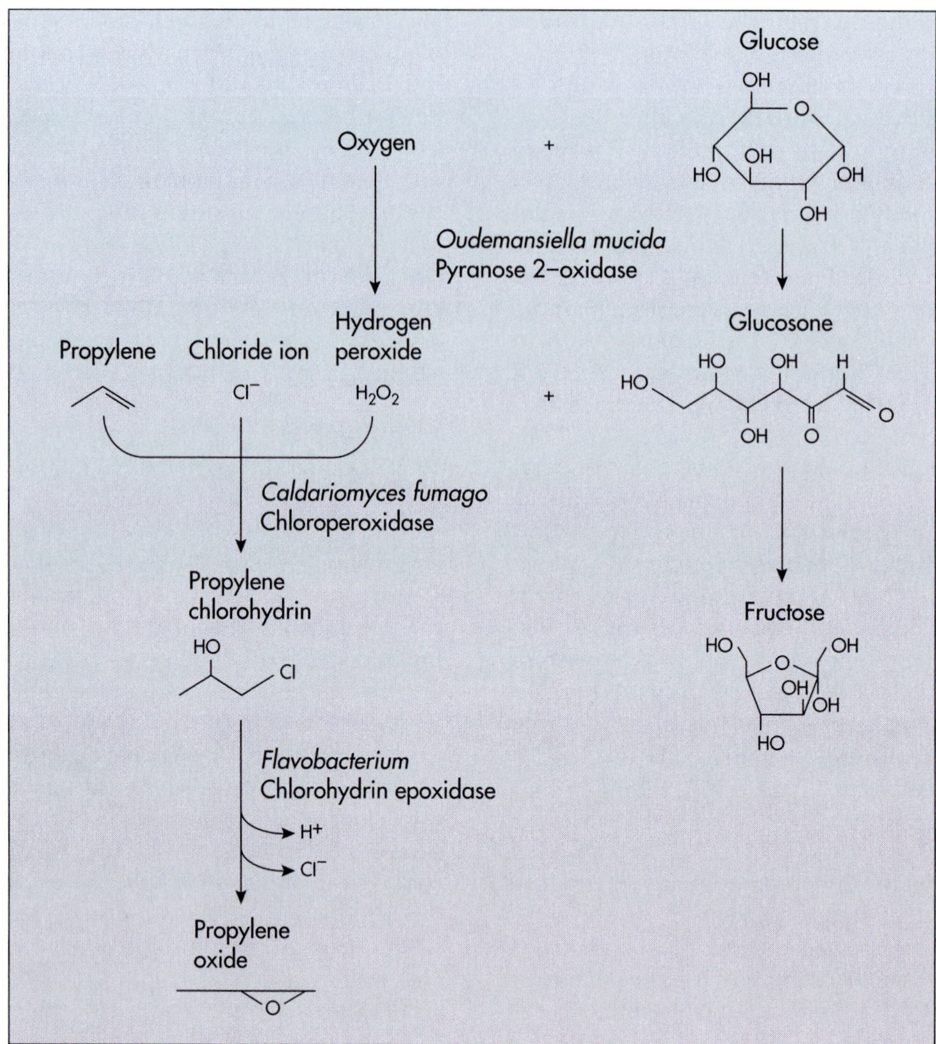

FIG. 15-26 Plastics can be produced from microorganisms that can synthesize propylene oxide.

PRODUCTION OF SOLVENTS

Several organic solvents can be produced by using microbial fermentation but generally organic solvents are produced today by chemical synthesis. For example, although ethanol is produced by fermentation for beverages and fuel, industrial alcohol for use as a solvent is mostly produced by chemical synthesis. Fermentation processes were important in the past in the industrial production of organic solvents and, as economic conditions change, will likely be used again in the future.

The process for producing acetone and butanol by fermentation, for example, was discovered by Chaim Weizmann (1874-1952), a Polish-born chemist then working in England. The discovery he made was influential in the British willingness to permit the establishment of a Jewish homeland in Palestine, and Weizmann later became the first president of the new State of Israel. During World War I, the microbial production of acetone was important for the production of the propellant cordite, and microbially produced butanol was converted to butadiene and used in making synthetic rubber. Until the development of a fermentation process, the German petrochemical industry was the major producer of acetone. After the war the demand for acetone declined, but the need for *n*-butanol increased for its use in brake fluids, urea-formaldehyde resins, and the production of protective coatings, such as lacquers used on automobiles.

The microbial production of acetone and butanol uses anaerobic *Clostridium* species. The fermentation process discovered by Weizmann was based on the conversion of starch to acetone by *C. acetobutylicum.* Other species, such as *C. saccharoacetobutylicum,* are able to convert the carbohydrates in molasses to acetone and butanol. These *Clostridium* species synthesize butyric and acetic acids, which are then converted to butanol and acetone. The yields of these neutral solvents are typically low, approximately 2% by weight of the fermentation broth, representing a 30% conversion of carbohydrates to neutral solvents. The accumulation of higher concentrations of these solvents is limited by the toxicity of the compounds. The solvents produced by fermentation are recovered by distillation. In South Africa, because of the scarcity of petroleum and the abundance of plant residues as substrates for fermentation, butanol and acetone are produced today by microbial fermentation employing this process. Elsewhere, these solvents are currently produced from petroleum. However, if the costs of petrochemicals increase, the production of *n*-butanol by fermentation may become more economically attractive.

Like butanol, glycerol is also produced today primarily by chemical synthesis, based on the saponification of fats and the chemical oxidation of propane and propylene. Glycerol is used as (1) a solvent in flavorings and food coloring agents; (2) a lubricant in the manufacture of pet food, candy, cake icings, toothpaste, glue, cellophane, and other products; and (3) a softening agent and a smoothing agent in pharmaceuticals and cosmetics. Glycerol is also used in the production of explosives and propellants. The production of glycerol by fermentation in Germany was an important factor during World War I because it was used in the production of munitions. The microbial production of glycerol is accomplished by adding sodium sulfite to a yeast–ethanol fermentation process. The sodium sulfite reacts with the carbon dioxide to produce sodium bisulfite, which prevents the reduction of acetaldehyde to ethanol. This blockage results in a divergence of the metabolic pathway with the accumulation of glycerol. Glycerol can be produced by using yeasts, such as *Saccharomyces cerevisiae,* and bacteria, such as *Bacillus subtilis.* The microbial production of glycerol may be renewed as a result of the finding that some yeasts can synthesize glycerol without the need to add sodium sulfite, thus making the process economically competitive with chemical methods of glycerol production.

PRODUCTION OF FUELS

Limited petroleum resources are forcing many industrialized nations to seek alternative fuel resources. Microbial production of *synthetic fuels* has the potential for helping to meet world energy demands. Useful fuels produced by microorganisms include ethanol, methane, hydrogen, and hydrocarbons. The use of microorganisms to produce commercially valuable fuels depends on finding the right strains of microorganisms that are able to produce the desired fuel efficiently and having an inexpensive supply of substrates

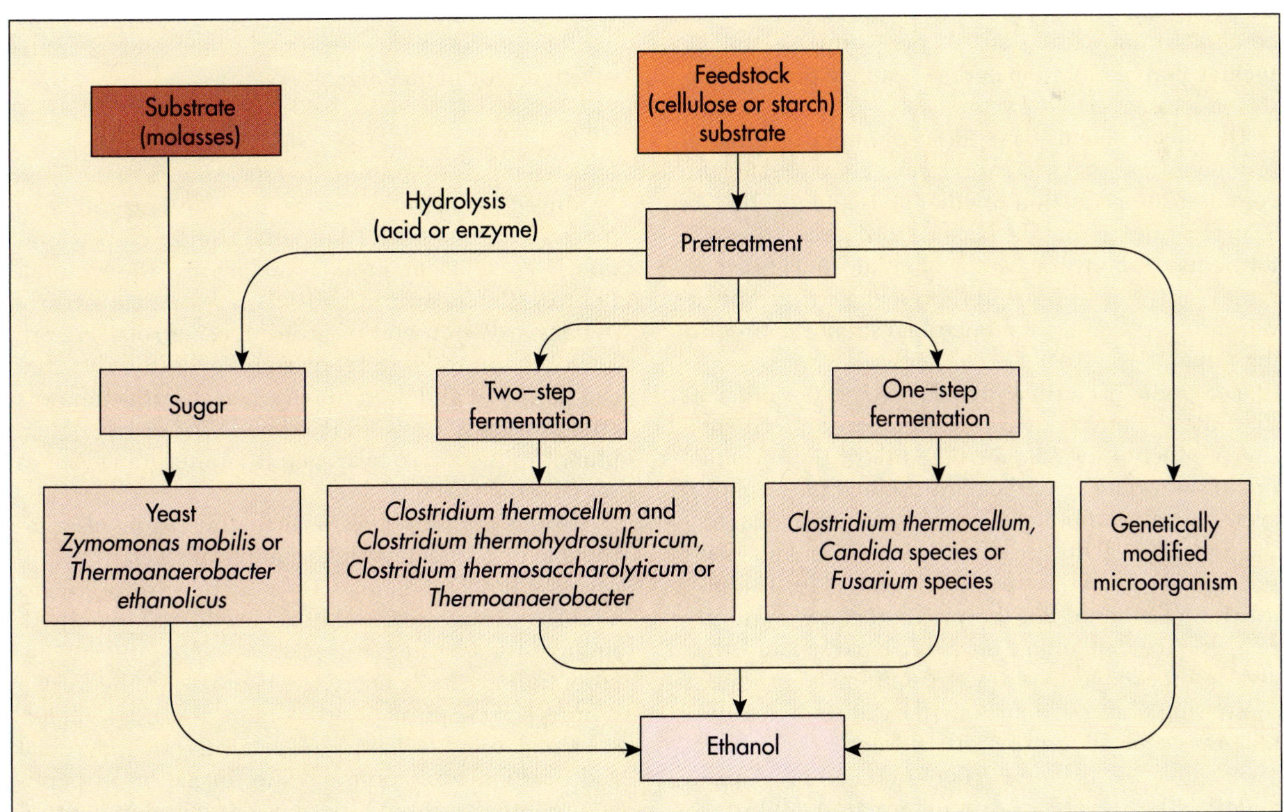

FIG. 15-27 Ethanol is commerically produced from various substrates. Yeast fermentation of molasses is commonly used for the production of alcoholic beverages and ethanol as fuel. Several bacteria and fungi can be used to produce ethanol from cellulose.

available for the fermentation process. It is obviously imperative that the production of synthetic fuels not consume more natural fuel resources than are produced. Microbial production of fuels can be a particularly attractive process when waste materials such as sewage and municipal garbage are used as the fermentation substrate.

Ethanol

The microbial production of ethanol has become an important source of a valuable fuel, particularly in regions of the world that have abundant supplies of plant residues. Brazil produces and uses large amounts of ethanol as an automotive fuel. Mixing gasoline and ethanol in a 9:1 ratio, has become a popular fuel in the midwestern United States. Ethanol combustion produces lowered air pollutants compared to gasoline combustion. At present about 100 million gallons of ethanol per year are used as a fuel, but 12 billion gallons per year would be required to completely replace gasoline use in the United States. There are three major limitations to the successful production of sufficient quantities of ethanol to serve as a major fuel source: (1) ethanol is relatively toxic to microorganisms, and therefore only limited concentrations of ethanol can accumulate in a fermentation process; (2) carbohydrate substrates normally used for the production of ethanol in the food industry are relatively expensive, making the cost of fuel produced by fermentation high; and (3) distillation to recover ethanol requires a substantial energy input, reducing the net gain of fuel as an energy resource produced in this process.

Despite problems with the economics of ethanol production, several processes can be employed for the commercial production of ethanol as a fuel (FIG. 15-27). The finding that the bacterium *Zymomonas mobilis* ferments carbohydrates, forming alcohol twice as rapidly as yeasts, appears to represent a significant advance in the search for a microbial strain for producing ethanol as a fuel. *Thermoanaerobacter ethanolicus,* a thermophilic bacterium, may be even more efficient than the organisms currently used for the fermentative production of ethanol. The use of thermophilic organisms would be particularly useful if the organism grew above the boiling point of ethanol, facilitating the recovery of the product. Corn sugar and plant starches are currently used as substrates for the production of ethanol but the prices of these substrates vary greatly, depending on plant harvests, and they also are needed as food resources. Biomass produced by growing photosynthetic microorganisms is a potential source of an inexpensive substrate for ethanol production, but cellulose from wood and other plant materials is probably the most promising substrate. Cellulose, however, is difficult to convert into fermentable sugars. A two-step fermentation process can be used for the conversion of cellulose to ethanol, in which cellulose is first converted to sugars, generally by *Clostridium* species, and the carbohydrates are then converted to ethanol by yeasts, *Zymomonas* species, or *Thermoanaerobacter* species. It is very likely that genetic engineering can create a microbial species that can efficiently convert cellulose directly to ethanol and that will also tolerate high concentrations of ethanol. Such an organism should permit the commercial production of ethanol as a fuel.

Methane

Methane produced by methanogenic bacteria is another important potential energy source. Methane can be used for the generation of mechanical, electrical, and heat energy. Large amounts of methane can be produced by anaerobic decomposition of waste materials. Many sewage treatment plants meet all or part of their own energy needs from the production of methane in their anaerobic sludge digesters. Excess methane produced in such facilities is sufficient to supply power for some municipalities. Efficient generation of methane can be achieved by using algal biomass grown in pond cultures, sewage sludge, municipal refuse, plant residue, and animal waste.

Methanogenic bacteria are members of the archaebacteria; they are obligate anaerobes and produce methane from the reduction of acetate and/or carbon dioxide. The production of methane generally requires a mixed microbial community, with some bacterial populations converting the available organic carbon into low molecular weight fatty acids that are substrates for methanogens.

Other Fuels

Hydrogen is another potential fuel source that can be produced by microorganisms. It is not currently employed as a major fuel but could be developed into one if an efficient production process were found. Photosynthetic microorganisms are capable of producing hydrogen and of growing using solar energy. Such organisms convert solar energy into a fuel that can be stored and used to power electrical generators and provide a conventional source of energy. Such photoproduction of hydrogen is an intriguing, but as yet far from practical, idea.

Various microorganisms, including algae, also are capable of producing higher molecular weight hydrocarbons, but the potential use of such hydrocarbons as a fuel source has received relatively little attention. Although physicochemical processes are crucial, microorganisms are believed to play a role in the formation of petroleum deposits. A more thorough understanding of the basic mechanisms of microbial hydrocarbon formation and the formation of petroleum deposits should permit the development of genetically engineered microorganisms and fermentation processes to produce synthetic sources of petroleum hydrocarbons.

15.2 ENVIRONMENTAL BIOTECHNOLOGY

BIOLEACHING

As the technological level of an ever-increasing world population rises, so does the need for industrially important minerals. As easily accessible, high-grade deposits of ores are depleted, it becomes increasingly important to find innovative and economical methods to recover such metals from lower-grade deposits, which for technical or economic reasons have not been used. Microorganisms can play an important role in recovering valuable minerals from low-grade ores, meeting some of the needs of industrialized society. Such recovery processes employ microbial metabolic activities to gain access to, rather than to actually produce, desired products; this process is called **bioleaching.**

Recovery of Metals

Bioleaching for the recovery of metals uses microorganisms to alter the physical or chemical properties of a metallic ore so that the metal can be extracted. This process is used to recover metals from ores that are not suitable for direct smelting because of their low metal content (FIG. 15-28). Metals can be extracted economically from low-grade sulfide or sulfide-containing ore by exploiting the metabolic activities of thiobacilli, particularly *Thiobacillus ferrooxidans.* Under optimal conditions in the laboratory, as much as 97% of the copper in low-grade ores has been recovered by bioleaching, but such high yields are seldom achieved in actual mining operations. Even a 50% to 70% recovery of copper by bioleaching from an ore that would otherwise be completely unproductive would be an important achievement. The process is currently applied on a commercial scale to low-grade copper and uranium ores, and laboratory experiments indicate that it also has promise for the recovery of nickel, zinc, cobalt, tin, cadmium, molybdenum, lead, antimony, arsenic, and selenium from their low-grade sulfide-containing ores. The leaching process can also be used to separate the insoluble lead sulfate ($PbSO_4$) from other metals that occur in the same ore.

The equation for the general process carried out by *T. ferrooxidans* and related species is:

$$MS + 2\,O_2 \rightarrow MSO_4$$

where M represents a divalent metal. Because the metal sulfide (MS) is insoluble and the metal sulfate (MSO_4) is usually water soluble, this transformation produces a readily leachable form of the metal. *T. ferrooxidans* is a chemolithotrophic bacterium that derives energy through the oxidation of either a reduced sulfur compound or ferrous iron. It exerts its bioleaching action by oxidizing the metal sulfide be-

FIG. 15-28 Large bioleaching operations are used for the recovery of copper. A solution of sulfur oxidizing bacteria *(Thiobacillus)* is sprayed over the copper bearing rocks. The leachate is drained into a pond and the copper is recovered.

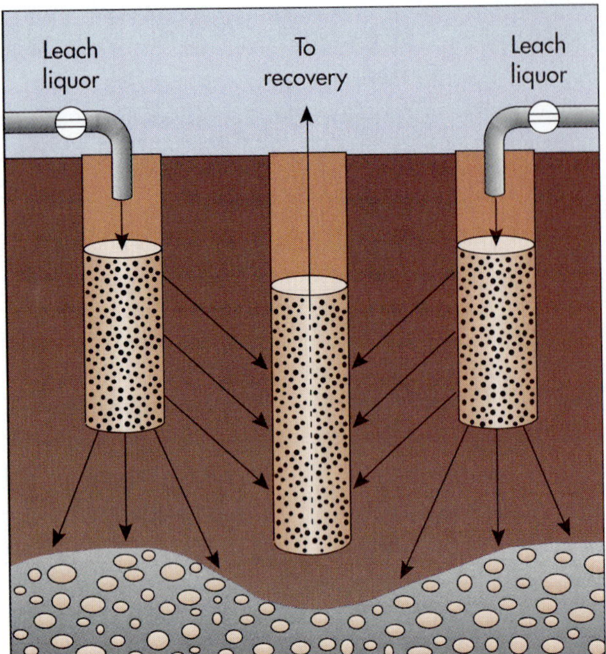

FIG. 15-29 In the hole-to-hole leaching process the leach liquor is added to peripheral holes; it migrates to a central hole from which the mineral is recovered.

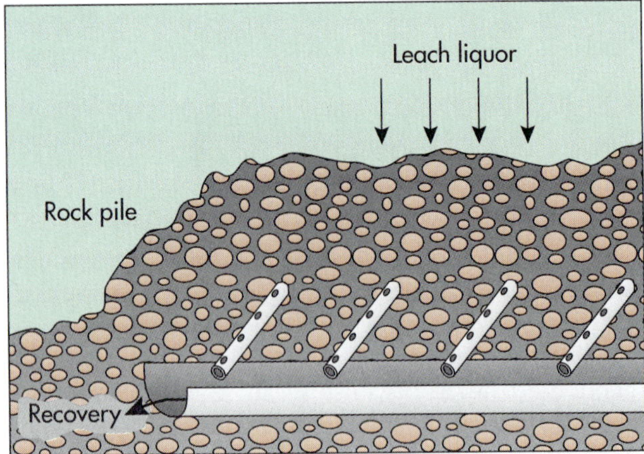

FIG. 15-30 In the heap bioleaching process, the ore is mined and piled over a series of perforated recovery pipes. The leach liquor is poured over the surface of the heap and the mineral is recovered from the leachate.

ing recovered directly, converting S^{2-} to SO_4^{2-}, and/or indirectly by oxidizing the ferrous iron content of the ore to ferric iron. The ferric iron, in turn, chemically oxidizes the metal to be recovered to a soluble form that can be leached from the ore.

If the ore formation is sufficiently porous and overlays a water-impermeable stratum, it is possible to leach the ore *in situ* without first mining it. An appropriate pattern of boreholes is established, with some of the holes used for the injection of the leaching liquor and others for the recovery of the leachate (FIG. 15-29). More frequently, though, this bioleaching process is accomplished after the ore is mined, broken up, and piled in heaps on a water-impermeable formation or on a specially constructed apron (FIG. 15-30). Water is then pumped to the top of the ore heap and trickles down through the ore to the apron. A continuous reactor leaching operation for recovery of copper from its low-grade sulfide ore is shown in FIG. 15-31. The leaching water and ore usually supplies enough dissolved mineral nutrients to satisfy the needs of *T. ferrooxidans*, but in some cases mineral nutrients such as ammonia and phosphate must be added. In most of these bioleaching operations, the leached metal is then extracted with an organic solvent and subsequently removed from the solvent by stripping. The leaching liquor and the solvent are recycled.

The characteristics of the ore have an important effect on its susceptibility to bioleaching. The rate of leaching is determined in large part by the size of the mineral particles. Increasing the surface area, accomplished by crushing and/or grinding, generally increases production efficiency. Environmental factors must also be conducive for efficient bioleaching to occur. Optimal conditions for bioleaching use *T. ferrooxidans* area temperature of 30° to 50° C, a pH of 2.3 to 2.5, and an iron concentration of 2 to 4 g/L of leach liquor. Available oxygen and nutrients, such as ammonium, nitrogen, phosphorus, sulfate, and magnesium, are essential for the growth of *T. ferrooxidans.*

The oxidative activities of *Thiobacillus* can produce high temperatures in some mineral deposits, which may exceed the tolerance limits of the species being used. Obviously, this would lead to decreased bioleaching activity and mineral production. Because of these high temperatures, thermophilic sulfur-oxidizing microorganisms may be useful for some bioleaching processes. Members of the genus *Sulfolobus* are obligate thermophiles that can oxidize ferrous iron and

FIG. 15-31 In a continuous reactor, the bacterial culture is continuously pumped through a pile of ore. The leached mineral is recovered by precipitation from the leachate.

sulfur in a manner similar to that of the members of the genus *Thiobacillus*. These acid-tolerant thermophilic bacteria can oxidize inorganic substrates and are used in the bioleaching of metallic sulfides. *Sulfolobus* has been used for the bioleaching of molybdenite (molybdenum sulfide), whereas *Thiobacillus* is intolerant of high concentrations of molybenum, mercury, and silver.

Copper Bioleaching Copper, which is in high demand for the electrical industry, is generally in short supply. A typical low-grade copper ore contains 0.1% to 0.4% copper. The "pregnant" leaching solution may contain 1 to 3 g of copper per liter. In copper leaching operations, the action of *Thiobacillus* involves both direct oxidation of copper sulfide (CuS) and indirect oxidation of CuS via generation of ferric ions from ferrous sulfide. Ferrous sulfide is present in most of the important copper ores, such as chalcopyrite ($CuFeS_2$). The copper is recovered by solvent extraction or by using scrap iron. In the latter case, copper replaces iron according to the equation $CuSO_4 + Fe^\circ \rightarrow Cu^\circ + FeSO_4$ and is more advantageous for bioleaching because the organic solvent residues in the leaching liquor may inhibit the continued activity of *T. ferrooxidans.*

Uranium Bioleaching The recovery of uranium, a fuel required by the nuclear power generation industry, can also be enhanced by microbial activities. The microbial recovery of uranium from otherwise useless low-grade ores is helpful in overcoming the international energy shortage. Nuclear safety and waste disposal problems, as well as the limited supply of uranium, render current nuclear fission generators controversial; for all of these reasons, they may very well be only a stopgap solution to the international energy problem. Although bioleaching cannot influence safety considerations, this process can have an immediate and direct bearing on the economics of nuclear power production by providing a mechanism for commercial use of low-grade uranium deposits and for the recovery of uranium from low-grade nuclear wastes. Recovery of uranium from radioactive wastes is extremely important because it overcomes the problem of waste disposal, a major shortcoming of using nuclear power generators.

Insoluble tetravalent uranium oxide (UO_2) occurs in low-grade ores. Although there is no evidence for the direct oxidation of UO_2 by *T. ferrooxidans,* UO_2 can be converted to the leachable hexavalent form (UO_2SO_4) indirectly by the action of this microorganism. *T. ferrooxidans* oxidizes the ferrous iron in pyrite (FeS_2), which often accompanies uranium ores, to ferric iron. The oxidized iron acts as an oxidant, converting UO_2 chemically to UO_2SO_4, which can be recovered by leaching. The technical and economic feasibility of employing *Thiobacillus* for the recovery of uranium and copper minerals depends on various factors. The particular form of the naturally occurring mineral is important. Bacterial leaching of uranium is most feasible in geological strata where the ore is in the tetravalent state and is pyritic, that is, closely associated with reduced sulfur and iron minerals. The geological formation in which the minerals occur is also important in determining the suitability of the bioleaching process. *In situ* bioleaching is ideal when there is a natural drainage system, as through a fault with an impermeable basin, that will permit economical recovery of the minerals. If these conditions do not exist, mining must precede the heap leaching process described previously.

Oil Recovery

Bioleaching of oil shales also has the potential to enhance the recovery of hydrocarbons. Many oil shales contain large amounts of carbonates and pyrites, and the removal of these minerals increases the porosity of the shale, enhancing recovery of the oil. Acid dissolves the carbonates and can be produced by *Thiobacillus* species growing on the sulfur and iron in the pyrite. Such microbial leaching appears to have the potential for making recovery of hydrocarbons from oil shales economically feasible.

The *tertiary recovery of petroleum,* that, is the use of biological and chemical means to enhance oil recovery, and the enhanced recovery of hydrocarbons from oil shales are important because readily recoverable oil supplies have diminished. Tertiary recovery of oil employs solvents, surfactants, and polymers to dislodge oil from geological formations. The use of tertiary recovery methods has the potential for recovering 60 to 120 billion barrels of oil in United States reserves alone that otherwise could not be recovered. Xanthan gums produced by bacteria, such as *Xanthomonas campestris,* are promising compounds for the tertiary recovery of oil. These polymers have high viscosity and flow characteristics that allow them to pass through small pores in the rock layers containing oil deposits. When added during water flooding operations, that is, when water is pumped into petroleum reservoirs to force out the oil, xanthan gums help push the oil toward the production wells. These polymers are produced by conventional fermentation processes in which *X. campestris* is grown and the xanthan gums are recovered.

BIOREMEDIATION

Bioremediation is the utilization of microorganisms to remove pollutants from the environment. It is an acceleration of the natural fate of biodegradable pollutants and hence a natural, or "green solution," to the problem of oil pollutants that causes minimal, if any, additional ecological effects. The most cost effective methods are generally *in situ* because these avoid costly movement of contaminated soils and waters.

Bioremediation has become an important method for oil spill cleanup. Populations of hydrocarbon degraders generally are less than 1% of the total microorganisms in unpolluted environments but increase to 1% to 10% in environments exposed to petroleum pollutants. Mixed cultures of nongenetically engineered microorganisms are commonly proposed as inocula for seeding to bioremediate oil contaminated soils and waters. A genetically engineered hydrocarbon-degrading pseudomonad was the first patented organism in a landmark decision of the U. S. Supreme Court that greatly increased the economic potential of biotechnology. There is considerable controversy surrounding deliberate environmental release of genetically engineered microorganisms, and given the current worldwide regulatory framework for the deliberate release of genetically engineered microorganisms, it is unlikely that any such organism could currently gain the necessary regulatory approval in time to be of much use in treating an oil spill.

The bioremediation of oil pollutants generally relies on modifying the environment so that the growth of indigenous hydrocarbon-degrading microorganisms is stimulated. Since microorganisms require nitrogen, phosphorus, and other mineral nutrients for incorporation into biomass, the availability of these nutrients within the area of hydrocarbon degradation is critical. Concentrations of available nitrogen and phosphorus generally are severely limiting to microbial hydrocarbon degradation. Various fertilizer formulations are used to supply these necessary nutrients. Molecular oxygen also is necessary for rapid hydrocarbon degradation because the initial steps in the biodegradation of hydrocarbons by most microorganisms is obligately aerobic. Forced aeration has been successfully used for the bioremediation of oil contaminated aquifers. Hydrogen peroxide is often used to supply oxygen for the bioremediation of soils and groundwaters.

The *Exxon Valdez* spill formed the basis for a major study on bioremediation through fertilizer application and was the largest application of this emerging technology. Inipol (an oleophilic microemulsion with urea as a nitrogen source, laureth phosphate as a phosphate source, and oleic acid as a carbon source) and Customblen (a slow-release fertilizer composed of calcium phosphate, ammonium phosphate, and ammonium nitrate within a polymerized vegetable oil coating) were used. Within approximately 2 to 3 weeks, oil on the surfaces of cobble shorelines treated with Inipol and Customblen was degraded so that these shorelines were visibly cleaner than non-bioremediated shorelines (FIG. 15-32). Monitoring of the oil-degrading microbial populations and measuring the rates of oil degradation activities by a joint Exxon, United States Environmental Protection Agency (USEPA), and State of Alaska Department of Conservation team showed that a fivefold increase in rates of oil biodegradation typically followed fertilizer application. The addition of fertilizers caused no eutrophication, no acute toxicity to sensitive marine test species, and did not cause the release of undegraded oil residues from the beaches. Because of its effectiveness, bioremediation became the major treatment method for removing oil pollutants from the impacted shorelines of Prince William Sound. The success of the field demonstration program introduces the consideration of bioremediation as a key component (but not the sole component) in any cleanup strategy developed for future oil spills.

FIG. 15-32 The shorelines contaminated by oil spilled by the *Exxon Valdez* were cleaned through bioremediation. Nutrients were added to stimulate the growth of indigenous oil-degrading bacteria. This test plot shows the dramatic results that demonstrated the efficacy of bioremediation.

15.3 BIOTECHNOLOGY AND THE PRODUCTION OF FOOD

Microorganisms are used beneficially in the food industry for food production. Many of the foods and beverages we commonly enjoy, such as wine and cheese, are the products of microbial enzymatic activity. For the most part, it is the fermentative metabolism of microorganisms that is exploited in the production of food products. The accumulation of fermentation products, such as ethanol and lactic acid, is desirable because of their characteristic flavors and other properties. Only a few processes, such as the production of vinegar, make use of microbial oxidative metabolism. The microbial production of foods can be viewed as an exercise in harnessing microbial biochemistry to produce desired, rather than adverse, changes in food products.

The production of fermented foods requires the proper substrates, microbial populations, and environmental conditions to obtain the desired end product. Quality control is essential in food fermentation to ensure that the product is of high quality. A fermented food may require additional preservation to prevent spoilage because further uncontrolled microbial growth could render it inedible. For example, once wine is produced, it must be maintained under anaerobic conditions to prevent its oxidation to vinegar.

Microbial processes used in food production traditionally employ microbial enzymatic activities to transform one food into another, with the microbially produced food product having properties vastly different from those of the starting material. In addition to the use of microorganisms to produce fermented food products, microbial biomass is now considered a potential source of protein for meeting the food needs of an expanding world population. Some microorganisms such as mushrooms have been used as food products for centuries. The growth of bacteria, algae, and fungi as proteinaceous food, however, is not yet a generally accepted concept. Microbial biomass can be used as an animal feed supplement or may be developed as a direct source of protein for human consumption.

FERMENTED DAIRY PRODUCTS

Numerous products are made by the microbial fermentation of milk, including buttermilk, yogurt, and many cheeses. The fermentation of milk is primarily carried out by lactic acid bacteria. The lactic acid fermentation pathway and the accumulation of lactic acid from the metabolism of the milk sugar lactose are common to the production of fermented dairy products. The accumulated lactic acid in these products acts as a natural preservative. The differences in the flavor and aroma of the various fermented dairy products are due to additional fermentation products that may be present in only relatively low concentrations.

Buttermilk, Sour Cream, Kefir, and Koumis

Different fermented dairy products are produced by using different strains of lactic acid bacteria as starter cultures and different fractions of whole milk as the starting substrate (Table 15-9). Sour cream, for example, uses *Streptococcus cremoris* or *S. lactis* for the production of lactic acid, and *Leuconostoc cremoris* or *S. lactis diacetilactis* for the production of the characteristic flavor compounds. Cream is the starting substrate for this product. If skim milk is used as the starting material, cultured buttermilk is produced. Bulgarian buttermilk is made by using *Lactobacillus bulgaricus* for the production of both lactic acid and flavor compounds.

TABLE 15-9 Some Foods Produced from Fermented Milks

FERMENTED PRODUCT	MICROORGANISMS RESPONSIBLE FOR FERMENTATION	DESCRIPTION
Sour cream	*Streptococcus* sp., *Leuconostoc* sp.	Cream is inoculated and incubated until the desired acidity develops.
Cultured buttermilk	*Streptococcus* sp., *Leuconostoc* sp.	Made with skimmed or partly skimmed pasteurized milk.
Bulgarian buttermilk	*Lactobacillus bulgaricus*	Product differs from commercial buttermilk in having higher acidity and lacking aroma.
Acidophilus milk	*Lactobacillus acidophilus*	Milk for propagation of *L. acidophilus* and the milk to be fermented are sterilized and then inoculated with *L. acidophilus.* This milk product is used for its medicinal therapeutic value.
Yogurt	*Streptococcus thermophilus, Lactobacillus bulgaricus*	Made from milk in which solids are concentrated by evaporation of some water and addition of skim milk solids. Product has consistency resembling custard.
Kefir	*Streptococcus lactis, Lactobacillus bulgaricus,* yeasts	A mixed lactic acid and alcoholic fermentation; bacteria produce acid, and yeasts produce alcohol.

Butter is normally made by churning cream that has been soured by lactic acid bacteria. *S. cremoris* or *S. lactis* is used to produce lactic acid rapidly, and *Leuconostoc citrovorum* produces the necessary flavor compounds. The *Leuconostoc* enzymes attack citrate in milk, producing diacetyl, which gives butter its characteristic flavor and aroma. Kefir and koumis, which are popular in some European countries, are fermentation products of *S. lactis, S. cremoris,* other *Lactobacillus* species, and yeasts. Lactic acid, ethanol, and carbon dioxide are formed during the fermentation and give these products their characteristic flavors.

Yogurt

Over 550,000 pounds of yogurt are produced annually in the United States. Yogurt is made by fermenting milk with a mixture of *L. bulgaricus* and *S. thermophilus.* Yogurt fermentation is carried out at 40° C. The characteristic flavor of yogurt is due to the accumulation of lactic acid and acetaldehyde produced by *L. bulgar-*

TABLE 15-10 Classification of Some Cheeses

CHEESE	MICROORGANISMS		
SOFT, UNRIPENED			
	Streptococcus lactis, Leuconostoc citrovorum *Streptococcus cremoris* *Streptococcus diacetilactis*		
SOFT, RIPENED, 1-5 MONTHS			
Brie	*Streptococcus lactis, Streptococcus cremoris*	*Penicillium candidium, Penicillium camemberti*	*Brevibacterium linens*
Camembert	*Streptococcus lactis, Streptococcus cremoris*	*Penicillium candidium, Penicillium camemberti*	
Limburger	*Streptococcus lactis, Streptococcus cremoris*	*Brebacterium linens*	
SEMISOFT, RIPENED, 1-12 MONTHS			
Blue	*Streptococcus lactis, Streptococcus cremoris*	*Penicillium roqueforti, Penicillium glaucum*	
Brick	*Streptococcus lactis, Streptococcus cremoris*	*Brevibacterium linens*	
Gorgonzola	*Streptococcus lactis, Streptococcus cremoris*	*Penicillium roqueforti, Penicillium glaucum*	
Monterey Jack	*Streptococcus lactis, Streptococcus cremoris*		
Muenster	*Streptococcus lactis, Streptococcus cremoris*	*Brevibacterium linens*	
Roquefort	*Streptococcus lactis, Streptococcus cremoris*	*Penicillium roqueforti, Penicillium glaucum*	
HARD, RIPENED, 3-12 MONTHS			
Cheddar	*Streptococcus lactis, Streptococcus cremoris, Streptococcus durans*	*Lactobacillus casei*	
Colby	*Streptococcus lactis, Streptococcus cremoris, Streptococcus durans*	*Lactobacillus casei*	
Edam	*Streptococcus lactis, Streptococcus cremoris*		
Gouda	*Streptococcus lactis, Streptococcus cremoris*		
Gruyère	*Streptococcus lactis, Streptococcus thermophilus*	*Lactobacillus helveticus*	*Propionibacterium shermanii* or *Lactobacillus bulgaricus* and *Propionibacterium freudenreichii*
Swiss	*Streptococcus lactis, Streptococcus thermophilus*	*Lactobacillus helveticus*	*Propionibacterium shermanii* or *Lactobacillus bulgaricus* and *Propionibacterium freudenreichii*
VERY HARD, RIPENED, 12-16 MONTHS			
Parmesan	*Streptococcus lactis, Streptococcus cremoris, Streptococcus thermophilus*	*Lactobacillus bulgaricus*	
Romano	*Lactobacillus bulgaricus*	*Streptococcus thermophilus*	

icus. Because of the tart taste of acetaldehyde, most yogurt produced in the United States is flavored by adding fruit.

Cheese

Various cheeses are produced by microbial fermentation. Cheeses consist of milk curds that have been separated from the liquid portion of the milk (whey). The curdling of milk is accomplished by using the enzyme rennin (casein coagulase or chymosin) and lactic acid bacterial starter cultures. Rennin is obtained from calf stomachs or by microbial production. Cheeses are classified as (1) soft if they have a high water content (50% to 80%), (2) semihard if the water content is about 45%, and (3) hard if they have a low water content (less than 40%). Cheeses are also classified as unripened if they are produced by single-step fermentation or as ripened if additional microbial growth is required during maturation of the cheese to achieve the desired taste, texture, and aroma (Table 15-10). Processed cheeses are made by blending various cheeses to achieve a desired product. If the water content is elevated during processing, thereby diluting the nutritive content of the product, the product is called a *processed food* rather than a cheese.

The natural production of cheeses involves lactic acid fermentation, with various mixtures of *Streptococcus* and *Lactobacillus* species used as starter cultures to initiate the fermentation. The flavors of different cheeses result from the use of different microbial starter cultures, varying incubation times and conditions, and the inclusion or omission of secondary microbial species late in the fermentation process.

Ripening of cheeses involves additional enzymatic transformations after the formation of the cheese curd, using enzymes produced by lactic acid bacteria or enzymes from other sources. Unripened cheeses do not require the additional enzymatic transformations. Cottage cheese and cream cheese are produced by using a starter culture similar to the one used for the production of cultured buttermilk and are soft cheeses that do not require ripening. Sometimes a cheese is soaked in brine to encourage the development of selected bacterial and fungal populations during ripening. Limburger is a soft cheese produced in this manner. During ripening the curds are softened by proteolytic and lipolytic enzymes, and the cheese acquires its characteristic aroma. The production of Parmesan cheese also involves brine curing.

Swiss cheese formation involves a late propionic acid fermentation, with ripening accomplished by *Propionibacterium shermanii* and *P. freudenreichii*. The propionic acid yields the characteristic aroma and flavor, and the carbon dioxide produced during this late fermentation forms the holes in Swiss cheese. Various fungi are also used in the ripening of different cheeses. The unripened cheese is normally inoculated with fungal spores and incubated in a warm, moist room to promote the growth of filamentous fungi. For example, blue cheeses are produced by using *Penicillium* species. Roquefort cheese is produced by using *P. roqueforti*, and camembert and brie are produced by using *P. camemberti* and *P. candidum*.

FERMENTED MEATS

Several types of sausage, such as Lebanon bologna, the salamis, and the dry and semidry summer sausages, are produced by allowing the meat to undergo heterolactic acid fermentation during curing. The fermentation has a preservative effect and also adds a tangy flavor to the meat. Various lactic acid bacteria are normally involved in the fermentation, but *Pediococcus cerevisiae* can be used for controlled production of these types of meats.

LEAVENING OF BREAD

Yeasts are added to bread dough to ferment the sugar, producing the carbon dioxide that leavens the dough and causes it to rise. The principal yeast used in bread baking is *Saccharomyces cerevisiae*, known as *bakers' yeast*. Bakers' yeast is produced in large quantities for the baking industry (FIG. 15-33, p. 632). The yeast is normally grown in a molasses-mineral salts medium at a pH of 4.3 to 4.5 and temperature of 30° C, with the molasses substrate added gradually to maintain a sugar concentration of 0.5% to 1.5%. The concentration of sugar in the fermentor is critical because too high a concentration represses respiratory enzymes and alcohol production even under highly aerobic conditions. The yeasts are generally collected by centrifugation and pressed through a filter to remove excess liquid. For the baking industry, the yeasts are normally formed into cakes or are dried further to form active dry yeast. Packages of active dry yeast, containing less than 8% water, are frequently used for home baking purposes.

In the baking process, the yeast is used strictly as a source of enzymes to carry out alcoholic fermentation. The yeast does not grow during the first 2 hours after addition to the dough, by which time the leavening process is normally completed. Amylases in the dough convert starch to sugars, and the yeasts metabolize the sugars that are formed, producing carbon dioxide and ethanol. Besides *S. cerevisiae*, various other microorganisms, including coliform bacteria and *Clostridium* species, can be employed for leavening bread. The microorganisms used for bread leavening must produce carbon dioxide from the fermentation of sugars to be useful.

In modern home and commercial baking processes, excess amounts of yeast are normally added so that the fermentation time is short. Older, more traditional bread-making processes use less yeast and longer fermentation times. However, when the pro-

Cane molasses
Beet molasses
Additional nutrients
In laboratory
Mixing and cooking
Filter
Culture "scale–up"
Finished mash storage
Stock inoculum
Scale–up of large volume of inoculum
A
Large–scale fermentor
Removal of yeast cell crop
Filter
Mixer and extruder
Conversion of cell paste to yeast cakes
Packaging

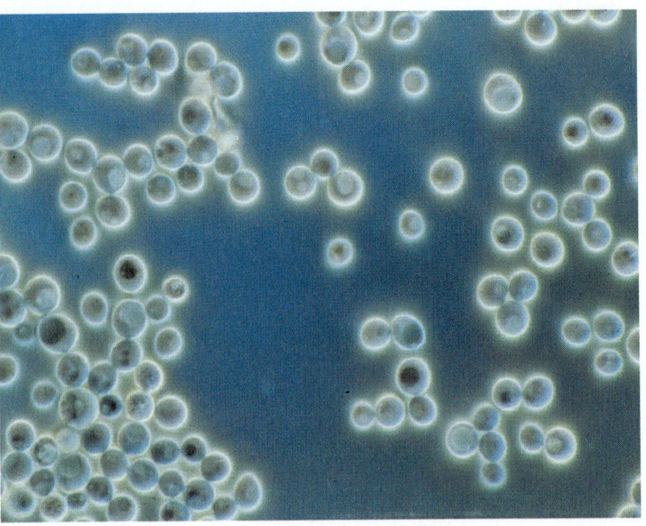

B

FIG. 15-33 **A,** To produce baker's yeast, cultures of *Saccharomyces* are grown on molasses. The yeasts are recovered by centrifugation and pressed into yeast cakes or freeze dried. **B,** Large quantities of yeast are grown for bread production and the brewing industry.

cessing time exceeds 2 hours, there can be an undesirable growth of fungi and bacteria. During fermentation the dough becomes conditioned as a result of the action of proteases on the flour protein, gluten. Enzymes are produced by the yeasts or may be added from other sources. As a result of this conditioning, the gluten matures, becoming elastic and capable of retaining the carbon dioxide gas produced by the yeasts during fermentation. Sugar, or amylase to convert starches to sugar, is normally added to the flour to increase the rate of gas production by the yeast. Addition of increased amounts of yeast and various salts to support yeast metabolism also increases the rate of gas production. The leavening process is normally carried out at 27° C, which is optimal for fermentation. Too high or too low a temperature can result in reduced rates of gas production.

After leavening, the bread is baked. Carbon dioxide bubbles are trapped in the dough and give rise to the honeycomb texture and increased volume of the baked bread. Although the interior of the bread does not reach 100° C, the heating is sufficient to kill the yeasts, inactivate their enzymes, expand the gas, evaporate the ethanol produced during the fermentation, and establish the structure of the bread loaf. During baking there is also a gelatinization of the starch, which results in setting of the bread. In the dough the gluten gives structural support, but in the baked bread the structural support comes from the gelatinized starch.

In addition to leavening bread, microorganisms produce the characteristic flavors of some breads. For example, the production of San Francisco sourdough bread uses the yeast *Torulopsis holmii* and a heterofermentative *Lactobacillus* species to sour the dough and give this bread its characteristic sour flavor. Rye bread is also produced by initially souring the dough; cultures of *Lactobacillus plantarum, L. brevis, L. bulgaricus, Leuconostoc mesenteroides,* and *Streptococcus thermophilus* are employed as starter cultures in making different rye breads. The action of heterofermentative lactic acid bacteria produces the bread's characteristic flavor.

ALCOHOLIC BEVERAGES

Microorganisms, principally yeasts in the genus *Saccharomyces,* are used to produce various types of alcoholic beverages. The production of alcoholic beverages relies on *alcoholic fermentation,* that is, the conversion of sugar to alcohol by microbial enzymes. The flavor and other characteristic differences between various types of alcoholic beverages reflect differences in the starting substrates and the production process, rather than differences in the microbial culture or the primary fermentation pathways employed in the production of alcoholic beverages.

Beer and Ale

Beer is a popular beverage with a high per capita consumption rate. The worldwide production of beer is over 18 billion gallons per year. Beer and ale are malt beverages, so named because the initial preparation of the substrate for microbial fermentation involves barley malt and the production of beer begins with the *malting* of the barley (FIG. 15-34). Malt contains a mixture of amylases and proteinases prepared by germinating barley grains for about a week and crushing the grains to release the plant enzymes. Some beers, particularly those produced in Europe, are prepared entirely from malted barley. In the production of most beers, however, the malt is added to adjuncts in a process known as *mashing.* The malt *adjuncts,* such as corn, rice and wheat, provide carbohydrate substrates for ethanol production. During the mashing process, the amylases from the barley malt hydrolyze the starches and other polysaccharides, as well as the proteins in the malt adjunct. The mash is heated to reach temperatures of about 70° C, which facilitate the rapid enzymatic conversion of starch to sugars. The insoluble materials are allowed to settle from the mash and serve as a filter. The clear liquid that is produced in this process is called *wort.*

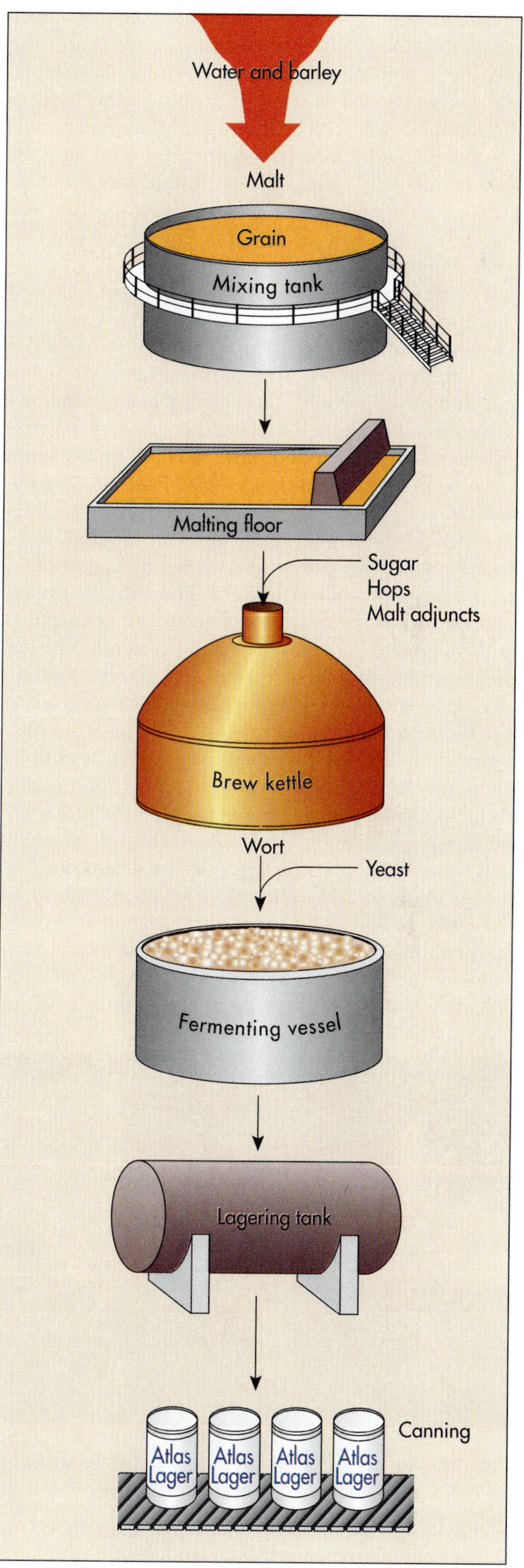

FIG. 15-34 Beer is produced by mixing water and barley to produce malt (active enzymes). The malt is added to grain (e.g., corn), which produces simple fermentable sugars from the plant carbohydrates of the grain. The mash produced in this process is used as a substrate for the growth of *Saccharomyces.* The yeast produces alcohol (beer).

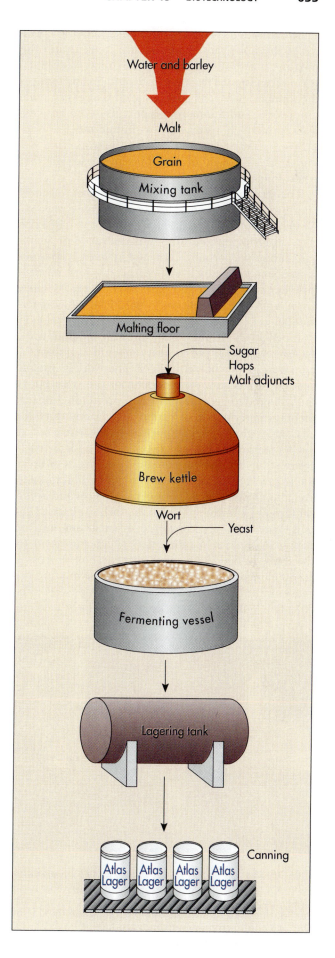

The wort is then cooked with hops, the dried flowers of the hop plant. This cooking concentrates the mixture, inactivates the enzymes, extracts soluble flavoring compounds from the hops, and greatly reduces the number of microorganisms prior to the fermentation process. Additionally, compounds in the hops extract, principally resins such as humulone, have antibacterial properties and protect the wort from the undesirable growth of Gram-positive bacteria that could sour the beer.

The fermentation of wort to produce beer in most countries is carried out by the yeast *Saccharomyces carlsbergensis,* a bottom fermenter. This means that at a late stage in fermentation, the yeasts flocculate or aggregate and settle, partially clarifying the beer. *S. cerevisiae* is also sometimes used in beer production, particularly in Great Britain and parts of the United States, but it is a top yeast and rises to the surface during fermentation.

Inoculation of the yeast into the cooled wort, known as *pitching,* uses a heavy inoculum of about 1 pound yeast per barrel of beer. The wort is initially aerated to facilitate reproduction of the yeast but is then allowed to become anaerobic, promoting the fermentative production of alcohol and carbon dioxide.

Usually the fermentation process is carried out at low temperatures and may take 1 to 2 weeks to reach completion. During fermentation the yeasts convert the sugars in the wort to alcohol and carbon dioxide and also produce small amounts of glycerol and acetic acid from the fermentation of the carbohydrates. Proteins and lipids are converted to small amounts of higher alcohols, acids, and esters, which contribute to the flavor of beer. The active fermentation process is accompanied by extensive foaming of the mixture because of the production of carbon dioxide (FIG. 15-35). The product is then known as a *green beer* and requires aging to achieve the characteristic flavor and aroma of the finished product.

FIG. 15-35 Beer producing facility. Copper brew kettles often are used for preparing the substrate for yeast fermentation (mash production). The fermentation often is carried out in open fermentors. Bubbles of carbon dioxide in the fermentor accompany ethanol production.

The commercial production of beer is usually a *batch process,* in which the substrates and inoculum are added to a brewing kettle. When the fermentation is completed, the products are collected as a single batch. In some countries the production of beer is carried out in a *continuous flow-through process,* in which fresh substrate is continuously or periodically added to the fermentation and product is continuously collected. This production process is analogous to the operation of a chemostat.

During the aging process, precipitation of proteins, yeasts, and resins occurs, resulting in a mellowing of the flavor. The mature beer is removed and filtered. The finished product is carbonated to achieve a carbon dioxide content of 0.45% to 0.52%. In the commercial production of beer, the carbon dioxide is normally collected during the fermentation phase and reinjected during the finishing process. In home production of beer, a small additional amount of sugar is usually added to each bottle to permit limited additional fermentative production of CO_2, achieving carbonation within the bottle. Most bottled or canned beers are pasteurized at 60° to 61° C or filtered to remove viable yeasts. Commercially produced beer in the United States has an alcohol content of about 3.8%. In Canada it is 5%.

In addition to normal beer, there are several other malt beverages. *Light beers* are low carbohydrate beers produced by using a wort prehydrolyzed with fungal glucoamylases and amylases. The prehydrolysis of dextrin in the wort to maltose and glucose permits the yeasts to ferment the carbohydrates completely to alcohol and carbon dioxide, greatly reducing the concentration of residual carbohydrates in the beer. These low-calorie beers are particularly popular today for those who consume large amounts of beer and don't wish to develop a "beer belly."

Ale is produced by using *Saccharomyces cerevisiae.* The fermentation is carried out at temperatures of 12° to 25° C, permitting the fermentation to reach completion in only 5 to 7 days. The yeast cells are carried upward with the carbon dioxide, and excess cells are skimmed off the top during the fermentation period. A higher concentration of hops is used in the production of ale than in beer, contributing to the particularly tart taste of ale; some ales have higher alcohol concentrations than most beers.

Saki, a Japanese beverage, is a rice beer. Its alcohol concentration normally is 14% to 17%. In the production of saki, a starter culture (normally *Aspergillus oryzae*) is used as a source of fungal enzymes to hydrolyze the rice starch to sugars that can then be converted to alcohol by *Saccharomyces* species during fermentation. The *Aspergillus* spores are mixed with steamed rice and incubated at approximately 35° C for 5 to 6 days before inoculation with yeast. The yeast fermentation of the rice mash to produce saki takes several weeks. Sonti, a similar product produced in India, uses the fungus *Rhizopus sonti* to convert the rice starch to sugars, which are subsequently fermented by yeasts.

Distilled Liquors

Distilled liquors or spirits are produced in a manner similar to that of beer, except that after the fermentation process the alcohol is collected by distillation, permitting the production of beverages with much higher alcohol concentrations than could be achieved during the fermentation process (FIG. 15-36). The initial steps in the production of distilled spirits are analogous to those in beer production, beginning with a mashing process in which the polysaccharides and proteins in a starting plant material are converted to sugars and other simple organic compounds that can be readily fermented by yeasts to form alcohol.

Various starting plant materials are used for the production of different distilled liquor products. Rum is produced by using sugar cane syrup or molasses as the initial substrate; rye whiskey is produced from the fermentation of a rye mash; bourbon or corn whiskey uses corn mash; and brandy comes from the fermentation of grapes. The yeasts used in the production of distilled liquors typically are special distiller strains of *S. cerevisiae,* which yield relatively high concentrations of alcohol. The yeasts produced during fermentation are collected, dried, and used as animal feed. The mash is sometimes soured prior to the yeast fermentation process by allowing lactic acid fermentation to occur initially to prevent the growth of undesired microorganisms that might interfere with the fermentative action of the yeast.

The alcoholic product formed from the fermentation of wort, known as a *beer* or *wine,* is heated in a still and alcohol is collected. In addition to alcohol, various volatile organic compounds, fusel oils, are collected with the distillate and contribute to the characteristic flavors of the different distilled liquor products. Distilled products also differ from one another in the nature of the distillation process; Scotch whiskey, for example, is distilled in batches by using small pot stills, whereas many other distilled whiskeys are produced by using continuous distillation processes. The distilled alcohol product is normally aged to yield a mellow-tasting alcoholic beverage.

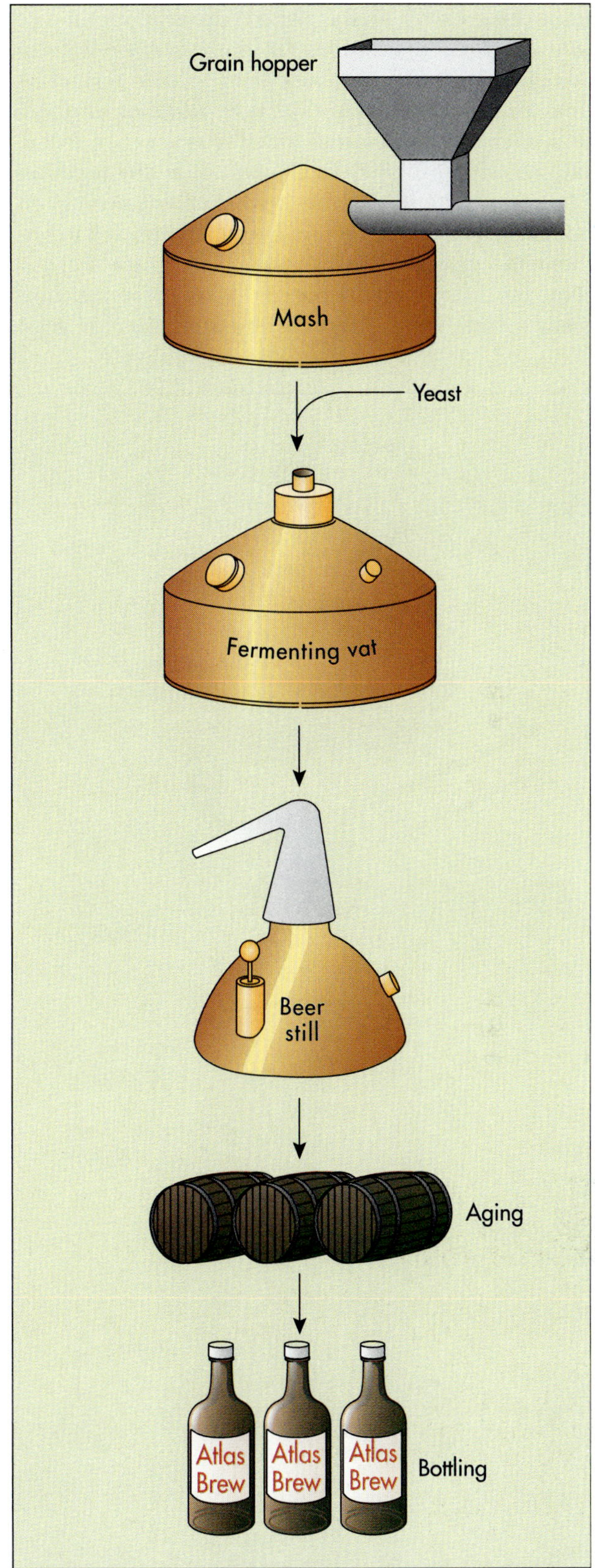

FIG. 15-36 To produce distilled spirits a beer produced by fermentation is subjected to distillation. This removes water and produces concentrated alcohol. The alcohol can be aged to bring about additional chemical reactions. Bourbon, for example, is aged in Kentucky in charred oak casks.

Wines

Wine is fermented primarily from grapes, although other fruits are sometimes used. Red wines are produced by using whole red grapes, whereas white wines are made from white grapes or from red grapes that have had their skins removed. The production of wine begins when the grapes are crushed to form a juice or must (FIG. 15-37). In the classic European method of wine production, wild yeasts from the surface skins of the grapes are the only inoculum for the fermentation. In modern wine production, however, the natural microbiota associated with the grapes are inactivated by sulfur dioxide fumigation or by the addition of metabisulfite so that the "wild microorganisms" do not compete with the defined yeast strains used to ferment the grapes in this process. The grape must is then inoculated with a specific strain of yeast, normally a variety of *S. cerevisiae*. By using specific yeast strains and controlled fermentation conditions, a product of consistent quality can be produced.

Initially, the grape must and yeasts are stirred to increase aeration and permit the proliferation of the yeasts. The mixing is later discontinued, permitting anaerobic conditions to occur that favor the production of alcohol. The sugar content of the grapes and the alcohol tolerance limit of the yeasts determine the final ethanol concentration. The sugar content of the grapes depends on the grape variety and its ripeness and varies from season to season, accounting in part for the fact that some years and vineyards are better than others for the production of quality wines.

The fermentation of red wines typically is carried out at 24° to 27° C for 3 to 5 days, and white wines take 7 to 14 days at 10° to 21° C. During fermentation wine is periodically racked, that is, it is filtered through the bottom sediments and added back to the top of the fermentation vat. Carbon dioxide produced during the fermentation process forces the skins and other debris to the surface. The color of red wine is due to extraction of the pigments from the grape skin by the alcohol produced during the fermentation. At the end of fermentation, wines typically have an alcohol content of 11% to 16% by volume. They are then aged to achieve their final bouquet and essence of flavor. During aging, some fermentation of the malic acid of grape juice is carried out by lactobacilli (malolactic fermentation), reducing the acidity of the wine.

By using similar processes, various wines can be produced. Dry wines contain little or no sugar, whereas sweet wines contain some residual unfermented sugar. Distillation is used to achieve the high alcohol content (19% to 21%) of fortified or dessert wines. Normally, the carbon dioxide produced during alcoholic fermentation is allowed to escape and the wine is, therefore, still. In the case of champagne and other sparkling wines, however, the carbonation is essential. In some commercially produced champagne,

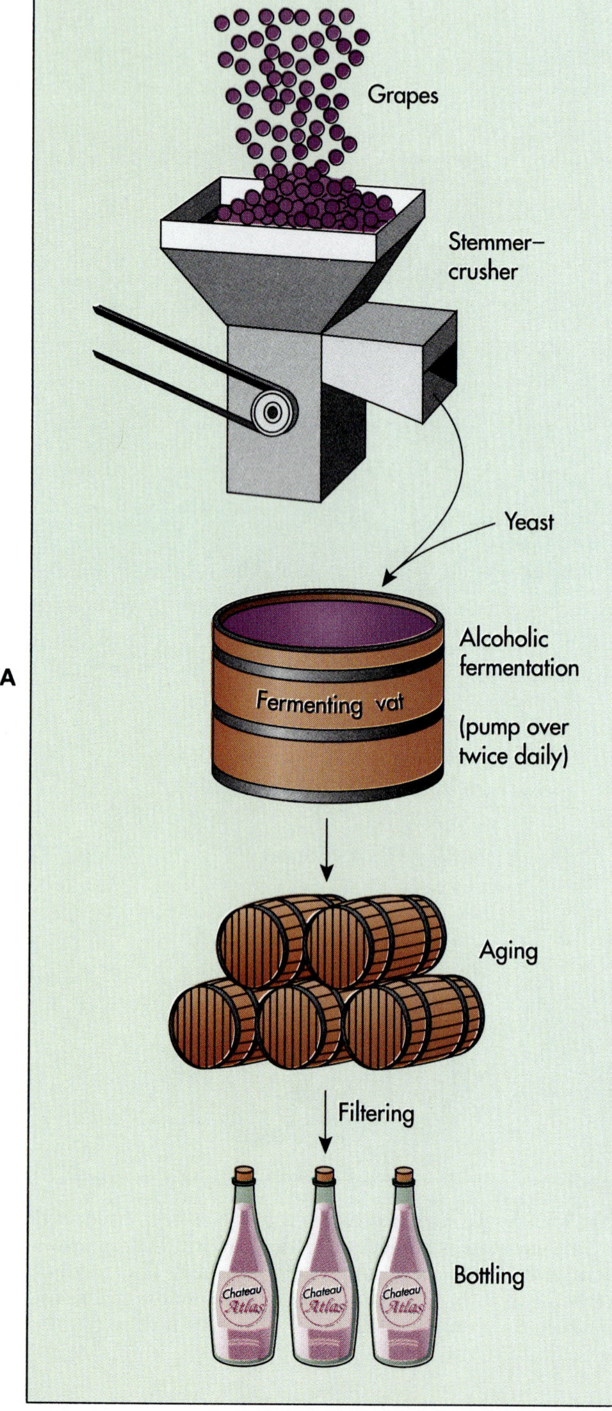

FIG. 15-37 **A,** Wine is produced by the fermentation of grapes. **B,** Numerous types of wines are produced.

carbon dioxide is reinjected into the wine after fermentation. In the classic French method of producing champagne, the wine is fermented in the bottle. After fermentation is complete, the bottles are inverted, and the yeast sediments into the neck of the specially shaped champagne bottles. The yeasts are frozen and removed as a plug without excessive loss of carbon dioxide. Wines stoppered with a cork must be stored on their side to prevent the cork from drying out, which would permit air to enter and allow the alcohol to be oxidized by bacteria to form acetic acid. The spoilage of wines, with the formation of vinegar (sour wine) is a serious problem. In the United States, most wine bottles are sealed with a plastic stopper and therefore need not be stored on their side to preclude the souring of the wine.

VINEGAR

The production of vinegar involves an initial anaerobic fermentation to convert carbohydrates by *S. cerevisiae* to alcohol, followed by a secondary oxidative transformation of the alcohol to form acetic acid by *Acetobacter* and *Gluconobacter* or the direct conversion of glucose to acetate by *Clostridium* species. The starting materials for the production of vinegar may be fruits such as grapes, oranges, apples, pears; vegetables such as potatoes; malted cereals such as barley, rye, wheat, and corn; and sugary syrups such as molasses, honey, and maple syrup. The type of vinegar is determined by the starting material. For example, wine vinegar comes from grapes and cider vinegar from other fruits.

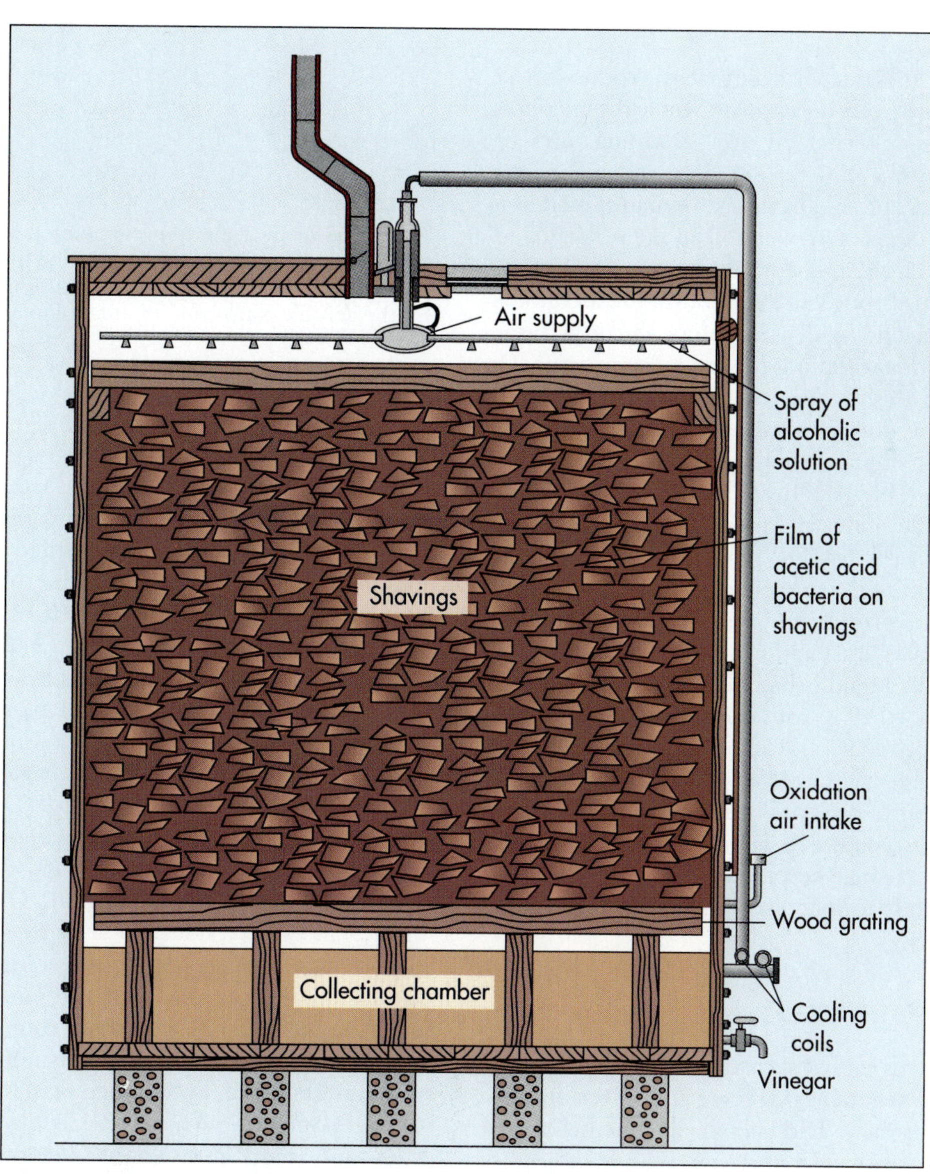

FIG. 15-38 In the classic vinegar generator, a biofilm of *Acetobacter* grows on wood shavings. An aerated alcoholic solution drips past these bacteria, which aerobically convert ethanol to acetic acid.

The history of the commercial production of vinegar shows an interesting progression in fermentor design to accomplish the necessary transfer of oxygen to the bacteria. In slow methods for the production of vinegar, still used in some small European operations, an initial natural alcoholic fermentation achieves an alcohol concentration of 11% to 13%. After production of the alcoholic liquid, acetic bacteria are seeded into the solution and allowed to convert the alcohol slowly to acetic acid. In the *Orleans process* for producing vinegar, a barrel is filled about one-fourth full with raw vinegar from a previous run to provide the active inoculum. A wine, hard cider, or malt liquor is then added as a substrate. Sufficient air is left in the barrel to permit oxidative metabolism, acetic acid bacteria grow as a film on the top of the liquid, and the conversion of alcohol to acetic acid takes several weeks to several months to complete at 21° to 29° C. The rate of vinegar production is limited primarily by the transfer of oxygen.

To increase the rate of acetic acid production, a vinegar generator can be used in which the alcohol-containing liquid is trickled over a surface film of acetic acid bacteria (FIG. 15-38). In a typical vinegar generator, the acetic acid bacteria are maintained as a film on wood chips. The alcohol liquid is sprinkled over the wood chips, and during the slow trickling of the liquid down through the generator, the alcohol is converted to acetic acid. Air enters the generator from the bottom, facilitating the oxidative process. To control any excessive heat that may be generated, cooling coils are normally required. One or two runs of the alcoholic liquid through the generator is sufficient to produce high-quality vinegar.

Today, though, industrial producers of vinegar use *submerged culture reactors* (FIG. 15-39). Forced aeration is used to maximize the rate of acetic acid production, and the bacteria grow in the fine suspension created by the air bubbles and the fermenting liquid. An 8% to 12% alcoholic liquid is inoculated with an *Acetobacter* species at 24° to 29° C with carefully controlled aeration. Using a 10% alcohol solution as substrate, the acetic acid yield can be 13%. Once the vinegar is formed, it is clarified by passage through a filter and allowed to age to achieve its final body, taste, and bouquet. The vinegar may be pasteurized at 60° to 66° C for a few seconds to inactivate any remaining viable bacteria.

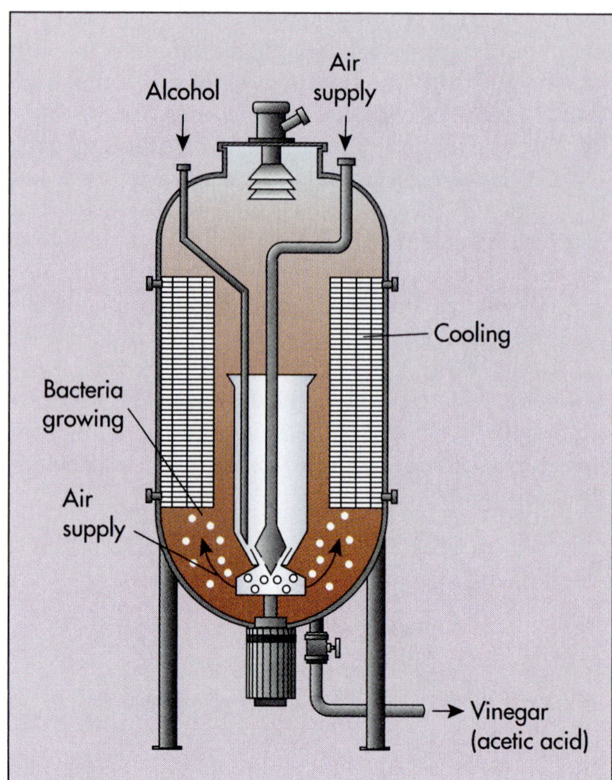

FIG. 15-39 In a modern submerged vinegar generator, small air bubbles are forcefully injected into a fermentor. As they rise and mix through the fermentor they supply oxygen for the aerobic conversion of ethanol to acetic acid by *Acetobacter.*

Fermented Vegetables

Vegetables such as cabbage, carrots, cucumbers, green tomatoes, leafy vegetables, greens, and olives are fermented by using lactic acid bacteria as a means of creating new food products that are not readily subject to spoilage. Other fermentations, particularly of soybeans, are carried out to produce specially desired flavors, aromas, and textures in food products.

Sauerkraut

Sauerkraut is produced from a lactic acid fermentation of wilted, shredded cabbage (FIG. 15-40). Salt, 2.25% to 2.5%, is added to shredded cabbage to help extract plant juices, control the microbiota during fermentation, and maintain an even dispersal of bacteria. Anaerobic conditions develop in the salted, shredded cabbage and surrounding juice, primarily as a result of continued respiration of plant cells but also because of some bacterial metabolism.

The production of sauerkraut involves a succession of bacterial populations (FIG. 15-41). Coliform bacteria, such as *Enterobacter cloacae,* are prominent in the initial mixed community and produce gas and volatile acids, as well as some lactic acid. The accumulating lactic acid exerts a selective pressure on the microbial community, causing population shifts and continued succession. As a result, after the initial fermentation there is a shift in the microbial community, and *Leuconostoc mesenteroides,* which grows well at 21° C and is not inhibited by 2.5% salt, becomes the dominant microbial population. Up to 1% lactic acid may accumulate—and yeasts and various bacteria may grow as a surface film—during this phase of the fermentation.

The continuing succession of bacterial populations next favors the development of *Lactobacillus plan-*

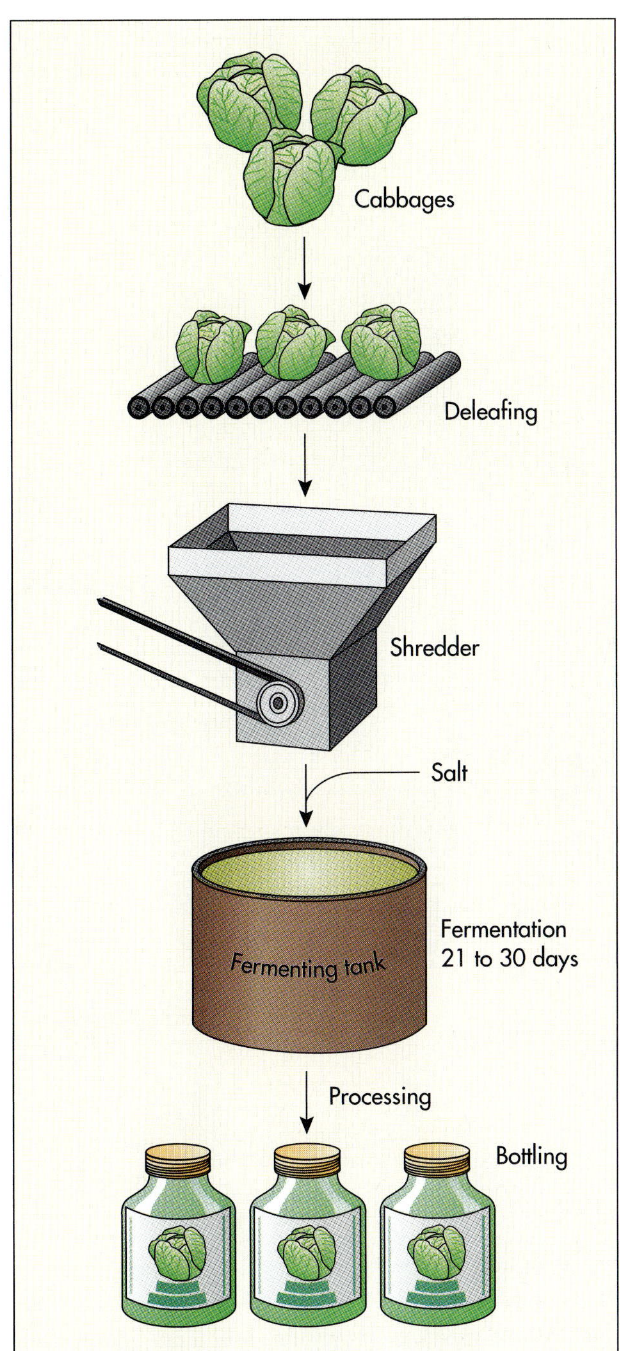

FIG. 15-40 Sauerkraut is produced from cabbage by a heterolactic acid fermentation.

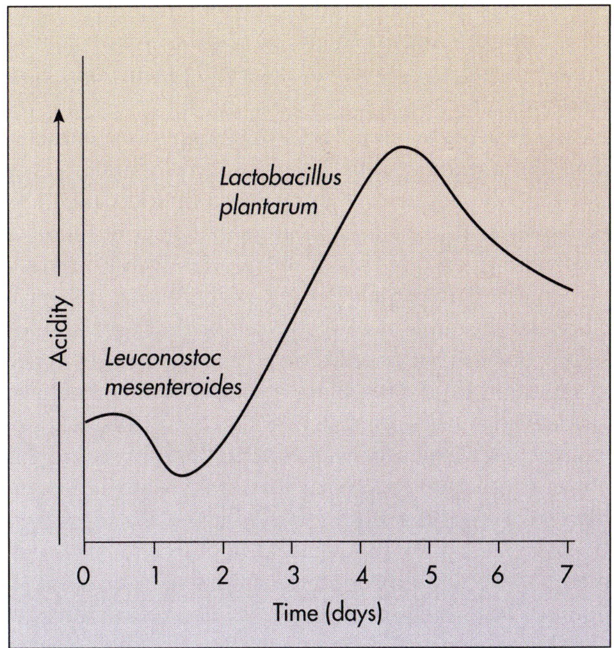

FIG. 15-41 During the early phase of sauerkraut production, *Leuconostoc mesenteroides* grows, producing relatively little lactic acid. Then there is a population succession to *Lactobacillus plantarum*, which produces significant amounts of lactic acid.

tarum, which produces acid but no gas. During this phase of the fermentation, the concentration of lactic acid reaches 1.5% to 2%. Growth of *L. plantarum* also removes mannitol, which is produced by *Leuconostoc* and has an undesirable bitter flavor. The fermentation can be stopped at this stage by canning or refrigerating the sauerkraut. If there is any residual sugar and mannitol after the action of *L. plantarum,* the successional process can continue with the development of *Lactobacillus brevis,* a gas-producing species. The growth of *L. brevis* can increase the lactic acid concentration to 2.4% and also imparts a bitter acid flavor to the sauerkraut. High-quality sauerkraut has a lactic acid concentration of about 1.7% and a clean acid flavor, with low concentrations of diacetyl contributing to the aroma and flavor of the final product.

Pickles

The traditional method for producing pickles by fermenting cucumbers uses the natural microbiota associated with the cucumber, and controlled temperature and salt concentrations, to regulate the fermentation process. Controlled fermentation of pickles can also be achieved by inoculation with *L. plantarum* and *Pediococcus cerevisiae.* The traditional process takes 6 to 9 weeks to reach completion. During this period, the salt concentration is gradually increased to reach a final level of about 15.9% NaCl. At the beginning of the fermentation, when the salt concentration is low, many bacterial genera are able to grow, including *Pseudomonas, Flavobacterium,* and *Bacillus.* As the salt concentration is increased, the populations that become favored include the lactic acid bacteria *Leuconostoc mesenteroides, Enterococcus faecalis,* and *P. cerevisiae.* As the lactic acid and salt concentrations increase, *L. plantarum* becomes the dominant bacterium, beginning several days after the fermentation and continuing until the salt concentration surpasses 10%. Completion of the fermentation process involves yeasts that grow at high salt concentrations. During the final yeast fermentation stage, some carbohydrates are converted to alcohol. The growth of film-forming yeasts, such as *Debaryomyces, Pichia, Endomycopsis,* and *Candida,* lowers the lactic acid concentration.

Because of the complexity of changes in the microbial community during this natural fermentation, the process often goes awry and yields unmarketable pickles, such as floaters and bloaters that float because of excessive gas accumulation within the cucumber; hollow pickles, in which the cucumber contents have shriveled because of excessive salt or the formation of high concentrations of acetic acid; stinkers, due to the accumulation of H_2S; black pickles, due to bacterial pigment production; soft pickles, due to fungal proteases; and slippery pickles, due to the surface growth of encapsulated bacteria. Controlled fermentation conditions—and a pure inoculum of *P. cerevisiae* and *L. plantarum* after the removal of the natural microbiota by fumigation or chlorination—can be used to increase the likelihood of producing a quality pickle.

The sourness of the pickle reflects the amount of lactic acid that accumulates during the fermentation. Several varieties of pickles are produced by a modification of the basic fermentation process. In the production of dill pickles, a brine of 7.5% to 8.5% NaCl is used. The dill herb is added for flavoring, and vinegar also is normally added to prevent undesirable fermentation reactions. Because of the low concentration of salt, various indigenous soil bacteria on cucumber surfaces grow during the initial stages of fermentation. As lactic acid accumulates, the bacterial community becomes dominated by *L. mesenteroides, E. faecalis, P. cerevisiae,* and *L. plantarum.* The final concentration of lactic acid in dill pickles is in the range of 1% to 1.5%.

Olives

The production of green olives involves lactic acid fermentation. The harvested olives are washed with a solution of sodium hydroxide that removes most of the oleuropein, a bitter phenolic glucoside that gives unfermented olives a very undesirable flavor. The olives are then placed in a brine solution, and a lactic acid fermentation lasting for 2 to 10 months is permitted to occur. During the first 2 weeks of the fermentation, the brine becomes stabilized as compounds are leached from the olives and microbial populations begin to multiply. At the intermediate stage, which occurs during the following 2 to 3 weeks, *Leuconostoc* is the dominant bacterial species and lactic acid accumulates. The final stage of fermentation is dominated by *L. plantarum* and *L. brevis*; yeasts and various bacteria also occur during this stage. The final acidity of the olives is approximately 7.1% lactic acid.

Soy Sauce

Several oriental foods are prepared by fermenting soybeans or rice. Soy sauce, a brown, salty, tangy sauce, which in Japanese is called *shoyu,* is produced from a mash consisting of soybeans, wheat, and wheat bran. Soy sauce is used as a condiment or as an ingredient in other sauces (FIG. 15-42). The starter culture for the production of soy sauce is produced by *koji fermentation,* a dry fermentation in which a mixture of soybeans and wheat is inoculated with spores of *Aspergillus oryzae* (FIG. 15-43). The mixture is moistened but is not submerged in liquid. The fungi grow on the surface of the soybeans and wheat, accumulating various enzymes, including proteinases and amylases. Various bacterial populations, normally dominated by

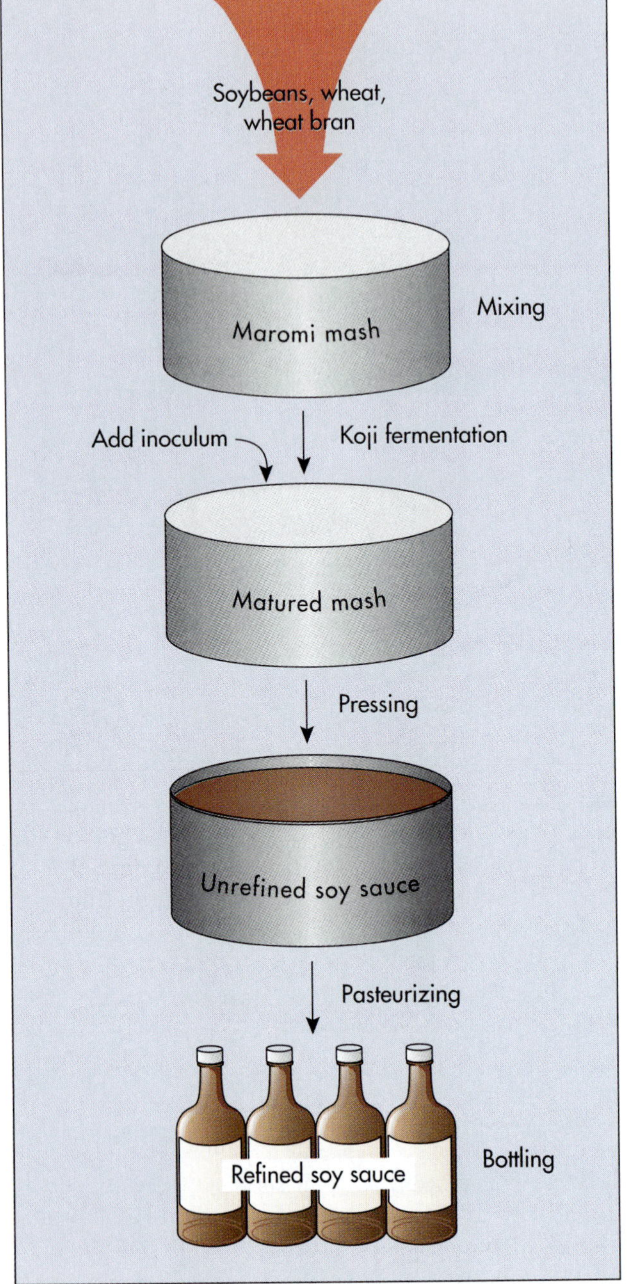

FIG. 15-42 Soy sauce is produced by a dry bran fermentation (koji fermentation) in which fungi grow on wheat and soybeans in a brine.

FIG. 15-43 Micrograph showing growth of *Aspergillus oryzae* on bran during koji fermentation.

lactic acid bacteria, also develop during this koji fermentation. After the starter culture develops, it is dried and extracted.

The extract is mixed with a mash consisting of autoclaved soybeans, autoclaved and crushed wheat, and steamed wheat bran. The mash with the koji is incubated in flat trays for several days at approximately 30° C and is then soaked with concentrated brine. The resulting mixture is called *maromi.* The mash is then incubated for a period ranging from 10 weeks to over 1 year, depending on the incubation temperature. During this incubation period the proteinases, amylases, and other enzymes of the koji are active, and there is a succession of microbial populations. The maturation begins with lactic acid bacteria, including lactic acid production by *Pediococcus soyae,* and later involves alcoholic fermentations by yeasts such as *Saccharomyces rouxii, Zygosaccharomyces soyae,* and *Torulopsis* species. The most important organisms during the fermentation process are *A. oryzae,* which produces proteinases and amylases; *Lactobacillus* species, which produce sufficient amounts of lactic acid to prevent spoilage by other microorganisms; and yeasts, which produce sufficient alcohol to increase the flavor.

An interesting problem was encountered when soy sauce production was begun in the United States. In Japan the maturation process is carried out in concrete tanks and the necessary microbial populations are maintained in the porous concrete surface. In the United States, where sterilized stainless steel tanks are used for the secondary fermentation process, it was difficult to define, maintain, and add at the proper times the cultures that are needed for the successional process involved in producing quality soy sauce. Eventually, the process was perfected, and only a soy sauce connoisseur can tell the difference between the U.S. and Japanese products.

Miso

Miso is also produced by using a koji fermentation with *Aspergillus oryzae.* Steamed polished rice, placed in shallow trays, is used in the production of the starter culture. The koji is mixed with a mash of steamed soybeans and, after the addition of salt, the fermentation is allowed to proceed at 28° C for 1 week, at 35° C for 2 months, and at room temperature for several additional weeks. The miso is normally ground into a paste, to be combined with other food before eating.

Tempeh

Tempeh is an Indonesian food produced from soybeans. The soybeans are soaked at 25° C, dried, and inoculated with spores of various species of *Rhizopus.* The mash is incubated at 32° C for 20 hours, during which mycelial growth occurs. The product is then salted and fried before eating.

Tofu and Sofu

Tofu (Japanese) or sofu (Chinese) is a cheese-like product produced by fermenting soybeans with *Mucor* species. The soybeans are soaked, ground to a paste, and curdled by adding calcium or magnesium salts. The pressed curd blocks are placed in trays at 14° C and incubated for 1 month, during which time the fungal populations develop.

Natto

Natto also is produced from boiled soybeans and involves the incubation of *Bacillus subtilis* with soybeans for 1 to 2 days, during which time proteinase enzymes soften and add flavor compounds to the soybeans. Various other oriental foods are also produced by similar fermentations.

Poi

Poi is a fermented food product from the islands of Polynesia. In the production of poi, the stems of the taro plant are steamed, ground, and subjected to fermentation for 1 to 6 days. During the first few hours, coliforms, *Pseudomonas,* and various other microorganisms predominate. Then a successional process occurs, with *Lactobacillus, Streptococcus,* and *Leuconostoc* becoming the dominant populations. Finally, yeasts and the fungus *Geotrichum candidum* flourish. The fermentation products, principally lactic acid, acetic acid, formic acid, ethanol, and carbon dioxide, contribute to the characteristic texture, flavor, and aroma of poi.

SINGLE CELL PROTEIN

Microorganisms can be grown as a source of *single cell protein (SCP),* so named because the microorganisms are single-celled organisms rich in protein. Microorganisms grow rapidly and produce a high-yield, high protein food crop. The proteins of selected microorganisms contain all of the essential amino acids. Various bacteria, fungi, and algae are potential sources of large amounts of SCP. The algae *Scenedesmus* and *Spirulina,* for example, have been cultured in various warm ponds as a food source. The production of SCP from algae is advantageous because these organisms utilize solar energy, greatly reducing the amount of fuel resources required to produce SCP. Some algae currently are harvested as a source of food.

Research on the concept of SCP production was begun during the 1960s by oil companies when petroleum was inexpensive and appeared to be an economically attractive substrate for growing SCP. The Imperial Chemical Works in Britain produces Pruteen, the SCP product of *Methylophilus methylotrophus,* a bacterium that grows on C1 compounds. *M. methylotrophus* is grown on methanol, derived from methane, and the cell crop is harvested, centrifuged, dried, and sold in pellet or granular form (FIG. 15-44). Because of dramatic increases in the price of oil, petroleum hydrocarbons are no longer considered as the primary substrates for producing SCP. The product simply could not be economically competitive with soybean and fish meal. Future less expensive sources of methanol, perhaps derived from cellulose, will likely revive the prospects for large-scale production of microbial SCP.

Yeasts are excellent candidates for development as commercial sources of SCP. Yeast-based SCP has a high vitamin content. Various species of yeast, including members of the genera *Saccharomyces, Candida,* and *Torulopsis,* can be grown on waste materials, recycling these substances into useful sources of food. The growth of yeasts on waste materials serves a dual function: the removal of the unwanted substances and the production of much needed protein-rich foods. In Russia there is huge commercial production of *Candida* yeast protein from hydrolyzed peat. Approximately 1.1 million tons of yeast protein per year are being produced in a rapidly expanding Russian industry that aims to reduce Russian dependence on imported grain.

SCP is primarily produced as an animal feed. There are problems with using SCP for direct human consumption because of high concentrations, 6% to 11%, of nucleic acids. This may result in increased serum levels of uric acid, causing kidney stone formation or gout, possible allergic reactions, and possible gastrointestinal reactions, including diarrhea and vomiting. Chickens and other animals, however, can be grown on SCP rather than on plant materials, helping to meet world food needs. Researchers are still trying to find the proper microorganism and set of production conditions to produce SCP that can be fed directly to humans.

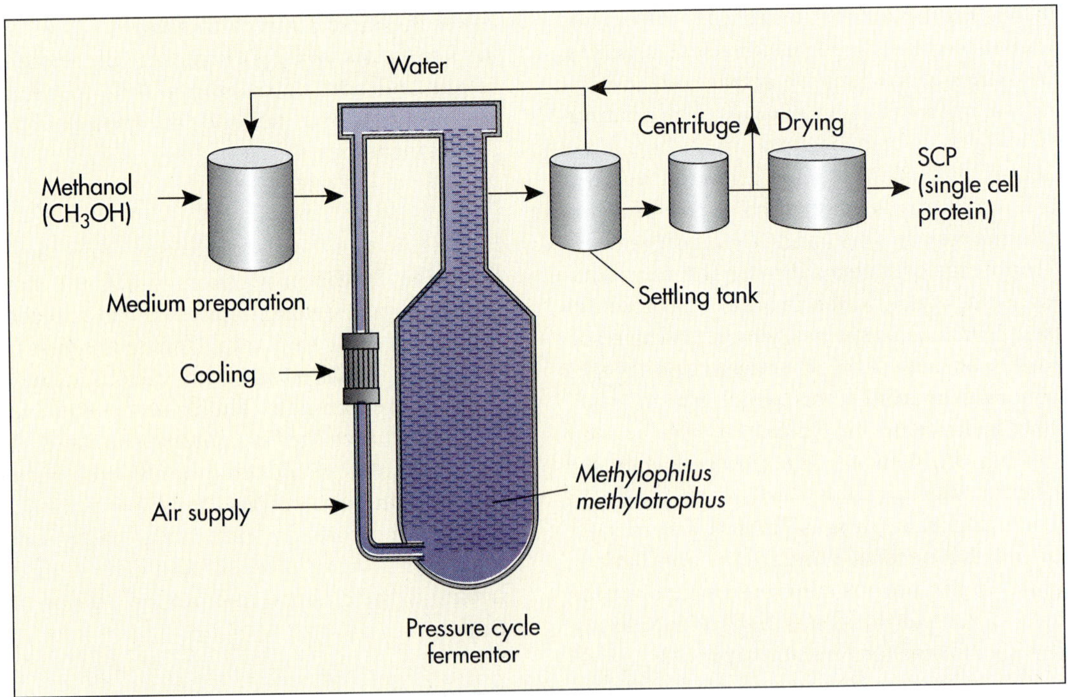

FIG. 15-44 Bacterial cells can be grown in large aerated fermentors as a source of single cell protein for animal feed. *Methylophilus methylotrophus* can be grown on methanol for SCP production.

CHAPTER REVIEW

STUDY QUESTIONS

1. What are the differences in the methods used to produce beer, wine, and distilled liquors?
2. How is cheese made?
3. What is ripening?
4. When we consider the great variety of cheeses, how can they all be made from essentially the same starting material?
5. How is sauerkraut produced? Discuss the role of microbial succession in the production of sauerkraut.
6. What can go wrong in the production of pickles?
7. What is a chemical food preservative? What are the advantages and disadvantages of the use of chemical preservatives? Should they be added to food products?
8. What is single-cell protein (SCP)? What are the useful candidate substrates for SCP production? How could SCP be used to alleviate world food shortages?
9. Can recombinant DNA technology help create a microbial strain that will solve world hunger? Discuss.
10. How does the industrial use of the term *fermentation* differ from its use to describe microbial metabolism?
11. How are antibiotic-producing microorganisms found?
12. How is it determined if microorganisms are producing substances of industrial importance?
13. Discuss the role of mutation and selection in the history of penicillin production. Why would a similar approach not be suitable for finding an insulin-producing strain of *E. coli*?
14. Why are microorganisms especially important in the production of steroids?
15. What is an immobilized enzyme?
16. Discuss the role of such enzymes in industrial microbiology.
17. What is a fermentor? How are aeration and pH controlled in fermentors?
18. What are the essential properties of a substrate for an industrial fermentation?
19. How was the microbial production of butanol critical in determining the outcome of World War I?
20. How are microorganisms involved in the corrosion of metals?
21. What is bioleaching?
22. How is bioleaching used for the recovery of uranium?
23. Discuss several ways in which microorganisms can help meet the current fuel shortage.
24. What is bioremediation?
25. How is bioremediation used to treat oil pollutants?

SITUATIONAL PROBLEMS

1. Planning a Party with Foods and Beverages Produced by Microorganisms

Congratulations! You have been chosen as chairperson of the annual summer Biology Department picnic. Each year the party has a special biological theme. This year the theme is "The Fungi." In keeping with this theme, you decide that the foods and beverages served should be produced by fungi.

1. Plan the menu for this picnic. Assume that the food will be served outdoors and that there will be only minimal refrigeration available for several hours before and during the picnic.

2. You also feel that the picnickers should know how fungi contributed to the production of each of the items served. So the decorations will include posters that explain the role of the fungi. Prepare sketches of the posters to display with each of the foods and beverages at the picnic.

3. Because the picnic was a tremendous success, you have been asked to do an encore for the winter break party. This time the theme is "The Bacteria." Prepare a menu and sketches of appropriate posters illustrating the role of bacteria in the production of each of the foods and beverages that you would serve.

2. Entrepreneurial Advice on Biotechnology

Biotechnology is one of the more exciting applied fields of science and has major potential for economic growth that has yet to be realized. Several corporations have been formed to capitalize on recombinant DNA technology. Stock in these companies has been actively traded, but major product successes have been limited to date. Nevertheless, in an era of individualistic entrepreneurial enthusiasm, biotechnology is an appealing area of investment. Although genetic engineering clearly dominates the headlines in this field, biotechnology encompasses a broad field that combines the biological and engineering sciences for economic (applied) purposes. The application of microorganisms, whether created by genetic engineers or discovered in nature—to produce economically valuable products such as antibiotics, or to control detrimental situations such as environmental pollution—is the mainstay of biotechnology.

Suppose your friend unexpectedly inherited a large sum of money and asked you to join him in starting a biotechnological enterprise. What projects would you suggest? How would you know what work had already been done on that project? How could you realistically determine the economic investment needed and the potential profits that could be realized? Compose a proposal that could serve as a prospectus for additional investors.

Suggested Supplementary Readings

Aharonowitz Y and G Cohen: 1981. The microbiological production of pharmaceuticals, *Scientific American* 245(3):140-152.

Atlas RM (ed.): 1983. *Petroleum Microbiology,* Macmillan, New York.

Ball C (ed.): 1984. *Genetics and Breeding of Industrial Microorganisms,* CRC Press, Inc., Boca Raton, FL.

Brierley CL: 1982. Microbiological mining, *Scientific American* 247(2):44-53.

Bu'Lock JD and B Kristiansen (eds.): 1987. *Basic Biotechnology,* Academic Press, London.

Coombs J (ed.): 1985. *Dictionary of Biotechnology,* Elsevier Science Publishing Co., Inc., New York.

Crueger W and A Crueger: 1990. *Biotechnology: A Textbook of Industrial Microbiology,* ed. 2, Sinauer Associates, Sunderland, MA.

Demain AL: 1981. Industrial microbiology, *Science* 214:987-995.

Demain AL and NA Solomon: 1981. Industrial microbiology, *Scientific American* 245(3):66-76.

Demain AL and NA Solomon (eds.): 1985. *Biology of Industrial Microorganisms,* Butterworth, Stoneham, MA.

Demain AL and NA Solomon: 1986. *Manual of Industrial Microbiology and Biotechnology,* American Soc. for Microbiology, Washington, D.C.

Ehrlich HL and CL Brierley (eds.): 1990. *Microbial Mineral Recovery,* McGraw-Hill, New York.

Eveleigh DE: 1981. The microbiological production of industrial chemicals, *Scientific American* 245(3):154-178.

Frazer WC and DC Westhoff: 1988. *Food Microbiology,* ed. 4, McGraw-Hill, New York.

Hopwood DA: 1981. The genetic programming of industrial microorganisms, *Scientific American* 245(3):91-102.

Hutchins S, S Davidson, J Brierly, C Brierly: 1986. Microorganisms in reclamation of metals, *Annual Review of Microbiology* 40:311-366.

Jay JM: 1991. *Modern Food Microbiology,* ed. 4, Van Nostrand Reinhold Co., New York.

Jones DT and DR Woods: 1986. Acetone-butanol fermentation revisited, *Microbiological Reviews* 50:484-524.

Moo-Young M (ed.): 1985. *Comprehensive Biotechnology: The Principles, Applications, and Regulations of Biotechnology in Industry* (4 volumes), Pergamon Press, Oxford, England.

Nakas JP and C Hagedorn (eds.): 1990. *Biotechnology of Plant-Microbe Interactions,* McGraw-Hill, New York.

Phaff H: 1981. Industrial microorganisms, *Scientific American* 245(3):77-89.

Primrose SB: 1991. *Molecular Biotechnology,* ed. 2, Blackwell Scientific Publishers, Oxford, England.

Primrose SB: 1987. *Modern Biotechnology,* Blackwell Scientific Publishers, Oxford, England.

Rehm H and G Reed (eds.): 1981-1988. *Biotechnology: A Comprehensive Treatise* (8 volumes), Verlag Chemie International, Inc., Deerfield Beach, FL.

Rose AH: 1977-. *Economic Microbiology* (a multivolume treatise), Academic Press, New York.

Rose AH: 1981. The microbiological production of food and drink, *Scientific American* 245(3):126-139.

Rose AH (ed.): 1983. *Food Microbiology,* Academic Press, London.

Saunders VA and JR Saunders: 1987. *Microbial Genetics Applied to Biotechnology,* Croom Helm, London.

Silver S (ed.): 1986. *Biotechnology: Potentials and Limitations,* Springer-Verlag, Berlin.

Vanek Z and Z Hostalek (eds.): 1986. *Overproduction of Microbial Metabolites: Strain Improvement and Process Control Strategies,* Butterworth, Stoneham, MA.

THE SIREN CALL OF THE SEA—MARINE MICROBIOLOGY

RITA R. COLWELL

Rita R. Colwell was born in Beverly, Massachusetts, in 1936. She was educated at Purdue University and the University of Washington, Seattle. She is a professor of microbiology and director of the Maryland Biotechnology Institute at the University of Maryland. She is a past president of the American Society for Microbiology and Sigma Xi, the honorary society for science. She is head of the American Academy of Microbiology. She is President of the American Association for the Advancement of Science and viewed as the most influential woman in science today. Her research relates to marine microbiology, biotechnology, and ecology.

The history of Marine Microbiology traces to the early voyages in the late 1800s, particularly the studies of a ship's doctor who was intrigued by the luminescence of the sea on moonless nights. Dr. Fischer isolated bacteria from the sea that indeed did luminesce, i.e., glow in the dark, when grown in artificial medium. Subsequent questions that were asked concerned life at the deepest parts of the ocean. The prevailing notion was that there was no life in the deep sea, that it was azoic, but in the 1950s Dr. Claude ZoBell and his then student, Dr. Richard Y. Morita, collected samples from the deepest trench of the Pacific Ocean and were able to culture microorganisms. The interest in marine microbiology until recently has been more or less exploratory and descriptive. What is there, what microorganisms are present, and what they do. In fact, many of the studies were simply measurements of processes. How much carbon was cycled, and how much CO_2 was taken up. Such questions considered microorganisms as inhabitants of a "black box." In the early 1960s, a serious effort was made to bring marine microbiology to a quantitative point of development.

Thus work was begun on identifying species of marine bacteria, isolating marine viruses, and attempting to answer the questions of what is a "marine microorganism." Just about this time the use of computers in biology was beginning to take hold.

I grew up in Massachusetts a stone's throw from the ocean and a block from the Lighthouse in Beverly Harbor in the village of Beverly Cove, Massachusetts, and the ocean has always held a mysterious attraction for me. I enjoyed long walks along the beaches from Beverly Cove to Manchester, Rockport, and Glouster in the days when the beaches were open to all and not partitioned off as "private property." The lure of the sea was strong. Having come from a family of modest means, the offer from Purdue University for full tuition scholarship and residence on campus was too good to turn down. The result was an extraordinarily good grounding in science at an institution where undergraduates truly mattered. At the time, it seemed as though medicine was the path to choose and I applied and was admitted to several medical schools. However, a fateful meeting late in my senior year with a graduate student in physical chemistry, who was to become my husband, resulted in an additional year at Purdue University studying classical genetics instead. From Purdue, my husband and I adventurously attended the University of Washington in Seattle, where we worked together to earn our doctorates. The work at the University of Washington was a dual track with all of the coursework in Microbiology being taken through the School of Medicine, Department of Microbiology, but the chance meeting with an extraordinary individual, at the time a newly hired young Professor from Scotland, Dr. John Liston, led to thesis work in Marine Microbiology. The field was new. In fact, it was a raw, unfinished science with many paths to follow. My work focussed on bacteria associated with marine animals, specifically, invertebrates, including shell fish, both mollusks and crustaceans. One of the studies was a comparative study of microorganisms associated with marine animals from the Rongelap and Eniwetok atolls after the atomic bomb tests. This was a fascinating study because it demonstrated concentration of radioactive elements by microorganisms, work that was shown by other investigators in later years to be important and which has relevance in today's society regarding bioremediation, that is, in radioactive wastes, microorganisms can be employed to concentrate and remove radioactive elements.

The work at the University of Washington was exciting, and clearly pioneering. At that time, women were not welcome on board ship for oceanographic and fisheries work—certainly not overnight. Several cruises were undertaken but these were always 1-day cruises. One of the most exciting trips was a fishing expedition using experimental nets to catch salmon. I had never seen salmon of the size we collected that day. Each of us was allowed to take home a "trophy," which in my case was a 16 lb. salmon that grilled beautifully in the fireplace of the wee apartment in the University housing complex.

My interest in marine microbiology expanded to a curiosity about the genetics of marine microorganisms. Very little was known about microbial genetics at the time, and, of course, in the ensuing 2 decades an incredible

Continued.

Research vessel operated by the National Oceanographic and Atmospheric Administration (NOAA).

explosion of information has occurred. The initial work was done, demonstrating the presence of plasmids in marine bacteria, especially bacteria found in harbors in coastal areas receiving effluent from sewage treatment plants and industry. My students and I demonstrated the association of plasmids with metal resistant marine bacteria, and we were able to demonstrate transfer amongst marine bacteria of plasmids, not only between marine bacteria but also between terrestial bacteria entering estuaries and the naturally occurring bacteria found therein.

The most exciting aspect of the work evolved around the systematics of marine bacteria. We were able to show that of the bacteria able to be cultured, dominate forms were a *Vibrio* species. These bacteria included causative agents of disease in fish, as well as in humans, the most notorious of which, of course, is *Vibrio cholerae.* The questions of *Vibrio cholerae* as an aquatic bacteria was raised by my students and I in the late 1960s and early 1970s. Of course it was not accepted, and the prevailing dogma was that *Vibrio cholerae* was transmitted from case to case or perhaps carrier to case. Fortunately, we were able to develop antibodies, first highly absorbed polyclonal antibodies and, subsequently, monoclonal antibodies, to demonstrate the presence of *Vibrio cholerae* in samples in which we could not isolate it.

A major limitation to research in microbial ecology has been the inability to isolate, grow, and culture the vast majority of bacteria that occur in nature. The occurrence of nonculturable bacteria has long been known because direct staining has always demonstrated larger numbers of bacteria than could be cultured from wa-

Laboratory aboard a research ship where samples are processed.

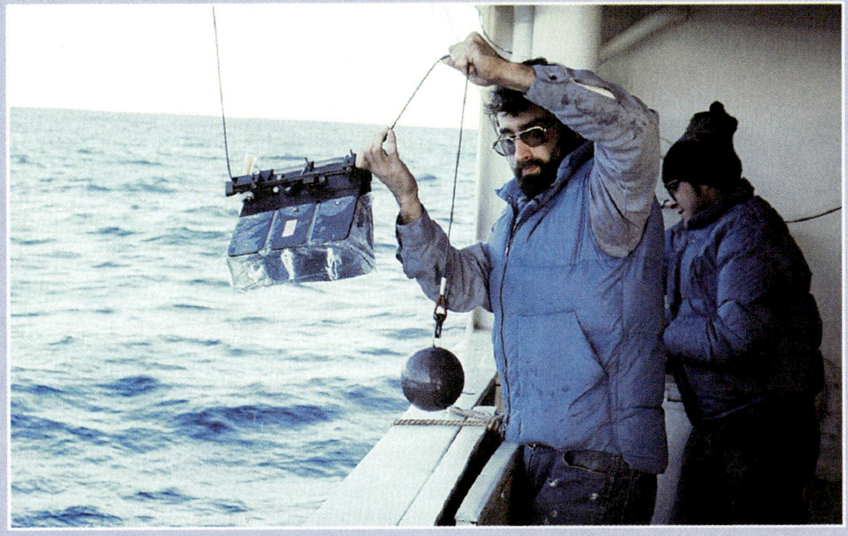

Lowering a Niskin sterile water sampler over the side of a ship to collect water samples from a specified depth.

ter samples, but the nature of the phenomenon was not determined. We reported that some pathogenic bacteria, like *Vibrio cholerae,* lost the ability to grow on laboratory media after incubation in oligotrophic ocean water or in laboratory flasks for short periods of time (less than 1 day to 3 weeks), while cell numbers, by direct microscopic counts, changed little. The implications of these observations proved far reaching in that pathogens survive in the environment but may not be detected by standard methods. The results of our studies showed that waterborne pathogens that elude detection in the laboratory can retain their pathogenicity and may be "revived" to be culturable by animal passage. We showed that animal studies, i.e., rabbit ileal loop studies, that viable but nonculturable *Vibrio cholerae* could be "revived" to the culturable state. Thus bacteria may not only survive exposure to the marine environment, previously believed to lead to rapid die off, but they retain important properties, including potential pathogenicity. Therefore we proposed a resting cell stage for Gram-negative bacteria, analogous to spore formation in some Gram-positive bacteria.

Much of the work with nonculturable bacteria requires direct counting methods that assay the total numbers of cells in a sample. The direct viable count (DVC) method has been employed as a means of estimating metabolically active bacteria populations. DVC counts are generally much higher than counts obtained by plate count on agamedia and lower than aquadine orange direct counts (AODC). We were able to show a strong correlation between DVC counts, heterotrophic activity in natural samples, and metabolic activity by micro-autoradiography, leaving us to conclude that the DVC method provides a reasonable estimate of viable bacterial populations, which strongly substantiates the existence of viable but nonculturable microorganisms in the environment. The new

Trawl collection of animals and plankton for marine studies.

Continued.

methods of polymerase chain reaction (PCR) allows direct detection of viable but nonculturable bacteria and, more recently, using radiolabeled sulphur substraits, we have been able to demonstrate metabolic activity, i.e., protein incorporation of radiolabeled self-containing amino acids.

Thus the work has been very exciting, and most recently the field of marine biotechnology has developed extraordinarily quickly. In 1983, biotechnology was taking off in a meteroritic way but nothing was being directed toward the potential of marine biotechnology. This seemed to me a serious shortcoming and I published a paper in *Science* describing the potential of marine biotechnology. Ten years later, marine biotechnology is now internationally recognized and pursued with vigor by many countries, including Japan, Norway, France, Thailand, Taiwan, and other countries of Europe, Asia, and Latin America. In the United States, a Center of Marine Biotechnology has been established in Baltimore with construction of a facility on the Inner Harbor of Baltimore, The Columbus Center, opening in early 1995. The Columbus Center will house a major research enterprise focussed on marine bio-technology and will also provide an opportunity for public exhibits that describe the excitement of and developments in marine biotechnology.

When one begins one's career, it is not clear where the chosen path will lead. Only a relatively small percentage of graduate students are fortunate enough to spend the rest of their career in the area in which they did their doctoral thesis. I was one of the lucky ones. Furthermore, the areas of choice, although unforseen at the time of choosing, proved exciting and at the cutting edge. The message, or perhaps the moral of this story, is that you must choose the path that interests you and that allows fulfillment of your interest and capabilities and intellectual challenge. By making that choice you will more likely, with luck, find yourself in a rich, rewarding, and exciting lifetime career.

The Maryland Marine Biotechnology Institute, headed by Dr. Colwell, is located at Baltimore Harbor. This new institute will meet research and educational needs into the twenty-first century.

P A R T S E V E N

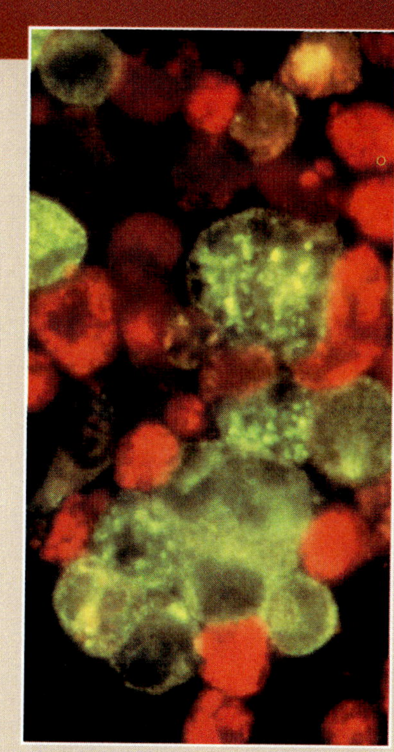

Survey of Microorganisms

CHAPTER 16

Prokaryotes

Chapter Outline

The prokaryotes (eubacteria and archaebacteria) evolved along different evolutionary lines. Modern classification systems for the prokaryotes reflect phylogenetic relationships, placing some prokaryotes in the Kingdom Eubacteria and others in the Kingdom Archaea. All prokaryotes are unicellular and their cells lack nuclei. Both phenotypic and genetic characteristics are used for the classification and identification of the prokaryotes. RNA and DNA homologies have become especially important for classifying prokaryotes. Various morphological and physiological features are used to identify prokaryotes. Eubacteria are grouped according to such criteria as the Gram stain reaction, cell shape, aerobic or anaerobic metabolism, and phototrophic, chemolithotrophic, and organotrophic modes of metabolism. Archaebacteria (Archaeobacteria or Archaea) are grouped according to physiological characteristics; the archaebacteria include the methanogens, halophiles, and thermophilic sulfur bacteria that tolerate extreme environmental conditions. There is enormous diversity among the prokaryotes. Their metabolic versatility makes them essential for life on Earth but infections with specific bacteria cause disease.

16.1 SYSTEMATICS OF PROKARYOTIC MICROORGANISMS

Because of the great diversity of prokaryotes there is a need to group them into an organizational system that facilitates their study and communication about them. **Systematics** is the comparative study of the diversity of organisms, with the aim of establishing an orderly (logical) system within which organisms can be described and classified. The systematics of prokaryotes is always in a state of flux, with descriptions of new bacterial and archaebacterial genera and species and revisions of older taxonomic classifications frequently appearing in the *International Journal of Systematic Bacteriology.* Periodically, the status of bacterial and archaebacterial taxonomy is summarized in a comprehensive volume, *Bergey's Manual of Determinative Bacteriology,* which is usually referred to simply as *Bergey's Manual.* The ninth edition of *Bergey's Manual,* published in 1994, is the most recent comprehensive volume produced. As stated in *Bergey's Manual,* "The manual is meant to assist in identification of . . . No attempt has been made to provide a complete hierarchy because a complete and meaningful hierarchy is impossible."

In addition to *Bergey's Manual of Determinative Bacteriology, Bergey's Manual of Systematic Bacteriology* gives the descriptions of the eubacteria and archaebacteria. The latter manual is a multivolume treatise: Volume 1 covers the Gram-negative bacteria of general, medical, or industrial importance; Volume 2 covers the Gram-positive bacteria other than actinomycetes; Volume 3 covers the archaebacteria, cyanobacteria, and remaining Gram-negative bacteria; and Volume 4 covers the actinomycetes. These volumes emphasize the systematics of the prokaryotes, including information on the ecology, cultivation, and descriptions of archaebacteria and eubacteria. *The Prokaryotes,* which also is a multivolume treatise, similarly gives excellent coverage of the systematics of these organisms. It considers phylogeny, which distinguishes it from *Bergey's Manuals* that are designed to assist identification.

TAXONOMY

Taxonomy is the process, based on established procedures and rules, of describing groups of organisms, their interrelationships, and the boundaries between groups of organisms. Although some individuals find such studies tedious, others are fascinated by the comparisons that can be made. Two functions of taxonomy are (1) to identify and describe the basic taxonomic units and (2) to devise an appropriate way of arranging and cataloging these units. The cardinal principles of taxonomy are that organisms exist as real, separate groups and that there is a natural ordering of these groups. A taxonomist is concerned with **classification** (ordering or placing organisms into groups based on their relationships), **nomenclature** (assigning names to the units described in a classification system), and **identification** (applying the system of classification and nomenclature to assign the proper name to an unknown organism and to place it in its proper position within the classification system).

NOMENCLATURE

Because one function of a taxonomic system is to establish unambiguous names for organisms, a logical system of nomenclature is required. Organisms are normally named according to a binomial system in which the organism is identified by its genus and species. Bacteria, like other organisms, are referred to by their unique *binomial name,* consisting of the *genus* and *species* names of each organism. The names of bacteria and all other organisms are given in Latin. This is because Latin was the classical language of science when early classification systems were developed and formal names were first given to organisms on a systematic basis. When typed or handwritten, genus and species names are underlined to indicate that they are in Latin. In print the genus and species names are italicized. The first letter of the genus name is capitalized and the species name is written in all lowercase letters. For example, we have already made frequent reference to the bacterial species *Escherichia coli.* If the genus name is understood (for example, known to be *Escherichia*), the species name can be abbreviated by using only the first letter of the genus (for example, *E. coli*).

The rules of nomenclature for microorganisms are established by international committees. Different codes of nomenclature are used for different microbial groups. The code of nomenclature of bacteria applies to all bacteria; fungi and algae are covered by the botanical code; protozoa are named according to the zoological code; and viruses are named according to the virological code. In general, the codes of nomenclature attempt to avoid ambiguity and ensure that the name of a microorganism specifically and unambiguously designates that organism. The name sometimes reflects the physiology or ecology of the organism. As examples, *Legionella pneumophila* is a name given to a bacterial species that grows in the lung (*pneumophila* indicates lung loving); *Pseudomonas marina* is a bacterial species that grows in the oceans (*marina* indicates marine); *Thermus aquaticus* is the name given to the bacterial species that grows in hot aquatic environments (*Thermus* indicates hot and *aquaticus* indicates aquatic). In other cases, the bacterial name may indicate the name of the individual who discovered it or may be given to honor a microbiologist. The genus *Beijerinckia,* for example, is named after the microbiologist Martinius Beijerinck. Once the name is assigned it cannot be changed unless a mistake was made in classification. In the field of bacteriology, a summary list of the approved names of bacteria has been published. Only names published in that listing and those validated and published individually as supplements to the list in that journal are considered valid.

CLASSIFICATION OF MICROORGANISMS

The second objective of taxonomy, *classification,* attempts to differentiate microbial taxa into structured groups so that the members of a group are more closely related to each other than they are to members of any other group. Classification is a coherent scheme by which a collection of organisms is arranged so as to reflect the relationships between individuals and groups. The ordering of organisms into groups is based on an assessment of their similarities. Ideally, the classification of microorganisms should follow the natural ordering established by evolutionary processes, and therefore taxonomic systems should be based on the genetic interrelationships among groups of microorganisms. Many classification systems used for microorganisms are artificial rather than natural. They are based on observable phenotypic features and not on evolutionary (genetic) relatedness. However, the situation is changing rapidly; modern molecular genetic approaches are making it possible for classification based on genetic relatedness. Even artificial systems help give a coherent overview of a group of related or similar organisms.

Taxonomists frequently debate the validity of a taxonomic system, questioning whether it truly reflects the evolutionary relationships of the organisms and sometimes arguing vehemently whether the structure of the system contains the proper taxonomic units and reflects the appropriate ordering of the units. As a result, taxonomic systems are frequently revised. In Chapter 1 we considered the taxonomic position of microorganisms and examined three different classification systems that at one time or another were considered to define properly the primary kingdoms and reflect the evolutionary relationships of living organisms. Obviously, the classification systems proposed by Whittaker and Woese show the development of our understanding of **phylogenetic relationships (evolutionary relationships).** The use of genetic analyses for assessing similarity holds great promise for the development of a valid natural classification system.

Although biological classification systems should reflect genetic similarities, the classification of bacteria has been traditionally based on phenotypic characteristics. Phenotypic characteristics are readily determined by observing bacteria growing in pure culture, whereas, until recently, methodology for directly analyzing the genome did not exist. Taxa based on observed phenotypic characteristics may not accurately reflect genetic similarities and such a classification may not correspond to the evolutionary flow of events. It is possible for genetically dissimilar microorganisms *(homologously dissimilar)* to resemble each other phenotypically *(analogously similar).* For example, many genetically dissimilar bacteria produce yellow pigments, and a classification scheme based on such a phenotypic characteristic could produce a taxonomic group of genetically unrelated bacteria. In fact, classification systems are filled with errors made by using such phenotypic characteristics. Various groups of bacteria that have been defined on the basis of their apparent phenotypic relationship are now considered to be "groups of uncertain taxonomic affinity" because the taxonomic group may not be homologously similar and therefore may not accurately represent genetic similarities.

Hierarchical Organization of Classification Systems

Although the hierarchical organization of a classification system should reflect the natural consequence of evolution, evolutionary affinities among microorganisms are difficult to discern because there is no fossil record of most microorganisms. The lack of a fossil record makes examination of the remains of most ancient microorganisms impossible. Additionally, the examination of bacteria requires their culture in the laboratory, and many bacteria that may prove to be critical evolutionary links have yet to be grown on defined media. This limitation is being overcome, in part, by using genetic analyses and analyses of ribosomal RNA.

Despite the increased use of DNA and RNA analyses in classifying microorganisms, bacterial taxonomy generally requires many subjective decisions, resulting in an artificial classification scheme. Some taxonomists are "lumpers," tending to lump many similar organisms into large taxonomic units. In contrast, other taxonomists are "splitters," favoring small taxonomic groups that emphasize even minor differences between organisms. Arguments over the proper taxonomic position of a microorganism can be quite heated, and these debates enhance the interest of microbiologists in the field of microbial taxonomy.

When classifying organisms, taxonomists use a hierarchy consisting of different organizational levels. The usual levels of a **taxonomic hierarchy,** from the highest to the lowest, are kingdoms, phyla, classes, orders, families, genera, and species (Table 16-1). Ideally, each level represents a different degree of homology, that is, of genetic and evolutionary similarity. In reality, many levels represent varying degrees of

TABLE 16-1 Hierarchy of Taxonomic Organization

LEVEL	DESCRIPTION	EXAMPLE
Kingdom	A group of related divisions or phyla	Eubacteria
Division	A group of related classes	Gracilicutes
Class	A group of related orders	Scotobacteria
Order	A group of related families	Rickettsiales
Family	A group of related tribes or genera	Rickettsiaceae
Tribe	A group of related genera	—
Genus	A group of related species	*Rickettsia*
Species	A group of organisms of the same kind	*R. typhi*
Subspecies or type	Variants of a species	*R. typhi* ATCC VR-144

analogous (phenotypic) similarity. The higher the taxonomic level, the greater the diversity of the organisms classified as belonging to that group.

Tremendous ambiguity exists relative to the higher taxonomic levels of prokaryotes because of their great diversity. Hence, bacteriologists usually ignore the phylum, class, and order and focus on the genus and species. The **species** is considered to be the basic taxonomic unit of a classification system. Species of higher organisms are readily recognized as a result of their reproductive isolation, but a bacterial species is difficult to define objectively. Implicit in the definition of a species for higher organisms is a similar and shared gene pool. The asexual means of reproduction typically exhibited by bacteria that gives rise to clones of genetically nearly identical cells limits the diversity of the gene pool, but closely related bacteria do exchange genetic information by several mechanisms. Recombination among closely related bacteria gives rise to a limited degree of genetic diversity within the population of a bacterial species.

A eubacterial or archaebacterial species can be considered as a group of strains that have an overall similarity and are significantly different from other similarly defined groups. In defining a new eubacterial or archaebacterial species, the organism must be a pure culture, described, named, and shown to be different from previously described species. International committees have been established to rule on the validity of defining new species. Once an organism is defined as representing a new species, a culture should be deposited in an appropriate culture collection as the **type culture.** That type culture and its description become the reference for future identification.

Although species are the basic taxonomic units, the genetic variability of microorganisms permits a further division into *subspecies* or *types* that describe the specific clone of cells. The subspecies or type may differ physiologically **(biovar),** morphologically **(morphovar),** or antigenically **(serovar).** It is often important to identify the subspecies of a given microorganism. For example, one strain of a bacterial species may produce a toxin and be a virulent pathogen, and other strains of the same species may be nonpathogenic. A **strain** is a population of cells that are descendents of a single cell. Pure cultures grown in the microbiology laboratory represent individual strains of a species. The ability to distinguish correctly between such strains and subspecies of a particular microbial species is of obvious importance in medical and industrial microbiology.

Approaches to the Classification of Microorganisms

Several approaches are used in microbiology for developing classification systems and establishing hierarchical relationships. Early approaches grouped microorganisms on the basis of the similarity of their morphologies. Later, physiological properties dominated microbial classification. Modern microbial classification systems still include morphological and physiological characteristics, but molecular-level similarity, that is, genetic relatedness, is given greater emphasis.

Classification systems may be *phenetic* (assessing similarity) or *phylogenetic* (assessing evolutionary relationships). Because organisms could evolve quite differently and still develop similar characteristics, microorganisms that are distantly related in evolutionary terms may still be similar and grouped together in a phenetic but not a phylogenetic classification system. Phenetic approaches require quantification and explicitness and do not permit *a priori* weighting of features. Such systems persist because of their utility in identification. In contrast, phylogenetic approaches may consider evolutionary evidence and give added importance to those key features viewed as indicative of different evolutionary paths. Such systems are not exactly used in routine identification as, for example, in a clinical microbiology laboratory.

In a conventional or classical approach to classification, several features of organisms are examined and organisms are grouped on the basis of their similarity with respect to selected features. In the development of such classification systems, certain features are generally considered more important than others for defining taxonomic units. These key features are those considered to be of primary importance in the separation of species. For example, the Gram stain reaction is considered a key test in many bacterial classification systems. A taxonomic system based on this approach employs a sequential series of hierarchical decisions to separate the taxonomic units called *taxa* or *taxons.* This type of classification system emphasizes the branch

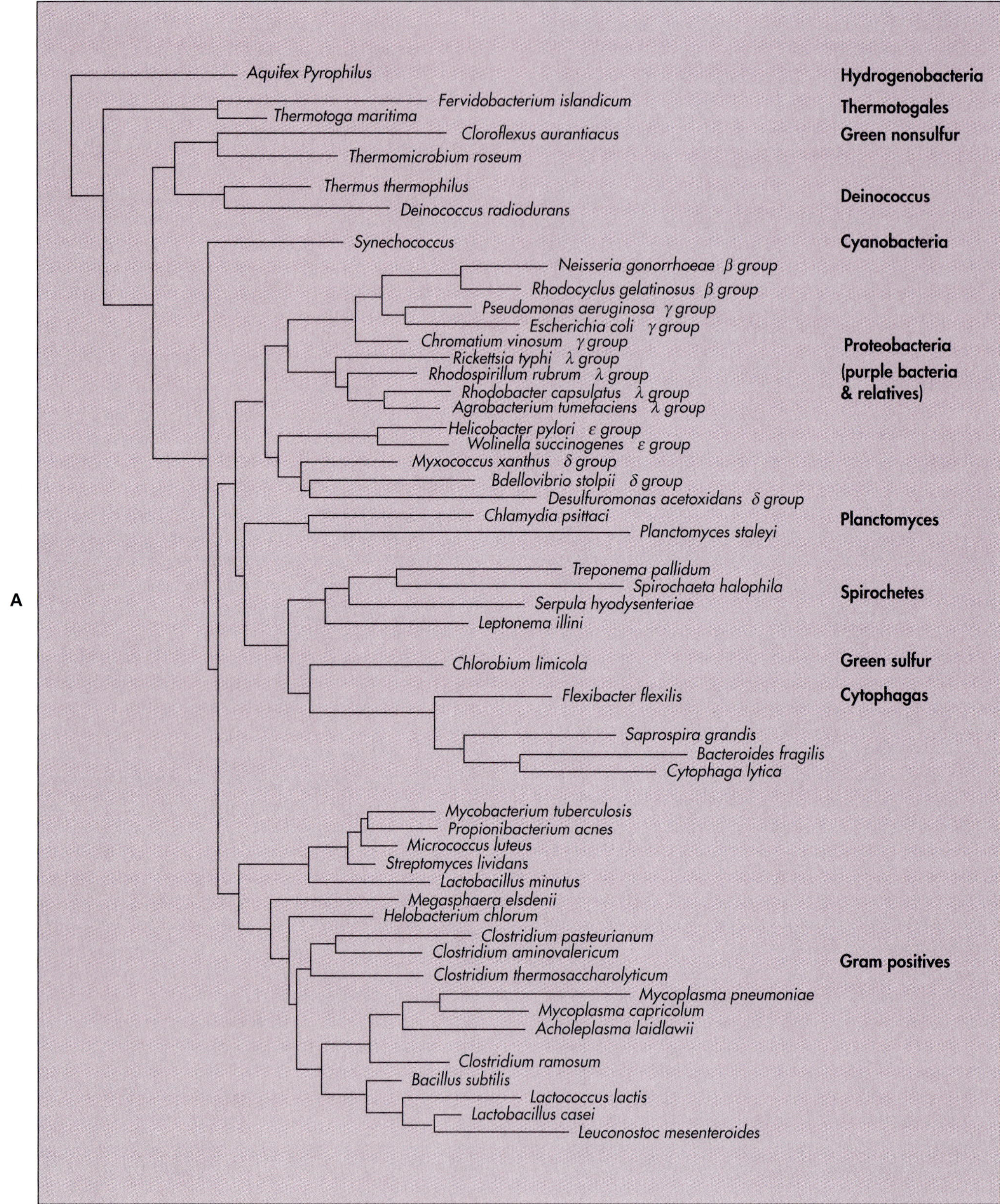

FIG. 16-1 The classification of bacteria is often represented as a tree that shows the branching of one taxon from another. **A,** This branching is shown as a dendrogram of the classification of eubacteria based on the analyses of 16S rRNA sequences that represent phylogenetic relationships.

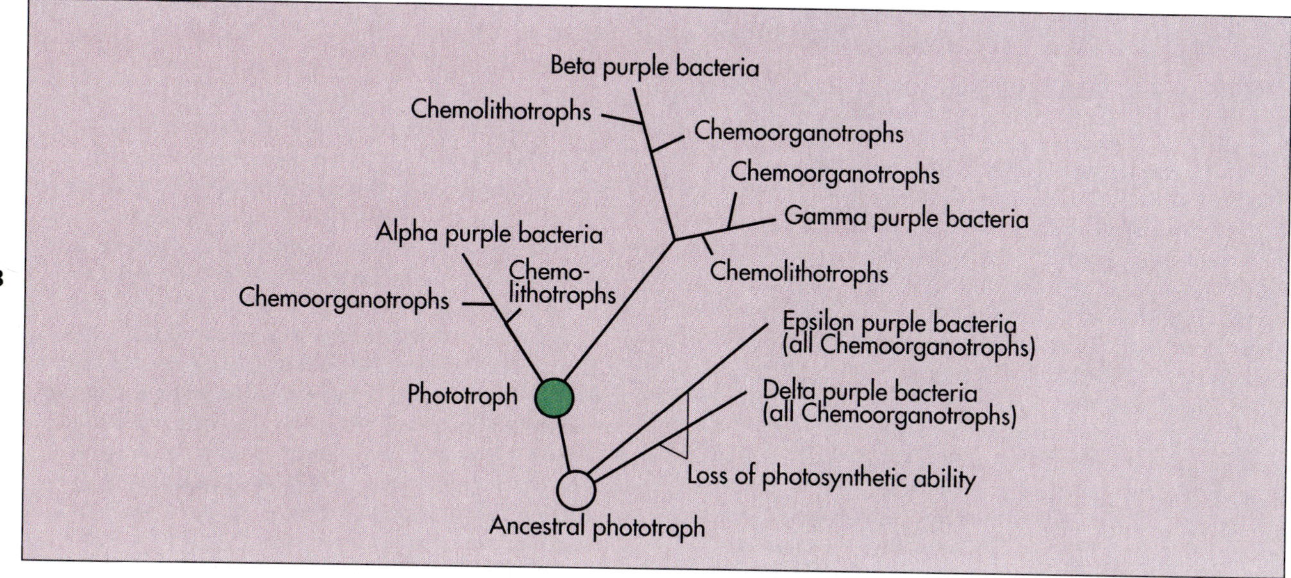

FIG. 16-1, cont'd **B,** A phylogenetic tree showing the evolution of the various groups of Proteobacteria (purple bacteria).

points between groups that are presumed to represent fundamental differences between taxa. Often the classification system is represented as a tree diagram showing the various key branch points and the individual taxa at the ends of the branches (FIG. 16-1).

An alternative approach, *numerical taxonomy,* does not emphasize points of branching but uses overall degrees of similarity between organisms to establish a taxon. In numerical taxonomy a single characteristic does not determine the taxonomic position of an organism. Instead, overall similarity and the definition of the taxa are based on statistical analyses using a large number of characteristics that are examined. Equal weight is given to each characteristic to ensure that no single one is more important in defining the taxa.

Various measures can be applied to assess similarity. These measures are often expressed as indices of similarity, or similarity coefficients (FIG. 16-2). The most common indices of similarity used in microbiology are the simple matching coefficient, which includes positive and negative matches, and Jaccard coefficient, which includes only positive matches to assess similarity. The *simple matching coefficient* (S_{SM}) is based on all of the measured characteristics. In contrast, the calculation of the *Jaccard coefficient* (S_J) does not use a characteristic when the organisms being compared are both negative for that feature; the assumption is made that such a feature may be an inappropriate description for the group under consideration. For example, a weight of over 1 ton may be an appropriate descriptive characteristic for elephants but is clearly inappropriate for microorganisms. When the simple matching coefficient is used, the inclusion of such an irrelevant feature in a classification system would artificially, even nonsensically, make organisms appear more similar than they really are; the Jaccard coefficient eliminates this problem.

The classification of organisms by the use of numerical taxonomy is normally represented graphically

$$S_m = \frac{(++)+(--)}{(++)+(--)+(+-)+(-+)}$$

Where

S_m = simple matching coefficient
++ = positive matches
− − = negative
(+ −) + (+ −) = mismatches

$$S_J = \frac{(++)}{(++)+(+-)+(-+)}$$

Where

S_J = Jaccard coefficient
+ + = positive matches
(+ −) + (− +) = mismatches

FIG. 16-2 The similarities of microorganisms can be determined by comparing the positive and negative results for specific features. In the simple matching coefficient, all features examined are used in the calculation. In the Jaccard coefficient, features that are negative for both organisms being com[illegible]red are omitted from the calculation.

BOX 16-1

RIBOSOMAL RNA (rRNA) AND PHYLOGENY

Ribosomal RNAs (rRNAs) have been relatively conserved during evolution. As such, changes in RNA nucleotide sequences are indices of evolutionary change. The comparison of rRNA molecules isolated from different organisms is useful for determining the evolutionary relationships of all living things. There are many possible nucleotide sequences of rRNA molecules. Any similarity in two nucleotide sequences suggests some phylogenetic relationship between these nucleotide sequences and the organisms that contain them. In particular, the 16S rRNA of Eubacteria and Archaea is used to determine the phylogenetic relationships among these microorganisms (see FIG., p. 658). For eukaryotes, 18S rRNA is analyzed. The use of 16S rRNA in the field of phylogenetic analyses was advanced by Carl Woese at the University of Illinois in the early 1970s. This technique to determine phylogenetic relationships has revolutionized systematics.

To analyze rRNA, cells are ruptured in the presence of DNase to degrade all DNA. The RNA is then extracted with phenol/water. Large RNA molecules are separated in the aqueous phase. After precipitation of the RNA with alcohol and salt, a DNA primer that is complementary to a conserved region of the 16S rRNA is added. Reverse transcriptase can then be used to generate cDNAs. The sequence of nucleotides of the cDNAs is determined and the sequence of nucleotides of the original 16S rRNA is deduced. The polymerase chain reaction (PCR) also can be used to amplify the DNA encoding the rRNA genes. This procedure uses synthetically produced primers that are complementary to conserved sequences in rRNA as PCR templates. Use of PCR amplification of the DNA coding for rRNA requires fewer cells than direct rRNA sequencing. It is also faster and more convenient for large-scale studies.

Comparisons of nucleotide sequences of 16S rRNA determined in this manner allow the construction of phylogenetic trees that show relative evolutionary positions and relationships. The resultant phylogeny based on 16S rRNA analyses revealed that there are separate domains of the Eubacteria, Archea, and Eukaryotes; this was quite different from previously held beliefs based on phenotypic relationships. The branches of the trees indicate evolutionary divergences to form new species. The distance matrix method is used to generate phylogenetic trees from rRNA sequences. An evolutionary distance can be calculated by recording the number of positions at which two aligned rRNA sequences differ. The evolutionary distance separating organisms is directly proportional to the total length of the branches separating them.

Based on these phylogenetic analyses of 16S rRNA, at least 12 different groups of eubacteria have been shown to exist (see Table). These groups represent major evoluationary divergences. Each group contains specific nucleotide sequences that act as *signature sequences* that help define the group.

Phylogenetic Relationships of the Bacteria

GROUP	EXAMPLES	CHARACTERISTICS	CONSERVED 16S rRNA SEQUENCE
Purple bacteria	*Rhodobacter, Nitrobacter, Beggiatoa, Escherichia, Enterobacter, Pseudomonas, Rhizobium, Legionella*	Contains most of the Gram-negative bacteria. Subdivided into alpha, beta, gamma, delta, and epsilon subgroups. Many members of the alpha, beta, and gamma subgroups are phototrophic. This group also contains the free-living and symbiotic nitrogen-fixing bacteria.	AAAUUCG—alpha CPy*UUACACAUG—beta ACUAAAACUCAAAG—delta
Green sulfur bacteria	*Chlorobium*	Phototrophic bacteria with light harvesting pigments in chlorosomes.	AUACAAUG
Green nonsulfur bacteria	*Chloroflexus, Herpetosiphon,* and *Thermomicrobium*	Most bacteria in this group are phototrophic; some are thermophilic.	CCUAAUG

*Py refers to any pyrimidine.

Phylogenetic Relationships of the Bacteria—cont'd

GROUP	EXAMPLES	CHARACTERISTICS	CONSERVED 16S rRNA SEQUENCE
Cyanobacteria	*Nostoc, Anabena, Oscillatoria*	Metabolism is by oxygenic photosynthesis.	AAUUUUPyCG
Planctomyces—Pirella group	*Planctomyces, Pirella*	Budding bacteria that lack peptidoglycan and contain a protein cell wall. Many cells contain stalks or holdfasts.	CUUAAUUCG
Spirochete	*Spirochaeta, Borrelia,* and *Treponema; Leptospira*	Unique spiral-shaped cells and corkscrew motility.	AAUCUUG—a few spirochetes UCACACPyAPyCPyG—most spirochetes
Bacteroides—Flavobacterium group	*Bacteroides, Fusobacterium, Cytophaga,* and *Flavobacterium*	Divided into two subgroups: the *Bacteroides* and *Fusobacterium* subgroup containing fermentative, rod-shaped anaerobes and the *Flavobacterium* subgroup containing respiring rod-shaped to filamentous bacteria with gliding motility.	UUACAAUG—*Bacteroides* group CCCCCACACUG—gliding group
Chlamydia	*Chlamydia*	Cells lack peptidoglycan and are obligate intracellular parasites.	
Deinococcus—Thermus	*Deinococcus, Thermus*	*Deinococcus*—Gram-positive, radiation resistant cells. *Thermus*—Gram negative, thermophilic cells. Both bacterial groups contain atypical cell walls with ornithine instead of diaminopimelic acid.	CUUAAC
Gram-positive bacteria	*Clostridium, Bacillus, Staphylococcus, Mycoplasma, Actinomyces, Streptomyces, Corynebacterium, Mycobacterium,* and *Heliobacterium*	Contain most Gram-positive bacteria, including endospore-forming bacteria, lactic acid bacteria, anaerobic and aerobic cocci, coryneforms, actinomycetes, and mycoplasmas. Divided into three subgroups: a low GC group containing *Clostridium* and related bacteria, a high GC group containing *Actinomycetes* and related bacteria, and a phototrophic group containing *Heliobacterium*.	CUAAAACUCAAAG—high GC group
Thermotoga—Thermosipho	*Thermotoga* and *Thermosipho*	Extremely themophilic bacteria.	
Aquifex—Hydrogenobacter	*Aquifex* and *Hydrogenobacter*	Extremely themophilic bacteria.	

Continued.

BOX 16-1

Ribosomal RNA (rRNA) and Phylogeny—cont'd

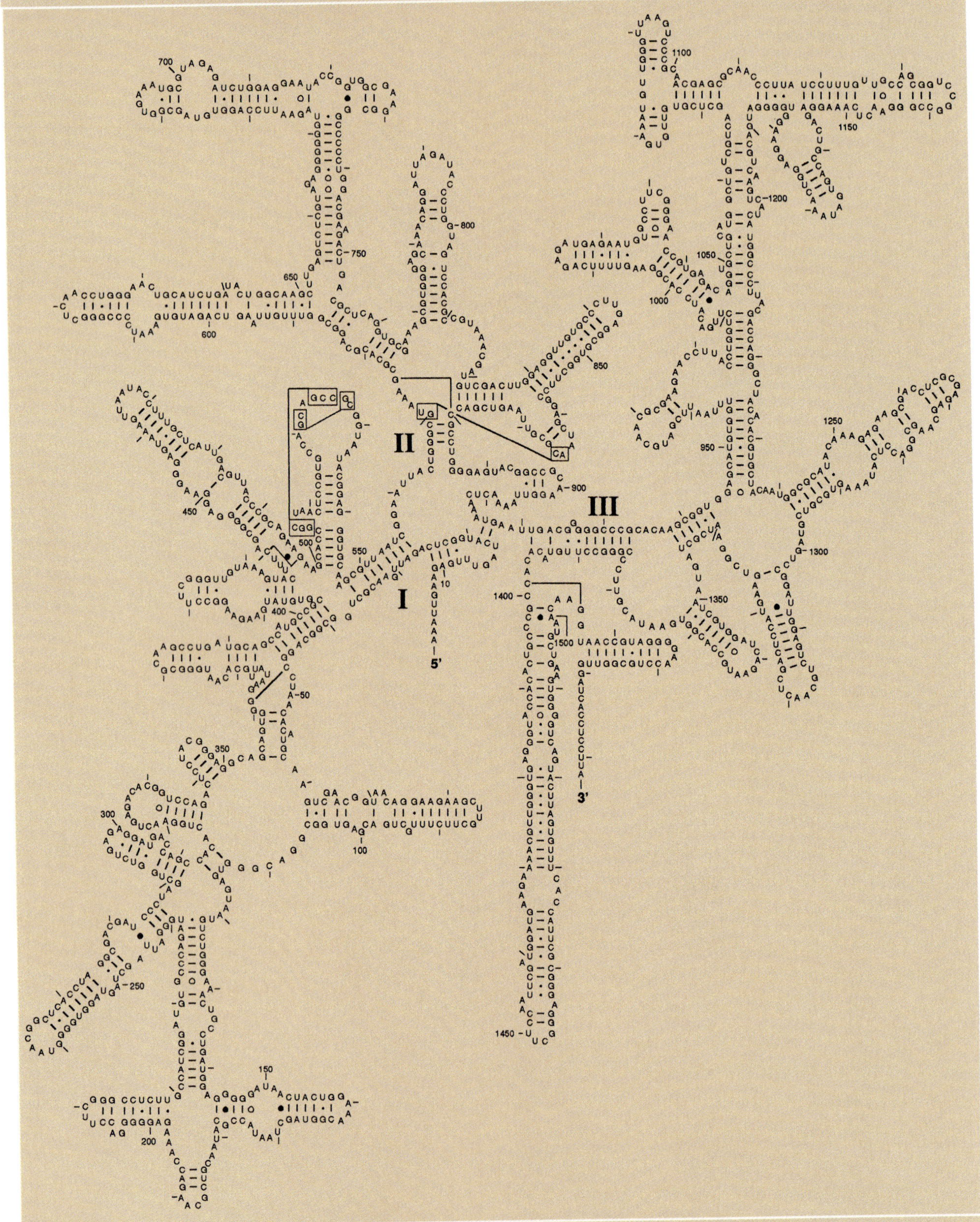

Representation of the 16S rRNA molecule on which today's phylogenetic relationships of eubacteria and archaebacteria (Archaea) are based.

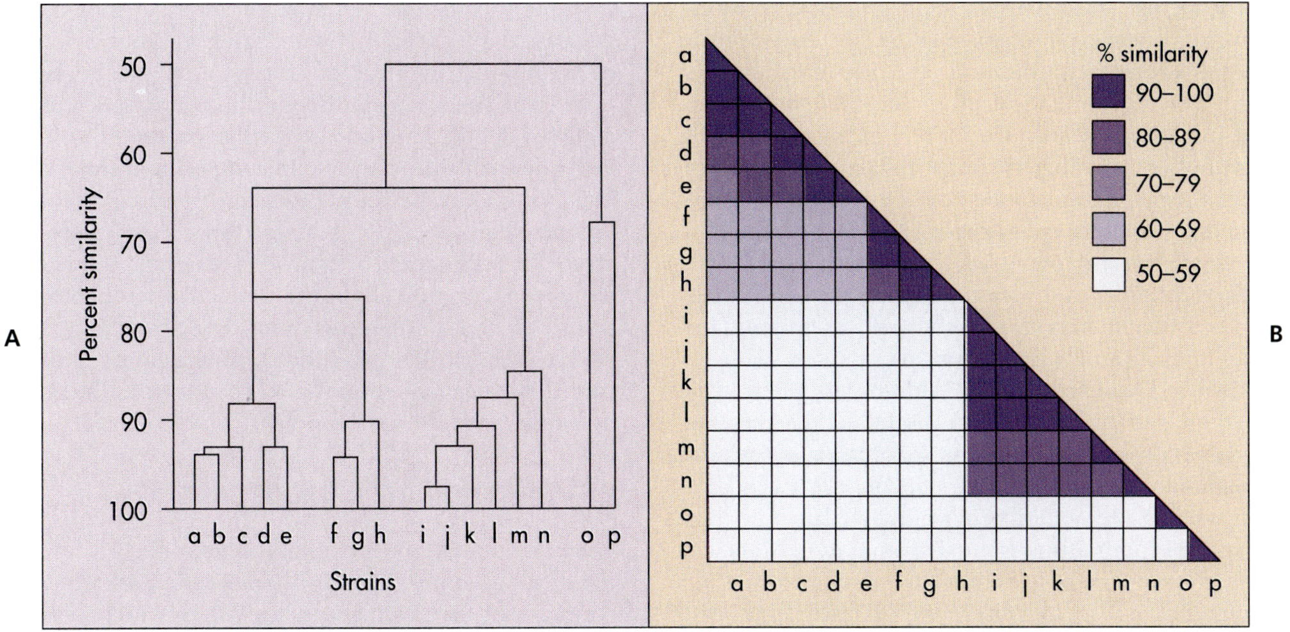

FIG. 16-3 The similarities among organisms are represented as matrices of the calculated similarity coefficients. **A,** The data is then graphically represented as a dendrogram that shows the similarity relationships among the organisms. Each organism is represented as a vertical line. Organisms that are most closely related are located adjacent to each other. The levels of similarity are represented by the horizontal lines. **B,** The data can also be represented as a similarity triangle.

by a similarity matrix, or a dendrogram (FIG. 16-3). Organisms are grouped on the basis of the overall similarity of all of the tested characteristics by using a type of statistical analysis known as *cluster analysis.* In the graphic representations of these analyses, organisms of high similarity occur in close geometric proximity, whereas organisms of low similarity are separated.

Criteria for Classifying Microorganisms

Regardless of the classification approach employed, it is necessary to characterize organisms to assess their similarity. To characterize a microorganism, it is important to isolate and to maintain *pure cultures* of the organism. Otherwise one might examine the combined features of several unrelated organisms or an anomaly based on environmental variations. Determining the characteristics of a pure culture of a microorganism permits the description of that organism so that it can be classified. To exemplify the types of characteristics employed as microbial descriptors, some of the criteria frequently used in bacterial classification are listed in Table 16-2. The various criteria used in classifying microorganisms represent a continuum from the analysis of the genome itself to the phenotypic expression of genetic information. Presumably, classification systems based on genetic analyses reflect a natural evolutionary hierarchy more accurately than other artificial classification systems based on phenotypic characteristics.

TABLE 16-2 Some Criteria for Classifying Bacteria

CRITERION	EXAMPLE
Cellular characteristics Morphology	Cell shape, cell size, arrangement of cells, arrangement of flagella, capsule, endospores
Staining reactions	Gram stain, acid-fast stain
Growth and nutritional characteristics	Appearance in liquid culture, colonial morphology, pigmentation, energy sources, carbon sources, nitrogen sources, fermentation products, modes of metabolism (autotrophic, heterotrophic, fermentative, respiratory)
Biochemical characteristics	Cell wall constituents, pigment biochemicals, storage inclusions, antigens, RNA molecules
Physiological and ecological characteristics	Temperature range and optimum, oxygen relationships, pH tolerance range, osmotic tolerance, salt requirement and tolerance, antibiotic sensitivity
Genetic characteristics	DNA mole % G + C, DNA hybridization

Phenotypic Characteristics For practical reasons, however, phenotypic characteristics are employed in most microbial classification and identification systems. The morphological, physiological, biochemical, and nutritional features normally examined include morphology, staining reactions, ability to form spores, motility, specific metabolic activities, mode of reproduction, and life cycle stages. Analysis of the biochemical constituents of the cell and cell structures, such as cell walls and membranes, among others, may also be valuable in revealing major differentiating features of groups of microorganisms.

Genetic Characteristics In addition to phenotypic analyses, genetic analyses are useful in the development of classification schemes for microorganisms; genetic analyses are necessary for modern classification systems. One of the genetic analyses used for classifying microorganisms is the determination of the relative proportion of guanine (G) and cytosine (C) compared to the total number of nucleotide base pairs in the DNA. Because there is pairing between complementary bases in DNA, specifying G + C also specifies adenosine + thymine (A + T). Therefore the composition of the DNA is normally described by specifying the *mole % G + C*, that is the proportion of the DNA macromolecule composed of G + C base pairs. Measuring the proportion of G + C in the DNA is a crude way of analyzing the microbial genome. Closely related organisms should have similar proportions of G + C in their DNA, and organisms with significantly differing proportions of G + C in their DNA can safely be said to be unrelated. Microorganisms that are otherwise similar, but differ by 2% to 3% G + C content in their genomes, may represent different species. However, a similarity of G + C ratios does not necessarily establish the relatedness of organisms because the sequence of genes may be different even when the mole % G + C content is the same.

Genetic analyses can also be extended to the analysis of gene products, namely, RNA molecules and proteins. The subunits of these macromolecules can be described explicitly. Proteins can be separated and analyzed by using electrophoresis and other analytical methods. Because RNA such as 16S RNA are highly conserved molecules, any changes represent points of evolutionary divergence. The greater the dissimilarity, the longer ago that divergence began. Hence, 16S RNA is useful as a *chronometer* of bacterial evolution.

The nucleotide sequences of RNA molecules can be determined and the similarity between these molecules assessed. Because the order of nucleotides in RNA and amino acids in proteins is directly controlled by the genome, analyses of these gene products should permit the combining of phenetic and phylogenetic approaches to microbial taxonomy.

Such comparisons of gene products represent an intermediary stage between the analysis of genotype and phenotype. The examination of rRNA molecules is particularly useful for establishing the higher levels of taxonomic organization, for example, at the kingdom level. As has been discussed in previous sections, analyses of rRNA molecules have been used to establish a new classification system composed of three primary kingdoms: Archaea, Eubacteria, and Eukaryotes. Similar analyses of rRNA molecules are now used to assess the relatedness of microbial genera and species. As more is learned about the molecular-level composition of microorganisms and theories about the course of evolution are revised, phylogenetic classification systems will continue to change to reflect the prevailing evolutionary concepts.

IDENTIFICATION OF MICROORGANISMS

Classification attempts to establish an orderly arrangement of taxonomic groups. **Identification** attempts to compare an unknown organism with previously established groups to determine whether it should be considered as a member of one of these groups. The two processes, classification and identification, are not synonymous. Classification defines taxonomic groups. Identification assigns an organism of unknown taxonomic affinity to the correct group.

One can view identification as a practical application of classification, permitting the correct recognition of an unknown microorganism as a member of a pre-existing taxonomic group. An identification system should permit the efficient and reliable distinguishment of microorganisms. For identification purposes, any artificial classification system will suffice, providing that it permits the organism to be identified with others that have previously been placed in the system.

Although classification and identification of microorganisms are distinct processes, both generally require that pure cultures be examined and characterized. The characteristics used in an identification system are limited to the significant features that distinguish one group from another. As a rule, identification systems try to use the minimal number of characteristics that will produce a reliable identification. Because the purpose of these systems is to make a correct identification efficiently, the features included in the identification system are often different from those used in the classification system.

Identification Keys and Diagnostic Tables

The classical approach to microbial identification involves the development of keys or diagnostic tables. An **identification key** consists of a series of questions that lead through a classification system to the determination of the identity of the organism. In a *dichotomous key* a series of yes–no questions is asked that leads through the branches of a flow chart to the identification of a microorganism as a member of a specified microbial group (Table 16-3; see FIG. 16-1). The path to an identification in a true dichotomous key is unidirectional, and a single atypical feature or error in determining a feature will result in a misidentification. Most students in introductory microbiology laboratory courses use dichotomous keys for the identification of an unknown organism. Although dichotomous keys are frequently used in identification systems, other keys based on multiple-choice questions also can be used. Regardless of whether the choices are dichotomous or not, the characteristics used in establishing an identification key must be constant for the particular group. For example, if the Gram stain is employed as a key feature in a dichotomous key, the groups separated by this characteristic must be either Gram-positive or Gram-negative; a group cannot contain both Gram-positive and Gram-negative members.

Diagnostic tables can be developed to aid in microbial identification (Table 16-4). Such tables summarize the characteristics of the taxonomic groups but do not indicate a hierarchical separation of the taxa. Diagnostic tables generally appear to be far more complicated than keys for the identification of microorganisms because they contain more information. However, in cases where some features are variable for different groups, diagnostic tables are better than keys for the successful identification of an unknown microorganism.

TABLE 16-3 Dichotomous Key for the Diagnosis of Species of the Genus *Psuedomonas*

1. Oxidase negative (Go to 2)	
Oxidase positive (Go to 4)	
2. Lysine positive	*P. maltophilia*
Lysine negative (Go to 3)	
3. Motile	*P. paucimobilis*
Nonmotile	*P. malleii*
4. Fluorescent (Go to 5)	
Nonfluorescent (Go to 8)	
5. Pyocyanin and pyorubin positive	*P. aeruginosa*
Pyocyanin and pyorubin negative (Go to 6)	
6. Growth at 42° C	*P. aeruginosa*
No growth at 42° C (Go to 7)	
7. Gelatinase positive	*P. fluorescens*
Gelatinase negative	*P. putida*
8. Nonmotile	(probably not a pseudomonad)
Motile (Go to 9)	
9. Petrichous	(not a pseudomonad)
Polar (Go to 10)	
10. Glucose oxidation negative (Go to 11)	
Glucose oxidation positive (Go to 13)	
11. Two or more flagella	*P. diminuta*
One flagellum (Go to 12)	
12. PHB positive	*P. testosterioni*
PHB negative	*P. alcaligenes*
13. Mannose negative (Go to 14)	
Mannose positive (Go to 16)	
14. Ornithine positive	*P. putrefaciens*
Ornithine negative (Go to 15)	
15. Mannitol positive	*P. acidovorans*
Mannitol negative	*P. pseudoalcaligenes*
16. Arginine positive (Go to 17)	
Arginine negative (Go to 19)	
17. 6.5% NaCl positive	*P. mendocina*
6.5% NaCl negative (Go to 18)	
18. Gelatinase positive	*P. fluorescens*
Gelatinase negative	*P. putida*
19. Galactose negative (Go to 20)	
Galactose positive (Go to 21)	
20. Mannose positive	*P. maltophilia*
Mannose negative	*P. vesicularis*
21. Lactose negative (Go to 22)	
Lactose positive (Go to 23)	
22. 6.5% NaCl positive	*P. stutzeri*
6.5% NaCl negative	*P. pickettii*
23. Nitrogen production	*P. pseudomallei*
No nitrogen production (Go to 24)	
24. Citrate positive	*P. cepacia*
Citrate negative	*P. paucimobilis*

TABLE 16-4 Diagnostic Table for Differentiating the Species *Pseudomonas aeruginosa, P. fluorescens,* and *P. putida*

CHARACTERISTIC	*P. aeruginosa*	*P. fluorescens*	*P. putida*
Monotrichous polar flagella	+	−	−
Pyocyanin	+	−	−
Growth at 4° C	−	+	+
Growth at 42° C	+	−	−
Denitrification	d	−	−
Lecithinase	−	+	−
Gelatinase	d	+	−
Utilization			
Acetamide	+	−	
Creatinine	−		+
Benzylamine	−	−	+
Geranitol	+	−	−
Hippurate	−	−	+
Inositol	−	+	−
Phenylacetate	−		+
Trehalose	−	+	−

+, Over 90%; −, less than 10%; d, 10% to 90% of strains tested are positive.

Computer-assisted Identification

Computers facilitate the identification of microorganisms. When computers are used, the data gathered on an unknown microorganism can rapidly be compared to a data bank containing information on the characteristics of defined taxa. Keys and diagnostic tables can readily be programmed for *computer-assisted identification* of unknown isolates. Because computers rapidly perform large numbers of calculations and comparisons, computerized identification systems have also been developed to assess the statistical probability of correctly identifying a microorganism. In these methods the results of a series of phenotypic tests are scored and compared to the test results of organisms that have been classified as belonging to a particular taxonomic group. Unlike keys in which in-

BOX 16-2

COMMERCIAL SYSTEMS FOR RAPID IDENTIFICATION OF BACTERIA

Several commercial systems were developed for the identification of members of the family Enterobacteriaceae and other pathogenic microorganisms. These systems are widely used in clinical microbiology laboratories because of the high frequency of isolation of Gram-negative rods indistinguishable except for characteristics determined by detailed biochemical or serological testing. Systems commonly used in clinical laboratories include the Enterotube, API, Minitek, Micro-ID, Enteric Tek, and r/b enteric systems. The pattern of test results obtained in these systems is converted to a numerical code that can be used to calculate the identity of the isolate. The numerical code describing the test results obtained for a clinical isolate is compared with results in a data bank describing test reactions of known organisms. Some of the commercial systems list a series of possible identifications indicating the statistical probability that a given organism (biotype) could yield the observed test results. All of the commercial systems employ miniaturized reaction vessels, and some are designed for automated reading and computerized processing of test results. The systems differ in how many and which specific biochemical tests are included. They also differ in whether they are restricted to identifying members of the family Enterobacteriaceae or whether they can be used for identifying other Gram-negative rods. The test results obtained with all of these systems show excellent correlation with conventional test procedures. They are completed rapidly, are cost-effective, and these package systems yield reliable identifications as long as the isolate is one of the organisms that the system is designed to identify.

The *Enterotube system* contains 8 solid media from which 11 different features can be determined (see FIG. 13-9). This system has a self-contained inoculating needle that is touched to a colony on the isolation plate and drawn through the tube. The characteristics determined in the Enterotube are used to generate a five-digit biotype number from which bacterial identifications can be made. The identification is made by comparing the biotype number of an unknown organism with those of previously identified organisms.

The *API-20 E system,* as the name implies, uses 20 miniature capsule reaction chambers. However, 21 tubes are run in this system (see FIG. 13-10). A suspension of bacteria is used to inoculate each of the reaction chambers. The results of the API-20 E test system yield a seven-digit biotype number from which a computer-assisted identification can be made. The results of the API system can also be used in the identification of some nonfermentative, Gram-negative rods and for the identification of anaerobic bacteria. For the identification of nonfermentative, Gram-negative rods, six additional tests are run to generate a nine-digit biotype identification number. Over 100 taxa of Gram-negative rods can be identified by using the API-20E system.

The *Minitek system* consists of reagent-impregnated paper discs to which a broth suspension is added for the determination of characteristic reactions. The number of discs and tests employed is variable; generally, 17 tests at a time are used to differentiate clinical isolates. The profile of test results obtained with the Minitek system is useful in identifying obligate anaerobes, as well as facultative enteric bacteria.

The *Micro-ID system,* which is based on constitutive enzymes, is designed primarily for identifying members of the Enterobacteriaceae, although it can also be used for biotyping *Haemophilus influenzae* and *H. parainfluenzae.* Bacteria must be screened for oxidase activity, and only oxidase-negative strains are tested with this system. All commercial ID systems actually recommend performing the oxidase test before attempting an identification. This system employs 15 reaction chambers, and the test results are used to generate a five-digit identification code number. The Micro-ID system lists possible identifications and probabilities based on the results of the 15 biochemical test reactions. Identifications with the Micro-ID system can be accomplished in as little as 4 hours.

The API-20E and Minitek systems were expanded to identify obligate anaerobes. To use these systems to identify anaerobes, the isolates are grown in a liquid culture medium suitable for the growth of anaerobes, and the tests are carried out under anaerobic conditions. There is also a 20 test-API-20C system and a Uni-Yeast-Tek system with 11 test chambers that can be used in clinical laboratories for yeast identification. Several other systems are also available for the identification of nonfermentative, Gram-negative rods, such as the Automicrobic (AMS), Oxi-Ferm, and Oxitech systems. The Oxi-Ferm system is similar in design to the Enterotube, but eight different media are used in the tube for the identification of nonfermentative bacteria.

dividual tests are critical in achieving proper diagnostic identification, these identification systems assess the statistical likelihood of obtaining a particular pattern of test results.

Computerized identification systems often involve the development and use of *probabilistic identification matrices,* which are compilations of the frequencies of occurrence of individual features within separate taxonomic groups (FIG. 16-4). These probability matrices are developed by characterizing large numbers of strains belonging to each taxonomic group. In this way, the variability of the group for a particular feature can be determined. Many commercial identification systems used in clinical laboratories for diagnosing infectious disease agents are based on such probabilistic identification matrices. These systems permit fast and accurate identification of bacteria, which is essential for rapid diagnosis of infectious diseases. In many of these systems, the test results of an isolated organism are rapidly compared with a previously developed probability matrix (FIG. 16-5). Such multiple comparisons require the use of a computer, which generally also computes the statistical probability that the identification is correct.

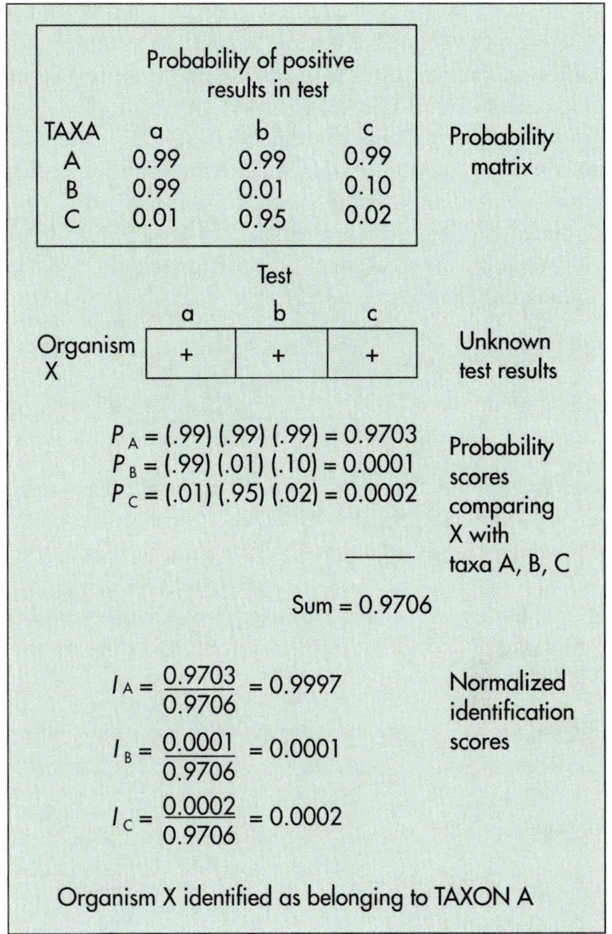

FIG. 16-4 The probabilistic matrix approach to organism identification allows organisms of unknown affiliation to be identified as members of established taxa.

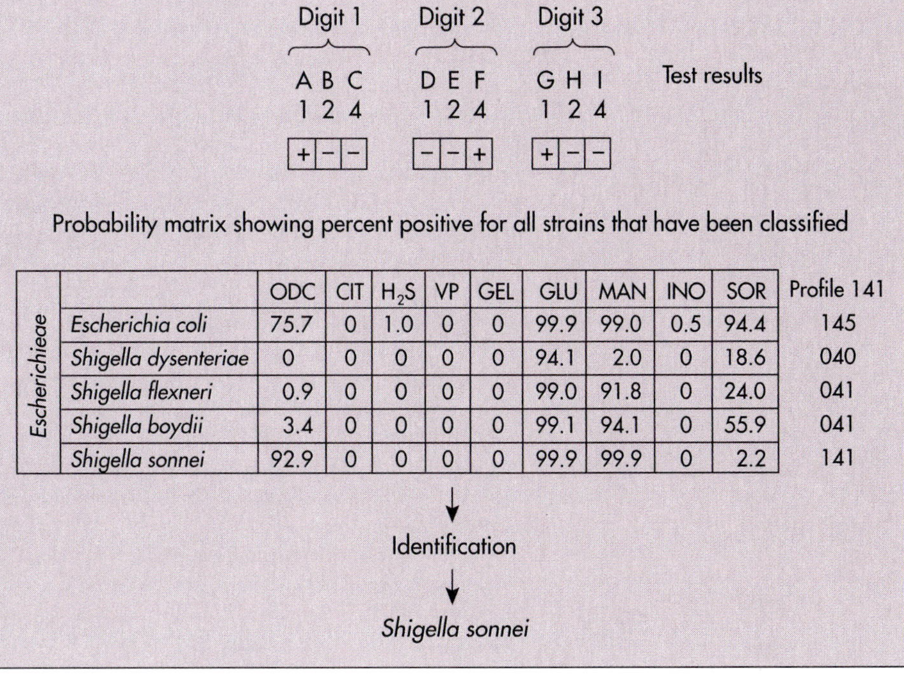

	ODC	CIT	H_2S	VP	GEL	GLU	MAN	INO	SOR	Profile 141
Escherichia coli	75.7	0	1.0	0	0	99.9	99.0	0.5	94.4	145
Shigella dysenteriae	0	0	0	0	0	94.1	2.0	0	18.6	040
Shigella flexneri	0.9	0	0	0	0	99.0	91.8	0	24.0	041
Shigella boydii	3.4	0	0	0	0	99.1	94.1	0	55.9	041
Shigella sonnei	92.9	0	0	0	0	99.9	99.9	0	2.2	141

FIG. 16-5 A numerical profile can be created to identify an unknown organism. This approach is employed in several widely used commercial systems for the identification of clinical isolates.

Because of the critical need to make correct identifications in medical microbiology, a positive identification in a clinical identification system generally requires that the unknown organism be far more similar to the group to which it is identified as belonging than to any other group. For example, in some identification systems, an unknown microorganism must be a thousand times more similar to one group than to all other groups in the system for a positive identification to be established.

Several of the commercial systems simplify the process of identification by calculating a numerical profile to describe unambiguously the pattern of test results (see FIG. 16-5). The numerical profile is simply a way of compressing the data so that they can easily be compared to the data collected on other organisms. The numerical profile of an unknown organism can be compared with the test pattern of a defined group to determine the probability that the test results represent a member of that taxon.

16.2 EUBACTERIA

Following the lead of *Bergey's Manual,* the major groups of eubacteria (true bacteria) and archaebacteria will be discussed without attempting to place them into a hierarchical classification system (Table 16-5). These groups of bacteria are defined primarily on the basis of physiological and morphological criteria that represents the phenotype seen in test observations. In the remainder of this chapter, we will consider the diversity of these organisms. For the most part, the order in which they are described follows the ninth edition of *Bergey's Manual of Determinative Bacteriology,* and includes a brief description of each group.

TABLE 16-5 Groups of Prokaryotic Microorganisms

GROUP	GENUS
Spirochetes	*Borrelia, Brachyspira, Cristispira, Leptonema, Leptospira, Serpulina, Spirochaeta, Treponema*
Gram-negative, aerobic/microaerophilic, motile, helical/vibrioid bacteria	*Alteromonas, Aquaspirillum, Azospirillum, Bdellovibrio, Campylobacter, Cellvibrio, Halovibrio, Helicobacter, Herbaspirillum, Marinomonas, Micavibrio, Oceanospirillum, Spirillum, Sporospirillum, Vampirovibrio, Wolinella*
Gram-negative curved bacteria, nonmotile (or rarely motile)	*Ancylobacter, Brachyarcus, Cyclobacterium, Flectobacillus, Meniscus, Pelosigma, Runella, Spirosoma*
Gram-negative aerobic/microaerophilic rods and cocci	*Acetobacter, Acidiphilium, Acidomonas, Acidothermus, Acidovorax, Acinetobacter, Afipia, Agrobacterium, Agromonas, Alcaligenes, Alteromonas, Aminobacter Azomonas, Azorhizobium Azotobacter, Beijerinckia, Bordetella, Bradyrhizobium, Brucella, Chromohalobacter, Chryscomonas, Comamonas, Cupriavidus, Deleya, Derxia, Ensifer, Erythrobacter, Flavimonas, Flavobacterium, Francisella, Frateuria, Halomonas, Hydrogenophaga, Janthinobacterium, Kingella, Lampropedia, Legionella, Marinobacter, Marinomonas, Mesophilobacter, Methylobacillus, Methylobacterium, Methylococcus, Methylomonas, Methylophaga, Methylophilus, Moraxella, Morococcus, Neisseria, Ochrobactrum, Oligella, Paracoccus, Phenylobacterium, Phyllobacterium, Pseudomonas, Psychrobacter, Rhizobacter, Rhizobium, Rhizomonas, Rochalimaea, Roseobacter, Rugamonas, Serpens, Sinorhizobium, Sphingobacterium, Taylorella, Thermoleophilum, Thermomicrobium, Thermus, Variovorax, Volcaniella, Weeksella, Wolinella, Xanthobacter, Xanthomonas, Xylella, Xylophilus, Zoogloea*
Gram-negative rods, facultatively anaerobic	*Actinobacillus, Aeromonas, Arsenophonus, Budvicia, Buttiauxella, Calymmatobacterium, Cardiobacterium, Cedecea, Chromobacterium, Citrobacter, Edwardsiella, Eikenella, Enhydrobacter, Enterobacter, Erwinia, Escherichia, Ewingella, Gardnerella, Haemophilus, Hafnia, Klebsiella, Kluyvera, Leclercia, Leminorella, Moellerella, Morganella, Obesumbacterium, Pantoea, Pasteurella, Photobacterium, Plesiamonas, Pragia, Proteus, Providencia, Rahnella, Salmonella, Serratia, Shigella, Streptobacillus, Tatumella, Vibrio, Xenorhabdus, Yersinia, Yokenella*
Gram-negative, anaerobic, straight, curved, and helical bacteria	*Acetivibrio, Acetoanaerobium, Acetofilamentum, Acetogenium, Acetomicrobium, Acetothermus, Acidaminobacter, Anaerobiospirillum, Anaerohabdus, Anaerovibrio, Bacteroides, Butyrivibrio, Centipeda, Fervidobacterium, Fibrobacter, Fusobacterium, Haloanaerobium, Halobacteroides, Ilyobacter, Lachnospira, Leptotrichia, Malonomonas, Megamonas, Oxalobacter, Pectinatus, Pelobacter, Porphyromonas, Prevotella, Propionigenium, Propionispira, Rikenella, Roseburia, Ruminobacter, Sebaldella, Selenomonas, Sporomusa, Succinomonas, Succinivibrtio, Syntrophobacter, Syntrophomonas, Thermobacteroides, Thermosipho, Thermotoga, Tissierella, Wolinella, Zymophilus*

TABLE 16-5 Groups of Prokaryotic Microorganisms—cont'd

GROUP	GENUS
Dissimilatory sulfate or sulfur-reducing bacteria	*Desulfobacter, Desulfobacterium, Desulfobulbus, Desulfococcus, Desulfomicrobium, Desulfomonas, Desulfomonile, Desulfonema, Desulfosarcina, Desulfotomaculum, Desulfovibrio, Desulfurella, Desulfuromonas, Thermodesulfobacterium*
Gram-negative anaerobic cocci	*Acidaminococcus, Megasphaera, Syntrophococcus, Veillonella*
Rickettsias and Chlamydias	*Aegyptianella, Anaplasma, Bartonella, Chlamydia, Cowdria, Coxiella, Ehrlichia, Grahamella, Neorickettsia, Rickettsia, Rickettsiella, Rochalimaea, Wolbachia*
Anoxygenic phototrophic bacteria	*Amoebobacter, Ancalochloris, Chlorobium, Chloroflexus, Chloroherpeton, Chloronema, Chromatium, Ectothiorhodospira, Erythrobacter, Heliobacillus, Heliobacterium, Heliothrix, Lamprobacter, Lamprocystis,, Oxcillochloris, Pelodictyon, Prosthecochloris, Rhodobacter, Rhodocyclus, Rhodomicrobium, Rhodopila, Rhodopseudomonas, Rhodospirillum, Thiocapsa, Thiocystis, Thiodictyon, Thiopedia, Thiospirillum*
Oxygenic phototrophic bacteria	*Anabaena, Aphanizomenon, Athrospira, Calothrix, Chamaesiphon, Chlorogloeopsis, Chroococcidiopsis, Crinalium, Cyanothece, Cylindrospermum, Dermocarpa, Dermocarpella, Fischerella, Geitleria, Gloeobacter, Gloeocapsa, Gloeothece, Lyngbya, Microcoleus, Microcystis, Myxobaktron, Myxosarcina, Nodularia, Nostoc, Oscillatoria, Pleurocapsa, Prochloron, Prochlorothrix, Pseudanabaena, Scytonema, Spirulina, Starria, Stigonema, Synechococcus, Synechocystis, Trichodesmium, Xenococcus*
Aerobic, chemolithotrophic bacteria and associated organisms	*Acidiphilium, Gallionella, Leptospirillum, Macromonas, Metallogenium, Naumanniella, Nitrobacter, Nitrococcus, Nitrosococcus, Nitrosolobus, Nitrosomonas, Nitrosospira, Nitrosovibrio, Nitrospina, Nitrospira, Ochrobium, Siderocapsa, Siderocapsaceae, Siderococcus, Sulfobacillus, Thermothrix, Thiobacillus, Thiobacterium, Thiodendron, Thiomicrospira, Thiosphaera, Thiospira, Thiovulum*
Budding and appendaged bacteria	*Ancalomicrobium, Angulomicrobium, Asticcacaulis, Blastobacter, Caulobacter, Dichotomicrobium, Ensifer, Filomicrobium, Gallionella, Gemmata, Gemmiger, Hirschia, Hyphomicrobium, Hyphomonas, Isosphaera, Labrys, Nevskia, Pedomicrobium, Pirellula, Planctomyces, Prosthecobacter, Prosthecomicrobium, Seliberia, Stella, Verrucomicrobium*
Sheathed bacteria	*Clonothrix, Crenothrix, Haliscomenobacter, Leptothrix, Lieskeella, Phragmidiothrix, Sphaerotilus*
Nonphotosynthetic, nonfruiting gliding bacteria	*Achromatium, Achroonema, Agitococcus, Alysiella, Beggiatoa, Capnocytophaga, Chitinophaga, Cytophaga, Desmanthos, Desulfonema, Flexibacter, Flexithrix, Herpetosiphon, Isosphaera, Leucothrix, Lysobacter, Microscilla, Pelonema, Peloploca, Saprospira, Simonsiella, Sporocytophaga, Thermonema, Thioploca, Thiospirillopsis, Thiothrix, Toxothrix, Vitreoscilla*
Fruiting, gliding bacteria: the myxobacteria	*Angiococcus, Archangium, Chondromyces, Corallococcus, Cystobacter, Haploangium, Melittangium, Myxococcus, Nannocystis, Polyangium, Sorangium, Stignatella*
Gram-positive cocci	*Aerococcus, Coprococcus, Deinobacter, Deinococcus, Enterococcus, Gemella, Lactococcus, Leuconostoc, Marinococcus, Melissococcus, Micrococcus, Pediococcus, Peptococcus, Peptostreptococcus, Planococcus, Ruminococcus, Saccharococcus, Salinococcus, Sarcina, Staphylococcus, Stomatococcus, Streptococcus, Trichococcus, Vagococcus*
Endospore-forming Gram-positive rods and cocci	*Amphibacillus, Bacillus, Clostridium, Desulfotomaculum, Oscillospira, Sporohalobacter, Sporolactobacillus, Sporosarcina, Sulfobacillus, Syntrophospora*
Regular nonsporing Gram-positive rods	*Brochothrix, Carnobacterium, Caryophanon, Erysipelothrix, Kurthia, Lactobacillus, Listeria, Renibacterium*
Irregular, nonsporing Gram-positive rods	*Acetobacterium, Acetogenium, Actinomyces, Aeromicrobium, Agromyces, Arachnia, Arcanobacterium, Arthrobacter, Aureobacterium, Bifidobacterium, Brachybacterium, Brevibacterium, Butyrivibrio, Caseobacter, Cellulomonas, Clavibacter, Coriobacterium, Corynebacterium, Curtobacterium, Dermabacter, Eubacterium, Exiguobacterium, Falcivibrio, Gardnerella, Jonesia, Lachnospira, Microbacterium, Mobiluncus, Pimelobacter, Propionibacterium, Rarobacter, Rothia, Rubrobacter, Sphaerobacter, Terrabacter, Thermoanaerobacter*
Mycobacteria	*Mycobacterium*
Nocardioform actinomycetes	*Actinobispora, Actinokineospora, Amycolata, Amycolatopsis, Gordona, Jonesia, Kibdelosporangium, Nocardia, Nocardioides, Oerskovia, Promicromonospora, Pseudoamycolata, Pseudonocardia, Rhodococcus, Saccharomonospora, Saccharopolyspora, Terrabacter, Tsukamurella*
Genera with multiocular sporangia	*Dermatophilus, Frankia, Geodermatophilus*
Actinoplanetes	*Actinoplanes, Ampullariella, Catellatospora, Dactylosporangium, Micromonospora, Pilimelia*
Streptomycetes and related genera	*Intrasporangium, Kineosporia, Sporichthya, Streptomyces, Streptoverticillum*

Continued.

TABLE 16-5 Groups of Prokaryotic Microorganisms—cont'd

GROUP	GENUS
Maduromycetes	*Actinomadura, Microbispora, Microtetraspora, Planobispora, Planomonospora, Spirillospora, Streptosporangium*
Thermomonospora and related genera	*Actinosynnema, Nocardiopsis, Streptoalloteichus, Thermomonospora*
Thermoactinomycetes	*Thermoactinomyces*
Other genera	*Glycomyces, Kitasatosporia, Saccharothrix*
Mycoplasmas (or mollicutes): cell wall-less bacteria	*Acholeplasma, Anaeroplasma, Asteroleplasma, Mycoplasma, Spiroplasma, Ureaplasma*
Methanogens	*Methanobacterium, Methanococcoides, Methanococcus, Methanocorpusculum, Methanoculleus, Methanogenium, Methanohalobium, Methanohalophilus, Methanolacinia, Methanolobus, Methanomicrobium, Methanoplanus, Methanosarcinia, Methanosphaera, Methanospirillum, Methanothermus, Methanothrix*
Archaeal sulfate reducers	*Archaeoglobus*
Extremely halophilic, aerobic archaeobacteria (Halobacteria)	*Haloarcula, Halobacterium, Halococcus, Haloferax, Natronobacterium, Natronococcus*
Cell wall-less archaebacteria	*Thermoplasma*
Extremely thermophilic and hyperthermophilic S^0-metabolizers	*Acidianus, Desulfurococcus, Desulfurolobus, Hyperthermus, Metallosphaera, Pyrobaculum, Pyrococcus, Pyrodictium, Staphylothermus, Sulfolobus, Thermococcus, Thermodiscus, Thermofilum, Thermoproteus*

SPIROCHETES

The spirochetes are helically coiled rod-shaped cells that are wound around one or more central axial fibrils (endoflagella) (FIG. 16-6). The cell length varies in different genera from 3 to 500 μm. In addition to their characteristic morphology, the spirochetes exhibit a unique mode of motility. These bacteria move by a flexing motion of the cell and exhibit their greatest velocities in very viscous solutions where motility by bacteria with external flagella is slowest. Five genera are recognized in the family Spirochaetaceae, and several more have been proposed (Table 16-6). Members of the genus *Spirochaeta* are nonpathogenic, occurring in aquatic environments, in mud containing

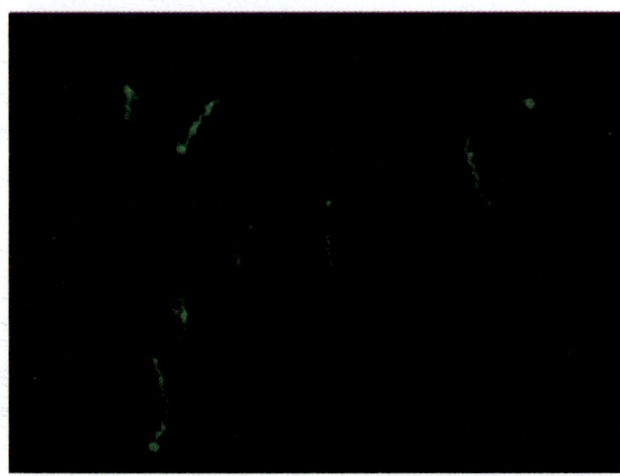

FIG. 16-6 Micrograph of the spirochete *Treponema pallidum (green)* after fluorescent antibody staining. This bacterium causes syphilis.

TABLE 16-6 Spirochetes

TAXON	DESCRIPTION
Order Spirochetales	
Family Spirochaetaceae	
Spirochaeta	5-500 μm long, 0.2-0.75 μm wide; free living; anaerobic or facultative
Cristispira	30-150 μm long, 0.5-3.0 μm wide with 3 to 10 complete turns; not free living
Treponema	5-15 μm long, 0.09-0.5 μm wide, not free living; anaerobic
Borrelia	3-15 μm long, 0.2-0.5 μm wide; not free living; anaerobic
Leptospira	6-20 μm long, 0.1 μm wide; aerobic

hydrogen sulfide, in sewage, and in polluted waters. Many spirochetes, though, are human pathogens. Several members of the genus *Treponema,* for example, are human pathogens, with *T. pallidum* causing syphilis and *T. pertenue* causing yaws. *Borrelia burgdorferi* causes Lyme disease. Likewise, some members of the genera *Cristispira* and *Leptospira* are animal and human pathogens.

Gram-Negative Aerobic or Microaerophilic Spiral and Curved Bacteria

Members of the heterogeneous group of aerobic or microaerophilic Gram-negative, spiral and curved bacteria are helically curved rods that may have less than one complete turn (vibroid or comma-shaped) or many turns (helical). Unlike the spirochetes, the cells are not wound around a central axial filament. The cells of members of this group are motile by means of polar flagella. Members of *Spirillum,* for example, have multiple polar flagella, usually at both ends (FIG. 16-7). The original genus *Spirillum* has been divided into several genera—*Aquaspirillum, Spirillum, Azospirillum,* and *Oceanospirillum*—based on genetic analyses that showed the mole % G + C for these genera to be 38, 70, 42-51, and 30-38, respectively.

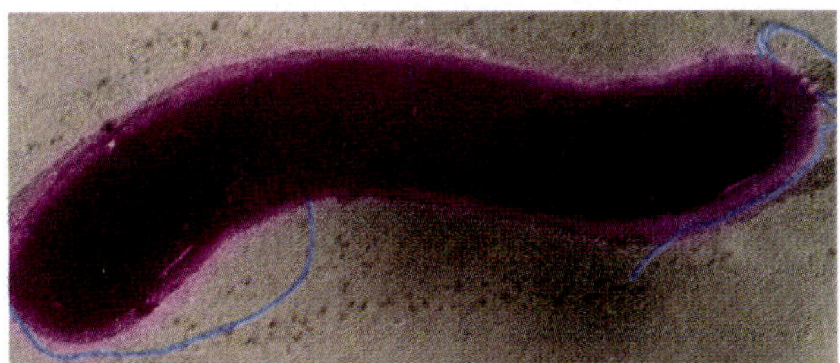

FIG. 16-7 Colorized micrograph of the spiral bacterium *Aquaspirillum bengal.*

Some members of *Campylobacter,* another genus affiliated with this group, are important pathogens of humans and other animals. *Bdellovibrio,* a genus of uncertain affiliation within this group, has the outstanding characteristic of being able to penetrate and reproduce within prokaryotic cells (FIG. 16-8). All naturally occurring strains of *Bdellovibrio* have been found to be bacterial parasites. *Bdellovibrio* do not lose their integrity when they reproduce within host cells. Within host cells, bacteria in the genus *Bdellovibrio* reproduce by binary fission. After reproduction of *Bdellovibrio* within a host cell, the host cell lyses, releasing the *Bdellovibrio* progeny.

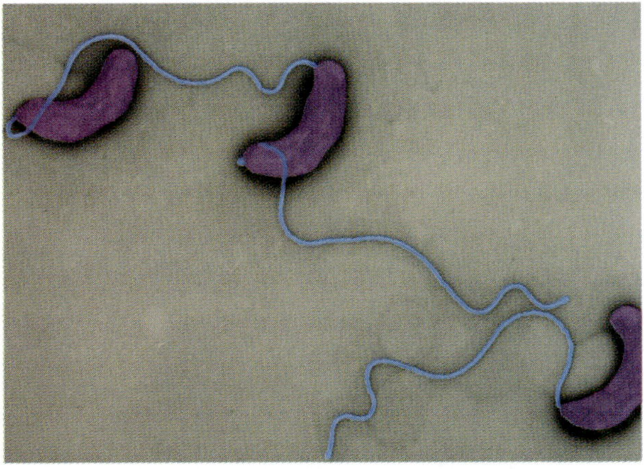

FIG. 16-8 Colorized micrograph of the comma-shaped bacterium *Bdellovibrio bacteriovorus.* (17,000×).

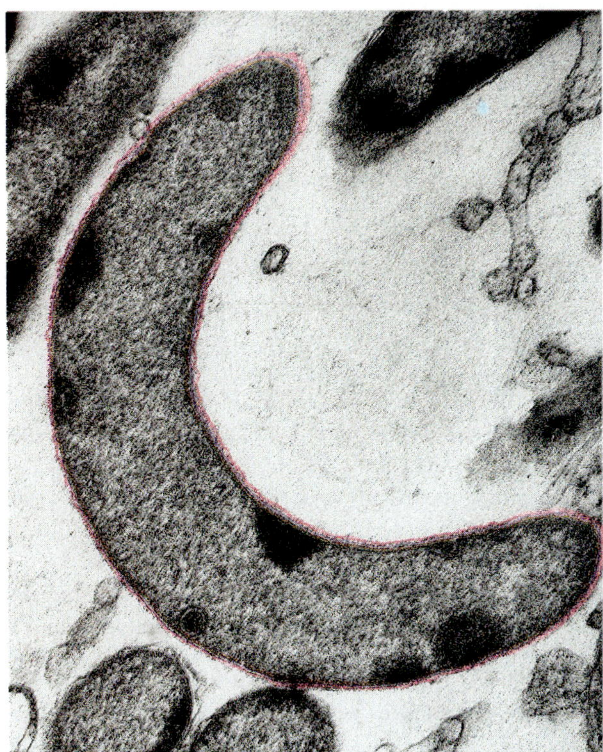

FIG. 16-9 Colorized micrograph of the ring-shaped bacterium *Microcyclus aquaticus.*

Another curved bacterium, *Microcyclus,* forms unique closed, ring-shaped cells (FIG. 16-9); these bacteria differ from the other spiral and curved bacteria in that they are nonmotile and are considered in the latest edition of *Bergey's Manual* to be part of a separate group that also includes *Spiromonas, Runella, Flectobacillus, Meniscus, Brachyarcus,* and *Pelosigma.*

GRAM-NEGATIVE AEROBIC RODS AND COCCI

The Gram-negative aerobic rods and cocci encompass a large number of taxonomic units. Several major families are included in this group: Pseudomonadaceae, Azotobacteraceae, Rhizobiaceae, Methylomonadaceae, Halobacteriaceae, Acetobacteriaceae, Legionellaceae, and Neisseriaceae (Table 16-7). Members of the family Pseudomonadaceae are Gram-negative, straight, or curved rods that are motile by means of polar flagella. Because their metabolism is respiratory, members of this family cannot carry out fermentative metabolism. Whereas the metabolism of the Pseudomonadaceae is obligately aerobic, some strains are able to carry out anaerobic respiration. For example, some pseudomonads use nitrate as a terminal electron acceptor in anaerobic respiration, forming molecular nitrogen in a process called *denitrification.* The Pseudomonadaceae are unable to fix atmospheric nitrogen.

Many *Pseudomonas* species are nutritionally versatile and are capable of degrading many natural and synthetic organic compounds. Some *Pseudomonas* species produce characteristic fluorescent pigments, but others do not. For example, *P. aeruginosa* produces yellow-green diffusible pigments that fluoresce when excited at a wavelength of less than 260 nm. *Pseudomonas* species are widely distributed in soil and aquatic ecosystems, occurring as free-living bacteria or in association with plants and animals, and some species are plant and animal pathogens. *P. aeruginosa,* for example, can be a human pathogen and is commonly isolated from wound, burn, and urinary tract infections. All recognized species of *Xanthomonas,* a genus included in the Pseudomonadaceae, are plant pathogens. *Xanthomonas* species are Gram-negative rods that are motile by means of polar flagella and in most cases produce yellow pigments.

Although nitrogen fixation does not occur in the Pseudomonadaceae, the family Azotobacteraceae is characterized by its capacity to fix molecular nitrogen. This family consists of Gram-negative rods exhibiting pleomorphic morphology. The genera *Azotobacter* and *Beijerinckia* are particularly important free-living, nitrogen-fixing bacteria. The practical importance of these bacteria is discussed in the section on environmental microbiology (Chapter 14). The Rhizobiaceae are also capable of fixing atmospheric nitrogen. *Rhizobium* and slower-growing *Bradyrhizobium* species can infect leguminous plant roots, causing the formation of tumorous growths called *nodules.* Free-living cells of these bacteria are rod-shaped, but within the nodules they occur as pleomorphic (irregularly shaped) cells termed *bacteroids. Rhizobium* can fix atmospheric nitrogen only within root nodules and thus is considered an obligately symbiotic nitrogen fixer, whereas some strains of *Bradyrhizobium* can fix nitrogen nonsymbiotically under defined laboratory conditions. Unlike *Rhizobium* and *Bradyrhizobium, Agrobacterium* species do not fix molecular nitrogen. *Agrobacterium* species, however, produce tumorous growths on infected plants known as galls. *Agrobacterium tumefaciens* causes galls of many different plants and is an extremely important plant pathogen causing large economic losses in agriculture.

The family Methylomonadaceae are bacteria that can utilize carbon monoxide, methane, or methanol as their sole source of carbon. The ability to use 1-carbon-containing (C1) organic compounds as the sole source of carbon and energy requires a special metabolic capability. Some of these bacteria are restricted to growth on C1 compounds. The metabolism of these organisms is respiratory, using molecular oxygen as the terminal electron acceptor. Members of this group are of interest to industry as a potential source of protein for animal feed or as a human dietary supplement. The C1 compounds, such as methane and methanol, are considered prime candidates as substrates for industrial processes aimed at growing microorganisms as a source of protein.

The Legionellaceae includes only one genus, *Legionella.* Species of *Legionella* have unique physiologi-

TABLE 16-7 Gram-negative Aerobic Rods and Cocci

TAXONOMIC GROUP	FLAGELLA	CARBON SOURCE	N_2 FIXATION	SALT REQUIREMENT
Pseudomonadaceae	Polar	Numerous	No	3% NaCl for marine species
Azotobacteraceae	Peritrichous or polar	Numerous	Yes	None
Rhizobiaceae	Peritrichous or polar	Numerous	Yes	None
Methylococcaceae	Polar or none	1-carbon compounds only; methane oxidized	Yes (some)	None
Acetobacteraceae	Peritrichous or polar	Various; ethanol oxidized to acetic acid	No	None
Legionellaceae	Polar and lateral	Various; requires growth factors	No	None
Neisseriaceae	None	Various	No	None

cal properties; they are Gram-negative, nonfermentative rods that exhibit a requirement for iron and cysteine as growth factors, and form predominantly branched chain fatty acids. *Legionella pneumophila,* which causes Legionnaire's disease, frequently is associated with breathing aerosols formed from rapidly evaporating water bodies, including air-conditioning cooling towers.

Only one family of Gram-negative cocci and coccobacilli, Neisseriaceae, is recognized (FIG. 16-10). The family Neisseriaceae includes the genera *Neisseria, Branhamella, Moraxella,* and *Acinetobacter.* The cells of *Neisseria* and *Branhamella* are cocci; the cells of *Moraxella* and *Acinetobacter* are coccobacilli (oval-shaped) (Table 16-8). Members of the genera *Neisseria, Branhamella,* and *Moraxella* are parasitic, and some are important human pathogens. *Acinetobacter* species are saprophytic, although some are opportunistic pathogens. Members of the genus *Acinetobacter* are nutritionally versatile and can utilize various organic compounds as their sole source of carbon and energy. Several species of the genus *Neisseria* are important human pathogens. For example, *N. gonorrhoeae* causes gonorrhea and *N. meningitidis* causes meningitis.

Several genera of uncertain affiliation are Gram-negative, aerobic rods. These include *Brucella, Bordetella,* and *Francisella.* Some members of these three genera are important human pathogens; *Bordetella pertussis* is the causative agent of whooping cough and *Francisella tularensis* is the causative agent of tularemia. Other genera of uncertain affiliation in this group are *Alcaligenes, Acetobacter,* and *Thermus. Thermus* is an ecologically interesting genus that grows well at temperatures over 70° C. Strains of this organism have been isolated from hot springs and the hot water tanks of laundromats.

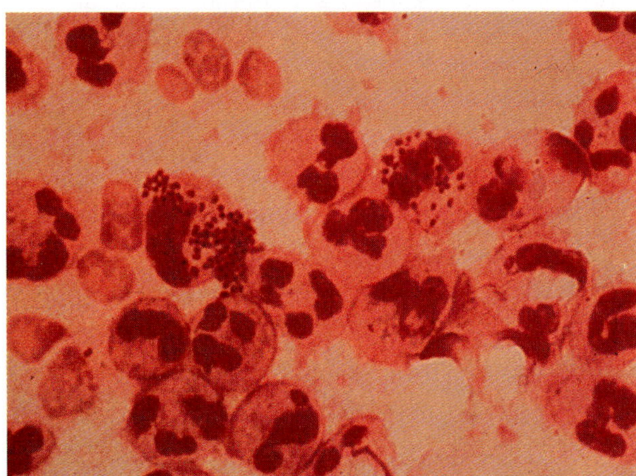

FIG. 16-10 Micrograph of intracellular, Gram-negative diplococci. The presence of these bacteria in a urethral discharge is diagnostic for gonorrhea and in a vaginal discharge is presumptive for gonorrhea.

TABLE 16-8 Descriptions of Some Genera of Gram-negative Cocci and Coccobacilli

GENUS	DESCRIPTION
Neisseria	Cocci; divide in two planes; sensitive to penicillin; oxidase positive; mole % G + C 47-52
Branhamella	Cocci; divide in two planes; oxidase positive; reduce nitrates; mole % G + C 40-45
Moraxella	Coccobacilli; divide in one plane; oxidase positive; sensitive to penicillin; mole % G + C 40-46
Acinetobacter	Coccobacilli; divide in one plane; oxidase negative; penicillin resistant; mole % G + C 39-47
Paracoccus	Cocci; divide in one plane; aerobic; mole % G + C 64-67
Lampropedia	Cells rounded or cubical; aerobic; divide in two planes; mole % G + C 61

GRAM-NEGATIVE FACULTATIVELY ANAEROBIC RODS

There are two major families of Gram-negative, facultatively anaerobic rods: the Enterobacteriaceae, which, if motile, are motile by means of peritrichous flagella, and the Vibrionaceae, which, if motile, are motile by means of polar flagella. The family Enterobacteriaceae includes the genera *Escherichia, Edwardsiella, Citrobacter, Salmonella, Shigella, Klebsiella, Enterobacter, Hafnia, Serratia, Proteus, Yersinia,* and *Erwinia* (FIG. 16-11). Members of the genus *Escherichia* occur in the human intestinal tract. Many of the bacteria, such as *E. coli,* studied in introductory microbiology laboratory courses, are such enteric bacteria.

E. coli has achieved a special place in microbiology. It is used as the test organism in many metabolic and genetic studies, and much of what we know about bacterial metabolism and genetics was elucidated in studies using *E. coli.* In addition, *E. coli* is employed as an indicator of fecal contamination in environmental microbiology.

The genera *Salmonella* and *Shigella* contain numerous species, many of which are important human pathogens. In particular, typhoid fever and various gastrointestinal upsets are caused by *Salmonella* species, and bacterial dysentery is caused by *Shigella. Serratia marcescens,* once thought to be a nonpathogen, is now recognized as causing insect diseases and as an opportunistic human pathogen. *Serratia* strains can produce a red pigment known as *prodigiosin.* All members of the genus *Erwinia* are plant pathogens. *Erwinia amylovora,* for example, causes fire blight of pears and apples.

The family Vibrionaceae includes the genera *Vibrio, Aeromonas, Plesiomonas,* and *Photobacterium.* Many of

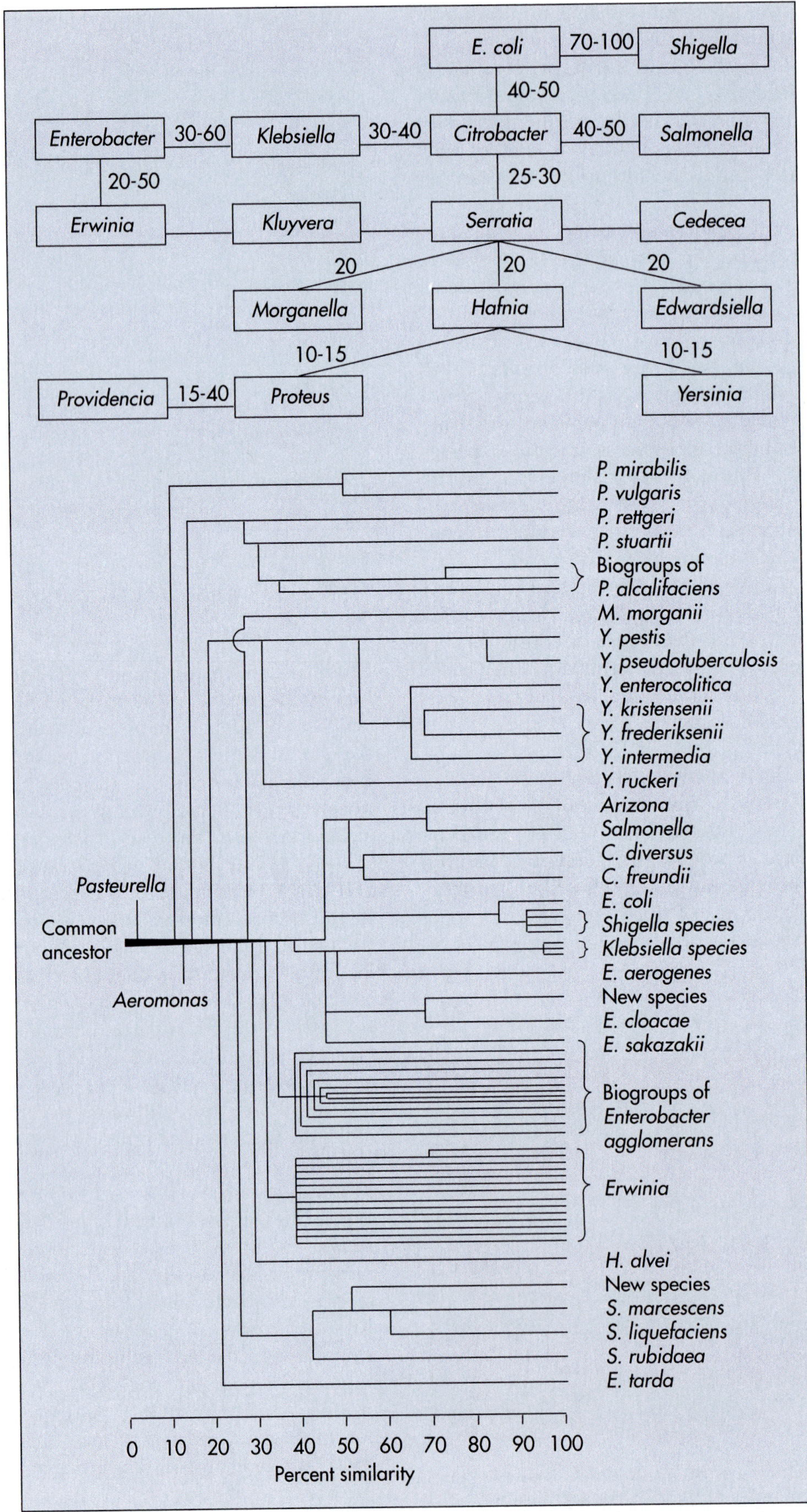

FIG. 16-11 Genetic relationships among the genera of Enterobacteriaceae. The numbers represent the approximate percentage of relatedness based on DNA hybridization analyses.

the *Vibrio* have curved, rod-shaped cells. The habitat of *Vibrio* species is generally aquatic. *V. cholerae* is an important human pathogen that causes cholera. *Photobacterium* species are interesting because of their ability to luminesce. Bioluminescence, discussed in Chapter 14, involves an ATP-driven reaction, an electron transport system, and the enzyme luciferase. Some species of luminescent bacteria occur in association with fish; some of these fish are known as *flashlight fish* because of the light emitted by these bacteria. The association of luminescent bacteria with these fish is important in various behavioral aspects of these fish, including mating activities.

Several genera of uncertain affiliation are Gram-negative, facultatively anaerobic rods. These include the genus *Chromobacterium,* which produces violet pigments. *Flavobacterium,* which produces various insoluble yellow, orange, red, or brown pigments, has been associated with this group, but, based on its mole % G + C, *Flavobacterium* clearly represents more than one group; in group I it is = 30-42 and in group II it is = 63-70. Also included in this group are the genera *Zymomonas, Cardiobacterium, Streptobacillus,* and *Calymmatobacterium.* Various species in these genera are important human pathogens.

TABLE 16-9 Gram-negative Anaerobic Bacteria

TAXON	DESCRIPTION
FAMILY BACTERIODACEAE	
Bacteroides	Produce mixtures of acids, including succinic, acetic, formic, lactic, and propionic
Fusobacterium	Produce butyric acid as the major product
Leptotrichia	Produce lactic acid as the only major fermentation acid
GENERA OF UNCERTAIN AFFILIATION	
Butyrovibrio	Curved rods, fermentative, produce butyrate
Succinovibrio	Curved rods, fermentative, produce succinate and acetate
Succinomonas	Straight rods, fermentative, produce large amounts of succinate and some acetate
Lachnospira	Curved rods, fermentative, produce mixture of acids
Selenomonas	Curved rods; fermentative; produce acetate, propionate, and lactate

GRAM-NEGATIVE ANAEROBIC RODS

There is only one family, Bacteroidaceae, and relatively few genera in the Gram-negative, anaerobic bacteria group (Table 16-9). The genera include *Bacteroides, Fusobacterium,* and *Leptotrichia. Bacteroides* are important members of the normal microbiota of humans and may be the dominant microorganisms in the intestinal tract. *Bacteroides* species characteristically form pleomorphic rods (FIG. 16-12). Some members of the family Bacteroidaceae are human pathogens. Various *Bacteroides* and *Fusobacterium* species cause human infections.

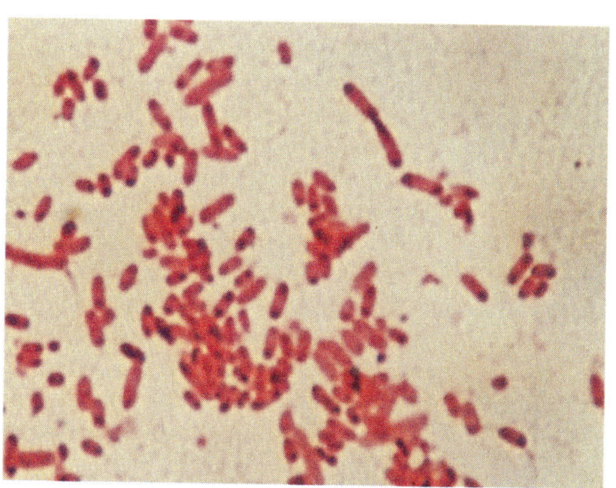

FIG. 16-12 Micrograph of *Bacteroides fragilis.*

Other genera affiliated with the Gram-negative, anaerobic rods include *Butyrovibrio, Lachnospira, Succinovibrio, Succinimonas,* and *Selenomonas.* Species of these genera occur in the rumen (a compartment of the stomach of cows and related animals), where they play critical roles in the digestion of cellulosic materials and the nutrition of the animal, producing low molecular weight fermentation substrates.

BOX 16-3

IDENTIFICATION OF ANAEROBES

A novel approach to the identification of obligate anaerobes used in clinical laboratories involves the gas liquid chromatographic (GLC) detection of metabolic products. The anaerobes are grown in a suitable medium, and the short chain, volatile fatty acids produced are extracted in ether. Fatty acids detected in this procedure include acetic, propionic, isobutyric, butyric, isovaleric, valeric, isocaproic, and caproic acids (see FIG. 13-11). The pattern of fatty acid production can be used to differentiate and identify various anaerobes. When coupled with observations of colony and cell morphology and a limited number of biochemical tests, the common anaerobes isolated from clinical specimens can be identified.

TABLE 16-10 Sulfate- and Sulfur-reducing Bacteria

GENUS	DESCRIPTION
Desulfovibrio	Curved rods; motile; anaerobic respiration using sulfate or other sulfur compounds as terminal electron acceptors and producing hydrogen sulfide; mole % G + C 46.1-61.2
Desulfuromonas	Acetate completely oxidized to CO_2 using elemental sulfur as the electron acceptor; sulfate never reduced; dissimilatory reduction of sulfur; straight or slightly curved rods; motile; mole % G + C 50-63
Desulfomonas	Straight rods; nonmotile; reduce sulfate to hydrogen sulfide; incomplete oxidation of pyruvate to acetate and CO_2; mole % G+ C 66-67
Desulfococcus	Spherical cells; nonmotile; completely oxidize fatty acids or benzoate; sulfate and other oxidized sulfur compounds serve as terminal electron acceptors and are reduced to hydrogen sulfide; ferment lactate or pyruvate to acetate and propionate; mole % G + C 57.4
Desulfobacter	Ellipsoidal to rod-shaped cells with rounded ends; nonmotile or motile by polar flagellum; oxidize acetate to CO_2; sulfate or other oxidized sulfur compounds serve as terminal electron acceptors and are reduced to hydrogen sulfide; mole % G + C 45.9
Desulfobulbus	Ellipsoidal cells with pointed ends; motile by polar flagellum; incompletely oxidize propionate or lactate to acetate and CO_2; in absence of an external electron acceptor, ferment pyruvate or lactate to propionate and acetate; sulfate or other oxidized sulfur compounds serve as terminal electron acceptors and are reduced to hydrogen sulfide; mole % G + C 59.9
Desulfosarcina	Irregularly shaped cells that tend to be coccoid after extended growth; usually nonmotile; benzoate can serve as electron donor for anaerobic respiration; chemoautotrophic growth using molecular hydrogen as electron donor and CO_2 as carbon source; sulfate or other oxidized sulfur compounds serve as terminal electron acceptors and are reduced to hydrogen sulfide; ferment pyruvate or lactate to propionate and acetate; mole % G + C 51.2
Desulfotomaculum	Anaerobic endospore former; sulfate or other oxidized sulfur compounds serve as terminal electron acceptors and are reduced to hydrogen sulfide
Desulfonema	Rod shaped; gliding motility; sulfate or other oxidized sulfur compounds serve as terminal electron acceptors and are reduced to hydrogen sulfide

DISSIMILATORY SULFATE- OR SULFUR-REDUCING BACTERIA

Several genera of bacteria are characterized by their ability to reduce sulfate, other oxidized sulfur-containing compounds, or elemental sulfur (Table 16-10). Members of the genus *Desulfovibrio* are curved, Gram-negative rods capable of reducing sulfates, or other reducible sulfur compounds, to hydrogen sulfide. Sulfate-reducing bacteria, including *D. desulfuricans,* are normally found in anaerobic soils and sediments (such as those found in bogs and marshes) where they are important in the biogeochemical cycling of sulfur.

GRAM-NEGATIVE ANAEROBIC COCCI

The Gram-negative, anaerobic cocci include the genera *Veillonella, Acidaminococcus, Megasphaera,* and *Gemmiger.* Each of these genera contains very few species. The cells of species in all of these genera typically occur as diplococci (pairs of cocci). *Veillonella* species have complex nutritional requirements and are unable to grow on individual organic substrates. They also require carbon dioxide for growth. Although these organisms are fastidious in their nutritional requirements, they comprise part of the normal human microbiota, representing, for example, 5% to 16% of the bacteria in the oral cavity. Some *Veillonella* species are human pathogens, causing infections in the oral cavity and the intestinal and respiratory tracts.

RICKETTSIAS AND CHLAMYDIAS

The rickettsias are intracellular parasites. The majority of members of the Rickettsiales are Gram negative and multiply only within host cells. They are small for bacteria but larger than viruses. Within host cells the rickettsias reproduce by binary fission. They lack the enzymatic capability to produce sufficient amounts of ATP to support their reproduction; they are able to obtain the ATP from the host cells in which they grow.

Many species of Rickettsiales cause disease in humans and other animals. Some members of the family Rickettsiaceae are adapted to existence in arthropods but can infect vertebrate hosts, including humans. For example, many members of the genus *Rickettsia* are carried by insect vectors and cause diseases in humans; *R. rickettsii* is transmitted by ticks and causes Rocky Mountain spotted fever.

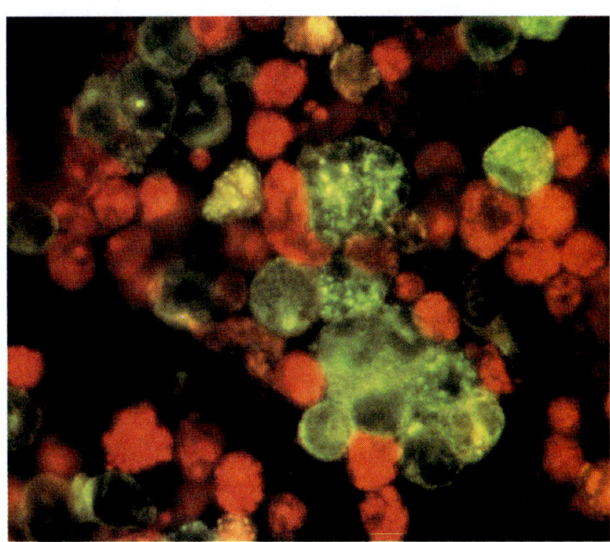

FIG. 16-13 Micrograph showing fluorescent-antibody–stained inclusions of *Chlamydia trachomatis (light yellow)* within McCoy cells.

The chlamydias are obligate intracellular parasites whose reproduction is characterized by the change of the small, rigid-walled infectious form of the organism *(elementary body)* into a larger, thin-walled, noninfectious form *(initial body)* that divides by fission (FIG. 16-13). Members of the order Chlamydiaceae are metabolically limited. These organisms are unable to generate sufficient ATP to support their reproduction. The chlamydias have sometimes been referred to as *large viruses* but they are truly bacteria. Members of the genus *Chlamydia* are Gram negative. The reproductive cycle for these organisms takes about 40 hours. *Chlamydia* cause human respiratory and genitourinary tract diseases, and in birds they cause respiratory diseases and generalized infections. For example, the disease psittacosis (parrot fever) is caused by *C. psittaci.*

PHOTOTROPHIC BACTERIA

The phototrophic bacteria (Table 16-11) are distinguished from other bacterial groups by their ability to use light energy to drive the synthesis of ATP. Most of the organisms included in this group are autotrophs capable of using carbon dioxide as the source of cellular carbon. Some of the phototrophic bacteria use water as an electron donor and liberate oxygen. These bacteria can be considered as belonging to the Oxyphotobacteria. The remainder of the photobacteria do not produce oxygen and, with one exception, can be classified as belonging to the Anoxyphotobacteria. The exception, *Halobacterium,* belongs to the Archaebacteria and has a unique mode of phototrophic metabolism. *Halobacterium* will be considered with the Archaebacteria later in this chapter.

Anoxygenic Phototrophic Bacteria

The *anoxygenic phototrophic bacteria* (Anoxyphotobacteria) are photosynthetic but do not produce oxygen. They require an electron donor other than water and carry out only one form of oxidative photophosphorylation. Physiologically, these bacteria carry out photosynthesis anaerobically. The anaerobic photosynthetic bacteria typically occur in aquatic habitats, often growing at the sediment–water interface of shallow lakes where there is sufficient light penetration to permit photosynthetic activity, anaerobic conditions are sufficient to permit the existence of these organisms, and there is a source of reduced sulfur or organic compounds to act as electron donors for the generation of reduced coenzymes.

TABLE 16-11 Characteristics of the Major Groups of Phototrophic Bacteria

METABOLISM	TAXONOMIC GROUP	PHOTOSYNTHETIC PIGMENTS	ELECTRON DONORS	CARBON SOURCE
Anoxygenic photosynthesis	Purple bacteria	Bacteriochlorophyll *a* or *b*, carotenoids	H_2, H_2S, S	Organic C or CO_2
Anoxygenic photosynthesis	Green bacteria	Bacteriochlorophyll *a* or *b*, carotenoids	H_2,H_2S, S	CO_2
Oxygenic photosynthesis*	Cyanobacteria	Chlorophyll *a*, phycobiliproteins	H_2O	CO_2
Oxygenic photosynthesis	Prochlorobacteria	Chlorophyll $a + b$, β-carotenes	H_2O	CO_2
Purple membrane mediated	Halobacterium†	Bacteriorhodospin	—	Organic C

*Under some conditions, photosynthesis is anoxygenic, and H_2S serves as the electron donor.
†A nonautotrophic archaebacterium.

TABLE 16-12 Phototrophic Bacteria

TAXON	DESCRIPTION
Order Rhodospiralles	Cells capable of photosynthetic anaerobic metabolism
Suborder Rhodospirillineae (purple bacteria)	Cells contain bacteriochlorophyll *a* or *b*
Family Rhodospirillaceae (purple nonsulfur bacteria)	Cells photoassimilate simple organic substrates; most species unable to grow with sulfide as the sole electron donor
Genera: *Rhodospirillum, Rhodobacter, Rhodomicrobium*	
Family Chromatiaceae (purple sulfur bacteria)	Cells able to grow with sulfide and sulfur as the sole electron donor; sulfur deposited inside or outside of cell
Genera: *Chromatium, Thiocystis, Thiosarcina, Thiospirillum, Thiocapsa, Lamprocystis, Thiodictyon, Thiopedia, Amoebobacter, Ectothiorhodospira*	
Suborder Chlorobiineae (green bacteria)	Cells contain bacteriochlorophyll *a, b,* or *c*
Family Chlorobiaceae (green sulfur bacteria)	Cells able to grow with sulfide and sulfur as the sole electron donor; sulfur deposited only outside of cell
Genera: *Chlorobium, Prosthecochloris, Chloropseudomonas, Pelodictyon, Clathrochloris*	
Family Chloroflexaceae (green flexibacteria)	Cells have flexible walls, gliding motility; form filaments and utilize organic C sources
Genera: *Chloroflexus, Chloronema, Oscillochloris*	

The pathways of anoxygenic photosynthesis are discussed in Chapters 4 and 5. The anoxygenic phototrophic bacteria include the Rhodospirillaceae (purple nonsulfur bacteria), Chromatiaceae (purple sulfur bacteria), Chlorobiaceae (green sulfur bacteria), and Cloroflexaceae (green flexibacteria) (Table 16-12). The green and purple sulfur bacteria utilize reduced sulfur compounds, such as hydrogen sulfide, as electron donors for generating reducing power. Most of the purple nonsulfur bacteria and green flexibacteria are unable to use reduced sulfur compounds; these organisms utilize organic compounds to support photosynthetic growth.

Members of the family Chromatiaceae produce carotenoid pigments and may appear orange-brown, red-brown, purple-red, or purple-violet. They deposit elemental sulfur as a consequence of their utilization of reduced sulfur compounds as electron donors for generating reducing power (FIG. 16-14). Because of their color and sulfur metabolism, the Chromatiaceae are called the *purple sulfur bacteria.* In all but one genus of organisms within this large family, the sulfur accumulates intracellularly. Members of the Chromatiaceae are potentially mixotrophic, that is, they are capable of photoautotrophic and heterotrophic growth, and all strains are capable of photoassimilating simple organic substrates such as acetate. The cells of *Chromatium, Thiocystis, Thiosarcina, Thiospirillum,* and *Thiocapsa* do not contain gas vacuoles, but some genera of the family Chromatiaceae, such as *Thiodictyon* and *Thiopedia,* do contain gas vacuoles that permit an adjustment of cell buoyancy in a water column to a

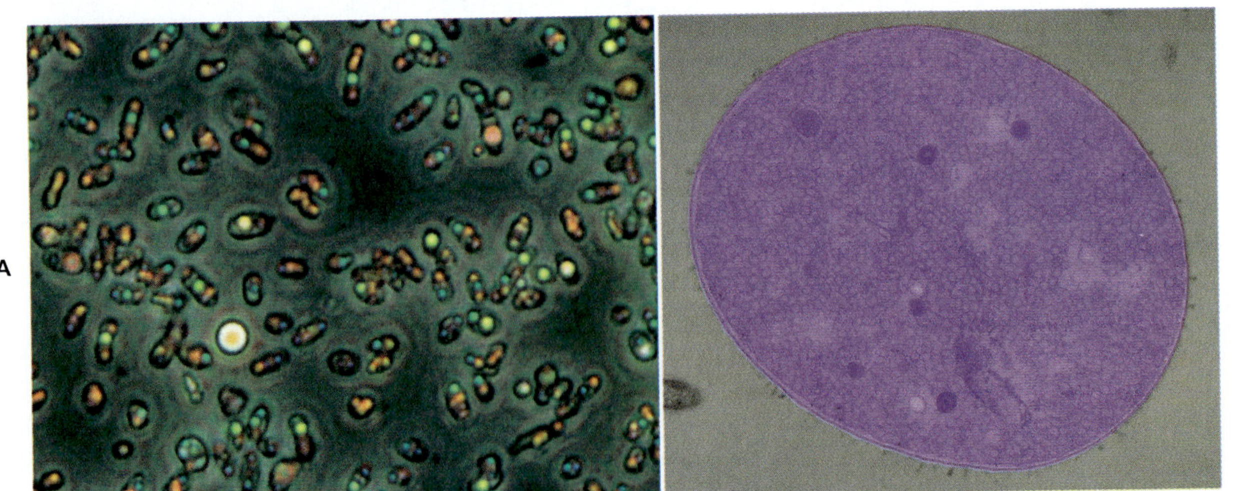

FIG. 16-14 **A,** Micrograph of *Chromatium* showing sulfur granules that refract light. **B,** Colorized micrograph of a thin-section of the purple sulfur bacterium *Chromatium* species. (31,000×). These bacteria contain intracytoplasmic membranes of the vesicular type.

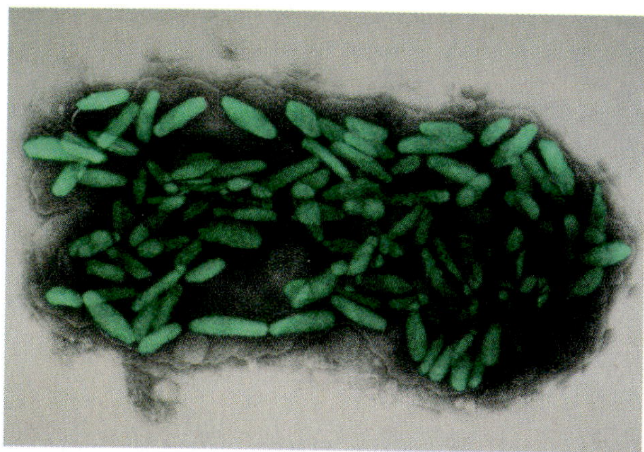

FIG. 16-15 Colorized micrograph of negatively-stained vesicles (identical to *Chlorobium* vesicles) isolated from the green sulfur phototrophic bacterium *Chloropseudomonas ethylica.*

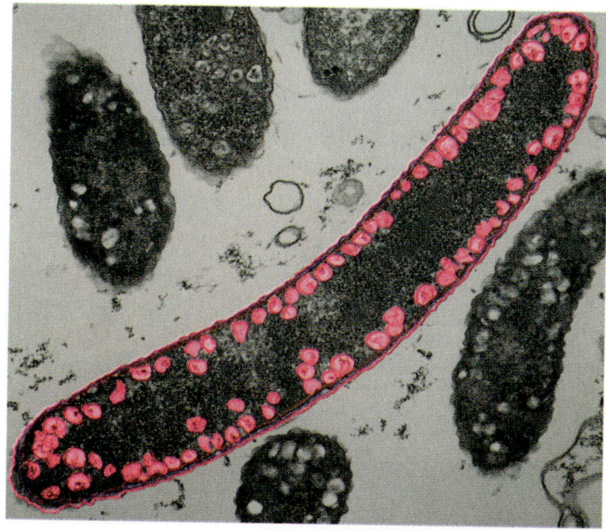

FIG. 16-16 Colorized micrograph of the photosynthetic bacterium *Rhodospirillum rubrum* grown anaerobically in the light. (28,400×). The cells contain numerous intracytoplasmic vesicles *(red).*

depth appropriate for light intensity and oxygen concentration, making anaerobic photosynthetic metabolism possible.

The Chlorobiaceae produce green or green-brown carotenoid pigments and are obligately phototrophic. They assimilate carbon dioxide, utilizing sulfide or elemental sulfur as electron donors, and they deposit sulfur granules extracellularly. Because of their color and sulfur metabolism, the Chlorobiaceae are called the *green sulfur bacteria.* Some genera of Chlorobiaceae, such as *Pelodictyon,* have gas vacuoles, but others, such as *Chlorobium* and *Chloropseudomonas,* do not (FIG. 16-15). All members of the Chlorobiaceae are nonmotile. These bacteria often occur in ecological situations similar to those of the Chromatiaceae.

The Rhodospirillaceae generally produce red-purple carotenoid pigments. Three genera are recognized: *Rhodospirillum* has spiral-shaped cells; *Rhodopseudomonas* has spherical or rod-shaped cells that do not form filaments; and *Rhodomicrobium* has oval cells that do form filaments and exhibit budding division (FIG. 16-16). Members of the genera *Rhodospirillum* and *Rhodopseudomonas* are motile by means of polar flagella, whereas those of the genus *Rhodomicrobium* are peritrichously flagellated. Their photosynthetic development depends on the ability of the cells to photoassimilate simple organic compounds. When sulfide or thiosulfate is utilized as an electron donor, elemental sulfur is not deposited within the cell. The organic substrates utilized by the Rhodospirillaceae may serve as electron donors for generating reducing power or may be photoassimilated. Because they generally require preformed organic matter for growth and are able to utilize light energy for generating ATP, the type of metabolism they carry out is sometimes referred to as *photoheterotrophic metabolism* and the organisms are called the *purple nonsulfur bacteria.*

The Rhodospirillaceae convert carbon dioxide to organic matter by means of the Calvin cycle pathway. Members of the Rhodospirillaceae can grow heterotrophically and aerobically in the dark. In the light under anaerobic conditions, typical members of the Rhodospirillaceae use molecular hydrogen or sulfide as an electron donor and can grow without organic compounds. As such, these organisms may be viewed as photoheterotrophs or as photoautotrophs, generally requiring organic growth factor compounds. Indeed, most strains in the Rhodospirillaceae require one or more vitamins. Clearly, the Rhodospirillaceae occupy a boundary position between autotrophs and heterotrophs. The basic metabolic pathways of the Rhodospirillaceae are the same as those of other autotrophic microorganisms. Their ability to assimilate organic compounds and the requirement of many members of the Rhodospirillaceae for such compounds establish the resemblance of these organisms to heterotrophs.

In terms of physiology and morphology, the Chloroflexaceae exhibit unique combinations of characteristic features of other phototrophic bacteria. These bacteria have flexible walls, form filaments, and exhibit gliding motility. Among phototrophic bacteria, gliding motility and formation of filaments were previously thought to be restricted to the cyanobacteria. Photosynthesis is anoxygenic, and some organic compounds are needed to achieve optimal growth. *Chloroflexus,* which resembles a green sulfur bacterium in cell ultrastructure and photosynthetic pigments but resembles a nonsulfur purple bacterium in its photosynthetic and catabolic metabolism, is the only genus in this family that has been characterized in pure culture, although other genera have been assigned to the Chloroflexaceae based on field observations. *C. aurantiacus* has been isolated from alkaline hot springs in various parts of the world.

Oxygenic Phototrophic Bacteria

The *oxygenic phototrophic bacteria* (Oxyphotobacteria) split water to form oxygen as part of their photosynthetic metabolism. Two orders are contained in this subclass of the Photobacteria: Cyanobacteriales and Prochlorales. Both of these orders occupy intermediary positions between the phototrophic bacteria and the eukaryotic algae, indicating a probable evolutionary link to these higher photosynthetic organisms. The primary photosynthetic pigment in both cases is chlorophyll a, but the prochlorophytes also possess chlorophyll b, making them very similar to the green algae. Presumably, the prochlorobacteria are more closely related to the green algae than are the cyanobacteria. Some cyanobacteria, on the other hand, are capable of anoxygenic photosynthesis, making them closely related to the Anoxyphotobacteria. Clearly, there is a phylogenetic relationship among the photosynthetic organisms, with the Oxyphotobacteria occupying an intermediate position between the Anoxyphotobacteria and the algae. Chloroplasts of plants and some algae are phylogenetically related to cyanobacteria and arose by endosymbiosis. Phycobilisomes are associated with red algae.

The *cyanobacteria*, or blue-green bacteria, are the most diverse and widely distributed group of photosynthetic bacteria. Over 1,000 species of cyanobacteria have been reported, based largely on field observations. Field observations, however, leave many uncertainties about the variability of particular features and ambiguities concerning the separation of taxa. Examination of pure cultures indicates that by eliminating ambiguous features, the 170 genera described on the basis of field observations can be reduced to 22 genera. Among the cyanobacteria some genera characteristically are unicellular, whereas others are filamentous (FIG. 16-17). The cell wall structures of cyanobacteria are of the Gram-negative type. The cytoplasm of cyanobacteria is filled with photosynthetic membranes (thylakoids) containing the primary photosynthetic pigment—chlorophyll *a*. The outer surfaces of the photosynthetic membranes have associated granules known as *phycobilisomes*, which are composed of auxiliary photosynthetic pigments.

There are four major subgroups of cyanobacteria (Table 16-13). The chroococcacean cyanobacteria are unicellular rods or cocci. They reproduce by binary fission (family Chroococcaceae) or by budding (family Chamesiphonaceae). Chroococcacean cyanobacteria are generally nonmotile. *Synechococcus, Synechocystis*, and *Chamaesiphon* are representative genera. One interesting genus in this group, *Gloeobacter*, lacks thylakoids and is purple in color. *Gloeobacter* can easily be confused with the anaerobic phototrophs, but in pure culture studies its biochemistry and metabolism are typical of those of cyanobacteria.

FIG. 16-17 Micrograph of the cyanobacterium *Aphanizomenon flos-aquae* with gas vacuoles.

The pleurocapsalean cyanobacteria are distinguished from the chroococcacean cyanobacteria by the fact that they exhibit multiple fission to produce small coccoid reproductive cells. In the phycological literature these reproductive cells are referred to as *endospores*, but to avoid confusion with endospore-forming bacteria, it has been proposed that the term *baeocyte* be used to describe the reproductive cells of the pleurocapsalean cyanobacteria. These pleurocapsalean cyanobacteria are unicellular, but the cells generally fail to separate completely following binary fission. Because binary fission does not result in complete separation of the cells, the pleurocapsalean cyanobacteria form multicellular aggregates.

TABLE 16-13 Subgroups of the Cyanobacteria

GROUP	DESCRIPTION
Chroococcacean	Unicellular rods or cocci reproducing by binary fission or budding
Pleurocapsalean	Single cells enclosed in a fibrous layer; reproduce by multiple fission, producing baeocytes
Oscillatorian	Cells form trichomes but not heterocysts
Heterocystous	Form trichomes with vegetative cells and heterocysts

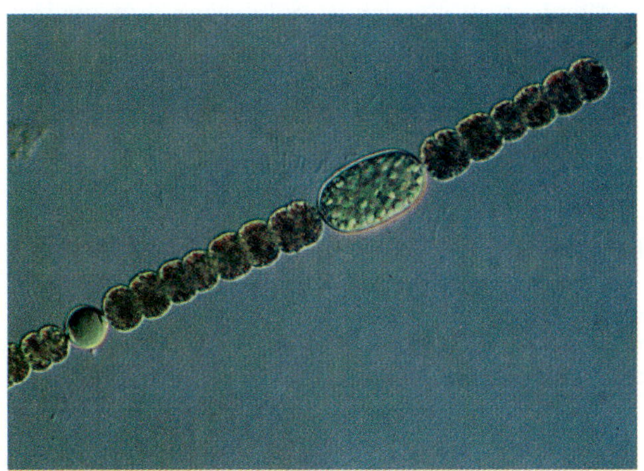

FIG. 16-18 Micrograph of the cyanobacterium *Anabaena cylindrica* showing vegetative cells and a heterocyst (enlarged cell) in which nitrogen fixation occurs.

The oscillatorian cyanobacteria form filamentous structures, composed exclusively of vegetative cells, known as *trichomes.* In some cases, the trichomes are straight, and in others they are helical. *Spirulina, Oscillatoria,* and *Pseudanabaena* are representative genera of oscillatorian cyanobacteria.

Like the oscillatorian cyanobacteria, the heterocystous cyanobacteria are filamentous. Unlike the oscillatorian cyanobacteria, however, the heterocystous cyanobacteria form differentiated cells known as heterocysts when growing in the absence of fixed forms of nitrogen. *Heterocysts* are nonreproductive cells that are distinguished from the adjoining vegetative cells by the presence of refractory polar granules and a thick outer wall (FIG. 16-18). The ability to form heterocysts is associated with the physiological capability of fixing atmospheric nitrogen. The physiologically specialized heterocyst cells appear to be the anatomical site of nitrogen fixation in heterocystous cyanobacteria. *Nostoc* and *Anabaena* are probably the best-known genera among the heterocystous cyanobacteria. The ability to carry out oxygen-yielding photosynthesis and nitrogen fixation is a unique characteristic of cyanobacteria principally found among the heterocystous cyanobacteria. The heterocystous cyanobacteria are ecologically important because they can form organic carbon and fixed forms of nitrogen that can support the nutritional requirements of other organisms. Some cyanobacteria are thermophilic. As such, they sometimes are the first colonizers of cooled lava flows, paving the way for additional biological succession.

The prochlorales are similar to the cyanobacteria except that they also synthesize chlorophyll *b.* Although they originally were considered to be cyanobacteria, their unique ability as prokaryotes to produce chlorophyll *b* is now considered significant enough to separate them into their own order. The only known genus, *Prochloron,* occurs as single-celled, extracellular symbionts of marine invertebrates. These bacteria appear bright green on the surfaces of the animals with which they are associated. Various species of *Prochloron* have been recognized in field studies, but until the organisms are grown in pure culture, the validity of these species remains ambiguous.

CHEMOLITHOTROPHIC BACTERIA

The metabolic activities of the *chemolithotrophic bacteria* are extremely important in biogeochemical cycling reactions (Table 16-14). These bacteria oxidize inorganic compounds to generate ATP. Because their ATP-generating metabolism is inefficient, they must metabolize large amounts of substrate to meet their energy requirements. The metabolic transformations of inorganic compounds mediated by these organisms cause global-scale cycling of various elements, moving substances between the air, water, and soil.

The family Nitrobacteraceae oxidizes ammonia or nitrite to generate ATP. Organisms in this family, commonly referred to as *nitrifying bacteria,* are commonly found in soil, fresh water, and seawater. Many of the nitrifying bacteria have extensive internal membrane

TABLE 16-14 Chemolithotrophic Bacteria

FAMILY NITROBACTERACEAE	Oxidize ammonia or nitrite
Nitrobacter	Oxidize nitrite to nitrate
Nitrospina	
Nitrococcus	
Nitrosomonas	Oxidize ammonia to nitrite
Nitrospira	
Nitrosococcus	
Nitrosolobus	
CHEMOLITHOTROPHIC SULFUR OXIDIZERS	Oxidize sulfur and sulfur compounds
Thiobacillus	
*Sulfolobus**	
Thiobacterium	
Macromonas	
Thiovulum	
Thiospira	
FAMILY SIDEROCAPSACEAE	Oxidize iron or manganese
Siderocapsa	Iron or manganese oxides deposited
Naumanniella	
Ochrobium	
Siderococcus	Iron but not manganese deposited

*An archaebacterium.

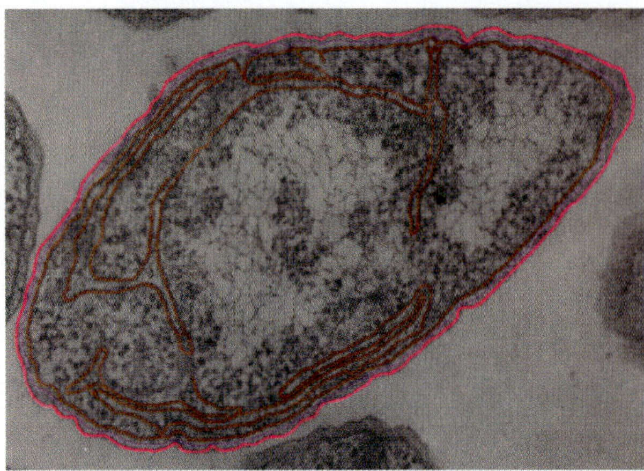

FIG. 16-19 Colorized micrograph of membrane systems of the nitrifying bacterium *Nitrosomonas europa.*

systems (FIG. 16-19). There are two physiological groups in the family Nitrobacteraceae; the first group oxidizes nitrite to nitrate, and the second group oxidizes ammonia to nitrite. Most members of this family are obligate chemolithotrophs. There are seven genera: *Nitrobacter, Nitrospina, Nitrococcus, Nitrosomonas, Nitrosospira, Nitrosococcus,* and *Nitrosolobus.* The first three genera, whose names begin with the prefix *nitro-*, oxidize nitrite to nitrate; the remaining four genera, whose names begin with the prefix *nitroso-*, oxidize ammonia to nitrite. *Nitrobacter* species are extremely important nitrifiers in soil, oxidizing nitrite to nitrate. *Nitrosomonas* species, likewise, are important nitrifiers in soil, oxidizing ammonia to nitrite. The combined actions of the members of the genera *Nitrosomonas* and *Nitrobacter* permit the conversion of ammonia to nitrate. The change in electronic charge between NH_4^+ and NO_3^- alters the mobility of these nitrogenous ions in soil and has a major influence on soil fertility.

Several genera of chemolithotrophic bacteria metabolize sulfur and sulfur-containing inorganic compounds. *Thiobacillus* derives energy from the oxidation of reduced sulfur compounds; its members are Gram-negative rods, motile by means of polar flagella. Some members of the genus *Thiobacillus* oxidize only sulfur compounds, and others, such as *T. ferrooxidans,* also oxidize ferrous to ferric iron to generate ATP. *Thiobacillus* species can be used in the recovery of minerals, including uranium, and their oxidation of reduced iron and sulfur compounds mobilizes various metals so that they can be extracted from even low-grade ores. *T. thiooxidans,* frequently used in biological metal recovery, is an acidophile, with optimum growth occurring in the pH range of 1 to 3.5. The metabolic activities of *T. thiooxidans,* often found in association with waste coal heaps, produce acid mine drainage, a serious ecological problem associated with some coal mining operations.

Members in the family Siderocapsaceae oxidize iron or manganese, depositing iron and/or manganese oxides in capsules or extracellular material. Members of the genus *Siderocapsa,* for example, have spherical cells embedded in a common capsule partially encrusted with iron and/or manganese oxides. The taxonomic status of the entire family, and of the genus *Siderocapsa* in particular, has been questioned frequently. The description of these bacteria as unicellular, non-thread-forming or non-stalk-forming iron or manganese bacteria that under natural conditions deposit metal oxides on or in extracellular mucoid material is taxonomically imperfect and undoubtedly the source of the controversy. Although their proper taxonomic position is in doubt, these bacteria are ecologically important. They are widely distributed in nature, and their metabolic activities are of geologic importance. Members of this family are found in iron-bearing waters, forming high concentrations in the lower portions of some lakes.

BUDDING AND APPENDAGED BACTERIA

The budding and appendaged bacteria represent a heterogeneous group on the basis of a particular morphological feature. These bacteria have in common the formation of extensions or protrusions from the cell (FIG. 16-20). In some cases, the cellular extensions have a reproductive function, but in others they have a physiological purpose. Some bacteria in this group reproduce by budding, others by binary fission (Table 16-15). Several budding bacteria, such as *Rhodomicrobium,* are associated primarily with other groups on the basis of their characteristic modes of

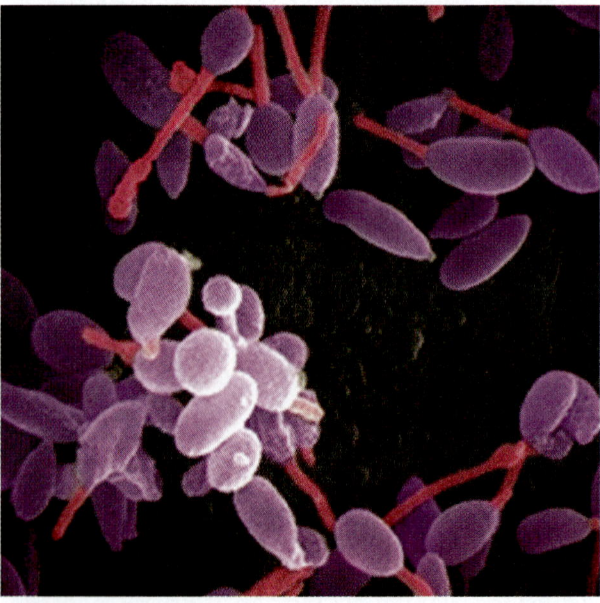

FIG. 16-20 Colorized micrograph of the stalked bacterium *Hyphomicrobium.*

TABLE 16-15 Budding and Appendaged Bacteria

DESCRIPTION	GENUS
PROSTHECATE BACTERIA	
Prosthecate with reproductive function; form new cells by budding	*Hyphomicrobium*
	Hyphomonas
	Pedomicrobium
	Thiodendron
Prosthecate with no reproductive function	*Caulobacter*
	Asticcacaulis
	Ancalomicrobium
	Prosthecobacter
	Prosthecomicrobium
	Stella
NONPROSTHECATE BACTERIA—REPRODUCE BY BUDDING	
	Pasteuria
	Blastobacter
	Seliberia
BACTERIA WITH EXCRETED APPENDAGES AND HOLDFASTS	
Reproduce by binary fission only	*Gallionella*
	Nevskia
Reproduce by budding	*Planctomyces*
GENERA OF UNCERTAIN AFFILIATION	
	Metallogenium
	Caulococcus
	Kusnezovia

metabolism. Budding and appendaged bacteria occur in all nutritional categories. Members of the genus *Gallionella* are capable of chemolithotrophic metabolism; they are probably facultatively chemolithotrophic because they oxidize ferrous to ferric iron and fix carbon dioxide. *Gallionella* are sometimes considered to be sheathed bacteria because their "stalks" may be covered with iron hydroxide. The growth of *Gallionella* species often causes problems in iron pipes of water delivery systems.

The cell appendages of the bacteria in this group, known as *prosthecae*, provide greater efficiency in concentrating available nutrients. Many of the appendaged bacteria grow well at low nutrient concentrations. The appendages provide sufficient membrane surface to transport adequate nutrients into the cell to support the metabolic requirements of the organism. Many of the bacteria in this group primarily occur in aquatic habitats where concentrations of organic matter typically are low. *Caulobacter*, for example, grows in very dilute concentrations of organic matter in lakes and even in distilled water. Its appendages are referred to as *stalks*. In some cases, the stalks of individual cells provide a *holdfast* by which the organisms can attach to a substrate. In other cases, stalks do not function in attachment but may permit cells to adhere to each other, forming rosettes.

Some of the appendaged bacteria form bizarre-looking cells. For example, members of the genus *Prosthecomicrobium* form prosthecae extending in all directions from the cell. *Seliberia* form radial clusters (star-like aggregates) of rod-shaped bacteria with a screw-like twisting of the rod surface and the formation of round reproductive cells by budding. At low nutrient concentrations, *Stella* forms flat cells resembling six-pronged stars. The isolation of various new types of appendaged bacteria has greatly increased our knowledge of the morphological diversity among the bacteria and the relationship between morphology and nutritional status. Many of the varied morphological forms of these bacteria are observed only at very low nutrient concentrations.

SHEATHED BACTERIA

The sheathed bacteria comprise bacteria whose cells occur within a filamentous structure known as a *sheath* (FIG. 16-21). The sheathed bacteria include the genera *Sphaerotilus, Leptothrix, Haliscomenobacter, Lieskeella, Phragmidiothrix, Crenothrix,* and *Clonothrix*. The formation of a sheath enables these bacteria to attach to solid surfaces. This is important to the ecology of these bacteria because many sheathed bacteria live in low nutrient aquatic habitats. By absorbing nutrients from the water that flows by the attached cells, these bacteria conserve their limited energy resources. Additionally, the sheaths afford protection against predators and parasites. In some cases, the sheaths may be covered with metal oxides. For example, in the genus *Leptothrix*, sheaths are encrusted with iron or manganese oxides. In other genera, such as *Haliscomenobacter*, this does not occur. In the genus *Sphaerotilus*, the sheath is sometimes encrusted with

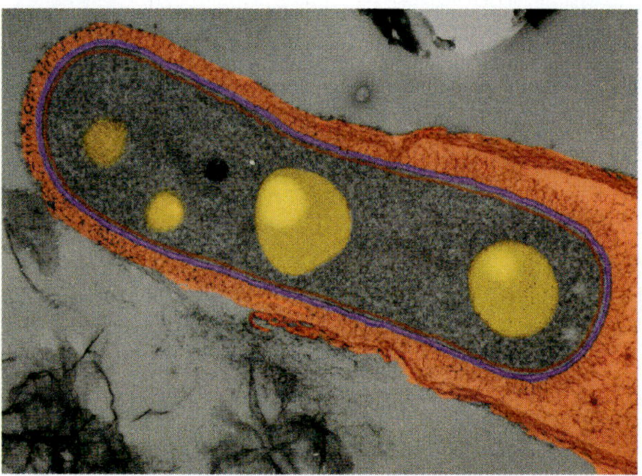

FIG. 16-21 Colorized micrograph of the bacterium *Leptothrix discophora*. The cell is coming out of a sheath *(orange)*, which is covered with manganese oxide deposits *(black)*. Polyhydroxybutyrate *(yellow)* is stored inside the cell.

iron oxides. *S. natans,* often referred to as the *sewage fungus,* is the only species in the genus *Sphaerotilus.* This organism normally occurs in polluted flowing waters, such as sewage effluents, where it may be present in high concentrations just below sewage outfalls.

Gliding Bacteria

We have already seen that some phototrophic bacteria are capable of gliding motility. In addition to the cyanobacteria and Chloroflexaceae, the Myxobacterales (fruiting myxobacteria) and the Cytophagales are grouped on the basis of their *gliding motility* on solid surfaces (Table 16-16). The mole % G + C of the gliding bacteria covers the entire range from 30% to 70%, and, in all likelihood, the gliding bacteria represent a phylogenetically heterogeneous group.

Myxobacteriales

The myxobacteria are small rods that are normally embedded in a slime layer. They lack flagella but are capable of gliding movement. A unique feature of the myxobacteria is that under appropriate conditions they aggregate to form *fruiting bodies* (specialized structures bearing spores) (FIG. 16-22). The taxonomy of the myxobacteria is based largely on the fruiting body structures, which are often brightly colored and visible without the aid of a microscope. Frequently, the fruiting bodies of myxobacteria occur on decaying plant material, on the bark of living trees, or on animal dung, appearing as highly colored, slimy growths that may extend above the surface of the substrate. Within the fruiting body, the cells of the myxobacteria are dormant and are called *myxospores.* In some genera of myxobacteria, the myxospores cannot be distinguished from vegetative cells, but in others the myxospores are refractile and encapsulated, in which case they are known as *microcysts.* Most of the myxobacteria produce various hydrolytic enzymes, such as cellulases, and many are capable of lysing other microorganisms.

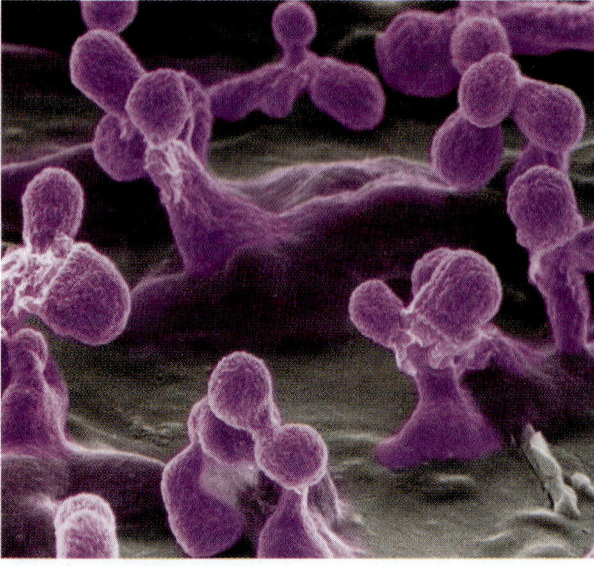

FIG. 16-22 Colorized micrograph of the fruiting myxobacterium *Stigmatella auranticaca.*

Cytophagales

In contrast to the Myxobacterales, the Cytophagales do not produce fruiting bodies. Members of both groups, however, do exhibit gliding motion. Genera in

TABLE 16-16 Gliding Bacteria

TAXON	DESCRIPTION
Order Myxobacterales—Produce Fruiting Bodies	
Family Myxococcaceae	Vegetative cells tapered; microcysts spherical or oval
Genus: *Myxococcus*	
Family Archangiaceae	Vegetative cells tapered; microcysts rod-shaped, not in sporangia
Genus: *Archangium*	
Family Cystobacteraceae	Vegetative cells tapered; microcysts rod-shaped, in sporangia
Genera: *Cystobacter, Melittangium, Stigmatella*	
Family Polyangiaceae	Myxospores resemble vegetative cells
Genera: *Polyangium, Nannocystis, Chondromyces*	
Order Cytophagales—Fruiting Bodies Not Produced	
Family Cytophagaceae	Pigmented; filaments not attached
Genera: *Cytophaga, Flexibacter, Herpetosiphon, Flexithrix, Saprospira, Sporocytophaga*	
Family Beggiatoaceae	Nonpigmented; filaments not attached; cells in cylindrical filaments
Genera: *Beggiatoa, Vitreoscilla, Thioploca*	
Family Simonsiellaceae	Nonpigmented; filaments attached, cells in flat filaments
Genera: *Simonsiella, Alysiella*	
Family Leucotrichacea	Filaments attached at one end
Genera: *Leucothrix, Thiothrix*	

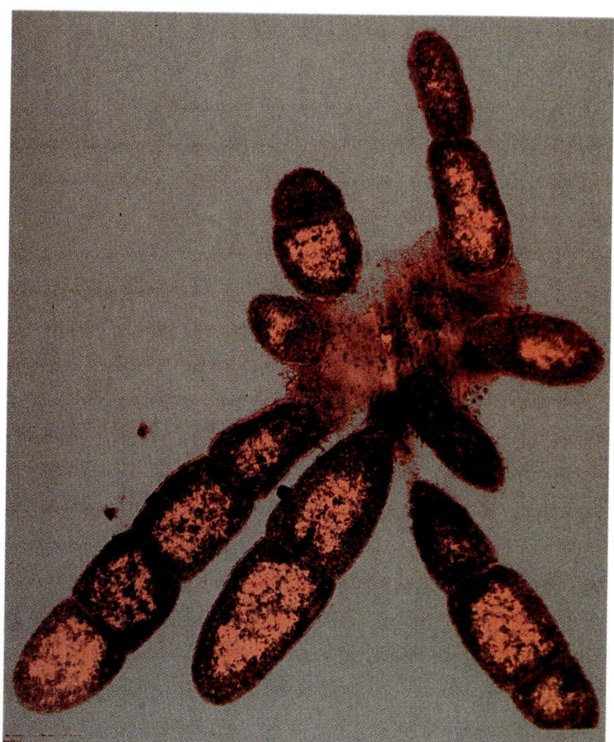

FIG. 16-23 Micrograph of *Leucothrix mucor.*

the order Cytophagales exhibit widely differing morphological forms (FIG. 16-23) and modes of metabolism. They are unified only by the presence of gliding motion and lack of fruiting body formation. Some Cytophagales form filaments and others do not. Some *Flexibacter* species, for example, may form filaments measuring as much as 100 μm in length. Some of the Cytophagales are chemolithotrophs. For example, *Beggiatoa* forms filaments, oxidizes hydrogen sulfide, and deposits sulfur intracellularly when growing on hydrogen sulfide. *Cytophaga* species, on the other hand, do not form filaments. Cells of *Cytophaga* contain deep yellow-orange or red pigments and hydrolyze agar, cellulose, and chitin. As a consequence of their hydrolytic activities, these gliding bacteria are important ecologically in the decomposition of organic matter.

Gram-positive Cocci

The Gram-positive cocci include the families Micrococcaceae, Streptococcaceae, and Peptococcaceae (Table 16-17). The coccoid cells of the Micrococcaceae may occur singly or as irregular clusters (FIG. 16-24). For example, the genus *Staphylococcus* typically forms grape-like clusters. Most strains of *Staphylococcus* can grow in the presence of 15% NaCl. Species of *Staphylococcus* commonly occur on skin surfaces. *S. au-*

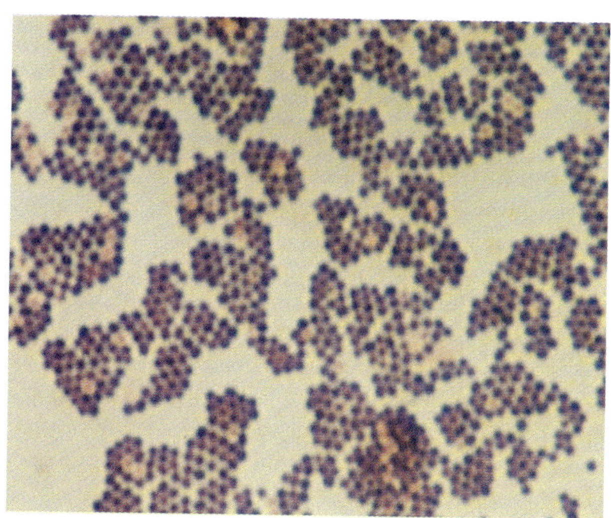

FIG. 16-24 Micrograph of *Staphylococcus aureus.*

TABLE 16-17 Gram-positive Cocci

TAXON	DESCRIPTION
Family Micrococcaceae	
Micrococcus	Irregular clusters; % G + C 60-75
Staphylococcus	Irregular clusters; % G + C 30-40
Planococcus	Tetrads; % G + C 39-52
Family Streptococcaceae	
Streptococcus	Pairs or chains; homofermentative; % G + C 33-42
Leuconostoc	Pairs or chains; heterofermentative; % G + C 38-44
Pediococcus	Pairs or tetrads; homofermentative; % G + C 34-44
Aerococcus	Pairs or tetrads; heterofermentative; % G + C 36-40
Gemella	Single or pairs; % G + C 31-53
Family Peptococcaceae	
Peptococcus	Irregular clusters; no growth at pH 2.5; cellulose not degraded; % G + C 33-34
Peptostreptococcus	Chains; no growth at pH 2.5; cellulose not degraded; % G + C 40-46
Ruminococcus	Irregular clusters or chains; no growth at pH 2.5; cellulose degraded; % G + C 40-46
Sarcina	Tetrads or octads; growth at pH 2.5; cellulose not degraded; % G + C 28-31

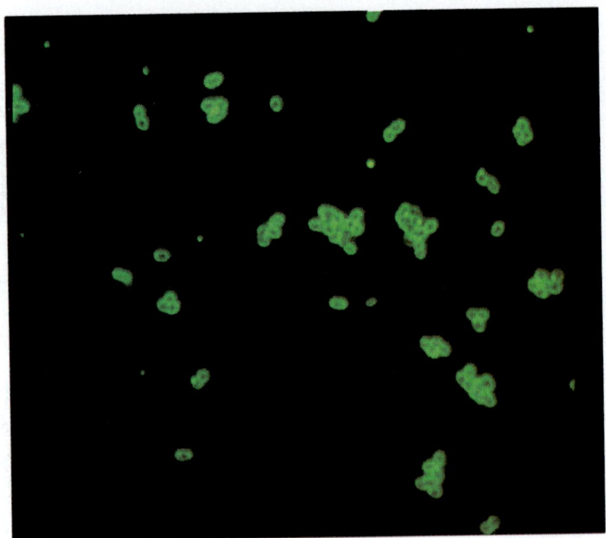

FIG. 16-25 Micrograph of group A streptococci after fluorescent antibody staining, examined with ultraviolet light. The bacteria appear as rings with dark centers.

reus is a potential human pathogen, infecting wounds and causing food poisoning.

In the family Streptococcaceae, Gram-positive cocci occur as pairs or chains (FIG. 16-25). The metabolism of the Streptococcaceae is fermentative. Even though their metabolism is anaerobic, the Streptococcaceae are listed as being facultatively anaerobic because they grow in the presence of air. Indeed, many species of *Streptococcus* occur in the oral cavity, where—although continuously exposed to air—they grow, and some cause formation of dental caries. Other streptococci cause more serious diseases, such as pneumonia due to *S. pneumoniae* infections and rheumatic fever associated with *S. pyogenes* infections.

The Peptococcaceae have complex nutritional requirements. Cells of organisms of this family may occur singly, in pairs, or in regular or irregular masses. They are obligately anaerobic and produce low molecular weight volatile fatty acids, carbon dioxide, hydrogen, and ammonia as the main products of amino acid metabolism.

GRAM-POSITIVE ENDOSPORE-FORMING RODS AND COCCI

The endospore-forming rods and cocci are extremely important because of the heat resistance of the endospore structure. The genera *Bacillus, Sporolactobacillus, Clostridium, Desulfotomaculum, Sporosarcina,* and *Thermoactinomyces* are all characterized by the formation of endospores (Table 16-18). These genera occur in the family Bacillaceae. Most endospore formers are Gram-positive rods. Only members of the genus *Desulfotomaculum* are Gram-negative endospore formers.

TABLE 16-18 Endospore Producers

TAXON	DESCRIPTION
FAMILY BACILLACEAE	
Bacillus	Rods, aerobic or facultative, catalase usually produced
Sporolactobacillus	Rods, microaerophilic, catalase not produced
Clostridium	Rods, anaerobic, sulfate not reduced to sulfide
Desulfotomaculum	Rods, anaerobic, sulfate reduced to sulfide
Sporosarcina	Cocci, tetrads or octads
FAMILY MICROMONOSPORACEAE	
Thermoactinomyces	Filamentous thermophile

The two most important genera of endospore-forming bacteria are the genera *Bacillus* and *Clostridium. Bacillus* species are strict aerobes or facultative anaerobes. *Clostridium* species are obligately anaerobic. The endospore-forming bacteria are extremely important in food, industrial, and medical microbiology. Food spoilage by *Bacillus* and *Clostridium* species is of great economic importance. Several *Clostridium* species are important human pathogens. For example, *C. botulinum* is the causative agent of botulism, *C. tetani* causes tetanus, and *C. perfringens* causes gas gangrene.

GRAM-POSITIVE ASPOROGENOUS RODS OF REGULAR SHAPE

The Gram-positive, asporogenous (nonsporulating), rod-shaped bacteria include the family Lactobacillaceae. These are Gram-positive rods that produce lactic acid as the major fermentation product; they occur in fermenting plant and animal products that have available carbohydrate substrates. They are also found as part of the normal human microbiota in the oral cavity, vaginal tract, and intestinal tract. *Lactobacillus,* the only genus in the family Lactobacillaceae, is extremely important in the dairy industry. Cheese, yogurt, and many other fermented products are made by the metabolic activities of *Lactobacillus* species.

There are several genera of uncertain affiliation that are Gram-positive, nonspore-forming, rod-shaped bacteria. These include *Listeria, Erysipelothrix,* and *Caryophanon.* The *Listeria,* which are Gram-positive rods that tend to produce chains, include several species that are animal pathogens. Some recent outbreaks of human foodborne infections have been caused by *Listeria*-contaminated milk and cheeses. *Caryophanon latum,* another bacterium in this group, produces large rods or filaments up to 3 μm in diameter. This bacterium is normally found colonizing

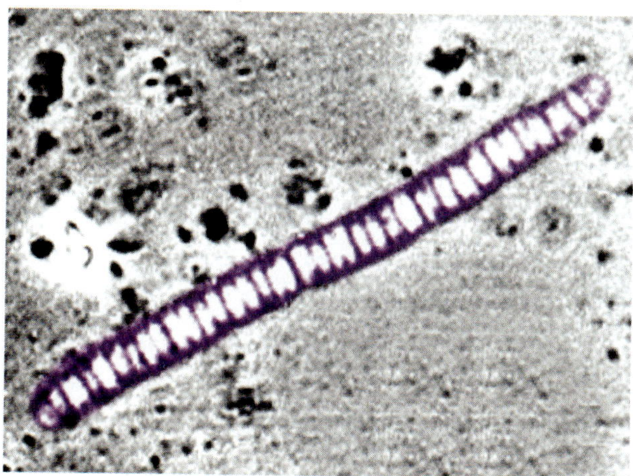

FIG. 16-26 Colorized micrograph of *Caryophanon latum.*

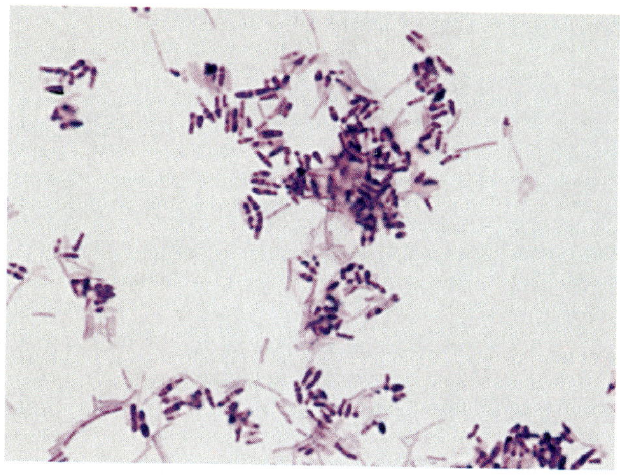

FIG. 16-27 Micrograph of the Gram-positive pleomorphic rod-shaped bacterium *Corynebacterium diphtheriae.*

animal fecal matter. The filaments of *C. latum* are divided by closely spaced cross walls into numerous disk-shaped cells less than 1 μm long, giving them an unusual morphology that is quite striking (FIG. 16-26).

GRAM-POSITIVE RODS OF IRREGULAR SHAPE

The coryneform group of bacteria is a heterogeneous group defined by the characteristic irregular morphology of the cells and their tendency to show incomplete separation following cell division. The coryneform bacteria exhibit pleomorphic morphology. They do not form true filaments. The irregular morphology and the association of the cells after division, however, indicate a relationship to the filament-forming actinomycetes. This group includes the genera *Corynebacterium, Arthrobacter, Brevibacterium, Cellulomonas,* and *Kurthia* (Table 16-19). Many species of *Corynebacterium* are plant or animal pathogens. For example, *Corynebacterium diphtheriae* is the causative agent of diphtheria. As noted in an earlier chapter, *C. diphtheriae* causes diphtheria only when it is infected with a specific temperate phage. Cells of *Corynebacterium* exhibit *snapping division;* that is, after binary fission the cells do not completely separate (FIG. 16-27) and appear to form groups resembling "Chinese letters" when viewed under the microscope.

The genus *Arthrobacter,* which is widely distributed in soils, is interesting because it exhibits a simple life cycle (FIG. 16-28) in which there is a change from rod-shaped cells to coccoid cells. The sequence of morphological changes in the growth cycle distinguishes *Arthrobacter* from other genera. The coccoid cells present during the stationary growth phase are sometimes referred to as *arthrospores* and *cystites.* The formation of arthrospores represents the beginning of a regular life cycle that is characteristic of eukaryotic microorganisms but is rare among the prokaryotes.

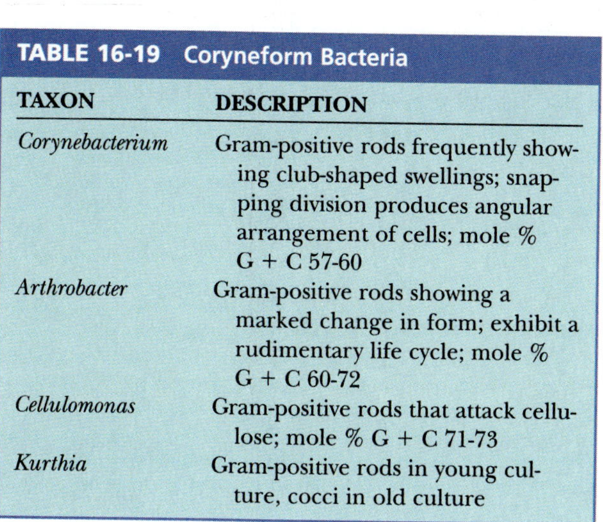

TABLE 16-19 Coryneform Bacteria

TAXON	DESCRIPTION
Corynebacterium	Gram-positive rods frequently showing club-shaped swellings; snapping division produces angular arrangement of cells; mole % G + C 57-60
Arthrobacter	Gram-positive rods showing a marked change in form; exhibit a rudimentary life cycle; mole % G + C 60-72
Cellulomonas	Gram-positive rods that attack cellulose; mole % G + C 71-73
Kurthia	Gram-positive rods in young culture, cocci in old culture

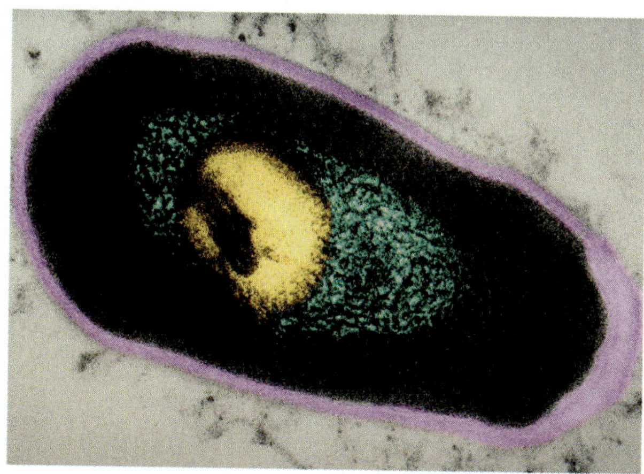

FIG. 16-28 Colorized micrograph of *Arthrobacter globiformis* showing vegetative rod. In late culture this bacteria forms spherical cysts.

MYCOBACTERIA

The mycobacteria, members of the genus *Mycobacterium,* are slow-growing, aerobic rod-shaped bacteria. Mycobacterial cells are difficult to stain by the Gram procedure. They are acid fast; that is, stained cells resist decolorization with acid alcohol. Because of many similarities, including acid-fastness, mycobacteria have traditionally been considered as related to *Corynebacterium* and *Nocardia* and referred to as the CNM group. Recently, *Rhodococcus* was added to this grouping. The acid-fast property is associated with the presence of waxy *mycolic acids* that are associated with their cell walls.

The morphology of the mycobacteria is highly pleomorphic. Cells may be slightly curved or straight rods, and filamentous or mycelial growth may occur. The genus can be divided into slow-growing species that typically may have a doubling time of up to 20 hours and fast-growing species that may double every 2 hours. Colonies of slow-growing species such as *Mycobacterium tuberculosis* may not be visible on solidified medium for days or even weeks after inoculation.

Many species produce yellow carotenoid pigments that render the colonies a characteristic color. Mycobacteria are divided into nonpigmented species such as *M. tuberculosis* and *M. smegmatis,* photochromogenic species such as *M. kansasii* that form pigment only when cultured in the light, and scotochromogenic species such as *M. gordonae* that can form pigment when cultured in the dark.

Several mycobacteria are important human pathogens that establish persistent infections. *M. tuberculosis* is the causative agent of tuberculosis and *M. leprae* causes Hansen disease (leprosy). Mycolic acids contribute to their resistance to phagocytosis and allow these bacteria to persist inside of macrophages and neutrophils as intracellular parasites.

ACTINOMYCETES

The Gram-positive bacteria have been traditionally divided into two major groups that are differentiated on the basis of DNA base composition. Bacteria with a low mole % G + C composition have been included in the *Bacillus-Clostridium-Streptococcus* branch, and bacteria with a high mole % G + C composition have been associated as actinomycetes. The group actinomycetes contains Actinobacteria, Actinoplanetes, Maduromycetes, Micropolysporas, Nocardioforms, Streptomycetes, Thermomonosporas, and others. Actinomycetes are characterized by the formation of branching filaments. These filaments form intertwining masses called mycelia that superficially resemble the mycelia of filamentous fungi. The actinomycete filament, however, is of bacterial dimensions; the cells are prokaryotic, and they are clearly eubacteria.

The families in the order Actinomycetales include Frankiaceae, Actinoplanaceae, Dermatophilaceae, Streptomycetaceae, and Micromonosporaceae (Table 16-20). The various families of the order Actinomycetales are distinguished from one another by the nature of their mycelia and spores (FIG. 16-29).

TABLE 16-20 Actinomyces

TAXON	DESCRIPTION
Family Frankiaceae Genera: *Frankia*	Mycelium formed; symbionts in plant nodules with free stage in soil
Family Actinoplanaceae Genera: *Actinoplanes, Spirillospora, Streptosporangium, Amorphosporangium, Ampullariella, Pilimelia, Planomonospora, Planobispora, Dactylosporangium, Kitasatoa*	Mycelium formed; saprophytes or facultative parasites; spores borne inside sporangia
Family Dermatophilaceae Genera: *Dermatophilus, Geodermatophilus*	Mycelium divides transversely to form motile cocci; saprophytes or facultative parasites; spores not borne in sporangia
Family Streptomycetaceae Genera: *Streptomyces, Streptoverticillium, Sporichthya, Microellobosporia*	Mycelium tends to remain intact; saprophytes or facultative parasites; spores not borne in sporangia; usually abundant aerial mycelia and long spore chains
Family Micromonosporaceae Genera: *Micromonospora, Thermoactinomyces, Actinobifida, Thermomonospora, Microbispora, Micropolyspora*	Mycelium remains intact; saprophytes or facultative parasites; spores not borne in sporangia; spores formed singly or in short chains

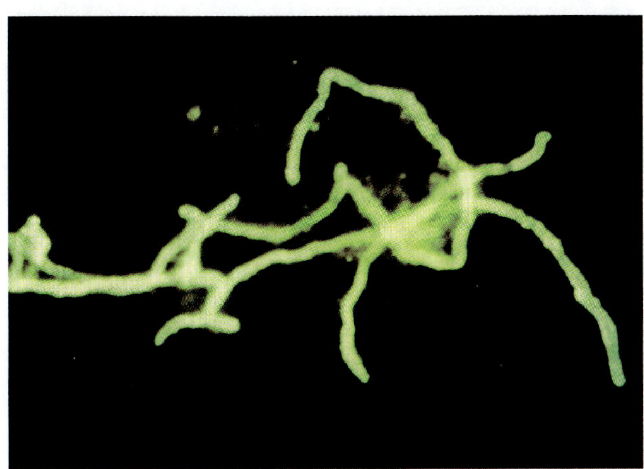

FIG. 16-29 Micrograph of the actinomycete *Actinomyces israelii* showing hyphae formation.

Nocardioform Actinomycetes

The nocardioforms typically produce fungal-like filaments that fragment into nonmotile cells. Some bacteria in this group form mycelia (filaments) that do not readily fragment. All bacteria in this group are aerobic Gram-positive cells and are differentiated based on cell wall composition, lipid composition, and whole-cell sugar patterns. Some genera produce aerial mycelia; others do not. Often, the nocardioforms produce brightly colored pigments. *Nocardia* is a representative genus of this group.

Streptomycetes

The streptomycetes are a large group of filamentous, Gram-positive actinomycetes that do not fragment into rods or coccoid elements. The formation of aerial filaments with spore production and spore morphology are important diagnostic characteristics for the identification of these actinomycetes. These spores are not heat-resistant structures as are the endospores of *Bacillus* and *Clostridium*. Various types of spores are produced by actinomycete species, many of which are involved in the dispersal of actinomycetes; only *Thermoactinomyces* produces endospores.

The streptomycetes are widely distributed in nature. The oxidative forms are numerous and occur primarily in soils. The main ecological role of actinomycetes is the decomposition of organic matter in soil. Fermentative types are primarily found in association with humans and other animals. Many of the Streptomycetes, such as *Streptomyces griseus,* produce antibiotics that are extremely important in the pharmaceutical industry. Nearly 75% of the antibiotics currently available have been isolated from *Streptomyces* species. The production and use of such antibiotics have revolutionized medical practice, and many previously fatal diseases are now more easily controlled.

Mycoplasmas

The mycoplasmas are classified as mollicutes (meaning soft skin) because they lack a cell wall. They are bacteria that are bounded by a single triple-layered membrane. Phylogenetic studies show that the mollicutes are closely related to a grouping of *Clostridium* species and are undoubtedly cell wall-less derivatives. They are the smallest organisms capable of self-reproduction. When growing on artificial media, mycoplasmas form small colonies that have a characteristic "fried-egg" appearance (FIG. 16-30). Most members of the genus *Mycoplasma* require sterols for growth. Several of them cause diseases in humans. For example, some forms of pneumonia are caused by *Mycoplasma* species.

Like the colonies of *Mycoplasma,* the colonies of *Spiroplasma* species exhibit a typical biphasic fried-egg appearance. *Spiroplasma* is considered a genus of uncertain affiliation in the class Mollicutes. *Spiroplasma* species lack a cell wall, have a triple-layered cytoplasmic membrane, and require sterols for growth. They cause diseases in plants and animals. For example, *S. citri* causes "stubborn" disease of citrus plants. Suckling mouse cataract disease is also caused by a *Spiroplasma* species.

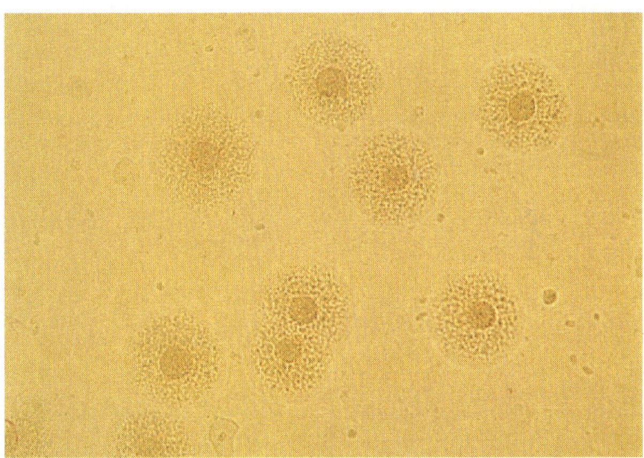

FIG. 16-30 Colonies of *Mycoplasma hominis* with characteristic "fried-egg" appearance.

Anaerobic Nonfilamentous or Filamentous Rods

The family Propionibacteriaceae contains Gram-positive rods that produce propionic acid, acetic acid, or mixtures of organic acids by fermentation; lactic acid is not a major fermentation product but is used as a fermentation substrate. There are two genera in the family Propionibacteriaceae: *Propionibacterium* and *Eubacterium.* Species of *Propionibacterium* are important in the dairy industry; they normally carry out propionic acid fermentation. Species of *Eubacterium* usually produce mixtures of organic acids, including large amounts of butyric, acetic, and formic acids; they do not produce propionic, lactic, succinic, or acetic acids as major fermentation products.

ENDOSYMBIONTS

Several bacterial genera are obligate endosymbionts of invertebrates; that is, they live within the cells of invertebrate animals without adversely affecting the host. For example, the protozoan *Paramecium aurelia* can harbor various endosymbiotic bacteria (Table 16-21). Additionally, new genera of endosymbionts have recently been described for other protozoa, insects, and various other invertebrates. *Mycoplasma*-like organisms have been found in plants. Although these bacteria can be readily seen within host cells, difficulties in culturing them outside of the host hampers efforts to determine their proper taxonomic status. Developing an understanding of the nutritional requirements of these bacteria will permit the creation of complex media for their culture and identification.

TABLE 16-21 Symbionts of *Paramecium aurelia*

GENUS	COMMON NAMES	DESCRIPTION
Caedibacter	Kappa	Varying in size and distinguished by the presence of a 0.5 mm diameter inclusion within the host cell; exhibits killing of sensitive strains
Pseudocaedibacter	Pi	Slender rod until recently considered as a mutant of kappa; nonkilling symbiont
	Nu	A nonkilling symbiont similar in appearance to pi and mu
	Mu	Slender rod, often elongated; distinguished because its killing action is wholly dependent on cell–cell contact between mating paramecia
	Gamma	A diminutive bacterium, frequently appearing as doublets; strong killing of other strains is shown by gamma bearers
Tectibacter	Delta	Rod distinguished by an electron-dense material surrounding the outer of its two membranes
Lyticum	Lambda	Appears as a typical motile bacterium with peritrichous flagella, although its movement within the cytoplasm has not been observed
	Sigma	Largest of all endosymbionts of *Paramecium aurelia;* curved, flagellated rod resembling lambda
Hotospora	Omega	Present in the micronucleus existing in two forms, a short reproductive form and a long infective form with rounded ends
	Iota	Present in the macronucleus existing in two forms, a short reproductive form and a long infective form with rounded ends
	Alpha	Present in the macronucleus existing in two forms, a short reproductive form and a long infective form with spiral tapered ends

16.3 ARCHAEBACTERIA

Members of the archaebacteria, which are also called archaeobacteria, are phylogenetically related to each other on the basis of analysis of their 16S rRNA molecules (signature sequences) (FIG. 16-31), and are distinct from eubacterial and eukaryotic species (see Chapter 1). They are placed in the separate Kingdom Archaea. The archaebacterial species share several morphological and physiological features that make them distinct from other prokaryotic microorganisms, including the lack of murein in their cell walls and the unusual ether linkage that occurs in their phospholipid molecules. Many archaebacteria possess a multicomponent RNA polymerase that is resistant to rifampicin and streptolydigin. Members of the Kingdom Archaea are considered to be distantly related to other prokaryotes.

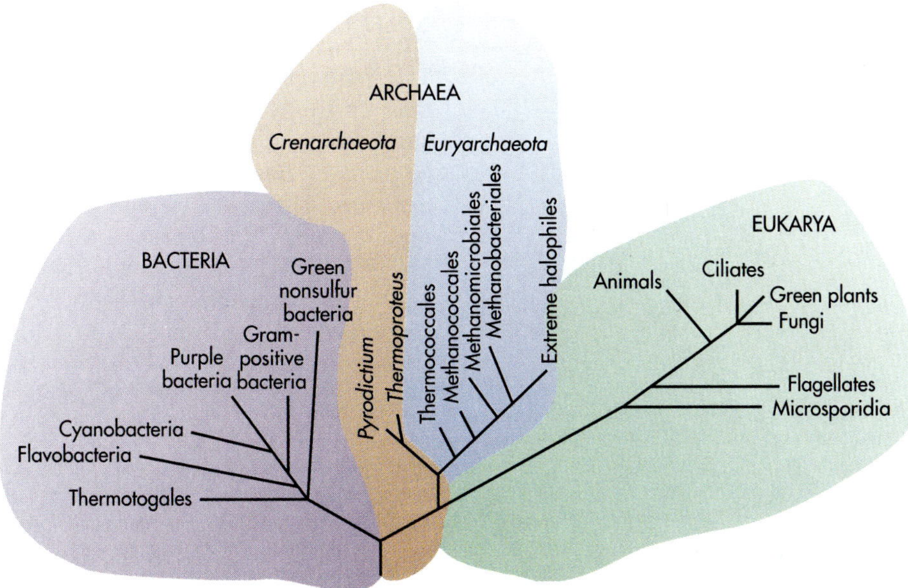

FIG. 16-31 Phylogenetic tree of the Archaea showing evolutionary relationships.

METHANE-PRODUCING BACTERIA

The methane-producing bacteria, or methanogens, represent a highly specialized physiological group. Members of the family Methanobacteriaceae obtain energy for growth from the reduction of specific substrates to methane. Commonly, H_2 serves as an electron donor and CO_2 is the electron acceptor. Other methanogens can utilize formate or acetate as the substrate for generating ATP. Methanogenic bacteria are unable to use carbohydrates, proteins, or other complex organic substrates. Improvements in anaerobic isolation techniques permit the isolation of many new species of methanogens.

The family Methanobacteriaceae has been extensively revised recently to accommodate several new taxa. These genera of methane-generating bacteria can be differentiated on the basis of relatively few morphological and physiological features (Table 16-22). The cell wall of many methanogens is composed

TABLE 16-22 Methanogenic Bacteria

TAXON	DESCRIPTION
Family Methanobacteriaceae	
Order Methanobacteriales	Cells short, lancet-shaped cocci to long filaments; cells appear Gram-positive but lack murein; strict anaerobes; oxidize hydrogen; reduce CO_2 to methane
Family Methoaobacteriaceae	
Genera *Methanobacterium*	Slender rods, often forming filaments
Methanobrevibacter	Short rods or lancet-shaped cocci often in pairs or chains
Order Methanococcales	Cells cocci; oxidize hydrogen or formate; reduce CO_2 to methane or form methane via fermentation of methanol and related compounds
Family Methanococcaceae	
Genus *Methanococcus*	Cocci single, in pairs, or clumps
Order Methanomicrobiales	Cells cocci to rods; Gram-negative or Gram-positive; motile or nonmotile; strict anaerobes; oxidize hydrogen or formate; reduce CO_2 to methane or form methane via fermentation of methanol and related compounds
Family Methanomicrobiaceae	Gram-negative cocci to rods
Genera: *Methanomicrobium*	Short motile rods
Methanogenium	Irregular coccoid cells
Methanospirillum	Curved, slender motile rods, often forming filaments
Family Methanosarcinaceae	Gram-positive coccoid cells occurring in packets
Genus: *Methanosarcina*	

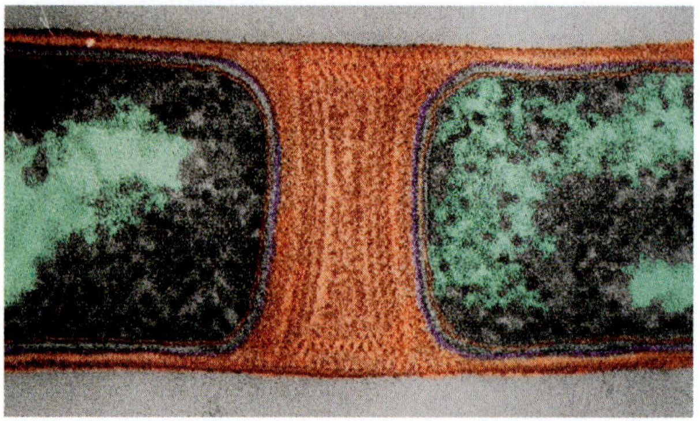

FIG. 16-32 Colorized micrograph of *Methanospirillum hungatei* cells within a sheath (orange). (78,750×). The cells are separated by a cell spacer.

of a chemically unique molecule, pseudomurein, that differs from eubacterial peptidoglycan in several ways (see Chapter 3 for a discussion of the morphological characteristics of archaebacteria and their wall structures). Other methanogen cell walls are composed of protein. Among the methanogens, *Methanobacterium* consists of rods or lancet-shaped cocci, *Methanosarcina* consists of large cocci occurring in packets, and *Methanococcus* species occur as cocci arranged singly or in irregular clusters (FIG. 16-32). With such structural and chemical diversity, the comparisons of 16S ribosomal RNA homologies still remain the best criteria for classifying methanogens.

The conversion of CO_2 to CH_4 requires the activity of some reducing enzymes that are unique to methanogens. These include the coenzymes F_{420} and the nickel-containing coenzyme F_{430}, Methanofuran, Methanopterin, and coenzyme M. The details of autotrophic methanogenesis were previously discussed (see Chapter 4 for a discussion of methanogenic metabolism).

The methanogens often form consortia in association with other microorganisms. The microorganisms associated with the methanogens maintain the low oxygen tensions and provide the carbon dioxide and fatty acids required by the methanogenic bacteria. Such associations are extremely important in the rumen of animals such as cows. A major source of atmospheric methane is the rumen of such animals. The United States Environmental Protection Agency once issued an indelicate report stating that the burping cow was the major source of atmospheric hydrocarbon pollutants. Clearly, though, in urban areas, hydrocarbon pollutants originate primarily from automotive exhausts and not cows. The anaerobic decomposition of cellulosic plant debris that occurs in the sediments of lakes, rivers, and bogs results in formation of methane and carbon dioxide (biogas or marsh gas).

SULFATE REDUCERS

The genus *Archaeoglobus* contains archaebacterial sulfate reducers. These microorganisms have been isolated from anaerobic submarine hydrothermal regions and have a requirement for salt and high temperature. The cell envelope lacks a rigid structure, pseudomurein is absent, and the cell is covered by a polypeptide S layer (regularly structured protein assembly, which is the only cell wall structure). *Archaeoglobus* cells grow at 65° to 90° C and 1% to 4% salt. During growth, sulfate (SO_4^{2-}), sulfite (SO_3^{2-}), or thiosulfate ($S_2O_3^{2-}$) is reduced to hydrogen sulfide.

HALOBACTERIACEAE

The genera *Halobacterium* and *Halococcus,* included in the family Halobacteriaceae, have the characteristic properties of the archaebacteria. The unusual bacteriorhodopsin-mediated phototrophic metabolism of *Halobacterium* was discussed earlier. In addition to this unique feature, all members of the family Halobacteriaceae are obligate halophiles, growing only in media containing at least 15% NaCl. Halobacteria may be divided into alkaliphilic and neutrophilic (nonalkaliphilic) groups. Alkaliphilic members such as *Natronobacterium* and *Natronococcus* grow optimally at low magnesium concentrations and pH around 10. The members of the neutrophilic group, represented by *Halobacterium* and *Halococcus,* grow well under conditions of high magnesium concentration (0.5 M), high sodium concentration (4.0 M), and neutral pH.

The majority of members of the Halobacteriaceae are colored purple by the presence of intracellular bacteriorhodopsin or red, pink, or orange by the presence of carotenoid pigments. Members of this family are found in ecosystems that have extremely high sodium chloride concentrations, such as some salt lakes, the Dead Sea, and foods preserved by salting. *Halobacterium* species are normally aerobic microorganisms but can grow anaerobically in the light. Under anaerobic conditions in the light, the "purple membrane" (cytoplasmic membrane that contains bacteriorhodopsin) functions as a proton pump and drives ATP synthesis (see Box 4-2).

CELL WALL-LESS ARCHAEBACTERIA

The archaebacterium *Thermoplasma* is acidophilic, thermophilic, and lacks a cell wall. With respect to the last characteristic, this organism is similar to the eubacterial *Mycoplasmas.* Because they lack a rigid outer structure, cells of *Thermoplasma* vary in size (0.2 μm to 5.0 μm) and shape (filamentous, club-shaped, and coccoid). *Thermoplasma* is found in nature growing in coal refuse piles that through self-combustion and leaching of organic compounds result in an acidic and moderately warm environment. In addition, these archaebacteria have been isolated from hot, acidic sulfur-rich fields. Since coal refuse piles are man-made, growth in solfataras may represent the more natural habitat of *Thermoplasma* species.

Thermoplasma grow optimally about 59° C and pH 2. They grow both aerobically and anaerobically. Under anaerobic conditions, there is a requirement for sulfur, which is reduced to hydrogen sulfide. In spite of this metabolism, the 16S ribosomal RNA sequence homology suggests that *Thermoplasma* is more closely related to the methanogen/halophile branch of the archaebacterial phylogenetic tree than to sulfur-metabolizing thermophiles (see FIG. 16-31).

Extremely Thermophilic Sulfur Metabolizers

One of the distinct branches of the Archaea contains microorganisms that metabolize sulfur and grow at very high temperatures. These extremely thermophilic sulfur metabolizers convert elemental sulfur to hydrogen sulfide using organic compounds or hydrogen as electron donors. This group consists of three orders: Thermoproteales, Sulfolobales, and Thermococcales: Members of the order Thermoproteales are extreme thermophiles and have optimal growth temperatures between 85° and 105° C. Most species in this group cannot grow at temperatures below 60° C. These Gram-negative cells are strict anaerobes.

Sulfolobus and *Acidianus,* members of the Sulfolobales, are extreme acidophiles in addition to being extreme thermophiles. They will not grow above pH 5.5 and prefer to grow between pH 2 to 3. *Sulfolobus* species occur in high temperature, acidic environments such as sulfur-rich hot springs in volcanic areas. On the basis of their staining reactions, the bacteria in the sulfur-oxidizing genus *Sulfolobus* have been characterized as Gram-negative spherical cells (FIG. 16-33). The cell walls of *Sulfolobus,* however, lack peptidoglycan and also share other properties with the Archaebacteria, including rRNA homology and membrane structure. *Sulfolobus* is a strict aerobe and *Acidianus* is a facultative aerobe. Both genera contain cells that can oxidize elemental sulfur to sulfuric acid in the presence of O_2.

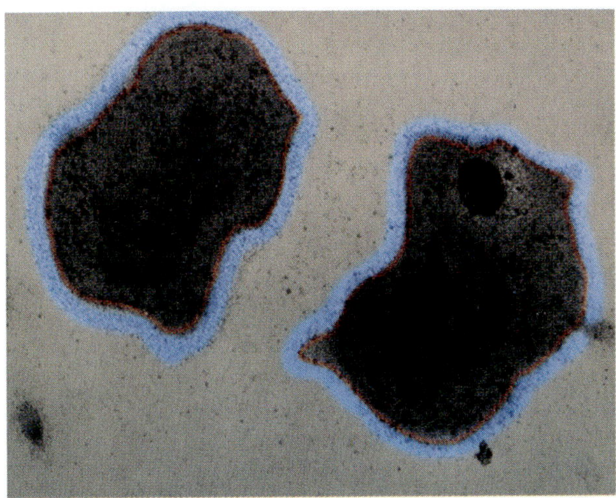

FIG. 16-33 Colorized micrograph of the sulfur-oxidizing archaebacterium *Sulfolobus brierleyi.*

Thermococcus and *Pyrococcus,* the two genera of the Thermococcales, are anaerobic cells found in marine and terrestrial sulfur-rich regions. They are extreme thermophiles that live near geothermal vents. They utilize organic carbon from peptides or amino acids and sometimes carbohydrates. Elemental sulfur serves as an electron acceptor, thus forming H_2S. *Pyrodictium brockii* has an optimal growth temperature of 105° C. This clearly approaches the upper temperature limits for life.

Chapter Review

Study Questions

1. How are bacteria named?
2. What is the difference between classification and identification?
3. Compare phenetic and phylogenetic approaches to microbial classification.
4. Why has DNA homology caused the reclassification of many bacterial species? Why is DNA homology a better measure of relatedness than phenotypic characteristics for developing classification systems?
5. Why does comparison of the mole percent G + C permit the assessment of genetic relatedness? Why does DNA homology better describe genetic relatedness than the proportion of G + C in the DNA?
6. What is an identification key? How is a dichotomous key used in identifying an unknown?
7. How do computers aid in the identification of bacteria?
8. Describe the similarities and differences between cyanobacteria and other phototrophic bacteria.
9. How are the archaebacteria different from other bacterial groups? How has rRNA analysis helped define the relationships among these organisms?
10. Which bacterial genera are characterized by endospore formation?
11. What phenotypic characteristics distinguish major groups of bacteria?
12. Where would you find a description of a bacterial genus that was described 10 years ago? A description of one that had been described for the first time this year?

SITUATIONAL PROBLEMS

Designing an Identification Scheme

One of the simplest and most efficient methods of identifying a bacterial isolate that is one of a very limited number of possible species is the use of a dichotomous key. The dichotomous, or two-branching, key facilitates the separation of bacteria into increasingly smaller groups until only one bacterium remains (see FIG. 16-1). This process of separation and identification is based on determining a series of physical and biochemical characteristics of the bacterium, including its morphology, growth requirements, and enzymatic processes. Suppose you are asked to help design an identification scheme for a limited number of common bacterial isolates that are expected to be found in the specimens to be examined. The positive identification of particular organisms in the specimens is critical. Because of limited funds, you decide to design a dichotomous key rather than to advise the selection of a miniaturized commercial identification system that would be far more costly per specimen.

The first step in the development of a dichotomous key involves the characterization of all of the possible bacterial isolates. By referring to a taxonomic guide such as *Bergey's Manual,* you find the characteristics of most known bacteria. Once the characteristics of the bacteria have been determined, the construction of the key can begin. The most efficient dichotomous keys use tests that divide a group of bacteria into two groups of equal size. Each group, in turn, should be divided into two smaller groups—again preferably of equal size—and the process of division repeated until only one organism remains in each of the subgroups. The tests should be selected so that there are only two possible results, one positive and the other negative. Ideally, the dichotomous key separates bacteria into individual families, which are subsequently divided into one or more genera, which in turn are divided into species.

The first test in many such keys is the Gram stain. This divides most bacteria into two groups, which may be further divided into individual families according to shape, endospore production, or some other characteristic. Each family is divided into its respective genera by other tests that depict more specific differences between the organisms, and each genus is divided by still more specific characteristics until only one species remains at the end of each branch. Thus, with the use of a dichotomous key, the identity of most common bacterial isolates can be determined quickly, accurately, and efficiently.

1. Given the results for the following 10 Gram-positive bacteria, design a dichotomous key for their identification using the minimum number of tests.

Bacterial Species

0. *Bacillus anthracis*
1. *Bacillus cereus*
2. *Clostridium perfringens*
3. *Clostridium tetani*
4. *Corynebacterium diphtheriae*
5. *Mycobacterium tuberculosis*
6. *Staphylococcus aureus*
7. *Staphylococcus epidermidis*
8. *Streptococcus pneumoniae*
9. *Streptococcus pyogenes*

Characteristics Tested

A. Rods
B. Cocci
C. Endospores
D. Endospores central
E. Endospores subterminal
F. Endospores terminal
G. Acid fast
H. Growth in presence of air
I. Growth in absence of air
J. Acid from glucose
K. Gas from glucose
L. Acid from mannitol
M. Catalase
N. Oxidase
O. Nitrate reduced
P. Motile
Q. Snapping division
R. Coagulase
S. Beta hemolysis
T. Growth at 45° C
U. Growth at 6.5% NaCl

Test Results

Test

ORGANISM	A	B	C	D	E	F	G	H	I	J	K	L	M	N	O	P	Q	R	S	T	U
0	+	−	+	+	−	−	−	+	+	+	−	−	+	+	+	−	−	−	−	−	
1	+	−	+	+	−	−	−	+	+	+	−	−	+	+	+	−	−	−	−	+	
2	+	−	+	−	+	−	−	−	+	+	+	−	−	−	−	−	−	−	−	+	
3	+	−	+	−	−		+	−	−	+	−	−	−	−	−	−	+	−	−	+	−
4	+	−	−	−	−	−	−	+	+	+	−	−	+	+	+	−	−	+	+	−	
5	+	−	−	−	−	−	+	+	+	−	−	−	+	+	+	−	−	−	−	−	−
6	−	+	−	−	−	−	−	+	+	+	−	+	+	+	+	−	−	+	+	−	+
7	−	+	−	−	−	−	−	+	+	+	−	−	+	+	+	−	−	−	−	+	+
8	−	+	−	−	−	−	−	+	+	+	−	−	−	−	−	−	−	−	−	+	−
9	−	+	−	−	−	−	−	+	+	+	−	−	−	−	−	−	−	−	+	−	−

+, Positive test result; −, negative test result; blank, indeterminate test result.

2. Given the results for the following 10 Gram-negative bacteria, design a dichotomous key for their identification using the minimum number of tests.

Bacterial Species

0. *Citrobacter freundii*
1. *Enterobacter aerogenes*
2. *Escherichia coli*
3. *Klebsiella pneumoniae*
4. *Proteus vulgaris*
5. *Pseudomonas aeruginosa*
6. *Salmonella typhimurium*
7. *Serratia marcescens*
8. *Shigella flexnerii*
9. *Yersinia enterocolitica*

Characteristics Tested

A. Rods
B. Acid from glucose
C. Gas from glucose
D. Catalase
E. Oxidase
F. Nitrates reduced
G. Methyl Red
H. Voges-Proskauer reaction
I. Citrate
J. β-Galactosidase
K. Acid from lactose
L. Hydrogen sulfide
M. Urease
N. Gelatinase
O. Indole
P. Lysine decarboxylase
Q. Ornithine decarboxylase
R. Phenylalanine deaminase
S. Motile
T. Red pigments
U. Fluorescent pigments
V. Growth at 37° C

Test Results

Test

ORGANISM	A	B	C	D	E	F	G	H	I	J	K	L	M	N	O	P	Q	R	S	T	U	V
0	+	+	+	+	−	+	+	−	+	+	+	+	+	−	−	−	−	−	+	−	−	+
1	+	+	+	+	−	+	−	+	+	+	+	−	−	+	+	+	+	−	+	−	−	+
2	+	+	+	+	−	+	+	−	−	+	+	−	−	−	+	+	−	−	+	−	−	+
3	+	+	+	+	−	+	−	+	+	+	+	−	+	−	−	+	−	−	−	−	−	+
4	+	+	+	+	−	+	+	−	+	−	−	+	+	+	+	−	−	+	+	−	−	+
5	+	−	−	+	+	+	−	−	−	−	−	−	+	+	−	−	−	−	+	−	+	+
6	+	+	+	+	−	+	+	−	+	−	−	+	−	−	−	+	+	−	+	−	−	+
7	+	+	−	+	−	+	−	+	+	+	−	−	−	+	−	+	+	−	+	+	−	+
8	+	+	−	+	−	+	+	−	−	−	−	−	−	−	−	−	−	−	−	−	−	+
9	+	+	−	+	−	+	+	−	−	+	−	−	+	−	−	−	+	−	+	−	−	+

+, Positive test result; −, negative test result; blank, indeterminate test result.

3. Create a key for separating the following bacterial genera: *Bacillus, Clostridium, Escherichia, Enterobacter, Streptococcus,* and *Staphylococcus.*
4. Consider that the following 30 bacterial species represent all the possible bacteria that may occur in the specimens received by a laboratory for identification.

Bacillus cereus
Bacillus firmus
Bacillus licheniformis
Bacillus stearothermophilus
Bacillus subtilis
Citrobacter freundii
Clostridium perfringens
Clostridium sporogenes
Enterobacter aerogenes
Enterobacter cloacae
Escherichia coli
Micrococcus luteus
Micrococcus roseus
Mycobacterium gastri
Mycobacterium phlei
Mycobacterium smegmatis
Mycobacterium terrae
Planococcus citreus
Proteus mirabilis
Proteus vulgaris
Pseudomonas aeruginosa
Pseudomonas flava
Pseudomonas fluorescens
Salmonella typhimurium
Serratia marcescens
Shigella flexneri
Staphylococcus aureus
Staphylococcus epidermidis
Streptococcus faecalis
Streptococcus lactis

Using any edition of *Bergey's Manual,* look up the characteristic features of these species. The tests that you probably want to consider are as follows:

Morphological features
Colony color
Cell shape
Cell arrangement
Gram-stain reaction
Acid-fast stain reaction
Endospore stain reaction
Capsule stain
Motility
Physiological features
Aerobic growth
Anaerobic growth
Catalase production
Cytochrome oxidase production
Growth temperature range and optimum
pH growth range
Glucose fermentation (acid and gas)
Galactose fermentation (acid and gas)
Lactose fermentation (acid and gas)
Maltose fermentation (acid and gas)
Sucrose fermentation (acid and gas)
Amylase production (starch hydrolysis)
Citrate utilization
DNase
Gelatinase
Blood hemolysis reactions (alpha and beta hemolysis)
Indole production
Lysine decarboxylase
Methyl Red reaction
Voges-Proskauer reaction
Ornithine decarboxylase
Phenylalanine deaminase
Hydrogen sulfide production

Beginning with the Gram-stain reaction, select the features that will enable you to separate the species in the most efficient manner, that is, using the fewest number of tests, and construct an unambiguous dichotomous key that can be used to identify any of these bacteria that may occur in the specimen.

Suggested Supplementary Readings

Balows A, HG Truper, M Dworkin, W Harder, K-H Schleifer: 1992. *The Prokaryotes,* ed. 2, Springer-Verlag, New York.

Baumann P, L Baumann, MJ Woolkalis, SS Bang: 1983. Evolutionary relationships in *Vibrio* and *Photobacterium:* A basis for a natural classification, *Annual Review of Microbiology* 37:369-398.

Campbell I and JH Duffus (eds.): 1988. *Yeast: A Practical Approach,* IRL Press, Oxford, England.

Delwiche EA, JJ Pestka, ML Tortorello: 1985. The Veillonellae: Gram-negative cocci with a unique physiology, *Annual Review of Microbiology* 39:175-193.

Gerhardt P (ed.): 1994. *Manual of Methods for General Bacteriology,* American Society for Microbiology, Washington, D.C.

Ghiorse WC: 1984. Biology of iron- and manganese-depositing bacteria, *Annual Review of Microbiology* 38:515-550.

Harwood CS and E Canale-Parola: 1984. Ecology of spirochetes, *Annual Review of Microbiology* 38:161-192.

Holt J (ed.): 1994. *Bergey's Manual of Determinative Bacteriology,* ed. 9, Williams & Wilkins Co., Baltimore.

Jones WJ, DP Nagle Jr, WB Whitman: 1987. Methanogens and the diversity of archaeobacteria, *Microbiological Reviews* 51:135-77.

Krieg NR and J Holt (eds.): 1984. *Bergey's Manual of Systematic Bacteriology,* Volume 1, Williams & Wilkins Co., Baltimore.

Larkin JM and WR Strohl: 1983. *Beggiatoa, Thiothrix,* and *Thioploca, Annual Review of Microbiology* 37:341-367.

Moore RL: 1983. The biology of *Hyphomicrobium* and other prosthecate, budding bacteria, *Annual Review of Microbiology* 37:567-594.

Poindexter JS: 1981. The caulobacters: Ubiquitous unusual bacteria, *Microbiological Reviews* 45:123-179.

Reichenbach H: 1983. Taxonomy of the gliding bacteria, *Annual Review of Microbiology* 37:339-364.

Schlegel HG and B Bowien: 1989. *Autotrophic Bacteria,* Science Tech Publishers, Madison, WI.

Schleifer KH and E Stackebrandt: 1983. Molecular systematics of prokaryotes, *Annual Review of Microbiology* 37:143-187.

Shewan JM and TA McMeekin: 1983. Taxonomy (and ecology) of *Flavobacterium* and related genera, *Annual Review of Microbiology* 37:233-252.

Skerman VBD, V McGowan, PHA Sneath (eds.): 1980. Approved lists of bacterial names, *International Journal of Systematic Bacteriology* 36:225-420.

Skinner FA and DW Lovelock: 1980. *Identification Methods for Microbiologists,* Academic Press, New York.

Sneath PHA, NS Mair, ME Sharpe, J Holt (eds.): 1986. *Bergey's Manual of Systematic Bacteriology,* Volume 2, Williams & Wilkins Co., Baltimore.

Sneath PHA: 1992. *International Code of Nomenclature of Bacteria,* American Society for Microbiology, Washington, D.C.

Sokatch JR (ed.): 1986. *The Biology of* Pseudomonas, Academic Press, Orlando, FL.

Staley JT, MP Bryant, N Pfennig, J Holt (eds.): 1989. *Bergey's Manual of Systematic Bacteriology,* Vol. 3, Williams & Wilkins, Baltimore.

Starr MP, H Stolp, HG Truper, A Ballows, HG Schlegel (eds.): 1981. *The Prokaryotes: A Handbook on Habits, Isolation, and Identification of Bacteria,* Springer-Verlag, Berlin.

Thornsberry C, A Balows, JC Feeley, W Jakubowski: 1984. *Legionella,* American Society for Microbiology, Washington, D.C.

Weiss E: 1984. The biology of rickettsiae, *Annual Review of Microbiology* 36:345-370.

Whitcomb RF: 1980. The genus *Spiroplasma, Annual Review of Microbiology* 34:677-709.

Williams ST, ME Sharpe, J Holt (eds.): 1989. *Bergey's Manual of Systematic Bacteriology,* Volume 4, Williams & Wilkins Co., Baltimore.

Woese CR: 1981. Archaebacteria, *Scientific American* 244(6):98-122.

Woese CR: 1985. Why study evolutionary relationships among bacteria? In *Evolution of Prokaryotes,* FEMS Symposium 29, (KH Scheifer and E Stackebrandt, eds.), pp. 1-30, Academic Press, London.

Woese CR and RS Wolfe (eds.): 1985. *The Archaebacteria,* Academic Press, Orlando, FL.

CHAPTER 17

Eukaryotes

Chapter Outline

Fungi, algae, and protozoa, which are the eukaryotic microorganisms, evolved along three distinct lines of nutrient and cellular energy acquisition. The algae carry out photosynthesis to form cellular ATP. Protozoa acquire nutrients and energy through ingestion of organic compounds, often using phagocytosis to bring nutrients into the cell. The fungi absorb nutrients.

The eukaryotic microorganisms evolved extensive intracellular compartmentalization, multicellularity, and sexuality. Many of these microorganisms exhibit asexual and sexual reproduction, producing various sexual and asexual spores. Fungi typically form filamentous mycelia, but one group, the yeasts, are characteristically unicellular. The fungi are classified largely on the basis of their modes of reproduction. The sexual spores of fungi are the most important features used in their classification and identification. The algae are classified largely on the basis of pigment production and the biochemical nature of the storage reserve materials. The protozoa are classified largely on their modes of locomotion.

17.1 FUNGI

Fungi are heterotrophic eukaryotic microorganisms. They are nonphotosynthetic and typically form reproductive spores. The mitochondria of fungal cells, which are sites of energy transformations, are derived from eubacteria probably as a result of symbiotic relations in which purple nonsulfur bacteria lived within the early eukaryotic cells.

Most fungi obtain their nutrition by absorption of nutrients that are transported across the cytoplasmic membrane into the cell. Most are *saprophytes,* obtaining their nutrients from dead organic material. In nature, fungi are important decomposers. Trees and leaves that fall in the forest are decomposed in large part by fungi. Many fungi produce enzymes that attack plant polymers, such as cellulose and lignin. They also can grow in relatively dry locations. This enables them to decompose complex materials that are difficult for bacteria to attack. They can be observed growing fuzzy mats on rotting bread, fruits, and vegetables, and various other plant materials.

Vegetative structures (structures involved in nutrition and growth that are not specialized reproductive or dormant forms) of fungi are called *thalli* (singular, *thallus*). Some fungi are unicellular and others are multicellular. **Yeasts** are fungi that exist predominantly as unicellular organisms. The **filamentous fungi** or **molds** develop multicellular branching structures known as **hypha,** which are connected filaments of vegetative cells. Integrated masses of hyphae are called a **mycelium.** Hyphae may be separated into individual compartments by the formation of cross walls called *septa.* The hyphae usually exhibit branching and are typically surrounded by cell walls containing chitin or cellulose.

Fungi exhibit various reproductive strategies. Many fungi exhibit sexual and asexual forms of reproduction. The asexual reproduction of fungi may involve division of the parent cell into two equal sized cells, budding of the parent cell to form a smaller daughter cell, and the formation of spores. Most fungi exhibit life cycles in which various spores may be produced. Asexual spore formation occurs through mitosis and subsequent cell division.

GROWTH AND REPRODUCTION OF FUNGI

Most fungi are aseptate or have partially completed cross walls. When reproduction begins, specialized structures form that are cut off from the rest of the hypha by complete septa. These reproductive structures are **sporangia,** which form asexual spores, or **gametangia,** in which sexual gametes form. Spores may be formed as a result of asexual or sexual processes. They may be motile or nonmotile. Nonmotile spores released from the mother cell may remain suspended in the air for quite some time due to their light weight and small size. If a spore lands in an environment that can support growth, it germinates into a new fungal hypha.

Fungal nuclei are usually haploid, except during reproduction. There may be many hybrid nuclei in the cytoplasm of nonseptated (aseptate) hyphae or a period in the life cycle during which the fungus is diploid. Sexual reproduction in fungi involves the fusion of two genetically different nuclei. In some fungal groups, the two genetically different nuclei may co-exist in the cytoplasm and not fuse immediately. Hyphae that contain genetically different nuclei are called *heterokaryotic* and hyphae that contain genetically similar nuclei are called *homokaryotic.* In septate hyphae, individual cells that contain two genetically different nuclei are *dikaryotic* and individual cells that contain one nucleus are *monokaryotic.*

Fungal mitosis is different from mitosis in other eukaryotic cells. The chromosomes are retained in the nucleus—the nuclear membrane does not break down—and spindle fibers form within the nucleus. All fungi lack centrioles. They produce microtubules from small structures called spindle plaques.

Yeasts

The most common mode of reproduction for yeasts is *budding*—a process in which a daughter cell is formed by pinching off a segment of the mother cell (FIG. 17-1). Budding involves the formation of a cross wall that separates the bud from the mother cell. The cross wall of *Saccharomyces,* for example, consists of chitin, which does not occur elsewhere in the cell wall. Budding follows mitotic division, so that both the progeny and the parent cell contain a complete genome. Budding can occur all around the mother cell *(multilateral budding)* or may be restricted to the end *(polar budding)* (FIG. 17-2). The budding process leaves a bud scar on the mother cell, and consequently, only a limited number of progeny may be derived from an individual yeast cell. Although budding is the most common form of reproduction, various other reproductive strategies exist among the yeasts, including sexual reproduction and fission.

Filamentous Fungi

The growth of the filamentous fungi involves the elongation of the hyphae, generally with the formation of branches and cross walls separating individual cells. Some fungi, however, form multinucleate **coenocytic mycelia** that lack cross walls; therefore these fungi are actually one-celled, multinucleate organisms. Some fungi reproduce as a unicellular organism, appear

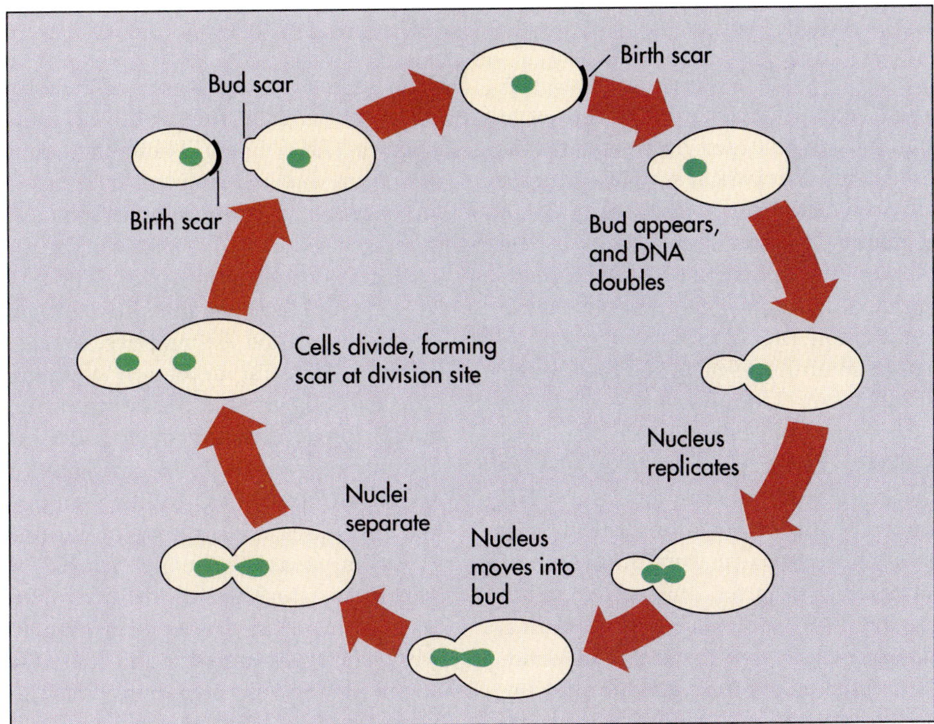

FIG. 17-1 Asexual reproduction in yeast by budding.

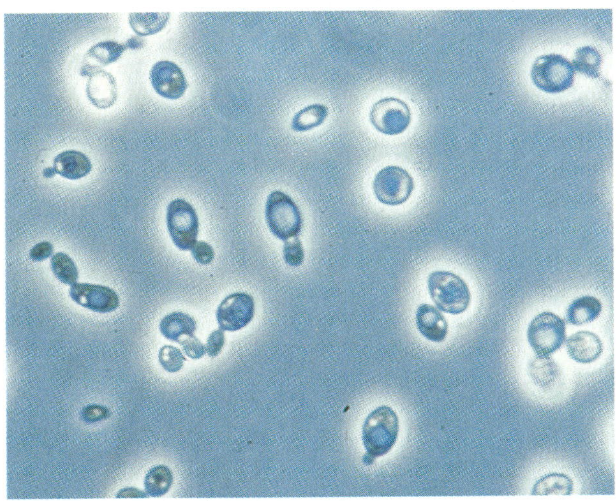

FIG. 17-2 Micrograph of *Saccharomyces cerevisiae* showing multilateral budding.

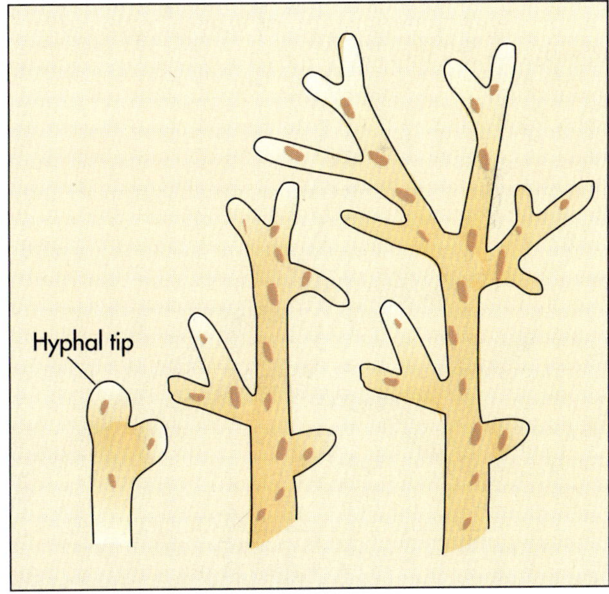

FIG. 17-3 Filamentous fungi reproduce by hyphal extension. Here, growth (illustrated at 30-minute intervals) of a hyphal tip of *Gelasinospora autosteira.*

yeast-like under some conditions, and grow as a filamentous form under other conditions. This alternating growth is called **dimorphism.** Dimorphism is especially common among fungi that cause human diseases.

Because filamentous fungi form elongated filaments, growth can occur in the absence of reproduction. Growth requires an increase in biomass, but unlike reproduction, cellular division does not always occur. In filamentous fungi, growth normally originates from the hyphal tip (FIG. 17-3). The apical growth of a fungal hypha requires that the necessary polymers be transported to the area of new cell wall synthesis, and in eukaryotes this area generally contains a large number of microfibrils that are involved in cell wall synthesis.

Enumeration of Fungi

Defining the number of fungi is often a difficult task because individual organisms frequently represent multicellular aggregations that can be considered as one or many individuals. The task is simplest when it involves yeasts that can be enumerated by using viable count or direct count procedures analogous to the procedures for the enumeration of bacteria. Enumeration of the filamentous fungi is far more difficult. Plate count enumeration procedures are biased toward fungal spores and underestimate the number of cells in a hyphal filament. The enumeration of filamentous fungi can be accomplished by determining the length of hyphae, which is considered a measure of fungal biomass, rather than the number of individual cells. Direct microscopic observations with the aid of a micrometer can be used to measure the length of hyphae. This approach, however, has some limitations. Fungi growing in an aqueous solution lacking growth nutrients can exhibit rapid growth of individual hyphae but minimal change in total biomass because the density of the hyphae is sparse. It is probably best, therefore, to determine the biomass of filamentous fungi by measuring the dry weight or a specific biochemical component of the cell walls, such as chitin. With filamentous fungi, a change in biomass is the appropriate measure of growth, rather than a change in cell numbers.

Fungal Spores

During the asexual phase of fungal reproduction, various spores may be produced, depending on the species (FIG. 17-4). These include various **conidia,** which are asexual spores borne externally on hyphae or specialized **conidiophore** structures. Conidia are not enclosed in a specialized structure but are formed at the tips or sides of hyphae. The conidia can be separated from the fungal hypha as single cells. One type of conidium, the **arthrospore,** represents fragmented hyphae. The fragmentation of multicellular eukaryotic microorganisms constitutes a form of reproduction because the individual fragments are each capable of reproducing the original organism. These spores are not resistant to heat and desiccation as are the endospores of some bacterial species.

Other asexual fungal spores include **sporangiospores,** which are produced within a sac-like structure known as the **sporangium; chlamydospores,** which are thick-walled spores that occur within hyphal segments; and **blastospores,** which are produced by budding. These fungal spores can be dispersed from the fungal hyphae and later germinate to form new mycelia.

Fungi also can produce various types of sexual reproductive spores. Some sexual spores of fungi, **ascospores,** are formed within a specialized structure known as the **ascus** (FIG. 17-5). The ability to produce

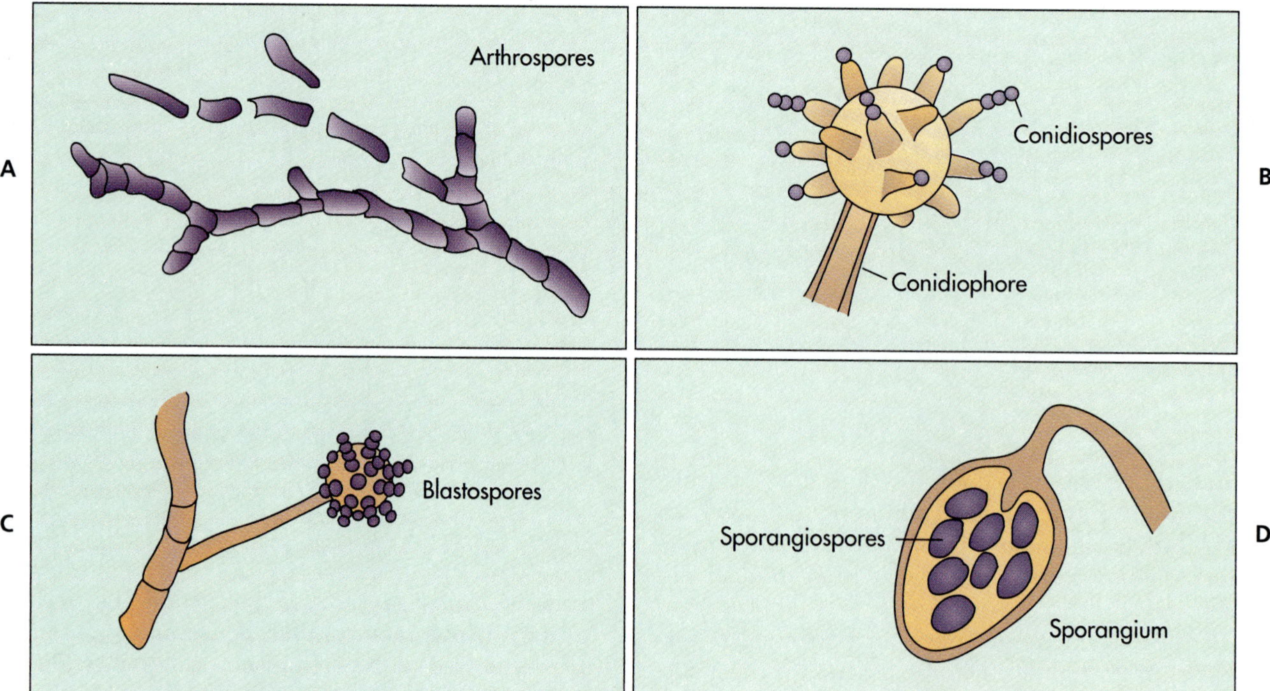

FIG. 17-4 Various asexual spores produced by fungi. **A,** Arthrospores; **B,** conidiophore and conidiospores; **C,** blastospores; and **D,** sporangium and sporangiospores.

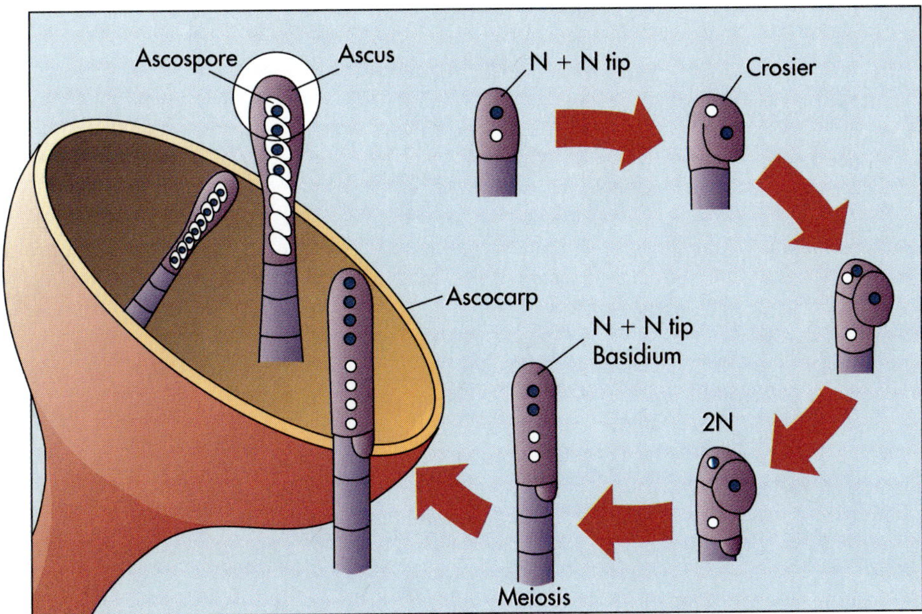

FIG. 17-5 Sexual reproduction in ascomycete fungi is characterized by the formation of ascospores. The diagram shows the formation of ascospores within a heterothallic ascomycete, an orange-cup fungus. Dark and light *(purple)* nuclei *(N)* represent the two compatible mating types.

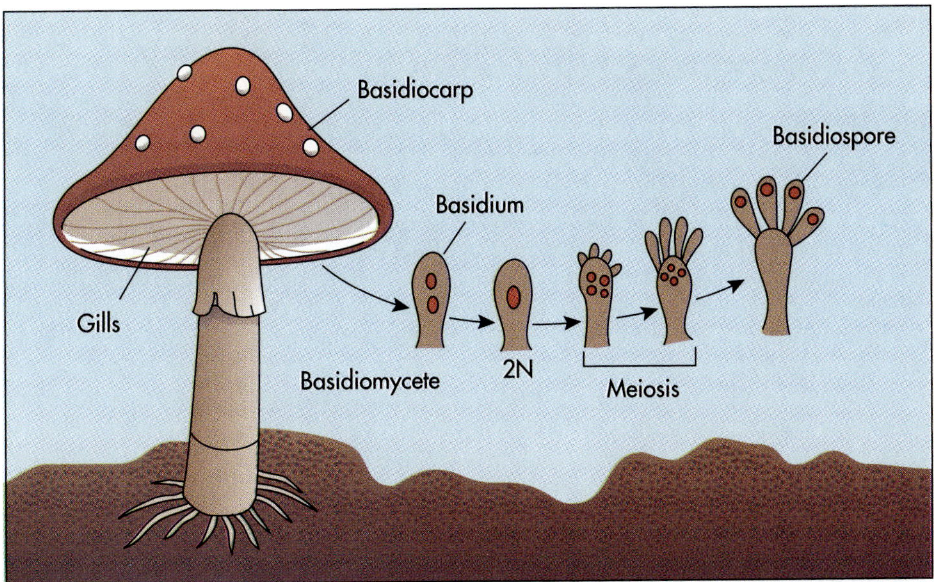

FIG. 17-6 Sexual reproduction in basidiomycete fungi is characterized by the formation of basidiospores. These sexual spores are formed on a basidium.

ascospores distinguishes the Ascomycetes, which includes yeasts and filamentous fungi, from other fungi. In another major group of fungi, the **Basidiomycetes,** the sexual spores **(basidiospores)** are produced on a specialized structure known as the **basidium** (FIG. 17-6). The sexual reproduction of Basidiomycetes usually involves the fusion of hyphal cells. In several other fungal groups, sexual reproduction generally occurs by fusion of *gametes* (FIG. 17-7, p. 698). These gametes are haploid, and their fusion reestablishes a diploid state. In some cases, the gametes are motile; in other cases, such as bread molds, only nonmotile reproductive gametes are formed. The Deuteromycetes, or *Fungi Imperfecti,* have no known sexual reproductive phase, and as far as we know, they are restricted to asexual means of reproduction. If a sexual stage is discovered for a fungus that has been classified among the *Fungi Imperfecti,* it is reclassified into one of the other major fungal groups on the basis of the type of sexual spores that are produced.

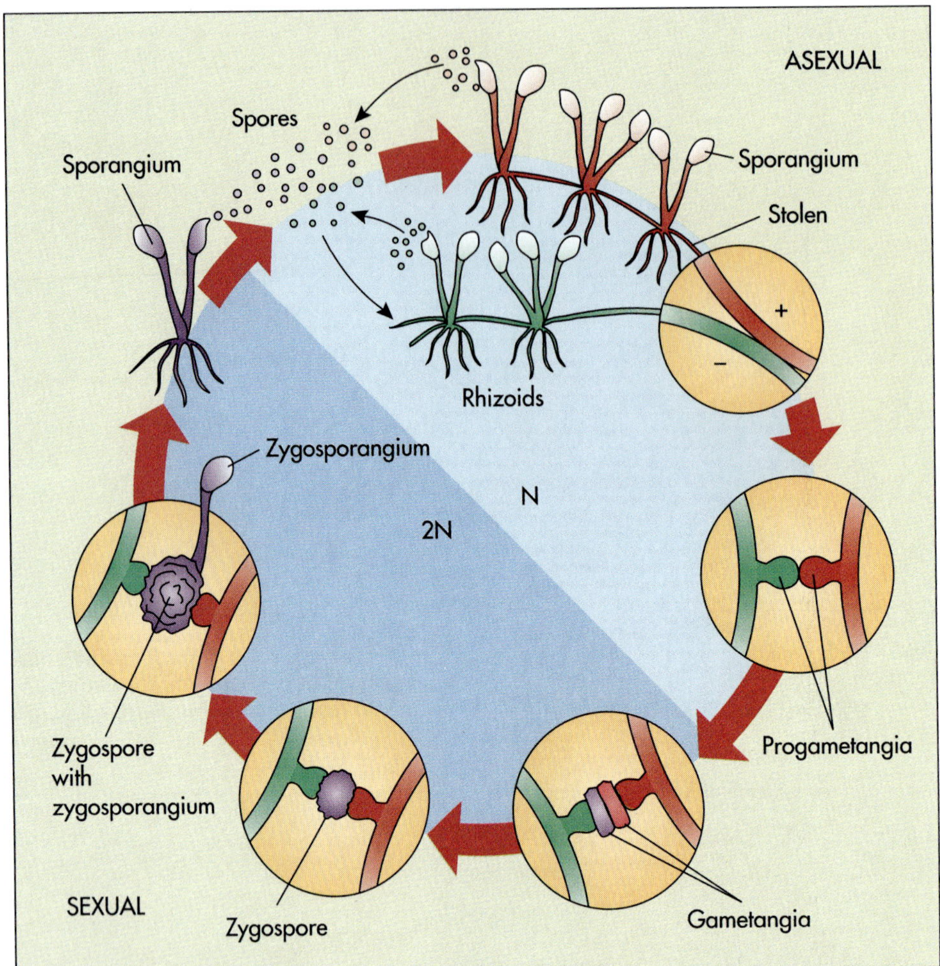

FIG. 17-7 The life cycle of *Rhizopus stolonifer* showing asexual and sexual reproduction. During asexual reproduction, a mycelium arises from the outgrowth of a fungal spore. When the mycelium reaches a specific size, aerial hyphae form bearing sporangia filled with haploid spores. After dissemination, these spores give rise to new mycelial mats. During sexual reproduction, when the subsurface hyphae of two different mating types meet, they fuse together and form a zygospore.

Classification of Fungi

By a concise definition, the fungi are achlorophyllous, saprophytic or parasitic, with unicellular or more typically filamentous vegetative structures usually surrounded by cell walls composed of chitin or other polysaccharides; propagation is by spores, and fungi normally exhibit both asexual and sexual reproduction. If this definition seems complex and vague, it is; a broad definition is necessary to accommodate all of the morphological and physiological anomalies that occur among the fungi.

The classification of fungi is based largely on the means of reproduction, including the nature of the life cycle, reproductive structures, and reproductive spores. The primary taxonomic groupings are based on the sexual reproductive spores. To a lesser extent, the classification of fungi relies on the morphological characteristics of the vegetative cells. Most classical approaches to fungal classification are based largely on observation of the morphology of the reproductive forms, but physiological, biochemical, and genetic characteristics are included in some modern classification systems. Physiological features are particularly important in the classification of yeasts, which are primarily unicellular fungi.

In a formal systematic sense, yeasts are not recognized as being separate from the rest of the fungi and are classified with their filamentous counterparts. In practice, however, the yeasts are typically treated separately from the filamentous fungi in classification and identification systems. Separate classification and identification systems, for example, have been developed that include only the yeasts. Revisions of yeast systematics are published in the *International Journal of Systematic Bacteriology* rather than in the mycological lit-

BOX 17-1

History of Mycology

Some fungi form macroscopic structures, which made it possible to observe them before the invention of the microscope. Fungi were used and studied from early times. The ancient Romans knew which fungi were epicurean delicacies, which were lethal, and which had hallucinogenic effects. Hooke's *Micrographia* (1665) included illustrations of microscopic fungi. Yeasts are recognizable in the drawings of Leeuwenhoek. The first book solely about fungi was the *Theatrum Fungorum* by Johannes Franciscus Van Starbeeck in 1675, using the drawings Charles de l'Escluse (also known as Clusius) prepared in 1601. The fungi *Rhizopus, Mucor,* and *Penicillium* are identifiable in the 1679 drawings of Marcello Malpighi.

The science of mycology (the study of fungi) however, probably owes its origins to Pier Antonio Micheli, an Italian botanist who, in 1729, published *Nova Plantarum Genera,* which included his studies on fungi. Almost half of the plants Micheli described were fungi, and many of the generic names still used today were first presented in this study. Micheli's most important contribution was the observation of the production of spores and the demonstration that the spores reproduced plants similar to their parent. Heinrich Anton deBary made major contributions to the field of mycology in his studies on plant pathology. He elucidated the life cycles of many rusts. In 1885, deBary proved that the blight that caused the great Irish potato famine of the preceding decade was caused by a fungus; this was one of the earliest demonstrations that a specific fungus can be the causative agent of plant disease.

A practical system of classification of the *Fungi Imperfecti* (fungi that do not exhibit sexual reproductive phases according to spore groups) was developed by Pier Andrea Saccardo, who also collaborated on the 25-volume *Sylloge Fungorum* (1882–1925), which critically compiled most of the literature on fungal systematics published before 1920. In the early twentieth century, A. H. R. Buller also published a major monograph on fungal systematics. The first major compilation of yeast systematics was published in 1896 by Emil Hansen; this taxonomic system was greatly revised by A. Guilliermond between 1920 and 1928. The systematics proposed by Hansen and Guilliermond included the use of physiological, sexual, and phylogenetic relationships, as well as morphological observations, to determine classification. These characteristics, supplemented by direct analyses of fungal genetic information, form the basis of today's classification of the fungi.

The investigation of fungal genetics by Beadle and Tatum in the 1940s greatly advanced the understanding of chromosomes and their functioning. *Neurospora crassa,* a member of the Ascomycetes, forms sexual spores in a specialized structure called an ascus. The nuclei from male and female (or sexually compatable) cells unite in the ascus and, through meiotic and mitotic divisions of the DNA, form eight linearly ordered ascospores—a pair of duplicate nuclei (spores) in a tetrad derived from the meiotic division of each zygote nucleus. Tetrad analysis allows an understanding of the process of crossing-over and recombination between DNA strands and an important system for studying the segregation of genetic factors after meiosis.

Fungi, such as the yeast, *Saccharomyces cerevisiae,* the molds, *Neurospora crassa* and *Aspergillus flavus* and others have been examined to further the understanding of eukaryotic molecular genetics. More recently, the yeast, *Saccharomyces cerevisiae,* have been used as host cells for the expression of viral, prokaryotic, and eukaryotic genes by recombinant DNA technology (see Chapter 15). This is especially useful for the development of recombinant vaccines such as for Hepatitis B.

erature. Commercial clinical systems are also available for identifying pathogenic yeasts. Similarly, separate classification and identification systems have been developed for other groups of fungi, such as the mushrooms. Such systems are very important because of their functional utility for identification purposes, even if they do not follow a formal taxonomic scheme based on phylogenetic relationships.

Chytridiomycetes

Chytridiomycetes produce zoospores, which are motile with a single posterior flagellum of the whiplash type. Some, such as *Olpidium brassicae,* which infects cabbage roots, cause plant diseases. Some are obligate parasites of other fungi, algae, and plants. They cause abnormally swollen structures called *galls,* which are the result of *hypertrophy* (increase of size of cells), hyperplasia (increase in number of cells), or both. Some of these fungi develop within the host cells of plants. Some cause diseases of plants that are of economic significance. For example, *Plasmodiophora brassicae* causes clubfoot of cabbage and *Spongospora subterranea* causes powdery scab of potatoes.

Oomycetes

Oomycetes, known as the *water molds,* reproduce by using flagellated zoospores. The zoospores typically have two flagella, each with a different morphology. Sexual reproduction in the oomycetes typically involves the formation of *oospores,* which are thick-walled spores that develop by contact with specialized *gametangia* (structures containing differentiated cells in-

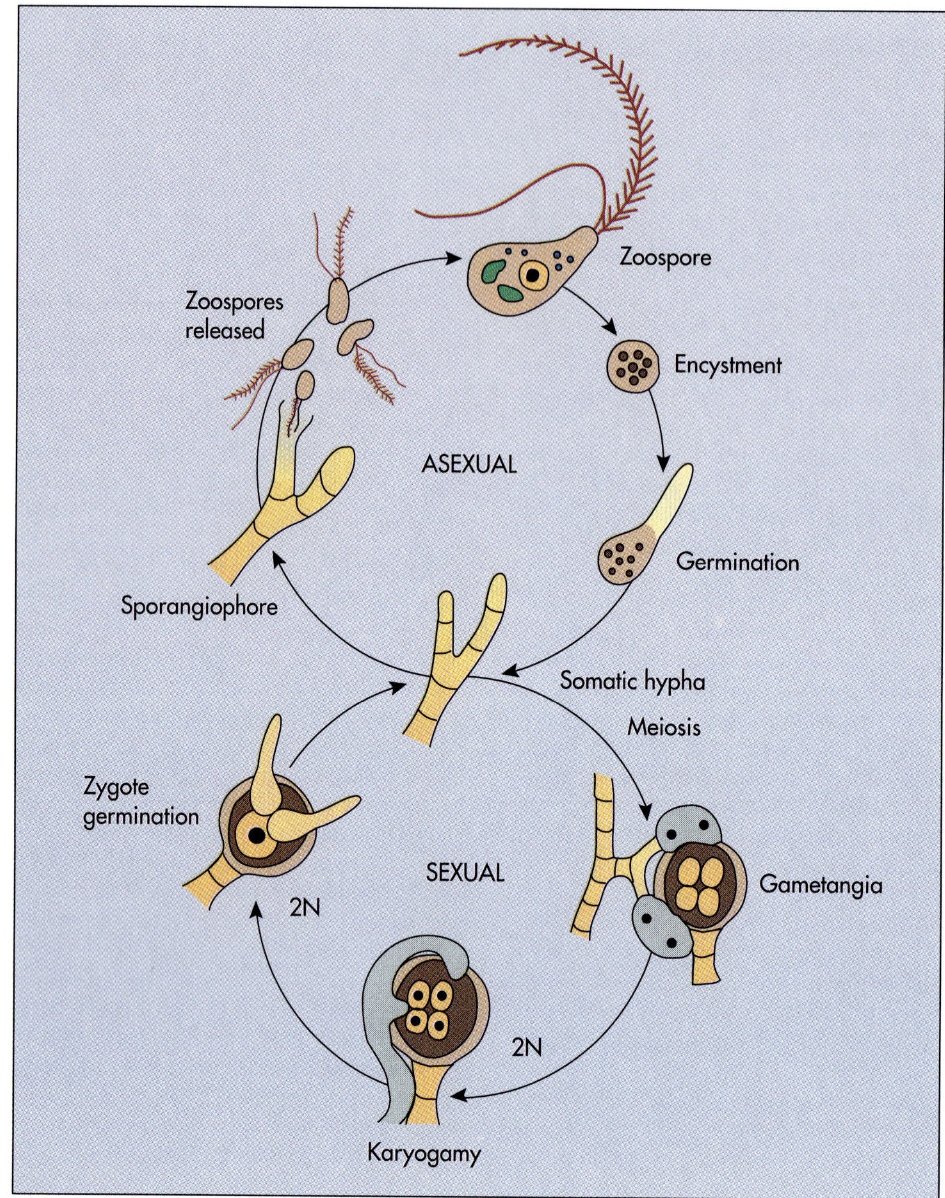

FIG. 17-8 The life cycle of the oomycete (water molds) fungus *Phytophthora infestans.*

volved in sexual reproduction). The gametangia of oomycetes normally occur at the terminal ends of the mycelia. During gametangial contact, male gametes pass through a fertilization tube into the female gametangia (FIG. 17-8). The male gametangium is referred to as an *antheridium* and the female gametangium as an *oogonium.* Several species in this order are animal and plant pathogens. For example, *Phytophthora infestans* causes potato blight and was responsible for the great Irish potato famine of 1845 and 1846, which resulted in the great wave of immigration from Ireland to the United States.

Zygomycetes

Zygomycetes typically have coenocytic mycelia, that is, mycelia that lack septa and, hence, contain multiple nuclei within the cytoplasm. This group is characterized by the formation of a zygospore, a sexual spore that results from the fusion of gametangia. For sexual reproduction (zygote formation), some species require gametangia of two different mating types (*heterothallic*) and others require only one type (*homothallic*). In addition to sexual reproduction, the Zygomycetes characteristically produce asexual sporangiospores within a sporangium. Many are plant or animal pathogens.

Rhizopus stolonifer is a common bread mold (FIG. 17-9). Some *Rhizopus* species are important in the food industry. For example, *R. oryzae* is used for the production of fermented Oriental foods such as tempeh. Other *Rhizopus* species are important causes of food spoilage, such as the rotting of strawberries.

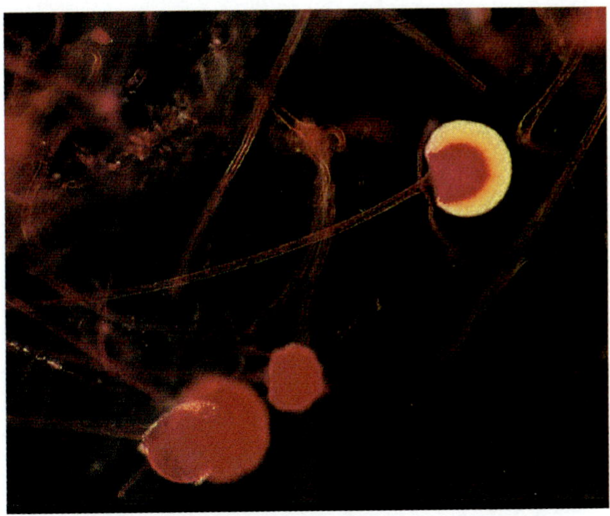

FIG. 17-9 Micrograph of *Rhizopus* species.

Several species of Mucorales exhibit *dimorphism.* For example, *Mucor rouxii* grows in a yeast-like form in atmospheres with a high percentage of carbon dioxide but produces filamentous mycelia at normal atmospheric concentrations of CO_2. *Mucor* species are important opportunistic human pathogens and can cause serious infections in burn wounds. The genus *Pilobolus* also occurs in the order Mucorales. *Pilobolus* species are interesting because of their forceful mode of spore discharge, shooting their spores several meters into the air, with the entire spore cluster ejected in the direction of highest light intensity (FIG. 17-10).

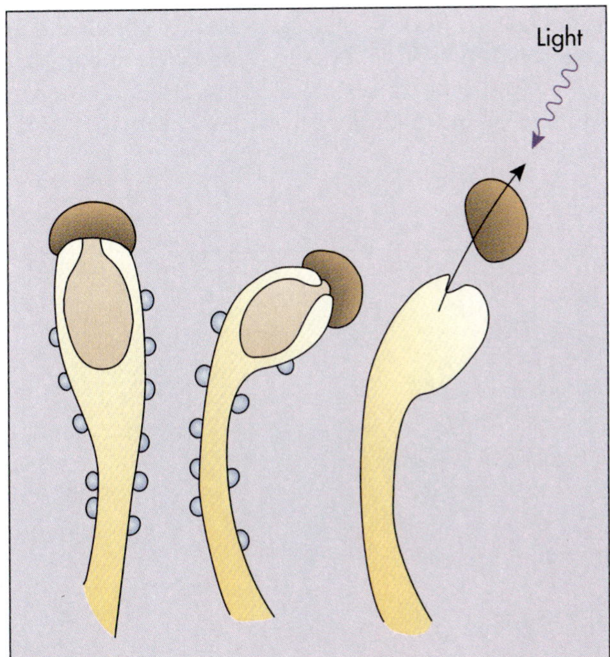

FIG. 17-10 During the spore discharge by *Philobolus,* the spore mass is forcefully ejected toward an area of high light intensity.

In this way, the spores of *Pilobolus* are released to an area of open air where air currents are likely to disperse them further.

Some Zygomycete species are obligately associated with arthropods and normally grow within the guts of these animals, where they attach to the chitinous lining of the gut by means of a specialized structure known as a *holdfast.*

Ascomycetes

Ascomycetes produce sexual spores within a specialized sac-like structure known as the **ascus.** They are sometimes called the sac fungi. Normally they produce a specific number of ascospores within the ascus. During sexual reproduction the Ascomycetes normally exhibit a short-lived dikaryotic stage (having cells containing two nuclei) between the time of fusion of gametes *(plasmogamy)* and the time of fusion of the two nuclei *(karyogamy).*

The mycelia of Ascomycetes is composed of septate hyphae, and the cell walls of the hyphae of most Ascomycetes contain chitin. Asexual reproduction in the Ascomycetes may be carried out by fission, fragmentation of the hyphae, formation of *chlamydospores* (thick-walled spores within the hyphal filaments), and production of conidia (nonmotile spores produced on a specialized spore-bearing cell).

Many yeasts are Ascomycetes (FIG. 17-11). The morphology of the ascospore is a critical taxonomic feature in classifying yeasts at the genus level (Table 17-1, p. 702). Classification of the yeasts at the species level normally employs numerous biochemical and physiological characteristics, as well as morphological features. The metabolic activities of the ascosporogenous yeasts have many industrial applications. *Saccharomyces cerevisiae* is used as baker's yeast. Many fer-

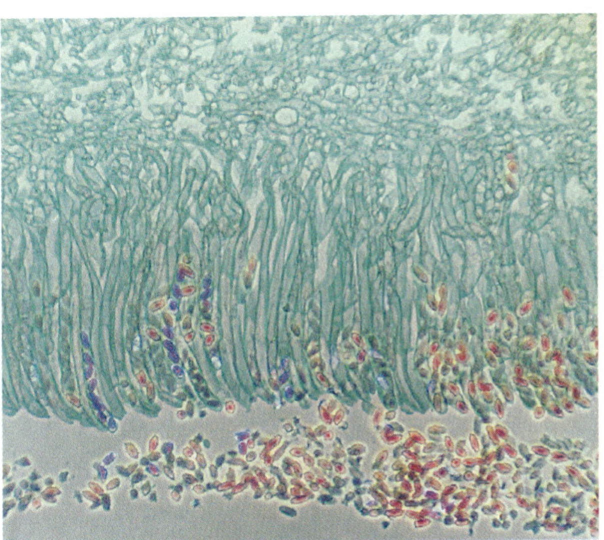

FIG. 17-11 Asci and ascospores of the black morel *Morchella elata.*

TABLE 17-1 Descriptions of Ascospores in Different Genera of Yeasts

GENUS	NUMBER OF ASCOSPORES	SHAPE OF ASCOSPORES
Citeromyces	1	Spheroidal
Coccidiascus	8	Fusiform
Debaryomyces	1-4	Spheroidal, ovoidal, warty
Dekkera	1-4	Hat-shaped
Endomycopsis	1-4	Spheroidal, hat-shaped, Saturn-shaped, sickle-shaped
Hanseniaspora	1-4	Hat-shaped, helmet-shaped, walnut-shaped
Hansenula	1-4	Hat-shaped, spheroidal, hemispherical, Saturn-shaped
Kluyveromyces	1-many	Crescentiform, reniform, spheroidal, ellipsoidal
Lipomyces	1-16	Ellipsoidal, lenticular
Lodderomyces	1-2	Oblong, ellipsoidal
Metschnikowia	1-2	Needle-shaped
Nadsonia	1-2	Spheroidal, warty
Nematospora	8	Spindle-shaped
Pachysolen	4	Hemispherical
Pichia	1-4	Spheroidal, hat-shaped, Saturn-shaped, warty
Saccharomyces	1-4	Spheroidal, ellipsoidal
Saccharomycodes	4	Spheroidal
Saccharomycopsis	1-4	Ovoidal, double-walled
Schizosaccharomyces	4-8	Spheroidal, ovoidal
Schwanniomyces	1-2	Walnut-shaped, warty
Wickerhamia	1-16	Cap-shaped
Wingea	1-4	Lens-shaped

mented beverages are also produced by using members of the genus *Saccharomyces.* Most commonly, *S. carlsbergensis* and *S. cerevisiae* are used for the production of beer, wine, and spirits.

The Taphrinales resemble yeasts in that they reproduce asexually by budding and sexually by producing ascospores but differ from the yeasts in that they produce a definite true mycelium. Members of the Taphrinales are parasitic on plants. For examples, *Taphrina deformans* causes peach leaf curl, *T. cerasi* causes witches' broom of cherries, *T. pruni* causes prune pockets, and *T. coerulescens* causes puckering of oak leaves.

The *true Ascomycetes* produce *asci* that normally develop from dikaryotic hyphae. The asci are produced in or on a structure known as the *ascocarp.* The Euascomycetes are divided according to the structure of the ascocarp into the Plectomycetes, in which the ascocarp has no special opening; the Pyrenomycetes, in which the ascocarp is shaped like a flask; and the Discomycetes, in which the ascocarp is cup-shaped (FIG. 17-12).

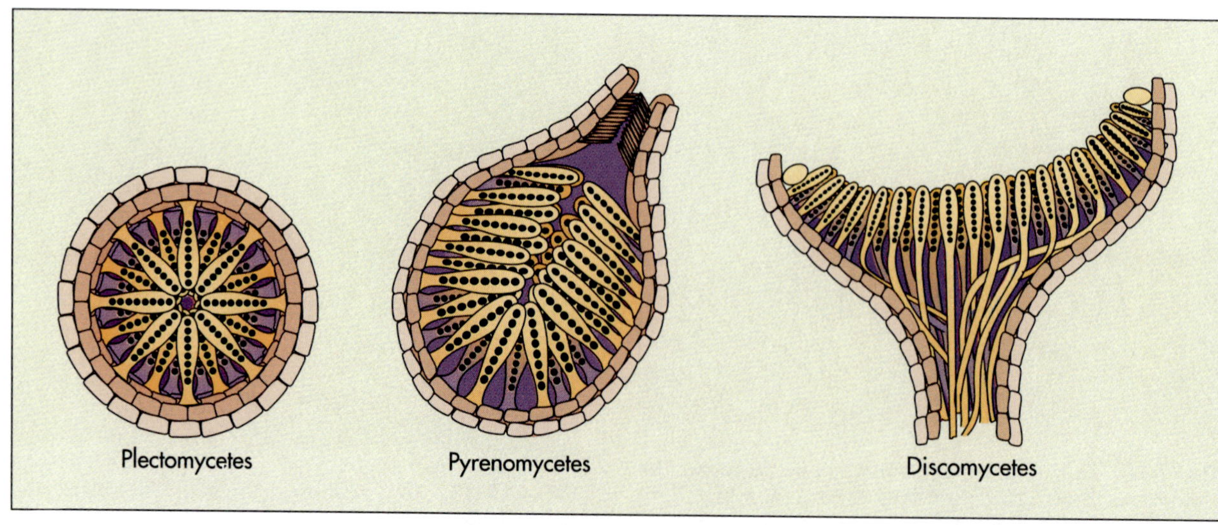

FIG. 17-12 Various ascocarps formed by different ascomycete fungi.

Species of Pyrenomyctes are important for their roles in basic scientific investigations. For example, studies on the genetics of *Neurospora*, a Pyrenomycete, have greatly added to our understanding of recombinational processes. *Neurospora* is useful in genetic studies because the spores can be isolated from the ascus and the genotypes readily determined. Some Pyrenomycetes are important plant and animal pathogens—the powdery and black mildews, for example, that occur in this taxonomic group. *Claviceps purpurea* causes ergot of rye; cattle and other animals are poisoned when grazing on grasses contaminated with the resting bodies—*sclerotia*—of the fungus. Sclerotia are hard resting bodies that are resistant to unfavorable conditions and may remain dormant for prolonged periods. Various alkaloid biochemicals are produced by *C. purpurea:* some have hallucinogenic properties and others are useful medicinals, such as those used to induce labor for childbirth. *Endothia parasitica*, another Pyrenomycete, is the causative agent of chestnut blight. This organism was introduced into North America from eastern Asia in the early twentieth century and quickly devastated the chestnut trees of the United States and Canada.

The Plectomycetes also include some important plant and animal pathogens, such as the black molds, blue molds, and ringworms. Several species of *Ceratocystis* are responsible for blue stain, which reduces the commercial value of lumber. *C. ulmi* is the causative agent of Dutch elm disease, a great threat to elm trees in North America. The fungus that causes the human disease histoplasmosis, *Emmonsiella capsulata*, also belongs to the subclass Plectomycetes. *Emmonsiella capsulata* was formerly known as *Histoplasma capsulatum* before the sexual reproductive stage of the organism was known, and some medical mycologists still retain the name of the imperfect (nonsexual) form when referring to this organism. This fungus commonly occurs in soils that are contaminated with fecal droppings from birds. Other fungi known by the names of their imperfect forms associated with the Plectomycetes include the well-known genera *Penicillium* and *Aspergillus*.

FIG. 17-13 The yellow morel *Morchella esculenta.*

The Discomycetes include the cup fungi, morels, and truffles. Species of the genus *Morchella* (morels) are gastronomical delights (FIG. 17-13). All morels are edible and delicious. (False morels that may be mistaken for morels are poisonous and nonedible.) Truffles occur in the order Tuberales and, like morels, are considered edible delicacies.

Basidiomycetes

Basidiomycetes are the most complex fungi. They include the smuts, rusts, jelly fungi, shelf fungi, stinkhorns, bird's nest fungi, puffballs, and mushrooms. The Basidiomycetes are distinguished from other fungi by the fact that they produce sexual spores, known as **basidiospores,** on the surfaces of specialized spore-producing structures, known as **basidia** (FIG. 17-14).

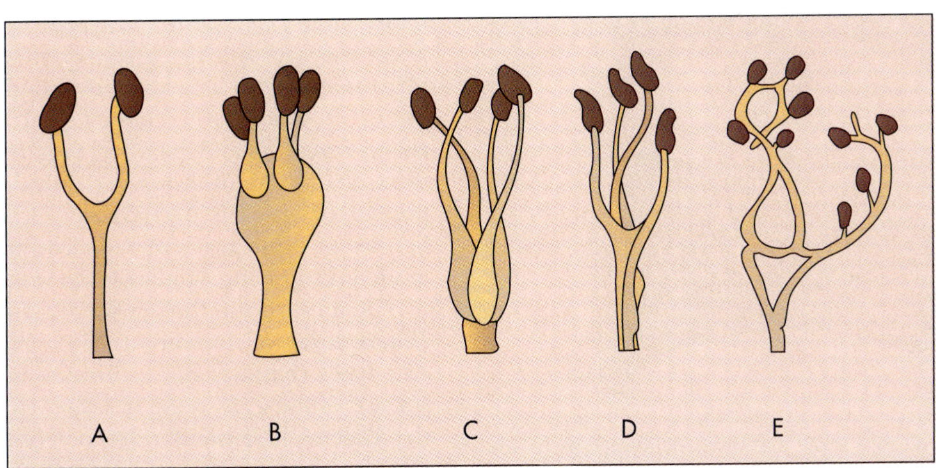

FIG. 17-14 Various basidia. **A,** tuning fork basidium of *Dacrymyces;* **B,** basidium of *Tulasnella;* **C,** basidium of *Tremella;* **D,** basidium of *Auricularia;* **E,** basidium of *Puccinia.*

Continued.

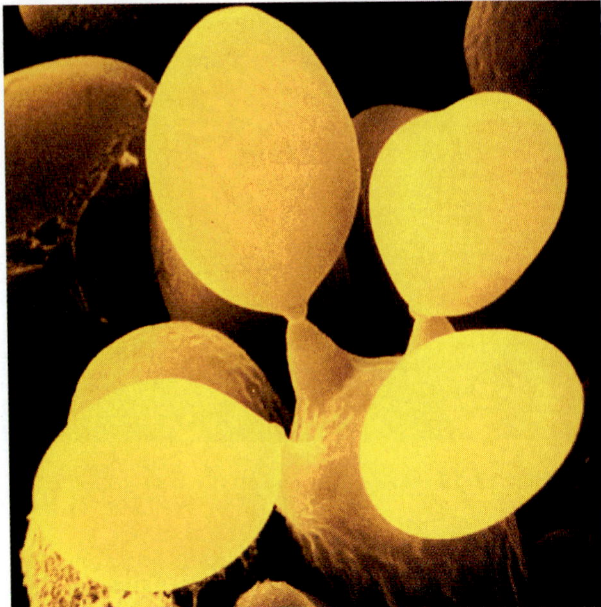

FIG. 17-14, cont'd F, Micrograph of the basidium and basidiospores of *Psilocybe mexicana*.

The Basidiomycetes are also known as the *club fungi* because of the typical shape of the basidia. The mycelia of Basidiomycetes typically form **clamp connections** between cells. The clamp cell connections are generally indicative of a dikaryotic mycelium. Additionally, the mycelia of many Basidiomycetes are characterized by specialized cross walls between connecting cells, known as *dolipore septa* (FIG. 17-15). The dolipore septum has a central pore surrounded by a barrel-shaped swelling of the cross wall. Effectively, the clamp cell connections and the dolipore septa permit enhanced chemical communication through the mycelia of the organism.

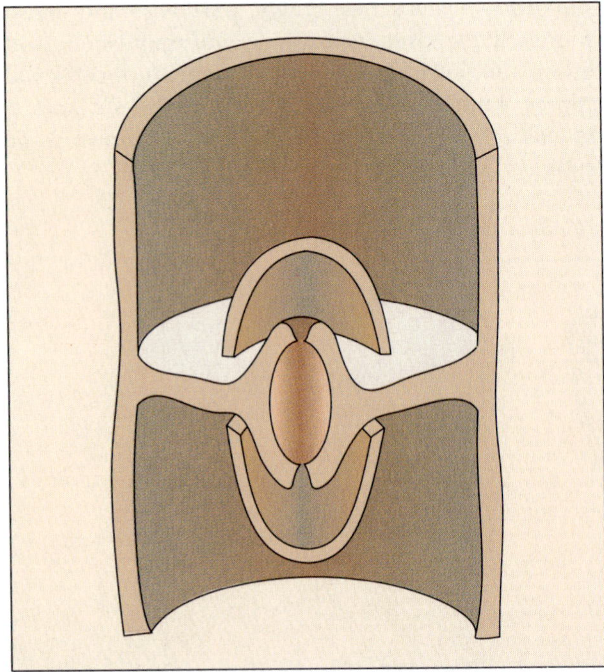

FIG. 17-15 Dolipore septa are formed by various basidiomycetes. A pore in the septum permits the flow of material from one cell to another.

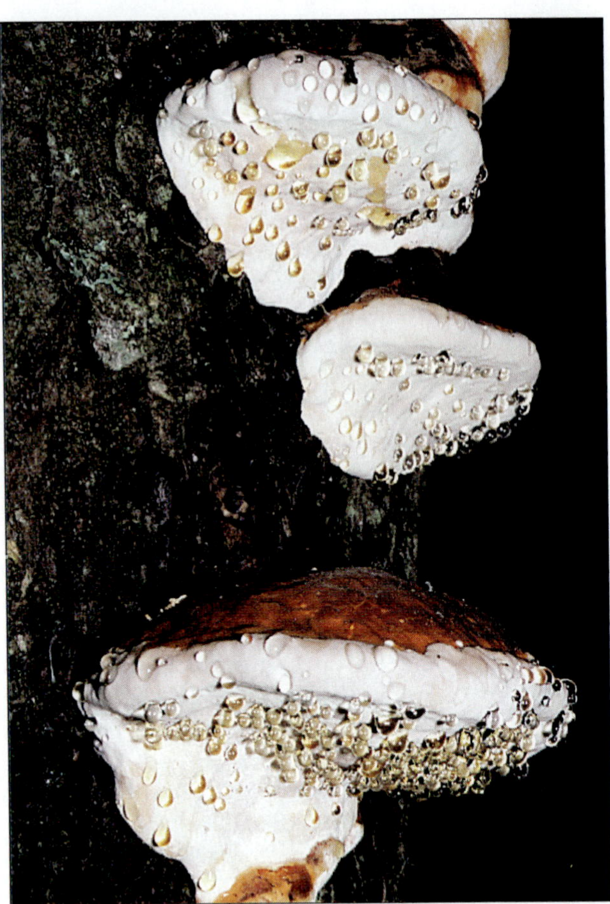

FIG. 17-16 The bracket fungus *Ischnoderma resinosum*.

The *shelf fungi* or *bracket fungi* are some of the most conspicuous fungi, often seen growing on trees (FIG. 17-16). The fruiting bodies of these fungi are tough and leathery. In addition to the bracket fungi, the Aphyllophorales includes cantharelles, coral fungi, tooth fungi, and pore fungi. The majority of these fungi are saprophytic, growing on dead and living plant materials. The growth on wood of fungi in this group results in two characteristic types of decay, called *brown rots* and *white rots* because of the color of the rotted wood. In brown rot, only the cellulose component of wood is decomposed, leaving the brown lignins. In white rot, both cellulose and lignin are degraded, producing white-colored wood.

The mushrooms that we see are the fruiting bodies *(basidiocarps)* of Basidiomycetes. The spore-bearing structures (basidia) of mushrooms are borne on the surface of the gills of the basidiocarp (FIG. 17-17). In the Boletes, the basidia are not borne on gills but rather within tubes. Some mushrooms are edible but others are extremely poisonous—making the proper

FIG. 17-17 The ink cap mushroom *Coprinus atrameutarius.*

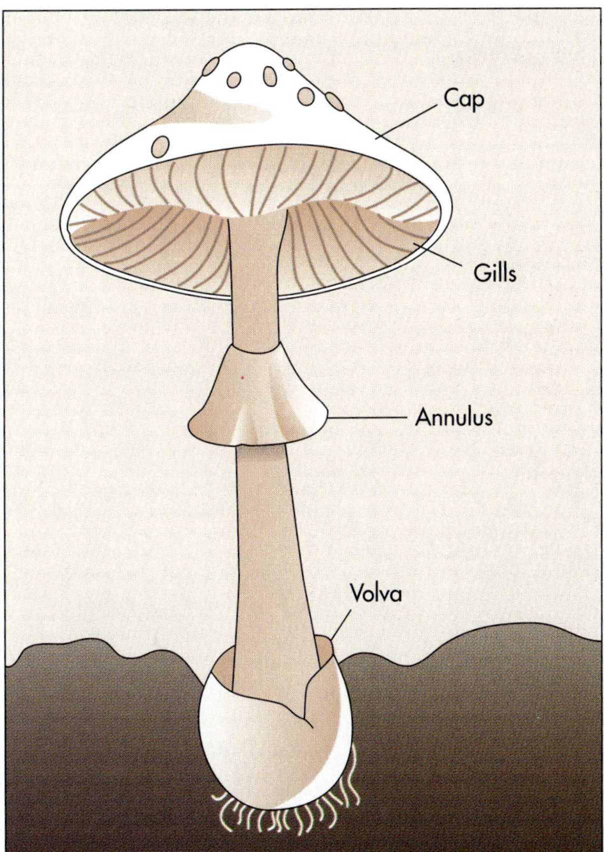

FIG. 17-18 The poisonous mushroom *Amanita* has a sac-like cup (volva) at its base and a skirt-like ring (annulus) on the stalk.

identification of mushrooms critical, lest one become the victim of mushroom poisoning. It is sometimes easy to confuse an edible species with one that is deadly.

Russula species produce white spores and brittle fruiting bodies, and many species produce brilliantly colored, beautiful caps. Some of these attractive *Russula* species are poisonous. *Amanita,* which is characterized by free gills and the presence of an annulus and a volva, are quite beautiful, but most are deadly (FIG. 17-18). *Amanita phalloides* is known as the *death cap* because most deaths due to mushroom poisoning have been attributed to its ingestion. *Agaricus* species, which occur in the family Agaricaceae, produce white to brown mushrooms with free gills and an annulus but no volva. Several mushrooms of this genus, such as *Agaricus bisporus,* are grown commercially for human consumption. *Coprinus* is known as the *ink cap* mushroom because autodigestion (self-decomposition) causes it to dissolve into a black, ink-like liquid.

The *Gastromycetes* include puffballs, earthstars, stinkhorns, and bird's nest fungi. Unlike other Basidiomycetes, the spores of the Gastromycetes are not forcefully discharged. The order Phallales (stinkhorns) produces a green gelatinous ooze and a foul smell when the basidiocarp undergoes autodigestion, releasing the basidiospores. Although humans find the odor offensive, flies are attracted to it. Some of the ooze containing the basidiospores adheres to the flies, providing a mechanism for the dissemination of the basidiospores of these fungi.

The numerous species of rust and smut fungi are the most serious fungal plant pathogens. There are over 20,000 species of rust fungi and over 1,000 species of smut fungi. Rusts and smuts are characterized by the production of a resting spore known as a *teliospore,* which is thick-walled and binucleate. The rusts, all of which are plant pathogens, occur in the order *Uredinales.* The rust fungi require two unrelated hosts for the completion of their normal life cycle. For example, white pine blister rust uses gooseberry bushes as its alternate host. Important plant diseases are caused by rust fungi, and these fungal plant pathogens cause great economic losses in agriculture. Rust of cereals is caused by members of the genus *Puccinia,* rust of beans by *Uromyces* species, and pine blister rust by a *Cronartium* species. The smuts occur within the order Ustilaginales. The smut fungi cause serious economic losses in agriculture. Members of the genus *Ustilago* cause smut of corn, wheat, and other plants; *Tilletia* species cause stinking smut of wheat; *Sphacelotheca* species cause loose smut of sorghum; and *Urocystis* species cause smut of onion. These are only a few examples of the common plant diseases caused by smut fungi.

Deuteromycetes

Deuteromycetes or ***Fungi Imperfecti*** are fungi that have not been observed to produce sexual spores. Either sexual forms of reproduction in the Deuteromycetes do not occur or they simply have not been detected. There are about 15,000 species in the *Fungi Imperfecti.*

TABLE 17-2 Some Representative Genera of Deuteromycetes

Alternaria	Soil saprophytes and plant pathogens; muriform spores fit together like bricks of a wall
Arthrobotrys	Soil saprophytes; some form organelles for the capture of nematodes
Aspergillus	Common molds; radically arranged; colored, often black, conidiospores
Aureobasidium (Pulullaria)	Short mycelial filaments, lateral blastospores; often damage painted surfaces
Candida	Common yeasts; some cause mycoses; some species grow in concentrated sugar solutions; others grow on hydrocarbons
Coccidioides	*C. immitis* causes mycotic infections in humans and animals
Cryptococcus	Yeasts; saprophytic in soil, but some may cause mycoses in animals and humans
Geotrichum	Common soil fungus; older mycelial filaments break up into arthrospores
Helminthosporium	Cylindrical, multiseptate spores; many are economically significant plant pathogens
Penicillum	Common mold with colored, often green, conidiospores arranged in a brush shape
Trichoderma	Common soil saprophyte with highly branched conidiophores

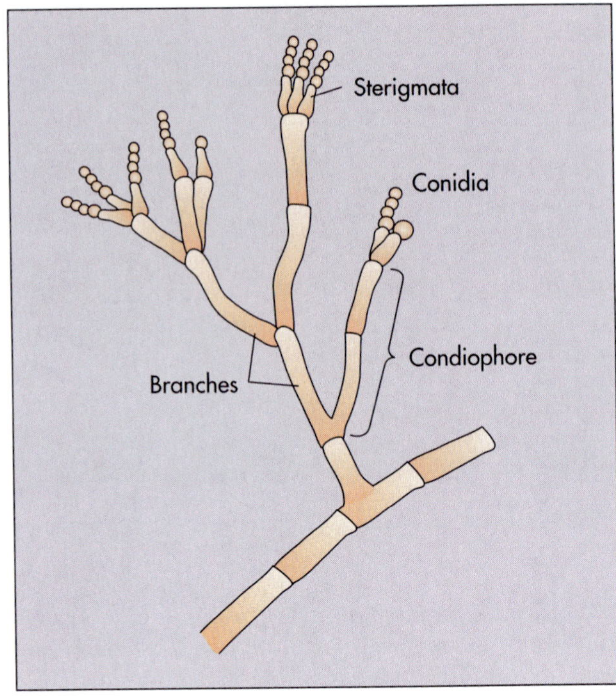

FIG. 17-19 The fungus *Penicillium* produces chains of asexual spores (conidia).

Representative genera of the Deuteromycetes are listed in Table 17-2.

The Deuteromycetes are classified largely on the basis of the morphological structure of the vegetative phase and the types of asexual spores produced (FIG. 17-19). They include many important genera of filamentous fungi, such as *Penicillium,* and yeasts, such as *Candida.* Some species of *Fungi Imperfecti* are important in food and industrial microbiology. The antibiotic penicillin, for example, is produced by *Penicillium* species, and *Aspergillus* and *Penicillium* species are used in the production of various foods, such as soy sauce and blue cheese.

Without observation of the sexual reproductive stage, it is impossible to place members of the Deuteromycetes into the Ascomycetes or Basidiomycetes, although many *Fungi Imperfecti* are clearly closely related to the Ascomycetes or Basidiomycetes. Although the sexual stages of several fungi have now been detected, a wholesale reclassification of fungi that have traditionally been placed in the Deuteromycetes has fortunately been avoided. For example, the sexual or perfect stages for several members of the genera *Penicillium* and *Aspergillus* have been found to involve the production of ascospores, but the members of these genera are still classified among the *Fungi Imperfecti.* It is likely, though, that many genera of Deuteromycetes will eventually be reclassified into other subdivisions.

17.2 ALGAE

The **algae** are photosynthetic eukaryotic organisms. Their photosynthetic metabolism differentiates them from other eukaryotic microorganisms and their lack of tissue differentiation separates them from plants. Algae exhibit sexual and asexual reproduction. In some cases, the vegetative structure (thallus) fragments into pieces and each piece grows into a new algal thallus. In other cases, asexual reproduction involves spore formation, including formation of *aplanospores* (nonmotile spores) and *zoospores* (motile spores). Sexual algal reproduction typically involves formation of a female gamete in an *oogonium* and a male gamete in an *antheridium;* fusion of the haploid gametes produces a diploid *zygote.*

TABLE 17-3 Major Division of Agae

Division	Characteristics
Chlorophycophyta (green algae)	Photosynthetic pigments: chlorophylls *a* and *b*, carotenes, several xanthophylls. Storage product: starch. Cell wall: cellulose, xylans, mannans, absent in some, calcified in others. Flagella: 1, 2-8, many, equal, apical. Some are nonmotile.
Chrysophycophyta (golden and yellow-green algae, including diatoms)	Photosynthetic pigments: chlorophylls *a* and *c*, carotenes, fucoxanthin, and several other xanthophylls. Storage product: chrysolaminarin. Cell wall: cellulose, silica, calcium carbonate. Flagella: 1-2, unequal or equal, apical.
Cryptophycophyta (cryptomonads)	Photosynthetic pigments: chlorophylls *a* and *c*, carotenes, xanthophylls (alloxanthin, crocoxanthin, monadoxanthin), phycobilins. Storage product: starch. Cell wall: absent. Flagella: 2, unequal, subapical.
Euglenophycophyta (euglenoids)	Photosynthetic pigments: chlorophylls *a* and *b*, carotenes, several xanthophylls. Storage product: paramylon. Cell wall: absent. Flagella: 1-3, apical, subapical.
Phaeophycophyta (brown algae)	Photosynthetic pigments: chlorophylls *a* and *c*, carotenes, fucoxanthin, and several other xanthophylls. Storage product: laminarin. Cell wall: cellulose, alginic acid, sulfated mucopolysaccharides. Flagella: 2, unequal, lateral.
Pyrrophycophyta (dinoflagellates)	Photosynthetic pigments: chlorophylls *a* and *c*, carotenes, several xanthophylls. Storage product: starch. Cell wall: cellulose or absent. Flagella: 2, one trailing, one girdling.
Rhodophycophyta (red algae)	Photosynthetic pigments: chlorophyll *a* (also *d* in some), phycocyanin, phycoerythrin, carotenes, several xanthophylls. Storage product: Floridian starch. Cell wall: cellulose, xylans, galactans. Flagella: absent.

The algae are classified into seven major divisions, largely on the basis of the types of photosynthetic pigments produced, the types of reserve materials stored intracellularly, and the morphological characteristics of the cell (Table 17-3). The relative concentrations of photosynthetic pigments give the algae their characteristic colors. Many of the major algal divisions have common names based on these characteristic colors, such as the green algae, red algae, and brown algae. The chloroplasts of the red algae probably arose from symbiotic cyanobacteria. These chloroplasts contain chlorophyll *a*, carotenoids, and phycobilins. The

BOX 17-2

HISTORY OF PHYCOLOGY

Many algae form macroscopic structures that are visible to the naked eye, and references to algae are found in early Eastern and Western literature. It was not until the mid-eighteenth century, though, that microscopic methods were used to examine algae. After the reproductive phases of algae were recognized, life history studies proceeded and taxonomic systems of classification were developed. The elucidation of algal sexual reproductive cycles was pioneered by Gustave Thuret, a wealthy Parisian amateur scientist, in studies conducted from 1840 to 1854 with *Fucus*. Nathaniel Pringsheim, working with *Vaucheria* during the same period, described the growth of algae and the development of sexual stages, allowing algal classification based on reproductive systems rather than just on superficial resemblances. During the early nineteenth century, many phycologists (algologists) published works that advanced the taxonomic classification of algae.

At the end of the nineteenth century, phycologists used their accumulated knowledge of algal morphology and reproduction to revise the classification schemes for the taxonomy of algae. Many of today's views on the systematics of the algae date from the late nineteenth and early twentieth centuries. In Whittaker's five-kingdom classification system, some of the algae are placed in the Kingdom Protista along with the protozoa, and other algae exhibiting more extensive organizational development are placed in the Kingdom Plantae.

Some organisms that are classified as algae are borderline cases with higher plants and others are borderline cases with protozoa. There are some algae that lose their ability to carry out photosynthetic metabolism, rendering them indistinguishable from the protozoa. Some motile, unicellular algae have traditionally been studied by both protozoologists and phycologists. This situation has led to an inevitable confusion in the literature because zoologists and botanists typically use different features and criteria for establishing classification systems. Most traditional algal classification systems include the blue-green algae, but these organisms are properly considered as cyanobacteria because of their prokaryotic cells. The reclassification of the blue-greens as cyanobacteria is still considered controversial and is opposed by many phycologists.

chloroplasts of diatoms, dinoflagellates, and brown algae are related to the photosynthetic bacterium *Heliobacterium.* These chloroplasts contain chlorophylls *a* and *c* and carotenoids. The chloroplasts of the euglenoids and green algae are closely related to the photosynthetic bacterium, *Prochloron.* These chloroplasts contain chlorophylls *a* and *b* and carotenoids. Multicellularity in the green, red, and brown algae was achieved through separate lines of evolution. The green algae includes both unicellular and multicellular organisms. All of the red and brown algae are multicellular and several of them are conspicuous seaweeds.

FIG. 17-20 The green alga *Volvox aureus.*

Green Algae

The *green algae (Chlorophycophyta)* contain chlorophylls *a* and *b* and appear green. They are widely distributed in aquatic ecosystems. These algae may be unicellular, colonial, or filamentous. Most cells are uninucleate, but several orders of green algae are characterized by the formation of coenocytic filaments. The chloroplasts of many unicellular green algae contain a red pigmented region known as the *stigma* or *eyespot.* Some green algae contain contractile vacuoles that serve an osmoregulatory function, protecting the cell against osmotic shock. The green algae normally store starch as a reserve material. The cell walls of different species of Chlorophycophyta are composed of cellulose, mannans, or xylans, but a high proportion of the cell wall also may be composed of protein.

The unicellular green algae, which are normally motile by means of flagella, include the genera *Chlamydomonas* and *Volvox. Chlamydomonas* contains several hundred species. Members of this genus are unicellular and biflagellate. *Volvox* species form spheroidal colonies (FIG. 17-20). The colonies contain many small vegetative cells and relatively few reproductive cells. The reproductive cells lack flagella and are called *gonidia.* The cells within a colony of *Volvox* act in a cooperative fashion so that the entire colony behaves as a superorganism. The flagella of the vegetative cells face outward and can move the entire colony in a unified manner. Individuals in the colonies act as gametes, some producing male gametes and others producing female gametes. The colonies of some species thus exhibit sexual differentiation. Reproduction is dependent on the intact colony. The colonies of *Volvox* approach the level of tissue differentiation. It would appear that algae, having such complex levels of organization, represent an evolutionary link between microorganisms and higher plants. Based on ultrastructural analyses of the microtubules involved in mitotic division, however, *Volvox* does not appear to represent the missing evolutionary link between the green algae and green plants.

There are several nonmotile types of green algae. These include members of the genera *Chlorococcum* and *Chlorella,* which are unicellular types, and members of the genus *Scenedesmus,* which form colonies of four to eight laterally united cells. There are several green algae that form filaments, including members of the genera *Ulothrix* and *Spirogyra.* Probably the best-known genus of filamentous green algae, *Spirogyra,* occurs in the order Zygnemales. *Spirogyra* is an example of a filamentous green alga. The walls of the filament are continuous. The chloroplasts of *Spirogyra* form a spiral within the filaments (FIG. 17-21). Another well-

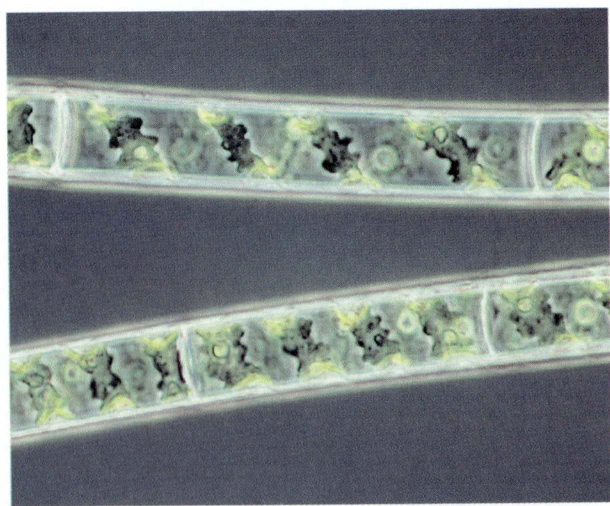

FIG. 17-21 Detail of spiral chloroplasts of the green alga *Spirogyra* species.

FIG. 17-22 The tubular green alga *Acetabularia.*

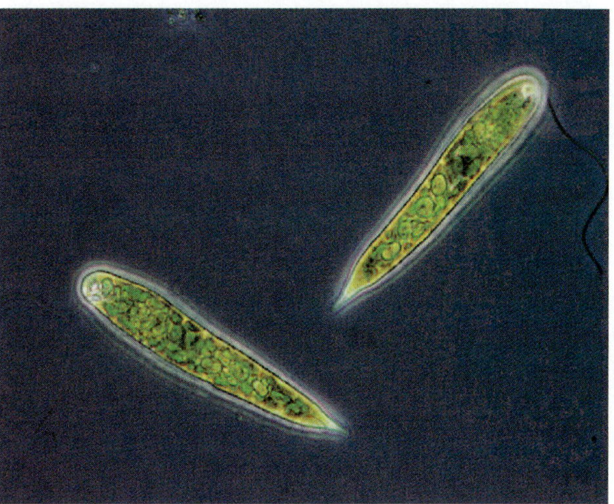

FIG. 17-23 Micrograph of *Euglena* species.

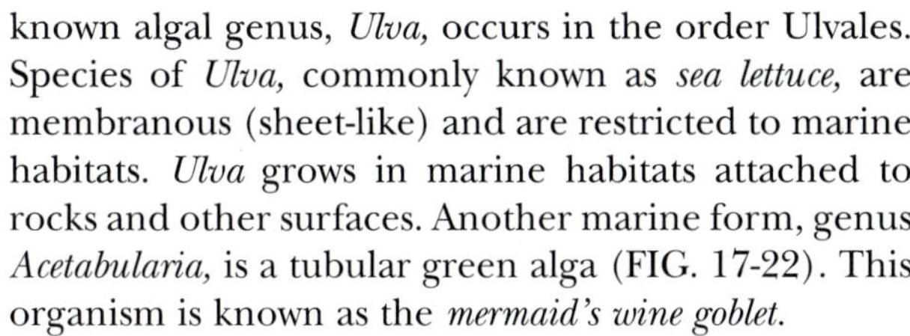

known algal genus, *Ulva,* occurs in the order Ulvales. Species of *Ulva,* commonly known as *sea lettuce,* are membranous (sheet-like) and are restricted to marine habitats. *Ulva* grows in marine habitats attached to rocks and other surfaces. Another marine form, genus *Acetabularia,* is a tubular green alga (FIG. 17-22). This organism is known as the *mermaid's wine goblet.*

The great range of organization that exists among the green algae shows a clear tendency toward the formation of complex tissues (parenchyma) and multicellular organs. This indicates a possible line of evolution to higher plants.

Euglenoid Algae

The *Euglenoid algae (Euglenophycophyta)* contain chlorophylls *a* and *b* and typically appear green but differ from the green algae with respect to their cellular organization and their intracellular reserve storage products. They are unicellular. They lack a cell wall but normally are surrounded by an outer layer, known as a *pellicle,* composed of lipid and protein. The Euglenophycophyta do not store starch like the green algae, but rather paramylon, a β-1,3-glucose polymer.

The Euglenophycophyta appear to be closely related to the protozoa (FIG. 17-23). Members of this division that lose their photosynthetic apparatus are indistinguishable from protozoa. Reproduction in the Euglenophycophyta is normally by longitudinal division. These algae are widely distributed in aquatic and soil habitats. *Euglena* is the best-known genus of Euglenophycophyta. *Euglena* species have two flagella for locomotion and normally contain a contractile vacuole to protect it against osmotic shock.

Yellow-Green Algae, Golden Algae, and Diatoms

The *yellow-green algae (Xanthophyceae), golden algae (Chrysophyceae),* and the *diatoms (Bacillariophyceae)* form a group of algae called the *Chrysophycophyta.* The Chrysophycophyta are unified by the production of the same reserve storage material, chrysolaminarin. Chrysolaminarin is a β-linked polymer of glucose. Chrysophycophyta species produce carotenoid and xanthophyll pigments that tend to dominate over the chlorophyll pigments; this confers golden-brown hues on members of this division. Most members of the Chrysophycophyta are unicellular, although some are colonial.

Yellow-green and Golden Algae

Genera in the family Xanthophyceae include *Botrydiopsis,* a unicellular form; *Tribonema,* a filamentous form; and *Vaucheria,* a coenocytic tubular form. *Vaucheria* is known as the *water felt* and is widely distributed in moist soils and aquatic habitats. The Xanthophyceae generally reproduce asexually by zoospores (motile spores) or aplanospores (nonmotile spores). The Chrysophyceae are typically motile by means of flagella. Asexual reproduction in the Chrysophyceae is by cell division, zoospores, or statospores (silicified cysts). Many members of the Chrysophyceae form siliceous or calcareous walls.

Diatoms (Bacillariophyceae)

The **diatoms** (Bacillariophyceae) produce distinctive cell walls known as *frustules.* There are approximately 200 genera of diatoms. The diatoms typically are golden brown in color.

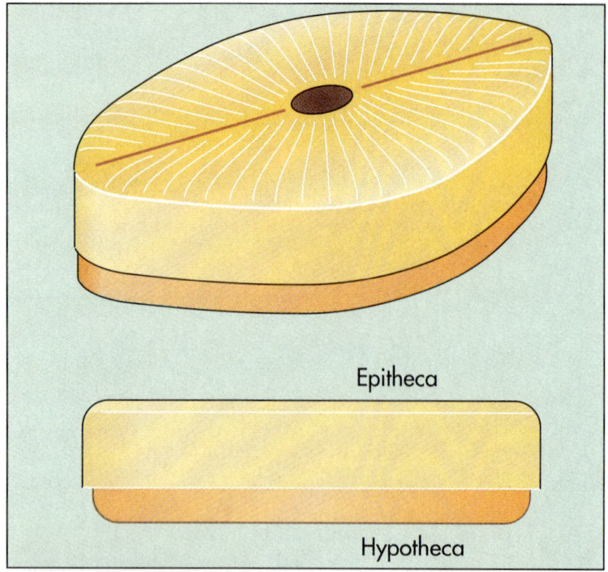

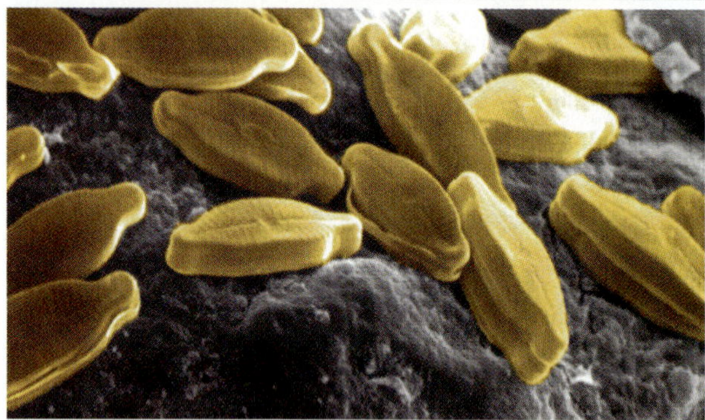

FIG. 17-24 Diatoms produce frustules (walls) composed of silicon dioxide. The walls form overlapping halves.

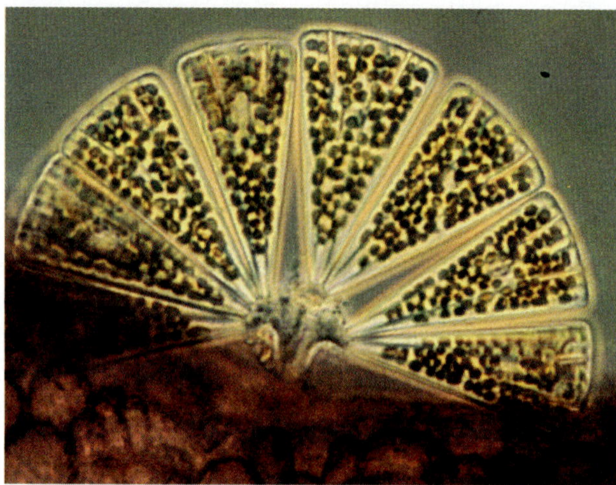

FIG. 17-25 Micrograph of the marine diatom *Licmophora.*

The frustules of diatoms, also known as *valves,* have two overlapping halves; the larger portion is referred to as the *epitheca* and the smaller one as the *hypotheca* (FIG. 17-24). The halves of the frustule fit together like a Petri dish. The geometric appearance of diatoms renders them aesthetically attractive (FIG. 17-25). Pennate diatoms have bilateral symmetry and centric diatoms have radial symmetry. Some diatoms are benthic, living at the bottom of aquatic ecosystems at the sediment layer, and other diatoms are planktonic, living suspended in open water bodies. The growth of diatoms depends on the concentrations of available silica because the cell walls of diatoms are impregnated with silica. Holes in the silica walls, called *puntae,* allow exchange of nutrients and metabolic wastes between the cell and its surroundings.

The frustules of diatoms are resistant to natural degradation and accumulate over geologic periods. As a result, diatoms are preserved in fossil records dating back to the Cretaceous period 65 million years ago. There are significant deposits of diatom frustules in the world. Such deposits are known as *diatomaceous earth* and are mined for numerous commercial uses. Diatomaceous earth is sometimes used as an abrasive in toothpaste and metal polish. The most extensive use of diatomaceous earth is in the filtration of liquids, especially those from sugar refineries.

Reproduction in diatoms is normally by the formation of uneven-sized cells. Asexual reproduction involves the synthesis of a new cell wall structure in which each daughter cell reconstructs the smaller segment of the frustule, regardless of which segment of the parent frustule it receives. Therefore continued asexual reproduction tends to result in diatoms of progressively smaller size. Occasionally, environmental conditions or the severe reduction in cell size leads to sexual reproduction with the production of auxospores, which are larger cells that act to reestablish larger diatoms. The valves of some diatoms have an opening along the apical axis known as the *raphe.* Diatoms that have a raphe exhibit gliding motility, with the direction of movement depending on the shape of the raphe. For example, due to differences in the shapes of their raphes, *Navicula* species exhibit straight movement and those of *Nitzschia* exhibit curved movement. The gliding motility of diatoms permits these organisms to exhibit phototaxis, allowing them to move toward or away from light.

Fire Algae

The *fire algae (Pyrrophycophyta)* are generally brown or reddish-brown because of the presence of xanthophyll pigments. These algae are unicellular and biflagellate, and store starch or oils as their reserve material. Reproduction is primarily by cell division. The cell walls of Pyrrophycophyta contain cellulose and sometimes form structured plates, called *theca.*

The **dinoflagellates** are characterized by the presence of a transverse groove that divides the cell into two semicells (FIG. 17-26). The two flagella of the dinoflagellates emerge from an opening in the groove. Because of their cell wall structures, some dinoflagellates that produce thecal plates are referred to as *armored dinoflagellates.*

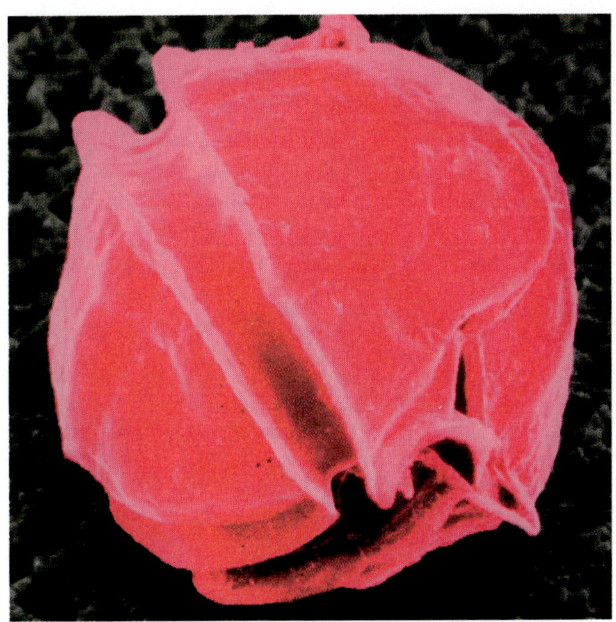

FIG. 17-26 Colorized micrograph of the dinoflagellate *Gonyaulax tamarensis* that causes red tide. (30,700×).

Several dinoflagellates exhibit *bioluminescence,* the characteristic on which the designation *fire algae* is based. Some species also exhibit regular 24-hour behavioral patterns, known as *circadian rhythms.* For example, *Gonyaulax polyedra* exhibits a cyclic expression of luminescence, with peak luminescence occurring in the middle of the dark period. The luminescent capacity of *G. polyedra* allows this organism to glow at night. The glow rhythm is associated with a nightly increase in the level of luciferin and luciferase, the same enzyme substrate system that is operative in fire flies and luminescent bacteria. *G. polyedra* also exhibits circadian rhythms in its photosynthetic activities and cell division, with maximal cell divisions occurring at dawn and maximal photosynthesis occurring at midday.

Species of *Gonyaulax* and other dinoflagellates are economically important because they produce the toxic blooms known as *red tides* that tend to color the seawater red or red-brown. The toxins of dinoflagellates during such blooms may kill invertebrate organisms. They also result in dieoffs of dolphins and whales. Although the blooms kill relatively few marine organisms, their toxins are concentrated in the tissues of filter-feeding molluscs such as clams and oysters. Ingestion of shellfish containing dinoflagellates results in paralytic shellfish poisoning, a serious form of food poisoning. To prevent such outbreaks in humans, collection of shellfish is banned during occurrences of red tide.

Some dinoflagellates enter into mutually beneficial (symbiotic) relationships with various marine invertebrates. Such associations are termed *zooxanthellae.* Within such associations, the animal cell provides protection and carbon dioxide for photosynthesis for the dinoflagellates and the algae provide the animal with oxygen and organic carbon for its nutritional needs. Often dinoflagellates grow on ingested bacteria and algal species. As such, dinoflagellates are *mixotrophic,* capable of chemoorganotrophic and photolithotrophic metabolism. Some microbiologists hypothesize that such symbiotic relationships are responsible for the evolution of higher organisms.

CRYPTOMONADS

The *Cryptomonads (Cryptophycophyta)* are a small group of unicellular algae that normally reproduce by longitudinal cell division, typically producing two flagella of equal lengths. These algae normally appear brown in color. The cryptomonads have asymmetric cells that are flattened and bounded by an outer covering called the *periplast.* Representative genera of this group are *Cryptomonas* and *Chroomonas.*

RED ALGAE

Red algae, (Rhodophycophyta) exhibit tissue differentiation and should be classified as plants. They contain *phycocyanin* and *phycoerythrin* in addition to chlorophyll pigments. The red color of the Rhodophycophyta is due to the phycoerythrin. The primary reserve material in the Rhodophycophyta is *Floridean starch,* a polysaccharide similar to amylopectin in higher plants. Rhodophycophyta exhibit a specialized type of oogamous sexual reproduction involving specialized female cells called *carpogonia* and specialized male cells called *spermatia.* Tetraspores, which are spores produced in a tetrasporangium, are formed during the life cycle of some red algae, and the tetraspores eventually differentiate into the male and female gametes. *Nemalion, Callithamnion, Delesserica, Anthithamnion, Callophyllis,* and *Porphyridium* are representative genera of red algae (FIG. 17-27).

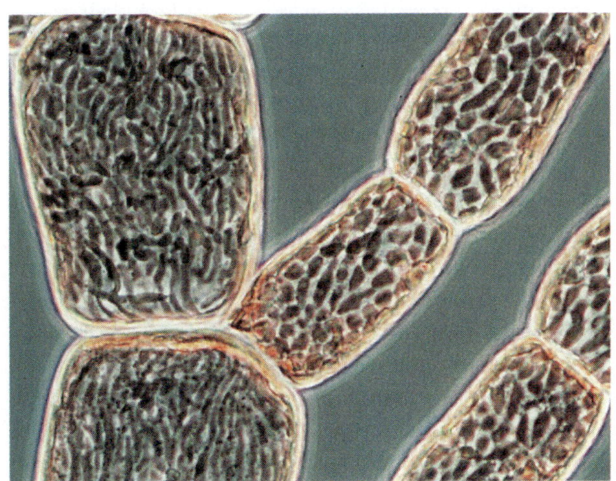

FIG. 17-27 The red alga *Callithamnion.*

Most red algae occur in marine habitats. They typically have a bilayered cell wall with an inner microfibrillar, rigid layer and an outer mucilaginous layer. Various biochemicals, including agar and carrageenin, occur in the cell walls of red algae. The agar and carrageenin of red algae are widely used as thickening agents and binders in various food products. Agar is also used as a solidifying agent in culture media, upon which the cultivation of bacteria largely depends. The carrageenin of *Chondrus crispus* is used in puddings. The red alga *Porphyra* is cultivated and harvested by the Japanese as a source of food.

Brown Algae

Brown algae (Phaeophycophyta) produce *xanthophylls* that dominate over the carotenoid and chlorophyll pigments and impart a brown color to these organisms. The main reserve materials for the brown algae are laminarin and mannitol. The cell walls of the Phaeophycophyta are generally composed of two layers: an inner cellulosic layer and an outer mucilaginous layer. Alginic acid is normally found as a biochemical constituent of the cell wall.

The brown algae includes over 200 genera and 1,500 species of almost exclusively marine organisms and are found primarily in coastal zones. These are the *kelps,* which are brown algae, that can form macroscopic structures up to 50 m in length (FIG. 17-28). It is difficult to consider organisms of this size as members of the microbial world. Most kelps have vegetative structures consisting of a holdfast, stem, and blade. These are histologically complex organisms that exhibit some cellular differentiation.

FIG. 17-28 The brown algal kelp *Heterocystis.*

The genera *Fucus* and *Sargassum* are abundant brown algae. Large populations of *S. natans* occur in the Atlantic Ocean in the region known as the Sargasso Sea. Species of *Fucus* commonly occur along rocky shores, attached to the rocks by disc-like holdfasts. These brown algae clearly are the most complex organisms classified as algae, or for that matter, as microorganisms, representing a borderline case between algae and plants. Green plants, however, do not appear to have evolved directly from brown algae. Rather, parallel evolution appears to have occurred in which organisms in different evolutionary lines developed similar adaptive, organized structures.

17.3 PROTOZOA

Protozoa are unicellular nonphotosynthetic eukaryotic microorganisms. They generally lack cell walls. There are over 65,000 species of protozoa. A few protozoa lack mitochondria. *Pelomyxa palustris* is a protozoan that has endosymbiotic bacteria and no energy transforming organelles of its own. This organism may represent an evolutionary stage in the formation of the contemporary eukaryotic cell. *P. palustris* does not carry out mitosis as occurs in other eukaryotic cells.

Most protozoa are chemoheterotrophic. Some exhibit *holozoic nutrition,* obtaining nutrients by phagocytosis of bacterial cells, and others exhibit *saprozoic nutrition,* obtaining nutrients by diffusion, active transport, or pinocytosis from nonliving sources. Some protozoa, such as *Paramecium,* have a specialized structure for phagocytosis called the *cytostome.* Most protozoa are aerobic but some are anaerboes. The anaerobic protozoa typically lack mitochondria and do not have an active Krebs cycle. Hydrogenase catalyzes the transfer of electrons to protons that act as terminal electron acceptors in a unique electron transport pathway. The hydrogenase is localized in organelles called *hydrogenosomes.*

Many protozoa form a resting stage, called a **cyst,** during their life cycle. A cyst is a dormant stage that has very low metabolic activity. In protozoa, a cyst usually has a wall, whereas vegetative protozoan cells typically lack a wall. Cyst formation is a mechanism for withstanding adverse conditions, such as low nutrient concentrations, desiccation, low pH, and lack of oxygen. Cysts are important in the transmission of disease-causing protozoa to humans. Under appropriate conditions, cysts return to actively growing vegetative forms, a process called *excystation.*

Some protozoa have one nucleus, but others have two or more nuclei. In some cases, the multiple nuclei are identical. However, some protozoa have a macronucleus (larger nucleus) and one or more micronuclei (smaller nuclei). The macronucleus usually directs the activities of the protozoan cell. The micronucleus is involved in reproduction (genetic recombination) and regeneration of the macronucleus. Most protozoa reproduce asexually, most often by binary fission. Some protozoa also exhibit sexual reproduction, usually by conjugation. During conjugation, there is an exchange of gametes between mating protozoa.

The protozoa traditionally are classified into major groups largely on the basis of their means of locomotion. Some protozoa form extensions of the cytoplasm known as *pseudopodia* or *false feet,* involved in locomotion and the ingestion of food. Others are motile by means of cilia. Yet others are motile by means of flagella. Some protozoa, including some parasitic spore formers, are nonmotile. The four traditional groups of protozoa are the *Mastigophora (flagellates), Sarcodina (pseudopodia formers), Ciliophora (ciliates),* and *Sporozoa (spore formers).*

In 1980, the Committee on Systematics and Evolution of the Society of Protozoologists developed a new classification system in which the protozoa are divided into seven phyla (Table 17-4). This new system encompasses the classification of several groups claimed by other disciplines, including most of the algae and the lower fungi. The protozoologists felt that unicellular eukaryotic organisms should be classified as protozoa. Genetic studies support some of the changes in classifying protozoa, such as the inclusion of slime molds, which are much more closely related phylogenetically to protozoa than to fungi.

There are several noteworthy aspects of the new protozoa classification system. First, the Sarcodina and the Mastigophora are included in one phylum, the Sarcomastigophora. Within this phylum, the Mastigophora and Sarcodina are treated as separate subphyla. The other major change in this classification system is the division of the Sporozoa into four separate phyla: the Apicomplexa, Microspora, Acetospora, and Myxospora. The last three have spores but many members of the Apicomplexa do not; the Apicomplexa have an apical complex visible by electron microscopy.

TABLE 17-4 Classification of the Protozoa

Old System	
Ciliophora	Locomotion: cilia. Reproduction: asexual, transverse fission; sexual, conjugation. Nutrition: ingestive
Mastigophora	Locomotion: usually paired flagella. Reproduction: asexual, longitudinal fission. Nutrition: heterotrophic, absorptive
Sarcodina	Locomotion: pseudopodia (false feet). Reproduction: asexual, binary fission. Nutrition: phagocytic
Sporozoa	Locomotion: usually none; some stages with flagella. Reproduction: asexual, multiple fission; sexual, within host; spores formed. Nutrition: absorptive
New System	
Sarcomastigophora	Locomotion: flagella, pseudopodia, or both. Reproduction: when sexual, essentially syngamy. Representative genera: *Monosiga, Bodo, Leishmania, Trypanosoma, Giardia, Opalina, Amoeba, Entamoeba, Diffugia*
Labyrinthomorpha	Synonymous with the net slime molds. Produce an ectoplasmic network with spindle-shaped or spherical nonamoeboid cells; in some genera, amoeboid cells move within a network by gliding
Apicomplexa	Produce an apical complex visible with the electron microscope; all species parasitic. Representative genera: *Eimeria, Toxoplasma, Babesia, Theileria, Plasmodium*
Microspora	Unicellular spores, each with an imperforate wall; obligate intracellular parasites. Representative genus: *Metchnikovella*
Ascetospora	Multicellular spore; no polar capsules or polar filaments; all species parasitic. Representative genus: *Paramyxa*
Myxospora	Spores of multicellular origin with one or more polar capsules; all species parasitic. Representative genera: *Myxidium, Kudoa*
Ciliophora	Cilia produced at some stage in the life cycle. Reproduce by binary transverse fission; budding and multiple fission also occur. Sexuality involving conjugation, autogamy, and cytogamy; most are free-living heterotrophs. Representative genera: *Didinium, Tetrahymena, Paramecium, Stentor*

BOX 17-3

HISTORY OF PROTOZOOLOGY

Protozoa were among the first microscopic organisms observed. The protozoa *Vorticella* is shown in the 1677 sketches of van Leeuwenhoek. *Paramecium,* as well as other protozoa, were described in 1678 by Christian Huygens. Leeuwenhoek continued to report his drawings of protozoa and in 1681 described what appears to be *Giardia intestinalis,* thus discovering parasitic protozoa. Louis Joblot, a professor of mathematics with an interest in optics that led him to microscopy, published the first treatise on protozoa in 1718. G. A. Goldfuss introduced the term *protozoan* in 1817, and a chapter about this group of organisms appeared in a book on the comparative anatomy of invertebrates in 1848 by Karl T. E. von Siebold. The term *protozoan* is derived from the Greek *protos,* meaning first, and *zoon,* meaning animal. In 1838 Christian Ehrenberg published a major monograph on the protozoa, describing more than 500 species, including their digestive and reproductive systems. Felix Dujardin, a French professor of zoology, published in 1841 a classification system for the protozoa using primarily morphological features. Dujardin was an accurate observer and his classification system was sounder than that of Ehrenberg.

Medical protozoology began in the mid-1800s. Pasteur, in 1870, reported that a protozoan was responsible for a disease of silkworms that devastated the French silk industry during the 1800s. Also in 1870, T. R. Lewis observed *Amoeba* in the stools of individuals suffering from choleric symptoms and, shortly thereafter, F. Losch described *Entamoeba histolytica* as the causative agent of dysentery in man. Transmission of this disease by ingestion of *E. histolytica* was shown by E. L. Walker and A. W. Sellards in 1913. The discovery that disease-causing microorganisms could be transmitted by animal vectors, which was made by Theobold Smith, represented a major advance in medical protozoology and in our understanding of the mechanisms of disease transmission. Smith and co-workers (1893) proved that Texas cattle fever was caused by a protozoan and that transmission of the disease involved a tick vector. This proof led to the discovery that a number of other diseases are transmitted by arthropod vectors. Alphonse Laveran and Camillo Golgi (1881–1886) showed that malaria was caused by a parasitic protozoan. Ronald Ross, in 1897–1898, found that the malarian parasite was transmitted in birds by a mosquito vector. The mode of transmission of the protozoan that caused malaria in humans was discovered by Battista Grassi, who disputed with Ross the priority of discovery of vector transmission of this disease. Joseph Dutton (1902) found that a trypanosome protozoon caused African sleeping sickness and was transmitted by the tsetse fly. William B. Leishman and C. Donovan (1903) discovered that kala-azar disease was caused by a protozoan that subsequently was named *Leishmania donovani*—many microbial species names are derived from the names of the individuals who studied them.

SLIME MOLDS

Slime molds traditionally have been studied by mycologists. Hence their name as molds. However, RNA analyses show that these organisms are an evolutionary branch from protozoa and not fungi. Their nutrition is phagotrophic, that is, they engulf and ingest nutrients. The phagotrophic mode of obtaining nutrients exhibited by the slime molds is characteristic of protozoa and not fungi. Further, the vegetative cells of the slime molds are amoeboid and lack a cell wall, making them similar to protozoa. The resemblance of the slime molds to the fungi is based on the production of spores that are surrounded by wall structures. All slime molds exhibit characteristic fungal-like life cycles, a feature used to subdivide this division (FIG. 17-29). Typically, slime molds, like chitrids and Oomycetes, bear asexual spores within sporangia.

Cellular Slime Molds

Cellular slime molds (Acrasiales) form a fruiting (spore-bearing) body known as a *sporocarp* or *sorocarp.* The sporocarp is a special type of fruiting body that bears a mucoid droplet at the tip of each branch, containing spores with cell walls. The sporocarps of slime molds are generally stalked structures. The stalks normally consist of walled cells, and this characteristic forms the basis for designating these organisms as the cellular slime molds. The sporocarp releases spores that germinate, forming *myxamoebae,* which are amoeboid cells that form pseudopodia. The myxamoebae swarm together or aggregate to form a structure called a *pseudoplasmodium.* Within the pseudoplasmodium, the cells of the cellular slime molds do not lose their integrity. The pseudoplasmodium undergoes a developmental sequence (differentiation), culminating in the formation of a sporocarp.

The pseudoplasmodium formation of slime molds, such as *Dictyostelium discoideum,* is of special interest because of the biochemical communication involved in initiating swarming activity. Myxamoebae of *D. discoideum* feed largely on bacteria, using them as a food-source for growth and multiplication. Under appropriate conditions, when food sources become limited,

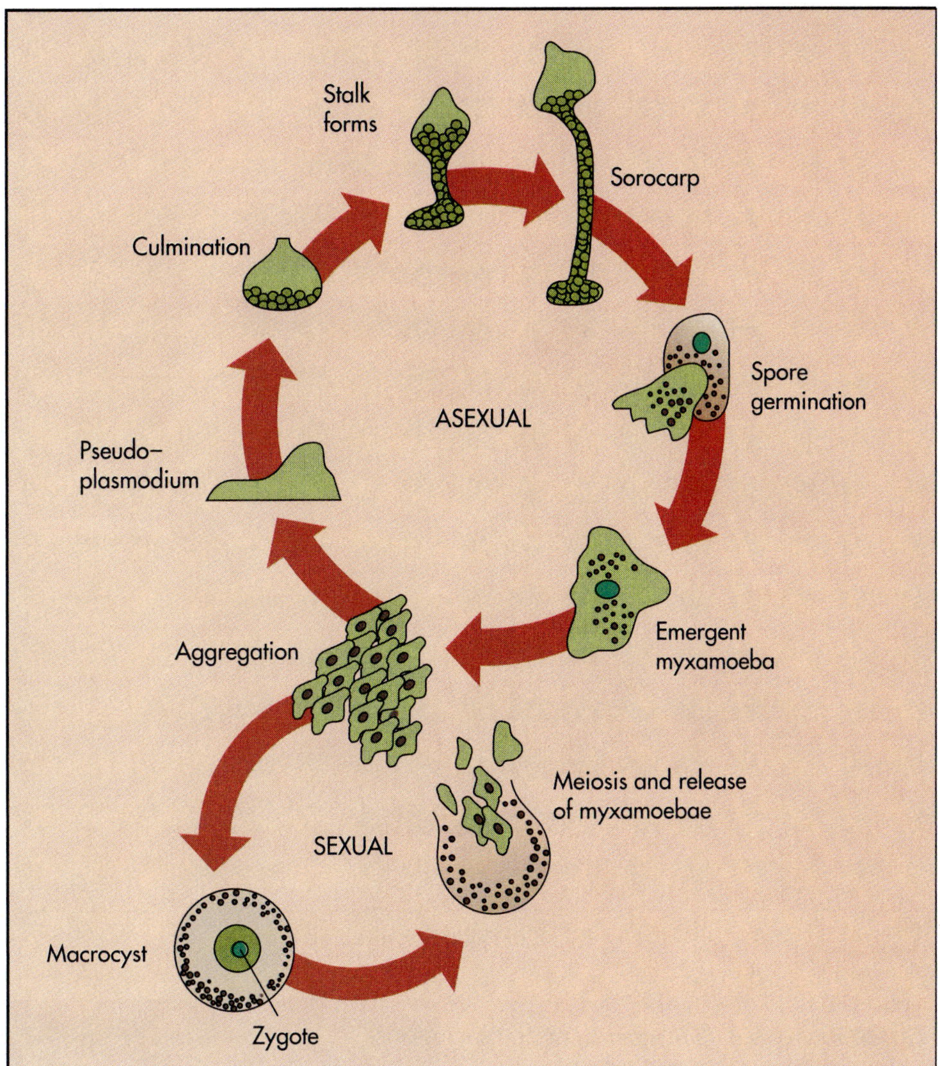

FIG. 17-29 The slime mold *Dictyostelium* exhibits a life cycle during which myxamoebae swarm together and aggregate in response to a chemical signal to form a vertical stalk. Spores are released from the stalk and germinate to form new myxamoebae.

the myxamoebae cease their feeding activity and swarm to an aggregation center. The swarming activity is initiated when one or more cells at the aggregation center release cyclic AMP *(acrasin)*. Cyclic AMP is responsible for communication between the myxamoebae. The myxamoebae move along the concentration gradient of cyclic AMP until they reach the center of aggregation. They then mass together, myxamoebae piling up to form a pseudoplasmodium. Swarming occurs as a pulsating wave motion in which the chemical stimulus, cyclic AMP, is transmitted from cells that are proximal to the aggregation center to distant cells. Different species of Acrasiomycetes exhibit different waveforms in their swarming behavior, some moving in linear wave-like motion and others exhibiting spiral wave motion.

True Slime Molds

True slime molds (Myxomycetes) form either *myxamoebae* or flagellated cells known as *swarm cells*. The myxamoebae or swarm cells fuse to form a **plasmodium,** which is a multinucleate protoplasmic mass that is devoid of cell walls that is enveloped in a gelatinous slime sheath. The classification of the Myxomycetes is based largely on the structure of the fruiting body. In many species of Myxomycetes, spores are formed inside the fruiting body. These spores are sometimes referred to as *endospores* but they do not bear any resemblance to the endospores of bacteria. The spores of Myxomycetes generally have a definite thick wall.

During the life cycle of true slime molds, the spores are released from the sporangia and disseminated. At a later time they germinate, producing myxamoebae

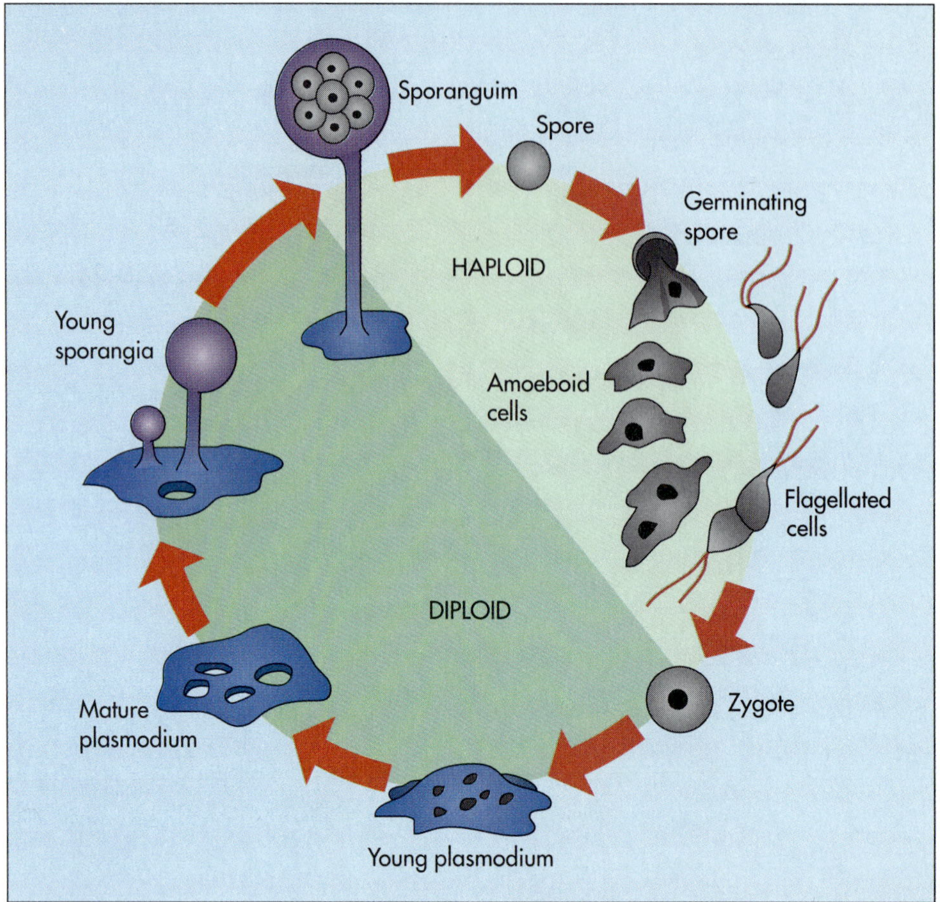

FIG. 17-30 Life cycle of a myxomycete.

and/or swarm cells (FIG. 17-30). These structures later unite by sexual fusion to initiate formation of the plasmodium. The plasmodium gives rise to brilliantly colored fruiting bodies.

The brightly colored fruiting bodies of myxomycetes are often seen on decaying logs or other moist areas of decaying organic matter (FIG. 17-31). Myxomycetes are often conspicuous on grass lawns, often appearing as large blue-green colonies. To remove these unsightly blemishes from an otherwise luxuriant lawn, simply mow the grass.

SARCODINA

Sarcodina are motile by means of pseudopodia. These are extensions of the cytoplasm sometimes called *false feet.* The pseudopodia are used for engulfing and ingesting food, as well as for locomotion. Members of the Sarcodina may move at rates of 2 to 3 cm per hour under optimal conditions. The false feet may occur in various forms, including extensions of the ectoplasm that encompass the flow of endoplasm *(lobopodia);* filamentous projections composed entirely of ectoplasm *(philopodia);* filamentous projections with branching *rhizopodia;* and axial rods within a cytoplasmic envelope *(axopodia)* (FIG. 17-32). Some members of the Sarcodina are important because they cause human diseases. For example, *Entamoeba histolytica* causes amoebic dysentery, a serious, debilitating disease.

FIG. 17-31 Photograph of the myxomycete *Lycogola epidendron.*

Members of the genus *Amoeba* form lobopodia. They have no distinct shape because they lack a skeletal structure. The flow of cytoplasm continuously changes the shape of true amoebae. The giant

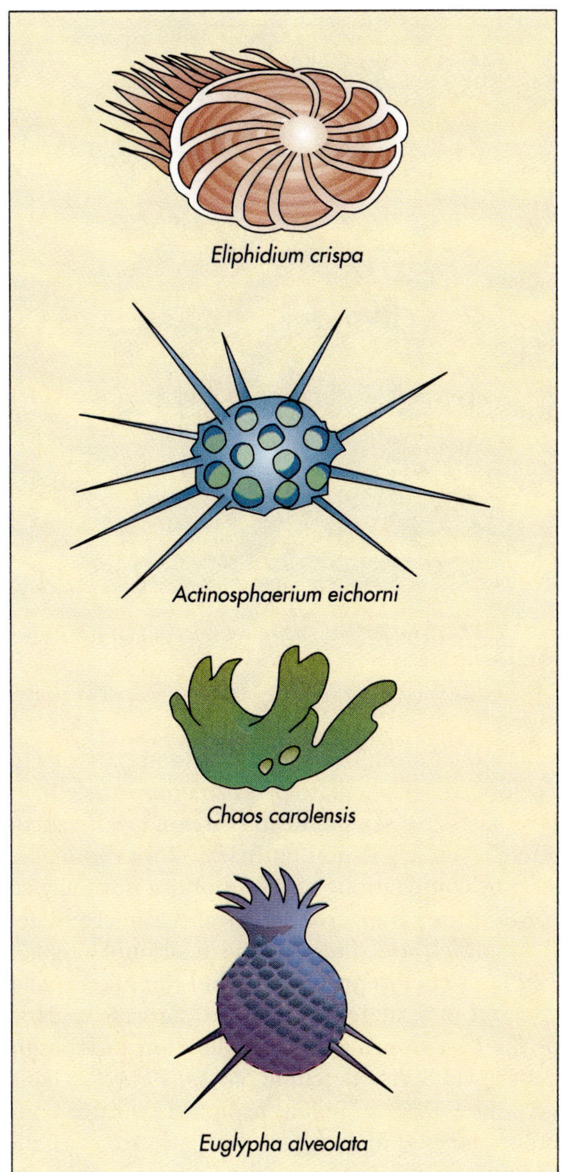

FIG. 17-32 Sarcodina are protozoa that move by extending the cytoplasm (false foot formation).

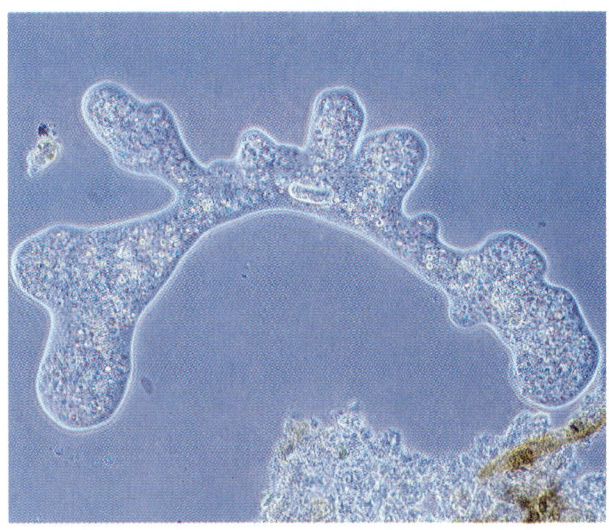

FIG. 17-33 Micrograph of Amoeba proteus.

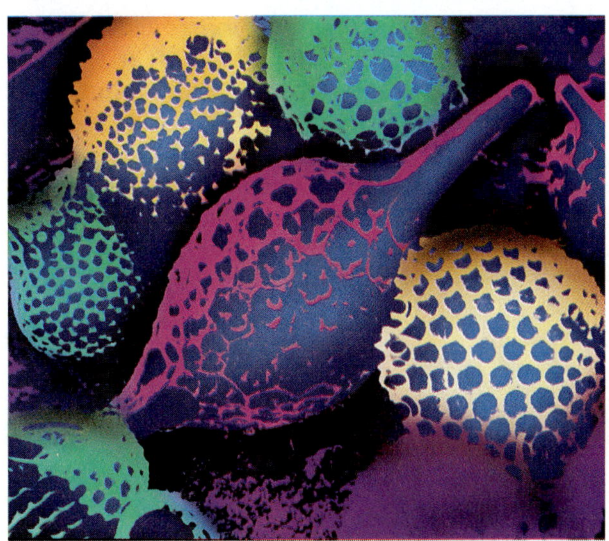

FIG. 17-34 Micrograph of fossil radiolarian shells.

FIG. 17-35 The fossil foraminiferan, *Elphidium.*

amoeba, *A. proteus,* is normally about 250 μm in length (FIG. 17-33). This organism is readily found and visualized microscopically in pond water samples. *Amoeba* feed on smaller organisms, including bacteria and other protozoa. For example, *A. proteus* can ingest the protozoa *Tetrahymena* and *Paramecium.*

Heliozoans are freshwater forms that typically produce numerous radiating axopodia. Radiolarians typically have axopodia, with a skeleton of silicon or strontium sulfate (FIG. 17-34). They occur in marine ecosystems. The silica-containing exoskeletons of radiolarians are quite attractive when viewed microscopically.

Foraminiferans form one or many chambers composed of siliceous or calcareous tests (FIG. 17-35, p. 718). A *test* is a skeletal or shell-like structure. Tests of the Foraminiferida accumulate in marine sediments and are preserved in the geologic record. The white cliffs of Dover are composed largely of the test structures of foraminiferans. Many of the foraminiferans are recognized in fossil records, but there are no fossil records for many microorganisms.

Mastigophora

Mastigophora are the flagellate protozoa. Because some members of the Mastigophora produce pseudopodia in addition to flagella, these organisms are now classified with the Sarcodina. It is in this subphylum that protozoologists place the dinoflagellates, euglenoids, and other algae.

Many members of the Mastigophora are plant and animal parasites. The genera *Trypanosoma* and *Leishmania* contain species that produce serious human diseases (FIG. 17-36). *Trypanosoma gambiense,* for example, causes African sleeping sickness, and *T. cruzi* is the causative agent of Chagas disease. Infections with the flagellate protozoan *Giardia* can cause severe diarrhea. This protozoan is transmitted by contaminated water. *Leishmania donovani* is the causative agent of kala-azar disease, also known as *dum dum fever.* Human diseases caused by these flagellate protozoa are normally transmitted by arthropods, and control depends on controlling the carrier rather than eliminating the disease-causing protozoa.

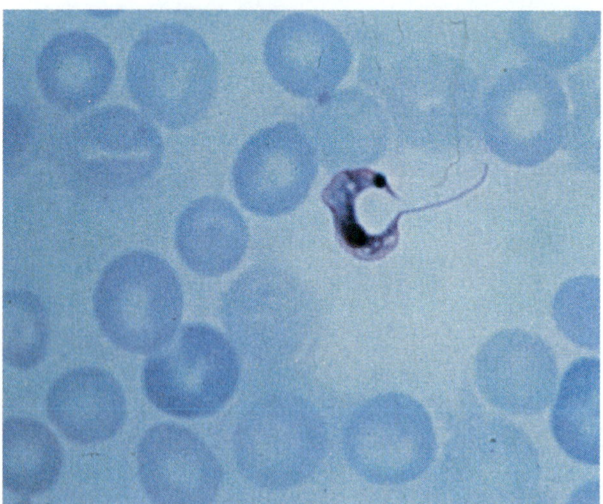

FIG. 17-36 Micrograph of the trypomastigote form of *Trypanosoma cruzi.*

Ciliophora

Ciliophora are motile by means of cilia. Some members of the Ciliophora have a mouth-like region known as a *cytostome* (FIG. 17-37). In addition to their role in locomotion, the cilia move food particles into the cytostome. The ciliate protozoa reproduce by various asexual and sexual means. Asexual reproduction is often by binary fission, and sexual reproduction is usually by conjugation. The Ciliophora normally contain two nuclei, a macronucleus and a micronucleus, both of which are diploid. The macronucleus is involved in asexual reproduction and the micronucleus is involved in sexual reproduction. *Paramecium* is perhaps the best-known genus of ciliate protozoa. Other genera of Ciliophora include *Stentor, Vorticella, Tetrahymena,* and *Didinium.* Ciliate protozoa consume other microorganisms, including other protozoa, as their food source. For example, the genus *Didinium* can consume *Paramecium* species, providing a dramatic picture of the microbial world when viewed by scanning electron microscopy (FIG. 17-38).

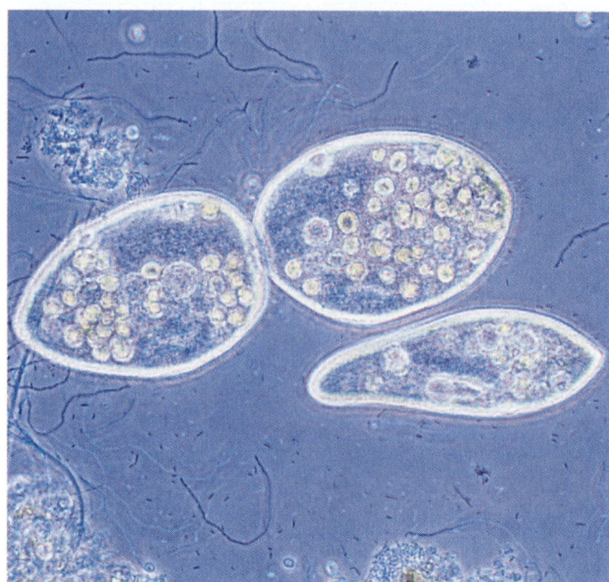

FIG. 17-37 The ciliate *Paramecium caudatum* showing transverse fission.

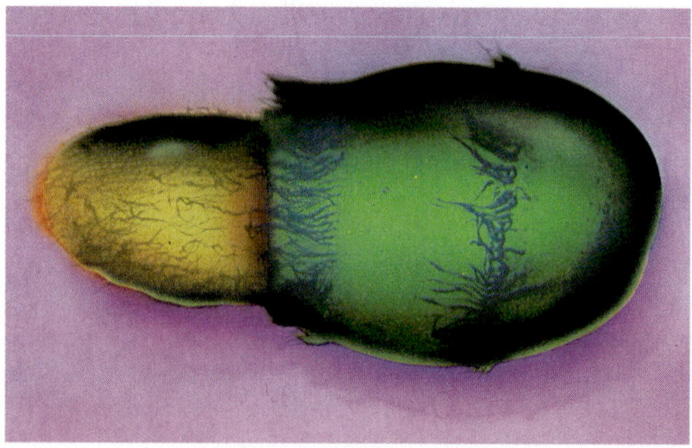

FIG. 17-38 Micrograph of the protozoan *Didinium* consuming the protozoan *Paramecium.*

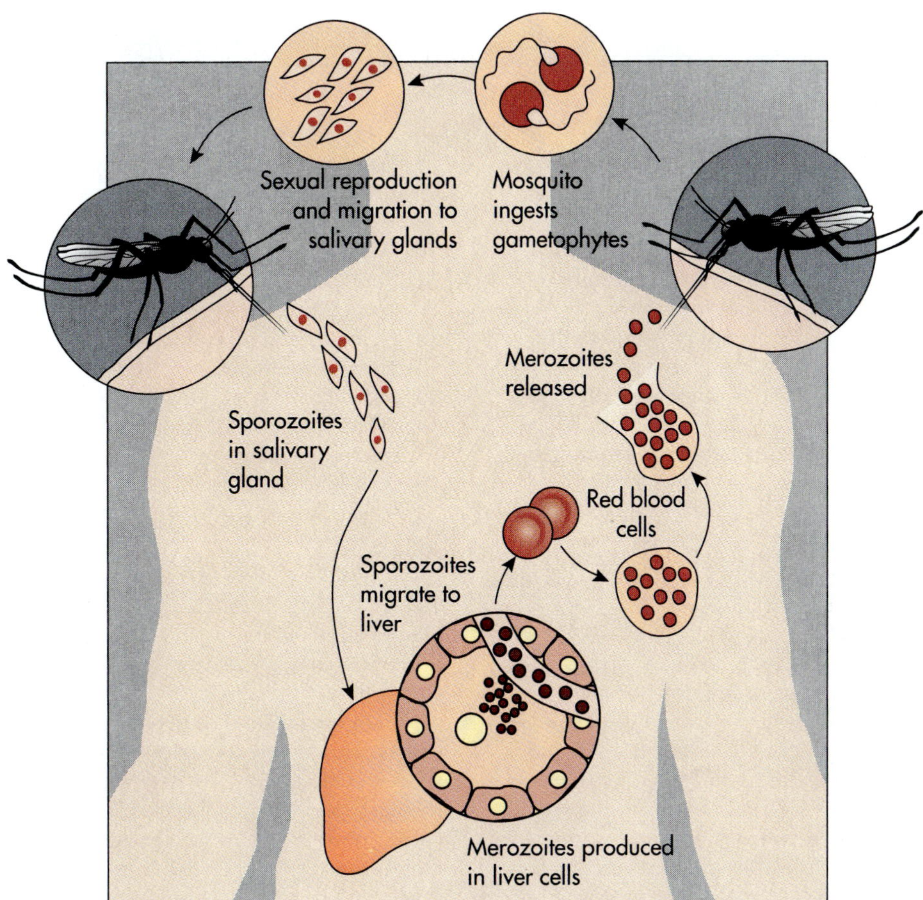

FIG. 17-39 Life cycle of *Plasmodium,* the protozoan that causes malaria.

Sporozoa

Sporozoa are parasites, exhibiting complex life cycles. The adult forms are nonmotile but immature forms and gametes may be motile. The sporozoans derive nutrition by absorbing nutrients from the host cells they inhabit. The immature stages are referred to as *sporozoites.* Reproduction of the *trophozoite,* the adult stage of a sporozoan, occurs asexually by multiple fission in which the mother cell divides into many daughter cells (FIG. 17-39). The cells produced by multiple fission eventually mature into gametes that can be involved in sexual reproduction. The multiple fission process can result in the production of thousands of spores. *Plasmodium vivax* and various other species of *Plasmodium* cause malaria. During the course of a malarial infection, life cycles of *Plasmodium* involve reproduction within human red blood cells, with the periodic release of numerous protozoa. As discussed earlier, members of the Apicomplexa, which include *Plasmodium* species, are characterized by the formation of an apical complex (FIG. 17-40). It is interesting that such morphological observations, achievable only by using electron microscopy, are now employed for defining major taxonomic groupings.

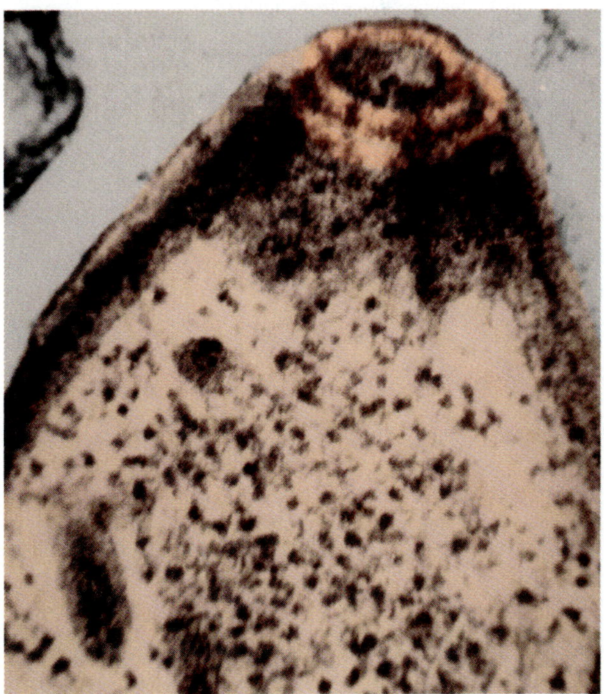

FIG. 17-40 Colorized micrograph showing the apical complex structure of the protozoan, a member of the apicomplexa.

CHAPTER REVIEW

STUDY QUESTIONS

1. On what basis are the major groups of fungi defined?
2. What is the importance of spore formation in fungal classification?
3. On what basis are the major groups of algae defined?
4. What is the importance of photosynthetic pigments and reserve materials in algal classification?
5. On what basis are the major groups of protozoa defined?
6. What is the importance of mode of locomotion to protozoan taxonomy?
7. Why are dinoflagellates treated by both protozoan and algal taxonomists?
8. What are the differences between the Ascomycetes and the Basidiomycetes?
9. What is a diatom?
10. What is unique about the structure of a diatom?
11. Should the brown algae be considered as plants or microorganisms?
12. Compare the reproduction of a yeast with that of a filamentous fungus.
13. How are yeasts and filamentous fungi enumerated?
14. What is the role of sexual reproduction in eukaryotic microorganisms?
15. Are slime molds fungi or protozoa?

SITUATIONAL PROBLEMS

Identifying Mushrooms

The ability to identify mushrooms can be a matter of life and death because some mushrooms are deadly poisonous. Mushrooms should never be eaten unless you are absolutely certain that they are not among the poisonous varieties. Many tragic stories appear in the news media when someone errs and eats a poisonous mushroom. In some cases, immigrants to the United States find and pick mushrooms that look just like the ones in their native country, only to discover that they are poisonous. Even knowledgeable people, such as the White House chef during the administration of President John Kennedy, have unfortunately mistaken the identity of a poisonous mushroom for one that they considered to be an edible delicacy. Hospitals and poison control centers have expert mycologists as consultants whom they contact in cases of suspected fungal poisoning to aid in the identification of the fungus and thus in the determination of the appropriate treatment process.

Suppose you want to collect mushrooms and serve them at a meal. You should compare the mushrooms you collect with an identification guide that is pertinent to your specific region. To determine what is involved in this task, assuming the season is appropriate, find and collect mushrooms in your local vicinity; otherwise, obtain several different types of mushrooms from your local supermarket or produce supplier. Then, using an identification guide, which should be available in your library, try to identify the species of these mushrooms. If the mushrooms you identify are store bought, you can check your identification and actually eat the mushrooms. Do not eat any of the wild mushrooms you have collected, just in case you are not yet enough of an expert on mushroom identification.

Suggested Supplementary Readings

Adam R: 1991. The biology of *Giardia* spp., *Microbiological Reviews* 55(4):706-32.

Ainsworth GC and AS Sussman (eds.): 1965-1973. *The Fungi: An Advanced Treatise* (4 volumes), Academic Press, New York.

Alexopoulos CJ and CW Mims: 1979. *Introductory Mycology*, John Wiley & Sons, Inc., New York.

Barnett JA, RW Payne, D Yarrow: 1979. *A Guide to Identifying and Classifying Yeasts*, Cambridge University Press, New York.

Bold HC and MJ Wynne: 1985. *Introduction to the Algae*, ed. 2, Prentice-Hall, Englewood Cliffs, NJ.

Bold HC and MJ Wynne: 1978. *Introduction to the Algae: Structure and Reproduction*, Prentice-Hall, Inc., Englewood Cliffs, NJ.

Chapman VJ and DJ Chapman: 1975. *The Algae*, St. Martin's Press, New York.

Cole GT and B Kendrick (eds.): 1981. *Biology of Conidial Fungi*, Academic Press, New York.

Corliss JO: 1979. *The Ciliated Protozoa: Characterization, Classification and Guide to the Literature*, Pergamon Press, New York.

Farmer JN: 1980. *The Protozoa: Introduction to Protozoology*, C.V. Mosby Co., St. Louis.

Fenchel T: 1987. *Ecology of Protozoa*, Springer-Verlag, New York.

Gall JG (ed.): 1986. *The Molecular Biology of Ciliated Protozoa*, Academic Press, Orlando, FL.

Jahn TL, EC Bovee, FF Jahn: 1979. *How to Know the Protozoa*, Wm. C. Brown Co., Dubuque, IA.

Kudo RR: 1977. *Protozoology*, Charles C. Thomas, Publisher, Springfield, IL.

Lee RE: 1989. *Phycology*, ed. 2, Cambridge University Press, NY.

Levine ND, JO Corliss, FEG Cox, G Deroux, J Grain, BM Honigberg, GF Leedale, AR Loeblich, J Lom, D Lynn, EG Meringeld, FC Page, G Poljansky, V Sprague, J Vavra, FG Wallace: 1980. A newly revised classification of the protozoa, *Journal of Protozoology* 27:37-58.

Lodder J and N Kreger-van Rij: 1970. *The Yeasts: A Taxonomic Study*, North Holland Publications, Amsterdam.

Margulis L, JO Corliss, M Melkonian: 1990. *Handbook of Protoctista*, Jones and Bartlett, Boston.

Miller OK: 1979. *Mushrooms of North America*, E.P. Dutton Co., NY.

Moore-Landecker E: 1991. *Fundamentals of Fungi*, ed. 3, Prentice-Hall, Englewood Cliffs, NJ.

Phaff HJ, MW Miller, EM Mrak: 1978. *The Life of Yeasts*, Harvard University Press, Cambridge, MA.

Rose AH and JS Harrison (eds.): 1986. *The Yeasts*, Academic Press, Orlando, FL.

Trainor FR: 1978. *Introductory Phycology*, John Wiley & Sons, Inc., New York.

THE STRUCTURED LIFE OF A BACTERIAL TAXONOMIST

R.G.E. Murray
University of Western Ontario

Robert George Everett (RGE) Murray was born in England in 1919 and educated at Cambridge and McGill University. He is emeritus professor of bacteriology and immunology at the University of Western Ontario, London, Ontario, Canada. Dr. Murray has edited the Canadian Journal of Microbiology, Bacteriological Reviews, *and* International Journal of Systematic Bacteriology. *He served on* Bergey's Manual *Trust, the International Committee on Bacteriological Nomenclature, the Biology Council of Canada, and the International Union of Microbiological Societies. He has been president of both the American and Canadian Societies for Microbiology. His research concerns bacterial cytology and physiology, the ultrastructure of bacteria, and the relationship of structure to function with emphasis on the cell wall and macromolecular arrangement.*

Most of my working life involved the study of the structure of bacteria and in trying to come to terms with their classification. Cytology and taxonomy have not been popular aspects of bacteriology, despite obvious utility, which was fortunate because my research has never been hampered by the overzealous competition that plagues popular fields. I grew up with and came naturally to studying microorganisms because my father was a professor of microbiology, full of enthusiasm for science and bacteria in particular, and introduced me as a child to an old brass microscope and the joy's of pond water and infusions of hay, leaves, and mud. There was very little science at school so I looked forward keenly to university studies. After some years of basic biology followed by medical studies, a year of pathology and bacteriology gave me the chance to study various aspects of disease. Despite the temptations of other subjects and exposure to a diversity of stimulating teachers at Cambridge University and McGill University, the lure of the bacteria had to be accepted, and in the end I spent my intership year in clinical bacteriology and infectious diseases.

After a brief time as a medical officer in the army I was offered a junior posting in the Department of Bacteriology and Immunology of the university which still houses me. This began my teaching (the best way to learn a subject!) with responsibility for diagnostic medical bacteriology, with all the attendant problems and rewards involved in isolating and identifying a variety of bacteria. The "baptism of fire" continued because within 4 years the professor left for another job and, remarkably, I was appointed a professor and head of a department at an early age. These were formative years and busy because Professor Asheshov had given me increasing responsibilities, as well as the encouragement and freedom to begin experimental work. His long-term interest in bacteriophage and my interest in making good use of the light microscope were combined when he suggested in 1948 that it would be interesting to know what a phage infection did to the structure of a bacterium. It was a stimulating time to do this because the new approaches to understanding virus infections by the study of phage infections of bacteria began in 1945 and exciting results were frequent and quickly shared among "phage workers." Light microscopy and simple cytochemical methods told us that infection led to a sequence of changes to the host cell nucleoids, essentially the loss of host chromatin (DNA) followed by the appearance of new DNA related to phage, and by changes in cytoplasmic basiphilia related to ribosomes and protein synthesis. The foremost exponent of bacterial cytology, C.F. Robinow, visited us, taught us many procedures, and, to our great benefit, agreed to stay and is still with us. This was exciting work because it gave visible dimensions to the new understanding of virus infections arising from model systems using the T-phages acting on *Escherichia coli*. It became obvious that we needed to know a lot more about the host cell structure and the functions of the discernable elements revealed by improved electron microscopy at a much higher resolution than light microscopy could provide.

We obtained our first electron microscope (EM) in 1954 and made mistakes but learned by consulting more experienced colleagues. Preparation of bacteria for electron microscopy had requirements different from those for animal tissues and to those we had learned laboriously for light microscopic cytology. In concert with colleagues around the world we had to design or discover appropriate chemical fixation regimes, resins for embedding, sectioning methods, means of improving contrast by "staining" with heavy metals, improvements in microscopy and the recording of images, and how to monitor the fractionation of cells. Along the way, many discoveries were made using sections of embeddings that gave us a view of differential cell wall profiles, plasma membrane, specialized functional membranous intrusions, flagella, and surface structure. However, crucial to development was the introduction of negative staining using heavy metal salts, which allowed the characterization of cell fragments so that we could follow the fractionation of cells for biochemical analysis and the relation of structures and functions. All this work was exciting because it fit into the overwhelming development of cell biology and molecular biology.

There was a mundane but no less important consequence because, by the end of the 1950s, we knew enough for a reasonably accurate structural description of bacteria as cells and there was progress toward adding unique features in a molecular and genetic description. These developments were significant for bacterial taxonomy. Textbooks and compendia such as *Bergey's Manual* up to 1957 classified bacteria as Schizomycetes and defined them as "typically unicellular plants," despite the publication of a Bacteriological Code in 1948. This judgement was considered by my father (an Editor-Trustee of the *Bergey's Manual* Trust) as an inaccurate and unfortunate treatment of a group likely to belong to a Kingdom of their own given adequate characterization. We discussed this often and knew in the mid-50s that a suitable description should be possible, but it was 10 years or more before R.Y. Stanier and C.B. van Niel wrote in 1962 about "the concept of a bacterium" and 1968 when I named a Kingdom *Procaryotae* based on the description of bacteria as cells.

Research and the decisions that arise are often slow and plodding even with excitements and maybe inexplicable obstructions along the way. In this case, much of the 10 years allowed for great improvements and included the delaying effect of an extended polemic, which played to full houses in major meetings on both sides of the Atlantic, about the behavior of segregating bacterial nuclei and the function of mesosomes (i.e., whether or not the constellations of bits of chromatin in certain bacteria represented a phase in mitosis and whether or not some intrusions of plasma membrane into cytoplasm represented the bacterial equivalent of mitochondria). Although the debates today seem trivial and without foundation they forced me and my colleague, C.F. Robinow (who bore the brunt of our side of the argument), even further into high standards for light and electron microscopic cytology. Putting structure with genetics (single linkage group in the nucleoid), the biochemical and physiological characterization of components (walls, membranes, functional intrusions and inclusions, ribosomes, flagella, to say nothing of the nucleic acids), and a still growing appreciation of energy mechanisms and metabolic transformations brought new aspects to considering bacterial diversity in the context of taxonomy and biotechnology. One of the many consequences of all this work was that textbooks and *Bergey's Manual* (Edition 8, 1974) could define bacteria as "unicellular procaryotic organisms," forming part of a "Kingdom defined by cellular, not organismal, properties." Another personal consequence was that I became a Trustee of *Bergey's Manual.*

The phylogenetic studies of today, initiated by C.R. Woese in the mid-70s, has identified a dozen or so major lineages of Bacteria and the distinct set of lineages for the Archaea. It is evident that one bacterial lineage is special because of the great variety of distinct morphological and physiological forms found in the five main branches within it, and it presented problems to us as taxonomists. Two branches include the purple, anoxygenic, photosynthetic bacteria, and all branches include a selection of the important fermentative and oxidative gram-negative bacteria we all know from medical and general bacteriology. After some time of referring to the entire lineage as "the purple photosynthetic bacteria and relatives" it became necessary to give them an ordinal name, *Proteobacteria* (with group *alpha, beta,* etc., for the main branches) so that there was some convenience in talking or writing about them. Fortunately, most of the other lineages are more consistent, and integration into bacterial taxonomy will be less stressful and will be effective as more and more molecular data is accumulated.

I learned about this taxonomic revolution in an interesting way. In 1957 a pretty, red-pigmented, gram-positive but structurally gram-negative coccal bacterium was isolated as a plate contaminant and we used it for teaching because it made elegant tetrads. Our first trial of phosphotungstic acid as a negative stain displayed a remarkable paracrystalline surface layer on the cell wall, which began our studies of S-layers. We were sure it was no ordinary coccus but could not prove it. We learned it was *"Micrococcus radiodurans,"* which had been isolated from irradiated canned meat and which, 20 years later and after a lot of taxonomic studies, we named *Deinococcus radiodurans.* It was extraordinary not only because of its extreme resistance to radiation but because, in collaboration with C.R. Woese, we found that the sequences in its 16S rRNA put it in one of the earliest phylogenetic lineages of the bacteria. This genus stands alone, although it must have been in development for a very long time; no fairly close relatives have yet been found and *Thermus* is a very distant relative.

The most exciting part of watching and having a small part in the taxonomic revolution brought on by reading the documents of evolution as written in highly conserved macromolecules such as ribosomal RNA and ATPase is the clear evidence of life forms being evolved as the derivatives of a single stem. We deal now with only the tips of the surviving branches of an evolutionary tree and have to infer order from the statistical assessment of sequences in semantide macromolecules.

Our exploration of bacterial structure over about 30 years (1960 to 1990) involved the diversity of forms of bacteria and the study in model systems of dynamic events such as the behavior of envelope components in cell division, functional entities such as flagella, special wall components such as the regularly structured S-layers, and some interactions with the environment such as the trapping of metal ions by envelope biopolymers. The "model systems" were not usually *E. coli* or *Bacillus subtilis* but more often an exemplary bacterium with diverse interesting features. For example, *Spirillum serpens* gave us the initial impetus to go further with a very long continued study of the paracrystalline, protein S-layers. These assemblies encrust the outer surface of the cell walls of many bacteria and archaea in nature and protect them from calamitous events (such as predation by *Bdellovibrio bacteriovorus* or damage to their polymers by stray enzymes) so there is a strong selection in favor of making sure they are not lost. It was not just the structure and the variety of symmetries within and between species that was fascinating to us. The essential information for assembly is provided in the structure of the macromolecule and is entropy driven to form crystalline sheets; some alone and others on the template of the underlying membrane; some formed of two different proteins making a double layer, and some extraordinary organisms (e.g., *Lampropedia hyalina*) have S-layers with units that are themselves a complex assembly of three or more proteins. So these are not only functional extra-wall components but also were of use as models of the assembly of cellular structures. To give added pleasure, other groups have joined the research and there have been three international workshop meetings in recent years that demonstrate the possibilities of structural analysis, diversity of functions, and biological significance regarding S-layers. Research progresses slowly and requires the development of suitable technology and of understanding, which is assisted by recognition of the natural variants expressed in biological diversity.

I have learned in my life that there are good reasons to be interested in bacterial structure and physiology and in the taxonomy and systematic study of bacteria. A detailed knowledge of structure assists in the recognition of what distinguishes bacteria from other forms of life, and this distinction is made more precise by the correlation of structure down to molecular levels with the biochemistry, physiology, and molecular genetics of the cells. Nowadays, we use all these latter features to classify bacteria and to place them in taxa with names so that we can talk about them and identify them by their properties when we cultivate them from nature. This represents in systematic form what we know of bacterial diversity. This kind of correlative study, taxonomy, makes use of *all that we know or think we know* and is the real basic bacteriology. The level of understanding available for a scientific basis for classifying bacteria was very primitive until an entire new set of approaches to thinking about bacteria became possible following the great innovative spurt (1945 and there after) in what came to be called cell biology, which affected all the biological disciplines in the past 50 years. I am fortunate that my time as a bacteriologist came at this exciting time and that I was involved in the progressive stages of a revolution in bacterial systematics. The stages involve answering a few direct questions:

What are bacteria?

Can bacteria be described more effectively?

Can we define relationships within bacterial taxa?

Where do bacteria belong among living things?

We have come a long way in answering these questions and it has been a very interesting journey.

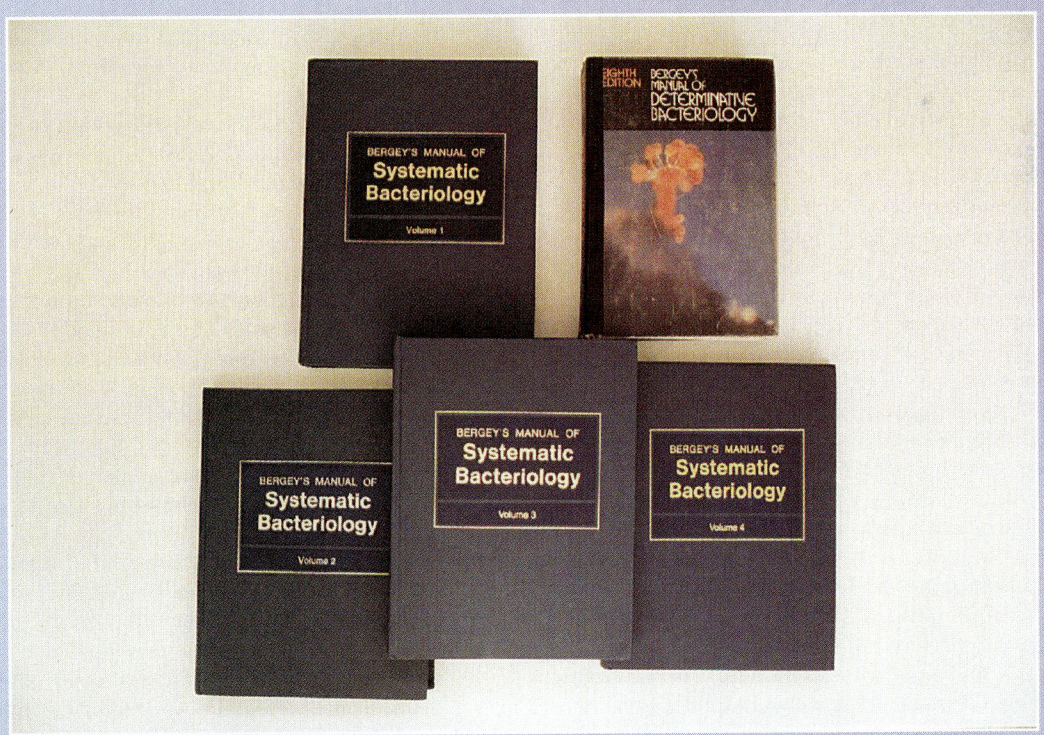

The multivolume *Bergey's Manual* is the standard taxonomic reference for bacterial identification.

STUDY OUTLINES

CHAPTER 1

CONTEMPORARY MICROBIOLOGY

A. Microbiology is the science that studies microorganisms, which are small life forms requiring magnification to be observed.
B. Modern microbiology is a fundamental science, often using microorganisms to examine molecular and biochemical questions, and an applied science, often using microorganisms or their control to solve human and global problems.
C. Contemporary subdisciplines of microbiology include medical microbiology, immunology, agricultural microbiology, plant pathology, microbial ecology, sanitary engineering, industrial microbiology, food microbiology, and biotechnology.

MICROORGANISMS

A. The microorganisms include the bacteria, viruses, fungi, algae, and protozoa.
B. Most microorganisms are unicellular; all lack tissue differentiation.
C. Cells are the fundamental units of living systems.
   1. Cells are organized, grow, metabolize, reproduce, and pass on their genetic information.
   2. Each cell is delimited by a boundary cytoplasmic membrane.
   3. Cells are prokaryotic or eukaryotic.
      a. Eukaryotic cells have membrane-bound compartments called organelles that serve specific functions.
      b. The nucleus is the organelle that contains the DNA (hereditary information) within a eukaryotic cell.
      c. Prokaryotic cells do not have a nucleus or other membrane-bound organelles.
D. Microorganisms evolved from a common ancestor along three distinct paths to form the archaebacteria (Archaea), eubacteria, and eukaryotes (fungi, algae, and protozoa).
E. The archaebacteria (Archaea) and eubacteria (commonly called simply bacteria) have prokaryotic cells.
   1. The archaebacteria are physiologically highly specialized prokaryotes and include methanogens, halophiles, thermophiles, and acidophiles.
   2. The eubacteria are morphologically and physiologically diverse.
F. The fungi, algae, and protozoa have eukaryotic cells as do plants and animals.
   1. Fungi have cell walls and form spores.
      The yeasts are unicellular fungi.
      The molds are filamentous fungi that form hyphae.
   2. Algae are photosynthetic.
   3. Protozoa are unicellular and typically motile by various means.
G. Viruses are microorganisms that lack cellular organization.
   1. Viruses cannot carry out life functions independently.
   2. Viruses can only replicate within the cells of living organisms.

SCIENCE OF MICROBIOLOGY

A. The scientific method is used to advance knowledge in microbiology.
   1. The scientific method starts with a question to which a tentative answer (hypothesis) is proposed.
   2. Controlled experiments are done to test the hypothesis.
B. The observation of microorganisms is essential for their scientific study.
   1. The invention of the microscope made the observation of microorganisms possible.
   2. Antonie van Leeuwenhoek reported the first observations of microorganisms from water in 1674.
C. Bacteria and other cellular microorganisms are living organisms.
   1. Louis Pasteur in the mid-nineteenth century demonstrated that microorganisms do not arise spontaneously from nonliving matter.
   2. Pasteur showed that microorganisms have the same essential properties as other living organisms.
   3. Pasteur established microbiology as a true science by demonstrating that the scientific method could be applied to the study of microorganisms.
   4. Pasteur showed that fermentation and putrefaction were caused by the actions of different microorganisms and that heat could be used to kill microorganisms.
D. Some microorganisms cause human diseases.
   1. The germ theory of disease was proved by Robert Koch in the nineteenth century.
   3. Koch's postulates established the steps needed to prove scientifically that a specific microorganism causes a particular disease.
   3. Koch and his co-workers developed the methods for growing (culturing) individual types of microorganisms in the laboratory—a necessary step for identifying disease-causing microorganisms.
E. Chemicals can be used to control microorganisms.
   1. Lister introduced antiseptic principles to surgical practice, significantly reducing the rate of postoperative infection.
   2. The first antimicrobial agents for treating disease came from the work of Koch's co-workers.

3. Penicillin was discovered in 1929 by Alexander Fleming; since then numerous antibiotics have been discovered that are useful for treating disease.

F. The immune response is the system of body defenses against infection.
   1. Immunization artificially stimulates this natural immune defense system.
   2. Edward Jenner used vaccination with cowpox as a means of protection against smallpox. Pasteur developed a vaccine against anthrax and rabies.
   3. The immune response is a complex network of cellular and chemical responses.
   4. Eli Metchnikoff discovered that phagocytic cells migrate to areas of infection and digest infecting microorganisms.
   5. Antibodies are made in response to an infection—antibodies are proteins made in response to antigens; antigens stimulate the body to form antibodies with which they react.

G. Microorganisms play critical roles in nature that recycle substances and maintain ecological balance.
   1. Microbial ecology examines the interactions of microorganisms with their biotic and abiotic surroundings.
   2. Sergei Winogradsky and Martinus Beijerinck opened the field of microbial ecology with their discoveries on the microbial transformations of inorganic compounds.

H. DNA is the molecule that stores and transmits hereditary information.
   1. The discovery that DNA is the substance of heredity was made in the 1940s when Oswald, Avery, and coworkers demonstrated that DNA was capable of transforming *Streptococcus pneumoniae.*
   2. James Watson and Francis Crick proposed a double helical structure for DNA that permitted further discoveries of the ways in which genetic information is stored and expressed.
   3. The operon theory explains the control of protein synthesis by the expression of specific genes.
   4. Recombinant DNA technology permits the cloning and transfer of genes.

CHAPTER 2

MICROSCOPY

A. Microscopes magnify the size of the apparent image of an object.

B. Magnification is the enlargement of the image of an object.

C. Light Microscopy.
   1. Microscope lenses and properties of light.
      a. Ground glass lenses bend and focus light on the focal point.
      b. Compound microscopes have ocular and objective lenses.
      c. Spherical and chromatic aberrations are distortion problems associated with convex-convex lenses that are corrected with the use of achromatic, apochromatic, or flat-field lenses.
   2. Magnification is the product of the individual magnifying capacities of the objective and ocular lenses.
   3. Resolution is the degree to which the detail in a specimen is revealed in its magnified image.
      a. Resolving power is the closest space between two points at which the points can still be seen as separate entities through a microscope.
      b. Resolving power is improved by shorter wavelengths of light and higher numerical apertures.
      c. Numerical aperture is the property of a lens that describes the amount of light that can enter it.
      d. Numerical aperture is determined by the refractive index of the medium in the space between the specimen and the objective lens and the angle of the most oblique light rays that can enter the objective lens.
      e. The refractive index, and thus resolving power, can be improved with the use of an oil immersion lens and immersion oil.
   4. Staining is necessary to provide enough contrast to distinguish specimen and background under the light microscope.
      a. Stains can be positive or negative.
      b. Differential stains, such as the Gram and acid-fast stains, permit specific types of microorganisms and their particular structures to be distinguished.
   5. In the bright-field microscope, light is transmitted through the specimen.
   6. Fluorescent dyes stain antibodies and make fluorescence microscopy useful for identifying specific microorganisms.
   7. Specimens observed with dark-field microscopes do not have to be stained.
   8. Phase contrast microscopes are used to visualize unstained living microorganisms.
   9. Interference microscopes take advantage of changes in intensity that occur when differing waves of light are combined; the Nomarski differential interference microscope produces a pseudo three-dimensional image.
   10. A scanning confocal microscope eliminates blur due to out of focus light; a laser scanning confocal microscope produces a three-dimensional image from a series of scanned images.

D. Electron Microscopy.
   1. Electron microscopes can magnify an image up to a million times larger than the object.
   2. Electron microscopes have the highest resolving power because they use electron beams that have very short wavelengths.
   3. Artifacts sometimes occur in transmission electron microscopy because specimens must be specially prepared.
   4. Sample preparation involves dehydration; it may also involve thin sectioning and freeze etching to reveal detailed structures.
   5. Transmission electron microscopes focus electron beams on specimens with electromagnetic condenser lenses.
   6. In scanning electron microscopy an electron beam is scanned across a heavy metal–coated specimen surface; secondary electrons are emitted.

7. Secondary electrons are thus produced that are transmitted to a collector and then to a detector that emits light when struck by electrons.
8. The emitted light is converted to an electron current that controls the brightness of the image on a cathode ray tube screen.
9. The intensity of the image on the CRT screen reflects the composition and topography of the specimen surface.

CULTURE OF MICROORGANISMS

A. Pure cultures of microorganisms contain only a single type of microorganism.
B. Isolation methods separate microorganisms into individual cells that reproduce to form clones.
C. Culture media provide nutrition for microorganisms.
D. In a defined medium, all the components are known. In complex media, some of the chemical components are unknown.
E. Growth media usually contain a source of nitrogen, phosphate, sulfate, iron, magnesium, sodium, potassium, and chloride ions.
F. Heterotrophic microorganisms require organic carbon compounds.
G. Enrichment culture technique isolates specific groups of microorganisms based on the culture medium and incubation conditions, such as temperature, aeration, and pH, that preferentially support the growth of specific microorganisms.
H. Sterilization can be accomplished with filtration or heat. Microbial cultures are kept sterile by using aseptic technique when working with them.
I. The streak, spread, and pour plate techniques isolate pure cultures of bacteria on or in culture media.
J. Pure cultures of bacteria can be preserved by refrigeration, freezing, or lyophilization.

CHARACTERIZATION AND IDENTIFICATION

A. Physiological growth characteristics and an array of metabolic reactions are used to characterize microorganisms so they can be identified.
B. Serological procedures are used to identify microorganisms based on specific antigen–antibody reaction.
   1. Fluorescent antibody stains are used to detect specific microorganisms.
   2. The enzyme-linked immunosorbant assay (ELISA) is a rapid, sensitive, and specific method for identifying microorganisms.
C. Gene probes are used to identify microorganisms based on their genetic composition.
   1. Hybridization artificially constructs a double-stranded nucleic acid by complementary base pairing of two single-stranded nucleic acids.
   2. Hybridization of gene probes is used to detect specific DNA sequences.

ENUMERATION

A. The viable plate count and direct counting techniques are used to enumerate bacteria.
B. Bacteria are also counted by using machines, such as a particle counter or spectrophotometer (to measure turbidity).
C. The most probable number technique uses probability theory to enumerate bacteria.

CHAPTER 3

CELLS

A. The cell is the fundamental structural unit of all living organisms.
B. Cells are surrounded by cytoplasmic membranes and contain cytoplasm, DNA, and ribosomes.
C. Cells process genetic information, form proteins, and use energy from ATP.
D. Prokaryotic cells are simply organized without organelles, which are membrane-bound compartments that serve specialized functions.
E. Eukaryotic cells have organelles, including a nucleus, which is the specialized eukaryotic organelle that contains the cell's DNA.

CYTOPLASMIC MEMBRANE

A. A cell's cytoplasmic membrane is a differentially permeable barrier, selectively restricting the movement of specific molecules in and out of the cell.
B. The cytoplasmic membrane is composed of hydrophobic and hydrophilic portions.
   1. Cytoplasmic membranes of eukaryotic and eubacterial cells contain phospholipids arranged in a bilayer and straight chain fatty acids linked to glycerol by ester bonds.
   2. The cytoplasmic membrane of eubacterial cells is made of phospholipids with unbranched fatty acids and phosphate bonded to glycerol with proteins interspersed in the matrix.
   3. Eukaryotic cell cytoplasmic membrane contains sterols, which make it stronger.
   4. According to the fluid mosaic model, proteins in cytoplasmic membranes are arranged in a mosaic-like pattern on the surface and within the lipid bilayer.
   5. Proteins establish channels through which substances can move across the membrane.
   6. The cytoplasmic membranes of archaebacteria contain branched lipids linked to glycerol by ether bonds.
      a. Major lipids of archaebacteria are not phospholipids, but diverse polar and nonpolar lipids.
      b. Cytoplasmic membranes of archaebacterial cells may be mono- or bilayers. This diversity in the archaebacterial cytoplasmic membrane may be environmentally related because these organisms tend to live in extreme environments.
C. Various transport mechanisms move substances into and out of cells across the cytoplasmic membrane.
   1. Diffusion is the movement of molecules from a region of higher concentration to one of lower concentration until equal concentrations are established of a substance on opposing sides of a cytoplasmic membrane.
      a. Diffusion is passive when the movement is unassisted.

b. The rates of passive diffusion are slow, determined by the concentration gradient and the membrane's permeability.
c. Glycerol is transported by facilitated diffusion, an enhanced rate of diffusion that depends on facilitator or membrane transport proteins, which increase the permeability of the membrane for specific solutes.

2. Osmosis is the process by which water crosses the membrane in response to the concentration gradient.
   a. Osmotic pressure is the pressure exerted by the movement of water by osmosis.
   b. Osmotic pressure is the force that must be exerted to maintain the concentration differences between solutions on opposite sides of the membrane.
   c. Solute concentrations are isotonic, hypotonic, or hypertonic.
   d. Osmotic shock is cell lysis due to osmosis.
3. Active transport is the movement across the cytoplasmic membrane that requires the expenditure of energy and does not modify the transported material.
   a. Permeases act as carriers; uniporters carry only one substance and co-transporters can carry more than one substrate.
      (i). Substrates can be carried in the same or opposite directions.
      (ii). The energy is from ATP or an electrochemical gradient.
      (iii). Protonmotive force is the energy used in archaebacterial and eubacterial cells that comes from the electrochemical concentration gradient of protons across the cytoplasmic membrane.
      (iv). In some eukaryotic cells the gradient is between sodium and potassium ions.
   b. In group translocation the transported substance is chemically altered during passage through the membrane.
      (i). The phosphoenolpyruvate phosphotransferase system (PEP:PTS) adds a phosphate group to a sugar as it crosses the cytoplasmic membrane of some prokaryotic cells.
   c. Gram-negative bacteria can use binding protein transport (also known as shock-sensitive transport) that involves a second, outer membrane and the periplasmic space between the two membranes.
   d. Cytosis is an energy-requiring transport process in which a substance is engulfed by the cytoplasmic membrane forming a vesicle.
      (i). Endocytosis is the movement of materials into the cell and exocytosis is movement out of the cell.
      (ii). During phagocytosis a cell engulfs a smaller cell or particle.

EXTERNAL STRUCTURES THAT PROTECT THE CELL

A. Most eubacterial cells are surrounded by firm, flexible, porous cell walls made of peptidoglycan (murein or mucopeptide) that protect the cell from osmotic shock.
   1. Lysozyme is an enzyme that can destroy cell walls by breaking the bonds of the glycan backbone of peptidoglycan.
      a. Spheroplasts are the remnants of a cell with a portion of the cell wall remaining after lysozyme treatment.
      b. An intact bacterial cell without a cell wall is called a protoplast.
   2. Penicillin prevents the formation of peptide cross-linkages in peptidoglycan, creating defective cell walls that cannot protect the cell against osmotic shock; it binds to penicillin-binding proteins; autolysins break specific bonds in the peptidoglycan.
   3. Gram-positive eubacterial cell walls have thick peptidoglycan layers bonded to teichoic acids, which can bind protons and thus keep the cell wall at low pH and prevent autolytic degradation of the wall.
   4. Gram-negative cell walls have thin peptidoglycan layers with lipoproteins bonded to the peptidoglycan and layers of lipopolysaccharide, phospholipids, and proteins outside the peptidoglycan layer.
      a. Gram-negative cells have outer membranes, lipid bilayers that are joined to the cytoplasmic membrane at adhesion sites (Bayer junctions) around the cell at which some material is moved from inside the cell.
      b. The outer membrane contains lipopolysaccharides, which act as endotoxins.
      c. The outer membrane is a coarse molecular sieve through which hydrophilic and hydrophobic molecules can diffuse.
      d. Porins form cross channels through which some molecules can diffuse.
      e. The periplasmic space (or gel) is the space between the cytoplasmic and outer membranes.
      f. Binding proteins, chemoreceptors, and hydrolytic enzymes are found in the periplasmic space.

B. Cell walls of methanogenic and halophilic Archaebacteria are made of pseudopeptidoglycan.
C. Algal cell walls are made of cellulose; some have tests or frustules made of calcium or silicon.
D. Most fungi have cell walls that are often composed of chitin.
E. Protozoa do not have true cell walls; they are surrounded by thin pellicles that maintain their shapes.
F. Some bacteria have protective capsules or slime layers made of polysaccharides surrounding the cell wall.
   1. Capsules protect the cell against phagocytosis.
   2. Encapsulated bacteria tend to be more pathogenic.
   3. Capsules protect against dehydration and loss of nutrients and also trap nutrients.
   4. Slime layers are more loosely attached to cells than capsules.

CELLULAR GENETIC INFORMATION

A. The bacterial chromosome contains the genetic information of archaebacteria and eubacteria.
   1. It is a highly twisted, circular DNA molecule that occurs in the nucleoid region.
   2. Cell division must be synchronized with chromosome replication.

B. Bacteria reproduce by binary fission.
   1. Septa formation separate the two complete bacterial chromosomes.
   2. Cross walls (septae) cut the bacterial chromosome and distribute them to the daughter cells.
C. Plasmids are small, circular macromolecules of DNA occurring in bacteria that contain specific genetic information in addition to the chromosome and can be used in genetic engineering.
D. Eukaryotic cells have an organelle called a nucleus that holds the genetic information of the cell.
   1. The nucleus is bound by a double layer phospholipid nuclear membrane.
   2. Chromosomes, made of chromatin (DNA and protein), hold the genetic information in the nucleus.
      a. Chromatin proteins consist of histones ionically bound to the DNA.
      b. Nucleosomes are subunits of DNA coiled around the histones, composed of 200 nucleotides.

RIBOSOMES AND PROTEIN SYNTHESIS

A. Ribosomes, made of rRNA, are the sites of protein synthesis.
B. Ribosomes are sized in Svedburg units, which are a measure of sedimentation in an ultracentrifuge.
C. Prokaryotic cells have 70S ribosomes composed of 30S and 50S subunits.
D. Eukaryotic cells have 80S ribosomes composed of 40S and 60S subunits.

SITES OF CELLULAR ENERGY TRANSFORMATIONS

A. Chemiosmosis is the generation of ATP by the flow of protons across a membrane.
B. Synthesis of ATP by chemiosmosis is driven by the establishment of a hydrogen ion gradient across membranes.
C. Nitrifying and photosynthetic bacteria have extensive internal membranes.
D. Cyanobacteria have multilayered membrane structures called thylakoids.
E. Chemiosmotic generation of ATP occurs in the mitochondria of eukaryotes.
   1. Mitochondria have inner and outer membranes.
   2. Cristae are the convolutions of the inner membrane that extend into the interior of the mitochondrion.
F. Photosynthetic ATP synthesis and carbon dioxide fixation occur in the chloroplasts of algal and plant cells.
   1. Chloroplasts are plastids, large cytoplasmic organelles containing pigment or other cellular products occurring within the cytoplasm of algae.
   2. The stroma is the inner compartment of the chloroplast and the site of carbon dioxide fixation during photosynthesis.
   3. Thylakoids are the internal membranous system of chloroplasts.
   4. Grana are stacked thylakoids.

MATERIAL MOVEMENT AND STORAGE IN CELLS

A. Exoenzymes are extracellular enzymes that degrade large substances outside the cell so smaller molecules can be transported across the cell membrane.
   1. Exoenzymes destroy harmful substances.
   2. A signal sequence in an enzyme is a segment at the amino terminal end that acts as a signal to begin the secretion process.
B. Inclusion bodies are unbounded accumulations of reserve materials in the cytoplasm.
   1. Polyphosphate granules (volutin or metachromatic granules) are stored for later generation of ATP and cell constituents.
   2. Poly-β-hydroxybutyric acid is the most common bacterial carbon reserve material.
C. Many eukaryotic organelles are linked for coordinated functioning.
   1. The endoplasmic reticulum, a membranous network of fluid-filled sacs, provides a large surface area for enzymatic activity and a source of lipids and membranes for other organelles.
   2. Golgi bodies, the sites of synthetic activity, are flattened membranous sacs stacked to form the Golgi apparatus, which is continuous with the rough endoplasmic reticulum.
   3. Proteins and lipids are repackaged into secretory vesicles at the Golgi apparatus, they move to the cytoplasmic membrane and release their contents by exocytosis.
   4. Lysosome organelles contain digestive enzymes.
   5. Microbodies contain catalase and isolate metabolic reactions involving hydrogen peroxide.
   6. The peroxisome microbody is the site of amino acid oxidation; isolation of the process within the microbody protects the cell.
   7. Vacuoles are membrane-bound organelles involved in storage and movement.
   8. The cytoskeletal network, composed of microtubules and microfilaments, determines the eukaryotic cell's ability to move and maintain its shape; it also links the components of the cytoplasm into a unified cytoplast, giving the necessary rigidity to maintain the various structures in place.

MOVEMENT OF CELLS

A. Bacterial flagella are long projections from the cytoplasmic membrane.
   1. Bacterial flagella are made of protein (flagellin).
   2. Bacterial flagella are attached to the cell by a hook and basal body.
   3. Flagella propel bacteria by rotating.
   4. Polar flagella originate from the end of the cell.
   5. Peritrichous flagella surround the cell.
B. Chemotaxis is movement in response to chemical stimuli.
   1. Chemicals can be chemoattractants or chemorepellents.
   2. Bacteria run and tumble (twiddle) in response to stimuli.
   3. Methyl-accepting chemotaxis proteins (MCPs) control the direction of flagellar rotation.
   4. MCPs alternate between excited and adapted states.
C. Magnetosomes are bacterial inclusions of iron granules that allow bacteria to orient themselves in response to magnetic fields (magnetotaxis).

D. Phototaxis is the response to differences in light intensity.
   1. Gas vacuoles enable some bacteria to respond to light.
   2. They also adjust cell buoyancy because they are filled with hydrogen gas.
E. Eukaryotic flagella are polar structures whereas cilia surround the eukaryotic cell.
   1. Flagella and cilia consist of a series of hollow cylinders made of tubulin protein surrounded by a membrane (microtubules).
   2. There are nine pairs of microtubules forming a circle and surrounding two single central microtubules connected by radial spokes of protein microfilaments.

STRUCTURES INVOLVED IN ATTACHMENT

A. The glycocalyx is a bacterial attachment structure made of a mass of tangled fibers of polysaccharides or branching sugar molecules surrounding a cell or colony of cells.
B. Pili are proteinaceous bacterial attachment structures emanating from some bacterial surfaces.
   1. The F or fertility pilus is involved in bacterial mating.
   2. Pili act as receptor sites for some bacteriophages.
   3. Other pili act as adhesins.

SPORES

A. Spores are specialized, resistant structures produced by some bacteria and fungi. Spores are involved in the ability to reproduce, to disperse, or to withstand adverse environmental conditions.
B. Bacterial endospores are multilayered, heat resistant spores made of peptidoglycan and calcium dipicolinate.
   1. Sporulation occurs under unfavorable environmental conditions.
   2. When conditions are favorable, the endospore germinates; the spore swells, breaks out of the spore coat, and elongates; and the organism renews normal vegetative growth.

CHAPTER 4

CELLULAR ENERGY AND METABOLISM

A. Conservation of energy.
   1. The principle of energy conservation says that chemical reactions can neither create nor destroy energy.
   2. Energy can be transformed from one form to another.
   3. The change in free energy (ΔG) is the change in energy that is available to do work.
      a. ΔG is a function of the change of the heat of reaction, temperature, and the change in entropy between the reactants and the products of the chemical reaction.
      b. The enthalpy change (ΔH) of a biochemical reaction indicates the difference between the energy stored within the reactants and the energy stored within the products of the reaction.
      c. The change in free energy (ΔG) of a reaction is the change in the energy available for doing work.
      d. Only reactions with negative ΔG values can proceed spontaneously.
      e. Reactions with negative ΔG values are called exergonic reactions.
      f. Reactions with positive ΔG values are called endergonic reactions and will only proceed if energy from another source is supplied to make them proceed.
      g. Endergonic reactions can be made to proceed if they are coupled with a sufficiently exergonic reaction, so that the net coupled reaction is exergonic overall.
      h. The ΔG of a reaction is a function of the relative concentrations of the reactants and products and the standard free energy change (ΔG) of the reaction.
      i. The ΔG is the difference between the sum of the standard free energies of all the products and the sum of the standard free energies of all the reactants.
      j. The ΔG values themselves depend on the chemical nature of the reactants and products.
   4. Cellular metabolism is the collection of chemical reactions cells carry out to transform energy to generate ATP and to use that ATP to power the many energy-requiring reactions on which all cells depend.
      a. The constant interconversion of ADP and ATP is fundamental to cellular energetics.
      b. Cells must continuously form and consume ATP.
      c. ATP contains high energy phosphate ester bonds that release −7.3 kcal/mole of free energy when ATP is hydrolyzed to ADP and P_i.
B. Enzymes and activation energy.
   1. An input of activation energy is required for a chemical reaction to occur.
   2. Activation energy is the amount of energy required in a collision between two reactants to initiate a chemical reaction between them.
   3. Enzymes are the biological catalysts that speed up almost all of the chemical reactions of life.
      a. Enzymes lower the activation energy of the reactions they catalyze, allowing the reactions to occur more quickly and at lower temperatures.
      b. Almost all enzymes are proteins.
      c. Enzymes are substrate specific.
         (i). Enzyme and substrate must fit together in a specific way for the enzyme to lower the activation energy.
         (ii). Enzymes have specific active sites at which specific substrates bind, forming weak bonds that strain the substrate molecule sufficiently to lower the activation energy of the catalyzed reaction and allow it to occur.
      d. Rates of enzymatic reactions depend on temperature, concentrations of enzyme and substrate, and the affinity of enzyme for the substrate.

e. Heat-denatured enzymes are nonfunctional due to the distortion of the shape of an enzyme at high temperature.
f. Enzymatic reactions can reach a point of saturation when all of the enzyme's active sites are occupied all of the time; at this point, further increasing the concentration of substrate does not alter the rate of reaction. V_{max} is the maximal reaction rate of the enzyme.
g. The Michaelis constant (K_m) is the substrate concentration at one-half V_{max} and is a measure of the affinity of the enzyme for the substrate.

4. Allosteric effectors bind to and alter the shape of enzymes and may activate or inhibit the enzymes they bind to, depending on the effectors and enzymes involved.
   a. Feedback (or end product) inhibition by allosteric effectors slows down the affected reaction pathway when excessive product is present.
   b. Allosteric activation speeds up the activity of the enzymes concerned.

C. Oxidation-reduction reactions.
1. Oxidation (loss of electrons) and reduction (gain of electrons) reactions are always coupled to form oxidation-reduction reactions.
2. Coenzymes are small, nonprotein organic compounds that participate in many enzymatic oxidation-reduction reactions, where they accept, hold, or donate electrons.
3. Reduction potential is a substance's relative susceptibility to oxidation or reduction; it is the relative voltage (electromotive force) required to remove an electron from a given compound compared to the voltage required to remove an electron from H_2 under standard conditions.
4. Reducing agents have more negative reduction potentials than oxidizing agents and donate electrons to oxidizing agents.
5. Oxidizing agents have more positive reduction potentials than reducing agents and accept electrons from reducing agents.
6. The greater the difference in voltage between the half-reactions of an oxidation-reduction reaction, the greater the free energy change of the reaction.

METABOLIC STRATEGIES FOR GENERATING ATP

A. The synthesis of ATP can be autotrophic (through metabolism of inorganic substrates or through conversion of light energy to chemical energy) or heterotrophic (through the utilization of organic substrates).

B. A metabolic pathway is a specific series of chemical reactions that converts a starting substrate into an end product.

C. Many metabolic pathways involve the transformation of energy to either generate or utilize ATP. Substrate-level phosphorylation generates ATP by the direct transfer of phosphate onto ADP in an exergonic reaction that couples the phosphorylation with a reaction that releases sufficient free energy to drive the phosphorylation.

D. Cellular metabolism is used to pump protons across a membrane to establish a proton gradient that can then drive the chemiosmotic generation of ATP.
1. The proton gradient generates a force (the protonmotive force) that pushes protons through any suitable channel through the membrane.
2. ATPase is a proton-conducting membrane-bound enzyme that couples the movement of protons driven by the protonmotive force with the synthesis of ATP.

E. Autotrophic metabolism does not require preformed organic matter to drive the conversion of ADP + P_i to ATP.
1. Photoautotrophic (photosynthetic) metabolism uses light energy to drive the conversion of ADP + P_i to ATP.
2. Chemoautotrophic (chemolithotrophic) metabolism uses the energy released by reactions of inorganic compounds to drive the conversion of ADP + P_i to ATP.

F. In heterotrophic (chemoorganotrophic) metabolism, organic substrate molecules are converted to end products via a metabolic pathway of oxidation-reduction reactions that has sufficient free energy to be coupled with the synthesis of ATP.
1. Catabolism is the breakdown of organic molecules to smaller molecules.
2. Glycolysis is sugar catabolism that yields pyruvate and ATP.
3. Glycolysis is a core pathway in cellular metabolism.
4. Respiratory pathways require an external molecule, usually molecular oxygen, to act as the final electron acceptor whose reduction balances the oxidation of an organic substrate.
5. When molecular oxygen is the terminal electron acceptor, the pathway is aerobic respiration. Anaerobic respiratory pathways involve other chemicals (such as nitrates or sulfates) serving as the terminal electron acceptor.
6. In fermentation, an organic substrate acts as an electron donor and a product derived from the substrate acts as the electron acceptor, there is no net change in oxidation states of substrates or products in fermentation pathways, and there is no requirement for oxygen.
7. Fermentation yields much less ATP per substrate molecule than respiration so fewer substrate molecules must be metabolized during respiration than during fermentation to support the metabolic requirements of the same number of cells.

RESPIRATORY METABOLISM

A. The completion of the aerobic respiration pathway results in the formation of carbon dioxide (whose carbon atoms are derived from an organic substrate molecule), water (derived from the reduction of oxygen), and ATP (derived from ADP and P_i).

B. The pathway for the aerobic respiration of glucose and other substrates consists of an initial catabolic pathway, followed by the tricarboxylic acid cycle, and then oxidative phosphorylation.

C. Carbohydrates are initially broken down via a glycolytic pathway that produces pyruvate.
1. The Embden-Meyerhof pathway of glycolysis converts glucose to two pyruvate molecules, two ATP molecules, and two reduced coenzyme molecules.
2. The Embden-Meyerhof pathway uses two ADP mole-

cules, two inorganic phosphate ions, and two molecules of coenzyme NAD^+. Phosphofructokinase is the key enzyme in the regulation of glycolysis.
3. Catabolism of glucose by the Entner-Doudoroff pathway by eubacteria (which lack the key enzyme 6-phosphofructokinase used in the Embden-Meyerhof pathway) produces only 1 ATP molecule per mole of glucose; the Entner-Doudoroff pathway is an important source of reduced coenzyme and 3-carbon molecules.
4. The pentose phosphate pathway generates ATP, reduced coenzymes, and small precursor molecules for biosynthesis; variations on the pathway depend on the need for NADPH, ATP, and precursor molecules.
5. The methyl glyoxal pathway is an alternate to the Embden-Meyerhof pathway under low phosphate conditions.

D. Lipids can be substrates providing the energy for the cellular production of ATP.
1. Lipases cleave fatty acids from the glycerol portion of a triglyceride lipid molecule.
2. Glycerol can then be metabolized to enter the glycolytic pathways.
3. Phospholipase cleaves fatty acid and phosphate groups from glycerol molecules.
4. Fatty acids are broken down into small 2-carbon acetyl-CoA molecules by β-oxidation, which also yields NADH and $FADH_2$.

E. Proteins can be used by some bacteria as the substrates providing the energy for the synthesis of ATP.
1. Proteins are broken down by proteases into smaller peptides and amino acids.
2. Deaminases and decarboxylases remove amino groups and carboxylic acid groups from amino acids.

F. The tricarboxylic acid (TCA) cycle is also known as the citric acid or Krebs cycle.
1. The TCA cycle supplies precursors to many biosynthetic pathways.
2. In the TCA cycle, 2 pyruvate molecules, generated from glucose, 2 ADP molecules, 2 flavin adenine dinucleotide enzyme molecules, and 8 NAD^+ coenzyme molecules are converted to 6 carbon dioxide molecules, 2 ATP molecules, 2 molecules of reduced flavin adenine dinucleotide, and 8 NADH molecules.

G. Oxidative phosphorylation uses the reoxidation of reduced coenzymes generated during glycolysis and the TCA cycle to generate ATP by chemiosmosis.
1. An electron transport chain is formed by the transfer of electrons from the reduced coenzymes NADH and $FADH_2$ to a series of membrane-bound carriers.
   a. The reduced coenzymes are reoxidized and reused as electron acceptors.
   b. The carriers in the electron transport chain participate in a series of reactions of increase in E'_0 values (between that of the primary electron donor and the terminal electron acceptors).
   c. Within the electron transport chain, some carriers transport hydrogen atoms and others transport only electrons.
2. The transfer of electrons from the reduced coenzyme to the terminal electron acceptor establishes a proton gradient across the membrane that is critical for the generation of ATP.
   a. The carriers of the electron transport chain are asymmetrically distributed through the membrane, and the movement of protons across the membrane, as a result of electron transport, forms an electrochemical proton gradient that is used to make ATP.
   b. The orientation of the carriers in the bacterial cytoplasmic membrane is such that proton carriers transport toward the outside of the cell while electron carriers transport toward the inside.
   c. At each conjunction in the electron transport chain of a proton carrier and an electron carrier, a proton is transported out of the cell.
3. A portion of the chemical energy released by the net reaction of the electron transport chain is trapped in the form of a protonmotive force that can be used to generate ATP or perform work.
4. Three ATP molecules can be synthesized for each NADH molecule oxidized to NAD^+, and two ATP molecules can be made for each $FADH_2$ oxidized to FAD, as a result of the protonmotive force established by the electron transport chain.

FERMENTATION

A. The synthesis of ATP in fermentation is due to substrate level phosphorylation and is largely restricted to the amount formed during glycolysis.

B. All fermentation pathways are anaerobic and all microorganisms that generate energy by fermentation carry out anaerobic metabolism.

C. Fermentation pathways are named for the characteristic end products formed.
1. In the lactic acid fermentation pathway, pyruvate is reduced to lactic acid, coupled with the reoxidation of NADH to NAD^+.
   a. When the Embden-Meyerhof pathway of glycolysis is used in the lactic acid fermentation pathway, the overall pathway is a homolactic fermentation because the only end product is lactic acid.
   b. In a heterolactic fermentation the pentose phosphate pathway rather than the Embden-Meyerhof pathway of glycolysis is used.
   c. Ethanol, carbon dioxide, and lactic acid are produced along with only 1 molecule of ATP per molecule of glucose substrate metabolized.
2. The ethanolic fermentation pathway produces ethanol and carbon dioxide.
   a. In the ethanolic fermentation pathway, pyruvate is converted to ethanol and carbon dioxide and NADH is converted to NAD^+.
   b. It is carried out by many yeasts and is important in food and industrial microbiology for the production of beer, wine, and distilled spirits.
3. Propionic acid bacteria carry out propionic acid fermentation using lactic acid as the substrate to produce propionic acid; this fermentation pathway is used in the production of cheese.
4. In mixed acid fermentation, the pyruvate formed during glycolysis is converted to ethanol, acetate, formate, lactate, succinate, molecular hydrogen, or carbon dioxide.

a. Mixed acid fermentation is carried out by members of the family Enterobacteriaceae.
b. The Methyl Red test detects the occurrence of mixed acid fermentation.

5. Butanediol fermentation produces butanediol, releasing carbon dioxide and reoxidizing NADH to NAD^+ with no additional ATP generated.
   a. The Voges-Proskauer test detects the presence of the butanediol fermentation pathway.
   b This test is used to distinguish between *Enterobacter aerogenes* (VP positive) and *Escherichia coli* (VP negative).
6. *Clostridium* species carry out the butyric acid (butanol) fermentation pathway; different species produce different end products, with pyruvate being converted to either acetone and carbon dioxide, isopropanol and carbon dioxide, butyrate, or butanol. Individual amino acids can be fermented by some bacteria.
7. Amino acids can also be metabolized by a mixed amino acid fermentation when there is extensive protein degradation within the cell.
   a. One amino acid serves as an electron donor and another serves as an electron acceptor.
   b. The coupling of oxidation-reduction reactions between pairs of amino acids is called the Stickland reaction and results in the deamination and decarboxylation of the amino acids.
8. Some archaebacteria carry out methanogenesis, forming methane from fermentation of acetate.

CHEMOAUTOTROPHY (CHEMOLITHOTROPHY)

A. The respiration of chemoautotrophs is based on the metabolism of inorganic compounds, coupling the oxidation of an inorganic compound with the reduction of a suitable coenzyme.
B. The transfer of electrons from the reduced coenzyme molecules through an electron transport chain of membrane-bound carriers establishes a proton gradient that can drive the synthesis of ATP by chemiosmosis.
C. Molecular hydrogen, reduced sulfur compounds, reduced iron compounds and nitrogen compounds can serve as the basis for autotrophic metabolism.
D. The metabolic activities of chemoautotrophic bacteria are important in biogeochemical cycling.
E. Homoacetogenic bacteria oxidize hydrogen and couple this reaction with the reduction of carbon dioxide to form acetate via the acetyl-CoA pathway.
F. Methanogens are chemoautotrophic archaebacteria that form methane by using electrons from molecular hydrogen to reduce CO_2 in an exergonic reaction.
   1. Methanogens use a specialized anaerobic pathway to convert CO_2 to CH_4.
   2. The synthesis of ATP in methanogens is based on chemiosmosis rather than direct substrate-level phosphorylation.
   3. One molecule of ATP can be synthesized for every molecule of CO_2 converted to CH_4; NADPH is also generated.
G. Sulfur-oxidizing bacteria can use reduced sulfur compounds as energy sources.
   1. The electrons derived from these enter the electron transport chain via a lower energy level cytochrome carrier molecule.
   2. *Thiobacillus ferrooxidans* oxidizes both reduced sulfur and reduced iron for generating ATP.
   3. *Thiobacillus* can generate ATP by using the low acidic environment in which it lives to supply its protonmotive force.
H. Nitrifying bacteria are eubacteria that oxidize ammonia or nitrite ions to generate ATP by chemiosmosis; their metabolic activities are important in soil.

PHOTOAUTOTROPHY

A. Algae and photosynthetic bacteria carry out photoautotrophic metabolism.
B. Photosynthetic microorganisms have chlorophylls and accessory pigments that allow them to absorb light and use it to power ATP generation.
C. The photosynthetic apparatus consists of light-harvesting pigments (chlorophylls, carotenoids, and phycobiliproteins), a photosynthetic reaction center, and an electron transport chain.
D. Light-harvesting pigments absorb light energy of particular wavelengths and transmit energy to the photosynthetic reaction center, which has a chlorophyll molecule that can release electrons when excited by the energy arriving from the light-harvesting pigments.
E. In photophosphorylation, chlorophyll molecules absorb light energy, become energetically excited, and emit an electron that is transferred through an electron transport chain.
   1. The transfer of electrons through the carriers of the electron transport chain establishes a proton gradient across the membrane that can be used to power the generation of ATP.
   2. This pathway of electron transfer makes up a photosystem.
F. Photosystem I or cyclic photophosphorylation is used by anaerobic green and purple sulfur bacteria.
   1. The primary pigment is bacterial chlorophyll, which acts as an internal electron donor and acceptor.
   2. In the course of returning the excited electron to the oxidized chlorophyll, a sufficient energy gradient is established to permit the synthesis of 1 ATP molecule. Reduced coenzyme is not generated.
G. Photosystem II is a noncyclic photophosphorylation pathway.
   1. The photoreceptor is P_{680}.
   2. A proton gradient is established across the specialized photosynthetic membranes of the cyanobacteria and the membranes of algal chloroplasts.
   3. The protonmotive force is used to generate ATP by chemiosmosis.
   4. A water molecule is split and oxygen is formed (oxygenic photosynthesis).
H. The Z pathway of photophosphorylation links photosystems I and II into a unified pathway that generates ATP and reduced coenzyme for biosynthesis.
   1. Chlorophyll *a* is the primary photosynthetic pigment.
   2. In photosystem I, it absorbs light at a wavelength of 700 nm, and in photosystem II, it absorbs light at a wavelength of 680 nm.

I. At low light intensities, cyanobacteria carry out anoxygenic photosynthesis; photosystem I then acts as a cyclic oxidative photophosphorylation system that produces an increased ATP yield. Photosystem II is inoperative.

CHAPTER 5

BIOSYNTHESIS (ANABOLISM)

A. Overall metabolism of the cell can be subdivided into catabolism and anabolism.
B. Catabolism involves the breakup of substrates to provide energy, reducing power and the small precursor molecules needed for biosynthesis; in catabolism, NAD^+ serves as an oxidizing agent and is reduced to NADH.
C. In anabolism, also known as biosynthesis, the molecules of the cell, including several types of macromolecules, are built up from the small precursors using the energy and reducing power supplied by catabolism.
   1. Biosynthetic pathways always require reducing power and ATP.
   2. The reducing power of NADH can be converted into the form of NADPH, and some microbial metabolic activities generate NADPH directly.
   3. In anabolism, coenzyme NADPH serves as the reducing agent and is converted to $NADP^+$.
D. Central metabolic pathways are amphibolic.
   1. Compounds are siphoned off from these pathways to make biomass.
   2. The central pathways permit the interconversion of the main classes of compounds in the cell.

CARBON DIOXIDE FIXATION

A. Autotrophs form organic molecules from CO_2.
B. The autotrophic reduction of CO_2 to organic carbon requires NADPH and ATP.
   1. In chemoautotrophs, (chemolithotrophs), ATP and NADPH are generated by the oxidation of inorganic compounds.
   2. In photoautotrophs ATP and NADPH are generated by reaction driven by light energy.
C. The fixation of CO_2 occurs in the Calvin cycle (C_3 pathway), a series of reactions that is three different, integrated metabolic sequences.
   1. Three turns of the Calvin cycle synthesize one molecule of glyceraldehyde-3-phosphate. In photoautotrophs, ATP and NADPH are generated by the light reactions of photosynthesis.
   2. The Calvin cycle is a *dark reaction* because none of its reactions needs to be coupled with the input of light energy.
   3. The Calvin cycle begins with the reaction of CO_2 with ribulose-1,5-bisphosphate; this forms an unstable compound that splits to form 3-phosphoglycerate.
   4. Some of the 3-phosphoglycerate is reduced to form glyceraldehyde-3-phosphate.
   5. The remaining 3-phosphoglycerate is used to regenerate ribulose-1,5-bisphosphate.
   6. Three CO_2 molecules produce one molecule of glyceraldehyde-3-phosphate.
D. Ribulose-1,5-bisphosphate carboxylase occurs on the surfaces of the thylakoid membranes of photosynthetic microorganisms and determines the rates of the Calvin cycle.
   1. Ribulose-1,5-bisphosphate carboxylase catalyzes the reaction of CO_2 with ribulose-1,5-bisphosphate.
   2. Ribulose-1,5-bisphosphate carboxylase enzyme is subject to allosteric control.
   3. Ribulose-1,5-bisphosphate carboxylase is more active at alkaline pH values than at neutral pH.
   4. Many autotrophs store ribulose-1,5-bisphosphate carboxylase as carboxysomes within the cell.
E. Some photoautotrophs fix carbon dioxide via a reverse (reductive) TCA cycle pathway.
   1. Four CO_2 molecules are fixed into oxaloacetate at the expense of 3 ATPs.
   2. In most of these reactions normal enzymes of the TCA cycle work in reverse of the normal oxidative direction.
F. Two CO_2 molecules are fixed and converted into one acetyl-CoA via the hydroxypropionate pathway, carried out by *Chloroflexus*; the net result is that every 3 CO_2 molecules can be converted into one pyruvic acid molecule.
G. In the C_4 pathway of CO_2 fixation the product is the 4-carbon molecule oxaloacetate.
   1. The oxaloacetate is used in amino acid and nucleic acid biosynthesis.
   2. Pyruvate or phosphoenolpyruvate, metabolites of the glycolytic pathway, react with CO_2 to form the oxaloacetate, which is an intermediate metabolite of the TCA cycle.

ASSIMILATION OF ORGANIC C-1 COMPOUNDS

A. Methane oxidation begins with a methane monooxygenase enzyme that catalyzes the addition of oxygen to methane to form methanol.
   1. This reaction requires NADH or cytochrome c to act as electron donor.
   2. The methanol formed is further oxidized to formaldehyde.
B. Type I methanotrophs use the ribulose monophosphate cycle to assimilate formaldehyde into organic molecules; rearrangement reactions regenerate ribulose-5-phosphate.
C. Type II methanotrophs and methylotrophs utilize a serine pathway for carbon assimilation, which, overall, forms a two-carbon acetyl-CoA from the reaction of formaldehyde with a CO_2.
D. Methylotrophs are heterotrophic aerobes that can utilize one-carbon molecules as their sole source of carbon.
   1. Some methylotrophs can use methane as their sole carbon source (methanotrophs).
   2. Not all methylotrophs are also methanotrophs.

CARBOHYDRATE BIOSYNTHESIS

A. Biosynthesis of glucose from noncarbohydrate molecules is called gluconeogenesis.
B. Gluconeogenesis reverses the flow of carbon during glycolysis while utilizing the same intermediary metabolites.

1. In each direction there is a critical irreversible enzymatic step, at which each enzyme catalyzes a unidirectional flow of carbon.
2. These enzymes involved in these steps each have different allosteric inhibitors that regulate the direction of carbon flow.
3. Biosynthesis of carbohydrates is favored when the cell has an adequate supply of ATP; catabolism is favored when ATP concentrations are low.
4. Gluconeogenesis requires the input of carbon skeletons containing three or more carbon atoms.

C. Fatty acid metabolism forms acetyl groups that contain only two carbon atoms.
   1. To convert fatty acids or acetate to carbohydrates, some microorganisms utilize the glyoxylate cycle.
   2. The glyoxylate is actually a shunt across the TCA cycle that replenishes the supply of oxaloacetate in the cell.

D. Reactions in a cell that serve to replenish the supplies of key molecules are called anaplerotic sequences.

E. Formation of a 6-carbon carbohydrate from a fatty acid requires the use of four acetyl-CoA molecules, two carbons of which are released as carbon dioxide.

F. Carbohydrates formed by gluconeogenesis can be converted to larger polysaccharide molecules.

G. Some polysaccharides synthesized under nutritionally rich conditions are stored as supplies of materials and energy within the cell.

H. The peptidoglycan of cell walls is essential for cell growth and division.

I. New peptidoglycan must be inserted into the existing cell wall without disrupting its structure. The backbone of the eubacterial cell wall is a disaccharide of *N*-acetylglucosamine and *N*-acetylmuramic acid.
   1. The formation of *N*-acetylglucosamine involves the conversion of glucose to fructose-6-phosphate and subsequent reactions with glutamic acid and acetyl-CoA.
   2. To form *N*-acetylmuramic acid, *N*-acetylglucosamine reacts with UTP to form *N*-acetylglucosamine-UDP, which reacts with phosphoenolpyruvate to form *N*-acetylmuramic acid-UDP.
   3. In the first stage of cell wall synthesis, the precursors of peptidoglycan are assembled in the cytoplasm to form a uridine diphosphate (UDP)-*N*-acetylmuramic acid-pentapeptide.
      a. The pentapeptide is composed of a tetrapeptide found in the wall of that bacterium with an additional D-alanine unit added onto the carboxyl end of the chain.
      b. Each amino acid of the pentapeptide is added in the appropriate place by specific adding enzymes or "ligases," which activity requires ATP.
   4. The second stage of cell wall synthesis occurs in the cytoplasmic membrane.
      a. The *N*-acetylmuramic acid-pentapeptide is transferred to a membrane-bound carrier molecule (C_{55} carrier lipid, undecaprenylphosphate or bactoprenol).
      b. *N*-acetylglucosamine is transferred to the bactoprenol–*N*-acetylmuramic acid-pentapeptide to form bactoprenol–*N*-acetylglucosamine–*N*-acetylmuramic acid pentapeptide, which moves across the cytoplasmic membrane to the outside of the cell (translocation).
      c. This precursor is transferred to a growing chain of the cell wall structure (nascent peptidoglycan).
      d. The nascent peptidoglycan is covalently bound to the existing cell wall by transpeptidation, the formation of cross-bridges.
      e. All these reactions must be exergonic.

J. In Gram-negative cell wall construction, the synthesis and addition of lipopolysaccharide (LPS) involves undecaprenylphosphate as a carrier, occurs at the cytoplasmic membrane, and involves the initial addition of fatty acids to a glucosamine disaccharide phosphate, followed by successive sugar additions.

LIPID BIOSYNTHESIS

A. Lipids contain fatty acids, which are synthesized by the sequential addition of two carbon units derived from acetyl-CoA.
   1. During fatty acid biosynthesis, reactants are bound to the *acyl carrier protein* (ACP). Malonyl-CoA is formed from the reaction of acetyl-CoA with CO_2, which requires ATP and biotin.
   2. The 3-carbon malonyl-CoA unit successively contributes two carbon units for the elongation of the fatty acid, releasing CO_2.
   3. Energy in the form of ATP and reducing power as NADPH are required.

B. Poly-β-hydroxybutyric acid is a common storage product of bacteria.
   1. Its biosynthesis begins with the reaction of acetyl-CoA to form acetoacetyl-CoA.
   2. Repetitive sequential addition of acetyl-CoA results in chain length elongation. Eventual removal of the CoA portion of the molecule forms the poly-β-hydroxybutyric acid.

C. Phospholipids are required in prokaryotic and eukaryotic membranes.
   1. Formation of phospholipids involves the addition of fatty acids to glycerol-3-phosphate.
   2. Dihydroxyacetone phosphate is reduced by NADPH to glycerol-3-phosphate, which then reacts with acylated-ACP to form phosphatidic acid.
   3. Phosphatidic acid is activated by CTP to form a CDP-diacylglycerol molecule and the CDP is displaced by alcohols to produce a completed phospholipid.

D. Sterols are made up of repeating units of the unsaturated hydrocarbon isoprene and are found in the membranes of eukaryotic cells.
   1. Isoprenoid hydrocarbons are synthesized from activated acetyl-CoA molecules.
   2. The synthesis of mevalonic acid from 3-hydroxy-3-methylglutaryl-CoA, derived from the reaction of acetyl-CoA with acetoacetyl-CoA, is the key step in the formation of cholesterol.

BIOSYNTHESIS OF AMINO ACIDS FOR PROTEINS

A. Protein biosynthesis involves the formation of the 20 essential amino acids found in proteins, and the linkage of the appropriate amino acids in the correct sequences to form the primary structures of specific proteins.

B. Amino acids are organic molecules that contain nitrogen.
C. Most organisms are unable to use N_2 as a source of nitrogen.
D. A few prokaryotes that have nitrogenase enzyme complex, however, can transform N_2 into ammonium nitrogen.
E. The transformation of N_2 into ammonium nitrogen is endergonic, requiring reducing power and ATP.
F. There are two pathways for the incorporation of inorganic ammonium nitrogen into organic amino acids.
   1. Ammonium ions can be assimilated to form the amino acid L-glutamate, which can then be transformed into other amino acids, and can supply nitrogen needed for formation of all other amino acids.
   2. L-Glutamate can be formed from ammonium ions and α-ketoglutarate in a reductive amination pathway.
      a. This is catalyzed by the enzyme glutamate dehydrogenase and requires NADPH or NADH.
      b. Ammonium ions are combined directly with an α-ketocarboxylic acid when they are in relatively high concentrations.
   3. When the ammonium ion concentration is low, the alternative glutamine synthetase/glutamate synthase pathway is used.
      a. In this pathway, pre-existing L-glutamate reacts with ammonium ions in an ATP driven reaction to form L-glutamine, then the L-glutamine reacts with α-ketoglutarate to form two molecules of L-glutamate.
      b. Glutamine synthetase is a key enzyme regulating the rate of intermediary metabolism.
         (i). It is subject to cumulative feedback inhibition by each of the products of glutamine metabolism.
         (ii). Each of the eight allosteric inhibitors has its own binding site on the enzyme, and when all eight inhibitors are bound to the enzyme, the activity of glutamine synthetase is shut off.
G. There are six biosynthetic families of amino acids.
   1. L-Glutamate is the parent molecule of one family and can be further metabolized to form the amino acids L-glutamine, L-proline, and L-arginine.
   2. L-Glutamate serves as the nitrogen source for other amino acids.
   3. The carbon skeletons for the various amino acids come from glycolytic, pentose phosphate, or TCA cycle pathway intermediates.
H. The ability to transfer the amino group of one amino acid to form another amino acid (transamination) is essential for the synthesis of all of the amino acids.
   1. Transamination involves specific transaminase enzymes and the coenzyme pyridoxal phosphate.
   2. Glutamate transaminase catalyzes the transfer of the amino group from L-glutamate to form the parental amino acids of the various amino acid families.
   3. L-Aspartate, made by transamination with L-glutamate, is the parent molecule of another family of amino acids and can be further metabolized to form L-asparagine, L-methionine, L-threonine, L-lysine, or L-isoleucine.
   4. Transamination reactions involving pyruvate can also generate the amino acids L-alanine, L-valine, and L-leucine.
I. L-Serine is a precursor for the amino acids L-glycine and L-cysteine.
J. L-Cysteine contains sulfur, and the transformation of L-serine to L-cysteine involves a reaction with hydrogen sulfide.
K. The formation of L-phenylalanine, L-tyrosine, and L-tryptophan originates with phosphoenolpyruvate and erythrose-4-phosphate.
L. Histidine and nucleic acid purines arise from ribose-5-phosphate.
   1. The adenine unit of ATP provides one nitrogen and one carbon atom for the ring of L-histidine; the other nitrogen atom of the ring comes from the side chain of the amino acid L-glutamine.
   2. The amino group of L-histidine comes from a transamination reaction with L-glutamate.
M. The rates of amino acid biosynthesis reactions are regulated by feedback inhibition. These rates depend on the activities of the enzymes catalyzing the regulatory steps in the pathways, and the final product of a pathway often acts as an allosteric inhibitor of the enzyme catalyzing the critical regulatory step.

BIOSYNTHESIS OF NUCLEOTIDES FOR NUCLEIC ACIDS

A. There are two classes of nucleic acid bases: purines and pyrimidines.
   1. Purines and pyrimidines are key components of the nucleotides that serve as the precursors of RNA, DNA, ATP, NAD^+, $NADP^+$, and CoA. ATP, NAD^+, $NADP^+$, and CoA are all derived from adenine nucleotides.
   2. Nucleotides are also important activators and inhibitors of regulatory enzymes, thus serving to regulate the rates of many metabolic pathways within cells.
B. The precursors of the atoms of the pyrimidine ring are NH_3, CO_2, and L-aspartate.
   1. Pyrimidine synthesis begins with the formation of carbamoyl aspartate, catalyzed by aspartate transcarbamoylase. This is the key regulatory step in this synthesis.
   2. Aspartate transcarbamoylase is subject to allosteric feedback inhibition and to allosteric activation by ATP.
   3. Succeeding steps of the pathway eventually form orotate.
   4. After the ring is synthesized, ribose and phosphate are added.
   5. Decarboxylation forms UMP, which is phosphorylated to form UTP. UTP can be modified to form CTP, a nucleotide in both RNA and DNA.
   6. Ribose is reduced to the deoxyribose form of the nucleotide for DNA.
   7. UTP is also the precursor for the TTP in DNA.
C. Purine nucleotides have two rings synthesized from various amino acids.
   1. Carbon dioxide and a methyl group donated by folic acid are needed.

2. The biosynthesis of the adenine ring involves the substitution of an amino group for a keto group.
3. The adenosine phosphate molecule that is formed serves not only as a nucleotide base in DNA and RNA but also in the ATP, NAD^+, $NADP^+$, CoA, and FAD molecules.
4. The biosynthesis of the guanine ring involves the addition of an amino group without the removal of a keto group.

CHAPTER 6

DNA STRUCTURE

A. DNA is made up of deoxyribonucleotides.
   1. Each deoxyribonucleotide consists of a nucleic acid base, deoxyribose, and phosphate.
   2. The nucleic acid bases in DNA are adenine, guanine, cytosine, and thymine.
      a. Adenine (A) and guanine (G) are purines.
      b. Cytosine (C) and thymine (T) are pyrimidines.
   3. The nucleic acid bases are attached to the deoxyribose sugars to form deoxyribonucleosides.
   4. Deoxyribonucleosides are joined to a phosphate group on carbon 5′ of the sugar to form a deoxyribonucleotide.
   5. The deoxyribonucleotides in DNA are linked together by 3′-5′ phosphodiester bonds.
      a. At one end of the nucleic acid molecule, there is no phosphodiester bond to the 3′-carbon of the deoxyribose, and thus there is an unattached or free hydroxyl group at the 3′-carbon position (3′-OH free end).
      b. At the other end of the molecule, the 5′-carbon is not involved in forming a phosphodiester linkage, and there is a free phosphate ester group at the 5′-carbon position (5′-P free end).
      c. This permits directional recognition at the biochemical level.

B. DNA is a double helix composed of two primary polynucleotide chains held together by weak hydrogen bonding.
   1. The hydrogen bonds that hold together the primary chains occur between complementary nucleic acid bases.
   2. Adenine pairs with thymine, and guanine pairs with cytosine.
   3. Hydrophobic interactions stabilize the DNA double helix.
   4. Grooves along the DNA helical axis are the sites where DNA-protein interactions occur.
   5. The most common form of the DNA helix is called B-DNA.
   6. Palindromic sequences are regions of DNA in which the sequence of nucleotides is symmetrical about an axis, that is, the same nucleotide sequences occur in opposite directions.
      a. They are called inverted repeats because they are repeated in inverse order.
      b. They permit base pairing and stabilized folding of the DNA.
   7. Bacterial DNA is supercoiled.
      a. Relaxed DNA is DNA in simple circular form.
      b. Relaxed, circular DNA with one broken strand twisting in the direction of the helix is positively supercoiled.
      c. Relaxed, circular DNA with one broken strand twisting in the opposite direction of the helix turns is negatively supercoiled.
      d. DNA is normally found in the cell in a negatively supercoiled state.
      e. Histones are proteins that stabilize the supercoiling of eukaryotic DNA.
         (i). Eukaryotes have histones; prokaryotes do not. There are five types of histone molecules: H1, H2A, H2B, H3, and H4.
         (ii). The nucleosome is the histone-DNA complex, a bead-like structure.

DNA REPLICATION

A. Prokaryotic and eukaryotic cells transmit their hereditary information via deoxyribonucleic acid molecules.

B. The replication of a DNA molecule is a semiconservative process because when a DNA molecule is replicated to form two double helical DNA molecules, each of the new daughter DNA molecules consists of one intact (conserved) strand from the parental double helical DNA and one newly synthesized complementary strand.

C. DNA replication begins at the origin of replication, where specific initiation proteins attach.

D. The double helix must be unwound and separated into single strands so that each strand can be copied as a template into complementary strands.

E. A replication fork is the region of DNA helix where unwinding, strand separation, and DNA synthesis is localized.
   1. Here, free nucleotide bases are aligned opposite their base pairs in the parental DNA molecules, A opposite T and G opposite C.
   2. There are four strands of DNA at this point: two are conserved and two are newly synthesized.
   3. Bacteria have a single point of origin of DNA replication (*ori*C).
   4. DNA polymerases move bidirectionally from the origin to the terminus of DNA replication (*tre*), so that there are two replicating forks moving in opposite directions.
   5. The bidirectional replication of the DNA proceeds at identical speeds after initiation, and both replication forks meet precisely at the termination site.
   6. Two replication forks are formed as a result of initiation.
      a. Both forks move along the double helix away from the origin of replication in opposite directions and around the circular chromosome.
      b. Theta structures are formed with a loop of DNA.
   7. Eukaryotic DNA replication begins at multiple points of origin and proceeds bidirectionally.
      a. The rate of synthesis of DNA along a replicating fork may be slower in eukaryotes than in prokaryotes.
      b. The rate of DNA synthesis can vary in a eukaryote.
      c. The overall rate of DNA replication is higher in

eukaryotes than in prokaryotes because the DNA of eukaryotes has multiple replicons (segments of a DNA macromolecule having their own origin and termini) compared to the single replicon of the bacterial chromosome, a fundamental difference between prokaryotic and eukaryotic microorganisms.

F. Replication of the DNA involves a series of enzymatic reactions.
   1. The DNA strands must be uncoiled or "relaxed" by topoisomerase I, which breaks the phosphodiester linkage of one of the strands and passes the strand through the other.
   2. Topoisomerase II (DNA gyrase) introduces negative supercoiling into relaxed DNA and returns the DNA into its negatively-supercoiled, condensed state.
   3. The gyrase nicks or breaks both strands of DNA, passes the strands around another part of the double helix, and reseals the nicks. Energy from ATP is required to nick and reseal the DNA strands.
   4. The double helix must be separated into single-stranded regions before each single strand can be used as a template.
      a. DNA helicases and Rep protein are unwinding proteins and use energy from ATP to break the hydrogen bond between the two strands of DNA together.
      b. Separated strands are prevented from reassociating by single-stranded binding proteins that attach to single-stranded regions of the DNA and stabilize them.
   5. DNA polymerases link nucleotide bases with phosphodiester bonds to establish new strands of DNA.
      a. DNA polymerases add deoxyribonucleotides only to the free 3′-OH end of an existing nucleic acid polymer.
      b. These enzymes require an RNA primer molecule with a 3′-OH free end.
      c. The RNA primer is synthesized by RNA polymerase or DnaG protein.
      d. The direction of DNA synthesis is 5′-P to 3′-OH because a DNA polymerase can add deoxyribonucleotides only to the 3′-OH free end of a nucleic acid primer.
      e. The two strands of the double helical DNA molecule are antiparallel, one strand running from the 5′-P to the 3′-OH free end and the other complementary strand running from the 3′-OH to the 5′-P free end.
      f. Synthesis of complementary strands requires that DNA synthesis proceed in opposite directions, while the double helix is progressively unwinding and replicating in only one direction.
         (i). One DNA strand can be continuously synthesized (continuous or leading strand of DNA) because it runs in the appropriate direction for the continuous addition of new free nucleotide bases to the free 3′-OH end of the primer molecule.
         (ii). This occurs simultaneously with the unwinding of the double helical molecule and progresses toward the replication fork.
         (iii). The other strand of DNA (discontinuous or lagging strand of DNA) must be synthesized discontinuously.
         (iv). Initiation of its synthesis begins only after some unwinding of the double helix has occurred and lags behind the synthesis of the continuous strand.
      g. DNA replication is semidiscontinuous.
         (i). Short segments of DNA (Okazaki fragments) are formed by the DNA polymerase running opposite to the direction of unwinding of the parental DNA molecule.
         (ii). They are joined together by DNA ligase, which establishes a phosphodiester bond between the 3′-OH and 5′-P ends of chains of nucleotides.
   6. Ligases act as repair enzymes for sealing "nicks" within the DNA molecule.
   7. Processivity is the movement of DNA polymerase and its associated proteins along the DNA template, adding nucleotides without dissociating and reassociating at each step.
   8. There are four different types of eukaryotic DNA polymerases, α, β, γ, and δ.
      a. The α form is the major form used for replication of DNA within the nucleus.
      b. The δ form also functions within the nucleus.
      c. The γ form is found in the mitochondria.
      d. The β form is involved in DNA repair.
   9. Bacterial DNA polymerases can remove the RNA primers from the DNA strand; a ribonuclease accomplishes this in eukaryotes.
   10. Bacterial DNA polymerases also exhibit exonuclease activity, degrading or depolymerizing a nucleic acid chain.
      a. This activity permits correction of errors in the DNA molecule.
      b. This function is called proofreading.
      c. A gap results from the removal of nucleotides from a strand of DNA.
      d. Gaps are filled in by the action of DNA polymerase I.
   11. Post-replication of DNA occurs.
      a. DNA methylases add methyl groups to specific nucleotides.
      b. Methylation protects against endonuclease digestion.

GENETIC EXPRESSION

A. The genotype is the informational capacity of a cell contained within its DNA.

B. The genome is a single copy of the genetic information of a cell.

C. Genes are segments of the genome.
   1. Each gene has a specific function.
   2. Structural genes (cistrons) code for the synthesis of RNA and proteins.
   3. Regulatory genes act to control the activities of the cell.
   4. Structural and regulatory genes constitute the cell's genotype and determine its phenotype.

D. Expression of genetic information involves using information encoded within the DNA to effect the synthesis of proteins.

E. The sequence of nucleotides within the genome determines the sequence of amino acids within protein molecules and thus the functional properties of microbial enzymes.
F. The expression of the genetic information of the organisms is reflected in its phenotypic features.
G. Transcription and translation accomplish the transfer of information contained in DNA to form a functional enzyme through protein synthesis.
   1. Reading the sequence of nucleotides in the appropriate order is essential for converting stored genetic information into the functional activities of the organism.
   2. There are recognition sequences encoded within the DNA molecule that designate which chain to read, where to begin, and where to end.
   3. The order of nucleotides in the DNA specifies the order of amino acids in a protein.
   4. The information in the DNA molecule is initially transferred to ribonucleic acid molecules by transcription.
   5. The information encoded in the mRNA molecule is then translated into the sequence of amino acids that comprise the protein.

TRANSCRIPTION: TRANSFERRING INFORMATION FROM DNA TO RNA

A. Transcription is the process in which the information stored in the DNA is used to code for the synthesis of RNA.
   1. DNA serves as a template for synthesis of RNA, transferring information for the eventual expression of genetic information.
   2. The transcription of DNA results in the production of three types of RNA: rRNA, tRNA, and mRNA.
   3. RNA is a macromolecule composed of nucleotides.
      a. It is a strand of ribonucleotides linked by 3′-5′ phosphodiester bonds.
      b. RNA usually is single stranded with a 3′-OH free end and a 5′-P free end.
      c. Ribose instead of deoxyribose occurs in RNA nucleotides.
      d. RNA contains adenine, guanine, cytosine, and uracil.
      e. RNA is less stable than DNA.
   4. There are three types of RNA.
      a. Messenger RNA contains the code copied from the DNA to specify a sequence of amino acids in protein synthesis.
         (i). mRNA molecules formed by transcription actually encode the information for protein synthesis.
         (ii). Prokaryotes usually have only one DNA sequence coding for a particular mRNA.
         (iii). Eukaryotes often have multiple copies.
         (iv). In prokaryotes and eukaryotes there can be multiple sites of synthesis for identical proteins using the multiple copies of the mRNA molecule.
         (v). Prokaryotic mRNA molecules last for only a few minutes. Eukaryotic mRNA can remain functional for hours or days.
      b. Transfer RNA (tRNA) decodes the mRNA sequence, helping to translate it into a correct amino acid sequence.
         (i). Transfer RNA molecules are short, three-dimensional structures.
         (ii). Each of the four tRNA lobes has a characteristic nucleotide sequence and function. tRNA is enzymatically modified after RNA synthesis.
         (iii). Specific nucleotides are methylated, hydrogenated, or rearranged to form unusual ribonucleotides.
         (iv). The fourth lobe is the amino acid stem to which a specific amino acid is attached and carried to the ribosome during protein synthesis.
         (v). The anticodon loop contains three variable nucleotides, the anticodon, which can form complementary base pairs with the three nucleotides in the mRNA codon.
      c. Ribosomal RNA (rRNA) combines with ribosomal proteins to form a ribosome.
         (i). In prokaryotes, the 30S small ribosomal subunit contains one 16S rRNA molecule that contains about 1,540 nucleotides and the 50S large ribosomal subunit contains one 23S rRNA molecule (2,900 nucleotides) and one 5S rRNA (120 nucleotides).
         (ii). In eukaryotes, the 40S small subunit contains one 18S (1,900 nucleotides) rRNA and the 60S large subunit contains one each of 28S (4,800 nucleotides), 5.8S (160 nucleotides) and 5S (120 nucleotides) rRNA molecules.

B. Synthesis of RNA.
   1. There are several similarities between DNA replication and synthesis of RNA during transcription.
      a. The RNA molecule that is synthesized in transcription is antiparallel to the strand of DNA that serves as a template.
      b. Transcription involves unwinding of the double helical DNA molecule for a short sequence of nucleotide bases, alignment of complementary ribonucleotides by base pairing opposite the nucleotides of the DNA strand being transcribed, and linkage of these nucleotides with phosphodiester bonds by a DNA-dependent RNA polymerase.
      c. RNA polymerases link nucleotides only to the 3′-OH free end of the polymer.
   2. There are also major differences between RNA and DNA synthesis.
      a. Synthesized RNA is single stranded.
      b. Only one strand of DNA serves as a template (sense strand).
      c. Different regions of either DNA strand can serve as the sense strand.
   3. RNA polymerase is the enzyme that synthesizes RNA from ribonucleotides.
      a. It is capable of forming phosphodiester bonds between two ribonucleotides only when they are aligned opposite the complementary DNA template nucleotides.

b. RNA synthesis does not require a primer.
c. Eubacteria have one basic type of RNA polymerase that produces all three classes of RNA molecules.
d. Eubacterial RNA polymerase is a complex of four protein subunits that form the core enzyme.
e. Archaebacterial cells have their own unique RNA polymerases.
f. Eukaryotic cells have three distinct RNA polymerase enzymes that synthesize the three different classes of RNA.
g. RNA polymerase I synthesizes rRNA, RNA polymerase II synthesizes mRNA, and RNA polymerase III synthesizes tRNA and 5S rRNA.

4. Transcription must begin at precise locations.
   a. There are multiple initiation sites for transcription for the synthesis of different classes of RNA and the synthesis of RNA for different polypeptide sequences.
   b. The promoter region is the sequence of DNA nucleotides that specifies both the site of transcription initiation and which of the two DNA strands is to serve as the sense strand for transcription.
      (i). Bacterial promoter regions consist of about 40 nucleotides and contain a seven-nucleotide sequence (Pribnow sequence), a part of the recognition signal about 5 to 8 bases upstream from the beginning of transcription.
      (ii). Pribnow sequences are consensus sequences with high nucleotide sequence homology.
   c. The initial binding of eubacterial RNA polymerase core enzyme ($\alpha_2\beta\beta'$) to the promoter region requires a σ factor to ensure that RNA synthesis begins at the correct site.
      (i). The holoenzyme is the complete RNA polymerase (core + sigma unit). The RNA polymerase holoenzyme first binds to the DNA promoter at the −35 consensus sequence, forming a closed complex, then shifts its binding to the −10 Pribnow sequence, unwinding the DNA helix to form a single-stranded region and an open complex.
      (ii). The RNA polymerase holoenzyme begins transcription and the first nucleotide added is usually a purine.
      (iii). After formation of about 10 phosphodiester bonds between ribonucleotides, the sigma subunit dissociates from the RNA polymerase and the remainder of the RNA molecule is synthesized or elongated by the core RNA polymerase.
      (iv). The sigma subunit is then free to associate with another RNA polymerase molecule.
   d. Eubacteria actually have multiple σ factors, each of which is responsible for the recognition of specific promoter initiation sequences.
      (i). Regulation of the concentrations of the different σ factors leads to the specific or preferential transcription of certain genes and not others.
      (ii). Eukaryotic transcription factors bind to DNA at specific promoter sites for the initiation of transcription.
      (iii). The TATA factor is a protein transcription factor that preferentially binds to a conserved A-T rich DNA sequence (TATA box), an important recognition site for initiation of transcription that leads to synthesis of the proteins of the cell.
5. The rate of RNA polymerization is not constant during the elongation phase of synthesis.
6. Specific termination sites (sequences of nucleotides) act as a signal to stop transcription.
   a. These sequences cause the RNA polymerase to pause and terminate RNA synthesis.
   b. In some cases, termination of transcription requires the presence of a rho (ρ) protein.
7. Bacterial mRNA is not modified between the time it is synthesized, through transcription of the DNA, and the time it is translated into the amino acid sequence of a polypeptide at the ribosome.
   a. Eubacterial mRNA is colinear with the corresponding genes in the DNA.
   b. Polycistronic bacterial mRNA contains the information for several proteins—often with related functions—coded for by a continuous region of the DNA.
8. rRNA and tRNA molecules are substantially modified in prokaryotes and eukaryotes. RNA molecules are single stranded, but can fold back on themselves, establishing double-stranded regions.
   a. Both tRNA and rRNA molecules have extensive double-stranded regions.
9. Precursor rRNA molecules must be processed to form rRNA molecules because the RNA molecules transcribed from DNA are larger that the rRNA in ribosomes.
   a. Prokaryotic ribosomes contain 5S, 16S, and 23S RNA but the initial transcript from the DNA is a large 30S molecule that can be cleaved by nuclease enzymes to form these different-sized RNA molecules.
   b. tRNA molecules are synthesized as high molecular weight precursors that are processed to produce mature tRNA molecules.
10. RNA molecules of eukaryotic cells are generally modified extensively after transcription from DNA to form mRNA.
   a. Heterogeneous nuclear RNA is several times larger than the final mRNA molecule and is subjected to post-transcriptional modification within the nucleus to form the mRNA, involving removing, adding, and rearranging sequences of nucleotides.
   b. Introns are intervening sequences.
   c. The regions that code for amino acid sequences are exons.
   d. hnRNA processing of hnRNA involves the excision of introns to form the mature mRNA molecule.
   e. Eukaryotes have split genes because the nucleotides that comprise the gene that codes for a specific protein are separated in the DNA.

some cases physical disruption, such as sonication or freezing and thawing, is used to break them open.

2. The released DNA is treated with ribonuclease and precipitated with cold ethanol. Repeated washing and reprecipitation produces purified DNA.
3. Further purification is done by cesium-chloride buoyant density ultracentrifugation, electrophoresis, and column chromatography.
4. mRNA can also be isolated as a template and a copy DNA synthesized.
5. cDNA is used for cloning.
6. DNA sequences can also be produced by chemical or automated nucleotide synthesizing systems, producing DNA sequences up to several hundreds of nucleotides in length.

D. Restriction endonucleases (restriction enzymes) and ligases permit the cutting and splicing of DNA.

1. Restriction endonucleases normally function to prevent the incorporation of foreign DNA into the genome of a cell by cutting both strands of a foreign DNA molecule.
2. Bacteria protect themselves against their own endonucleases by modifying DNA bases at the recognition sites where the endonucleases act.
3. Endonucleases are named using a system whereby the first letter indicates the genus from which it was isolated, the next two letters indicate the species, the fourth letter (when needed) indicates the strain, and the number indicates the order of discovery of endonucleases from that strain.
4. Different types of endonucleases vary with respect to the site at which they cut DNA.
   a. Type I restriction endonucleases cleave DNA at a random distance from a recognition site in the DNA nucleotide sequence.
   b. Type II restriction endonucleases cleave the DNA at the recognition site.
      (i). A type II restriction endonuclease cuts the DNA at a palindromic sequence of bases, which is a sequence of nucleotide bases that can be read identically in the 3′-OH → 5′-P and 5′-P → 3′-OH directions.
      (ii). Type II restriction endonucleases frequently produce DNA with staggered single-stranded ends; these staggered DNA ends can act as cohesive or sticky ends during recombination, making them suitable for splicing with segments of foreign source DNA.
      (iii). Some type II restriction endonucleases cut the DNA in both strands at the same site.
   c. Type III endonucleases cut the DNA at some precise distance from the recognition site.
5. The enzyme terminal deoxynucleotidyl transferase can be used to create artificial homology at the terminal ends of two different DNA molecules.
   a. This can be accomplished by adding polyadenine tails to one fragment and polythymine tails to the other.
   b. Pairing occurs between homologous regions of complementary bases.
   c. Blunt end ligation is also encountered when two different endonucleases are used.
      (i). One opens a plasmid ring and the other forms a segment of donor DNA.
      (ii). Artificial homology at the terminal ends of the donor and plasmid DNA molecules must be synthesized.
      (iii). Homologous regions of complementary bases pair.
      (iv). Ligases seal the circular plasmid.
      (v). The tails left by the action of the endonuclease are cleaved *in vitro*, using exonucleases.
      (vi). By adding a polyT tail to the donor DNA after its excision with an endonuclease, the donor DNA can be made complementary to the polyA tails of the plasmid DNA, permitting the formation of a circular plasmid molecule.

E. A cloning vector is used to clone a segment of DNA.

1. Cloning vectors should replicate autonomously in a suitable host cell, be separable from the host DNA so that it can be purified, should have regions that can accept source DNA without losing self-replication capacity, should also be able to enter a host cell and replicate to a high copy number (large number of repetitive copies of the genes, such as can be achieved by having multiple identical plasmids), and should be stable in the host.
2. Plasmids, bacteriophage, and phage–plasmid artificial hybrids (cosmids) are frequently used as cloning vectors.
3. Cloning vectors are constructed so that they can function in several different types of cells and permit the transfer of recombinant DNA from one cell type to another.
4. Cloning vectors usually have several single restriction enzyme cleavage sites.
   a. These sites permit circular DNA to be opened (linearized).
   b. The linearized DNA of the cloning vector can be joined with the DNA to be cloned by ligation.
   c. If the insertion occurs at the antibiotic resistance site, resistance is lost because the nucleotide sequence of the antibiotic resistance gene is disrupted.
   d. This insertional inactivation is useful for detecting the presence of foreign DNA within a plasmid.
5. A collection of clones of individual genes from a specific organism constitutes a genomic library.
6. The construction of a genomic library involves obtaining copies of the nucleotide sequences of the genome and cloning these into a suitable vector.

F. Site-directed mutagenesis can be brought about through reconstruction with phage.

G. The expression of the foreign genetic information requires that the appropriate reading frame be established and the transcriptional and translational control mechanisms turned on to permit the expression of the DNA.

1. Often the genes produced using a cloning vector must be transferred to an expression vector that contains the desired gene and the necessary regulatory sequences that permit control of the expression of that gene.
2. There should be a strong promoter associated with

on the ribosome. After GTP hydrolysis to GDP, EF-Tu–GDP is released.
   b. Elongation factor EF-Ts is required to recycle the EF-Tu–GDP back to EF-Tu–GTP.
4. eEF1 is the elongation factor in eukaryotes.
5. When tRNA molecules move to the aminoacyl site, the proper anticodon pairs with its matching codon on the mRNA.
6. The polypeptide chain is then transferred from the tRNA occupying the peptidyl site to the aminoacyl site.
7. A peptide bond is formed between the amino group of the amino acid attached at the aminoacyl site and the carboxylic acid group of the last amino acid that was added to the peptide chain; this reaction is mediated by peptidyl transferase; energy is not required.
8. At the initiation of protein synthesis, f-Met in prokaryotes and Met in eukaryotes are transferred to the aminoacyl site, forming a peptide bond with the second amino acid coded for by the mRNA molecule.
9. Translocation is the movement of the mRNA, tRNA, and growing polypeptide chain along the ribosome.
   a. It requires energy from GTP.
   b. Translocation moves the tRNA molecule with an attached peptide chain to the peptidyl site, leaving the aminoacyl site open for the anticodon of the next charged tRNA molecule to pair with the next codon of the mRNA.
   c. Translocation requires elongation factor EF-G in prokaryotes or EF-2 in eukaryotes.
   d. During translocation the uncharged tRNA molecule returns to the cytoplasm, where it can be recycled.

G. The process of peptide elongation is repeated, forming the polypeptide chain until one of the nonsense codons appears at the aminoacyl site to signal termination.
   1. Two bacterial release factors help catalyze termination of peptide bond formation.
   2. Eukaryotes have one release factor.
   3. At termination, the carboxyl end of the nascent protein is transferred to H_2O, releasing the polypeptide chain into the cytoplasm.

REGULATION OF GENE EXPRESSION

A. The cell's genome codes the information that regulates its own expression.

B. Controlling which genes are to be translated into functional enzymes controls the cell's metabolic activities.
   1. In some cases, gene expression is not subject to specific genetic regulatory control, and the enzymes coded for by genes to subject to specific genetic regulatory control are continuously synthesized (constitutive).
   2. Some enzymes are synthesized only when the cell requires them.
      a. Some enzymes are only produced in response to a specific inducer substance (inducible).
      b. Some enzymes are made unless stopped by the presence of a specific repression substance (repressible).
   3. Induction and repression are based on a regulator gene producing a regulator protein that controls transcription.
      a. Regulation of transcription may be under negative control, when mRNA for a particular set of genes is synthesized unless it is turned off by the regulator protein.
      b. Transcription may be regulated by the control of mRNA synthesis by the presence of a regulator protein that binds to the DNA (positive control).

C. Control of the expression of the structural genes for lactose metabolism in *E. coli* is explained in part by the operon model.
   1. The operon for lactose metabolism *lac* operon includes a promoter region where RNA polymerase binds, a regulatory gene that codes for the synthesis of a repressor protein, and an operator region that occurs between the promoter and the three structural genes involved in lactose metabolism.
      a. The regulatory gene codes for a repressor protein, which in the absence of lactose binds to the operator region of the DNA.
      b. The binding of the repressor protein at the operator region blocks the transcription of the structural genes.
      c. In the absence of lactose, the three structural *lac* genes are not transcribed.
      d. The binding of the repressor protein at the operator region interferes with the binding of RNA polymerase at the promoter region.
      e. An inducer binds to the repressor protein and alters the conformation of the repressor protein, so that it is unable to interact with and bind at the operator region.
   2. Transcription of the *lac* operon is derepressed, and the synthesis of the three structural proteins needed for lactose metabolism proceeds.
      a. As the lactose is metabolized and its concentration diminishes, the concentration of the derivative allolactose also declines, making it unavailable.
      b. Active repressor protein molecules are again available for binding at the operator region and the transcription of the *lac* operon is repressed.

D. Catabolite repression is regulation by positive control that simultaneously shuts off several operons.
   1. Efficient binding of RNA polymerase to promoter regions subject to catabolite repression requires a catabolite activator protein.
   2. In the absence of catabolite activator protein, the RNA polymerase enzyme has a greatly decreased affinity to bind.
   3. The CAP cannot bind to the promoter region unless it is bound to cyclic adenosine monophosphate.
   4. There is an inverse relationship between the concentrations of cAMP and ATP; intracellular levels of cAMP are low when rapidly metabolizable substrates are used. In the presence of glucose, cAMP levels are greatly reduced and the CAP is unable to bind at the promoter region.
   5. RNA polymerase enzymes then are unable to bind to catabolite-repressible promoters, and transcription of some regulated structural genes ceases.
   6. In the absence of glucose, cAMP is synthesized from

ATP and there is an adequate supply of cAMP to permit the binding of RNA polymerase to the promoter region.

7. When glucose levels are low, cAMP stimulates the initiation of many inducible enzymes.

E. Repressible operons are regulatory genes that can be shut off under specific conditions.
   1. The *trp* operon is repressible.
   2. The *trp* repressor protein is normally inactive and unable to bind at the operator region, but tryptophan can act as an allosteric effector or corepressor.
   3. In the presence of excess tryptophan, the *trp* repressor protein binds with tryptophan and is then able to bind to the *trp* operator region.
   4. When the tryptophan complex binds at the *trp* operator region, the transcription of the enzymes involved in the biosynthesis of tryptophan is repressed.
   5. End product repression is the process of shutting off transcription by a by-product of the metabolism coded for by the genes in that operon.
F. Attenuation is a mode of regulating gene expression in which the events that occur during translation affect the transcription of an operon region of the DNA.
   1. There is a redundancy in the control mechanisms for the biosynthesis of amino acids such as tryptophan. The leader sequence and the associated attenuator site provide a mechanism for even finer control of transcription and the expression of genetic information than the operator region.
   2. In the case of the *trp* operon, there is an attenuator site between the operator region and the first structural gene of the operon (at or near the end of the leader sequence) where transcription can be interrupted.
      a. Whether or not termination occurs is determined by the secondary structure of the mRNA at the attenuator region.
      b. If mRNA folds to establish a double-stranded region (terminator hairpin), that causes termination of transcription.
      c. When tryptophan is available, the peptide sequence coded for by this leader sequence can be translated.
      d. When tryptophan is low, translation is delayed at the leader codons that code for the insertion of tryptophan into the polypeptide.
      e. When translation is slowed, the mRNA is in the form that permits transcription to proceed through the entire sequence of the *trp* operon.
      f. If there is sufficient tryptophan to permit rapid translation to proceed through the attenuator site, the mRNA forms the terminator hairpin structure and transcription of the *trp* operon ceases.
      g. The histidine and phenylalanine operons in *E. coli* also contain attenuator regions.
      h. Only when the concentrations of these amino acids are very low does translation stall, allowing transcription to proceed through the attenuator site.
G. Under poor growth conditions the cell has the ability to shut down several energy-draining activities (the stringent response).
   1. It involves the production of unusual guanosine phosphates: guanosine pentaphosphate (pppGpp) and guanosine tetraphosphate (ppGpp).
   2. Bacteria that exhibit the stringent response produce a stringent factor protein.
   3. Under conditions of amino acid starvation, uncharged tRNAs can enter the ribosomal aminoacyl site.
   4. When this occurs, stringent factor catalyzes the transfer of a pyrophosphate group from ATP to GTP or GDP, which are involved in protein synthesis.
      a. The pyrophosphorylation of GTP (pppG) produces pppGpp and the pyrophosphorylation of GDP (ppG) or dephosphorylation of pppGpp produces ppGpp.
      b. The effector molecule ppGpp may specifically bind to promoters of rRNA and tRNA sequences and inhibit their transcription by RNA polymerase or ppGpp may cause increased pausing of the translation process and premature termination of specific polypeptides.
   5. Some bacterial strains that have mutations in the *relA* gene and do not exhibit a stringent response under conditions of amino acid starvation are said to be relaxed.
H. There are various control mechanisms in eukaryotic cells.
   1. Each eukaryotic mRNA generally contains the information for only one protein (monocistronic).
   2. Control over several different mRNA molecules may be required to achieve coordinated control.
   3. The sequence of codons of a given gene in eukaryotic microorganisms is not colinear with the mRNA molecule or with the polypeptide sequence of the protein, making operator region regulation of transcription unlikely.
   4. Control mechanisms for genetic expression in eukaryotic microorganisms include the loss of genes, gene amplification, rearrangement of genes, differential transcription of genes, post-transcriptional modification of RNA, and translational control.
   5. The elimination of some of the genetic information restricts the number of genes that can be expressed. Some eukaryotic cells amplify gene expression, thereby producing large amounts of the enzyme coded for by a given gene and increasing the amount of rRNA and thus the number of ribosomes that can be used to translate the information in a stable mRNA molecule.
   6. The rearrangement of genes (change in relative position within the chromosome) can alter the expression of the information contained in those genes.

CHAPTER 7

GENETIC VARIATION

A. Genetic variability comes from changes in the cells hereditary molecules resulting from mistakes made during DNA replication or exchanges of DNA.

B. Eukaryotic cells usually contain multiple copies of genes.
   1. Eukaryotic cells generally have pairs of matching chromosomes (diploid) and two sets of genes.
   2. Alleles are corresponding genes of chromosomal pairs.
      a. Alleles may be identical or contain different genetic information, coding for different amino acid sequences in polypeptides.
      b. Homozygous cells contain identical copies of the gene.
      c. Heterozygous cells have different corresponding copies of the gene.
      d. Genes may be dominant or recessive.
      e. Codominant alleles produce a hybrid state within an intermediate phenotype.
      f. There may be more than two allelic forms of a given gene in the entire population.
      g. The number of alleles determines the number of potential genotypes for a given gene locus.
   3. The number of different genotypes that can arise from multiple alleles raises the potential degree of heterogeneity within the gene pool of a population.

C. Prokaryotes have a single bacterial chromosome (haploid).

D. Prokaryotes may have small extrachromosomal genetic elements (plasmids).
   1. Plasmids generally contain genetic information for specialized features such as resistance to heavy metals and antibiotics.
   2. They are small genetic elements with 1 to 30 kb pairs capable of self-replication.
   3. Plasmids can be exchanged between cells.
   4. Transmissibility of some plasmids is controlled by *tra* genes.
   5. Curing is the loss of plasmids.
      a. Acridine dyes, ultraviolet light, and heavy metals increase the rates of plasmid curing.
      b. Retention or loss of plasmids often depends on selective pressure to possess the genes encoded within that plasmid.
   6. Certain pairs of plasmids cannot be stably replicated in the same bacterial cell.
      a. Incompatible plasmids do not co-exist in the same cell and belong to an incompatibility group.
      b. The incompatibility group of a plasmid is designated *Inc* followed by a capital letter and sometimes also a number.
      c. Plasmids of the same incompatibility group are closely related and have similar properties.
   7. Plasmids can contain various types of information that determine the ability of bacteria to survive.
      a. Some plasmids are involved in mating, determining whether a bacterial strain donates DNA during mating.
         (i). The F (fertility) plasmid codes for mating behavior in *E. coli.* Strains with the F plasmid are donor strains, and those without it are recipient strains.
         (ii). Bacteria with the F plasmid form pili of the F type involved in establishing mating pairs.
      b. Colicinogenic plasmids carry genes for a protein toxic to closely related bacteria. Colicins are toxins produced by *E. coli.*
         (i). Colicinogenic plasmids have genes that protect the host cell.
         (ii). They also may carry the information necessary for bacterial conjugation.
         (iii). Colicinogenic plasmids enable bacterial strains to enter into antagonistic relationships with other bacterial strains.
      c. Some plasmids contain the information that codes for resistance to antibiotics and other chemicals.
         (i). R (resistance) plasmids carry genes that code for antibiotic resistance or mating.
         (ii). The enzymes coded for by R plasmid genes degrade antibiotics.
         (iii). R factors can be passed among bacteria.
      d. Some plasmids encode the information for the degradation of various complex organic compounds.
      e. Some plasmids have the information for toxin production that renders some bacteria pathogenic to humans.
      f. The genes responsible for nitrogen fixation and the formation of root nodules on leguminous plants occur on plasmids.

MUTATIONS

A. A mutation is a heritable change in the nucleotide sequence of a cells DNA.
   1. Mutations alter a cell's genotype.
   2. Changing the nucleotide sequence (genotype) can alter the ability of the cell to produce properly functioning proteins, changing the functions of regulatory or structural genes.
   3. There are various types of mutations, described by the nature of the change in the DNA or the effect of the mutation on the phenotype.
      a. A base substitution mutation occurs when one pair of nucleotide bases in the DNA is replaced by another.
         (i). Transition base substitutions involve the replacement of a purine on one strand by a different purine and the replacement of a pyrimidine on the other strand by a different pyrimidine.
         (ii). Transversions are base substitutions in which purines replace pyrimidines and pyrimidines replace purines.
      b. Missense mutations are base substitutions that result in a change in the amino acid inserted into the polypeptide chain specified by the gene in which the mutation occurs, resulting in the production of an inactive enzyme or may have no effect on the phenotype.
         (i). Silent mutations do not alter the phenotype of the organism and go undetected.
         (ii). A silent mutation results in the production of proteins with exactly the same amino acid sequences as the nonmutant cell.
         (iii). Changes in the nucleotide sequence that alter the third base of codon are most likely to produce silent mutations because this is

where most of the redundancy in the genetic code occurs.

(iv). The wobble hypothesis states that changes in the third position of the codon often do not alter the amino acid sequence of the polypeptide.

c. A nonsense mutation is an alteration in the base sequence of the DNA that results in the formation of a codon that does not code for an amino acid.

(i). Nonsense codons act as terminator signals during protein synthesis, preventing the formation of a functional enzyme molecule.

(ii). Nonsense mutations near the beginning of translation (the 5′-P end) will terminate translation of all the successive genes; nonsense mutations farther down will have fewer effects.

d. Polar mutations prevent the translation of subsequent polypeptides coded for in the same mRNA molecule.

e. A deletion mutation involves the removal of one or more nucleotide base pairs from the DNA.

f. An insertion mutation involves the addition of one or more base pairs.

g. Deletions of large numbers of base pairs (deficiencies) can result in the loss of genetic information for one or more complete genes.

h. Frame shift mutations can result in the misreading of large numbers of codons.

i. A suppressor mutation reestablishes a reading frame.

(i). An intragenic suppressor mutation is a mutation within one gene that permits the successful synthesis of the polypeptide specified by the gene in which the mutation occurs.

(ii). An intergenic mutation is a mutation within one gene that affects another gene.

j. A lethal mutation results in the death of the microorganism or its inability to reproduce.

(i). A conditionally lethal mutation causes a loss of viability only under some specified conditions in which the organism would normally survive.

(ii). Temperature-sensitive mutations alter the range of temperatures over which the microorganism may grow when using specific substrates.

k. Nutritional mutations occur when a mutation alters the nutritional requirements for the progeny of a microorganism.

(i). Often, nutritional mutants are unable to synthesize essential biochemicals.

(ii). Auxotrophs are nutritional mutants that require growth factors that are not needed by the parental or wild type (prototroph) strain.

B. There are several methods for detection of mutations.

1. The replica plating technique is used to detect mutants by observing microorganisms under a series of growth conditions.

a. A piece of sterile velvet is touched to the surface of an agar plate containing surface bacterial colonies.

b. The velvet with its attached microorganisms is then touched to the surface of a sterile agar plate, inoculating it and stamping microorganisms onto different media.

c. The distribution of colonies will be the same on each plate unless the colonies have different genetic compositions.

d. A nutritional mutation is indicated when a colony that develops on a complete medium fails to develop on a minimal medium without a specific growth factor.

e. Auxotrophs are microorganisms that do not grow on the minimal medium.

2. The complementation method determines whether mutations are in the same or different locations.

a. The procedure involves genetically crossing (mating) two different mutant strains to determine whether the two mutations complement each other.

b. If the two mutations are in the same gene, the resulting progeny should still be mutant.

c. If the mutations are in different genes, the mutant phenotype should be eliminated in the progeny.

d. A *cis/trans* complementation test is used to determine whether two mutations are in the same gene.

(i). If the two mutations are on separate DNA molecules, they are in the *trans* configuration.

(ii). If they are on the same molecule, they are in the *cis* configuration.

C. The mutation rate is the probability that any one cell will mutate during the period of time required by a cell to divide to form a new generation of cells.

1. The mutation rate is equal to the average number of mutations per cell generation.

2. Mutations occur spontaneously only at relatively low rates.

3. This spontaneous rate varies among different bacterial species.

4. Mutagens are chemical or physical agents that increase the incidence of mutation.

5. High-energy radiation causes mutations because it produces breaks in the DNA molecule.

a. Exposure to gamma radiation sterilizes objects because sufficient exposure to ionizing radiation results in lethal mutations and the death of all exposed microorganisms.

b. The time and intensity of exposure determine the number of lethal mutations that occur and establishes the required exposures for ionizing radiation for sterilization.

6. Ultraviolet light can cause base substitutions by creating covalent linkages between adjacent thymidines on the same strand of the DNA.

a. A thymine dimer cannot act as a template for DNA polymerase.

b. These dimers prevent the proper functioning of polymerases.

7. Various chemicals modify nucleotides and act as mutagens, increasing rates of mutations.

a. Base analogs are chemicals that resemble DNA nucleotides but do not function in the same manner.

b. Several chemical mutagens result in base deletion or base addition mutations and cause frame shift mutations.
c. Other mutagens form covalent cross-linkages between base pairs, preventing the replication of the DNA molecule.

8. The Ames test is used to detect chemical mutagens and carcinogens. It is based on determining whether exposure to a particular chemical alters the mutation rate of strains of auxotrophic *Salmonella typhimurium* that require the amino acid histidine for growth.
   a. The organisms are exposed to a concentration gradient of the chemical being tested on a solid growth medium that contains only a trace of histidine.
   b. Normally no colonies develop because the test strain bacteria cannot grow sufficiently due to the lack of histidine.
   c. If the chemical is a mutagen, mutations will occur in the areas of high chemical concentration.
   d. No growth will occur if these are lethal mutations.
   e. At lower chemical concentrations some of the mutants will be revertants to the prototrophs that do not require histidine.
   f. The appearance of bacterial colonies demonstrates that histidine prototrophs have been produced and a high rate of formation of such mutants suggests that the chemical has mutagenic properties.
9. The Ames test is used to determine if a chemical is a potential carcinogen.
   a. There is a high correlation between mutagenicity and carcinogenicity. In testing for potential carcinogenicity, the chemical is incubated with a preparation of rat liver enzymes to simulate what normally occurs in the liver, where many chemicals are inadvertently transformed into carcinogens in an apparent effort by the body to detoxify the chemical.
   b. Various concentrations of the transformed chemical are incubated with the *Salmonella* auxotroph to determine whether it causes mutations.
   c. Further testing for carcinogenicity is done on these chemicals.

D. Cells have several mechanisms for repairing DNA.
   1. Mismatch repair removes improperly inserted bases by the action of mismatch correction enzyme.
   2. Excision repair corrects damaged DNA by removing nucleotides and then resynthesizing the region.
   3. Photoreactivation breaks the covalent linkages between the thymine bases to remove them. It depends on an enzyme that functions only in the presence of light.
   4. Recombination repair uses recA protein and a segment of DNA from a compatible DNA molecule to replace a damaged or missing segment.
   5. The SOS system is a generalized multifunctional process for repair of damaged DNA.
      a. The SOS system is induced after a delay during which incomplete DNA replication has occurred.
      b. Cell division ceases and filamentous growth occurs.

RECOMBINATION

A. Recombination occurs when there is an exchange of genetic information among different DNA molecules that results in a reshuffling of genes.

B. Recombination is a mechanism for redistributing the informational changes that occur in DNA that produces progeny that contain genetic information derived from two potentially different genomes.

C. Recombination results in an exchange of allelic forms of genes that can produce new combinations of alleles.

D. Homologous recombination occurs between regions of DNA containing the same or nearly the same nucleotide sequences.
   1. It is seen in the crossing over of chromosomes where pairs of chromosomes containing the same gene loci pair and exchange allelic portions of the same chromosomes.
   2. In eukaryotic cells this often occurs during meiosis.
   3. Homologous recombination can be initiated by an endonuclease that produces a short single-stranded segment by nicking one of the strands of DNA.
      a. The free 3′-OH end acts as a primer for DNA synthesis.
      b. The newly synthesized region pairs with the corresponding region of the homologous chromosome.
      c. A heteroduplex is formed when two strands of DNA that are complementary over only part of their lengths join together.
         (i). The homologous regions form a duplex (double-stranded complementary segment) and the noncomplementary segments remain single-stranded.
         (ii). An endonuclease cleaves out the unpaired section of the DNA macromolecule.
         (iii). Ligases join the free ends of the DNA strands.
         (iv). Heteroduplex formation is catalyzed by enzymes coded for by *rec* (recombination) genes.
         (v). A bridge between the two homologous DNA strands is formed.
         (vi). Chromosomes joined at a homologous region establish a chi form.
         (vii). The chromosomes then rotate so that the two strands no longer cross each other (they are still held together by covalent linkages).
         (viii). An endonuclease cleaves the DNA strands, breaking the heteroduplex.
         (ix). Two independent chromosomes are made.

E. Nonhomologous recombination (nonreciprocal recombination) occurs when the extent of homologous regions is limited.
   1. It can be a site-specific exchange process, that is, DNA exchange occurs only at a given location within the genome.
   2. Nonhomologous recombinations permit the joining of DNA molecules from different sources.
   3. Transposable genetic elements have nucleotide sequences that enable them to undergo nonreciprocal recombination.
      a. Transposons can move "jumping jack genes" from one location to another.

b. The ends of the transposable genetic elements often contain inverted repetitive sequences of nucleotide bases that permit the folding of DNA stabilized by hydrogen bonding between complementary bases within the DNA macromolecule.

4. An insertion sequence (IS) is a small transposable genetic element that can move around bacterial chromosomes, occurring at different times at different locations on the chromosome.
   a. An IS is not homologous with the regions of the plasmids or the chromosomes into which it is inserted.
   b. The IS has an identical nucleotide sequence repeated at each end, allowing for base pairing for transposition.
5. Transposons are transposable genetic elements that contain genetic information for the production of structural proteins.
   a. They may be constructed by the attachment of ISs to structural genes.
   b. Recombination can occur between an IS on a bacterial chromosome and an IS on a transposon.
   c. In conservative transposition, the transposon is excised from one location and inserted at another.
   d. In replicative transposition a copy of the transposable DNA is made and inserted at a new location.
      (i). The source transposon is retained and does not move.
      (ii). The copy number of the transposon increases.
   e. In some cases, the transposon inserts at the same site but in the reverse direction, inverting the order of nucleotides and altering gene expression.
   f. Transposons provide a mutation mechanism.
6. Lysogeny is the process by which a viral genome may be incorporated into a bacterial chromosome.
   a. The genes of temperate bacterial viruses can be expressed by the bacterial host.
   b. The bacterium produces proteins coded for by the viral genes by the process of lysogenic conversion.

DNA TRANSFER IN PROKARYOTES

A. Bacterial genetic exchange followed by recombination occurs by transformation, transduction, or conjugation (mating); these mechanisms differ in the way DNA is transferred between donor and recipient cells.

B. In transformation a free DNA molecule is transferred from a donor to a recipient bacterium when the donor leaks its DNA and the recipient bacterium is able (competent) to take it up, that is, it must have a site for binding the donor DNA at the cell surface and its cytoplasmic membrane must be in a state so that free DNA can pass across it.
   1. This is a reciprocal recombinational event.
   2. If the allelic forms of the donor and recipient genes are not identical, the progeny of the recipient cell may have a composite (hybrid) genome.
   3. The competency of a cell depends on its growth phase and environmental conditions.
   4. Relatively few bacterial genera have been demonstrated to be capable of taking up naked DNA.
   5. A competence-specific protein associates with the intact DNA and protects it from nuclease digestion.
   6. The intact strand of DNA forms a heteroduplex with the bacterial chromosome of the recipient bacterium.
   7. A nuclease degrades the corresponding region of DNA in one of the strands of the recipient cell, and ligases join the donor DNA with the DNA of the recipient bacterial chromosome.

C. In transduction, DNA is transferred from a donor to a recipient cell by a viral carrier. Generalized transduction brings about the general transfer of genes and can result in the exchange of any of the homologous alleles.
   1. Pieces of bacterial DNA are accidentally acquired by developing bacteriophage during their normal replication within a host bacterial cell.
   2. Defective (temperate) phage do not cause death of a host cell.
   3. Inside the recipient cell, DNA may be degraded by nucleases or may undergo homologous recombination.
   4. Specialized transduction results in transmission of a specific bacterial DNA region.
      a. Lambda and mu bacteriophage are capable of specialized transduction.
         (i). When these phage establish lysogeny, the phage DNA occasionally carries with it adjacent bacterial genes when viral replication occurs and leaves behind some of the viral genes.
         (ii). This makes the phage defective in some viral genes.
      b. The formation of defective phage establishes a viral carrier of bacterial DNA.
      c. Only the genes that are adjacent to the site of insertion of the viral genome may be transferred by specialized transduction.
   5. Generalized transduction occurs when a large number of genes are transferred by a phage.

D. Conjugation (mating) requires the establishment of physical contact between the donor and recipient bacterial cells of the mating pair.
   1. The physical contact between mating cells of *E. coli* is established through the F pilus.
   2. The F plasmid confers the ability to produce the F pilus.
   3. Gram-negative bacterial strains that produce F pili act as donors during conjugation; those lacking the F plasmid are recipient strains.
   4. The F plasmid contains *rep* genes that allow it to be replicated by the host cell.
   5. Recipient bacterial strains are F^- and donor strains are F^+ if the F plasmid is independent or Hfr (high frequency recombination strain) if the F plasmid DNA is incorporated into the bacterial chromosome.
   6. Conjugative plasmids encode for self-transfer.
   7. The donor cell replicates one strand of DNA using rolling circle DNA replication, a process in which one of the strands of the double helical DNA is nicked and replicated, using the unnicked strand as a template.

8. The original nicked strand becomes displaced as the replication fork "rolls" around the circular DNA.
9. The F plasmid mediates the transfer of other plasmids that are incapable of self-transfer.
   a. The ability to mobilize chromosomal DNA rests with its complement of insertion sequences.
   b. The F plasmid can replicate only in Gram-negative enteric bacteria, but other conjugative plasmids can self-transfer in other Gram-negative bacteria.
10. Normally, only a portion of the donor bacterial chromosome is transferred during bacterial mating.
   a. The precise portion of the transferred DNA depends on the time of mating.
   b. When an F^+ cell is mated with an F^- cell, the F plasmid DNA is usually transferred from the donor to the recipient.
   c. The F plasmid does not normally recombine with the bacterial chromosome of the recipient bacterium.
   d. The transferred single-stranded linear DNA molecule acts as a template for the synthesis of a complementary strand of DNA.
   e. F genes of the bacterial chromosome usually are not transferred when Hfr strains are mated with F^- strains.

GENETIC MAPPING

A. Genetic mapping involves the use of recombinants formed from different allelic forms of multiple genes to determine the relative locations of genes.
B. The occurrence of recombinants that result from mating is used to establish a map showing the order and relative locations (loci) of genes.
C. By vibrating a culture of mating bacteria, one can interrupt mating by breaking the F pilus, stopping DNA transfer, and the order of genes on the bacterial chromosome can be determined by examining the times at which recombinants for given genes are found.
   1. The recovery of recombinants of marker genes is normally used as a reference point for establishing the fine structure of the genome.
   2. If a gene of unknown location shows a high frequency of recombination along with the marker gene, it is likely that the marker and unknown genes are closely associated in the chromosome.
   3. If the genes are far apart, it is unlikely that recombinants of both the marker gene and the gene of unknown location will occur in the progeny.
D. Transduction and cotransformation can also be used to establish the fine structure of the bacterial genome.
   a. In generalized transduction, it is unlikely that genes will undergo cotransduction unless they are closely associated in the bacterial chromosome.
   b. The locations of genes can be determined by the transfer times for recombination as determined by interrupted mating.
E. Superscript + indicates that the organism has the genes for biosynthesis or utilization; superscript − indicates that the organism lacks these genes; superscript R indicates resistance; and superscript S indicates sensitivity.

GENETIC MODIFICATION AND MICROBIAL EVOLUTION

A. The introduction of diversity into the gene pools of microbial populations establishes a basis for selection and evolution.
B. The basis of evolution lies in the ability to change the gene pool and to maintain favorable new combinations of genes.
C. Mutation and general recombination provide a basis for the gradual selection of adaptive features.
   1. Reciprocal recombination produces evolutionary links between closely related organisms, and nonreciprocal recombinational events appear to provide a mechanism for rapid, stepwise evolutionary changes.
   2. Mutations introduce variability into genomes, resulting in changes in the enzymes that the organism synthesizes.
   3. Changes in the genetic information of microorganisms can be widely and rapidly disseminated.
D. The occurrence of favorable mutations introduces information into the gene pool that can make an organism more fit to survive in its environment and compete with other microorganisms for available resources.
   1. Change toward more favorable variants in a particular environment is the essence of evolution.
   2. Recombination creates new allelic combinations that may be adaptive.
   3. The long-term stability of a population depends on its incorporating adaptive genetic information into its chromosomes.
E. Plasmids and other transposable genetic elements may contribute to rapid changes in the genetic composition of a population.

RECOMBINANT DNA TECHNOLOGY

A. Recombinant DNA technology is the intentional recombination of genes from different sources by artificial means.
   1. This is the basis for genetic engineering.
   2. The replication of recombinant DNA is accomplished by gene cloning, which involves isolation of the DNA to be cloned; incorporation of the source DNA into a segment of DNA used for replication of foreign DNA fragments to form a recombinant DNA molecule; incorporation of the recombinant DNA in the cloning vector into a recipient cell that can replicate the cloning vector; detection of the newly transformed cells containing recombinant DNA; and growth of cultures of cells containing the cloned DNA fragment.
B. Cells can be artificially fused by protoplast fusion.
   1. Protoplasts are cells that have had their walls removed by enzymatic or detergent treatment.
   2. Protoplast membranes can fuse to form a single cell.
   3. The basic procedure involves polyethylene glycol–induced fusion of protoplasts followed by the regeneration of normal cells, establishing a transient quasi-diploid state, and permitting recombination to occur between complete bacterial chromosomes.
C. DNA is isolated from bacterial cells for cloning by lysing the cells and recovering and purifying the DNA.
   1. Gram-positive cells are more difficult to lyse and in

some cases physical disruption, such as sonication or freezing and thawing, is used to break them open.

2. The released DNA is treated with ribonuclease and precipitated with cold ethanol. Repeated washing and reprecipitation produces purified DNA.
3. Further purification is done by cesium-chloride buoyant density ultracentrifugation, electrophoresis, and column chromatography.
4. mRNA can also be isolated as a template and a copy DNA synthesized.
5. cDNA is used for cloning.
6. DNA sequences can also be produced by chemical or automated nucleotide synthesizing systems, producing DNA sequences up to several hundreds of nucleotides in length.

D. Restriction endonucleases (restriction enzymes) and ligases permit the cutting and splicing of DNA.
   1. Restriction endonucleases normally function to prevent the incorporation of foreign DNA into the genome of a cell by cutting both strands of a foreign DNA molecule.
   2. Bacteria protect themselves against their own endonucleases by modifying DNA bases at the recognition sites where the endonucleases act.
   3. Endonucleases are named using a system whereby the first letter indicates the genus from which it was isolated, the next two letters indicate the species, the fourth letter (when needed) indicates the strain, and the number indicates the order of discovery of endonucleases from that strain.
   4. Different types of endonucleases vary with respect to the site at which they cut DNA.
      a. Type I restriction endonucleases cleave DNA at a random distance from a recognition site in the DNA nucleotide sequence.
      b. Type II restriction endonucleases cleave the DNA at the recognition site.
         (i). A type II restriction endonuclease cuts the DNA at a palindromic sequence of bases, which is a sequence of nucleotide bases that can be read identically in the 3′-OH → 5′-P and 5′-P → 3′-OH directions.
         (ii). Type II restriction endonucleases frequently produce DNA with staggered single-stranded ends; these staggered DNA ends can act as cohesive or sticky ends during recombination, making them suitable for splicing with segments of foreign source DNA.
         (iii). Some type II restriction endonucleases cut the DNA in both strands at the same site.
      c. Type III endonucleases cut the DNA at some precise distance from the recognition site.
   5. The enzyme terminal deoxynucleotidyl transferase can be used to create artificial homology at the terminal ends of two different DNA molecules.
      a. This can be accomplished by adding polyadenine tails to one fragment and polythymine tails to the other.
      b. Pairing occurs between homologous regions of complementary bases.
      c. Blunt end ligation is also encountered when two different endonucleases are used.
         (i). One opens a plasmid ring and the other forms a segment of donor DNA.
         (ii). Artificial homology at the terminal ends of the donor and plasmid DNA molecules must be synthesized.
         (iii). Homologous regions of complementary bases pair.
         (iv). Ligases seal the circular plasmid.
         (v). The tails left by the action of the endonuclease are cleaved *in vitro*, using exonucleases.
         (vi). By adding a polyT tail to the donor DNA after its excision with an endonuclease, the donor DNA can be made complementary to the polyA tails of the plasmid DNA, permitting the formation of a circular plasmid molecule.

E. A cloning vector is used to clone a segment of DNA.
   1. Cloning vectors should replicate autonomously in a suitable host cell, be separable from the host DNA so that it can be purified, should have regions that can accept source DNA without losing self-replication capacity, should also be able to enter a host cell and replicate to a high copy number (large number of repetitive copies of the genes, such as can be achieved by having multiple identical plasmids), and should be stable in the host.
   2. Plasmids, bacteriophage, and phage–plasmid artificial hybrids (cosmids) are frequently used as cloning vectors.
   3. Cloning vectors are constructed so that they can function in several different types of cells and permit the transfer of recombinant DNA from one cell type to another.
   4. Cloning vectors usually have several single restriction enzyme cleavage sites.
      a. These sites permit circular DNA to be opened (linearized).
      b. The linearized DNA of the cloning vector can be joined with the DNA to be cloned by ligation.
      c. If the insertion occurs at the antibiotic resistance site, resistance is lost because the nucleotide sequence of the antibiotic resistance gene is disrupted.
      d. This insertional inactivation is useful for detecting the presence of foreign DNA within a plasmid.
   5. A collection of clones of individual genes from a specific organism constitutes a genomic library.
   6. The construction of a genomic library involves obtaining copies of the nucleotide sequences of the genome and cloning these into a suitable vector.

F. Site-directed mutagenesis can be brought about through reconstruction with phage.

G. The expression of the foreign genetic information requires that the appropriate reading frame be established and the transcriptional and translational control mechanisms turned on to permit the expression of the DNA.
   1. Often the genes produced using a cloning vector must be transferred to an expression vector that contains the desired gene and the necessary regulatory sequences that permit control of the expression of that gene.
   2. There should be a strong promoter associated with

the gene to ensure binding of RNA polymerase.
   3. The early part of the RNA transcript must contain a ribosome-binding site that establishes the appropriate reading frame.

H. To detect the presence of foreign DNA, probes can be radioactively labelled with synthetically produced DNA or RNA molecules complementary to the sequence one wishes to detect, or reporter genes can be used.
   1. If the probe binds to a region of DNA isolated from a specific clone, this indicates that the DNA sequence of interest is present.
   2. Reporter genes code for an easily detectable trait in the cell in which they are placed.

I. Bacteria do not possess the capacity to remove introns from eukaryotic DNA to form the mRNA needed to produce functional protein molecules.
   1. Eukaryotic DNA must be cut and spliced artificially to establish a contiguous sequence of nucleotide bases to define the protein to be expressed.
      a. An mRNA molecule and a reverse transcriptase enzyme are used to produce a DNA molecule that has a contiguous sequence of nucleotide bases containing the complete gene.
      b. The single-stranded DNA molecule formed is complementary to the complete mRNA molecule. It is called complementary or copied DNA (cDNA).
      c. The RNA can be removed using ribonuclease and the second complementary strand of DNA synthesized.
      d. The double-stranded DNA molecule formed in this manner can then be inserted into a carrier plasmid.
   2. Proper expression and stability of the product must be ensured.
      a. One method of providing a ribosome-binding site in the proper reading frame when a mammalian DNA sequence is added to a bacterial host cell is to establish a nucleotide sequence that produces a fusion protein that contains a short prokaryotic sequence at the amino end and the desired eukaryotic sequence at the carboxyl end.
      b. Fusion proteins are often more stable in bacteria.
      c. Also, the bacterial portion can contain the bacterial sequence coding for the signal peptide that enables transport of the protein across the cell membrane.

J. Recombination involving plasmids, as well as other vectors, provides a mechanism for the particularly rapid dissemination of genes through a population.

K. Plasmids are quite useful as carriers of foreign genetic information in genetic engineering.

L. Recombinant DNA technology can be employed to create organisms that contain combinations of genetic information that do not occur naturally.
   1. Bacteria containing genetically engineered plasmids can synthesize proteins that are normally produced only in eukaryotic organisms.
   2. Recombinant DNA technology can be used to engineer organisms that can produce any desired combination of proteins.
   3. Genetic engineering can create novel living systems that can be patented as inventions.

M. The problem of safety has been temporarily solved by using mutation and selection procedures to develop a fail-safe strain of *E. coli* that is unable to grow outside a carefully defined culture medium.

N. The questions of whether novel genomes will survive in the environment, whether they will transfer to other microorganisms and spread, and whether this dissemination could represent a serious biological hazard are being actively debated.

CHAPTER 8

STRUCTURE OF VIRUSES

A. A virus consists of a central genetic nucleic acid core, RNA or DNA, surrounded by a protein coat.

B. The nucleocapsid is the combined genome and capsid.

C. The capsid is the coat structure surrounding the nucleic acid genome of a virus.
   1. A capsid is composed of capsomers.
   2. Capsids can have helical or isometric symmetry.
      a. Helical capsids form helical coils around the nucleic acid.
      b. Isometric capsids are geometric, often icosahedrons.
      c. In simple capsids the proteins aggregate into pentamers.
      d. In large isometric viruses the capsomers may bind into pentamerous and hexamerous arrangements.

D. The viral genome is enclosed within the capsid.
   1. The genome may consist of linear or circular double-stranded DNA, single-stranded DNA, single-stranded RNA, or double-stranded RNA.
   2. Complete genetic maps for various viruses have been developed.
   3. Viral genes may be contained within a single chromosome or the virus may have a segmented genome.
   4. A segmented viral genome has multiple nucleic acid molecules as separate chromosomes.
   5. Viral genes are clustered according to their function.
   6. Some viruses maximize the amount of information that is stored within the genome by using overlapping genes and transcription of both strands of the DNA in opposite directions to code for different protein products.

E. Some viruses have an envelope composed of host cell cytoplasmic membrane.
   1. The viral envelope has phospholipid and proteins.
   2. On leaving the host cell, the virus picks up a portion of the nuclear or cytoplasmic membrane, which can surround the viral capsid, forming the lipid portion of the envelope.
   3. The hydrophilic carbohydrate ends of glycosylated proteins may protrude from the viral particle, appearing as spikes.
   4. The carbohydrate moieties of the glycoproteins and the lipid components are obtained from the host cell.
   5. Envelope proteins are specified by the viral genome.

a. Some of these proteins are involved in binding the virus to a host cell; others cause cell lysis.
b. Some envelope proteins form a matrix layer that attaches the envelope to the capsid.

VIRAL REPLICATION

A. In viral replication, copies of the viral genome and protein coat are made and assembled into new viruses.
B. Viruses are not capable of independent activity outside of a host cell.
C. Replication can only occur within a host cell.
D. For a specific virus to replicate within a host cell: the host cell must be permissive, and the virus must be compatible with the host cell; the host cell must not degrade the virus; the viral genome must possess the information for modifying the normal metabolism of the host cell; and the virus must be able to use the metabolic capabilities of the host cell to produce new virus particles containing replicated copies of the viral genome.
E. The stages in viral replication include (1) adsorption, the attachment of the virus to the outer surface of a suitable host cell; (2) penetration into the host cell; (3) uncoating, the release of the viral genome from the capsid; (4) synthesis of viral proteins; (5) synthesis of viral nucleic acid; (6) assembly of viral progeny; and (7) release of viruses from the host cell.
   1. Viral replication begins with the attachment of a virus to the surface of a susceptible host cell.
   2. The virus or only its nucleic acid enters the host cell.
   3. The nucleic acid codes for the production of viral proteins and nucleic acid.
   4. The viral genome controls the cell's metabolic activities.
      a. Often host-cell reproduction metabolic activities are shutdown.
      b. The virus uses the host cell's ribosomes for producing viral proteins and the cell's ATP and reduced coenzymes for carrying out biosynthesis and replication.
      c. Either transcription of host cell genes is inhibited or viral mRNAs are translated more efficiently than host cell mRNAs so that viral protein synthesis dominates over synthesis of normal host cell proteins.
      d. After infection by many viruses, inhibition of host-cell mRNA translation occurs.
      e. Viral proteins are made that alter host cell functions so that the host cell produces viral capsid proteins, proteins for the replication of viral genomes, and proteins for the packaging of the genome into virus particles.
      f. Some viruses use host enzymes to replicate the viral genome.
      g. Most viruses use viral proteins to replicate the viral genome and to assemble viruses.
   5. New viruses are assembled from the viral genome and the viral capsid.
   6. The assembled virions are then released from the host cell.
   7. Sometimes they kill the host cell in the process.
   8. Sometimes they acquire a portion of host cell cytoplasmic membrane as an envelope surrounding the virus.
   9. Many virions are produced within a single host cell and are released together.
   10. The replication of a virus results in changes in the host cell, often causing death.
   11. Viruses only replicate within compatible host cells.
      a. The host range of a virus is defined by the types of cells within which replication of that virus occurs.
      b. Bacteriophage are viruses that replicate only within bacterial cells. Phage are further restricted to replication only within certain bacterial species.
      c. Animal viruses replicate only within animal cells.
      d. Plant viruses only replicate within plant cells.
   12. Viral infections can have several outcomes.
      a. Productive infection occurs in permissive cells and results in viral replication.
      b. Abortive infections occur when the host cell is nonpermissive, replication does not occur or produces viral progeny that are not capable of infecting other host cells.
      c. Host cells may be only transiently permissive.
      d. Either the virus persists in the cell until the cell becomes permissive, or only a few of the cells produce viral progeny.
      e. Restrictive infections occur when the host cell is transiently permissive; infective viral progeny are sometimes produced and at other times the virus persists in the infective cell without the production of infective viral progeny.
F. Attachment of a virus to a host cell involves binding specific sites on the surface of the virus to specific sites on the surface of the host cell.
   1. Attachment does not require energy but does require ions to reduce electrostatic repulsion.
   2. Cell susceptibility to viral infection is limited by the availability of appropriate receptors.
   3. The receptor is the binding constituent on the host cell surface, typically a glycoprotein.
   4. More than one receptor on a cell surface may be involved in attachment.
   5. The ability of an antireceptor to bind only at a particular receptor explains the specificity between virus and host.
   6. Once most viruses attach to a cell surface they cannot detach, but some viruses can readsorb.
   7. Attachment of viruses to cells often leads to irreversible changes in the structure of the virion.
G. Penetration occurs shortly after attachment.
   1. Penetration requires energy.
   2. It may involve: transfer of only the viral genome across the cytoplasmic membrane; endocytosis, transport of the entire virus across the cytoplasmic membrane; or fusion of a viral envelope with the cytoplasmic membrane of the host cell.
   3. Some bacteriophage inject their DNA genomes into the host cell while their capsids remain outside the cell.
   4. Others are engulfed by the host cell cytoplasmic

membrane and remain intact until inside the host cell. Most enveloped viruses enter by endocytosis.

5. After binding, a clathrin-coated pit, an invagination of the cytoplasmic membrane, is formed.
   a. The pit with its attached virion is internalized inside the cell and pinches off, forming a clathrin-coated vesicle.
   b. This vesicle fuses with endosomes.
   c. Endosomes are smooth cytoplasmic vesicles.
   d. The virion lipid envelope and the vesicle membrane fuse, releasing the nucleocapsid into the cytoplasm.
   e. A few enveloped viruses penetrate by fusion of their envelopes with the host cytoplasmic membrane.

H. Uncoating is the process by which the viral genome is released from the capsid.
   1. The cytoskeleton of the eukaryotic cell plays a role in the transport of the viral nucleocapsid to the nucleus.
   2. Uncoating occurs at the nuclear pores.
   3. The viral DNA or a DNA-protein complex is transported into the nucleus.
   4. The capsid breaks down and is eliminated.

I. The genomes of viruses can be single-stranded RNA, double-stranded RNA, single-stranded DNA, or double-stranded DNA.
   1. Plus strand viruses are viruses whose RNA genomes serve as mRNAs.
      a. These viruses do not need RNA polymerase to initiate viral gene expression.
      b. The RNA genome of single-stranded (+) RNA viruses also serves as a template for synthesis of a complementary (−) strand RNA.
      c. The synthesis of the (−) strand RNA uses a viral RNA polymerase derived from cleavage of the polypeptide.
      d. The (−) strand RNA serves as a template to make more (+) strands.
      e. The progeny (+) strands can then serve as mRNAs, templates to make more (−) strands, and genomes of progeny virions.
   2. The genome of a single-stranded (−) RNA virus does not serve as an mRNA.
      a. Transcription must occur to form mRNAs.
      b. All (−) RNA viruses carry an RNA polymerase within the virion for transcription.
      c. Transcription yields functionally monocistronic (+) strand mRNAs, each specifying a single protein.
      d. The (−) strand RNA alternately serves for the transcription of specific mRNAs and as a complete template for the synthesis of (+) RNA that can serve as the template for the production of (−) RNA genomes.
      e. Splicing of the (+) RNA can produce multiple mRNAs, each specifying a different protein.
   3. Retroviruses are single-stranded RNA viruses that form DNA as a template for the production of viral RNA.
      a. Their genomic RNA serves as the template for the synthesis of viral DNA.
      b. Typically the retrovirus genome consists of two strands of partially hydrogen-bonded RNA.
      c. Retroviruses also contain an RNA-dependent DNA polymerase (reverse transcriptase), a primer to initiate DNA synthesis, and a mixture of tRNAs.
      d. The key steps of retrovirus replication are: binding of the primer–reverse transcriptase complex to the genomic RNA; synthesis of a DNA copy complementary to the RNA to produce a DNA-RNA hybrid; digestion of genomic RNA by ribonuclease H; and synthesis of the complementary strand of the viral DNA to produce linear double-stranded DNA.
      e. The products of transcription are genome-length RNA molecules and mRNAs that are translated to form viral polypeptides that are subsequently cleaved to produce individual viral proteins.
   4. Only a few viruses have double-stranded RNA genomes.
      a. The double-stranded RNAs of reoviruses are transcribed by an RNA-dependent RNA polymerase contained within the virion.
      b. The RNAs formed serve as mRNAs for protein synthesis and also as templates for synthesis of complementary strands of RNA.
   5. The replication of a DNA viral genome can occur by several mechanisms.
      a. DNA replication may be bidirectional from a single point of origin, from multiple initiation points, or follow a rolling circle model.
      b. The genes of some DNA viruses are expressed within the nuclei of eukaryotic host cells.
      c. These viruses use host cell DNA-dependent RNA polymerases for transcription to produce viral mRNAs.
      d. Early proteins are formed for the synthesis of new viral genomes and as regulators of gene expression.
      e. A few viruses require the help of a second virus to complete their replication.

J. Viruses have evolved three fundamental strategies for their assembly, maturation, and release from the infected host cell.
   1. One strategy involves intracellular assembly and maturation.
      a. Multiple copies of the virion proteins assemble in the cytoplasm into a procapsid.
      b. Viral RNA then wraps around the procapsid, and one protein is cleaved to yield two polypeptides.
      c. This probably causes rearrangement of the capsid into a thermodynamically stable structure in which the RNA is shielded from access by nucleases.
   2. In the strategy employed by enveloped viruses the assembled viral nucleocapsids become wrapped in portions of the cytoplasmic membrane as the virus particle is expelled from the cell.
   3. The third strategy is nucleocapsid assembly in the nucleus.
      a. Envelopment and maturation occur at the inner nuclear membrane.
      b. Viral replication proteins and assembled virions

accumulate in specific regions of the nucleus or cytoplasm, often displacing host-cell components from specific regions of the cell and leading to a cytopathic effect.

K. Assembled viruses are released from host cells.
   1. Lysozyme is a late protein coded for by the phage genome that catalyzes the breakdown of the bacterial peptidoglycan wall.
   2. Lysis of the bacterial cell releases phage particles into the surrounding medium.
   3. Nonenveloped animal viruses that assemble and acquire infectivity inside the cell depend largely on the disintegration of the infected cell for release from the host.
   4. The enveloped herpesviruses are assembled in the nucleus and accumulate in the space between the inner and outer lamellae of the nuclear membrane, in the cisternae of the cytoplasmic reticulum, and in vesicles carrying the virus to the cell surface.
   5. Enveloped viruses exit from the infected cell by budding through the cytoplasmic membrane or by fusion of vesicles containing virus particles with the host's cytoplasmic membrane.
   6. Some viruses are released when their assembled nucleocapsids bud directly through the cytoplasmic membrane, producing extracellular enveloped virions.
   7. Other viruses bud through internal membranes or inner nuclear membrane forming vesicles; the vesicles containing the assembled viruses migrate to the inner surface of the cytoplasmic membrane and fuse with it, effectively releasing intact virions to the outside.

REPLICATION OF BACTERIOPHAGE

A. Temperate bacteriophage are capable of lysogeny in which the phage genome is incorporated into the bacterial chromosome.
   1. In lysogeny, only the integrated phage genome is replicated with the replication of host cell DNA.
   2. The host cell is not killed.
   3. Incorporation of the phage genome into a bacterial chromosome is an example of nonreciprocal recombination.
   4. The incorporated prophage is replicated along with the bacterial DNA during normal host cell DNA replication.

B. Lytic phage kill the host cell as a result of phage replication.
   1. Lysis of bacterial cells releases a large number of phage simultaneously.
   2. This is a one-step growth curve.
   3. The growth curve for lytic phage begins with an eclipse period, the time between entry of the phage DNA and formation of the first complete phage within the host cell.
   4. Both the latent period and the eclipse period begin when the phage injects DNA into a host cell.
   5. The latent period ends when the first assembled phage from the infected cells appear extracellularly, about 15 minutes.
   6. The burst size is the average number of infectious phage units produced per cell.
   7. As a result of the simultaneous release of infective phage, the number of phages that are able to initiate a lytic replication cycle increases greatly in a single step.
   8. The entire lytic growth cycle for some T-even phage can occur in less than 20 minutes under optimal conditions.

C. The complete replication cycle of the T-even bacteriophage, such as bacteriophage T4, results in the lysis of the host cell when the phage are released.
   1. Replication of T4 begins with the attachment of phage tail fibers to the outer surface of a host cell.
   2. The phage injects its DNA into the bacterial cell, using its tail structure like a syringe.
      a. The tail does not penetrate the cytoplasmic membrane.
      b. Contraction of the tail forces the phage DNA into the periplasmic space. It migrates across the cytoplasmic membrane into the cell.
   3. The phage genome is not degraded by the host's endonucleases because the phage DNA contains glucosylated 5-hydroxymethylcytosine instead of cytosine—a chemical modification of the DNA that prevents the nucleases of the bacterium from degrading the phage genome.
   4. T-even phage codes for a nuclease that degrades the host cell DNA.
   5. The deoxynucleotides released by the degradation of the bacterial chromosome are used as precursors for the synthesis of phage DNA.
   6. Early proteins are involved in the penetration of phage DNA into the bacterial cell and the stoppage of host cell macromolecular synthesis.
      a. The entire sequence of penetration, shutting off host cell transcription and translation, and the degradation of the bacterial chromosome takes only a few minutes.
      b. The early genes coded for by the phage genome include large amounts of enzymes involved in the replication of the phage DNA.
      c. Phage DNA is initially transcribed by a bacterial RNA polymerase.
      d. Proteins for the modification of the bacterial RNA polymerase are among the first proteins to be coded.
         (i). The phage-coded polypeptides replace or modify the sigma subunits of the bacterial RNA polymerase.
         (ii). They alter the recognition sequence.
         (iii). Further modification of the RNA polymerase ends synthesis of early phage proteins.
      e. A shift in the recognition site of the RNA polymerase coincides with the beginning of the synthesis of middle and late proteins. Middle genes are transcribed along the same DNA strand as the early genes. Late genes are transcribed along the opposite strand. The transition from early to late gene transcription in T4 phage involves a shift with regard to which of the two DNA strands of the phage genome serves as the sense strand. The change from counterclockwise to clockwise must mean that the opposing strands of the phage DNA

code for the early and late proteins. The late phage genes code for the various proteins that make up the capsid structure of the phage.

7. The phage is assembled with the nucleic acid genome packaged within the protein capsid.
   a. Assembly of the head and tail structures requires enzymes coded for by the phage genome.
   b. The head, tail, and tail fiber units of the T-even phage capsid are assembled separately.
   c. Tail fibers are added after the head and tail structures are combined. DNA is tightly packed within the phage head assembly.
   d. The viral head is stuffed with DNA and the excess is cleaved by a nuclease.
8. Phage-coded T4 lysozyme attacks host cell peptidoglycan and causes cell lysis.
   a. Lower numbers of phage progeny are associated with early lysis.
   b. Slower lysis leads to higher numbers of phages released. The T4 phage lytic cycle takes about 25 minutes.
9. Lysis inhibition is exhibited by wild type phage that release large numbers of phages.

D. Bacteriophage T7 has a small, linear double-stranded DNA genome, and its replication results in lysis of the host cell.
   1. The DNA is injected linearly into bacterial cells.
   2. Transcription begins immediately at closely spaced promoters using host cell RNA polymerase.
   3. It generates a set of overlapping polygenic mRNA molecules that are cut by a specific host cell RNase, generating smaller mRNA molecules, which code for one to four proteins each.
      a. One protein is an RNA polymerase that copies double-stranded DNA.
      b. Two others code for proteins that stop host RNA polymerase action, ending early gene transcription and translation of host genes.
   4. Host RNA polymerase is used to copy the first few genes and to make mRNA for the phage-specific RNA polymerase that is used in RNA transcription during phage replication.
   5. Negative control of T7 gene expression is by the formation of proteins that stop host RNA polymerase and shut off early T7 gene transcription.
   6. Positive control is by the formation of new RNA polymerase that recognizes the rest of the T7 promoters.
   7. The T7 phage strongly affects host transcription and translation processes by producing proteins that turn off transcription of host genes.
   8. This phage has genes coding for enzymes that degrade host cell DNA.
   9. T7 DNA is replicated within the host cell to make new copies of the phage genome.
      a. T7 DNA replication begins at an origin of replication.
      b. It proceeds bidirectionally and involves an RNA primer.
      c. The enzymes involved in the synthesis of this primer for the left and right are different.
      d. T7 polymerase elongates both primers.
      e. RNA primer molecules must be removed before replication is complete to replicate the DNA at the 5′-P terminus.
      f. There is an unreplicated portion of T7 DNA at the 5′-P terminus of each strand.
      g. The complementary 3′-OH ends on separate DNA molecules pair with these 5′-P ends to form a DNA molecule. The product is a linear bimolecule called a concatamer.
      h. An endonuclease cuts each concatamer at a specific site, producing linear molecules with repetitious ends.

E. The genome of phage ϕX174 consists of a circular single-stranded 5.3 kb DNA molecule.
   1. Its single-stranded DNA is a plus sense strand.
   2. It separates from the protein coat on infection. It is converted into a doubled-stranded form called replicative form DNA.
   3. Replicative form is a closed, supercoiled, double-stranded circular DNA.
   4. Replication begins at one or more specific initiation sites.
   5. DNA replication around the closed circle forms the complete double-stranded replicative form.
   6. DNA replication then occurs by conventional semi-conservative replication of the replicative form.
   7. Replicative form DNA directs phage mRNA synthesis. mRNA synthesis begins at several promoters and terminates at several sites.
   8. Asymmetric rolling circle replication produces single-stranded phage progeny.
   9. Protein A cleaves and ligates the two ends of the newly synthesized strand to give a circular single-stranded DNA when the growing phage strand reaches unit length.

F. Filamentous DNA phages have circular DNA and a helical capsid.
   1. They attach to the specific receptor on the pilus of a donor host cell.
   2. The adjacent halves of the genome run up and down the phage and form loops at the ends.
   3. They exhibit little base pairing.
   4. Bacteriophage M13 virion is released without killing the host cell.
   5. Release occurs by budding.
   6. Cells infected with phage M13 continue to grow slowly while releasing phage particles.

G. Bacteriophage MS2 has a single-stranded RNA genome.
   1. In the host cell ribosome, MS2 is translated into four proteins: maturation protein, coat protein, lysis protein, and RNA replicase.
   2. The phage RNA is a plus strand. It can act as a mRNA. It is translated to produce a phage RNA polymerase.
   3. This RNA polymerase or RNA replicase can synthesize minus strand RNA using infecting RNA as the template.
   4. More plus RNA is made from this minus RNA.
   5. New plus RNA strands serve as mRNAs for continued phage protein synthesis.
   6. Translation of this gene occurs only from the nascent form of the plus strand.
   7. As the phage RNA is made, it folds into a complex

extensive secondary and tertiary structure.

8. The most accessible AUG start site for translation is on the coat protein.
9. Coat protein molecules increase and combine with the RNA around the AUG start site for the replicase protein, turning off RNA replicase synthesis.
10. The major phage protein synthesized is coat protein.
11. A shift in the reading frame must occur as the ribosome passes over the coat protein for the lysis gene to be read.
12. This prevents premature cell lysis.
13. When sufficient coat protein is available for mature phage particle assembly, lysis begins.

H. Bacteriophage lambda alternates between lytic and lysogenic replication cycles.
   1. Molecular level regulation of lambda replication determines whether the replication cycle is lytic or lysogenic.
      a. In lytic replication, transcription begins at two promoter sites, for clockwise and counterclockwise transcription.
      b. Completion of the clockwise transcription requires the expression of a *Q* gene, which codes for a Q protein required for late gene expression.
      c. Complete counterclockwise transcription requires expression of the *N* gene that codes for an N protein.
   2. Expression of the N and Q proteins can be repressed.
      a. Without the N protein, transcription of the genes involved in the delayed early stage of phage replication cannot occur.
      b. The lambda phage genome contains a *cI* gene that codes for a repressor protein that binds to the operator region of the phage genome, which then controls the expression of the N protein, blocking the lytic replicative cycle.
      c. The repressor protein also binds to another operator region, blocking the clockwise transcription of the lambda phage DNA and, thus, the production of the Q protein.
      d. This leads to a conversion to lysogenic replication.
   3. Homologous overlapping ends of the linear lambda genome join to form a circular DNA molecule for integration of the lambda phage genome.
      a. This circular DNA then is integrated into a specific chromosome site.
      b. Integration requires a site-specific topoisomerase.
      c. During cell growth, the lambda repression system prevents the expression of the integrated lambda genes except for the gene *cI*, which codes for the lambda repressor.
   4. Expression of the *cI* gene is subject to regulation.
      a. If the concentration of lambda repressor protein declines sufficiently to permit further transcription of the phage genome, a Cro protein is produced.
      b. The Cro protein represses transcription of the *cI* gene, stopping synthesis of the repressor protein responsible for preventing complete expression of the phage genome.
      c. Then the phage can carry out a lytic replication cycle.
   5. Expression of the lambda phage genes then leads to formation of complete phages and their lytic release from the host cell.

I. Bacteriophage P1 DNA does not become integrated into the bacterial chromosome following infection.
   1. The P1 genome is maintained like a plasmid within the cytoplasm.
   2. Only one copy of the prophage is maintained in a host cell.
   3. The phage repressor genes closely coordinate the replication of the phage genome with the replication of host cell DNA.

J. Bacteriophage Mu is a DNA phage that can act as a transposon within a host cell.
   1. The Mu genome is not digested by nuclease in an *E. coli* host cell.
   2. The Mu genome is integrated into the bacterial chromosome through the action of a transposase encoded by the phage.
   3. Mu inserts phage DNA within bacterial genes, causing mutations.
   4. Production of *c* gene repressor prevents complete expression of the Mu genome.
   5. As long as the C protein production is repressed the Mu phage DNA is maintained as a prophage and replicated along with host cell DNA during bacterial cell reproduction.

REPLICATION OF PLANT VIRUSES

A. The stages of plant viral replication involve penetration by the virus of a susceptible plant cell; uncoating of the viral nucleic acid within the plant cell; assumption by the viral genome of control of the synthetic activities of the host cell; expression of the viral genome so that viral nucleic acid and capsid components are synthesized; assembly of the viral particles within the host cell; and release of the complete viral particles from the host plant cell.

B. Most plant viruses exhibit great host cell specificity and cause various symptoms in the plants they infect.

C. Tobacco mosaic virus (TMV) is a plant virus that infects tobacco.
   1. It has a single-stranded RNA genome contained within a helical array of protein subunits that comprise the viral capsid.
   2. Replication occurs within the cytoplasm of the infected cell.
   3. The RNA genome codes for an RNA-dependent RNA replicase for the synthesis of a complementary RNA (minus strand) to serve as a template for the synthesis of the RNA genome (plus strand) of TMV.
   4. The complementary RNA acts as a template for the synthesis of mRNA, which is subsequently translated at the plant cell ribosomes for the production of the protein coat subunits. TMV is self-assembled.
   5. Assembly initiation involves attachment of the viral RNA to a protein disc subassembly of the core structure.

6. The RNA molecule forms a loop, and protein disc subunits are added continuously to the looped end.
7. Within infected plant cells TMV particles form crystalline cytoplasmic inclusions.
8. The chloroplast of a TMV-infected leaf becomes chlorotic and the cell dies, releasing completely assembled TMV particles and unpackaged viral nucleic acid.
9. Within plants, both completely assembled viral particles and viral RNA can move from one cell to another, establishing new sites of infection.

D. Viroids have very small RNA genomes and no other structures; a viroid is an RNA macromolecule that can be preserved and transmitted to cells, where it is replicated.

REPLICATION OF ANIMAL VIRUSES

A. There are many types of animal viruses and many variations in the details of their replication.
B. In some cases, the replicative cycle of animal viruses closely resembles that of lytic bacteriophage, with a stepwise growth curve and the simultaneous release of a large number of viruses.
C. This single-step growth curve for animal viruses occurs within hours not minutes.
D. Some animal viruses characteristically do not kill the host cell and instead reproduce with a gradual, slow release of intact viruses.
E. Some animal viruses transform the host cells, resulting in tumor formation rather than death.
F. The essential steps of the replicative cycle for animal viruses are: attachment, the adsorption of the virus to the surface of the animal cell; penetration, the entry of the intact virus or viral genome into the host cell; uncoating, the release of the viral genome from the capsid; transcription to form viral mRNA; translation using viral-coded mRNA to form early proteins; (6) replication of viral nucleic acid to form new viral genomes; translation of mRNA to form late proteins needed for structural and other functions; assembly of complete viral particles; and release of new viruses.
G. Animal viruses adsorb onto specific receptor sites on animal cell surfaces.
H. The entire virion typically enters the cell, often by endocytosis.
I. Uncoating of animal viruses varies.
   1. Viral nucleic acids may be released at the cytoplasmic membrane.
   2. The virus may be uncoated in a series of complex steps within the host cell.
   3. The virus may never be completely uncoated.
J. The uncoated genome of a DNA animal virus generally enters the nucleus, where it is replicated.
K. The genome of most RNA animal viruses enters the cytoplasm of the animal cell to be replicated.
L. Cytopathic effects are visible changes in the appearance of virus-infected animal cells.
   1. Some common morphological changes that occur in virally infected cells are cell rounding and detachment from the substrate, cell lysis, syncytium formation, and inclusion body formation.
   2. Many of the CPEs or cell injuries are secondary effects of viral replication.
M. The DNA produced during the replication of retroviruses and some other viruses can be incorporated into the host cell's chromosomes.
   1. Within host chromosomes, the viral genome can be transcribed, resulting in the production of virus-specific RNA and viral proteins.
   2. Incorporated viral DNA can be passed from one generation of animal cells to another. It can also transform the animal cell.
   3. Transformed cells have altered surface properties and continue to grow even when they contact a neighboring cell.
   4. Oncogenic viruses transform cells and cause cancerous growth.
      a. They replicate in permissive hosts.
      b. In nonpermissive host cells, part of the viral genome is incorporated into the host cell genome, resulting in the transformation of the host cell.
N. Adenoviruses are medium-sized double-stranded DNA viruses.
   1. They exhibit cubic symmetry, have 252 capsomers and spikes projecting from the capsid that are involved in the adsorption of the virus to the host cell.
   2. They multiply within the nuclei of infected cells, where they produce an array of crystalline particles.
   3. Uncoating takes several hours, during which the viral nucleic acid is released from the capsid, entering the nucleus possibly through a nuclear pore.
   4. Within the nucleus, the viral genome codes for the inhibition of normal host cell synthesis of macromolecules and acts as a template for its own replication.
   5. The assembly of the adenovirus particles occurs within the nucleus, and therefore the nucleus of an infected animal cell contains inclusion bodies consisting of crystalline arrays of densely packed adenovirus particles.
O. Hepatitis B virus particles consist of a double-stranded DNA genome composed of a complete strand and an incomplete strand.
   1. The virions contain one DNA polymerase molecule. The HBV polymerase completes the synthesis of a closed circular strand DNA that is then transcribed into (+) strand RNA and mRNA.
   2. The mRNAs are translated into the respective proteins of the virus, and the (+) strand RNA then gets packaged into cores.
   3. Within the core, the (+) strand RNA is transcribed into (−) strand DNA by the HBV polymerase and the RNA template is degraded.
   4. The cores are coated with the envelope surface layer and surface proteins and the (−) strand DNA is partly transcribed into (+) strand DNA.
   5. Intact virions are released by lysis.
P. Herpesviruses are medium-sized viruses containing linear, double-stranded DNA.
   1. The capsid has cubical symmetry with 162 capsomers.
   2. It is surrounded by a lipid-containing envelope.
   3. Herpesviruses probably enter the host cell by fusion

of the cytoplasmic membrane of the cell with the viral envelope.
4. The double-stranded DNA is uncoated at the nuclear pores.
5. The viral genome proceeds into the nucleus.
6. The viral DNA is replicated by a virus-specified DNA polymerase.
7. The genome is transcribed and translated by host-specified RNA polymerase II and ribosomes respectively.
8. After the protein capsids are assembled, the newly synthesized DNA is spliced and packaged into them.
9. The virions bud out of the nuclear membrane and are transported through the cytoplasm of the cell to the cell surface.

Q. Poxviruses are large double-stranded DNA viruses.
1. They contain over 100 proteins.
2. They replicate in host cytoplasm and code for their own transcription enzymes.
3. Poxviruses are taken up into the cell by coated pits in the cytoplasmic membrane and liberated into the cytoplasm, where they are seen microscopically as inclusions in which viral synthesis occurs.
4. After packaging of the replicated DNA into their complex cores, outer coats, envelopes, and surface fibers, they are released from the cell when it disintegrates.

R. Picornaviruses are small, single-stranded RNA animal viruses.
1. The nonencapsulated nucleocapsid has cubical symmetry.
2. Maturation occurs in host cell cytoplasm. Poliovirus is very specific in its adsorbtion to cells.
3. The virions are internalized by endocytosis and RNA is released into the cytoplasm.
4. The poliovirus RNA codes for a polyprotein, which is cleaved by proteases encoded by both the virus and the host cell, to form many different proteins, including an RNA-dependent RNA polymerase and four proteins of the viral capsid.
5. The RNA polymerase is used to produce a complementary replicative RNA strand that can act as a template for new viral genomes.
6. The proteins assemble into pentamers that condense into capsids.
7. The assembly of the capsid and insertion of the RNA genome is followed by the release of viral particles, which occurs because blockage of cellular protein synthesis leads to breakdown of lysosomes.
8. The digestive enzymes released from the lysosomes cause cell lysis.

S. Orthomyxoviruses are single-stranded, enveloped RNA viruses that exhibit helical symmetry.
1. Influenza viruses have a segmented genome, consisting of eight different RNA molecules, each of which codes for a different monocistronic mRNA molecule.
2. There are two types of protein spikes on the influenza virus envelope.
   a. Hemagglutinin is responsible for the attachment of the viral particle to the cell and brings about the fusion of the viral envelope with the cytoplasmic membrane of the host cell.
   b. Neuraminidase cleaves neuraminic acid residues from the cell surface and may facilitate the release of newly formed virus from the host cell.
3. Influenza mRNA transcription from the genomic RNA segments occurs in the host-cell nucleus. The replication of the viral (−) strand RNA genome involves the production of a complementary (+) strand RNA that then serves as a template for the synthesis of new viral (−) strand RNA genomes.
4. The newly synthesized (−) strand RNAs are assembled by random assortment of the eight different RNA segments into capsid proteins.
5. Mature particles exit the host cell by budding.

T. Reoviruses contain segmented double-stranded RNA genomes.
1. Reoviruses initially attach to cells via a hemagglutinin and a surface protein.
2. The genome must first be converted to (+) strand RNA and then translated.
3. Reoviruses have an RNA polymerase for the synthesis of new viral genome molecules and other enzymes that post-transcriptionally modify the RNA molecules.
4. Each of these RNA molecules codes for a different protein that is then assembled into the viral capsid.
5. The RNA genome is inserted before release of the completed reoviruses.

U. Retroviruses are RNA viruses that use a reverse transcriptase to produce a DNA molecule within the host cell. DNA production requires an RNA-dependent DNA polymerase to carry out reverse transcription of the viral RNA.
1. DNA "transcribed" from the viral RNA genome codes for viral replication within the host cell.
2. Retroviruses contain a central core surrounded by an inner shell and an outer lipid-containing envelope to which protein spikes are attached.
3. Retroviruses adsorb to specific receptors on host cells.
4. Penetration occurs by endocytosis.
5. The single-stranded RNA genome is transcribed by reverse transcriptase into double-stranded DNA.
6. This proviral DNA is transported into the host cell nucleus where it becomes integrated with the host genome at specific sites on the chromosome.
7. Mature viral particles are released slowly and continuously from infected host cells by budding.
8. Some retroviruses carry an additional gene that codes for a protein that causes the host cell to be transformed from a normal cell into a cancer cell.
9. These retroviruses are oncogenic and cause animal cell transformations.

V. Prions may be composed only of protein; they may be nothing more than specific infectious protein molecules that contain the information that codes for their own replication.
1. Prions actually could be encoded by acellular genes and their action could result from their binding to a cell membrane.

2. They could also be the product of an earlier undetected viral infection.
3. We do not know exactly how prions reproduce or how prevalent they are.
4. Prions were discovered during the search for the cause of scrapie.
    a. This disease was known to be caused by an agent that could pass through a bacteriological filter.
    b. It was believed to be a slow virus.
    c. However, no virus could be found and the cause of scrapie was attributed to a prion.

CHAPTER 9

BACTERIAL CELL CYCLE

A. Most bacterial cells reproduce asexually by binary fission.
    1. In this process, a cell divides to produce two equal-sized progeny cells.
    2. The number of viable bacterial cells is doubled.

B. Increases in cell size requires growth of the cell wall by the insertion of new cell wall material at specific sites in the pre-existing cell wall.

C. A new round of replication of the bacterial chromosome is initiated every time the cell divides.

D. The cell partitions the DNA and cytoplasmic components by synthesizing a septum, or crosswall, consisting of cytoplasmic membrane and cell wall peptidoglycan.

E. The doubling or generation time is the time required to achieve a doubling of the population size.
    1. It is the unit of measure of the bacterial growth rate.
    2. Bacteria reproduce more rapidly than higher organisms.

F. The relationship between population size, time, and generation time can be expressed mathematically:

If N_0 = the initial population number
then N_t = the population at time t
and n = the number of generations in time

Then,

$$N_t = N_0 \times 2^n$$

Solving for n (the number of generations):

$$\log N_t = \log N_0 + n \times \log 2$$

$$n = \frac{\log N_t - \log N_0}{\log 2} = \frac{\log N_t - \log N_0}{0.301}$$

PHASES OF BACTERIAL GROWTH

A. The typical bacterial growth curve begins with the lag phase.
    1. There is no increase in cell numbers.
    2. Bacteria are preparing for reproduction, synthesizing DNA and various inducible enzymes needed for cell division.

B. In the log growth phase (exponential growth phase) bacterial cell division begins and proceeds as a geometric progression.
    1. The logarithm of the bacterial biomass increases linearly with time.
    2. Bacterial reproduction occurs at a maximal rate for a specific set of growth conditions.
    3. The number of cells increases as an exponential function of 2^n.
    4. Growth is balanced, all properties of the cell are increasing at the same rate.
    5. The average composition of the cells remains constant.
    6. The growth rate of a bacterium is proportional to the biomass of bacteria that is present.

C. The stationary growth phase begins when there is no further net increase in bacterial cell numbers of a bacterial culture.
    1. The various cellular components are synthesized at unequal rates during the transition between the exponential and stationary phases.
    2. Cells in this phase have a different chemical composition from cells in the exponential phase.
    3. The growth rate is exactly equal to the death rate.
    4. A bacterial population may reach stationary growth when a required nutrient is exhausted, when inhibitory end products accumulate, or when physical conditions are appropriate.
    5. A feedback mechanism regulates the bacterial enzymes involved in key metabolic steps.
    6. The duration of the stationary phase varies.
    7. Cells in stationary phase have distinct characteristics.
    8. The formation of arthrospores represents the beginning of a regular life cycle that is characteristic of eukaryotic microorganisms but is rare among prokaryotes.

D. The onset of the death phase begins with a decline in the number of viable bacterial cells.
    1. The kinetics of bacterial death are exponential because the death phase really represents the result of the inability of the bacteria to carry out further reproduction.
    2. The rate of death is proportional to the number of survivors.

GROWTH OF BACTERIAL CULTURES

A. In both laboratory and natural situations, some environmental parameter or interaction of environmental parameters controls the rate of growth of a given bacterial species.

B. The normal bacterial growth curve is characteristic of bacteria in batch culture.
    1. In batch culture, fresh medium is inoculated with a bacterium, growth nutrients are expended, and metabolic products accumulate in a closed environment.
    2. Chemostats and turbidostats are continuous culture systems.
        a. A turbidostat has an optical sensing device that measures the turbidity of the culture and generates an electrical signal that is used to regulate the flow of fresh medium into the vessel and the flow of spent medium and cells out it.
            (i). The number of cells in the culture controls the flow rate.

(ii). The rate of growth of the culture adjusts to this flow rate.

b. In a chemostat the flow rate is set at a particular value and the rate of growth of the culture adjusts to this flow rate.
   (i). End products do not accumulate.
   (ii). Nutrients are not completely expended.
   (iii). Bacteria never reach stationary phase but are maintained in the exponential growth phase.
   (iv). Liquid medium, containing some nutrient in growth-limiting concentration, is continuously fed into the bacterial culture.
   (v). The concentration of the limiting nutrient in the growth medium determines the rate of bacterial growth.
   (vi). Because the rate of cell washout is equal to the growth rate, the dilution rate is equal to the growth rate of a bacterium growing in a chemostat.

C. Synchronous growth of bacteria occurs when all cells divide at the same time.
   1. Adjusting environmental conditions can induce synchronous growth.
   2. A synchronous population of bacterial cells also can be obtained by physical separation procedures.

EFFECTS OF NUTRIENT CONCENTRATIONS ON BACTERIAL GROWTH

A. Oligotrophs are bacteria that grow at low nutrient concentrations.
   1. Most have low growth rates.

B. Copiotrophs, bacteria that grow at high nutrient concentration, exhibit high rates of reproduction.

C. Under conditions of starvation many bacteria degrade their existing proteins and RNA and then synthesize new protein that better enables them to scavenge for low amounts of nutrients and to survive under conditions of stress, in general.

D. Several bacteria have complex life cycles to cope with alternating conditions of sufficient nutritional resources and starvation.
   1. Myxobacteria, gliding Gram-negative bacteria that can consume bacterial cells as well as obtain nutrients from dead plants or animals, grow on rotting plant materials or animal wastes.
   2. During growth on the nutrient-rich animal or plant material, vegetative cells divide by binary fission.
      a. Before total consumption of that nutrient, binary fission ceases and up to 1,000 cells fuse to form a fruiting body.
      b. The fruiting body rises up from the surface and myxospores form within it.
         (i). Myxospores are cells surrounded by a thick layer of polysaccharide.
         (ii). Myxospores are released from the fruiting body.
         (iii). When a myxospore reaches a favorable environment, the myxospores germinate and produce vegetative cells.
   3. Oligotrophic low-nutrient bacteria conserve available resources.
      (i). Many have appendages or form very small cells so that they have a high surface area to volume ratio, enabling them to accumulate nutrients efficiently from dilute solutions.
      (ii). One group forms appendages, called prosthecae, that increase the surface area to volume ratio.
      (iii). Some bacteria form a stalk, which is a prostheca structure by which they attach to solid substrates.
      (iv). The tip of the stalk establishes a holdfast through which the cell can affix to a surface, enabling the bacteria to conserve energy, remaining sessile (nonmoving) while nutrients flow by its surface and can be absorbed.
   4. Some bacterial genera form endospores when an essential growth nutrient is exhausted.
      a. Endospore formation is initiated when exhaustion of a growth substrate causes exponential growth to cease.
      b. Once started, the process of endospore formation is irreversible, and sporulating bacteria continue to form spores even when starvation is relieved.
         (i). In sporulation, the cytoplasmic membrane invaginates to establish the site of endospore formation.
         (ii). A copy of the bacterial chromosome is incorporated into the endospore, and the various layers of the endospore are then synthesized around the bacterial DNA.
      c. Endospore-forming bacteria have large numbers of spore specific genes.
         (i). During sporulation, the cell makes spore specific proteins rather than synthesizing proteins involved in cell growth.
         (ii). Expression of spore specific genes involves production of new sigma factors that alter the promoter recognition sites of RNA polymerase.
         (iii). Sporulation is controlled by sequential activation of sigma factors, each sigma factor directing the synthesis of a particular set of genes.
      d. An endospore is a very resistant body that can withstand adverse conditions of desiccation and elevated temperature.
         (i). Endospores can retain viability for millennia.
         (ii). Under favorable conditions, the endospore can germinate and give rise to an active vegetative cell of the bacterium.
      e. During germination the spore swells, breaks out of the spore coat, and elongates.
      f. Endospores are metabolically self-sufficient.
      g. After spore germination, the organism renews normal vegetative growth.

EFFECTS OF TEMPERATURE ON BACTERIAL GROWTH RATES

A. Temperature influences the rate of chemical reactions and the three-dimensional configuration of proteins.
   1. A rise of 10° C generally results in the approximate doubling of the rate of its reaction.

2. The Q_{10} of a reaction describes the change in reaction rate that occurs when the temperature is increased by 10° C.
   a. Enzymatic reactions typically exhibit Q_{10} values near two.
   b. Enzymes have optimal temperatures that vary. At some temperature above optimal, denaturation occurs.
   c. Enzymatic activities decline above the specific temperature that is characteristic of the heat stability of the enzyme.
3. There is an upper temperature limit for bacterial growth because of protein denaturation at elevated temperatures and the resultant change in membrane fluidity.

B. The heat shock response is a rapid change in gene expression that occurs when there is a temperature shift to an elevated temperature.
   1. Between ten and thirty new heat shock proteins are synthesized at the higher temperature that are not otherwise expressed.
   2. Heat shock proteins perform diverse functions and are necessary for the survival of the cell at the higher temperature.

C. The minimum and maximum temperatures at which a bacterium can grow establish the temperature growth range for that bacterium.
   1. At the optimal growth temperature the highest rate of reproduction occurs.
   2. The optimal growth temperature is defined by the maximal growth rate, not the maximal cell yield.
   3. The shortest generation time occurs at the optimal temperature.
      (i). Psychrophiles are bacteria that grow best at low temperatures.
      (ii). Mesophiles are bacteria that reproduce fastest at moderate temperatures.
      (iii). Thermophiles are bacteria with fastest growth rates at high temperatures.

D. The differences in optimal growth temperatures and temperature growth ranges among bacteria result in a spatial separation of these different classes of organisms in nature.
   1. Stenothermal bacteria grow only at temperatures near their optimal growth temperature.
   2. Eurythermal bacteria grow over a wider range of temperatures.

E. Laboratory incubators are controlled-temperature chambers used to establish conditions that permit the growth of a bacterial culture at temperatures favoring optimal growth rates.

F. Psychrophiles have optimal growth temperatures under 20° C.
   1. They may have enzymes that are inactivated at even moderate temperatures or may have proteases that are activated at these temperatures.
   2. The membrane fluidity of psychrophiles may be altered at moderate temperature.

G. Mesophiles have optimal growth temperatures between 20° C and 40° C.
   1. Many mesophiles have an optimal temperature of about 37° C, human body temperature.
   2. Many of the normal resident bacteria of the human body are mesophiles.
   3. Most human pathogens are mesophiles. Bacteria can generally actively reproduce over a wider range of temperatures below the optimal growth temperature than above it.
   4. Thermophiles have optimal growth temperatures above 40° C.
      a. The upper growth temperature for thermophilic bacteria is about 99° C.
      b. Many thermophilic bacteria have optimal growth temperatures of about 55° to 60° C.
      c. The highest temperature at which bacterial growth can occur is not known.
      d. Obligate thermophiles are restricted to growth at high temperatures.
      e. Many produce enzymes that are not readily denatured at high temperatures; some have unusual amino acids with their proteins that act as stabilizers; their membranes have high molecular weight and branched fatty acids that maintain semipermeable properties; they have high proportions of guanine and cytosine that raise the melting point; they occur in high temperature habitats.

EFFECTS OF OXYGEN CONCENTRATION—REDUCTION POTENTIAL

A. A positive reduction potential (E_h) value favors oxidation.

B. A negative E_h indicates a reducing environment.

C. In a complex system the reduction potential is influenced by the strongest oxidant or reductant in that system, as well as by the concentration of that compound.

D. The reduction potential is greatly influenced by the presence or absence of molecular oxygen. Some essential nutrient elements, such as iron and manganese, are soluble at low reduction potentials but precipitate in oxidizing environments.

E. Lower reduction potentials may be caused by the extensive growth of heterotrophic bacteria that scavenge all available oxygen.

F. Microorganisms grow under specific oxygen concentrations.
   1. Aerobes grow in the presence of oxygen.
   2. Microaerophiles grow only at reduced oxygen concentrations.
   3. Facultative anaerobes grow with and without oxygen.
   4. Anaerobes grow in the absence of oxygen.

G. Oxygen is toxic to microorganisms.
   1. Microorganisms that grow in the presence of air have enzymes that detoxify oxygen.
   2. Catalase and superoxide dismutate are important oxygen detoxifying enzymes.

EFFECTS OF WATER ACTIVITY

A. Water activity is an index of the amount of water that is free to react.
   1. Adsorption and solution factors can reduce the availability of water and lower the water activity.
   2. Pure distilled water has a water activity of 1.0.
   3. In the atmosphere, the availability of water is expressed as relative humidity.

4. The relatively low availability of water in the atmosphere accounts for the inability of bacteria to grow in the air.
5. Water activity is an index of the water that is actually available for utilization by bacteria.
   a. Bacteria are unable to grow on dry surfaces except when the relative humidity is high.
   b. Most bacteria require an A_w above 0.9 for active metabolism.

B. Xerotolerant organisms can grow at much lower water activities.
C. Fungi are able to grow at lower water activities than bacteria.
D. The ability to withstand drying can have important consequences for survival of microorganisms and disease transmission.
   1. Some bacteria are unable to survive desiccating conditions for even a short period of time.
   2. Bacteria living in dry desert soils must be able to tolerate long periods of desiccation.
E. Some microorganisms produce specialized spores that can withstand the desiccating conditions of the atmosphere.
   1. Spores generally have thick walls that retain moisture within the cell.
   2. Many fungal spores can be transmitted over long distances through the atmosphere.

EFFECTS OF PRESSURE

A. Osmotic pressure.
   1. Solute concentration affects the availability of water and osmotic pressure.
   2. Bacterial cell walls make them relatively resistant to changes in osmotic pressure.
   3. Extreme osmotic pressures can result in the death of bacteria.
   4. In hypertonic solutions, bacteria may shrink and become desiccated, and in hypotonic solutions the cell may burst.
   5. Osmotolerant organisms grow in solutions with high solute concentrations, withstanding high osmotic pressures and growing at low water activities.
   6. Osmophilic bacteria require high solute concentrations for growth.
B. Salinity.
   1. The degree of sensitivity to salt varies among different bacterial species.
   2. Many bacteria will not grow at a salt concentration of 3%.
   3. Halophiles require NaCl for growth.
      a. Moderate halophiles grow best at salt concentrations of about 3%.
      b. Extreme halophiles exhibit maximal growth rates in saturated brine solutions, at salt concentrations of greater than 15%.
      c. Since high salt concentrations normally disrupt membrane transport systems and denature proteins, extreme halophiles possess physiological mechanisms for tolerating high salt concentrations.
      d. Halophilic bacteria have high internal concentrations of potassium chloride.
      e. High concentrations of salt are required by halophiles to maintain their enzymatic activities.
      f. Many halophiles have unusual membranes.
C. Effects of hydrostatic pressure.
   1. Hydrostatic pressure is the pressure exerted by a water column as a result of the weight of the column; each 10 m of water depth is equivalent to approximately 1 atm.
   2. Hydrostatic pressures of more than 200 atm generally inactivate enzymes and disrupt membrane transport processes.
   3. Barotolerant bacteria can grow at high hydrostatic pressures. Barophiles grow best at such pressures.

EFFECTS OF ACIDITY AND PH

A. pH is equal to $-\log H^+$ or $1/\log H^+$.
B. A neutral solution has a pH of 7.0; acidic solutions have pH values below 7; and alkaline or basic solutions have pH values greater than 7.
C. Bacterial growth rates are greatly influenced by pH values and are based largely on the nature of proteins.
D. Because charge interactions within the amino acids of a polypeptide chain greatly influence the structure and function of proteins, enzymes are normally inactive at very high and very low pH values.
E. Bacteria are generally less tolerant of higher temperatures at low pH values than they are at neutral pH value.
F. Buffers are salts of weak acids or bases that keep the hydrogen ion concentration constant by maintaining an equilibrium with the hydrogen ions of the solution.
G. Microorganisms vary in their pH tolerance ranges.
   1. Fungi generally exhibit a wider pH range, compared to most bacteria.
   2. Some protozoa and algae are able to grow at low pH values.
   3. Differences in tolerance to acidic pH values can be used in designing selective growth media.
H. Acidophiles are restricted to growth at low pH values.
   1. Acidophiles grow at pH values less than 2.
   2. Acidophiles possess physiological adaptations that permit enzymatic and membrane transport activities.
I. Alkalophiles grow best at high pH.

EFFECTS OF LIGHT

A. Photosynthetic bacteria may regulate the amount of light they receive by synthesizing gas vesicles that adjust the position of the cell in an aqueous environment.
B. Phototaxis or movement in response to light helps the bacterium receive the optimal amount of light for photosynthesis.

CHAPTER 10

TEMPERATURE

A. At high temperatures, microbial proteins are denatured.
   1. The decimal reduction time is the exposure time at a given temperature needed to reduce the number of viable microorganisms by 90%.
   2. Death rates increase with temperature.

3. High temperature exposure methods to kill microorganisms include incineration, dry heat, and moist heat.
   a. Incineration means complete combustion.
   b. Dry heat methods use the conventional convection oven.
   c. Exposure at 100° C in boiling water for just a few minutes kills all vegetative cells.
   d. Endospores can survive, but are killed in an autoclave at 121° C and 15 psi pressure.
   e. Moist heat sterilization using steam under pressure kills microorganisms more rapidly and at lower temperatures.
4. The ability to use high-temperature preservation methods for food is dependent on the temperature sensitivity of that food.
5. Ultra high-temperature sterilization, exposure to 141° C for 2 seconds, sterilizes milk without destroying flavor or texture.

B. Canning uses heat for sterilizing food and hermetic sealing under anaerobic conditions to prevent spoilage.
   1. High-temperature exposure kills all of the microorganisms, the can or jar acts as a physical barrier to prevent recontamination and anaerobic conditions inside prevent oxidation of chemicals in the food.
   2. In commercial canning, *Bacillus stearothermophilus* or *Clostridium sporogenes* PA 3679 is used for determining an acceptable D value.
   3. Exposure to 115° C for 15 minutes kills endospore formers.
   4. Since endospores of *C. botulinum* have a D value of 0.21 minute at 121° C, heating a food for 2.52 minutes at 121° C reduces the probability of the survival of *C. botulinum* endospores to 10^{-12}.

C. Pasteurization uses brief exposures to moderately high temperatures to reduce the number of viable microorganisms and to eliminate human pathogens.
   1. The low temperature–long time process employs exposure to 62.8° C for 30 minutes.
   2. The high temperature–short time process uses 71.7° C for 15 seconds.
   3. Pasteurization increases shelf life and is aimed at eliminating some nonspore-forming pathogenic bacteria, namely, *Brucella* species, *Coxiella burnetii*, and *Mycobacterium bovis.*

D. Low temperatures restrict the rates of growth and enzymatic activities of microorganisms.
   1. Most pathogenic microorganisms are mesophilic and unable to grow in refrigerated foods at 5° C.
   2. Freezing at −20° C or less precludes microbial growth entirely.
   3. Freezing does not kill all microorganisms.
   4. Some microbial death occurs during freezing and thawing as a result of ice crystal damage to microbial membranes.

RADIATION

A. Gamma rays and X-rays increase the death rate of microorganisms.
   1. High energy, short wavelength forms of radiation have high penetrating power and kill microorganisms by inducing or forming toxic free radicals.
   2. Free radicals can lead to polymerization and other chemical reactions that disrupt microbial chemical organization.
   3. Endospores are more resistant than vegetative cells.
   4. Exposure to 0.3-0.4 Mrad causes a tenfold reduction in viable bacterial endospores.
   5. *Micrococcus radiodurans* is particularly resistant to ionizing radiation.
   6. Exposure to ionizing radiation sterilizes materials that are destroyed by heat.
      a. Radiation exposure can be used to increase the shelf life of various foods.
      b. Radiation can inactivate enzymes involved in autocatalytic spoilage.
   7. Most gamma radiation food sterilization procedures use gamma radiation from ^{60}Co or ^{137}Ce at levels of 100 to 200 krads.

B. Ultraviolet radiation is sometimes used to kill microorganisms.
   1. UV kills only on or near the surface of a clear solution.
   2. The greatest effectiveness for killing microorganisms occurs at a wavelength of 260 nm, the absorption maxima of DNA.

FILTRATION

A. Microorganisms can be removed from gases and liquids by filtration.
B. HEPA filters are used to sterilize air.
C. Filters with pore sizes of 0.2 μm trap bacteria and are used to sterilize liquids.

DESICCATION

A. Desiccation prevents microbial reproduction but does not kill microorganisms.
B. Freeze drying preserves microbial cultures.
C. Bacteria generally will not grow below a water activity level of 0.9.
D. Fungi generally will not grow below an A_w of 0.65.
E. Maintenance of an A_w value of 0.65 or less prevents microbial growth.
F. Foods preserved by drying do not spoil for years.

OXYGEN

A. Oxygen is toxic to strict anaerobes.
B. Removal of oxygen prevents growth of aerobic microorganisms.
C. Anaerobiosis is the packaging of food products under anaerobic conditions.
   1. It prevents aerobic spoilage.
   2. Vacuum packing in an airtight container eliminates air.
   3. The absence of oxygen prevents autoxidation of the food as a result of intrinsic enzymatic activities, greatly increasing product shelf life.
D. Anaerobic conditions are ideal conditions for the growth of obligate anaerobes, such as *C. botulinum.*
E. Oxygen concentrations can be increased to kill strict anaerobes.
F. Hyperbaric oxygen is used to treat gas gangrene caused by the strict anaerobe *Clostridium perfringens.*

CHEMICAL CONTROL OF MICROORGANISMS

A. Antimicrobial agents are chemicals that kill or prevent growth of microorganisms.
B. Concentration and contact time determine the effectiveness of an antimicrobial agent against a particular microorganism.
C. Microorganisms vary in their sensitivity to antimicrobial agents.
   1. Growing microorganisms are more sensitive than organisms in dormant stages.
   2. Many antimicrobial agents block active metabolism.
   3. Viruses and resting stages (e.g., endospores) are metabolically dormant, not reproducing, and are not affected by such antimicrobial agents.
D. Antimicrobial agents are classified according to their application and spectrum of action.
   1. Germicides kill microorganisms, but not necessarily bacterial endospores.
   2. Agents that inhibit growth of microorganisms are given the suffix -cidal.
   3. Agents that inhibit growth of microorganisms are given the suffix -static.
E. Disinfectants.
   1. Disinfectants can kill or prevent the growth of pathogenic microorganisms.
      a. Agents that oxidize biological macromolecules are effective disinfectants.
      b. Disinfectants are applied only to inanimate objects.
      c. Ammonia and bleach are widely used disinfectants.
      d. Ethylene oxide gas is a sterilizing agent for prepackaged disposable plasticware.
   2. Several standardized test procedures evaluate the effectiveness of disinfectants.
      a. The phenol coefficient test compares the activity of a given product with the killing power of phenol under the same test conditions.
      b. The Association of Official Analytical Chemists (AOAC) use-dilution method establishes appropriate dilutions of a germicide for actual conditions.
         (i). Disinfectants are tested against *Staphylococcus aureus* strain ATCC 6538, *Salmonella cholerasuis* strain ATCC 10708, and *Pseudomonas aeruginosa* strain ATCC 15442.
         (ii). Small stainless steel cylinders are contaminated with test bacteria.
         (iii). The cylinders are dried and placed in specified dilutions of the test disinfectant.
         (iv). The cylinders are exposed to the disinfectant for 10 minutes, allowed to drain, transferred to appropriate culture media, incubated for 2 days, and examined for growth of the test bacteria.
         (v). No growth should occur if the disinfectant was effective at the test concentration.
         (vi). An acceptable use dilution is one that kills all test organisms at least 95% of the time.
   3. Chlorination is the traditional method for disinfecting municipal water.
      a. It is relatively inexpensive, and the free residual chlorine content of the treated water represents a built-in safety factor against pathogens surviving the actual treatment period and causing recontamination.
      b. The disadvantage is the incidental production of trace amounts of organochlorine compounds.
      c. Chloramination is the least expensive way to reduce trihalomethane (THM) formation.
      d. Disinfection by monochloramine is effective but produces much lower amounts of THMs.
      e. Monochloramine may be generated in the water by adding ammonium prior to or simultaneously with chlorine or hypochlorite.
   4. Ozone (O_3) is a more expensive water disinfecting alternative.
      a. It kills pathogens reliably and does not produce undesirable trace organochlorine contaminants, but it does not have any residual antimicrobial activity and is more prone to chance recontamination than chlorinated water.
      b. Ozone is generated from air on site in ozone reactors, using an electrical corona discharge.
F. Food Preservatives.
   1. Effective food preservation prevents spoilage and the transmission of foodborne diseases.
   2. The addition of salt to food reduces the amount of available water and alters the osmotic pressure.
      a. High salt concentrations are bacteriostatic, and the shrinkage of microorganisms in brine solutions can cause loss of viability.
      b. Salting is used to preserve fish, meat, and other foods.
   3. The high osmotic pressure and low water availability of a high sugar solution prevents microbial growth.
   4. Some foods are preserved naturally by their high sugar content.
   5. Various low molecular weight carboxylic acids are inhibitors of microbial growth.
      a. The effectiveness of a particular acidic compound depends on the pH of the food, which determines the degree of dissociation of the acid.
      b. Lactic, acetic, propionic, citric, benzoic, and sorbic acids or their salts are effective food preservatives.
   6. Nitrates and nitrites are added to cured meats to preserve red meat color and to protect against the growth of food spoilage and poisoning microorganisms.
   7. Nitrates effectively inhibit *C. botulinum.*
   8. Sulfur dioxide and various sulfites have antimicrobial activities.
   9. Ethylene and propylene oxides are microbicidal and can be used to sterilize food products.
G. Antiseptics.
   1. Antiseptics are antimicrobial agents that can be applied safely to living tissues.
   2. The use of antiseptics in surgical practice was introduced by Joseph Lister.
   3. In the tissue toxicity test, agents are tested for their ability to kill bacteria and their toxicity to chick-heart tissue cells.
      a. The toxicity index is the ratio of the greatest dilution of the product that can kill the animal cells in 10 minutes to the dilution that can kill the bacter-

ial cells in the same period of time under identical conditions.
   b. An antiseptic should have a toxicity index of less than 1.0, that is, it should be more toxic to bacteria than to human tissue.
4. Alcohol is the most widely used antiseptic and is used to reduce the number of microorganisms on the skin surface in the area of a wound.
   a. Alcohol denatures proteins, extracts membrane lipids, and acts as a dehydrating agent.
   b. Viruses are also inactivated by alcohol.
5. Iodine kills all types of bacteria, including spores.
6. Heavy metals, such as mercuric chloride, copper sulfate, and silver nitrate, are used to kill microorganisms.
7. Phenolics and related compounds are used as surgical scrubs.
8. Cationic and anionic detergents are also used as antiseptics.

H. Antibiotics.
1. Antibiotics eliminate infecting microorganisms or prevent the establishment of an infection.
2. They are antimicrobial substances produced by microorganisms.
3. They were discovered by Sir Alexander Fleming.
4. Some antibiotics are produced partly or entirely by chemical synthesis.
5. Some antimicrobics are produced by several companies under several different trade names.
6. Some antimicrobial agents are microbicidal and others are microbiostatic, inhibiting the growth of microorganisms but not actually killing them.
7. Microbiostatic agents prevent the proliferation of infecting microorganisms, holding populations of pathogens in check until the normal immune defense mechanisms are activated.
8. A therapeutically useful antimicrobic must inhibit infecting microorganisms and exhibit greater toxicity to the infecting pathogens than to the host organism.

SELECTION OF ANTIMICROBIAL AGENTS

A. The selection of a particular antimicrobial agent for treating a given disease depends on the sensitivity of the infecting microorganism to the particular antimicrobial agent; the side effects of the antimicrobial agent with regard to direct toxicity to mammalian cells and to the normal microbiota; the biotransformations of the antimicrobial agent that occur *in vivo*, relative to how long the agent will remain in its active form; and the chemical properties of the antimicrobial agent that determine its distribution within the body, relative to the concentration levels of the active antimicrobial chemical that reach the site of infection.

B. Antimicrobics exhibit specific distribution patterns within the body because of differential solubilities.

C. Antimicrobial agents can influence the effects of other antimicrobials.

D. Narrow spectrum antibiotics are targeted at particular pathogens or particular bacterial species.

E. Broad spectrum antibiotics inhibit a relatively wide range of bacterial species.
1. Concern is mounting about the overuse of antibiotics because of the selection for disease-causing antibiotic-resistant strains.
2. Numerous bacterial strains have acquired the ability to resist the effects of some antibiotics.
3. Some bacterial strains containing R plasmids have multiple antibiotic resistance.
4. Particular strains produce enzymes that degrade the antibiotic.
5. Resistance may also be due to decreased drug uptake, decreased transformation of the drug to its active form, or decreased sensitivity of the microbial structure against which the drug is directed.

F. Determination of the pathogen's antimicrobial susceptibility aids the clinician in selecting the most appropriate therapeutic agent.
1. The clinical microbiology laboratory provides information about the activities of antimicrobial agents against microorganisms that have been isolated and identified as probable etiological agents.
2. Antibiotic susceptibility testing relies on the observation of antibiotics inhibiting the growth and/or killing cultures of microorganisms *in vitro*.

G. The Bauer-Kirby test system is a standardized antimicrobial susceptibility procedure.
1. A culture is inoculated onto the surface of Meuller-Hinton agar with antibiotic impregnated discs.
2. The antibiotics diffuse into the agar, establishing a concentration gradient. Inhibition of microbial growth is indicated by a clear zone of inhibition around the antibiotic disc.
3. The diameter of the zone of inhibition reflects the solubility properties of the particular antibiotic—that is, the concentration gradient established by diffusion of the antibiotic into the agar—and the sensitivity of the given microorganism to the specific antibiotic.
4. Standardized zones for each antibiotic disk determine whether the microorganism is sensitive, intermediately sensitive, or resistant to the particular antibiotic.
5. The results of this test indicate whether a particular antibiotic might control an infection by a particular pathogen.
6. It is designed for use with rapidly growing bacteria.
7. It is not directly applicable to filamentous fungi, anaerobes, or slow growing bacteria.

H. Light scattering or equivalent automated liquid diffusion methods are also used for antibiotic sensitivity testing.

I. Automated systems available for performing this procedure include the Autobac, Microscan, BBL sceptre, Vitek AMS, and Abbott MSII.

J. The minimum inhibitory concentration test uses dilutions of the antimicrobic to determine the lowest concentration of the antimicrobic that prevents growth of the pathogen.
1. Standardized microbial inoculum is added to tubes with serial dilutions of an antibiotic. Microbial growth is monitored as a change in turbidity.
2. The MIC indicates the minimal concentration of the antibiotic at the site of infection that inhibits microbial growth.
3. The MIC and the theoretical level of the antibiotic

that may be achieved in body fluids determines the appropriate antibiotic, dosage schedule, and route of administration.

K. The minimal bactericidal concentration (MBC) is the lowest concentration of an antibiotic that will kill a defined proportion of viable organisms in a bacterial suspension during a specified exposure period.
   1. A 99.9% kill of bacteria at an initial concentration of 10^5 to 10^6 cells/mL during an 18 to 24-hour exposure period is used to define the MBC.
   2. To determine the MBC, tube suspensions showing no growth in MIC tests are plated onto an agar growth medium to determine whether the bacteria are killed or survive exposure to the antibiotic at the concentration being tested.

L. Serum killing power is determined by adding a bacterial suspension to dilutions of the patient's serum.
   1. No bacterial growth should occur if the patient is being treated with an antibiotic.
   2. The breakpoint in the dilutions where bacterial growth occurs reflects the concentration of the antibiotic in the patient's blood and the effectiveness of the antibiotic.
   3. Inhibition at dilutions of the patient's serum of to 1:8 or more is considered an acceptable level.

ANTIBACTERIAL ANTIMICROBICS

A. Penicillins and cephalosporins inhibit the formation of bacterial cell walls.
   1. Penicillins are synthesized by strains of the fungus *Penicillium.*
   2. Cephalosporins are produced by members of the fungal genus *Cephalosporium.*
   3. They both contain a β-lactam ring and inhibit the formation of peptide cross-linkages within the peptidoglycan backbone of the cell wall.
   4. These antibiotics specifically inhibit the enzymes involved in the cross-linkage for transpeptidase reactions, and bacterial cell walls lacking the normal cross-linking peptide chains are subject to attack by autolysins.
   5. Many penicillins have a relatively narrow spectrum of activity and are most effective against Gram-positive cocci.
   6. Ampicillin has a broader spectrum of activity based on its ability to penetrate to the site of action of the transpeptidase enzyme.
   7. Penicillin G and other β-lactam antibiotics are inactivated by penicillinase enzymes because penicillinase-producing bacterial strains degrade the β-lactam ring structure of many penicillins.
   8. Cephalosporins generally have a broad spectrum of action and many of them are relatively resistant to penicillinase.
      a. Cephalosporins are used as alternatives to penicillins for allergic patients and for pathogens that are not penicillin sensitive.
      b. Cephalothin is used to treat severe staphylococcal infections.

B. Vancomycin, bacitracin, and cycloserine inhibit cell-wall synthesis.
   1. Cycloserine is a structural analog of D-alanine and can prevent the incorporation of D-alanine into the peptide units of the cell wall.
   2. Vancomycin and bacitracin prevent the linkage of the *N*-acetylglucosamine and *N*-acetylmuramic acid moieties that compose the peptidoglycan molecule.
   3. Bacitracin is produced by strains of *Bacillus subtilis.*
   4. Bacitracin is restricted to topical application.
   5. Vancomycin is produced by *Streptomyces orientalis* and is especially effective against strains of *S. aureus.*
   6. It is used to treat only serious infections caused by penicillin-resistant strains of *Staphyloccocus* or when the patient exhibits allergic reactions to penicillins and cephalosporins.

C. Aminoglycoside antibiotics, which include streptomycin, gentamicin, neomycin, kanamycin, tobramycin, and amikacin, are inhibitors of bacterial protein synthesis.
   1. They are used in the treatment of Gram-negative bacterial infections.
   2. They are produced by actinomycetes.
   3. Aminoglycosides bind to the 30S ribosomal subunit of the 70S prokaryotic ribosome, blocking protein synthesis and decreasing the fidelity of translation of the genetic code.
   4. They disrupt the normal functioning of the ribosomes by interfering with the formation of initiation complexes.
   5. They induce misreading of the mRNA molecules, leading to the formation of nonfunctional enzymes.
   6. Aminoglycoside antibiotics must be transported across the cytoplasmic membrane.
   7. Resistant strains lack a mechanism for aminoglycoside transport across the membrane and may produce enzymes that degrade or transform the aminoglycoside molecules. Mutations alter the aminoglycoside binding site at the bacterial ribosome.
   8. Streptomycin is used to treat brucellosis, tularemia, endocarditis, plague, and tuberculosis.
   9. Gentamicin is extremely toxic, used only in severe infection, and is effective in treating urinary tract infections, pneumonia, and meningitis.
   10. *Pseudomonas aeruginosa* is particularly sensitive to tobramycin.
   11. Neomycin is primarily used in topical application for various infections of the skin and mucous membranes.
   12. Kanamycin, a narrow-spectrum antibiotic, is frequently used by pediatricians for infections due to *Klebsiella, Enterobacter, Proteus,* and *E. coli.*
   13. Amikacin, which has the broadest spectrum of activity of the aminoglycosides, is the antibiotic of choice for treating serious nosocomial infections caused by Gram-negative bacteria.

D. Tetracyclines bind specifically to the 30S ribosomal subunit, apparently blocking the receptor site for the attachment of aminoacyl tRNA to the mRNA ribosome complex and thus preventing the addition of amino acids to the peptide chain.
   1. Sensitivity to tetracyclines depends on the transport of the tetracycline molecules across the cytoplasmic membrane.
   2. Resistance to tetracyclines develops because of the

movement of a transposon between a plasmid and the bacterial chromosome.

3. It involves an alteration in the membrane transport mechanism of tetracycline molecules.
4. Tetracyclines are effective against various pathogenic bacteria, including rickettsia and chlamydia species.

E. Chloramphenicol acts primarily by binding to the 50S ribosomal subunit, preventing the binding of tRNA molecules to the aminoacyl and peptidyl binding sites of the ribosome.
   1. Peptide bonds are not formed in the presence of chloramphenicol.
   2. Chloramphenicol is produced by *Streptomyces venezuelae.*
   3. It is a fairly broad-spectrum antibiotic active against many species of Gram-negative bacteria.
   4. Chloramphenicol resistance is associated with an R plasmid that codes for enzymes able to transform the chloramphenicol molecule.
   5. It has several toxic effects but is used for treating typhoid fever and other *Salmonella* infections; it is also effective against anaerobic pathogens.

F. Erythromycin is a macrolide antibiotic.
   1. It acts by binding to 50S ribosomal subunits, blocking protein synthesis.
   2. It is produced by *Streptomyces erythreus.*
   3. This antibiotic is most effective against Gram-positive cocci and is used for the treatment of Legionnaire's disease, diphtheria, whooping cough, and the type of pneumonia caused by *M. pneumoniae.*
   4. Erythromycin is also used as an alternative to penicillin in treating staphylococcal and streptococcal infections, tetanus, syphilis, and gonorrhea.

G. Lincomycin and clindamycin bind to the 50S ribosomal subunit, blocking protein synthesis.
   1. Lincomycin is produced by *Streptomyces lincolnensis.* Clindamycin is a semisynthetic derivative of lincomycin.
   2. The use of these antibiotics is restricted by their side effects.

H. Rifampin inhibits DNA-dependent RNA polymerase enzymes and thus can block transcription. It is more effective against bacterial RNA polymerase enzymes than mammalian RNA polymerases and is used therapeutically in treating some bacterial diseases.

I. Polymyxins interact with the plasma membrane, causing changes in the structure of the bacterial cell membrane and leakage of cell contents.
   1. Polymyxin B is bactericidal only to Gram-negative bacteria.
   2. Its action is related to the phospholipid content of the cell wall and the membrane complex.
   3. Polymyxin B and colistin treat infections caused by *Pseudomonas* species and other Gram-negative bacteria that are resistant to penicillins and the aminoglycoside antibiotics.

J. Some antimicrobial agents act by blocking normal DNA replication.
   1. Quinolones interfere with DNA gyrase, preventing the establishment of a replication fork.
   2. Bacteria exposed to quinolones elongate rather than divide normally.
   3. They are effective against a broad range of Gram-positive and Gram-negative bacteria, including some that are resistant to many other compounds.

K. Sulfonamides, sulfones, and para-aminosalicylic acid are structural analogs of the vitamin para-aminobenzoic acid.
   1. A cell mistakenly using an analog in place of the normal substance forms molecules that are unable to perform their metabolic functions.
   2. The analogs of para-aminobenzoic acid are effective competitors with the natural substrate for the enzymes involved in the synthesis of folic acid and inhibit the formation of this required coenzyme, causing a bacteriostatic effect.
   3. Sulfones are used in treating leprosy.

L. Trimethoprim is an inhibitor of dihydrofolate reductase, especially in bacteria.
   1. It is effective in blocking bacterial growth by preventing the formation of the active form of the required dihydrofolic acid coenzyme.
   2. It is a broad-spectrum antibacterial agent and is effective in the treatment of many urinary and intestinal tract infections.
   3. Trimethoprim is an antiseptic because these substances actually wash the surface of the urinary tract.
   4. Trimethoprim becomes concentrated in the urinary tract tissues and thus can act as antiseptics at this location.

ANTIFUNGAL ANTIMICROBICS

A. Antifungal polyene antibiotics act by altering the permeability properties of the cytoplasmic membrane, leading to death of the affected cells.
   1. Interactions of polyenes with the sterols in the cytoplasmic membranes of eukaryotic cells form channels or pores in the membrane, allowing leakage of small molecules.
   2. Differences in the sensitivity of various organisms are determined by the concentrations of sterols in the membrane.

B. Polyene antibiotics cause alterations in the membrane permeability of mammalian cells and toxicity to mammalian tissue, as well as the death of fungal pathogens.
   1. Amphotericin B is a broad spectrum polyene antibiotic produced by *Streptomyces nodosus.*
   2. It is the most effective therapeutic agent for treating systemic yeast and fungal infections.
   3. Amphotericin B is used to treat cryptococcosis, histoplasmosis, coccidioidomycosis, blastomycosis, sporotrichosis, and candidiasis.

C. Imidazole derivatives have a broad spectrum of antifungal activities and are used in the topical treatment of superficial mycotic infections; they appear to alter membrane permeability.

D. Griseofulvin is effective against some fungal infections.
   1. It is produced by *Pencillium griseofulvum* and causes a disruption of mitotic spindles.
   2. Griseofulvin is used in the treatment of fungal diseases of the skin, hair, and nails caused by various species of dermatophytic fungi.

ANTIPROTOZOAN ANTIMICROBICS

A. Different antimicrobial agents are used against different forms of the same pathogenic protozoan, depending on the stage of the life cycle and the involved tissues.

B. Antimalarial agents interfere with DNA replication by rapid schizontocidal action.
   1. Chloroguanide is used in the suppression of malaria.
   2. For the radical cure of malaria, that is, the eradication of the erythrocytic and liver stages of the protozoan, primaquine is used in conjunction with chloroquine and chloroguanide.
   3. Quinacrine hydrochloride and metronidazole are used to treat *Giardia lamblia.*

C. Metronidazole interferes with hydrogen transfer reactions, specifically inhibiting the growth of anaerobic microorganisms, including anaerobic protozoa.

D. Pentamidine and related diamidine compounds are useful in treating infections by members of the protozoan genus *Trypanosoma* because they interfere with DNA metabolism.

E. Melarsoprol is an arsenical that is useful in treating some stages of human trypanosomiasis because it penetrates into cerebrospinal fluid.

F. Arsenicals react with the sulfhydryl groups of proteins, inactivating a large number of enzymes.

G. Sodium stibogluconate, an antimony-containing compound, is useful in treating diseases caused by members of the protozoan genus *Leishmania.*

ANTIVIRAL ANTIMICROBICS

A. Vidarabine treats herpes simplex encephalitis and keratoconjuntivitis. It acts as an inhibitor of viral DNA polymerase, thus blocking viral DNA replication.

B. Acyclovir is the best antiherpes drug so far discovered because an enzyme coded for by the herpes virus is required to activate acyclovir, this compound exhibits selective antiviral activity, making it therapeutically valuable.

C. Zidovudine (azidothymidine) and dideoxyinosine are effective in the treatment of AIDS.
   1. DNA nucleotide analogs are effective in preventing the reverse transcriptase of the HIV retrovirus from forming viral-directed DNA that is needed for the successful replication of the virus.
   2. Both antiviral agents also interfere with normal human cell DNA replicaton and both have serious side effects with prolonged usage.
   3. They are effective in limiting viral replication and delaying the onset of AIDS.

CHAPTER 11

NONSPECIFIC DEFENSES

A. Nonspecific defenses against microbial infections include physical barriers and antimicrobial chemical and cellular responses that limit the abilities of microorganisms to enter and to reproduce or replicate within the body.

B. The physical barrier provided by intact body surfaces defends the body against microorganisms.
   1. Most microorganisms are not invasive and cannot penetrate the skin or degrade the skin's outer layer of keratin.
   2. Mucous membranes line many body surfaces and secrete mucus, which traps microorganisms and prevents them from entering the body.
   3. The mucociliary escalator system of the respiratory tract is a lining of mucous membranes that move in a wave-like motion and acts to filter out potential pathogens.
   4. Saliva, tears, and urine all remove microorganisms from the body.

C. Various body fluids have antimicrobial substances that combat infections.
   1. Lysozyme, an enzyme that degrades bacterial cell walls, is found in body fluids.
   2. Areas of high acidity in the body, such as the skin, the vagina, and the stomach, provide environments in which pathogenic microorganisms cannot grow.
   3. Lactoferrin and transferrin are proteins in body fluids that prevent pathogens from getting the iron they need for growth.
   4. Interferons are a family of inducible glycoproteins produced by infected eukaryotic cells in response to viral infections that migrate to uninfected cells and protect them from infection.
   5. Complement is the group of 11 glycoproteins in the blood that augment other defenses against microbial infection in an autocatalytic cascade, with each component activating the next, initiated by the alternate or classical pathways, and leading to various nonspecific host defense responses.

D. The normal microbiota help defend the body against pathogens.
   1. Distinct nonpathogenic microbial populations, normal microbiota, inhabit the surface tissues of the skin, oral cavity, respiratory tract, gastrointestinal tract, and genitourinary tract.
   2. The normal microbiota produce allelopathic substances that inhibit or kill microorganisms.

E. Phagocytosis, a host defense mechanism, is the engulfment and ingestion of cells, generally followed by the destruction of the engulfed cells.
   1. Phagocytic blood cells can have numerous lysosomes that contain hydrolytic enzymes that can degrade microorganisms when they are engulfed by a phagocyte's pseudopods, transported by exocytosis across the cell membrane, and contained within a phagosome that fuses with a lysosome and is degraded.
   2. Neutrophils are phagocytic leukocytes made in bone marrow that are chemically attracted to invading pathogens that they then engulf and digest.
   3. Monocytes are mononuclear phagocytes that move out of the blood to infected tissues where they become enlarged and form phagocytic macrophages that are capable of reproducing.
   4. The mononuclear phagocyte system is a systemic network of phagocytic macrophage cells distributed through a network of loose connective tissue and the

endothelial lining of the capillaries and sinuses of the human body.

F. The inflammatory response is a generalized response to infection or tissue damage characterized by redness, swelling, pain, and elevated temperature, designed to localize invading microorganisms and stop the spread of infection.
   1. Blood vessels in an inflamed area dilate, increasing blood circulation and allowing increased numbers of phagocytic blood cells to reach the affected area.
   2. When phagocytic cells die they release chemicals that increase the internal diameter of blood vessels.
   3. Inflamed areas become walled off by the deposit of fibrin in clots, cutting off circulation and allowing pus to accumulate.
   4. The fever of an inflammation, produced by pyrogens that enter the blood as the result of the death of microorganisms or are released by phagocytes, allows enzymatic reactions to occur faster at higher temperatures and kills heat sensitive pathogens.

IMMUNE RESPONSE

A. The immune response, characterized by specificity, memory, and the acquired ability to detect foreign substances, recognizes foreign substances and acts to eliminate them.

B. Once a response to a particular macromolecule, an antigen, is made, a memory system is established that permits a rapid and specific secondary response on re-exposure to that same substance and an acquired immunity has been established.
   1. Active immunity is the response established by an individual's immune system to a foreign antigen.
   2. Passive immunity is established by the transfer antibodies, serum or immune cells from another individual that makes the recipient immune to specific foreign antigens without their own immune system being activated.

C. Various lymphocytes form the basis of the immune response
   1. Lymphocytes differentiate during maturation into B cells in the bone marrow and T cells in the thymus gland.
   2. T helper cells interact with B lymphocytes; they are required for B cells to produce antibody.
   3. Cytotoxic T cells recognize intracellular parasites and tumors, which they lyse.
   4. Suppressor T cells are involved in the regulation of the immune response.
   5. Natural killer cells are responsible for the lysis of tumor cells.

ANTIBODY-MEDIATED IMMUNITY

A. In antibody-mediated immunity, antibodies are made in serum when foreign antigens are detected.

B. An antigen is any macromolecule that elicits the formation of antibody and can react with antibody.
   1. Antigens are characterized by the ability to stimulate antibody formation (immunogenicity) and specific reactivity with antibody molecules.
   2. The reactive portion of an antigen is called the epitope or antigenic determinant.
   3. Antigens may have one or many reactive sites.
   4. Surface antigens are associated with cell surfaces.
   5. Toxins are highly antigenic, causing the production of high titers of antibodies called antitoxins.

C. Immunoglobulins (antibodies) are glycoproteins found in blood serum synthesized by plasma cells in response to the detection of a foreign antigen.
   1. There are five classes of immunoglobulins.
      a. IgG is the largest fraction and stimulates the attraction of phagocytes to pathogens.
      b. IgA occurs in body secretions and protects surface tissues.
      c. IgM has a high number of binding sites and is effective in attaching to multiple cells with the same surface antigens.
      d. The role of IgD is unknown.
      e. IgE protects external mucosal surfaces.
   2. All immunoglobulins have the same molecular structure.
      a. An immunoglobulin molecule has four peptide chains: two identical heavy chains and two identical light chains joined by disulfide bridges.
      b. The light chains are either kappa or lambda.
      c. There are five types of heavy chains that determine the major classes of immunoglobulins.
   3. There are variable and constant regions of antibodies encoded by separate groups of genes.
      a. Recombination permits shuffling and joining of the components so that billions of combinations can occur.
      b. Recombination forms numerous combinations of varieties of light and heavy chains for immunoglobulins that respond to the vast variety of antigens.

D. B cell activation leads to the formation of B memory cells and antibody secreting plasma cells.
   1. When a B lymphocyte with a surface immunoglobulin receptor encounters its specific foreign antigen, the reaction between the immunoglobulin and the antigen initiates B cell activation.
      a. Heavy chain class switching is the process by which the same variable region on a B lymphocyte appears in association with different heavy-chain constant regions.
   2. After activation and maturation, B lymphocytes differentiate into plasma cells that secrete large amounts of antibody specific for the stimulating antigen.
   3. The reaction of B cells with antigen results in an increased population of memory cells.
   4. The response to first exposure to an antigen, the primary response, is slow because relatively few B cells with appropriate receptors producing relatively low yields of antibody are present.
   5. The response to second or other exposures to an antigen, the secondary or anamnestic response, is generally faster, longer lasting, and produces more antibody than the primary response.

E. There are various types of antigen–antibody reactions.

1. Opsonization is the increased phagocytosis associated with antibody-bound antigen.
2. Precipitin reactions occur when antibodies combine with soluble multivalent antigens and precipitate the antigen out of solution.
3. Agglutination is the aggregation or clumping of antibody molecules with surface antigens or insoluble particles.
   a. Agglutinins are antibodies that combine with particulate antigens.
   b. Hemagglutination is clumping of cells caused by the addition of antibody to antigens on the surface of red blood cells.
4. Enzyme-linked immunosorbent assays use enzymatic reactions to identify antigen–antibody complexes.
5. Radioimmune assays use radioisotopes to identify antigen–antibody complexes.

CELL-MEDIATED IMMUNITY

A. In the cell-mediated immune response, T cells detect foreign cells.
B. The cell-mediated immune response includes delayed type hypersensitivity reactions; cytotoxic T lymphocyte responses to viral infections, tissue transplants, and tumors; and responses to tumor cells and tissue grafts by natural killer cells.
C. Foreign antigen activated T_H lymphocytes can secrete cytokines that lead to activation of neutrophils, eosinophils, macrophages, and NK cells, which causes localized inflammation.
D. The cell-mediated immune response can eliminate cells infected with viruses.
E. T_H helper lymphocytes are necessary for the activation of T and B lymphocytes.
F. The genes of the major histocompatibility complex encode for molecules in the cell membrane that activate T cells.
G. T cell receptor along with CD4 or CD8 is responsible for MHC-restricted antigen recognition.
H. T cells secrete lymphokines in response to antigen stimulation.
   1. Lymphokines (cytokines) are small effector molecules secreted by activated T lymphocytes, macrophages, and fibroblasts in response to antigen recognition and serve communication and regulatory functions.
   2. Macrophage chemotactic factor, migration inhibition factor, macrophage activating factor, skin reactive factor, and immune interferon are lymphokine effector molecules produced by T cells.
I. Immunologic tolerance is a normal unresponsiveness to self-antigens.

DYSFUNCTIONAL IMMUNITY

A. There are occasional failures of the immune response (dysfunctional immunity).
B. Autoimmunity occurs when there is a failure of the immune response to recognize self-antigens.
   1. Failure to expose T and B cells to particular human antigens during fetal development allows these cells programmed for reaction with self-antigens to survive.
   2. Autoimmune diseases include systemic lupus erythematosus and myasthenia gravis.
C. Immunodeficiencies occur when the body fails to produce function T lymphocytes or B lymphocytes.
   1. Severe combined immunodeficiency is the result of the failure of stem cells to differentiate properly, and individuals with this condition are incapable of any immunological response.
   2. DiGeorge syndrome results from the failure of the thymus to develop correctly so that T lymphocytes are not properly differentiated, making cell-mediated immunity nonfunctional.
   3. Bruton congenital agammaglobulinemia is a sex-linked syndrome that affects only males and results in the failure of B cells to differentiate and produce antibodies.
   4. Late onset hypogammaglobulinemia is a deficiency of circulating B cells or B cells with IgG surface receptors.
   5. Individuals with AIDS, which is caused by a retrovirus (the human immunodeficiency virus), exhibit immunosuppression with depressed levels of T_H cells that effectively shuts off the immune response network.
D. Hypersensitivity is an excessive immunological response to an antigen that occurs when an individual sensitized to an antigen has contact with that antigen that results in an elevated immune response.
   1. Anaphylactic hypersensitivity occurs when an antigen reacts with antibody bound to mast or basophil blood cells that causes a release of vasoactive mediators causing an immediate, systemic, potentially life-threatening condition.
   2. Allergies are a type 1 hypersensitivity that are specific because IgE is specific and involve the sudden release of histamine and other pharmacologically active compounds that can produce anaphylactic shock.
   3. Atopic allergies, such as hay fever and food allergies, can be diagnosed by skin tests and result from localized expression of type 1 hypersensitivity reactions.
   4. In antibody-dependent cytotoxic (type 2) hypersensitivity reactions, an antigen on a cell surface combines with an antibody, resulting in the death of that cell by stimulating phagocytic attack or by initiating the complement pathway that results in cell lysis.
      a. Transfusions with incompatible blood types produce an antibody-dependent cytotoxic response; type O persons can be universal donors and type AB persons are universal recipients.
      b. Rh incompatibility occurs when the father is Rh positive, the mother is Rh negative, and the fetus is Rh positive, causing the mother to produce Rh antibodies in response, generally after the birth of the baby so that in subsequent pregnancies the mother has circulating anti-Rh antibodies that might cross the placenta and attack fetal cells, causing hemolytic disease of the newborn.
      c. Hemolytic disease of the newborn can be prevented by passive artificial immunization of the mother with anti-Rh antibodies at each birth.
   5. Complex-mediated (type 3) hypersensitivity reactions occur when the formation of antibody–antigen complexes triggers an inflammatory response.

a. If large amounts of antigen are produced, the antigen-antibody–complement complexes may circulate and deposit in tissues, causing damage to kidneys, joints, and skin.
b. Serum sickness is the result of large doses of foreign serums whose antigens stimulate an immune response.
6. Cell-mediated or delayed (type 4) hypersensitivity reactions, such as contact dermatitis, occur after exposure to the antigen.
7. The immune response must be suppressed to prevent rejection of transplanted tissues and organs; this leaves the patient susceptible to infection.

CHAPTER 12

SCIENCE OF EPIDEMIOLOGY

A. Epidemiology is the science that studies the occurrence of disease, the factors that determine incidence and spread, and the prevention and control of disease.
B. Epidemiology is based on the statistical probabilities that the exposure of a susceptible individual to a pathogen will result in the transmission of an infectious disease.
C. Incidence of disease is measured as morbidity; death rates are measured as mortality.
D. The concentration and virulence of the pathogen, the distribution of susceptible individuals, and the sources of exposure to the pathogen determine the probability of a disease outbreak.
E. Etiology is the study of the underlying cause of disease; for infectious diseases, this is determining the pathogen and its source.
F. A cohort study is an analytical epidemiological study over time for the development of a disease of groups of persons with and without various suspected risk factors.
G. Case-control studies compare persons with a disease with a disease-free control group to determine possible risk factors.

DISEASE OUTBREAKS

A. Sporadic disease occurrences are those where individual disease cases are geographically remote from each other.
B. A common source disease outbreak is characterized by a sharp rise and rapid decline in the number of cases.
C. A person-to-person disease outbreak is characterized by a relatively slow, prolonged rise and decline in the number of cases.
D. A reservoir is a source of an infectious agent; it can be living or nonliving, for example, soil, water, food, humans, or other animals.
E. A contagious disease is one whose infectious agent moves from an infected individual to other potential hosts.
F. Asymptomatic carriers are infected individuals who do not develop the symptoms associated with the disease their infectious agent causes; they are reservoirs.
G. Endemic diseases are constantly present in low numbers in a population.
H. Epidemic outbreaks of disease involve high numbers of individuals in a population.
I. Pandemic outbreaks affect large numbers of people in a large geographical region or consist of epidemics of the same disease occurring simultaneously in different parts of the world.
J. In a common source epidemic, many individuals simultaneously acquire the infectious agent from the same source.
K. In a person-to-person epidemic, the infectious agent is transmitted from an infected individual to an uninfected individual.
L. In propagated transmission, the infectious agent is spread from one individual to another in a progressive chain of infection, as in sexually transmitted diseases.

DISEASE PREVENTION

A. The study of epidemiology has led to the institution of public health measures for the control of public sanitation and hygiene and mass immunization that has reduced the incidence of many infectious diseases.
B. Proper sewage treatment and drinking water disinfection programs reduce the likelihood of contracting a disease from contaminated water.
C. The control of animal and insect vector populations, (especially mosquitoes, lice, ticks, and fleas) and their reservoirs is important for the control of the transmission of infectious diseases.
D. Quarantine is the enforced separation of infected individuals from healthy individuals.
E. Immunization is the intentional exposure of susceptible individuals to antigens to solicit an immune response.
1. Immunization results in the proliferation of memory cells and the ability to exhibit a secondary memory or anamnestic response on subsequent exposure to same antigens.
2. The number of individuals who must be immune to prevent an epidemic outbreak of disease is a function of the infectivity of the disease, the duration of the disease, and the proportion of susceptible individuals in the population.
3. Herd immunity is the protection against an infectious disease that occurs when 70% of the population is immune.
4. Vaccination is widely used to prevent disease.
a. Toxoids are denatured toxins produced by microorganisms; they are antigenically active, can elicit an antibody-medicated immune response, and can be used as vaccines.
b. Pathogenic microorganisms that are killed or inactivated by treatment with chemicals, radiation, or heat retain their antigenic properties and can be used in vaccines.
c. Pathogenic microorganisms can be attenuated by moderate use of heat, chemicals, desiccation, and growth in nonhost tissues and used in vaccines; small amounts of antigens can be used because the microorganisms multiply after the vaccine is inoculated.
d. Specific components of a pathogen can be used in a vaccine to elicit an immune response.
e. Booster vaccinations or multiple exposures to the

antigens in vaccines are sometimes necessary to establish and/or maintain a memory response.
   f. Vaccines can be introduced into the body intradermally, subcutaneously, intramuscularly, intravenously, orally, or via inhalation.
   g. Adjuvants are chemicals added to vaccines that enhance the antigenicity of other biochemicals.
   h. Some vaccines are administered after suspected exposure to a pathogen to elicit an immune response before disease symptoms begin.
5. Antitoxins are antibodies that neutralize toxins that can be used to prevent microbial or other toxins from causing the symptoms of disease and establish passive artificial immunity.
6. Short-term passive immunity can also be established by the administration of IgG.

DISEASE TRANSMISSION

A. Transmission of infectious agents involves escape from the host, travel, and entry into a new host via different routes of transmission.
B. The portals of entry of the human body provide access to the body to pathogenic microorganisms.
   1. The portals are the respiratory tract, the gastrointestinal tract, the genitourinary tract, skin, and wounds.
   2. To establish an infection, the pathogen must enter via the proper portal.
C. The infectious dose is the number of pathogens needed to establish a disease.

AIRBORNE DISEASE TRANSMISSION

A. Airborne transmission, the main route of transmission of pathogens that enter via the respiratory tract, occurs when droplets containing pathogens are transferred from an infected individual to a susceptible individual.
B. Phagocytic cells in the lower respiratory tract, cilia, and mucus protect the respiratory tract from infection.
   1. Viruses that cause the common cold infect the cells lining the nasal passages and pharynx. Cold-causing viruses produce an inflammatory response with associated tissue damage in the infected region.
   2. There are over 100 different rhinoviruses that cause 25% of colds in adults and 10% of colds in children.
C. Influenza is transmitted by the inhalation of droplets containing influenza viruses contained in droplets from the respiratory tracts of infected individuals.
   1. Changes in the combinations of genes that cause antigenic shifts and the production of new strains of influenza viruses are associated with changes in the biochemistry of spikes that protrude from these viruses.
   2. Groups of influenza viruses are designated according to the antigens associated with their capsids.
   3. Antigenic drift occurs because of accumulated genetic mutations and recombinations.
   4. Antigenic shift produces new strains of influenza viruses from the addition of new genes.
   5. Reye syndrome is an acute pathological syndrome that affects the central nervous system, mostly of children who have taken aspirin when they had a viral infection.
D. *Legionella* species inhabit bodies of water, such as air-conditioning cooling systems, and when the water evaporates quickly they become airborne in aerosols, causing Legionnaire's disease.
E. Tuberculosis, caused by *Mycobacterium tuberculosis* and other *Mycobacterium* species, is transmitted via droplets to the respiratory tract where it generally infects the pulmonary system, inflaming and causing lesions in the lungs.
F. Histoplasmosis is caused by the fungus *Histoplasma capsulatum,* which enters the respiratory tract via the inhalation of spores that deposit in the lungs, producing the symptoms of a mild cold.
G. Coccidioidomycosis is caused by the conidia of *Coccidioides immitis* deposited in the bronchi or alveoli.

FOOD AND WATERBORNE DISEASE TRANSMISSION

A. In cases of food poisoning, there is no true infectious agent; ingestion of microbially produced toxins causes the disease process.
   1. *Staphylococcus aureus* strains cause food poisoning.
   2. Botulism results from the ingestion of toxin-containing foods.
      a. *Clostridium botulinum* grows and produces toxin in low-acid canned foods.
      b. Ingestion of spores of *C. botulinum* by infants can cause a fatal infection.
B. Gastroenteritis can be caused by the ingesting of various viruses and bacteria and involves the inflammation of the lining of the gastrointestinal tract.
   1. Salmonellosis is caused by various *Salmonella* species that adhere to the lining of the gastrointestinal tract; when they enter the circulatory system, they cause bacteremia.
   2. *Vibrio parahaemolyticus* occurs in marine environments and causes bacterial gastroenteritis when ingested in contaminated seafood.
C. Typhoid fever is a systemic infection caused by *Salmonella typhi* that is transmitted via contaminated water and food.
D. Shigellosis, also called bacterial dysentery, is an acute inflammation of the intestinal tract caused by species of *Shigella.*
E. Yersiniosis is caused by *Yersinia enterocolitica* transmitted by contaminated foods.
F. Hepatitis A virus is transmitted by the fecal-oral route, affects the liver, and is prevalent in areas with inadequate sewage treatment.
G. Giardiasis is caused by *Giardia lamblia,* a waterborne protozoan, that causes a diarrhea-type disease.

SEXUALLY TRANSMITTED DISEASES

A. Sexually transmitted diseases are contracted by direct physical contact with an infected individual, generally during sexual intercourse.
B. AIDS, genital herpes, genital warts, gonorrhea, syphilis, and nongonococcal urethritis, are sexually transmitted diseases.
   1. AIDS is caused by the human immunodeficiency virus (HIV) and is characterized by a loss of immunity because of death of infected CD4-T lymphocytes.
   2. Genital herpes is caused by a herpes virus and is characterized by periods of lesions and remission.

3. Genital warts is caused by a papilloma virus and is characterized by the formation of benign tumors.
4. Gonorrhea is caused by *Neisseria gonorrhoeae* and can cause infertility in females.
5. Syphilis is caused by *Treponema pallidum* and is characterized by stages that eventually can be fatal.
6. Nongonococcal urethritis is caused by any bacteria other than *N. gonorrhoeae* that causes an inflammation of the urethra.

ZOONOSES AND VECTOR TRANSMISSION OF HUMAN DISEASES

A. Zoonoses are disease outbreaks that primarily affect wild and domestic animals, some of which can be transmitted to humans, usually by vectors.
B. Vectors are carriers of infectious microorganisms.
   1. The bite of a vector provides the portal of entry and the source of inoculum for causing a disease.
   2. Yellow fever is transmitted by mosquito vectors.
   3. Plague is caused by *Yersinia pestis* maintained in populations of wild rodents infected by fleas.
   4. In bubonic plague, *Y. pestis* becomes localized and inflames the lymph nodes, causing buboes; sometimes the tissues become necrotic and the skin blackens.
   5. Rocky Mountain spotted fever is caused by *Rickettsia rickettsii* transmitted to humans by tick bites, causing vascular lesions and skin rashes.
   6. The various typhus fevers are caused by rickettsias transmitted to humans via biting arthropods such as fleas and body lice.
   7. Lyme disease is an inflammatory response to an infection with *Borrelia burgdorferi* that is transmitted by ticks.
   8. Malaria is one of the most common human infectious diseases in the world; it is caused by four species of *Plasmodium* transmitted to humans via the *Anopheles* mosquito.
   9. Leishmaniasis is caused by the protozoan *Leishmania* and is transmitted to humans by sand fly vectors
   10. *Trypanosoma cruzi* causes American trypanosomiasis (Chagas disease), is a major cause of heart disease in Latin America, and is transmitted to humans by cone-nosed bugs.
   11. African trypanosomiasis (African sleeping sickness) is caused by *Trypanosoma* species transmitted by tsetse flies.

DISEASES TRANSMITTED THROUGH DIRECT SKIN CONTACT

A. Warts are benign tumors of the skin caused by papillomaviruses transmitted primarily by direct contact.
B. Hansen disease (leprosy) is caused by *Mycobacterium leprae* and is transmitted by direct skin contact.
C. Superficial infections of the skin, including athlete's foot, caused by various fungal species (dermatophytes) are called tinea or ringworm.

NOSOCOMIAL INFECTIONS

A. Nosocomial infections are hospital acquired infections.
B. Serum hepatitis is caused by contamination of transfusion blood with hepatitis B and C (nonA-nonB) viruses.
C. Puerperal or childbed fever is a systemic bacterial infection caused by beta-hemolytic group A and group B *Streptococcus* species acquired via the genital tract during childbirth or abortion.
D. The exposure of deep body tissues during surgical procedures can sometime lead to infection despite stringent efforts to avoid microbial contamination.

CHAPTER 13

INFECTION AND DISEASE

A. Infection is the growth or replication of microorganisms within the body.
B. Disease is the result of an infection producing a change in normal body physiology.
C. Pathogens are disease-causing microorganisms.
   1. Pathogens typically invade the body and disrupt normal functions.
   2. Pathogens have virulence factors that enhance their ability to cause disease.
      a. Invasiveness is the ability of pathogens to invade human cells and tissues and to establish infection.
      b. Toxins are microbially produced substances that disrupt normal cells functions and/or destroy cells and tissues.
   3. Pathogenicity is the qualitative ability to cause disease.
   4. Virulence quantitatively describes the extent of an organism's ability to cause disease.
D. Establishment of a microbially caused disease is a function of the virulence of the pathogen, the dosage of the microorganisms, and the resistance of the host.
E. There is a characteristic pattern to the course of a disease.
   1. Signs are objective changes of the body, such as a rash or fever, that can be observed associated with a disease.
   2. Symptoms are subjective changes in body function, such as pain or malaise, experienced by a patient.
   3. A disease syndrome is a characteristic group of signs and symptoms.
   4. The progress of an infectious disease follows a characteristic pattern that occurs in distinct stages: incubation period, prodromal stage, period of illness, and period of decline.
      a. An acute disease is characterized by the rapid development of signs and symptoms that after reaching a height of intensity end quickly.
      b. Chronic diseases are characterized by the long-term persistence of symptoms.

DIAGNOSIS OF INFECTIOUS DISEASES

A. Infections elicit nonspecific and specific immune defenses reflected in shifts in relative quantities and types of white blood cells, permitting the use of a differential blood count to determine if a disease is of microbial origin.
   1. Leukocytosis, an elevated white blood cell count, is characteristic of a systemic bacterial infection.

2. Neutrophilia is an increase in neutrophil cells, especially young stab or band cells.
3. Neutropenia is a persistent depression in numbers of white blood cells, usually caused by a viral infection; anemia is decreased numbers of red blood cells.
4. Eosinophilia, an increase in numbers of eosinophils, is characteristic of allergies and parasitic infections.

B. Skin testing based on delayed hypersensitivity reactions can be used as screening methods or diagnostic aids in which signs of redness are evidence of infection after injection of antigens derived from a test organism are injected intradermally.

C. The increase in antibody titer against a pathogen can be used as the basis of a diagnosis.

D. For identification and disease diagnosis, pathogens generally must be isolated.
1. Throat and nasopharyngeal cultures are collected using sterile cotton swabs to isolate pathogens from the upper respiratory tract, streaked onto blood agar plates, and incubated under CO_2 to permit the detection of alpha, beta, and gamma hemolysis of streptococci; other agars are used for the detection of other upper respiratory tract pathogens.
2. Acceptable sputum samples with high numbers of neutrophils, mucus, and low numbers of squamous epithelial cells obtained by transtracheal aspiration or bronchoscopy can be used for the culture of lower respiratory tract pathogens.
3. Cerebrospinal fluid collected by lumbar puncture is examined for infection of the central nervous system.
4. Blood can be collected for culture by aseptic venal puncture and cultured aerobically and anaerobically.
5. A midstream catch of voided urine is used to detect urinary tract infections and qualitatively and quantitatively cultured.
6. Urethral and vaginal exudates are examined for microorganisms that cause sexually transmitted diseases.
7. Stool specimens are used for the isolation of microorganisms that cause intestinal tract infections using selective, differential, and enrichment media.
8. Fluids from eye and ear tissues and material from skin lesions can be collected and cultured.

E. Miniaturized pathogen identification systems perform about 20 tests that can differentiate most pathogenic bacteria based on the substrates they use and the products of their metabolism; the pattern of test results is compared to test results of known organisms.

F. Gas-liquid chromatography is used to detect characteristic patterns of production of fatty acids and other metabolites to differentiate and identify various anaerobes.

G. Serological tests and nucleic acid probes are also used for the identification of microbial pathogens.

BACTERIAL TOXIGENICITY

A. Endotoxins are lipopolysaccharides of the bacterial cell wall structure that act as toxins only after release from the outer layer of the cell when they can trigger the complement cascade by the alternative pathway.

B. Exotoxins are microbe-specific protein toxins composed of a receptor protein component that attaches to a target cell and a toxic component that enters and disrupts cells and cause distinctive clinical symptoms.
1. Botulism is caused by neurotoxins produced by *Clostridium botulinum* that bind to nerve synapses, causing loss of motor function.
2. Tetanus is caused by neurotoxins produced by *Clostridium tetani* that interfere with the peripheral nerves of the spinal cord, causing spastic paralysis.
3. Shiga toxin is the neurotoxin produced by *Shigella dysenteriae* and interferes with the circulatory vessels that supply blood to the central nervous system.
4. *Clostridium perfringens* produces toxins that cause food poisoning.
5. Cholera is caused by the enterotoxin choleragen produced by *Vibrio cholerae,* which causes the movement of large amounts of water into the lumen of the colon, leading to dehydration.
6. Enterocolitis is caused by enterotoxin-producing strains of *Escherichia coli* that result in diarrhea.
7. Diphtheria is caused by the action of a protein toxin produced by *Corynebacterium diphtheriae* that inhibits protein synthesis in most mammalian cells.
8. Whooping cough (pertussis) is caused by several toxins produced by *Bordetella pertussis.*
9. Hemolysins are cell-killing toxins produced by streptococcal species that cause lysis of erythrocytes and produce zones of clearing around bacterial colonies growing on blood agar plates.
10. Toxic shock syndrome is caused by shock syndrome toxin-1 producing strains of *Staphylococcus aureus.*
11. Anthrax, which primarily affects animals other than humans, is caused by *Bacillus anthracis* whose major virulence factors are capsule and exotoxin production.

BACTERIAL INVASIVENESS

A. Some microbially produced enzymes contribute to the virulence of pathogens.
1. Gas gangrene is the result of the deposition of the endospores of toxin-producing *Clostridium* species in the anaerobic conditions of a wound area; these toxins are necrosins and hemolysins.
2. The fibrinolytic enzymes staphylokinase and streptokinase catalyze the lysis of fibrin clots, enhancing the invasiveness of pathogenic strains of *Staphylococcus* and *Streptococcus* by preventing host fibrin from walling off the area of infection.
3. Coagulase, hyaluronidase, and collagenase are toxic enzymes that contribute to the virulence of pathogens by enhancing the ability of the microorganisms to proliferate within body tissues and to interfere with normal host defense mechanisms.

B. Some microorganisms produce factors that interfere with phagocytosis.
1. Pneumonia is an inflammation of the lungs involving the alveoli, usually occurring as a complication of other diseases, caused most frequently by capsule-forming *Streptococcus pneumoniae.*
2. Primary atypical pneumonia is caused by the encapsulated bacterium *Mycoplasma pneumoniae,* which produces hydrogen peroxide that causes cell damage.

C. Adhesins are factors that enhance the ability of a microorganism to attach to the surfaces of mammalian cells.

1. Pili and their associated adhesins permit bacteria to adhere to host cells and interfere with phagocytosis.
2. Dental caries are initiated at the tooth surface as a result of the growth of *Streptococcus* species that can adhere to the tooth surface, produce enamel-dissolving lactic acid, and produce a polymeric substance that keeps the acid in contact with the tooth surface.

D. The limitation on bacterial growth in blood due to lack of available iron is overcome by pathogens that can sequester iron in siderophores.

FUNGAL AND ALGAL TOXINS

A. Several fungi produce cell-killing cytotoxins, including mycotoxins that cause food poisoning, aflatoxins produced by *Aspergillus* species, and ergot alkaloids produced by *Claviceps purpurea* that contaminate grain.

B. Paralytic shellfish poisoning is caused by toxins produced by the dinoflagellate *Gonyaulax* that causes red tides.

VIRAL PATHOGENESIS

A. Some viruses have external spikes that aid in their attachment to host cells.

B. Cytopathic effects, including inclusions, fusions, and conversions to malignancies, are observable changes in the appearance of cells infected with viruses.

C. Measles virus causes infected human cells to fuse, forming giant cells and syncytia.

D. Rubella viruses multiply in the mucosal cells of the upper respiratory tract and disseminate systemically through the blood, causing German measles.

E. The ribonucleic acid-protein core of the mumps virus contains a complement-fixing antigen, and the viral envelope of the mumps virus has two glycoproteins that aid in adsorption of the virus to the host cell and the penetration of the viral nucleocapsid through the host cell membrane.

F. Chickenpox is caused by the varicella-zoster virus that produces local skin lesions after it is disseminated throughout the body.

G. Shingles is the result of the reactivation of a latent varicella-zoster virus.

H. Infectious mononucleosis is caused by the Epstein-Barr virus, which infects B lymphocytes and some epithelial cells where it leads to the formation of antigenic proteins that elicit a cell-mediated immune response, causing swelling of the lymph glands and enlargement of the spleen and liver.

I. Polioviruses, which adsorb via viral surface capsid proteins to poliovirus receptors located only on cells in the nasopharynx, intestinal tract lining, and anterior horn of the spinal cord, are taken up inside the cell by endocytosis, disseminated through the blood stream, and cross the blood-brain barrier, damaging the central nervous system and causing poliomyelitis.

J. Negri bodies are cytoplasmic inclusion bodies that develop within the neurons of the brain when rabies viruses migrate to the central nervous system.

K. Dengue virus replicates within circulatory system cells, causing dengue fever and vascular damage.

L. Encephalitis is a disease syndrome defined by inflammation of the brain, caused by various viruses with different arthropod vectors and geographical distributions.

CHAPTER 14

POPULATION INTERACTIONS

A. Interactions among diverse populations may be beneficial or harmful.

B. Neutralism is the absence of interaction between populations and is likely to exist when there are low population densities, dormant resting stages, and/or minimal metabolic activity.

C. Commensalism is a unidirectional relationship between populations in which one population benefits and the other is unaffected and can be based on microbial produced changes in habitat or production of growth factors.

1. Cometabolism is a specific type of commensal relationship that occurs when an organism growing on a substrate gratuitously oxidizes another substrate that a second organism can use.
2. Epiphytic organisms have a commensal relationship in which one organism grows on the surface of another.

D. Synergism (proto-cooperation) is a nonobligatory relationship in which both populations benefit.

1. Syntrophism is a synergistic relationship that occurs as a result of cross-feeding where two populations supply each other's nutritional needs.
2. The rhizosphere is the soil region in close contact with plant roots that influences soil bacteria, causing increased microbial populations and enhanced plant growth; this is known as the rhizosphere effect.

E. Mutualism (symbiosis) is an obligatory relationship between two populations in which both populations benefit.

1. Lichens are composed of a primary producer (phycobiont) and a consumer (mycobiont) and represent a mutualistic relationship between a heterotrophic fungus and photosynthetic algae or cyanobacteria that forms an essentially new organism.
2. Some protozoa contain endosymbiotic bacteria.
3. A symbiotic relationship exists between members of the bacterial genera *Rhizobium* and *Bradyrhizobium* and leguminous plants that aids in the maintenance of soil fertility because the bacterial invasion of the plant roots causes the formation of nodules in which the bacteria fix atmospheric nitrogen, eliminating the need for nitrogen fertilizers.
4. Mycorrhizae are mutualistic relationships, present in 95% of all plants, between fungi and plant roots involving their integration into a unified morphological unit.
5. Some insects grow and maintain fungal populations as a food source.
6. Ruminant animals establish mutualistic relationships with microbial populations in their rumens that degrade the cellulosic materials they consume.

7. Some fish and marine invertebrates maintain mutualistic relationships with populations of luminescent bacteria that glow blue-green continuously.

F. Competition occurs when two populations compete for the same resource, such as nutrients, light, or space, and leads to ecological separation of related populations; competitive exclusion prevents two populations from occupying the same ecological niche.

G. Amensalism (antagonism) occurs when one population produces a substance inhibitory to another.

H. Predation, an important factor in the establishment of food webs, is the consumption of a prey species by a predator population.

I. In a parasitic relationship, the parasite population benefits and the host population is harmed.
   1. Plant pathogens are microorganisms that cause diseases in plants by weakening or destroying plant cells and tissues, reducing or eliminating the ability of the plant to perform normal physiological functions and resulting in disease symptoms and reduced plant growth or death.
   2. Mosaics and ringspots are common symptoms of viral plant infection.
   3. Viroids are naked RNA molecules that are the causative agents of several plant diseases, including potato spindle disease, chrysanthemum stunt, and citrus exocortis disease.
   4. Plant pathogenic bacteria occur in the genera *Mycoplasma, Spiroplasma, Corynebacterium, Agrobacterium, Pseudomonas, Xanthomonas, Streptomyces,* and *Erwinia* and cause hypertrophy, wilts, rots, blights, and galls.
   5. Most plant diseases are caused by pathogenic fungi; the most economically damaging fungal plant diseases are caused by rusts and smuts.
   6. Plant pathogens can be controlled by quarantine, sanitary practices, use of resistant crop varieties, crop rotation, pesticides, and microbial amensalism and parasitism.

J. Biological control is the use of microbial populations (microbial pesticides) to control plant and animal pest populations.
   1. Microbial pesticides must be virulent, adaptable to environmental variations, not affect nontarget populations, and be specific for the target pest population in which it should rapidly cause disease.
   2. Epizootics are disease epidemics in insects caused by viruses, and therefore viruses can be used to control outbreaks of many insect pests.
   3. *Bacillus thuringiensis* is widely used for bacterial control of insect pests.

BIOGEOCHEMICAL CYCLING

A. Biogeochemical cycling is the movement of materials via biochemical reactions through the global biosphere.

B. Carbon is cycled between inorganic carbon dioxide and the variety of organic compounds that compose living organisms.
   1. Autotrophic metabolism of photosynthetic and chemolithotrophic organisms is responsible for primary production: the conversion of inorganic carbon dioxide to organic carbon.
   2. Gross primary production is the total amount of organic matter produced by the autotrophic biological community in a given habitat; it is the carbon dioxide converted into organic carbon by the habitats' primary producers.
   3. Net primary production is the gross primary production minus the organic carbon taken by the primary producers for respiration and represents the organic carbon available for heterotrophic consumers.
   4. Feeding relationships between organisms establish the trophic structure: the routes by which energy and materials are transferred in an ecosystem.
   5. A food web is an integrated feeding structure formed by the transfer of energy stored in organic compounds between organisms in a community; primary producers are the base of the food web; grazers feed on primary producers and predators eat grazers.
   6. Microorganisms control the decay portions of food webs, converting organic matter to carbon dioxide and reinjecting inorganic CO_2 into the atmosphere.
   7. Rates of mineralization of organic matter depend on environmental conditions and the chemical nature of the organic matter; some compounds are recalcitrant.

C. The conversion of nitrogen compounds primarily by microorganisms changes the oxidation states of nitrogenous compounds and establishes a nitrogen cycle, moving nitrogen from the atmosphere through the biota, soil, and aquatic habitats.
   1. Nitrogen fixation is the conversion of N_2 to ammonia or organic nitrogen.
      a. Nitrogen fixation depends on the nitrogenase enzyme system.
      b. Only a few bacterial species are capable of nitrogen fixation; other microorganisms, plants, and animals are unable to use atmospheric nitrogen directly and need fixed forms of nitrogen for incorporation into cellular biomass.
   2. Ammonification, the conversion of organic amino nitrogen to inorganic ammonia, is done by many microorganisms, plants, and animals.
   3. Nitrification is the oxidation of ammonium ions to nitrite ions and then to nitrate ions.
      a. Nitrification is an aerobic respiration process that yields energy for chemolithotrophic bacteria.
      b. Different microbial populations oxidize ammonia and nitrite.
      c. The change of the positively charged ammonium ions to negatively charged nitrate and nitrite ions mobilizes nitrogen in soil.
         (i). The transfer of nitrate and nitrite ions from surface soil to groundwater is important because it represents an important loss of nitrogen needed to support plant growth from soil.
         (ii). High concentrations of nitrate and nitrite in drinking water is hazardous to humans.
   4. Nitrite ammonification is the reduction of nitrite to ammonium ions by *Clostridium* species.
   5. Denitrification, an anaerobic process that converts fixed forms of nitrogen to molecular nitrogen, is mediated by microorganisms.

D. Changes in the oxidation states of sulfur caused by oxidation-reduction reactions mediated by microorganisms establish the sulfur cycle.
   1. Desulfurization is the removal of sulfur from organic compounds and results in the formation of sulfate.
   2. Photosynthetic sulfur bacteria use hydrogen sulfide for generating reduced coenzymes during metabolism; some bacteria generate ATP by oxidizing hydrogen sulfide.
   3. Acid mine drainage is the result of the metabolism of sulfur and iron-oxidizing bacteria on pyrite ores exposed to atmospheric oxygen as a result of strip mining.

E. Microorganisms assimilate inorganic phosphate and mineralize organic phosphorus compounds and are involved in the solubilization or mobilization of phosphate compounds; microorganisms do not oxidize or reduce phosphorus; the phosphorus cycle is the physical movement of phosphates without alteration of the oxidation level.

F. Iron is transformed between the ferrous and ferric oxidation states by microorganisms.

G. Calcium cycles between soluble and nonsoluble forms.

H. Microbial biogeochemical cycling of heavy metals alters the mobility and toxicity of the metals.

BIOLOGICAL TREATMENT OF WASTES AND POLLUTANTS

A. Microorganisms are used to degrade wastes and pollutants.

B. Organic and inorganic solid waste deposited in low-lying land forms a landfill; covering each day's waste deposit with soil creates a sanitary landfill.

C. Composting is the process by which solid heterogeneous organic matter is degraded by aerobic microorganisms.
   1. Mesophilic and thermophilic microorganisms under controlled conditions of temperature, moisture, and carbon:nitrogen ratio yield a stable, sanitary, humus-like product.
   2. Composting processes include the windrow method, the aerated pile method, and the continuous feed composting process.

D. A high biological oxygen demand (BOD) indicates the presence of excessive amounts of organic carbon, making oxygen depletion and the death of obligately aerobic organisms, such as fish, a likely result in waters into which wastes are dumped.

E. Sewage treatment uses physical, chemical, and microbiological methods to lower the BOD.
   1. Primary treatments rely on physical separation.
   2. Secondary treatments, such as oxidation ponds, trickling filters, rotating biological contactors (biodiscs), activated sludge, septic tanks, and anaerobic digesters, rely on microbial biodegradation to reduce concentrations of organic compounds.
   3. Tertiary treatments use chemical methods to remove inorganic compounds, nonbiodegradable organic pollutants, and pathogenic microorganisms.
   4. Disinfection, the final step in the sewage treatment process, is designed to kill enteropathogenic bacteria and viruses and is commonly accomplished by chlorinations using chlorine gas or hypochlorite.
   5. Fecal coliform counts are used to establish the safety of water.

F. Biodegradation is the decomposition of compounds by living organisms, generally by microorganisms.
   1. Recalcitrance is the resistance to biodegradation.
   2. Microbial degradation of oil pollutants is the major process responsible for the ecological recovery of oil spill areas.
   3. Biological magnification (biomagnification) is the increase in concentration of a chemical in biological organisms compared to its concentration in the environment that occurs when the pollutant is persistent and lipophilic.
   4. Pesticides are subject to biomagnification.

CHAPTER 15

BIOTECHNOLOGY

A. Biotechnology is concerned with the practical uses of microorganisms.

B. Traditional biotechnological processes are used to produce foods, pharmaceuticals, and other products of economic value, and for the degradation of wastes.

C. Modern biotechnological processes use recombinant DNA technology.

FERMENTATION INDUSTRY

A. Enzymatic activities of microorganisms are used to produce substances of commercial value for the fermentation industry, which defines fermentation as any chemical transformation of organic compounds carried out by microorganisms and their enzymes.

B. Industrial microbiologists find or create strains of microorganisms that will carry out biotransformations that will yield large amounts of a desired product and determine the optimal production process using the least expensive substrates and fermentors that optimize environmental conditions for maximal yields and efficient recovery methods.
   1. Microorganisms are screened for their abilities to produce substances of commercial value.
      a. Assays are performed as primary screening procedures on microorganisms to determine their industrial potential.
      b. Secondary screening procedures include qualitative and quantitative assays; screening should identify the optimal incubation conditions for maximal economic yield of a product.
   2. The development of a commercial process begins using small flasks, then small fermentors, intermediate-size fermentors, and finally large-scale fermentors at each stage, determining the organic and inorganic composition of the medium (including sources of carbon nitrogen, and phosphorus), pH, temperature, and oxygen concentration (sometimes using forced aeration and/or mechanical mixing) that will maximize the efficiency and output of the production process.
   3. In processes using immobilized enzymes, microbial

enzymes are adsorbed or bonded to a solid support and act as a solid-surface catalyst as a solution is passed across the solid surface.

C. Many antibiotics and other pharmaceuticals are produced by microorganisms.
   1. To manufacture penicillin, a dense suspension of *Penicillium chrysogenum* is inoculated onto a wheat brannutrient solution, allowed to incubate for one week at 24° C, transferred to an inoculum tank where it is agitated with forced aeration for 1 to 2 days to produce a heavy mycelium growth that is inoculated into a production tank; when the fermentation is complete the liquid medium containing the penicillin is separated from the fungal cells and the penicillin is recovered from the filtrate.
   2. Cephalosporin C is the clinically weak fermentation product of *Cephalosporium acremonium,* which is transformed by removing and adding side chains to form clinically useful products.
   3. Streptomycin is produced by strains of *Streptomyces griseus*: mycelial biomass is produced during rapid growth of *S. griseus*; accumulation of streptomycin then occurs; finally there is depletion of carbohydrates and cessation of streptomycin production.
   4. Production of steroids requires the exact positioning of chemical constituents on the basic steroid ring; this can be accomplished by microorganisms.
   5. Using recombinant DNA technology, human DNA sequences that code for various proteins can be incorporated into bacterial genomes, which when grown in fermentors can produce human proteins such as insulin, human growth factors, interferon, and interleukin-2.
   6. Vaccines are produced by mutant strains of pathogens or by attenuating or inactivating pathogens without removing the antigens necessary for eliciting the immune response.
   7. Viruses for vaccines are often grown in embryonated eggs or tissue culture.
   8. Vitamin B_{12} and riboflavin are examples of vitamins that can be produced by microbial fermentation; B_{12} is a by-product of *Streptomyces* antibiotic fermentation, and riboflavin is a by-product of acetone butanol fermentation, produced by various *Clostridium* species or direct fermentation of *Eremothecium ashbyi* or *Ashbya gossypii.*

D. Acetic, gluconic, citric, itaconic, gibberellic, and lactic acid (organic acids) and lysine and glutamic acid (amino acids) are produced by microbial fermentation.
   1. Lysine is produced directly from carbohydrates, using an auxotroph of *Corynebacterium glutamicum.*
   2. Glutamic acid and MSG can be produced by direct fermentation with strains of *Brevibacterium, Arthrobacter,* and *Corynebacterium.*
   3. Leaky membranes must be induced in the production of glutamic and other amino acids to permit excretion of the amino acid product from the cell.
   4. Gluconic acid is produced by various bacteria and several fungi; its commercial production using *Aspergillus niger* employs a submerged culture process.
   5. Citric acid is produced by cultures of *Aspergillus niger* and is used as a food additive, a metal chelating and sequestering agent, and as a plasticizer.
   6. Itaconic acid is produced by the transformation of citric acid by *Aspergillus terreus.*
   7. Gibberellic acid is formed by the fungus *Gibberella fujikuroi* and is produced commercially using aerated submerged culture.
   8. *Lactobacillus delbrueckii* is used in the commercial production of lactic acid.

E. Various enzymes are produced by microorganisms for commercial applications.
   1. Proteases are enzymes that attack the peptide bonds of protein molecules forming small peptides and are produced by different bacterial species and used for different industrial purposes, including in laundry detergent and in baking to alter the gluten properties of flour to reduce mixing time and improve product quality.
   2. Fungal production of alpha, beta, and glucamylase amylases uses *Aspergillus* species; bacterial amylases are made with *Bacillus subtilis* and *B. diastaticus.*

F. Organic solvents can be produced by microbial fermentation but are currently more cheaply produced by chemical synthesis.

G. Microorganisms are involved in the production of synthetic fuels such as ethanol, methane, hydrogen, and hydrocarbons. *Saccharomyces cerevisiae* is used to produce ethanol from sugars and hydrolyzed starch from corn.
   1. Corn sugar and plant starch and *Zymomonas mobilis* and *Thermoanaerobacter ethanolicus* are used in the production of methanol.
   2. Methane is produced by the anaerobic decomposition of waste materials by methanogenic bacteria.

ENVIRONMENTAL BIOTECHNOLOGY

A. Bioleaching is the use of microorganisms, particularly *Thiobacillus ferrooxidans,* in the recovery of minerals from low-grade ores by altering the physical or chemical properties of a metallic ore so that the metal can be extracted.
   1. Copper and uranium are recovered by bioleaching.
   2. Bioleaching of oil shales has potential for enhancing the recovery of hydrocarbons.
   3. Tertiary recovery of petroleum is the use of biological and chemical means to enhance oil recovery and include the use of xanthan gums produced by bacteria.

B. Bioremediation is the use of microorganisms to remove pollutants from the environment, accelerating the natural fate of biodegradable pollutants.
   1. Microorganisms may be selected or engineered for use *in situ* for bioremediation.
   2. Bioremediation is used in the cleanup of oil spills by stimulating the growth of indigenous hydrocarbon-degrading microorganisms by supplying nitrogen and phosphorus fertilizers.

BIOTECHNOLOGY AND THE PRODUCTION OF FOOD

A. Microbial processes yield fermented foods, require proper substrates, microbial populations, and environmental conditions, and employ microbial enzymatic activities to transform one food into another.

B. Fermentation of milk to produce buttermilk, yogurt, and cheeses is the result of the metabolism of the milk sugar lactose carried out primarily by lactic acid bacteria such as *Streptococcus cremoris, S. lactis, S. thermophilus,* and *Lactobacillus bulgaricus.*
   1. The natural production of cheeses involves lactic acid fermentation with various mixtures of *Streptococcus* and *Lactobacillus* species used as starter cultures to initiate fermentation.
   2. The flavors of cheeses result from the use of different microbial starter cultures, varying incubation times and conditions, and the inclusion or omission of secondary microbial species late in the fermentation process.
   3. Ripening of cheeses involves additional enzymatic transformations after the formation of the cheese curd, using enzymes produced by lactic acid bacteria or enzymes from other sources.

C. Yeasts, principally *Saccharomyces cerevisiae,* are added to bread dough to ferment the sugar in an alcoholic fermentation, producing carbon dioxide that leavens the dough and causes it to rise.

D. Production of alcoholic beverages is based on an alcoholic fermentation of sugar to alcohol by microbial enzymes.
   1. The fermentation of wort to produce beer is carried out by the yeast *Saccharomyces carlsbergensis* or *S. cerevisiae.*
   2. In the production of distilled liquors after fermentation the alcohol is collected by distillation, permitting the production of higher alcohol concentrations.
   3. Wine is fermented from grapes and other fruits using wild microorganisms or a variety of *S. cerevisiae.*

E. Production of vinegar involves an initial anaerobic fermentation to convert carbohydrates from fruits, vegetables, malted cereals, or sugary syrups by *S. cerevisiae* to alcohol, followed by a secondary oxidative transformation of the alcohol to acetic acid by *Acetobacter* and *Gluconobacter.*

F. Vegetables such as cabbage, carrots, green tomatoes, greens, and olives are fermented using lactic acid bacteria to create new food products that are not readily subject to spoilage.

G. Sauerkraut is produced from a lactic acid fermentation of wilted, shredded cabbage, involving a succession of bacterial populations, including *Enterobacter cloacae, Leuconostoc mesenteroides, L. plantarum,* and *L. brevis.*

H. Traditional pickle production is by fermenting cucumbers using the natural microbiota associated with the cucumber and controlling temperature and salt concentration, or by inoculation with *Leuconostoc plantarum* and *Pediococcus cerevisiae.*

I. Olive production involves lactic acid fermentation in a brine solution.

J. Soy sauce is produced from a soybean, wheat, and wheat bran; the starter culture is produced by koji fermentation with *Aspergillus oryzae* inoculated into a mixture of soybeans and wheat; other bacteria involved in the production of soy sauce are *Pediococcus soyae, Saccharomyces rouxii, Zygosaccharomyces soyae,* and *Torulopsis* and *Lactobacillus* species.

K. Microorganisms can be grown as a source of single-cell protein, a high yield, high protein food crop that contains all essential amino acids and is used primarily as animal feed; SCP can be grown on hydrocarbons or waste materials.

CHAPTER 16

SYSTEMATICS OF PROKARYOTIC MICROORGANISMS

A. Systematics attempts to arrange organisms in an orderly manner by studying their diversity and interrelationships.

B. Taxonomy attempts to identify and describe the taxonomic units and devise an appropriate way of arranging and cataloging these units and is the process, based on established procedures and rules, of describing the groups of organisms, their interrelationships, and the boundaries between the organisms.

C. Classification is the ordering or placing of organisms into groups based on their genetic interrelationships and reflecting their evolutionary (phylogenetic) relationships.

D. Nomenclature is the assignment of names to the units described in the classification system.

E. Identification is the application of the systems of classification and nomenclature to assign the proper name to an unknown organism and to place it in its proper position within the classification system.

F. Each microorganism has a unique binomial name consisting of its genus and species names.

G. The levels of taxonomic hierarchy are kingdom, phyla, class, order, family, genera, species, subspecies (type) and strain; species is the basic taxonomic unit.

H. Classification systems have been based on morphology, physiology, and genetic relatedness.
   1. When the classification system is based on similarity of features, it separates the taxonomic units into taxa and emphasizes the branch points between groups that are presumed to represent fundamental differences between taxa.
   2. In numerical taxonomy, many characteristics are examined and measured to assess similarities that are expressed as indices of similarity (similarity coefficients).
   3. The relative proportion of guanine and cytosine compared to the total number of nucleotide base pairs in DNA (mole % G + C) crudely analyzes the microbial genome and is used in genetic analyses to classify microorganisms; RNA and proteins can also be analyzed as direct genetic products.

I. Identification compares unknown microorganisms with previously established groups to determine whether they belong in one of these groups.
   1. An identification key is a series of questions that lead through a classification system to the determination of the identity of an organism; in a dichotomous key, the answers to the yes–no questions lead through

the branches of a flow chart to the identification of a microorganism as part of a specific group.
2. Diagnostic tables summarize the characteristics of taxonomic groups but do not indicate a hierarchical separation of the taxa.
3. Computers facilitate the rapid comparison of the data on an unknown microorganism with a data band of microbial taxa and assess the statistical probability of obtaining a particular pattern of test results; probabilistic identification matrices are compilations of the frequencies of occurrence of individual features within separate taxonomic groups.

J. *Bergey's Manual of Systematic Bacteriology* summarizes the status of bacterial taxonomy.
K. *Bergey's Manual of Determinative Bacteriology* assists in the identification of bacteria.

EUBACTERIA

A. Spirochetes are helically coiled rod-shaped cells that are wound around one or more central axial fibrils, motile by a flexing motion of the cell.
B. Gram-negative aerobic or microaerophilic spiral and curved bacteria are helically curved rods not curved around a central axial filament and are motile by means of polar flagella.
C. Gram-negative aerobic rods and cocci include many common bacterial genera.
 1. Pseudomonadaceae are Gram-negative straight or curved respiratory, aerobic rods that are motile by means of polar flagella.
 2. Azotobacteraceae are Gram-negative aerobic, pleomorphic, nitrogen-fixing rods.
 3. Rhizobiaceae are Gram-negative aerobic rods that can fix atmospheric nitrogen.
 4. Methylomonadaceae are Gram-negative aerobic rods that can utilize carbon monoxide, methane, or methanol as their sole source of carbon.
 5. Halobacteriaceae and Acetobacteriaceae are Gram-negative aerobic rods.
 6. Legionellaceae are Gram-negative, nonfermentative aerobic rods that require iron and cysteine and form branched chain fatty acids.
 7. Members of the family Neisseriaceae are Gram-negative aerobic cocci and coccobacilli and many are parasitic or human pathogens.
D. Gram-negative facultatively anaerobic rods belong to the families Enterobacteriaceae, which move with peritrichous flagella, and Vibrionaceae, which move with polar flagella.
E. Bacteroidaceae are Gram-negative anaerobic rods.
 1. *Bacteroides, Fusobacterium,* and *Leptotrichia* are representative Gram-negative anaerobes.
F. Dissimilatory sulfate- or sulfur–reducing bacteria.
 1. Members of the genus *Desulfovibrio* are curved, Gram-negative rods capable of reducing sulfates or other reducible sulfur compounds to hydrogen sulfide.
G. Gram-negative anaerobic cocci include the genera *Veillonella, Acidaminococcus, Megasphaera,* and *Gemmiger.*
H. Rickettsias are intracellular parasites, most of which are Gram negative and multiply only within host cells by binary fission.
I. Chlamydias are obligate intracellular parasites whose reproduction is characterized by change from an elementary body into an initial body that divides by fission.
J. Phototrophic bacteria use light energy to drive the synthesis of ATP.
 1. Anoxyphotobacteria are anoxygenic photosynthetic bacteria that do not produce oxygen, require an electron donor other than water, typically occur in aquatic habitats, and include the Rhodospirillaceae (purple nonsulfur bacteria), Chromatiaceae (purple sulfur bacteria), Chlorobiaceae (green sulfur bacteria), and Chloroflexaceae (green flexibacteria).
 2. Oxyphotobacteria are oxygenic phototrophic bacteria that split water to form oxygen as part of their photosynthetic metabolism and include the orders Cyanobacteriales (blue-green bacteria) and Prochlorales.
 3. Cyanobacteria include four major subgroups: chroococcacean cyanobacteria, pleurocapsalean cyanobacteria, oscillatorian cyanobacteria, and heterocystous cyanobacteria.
K. Chemolithotrophic bacteria oxidize large amounts of inorganic compounds to generate ATP, causing global scale biogeochemical cycling of various elements.
 1. Nitrobacteraceae (nitrifying bacteria) oxidize ammonia or nitrite to generate ATP.
 2. Siderocapsaceae oxidize iron or manganese and deposit iron or manganese oxides in capsules or extracellular material.
L. The budding and appendaged bacteria are grouped based on the formation of extensions or protrusions (prosthecae) that have either reproductive or physiological functions.
M. The sheathed bacteria are those whose cells occur within a filamentous sheath that enables them to attach to solid surfaces and conserve energy.
N. The bacteria that are capable of gliding motility are the Myxobacterales (fruiting myxobacteria) and the Cytophagales.
 1. Myxobacteria are small rods usually embedded in a slime layer that form fruiting bodies that contain dormant myxospores.
 2. Cytophagales have gliding motion and do not produce fruiting bodies.
O. Gram-positive cocci include the Micrococcaceae (single cells or irregular clusters), Streptococcaceae (pairs of chains of cells with fermentative metabolism), and Peptococcaceae (single cells, pairs, regular or irregular clusters).
P. Gram-positive endospore-forming rods and cocci have heat resistant endospores and include the genera *Bacillus* and *Clostridium.*
Q. Gram-positive asporogenous rods of regular shape do not form spores and produce lactic acid as its fermentation product.
R. Gram-positive rods of irregular shape (coryneform bacteria) are a heterogeneous group with irregular cell morphology and incomplete separation following cell division.
S. Mycobacteria are slow-growing, aerobic, rod-shaped, acid-fast, pleomorphic bacteria.
T. Actinomycetes are Gram-positive bacteria with a high mole % G + C.

1. Norcardioform actinomycetes produce fungal-like filaments that fragment into nonmotile cells.
2. Streptomyces are Gram-positive, filamentous, spore-producing actinomycetes that do not fragment into rods or coccoid elements.

U. Mycoplasmas lack a cell wall, are bounded by a single triple-layered membrane, are the smallest organisms capable of self-reproduction, and form small colonies with a characteristic "fried-egg" appearance.

V. The family Propionibacteriaceae are anaerobic nonfilamentous or filamentous Gram-positive rods that produce propionic acid, acetic acid, or mixtures of organic acids by fermentation.

W. Endosymbionts live within the cells of invertebrates, protozoa and insects, without adversely affecting the host.

ARCHAEBACTERIA (ARCHAEA)

A. Archaebacteria are phylogenetically related based on 16S rRNA molecules, lack murein in their cell walls, and have an unusual ether linkage in their phospholipid molecules.

B. Methanogens (Methanobacteriaceae) are methane-producing bacteria that obtain energy by reducing H_2, formate, or acetate.

C. *Archaeoglobus* are archaebacterial sulfate reducers and require salt and high temperature.

D. Halobacteriaceae are obligate halophiles.

E. *Thermoplasma* are acidophilic, thermophilic archaebacteria that lack cell walls and are found in coal refuse piles.

F. Some archaebacteria are extremely thermophilic sulfur metabolizers that convert elemental sulfur to hydrogen sulfide.

CHAPTER 17

FUNGI

A. Fungi are eukaryotic, heterotrophic, nonphotosynthetic microorganisms that form reproductive spores and absorb nutrients; they live saprophytically or parasitically.

B. Yeasts are fungi that exist as unicellular organisms and reproduce by budding.
   1. In budding, daughter cells are formed by pinching off segments of mother cells and forming cross walls.
   2. After budding, progeny and parent both have complete genomes.
   3. A bud scar is formed and may be polar or multilateral.

C. Filamentous fungi or molds form hyphae.
   1. The growth of filamentous fungi (molds) involves the development and elongation of multicellular hyphae, which are connected lines of vegetative cells that exhibit branching and that are surrounded by cell walls.
   2. Mycelia are integrated masses of hyphae.

D. Fungi produce various sexual and asexual spores.
   1. Conidia are asexual fungal spores borne externally on hyphae or specialized conidiophore structures.
      a. Arthrospores are fragmented hyphae.
      b. Sporangiospores are produced within the sporangium.
      c. Chlamydospores occur within hyphal segments.
   2. Blastospores are asexual spores produced by budding.
   3. Ascospores are sexual fungal spores formed within the sac-like ascus of ascomycetes (sac fungi).
   4. Sexual spores of basidiomycetes are produced on the basidium.

E. Classification of fungi is based largely on means of reproduction.
   1. Chytrdiomycetes (chytrids) are zoospore-producing fungi that often cause plant disease, including hypertrophy (enlargement of host cells) and hyperplasia (multiplication of host cells).
   2. Oomycetes are water molds that reproduce using flagellated zoospores and form oospores that develop by contact with gametangia at the ends of mycelia.
   3. Zygomycetes are saprophytes or plant and animal pathogens that have coenocytic mycelia and form zygospores from fusion of gametangia.
   4. Ascomycetes reproduce asexually by fission, fragmentation of hyphae, formation of chlamydospores, and production of conidia.
      a. Many yeasts are ascomycetes and the morphology of the ascospore is the defining feature in classifying yeasts at the genus level.
      b. True ascomycetes produce asci in the ascocarp.
   5. Basidiomycetes (club fungi) produce sexual basidiospores on basidia and include smuts, rust, jelly fungi, shelf fungi, stinkhorns, bird's nest fungi, puffballs, and mushrooms.
      a. Basidiomycete mycelia form clamp connections between cells.
      b. Dolipore septa are specialized cross walls between connecting cells of basidiomycetes.
      c. Shelf or bracket fungi are saprophytic, have tough, leathery fruiting bodies, and cause brown and white rot decay.
      d. Mushrooms are the basidiocarps of basidiomycetes.
      e. Gastromycetes do not forcibly eject their spores.
      f. Rusts and smuts produce a resting spore (teliospore).
   6. Deuteromycetes (Fungi Imperfecti) do not produce sexual spores and are classified based on the morphological structure of the vegetative phase and the types of asexual spores produced.

ALGAE

A. Algae are photosynthetic eukaryotic microorganisms whose classification is based on types of photosynthetic pigments produced, the types of intracellularly stored reserve materials, and cell morphology.

B. Chlorophycophyta (green algae) contain chlorophylls *a* and *b*, live in aquatic ecosystems, are motile by means of flagella, and may be unicellular, colonial, or filamentous and quite complex; higher plants may have evolved from them.

C. Euglenophycophyta contain chlorophylls *a* and *b*, are green, unicellular, and surrounded by a pellicle.

D. Chrysophycophyta are the yellow-green and golden algae and the diatoms; they produce chrysolaminarin as the reserve storage material, and carotenoid and xanthophyll pigments.

1. Bacillariophyceae (diatoms) produce frustules (valves).
2. Frustules have an epitheca and a hypotheca.
3. The cell walls of diatoms are impregnated with silica.
4. Diatoms reproduce asexually by the formation of uneven-sized cells.

E. Pyrrophycophyta (fire algae) produce xanthophyll pigments, making them brown or red.
   1. Fire algae are unicellular and biflagellate.
   2. Fire algae store starch or oils, reproduce by cell division, and their cell walls contain cellulose.
   3. Dinoflagellates are fire algae that have transverse grooves that divide them into semicells and two flagella.
      a. Some dinoflagellates are bioluminescent.
      b. Red tides are toxic blooms of *Gonyaulax* and other dinoflagellates that kill invertebrates and are poisonous to humans as well.

F. Cryptophycophyta (Cryptomonads) are brown algae with asymmetric cells bounded by a periplast that reproduce by longitudinal cell division.

G. Rhodophycophyta (red algae) exhibit tissue differentiation and may be classified as plants.
   1. Red algae contain the pigments phycocyanin, phycoerythrin, and chlorophyll.
   2. The reserve material of red algae is Floridean starch.
   3. Red algae reproduce by oogamous sexual reproduction involving carpogonia and spermatia.
   4. Red algae are marine.

H. Phaeophycophyta (brown algae) exhibit tissue differentiation and should be classified as plants.
   1. Brown algae include the kelps and giant seaweeds.
   2. Brown algae produce xanthophylls. The reserve materials of brown algae are laminarin and mannitol.

PROTOZOA

A. Protozoa are unicellular nonphotosynthetic eukaryotic microorganisms lacking cell walls that are classified based on locomotion, being nonmotile or using pseudopodia, cilia, or flagella.

B. Slime molds are evolutionarily related to protozoa; they are phagotrophic; their vegetative cells are amoeboid and lack a cell wall.
   1. Cellular slime molds (Acrasiales) form stalked sporocarps as fruiting bodies that release spores that germinate, forming myxamoebae that swarm to form a pseudoplasmodium.
   2. Myxomycetes (true slime molds) form myxamoebae or swarm cells that fuse to form a plasmodium.

C. Sarcodina ingest food and are mobile via pseudopodia.
   1. Pseudopodia (false feet) are extensions of cytoplasm involved in locomotion and ingestion of food.
   2. Pseudopodia have different shapes (lobopodia, philopodia, rhizopodia, and axopodia).

D. Mastigophora are flagellate protozoa that may also produce pseudopodia.

E. Ciliophora use cilia for mobility.
   1. Some ciliate protozoa have cytosomes, a mouth-like region.
   2. Ciliate protozoa reproduce by various sexual and asexual means, such as binary fission and conjugation.

F. Sporozoa are parasites with complex life cycles: immature stages are called sporozoites and adult stages are called trophozoites.

APPENDIX

Chemistry for the Microbiologist

ORGANIZATION OF MATTER

Early biological studies centered on the observation of living organisms—what they looked like, where they lived, what they ate. Naturalists cataloged the species of plants and animals in a region, recorded their distributions, and observed their appearances and behaviors. Early microbiologists continued in this tradition, looking at microorganisms and describing their morphologies and movements. Antonie van Leeuwenhoek, for example, recorded the shapes and movements of the "animalcules" he observed. Such microscopic observations revealed the existence of the living microbial world, but gave only limited insight into how microorganisms interact with their environment, or how they obtain the matter and energy needed to sustain life.

In the first half of the nineteenth century chemists developed a fundamental understanding of matter—the physical material of the universe. With the recognition that all matter in the universe has certain unifying chemical and physical properties and that living organisms are manifestations of their underlying chemical composition and the chemical reactions that they carry out, the fields of chemistry, physics, and biology began to be drawn together. Biologists soon recognized that to understand living organisms they had to investigate the chemistry of life. Microbiologists realized that the scientific understanding of the microorganisms, what they are and what they can do, necessitates the understanding of their underlying chemistry. So they incorporated chemistry as an integral part of the field of microbiology. To understand the chemistry of living systems, it is necessary to learn the "language" that chemists use for communicating information about chemicals. It is necessary to become conversant with the chemical terms and principles that are applied to the descriptions of microorganisms and their activities.

CHEMICAL ELEMENTS

An **element** is the fundamental unit of a chemical that cannot be broken down further without destroying the properties of that pure chemical substance. There are 92 different naturally occurring elements—such as carbon, hydrogen, nitrogen, and oxygen. Chemists have assigned each element a **chemical symbol** that is a one- or two-letter abbreviation of its English or Latin name. The chemical symbol for the element hydrogen is H, oxygen is O, carbon is C, and so forth. The same chemical symbol is used regardless of the element's name in the language of the country in which it is being used. Thus, even though nitrogen is called *azoto* in Italy and *stickstoff* in Germany, its chemical symbol is always N. These symbols for the chemical elements form the "alphabet" of the language of chemistry. Biologists, generally, are only concerned with the 26 elements that form the major components of living systems. The most abundant elements in living systems are carbon (C), hydrogen (H), oxygen (O), nitrogen (N), phosphorus (P), sulfur (S), sodium (Na), potassium (K), magnesium (Mg), calcium (Ca), iron (Fe), and chlorine (Cl). Of these, carbon is the element that forms the backbone of all molecules that comprise living organisms.

STRUCTURE OF ATOMS

The smallest unit of an element that still retains the chemical properties of that element is called an **atom** (Greek, meaning that which cannot be cut). Atoms were thought to be the smallest particles into which matter could be divided. It was not until the twentieth century that physicists showed that atoms are composed of yet smaller subatomic particles. Chemists subsequently discovered that the number of an atom's

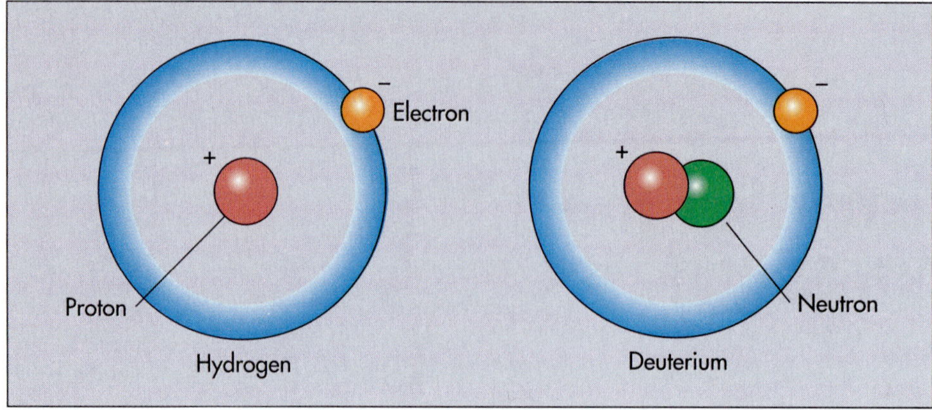

FIG. 1 Atoms are the fundamental units of chemical elements. They are composed of subatomic particles (negatively charged electrons, positively charged protons, and, with the exception of hydrogen, neutrally charged neutrons)

constituent subatomic particles determines the characteristic properties of the atoms of different elements, such as their capacities to combine with other atoms.

These subatomic particles of atoms carry a positive or a negative charge, or no charge (FIG. 1). Positively charged particles are called **protons,** uncharged neutral particles are called **neutrons,** and negatively charged particles are called **electrons.** The atom is organized with the protons and neutrons in a central region called the **nucleus.** The electrons move in regions of space around the nucleus.

The nucleus of an atom has a net positive charge because it contains positively charged protons. However, because the number of protons in each nucleus is equal to the number of electrons, the total positive charge of the nucleus's protons equals the total negative charge of the electrons. Therefore each atom has a net charge of zero. An atom is said to be neutral. As discussed later, the chemical properties of atoms, which allow them to participate in chemical reactions, depend on the number and arrangements of their electrons.

Atoms, which are the smallest units of elements, contain positively charged protons, uncharged neutrons, and negatively charged electrons; an atom has a net electronic charge of zero because it contains equal numbers of protons and electrons.

Ions

The number of electrons moving around the nucleus of an atom can increase or decrease. Some atoms have a tendency to lose one or more electrons. Others tend to gain electrons. An atom that has lost or gained an electron is called an **ion.** It is no longer neutral. When a sodium (Na) atom loses an electron, it becomes a positively charged sodium ion (Na^+). Such a positively charged ion is called a **cation.** Other examples of cations are the potassium ion (K^+), magnesium ion (Mg^{2+}), and calcium ion (Ca^{2+}). Atoms of hydrogen can lose an electron and become a stable positive ion (H^+). The formation of hydrogen ions is important because this is what causes acidity in the watery solutions that are an integral part of biological systems.

When a chlorine (Cl) atom gains an electron, it becomes a negatively charged chloride ion (Cl^-). Such a negatively charged ion is called an **anion.** Other examples of anions are the iodide ion (I^-) and sulfide ion (S^{2-}). Notice that the symbol for an ion is the chemical abbreviation followed by a superscript designating the ion's number of positive (+) or negative (−) charges.

An ion is an atom that has gained or lost one or more electrons.

Atoms that gain electrons form negatively charged ions (anions) and atoms that lose electrons form positively charged ions (cations).

Atomic Number and Weight

Chemists have assigned each element a unique atomic number. The **atomic number** of an element is determined by the number of protons in its nucleus. No two elements have the same number of protons. Therefore each chemical element has a different atomic number.

The atomic number of an atom of an element is the number of protons in the nucleus.

The **atomic weight** of an element is the total number of protons and neutrons in each atom of that element. Each proton and each neutron has one unit of atomic weight. Electrons contribute only negligibly to the weight of an atom. Therefore the atomic weight is calculated by adding only the numbers of protons and neutrons.

The atomic weight of an atom of an element is the sum of the numbers of protons and neutrons in its nucleus.

Isotopes

Isotopes of an element have varying numbers of neutrons. All isotopes of a given element have the same number of protons in their nuclei. Hence, they all have the same atomic number. Their atomic weights differ because they have different numbers of neutrons. The most abundant isotope of carbon (^{12}C), for example, has six protons and six neutrons. Another isotope of carbon (^{14}C) has six protons and eight neutrons.

Many isotopes are stable. They do not change spontaneously into other atomic forms. Some isotopes, though, have unstable combinations of protons and neutrons in their nuclei. Such isotopes are called **radioactive isotopes.** A radioactive isotope breaks down or decays by giving off subatomic particles and energy (radiation). For example, carbon-14 (^{14}C) is a radioisotope of carbon because it has too many neutrons in its nucleus to be stable. The instability within the nucleus of ^{14}C results in the breaking apart of a neutron. Energy and a beta particle (an electron formed by the decomposition of a neutron) are emitted from the nucleus. Radioactive isotopes, such as ^{14}C, are useful for labelling biological substances because beta particles can be easily detected. Caution must be used, however, whenever handling radioisotopes because the energy they give off can damage biological systems.

Atoms of the same element that have different numbers of neutrons are called isotopes.

Electron Arrangements and Chemical Reactivity

The protons and neutrons in the nucleus determine the atomic weight of an atom, but electrons of the atom determine its chemical properties. It is the electrons that actually participate in chemical reactions. Each element's atoms differ from those of all other elements in the number and arrangement of their electrons. Electrons move in regions of space around the nucleus.

The regions of space where electrons are likely to be found are called **shells.** Each electron shell represents an energy level. Shells closest to the nucleus have the lowest energy. Shells furthest from the nucleus have the greatest energy. Each shell has a maximal number of electrons that it can hold. The further away from the nucleus a shell is located, the greater the number of electrons that can occupy that shell (FIG. 2). The shell closest to the nucleus can hold only two electrons. Electrons first occupy the shells closest to the nucleus. Only after these shells are filled do electrons occupy the shells with higher energy levels.

The outermost shell is called the **valence shell.** The number of electrons that can occupy the valence electron shell establishes in large part the capacity of that atom to combine with other atoms. The basic principle of atomic reactivity is that when its outermost electron shell is completely full an atom is stable. It will not react with other atoms. By interacting, atoms gain, lose, or share electrons to fill their outer shells. The outer electron shells of the atoms of the major elements in biological systems—hydrogen, carbon, nitrogen, oxygen, phosphorus, and sulfur—are all incomplete. The atoms of these elements, therefore, readily react with other atoms to achieve stable outer electron shells.

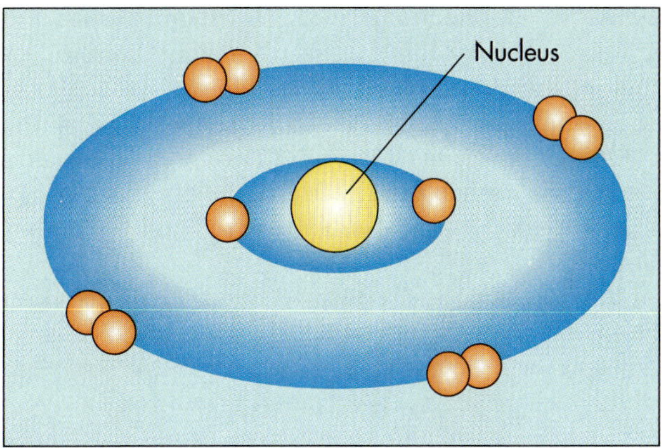

FIG. 2 The electrons of an atom are arranged in shells. Each shell represents a different energy level.

The fullness of the outer electron shell (valence shell) of an atom determines the capacity of that atom to combine with other atoms.

Atoms react with each other by losing, gaining, or sharing electrons to fill their outer electron shells.

Molecules and Chemical Bonds

When elements combine with each other they form compounds. A **compound** is a specific combination of elements in which the elements are present in a fixed and unvarying proportion. For example, water (H_2O) is a compound that has a fixed 2:1 proportion of two elements: hydrogen and oxygen. Because the proportion of elements in compounds never varies, they are distinct from **mixtures.** In a mixture two or more elements can be present in different and varying proportions. A mixture can be separated by physical means, such as filtering or sorting. A compound cannot be split into its component parts by such means.

A **molecule** is the simplest form of a compound that still retains the properties of that compound. A molecule is formed when atoms combine with each other. Chemists write **molecular formulas** to describe how many and which specific atoms form a molecule. For example, the molecular formula for water (H_2O) communicates the fact that this molecule is formed when two atoms of hydrogen and one atom of oxygen combine. Likewise the molecular formula for glucose ($C_6H_{12}O_6$) tells us that this sugar is formed by combining six carbon atoms, twelve hydrogen atoms, and six oxygen atoms. If the atoms of elements are the "letters" of the chemical alphabet, then the molecules of compounds are the "words" in the language of the chemist. Like atoms, molecules have specific physical properties, such as density. Molecules also have chemical properties, such as the ability to react with other molecules.

Chemical bonds are formed between atoms when atoms combine by transferring or sharing electrons. Stable bonds occur when atoms establish complete outer valence shells. The chemical bonds of a molecule hold together the constituent atoms that make up that molecule. The number of bonds that an atom can form depends on the number of electrons required by that atom to fill its outer electron shell. A carbon atom, for example, has four electrons in its outer electron shell that can hold a maximum of eight electrons. A carbon atom, therefore, can establish up to four bonds with other elements.

Stable chemical bonds occur when atoms fill their outer shells with electrons.

Molecules—the fundamental units of compounds—are specific combinations of atoms formed when atoms form chemical bonds. They form these bonds by sharing or transferring electrons.

A molecular formula specifies the numbers and kinds of atoms of elements that are bonded together to form a molecule of a compound.

Three types of chemical bonds can form between atoms. **Ionic bonds** are based on attractions of ions with opposite electronic charges. **Covalent bonds** are based on sharing of electrons. **Hydrogen bonds** are based on interactions of hydrogen atoms with weak opposing electronic charges. Each type of bond is important in establishing and determining the properties of the molecules that make up living systems.

Ionic Bonds

Two ions with different charges can be held together by the mutual attraction of these charges. These are called electrostatic forces. A chemical bond based on such electrostatic forces is called an **ionic bond.** This is the type of bonding that holds sodium and chloride ions together in table salt (NaCl) (FIG. 3). Similarly, positively charged hydrogen ions can form ionic bonds with negatively charged chloride ions to form hydrochloric acid. The atoms of certain other elements similarly can lose or gain electrons and thereby establish ionic bonds.

In an ionic bond, two ions with different charges are held together by the mutual attraction of the opposite charges of the two ions.

Ionic bonds readily dissociate (break apart) in water. This is because of the interactions with water molecules. Hydrochloric acid, for example, readily dissociates in water into H^+ and Cl^-. The concentration or relative amount of H^+ formed by such dissociation of acids is what determines the acidity of a solution.

Ionic bonds typically dissociate in water.

Covalent Bonds

Covalent bonds are formed when atoms are held together by sharing electrons. Many of the molecules in living systems are based on the ability of carbon atoms to form covalent bonds. The covalent bonds between carbon atoms is what holds together the molecules that make up the structures of all living systems. The outer shell of carbon contains four electrons and is completed by the addition of four more electrons. Carbon atoms can form four covalent bonds. A carbon atom, for example, can combine with four hydro-

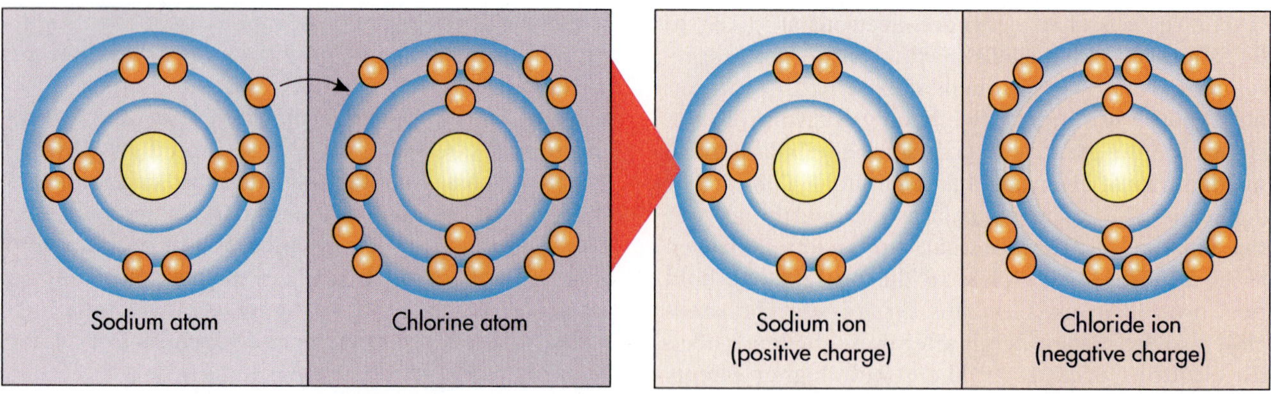

FIG. 3 The formation of ionic bonds involves the loss and gain of electrons. In the formation of NaCl, the chlorine atom gains an electron to fill its outer electron shell and the sodium atom loses an electron, so that all the remaining electron shells are filled. After the formation of the ionic bond, the sodium ion has a positive charge and the chloride ion a negative charge.

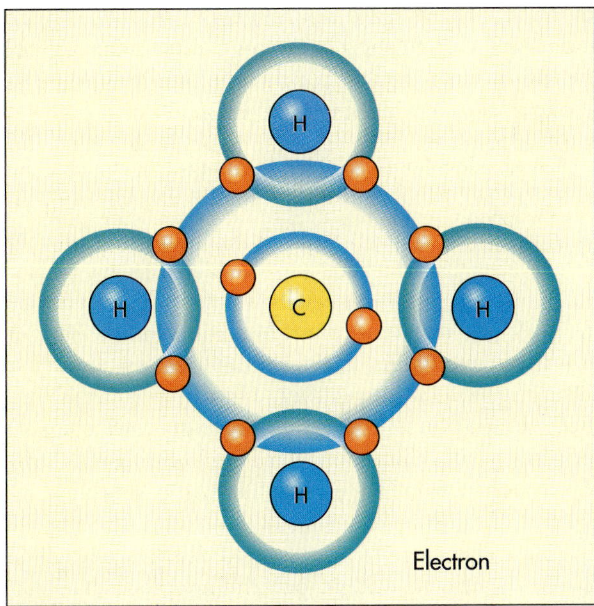

FIG. 4 The formation of the covalent bond involves the sharing of electrons. In methane, each hydrogen atom shares an electron with a carbon atom, completing the orbitals of the carbon and hydrogen atoms.

gen atoms to form methane (CH_4) (FIG. 4). Methane is a simple **organic compound,** that is, a molecule that contains carbon and hydrogen. In the methane molecule, the carbon atom shares four electrons to complete its outer shell. It shares one electron with each of the four hydrogen atoms. A hydrogen atom has one electron and can hold two in its only shell. Each hydrogen atom completes its shell by sharing one electron from the carbon atom. A carbon atom can also form a covalent bond with another carbon atom, as well as with hydrogen atoms to form a chain of carbon atoms linked to each other. A chain of carbon atoms with hydrogen atoms attached to the carbon atoms is called a hydrocarbon. Similarly, carbon forms covalent bonds with other atoms to establish the large and complex molecules of living systems.

Stable covalent bonds are formed when atoms completely fill their outer electron shells as a result of sharing electrons with other atoms.

The number of covalent bonds that a particular atom can form depends on the number of electrons in its outer electron shell and the number of electrons needed to complete that shell.

Water is an essential molecule for life. When water (H_2O) forms from the elements hydrogen and oxygen, the outer electron shells in both elements reach a stable configuration (FIG. 5). The oxygen atom initially has six electrons in the outer electron shell that can hold eight electrons. It completes its outer shell by sharing two electrons—one with each of the two hydrogen atoms. The hydrogen atoms each share an electron with oxygen so that they completely fill their outer electron shells.

In most cases only one pair of electrons is shared to form a **single bond.** A covalent single bond is represented as a line (—). In some cases, atoms share two pairs of electrons. This gives rise to a **double bond,** which is expressed as two lines (=). Double bonds occur most frequently when carbon is double bonded to carbon (C=C) or when carbon is double bonded to oxygen (C=O). They are found in many biologically important molecules. Carbon dioxide (CO_2), for example, is the molecule from which plants, algae, and most photosynthetic bacteria obtain the carbon to build cellular structures. It contains two double bonds between carbon and oxygen (O=C=O).

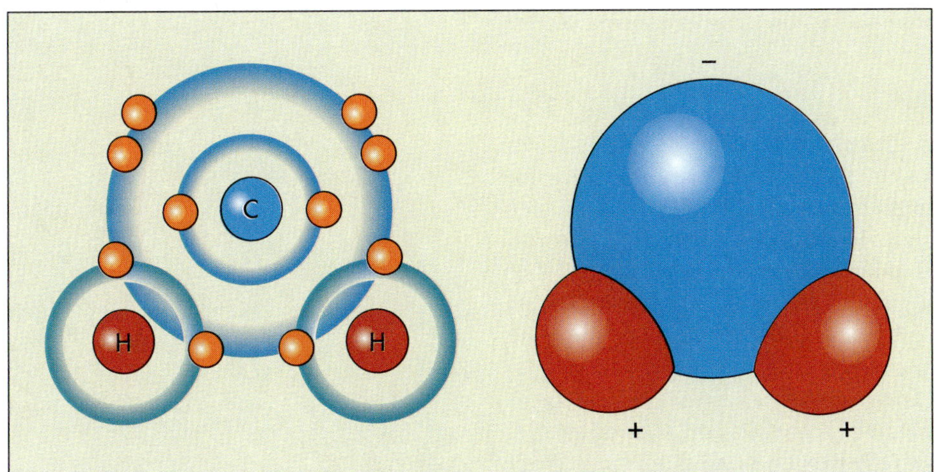

FIG. 5 The spatial arrangement of atoms in a water molecule *(left)* results in a dipole moment because of unequal distribution of electrons between hydrogen and water *(right)*. As a result, water is a good polar solvent because water can surround both positively and negatively charged ions.

Three pairs of electrons can form a **triple bond.** To form a triple bond, three electron pairs are shared between two atoms. A triple covalent bond is expressed as three single lines (≡). Molecular nitrogen (N_2) is an example of a biologically important molecule with a triple bond (N≡N) This triple bond structure is very stable and difficult to break. Although it constitutes 78% of the atmosphere, molecular nitrogen cannot be used by most organisms in their metabolism. A few bacterial species, however, are able to use molecular nitrogen. Such species are called nitrogen-fixing bacteria. They incorporate the nitrogen atoms from N_2 into proteins and other chemicals that make up their cellular structures. These nitrogen-fixing bacteria are extremely important because they form nitrogen-containing nutrients that can be used by other bacteria and higher organisms.

By sharing one, two, or three pairs of electrons, atoms can form single, double, and triple covalent bonds.

Covalent bonds are strong. A relatively large amount of energy is required to break them. Atoms held by covalent bonds generally do not dissociate in water as do ionic bonds. The covalent bonds between carbon atoms are strong enough to form the backbones of the major molecules of living systems. The fact that carbon atoms can form four single covalent bonds is important. This allows carbon to form backbone chains of covalently bonded carbon molecules. It also allows carbon to bond with other atoms, such as hydrogen, oxygen, or nitrogen. Covalent carbon-carbon bonds provide much of the stability needed to establish the very large molecules essential to the operation and reproduction of microorganisms and other living organisms. Such large molecules are called **macromolecules** and include DNA and proteins.

Biochemists have concluded that of all the naturally occurring elements only carbon atoms can form the bonds that will hold together the large molecules of living systems.

Hydrogen Bonds

When hydrogen forms a covalent bond with atoms of oxygen or nitrogen, the relatively large positive nucleus of these larger atoms attracts the hydrogen electron more strongly than the single hydrogen proton. This establishes **polarity** within the molecule. This means that one end of the molecule has a positive charge and the other a negative charge. The positively charged end of the molecule is the end with the hydrogen atoms. The positively charged end can be attracted to the negatively charged end of another molecule. In this way a **hydrogen bond** is formed. When molecules of water (H_2O), for example, come close to each other, a hydrogen atom of one of the water molecules is attracted to the negatively charged oxygen atoms of another (FIG. 6). The result is a lattice of water molecules that are held together by these hydrogen bonds established by charge interactions. Such hydrogen bonds do not link atoms together as strongly as do covalent bonds.

A hydrogen bond is formed when a hydrogen atom that is covalently bonded to an oxygen or a nitrogen atom is attracted to a polar atom in another molecule.

A hydrogen bond has only about 5% of the strength of a covalent bond. Although such hydrogen bonds are weak, they are important because they hold different molecules together. They help establish the three-dimensional structures of large molecules by forming weak bonds between atoms with long chains of covalently bonded atoms. They also establish important chemical properties of various molecules. For example, the capacity of water to dissolve many substances is due to water's polarity and its capacity to form hydrogen bonds with ions and polar molecules. Hydrogen bonds are also important in the formation of helical molecules.

Hydrogen bonds are relatively weak bonds that help establish important properties of molecules.

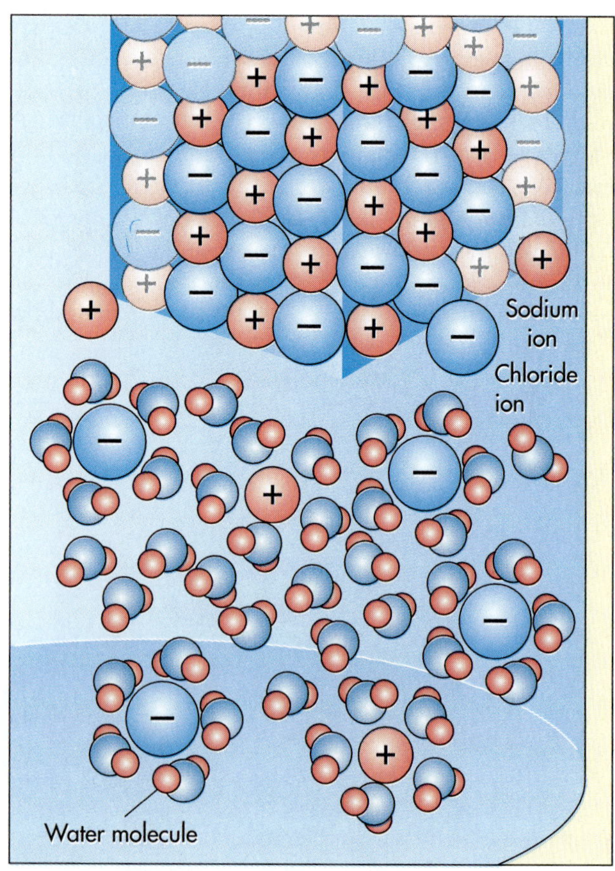

FIG. 6 Water forms hydrogen bonds with polar compounds. This allows water to act as a solvent. Most polar substances readily dissolve in water. The figure represents NaCl *(top)* dissolving in water.

Isomers and the Three-dimensional Structures of Molecules

Molecules that contain identical types and numbers of atoms, but that have different arrangements of those atoms, are called **isomers.** The isomers of a molecule can have very different properties because the ability of each isomer to interact with other chemicals depends in part on the precise position of its constituent atoms in three-dimensional space. For example, glucose and fructose—both of which have the molecular formula $C_6H_{12}O_6$—are isomers that have different chemical properties (FIG. 7). Some bacteria can use glucose but not fructose as a source of energy for their metabolism. Other isomers can be distinguished based on how they rotate light: those rotating light to the left are called L-isomers and those rotating light to the right are called D-isomers (L stands for levorotary [left turning] and D for dextrorotary [right turning]. The amino acids that make up proteins are all L-amino acids; D-amino acids occur only in rare and special molecules of living organisms, such as the cell walls of bacteria.

Molecules with different arrangements of the same atoms (isomers) often have different chemical and physical properties.

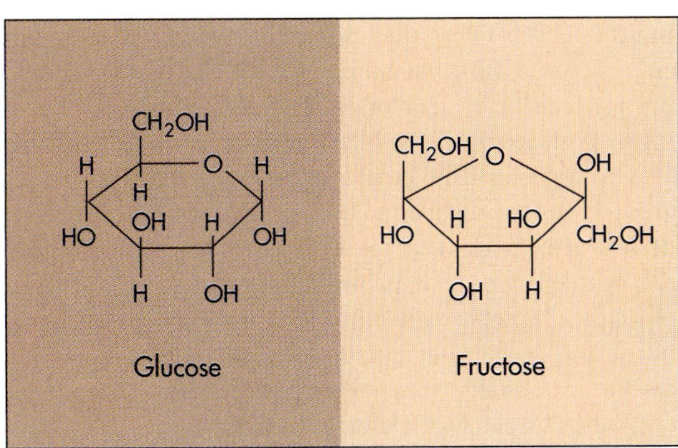

FIG. 7 The sugars glucose and fructose are isomers. They have the same elemental composition but their atoms are arranged differently.

Functional Groups

When certain atoms are bound together and behave chemically as a unit that is part of a larger molecule, they are called a functional group. **Functional groups** act in the same way regardless of the molecules in which they occur (FIG. 8). Functional groups determine some of the characteristics, such as solubility, and chemical reactivity of the molecules to which they are attached.

Bonding of specific atoms that behave as a unit form a functional group within a molecule.

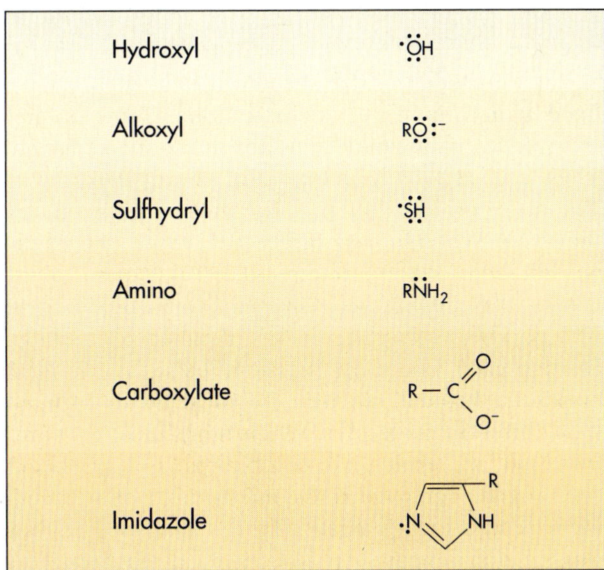

FIG. 8 The chemical characteristics of a substance are determined in large part by its functional groups.

Functional groups have specific chemical properties, even when they are attached to very different molecules.

The bonding of an oxygen atom to a hydrogen atom forms a polar **hydroxyl (-OH) functional group.** The hydroxyl group has polarity because shared electrons of a covalent bond are drawn closer to the oxygen atom than to the hydrogen atom. This gives the hydroxyl group a slightly negative oxygen atom and a slightly positive hydrogen atom. Alcohols such as ethanol and glycerol are organic molecules that have hydroxyl functional groups. They tend to be relatively soluble in water. Alcohols dissolve in water because of the hydrogen bonding between water molecules and the hydroxyl group of the alcohol.

The bonding of a nitrogen atom with two hydrogen atoms forms a polar functional group, called an **amino (-NH_2) functional group.** The bonding of carbon with oxygen and a hydroxyl group forms a polar **carboxyl (-COOH) functional group.** Amino acids, which are the building blocks of proteins, have both amino and carboxyl functional groups.

Functional groups are important because they permit molecules to react with each other in predictable ways. In some cases, reactions between functional groups form bonds that link molecules together. This is how small molecules can be joined to form large molecules. Proteins, for example, are large molecules that are assembled by linking smaller amino acid molecules. Other functional groups have characteristic properties and engage in chemical reactions that are essential for sustaining microorganisms and other living systems.

CHEMICAL REACTIONS

So far we have considered molecules as if they were fixed structures that remain stationary and do not change. In reality, molecules are in constant motion. They possess **kinetic energy,** the energy of motion. The faster molecules move, the more kinetic energy they have. When moving molecules collide, there may be sufficient kinetic energy to break bonds apart. When this occurs, the atoms can form new bonds. This permits new arrangements of molecules to form. During each chemical reaction, existing chemical bonds are broken and new chemical bonds form to yield different molecules. When molecules react and form new molecules, the combinations of atoms get rearranged. The total kinds and number of atoms always remain unchanged. Atoms can be neither formed nor destroyed in any chemical reaction. This **conservation of matter** is a fundamental law governing the universe.

Kinetic energy, the energy of motion, is used to break chemical bonds.

The law of conservation of matter states that atoms cannot be created or destroyed in chemical reactions.

CHEMICAL EQUATIONS

The conservation of matter always applies to all chemical reactions, including the chemical reactions occurring in living systems. There must be a balance between what goes into a chemical reaction, the **reactants,** and what is produced by that reaction, the **products.** The **chemical equation** describes the relationship between the reactants and products. The reactants are shown on the left side and the products are shown on the right side of the equation. If elements are the "letters" of chemistry and molecules are the "words," then chemical equations are the "sentences" in the language of chemistry. A chemical equation identifies the reactants and products by name or chemical formula. It permits chemists to describe the changes that occur during chemical reactions.

In a **balanced chemical equation,** the number of atoms of each element in the reactant molecules must equal the number of product molecules of that element. For example, the equation for the reaction of sodium chloride (NaCl) in water to form sodium (Na^+) and chloride (Cl^-) ions is written:

$$NaCl \longrightarrow Na^+ + Cl^-$$

The numbers of sodium and chlorine atoms on both sides of the equation are the same. The equation is properly balanced. Water is required for this reaction to occur. It is not shown in the equation because it is not changed or transformed in the process of the reaction. When a substance acts as a solvent and does not participate directly in the reaction, it is not shown within the equation. Sometimes, however, the solvent is indicated above the arrow to show that its presence is necessary for the reaction to occur.

$$NaCl \xrightarrow{\text{water}} Na^+ + Cl^-$$

Chemical equations show the changes that occur during a chemical reaction.

The chemical equation shows the balance between reactants and products.

EQUILIBRIUM

Virtually all chemical reactions are reversible. In a reversible reaction, the reactants can become the products and the products the reactants. The direction of the reaction depends in part on the concentrations of reactants and products. The likelihood of molecules colliding with sufficient kinetic energy to break bonds depends on the relative abundances of molecules with sufficient kinetic energies to react. Concentrations of reactants and products are expressed in units called moles. A **mole** is a measure of the number of molecules (6×10^{23} molecules). A mole is equal to the weight in grams of the molecular weight of a molecule. Thus, 1 mole of water weighs 18 grams because the molecular weight of water is 18, the sum of the molecular weights of two ^{1}H atoms and one ^{16}O atom.

The greater the concentration of reactants, the greater the opportunity for collisions to occur and, hence, the faster the forward reaction. The greater the concentration of products, the faster the reverse reaction. As more and more product molecules form, fewer and fewer reactant molecules remain. This lowers the rate of the forward reaction. As the concentration of product molecules increases, they will collide more frequently with each other than before. In some cases the reaction is reversed so that the original reactants are reformed. Eventually, a balance—called **equilibrium**—is achieved between the reactants and products of the forward and reverse reactions. At equilibrium the rates of the forward and reverse reactions are equal. This does not mean that the amounts of the products and reactants are equal. In this state there is no net change in the concentrations of reactants and products even though the molecular reactions are still continuing.

Chemical reactions are reversible and chemical reactions tend toward a state of equilibrium.

At equilibrium, the rates of the forward and the reverse reactions are equal and there is no further net change in the concentrations of reactants and products.

Energy and Chemical Reactions

There is only a finite amount of energy in the universe. This energy cannot be created or destroyed. Energy, however, can be converted from one form to another. The various forms of energy include the chemical energy stored in molecular bonds (*potential* or *stored energy*), kinetic energy (energy of motion), electrical energy (energy produced by movement of electrons), and radiant energy (heat or light energy) from the sun. During chemical reactions chemical bonds are broken and new bonds are formed. Energy is transformed during these reactions. In a chemical reaction there always is a net balance between the energy required to break chemical bonds, the energy released by the new bonds that are formed, and the energy—such as heat energy—that is exchanged with the surroundings.

Energy is neither created nor destroyed in chemical reactions; however, energy can be converted from one form to another.

The products of chemical reactions can end up with either less or more energy than the reactants had. Some chemical reactions release energy. Others require the input of energy. Energy-requiring reactions can occur only when extra energy enters into the reaction. The extra energy must come from some other system.

Chemical reactions involve energy changes.

Most often the energy needed to drive energy-requiring chemical reactions in living systems is supplied by **ATP (adenosine triphosphate).** ATP is called an energy-rich or high-energy compound. It contains chemical bonds that can release a relatively large amount of energy (FIG. 9). The release of this energy from the ATP molecule can be coupled to energy-requiring reactions. In this fashion, energy-releasing reactions drive the energy-requiring reactions of cell growth, movement, and transport. ATP serves almost universally in biological systems as the energy source for energy-requiring reactions. Cellular processes requiring energy most likely depend on the use of ATP. As such, ATP can be termed the *universal currency of energy* in biological systems.

ATP has a central role in the flow of energy through living systems.

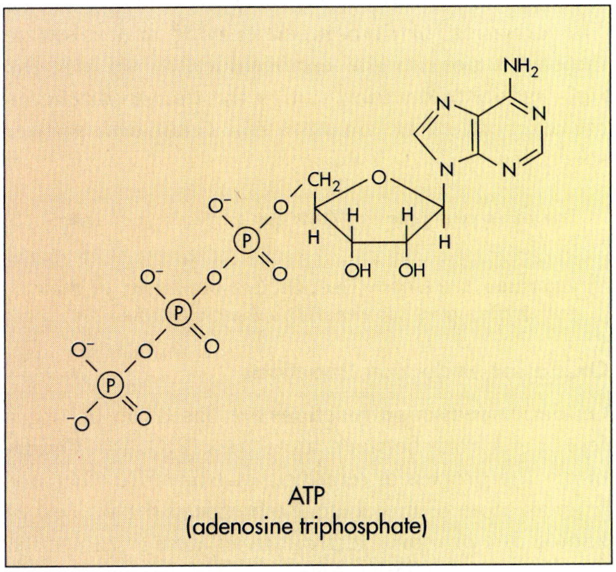

FIG. 9 ATP is a compound with high-energy phosphate bonds.

Types of Chemical Reactions

Enzymatic Reactions

For a chemical reaction to occur, the reactant molecules must collide with sufficient kinetic energy to bring about the reaction. The amount of energy needed is called the **activation energy.** The activation energy is the amount of energy needed to start the reaction. It is not the amount consumed or released by the breaking and forming of chemical bonds. A chemical reaction can occur only when the energy of activation is provided to start the reaction. Chemists often heat chemicals with a Bunsen burner to provide the energy needed for chemical reactions to occur. But cells operate at nearly constant temperatures. Cells employ other methods to overcome the energy barrier to starting a chemical reaction presented by the activation energy.

Biological systems depend on enzymes to lower the activation energy of a chemical reaction (FIG. 10). **Enzymes** are proteins that act as biological catalysts; some RNA molecules, called ribozymes, can similarly

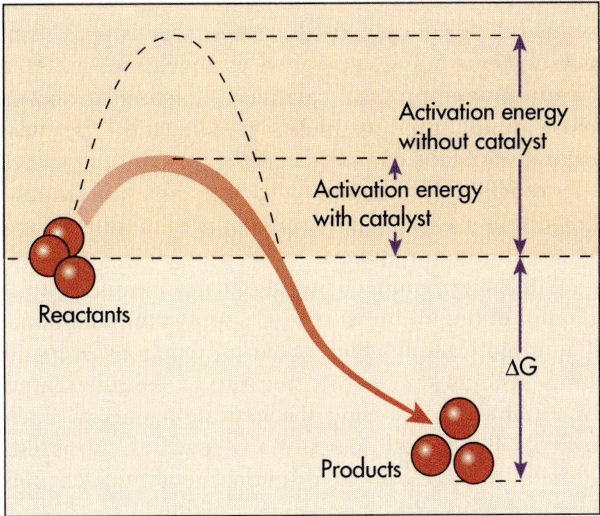

FIG. 10 An input of energy called the activation energy is needed to start a chemical reaction. A catalyst lowers the activation energy. In biological systems, enzymes serve as the catalysts to lower the activation energy.

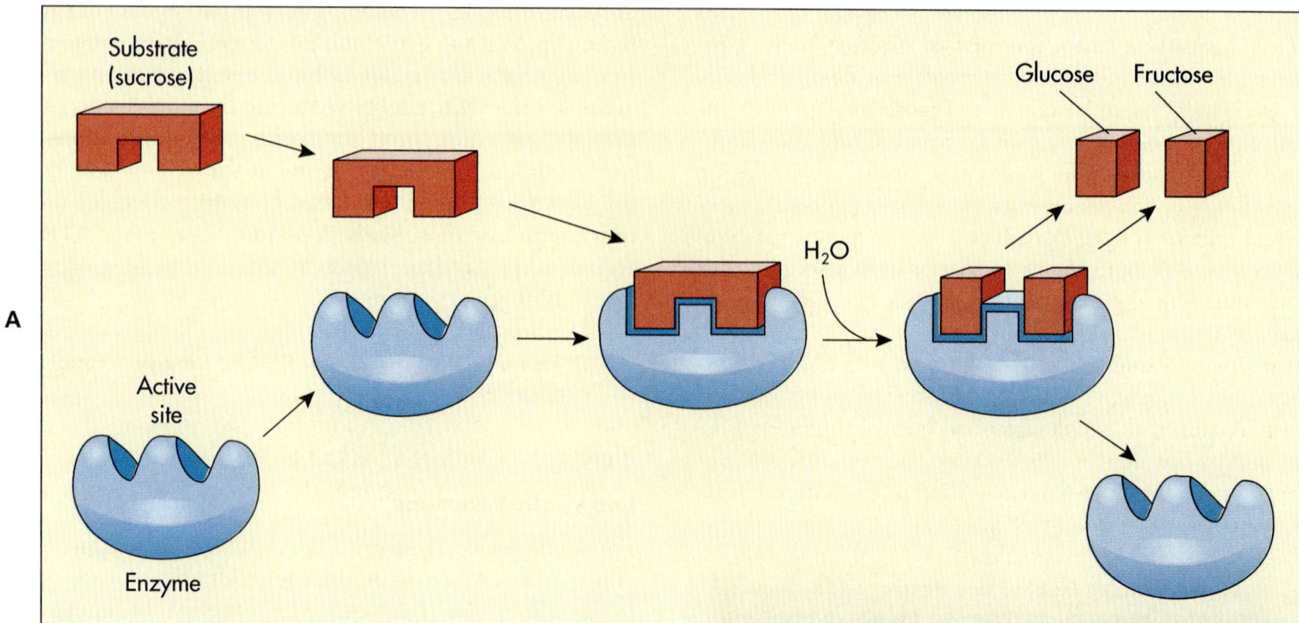

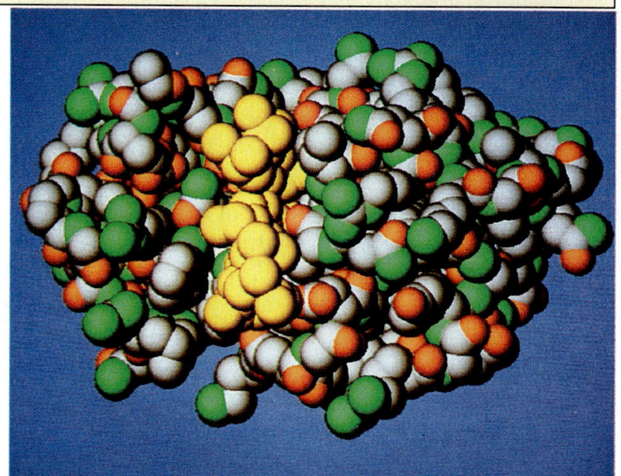

FIG. 11 **A,** The fit between the enzyme and the substrate to form an enzyme-substrate complex has been likened to that of a lock and key. Actually, this interaction modifies the three-dimensional structure of the enzyme so that the substrate induces its fit to the enzyme. The precision of fit is responsible for the high degree of specificity of enzymes for particular substrates. **B,** Model showing the fit between the *polysaccharide* component of a bacterial cell wall *(yellow substrate)* and the active site of the enzyme lysozyme that catalyzes the breakdown of the bacterial cell wall.

act as biological catalysts. A catalyst speeds up a reaction without being consumed in that reaction. At a given temperature, a catalyzed reaction proceeds more rapidly than an uncatalyzed reaction. Because catalysts are not consumed in the reaction, enzymes theoretically may continue to function indefinitely. Since they can be reused, only small amounts of enzymes are often required.

Without enzymes, chemical reactions would not occur fast enough within a cell to support life functions. The rapid rates at which chemical reactions occur in living systems are possible because of the role played by enzymes in lowering the activation energy. Each microbial cell must possess many enzymes, thousands in fact, to carry out the essential metabolic activities involved in its growth and reproduction.

An enzyme works by binding with a molecule called the **substrate.** An enzyme can bond only to a specific substrate. The degree of substrate specificity exhibited by enzymes reflects the fact that the enzyme and the substrate must fit together in a specific way (FIG. 11). The precision of fit between enzyme and substrate molecules permits the establishment of exactly the right spatial orientation so that the numerous chemical reactions of an organism can occur with greater speed.

Enzymes are proteins that act as biological catalysts.

Enzymes are highly specific, both in terms of their substrates and the reactions they catalyze.

Oxidation-reduction Reactions

Oxidation-reduction reactions are based on the transfers of electrons between molecules (FIG. 12). **Oxidation** is the process of removing one or more electrons from an atom or molecule. **Reduction** is the process of adding one or more electrons to an atom or molecule. Oxidation and reduction are coupled because they involve the simultaneous removal of an electron from

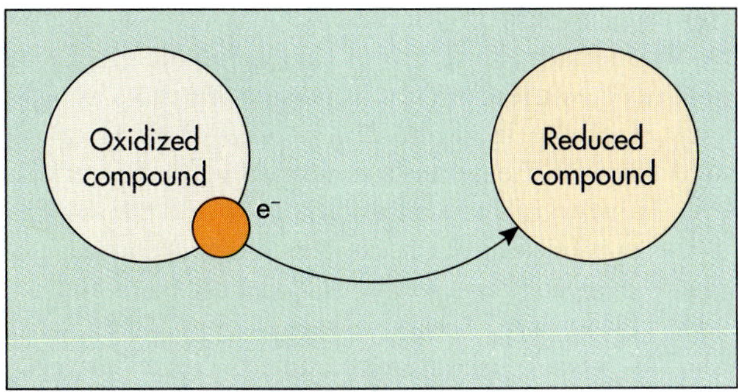

FIG. 12 Oxidation-reduction reactions involve an exchange of electrons. The substance that accepts an electron becomes reduced and the substance that donates an electron becomes oxidized.

one substance and the addition of that electron to another. Often in biological systems a proton or hydrogen ion (H^+) is transferred with the electron during oxidation-reduction reactions. Oxidation reactions that involve the removal of an electron and hydrogen ion are called *dehydrogenation reactions.* Reduction reactions that involve the addition of an electron and hydrogen ion are called *hydrogenation reactions.*

An example of biological oxidation-reduction reactions is shown in the following equation:

$$X_{reduced} + NAD^+ \longrightarrow X_{oxidized} + NADH + H^+$$

In this example, molecule X serves as the source of two electrons and two protons that are transferred to a molecule of nicotinamide adenine dinucleotide (NAD^+). Molecule X becomes oxidized (two electrons are removed) and NAD^+ becomes reduced (two electrons are added). At the same time, two protons are removed from molecule X. One of these is added to NAD^+ (so that the reduced form of NAD^+ is written as NADH) and the other proton (H^+) is released into the medium.

Oxidation is the removal of electrons and reduction is the addition of electrons.

The oxidation of one substance must always be coupled with the reduction of another.

Oxidation-reduction reactions are important in the metabolism of cells for energy changes and the formation of new cellular material. Oxidation-reduction reactions can release energy that is used to form ATP. For example, during cellular respiration the oxidation of glucose to form carbon dioxide is coupled with the reduction of oxygen to form water. This provides the energy to drive ATP production. Living organisms use the energy released from such oxidation-reduction reactions for growth, reproduction, and other life processes—such as movement.

Oxidation-reduction reactions also are used by living systems to store energy. Thus, when carbon dioxide is reduced to glucose during photosynthesis, energy is stored within the organic molecules of the organism. This stored energy can later be released when organisms oxidize sugars during cellular respiration.

Oxidation-reduction reactions can release energy and are used to fuel cellular reactions, to store energy, and for biosynthesis of the macromolecules of the cell.

Acid-base Reactions

Another important type of chemical reaction is the acid-base reaction. An **acid** is a substance that dissociates into one or more hydrogen ions (H^+) and one or more negative ions (anions). Thus an acid can also be defined as a proton (H^+) donor. A **base,** on the other hand, is a substance that dissociates into one or more positive ions (cations), plus one or more anions that can accept or combine with protons. Thus sodium hydroxide (NaOH) is a base because in water it dissociates to release hydroxyl ions (OH^-), which have a strong attraction for protons. Bases that produce hydroxyl ions are among the most important proton acceptors.

Acids increase the concentration of hydrogen ions in solution.

Bases decrease the concentration of hydrogen ions in solution.

The amount of H^+ in a solution is expressed by a logarithmic pH scale that ranges from 0 to 14 (FIG. 13). The **pH** of a solution is the negative logarithm to the base 10 of the hydrogen ion concentration.

$$pH = -\log[H^+]$$

The greater the hydrogen ion concentration the lower the pH. Because the pH scale is logarithmic, a change of one whole pH unit represents a tenfold change from the previous concentration of hydrogen ions. Thus a solution with a pH 1 has 10 times more H^+ ions than one with a pH 2 and 100 times more H^+ ions than a solution with a pH 3. Acidic solutions contain more H^+ ions than OH^- ions and have a pH lower than 7. Basic or alkaline solutions have more OH^- ions than H^+ ions and a pH higher than 7. In pure water the concentrations of H^+ and OH^- are equal and the pH is 7. This pH level is called **neutral.**

pH describes the concentration of hydrogen ions.

Acidic solutions have pH values less than 7; basic solutions have pH values greater than 7; water is neutral (pH = 7).

When an acid reacts with a base, there is a reaction between the hydrogen ions produced by the acid and the hydroxyl ions produced by the base. Acid-base reactions result in the formation of water and a salt. For example, when hydrochloric acid reacts with sodium hydroxide, the products are sodium chloride and water.

$$HCl + NaOH \longrightarrow NaCl + H_2O$$

$$H^+ + Cl^- + Na^+ + OH^- \longrightarrow Na^+ + Cl^- + H_2O$$

If the amounts of acid and base are balanced, all the free hydrogen ions react with all the free hydroxyl ions. This is known as a **neutralization reaction** because it results in a neutral solution of the salt. The hydrogen ion and hydroxyl ion concentrations are balanced and thus achieve a neutral pH of 7.

As living organisms take up nutrients, carry out chemical reactions, and excrete wastes, they may change the balance of acids and bases. This change may occur both within their cells and in the surrounding solution. When bacteria are grown in laboratory medium, for example, some of the chemicals produced by their metabolism are acids that can alter the pH of the medium. Unchecked, the pH of the medium would become too acidic for the bacteria to live. To prevent this, microbiologists add pH buffers to the culture medium. A **buffer** limits the change of pH by reacting with acids or bases to form neutral salts. Phosphate buffer containing K_2HPO_4 and KH_2PO_4 is often used to maintain a pH near 7.0 in culture media.

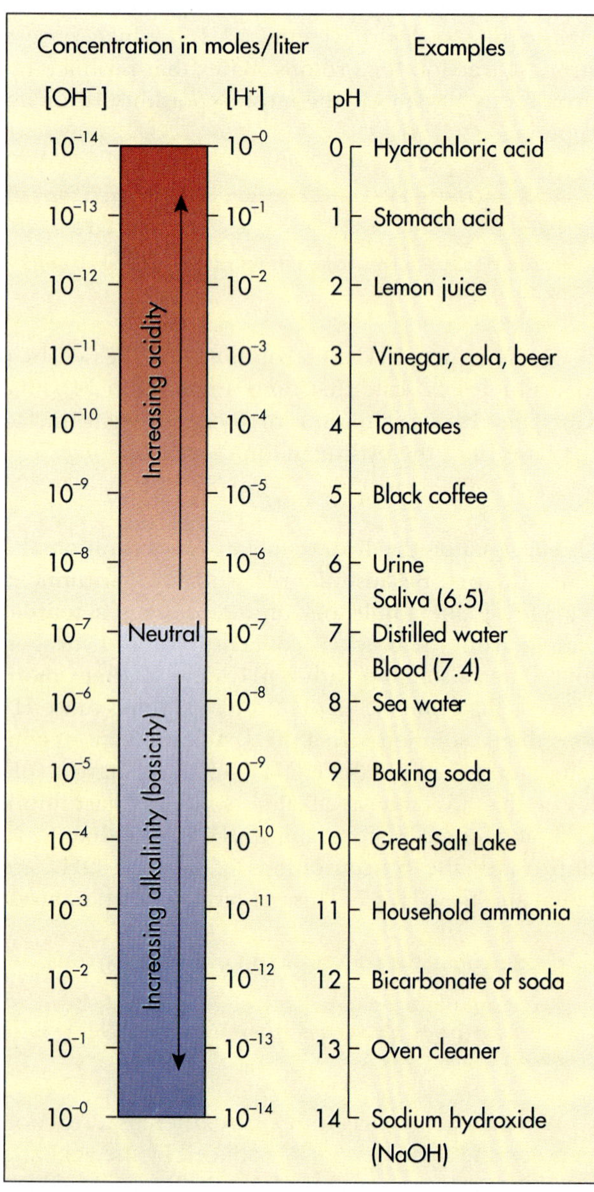

FIG. 13 The pH scale showing pH values of some common substances.

Condensation and Hydrolysis Reactions

Condensation reactions involve the bonding of two molecules into one. Condensation reactions are very important in forming the large molecules of living systems. In a **condensation reaction,** a hydrogen ion (H^+) removed from one functional group of a molecule and a hydroxyl ion (OH^-) from another combine to form a molecule of water (H_2O). The component molecules are joined by a covalent bond (FIG. 14). For example, glucose molecules combine into larger molecules containing multiple glucose subunits. Large molecules formed from the bonding of many subunit molecules are called **polymers.** The polymers produced by condensation reactions may contain millions of individual subunit molecules, called **monomers**, which may or may not be identical. As a rule polymers are less soluble and more stable (long-lived) than monomers. Polymers are important components of many biological structures.

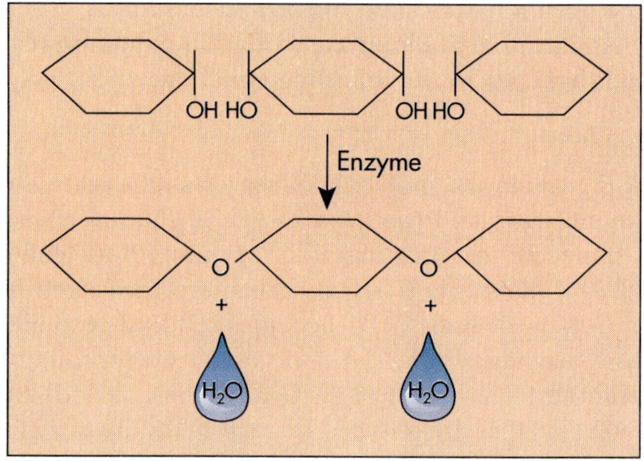

FIG. 14 Polymers are formed when smaller chemical units join together in a condensation reaction.

The reverse reaction is **hydrolysis.** A hydrolytic reaction breaks down polymers into their component monomers (FIG. 15). Covalent bonds between parts of molecules are broken and H^+ and OH^- ions from water become attached to the component subunit molecules. Hydrolysis reactions, such as the hydrolysis

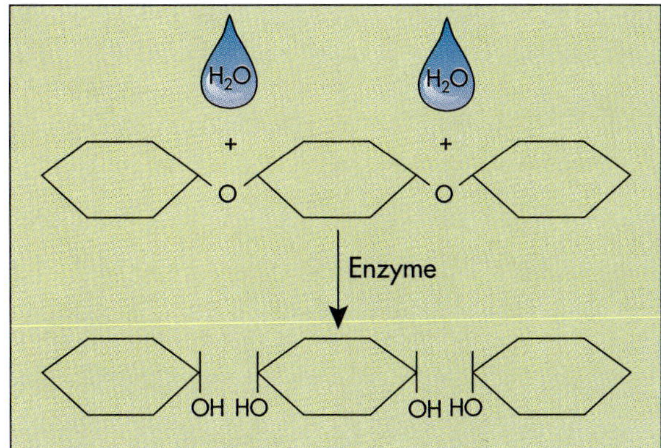

of ATP, are important for the extraction of energy from molecules. They yield the energy needed to support energy-requiring reactions in cells. Hydrolysis reactions also produce the small molecules that are used by cells for the synthesis of the large molecules that make up the structures of organisms.

Condensation and hydrolysis reactions permit the linking and breaking apart of molecules, including some of the very large molecules of living systems.

FIG. 15 Large molecules are broken down into smaller molecules in hydrolysis reactions.

MOLECULES OF LIVING SYSTEMS

A common feature of all living systems is that they are based on carbon atoms. Organic molecules that contain carbon form the essential components of all living organisms. Carbon, hydrogen, oxygen, and nitrogen atoms comprise 99% of the mass of living organisms. Carbon atoms are able to establish strong bonds with these atoms, as well as with other carbon atoms. Therefore carbon is well suited for uniting the atoms of living systems into stable macromolecules. Microorganisms are composed of various organic macromolecules representing four major classes of chemicals: carbohydrates, lipids, proteins, and nucleic acids. In addition, microorganisms are also composed largely of water. All living systems depend on the availability of water and various other inorganic molecules, such as carbon dioxide and phosphate.

WATER

Of the inorganic compounds of living systems, water is without doubt the most abundant and important. Life cannot exist in the absence of water. Water usually comprises over 75% of the weight of a living cell. Water serves as a solvent that permits the dissociation of chemicals, allowing chemical reactions of many molecules to occur within living cells that produce numerous new combinations of molecules.

Water's structural and chemical properties make it particularly suitable for living cells (FIG. 16). The hydrogen (H^+) and hydroxyl (OH^-) portions of water (HOH) can split apart and later rejoin. This enables water to participate as a reactant or a product in many chemical reactions. Water molecules, for example, are

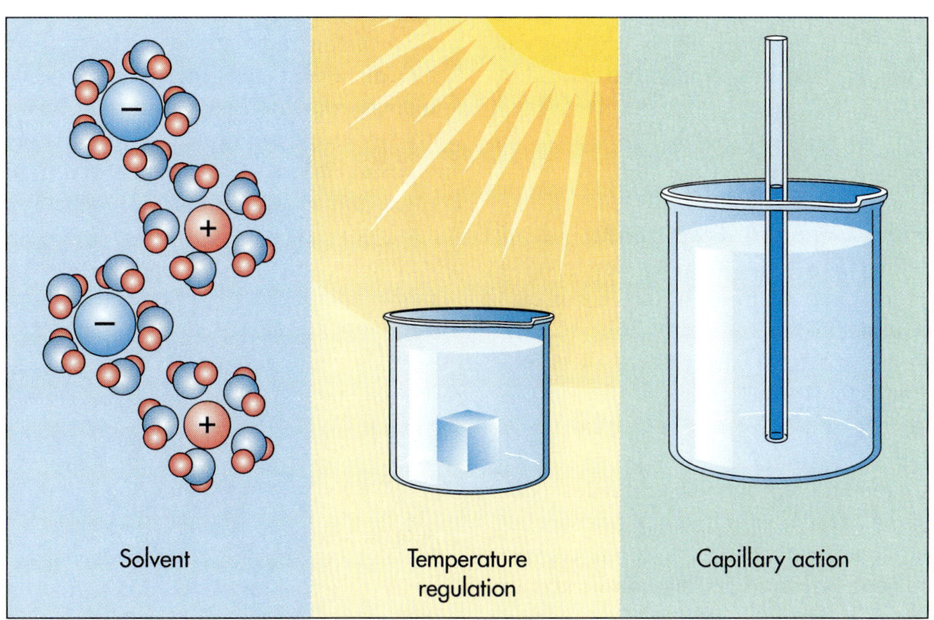

FIG. 16 Water is essential for life. It has critical roles in life's functions, including its ability to regulate temperature and to act as a solvent, that are based largely on its ability to form hydrogen bonds.

involved in many chemical reactions as an important source of the hydrogen and oxygen atoms that are incorporated into the numerous organic compounds that make up living cells.

Because the oxygen region of the water molecule has a slightly negative charge and the hydrogen region has a slightly positive charge, water has a **polar** nature. The polarity of water means that many charged or polar substances dissolve in water by dissociating into individual molecules. Molecules dissolved in water are called **solutes.** The negatively charged part of the water molecule is attracted to the positively charged part of the solute molecule. At the same time the positively charged part of the water molecule is attracted to the negatively charged part of the solute molecule. Solid NaCl, for example, dissolves in water by dissociating into the positively charged sodium ions (Na^+) and chloride ions (Cl^-). The positive sodium ions are attracted to the negatively charged oxygen atom of water. The negative chloride ions are attracted to the positively charged hydrogen atoms of water. Thus the Na^+ and Cl^- ions of solid NaCl are separated by the water molecule and table salt dissolves in water.

This polarity of the water molecule also means that hydrogen bonds are formed between nearby water molecules. The hydrogen bonds between water molecules make water an excellent temperature regulator. Cells are mostly water and live surrounded by water. Water readily maintains a constant temperature and tends to protect cells from sudden environmental temperature changes. Also, a great deal of heat energy is required to separate water molecules—held together by hydrogen bonds—from each other to form water vapor, that is, to convert liquid water into gaseous steam. Water exists in the liquid state at temperatures of 0° to 100° C. Liquid water is available on most of the Earth's surface and readily available for use as a solvent.

CARBOHYDRATES

Carbohydrates are a large and diverse group of organic compounds. This group includes sugars and compounds such as starch that are derived from sugars. Each sugar molecule has a fixed ratio of carbon:hydrogen:oxygen of 1:2:1. Therefore, all **carbohydrates** have the same basic chemical formula—$C_n(H_2O)_n$, where n is a whole number equal to or greater than 3.

Carbohydrates include the **monosaccharides** (saccharide is the Greek word for sugar). Monosaccharides are simple sugars with three to seven carbon atoms (FIG. 17). Monosaccharides may be linked to form larger carbohydrate molecules. A **disaccharide** contains two monosaccharide units, an **oligosaccharide** contains three to ten monosaccharide units, and a **polysaccharide** contains more than ten monosaccharide units. Monosaccharides with five or more carbon atoms tend to form ring structures when dissolved in water. Thus, within cells, **pentoses,** which have five carbon atoms, and **hexoses,** which have six carbon atoms, form molecules with ring structures. Pentoses and hexoses are biologically significant. They both serve as energy sources and as the structural backbones of large informational molecules. Deoxyribose is a pentose found in deoxyribonucleic acid (DNA), the genetic material of the cell. Ribose, another pentose, is found in ribonucleic acid (RNA). RNA is the molecule used to transfer genetic information within cells for the expression of genetic information. Glucose is a common hexose and the main energy-supplying molecule of living cells.

Disaccharides are formed when two monosaccharides join in a condensation reaction (FIG. 18). For

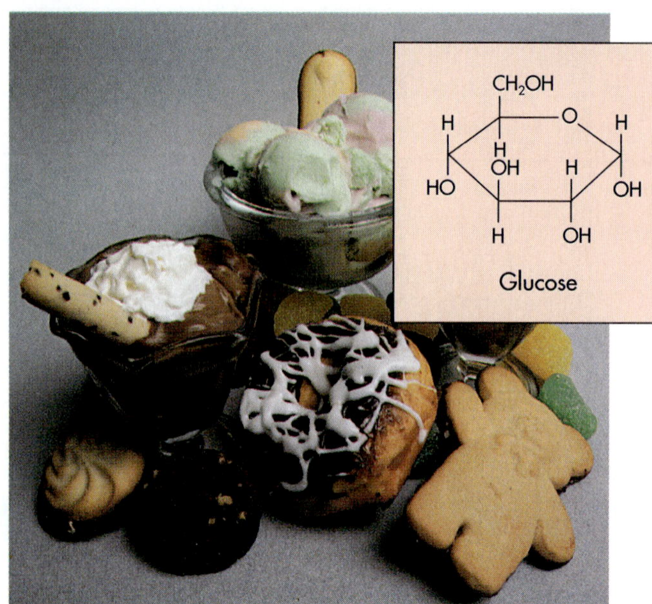

FIG. 17 A monosaccharide is the fundamental chemical unit of carbohydrates.

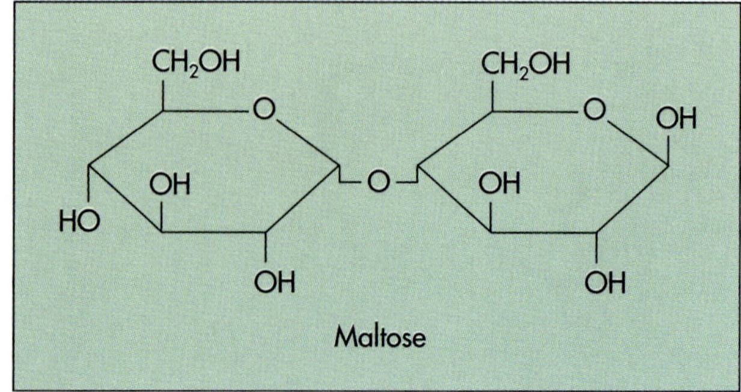

FIG. 18 A disaccharide is composed of two monosaccharides.

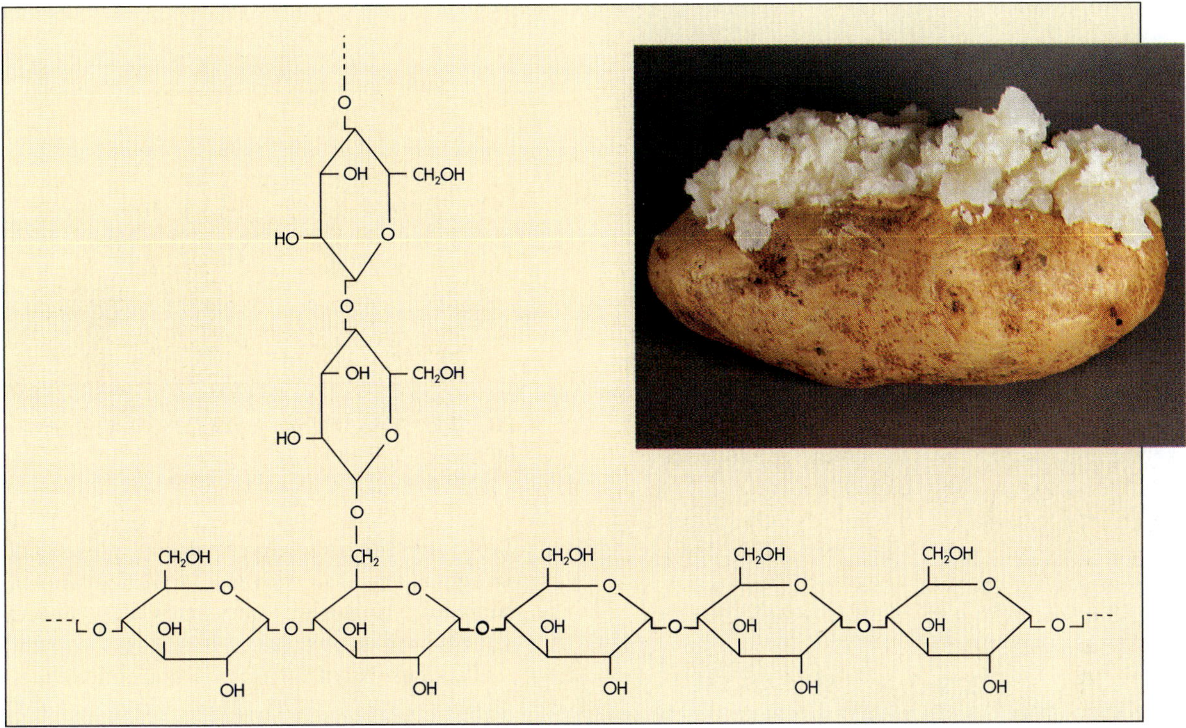

FIG. 19 A polysaccharide is composed of numerous monosaccharides.

example, molecules of two monosaccharides, glucose and fructose, combine to form a molecule of the disaccharide sucrose (table sugar). Sucrose is the form in which carbohydrates are transported through plants. The disaccharide lactose is formed by the bonding of one glucose and one galactose subunit. Lactose occurs in the milk of mammals. The bond linking the monosaccharides in these disaccharides is a type of covalent bond known as a glycosidic bond. In a **glycosidic bond** an oxygen atom forms a bridge between two carbon atoms.

Many monosaccharide units can likewise be linked to form **polysaccharides** (FIG. 19). Polysaccharides, like starch and glycogen, are composed of many units of glucose that are linked together. They function as important carbon and energy reserves in bacteria, plants, and animals. Other polysaccharides, such as cellulose, function as structural supports as in the cell walls of algal and plant cells.

Carbohydrates serve as sources of energy for cells and make up key structures, such as the walls that surround some cells.

LIPIDS

Like carbohydrates, **lipids** are organic compounds composed of atoms of carbon, hydrogen, and oxygen. Lipids, however, are mostly made up of carbon and hydrogen. They have very little oxygen compared to carbohydrates. Therefore lipids are nonpolar and **hydrophobic.** Being hydrophobic means that they do not readily dissolve in water. Although most lipids are insoluble in water, they dissolve readily in nonpolar solvents such as ether, chloroform, and alcohol. Some lipids function in the storage and transport of energy. Others are key components of membranes, protective coats, and other structures of cells.

Lipids are hydrophobic nonpolar molecules

Many lipids have fatty acid components (FIG. 20). A **fatty acid molecule** consists of a carboxyl (–COOH) functional group attached to the end of a long hydrocarbon chain composed only of carbon and hydrogen atoms. Thus fatty acids contain a highly hydrophobic hydrocarbon chain, usually 16 to 18 carbon atoms long, and a carboxyl functional group that is highly hydrophilic. Being hydrophilic means that it is attracted to water molecules. This gives fatty acids interesting chemical properties, such as the ability of part of the fatty acid molecule to associate with water molecules while the other part is pushed away. The carboxyl functional group can donate hydrogen ions in a chemical reaction with the alcohol group of another molecule. In this way fatty acids can combine with alcohols such as glycerol to form fats.

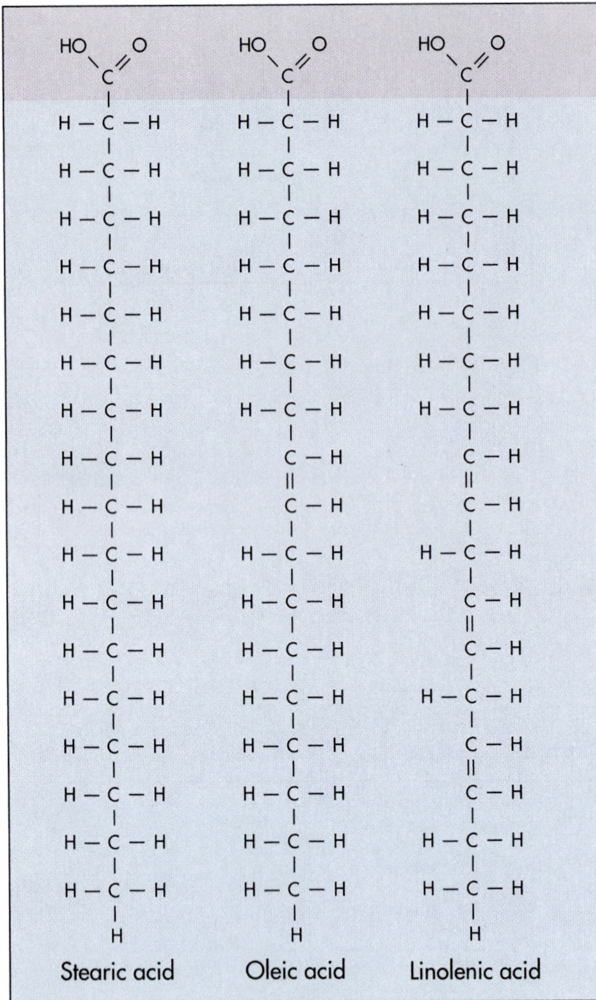

FIG. 20 A fatty acid is an organic acid. The portion of the fatty acid with the functional carboxylic acid group is polar and hydrophilic (attracted to water) whereas the remaining hydrocarbon portion is hydrophobic (repelled by water).

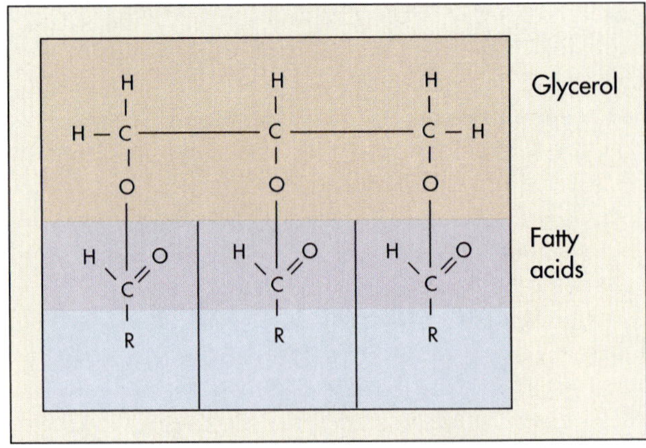

FIG. 21 A triglyceride is composed of glycerol and three fatty acids.

boxyl functional group can donate hydrogen ions in a chemical reaction with the alcohol group of another molecule. In this way fatty acids can combine with alcohols such as glycerol to form fats.

Fats consist of fatty acids bonded to the 3-carbon alcohol glycerol (FIG. 21). In the fat molecule the fatty acid is usually stretched out like a flexible tail. A fat molecule is formed when a molecule of glycerol combines with one, two, or three fatty acid molecules to form a **monoglyceride, diglyceride,** or **triglyceride,** respectively. The chemical bond formed between a fatty acid and an alcohol group of glycerol is called an **ester linkage.** Plants and animals store lipids as triglycerides. Glycerides are the most abundant lipids and the richest source of energy in the human body. They are insoluble in water and tend to clump into fat globules.

Complex lipids have additional components such as phosphate, nitrogen, or sulfur, or small hydrophilic

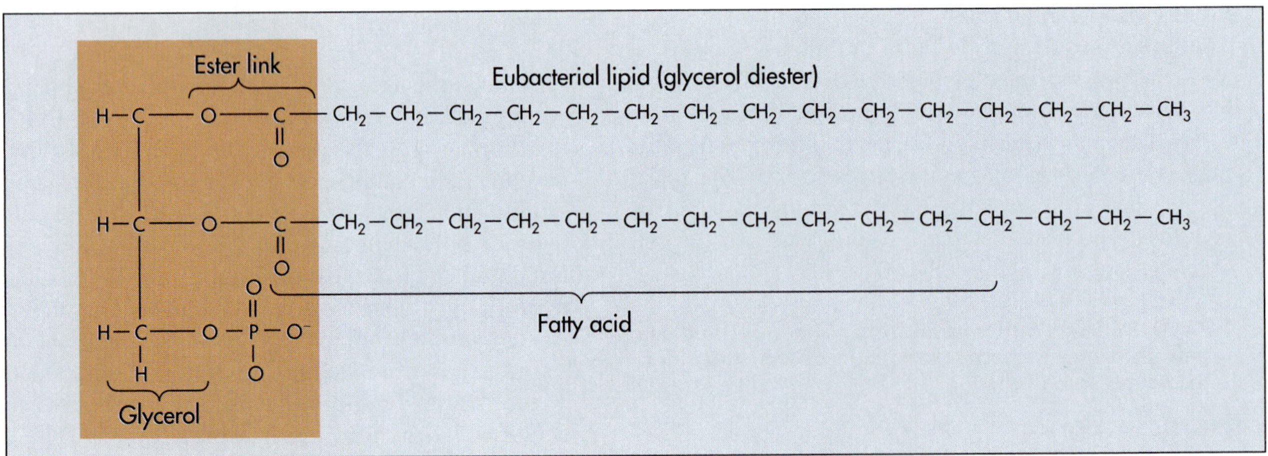

FIG. 22 Phospholipids are composed of glycerol linked to two fatty acids and a phosphate group.

joined to lipids). These glycolipids give the bacterium a wax-like covering that contributes to its distinctive acid-fast staining characteristic.

Phospholipids are complex lipids made up of glycerol, two fatty acids, and a phosphate functional group (FIG. 22). Phospholipids are the major chemical component of biological membranes, including the plasma membrane. Their molecules contain both hydrophobic and hydrophilic portions. This enables phospholipids to aggregate into bilayers in which the hydrophobic components of each layer interact with each other and the hydrophilic components are exposed to the aqueous interior or exterior of the cell. The chemical properties of phospholipids make them effective structural components of a cell's plasma membrane. Water soluble (polar) substances are unable to flow through the hydrophobic fatty acid portion of the bilayer. Phospholipids, thus, enable the plasma membrane to restrict the flow of materials into and out of the cell.

Phospholipids, which have hydrophilic and hydrophobic portions, form an integral part of the plasma membrane.

Steroids are also lipids but they are structurally very different from the lipids described previously. Cholesterol is a steroid compound that contains a —OH group, making it a **sterol** (FIG. 23). Cholesterol is an important component of the plasma membrane of eukaryotic animal cells. Other eukaryotic cells such as fungal cells contain different sterols in their plasma membranes. Cholesterol and other sterols wedge between phospholipids in the plasma membrane, maintaining membrane fluidity. Cholesterol and other sterols generally are absent from the plasma membrane of a prokaryotic cell.

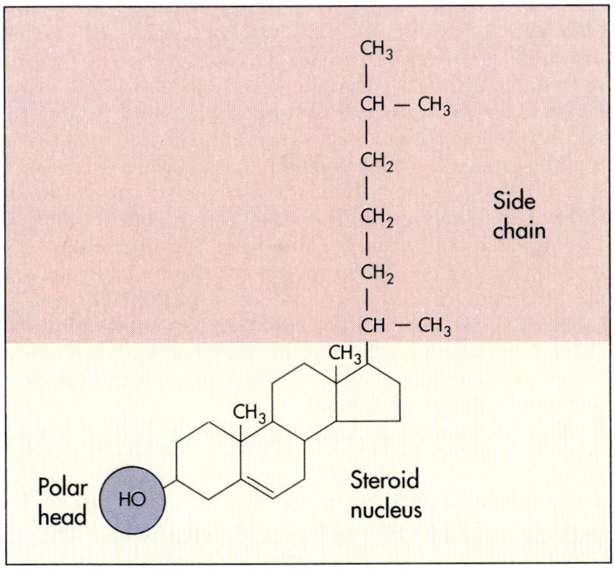

FIG. 23 A steroid is a nonpolar lipid with four rings. Cholesterol is an example of a steroid.

PROTEINS

Proteins are large molecules made up of hundreds or thousands of amino acid subunits. **Amino acids** are the building blocks of proteins. An amino acid contains at least one carboxyl (—COO^-) functional group and one amino (—NH_3^+) functional group attached to the same carbon atom. This carbon atom is called the alpha-carbon (α-carbon). There are only 20 amino acids naturally found in proteins (FIG. 24).

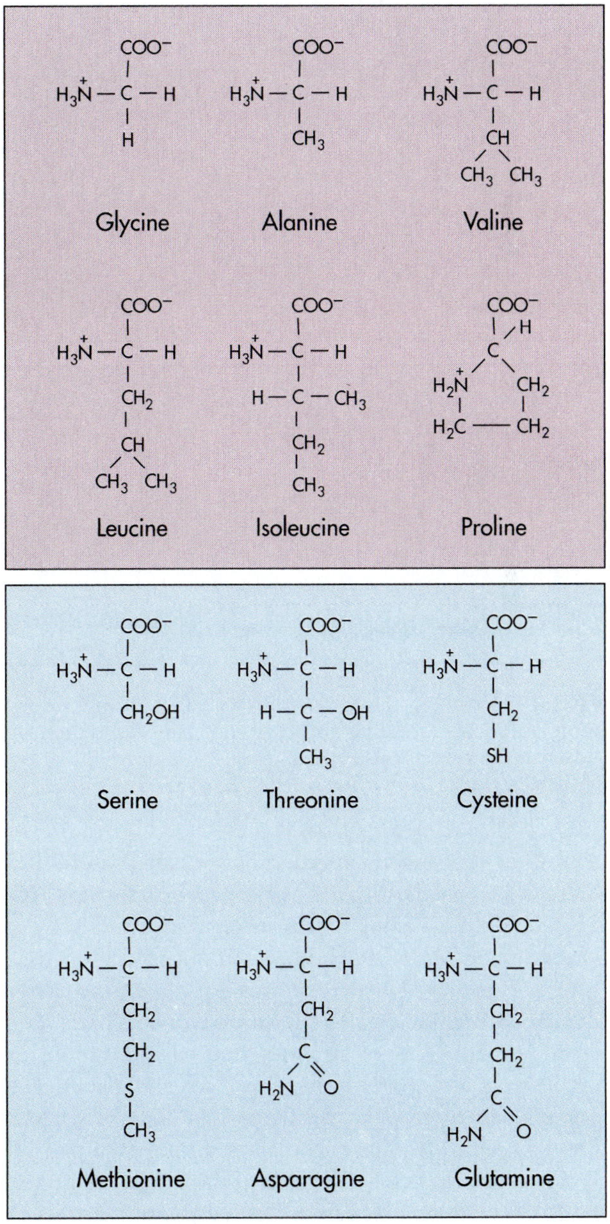

FIG. 24 The structural formulas of twelve common amino acids. Each is an L-α-amino acid. The structures differ in the other constituents. *Continued.*

Phenylalanine Tyrosine Tryptophan

Lysine Arginine Histidine

Aspartate Glutamate

FIG. 24, Cont'd The structural formulas of eight common amino acids. Each is an L-α-amino acid. The structures differ in the other constituents.

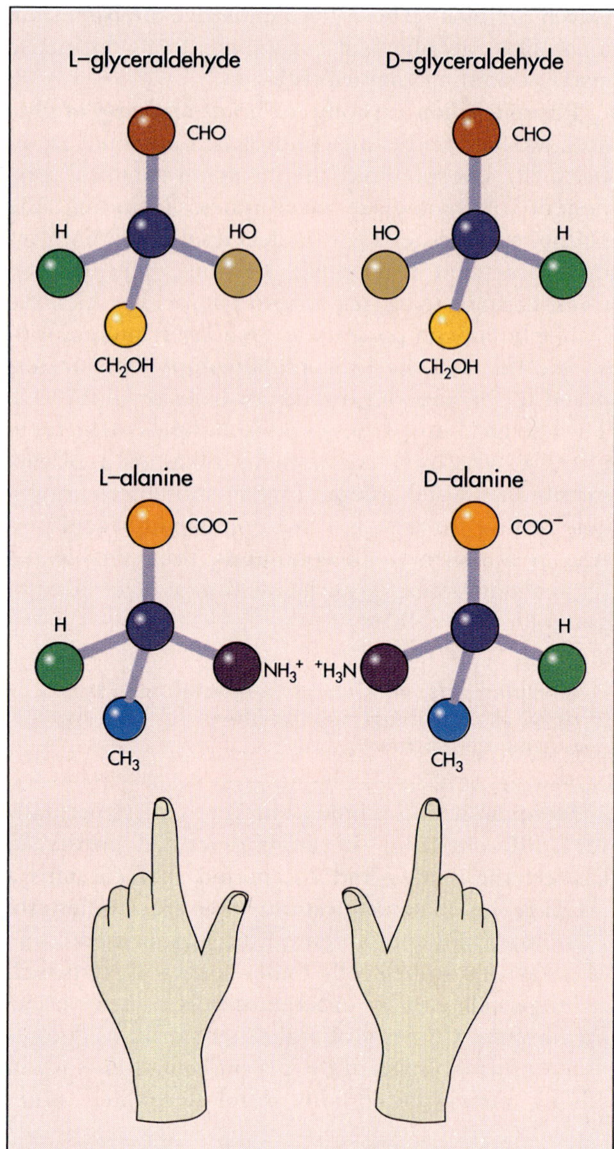

FIG. 25 An asymmetric carbon allows molecules to exist in two different forms, or isomers, that are mirror images: the D and L forms of gylceraldehyde molecules and their relation to L-alanine. In determining the absolute configuration of a carbohydrate, the D designation is used to indicate that the groups H, CHO, and OH, in that order, are situated in a clockwise fashion about the asymmetric carbon atom, when the CH_2OH group is directed away from the viewer. The designation L is used if the order is counterclockwise. In determining the configurations of amino acids, we still use glyceraldehyde as the reference, with the NH_3^+ group substituting for OH and the COO^- group substituting for CHO. Note that according to this system some D forms are levorotatory, designated D- (−), and some L forms are dextrorotatory, designated L- (+).

Amino acids exist in mirror images called **stereoisomers.** They are designated as either *L* or *D* forms (FIG. 25). The amino acids found in proteins are always **L-amino acids.** Also attached to the alpha-carbon is a side or **R group.** These R groups are the amino acid's distinguishing factors. The R group can be a hydrogen atom, an unbranched or branched carbon chain, or cyclic ring structure. It can also contain functional groups—such as the sulfhydryl (—SH), hydroxyl (—OH), or additional carboxyl or amino groups.

The L-amino acids of a protein molecule are linked by covalent bonds. These are called peptide bonds. A **peptide bond** forms between the amino group of one amino acid and the carboxyl group of another. The bonding of two amino acids by a peptide bond forms a dipeptide. Three or more amino acids linked by peptide bonds form a **polypeptide chain** (FIG. 26).

A protein is composed of a chain of L-amino acids held together by peptide linkages.

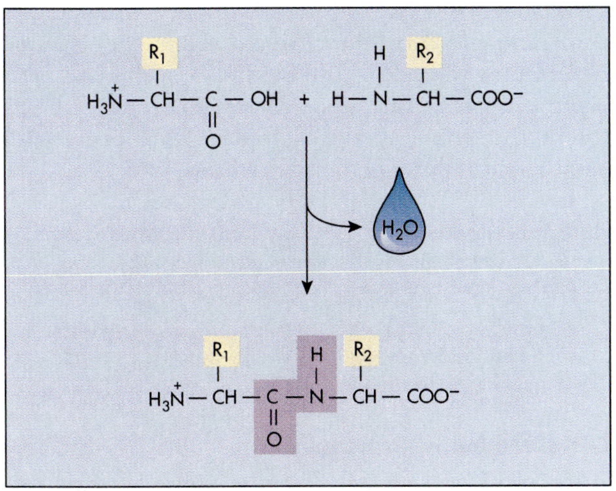

FIG. 26 A polypeptide has a free amino end and a free carboxyl end. The shaded area *(purple)* is the peptide bond.

Protein Structure

Proteins have very highly organized three-dimensional structures (FIG. 27). Both the number and order of the specific amino acids within the polypeptide chain are important. They establish the structure and functional properties of protein molecules. Proteins have different lengths, different quantities of the various amino acid subunits, and different specific sequences in which the amino acids are bonded. Hence, the number of proteins is practically endless. Every living cell produces many different proteins.

There are only 20 different L-amino acids found in proteins, and virtually every protein contains the same amino acids. Yet each different protein has a unique sequence of amino acids. This sequence of amino acids forms the **primary structure** of a protein. The primary structure influences the three-dimensional shape of a protein, its function, and how it will interact with other substances. Alterations in amino acid sequences can have profound metabolic effects. For example, a single incorrect amino acid in a blood protein can produce the deformed hemoglobin molecule characteristic of sickle cell anemia.

The primary structure of a protein is the sequence of amino acids in its polypeptide chain.

The primary structure of a polypeptide determines how the molecule can fold and twist. The positioning of the R groups of the amino acids is dictated by the primary structure of the peptide chain. The R group position forces the polypeptide to twist and fold in a specific way. The term **secondary structure** refers to the helical or extended protein structures that result when different amino acids are positioned close enough to allow hydrogen bonding to occur. Most often, hydrogen bonds form between every fourth amino acid. They hold the chain in a specific struc-

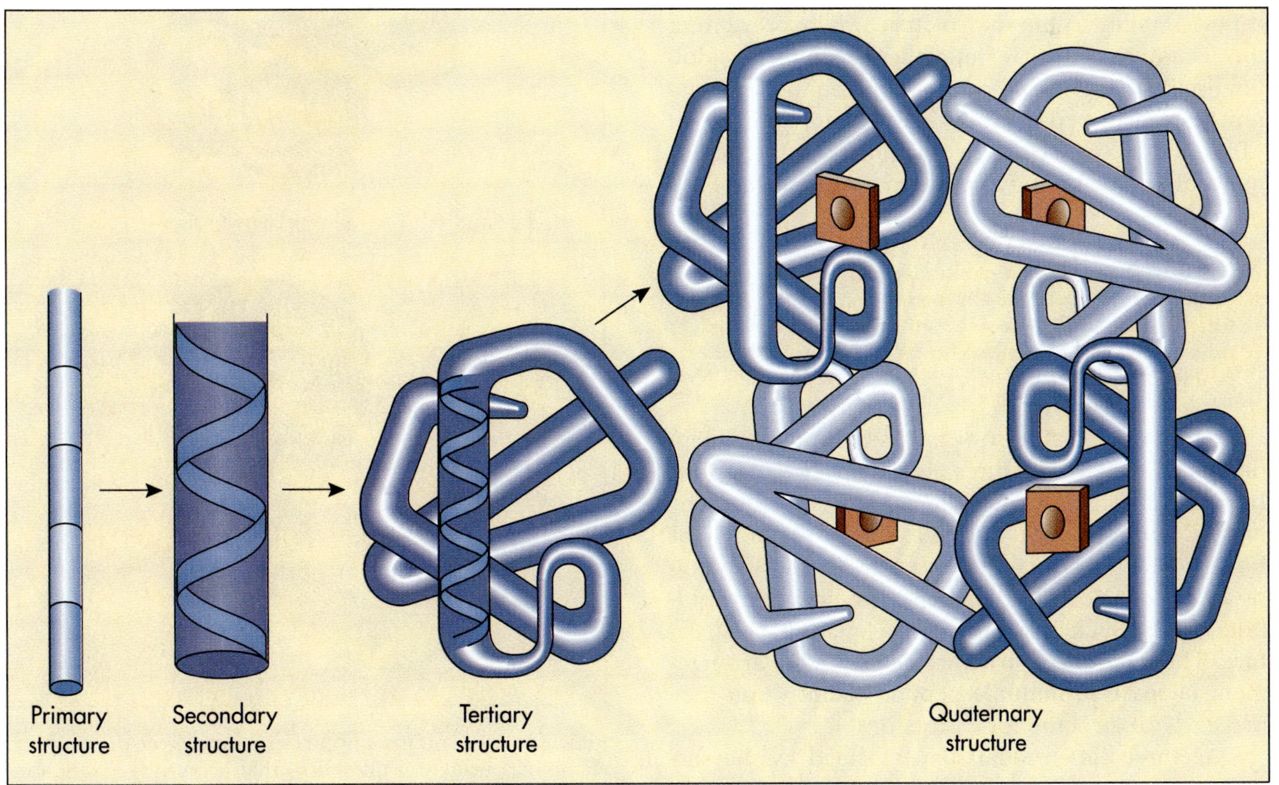

FIG. 27 Proteins have primary, secondary, tertiary, and quaternary structures.

ture, called the α-helix, in which a helical coil is wound about its own axis. In other cases the chain is almost fully extended and hydrogen bonds form between different chains. These bonds hold many chains side by side in a sheetlike structure. In the β-sheet or pleated sheet, the chain of amino acids in the polypeptide folds back and forth on itself. R groups are thus exposed that can undergo extensive hydrogen bonding. The R groups of some amino acids tend to favor helical patterns; others tend to favor sheetlike patterns.

The secondary structure of a protein is stabilized by hydrogen bonding between the amino acids of the polypeptides.

Most helically coiled chains become further folded into some characteristic shape. The folding of polypeptide chains is called **tertiary structure.** Folding of a helical polypeptide accomplishes two things. The polypeptide becomes a unique shape that is compatible with a specific biological function, and the folding process converts the molecule into its most chemically stable form. The tertiary structure is based on interactions between various R groups of specific amino acids. Hydrophobic R groups associate with each other at the interior of folded chains. Hydrophilic R groups assume exterior positions where they can form weak bonds with other polar R groups or with water. The highly nonpolar regions of the polypeptide are brought close together by tertiary folding. They contribute stability to the folded structure by preventing the penetration of water into these regions. In addition, sulfhydryl groups (—SH) on two amino acid subunits can form a covalent, disulfide bond (—S—S—). This bond further stabilizes the folding of the protein molecule, contributing to the tertiary structure of the protein.

The actual shape of a protein is the result of the interactions of the polar covalent bonds of the peptide linkage and the combined interactions of the polar and nonpolar side chains of the individual amino acids.

Some proteins consist of more than one polypeptide chain. Their structures are even more complex. In some cases, the polypeptide chains are linked by disulfide bridges. For example, the antibodies that help protect the human body against disease are composed of four peptide chains that are linked by disulfide bonds. Such proteins have a quaternary structure. The **quaternary structure** describes the arrangement in space of multiple peptide chains when they make up the structure of a protein.

The three-dimensional shape formed by the secondary, tertiary, and quaternary structure of a protein is essential for the function of all proteins, including those that act as enzymes. The sequence of the amino acids and the three-dimensional shape they assume determines where a substrate can bind and the catalytic properties of the active site. Enzymes with different three-dimensional shapes at their active sites catalyze different metabolic reactions.

Primary, secondary, tertiary, and quaternary structures contribute to the three-dimensional shape of a protein that is essential for its proper functioning.

The ability of a protein to function as an enzyme and catalyze chemical reactions depends on its three-dimensional shape.

Denaturation of Proteins

If the three-dimensional structure of a protein is disrupted, the protein is **denatured** (FIG. 28). Denaturation occurs when there is a change in the three-dimensional structure of the protein that results in

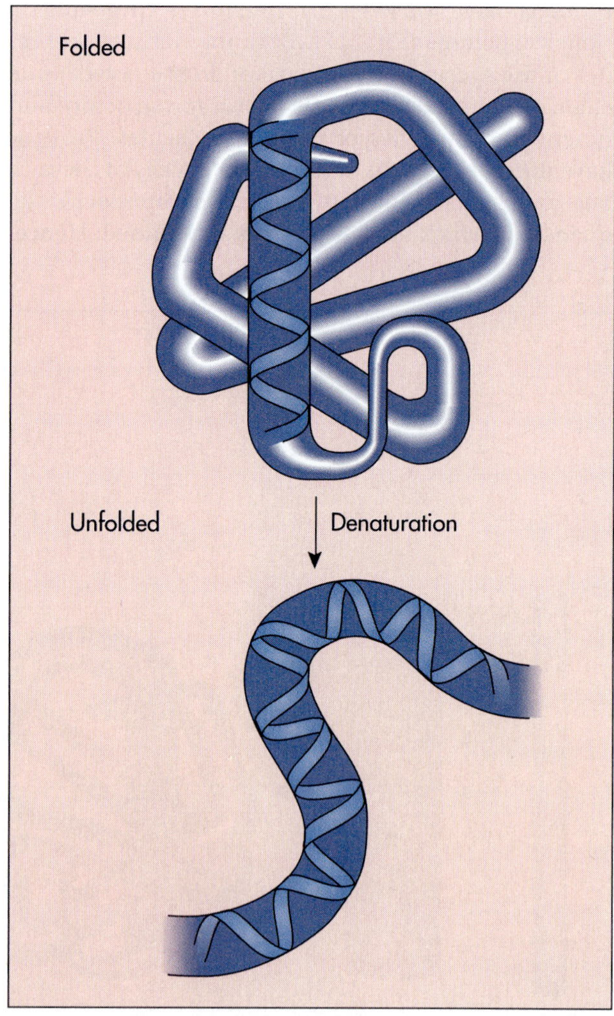

FIG. 28 Denaturation occurs when the three-dimensional shape of a protein is altered so that it no longer functions properly. Heat, salt, and various other factors can disrupt the tertiary structure of a protein, denaturing it.

the loss of proper function of the protein. If the protein is an enzyme, denaturation results in the loss of catalytic capacity. The critical three-dimensional configuration of a protein can be disrupted without breaking the covalent peptide bonds of the polypeptide chain. Exposure to high temperatures, typically above 60° C, or certain chemical agents can disrupt the hydrogen bonds, sulfhydryl bonds, and hydrophobic interactions on which secondary, tertiary, and quaternary structures are based. This is one reason that high temperatures can be used to kill microorganisms. High salt or high H^+ concentrations can also denature proteins. They alter the weak bond interactions that maintain the structure of the protein molecule.

Proteins lose their functional capabilities when they are denatured because denaturation disrupts critical three-dimensional structures.

Nucleic Acids

Nucleic acids are polymers composed of monomeric **nucleotides.** Each nucleotide has three different parts: a nitrogen-containing base, a pentose, and a phosphate group (FIG. 29). These three parts of the nucleotide are joined by covalent bonds. The nitrogen-containing base is either adenine, guanine, cytosine, thymine, or uracil. Adenine and guanine are double-ring structures. Collectively they are referred to as **purines.** Thymine, uracil, and cytosine are smaller, single-ring structures. They are called **pyrimidines.**

A single strand of a nucleic acid consists of nucleotide units strung into long chains. A phosphate bridge connects their sugars. Bases stick out to the side. The type of bond that links the nucleotides in a nucleic acid is called a **phosphodiester bond** (FIG. 30). The backbone of the nucleic acid molecule is always the same. It consists of alternating sugar and phosphate units. The nitrogenous bases attached to the sugar portion of the nucleotides vary in the chain. Hence, when chemists refer to a specific sequence of nucleotides in a nucleic acid, they really are describing the sequence of nitrogenous bases. The sequence of bases in a DNA or RNA molecule carries the genetic information necessary to produce the proteins required by the organism.

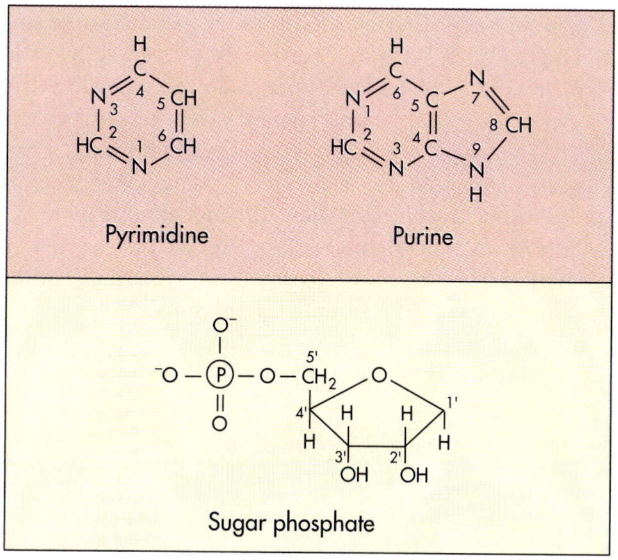

Pyrimidine

Purine

Sugar phosphate

FIG. 29 A nucleotide consists of a pyrimidine or purine (nitrogenous base) attached to a sugar phosphate.

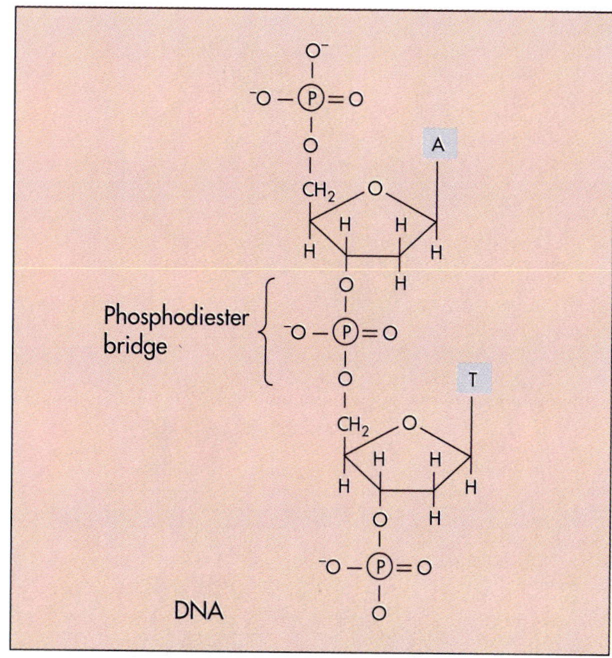

FIG. 30 Nucleotides are linked by phosphate diester bonds to form dimers and polymeric units.

Nucleic acids are polymers composed of nucleotide monomers held together by phosphodiester linkages.

DNA

All cells contain hereditary material called genes. Each gene is a segment of a **deoxyribonucleic acid (DNA)** molecule. Genes determine all hereditary traits. They control all the potential activities that take place within living cells. When a cell divides, its hereditary information is passed on to the next generation. This transfer of information is possible because of DNA's unique structure. DNA contains four nucleotides that each contain one of four nucleic acid bases: adenine (A), guanine (G), cytosine (C), and thymine (T). The ordering of the nucleotides determines the hereditary information contained in DNA. Nucleotides are held together by phosphodiester

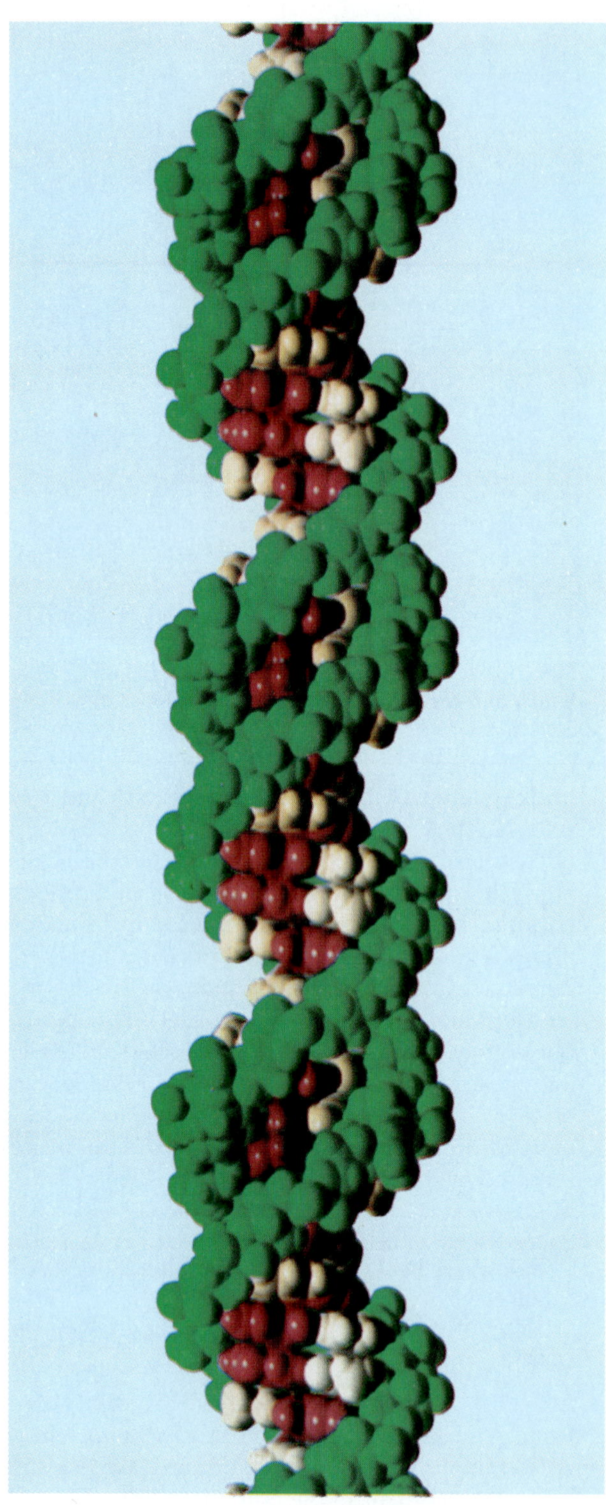

FIG. 31 A model of a DNA double helix.

bonds between deoxyribose, the sugar found in the backbone of DNA. There are two strands of DNA held together by hydrogen bonds to form a coiled molecule called a **double helix** (FIG.31). Hydrogen bonds can form between adenine (A) and thymine (T) or between guanine (G) and cytosine (C).

The four nucleic acid bases in DNA are adenine, guanine, cytosine, and thymine.

RNA

Ribonucleic acid (RNA) differs from DNA in several respects. The five-carbon sugar in the RNA nucleotide is ribose. Ribose has one more oxygen atom than does the deoxyribose in DNA. One of RNA's bases is uracil (U) instead of thymine. Whereas DNA is normally double stranded, RNA is usually single stranded.

The four nucleic acid bases in RNA are adenine, guanine, cytosine and uracil.

Other Nucleotides

The nucleotide **adenosine triphosphate (ATP)** is the principal energy-carrying molecule of all cells. It stores the chemical energy released by some chemical reactions. It also provides the energy for energy-requiring reactions when needed. ATP consists of adenine, ribose, and three phosphate groups. ATP is called a high-energy molecule because it releases a large amount of usable energy upon hydrolysis of a phosphate group. The product is **adenosine diphosphate (ADP)**. The production and utilization of ATP are essential to the bioenergetics of the cell. All of the metabolic pathways of microorganisms are involved in producing or consuming ATP.

Nucleotides also serve as coenzymes. A **coenzyme** is a temporary carrier of substances such as electrons. During metabolism, coenzymes transport hydrogen atoms and electrons. Nicotinamide adenine dinucleotide (NAD^+) and flavin adenine dinucleotide (FAD) are two of these coenzymes. These coenzymes gain electrons and hydrogen during some chemical reactions and donate them during other chemical reactions. Much of the metabolism of microorganisms involves chemical reactions requiring ATP and/or coenzymes. This accounts for the importance of these nucleotide molecules in the chemical reactions of living systems.

GLOSSARY

A

aberrations Distortions that occur in a magnifying lens

abiotic Referring to the absence of living organisms

abortive infections A viral infection in which viral replication does not occur or does not produce viral progeny that are capable of infecting other host cells

abrasion An area denuded of skin, mucous membrane, or superficial epithelium by rubbing or scraping

abscess A localized accumulation of pus

absorption The uptake, drinking in, or imbibing of a substance; the movement of substances into a cell; the transfer of substances from one medium to another (e.g., the dissolution of a gas in a liquid); the transfer of energy from electromagnetic waves to chemical bond and/or kinetic energy (e.g., the transfer of light energy to chlorophyll)

accessory pigments Pigments that harvest light energy and transfer it to the primary photosynthetic reaction centers

acellular Lacking cellular organization; not having a delimiting cytoplasmic membrane; organizational description of viruses, viroids, and prions

acetyl-CoA Acetyl-coenzyme A; a condensation product of coenzyme A and acetic acid; an intermediate in the transfer of 2-carbon fragments, notably in their entrance into the tricarboxylic acid cycle

acetylene reduction assay Assay for nitrogen fixation based on the conversion of acetylene to ethylene by nitrogenase, the enzyme responsible for nitrogen fixation

achromatic lens An objective lens in which chromatic aberration has been corrected for two colors and spherical aberration for one color

acid-fast The property of some bacteria, such as mycobacteria, that retain their initial stain and do not decolorize after washing with dilute acid-alcohol

acid foods Foods with a pH value less than 4.5

acid mine drainage Consequence of the metabolism of sulfur- and iron-oxidizing bacteria when coal mining exposes pyrite to atmospheric oxygen and the combination of autoxidation and microbial sulfur and iron oxidation produces large amounts of sulfuric acid, which kills aquatic life and contaminates water

acidic stains Stains with a positively charged chromophore (colored portion of the dye) that are attracted to negatively charged cells

acidophiles Microorganisms that show a preference for growth at low pH, e.g., bacteria that grow only at very low pH values, ca. 2.0

acidulant Acidic compound used as a chemical food preservative

acquired immune deficiency syndrome (AIDS) An infectious disease syndrome caused by HIV retrovirus, characterized by the loss of normal immune response system functions, followed by various opportunistic infections

acquired immunity The ability of an individual to produce specific antibodies in response to antigens to which the body has been previously exposed based on the development of a memory response

acrasin Substance (3′-5′ cyclic AMP) secreted by a slime mold that initiates aggregation to form a fruiting body

Actinomycetales Order of bacteria characterized by the formation of branching filaments whose families are distinguished on the basis of the nature of their mycelia and spores

actinomycetes Members of an order of bacteria in which species are characterized by the formation of branching and/or true filaments

activated sludge The active microorganisms formed during the activated sludge secondary sewage treatment process that are used as an inoculum for the next batch treatment

activated sludge process An aerobic secondary sewage treatment process using sewage sludge containing active complex populations of aerobic microorganisms to break down organic matter in sewage

activation energy The energy in excess of the ground state that must be added to a molecular system to allow a chemical reaction to start

active immunity Immunity acquired as a result of the individual's own reactions to pathogenic microorganisms or their antigens; attributable to the presence of antibody or immune lymphoid cells formed in response to an antigenic stimulus

active site The site on the enzyme molecule at which the substrate binds and the catalyzed reaction actually proceeds

active transport The movement of materials across cell membranes from regions of lower to regions of higher concentration, requiring the expenditure of metabolic energy

acute Referring to a disease of rapid onset, short duration, and pronounced symptoms

acute disease A disease characterized by rapid development of symptoms and signs, reaching a height of intensity, and ending fairly quickly

acute stage Stage of a disease when symptoms appear and the disease is most severe

acyclovir Antiviral agent used in the treatment of diseases caused by herpes simplex

adaptive enzymes Enzymes produced by an organism in response to the presence of a substrate or a related substance; also called *inducible enzymes*

adenine A purine base component of nucleotides, nucleosides, and nucleic acids

adenosine diphosphate (ADP) A high-energy derivative of adenosine containing two phosphate groups, one less than ATP; formed upon hydrolysis of ATP

adenosine monophosphate (AMP) A compound composed of adenosine and one phosphate group formed upon the hydrolysis of ADP

adenosine triphosphatase (ATPase) An enzyme that catalyzes the reversible hydrolysis of ATP; the membrane-bound form of this enzyme is important in catalyzing the formation of ATP from ADP and inorganic phosphate

adenosine triphosphate (ATP) A major carrier of phosphate and energy in biological systems, composed of adenosine and three phosphate groups; the free energy released from the hydrolysis of ATP is used to drive many energy-requiring reactions in biological systems

adhesion factors Substances involved in the attachment of microorganisms to solid surfaces; factors that increase adsorption

adhesion sites Sites of association in Gram-negative bacteria between the cytoplasmic membrane and the outer membrane; also called Bayer junctions

adjuncts Starchy substrates, such as corn, wheat, and rice, that provide carbohydrates for ethanol production and are added to malt during the mashing process in the production of beer

adjuvants Substances that increase the immunological response to a vaccine and, for example, can be added to vaccines to slow down absorption and increase effectiveness; substances that enhance the action of a drug or antigen

ADP Adenosine diphosphate

adsorption A surface phenomenon involving the retention of solid, liquid, or gaseous molecules at an interface

aer- Combining form meaning air or atmosphere

aerated pile method Method of composting for the decomposition of organic waste material where the wastes are heaped in separate piles and forced aeration provides oxygen

aerial mycelia A mass of hyphae occurring above the surface of a substrate

aerobactin A siderophore

aerobes Microorganisms whose growth requires the presence of air or free oxygen

aerobic Having molecular oxygen present; growing in the presence of air

aerobic bacteria Bacteria requiring oxygen for growth

aerobic respiration Metabolism involving a respiration pathway in which molecular oxygen serves as the terminal electron acceptor

aerosol A fine suspension of particles or liquid droplets sprayed into the air

aflatoxin A carcinogenic poison produced by some strains of the fungus *Aspergillus flavus*

agar A dried polysaccharide extract of red algae used as a solidifying agent in various microbiological media

agglutinating antibody Agglutinin

agglutination The visible clumping or aggregation of cells or particles due to the reaction of surface-bound antigens with homologous antibodies

agglutinin An antibody capable of causing the clumping or agglutination of bacteria or other cells

agricultural microbiology The study of the role of microorganisms in agriculture

AIDS Acquired immune deficiency syndrome

airborne transmission Route by which pathogens are transported to a susceptible host via the air; main route of transmission of pathogens that enter via the respiratory tract through the air

akinetes Thick-walled resting spores of cyanobacteria and green algae

alcoholic fermentation Conversion of sugar to alcohol by microbial enzymes; fermentation that produces alcohol (ethanol) and carbon dioxide from glucose; also known as *ethanolic fermentation*

ale Alcoholic beverage produced with top-fermenting *Saccharomyces cerevesiae* and a high concentration of hops to produce a tart taste and a high alcohol concentration

algae A heterogeneous group of eukaryotic, photosynthetic, unicellular, and multicellular organisms lacking true tissue differentiation

algicides Chemical agents that kill algae

alkalophiles Bacteria that live at very high pH; bacteria that live under extremely alkaline conditions, having developed mechanisms for keeping sodium and hydroxide ions outside the cell

allele One or more alternative forms of a given gene concerned with the same trait or characteristic; one of a pair or multiple forms of a gene located at the same locus of homologous chromosomes

allelopathic substance A substance produced by one organism that adversely affects another organism

allergen An antigen that induces an allergic response, i.e., a hypersensitivity reaction

allergy An immunological hypersensitivity reaction; an antigen–antibody reaction marked by an exaggerated physiological response to a substance in sensitive individuals

allochthonous An organism or substance foreign to a given ecosystem

allochthonous population A population of allochthonous organisms

allosteric activation The acceleration of the rate of an enzymatic reaction as a result of an allosteric effector binding to an enzyme

allosteric effector Substance that can bind to the regulatory site of an allosteric enzyme, resulting in the alteration of the rate of activity of that enzyme

allosteric enzymes Enzymes with a binding and catalytic site for the substrate and a different site where a modulator (allosteric effector) acts

allosteric inhibitor An allosteric effector that results in reduced rates of activity of an allosteric enzyme

allotypes Antigenically different forms of a given type of immunoglobulin that occur in different individuals of the same species

alpha hemolysis (α hemolysis) Partial hemolysis of red blood cells as evidenced by the formation of a zone of partial clearing (greening) around certain bacterial colonies growing on blood agar

amastigotes Rounded protozoan cells lacking flagella; a form assumed by some species of Trypanosomatidae, e.g., *Plasmodium,* during a particular stage of development

amensalism An interactive association between two populations that is detrimental to one while not adversely affecting the other

Ames test Test for the detection of chemical mutagens and potential carcinogens

amino acids A class of organic compounds containing an amino ($-NH_2$) group and a carboxyl ($-COOH$) group

amino end The end of a peptide chain or protein with a free amino group, i.e., an alpha amino group not involved in forming the peptide bond

aminoacyl site Site on a ribosome where a tRNA molecule attached to a single amino acid initially binds during translation

aminoglycosides Broad-spectrum antibiotics containing an aminosugar, an amino- or guanido-inositol ring, and residues of other sugars that inhibit protein synthesis, e.g., kanamycin, neomycin, and streptomycin

ammonification The release of ammonia from nitrogenous organic matter by microbial action

amoebida Protozoa having no distinct shape that form lobopodia and lack a skeletal structure

AMP Adenosine monophosphate

amphibolic pathway A metabolic pathway that has catabolic and anabolic functions

amphotericin B Broad-spectrum antifungal agent used for treating systemic infections

amplifying gene expression Activity by which eukaryotes can increase the amount of rRNA and thus the number of ribosomes that can be used to translate the information in a stable mRNA molecule, thus producing large amounts of the enzyme coded for by a given gene

amylases Enzymes that hydrolyze starch

anabolism Biosynthesis; the process of synthesizing cell constituents from simpler molecules, usually requiring the expenditure of energy

anaerobes Organisms that grow in the absence of air or oxygen; organisms that do not use molecular oxygen in respiration

anaerobic The absence of oxygen; able to live or grow in the absence of free oxygen

anaerobic culture chamber Enclosures designed to exclude oxygen from the atmosphere, generally by generating hydrogen, which reacts with available oxygen as a catalyst to produce water

anaerobic digestor A secondary sewage treatment facility used for the degradation of sludge and solid waste

anaerobic life Life in the absence of air

anaerobic photosynthetic bacteria Bacteria that carry out the reactions of photosystem I

anaerobic respiration The use of inorganic electron acceptors other than oxygen as terminal electron acceptors for energy-yielding oxidative metabolism

anaerobiosis The state or condition characterized by the absence of air; anaerobic; lack or removal of oxygen from the atmosphere

analogously similar Phenotypically similar

anamnestic response A heightened immunological response in persons or animals to the second or subsequent administration of a particular antigen given some time after the initial administration; a secondary or memory immune response characterized by the rapid reappearance of antibody in the blood due to the administration of an antibody to which the subject had previously developed a primary immune response

anaphylactic hypersensitivity An exaggerated immune response of an organism to foreign protein or other substances, involving the degranulation of mast cells and the release of histamine

anaphylactic shock Physiological shock resulting from an anaphylactic hypersensitivity reaction, e.g., to penicillin or bee bites; in severe cases, death can result within minutes

anaplerotic sequences Reactions in a cell that serve to replenish the supplies of key molecules

anemia A condition characterized by having less than the normal amount of hemoglobin, reflecting a reduced number of circulating red blood cells

anergic Unresponsive to antigens

anergic B cell clones B cells that do not respond to antigenic stimulation

animal viruses Viruses that multiply within animal cells

anions Negatively charged ions

anisogametes Gametes differing in shape, size, and/or behavior

annulus A ring-shaped structure; a transverse groove in the cellular envelope of dinoflagellates

anode The positive terminal of an electrolytic cell

anorexia Absence of appetite

anoxic Absence of oxygen; anaerobic

anoxygenic photosynthesis Photosynthesis that takes place in the absence of oxygen and during which oxygen is not produced; photosynthesis that does not split water and evolve oxygen

anoxygenic phototrophic bacteria (anoxyphotobacteria) Bacteria that can carry out only anoxygenic photosynthesis; a group of photosynthetic, phototrophic bacteria occurring in aquatic habitats that do not evolve oxygen

antagonism The inhibition, injury, or killing of one species of microorganism by another; an interpopulation relationship in which one population has a deleterious (negative) effect on another

antheridium A specialized structure where male gametes are produced; the male gametangium of oomycete fungi

anti- Combining form meaning opposing in effect or activity

antibacterial agents Agents that kill or inhibit the growth of bacteria, e.g., antibiotics, antiseptics, and disinfectants

antibiotics Substances of microbial origin that in very small amounts have antimicrobial activity; current usage of the term extends to synthetic and semisynthetic substances that are closely related to naturally occurring antibiotics and that have antimicrobial activity

antibodies Glycoprotein molecules produced in the body in response to the introduction of an antigen or hapten that can specifically react with that antigen; also known as *immunoglobulins,* which are part of the serum fraction of the blood formed in response to antigenic stimulation and which react with antigens with great specificity

antibody-dependent cytotoxic hypersensitivity Type 2 hypersensitivity; reaction in which an antigen on the surface of a cell combines with an antibody, resulting in death of that cell by stimulating phagocytic attack or initiating the complement pathway; examples include blood transfusions between incompatible types and Rh incompatibility

antibody-mediated immunity Immunity produced by the activation of the B-lymphocyte population, leading to the production of several classes of immunoglobulins

anticodon A sequence of 3 nucleotides in a tRNA molecule that is complementary to the codon triplet in mRNA

antifungal agents Agents that kill or inhibit the growth and reproduction of fungi; may be fungicidal or fungistatic

antigen Any agent that initiates antibody formation and/or induces a state of active immunological hypersensitivity and that can react with the immunoglobulins that are formed

antigen presenting cell Cells with small polypeptide antigens attached to the MHC class II proteins on outer cell membrane surfaces such that the antigen is presented, or shown, to T_H cells

antigen–antibody complex The molecular combination that results from the reaction between antigen and complementary antibody molecules

antigenic drift Major antigenic changes, typically seen in influenza viruses and other pathogens, that occur because of accumulated genetic mutations and recombinations; process of antigenic change that can cause gene reassortment between an animal and a human strain; a gradual and cumulative process of antigenic changes that only become apparent with time

antigenic shift Genetic mutation caused by the addition of new genes that produces new strains of influenza viruses

antihistamines Compounds used for treating allergic reactions and cold symptoms that work by inactivating histamine that is released as part of the immune response

antimalarial drugs Agents effective against the erythrocytic stage of the *Plasmodium* life cycle

antimicrobial agents Chemical or biological agents that kill or inhibit the growth of microorganisms

antimicrobics Antimicrobial agents; chemicals that inhibit or kill microorganisms and can be safely introduced into the human body; include synthetic and naturally produced antibiotics; term generally used instead of *antibiotic*

antiport A mechanism in which different substances are actively transported across the cytoplasmic membrane simultaneously in opposite directions

antisense mRNA An mRNA that is complementary to another mRNA forming a double-stranded RNA that is not translated

antiseptics Chemical agents used to treat human or animal tissues, usually skin, to kill or inactivate microorganisms capable of causing infection; not considered safe for internal consumption

antisera Blood sera that contain antibodies

antitoxin Antibody to a toxin capable of reacting with that poison and neutralizing the toxin

antiviral agents Substances capable of destroying or inhibiting the reproduction of viruses

APC Antigen presenting cell

aplanospores Nonmotile, sexual spores

apochromatic lens An objective microscope lens in which chromatic aberration has been corrected for three colors and spherical aberration for two colors

appendaged bacteria Budding bacteria

aqueous Of, relating to, or resembling water; made from, with, or by water; solutions in which water is the solvent

arbuscules Specialized inclusions in root cortex in the vesicular-arbuscular type of mycorrhizal association

Archaea The kingdom of organisms that contains the archaebacteria

archaebacteria Archaea; archaeobacteria; prokaryotes with cell walls that lack murein, having ether bonds in their membrane phospholipids; analysis of rRNA indicates that the archaebacteria represent a primary biological kingdom related to both eubacteria and eukaryotes; considered to be a primitive group of organisms that were among the earliest living forms on Earth

armored dinoflagellates Dinoflagellates that produce thecal plates

arthropods Animals of the invertebrate phylum Arthropoda, many of which can be vectors of infectious diseases

arthrospores Spores formed by the fragmentation of hyphae of certain fungi, algae, and cyanobacteria; coccoid cells present during the stationary growth phase of *Arthrobacter* species

Arthus immune-complex reaction Complex-mediated hypersensitivity; type 3 hypersensitivity

artifact The appearance of something in an image or micrograph of a specimen that is due to causes within the optical system or preparation of the specimen and is not a true representation of the features of the specimen

asci Plural of *ascus*

ascocarp Structure on true ascomycetes that produces asci

Ascomycetes Members of a class of fungi distinguished by the presence of an ascus, a sac-like structure containing sexually produced ascospores

ascospores Sexual spores characteristic of ascomycetes, produced in the ascus after the union of two nuclei

ascus The sporangium or spore case of fungi, consisting of a single terminal cell

-ase Suffix denoting an enzyme

asepsis State in which potentially harmful microorganisms are absent; free of pathogens

aseptic techniques Precautionary measures taken in microbiological work and clinical practice to prevent the contamination of cultures, sterile media, etc., and/or infection of persons, animals, or plants by extraneous microorganisms

asexual Lacking sex or functional sexual organs

asexual reproduction Reproduction without union of gametes; formation of new individuals from a single individual

assay Analysis to determine the presence, absence, or quantity of one or more components

assembly Stage of viral replication during which packaging of a nucleic acid genome within a protein capsid occurs

assimilation The incorporation of nutrients into the biomass of an organism

asthma Type 1 hypersensitivity reaction that primarily affects the lower respiratory tract; the condition is characterized by shortness of breath and wheezing

asymptomatic carriers Individuals infected with a pathogen who do not develop disease symptoms

ataxia The inability to coordinate muscular action

athlete's foot Disease caused by dermatophytic fungi affecting chronically wet feet with skin abrasions; tinea or ringworm of the feet

atmosphere The mass of air surrounding the Earth; a unit of pressure approximating 1×10^6 dynes/cm^2

ATP Adenosine triphosphate

ATPase Adenosine triphosphatase

attenuation Any procedure in which the pathogenicity of a given organism is reduced or abolished; reduction in the virulence of a pathogen; control of protein synthesis involving the translation process

attenuator site The site between the operator region and the first structural gene of the operon where transcription can be interrupted, as in the *trp* operon

attractants Chemicals that cause bacteria to move toward them; chemicals that cause phagocytic white blood cells to move toward them

autochthonous Microorganisms or substances indigenous to a given ecosystem; the true inhabitants of an ecosystem; term often used to refer to the common microbiota of the body or species of soil microorganisms that tend to remain constant despite fluctuations in the quantity of fermentable organic matter in the soil

autochthonous populations Populations of autochthonous organisms

autoclave Apparatus in which objects or materials may be sterilized by air-free saturated steam under pressure at temperatures in excess of 100° C

autoimmune diseases Diseases that result from the failure of the immune response to recognize self-antigens so that the immune system attacks the body's own cells, resulting in the progressive degeneration of tissues

autoimmunity Immunity or hypersensitivity to some constituent in one's own body; immune reactions with self-antigens

autolysins Endogenous enzymes involved in the breakdown of certain structural components of the cell during particular phases of cellular growth and development

autolysis The breakdown of the components of a cell or tissues by endogenous enzymes, usually after the death of the cell or tissue

autospores Sexually formed, nonmotile spores resembling the parent cell morphologically

autotrophs Organisms whose growth and reproduction are independent of external sources of organic compounds, the required cellular carbon being supplied by the reduction of CO_2 and the needed cellular energy being supplied by the conversion of light energy to ATP or the oxidation of inorganic compounds to provide the free energy for the formation of ATP

autoxidation The oxidation of a substance on its exposure to air

auxotrophs Nutritional mutants that require growth factors not needed by the parental strain

avirulent Lacking virulence; a microorganism lacking the properties that normally cause disease

A_w Water activity

axopodia Semipermanent pseudopodia, e.g., the pseudopodia that emanate radially from the spherical cells of heliozoans and some radiolarian species

Azobacteraceae Family of Gram-negative bacteria that exhibit pleomorphic morphology and fix molecular nitrogen—free-living soil bacteria

B

B cell B lymphocytes

B lymphocytes A differentiated lymphocyte involved in antibody-mediated immunity; white blood cells that produce specific immunoglobulins; their surfaces carry specific immunoglobulin antigen-binding receptor sites

B memory cells Specifically stimulated B lymphocytes not actively multiplying but capable of multiplication and production of plasma cells on subsequent antigenic stimuli

Bacillaceae Family of Gram-negative, endospore-forming, rod- and coccal-shaped bacteria

Bacillariophyceae A group of Chrysophycophyta algae containing the diatoms

bacilli Bacteria in the shape of cylinders

bacitracin Antibiotic that inhibits bacterial cell wall synthesis

bacteremia Condition in which viable bacteria are present in the blood

bacteria Members of a group of diverse and ubiquitous prokaryotic, single-celled organisms; organisms with prokaryotic cells, i.e., cells lacking a nucleus

bacterial chromosome The single circular DNA macromolecule that contains the genetic information of bacterial cells

bacterial dysentery Dysentery caused by *Shigella* infections; also called *shigellosis*

bacterial endotoxin Endotoxin

bactericidal Any physical or chemical agent able to kill some types of bacteria

bactericide A chemical that kills microorganisms

bacteriochlorophyll Photosynthetic pigment of green and purple anaerobic photosynthetic bacteria

bacteriological filter A filter with pores small enough to trap bacteria, about 0.45 μm or smaller, used to sterilize solutions by removing microorganisms during filtration

bacteriology The science of dealing with bacteria, including their relation to medicine, industry, and agriculture

bacteriophage A virus whose host is a bacterium; a virus that replicates within bacterial cells

bacteriostatic An agent that inhibits the growth and reproduction of some types of bacteria but need not kill the bacteria

Bacteroidaceae Family of Gram-negative anaerobic bacteria, many of which are important in the normal microbiota of humans

bacteroids Irregularly shaped (pleomorphic) forms that some bacteria can assume under certain conditions, e.g., *Rhizobium* in root nodules

baeocytes Endospores of pleurocapsalean cyanobacteria

baker's yeast *Saccharomyces cerevisiae;* yeast used in the baking industry

band cells Stab cells

barophiles Organisms that grow best or only under conditions of high pressure, e.g., in the ocean's depths

barotolerant Organisms that can grow under conditions of high pressure but do not exhibit a preference for growth under such conditions

base analogs Chemicals that structurally resemble the DNA nucleotides and therefore may substitute for them but do not function in the same manner

base substitutions Mutations that occur when one pair of nucleotide bases in the DNA is replaced by another pair

basic stains Dyes whose active staining parts consist of a cationic, negatively charged group that may be combined with an acid, usually inorganic, that has affinity for nucleic acids

basidia Specialized sexual spore-producing structures found in Basidiomycetes

basidiocarps The fruiting bodies of basidiomycetes

basidiomycetes A group of fungi distinguished by the formation of sexual basidiospores on a basidium

basidiomycotina Club fungi; fungal subdivision of Amastigomycota; includes smuts, rusts, jelly fungi, shelf fungi, stinkhorns, bird's nest fungi, puffballs, and mushrooms; produce sexual basidiospores on the surfaces of basidia

basidiospores Sexual spores formed on basidiocarps by basidiomycetes

basidium Club-like structure of basidiomycetes on which basidiospores are borne

basophils White blood cells containing granules (granulocytes) that readily take up basic dye

batch culture Growth of microorganisms under conditions in which a medium in a reaction vessel is inoculated and further additions of organisms or growth substrates are not made

batch process Common simple form of culture in which a fixed volume of liquid medium is inoculated and incubated for an appropriate period of time; cells grown this way are exposed to a continually changing environment; when used in industrial processes, the culture and products are harvested as a batch at appropriate times

Bauer-Kirby test A standardized antimicrobial susceptibility procedure in which a culture is inoculated onto the surface of Mueller-Hinton agar, followed by the addition of antibiotic impregnated discs to the agar surface

Bayer junctions Adhesion sites between the cytoplasmic membrane and outer membrane of Gram-negative bacteria

beer Beverage produced by microbial alcoholic fermentation and brewing of cereal grains

benthos The bottom region of aquatic habitats; collective term for the organisms living at the bottom of oceans and lakes

Bergey's Manual Reference book describing the established status of bacterial taxonomy; describes bacterial taxa and provides keys and tables for their identification

beta-galactosidase (β-galactosidase) An enzyme catalyzing the hydrolysis of β-linked galactose within dimers or polymers

beta-hemolysis (β-hemolysis) Complete lysis of red blood cells, as shown by the presence of a sharply defined zone of clearing surrounding certain bacterial colonies growing on blood agar

beta-lactamase (β-lactamase) An enzyme that attacks a β-lactam ring, such as a penicillinase that attacks the lactam ring in the penicillin antimicrobials, inactivating such antibiotics

beta-oxidation (β-oxidation) Metabolic pathway for the oxidation of fatty acids resulting in the formation of acetate and a new fatty acid that is two carbon atoms shorter than the parent fatty acid; the pathway in which fatty acids are metabolized in cells by being broken down into small 2-carbon acetyl-coenzyme A units

bilateral parotitis Swelling of salivary glands on both sides in a case of mumps

binary fission A process in which two similarly sized and shaped cells are formed by the division of one cell; process by which most bacteria reproduce

binding protein transport A mechanism for transporting substances across the Gram-negative bacterial cytoplasmic membrane that involves the cooperative activities of periplasmic binding proteins and cytoplasmic permeases; shock-sensitive transport

binding proteins Chemosensors in the cell envelope that bind specifically and tightly to substances in the membrane transport process, detect certain chemicals, and signal the flagella to respond

binomial nomenclature The scientific method of naming plants, animals, and microorganisms composed of two names consisting of the species and genus

bioassay The use of a living organism to determine the amount of a substance based on the growth or activity of the test organism under controlled conditions

biochemicals Substances produced by or involved in the metabolic reactions of living organisms

biodegradation The process of chemical breakdown of a substance to smaller products caused by microorganisms or their enzymes

biodeterioration The chemical or physical alteration of a product that decreases the usefulness of that product for its intended purpose

biodisc system A secondary sewage treatment system employing a film of active microorganisms rotated on a disc through sewage

bioenergetics The transfer of energy through living systems; energy transformations in living systems

biogeochemical cycling The biologically mediated transformations of elements that result in their global cycling, including transfer between the atmosphere, hydrosphere, and lithosphere

bioleaching The use of microorganisms to transform elements so that the elements can be extracted from a material when water is filtered through it

biological control Deliberate use of one species of organism to control or eliminate populations of other organisms; used in the control of pest populations

biological magnification Biomagnification

biological oxygen demand (BOD) The amount of dissolved oxygen required by aerobic and facultative microorganisms to stabilize organic matter in sewage or water; also known as *biochemical oxygen demand*

bioluminescence The generation of light by certain microorganisms

biomagnification An increase in the concentration of a chemical substance, such as a pesticide, as the substance is passed to higher members of a food chain

biomass The dry weight, volume, or other quantitative estimation of organisms; the total mass of living organisms in an ecosystem

bioremediation The use of biological agents to reclaim soils and waters polluted by substances hazardous to human health or the environment; it is an extension of biological treatment processes that have traditionally been used to treat wastes in which microorganisms typically are used to biodegrade environmental pollutants

biosphere The part of the Earth in which life can exist; all living things with their environment

biosynthesis The production (synthesis) of chemical substances by the metabolic activities of living organisms

biotechnology The modern use of biological systems for economic benefit

biotic Of or relating to living organisms, caused by living things

biotype A variant form of a given species that may be distinguished based on physiology, morphology, or serology

biovar A biotype of a given species that is differentiated based on physiology

biphasic growth curve Growth curve reflecting diauxie, i.e., the preferential utilization of one substrate at a given rate before another substrate is metabolized at a different rate

black death Death due to plague in which there is severe tissue necrosis so that the skin appears blackened

blastospores Spores produced by budding

blight Any plant disease or injury that results in general withering and death of the plant without rotting

blood plasma The fluid portion of the blood minus all blood corpuscles

blood serum The fluid expressed from clotted blood or clotted blood plasma

blood type An immunologically distinct, genetically determined set of antigens on the surfaces of erythrocytes (red blood cells), defined as A, B, AB, and O

bloodstream The flowing blood in a circulatory system

bloom A visible abundance of microorganisms, generally referring to the excessive growth of algae or cyanobacteria at the surface of a body of water

BOD Biological oxygen demand

booster vaccines Vaccine antigens administered to elicit an anamnestic response and to maintain extended active immunity

botulinum toxins Neurotoxins produced by *Clostridium botulinum*

botulism Food intoxication or poisoning that is severe and often fatal, caused by *Clostridium botulinum*

bracket fungi Shelf fungi

bradykinin A mediator of pain that acts by lowering the threshold for firing of nerve cells

breakpoint chlorination Procedure for the removal and oxidation of ammonia from sewage to molecular nitrogen by the addition of hypochlorous acid

bright-field microscope A microscope that uses visible light transmitted through a specimen to illuminate that specimen

broad-spectrum antibiotic Antibiotics capable of inhibiting a relatively wide range of bacterial species, including Gram-negative and Gram-positive types

bronchitis Inflammation occurring in the mucous membranes of the bronchi, often caused by *Streptococcus pneumoniae, Haemophilus influenzae,* and certain viruses

brown algae Members of the division Phaeophycophyta; Phaeophycophyta

Bruton congenital agammaglobulinemia An immunodeficiency disease affecting males in which all immunological classes are totally or partially absent

buboes Enlarged lymph nodes that are symptomatic of plague

bud scar Site on a yeast cell produced by the process of fungal budding, which limits the number of progeny that can be derived from a mother cell

budding A form of asexual reproduction in which a daughter cell develops from a small outgrowth or protrusion of the parent cell; the daughter cell is smaller than the parent cell

budding bacteria Heterogeneous group of bacteria that form extensions or protrusions from the cell; these bacteria have reproductive or physiological functions; some reproduce by budding, others by binary fission

buffer A solution that tends to resist the change in pH when acid or alkali is added

burst size The average number of infectious viral units released from a single cell

butanediol fermentation pathway Metabolic sequence during which acetoin is produced, carbon dioxide is released, and NADH is reoxidized to NAD^+; the end product is butanediol

butanol fermentation pathway Metabolic sequence carried out by certain *Clostridium* species, with pyruvate converted to either acetone and carbon dioxide, isopropanol and carbon dioxide, butyrate, or butanol

butyric acid fermentation pathway Butanol fermentation pathway

C

C_4 pathway A carbon dioxide fixation pathway in heterotrophs and autotrophs that produces oxaloacetate

calcium dipicolinate Chemical component of bacterial endospores contained within the core and involved in conferring heat resistance on endospores

Calvin cycle The primary pathway for carbon dioxide fixation (conversion of carbon dioxide to organic matter) in photoautotrophs and chemolithotrophs

cankers Plant diseases, or conditions of the diseases, that interfere with the translocation of water and minerals to the crown of the plant

canning Method for the preservation of foodstuffs in which suitably prepared foods are placed in metal containers that are heated, exhausted, and hermetically sealed

capillary One of a network of tiny hair-like blood vessels connecting the arteries to the veins

capnophiles Microaerophiles that grow at elevated concentrations of carbon dioxide (5% to 10% CO_2)

capsid A protein coat of a virus enclosing the naked nucleic acid

capsomere The individual protein units that form the capsid of a virus

capsule A mucoid envelope that is composed of polypeptides or carbohydrates surrounding certain microorganisms; a gelatinous or slimy layer external to the bacterial cell wall

carbohydrates A class of organic compounds consisting of many hydroxyl (–OH) groups and containing either a ketone or an aldehyde

carbolic acid Phenol

carbon cycle The biogeochemical cycling of carbon through oxidized and reduced forms, primarily between organic compounds and inorganic carbon dioxide

carboxyl end The terminus of a polypeptide chain with a free alpha carboxyl group not involved in forming a peptide linkage; also known as the *C terminal end*

carboxysomes Inclusions within some autotrophic bacteria containing ribulose-1,5-bisphosphate carboxylase

carcinogen Cancer-causing agent

carditis Inflammation of the heart

caries Bone or tooth decay with the formation of ulceration; also known as *dental caries* or *cavities*

carotenoid pigments A class of pigments, usually yellow, orange, red, or purple, that are widely distributed among microorganisms

carpogonia The basal bodies bearing female gametes in some red algae

carpospore Red algal spore produced during fertilization

carriers Individuals who harbor pathogens but do not exhibit any signs of illness

case–control studies Studies where persons with a disease are compared with a disease-free control group for various possible risk factors

catabolic pathway A degradative metabolic pathway; a metabolic pathway in which large compounds are broken down into smaller ones

catabolism Metabolic reactions involving the enzymatic degradation of organic compounds to simpler organic or inorganic compounds with the release of free energy

catabolite repression Repression of the transcription of genes coding for certain inducible enzyme systems by glucose or other readily utilizable carbon sources

catalases Enzymes that catalyze the decomposition of hydrogen peroxide (H_2O_2) into water and oxygen and the oxidation of alcohols to aldehydes by hydrogen peroxide

catalyst Any substance that accelerates a chemical reaction but itself remains unaltered in form and amount

catheterization Insertion of a hollow tubular device (a catheter) into a cavity, duct, or vessel to permit injection or withdrawal of fluids

cathode The electrode at which reduction takes place in an electrolytic cell; a negatively charged electrode

cations Positively charged ions

cauldoactive bacteria Extreme thermophiles that often fail to grow at temperatures below 50° C and are able to grow at temperatures above 100° C

cDNA Complementary DNA; copied DNA

cell The functional and structural subunit of living organisms, separated from its surroundings by a delimiting membrane

cell envelope Structure found only in Gram-negative cell walls, extending outward from the cytoplasmic membrane to the outer membrane

cell wall Structure outside of and protecting the cell membrane, generally containing murein in prokaryotes and composed chiefly of various other polymeric substances, e.g., cellulose or chitin, in eukaryotic microorganisms

cell-mediated hypersensitivity Type 4 hypersensitivity or delayed hypersensitivity; reaction involving T lymphocytes and occurring 24 to 72 hours after exposure to the antigen; contact dermatitis, including poison ivy, is an example

cell-mediated immune response Cell-mediated immunity

cell-mediated immunity Specific acquired immunity involving T cells, primarily responsible for resistance to infectious diseases caused by certain bacteria and viruses that reproduce within host cells

cellular metabolism The collective process of chemical reactions that accompanies the flow of energy through a cell

cellular slime molds Members of the Acrasiales that form a sporocarp fruiting body

cellulase An extracellular enzyme that hydrolyzes cellulose

cellulose A linear polysaccharide of *β*-D-glucose

central metabolic pathways Metabolic sequences that play key roles in both catabolism and biosynthesis

centrifugation Process in which particulate matter is sedimented from a fluid, or fluids of different densities are separated, using a centrifuge

centrifuge An apparatus used to separate by sedimentation particulate matter suspended in a liquid by centrifugal force

cephalosporins A heterogeneous group of natural and semisynthetic β-lactam antibiotics that act against a range of Gram-positive and Gram-negative bacteria by inhibiting the formation of cross-links in peptidoglycan

cerebrospinal fluid (CSF) The fluid contained within the four ventricles of the brain, the subarachnoid space, and the central canal of the spinal cord

CFU Colony forming unit

chancre The lesion formed at the site of primary inoculation by an infecting microorganism, usually an ulcer

change in free energy (ΔG) The change in the usable energy that is available for doing work

charging The attachment of an amino acid to its specific tRNA molecule

chemical mutagens Chemical substances that can modify nucleotide bases; chemicals that increase the rate of mutation

chemical oxygen demand (COD) The amount of oxygen required to oxidize completely the organic matter in a water sample

chemical preservative Chemical substances added to prevent the spoilage of a food or the biodeterioration of any substance by inhibiting microbial growth or activity

chemiosmosis The generation of ATP by the movement of hydrogen ions into pores in the cytoplasmic membrane that are associated with the ATPase system

chemiosmotic hypothesis The theory that the living cell establishes a proton and electrical gradient across a membrane and that, by controlled reentry of protons into the region contained by that membrane, the energy to carry out different types of endergonic processes may be obtained, including the ability to drive the formation of ATP

chemoattractants Substances that attract motile bacteria—bacteria move through their environment toward higher concentrations of a chemoattractant

chemoautotrophic metabolism A type of metabolism in which inorganic molecules serve as electron donors and energy source and inorganic CO_2 serves as carbon source

chemoautotrophs Microorganisms that obtain energy from the oxidation of inorganic compounds and carbon from inorganic carbon dioxide; organisms that obtain energy through chemical oxidation and use inorganic compounds as electron donors; also known as *chemolithotrophs*

chemoheterotrophs Heterotrophs

chemolithotrophic metabolism Chemoautotrophic metabolism

chemolithotrophs Microorganisms that obtain energy through chemical oxidation and use inorganic compounds as electron donors and cellular carbon through the reduction of carbon dioxide; also known as chemoautotrophs

chemoorganotrophic metabolism A type of metabolism in which organic molecules serve as electron donors, energy source, and carbon source

chemoorganotrophs Organisms that obtain energy from the oxidation of organic compounds and cellular carbon from preformed organic compounds

chemorepellents Substances that repel motile bacteria—bacteria move through their environment away from higher concentrations of chemorepellents

chemostat An apparatus used for continuous-flow culture to maintain bacterial cultures in the log phase of growth, based on maintaining a continuous supply of a solution containing a nutrient in limiting quantities that controls the growth rate of the culture

chemotaxis A locomotive response in which the stimulus is a chemical concentration gradient; movement of microorganisms toward or away from a chemical stimulus

chemotherapy The use of chemical agents for the treatment of disease, including the use of antibiotics to eliminate infecting agents

chi (χ) form The joining of chromosomes at a homologous region during recombination

chitin A polysaccharide composed of repeating *N*-acetylglucosamine residues, abundant in arthropod exoskeletons and fungal cell walls

chlamydias Obligate intracellular parasites whose reproduction is characterized by a change of the small, rigid-walled, infectious form of the organism into a larger, thin-walled, noninfectious form that divides by fission

chlamydospores Thick-walled, typically spherical or ovoid resting spores produced asexually by certain types of fungi from cells of the somatic hyphae

chlor- Combining form indicating chlorine substituted for hydrogen

chloramination The use of chloramines to disinfect water

chloramphenicol Aminoglycoside antibiotic that inhibits bacterial protein synthesis; it acts by binding to the 50S ribosomal subunit, preventing the binding of tRNA

chlorination The process of treating with chlorine, as in disinfecting drinking water or sewage

Chlorobiaceae Green sulfur bacteria; family of nonmotile, obligately phototrophic bacteria that produce green or green-brown carotenoid pigments

Chloroflexaceae Family of anaerobic phototrophic bacteria; its members have flexible walls, form filaments, and exhibit gliding motility

Chlorophycophyta Green algae; may be unicellular, colonial, or filamentous; most cells are uninucleate; some form coenocytic filaments, contain contractile vacuoles, or store starch as reserve material; their cell walls are composed of cellulose, mannans, xylans, or protein

chlorophyll The green pigment responsible for photosynthesis in plants; the primary photosynthetic pigment of algae and cyanobacteria

chloroplasts Membrane-bound organelles of photosynthetic eukaryotes where the biochemical conversion of light energy to ATP occurs; the sites of photosynthesis in eukaryotic organisms

chlorosis The yellowing of leaves or plant components due to bleaching of chlorophyll, often symptomatic of microbial disease

chlorosomes Vesicles that contain photosynthetic antenna pigments in some green photoautotrophic bacteria

choleragen Enterotoxin produced by *Vibrio cholerae* that blocks the conversion of cyclic AMP to ATP

Chromatiaceae Purple sulfur bacteria; family of phototrophic bacteria that produce carotenoid pigments, appear orange-brown, purple-red, or purple-violet, and deposit elemental sulfur

chromatic aberration An optical lens defect causing distortion of the image because light of differing wavelengths is focused at differing points instead of at a single focal point

chromatids Fibrils formed from a eukaryotic chromosome when it replicates before meiosis or mitosis

chromatin The deoxyribonucleic acid–protein complex that constitutes a chromosome; the readily stainable protoplasmic substance in the nuclei of cells

chromatophore Internal membranes in some photosynthetic bacteria that contain the pigments and accessory molecules utilized in photosynthesis

chromosomes Structures that contain the nuclear DNA of a cell

chronic A disease condition in which the symptoms persist for a long time

chronic disease A persistent disease

chronometer A device for measuring time

chroococcecean cyanobacteria Subgroup of cyanobacteria, unicellular rods or cocci that reproduce by binary fission or budding; generally nonmotile

Chrysophyceae A group within the Chrysophycophyta that contains the golden algae

Chrysophycophyta Division of algae that includes the yellow-green algae, golden algae, and diatoms; all produce chrysolaminarin; most are unicellular and some are colonial

chytrids Members of the Chytridiales, which are mainly aquatic fungi that produce zoospores with a single posterior flagellum

-cide Suffix signifying a killer or destroyer, as in a chemical that kills microorganisms

cilia Thread-like appendages having a 9 + 2 arrangement of microtubules occurring as projections from certain cells that beat rhythmically, causing locomotion or propelling fluid over surfaces

ciliated epithelial cells Cells that line the respiratory tract and act as filters by sweeping microorganisms out of the body with a wave-like motion

Ciliophora Group of one subphylum of protozoa that possess simple to compound ciliary organelles in at least one stage of their life cycle; these protozoa are motile by means of cilia

circadian rhythm Daily cyclical changes that occur in an organism even when it is isolated from the natural daily fluctuations of the environment

circulatory system The vessels and organs comprising the cardiovascular and lymphatic systems of animals

***cis* configuration** Genetic elements that have an effect on the same DNA molecule

***cis/trans* complementation test** A test to determine whether two mutations are in the same gene and on the same DNA molecule

cistron The functional unit of genetic inheritance; a segment of genetic nucleic acid that codes for a specific polypeptide chain; synonym for *gene*

citric acid Intermediary metabolite in the Krebs cycle, and organic acid, produced by *Aspergillus niger,* used as a food additive, a metal chelating and sequestering agent, and a plasticizer

citric acid cycle Krebs cycle

clamp cell connections Hyphal structures in many basidiomycetes formed during cell division by dikaryotic hyphal cells, i.e., formed by hyphal cells containing two nuclei of different mating types

classical complement pathway Series of reactions initiated by the formation of a complex between an antigen and an antibody that lead to the lysis of microbial cells or the enhanced ability of phagocytic blood cells to eliminate such cells

classification The systematic arrangement of organisms in groups or categories according to established criteria

clonal deletion Elimination of clones of T cells in the thymus gland that would attack the body's own normal cells

clonal selection theory A theory that accounts for antibody formation by supposing that during fetal development a complete set of lymphocytes are developed, with each lymphocyte containing the genetic information for initiating an immune response to a single specific antigen for which it has only one type of receptor; B cells that react with self-antigens during this period are destroyed

clone A population of cells derived asexually from a single cell, often assumed to be genetically homologous; a population of genetically identical individuals

cloning vector Segment of DNA used for the replication of foreign DNA fragments

club fungi Members of the Basidiomycotina

cluster analysis A statistical method for grouping (clustering) organisms based on their degree of similarity; method used in numerical taxonomy for defining taxonomic groups

coagglutination An enhanced agglutination reaction based on using antibody molecules whose Fc fragments are attached to cells so that a larger matrix is formed when the Fab portion reacts with other cells for which the antibody is specific

coagulase An enzyme produced by pathogenic staphylococci, causing coagulation of blood plasma

cocci Spherical or nearly spherical bacterial cells, varying in size and sometimes occurring singly, in pairs, in regular groups of four or more, in chains, or in irregular clusters

coccidioidomycosis A disease of humans and domestic animals caused by *Coccidioides immitis*, usually occurring via the respiratory tract

codominance The partial expression of the genetic information contained in both the recessive and dominant alleles of a gene

codon A triplet of adjacent bases in a polynucleotide chain of an mRNA molecule that codes for a specific amino acid; the basic unit of the genetic code specifying an amino acid for incorporation into a polypeptide chain

coenocytic Referring to any multinucleate cell, structure, or organism formed by the division of an existing multinucleate entity or when nuclear divisions are not accompanied by the formation of dividing walls or septa; multinucleate hyphae

coenzymes The nonprotein portions of enzymes; small, nonprotein organic chemicals that are not tightly bound to the enzymes with which they function and that act as acceptors or donors of electrons or functional groups during enzymatic reactions

cofactors Inorganic substances, such as minerals, required for enzymatic activity

cohort study The most definitive type of analytical epidemiological study based on comparisons with a defined group (cohort)

cold pack method A method of canning uncooked high-acid food by placing it in hot jars or cans and sterilizing in a bath of boiling water or steam

colicinogenic plasmids Plasmids that code for colicins

colicins Proteins produced by some bacteria that inhibit closely related bacteria

coliform count Enumeration of coliform bacteria, especially *Escherichia coli*, that is commonly used as an indicator of water quality and potential fecal contamination

coliforms Gram-negative, lactose-fermenting, enteric rods, e.g., *Escherichia coli*

colinear Two related linear information sequences arranged so that the unit may be moved from one to the other without rearrangement; RNA and DNA molecules with precisely matching base pairs

coliphage A virus that infects *Escherichia coli*

collagenase An enzyme that breaks down the proteins of collagen tissues

colonization The establishment of a site of microbial reproduction on a material, animal, or person without necessarily resulting in tissue invasion or damage

colony The macroscopically visible growth of microorganisms on a solid culture medium

colony forming units (CFU) Number of microorganisms that can replicate to form colonies, as determined by the number of colonies that develop

colony hybridization A technique that can be used to detect the presence of a specific DNA sequence in a cell by transferring cells from a colony to a filter, lysing the cells, and identifying a target DNA sequence by hybridization with a gene probe

coma A state of unconsciousness

cometabolism The gratuitous metabolic transformation of a substance by a microorganism growing on another substrate; the cometabolized substance is not incorporated into an organism's biomass, and the organism does not derive energy from the transformation of that substance

commensalism An interactive association between two populations of different species living together in which one population benefits from the association, while the other is not affected

common source epidemic An epidemic where many individuals simultaneously acquire an infectious agent from the same source

common source outbreak Disease outbreak characterized by a sharp rise and a rapid decline in the number of cases

communicable disease A disease in which a pathogen will move with ease from one individual to the next

community Highest biological unit in an ecological hierarchy composed of interacting populations

competent In transformation, the state of a recipient cell in which DNA can pass across its membrane, depending on environmental conditions and the cell growth phase

competition An interactive association between two species, both of which need some limited environmental factor for growth and thus grow at suboptimal rates because they must share the growth-limiting resource

competitive exclusion Competitive interactions tend to bring about the ecological separation of closely related populations and precludes two populations from occupying the same ecological niche

competitive inhibition The inhibition of enzyme activity caused by the competition of an inhibitor with a substrate for the active (catalytic) site on the enzyme; impairment of the function of an enzyme due to its reaction with a substance chemically related to its normal substrate

complement Group of proteins normally present in plasma and tissue fluids that participates in antigen–antibody reactions, allowing reactions such as cell lysis to occur

complement fixation The binding of complement to an antigen–antibody complex so that the complement is unavailable for subsequent reactions

complement fixation test Test that measures the degree of complement fixation for diagnostic purposes

complementary DNA (cDNA) In cloning eukaryotic genes in bacteria, a single-stranded DNA molecule that is complementary to the complete mRNA; copy DNA

complementation A method for determining whether mutations are in the same or different locations

completed test In assays for assessing water safety, gas formation by subcultured colonies showing a greenish metallic sheen on EMB agar grown on lactose broth incubated at 35° C; positive test for fecal coliforms

complex-mediated hypersensitivity Type 3 hypersensitivity; reaction that occurs when excess antigens are produced during a normal inflammatory response and antibody–antigen–complement complexes are deposited in tissues

complex medium A medium made with constituents whose compositions are not fully known and may vary

composting The decomposition of organic matter in a heap by microorganisms; a method of solid waste disposal

computer-assisted identification Rapid identification of microorganisms by a computer based on a large number of calculations and comparisons of data and assessment of the probability of correctly identifying a particular microorganism

concentration gradient Condition established by the difference in concentration on opposite sides of a membrane

condenser lenses The lenses on a microscope used for focusing or directing light from the light source onto the object

conditionally lethal mutations Mutations that cause the loss of microbial viability only under certain environmental conditions

confirmed test In assays for assessing water safety, the formation of greenish, metallic colonies of fecal coliforms on EMB agar or brilliant green lactose–bile broth

conidia Thin-walled, asexually derived spores, borne singly or in groups or clusters in specialized hyphae

conidiophores Branches of mycelia-bearing conidia

conjugated fluorescent dyes Fluorescent dyes coupled with antibody molecules used to tag antibodies

conjugation The process in which genetic material is transferred from one microorganism to another, involving a physical connection or union between the two cells; a parasexual form of reproduction sometimes referred to as *mating*

conjugative plasmids F and other plasmids that encode for self-transfer from one cell to another

conjunctivitis Inflammation of the mucous membranes covering the eye, the conjunctiva

consensus sequence Conserved DNA sequence that characterizes the bacterial promoter where there is a high nucleotide sequence homology among most promoters

conservation of energy Maintenance of energy during chemical reactions: transfer of energy without destruction

conservative transposition Excision and insertion of a transposon from one location to another without a change in copy number

consortium An interactive association between microorganisms that generally results in combined metabolic activities

constant region The carboxyl terminal end of an immunoglobulin molecule that has a relatively constant amino acid sequence

constipation A condition in which the bowels are evacuated at long intervals or with difficulty; the passage of hard, dry stools

constitutive enzymes Enzymes whose synthesis is not altered in response to changes in the environment but rather are continuously synthesized

contact dermatitis Delayed hypersensitivity reaction resulting from exposure of the skin to chemicals; poison ivy is an example

contact diseases Diseases caused by agents that are able to enter the subcutaneous layers of the skin through hair follicles

contagion The process by which disease spreads from one individual to another

contagious disease An infectious disease that is communicable to healthy, susceptible individuals by physical contact with someone suffering from that disease, contact with bodily discharges from that individual, or contact with inanimate objects contaminated by that individual

contamination The process of allowing the uncontrolled addition of microorganisms to an area or substance

continuous feed composting process A composting process that uses a reactor to establish the environmental parameters that maximize the degradation process

continuous flow process A process for growing microorganisms without interruption by continual addition of substrates and recovery of products

continuous flow-through process Continuous flow process

continuous strand of DNA The strand of DNA that can be synthesized continuously because it runs in the appropriate direction for the continuous addition of new free nucleotide bases; also referred to as the *leading strand of DNA*

contractile vacuoles Pulsating vacuoles in certain protozoa used for the excretion of wastes and the exclusion of water for the maintenance of proper osmotic balance

contrast In microscopy, the ability to visually distinguish an object from the background

control group The reference point in a controlled experiment in which a set of conditions does not vary

controlled experiment An experiment in which results from an experimental group with variable conditions is compared with a control group with nonvariable conditions

convalescence Recovery period of a disease during which signs and symptoms disappear

copiotrophs Bacteria that grow at high nutrient concentrations, such as the nutrient concentration in most culture media

coprophagous Capable of growth on fecal matter; feeding on dung or excrement

copy DNA Complimentary DNA

cornsteep liquor The concentrated water extract by-product resulting from the steeping of corn during the production of cornstarch; used as a medium adjunct to supply nitrogen and vitamins in industrial fermentations

cortex A layer of a bacterial endospore, important in conferring heat resistance on that structure

coryneform group Bacterial group of Gram-positive, irregularly shaped rods with a tendency to show incomplete separation after cell division and to exhibit pleomorphic morphology

coryza An inflammation of the mucous membranes of the nose, usually marked by sneezing and the discharge of watery mucus

cosmid Phage–plasmid artificial hybrids; a genetically engineered hybrid of bacteriophage λ and plasmid genes that contains *cos* sites needed to package λ DNA into its particles

co-transporters Permeases in the cytoplasmic membrane that transport more than one type of substrate at the same time

countercurrent immunoelectrophoresis A technique based on the immunological detection of substances that relies on the movement of an antibody and an antigen toward each other in an electric field, resulting in the rapid formation of a detectable antigen–antibody precipitate

counterstain In microscopy, the use of a secondary stain to visualize objects differentially from those stained with a primary stain

covalent bond A strong chemical bond formed by the sharing of electrons

CPE Cytopathic effects

cristae Convolutions of the inner membrane that extend into the interior of the mitochondria of eukaryotic cells

critical point drying A method for removing liquids from a microbiological specimen by adjusting the temperature and pressure so that the liquid and gas phases of the liquid are in equilibrium with each other; used to minimize disruption of biological structures for viewing by scanning electron microscopy

crop rotation The alternation of the types of crops planted in a field

cross-feeding The phenomena in which the growth of an organism is dependent on the provision of one or more metabolic factors or nutrients by another organism growing in the vicinity; also termed *syntrophism*

cross-reactive antibodies Heterophile antibodies

cross walls Septa

crossing over The process in which, in effect, a break occurs in each of the two adjacent DNA strands and the exposed 5′-P and 3′-OH ends unite with the exposed 5′-P and 3′-OH ends of the adjacent strands so that there is an exchange of homologous regions of DNA

crown gall Plant disease caused by *Agrobacterium tumefaciens* that infects fruit trees, sugar beets, and other broad-leafed plants, manifested by the formation of a tumor growth

cruciform loops A region of DNA that forms a loop because it contains inverted repeat nucleotide sequences that form hydrogen-bonded hairpin structures

Cryptophycophyta Group of unicellular brown algae that reproduce by longitudinal division, producing 14 flagella of equal length

culture To encourage the growth of particular microorganisms under controlled conditions; the growth of particular types of microorganisms on or within a medium as a result of inoculation and incubation

culture medium A liquid or solidified nutrient material that is suitable for the cultivation of a microorganism

curing The loss of plasmids from a bacterial cell

curvature of field Distortion of a microscopic field of view in which specimens in the center of the field are in clear focus, while those in the peripheral region are out of focus

cutaneous Pertaining to the skin

cyanobacteria Prokaryotic, photosynthetic organisms containing chlorophyll *a*, capable of producing oxygen by splitting water; formerly known as *blue-green algae*

Cyanobacteriales Order of Oxyphotobacteria whose primary bacterial photosynthetic pigment is chlorophyll *a*; the blue-green algae, or cyanobacteria

cyclic oxidative photophosphorylation Cyclic photophosphorylation

cyclic photophosphorylation A metabolic pathway involved in the conversion of light energy to chemical energy, with the generation of ATP that does not produce the reduced coenzyme, NADPH

cycloserine Antibiotic that inhibits bacterial cell wall synthesis

cyst A dormant form assumed by some microorganisms during specific stages in their life cycles, or assumed as a response to particular environmental conditions in which the organism becomes enclosed in a thin- or thick-walled membranous structure, the function of which is either protective or reproductive; a normal or pathological sac with a distinct wall containing fluid; a protozoan resting stage that has a wall

cystites Arthrospores of *Arthrobacter* species

cystitis An inflammation of the urinary bladder

cytochromes Reversible oxidation-reduction carriers in respiration

cytokines Substances that stimulate cell growth, particularly lymphocyte proliferation

cytokinesis The division of cytoplasm following nuclear division

cytolysis The dissolution or disintegration of a cell

cytopathic effects Generalized degenerative changes or abnormalities in the cells of a monolayer tissue culture due to infection by a virus

Cytophagales Gliding bacteria exhibiting widely differing morphological forms and modes of metabolism that do not form fruiting bodies; however, some form filaments and others are chemolithotrophs

cytoplasm The living substance of a cell, exclusive of the nucleus

cytoplasmic membrane The selectively permeable membrane that forms the outer limit of the protoplast, bordered externally by the cell wall in most bacteria

cytoplasmic polyhedrosis virus A type of virus used as a viral pesticide that develops in the cytoplasm of host midgut epithelial cells

cytoplast The unified structure that provides the rigidity needed to hold the various structures of the eukaryotic cell in their appropriate locations

cytosine A pyrimidine base found in nucleic acids

cytosis The movement of materials into or out of a cell, involving the engulfment and formation of a membrane-bound structure rather than passage through a membrane

cytoskeleton Protein fibers composing the structural support framework of a eukaryotic cell

cytostomes Mouth-like openings of some protozoa, particularly ciliates; structure found in some protozoa that acts as specialized structure for phagocytosis

cytotoxic T cells Specialized class of T lymphocytes that are able to kill cells as part of the cell-mediated immune response

cytotoxins Substances capable of injuring certain cells without causing cell lysis

D

D value Decimal reduction time

dark-field microscope A microscope in which the only light seen in the field of view is reflected from the object under examination, resulting in a light object on a dark background

deaminase An enzyme involved in the removal of an amino group from a molecule, liberating ammonia

deamination The removal of an amino group from a molecule, especially an amino acid

death phase The part of the normal growth curve that represents the inability of microorganisms to reproduce

decarboxylase An enzyme that liberates carbon dioxide from the carboxyl group of a molecule by hydrolysis

decarboxylation The splitting off of one or more molecules of carbon dioxide from organic acids, especially amino acids

decimal reduction time The time required at a given temperature to heat inactivate or kill 90% of a given population of cells or spores; the time needed to reduce the number of visible microorganisms under a specified set of conditions by an order of magnitude

decimal reduction value Decimal reduction time

decolorization Removal of a colored stain from an object

decomposers Organisms, often bacteria or fungi, in a community that convert dead organic matter into inorganic nutrients

deductive reasoning A logical process in which a conclusion drawn from a set of premises contains no more information than the premises taken collectively

defective phage A bacteriophage that carries some bacterial DNA instead of viral DNA and therefore cannot cause lysis in an infected bacterial cell

deficiencies Deletions of large numbers of base pairs that can result in the loss of genetic information for one or more complete genes

defined medium The material supporting microbial growth in which all of the constituents, including trace substances, are quantitatively known; a mixture of known composition for culturing microorganisms

degenerate Describes the redundancy inherent in the genetic code that occurs because there are several codons coding for the insertion of the same amino acid into the polypeptide chain

dehydration Removal of water; drying

dehydrogenase An enzyme that catalyzes the oxidation of a substrate by removing hydrogen

delayed hypersensitivity Cell-mediated hypersensitivity

deletion mutations Mutations caused by the removal of one or more nucleotide base pairs from the DNA

Delta G (ΔG) Change in free energy

denaturation Alteration in the characteristics of an organic substance, especially a protein, by physical or chemical action; the loss of enzymatic activity due to modification of the tertiary protein structure

dendrograms Graphic representations of taxonomic analyses, showing the relationships between the organisms examined

denitrification The formation of gaseous nitrogen or gaseous nitrogen oxides from nitrate or nitrite by microorganisms

dental plaque Matrix of microbial cells and microbially produced extracellular polysaccharides that forms on the tooth surface and can be removed by brushing and flossing

deoxyribonucleic acid The carrier of genetic information; a type of nucleic acid occurring in cells, containing adenine, guanine, cytosine, and thymine, and D-2-deoxyribose linked by phosphodiester bonds

deoxyribose A 5-carbon sugar having one oxygen less than the parent sugar ribose; a component of DNA

derepress The regulation of transcription by reversibly inactivating a repressor protein

dermatitis An inflammation of the skin

dermatophytes Fungi characterized by their ability to metabolize keratin and capable of growing on the skin surface, causing disease

desert A region of low rainfall; a dry region; a region of low biological productivity

desiccation Removal of water; drying

desulfurization Removal of sulfur from organic compounds

detergent A synthetic cleaning agent containing surface-active agents that do not precipitate in hard water; a surface-active agent having a hydrophilic and a hydrophobic portion

detrital food web A food web based on the biomass of decomposers rather than on that of primary producers

detritus Waste matter and biomass produced from decompositional processes

Deuteromycetes A group of fungi with no known sexual stage; also known as *Fungi Imperfecti*

Deuteromycotina *Fungi Imperfecti*

diagnostic table A table of distinguishing features used as an aid in the identification of unknown organisms

diapedesis The process by which leukocytes move out of blood vessels

diarrhea Common symptom of gastrointestinal disease, characterized by increased frequency and fluid consistency of stools

diatomaceous earth A silicaceous material composed largely of fossil diatoms, used in microbiological filters and industrial processes

diatoms Unicellular algae having a cell wall composed of silica, the skeleton of which persists after the death of the organism

diauxic growth Biphasic growth; growth exhibiting diauxie

diauxie The phenomenon in which, given two carbon sources, an organism preferentially metabolizes one completely before utilizing the other

dichotomous key A key for the identification of organisms, using steps with opposing choices until a final identification is achieved

dictysomes The individual stacks of membranes in a Golgi apparatus

differential blood count Procedure for finding the ratios of various types of blood cells, used to determine the relative numbers of white blood cells as a diagnostic indication of an infectious process

differential medium Bacteriological medium on which the growth of specific types of organisms leads to readily visible changes in the appearance of the medium so that the presence of these organisms can be determined

differential stain The use of multiple staining reactions to differentiate one part of a cell from another or one cell type from another

differentially permeable membrane A membrane that selectively restricts the movement of molecules

diffraction The breaking up of a beam of light into bands of differing wavelength due to interference

diffusion Movement of molecules across a concentration gradient from the area of higher concentration to the area of lower concentration

DiGeorge syndrome Immune disorder caused by the partial or total absence of cellular immunity, resulting from a deficiency of T lymphocytes because of incomplete fetal development of the thymus

digestive vacuoles Membrane-bound organelles formed when a eukaryotic cell engulfs a food source and then fuses with lysosomes, permitting digestion of the contents

dikaryotes Cells with two different nuclei resulting from the fusion of two cells

dimorphism The property of existing in two distinct structural forms, e.g., fungi that occur in filamentous and yeast-like forms under different conditions

dinitrogenase One of the two proteins that comprise nitrogenase; protein of nitrogenase that has attached iron and molybdenum or vanadium cofactor

dinitrogenase reductase One of the two proteins that comprise nitrogenase; protein of nitrogenase that has only attached iron cofactor

dinoflagellates Algae of the class Pyrrhophyta, primarily unicellular marine organisms, possessing flagella

diphtheria An acute, communicable human disease caused by strains of *Corynebacterium diphtheriae*

diphtheria toxin Cytotoxin produced by *Corynebacterium diphtheriae* that inhibits protein synthesis in mammalian cells by blocking transferase reactions during translation

diplococci Cocci occurring in pairs

diploid Having double the haploid number of chromosomes; having a duplication of genes

direct counting procedures Methods for the enumeration of bacteria and other microbes that do not require the growth of cells in culture but rather rely on direct observation or other detection methods by which the undivided microbial cells can be counted

direct fluorescent antibody staining (FAB) Method used to detect the presence of an antigen by staining with a specific antibody linked with a fluorescent dye; the conjugated fluorescent antibody reacts directly with the antigens

disaccharides Carbohydrates formed by the condensation of two monosaccharide sugars

discontinuous strand of DNA The strand of DNA that lags behind the replication of the continuous strand because DNA polymerases can add nucleotides in only one direction; therefore synthesis of this strand can begin only after some unwinding of the double strand has occurred and takes place via the synthesis of short segments that run in the opposite direction to the overall direction of synthesis; also referred to as the *lagging strand of DNA*

disease Condition of an organ, part, structure, or system of the body in which there is incorrect functioning due to the effect of heredity, infection, diet, or environment; a physiologically impaired state of a plant or animal resulting from microbial infection, microbial products, or microbial activities; a physiological condition that occurs when microorganisms overcome host defense systems

disease syndrome Stages in the course of a disease

disinfectants Chemical agents used for disinfection

disinfection The destruction, inactivation, or removal of microorganisms likely to cause infection or produce other undesirable effects

dispersal Breaking up and spreading in various directions, e.g., the spread of microorganisms from one place to another

dissemination The scattering or dispersion of microorganisms or disease, e.g., the spread of disease associated with the dispersal of pathogens

dissociation Separation of a molecule into two or more stable fragments; a change in colony form often occurring in a new environment, associated with modified growth or virulence

distilled liquor Alcoholic beverage produced by microbial alcoholic fermentation followed by chemical distillation to achieve a high alcohol concentration

DNA Deoxyribonucleic acid

DNA double helix The two primary polynucleotide chains of DNA held together by hydrogen bonding between complementary nucleotide bases

DNA gyrase An enzyme that introduces negative supercoiling into relaxed DNA; topoisomerase II; enzyme that breaks the phosphodiester linkage of one of the strands of DNA, passing that strand through the other, which results in a localized uncoiling effect

DNA helicases Unwinding proteins that catalyze the breaking of the hydrogen bonding that hold the two strands of DNA together

DNA homology The degree of similarity of base sequences in DNA from different organisms

DNA ligase Enzyme that establishes a phosphodiester bond between the 3′-OH and 5′-P ends of chains of nucleotides; functions naturally as a repair enzyme and is used in genetic engineering to join chains of nucleotides

DNA methylases Enzymes that add methyl groups to some nucleotides of DNA after the nucleotides have been incorporated by DNA polymerases

DNA polymerases Enzymes that catalyze the phosphodiester bonds in the formation of DNA

DnaG protein RNA polymerase that makes an RNA primer of about 3 to 5 bases long; primase

dolipore septae The thick internal transverse openings between cell walls of basidiomycetes

domestic sewage Household liquid wastes

dominant allele The allelic form of a gene whose information is preferentially expressed

donor Any cell that contributes genetic information to another cell

dormant An organism or spore that exhibits minimal physical and chemical change over an extended period of time but remains alive

double diffusion method Precipitin reaction technique in which an antigen and an antibody diffuse toward each other from separate wells cut into an agar gel

double helix Two primary polynucleotide strands of DNA held together by hydrogen bonds and twisted like a spiral staircase

doubling time Generation time

drugs Substances used in medicine for the treatment of disease

Durham tubes Small inverted test tubes used to detect gas production during fermentation

dust cells Macrophage cells fixed in the alveolar lining of the lungs

dwarfism Plant condition resulting from degradation or inactivation of plant growth substances by pathogens

dysentery An infectious disease marked by inflammation and ulceration of the lower part of the bowels, with diarrhea that becomes mucous and hemorrhagic; disease condition characterized by diarrhea

dysfunctional immunity An immune response that produces an undesirable physiological state, e.g., an allergic reaction, or the lack of an immune response resulting in a failure to protect the body against infectious or toxic agents

E

early proteins Proteins that are made early in viral replication

ECHO virus group Group of viruses frequently found as causative agents of gastroenteritis

eclipse period Period in the lytic reproduction cycle in which complete infective viruses are not present

ecology The study of the interrelationships between organisms and their environments

ecosystem A functional self-supporting system that includes the organisms in a natural community and their environment

ectomycorrhizae Stable, mutually beneficial (symbiotic) association between a fungus and the root of a plant where the fungal hyphae occur outside the root and between the cortical cells of the root

ectopic pregnancy Fertilization and development of an egg that occurs outside the uterus

effluent The liquid discharge from sewage treatment and industrial plants

Eijkman test For assessing water safety; gas formation from dilutions of water samples incubated in lactose broth at 45° C demonstrates the presence of fecal coliforms

electromagnetic spectrum A range of energy in the form of waves of differing lengths that produces varying electric and magnetic fields as it travels through space from its source to a receiver

electron A negatively charged subatomic particle that orbits the positively charged nucleus of an atom

electron acceptors Substances that accept electrons during oxidation-reduction reactions

electron donors Substances that give up electrons during oxidation-reduction reactions

electron microscope A type of microscope with very high magnification ability that uses an electron beam; focuses by magnetic lenses instead of rays of light, the magnified image being formed on a phosphorescent screen or recorded on a photographic film

electron transport chain A series of oxidation-reduction reactions in which electrons are transported from a substrate through a series of intermediate electron carriers to a final acceptor, establishing an electrochemical gradient across a membrane that results in the formation of ATP

electrophoresis Movement of charged particles suspended in a liquid under the influence of an applied electron field

elementary body Small, rigid-walled, infectious form of chlamydias

elevated temperature Higher than normal temperature; characteristic symptom of the inflammatory response associated with the high metabolic activities of neutrophils and macrophages

ELISA Enzyme-linked immunosorbent assay

elongation factor (EF-Tu) Factor involved in placement of charged tRNA molecules into the aminoacyl site that initially forms a complex with GTP, which then binds to charged tRNA to form a ternary complex of aminoacyl-tRNA–EF-Tu–GTP

EMB agar Eosin methylene blue agar

Embden-Meyerhof pathway A specific glycolytic pathway; a sequence of reactions in which glucose is broken down to pyruvate

Embden-Meyerhof-Parnas pathway Embden-Meyerhof pathway

embryonated eggs Hen or duck eggs containing live embryos, used for culturing viruses and preparing tissue cultures

encephalitis An inflammation of the brain

end- Combining form indicating within

end product The chemical compound that is the final product in a particular metabolic pathway

end product inhibition Feedback inhibition

end product repression The process of shutting off transcription when a by-product of the metabolism coded for by the genes in that transcription region accumulates

endemic Peculiar to a certain region, e.g., a disease that occurs regularly in an area

endergonic A chemical reaction with a positive ΔG; a chemical reaction requiring input of free energy

endocarditis Infection of the endocardium or heart valves caused by bacteria or, in the cases of intravenous drug abusers, fungi

endocardium Membrane lining the interior of the heart

endocytosis Movement of materials into a cell by cytosis

endogenous Produced within; due to internal causes; pertaining to the metabolism of internal reserve materials

endomycorrhizae Mycorrhizal association in which there is fungal penetration of plant root cells

endonuclease An enzyme that catalyzes the cleavage of DNA, normally cutting it at specific sites

endoparasitic slime molds Plasmodiophoromycetes

endophytic A photosynthetic organism living within another organism

endoplasmic reticulum The extensive array of internal membranes in a eukaryotic cell involved in coordinating protein synthesis

endospores Thick-walled spores formed within a parent cell; in bacteria, heat-resistant spores; spores of myxomycetes; small, coccoid reproductive cells of pleurocapsalean cyanobacteria

endosymbiotic A symbiotic (mutually dependent) association in which one organism penetrates and lives within the cells or tissues of another organism

endosymbiotic bacteria Bacteria that live symbiotically within eukaryotic cells; bacteria that obligately live within protozoa

endosymbiotic evolution Theory that bacteria living as endosymbionts within eukaryotic cells gradually evolved into organelle structures

endothelium A single layer of thin cells lining internal body cavities; the inner layer of the seed coat of some plants

endothermic A chemical reaction in which energy is consumed; a chemical reaction requiring an input of heat energy

endotoxins Toxic substances found as part of some bacterial cells; the lipopolysaccharide component of the cell wall of Gram-negative bacteria

energy charge Measure of the energy status of a cell, describing its relative proportions of ATP, ADP, and AMP

enrichment culture Any form of culture in a liquid medium that results in an increase in a given type of organism while minimizing the growth of any other organism present

enter- Combining form meaning the intestine

enteric Of or pertaining to the intestines

enteric bacteria Bacteria that live within the intestinal tract

Enterobacteriaceae Family of Gram-negative, facultatively anaerobic rods, motile by means of peritrichous or polar flagella, divided into five tribes

enterobactin Siderophore synthesized by enteric bacteria

enterocolitis Infection of the lower gastrointestinal tract, lower small intestine and colon, characterized by abdominal pain and diarrhea, often with blood in the stools

enterotoxins Toxins specific for cells of the intestine, causing intestinal inflammation and producing the symptoms of food poisoning

enthalpy The total heat of a system; ΔH

Entner-Doudoroff pathway Glycolytic pathway that results in the net production of only one ATP molecule per molecule of glucose substrate metabolized

entomogenous fungi Fungi living on insects; fungal pathogens of insects

entropy That portion of the energy of a system that cannot be converted to work; ΔS

enumeration Determination of the number of microorganisms

envelope The outer covering surrounding the capsid of some viruses

enzymatic reactions Chemical reactions catalyzed by enzymes

enzyme kinetics The study of the rates at which enzymatic reactions proceed

enzyme-linked immunosorbent assay (ELISA) Technique used for detecting and quantifying specific serum antibodies based on tagging the antigen–antibody complex with a substrate that can be enzymatically converted to a readily quantifiable product by a specific enzyme

enzymes Proteins that function as efficient biological catalysts, increasing the rate of a reaction without altering the equilibrium constant by lowering the energy of activation

eosin methylene blue agar A medium used for the detection of coliform bacteria; the growth of Gram-positive bacteria is inhibited on this medium, and lactose fermenters produce colonies with a green metallic sheen

eosinophil A white blood cell having an affinity for eosin or any acid stain

eosinophilia An increase above normal in the number of eosinophils in the peripheral blood

epi- Prefix meaning upon, beside, among, above, or outside

epidemic An outbreak of infectious disease among a human population in which, for a limited time, a high proportion of the population exhibits overt disease symptoms

epidemiology The study of the factors and mechanisms that govern the spread of disease within a population, including the interrelationships between a given pathogenic organism, the environment, and populations of relevant hosts

epifluorescence microscopy A form of microscopy employing stains that fluoresce when excited by light of a given wavelength, emitting light of a different wavelength; exciter filters are used to produce the proper excitation wavelength, and barrier filters are used so that only the fluorescing specimens are visible

epigenetic Direct products derived from an organism's genome, e.g., ribosomal RNA

epilimnion The warm upper surface layer of an aquatic environment

epiphytes Organisms growing on surfaces of other organisms, e.g., bacteria growing on the surface of an algal cell

episomes Segments of DNA capable of existing in two alternate forms, one replicating autonomously in the cytoplasm, the other replicating as part of the bacterial chromosome

epitheca The larger of the two parts of the cell wall (frustule) of a diatom

epizootic An epidemic outbreak of infectious disease among animals other than humans

Epstein-Barr virus A member of the herpesvirus group; the causative agent of infectious mononucleosis

equilibrium A state of balance, a condition in which opposing forces equalize with one another so that no movement occurs; in a chemical reaction, the condition where forward and reverse reactions take place at equal rates so that no net change occurs; when a reaction is at equilibrium, the amounts of reactants and products remain constant

equilibrium constant The relationship among concentrations of the substances within an equilibrium system regardless of how the equilibrium condition is achieved

ergotism A condition of intoxication that results from the ingestion of grain contaminated by ergot alkaloids produced by the fungus *Claviceps purpurea*

erythema Abnormal reddening of the skin due to local congestion, symptomatic of inflammation

erythrocytes Red blood cells

erythromycin An antibiotic produced by a strain of *Streptomyces* that inhibits protein synthesis

estuary A water passage where the ocean tide meets a river current; an arm of the sea at the lower end of a river

ethanolic fermentation A type of fermentation in which glucose is converted to ethanol and carbon dioxide

etiological agent An agent, such as a microorganism, that causes a disease

etiology The study of the causation of disease

Euascomycetidae True ascomycetes; fungi that produce asci in ascocarps that develop from dikaryotic hyphae

eubacteria Prokaryotes other than archaebacteria; prokaryotes whose cytoplasmic membranes contain phospholipids linked by ester bonds

eugenotes Theoretical primitive versions of prokaryotes

euglenoid algae Members of the Euglenophycophyta

Euglenophycophyta Division of unicellular algae that contain chlorophylls *a* and *b*, appear green, lack a cell wall, and are surrounded by a pellicle; they store paramylon as reserve material and reproduce by longitudinal division; they are widely distributed in aquatic and soil habitats

eukaryotes Cellular organisms having a membrane-bound nucleus within which the genome of the cell is stored as chromosomes composed of DNA; eukaryotic organisms include algae, fungi, protozoa, plants, and animals

euphotic The top layer of water, through which sufficient light penetrates to support the growth of photosynthetic organisms

eurythermal Microorganisms that grow over a wide range of temperatures

eutrophication The enrichment of natural waters with inorganic materials, especially nitrogen and phosphorus compounds, that support the excessive growth of photosynthetic organisms

evolution Directional process of change of organisms by which descendants become distinct in form and/or function from their ancestors

evolutionary relationships The degree of relatedness of organisms based on their ancestry

excision repair A mechanism found in bacteria that corrects damaged DNA by removing nucleotides and then resynthesizing the region

excystation Conversion of cysts to actively growing vegetative forms

exergonic A reaction accompanied by a liberation of free energy

exo- Prefix indicating outside, an outside layer, or out of

exocytosis Movement of materials out of a cell

exoenzymes Enzymes that occur attached to the outer surface of the cell membrane or in the periplasmic space; enzymes released into the medium surrounding a cell, including enzymes that attack extracellular polymers by sequentially removing units from one end of a polymer chain

exogenous Due to an external cause; not arising from within the organism

exon The region of a eukaryotic genome that encodes the information for protein or RNA macromolecules or regulation of gene expression; a segment of eukaryotic DNA that codes for a region of RNA that is not excised during post-transcriptional processing

exonucleases Enzymes that progressively remove the terminal nucleotides of a polynucleotide chain

exothermic A chemical reaction that produces heat

exotoxins Protein toxins secreted by living microorganisms into the surrounding environment

experimental group The condition in a controlled experiment in which a factor or factors vary

exponential growth phase The period during the growth cycle of a microbial population when growth is maximal and constant and there is a logarithmic increase in population size

expression vector In gene cloning, a genetic vector that contains the desired gene and the necessary regulatory sequences that permit control of the expression of that gene

extracellular External to the cells of an organism

extraterrestrial Originating or existing outside of the Earth or its atmosphere

extreme environments Environments characterized by extremes in growth conditions, including temperature, salinity, pH, and water availability, among others

extreme thermophiles Thermophilic archaebacteria that have optimal temperatures above 80° C

exudate Viscous fluid containing blood cells and debris that accumulate at the site of an inflammation or lesion

F

F pilus Attachment structure that projects from cells of certain bacteria involved in mating, found on cells that donate DNA

F plasmid Fertility plasmid coding for the donor strain that includes genes for the formation of the F pilus

F value The number of minutes required to heat inactivate or kill an entire population of cells or spores in an aqueous solution at 121° C

Fab (antigen-binding fragment) Either of two identical fragments produced when an immunoglobulin is cleaved by papain; the antigen-binding portion of an antibody, including the hypervariable region

facilitated diffusion Diffusion at an enhanced rate; movement from a region of high concentration to one of low concentration that occurs more rapidly than it would on the basis of the concentration gradient

facilitator protein A cytoplasmic membrane-bound protein that carries out facilitated diffusion of substrates

facultative anaerobes Microorganisms capable of growth under either aerobic or anaerobic conditions; bacteria capable of both fermentative and respiratory metabolism

FAD Flavin adenine dinucleotide

$FADH_2$ Reduced flavin adenine dinucleotide

false feet Pseudopodia of some protozoa

family A taxonomic group; the principal division of an order; the classification group above a genus

fastidious An organism difficult to isolate or culture on ordinary media because of its need for special nutritional factors; an organism with stringent physiological requirements for growth and survival

fatty acids Straight chains of carbon atoms with a COOH at one end in which most of the carbons are attached to hydrogen atoms

Fc (crystallizable) fragment The remainder of the molecule when an immunoglobulin is cleaved and the Fab fragment separated; the crystallizable portion of an immunoglobulin molecule containing the constant region; the end of an immunoglobulin that binds with complement

feedback activation The binding of a substance to an allosteric site, thus activating the enzyme and increasing its activity

feedback inhibition A cellular control mechanism by which the end product of a series of metabolic reactions inhibits the activity of an earlier enzyme in the sequence of metabolic transformations; thus, when the end product accumulates, its further production ceases

FeMoco Cofactor for nitrogenase that contains iron and molybdenum

ferment To cause fermentation in; that which causes fermentation

fermentation A mode of energy-yielding metabolism that involves a sequence of oxidation-reduction reactions in which an organic substrate and the organic compounds derived from that substrate serve as the primary electron donor and the terminal electron acceptor, respectively; in contrast to respiration, there is no requirement for an external electron acceptor to terminate the metabolic sequence

fermentation pathways Metabolic sequences for the oxidation of organic compounds to release free energy to drive the formation of ATP in which the organic substrate acts as electron donor and a product of that substrate acts as an electron acceptor

fermented food Food product of microbial fermentation

fermenter An organism that carries out fermentation

fermentor A reaction chamber in which a fermentation reaction is carried out; a reaction chamber for growing microorganisms used in industry for a batch process

fertility Fruitfulness; the reproductive rate of a population; the ability to support life; the ability to reproduce

fertility pilus Structure involved in cell-to-cell contact between mating bacteria; F pilus

fertility plasmid F plasmid

fever The elevation of body temperature above normal

fibrin The insoluble protein formed from fibrogen by the proteolytic action of thrombin during normal blood clotting

fibrinogen A protein in human plasma synthesized in the liver; it is the precursor of fibrin, which is used to increase coagulability of blood

fibrolysin A proteolytic enzyme capable of dissolving or preventing the formation of a fibrin clot

filament Any elongated, thread-like bacterial cell

filamentous fungi Fungi that develop hyphae and mycelia; also called *molds*

filterable virus Obsolete term used to describe infectious agents that can pass through bacteriological filters

filtration Separation of microorganisms from the medium in which they are suspended by passage of a fluid through a filter with pores small enough to trap the microorganisms

fire algae Members of the Pyrrophycophyta algae

fission A type of asexual reproduction in which a cell divides to form two or more daughter cells

fixation of carbon dioxide The conversion of inorganic carbon dioxide to organic compounds

flagella Flexible, relatively long appendages on cells used for locomotion

flagellates Organisms having flagella; one of the major divisions of protozoans, characterized by the presence of flagella

flagellin Soluble, globular proteins constituting the subunits of bacterial flagella

flashlight fish Fish of the genus *Anomalops* that have organs in which they maintain populations of luminescent bacteria as a source of light

flat-field objective A microscope lens that provides an image in which all parts of the field are simultaneously in focus; an objective lens with minimal curvature of field

flat-sour spoilage A type of microbially caused spoilage that occurs in canned foods in which acid but no gas is produced

flavin adenine dinucleotide A coenzyme involved in transfers of electrons during oxidation-reduction reactions of the Krebs cycle and oxidative phosphorylation

floc A mass of microorganisms caught in a slime produced by certain bacteria, usually found in waste treatment plants

Floridean starch Primary carbohydrate reserve material of Rhodophycophyta

fluid mosaic model The currently accepted model of the structure of the cytoplasic membrane that describes this membrane as a bilipid layer of proteins that is distributed in a mosaic-like pattern on the surface and in the interior of the membrane, with lateral as well as transverse movement of proteins occurring throughout the structure

fluorescence The emission of light by certain substances after absorption of an exciting radiation; the wavelength of the emitted light is different from that of the excitation radiation

fluorescence microscope A microscope in which the microorganisms are stained with a fluorescent dye and observed by illumination with short-wavelength light, e.g., ultraviolet light

fomes Inanimate objects that can act as carriers of infectious agents

fomites Objects and materials associated with infected persons or animals and that potentially harbor pathogenic microorganisms

food additive A substance or mixture of substances other than the basic foodstuff that is intentionally present in food as a result of any aspect of production, processing, storage, or packaging

food infection Disease resulting from the ingestion of food or water containing viable pathogens that can establish an infectious disease, e.g., gastroenteritis, from ingestion of food containing *Salmonella*

food intoxication Disease resulting from the ingestion of toxins produced by microorganisms that have grown in a food

food poisoning General term applied to all stomach or intestinal disorders due to food contaminated with certain microorganisms, their toxins, chemicals, or poisonous plant materials; disease resulting from the ingestion of toxins produced by microorganisms that have grown in a food

food preservation The prevention or delay of microbial decomposition or self-decomposition of food and prevention of damage due to insects, animals, mechanical causes, etc.; the delay or prevention of food spoilage

food spoilage Deterioration of a food that lessens its nutritional value or desirability, often due to the growth of microorganisms that alter the taste, smell, or appearance of the food or the safety of ingesting it

food web An interrelationship among organisms in which energy is transferred from one organism to another; each organism consumes the preceding one and in turn is eaten by the following member in the sequence

Foraminiferida Marine members of the protozoan class Sarcodina that form one or more chambers composed of silicareous or calcareous tests

foreign populations Allochthonous populations

formalin A 40% solution of formaldehyde; a pungent-smelling, colorless gas used for fixation and preservation of biological specimens and as a disinfectant

forssman antigen A heat-stable glycolipid; a heterophile antigen, an immunologically related antigen found in unrelated species

frameshift mutation A type of mutation that causes a change in the three base sequences read as codons, i.e., a change in the phase of transcription arising from the addition or deletion of nucleotides in numbers other than three or multiples of three

free energy The energy available to do work, particularly in causing chemical reactions; ΔG

freeze etching A technique used to examine the topography of a surface that is exposed by fracturing or cutting a deep-frozen cell, making a replica, and removing the biological material; used in transmission electron microscopy

freeze-drying Lyophilization

freezing Conversion of a liquid to a solid by reducing the temperature; a method used for the preservation of food by storage at −20° C, based on the fact that low temperatures restrict the rate of growth and enzymatic activities of microorganisms

freshwater habitats Lakes, ponds, swamps, springs, streams, and rivers

fruiting body A specialized microbial structure that bears sexually or asexually derived spores

frustules The silicaceous cell walls of a diatom

fungal gardens Fungi grown in pure culture by insects

fungi A group of diverse, widespread unicellular and multicellular eukaryotic organisms, lacking chlorophyll and usually bearing spores and often filaments

Fungi Imperfecti Fungi with septate hyphae that reproduce only by means of conidia, lacking a known sexual stage; Deuteromycetes

fungicides Agents that kill fungi

fungistasis The active prevention or hindrance of fungal growth by a chemical or physical agent

G

galls Abnormal plant structures formed in response to parasitic attack by certain insects or microorganisms; tumor-like growths on plants in response to an infection

gametangium A structure that gives rise to gametes or that in its entirety functions as a gamete

gametes Haploid reproductive cells or nuclei, the fusion of which during fertilization leads to the formation of a zygote

gamma globulin Immunoglobulin G

gamma interferon (IF-γ) Immune interferon

gap Region of the double helix in which there are no complementary nucleotides opposite one of the strands

gas vacuoles Membrane-limited, gas-filled vacuoles that occur commonly in groups in the cells of a number of cyanobacteria and certain other bacteria

gasohol A mixture of gasoline and ethanol used as a fuel

gastroenteritis Inflammation of the stomach and intestine

gastroenterocolitis Inflammation of the gastrointestinal tract accompanied by the formation of pus and blood in the stools

gastrointestinal syndrome Gastroenteritis associated with nausea, vomiting, and diarrhea

gastrointestinal tract The stomach, intestines, and accessory organs

Gastromycetes Basidiomycete group that includes the puffballs, earthstars, stinkhorns, and bird's nest fungi

gelatin A protein obtained from skin, hair, bones, tendons, etc.; used in culture media for the determination of a specific proteolytic activity of microorganisms

gelatinase A hydrolytic enzyme capable of liquefying gelatin

gene A sequence of nucleotides that specifies a particular polypeptide chain or RNA sequence or that regulates the expression of other genes

gene cloning Replication of foreign DNA inserted by recombinant DNA technology

gene pool Set of genes of an organism

gene probe A small molecule of single-stranded RNA or DNA with a known sequence of nucleotides that is used to detect or identify a homologous complementary nucleotide sequence

generalized transduction A form of recombination in which a phage carries bacterial DNA from a donor to a recipient cell, resulting in the exchange of any homologous genes

generation time The time required for the cell population or biomass to double

genetic code Code for specific amino acids formed by three sequential nucleotides in mRNA; the 64 codons formed by sequences of three nucleotides that specify the genetic information of all organisms

genetic engineering The deliberate modification of the genetic properties of an organism either through the selection of desirable traits, the introduction of new information on DNA, or both; the application of recombinant DNA technology

genetic mapping Determination of the relative positions of genes in DNA or RNA

genetics The science dealing with inheritance

genitourinary tract The combined urinary and genital systems; the combined reproductive system and urine excretion system, including the kidneys, ureters, urinary bladder, urethra, penis, prostate, testes, vagina, fallopian tubes, and uterus

genome The complete set of genetic information contained in a haploid set of chromosomes

genomic library A collection of clones of individual genes from a specific organism

genotype The genetic information contained in the entire complement of alleles

genus A taxonomic group directly above the species level, forming the principal subdivisions of the family

germ Any microorganism, especially any of the pathogenic bacteria

germ theory of disease Theory that infectious and contagious diseases are caused and transmitted by the activity of microorganisms

germ-free animal An animal with no normal microbiota; all of its surfaces and tissues are sterile, and it is maintained in that condition by being housed and fed in a sterile environment

germicide A microbicidal disinfectant; a chemical that kills microorganisms

germination A degradative process in which an activated spore becomes metabolically active, involving hydrolysis and depolymerization

gibberellic acid Organic acid used as a plant growth hormone, formed by the fungus *Gibberella fujikuroi* in aerated submerged culture

gingivitis Inflammation of the gums

gliding motility Movement that occurs when some bacteria are in contact with solid surfaces

global cycling Biogeochemical changes in the chemical forms of various elements that can lead to the physical translocations of materials, sometimes mediating transfers between the atmosphere (air), hydrosphere (water), and lithosphere (land); biogeochemical cycling that moves materials throughout global ecosystems

globular protein General name for a group of water-soluble proteins

gluconeogenesis The biosynthesis of glucose from noncarbohydrate substrates

gluconic acid Organic acid produced by a submerged culture process from mycelia of *Aspergillus niger*

glucose Monosaccharide sugar $C_6H_{12}O_6$

glutamine synthetase/glutamate synthase pathway Pathway for the formation of L-glutamate used when ammonium concentrations are low

glycocalyx Specialized bacterial structure with an attachment function composed of a mass of tangled fibers of polysaccharides or branching sugar molecules surrounding a cell or colony of cells

glycogen A nonreducing polysaccharide of glucose found in many tissues and stored in the liver, where it is converted when needed into sugar

glycolysis An anaerobic process of glucose dissemination by a sequence of enzyme-catalyzed reactions to a pyruvic acid

glycolytic pathways The catabolic pathways of sugar metabolism

glycoproteins A group of conjugated proteins that, on decomposition, yield a protein and a carbohydrate

glycosidic bonds Bonds in disaccharides and polysaccharides formed by the elimination of water

glyoxylate cycle A metabolic shunt within the Krebs cycle involving the intermediate glyoxylate

golden algae Members of the Chrysophyceae

Golgi apparatus A membranous organelle of eukaryotic organisms involved in the formation of secretory vesicles and the synthesis of complex polysaccharides

gonidia Reproductive cells of unicellular green algae *Volvox* that lack flagella

gonococcal urethritis Inflammation of the urethra caused by a gonococcal infection

gonorrhea A sexually transmitted disease caused by *Neisseria gonorrhoeae;* infectious inflammation of the mucous membrane of the urethra and adjacent cavities

graft-versus-host (GVH) disease Disease that occurs when transplanted or grafted tissue contains immunocompetent cells that respond to the antigens of the recipient's tissues

Gram-negative cell wall Bacterial cell wall composed of a thin peptidoglycan layer, lipoproteins, lipopolysaccharides, phospholipids, and proteins

Gram-positive cell wall Bacterial cell wall composed of a relatively thick peptidoglycan layer and teichoic acids

Gram stain Differential staining procedure in which bacteria are classified as Gram-negative or Gram-positive, depending on whether they retain or lose the primary stain when subject to treatment with a decolorizing agent; the staining procedure reflects the underlying structural differences in the cell walls of Gram-negative and Gram-positive bacteria

grana A membranous unit formed by stacks of thylakoids

granules Small intracellular particles that usually stain selectively

granulosis virus Viral pesticide that develops in the nucleus or the cytoplasm of host fat, tracheal, or epidermal cells

grazers Organisms that prey on primary producers; protozoan predators that consume bacteria indiscriminately; filter-feeding zooplanktons

green algae Members of the Chlorophycophyta algae

green beer The product of an alcoholic fermentation of grain that has not been aged or distilled

green sulfur bacteria Members of the Chlorobiaceae anoxygenic phototrophic bacteria that utilize reduced sulfur compounds as electron donors

greenhouse effect Rise in the concentrations of atmospheric CO_2 and a resulting warming of global temperatures

gross primary production Total amount of organic matter produced in an ecosystem

groundwater All subsurface water

group translocation The transfer of materials across the cytoplasmic membrane of a bacterial cell that results in chemical modification of the substance as it moves across the membrane

growth Any increase in the amount of actively metabolic protoplasm accompanied by an increase in cell number, cell size, or both

growth curve A curve obtained by plotting the increase in the size or number of microorganisms against the elapsed time

growth factors Any compound, other than the carbon and energy source, that an organism requires and cannot synthesize

growth rate Increase in the number of microorganisms per unit time

guanine A purine base that occurs naturally as a fundamental component of nucleic acids

Gymnomycota Slime molds; a group of protozoa that have several characteristics of fungi; their vegetative cells lack cell wall and exhibit a phagotrophic mode of nutrition

H

H^+ Hydrogen ion or proton; a hydrogen ion concentration described by the pH that is the negative logarithm of the hydrogen ion concentration

H antigen A flagellar antigen found in certain bacteria

H peplomers Hemagglutinin peplomers

habitat A location where living organisms occur

hairpin loops Regions of DNA or RNA, part of which are single-stranded regions and part of which are double-stranded so that there is a loop with three-dimensional topology

halophiles Organisms requiring NaCl for growth; extreme halophiles grow in concentrated brines

haploid A single set of homologous chromosomes; having half of the normal diploid number of chromosomes

hapten A substance that elicits antibody formation only when combined with other molecules or particles but that can react with preformed antibodies

heat-labile A form that is likely to be changed or destroyed by exposure to heat

heat-resistant A form that is not likely to be changed or destroyed by exposure to heat

heat shock proteins Proteins that are synthesized at high temperature that are not otherwise expressed

heat shock response A rapid change in gene expression that occurs when there is a temperature shift to an elevated temperature

heavy chain class switching In lymphocyte maturation, the process in which the same variable region of antibodies appears in association with different heavy-chain constant regions

Heliozoida Protozoa that produce numerous radiating axopodia found in fresh water

helix A spiral structure

helper T cells T helper cells; T_H cells

hemagglutination Agglutination or clumping of red blood cells

hemagglutination inhibition (HI) The inhibition of hemagglutination (antibody-mediated clumping of red blood cells), usually by means of specific immunoglobulins or enzymes, used to determine whether a patient has been exposed to a specific virus

hemagglutinin peplomers (H peplomers) Peplomer spikes of an influenza virus that cause agglutination of red blood cells

hemagglutinin spikes Projections from surfaces of influenza viruses that cause agglutination of red blood cells; they increase the ability of influenza viruses to attach to human cells

heme An iron-containing porphyrin ring occurring in hemoglobin

hemocytometer A counting chamber used for estimating the number of blood cells

hemoglobin The iron-containing, oxygen-carrying molecule of red blood cells, containing four polypeptides in the heme group

hemolysin A substance that lyses erythrocytes (red blood cells)

hemolysis Lytic destruction of red blood cells and the resultant escape of hemoglobin

hemolytic disease of the newborn Disease that stems from an incompatibility of fetal (Rh-positive) and maternal (Rh-negative) blood, resulting in maternal antibody activity against fetal blood cells; also known as *erythroblastosis fetalis*

hemorrhagic Showing evidence of bleeding; the tissue becomes reddened by the accumulation of blood that has escaped from capillaries into the tissue

hepatitis Inflammation of the liver

herbicides Chemicals used to kill weeds

herd immunity Concept that an entire population is protected against a particular pathogen when 70% of the population is immune to that pathogen

heritable Any characteristic that is genetically transmissible

hetero- Combining form meaning other, other than usual, different

heterocysts Cells that occur in the trichomes of some filamentous cyanobacteria that are the sites of nitrogen fixation

heteroduplex An intermediate form of DNA occurring during homologous recombination

heterogamy Conjugation of unlike gametes

heterogeneous Composed of different substances; not homologous

heterogeneous nuclear RNA (hnRNA) Heterogeneous RNA

heterogeneous RNA (hnRNA) High molecular weight RNA formed by direct transcription in eukaryotes that is then processed enzymatically to form mRNA

heterokaryotic Containing genetically different nuclei, as in some fungal hyphal cells

heterolactic fermentation Fermentation of glucose that produces lactic acid, acetic acid, and/or ethanol, and carbon dioxide, carried out by *Leuconostoc* and some *Lactobacillus* species

heterologous antigen Multivalent antigen; Forssman antigen

heterophile antibodies Antibodies that react with heterophile antigens; commonly found in sera of individuals with infectious mononucleosis

heterophile antigens Immunologically related antigens in unrelated species; multivalent antigen; Forssman antigen

heterotrophic metabolism A type of metabolism in which an organic molecule serves as carbon source; a type of metabolism in which an organic molecule serves as carbon source and energy source—often used to describe chemoheterotrophic metabolism

heterotrophs Organisms requiring organic compounds for growth and reproduction, the organic compounds serve as sources of carbon and energy

heterozygous A microorganism whose allelic forms of a gene differ

Hfr High frequency recombinant

high copy number In gene cloning, a large number of repetitive copies of a gene that are produced

high frequency recombinant A bacterial strain that exhibits a high rate of gene transfer and recombination during mating; the F plasmid is integrated into the bacterial chromosome

high temperature–short time process HTST process

histamine A physiologically active amine that plays a role in the inflammatory response

histiocytes Macrophages that are located at a fixed site in a certain organ or tissue

histocompatibility antigens Genetically determined isoantigens on the lipoprotein membranes of nucleated cells of most tissues that cause an immune response when grafted onto a genetically disparate individual and thus determine the compatibility of tissues in transplantation

histones Basic proteins rich in arginine and lysine that occur in close association with the nuclear DNA of most eukaryotic organisms

HIV Human immunodeficiency virus

hnRNA Heterogeneous nuclear RNA

holdfast A structure that allows certain algae and bacteria to remain attached to the substratum

holozoic nutrition Type of nutrition exhibited by some protozoa that obtain nutrients by phagocytosis of bacterial cells

homo- Combining form denoting like, common, or same

homokaryotic Containing genetically similar nuclei, as in some fungal hyphal cells

homolactic fermentation The fermentation of glucose that produces lactic acid as the sole product, carried out by certain species of *Lactobacillus*

homologous Pertaining to the structural relation between parts of different organisms due to evolutionary development of the same or a corresponding part; a substance of identical form or function

homologous recombination Recombination of regions of DNA containing alleles of the same genes

homologously dissimilar Genetically dissimilar microorganisms

homology Genetic relatedness

homozygous Microorganism whose allelic forms of a gene are identical

host A cell or organism that acts as the habitat for the growth of another organism; the cell or organism on or in which parasitic organisms live

host cell A cell within which a virus replicates

host cell range The types of cells within which replication of a virus occurs

host-range mutation Viral mutation that alters the host that the virus can infect

hot springs Thermal springs with a temperature above 98° C

HTST process High temperature–short time pasteurization process at a temperature of at least 71.5° C for at least 15 seconds; the most widely used form of commercial pasteurization

human immunodeficiency virus Retrovirus that causes AIDS

humic acids Any of the various organic acids obtained from humus, the soil matter whose origin is no longer identifiable; complex polynuclear aromatic compounds comprising the soil organic matter

humoral Referring to the body fluids

humoral immune defense system Antibody-mediated immunity

humus Organic portion of the soil remaining after microbial decomposition

hyaluronidase Enzyme that catalyzes the breakdown of hyaluronic acid

hybridization of nucleic acids Artificial construction of a double-stranded nucleic acid by complementary base pairing of two single-stranded nucleic acids

hybridomas Cells formed by fusion of lymphocytes (antibody precursors) with myeloma (tumor) cells that produces rapidly growing cells that secrete monoclonal antibodies

hydr- Combining form meaning water

hydrocarbons Compounds composed only of hydrogen and carbon that are the major compounds in petroleum

hydrogen bond A weak attraction between an atom that has a strong attraction for electrons and a hydrogen atom that is covalently bonded to another atom that attracts the electron of the hydrogen atom

hydrogenosomes Organelle containing hydrogenase in some protozoa

hydrolase Enzyme that hydrolyzes a molecule by adding water

hydrolysis The chemical process of decomposition involving the splitting of a bond and the addition of the elements of water

hydrophilic A substance having an affinity for water

hydrophobia Fear of water, one of the symptoms of rabies

hydrophobic A substance lacking an affinity for water; not soluble in water

hydrosphere The aqueous envelope of the Earth, including bodies of water and aqueous vapor in the atmosphere

hydrostatic pressure Pressure exerted by the weight of a water column; it increases approximately 1 atm with every 10 m/in depth

hydroxypropionate pathway A metabolic pathway in which two CO_2 molecules are fixed and converted into one acetyl-CoA

hyperbaric oxygen Pure oxygen under pressure

hyperchromatic shift The change in absorption of light exhibited by DNA when it is melted, forming two strands from the double helix

hyperplasia The abnormal proliferation of tissue cells, resulting in the formation of a tumor or gall

hypersensitivity An exaggerated immunological response after re-exposure to a specific antigen

hypertonic A solution whose osmotic pressure is greater than that of a standard solution

hypertrophy An increase in the size of an organ, independent of natural growth, due to enlargement or multiplication of its constituent cells

hypervariable region A region of immunoglobulins that accounts for the specificity of antigen–antibody reactions; genetically specified terminal regions of the Fab fragments

hyphae Branched or unbranched filaments that constitute the vegetative form of an organism, occurring in filamentous fungi, algae, and bacteria

Hyphochytridiomycetes Class of Mastigomycota; fungi that produce uniflagellate zoospores of the tinsel type

hypolimnion The deeper, colder layer of an aquatic environment; the zone below the thermocline

hypotheca The smaller of the two parts of the cell wall of a diatom

hypothesis In the scientific method, a tentative answer to a question that has been asked

hypotonic A solution whose osmotic pressure is less than that of a standard solution

I

icosahedral virus A virus having cubical symmetry and a complex, 20-sided capsid structure

icosahedron A solid figure contained by 20 plane faces

identification Process of determining the closest relationship of an unknown organism to a group that has already been defined

identification key A series of questions that leads to the unambiguous identification of an organism

idiolite A secondary metabolite in the production of penicillin that is not required for the growth of the fungus

idiophase The phase of metabolism in batch culture in which secondary metabolism is dominant over primary growth-directed metabolism; the phase of antibiotic or other secondary product accumulation

idiotypes Immunoglobulin molecules with distinct variable regions determining the specificity of the antigen–antibody reaction

IF-γ Immune interferon

IgA (immunoglobulin A) An antibody that occurs primarily in mucus, semen, and secretions such as saliva, tears, and sweat; an immunoglobulin that plays a major role in protecting mucous membrane surface tissues against microbial infection

IgD (immunoglobulin D) An immunoglobulin that is present on the surface of some lymphocytes, along with IgM, and appears to have a regulatory role in lymphocyte activity

IgE (immunoglobulin E) An immunoglobulin that normally is present in blood serum in very low concentrations but that becomes elevated in individuals with allergies; an immunoglobulin that attaches to mast and basophil cells and triggers an allergic response when it reacts with allergens in sensitized individuals

IgG (immunoglobulin G) The largest fraction of the body's immunoglobulins and a major antibody that circulates through the body; an immunoglobulin that has a major role in protecting the body against systemic microbial infections

IgM (immunoglobulin M) A high molecular weight immunoglobulin occurring as a pentamer that is formed prior to IgG in response to exposure to an antigen; an immunoglobulin that is important in the early response to a microbial infection

IL-2 Interleukin-2

immediate hypersensitivity Anaphylactic hypersensitivity (Type I hypersensitivity); a systemic, potentially life-threatening condition that occurs when an antigen reacts with antibody bound to mast or basophil blood cells, leading to disruption of these cells with the release of vasoactive mediators, such as histamine—it occurs shortly (5 to 30 minutes) after exposure to the antigen that triggers this response

immobilization The binding of a substance so that it is no longer reactive or able to circulate freely

immobilized enzyme An enzyme bound to a solid support

immune The condition following initial contact with a given antigen in which antibodies specific for that antigen are present in the body; the innate or acquired resistance to disease

immune adherence Opsonization

immune interferon (IF-γ) A lymphokine secreted by lymphocytes in response to a specific antigen that has antiviral activity and may kill tumor cells

immune response system The integrated mechanisms for responding to the invasion of the body by particular pathogenic microorganisms and other foreign substances; the specific immune response is characterized by specificity, memory, and the acquired ability to detect foreign substances

immunity The relative insusceptibility of a person or animal to active infection by pathogenic microorganisms or the harmful effects of certain toxins; resistance to disease by a living organism

immunization Any procedure in which an antigen is introduced into the body to produce a specific immune response

immunodeficiency Lack of an adequate immune response due to inadequate B- or T-cell recognition and/or response to foreign antigens; a lack of antibody production

immunoelectrophoresis A two-stage procedure used for the analysis of materials containing mixtures of distinguishable proteins, e.g., serum using electrophoretic separation and immunological detection

immunofluorescence Any of various techniques used to detect a specific antigen or antibody by means of homologous antibodies or antigens that have been conjugated with a fluorescent dye

immunogenicity The ability of a substance to elicit an immune response

immunoglobulins (antibodies) A varied class of proteins in plasma and other body fluids, including all known antibodies; the antibody fraction of serum; the five classes of antibodies IgA, IgD, IgE, IgG, and IgM

immunological Referring to the immune response

immunological tolerance The unresponsiveness to self antigens

immunology The study of immunity

immunosuppressant A drug that depresses the immune response

IMViC test A group of tests (indole, Methyl Red, Voges-Proskauer, citrate) used in the identification of bacteria of the Enterobacteriaceae family

inclusion bodies Accumulations of reserve materials in bacteria

incompatibility group Incompatible plasmids that do not co-exist in the same cell

incompatible plasmids Pairs of plasmids that cannot be replicated with stability in the same cell

incubation The maintenance of controlled conditions to achieve the optimal growth of microorganisms

incubation period The period of time between the establishment of an infection and the onset of disease symptoms

indicator organism An organism used to indicate a particular condition, commonly applied to coliform bacteria, e.g., *Escherichia coli* or *Enterococcus faecalis,* when their presence is used to indicate the degree of water pollution due to fecal contamination

indigenous population A population that is native to a particular habitat; an autochthonous population; normal microbiota or microflora

indirect immunofluorescence test Used in identifying bacteria such as *Treponema pallidum* by adding dead cells to the patient's serum and adding fluorescent anti-immunoglobulin; if the bacteria stain, the test is positive

induced mutations Mutations that result from the exposure of the cell to exogenous DNA modifiers such as radiation or chemical substances

inducers Substances responsible for activating certain genes, resulting in the synthesis of new proteins

inducible enzymes Enzymes that are synthesized only in response to a particular substance in the environment

induction An increase in the rate of synthesis of an enzyme; the turning on of enzyme synthesis in response to environmental conditions

inductive reasoning A logical process in which a conclusion is proposed that contains more information than the observations or experience on which it is based

induration Hardening of the skin, a positive hypersensitivity reaction

infantile paralysis Poliomyelitis

infection A condition in which pathogenic microorganisms have become established in the tissues of a host organism

infectious disease A disease-causing agent or disease that can be transmitted from one person, animal, or plant to another

infectious dose The number of pathogens that are needed to overwhelm host defense mechanisms and establish an infection

infectious mononucleosis Glandular fever, an acute infectious disease that primarily affects the lymphoid tissues; caused by Epstein-Barr virus, which enters the body via the respiratory tract

inflammation The reaction of tissues to injury characterized by local heat, swelling, redness, and pain

inflammatory exudate Pussy material from blood vessels deposited in tissues or on tissue surfaces as a defensive response to injury or irritation

inflammatory response A nonspecific immune response to injury characterized by redness, heat, swelling, and pain in the affected area; inflammation

infusoria Archaic term for microorganisms

inhibition Prevention of growth or multiplication of microorganisms; reduction in the rate of enzymatic activity; repression of chemical or physical activity

inhibitors Substances that repress or stop a chemical action

initial body Larger, thin-walled, noninfectious form of chlamydias

initiation In protein synthesis, the stage at which the translating complex of mRNA, ribosome, and tRNA first assembles

inoculate To deposit material, an inoculum, onto medium to initiate a culture, carried out with an aseptic technique; to introduce microorganisms into an environment that will support their growth

inoculum The material containing viable microorganisms used to inoculate a medium

insecticides Substances destructive to insects; chemicals used to control insect populations

insertion A type of mutation in which a nucleotide or two or more contiguous nucleotides are added to DNA

insertion mutations A mutation in which one or more nucleotides are inserted into a gene

insertion sequence (IS) A transposable genetic element that can move around bacterial chromosomes, occurring at different locations on the chromosome

insertional inactivation In gene cloning, insertion of foreign DNA at an antibiotic-resistant site, causing loss of resistance because the nucleotide sequence of the antibiotic resistance gene is disrupted

in situ In the natural location or environment

interference microscope A microscope that relies on destructive and/or additive interference of light waves to achieve contrast

interferons Glycoproteins produced by animal cells that act to prevent the replication of a range of viruses by inducing resistance

intergenic mutations Mutations within a single gene that affect other genes

interleukin-2 (IL-2) A cytokine formed by T lymphocytes that stimulates the growth of T lymphocytes and cytokine production by T cells

intermediary metabolism Intermediate steps in the cellular synthesis and breakdown of substances

interspecies hydrogen transfer A series of reactions that results in supplying hydrogen from complex polymers by one or more bacterial populations for the reduction of CO_2 to CH_4 by methanogenic archaebacteria

intoxication Poisoning, as by a drug, serum, alcohol, or any poison

intracellular Within a cell

intradermal Within the skin

intragenic Occurring within a gene

intragenic suppressor mutations Suppressor mutations that occur within a single gene

intramuscular Within the substance of a muscle

intravenous Within or into the vein

intron An intervening region of the DNA of eukaryotes that does not code for a known protein or a regulatory function

invasiveness Ability of a pathogen to spread through a host's tissues

inverted repeats Palindromic sequences in which the sequences of nucleotides in complementary strands of DNA are in exact opposite directions

in vitro In glass; a process or reaction carried out in a culture dish or test tube

in vivo Within the living organism

ion An atom that has lost or gained one or more orbital electrons and therefore is capable of conducting electricity

ionic bond A chemical bond resulting from the transfer of electrons between metallic and non-metallic atoms; positive and negative ions are formed and held together by electrostatic attraction

ionization The process that produces ions

ionizing radiation Radiation, such as gamma and X-radiation, that induces or forms toxic free radicals, which cause chemical reactions disruptive to the biochemical organization of microorganisms

IS Insertion sequence

iso- Combining form meaning for or from different individuals of the same species

isogamete A reproductive cell similar in form and size to the cell with which it unites; found in certain protozoas, fungi, and algae

isogamy Fertilization in which the gametes are similar in appearance and behavior

isolation methods Aseptic procedures used for the establishment of pure cultures, usually involving the separation of microorganisms on a solid medium into individual cells that are then allowed to reproduce to form clones of single microorganisms

isomer One of two or more compounds having the same chemical composition but differing in the relative positions of the atoms within the molecules

isomerase Enzyme that rearranges groups within a molecule

isotope An element that has the same atomic number as another element but a different atomic weight

isotypes Antibodies differing in heavy chain constant regions associated with different classes and subclasses of immunoglobulins

itaconic acid An organic acid used as a resin in detergents; made by the transformation of citric acid by *Aspergillus terreus*

-itis Suffix denoting a disease; specifically, an inflammatory disease of a specified part

J

Jaccard coefficient A measure of similarity used in cluster analysis to show the relationship between individuals; it does not consider negative matches

jaundice Yellowness of the skin, mucous membranes, and secretions resulting from liver malfunction

K

kappa particles Bacterial particles that occur in the cytoplasm of certain strains of *Paramecium aurelia;* such strains have a competitive advantage over other strains of *Paramecium* and are known as killer strains

karyogamy The fusion of nuclei, as of gametes in fertilization

kelp Brown algae with vegetative structures consisting of a holdfast, stem, and blade; it can form large macroscopic structures

K_{eq} Equilibrium constant

keratin A highly insoluble protein that occurs in hair, wool, horn, and skin

kinase Fibrinolysin

kingdom A major taxonomic category consisting of several phyla or divisions; the primary divisions of living organisms

Kirby-Bauer test Bauer-Kirby test

K_m The Michaelis constant; describes the affinity of an enzyme for a substrate; the substrate concentration at half of the maximal velocity of an enzyme

Koch's postulates A process for elucidating the etiological (causative) agent of an infectious disease

Koji fermentation Dry fermentation — a mixture of soybeans and wheat is inoculated with spores of *Aspergillus oryzae* and moistened, not submerged in liquid, so that fungi grow on the surface; used in soy sauce production

Koplik spots Small red spots surrounded by white areas occurring on the mucous membranes of the mouth during the early stages of measles

Krebs cycle The tricarboxylic acid cycle; the citric acid cycle; the metabolic pathway in which acetate derived from pyruvic acid is converted to carbon dioxide and reduced coenzymes are produced

Kupffer cells Macrophages lining the sinusoids of the liver

L

-labile Unstable, readily changed by physical, chemical, or biological processes

***lac* operon** Inducible enzyme system of *Escherichia coli* for the utilization of lactose

lactam An organic compound containing an -NH-CO- group in ring form

lactamase An enzyme that breaks a lactam ring

lactic acid Organic acid with antimicrobial activity produced by lactic acid bacteria *(Lactobacillus, Streptococcus, Leuconostoc)* involved in antagonistic relationships among microorganisms and used as a preservative

lactic acid fermentation Fermentation that produces lactic acid as the primary product

Lactobacillaceae Family of Gram-positive, asporogenous, regularly shaped rods that produce lactic acid as a major fermentation product

lactoferrin An iron-containing compound that binds the iron necessary for microbial growth, resulting in a slight antimicrobial action

lactose A disaccharide in milk; when hydrolyzed, it yields glucose and galactose

lag phase A period following inoculation of a medium during which the number of microorganisms does not increase

lagging strand of DNA Discontinuous strand of DNA

lagoons Ponds used for the secondary treatment of sewage and industrial effluents

laminar flow The flow of air currents in which streams do not intermingle; the air moves along parallel flow lines; used in a laminar flow hood to provide air free of microbes over a work area

landfill A site where solid waste is dumped and allowed to decompose; a process in which solid waste containing organic and inorganic material is added to soil and allowed to decompose

late proteins Proteins coded for late in the developmental sequence of a virus

late syphilis Tertiary phase of syphilis that can damage any body organ, occurring several years after the initial infection

latent Potential; not manifest; present but not visible or active

latent period The period of time following infection of a cell by a virus before new viruses are assembled

late-onset hypogammaglobulinemia Immunodeficiency disorder characterized by a shortage of circulating B cells and/or B cells with IgG surface receptors

leach To wash or extract soluble constituents from insoluble materials

leader sequence The beginning sequence of nucleotides in an mRNA molecule involved in the initiation of protein synthesis at the ribosomes

leading strand of DNA Continuous strand of DNA

leaf spots Plant diseases in which infection of the foliage interferes with photosynthesis

leavening Substance used to produce fermentation in dough or liquid; the production of CO_2 that results in the rising of dough

lecithinases Extracellular phospholipid-splitting enzymes

Legionellaceae Family of Gram-negative, fermentative, rod-shaped bacteria that require iron and cysteine as growth factors

Legionnaire's disease A form of pneumonia caused by *Legionella pneumophila*

lesion A region of tissue mechanically damaged or altered by any pathological process

lethal dose The amount of a toxin that results in the death of an organism

lethal mutations Mutations that result in the death of a microorganism or its inability to reproduce

leukocidin An extracellular bacterial product that can kill leukocytes

leukocyte A type of white blood cell characterized by a beaded, elongated nucleus

leukocytosis An increase above the normal upper limits of the leukocyte count

leukopenia A decrease below the normal lower limit of the leukocyte count

lichens A large group of composite organisms, each consisting of a fungus in symbiotic association with an alga or cyanobacterium

life A state that characterizes living systems, encompassing the complex series of physicochemical processes essential for maintaining the organization of the system and the ability to reproduce that organization

ligases Enzymes that catalyze reactions in which a bond is formed between two substrate molecules using energy obtained from the cleavage of a pyrophosphate bond; enzyme that joins two molecules using energy from ATP

light beer Beer with a low calorie content produced with fungal enzymes to ensure that simple substrates are available for alcoholic fermentation

light microscope A microscope in which visible light is used to illuminate the specimen; often referred to as a bright-field microscope

light scattering Dispersion of light when it strikes particles; used in some instruments for estimating quantities of suspended particles, including microorganisms

lignins A class of complex polymers in the woody material of higher plants

Limulus amoebocyte assay Assay that uses aqueous extracts from the blood cells (amoebocytes) of the horseshoe crab *(Limulus)* to detect endotoxin

linear alkyl benzyl sulfonate (ABS) Synthetic molecule with a straight hydrocarbon chain, benzene ring, and sulfate group designed as a component of anionic laundry detergent that is easily biodegraded

lipases Fat-splitting enzymes; enzymes that break down lipids

lipids Fats or fat-like substances that are insoluble in water and soluble in nonpolar solvents

lipophilic Preferentially soluble in lipids or nonpolar solvents

lipopolysaccharide toxin (LPS toxin) Endotoxin

lipopolysaccharides Molecules consisting of covalently linked lipids and polysaccharides; a component of Gram-negative bacterial cell walls

liquid diffusion method A method for detecting of a substance based on the diffusion of that substance into a medium to achieve the appropriate concentration for a reaction to occur; a method used in serology for detection of antigens and antibodies based on its ability to achieve a zone of equivalence in which antigen–antibody reactions can occur

liquid wastes Waste material in liquid form, the result of agricultural, industrial, and all other human activities

liter A metric unit of volume equal to 1000 milliliters; approximately equal in volume to a quart

lithosphere Solid part of the Earth

lithotrophs Microorganisms that live in and obtain energy from the oxidation of inorganic matter; autotrophs

litmus Plant extract dye used as an indicator of pH and of oxidation or reduction

living system A system separated from its surroundings by a semipermeable barrier; composed of macromolecules, including proteins and nucleic acids, having lower entropy than its surroundings, and thus requiring inputs of energy to maintain its high degree of organization, capable of self-replication and normally based on cells as the primary functional and structural unit

lobopodia False feet that are extensions of ectoplasm, which includes the flow of endoplasm

lockjaw Tetanus

locus The point on a chromosome occupied by a gene

logarithmic growth phase Exponential phase

low-acid food Food with a pH above 4.5

low-nutrient bacteria Oligotrophic bacteria; bacteria that grow at low nutrient concentrations

low temperature–long-time pasteurization process (LTH) Pasteurization process at 63° C for 30 minutes

LPS Lipopolysaccharides

LTH process Low temperature–long-time pasteurization process

luciferase Enzyme that catalyses light-producing reaction in bioluminescent bacteria

luminescence The emission of light without production of heat sufficient to cause incandescence, produced by physiological processes or by friction, chemical, or electrical action

luminescent bacteria Bacteria that carry out light-producing metabolism

ly-, lys-, lyt- Combining forms meaning to loosen or dissolve

lyase Enzyme that removes groups from a molecule to form double bonds or adds groups to double bonds

lymph A plasma filtrate that circulates through the body

lymph nodes An aggregation of lymphoid tissues surrounded by a fibrous capsule found along the course of the lymphatic system

lymphocytes Lymph cells

lymphokines A varied group of biologically active extracellular proteins formed by activated T lymphocytes involved in cell-mediated immunity

lyophilization The process of rapidly freezing a substance at low temperature and then dehydrating the frozen mass in a high vacuum; a process in which water is removed by sublimation, moving from the solid to the gaseous phase

lysins Antibodies or other entities that under appropriate conditions are capable of causing the lysis of cells

lysis The rupture of cells

lysogenic conversion The process in which the genes of temperate bacterial viruses (viruses capable of lysogeny) can be expressed by the bacterial host, with the bacterium producing proteins that are coded for by the viral genes

lysogeny Nondisruptive infection of a bacterium by a bacteriophage

lysosomes Organelles containing hydrolytic enzymes involved in autolytic and digestive processes

lysozymes Enzymes that hydrolyze peptidoglycan; act as bactericidal agents when they degrade bacterial cell walls

lytic Of or relating to lysis or a lysin; viruses that cause lysis of cells within which they reproduce

lytic phage Phage that kill host bacterial cells when they are released; bacteriophage the replication of which causes lysis of the host bacterial cell

M

MacConkey agar A solid medium used for the growth of enteric bacteria

macro- Combining form meaning long or large

macromolecules Very large organic molecules having polymeric chain structures, as in proteins, polysaccharides, and other natural and synthetic polymers

macronucleus Larger nucleus in multinucleate protozoa

macroorganisms Organisms that are large enough to be visible to the naked eye

macrophages Mononuclear phagocytes; large, actively phagocytic cells found in spleen, liver, lymph nodes, and blood; important factors in nonspecific immunity

macroscopic Of a size visible to the naked eye

magnetosomes Dense inclusion bodies within bacterial cells that contain iron granules and act as magnetic compasses, permitting bacteria to move in response to the Earth's magnetic field

magnetotaxis Motility directed by a geomagnetic field

magnification The extent to which the image of an object is larger than the object itself

major histocompatibility complex (MHC) Proteins found on almost all cells in the body that are responsible for showing processed foreign protein antigens to T_H cells or cytotoxic T cells; they were first identified as the main determinants of tissue or graft rejection when tissue from one individual is transplanted to a second individual

malaise A general feeling of illness, accompanied by restlessness and discomfort

maltase An enzyme that converts maltose to glucose

malting Enzymatic conversion of barley by plant amylases and proteases that is used to prepare grain for microbial alcoholic fermentation

maltose A disaccharide formed on hydrolysis of starch or glycogen and metabolized by a wide range of fungi and bacteria

manganese nodules Nodules (round, irregular mineral masses) produced by microbial oxidation of manganese oxides

marine Of or relating to the oceans

maromi A mixture of a starter culture and a mash consisting of autoclaved soybeans, autoclaved crushed wheat, and steamed wheat bran after incubation and soaking in concentrated brine

mash Crushed malt or grain meal steeped and stirred in hot water with amylases to produce wort as a substrate for microorganisms

mashing Process in the production of beer in which adjuncts are added to malt

mast cells Cells that contain granules of histamine, serotonin, and heparin, especially in connective tissues involved in hypersensitivity reactions

Mastigomycota True fungi; some are unicellular, whereas others form extensive filamentous, coenocytic mycelia to produce motile cells with flagella; asexual reproduction involves zoospores, nutrition provided by the absorption of nutrients

Mastigophora A subclass of protozoans characterized by the presence of flagella

mastitis Inflammation of the breast

mating The meeting of individuals for sexual reproduction

maturation The process in the replication of some viruses in which an envelope is added

MBC Minimal bactericidal concentration

MCPs Methyl-accepting chemotaxis proteins

measles An acute, contagious systemic human disease caused by a paramyxovirus that enters via the oral and nasal routes, characterized by the presence of Koplik spots

medical microbiology The study of medical science as it relates to microorganisms

medium Material that supports the growth/reproduction of microorganisms

meiosis Cell division that results in a reduction of the state of ploidy, normally from diploid to haploid during the formation of the germ cells

melting temperature of DNA Midpoint temperature of a denaturation curve used in the analysis of DNA composition in which DNA is heated and the double-stranded helix is converted to single-stranded DNA

membrane filter A cellulose–ester membrane used for microbiological filtrations

memory cells Clones of lymphocytes with receptors of high affinity for a particular antigenic molecule

memory response Anamnestic response

meninges Membranes covering the brain and spinal cord

meningitis Inflammation of the membranes of the brain or spinal cord

merozoites Progeny cells of a protozoan formed from a sporozoite by schizogony

mesophiles Organisms whose optimum growth is in the temperature range of 20° to 45° C

mesosomes Intracellular membranous structures observed as infoldings of bacterial cell membranes in electron microscopy; their function is unknown, and in fact they now appear to be artifacts of specimen preparation

messenger RNA (mRNA) The RNA that specifies the amino acid sequence for a particular polypeptide chain

metabolic pathway A sequence of biochemical reactions that transforms a substrate into a useful product for carbon assimilation or energy transfer

metabolism The total of all chemical reactions by which energy is provided for the vital processes and new cell substances are assimilated

metabolites Chemicals participating in metabolism; nutrients

metabolize To transform by means of metabolism

metachromatic granules Cytoplasmic granules of polyphosphate occurring in the cells of certain bacteria that stain intensively with basic dyes but appear a different color

methane monooxygenase Enzyme that catalyzes the initial step in the utilization of methane, namely its oxidation by reaction with O_2

methanogenesis A type of anaerobic metabolism that results in methane production

methanogens Methane-producing prokaryotes; a group of archaebacteria capable of reducing carbon dioxide or low molecular weight fatty acids to produce methane

methanotrophs Bacteria that have the ability to use methane as their sole carbon source

Methyl Red test (MR) A diagnostic test used to detect significant acid production by bacterial metabolism, particularly by mixed-acid fermentations

methyl-accepting chemotaxis proteins (MCPs) Cytoplasmic membrane-bound proteins in bacteria that are involved in transmitting signals to the flagellum that dictate its direction of rotation and therefore the movement of the cell; these proteins are alternately methylated and demethylated by specific enzymes

methylation The process of substituting a methyl group for a hydrogen atom

Methylonionadaceae A family of Gram-negative bacteria that can utilize carbon monoxide, methane, or methanol as the sole source of carbon; they also utilize respiratory metabolism

methylotrophs Bacteria that can utilize organic C-1 compounds other than methane as their sole source of carbon

MHC Major histocompatibility complex

MIC Minimum inhibitory concentration

Michaelis-Menten equation Mathematical description of the relationship between the rate of an enzymatic reaction and the substrate concentration

micro- Combining form meaning small

microaerophiles Aerobic organisms that grow best in an environment with less than atmospheric oxygen levels; oxygen-requiring microorganisms that grow only at reduced oxygen concentrations

microbes Microscopic organisms; microorganisms

microbial ecology The field of study that examines the interactions of microorganisms with their biotic and abiotic surroundings

microbial mining A mineral recovery method that uses bioleaching to recover metals from ores not suitable for direct smelting

microbial pesticides Preparations of populations of pathogenic or predatory microorganisms that are antagonistic toward a particular pest population

microbicidal Any agent capable of destroying, killing, or inactivating microorganisms so that they cannot replicate

microbiology The study of microorganisms and their interactions with other organisms and the environment

microbiota The totality of microorganisms associated with a given environment

microbistatic Chemical agents that inhibit the growth of microorganisms but do not kill them; when the agent is removed, growth is resumed

microbodies Organelles within a cell containing specialized enzymes whose functions involve hydrogen peroxide

microcidal Microbicidal

Micrococcaceae Family of Gram-positive cocci whose cells occur singly or as irregular clusters

microcysts Refractile, encapsulated myxospores

microfibrils Thread-like structures in the cell walls of filamentous fungi, consisting of chitin

microfilament An elongated structure composed of protein subunits

microglia Macrophages of the central nervous system

microhabitat The location where microorganisms live defined on a small scale

micro-ID system A miniaturized commercial identification system

micrometer One millionth (10^{-6}) of a meter; one thousandth (10^{-3}) of a millimeter

micronuclei Smaller nuclei in multinucleate protozoa

microorganisms Microscopic organisms, including algae, bacteria, fungi, protozoa, and viruses

microscope An optical or electronic instrument for viewing objects too small to be visible to the naked eye

microtome An instrument used for cutting thin sheets or sections of tissues or individual cells for examination by light or electron microscopy

microtubules Cylindrical protein tubes that occur within all eukaryotic organisms; they aid in maintaining cell shape, comprise the structure of organelles of cilia and flagella, and serve as spindle fibers in mitosis

mildew Any of various plant diseases in which the mycelium of the parasitic fungus is visible on the affected plant; biodeterioration of a fabric due to fungal growth

mineralization Microbial breakdown of organic materials into inorganic materials brought about mainly by microorganisms

miniaturized commercial identification systems Small devices containing multicompartmentalized chambers that each perform separate biochemical tests, used for the identification of bacterial species

minimal bactericidal concentration (MBC) Lowest concentration of an antibiotic that will kill a defined proportion of viable organisms in a bacterial suspension during a specified exposure period

minimum inhibitory concentration (MIC) Concentration of an antimicrobial drug necessary to inhibit the growth of a particular strain of microorganism

Minitek system Miniaturized commercial identification system

mismatch correction enzyme The gene products of *mut*H, *mut*L, *mut*S and *mut*U that form an enzyme that recognizes and excises improperly inserted nucleotides in a DNA double helix

mismatch repair A mechanism found in bacterial cells that corrects incorrectly matched base pairs in the DNA

miso Product of Koji fermentation of rice with *Aspergillus oryzae,* it is ground into a paste and combined with other foods

missense mutations Type of base substitution that results in the change in the amino acid inserted into the polypeptide chain specified by the gene in which the mutation occurs

mitochondrion A semiautonomous organelle in eukaryotic cells, the site of respiration and other cellular processes; consists of an outer membrane and an inner one that is convoluted

mitosis The sequence of events resulting in the division of the nucleus into two genetically identical cells during asexual cell division; each of the daughter nuclei has the same number of chromosomes as the parent cell

mixed acid fermentation A type of fermentation carried out by members of the Enterobacteriaceae that converts glucose to acetic, lactic, succinic, and formic acids

mixed amino acid fermentation pathway Metabolism of amino acids resulting in their deamination and decarboxylation

mixotrophic Capable of utilizing both autotrophic and heterotrophic metabolic processes, e.g., the concomitant use of organic compounds as sources of carbon and light as a source of energy

modification The methylation of nucleotide residues in DNA; modification of newly synthesized DNA by specific enzymes in a manner characteristic of the particular bacterial strain

moiety A part of a molecule having a characteristic chemical property

mold Type of fungus having a filamentous structure

mole % G + C The proportion of guanine and cytosine in a DNA macromolecule

Mollicutes A class of prokaryotic organisms that do not form cell walls, e.g., *Mycoplasma*

Monera Prokaryotic protists with a unicellular, simple colonial organization; bacteria

mono- Combining form meaning single, one, or alone

monocistronic mRNA that contains the information for only one polypeptide sequence

monoclonal antibody An antibody produced from a clone of cells making only that antibody

monocytes Ameboid, agranular, phagocytic leukocytes derived from the bone marrow

monokaryotic Containing one nucleus per cell in fungal septate hyphae

mononuclear Having only one nucleus

mononuclear phagocyte system The macrophage system of the body, including all phagocytic white blood cells except granular white blood cells; the reticuloendothelial system

monosaccharide Any carbohydrate whose molecule cannot be split into simpler carbohydrates; a simple sugar

Montoux test Test for tuberculosis in which an appropriate dilution of purified protein derivative is injected intradermally into the superficial layers of the skin of the forearm

morbidity The state of being diseased; the ratio of the number of sick individuals compared to the total population of the community; the conditions that induce disease

morbidity rate Number of diseased individuals per unit population per unit time

mordant A substance that fixes the dyes used in staining tissues or bacteria; a substance that increases the affinity of a stain for a biological specimen

morphogenesis Morphological changes, including growth and differentiation of cells and tissues during development; the transformations involved in the growth and differentiation of cells and tissues

morphology The study of the shape and structure of microorganisms

morphovar A biotype of a given species that is differentiated based on morphology

mortality Death; the proportion of deaths within a population

mortality rate Death rate; number of deaths per unit population per unit time

mosaics A plant disease in which a patchy pattern of symptoms develop

most probable number (MPN) The statistical estimate of a bacterial population through the use of dilution and multiple tube inoculations

motility The capacity for independent locomotion

MPN Most probable number

MR test Methyl Red test

mRNA Messenger RNA

mucociliary escalator system Defense system that lines the upper respiratory tract and protects it against pathogens; the system consists of mucous membranes and cilia; mucous secretions trap microorganisms and cilia beat with an upward wave-like motion to expel microorganisms from the respiratory tract

mucopeptide Peptidoglycan component of bacterial cell walls

mucosa Mucous membrane, the lining of body cavities that communicate with the exterior

mucous membrane The type of membrane lining body cavities and canals that have communication with air

mucus Viscid fluid secreted by mucous glands consisting of mucin, water, inorganic salts, epithelial cells, and leukocytes

multicellular Composed of or containing more than one cell

multilateral budding In fungi, budding that occurs all around the mother cell

multiple antibiotic resistance The ability to resist the effects of two or more unrelated antibiotics by bacterial strains generally containing R plasmids

murein Peptidoglycan; the repeating polysaccharide unit that comprises the backbone of the cell walls of eubacteria

mushrooms Fungi that are members of the Agaricales; the basidiocarps of basidiomycetes

must Fluid extracted from crushed grapes; the ingredients, e.g., fruit pulp or juice, used as substrate for fermentation in wine making

mutagen Any chemical or physical agent that promotes the occurrence of mutation; a substance that increases the rate of mutation above the spontaneous rate

mutant Any organism that differs from the naturally occurring type because its base DNA has been modified, resulting in an altered protein that gives the cell properties different from those of its parent

mutation A stable, heritable change in the nucleotide sequence of the genetic nucleic acid, resulting in an alteration in the products coded for by the gene

mutation rate The average number of mutations per cell generation

mutualism A stable condition in which two organisms of different species live in close physical association, each organism deriving some benefit from the association; symbiosis

myc- Combining form meaning fungus

mycelia The interwoven mass of discrete fungal hyphae

mycobiont Fungal partner in a lichen

mycolic acids Fatty acids in the cell walls of *Mycobacterium* and several other bacteria related to the actinomycetes

mycology The study of fungi

mycoplasmas Members of the group of bacteria that are composed of cells lacking cell walls, bounded by a single triple-layered membrane, exhibiting a variety of shapes; the smallest organisms capable of self-reproduction

mycorrhizae A stable, symbiotic association between a fungus and the root of a plant; the term also refers to the root–fungus structure itself

mycosis Any disease in which the causal agent is a fungus

mycotoxins Toxic substances produced by fungi, including aflatoxin, amatoxin, and ergot alkaloids

mycovirus A virus that infects fungi

myocarditis Infection of the myocardium; can result from viral, bacterial, helminthic, or parasitic infections, hypersensitivity immune reactions, radiation therapy, or chemical poisoning

myocardium Muscular tissue of the heart wall

myx- Combining form meaning mucus

myxamoebae Nonflagellated ameboid cells that occur in the life cycle of the slime molds and members of the Plasmodiophorales

Myxobacterales Fruiting myxobacteria; gliding, small, rod-shaped bacteria normally embedded in a slime layer; under appropriate conditions they aggregate to form fruiting bodies

myxobacteria Myxobacterales

Myxomycetes True slime molds, class of Plasmodiogymnomycotina; some form myxamoebae, others form swarm cells; their classification is based on the structure of the fruiting body

myxospores Resting cells in the fruiting bodies of members of the Myxobacteriales

N

N peplomers Neuraminidase peplomers

NAD$^+$ Oxidized nicotinamide adenine dinucleotide

NADH Reduced nicotinamide adenine dinucleotide

NADP$^+$ Oxidized nicotinamide adenine dinucleotide phosphate

NADPH Reduced nicotinamide adenine dinucleotide phosphate

narrow-spectrum antibiotic Antibiotics that are relatively selective and are usually targeted at a particular pathogen

nasopharynx Upper part of the pharynx continuous with the nasal passages

natto Food product from the Orient; the fermentation product of boiled soybeans and *Bacillus subtilis*

natural killer cells A special subset of lymphocytes that are neither T nor B cells; natural killer (NK) cells are responsible for lysis of tumor cells

necrosis Pathological death of a cell or group of cells in contact with living cells

negative interactions Interactions between populations that act as feedback mechanisms and limit population densities

negative stain A stain with a negatively charged chromophore

negative staining The treatment of cells with dye so that the background, rather than the cell, is made opaque; used to demonstrate bacterial capsules or the presence of parasitic cysts in fecal samples

negatively supercoiled Underwound DNA that is twisted in the opposite direction that the helix turns

Negri bodies Acidophilic, intracytoplasmic inclusion bodies that develop in cells of the central nervous system in cases of rabies

Neisseriaceae Family of Gram-negative cocci and coccobacilli, including the genera *Neisseria, Branhamella, Moraxella,* and *Acinetobacter*

nematodes Worms of the class Nematoda

neoplasm Result of the abnormal and excessive proliferation of the cells of a tissue; if the progeny cells remain localized, the resulting mass is called a *tumor*

net primary production Amount of organic carbon in the form of biomass and soluble metabolites available for heterotrophic consumers in terrestrial and aquatic habitats

neuraminidase peplomers (N peplomers) Projections from surfaces of influenza viruses that split neuraminic acid from polysaccharides and are involved in the release of viruses from infected cells following viral replication

neurotoxin A toxin capable of destroying nerve tissue or interfering with neural transmission

neutralism The relationship between two different microbial populations characterized by the lack of a recognizable interaction

neutralization Reaction of antitoxin with toxin that renders the toxin harmless

neutralization of toxic materials Conversion of toxic materials to nontoxic forms

neutralophiles Bacteria that tend to thrive under neutral pH conditions

neutropenia A decrease below the normal standard in the number of neutrophils in the peripheral blood

neutrophilia (neutrophilic leukocytosis) An increase above the normal standard in the number of neutrophils in the peripheral blood

neutrophils Large granular leukocytes with highly variable nuclei consisting of three to five lobes and cytoplasmic granules that stain with neutral dyes and eosin

niche The functional role of an organism within an ecosystem; the combined description of the physical habitat, functional role, and interactions of the microorganisms occurring at a given location

nicotinamide adenine dinucleotide (NAD^+) A coenzyme used as an electron acceptor in oxidation-reduction reactions

nicotinamide adenine dinucleotide phosphate ($NADP^+$) The phosphorylated form of NAD^+ formed when NADPH serves as an electron donor in oxidation-reduction reactions

***nif* genes** Genes that code for nitrogenase; genes that code for nitrogen fixation

nine + two (9 + 2) system The arrangement of microtubules in eukaryotic flagella and cilia, consisting of nine peripheral pairs of microtubules surrounding two single central microtubules

nitrate reduction The reduction of nitrate to reduced forms; for example, under anaerobic and microaerophilic conditions, bacteria use nitrate as a terminal electron acceptor for respiratory metabolism

nitrification The process in which ammonia is oxidized to nitrite and nitrite to nitrate; a process primarily carried out by the strictly aerobic, chemolithotrophic bacteria of the family Nitrobacteraceae

nitrifying bacteria Nitrobacteraceae; Gram-negative, obligately aerobic, chemolithotrophic bacteria occurring in fresh and marine waters and in soil that oxidize ammonia to nitrite or nitrite to nitrate

nitrite A salt of nitrous acid; NO_2^-; nitrites of sodium and potassium are used as food additives and preservatives

nitrite ammonification Reduction of nitrite to ammonium ions by bacteria; does not remove nitrogen from the soil

Nitrobacteriaceae Nitrifying bacteria; family of chemolithotrophic bacteria that oxidize nitrite or ammonia to generate ATP; found in soil, fresh water, and sea water

nitrogen cycle The biogeochemical cycling of nitrogen through oxidized and reduced forms, including the fixation of nitrogen (conversion of molecular nitrogen to ammonia), nitrification (conversion of ammonia to nitrite and nitrate), and denitrification (conversion of nitrate to molecular nitrogen)

nitrogen fixation The reduction of gaseous nitrogen to ammonia, carried out by certain prokaryotes

nitrogenase The enzyme that catalyzes biological nitrogen fixation

nitrogenous Containing nitrogen

nitrogen-rich fertilizers Products containing fixed forms of nitrogen that can serve as plant nutrients when applied to crop fields to support increased production

NK cells Natural killer cells

nodules Tumor-like growths formed by plants in response to infections with specific bacteria within which the infecting bacteria fix atmospheric nitrogen; a rounded, irregularly shaped mineral mass

nodulin genes Genes involved in root nodule formation

Nomarski differential interference microscope A specialized type of interference microscope that produces high-contrast images of unstained specimens with a three-dimensional appearance; its special features are a polarizing filter, an interference contrast condenser, and a prism analyzer plate

nomenclature The naming of organisms, a function of taxonomy governed by codes, rules, and priorities laid down by committees

noncompetitive inhibition Inhibition of enzyme activity by a substance that does not compete with the normal substrate for the active site and thus cannot be reduced by increasing the substrates concentration

noncyclic photophosphorylation A metabolic pathway involved in the conversion of light energy for the generation of ATP in which an electron is transferred from an electron donor, normally water, by a series of electron carriers, with the eventual formation of a reduced coenzyme, normally NADPH

nongonococcal urethritis Any inflammation of the urethra not caused by *Neisseria gonorrhoeae*

nonhomologous recombination Recombination that involves little or no homology between the donor DNA and the region of the DNA in the recipient where insertion occurs

nonlinear alkyl benzyl sulfonate (ABS) Component of anionic laundry detergent that contains a braided alkane chain, is resistant to biodegradation, and causes foaming of receiving waters; banned because of its persistence in groundwater

nonperishable foods Food products that are not subject to spoilage by microorganisms under normal storage conditions and consequently have an extended shelf life as long as those conditions are maintained

nonreciprocal recombination Nonhomologous recombination

nonsense codon A codon that does not specify an amino acid but acts as a punctuator of mRNA

nonsense mutation A mutation in which a codon specifying an amino acid is altered to a nonsense codon

nonspecific urethritis (NSU) A sexually transmitted disease that results in inflammation of the urethra caused by bacteria other than *Neisseria gonorrhoeae*

normal microbiota Microbial populations most frequently found in association with particular tissues that typically do not cause disease; also known as indigenous microbial populations

normal microflora Normal microbiota

Northern blotting A technique that permits the separation and identification of specific RNA sequences

Norwalk agent Small DNA virus responsible for an outbreak of winter vomiting disease in Norwalk, Ohio, in 1968

nosocomial infection An infection acquired while in the hospital

NSU Nonspecific urethritis

nuclear membrane A double layer with a distinct space between the two membranes surrounding the genomes of eukaryotic cells

nuclear polyhedrosis virus Viral pesticide that develops in host-cell nuclei

nuclease An enzyme capable of splitting nucleic acids to nucleotides, nucleosides, or their components

nucleic acid A large, acidic, chain-like macromolecule containing phosphoric acid, sugar, and purine and pyrimidine bases; the nucleotide polymers RNA and DNA

nucleocapsid The combined viral genome and capsid

nucleoid region The region of a prokaryotic cell in which the genome occurs

nucleolus An RNA-rich intranuclear body not bounded by a limiting membrane that is the site of rRNA synthesis in eukaryotes

nucleoprotein A conjugated protein closely associated with nucleic acid

nucleosome The fundamental structural unit of DNA in eukaryotes, having approximately 190 base pairs folded and held together by histones

nucleotide The combination of a purine or pyrimidine base with a sugar and phosphoric acid; the basic structural unit of nucleic acid

nucleus An organelle of eukaryotes in which the cell's genome occurs; the differentiated protoplasm of a cell that is rich in nucleic acids and is surrounded by a membrane

numerical aperture (NA) The property of a lens that describes the amount of light that can enter it

numerical taxonomy A system that uses overall degrees of similarity and large numbers of characteristics to determine the taxonomic position of an organism; allows organisms of unknown affiliation to be identified as members of established taxa

nutrient A growth-supporting substance

nutritional mutations Mutations that alter the nutritional requirements of the progeny of a microorganism

nutritional requirements Essential growth substances needed for metabolism and reproduction

nystatin Polyene antibiotic used in the treatment of topical *Candida* infections

O

O antigens Polysaccharide antigens occurring in the cell walls of Gram-negative bacteria

objective lens The microscope lens closest to the object

obligate aerobes Organisms that grow only under aerobic conditions, i.e., in the presence of air or oxygen

obligate anaerobes Organisms that cannot use molecular oxygen; organisms that grow only under anaerobic conditions, i.e., in the absence of air or oxygen; organisms that cannot carry out respiratory metabolism

obligate intracellular parasites Organisms that can live and reproduce only within the cells of other organisms, such as viruses, all of which must find suitable host cells for their replication

obligate thermophiles Organisms restricted to growth at high temperatures

occluded Closed or shut up

oceans The body of salt water that covers nearly three fourths of the Earth's surface

ocular lens The eyepiece of a microscope; the lens closest to the eye

3′-OH free end Unattached hydroxyl group at the 3-carbon position at one end of a nucleic acid molecule

-oid Combining form meaning resembling

oil immersion lens A high-power objective lens of a microscope designed to work with the space between the objective and the specimen, filled with oil to enhance resolution

oil pollutants Petroleum hydrocarbons that contaminate the environment

Okazaki fragments The short segments of newly synthesized DNA along the trailing or discontinuous strand that are linked by a ligase to form the completed DNA

oligotrophic Pertaining to lakes and other bodies of water that are poor in nutrients that support the growth of aerobic, photosynthetic organisms; microorganisms that grow at very low nutrient concentrations

oligotrophic bacteria Bacteria that possess physiological properties that permit them to grow at low nutrient concentrations

oncogenes Genes that can lead to malignant transformations of animal cells

oncogenic viruses Viruses capable of inducing tumor formation, i.e., animal cell transformations

one gene–one enzyme hypothesis An hypothesis developed in the 1940s, which states that one gene codes for a specific protein

one-step growth curve Curve that describes the lytic reproduction cycle that releases a large number of phage simultaneously

oogamy A form of fertilization that involves a motile male gamete and a relatively large, nonmotile female gamete or gametangial contact in which the gametangia are morphologically different

oogonium A specialized structure where female gametes are produced; the female gametangium of oomycete water molds

oomycetes Water molds, class of Mastigomycota; fungi that reproduce using flagellated zoospores

oospores Thick-walled, resting spores of fungi

operator region A section of an operon involved in the control of the synthesis of the gene products encoded within that region of DNA; a regulatory gene that binds with a regulatory protein to turn on and off transcription of a specified region of DNA

operon A group or cluster of structural genes whose coordinated expression is controlled by a regulator gene

operon model A model that explains control of the expression of structural genes, such as for lactose metabolism, by regulation of the transcription of the mRNA directing synthesis of the products of the structural genes

opportunistic pathogens Organisms that exist as part of the normal body microbiota but that may become pathogenic under certain conditions, e.g., when the normal antimicrobial body defense mechanisms have been impaired; organisms that are not normally considered pathogens but that cause disease under some conditions

opsonization The process by which a cell becomes more susceptible to phagocytosis and lytic digestion when a surface antigen combines with an antibody and/or other serum component

optimal growth temperature Temperature at which microbes exhibit the maximal growth rate

optimal oxygen concentration The oxygen concentration at which microbes exhibit the maximal growth rate with maximal product yield

orally Ingestion into the gastrointestinal tracts

orchitis Inflammation of the testes

organelle A membrane-bound structure that forms part of a microorganism and that performs a specialized function

Orleans process Method for the production of vinegar in which raw vinegar from a previous run provides the active inoculum; classic slow process for producing vinegar that relies on a microbial surface film

oscillatorian cyanobacteria Subgroup of cyanobacteria that form filamentous structures composed of straight or helical vegetative cells

-ose Combining form denoting a sugar

osmophiles Organisms that grow best or only in or on media of relatively high osmotic pressure

osmosis Passage of a solvent through a membrane from a dilute solution into a more concentrated one

osmotic pressure The force resulting from differences in solute concentrations on opposite sides of a semipermeable membrane

osmotic shock Any disturbance or disruption in a cell or subcellular organelle that occurs when it is transferred to a significantly hypertonic or hypotonic medium, with lysis of cells resulting from osmotic pressure

osmotolerant Capable of withstanding high osmotic pressures and growth in solutions of high solute concentrations

outer membrane A structure found in Gram-negative cell walls that acts as a coarse molecular sieve and allows the diffusion of hydrophilic and hydrophobic molecules

overgrowths A plant disease condition characterized by excessive growth

oxidase An enzyme (oxidoreductase) that catalyzes a reaction in which electrons removed from a substrate are donated directly to molecular oxygen

oxidation An increase in the positive valence or a decrease in the negative valence of an element resulting from the loss of electrons that are taken on by some other element

oxidation pond A method of aerobic waste disposal employing biodegradation by aerobic and facultative microorganisms growing in a standing water body

oxidation-reduction potential A measure of the tendency of a given oxidation-reduction system to donate electrons, i.e., to behave as a reducing agent, or to accept electrons, i.e., to act as an oxidizing agent; determined by measuring the electrical potential difference between the given system and a standard system

oxidation-reduction reactions Coupled reactions in which one substrate loses an electron (oxidation) and a second substrate gains that electron (reduction)

oxidative phosphorylation A metabolic sequence of reactions occurring within a membrane in which an electron is transferred from a reduced coenzyme by a series of electron carriers, establishing an electrochemical gradient across the membrane that drives the formation of ATP from ADP and inorganic phosphate by chemiosmosis

oxidative photophosphorylation A metabolic sequence of reactions occurring within a membrane in which light initiates the transfer of an electron by a series of electron carriers, establishing an electrochemical gradient across the membrane that drives the formation of ATP from ADP and inorganic phosphate by chemiosmosis

oxidize To produce an increase in the positive valence through the loss of electrons

oxidoreductase Enzyme that carries out oxidation-reduction reactions

oxygenic photosynthesis A type of photosynthesis carried out by plants, algae, and cyanobacteria in which oxygen is produced from water

oxygenic phototrophic bacteria (oxyphotobacteria) Subclass of Photobacteria; bacteria capable of splitting water to form oxygen as part of photosynthetic metabolism; bacteria capable of producing oxygen during photosynthesis

ozonation Killing of microorganisms by exposure to ozone

P

5′-P free end Unattached phosphate ester group at the 5-carbon position at one end of a nucleic acid molecule

pain Characteristic of the inflammatory response, an unpleasant sensation due to lysis of blood cells, triggering the production of bradykinin and prostaglandins that alter the threshold and intensity of the nervous system's response to pain

palindrome (palindromic sequence) A word reading the same backward and forward; a base sequence the complement of which has the same sequence; a nucleotide sequence that is the same when read in the antiparallel direction

pandemic An outbreak of disease that affects large numbers of people in a major geographical region or that has reached epidemic proportions simultaneously in different parts of the world

papilloma viruses Small, icosahedral DNA viruses that cause warts

parasites Organisms that live on or in the tissues of another living organism, the host, from which they derive their nutrients

parasitism An interactive relationship between two organisms or populations in which one is harmed and the other benefits; generally, the population that benefits, the parasite, is smaller than the population that is harmed

parfocal Pertaining to microscopic oculars and objectives that are so constructed or so mounted that in changing from one to another, the image remains in focus

parotitis Inflammation of the parotid gland, as in mumps

passive agglutination A procedure in which the combination of an antibody with a soluble antigen is made readily detectable by the prior adsorption of the antigen to erythrocytes or to minute particles of organic or inorganic materials

passive diffusion Unassisted movement of molecules from areas of high concentration to areas of low concentration

passive immunity Short-term immunity brought about by the transfer of preformed antibody from an immune subject to a nonimmune subject

Pasteur effect The slower rate of glucose utilization by a microorganism growing aerobically by respiratory metabolism than by the same organism growing anaerobically, reflecting feedback inhibition; in organisms capable of both fermentative and respiratory metabolism, the inhibition of glucose utilization in anaerobically grown cells on exposure to oxygen

pasteurization Reduction in the number of microorganisms by exposure to elevated temperatures but not necessarily killing all microorganisms in a sample; a form of heat treatment that is lethal for the causal agents of a number of milk-transferable diseases, as well as for a proportion of normal milk microbiota, which also inactivates certain bacterial enzymes that may cause deterioration in milk

pathogenicity The ability of an organism to cause disease in the host it infects

pathogens Organisms capable of causing disease in animals, plants, or microorganisms

pathology The study of the nature of disease through the study of its causes, processes, and effects, along with the associated alterations of structure and function

PBP Penicillin-binding protein

pellicle A thin protective membrane occurring around some protozoa, also known as a *periplast;* a continuous or fragmentary film that sometimes forms at the surface of a liquid culture; it consists entirely of cells or may be largely extracellular products of the cultured organisms

pelvic inflammatory disease (PID) Inflammation that results from a generalized bacterial infection of the uterus, pelvic organs, uterine tubes, and ovaries

penetration Entry of the phage genome into the host cell

penicillin-binding proteins Bacterial cytoplasmic membrane-bound proteins that are involved in some of the reactions in peptidoglycan biosynthesis; these proteins irreversibly bind penicillins

penicillins A group of natural and semisynthetic antibiotics with a β-lactam ring that are active against Gram-positive bacteria inhibiting the formation of cross-links in the peptidoglycan of growing bacteria

pentose A class of carbohydrates containing five carbon atoms

pentose phosphate pathway Metabolic pathway that involves the oxidative decarboxylation of glucose 6-phosphate to ribulose 5-phosphate, followed by a series of reversible, nonoxidative sugar interconversions

peplomers Protruding peptide spikes of a virus that affect pathogenicity and antigenicity of the particular viral strain

PEP:PTS Phosphoenolpyruvate:phosphotransferase system

pepsin A proteolytic enzyme

peptidase An enzyme that splits peptides to form amino acids

peptide bond A bond in which the carboxyl group of one amino acid is condensed with the amino group of another amino acid

peptides Compounds of two or more amino acids containing one or more peptide bonds

peptidoglycan The rigid component of the cell wall in most bacteria, consisting of a glycan (sugar) backbone of repetitively alternating *N*-acetylglucosamine and *N*-acetylmuramic acid with short, attached, cross-linked peptide chains containing unusual amino acids; also called murein

peptidyl site Site on the ribosome where the growing peptide chain is moved during protein synthesis

Peptococcaceae Family of Gram-positive cocci with complex nutritional requirements whose cells occur singly or in pairs, or in regular or irregular masses; they are obligately anaerobic, producing low molecular weight fatty acids, carbon dioxide, hydrogen, and ammonia

peptones A water-soluble mixture of proteases and amino acids produced by the hydrolysis of natural proteins by an enzyme or by an acid

period of decline Stage of disease after the period of illness during which the signs and symptoms of the disease disappear

period of illness Acute phase of a disease during which the patient experiences characteristic symptoms

periodontal pockets Holes in the gums deepened by periodontal disease

periodontitis Inflammation of the periodontium, the tissues surrounding a tooth

periodontosis Juvenile periodontitis, noninflammatory degeneration of the periodontium leading to bone regression

periplasm The region between the cytoplasmic and the outer cell wall membranes of Gram-negative bacteria

periplasmic space In Gram-negative bacterial cells, the area between the outer cell wall membrane and the cytoplasmic membrane

periplast Pellicle of cryptomonad algae

perishable foods Food products that are readily subject to spoilage by microorganisms and consequently have a short shelf life

peritonitis Inflammation of the peritoneum

peritrichous flagella Referring to the arrangement of a cell's flagella in a more or less uniform distribution over the surface of the cell

permeability The property of cell membranes that permits transport of molecules and ions in solution across the membrane

permease An enzyme that increases the rate of transport of a substance across a membrane

peroxidase An oxidoreductase that catalyzes a reaction in which electrons removed from a substrate are donated to hydrogen peroxide

peroxide The anion O_2^- or HO_2^-, or a compound containing one of these anions

peroxisomes Microbodies that contain D-amino acid oxidase, α-hydroxy acid oxidase, catalase, and other enzymes, found in yeasts and certain protozoa

person-to-person epidemic Epidemiological disease pattern characterized by a relatively slow, prolonged rise and decline in the number of cases; an epidemic in which there is a chain of transmission from one infected individual to an uninfected individual

pest A population that is an annoyance for economic, health, or aesthetic reasons

pesticides Substances destructive to pests, especially insects

Petri dish A round, shallow, flat-bottomed dish with a vertical edge with a similar, slightly larger structure that forms a loosely fitting lid, made of glass or plastic, widely used as receptacles for various types of solid media

pH An expression of the hydrogen ion (H^+) concentration; the logarithm to the base 10 of the reciprocal of the hydrogen ion concentration

Phaeophycophyta Brown algae that produce xanthophylls; algae where the primary reserve materials are laminarin and mannitol and the cell wall is two-layered cell and composed of alginic acid

phage Bacteriophage

phagocytes Any of various cells that ingest and break down certain categories of particulate matter

phagocytosis The process in which particulate matter is ingested by a cell, involving the engulfment of that matter by the cell's membrane

phagosomes Membrane-bound vesicles in phagocytes formed by the invagination of the cell membrane and the phagocytized material

phagotrophic Referring to the ingestion of nutrients in particulate form by phagocytosis

pharmaceutical A drug used in the treatment of disease

pharyngitis Inflammation of the pharynx

phase contrast microscope A microscope that achieves enhanced contrast of the specimen by altering the phase of light that passes through the specimen relative to the phase of light that passes through the background, eliminating the need for staining to view microorganisms and making the viewing of live specimens possible

PHB Poly-β-hydroxybutyric acid

phenetic Pertaining to the physical characteristics of an individual organism without consideration of its genetic makeup; in taxonomy, a classification system that does not take evolutionary relationships into consideration; a classification system that assesses similarity based on appearance

phenol coefficient A number that expresses the antibacterial power of a substance relative to that of the disinfectant phenol

phenotype The totality of observable structural and functional characteristics of an individual organism, determined jointly by combination of its genotype and the environment

-phile Combining form meaning similar to or having an affinity for

philopodia False feet that are filamentous projections composed entirely of ectoplasm

-phobic Combining form meaning having an aversion for or lacking affinity for

phosphatases Enzymes that hydrolyze esters of phosphoric acid

phosphatidylcholine phosphohydrolase The alpha toxin of *Clostridium perfringens* that is a lecithinase

phosphodiester bond Bonding of two moieties by a phosphate group; each moiety is held to the phosphate by an ester linkage

phosphoenolpyruvate:phosphotransferase system (PEP: PTS) A type of group translocation in which a phosphate group is added to a sugar as it is transported through the cytoplasmic membrane of some bacteria

phosphofructokinase An enzyme that mediates the addition of a phosphate group to glucose 6-phosphate, with the formation of glucose-1,6-diphosphate, a key step during glycolysis

phospholipase An enzyme that catalyzes the hydrolysis of a phospholipid

phospholipase C The alpha toxin of *Clostridium perfringens* that is a lecithinase

phospholipid A lipid compound that is an ester of phosphoric acid and also contains one or two molecules of fatty acid, an alcohol, and sometimes a nitrogenous base

phosphorylation The esterification of compounds with phosphoric acid; the conversion of an organic compound into an organic phosphate

photo- Combining form meaning light

photoautotrophic metabolism A type of metabolism in which inorganic molecules serve as electron donors and carbon source and light serves as energy source

photoautotrophs Organisms whose source of energy is light and whose source of carbon is carbon dioxide; characteristic of algae and some prokaryotes

photoheterotrophs Organisms that obtain energy from light but require exogenous organic compounds for growth

photolithotrophic metabolism Photoautotrophic metabolism

photolithotrophs Photoautotrophs

photolysis Liberation of oxygen by splitting of water during photosynthesis

photoorganotrophic metabolism A type of metabolism in which organic molecules serve as electron donors and carbon source and light serves as energy source

photophosphorylation A metabolic sequence by which light energy is trapped and converted to chemical energy, with the formation of ATP

photoreactivation A mechanism whereby the effects of ultraviolet radiation on DNA may be reversed by exposure to radiation of wavelengths in the range 320-500 nm; an enzymatic repair mechanism of DNA in many microorganisms

photosynthesis The process in which radiant (light) energy is absorbed by specialized pigments of a cell and is subsequently converted to chemical energy; the ATP formed in the light reactions is used to drive the fixation of carbon dioxide, with the production of organic matter

photosynthetic membranes Specialized membranes in photosynthetic bacteria that are the anatomical sites where light energy is converted to chemical energy in the form of ATP during photosynthesis

photosynthetic metabolism Photosynthesis

photosystem I Cyclic photophosphorylation

photosystem II Noncyclic photophosphorylation

photosystems Pathways of electron transfer initiated by light energy; pathways of ATP synthesis that are used to convert light energy to chemical energy in photosynthetic bacteria

phototaxis The ability of bacteria to detect and respond to differences in light intensity, moving toward or away from light

phototrophs Organisms whose sole or principal primary source of energy is light; organisms capable of photophosphorylation

phycobilisomes Granules found in cyanobacteria and some algae on the surface of their thylakoids

phycobiont Algal partner of a lichen

phycocyanin Type of pigment in cyanobacteria and some algae that confers blue color

phycoerythrin Type of pigment in cyanobacteria and red algae that confers red color

phycology The study of algae

phycomycete A group of true fungi that lack regularly spaced septae in the actively growing portions of the fungus and produce sporangiospores by cleavage as the primary method of asexual reproduction

phycovirus Any virus whose host cell, within which it replicates, is a cyanobacterium or alga

phylogenetic Referring to the evolution of a species from simpler forms; in taxonomy, a classification based on evolutionary relationships

phylum A taxonomic group composed of groups of related classes

physiology The study of the functions of living organisms and their physicochemical parts and metabolic reactions

phytoalexin Polyaromatic antimicrobial substances produced by higher plants in response to a microbial infection

phytoplankton Passively floating or weakly motile photosynthetic aquatic organisms, primarily cyanobacteria and algae

phytoplankton food web A food web in aquatic habitats based on the grazing of primary producers

PID Pelvic inflammatory disease

pili Filamentous appendages that project from the cell surface of certain Gram-negative bacteria apparently involved in adsorption phenomena; filamentous appendages involved in bacterial mating

pilin A chain of proteins, the subunits of pili

pilot plant Facility with small-intermediate size fermentors that is used during scale up to determine appropriate fermentation conditions for full scale commercial production

pitching Inoculation of yeast into cooled wort or grape must during the production of beer or wine, respectively

plague A contagious disease often occurring as an epidemic; an acute infectious disease of humans and other animals, especially rodents, caused by *Yersinia pestis* that is transmitted by fleas

planapochromatic lens A flat-field apochromatic objective microscope lens

plankton Collectively, all microorganisms that passively drift in the pelagic zone of lakes and other bodies of water, chiefly microalgae and protozoans

plant pathogens Microorganisms that cause plant diseases

plant pathology The study of the diseases of plants

plant pests Plant pathogenic bacteria

plant viruses Viruses that replicate within plant cells

plaques Clearings in areas of bacterial growth due to lysis by phage; also, the accumulation of bacterial cells within a polysaccharide matrix on the surfaces of teeth; also known as *dental plaque*

plasma cells Cells that are able to synthesize a specific antibody and secondary B cells

plasma membrane Cytoplasmic membrane

plasmids Extrachromosomal genetic structures that can replicate independently within a bacterial cell

Plasmodiogymnomycotina Subdivision of Gymnomycota; includes two classes, Protostetliomycetes and Myxomycetes

Plasmodiophoromycetes Endoparasitic slime molds, class of Mastigomycota; protozoa that are obligate parasites of plants, algae, and fungi, forming a plasmodium within host cells

Plasmodium Genus of malaria-causing protozoa; the life stage of acellular slime molds, characterized by a motile, multinucleate body

plasmogamy Fusion of cells without nuclear fusion to form a multinucleate mass

plastids A class of membrane-bound organelles in cells of higher plants and algae, containing pigments and/or certain products of the cell, e.g., chloroplasts

plate counting Method of estimating numbers of microorganisms by diluting samples, culturing on solid media, and counting the colonies that develop to estimate the number of viable microorganisms in the sample

pleomorphism The variation in size and form among cells in a clone or a pure culture

pleurocapsalean cyanobacteria Unicellular subgroup of cyanobacteria, exhibiting multiple fission to produce coccoid reproductive cells that fail to separate completely following binary fission, forming multicellular aggregates

ploidy In a eukaryotic nucleus or cell, the number of complete sets of chromosomes

plus (+) strand viruses Viruses whose RNA genomes can serve as mRNAs

PMNs Neutrophils

pneumonia Inflammation of the lungs

poi Hawaiian fermented food product made from the root of the taro plant

polar budding In fungi, budding that occurs at only one end of the mother cell

polar flagella Flagella emanating from one or both polar ends of a cell

polar mutations Mutations that prevent the translation of subsequent polypeptides coded for in the same mRNA molecule

polarized light Light vibrating in a defined pattern

pollutant A material that contaminates air, soil, or water; substances—often harmful—that foul water or soil, reducing their purity and usefulness

poly-β-hydroxybutyric acid A polymeric storage product formed by some bacteria

polycistronic Coding for multiple cistrons; mRNA molecules that code for the synthesis of several proteins, often the proteins are functionally related and under the control of a specific operon

polyene antibiotics A group of antibiotics used to treat fungal diseases; they act by altering the permeability properties of cytoplasmic membranes

polymerase An enzyme that catalyzes the formation of a polymer

polymers The products of the combination of two or more molecules of the same substance

polymorph A leukocyte with granules in the cytoplasm; also known as a polymorphonuclear leukocyte (PMN)

polymorphonuclear Having a nucleus that resembles lobes connected by thin strands of nuclear substance

polymorphonuclear neutrophils (PMNs) Neutrophils

polypeptide A chain of amino acids linked by peptide bonds, but of lower molecular weight than a protein

polyphosphate Reserves of organic phosphate that can be used in the synthesis of ATP

polysaccharides Carbohydrates formed by the condensation of monosaccharides, e.g., starch and cellulose, that have multiple monosaccharide subunits

polysomes Complexes of ribosomes bound together by a single mRNA molecule; also known as *polyribosomes*

population An assemblage of organisms of the same type living at the same location; a clone of organisms

porins Proteins found in the outer membranes of Gram-negative cells in groups of three, they form cross-membrane channels through which small molecules can diffuse

portals of entry Sites through which pathogens can gain access and entry to the body

positive interactions Between biological populations, interactions that enhance the ability of the interacting populations to survive within the community, a particular habitat

positive staining procedures Use of a basic, positively charged chromophore to stain a negatively charged structure

positively supercoiled Overwound DNA that is twisted in the same direction that the helix turns

post-transcriptional modification Action on hnRNA within the nucleus to form mRNA

potable Fit to drink

pour plate A method of culture in which the inoculum is dispersed uniformly in molten agar or other medium in a petri dish; the medium is allowed to set and is then incubated

precipitation Separation of a substance in solid form from a solution, as by means of a reagent

precipitin Reaction of a serological test in which the interaction of antibodies with soluble antigens is detected by the formation of a precipitate

predation A mode of life in which food is primarily obtained by killing and consuming animals; an interaction between organisms in which one benefits and one is harmed, based on the ingestion of the smaller organism, the prey, by the larger organism, the predator

predators Organisms that practice predation

pre-emptive colonization Alteration of environmental conditions by pioneer organisms in a way that discourages further succession

presumptive test In assays for assessing water safety, gas formation in Durham tubes containing lactose broth and water samples is positive evidence of fecal contamination exists

prey An animal taken by a predator for food

Pribnow sequence A sequence within nucleotide bases in DNA that determines the site of transcription initiation

primary immune response The first immune response to a particular antigen that has a characteristically long lag period and a relatively low titer of antibody production

primary producers Organisms capable of converting carbon dioxide to organic carbon, including photoautotrophs and chemoautotrophs

primary production The autotrophic conversion of inorganic carbon dioxide to organic carbon

primary sewage treatment The removal of suspended solids from sewage by physical settling in tanks or basins

primary staining Use of the first or primary stain in a differential staining procedure

principle of energy conservation Principle stating that energy involved in chemical reactions is never created or destroyed

prions Protein substances that are infectious and reproduce within living systems; they appear to be proteinaceous, based on degradation by proteases, and to lack nucleic acids based on resistance to digestion by nucleases

probabilistic identification matrices Combinations of characteristics of organisms used to characterize large numbers of strains of a taxonomic group to establish the variability of a particular feature within a group; data matrices used to allow organisms of unknown affiliation to be identified as members of established taxa

processed foods Cheese products to which water has been added, thereby diluting their nutritional value

processivity A mechanism in which an enzyme or enzyme complex that copies a long message maintains an uninterrupted contact with the template until the copying is terminated

Prochlorales Order of Oxyphotobacteria; the primary photosynthetic pigments are chlorophyll *a* and *b*, only members of the genus *Prochloron* occur as green, single-celled, extracellular symbionts of marine invertebrates

prodigiosin A red pigment produced by some *Serratia* species

prodromal stage Time period in the infectious process following incubation when the symptoms of the illness begin to appear

productive infection An infection that results in viral replication with the production of viruses that can infect other compatible host cells

progenotes Theoretical primitive, self-replicating, protein-containing, cell-like structures

progeny Offspring

projector lens The lens of an electron microscope that focuses the beam on the film or viewing screen

prokaryotes Cells whose genomes are not contained within a nucleus; the bacteria and archaebacteria

prokaryotic cells Eubacterial and archaebacterial cells

promastigote An elongated, flagellated form assumed by many species of the Trypanosomatidae during a particular stage of development

promoter region Specific initiation site of DNA where the RNA polymerase enzyme binds for transcription on the DNA

proofreading The 3′-OH → 5′-P exonuclease activity of DNA polymerases; the excision of improperly inserted nucleotides by DNA polymerases during DNA replication

propagated transmission Person-to-person transmission

propagules The reproductive units of microorganisms

prophage The integrated phage genome formed when this genome becomes integrated with the host's chromosome and is replicated as part of the bacterial chromosome during subsequent cell division

prophylaxis The measures taken to prevent the occurrence of disease

Propionibacteriaceae Family of Gram-positive rods that produce propionic acid, acetic acid, or mixtures of organic acids by fermentation; consists of the genera *Propionibacterium* and *Eubacterium*

propionic acid fermentation pathway Metabolic sequence carried out by the propionic bacteria that produces propionic acid

prosthecae A cell wall–limited appendage forming a narrow extension of a prokaryotic cell

proteases Exoenzymes that break down proteins into their component amino acids
protein A class of high molecular weight polymers composed of amino acids joined by peptide linkages
protein toxins Exotoxins of bacteria; proteins secreted by bacteria that act as poisons
proteinase One of the subgroups of proteases or proteolytic enzymes that act directly on native proteins in the first step of their conversion to simpler substances
proteolytic enzymes Enzymes that break down proteins
Protista In one proposed classification system, a Kingdom of organisms that lacks true tissue differentiation, i.e., the microorganisms; in another classification system, a Kingdom that includes many of the algae and protozoa
protobionts Progenotes
proto-cooperation Synergism; a nonobligatory relationship between two microbial populations in which both populations benefit
protonmotive force Potential chemical energy in a gradient of hydrogen ions and electrical energy across the bacterial cytoplasmic membrane
protoplasm The viscid material constituting the essential substance of living cells on which all the vital functions of nutrition, secretion, growth, reproduction, irritability, and locomotion depend
protoplasts Spherical, osmotically sensitive structures formed when cells are suspended in an isotonic medium and their cell walls are completely removed; a bacterial protoplast consists of an intact cell membrane and the cytoplasm it contains
prototrophs Parental strains of microorganisms that give rise to nutritional mutants known as *auxotrophs*
protozoa A group of diverse eukaryotic, typically unicellular, nonphotosynthetic microorganisms generally lacking a rigid cell wall
protozoology The study of protozoa
provirus A viral genome that integrates with the host genome
Pseudomonadaceae Family of Gram-negative, straight or curved rods that are motile by means of polar flagella; most strains carry out obligately aerobic respiration, unable to fix atmospheric nitrogen; nutritionally versatile; some produce characteristic fluorescent pigments; widely distributed in soil and water
pseudopeptidoglycan Component of archaebacterial cell walls
pseudoplasmodium Structure formed by swarming together or aggregation of myxamoebae; undergoes a developmental sequence to form a sporocarp
pseudopodia False feet formed by protoplasmic streaming in protozoa; used for locomotion and the capture of food
psychro- Combining form meaning cold
psychroduric Capable of surviving but not of growing at low temperatures
psychrophile An organism that has an optimum growth temperature below 20° C
psychrotroph A mesophile that can grow at low temperatures
puntae Holes in the silica walls of diatoms that allow exchange of nutrients and metabolic wastes between the cell and its surroundings
pure culture A culture that contains cells of one kind; the progeny of a single cell
purine $C_5H_4N_4$, a cyclic nitrogenous compound, the parent of several nucleic acid bases
purple membrane The portion of the cytoplasmic membrane that contains bacteriorhodopsin, found in *Halobacterium*
purple nonsulfur bacteria Members of the Chromatiaceae anoxygenic phototrophic bacteria that do not oxidize sulfur to sulfate
pus A semifluid, creamy yellow or greenish-yellow product of inflammation composed mainly of leukocytes and serum
putrefaction The microbial breakdown of protein under anaerobic conditions
pyelonephritis Inflammation of the kidneys
pyknosis A condition in which the nucleus is contracted
pyoderma A pus-producing skin lesion
pyogenic Pus producing
pyorrhea Periodontitis
pyrimidine A six-membered cyclic compound containing four carbon and two nitrogen atoms in a ring; the parent compound of several nucleotide bases
pyrite A common mineral containing iron disulfite
pyrogenic Fever producing
pyrogens Fever-producing substances
Pyrrophycophyta Fire algae; generally brown or red because of xanthophyll pigments; unicellular and biflagellate; store starch or oils as the reserve material; the cell walls contain cellulose

Q

Q_{10} Describes the actual change in the rate at which a reaction proceeds when the temperature is increased by 10° C; for enzymatic reactions the Q_{10} usually is about 2
quality control A system for verifying and maintaining a desired level of quality in a product or process by careful planning, use of proper equipment, continued inspection, and corrective action when required; in fermentation processes, quality is determined by the yield and purity of the product
quarantine Isolation of persons or animals suffering from an infectious disease to prevent transmission of the disease to others
quick freezing Subjecting cooked or uncooked foods to rapid refrigeration, permitting them to be stored almost indefinitely at freezing temperatures
quinolones Antimicrobial agents that act by blocking normal DNA replication by interfering with DNA gyrase

R

R plasmid A plasmid encoding for antibiotic resistance
racking A step in the fermentation of wine in which the wine is filtered through the bottom sediments and added back to the top of the fermentation vat
radappertization Reduction in the number of microorganisms by exposure to ionizing radiation
radioimmunoassay (RIA) A highly sensitive serological technique used to assay specific antibodies or antigens, employing a radioactive label to tag the reaction
radioisotopes Radioactive isotopes; isotopes emitting radiation

radiolaria Free-living protozoa occurring almost exclusively in marine habitats; they contain axopodia, with a skeleton of silicon or strontium sulfate

radurization Sterilization by exposure to ionizing radiation

rancid Having the characteristic odor of decomposing fat, chiefly due to the liberation of butyric and other volatile fatty acids

raphe A slit or pore in the cell wall of a diatom

rDNA Recombinant DNA

reading frame Groups of three nucleotide sequences

reagins A group of antibodies in serum that react with the allergens responsible for the specific manifestations of human hypersensitivity; a heterophile antibody formed during syphilis infections

reaneal To reestablish double-stranded DNA

rearrangement of genes Change in the relative positions of genes within the chromosome, thus altering the expression of the information contained in the genes

***rec* genes** Recombination genes

recalcitrant A chemical that is totally resistant to microbial attack

receptor The binding constituent on a surface

recessive allele The allelic form of a gene whose information is not expressed

recipient strain Any strain that receives genetic information from another strain

reciprocal recombination Occurs as a result of crossing-over in which a symmetrical exchange of genetic material takes place, i.e., the genes lost by one chromosome are gained by the other, and vice versa

recombinant Any organism whose genotype has arisen as a result of recombination; also, any nucleic acid that has arisen as a result of recombination

recombinant DNA technology Genetic engineering

recombination The exchange and incorporation of genetic information into a single genome, resulting in the formation of new combinations of alleles

recombination genes Genes that code for heteroduplex formation during homologous recombination

recombination repair A mechanism found in bacteria that is used to repair damaged DNA that involves cutting and splicing a piece of template DNA from a complementary strand

recovery The end of a disease syndrome

red algae Members of the Rhodophycophyta algae

red eyespot The stigma or pigmented region of many unicellular green algae

red tides Aquatic phenomenon caused by toxic blooms of *Gonyaulax* and other dinoflagellates that color the water and kill invertebrate organisms; the toxins concentrate in tissues of filter-feeding molluscs, causing food poisoning

redness Characteristic of the inflammatory response resulting from capillary dilation

reducing power The capacity to bring about reduction

reduction An increase in the negative valence or a decrease in the positive valence of an element resulting from the gain of electrons

reduction potential The relative susceptibility of a substrate to oxidation or reduction

reductive amination The reaction of an α-carboxylic acid with ammonia to produce an amino acid

reductive tricarboxylic acid cycle A metabolic pathway in some photoautotrophs for the fixation of carbon dioxide in which oxaloacetate is reduced to malate, converted to fumarate, and then reduced again to succinate; the succinate is converted to α-ketoglutarate, and a second molecule of CO_2 is reductively added to the α-ketoglutarate to form isocitric acid and then citric acid that is split into oxaloacetate and acetyl-CoA

refraction The deviation of a ray of light from a straight line in passing obliquely from one transparent medium to another of different density

refractive index An index of the change in velocity of light when it passes through a substance causing a deviation in the path of the light

refrigeration Method used for the preservation of food by storage at 5° C, based on the fact that low temperatures restrict the rates of growth and enzymatic activities of microorganisms

regulatory genes Genes that serve a regulatory function; genes that do not code for specific peptides but instead regulate the expression of structural genes

relative humidity (RH) The availability of water in the atmosphere

relaxed DNA A circular double-helix of DNA that does not have additional supercoiling and can lie flat on a planar surface without being contorted

relaxed strains Bacterial strains that have mutations in the *relA* gene and, therefore, do not exhibit a stringent response under conditions of amino acid starvation

release factors Bacterial proteins, RF1 and RF2, that help catalyze the termination of peptide bond formation and end translation

rennin Enzyme obtained from a calf's stomach that can hydrolyze proteins

Rep protein An unwinding protein in bacteria that catalyzes breaking the hydrogen bonding that holds the two strands of DNA together

repellents Chemicals that push substances away from them; chemicals that cause microorganisms to move away from them

replica plating A technique by which various types of mutants can be isolated from a population of bacteria grown under nonselective conditions, based on plating cells from each colony onto multiple plates and noting the positions of inoculation

replication Multiplication of a microorganism; duplication of a nucleic acid from a template; the formation of a replica mold for viewing by electron microscopy

replication fork The Y-shaped region of a chromosome that is the growing point during replication of DNA

replicative form DNA (RF DNA) Doubled-stranded DNA that is formed during the replication of a single-stranded DNA virus and that serves as a template for the formation of new viral genomes

replicative RNA strands Templates for the synthesis of new viral genomes produced by RNA polymerase

replicative transposition Insertion of a transposon from one location to another by copying the original sequence and inserting the copy at another site—the source transposon is retained and does not move from its site

replicon Segments of a DNA macromolecule having their own origin and termini; a nucleic acid molecule that possesses an origin and is therefore capable of initiating its own replication

replisome The complex of DNA polymerase and accessory proteins that are involved in DNA replication

reporter genes Genes that code for an easily detectable trait in the cell in which they are placed and can be used to identify recombinant DNA

repressible A characteristic of enzymes that allows them to be made unless stopped by the presence of a specific repression substance

repressible operons Genetic system with regulatory genes that can be shut off under specific conditions

repression The blockage of gene expression

repressor protein A protein that binds to the operator and inhibits the transcription of structural genes

reproduction A fundamental property of living systems by which organisms give rise to other organisms of the same kind

reservoirs The constant sources of infectious agents found in nature

resistance plasmid R plasmid

resistant crop varieties Species of agricultural plants that are not susceptible to particular plant pathogens

resolution The fineness of detail observable in the image of a specimen

resolving power A quantitative measure of the closest distance between two points that can still be seen as distinct points when viewed in a microscope field; depends largely on the characteristics of the microscope's objective lens and the optimal illumination of the specimen

respiration A mode of energy-yielding metabolism requiring a terminal electron acceptor for substrate oxidation; oxygen is frequently used as the terminal electron acceptor

respiration pathways Metabolic sequences for the oxidation of organic compounds to release free energy to drive the formation of ATP that require an external electron acceptor

respiratory tract The structures and passages involved in the intake of oxygen and the expulsion of carbon dioxide in animals

restriction endonuclease A bacterial enzyme that cuts double-stranded DNA at specific locations

restriction enzymes Restriction endonucleases; enzymes capable of cutting DNA macromolecules

restriction map A map of a genome indicating sites where specific restriction endonucleases will cut

restrictive infections Viral infections that occur when the host cell is transiently permissive so that infective viral progeny are sometimes produced and at other times the virus persists in the infective cell without the production of infective viral progeny

reticuloendothelial system Mononuclear phagocyte system

Retroviruses Family of enveloped RNA animal viruses that use reverse transcriptase to form a DNA macromolecule needed for their replication

reverse transcription Mechanism for RNA synthesis in which the RNA viruses use their RNA genome as a template for an RNA-directed DNA polymerase; RNA-directed synthesis of DNA that is the reversal of normal informational flow within a cell

reverse tricarboxylic acid cycle Reductive tricarboxylic acid cycle

reversion mutations Genotypically double mutants that appear phenotypically like wild type cells because the second mutation cancels out the first

RF DNA Replicative form DNA

RH Relative humidity

Rh incompatibility Type 2 hypersensitivity reaction that occurs when a mother is Rh negative and the father and fetus are Rh positive; during birth of the infant, the mother develops Rh antibodies that may cross the placenta and cause anemia in her next Rh-positive fetus

rhinoviruses Causal agents of 25% of all common colds in adults

Rhizobiaceae Gram-negative family of rod-shaped bacteria capable of fixing atmospheric nitrogen

rhizopodia Root-like pseudopodia of some protozoa

rhizosphere An ecological niche that comprises the surfaces of plant roots and the region of the surrounding soil in which the microbial populations are affected by the presence of the roots

rhizosphere effect Evidence of the direct influence of plant roots on bacteria, demonstrated by the fact that microbial populations usually are higher within the rhizosphere (the region directly influenced by plant roots) than in root-free soil

rho (ρ) protein Protein required to interrupt transcription; a factor that is involved in some types of termination (ρ-dependent) of transcription in bacteria

Rhodophycophyta Red algae that occur in marine habitats and contain phycocyanin, phycoerythrin, and chlorophyll pigments; the primary reserve material is Floridean starch; exhibit a specialized type of oogamous sexual reproduction; some produce tetraspores and have a bilayered cell wall

Rhodospirillaceae Purple, nonsulfur bacteria; family of phototrophic bacteria that produce red-purple carotenoid pigments; consist of the genera *Rhodospirillum, Rhodopseudomonas,* and *Rhodomicrobium;* carry out photoheterotrophic metabolism, converting carbon dioxide to organic matter by the Calvin cycle

RIA Radioimmunoassay

ribonucleic acid (RNA) A linear polymer of ribonucleotides in which the ribose residues are linked by 3′-5′-phosphodiester bridges; the nitrogenous bases attached to each ribose residue may be adenine, guanine, uracil, or cytosine

ribosomal RNA (rRNA) RNA of various sizes that makes up part of the ribosomes, constituting up to 90% of the total RNA of a cell; single-stranded RNA, but with helical regions formed by base pairing between complementary regions within the strand

ribosomes Cellular structures composed of rRNA and protein; the sites where protein synthesis occurs within cells

70S ribosomes Sites of protein synthesis in bacterial cells, mitochondria, and chloroplasts

80S ribosomes Sites of protein synthesis in the cytoplasm of eukaryotic cells

ribozyme RNA molecule that is capable of catalyzing a reaction

ribulose 1,5-bisphosphate carboxylase (RuBisCo) Enzyme that determines the rates of the Calvin cycle

ribulose monophosphate cycle A metabolic pathway in which formaldehyde initially reacts with ribulose-5-phosphate to form hexulose-6-phosphate, and the hexulose-6-

phosphate is then split to form glyceraldehyde-3-phosphate

rickettsias Members of the family Rickettsiaceae; Gram-negative bacterial parasites or pathogens of vertebrates and arthropods that reproduce within host cells by binary fission

ringspots Symptom of viral plant disease characterized by the appearance of chlorotic or necrotic rings on the leaves

ringworm Any mycosis of the skin, hair, or nails in humans or other animals in which the causal agent is a dermatophyte; also called *tinea*

ripen To bring to completeness or perfection; to age or cure, as in cheese; to develop a characteristic flavor, odor, texture, and color

RNA Ribonucleic acid

RNA polymerase An enzyme that catalyzes the formation of RNA macromolecules

RNA replicase RNA-dependent RNA polymerase used in replication of some RNA viruses

rods Bacteria in the shape of cylinders; bacilli

roll tube method Technique used to create anaerobic conditions in which a prereduced, sterilized medium is rolled during cooling so that it covers the inside of the test tube and inoculation is accomplished under a stream of carbon dioxide or nitrogen

rolling circle model Replication pattern of viral DNA in which a circular DNA model is used to spin off unidirectionally a linear DNA molecule

rot Any of various unrelated plant diseases characterized by primary decay and disintegration of host tissue

rotating biological contactor Biodisc system

rotavirus A large DNA virus, the common etiological agent for diarrhea in infants

rough endoplasmic reticulum (ER) A network of interconnected closed internal membrane vesicles in eukaryotic cells where ribosomes synthesize certain membrane and secreted proteins

rRNA Ribosomal ribonucleic acid

RuBiCo Ribulose-1,5-bisphosphate carboxylase

rumen One of the four compartments that form the stomach of a ruminant animal where anaerobic microbial degradation of plant residues occurs, producing nutrients that can be metabolized by the animal

runs Straight-line movements by motile bacteria

rusts Plant diseases caused by fungi of the order Uredinales, so called because of the rust-colored spores formed by many of the causal agents on the surfaces of the infected plants

S

S layer In some bacteria, a crystalline protein layer surrounding the cell

Sabin vaccine Attenuated live viral antigenic preparation administered for the prevention of polio

sac fungi Members of the Ascomycotina

sacculus The cross-linked peptidoglycan molecule that forms a little sac around the eubacterial cell

saki Yellow rice beer made in Japan

salinity The concentration of salts dissolved in a solution

Salk vaccine Inactivated viral antigenic preparation administered for the prevention of polio

salpingitis Inflammation of the Fallopian tubes

salt lake An inland water body with a high salt concentration normally approaching saturation

salt-tolerant bacteria Bacteria that can grow at concentrations of NaCl of 3% to 15%, which most bacteria cannot tolerate

sanitary engineering The science dealing with the removal of waste materials

sanitary landfill A method for disposal of solid wastes in low-lying areas, with wastes covered with a layer of soil each day

sanitary methods Techniques that prevent contamination of food or objects with pathogenic and spoilage organisms, including washing, sanitizing, and packaging

sanitary practices Any practice that produces sanitary conditions, such as by cleaning and sterilizing, or removes microorganisms or the substances that support microbial growth

sanitize To make sanitary, as by cleaning or sterilizing

sanitizing agents Compounds that reduce the number of microbes without necessarily killing them or inhibiting their growth

saprophytes Organisms, e.g., bacteria and fungi, whose nutrients are obtained from dead and decaying plant or animal matter in the form of organic compounds in solution

saprozoic nutrition Type of nutrition exhibited by some protozoa that obtain nutrients by diffusion, active transport, or pinocytosis from nonliving sources

Sarcodina A major taxonomic group of protozoa characterized by the formation of pseudopodia

saturation Phenomenon in enzyme kinetics in which raising the concentration of a substrate does not continue to increase the rate of the reaction; the maximal concentration of a substance that will dissolve in a given solvent

scale-up A stepwise process of going from small laboratory flasks to large production fermentors

scanning electron microscope (SEM) An electron microscope in which a beam of electrons systematically sweeps over the specimen, and the intensity of secondary electrons generated at the specimen's surface where the beam's impact is measured and the resulting signal is used to determine the intensity of a signal viewed on a cathode ray tube that is scanned in synchrony with the scanning of the specimen

scanning electron microscopy A form of electron microscopy in which the image is formed by a beam of electrons that has been reflected from the surface of a specimen

schizogamy A form of asexual reproduction characteristic of certain groups of sporozoan protozoa; coincident with cell growth; nuclear division occurs several or numerous times, producing a schiziont that then further segments into other cells

schizontocidal action Effect of antimalarial drugs that rapidly interrupts schizogony within red blood cells

SCID Severe combined immunodeficiency

scientific method A method of research in which a problem is identified, relevant data are gathered, a hypothesis is formulated from these data, and the hypothesis is empirically tested

sclerotia Hard resting bodies that are resistant to unfavorable conditions and may remain dormant for prolonged periods

SCP Single cell protein

screening A discovery process of searching for microorganisms with desired metabolic capabilities that can be used in a commercial process

screening methods Diagnostic tests used to determine the likelihood that an individual has an infectious disease; initial tests used to direct the course of further diagnosis; tests used to identify a microorganism with a desired metabolic feature

sebum The secretion of the sebaceous gland containing unsaturated free fatty acids that act as antimicrobics

secondary B lymphocytes Memory B-lymphocyte cells capable of initiating the antibody-mediated immune response for which they are genetically programmed

secondary immune response Anamnestic response; the response of an individual to the second or subsequent contact with a specific antigen, characterized by a short lag period and the production of a high antibody titer

secondary productivity The heterotrophic recapture of dilute nutrients; formation of bacterial biomass from utilization of nutrients at low concentrations

secondary sewage treatment The treatment of the liquid portion of sewage containing dissolved organic matter, using microorganisms to degrade the organic matter that is mineralized or converted to removable solids

secretory Pertaining to the act of exporting a fluid from a cell or organism

secretory vesicles Vesicles containing proteins destined for secretion that bud off of the Golgi apparatus in eukaryotic cells

sedimentation The process of settling, commonly of solid particles from a liquid

segmented genome A viral genome composed of several separate RNA molecules

selective medium An inhibitory medium or one designed to encourage the growth of certain types of microorganisms in preference to any others that may be present

selective toxicity The toxic effect of some antimicrobial agents on some microorganisms but not on others

self-limiting A disease that normally does not result in mortality even without medical intervention; an infection that is eliminated by natural host immune defenses prior to mortality and without the need for antimicrobics to curtail progression of the infection

self-purification Inherent capability of natural waters to cleanse themselves of pollutants based on biogeochemical cycling activities and interpopulation relationships of indigenous microbial populations

SEM Scanning electron microscope

semiconservative replication The production of double-stranded DNA containing one new strand and one parental strand

semidiscontinuous replication A term used to describe the mechanism of DNA replication because the leading strand is replicated continuously and the lagging strand is replicated discontinuously

semiperishable foods Food products that are not readily subject to spoilage by microorganisms and consequently have a long shelf life unless improperly handled

sense strand The strand of DNA that codes for the synthesis of RNA

sensitization A process in which specific IgE antibodies are synthesized in response to an allergen, move through the bloodstream to mast cells in connective tissue, and become firmly fixed to receptors so that the next time the individual is exposed to the same allergen, that allergen can react directly with the IgE fixed to the mast cells

septate Separated by septa or cross walls

septic tank A simple anaerobic treatment system for waste water where residual solids settle to the bottom of the tank and the clarified effluent is distributed over a leaching field

septicemia A condition in which an infectious agent is distributed throughout the body via the bloodstream; blood poisoning, the condition attended by severe symptoms in which the blood contains large numbers of bacteria

septum In bacteria, the partition or cross wall formed during cell division that divides the parent cell into two daughter cells; in filamentous organisms, e.g., fungi, one of a number of internal transverse cross walls that occur at intervals within each hypha

septum formation In binary fission, the inward movement of the cytoplasmic membrane and cell wall that establishes the separation of the two complete bacterial chromosomes

serine pathway A metabolic pathway in type II methanotrophs, the first step of which is the reaction of formaldehyde with glycine to form serine—the serine is then deaminated to form pyruvate, which is subsequently reduced to form glycerate

serology The *in vitro* study of antigens and antibodies and their interactions; immunological (antigen–antibody) reactions carried out *in vitro*

serotypes The antigenically distinguishable members of a single species; serovar

serotyping Tests to identify microorganisms based on serological procedures that detect the presence of specific characteristic antigens

serovar A biotype of a given species that is differentiated based on serology (antigenic characteristics)

serum The fluid fraction of coagulated blood

serum killing power The antimicrobial activity of the serum of a patient receiving antibiotics; an *in vivo* measure of antibiotic activity

serum sickness A hypersensitivity reaction that occurs 8 to 12 days after exposure to a foreign antigen; symptoms caused by the formation of immune complexes include a rash, joint pain, and fever

severe combined immunodeficiency (SCID) A genetically determined type of immunodeficiency caused by the failure of stem cells to differentiate properly; victims are incapable of any immunological response

sewage Refuse liquids or waste matter carried by sewers

sewage fungus The bacterium *Sphaerotilus natans;* grows beneath sewage outfalls and forms filaments, giving it a fungal-like appearance

sewage treatment The treatment of sewage to reduce its biological oxygen demand and to inactivate the pathogenic microorganisms present

sex pilus F pilus

sexual reproduction Reproduction involving the union of gametes from two individuals

sexual spore A spore resulting from the conjugation of gametes or nuclei from individuals of different mating type or sex

sexually transmitted diseases (STDs) Diseases whose transmission occurs primarily or exclusively by direct contact during sexual intercourse

sheath A tubular structure formed around a filament or bundle of filaments, occurring in some bacteria

sheathed bacteria Bacteria whose cells occur within a filamentous sheath that permits attachment to solid surfaces and affords protection

shelf fungi Members of the order Aphyllophorales; fungi that grow on trees with tough leathery fruiting bodies

shelf life Period of time during which a stored product remains effective, useful, or suitable for consumption

shift to the left An increase in stab cells, indicative of neutrophilia, that refers to a blood cell classification system in which immature blood cells are positioned on the left side of a standard reference chart and mature blood cells are placed on the right

Shine-Dalgarno sequence A polypurine consensus sequence on bacterial mRNA that helps position the mRNA on the 30S ribosomal subunit by forming a base-paired region to a complementary sequence on the 16S rRNA

shock-sensitive transport Binding-protein transport

shotgun cloning A technique used to randomly clone DNA when the sequence is unknown by breaking an entire genome into fragments that are individually cloned

shoyu Soy sauce

shunt A diversion from the normal path as an alternative pathway in metabolism

shuttle vectors Cloning vectors that permit the transfer of recombinant DNA from one cell type to another

Siderocapsaceae A unicellular family of chemolithotrophic bacteria that oxidizes iron or manganese, depositing iron or manganese oxides in capsules or extracellular material

siderophores Iron chelators that solubilize ferric hydroxide, making soluble iron available

sigma unit A subunit of RNA polymerase that helps to recognize the promoter site

signal sequence A region of nucleotides at the beginning of an mRNA molecule and the corresponding sequence of amino acids in the synthesized protein that indicates that the protein is an exoprotein and is responsible for initiating the export of that protein across the cytoplasmic membrane

signs Observable and measurable changes in a patient caused by a disease

silent mutations Mutations that do not alter the phenotype of an organism and therefore go undetected

simple matching coefficient A similarity measure used in taxonomic analysis that includes both negative and positive matches in its calculation

simple staining procedure A method using a single stain that does not differentiate parts of a cell or different types of cells

single cell protein (SCP) Protein that is produced by microorganisms and primarily composed of microbial cells; sources of this protein include bacteria, fungi, and algae

single diffusion method Precipitin reaction technique in which an antigen is allowed to diffuse unidirectionally into a tube containing a uniform concentration of soluble antibody so that the antigen establishes a concentration gradient through the tube

single-stranded binding proteins Bacterial proteins that preferentially bind to regions of single-stranded DNA and prevent association of the strand to other strands

singlet oxygen Form of oxygen in which two of the electrons in the valence shell have antiparallel spins chemically reactive with and lethal to microorganisms

site-directed mutagenesis A technique in which a single and specific base is altered in a gene sequence, producing a mutation at a desired site

site-specific recombination Nonhomologous recombination

SJ The Jaccard coefficient

skin rash Cutaneous eruption; sign of a disease condition

skin surfaces An environment characterized by lack of available water, high salt concentrations, low water activity, and the presence of antimicrobial agents; generally an unfavorable habitat for microbial growth

skin testing Testing procedure based on delayed hypersensitivity reactions useful in the presumptive diagnosis of some diseases

SLE Systemic lupus erythematosus

slime layer An external polysaccharide layer surrounding microbial cells composed of diffuse secretions that adhere loosely to the cell surface

slime molds Members of the Gymnomycota fungi

slow-reacting substance of anaphylaxis (SRS-A) A mixture of leukotrienes that acts as a potent bronchial constrictor

sludge The solid portion of sewage

smooth endoplasmic reticulum (ER) A network of interconnected closed internal membrane vesicles in eukaryotic cells where fatty acids and phospholipids are synthesized and metabolized

smuts Plant diseases caused by fungi of the order Ustilaginales; typically involve the formation of masses of dark-colored teliospores on or within the tissues of the host plant

snapping division After binary fission, cells do not completely separate; they appear to form groups resembling Chinese ideographs

sneeze A sudden, noisy, spasmodic expiration through the nose, caused by the irritation of nasal nerves

sodium-potassium pump A mechanism in eukaryotic cells by which Na^+ is pumped out of the cell and K^+ is pumped into the cell by the enzyme Na^+/K^+ ATPase

soft spots Evidence of microbial spoilage of fruits and vegetables resulting from the action of microbially produced pectinesterases and polygalacturanases

sofu Chinese word for tofu; tofu

soil fungistasis The inhibition of fungi by soil which is believed by some to be due to microbial activities

solenoid A structure found in eukaryotic cells in which chromatin is wound into a secondary helix with about six nucleosomes per turn

solid waste refuse Waste material composed largely of inert materials—glass, plastic, metal—and some decomposable organic wastes, i.e., paper and kitchen scraps

somatic antigens Anitgens that form part of the main body of a cell, usually at the cell surface; distinguishable from antigens that occur on the flagella or capsule

somatic cell gene therapy Introduction of genes into somatic cells of an individual through genetic engineering that overcomes a genetic defect

somatic cells Any cell of the body of an organism except the specialized reproductive germ cell

sonti Indian rice beer made with *Rhizopus sonti*

SOS system Radical, complex, multifunctional system for repairing DNA damage

Southern blotting A technique that permits the separation and identification of specific DNA sequences

soy sauce Brown, salty, tangy sauce made in Japan from soybeans, wheat, and wheat bran fermented with *Aspergillus oryzae*

specialized transduction Form of gene transfer and recombination accomplished by the transmission of bacterial DNA from a donor to a recipient cell by a temperate phage in which only a small amount of genetic information is transferred; the transferred genes occur at specific locations

species A taxonomic category ranking just below a genus; includes individuals that display a high degree of mutual similarity and that actually or potentially inbreed

specific immune response Defense system of the body characterized by a high degree of specificity to different antigens; the ability to distinguish self from non-self and the development of memory to recognize and react with foreign substances

specificity The restrictiveness of interaction; of an antibody, refers to the range of antigens with which an antibody may combine; of an enzyme, refers to the substrate that is acted on by that enzyme; of a pathogen or parasite, refers to the range of hosts

spectrophotometer An instrument that measures the transmission of light as a function of wavelength, allowing quantitative measure of the intensity of two sources or wavelengths

spectrum A range, e.g., of frequencies within which radiation has some specified characteristic, such as the visible light spectrum

spectrum of action The range of bacteria against which an antibiotic may be targeted; may be narrow or broad

spermatia In certain ascomycetes and basidiomycetes, nonmotile, male reproductive cells

spherical aberration A form of distortion of a microscope lens based on the differential refraction of light passing through the thick central portion of a convex-convex lens and the light passing through the thin peripheral regions of the lens

spheroplasts Spherical structures formed from bacteria, yeasts, and other cells by weakening or partially removing the rigid component of the cell wall

spirilli Bacteria in the shape of spirals

spirochetes Bacterial group characterized by the presence of helically coiled rods wound around one or more central axial filaments; mobile by a flexing motion of the cell

split genes Genes coded for by noncontiguous segments of the DNA so that the mRNA and the DNA for the protein product of that gene are not colinear; genes with intervening nucleotide sequences not involved in coding for the gene product

spontaneous generation Formation of living organisms from nonliving entities by natural processes, a now proven impossibility

spontaneous mutations Naturally occurring changes in the DNA sequence in cells

sporadic Occurrences of cases of a disease in areas geographically remote from each other or temporally separated, implying that the occurrences are not related

sporangiospores Asexual fungal spores formed within a sporangium

sporangium A sac-like structure within which numbers of motile or nonmotile, asexually derived spores are formed

spore An asexual reproductive or resting body that is resistant to unfavorable environmental conditions, capable of generating viable vegetative cells when conditions are favorable; resistant and/or disseminative forms produced asexually by certain types of bacteria by a process that involves differentiation of vegetative cells or structures; characteristically formed in response to adverse environmental conditions

sporocarp Special type of fruiting body that bears a mucoid droplet at the tip of each branch containing spores with cell walls

Sporozoa A subphylum of parasitic protozoa in which mature organisms lack cilia and flagella, characterized by the formation of spores

sporozoite A motile infective stage of a protozoan; the cells produced by the division of the zygote of a sporozoan

sporulation The process of spore formation

spread plate technique A method of microbial inoculation whereby a small volume of liquid inoculum is dispersed with a glass spreader over the entire surface of an agar plate

spreading factor Hyaluronidase, an enzyme that allows pathogens to spread through the body

sputum The material discharged from the surface of the air passages, throat, or mouth, consisting of saliva, mucus, pus, microorganisms, fibrin, and/or blood

SRS-A Slow reactive substance of anaphylaxis

SSM The simple matching coefficient

stab cells Immature leukocytes

stabilization ponds Ponds used for the secondary treatment of sewage and industrial effluents

stain A substance used to treat cells or tissues to enhance contrast so that specimens and their details may be detected by microscopy

stalks Relatively wide bacterial appendages that can attach to a substrate or to other cells; may serve to increase the efficiency of nutrient acquisition

staphylokinase A fibrinolytic enzyme that catalyzes the lysis of fibrin clots produced by *Staphylococcus* species

stationary growth phase A growth phase during which the death rate equals the rate of reproduction, resulting in a zero growth rate in batch cultures

statospore A resting spore of some algae, consisting of two pieces

STD Sexually transmitted disease

stem cell A formative cell; a blood cell capable of giving rise to various differentiated types of blood cells

stenothermophiles Microorganisms that grow only at temperatures near their optimal growth temperature

sterilization Process that results in a condition totally free of microorganisms and all other living forms

sterilize To render incapable of reproducing or free from microorganisms

sterol A polycyclic alcohol such as cholesterol or ergosterol

Stickland reaction The coupling of oxidation-reduction reactions between pairs of amino acids

stigma Red eyespot, a pigmented region in the chloroplasts of many unicellular green algae

stock culture A culture that is maintained as a source of authentic subcultures; a culture whose purity is ensured and from which working cultures are derived

storage vacuoles Membrane-bound organelles involved in maintaining accumulated reserve materials segregated from the cytoplasm within eukaryotic cells

strain A population of cells derived by asexual reproduction from a single parental cell; a cell or population of cells that has the general characteristics of a given type of organism, e.g., a bacterium or fungus, or of a particular genus, species, and serotype

streak plate technique A method of microbial inoculation whereby a loopful of culture is scratched across the surface of a solid culture medium so that single cells are deposited at a given location

Streptococcaceae Family of Gram-positive cocci whose cells occur as pairs or chains, exhibiting facultative, anaerobic, fermentative metabolism

streptokinase A fibrinolytic enzyme that catalyzes the lysis of fibrin clots produced by *Streptococcus* species

streptomycin An aminoglycoside antibiotic produced by *Streptomyces griseus,* affecting protein synthesis by inhibiting polypeptide chain initiation

strict anaerobes Microorganisms that cannot tolerate molecular oxygen and are inhibited or killed in its presence; microorganisms that cannot use oxygen or survive in its presence

stringent response A response in bacteria that enables them to shut down several energy-draining processes (RNA synthesis and protein synthesis) during poor growth conditions (amino acid starvation)

stroma The interior compartment of the chloroplast where carbon dioxide fixation occurs during photosynthesis

structural gene A gene whose product is an enzyme, structural protein, tRNA, or rRNA, as opposed to a regulator gene whose product regulates the transcription of structural genes; genes that code for polypeptides

structural RNA Ribosomal RNA

subcutaneous Beneath the skin

submerged culture reactors Used for the commercial production of vinegar, using forced aeration to maximize the rate of acetic acid production, with bacteria growing in a fine suspension created by the air bubbles and the fermenting liquid

subspecies Division of species that describes a specific clone of cells

substrate A substance on which an enzyme acts

substrate-level phosphorylation Reaction in which ATP is formed from ADP by the direct transfer of a high-energy phosphate group from an intermediate substrate in a metabolic pathway, as opposed to chemiosmotic generation of ATP

substrate specificity A characteristic of enzymes reflecting the fact that the enzyme and substrate must fit together in a specific way for the enzyme to lower the activation energy

succession The replacement of populations by other populations better adapted to fill the ecological niche

sulfate-reducing bacteria Bacteria that can utilize sulfate as a final electron acceptor, thereby converting it to sulfide; they are important in the cycling of sulfur compounds in soil, sediment, and water

sulfide A compound of sulfur with an element or basic radical

sulfide stinker A type of microbially caused spoilage that occurs in canned foods, producing the noxious odor of hydrogen sulfide from putrefying proteins

sulfur cycle Biogeochemical cycle mediated by microorganisms that changes the oxidation state of sulfur within various compounds

sulfur granules Internal or external deposits of elemental sulfur formed by some photosynthetic bacteria

superoxide dismutase An enzyme that catalyzes the reaction between superoxide anions and protons, the products being hydrogen peroxide and oxygen

superoxide radical A toxic free radical of oxygen (O_2^-)

suppressor mutation A mutation that alleviates the effects of an earlier mutation at a different locus

suppressor T cells T cells usually with CD8 that tend to suppress the immune response

surface antigens Antigens associated with cell surfaces

surfactant A surface-active agent

susceptibility The likelihood that an individual will acquire a disease if exposed to the causative agent

Svedberg unit (S) The unit in which the sedimentation coefficient of a particle is commonly expressed; when values are given in seconds, the basic unit is 10 to 13 seconds

swan-necked flasks Flasks whose necks were curved by Pasteur for use in his experiments disproving the theory of spontaneous generation

swarm cells Flagellated cells of Myxomycetes that fuse together to form a true plasmodium

swelling Characteristic of the inflammatory response associated with the accumulation of fluids in the bases surrounding tissue cells

symbiosis An obligatory interactive association between members of two populations, producing a stable condition in which the two organisms live together in close physical proximity, to their mutual advantage

symbiotic nitrogen fixation Fixation of atmospheric nitrogen by bacteria living in mutually dependent associations with plants

symport A mechanism in which different substances are actively transported across the cytoplasmic membrane simultaneously in the same direction

symptom A physiological disorder that results in a detectable deviation from the normal healthy state and is usually indicated by complaints from a patient

symptomatology The combined symptoms of a disease

synchronous growth Growth that occurs when all cells divide at the same time

synchrony A state or condition of a culture in which all cells are dividing at the same time

synergism In antibiotic action, when two or more antibiotics are acting together, the production of inhibitory effects on a given organism that are greater than the additive effects of those antibiotics acting independently; an interactive but nonobligatory association between two populations in which each population benefits

syngamy The union of gametes to form a zygote

synthetic fuels Fuels, such as ethanol, methane, hydrogen, and hydrocarbons, produced by microorganisms

syntrophism A phenomenon in which the extent of growth of an organism depends on the provision of one or more metabolic factors or nutrients by another organism growing in the vicinity

systematics A system of taxonomy; the range of theoretical and practical studies involved in the classification of organisms

systemic infections Infections that are disseminated throughout the body via the circulatory system

systemic lupus erythematosus (SLE) Autoimmune disease resulting from the failure of the immune response to recognize self antigens; results in kidney failure

T

T cell receptor (TCR) A receptor on the surface of a T cell that in association with either CD4 or CD8 is responsible for MHC-restricted antigen recognition (the TCR on most cells is a heterodimer of two polypeptide chains that are anchored to the T cell membrane and contain immunoglobulin-like constant domains and amino-terminal variable domains)

T cells T lymphocytes; lymphocyte cells that are differentiated in the thymus and are important in cell-mediated immunity, as well as in the modulation of antibody-mediated immunity

T helper cells (T_H) A class of T cells with CD4 markers that enhance the activities of B cells in antibody-mediated immunity

T lymphocytes T cells

T suppressor cells (T_S) A class of T cells that depress the activities of B cells in antibody-mediated immunity

TATA box A conserved consensus sequence in eukaryotic cells that is recognized by TFIID and assists RNA polymerase II in initiating transcription

taxis A directional locomotive response to a given stimulus exhibited by certain motile organisms or cells

taxon A taxonomic group, e.g., genus, family, or order

taxonomic hierarchy Organizational levels used to group living things; the levels are Kingdom, phylum, class, order, family, genus, and species

taxonomy The science of biological classification; the grouping of organisms according to their mutual affinities or similarities

T_C cells Cytotoxic T cells

TCA cycle Krebs cycle

TCR T cell receptor

teichoic acids Polymers of ribitol or glycerol phosphate in the cell walls of Gram-positive bacteria

teichuronic acids Polymers containing uronic acids and *N*-acetylglucosamine in the cell walls of Gram-positive bacteria that are growing at limiting phosphate concentrations

teliospores Thick-walled, binucleate resting spores of rusts and smuts

TEM Transmission electron microscope

tempeh Food from Indonesia made from soybeans fermented with spores of *Rhizopus*

temperate phage Bacteriophage with the ability to form a stable, nondisruptive relationship within a bacterium; a prophage in which the phage DNA is incorporated into the bacterial chromosome

temperature Degree of heat or coldness of a body or substance, as measured by a thermometer or other graduated scale; environmental parameter that influences the rates of chemical reactions and the three-dimensional configuration of proteins

temperature growth range The range between the maximum and minimum temperatures at which a microorganism can grow

temperature sensitive mutations Mutations that alter the range of temperatures over which a microorganism may grow, using specific substrates

template A pattern that acts as a guide for directing the synthesis of new macromolecules

termination The cessation of strand elongation as in DNA replication, RNA transcription, or protein synthesis

termination codons Three codons, UGA, UAG and UAA, which do not code for a particular amino acyl–tRNA anticodon and bring about the release of a nascent polypeptide from the ribosome (termination of protein synthesis)

termination sites Sequences of nucleotides in the DNA that act as signals to stop transcription

terrestrial Relating to or consisting of land, as distinct from water or air

tertiary recovery of petroleum The use of biological and chemical means to enhance oil recovery

tertiary sewage treatment A sewage treatment process that follows a secondary process, aimed at removing nonbiodegradable organic pollutants and mineral nutrients

test Algal cell wall structure containing calcium or silicon; the outer protective covering or shell formed by some protozoa

tetanospasmin Neurotoxin produced by *Clostridium tetani* that interferes with the ability of peripheral nerves of the spinal column to properly transmit signals to the muscle cells

tetracyclines A group of natural and semisynthetic antibiotics that have in common a modified naphthalene ring; bacteriostatic, with a broad spectrum of activity

TFs Transcription factors

thallus The vegetative body of a fungus or alga

theca A layer of flattened, membranous vesicles beneath the external membrane of a dinoflagellate; an open or perforated shell-like structure that houses part or all of a cell

theory of spontaneous generation Nonscientific theory that held that living organisms could arise without external cause from nonliving matter

thermal death time The time required at a given temperature for the thermal inactivation or killing of a specified number of microorganisms

thermal vents Hot areas located at depths 800 to 1000 m on the sea floor, where spreading allows seawater to percolate deeply into the crust and react with hot core materials; life around the vents is supported energetically by the chemoautotrophic oxidation of reduced sulfur

thermoacidophiles Microorganisms in the kingdom Archaea that grow optimally at low pH and high temperatures

thermocline Zone of water characterized by a rapid decrease in temperature, with little mixing of water across it

thermoduric Microorganisms capable of surviving but not growing at high temperatures

thermodynamics The basic relationships between properties of matter, especially those affected by changes in temperature, and a description of the conversion of energy from one form to another

thermophiles Microorganisms with optimal growth temperatures above 45° C

theta (θ) structure A structure formed during replication of circular DNA molecules that appears like the Greek letter, θ

thin sectioning Preparation of specimens for viewing in a transmission electron microscope by cutting them into thin slices with a microtome

thylakoids Flattened, membranous vesicles that occur in the photosynthetic apparatus of cyanobacteria and algae; the thylakoid membrane contains chlorophylls, accessory pigments, and electron carriers and is the site of light reaction in photosynthesis

thymine A pyrimidine component of DNA

thymine dimers Structures formed by base substitutions creating covalent linkages between pyrimidine bases on the same strand of the DNA, caused by exposure to ultraviolet light—they cannot act as templates for DNA polymerase and so prevent the proper functioning of polymerases

thymocytes T cells

Ti plasmid Tumor-inducing plasmid of *Agrobacterium tumefaciens*

Tine test Test for tuberculosis in which a mechanical device makes multiple punctures in the skin to expose the individual to the antigen

tinea The lesions of dermatophytosis; also called ringworm

tinsel flagellum Flagellum of eukaryotic organisms that bear fine, filamentous appendages along their lengths

tissue culture The maintenance or culture of isolated tissues and of plant or animal cell lines *in vitro*

tissue toxicity test A test in which germicides are examined for their ability to kill bacteria and their toxicity to chick-heart tissue cells

tissues In plants and animals, a group of similar cells performing the same function

titer The concentration in a solution of a dissolved substance or particulate substance

tofu Japanese cheese-like food product made by fermenting soybeans with *Mucor* species

tonsilitis Inflammation of the tonsils, commonly caused by *Streptococcus pyogenes*

topoisomerase I An enzyme that converts negatively supercoiled DNA into relaxed DNA by uncoiling the helix

topoisomerase II An enzyme that introduces negative supercoiling into relaxed DNA

toxicity The quality of being toxic; the kind and quantity of a poison produced by a microorganism or possessed by a nonbiological chemical

toxicity index A relative measure of the ability of a chemical to kill microorganisms and its toxicity to mammalian cells that is useful for determining the suitability of antiseptics for use on human tissues

toxigenicity The ability to produce toxins

toxin Any organic microbial product or substance that is harmful or lethal to cells, tissue cultures, or organisms; a poison

toxoid A modified protein exotoxin that has lost its toxicity but has retained its specific antigenicity

***trans* configuration** Genetic elements that have an effect on different DNA molecules

transamination The transfer of one or more amino groups from one compound to another; the formation of a new amino acid by the transfer of the amino group from another amino acid

transcription The synthesis of mRNA, rRNA, and tRNA from a DNA template

transcription factors Eukaryotic proteins that bind to DNA and are responsible for binding the correct RNA polymerases to their correct promoters

transduction The transfer of bacterial genes from one bacterium to another by bacteriophage; transfer of DNA from a donor to a recipient cell by a viral carrier

transfer RNA (tRNA) A type of RNA involved in carrying amino acids to the ribosomes during translation; for each amino acid there are one or more corresponding tRNAs that can bind it specifically

transferase Enzyme that transfers a part of one molecule to another molecule

transferrin Serum beta-globulin that binds and transports iron

transformation A mode of genetic transfer in which a naked DNA fragment derived from one microbial cell (typically bacterial) is taken up by another and subsequently undergoes recombination with the recipient's chromosome; transfer of a free DNA molecule from a donor to a recipient bacterium; in tissue culture, the conversion of normal cells to cells that exhibit some or all of the properties typical of tumor cells; morphological and other changes that occur in both B and T lymphocytes on exposure to antigens to which they are specifically reactive

transformed cells Cells produced *in vitro* that have altered surface properties and continue to grow even when they contact a neighboring cell; microbial cells that have undergone transformation; cancer cells; malignant cells; bacterial cells that have incorporated DNA by transformation

transgenic plants Plants that gain new genetic information from foreign sources

transition A point mutation in which one purine or one pyrimidine is replaced by another

translation The assembly of polypeptide chains with mRNA serving as the template, a process that occurs at the ribosomes

translocation Nonhomologous recombination

transmission electron microscope (TEM) An electron microscope in which the specimen transmits an electron beam focused on it; image contrasts are formed by the scattering of electrons out of the beam, and various magnetic lenses perform functions analogous to those of ordinary lenses in a light microscope

transposable genetic elements Specific segments of DNA that can undergo nonreciprocal recombination and thus move from one location to another

transposons Translocatable genetic elements; genetic elements that move from one locus to another by nonhomologous recombination, allowing them to move around a genome

transversion A point mutation in which a purine is replaced by a pyrimidine or a pyrimidine by a purine

tricarboxylic acid cycle Krebs cycle

trichome A chain or filament of cells that may or may not include one or more resting spores

trickling filter system A simple, film-flow aerobic sewage treatment system; the sewage is distributed over a porous bed coated with bacterial growth that mineralizes the dissolved organic nutrients

triplet code Describes the genetic code because three sequential nucleotides in mRNA are needed to code for a specific amino acid

trismus Tetanus; name given to tetanus indicating the jaw and neck contract convulsively so that the mouth remains locked closed, making swallowing difficult

tRNA Transfer RNA

-troph Combining form indicating a relation to nutrition or nourishment

trophic level Steps in the transfer of energy stored in organic compounds from one organism to another

trophic structure Steps in the transfer of energy stored in organic compounds from one organism to another

trophophase The growth phase during a fermentation process when biomass forms, but during which the desired secondary metabolite is not yet accumulating; during batch culture of a fungus, that phase in which growth-directed metabolism is dominant over secondary metabolism

trophozoite A vegetative or feeding stage in the life cycle of certain protozoa

***trp* operon** Contains the structural genes that code for the enzymes required for the biosynthesis of the amino acid tryptophan and the regulatory genes that control the expression of these structural genes

tuberculin reaction Classic skin test for detecting probable cases of tuberculosis in which a purified protein derivative of *Mycobacterium tuberculosis* is injected subcutaneously and the area near the injection site is observed for evidence of a delayed hypersensitivity reaction

tumbles Turning movements that occur when bacteria stop traveling in a straight line

tumor-inducing (Ti) plasmid Plasmid found in *Agrobacterium tumefaciens* that codes for tumorous plant growths (galls) when this bacterium infects plants

turbidity Cloudiness or opacity of a solution

turbidostat A system in which an optical sensing device measures the turbidity of the culture in a growth vessel and generates an electrical signal that regulates the flow of fresh medium into the vessel and the release of spent medium and cells

twiddles Tumbles

tyndallization A sterilization process designed to eliminate endospore formers in which the material is heated 80° to 100° C for several minutes on each of 3 successive days and incubated at 37° C during the intervening periods

type A subdivision of a species; subspecies

type culture Collections; centralized storage depositories for the preservation of all microbial species

type 1 hypersensitivity Anaphylactic hypersensitivity

type 2 hypersensitivity Antibody-dependent hypersensitivity

type 3 hypersensitivity Complex-mediated hypersensitivity; Arthus hypersensitivity; serum sickness

type 4 hypersensitivity Cell-mediated hypersensitivity; delayed type hypersensitivity

type strain Specific microbial strain deposited in a culture collection

U

UHT sterilization Ultra high-temperature sterilization

ultra high-temperature sterilization Sterilization using very high temperatures and short exposure times, such as 141° C for 2 seconds

ultracentrifuge A high-speed centrifuge that produces centrifugal fields up to several hundred thousand times the force of gravity; used for the study of proteins and viruses, for the sedimentation of macromolecules, and for the determination of molecular weights

ultraviolet light Short wavelength electromagnetic radiation in the range 100 to 400 nm

uncoating Stage in viral replication in which the nucleic acid is released from the capsid; the removal of a viral capsid

unicellular Having the form and characteristics of a single cell

uniporters Permeases that transport only one kind of molecule

universal donors Persons with type O blood

universal recipients Individuals with type AB blood

uracil A pyrimidine base, a component of nucleic acids

ureases Enzymes that split urea into carbon dioxide and ammonia

urethra The canal through which urine is discharged

urethritis Inflammation of the urethra

urinary tract The system that functions in the elaboration and excretion of urine

urkaryote The proposed progenitor of prokaryotic and eukaryotic cells; the primordial living cell

use-dilution method Method of the Association of Official Analytical Chemists (AOAC) for evaluating the effectiveness of disinfectants that establishes appropriate dilutions of a germicide for actual conditions—this method gauges the effects of disinfectants by comparing them to each other, not to phenol and it tests nonphenol-like disinfectants

UV Ultraviolet light

V

V_{max} The maximal velocity of an enzymatic reaction occurring when the enzyme is saturated with substrate

VA mycorrhizae Vesicular-arbuscular mycorrhizae

vaccination The administration of a vaccine to stimulate the immune response to protect an individual from a pathogen or toxin

vaccine A preparation of antigens used for vaccination

vacuole A membrane-bound cavity within a cell that may function in digestion, secretion, storage, or excretion

vaginal tract A region of the female genital tract, the canal that leads from the uterus to the external orifice of the genital canal

vaginitis Inflammation of the vagina
valves Frustules of diatoms
vancomycin Antibiotic that inhibits bacterial cell wall synthesis
variable region The amino terminal end of an immunoglobulin molecule that is characterized by a high degree of variability
variant A strain that differs in some way from a particular organism
variolation A historically old procedure used by some cultures to protect individuals from smallpox; inoculation of an individual with smallpox virus
vector vaccines Vaccines that act as carriers for antigens associated with pathogens other than the one from which the vaccine was derived; created through recombinant DNA technology
vectors Organisms that act as carriers of pathogens and are involved in the spread of disease from one individual to another
vegetative cells Cells that are engaged in nutrition and growth; they do not act as specialized reproductive or dormant forms
vegetative growth Production of a new organism from a portion of an existing organism exclusive of sexual reproduction
vegetative structures Structures involved in nutrition and growth that are not specialized reproductive or dormant forms
venereal disease Sexually transmitted disease
vesicle A membrane-bounded sphere; specialized inclusion in root cortex in the vesicular-arbuscular type of mycorrhizal association
vesicular arbuscular mycorrhizae A common type of mycorrhizae characterized by the formation of vesicles and arbuscules
viability The ability to grow and reproduce
viable plate count method Procedure for the enumeration of bacteria whereby serial dilutions of a suspension of bacteria are plated onto a suitable solid growth medium, the plates are incubated, and the number of colony-forming units is counted
Vibrionaceae Family of Gram-negative, facultatively anaerobic rods consisting of the genera *Vibrio, Aeromonas, Plesiomonas,* and *Photobacterium*
***vir* genes** Genes that code for proteins required for the transfer of T-DNA (transforming DNA) of *Agrobacterium tumefaciens*
viral Of or pertaining to a virus
viremia Viral infection of the bloodstream
viricides Chemicals capable of inactivating viruses so that they lose their ability to replicate
virion A single, structurally complete, mature virus
viroids The causal agents of certain diseases, resembling viruses in many ways but differing in their apparent lack of a virus-like structural organization and their resistance to a wide variety of treatments to which viruses are sensitive; naked infective RNA
virology The study of viruses and viral diseases
virulence Capacity of a pathogen to cause disease, broadly defined in terms of severity of disease in the host
virulence factors Special inherent properties of disease-causing microorganisms that enhance their pathogenicity, allowing them to invade human tissue and disrupt normal body functions
virulent pathogen An organism with specialized properties that enhance its ability to cause disease
virus A noncellular entity that consists minimally of protein and nucleic acid and that can replicate only after entry into specific types of living cells; it has no intrinsic metabolism, and its replication depends on the direction of cellular metabolism by the viral genome; within the host cell, viral components are synthesized separately and are assembled intracellularly to form mature, infectious viruses
visible light Radiation in the wavelength range of 400 to 800 nm that is required for photosynthesis but can be lethal to nonphotosynthetic microorganisms
vital force The force that animates and perpetuates living organisms
vitamins A group of unrelated organic compounds, some or all of which are necessary in small quantities for the normal metabolism and growth of microorganisms
Voges-Proskauer test (VP) A diagnostic test to detect acetoin production by bacterial butanediol fermentation
volutin Metachromatic granules
volva A cup-shaped remnant of the universal veil that surrounds the base of the stalk in mature fruiting bodies of certain fungi
vomiting The forcible ejection of the contents of the stomach through the mouth
VP test Voges-Proskauer test
vulvovaginitis Inflammation of the vulva and vagina, usually caused by *Candida albicans,* herpes viruses, *Trichomonas vaginalis,* or *Neisseria gonorrhoeae*

W

wandering cells Cells capable of ameboid movement, including free macrophages, lymphocytes, mast cells, and plasma cells
warts Small, benign tumors of the skin, caused in humans by the human papilloma virus
water activity (A_w) A measure of the amount of reactive water available, equivalent to the relative humidity; the percentage of water saturation of the atmosphere
water molds Members of the oomycetes fungi
Weil-Felix test Serological test for the diagnosis of some diseases caused by *Rickettsia* species, especially typhus fever, using heterophile antibodies
whiplash flagella Smooth flagella of algae and fungi
Widal test Agglutination test for the diagnosis of typhoid fever, using antigens from *Salmonella* species
wild type Cells that contain the most common form of DNA sequences
wilts Plant diseases that are characterized by a reduction in host tissue turgidity, commonly affecting the vascular system; common causal agents are species of the fungi *Fusarium* and *Verticillium* and the bacteria *Erwinia* and *Pseudomonas*
windrow method A slow composting process that requires turning and covering with soil or compost
wine An alcoholic beverage produced by microbial fermentation of grapes and other fruit
wobble hypothesis Proposed by Frances Crick, this hypothesis accounts for the observed pattern of degeneracy

in the third base of a codon and states that this base can undergo unusual base pairing with the corresponding first base in the anticodon

wort In brewing, the liquor that results from the mixture of mash and water held at 40° to 65° C for 1 to 2 hours, during which the starch is broken down by amylases to glucose, maltose, and dextrins, and proteins are degraded to amino acids and polypeptides

X

Xanthophyceae Members of the Chrysophycophyta algae; yellow-green algae

xanthophyll A pigment containing oxygen and derived from carotenes; a yellow photosynthetic accessory pigment in some algae

xenobiotic A synthetic product that is not formed by natural biosynthetic processes; a foreign substance or poison

xerotolerant Able to withstand dryness; an organism capable of growth at low water activity

Y

yeasts A category of fungi defined in terms of morphological and physiological criteria; typically, unicellular, saprophytic organisms that characteristically ferment a range of carbohydrates and in which asexual reproduction occurs by budding

yellow-green algae Members of the Xanthophyceae

Z

Z pathway of oxidative photophosphorylation The combination of the cyclic and noncyclic photophosphorylation pathways in oxygenic photosynthetic organisms describing the metabolic reactions accounting for the trapping of light energy, and the generation of ATP, oxygen, and NADPH during photosynthesis

***z* value** The number of degrees Fahrenheit required to reduce the thermal death time tenfold

zone of greening Area of green discoloration with partial clearing around the colony resulting from α hemolysis

zoology The study of animal life, including its origin, development, structure, function, and classification

zoonoses Diseases of lower animals

zoospores Motile, flagellated spores

zooxanthellae Symbiotic relationships between dinoflagellates and other marine invertebrates

Zygomycotina Fungal subdivision of Amastigomycota; its members have coenocytic mycelia and form zygospores, exhibit sexual reproduction, or produce asexual sporangiospores

zygospore Thick-walled resting spores formed after gametangial fusion by members of the zygomycetes

zygote A single diploid cell formed from two haploid parental cells during fertilization; diploid reproductive form produced by union of haploid gametes

Zymogenous Term used to describe soil microorganisms that grow rapidly on exogenous substrates

ILLUSTRATION CREDITS

Chapter 1

Fig. 1-1, **A,** John J. Cardamone, Jr., University of Pittsburgh/Biological Photo Service; **B,** William L. Dentler, University of Kansas/Biological Photo Service

Box 1-1, **B,** Bob McKeever/Tom Stack & Associates

Fig. 1-3, **A** and **C,** GW Willis, Ochsner Medical Institution/Biological Photo Service; **B,** Paul W. Johnson/Biological Photo Service

Fig. 1-4, From Baron EJ, Peterson LR, and Finegold SM: *Bailey & Scott's Diagnostic Microbiology,* ed 9, St. Louis, Mosby, 1994

Fig. 1-6, **A,** Robert Brons/Biological Photo Service; **B,** J. Robert Waaland, University of Washington/Biological Photo Service

Fig. 1-7, Robert Brons/Biological Photo Service

Fig. 1-8, Terry J. Beveridge, University of Guelph/Biological Photo Service

Fig. 1-10, The Bettmann Archive

Fig. 1-12, The Bettmann Archive

Fig. 1-14, The Bettmann Archive

Fig. 1-16, The Bettmann Archive

Fig. 1-17, The Bettmann Archive

Fig. 1-18, The Bettmann Archive

Fig. 1-19, The Bettmann Archive

Fig. 1-22, Cold Springs Laboratory Archives

Fig. 1-23, David M. Dennis/Tom Stack & Associates

Chapter 2

Fig. 2-7, **B,** GW Willis, Ochsner Medical Institution/Biological Photo Service

Fig. 2-9, **B,** GW Willis/Biological Photo Service

Fig. 2-9, **C,** GW Willis/Biological Photo Service

Fig. 2-10, GW Willis, Ochsner Medical Institution/Biological Photo Service

Fig. 2-11, GW Willis, Ochsner Medical Institution/Biological Photo Service

Fig. 2-13, **B,** From Baron EJ, Peterson LR, and Finegold SM: *Bailey & Scott's Diagnostic Microbiology,* ed 9, St. Louis, Mosby, 1994

Fig. 2-14, **B,** From Immunology slide set, UpJohn, Kalamazoo, MI

Fig. 2-15, **B,** Robert Brons/Biological Photo Service

Fig. 2-16, **B,** J. Robert Waaland, University of Washington/Biological Photo Service

Fig. 2-17, **B,** Courtesy William Ghiorse, Cornell University

Fig. 2-18, **B,** John J. Cardamone, Jr., University of Pittsburgh and BK Pugashetti, University of Pittsburgh/Biological Photo Service

Fig. 2-20, **B,** Stanley C. Holt, University of Texas Health Center, San Antonio/Biological Photo Service

Fig. 2-21, **B,** Kennedy/Biological Photo Service; **C,** John J. Cardamone, Jr., University of Pittsburgh/Biological Photo Service

Fig. 2-22, **A,** Garry T. Cole, University of Texas at Austin/Biological Photo Service; **C,** Lara Hartley/Terraphotographics

Fig. 2-23, **B,** Courtesy Exxon Research and Engineering Company

Fig. 2-26, **B,** From Baron EJ, Peterson LR, and Finegold SM: *Bailey & Scott's Diagnostic Microbiology,* ed 9, St. Louis, Mosby, 1994

Fig. 2-31 From Baron EJ, Peterson LR, and Finegold SM: *Bailey & Scott's Diagnostic Microbiology,* ed 9, St. Louis, Mosby, 1994

Fig. 2-33, **B,** From Baron EJ, Peterson LR, and Finegold SM: *Bailey & Scott's Diagnostic Microbiology,* ed 9, St. Louis, Mosby, 1994

Part Two Opener Eldon H. Newcomb and TD Pugh, University of Wisconsin/Biological Photo Service

Chapter 3

Fig. 3-3, **B,** Terry J. Beveridge, University of Guelph/Biological Photo Service

Fig. 3-14, **B,** Charles L. Sanders/Biological Photo Service

Box 3-3, Terry J. Beveridge, University of Guelph/Biological Photo Service

Fig. 3-15, Terry J. Beveridge, University of Guelph/Biological Photo Service

Fig. 3-20, Terry J. Beveridge, University of Guelph/Biological Photo Service

Fig. 3-21, **B,** Terry J. Beveridge, University of Guelph/Biological Photo Service

Fig. 3-24, Cathy M. Pringle/Biological Photo Service

Fig. 3-25, Terry J. Beveridge, University of Guelph/Biological Photo Service

Fig. 3-26, Terry J. Beveridge, University of Guelph/Biological Photo Service

Fig. 3-27 Recolorized from an image by Gopal Murti/Photo Researchers

Fig. 3-29, Terry J. Beveridge, University of Guelph/Biological Photo Service

Fig. 3-30, **B,** Richard Rodewald, University of Virginia/Biological Photo Service

Fig. 3-31, **B,** Ada L. Olins, University of Tennessee/Biological Photo Service

Fig. 3-34, Eldon H. Newcomb and TD Pugh, University of Wisconsin/Biological Photo Service

Fig. 3-35, **B,** Barry F. King, University of California School of Medicine/Biological Photo Service

Fig. 3-36, **B,** Paul W. Johnson/Biological Photo Service

Fig. 3-38, Terry J. Beveridge, University of Guelph/Biological Photo Service

Fig. 3-39, Paul W. Johnson and John Sieburth, University of Rhode Island/Biological Photo Service

Fig. 3-41, **B,** Paul W. Johnson/Biological Photo Service

Fig. 3-43, **A,** Paul W. Johnson/Biological Photo Service; **B,** William L. Dentler, University of Kansas/Biological Photo Service

Fig. 3-46, Terry J. Beveridge, University of Guelph and Y. Gorby and D. Blakemore, University of Kansas/Biological Photo Service

Fig. 3-47, H. Stuart Pankratz, Michigan State University/Biological Photo Service

Fig. 3-48, **B,** William L. Dentler, University of Kansas/Biological Photo Service

Fig. 3-49, **B,** Paul W. Johnson/Biological Photo Service

Fig. 3-50, **B,** Terry J. Beveridge, University of Guelph/Biological Photo Service

Fig. 3-51, **B,** S Abraham and EH Beachey, VA Medical Center, Memphis, TN/Biological Photo Service

Fig. 3-52, Recolorized from an image by L. Caro/Science Photo Library/Photo Researchers

Fig. 3-53, **B,** Terry J. Beveridge, University of Guelph/Biological Photo Service

Fig. 3-54, **B,** Stanley C. Holt, University of Texas Health Center, San Antonio/Biological Photo Service

Chapter 5

Fig. 5-3, Paul W. Johnson/Biological Photo Service
Fig. 5-20, L. Evans Roth, University of Tennesee/Biological Photo Service

Part Three Opener Courtesy Richard J. Feldman, National Institutes of Health

Chapter 6

Fig. 6-3, Courtesy Richard J. Feldmann, National Institutes of Health

Chapter 7

Fig. 7-2, R. Welch, University of Wisconsin Medical School/Biological Photo Service
Fig. 7-9, Barbara J. Miller/Biological Photo Service
Fig. 7-20, Courtesy Huntington Potter and David Dressler Harvard Medical School
Fig. 7-29, David P. Allison, Oak Ridge National Laboratory/Biological Photo Service
Fig. 7-42, Paul W. Johnson/Biological Photo Service
Fig. 7-44, **B,** VU/SIU/Visuals Unlimited
Fig. 7-44, **C,** Hank Morgan/Photo Researchers
Author Essay photo, Agracetus/Biological Photo Service

Part Four Opener From Mims CA, Playfair JHL, Roitt IM et al: *Medical Microbiology,* St. Louis, Mosby Wolfe, 1993. Courtesy D Hockley

Chapter 8

Fig. 8-2 Nelson L. Max, University of California/Biological Photo Service
Fig. 8-3, **B,** Bernard Roizman, University of Chicago/Biological Photo Service
Fig. 8-4, GG Smith, NIH/Biological Photo Service
Fig. 8-7, Lee Simon/Photo Researchers
Fig. 8-9, Lee Simon/Photo Researchers
Fig. 8-13, From Mims CA, Playfair JHL, Roitt IM et al: *Medical Microbiology,* St. Louis, Mosby Wolfe, 1993. Courtesy D Hockley
Fig. 8-16, **A** and **B,** Photo Researchers
Box 8-2, Visuals Unlimited/Cabisco
Fig. 8-23, Leon J. Le Beau/Biological Photo Service
Fig. 8-25, **B,** From Baron EJ, Peterson LR, and Finegold SM: *Bailey & Scott's Diagnostic Microbiology,* ed 9, St. Louis, Mosby, 1994
Fig. 8-25, **C,** From Baron EJ, Peterson LR, and Finegold SM: *Bailey & Scott's Diagnostic Microbiology,* ed 9, St. Louis, Mosby, 1994
Fig. 8-26, C Garon and J. Rose, National Institutes of Health/Biological Photo Service
Box 8-3, **B,** From Baron EJ, Peterson LR, and Finegold SM: *Bailey & Scott's Diagnostic Microbiology,* ed 9, St. Louis, Mosby, 1994
Fig. 8-28, **B,** John J. Cardamone, Jr., University of Pittsburgh/Biological Photo Service
Fig. 8-29, **B,** John J. Caramone, Jr., University of Pittsburgh/Biological Photo Service
Fig. 8-32, Centers for Disease Control/Biological Photo Service

Chapter 9

Fig. 9-1, Stanley C. Holt, University of Texas Health Center, San Antonio/Biological Photo Service
Fig. 9-3, Terry J. Beveridge, University of Guelph/Biological Photo Service
Fig. 9-4, Stanley C. Holt, University of Texas Health Center, San Antonio/Biological Photo Service
Fig. 9-8, Terry J. Beveridge, University of Guelph/Biological Photo Service
Fig. 9-9, Terry J. Beveridge, University of Guelph/Biological Photo Service
Fig. 9-10, H. Stuart Pankratz, Michigan State University/Biological Photo Service
Fig. 9-11, **B,** Karen Stephens, University of Washington/Biological Photo Service
Fig. 9-15, Helen Carr, Ecofilms/Biological Photo Service
Fig. 9-16, Courtesy Holger Jannasch, Woods Hole Oceanographic Institution
Fig. 9-18, Terry J. Beveridge, University of Guelph and G Patel National Research Council of Canada, Ottawa/Biological Photo Service
Fig. 9-19, Courtesy E. Imre Friedman, Florida State University; AAAS, Science 215:1045
Fig. 9-21, Courtesy Paul Zahn; National Geographic August 1967, pp. 258-259
Fig. 9-23, J. Robert Waaland, University of Washington/Biological Photo Service

Chapter 10

Fig. 10-4, Courtesy American Can Company, Barrington, IL
Fig. 10-9, Leon J. Le Beau/Biological Photo Service
Fig. 10-11, RM Atlas, University of Louisville
Fig. 10-13, Leon J. Le Beau/Biological Photo Service

Part Five Opener From Mims CA, Playfair JHL, Roitt IM et al: *Medical Microbiology,* St. Louis, Mosby Wolfe, 1993. Courtesy T Yamamoto

Chapter 11

Fig. 11-1, RM Atlas, University of Louisville
Fig. 11-6, Leon J. Le Beau/Biological Photo Service
Fig. 11-7, From Roitt IM, Brostoff J, and Male DK: *Immunology,* ed 3, St. Louis, Mosby Wolfe, 1993. Courtesy H. Validimarsson
Fig. 11-11, From Roitt IM, Brostoff J, and Male DK: *Immunology,* ed 3, St. Louis, Mosby Wolfe, 1993. Courtesy D. McLaren
Fig. 11-16, From Roitt IM, Brostoff J, and Male DK: *Immunology,* ed 3, St. Louis, Mosby Wolfe, 1993
Fig. 11-24, From Mims CA, Playfair JHL, Roitt IM et al: *Medical Microbiology,* St. Louis, Mosby Wolfe, 1993
Fig. 11-35, UPI/The Bettmann Archive
Fig. 11-38, From Cerio R and Jackson WF: *A Colour Atlas of Allergic Skin Disorders,* London, Mosby Wolfe, 1992

Chapter 12

Fig. 12-4, From Potter P and Perry A: *Fundamentals of Nursing: Concepts, Process, and Practice,* ed 3, St. Louis, Mosby, 1993
Fig. 12-10, RM Atlas, University of Louisville
Fig. 12-11, **A,** Centers for Disease Control/Biological Photo Service
Fig. 12-12, Courtesy James Snyder, University of Louisville Hospital
Fig. 12-13, RB Morrison, MD, Austin, TX/Biological Photo Service
Fig. 12-16, From Farrar WE, Wood MJ, Innes JA et al: *Infectious Diseases: Text and Color Atlas,* ed 2, London: Gower Medical Publishing, 1992, Courtesy S. Knutton
Fig. 12-18, JJ Pauline, University of Georgia/Biological Photo Service
Fig. 12-23, From Farrar WE, Wood MJ, Innes JA et al: *Infectious Diseases: Text and Color Atlas,* ed 2, London: Gower Medical Publishing, 1992, Courtesy RD Catterell
Fig. 12-25, **A,** The Bettmann Archive
Fig. 12-33, From Farrar WE, Wood MJ, Innes JA et al: *Infectious Diseases: Text and Color Atlas,* ed 2, London: Gower Medical Publishing, 1992, Courtesy AE Prevost

Chapter 13

Fig. 13-3, From Farrar WE, Wood MJ, Innes JA et al: *Infectious Diseases: Text and Color Atlas,* ed 2, London: Gower Medical Publishing, 1992
Fig. 13-4, RM Atlas, University of Louisville
Fig. 13-6, From Mims CA, Playfair JHL, Roitt IM et al: *Medical Microbiology,* St. Louis, Mosby Wolfe, 1993. Courtesy PJ Watt

Fig. 13-7, From Mims CA, Playfair JHL, Roitt IM et al: *Medical Microbiology,* St. Louis, Mosby Wolfe, 1993
Fig. 13-8, From Mims CA, Playfair JHL, Roitt IM et al: *Medical Microbiology,* St. Louis, Mosby Wolfe, 1993. Courtesy JE Banatvala
Fig. 13-11, **A,** From Baron EJ, Peterson LR, and Finegold SM: *Bailey & Scott's Diagnostic Microbiology,* ed 9, St. Louis, Mosby Wolfe, 1994
Fig. 13-15, From Emond RTD and Rowland HAK: *A Colour Atlas of Infectious Diseases,* ed 2, London, Mosby Wolfe, 1987. **A,** Courtesy GDW McKendrick/ **B,** Courtesy JA Forbes
Fig. 13-18, **A,** Leodocia M. Pope, University of Texas/Biological Photo Service; **B,** James Snyder, University of Louisville Hospital
Fig. 13-20, Leon J. Le Beau/Biological Photo Service
Fig. 13-22, From Mims CA, Playfair JHL, Roitt IM et al: *Medical Microbiology,* St. Louis, Mosby Wolfe, 1993. **A,** Courtesy ET Nelson; **B,** Courtesy T Yamamoto
Fig. 13-23, Max Listergarten, University of Pennsylvania/Biological Photo Service

Part Six Opener

Courtesy Jeffrey C Burnham, Medical College of Ohio and Sam F. Conti, University of Massachusetts; American Society for Microbiology, *J Bacteriology,* 96:1374, 1968

Chapter 14

Fig. 14-3, Paul W. Johnson/Biological Photo Service
Fig. 14-4, **A,** John NA Lott, McMaster University/Biological Photo Service; **B,** Varley Weideman, University of Louisville
Fig. 14-6, Phil Gates, University of Durham/Biological Photo Service
Fig. 14-7, EH Newcomb and SR Tandon, University of Wisconsin/Biological Photo Service
Fig. 14-11, Ken Lucas/Biological Photo Service
Fig. 14-13, H. Stuart Pankratz, Michigan State University/Biological Photo Service
Fig. 14-14, **A,** N. Allin and GL Barron, University of Guelph/Biological Photo Service. **B,** B. Norbring-Hertz, University of Lund
Fig. 14-16, Courtesy Jeffrey C Burnham, Medical College of Ohio and Sam F. Conti, University of Massachusetts; American Society for Microbiology, *J Bacteriology,* 96:1374, 1968
Fig. 14-21, **A,** Courtesy William Merrill, Pennsylvania State University
Fig. 14-24, John NA Lott, McMaster University/Biological Photo Service
Fig. 14-26, **A,** Stanley C. Holt, University of Texas Health Center, San Antonio/Biological Photo Service; **B,** Courtesy Dr. Guggenheim, Laboratory for Scanning Electron Microscopy, University of Basel, Switzerland
Fig. 14-28, Courtesy Holger Jannasch, Woods Hole Oceanographic Institution
Box 14-3, Visuals Unlimited/Christine L. Case
Fig. 14-31, **A,** William E. Schadel, Small World Enterprises/Biological Photo Service; **B,** Orson K. Miller, Jr., Virginia Polytechnic Institute
Fig. 14-34, Recolorized from an image by Science Vu-RGE Murray/Visuals Unlimited
Fig. 14-38, Paul W. Johnson/Biological Photo Service
Box 14-5, **A,** Courtesy Holger Jannasch, Woods Hole Oceanographic Institution
Fig. 14-39, John NA Lott, McMaster University/Biological Photo Service
Fig. 14-42, **A,** Courtesy Diana Lyn Laulainen; **B,** Courtesy Gary B. Collins, US Environmental Protection Agency
Fig. 14-43, Terry J. Beveridge, University of Guelph/Biological Photo Service
Fig. 14-46, Stewart Halperin
Fig. 14-48, Judith FM Hoeniger, University of Toronto/Biological Photo Service
Fig. 14-55, Courtesy Autotrol Corporation, Milwaukee, WI
Fig. 14-56, John NA Lott, McMaster University/Biological Photo Service
Box 14-7, 3 Visuals Unlimited/Christone L Case

Chapter 15

Fig. 15-3, Visuals Unlimited/Science Vu-URSCIM
Fig. 15-16, Hank Morgan/Photo Researchers
Fig. 15-28, Courtesy KC Hochstetler, Salt Lake City
Fig. 15-32, Courtesy Exxon Research & Engineering Company
Fig. 15-33, **B** and **C,** Photos courtesy of Anheuser-Busch Companies, Inc.
Fig. 15-35, Photo courtesy of Anheuser-Busch Companies, Inc
Fig. 15-37, **B,** Stewart Halperin
Fig. 15-43, **B,** Courtesy Shigeomi Ushijima, Kikkoman Corporation, Noda City, Chiba Prefecture, Japan

Part Seven Opener

From Baron EJ, Peterson LR, and Finegold SM: *Bailey & Scott's Diagnostic Microbiology,* ed 9, St. Louis, Mosby, 1994. Courtesy Ellena Patterson, University of California, Irvine

Chapter 16

Fig. 16-6, From Baron EJ, Peterson LR, and Finegold SM: *Bailey & Scott's Diagnostic Microbiology,* ed 9, St. Louis, Mosby, 1994
Fig. 16-7, Terry J Beveridge, University of Guelph/Biological Photo Service
Fig. 16-8, Linda S. Thomashow, Washington State University/Biological Photo Service
Fig. 16-9, Terry J Beveridge, University of Guelph/Biological Photo Service
Fig. 16-10, From Baron EJ, Peterson LR, and Finegold SM: *Bailey & Scott's Diagnostic Microbiology,* ed 9, St. Louis, Mosby, 1994
Fig. 16-12, Leon J. Le Beau/Biological Photo Service
Fig. 16-13, From Baron EJ, Peterson LR, and Finegold SM: *Bailey & Scott's Diagnostic Microbiology,* ed 9, St. Louis, Mosby, 1994. Courtesy Ellena Patterson, University of California, Irvine
Fig. 16-14, **A,** and **B,** Paul W. Johnson/Biological Photo Service
Fig. 16-15, Stanley C. Holt, University of Texas Health Center, San Antonio/Biological Photo Service
Fig. 16-16, H Stuart Pankratz and RL Uffen, Michigan State/Biological Photo Service
Fig. 16-17, J. Robert Waaland, University of Washington/Biological Photo Service
Fig. 16-18, Paul W. Johnson/Biological Photo Service
Fig. 16-19, Recolorized from an image from Science Vu-SW Watson/Visuals Unlimited
Fig. 16-20, Richard L. Moore/Biological Photo Service
Fig. 16-21, Terry J. Beveridge, University of Guelph/Biological Photo Service
Fig. 16-22, Karen Stephens, University of Washington/Biological Photo Service
Fig. 16-23, Visuals Unlimited/HD Raj
Fig. 16-24, Leon J. Le Beau/Biological Photo Service
Fig. 16-25, From Baron EJ, Peterson LR, and Finegold SM: *Bailey & Scott's Diagnostic Microbiology,* ed 9, St. Louis, Mosby, 1994
Fig. 16-26, Courtesy William Trentini, Mount Allison University, Sackville, New Brunswick, Canada
Fig. 16-27, GW Willis, Ochsner Medical Institution/Biological Photo Service
Fig. 16-28, Terry J. Beveridge, University of Guelph/Biological Photo Service
Fig. 16-29, Visuals Unlimited/Science Vu
Fig. 16-30, From Baron EJ, Peterson LR, and Finegold SM: *Bailey & Scott's Diagnostic Microbiology,* ed 9, St. Louis, Mosby, 1994
Fig. 16-32, Terry J. Beveridge, University of Guelph and GD Sprott, National Research Council of Canada/Biological Photo Service

Fig. 16-33, Courtesy CL and JA Brierly, New Mexico Technical University

Chapter 17

Fig. 17-2, Courtesy CP Kurtzman/US Department of Agriculture
Fig. 17-9, Jim Solliday/Biological Photo Service
Fig. 17-11, William E. Schadel, Small World Enterprises/Biological Photo Service
Fig. 17-13, Barbara J. Miller/Biological Photo Service
Fig. 17-14, **B,** Visuals Unlimited/Stanley Flegler
Fig. 17-16, Barbara J. Miller/Biological Photo Service
Fig. 17-17, Courtesy Orson K. Miller, Jr., Virginia Polytechnic Institute
Fig. 17-20, Alfred Oxczarazk/Biological Photo Service
Fig. 17-21, Paul W. Johnson/Biological Photo Service
Fig. 17-22, Visuals Unlimited/LL Sims
Fig. 17-23, Paul W. Johnson/Biological Photo Service
Fig. 17-25, J. Robert Waaland, University of Washington/Biological Photo Service
Fig. 17-26, Paul W. Johnson/Biological Photo Service
Fig. 17-27, J. Robert Waaland, University of Washington/Biological Photo Service
Fig. 17-28, David J. Wrobel/Biological Photo Service
Fig. 17-31, Orson K. Miller, Jr., Virginia Polytechnic Institute
Fig. 17-33, Robert Brons/Biological Photo Service
Fig. 17-34, Omikron/Science Source/Photo Researchers
Fig. 17-35, Robert Brons/Biological Photo Service
Fig. 17-36, From Baron EJ, Peterson LR, and Finegold SM: *Bailey & Scott's Diagnostic Microbiology,* ed 9, St. Louis, Mosby, 1994
Fig. 17-37, Robert Brons/Biological Photo Service
Fig. 17-38, Biophoto Associations/S.S./Photo Researchers
Fig. 17-40, Courtesy T. Varghese; From J Protozoology 22:68, 1975

INDEX

D

E

G

T

Emerging Infectious Diseases

Disease	Deaths
Pneumonia	4,300,000
Diarrheal diseases	3,200,000
Tuberculosis	3,000,000
Hepatitis B	1–2,000,000
Malaria	1,000,000
Measles	880,000
Neonatal tetanus	600,000
AIDS	550,000

AIDS cases

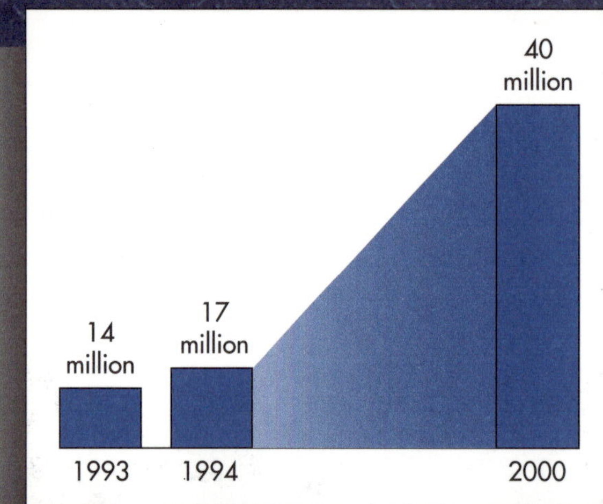

HIV infections

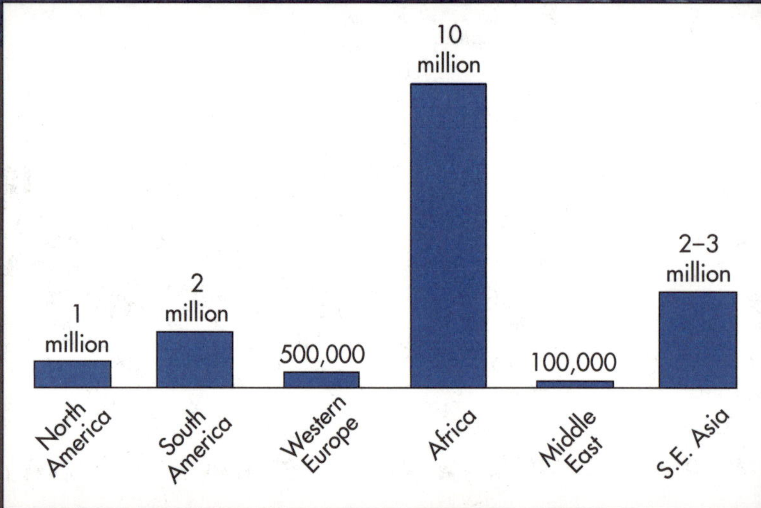